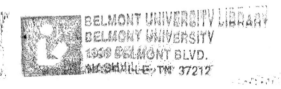

International Directory of

COMPANY HISTORIES

International Directory of

COMPANY HISTORIES

VOLUME 94

Editor

Tina Grant

ST. JAMES PRESS
A part of Gale, Cengage Learning

GALE
CENGAGE Learning™

Detroit • New York • San Francisco • New Haven, Conn • Waterville, Maine • London

GALE
CENGAGE Learning

International Directory of Company Histories, Volume 94

Tina Grant, Editor

Project Editor: Miranda H. Ferrara

Editorial: Virgil Burton, Donna Craft, Louise Gagné, Peggy Geeseman, Julie Gough, Linda Hall, Sonya Hill, Keith Jones, Lynn Pearce, Holly Selden, Justine Ventimiglia

Production Technology Specialist: Mike Weaver

Imaging and Multimedia: Lezlie Light

Composition and Electronic Prepress: Gary Leach, Evi Seoud

Manufacturing: Rhonda Dover

Product Management: David Forman

Cover Photograph: Vectren headquarters, Evansville, Indiana © photographer: TJ Thompson.

Gale
27500 Drake Rd.
Farmington Hills, MI, 48331-3535

LIBRARY OF CONGRESS CATALOG NUMBER 89-190943
ISBN-13: 978-1-55862-615-7
ISBN-10: 1-55862-615-8

This title is also available as an e-book
ISBN-13: 978-1-4144-2978-6 ISBN-10: 1-4144-2978-9
Contact your Gale, a part of Cengage Learning sales representative for ordering information.

BRITISH LIBRARY CATALOGUING IN PUBLICATION DATA
International directory of company histories, Vol. 93
Jay P. Pederson
33.87409

Printed in the United States of America
1 2 3 4 5 6 7 12 11 10 09 08

Contents

Preface vii
Notes on Contributors ix
List of Abbreviations xi

Actuant Corporation 1
Alfred Kärcher GmbH & Co KG 9
Align Technology, Inc. 15
Allied Irish Banks plc 19
Alside Inc. 25
Anacomp, Inc. 30
Arkansas Best Corporation 35
Ash Grove Cement Company 41
Autoridad del Canal de Panamá 45
B.W. Rogers Company 49
Bally Total Fitness Corporation 53
Balmac International, Inc. 58
The Bartell Drug Company 62
Besix Group S.A./NV 66
Beth Abraham Family of Health Services 70
BJ's Wholesale Club, Inc. 75
Boizel Chanoine Champagne S.A. 79
Borealis AG 83
Buffalo Grill S.A. 87
Bugatti Automobiles S.A.S. 91
The Burton Corporation 95
Carl Kühne KG (GmbH & Co.) . . 101
Carver Bancorp, Inc. 106
Cerner Corporation 111
Cheung Kong (Holdings) Ltd. 117
Claire's Stores, Inc. 125
Companhia Suzano de Papel e Celulose S.A. 130
Cora S.A./NV 134
Corporación Multi-Inversiones 138
Dairy Farmers of America, Inc. 143
Delphax Technologies Inc. 147
Devoteam S.A. 151
Dirk Rossmann GmbH 155
Dolan Media Company 160
Draftfcb 164
DTE Energy Company 169
Duferco Group 177
Duncan Aviation, Inc. 181
Egan Companies, Inc. 185
8x8, Inc. 189
Element K Corporation 193
Elite World S.A. 197
Fairfax Media Ltd. 202
Gartner, Inc. 209
Granite City Food & Brewery Ltd. 214
Grupo Planeta 218
The Haartz Corporation 223

Harkins Amusement Enterprises, Inc. 227
Harland Clarke Holdings Corporation 232
Hobie Cat Company 236
ICF International, Inc. 240
IKEA Group 248
Image Entertainment, Inc. 254
Jack Henry and Associates, Inc. . . .258
John D. Brush Company Inc. 264
Just Bagels Manufacturing, Inc. . . .268
Lewis Drug Inc. 272
LG Corporation 277
Macy's, Inc. 284
MAN Roland Druckmaschinen AG 294
Mark T. Wendell Tea Company . . .299
MBK Industrie S.A. 303
McAfee Inc. 307
Microsemi Corporation 311
MoneyGram International, Inc. . . .315
National Frozen Foods Corporation 319
Nebraska Furniture Mart, Inc. 323
Neogen Corporation 327
Newmont Mining Corporation . . .331
Pacific Coast Building Products, Inc. 338
Paramount Pictures Corporation . .342
PCC Natural Markets 348
Peavey Electronics Corporation . . .352
Quick Restaurants S.A. 357
Reiter Dairy, LLC 361
Ritz-Craft Corporation of Pennsylvania Inc. 365
Röchling Gruppe 369
Rudolph Technologies Inc. 375
Scherer Brothers Lumber Company .379
Schouw & Company A/S 384
Scope Products, Inc. 388
Smart & Final LLC 392
South Dakota Wheat Growers Association 397
Sport Chalet, Inc. 402
Stemilt Growers Inc. 407
Technology Research Corporation 411
Technology Solutions Company . . .415
Terra Industries, Inc. 420
United Parcel Service, Inc. 425
Valhi, Inc. .431
Varsity Brands, Inc. 436
Velocity Express Corporation 441
Virginia Dare Extract Company, Inc. 447
Vitasoy International Holdings Ltd. 451
Vocento 455
Wilh. Wilhelmsen ASA 459
Wilhelm Karmann GmbH 463
World Wide Technology, Inc. 469
Xerium Technologies, Inc. 473
Yara International ASA 477

Index to Companies 483
Index to Industries 655
Geographic Index 719

Preface

The St. James Press series *The International Directory of Company Histories* (*IDCH*) is intended for reference use by students, business people, librarians, historians, economists, investors, job candidates, and others who seek to learn more about the historical development of the world's most important companies. To date, *IDCH* has covered over 9,150 companies in 94 volumes.

INCLUSION CRITERIA

Most companies chosen for inclusion in *IDCH* have achieved a minimum of US$25 million in annual sales and are leading influences in their industries or geographical locations. Companies may be publicly held, private, or nonprofit. State-owned companies that are important in their industries and that may operate much like public or private companies also are included. Wholly owned subsidiaries and divisions are profiled if they meet the requirements for inclusion. Entries on companies that have had major changes since they were last profiled may be selected for updating.

The *IDCH* series highlights 25% private and nonprofit companies, and features updated entries on approximately 35 companies per volume.

ENTRY FORMAT

Each entry begins with the company's legal name; the address of its headquarters; its telephone, toll-free, and fax numbers; and its web site. A statement of public, private, state, or parent ownership follows. A company with a legal name in both English and the language of its headquarters country is listed by the English name, with the native-language name in parentheses.

The company's founding or earliest incorporation date, the number of employees, and the most recent available sales figures follow. Sales figures are given in local currencies with equivalents in U.S. dollars. For some private companies, sales figures are estimates and indicated by the abbreviation *est.* The entry lists the exchanges on which the company's stock is traded and its ticker symbol, as well as the company's NAICS codes.

Entries generally contain a *Company Perspectives* box which provides a short summary of the company's mission, goals, and ideals; a *Key Dates* box highlighting milestones in the company's history; lists of *Principal Subsidiaries*, *Principal Divisions*, *Principal Operating Units*, *Principal Competitors*; and articles for *Further Reading.*

American spelling is used throughout *IDCH*, and the word "billion" is used in its U.S. sense of one thousand million.

SOURCES

Entries have been compiled from publicly accessible sources both in print and on the Internet such as general and academic periodicals, books, and annual reports, as well as material supplied by the companies themselves.

CUMULATIVE INDEXES

IDCH contains three indexes: the **Index to Companies**, which provides an alphabetical index to companies discussed in the text as well as to companies profiled, the **Index to Industries**, which allows researchers to locate companies by their principal industry, and the **Geographic Index**, which lists companies alphabetically by the country of their headquarters. The indexes are cumulative and specific instructions for using them are found immediately preceding each index.

SUGGESTIONS WELCOME

Comments and suggestions from users of *IDCH* on any aspect of the product as well as suggestions for companies to be included or updated are cordially invited. Please write:

The Editor
International Directory of Company Histories
St. James Press
Gale, Cengage Learning
27500 Drake Rd.
Farmington Hills, Michigan 48331-3535

St. James Press does not endorse any of the companies or products mentioned in this series. Companies appearing in the *International Directory of Company Histories* were selected without reference to their wishes and have in no way endorsed their entries.

Notes on Contributors

Gerald E. Brennan
Writer and musician based in Germany.

M. L. Cohen
Novelist, business writer, and researcher living in Paris.

Ed Dinger
Writer and editor based in Bronx, New York.

Paul R. Greenland
Illinois-based writer and researcher; author of two books and former senior editor of a national business magazine; contributor to *The Encyclopedia of Chicago History*, *The Encyclopedia of Religion*, and the *Encyclopedia of American Industries.*

Robert Halasz
Former editor in chief of *World Progress* and *Funk & Wagnalls New Encyclopedia Yearbook*; author, *The U.S. Marines* (Millbrook Press, 1993).

Evelyn Hauser
Researcher, writer and marketing specialist based in Germany.

Frederick C. Ingram
Writer based in South Carolina.

Micah L. Issit
Philadelphia-based writer, historian, ecologist and humorist.

Carrie Rothburd
Writer and editor specializing in corporate profiles, academic texts, and academic journal articles.

Daniel Thurs
Writer and researcher specializing in issues related to science and technology.

Frank Uhle
Ann Arbor-based writer; movie projectionist, disc jockey, and staff member of *Psychotronic Video* magazine.

Ellen D. Wernick
Florida-based writer and editor.

A. Woodward
Wisconsin-based writer.

List of Abbreviations

¥ Japanese yen
£ United Kingdom pound
$ United States dollar

A

AB Aktiebolag (Finland, Sweden)
AB Oy Aktiebolag Osakeyhtiot (Finland)
A.E. Anonimos Eteria (Greece)
AED Emirati dirham
AG Aktiengesellschaft (Austria, Germany, Switzerland, Liechtenstein)
aG auf Gegenseitigkeit (Austria, Germany)
A.m.b.a. Andelsselskab med begraenset ansvar (Denmark)
A.O. Anonim Ortaklari/Ortakligi (Turkey)
ApS Amparteselskab (Denmark)
ARS Argentine peso
A.S. Anonim Sirketi (Turkey)
A/S Aksjeselskap (Norway)
A/S Aktieselskab (Denmark, Sweden)
Ay Avoinyhtio (Finland)
ATS Austrian shilling
AUD Australian dollar
ApS Amparteselskab (Denmark)
Ay Avoinyhtio (Finland)

B

B.A. Buttengewone Aansprakeiijkheid (Netherlands)
BEF Belgian franc
BHD Bahraini dinar
Bhd. Berhad (Malaysia, Brunei)
BRL Brazilian real
B.V. Besloten Vennootschap (Belgium, Netherlands)

C

C.A. Compania Anonima (Ecuador, Venezuela)
CAD Canadian dollar
C. de R.L. Compania de Responsabilidad Limitada (Spain)
CEO Chief Executive Officer
CFO Chief Financial Officer
CHF Swiss franc
Cia. Companhia (Brazil, Portugal)
Cia. Compania (Latin America (except Brazil), Spain)
Cia. Compagnia (Italy)
Cie. Compagnie (Belgium, France, Luxembourg, Netherlands)
CIO Chief Information Officer
CLP Chilean peso
CNY Chinese yuan
Co. Company
COO Chief Operating Officer
Coop. Cooperative
COP Colombian peso
Corp. Corporation
C. por A. Compania por Acciones (Dominican Republic)
CPT Cuideachta Phoibi Theoranta (Republic of Ireland)
CRL Companhia a Responsabilidao Limitida (Portugal, Spain)
C.V. Commanditaire Vennootschap (Netherlands, Belgium)
CZK Czech koruna

D

D&B Dunn & Bradstreet
DEM German deutsche mark
Div. Division (United States)
DKK Danish krone
DZD Algerian dinar

E

EC Exempt Company (Arab countries)
Edms. Bpk. Eiendoms Beperk (South Africa)
EEK Estonian Kroon
eG eingetragene Genossenschaft (Germany)
EGMBH Eingetragene Genossenschaft mit beschraenkter Haftung (Austria, Germany)
EGP Egyptian pound
Ek For Ekonomisk Forening (Sweden)
EP Empresa Portuguesa (Portugal)
E.P.E. Etema Pemorismenis Evthynis (Greece)
ESOP Employee Stock Options and Ownership
ESP Spanish peseta
Et(s). Etablissement(s) (Belgium,

France, Luxembourg)
eV eingetragener Verein (Germany)
EUR euro

F
FIM Finnish markka
FRF French franc

G
G.I.E. Groupement d'Interet Economique (France)
gGmbH gemeinnutzige Gesellschaft mit beschraenkter Haftung (Austria, Germany, Switzerland)
G.I.E. Groupement d'Interet Economique (France)
GmbH Gesellschaft mit beschraenkter Haftung (Austria, Germany, Switzerland)
GRD Greek drachma
GWA Gewerbte Amt (Austria, Germany)

H
HB Handelsbolag (Sweden)
HF Hlutafelag (Iceland)
HKD Hong Kong dollar
HUF Hungarian forint

I
IDR Indonesian rupiah
IEP Irish pound
ILS new Israeli shekel
Inc. Incorporated (United States, Canada)
INR Indian rupee
IPO Initial Public Offering
I/S Interesentselskap (Norway)
I/S Interessentselskab (Denmark)
ISK Icelandic krona
ITL Italian lira

J
JMD Jamaican dollar
JOD Jordanian dinar

K
KB Kommanditbolag (Sweden)
KES Kenyan schilling
Kft Korlatolt Felelossegu Tarsasag (Hungary)
KG Kommanditgesellschaft (Austria, Germany, Switzerland)
KGaA Kommanditgesellschaft auf Aktien (Austria, Germany, Switzerland)
KK Kabushiki Kaisha (Japan)
KPW North Korean won
KRW South Korean won
K/S Kommanditselskab (Denmark)
K/S Kommandittselskap (Norway)
KWD Kuwaiti dinar
Ky Kommandiitiyhtio (Finland)

L
LBO Leveraged Buyout
Lda. Limitada (Spain)
L.L.C. Limited Liability Company (Arab countries, Egypt, Greece, United States)
L.L.P. Limited Liability Partnership (United States)
L.P. Limited Partnership (Canada, South Africa, United Kingdom, United States)
Ltd. Limited
Ltda. Limitada (Brazil, Portugal)
Ltee. Limitee (Canada, France)
LUF Luxembourg franc

M
mbH mit beschraenkter Haftung (Austria, Germany)
Mij. Maatschappij (Netherlands)
MUR Mauritian rupee
MXN Mexican peso
MYR Malaysian ringgit

N
N.A. National Association (United States)
NGN Nigerian naira
NLG Netherlands guilder
NOK Norwegian krone
N.V. Naamloze Vennootschap (Belgium, Netherlands)
NZD New Zealand dollar

O
OAO Otkrytoe Aktsionernoe Obshchestve (Russia)
OHG Offene Handelsgesellschaft (Austria, Germany, Switzerland)
OMR Omani rial
OOO Obschestvo s Ogranichennoi Otvetstvennostiu (Russia)
OOUR Osnova Organizacija Udruzenog Rada (Yugoslavia)
Oy Osakeyhtî (Finland)

P
P.C. Private Corp. (United States)
PEN Peruvian Nuevo Sol
PHP Philippine peso
PKR Pakistani rupee
P/L Part Lag (Norway)
PLC Public Limited Co. (United Kingdom, Ireland)
P.L.L.C. Professional Limited Liability Corporation (United States)
PLN Polish zloty
P.T. Perusahaan/Perseroan Terbatas (Indonesia)
PTE Portuguese escudo
Pte. Private (Singapore)
Pty. Proprietary (Australia, South Africa, United Kingdom)
Pvt. Private (India, Zimbabwe)
PVBA Personen Vennootschap met Beperkte Aansprakelijkheid (Belgium)

Q
QAR Qatar riyal

R
REIT Real Estate Investment Trust
RMB Chinese renminbi
Rt Reszvenytarsasag (Hungary)
RUB Russian ruble

S
S.A. Société Anonyme (Arab countries, Belgium, France, Jordan, Luxembourg, Switzerland)
S.A. Sociedad Anónima (Latin America [except Brazil], Spain, Mexico)
S.A. Sociedades Anônimas (Brazil, Portugal)
SAA Societe Anonyme Arabienne (Arab countries)
S.A.C. Sociedad Anonima Comercial (Latin America [except Brazil])
S.A.C.I. Sociedad Anonima Comercial e Industrial (Latin America [except Brazil])
S.A.C.I.y.F. Sociedad Anonima Comercial e Industrial y Financiera (Latin America [except Brazil])

S.A. de C.V. Sociedad Anonima de Capital Variable Mexico)
SAK Societe Anonyme Kuweitienne (Arab countries)
SAL Societe Anonyme Libanaise (Arab countries)
SAO Societe Anonyme Omanienne (Arab countries)
SAQ Societe Anonyme Qatarienne (Arab countries)
SAR Saudi riyal
S.A.R.L. Sociedade Anonima de Responsabilidade Limitada (Brazil, Portugal)
S.A.R.L. Société à Responsabilité Limitée (France, Belgium, Luxembourg)
S.A.S. Societá in Accomandita Semplice (Italy)
S.A.S. Societe Anonyme Syrienne (Arab countries)
S.C. Societe en Commandite (Belgium, France, Luxembourg)
S.C.A. Societe Cooperativa Agricole (France, Italy, Luxembourg)
S.C.I. Sociedad Cooperativa Ilimitada (Spain)
S.C.L. Sociedad Cooperativa Limitada (Spain)
S.C.R.L. Societe Cooperative a Responsabilite Limitee (Belgium)
Sdn. Bhd. Sendirian Berhad (Malaysia)
SEK Swedish krona
SGD Singapore dollar
Sdn. Bhd. Sendirian Berhad (Malaysia)
S.L. Sociedad Limitada (Latin America (except Brazil), Portugal, Spain)
S/L Salgslag (Norway)
S.N.C. Société en Nom Collectif (France)
Soc. Sociedad (Latin America (except Brazil), Spain)
Soc. Sociedade (Brazil, Portugal)
Soc. Societa (Italy)
S.p.A. Società per Azioni (Italy)
Sp. z.o.o. Spólka z ograniczona odpowiedzialnoscia (Poland)
S.R.L. Sociedad de Responsabilidad Limitada (Spain, Mexico, Latin America [except Brazil])
S.R.L. Società a Responsabilità Limitata (Italy)
S.R.O. Spolecnost s Rucenim Omezenym (Czechoslovakia
S.S.K. Sherkate Sahami Khass (Iran)
Ste. Societe (France, Belgium, Luxembourg, Switzerland)
Ste. Cve. Societe Cooperative(Belgium)
S.V. Samemwerkende Vennootschap (Belgium)
S.Z.R.L. Societe Zairoise a Responsabilite Limitee (Zaire)

T

THB Thai baht
TND Tunisian dinar
TRL Turkish lira
TWD new Taiwan dollar

U

U.A. Uitgesloten Aansporakeiijkheid (Netherlands)
u.p.a. utan personligt ansvar (Sweden)

V

VAG Verein der Arbeitgeber (Austria, Germany)
VEB Venezuelan bolivar
VERTR Vertriebs (Austria, Germany)
VND Vietnamese dong
V.O.f. Vennootschap onder firma (Netherlands)
VVAG Versicherungsverein auf Gegenseitigkeit (Austria, Germany)

W–Z

WA Wettelika Aansprakalikhaed (Netherlands)
WLL With Limited Liability (Bahrain, Kuwait, Qatar, Saudi Arabia)
YK Yugen Kaisha (Japan)
ZAO Zakrytoe Aktsionernoe Obshchestve (Russia)
ZAR South African rand
ZMK Zambian kwacha
ZWD Zimbabwean dollar

Actuant Corporation

13000 West Silver Spring Drive
Butler, Wisconsin 53007
U.S.A.
Telephone: (414) 352-4160
Fax: (414) 247-5550
Web site: http://www.actuant.com

Public Company
Incorporated: 1910 as American Grinder and Manufacturing Company
Employees: 7,500
Sales: $1.45 billion (2007)
Stock Exchanges: New York
Ticker Symbol: ATU
NAIC: 326199 All Other Plastics Product Manufacturing; 332439 Other Metal Container Manufacturing; 332999 All Other Miscellaneous Fabricated Metal Product Manufacturing; 335999 All Other Miscellaneous Electrical Equipment and Component Manufacturing; 326291 Rubber Product Manufacturing for Mechanical Use; 332912 Fluid Power Valve and Hose Fitting Manufacturing; 333515 Cutting Tool and Machine Tool Accessory Manufacturing; 333995 Fluid Power Cylinder and Actuator Manufacturing; 333996 Fluid Power Pump and Motor Manufacturing; 336399 All Other Motor Vehicle Parts Manufacturing; 336413 Other Aircraft Parts and Auxiliary Equipment Manufacturing

■ ■ ■

Actuant Corporation is a global manufacturer of niche consumer and industrial products. Originally part of Applied Power Inc., Actuant was known as APW Industrial until the 2000 spinoff that separated the industrial business from APW Electronics Ltd., a maker of electronics enclosures. Actuant possesses a large stable of brand names, including Acme Electric, Enerpac, Kwikee, Milwaukee Cylinder, Gardner Bender, and Power-Packer. The company has manufacturing operations in the United States, Europe, and Asia and has grown its international distribution through acquisitions. Nearly half of its sales were coming from outside the United States by 2007. Europe was its second largest market, accounting for 39 percent of its business. Key markets are tools for do-it-yourselfers, bolting products for the energy industry, convertible tops and recreational vehicle (RV) products, and electrical components for the boating industry.

EARLY HISTORY: HAND TOOLS AND ENGINE PUMPS

The company that would one day be known as Actuant Corporation was founded in 1910 in Milwaukee, Wisconsin. The company got its start as American Grinder and Manufacturing Company, a producer of hand grinders that sharpened tools used in agriculture and other fields. The company's advertisements claimed that its products were suitable for use in "Ship Yards, Construction Work, Lumber Camps, Mining and Engineering, Signal and Line Repair Work, Machine Shops, Garages, etc." When the United States entered World War I, American Grinder began to manufacture water and oil pumps for use in engines that powered trucks and other military vehicles. At the end of the war, the company decided to continue its manufacture of

> **COMPANY PERSPECTIVES**
>
> Our global diversity is a critical advantage as we seek to deliver consistent future growth. This diversity protects Actuant from the ups and downs of individual markets, geographies or customers. It also allows us to participate in many areas of the world that are growing more rapidly than the United States.

these products, offering them to the general automotive market that was then beginning to take root and grow.

By the end of its first decade, American Grinder had expanded its line to include hand tools as well as pumps, a move made at the behest of the company's distributor. For this new line, American Grinder chose the trade name "Blackhawk," in reference to the Blackhawk Army Division, which had fought with distinction in World War I. The line's logo featured an arrowhead with the silhouette of an Indian and the slogan "Service, Quality, Finish." Many of the tools sold, such as sets of socket wrenches in different sizes, were designed for use in automobile repairs.

BLACKHAWK REPUTATION GROWS

After American Grinder chose to call its engine pumps and mechanic's tools Blackhawk, this trade name began to establish a reputation in the automotive field. In 1925 American Grinder officially changed its company name to Blackhawk, and, shortly thereafter, the company sold its line of tool grinders, as it reoriented itself toward the automobile industry. Eventually, however, Blackhawk water pumps were made obsolete, as car manufacturers began to include this equipment in their vehicles as a matter of course.

After discontinuing its pump operations, Blackhawk sought out a replacement business. In 1927 the company purchased a small hydraulic jack manufacturer, the Hydraulic Tool Company, in Los Angeles, California, which fit the bill. After acquiring these operations, Blackhawk marketed the Hydraulic Tool Company's products under the Blackhawk trade name.

As Blackhawk grew, its products gained a wider reputation, and its trade name became known across the country. In the late 1920s, Blackhawk expanded its line further when a snowplow manufacturer asked the company to help it develop a hydraulic pump to replace the hand winch then used to raise and lower the plow. In response to this request, Blackhawk developed a hydraulic system, made up of a hand pump, a long bending hose, and a hydraulic cylinder, which it marketed under the name Power-Packer. This line was soon expanded to include other remote-control hydraulic systems for use in different kinds of equipment. By the end of the 1920s, the company's logo—placed on its expanded line of products—had evolved to feature an Indian's profile in a large feathered headdress, placed inside an abstract representation of an arrowhead.

In the mid-1930s Blackhawk further expanded its product offerings when it used the technology developed for use in snow plows to make products for the collision repair market. Calling this line "Porto-Power," Blackhawk marketed hydraulic tools to be used in repairing auto bodies. The Porto-Power line featured a set of pumps and cylinders, with a variety of attachments that could be used to perform different pulling, pushing, and straightening tasks to fix damaged cars. In the late 1930s, Blackhawk marketed its Porto-Power line of products to a wider pool of customers, offering them for use in industrial and construction fields, through various distributors. The company tailored its products to different tasks and industries, creating special pumps and cylinders that could be used as building blocks for different applications.

INTERNATIONAL EXPANSION IN THE POSTWAR ERA

In 1955 Blackhawk sold its original line of hand tools, as its business evolved away from that area into more complicated systems. Late in that decade, the company decided to further restructure itself to provide more definition for each of its different parts. The two lines of products, Blackhawk and Power-Packer, became separate business units within the company. In 1960 the company's industrial and construction lines were set apart and given the name Enerpac in an effort to strengthen their identity within their respective markets.

Also in 1960, Blackhawk began an effort to expand its markets beyond the borders of the United States. Although its products had long been sold in other countries through importers and distributors, Blackhawk began to set up its own direct overseas operations, to both sell and manufacture goods. Its first targets for growth were the United Kingdom and continental Europe.

BLACKHAWK EXPANDS UNDER NEW NAME

In 1961 Blackhawk changed its corporate name to Applied Power Industries, Inc., in an effort to better reflect

KEY DATES

1910: Company is founded in Milwaukee, Wisconsin.
1925: Company changes its name to Blackhawk.
1927: Hydraulic Tool Company, a maker of hydraulic jacks, is purchased.
1955: Company sells its original line of hand tools.
1960: Foreign expansion is stepped up with the establishment of the first direct overseas operations; Europe is the first area targeted for growth.
1961: Company changes its name to Applied Power Industries, Inc.
1973: Company changes its name to Applied Power Inc.
1985: Richard G. Sim, a former General Electric Company executive, is brought in as president and CEO; revenues reach $100 million.
1986: The Blackhawk automotive division is sold to Hein-Werner Company.
1987: Company goes public through an IPO, with a listing on the NASDAQ.
1989: Company engineers a $147 million hostile takeover of Barry Wright Corporation, maker of electronic control equipment; revenues increase to $245 million.
1992: In a recessionary environment, company reports loss of $24.4 million.
1993: Stock begins trading on the New York Stock Exchange.
1995: Revenues surpass $500 million for the first time.
1998: Company acquires VERO Group plc for $191.7 million, ZERO Corporation for $386 million, and Rubicon Group plc for $371 million; revenues surpass $1 billion for the first time.
1999: A restructuring organizes the company's operations into two segments: APW Electronics and APW Industrial.
2000: APW Electronics spun off as APW Ltd.; APW Industrial begins trading as Actuant Corporation.
2005: Purchase of Key Components, Inc., adds Gits, Marinco, Acme, and Elliott brands.
2006: Multiyear buying spree helps push post-spinoff revenues past $1 billion.

the different aspects of its operations. In the 1960s the company expanded through acquisitions of other companies in its field. In January 1966 it bought Rivett, Inc., and two years later, Applied Power purchased Branick Manufacturing, Inc. In 1969 the company acquired the Big Four division of the Studebaker Company. In May 1970 Applied Power added the operations of the Bear Manufacturing Company, and later that year, the company added another business unit to its corporate profile, taking over the Marquette Corporation. This company was a maker of diagnostic systems and service equipment, including products designed especially for use with batteries, for automobiles.

Also in 1970, Applied Power increased its geographical scope further when it opened a subsidiary in the Netherlands. This trend continued the following year, when Applied Power made a number of purchases that increased its international holdings. The company acquired Bear Equipment & Services, Ltd., of Scarborough, Canada, and renamed it Applied Power Automotive Canada, Ltd. In addition, Applied Power bought 80 percent of two French companies, Matairco, which eventually became a separate business unit of its parent company, and Société-Hydro-Air S.a.r.L. Three years later, Applied Power increased its stake in these properties to 100 percent.

Applied Power Industries became Applied Power Inc. in January 1973. Following the simplification of its name, Applied Power also streamlined its corporate structure and operations, shedding businesses that did not fit with its larger corporate identity, or that were not as profitable as others. In 1975 the company sold Hydralique Gury S.A. to a group of French investors for $2.1 million. Five years later, the company divested itself of its Bear Wheel Service and Marquette Engine Diagnostic Equipment Product Lines, reaping $8 million.

In 1981 Applied Power added another major brand group when it purchased Electro-Flo, Inc. This company supplemented Applied Power's Power-Packer unit in providing specialized hydraulic products for use in the manufacture of other kinds of heavy equipment. Electro-Flo used electronic controls of hydraulic systems to enable precise movement and positioning of machinery. Electro-Flo technology, which included microprocessors, flow control valves, and electronic sensors, was used in the precise laying of asphalt by road-reconditioning equipment and in the movement of booms on materials-handling machinery.

ACQUISITIONS FOR GROWTH

By 1985, Applied Power's 75th year in business, the company had become a solid operation closely held by the members of its founding family. Lacking new blood, however, the company had begun to stagnate. While its operations returned a steady profit, the company had ceased growing. In an effort to remedy this situation and increase Applied Power's financial returns, company leaders brought an outside executive aboard, hiring Richard G. Sim, a former General Electric Company executive, as president and CEO.

Among the first steps taken in the mid-1980s were a series of acquisitions. The company bought the half of the Toyo Hydraulic Equipment Company which it did not already own and also added Electro-Hydraulic Controls, Inc., for which it paid $2.6 million in cash. In 1986 Applied Power divested itself of one of its core businesses—and the line of products with the longest heritage of any made by the company—when it sold its Blackhawk automotive division to the Hein-Werner Company for $9.3 million. One year later, in August 1987, the newly defined Applied Power offered stock to the public for the first time, tendering 1.8 million shares, which traded on the NASDAQ. With the proceeds from this sale, the company moved to reduce part of the debt it had amassed through its long string of acquisitions. At the end of 1987, Applied Power reported a loss of $1.6 million.

In 1988 Applied Power returned to its roots, reentering the field that had launched the company decades before, when it purchased a manufacturer of hand tools, Garner-Bender, Inc., for $31.4 million. This company was subsequently renamed GB Electrical, Inc.

The next year, Applied Power made its most ambitious purchase to date, when it engineered the hostile takeover of the Barry Wright Corporation for $147 million. This purchase doubled the size of Allied Power and increased its debt sixfold. Barry Wright, an ailing manufacturer based in Watertown, Massachusetts, made equipment for use in computer rooms and devices that controlled vibration. The company's earnings had dropped in the previous year from $8.4 million to $1.3 million as sales stagnated. Applied Power's executives hoped that their acquisition could come to dominate certain niche markets profitably. Such previous successes helped Applied Power post sales of $245 million in 1989, up from $100 million just four years earlier.

RESTRUCTURING FOR STABILITY

In integrating Barry Wright with the rest of its operations, Applied Power faced a challenging task—it sought to streamline Barry Wright's product line and cut its manufacturing costs. The first of the new acquisition's units to face the ax was Barry Wright's Wright Line division, a maker of furnishings and enclosures for technical environments. Applied Power attempted to sell this business in 1992, taking a $25 million write-down charge, but ended up selling only portions of it. These developments followed a year of lackluster results in 1991, when earnings fell to $12 million, hurt by the overall high costs of absorbing the Barry Wright operations and by a general recession. As a maker of tools for use in construction, Applied Power was hurt in particular by the slump in that industry. While its GB Electrical unit and its Enerpac operations continued to contribute strongly, another company unit, Apitech, which had been founded to develop high-tech valves and other equipment to improve automobile suspensions, continued to eat up millions of dollars in research and development costs.

This trend continued in 1992, as Applied Power reported a loss of $24.4 million. In an effort to strengthen its positions, Applied Power reorganized certain aspects of its operations, altering the structure of its Barry Controls division in California and changing the nature of its Power-Packer operations in Europe. In addition, the company moved forward aggressively in foreign markets, purchasing the remaining portions of its joint venture operations in Mexico and Germany. Anticipating dramatic growth in Asia, Applied Power hired a new executive to run its Asian operations in Korea and Japan, with the intention of intensifying marketing efforts in those countries.

This thrust toward foreign markets continued in 1993, as Applied Power entered into a joint project with the Detec Design and Industrie Company in Germany to manufacture hydraulic products. That year the company's stock moved from the NASDAQ to the New York Stock Exchange. Applied Power began recovering from its early 1990s doldrums in 1994, when it posted profits of $16.6 million, its best year since 1990. The following year, revenues surpassed the $500 million mark for the first time, and the company began pursuing larger acquisitions again. San Diego-based Vision Plastics Manufacturing Co. was acquired that year for $21.5 million. Vision was a producer of plastic cable ties that GB Electrical distributed. In early 1996 Applied Power spent about $10 million to acquire CalTerm Inc., a supplier of electrical products for do-it-yourself automotive repairs, based in El Cajon, California. Like

Vision, CalTerm fit in well alongside the GB Electrical unit.

THE RISE OF ELECTRONIC ENCLOSURES

The late 1990s were marked by Applied Power's rapid acquisition-led expansion into the electronic enclosure products and systems sector. Unlike many of the company's other businesses—including Enerpac, Barry Controls, and Power-Packer—which were cyclical in nature, the enclosures business was growth-oriented, expanding at an annual rate of 35 percent in the late 1990s. The enclosures sector also offered higher margins than other Applied Power sectors, and was a highly fragmented industry, rife for consolidation. Applied Power set out to be the enclosure consolidator.

Ironically, given that the company had attempted to sell it in 1992, Wright Line was Applied Power's entrance into this sector. By the mid-1990s Wright Line had sales of $95 million, representing about 18 percent of overall sales, and was one of Applied Power's fastest-growing and most profitable units. The company then made a number of acquisitions in the late 1990s, most of which were enclosure-related. In September 1996 Applied Power completed its largest purchase since 1989 when it spent $52 million for Everest Electronic Equipment, Inc., a maker of custom and standard electronic enclosures based in Anaheim, California. For the fiscal year ending in August 1997, Applied Power posted revenues of $672.3 million, 28 percent of which was generated by the company's enclosure products and systems unit.

ACQUISITIONS TO BROADEN PRODUCT LINES

Applied Power acquired Racine, Wisconsin-based Versa Technologies, Inc., (Versa/Tek) in October 1997 for $141 million. Versa/Tek included several businesses, some of which fit in with Applied Power's engineered solutions unit, which included Barry Controls and Power-Packer. These were Power Gear, maker of hydraulic leveling systems for the RV market; and Mox-Med, which made silicone rubber products for medical equipment. Other Versa/Tek units included Milwaukee Cylinder, a maker of hydraulic cylinders that fit alongside Enerpac and the company's tools and supplies division; and Eder Industries, a maker of electronic control systems for a variety of industries. Eder Industries had synergies with both the engineered solutions and the enclosures segments, but was initially placed within engineered solutions.

Applied Power next acquired VERO Group plc in June 1998 for $191.7 million (fending off a competing bid by Pentair, Inc.) and ZERO Corporation the following month in a merger valued at $386 million. Based in the United Kingdom, VERO manufactured electronic enclosures and related products, including racks, backplanes, and power supplies. VERO, which in 1997 had sales of $170 million and earnings of $17 million, helped Applied Power broaden its line of products in the European market.

ZERO, which was based in Los Angeles and had 1997 revenues of $260 million, was also active in the electronic enclosures market; its system packaging, thermal management, and engineered cases served the telecommunication, instrumentation, and data-processing markets. These major acquisitions helped increase Applied Power's fiscal 1998 revenues to $1.23 billion, an increase of 37 percent over 1997 results. The company's enclosure products segment was its largest segment, accounting for 39 percent of overall sales. Net income for 1998 was reduced to $26.7 million because of a $52.6 million charge relating to acquisition costs, plant consolidations, and other restructuring costs.

TOP SUPPLIER STATUS ACHIEVED

In September 1998 Applied Power completed its third major enclosure acquisition in the span of four months, with the $371.5 million purchase of U.K.-based Rubicon Group plc, one of the leading manufacturers of electronic enclosures in Europe. Rubicon brought to Applied Power a new segment of the enclosure market—automated teller machines (ATMs)—and it manufactured safes, the surrounding enclosure, and other ATM component parts as well as providing assembly services. With this latest acquisition, Applied Power was the number one worldwide supplier of custom electronic enclosures, a position it had attained in an astonishingly short period.

In early 1999 the company received another boost when it landed a ten-year, $200 million contract to supply electronic enclosure systems for wireless base station equipment to Sweden-based Telefonaktiebolaget LM Ericsson. Applied Power announced a restructuring of its operations in May of that year, which involved the organizing of its operations into two segments: APW Electronics and APW Industrial. The former included all of the enclosure products and systems businesses along with McLean Thermal Management and Eder Industries. Applied Power's remaining operations, including most of its engineered solutions and tools and supplies units were grouped within APW Industrial. For the fiscal year ending in August 1999, APW Electronics generated $1.06 billion in revenues (60 percent of overall revenues), while APW Industrial contributed

$696 million. Overall profits reached a record $79.4 million.

2000 SPINOFF

APW Electronics was spun off as APW Ltd. in July 2000. To remove any confusion in the mind of the investing public, the company's remaining unit, APW Industrial, began trading under the name Actuant Corporation. It was formally renamed in fiscal 2001.

Although the electronics unit, APW Ltd., was formed in order to reap the benefits of the "new economy," the tech sector soon crashed, prompting the newly independent company to declare bankruptcy in March 2002. A Los Angeles investment group, Oaktree Capital Management, bought APW a few months later.

Meanwhile, Actuant was preparing to enter a growth period as it acquired or built up an array of thriving niche businesses. Revenues for the 2000 fiscal year were $681 million, when the company recorded net earnings of $67.1 million. It would take a couple of years for figures to return to these levels.

Under the guidance of new CEO Robert C. Arzbaecher, the company held an initial public offering in February 2002, taking in $99 million. Most of this was earmarked toward paying down the $451 million debt it had had since the spinoff of APW Ltd. Revenues slipped from $482 million to $463 million in fiscal 2002, as the company posted a net loss of $2.6 million after earning $23.6 million the previous year.

Acquisitions continued with the 2001 purchase of Dewald Manufacturing Inc., a Mishawaka, Indiana, manufacturer of RV slideout systems. Dewald's revenues were about $20 million a year. Actuant also ditched some operations, divesting its Mox-Med and Quick Mold Change operations during the year.

Actuant further bolstered its RV business by buying Kwikee Power Products Co. in September 2003. Kwikee, based in Cottage Grove, Oregon, produced slide-outs, levelers, and step systems. It had 115 employees; sales were about $24 million a year. Actuant paid $30 million for the unit.

In fiscal 2003 Actuant bought a majority holding in Heinrich Kopp A.G. for $17 million. Kopp, headquartered near Frankfurt, Germany, made electrical supplies and had 1,200 employees in several countries. Actuant continued to build its European business by adding a Netherlands-based hardware supplier, Dresco B.V., the next year. The price was $30 million.

Revenues continued their steady climb, reaching $585.4 million in 2003 and $726.9 million the next year. By 2005 they were up to $976.1 million and Actuant was virtually a $1 billion company again.

A KEY ACQUISITION IN 2005

Actuant's typical acquisition cost less than $50 million, but the company did splurge on the $315 million purchase of Key Components, Inc., in 2005. This brought a handful of brands to the stable: Gits (air handling components/turbochargers), Marinco, Acme (power distribution products and engineered aerospace/defense products), B.W. Elliott (flexible shafts), and Turner Electric. Key was based in Tarrytown, New York.

Actuant then added Hauppauge, New York's A.W. Sperry Instruments, Inc., a 35-person outfit making electrical test equipment. The cost was $12.5 million. In 2005 Actuant also augmented its Enerpac unit with the acquisition of Hedley Purvis Holdings, Ltd., whose operating companies produced torque wrenches and other specialized tools.

Hydratight Sweeney Ltd., formerly part of Dover Corp.'s Waukesha Bearings Corp. unit, was added toward the end of fiscal 2005 at a cost of $93 million. It made bolting products for power plants and chemical facilities and had several manufacturing facilities around the world.

Other acquisitions in fiscal 2005 included Paris-based Yvel S.A., acquired early in the year for $9 million. Yvel made hydraulic latches used in tractor-trailer cabs, a complement to Actuant's existing Power-Packer line.

ACQUISITIONS TO DIVERSIFY BUSINESS IN 2006

The pace of acquisitions continued in fiscal 2006 with the addition of D.L. Ricci, which made portable machining equipment for the energy industry. Based in Red Wing, Minnesota, Ricci had annual sales of $25 million and 75 employees.

Precision Sure-Lock, maker of products used in concrete construction, was acquired at a cost of $43 million. It had sales of $25 million and a 75-person workforce. Another 2006 purchase was Actown Electrocoil, Inc., a Spring Grove, Illinois, manufacturer of transformers and coils, acquired for $24 million. Actown had $36 million sales and 300 employees.

Actuant continued to evolved by developing new niches. In 2006, it bought B.E.P. Marine Limited of Auckland, New Zealand, which made electrical components for the marine industry and had annual sales of $10 million. Actuant paid $8 million plus a performance-based incentive. The next year, it paid $30 million for BH Electronics (BHE), a producer of electronic assemblies for boats. Based in Munford, Tennessee, the company had 450 employees and annual revenues of about $35 million. Actuant was planning to introduce some of its boating products into new sectors such as RVs.

Total revenues were up to $1.2 billion in 2006 and were still growing at a double-digit rate. Net income was $92.6 million. Sales rose 21 percent in fiscal 2007 to $1.5 billion as net earnings passed the $100 million mark. Although high costs at the operations in Europe prompted a restructuring there, Actuant continued to buy smaller companies in fiscal 2007.

ACQUISITIONS IN 2007

Actuant complemented its Hydratight business by adding Injectaseal Deutschland GmbH for about $13 million. Based in Kerpen, Germany, Injectaseal specialized in leak management services for the energy industry. It had annual revenues of about $10 million.

Maxima Technologies, a Lancaster, Pennsylvania-based electronic instrumentation specialist, was acquired at a cost of about $91 million. Maxima had 500 employees and annual revenues of $65 million.

Actuant continued to invest in Europe, buying T.T. Fijnmechanica (TTF) for $20 million. Based in Holland, TTF produced heavy-duty lifts used in construction. Actuant bought another Dutch company during the year, Veha Haaksbergen B.V., a small ($5 million) maker of hydraulic cylinders.

In September 2007 Actuant acquired hydraulic pump and tool manufacturer Templeton Kenly of Illinois for $48 million. This added the Simplex, Uni-Lift, and Pow'r Riser brands to the stable. Templeton Kenly had 120 employees and sales exceeding $30 million a year.

In just a few years since the spinoff, Actuant's market capitalization had increased from $113 million to more than $1.8 billion, and the company was aiming to double in size within five years. Its many acquisitions had raised its total debt level to $561.7 million. Actuant projected sales to rise 20 percent to $1.6 billion in fiscal 2008.

Elizabeth Rourke
Updated, David E. Salamie; Frederick C. Ingram

PRINCIPAL SUBSIDIARIES

Actuant China Ltd.; New England Controls, Inc.; Nielsen Hardware Corporation; Atlantic Guest, Inc.; Kwikee Products Company, LLC; Versa Technologies, Inc.; Actuant France SA; Pivicat SAS (France); Yvel S.A. (France); Barry Controls GmbH (Germany); Brunnquell GmbH (Germany); Condor Installationstechnik GmbH (Germany); Heinrich Kopp GmbH (Germany); Injectaseal Deutschland GmbH (Germany); Kopp Properties KG (Germany); Dresco BV (Netherlands); T.T. Fijnmechanica BV (Netherlands); Veha Haaksbergen BV (Netherlands); A.W. Sperry Instruments, Inc.; Acme Electric Corporation; BW Elliott Mfg. Co., LLC; Gits Mfg. Co. LLC; Key Components, Inc.; Hypur-Mate Norge AS (Norway); Maxima Technologies; BH Electronics; Amveco Magnetics, Inc.; HEKO Electrotechnique SARL (Tunisia); Ergun Kriko San, AA (Turkey); Hedley Purvis Group Ltd. (U.K.); Hevilift Limited (U.K.); Hydratight Sweeney Ltd. (U.K.); Pertesco Ltd (U.K.); Columbus Manufacturing, LLC; Enerpac Corp.; GB Tools and Supplies, Inc.

PRINCIPAL DIVISIONS

Industrial; Electrical; Actuation Systems; Engineered Products.

PRINCIPAL OPERATING UNITS

Enerpac; Hydratight; Simplex; Injectaseal; Precision Sure-Lock, LP; Gardner Bender; Kopp; Dresco; Marinco; Ancor; BH Electronics; BEP Marine; Guest; Power-Packer; Power Gear; Kwikee; Gits Mfg. Co.; Elliott; Maxima Technologies; Nielsen Sessions; Turner Electric LLC; Acme Electric Corporation—Aerospace Division.

PRINCIPAL COMPETITORS

Eaton Corporation; Parker Hannifin Corporation; The Stanley Works; Steelcase Inc.; Kennametal Inc.

FURTHER READING

"Actuant Completes Public Offering," *Business Journal of Milwaukee,* February 15, 2002.

"Actuant Finalizes $93M Purchase of Hydratight Sweeney," *Business Journal of Milwaukee,* May 18, 2005.

"Actuant Plans European Restructuring; Shares Plunge," *Business Journal of Milwaukee,* June 20, 2006.

Byrne, Harlan S., "Applied Power: Struggling Past a Big Acquisition," *Barron's,* October 12, 1992.

Content, Thomas, "Actuant to Delay Its Annual Report: SEC Wants More Data; Auto Parts Maker Says Sales, Income Numbers Won't Change," *Milwaukee Journal Sentinel,* November 17, 2006.

Daykin, Tom, "Applied Power Has Value, Growth Potential, Analyst Says," *Milwaukee Journal Sentinel,* October 5, 1998, p. 10.

———, "Applied Power Sells New Headquarters," *Milwaukee Journal Sentinel,* December 1, 1999, p. 2.

———, "Applied Power to Buy British Company: Butler-Based Company to Pay $347.8 Million for One of Europe's Largest Manufacturers of Electronic Enclosures," *Milwaukee Journal Sentinel,* September 2, 1998, p. 1.

Gallun, Alby, "Airline Business Propels Applied Power," *Business Journal-Milwaukee,* September 19, 1997, p. 1.

———, "Applied Power at Crossroads After Spinoff," *Business Journal-Milwaukee,* February 18, 2000, p. 5.

———, "Applied Power Continues Binge of Acquisitions," *Business Journal-Milwaukee,* December 12, 1997, p. 9.

———, "Applied Power to Take $52.6 Million Charge," *Business Journal-Milwaukee,* October 2, 1998, p. 3.

Harlin, Kevin, "Actuant Seeks Out Niches to Make It Big Fish in Pond," *Investor's Business Daily,* July 10, 2007.

Hawkins, Lee, Jr., "Applied Power Lands 10-Year Deal Worth More Than $200 Million," *Milwaukee Journal Sentinel,* February 25, 1999, p. 7.

Holley, Paul, "A Selective Applied Power Goes on the Prowl Again," *Business Journal-Milwaukee,* May 4, 1996, p. 5.

Kirchen, Rich, "Applied's Mathematics: Manufacturer Figures to Be 'On Way Back,'" *Business Journal-Milwaukee,* July 9, 1994, p. 1.

Kurowski, Jeff, "RV Supplier Actuant Acquires Competitor Dewald," *RV Business,* May 2001, p. 10.

———, "Supplier Actuant Acquires Kwikee," *RV Business,* November 2003, p. 103.

Rovito, Rich, "Actuant Morphs into Swan," *Business Journal-Milwaukee,* October 10, 2003, pp. A1f.

———, "Actuant, MSOE Pair Up to Teach Lean Principles," *Business Journal of Milwaukee,* March 24, 2006.

Savage, Mark, "Applied Power Boosts Bid for British Company," *Milwaukee Journal Sentinel,* May 13, 1998, p. 1.

———, "Applied Power Deal Lures Competitor," *Milwaukee Journal Sentinel,* May 6, 1998, p. 1.

———, "Applied Power Sets $52 Million Deal," *Milwaukee Journal Sentinel,* August 29, 1996, p. 1.

———, "Applied Power to Buy ZERO Corp.," *Milwaukee Journal Sentinel,* April 7, 1998, p. 1.

Serant, Claire, "APW Prepares for Spinoff," *Electronic Buyers' News,* February 21, 2000, p. 84.

Sharma-Jensen, Geeta, "Applied Power Agrees to Deal," *Milwaukee Journal Sentinel,* September 4, 1997, p. 1.

Alfred Kärcher GmbH & Co KG

Alfred-Kärcher-Strasse 28-40
Winnenden, D-71364
Germany
Telephone: (49 7195) 14-0
Fax: (49 7195) 14-2212
Web site: http://www.kaercher.com

Private Company
Incorporated: 1935 as Maschinenfabrik Alfred Kärcher
Employees: 6,591
Sales: EUR 1.4 billion ($1.9 billion) (2007)
NAIC: 333319 Other Commercial and Service Industry Machinery Manufacturing; 335212 Household Vacuum Cleaner Manufacturing

■ ■ ■

Alfred Kärcher GmbH & Co KG bills itself as the world's largest manufacturer of cleaning devices, equipment, and accessories for commercial, industrial, and domestic use. Kärcher leads the world market for high-pressure washers, which are used outdoors, mainly for cleaning vehicles and buildings. The company also makes vacuum and steam cleaners, sweepers and scrubber-driers, vehicle washers, and industrial cleaning equipment. In addition, the company supplies cleaning agents, makes water pumps for domestic use, and provides equipment for the treatment of waste and drinking water and decontamination equipment for the military. Kärcher production plants are located in Germany, Italy, the United States, Mexico, Brazil, Romania, and China. Primary markets include the United States, Germany, and France; consumer products sales account for roughly half of Kärcher's total business. Headquartered in Winnenden near Stuttgart in Germany, Kärcher is owned by Johannes Kärcher and Susanne Zimmermann von Siefart, the son and daughter of Alfred Kärcher, who founded the enterprise in 1935.

INDUSTRIAL SALT SMELTERS AND AIR HEATERS

Alfred Kärcher joined his father's sales agency in Stuttgart-Bad Cannstatt in southwestern Germany in 1924 with a master's degree in engineering from Stuttgart Technical University. Putting his newly acquired skills to work right away, the 23-year-old soon transformed the business into an engineering firm. The young Kärcher was fascinated by technology and he devoted his exceptionally inventive mind and technical problem-solving abilities to two overriding subjects: water and fire; or, more specifically, the use of water and fire in heating and cleaning.

Among his first engineering projects were industrial laundering equipment, industrial boilers, and water purification equipment. In the early 1930s Kärcher began to focus on the design of electrically heated basins for industrial use. In 1934 the German airline Lufthansa asked Kärcher to develop a device for warming up airplane motors in the wintertime.

In addition to his technical genius, Kärcher had the vision of a successful businessman. Encouraged by the contracts he had received, the entrepreneurially minded inventor foresaw the market potential of his creations and founded his own industrial heating equipment

COMPANY PERSPECTIVES

In terms of quality and technology we are the world's leading provider of cleaning systems, cleaning products and services for recreation, household, trade and industry. Our products enable our customers to solve their cleaning tasks in an economical and environmentally-friendly manner. We have extremely satisfied and enthusiastic customers!

company in Bad Cannstatt in 1935. Funded with seed capital from Kärcher's father, who remained a partner in the firm until his death in 1938, the firm began to manufacture the electric heaters and custom-designed heating equipment Kärcher developed. His first "best-sellers" were industrial salt smelters—huge salt bathtubs, up to 11 meters long, with an inbuilt electric heating system, which were used for firing up steel smelter furnaces and for electroplating.

Kärcher patented the Kärcher Salt-Bath Furnace, an optimized standard version of a hardening furnace for alloys. Kärcher engaged the Frankfurt am Main-based gold and silver refinery Degussa to produce the furnace. The license deal provided the cash necessary to acquire a large industrial site with spacious production halls, warehouses and storage areas in Winnenden, about 15 miles northeast of Stuttgart, where Kärcher relocated his company to in 1939.

Within two short years, Kärcher and his engineers developed a production-ready model of a new kind of gasoline-fueled hot-air heater for Lufthansa, to be produced in Winnenden. Engine and cabin heaters for aircraft became one of Kärcher's mainstay products for many years. During World War II the company also developed and manufactured atomizing nozzles for high-performance engines, impact burners, and vehicle trailers.

HEATING KITCHENS, CARS, AND AIRCRAFT

After World War II, which left the company premises undamaged, Kärcher and his remaining staff of 40 once again proved their creativity. They took whatever materials they could acquire and turned them into items that were in high demand at the time. They made round iron ovens and heater coverings from artillery shells, and sieves, large paper trays, containers, and a variety of metal kitchen stoves from spare metal parts. Demand for such basic goods was high from refugees who had fled in large numbers from the easternmost regions of the former Germany.

Until 1954, Kärcher also continued to produce vehicle trailers, small and large, from handcarts to canvas-covered trailers for passenger cars and trucks, which were in high demand during the postwar years in Germany. Because gasoline was scarce, however, many vehicles were fueled by gas generated from burning wood, for which Kärcher built special devices.

The second of Kärcher's major product lines in the second half of the 1940s and early 1950s was hot-air heaters of different kinds and sizes. Kärcher put out stationary and portable models designed to heat any enclosed space, from small rooms to large halls. The company also continued to manufacture aircraft motor and cabin heaters, for the U.S. military administration. During the 1950s Kärcher's engineers adapted their heating know-how to other vehicles as well. In 1951 Kärcher launched an air heater for buses and designed a cabin heating system for the popular Volkswagen Käfer passenger car, which was introduced in 1952. Four years later the company launched a mobile fresh-air heater that was used in construction, industry, and agriculture for heating halls, livestock stalls, and buildings, as well as large tents and other temporary structures.

REINVENTING THE STEAM CLEANER

In the late 1940s Kärcher was approached by the U.S. occupation forces to help them fix the broken burners of the steam cleaners they were using. Fixing the appliances was one thing. Alfred Kärcher, however, placed every piece of the technology from the 1920s under scrutiny and decided to build a much improved version for the German market. By 1950 Kärcher had developed and patented his own brand of hot-water high-pressure cleaner. The burners, pumps, and security features incorporated into the new design were much simpler and the highest operating temperature was pushed below the boiling point.

Although the presentation of his invention at the 1951 Hannover Trade Fair did not generate much interest, Alfred Kärcher foresaw its future market potential. Consequently, he continued to invest in the further development of the technology, creating a variety of prototypes for different uses. Kärcher's vision proved correct; the technology he had developed would be a fundamental element of many generations of Kärcher high-pressure cleaners. Yet, it took much longer than he had expected for the market to develop—so long, in fact, that Alfred Kärcher was not able to witness it

KEY DATES

1935: Engineer Alfred Kärcher establishes an industrial heating equipment company.
1939: The company is relocated to Winnenden near Stuttgart.
1950: Kärcher introduces high-pressure hot-water cleaners in Europe.
1962: The company establishes a subsidiary in France.
1974: High-pressure washers become the company's major focus.
1980: Strategic decision to concentrate on cleaning equipment.
1982: The company sets up Alfred Karcher, Inc., in the United States.
1984: Kärcher launches the world's first portable high-pressure washer for consumers.
1989: Kärcher develops its first car wash for passenger cars.
1993: The company adds consumer appliances for use indoors to its product line.
2003: Kärcher introduces an automatic cleaning robot for private homes.
2007: The company launches a range of water pumps for domestic use.

himself. In the fall of 1959 the company founder died from a heart attack at age 58. By that time his enterprise employed a workforce of over 250 and generated DEM 7 million in annual revenues.

NEW COMPANY LEADERSHIP

After the company founder's death, his wife Irene took on the responsibility for managing the family business. Under her leadership Kärcher made the transition from a manufacturer of mainly industrial heating equipment to cleaning devices for both commercial clients and consumers. However, the demand for the company's high-pressure cleaners increased only slowly at first, and the company looked for alternatives.

One of Kärcher's main product lines of the 1960s was steam generators for use in a broad variety of industries. In construction they were useful for warming up various materials in the wintertime; in transportation they heated up diesel locomotives; in agriculture they were used for preparing the soil in large greenhouses. Steam generators were also used in the textile industry for fabric dying and commercial laundering. Most were mounted on trailers with wheels. Other models had runners and could be used outdoors in the wintertime, for example, to melt the ice in sewers.

In addition to marketing steam generators and fresh-air heaters, Kärcher ventured into several new markets in the 1960s and early 1970s. The company's product line of that era included equipment for cleaning large containers, casings for the construction industry, boats, and even playground equipment made from plastics.

SPECIALIZING IN CLEANING EQUIPMENT

Demand for Kärcher's high-pressure cleaners increased significantly in the early 1970s. In 1974 Kärcher's management decided to focus its efforts on the product line that Alfred Kärcher had seen as one of high strategic importance 15 years earlier: high-pressure cleaners. The company offered different models for various purposes. The principle, however, was the same. Water is put under high pressure using a pump, and sprayed out in a focused stream through a portable nozzle. In addition, in a hot-water high-pressure cleaner, the water is heated while passing through a boiler, where it is heated to a maximum of 302 degrees Fahrenheit. In the early 1970s, Kärcher's boiling-water high-pressure cleaners HDS 800 and HDS 1200 became very popular for vehicle cleaning. Later in the decade, the company's cold-water high-pressure cleaner, the HD 1000, which was mainly used in agriculture, was added to the product range.

For many years following the decision to focus on high-pressure cleaners, Kärcher enjoyed robust two-digit growth annually, growing more than 40 percent in peak years. In 1978 Kärcher discontinued the production of hot-air heaters. The company also stopped making steam generators, its main cash cow of the 1960s. In 1980 Kärcher's management made another far-reaching strategic decision. Convinced that cleaning appliances offered a very promising growth market, the company withdrew from most of its activities and concentrated solely on making devices for all kinds of cleaning purposes. Beginning in the 1980s Kärcher extended its line of commercial cleaning products to vacuum cleaners, spray-extraction cleaners, and street sweepers.

ENTERING THE CONSUMER MARKET

While the company's main focus during the 1970s and early 1980s was on the business-to-business market,

Kärcher ventured into the consumer market in 1984. Kärcher's engineers came up with the world's first portable high-pressure cleaner for private users, creating a market that had not previously existed. After Irene Kärcher's death in 1989, her son Johannes became managing partner. The company was reorganized into three business divisions, for commercial, industrial, and consumer products. In the years that followed, consumer products became more and more important for Kärcher.

Based on thorough market research that projected a market potential of one-quarter of all homeowners in Germany, the company targeted male homeowners with a variety of appliances for cleaning jobs around the house and the backyard. With the slogan "Cleaning like the pros," the company appealed to technology-savvy men to use Kärcher's high-pressure cleaners, which in the beginning were most popular for washing their cars. While high-pressure cleaners were pitched mainly to men, Kärcher began to target female consumers as well with a line of cleaning appliances for use indoors in 1993.

Kärcher later added a number of additional appliances for cleaning bathrooms, windows and carpets. To set them apart from existing products, however, Kärcher positioned itself as a provider of innovative and environmentally friendly solutions under the slogan "Cleaning without Chemicals." One of the company's early novelties was a battery-powered window cleaner.

CREATIVITY IN MARKETING

If short innovation cycles were one of Kärcher's hallmarks—its R&D department made sure that some four-fifths of the company's products were less than four years old—creative thinking did not stop there. Innovative, original marketing efforts became another major success factor for the company.

Kärcher's ad campaigns in home improvement and sports magazines, women's magazines, and TV guides promoted the idea that cleaning one's house or car could be fun, not drudgery, with Kärcher's innovative appliances. In the mid-1980s, a theater group toured Germany's home improvement outlets, with actors demonstrating that Kärcher products were effective and fun to use. Later the company offered special training for sales personnel and used video presentations and large displays along the shelves of large chain stores to educate consumers. In the second half of the 1990s Kärcher began selling its products via shopping TV in up to 15-minute infomercials.

Sports sponsorships began in the late 1980s, when Kärcher started supporting national league soccer teams. For example, when the sponsored VfB Stuttgart had a home game, dirty cars were driven into Stuttgart's Gottlieb-Daimler Stadium and rapidly cleaned by Kärcher men in bright yellow uniforms, which highlighted the new company color. Later the company sponsored a national league soccer team and the German ice skating association.

The company became most famous, however, for its spectacular cleaning of well-known landmarks without charge. In exchange for cleaning these sites, Kärcher received free worldwide media coverage. Kärcher's team of cleaners removed the grime from the world-famous Brandenburg Gate in then–East Berlin in 1990. The contract was still signed with the East German government. The company also scrubbed the statue of Christ overlooking Rio de Janeiro and the 284 columns of the Bernini colonnades on St. Peter's Square in Rome, a feat that earned Kärcher an entry in the *Guinness Book of Records.*

The company's marketing efforts paid off. In 1997 Kärcher received the German Marketing Award for its successful diversification strategy and entrance into the consumer market. Within just over a decade, the company's output of consumer appliances had grown 240-fold, from 5,000 in 1984 to 1.2 million in 1996. When asked if they knew the Kärcher brand, roughly eight out of ten German men and approximately two out of three German women answered "Yes" by the late 1990s. By that time, consumer product sales accounted for two-fifths of Kärcher's total revenues. At the Marketing Awards ceremony, Kärcher offered another taste of its creativity when a group of musicians used high-pressure cleaners to create a grooving sound.

MEETING CHALLENGES IN THE 21ST CENTURY

By 2000, Kärcher had grown to a large enterprise with about 5,000 employees generating roughly DEM 1 billion in sales. Although Germany was still the most important single market, the company had established 32 foreign subsidiaries. In the high-pressure cleaner segment, however, Kärcher's success attracted a growing number of competitors that offered similar devices for much less. Since their market introduction in 1984, prices for high-pressure cleaners for consumer use had decreased by more than four-fifths. To keep up with the aggressive nonbrand competition in the low-price segment, Kärcher regularly introduced new, less expensive models.

In 2001 Johannes Kärcher became head of Kärcher's administrative board, while and executive management team took over the day-to-day management of the company. To meet the challenges of an increasingly competitive environment, they focused on broadening Kärcher's product portfolio, on geographic expansion, particularly in the United States, and on creating new and innovative cleaning technologies and devices.

In the area of commercial cleaning products, Kärcher developed vehicle washers for cars, trucks, and buses which recycled 85 percent of the water used in the process and launched innovative sweepers and scrubber-driers that swept and scrubbed commercial floor space in a single cycle. The company also invented a new cleaning technology for hard-to-remove stains using dry-ice pellets—that is, solid carbon dioxide snow—as an abrasive. Kärcher's engineers also worked to develop cleaning devices that extracted difficult-to-remove dirt, such as wax, paints, oil, or chewing gum, by cooling it down to minus 79 degrees Celsius, where anything comes off easily.

Kärcher's new CEO Hartmut Jenner, who had been with the company since 1991, foresaw the development of smart technical solutions for cleaning windows, heaters, and air conditioners. In addition, the company ventured into the growing market for the treatment of waste and drinking water. A new subsidiary for government agencies, Kärcher Futuretech, began developing water filtering equipment, cleaning devices, and decontamination equipment for the military.

GLOBAL GROWTH AND VISIBILITY

Early in the 21st century Kärcher set its sights on becoming a major player in the world's largest market for cleaning products: the United States. In 2004 the company acquired C-Tech Industries, then the leading U.S. manufacturer of high-pressure cleaners for commercial use with annual sales of almost $100 million. Two years later Kärcher took over Castle Rock Industries Inc. in Englewood, Colorado, the U.S. market leader for commercial carpet cleaning under the Windsor, Prochem, and Century 400 brands, with about $130 million in sales annually. The acquisition strengthened Kärcher's position in commercial floor care and included parts supplier Graco and service arm TecServ. By 2007 the United States had become Kärcher's single most important market, followed by Germany and France, where the company's brand name had led to the coining of the word *karchériser,* a popularly used verb meaning "to clean thoroughly with high pressure." In addition, the company intensified its activities in Asia and Eastern Europe.

The number of competitors trying to get a piece of the consumer market action in high-tech cleaning equipment had grown to about 50. None of them, however, was as well-known as Kärcher. With its program of cleaning historical sites at no charge, the company continued to make international headlines. In 2003 Kärcher cleaned the more than 3,300-year-old Colossi of Memnon in Egypt. Just in time for the Olympic Games in Greece, the company removed layers of paint, soot, and graffiti from the National Library in Athens. Most spectacular, however, was the "facial" the four U.S. presidents of the Mount Rushmore Monument in South Dakota received from Kärcher specialists, beginning on the Fourth of July, 2005. In cooperation with the U.S. National Park Service, they freed the 60-foot-high presidential heads of lichen, algae, and moss, using five high-pressure washers, with each weighing 180 kilograms.

ROBOT TECHNOLOGY FOR THE FUTURE

One of Kärcher's 21st-century additions to the consumer segment came in 2003 with the launch of RoboCleaner RC3000, a cleaning robot that cleans the floors in people's homes while they are out at work or shopping. About the size and shape of an apple pie, the infrared-controlled vacuum independently moves through the rooms in the house, travels over small obstacles such as cables, and finds its way back to the docking station to put away the dirt it collected and to reload its battery. Suitable for any kind of floor, including stone, linoleum, parquet flooring, laminate, and carpets up to two centimeters high, the robot senses the amount of dust or dirt and activates one of four cleaning programs. It cleans all floors on one level—assuming it finds all doors open—up to 15 square meters per hour. Kärcher's marketing efforts were aimed at making these appliances one day as common for cleaning one's house as high-pressure washers were for cleaning one's car in 2007.

Evelyn Hauser

PRINCIPAL SUBSIDIARIES

Alfred Karcher Holdings, Inc. (U.S.A.); Alfred Kärcher Vertriebs-GmbH (Germany); Kärcher Leasing GmbH (Germany); Kärcher S.A.S. (France); Kärcher AG (KS Karcher México), S.A. de C.V.; C-Tech Industries de México, S. de R.L. de C.F.; Kärcher Indústria e Comérció Ltda. (Brazil); Kärcher B.V. (Belgium); Kärcher B.V. (Netherlands); Kärcher, S.A. (Spain); Alfred Kärcher Ges.m.b.H. (Austria); Kärcher A/S (Denmark); Kärcher Oy (Finland); Kärcher AS (Norway); Kärcher AB (Sweden); Kärcher (U.K.) Ltd.; Karcher Ltd (Ireland);

Kärcher Cleaning Systems A.E. (Greece); Kaercher (Shanghai) Cleaning Systems Co., Ltd. (China); Kärcher (Japan) Co., Ltd.; Kärcher Co., Ltd (South Korea); Kärcher (Pty) Ltd. (South Africa); Karcher Cleaning Systems Sdn. Bhd. (Malaysia); Karcher Asia-Pacific Pte. Ltd. (Singapore); Kärcher Pty.Ltd. (Australia); Karcher Canada, Inc.; Kärcher Poland Ltd. Sp.z. o.o.; Karcher Ltd. (Russia); Kärcher Servis Ticaret A.S. (Turkey); Kärcher spol. s r.o. (Czech Republic); Kärcher TOV (Ukraine); Kärcher Hungaria Kft.; CER Cleaning Equipment S.R.L. (Romania).

PRINCIPAL COMPETITORS

Hako Holding GmbH & Co. KG; IP Cleaning S.p.A.; Minuteman International Inc.; TTI Floor Care North America; Vorwerk Group.

FURTHER READING

"Bei minus 79 Grad lässt sich jeder Kaugummi lösen; Innovation ist der Wachstumstreiber des Familienunternehmens Kärcher; 1,25 Milliarden Euro Umsatz mit Hochdruckreinigern," *Frankfurter Allgemeine Zeitung,* May 22, 2007, p. 17.

Deckstein, Dagmar, "Gesichtspflege für Ex-Präsidenten," *Süddeutsche Zeitung,* August 7, 2006, p. 21.

"Engineered Support Signs Pact; Receives $2.5 Million NBC Defense Contract," *PR Newswire,* July 2, 2003.

"Germany: Karcher Counts On Indoor Appliances," *Frankfurter Allgemeine Zeitung,* October 11, 2000, p. 56.

"Heads Up for Hot-Water Surface Treatment," *Concrete Products,* September 1, 2005.

"Heritage Partners Sells Castle Rock Industries to Alfred Karcher GmbH; Investment Employed Private IOP(R) Structure," *Business Wire,* June 21, 2006.

Kärcher-Museum, Eine Bilddokumentation, Winnenden, Germany: Alfred Kärcher GmbH & Co., 2000, 35 p.

"Mit Hochdruck aus der Absatzflaute," *Lebensmittel Zeitung,* October 1, 1999, p. 121.

Neidhart, Thilo, "Saubermaenner polieren an ihrem Image," *Horizont,* October 23,1997, p. 24.

"Optimizing Flow Characteristics Under High Pressure Using Fluent for Catia Software," *CA Group,* November 21, 2006.

Paul, Peralta C., "Duluth Gains 45 Jobs in Headquarters Move," *Atlanta Journal-Constitution,* May 23, 2002, p. F4.

"Product News: Dual Cycle Tandem Washing," *Asia Pacific Rail,* March 2001, p. 24.

Sims, Stephanie, "Karcher Cleans Up in Different Markets," *Manufacturing Today,* July/August 2006, p. 80.

"Spring Cleaning; Brand Management," *Economist,* March 17, 2007, p. 72.

"System Filters on the Spot," *Water Technology News,* May 1999.

Align Technology, Inc.

881 Martin Avenue
Santa Clara, California 95050
U.S.A.
Telephone: (408) 470-1000
Toll Free: (888) 822-5446
Fax: (408) 470-1010
Web site: http://www.aligntech.com

Public Company
Incorporated: 1997
Employees: 1,253
Sales: $206.4 million (2006)
Stock Exchanges: NASDAQ
Ticker Symbol: ALGN
NAIC: 339113 Surgical Appliance and Supplies Manufacturing

■ ■ ■

Santa Clara, California-based Align Technology, Inc., manufactures the well-known "invisible" orthodontic product named Invisalign. An alternative to traditional braces, the Invisalign system consists of clear, removable aligners that patients use to straighten their teeth. Heading into 2008, Align Technology claimed that some 30,000 orthodontists and dentists had prescribed Invisalign for approximately 250,000 patients. In addition to manufacturing in excess of ten million aligners, the company also has developed a number of proprietary technologies and processes related to Invisalign, including special software that customizes the aligners for each patient.

ORTHODONTIC START-UP

Align Technology's roots can be traced back to the mid-1990s, when classmates Kelsey Wirth, a Washington, D.C., native, and Zia Chishti, a native of Pakistan, met one another at the Stanford University Graduate School of Business.

Neither Chishti, a former Morgan Stanley Dean Witter & Co. investment banker and McKinsey & Co. consultant, nor Wirth, an investment banker and environmental consultant, had any professional experience in the field of orthodontics or dentistry. However, both had firsthand experience with the rigors of wearing traditional braces.

Although orthodontists had been mulling the idea of using plastic appliances to move teeth since the mid-1940s, doing so on a mass scale had proved to be an elusive challenge. Chishti and Wirth, who formed Align Technology in April 1997, decided to apply computer science to the problem. As writer Barnaby J. Feder wrote in the August 18, 2000, issue of the *New York Times:* "Not only could computers be used to design the sequence of aligners, they realized, but stereolithography, a computer-driven process widely used by design engineers in industry for building plastic models layer by layer, could be the key to inexpensive automated production."

According to the aforementioned article, Wirth's desire to "build a company and revolutionize an industry" dovetailed nicely with Chishti's idea of applying computers to orthodontics. However, when the classmates-turned-entrepreneurs sought a means of developing their new idea, they received a cold response

COMPANY PERSPECTIVES

Align Technology is committed to bringing Invisalign to doctors and patients everywhere and to building a great company for our customers, employees and shareholders.

from industry manufacturers and venture capitalists alike. Good fortune eventually came their way when Joseph S. Lacob, a partner at the Menlo Park, California-based venture capital firm Kleiner Perkins Caufield & Byers, was receptive to their idea, resulting in $2.2 million of initial funding in August 1997.

Before the close of the 20th century, Align Technology completed two additional rounds of funding. The company secured $10 million in July 1998 in an effort that included Princeton, New Jersey-based Domain Associates, LLC, and Gund Investment Corp. Finally, in October 1999 a campaign headed by Baltimore-based QuestMark Partners, and involving Bayview Investors, LLP, Vector Fund Management, and Deerfield Management, raised another $26 million.

Initially based in Sunnyvale, California, Align Technology began operations with Chishti as chairman and CEO, and Wirth as president. The company reported a loss of $3.78 million for 1998, the year the U.S. Food and Drug Administration granted its approval of Invisalign, and no revenues. Although Align Technology was cleared to prescribe its product to patients of all ages, the company decided to target teenagers and adults who were past the growth phase.

Align Technology's workforce had grown to include 282 employees by 1999. That year, losses totaled $15.42 million on revenues of $410,000. For 2000, the company lost approximately $70.9 million on revenues of roughly $4.3 million.

INITIAL GROWTH

Rapid growth unfolded at Align Technology at the beginning of the 21st century, and the company's workforce swelled to approximately 900 workers by mid-2000. By this time the firm had manufactured approximately 3,000 Invisalign systems. That year, the company secured a fourth wave of venture capital funding. In an effort headed by Oak Hill Capital Partners LP, Align Technology raised about $86 million. Then, in November the company filed for a $200 million initial public offering.

While Align Technology had provided Invisalign training to approximately 75 percent of North America's 8,500 orthodontists as of early 2001, the company had not marketed the system to general dentists. This situation led general practice dentists in the United States to file a class-action lawsuit against the company in February, alleging that the practice violated antitrust laws. A settlement was reached in July, with Align Technology agreeing to pay $400,000 and offer training and certification to 5,000 general practice dentists annually over a four-year period.

In 2001 patients paid between $2,000 and $8,000 for Invisalign, depending on their particular needs. Of this amount, orthodontists paid $1,000 to $3,000 to Align for various fees and lab work. Demand for the product was evident when the company shipped its one-millionth aligner on August 30.

Two months later, Align Technology's manufacturing sites in Santa Clara, California, and Lahore, Pakistan, received ISO 9001 certification for meeting the quality standards set by the International Organization for Standardization. Commenting on the accomplishment in an October 19, 2001, news release, Zia Chishti said: "This certification supports our global expansion and marketing efforts. Doctors and consumers worldwide will recognize that this endorsement assures them the highest standards of quality control."

Days after announcing the ISO 9001 achievement, cofounder Kelsey Wirth announced that she would resign as the company's president in November, in order to return to the fields of education and environmental protection. Wirth remained with the company as a consultant and board member.

Heading into the early years of the new century, Align Technology and its investors stood to benefit from a large, untapped market for orthodontic treatment. In its June 2, 2000, issue, the *Daily Deal* had reported that, based on American Dental Association figures, approximately 66 percent of U.S. adults were potential candidates for orthodontic services. This was supported by American Association of Orthodontists data, which revealed that while some 400,000 adults received braces each year and 100 million were orthodontic candidates, according to the August 18, 2000, issue of the *New York Times*.

In order to build the Invisalign brand, Align Technology launched a massive marketing effort that cost roughly $40 million. A side effect of the campaign was the general awareness that it created, thereby breathing some fresh air into the somewhat stagnant orthodontic industry.

Following Wirth's exit from Align Technology, more leadership changes occurred in early 2002. On

KEY DATES

1997: Stanford University Graduate School of Business classmates Kelsey Wirth and Zia Chishti establish Align Technology.

1998: The FDA grants approval of the Invisalign system.

2000: The company files for its $200 million initial public offering.

2001: Align Technology settles a class-action lawsuit filed by general dentists in the United States and begins training them on the use of Invisalign, in addition to orthodontists; cofounder Kelsey Wirth announces her resignation as president.

2006: Align Technology acquires the intellectual property of San Francisco-based competitor OrthoClear, Inc., for $20 million.

March 27 Thomas Prescott, formerly the president and CEO of Sunnyvale, California-based Cardiac Pathways, Inc., was named CEO, succeeding Zia Chishti, who remained with the company as chairman.

According to *Investor's Business Daily,* during the early years of the new century, Align Technology devoted virtually all of its revenue to marketing, which came at the expense of product support. Prescott quickly implemented corrective measures. The portion of revenues spent on marketing, which totaled 100 percent in 2001, was cut to 34 percent by 2003. In addition, Prescott focused the company's growth efforts on the North American market.

As the industry became more familiar with the Invisalign system, Align Technology was recognized with several awards. These included the Stereolithography Excellence Award in 2001 and the Medical Design Excellence Award in 2002. In 2003 Align Technology shipped its five-millionth aligner. That year, U.S. orthodontists bought approximately $123 million worth of the company's products, helping it to generate a profit during the second half of the year. Subsequently, the population of Invisalign patients swelled from 80,000 in 2002 to about 175,000 by mid-2004.

BECOMING AN INDUSTRY LEADER

By 2005 North America accounted for approximately 85 percent of Align Technology's sales. The company, which claimed a market share of 6 percent, had made strong inroads with the orthodontic community, providing training to about 90 percent of U.S. orthodontists and about 10 percent of U.S. dentists. A strong indication of Align Technology's growth was a revenue increase of 2,464 percent between 2000 and 2004.

Several positive developments unfolded in 2005. One was the acquisition of San Francisco-based General Orthodontic, LLC. The $2.4 million deal gave Align Technology a company that, for two years, had been offering clinical support to dentists and orthodontists using the Invisalign system. In October of that year, the company announced the launch of Invisalign in Japan at the Japanese Orthodontic Society's 64th Annual Meeting. Plans were formed to offer certification to Japanese orthodontists and to launch Japanese versions of the company's VIP and ClinCheck applications.

It also was in October 2005 that the Harvard School of Dental Medicine added Invisalign certification to its required coursework, and the company made the 2005 Deloitte Technology Fast 500 list. Among the listing of North America's 500 fastest-growing technology firms, Align Technology was ranked at 94. The company also was named to Deloitte & Touche USA, LLP's, Technology Fast 50 Program for Silicon Valley, which recognized the area's fastest-growing scientific, medical equipment, and biotechnology firms.

Align also faced a number of difficulties during the middle of the decade, including a lawsuit against San Francisco-based OrthoClear, Inc., a company started by former Align Technology employees in January 2005. OrthoClear introduced its own invisible orthodontic product during the second quarter of that year, and Align quickly sued the new competitor for alleged false advertising and trademark infringement, and for violating both California's Unfair Practices Act and the federal Lanham Act. By August 2006, Align had filed a second lawsuit, and the two companies were tied up in a legal battle.

OrthoClear was a real competitive threat to Align Technology. According to the August 9, 2006, issue of the *Daily Deal,* the two companies essentially controlled the entire "invisible" braces market, with OrthoClear claiming to have a 20 percent share of business in North America. Despite the legal battle, investors were willing to pump money into OrthoClear, which had garnered $10 million in venture capital funding.

To settle the matter, a hearing was set with the International Trade Commission for November 2006. However, the companies reached a settlement in September, which called for Align Technology to acquire

OrthoClear's intellectual property for $20 million, and for OrthoClear to stop marketing its invisible orthodontic products. Following the settlement, Align Technology's stock rose 44 percent.

By December 2006, the number of Invisalign patients had grown to more than 250,000. In early 2007, the company set the stage for further expansion by inking an exclusive distribution agreement for both Australia and Hong Kong. The deal involved former Asia Pacific Managing Director Mark van Weelde acquiring Invisalign Australia Pty. Ltd. and Invisalign Hong Kong Pty. Ltd.

In August 2007 Align Technology had reason to celebrate when the Federal Circuit Court of Appeals sided with the company on 86 of 92 patent infringement claims made by Ormco Corp., regarding the automatic computer design of orthodontic appliances. The court agreed with an earlier ruling by the District Court for the Central District of California.

Heading into the 21st century's second decade, Align Technology's prospects were bright in the way of opportunity. According to data from The Freedonia Group, cited in the August 13, 2007, issue of the *Fort Worth Star-Telegram,* 6 percent annual growth was forecast for orthodontic devices through 2010, by which time the market was expected to be worth $3.7 billion.

Paul R. Greenland

PRINCIPAL SUBSIDIARIES

Align Technology De Costa Rica SRL (Costa Rica); Align Technology GmbH (Germany); Align Technology B.V. (Netherlands).

PRINCIPAL COMPETITORS

3M Co.; DENTSPLY International, Inc.; Sybron Dental Specialties, Inc.

FURTHER READING

Bonanos, Paul, "3i Backs OrthoClear with $10M," *Daily Deal,* August 9, 2006.

Feder, Barnaby J., "Orthodontics Via Silicon Valley; A Start-Up Uses Computer Modeling and Venture Capital to Reach Patients," *New York Times,* August 18, 2000.

Huget, Jennifer, "Seen Up Close, Invisalign's Smile Isn't Perfect; The 'Invisible' Braces Are Pricey and Not Right for Everyone. But They Can Make Dentists Rich," *Washington Post,* April 10, 2001.

Lau, Gloria, "It Has a Bracing Impact on Patients; Align Technology, Santa Clara, California," *Investor's Business Daily,* May 3, 2004.

Menlow, David, "IPO Pick of the Week: Align Technology (ALGN)," *Daily Deal,* January 24, 2001.

Perotin, Maria M., "All Smiles: Patients in Search of Perfect Grin Have Options as Braces and Other Devices Become More Common," *Fort Worth Star-Telegram,* August 13, 2007.

Tenorio, Vyvyan, "Align Technology Reports $105M Fourth Round," *Daily Deal,* June 2, 2000.

Allied Irish Banks plc

AIB Bankcentre
P.O. Box 452
Ballsbridge, Dublin 4
Ireland
Telephone: (353 1) 660 0311
Fax: (353 1) 660 9137
Web site: http://www.aibgroup.com

Public Company
Incorporated: 1966 as Allied Irish Banks Limited
Employees: 24,000
Total Assets: EUR 158.52 billion ($208.77 billion) (2006)
Stock Exchanges: Dublin London New York
Ticker Symbol: AIB
NAIC: 522110 Commercial Banking

■ ■ ■

Allied Irish Banks plc (AIB) is the largest bank in Ireland, and its significant investments in Great Britain, Poland, and the United States make it important internationally. It is also one of the Emerald Isle's largest publicly owned firms and one of the world's 200 largest banks, placing it among the *Financial Times* 500 Top Global Companies. Although AIB's international involvement is growing, the Republic of Ireland still accounts for nearly 70 percent of assets and half of pretax profits. AIB has more than 750 offices in all.

ORIGINS

Allied Irish Banks Limited was formed in 1966 as an amalgamation of three banks: the Royal Bank of Ireland Ltd. (founded 1836), the Provincial Bank of Ireland Ltd. (founded 1825), and the Cork-based Munster and Leinster Bank Ltd. (founded in 1885 to take over the failed Munster Bank). Munster and Leinster Bank was the largest of the three independent banks remaining in Ireland and contributed more than half of the shares of the new holding company. The heritage of these banks could be traced back even further; Munster and Leinster's holdings included those of a private bank dating to the days of William of Orange. The banks, when combined, provided thorough coverage of the island, both geographically and economically. Altogether, their combined assets were worth £250 million. After operating in a type of loose "Trinity" arrangement, in 1968 the banks began to trade as one company. This integration was fully completed in 1972.

Many industries in the British Isles faced consolidation during the 1960s. For the Irish banking industry, this reduction in numbers first affected the numerous private banks. The *Economist* reported that the island had a thousand branch offices to serve less than five million people; it was felt that fewer larger banks would be able to provide more modern and efficient service. The bank employees union, which had held a strike just before AIB's creation, was another factor.

Both Allied Irish Banks and its slightly larger rival, the Bank of Ireland, entered this phase of consolidation under pressure from North American competitors,

COMPANY PERSPECTIVES

AIB's principal countries of operation are Ireland, Poland, the UK and the US. These were chosen as they are economies with strong potential, are politically stable, have a good spread of industrial and service sectors and they have high standards of regulation. AIB's dominant business strategy is to develop mutually rewarding customer relationships offering high quality banking advice, services and products. Relationship banking and investment management businesses account for more than 90% of AIBs activity.

which first entered the Irish market in 1965, beginning with First National City Bank. Both the Bank of Ireland and AIB began offering new services and forming international strategic alliances; AIB showed itself to be more dedicated to merchant and industrial banking. In a March 1968 company statement, Chairman Edmond M. R. O'Driscoll reported on a newly formed alliance between AIB and Toronto-Dominion Bank, strengthening AIB's international stance. At the same time, a devalued pound stimulated growth on the home front.

AIB continued to standardize its three families of branch offices, which in 1971 numbered 281 in the Irish Republic and 46 in Northern Ireland; only 11 branches had been closed after the merger. During this time, several subsidiaries specialized in various areas of business finance: the Hire-Purchase Company of Ireland and its Northern Ireland counterpart (brought to the group by the Munster and Leinster Bank); Mercantile Credit Co. of Ireland (a hire-purchase bank in which Provincial Bank had a 40 percent stake); Allied Irish Leasing Ltd., which financed industrial expansion; and the Allied Irish Investment Corporation, a merchant bank formed in association with Hambros Bank, Toronto-Dominion, and the Irish Life Assurance Company. In 1967, the group boasted assets of £318 million. The late 1960s were booming years for Irish industry and for AIB.

A NEW WAY OF DOING BUSINESS

In the early 1970s, Allied Irish Banks, which formerly derived income only from interest on loans, began charging fees for services, such as five pence per transaction and five pence per £100 withdrawal of cash. The competitive situation inspired the new way of doing business.

Wages accounted for three-quarters of a bank's costs; in the 1970s, bank employees, among the most highly paid workers in the country, lobbied for increases in salaries. The Irish Bank Officials Association, spurred by staff alienation after the merger, called a devastating eight-month strike in 1970, which sent customers scrambling to the smaller, nonassociated banks. Two other strikes were called during the decade. As Mary Campbell reported in the *Banker,* "The Union's strength is reflected ... in the incredible facts that these banks cannot employ married women or take on new staff (except in certain specialized cases) who are 21 years of age; starting salaries are the same at all ages." To make matters more expensive, the banks often sent promising staff members to earn an M.B.A. Both AIB and the Bank of Ireland succeeded in reforming staff grades in 1989, resulting in some cost savings and better utilization of especially skilled employees without significant layoffs. As AIB Chief Executive Gerald Scanlan told the *Banker:* "We're no longer paying people IR £24,000 for an IR £8,000 job." At the same time, AIB continued to fight for longer hours; its Irish branches were open only half the hours of its U.S. ones.

A common language and a history of Irish immigration made America an attractive overseas market. AIB's first New York branch opened in 1978, specializing in serving companies from the British Isles. In 1983, AIB Group invested in a 43 percent share of America's First Maryland Bancorp, with its 1820s roots making it even more venerable than the original three Allied Irish Banks. After increasing its stake in First Maryland to 49.7 percent in 1988, AIB offered to buy the rest of the shares and by March 1989 the company had done so, for a total investment of US$522 million. At the end of 1991, AIB's subsidiary First Maryland Bancorp bought the York Bank and Trust Company, entering AIB in the southern Pennsylvania market. First Maryland Bancorp offered credit cards through another subsidiary, First Omni Bank NA.

AIB restructured itself in 1986. It introduced stockbroker services in 1987 with the opening of Allied Irish Securities, a few weeks before the market collapsed on infamous Black Monday. Two years later, after agreeing to buy Ireland's second largest stockbroker, Goodbody James Capel (the Bank of Ireland owned 49 percent of the largest, J. and E. Davy), it formed the Capital Markets division to manage its entire treasury, international, corporate banking, and investment banking operations. Insurance and stock brokering interested both AIB and its chief rival.

KEY DATES

1966: Company is founded upon the alliance of Royal Bank of Ireland, Provincial Bank of Ireland Ltd., and Munster and Leinster Bank.
1970: Company introduces banking services in Great Britain.
1972: Company adopts the name Allied Irish Banks plc.
1978: Opens first U.S. branch in New York.
1987: Company offers stockbroker services with the opening of Allied Irish Securities.
1989: Company acquires full ownership of First Maryland Bancorp, forms Capital Markets division.
1991: Acquires TSB Bank Northern Ireland, creating First Trust Bank.
1997: Acquires majority ownership of Poland's Wielkopolski Bank Kredytowy.
1999: First Maryland Bancorp and Mid-Atlantic holdings renamed Allfirst Financial, Inc.; acquires majority ownership of Poland's Bank Zachodni; secures option to buy almost 25 percent of Keppel Tatlee Bank (KTL).
2001: Bank Zachodni WBK formed by merger of two Polish subsidiaries.
2002: A rogue currency trader is found to have hidden $691 million in losses for AIB's Allfirst subsidiary.
2003: M&T Bank acquires Allfirst, giving AIB a minority stake in M&T, a leading U.S. regional bank.

INTERNATIONAL EXPANSION

Early in 1991, AIB merged with TSB Northern Ireland plc. The company's operations in Northern Ireland, known as First Trust Bank, numbered nearly 100 branches with 1,400 employees. Although AIB spent much effort in developing its successful overseas business, it (like the Bank of Ireland) seemed to fare best in its home territory. This was largely because of the Irish economy, which performed relatively well, with a less intense downturn early in the 1990s than that of Britain, where AIB also had a long-established presence. In 1992, Allied Irish lost IR £26 million in Britain; the next year it succeeded in reclaiming a profit of IR £7 million. Ireland, quite dependent on England for trade, suffered its own recession a couple of years later, enduring high unemployment and high interest rates.

In the mid-1990s, Ireland accounted for just under half of the group's income and the United States accounted for about 30 percent. In addition to its subsidiary First Maryland Bancorp, the group maintained an AIB branch in New York City. Other locations included Brussels, the Cayman Islands, the Channel Islands, Frankfurt, and the Isle of Man. The company also obtained a 16.3 percent shareholding (worth about IR £13 million) in the Polish bank Wielkopolski Bank Kredytowy. AIB had been advising the 63-branch bank since 1991. Neither AIB nor the Bank of Ireland appeared especially optimistic about continental prospects, with the exception of Eastern Europe. In 1994, AIB bid for the state-owned Budapest Bank; AIB would later concentrate its Eastern European expansion efforts on Polish markets alone.

The Pacific Rim was also an important venue. By the late 1980s, offices were operational in Singapore, Sidney, and Tokyo. In 1995, the company's partnership with Phillip Securities in Singapore was mirrored by a new Malaysian partnership involving both Phillip and Grand Care. Both ventures shared the name Allied Phillip Capital Management and offered investment management services in the emerging Pacific market.

CONTINUED GROWTH AND EXPANSION

AIB earned admiration for its innovative management and quality assurance practices. In the late 1980s, it implemented an "action learning" program to set management priorities in the large and evolving market in Great Britain. Although Ireland, with a population of only 3.5 million, not much larger than South Carolina's, seemed to provide only limited opportunities for growth, Allied Irish Banks was one of the few foreign banks to expand successfully into the United States. Its conservative approach, cultivated in light of its size and regional origins, seemed sure to offer similar returns in the future. AIB's balance sheet remained healthy as the company continued to orchestrate its international growth, in its reserved manner, while also maintaining its loyal domestic customer base. Its three main divisions, AIB Banking, USA, and Capital Markets, gained strength and vitality.

The USA division continued to expand throughout the Mid-Atlantic region through strategic acquisitions and investments of First Maryland Bancorp, and by the late 1990s, had added National Bank of Maryland, Dauphin Deposit Corporation, the York Bank, Farmers Bank, Bank of Pennsylvania, and Valley Bank to the family. The acquisition of Dauphin Deposit in 1997 transformed First Maryland Bancorp into one of America's top 50 banks. In 1999, the entire Mid-Atlantic group was renamed Allfirst Financial, Inc., and given a new logo. By 2000, Allfirst's assets climbed to US$18.4 billion. AIB's own brand operations, located in New York, Philadelphia, Los Angeles, Chicago, and San Francisco, reported a net income of US$184.4 million in 2000, representing a 7 percent increase from 1999. AIB added to its portfolio Community Counseling Service Co., a privately owned consulting firm to the not-for-profit sector, to complement its existing array of financial services already dedicated to nonprofit organizations. In all, the USA division profits grew 10 percent in 2000.

The Capital Markets division, comprised of three main units, Corporate Banking, Investment Banking, and Treasury and International, also enjoyed steady profits. In 1999, AIB secured the rights to acquire a 24.9 percent equity stake in Singapore-based Keppel Tatlee Bank Limited (KTL), an alliance that would enhance the positioning of both AIB and KTL as key players in Singapore's financial market. AIB's private banking and treasury operations in Singapore were sold to KTL as well.

PACING ITSELF IN THE NEW MILLENNIUM

In preparation for the 2002 conversion to the European Monetary Unit (EMU), AIB invested heavily in systems development, communications, and education programs, and began offering euro-based banking services well in advance. While Ireland enjoyed a more buoyant economy than most of its European neighbors, the combination of a somewhat decelerated European market and the imminent arrival of a single currency fueled speculation of cross-border mergers that would affect banks throughout Europe.

Profits from AIB's Banking division grew 19 percent in 2000, with retail and commercial outlets numbering 300 in Ireland, 70 in Northern Ireland, and 35 in Great Britain. In addition to its traditional services, AIB also offered online banking services, including home mortgaging. Banking services in the United Kingdom focused on small- to medium-sized business and professional markets as the company successfully endeavored to cultivate long-lasting relationships with its customers. In 2000, AIB paid EUR 114.33 million to the Irish Revenue Commissioners to settle its portion of a banking scandal involving falsified nonresident savings accounts that enabled account holders to avoid paying the Deposit Interest Retention Tax, which was otherwise collected from resident account holders. Other Irish banks were implicated as well; the scandal was not confined to AIB.

A fourth division was formed in the late 1990s to support AIB's Eastern European interests and specifically, its investments in Poland's banking sector. In 1996, AIB acquired an additional 20 percent interest in Wielkopolski Bank Kredytowy; by 1997, AIB had attained majority (60.14 percent) ownership. Allied Irish also acquired majority ownership (80 percent) of a second Polish bank, Bank Zachodni, S.A., in 1999. AIB's banking operations in Poland gained momentum with the merger of Wielkopolski Bank Kredytowy and Bank Zachodni, which when completed in June 2001, established Bank Zachodni WBK as the fifth largest bank in Poland. AIB retained a majority (70.5 percent) holding of the newly formed bank. As one of the largest banks quoted on the Warsaw Stock Exchange, Bank Zachodni WBK would be attractive to both domestic and international investors as it streamlined and expanded banking services to meet traditional and high-tech customer needs in an emerging market.

As an increasingly international company, over half of its profits and assets in 2000 were either made or held outside the Republic of Ireland. With a domestic economy stronger than the European average, AIB eagerly anticipated achieving growth projections and continued to thrive amid increasing competition and rising costs from accelerating business programs, technology, and e-business services. Its commitment to customer satisfaction and conservative approach to expansion enabled the company to maintain its healthy balance sheet and deliver long-term shareholder value. Although limited geographically, AIB's domestic presence remained a strong and steadfast anchor to its international operations. Boasting over five million retail, corporate, and commercial customers, AIB found itself consistently winning consumer accolades, such as the "Best Business Bank in Great Britain," and steadily advancing in the *Financial Times* rankings of Europe's largest companies.

In June 2002, AIB and Bank of Ireland proposed a 50-50 joint venture to link some of their information technology operations, but this was quickly withdrawn in the face of antitrust concerns. The idea was to reap efficiencies from the combination, as an alternative to outsourcing. However, the prospect of cooperation between Ireland's two largest banks made some in the government uneasy, as together they accounted for 80 percent of the country's current accounts.

INCREASING INTERNATIONAL INVOLVEMENT

A serious scandal emerged at the Allfirst subsidiary in 2002. A rogue trader at AIB's Allfirst subsidiary, John Rusnak, was found to have hidden $691 million in currency losses over the course of five years. AIB had been planning to merge its U.S. interests into another bank, but the damage was considerable and far-reaching. It had to restate several years' results, and recorded a $36.8 million net loss for 2001.

By the end of 2002, AIB had agreed to merge Allfirst into M&T Bank Corporation, a leading regional bank based in Buffalo, New York. Officials stressed that this arrangement had been in the making since October 2001, well before the trouble at Allfirst surfaced.

The deal, which closed in April 2003, was worth $3.1 billion altogether. AIB gained a 23.5 percent holding in M&T, making it the largest shareholder, in addition to $886 million in cash. Half of the proceeds were earmarked for a stock buyback, a move seen as a takeover defense against the likes of Royal Bank of Scotland plc which was also active in the U.S. market.

The combined operations of M&T and Allfirst included more than 700 branches, although some of these would be closed. The merger made M&T one of the 20 largest banks in the United States. This was not AIB's only presence in the country. It had a small unit called Allied Irish America that served nonprofit groups.

AIB absorbed the impact of the trading scandal as a momentary blip. Pretax income doubled to EUR 1 billion in 2002, and within four years would exceed EUR 2 billion. The company was soon again reporting growth on all fronts.

There were other controversies closer to home, however. A handful of executives were tainted by a tax evasion situation. In 2004 AIB agreed to refund fees on millions of foreign exchange transactions on which it had overcharged customers.

AIB's involvement in Poland proved less dramatic than its U.S. adventure. The company was well positioned for Poland's entrance into the European Union in 2004. In the United States, market conditions deteriorated as a result of a growing subprime lending crisis.

DOMESTIC DEVELOPMENTS

Whatever was happening overseas, AIB could still bank on the surging economy at home. Net profit rose from EUR 1.3 billion in 2005 to EUR 2.2 billion ($2.9 billion) in 2006. AIB cashed in on Ireland's frenzied real estate market through the sale and leaseback of its headquarters building.

The Emerald Isle's growing wealth was attracting more competition from foreign banks, however, in the areas of mortgages and private banking for high net worth individuals. AIB had little exposure to a slowdown of the domestic housing market in 2007, as residential mortgages accounted for only 6 percent of pretax profits.

Frederick C. Ingram
Updated, Suzanne P. Selvaggi; Frederick C. Ingram

PRINCIPAL SUBSIDIARIES

AIB Capital Markets plc; AIB Corporate Finance Ltd.; AIB Finance Ltd.; AIB Group (UK) plc; AIB International Financial Services Ltd.; AIB Leasing Ltd.; Bank Zachodni WBK S.A. (Poland; 70.5%); M&T Bank Corporation (United States; 25%).

PRINCIPAL DIVISIONS

AIB Bank Republic of Ireland; AIB Bank Great Britain & Northern Ireland; Capital Markets; Poland.

PRINCIPAL COMPETITORS

Bank of Ireland; Barclays plc (U.K.); Lloyds TSB Group plc (U.K.); Royal Bank of Scotland plc; Anglo Irish Bank Corporation.

FURTHER READING

"AIB Appoints Trouble-Shooter Sheehy as CEO Designate," *European Banker,* March 31, 2005, p. 2.

"AIB's Allied Front," *Euromoney,* June 2000, p. 224.

"Allied Irish Open for Business, Collects EUR 1.5bn in a Day," *Euroweek,* August 6, 2004, p. 3.

"Banks Face Squeeze on Profits," *Banker,* February 1979, pp. 87–92.

Barrow, G. L., *The Emergence of the Irish Banking System 1820–1845,* New York: Gill and Macmillan, 1975.

Bee, Robert N., "Buying into a US Bank: The Allied Irish Experience," *Banker,* July 1986, pp. 32–35.

Blanden, Michael, "Back to the Home Turf," *Banker,* February 1990, pp. 61–62.

———, "Celtic Tiger on the Prowl," *Banker,* February 1995, pp. 35–38.

———, "Green, Green Grass of Home," *Banker,* February 1992, p. 19.

———, "Victim of Its Success," *Banker,* March 2000, pp. 40–41.

Bourke, Kevin J., "Implementing a Marketing Action: A Programme for AIB Group," *Long Range Planning,* December 1992.

Bray, Nicholas, "Allied Irish Banks Looking to Resume International Expansion Begun in '80s," *Wall Street Journal,* February 3, 1995, p. B6.

———, "Analysts Point to Bank of Ireland, A.I.B. as Top Choices Among European Stocks," *Wall Street Journal,* May 16, 1994, p. A11.

Brown, John Murray, "Global Eye: Helping AIB to Make a New Start," *Financial Times* (London), November 17, 2003, p. 7.

———, "How to Survive a Rogue Trader's Ravages," *Financial Times* (London), August 21, 2003, p. 10.

———, "Market Focus: Banks and Builders Buoy Dublin," *Financial Times,* June 5, 2001.

"Business Buzz: Coming Cash Tsunami," *Banker,* July 6, 2000, p. 1.

Campbell, Mary, "Irish Banking Today," *Banker,* November 1972.

"First Maryland Getting New Brand," *Bank Advertising News,* March 8, 1999, pp. 1, 17.

Fuerbringer, Jonathan, "Bank Report Says Trader Had Bold Plot," *New York Times,* March 15, 2002, p C1.

Gilbart, James William, *The History of Banking in Ireland,* London: Longman, 1836.

Kimbell, Lucy, and Grog Smosarski, "Wielkopolski Grows with Polish Economy," *Central European,* April 1994, p. 37.

Kline, Alan, and John Reosti, "Allfirst CEO Stays but Six Managers Get Ax," *American Banker,* March 15, 2002, p. 5.

Lavery, Brian, "6 Fired as Irish Bank Acts on U.S. Trading Loss," *New York Times,* March 14, 2002, p. W1.

———, "Irish Sell Troubled U.S. Bank but Maintain Some Influence," *New York Times,* September 27, 2002, p. W1.

Leighton, Oonagh, "Good Crack at Poland," *Central European,* February 1999, pp. 17–20.

McConnell, Kevin, and David Odlum, "Still the Nation's Favourite Bank," *Sunday Times* (London), August 5, 2007, Bus. Sec., p. 8.

———, "The Sums Add Up for Irish Bank Giant," *Sunday Times* (London), February 26, 2006, Bus. Sec., p. 8.

McRae, Hamish, "Irish Banks Consolidate," *Banker,* August 1968.

Merrell, Caroline, "AIB Sues US Banks to Recover Fraud Loss," *Times* (London), February 20, 2003, Bus. Sec., p. 27.

Murphy, Paul, "Gloves Off and Come Out Fighting," *Banker,* February 1989, pp. 43–48.

———, "Seconds Out, Round One," *Banker,* February 1988, pp. 42–49.

Murphy, Seamus, "Irish Banks Dragged Through the DIRT," *European Banker,* January 2000, p. 2.

Murray, Brendan, "And Then There Were Two," *European Banker,* October 2002, p. 6.

O'Hara, Terrence H., "Perpetual to Sell Credit Card Unit to Irish Bankers," *Washington Business Journal,* April 1, 1991, p. 4.

Panday, Mark, "Irish Banks Set Priority Markets," *Euromoney,* July 1989, pp. 99–100.

"Private Banks Push into Ireland's Booming Wealth Markets," *Private Banker International,* April 10, 2007, p. 1.

"Ready for a New Brew," *Banker,* February 1993, pp. 13–16.

Ring, Niamh, "RBS to Buy AIB? Makes Sense in U.S.," *American Banker,* February 26, 2002, p. 1.

Shapiro, Stacy, "Irish Government Takes Control of Insurer," *Business Insurance,* March 25, 1985.

"Small Is Beautiful," *Euromoney,* January 1990, pp. 29, 32.

Spender, Barnabas, "De Buitleir Sees an Allied Vision," *International Tax Review,* July/August 1993, pp. 44–46.

Stewart, Kathryn, "Corporate Identity: A Strategic Marketing Issue," *International Journal of Bank Marketing,* 1991, pp. 32–39.

Thackray, John, "Curate's Egg for Foreign Bankers," *Euromoney,* November 1989, pp. 121–37.

Webb, Sara, "Allied Irish Gets Right to Buy Stake in Singapore Bank," *Wall Street Journal,* June 3, 1999, p. A23.

Wills, Gordon, "What Manager Doesn't Study at Home?" *European Journal of Marketing,* 25, no. 4, 1991, pp. 128–32.

Wilson, Brian, "Organisation and Business Development Through Action Learning," *International Journal of Bank Marketing,* 1988, pp. 57–66.

Alside Inc.

P.O. Box 2010
Akron, Ohio 44309-2010
U.S.A.
Toll Free: (800) 922-6009
Web site: http://www.alside.com

Wholly Owned Subsidiary of Associated Materials Inc.
Incorporated: 1947
Employees: 3,000
Sales: $670 million (2004 est.)
NAIC: 332321 Metal Window and Door Manufacturing

■ ■ ■

Alside Inc., a subsidiary of Associated Materials Inc., is a Cuyahoga Falls, Ohio-based manufacturer of vinyl siding, windows, doors, fencing, and railing products for the new construction and residential remodeling markets. The company's flagship product is siding, which in addition to vinyl includes steel siding, trim, and such accessories as fluted corner posts and gable vents. Alside insulation products are designed to be installed beneath the siding products. Alside's vinyl-resin windows are available in a wide variety of styles, from single-hung to bay, bow, and garden. The company's railing and fencing products emulate the look of wood, but are free of the maintenance demands of wood. Alside also offers rainware systems, including gutters, spouts, elbows, and miters. In addition to being available through remodeling contractors and homebuilders, Alside products are sold through authorized distributors and a network of about 100 Alside Supply Centers. Manufacturing is done at seven plants located in Ohio, Iowa, Texas, North Carolina, Washington, and Arizona.

POST–WORLD WAR II ORIGINS

Alside grew out of the aluminum siding industry, which began to take shape after World War II came to an end in 1945 and a population boom led to the growth of the suburbs, a prime market for the new easy-to-maintain siding. Steel and aluminum cladding products had been available for years from such well-known companies as Sears and Alcoa, but these products had a tendency to warp, creating gaps that could be breached by water and lead. In 1937 an Indiana machinist named Frank Hoess tackled this problem by experimenting with steel siding that imitated wooden clapboards, work that resulted in the development of a locking joint for which he received a patent two years later.

Hoess formed a company and began covering houses in the Chicago area with his new siding when World War II intervened and material shortages put his business on hold. After the war his weatherboard siding was sold through Detroit's Metal Building Products and began to be used in the building of suburbs in the northeastern United States. Soon Sears and Reynolds Metals Company began offering their own aluminum panels, and Kaiser Aluminum and Chemical Corporation got involved in the business, acquiring the rights to a panel using a new kind of locking joint, developed by Canadian inventor Charles Kinghorn, which offered improvements over the Hoess design.

COMPANY PERSPECTIVES

Alside represents nearly six decades of inspired innovation. Founded in 1947, Alside is a leading manufacturer of vinyl siding and accessories, vinyl windows and patio doors, and fencing and railing products for the residential and commercial remodeling and new construction markets.

The siding that came on the market shortly after World War II was unpainted, intended to weather to a gray-white color. Customers were also told that the panels could be painted like wood and would last longer, but Akron, Ohio, businessman Jerome J. Kaufman had a better idea. He had seen firsthand during the war how paint could be bonded to the aluminum fuselages of aircraft, and while running one of the country's largest retail home improvement dealerships in Akron he became aware of the growing demand for more attractive siding products. After some experimentation he developed a method to bake a coat of paint directly onto an aluminum siding panel in the factory. The sheets were placed on a conveyor and carried through an electrostatic spray paint booth, then taken to a gold-lined oven where the paint was baked on using one thousand 500-watt infrared lightbulbs.

ALSIDE FORMED: 1947

In 1947 Kaufman assembled a group of investors, including his brother Manual, raising $100,000 to form a company under the name Alside. The company's first products were available in white, cream, or gray. The factory-painted panels, able to fit over wood and stucco exteriors to brighten up a home instantly and thus increase resale value, proved extremely popular. Alside's success led to an alliance with Reynolds Metals, which bought a stake in the company, soon making Alside one of the largest end-users of sheet aluminum in the United States. In fact, the company ran afoul of the U.S. government in 1951 when it exceeded its allocation of aluminum at a time when restrictions had been put in place to conserve aluminum for military use during the Korean War. The year before, Alside had used more than 13 million pounds of aluminum to produce paneling that resulted in revenues of about $6 million. The company was punished by the National Production Authority, and was forbidden for six months from using any controlled materials.

The company's success also resulted in Reynolds and Kaiser introducing their own pre-painted aluminum siding products, and within a few years virtually all siding was painted at the factory. Alside became involved in the distribution side of the business in 1952 when it opened Supply Centers in Chicago, Indianapolis, and Pittsburgh. The 1950s also brought a third Kaufman brother, Donald, into the business. After graduating from law school at Ohio State University he became part of Alside's legal department in 1955.

TAKEN PUBLIC: 1960

A fire in 1958 destroyed the Akron plant, and two years later a new $3.5 million modern plant and corporate offices were erected in a former cornfield in Northampton Township, which later became part of Cuyahoga Falls and remained Alside's headquarters. Also in the summer of 1960, Alside was taken public, with Reynolds and stake-holding investment banks selling 300,000 shares of common stock at $11 a share. When the company's fiscal year came to a close on September 30, 1960, Alside tallied sales of $23 million, a significant increase over the prior year's $19.7 million. Net income also grew from $1.2 million to $1.6 million.

After its initial public offering, Alside shares quickly grew in value, landing the stock a place on the New York Stock Exchange in 1961. The price peaked at $49.75 per share in 1962, and then began to recede as the aluminum siding industry was hurt by increased competition that resulted in lower prices. Exaggerated advertising claims for aluminum siding had also tarnished the product's image, helped in large measure by attacks from the paint industry, which had lost a good deal of business to siding companies over the past dozen years. Moreover, the aluminum siding business became populated by quick-buck operators whose makeshift operations turned out aluminum siding as well as doors and windows. Kaiser, Reynolds, and Alcoa did not help matters by extending easy credit to these operations to drive up sales for aluminum. Not only did these hastily installed slipshod products tarnish the image of the entire aluminum fabrication industry, they created ruinous competition and low prices that crippled more reputable companies. To help rectify the matter, the Federal Trade Commission adopted a code offered by the Aluminum Siding Association intended to curb the abuse of advertising claims.

After dipping to $16.625 a share in 1962, Alside stock mounted a comeback as a shakeout took place in the crowded aluminum siding field. The price of aluminum siding also began to increase. Due to higher aluminum costs, labor, and other expenses, all the major players in the industry boosted prices by the fall of

KEY DATES

1947: Jerome Kaufman founds Alside to produce aluminum siding.
1952: First Supply Centers open.
1960: Company taken public.
1968: U.S. Steel acquires Alside.
1979: Alside begins producing vinyl siding.
1984: Associated Materials acquires company.
1989: Alside ceases aluminum siding manufacturing.
1996: Charter Oak siding product introduced.
2002: Harvest Partners acquires Associated Materials.

1963. Alside's revenues improved to $25.3 million in fiscal 1963, and net income approached $1.8 million. Late in the fiscal year the company established Alside Homes Corporation to enter the manufactured housing field. The subsidiary opened model homes in a number of states but sales were disappointing, and the effort was soon liquidated. Alside's revenues dipped to $24.2 million, with a net loss of $5.6 million in fiscal 1964. The failed venture at least jump-started an effort at Alside to find ways to better control costs. Alside tried some other ventures in the mid-1960s to become less dependent on aluminum. It formed Alside International, based in Puerto Rico, to produce stone siding, followed by brick panels. Alside also dabbled in steel siding.

U.S. STEEL ACQUIRES ALSIDE: 1968

After 20 years of operating Alside as a major independent company, Kaufman decided to align the business with a deep-pocketed corporate parent. In 1968 he agreed to sell his controlling share in Alside to the United States Steel Corporation for about $20 million. Altogether U.S. Steel paid about $37 million to acquire all of Alside's outstanding shares. After the sale Jerome Kaufman continued to run the business he founded.

With the backing of its new owner, Alside made inroads within the construction industry and became the leader in the aluminum siding industry as well as the steel siding industry. Early in the 1970s Alside began distributing aluminum storm doors and windows. In 1978 the company began manufacturing aluminum replacement windows, opening a new manufacturing plant in Wadsworth, Ohio. However, with a giant corporate parent also came some drawbacks. U.S. Steel took a hard line when it came to labor unions, in particular Local 5144 of the United Steelworkers who bargained for Alside employees. The two parties locked horns in 1973, resulting in an 11-week strike. Just three years later negotiations broke down again, and this time the strike lasted for 22 weeks.

Although aluminum siding had always been Alside's signature product, another material, vinyl, had been gaining in popularity since the 1960s. Unlike aluminum, which eventually had to be painted, vinyl siding had its color embedded in the sheet, making the color permanent. The greatest drawback was the higher cost of vinyl, both in terms of material and installation, but that would change in the late 1970s as aluminum prices soared, making vinyl cost-competitive with the better grade of aluminum siding. In addition, installers were becoming more familiar with vinyl and began to charge less to install the siding. Rather than be left behind, in 1979 Alside decided to enter the vinyl siding business by opening a new manufacturing plant to produce the material in Ohio. A year later the company made a further commitment to vinyl, its researchers developing the company's first vinyl replacement window.

Jerome Kaufman retired as chairman in 1983 and was succeeded by his brother, Donald, who also became chief executive officer of Alside, which by this point was generating annual sales of about $200 million. In that same year U.S. Steel decided to sell Alside along with some other assets in order to trim debt taken on to acquire Marathon Oil Co. the previous year. In March 1983 a letter of intent was signed with William W. Winspear, the former president of Chaparral Steel Co., who formed a new company called Associated Materials Incorporated to acquire Alside along with a Georgia tire cord company and an Arkansas electrical cable business. The deal fell apart, but was later rekindled, and the sale was finally completed in March 1984.

ALUMINUM ASSETS SOLD: 1989

No longer part of U.S. Steel, Alside improved its relationship with its unionized employees. The company did not experience a loss of contractor-customers, and expanded in a number of directions through the rest of the 1980s. With vinyl products increasing in popularity, a plant was opened in Ennis, Texas, in 1985 to produce vinyl siding and accessories. A year later a kitchen cabinet division called UltraCraft was formed, supplied by a new plant in Liberty, North Carolina. In 1987 a plant dedicated to vinyl window manufacturing was added in Cedar Rapids, Iowa, and Alside closed the decade by opening a second vinyl window plant in Kinston, North Carolina. While the company was turning its focus to vinyl, the sale of aluminum products eroded steadily, so that in 1989 Alside sold its aluminum siding equipment and machinery to Alcan Aluminum Corp., which also agreed to produce residential siding to Alside's specification to meet Alside's distribution needs.

Long associated with aluminum, Alside was not able easily to duplicate its success with vinyl. In the early 1990s Donald Kaufman reached a turning point in his life. He took the time while recovering from surgery to take stock of his life and the company. Concluding that he was not yet ready for retirement, he read some books on corporate reengineering and decided to make significant changes to the way Alside operated. Once he was back at work, he sought an outside perspective and hired some consultants, who told him to pay more attention to customers, whose needs had changed over time. The sales force was then trained to ease up on the hard-sell approach and to seek solutions for customers. Less than half the salespeople were able, or were willing, to make the transition, resulting in a major recasting of the force. In another bid to make it easier for customers to deal with Alside, many functions were taken away from the headquarters and put in the field, a move that trimmed overhead by several million dollars.

Alside also made significant investments in product development to provide customers with the kind of products they wanted. In 1993, for example, Alside's new division, UltraGuard, began offering vinyl fence products, and subsidiary Premium Garage Door Company began an effort to develop vinyl garage doors. Two years later the company moved into the new construction market by introducing the Performance Series vinyl window line.

Another new product that would prove extremely popular, Charter Oak Premium Vinyl Siding, was unveiled in 1996, offering the winning combination of beauty, wear, and ease of installation. In addition to many houses and apartment buildings, Charter Oak would find customers that included Marriott hotels and Long John Silver's restaurants. Other important new products were introduced in 1998, including CenterLock, a premium vinyl siding that brought together a double-lock design with pieces that looked like wood boards, and Architectural Shakes, a decorative ornamental siding product.

To keep pace with demand for its vinyl products, Alside opened a new vinyl extrusion operation in Freeport, Texas, in 1999 that operated under the name Freeport Vinyl Technologies. At the same time, Alside Supply Centers added several new locations, including Southgate, Michigan, and Pawtucket, Rhode Island. When the decade came to a close, Alside's revenues totaled more than $410 million.

The Supply Centers continued to expand in the new century, with nine units opening in 2000 alone, five more the following year, and seven in 2002. Another window manufacturing plant was added in 2000 through the purchase of Bothell, Washington-based Alpine Window, a deal that also provided Alside with a West Coast presence. The parent company, in the meantime, was not faring as well, and in late 2001 was put on the block. In March 2002 the private equity firm Harvest Partners Inc. agreed to buy Associated Materials for $436 million in cash and debt. Alside's chief executive officer, Michael Caporale, was named Associated Materials CEO and the Dallas headquarters were relocated to Alside's offices.

Little changed under new ownership, as Alside continued a steady launch of new products. In 2002 the company unveiled Pelican Bay Polypropylene Shakes and Scallops, and the Architectural Color Collection of six dark colors for its siding and accessories. The following year brought the Platinum Series insulation line of premium fanfold and insulation board products, and in 2004 Charter Oak Energy Elite, Pelican Bay Hand-Split Shakes and Scallops, and redesigned Excalibur Window products were introduced. In 2005 specialized siding accessories and shutters debuted under the Exterior Accents banner, and Prodigy Next Generation Insulated Siding was rolled out. Alside's company-owned Supply Centers were also increasing, with three locations added in both 2003 and 2004, and four in 2005. In addition Alside opened a new window plant in Yuma, Arizona, to support further growth on the West Coast.

Ed Dinger

PRINCIPAL OPERATING UNITS

Siding; Windows; Railing; Fencing; Rain Systems; Insulation.

PRINCIPAL COMPETITORS

NTK Holdings, Inc; Owen Corning Sales, LLC; Royal Group, Inc.

FURTHER READING

"Alside, Inc. Is Suspended by N.P.A. for Exceeding Priorities on Aluminum Use," *New York Times*, December 1, 1951.

Fernandez, Robert, "Alside Inc. Founder Kaufman Dies," *Akron Beacon Journal*, January 17, 1992, p. B8.

Orol, Ron, "Harvest to Pay $436M for Associate Materials," *Daily Deal*, March 18, 2002.

Pantages, Larry, "Alside to Close Falls Factory, Laying Off 300," *Akron Beacon Journal*, May 25, 1989, p. A1.

Reiff, Rick, "A Record of Running the Show," *Akron Beacon Journal,* August 18, 1986, p. D1.

Russell, John, "Alside Has Changes Covered," *Akron Beacon Journal,* May 6, 1999, p. C8.

"Siding Makers Are Overcoming the Problems of Rapid Growth," *New York Times,* July 7, 1963.

"Stock of Alside Marketed Today," *New York Times,* June 21, 1960.

Thomas, Dana L., "Aluminum Fabricators Are Finally Showing Their Competitive Mettle," *Barron's National Business and Financial Weekly,* March 7, 1966, p. 3.

Anacomp, Inc.

15378 Avenue of Science
San Diego, California 92128-3407
U.S.A.
Telephone: (858) 716-3400
Toll Free: (800) 350-3044
Fax: (858) 716-3775
Web site: http://www.anacomp.com

Public Company
Incorporated: 1968
Employees: 1,000
Sales: $151.7 million (2006)
Stock Exchanges: NASDAQ
Ticker Symbol: ANCPA
NAIC: 561410 Document Preparation Services; 493190 Other Warehousing and Storage; 333315 Photographic and Photocopying Equipment Manufacturing

■ ■ ■

Based in San Diego, California, Anacomp, Inc., is a leading provider of document management and business process management services, as well as information technology equipment service and support. The company is a global enterprise, with an international headquarters facility in Wokingham, United Kingdom. According to Anacomp, its customer base includes most *Fortune* 100 and *Fortune* 500 firms.

In addition to its two headquarters facilities, Anacomp's 1,000 employees work from domestic offices in Atlanta, Boston, Dallas, Los Angeles, Nashville, New York, Sacramento, and Washington, D.C. The company has additional international offices in Wiesbaden, Germany; Milan, Italy; and Paris, France.

Anacomp's product offerings include a document preparation, scanning, indexing, process management, and storage service called docHarbor Solutions-as-a-Service, as well as a litigation software and support service named CaseLogistix. Finally, the company's Multi-Vendor Services offers authorized vendor-neutral support of storage equipment, network devices, specialty systems and peripherals.

COM PIONEER

Anacomp's origins date back to April 16, 1968, when three Purdue University professors, including Ronald D. Palamara, established the first local computer services business in Indianapolis, Indiana. According to Anacomp, the company's name was formed by joining portions of the words "analyze" and "compute."

Anacomp went public in 1970 and immediately embarked upon a path of acquisition-based growth. The firm's earliest acquisitions secured it a position in the emerging computer output to microfiche (COM) industry, otherwise known as micrographics, which involves converting computer data into microfilm and other storage media. In early 1970 Anacomp acquired a 50 percent stake in Learning Foundations of Denver, Inc., as well as a 57 percent interest in International Health Resources Development Corp. In an all-cash deal, Anacomp acquired Computer Techniques, Inc., in March, followed by Micromation, Inc., in November for 15,004 shares of common stock.

COMPANY PERSPECTIVES

Customer service is the core of Anacomp's business model. Our docHarbor, CaseLogistix and Multi-Vendor Support services strive to deliver quality service to our customers in a personal and timely manner. This customer-based service model reflects the efforts of all Anacomp associates to meet the needs of our partners and customers every day.

Anacomp sold Learning Foundations of Denver in 1972 and acquired two additional businesses the following year. Micrographix Data Services, Inc., was acquired in August, followed by Electronic Data Preparation Corp. two months later. Indiana-based Computer Accounting, Inc., was acquired in 1975.

After buying VElectronic Data Preparation Corp. and Computer Techniques, Inc., in June 1977, Anacomp continued on the acquisition path during the late 1970s. Sci-Tek Associates was acquired in August 1978, followed by Escom, Inc., in September. The company capped off the year by acquiring an 84 percent stake in Detroit-based Computer Services Corp., along with the payroll service and computer output microfilm divisions of Wachovia Services, Inc.

Anacomp kicked off 1979 with the purchase of the Phoenix-based credit union services firm Access Data Systems, Inc., followed by the Dayton, Ohio-based credit union processor ERCO, Inc., in April. That same month, the company agreed to acquire Richmond, Virginia-based United Virginia Bank's data processing arm. Around this time, international growth was furthered when Anacomp inked a deal to supply its customer integrated reference file (CI/RF) software to the Savings Bank of South Australia. Rapid growth caused the company's revenues to reach $38.1 million in June, an increase of 76 percent from June 1978. Anacomp rounded out the year by acquiring Torrance, California-based Computer Micrographics, Inc., in September.

Anacomp had essentially evolved from a micrographics services firm that also marketed retail banking software into a major player in the financial data services sector. The company served some 250 bank locations from processing centers in San Francisco and Fresno, California, as well as Winston-Salem, North Carolina. Anacomp had become a provider of data processing services to both banks and credit unions, with assets of roughly $21 million. According to President and Chairman Ronald D. Palamara, among a field of some 3,000 computer services firms, the company ranked in the top 20 in terms of size. By December 1979, Anacomp had managed to triple both its revenues and workforce in the course of only 18 months.

FINANCIAL DATA SERVICES PLAYER

Growth continued at a fervid pace throughout the 1980s. Acquisitions continued to be a principal means of expansion, with Anacomp acquiring at least two companies in all but three years of the decade. Activity was especially heavy during the first half of the 1980s.

Anacomp ushered in the decade by acquiring Cherry Hill, New Jersey-based Kranzley & Co., a systems development enterprise serving some 33 percent of U.S. banks with deposits exceeding $1 billion. Because Kranzley had developed software systems that supported large-scale point-of-sale and ATM-related transfers between banks, the deal gave Anacomp a boost in the electronic funds transfer (EFT) sector.

Transamerica Corp.'s former Synergraphics subsidiary was acquired in June 1980, followed by a majority stake in Eikon Technology, Inc., three months later. Four acquisitions occurred in 1981, beginning with International N.V. and Micro-Land Corp. in January and February, respectively. It also was around this time that Anacomp purchased a number of General Computing Corp.'s assets.

After acquiring Microfilm Communication Systems, Inc., in mid-1981, DSI Corp. was acquired the following year for approximately $19.95 million in cash, along with Cleveland, Ohio-based Computer Management Group, Inc., and Kal Var's NMI Reader Manufacturing Division.

In April 1982 Anacomp moved forward with an application to list its stock on the New York Stock Exchange. In May, the company announced a deal with R.T.S. Associates to acquire an interactive, online retail banking database application named the Continuous Integrated System (CIS), which it had been developing in tandem with a number of banks since 1979.

Anacomp's growth in the EFT market was furthered by the release of its Bankserv 10800 transaction-switching and processing system in late 1982. In addition, the company announced that it had been tapped by the Regional Interchange Association to supply a switch for an EFT network connecting some 13,000 point-of-sale locations and ATMs in 27 states.

Rounding out the early 1980s, Anacomp snapped up two Florida-based COM service providers in 1983

KEY DATES

1968: Three Purdue University professors establish Anacomp as the first local computer services business in Indianapolis, Indiana.
1970: Anacomp goes public and immediately embarks upon a path of acquisition-based growth.
1982: Anacomp moves forward with an application to list its stock on the New York Stock Exchange.
1985: Founder Ronald D. Palamara dies of cancer in January.
1996: The company reorganizes and emerges from bankruptcy; revenues total $460 million.
1998: The company's Internet Document Services business is introduced.
2000: Anacomp begins focusing heavily on web-based document delivery and storage.
2002: Corporate headquarters relocate to a new facility in San Diego, California.

and introduced its Videoserv 2000 terminal system. That year, the company lost $3.9 million on record sales of $172.2 million. In the first quarter of fiscal year 1984, sales fell 25 percent, to $36 million, and losses swelled to $12 million. As conditions soured, some industry observers predicted Anacomp would either fold or be acquired. Conditions worsened, and when the company was about to default on a $44.6 million revolving credit loan, five banks restructured the debt into a term loan.

Anacomp pinned its difficulties on the CIS "supersystem," which it was late in delivering to banking customers. In its June 4, 1984, issue, *Computerworld* cited a report from the research firm International Data Corp. (IDC) that explored the impact of the company's woes on the larger financial industry. According to the publication, "IDC concluded that Anacomp tried to do too much at one time; did not clearly define its target market; lost control of development to clients; and did not efficiently manage its resources." In fiscal year 1984, Anacomp's losses totaled $116 million on revenues of nearly $132 million.

In May 1984 Louis P. Ferrero, a senior executive at the company since 1979, succeeded founder Ronald Palamara as president. In November, Ferrero began sharing chairman duties with Palamara, who died of cancer the following January. Ferrero was at the helm when Anacomp inked an agreement with creditors to cut the balance of its term loan to $33 million.

In order to cut costs and generate savings of approximately $6 million per year, Anacomp canceled plans to relocate its headquarters from Indiana to Atlanta in 1985. Not only did the company remain in Indiana, it relocated a number of its operations there, including data processing, micrographics, and accounting operations that were based in Long Beach, California.

After selling its U.S.A Communications, Inc., business in early 1985 for $6.7 million in cash, Anacomp spent $2.1 million to acquire three additional COM centers later that year. Two additional micrographics service centers were purchased in 1986 for roughly $1.6 million.

REFOCUSING ON MICROGRAPHICS

The most significant development at Anacomp during the mid-1980s was its exit from the banking software industry, which allowed the company to refocus on micrographics. In 1985 Anacomp had netted almost $24 million on micrographics-related revenues of $97 million. In 1986 the company sold its Bankserv funds transfer and transaction processing arm to Arlington, Virginia-based American Management Systems, Inc. The company's exit from banking software was completed that year with the additional sale of CIS to Dallas, Texas-based Electronic Data Systems Corp., as well as the sale of the Customer Integrated/Reference File (CI/RF) to Sarasota, Florida-based Michael Shade & Associates.

After divesting its banking software businesses, Anacomp's net income surged 1,025 percent for the fiscal year ending September 30, 1986. In all, the company earned $10.1 million on sales of $239 million that year.

In March 1987 Anacomp acquired DatagraphiX, Inc., from General Dynamics Corp. in a $128 million cash deal. Three months later, the company spent another $14.1 million in cash to acquire a number of Consolidated Micrographics, Inc.'s, assets. By this time, Anacomp had expanded far beyond the United States, with footholds in Belgium, Canada, France, the Netherlands, the United Kingdom, and West Germany.

Anacomp's sales increased 63 percent in 1988, reaching $450.5 million, and net income jumped 64 percent, to $43.6 million. The company proceeded to acquire a number of micrographics service centers throughout the remainder of the 1980s. In addition, Anacomp expanded its product lineup to include floppy and rigid disks, magnetics, reader/printers, and more via the acquisition of Xidex Corp. for $400.45 million in cash. Finally, the acquisition of Realist, Inc.'s, Micrographic Systems Division in 1989 bolstered Anacomp's offerings in the area of microfilm reading equipment.

Activity during the first half of the 1990s included the sale of Anacomp's flexible disc business to Hanny Magnetics Ltd. in 1990, the acquisition of National Business Systems' micrographics operations for $13.5 million in 1993, and the purchase of Graham Magnetics, Inc., the following year. A milestone was reached on June 4, 1996, when Anacomp reorganized and emerged from bankruptcy. That year, the company's revenues totaled $460 million.

FOCUS ON DOCUMENT MANAGEMENT

During the second half of the 1990s, Anacomp began concentrating more heavily on document management. In December 1996 the company acquired Data/Ware Development, Inc., giving it capabilities in the area of high-volume CD production. In 1997 Ralph W. Koehrer was named president and CEO. That year, Cambridge Technology Group, Inc., an East Brunswick, New Jersey-based multicurrency accounting software enterprise, was acquired. The addition of First Data Corp.'s First Image Management Co. division followed in mid-1998, strengthening Anacomp's document management business.

The company's Internet Document Services business was introduced toward the end of 1998. In mid-1999, Windward Capital bought Anacomp's Magnetics Solutions Group as the company continued to sharpen its focus on document management. In keeping with this strategy was the acquisition of Litton Industries' Adesso Software business in a $17 million deal. Anacomp rounded out the 1990s by acquiring Switzerland's Bgin Holdings AG in September.

Anacomp ushered in the new millennium with a number of major changes. On May 2, 2000, the company announced the resignation of President and CEO Ralph Koehrer. A new leadership approach was then revealed, in which two CEOs would be hired. One CEO would focus on the company's traditional business, with the other concentrating on Internet-based operations. The latter was becoming especially important at Anacomp, as it put more and more emphasis on web-based document delivery and storage.

It was at this time that Anacomp created a web-based document management offering called docHarbor by taking technology from the Adesso acquisition and melding it with the company's existing Internet Document Services arm. In September, Anacomp restructured operations into three independent business units. Operations then consisted of Anacomp Technical Services and Anacomp Document Solutions, as well as the newly formed docHarbor, which was absorbed into Anacomp Document Solutions midway through 2001.

Difficult times led Anacomp to file for Chapter 11 bankruptcy in October 2001, when the company's debt ($469.2 million) outweighed its assets ($211.8 million) by more than two to one. When Anacomp emerged from bankruptcy in early January 2002, restructuring gave bondholders a 99.9 percent stake in the company. Anacomp's two business units were merged into one that year.

Significant developments continued to unfold as Anacomp headed into the middle of the first decade of the new century. In December 2002 the company relocated its corporate headquarters to a new facility in San Diego. Two years later, the cost of complying with various regulatory requirements prompted Anacomp's announcement that it would deregister its securities.

Anacomp experienced more difficult times in fiscal year 2004, losing $9.9 million on revenues of $184 million. In addition to a major restructuring of its data centers, the company was forced to implement major cost-cutting measures. As CEO Jeff Cramer explained in a December 21, 2004, *PR Newswire* release: "In total, we closed 30 facilities, decreased our number of employees by 246 worldwide and incurred $9.1 million in restructuring charges."

Despite these difficulties, Anacomp pressed onward, rolling out docHarbor Document Services in 2005 and then acquiring Warrenton, Virginia-based scanning and document services firm Imaging Acceptance Corp. (IAC) in October of the following year. Because IAC dealt extensively in the government sector, the deal gave Anacomp's business a major boost in that area.

By 2007, Howard Dratler was in the CEO seat at Anacomp. Midway through the year, the company acquired the evidence and litigation management software firm CaseLogistix and made inroads into the legal industry. In a May 30, 2007, *PR Newswire* release, Dratler explained: "This is the latest in a series of strategic actions to extend our core competencies in document and business process management, enterprise capture, conversion and archiving to create significant value in a new market segment."

Over the course of 40 years, Anacomp's evolution from a tiny computer services business to a major document management firm had unfolded at a dizzying pace. Despite several rough patches, the company moved forward toward the 21st century's second decade with experience, focus, and a good chance of celebrating 50 years of operations.

Paul R. Greenland

PRINCIPAL SUBSIDIARIES

Anacomp GmbH (Germany); Anacomp Ltd. (United Kingdom); Anacomp S.A. (France).

PRINCIPAL COMPETITORS

FileNet Corporation; Lason, Inc.; Sourcecorp, Inc.

FURTHER READING

"Anacomp Announces Plans to Deregister Its Securities; Repurchases to Continue Under Its Repurchase Plan," *PR Newswire US,* December 21, 2004.

"Anacomp Completes Acquisition of CaseLogistix; Enters Litigation Support Market," *PR Newswire US,* May 30, 2007.

"Anacomp Inc.," *Mergent Online,* December 5, 2007, http://www.mergentonline.com.

"Anacomp's Problems Cripple Industry," *Computerworld,* June 4, 1984.

"Anacomp, Through Aggressive Acquisitions, Becomes Major Data Services Competitor," *American Banker,* May 25, 1979.

Kutler, Jeffrey, "Anacomp Sells Bank Software to Electronic Data Systems," *American Banker,* September 10, 1986.

Arkansas Best Corporation

3801 Old Greenwood Road
Fort Smith, Arkansas 72903-5937
U.S.A.
Telephone: (479) 785-6000
Fax: (479) 785-6009
Web site: http://www.arkbest.com

Public Company
Incorporated: 1923
Employees: 12,667
Sales: $1.9 billion (2006)
Stock Exchanges: NASDAQ
Ticker Symbol: ABFS
NAIC: 551112 Offices of Holding Companies; 484121 General Freight Trucking, Long-Distance, Truckload; 488510 Freight Transport Arrangement

■ ■ ■

Arkansas Best Corporation (ABC) is a holding company with diverse interests in all aspects of the national and international freight industry. The company's primary subsidiary, ABF Freight Systems, accounts for more than 80 percent of the company's annual revenues and provides shipping services with a fleet of more than 4,000 tractors and 20,000 trailers, with 250 shipping ports in over 150 countries. Through its other principal subsidiaries, FleetNet America and Data-Tronics Corporation, ABC also provides trailer repair and services and data and logistics management for ABF and other national freight companies.

FOUNDATION AND GROWTH: 1923–70

Arkansas Best Corporation has its roots in the ABF Freight Systems company, its largest subsidiary, which was founded in 1923 under the name OK Transfer. From the company's beginnings, hauling freight within the Arkansas borders, the company grew through several strategic mergers to expand gradually into the surrounding states. In 1935, the company completed its first major merger, combining with Arkansas Motor Freight to expand operations into Texas and the Midwest. The combined company, taking the name Arkansas Motor Freight, continued to grow rapidly, completing nine further acquisitions by 1950 and becoming one of the most profitable shipping companies in Arkansas.

In 1951, Fort Smith attorney Robert A. Young, Jr., purchased Arkansas Motor Freight and developed an aggressive business strategy that would bolster profits and help to make the company the dominant shipping concern in the region within a decade. In 1957, the company acquired Best Motor Freight and Young changed the company's name to Arkansas-Best Freight Systems. Young continued to grow his company through strategic acquisitions and eventually the senior management team decided to expand the business by forming a holding company to manage their various acquired subsidiaries.

Arkansas Best Corporation (ABC) was formally established in 1966, marking a new era for the 43-year-old trucking business. One of Young's oldest and closest business associates, H. L. Hembree, was selected to lead ABC as president, having previously worked his way

COMPANY PERSPECTIVES

We will adequately serve the needs of the shipping public by meeting the agreed-upon requirements of our customers. With consistency in pickup and delivery a priority, we will handle information requests quickly. Our sales representatives' high degree of professional knowledge will assist customers in every phase of their logistics needs.

through the company to the position of finance manager. Along with Young, who remained chairman of the board, Hembree helped to organize more than a dozen mergers and acquisitions over the following decade, significantly expanding the reach and influence of ABC's business.

In the months leading up to the formation of ABC, Young and the rest of ABF Freight's management had decided to diversify into business areas other than trucking, resolving to acquire interests that would move the company into business areas not regulated by the Interstate Commerce Commission, the federal regulatory organization responsible for supervising the railroad and carrier industries.

The company completed its first major acquisition seven months after ABC was incorporated. In December 1966, the company purchased Riverside Furniture Corporation and Twin Rivers Furniture Corporation, both of which had been established in 1946. The next acquisition moved ABC farther afield, both geographically and in business scope. In June 1968, ABC purchased a 64 percent stake in a Dallas, Texas-based financial institution, National Bank of Commerce, adding financial services to the company's widening roster of business interests. With these new additions rounding out ABC's major business interests, the company's management embarked on their new course, intent on applying their business skills to engender optimum profitability in the disparate business interests they maintained.

Within a few short years, ABC's management team had earned a solid reputation in the minds of analysts, drawing praise from nationally distributed publications that characterized the young cadre of managers as "ambitious, goal-oriented, and alert to opportunities for corporate growth." Heading this group and in charge of the day-to-day operations of the company was Hembree, who governed the company much like a former finance director would, with an emphasis on profitability and sound fiscal performance. "If you don't watch your costs," Hembree would explain later to a *Forbes* reporter about managing a trucking concern, "you can run up and down the highway with full loads and still go broke." Hembree, in the years ahead, would keep his eyes on costs, as they applied not only to ABF Freight, but to the three new additions as well. His was a perspective that placed a premium on profitability and gave ABC, which was described simply and accurately by industry pundits as a "management company," the task of stewarding each of its business segments in the right direction.

By the time the dust had settled from the acquisition of the National Bank of Commerce in June 1968, ABC was recording success in managing its new furniture business, having organized the Twin Rivers Furniture Corporation as a subsidiary of its Riverside Furniture subsidiary. By far the parent company's most important business, however, was its trucking concern, ABF Freight. By the late 1960s, ABF Freight was covering 12,500 route miles, transporting food, textiles, apparel, furniture, appliances, chemicals, and machinery, along with a host of other goods, with no single type of commodity accounting for more than 3 percent of the company's total traffic. The nearly 40-year-old trucking line hauled its freight through a 14-state area, servicing major commercial hubs throughout the Midwest and the southern United States, stopping throughout much of its service territory at company-owned terminals that were operated by another ABC subsidiary, Arkansas Bandag Corp., which also retreaded tires under a patented German process.

ABF Freight's service territory expanded before the end of the decade, moving into Pennsylvania and New York after ABC acquired Fast Freight, Inc., in November 1969. Although ABC collected roughly 80 percent of its annual revenues from its trucking business, the most promising segment of its business, at least in terms of financial growth, was its newly acquired furniture company. Riverside Furniture, which generated approximately 18 percent of its parent company's annual revenues during the late 1960s, manufactured popularly priced wood occasional tables, exposed wood living room furniture, and rocking chairs, marketing its products through the efforts of more than 50 salespeople. With roughly 5,000 wholesale and retail accounts and permanent showrooms in North Carolina, Los Angeles, San Francisco, and Seattle, Riverside Furniture ranked as one of the five largest table manufacturers in the United States, an enviable market position that was expected to grow stronger as the company benefited from the "ambitious and goal-oriented" management of ABC.

KEY DATES

1923: OK Transfer company is founded in Fort Smith, Arkansas.
1935: Combines with Arkansas Motor Freight.
1951: Company purchased by Robert A. Young, Jr.
1957: Company acquires Best Motor Freight, Inc.; name change to Arkansas-Best Freight Systems.
1966: Arkansas Best Corporation (ABC) established with H. L. Hembree as president; company purchases Riverside Furniture Corporation and Twin Rivers Furniture Corporation.
1969: Acquires Fast Freight, Inc.; moves into New York and Pennsylvania.
1978: Acquires Denver-based Navajo Freight Line.
1982: Acquires East Texas Motor Freight.
1988: Hostile takeover avoided; company taken private.
1989: Divests interest in Riverside Furniture.
1992: Company goes public, trades on NASDAQ.
1993: Company's revenues exceed $1 billion.
1995: Acquires WorldWay Corporation.
1997: FleetNet America developed as major operating division.
1999: Purchases controlling interest in Treadco, Inc.
2000: Treadco joins with Goodyear to open Wingfoot Commercial Tire Systems, LLC.
2004: Robert Davidson named president of ABC.
2006: Davidson replaces Robert A. Young III as CEO of ABC.

Early on, ABC's management was credited with staging two dramatic turnarounds, the reports of which induced financial analysts to recommend the company to prospective investors. Riverside Furniture recorded $9 million in annual sales in 1968, 26 percent more than the previous year's total. More impressive, however, was the growth achieved by National Bank of Commerce. Ranking as the fifth largest bank in Dallas County, Texas, National Bank of Commerce posted net operating earnings of nearly $850,000 in 1968, which represented an increase of 104 percent from the total recorded in 1967, giving senior management in Fort Smith every expectation that all three of their primary businesses would flourish during the decade ahead. As Hembree and the rest of his team prepared for the 1970s, plans were being made to bolster ABC's interests in each of its three major businesses, as the company searched for acquisitions in the transportation, consumer products, and financial services industries.

CHANGING BUSINESS STRATEGIES: 1970–80

During the first few years of the 1970s, ABC followed through on its plans to grow through acquisitions, purchasing Flanders Manufacturing Co. and Coffey Furniture Industries, Inc., both of which were merged into Riverside Furniture's operations. The company also added to its trucking service territory by acquiring Youngblood Truck Lines, which extended ABF Freight's presence in the southeastern United States from 16 to 19 states. After this initial spurt of acquisition activity to start the decade, the company was enjoying encouraging success, with nearly every facet of its business demonstrating vibrant growth. By the end of 1973, ABC's furniture segment was accounting for roughly 30 percent of the company's total yearly sales, up from the 18 percent it contributed five years earlier, and the profits derived from furniture manufacturing had registered a greater leap, jumping from 12 percent to 32 percent during the five-year span.

ABF Freight, meanwhile, had exhibited a vitality of its own, consistently ranking as one of the most profitable operations in the trucking industry. The 31st largest trucking concern in the country in terms of total revenues, ABF Freight operated in a 19-state territory, bounded by Wisconsin, Ohio, Indiana, and New York on the north; Kansas, Oklahoma, and Texas on the west; Louisiana, Mississippi, and Georgia on the south; and North and South Carolina on the east.

Conspicuously absent from the series of acquisitions during the early 1970s were any additions to ABC's financial services segment. Despite increasing its net income two and a half times in its first five years as a partly owned ABC subsidiary, National Bank of Commerce had proved to be an ill-advised acquisition. The bank, as one company observer noted, had "serious collateral problems in its loan portfolio," but Hembree did not become aware of such problems until 1972, four years after he had invested in the bank. Once alerted to the problem, Hembree disposed of ABC's interest, explaining, "Autonomy was the problem with [National Bank of Commerce]. It was also the only subsidiary in which we had less than 100 percent interest." After writing off $22 million over a three-year period, Hembree had learned a valuable lesson, vowing, "We will never make that mistake again."

While the National Bank of Commerce was being divested, ABC continued to strengthen its trucking concern's business, completing a string of acquisitions during the mid-1970s that gave ABF Freight the operating authority to service a larger territory. By 1977, however, the value of operating authority for additional territories was becoming questionable as the U.S. Congress was debating deregulating interstate trucking, which would open routes to any interested trucking company. Mindful that federal intervention would dramatically alter the dynamics of his company's mainstay business, Hembree knew a decision had to be made about the future course of ABF Freight and ABC if the government did indeed deregulate the trucking industry. For help, Hembree turned to his four full-time economic forecasters for advice on what the company should do in the event of deregulation.

Hembree's economic forecasters and their computers came up with three possible options: scale back expansion and become a regional trucker in the Midwest, sell the company to a larger competitor, or buy another trucking company and make a bid to become a major national carrier. In Hembree's mind, the first two options assured survival, but as he later explained to a *Forbes* reporter, "I didn't want to be just a survivor—makes it sound like you're going to a funeral. I wanted to achieve." Accordingly, he adopted the third option as the company's strategy, deciding that before deregulation opened the floodgates to the trucking industry ABF Freight would become a major national competitor. The first step toward national prominence was taken in 1978, when Hembree authorized the acquisition of Denver-based Navajo Freight Line for roughly $15 million. The move immediately transformed ABF Freight from the country's 22nd largest trucking company into the eighth largest concern.

DEREGULATION AND ADJUSTMENT: 1980–2000

In the early 1980s, ABC continued its growth strategy with the acquisition, in 1982, of East Texas Motor Freight, Inc. With the addition of East Texas and Navajo Freight, the company had access to 90 percent of the nation's major metropolitan markets. Still the major engine driving ABC's growth, ABF Freight contributed the bulk of what its parent company declared in annual sales, a figure that had grown exponentially between the mid-1970s and mid-1980s, soaring from roughly $150 million to more than $500 million.

The U.S. trucking industry, as expected, was deregulated early in the decade, making the operating rights ABC had obtained through more than 30 acquisitions essentially worthless. The passage of the 1980 Motor Carrier Act also precipitated another change in ABF Freight's business, one that would change the way in which the company operated and opened the doors to a flourishing segment of the carrier market. The number of licensed trucking companies doubled in the first few years after deregulation; then, just as quickly, a majority of the new entrants fell into financial ruin. The rising number of bankruptcies created more than $1 billion worth of extra business for those who survived, with the biggest profits going to those companies that operated as less-than-truckload (LTL) carriers. Aware of the shifting dynamics in its industry, ABC changed from being a truckload operator to an LTL carrier, ranking by the mid-1980s as one of the five leading competitors in the lucrative industry niche market.

In 1988, Emanuel Pearlman's Razorback Acquisition Corporation attempted a hostile takeover of Arkansas Best. The company avoided the takeover through a partnership with Kelso & Co., a New York-based private equity company that conducted a leveraged buyout, thereby making ABC a private company. ABC repaid its debt, under the leadership of Robert A. Young III, and engaged in a number of fund raising measures, which included selling its subsidiary, USA Truck, and its furniture business in 1989. In 1992, the company returned to public status, trading its shares on the NASDAQ.

By the end of 1993, ABC could rightly call itself a $1 billion company, generating $1.009 billion in sales and posting more than $50 million in operating income. Growth continued over the next several years and, in 1995, ABC was posting annual sales in excess of $1.4 billion. As the company prepared for the beginning of the 21st century, Robert A. Young III, the son of ABC's founding chairman, was leading the way as chief executive officer, hoping to continue the robust growth that had transformed the company's mainstay business from the 48th largest trucking company into the country's fourth largest.

The 1995 acquisition of WorldWay Corporation, a holding company similar to ABC, gave the company control of two of their major competitors, Carolina Freight Carriers Corporation and Red Arrow Freight Lines, Inc. Carolina Freight Carriers Corporation also had a subsidiary company, known as Carolina Breakdown Service, that provided breakdown assistance and repair for the company's vehicles. After the integration of Carolina's companies into ABC, the company bolstered their investment in the breakdown service, transforming it into one of the company's major operating divisions. The company was renamed FleetNet America in 1997 and began offering its services to truckers working with other shipping companies and for privately owned trucks.

While the company diversified its vehicle repair operations, significant resources were also invested in Data-Tronics Corp. (DTC), the company's logistics and computer services division, which was established in 1962 and had grown along with ABC to handle the needs of the company's rapidly expanding shipping divisions. By the end of the 1990s, DTC was one of the company's three largest divisions and had successfully shifted toward an Internet system for managing shipping and logistics. DTC's programming and development teams were recognized within the industry for their innovative design solutions, which played a major role in helping ABC's shipping companies to become leaders in the national market.

ABC ENTERS THE 21ST CENTURY

Arkansas Best achieved its third year of record income in 2000, recording over $1.8 billion in revenues for the year, and was recognized by *Forbes* magazine as one of the nation's 400 leading companies. ABF Freight Systems continued to be the company's largest and most profitable subsidiary, accounting for more than 75 percent of revenues. Among the notable accomplishments of the year, ABC's subsidiary Treadco, which the company purchased in 1999, entered into a joint venture with Goodyear, Inc., to create Wingfoot Commercial Tire Systems, LLC, which was the largest network of tire sales and service in the nation.

The following year, ABC's business suffered during a recession that extended into nearly every national industry. Revenues fell from $1.8 billion to $1.5 billion in 2001 and $1.4 billion in 2002. The company responded by selling some of its less-profitable divisions and paying down company debt. In 2003, revenues returned to the $1.5 billion mark and the company had successfully eliminated its long-term debt (estimated in 1995 at over $400 million). Despite two years of financial difficulties, ABC was still recognized by analyst organizations, such as *Forbes* magazine, as one of the leading companies in the nation. Revenues increased again in 2004, reaching $1.7 billion by the end of the year.

As Robert Young III planned for his eventual retirement, the company made changes to its management and executive staff. Robert A. Davidson, who joined the company in 1972 in the company's economic analysis department and later served as president of ABF Freight System, Inc., was named to the ABC Board of Directors in December 2003. In January 2004, Davidson was promoted to president and chief operating officer. With a history of prudent economic analysis and management, Davidson helped to develop strategies that continued the two-year pattern of growth for ABC and its largest affiliates. After Davidson's first full year at the company's helm, ABC reported revenues exceeding $1.8 billion. It was reported in October 2005 that Robert A. Young III would retire, effective in 2006, and that Davidson had been named as his replacement to serve as ABC's CEO.

In 2006, the board completed the sale of Clipper Exxpress, the company's intermodal transportation subsidiary, for a reported price of $19 million. Although Clipper had been a strong contributor to the company's past successes, the company had come to represent less than 10 percent of incoming revenues and had declined in profitability over the course of ABC's ownership. In addition, Davidson cited a "lack of synergy" between Clipper and the rest of ABC's subsidiary businesses as a key reason for the sale. In 2006, ABC recorded approximately $1.9 billion in revenues and had achieved a steady pattern of growth. As in previous years, ABF was consistently the most profitable subsidiary, representing over 90 percent of the company's revenues.

In the company's transition from local shipping management to nationwide shipping and logistics leader, ABC's success relied on shrewd industry analysis and confident management. By the third quarter of 2007, ABC had experienced a net reduction in profits, largely related to fluctuations within the industry and changes to tonnage levels and costs. Third-quarter revenues were estimated at $479.8 million compared to third-quarter 2006 revenues of $507.3 million. Although industry changes again posed a challenge, Davidson and his fellow managers remained confident that the company's financial outlook was positive.

Jeffrey L. Covell
Updated, Micah L. Issitt

PRINCIPAL SUBSIDIARIES

ABF Freight System, Inc.; Data-Tronics Corp.; FleetNet America, Inc.

PRINCIPAL COMPETITORS

Con-way Freight; FedEx Freight; YRC Worldwide, Inc.

FURTHER READING

"Arkansas Best Unit Acquisition," *Wall Street Journal,* December 29, 1978, p. 24.

Bagamery, Anne, "We Want to Achieve," *Forbes,* August 17, 1981, p. 58.

"Bid Made for Arkansas Best," *New York Times,* May 3, 1988.

"Concern Concedes to Kelso, Drops Bid for Arkansas Best," *Wall Street Journal,* June 27, 1988, p. 17.

"Kelso Adding Arkansas Best," *New York Times,* June 18, 1988.

Mitchell, Ruth, "Truckin' On," *Arkansas Business,* July 15, 1991, p. 25.

Myers, Randy, "Growth Trucker," *Barron's,* November 11, 1985, p. 85.

Power, Christopher, "What Can You Buy with $116,325 and a Good Idea," *Business Week,* June 13, 1988, p. 38.

Smith, David, "Treadco Investors Know What's Best," *Arkansas Business,* April 1999.

Turner, Lance, "Arkansas Best to Sell Clipper Unit for $20 Million," *Arkansas Business,* May 2006.

Ash Grove Cement Company

11011 Cody Street
Overland Park, Kansas 66210
U.S.A.
Telephone: (913) 451-8900
Toll Free: (800) 545-1882
Fax: (913) 451-5697
Web site: http://www.ashgrove.com

Private Company
Incorporated: 1882 as Ash Grove White Lime Association
Employees: 2,600
Sales: $1.2 billion (2006 est.)
NAIC: 327310 Cement Manufacturing

■ ■ ■

Ash Grove Cement Company is one of the leading cement manufacturing companies in the United States and the largest American-owned company in the field. Spread across nine states, the privately held, Overland Park, Kansas-based business operates nine cement plants with a combined annual production capacity of nearly nine million tons and also operates one lime plant in Portland, Oregon, 20 cement terminals, and aggregate quarries in Canada and the United States. Ash Grove offers a full range of cement products used in construction, as well as masonry cement and oil well cement. In addition, Ash Grove produces ready-mix concrete and aggregates, and through subsidiary Ash Grove Packaging offers a wide range of building products for the contractor and do-it-yourself market, including general purpose portland cement, repair cements, sealers and additives, caulks, sand, stucco, mortar, and decorative rocks. Ash Grove is owned and headed by the fourth generation of the Sunderland family.

ORIGINS IN THE 19TH CENTURY

Ash Grove was not founded by the Sunderland family. Rather, it was established in Ash Grove, Missouri, in 1882 by businessmen James H. Barton, Charles W. Goetz, and W. B. Hill, according to documents held by the Springfield-Greene County Library in Missouri. The leader of the group was Barton. Born in St. Louis in 1844, he was sent to Boston to be raised by an aunt after his mother died and his father headed west to become one of the "forty-niners" who tried their luck in the newly discovered gold fields of northern California. After serving in the Union army during the Civil War, Barton returned to St. Louis and ran an itinerant supply store that followed the construction crews of the St. Louis & San Francisco Railroad Company as they laid tracks toward the West Coast. Barton moved only as far as Pierce City, Missouri, opening a lumber business that he ran for several years before opening a lime kiln, which was fired by large quantities of wood. In 1880 he moved to Ash Grove, where construction for the Springfield & Western Missouri Railroad had uncovered the purest seam of limestone in the United States. Along with partners Goetz and Hill, Barton formed the Ash Grove White Lime Association.

According to contemporaneous accounts, the business was established in 1880. The limestone was crushed, and then cooked in the company's lone kiln,

> COMPANY PERSPECTIVES
>
> The Ash Grove Cement Company has a strong and longstanding tradition of service, reliability, and quality that reaches back more than 125 years.

producing an exceptional grade of white lime, the first shipment of which was made in May 1881. During this period lime had a number of uses. It was needed to make plaster as well as the mortar used in the construction of brick and stone buildings. Lime was also a household product used to sanitize outhouses.

COMPANY INCORPORATED

According to Ash Grove Cement documentation, Ash Grove White Lime was incorporated in 1882 with a capital of $10,000. The company expanded steadily until there were 11 kilns in operation. In addition, Ash Grove White Lime opened a two-kiln plant in Galloway, Missouri, a depot town of the St. Louis & San Francisco Railroad Company. In 1891 the company moved its headquarters to Kansas City, Missouri, a key midwestern rail center.

The demand for traditional uses of lime began to decline late in the decade. Not only did the rise of indoor plumbing lower the need for household lime, but portland cement became the building material of choice, superseding brick and stone construction, thus putting a crimp on the demand for lime used to make mortar. In 1907 Barton died at the age of 64 and in that same year Ash Grove White Lime was reorganized and incorporated as Ash Grove Lime and Portland Cement Company with a capital stock $2.75 million. Some of those funds were used to make the transition to cement production and in 1908 a portland cement plant was opened in Chanute, Kansas.

The company soon ran into financial difficulties, however, and one of its customers, the Sunderland Brothers Company of Omaha, Nebraska, believed it was in its best interest to make sure the business survived. Sunderland had been founded by James A. Sunderland in 1883 to supply coal, cement, lime, and other building materials needed by the fast-growing city of Omaha. Four years later he was joined by his 20-year-old brother, Lester T. Sunderland, who had been working in the coal business in Ottumwa, Iowa, since leaving school at the age of 14.

SUNDERLAND FAMILY BECOMES INVOLVED

By the start of the 1900s, Sunderland Brothers was supplying 80 percent of Omaha's building supplies, including Ash Grove white lime. When Ash Grove Lime and Portland Cement began to falter, the Sunderland brothers did not want to lose its business. In 1909 they formed a new company to keep their Omaha business separate and took an ownership position in Ash Grove Lime and Portland Cement. Lester was then dispatched to Kansas City to become vice-president and general manager of this new entity. In 1913 he was elected president of the company.

Under Lester Sunderland's leadership, Ash Grove rebounded and resumed growth, especially prospering during the years of World War I. He also became a respected industry figure. In 1921 he was named president of the Portland Cement Association. During the Roaring Twenties Ash Grove continued to grow and in 1929 the company opened its second cement plant, located in Louisville, Nebraska. However, that was also the year of the stock market crash that precipitated the Great Depression of the 1930s. Poor economic conditions and tight money resulted in a dearth of new construction and a drop in demand for portland cement and lime. The original lime plant in Ash Grove was closed, severing ties with the company's birthplace. Ash Grove Cement was barely able to scrape by during this difficult period, but was still in business when the economy roared back to life in the 1940s, fueled by military spending after the United States entered World War II in late 1941. To help meet demand, a quarry in Springfield, Missouri, was acquired in 1941.

Lester Sunderland continued to head Ash Grove Cement until 1946, when he turned over the presidency to his 50-year-old son, Paul Sunderland. The younger Sunderland had been born in Omaha in 1896 and moved with his parents to Kansas City in 1910. After enrolling at the University of Wisconsin, he left school to enlist in the U.S. Navy during World War I, serving as a mechanic on an escort cruiser that accompanied North Atlantic convoys. Upon his discharge he went to work for the family company at the Springfield, Missouri, operation until returning to Kansas City in 1946 to replace his father, who stayed on as chairman of the executive committee until his death in 1955. Another son, Allan B. Sunderland, four years younger than Paul, also worked for Ash Grove Cement. When their father died, Allan became president and Paul assumed the chairmanship. Just a year later, however, Allan Sunderland died as well.

KEY DATES

1882: Ash Grove White Lime Association incorporated in Ash Grove, Missouri.
1891: Headquarters moved to Kansas City, Missouri.
1907: Business reorganized as Ash Grove Lime and Portland Cement Company.
1909: Sunderland family buys into company.
1929: Louisville, Nebraska, cement plant opens.
1946: Second generation of Sunderland family takes charge.
1968: Name changed to Ash Grove Cement Company.
1983: Portland Cement Co. acquired.
1992: Seattle plant expanded.
2000: Lyman-Richey Corp. acquired.
2003: New headquarters opened in Overland Park, Kansas.

Ash Grove Cement took advantage of the postwar economic boom that resulted in an abundance of construction projects that required cement. New housing was needed for returning servicemen and their wives, who gave birth to the baby-boom generation that in turn required new hospitals and new schools. New security concerns arising out of the Cold War with the Soviet Union led to the building of the interstate highway system, intended to transport men and materials in the case of war. To keep pace with increasing demand, Ash Grove Cement installed a new kiln in its Louisville plant in 1949, increasing annual production to 375,000 tons.

NAME SHORTENED

The 1960s would bring a host of upgrades to Ash Grove Cement. In 1962 a transfer station was added in Kansas City to accommodate truck deliveries. Two years later the Chanute plant received a much-needed modernization, which increased production capacity from 164,500 tons to 574,000 tons. Also in 1964 the company's present-day lime plant was opened in Portland, Oregon, originally intended as just a Pacific Northwest supplier. During this time the Springfield quarry was abandoned after it had supplied more than six billion pounds of material during nearly 80 years in operation. Moreover, in 1968 the company shortened its name to Ash Grove Cement Company. A year earlier the third generation of the Sunderland family took charge when Paul Sunderland retired as chairman in his early 70s. By this time honorary chairman, he remained active in the business and lived until the age of 107, passing away in 2004 as one of the country's oldest living World War I veterans.

After difficult economic times in the 1970s, Ash Grove Cement resumed its growth in the 1980s. The Louisville plant was expanded in 1982, increasing its annual production capacity to one million tons. The following year the company grew externally, acquiring Durkee, Oregon-based Oregon Portland Cement Co., with plants Durkee, Oregon, and Inkom, Idaho, as well as in British Columbia, Canada. In 1984 a cement plant in Seattle, Washington, was acquired for $23 million from Lone Star Industries, which also included its limestone reserves at Dall Island, Alaska. The following year Ash Grove Cement paid $38 million to Arkla, Inc., for a cement plant in Foreman, Arkansas. The company paid an estimated $25 million in 1987 to acquire a Montana City, Montana, plant, and two years bought another plant in Leamington, Utah.

More changes were to follow in the 1990s. The Seattle plant was expanded and modernized in 1992, and a year later a stake was acquired in North Texas Cement Company, which owned a plant in Midlothian, Texas. By the middle of the decade sales reached $400 million. To maintain production, Ash Grove Cement required massive amounts of fuel to keep its kiln furnaces running. This problem was turned into an opportunity in the 1990s when the company developed a new revenue stream by collecting other companies' flammable wastes, such as industrial cleaners, paint residues, and printing solvents—items that were not permitted to be buried in landfills. The materials were burned to supplement the usual coal, providing a significant savings on fuel bills. When flammable wastes became scarcer, Ash Grove Cement turned its attention to old tires, for which the company was paid between 50 cents and $1 to remove. The kilns, burning at 3,500 degrees Fahrenheit, were able to consume virtually the entire tire, even vaporizing the steel in steel-belted radials.

BUILDING TOWARD THE FUTURE

Ash Grove Cement took advantage of a building boom that began in the 1990s and extended into the new century, when the company continued to invest in expansion. Ground was broken in October 1999 on a $160 million modernization and expansion project in Chanute. In 2000 the company acquired Lyman-Richey Corp., an Omaha, Nebraska-based concrete company with a history almost as long as Ash Grove Cement. It was established in Lawrence, Kansas, in 1884, moved to

Nebraska eight years later, and began operating in Omaha in 1929. Ash Grove Cement bolstered its position in the Texas market in 2002 when the rest of the Midlothian plant was acquired. In the meantime, the Chanute project was completed, resulting in a new dry process plant, which replaced a wet process plant that had been in operation for close to a century. In addition the facility received a 40,000-square-foot core building, a massive geodesic storage dome, bins, mills, and silos.

A new headquarters was opened in Overland Park, Kansas, in 2003, followed by a number of other advances. The company joined forces with San Antonio, Texas-based Alamo Cement Co. and Texas Lehigh Cement Company in 2004 to build a terminal on the Port of Houston, a facility that opened in August 2006, the same year that the Portland terminal was upgraded. For the first time since 1929 Ash Grove decided to build a plant, rather than acquire, announcing in 2005 that it planned to construct a plant in Moapa, Nevada. Although the construction industry was turning soft, Ash Grove cement was undeterred about building the new plant because it viewed the investment from a long-term perspective, the growth potential of the region for the next half-century. It was that same mind-set taken by the company in 2007 when it began work on a $190 million expansion of the Foreman, Arkansas, plant.

Ed Dinger

PRINCIPAL SUBSIDIARIES

Ash Grove Packaging; Kansas City Ready-Mix Group; Lyman-Rich Corp.; Permanent Paving, Inc.

PRINCIPAL COMPETITORS

Cemex, S.A. de C.V.; Holcim (US), Inc.; Lafarge North America, Inc.

FURTHER READING

"Ash Grove Celebrates Plant Upgrade with Open House," *Concrete Products,* November 2001, p. 55.

"Ash Grove Cement Will Build HQ in Overland Park," *Kansas City Business Journal,* March 20, 2001.

Crumpley, Charles R. T., "Cement Is Not Firm's Sole Trade," *Kansas City Star,* August 19, 1997, p. D7.

Hillix, Danielle, "Area's Last Known WWI Vet Dies at 107," *Kansas City Star,* January 13, 2004, p. B1.

Wilkerson, Jan, "New Players Churn Up Cement, Concrete Market," *Business Journal-Portland,* May 11, 1987, p. 8.

Autoridad del Canal de Panamá

Balboa Ancón
Panama City,
Panama
Telephone: (50 7) 272-7877
Fax: (50 7) 272-2122
Web site: http://www.pancanal.com

State-Owned Company
Incorporated: 1997
Employees: 9,210
Sales: $1.76 billion (2007)
NAIC: 221121 Electric Bulk Transmission and Control; 221310 Water Supply and Irrigation Systems; 488330 Navigational Services to Shipping; 488390 Other Support Activities for Water Transportation

■ ■ ■

The Autoridad del Canal de Panamá (ACP), or Panama Canal Authority, is an autonomous public body of the Republic of Panama whose function is to administer, conserve, maintain, and modernize the Panama Canal, with the aim of operating the canal in a secure, continuous, efficient, and profitable manner. It is also responsible, in coordination with other government agencies, for the administration, maintenance, use, and conservation of the water resources—rivers and lakes—linked to the canal.

The ACP is governed by an appointed 11-member board whose chairman is appointed by the president of the republic and who is a cabinet member with the title minister of canal affairs. It is, however, an autonomous body with its own assets and budget. The ACP maintains itself from its own profits. While it pays no taxes, it provides the Republic of Panama with surplus funds after meeting its own needs. It also forwards part of what it collects in tolls to the Panamanian state. ACP is, in terms of revenue, one of the biggest businesses in Central America. According to some estimates, the Panama Canal and businesses dependent on it are responsible for 40 percent—and perhaps more—of Panama's gross domestic product.

THE FIRST YEARS

The 51-mile-long Panama Canal, linking the Atlantic and Pacific oceans, was built by the United States and began operation in 1914. A 1977 treaty ceded the Canal Zone, over which the United States had exercised sovereignty, to Panama. It was turned over to Panama in 1979, but the canal itself, and use of about 40 percent of the land in the former zone for maintenance of the canal, remained with the United States until the last day of 1999. During this period the canal was administered by the nine-member Panama Canal Commission, which was a U.S. agency, although it included Panamanian members and had a Panamanian administrator from 1990. The Autoridad del Canal de Panamá (ACP), the successor agency, was created by Panama in 1997 to administer, operate, maintain, and modernize the canal after the turnover on December 31, 1999. Among its provisions was a prohibition of strikes by its employees.

The ACP inherited aging infrastructure, with problems such as cracks in the concrete of the locks and deterioration of the machinery that opened and closed

KEY DATES

1997: Panama establishes the Autoridad del Canal de Panamá (ACP) to administer the Panama Canal after 1999.

1999: The United States turns over the canal to Panama on the last day of the year.

2002: The ACP completes widening of the part of the canal called the Gaillard Cut.

2004: Toll revenues pass $1 billion a year for the first time.

2006: Panama's electorate approves a plan to widen the canal over a seven-year period.

the locks. Leading up to this time, the canal had been closed for repairs more and more frequently. An even more serious problem was traffic congestion. It was agreed that the Culebra, or Gaillard, Cut at the narrowest part of the canal needed to be widened and deepened so that two-way traffic could pass at all hours. The widening of this part of the canal was completed in 2002; dredging to deepen the channel began later.

An expansion of the canal's waterway and the building of a larger third set of locks at either end of the canal were also envisioned. Although the ACP received $160 million from tolls that the former Panama Canal Commission had held on reserve, an increase in the toll rate was considered inevitable, since the commission, a nonprofit body, was running a deficit, although a small one. There had been little incentive for the commission to operate in the black, since any profit had to be spent during the same fiscal year.

The ACP, by contrast, was expected to turn a profit. Ricardo Martinelli, its chairman, told Lisa K. Wing of *LatinFinance* in 1999, "The canal's main objective was to pass ships through the canal, it was a strategic and military operation for the U.S. We now want to continue providing reliable and efficient services, but also make a profit on the side." While tolls were the main source of income, transit-related services also brought in a significant sum, and some revenue came from electric power and water sales, plus rental fees. Martinelli said that selling electricity and water to Panamanian cities and corporations could bring in more money if the authority realized plans to build three hydroelectric plants in the canal watershed. He also cited tourism, including visitors aboard cruise ships, as a potentially growing source of funds. The average ship toll was $65,000 in 2005, but the largest cruise ships were paying about $250,000.

PREPARING FOR EXPANSION

The ACP slimmed down its operations by selling what an U.S. businessman and former naval officer told Richard Lapper of the *Financial Times* was "beautifully maintained antique equipment." Employment was trimmed, and productivity levels increased noticeably. The businessman who spoke to Lapper said, "They are doing a better job of it than the Americans did." In 2002 the authority opened an information system available for rent to telecommunications companies. It offered broadband data transmission services in the area through its fiber-optic network.

The ACP quickly proved financially capable, earning a profit of about $90 million in fiscal 2002 (the year ended September 30, 2002). It also proved operationally capable, setting a record in 2003 for consecutive days without an accident. Tolls were revised so that oil tankers, container and other cargo vessels, and cruise ships were, for the first time, charged different rates. Toll revenues passed $1 billion for the first time in fiscal 2004. Tolls on container ships—which in 2002 became the canal's chief users—were increased in 2005, 2006, and 2007. By the end of fiscal 2006, income from tolls and dividends had risen more than fivefold since 1999.

Higher tolls did not discourage shippers from directing merchant traffic through the Panama Canal. The percentage of container traffic through the canal from Asia to the U.S. Atlantic seaboard grew from 11 percent in 2000 to 40 percent in 2007. Business was so good that in the last week of March 2006, the number of ships waiting in line to pass through the canal reached 78, resulting in delays of up to five days to cross, far more than the average of about 26 hours.

This traffic congestion was one reason the ACP was anxious to widen the waterway. Another was to win the trade carried by the growing number of vessels too large to be accommodated by the existing canal. A study found that the proportion of the world's sea cargo passing through the Panama Canal had fallen from 5.6 percent in 1970 to 3.4 percent in 2004. In a 2006 referendum, Panama's voters approved, by a 4-to-1 margin, the ACP's plan for a third set of parallel three-step locks on both the Atlantic and Pacific ends of the canal so that many of the 20 percent of the world's ships too long and/or too wide to pass through the canal could do so in the future. Some container ships were at that time twice as big as the canal could accommodate, and there were oil tankers that were five times as large.

Construction began September 3, 2007 and was planned to be completed in 2014 (the canal's centennial), at an estimated expense of $5.25 billion. Part of this cost would be borne by container ships, but, for the first time since 2002, the tolls for general cargo ships, bulk-cargo barges, refrigerated vessels, car carriers, and oil tankers would be raised. The authority's administrator had declared that the ACP intended to double the toll rate over 20 years, at an annual rate of 3.5 percent. The increased capacity of the canal was projected to increase annual revenue more than fourfold, to $6 billion, over this period.

REMAINING COMPETITIVE

ACP officials realized, however, that tolls might rise beyond a competitive rate. Other alternatives were available to shippers receiving goods from, or sending goods to, the eastern coast of the United States, which together accounted for almost two-thirds of traffic passing through the Panama Canal.

Rail and road links were available to connect North American Atlantic, Pacific, and Gulf Coast ports with one another and to the continental midsection. Another possible alternative would be proposed rail and road lines through Mexico's Isthmus of Tehuantepec, the narrow band of land dividing the Pacific Ocean and the Gulf of Mexico.

Still another alternative for East Asian shipping, such as the many vessels bearing Chinese merchandise to the eastern United States, was westward through the Indian Ocean, Suez Canal, Mediterranean Sea, and Atlantic Ocean to East Coast ports, rather than across the Pacific Ocean and through the canal into the Atlantic. Because of economy of scale, some vessels would be too big to pass through even a widened Panama Canal but would still be competitive in price despite the long voyage around South America.

Tolls accounted for 69 percent of the ACP's revenues of $1.49 billion in fiscal 2006. Transit related services accounted for another 21 percent. Of the authority's $675.93 million in net income, almost half was forwarded to the national treasury. Its revenues grew to $1.76 billion in fiscal 2007, and its net income to $806.65 million.

In 2007 the ACP was holding talks with international banks to provide $1.5 billion to $2.3 billion for the project in the form of extending loans or purchasing bonds. Meanwhile, it had begun to spend more than $1 billion on various other improvements. These included purchasing 14 new tugboats; turntables at each end of the locks so that the locomotives (or "mules") guiding ships through the locks would not need to be changed; two waiting area mooring stations at the Pacific end of the locks; and new lighting systems at the locks for greater reliability. The improvements, completed in 2007, were regarded as needed to service vessels properly before the opening of the new set of locks. They made it possible for the canal to continue accommodating about 14,000 ship transits each year.

THE PROPOSED EXPANSION

The long range project called for new locks more than three times the size of the existing ones in order to accommodate supertankers and container ships as much as four football fields in length. The locks would be able to accommodate vessels with a draft of almost as much as 60 feet and a weight almost two and a half times the existing limit. As many as 12,000, 20-foot containers could be carried on a single ship passing through the expanded canal, compared to a maximum of fewer than 5,000 on ships traveling through the existing locks.

Nearly five miles of new channels in all, on both the Atlantic and Pacific sides, would be dug into the earth for the locks, which, like the existing ones, would lift ships up from one end to the level of 166-square-mile Lake Gatún about 90 feet above sea level and lower them at the other end. The locomotives used to guide ships through the existing locks would be replaced by a computerized guidance system. However, the amount of water needed for the enormous locks would strain the resources of Lake Gatún in the dry season, requiring a huge amount of dredging to increase the capacity of this artificially created reservoir, also used for Panama City's drinking water.

In order to conserve Panama's water resources, the plan called for each new lock to contain a basin allowing displaced water to be reused rather than escaping to the sea. According to an ACP manager, the waters of the Chagres River flowing into Lake Gatún would be sufficient to meet the canal's increased needs. However, other environmentalists questioned this assessment, at least in years of extreme drought. Under consideration was a proposal to create another reservoir from the waters of two rivers to the west of the canal.

The excavation of earth for the new channels, plus the added dredging of existing bodies of water, would entail the destruction of almost three square miles of mangrove forest lining the canal, threatening the welfare of many bird and fish species. Because of the loss of mangrove forest, plus the existing deforestation in the area due to logging and clearing of land for agriculture and cattle raising, there would be a greater prospect of havoc inducing floods during the rainy season. The huge amount of earth and rock excavated would have to be dumped somewhere else in the canal watershed, creating another environmental challenge.

Robert Halasz

FURTHER READING

"Aprueba asamblea ley sobre el Canal," *Reforma* (Mexico City), May 16, 1997, p. 21.

Brooks, Mark, "The Bigger Ditch," *Globe and Mail* (Toronto), July 23, 2005, Sec. F, p. 6.

"Challenges Ahead for Canal," *LatinFinance,* February 2002, p. 51.

Dean, Cornelia, "To Save Its Canal, Panama Fights for Its Forests," *New York Times,* May 24, 2005, pp. F1, F4.

Fahey, Michael, "El canal usado," *AméricaEconomía,* December 1997, pp. 54–55.

Lapper, Richard, and Adam Thomson, "Panama Gates Unlocked to Surprise Prosperity," *Financial Times,* July 24, 2007, p. 4.

Leach, Peter T., "Building Bridges," *Journal of Commerce,* August 6, 2007, p. 40.

———, "How High the Sky?" *Journal of Commerce,* February 12, 2007, p. 38.

Schexnayder, C. J., "Panama Canal Construction Shapes the Future for Shipping," *ENR/Engineering News Record,* April 30, 2007, pp. 26–30.

"Tomorrow's Canal," *LatinFinance,* February 2005, pp. 72–73.

Wing, Lisa K., "Raising Revenues," *LatinFinance,* December 1999/January 2000, pp. 25–26, 28.

B.W. Rogers Company

380 Water Street
Akron, Ohio 44308-1045
U.S.A.
Telephone: (330) 762-0251
Fax: (330) 762-5505
Web site: http://www.bwrogers.com

Private Company
Incorporated: 1929
Employees: 95
Sales: $30 million (1995 est.)
NAIC: 423840 Industrial Supplies Merchant Wholesalers; 423610 Electrical Apparatus and Equipment, Wiring Supplies, and Related Equipment Merchant Wholesalers

■ ■ ■

The subsidiaries and affiliates of Akron, Ohio-based B.W. Rogers Company supply fluid connectors, motion control, and process equipment for a wide variety of industries, including automotive, biomedical, construction machinery, conveyors, food products machinery, glass, fabricated metals, life sciences, metalworking machinery, packaging, rubber and plastic, special machinery, and steel. Rogers operates in more than 20 locations in Ohio, Pennsylvania, West Virginia, Indiana, and Kentucky, doing business under the B.W. Rogers name as well as those of its sister units.

The Indianapolis-based HydraAir division serves Indiana, Kentucky, Ohio, and Pennsylvania, specializing in hoses and fittings. Kentucky Pneumatics Inc. is a Louisville, Kentucky-based distributor of fluid power valves, cylinders, power tools, accessories, and automated controls. Based in Pittsburgh, Pennsylvania, Exonic Systems focuses on electromechanical automation products, including motion control, process control, sensors, and pneumatic and vacuum products, as well as repair, engineering services, and training. Pennsylvania Hose & Fittings is a Monroeville, Pennsylvania, distributor of fluid connector parts and other hydraulics, pneumatics, and filtration products to makers of fluid connectors and to other small and medium users.

Another Louisville-based unit, Fluid Power Products, supplies industrial customers with automation, connector, hydraulic, pneumatic, process equipment, and industrial power tools products. Based in Wheeling, West Virginia, Scott Fluid Power supplies industrial customers with hoses and fittings. Finally, Machine Drive Company maintains operations in Indianapolis, Cincinnati, and Wapakoneta, Ohio, providing variable speed, motion control, motor control, and industrial automotive products and design, repair, and project management services. B.W. Rogers is a private company owned by the Rogers family and headed by a third-generation chief executive officer, Richard "Rick" Rogers.

COMPANY FOUNDED

The man behind the establishment of B.W. Rogers was Bruce W. Rogers, Sr. A trained engineer, Rogers was employed by the Akron rubber company, B.F. Goodrich, when he decided to go into business for himself in

COMPANY PERSPECTIVES

Through the years, the B.W. Rogers Company has grown through affiliations and acquisitions. But through our growth, we've always remained focused on our core business and a singular goal of providing you with the quality products, services and dependability that your endeavor demands.

1928. He started out as an independent sales representative for makers of power transmission and process equipment, pitching his wares to industrial customers in northeast Ohio. A year later he established a distributorship in Akron under the name B.W. Rogers Company.

The year 1929 was not a particularly good time to start a business of any kind. In October the stock market crashed, leading to a financial crisis and the Great Depression that encompassed all of the 1930s. Tough times would not be fully overcome until defense spending from the United States' entry into World War II spurred an economic boom. B.W. Rogers managed to scrape by during the early years of the Depression until he was able to establish regular customers among Akron's rubber and tire companies and machine builders.

POSTWAR EXPANSION

In the postwar era Rogers expanded his slate of products beyond power transmission and process equipment by becoming the initial distributor of the hydraulic tube fittings produced by the Parker Appliance Company, which would later be known as the Parker Hannifin Corporation. Parker Appliance had been founded in Cleveland in 1918 by Arthur L. Parker, who developed a pneumatic brake system for trucks and buses. He later developed pneumatic seals used in aircraft, including the plane Charles Lindbergh used to cross the Atlantic Ocean. The business was converted to produce war materials during World War II but soon after the war ended in 1945 Parker died from a heart attack.

A brief recession that followed the war crippled Parker Appliance, which was at the edge of bankruptcy. Parker's widow invested the $1 million she received from his life insurance policy to rebuild the business. A new management team was installed to expand the company's fluid components products. The relationship with B.W. Rogers as distributor played a large role in revitalizing Parker's business. Both companies prospered from a mutually beneficial relationship that would endure.

A SECOND GENERATION JOINS THE COMPANY

Soon after the affiliation with Parker, B.W. Rogers was poised to expand beyond northeast Ohio into other parts of the state. Business was strong enough in Cleveland that Rogers opened a second office in the city to better serve its customers there. The Rogers company remained a two-city operation through the 1950s. During this period a second generation of the Rogers family became involved with the business. In 1956 Bruce W. Rogers, Jr., joined the company after graduating from the University of Akron with a degree in engineering. The younger Rogers started out as a salesman, a position for which he was not particularly suited, yet he heeded the advice his father had to offer, words that he would offer others later in life: "Work harder than you're expected to work. Work harder than you're paid to work, and work harder than the guy sitting next to you."

B.W. Rogers continued to expand in the 1960s. It extended its footprint southward to the central Ohio markets, opening an office in Columbus in 1960. By the end of the decade B.W. Rogers was doing well enough in northern and central Ohio to venture into the southwest corner of the state, to serve southern Ohio as well as stake a claim in northern Kentucky by adding an office in Cincinnati in 1969.

DEATH OF FOUNDER SLOWS COMPANY GROWTH

In 1971 Bruce W. Rogers died unexpectedly, leaving the company in a state of uncertainty. While he may have offered advice to his son about the value of hard work, he was less generous about providing management training or sharing information about the company's finances. "My grandfather kept the cards close to his chest," Rick Rogers told trade newsletter *Modern Distribution Management* many years later. "He left no information regarding his desires for the company or the financial condition of the business."

Thus, Bruce Rogers, Jr., who was a trained salesman, found himself thrust into the role of chief executive with little training. As a result, he spent a good bit of time adjusting to the job instead of growing the business as effectively as he might. Nevertheless, in 1973 he opened an office in Dayton, Ohio, filling in the gap between the Columbus and Cincinnati markets.

KEY DATES

1929: B.W. Rogers Company is founded in Akron, Ohio.
1950: Cleveland office opens.
1960: Columbus office opens.
1971: Founder Bruce Rogers dies.
1992: Youngstown office opens.
1995: Rick Rogers is named president.
2002: Merger is completed with Exonic Systems.
2006: Fluid Power Products is acquired.

B.W. Rogers added no new offices from the mid-1960s through the 1980s. The company did, however, attempt to improve its operations to better serve customers. In 1983 a new software system was installed to improve the handling of inventory and distribution. By the end of the decade the company's lines included about 8,000 products. This required not only required a new warehouse in Cleveland but a more efficient way to shelve and pick the items.

When a new warehouse building was added in 1990, B.W. Rogers eschewed regular shelving in favor of eight-foot-high carousels, a system that kept the size of the addition to a minimum while reducing the picking time per item from three or four minutes to about 30 seconds. As a result of this time savings, the company was able to drastically improve its same-day shipping statistics. When the company expanded the facility again in 1995, adding a conference room, extra space for the engineering department, and more office space, it was able to increase warehousing capabilities without increasing square footage by simply stacking three six-foot horizontal carousels on top of the other carousels.

Improving its warehousing capabilities was not the only challenge facing the company in the early 1990s. B.W. Rogers also had to contend with competition from larger companies. "Being a small, local distributor, we weren't sure we would make the cut," Bruce Rogers, Jr., explained to the *Akron Beacon Journal.* "We had to look at ways to improve our efficiencies." The company developed a plan that called for the development of new products, to be accomplished in part through mergers and acquisitions, in order to drive higher sales.

PLANNING FOR A NEW GENERATION OF LEADERSHIP

At the same time the company was gearing up for strategic change, Bruce Rogers, Jr., was grooming his son, Richard (Rick), to succeed him, making an effort to correct the oversights of his own father. In his mid-30s at the start of the 1990s, Rick Rogers had already held a number of positions in the company. He began working closely with his father to prepare for taking over the business, and in 1995 was named president.

By this stage in the company's history, annual revenues were in the $30 million range. Three years later Rick Rogers became chief executive officer. His father remained chairman of the company but the torch had been passed to the next generation. Moreover, the company took steps to retain talented managers and perhaps groom a replacement for Richard Rogers from the ranks of the company by offering stock plans to key personnel to keep them invested in the future of B.W. Rogers.

During this transitional phase in the 1990s, B.W. Rogers was still able to expand the business in order to fend off larger competition. An office was opened in the northeast corner of Ohio near the Pennsylvania border in Youngstown in 1992. The decade also saw B.W. Rogers expanding through what it called partnerships, bringing other companies into the fold to increase product offerings and expand market share. In 1996 the business of HydraAir, Inc., was added. The Indianapolis-based company had been founded 20 years earlier by William C. Myrvold and William A. Newton, a former territory manager for Parker Hannifin. In 1998 Kentucky Pneumatics Inc. of Louisville was brought into the fold.

GROWTH THROUGH ACQUISITIONS AND PARTNERSHIPS

The expansion program continued in the new century. A major step came in July 2002 when B.W. Rogers and Exonic Systems, Inc., merged. The Pittsburgh, Pennsylvania-based Exonic had been founded in 1978 by Jay Jones and Robert Burig. The addition of Exonic gave B.W. Rogers entry into the field of electromechanical motion control systems, thus providing customers with a wider range of automation solutions. As a result, B.W. Rogers could offer solutions without customers worrying that the company had an incentive to favor one technology over the other. Exonic also maintained an office in Philadelphia. Another Pennsylvania company, Monroeville-based Pennsylvania Hose & Fittings, provider of hydraulics, pneumatics, and filtration components, was also added in the early 2000s.

Further growth to the B.W. Rogers family of companies came in 2005 when Scott Fluid Power joined the group. In business since 1946, Scott was based in

Wheeling, West Virginia. It supplied industrial customers with pneumatics, hydraulics, and hose assemblies.

In July 2006 B.W. Rogers acquired Fluid Power Products Inc. of Louisville, supplying industrial customers with pneumatic, hydraulic, connector, and systems solutions. Fluid Power was established in 1965 by engineer Bill Thompson, who used his experience in the pneumatic fluid power manufacturing field to start a business from his Paris, Kentucky, home, where he converted his garage into a warehouse. As the business grew he put up a structure behind his house to serve as a warehouse, and in time expanded his reach throughout Louisville and beyond, ultimately spreading to West Virginia and Indiana.

B.W. Rogers grew further in 2007 when it acquired Machine Drive Company. The Cincinnati-based company was founded in 1947, serving automakers and specialty machine builders, especially the waste water and pumping market, with a broad range of value-added machine control products and services, including design, building, and project management. Well entrenched in five states, the B.W. Rogers family of companies was positioned to maintain its growth in the years ahead.

Ed Dinger

PRINCIPAL SUBSIDIARIES

HydraAir; Exonic Systems; Pennsylvania Hose & Fittings; Fluid Power Products; Scott Fluid Power; Machine Drive Company; Kentucky Pneumatics Inc.

PRINCIPAL COMPETITORS

Applied Industrial Technologies; Babson Fluid Power Inc.; Scott Industrial Systems; SunSource Technology Services Inc.

FURTHER READING

Evans, Diane, "Family's Values Applauded by Group; B.W. Rogers Co. Proves Community Service Matters," *Akron Beacon Journal,* May 14, 2000, p. G1.

"Horizontal Carousels Provide Needed Storage Without Expansion," *Material Handling Engineering,* September 1996, p. 73.

McEnaney, Laura, "Award Honors Hard Worker; Warehousing Company Also Noted for Growth into Multifaceted Corporation," *Akron Beacon Journal,* May 11, 1995, p. B1.

Young, Lindsay, "Make Transition to Next Generation as Seamless as Possible," *Modern Distribution Management,* September 10, 2006.

Bally Total Fitness Corporation

8700 West Bryn Mawr Avenue
Chicago, Illinois 60631
U.S.A.
Telephone: (773) 380-3000
Toll Free: (800) 515-CLUB (2582)
Fax: (773) 693-2982
Web site: http://www.ballyfitness.com

Private Company
Incorporated: 1983 as Bally's Health & Tennis Corporation
Employees: 19,200
Sales: $800 million (2007 est.)
NAIC: 339920 Sporting and Athletic Goods Manufacturing; 611620 Sports and Recreation Instruction; 713940 Fitness and Recreational Sports Centers

■ ■ ■

Bally Total Fitness Corporation is the second largest commercial operator of fitness centers in the United States. The company has about four million members and operates 375 facilities in 26 states and a handful of foreign countries. Bally Total Fitness offers a variety of services in their fitness centers, including personal training services and BFIT Rehab, a physical rehabilitation service. They also sell a variety of health, fitness, and nutritional products. Facilities offer cardiovascular and strength training, as well as a variety of aerobic programs, from spinning and step to low impact and yoga. Club members may purchase either single club memberships or premier memberships, allowing the use of Bally Total Fitness Centers nationwide. Laden with debt and bruised by accounting problems, in 2007 Bally Total Fitness went through a prepackaged bankruptcy reorganization from which it emerged a private company.

THE ORIGINS OF BALLY TOTAL FITNESS

Bally Total Fitness has roots that extend all the way back to 1931 to a company by the name of Lion Manufacturing. Lion Manufacturing, which later became Bally Manufacturing, was formed as and expanded as one of the largest producers of coin-operated amusement games. Bally Manufacturing continued its growth in the entertainment industry for the next 50 years, developing and producing products such as slot machines, video games, and pinball machines. Bally Manufacturing also entered into the casino business by becoming the owner of a series of a few different gaming hotels.

In a push to become a leader in the recreation industry, in 1983 Bally Manufacturing purchased Health and Tennis Corporation of America, which had formed in Detroit and Chicago about two decades earlier. The deal created Bally Health and Tennis Corporation, which became a subsidiary of the Bally parent company, then named Bally Entertainment. Bally also acquired Lifecycle, Inc., an exercise bicycle manufacturer, renaming it Bally Fitness Products Corporation. With this expansion, Bally became the world's largest owner and operator of fitness centers by the year 1987. With the purchase of the American Fit-

COMPANY PERSPECTIVES

Shaping a better future. Bally Total Fitness is committed to building upon its position and brand as the leading provider of fitness services. Bally is helping our members achieve their fitness goals by providing the highest quality service, facilities and products in a fun, friendly, safe and welcoming environment. As a result, Bally operates our business in a manner designed to ensure our long-term success and maximize returns to shareholders.

ness Centers business and 19 Nautilus Fitness Centers, Bally Health and Tennis Corporation continued to grow throughout the remainder of the 1980s and into the 1990s, at one point operating a total of almost 400 fitness centers in the United States and Canada.

The Bally Total Fitness name was developed in 1995, as Bally Health and Tennis Corporation consolidated all of its various health clubs under one name. Before the consolidation, the Bally clubs were operated under several different names, such as Bally's Health and Fitness, Vic Tanny, and Jack LaLanne. The move to consolidate under the Bally Total Fitness name was done in an attempt to unify the clubs and to increase Bally's already recognizable national image. Bally marketed this change with a promotional campaign featuring the slogan, "Turn on Your Life," and television's Teri Hatcher from the hit television show *Lois and Clark.*

NEW LEADERSHIP FOR BALLY TOTAL FITNESS IN 1996

In January 1996, Bally Total Fitness Holding Corporation emerged from Bally Health and Tennis Corporation after being spun off from Bally Entertainment. This move completely separated the health and fitness arm of the Bally operation from that of the Bally gaming and entertainment arm. On its own, Bally Total Fitness Holding Corporation began to institute a strong campaign to improve its operations.

In October 1996, Lee Hillman was named president and chief executive officer of Bally Total Fitness, and was put in charge of paving the way for Bally's growth. Hillman took over for the retiring Michael Lucci, Sr., who had decided to step down after leading the company through the early 1990s. Hillman, tasked with making Bally Total Fitness profitable after years of muddled fitness and gaming operations had eroded profitability somewhat, had helped Bally Entertainment CEO Arthur Goldberg turn that company around several years earlier. Hillman's main focus was to increase the shareholders' value, through efforts at expansion, increasing revenues per square foot, and increasing operating margins.

The company operated over 340 fitness centers in the United States and Canada, so the focus of Bally's expansion was not to increase the number of fitness centers, but to expand the variety of products that the company had to offer. Selling only one product—memberships—the company had well over 120 million visitors each year. With the desire to sell a variety of products, Hillman looked to his customers for ideas. He noticed that the customers all came into the fitness centers with T-shirts, sweatsuits, shoes, and socks, yet Bally did not sell any of those items. He also noticed the tremendous opportunity in the market of vitamins, nutritional supplements, and protein bars. He saw all of these items as avenues for increased product offerings from Bally Total Fitness.

Another avenue for increased exposure of the Bally name became the use of strategic partnerships. Bally entered into a deal with Florida-based ContinueCare Corporation to operate physical rehabilitation services in its fitness centers. The partnership was a perfect match for Bally, because the fitness centers had the necessary equipment and the demand for physical therapy often occurred between 10:00 A.M. and 5:00 P.M., the least busy time for Bally fitness centers.

Another partnership was developed with Metris Companies to deliver a cobranded MasterCard to Bally customers. The MasterCard, another step by Hillman to expand the range of products and services, offered a competitive interest rate, and customers who used the card could take advantage of significant travel benefits and savings while also collecting valuable savings on Bally memberships.

The last of the initial changes started by Hillman was to shift the company's marketing focus away from heavily discounting memberships as a means to attract new customers. Instead, the company began focusing more on people who were serious about their health. Bally stopped offering deep discounts to customers who paid cash up front for long-term memberships and they soon saw new membership revenue begin to rise.

BUILDING A STRONG FOUNDATION FOR GROWTH IN 1997

Bally Total Fitness returned a profit of $2.5 million for the first quarter of 1997. According to Hillman, the

KEY DATES

1931: Lion Manufacturing, the precursor to Bally Manufacturing, begins by making coin-operated amusements.
1962: Health & Tennis Corporation of America opens in Detroit and Chicago.
1983: Bally acquires Health and Tennis Corporation of America.
1995: Bally unifies its various health clubs under the Bally Total Fitness brand.
1996: Bally Total Fitness Holding Corporation is spun off as an independent company.
2004: Discovery of an accounting problem prompts five years of restated results.
2007: Laden with debt, Bally Total Fitness goes through bankruptcy reorganization, and then is taken private again.

profit was not so much a sign of the changes starting to take effect, but more a sign that the company was still solid. He felt that the changes made would serve only to further increase profitability. With the prospect of bright days ahead, the income earned during that quarter marked an important step for Bally Total Fitness.

With initial plans working well, Bally continued to expand its operations in step with Hillman's five-year plan. Part of this included closing some of the less-profitable fitness centers, redesigning other existing centers, and building newly designed facilities. New clubs were built with more space for weight machines and cardiovascular areas and less space for the lesser-used swimming pools and basketball and racquetball courts. The new design cost 60 percent less to build, while providing space for 40 percent more people.

Also introduced in 1997 were 40 BFIT Essentials retail stores. These stores operated inside the fitness centers, and offered items ranging from vitamins to T-shirts to gym bags. The fitness centers were thus offering the products that customers traditionally had been purchasing away from the Bally Total Fitness Centers, another step toward increasing overall profits.

Despite all of the changes, Bally Total Fitness still showed a net loss for the overall year of 1997. Several signs pointed in the right direction, however, as membership revenues continued to increase. The company's goal for the following year was not only to increase revenue, but also to introduce new profit centers. With the addition of personal training centers in the facilities, BFIT Essentials retail stores, and the rehabilitation services, Bally was poised to build on strong profit centers that were ready to show results in the future.

RETURN TO PROFITABILITY IN 1998

The start of 1998 marked the real move of Bally Total Fitness toward becoming a profitable entity. Bally Total Fitness once again experienced growth in membership fees, bolstered by sales of all-club premier memberships. These memberships allowed customers to use their Bally memberships at any Bally location around the country, which was a very appealing feature to businesspeople who tended to travel a lot but did not want to sacrifice their workout schedules to do so. Continued growth in revenues from personal training, BFIT Nutritionals, and BFIT Essentials retail stores also helped the centers to raise profits.

In early 1998 Bally Total Fitness introduced its new BFIT Energy Bar, a snack bar designed to act as an energy source during and after workouts. This product became the 12th in a growing line of BFIT Nutritionals, including BFIT-RX, a meal replacement shake, BFIT for men and women, a daily multivitamin, and SnackFit—snack crackers that were intended to reduce between-meal cravings. Sales of these nutritional products reached nearly $1 million per month after fewer than 18 months in existence.

Bally's next move was to increase brand visibility and perception. Bally signed an agreement with Baywatch Production Company, owner of *Baywatch,* the most watched television show in the world. The deal included several promotions throughout the year, including an episode to be filmed at a Bally Total Fitness Center. Bally also penned an agreement with Quintana Roo to become the official sponsor of the United States Triathlon Series, in an effort to attract the serious athlete to the fitness centers.

As growth continued, Bally looked to outside sources to fund the development. In May 1998, Bally sold 2.8 million shares of common stock, with the proceeds of $83 million being used to build new fitness centers and acquire club-related real estate. The expansion came rapidly as Bally acquired nine new clubs, including entering into the densely populated San Francisco Bay area with the acquisition of the Pinnacle Fitness and Gorilla Sports Club chains.

As new centers were acquired through construction and aggressive acquisition, and the new programs and services became successful, Bally Total Fitness announced revenues of $365.4 million for the first half of

1998. Revenues from the new products—personal training services, BFIT Nutritionals, BFIT Essentials retail stores, and BFIT Rehab Centers—also surpassed 1997 levels.

Plans for the future included opening close to 110 new BFIT Essentials retail stores by the end of 1999, while also continuing to expand the number of BFIT Rehab Centers to over 100 and building more fitness centers in the coming years. With these plans in place, and with revenues from memberships and other products continuing to grow while the fitness centers operated more effectively and efficiently, Bally Total Fitness moved closer to being the biggest operator of fitness centers in not only quantity, but in quality as well.

FINDING ROOM TO GROW

Bally increased its holdings north of the border in 1999, acquiring a ten-unit chain in Toronto called The Sports Clubs of Canada. Crunch, a trendy chain of 19 fitness centers in major U.S. metropolitan areas, was added in 2000 in a deal worth $90 million, most of it in stock. The latter purchase was credited not just with adding an affluent urban demographic, but with infusing the rest of the Bally system with innovative workout ideas.

Apart from these acquisitions, Bally was looking to slow its rate of growth following its expansion spree in the late 1990s. It did, however, enter a number of agreements to spread the Bally brand overseas in China, Europe, and the Caribbean via joint ventures and franchises.

With its membership base losing about as many subscribers annually as were signed up, Bally turned to underexploited demographic groups for new customers. These included suburban baby boomers, Hispanics, and seniors. However, 18-to-34-year-olds remained the central focus of its marketing efforts.

Bally was tainted by a number of scandals in the first few years of the 21st century. The company unsuccessfully tried a merger with Healthsouth, itself embroiled in some fraud scandals. Lee Hillman subsequently resigned in 2002 after six years as Bally's CEO. The board designated Chief Operating Officer Paul Toback to be his replacement. Struggles to comply with required tax filings ensued, however. In 2004 an accounting problem was discovered that prompted the company to restate five years of results. Bally had lost a staggering $450 million in that time.

2007 BANKRUPTCY REORGANIZATION

After losing almost $40 million in the previous two years, Bally regained profitability in 2006, showing a $43 million surplus on revenues of $1.06 billion; however, the company was teetering under a hefty $740 million debt. Toback stepped down as CEO in August 2006 after an effort to find a buyer proved fruitless. Don Kornstein, formerly an investment banker, was then named interim chairman. Although he was backed by activist shareholders, he would soon lead the company through a bankruptcy reorganization.

In May 2007, Bally lost its listing on the New York Stock Exchange as its share price plummeted. At the end of July 2007, it filed for bankruptcy reorganization via a prepackaged Chapter 11 Plan. Existing shareholders, led by Pardus Capital Management, LP, and Liberation Investment Group, LLC, saw the value of their holdings erased. Harbinger Capital Partners then acquired all the equity of the reorganized Bally Total Fitness for $233.6 million. This made Bally a private company again after 11 years of being publicly traded.

The cash-strapped company had sold some newly acquired assets. Fitness-club entrepreneur Marc Tascher bought Crunch for $45 million. Bally also sold off the Gorilla chain. Also divested were Bally's Canadian clubs, which went to two Toronto chains, Extreme Fitness, Inc., and GoodLife Fitness Centres, Inc. The proceeds were about $18 million in cash.

Bally was still bulky, even after trimming down somewhat. In 2006, its last year as a public company, Bally's revenues were $1.06 billion from its 375 health clubs and other ventures. There were 19,200 employees. The next year, in the trade journal *Club Industry's Fitness Business Pro,* an industry source pegged revenues for a slimmed down Bally at $800 million.

Robert Alan Passage
Updated, Frederick C. Ingram

PRINCIPAL COMPETITORS

24 Hour Fitness Worldwide, Inc.; Gold's Gym International, Inc.; YMCA of the USA; Curves International, Inc.; PFIP, LLC.

FURTHER READING

Borden, Jeff, "Bally Total Fitness CEO Flexed Product, Partnership Muscles," *Crain's Chicago Business,* February 24, 1997, p. 6.

Curtis, Richard, "For-Profit Facilities Set Counterattack," *Cincinnati Business,* March 31, 1997, p. 6.

Fischbach, Amy Florence, "Balancing Bally," *Club Industry's Fitness Business Pro,* September 2006, pp. 22, 24–28.

———, "War and Peace," *Club Industry's Fitness Business Pro,* February 2006, pp. 20–22, 24–25.

"Fitness Chains Are Going Global," *Club Industry Magazine,* June 2002, p. 10.

Frank, John N., "Corporate Case Study: Bally Works Out Reputation Woes by Committing to PR," *PR Week US,* May 26, 2003.

Goldman, Stuart, "The Waiting Game," *Club Industry's Fitness Business Pro,* July 2007, pp. 20–22, 24.

Kirk, Jim, "Bally's Brand Workout," *Adweek,* June 6, 1995, p. 1.

———, "Bally Total Fitness Gets New President," *Chicago Sun-Times,* October 9, 1996, p. 64.

Kufahl, Pamela, "Time Ticking on Bally Turnaround," *Club Industry's Fitness Business Pro,* March 2005, p. 18.

Meyer, Gregory, "At Bally, Activist Gets Boxed Out," *Crain's Chicago Business,* June 18, 2007, pp. 1, 10.

———, "Critics Now in Charge of Bally: So What's the Plan?" *Crain's Chicago Business,* January 1, 2007, p. 2.

Meyers, Lawrence, "Tug of War," *Club Industry's Fitness Business Pro,* January 2006, pp. 20–25.

Murphy, H. Lee, "To Get in Shape, Bally Pumps Up Expansion: Health Club Chain Debuts Products, Buys Competitors," *Crain's Chicago Business,* July 26, 1999, p. 4.

"Paul Toback, President and CEO, Bally Total Fitness," *Club Industry Magazine,* January 2003, pp. 34–35, 37.

Pauly, Heather, "Bally Total Fitness CEO Gets Firm Back in Shape," *Chicago Sun-Times,* December 9, 1997, p. 57.

Balmac International, Inc.

61 Broadway, Suite 1900
New York, New York 10006-2706
U.S.A.
Telephone: (212) 898-9600
Fax: (212) 898-9641
Web site: http://www.balmacinternational.com

Private Company
Incorporated: 1986
Employees: 32
Total Assets: $1.31 billion (2007 est.)
NAIC: 523999 Miscellaneous Financial Investments Activities

■ ■ ■

Balmac International, Inc., is a privately held New York City-based trading company operating in the heart of the financial district in lower Manhattan. The firm deals in cocoa, coffee, and cotton, involved in both New York and London's cash market (physical commodity) and the commodity futures market, and the shifting relationships between the two markets. The firm's cocoa business involves beans, butter, cake, and powder from Indonesia, Côte d'Ivoire, Ecuador, Haiti, China, Nigeria, and Peru. Trading partners include cocoa merchants as well as producers and manufacturers. Balmac's cotton division is mostly involved in the global trade of extra-long staple cotton, produced in the United States from pima cotton and similar strains grown in China, Egypt, India, and Peru.

A German affiliate in which Balmac holds a financial interest, Otto Stadtlander GmbH, is a raw cotton merchant that trades a variety of cotton types in Europe and to a lesser extent in Eastern and Southern markets. The business of Balmac's coffee division is handled by subsidiary Van Ekris & Company, which trades in green coffee in the United States and global markets. In addition to the trading of commodities, Balmac is involved in refrigeration. Subsidiary BMIL International, Inc., supplies a variety of turnkey prefabricated refrigeration units, including refrigerated warehouses, blast freezers, and basic walk-in coolers and freezers. Chairman Anthonie C. van Ekris owns 75 percent of Balmac. Swiss investor Jörg G. Bucherer owns the remaining 25 percent.

VAN EKRIS MOVES TO UNITED STATES: 1963

While some elements of Balmac's trading operations date back to the 1800s and at one time were part of the same company that operated one of the United States' leading jewelry store chains in addition to a vision wear chain, the common element is Anthonie C. van Ekris. He was born in Rotterdam, Netherlands, in 1934. Following a two-year stint in the Royal Dutch Navy that ended in 1953, he joined the Rotterdam firm of Van Rees Ltd. as a trainee, learning the commodities training business. In 1957 he became a coffee trader, moving to Kenya to serve as the manager of the African Coffee Trading Operations.

He relocated to New York City in 1963 to serve as manager of Ralli Trading Company, a subsidiary of the

> **COMPANY PERSPECTIVES**
>
> Balmac believes that the success of its business is to a greater or lesser extent dependent on its willingness to take positions as a principal.

United Kingdom's venerable cotton merchant and jute trader, Ralli Brothers. Van Ekris then struck out on his own in 1967, forming Van Ekris & Stoett, Ltd., a New York coffee-trading firm. Three years later he returned to Ralli, which had become Ralli International, put together by Slater Walker Security along with Oriental Carpet Manufacturers and then taken public. In order to achieve growth to satisfy shareholders Ralli was eager to expand into metal brokering and coffee trading, hence the acquisition of Van Ekris & Stoett.

VAN EKRIS NAMED RALLI AMERICA'S PRESIDENT

Van Ekris was made president of Ralli America Inc. in 1970. In addition to Van Ekris & Stoett, the company was comprised of subsidiaries R.E.B. Willcox & Co., Fritz & LaRue Co., and Naumann, Gepp & Co., but its main unit was Balfour Maclaine International Ltd., an old-line Manhattan trading firm whose name would one day be truncated to Balmac International.

Balfour Maclaine included a number of subsidiaries that were involved in the worldwide trading of coffee, tea, spices, rubber, oil, and chemicals. All told, the Ralli America units combined to generate revenues of $110 million in 1971.

Van Ekris began looking for a way to access the U.S. capital markets, and in 1972 found it in Kay Jewelry Stores, Inc. Not only did Kay possess an American Stock Exchange listing, its chain of 155 stores offered steady cash flow to support Ralli's more volatile commodities trading business, provided that the 37-year-old Van Ekris could turn around the stores. Moreover, as a commodities trader, he took an interest in precious metals, making the jewelry business a natural fit.

KAY JEWELRY'S GROWTH AND DECLINE

Kay Jewelry was established by brothers Sol and Edmund Kaufmann in 1916 in Reading, Pennsylvania, where they initially set up shop in their father's furniture store. They soon began opening branches that in addition to jewelry offered a variety of household goods, including eyeglasses and later radio and kitchen appliances. In 1919 a store was opened in Washington, D.C., and in time the growing chain would establish its headquarters there. Following the death of the founders, Sol's son Cecil D. Kaufmann took charge and expanded the chain further. In 1954 he acquired 67 stores in a single stroke, bringing the total number of units to 82, which combined for sales of $27.4 million, making it the largest jewelry store chain in the United States.

To pay down debt taken on to complete this transaction, Kay made an initial public offering of stock in 1956, giving the company its listing on the American Stock Exchange that van Ekris would later covet. The chain grew to 216 units in 1968, but by that time it was eclipsed in size by the Zales Jewelers store chain. Worse yet, a number of the stores were performing poorly and as the company began to close them, revenues plummeted. By 1971 cash was so tight that the company was unable to adequately stock their stores with merchandise during the critical holiday season, leading to a loss of $608,317 in fiscal 1971 and a further $1.4 million in fiscal 1972. The elderly Kaufmann was ready to sell the business.

RALLI AMERICA REJUVENATES THE KAY NAME

Kaufmann insisted that the Kay name be retained as long as he lived, and so Ralli America changed its name to Kay Corporation and made its headquarters in Alexandria, Virginia, although much of the company's operations were housed in New York City. Ralli International owned 70 percent of Kay's stock, and itself was subsequently taken over by another United Kingdom firm, Bowater Corp. Gradually, van Ekris and other members of management and their friends bought out the stock of the parent company and became a stand-alone company. In 1977 Kaufmann died, and since it no longer made sense to reassume the Ralli America name, the company was content to remain Kay Corporation.

Under van Ekris, who served as president and chief executive officer, Kay enjoyed strong growth in the 1970s, both with the jewelry stores and the trading operations. Although the commodities business provided the lion's share of revenues, the jewelry business proved more profitable. Net revenues grew from $213 million in 1975 to $765 million in 1979, and of that latter amount $110 was contributed by the jewelry stores, whose operating profit was $14.3 million. The commodities business, on the other hand, produced just $5.8 million in operating profits.

KEY DATES

1956: Kay Jewelry Stores, Inc., becomes public company.
1972: Ralli America Inc. acquires Kay Jewelry Stores, Inc., and becomes Kay Corporation.
1984: Jörg Bucherer invests in Kay Corporation.
1986: Following Kay Jewelry spinoff, Kay Corporation becomes Balfour Maclaine Corporation.
1990: Anthonie C. van Ekris resigns as CEO and chairman.
1992: Balfour Maclaine declares bankruptcy.
1993: Balfour Maclaine emerges from bankruptcy as Balmac International, Inc.
2000: Rubber Division is launched.

Kay continued to build its commodities business in the 1980s. Balfour Maclaine Inc. was formed as a brokerage firm to trade commodities futures in New York, and in 1981 it opened an office in Chicago to do business on the Chicago Mercantile Exchange. Kay stores, in the meantime, were also prospering, the result of an aggressive expansion program launched in 1974 that targeted middle-class consumers, especially in enclosed shopping malls in such new territories for the chain as Arizona, California, and Texas. Kay also leased space in dozens of department stores and reactivated the dormant Black, Starr & Frost brand it had picked up through an earlier acquisition. Although it was one of the United States' oldest names in jewelry retail, Black, Starr & Frost had not been in operation since the early 1960s after its flagship Fifth Avenue store closed. The venerable name was applied to an upscale jewelry retail concept within the Kay Corporation.

BUCHERER BECOMES INVESTOR: 1984

In 1984 Swiss investor Jörg G. Bucherer, owner of a quarter interest in Balmac International, began investing in Kay through Lucerne, Switzerland-based Bucherer AG. It was the jewelry business of Kay and Black, Starr & Frost more so than the commodities operation that likely attracted his attention. His grandfather, Carl-Friedrich, had founded the family company in 1888 when he opened a watch and jewelry store in Lucerne. Out of that grew a chain of high-end watch and jewelry stores.

By the mid-1980s the jewelry business was accounting for $189 million of Kay's total revenues and continued to generate much higher operating profits. Because the more speculative trading business overshadowed the strong results of Kay Jewelry stores, investors were reluctant to buy the stock of Kay Corporation, leading to talk of spinning off the jewelry chain.

NAME CHANGED TO BALFOUR MACLAINE CORP.

In 1985 Kay Jewelers was taken public when the parent company sold 20 percent of its stock to the public. Late in the year Kay Corp. expanded the trading side into base metals, such as copper, lead, and zinc concentrates through the creation of Balfour, Maclaine Metals & Minerals Inc. A few months later, in April 1986, Kay Corp. announced plans to spin off Kay Jewelry to its shareholders in order to focus on Balfour Maclaine's commodities activities. In 1987 the jewelry company was renamed Kay Jewelers, Inc.

More than a year would elapse before the stock was distributed, and in 1988 Kay Corp. changed its name to Balfour Maclaine Corp., with van Ekris serving as president, CEO, and chairman. It would not be a pure-play commodities business, however. In 1987 the company had acquired a controlling interest in American Vision Centers and its chain of 92 company-owned and franchised stores, reminiscent of the approach the company had taken with Kay Jewelry in the early 1970s.

BALFOUR MACLAINE FALTERS

With the economy struggling in the late 1980s, Balfour Maclaine began running into trouble, especially with its metal ores and concentrates business, which experienced steep losses in the first half of 1990. About 100 employees were laid off in Chicago and New York, fueling rumors that the company was in severe trouble. The situation was exacerbated by word that a major coffee supplier that dealt with Balfour had suffered a massive loss. Balfour called the rumors "vicious" and "contrived." But it was clear that Balfour was facing some serious problems. Soon rumors were circulating that Van Ekris & Stoett Inc., Balfour's coffee trading unit, was on the verge of bankruptcy.

At the same time that he had to contend with problems at Balfour, van Ekris had his share of trouble with Kay Jewelers. The price of its stock was being hammered, a situation he blamed on short sellers. At the company's annual meeting, van Ekris urged shareholders to "keep the faith." A few weeks later he sold the company to Ratners Group PLC, receiving $16.8 million for his shares plus another $10 million in a five-year noncompetition and consulting agreement.

With Kay Jewelers situation behind him, van Ekris focused on Balfour, which in November 1990 found itself in technical default after reporting a $7 million operating loss for the third quarter of the year, plus further losses from discontinued businesses. A restructuring plan was then put forth that called for several units to be shed. Unable to be spun off, the metals division was sold, as was Balfour Maclaine Capital Markets Inc., American Vision Centers, Balfour Maclaine Futures Inc., and some assets of its London-based commodities trading unit. Negotiations were also begun with lenders and debt holders in an attempt to recapitalize the company. In the meantime, van Ekris resigned as president, CEO, and chairman, although he stayed on as a director and consultant.

BALFOUR DECLARES BANKRUPTCY: 1992

Balfour Maclaine International Ltd. and Van Ekris & Stoett Inc. filed for Chapter 11 bankruptcy protection, and parent company Balfour Maclaine Corp. followed suit in September 1992. In the meantime, van Ekris had to deal with a class-action lawsuit filed by Kay Jewelers' shareholders who charged that he and other company officers had misled them and used artificial means to inflate the price of the stock. The case went to trial in August 1991, but during the proceedings the two sides agreed to a $3 million settlement.

When Balfour Maclaine emerged from bankruptcy in 1993 van Ekris was in charge, along with Bucherer, who held a minority stake. The company operated under the Balmac International name and Balfour Maclaine International Ltd became BMIL International, Inc., focusing on a refrigeration sideline. Balmac and van Ekris kept a low profile, doing business from a suite in lower Manhattan and rebuilding the trading business. The company focused on cocoa, coffee, and cotton.

In 2000 it launched a new rubber division, picking up on an activity that Balfour Maclaine had pursued from the 1960s until 1987. The goal was to source product from Southeast Asia and West Africa. By 2004, however, the division was no longer listed on the company's web site. Since it was privately held, van Ekris and Balmac were under no obligation to make public the state of their finances. There was also no effort to publicize the company's activities. With van Ekris still in charge but well into his 70s, the future of Balmac was uncertain.

Ed Dinger

PRINCIPAL SUBSIDIARIES

Van Ekris & Company; BMIL International, Inc.

PRINCIPAL DIVISIONS

Cocoa; Coffee; Cotton; Refrigeration.

PRINCIPAL COMPETITORS

Armajaro Group; Drachenberg Trading Company; Olam Americas Inc.

FURTHER READING

Abrahams, Doug, "Kay Officers Settle Suit by Shareholders," *Washington Business Journal,* August 19, 1991, p. 1.

"Balfour Maclaine Says Loss Will Put Firm in Technical Default," *Wall Street Journal,* November 12, 1990, p. C17.

"Balfour Maclaine's Van Ekris Resigns Three Top Positions," *Wall Street Journal,* November 30, 1999, p. B10.

"Balfour Rejects Further Rumors About Impending Financial Problems," *Securities Week,* October 15, 1990, p. 7.

Jones, William H., "British Firm Buys Control of Kay Jewelry Store Chain," *Washington Post,* February 15, 1972.

Mayer, Caroline E., "Kay Jewelry Chain Stages a Sparkling Comeback," *Washington Post,* November 12, 1984.

Peers, Alexandra, and Vindu P. Goel, "Kay Jewelers Chairman Sells Shares in Firm," *Wall Street Journal,* August 29, 1990, p. C1.

"Ralli International: Tough Challenge for the Ace," *Economist,* November 15, 1969, p. 79.

Rowe, James L., "Kay Jewelers: Hot Commodity for U.K. Ralli," *Washington Post,* February 2, 1981.

Yafie, Roberta C., "Kay to Spin Off Jewelry Business to Concentrate on Commodities," *American Metal Market,* April 9, 1986, p. 2.

The Bartell Drug Company

4727 Denver Avenue South
Seattle, Washington 98134
U.S.A.
Telephone: (206) 763-2626
Fax: (206) 763-2062
Web site: http://www.bartelldrugs.com

Private Company
Incorporated: 1904
Employees: 1,600
Revenues: $300 million (2007 est.)
NAIC: 446110 Pharmacies and Drug Stores

■ ■ ■

The Bartell Drug Company is the nation's oldest continuously held drugstore chain. In addition to selling over-the-counter medications, personal products, and convenience items at its 56 stores in King, Snohomish, and Pierce counties, Washington, all Bartell Drugs locations house a full-service pharmacy. Some stores also provide a drive-through pharmacy and free blood pressure testing. The family-owned chain also sells some electronics and offers digital photo-processing services and home delivery.

SEATTLE'S FIRST DISCOUNT DRUGSTORES

In 1890, George H. Bartell, Sr. bought his first drugstore at 27th Street and Jackson Avenue in Seattle. Bartell had grown up on his family's farm in Kansas; he left home and moved to Lincoln, Kansas, in 1883 at age 14, where he apprenticed as a pharmacist at a local drugstore until 1887. That year Bartell left for Seattle, Washington, making the monthlong trip onboard the Milwaukee Railroad. For the next three years, Bartell worked as a real estate broker and as a fill-in pharmacist in Seattle. Two weeks after being hired at the Lake Washington Pharmacy in Seattle in 1890, he purchased the store from the physician who owned it.

Bartell lived behind the store and worked long hours. Business was reasonably good despite a slow economy, but his health and interest in the business both began to flag. After the steamer the S.S. *Portland* docked in Seattle, filled with what the local press described as "tons of Klondike gold," Bartell left his business in the care of assistants and headed to the Yukon Territory in search of gold. He returned a year later with only enough gold to pay for most of his trip expenses and a plan to open several drugstores offering products at reduced prices in downtown Seattle, then the fastest-growing city on the Pacific Coast.

Bartell opened the first Bartell's Owl Drug store in 1898. His competitors, upset with Bartell for his discount plan, at first disrupted his access to wholesalers; Bartell dodged their interference, however, and began buying directly from manufacturers. Customers were drawn to Bartell's Owl Drug, and the store grew steadily. In 1904, The Bartell Drug Company incorporated, and in 1909, Bartell opened a second store, called simply Bartell Drugs. During the next 35 years, Bartell added another 17 stores throughout Seattle providing prescription drugs and, early on, horse medicine.

COMPANY PERSPECTIVES

We believe the primary reason for our success and longevity is encompassed in our basic philosophy of doing business. We believe that we provide our customers with the best possible selection of quality merchandise and friendly, courteous service at competitive prices in pleasant surroundings, and that we must provide our employee associates with a pleasant and rewarding employment.

Bartell's second store had a soda fountain, an unusual feature at that time for a drugstore. Two stores also had tea rooms. The soda fountain soon became a staple in all Bartell Drugs locations. After Prohibition went into effect in January 1920, and throughout the 1920s, 1930s, and 1940s, this feature helped the company prosper. As Bartell Drugs expanded, stores also began to add lunch counters and commissaries; the company began to operate a photo lab, candy factory, medical laboratory, and warehouse that serviced all of its stores. Bartell Drugs began to advertise using the slogan "Prescriptions Carefully Compounded at All Hours."

A NEW STRATEGY FOR GROWTH

The early success of Bartell Drugs attracted attention beyond Seattle. In 1925, rumors spread that Bartell was going to sell his stores to a large international pharmaceutical company for the amazing sum of $1 million. Bartell confirmed that he had in fact received such an offer, but rejected it. He also took the opportunity to reaffirm his company's continuing commitment to the Seattle area.

George H. Bartell, Jr., became president of The Bartell Drug Company in 1939. The younger Bartell had worked his way through the company ranks, starting out as a warehouse worker. In the years following World War II, he oversaw the opening of several more stores. In 1950, under his direction, Bartell Drugs became the first drugstore company in Seattle to open a store in a major regional shopping center, the Northgate Mall.

The 1950s were also a decade during which the company shuttered some of its stores. Many of the company's downtown locations had become obsolete due to Seattle's postwar expansion into suburbia and the shift from mass transit to the automobile as a main method of transportation. Additionally, the soda fountain had become a thing of the past with the rise of fast-food restaurants. As a result, the company changed its strategy: it closed stores that lacked off-street parking, opened stores in the suburbs, and remodeled stores to remove soda fountains and install more self-serve items. By the time Bartell, Sr., died in 1956, the number of company stores had dropped to 12.

Over the next several decades, however, Bartell's recovered and began once again to expand. By the mid-1980s, the company had begun to move beyond its traditional base in King County, opening stores in Snohomish and Pierce counties. Bartell stores also found themselves in increased competition with a number of new challengers. Grocery stores began to open their own pharmacies and discount pharmacies began to proliferate. Bartell's responded in part by continuing to focus on its local, corner drugstore image.

INNOVATION AND TRADITION

The Bartell Drug Company entered the 1990s rooted in its traditional identity, but also ready for change. In 1990 the company celebrated its 100th anniversary with birthday cakes at various locations. The same year also witnessed the third new president and chief executive in the company's history, George D. Bartell, the son of George H. Bartell, Jr. The youngest Bartell had begun working at one of the company's locations in downtown Seattle in 1983, but unlike his forebears, he did not have a pharmacist's license. Instead he had completed his undergraduate education at Bowdoin College and earned a graduate degree in business at Harvard. For the next seven years, Bartell held a variety of positions within the store and in the company's administration. He became company chairman in 2001.

George D. Bartell continued the traditions established by his father and grandfather. All Bartell stores were of a small size in order allow staff to respond quickly to customers' needs and to be able to quickly offer new product innovations. Bartell Drugs participates annually in a number of local community events, such as the Northwest Women's Show, the Annual Super Pet Photo Contest for the Seattle Animal Shelter, and several fund-raising walks, runs, and health-related programs in the Puget Sound area. At The Bartell Drug Company's web site, Jean Bartell Barber, chief financial officer and granddaughter of the company's founder, explains, "All of our stores have a strong neighborhood focus. That is why we feel it is important to support and sponsor organizations that benefit the members of the communities in which we do business."

Bartell Drugs also began to innovate. George D. Bartell inaugurated an analysis of the company's

KEY DATES

1890: George H. Bartell, Sr., buys the Lake Washington Pharmacy in Seattle, Washington.
1897: Bartell leaves to seek gold in the Yukon Territory.
1898: Bartell pioneers discount drugstore concept with the opening of the first Bartell's Owl Drug in the heart of downtown Seattle.
1904: The company incorporates as The Bartell Drug Company.
1909: Bartell adds a second drugstore in Seattle.
1939: George H. Bartell, Jr., becomes president of The Bartell Drug Company when Bartell, Sr., retires.
1956: George H. Bartell, Sr., dies.
1983: George D. Bartell, grandson of Bartell, Sr., joins the company.
1990: George D. Bartell becomes president and chief executive of the company when Bartell, Jr., retires.
2001: George D. Bartell becomes chairman of the company.

management. Under his direction, the company also continued to build larger stores at more widely distributed locations. In 1992, the size of the store in Seattle's Magnolia district was doubled from 8,000 square feet to 17,000 square feet. In 1995, Bartell Drugs opened its first modern 24-hour location. Three years later a centralized information department was created to disseminate up-to-date pricing information to individual store computers. Also in 1998, a web site was introduced. At first this was primarily devoted to posting employment information. In 1999 the company entered into a relationship with DailyShopper.com, a Seattle-based web site that provided information on specials and sales in participating stores. By the end of the decade, the company had opened its 49th store.

CHALLENGES IN THE MARKETPLACE

Bartell's innovations were partly due to increased pressure on the company from a number of different directions. The growing influence of managed care reduced the compensation that drugstores received for prescription drugs, which had become a mainstay of Bartell's business. Reversing a longtime avoidance of politics, the company became more politically active in the mid-1990s to ensure that independent drugstores would continue to receive state reimbursement for prescriptions.

Bartell Drugs also found itself increasingly in competition with mail-order pharmacies and the large national chains. Wal-Mart and Walgreens each opened a first store in the Seattle area in 1995. A month after Walgreens announced its plans to enter the local market, Bartell Drugs hired a marketing firm to help it promote its longstanding brand.

Despite these limits on growth, the company continued to expand in very measured ways. The changing landscape of the prescription drug market also nudged Bartell into court. In 1990, a King County Superior Court judge ordered Bartell Drugs to end its arrangement with an Ohio-based mail-order contact lens dispenser because of a challenge by the Washington Optometric Association. In 1993, the company joined a number of other independent drugstore chains to bring a lawsuit against several large pharmaceutical companies. Bartell and its litigation partners charged that they were being assigned higher rates for drugs than health maintenance organizations or hospitals, and they sought to end this practice.

A PERIOD OF NEW GROWTH

By the beginning of the 21st century, the company found itself in court once again for quite another reason. A landmark court case brought in 2000 by a Bartell employee, Jennifer Erickson, garnered the company unwanted attention. Erickson, who worked as a pharmacist, argued that Bartell's health insurance policy "singled out women and put them at a disadvantage because of their potential for pregnancy," when she discovered that contraceptives for female employees were not covered by the company's health plan. A district court judge ruled in 2001 that denial of prescription contraceptives discriminated against women, setting a precedent not just for Bartell, but for other companies as well.

During the first part of the decade, Bartell Drugs entered into a period of new growth, opening multiple new stores. It opened two new locations in 2000 and surpassed the 50-store mark in 2001, the year of the company's 111th anniversary. By 2004, the company, which could boast it was the nation's oldest drugstore chain and only one of five businesses in continuous existence in Seattle since the turn of the last century, was approaching an all-time high of more than 50 stores. That year, the company opened a new store in the heart of Seattle's downtown financial district, its second 24-hour store in Bellevue. The downtown boasted the company's first in-store espresso bar and plasma television screens displaying the latest financial news.

Between 2003 and 2004, the average chain drugstore experienced a 20 percent sales growth. Nonetheless as chief executive Bartell explained in a company press release, there were new challenges facing Bartell—competition from other large grocery store chains and mass merchants, shrinking profit margins, personnel shortages, insurance reimbursement requirements, and labor-intensive relationships with managed healthcare organizations. Smaller chains such as Bartell had to contend with a shortage of pharmacists, as did large regional and national chains. To be successful, Bartell Drugs had to reinvent itself as an effective partner in managed care with pharmacists who were involved in their customers' welfare.

By 2008, the company was operating 56 stores. In 2005 Bartell Drugs opened four in-store MinuteClinics, providing nursing care to customers. In that year's commemoration of the 115th anniversary of Bartell, Sr.'s purchase of the Lake Washington Pharmacy, George D. Bartell announced in a company press release, "My grandfather said [his business was] all about taking care of customers and their needs. We've taken it a step further, providing 24-hour stores, drive-thru pharmacy services or as the first major retailer here to offer on-site, self-service processing of prints from digital images." In 2006, the company began participation in a Washington State pilot program to safely dispose of unused prescription medications. In multiple ways, Bartell Drugs remained committed to keeping alive its founder's commitment to innovation and customer service in the greater Seattle community.

Carrie Rothburd

PRINCIPAL COMPETITORS

CVS/Caremark Corporation; Haggen Inc.; Walgreen Company.

FURTHER READING

Himanee, Gupta, "Bartell Drug Co.," *Seattle Times,* June 4, 1990, p. F2.

Kim, Nancy, "Bartell Watching Its Margins, Expanding Slowly," *Puget Sound Business Journal,* June 21, 1996, p. 55.

Liebman, Larry, "Bartell Drug Takes Slow but Steady Approach: The Longtime Family Drug Store Had Survived Where Others Have Not," *Puget Sound Business Journal,* June 26, 1998, p. 48.

———, "In '91, Bartell Expanded in Spite of Soft Economy," *Puget Sound Business Journal,* June 19, 1992, p. 30.

Besix Group S.A./NV

Avenue des Communautes 100
Brussels, B-1200
Belgium
Telephone: (32 02) 402 64 68
Fax: (32 02) 402 62 05
Web site: http://www.besixgroup.com

Private Company
Incorporated: 1909 as Société Belge de Betons
Employees: 16,000
Sales: EUR 1.28 billion ($1.74 billion) (2006)
NAIC: 236210 Industrial Building Construction; 236220 Commercial and Institutional Building Construction; 237310 Highway, Street, and Bridge Construction; 237990 Other Heavy and Civil Engineering Construction

■ ■ ■

Besix Group S.A./NV is Belgium's largest construction company, consisting of a group of industrial companies operating throughout the country. Belgium, and the wider Benelux market (including Belgium, the Netherlands, and Luxembourg), remain the company's primary source of sales, representing nearly one-half of total revenues of nearly EUR 1.28 billion ($1.75 billion) in 2006. The company's operations include major regional and nationally focused construction and real estate companies such as Besix Benelux-France, Vanhout, Wust, Jacques Delens, and Sud Construct. Through Besix Sanotec and holdings in GRWestkust, the company is present in the environmental sector; another significant subsidiary is Besix Real Estate Development. Since 2006, the company has also established itself in the road-building sector, through its acquisition of Socogetra and Cobelpa. These acquisitions also provide the group with its own quarrying and concrete production facilities.

Although a relatively minor player in the global market, Besix has nonetheless developed an extensive international presence. The company has been operating in the Persian Gulf region since the mid-1960s. This presence has given it the edge in competing for a number of the region's most high-profile construction projects, especially in the United Arab Emirates, where it operates as Besix International and Six Construct. Other Besix International operations are located in Oma, Qatar, France, Italy, Poland, Russia, Morocco, Algeria, Libya, Egypt, Cameroon, Congo, and Equatorial Guinea. The former public company known as SBB (Société Belge de Betons) became Besix after a management buyout, led by chairman and CEO Johan Beerlandt in 2004.

TURN OF THE 20TH-CENTURY ORIGINS

Besix traces its origins to the beginning of the 20th century and the founding of a small building supply business in Breda, in the Netherlands, in 1898. That company was established by brothers Frans, Jacques Marie, and Charles Stulemeijer, who had moved to Breda from Rotterdam with their mother after their father's death when they were still boys. The brothers' ambitions for their company, called FJ Stulemeijer, soon extended beyond sales of building materials.

COMPANY PERSPECTIVES

BESIX is an internationally-oriented industrial group focused primarily on construction, engineering and property development.

By 1901, the brothers had begun producing their own building supplies, creating FJ Stulemeijer & Co. The new operations then led the company into the construction sector proper. The new company specialized in the use of reinforced concrete, which was a novelty at the time. By 1918, the company had changed its name again, to Internationale Gewapend Beton Bouw (IGB), to underscore its expertise in the new material that was in the process of revolutionizing the construction industry.

In the meantime Charles Stulemeijer had recognized the potential of developing the family's construction interests beyond the Netherlands. In 1909 Charles and Jacques Marie Stulemeijer formed a new construction company, Société Belge de Beton (SBB), introducing its reinforced concrete expertise to Belgium. SBB quickly proved itself. By 1911 the company had completed its first high-prestige contract to construct the Horta stairway at Brussels' Palais des Beaux Arts.

SBB grew into a major construction player in Belgium following World War I. The company enjoyed strong growth in the postwar period as the country launched the widespread reconstruction of its devastated ports, bridges, and canals. The effort permitted SBB to expand its range of expertise, particularly into the hydraulics field. The company's diverse strengths allowed it to become a primary partner in the Belgian government's rebuilding of the country's infrastructure.

INTERNATIONAL EXPANSION

SBB once again turned to international expansion in the 1920s. In preparation for this the company went public, listing its stock on the Brussels Stock Exchange in 1920. Later that year the company established its first foreign operations, setting up Société Nord-France, based in Rijssel, near the Belgium border. The company next targeted Spain, setting up Sociedad Iberica de Construcciones y Obras Publicas S.A., or SICOP, in 1922. By then the company had also added new operations in Brussels as well, through S.A. des Ciments de Thieu, in 1921.

SBB's international interests continued to grow following the end of World War II. The company at first targeted expansion into Africa, especially the Belgian Congo. For this, SBB joined with fellow Belgian company Empain, forming Auxeltra Beton in 1947.

By the 1960s SBB had entered the Middle East region as well. The company's attention turned to the Persian Gulf region, especially the United Arab Emirates, where it established several companies in various markets. The launch of a major modernization effort in the region provided the group with strong growth prospects. In response, the company restructured its operations in the Middle East, combining its six existing companies in a single entity, called Six Construct, in 1967. Before long, SBB was a favored partner for the Emirates' increasingly large-scale construction projects.

SBB reorganized its holdings in 1973. A single holding company was created, called Les Entreprises Société Belge des Betons (SBBM), for both SBB and Six Construct. The restructuring came in response to the oil embargo of the early 1970s, one of the results of which was to transform the region's economies. The vast new wealth in turn brought about a new boom in the construction and engineering sector. SBB quickly expanded its operations in the region, winning major contracts throughout the Middle East and Africa.

ACQUISITION DRIVE BEGINS

The creation of the Belgian federal state and its corresponding regional structure forced SBB to adapt to a new marketplace. In order to ensure its national coverage, the company launched a series of acquisitions starting in 1982. Among the first to join SBB was Les Entreprises Jacques Delens, a company founded in Brussels in 1967. In 1980, Delens had expanded into the Walloon region, founding subsidiary Sud Construct. The acquisition also gave SBB operations in the Flanders region as well.

In 1985, SBB acquired Wust, based in Malmedy. Founded in the 1940s, Wust provided strengthened SBB's presence in the Walloon region. Wust also helped the company expand, enabling its entry into Luxembourg, and the border region of Germany. Next, SBB picked up Vanhout, founded in Turnhout in 1928. That acquisition also gave SBB an entry into the environmental market, through its Sanotec subsidiary. Vanhout provided SBB with a leading position in the Flanders region.

SBB's acquisition drive had enabled the company to consolidate its position in Belgium, where it became not only the largest construction group, but also the country's largest employer. The Belgium market, and the Benelux market in general, were to remain the company's core revenue base into the start of the 21st

KEY DATES

1909: Société Belge de Beton (SBB) is founded as a Belgian subsidiary of the Netherlands' FJ Stulemeijer & Co., which is later called Internationale Gewapend Beton Bouw.
1920: SBB goes public and expands into France and Spain.
1947: Company adds operations in Belgian Congo.
1967: Six Construct is created for company operations in the United Arab Emirates.
1982: An acquisition drive is launched to gain national status in Belgium.
1994: SBB and Six Construct are restructured to form Besix.
2004: Management buyout of SBB creates Besix Group.
2006: Launch of new multiservice strategy, including acquisition of Socogetra road-building business and launch of new environmental division.

century. Into the middle of the first decade of the 2000s, these markets continued to represent nearly two-thirds of the group's total revenues.

EARLY EASTERN EUROPEAN ENTRY

Despite its considerable international successes, SBB had continued to seek new horizons for its global operations. The company became one of the first to spot the opportunity for expansion into the "glasnost-era" Soviet Union. In Moscow, for example, the company completed a major hotel project five months ahead of schedule—quite a feat in the notoriously inefficient Soviet construction sector.

These efforts placed the company in position to take advantage of the collapse of the Soviet Empire at the end of the 1980s. The company quickly moved into Poland, establishing a subsidiary there, followed soon after by entry into the Czech Republic, Slovakia, and Bulgaria.

Yet the Middle East, especially the Persian Gulf region, remained the group's primary market outside of the Benelux region. The massive acceleration of the region's construction and engineering sector in the 1990s and into the new century provided the group with a new range of large-scale projects. The United Arab Emirates, Qatar, and Oman remained the group's focal point in the region, with major projects including the second Maqda bridge between the mainland and Dubai; the Al Aweer Power Station; the Dubai airport's second terminal; and a 310-meter hotel complex, also in Dubai.

A new restructuring in 1994 combined SBBM and Six Construct to form a new holding company, BESIX. That company was then placed under public listed holding company SBB. The company also expanded its reach, moving into North Africa. For this the company established new subsidiaries in Libya and Egypt, and then in Morocco and Algeria. The company was particularly successful in Egypt, where it completed a series of irrigation tunnels beneath the Suez Canal, built the Conrad Hotel in Cairo, and became a partner with Orascom in a $200 million office complex along the Nile. Not all of the company's expansion efforts were successful, however. In the early 1990s, the company had attempted an entry into Pakistan, where it completed a fish harbor at Gwadar. The company failed to find additional work in that country, however.

MANAGEMENT BUYOUT IN 2004

SBB remained in existence as the publicly listed holding company for Besix and its sister companies, including Jacques Delens, Six Construct, Vanhout, and Wust. A slump in the international construction sector had caused the group's revenues to drop sharply in the early 2000s, from a high of EUR 750 million to just EUR 525 million into 2004. In response, the management of the group's companies joined together, and, in partnership with Orascom Construction Industries, launched a management buyout of the company that year. SBB was then delisted, and renamed as Besix Group. Johan Beerlandt became the company's new chairman and CEO.

The change in ownership structure proved the prelude to a new period of impressive growth. Part of the company's strategy for its new phase was to boost its international business. By the end of 2006, the company had successfully transformed its revenue balance, with more than half of its total sales generated outside of the Benelux region. By then, the company's sales had rebounded, topping EUR 870 million in 2004, then jumping past EUR 1 billion for the first time at mid-decade. With a strong order book, Besix expected its revenues to top EUR 1.5 billion by the end of 2007.

By then Besix had begun to reposition itself from its longtime focus as a construction company to becoming a multiservice group. As part of that effort the company completed the acquisition of Socogetra in 2006. The addition of this Belgium-based company allowed Besix to establish itself in the road-building sector for the first time. The company acquired Cobelpa and its quarrying and concrete production assets. As part of its new multiservice strategy, Besix also set up a dedicated environmental services and waste management division. At the approach of its 100th anniversary, Besix appeared to have found the right mix for the new century.

M. L. Cohen

PRINCIPAL SUBSIDIARIES

B6SOMA (Morocco); BESIX France; BESIX Jamaica Ltd.; BESIX Nederland BV; BESIX Real Estate Development S.A.; BESIX Sanotec S.A.; Cobelba S.A.; Cocefi Polska; Ets. Jean Wust S.A.; GRWestkust; HBS NV; Investissement Léopold S.A.; Jacques Delens S.A.; Lux TP S.A. (Luxembourg); Proffund NV; S.G.T. S.A. (Luxembourg); Six Construct Ltd. (Dubai); Six International Ltd. (Cameroon); Sogepim S.A.; Sud Construct S.A.; Van Britsom NV; Vanhout NV; Verheye BVBA; Wust Construction Luxembourg SARL.

PRINCIPAL COMPETITORS

Compagnie d'Entreprises CFE S.A./NV; Compagnie Immobiliere de Belgique S.A.; Cordeel Invest S.C.A./CVA; Aannemingen Verelst S.C.A./CVA; Algemene Aannemingen Van Laere S.A./NV; Thomas and Piron S.A./NV; Les Entreprises Louis De Waele S.A./NV; Moury Construct S.A./NV; Democo Group S.A./NV.

FURTHER READING

"Belgian Contractor Besix Sharpens Its Focus," *International Construction,* March 1999.

"Besix, OCI Win Work on Nile City," *MEED Middle East Economic Digest,* August 19, 2005, p. 19.

"Besix Set for Burj al-Bahr," *MEED Middle East Economic Digest,* March 10, 2006, p. 20.

"Besix Subsidiary Sees Great Potential in Qatar Construction Sector," *Al Bawaba,* September 22, 2005.

"Besix Wins Culture Village Infrastructure," *MEED Middle East Economic Digest,* July 21, 2006, p. 17.

Marks, Jon, "Dynamic Duo Share a Gulf Orientation," *MEED Middle East Economic Digest,* March 3, 1995, p. 8.

Beth Abraham Family of Health Services

612 Allerton Avenue
Bronx, New York 10467
U.S.A.
Telephone: (718) 519-4000
Toll Free: (888) 238-4223
Fax: (718) 519-4010
Web site: http://www.bethabe.org

Not-for-Profit Company
Incorporated: 1918 as Beth Abraham Society
Employees: 829
Sales: $143.3 million (2007)
NAIC: 623990 Other Residential Care Facilities

■ ■ ■

Beth Abraham Family of Health Services is a not-for-profit company based in the Bronx, New York, providing long-term residential and community-based healthcare services. Residential programs include long-term medical care, subacute rehabilitation services to help patients make the transition from hospital to home, subacute medical care to provide clients with an alternative to a hospital stay, and a specialized unit to serve stroke victims. Rather than grouping clients in long-term residential care according to disease, Beth Abraham adheres to a "neighborhood" approach, bringing together residents who share lifestyle interests. The organization's community programs include housing for independent-living seniors, adult day healthcare services, a comprehensive care management program to help frail and elderly clients live outside of a nursing home, and an agency to provide in-home nursing rehabilitation and social services.

Aside from older people dealing with Alzheimer's disease, dementia, and other aging-related conditions, Beth Abraham's clients and residents include young people permanently disabled by traumatic injury, workers incapacitated by on-the-job accidents, the chronically disabled of all ages, retired educators and other professionals saddled with severe neurological conditions, and musicians who can no longer pursue their careers due to stroke or cardiac disease. Beth Abraham maintains branches in the Bronx, Brooklyn, and Westchester County. Through its affiliate, the Institute for Music and Neurological Function, Beth Abraham develops and offers ways to use music to heal and rehabilitate.

RAISING FUNDS TO FOUND AND EXPAND

Beth Abraham was founded by Bertha Alperstein, the wife of Talmudic scholar Rabbi Abraham Alperstein. A year after his death in 1917 she founded Beth Abraham ("The House of Abraham") Society in his honor to establish what would be the first Orthodox Jewish home for sufferers of incurable diseases in the United States, in particular indigent Jews who were being confined on what is now known as Roosevelt Island but was then called Blackwell Island or Welfare Island. A group of women who supported the society then formed the Beth Abraham Home for Incurables, which in January 1920 paid $115,000 for property at 612 Allerton Avenue in the Bronx, including a frame hotel, outbuildings, and 3½ acres of land.

COMPANY PERSPECTIVES

A voluntary, nonprofit organization, Beth Abraham has made life better for tens of thousands of New Yorkers from all backgrounds and walks of life. It first opened its doors to the poor, chronically ill and disabled just after the First World War.

Because the hotel was able to accommodate only 75 patients, two months later a $200,000 fund-raising campaign, directed by Joseph Marcus, president of the United States Bank, was launched to fund the construction of enough new buildings to accommodate 1,000 patients. According to the *New York Times,* at a celebration of the home's opening, Mrs. Alperstein initiated "the drive with the ingenious plan of auctioning off the keys to the different doors of the home. One thousand dollars was paid by Mrs. S. M. Rosenblatt for the front door key, and the rest also fetched record key prices, the total reaching $10,000."

A 1923 *Times* article indicated that the Beth Abraham home was still limited to 70 patients and that another fund-raising campaign—for $500,000—was underway, with $200,000 raised in the first ten days. The proposed new building was intended to care for 400 patients. The new home, the Farkas Pavilion, was ultimately built and dedicated in October 1925, and according to material provided by Beth Abraham, it served 250 residents.

More funds were raised at a dinner and dance held at the Hotel Astor in March 1926 to mark the fifth anniversary of the opening of the Home for Incurables and celebrate the opening of the new building. The *Times* noted at the time that the growing complex housed 225 "inmates," although a visit was slated "to Welfare Island to take as many incurables as possible from the city hospital to the new home before the advent of the Passover holidays."

FOUNDER DIES, WORK CONTINUES

Bertha Alperstein died in February 1929, but the work she began was continued by the more than 500 women of the Greater New York area who were members of the Beth Abraham Society. In June 1935 the home established a department of occupational therapy, providing patients with a chance to develop skills despite their afflictions, such as the young woman who crocheted with a needle in her mouth or the man who carved two model houses despite having no hands.

The following year the Beth Abraham Society was once again launching a new building fund to support further growth. In the fall of 1938 work began on a major expansion of the home, a four-story addition that brought the number of beds to 315. By this time, the home was not limited to Orthodox Jews, but open to all patients requiring "a highly specialized type of medical and nursing care for chronic conditions in addition to special religious and spiritual consideration."

The facilities for the Beth Abraham Home for Incurables continued to expand in the post–World War II years. In late 1949 the Federation of Jewish Philanthropies of New York recommended that $1.15 million of its $54 million building fund program be earmarked to add another wing to the home to house a further 100 patients as well as modernize the boiler plant, laundry, and kitchen.

Although seven years would pass before ground was finally broken, the scope of the project increased significantly. The budget grew to $3.25 million, provided by the Federation of Jewish Philanthropies, Beth Abraham's own capital expansion fund, $189,100 from the Ford Foundation, and nearly $350,000 in federal funding. The block-long, seven-story wing, which increased the number of beds from 319 to 530, was dedicated in 1958. It would eventually take the name Zahn Pavilion in honor of the home's president at the time, Mrs. Samuel Zahn, the wife of the owner of the International Dress Company and a trustee of the Federation of Jewish Philanthropies. The postwar era also brought a name change for the home, which in 1952 dropped the word "incurable" to become simply known as the Beth Abraham Home.

PICKETING LEADS TO WORKER LOCKOUT

Beth Abraham had to contend with labor difficulties in 1960. As a nonprofit organization it did not have to bargain with unions, according to both state and federal law, but Local 1199 of the Drug and Hospital Union began pressing the home for contract recognition. Rebuffed repeatedly, the union, which represented many of Beth Abraham's 200 nonmedical employees, picketed the home for several hours one morning. Only about 40 workers participated, but they prevented the rest of the nonmedical workers from reporting for work. When the demonstrators finally decided to report around 9:45, they were informed that everyone, union and nonunion employees, had been terminated for failing to report on time. The union declared the situation a lockout, and a

KEY DATES

1918: Bertha Alperstein founds Beth Abraham Society in honor of her husband.
1920: Beth Abraham Home for Incurables opens in the Bronx.
1925: The Farkas Pavilion opens.
1929: Bertha Alperstein dies.
1952: The Home drops "Incurables" from its name.
1958: The Zahn Pavilion is dedicated.
1983: Scheuer Gardens housing project opens.
1996: First Westchester program is established.
2002: Merger with CNR is completed.
2004: Work begins on $8 million renovation project.

number of assaults took place over the next few days before the home agreed to meet with the union to discuss their "problems."

Later in the year Local 1199 was able to bargain collectively with a group of three nonprofit institutions that included Beth Abraham. All of the parties involved agreed that the workers were underpaid but that the institutions lacked the funds to make much of an increase. In the end an arbitrator awarded the employees a $10 a month increase, noting that it was inadequate while explaining that "the financial burdens of these homes is such that to award any more at this time might seriously hamper their operations."

In 1968 work was begun to modernize and expand Beth Abraham. The centerpiece of the project was the $3.5 million Baum-Rothschild Pavilion, an eight-story structure. Dedicated in 1970, it brought the total number of beds to 520. In addition the main building was evacuated and renovated, and an apartment building was added to serve as a halfway house for patients no longer in need of daily medical and nursing services but lacking a place to live.

FAMOUS NEUROLOGY BREAKTHROUGH

Also in the late 1960s Beth Abraham gained notice because of the work of Dr. Oliver Sacks, who would go on to become a best-selling author. His book, *Awakenings,* chronicled his experiences at Beth Abraham (dubbed "Mount Carmel" in the book) and was made into a film starring Robin Williams. English-born and an Oxford-trained neurologist, Sacks came to the United States and eventually made his way to New York in 1965 to accept a fellowship at the Albert Einstein College of Medicine. Hopelessly lost in a laboratory, Sacks was dispatched to work with patients, which in 1966 led him to Beth Abraham where, according to the *New York Times,* he "came upon a strange community among the lost and seemingly lifeless souls. … About 80 patients had been stricken during the 1917–1926 pandemic of encephalitis lethargica, or 'sleeping sickness.'"

Aware of a drug called L-dopa that was being tried on non-encephalitis Parkinson's patients, Dr. Sacks used it with these patients to dramatic effect, essentially bringing them back to life. In 1969 Beth Abraham received permission from the U.S. Food and Drug Administration to use L-dopa to treat post-encephalitic patients. Dr. Sacks treated a number of patients at the home who had been extremely limited in movement and speech, but who had became quite animated.

Unfortunately, less desirable effects of L-dopa also became apparent and the drug lost effectiveness over time. Dr. Sacks reported both the good and the bad but soon found himself not taken seriously in the medical community, unable to publish his findings in medical journals, a situation that led to the writing of *Awakenings* in order to go over the heads of the medical community to reach a general audience. He would gain popular success and in time receive validation from the medical community.

NEW LABOR STRIFE

Beth Abraham suffered more labor difficulties in 1973, as did about 50 other New York–area hospitals and homes. This time a strike by Local 1199 was precipitated when a 7.5 percent wage increase that was awarded by a state arbitration panel and agreed to by the League of Voluntary Hospitals was shot down; the Cost of Living Council, which was established by the federal government to control inflation, refused to approve the deal. The resulting strike forced entire floors of hospitals to be closed and thousands of patients to be discharged. The impasse lasted a week before the council was forced to reconsider the situation by a federal court order. In the end, the union ended what was a medical crisis for the city by agreeing to a 6 percent raise.

Beth Abraham was caught up in an even more contentious strike in 1984, although the picket lines were peaceful. A confluence of events resulted in the longest healthcare strike in New York City's history, when almost 50,000 workers walked out on 27 private hospitals and 14 nursing homes. Local 1199 had broken away from its national organization, putting pressure on its leadership to deliver for members, while the League of Voluntary Hospitals and Homes of New York was under pressure from the city and state to hang tough because their agreement would impact the negotiations the city was initiating with 250,000 public employees and uniformed-services workers and the state with its 195,000 employees the following March.

The refusal of New York Governor Mario Cuomo to guarantee an increase in state aid to cover the cost of the settlement served only to make negotiations more contentious and difficult. After some six weeks the strike came to an end when workers agreed to a 5 percent wage increase.

EXPANDING LOCATIONS AND SERVICES

The early 1980s brought more expansion to Beth Abraham. In 1983 the skilled nursing facility was renovated, and the Beth Abraham Adult Day Health Care Program and Certified Home Health Agency were launched. In addition, the organization opened its first Health Service's housing project, Scheuer Gardens, which offered 115 apartments. The demand for the units was overwhelming, leading to another housing unit, Scheuer Plaza, which opened nearby at the end of the 1980s.

Also in the mid-1980s Beth Abraham established a Comprehensive Care Management (CCM) unit, the first long-term managed care program in the state of New York. Long-term care would become especially important in the 1980s because of the increasing number of AIDS cases and the demands of patients afflicted by the disease. Some of those patients would be cared for in Beth Abraham's Ritter-Scheuer Hospice, established in 1983 after hospices became eligible for Medicare coverage. Cuts in federal aid, however, led to the closing of the hospice at the end of the 1980s.

In 1993 Beth Abraham opened its third housing project, Weinberg Apartments, offering 95 units. It would be followed later in the decade by Weinberg Gardens and its 66 apartments. Also in the early 1990s the organization's Center for Research and Education was established.

In 1995 Beth Abraham established the Institute for Music and Neurologic Functions. Growing out of the work of Dr. Sacks and others, the institute provided patients with innovative music-based treatments. Patients trapped in isolation because of dementia, for example, could be reached through the singing of familiar songs and therapeutic drumming.

Beth Abraham branched out beyond the Bronx in 1995 when it acquired a former NCR warehouse in Greenburgh, Westchester County. The 15,200-square-foot facility was renovated to house an adult day health center for older disabled patients and a CCM program for Westchester County. Two other CCM sites would open in Manhattan and the Bronx in 1997. During this period Beth Abraham also took over management responsibilities for the 245-bed Schnurmacher Center for Rehabilitation and Nursing as part of a joint venture with Beth Israel Medical Center. Another joint venture was forged with Andrus Retirement Community in Westchester to codevelop retirement communities.

CNR MERGER

In 2002 Beth Abraham merged with CNR Health Care Network, leading to an expansion of home healthcare programs in the Bronx. The Bronx Long Term Health Care Program was opened in August 2004, and Beth Abraham's Best Choice Home Health Care Agency worked out of the location as well. Also in 2004 Beth Abraham's main facility on Allerton Avenue began work on an $8 million, two-phase renovation project. The first phase added a new lobby and first floor corridor, while the second phase addressed exterior restoration and some minor interior renovations to Zahn Pavilion and the Baum-Rothschild Pavilion.

Other developments in the 2000s included the 2005 opening of an adult day healthcare unit in Far Rockaway, New York, and the inclusion of the Margaret Tietz Nursing and Rehabilitation Center in Jamaica, New York, founded in 1971 by survivors of the Holocaust.

Ed Dinger

PRINCIPAL SUBSIDIARIES

Best Choice Home Health Care Inc.; Institute for Music and Neurologic Function.

PRINCIPAL COMPETITORS

Catholic Healthcare System; Eger Health Care Center; New York–Presbyterian Healthcare System.

FURTHER READING

Forgeron, Harry V., "Bronx Hospital to Be Modernized," *New York Times,* May 12, 1968.

"Home for Aged Expands," *New York Times,* November 12, 1956.

"Home for Incurables Drops 'Incurables' from Its Name," *New York Times,* January 11, 1952.

Kaufman, Michael, "Hospital Strike by 30,000 Ended," *New York Times,* November 13, 1973

"Mrs. Bertha Alperstein; Founder and President of Home for Incurables Dies," *New York Times,* February 20, 1929.

"Open Beth Abraham House," *New York Times,* March 22, 1920.

Purnick, Joyce, "A Strike Full of Errors," *New York Times,* August 28, 1984.

"$200,000 for Jewish Home," *New York Times,* May 22, 1923.

"Union and Hospital End Bronx Dispute," *New York Times,* February 25, 1960.

Webb, Andrew, "Seeing Sacks," *American Medical News,* June 15, 1990, p. 23.

BJ's Wholesale Club, Inc.

1 Mercer Road
Natick, Massachusetts 01760
U.S.A.
Telephone: (508) 651-7400
Toll Free: (800) 282-7239
Fax: (508) 651-6114
Web site: http://www.bjs.com

Public Company
Incorporated: 1997
Employees: 21,200
Sales: $8.3 billion (2006)
Stock Exchanges: New York
Ticker Symbol: BJ
NAIC: 452910 Warehouse Clubs and Superstores

■ ■ ■

Natick, Massachusetts-based BJ's Wholesale club, Inc., is the third largest membership warehouse club in the United States, trailing only Costco and Sam's Club, and is the market leader in New England. Unlike its larger rivals, which very much cater to small businesses, BJ's mostly serves individuals, primarily targeting middle-income households with children. With over 8.5 million members, the chain operates more than 170 clubs in 16 eastern states.

The stores offer apparel and accessories, consumer electronics, small appliances, jewelry, and groceries. Most units include an optical department and more than half sell gasoline. Club merchandise is also sold through the company's web site. A *Fortune* 500 company, BJ's is listed on the New York Stock Exchange.

MEMBERSHIP WAREHOUSE CONCEPT ESTABLISHED: 1976

The first membership warehouse club was opened in 1976 outside of San Diego by Sol Price, a pioneering retailer, and his son Robert. A lawyer by training, Price did not become involved in retailing until his late 30s. After inheriting a warehouse in Los Angeles he turned it into a retail operation in 1954 called FedMart, selling jewelry, furniture, and liquor to a select clientele: government employees willing to pay a $2 membership. The business thrived, growing into a chain of 45 stores.

Its success also inspired an Arkansas man named Sam Walton, who borrowed the idea to launch his own retail chain under the Wal-Mart banner. After selling FedMart to a German company in 1975, Price was soon ousted and looking for a new venture. After months of reflection and long walks through San Diego, during which they conversed with small business owners, Price and his son recognized that the wholesale distribution was failing to adequately serve this market. Thus in 1976 he converted an aircraft parts factory in San Diego into the first Price Club, tailored to the need of small business owners who were charged a $25 membership fee.

In order to keep prices low, selection was limited, items were sold in bulk, and little sales help was made available in the cavernous, unadorned facility. The business struggled until Price opened up membership to government employees and others, people who were not

COMPANY PERSPECTIVES

BJ's is dedicated to providing its members with high-quality, brand-name merchandise at prices that are significantly lower than the prices found at supermarkets, supercenters, department stores, drug stores and specialty retail stores.

likely to bounce checks. Not only did Price open other Price Clubs, he spawned a number of imitators in the early 1980s: Sam Walton opened Sam's Club, and a former Price Club executive helped launch Costco, which in time would acquire Price Club.

BJ's was the membership club entry of another respected retailer, Zayre Corporation. Its founders, Max and Morris Feldberg, were born in Russia and came to America in the early 1900s to avoid being conscripted into the army. They found work in a family variety store in Chelsea, Massachusetts, and in 1919 struck out on their own to launch a hosiery-jobbing company, and ten years later became involved in retailing by launching a chain of women's apparel stores, Bell Shoppes.

In the post–World War II era a second generation of the Feldberg family took charge and recognized the growing importance of the suburbs, where much of the baby boom generation was being raised, and looked to take advantage of the trend by opening a chain of discount department stores. The first opened in Massachusetts in 1956 under the name Zayre. By the late 1970s the Zayre discount stores were struggling, and a nonfamily member, former American Express Card executive Maurice Segall, was hired to turn the company around. He grew a small retail chain called T.J. Maxx, launched an off-price women's apparel mail-order catalog business, and decided to take a crack at the membership warehouse club idea.

BJ'S LAUNCHED: 1983

In 1983 Segall appointed a Zayre's computer-management executive, Mervyn Weich, to start a wholesale club. The first unit opened a year later in Medford, Massachusetts, under the name BJ's Wholesale Club, the initials drawn from Weich's daughter, Beverly Jean. Membership was opened to government workers and employees of hospitals, banks, educational institutions, and public utilities, as well as credit union members. Some large companies also provided memberships to their employees as a fringe benefit. BJ's focused on high demand, high price products, skewed toward such opportunistic categories as gold and diamonds, soft goods, and frozen foods. Before the end of 1984 two more 100,000-square-foot stores were opened. Zayre's warehouse club division expanded further in 1985 with the acquisition of HomeClub, Inc., a home improvement store chain.

By early 1986 BJ's had a dozen stores in the fold and hoped to have 50 by the end of the decade. The company ventured into the Chicago market in 1986, opening three stores, but they did not perform well and lost money. While the other stores performed reasonably well, the overall performance of BJ's was deemed disappointing. In July 1987 Weich resigned, citing a desire "to pursue other interests."

BJ'S SPUN OFF AS PART OF WABAN, INC.

The parent company had other pressing problems to deal with as well. The Zayre discount chain was suffering severe losses, and in the autumn of 1988 management elected to sell the 400 Zayre stores to Ames Department Stores, Inc., in order to focus on the emerging T.J. Maxx unit. A further step in this direction was taken in June 1989 when the warehouse club division, which included BJ's and HomeClub, was spun off as Waban, Inc.

By this point, BJ's was operating 22 stores, 16 of them in the Northeast, where it faced increasing competition from Sam's Club and invasion by three other warehouse clubs: Price Club, Pace, and Makro. BJ's looked to protect its position in the Northeast by stepping up its expansion plans in the region. It also looked to eliminate free group members from its ranks to become a paid-member-only wholesale club. Paid members were more loyal, and shopped more often and spent more money than free group members, who only shopped on occasion and simply created congestion in the parking lot and in the stores, hindering the big spenders from spending.

BJ's began the 1990s with a new president, Herb Zarkin, a 29-year Zayre veteran who was also Home-Club's president, and a major expansion program. Seven new stores opened in 1990, more than any prior year, including the chain's first store in Virginia and units in Hamburg, New York; Fairfield, Connecticut; Allentown, Pennsylvania; Sunrise, Florida; Harrisburg, Pennsylvania; and Niles, Illinois. All told the chain numbered 30 stores. Going forward, the company looked to focus on three areas, the Northeast, Florida, and Chicago. The idea was to cluster the clubs in order to save on overhead by sharing management support, distribution

KEY DATES

1983: Zayre Corp. establishes wholesale club division.
1984: First BJ's Wholesale Club opens in Medford, Massachusetts.
1985: Zayre acquires HomeClub, Inc.
1989: BJ's and HomeClub spun off as Waban, Inc.
1997: Waban spins off BJ's.
2003: New-concept club opens in Kissimmee, Florida.
2005: Second research and development club opens in Cape Coral, Florida.

centers, and marketing efforts. A year later, however, management decided to exit the Chicago market, which had always offered more promise than profit. Three of the four BJ's stores in the area were converted into HomeClubs while the fourth was simply closed.

Despite the problems in Chicago, BJ's began to see improvement in its core Northeast market, where consumers were finally becoming more comfortable with the warehouse club format. As a result, BJ's annual revenues grew at a 25 percent rate in the early 1990s, reaching $1.8 billion in 1992, but profit margins were thin, the company netting just $21.1 million. In truth, much of the gains enjoyed by BJ's, and Waban in general, were the result of new store openings. Stores in operation for more than a year actually experienced declines. Because Waban was not performing up to the board's expectations, the company's chief executive, John F. Levy, resigned in May 1993. He was replaced by Zarkin.

BJ's opened 13 new clubs in 1993, bringing the total to 52. Revenues topped $2 billion in 1993 while net income improved modestly to $22.3 million. Ten stores were added to the chain in 1994, nine in 1995, and another ten in 1996. Total revenues during this period increased to $2.92 billion and net income grew to $53.6 million. A key to the chain's success was its thriving fresh food business. By making quality meats and international cheeses available, BJ's provided customers with a compelling reason to shop more frequently.

Despite BJ's improvement, the price of Waban's stock did not fare well, depressed because of the less-than-stellar performance of HomeClub. In order to increase shareholder value, the company decided in late 1996 to spin off BJ's as a separate public company to allow both BJ's and HomeClub to devote more attention to their particular goals and thereby increase the value of both chains.

BJ'S GOES SOLO

The BJ's spinoff was completed in July 1997 as a special, tax-free dividend to Waban shareholders who received BJ's new stock on a one-to-one basis. Zarkin remained chairman of BJ's while President John Nugent became the new CEO. The chain opened just four clubs in 1997 while closing one, bringing the number in operation to 84. Revenues in the meantime reached $3.16 billion and net income improved to $68 million. The company also developed expansion plans that led to a dozen club openings in 1998 and BJ's entrance into the Cleveland, Ohio, market.

While the vast majority of the units were "big box" in size, averaging 112,000 square feet, 14 relied on smaller formats, about 69,000 square feet, more suitable for smaller markets. Also of importance, the company began adding gas stations and took steps to introduce private-label brands in 1999. BJ's closed the 1990s with 11 new store openings, including the first in North Carolina. Membership also increased 15 percent to 5.8 million. Total revenues increased to more than $4.1 billion and net income jumped to $111.1 million.

The BJ's chain grew to 130 clubs by the end of 2001, a year when the focus was on the Southeast. Five clubs opened in three markets in Florida, and two North Carolina markets that had been entered the previous year were bolstered by two new units. Of the company's $5.2 billion in total revenues for that year, more than 60 percent came from food sales (excluding gasoline, which was only available at 55 clubs). To support BJ's Southeast expansion a new 480,000-square-foot distribution center was opened in Jacksonville, Florida, in 2002, when 13 new clubs were added, including four prototype clubs in the Atlanta market. For the year, total revenues approached $5.9 billion and net income increased to $130.9 million.

The wholesale club business remained highly competitive, however, and the addition of difficult economic conditions served to dampen the price of BJ's stock. In September 2002 Nugent stepped down as CEO in favor of Michael Wedge, executive vice-president of club operations since 1997. While Wedge had been heir apparent for some time, the move was made because Nugent was undergoing some family concerns and Wedge was more suited to seeing BJ's through a period in which the focus would shift from expansion to technology and new marketing initiatives to stave off encroachments from Costco and Sam's Club.

Under Wedge's direction, BJ's began to improve greatly its selection of designer apparel, brand-name appliances, and consumer electronics, while introducing a line of premium prepared foods and improving the offerings in produce, baked goods, seafood, and international cheese. At the same time, some merchandise was pulled from the shelves, including large exercise equipment, automotive parts, and stationery. In addition, several new private labels were rolled out, including Wellsley Farms for fresh foods, Rozzano for Italian-style food, Willow Lane for furniture, Loving Home for housewares, Lanesborough for men's apparel, and Portsmouth Shores for outdoor furniture.

FOCUS ON NEW CONCEPTS FOR THE 21ST CENTURY

BJ's opened ten new clubs in 2003 while renovating 30 others, and established a new-concept club in Kissimmee, Florida, where new ideas could be tested, such as an enlarged consumer electronics department, a store-within-a-store jewelry department, and "BJ's Incredible Kids Club," a supervised area where children could play while their parents shopped. On the technology side, a price optimization program began to help in pricing decisions, leading to improved merchandise margins, and more self-checkout lanes were added to 100 clubs.

Total revenues improved to $6.72 billion in 2003, catching the attention of potential suitors. According to *Retail Merchandiser,* "reports began circulating in April [2003] that two offers had been made for the chain. One supposed offer came from an undisclosed buyer (rumored to be Albertson's, the Boise, ID-based supermarket chain), and the second from Wal-Mart Stores, parent of rival Sam's Clubs, which has been struggling."

A number of innovations tested in the Kissimmee club began making their way into the other units in 2004, leading to a second research and development club to be opened in 2005. This unit, located in Cape Coral, Florida, was tasked with focusing on food innovation, leaving general merchandise to Kissimmee. Total revenues grew to nearly $7.4 billion in 2004 and approached $8 billion in 2005, when net income improved to $128.5 million.

BJ's did not fare as well in 2006, however. Both sales and margins were down, leading to several months of disappointing results, fueling rumors that the company was on the block. Speculation grew even more heated after Wedge resigned in November 2006. Zarkin stepped in as CEO on an interim basis and in February 2007 took the position on a permanent basis. Although net income fell to $72 million in 2006, total revenues increased to $8.3 billion in 2006 when nine new clubs were opened as well as a new 618,000-square-foot distribution facility that replaced an older, smaller center in Massachusetts.

With Zarkin back in charge, BJ's showed a marked improvement in its performance in 2007, and the company took advantage of its low stock price to buy back well over $100 million of its shares. Late in the year the board of directors authorized another $250 million to be spent on the stock repurchase effort. BJ's also opened a new club located in Manchester, Connecticut, in 2007, and was poised for continued growth.

Ed Dinger

PRINCIPAL SUBSIDIARIES

Natick Security Corporation; Mormax Beverages Corporation; Mormax Corporation; Natick Reality Holdings, Inc.

PRINCIPAL COMPETITORS

Costco Wholesale Corporation; Wal-Mart Stores, Inc.; Family Dollar Stores, Inc.

FURTHER READING

"BJ's Wages Expansion Battle," *Discount Store News,* September 25, 1989, p. 7.

Bulkeley, William M., "Zayre to Split into Two Firms, Change Name," *Wall Street Journal,* December 6, 1988, p. 1.

Facenda, Vanessa L., "BJ's Growth Outpaces Larger Rivals," *Retail Merchandiser,* July 2003, p. 34.

Ferguson, Tim W., "A Revolution That Has a Long Way to Go," *Forbes,* August 11, 1997, p. 106.

Halverson, Richard, "BJ's Shows Its Strength as Stand-Alone Company," *Discount Store News,* August 18, 1997, p. 1.

Owen, Erica, "CEO of BJ's Wholesale Resigns As Firm Opts for 'Fresh' View," *Wall Street Journal,* November 24, 2006, p. B7.

Pereira, Joseph, "Waban's President, CEO Quits, Citing Financial Results," *Wall Street Journal,* May 26, 1993, p. B1.

Rudnitsky, Howard, "Making Money at the Low End of the Market; As a Discounter," *Forbes,* December 17, 1984, p. 42.

"Waban Looks to Bolster BJ's Profitability with Spin-Off," *Discount Store News,* November 4, 1996, p. 3.

Wedemeyer, Dee, "Those Low-Priced Price Clubs," *New York Times,* May 18, 1986, p. A4.

Boizel Chanoine Champagne S.A.

Allée du Vignoble
Reims, F-51100
France
Telephone: (33 03) 26 06 45 45
Fax: (33 03) 26 06 44 25
Web site: http://www.boizelchanoine.fr

Public Company
Incorporated: 1991 as Chanoine Champagne; 1996 as Boizel Chanoine Champagne
Employees: 645
Sales: EUR 311 million ($429 million) (2006)
Stock Exchanges: Euronext Paris
Ticker Symbol: 4027068 BOZ
NAIC: 312130 Wineries; 424820 Wine and Distilled Alcoholic Beverage Merchant Wholesalers

Boizel Chanoine Champagne S.A. is the second largest producer and distributor of champagne in the world, behind luxury products group LVMH. Boizel Chanoine, however, is entirely focused on its portfolio of champagne brands, making it the largest of the so-called pure-play champagne groups, which focus solely on champagne production. In 2006, the company sold nearly 21 million bottles of champagne. Boizel Chanoine operates as a holding company for its collection of champagne brands. These include Boizel, the leading French mail-order champagne specialist; Chanoine Frères and Burtin, both of which target the large-scale retail distribution channel; Philipponnat, Besserat de Bellefon, and de Venoge, all three of which are sold through the specialist retail channel; and Lanson, the group's largest brand and its main export brand. Boizel Chanoine also owns its own champagne vineyards, through subsidiary Alexandre Bonnet. Another subsidiary, Champenoise des Grands Vins (CGV) acts as champagne purchaser and distributor for third-party champagne labels. Boizel Chanoine is listed on the Euronext Paris Stock Exchange. Bruno Paillard, founder, chairman, and chief executive, leads the company, and also owns his own champagne house (not included in the Boizel Chanoine group). In 2006, the company posted revenues of EUR 311 million ($429 million).

STARTING A CHAMPAGNE HOUSE IN 1991

Champagne grower Bruno Paillard joined with Philippe Baijot to found a new champagne distribution company in 1991. Baijot had previously been a director at Marne et Champagne, which, as holder of the Lanson brand and others, was at that time one of the leading names in France's champagne sector. Paillard and Baijot launched the new company through the acquisition of two existing companies. The first was Champenoise des Grands Vins (CGV), which specialized in providing wholesale purchasing and distribution services to the retail distribution sector, notably through the development of private-label champagnes for the supermarket groups both in France and abroad. The second company, Champagne Chanoine Frères, provided the company with its first champagne label. Chanoine Frères was a long-established name in the exclusive champagne sector, having been founded in 1730 in the village of

COMPANY PERSPECTIVES

Responsible Development. For Boizel Chanoine Champagne, commitment is by its very nature long term, far removed from passing trends. Through its activities, the Group is committed to combining economic development, regional vitality and respect for the environment at all times.

Epinay. By the end of the 1990s, however, Chanoine Frères had ceased to operate.

The new company, named after Chanoine Frères, had relaunched champagne production under the Chanoine name by 1992. Paillard and Baijot then began scouting for other acquisition targets. The pair thus played a role in the rapidly developing consolidation of the champagne sector whereby a small number of large-scale production champagne houses emerged. These champagne houses maintained their own vineyards as a point of prestige, but they still needed to buy grapes from independent growers, and so the Champagne region's famed vineyards remained controlled by a large number of growers.

In 1994, Chanoine reached an agreement with Champagne Boizel, owned by the Roques-Boizel family, to acquire a majority stake in that famous brand. Boizel had been founded in 1834 by Auguste Boizel in the village of Epernay. By the middle of the 19th century, Boizel had become a leading export label. England became a major market for the champagne house, especially after 1887, when the company signed an exclusive contract with wine seller Hedges & Butler.

The third Boizel generation took over in 1920, and further expanded the company's export sales. Boizel also became one of the first in the region to introduce a Blanc de Blancs during this time. The company was forced to rebuild after World War I, and by the early 1960s had introduced a new vintage, called Joyau de France. Another generation of the Boizel family took over as head of the business under Evelyn Roques-Boizel and her husband Christophe.

Under their leadership, Boizel adopted a new distribution model, targeting the direct-mail channel in 1984. The company set up a toll-free telephone service—unusual in France—and quickly succeeded in becoming the leading direct-sales champagne brand.

Boizel recognized the opportunity to join forces with Paillard, a family friend, selling majority control of the family business to Chanoine Frères. By 1996, the families had agreed to transfer full control of Boizel to Chanoine, which then took on the new name of Boizel Chanoine Champagne. The Roques-Boizel family continued to direct the operations at the Boizel champagne house, while taking seats on Boizel Chanoine Champagne's board of directors.

GOING PUBLIC IN 1996

Following the merger with Boizel, the company went public, listing its shares on the Paris bourse in 1996. Boizel Chanoine had by then entered the top ten among the leading champagne companies. However, with revenues equivalent to EUR 30 million, and sales of approximately four million bottles—out of more than 250 million total—the company remained modest in size.

Paillard and Baijot had greater ambitions for the company. The public offering enabled the company to raise the capital to launch the next phase of its expansion strategy. The company then sought to develop a broader portfolio of champagne brands, targeting the sector's different distribution channels.

Acquisitions again formed a major part of the group's growth plans. In 1997, the company made its next purchase, of Champagne Philipponnat from drinks group Marie Brizard. That label traced its roots back to 1522, when the first champagne under the Philipponnat name was created in the village of Ay. At the end of the 20th century, Philipponnat had become a leading label in the upscale champagne segment, distributed through the specialist retail sector as well as through the restaurant sector. The purchase not only gave the company its own vineyard—the prestigious Le Clos des Goisses—but also gave it a distribution subsidiary, Philipponnat-Les Domaines Associés, which distributed the Domaines Barons de Rothschild (Lafite) label in France.

The next piece of the Boizel Chanoine puzzle fell into place in 1998, through the acquisition of Champagne Venoge, based in Epernay, which as part of the Rémy Cointreau drinks group had focused on the specialized retail channel. Venoge had been founded in 1837 and had built up a strong international reputation, both in Europe and abroad.

While the Venoge acquisition provided the company with a new prestigious label and significant reserves, the company remained hampered by the limited area of vineyard under its control. The late 1990s had seen a major shift in the champagne sector as the demand, particularly international demand, surged during the decade. The strictly limited Champagne region, however, meant that there was a finite amount of

KEY DATES

1991: Bruno Paillard and Philippe Baijot acquire Champagne Chanoine Frères and Champenoise des Grands Vins (CGV) to form Chanoine Champagne.
1994: Chanoine acquires majority control of Champagne Boizel.
1996: Full control of Boizel acquired, with name change to Boizel Chanoine Champagne; stock listed on Paris bourse.
1997: New prestige label Tsarine launched; Champagne Philipponnat acquired.
1998: Acquires Champagne de Venoge and Maison Bonnet.
2005: Revenues triple through acquisition of Marne & Champagne and its Lanson label.

available champagne grapes. With growing demand and limited supply, grape prices soared, leaving land-poor groups such Boizel Chanoine highly vulnerable to these price fluctuations.

PREPARING FOR THE MILLENNIUM EFFECT

With its survival at stake, Boizel Chanoine continued to seek new acquisitions. Relief came with the purchase of Maison Bonnet and its Alexandre Bonnet label in 1998. Bonnet was the youngest of the group's champagne houses, dating its origins to the pre–World War I era. The Bonnet purchase not only provided Boizel Chanoine with a strong traditional retail label, it also gave the company control of 65 hectares of vineyard in the area known as Les Riceys. Bonnet also brought Boizel Chanoine a strong reserve of more than one million bottles.

This latest acquisition placed Boizel Chanoine in strong shape to meet the so-called Millennium Effect—the expected surge in champagne sales in preparation for the celebration of the start of the new millennium. By the end of the 1990s, the company had succeeded in positioning itself as the world's seventh largest champagne group, with sales of more than 5.35 million bottles, worth EUR 69 million ($50 million) by the end of 1998.

The company had succeeded in boosting the vineyards under its control—either owned outright by the company or producing under contract—by more than 670 hectares. At the same time, Boizel Chanoine had continued to develop its strategy of broadening its distribution network. As part of this effort, the company sought to fill a gap in its portfolio by creating the Chanoine Tsarine label in 1997. The new champagne label enabled the company to gain a new place on supermarket shelves in the "affordable luxury" price segment.

NEW OPPORTUNITY IN 2005

During the early years of the new century, Boizel Chanoine continued to make inroads toward building up its distribution network. The company registered strong sales increases, building up a sales volume of more than seven million bottles by 2004. The steady demand, particularly from such emerging markets as China, India, and the Middle East, helped sustain high prices. The company's revenues climbed to more than EUR 93 million by 2005.

Up to that time, Boizel Chanoine remained a second-tier player, unable to fully compete with such prestigious rivals as Moët et Chandon, Pommery, Dom Perignon, Laurent-Perrier, and Piper Heidsieck. In comparison to Chanoine's seven million bottles, sector leader LVMH's volume neared 60 million bottles, while number two Vranken Pommery topped 20 million bottles. Nevertheless, Paillard remained determined to raise his company's profile.

Opportunity knocked at the end of 2005 amid the disastrous fortunes of Marne et Champagne, which controlled the Lanson label. Marne et Champagne had been founded in the 1920s by Gaston Burtin as a wine wholesaler. The company then began purchasing white wines and began assembling its own champagnes, developing a range of types that were marketed under a number of different labels.

Burtin recognized the opportunity presented by the rise of the supermarket sector in France, and became one of the first to begin supplying champagnes for the discount and private-label segments. By the end of the 1980s, the company, Maison de Champagne Marne & Champagne, had grown into one of the sector's largest, with a stock of some 45 million bottles in its cellars.

In the early 1990s, however, Marne & Champagne, led by Burtin's nephew-by-marriage François-Xavier Mora, adopted a new strategy of developing its own in-house brand portfolio. As part of this strategy, the company made its first acquisition in 1990, of Besserat de Bellefon, a champagne producer founded in 1843, for the equivalent of $30 million.

Marne & Champagne made an even larger acquisition the following year, paying LVMH more than $150 million for the Lanson champagne house. Founded in

1760, Lanson had grown into one of the leading champagne labels, with a particularly strong presence in the export market. The Lanson acquisition not only gave Marne & Champagne a prestigious brand, it also added stocks of more than 30 million bottles. However, the company had failed to negotiate the purchase of Lanson's vineyards, which remained under LVMH's control.

The lack of foresight in ensuring control over its grape supply cost the company dearly as grape and wine prices soared during the 1990s. At the same time, Marne & Champagne incorrectly read the market—which had increasingly moved upscale during the decade—and instead had attempted to position the Lanson brand toward lower-priced categories. Heavily indebted at the beginning of the 21st century, Marne & Champagne faced collapse by 2004. The company was rescued by the Caisse Nationale des Caisses d'Epargne, which provided a bridge loan of EUR 310 million in exchange for a 44 percent share of the company.

NUMBER TWO IN THE 21ST CENTURY

Caisse Nationale announced its intention to sell Marne & Champagne in 2005; by the end of that year, after other potential buyers backed out, Boizel Chanoine gained control of the company, including its Lanson label and other brands.

The acquisition of Marne & Champagne—subsequently renamed Maison Burtin—catapulted Boizel Chanoine into the champagne industry's second place, tripling its revenues past EUR 311 million and boosting its sales volume to nearly 21 million bottles. In this way, Boizel Chanoine Champagne claimed a market share of more than 6.5 percent.

The acquisition of Marne & Champagne was viewed as a highly risky move, as it raised the company's debt past EUR 400 million. At the same time, the company lost a number of important supply contracts. With its total acreage under contract reduced to just 1,200 hectares, the company appeared at risk of being unable to sustain its production volume.

However, Boizel Chanoine quickly set to work restructuring its new holdings. In particular, the company began repositioning the Lanson brand into the higher-priced segment. At the same time, the company began extending its other champagnes into higher-value segments. Through 2006, the company carried out a further restructuring, simplifying its operations into six primary champagne houses, along with its small CGV subsidiary.

Lanson's strong international business, which accounted for 72 percent of the label's sales, provided an opportunity to raise the export profiles of the company's other labels. For this the company turned especially toward its largest domestic label (after Lanson), Champagne Chanoine Frères, and its successful prestige label Tsarine. With sales expected to near EUR 370 million at the end of 2007, Boizel Chanoine Champagne had placed itself at the center of the world's most prestigious wine market.

M. L. Cohen

PRINCIPAL SUBSIDIARIES

Champagne Boizel; Champagne Chanoine Frères; Champagne de Venoge; Champagne Lanson; Champagne Philipponnat; Champenoise des Grands Vins, SA; Groupe Charmoy; Lanson International UK Ltd.; Maison Alexandre Bonnet; Maison Burtin; Vignobles Alexandre Bonnet.

PRINCIPAL COMPETITORS

LVMH; Vranken-Pommery Monopole; Laurent-Perrier S.A.; Lombard et Medot S.A.; Pol Roger & Compagnie S.A.; Yantai Changyu Pioneer Wine Company Ltd.; Schlumberger AG; Jeanjean S.A.; Sektkellerei J.Oppmann AG.

FURTHER READING

"Boizel Chanoine Sees H1 Profit Hit by Acquisitions," *just-drinks.com,* September 25, 2007.

"Boizel Chanoine Sees Q3 Sales Rise," *just-drinks.com,* November 7, 2007.

"Boizel Chanoine Toasts Burtin, Lanson Buys for Strong H1," *justdrinks.com,* August 21, 2007.

"Boizel Sales Triple After Burtin, Lanson Buys," *just-drinks.com,* February 13, 2007.

"Boizel Secures Lanson Deal," *just-drinks.com,* December 23, 2005.

"Bouyant Boizel Sounds Note of Caution," *just-drinks.com,* April 19, 2006.

"Corks Pop at Champagne Minnow After Lanson Deal," *Evening Standard,* December 22, 2005, p. 24.

Fallowfield, Giles, "Paillard More Keen on Own Brands Than Own Label," *just-drinks.com,* March 14, 2006.

Hollinger, Peggy, "Boizel Celebrates Lanson Acquisition," *Financial Times,* December 23, 2005, p. 18.

"Lanson Buy Weighs on Boizel Profits," *just-drinks.com,* October 24, 2006.

Sage, Adam, "Lanson Hopes to Toast New Deal As Suitors Walk Away," *Times,* December 14, 2005, p. 45.

BOREALIS

Borealis AG

Wagramerstrasse 17–19
Vienna, 1220
Austria
Telephone: (43 1) 22 400 300
Fax: (43 1) 22 400 333
Web site: http://www.borealisgroup.com

65% Owned by International Petroleum Investment Company (IPIC)
Incorporated: 1994
Employees: 4,500
Sales: EUR 5.74 billion ($6.6 billion) (2006 est.)
NAIC: 326113 Unsupported Plastics Film and Sheet (Except Packaging) Manufacturing; 326121 Unsupported Plastics Profile Shape Manufacturing

■ ■ ■

Borealis AG is a leading polyolefins specialist, producing polyethylene and polypropylene compounds for the global plastics industry. Headquartered in Vienna, Austria, Borealis operates production facilities in Belgium, Finland, Germany, Italy, Sweden, and the United States, and is a partner in several production joint ventures in Brazil and the United Arab Emirates. The group's manufacturing network includes steam crackers in Finland and Sweden, as well as a cracker operated under a joint venture with Abu Dhabi National Oil Company. Borealis also has its own propane dehydrogenation plant in Belgium. In 2006, the group's total production topped 3.5 million tons, including two million tons of polyolefins using its patented Borstar process.

In 2007 the company opened a new polypropylene plant in Germany and completed an expansion of its cracker in Finland. The company also began constructing a new low-density polyethylene plant in Sweden, with a capacity of 350,000 tons per year, slated for completion in 2009. The group is also building a Borstar-based polyethylene plant in partnership with OMV—one of two major shareholders and the group's primary source of olefins. That plant would add another 350,000 tons per year to the company's Austrian operations. Borealis is owned by International Petroleum Investment Company (IPIC), based in Abu Dhabi, which has a 65 percent stake, and OMV AG, of Austria, with 35 percent, since 2005. In 2006, the company moved its headquarters from Denmark to Austria. The company is led by Chief Executive Officer Mark Garrett.

ORIGINS IN NESTE IN 1948

Borealis was created in 1994 as a polyolefins joint venture between Finland's Neste and Norway's Statoil, as part of the privatization process of both state-owned oil companies. Under the agreement, Neste provided its industry-leading polyolefins technology—subsequently patented under the Borstar name—as well as its chemicals assets. Statoil, which had been set up to exploit the vast oil and gas reserves of the Norwegian continental shelf, supplied the joint venture with ethane, one of the raw materials used for the production of polyolefins, as well as funding capital. The new

COMPANY PERSPECTIVES

Our success is driven by responsiveness, operational excellence and innovation. Our mission: To be THE leading provider of innovative, value creating plastics solutions.

company immediately became Europe's largest producer of polyolefins, and the fifth largest in the world.

Neste's polyolefins production by then represented the largest part of the Finnish oil company's petrochemicals production. Neste had been established shortly after World War II. Finland had historically relied on imported oil for the country's petroleum needs. This dependence left the country highly vulnerable throughout the war years. The Finnish government began taking its first steps to develop its own oil reserves during the war, setting up a fuel reserve body, Pva, as part of the Ministry of Defense. Pva then created Naantali Central Storage (NKV), an oil company formed to construct storage facilities for the country's fuel oil and lubricant reserves.

Following the war, NKV was transferred to the Ministry of Trade and Industry. The company's mandate was also expanded at this time, calling for the company to develop its own oil-refining capacity. NKV's name was changed in 1948 to Neste, Finnish for "liquid."

Neste's early years were difficult ones for the company. The storage facilities constructed during the war proved unreliable and even dangerous. The company added its first oil tanker in 1948, yet found itself unable to generate profits from the operation. In the meantime, Neste's plans to enter oil refining met resistance from the major oil companies, which had traditionally controlled the sector in Finland and which enjoyed a great deal of influence on the Finnish government.

Neste's initial request in 1951 to build its own refinery was rejected by the government. However, the company's director, Uolevi Raade, continued to press for the refinery. Finally, in 1954, he managed to convince Dr. Urho Kekkonen, soon to become the country's president, of the importance of the project. The refinery, to be located in Naantali, gained approval that year. Construction of the refinery began in 1955 and initial launch of production began in 1957. By the time of the facility's inauguration in mid-1958, the refinery had increased production to 1.2 million tons of crude oil per year.

ENTERING PETROCHEMICALS IN 1972

Neste's production levels grew strongly through the 1960s. The expansion of the Naantali site boosted production levels to 2.5 million tons of crude oil per year. Neste then launched plans to build a second refinery, in Porvoo, doubling its total capacity. Production at the new facility began in 1967, and plans were quickly made to double capacity by the end of the decade.

The inauguration of the Porvoo facility enabled Neste to put into motion the second phase of its development strategy of entering petrochemicals production. From the outset, the Porvoo site had been designed to include a petrochemicals wing. Neste targeted the polyolefins market—the basic components of polyethylene and polypropylene, the world's most widely used plastics. Construction on two factories began in 1968. The first, an ethylene plant, was integrated directly into the Porvoo refinery, and operated as part of Neste itself. Construction of that unit was completed in 1972.

At the same time, Neste launched its polyethylene and polyvinylchloride (PVC) production unit. This operation was created as a joint venture company, Pekema. The new company was partly owned by a consortium of nine companies. These included eight leading Finnish industrial companies, which also became Pekema's main customers. Neste's share of the venture stood at 44 percent. At the end of the 1970s, however, Neste took full control of Pekema, which was then merged into its other petrochemicals businesses.

The absorption of Pekema came as part of Neste's move in the early 1980s to become Finland's dominant petrochemicals business. In 1981, the company absorbed another joint venture launched in the early 1970s, a producer of polystyrene founded near the Porvoo refinery. Over the next few years, the company took over many of the other petrochemicals and plastics businesses that had been founded in the Porvoo refinery's shadow. In this way, the company expanded its petrochemicals production to include benzine, acetone, and phenol, among others.

The group's polyolefins operations, however, remained the largest part of Neste's petrochemicals operations. Part of the impetus for this growth was the completion of a natural gas pipeline between Russia and Finland in the 1970s. Neste entered the natural gas market at that time, establishing its own distribution network. The access to natural gas also enabled the company to boost its production of polyolefins.

KEY DATES

1972: Neste of Finland inaugurates first ethylene plant in Porvoo as start of polyolefins production.
1985: Sweden's Statoil forms petrochemicals unit to begin production of polyolefins.
1994: Borealis is created through merger of polyolefins operations of Neste and Statoil.
1998: Borouge joint venture launched in Abu Dhabi; PCD Polymere acquired from Austria's OMV group to form world's fourth largest polyolefins producer.
2006: International Petroleum Investment Company (IPIC) and OMV AG take control of Borealis, which moves its headquarters to Austria.

EUROPEAN POLYOLEFINS LEADER IN 1994

During the 1980s, Neste also established itself as a major player in the global petrochemicals and plastics markets. The company established a wide-ranging network of production facilities, entering markets including Sweden, Belgium, France, and the United States. A significant boost to its polyolefins capacity came with the addition of an ethylene cracker in Sines, Portugal.

Through the 1980s and into the 1990s, Neste carried out a diversification strategy. The company added a variety of new businesses, including oil and gas trading, its own service station network, and composites and semifinished plastic products, among others. The company also built a strong research and development division. As a result, Neste was able to develop its own olefins production technology, later dubbed Borstar. In this way, Neste's polyolefins operations became not only its primary petrochemicals operation, but also the company's primary revenue generator.

In the early 1990s, Finland, like much of Europe, embarked on a privatization program for most of its state-owned businesses. In preparation for its own privatization, and future merger with Imatran Voima Oy (IVO), Neste launched a major restructuring of its operations. The centerpiece of this restructuring was the breakup of its petrochemicals business. The main part of this, the polyolefins division, was then spun off into a new joint venture with Norway's Statoil. The new company, called Borealis A/S and based in Copenhagen, became the leading polyolefins producer in Europe, and the fifth largest in the world.

Statoil, created in the early 1970s, had itself entered the petrochemicals market in the mid-1980s, creating Statoil Petrokemi AB in 1985. Statoil added its own polyolefins operations to the new company. However, Statoil's primary contribution to Borealis was its access to the vast oil and gas reserves off the coast of Norway, which had provided the foundation of its own fast-growing polyolefins operations since the launch of Statoil Petrokemi. The combination of the two companies' polyolefin production therefore created a giant in the global polyolefins industry, with first year sales of $2.6 billion. Neste later completed its merger with IVO, becoming Fortum Corporation.

LAUNCHING BORSTAR IN 1995

By 1995, Borealis had perfected its new polyolefins production technology, Borstar, building a dedicated plant for that at the company's main Porvoo site. Trial production of the first Borstar polyethylene began in October 1995, and the plant was officially inaugurated in March 1996.

Borealis entered a number of partnerships in 1996. As part of a joint venture agreement with Montell, Borealis took over the operations of Antwerp-based North Sea Petrochemicals (NSP) and its 250,000 tons-per-year polypropylene plant. Borealis took full control of NSP the following year. The company also formed a joint venture with Ashland Plastics, which began supplying small-scale orders across Europe. By then, the company had formed another highly significant joint venture with Abu Dhabi National Oil Company, to build a major petrochemicals complex in United Arab Emirates. The project, called Borouge, included the construction of a 600,000 tons-per-year ethylene cracker, as well as two Borstar-based polyethylene factories, with a combined capacity of 450,000 tons per year. The project was completed in 2001, at a cost of EUR 1.4 billion.

Borealis in the meantime continued to build its operations elsewhere. One of its most significant acquisitions came in 1998, when it acquired PCD Polymere from Austria's OMV group. The acquisition not only boosted Borealis into the number four spot among worldwide polyolefins producers, it also launched the company's relationship with the Austrian oil and gas group.

EXPANDING PRODUCTION IN THE 21ST CENTURY

Borealis continued to add to its own production capacity. The company completed its first Borstar polypropylene plant in Schwechat, in Austria, in 2000. The groundbreaking technology also attracted interest from outside the company. Borealis signed its first third-party license agreement with Shanghai Petrochemical Company, a subsidiary of China Petrochemical Company (Sinopec), which began producing Borstar-based polyethylene in 2002.

Borstar also enabled the company to expand its presence into Central and Eastern Europe, especially in the market for industrial and packaging film. In support of this, the company expanded its production capacity again, adding a 350,000 tons-per-year polyethylene plant in Schwechat. Borealis also expanded its Austrian polypropylene plant, adding capacity of another 90,000 tons. These projects, launched in 2004, were shortly joined by the announced expansion of the Borouge polyethylene plant to 580,000 tons per year by the following year. Other expansion planned by the company included its ethylene and propylene units in Porvoo, adding nearly 75,000 tons. In all, Borealis earmarked more than EUR 230 million for this phase of its expansion.

Borealis found new owners at the end of 2005, when Statoil agreed to sell its 50 percent stake in the company to OMV AG and Abu Dhabi's International Petroleum Investment Company (IPIC). As a result, IPIC's share stood at 65 percent, with OMV holding the remainder. The new owners quickly transferred their own chemicals operations into Borealis, further raising the company's profile on the world market.

Austria soon became the focal point of operations for Borealis, as the company launched a joint venture with OMV to build a new 350,000-ton Borstar polyethylene plant, as well as the expansion of the Schwechat polypropylene plant. OMV, for its part, raised production at its own cracker to 900,000 tons per year in support of production by Borealis. By 2006, Borealis had decided to transfer its own headquarters to Austria, becoming Borealis AG. In the meantime, the company benefited from its other major shareholder, IPIC, which backed the construction of a second Borouge cracker, a project estimated at $3.1 billion, launched in 2007. With powerful shareholders and industry-leading technology, Borealis had become a major polyolefins force in the 21st century.

M. L. Cohen

PRINCIPAL SUBSIDIARIES

AMI Agrolinz Melamine International GmbH; Borealis A/S (Denmark); Borealis AB (Sweden); Borealis Antwerpen Compounding N.V. (Belgium); Borealis Compounds LLC (USA); Borealis Deutschland GmbH; Borealis Financial Services N.V. (Belgium); Borealis Group Services AS (Norway); Borealis Italia S.p.A; Borealis Kallo N.V. (Belgium); Borealis Polymere GmbH (Germany); Borealis Polymers N.V. (Belgium); Borealis Polymers Oy (Finland); Borealis Polyolefine GmbH; Poliolefinas Borealis España S.A.

PRINCIPAL COMPETITORS

Basell; Ineos; Sabic; Total S.A.; Dow Corp.; Polimeri; ExxonMobil Inc.; Repsol S.A.; TVK Slovnaft; Chemopetrol; Plock; Polichim.

FURTHER READING

"Borealis Announces New Sales Strategies," *Nonwovens Industry,* December 2001, p. 16.

"Borealis AS Closing Compounding Plant," *Plastics News,* April 26, 1999, p. 29.

"Borealis Building Petchem Plants in UAE for Asian Penetration," *Japan Chemical Week,* February 10, 2000, p. 1.

"Borealis Completes Acquisition," *Nonwovens Industry,* September 1998, p. 18.

"Borealis Lands 'Borstar' Contract, Acquires Stake in Chem-Connect," *Nonwovens Industry,* March 2000, p. 17.

"Borealis Sells French Unit," *Plastics News,* October 28, 2002, p. 10.

Robinson, Simon, "Opportunities for Borealis," *ECN European Chemical News,* March 14, 2005, p. 6.

Buffalo Grill S.A.

Route Nationale 20
Avrainville, 91630
France
Telephone: (33 1) 60 82 54 00
Fax: (33 1) 64 91 38 01
Web site: http://www.buffalo-grill.fr

Public Company
Incorporated: 1981
Employees: 3,273
Sales: EUR 517.7 million ($640 million) (2006)
Stock Exchanges: Euronext Paris
Ticker Symbols: 4158061; BUF
NAIC: 722110 Full-Service Restaurants

■ ■ ■

Buffalo Grill S.A. is one of France's leading restaurant chains, taking second place only to McDonald's Corporation. The company is also the dominant player in the steak/grill restaurant segment, with a 49 percent market share. Buffalo Grill positions itself as a family restaurant, based on a "Far West" theme and food inspired by American-style steak houses. Prices are kept low—the entry-level meal costs less than EUR 10—by using imported beef. The company's restaurants are typically located on high-traffic edge-of-city sites along major arteries.

Buffalo Grill operates 275 restaurants across France. In that country, the company is one of the best-known brands, scoring recognition rates of more than 90 percent. There are an additional 15 Buffalo Grill restaurants, operating in Spain (seven restaurants), Belgium (three franchised restaurants), Luxembourg, and Switzerland. Approximately one-third of the group's restaurants are franchised. Altogether, Buffalo Grill serves more than 29 million meals per year, generating revenues of EUR 518 million in 2006. The company also operates its own meat processing subsidiary, Distri-coupe, which supplies the company's own restaurants, while generating additional revenues through contracted sales of meat to the company's franchisees. After a scandal—the company was accused of violating a ban on importing British beef—in the early 2000s, Buffalo Grill has renewed its growth. The company plans to add as many as 39 new restaurants each year through 2010, an expansion balanced by the closing of a number of existing stores. The company also operates a smaller chain of four Pizza Pub restaurants, remaining from an earlier attempt at diversification. Buffalo Grill is listed on the Euronext Paris Stock Exchange. Erich Harasymc-zuk is the company's chairman and CEO.

AMERICAN INSPIRATION IN 1981

After working in the restaurant sector in the United States during the 1970s, Christian Picart recognized the opportunity to import the American-style steak-house concept into his native France. Picart began developing his new restaurant concept, adopting a "Far West" motif and adapting the steak-house menu for the French palate. Picart named his new company Buffalo Grill, after Wild West legend Buffalo Bill Cody.

The first Buffalo Grill opened for business in Avra-inville, in the Essonne region near Paris, in 1981. The

KEY DATES

1981: Christian Picart founds Buffalo Grill and opens first "Far West" theme restaurant in Avrainville, France.
1984: The first Buffalo Grill franchise opens in Annecy.
1994: Establishes central meat processing and distribution subsidiary Districoupe.
1999: Buffalo Grill goes public on Paris Stock Exchange.
2002: Picart and three other employees arrested and accused of illegally importing British beef.
2003: All charges against the company dropped due to lack of evidence.
2005: Picart sells his 75 percent share in company to Colony Capital and Colyzeo investment funds.

concept represented something of a revolution in the French restaurant sector. While the country had already seen the opening of the first McDonald's, the idea of building a chain of family-style restaurants was quite new. Picart also departed from traditional architecture, developing a highly visible, red-roofed restaurant format. For its locations, the company chose sites on the outskirts of major urban centers but along major traffic arteries. Inside the restaurant, the company practiced a policy of providing low-priced meals. In support of this, the company developed a network of overseas suppliers instead of relying on higher-priced French beef.

The first Buffalo Grill was a strong success. The company quickly began opening new restaurants, at first focusing on the region around Paris. These first restaurants were entirely company owned. By 1984, however, the company had launched a franchise operation as well. The first Buffalo Grill franchise opened in Annecy that year. Franchises grew to represent approximately one-third of the group's total restaurants.

In the meantime, Buffalo Grill maintained its own expansion. This was aided by the arrival of a new major investor in 1983, the oil giant Total. With the financial backing of its new shareholder, Buffalo Grill began to plot its conquest of the French dining sector. By 1988, the company operated 16 restaurants.

BEEFING UP FOR GROWTH

Buffalo Grill's appearance and growth through the 1980s came at a time when the French retail sector was undergoing a major transformation. Traditionally concentrated in the city center, retailing had increasingly begun to shift to suburban commercial zones. This movement was largely driven by the major hypermarket groups, but also by a fast-growing number of specialist and "category killer" retail chains.

The creation of these large-scale shopping districts presented a major opportunity for Buffalo Grill. In 1988, the company launched a new and more ambitious expansion phase, adding an average of 17 new restaurants each year into the first half of the 1990s. By 1994, the company boasted nearly 115 restaurants and had become the clear leader in its category. The company's location along major roadways also led the company to explore a new sector, launching a chain of hotels under the Buffal'Hotel name. These hotels were located close to the company's restaurants. By the end of the decade, the hotel chain had grown to six locations, but nevertheless remained a small part of the company's operations.

In the meantime, the continued growth of the Buffalo Grill restaurant chain led the company to launch its own supply operation. In 1994, the company founded Districoupe, which took over as the central beef processing and distribution facility for the group. Instead of buying the whole cow, Districoupe focused on purchasing only those cuts required by the group's restaurant menus. By buying in bulk while eliminating wastage, the new subsidiary helped the group drive down its costs. Districoupe also provided a strong and steady source of revenues from the company's franchises, which were required to purchase all supplies from Districoupe. In this way, Buffalo Grill was also able to maintain control over the quality levels of the Buffalo Grill format.

The need for quality control became all the more urgent with the outbreak of bovine spongiform encephalopathy (BSE), or mad cow disease, in England, and the appearance of the first victims of Creutzfeldt-Jakob disease, the human form of the disease. By 1996, a ban on British beef imports had been put into place in France and the rest of Europe. The crisis, however, sparked a panic among consumers, prompting significant, if temporary, drops in beef consumption.

FACING THE MAD COW DISEASE CRISIS

Beef remained the focal point of the Buffalo Grill concept, placing the company at risk. In order to minimize its exposure to the possible fallout from the BSE crisis, the company was determined to diversify its restaurant operations. The company began developing a new restaurant format, called Victoria Pub, which launched in 1995. The Victoria Pub chain sought to attract a younger clientele than Buffalo Grill's family-based business. The new chain featured an international menu and an extensive beer selection, as well as large-screen televisions and table-based video screens.

Two years later, the company bought 15 restaurants that had been operating under the Chez Margot and Quai des Halles formats. The company at first maintained these operations. In 1998, however, the company bought up the Le Bistro d'Augustin restaurant chain. Following this acquisition, Buffalo Grill converted the Chez Margot and Quai des Halles formats to the Le Bistro d'Augustin brand. This format emulated a more traditional French wine bar, targeting an older and more upscale clientele.

The company was also preparing for a new growth phase for its core Buffalo Grill format. In 1998, the Picart family bought out Total's shareholding. The company went public in 1999, listing its stock on the Paris bourse. By then, the company had acquired the small chain of Pizza Pub restaurants, which were placed under the Victoria Pub chain. At the end of that year, the company counted more than 190 restaurants, included 135 owned by the company, and annual sales of EUR 245 million.

Meanwhile, Buffalo Grill made its first move into the international market, opening the first of seven restaurants in Spain in 1997. The following year, the company made another attempt to change its geographic profile. This time, the company targeted a move into the city center sector, buying ten Paris-area do-it-yourself (DIY) stores operating under the Batifol name.

NEW CRISIS IN THE 21ST CENTURY

Buffalo Grill celebrated the beginning of the new millennium with the opening of its 200th restaurant. However, things quickly soured for the company. By 2001, the company had been forced to acknowledge that its diversification effort had failed. In that year, the company sold seven of the Bistro d'Augustin restaurants, converting five others into Buffalo Grills. By 2002, the company had sold off most of its Victoria Pub restaurants as well. Nevertheless, the company itself was healthy, posting strong gains in both revenues and profits. With 258 restaurants in operation, the company's sales at that time neared EUR 300 million.

The appearance of the first cases of BSE and Creutzfeldt-Jakob disease in France placed the company under new pressure, as consumer panic once again threatened its sales. Then at the end of 2002, Buffalo Grill found itself at the center of a scandal when a number of former employees accused the company of continuing to import British beef despite the ban. Despite the lack of any evidence, the accusations caused a media frenzy in France and resulted in the arrest of Picart and three company employees. Buffalo Grill's fortunes appeared to decline even further when Picart and the other employees were charged with involuntary manslaughter in the deaths of four people who had died from Creutzfeldt-Jakob disease. Overnight, customer patronage rates at Buffalo Grill restaurants dropped by more than 40 percent. The loss in revenues came at an especially bad time for the company, which found itself struggling to meet its debts.

Another company might have collapsed under the pressure, but Buffalo Grill survived the crisis, launching a massive communications effort to win back its customers. The media campaign proved highly successful, especially in its ability to transform media coverage of the company. The company managed to position itself as a victim of the hysteria surrounding the BSE crisis and other crises affecting the agro-industrial industry at the beginning of the 21st century.

Buffalo Grill worked to restore its image through 2003. In April of that year, three of the company's restaurants, including the original Avrainville restaurant, were set on fire. The possibility that the attacks had been caused by a disgruntled employee helped earn new sympathy for the company from the consumer public. In October 2003, the courts dropped the involuntary manslaughter charges against Picart and the other employees. Finally, by the end of the year, all charges against the company had been dropped due to lack of evidence.

GROWTH TARGETS FOR THE FUTURE

Buffalo Grill emerged from the crisis even stronger than before, not only having won back its customer base, but having gained in name recognition. With more than 900 press articles and media reports about the company counted at the height of the crisis, it was difficult not to know about the company.

With the crisis behind it, Buffalo Grill turned its attention to further expansion of the chain. The company renewed interest in international expansion, entering the Belgian, Luxembourg, and Swiss markets. These efforts remained limited, however, and through the middle of the decade, the company's foreign operations stood at just 15 restaurants. In 2004, the company announced its intention to open a restaurant in the United States, in Florida, but that plan was shortly abandoned.

Christian Picart, who at that time held a 75 percent stake in the company, stepped down from day-to-day control of the company's operations in 2005. Picart had made known his intent to sell his interest in the company. By July of that year the company had located a buyer in the form of investment funds Colony Capital and Colyzeo. Erich Harasymczuk was named as company chairman and CEO. Picart remained on the group's board of directors.

In the meantime, Buffalo Grill was once again growing strongly. While the total number of restaurants remained just about level, the company restructured the network, shutting down less-profitable locations in favor of new, higher-traffic sites. As a result, the company's revenues built steadily, topping EUR 475 million in 2005, and nearing EUR 518 million at the end of 2006. The company announced plans to shut a further 20 restaurants, while adding 39 new locations through 2010, with ultimate plans to operate as many as 400 restaurants in France. As one of the best-known brands in the country, Buffalo Grill blazed the trail for success in the new century.

M. L. Cohen

PRINCIPAL SUBSIDIARIES

BABG S.A.; BG Belgium S.A.; BG Espana S.A.; BG Suisse S.A.; Buffalo Center SARL; Districoupe SAS; Hollande SAS; Lucky Steak House S.A.; Mega EURL; Victoria Pub S.A.

PRINCIPAL COMPETITORS

Casino Guichard-Perrachon S.A.; Groupe Auchan S.A.; Rallye S.A.; McDonald's Corporation; Sodexho Alliance S.A.; Quick Restaurants S.A.

FURTHER READING

Arnold, Martin, "Probe Gives Buffalo Grill Rough Ride," *Financial Times,* January 7, 2003, p. 24.

"Buffalo Grill Case Dropped," *Guardian,* October 2, 2003, p. 21.

"Buffalo Grill Sellers Cause Stampede," *Guardian,* January 9, 2003, p. 20.

Gless, Étienne, "Comment Buffalo Grill s'est Remis en Selle," *L'Enterprise,* April 3, 2006.

Jack, Andrew, "French Palates Adapt to American Steaks," *Financial Times,* November 16, 1995, p. S2.

Lichfield, John, "Arsonists with Beef Grudge Hit Series of French Restaurants," *Independent,* April 15, 2003, p. 13.

Lindberg, Anne, "French Steak House Picks Pinellas Park," *St. Petersburg Times,* July 13, 2004, p. 1.

Todd, Stuart, "Buffalo Grill to Be Sold," *just-food.com,* July 13, 2005.

Bugatti Automobiles S.A.S.

1, Château Saint Jean
Dorlisheim
Molsheim, 67120
France
Telephone: (33 3) 88 04 56 00
Web site: http://www.bugatti.com

Wholly Owned Subsidiary of Group Volkswagen France S.A.
Incorporated: 1998 as Bugatti S.A.S.
Employees: 25
Sales: $120 million (2008 est.)
NAIC: 336111 Automobile Manufacturing; 336211 Motor Vehicle Body Manufacturing; 541420 Industrial Design Services

■ ■ ■

Bugatti Automobiles S.A.S. makes some of the world's fastest and most expensive production cars. The Bugatti brand originally appeared at the beginning of the 20th century. A single-minded focus on the pursuit of speed resulted in the brand's dominance of the Grand Prix circuit in the years between World War I and World War II. The traditional factory in the Alsace region of France closed in 1956, several years after the passing of the firm's founder, Ettore Bugatti. The brand was revived three decades later by an Italian entrepreneur but this operation shut down after a few years. Volkswagen AG relaunched Bugatti in 1998 in Molsheim, France. The first contemporary production model, the Veyron 16.4, rolled off the assembly line several years later.

ART MEETS ENGINE

Ettore Bugatti was born on September 15, 1881, in Milan, Italy, to a family known for its artistic bent. The passion and creativity he inherited from a family of designers, painters, and sculptors would eventually be applied to the pursuit of speed. By the time he was 18, Bugatti was working as an apprentice for bicycle manufacturer Prinetti & Stucchi. There, he began experimenting with attaching motors to tricycles, ultimately creating a quadricycle by combining two bikes and four engines. By early in the 20th century he had produced a car of his own design.

In 1901 Bugatti's second automobile won a medal at an exhibition in his hometown, attracting the attention of the Baron de Dietrich, who hired him to work at his automobile operation in Alsace (then under German control). Production there ceased within three years, however. Bugatti then found work designing a car for Strasbourg auto agent Emile Mathis before going to Cologne to work for Deutz Gasmotoren Fabrik.

In his spare time, Bugatti completed the Type 10, which debuted in 1909. This is considered the first of the true, or "Pur Sang," Bugatti automobiles. In the same year, Bugatti moved his business to Molsheim in Alsace. With the advent of World War I he returned to Milan for a time, but Molsheim remained his firm's traditional base.

Bugatti was single-minded in the pursuit of speed. His name became synonymous with elegant engineering

COMPANY PERSPECTIVES

Bugatti has always been the epitome of exclusivity, luxury, elegance, style, extraordinary design, and a great passion for automobiles. Unique visions, the strong legacy of legendary sports cars, and high-precision engineering in development, construction, and manufacture distinguish this outstanding automotive brand. The elegant, individual, and independent character of Bugatti automobiles is reflected in the brand logo: the pearl-framed oval sporting 60 pearls, the stylized initials of the brand's founder Ettore Bugatti, and the elegantly simple Bugatti word mark have adorned each Bugatti model since 1909. The logo embodies the official statement and the tradition-conscious promise that Bugatti offers its discerning customers. All Bugatti brand values have been integrated in the Veyron, an aesthetic and engineering masterwork first introduced in 2005, which, like its predecessors, is a match for contemporary racing cars.

solutions and quality components. "Nothing is too beautiful, nothing is too expensive," decreed Bugatti, adding, "No matter what the price, one must win, working night and day if necessary." The company made only five cars its first year, but delivered 75 units in 1911. A French auto manufacturer licensed one of Bugatti's earliest designs for what became known as the *Bébé Peugeot.*

Bugatti started out with a dozen workers, and the workforce grew steadily to 200 people by 1914. A decade later, employment at the Molsheim plant was near its peak of 1,200 workers. Production of the cars could be measured in dozens. Surviving examples would later become some of the most sought-after collectible automobiles in the world, fetching millions at auction.

INTERWAR RACING DOMINANCE

Success came early as the cars racked up wins in local hill climbs and other racing events. Bugatti's cars tended to be light, fast, and packed with powerful engines. A monthlong, 14,000-kilometer crossing of the Sahara in 1927 by an intrepid French lieutenant in a Bugatti car helped build the maker's reputation for quality. One of Bugatti's most celebrated cars was the Type 35, which biographer Philippe Dejean called "the most glorious motor vehicle of all automotive history." Introduced in 1924, it racked up more than 2,000 racing titles.

Bugatti maintained a place among racing's top names throughout the 1920s, although the company sometimes had to respond to industry innovations as superchargers. After 1929, however, the faltering global economy put the brakes on the market for Bugatti's expensive sports cars. Jean Bugatti took over the plant when his father left Molsheim in 1936, a year marked by labor unrest. Jean Bugatti had been responsible for designing one of the firm's greatest examples, the Type 57SC Atlantic. Introduced in 1934, it won the 24-hour race at Le Mans in 1937. However, the younger Bugatti's leadership tenure was brief; he died in 1939 in a testing accident, when he struck a tree while dodging a bicyclist.

The operation was moved to Bordeaux during World War II. By the time Ettore Bugatti died in Paris in 1947, 7,950 automobiles had been crafted bearing the Bugatti name. In addition, Ettore Bugatti's influence was not limited to the automotive realm. In 1927 he helped launch the aerospace firm Messier-Bugatti, a leading manufacturer of landing gear and hydraulic systems for aircraft.

The Bugatti automotive company did not fully recover after its founder's death, although production continued at Molsheim until 1956. In the early 1960s Hispano-Suiza acquired Bugatti's plant in Molsheim. Hispano-Suiza was a venerable manufacturer of aircraft engines and had itself produced some of the most collectible automobiles of the 1930s. It later became part of French defense firm SNECMA (Groupe SAFRAN).

ITALIAN AUTOMOTIVE RENAISSANCE 1987–95

In 1987 a Luxembourg holding company called Bugatti International S.A.H., controlled by Romano Artioli, acquired the Bugatti brand from Hispano-Suiza. An operating company called Bugatti Automobili S.p.A. was created, and a new factory was built in Modena, Italy. The company's managing-technical director was Paolo Stanzani, the man behind the development of two of Automobili Lamborghini S.p.A.'s most celebrated sports cars, the Miura and the Countach. However, Stanzani was let go in 1990 after a failed takeover attempt.

Another Lamborghini vet, Marcello Gandini, drafted the design for the new Bugatti. Dubbed the EB 110, it boasted a 550-horsepower engine with 12 cylinders and two turbochargers. Production of the EB 110 sports car commenced in 1991, with 139 completed over the next four years. In 1993, Artioli acquired Lotus Cars Ltd., maker of the legendary British sports cars, from General Motors Corp. for $48 million. However, in an effort to raise cash, Artoli sold this

KEY DATES

1909: Ettore Bugatti establishes an automobile company in Molsheim, Alsace (now France).
1924: The legendary Type 35 debuts.
1956: The Molsheim plant closes several years after the passing of the company founder.
1963: Hispano-Suiza buys Bugatti's Molsheim plant.
1987: Italian entrepreneur establishes Bugatti Automobili S.p.A. in Modena, Italy.
1995: Bugatti Automobili S.p.A. folds.
1999: Volkswagen AG relaunches the brand via Bugatti S.A.S.
2004: VW renovates Bugatti's Molsheim headquarters.
2006: The first million-dollar Veyron 16.4 sports cars are delivered.

company a year and a half later, at a $10 million profit, to a U.K. investment group owned by Italy's Benetton and Bonomi families.

By mid-decade, Bugatti Automobili attained annual revenues of more than $40 million. During the Artoli years, some revenue came from the licensing of the Bugatti name for luxury items such as apparel, perfume, and wristwatches. This was accomplished through a joint venture called Ettore Bugatti s.r.l., led by Artioli's wife, Renata. There were plans for an initial public offering in London and New York to raise money to develop new offerings at both Bugatti and Lotus. However, the company slid into insolvency in 1995.

VW RELAUNCHES BUGATTI

Volkswagen AG acquired Bugatti Automobili S.p.A. and rights to the legendary brand in August 1998. The deal culminated a luxury buying spree orchestrated by VW chairman Ferdinand Piech that also included Lamborghini and Bentley (the latter, one of Bugatti's old racing rivals). In 1999 Volkswagen AG officially relaunched Bugatti S.A.S. as a unit of Volkswagen France. It was stabled at Bugatti's traditional quarters in Molsheim, Alsace.

VW had a prototype by this time, a luxury coupe called the Bugatti EB 118. Sculpted by Italdesign S.p.A., it was powered by an 18-cylinder, 555-horsepower engine made by Volkswagen. This was followed by plans for a four-door version called the Bugatti EB 218. In spite of the horsepower involved, the styling of these was understated and elegant, more suggestive of a night on the town than the 24-hour exertion of Le Mans racing.

A group of VW designers led by Hartmut Warkuss produced a couple more aggressively styled sports-car concepts. A prototype of the Bugatti 18.3 Chiron was introduced in 1999. Its streamlined curves, low profile, and large wheels gave it the look of a true racing machine; both it and its successor were named after Grand Prix champions. The VW team also designed the concept that first entered production, the Bugatti Veyron 16.4. With 1,000 horsepower and a top speed of more than 250 miles per hour, it was billed as the world's fastest production car.

A MILLION-DOLLAR CAR

The Veyron represented a groundbreaking design effort. The engine, a VW product, was essentially two V-8s joined together, along with four turbochargers. Among the custom systems developed were a seven-speed, dual-clutch transmission and a ten-radiator cooling system. The carbon fiber body was sourced from ATR, an Italian firm better known for its aerospace work. The Veyron was priced at EUR 1 million, or about $1.2 million to $1.6 million, depending on exchange rates. At $30,000, the sound system alone was roughly twice as expensive as a Ford Focus. The first models reached customers in 2006.

VW had renovated Bugatti's headquarters at Molsheim in 2004, after designating Thomas Bscher, a veteran of the banking industry, as the unit's new president. At a time when total Volkswagen Group production reached a record six million units, Bugatti delivered 81 automobiles in 2007. This represented a couple dozen more than Bugatti built the previous year, the result of efforts to speed deliveries to impatient customers, most of whom were from the United States.

In 2007 Thomas Bscher stepped down as president of Bugatti, to be replaced by Dr. Franz-Josef Paefgen, who had led the Veyron 16.4's development at Bugatti Engineering GmbH (a unit of Volkswagen Retail GmbH). Bugatti's production of the Veyron (limited to 300 models) was halfway done by 2007. According to *Automotive News,* Bugatti was contemplating the introduction of a less-expensive model at some point in the future.

Frederick C. Ingram

PRINCIPAL COMPETITORS

McLaren Automotive Ltd; Shelby SuperCars, LLC; Ferrari SpA; Koenigsegg Automotive AB; Automobili Lamborghini SpA; Aston Martin Lagonda Limited.

FURTHER READING

Batchelor, Dean, "Bugatti Type 10," *Road & Track,* February 1985, pp. 50–55.

Birch, Stuart, "Bugatti's Veyron Matures," *Automotive Engineering International,* February 2001, p. 25.

Borge, J., and N. Viasnoff, *Bugatti,* Paris: E.P.A., 1981.

Borgeson, Griffith, *Bugatti,* London: Osprey Ltd., 1981.

Bradley, W. F., *Ettore Bugatti,* Abingdon, England: Motor Racing Publications, 1948.

Browne, T. C., "The Last Bugatti: 101C Ghia Type Roadster," *Motor Trend,* September 1984, pp. 111–14.

Bugatti, L'Ebé, *The Bugatti Story,* London: Souvenir Press, 1967.

"Bugatti Plans Stock Offering," *Automotive News,* March 14, 1994, p. 44.

Callaway, Sue Zesiger, "Bachelor Meets Bugatti," *Fortune,* March 19, 2007, pp. 82–83.

Carter, Matthew, "Bugatti Unveils a Southern Bentley," *European,* October 5, 1998, p. 22.

Ciferri, Luca, "Lamborghini Designer Dreams of a New Bugatti Supercar," *Automotive News,* October 24, 1988, p. 28.

Dejean, Philippe, *Carlo-Rembrandt-Ettore-Jean Bugatti,* New York: Rizzoli, 1982.

Eaglesfield, B., and C. W. P. Hampton, *The Bugatti Book,* Abingdon, England: Motor Racing Publications, 1954.

"Fast Wheels on the Move," *Economist,* September 4, 1993, p. 85.

"G.M. Sells Its Lotus Group to Bugatti," *New York Times,* August 28, 1993.

Henning, Krogh, "Bugatti Speeds Up Veyron Output to Cut Wait Times," *Automotive News,* April 3, 2006, p. 28N.

Johnson, Richard, "Supercar Projects at Full Throttle: Europeans Not Slowing Despite Economic, Safety Potholes," *Automotive News,* March 4, 1991, pp. 3, 33.

Johnson, Richard, and Luca Ciferri, "Terra Firma: Bugatti Venture Appears Solid After a Failed Palace Coup," *Automotive News,* August 13, 1990, pp. 3, 26.

Kestler, P., *Bugatti,* Paris: E.P.A., 1981.

———, *Bugatti, l'evolution d'un style,* Lausanne, Switzerland: Edita, 1975.

Kurylko, Diana T., and Luca Ciferri, "Bugatti May Produce a Less-Expensive Car," *Automotive News,* September 3, 2007, p. 28.

———, "Bugatti Sells Lotus," *Automotive News,* April 3, 1995, p. 6.

Lewin, Tony, and Ruth Sullivan, "Creditors' Doubt over Bugatti Bid," *European,* September 14, 1995, p. 18.

Neher, Jacques, "Bugatti Weighs New Issue," *International Herald Tribune,* April 7, 1994, p. 13.

Ostmann, Bernd, "Simply No Comparison," *AutoWeek,* October 3, 2005, pp. 12–14.

Price, Barry, *Bugatti 57: The Last French Bugatti,* Dorchester, England: Veloce Publishing, 2000.

Rossant, John, "Bugatti's Back—And Only $350,000," *Business Week,* May 2, 1994.

Smith, Giles, "The Car Designer: Berliner Achim Anscheidt Leapt from Being a Motorbike Daredevil to Shaping the Future of One of the Most Advanced Supercars Ever," *Men's Vogue,* November 2007, pp. 140–43.

Sullivan, Ruth, "Bugatti Chief Signs Last-Minute 'Rescue' Deal," *European,* September 21, 1995, p. 17.

———, "Bugatti Drives Towards the U.S. Market," *European,* June 17, 1994, p. 32.

Sullivan, Ruth, Tony Patey, Nick Moss, and Sarah Cunningham, "'Prince' Claims to Have Paid $300m for Bugatti," *European,* August 3, 1995, p. 15.

Tagliabue, John, "Mr. Artioli's Dream Car Spins Out: Bugatti Maker Fights for Control of Insolvent Firm," *International Herald Tribune,* November 24, 1995, p. 13.

Tayman, John, "A Greed for Speed," *Business 2.0,* September 2006, pp. 118–20.

Tetzeli, Rick, "A $600,000 Car for Moral Buyers Only," *Fortune,* January 14, 1991, p. 13.

Tragatsch, Erwin, *Das Grosse Bugatti Buch,* Stuttgart, Germany: Motorbuch Verlag, 1967.

Venables, David, *Bugatti—A Racing History,* Sparkford, Yeovil, U.K.: Haynes Publishing, 2002.

Weernink, Wim Oude, "He Created First Serious Small Car," *Automotive News,* December 18, 2000, p. 20D.

———, "VW Begins Production of Bugatti Veyron; Automaker May Build a Second Model," *Automotive News,* September 12, 2005, p. 4.

Weisman, Katherine, "Bag War: Hermes Must Pay Bugatti for Use of Its Name," *WWD,* January 30, 1995, p. 9.

The Burton Corporation

80 Industrial Parkway
Burlington, Vermont 05401
U.S.A.
Telephone: (802) 862-4500
Toll Free: (800) 881-3138
Fax: (802) 660-3250
Web site: http://www.burton.com

Private Company
Incorporated: 1978
Employees: 650
Sales: $250 million (2007 est.)
NAIC: 339920 Sporting and Athletic Good Manufacturing

■ ■ ■

As one of the first snowboard companies in the world, The Burton Corporation designs, manufactures, and markets a full line of snowboarding equipment, clothing, and related accessories. Although snowboarding did not become a well-recognized sport until the early 1990s, Burton began manufacturing snowboards and bindings in 1977, when the company's founder started making his own boards in a borrowed woodworking shop in Stratton, Vermont. From these modest origins, Burton developed into a flourishing enterprise with offices in Europe and Japan. Recognized as an industry pioneer, Burton controls roughly 40 percent of the U.S. snowboarding market, but 60 percent of its sales come from abroad. Most of its manufacturing is handled outside the United States, although it still makes some high-end lines in Vermont. The company has diversified into snowboarding accessories, surfboards, lifestyle apparel, and footwear.

GENESIS OF SNOWBOARDING

Few individuals have had a greater effect on the creation and the development of the snowboarding industry than Jake Burton Carpenter, the founder of Burton Snowboards. Carpenter's pioneering influence is irrefutable, but in the history of snowboarding there was one key individual whose contributions preceded Carpenter's. His name was Sherman Poppen. Although Carpenter was recognized as a pioneer—and deservedly so—it was Poppen's innovative work that inspired him. Just as the hundreds of companies involved in the snowboarding industry during the 1990s were indebted to Carpenter, so too was Carpenter indebted to Poppen. Poppen never received the fanfare accorded to Carpenter, but in the history of Burton Snowboards, which framed the history of snowboarding itself, the origin of all that followed started in Poppen's garage in 1965.

A businessman residing in Muskegon, Michigan, Poppen was the inventor of the "Snurfer," the earliest version of the modern-day snowboard. Poppen assembled his first Snurfer on Christmas Day in 1965 when he nailed together two 36-inch skis with scraps of wood and gave the hastily created toy to his daughters. At first, Poppen was merely trying to create a diversion for his daughters to get them out of the house and away from his pregnant wife, but the toy proved to be an enormous hit among the neighborhood children,

> **COMPANY PERSPECTIVES**
>
> In 1977, Jake Burton Carpenter founded Burton Snowboards out of his Vermont barn. Since then, Burton has fueled the growth of snowboarding worldwide through its groundbreaking product lines, its team of top snowboarders and its grassroots efforts to get the sport accepted at boardsports and apparel brands.

prompting Poppen to refine the design of the first Snurfer.

Three months later, after tinkering with the design of the Snurfer and adding a rope to its front for the rider to grasp, Poppen had secured a patent for his invention and was ready to determine whether or not he had a marketable product. Poppen approached a friend of his who worked at Brunswick Bowling & Billiards Corp. and subsequently licensed the Snurfer to Brunswick. What followed was a renowned marketing disaster, but Poppen's misfortune proved to be the inspiration for Burton Snowboards.

Although the idea seemed logical, Brunswick never distributed Snurfers to sporting goods stores. Instead, the company distributed the snow toys to hardware stores, where they were sold for roughly $10. It was a major misstep, one that Harvard's business school used in later years as a case study to illustrate how not to market a new product. Even though 500,000 Snurfers eventually were sold before Brunswick abandoned production, the results were dismal. Poppen later realized his error, remarking, "They [Brunswick] knew the bowling industry, but they sure as hell didn't know consumer products." Much of the finger-pointing at Brunswick stemmed from the fact that Snurfers had considerable market appeal, but the company had failed to exploit consumer interest.

BURTON SNOWBOARDS TAKES SHAPE

One of those who recognized Brunswick's errors was Jake Carpenter. When Carpenter was 14 years old he received one of the Brunswick-made Snurfers, and from that moment forward, he had found his life's calling. Throughout high school and college, Carpenter labored to make improvements on the Snurfer, experimenting with one design after another during his hours away from classes. His devotion was tireless and his work was visionary.

"I felt there was an opportunity for it [the Snurfer] to be better marketed," Carpenter later told *Sports Illustrated,* continuing, "For serious technology to be applied to it, so Snurfing could become a legitimate sport instead of a cheap toy. I knew there was an opportunity there. I couldn't believe Brunswick never took advantage of it." Carpenter's father, Tim, a writer and former Wall Street broker, was impressed with his son's diligence: "He wasn't the type of kid who set up lemonade stands, but once he had the idea for this board in his head, he put every bit of his energy into it."

After earning a degree in economics from New York University, Carpenter took a position at a small Manhattan investment bank. His tenure there, however, was brief. A small inheritance from his grandmother enabled Carpenter to quit his job at the bank and move, in 1977, to Stratton Mountain, Vermont. There, with $20,000 as a nest egg, Carpenter founded Burton Snowboards at age 23, taking the company's name from his middle name. (The Burton Corporation was incorporated in Vermont in January 1978.)

Jake Burton Carpenter worked nights as a bartender at Stratton's ski resort and spent his days honing his skills as a snowboard maker in the woodworking shop of a friend, Emo Henrich, who was director of the Stratton Mountain ski school. Carpenter constructed more than 100 models in Henrich's shop, trying different shapes, different types of wood, and experimenting with various laminating materials and binding designs before settling on what he deemed a marketable product.

Although the improvements over the Snurfer design were vast, Carpenter's timing was off. "I was so naive," he later confided. "I thought I'd be selling boards and making money right away, but by the time I had a board ready, winter was over and nobody was interested." It was a frustrating start, but only the beginning in what would turn out to be an arduous undertaking. Carpenter was not only trying to develop a product and bring it to market, he also was trying to create the market in the first place. His perseverance, first displayed as a teenager in Cedarhurst, New York, would be tested for years to come.

TAKING THE PRODUCT TO MARKET

After his disappointing first attempt at selling his boards, Carpenter went to Europe and spent the summer of 1978 testing his boards on the glaciers in Austria. When the winter season neared, Carpenter returned to the United States and steeled himself for another go at selling his boards. This time he was more prepared, and spent endless weeks traveling around the

KEY DATES

1977: Jake Burton Carpenter launches Burton Snowboards in Vermont.
1984: Company breaks even on sales of $1 million.
1985: Burton sets up manufacturing facility in Innsbruck, Austria.
1997: Worldwide production totals 200,000 units.
1998: Snowboarding becomes an official Olympic sport.
1999: Burton launches Gravis Footwear.
2001: Burton forms Anon Optics.
2003: Analog Clothing line is introduced.
2004: Burton buys four California snowboard brands it renames "The Program."
2006: Burton acquires California surfboard company Channel Islands.

country attending trade shows. "I was afraid to go to the bathroom," Carpenter recalled. "I thought if I did, I might miss my only customer."

Compared to his first season of selling, Carpenter's next season was a success, thanks in large part to more thorough market research and the establishment of a mail-order department, whose telephone rang in Carpenter's bedroom. Offices were set up in a former electrician's store in Londonderry, Vermont, where Carpenter, with a few friends lending a hand, produced his four-foot-long, eight-inch-wide snowboards. By the end of the season, Carpenter had sold 300 boards, but he was far short of his breakeven point and was racking up debt with each passing day.

Snurfers at this point were more popular than ever, having transcended their ill-conceived marketing and distribution support to become a cult hit lionized at the National Snurfing Championships in Michigan. At the annual event in 1979, the Snurfer faithful gathered to compete in races on their boards, but their day of celebration was disrupted by the arrival of a newcomer: Jake Carpenter carrying one of his own snowboards.

After convincing race officials to let him race by creating an open division, Carpenter strapped into his bindings and proceeded to win the race. Carpenter's victory sounded the death knell for Snurfers, ushering in a new era of snowboarding that focused on the continual improvement of technology. In this new era, Carpenter and Burton Snowboards would rise above all other rivals to reign supreme in a market that a decade later represented the fastest-growing sport in the United States.

SLOW, MEASURED GROWTH

After his success at the Snurfing National Championships, Carpenter's problem was that the rampant growth of the snowboard market was still a decade away. Although there was palpable interest in the sport, there were not enough people willing to try snowboarding to support Carpenter and his business. By the end of the 1979–80 season, Carpenter had sold 700 boards, more than doubling his total during the previous season, but he still was well below his profitability point. Year by year, the financial loses mounted, leaving Carpenter $130,000 in debt by 1981.

Carpenter managed to move forward, however, and with the financial support of his wife's family he developed better bindings and a high-technology plastic base, and added steel edges to his boards, which improved maneuverability exponentially. Slowly but steadily the changes made by Burton and the handful of other snowboarding pioneers increased the demand for snowboards, enabling Carpenter to break even for the first time in 1984, when sales reached the $1 million mark.

The addition of steel edges to snowboards did much to persuade skiers to try snowboarding for the first time, but only a limited number of ski resorts allowed snowboards on their slopes. The battle to persuade resort operators to allow snowboards on their slopes raged for years, with economics proving to be the decisive factor in resolving the war.

The number of ski visits per year in the United States flattened out in 1979 and remained so for the ensuing two decades, forcing roughly half of the country's 1,000 ski resorts to close their operations by 1995. Accordingly, as business tapered off and snowboarding grew, resort operators were forced to embrace the new sport. In 1985, 93 percent of U.S. ski resorts banned snowboarding; by 1995, more than 90 percent of the resorts not only permitted snowboarding but also focused their marketing programs on attracting snowboarders. The chief benefactor of this development—of snowboarding's legitimacy—was Jake Carpenter and his promising company, Burton Snowboards.

MANUFACTURING OVERSEAS

On the heels of recording his first break-even year in 1984, Carpenter traveled to Europe and established a manufacturing plant in Innsbruck, Austria, in 1985.

Previously, Carpenter had fulfilled orders from Europe for his boards on an individual basis. By the end of the following year, Carpenter could point to his first profit, as Burton Snowboards, nearly a decade after its creation, began operating in the black.

For Carpenter and his company it was the beginning of lucrative times after years of trying to succeed with meager financial resources. In the years ahead, snowboard manufacturers would find a vast and exuberant audience for their products, although the emergence of this iconoclastic crowd of consumers came as a surprise to many of snowboarding's early proponents. Originally, Burton Snowboards and other manufacturers targeted their marketing efforts on experienced alpine skiers, hoping a considerable percentage of the veteran skiers would try snowboarding and stay with it. This market segment was referred to as the crossover market, but it never materialized in great numbers.

Instead, snowboarding received a greater boost to its ranks from skateboarding and surfer enthusiasts, people who typically had never visited a ski resort. These converts to winter recreation were the source of snowboarding's explosive growth, fueling the growth of Burton Snowboards and all those companies that followed in its wake. The arrival of snowboarding's lifeblood—primarily teenagers—began with a trickle in 1985. By the early 1990s, the trickle had turned into a voluminous river.

EXTREME YET MAINSTREAM

By the 1990s, snowboarding had moved into the mainstream, attracting headlines in newspapers, a perennially increasing number of participants, and a wave of start-up companies intent on grabbing a share of the lucrative, fast-growing market. Carpenter, who once operated in near isolation and generally was acknowledged only with bemused skepticism, found himself inundated with rivals on all flanks by the mid-1990s. More than 300 companies in the United States were competing for snowboard business in 1995, but all of the contenders took a backseat to Burton Snowboards. Operating in a highly fragmented industry, Burton Snowboards controlled an estimated 36 percent of the market, or twice as much as its nearest rival.

By 1997 Burton Snowboards was introducing its 1998 line of merchandise, the 20th year a new line of company-designed and -manufactured clothing, equipment, and accessories had debuted on the retail market. By this point, the company was selling more than 100,000 snowboards a year in North America, with sales in both Europe and Japan equal to the level registered in the United States. As the company charted its course past its 20th anniversary, the road ahead looked as promising as ever.

Industry consolidation was expected to take place during the late 1990s and the early 21st century, as the smaller companies either exited the business or sold their operations to larger competitors. When this inevitable industry shakeup occurred, Burton Snowboards was expected to benefit significantly, as the big companies became bigger and the smaller companies were weeded out of the market. Viewed from this perspective, Burton Snowboard's position as the industry giant appeared guaranteed in the years ahead.

SNOWBOARDING GOES TO THE OLYMPICS

Snowboarding was accepted as an official Olympic sport in time for the 1998 Nagano Winter Games. This was an appropriate venue for its debut, as Japan was home to one of the earliest snowboard companies, Pioneer Moss Pty., Ltd. The country was becoming one of Burton's most important international markets. It established a subsidiary there in 1995 and opened a store in Tokyo in 2006.

The sport received even more global media exposure at the 2002 Winter Games in Salt Lake City and the Torino Olympics four years later. An increasing number of other televised events, such as the X-Games, also kept the sport in the public eye both in the United States and abroad. At the same time, Burton's business was expanding internationally. By 2003, more than half of revenues were derived outside the United States.

Once the undisputed leader of the snowboarding world, Burton no longer had the market all to itself, however. The rival K2 stable of brands challenged it for market leadership. Burton was also facing pressure from a new class of competitor. After years of trying to ignore the scruffy outsider at their margins, mainstream ski manufacturers had begun to cater to snowboarding's youth-oriented market. In 2003, after a couple of years of below-average snowfall, Burton laid off nearly one-fifth of its workforce.

DIVERSIFICATION

Having created the market for snowboards, leading to the development of the sport of snowboarding, Burton continued to find new ways to build connections with the growing market of customers eager to buy equipment to support their interest. The 1996 creation of R.E.D.-Rider Engineered Devices brought Burton into the helmet manufacturing business. Seeking to add goggles—another critical piece of snowboarding gear—to its lineup, Burton formed Anon Optics in 2001.

Also, in spite of snowboarding's new levels of popularity, Burton believed it prudent to pursue diversification beyond the slopes. Connecting with skateboarders and surfers, as well as with snowboarders, could help offset the seasonal nature of Burton's core business; lifestyle apparel and accessories fit the bill. The Gravis Footwear brand debuted in 1999. It specialized in casual shoes, sandals, and accessories for the snowboarding, skateboarding, and surfing crowd. Gravis was producing revenues of $25 million or more within three years.

Burton introduced its fashion-oriented Analog Clothing line in 2003. Its products were not limited to the winter season and included such casual items as corduroy pants and sweaters. The plan for marketing Burton's lifestyle clothing brands included venturing outside resort towns into urban fashion centers. The company opened a store in New York City's SoHo district in 2005 and another one a couple of years later in Los Angeles.

Some acquisitions merely consolidated Burton's hold on the snowboard market. In 2004 Burton bought a collection of California snowboard brands—Forum Snowboards, Special Blend, Foursquare and Jeenyus—that together came to be known as "The Program."

Another buy brought Burton into the sister sport of surfing, which shared quite a few common participants with snowboarding. In 2006 the company acquired the legendary Santa Barbara, California, surfboard company known as Channel Islands. Formed in 1969 by Al Merrick, it had become the brand of choice for competitive surfers. The addition helped balance the seasonality of Burton's winter sports business.

Snowboards remained at the core of the brand, however, and Burton worked to maintain its edge. Following a pattern seen in other sporting goods industries, Burton experimented with new materials. A snowboard made mostly of aluminum was introduced in August 2003. Burton also produced models using graphite composites.

Expressive graphics remained a feature dear to the hearts of many snowboarders. Burton's Series 13 snowboards, introduced in 2005, gave customers unprecedented customization options via the Internet. They could even upload their own images to be printed on this line of boards, which were handmade in the United States. In 2007 Burton licensed some designs from The Andy Warhol Foundation for the Visual Arts, Inc., for use on snowboards, clothing, and accessories.

ATTRACTING NEW RIDERS

Attracting and retaining new enthusiasts is the key to positioning snowboarding as a sport with the potential for continued growth, yet the sport can be very difficult to learn. To address this problem, Burton formed its Learn to Ride Method Center in 1998. It had earlier created the Chill Foundation to introduce disadvantaged urban youth to the sport.

Changing the gender demographics of the sport's enthusiasts is another aspect of growing the market. While the typical snowboarder population had always been predominantly male, Burton has made a concerted effort to bring more females into the fold. The company debuted its first line of snowboards targeted to girls and young women in the late 1990s. In 2003 a creative director was hired to reshape the design of its offerings for women; according to *WWD,* these had earlier been based on a dubious "pink it and shrink it" philosophy.

Jeffrey L. Covell
Updated, Frederick C. Ingram

PRINCIPAL SUBSIDIARIES

Burton Sportartikel GmbH (Austria); Burton Snowboards (Japan); R.E.D.-Rider Engineered Devices; Gravis Footwear; Anon Optics; Analog Clothing; The Program; Channel Islands; Burton Canada Company; Burton Export Corporation.

PRINCIPAL OPERATING UNITS

Burton Snowboards USA; Burton Snowboards Europe; Burton Snowboards Japan; Burton Manufacturing Center.

PRINCIPAL COMPETITORS

K2 Corporation; Arbor Snowboards, Inc.; Quiksilver Inc.; Pioneer Moss Pty., Ltd.; adidas-Salomon AG.

FURTHER READING

Barna, Ed, "Burton Snowboards Catches Gnarly Production Process," *Vermont Business Magazine,* July 1, 2001, p. 23.

Bhonslay, Marianne, "Everything's Jake," *Sporting Goods Business,* January 2003, pp. 36–38.

Burton Snowboards Inc., *Back in the Day: An In-Depth Look at the History of Snowboarding and Burton Snowboards,* Burlington, Vt.: Burton Snowboards Inc., 2007.

Field, Alan M., "Dollars and $ense; Online Trade-Finance Tools Gain Acceptance as a Way to Cut Costs and Strengthen

Relationships," *Journal of Commerce,* January 17, 2005, pp. 18–20.

Finkel, Michael, "Chairman of the Board," *Sports Illustrated,* January 13, 1997, p. 9.

Gallagher, Leigh, "Balance of Powder," *Sporting Goods Business,* February 24, 1997, p. 26.

Horyn, Cathy, "To Balance a Business, He Rides a Snowboard," *New York Times,* Bus. Sec., August 24, 2003, p. 5.

Lane, Randall, "The Culture That Jake Built," *Forbes,* March 27, 1995, p. 45.

Olgeirson, Ian, "Snowboarding Craze Leaves Poppen Behind," *Denver Business Journal,* January 3, 1997, p. 19A.

Speer, Jordan K., "Burton Snowboard Performs on the Slopes," *Apparel Magazine,* September 13, 2007.

Tran, Khanh T. L., "Burton Courts Women with West Coast Flagship," *WWD,* November 29, 2007, p. 10.

Von Familie zu Familie.

Carl Kühne KG (GmbH & Co.)

Kühnehoefe 11
Hamburg, D-22761
Germany
Telephone: (49 40) 85305-0
Fax: (49 40) 85305-235
Web site: http://www.kuehne.de

Private Company
Incorporated: 1832 as Carl Kühne Company
Employees: 1,500
Sales: EUR 330 million ($376 million) (2003 est.)
NAIC: 311421 Fruit and Vegetable Canning; 311422 Specialty Canning

■ ■ ■

Headquartered in Hamburg, Germany, Carl Kühne KG (GmbH & Co.) is one of the largest manufacturers of vinegar and mustard in Europe. In Germany, Carl Kühne leads the market in its core areas of vinegar, pickled products, red cabbage, and dressings. The company's consumer division puts out a broad variety of premium-segment food products under the Kühne brand name, from specialty vinegars and mustards to gherkins, fine pickles, sauerkraut, red cabbage, and green kale to dressings, sauces, and even desserts. Kühne ships its delicacies to over 50 countries around the world—sauerkraut to the United States, gherkins to the United Kingdom, red cabbage to Spain, horseradish and dressings to Russia, vinegar to China, and dried fried onions to Japan. Kühne's commercial division supplies the European food industry with vinegar; fast-food chains in Germany such as Burger King and Subway with sauces for burgers and sandwiches, dips, and salad dressings; and restaurants and foodservice companies with vinegar, mustard, ketchup, mayonnaise, and seasonings.

Production facilities in Germany are located in Hagenow, Cuxhaven, Berlin, Hamm, Straelen, and Schweinfurt. In addition, the company manufactures vinegar in Denmark, Poland, and Turkey, and mustard in Poland and France. Exports account for roughly one-third of sales, while commercial customers contribute about one-tenth to the total. Kühne maintains its own logistics division and truck fleet to ship its products. Descendants of the Kühne family, who acquired it in 1761, own the company.

FROM SMALL-SCALE MANUFACTURING TO LARGE-SCALE PRODUCTION

When Friedrich Wilhelm Kühne's son-in-law, Daniel Friedrich Teichert, bought a vinegar distillery in Berlin in 1761, the small business had been in existence for almost 40 years. Founded in 1722 by Johann Daniel Epinius, it was sold by his wife after the founder's death. In the following 70 years, the business saw two generations of Kühne owners come and go, continuing output on a rather small scale. In 1795 the Kühne family expanded vinegar production and invested in a new and larger factory in Berlin's Alte Jacobstraße, where it remained for the next 40 years.

When Carl Ernst Wilhelm Kühne, Daniel Friedrich Teichert's cousin, took over the reins in 1832, the

COMPANY PERSPECTIVES

Innovation as a tradition: Yesterday, today and tomorrow. Tradition tells us how important values like curiosity, courage and an innovative spirit are. They are decisive for our development. Our tradition makes us dynamic, driving us on to develop our products further and innovate. Our customers and consumers are at the heart of our innovative force. In its leading position as a premium brand, Kühne is continuously developing its range, always giving the market vital impetus. Key factors for successful development are speed and the ability to succeed in the long-term, above all in fulfilling the customers' current requirements and creating real added value. Our future success is based on a responsible approach to human and environmental resources. As a traditional company, Kühne is aware of this responsibility. Kühne's understanding of its values means it will continue to stand for premium quality in the future. Because premium means long-term added value for all.

enterprise took off. The new owner renamed the company Carl Kühne Company and initiated the rapid transition from small-scale manufacturing to industrial-style production—at a time when industrialization was still in its infancy. The innovative technology Kühne introduced was called the Schützenbach high-speed vinegar production process. It enabled the company to produce large batches of vinegar at once and to speed up production significantly. The new technology was traditional in the sense that the vinegar still resulted from the same biological fermentation process. Instead of large barrels, however, it took place in enormous vessels made from oak or pitch pine with a holding capacity of 150,000 liters of liquid. Three years after the new technology was introduced, Kühne built a much larger vinegar factory at a new site in Berlin.

In 1867 Carl Ernst Wilhelm Kühne's son Carl took over the management of the company. Under his leadership, King Wilhelm I of Prussia awarded the company the honor of royal court supplier in 1876. When Carl Kühne died twelve years later, his son Wilhelm succeeded him and took on the task of leading the company into a new century, the age of industrial mass manufacturing of almost everything, including food products.

DIVERSIFICATION SPURS GROWTH IN GERMANY AFTER 1896

In 1896 Wilhelm Kühne set a process in motion that marked the next step in company growth, and that continued far into the 20th century. Although vinegar remained the company's main product, additional products that were made with vinegar were added to Kühne's line. Diversification began in 1896 when mustard became Kühne's second product. Then, in 1902, the company launched its first mayonnaise after Wilhelm Kühne discovered the sauce on a trip to England. Only one year later Kühne started manufacturing pickled gherkins, and sauerkraut was added to its product range in 1905.

In the following year, Kühne successfully registered its first brand-name product, Surol, with the German Imperial Patent Office. Surol was a special vinegar essence containing extracts of seven herbs. It was sold in a green bottle, which cost almost half as much as the contents, but could be redeemed when returned empty to the store. According to Kühne legend, the name was created from the German word for pickled cabbage, *Sauerkohl,* by deleting every other letter. Launched in 1905 and supported by massive advertising, Surol soon gained high popularity among Berlin housewives and chefs. Every one of the company's horse carriages that delivered goods to its customers had a large advertising display mounted to it, with "Surol," "Kühne Vinegar," or "Kühne Mustard" painted on it in large capital letters. In addition, the company used elements from its age-old family coat of arms—the head of a knight with a helmet on a shield—as a symbol for the Kühne brand. It symbolized reliability and honesty as well as courage and an unyielding spirit of determination.

Diversification and the commercial success of the company's new products were accompanied by Kühne's rapid expansion in Germany. Mustard was produced at a new factory in the center of Berlin. In the early 20th century the company moved closer to its main customers in the fish-processing industry on the northern German seacoast where it established additional production capacities. Vinegar was used, for example, to produce the popular pickled fish delicacy known in Germany as Bismarck Herrings. Kühne also bought a vinegar factory in Altona, a suburb of Hamburg that was later incorporated into the city. Growth continued through the 1920s and 1930s. In 1929 the company acquired Gundelsheim, located in the city of Gundelsheim, south of Heidelberg, a well-known Swabian manufacturer of brand-name pickles. Soon after, Gundelsheim pickles were exported to the United States for the first time, catering to the tastes of German immigrants who were

KEY DATES

1722: Johann Daniel Epinius founds a vinegar distillery in Berlin.
1761: Friedrich Wilhelm Kühne acquires the business.
1832: The company is renamed Carl Kühne Company.
1896: Mustard becomes Kühne's second product.
1906: The brand-name Surol is officially registered.
1929: Kühne acquires brand-name pickle manufacturer Gundelsheim.
1945: Company headquarters are moved to Hamburg.
1957: Pickled red cabbage is introduced.
1973: Kühne launches a range of salad dressings under the new Salatfix label.
1986: French mustard brands Bornier and Téméraire are acquired.
1991: A vinegar factory is set up in Turkey.
1995: The company's vinegar factory and headquarters in Hamburg are destroyed by fire.
1998: Kühne acquires Dutch pickled food manufacturer Uyttewaal.
2000: The company buys German vinegar manufacturer in Schlierbach.
2002: Kühne expands into Poland.
2003: The company takes over German competitor Johs. Oswaldowski.

glad to find a brand they knew from home at their local German bakery or butcher shop in America. By 1939, the year when World War II began, the Kühne family enterprise consisted of 20 subsidiaries stretching from northern to eastern Germany.

FROM FOOD STAPLES TO FOOD SPECIALTIES AFTER WORLD WAR II

Wilhelm Kühne, whose entrepreneurial capabilities had led the company to grow to a considerable size, did not witness the destruction of large parts of the thriving enterprise he had built, or the end of the devastating war. He passed away in 1943 and was succeeded by his nephew, Herbert Kühne, who together with his uncle's widow Therese Kühne, and later with his daughter Hildegard Preuss, steered the company through the postwar reconstruction years and the following economic upswing known as the German Economic Miracle.

The war left Kühne with less than half of its former production plants. The rest had been destroyed in bombing raids or expropriated by the Soviets. With Berlin in ruins and occupied by the victorious Allied forces, the Kühne family decided to move company headquarters from Berlin to Hamburg in 1945. What had been destroyed was rebuilt and modernized at the same time. Meanwhile, the company supplied the supermarkets at U.S. military bases with pickles from Gundelsheim and Kühne. After the introduction of a new currency in West Germany in 1948 and the foundation of the Federal Republic of Germany in 1949, Kühne invested heavily in new production plants and set up a tightly knit distribution network, including its own logistics division and truck fleet.

In addition to the company's mainstay products—vinegar, including Surol, mustard, gherkins, and sauerkraut—Kühne launched a number of new ones. In 1950 the company introduced pickled green-bean salad and red beets under the Kühne label. The label itself also underwent a series of modernizations, beginning around the same time. A green "cloud," resembling a stylized version of a three-leaf clover—another element of the historical family coat of arms—replaced the shield. The much smaller and streamlined knight's head in the upper part made space for a bright yellow handwritten "Kühne" signature in the center part of the logo.

Most notably, the company introduced ready-to-eat pickled red cabbage in 1957. This was no coincidence. Carl Wilhelm Kühne's mother, Lisel Kühne, had long complained about the red fingers she got from cutting up fresh red cabbage before cooking it—a problem experienced by many German women. When Kühne's preparation hit the shelves, it became an instant bestseller.

By 1960, pickled or specially seasoned vegetables and other delicacies accounted for roughly one-third of the company's product portfolio. In 1973 Kühne launched a range of salad dressings under the brand-name Salatfix. In 1981 the company introduced a range of barbecue and other seasoning sauces. Three years later the company followed up with *Rote Grütze,* a northern German sweet and fruity specialty dessert made from a variety of red berries.

NATIONAL AND INTERNATIONAL EXPANSION FOLLOWS GENERATION CHANGE

In 1975 Herbert Kühne's son, Carl Wilhelm Kühne, became a shareholder in the company. He set his sights on strengthening Kühne's market position in Germany as well as on expanding into Europe. A major step in that direction was the acquisition of a French mustard manufacturer based in Dijon, including the brands Bornier and Téméraire, in 1986. The reunification of Germany gave Kühne an unexpected boost in sales as East German consumers tried Western products in the supermarkets. With new prospects in Eastern Europe on the horizon, Kühne built a vinegar factory in Turkey in 1991. Four years later the company took the opportunity to acquire Danish vinegar and mustard manufacturer Ollerup.

November 30, 1995, became "Black Thursday" for Kühne. In the morning, a high-voltage cable caught fire. The fire quickly spread and eventually destroyed the company's vinegar factory and headquarters in Hamburg. Kühne's management decided to rebuild its headquarters, but to replace the vinegar production capacity lost through the fire at a different location. A brand-new vinegar factory was set up in the northeastern German city of Hagenow. According to Kühne, this was one of Europe's largest and most modern vinegar factories, with a capacity of 40 million liters of vinegar per year. The main goal of the DM 50 million investment—the largest one in the company's history—was to achieve cost leadership and to make Kühne Europe's top vinegar manufacturer. In addition, the company built two state-of-the-art distribution centers, one in Schweinfurt and one in Hagenow. All in all, distribution in Germany was centralized in four logistics and warehousing complexes.

After another generation change in 1996, Kühne continued to expand in Europe and to strengthen its leading market position as a vinegar producer. Axel Preuss-Kühne and Bernd Kühne-Oertel, two younger family members, assumed management responsibility—the former for key accounts, and the latter for Kühne's business with industrial clients. Supported by newly hired CEO Franz J. Empl, formerly with snack manufacturer Dany Snacks, and an executive management team of four that oversaw the day-to-day business, they steered the family enterprise into the 21st century.

In 1998 Kühne acquired Dutch pickled food manufacturer Uyttewaal, a former subsidiary of Fisher Quality Foods. Four years later the company expanded into Poland. The company's export business with the United States also continued to thrive as Gundelsheim and Kühne succeeded in getting their products—mainly pickled sauerkraut, gherkins, and red cabbage—on the shelves of national supermarket chains such as Kroger, Publix, Wal-Mart, and A&P.

In addition, Kühne managed to take over two domestic competitors. In 2000 the company acquired the vinegar factory in Schlierbach, near Göttingen, of the German firm Fr. Kauffmann GmbH & Co., which filed bankruptcy that year. With this strategic acquisition Kühne strengthened its presence in southern Germany, a region where per capita consumption of vinegar was twice that in northern Germany. Three years later Kühne took over the Hamburg-based firm Johs. Oswaldowski, a major manufacturer and distributor of vinegar and mustard products to the German food-processing industry and to retail chains with their own store brands, with additional production plants in Hamm, Cuxhaven, and Rostock. The deal propelled Kühne to the top of European vinegar manufacturers.

REORGANIZATION, FRESH MARKETING, AND INNOVATION

As the Kühnes celebrated the 275th anniversary of their family enterprise in 1997, the company had achieved German market leadership in vinegar products, salad dressings, and pickled red cabbage. In other core business areas the company held significant shares in the German market: about one-fifth of pickled vegetables, 18 percent of gherkins, and approximately 16 percent of mustard. All together there were more than 200 different Kühne products on the market. They were shipped to 70 different countries. Sales abroad accounted for over 10 percent of the total. However, rising cost pressure from industrial customers and growing competition from food retailers' own store brands in the stagnating and saturated German market called for action.

Kühne responded by streamlining its production capacities, by reorganizing its sales organization, and by focusing on strategic core product areas. For example, the manufacturing of mustard products, formerly performed in Hamburg, Berlin, and Straelen near the Dutch border, was moved in its entirety to Straelen, the new competence center for mustard and Kühne's base for exports to Belgium, Luxembourg, and the Netherlands. Large industrial customers were served by national key account managers. The store-brand business became a separate business unit. Eleven regional sales managers directed the company's sales force, which focused solely on the placement of Kühne brand products in large food retail stores and supermarkets. They tried to convince the stores to present Kühne's whole product range in one "brand bloc" on their shelves instead of placing them next to similar products made by other firms—with rising success. Most importantly, however, the company invested heavily in marketing and product innovation with a focus on revitalizing and strengthening the Kühne brand to attract younger target groups and to build a loyal following for its premium-priced goods.

Throughout the 1980s and up until the early 1990s, Kühne's investment in advertising was modest. In 1993 the company introduced television advertising and began to use the medium to revive the brand and to make it more appealing to younger consumers. During the next fourteen years Kühne worked with different advertising agencies on revitalizing the brand. Slogans changed from "*Kühne schmeckt*" (Kühne tastes good) in 1993 to "*Kühne weckt den Appetit*" (Kühne wakes up your appetite) in 1998 to "*Von Familie zu Familie*" (Keep it in the family) in 2006. Throughout that time period, the company put out product innovations at an impressive rate. Beginning with a staggering 18 percent of new products launched in 2001, the company swung back to an average of 5 percent annually later in the decade.

Based on thorough market research on brand recognition and consumer trends, Kühne introduced a wide variety of specialty food products. The vinegar range was extended to Italian-style balsamic vinegars. Sauces, dips, and dressings picked up on international trends, resulting in Mexican-, Asian-, Greek-, and American-style recipes. Pickled vegetables were presented in changing combinations, sour or sweet, herbal or fruity, mild or hot, in a more colorful and modern packaging. Seasonal products were created for the barbecue and holiday seasons. Kühne also launched a line of organic products, including vinegar, green kale, sauerkraut, and red cabbage, which was later extended to even more items. To promote product innovations with even more vigor, the company doubled its marketing budget. In addition to massive advertising, new product innovations were promoted intensely at the point of sale. As a result, Kühne's sales soared. In addition, the Kühne brand moved from a ranking of tenth to seventh on the national panel of Germany's most important food brands.

Andreas F. Schubert, former member of the board at German food manufacturer Bahlsen's snack food division Lorenz Bahlsen Snack-World, who succeeded Franz J. Empl as CEO in 2005, was optimistic about Kühne's future as a midsized brand-name manufacturer. He saw the serious challenges on the horizon: an increasingly consolidating market with rising cost pressure from discount stores and large international competitors as well as increasing prices for raw materials such as alcohol, mustard seeds, and cucumbers. On the other hand, he saw additional growth opportunities in extending the distribution of Kühne products in Germany to smaller food marts and gas stations as well as in expanding further into Europe, for example, in such countries as the United Kingdom, Switzerland, Austria, and Russia. He was also convinced that the market potential of the Kühne brand was strong enough to be extended to additional segments of the food market some time in the future. While the Kühne family traditionally refrained from publicizing annual sales figures, the heirs of Carl Kühne left no doubt about their determination to steer the company into the third century of its existence as an independent family-owned enterprise.

Evelyn Hauser

PRINCIPAL SUBSIDIARIES

DEP–Dansk Eddike Produktiion A/S (Denmark); Kühne Nordic A/S (Denmark); Kühne France EdC–Européenne de Condiments, S.A. (France); Kühne Benelux B.V. (Netherlands); Kühne Polska Sp. z o.o. (HQ & Factory) (Poland); Schwäbische Conservenfabrik Gundelsheim (Germany).

PRINCIPAL COMPETITORS

Rich. Hengstenberg GmbH & Co. KG; Luise Händlmaier Senf-Fabrikation GmbH & Co KG; Obst- und Gemüseverarbeitung Spreewaldkonserve Golßen GmbH; Develey Senf & Feinkost GmbH; Kraft Foods Deutschland GmbH; Unilever N.V.; Nestlé Deutschland AG.

FURTHER READING

"Am Anfang war alles Essig," *Lebensmittel Zeitung,* April 25, 1997, p. 91.

Ax, Martin, "Design statt Werbung: Das Credo der Familie Kühne," *Welt,* December 18, 2000.

Druck, Dieter, "Kühne: In Alten und neuen Feldern," *Lebensmittel Praxis,* October 2005, p. 72.

"Feinkost wird weiter ausgebaut," *Lebensmittel Zeitung,* March 16, 2007, p. 65.

"Fisher Sells Dutch Arm; Albert Fisher Group," *Times,* March 11, 1999, p. 32.

Hoos, Elisabeth, "Kühne ist zuversichtlich," *Lebensmittel Zeitung,* September 14, 2007, p. 20.

"Kühne hat den Grossbrand verdaut," *Lebensmittel Zeitung,* January 5, 1996, p. 12.

Kühne Jahre: Geschichte und Geschichten einer Marke, Hamburg, Germany: Carl Kühne KG (GmbH & Co.), 1997, 15 p.

"Kühne: Übernimmt Johs. Oswaldowski," *LZ.net,* May 8, 2003.

Reichardt, Holger, "Mit Emotionen und süssen Gürkchen," *Welt,* November 23, 2001, p. WS2.

"Starke Bündelung der Kräfte," *Lebensmittel Zeitung,* May 30, 1997, p. 72.

Carver Bancorp, Inc.

75 West 125th Street
New York, New York 10027-4512
U.S.A.
Telephone: (718) 230-2900
Fax: (212) 426-6162 or (212) 426-6123
Web site: http://www.carverbank.com

Public Company
Founded: 1948 as Carver Federal Savings and Loan Association
Employees: 160
Total Assets: $739.95 million (2007)
Stock Exchanges: NASDAQ
Ticker Symbol: CARV
NAIC: 522120 Savings Institutions; 522210 Credit Card Issuing; 522310 Mortgage and Other Loan Brokers; 522291 Consumer Lending; 551111 Offices of Bank Holding Companies

■ ■ ■

Carver Bancorp, Inc., the holding company for Carver Federal Savings Bank, a federally chartered savings bank, is the largest publicly traded financial institution in the United States operated by African and Caribbean Americans. It engages in a wide range of consumer- and commercial-banking services, including demand, savings, and time deposits for consumers, businesses, and governmental and quasi-governmental agencies in the New York City metropolitan area. Carver also offers a number of other products and services, including debit cards, online banking, and telephone banking. Its loan products include commercial and residential mortgages, construction loans, and business loans. The principal lending activity is the origination of mortgage loans for the purpose of purchasing or refinancing one- to four-family residential, multifamily residential, and commercial properties. Through a subsidiary, Carver participates in local economic development and other community-based activities. Located in the heart of Harlem, the bank has ten branches, all in New York City.

A PIONEER SAVINGS AND LOAN INSTITUTION

Carver Federal Savings and Loan Association was established in1948 as the result of a five-year effort by Harlem community leaders who were convinced that racial bias was keeping qualified black applicants from securing residential mortgage loans. After two years of waiting unsuccessfully for a response to its application to the state of New York, the group applied for, and received, federal approval. The charter, received on the basis of funds pledged to the undertaking, enabled Carver to obtain federal deposit insurance and become a member of the Federal Home Loan Bank of New York.

The first savings and loan association in the state of New York to be established by black people, it opened its doors on January 5 (the birth date of noted African American scientist George Washington Carver, for whom it was named) of the following year. Although Harlem residents pledged $250,000 to found the financial institution, only $14,000 was extended in the form of cash. Carver opened in a small storefront on

COMPANY PERSPECTIVES

Carver Federal Savings Bank is an urban community development bank dedicated to providing a full range of financial services to its customers. Carver is committed to meeting the credit needs of the communities it serves, increasing profitability and enhancing stockholder value.

125th Street—Harlem's main thoroughfare—with one desk, one cash register, and two employees.

Several men held leadership posts in Carver Federal Savings during its first two decades. Walter A. Miller was the first president, but its day-to-day manager was the executive vice-president, Joseph E. Davis. Miller, who died in 1950, was succeeded by William R. Hudgins. Hudgins, who later became first president of the rival Freedom National Bank, relinquished the post in 1958. Davis then held it until his death in 1968. The Rev. Dr. M. Moran Weston, an Episcopalian priest and one of Carver's founders, was appointed to fill out Davis' unexpired term, then continued as chairman into the 1990s.

In his obituary of Weston, Douglas Martin of the *New York Times* wrote, "Before Carver opened ... there was only one black above the rank of janitor working in a New York bank." That all changed, Weston told Robert Fleming for a *Black Enterprise* article in 1987, when banks realized they were losing African American depositors to Carver. "Without a doubt, our most significant contribution is that we broke the back of discrimination in the financial industry," he said. "Our success forced the white banks to hire blacks. They changed their policies to offset the drain of black dollars from their banks. We could save at their banks, but we couldn't get loans."

EARLY GROWTH AND EXPANSION

By 1952 Carver was affluent enough to move into a two story building at its present location. In 1961 it opened its first branch office, in the Bedford-Stuyvesant neighborhood of Brooklyn, which, like Harlem, was a predominantly black residential area. In late 1962 Carver had $31 million in assets and 32,000 depositors. It had lent more than $80 million to some 3,000 home buyers and, according to Lewis, had foreclosed on only one home loan—which had been made to a white family.

Carver opened another branch in 1963, in the racially integrated Penn Station South housing project, located in Chelsea, a predominantly white downtown Manhattan neighborhood. Davis told Layhmond Robinson of the *New York Times,* "We will not be operating down there as a Negro institution. We will be competing on the same basis as any other business." Davis was said to be proud of the varied ethnic background of the institution's tellers, who could serve customers in six languages besides English.

At Davis' death in 1968, Carver had some $40 million in assets and 40,000 depositors. It grew slowly in the 1970s, a decade marked by rising crime and economic decline in New York City, and continuing flight to the suburbs by blacks as well as whites, a migration that took its toll on Carver's middle-class base of depositors. Even so, the savings institution established more branches, in Brooklyn and the adjacent borough of Queens.

Richard T. Greene was president of Carver Federal Savings from 1969 to 1995. By 1982 the institution had assets of $88.5 million and five offices in Manhattan, Brooklyn, and Queens. In that year it absorbed Allied Federal Savings and Loan Association, a financial institution based in Jamaica, Queens. Allied had assets of $19.1 million, but its net worth had diminished to practically nothing in the economic recession of the early 1980s. Carver kept one Allied branch but closed the other. The merger made Carver the nation's second largest black-owned savings institution, trailing Family Savings and Loan Association of Los Angeles. In 1986 Carver converted to a savings bank and changed its name to Carver Federal Savings Bank. According to Greene, however, the change in status did not change the nature of the operation. Carver preferred to call itself a community development bank rather than a savings or commercial bank.

ROLLER-COASTER RIDE

Under Greene, Carver pursued a conservative policy, lending far less money than it had on deposit. Most of its loans were made on one- to four-family homes and to churches—more than 100 of them. Other assets went into safe but low-yielding investments such as money market funds and mortgage-based securities. This policy allowed the bank to avoid falling victim to the savings and loan crisis of the late 1980s and the problems created by the recession in the early 1990s. By contrast, Freedom National Bank, located only two blocks from Carver, was closed by federal regulators in 1990. By 1992, other than Carver, there were only four bank branches on 125th Street, compared to 14, representing 12 institutions, in 1960.

KEY DATES

1949: Carver Federal Savings and Loan Association opens.
1968: Carver has $40 million in assets and 40,000 depositors.
1986: The financial institution becomes Carver Savings Bank, a mutual bank.
1994: The bank converts from being owned by its depositors to stock ownership.
1999: Carver loses money, and its chief executive loses his job.
2006: Carver is chosen financial services company of the year by *Black Enterprise.*

If Carver seemed stingy in extending loans—and it did rank second-lowest for compliance with the Community Reinvestment Act—it nevertheless engaged in other means of serving African Americans in New York City. The bank was a popular field trip destination for groups of schoolchildren; it gave out dozens of college scholarships each year; employees were hired locally; and the bank published an annual black-history calendar.

By 1994 the number of Carver branches had grown to seven, including one in Roosevelt, Long Island, on the site of a former Anchor Savings Bank branch. All but the location in Chelsea were in minority neighborhoods, and most were in the former quarters of white-owned commercial banks that had left the area. Assets had passed $300 million, but Carver's management felt the bank had to grow faster in the more competitive, deregulated economic climate of the times. As a mutual savings bank, it was owned by its 44,000 depositors, but like many other such banks, it decided to change to stock ownership. After a considerable struggle, it won the necessary assent of more than half the depositors and went public, selling 2.4 million shares, about 90 percent to depositors, at $10 a share.

In 1993 the shares of banks converting from mutual to stock ownership had risen as much as 28 percent on the first day of trading. By 1994, when Carver followed this course of action, legislation had raised the capital requirement for such conversion, and the market had soured. Consequently Carver's stock, listed on the NASDAQ, sank by 22 percent on the first day of trading and seldom reached its original $10 mark until 2002. Another setback was the destruction by fire of Carver's headquarters in 1992, which forced depositors to visit a hastily assembled nearby office or take shuttle buses in order to conduct their business in the branches until the bank reopened in 1996 in a four story building on the same site.

NEW LEADERSHIP, MIXED SUCCESS

Greene was succeeded as president of Carver in 1995 by Thomas L. Clark, Jr., a former state banking regulator. Under Clark's leadership, Carver invested about 70 percent of its assets in mortgage loans and instituted a mortgage origination center making direct loans rather than buying lower-yielding but safer pools of mortgages. It also made good its claim to be a community development bank by lending $3.15 million to the Bedford Stuyvesant Restoration Corp. to help it renovate its commercial plaza, which was a neighborhood hub of business and cultural activity. In 1996 the magazine *Black Enterprise* chose Carver as financial company of the year. Also in that year, the bank completed a reorganization that made it the subsidiary of Carver Bancorp, Inc., a newly created Delaware-incorporated holding company. Federal Savings Bank shares were exchanged for Bancorp shares on a one-to-one basis.

One difficulty faced by Carver in the 1990s was a federal effort to prod banks into investing in inner-city neighborhoods. By 1999, Chase Manhattan Bank alone had three branches on 125th Street. Faced with increasing competition from outside, Carver began offering services such as unsecured credit cards and auto loans, interest-bearing checking accounts, and automated teller machines (ATMs). It also opened its first branch in suburban Westchester County, in predominantly African American Mount Vernon. However, the bank soon foundered on losses related to its consumer loan portfolio, many of the loans having proved of poor quality—including credit card and personal loans—and a badly implemented conversion of its data processing from an outside provider to an in-house system. Amid a $4.5-million loss in fiscal 1999, Clark was ousted and replaced by Deborah C. Wright, formerly a New York City housing commissioner.

RECOVERY IN THE 21ST CENTURY

Wright's first challenge was to keep her job, which had been threatened by a takeover bid from the Boston Bank of Commerce's Kevin Cohee, who, with his wife, had become one of Carver's largest shareholders. Cohee—a former classmate of Wright's at Harvard University—proposed that Carver acquire his bank and hire him and his wife to administer the joint operation. Wright parried the offer by persuading two downtown firms to purchase an equity stake larger than that held by the Cohees, who had sold their shares in Carver by 2002. By 2006 Wright was chairman and chief executive officer, as well as president, of the bank and holding company.

Wright next set out to improve Carver's bottom line by closing three unprofitable branches: Penn Station South and the two in the suburbs—Roosevelt and Mount Vernon. After writing off $8.3 million in nonperforming consumer loans, she reached out to powerful figures such as Henry Kravis of private equity Kohlberg Kravis Roberts & Co. for help in raising an additional $45 million in deposits. Carver invested in more ATMs; began selling life insurance, annuities, and other investments in its branches through other firms; and greatly increased its participation in nonresidential real estate loans, including $9 million for a housing project by Harlem's Abyssinian Baptist Church.

Under a 1998 state law, banks and thrift institutions in communities designated as underserved were eligible to receive state- and municipal-government deposits. In 2001 Carver opened a Harlem branch mainly to take advantage of the provision and received $55 million in state and city deposits. These funds, which remained on deposit for five years, helped tide the bank over the period it took for the branch to become profitable. Carver also opened a branch in a Queens area that was designated a banking development district in 2004. Two years later, the state designated part of northern Harlem as another banking development district. The immediate beneficiary was Carver, which was operating the only branch in this district.

One initiative that did not go well was Carver's attempt in 2004 to acquire Independence Federal Savings Bank of Washington, D.C., another big city financial institution founded and administered by African Americans. Carver was prepared to pay $30 million for Independence, which had assets of $195 million, but the federal Office of Thrift Supervision rejected the deal. Independence was losing money and was fighting three lawsuits relating to embezzlement of funds. Wright later conceded that the proposed acquisition had been a mistake. "I still feel bad about it," she told Philana Patterson and Tanisha A. Sykes in 2006 for a *Black Enterprise* article. "We spent a lot of money there."

POSITIONED FOR GROWTH

Black Enterprise again selected Carver as financial services company of the year in 2006. In that year the holding company entered a merger to acquire Community Capital Bank (CCB), a Brooklyn-based community bank, for $11.1 million cash. CCB had two branches, about $165 million in assets, and an award-winning small-business lending platform. In 2007 Carver forged an alliance with Merrill Lynch & Co. whereby two of Carver's branches allotted space to Merrill Lynch financial advisers, allowing the Wall Street firm to recruit bank customers for brokerage accounts, mutual funds, annuities, and other investment products. The two institutions also agreed to offer evening educational seminars at the Carver branches.

At the end of fiscal 2007 (the year ended March 31, 2007), Carver had ten offices, 46,034 deposit accounts, and assets of $740 million. Total loans of $609.19 million almost equaled deposits of $615.12 million. Return on average equity was 5.23 percent during the year. Revenues came to $44.61 million and net income to $2.58 million. The four leading holders of Carver's common stock were private equity firms; Wright came next, with 7.7 percent of the shares in March 2007.

Robert Halasz

PRINCIPAL SUBSIDIARIES

Carver Federal Savings Bank; Carver Statutory Trust I.

PRINCIPAL COMPETITORS

OneUnited Bank.

FURTHER READING

Eaton, Leslie, "A Shaky Pillar in Harlem," *New York Times,* July 11, 1999, pp. 21, 25.

Fairley, Juliette, "A New Lease on Banking," *Black Enterprise,* June 1996, pp. 174–75, 178, 180–81.

Fleming, Robert, "Carver Federal Carves Out Its Market Niche," *Black Enterprise,* June 1987, pp. 215–16, 218.

"Joseph E. Davis Is Dead at 58; Led Carver Savings and Loan," *New York Times,* May 8, 1968, p. 47.

Kennedy, Shawn G., "Defending the Territory," *New York Times,* October 16, 1994, City sec., p. 4.

Leuchter, Miriam, "Black S&L Endures, but Not by Lending," *Crain's New York Business,* April 19, 1993, pp. 3–4.

Mack, Gracian, "Carver Stock: Boon or Boondoggle?" *Black Enterprise,* January 1995, pp. 47, 50.

Martin, Douglas, "M. Moran Weston, 91, Priest and Banker of Harlem, Dies," *New York Times,* May 22, 2002, p. B7.

Mullins, Luke, "Varying Goals in Low-Income Neighborhoods," *American Banker,* January 13, 2006, pp. 1, 4.

Osuri, Laura Thompson, "Independence, Carver Face Futures Apart," *American Banker,* October 22, 2004, pp. 1, 4.

Patterson, Philana, and Tanisha A. Sykes, "Through the Fire," *Black Enterprise,* June 2006, pp. 180–86.

Robinson, Layhmond, "Negro Savings and Loan to Open First Unit Outside Negro Area," *New York Times,* May 11, 1963, p. 51.

———, "Savings Agency Gains in Harlem," *New York Times,* November 25, 1962, Sec. 3 (Business), p. 9.

Seals, Kimberly L., and Eric L. Smith, "The Wright Move," *Black Enterprise,* July 1999, p. 24.

Smith, Franklin L., "For Harlem Thrift, Housing Spells Success," *American Banker,* May 6, 1992, pp. 1, 8–9.

Spruell, Sakina P., "Carver vs. OneUnited," *Black Enterprise,* December 2004, pp. 96–105.

Stewart, Robert, "How Carver Federal Savings Began," *Amsterdam News,* July 2, 1975, p. D3.

Cerner Corporation

2800 Rockcreek Parkway
Kansas City, Missouri 64117-2551
U.S.A.
Telephone: (816) 221-1024
Fax: (816) 474-1742
Web site: http://www.cerner.com

Public Company
Incorporated: 1979
Employees: 7,419
Sales: $1.5 billion (2007)
Stock Exchanges: NASDAQ
Ticker Symbol: CERN
NAIC: 541511 Custom Computer Programming Services; 334611 Software Publishers; 541512 Computer Systems Design Services

■ ■ ■

Cerner Corporation is a leading global designer and provider of information systems for the healthcare industry. Founded in 1979 and headquartered in Kansas City, Missouri, Cerner's products are utilized by over 6,000 clients worldwide including hospitals, physician groups, HMO's, laboratories, pharmacies and other health clinics. The company packages its information solutions as a single platform, Cerner Millennium 2007, encompassing clinical, financial, and administrative data in a single system. The company also designs and manufactures software systems for applications ranging from records management to advanced document imaging, and customers are able to purchase all or part of Cerner's software package as needed to meet their specific needs. Cerner also provides installation, training, and consultation for its products, with in-house specialists on call to aid in implementation.

With 11 offices in the United States and 11 abroad, Cerner employs more than 7,000 full-time professionals and posts annual revenues in excess of $1.5 billion. Since 1980, Cerner has consistently been ranked among the nation's leading information technology providers and the company's healthcare products have won numerous awards. Cerner was ranked among *Forbes* magazine's 400 best big companies in America (2006 and 2007) and appeared on *Computerworld* magazine's top places to work during the same years. In the 21st century Cerner has expanded its services both nationally and internationally and, through strategic mergers, has emerged as a billion-dollar company.

COMPANY BEGINNINGS

In 1979 Neal Patterson, Clifford Illig, and Paul Gorup left the management information systems consulting division of Arthur Andersen's Kansas City office to found Cerner as a developer of laboratory information systems. Cerner was incorporated in 1980, as the company worked to perfect its first product.

By 1984 Cerner was ready to roll out its first application, the PathNet laboratory information system. PathNet provided a comprehensive information system for laboratory clinicians, allowing laboratories to automate their processes. PathNet, which grew to combine applications for general laboratory information, microbiology, blood bank transfusion and blood bank

> **COMPANY PERSPECTIVES**
>
> Cerner's mission is to connect the appropriate persons, knowledge and resources at the appropriate time and location to achieve the optimal health outcome. Cerner's vision of proactive healthcare management drives innovation in the development of effective solutions for today's healthcare challenges, while creating a foundation for tomorrow's healthy populations.

donation, and anatomic pathology, broke away not only from the traditional paper-based sharing of information, but also from the prevailing financial focus of data gathering systems.

PathNet proved to be an early success. First-year revenues were just under $2 million, with a net loss of $1.5 million. However, by the following year, Cerner turned a profit on $10.3 million in sales and was establishing itself as a leading provider of laboratory information systems. By 1986 PathNet became the market leader, with more than 30 client site placements generating $17.5 million in revenues for a $2.3 million net profit. In that year, Patterson and Illig took Cerner public, offering one million shares at $16 per share.

REDEFINING MEDICAL RECORDS PROCESSING

Through the end of the decade, PathNet remained Cerner's primary source of revenue, but by 1985 the company had begun to define what would become its Health Network Architecture (HNA). Cerner's goal was to automate the healthcare process by focusing all aspects of the process—from registration to clinical care to pharmacy services to outcomes measurement—around the individual patient.

With access to records across the continuum of a patient's care, the HNA system would achieve higher quality care, from prevention to treatment, as well as improved cost-effectiveness. Unlike paper-based medical charts, the medical records of a patient within Cerner's automated system could be made instantly available to each member of a healthcare network, including laboratory clinicians, nurses, general physicians, and such specialists as radiologists and surgeons, while also providing resources for patient input and information.

Cerner's vision of an HNA-based system would allow total management of a patient's care, including alerts and reminders to the patient of scheduled checkups, information to providers on patient clinical history, and medication allergies, and a means to provide routine and emergency care based on information uploaded by the patient. In this, Cerner anticipated the changing focus of the healthcare system, from a fee-for-service system, to the largely managed care-based system of the 1990s. Equally, Cerner's vision anticipated the mid-1990s trend toward integration that would sweep the healthcare system, as more and more hospitals, clinics, and other providers moved toward providing vertically integrated, complete healthcare services.

ADDING SOFTWARE COMPONENTS

Cerner's research and development (R&D) efforts began to show results as early as 1987, when it introduced two more components of its future HNA system: MedNet and Discern. MedNet joined PathNet in the clinical management family of Cerner products, offering support for pulmonary medicine, respiratory care, and other internal medicine departments. Discern formed the basis of Cerner's knowledge systems applications, offering retrospective and prospective databases and services that enabled providers to monitor patient care regimens and institute treatment and preventive protocols.

In 1988 Cerner added the next component of its clinical management system, RadNet, which focused on automating radiology department functions. The following year, pharmacy support was added with the PharmNet application. As with PathNet, each new component was based on the same application architecture, allowing applications to be seamlessly combined to share information across applications.

The flexibility of Cerner's HNA set it apart from its competitors as well. Through the 1980s and into the 1990s, hospitals, clinics, and their various departments typically purchased "best of breed" applications—individual products from many different vendors. As more and more hospitals and their departments began to forge the healthcare networks that slowly came to dominate the healthcare industry in the 1990s, they were faced with the task of forcing integration of their disparate information systems and products. This created not only confusion within each system but also the need to maintain costly support personnel to integrate the systems and maintain their functionality. With all of their applications based on a single architecture, Cerner offered advantages in functionality as well as cost-effective operation.

KEY DATES

1979: Cerner is founded in Kansas City, Missouri.
1984: Cerner debuts Pathnet Laboratory Information System.
1987: The MedNet and Discern software features are introduced.
1988: Company begins selling RadNet for radiology solutions.
1990: Company begins distributing patient care software solutions.
1991: First international subsidiaries are established in the United Kingdom and Australia.
1993: Cerner acquires Megasource, Inc., and integrated medication software.
1994: Cerner Alliance Program integrates administrative and financial functions.
1997: Cerner's HNA Millennium system is introduced, integrating all operational systems.
2000: Company adopts an ASP system for HNA Millennium.
2004: PathNet Helix is introduced to integrate genomic information into records.
2005: Cerner posts over $1 billion in revenues for a single year.
2006: Cerner Millennium 2007 system is implemented.

EXPANSION AND ACQUISITION

Cerner's client base grew steadily in the late 1980s, reaching 70 sites in 1987, 120 sites in 1988, 170 sites in 1989, and 250 sites in 1990. Installations were primarily of PathNet systems, and sales of systems made up the bulk of Cerner's revenues, which topped $57 million in 1990. However, recurring revenues, especially from support services and also from add-on applications sales, began to form an increasing share of Cerner's annual sales. Meanwhile, R&D spending grew from $4.2 million in 1987 to $10 million in 1990.

By 1990 more than 200 PathNet sites had been installed, solidifying Cerner's position as the leading maker of laboratory information systems. Cerner next moved to expand its product family beyond clinical management systems and into care management systems, with the introduction of its ProNet and CareNet products. ProNet provided automated support for patient management and registration, ordering, scheduling, and tracking processes. CareNet gave patient care planning, management, and measurement tools to nurses and other direct care providers.

Care management was meant to play a central role in gathering information needed for the care process. With Cerner's care management tools, providers could more easily manage the many pieces of patient information, including demographic and financial data, health status, operations data such as treatment procedures and protocols, while linking this information to ordering, tracking, scheduling, and patient, case, and health records management.

By the end of 1991 Cerner's client base had expanded to 320 sites, producing revenues over $77 million and net earnings of $4.7 million. These sales still centered primarily around PathNet. Yet in 1991 Cerner moved closer to its goal of creating the paperless patient medical record with the acquisition of Intellimetrics Instrument Corporation of Massachusetts, and with the launch of its repository product line with the introduction of its Open Clinical Foundation (OCF). The OCF was an enterprisewide, relational database with multimedia capabilities, which captured the information generated by the various clinical and core systems to form a computer-based patient record, while also supporting data extraction capabilities for medical and outcomes research.

INTERNATIONAL AND DOMESTIC GROWTH

In 1991 Cerner established its first international subsidiaries, in Australia and in the United Kingdom, marking the first implementation of its international strategy. In England, it took over service of PathNet systems originally installed in 15 hospitals through a licensing agreement with McDonnell Douglas Information Systems. In Australia, agreement had been reached to install PathNet in the New South Wales Health System. With client sites operating in Canada and Singapore, Cerner reached an agreement to install PathNet at the Riyadh Armed Forces Hospital in Saudi Arabia. International sales grew to $9 million by the end of 1991. By 1993 Cerner had established the first of its two German offices as well.

By the end of 1993 Cerner had completed the largest part of its product family, with the 1992 introduction of its SurgiNet and Open Management Foundation (OMF) products, and the 1993 introduction of its MRNet product. SurgiNet, part of Cerner's clinical management product line, offered information management support for operating room teams. OMF extended Cerner's repository line with tools for supporting management analysis and decision making based on process-related information. MRNet functioned to link the OCF and OMF products in automating the chart management process for the medical records department.

By this time Cerner's repository and care management products had begun to make significant contributions to the company's $120 million in revenues. Net earnings for 1993 reached $14.6 million.

In November 1993 Cerner acquired Megasource, Inc., in a stock-swap merger valued at approximately $6.7 million, creating the company's wholly owned Cerner Megasource, Inc., subsidiary. The Megasource merger added another product to Cerner's clinical management group, MSmeds, which provided information management capabilities to pharmacy operations. This merger was significant in that roughly 80 percent of all physician orders, both in inpatient and outpatient areas, went for either laboratory or pharmacy services. With Megasource, Cerner filled out a significant presence in both services. During 1993 Cerner also moved to expand its client support services, opening regional offices in Atlanta, Boston, Dallas, Kansas City, Los Angeles, and Washington, D.C., while providing 24-hour emergency support at its Kansas City headquarters.

STRATEGIC ALLIANCES

Strategic alliances contributed to Cerner's growth starting in the early 1990s. By 1991 Cerner had participated in a joint venture with Sony Corporation's medical electronics division to develop the Cerner Pathology PACS Workstation, which integrated Sony's color video capabilities with Cerner information technology. A second collaboration was formed with Beckman Instruments Inc. to introduce PathTrac, which coupled parts of PathNet with Beckman's chemistry analyzer. A third alliance, with APACHE Medical Systems, Inc., gave PathNet, ProNet, and CareNet capabilities through APACHE workstations.

In 1994 Cerner extended its alliance strategy with the formation of the Cerner Alliance Program. Initial partners were SDK Health Care Information Systems of Boston, MEDIC Computer Systems of Raleigh, North Carolina, and Amisys Managed Care Information Systems of Rockville, Maryland. With these alliances, Cerner moved to add administrative and financial functions, based on HNA, that fell outside of its own development efforts. In addition to collaborating on engineering, the alliances also profited from some shared marketing activities.

By year-end 1994 more than 30 clients had contracted with Cerner for the broad implementation of the complete HNA system, including five contracts in the fourth quarter alone; another 100 clients had purchased multiple system components. The company rolled out support for the IBM RISC System/6000 processor and announced support for Microsoft's Windows interface. Revenues reached $156 million, and net earnings grew to $19.5 million, representing increases from 1990 of 217 percent and 686 percent, respectively. An important component of Cerner's success had been its aggressive R&D spending—more than $80 million in the first half of the 1990s, with plans to spend another $200 million by 2000.

CERNER MILLENNIUM DEBUTS

In 1997 Cerner introduced Cerner Millennium, an upgrade to the previous HNA system that integrated all of Cerner's various product lines under a unified architectural system. Cerner's Millennium system was meant to be flexible, allowing organizations to purchase new features, online applications, and software that could be seamlessly integrated into the system. Cerner also offered previous customers an affordable "migration path," to help switch from the old systems to the millennium model without losing data or budgeting for extensive training.

In 1999 Cerner implemented the HNA Millennium architecture in over 349 institutions. "Today, Cerner Corporation's HNA Millennium base of installed applications has increased to nearly 100 clients at more than 150 locations around the world," said Glen Tobin, chief operating officer for Cerner, in official company press releases. Cerner achieved other important milestones in 1999, including the formation of a financial partnership with GE Healthcare to help provide clients with affordable options in purchasing Cerner's HNA system. Cerner also won a major contract toward the end of the year to implement their HNA system at Shriner's Children's Hospitals. At the end of the fourth quarter, revenues were estimated at $340.2 million, over a 3 percent increase from the previous year.

CERNER AT THE START OF THE 21ST CENTURY

In 2000 Cerner began offering its HNA systems through an applications service provider (ASP) model. The new structure allowed Cerner to deliver software, hardware, implementation, technical aid and automatic software upgrades from a single location and significantly simplified implementation and maintenance. "Unlike healthcare information technology companies that simply convert a provider's legacy system to operate over an ASP, our ASP delivers Cerner's fully functional HNA Millennium solutions with a convenient graphical user interface," explained Cerner CEO Neal Patterson. Cerner also debuted, in 2000, their first "e-health" division, IQHealth, designed to help health organizations to develop their own e-health consumer systems.

Cerner continued to expand its services through strategic partnerships, including partnering with DoctorQuality.com to integrate error management monitoring into the company's services and a partnership with LifeMetrix, Inc., to integrate cancer patient treatment programs into the system. Cerner also completed a number of strategic acquisitions, including purchasing Mitch Cooper & Associates, a company specializing in managing supply-line monitoring for health organizations and ADAC Health Care Information Systems, a company specializing in medical imaging. In April 2000, it was announced that Cerner's international division would expand with service to Saudi Aramco Medical Services Organization, a medical care group focusing primarily on the Saudi Arabian oil company employees.

In 2001 Cerner formed a partnership with IBM to integrate technology in hospitals, creating what the companies called "e-hospitals," with more integrated services, records, management and financial information to reduce costs and improve efficiency across the hospitals. As the company's list of products grew, it became clear that they would need more input from physicians to help direct the design and implementation of product lines. To this end, in 2002 Cerner appointed Jeff Rose, M.D., to serve as the company's first chief medical officer, helping to ensure that the company's products and development teams were designing systems that would meet the needs of physicians.

The year 2004 was one of the strongest growth years in Cerner's history, with revenues approaching $1 billion for the year and more than 3,000 implementations of the Cerner Millennium system. Bookings for new business increased by over 13 percent from the previous year. In 2004, Cerner added another revolutionary application to its list of programs, the PathNet Helix system, which was the first computer system to allow genomic information to be stored in patient records.

Growth continued in 2005, through key acquisitions, the expansion of partnerships, and the establishment of lucrative contracts, including a ten-year agreement to provide information services for the U.S. Department of Defense, through 100 hospitals and more than 400 clinics across the world. Cerner officially passed the $1 billion mark in 2005, with revenues of $1.16 billion, a 25 percent increase from the previous year.

From 2006 to 2008 Cerner continued to grow on a number of fronts and expanded both its domestic and international operations. In late 2006 the company released another expansion package for the Millennium architecture. "By far, our clients' participation in the design and process of Cerner Millennium 2007 is unparalleled in the industry," said Vice-President Jeff Townsend in a company announcement. The new software release featured over 8,600 new features, including an updated system for managing perioperative patient data and patient flow from the emergency department to all critical care departments.

In February 2008 Cerner released its financial data from the previous year, revealing over $1.5 billion in revenues and 10 percent growth. By the end of 2007 Cerner's Millennium architecture had been implemented at over 1,200 facilities worldwide, with over 339 successful implementations in 2007 alone.

In 2008 Cerner's healthcare services comprised three major areas. The company's Millennium 2007 architecture, its professional technology suite, incorporated 13 separate applications, with packages grouped as needed for use by emergency and radiology departments, as well as in critical care and record-keeping functions. Cerner also offered Cerner Learning, a group of applications and programs designed for student and staff training. Cerner's third major set of applications, called Cerner Devices, provided software and applications that integrate medical technology into electronic patient records.

Strategic partnerships and acquisitions have helped the company to expand geographically, reaching a total of 22 offices around the world. There are 11 international offices as well as partnerships with international clients, including the state of New South Wales in Australia; the NHS in the United Kingdom; the Canadian Infoway; the Ministry of Health in Malaysia; and the General Authority for Health Services for the Emirate of Abu Dhabi. With strong growth and products that are consistently acknowledged as innovative, Cerner was poised to remain a major force in health information technology.

M. L. Cohen
Updated, Micah L. Issitt

PRINCIPAL SUBSIDIARIES

Cerner Megasource, Inc.; Cerner Corporation Pty., Ltd. (Australia); Cerner Deutschland GmbH (Germany);

Cerner Arabia Co. Ltd. (Saudi Arabia); Cerner Ltd. (United Kingdom).

PRINCIPAL COMPETITORS

Eclipsys Corporation; GE Healthcare; McKesson Corporation.

FURTHER READING

Bond, Sarah, "MedStar Health Chooses Cerner Solutions to Drive Superior Health Outcomes," *Reuters,* January 23, 2008.

"Cerner Corporation (Members on the Move)," *Physician Executive,* May–June 2003, p. 68.

"Cerner Predicts Earnings Will Be Below Estimates," *New York Times,* April 4, 2003.

"Cerner Stock Jumps As Company Rejects Buyout Offers," *New York Times,* November 23, 1996.

DeCarlo, Scott, "America's Best Big Companies," *Forbes,* December 21, 2006.

Electronic Medical Record: Supporting Lifetime Health Management, Kansas City, Mo.: Cerner, 1995.

Intrarelation: Characterizing Cerner's Health Network Architecture, Kansas City, Mo.: Cerner, 1995.

McGill-Murphy, Richard, "49 Companies Batting a Billion," *Fortune,* April 27, 2006.

Meyer, Gene, "Diagnoses on Cerner: More Growth Ahead," *Kansas City Star,* September 26, 1995, p. E20.

"100 Best Places to Work in IT–Overall Rankings 2007," *Computerworld,* June 2007.

Rodengen, Jeffrey L., *Cerner: From Vision to Value,* Ft. Lauderdale, Fla.: Write Stuff Enterprises, 2006.

Tierney, Mary C., "Cerner Corporation," *Business Digest,* March 1996, p. 24.

Cheung Kong (Holdings) Ltd.

Cheung Kong Center, 7th Floor
2 Queen's Road Central
Hong Kong
Telephone: (852) 2128-8888
Fax: (852) 2845-2940
Web site: http://www.ckh.com.hk/eng/index.htm

Public Company
Incorporated: 1950
Employees: 7,400
Sales: HKD 18.54 billion ($2.37 billion) (2007)
Stock Exchanges: Hong Kong
Ticker Symbol: CHEUY
NAIC: 237210 Land Subdivision; 531120 Lessors of Nonresidential Buildings; 531110 Lessors of Residential Buildings and Dwellings

■ ■ ■

Cheung Kong (Holdings) Ltd. is among Hong Kong's leading property and investment development companies. The company's investments are centered in the Chinese and Hong Kong markets but the company owns business interests in a total of 55 countries. Cheung Kong is the flagship company for the property-to-telecommunications empire built up in Hong Kong by Li Ka-shing, who started his meteoric rise in business around 1960 by making plastic flowers. The company's subsidiaries and joint ventures are organized under five main listed companies, including Cheung Kong Holdings as the parent company. Hutchison Whampoa Ltd. (50 percent interest) is one of Hong Kong's major "hongs," or conglomerates, with holdings ranging from retailing to container terminals to telecommunications, energy, and property and financial investments. Cheung Kong Infrastructure (CKI) Holdings Limited, organized in October 1996, groups Cheung Kong's infrastructure subsidiaries and interests, primarily in road-building, toll roads and bridges, and power plants on the Chinese mainland. Cheung Kong also owns a controlling stake in the electric utility monopoly Hong Kong Electric (HKE) and CK Life Sciences Holdings Limited, founded in 2000, which invests in research and development in the biotechnology and life sciences industries.

FROM PLASTIC FLOWERS TO REAL ESTATE

Known to his colleagues as K. S. Li, Hong Kong tycoon Li Ka-shing was born in Chiu Chow in southern China in 1928 and later emigrated to Hong Kong. In 1950, Li set up Cheung Kong as a business manufacturing plastic flowers. The company's real growth started in the late 1960s, when Li bought his first building. In less than 30 years, Li built an empire controlling, through a series of interlocking stock market holdings, over 14 percent of stock registered on the Hong Kong exchange.

Cheung Kong (Holdings) also included highly profitable cement, quarrying, and ready-mixed concrete operations. At the end of 1972, after its first year on the Hong Kong stock market, the company had a total of 40 sites in its property portfolio, with a total floor area—after development—of about 2.4 million square feet of residential and commercial space.

COMPANY PERSPECTIVES

Cheung Kong Holdings is a property development and strategic investment company. The company is one of the largest developers in Hong Kong of residential, commercial and industrial properties. About one in twelve private residences in Hong Kong were developed by the company. The company's long-standing policy is to continuously enhance quality and introduce innovations and initiatives to cater to changing needs and trends in the property market, with the aim of bringing quality living to our customers.

Among the projects Cheung Kong had were a number of residential developments. Typical of these was the development of the Castle Peak Hotel, in Hong Kong's New Territories. Originally occupying a site of over 84,000 square feet, the former hotel was doubled in size and turned into several six-story expensive blocks of flats with a total floor area of over 167,000 square feet.

The company had plans to develop a number of warehouses and factories, as well as offices. Recognizing the static nature of the Hong Kong property market in 1973, Li Ka-shing informed his shareholders that his company would look to increase its supply of regular rental income from its properties, to protect their interests.

This increased effort at boosting rental income paid off a year later in 1974 when Hong Kong's property market slipped into depression. Cheung Kong's development plans continued undeterred, with a 10 percent rise in profits to HKD 48.2 million, against profits of HKD 43.7 million a year earlier.

This improved performance was encouraged by rent reviews that boosted income. One example was Regent House, on Queen's Road Central. Cheung Kong had planned to redevelop the property, but put off plans after the rental income increased to HKD 4.6 million, from about HKD 3 million, per year. Because it would take three years to develop the site, and would cost HKD 16 million, a loss of some HKD 13.8 million from leaving the building vacant was not thought feasible, particularly when depressed conditions in Hong Kong made the prospects of any future developments doubtful.

GROWING PROPERTY PORTFOLIO

The continuing downturn in fortunes hit Cheung Kong's profits in 1975, which dipped 6 percent to HKD 45.6 million. In that year, the company saw the fruits of a joint venture into which it had entered the previous year with the Canadian Imperial Bank of Commerce. The joint venture, Canadian Eastern Finance, acquired for HKD 85,000 a site along the Hong Kong harbor of some 864,000 square feet. On 53,000 square feet of the site, the company planned to build ten expensive residential units, each 24 stories high, and a parking garage. On the rest of the site, recreation facilities, including a swimming pool and sports ground, were planned.

At the end of 1975 Cheung Kong had some 5.1 million square feet of commercial and residential space. This property portfolio jumped by more than 20 percent in size over the next year to a total of 6.35 million square feet at the end of 1976. Of this space, 3.62 million square feet were said by the company to be in residential property, while 1.04 million square feet and 1.65 million square feet were bound up in commercial and industrial space, respectively.

Improving market conditions in Hong Kong in 1976 helped boost the company's profits that year to HKD 58.8 million, a rise of 29 percent over the previous year. The renown Li Ka-shing was gaining in the Hong Kong financial community was confirmed a year later, in 1977, when Cheung Kong announced its profits were up a further 45 percent to HKD 85.55 million. This improvement coincided with a 38 percent rise in total space in the company's property portfolio, to 10.2 million square feet in size.

Among the company's new properties was the celebrated Tiger Balm Gardens, a site of 150,000 square feet originally developed by the inventor of Tiger Balm, an ointment used to cure a number of minor ailments. Cheung Kong bought the site with the aim of building high-class residential units, a practice for which it was becoming widely known.

In 1977 the company also diversified into the hotel trade. It acquired Wynncor Ltd., which owned the 800-room Hong Kong Hilton Hotel and shopping arcade, and nearly all of the 400-room Bali Hyatt Hotel.

While Hong Kong's local property market was improving, Li Ka-shing warned in 1977 that various restrictions from the emerging European Common Market, based in Brussels, which included antidumping measures against Asian electronic products, were affecting export prospects for Cheung Kong. The reason was that Hong Kong's industry sector was felt to be tied in

KEY DATES

1950: Cheung Kong is founded by Li Ka-shing to manufacture plastic flowers.
1974: Canadian Eastern Finance Company created in joint venture.
1977: Company enters the hotel market.
1979: Company purchases interest in Hutchison Whampoa company.
1981: Begins purchasing commercial real estate in the United States.
1986: Cheung Kong splits Hong Kong Electric into two businesses and forms Cavendish International Holdings.
1989: All outstanding shares in Green Island Cement (Holdings) purchased by Cheung Kong.
1991: Enters broadcast industry with Star TV.
1998: Victor Li named Managing Director of Cheung Kong.
2000: Enters the biotechnology industry and starts CK Life Sciences Holdings.
2002: CK Life Sciences enters the Hong Kong stock market.
2006: Li Ka-shing donates one-third of his estimated HKD 18 billion in wealth to the Li Ka-shing Foundation.

fortunes to that of the local property market. When the first failed, the second was certain to feel the effects.

GAINING A WIDE REPUTATION

In 1978 the company's profits continued to rise. Total profits for the year reached HKD 132.6 million, a 55 percent increase over the previous year. In that year, Cheung Kong sold a number of properties not producing sufficient rental income, including sites in the Kwun Tong region of Kowloon, and on Hennessy Road. The company was gaining a wide reputation throughout Hong Kong, as demonstrated by the publicity given to each pre-let of its completed properties. The value of rents reached by each pre-letting—the practice whereby a property developer signs up a tenant for the building or property he is about to build—would give the local property market an indication of the going rates to follow.

As Li Ka-shing told his shareholders that year: "In both prestige and business expansion, the group has entered a new era, and it is my opinion that 1978 has been an exceptionally important year in the group's development." Li cautioned that the effects of high interest rates in Hong Kong and abroad would affect the local property market. He added, however, that mortgages and property developments would provide a useful hedge to investors against threatened inflation. Also in 1978, Cheung Kong acquired a 22 percent stake in Green Island Cement, increasing its holdings on the construction side.

In 1979 the company saw a 91.6 percent rise in profits to HKD 254.1 million. Among the developments then under construction was a joint-venture project with four other property companies to build an office development on the Hong Kong Macau Ferry Pier. With a 20 percent interest in the Shun Tak Centre, due for completion in 1984, the final complex was to include a total of 1.5 million square feet of office space.

In the same year, Cheung Kong purchased a substantial share stake in Hutchison Whampoa, a group whose interests included electricity, communications, wholesaling, and distribution. Hutchison was also involved in manufacturing, quarrying, and concrete markets. The initial stake in Hutchison was for 90 million shares in the group, or 24.4 percent of outstanding shares, bought for HKD 693 million. The company increased its stake in Hutchison to 30 percent by the end of the year.

At the same time, Li Ka-shing warned shareholders that continuing high interest rates and emerging rent control restrictions led him to believe that the local property market was showing signs of leveling off. Continuing economic difficulties in the Hong Kong economy continued to color the business climate for Cheung Kong in 1980. Li Ka-shing, nevertheless, maintained an optimistic air. "There is a slight slackening in the property market," he told shareholders. "But this phase will pass with a lowering of interest rates and an upturn in trade. I am, therefore, cautiously optimistic about the future of the Hong Kong property market."

FACING AN UNCERTAIN FUTURE

The 1980 profit rise of 176 percent, to HKD 701.3 million, gave grounds for this optimism, but also reflected first-time profit contributions from Hutchison Whampoa and Green Island Cement. In addition, the Hong Kong Hilton Hotel increased its profits for 1980 by 34 percent, compared with the previous year.

During 1981 Cheung Kong began amassing an overseas portfolio that would grow over the coming years. Overseas investments totaled HKD 125 million in value, or 3 percent of the group's total assets. These included a number of commercial buildings in the

United States with 950,000 square feet of space, and a shopping center with over 370,000 square feet of freehold space. This growing overseas portfolio was motivated by continuing recessionary conditions in the Hong Kong property market, and anxiety about any fallout from fears of 1997, when control of the colony would revert to China.

At the time, Li Ka-shing signaled to shareholders that it would be difficult, given the then-current trading conditions, to maintain in 1982 the same high level of profit recorded in 1981. In that year, profits rose 97 percent from the previous year's level, to HKD 1.38 billion.

Li Ka-shing's profit warning turned out to be timely. The company suffered a decline across the board at the end of 1982. Overall profits declined by 62 percent to HKD 525.6 million. Profits at the Green Island Cement company tumbled by 65 percent and were affected, according to the company, by a slowdown in Hong Kong's construction industry, bad weather, and large imports of Japanese cement. Even more difficult problems were projected for 1983.

Hutchison Whampoa, on the other hand, increased profits by 20 percent. Yet even here Cheung Kong forecast reduced profits for its subsidiary in 1983. At the Hong Kong Hilton Hotel, profits were 10 percent lower than in 1982, reflecting strong competition from new hotels in Hong Kong as well as a decline in the worldwide tourist trade owing to recessionary pressures in Europe and the United States.

Li Ka-shing had few words of consolation for his shareholders at the time. As he saw the local property market during 1982, "Property prices plunged and hesitation on the part of investors combined with generally weakening purchasing power left the market in a very depressed state from which appreciable recovery is unlikely in the short term."

CONTINUED DETERIORATION IN MARKET CONDITIONS

Matters did indeed deteriorate still further in 1983. The speculator-led boom in property prices and rents of the previous few years came to an abrupt halt, curbed by high interest rates and political tensions surrounding the future of the colony. As a result, Cheung Kong's annual profits fell 22 percent to HKD 408.8 million. Green Island Cement experienced losses as the Hong Kong construction industry faced depression conditions.

Investors in Hong Kong were maintaining a wait-and-see attitude as conditions in the United States and European markets began to improve. At the same time, the property market was expected to lag behind as lower interest rates allowed for growth worldwide, and therefore investment in commercial and residential properties throughout the colony would be delayed.

This situation was confirmed by Cheung Kong's 1984 profits of HKD 213.5 million, a decline of 47 percent compared with a year earlier. The company at this time was making fewer property acquisitions than usual for future developments. Two notable acquisitions were a site of 12,600 square feet on Queen's Road Central, destined to become a 130,000-square-foot office complex; and an 18,000-square-foot site in Repulse Bay, which was to provide space for a 12-story luxury residential complex.

A long-awaited improvement in earnings for the company came in 1985 when profits reached HKD 551.7 million, 158 percent higher than the previous year. The effects on earnings from the three-year-long recession appeared to be over. The company insisted that prices for residential property were on the rise, although the demand for commercial and industrial holdings had not yet meant substantially higher prices.

At this time, Hong Kong appeared to shed some of the anxiety that had gripped the colony after the signing of the Sino-British joint declaration in December 1984, signaling a return to Chinese sovereignty in 1997. Many Hong Kong residents had been hesitant to buy homes or rent offices until the ink on the newly signed agreement was completely dry.

For Li Ka-shing, fears over investing for the future in Hong Kong were partly allayed by his influence among Chinese leaders in Beijing. The entrepreneur was not a man to be ignored when, for example, Hutchison Whampoa imported each year 850,000 tons of coal from China, or 14 percent of the country's annual output. Li Ka-shing was also at this time working with China International Trust and Investment Corporation, China's investment bank, to build a $10 billion electricity plant in China's eastern province of Jiangsu.

Large profit gains resulted in 1986, when Hong Kong's economy grew 9 percent over the year. Cheung Kong reported earnings of HKD 1.28 billion, an increase of 128 percent over the year before. The improvements were helped by the completion of a number of developments, and by the company's sale of Hong Kong's Hilton Hotel for HKD 1.03 billion to Hong Kong Electric, which Li Ka-shing also owned.

MANAGEMENT REORGANIZATION

Cheung Kong announced at that time a reorganization of its management structure. In particular, Hong Kong

Electric's utility and nonutility businesses were to be split. The nonutility holdings—including the Hong Kong Hilton Hotel and a 43 percent stake in Husky Oil of Canada—were to become part of a new firm, Cavendish International Holdings.

The Cheung Kong/Hutchison/Electric group had become very important in Hong Kong by this time. Shares in Li Ka-shing's empire accounted for 15 percent of all shares traded on the Hong Kong stock market.

Cheung Kong moved ahead in 1987, producing profits of HKD 1.58 billion, 23 percent over earnings posted a year earlier. The number of properties for development that the company was acquiring continued to increase. They included an 8.8-hectare site and a 15. 5-hectare site, which together would require up to HKD 9 billion in investment before yielding more than 17,000 residential units, and two large shopping centers with total floor space of 1.22 million square feet. Profits at Hutchison Whampoa reached HKD 2.62 billion. The property market in Hong Kong suffered slightly from the effects of the worldwide stock market crash of October 1987, but the underlying strength of the Hong Kong economy helped steady the local property market and increase demand for residential and office space.

A shortage of office space in Hong Kong contributed to strong profits for Cheung Kong in 1989. Earnings were posted at HKD 2.09 billion, a 33 percent increase over the previous year. On the strength of improved earnings, the company announced that it would purchase all outstanding shares in Green Island Cement (Holdings) not already owned by Cheung Kong. Li Ka-shing told his shareholders in his 1989 accounts that he was optimistic about the outlook for the colony's property market, and that demand and prices for properties were likely to hold up.

PREPARING FOR CHINESE CONTROL

The Hong Kong government announced the building of a new airport for the colony, for which Cheung Kong received lucrative contracts. In 1989, the company posted profits of HKD 2.77 billion, up 33 percent over earnings a year earlier. At the same time, Li Ka-shing saw the colony's property market entering a period of consolidation. This was reflected in profits for the first six months of 1990 when Cheung Kong's earnings rose only 3 percent to HKD 948 million.

Around this time, Li Ka-shing, nicknamed "Superman" in the colony, made a HKD 484 million profit when Cheung Kong sold its 4.8 percent stake in Cable and Wireless, the U.K.-based telecommunications giant. The company, having bought the stake in 1987, profited from a rising Cable and Wireless share price, and the relative strength of sterling in the intervening period. By the beginning of the 1990s, Li's overseas holdings amounted to some 20 percent of his companies' assets, with forecasts to raise that stake to more than 30 percent. Meanwhile, Li, together with son Victor, ventured into satellite broadcasting, founding Star TV. In 1993, Li sold two-thirds of that company to Rupert Murdoch for $525 million.

As the 1990s began, Li pledged to remain in Hong Kong after the colony's handover to China in 1997. Cheung Kong's strategy leading to that event seemed to confirm this, as Cheung Kong stepped up its investments and projects on the mainland. In 1995, Li transferred more than 30 percent of the company's assets to the Cayman Islands; this move, however, was largely seen as a means to avoid Hong Kong's inheritance tax as Li prepared to hand over the company to his sons. In the previous year, Victor Li was named a deputy manager of Cheung Kong, while younger son Richard, engaged in building his own conglomerate in Singapore, was named a deputy manager of Hutchison Whampoa.

In 1993, Cheung Kong strengthened its economic, as well as political, position by teaming up with CITIC Pacific, the Hong Kong arm of the Chinese government-owned investment vehicle led by Larry Yung, son of Chinese Vice-President Rong Yiren, in a HKD 9.65 billion takeover of Miramar Hotel & Investment Co. At the same time, Li hedged his political bets by joining with Deng Zhifang, a son of the late Deng Xiaoping, and Shougang, the third largest steelmaker in China, to take over Kader Investment. Another investment, with China National Non-ferrous Metals Corp., allied Li with Deng's son-in-law, Wu Jianchang, a vice-president of that company. These deals helped boost Li's Chinese investments to nearly HKD 20 billion. On the basis of these and other deals, Cheung Kong's profits surged past $16 billion for 1993.

After adding the HKD 2.2 billion purchase of the 665 King's Road North Point site in 1994, Cheung Kong announced plans the following year to redevelop the colony's Hilton Hotel, as well as a purchase of 40 percent of the colony's last walled village, a 50,000-square-foot site targeted for redevelopment. Next, again working with CITIC Pacific, Cheung Kong won a HKD 7 billion contract to develop the Tsing Yi airport railway station near Kowloon. In late 1995, Cheung Kong, in a joint venture with Hutchison Whampoa and the Kowloon-Canton Railway Corporation, was awarded the property development rights, worth as much as HKD 8 billion, for the Hunghom area. Cheung Kong's earnings were rising steadily, climbing to HKD 10.11 billion in 1994 and to HKD 11 billion in 1995.

RESTRUCTURING FOR THE HANDOVER

Cheung Kong showed no signs of slowing down in 1996. The company won the rights to build the Tuen Mun River Terminal, a project worth HKD 1.14 billion. The company also received an exceptional gain of more than HKD 4 billion after the public listing of Hutchison Whampoa's U.K. mobile and telecommunications subsidiary, Orange. Nevertheless, Li also took steps to restructure the company for the impending handover. In June 1996, the company spun off its Hong Kong and mainland infrastructure holdings as a separately traded subsidiary, CKI, under leadership of Victor Li, which raised more than HKD 3.6 billion through sales of nearly 300 million shares. Then, in January 1997, Li restructured all of the holdings of the Cheung Kong Group in a series of ownership shifts among its four principal subsidiaries.

Under the restructured holding company, CKI became principally specialized in the company's Chinese infrastructure projects, including a nearly completed 140-kilometer toll highway running south of Shantao. Cheung Kong's share of Hutchison, meanwhile, advanced past the halfway mark, to 50.2 percent, while Hutchison's share of CKI moved up to 84.6 percent. This meant that Hutchison also added CKI's 35 percent of Hong Kong Electric (HKE), triggering a mandated takeover bid for full control of HKE. The restructuring was widely regarded as a shrewd repositioning of the company in the final months leading to the Hong Kong handover. Meanwhile, Victor Li's role as a principal architect in the restructuring signaled the coming to an end of Li Ka-shing's reign as Hong Kong's "Superman." The elder Li, who had previously suggested that he would retire prior to the July 1997 handover, instead indicated that he would step down in January 1998.

A NEW GENERATION OF LEADERSHIP

While Li Ka-shing remained executive chairman of the company into the new century, his eldest son, Victor Li, became the company's managing director in December 1998. Shortly before the announcement of Victor Li's promotion, both Cheung Kong and Hutchison Whampoa were awarded *Asiamoney* magazine's 1998 award for Best Managed Companies. The following year, *Far Eastern Economic Review* named both companies in their annual Review 200, a list of the leading companies in Hong Kong. Cheung Kong was ranked third in the list of Hong Kong's ten leading companies, while Whampoa was listed eighth. In addition, the companies were ranked first and second in the magazine's list of companies in which the management had a "long term vision."

In 1999, Victor Li was named deputy chairman of Cheung Kong. Li had been assisting his father in the chairman role for a number of years and was prepared to continue the projects initiated under his father's leadership. Among the various projects for 1999 was a series of mini-documentaries, titled *Knowledge Changes Fate,* funded and produced through Cheung Kong and Whampoa featuring stories that highlighted the value of education. The documentaries, which aired on television stations in both Hong Kong and Mainland China, featured stories about the education and achievements of some of the island's best known celebrities mixed with stories about everyday Hong Kong citizens who used their education and acquired knowledge to build better lives. The documentary series won three 4A Creative Awards for best promotional film and most creative documentaries. The awards were shared with the director of the series, Gu Chang-wei.

The timing of Cheung Kong's documentaries coincided with the establishment of the Cheung Kong Scholars Program, which awarded funds and support for international scholars to help establish and develop institutions and programs of higher learning in Hong Kong. Cheung Kong's program awarded grants to 127 scholars in 2000, working in conjunction with the Ministry of Education.

The first year of the new millennium was an important year for Cheung Kong as the company diversified its business through a number of strategic investments. In January, Cheung Kong and Hutchison Whampoa teamed with Hong Kong and Shanghai Banking Corporation and Hang Seng Bank to form IBusiness Corporation, an Internet-based commerce company intended to provide Internet portals and e-commerce services to companies in Hong Kong and the Chinese mainland. Cheung Kong's initial investment was estimated at HKD 3 billion. In March, IBusiness Corporation teamed with Excel Technology to create "i21," an enterprise that provided office applications for businesses.

In April 2000, one of Cheung Kong's subsidiary companies, Hong Kong Property Services Holdings Limited, merged with Midland Realty Holdings to form the largest property agency group in Hong Kong. Although both companies would remain separate from a general management standpoint, the merger increased potential profits for both companies and helped Cheung Kong to dominate the property market.

One of the most important developments for Cheung Kong in 2000 was the company's entrance into the life sciences market. Cheung Kong's newest subsidiary, CK Life Sciences Holdings Limited, was formed to take advantage of the growing life sciences, health, and sustainable development industries. Although the company was founded in 2000, it was not listed on the Hong Kong Stock Exchange until 2002.

CHEUNG KONG IN THE 21ST CENTURY

Cheung Kong grossed HKD 19.4 billion in 2000 but profits fell significantly over the following year, attributed to a global recession and residual effects from the terrorist attacks on the United States in 2001, which placed a constraint on global commerce and severely affected profits from the company's U.S. investments. In 2001, Cheung Kong's profits fell to HKD 7.2 billion. Although the company experienced a severe reduction in profit, projected growth from the expansion of the newly formed CK Life Sciences company was among the major projects intended to compensate for the losses.

In 2002, CK Life Sciences obtained patents for a number of new products, including a line of eco-friendly fertilizers. The fertilizers were intended to offer a solution to the common problem of acidification of soil, which reduces the fertility of arable land and leads to a reduction in productivity. Two of the company's ten fertilizers obtained patent approval in June 2002. In addition, CK Life Sciences announced the development of a system of animal feed additives for eco-friendly ranching and animal husbandry projects and a line of bioremediation products, used to treat degraded soil and replenish resources needed for productive agriculture.

Company profits rose significantly in 2002, from HKD 7.2 billion to 8.8 billion, attributable to improvements in the global economy and Cheung Kong's entrance into new markets, thereby encouraging increased investment. Cheung Kong and Hutchison Whampoa were again acknowledged as among Hong Kong's leading companies by *Far Eastern Economic Review,* placing fifth and third respectively. Growth continued over the following two years, with an increase to HKD 9.8 billion reported for 2003 and 12.3 billion for 2004. Property sales were among the key areas of growth, amounting to HKD 12.9 billion in 2003 and over HKD 17 billion in 2004.

Among the company's successes was CK Life Sciences, which was selected in the 2004 World Economic Forum as one of the world's 30 leading "Technology Pioneers." In 2004, the company strengthened its hold on Mainland China's growing fertilizer market, estimated at a HKD 85 billion industry in 2004. The company also began research and development on a number of products for the healthcare industry, including cancer and AIDS treatment programs. In 2004 and 2005, CK Life Sciences partnered with researchers at Massachusetts General Hospital to begin testing proposed treatments for AIDS patients, using CK Life Sciences' R&D Immunity product line to boost immune system performance.

COMMITMENT TO THE ENVIRONMENT

In the 21st century, Cheung Kong established itself as one of Hong Kong's environmentally conscious corporations. In December 2005, Cheung Kong worked with the World Wildlife Fund to establish a wetland preserve near existing fishponds at the Fung Lok Wai district. The company's commitment to conservation was furthered through the Cheung Kong Scholars Program, which since its inception had awarded funds and support for a number of important conservation programs.

In 2006, Li Ka-shing deepened his commitment to his charitable interests when he decided to donate one-third of his estimated HKD 18 billion in wealth to the Li Ka-shing Foundation. The foundation supported a number of interests including medical, environmental, cultural, and community welfare projects. In 2007, Li Ka-shing was listed by *Forbes* magazine as the tenth richest man in the world and was also the wealthiest man in Asia.

Cheung Kong's profits were estimated at HKD 13.9 billion in 2005, with growth reported in all of the company's major operating divisions and subsidiaries. The property business grew over 7 percent, while the company's revenues from life sciences investments increased from HKD 6.4 billion to HKD 7.1 billion over the course of the financial year. The property division fueled rapid growth in 2006, with estimated revenues exceeding HKD 18 billion and growth continued over the following year, with an estimated HKD 18.5 billion reached during the first six months of 2007. In the company's official press releases, Chairman Li Ka-shing, then 78 years old and still in control of the company he founded, praised efforts to stimulate economic growth in Mainland China as a major factor facilitating the continued success of Cheung Kong. With investments across a wide range of products and services and operations continuing in over 50 countries internationally, Cheung Kong was well positioned to remain one of Hong Kong's most influential companies.

Etan Vlessing
Updated, M. L. Cohen; Micah L. Issitt

PRINCIPAL SUBSIDIARIES

Hutchison Whampoa, Ltd.; Cheung Kong Infrastructure; Hong Kong Electric Holdings, Ltd.; Green Island Cement (Holdings) Limited Group; Anderson Asia Quarry Group; Hutchison Harbour Ring Limited; CK Life Sciences International Holdings, Inc.

PRINCIPAL COMPETITORS

Hang Lung Group; Sun Hung Kai Properties; Wharf, Inc.

FURTHER READING

"Bonds Point to Real Estate Bubble," *South China Morning Post,* January 15, 2008.

Hamlin, Kevin, "Superman in a Navy Suit," *Independent,* January 5, 1992, p. 9.

Hewett, Gareth, "Full Steam Ahead for Li's Flagships," *South China Morning Post,* October 25, 1996, p. 25.

Lau, Justine, and Tom Mitchell, "Li to Give Third of $18bn Wealth to Foundation," *Financial Times,* August 24, 2006.

Lee, Mark, "Li Ka-shing Raises Stake in Cheung Kong Holdings," *International Herald Tribune,* July 9, 2007.

"Li Builds Ties to Safeguard Future," *South China Morning Post,* June 27, 1993, p. 2.

"Li Ka-Shing: Preparing for China," *Economist,* January 11, 1997, p. 58.

"Li Ka-Shing Stays Ahead of the Game," *Financial Times,* January 7, 1997, p. 20.

Lucas, Louis, "Infrastructure Spin-off Helps Lift Cheung Kong," *Financial Times,* March 27, 1997, p. 24.

Lucas, Louis, and Dave Shellock, "Markets: Property Groups Drive Hong Kong Rally," *Financial Times,* October 26, 2007.

Mantel, Sukhmani, et al., "Cooperation for Environmental Reform: Business-NGO Partnerships in Hong Kong," *Journal of Corporate Citizenship,* Autumn 2007, p. 91.

Mitchell, Tom, "The Man Who Broke the Mold," *Financial Times,* October 27, 2007.

Nohria, Nitin, Anthony J. Mayo, and Mark Benson, "Li Ka-Shing and the Growth of Cheung Kong," *Harvard Business School Cases,* November 1, 2006, p. 1.

Rahul, Jacob, and Robert Budden, "Hong Kong's Dragon Enters the Third Generation," *Financial Times,* February 28, 2003.

"SHKP, Cheung Kong Seek Nod for Wetlands Housing Project," *Standard,* April 2007.

Sito, Peggy, and Josephine Ma, "CKI to Raise Mainland Profile After Reshuffle," *South China Morning Post,* March 4, 1997, p. 14.

Yeung, Henry Wai-chung, *Chinese Capitalism in a Global Era: Towards Hybrid Capitalism,* New York: Routledge Press, 2004.

Claire's Stores, Inc.

3 Southwest 129th Avenue
Pembroke Pines, Florida 33027
U.S.A.
Telephone: (954) 433-3900
Fax: (954) 433-3999
Web site: http://www.clairestores.com

Public Company
Founded: 1961
Employees: 18,500
Sales: $1.481 billion (2007)
Stock Exchanges: New York
Ticker Symbol: CLE
NAIC: 448150 Clothing Accessories Stores; 453998 Miscellaneous Retail Stores

■ ■ ■

A fixture in malls for more than three decades, Claire's Stores, Inc., and its subsidiaries lead the fashion accessory industry with over 3,000 stores in the United States, Canada, England, Japan, Puerto Rico, Scotland, and Wales. The company's perennially popular women's accessories, representing the company's primary product line, are marketed toward women in the 13 to 40 age range. Founder Rowland Schaefer grew the company from a modest success in the 1980s through shrewd acquisitions and calculated growth to become a world leader in women's accessories for the 21st century. After thirty years in the Schaefer family, Claire's Stores was sold to Apollo Management in 2007, marking a new era for the chain, which has continued to expand through franchise development into new international markets.

FROM WIGS TO ACCESSORIES

What became the Claire's Stores, Inc., of today emerged from two entirely separate companies. Schaefer formed a company named Fashion Tress Industries (FTI) in 1961 to service the increasingly popular wig marketplace in the South. FTI's quality hairpieces were a success with women of the early 1960s, and the company eventually became the world's largest retailer of fashion wigs. Meanwhile, in the Midwest, a small chain of retail outlets named Claire's Boutiques began selling a wide range of accessories from necklaces and earrings to evening bags and pins. Catering to women and teenaged girls, Claire's Boutiques had tapped a rare market niche—when times were tough and people had little to spend, women and teenaged girls could purchase a few trinkets and accessories to make an old outfit seem brand new. In plush times, these same consumers continued to enhance their wardrobes by purchasing accessories for both old and new outfits.

By the beginning of the 1970s America's fashion trends were changing and women began to turn away from wigs and to concentrate on their own tresses instead. As demand for wigs waned, Schaefer looked into diversification and found it in Claire's Boutiques. Based in Chicago with 25 retail outlets, Claire's was still a relatively young enterprise, yet with tremendous growth potential. Schaefer bought the midwestern chain and changed his company name from FTI to Claire's Stores, Inc., in 1973. The transition from wigs to acces-

COMPANY PERSPECTIVES

Our vision is for Claire's to be the world's most popular brand for girls, young adults and women in search of costume jewelry, fashion accessories and other products that enhance their lifestyle. To attain that objective, our mission is to provide customers with an unparalleled selection of fashion right and fun products at reasonable prices. Furthermore, within our stores, we strive to create an environment that is fun, welcoming and that encourages customers to tap into their creativity and explore their personal styles.

sories proved relatively smooth, and despite some rough times in the early 1980s, was a success. Yet few imagined just how successful Claire's Stores would become in the next decade and a half.

ACCESSORIZE, ACCESSORIZE, ACCESSORIZE

By fiscal 1985 (the company's fiscal year ended with the Saturday closest to January 31) sales for the Claire's chain reached $55.9 million with net income of $6.6 million. The following year, sales climbed to $74.5 million, income to $7.5 million, and stock traded as high as $15 on the New York Stock Exchange. Although sales continued to climb for fiscal 1987 to $87.2 million, net income fell to $5.3 million, an indicator of difficulties to come. From sales alone, Claire's appeared to be on the move, when fiscal 1988 brought in $103.4 million in sales, and income was back in the black to $6.2 million. Even Claire's Stores' stock held steady at $13, until fiscal 1989 when it plummeted to $2 despite strong sales of $127.3 million and income of $7.1 million.

During fiscal 1989 Claire's ambitious expansion plans took their toll on sales after a burst of openings and the acquisition of the Japanese chain Topkapi with 16 stores, bringing total stores to 580. Same-store sales and earnings floundered in red ink during the spring of 1988. Yet Schaefer, aware of the too-aggressive expansion and a temporary loss of control over his ever-growing empire, tightened the reins and initiated a turnaround by the last two quarters of 1988, with Claire's Stores' stock regaining some of its luster, trading at $7 by the end of the fiscal year.

Contributing to the company's turnaround was the implementation of a $5 million chainwide state-of-the-art computerized cash register and inventory system that linked Claire's stores with headquarters. Daily data capture rose to 99 percent as opposed to 70 percent when performed manually by the Claire's staff. The computer system and the hiring of Claire's Stores' first director of loss prevention further improved the company's numbers by reducing "shrinkage" or theft of the thousands of small items available in each store, with the company keeping this figure to 10 percent or less (the figure for 1986 was as high as 12 percent of sales). Lastly, an increase in Asian imports accelerated gross earnings, and new management selected by Schaefer completely stopped the company's hemorrhaging before any long-lasting or irreparable damage was done.

By May 1989, three months after the end of the previous fiscal year, Claire's posted an incredible sales surge of nearly 79 percent, with same-store increases of 58 percent. Although the company continued expanding, it did so carefully, and by July had 650 outlets in 47 states with some 4,000 employees, nearly two-thirds of whom worked part-time. Claire's finished the year (fiscal 1990) with $190.2 million and a very healthy $19.5 million in net income.

STAYING AHEAD OF COMPETITORS AND THRIVING

Sales for fiscal 1991 increased 35 percent to $255.2 million, and income was up to $20.5 million, partially due to a 7 percent rise in same-store sales. The company's stock was up again, too—trading at about $14—almost as high as 1985's all-time high of $15. Claire's hoped to add between 125 and 150 new stores by the end of the fiscal year and had revitalized its ordering system to facilitate keeping a better tab on trends and delivering merchandise to its stores in far less time. By the spring of 1992 there were a total of 1,006 company-owned stores in 47 states; of these 721 were Claire's, 113 were Topkapi, 32 Dara Michelle, 32 Arcadia, 20 Art Explosion, and another 90 were under the name Art Works or Picture Show. The latter four chains were a departure from Claire's Stores' general trade in women's and girls' accessories. Arcadia and Art Explosion stores were considered "trend" gifts shops stocking calendars, mugs, T-shirts, seasonal and stationery items, unframed posters, and other quick-sale products with a price range from $1 to $75 and an average sale of between $5 and $10. Art Works and Picture Show outlets carried graphic arts, such as framed posters and many other types of matted and framed artwork.

The end of the year, however, brought a vast turnaround as fiscal 1992 sales fell to $234.2 million, and Claire's suffered its first loss since 1981. Led by a

KEY DATES

1961: Rowland Schaefer creates Fashion Tress Industries (FTI).
1973: Schaefer merges FTI with Claire's Boutiques and forms Claire's Stores, Inc.
1989: Expands into Japan with purchase of Topkapi, Inc.
1996: Expands into the United Kingdom with purchase of Bow Bangles Plc.
1998: Claire's Stores expands into Zürich, Switzerland.
1999: Claire's Stores purchases Afterthoughts, Inc.
2000: Company expands into France with purchase of Cleopatre.
2003: Schaefer named director emeritus, executive control passes to his daughters.
2006: Claire's Stores begins franchising in the Middle East, Africa, and Turkey.
2007: Claire's Stores sold to Apollo Management.

same-store sales drop of 11 percent, the stunning loss of $8.7 million was blamed on several factors, including too-rapid expansion again (such as ill-fated stores in outlet malls which proved redundant), markdowns on excessive Christmas and Easter inventories which in turn compounded the problem by tying up space and keeping new merchandise from the shelves and racks, the discontinuation and disposal of the costly graphic arts line of stores (Art Works and Picture Show) for a sizable hit of nearly $12 million, and lastly, the cost of increased security as Claire's introduced cameras and locked display cases to lower theft rates.

While the company made adjustments to shore up losses and promote sales, Schaefer also looked into diversification. One option was a mail-order sideline with slightly higher-priced items; another was to duplicate the successful $130,000-prototype store that Claire's had opened in the Pembroke Pines Mall near headquarters, filled with black marble, mirrors, plenty of bright neon, mannequins, and several upscale items like earrings with a price tag of up to $50. Despite its difficulties in the early 1990s, Claire's was still considered a cash cow with some $22 million in cash in fiscal 1992.

Additionally, Schaefer, who at 76 had long passed the traditional age for retirement, sporadically talked about leaving the company or finding a buyer for his 41 percent share of Claire's Stores, Inc. If those on Wall Street were concerned, few showed it, for Schaefer was well liked and respected throughout the industry, and most knew he would never leave his company unstable. Fiscal 1993 brought good news as sales rose to $248 million, and income was back in good form at $14.5 million. By July total stores grew to 1,060, up from 1,040 the previous year, in 48 states.

Fiscal 1994 proved another successful year for Claire's with $281.7 million in sales and income of 7.9 percent or $23.6 million. Costume jewelry, generally Claire's Stores' biggest selling item, dominated the company's bottom line once again by accounting for $180.3 million or 64 percent of total sales. The same rang true in fiscal 1995 when costume jewelry sales reached $196.1 million of the year's $301.4 million total sales with income at 9 percent or $23.9 million. 1995's fiscal figures once again brought a red flag as same-store sales decreased 2 percent due to what the company deemed as the lack of a discernible "significant" fashion trend.

Near the end of fiscal year 1995, the company bought a $7.4 million new distribution facility in Hoffman Estates, Illinois, a suburb of Chicago. Claire's Stores' other distribution facility, originally leased in 1985 and located in Wood Dale (another Chicago suburb) continued to service the company's merchandising needs, with up to five shipments weekly to individual stores with the exception of imported goods like tote bags and costume jewelry, until the new facility was ready in June 1996.

NEW ACQUISITIONS AND INTERNATIONAL EXPANSION

In January 1996, just prior to the end of the company's fiscal year on February 3, a three-for-two stock split was declared by the board of directors in the form of a 50 percent stock dividend distribution (9.9 million shares of common stock and 653,807 shares of Class A common stock were given to stockholders of record). Also in January the company moved forward with the first of three major acquisitions, two in the United States and another in the United Kingdom. The first of the U.S. purchases (which counted towards fiscal 1996) involved assets from The Icing, Inc., which had filed for Chapter 7 protection. Assets included 85 property leases in prime locations, retail equipment, fixtures, and furniture.

After remodeling, Claire's planned to reopen the stores by May as either "Claire's Accessories" if no other Claire's store existed in the mall or as a refurbished "The Icing" if there was a Claire's store already in operation. The second acquisition was a British fashion chain known as Bow Bangles plc. Purchased assets included 48 stores throughout England, Scotland, and

Wales, as well as related fixtures, furniture, and equipment. Lastly, in April 1996 (fiscal 1997), the company acquired a third chain, Accessory Place, Inc., taking over 31 stores. This brought Claire's Stores' total number of outlets worldwide to over 1,500, with plans to open another 150 locations before fiscal 1997 ended—between 15 and 20 in Canada, 110 to 115 in the United States, and 30 more in Japan. Of the 1,500 stores, 142 were Claire's Accessories stores with each averaging 919 square feet in enclosed and "open-air" malls.

For a start-up cost of about $95,000, using specially-designed display systems, each Claire's Accessories store was ready for business within three months, a relatively short time in the retail industry, and well-stocked in women's and some unisex fashion accessories (usually in excess of 6,000 pieces of merchandise) such as costume jewelry (bracelets, earrings, hair ornaments, necklaces, pins, etc.), purses, sunglasses, tote bags, some trend gifts, and ear-piercing for a small fee. The other company-owned outlets under the names Bow Bangles, Dara Michelle (the more upscale outlet, with items priced from $5 to $75), The Icing, and Topkapi often operated within the same malls as Claire's Accessories stores. This clustering of stores in successfully tested geographical areas kept administrative supervision costs to a minimum and made it easier for refurbishing stores, which the company did on a regular basis.

Although the first quarter of fiscal 1996 found same-store sales lagging, a turnaround began in April and continued. By the third quarter (in October 1995), Schaefer and the company's management were jubilant over record sales and earnings. Stating that the year had proved to be "everything we expected it to be," Schaefer further explained that customer traffic was "excellent," average sales were higher, promotional costs were under budget, and markdowns had been unnecessary. Claire's Stores' finished fiscal 1996 with $344.9 million in sales, an increase of 14 percent over the previous year, and income of $30.9 million, including a rebound in same-store sales to 3 percent instead of 1995's decrease. Costume jewelry sales remained strong at $244.9 million for about 71 percent of sales, 6 percent over 1995 and 7 percent over 1994.

In 1998, Claire's Stores entered the men's clothing market, after purchasing Lux Corp., and its retail chain "Mr. Rags," for a reported price of $43 million. Claire's acquired 56 retail locations in the purchase and expanded the chain to 75 stores by the end of the year. In November, Claire's acquired 53 stores from Bijoux One, a privately held fashion chain headquartered in Zürich, Switzerland. By the end of the 1998 fiscal year, Claire's Stores had opened 48 stores and had expanded by over 170 stores in less than three years.

Near the end of 1999, Claire's Stores acquired rival clothing company Afterthoughts from the New York-based Venator Group (formerly Woolworth's, Inc.) for a reported $250 million. The purchase was the largest in Claire's Stores' history as the company acquired 768 retail stores and dramatically increased its customer and retail base. At the end of the fiscal year, Claire's Stores reported ownership of 2,027 stores in eight countries and the company was in preparations for further expansion in Europe and through subsidiaries in Asia. Marty Nealon, the former head of Afterthoughts for the Venator Group, was hired by Claire's and in December 1999 was named head of Claire's North America operations.

CLAIRE'S STORES IN THE 21ST CENTURY

By the end of the first financial quarter of 2000, Claire's Stores reported record growth for the eighth consecutive year in the company's history. The company continued its aggressive growth program with the acquisition of the French retail chain Cleopatre in February 2000, for a reported price of $11 million. Claire's gained 42 retail locations and a foothold in the French market. In September 2000, Claire's press department released information that Marty Nealon, the chief operating officer for the chain, had been released from the company and that Rowland Schaefer was assuming Nealon's duties until a replacement could be found.

According to company press statements, Claire's suffered during the first half of 2000 from difficulties in integrating the more than 700 retail locations acquired in the 1999 purchase of Afterthoughts. In addition, Claire's Stores suffered from an overall decline in same-store sales, although retail dividends remained steady. Sales began increasing in the 2003 fiscal year, with an 11 percent increase reported by November 2002. In May 2002, Claire's Stores announced that the company had decided to divest itself of its 154-store Mr. Rags division, which was based in Long Beach, California. A private investment company, headed by Ivan Spiers and Bruce Friedman, arranged to purchase controlling shares of the company and control of the retail outlets.

In November 2002, Rowland Schaefer suffered a mild stroke and took a leave of absence from his position as CEO of the company while his daughters Marla and Bonnie Schaefer, who served as board vice-chairpersons, took temporary control of their father's executive functions. In November 2003, the company announced that Rowland Schaefer would not return to his former positions and would be granted the position of chairman emeritus, en route to retirement, while his daughters Marla and Bonnie were elected by the board to serve as co-chairs and co-CEOs for the company. In the official press statement, Schaeffer stated, "For some time now, I have been thinking about passing the baton to Bonnie and Marla. Claire's Stores has delivered significant growth during the past year under their leadership, fully confirming my confidence in them." The board also released statements confirming the acceptance of a retirement package for Rowland Schaeffer valued at between $8 and $11 million.

At the close of the 2004 fiscal year, the company announced an increase in income of over 36 percent and a 13 percent increase in sales from the previous fiscal year. By the end of the year, Claire's Stores operated 2,810 retail locations in the United States, the Caribbean, Puerto Rico, Canada, the United Kingdom, Ireland, Switzerland, Austria, Germany, and France. In addition, the company maintained a 50 percent share in a joint venture with Aeon Corp., in its Claire Nippon line, which managed 150 stores in Japan.

Claire's Stores continued with European expansion in 2005, opening new stores in Spain and Holland. In contrast to previous expansion efforts, the company opted to open new stores without purchasing previously existing chains. Taking their expansion into account, Claire's Stores' sales increased by 7 percent in 2005 from 1.28 to 1.37 billion, with an additional 6–7 percent growth expected for 2006. In addition, the company conducted a buy back of approximately 215,000 shares of their common stock at a cost of over $6.5 million. In 2006, Claire's Stores entered into a franchising agreement with Al Shaya Co. to license 87 stores in the Middle East and Turkey. In addition, Claire's entered into an agreement to open franchises in South Africa under a partnership with the House of Busby Limited.

In March 2007, after several months of negotiations, Claire's Stores finalized an agreement to sell the company to Apollo Management L.P., a New York-based private equity company. The final price was negotiated at approximately $33 per share or a total of $3.1 billion. In a joint press release, Co-CEOs Bonnie and Marla Schaefer said of the sale, "The decision to sell the company that our father founded was reached after an enormous amount of soul searching over time and brings our strategic review to a successful conclusion. After reviewing the final bids, our Board of Directors unanimously concluded, after in-depth consideration, that this transaction with Apollo is in the best interests of our shareholders." The merger was formally approved by a majority vote among the shareholders in May 2007.

As Claire's Stores prepared for the 2008 calendar year, the company continued its record of sales growth and expansion. As of September 2007, the company owned 3,022 retail stores, half interest in 203 stores under the Claire Nippon division, and 153 franchises in the Middle East, Turkey, South Africa, Russia, and Poland. While the Schaefer family accepted a controlling buyout as part of the 2007 merger, many in the senior staff remained with the company, including Chief Financial Officer Ira D. Kaplan who was promoted to senior vice-president, while Eugene S. Kahn, of Apollo Management L.P., took the executive reins as chairman and CEO. With a history of growth and new leadership under an established corporate structure, Claire's Stores seemed prepared to head into a new decade as a leader in the retail market.

Taryn Benbow-Pfalzgraf
Updated, Micah L. Issitt

PRINCIPAL SUBSIDIARIES

CBI Distributing Corporation; Claire's Accessories U.K. Ltd.; Claire's Boutiques, Inc.; Claire's Canada Corp.; Claire's Nippon Co. Ltd. (50%); Claire's Puerto Rico Corp.; Afterthoughts, Inc.; Cleopatre, Inc.

PRINCIPAL COMPETITORS

Wet Seal, Inc.; Tween Brands, Inc.; Forever 21, Inc.

FURTHER READING

"Claire's Stores, Inc.," *South Florida Business Journal,* July 10, 1989, p. 21.

"Claire's Stores, Inc.," *South Florida Business Journal,* October 28, 1991, p. 18.

"Claire's Stores, Inc.," *South Florida Business Journal,* June 25, 1993, p. 25A.

Coletti, Richard J., "Claire's Renews Its Glitter," *Florida Trend,* February 1993, pp. 26–28.

Collins, Lisa, "Cheap and Cheerful Strategy Fuels Claire's Explosive Growth," *Crain's Chicago Business,* February 18, 1991, p. 16.

"Company News: Claire's Stores to Buy Rival Chain Afterthoughts," *New York Times,* November 3, 1999.

Forseter, Murray, "Shedding Light on Claire's Recovery," *Chain Store Age Executive,* July 1989, p. 6.

Marcial, Gene G., "A Costume Jeweler Regains Its Sparkle," *Business Week,* February 13, 1989, p. 88.

"Tempting Takeover Morsels That Could Gain 38%-Plus," *Money,* September 1994, p. 62.

Companhia Suzano de Papel e Celulose S.A.

Avenida Brigadeiro Faria Lima 1355
São Paulo, São Paulo 01452-919
Brazil
Telephone: (55 11) 3503-9061
Fax: (55 11) 3037-9557
Web site: http://www.suzano.com.br

Public Company
Incorporated: 1948 as Indústria de Papel Euclides Damiani, S.A.
Employees: 3,241
Sales: BRL 3.41 billion ($1.76 billion) (2007)
Stock Exchanges: Bolsa de Valores de São Paulo
Ticker Symbols: SUZB; SUZBY
NAIC: 321110 Pulp Mills; 322121 Paper (Except Newsprint); 322130 Paperboard Mills; 322222 Coated and Laminated Paper Manufacturing; 322224 Uncoated Paper and Multiwall Bag Manufacturing; 322226 Surface-Coated Paperboard Manufacturing

■ ■ ■

Companhia Suzano Papel e Celulose S.A. is, in terms of annual revenue, the second largest producer of paper and cellulose (wood pulp) in Brazil. Its paper products include printing and writing papers, paperboard (or cartonboard), colored paper, coated paper, and other papers. A vertically organized enterprise, it provides its basic raw material in the form of tracts of eucalyptus plantations in four states. Suzano has been a pioneer in the development of paper products made from eucalyptus.

UKRAINIAN IMMIGRANT BECOMES BRAZILIAN ENTREPRENEUR

The founder of Suzano, Leon Feffer, was born in 1902 in what is now Ukraine, in one of the innumerable Jewish rural villages called shtetels. His father immigrated to Brazil in 1910 with the object of finding work and then sending for his family. World War I intervened, resulting first in German occupation and then the Bolshevik Revolution. The family made its way across Europe and arrived in Brazil in 1921, settling in São Paulo. There Leon became friendly with the Klabin-Lafer clan: related Jewish families whose members sold him paper on credit. Ironically, their company, Klabin Irmãos & Cia., would, as Klabin S.A., become Suzano's principal rival.

Feffer soon began buying paper wholesale and selling it to stationery stores. With his brother-in-law as minority partner he registered his firm, Leon Feffer e Companhia, in 1923. The company began making envelopes and paper sacks in 1929. It also offered lithographic and typographic services. However, Brazilian paper companies were small, and the quantity and quality of Feffer's supplies was always uncertain. For three years he also purchased lead from old automobiles and railroad tracks, dissolving them with tin to make an alloy for Linotype machines. For two years he even supplemented his income by exporting oranges. In 1939, with the prospect of war threatening to cut off Brazil's paper imports, he took the daring step of selling

COMPANY PERSPECTIVES

The company's mission is to be one of the two largest and most profitable Brazilian companies in the sector. To win the admiration of the markets, and of the society that we live in.

the business, and even his home, to build a paper factory in São Paulo. Indústria de Papel Leon Feffer e Cia opened in 1941, but Feffer remained concerned for its future because of its dependence on imported wood pulp as the raw material.

Research conducted by Feffer's son, Max, convinced him that eucalyptus, rather than Brazilian pine, would make the best domestic wood pulp because of its rapid growth. Max identified a small firm in Suzano—a suburb of São Paulo—as the nucleus for a factory that would produce wood pulp from eucalyptus. Leon Feffer acquired it in 1955, renamed it Companhia Suzano de Papel e Celulose, and transformed it into the raw material supplier for a pilot plant that began turning out the world's first quality paper from 100 percent bleached eucalyptus pulp in 1957.

Suzano began planting its own eucalyptus in 1958. Feffer also, in 1960, bought control of Indústrias de Papel Rio Verde S.A., whose paper factories, along with the existing Feffer plant, became a unit for the consumption of Suzano's wood pulp. Rio Verde's paper mills were in Suzano and Pirituba.

BUILDING ON SUCCESS: 1974–86

Max Feffer's interest in science and technology led Suzano into a new field in 1974, when the firm participated in the creation of two petrochemical manufacturers, Politeno Indústria e Comércio S.A. and Polipropileno S.A. In 1992, as part of a government privatization program, Suzano became part-owner of Petroflex Indústria e Comércio S.A., a major producer of synthetic rubber. The company's petrochemical interests were separated from Suzano Papel e Celulose in 2001 as Suzano Petroquimica S.A.

In 1974 the U.S. paper products company Kimberly-Clark Corporation decided to enter the Brazilian market by means of a joint venture with Suzano. By late 1976 Suzano Kimberly was marketing Kleenex tissue in Brazil under the advertising slogan, "The end of the cold in your pocket." The joint venture was also making toilet tissues and table napkins. Suzano, which became a publicly traded company in 1980, sold its stake in the venture in 1982.

In the 1980s Suzano was obtaining eucalyptus for its four pulp mills from both its own plantations and from farms. Trucks, some of them company-owned, others contracted, hauled the trees—normally harvested after seven years and first stripped of bark—to conveyor belts transporting them to machinery that reduced the logs to wood chips before further processing. The company's pulp was being shipped to paper mills throughout Brazil as well as its own plants. Suzano's pulp and paper were being exported to dozens of foreign countries as well.

EXPANDING BEYOND SÃO PAULO: 1987–2000

All of the company's facilities were located in the state of São Paulo. In 1987, however, Suzano joined with Companhia Vale do Rio Doce (CVRD) in announcing a joint venture to build both a wood pulp and a paper mill in the state of Bahia. A large stake in this joint venture, Bahia Sul Celulose S.A., was taken by Brazil's development bank, but Suzano had a majority of the voting shares.

CVRD, the world's leading iron ore producer, had extensive forestry holdings. It contributed the raw material for wood pulp in the form of 97,000 hectares (about 240,000 acres) of forest in Bahia and Espíritu Santo states, of which almost 67,000 hectares (165,000) acres were in eucalyptus plantations. These trees in northeastern Brazil were typically harvested in six to seven years compared with 20 to 30 years for hardwood trees in the United States and Canada. And, unlike other hardwoods, eucalyptus trees could grow back from harvested stumps, sometimes more than once. For its part, Suzano pledged investment of $500 million to $700 million. Bahia Sul's pulp and paper mills, in Mucuri, Bahia, began production in 1992.

The Feffer group, Organizações Feffer, consisted of 43 companies in 1990. Companhia Suzano e Celulose was merely one unit, not even reporting directly to Organizações Feffer but through NemoFeffer S.A. (which became Suzano Holding S.A. in 2003). However, Suzano had seven units directly under its control, including the group's participation in Bahia Sul, Politeno, and Polipropileno, and its forestry subsidiary, Transurbes Agro Forestal Ltda.

Suzano entered a new joint venture in 1994, when it signed an agreement with Riverwood International Corp. to establish Igaras Papels e Embalagens S.A., a containerboard manufacturer. Suzano paid $100 million for a half-share of the enterprise. Suzano and Riverwood

KEY DATES

1923: Leon Feffer begins buying paper and selling it to stationery stores.
1941: Feffer opens a paper factory in São Paulo.
1955: Companhia Suzano begins as a plant converting lumber from eucalyptus trees to wood pulp (cellulose).
1957: A Suzano pilot plant turns out the world's first quality paper from bleached eucalyptus pulp.
1974: Suzano begins manufacturing petrochemical products.
1992: A joint venture, Bahia Sul Celulose, begins producing pulp and paper in the state of Bahia.
2001: The company's petrochemical units are diverted to another holding, Suzano Petroquimica.
2003: Suzano Papel e Celulose has acquired all of Bahia Sul Celulose.
2005: Suzano is Brazil's leading producer of paperboard and printed and writing paper.

sold Igaras to Suzano's rival, Industrias Klabin de Papel e Celulose S.A., in 2000 for $510 million.

NEW CENTURY, NEW DIRECTIONS: 2001–05

A broad-based restructuring of the Suzano group's holdings began in 1998, with the sale of assets in such segments as packaging, tissue papers, and telecommunications. This continued in 2001 with the separation of the petrochemical holdings from Suzano Papel e Cellulose. By this time both Leon and Max Feffer had died, the former in 1999, the latter in 2001. As an economy move, Max's son David cut employment in the holding company by about 30 percent and hired more professional managers to work throughout the group.

Suzano raised its share of the Bahia Sul joint venture in 2001, including purchase of all the common stock not previously in its hands, from CVRD for $320 million. It acquired the remaining shares in 2003. Suzano Papel e Celulose was merged into Bahia Sul Celulose in 2004, becoming Suzano Papel Bahia Sul Celulose S.A., but two years later, the company reverted to its former name. Bahia Sul became simply the Mucuri unit.

By 2005 Suzano was Brazil's leading producer of paperboard and both coated and uncoated printing and writing paper. In that year Suzano and a major competitor, Votorantim Celulose e Papel S.A., purchased a controlling stake of 60 percent, in equal portions, of another rival, Ripasa Celulose e Papel S.A.

GROWTH AND CHANGE: 2006 AND BEYOND

In 2006 Antonio Maciel Neto became president and chief executive officer of Suzano Papel e Celulose. Maciel, who had been in charge of Ford Motor Co.'s Brazilian subsidiary, was the first outsider to achieve so high a position at Suzano. He reported to David Feffer, who was chairman of the board. Maciel's principal task was to oversee the company's $1.3 billion investment in a new pulp mill in southern Bahia, intended to raise Suzano from eighth to second place in the world in wood pulp production from eucalyptus. Production began in 2007, with a completion date in 2009 set for this facility, which would more than double the company's wood pulp capacity. Three-quarters of Suzano's pulp-and-paper revenues were coming from paper and paperboard and only one-quarter from wood pulp.

The company prided itself on the management of its resources. The Mucuri unit, for example, cut its water consumption—through reuse—even while raising its production of wood pulp. In December 2006 Suzano's forests were 100 percent certified by the Forest Stewardship Council. This promised to foster the sale of not only the company's pulp but its paperboard cartons and paper for books, magazines, and the like, both in Brazil and abroad.

Suzano was rated by the Brazilian business magazine *Exame* as the best company in the country's pulp-and-paper sector in both 2005 and 2006. Maciel's goal was not only to raise the company's pulp production but to increase the proportion of exported pulp from 78 to 90 percent. In 2007 Suzano opened an office in Shanghai. Besides this unit, the company had subsidiaries in Argentina, Great Britain, Switzerland, and the United States.

Uncoated papers (48 percent), paperboard (17 percent), and coated papers (11 percent) accounted for three-quarters of Suzano's net sales in 2006. The company remained Brazil's leading producer of coated and uncoated printing and writing paper. It was also the leader in paperboard. Pulp sales accounted for 24 percent of sales but 43 percent of exports, which in 2007 came to almost half of net sales. Suzano owned 462,000 hectares (1.4 million acres) of land in five states, of which about half was in eucalyptus plantations.

It also leased a smaller amount of land containing pulpwood and had access to about 75,000 hectares (about 185,000 acres) of hardwood plantations that it had developed with third parties and that provided the wood for about 25 percent of Suzano's pulp production. Net company debt of BRL 4.29 billion ($2.42 billion) at the end of 2007 was seen as manageable by a rating service that affirmed Suzano's AA credit rating.

Suzano Petroquimica was sold in 2007 to Brazil's biggest enterprise, the state-owned oil and petrochemical company Petróleo Brasileiro S.A. (Petrobras), which paid BRL 2.7 billion ($1.4 billion), of which BRL 2.1 billion (about $1.1 billion) was due to Suzano Holding for its 76 percent stake. Suzano Holding held 50.1 percent of the total capital, and all of the voting shares, of Suzano Papel e Celulose. The Brazilian development bank BNDES held 11 percent of its shares, and about 35 percent was publicly traded.

Robert Halasz

PRINCIPAL SUBSIDIARIES

Bahia Sul Holding GmbH (Switzerland); Comercial e Agricola Paineiras Ltda.; Suzano America Inc. (64%); Suzano Trading Ltd.; Suzanopar Investimentos Ltd.

PRINCIPAL COMPETITORS

Aracruz Celulose S.A.; Klabin S.A.; Votorantim Papel e Celulose S.A.

FURTHER READING

Bechtos, Ramona, "Kimberly-Clark Makes Major Move in Brazil," *Advertising Age,* September 13, 1976, p. 88.

Cleber, Aquino, *História empresarial vivida,* São Paulo: Editora Atlas, 1991, Vol. 5, pp. 113–51.

"Fitch Affirms 'AA-(bra)' Rating on Suzano Papel e Celulose S.A.," *Business Wire,* November 30, 2007 (on Factiva database).

Mano, Cristiane, "Uma celebridade na Suzano," *Exame,* 2006, pp. 56–57.

Marcovitch, Jacques, *Pioneiros e emprendores,* São Paulo: Editora de Universidade de São Paulo, 2003, pp. 251–81.

Pastor, Luiza, "Cresceu e quer mais," *Exame Melhores e Maiores,* July 2006, pp. 198, 200.

Patrick, Ken L., "Bahia Sul Shifts Uncoated Free-Sheet Production to High Gear at Brazil Mill," *Pulp & Paper,* November 1997, pp. 51–56.

Rodden, Graeme, "Suzano Minds Its Ps and Qs," *Pulp & Paper International,* March 2006, pp. 29–31.

Sissell, Kara, "Petrobras to Acquire Suzano," *Chemical Week,* August 15, 2007, p. 9.

"Suzano, Riverwood to Sell Igaras," *Paperboard Packaging,* September 2000, p. 86B.

"Suzano-Feffer Maintains Volume Growth While Upgrading Product Value," *Paper,* November 1977, pp. 523, 535.

Vasconcelos, Lia, "Rumo á escala global," *Exame Melhores e Maiores,* August 2007, pp. 244, 246.

———, "Uma estratégia para o futuro," *Exame,* December 2007, pp. 70–71.

Cora S.A./NV

Zoning Industriel
Jumet, B-6040
Belgium
Telephone: (32 071) 25 88 83
Fax: (32 071) 25 88 20
Web site: http://www.cora.be

Wholly Owned Subsidiary of Louis Delhaize Group
Incorporated: 1968
Employees: 59,750
Sales: EUR 6 billion ($7.58 billion) (2006 est.)
NAIC: 452111 Department Stores (Except Discount Department Stores)

■ ■ ■

Cora S.A./NV is the leading operator of hypermarkets—large-scale retail centers combining both supermarket and department store formats—in Belgium. The company is also active in France, Hungary, Romania, the Antilles, and Luxembourg. In Belgium, Cora operates its seven hypermarkets as the anchor stores for a network of shopping malls also owned by the company. The company focuses primarily on French-speaking Belgium, with stores in Hornu, La Louvière, Rocourt, Messancy, and Châtelineau in the Walloon region, and in Woluwe St. Lambert and Anderlecht in Brussels.

The bulk of the company's operations are in France, where Cora oversees a network of 59 freestanding hypermarkets. Cora France is also responsible for the development of the company's operations in the Antilles, where the company has 23 hypermarkets. Cora has been building its presence in Eastern Europe since the late 1990s. The company operates seven hypermarkets in Hungary, and three in Romania, including two in Bucharest. Cora operates two stores in Luxembourg, in Foetz since 2002, and in Bertrange since 2004. Together, Cora's hypermarket operations generated approximately EUR 6 billion in revenues in 2006. The company is part of privately held Louis Delhaize Group. That company, not to be confused with the larger Delhaize Le Lion, operates more than 1,500 stores in a variety of retail formats, including Match, Ecomax, Profi, Louis Delhaize, Truffaut, Animalis, and the Internet-based Houra.fr. Louis Delhaize group reported revenues of more than EUR 11 million in 2006.

THE DELHAIZE RETAIL REVOLUTION IN THE 19TH CENTURY

The Delhaize family had been a pioneer in Belgium's retail sector long before opening the country's first hypermarket in the late 1960s. The family's retail empire originated as a Charleroi-based wine wholesaler founded in 1850 under Jacques Delhaize.

This background in wholesaling provided the basis for the retail empires founded by Delhaize's sons, Jules, Adolphe, Edouard, and Louis. Jules Delhaize played a particularly prominent role in the development of the family's fortunes. A commercial sciences professor, Jules Delhaize sought a means for testing a number of the retail theories he had conceived during the second half of the 19th century. Among these, Delhaize saw the potential for developing a branch-based network of

COMPANY PERSPECTIVES

At Cora, our business is to offer the widest choice at the best price, whether self-service or assisted by a salesperson, and with full guarantees: freshness guarantee, best price guarantee, "satisfaction or money-back" guarantee; and warranty guarantee.

stores supplied by a centralized warehouse. Such a system would permit the retailer to eliminate the many middlemen then involved in Belgium's grocery trade. The cost savings achieved could be used to lower prices. In addition, prices for all items were to be displayed.

Joined by brother Edouard and brother-in-law Jules Vieujant, both professors as well, Jules Delhaize launched the company Delhaize Frères in Charleroi in 1867. The brothers adopted the lion from Belgium's royal crest as the company's symbol. The lion later became incorporated in the company's name, which became known as Delhaize Le Lion. Soon after, Delhaize Frères moved their headquarters to Brussels. In 1883, the group moved their headquarters close to that city's Gare de l'Ouest train station, opening a state-of-the-art warehousing complex with its own rail link. In this way, the company gained ready distribution access to the rest of Belgium.

Delhaize Frères grew strongly, and by the end of the first decade of the 20th century boasted more than 500 stores in their network. The Delhaize brothers had also been precursors for the Belgian supermarket sector in other ways, notably in their expansion into manufacturing and the creation of their own store brand.

CREATING THE LOUIS DELHAIZE GROUP

The success of Delhaize Frères had in the meantime inspired the two other Delhaize brothers to enter the retail market. Adolphe established his own company in Brussels in the 1860s, and successfully developed his own store group. In 1950, Delhaize Frères merged with the Adolphe Frères group, and soon after the company took on the Delhaize Le Lion name.

In the meantime, the fourth brother, Louis Delhaize, had struck out on his own, developing a grocery business focused primarily on the Walloon region of southern Belgium. Louis Delhaize's sons, René and Georges, took over the business around the beginning of the 20th century. The success of the other branch of the Delhaize family in the rest of Belgium encouraged this pair of Delhaize brothers to seek growth outside of the country. Their focus naturally turned across the border, into France. René Delhaize traveled to France's eastern regions, buying the Sanal retail group in Nancy, and Sadal in Strasbourg. Georges Delhaize targeted France's northern region, and established his own store, Docks du Nord, in the city of Lille.

André Bouriez, a nephew of René Delhaize, joined his uncle's business in 1929. Sanal and Sadal later merged with rival Mielle, creating Mielle-Sanal-Sadal in 1945. By 1965, Bouriez had been named as that company's president. Under Bouriez the different components of the family's French retail operations, including Docks du Nord, were finally merged together into a single company within the Louis Delhaize Group.

LAUNCHING A HYPERMARKET FORMAT

The consolidation of the family's holdings came at a critical time in the history of the French and Belgian retail sectors. In the 1950s, Delhaize Le Lion had led the introduction of the American-style supermarket format in Belgium. The self-service supermarket concept had also appeared in France during this time. The new larger stores rapidly began to replace both countries' traditional grocery stores. In the meantime, by the end of the 1960s, a number of retailers, led by France's Carrefour, had begun to combine the supermarket concept with the nonfood offerings more usually found in department stores. The new vastly larger stores then became known as "hypermarkets."

The Louis Delhaize group responded by developing its own supermarket formats. By the late 1960s, the group had also become interested in the hypermarket format. For this, the company founded a new subsidiary, Cora, in 1968. Rather than immediately developing its own hypermarket format, Cora turned to upcoming French retail group Carrefour, signing a five-year franchise contract. Cora began opening its own shopping centers with the hypermarkets serving as anchor stores in Belgium. A separate company began developing the Louis Delhaize group's hypermarket network in France. The first of the group's French stores opened in Garges-lés-Gonesse in 1969.

The end of the franchise contract with Carrefour led to the rollout of the Cora hypermarket brand in 1974. By then, the group controlled a network of ten hypermarkets in France and Belgium. The following year, the group's direction was taken over by Philippe Bouriez.

Under its new president, Louis Delhaize launched a major expansion of its hypermarket subsidiary. Over the

KEY DATES

1867: Jules Delhaize launches Delhaize Frères in Charleroi.
1929: André Bouriez, nephew of the Delhaize brothers, joins the company.
1945: Sanal and Sadal merge with Mielle, forming Mielle-Sanal-Sadal.
1965: André Bouriez becomes company president and leads merger of Docks du Nord with Mielle-Sanal-Sadal, creating Louis Delhaize group.
1968: Founding of new company subsidiary, Cora.
1969: Opening of group's first hypermarket in France.
1974: Carrefour franchise agreement ends; hypermarkets in France are converted to Cora name.
1985: Company adds 15 new hypermarkets in France through acquisition of Radar retail group.
1997: First hypermarket opens in Hungary.
2002: Cora hypermarket opens in Luxembourg.
2004: Cora enters Romanian market.
2006: Louis Delhaize acquires full control of Cora France.
2007: Cora acquires majority control of its Hungarian franchisee, Magyar Hipermarket.

next decade, the company maintained a steady stream of new Cora openings, adding approximately two new stores each year. This expansion came despite the increasingly restrictive nature of both Belgian and French markets, as both governments adopted new rules limiting the number of new hypermarket openings. The competition for available locations added to the already intense rivalry for market share among supermarket groups in both countries.

GAINING IN SCALE

Cora nonetheless succeeded in developing a strong network of hypermarkets in Belgium. For this, the company maintained its focus on the Walloon region, opening five hypermarkets in the region. The company later ventured into the Brussels region, and continued to add new locations. The company added a store in Woluwe and then in 1998 opened its most modern hypermarket to date in a new company-owned shopping mall complex in Anderlecht.

France remained Cora's fastest-growing market. In that country, Cora operated as a subsidiary of holding company GMB, set up as a partnership between Louis Delhaize and Carrefour. The Belgian company nonetheless maintained majority control of its French operations, with a nearly 58 percent share.

Acquisitions enabled Cora to gain scale in the French market beginning in the mid-1980s, as the company continued to build up its presence in the northern and eastern regions of the country. In 1985, the company added 15 new hypermarkets through its acquisition of the Radar retail group. The next expansion came in 1989, when Louis Delhaize acquired *Société Européenne de Supermarchés.* That purchase gave the company control of another four hypermarkets. By 1997, the company had also added three former Mammouth hypermarkets as well. The company's French network ultimately expanded to nearly 60 hypermarkets in the new century.

Cora remained determined to maintain its independence, despite the ongoing consolidation of the French supermarket and hypermarket sectors in the late 1990s. The rising strength of the Carrefour retail empire in particular led Cora to begin seeking new partnerships in the 21st century. As part of that effort, the company established a joint buying venture, called Opera. The new business, headed by François Bouriez, then also head of Louis Delhaize, partnered Cora with Carrefour archrival Casino. In this way, Cora gained a stake in France's third largest buying group. At the same time, the agreement to place its buying operations within Opera served as a deterrent to the possibility that Carrefour might attempt to gain control of Cora.

TARGETING EASTERN EUROPE IN THE 21ST CENTURY

The company's effort to safeguard its independence in the face of Carrefour worked almost too well—in 2001 Carrefour announced its agreement to sell its stake in GMB to Deutsche Bank. The terms of that agreement, however, gave Deutsche Bank the option of selling the 42.39 percent stake to Casino. Louis Delhaize and Cora attempted to block the sale to Deutsche Bank, but in the end were unsuccessful.

Casino became the group's partner in GMB, but the acquisition put an end to the two companies' Opera venture, which had included an agreement that the two companies would not seek to build cross-shareholdings in each. Instead, Louis Delhaize established its own buying operation, Provera France, in order to supply the Cora network as well as its Match supermarket chain.

Casino's difficulties in the middle of the decade, as the retail group struggled to maintain profitability amid a price war launched by Carrefour, provided Louis Delhaize with the opportunity to consolidate its control of Cora. In 2006, Casino agreed to sell its stake in GMB to Louis Delhaize, which then became the sole owner of the entire Cora hypermarket network.

By then, that network had begun to develop new horizons. In the early 2000s, the group decided to enter neighboring Luxembourg, opening its first hypermarket in that country in the town of Foetz. The company added a second hypermarket in Luxembourg, in Bertrange, in 2004. The Luxembourg market's small size, dominated by homegrown retail group Cactus, limited Cora's growth prospects there, however.

Instead, the company placed its future growth goals farther east. In the late 1990s, the Louis Delhaize group had begun to explore expansion into the Eastern European market. Many of these markets had begun to exhibit strong economic growth toward the beginning of the 21st century, with most slated to join the European Union by around 2005. Cora followed the Louis Delhaize group's entry into these markets, with Hungary as its first target.

For its Eastern European expansion, Cora formed a franchise agreement with a local partner, Magyar Hipermarket Kft. Cora opened its first hypermarket in Hungary in 1997, in Törökbálint, in the Budapest region. By the end of 2000, the company had added four more stores in Hungary, in Budakalász, Fót, and Miskolc. These stores were then joined by two more, in Debrecen in 2002 and in Szolnok in 2004. All of the group's stores in Hungary targeted the Budapest area and the larger eastern region.

This eastern focus soon brought Cora into Romania as well, where it opened its first hypermarket in Bucharest in 2004. The company quickly added a second hypermarket serving the Romanian capital. By 2006, the group was ready to expand deeper into that country, opening a store in Cluj-Napoca in October 2006.

Cora integrated its Belgian and French operations, with the larger Cora France network becoming a subsidiary of Cora S.A. in Belgium. In 2007, the group gained control of its Hungarian network as well, with the purchase of a 72.9 percent stake in Magyar Hipermarket. The move came as part of the company's plan to extend its operations deeper into the Eastern European market through the end of the decade. With sales of approximately EUR 6 billion, Cora remained the flagship of the Louis Delhaize retail empire in the 21st century.

M. L. Cohen

PRINCIPAL DIVISIONS

Cora France; Cora Hungary; Cora Romania.

PRINCIPAL COMPETITORS

Carrefour S.A.; Casino S.A.; Auchan S.A.; E. LeClerc S.A.; Colruyt S.A.; Delhaize Le Lion.

FURTHER READING

"Belgian Retailer Delhaize Unit Cora to Expand in CEE, Keep 3% Hungarian Market Share," *Hungary Business News,* October 18, 2006.

"Carrefour Faces Legal Action," *Times,* January 5, 2002, p. 55.

Cordes, Rene, "Delhaize and Cora in Court," *Daily Deal,* January 4, 2002.

Deeny, Godfrey, "Bouriez Selloff: Trading Luxury for Hypermarkets," *WWD,* May 15, 1990, p. 1.

"EU Approves Belgian Louis Delhaize's Acquisition of Hungarian Cora Operator Magyar Hipermarket," *Hungary Business News,* July 10, 2007.

"Supermarket Clearance," *European Report,* July 12, 2007.

Willock, Rob, "Cora Goes to Casino to Win Independence," *Super Marketing,* April 30, 1999, p. 12.

Corporación Multi-Inversiones

Avenida Cinco y Calle 17
Guatemala City,
Guatemala
Telephone: (502) 2423-4000
Fax: (502) 2333-7109
Web site: http://www.corporacionmultiinversiones.com

Private Company
Founded: 1920s
Employees: 30,000
Sales: $3.8 billion (2006 est.)
NAIC: 112210 Hog and Pig Farming; 112320 Broilers and Other Meat-Type Chicken Production; 221111 Hydroelectric Power Generation; 236220 Commercial and Institutional Building Construction; 311221 Flour Milling; 311221 Wet Corn Milling; 311615 Poultry Processing; 311821 Cookie and Cracker Manufacturing; 311823 Pasta Manufacturing; 311830 Tortilla Manufacturing; 327310 Cement Manufacturing; 327331 Concrete Block and Brick Manufacturing; 531120 Lessors of Nonresidential Buildings (Except Miniwarehouses); 722211 Limited-Service Restaurants

■ ■ ■

Corporación Multi-Inversiones (CMI) is best known for its Pollo Campero fast-food chain, which it operates, through its own resources and franchisees, at hundreds of locations on four continents. However, within its native Guatemala, and more generally in Central America, the family-owned enterprise has much greater impact. Through one division, it builds and operates commercial and office centers and residential projects in Guatemala. Factories in Guatemala and El Salvador offer a wide range of products for home construction. The milling division turns out wheat flour, cornmeal, pasta, cookies, and crackers in four countries. The energy division has constructed hydroelectric projects in Guatemala. The animal husbandry division raises pigs and chickens on farms in four countries, and then processes them into food products. Pollo Campero forms the corporation's restaurant division. In all CMI encompasses about 100 companies, including a bank, and some industry analysts ranked it the largest enterprise in Central America.

POLLO CAMPERO IN CENTRAL AMERICA

Corporación Multi-Inversiones (CMI) got its start in the 1920s with a small store in San Cristóbal, Totonicapán, in Guatemala. El Molino Excelsior, founded by Juan Bautista Gutiérrez in 1936, was its first mill. The establishment of Granja Villalobos in 1964 initiated the enterprise's poultry raising activities. Pollo Campero (Country Chicken), founded in 1971 by Dionisio Gutiérrez and other businessmen, was Guatemala's first fast-food chain (although it did not consider itself as such, since it offered table service). Polo Campero opened its first unit outside Guatemala in neighboring El Salvador in 1972. Dionisio Gutiérrez died in 1974 in a plane crash, but the enterprise continued under the direction of family members and close associates, especially Francisco Pérez de Antón, who was one of the

COMPANY PERSPECTIVES

Mission: To be a multinational family Corporation that seeks excellence in its entrepreneurial activities. To compete in the production of goods and services of high significance in order to be leaders in the markets in which we participate. To seek in permanent form the development and integral well-being of the members of our organization. To be a significant factor in society by means of participating in the integral development of the countries where we operate.

founders. Dionisio's son Juan José Gutiérrez assumed direction of the enterprise in the early 1980s.

Pollo Campero's growth, although slow at first, was stimulated by changes in the economic life of Central America. A steady rural-to-urban migration and the entry of women into a paid workforce with fixed hours resulted in changed food consumption patterns. Instead of going home for lunch, many people started looking for places near their jobs where they could eat quickly and cheaply before returning to work. The basic product was being raised, slaughtered, and processed at Corporación Multi-Inversiones' own facilities in Guatemala and later in El Salvador.

Pollo Campero's business model, as Gutiérrez explained in 1997 to Crist Inman, a business administration professor in Costa Rica, was based not on the product, the location, or even the customer, but on the employee. "We pay attention to their training, their education and development, their health, their comfort," he said. "We work on the culture inside our organization and *they* take care of the customer." Since not many Pollo Campero workers had completed elementary school, let alone high school, the company established an institute to teach basic literacy and arithmetic skills.

Eventually the Campero Institute became the first business enterprise allowed by the Guatemalan government to issue diplomas to its employees, who attended classes on company premises. The institute, by the late 1990s, also offered a program in cooking, management, and related restaurant skills. Furthermore, a Campero "university" had been founded to provide three weeks of classes for all company workers and two months of training on the job. In addition, Pollo Campero paid its employees 15 percent more than the minimum wage and offered minimum cost medical and dental care. Little things were also important in fostering a motivated workforce: for example, employees were allowed to take their uniforms home, where they were admired by people not fortunate enough to hold a steady job.

The larger Pollo Campero units were freestanding, with ample parking, gardens, playgrounds, and a drive-through lane for motorists seeking takeout. In the cities, the units were usually located on the ground floors of buildings adjoining heavy pedestrian traffic. In food courts, shopping centers, and some central locations, express units offered only takeout service. Customers seeking delivery were accommodated by a routing system that processed orders and directed them to specially designed motorcycles with carrying cases to keep the food from becoming cold. Although chiefly a lunch establishment, Pollo Campero opened as early as 7 A.M. and in the 1990s introduced a variety of egg oriented breakfast choices. Units remained open until 10:30 P.M. The chain was aimed at working people, yet more than one-fifth of all sales were on Sunday, indicating its strength as a family establishment as well.

EXPANSION THROUGH FRANCHISING

Pollo Campero was so successful in Guatemala that it drove Kentucky Fried Chicken out of business there. The chain expanded into Honduras in 1989. After an unsuccessful foray in Miami, however, the company decided it was too expensive to export its business model, with high education and training costs, to other countries. It decided instead to expand through franchising. Pollo Campero offered partners a package that in addition to a recognized name included assistance in selecting sites and developing property; operations manuals and videos; auxiliary help in systems such as accounting, finance, and employee training; and participation in advertising, marketing, and promotions. The price for establishing such a unit was $25,000, plus a royalty fee of 5 percent on sales.

The first franchised unit opened in Panama City, Panama, in 1996, and the second in San José, Costa Rica, in 1997. By the end of 1998 there were five in Costa Rica, three each in Panama and Ecuador, and two in Nicaragua. The company owned units numbered 58 in Guatemala, 31 in El Salvador, and six in Honduras. By the fall of 2001 Pollo Campero had moved into Mexico. Of its 143 units there, 125 were franchised to Telepizza, a Spanish chain, which sold its pizza as well as its partner's chicken. Pollo Campero also opened an outlet in Madrid.

By this time Pollo Campero was well aware that there was a big market for its product among hungry,

KEY DATES

1920s: A small store in Guatemala marks the origins of Corporación Multi-Inversiones (CMI).
1971: Establishment of Pollo Campero, Guatemala's first fast-food chain.
1996: Pollo Campero opens its first franchised unit, in Panama.
2002: The fast-food chain opens its first restaurant in the United States, in Los Angeles.
2006: CMI is said to be the biggest enterprise in Central America.
2007: Pollo Campero has about 260 outlets in 12 countries, including China and Indonesia.

nostalgic Central Americans in the United States. The company's units in the airport terminals in Guatemala City and San Salvador were filled with customers ordering takeout in the company's bright orange cartons for the trip north—and for their relatives and friends. Pollo Campero sold three million takeout meals in 2001, many of them for such flights. The airlines flying to the United States complained that their planes reeked from the odor of chicken.

POLLO CAMPERO IN THE UNITED STATES

In 2002, when Pollo Campero opened its first restaurant, a franchised unit, in Los Angeles, Guatemalans and Salvadorans lined up as long as six hours before opening time, and customers continued to be served until 3:00 the next morning. More than 30,000 people visited the unit in the first five days even though there was no drive-through lane or delivery service. The phenomenon quickly inspired the opening of more Pollo Campero outlets, first in California, and then toward the end of the year in Houston, where an average of 5,000 people a day visited the first unit, many of them motorists patiently waiting for a place in the parking lot. Carlos Ortiz, the franchisee, said it was the first of 40 restaurants that he planned to open in south Texas.

Ortiz also revealed to the Latino weekly *Semana* the alleged recipe for Pollo Campero chicken, a secret closely guarded by the company. Ortiz said a mixture of spices was injected into the chicken, which was left to marinate and was then fried. Jennifer Olvera, an *Arlington (Ill.) Daily Herald* correspondent who visited a Chicago outlet in 2005, wrote that the chicken, which she called "moist" and "flavorful," was never frozen, and described the breading that preceded frying as "fiery."

Pollo Campero arrived in the Washington, D.C., area in the fall of 2003 and proved equally popular in that region, where half the Latino population was Central American. New York was next, in July 2004. Thousands of people stood in line for up to three hours for the opening of the first New York outlet, in Queens. Another soon opened in Brooklyn (but later closed), and Campero-approved franchisees prepared to introduce the chain to the Dallas and Chicago areas.

In December 2007, Campero USA announced that the chain would open about five to ten Pollo Campero outlets in Wal-Mart stores over the next 18 months. These units would be company-owned rather than franchised, with the first scheduled for a Chicago-area Wal-Mart in the second half of 2008. Campero USA's president said that the chain, while focusing on growth in existing locales, was planning on moving into a few more markets, including North Carolina and the Atlanta and Boston metropolitan areas. Although most of its restaurants would be franchised, Campero USA expected to operate eight company-owned stores by the end of 2008. It had a goal of placing about 500 outlets in the United States by 2013.

CATERING TO NORTH AMERICAN TASTES

Pollo Campero in the United States was not the same as in Central America. There was no table service. Many of the customers were other Latinos—Mexican, Puerto Rican, or Dominican—or non-Latinos. There were many dishes other than the fried chicken and ubiquitous french fries of the Central American outlets. Houston's first restaurant, for example, also offered the chicken extra crispy or roasted. It also offered "*camperitos*" (chicken nuggets), hamburgers, chicken sandwiches, salads, a salsa bar, and desserts such as flan, a custard popular throughout Latin America. Also available were typically Latino drinks such as *horchata*—a combination of rice, milk, and cinnamon—and *tamarindo,* a fruit drink. The outlet in Falls Church, Virginia, a predominantly Anglo area outside of Washington, D.C., offered mashed potatoes, iced tea, and U.S.-style soft drinks. Breakfast menus included, in addition to egg dishes, hotcakes, French toast, and croissants.

In her review of the Chicago outlet, Olvera wrote that she loved the cole slaw, which was sprinkled with lime and pepper, and smoky pinto beans dotted with cilantro and bacon bits. She also liked the caramelized mashed plantains, but not the green ones. Other side dishes included American-style cole slaw; thin, crisp, french fries and gravy topped mashed potatoes; and a salad with grilled chicken. Desserts included caramel or mango flan, rice pudding that she called "runny" and coconut pudding described as "too saccharine," and "intriguing" soft-serve cones filled with a choice of several toppings. In addition to the fried chicken, there was a chicken burrito available in two sizes, a bean burrito, and the usual chicken nuggets. "South-of-the-border sips" included *horchata, tamarindo,* and *marañón,* the last made from the fruit of the cashew tree.

According to the business magazine *AméricaEconomía,* Pollo Campero ranked second among Guatemala companies in 2005, with sales of $462.4 million (but only $345 million in 2006, a 25 percent drop). There were 218 outlets in 2006 and 260 in late 2007, including one in Shanghai, the first of many planned in China over the next six to eight years. A Pollo Campero in Jakarta, Indonesia, had already opened. In all, Pollo Campero by that time was in 12 countries. There were 36 units in the United States in late 2007.

THE PARENT COMPANY: CORPORACIÓN MULTI-INVERSIONES

Corporación Multi-Inversiones, Pollo Campero's parent, continued to thrive while Pollo Campero grew. A 2005 report by the research unit of the British magazine the *Economist* gave its annual revenue as $2.2 billion. The daily newspaper *ElPeriódico de Guatemala* ranked it first among Central American enterprises in 2006, with sales of $3.8 billion—roughly equivalent to one-tenth of Guatemala's gross domestic product.

CMI entered the construction field in 1988, with the intention of developing commercial centers, office complexes, and residential housing in various areas of Guatemala. By 2007 more than 700,000 square meters of such projects had been built. The Industrial and Commercial Unit made concrete and steel construction materials for other clients as well for the division's own use.

The milling division had manufacturing centers in Guatemala, El Salvador, Costa Rica, and the Dominican Republic. Wheat flour was used to make bread, pasta, crackers, biscuits, and cookies. The pastas were made and packed for CMI's own brands and those of other firms. Cornmeal was made for tortillas and other products. Wheat and corn breads were turned out as the prime material for snacks, and family and industrial-quantity premixes for food preparation. Pasta production included noodles for soups and Chinese foods. The division also made food packaging for other customers.

The animal husbandry division was active in Guatemala, El Salvador, Honduras, and Costa Rica. There were farms where eggs were laid, chicks incubated, and pigs and chickens raised, and processing plants for meat and poultry products. This division also produced animal feed and shrimp. CMI was one of the seven leading chicken producing companies in Latin America. The energy division included three hydroelectric plants with total installed capacity of 60 megawatts. CMI also owned a bank.

CMI was controlled by Juan José Gutiérrez Mayorga, his brother Dionisio Gutiérrez Mayorga, and their cousins Juan Luis Bosch Gutiérrez and Felipe Bosch Gutiérrez. Juan Luis Bosch, co-president of CMI, was known as a television commentator and host, a fierce opponent of President Hugo Chavéz's socialist regime in Venezuela, and a strong supporter of the Central America Free Trade Association. For his part, Dionisio Gutiérrez, the other co-president, had supported a movement that forced a Guatemalan president to resign his post in the early 1990s.

Juan Arturo Gutiérrez, who with his sister and brother, the deceased Dionisio Gutiérrez, helped found Pollo Campero, was pursuing a lawsuit in the United States against his four nephews who controlled CMI. He claimed that when his firm, Panama-based Lisa S.A., sold its one-third interest in Pollo Campero, they had cheated him by misrepresenting the chain's earnings. Furthermore, he claimed that his nephews had compounded the fraud by transferring assets to U.S.-based entities such as Campero Inc. and Campero USA Corporation and to Miami banks in case he won his suit.

Robert Halasz

PRINCIPAL DIVISIONS

Energy; Finances; Industrial Animal Husbandry; Modern Milling; Multi Projects; Pollo Campero.

PRINCIPAL COMPETITORS

Grupo Roble; KFC Corporation.

FURTHER READING

Anderson, Curt, "Judge in Miami Sends Feud Back to Guatemala," *Houston Chronicle,* September 2, 2006, p. 2.

"Un CEO con alas," *AméricaEconomía,* October 6, 2006, p. 118.

Chase, Randall, "Judge Stays Delaware Lawsuit in Pollo Campero Family Feud," *Associated Press Newswires,* October 29, 2007.

Contreras, Joseph, "Juan Jose Gutierrez," *Newsweek International,* June 20, 2005.

Fonseca, Diego, "Los otros bolivariano$," *AméricaEconomía,* July 15–August 18, 2005, pp. 136–39.

Haddix, Dar, "Faces of Globalization: Pollo Campero," *UPI Perspectives,* August 13, 2004.

Inman, Crist, "A Central American Approach to QSR Development," *Cornell Hotel and Restaurant Administration Quarterly,* June 1998, pp. 75–80.

"Las mayores empresas del istmo," *ElPeriódico,* http://www.elperiodico.com.gt, October 1, 2007.

"Mas Markets," *Restaurants & Institutions,* December 1, 2007, p. 12.

Olvera, Jennifer, "Move over Colonel Sanders, Pollo Campero Has Arrived," *Arlington (Ill.) Daily Herald,* October 7, 2005, p. 23.

"The People Behind Pollo Campero," *Latin American Economic and Business Report,* September 6, 2005.

Tunarosa, Andrea, "Pollo Cowboy," *AméricaEconomía,* December 10, 2007, pp. 64–65.

Vega, Elena, "Locura por pollo campero," *Semana,* January 17, 2003, p. 4.

Velásquez, Doménica, "El vuelo de Campero," *AméricaEconomía,* July 9–29, 2004, p. 120.

Dairy Farmers of America, Inc.

10220 North Ambassador Drive
Kansas City, Missouri 64153-2312
U.S.A.
Telephone: (816) 801-6455
Web site: http://www.dfamilk.com

Cooperative
Incorporated: 1998
Employees: 4,000
Sales: $11.1 billion (2007)
NAIC: 311512 Creamery Butter Manufacturing; 311423 Dried and Dehydrated Food Manufacturing; 311511 Fluid Milk Manufacturing; 311513 Cheese Manufacturing; 311514 Dry, Condensed, and Evaporated Dairy Product Manufacturing

■ ■ ■

Dairy Farmers of America, Inc. (DFA), is a Kansas City, Missouri-based dairy marketing cooperate serving about 18,000 dairy farmers in 48 states. It markets more than 60 billion pounds of fluid milk each year (61.85 billion in 2007), about a third of the U.S. supply, through joint ventures and shared ownership in milk bottling plants. The organization produces ice cream through joint ventures with several processing companies, and also owns more than 20 manufacturing plants to produce bottled dairy beverages, infant formulas, cream, butter oil, cheese, and other dairy items. DFA-owned brands include Borden Cheese, Keller's Creamery, Hotel Bar, Mid-America Farms, Enricco and Jacobo cheese, and Sport Shake. Product development is conducted in Springfield, Missouri, at DFA's state-of-the-industry Technical Center. DFA is organized into seven regional "councils," each headed by a chief operating officer and party to joint ventures with area partners, while offering specific services and programs to its member farmers, including dairy risk management services, financing, quality assurance, health insurance, and retirement plans.

ORIGINS IN FOUR DAIRY FARMER COOPERATIVES

Dairy Farmers of America, Inc., became operational on January 1, 1998, the result of the merger of four major dairy cooperatives: Mid-America Dairymen; the southern division of Associated Milk Producers, Inc.; Milk Marketing, Inc.; and Western Dairymen Cooperative, Inc. This combination was part of a longer pattern of consolidation and regional realignment among dairy cooperatives. The driving force behind the creation of DFA was Mid-America and its influential chief executive officer, Gary Hanman.

It had been through a series of mergers of small dairy cooperatives that Mid-America took shape in the late 1960s. Three Missouri and Illinois co-ops—Sanitary Milk Producers, the Producers Creamery Co., and Square Deal Milk Producers—agreed to merge in 1966 to create the St. Louis-Ozarks Marketing Agency (SLOMA). It operated under Associated Dairymen, a two-year-old federated cooperative, part of a move to address regional, as well as local, differences within the dairy industry. While the SLOMA merger was being finalized in 1968, another Missouri co-op, Producers

COMPANY PERSPECTIVES

First and foremost, DFA is a cooperative that serves the milk marketing needs of its dairy farmer owners. The co-op also provides the kind of services that an organization of DFA's size can deliver without diluting its primary mission.

Creamery Company, and newly formed Mid-America Dairymen of Kansas City, were brought into the fold, and rather than using the nondescriptive name SLOMA, the members chose to adopt the Mid-America Dairymen name.

Responsible for bringing the 1,000-member Square Deal co-op into Mid-America was its manager Gary Hanman. Born on a farm near Browning, Missouri, in 1934, he was educated in one of the state's last one-room schools, accommodating eight grades. Married at a young age, he supported his family and worked his way through college as a welder and a busboy. After attending Kirksville State Teacher's College for a year, he enrolled at the University of Missouri–Columbia, majoring in general agriculture, his goal to return home to become a farm manager. A dairy professor persuaded him to focus on the dairy field and stay in school for a master's degree, which Hanman completed in 1956. He then went to work in the Federal Milk Market Administrator's office in St. Louis, remaining there until 1964 when, looking for a new challenge, he joined Highland, Illinois-based Square Deal, becoming the co-op's first outside chief executive. After Mid-America was formed, Hanman had hoped soon to rise to the top of the organization, but would be passed over before finally taking over day-to-day control, and 20 years would pass before he was named CEO.

HANMAN TAKES CHARGE OF MID-AMERICA

Mid-America grew further in the early 1970s through the addition of about a dozen co-ops, but the organization suffered from serious growing pains. In addition to struggling with an internal restructuring, the organization had to contend with changes in farm legislation that led to an antitrust suit being filed against it by the U.S. Justice Department. To make matters worse, feed was commanding record high prices while a weak economy dampened consumer demand for dairy products, resulting in low commodity prices. Although recording sales of $625 million in 1974, Mid-America lost almost $10 million. Hemorrhaging members, it was on the verge of bankruptcy. To deal with the crisis, the 41-year-old Hanman was promoted in 1975 to general manager. He quickly took steps to clean house, asking for resignations from several top executives and cutting jobs, while also selling the company aircraft and eliminating company cars. He also sold factories and restructured Mid-America's operating divisions. In just one year Hanman returned the co-op to profitability, netting $1 million.

After he successfully righted the ship, Hanman in 1976 formed a marketing subsidiary, Mid-America Farms, to establish a brand to compete against the likes of Land O'Lakes and Kraft, and reduce the co-op's dependence on commodity sales, which at the time accounted for about 82 percent of sales but only about a third of the profits. Mid-America Farms soon found its niche in food ingredient sales.

Mid-America reached the $1 billion mark in annual sales in 1982. The organization continued to grow through joint ventures, and in order to compete against corporate food producers it looked to grow even larger through strategic mergers. In 1986 discussions were held with a future DFA member, Associated Milk Producers Inc., but plans for a merger were scrapped because at the time structural differences were considered too difficult to reconcile. Not only were there boards and large memberships to consider as well as differing ways of paying farmers, the co-ops also had complicated deals with suppliers and customers that would have to be untangled. Mid-America had more success in 1987 when it forged an alliance with Land O'Lakes, creating a joint venture to share production and marketing responsibilities for milk and whey in southeastern Minnesota, an arrangement that provided savings in overhead for both partners. They then discussed the possibility of a merger, which would have resulted in the creation of a $4 billion company, but unable to work out the details, they abandoned the idea in the fall of 1989.

Becoming Mid-America's CEO in 1988, Hanman led the organization into the 1990s and a time of significant change. Mid-America was still overly dependent on its commodities business and subject to price swings. At the start of the decade, for example, an overabundant supply of milk and cheese on the market caused a loss of more than $6 million for Mid-America. Hanman responded by consolidating divisions to reduce head count and divesting some real estate assets and operating facilities. He also looked to pursue mergers aggressively with other co-ops in order to grow large enough to act as a countervailing force to the clout of giant, ever-expanding retailers, who used their heft to

KEY DATES

1968: Mid-America Dairymen formed.
1975: Gary Hanman becomes Mid-America's general manager.
1988: Hanman named Mid-America's CEO.
1995: Through a series of mergers, Mid-America nearly doubles in size.
1996: Mid-America and three other co-ops begin merger discussions.
1998: Dairy Farmers of America (DFA) formed with Hanman as president and CEO.
1999: DFA and Suiza Food Corporation merge northeastern dairy operations.
2001: DFA acquires 11 Suiza and Dean Foods plants through joint venture.
2005: Hanman retires.

force concessions from suppliers.

BORDEN TRADEMARK ACQUIRED BY MID-AMERICA

From 1994 into the early months of 1995 Mid-America completed five mergers, almost doubling in size. Then, in 1997, Mid-America paid $435 million to acquire Borden/Meadow Gold Dairies, Inc., from Borden, Inc., adding 27 processing plants in 11 states. It also received some much needed help in branding. Not only did it acquire the Meadow Gold, Viva, Lite Line, and Mountain High dairy products brand names, it also received a license to use the Borden and iconic Elsie the Cow trademarks on some dairy products.

While Mid-America was working on the Borden deal, the groundwork for DFA was being laid. In late 1996 the four co-ops that would merge to create DFA began discussing what would become the largest cooperative merger in the dairy industry. Their long-term goals were to secure stable milk markets and achieve greater profitability. Moreover, they wanted to create a marketing cooperative strong enough to provide dairy farmers with control over their futures, especially important because price supports that had provided some measure of security for the past half-century were about to be phased out. What Hanman feared, as he expressed to *Forbes* in a 1999 profile, was "the dairyman going the way of poultry farmers, squeezed by processors. Purdue or Tyson supplies the chick, the feed, the trucks. The farmer supplies the slave labor. Ditto for cattle ranchers, choosing now among just four major meatpackers. 'In most of American agriculture, there are no entrepreneurs,' Hanman fumes. 'There are no farmers, just factory workers.'"

Members of the four co-ops voted to create DFA in the final months of 1997 and the new marketing cooperative began doing business on the first day of 1998, with Hanman serving as president and CEO from DFA's new corporate headquarters in Kansas City, Missouri. With 22,000 dairy farmer members in 42 states split between six regional councils, DFA was the largest dairy co-op in the United States. It produced 33 billion pounds of milk each year, or more than one-fifth of the country's milk production, and boasted revenues of $6.9 billion. DFA was as much a food manufacturer as agricultural co-op, and had to determine when it was in the best interests of its members to act as a hard-bargaining supplier or as an aggressive marketer. For example, DFA co-ops were the major supplier of raw milk to the plants of Leprino foods while at the same time an old Mid-America entity was Leprino's chief rival in the sale of fast-food restaurant dairy products. Because Leprino possessed better mozzarella technology, DFA opted to act just as a supplier. An arrangement was made with Schreiber Foods in which DFA supplied the company with shredded natural cheese, while Schreiber served as a supplier of American cheese slices to DFA. In the fluid milk business, DFA members sold three-quarters of their Class I milk to bottlers while at the same time DFA supplied milk to joint bottling ventures. Although DFA agreed not to manage the milk plants, it retained the right to sell milk to affiliated bottlers as long as the price was competitive.

In its first full year in operation, DFA recorded revenues of $7.3 billion, making it the country's third largest agribusiness cooperative. It also took a major step to increase that number in late 1998 by agreeing to a joint venture with Suiza Foods Corporation to combine their northeastern dairy operations, creating a $1.2 billion dairy doing business under the Suiza Fluid Dairy Group name. The venture included the $500 million in sales of DFA's Tuscan and Leigh dairy businesses and Suiza's Garelick Farms unit, which had sales of $720 million. After the joint venture was completed in 1999, Suiza and DFA joined forces again, merging their southern California operations, combining Suiza's $120 million Swiss Dairy with DFA's $150 million Adohr Farms.

TROUBLES WITH THE JUSTICE DEPARTMENT

DFA continued to grow larger as the new century dawned. However, one of its deals drew the scrutiny of the U.S. Justice Department, which in 2000 sued DFA to prevent it from acquiring Sodiaal North America Corporation, a Pennsylvania-based butter manufacturer whose brands included Hotel Bar and Keller's, contending that the merger could result in higher butter prices for consumers in Philadelphia and New York City. The transaction was eventually completed after an agreement was worked out with the Justice Department. Because the new DFA entity, Keller's Creamery, LLC, and Land O'Lakes held a virtual monopoly over the branded stick and branded whipped butter markets in both Philadelphia and New York City, DFA agreed not to coordinate its marketing efforts or share competitively sensitive information with Land O'Lakes in order to protect the interests of consumers.

More joint ventures were to follow in the early years of the new century. In 2001 DFA through half-owned Dairy Holdings LP acquired 11 dairy plants from Suiza. A year later a joint venture, DairiConcepts, LP, was created between DFA and New Zealand Milk Products, the ingredient business of New Zealand's Fonterra Cooperative Group, to produce milk protein concentrate. DFA also acquired a half-interest in Southern Belle Dairy Corporation in 2002, again raising the ire of the Justice Department, which filed suit because it deemed the purchase anticompetitive and might adversely affect milk pricing in more than 100 school districts in Kentucky and Tennessee. This time DFA was unable to reach a settlement and turned over control to the joint venture's co-owner, but this maneuver did not satisfy Justice. Finally, in November 2006, DFA agreed to sell Southern Belle Dairy to Prairie Farms Dairy, Inc.

HANMAN RETIRES, DFA LOOKS TO THE FUTURE

The dairy economy was robust in 2004 and 2005, when DFA recorded revenues of $8.94 billion and $8.91 billion respectively. In November 2005, 71-year-old Hanman announced that he would retire at the end of the year. Succeeding him as CEO on January 1, 2006, was Rick Smith, who had been groomed for the job for the past year serving as DFA's president and chief operating officer. He was a seasoned dairy executive with 23 years of experience at Dairylea Cooperative, Inc. Initially serving as general counsel in 1982, he became CEO in 1988, a post he held until joining DFA in 2005.

As Smith took charge of DFA the dairy economy cooled off, leading to higher production costs and lower milk prices, resulting in a dip in revenues to $7.9 billion in 2006. In response DFA took steps to better control costs and evaluate underperforming assets. At the same time it was willing to invest in wholly owned processing facilities to drive sales with important customers. In keeping with this strategy, DFA in 2007 closed its Lovington, New Mexico, cheese plant, transferring production to other DFA plants. A Corona, California, plant that produced large-bag shredded and packaged American cheese was shut down, and its production transferred to Schreiber Foods through a new alliance.

Ed Dinger

PRINCIPAL OPERATING UNITS

Borden Cheese; Keller's Creamery; Hotel Bar; Mid-America Farms; Enricco and Jacobo; Sport Shake.

PRINCIPAL COMPETITORS

Kraft Foods, Inc.; Land O'Lakes, Inc.

FURTHER READING

Aven, Paula, "Dairy Cooperatives Will Vote in Nov. on Merger," *Denver Business Journal,* October 17, 1997, p. 7A.

Behrendt, Cathy, "Getting Personal: On the Record with … Gary Hanman," *Dairy Field,* September 1998.

Clark, Gerry, and Dave Fusaro, "$1.2 Billion Power Play," *Dairy Foods,* February 1999, p. 20.

Condon, Bernard, "Bet the Farm," *Forbes,* May 3, 1999, p. 66.

Fusaro, Dave, "The Big Three of Fluid," *Dairy Foods,* March 1998, p. 9.

Markgraf, Sue, "Dairy Farmers of America," *Dairy Foods,* April 1998, p. 69.

———, "Mighty Mid-Am," *Dairy Foods,* December 1997, p. 36.

———, "New Mega Co-op Ready for Business," *Dairy Foods,* January 1998, p. 16.

Martin, Andrew, "Dairy Insider Has Clout in Setting Prices," *Chicago Tribune,* December 30, 2004.

Delphax Technologies Inc.

6100 West 110th Street
Bloomington, Minnesota 55438
U.S.A.
Telephone: (952) 939-9000
Toll Free: (877) 335-7429
Fax: (952) 939-1151
Web site: http://www.delphax.com

Public Company
Incorporated: 1981
Employees: 286
Sales: $44.6 million (2007)
Stock Exchanges: NASDAQ
Ticker Symbol: DLPX
NAIC: 333293 Printing Machinery and Equipment Manufacturing

■ ■ ■

Based in Bloomington, Minnesota, Delphax Technologies Inc. is a leading digital printing equipment manufacturer. The company's digital printing presses, which rely on its patented electron-beam imaging (EBI) technology, are sold in approximately 50 countries worldwide. According to Delphax, its presses deliver "continuous roll-fed and cut-sheet throughput for publishers, financial and form printers, direct mailers and other commercial printers."

EARLY STRUGGLES

Delphax Technologies got its start in January 1981 when data card engineers Jack Drillick, Roger McCumber, and Burt Quint established Check Technology Corp. (CTC) in Eden Prairie, Minnesota. With McCumber serving as the company's first president, CTC set out to sell machines that banks could use to print their own checks, thereby adding a new revenue source. The idea seemed good, but it was not well received in the market.

As Todd Nissen wrote in the November 1989 issue of *Corporate Report Minnesota,* "Many banks already had check printing contracts with market giants such as Deluxe Corporation of St. Paul and John H. Harland Company of Decatur, Georgia, and were reluctant to change. ... Check Tech's high-speed machines were models of efficiency, but the company's first systems could only print the checks; collating and binding them into booklets had to be done elsewhere. The $200,000 price tag also did not make sales easy. After three years of trying, Check Tech had sold only one of its check printers to a U.S. bank."

The same *Corporate Report Minnesota* article provided a detailed description of the company's equipment during the 1980s, explaining: "The machines combine non-impact alphanumeric printers that produce letters, numbers, logos, and signatures with impact printers that produce two kinds of machine-read code lines: magnetic ink character recognition (MICR) or optical character recognition (OCR). (MICR and OCR figures are used by banks and the Federal Reserve to monitor check flow. Because of this, the quality of the codes is crucial, and groups such as the American Banking Association and the American National Standards Association have only approved codes printed with impact printers.)"

COMPANY PERSPECTIVES

Delphax Technologies, Inc., will proactively continue advancing our electron-beam imaging (EBI) technology to ensure innovative, high performance digital imaging solutions. This will empower our customers and achieve global market leadership positions in the markets we serve and support.

After shipping the first Checktronic system in 1982, CTC relocated its headquarters to Eagan, Minnesota, in 1983. The company's machines were received warmly overseas, where banks in France and Great Britain printed smaller check runs. Global expansion began in 1983 with the formation of Check Technology Ltd. (United Kingdom). In 1984, McCumber was succeeded as president by Everett Carter.

FINDING A GLOBAL MARKET

Following a net loss of $1.7 million in 1986, 43 percent of CTC's stock was acquired by investor Craig-Hallum Inc. The following year, the company's international footprint expanded via the formation of Check Technology Espana S.A. (Spain), Check Technology France S.A., and Check Technology Pty. Ltd. (Australia). It also was in 1987 that CTC established two new companies: GTI Holdings and GTI Ventures. CTC recorded its first profit in 1987, netting $664,000 on sales of $13.1 million. For the 1988 fiscal year, CTC lost $2.4 million on sales of $12.9 million.

During the late 1980s some of the company's poor financial performance was tied to encoded financial document joint ventures that never developed as expected. The ventures, formed in tandem with De La Rue Company plc, I.C. Security Printers, and MarTech Corp., produced "encoded" financial documents such as accounts payable and insurance claim checks that included magnetically readable numbers on them. Ventures such as these generated a $439,000 loss for CTC in 1988, according to *Corporate Report Minnesota.*

CTC's early years were marked by frequent leadership changes. In June 1989, Chief Financial Officer Jay Herman, a former Gelco executive, was named as the company's fifth president and CEO, succeeding Frederic Sweeny. Sweeny had succeeded William Adams only a year before. The company ended the 1980s with foreign sales representing some 76 percent of total sales, which totaled nearly $17.6 million in 1989.

SEEKING PROFITABILITY

By May 1990 CTC had recorded six profitable quarters in a row, and was focusing on new products such as a continuous-form check printer, which expanded the capabilities of its equipment beyond sheet-fed printers and presented the company with new market opportunities. A stitching and binding machine that allowed for the creation of finished checkbooks also was introduced at this time.

CTC continued to introduce a wide array of computer-controlled coupon- and check-printing equipment during the mid-1990s. The Model 400 Foliotronic and Model 300 Foliotronic Mark II printers were introduced in 1994. In April of the following year, CTC inked a deal with Delphax to use the latter's Gemini digital technology in the new Imaggia MG20 line of check printing systems it was developing. That year, CTC relocated again to Minnetonka, Minnesota.

After successfully completing beta testing in 1996, CTC shipped its first Imaggia MG20 system to Paris, France-based François-Charles Oberthur in 1997. A sale to Davis+Henderson Intercheques, Canada's largest check printer, followed in 1998. The company began doing business with its 48th country—the People's Republic of China—in 1997 when it sold a Checktronic 450OX document production system to the Beijing Banknote Printing Co.

A stock buyback initiative, authorizing the company to repurchase 500,000 shares of its common stock, was announced in September 1999. CTC ended the 1990s with a net loss of $1.6 million on sales of $22.3 million, down from a profit of $199,000 on sales of $23.7 million in 1998.

DEVELOPMENTS AT THE START OF THE 21ST CENTURY

CTC ushered in the new millennium by securing its first major multisystem order of Imaggia MG20 systems. In 2001, a prototype of CTC's Imaggia II—which the company claimed was the fastest digital cut-sheet printer available, capable of printing 300 pages per minute—as introduced at an industry trade show.

A number of other important developments occurred in 2001. In September, the company closed its Australian subsidiary. The following month, President and CEO Jay Herman was named chairman. By this time the company had some 430 printing systems in place in 50 countries. For the fiscal year ending September 30, CTC reported that its revenues had increased 49 percent from 2000, reaching $42.8 million, and net income totaled $2.1 million, compared to a net

KEY DATES

1980: Delphax Systems is formed as a joint venture between Dennison Manufacturing Co. and Canada Development Corp. (CDC).
1981: Check Technology Corp. (CTC) is formed in Eden Prairie, Minnesota.
1984: Xerox Corp. buys out the CDC share of Delphax Systems.
1997: CTC ships its first Imaggia MG20 system to Paris, France-based François-Charles Oberthur.
2001: CTC finalizes the $14 million acquisition of Delphax Systems from Xerox Corp.
2002: CTC changes its name to Delphax Technologies Inc.
2008: The quantity of paper printed with the Imaggia Digital Print System is estimated to have reached 10 billion linear feet, equivalent to 1.9 million miles.

loss of $290,000 the previous year.

On December 20, 2001, CTC finalized what Herman called one of the "most significant events in our company's history," when it acquired Toronto, Ontario, Canada-based Delphax Systems in a $14 million deal with Xerox Corp.

In a December 3, 2001, *PR Newswire* release, Herman elaborated on the deal, commenting: "It not only strengthens our position in our served markets, but it represents a giant step in implementing our strategic plan for increasing our opportunities for market penetration beyond the check and financial document segment and enlarging our revenue base.

"A major element of our business plan is to increase our installed equipment base and generate a steady and growing stream of service revenue that, over time, will far outweigh revenue from the sale of equipment itself. The combination with Delphax will move us much closer to that objective, while fundamentally strengthening our position as a global provider of digital imaging solutions for specialized printing and publishing."

DELPHAX SYSTEMS CORPORATE ROOTS

Delphax Systems had formed in 1980 as a joint venture between Avery Dennison Corp. predecessor Dennison Manufacturing Co. and Canada Development Corp. (CDC). Four years later, CDC was bought out of the venture by Xerox Corp. Then based in Westwood, Massachusetts, Delphax embarked upon a path of international expansion in 1986, at which time the company established a European arm in Wiesbaden, Germany.

Delphax began the 1990s by opening another international office in London. At that time, Olympus Corp. secured an ownership stake in the company, joining Avery Dennison and Xerox. The following year, Delphax introduced EBI, which became the main marking technology used by its printers.

The early 1990s were filled with a number of other significant developments at Delphax. Avery Dennison's Imaging Systems Division was acquired in 1991, adding the Presidax line of high-speed on-press printing systems to the company's product base. A direct sales organization was also formed that same year when Delphax struck a deal with Bull HN Information Systems to buy Bull Printing Systems' large printing systems assets. Delphax ended the year by relocating to Canton, Massachusetts.

Delphax introduced the ImageFast Series 850 LE in 1993, which was recognized as the fastest roll-fed electronic printing system in the world. That same year, international expansion continued with the formation of a sales and service office in Helsinki, Finland, to serve the Scandinavian market, along with a new subsidiary in Paris, France. By this time the company claimed to have garnered a quarter of the market for telecommunications billing.

Prior to being acquired by CTC, Delphax recorded several other achievements. These included the introduction of Gemini, which the company called the fastest 600 dpi digital print engine on the market. (DPI is short for dots-per-inch, and is a measure of how many dots of ink a printing press can reproduce in one square inch. More dots result in a picture that is of higher quality or resolution.) One final development was the introduction of a system called the Publishing Factory, which marked Delphax's entrance into the print-on-demand industry.

MOVING INTO THE FUTURE AS DELPHAX TECHNOLOGIES

In keeping with its broader focus, CTC changed its name to Delphax Technologies Inc. in April 2002. The company set out to capture a share of Canada's $6.4 billion printing market via a distribution and service agreement with DocuPartners Inc., and ended the year by consolidating North American manufacturing and engineering operations, which were all relocated to Mississauga, Ontario. Delphax ended the 2002 fiscal year with sales of $52.4 million, a 22 percent increase from the previous year.

What Delphax billed as "the world's first fully integrated solution for digital book-on-demand production," was selected, in April 2004, by Muller Martini for use in its digital publishing system; according to a *PR Newswire* release, the system could perform everything from printing to binding. The following year, Delphax's line of CR Series Digital Web Presses were accredited by the Association of Payment and Clearing Services, an organization overseeing payment industry standards. The development allowed the equipment's use for financial document printing.

In April 2006 Delphax's client base grew with the addition of printing giant R.R. Donnelley, which added the company's CR2000 digital roll-fed press to its Financial Services Business. The following month, Dieter P. Schilling was named as Delphax's new president and CEO, succeeding Jay Herman, and Kenneth E. Overstreet was named chairman.

In the wake of declining sales, Delphax announced plans to trim its workforce by 15 percent in September 2006, resulting in the elimination of 52 jobs. A year later, in November 2007, the NASDAQ notified Delphax that it was in noncompliance with listing requirements after the minimum bid price of the company's common stock stayed below $1 per share for 30 consecutive days. The NASDAQ gave Delphax until April 28, 2008, to correct the situation. In a November 2, 2007, *PR Newswire* release, CEO Dieter Schilling expressed hope that new long-term financing and sales staff would enable the company to improve.

A positive development in 2007 was the introduction of the company's new CR2200 digital press, which Delphax said had a production capability of 500 feet per minute, a new speed standard for toner-based digital printing presses.

Delphax began 2008 by announcing that its customers had produced 10 billion feet of printed material with the Imaggia Digital Print System since it was first introduced, an amount equivalent to 1.9 million miles. The milestone was a noteworthy accomplishment for Delphax as the company prepared for the 21st century's second decade.

Paul R. Greenland

PRINCIPAL SUBSIDIARIES

Delphax Technologies Canada Ltd.; Delphax Technologies Ltd.; Delphax Technologies S.A.S.; Check Technology Pty Ltd.

PRINCIPAL COMPETITORS

International Business Machines Corporation; Océ North America Inc.; Xerox Corporation.

FURTHER READING

"Check Technology Announces Agreement to Acquire Delphax Systems from Xerox; Transaction Will Provide Ownership of Key Technology and Entry to New Markets," *PR Newswire,* December 3, 2001.

"Delphax Technologies' Imaggia Digital Print System Reaches Production Milestone of 10 Billion Feet of Output," *PR Newswire,* January 9, 2008.

"Muller Martini Partners with Delphax for Fully Integrated Book-on-Demand Printing Solution; First-of-a-Kind System Will Be Unveiled Next Month at the World's Largest Print Industry Trade Show," *PR Newswire,* April 29, 2004.

Nissen, Todd, "A Checkered Past, Another Chance," *Corporate Report-Minnesota,* November 1989.

Devoteam S.A.

86 rue Anatole France
Levallois-Perret, F-92300
France
Telephone: (33 01) 41 49 48 48
Fax: (33 01) 41 49 60 70
Web site: http://www.devoteam.com

Public Company
Incorporated: 1995
Employees: 2,836
Sales: EUR 267 million ($367.7 million) (2006)
Stock Exchanges: Euronext Paris
Ticker Symbol: 73793 DVT
NAIC: 541512 Computer Systems Design Services

■ ■ ■

Devoteam S.A. is one of the fastest-growing information technology (IT) services company in Europe. The Levallois Perret-based company claims to lead the European market in the information systems consultancy and engineering sector. Devoteam specializes in developing services and solutions for the networking, e-business, and IT architecture needs of many of Europe's largest corporations. Founded as a provider of IT services for the telecommunications sector, Devoteam successfully diversified its operations following the telecom crash of the early 2000s.

The company operates in three primary areas: Professional Services and Projects, which generates 65 percent of group revenues; Consulting, adding 22 percent; and Operations, at 13 percent. The telecommunications industry accounted for just 24 percent of the group's revenues of EUR 267 million. The finance industry added 24 percent to revenues, while the public sector and services, and industrial markets each add more than 17 percent.

The company has expanded widely outside of France, with European subsidiaries in Belgium, the Netherlands, Spain, the United Kingdom, Switzerland, the Scandinavian countries, Austria, the Czech Republic, and Poland. Devoteam has also begun to position itself in the Middle East and North African market, establishing operations in the United Arab Emirates, Saudi Arabia, Jordan, Morocco, and Algeria. Together, Devoteam's international operations generate 35 percent of sales. Devoteam is listed on the Euronext Paris stock exchange. The company is led by brothers, cofounders, and co-CEOs Stanislas and Godefroy de Bentzmann. The de Bentzmann family controls more than 25 percent of the group's shares.

TELECOMS IT PIONEER IN 1995

The deregulation of France's telecommunications sector in the mid-1990s launched a competitive market for the first time. The appearance of new telecom players, including Bouygues and SFR, among others, also created a new need for IT services to support not only the new companies, but the fast-developing mobile telephone market as well.

In 1995, brothers Stanislas and Godefroy de Bentzmann, both graduates of France's prestigious INSEEC, decided to launch a company dedicated to providing IT services to the telecommunications sector. Godefroy de

COMPANY PERSPECTIVES

Devoteam collaborates with its clients to help them meet their business challenges: value creation, risk management, operational excellence and cost reduction. To solve these issues we bring expertise in five major areas: The competitive and regulatory environment or how to help IT departments meet the expectations of business units that have to constantly adapt their offerings to competitive and regulatory changes; Information system alignment or how to help IT departments to adapt to the complexities of business needs; this involves supporting the IT departments in managing existing and legacy systems; Resources, or how IT departments should meet a triple requirement: find suitable skills, have the volume to deliver and have resources available; IT risk management, or the demands on IT departments to implement risk metrics, procedures, architectures, disaster recovery plans, etc.; Budgetary constraints, or how to help IT departments to carry out their tasks within the budget allocated.

Bentzmann began his career in the sector in the early 1980s, while brother Stanislas entered the field in 1987. The brothers were joined by cofounder Guy-Hubert Bourgeois, then a division director and CEO of another IT group, Sigle Informatique.

The new company, called Devoteam, focused especially on the development of core networks for the new telecom groups. The company not only pioneered the market, but also, with few rivals capable of matching its own expertise, gained a clear leading position in that market segment.

By 1996, Devoteam was ready to extend its base of operations, adding capacity in the enterprise networks segment. Supporting the company's growth was a policy of hiring only graduates of France's top schools, guaranteeing the company a pool of the best talent in the country. The company's head count topped 20 employees in 1996, then more than tripled the following year.

EXPANDING SERVICES

The rise in head count supported Devoteam's next expansion, into the provision of consultancy services, in 1997. For this the company founded a new subsidiary, Devoteam Système (subsequently renamed Devoteam SI), to focus on the information systems architecture and management market segments. The addition of consulting services allowed Devoteam to round out its operations, with both downstream (solutions) and upstream (consulting) services.

Devoteam took a new leap forward in 1998, as the company added another area of operations—the development and integration of e-business applications for the rapidly growing Internet market. For this move, the company added a second subsidiary, Dataverse. The company's workforce once again grew to meet the company's new ambitions, nearing 250 employees by 1998. In the meantime, the company's revenues had also been growing, from less than the equivalent of EUR 1 million in 1996, to EUR 3.4 million in 1997, and again to EUR 13 million in 1998.

INTERNATIONAL GROWTH BEGINS IN 1998

With its position in France's telecom sector already strong, Devoteam eyed a more ambitious expansion onto the wider European market. The boom in the telecommunications and Internet sectors, as well as the launch of the euro, provided a new range of opportunities for the company. In order to prepare for its expansion, the company went public in 1999, listing its shares on the Paris Stock Exchange's Nouveau Marché.

Acquisitions formed the foundation of Devoteam's international growth strategy. The company's first purchase came that same year, with the acquisition of MSB in Belgium, a company that specialized in information systems management services.

Devoteam next turned to Spain, where it acquired a minority stake in Fringes. That company, with offices in Madrid and Valencia, provided Devoteam with new capacity in Internet architecture and infrastructure, especially the management of IP-based networks, an important category at the end of the 20th century. Fringes was also one of Cisco's major partners in Spain. By the middle of 2000, Devoteam had taken majority control of Fringes; it acquired the company outright in 2001.

By then, Devoteam had staked out a new market, the Netherlands, through the acquisition of that country's Mainland Sequoia. The purchase not only gave the company a presence in that new market, it also strengthened its consultancy operations, while adding a further EUR 10 million to its revenues. The company continued to invest in the market, buying Wap Research, a France-based group that specialized in consulting services, especially financial applications for

KEY DATES

1995: Brothers Stanislas and Godefroy de Bentzmann, with Guy-Hubert Bourgeois, found Devoteam to provide IT services to the newly deregulated telecommunications industry in France.
1999: Devoteam goes public on the Paris Bourse's Nouveau Marché and launches international expansion strategy through acquisitions.
2002: Devoteam becomes an IT services company, adding new acquisitions, including Siticom and Fitec.
2004: Company expands beyond Europe with entry into Middle East and North African markets.
2007: Devoteam expands telecom sector operations through purchase of auSystems in France.

the mobile telecommunications sector.

At the end of 2001, the group boosted its consultancy operations with the acquisition of XP Conseil. This new operation also provided the company with its expertise in information systems security, a sector growing swiftly with the rollout of broadband Internet and high-speed mobile telephone technologies. These purchases enabled the group's revenues to grow dramatically, jumping past EUR 66 million in 2000, and over EUR 108 million by the end of 2001.

SURVIVING THE TELECOMS CRASH

Devoteam remained a highly focused company at the beginning of the 21st century. The telecommunications sector continued to represent more than 45 percent of the group's total sales. Yet the company's reliance on a single industry proved to be a detriment when the telecommunications sector crashed at the beginning of the 2000s.

With spending in the sector sharply reduced, Devoteam's growth slipped for the first time since it had been founded. Sales crept ahead through 2002, growing to EUR 136 million. By the end of 2003, the group's revenues had actually dropped, back to EUR 126 million, despite the company's continued stream of acquisitions.

At the same time Devoteam's acquisition drive, especially its strategy of developing international operations, formed a major part of its successful survival. Traditionally focused on single markets, and for most of its history dominated by state-controlled monopolies, the European telecommunications market became one of the world's most active at the turn of the century. A series of major acquisitions, mergers, and partnerships had broken down national barriers, and the first multinational telecom giants, such as Vodaphone, Orange, Deutsche Telekom, and others had begun to emerge.

Devoteam recognized the importance of strengthening its international presence. The company went in search of a major partner, and in early 2002 reached an alliance agreement with France's Siticom Group. That company was a major player in the European telecom and e-business infrastructures market, with operations in six countries. Shortly after the alliance agreement, Devoteam acquired majority control of Siticom. The addition of Siticom also gave the company control of Fischer & Lorenz, based in Denmark, and Austria's OSIconsult.

GROWTH IN THE UNITED KINGDOM IN 2002

Devoteam took additional steps to fill out its own multinational offering, particularly in the important U.K. market. The company had opened an office there in the late 1990s, while expanding its presence through Fischer & Lorenz's U.K. operations. In 2002, however, the company made a full entry into the United Kingdom, when it acquired FrontRunner Solutions Ltd. Founded in 1995, FrontRunner had become a major Cisco partner in the United Kingdom before extending its own operations into Germany in 2000. Following its acquisition by Devoteam, FrontRunner was renamed Devoteam UK; the company then took over the U.K.-based consulting operations from Siticom.

Devoteam's expansion had given it a pan-European presence and a position among the leaders in the telecommunications-based IT market. The company restructured its holdings into two core divisions, Solutions (downstream) and Consulting (upstream). At the same time, the company worked to achieve greater synergies from its expanded operations, enabling the company to lower its breakeven point. In this way the company maintained its profitability despite a drop in revenues.

DIVERSIFIED IT SERVICES OFFERING

Devoteam's acquisition drive during the bottoming out of the technology sector was another factor in the group's survival strategy. While Devoteam had earlier maintained focus on its position as a telecom specialist, the company moved to develop a wider range of operations as an IT services group. The company began developing business among other sectors, such as the Finance and Services industries. The company's sales once again began to move forward, topping EUR 150 million by the end of 2004. By then, the telecoms market accounted for just 34 percent of the group's sales.

The company had in the meantime continued to add new operations. The company bought Fitec, the France-based IT services subsidiary of the United Kingdom's Colt Telecom, in December 2003. The company also acquired two other Colt subsidiaries in France, Apogée Communications and Asthèa Ingenierie.

NEW INTERNATIONAL MARKETS 2004–06

At the beginning of 2004, Devoteam turned toward new geographic horizons and launched a subsidiary in Dubai. This came as part of the group's wider interest in the Middle East and North African markets. By the end of 2006, the company had extended its operations to include Saudi Arabia, Jordan, Morocco, and Algeria. The company also strengthened its presence in Eastern Europe, adding an office in the Czech Republic.

Back in France, the company bought Paris-based Cesmo, adding its IT consulting operations. The company then acquired SRIT, an integration specialist based in Lannion, with a strong partnership with Siemens. In 2005 the company expanded its operations again, adding IT outsourcing services capacity through a partnership with Pierre Fabre Informatique (PFI). As part of that partnership, Devoteam acquired a 51 percent stake in PFI. The company also bought Netherlands-based Ficie that year.

Devoteam remained on the lookout for new acquisition opportunities. The group solidified its Scandinavian presence with the purchases of Quaint, in Sweden, and daVinci, in Norway. The company also turned to the Benelux, adding Guidance, in Belgium, giving it an entry into Luxembourg. In the United Kingdom, the company acquired Tertio SMS. Lastly, the group expanded its North African presence with the purchase of Morocco's MIT, enabling the company to enter the 3G mobile network market there.

POSITIONED FOR FUTURE GROWTH

The company's active round of acquisitions helped boost its revenues to EUR 267 by the end of 2006. Yet the company showed no sign of slowing down in its drive to become one of Europe's largest IT services groups. The company completed a number of new deals in 2007, not least of which was the purchase of France's auSystems. That company added its expertise in the telecoms sector with a strong international presence, particularly in Italy, and revenues of more than EUR 50 million.

Devoteam continued to adapt its offering as well. In May 2007, the company created a new dedicated division, Enterprise Architecture Management, a move designed to enhance the company's profile in this major IT services segment. Under the leadership of the de Bentzmann brothers, Devoteam had emerged from the shadows to become one of the European IT industry's driving forces in the new century.

M. L. Cohen

PRINCIPAL SUBSIDIARIES

Devoteam Belgium S.A./NV; Devoteam Fischer and Lorenz A/S; Devoteam Nederland B.V.; Devoteam OSI-consult GmbH; Devoteam SRIT S.A.S.; Devoteam UK.

PRINCIPAL COMPETITORS

Vivendi S.A.; Thales S.A.; Cap Gemini S.A.; Thales Group; VINCI Energies S.A.; Philips France S.A.S.; Compagnie IBM France S.A.S.; Groupe Steria S.C.A.; MSX International SARL; Sopra Group S.A.; Atos Origin Integration SAS; GFI Informatique S.A.; Groupe Open S.A.

FURTHER READING

Capalar, Luc, "Devoteam Rachete daVinci," *Decision Distribution,* January 23, 2006.

"Devoteam Acquires Dutch Consultants Mainland Sequoia," *European Report,* November 22, 2000, p. 600.

"Devoteam Buys Colt Software Unit," *Computergram International,* December 23, 2003.

"Devoteam Tumbles After EU111m Issue," *Euroweek,* December 1, 2000, p. 22.

"Falling Share Price Threatens Devoteam EU140m Secondary," *Euroweek,* November 17, 2000, p. 21.

Kapko, Matt, "Nokia Siemens Offloads R&D Center," *RCR Wireless News,* September 24, 2007, p. 32.

"Nokia Siemens Devoteam Deal," *Total Telecom Online,* September 19, 2007.

Sicat, Armelle, "Devoteam poursuit sa croissance," *Decision Distribution,* May 28, 2007.

———, "Devoteam fait l'acquisition de Guidance," *Decision Distribution,* October 9, 2006.

ROSSMANN

Dirk Rossmann GmbH

Isernhägener Strasse 16
Burgwedel, D-30938
Germany
Telephone: (49 5139) 898-0
Fax: (49 5139) 898-4999
Web site: http://www.rossmann.de

Private Company
Incorporated: 1972 as Rossmann KG
Employees: 15,500
Sales: EUR 2.45 billion ($3.4 billion) (2007 est.)
NAIC: 446110 Pharmacies and Drug Stores

■ ■ ■

With over 1,270 outlets, Dirk Rossmann GmbH is Germany's third largest drugstore chain. Rossmann Central Europe B.V. is the company's Eastern European arm that operates more than 570 stores in Poland, Hungary, and the Czech Republic, generating about EUR 700 million in revenues annually. With the exception of pharmaceuticals, which in Germany are sold exclusively through *Apotheken,* the German term for pharmacies, consumers find an entire range of products at Rossmann drugstores, from vitamins to health food, from household chemicals to cosmetics, from baby care to cat food, from candy to alcoholic beverages. Rossmann markets its own range of more than 40 store brands. Roughly 1.2 million shoppers order via the company's online store. Headquartered in Burgwedel near Hannover, the company is majority-owned and managed by company founder Dirk Rossmann and his family. A.S. Watson Group holds a 40 percent stake in the company.

GERMANY'S FIRST DISCOUNT DRUGSTORE

When Dirk Rossmann, the son of a druggist, was growing up in post–World War II Germany, the world of drugstores still followed traditional rules. His father ran the small drugstore his grandfather had founded in Hannover in 1910. The modest profits yielded by the family business were barely enough to support his parents, grandparents, himself, and his older brother. After his father's early death, however, the then 11-year-old quickly had to come up with creative ideas to support his family financially. He went from door to door in his neighborhood and offered once-a-week home delivery of goods from the drugstore. He soon attracted a number of customers, and the number grew steadily. According to an agreement he had made with his mother, Dirk Rossmann could keep 10 percent of the sales he made delivering everything from soap to cough drops to his customers' doors on his bicycle. After graduating from school in 1960, Rossmann completed a four-year vocational training program as a druggist. At the same time he continued his delivery service business, which often grossed up to ten times more than the family drugstore. At the age of 16 he was able to buy a two-bedroom condominium from the proceeds of his small enterprise, where he and his mother lived for many years. The young man carefully saved all extra cash so that one day he would be able to open his own drugstore.

COMPANY PERSPECTIVES

In the drugstore sector we want to be the hunter, not the hunted.—Dirk Rossmann, CEO.

In the late 1960s the fixed price laws for brand-name products, which had kept retail prices fairly high while still allowing smaller drugstores like the Rossmann family's to survive, came under massive public pressure in Germany. At that time, Dirk Rossmann realized that the days of the traditional drugstore would soon be over and he decided that the time had come to put his idea of a new kind of drugstore into practice. In addition to the DEM 20,000 he had saved over the years for this purpose, his seed capital consisted of a personal loan from a neighbor—an older woman who entrusted to him her life savings of DEM 42,000—and a small bank loan. Rossmann's concept was simple and clear: generate high sales volumes by increasing store size and by attracting customers with low prices, while keeping costs as low as possible. The 25-year-old hired five of his friends and together they went to work. They rented and renovated the store, contacted wholesalers, ordered and picked up the goods, and stocked the shelves they had built themselves.

On May 17, 1972, Rossmann's *Markt für Drogerieewaren,* as his drugstore was called, opened its doors in Hannover's city center. Consumers embraced the self-service discount idea and stormed the shelves of Germany's first drugstore supermarket, filling their shopping baskets with products from Procter & Gamble, L'Oréal, Johnson & Johnson, Colgate-Palmolive, and Nestlé, among others, for about one-half to one-third the prices they were used to. The store was so crowded that in addition to the two regular cashiers, customers were checked out using simple adding machines and cash boxes to manage the long checkout lines. At the end of the day, Rossmann had grossed roughly DEM 20,000—ten times the amount he had expected.

MASSIVE ADVERTISING, ADDITIONAL STORES, AND RAPID GROWTH

Right from the beginning, Rossmann invested heavily in advertising, which contributed in a major way to his quick success. He placed whole-page ads in *Hannoversche Allgemeine Zeitung,* the city's daily newspaper, comparing manufacturers' recommended prices with Rossmann's discounted prices—a novelty at the time for a drugstore. The sharp price difference not only attracted many shoppers from Hannover, but also from the neighboring cities. In addition to advertisements, Rossmann ran special promotions to attract customers. For example, in 1972 he offered customers a rebate on a new toothbrush if they brought their old toothbrushes to the store. A large container had been filled with old toothbrushes when city authorities stopped the promotion. In 1974 Rossmann sponsored a Hannover-based singer-songwriter, who in return wrote the "Rossmann Song," a pop hymn that praised in four verses everything from the broad selection to the friendly staff. Of the 10,000 records produced, 90 were given to Rossmann's employees while the rest were given away to customers. Although not commercially successful at the time of its launch, the recording later became a collector's item. Early on, Rossmann created his first store brand of inexpensive sparkling wine, which became a standby.

Encouraged by the overwhelming success of his first drugstore supermarket, Dirk Rossmann used the incoming cash to open additional stores. In the beginning, new stores were set up in Hannover. Later, Rossmann expanded into other northern German cities such as Braunschweig, Hamburg, and Bremerhaven. By mid-October 1974, there were eight Rossmann stores and his staff had almost doubled from 45 in 1973 to 85 one year later. In 1976 Rossmann headquarters were moved to a former warehouse in Burgwedel near Hannover. In that same year, the first electronic data processing system, an IBM System 32, was purchased for processing store orders.

In the mid-1970s the number of new Rossmann stores grew at a tremendous pace. In 1976 alone, one new store was opened almost every week in northern German cities, the region Dirk Rossmann had chosen to focus his efforts. Renting, renovating, stocking, and opening a new store took a matter of three days at most. The company founder left store design up to the newly hired staff. There were no rules or guidelines, except one: "Do it fast!" Working conditions for Rossmann's employees, young people who ranged from truck drivers to fashion designers, were as improvised as the stores they ran. Office furniture was built from empty cartons and inventory was piled up to the ceiling on pallets. Everyone had to know how to do everything.

Opening days were the biggest challenge for Rossmann and his staff. Trucks with additional merchandise were parked in side streets around the new store to be able to refill shelves as quickly as possible. Sometimes stores were so crowded that additional personnel started selling products directly from the trucks. One opening

KEY DATES

1972: Dirk Rossmann opens Germany's first discount drugstore in Hannover.
1976: Rossmann headquarters are moved to Burgwedel.
1984: The company starts selling luxury perfumes at discounted prices.
1990: The first two Rossmann outlets in Eastern Germany are opened.
1993: Rossmann expands into Poland and Hungary.
1996: A joint venture with Dutch health and beauty chain Kruidvat for expansion to Eastern Europe is established.
1997: The company's first store brands Babydream and Sun-Ozon are launched.
1999: Rossmann opens online drugstore.
2000: More than 90 Idea drugstore outlets are taken over from Rewe Group.
2002: Kruidvat Beheer B.V. acquires a 40 percent stake in Rossmann.
2005: Rossmann acquires kd Kaisers Drugstore GmbH with 300 outlets from Tengelmann.
2007: German drugstore chain Kloppenburg GmbH & Co. KG is taken over by Rossmann.

day, when checkout lines crowded the store, Dirk Rossmann switched to "intuitive scanning." He looked at what customers had in their shopping baskets and quoted them a rounded-off, flat price on the spot. He would ask, for instance, "Would 20 marks for all of this be okay with you?" His new customers gladly accepted.

ADDITIONAL CAPITAL AND UPSCALE COSMETICS BOOST SALES

After an amendment in Germany in 1974 abolished the law that forbade drugstore owners to sell brand products below the manufacturers' recommended prices, the number of discount drugstores rose quickly. By 1982, the year of Rossmann's tenth anniversary, the company had grown to 100 outlets with about 700 employees, grossing some DEM 170 million per year. In addition, there were about 1,400 other discount drugstores in Germany. However, the rapid pace of growth in the mid-1970s had stretched Rossmann's financial resources to the limit. He found a financial investor, Hannover Finanz GmbH, a subsidiary of one of the world's largest reinsurers, Hannover Re. Hannover Finanz became a limited partner in Rossmann's enterprise and gave it a healthy capital boost of DEM 2 million to begin with, in exchange for a 30 percent share in the company and 10 percent of the profits. The influx of fresh capital and a reputable business partner for backing gave Rossmann the credibility he needed to launch his next coup.

To stay ahead of the growing competition, Rossmann took another bold step in 1984, when he decided to sell luxury brand-name perfumes and cosmetics at his stores. At that time, to preserve exclusivity and to ensure high profit margins, perfume manufacturers gave only a limited number of retail stores in Germany access to their upscale product lines. These specialized perfume stores signed contracts with manufacturers that guaranteed them exclusive distribution rights in a certain sales territory on one hand, but on the other hand, obliged them to guarantee an appropriate store design and qualified personnel, to carry items that were not as popular along with bestsellers, and most importantly, to sell these products at manufacturers' recommended prices. Perfume manufacturers also restricted stores to buying from a few general importers that received limited amounts of merchandise. The system had guaranteed healthy profits for those involved for many years, but Dirk Rossmann was ready to claim his share of the market.

Rossmann invested DEM 6 million in the complete remodeling of 50 stores and equipped them with special perfume sections where everything from Aramis to Yves St. Laurent was appropriately presented in polished and well-lit glass display cases behind a glass counter. The expensive merchandise was purchased from wholesalers in France, Belgium, Switzerland, and the Netherlands, who were paid in cash when the goods were received. The company's central warehouse in Burgwedel was enlarged to hold additional product, and 50 cosmeticians were hired to ensure competent customer service at Rossmann's new perfume sections.

In the fall of 1984, Rossmann opened luxury perfume sections in about half of his stores, most of them in larger cities such as Hamburg and Hannover. Rossmann's perfume departments carried about 700 different items at 10 to 20 percent less than in specialized perfume and department stores. While this caused bad industry press and resulted in several dozen legal battles—most of which were finally resolved in Dirk Rossmann's favor—German shoppers embraced the idea. Most popular were Rossmann's monthly special promotions, where consumers eagerly snatched up their favorite brand of *eau de toilette,* perfumed cream, lotion, or makeup from Chanel, Dior, Lancaster, or Rubinstein for up to 40 percent less than usual. The perfume shops drew new customers to the Rossmann stores and at the same time made buying brand-name cosmetics more attractive for regular Rossmann customers who would otherwise not shop at upscale perfume stores. The perfume business, which was run by Dirk Rossmann's wife Alice, generated an additional 10 percent in sales at half of Rossmann's outlets. Similar experiments with clothes, toys, and stationery were not nearly as successful and were therefore abandoned.

GEOGRAPHIC EXPANSION DRIVES FURTHER GROWTH

The sudden opening of the Berlin Wall also opened a new chapter in the history of Rossmann. After West Germany's hard currency had been introduced in Eastern Germany in June 1990, East Germans were eager, willing, and able to buy all the goods from the West, which many of them knew only from magazine or television advertising. Rossmann's potential market had grown by at least 20 percent almost overnight—an opportunity that the company founder seized quickly. On July 2, 1990, the first Rossmann store in the former Eastern German states was opened in Sondershausen, Thuringia. In 1991 and 1992 Rossmann conquered the East German market in a concerted action, the same way he had done it in the West before. Overseen by the newly founded subsidiary Rossmann Ost GmbH, based in Sondershausen, a total of 120 Rossmann stores were set up within two years. Their number more than doubled again within the next couple of years. In 1994 the company built a large distribution center to service the 260 Rossmann outlets in Eastern Germany. Rossmann's expansion, however, did not stop at the Eastern German border.

The year 1993 marked the company's first step abroad when it entered the Eastern European market. The first Rossmann stores outside of Germany were established in Lódz, Poland's second largest city, and in Debrecen, the second largest city in Hungary. Three years later the company teamed up with the Dutch health and beauty chain Kruidvat and founded R&R Oost Europa B.V., a joint venture for further expansion into Eastern Europe. By 1997, the company's 25th anniversary year, there were 499 Rossmann outlets, 55 of them in Poland, Hungary, and the Czech Republic, generating DEM 980 million in annual revenues.

GOING ONLINE

The advent of the Internet opened another sales channel for Rossmann. In 1999 the company opened Germany's first online drugstore supermarket, run by the new subsidiary Rossmann Online GmbH. Starting out with about 8,000 items in 1999, the store grossed more than DEM 8 million, about as much as four Rossmann stores, in its first year. In 2000 the company followed up with a 150-page mail-order catalog containing 3,500 basic items for potential customers who did not have a Rossmann store in their neighborhood and had no access to the Internet. Customers were able to choose the day of the week on which the merchandise was delivered to them at no extra shipping cost. Rossmann's range of products shipped to customers' homes was greatly expanded in 2005 when the company began cooperating with Deutsche Internet Apotheke, an online pharmacy offering prescription and nonprescription drugs at comparably low prices.

Throughout the 1990s Rossmann also continued to expand the range of products offered at the company's stores. In the 1970s, a Rossmann store carried about 1,700 items. By the end of the 1980s there were 5,000 items for sale. In the late 1990s, some 9,000 items were on display at a typical Rossmann store. For example, as the first rush for products from the West had cooled down in Rossmann's Eastern German stores, customers there started asking for the familiar products they used to buy before East and West Germany were reunited. Rossmann responded by adding about 200 products from East Germany, from baby food to cosmetics to laundry detergent, to its shelves.

A major step toward further increasing the company's earning power was the introduction of Rossmann's own store brands. In 1997 the company launched a line of baby food products under the brandname Babydream and a number of sun care products under the label Sun-Ozon. In the next two years, Rossmann invested heavily in the development and marketing of 22 additional store brands for everything from household cleaning products under the Domol brand to Perlodent toothpaste, including a total of about 520 items. High ratings from German consumer reports in the first years of their launch gave Rossmann's store brands an additional marketing boost.

ACQUISITIONS IN THE 21ST CENTURY

With the advent of the new millennium, Rossmann's growth was accelerated by a series of acquisitions. In order to be the undisputed market leader in northern Germany, Dirk Rossmann convinced large retail chains that he was able to run chain drugstores more efficiently and profitably than they could. In 2000 the company took over more than 90 Idea drugstore outlets from German retail group Rewe, all located in northern Germany. Three years later Rossmann sealed a deal with the German Tengelmann Group, another large retail conglomerate. Rossmann acquired 69 of Tengelmann's

Kaiser's Drugstore kd drugstore outlets in northern Germany and took over the management of the remaining 320 stores in the western and southern parts of the country, with the option to take over these outlets in the future as well. Between October 2003 and July 2005, all kd drugstore supermarkets were remodeled and reopened as Rossmann stores. In 2005 Rossmann formally acquired Tengelmann's drugstore subsidiary, kd Kaiser's Drugstore GmbH, with about 300 outlets. Finally, in November 2007 Rossmann announced the takeover of Kloppenburg GmbH & Co. KG, a regional drugstore chain in northwestern Germany, with 163 outlets in northern Germany and approximately EUR 290 million in annual sales. Kloppenburg became a new Rossmann subsidiary and, for the time being, the company's outlets kept their name, but Rossmann's store brands and other best-selling items were added to their range of products.

In addition to the acquisition of roughly 550 new stores, Dirk Rossmann, who by the early years of the new century had given up the idea to limit his activities to northern Germany, expanded in other regions as well, focusing on major cities. In May 2003, the 75th Rossmann outlet was opened in Berlin, where the company had become the most popular drugstore chain within ten years. In the following year, new stores were opened in Frankfurt am Main and Munich, and in the Ruhr. To handle the massive additional business volume, Rossmann invested heavily in expanding its logistics network. New distribution centers were set up in Landsberg near Halle in central Germany, in Berlin, and in Lódz, Poland. The company's main warehouse complex at Burgwedel headquarters was significantly enlarged.

In summer 2002 longtime investor Hannover Finanz sold its 38 percent share in Rossmann to Kruidvat Beheer B.V., the company's longtime joint venture partner, by then one of Europe's top three drugstore supermarket chains with revenues of about EUR 3.8 billion. Dirk Rossmann sold an additional 2 percent to Kruidvat, which was acquired by A.S. Watson, the retail and consumer division of the Hong Kong-based conglomerate Hutchison Whampoa Ltd., in 2002. Rossmann kept a 60 percent share in his company. By 2007 Rossmann Central Europe ran over 275 Rossmann outlets in Poland, almost 200 in Hungary, and more than 100 in the Czech Republic, grossing more than EUR 700 million annually. With solid financial backing, further expansion in Germany and Eastern Europe seemed to be the most promising growth strategy for Rossmann.

Evelyn Hauser

PRINCIPAL SUBSIDIARIES

Rossmann Online GmbH; Rossmann Logistik GmbH; Kloppenburg GmbH & Co. KG (Germany; 89.8%); Rossmann Central Europe B.V. (Netherlands).

PRINCIPAL COMPETITORS

Fa. Anton Schlecker, dm-Drogerie Markt GmbH + Co. KG; Beauty Alliance Deutschland GmbH & Co KG; TopCos GmbH; Parfümerie Douglas GmbH; Kaufhof Warenhaus AG; Hertie GmbH; Karstadt Warenhaus GmbH.

FURTHER READING

"A.S. Watson Acquires 40 Percent Stake in Rossmann," *Europe Intelligence Wire,* August 26, 2004.

"Chemist Chain Rossmann Cuts Loss in CzechRep to Kc2.6m in 2005," *Europe Intelligence Wire,* August 13, 2006.

"Discount erobert die edle Welt der Düfte," *Lebensmittel Zeitung,* December 7, 1984, p. F4.

"Fines Imposed on Two Companies for Price Fixing," *Cosmetics International,* February 23, 2007, p. 7.

Fries, Tanja, "Zukauf stärkt Rossmann im Norden," *Lebensmittel Zeitung,* December 7, 2007, p. 6.

Gillies, Peter, "Einfach mal angefangen," *Welt am Sonntag,* September 27, 1998.

"Hutchison Whampoa steigt bei der Drogeriekette Rossmann ein," *Frankfurter Allgemeine Zeitung,* August 26, 2004, p. 15

Kemper, Klaus, "Der erste 'Drogeriemarkt' war seine Idee," *Frankfurter Allgemeine Zeitung,* June 30, 1980.

"Parfüms zu Discountpreisen ein 'Bombengeschäft,'" *Frankfurter Allgemeine Zeitung,* February 15, 1985.

"Rossmann Acquires 69 kd Drugstores," *European Cosmetic Markets,* September 2003, p. 319.

"Rossmann Appeals Against Cartel Authority," *Europe Intelligence Wire,* March 12, 2007.

"Rossmann Enters into Agreement with Tengelmann," *Europe Intelligence Wire,* April 5, 2004.

"Rossmann Hoping to Gain Ground on DM," *Europe Intelligence Wire,* April 6, 2006.

"Rossmann to Take Over KD Completely on May 1," *Europe Intelligence Wire,* March 5, 2005.

Dolan Media Company

1200 Baker Building
706 Second Avenue South
Minneapolis, Minnesota 55402
U.S.A.
Telephone: (612) 317-9420
Fax: (612) 317-9434
Web site: http://www.dolanmedia.com

Public Company
Incorporated: 1992
Employees: 1,192
Sales: $111.6 million (2006)
Stock Exchanges: New York
Ticker Symbol: DM
NAIC: 511110 Newspaper Publishers

■ ■ ■

Dolan Media Company is a leading information services company. From its headquarters in Minneapolis, Minnesota, the company serves customers in the legal, financial, and real estate industries throughout the United States. Operating in approximately 20 markets nationwide, Dolan Media's Business Information division operates a variety of different publications, from court and commercial newspapers to business journals. In addition, the division offers web sites and events in connection with its printed publications. According to Dolan Media, each of its publishing franchises is considered a platform that is used to present market-specific business information products. Dolan Media's Professional Services division concentrates on the legal industry via American Processing Company (APC), a mortgage default processing services provider, as well as Counsel Press, which is the largest U.S. appellate services provider.

FORMATIVE YEARS

Dolan Media's roots date back to May 1992, when Jim Dolan, an award-winning journalist turned New York investment banker, established the company in partnership with Cherry Tree Investments. Dolan's career had started with a stint as a political reporter for the *San Antonio Express-News.*

According to the company, Dolan, who handled acquisitions for Rupert Murdoch's News Corp. after his journalism career, wanted to get back in the media business, and Cherry Tree wished to invest in an information business. After exploring possible investments for several years, Dolan and Cherry Tree finally discovered the right opportunity in *Finance and Commerce,* a daily business newspaper based in Minneapolis that served as the starting point for their new enterprise.

After acquiring *Finance and Commerce* in January 1993, Dolan Media embarked upon the acquisition path, with Jim Dolan serving as president and CEO. According to the June 10, 1994, issue of *Minneapolis-St. Paul CityBusiness,* Dolan Media doubled in size during its first year, and then tripled in size the following year.

Dolan was attracted to court and commercial newspapers because of their loyal subscriber bases, which made maintaining circulation easy. By early 1994 the company had added several publications to its lineup,

COMPANY PERSPECTIVES

The most concise way to summarize what we do at Dolan Media Company is this: We help our customers use information to succeed.

including another Minnesota publication titled *Appellate Courts Edition;* a national journal called *Nathan's Legal Markets;* and the *Daily Reporter,* a 97-year-old legal newspaper based in Milwaukee, Wisconsin.

In addition, Dolan Media offered a database of legal information gleaned from courthouses throughout the Midwest. According to the company, during its formative years Dolan Media made several efforts to sell public records data. Because of technical challenges, these early efforts proved difficult.

Profits in this business line eventually resulted when the company teamed with a public records research business named Heartland Information Services. Together, the companies acquired Minnesota Secured Transaction Reports and U.S. Secured Transaction Reports from St. Paul, Minnesota-based PLS Inc. in January 1995. A new business named Heartland Corporate Services LLC was established to operate these two enterprises.

By early 1995 Dolan Media had a staff of 180 people that ran 12 publications from offices in three cities. In January, the company acquired Baltimore, Maryland-based Longbranch Publishing Co., which offered publications such as *Maryland Family Law Monthly.* By this time, the five-figure investment Cherry Tree Investments had made to start Dolan Media had allowed the company to grow into an enterprise with revenues of more than $10 million. The company rounded out the year by launching *UCC & Lien Report,* a monthly publication connected with *Finance and Commerce* that listed UCC (Uniform Commercial Code) filings with the Minnesota Secretary of State, bankruptcy court filings, and state and federal tax liens.

GROWTH AND EXPANSION

After investing in new technology such as scanners and computers for digitizing public records, in the summer of 1996 Heartland Corporate Services moved from a location near the Minnesota state capitol to the Minnesota Building in downtown St. Paul. By this time the company claimed to serve virtually every major law firm and bank in the state.

Dolan Media's employee base continued to grow, reaching 225 in late 1996. By then the company's offerings had expanded to include approximately 50 print and electronic information products. As Dolan Media acquired legal and commercial newspapers in new markets, many of which were well-established publications that had been in the ownership of the same families for several generations, the company added related business newsletters aimed at the same market-specific readership. For example, a publication covering the oil and gas industry was created in Oklahoma City, Oklahoma. The company also began producing directories that listed the names of attorneys, court personnel, and construction firms.

During the late 1990s, Dolan Media expanded its offerings in the state of Wisconsin by acquiring the *Madison Business Journal,* adding to its Milwaukee-based publications, the *Daily Reporter* and *Wisconsin Opinions.* With the *Madison Business Journal* came sister papers in Pueblo and Colorado Springs, Colorado. In the 1998 fiscal year, Dolan Media's sales increased 38 percent, and profits climbed 54 percent, nearing the $50 million mark. By this time the company had 46 shareholders and had raised some $28 million through seven private placements.

Toward the decade's end, Dolan Media's empire had grown to include more than 100 business, construction, and legal publications in 17 different markets. These included the *Daily Record and Kansas City Daily News Press,* which was acquired in September 1999.

DATABASE FOCUS

It was at this time that Dolan Media made the first of several deals that would bolster its database businesses, collectively known as The National Group. In November 1999, the company struck an extensive, long-term data licensing deal with Omaha, Nebraska-based infoUSA, which allowed each company access to information from the other's databases. Dolan Media gained access to records on some 200 million individuals and 12 million businesses throughout the United States, while infoUSA gained access to 75 million public records from Dolan Media. The agreement involved infoUSA making a small equity investment in Dolan Media. In addition, Dolan Media agreed to pay a licensing fee to infoUSA. Beyond the immediate benefits, the deal set the stage for future product development initiatives.

Dolan Media ushered in the 21st century with another major deal on the electronic information front. In January 2000, the company acquired Oklahoma City, Oklahoma-based Hogan Information Services Co. from

KEY DATES

1992: Jim Dolan establishes Dolan Media in partnership with Cherry Tree Investments.
1993: The company acquires *Finance and Commerce,* its first publication.
2003: Dolan Media sells its database businesses, known collectively as The National Group, to Reed Elsevier plc's LexisNexis unit.
2007: The company's IPO, one of the largest in Minnesota history, generates more than $195 million from the sale of 13.5 million shares; Dolan Media begins trading on the New York Stock Exchange under the symbol DM.

First Data Corp. The acquisition was especially significant because Hogan was the largest public records gatherer in the United States.

Hogan's database of 75 million public records, which included everything from bankruptcies and civil judgments to federal, state, and county tax liens, was then growing at a daily rate of 50,000 records, thanks to a staff of 300 correspondents in 30 states, as well as systems to capture some records electronically.

Founded in the 1980s as the public records department of the *Journal Record,* a business newspaper in Oklahoma City, Hogan Information was made a sister firm to Banko, Dolan Media's bankruptcy information arm. In a January 6, 2000, *PR Newswire* release, James Dolan said Hogan would become the company's main national public records gathering and processing arm.

The National Group grew again in September 2000, when the Acollaid line of credit screening databases was acquired from Conway, Arkansas-based Acxiom Corp. In addition to Banko and Hogan Information, by this time The National Group—headed by Group President Brian K. Long—also included an identity theft prevention service named Identity Guardian, a probate information database called Probate Finder, and a document delivery service named Banko Document Retrieval. Dolan Media ended the year by establishing Dolan Information to oversee these businesses. James D. Farnham, a veteran of the credit industry, was named as president of the new group, reporting to Brian Long.

Acquisitions continued in 2002. On the traditional publication front, the 95-year-old *Colorado Springs Daily Transcript* was acquired from the Pioneer Printing & Publishing Co.'s Bernheim family. Around the same time, a minority stake was acquired in GovDocs, Inc., a company that provided web-based services to state and local governments.

Midway through the year, James Dolan was one of eight people to receive the Ernst & Young Entrepreneur of the Year Award for the Minnesota, North Dakota, and South Dakota region. By this time the company was operating a business-to-business Internet portal named Clickdata.com, which combined information from some 200 different sources with its own news and information.

In early 2003, Dolan Media's Journal Record Publishing Co. acquired Oklahoma Stateline, an online capitol news service, which it merged with *Oklahoma Business News* and renamed *Journal Record Legislative Report.* A related multimedia service was also introduced, which was the sole provider of real-time audio simulcasts of state legislative proceedings. The company also acquired the 92-year-old *Daily Journal of Commerce,* which was the South's largest daily construction newspaper.

A major development unfolded in mid-2003 when Dolan Media sold The National Group to Reed Elsevier plc, which added the operations to its well-known LexisNexis unit. Included in the sale were the businesses of Dolan Information, Dolan's U.S. Corporate Services business, and Clickdata.com. In all, some 200 employees were impacted by the sale of Dolan's public records arm, which was to be renamed LexisNexis Public Records Services.

CONTINUED RAPID GROWTH

Growth continued through the middle years of the decade, beginning with the September 2004 acquisition of 14 legal newspapers and web sites, with a total circulation of almost 93,000, from Lawyers Weekly Inc. for $33.4 million in cash. Early the next year, New York-based Counsel Press was acquired, giving Dolan Media the largest appellate services business in the nation.

In May 2005, electronic and print publisher Arizona News Service was acquired, giving Dolan Media several new publications and services, including the daily *Arizona Legislative Report;* the weekly *Arizona Capitol Times;* and an electronic legislative news service called Legislation On Line Arizona. In September, the company sold Greene & Associates, its business-to-business teleservices business, in a management buyout. By the year's end, Dolan Media had sales of roughly $100 million and employed approximately 800 people in 21 states.

In 2006 Dolan Media's revenues, which had climbed 116 percent in only two years, reached $111.6

million, with a net loss of $20.3 million. That year, the company formed a new business in conjunction with the Michigan law firm Trott & Trott P.C. Named American Processing Company LLC, the business was formed from Trott & Trott's existing default processing operations and aimed to provide law firms around the country with mortgage default processing services.

In March of the following year, the *Mississippi Business Journal* was acquired in a deal with Venture Publications. By this time Dolan Media had become one of the largest public notices carriers in the United States. In addition, it ranked as the country's second largest court and commercial publisher, as well as the third largest business journal publisher. In all, Dolan Media's publication holdings had grown to include about 60 titles.

In April 2007, Dolan Media filed for its initial public offering (IPO), indicating that it hoped to raise approximately $150 million. The IPO, which took place on August 1, was one of the largest in Minnesota history, generating more than $195 million from the sale of 13.5 million shares. The company's proceeds totaled $138 million from the sale of 10.5 million shares, with the remaining 3 million shares being sold by existing shareholders. Dolan Media began trading on the New York Stock Exchange on August 2, under the symbol DM. By early September, the company's stock had achieved a return rate of 38 percent.

Heading into 2008, Dolan Media was experiencing especially strong growth from its Professional Services Division, which the company attributed to its mortgage default processing business. In February, the company added another publication to its lineup after acquiring the *Mecklenburg Times,* a Charlotte, North Carolina-based court and commercial newspaper. Like others before it, the acquisition was but one example of the steady, measured growth that Dolan Media had pursued since acquiring its first publication 15 years before.

Paul R. Greenland

PRINCIPAL SUBSIDIARIES

American Processing Co.; Arizona News Service; Colorado Publishing Co.; Counsel Press; Daily Record Co.; Finance and Commerce Inc.; Kansas City Daily Record Co.; Lawyers Weekly Inc.; Long Island Commercial Review Inc.; Mississippi Business Journal; New Orleans Publishing Group; Oklahoma City Legal Ledger Inc.; Portland Legal Communications Corp.; St. Paul Daily Journal of Commerce Inc.; The Daily Record Co.; The Daily Reporter Publishing Company Inc.; The Idaho Business Review Inc.; The Journal Record Publishing Company Inc.; The Mecklenburg Times.

PRINCIPAL DIVISIONS

Business Information; Professional Services.

PRINCIPAL COMPETITORS

American City Business Journals Inc.; American Lawyer Media Holdings Inc.; MediaNews Group Inc.

FURTHER READING

"Dolan Media Acquires Major Public Records Company Hogan Information," *PR Newswire,* January 6, 2000.

"Dolan Media Forms New Processing Company with Trott & Trott," *PR Newswire US,* May 24, 2006.

Gilyard, Burl, "Finance and Commerce's Parent Company Goes Public," *Finance & Commerce,* August 3, 2007.

Kennedy, Patrick, "Dolan Media Gains from Mortgage Mess," *Star Tribune,* September 7, 2007.

Maler, Kevin, "IPOs Have Lost a Lot of Charm," *Minneapolis-St. Paul CityBusiness,* June 10, 1994.

DRAFTFCB

Draftfcb

633 North St. Clair Street
Chicago, Illinois 60611
U.S.A.
Telephone: (312) 944-3500
Fax: (312) 944-3566
Web site: http://www.draftfcb.com

Wholly Owned Subsidiary of the Interpublic Group of Companies, Inc.
Incorporated: 1978 as Kobs & Brady Advertising
Employees: 9,000
Revenues: $941.2 million (2006 est.)
NAIC: 541810 Advertising Agencies

■ ■ ■

Draftfcb is one of the top advertising agencies in the world, with operations in 110 countries and *Fortune* 500 clients such as Kmart, Citigroup, Qwest Communications, and Upjohn. The firm offers a wide range of services that include branding, advertising, direct and relationship marketing, and promotions. Draftfcb was created in 2006 by parent Interpublic Group through a merger of marketing specialist Draft and ad agency Foote, Cone & Belding. The firm is headed by Howard Draft, the longtime CEO of the firm that bore his name.

ORIGINS

Draftfcb was formed in 2006 by the merger of ad agency Foote, Cone & Belding and marketing services firm Draft. The latter traces its roots to 1978, when a marketing agency called Kobs & Brady was founded in Chicago as an outgrowth of Marshall John Advertising, which had in turn been created in 1963 by Bankers Life & Casualty Co. from direct-mail marketer Phillips & Cherbo. Under principals Marshall Edinger and John Egan, and with the backing of Bankers Life owner John D. MacArthur, Marshall John grew to encompass a printing operation, mailing list company, and marketing agency, with billings peaking at $15 million in the early 1970s.

When Edinger and Egan decided to retire, they recruited Jim Kobs from Chicago's top direct-marketing agency, Stone & Adler, who took the job with the provision that the agency become independent of Bankers Life, move to new quarters downtown, and be seen as a new agency, rather than a continuation of Marshall John. Although John D. MacArthur died during final negotiations and transfer of ownership was held up for several years by his estate, on April 1, 1978, Kobs & Brady Advertising opened on North Michigan Avenue. The agency's second namesake was Senior Vice-President Tom Brady.

The new firm had a dozen employees including Howard Draft, a philosophy and art history graduate of Ripon College in Wisconsin whom Kobs had originally recruited to Stone & Adler. Although the firm continued to work for Bankers Life, it quickly added other clients, doubling its billings to $26 million and boosting its staff to 60 by 1982. That year saw the exchange of ownership completed, with Kobs becoming majority shareholder.

COMPANY PERSPECTIVES

We are in the business of building business. We do it by transforming strategy, creativity and analytics into brilliant business-building ideas that have the greatest probability of selling our clients' products and building their brands.

In October 1982 the firm opened a New York office in partnership with Ted Bates Advertising, whose space it would share. Howard Draft was assigned to run the new operation, and it blossomed under his leadership, growing larger than the Chicago home office in less than two years. Starting with Bates client HBO, Draft boosted the firm's work with *Fortune* 500 companies such as Avis, Chesebrough-Ponds and Philip Morris. Unlike many in the field, Howard Draft viewed direct advertising as an integrated part of a modern ad campaign rather than a separate endeavor.

Howard Draft's success in New York brought him the titles of president and chief operating officer in 1986, when he returned to Chicago to grow the original agency. As he had done in New York, he began seeking large clients that would engage the firm on a contract basis, rather than for single projects. Kobs & Brady was by this time the sixth largest direct-marketing company in the United States with $70 million in billings.

FIRM BECOMES PART OF SAATCHI EMPIRE

The agency's rapid growth brought it many suitors including top ad firms like Leo Burnett, McCann-Erickson, and J. Walter Thompson, and in 1986 it was sold to Ted Bates Worldwide, Inc., for $10 million. Within six weeks Bates itself was acquired by advertising giant Saatchi & Saatchi.

The firm subsequently moved its Chicago staff of 100 to new quarters, and on April 1, 1988, exactly ten years after the founding of Kobs & Brady, its name was changed to Kobs & Draft. When Saatchi executives proposed moving Kobs to Europe to oversee development of operations there, he balked, taking a leave of absence before departing to found Kobs Gregory Passavant.

With Chairman and CEO Howard Draft fully in charge, the firm began opening small offices in foreign markets. A Spanish office had opened in 1987 and others were soon added in the United Kingdom, Canada, France, Germany, Norway, Australia, and Hong Kong under the leadership of Dan Ginsburg, who was subsequently named president of Kobs & Draft's global operations. Some were established via links with units of Bates (by then known as Backer Spielvogel Bates). New accounts of this period included the U.S. Mint, for which the firm was tapped to create a campaign to promote U.S. Congress Bicentennial commemorative coins; AT&T's international calling service; and Resorts International. Billings then stood at $120 million, a third of which was from foreign accounts.

Expansion to Asia proceeded in 1990 and 1991 with offices added in Malaysia, Singapore, and Thailand through mergers with Saatchi units. Kobs & Draft at that time was ranked the fifth largest marketing agency in the world.

In late 1991 Saatchi & Saatchi merged all of its international direct-marketing operations into Kobs & Draft, which boosted billings to $350 million. New York-based Saatchi & Saatchi Direct would remain independent initially, although it was later folded into the firm. Top clients included Time Warner, British Airways, and Primerica Financial Services.

In the early 1990s the agency continued its international expansion to Latin America and added clients such as Sprint Consumer Services Group, Dahlberg, Inc.'s, Miracle Ear brand, and Interactive Networks. New offices were also opened in Israel and Indonesia.

Saatchi & Saatchi was encountering financial difficulties at that time, and curtailed its expansion, and in December 1994 Howard Draft offered $22 million to buy the agency back. After eight months of negotiations with new Saatchi holding company Cordiant (during which Draft was offered the job of Saatchi CEO), a deal was struck to sell the firm for $27.2 million.

In September 1995 the again independent agency was renamed Draft Direct Worldwide. Total billings at that time stood at $500 million, and the firm employed 600 at 29 offices around the world. Draft Direct would be the world's largest independent direct-marketing agency.

During 1995 a new healthcare marketing unit called Draft Direct Healthcare Marketing Services was established to handle the Rogaine brand for Upjohn, and the firm added the $50 million account of CML Group's Nordic Track brand.

SALE TO INTERPUBLIC GROUP IN 1996

Though Howard Draft had long sought the independence the buyback brought, suitors were rife

KEY DATES

1873: Daniel Lord founds ad agency in Chicago, later known as Lord & Thomas.
1943: Lord & Thomas becomes Foote, Cone & Belding.
1978: Kobs & Brady direct-marketing agency founded in Chicago.
1988: Kobs & Brady, a part of Saatchi & Saatchi, becomes Kobs & Draft.
1995: Kobs & Draft bought by Howard Draft, renamed Draft Direct Worldwide.
1996: Draft sold to Interpublic Group.
2001: Foote, Cone & Belding becomes part of Interpublic Group.
2006: Interpublic merges Draft into Foote, Cone & Belding to create Draftfcb.

and in March 1996 the firm accepted an offer from Interpublic Group (IPG), the world's third largest advertising conglomerate after the WPP Group and Omnicom. The price was 1.8 million shares of IPG, then worth over $100 million, which eliminated the debt generated by the buyout and gave Draft and other senior executives handsome paydays.

With the backing of IPG, Draft quickly began making acquisitions, in 1997 buying D.L. Blair, Marketing Corp. of America, Lee Hill, Inc., and general ad agency Adler Boschetto Peebles & Partners. The four had combined billings of $400 million, which when added to Draft's own internal growth put the agency's total at more than $1.3 billion by the end of 1997. The firm's gross revenues stood at $141.8 million.

Late 1997 also saw the firm shorten its name to Draft Worldwide and move to new quarters in Chicago, near where Howard Draft had opened a restaurant and jazz club called 56 West. The firm had nearly 40 offices around the world and clients that included American Express, Bell Atlantic, Sprint, and the U.S. Postal Service.

Under the leadership of Jonathan Radnor, who had joined the firm in 1997 and was named president and chief operating officer of global operations in March 1998, Draft's acquisitions continued with the July purchase of Kevin Berg & Associates Marketing of Chicago, an event marketing specialist with clients such as Coca-Cola, Audi, Nike, and General Motors that had billings of $120 million. August saw the company buy M & V Gmbh of Germany, with billings of $78 million and clients including Volvo and Finland Tourism. Draft also continued to add accounts on its own, winning the $60 million U.S. work of Compaq Computer.

In late 1998 and early 1999 the firm bought Synthese Marketing of France, the Karamba Group of Belgium, Marketing Principles of the United Kingdom, and the Gingko Group of Canada. In May DRS Advertising of London was added and several months later Draft purchased an agency called Strategic Solutions. By the end of the year billings were estimated at $2.7 billion and the payroll had grown to 2,500 in 25 countries. Draft Worldwide was by then the largest direct-marketing agency in the United States.

The firm made its biggest deal to date in the spring of 2000 when it acquired a 55 percent stake in Peter Arnell's 20-year-old AG Worldwide of New York, London, and Tokyo, a brand strategy and advertising agency whose clients included Tommy Hilfiger, Donna Karan, and Banana Republic. The purchase would bring with it AG's digital marketing unit Surge Interactive.

In the summer of 2000 Draft also bought Group III Promotions and an e-business firm called Capita Technologies of Chicago and absorbed the IPG unit Lowe Lintas Columbian of Chicago. In September the company created a new division called Draft Digital to handle interactive technology, combining its Marketing Technologies division and its Internet strategy and design unit. Another Canadian firm, Fuel Technologies, was also acquired during September. Fall saw Verizon name Draft and Zenithmedia, Inc., as its advertising media buying agencies of record. For 2000 the firm had revenues of $285 million.

Howard Draft believed it was important to operate in an open manner with clients. The firm had for years been informing them about the number of staffers working on their accounts and their salaries, agreeing to a profit margin that each considered reasonable. A typical profit might be 20 percent of a total budget, with a bonus sometimes provided if the return was greater than anticipated. With new technological advances the firm was leaving the world of direct mail behind, using data mining to better target consumers and new media formats to develop more up-to-date pitches. A new concept called consumer relationship marketing was being utilized as well to build consumers' relationships with a brand and inspire long-term loyalty.

In early 2001 Burger King named Draft as its global promotion and merchandising agency for billings estimated at $150 million. The firm also formed a joint venture in Tokyo with several other agencies called Draft Worldwide Commons KK. In April Verizon awarded its $400 million-plus account to Draft and sister IPG agency Lowe Lintas & Partners. Draft had first begun working for Verizon six years earlier.

PROMOTIONS UNIT SURGE CREATED IN 2001

In May 2001 AG founder Peter Arnell bought back Draft's stake in his branding agency while selling the remainder of Surge Interactive. The latter was soon merged into the Draft Digital unit, while the company used the Surge name to bundle promotion subsidiaries KBA Marketing, Group 3, and Lee Hill, Inc., to form Surge at Draft Worldwide, under the leadership of Lee Hill. The growing field of promotion and event marketing services by this time accounted for about half of the Chicago office's revenues, and the move was expected to help streamline the experience of clients that included Burger King, Kellogg Co., R.J. Reynolds, and Sprint. A few months later a subunit, Premium Surge, was created to design and manufacture contest premiums.

In June 2002 Draft's U.K. office and sister IPG unit Lowe Live merged in a bid to boost the company's profile in the United Kingdom. With the weakened economy halting expansion plans, their chief architect Jonathan Radnor moved up the ladder to join IPG. Draft by this time had 60 offices in 29 countries and billings of $3.6 billion. During the year Quest Communications and Coors Brewing Company also began working with the agency.

In March 2003 the firm reached an agreement to form a global alliance with IPG unit Lowe Worldwide called Lowe & Draft. The two agencies would work together to pitch proposals and share back-office functions. Draft Worldwide shortened its name to Draft, and also renamed its digital unit Draft Data to reflect an ongoing shift to database and analytical services. The firm's efforts to expand overseas were not always as successful as its U.S. operations, however, and during the year its office in Edinburgh, Scotland, was shuttered. Owner IPG was also suffering from the effects of a number of poorly realized mergers and faulty accounting practices at that time.

In 2004 Draft created a unit that would market products to African Americans for client Bank of America, and in early 2006 Draft New York head Laurence Boschetto was named president and chief operating officer of global operations.

DRAFTFCB CREATED IN JUNE 2006

Though it had been assumed by some that Draft and Lowe would eventually merge, in June IPG announced that Draft would be combined with advertising agency Foote, Cone & Belding (FCB) to create Draftfcb. FCB, founded in 1943 but with roots dating to 1873, was one of advertising's most storied names, a full-service ad agency whose offerings would complement those of direct-marketing and database analysis experts Draft. Over the years FCB had been responsible for such industry icons as Planters' Mr. Peanut, the U.S. Forest Service's Smokey Bear, and Clairol's "Does she ... or doesn't she?" campaign, with top clients then including S.C. Johnson, Qwest Communications, Boeing, KFC, and Applebee's. FCB had become a part of IPG in 2001 and by this time had some 7,000 employees at 194 offices in 110 countries worldwide.

After the merger FCB head Steve Blamer would depart, with Howard Draft named to lead the merged organization as CEO and Laurence Boschetto continuing to serve as president and COO while the far-flung operations of the two companies were combined. The firms had some competing accounts, and FCB client Qwest Communications (a competitor of Draft client Verizon) was later shuttled to a newly created affiliate called Rivet, which was headed by Draft veteran Yvonne Furth. Over the next few months, work from both Verizon and Qwest diminished, however.

On October 15 the merger appeared to pay off in a major way when Draftfcb was chosen for the $570 million Wal-Mart account. The company was shocked less than two months later, however, when Wal-Mart announced it was reopening bidding for the work, after irregularities in the selection process had surfaced and two key Wal-Mart executives were dismissed. Draftfcb was asked not to participate in the new search, which was ultimately won by another IPG unit, the Martin Agency. For 2006 the firm had revenues estimated at $941.2 million.

Draftfcb rebounded in April 2007 when Kmart awarded the firm its $200 million account and it also won the $40 million Kraft Lunchables assignment. In addition to handling Kmart's print, television, and radio ads, the firm would perform customer relationship marketing to build loyalty among regular shoppers. In July Draftfcb announced it was cutting 50 jobs in New York after losing the account of Verizon, but in September the $200 million job of promoting the 2010 U.S. Census was secured. Several other specialized agencies would be asked to assist.

The loss of Verizon was tempered in December 2007 when Qwest Communications announced it would return its $95 million account to Draftfcb after shifting it for a time to McClain Finlon. In January 2008 the firm also won the U.K. account of Chevrolet and formed a new healthcare communications unit called Area 23. A sports and event marketing division, 361 Experiential, had been added as well. Both were formed by merging existing Draftfcb units.

With a long and storied history behind it, Draftfcb looked toward the future with a stable of major clients such as Kmart, Qwest Communications, and the U.S. Census. A team of seasoned industry professionals including Howard Draft and Laurence Boschetto headed the firm, and with the backing of top-three advertising conglomerate Interpublic Group, it appeared to be on a solid foundation for future growth.

Frank Uhle

PRINCIPAL SUBSIDIARIES

Draftfcb Healthcare; Draftfcb Chicago; Draftfcb New York; Draftfcb West Coast; Draftfcb London; 361 Experiential; Area 23.

PRINCIPAL COMPETITORS

Leo Burnett Worldwide; JWT; BBDO Worldwide; DDB Worldwide; TBWA Worldwide; Grey Worldwide; Ogilvy & Mather; Young & Rubicam; McCann Worldgroup; Lowe & Partners.

FURTHER READING

Baar, Aaron, "Direct from Chicago … It's Howard Draft!" *Adweek,* June 5, 2006.

Baar, Aaron, and Andrew McMains, "It's Official: Census to Draftfcb," *Adweek,* September 6, 2007.

Beardi, Cara, "Draft Surges Ahead with New Division," *Advertising Age,* June 18, 2001, p. 73.

Creamer, Matthew, "Draft Takes Command, Upends Old World Order," *Advertising Age,* June 5, 2006, p. 1.

Dougherty, Philip H., "Ted Bates Acquiring Kobs Unit," *New York Times,* March 10, 1986.

"Draft Has Big Plans in Asia, Goes on Acquisition Trail," *New Sunday Times,* February 4, 2001, p. 12.

Elliott, Stuart, "For an Agency, Life After Wal-Mart Is Called Kmart," *New York Times,* April 18, 2007, p. C3.

———, "In a Twist on the Consolidation Trend, a Direct-Marketing Concern Is Acquiring a General Agency," *New York Times,* August 6, 1997, p. D9.

———, "Interpublic Continues its Spate of Major Takeovers with Acquisition of Draft Direct Worldwide," *New York Times,* May 17, 1996, p. D6.

Gianatasio, David, "Qwest Selects Draftfcb," *Adweek,* December 14, 2007.

Helm, Burt, and David Kiley, "Wal-Mart Leaves Draft Out in the Cold," *BusinessWeek Online,* December 8, 2006.

Hume, Scott, and Kevin McCormack, "First Draft: Kobs & Draft Joins CME with a Buyback Bid," *Adweek Eastern Edition,* March 6, 1995, p. 1.

Kemp, Ed, "Chevrolet Awards UK Business to Draftfcb," *Marketing,* January 30, 2008.

Kiley, David, "Mad Ave's Man of the Hour," *BusinessWeek,* November 13, 2006, p. 42.

Laidlaw, Jennifer, "Interpublic Units Win Big Verizon Advertising Account," *Reuters News,* April 3, 2001.

Maddox, Kate, "Boschetto Heads Up Draftfcb," *B to B,* October 9, 2006, p. 12.

McDonough, John, "Draft at 20," *Advertising Age,* January 26, 1998, p. C1.

Millman, Nancy, "Kobs & Brady to Grow, Change as Kobs & Draft," *Chicago Sun-Times,* March 29, 1988, p. 57.

O'Leary, Noreen, "Wal-Mart Debacle Still Casts Shadow," *Adweek,* April 2, 2007.

Sampey, Kathleen, and Andrew McMains, "A Model for the Future or a Doomed IPG Merger?" *Adweek,* June 5, 2006.

Sanders, Lisa, "Draft Dealt Staggering Blow After Strutting Like a Champ," *Advertising Age,* December 11, 2006, p. 1.

DTE Energy

DTE Energy Company

2000 Second Avenue
Detroit, Michigan 48226-1279
U.S.A.
Telephone: (313) 235-4000
Fax: (313) 235-6743
Web site: http://www.dteenergy.com

Public Company
Incorporated: 1903 as Detroit Edison Company
Employees: 10,527
Sales: $9 billion (2006)
Stock Exchanges: New York
Ticker Symbol: DTE
NAIC: 221122 Electric Power Distribution; 221112 Fossil Fuel Electric Power Generation; 551112 Offices of Other Holding Companies

■ ■ ■

DTE Energy Company manufactures and distributes fossil fuel, hydroelectric, and nuclear energy. The company's largest subsidiaries, Detroit Edison and MichCon, provide energy and/or gas services to more than three million customers in Michigan, accounting for over half of Michigan's residents. DTE also owns over 840 miles of pipeline in 29 states for the transport and distribution of fossil fuels and owns a number of subsidiary companies involved in energy trading, transportation and the sale of unconventional gas products. With revenues exceeding $9 billion in 2006 and total assets in excess of $23 billion, DTE has grown rapidly during the first decade of the 21st century to become one of the largest energy supply companies in the nation.

ORIGINS

Electric companies sprang up throughout the United States after Thomas Edison's development of electric lighting in 1879. In Detroit alone, Brush Electric Light Company, Fort Wayne Electric Company, Commercial Electric Light Company, Detroit Electric Light and Power Company, Edison Illuminating Company of Detroit, and Peninsular Electric Light Company all simultaneously existed. Edison Illuminating had been formed on April 15, 1886, to supply alternating current to homes and businesses; and Peninsular Electric Light Company had been formed on June 16, 1891, to operate Detroit's street lights. It was not long before competition became so fierce that the less successful companies were swallowed up, and Peninsular Electric Light Company and Edison Illuminating were all that remained.

On January 1, 1903, Detroit Edison's founders purchased the securities of the Edison Illuminating Company and the Peninsular Electric Light Company and on January 17 The Detroit Edison Company was incorporated with Edison Illuminating as a subsidiary. For financial reasons, incorporation took place in New York rather than Michigan. Charles W. Wetmore became the company's first president and remained in that position until 1912. Detroit Edison's first general manager, Alex Dow, came to the company from its predecessor Edison Illuminating.

COMPANY PERSPECTIVES

More and more people look to DTE Energy every day to help turn their dreams into reality. They have good reason; DTE Energy helps them fuel the engine of progress.

At the time of the company's founding, Detroit Edison's customer base was larger than the company's supply capabilities. The first objective, therefore, was to increase generating and distribution capacity. In 1904, Detroit Edison finished construction on the Delray power house with two turbine generators together producing over 6,000 kilowatts of energy. The population of Detroit continued to grow, and the company was forced to add two additional turbines to the Delray power house in 1905 and again in 1906.

In 1905 Detroit Edison began to expand through acquisition in addition to construction. Among its purchases were Washtenaw Light and Power Company, Michigan Milling Company, and Ann Arbor Agricultural Company, making Detroit Edison the owner of the Argo, Barton, Geddes, and Superior generating dams on the Huron River. On July 24, 1906, the company formed a wholly owned subsidiary, Eastern Michigan Edison Company, which became the holding unit for the company's Huron River subsidiaries.

BUILDING NEW POWER SOURCES

As the company continued to suffer from insufficient supply, construction began on a second power station at Delray with a turbine capable of generating 14,000 kilowatts. The new turbine, completed in 1907, was a success but only temporarily alleviated supply issues. Two more 14,000-kilowatt turbines were added in 1910 and 1911 and the company's research and development division began looking into new technological developments to increase production capabilities.

In 1912 Dow became president of Detroit Edison. During his tenure Detroit Edison grew substantially. In 1913 a 15,000-kilowatt turbine was added to the new power house at Delray, and Detroit Edison began to construct a power plant at Conners Creek. For roughly the first decade of Detroit Edison's existence (the period ranging from 1903 until 1915) the company's subsidiary Edison Illuminating Company distributed, sold, billed for, and collected on, the energy produced by its parent, Detroit Edison. In 1915, under Dow, Detroit Edison began to serve its customers directly from the Connors Creek plant. Edison Illuminating survived as a company handling the parent company's real estate. Also in 1915, the company put two of the Conners Creek facility's three 20,000-kilowatt units into service, with the third becoming operational in 1917.

The Detroit Edison Company's generating capacity continued to grow under Dow, and in 1919 the company bought Port Huron Gas and Electric. In 1920 a 30,000-kilowatt generator was added to the plant at Delray. In 1922 Detroit Edison completed its first in suburban Marysville. Detroit Edison put its second at Trenton Channel in Trenton in July 1924. The Trenton Channel plant burned powdered coal, a technical innovation at the time, but also a process that tended to pollute the air because powdered coal is burned while suspended. Detroit Edison was aware of this fact and consequently equipped the plant, the first of its kind to use these pollution control devices, with electrostatic precipitators.

In addition to expanding its generating capacity, Detroit Edison expanded its service area. By 1929 the company supplied more than 4,582 square miles. In 1936 Detroit Edison purchased the Michigan Electric Power Company and acquired the entire "thumb" territory of southeastern Michigan, to increase its service area to 7,587 square miles.

NEW LEADERSHIP

In 1940 Alex Dow retired as company president; two years later he withdrew from the company's board of directors. Under Dow's leadership, not only had generating capacity and service area expanded, but Detroit Edison had developed its own engineering research department, founded in 1913, and improved customer service. This included instituting free light bulb service, financing the connection of electricity to customers previously using gas, and lending electrical motors.

From 1944 to 1954 former U.S. Senator Prentiss M. Brown held the post of first chairman of the board, while James W. Parker served as president and general manager. Walker Cisler, who joined Detroit Edison in 1943, became the company's first executive vice-president in 1948 and, in addition, worked with the U.S. government on the Marshall Plan, developing the economic and electric power of other nations.

When Parker retired in 1951, Cisler took over as president and general manager. Cisler's primary objectives for the company involved expanding generating capacity and improving transmission to the farthest reaches of Detroit Edison's service area, as well as exploring research opportunities. By 1954 the St. Clair

KEY DATES

1903: Detroit Edison is founded.
1905: Company purchases hydroelectric power facilities on the Huron River.
1915: The company's newly built Connors Power plant becomes operational.
1924: Company creates first powdered coal burning facility.
1955: Detroit Edison becomes headquarters for the Power Reactor Development Company (PRDC).
1963: Fermi 1, the first fast breeder nuclear reactor, becomes operational.
1966: Fermi 1 suffers partial core meltdown and is taken off-line.
1970: The Monroe Power Plant begins operations.
1976: Subsidiary Superior Midwest Energy Terminal is established.
1983: Company merges several subsidiaries in New York and Michigan.
1988: Fermi 2 goes into operation.
1991: Company named Electric Utility of the Year by *Electric Light and Power* magazine.
1996: DTE Energy is organized as a holding company for its largest subsidiaries.
1999: DTE Energy completes merger with MCN Energy.
2003: Michigan is hit by largest blackout in national history.

Power Plant was completely operational, with a total capacity of 624,000 kilowatts. That year Cisler became senior officer of Detroit Edison, which by then was looking into nuclear energy.

In 1952 Cisler assumed the leadership responsibilities for organizing electric utilities to explore the possibilities of nuclear energy, a development he named the Enrico Fermi Breeder Reactor Project. Among the companies he persuaded to join the project was the Public Service Electric and Gas Co. of Newark, New Jersey, and he convinced that company to assign one of its nuclear engineers, Walter J. McCarthy, to join the project as head of the nuclear and analytical division in October 1952. The project was headquartered at Detroit Edison. It was formally organized in 1955, with 34 companies participating, as the Power Reactor Development Company (PRDC). This consortium would eventually own and operate the Enrico Fermi Power Plant. Ground was broken on Fermi's first unit that year with Cisler as president and principal organizer of the PRDC.

As the possibilities of atomic energy were explored by the PRDC, Cisler continued to build conventional generating capacity. The River Rouge plant was completed in 1956, and by 1958 it had a capacity of 841,500 kilowatts. In 1961 St. Clair's capacity was upped to 1.35 million kilowatts when its sixth turbine generator went into operation. With its assets growing so rapidly, Detroit Edison authorized a two-for-one common stock split in December 1962.

THE ONSET OF NUCLEAR POWER DISTRIBUTION

In 1963 Walter McCarthy became general manager of the PRDC, with Cisler continuing as president. McCarthy also formally joined the Detroit Edison staff at this time, while continuing on loan to PRDC. On August 23 of that year, Fermi 1, the first commercial-sized fast breeder nuclear reactor, finally went into operation, beginning its first self-sustaining chain reaction. The plant used uranium to generate steam to produce electricity, and as part of the reaction process it produced plutonium, which was also an atomic fuel. In October 1966 a metal device that had been attached to the reactor's inside wall after it was built broke away. The device, whose purpose was to direct the flow of liquid sodium—used to transfer heat—through the nuclear core, ended up blocking the flow and caused the fuel to overheat and begin melting, damaging both the reactor and the fuel assemblies. After the partial core meltdown, Fermi I was taken off-line.

In spite of Walker Cisler's campaign for constant generating plant growth, demand still threatened to outstrip supply, and so, in 1966, peaking units were introduced into the generating system. Peaking generators burn gas and oil, are mobile, and can be brought on-line in ten minutes. The first peaking units were installed at the company's generating facility near Monroe, Michigan. By the time Detroit Edison's Harbor Beach Power Plant went on-line in 1968, nine peaking units were being used.

In the midst of repairs at Fermi 1 and the company's efforts to continue building generating capacity, Detroit Edison was reincorporated in Michigan on April 17, 1967. In that same year Detroit Edison requested its first electric rate increase in 20 years from the Michigan Public Service Commission (MPSC). The company sought the increase to help meet the expenses of building generating capacity.

In 1970 the first of the Monroe power plant's coal-fired units went online. At the time, the four-unit

Monroe plant was the largest in the world, and the company planned to add five more units: the two-unit Belle River coal-burning plant, the Greenwood Energy Center with its oil-burning plant, and two nuclear reactors, Fermi 2 and 3.

In November 1971 William G. Meese took over Cisler's position as chief executive officer while Cisler remained chairman. Meanwhile, the company was burdened with huge plant costs. It had taken four years to repair the reactor and fuel assemblies at Fermi 1, and when the repairs were finally completed the problem-plagued reactor remained operational only sporadically before being shut down again on September 22, 1972. In November of that year the PRDC executive committee decided to decommission the plant as of December 31, 1975.

FINANCIAL STRAIN AND THE MID-EAST OIL EMBARGO

By 1973, the Monroe power plant's four units had a total capacity of three million kilowatts. The Ludington storage plant began commercial operation, supplying 49 percent of its generating capacity to Detroit Edison, with the remainder going to Consumers Power, which supplied the area with natural gas. Then the Middle East oil embargo hit (also known as the OPEC oil embargo), striking the southeastern Michigan auto industry hard, and the demand for energy dropped as automobile production slumped and inflation and environmental protection costs continued to rise.

William Meese began to look for ways to cut Detroit Edison's overhead costs. The energy-efficient Ludington plant was part of this effort. In 1974 Meese began to implement other important practices, such as the increased hiring of minorities and women, as well as establishing a strategic planning procedure designed to help management anticipate future conditions. To deal with the new difficulties brought about by southeastern Michigan's economic recession, Meese also temporarily suspended all power plant construction and environmental modifications.

In 1975 Cisler retired and Meese assumed Cisler's position as chairman of the board. The company reorganized, setting up six divisions within Detroit Edison's service area, each headed by managers responsible for their division's business. That year, Walter McCarthy became executive vice-president of operations.

In 1976 another Meese cost-efficient measure was implemented when the Superior Midwest Energy Terminal was opened by a subsidiary of Detroit Edison. All of Detroit Edison's major power plants consumed coal, but the company did not mine or transport the coal itself. Realizing the company's dependence on reliable transport and supply of coal, Meese created the energy terminal at Superior, Wisconsin, to provide rail and water shipment of western low-sulfur coal. He also negotiated a 26-year contract for the purchase of coal from Montana, and had the company purchase its own coal cars to ensure shipment.

In 1977, the temporary suspension on power plant construction was lifted, the Greenwood power plant was set into operation, and construction was started on the Belle River power plant. In 1979, McCarthy became president and chief operating officer of Detroit Edison and John R. Hamann was elected to the newly created position of vice-chairman of the board. That was also the year that the company's Greenwood Power Plant became fully operational.

FEDERAL REGULATIONS SLOW NUCLEAR EXPANSION

In 1979, as Fermi 2 was in the midst of construction, the disaster at Three Mile Island hit. Two weeks later Detroit Edison had formed a 24-member safety review task force to review Fermi 2 again and recheck all its operating systems and safety features. Although the task force found everything to be entirely operational at Fermi 2, it took Detroit Edison several years of readjustments before the reactor could meet the new regulations that arose in response to the Three Mile Island incident. In fact, the added cost of meeting these new standards spun Detroit Edison into financial crisis.

The company began taking steps to help revive southeastern Michigan's economy. In 1979 it began the Energy Plus advertising campaign on a national and international level to interest companies in bringing their manufacturing facilities to Metro Detroit. With the Greater Detroit Chamber of Commerce, Michigan's Department of Commerce, and the Southeastern Michigan Council of Governments, Detroit Edison founded the Greater Detroit-Southeastern Michigan Business Attraction and Expansion Council. Detroit Edison also helped develop the Economic Alliance for Business, an organization aimed at improving Michigan's business climate. In September 1981 Meese retired and was succeeded by McCarthy as chairman and chief executive officer.

In April 1983, in order to consolidate the company, which was operating under dual incorporation in the states of New York and Michigan, Detroit Edison stockholders agreed to a merger plan. This plan was put into effect on June 30, 1983, when both the New York and the Michigan corporations merged with Detroit Edison's wholly owned inoperative subsidiary, Peninsular

Electric Light Company. The Detroit Edison Company was the merger's sole surviving company, and retained only its Michigan incorporation. All liabilities, capital, assets, and operations remained unchanged.

In 1985 Fermi 2 was completed, and low-power testing began. McCarthy, having been general manager of Fermi 1 during its early stages, felt experienced operating management was needed. With the delays involved in bringing in new plant management and in receiving approval of the Nuclear Regulatory Commission, Fermi 2 resumed low-power testing in July 1986.

In 1987 Detroit Edison's wholly owned subsidiary, Washtenaw Energy Corporation, was merged into the company. Later that year, the company bought the electric business and properties serving the city of Pontiac from Consumers Power and began to supply the people of Pontiac directly, increasing the company's total service area to 7,598 square miles. Consumers Power had served Pontiac with electricity bought from Detroit Edison.

On January 15, 1988, Fermi 2 began full-power operation. By November Fermi 2 had passed its warranty run and was on its way to long-term operation. However, after-tax write-offs of $968 million—resulting partially from the MPSC's disallowances of costs connected with the unit, dating from a 1986 rate case—caused Detroit Edison to post a net loss of $378.8 million in 1988.

McCarthy began to implement programs designed to increase sales and cut costs, keeping close watch on operating and maintenance expenses, capital expenditures, and the size of the company's staff, reducing it to its smallest size in 12 years—9,669 at the end of 1990. Perhaps most important was the resolution of rate-making issues involving Fermi 2. In December 1988 the MPSC had increased Detroit Edison's base rates by adding $29.5 million to a previously authorized $404.2 million—for a total of $433.7 million—to partly cover the cost of building Fermi 2. This increase was to be phased in over five years beginning January 1, 1989. That year Fermi 2 was taken off the Nuclear Regulatory Commission's list of plants requiring special attention. It completed its first scheduled shutdown for refueling in December 1989, and it produced more than 5 billion kilowatt-hours of electricity during the year. By June 1989 The Detroit Edison Company stock had risen to its highest price in 17 years, positioning Detroit Edison as one of the top-performing U.S. utilities.

In 1989 Fermi 2 had represented 31 percent of Detroit Edison's assets. In 1990 this grew to 33 percent as the company purchased the minority share of Fermi 2 from Wolverine Power Supply Cooperative, Inc., for $539.6 million, giving the company total ownership of the plant. On May 1, 1990, McCarthy retired as chairman and chief executive officer of Detroit Edison and John E. Lobbia was elected to replace him. As a result of strong lobbying in Washington, D.C., Detroit Edison was in compliance with the first phase of the requirements of the 1990 Clean Air Act amendments, scheduled to take effect in 1995.

TRANSITION AND GROWTH

By keeping ahead of federal regulations, in 1990 the company achieved record revenues as well as record earnings for its common stock. Detroit Edison's common stock hit its highest point in 23 years, when it reached $30.25, closing at $28.25, a full 11 percent higher than 1989's close. Sales during the year were reported at $3.31 billion, $104 million over 1989 levels.

However, things were soon to change. The recessionary economy of the early 1990s hit southeastern Michigan hard, slowing production at many automotive and steel plants and reducing demand for electricity from these industries. In response, Detroit Edison aggressively marketed its services to other industries, so much so that it had record sales to the commercial segment. In 1991, with record sales reaching $3.59 billion, the company received the "Electric Utility of the Year" award from the trade magazine *Electric Light & Power.* Based on the company's record revenues and earnings, in mid-December 1991 its common stock reached $35 per share, the highest price in 25 years.

Into the mid-1990s, Michigan's economy and state policy continued to be uncertain as its basic industries struggled to compete with foreign manufacturers. In addition, a new governor was redefining state goals. For these reasons, Detroit Edison continued to minimize staff levels, reduce its use of foreign crude, and cut its dependence on industrial sales, thereby maximizing the company's flexibility. Net income in 1993 reflected these efforts: $588 million, a jump of 14 percent over 1990's record levels.

As the decade advanced, it became increasingly clear that the utility industry was on the brink of major changes. In late 1992 Congress passed the Energy Policy Act, which allowed competition in the utility industry's wholesale sector by mandating existing utilities to transmit electricity generated by other producers through their lines. The company received another setback on Christmas Day 1993, when a turbine generator fire at Fermi 2 caused the high-production plant to close while repairs were made. The plant returned to partial service in 1995, as the company posted sales of $3.64 billion against net income of $406 million.

The Federal Energy Regulatory Commission (FERC) issued a new set of rules in April 1996 affecting transmission capacity and wholesale and retail competition. The following year, the industry was deregulated through the Public Utility Holding Company Act of 1935, which allowed utility companies such as Detroit Edison to operate as monopolies. Under the new federal law, other companies would be permitted to enter the area in as little at two years. Prior to deregulation, DTE's primary concern was to expand and maintain its plants and equipment. With deregulation looming, the company looked to its economic structure and attempted to streamline costs in preparation for competition in a larger field of competitors.

To supplement the new federal legislation, the MPSC designed a framework for the gradual restructuring of Michigan's electricity business. Beginning July 1, 1997, the state's utility load would be gradually opened to competition through a bidding process, with all customers able to select their energy supplier by January 1, 2002. Technical, environmental, and business-related issues would also be addressed and responded to during this five-year period.

In response to these industry-wide changes, Detroit Edison was reorganized in late 1995. On January 1, 1996, DTE Energy Company became the holding company for subsidiaries that included Detroit Edison and several nonutility assets, among them Biomass Energy Systems, Edison Energy Services, and Midwest Energy Resources. The new structure allowed the company greater financial flexibility in creating new energy-related businesses and separated regulated subsidiaries from those not under state or federal regulations.

The biggest challenge facing DTE and CEO John E. Lobbia in a competitive market was the company's high cost of production, as well as the huge investment the company had made in its Fermi 2 plant. With deregulation and competition from other providers, electrical rates would be sure to drop drastically, and DTE feared it would be priced out of the market it had controlled for decades. In preparation for full-scale deregulation in 2002, DTE signed its major commercial and industrial electricity customers (including the Big Three automakers) into ten-year contracts in order to help recover the company's high capital equipment costs. These capital costs would also diminish as a result of debt refinancing through the Michigan Legislature's approval of the issuance rate-reduction bonds in mid-1997.

DTE also began to leverage its extensive expertise in energy-related systems' engineering and installation. In an effort to increase consumption and attract new residential customers, new programs were developed, including an interruptible air conditioning program that promised to improve system management and also lower electricity rates by up to 20 percent. Over 250,000 customers were enrolled in the system in its first years of operation.

In 1999, DTE Energy completed a major merger with MCN Energy, in a deal estimated at $2.6 billion in cash and stock, creating the largest electric utility company in Michigan. The merger, the largest such acquisition in Detroit history at the time, represented another phase of DTE's efforts to strengthen the company in preparation for full industry deregulation in 2002. MCN Energy was a market leader in natural gas transport and storage, two key areas needed by DTE to maintain a hold on the Michigan power market.

DEREGULATION AND ADJUSTMENT

DTE was busy integrating MCN Energy subsidiaries into the company's administrative structure. In 2003, in efforts to comply with federal regulations, DTE sold part of its energy transmission subsidiary, International Transmission Co., to Kohlberg Kravis Roberts & Co, for a reported $610 million. While Michigan customers were free to choose from competing utility providers, the state of Michigan passed an additional regulation, in 2004, requiring that customers choosing to leave DTE Energy for a competitor were required to remain with their new choice for a period of no less than two years. The regulatory amendment was a positive change for DTE as many customers chose not to switch their service given the two-year commitment.

During this post-deregulation period, DTE sought to maximize its profits in some industry sectors not affected by deregulation, such as in methane gas extraction and coal reclamation. Another strategy included acquiring assets from energy companies that were struggling as competition among them increased. Economic downturns during this time further challenged DTE. According to the company's CEO, Anthony F. Earley, in an April 2004 *Crain's Detroit Business* article, tough economic times made collecting money owed from customers tough as well.

BLACKOUT AND RECOVERY

In August 2003 Michigan and large portions of the Midwest, Northeast, and parts of Ontario, Canada, were hit with a major power blackout. Initial fears were that the outage was the result of terrorism, and the U.S. Department of Homeland Security initiated an independent investigation. It was eventually discovered, however, that the outage was the result of a power plant failure in Ohio, linked to a relatively simple case of overdemand. The initial failure caused several cascade failures linked to problems with high-voltage power line obstructions that ultimately led to over 100 power plant failures, including those of DTE Energy.

DTE officials struggled to return power. Moreover, Michigan also soon suffered from water shortages, as pumping stations went offline. The blackout lasted for over two days, and Michigan's Governor Jennifer Granholm declared a state of emergency, ordering drinking water and gasoline to be brought into Detroit. In press statements, Earley urged those whose power had been restored to limit their usage in an effort to stretch supply while the company repaired production facilities. "Customers," he remarked in a press release, "hold the key to the speed of the restoration." By August 17, DTE had managed to restore power to its remaining customers although some distribution problems remained.

As federal investigations ensued, each utility company involved in the blackout conducted an internal investigation to ensure their own safe operating procedures. In one press release, Earley blamed a breakdown in communication between the Ohio facility and neighboring facilities as a key element in the blackout.

In 2005, Congress passed the Energy Policy Act, which gave FERC additional oversight authority over transactions and mergers between utility companies as well as to supplement state provisions governing transmission of energy between states. The new legislation also gave FERC increased control over the national energy grid to maintain quality standards in hopes of avoiding national emergencies like the 2003 blackout. Utility companies were forced to adjust to the new regulations, which included increased transparency in financial transactions.

In February 2005, DTE Energy hosted a conference on alternative energy, which was attended by environmental leaders and representatives of several major corporations, such as General Motors, with direct interest in alternative energy. The conference was one of several initiatives taken independently by DTE to address environmental concerns. DTE won its first award from the Environmental Awards Council for the company's emissions reduction program. In 2006, DTE became one of the first utility companies to offer customers the choice of using renewable energy for all or part of their energy services.

The company estimated that the average household could switch to using 100 percent renewable energy at a cost of roughly $10 to $15 per month. In 2008, DTE partnered with Wolverine Power Supply Cooperative, Inc., to provide wind energy for the company's GreenCurrents renewable energy program. In 2007, DTE commissioned McKinsey & Company, an environmental consulting firm to conduct research into the reduction of greenhouse gas emissions. The report, which recommended relatively minor steps that would enable the nation to cut greenhouse emissions by more than 28 percent, was conducted in cooperation with the National Resources Defense Council.

DTE posted revenues in excess of $9 billion in 2006, while the company's total assets exceeded $23 billion. In November 2006, the company announced a Non-Utility Monitization Plan, which involved selling some of the company's nonutility holdings as the companies matured to a sufficient size to maximize profit.

By 2008, DTE seemed to have successfully met the various challenges to the industry brought on by deregulation. In fact, it was the largest utility company in Michigan, servicing over 50 percent of the state's residential and commercial population. The company also operated peripheral subsidiaries in 29 states handling transportation and production of gas products.

Maya Sahafi
Updated, Pamela L. Shelton; Micah L. Issitt

PRINCIPAL SUBSIDIARIES

Detroit Edison; MichCon; DTE Energy Services, Inc.; DTE Biomass Energy; DTE Rail Services; Midwest Energy Resources.

PRINCIPAL COMPETITORS

CMS Energy Corporation; Integrys Energy Group, Inc.; Wisconsin Energy Corporation.

FURTHER READING

Bodipo-Memba, Alejandro, "DTE to Scrutinize Itself," *Detroit Free Press,* December 16, 2005.

Electric Utility Industry Overview: Introduction to the Restructuring Debate, Detroit: Detroit Edison, 1996.

Lane, Amy, "DTE Aims to Spark Growth Beyond Electricity," *Crain's Detroit Business,* April 14, 2003.

———, "Rate Concerns Drive DTE's Push to Cut Costs," *Crain's Detroit Business,* March 20, 2006.

"Major Power Outage Hits New York, Other Large Cities," *CNN News,* August 14, 2003.

McCarthy, Walter J., Jr., *Detroit Edison Generates More Than Electricity,* New York: Newcomen, 1983.

Serju, Tricia, "The Light on Utilities," *Detroit News,* December 2, 1996, p. 6F.

"A Short History of Detroit Edison," DTE corporate typescript, 1990.

Wald, Matthew L. "Study Details How U.S. Could Cut 28% of Greenhouse Gasses," *New York Times,* November 30, 2007.

Wald, Matthew L., and Carl Hulse, "Utilities Point Their Fingers at Each Other over Blackout," *New York Times*, September 3, 2003.

Wilgoren, Jodi, and Danny Hakim, "The Blackout: The Midwest: Detroit Sweats While It Waits for Electricity," *New York Times*, August 16, 2003.

Duferco Group

Via Bagutti 9
Lugano, CH-6900
Switzerland
Telephone: (41 091) 911 56 00
Fax: (41 091) 911 57 00
Web site: http://www.duferco.com

Private Company
Incorporated: 1979
Employees: 7,600
Sales: $8.43 billion (2006)
NAIC: 423510 Metals Service Centers and Other Metal Merchant Wholesalers; 331111 Iron and Steel Mills; 331221 Cold-Rolled Steel Shape Manufacturing; 331222 Steel Wire Drawing

■ ■ ■

Duferco Group is the world's largest steel trading concern. The Lugano, Switzerland-based company boasts trade volumes of 16.5 million metric tons (MT) per year, including more than 9.6 million MT of flat, long, and specialty steel products, and nearly seven million MT of iron ore, coal, coke, and other raw materials. Duferco is also a diversified steel group, with interests in production and distribution. The company produces nearly 7.2 million metric tons of steel and steel products each year, through subsidiaries in Italy (Duferdofin, Sertubi, Acciai Rivestiti Valdarno, Acciaierie Grigoli, and San Zeno Acciai Duferco); Belgium (Duferco Belgium-Carsid, Duferco La Louvière;, and Duferco Clabecq); France, Denmark, South Africa, Guatemala, Republic of Macedonia, and the United States (Duferco Farrell).

Europe and North and South America remain the company's core markets, although the company has also built a significant presence in the fast-growing Asian steel markets. Altogether the company operates in more than 40 countries, with more than 30 trading and distribution subsidiaries and 17 production facilities. Duferco Group is led by founder and chairman Bruno Bolfo. In 2006, the company posted sales of $8.43 billion.

EMERGING STEEL TRADER IN 1979

The late 1970s saw the beginning of a shift in steel production from its traditional base in the heavily industrialized West to fast-growing developing markets such as Brazil. These new sources of steel in turn provided new opportunities for the emergence of the globally operating steel trade sector. Among those spotting this potential was Bruno Bolfo. Born in Genova, in Italy's Liguria region, Bolfo's career included 16 years working for Italsider, later known as Ilva, one of the leading Italian steel groups. After a stint as head of the company's export division, Bolfo came to the United States, where he led Italsider's U.S. operations.

By 1978, Bolfo had decided to form his own company. Together with a number of partners, Bolfo founded Duferco in 1979. The company's initial operations were based in New York and in São Paolo, Brazil. Duferco quickly developed a strong network among Brazil's steel producers. Among the company's partners

COMPANY PERSPECTIVES

Duferco intends to focus on the highest level of service to its suppliers and customers wherever located in the world in combining the steel production/processing activities with the global trading knowledge for the benefit of its customers.

were such steel groups as Usiminas, Cosipa, and Acominas. Duferco at first focused on the U.S. market, setting up a number of sales offices around the country.

Yet the company quickly began expanding the scope of its distribution targets. In particular Duferco had spotted the growing importance of the Asian markets. Countries such as Korea, Taiwan, Singapore, Malaysia, and Thailand had launched major modernization and industrialization efforts, stimulating a boom in demand for steel. Duferco began shipping Brazilian steel to the Far East, and by 1980 had established its first subsidiary in the region, in Thailand.

Nonetheless, the West remained the world's primary steel consumer. With its U.S. base in position, Duferco next targeted the European market. The company set up its first European office in London in 1981. The company later expanded its European base to include Germany, Belgium, Italy, and other countries.

At the same time, Duferco sought to broaden its steel purchasing operations beyond Brazil. This brought the company into Venezuela, Argentina, and Mexico. Soon after, the company extended its trading and distribution operations to include North American steel producers. In the meantime, the company's London office served as a launching point for purchasing from European steel producers as well.

CORPORATE INTEGRATION IN THE NINETIES

By the end of the decade, Duferco had expanded its operations to include the Pacific Rim. Through the 1990s, the company's international network included offices in Singapore, the Philippines, Taiwan, China, Hong Kong, and South Korea. The company had also launched the first phase of a vertical integration effort and bought two steel mills in Brazil during the privatization of part of the country's steel sector. The first of these was Companhia Siderurgica de Mogi das Cruzes (Cosim), which operated a small, 25,000 ton-per-year mill in São Paolo state. The second was Companhia Ferro e Aco de Vitoria (Cofavi), acquired for $8 million plus $60 million in debt. The Cofavi purchase added more than 300,000 tons of production capacity per year. Duferco then announced plans to spend $30 million in order to boost its total Brazilian steel capacity past one million tons.

Duferco continued to adjust to changing markets into the next decade. The collapse of the Soviet Empire and the vast reconstruction effort needed to improve the Eastern European infrastructure opened new opportunities for the company, and it established operations in Russia, the Czech Republic, and other former Soviet bloc markets. The move into Eastern Europe also enabled the company to extend its trading operations beyond steel. Through the end of the decade Duferco developed a strong business in the trading and distribution of raw materials for the steel industry, including iron ore, coke, coal, and pig and scrap iron. By the middle of the first decade of the 2000s, raw materials represented more than 40 percent of the group's trading operations.

The move into raw materials formed only part of Duferco's strategy in the 1990s. The global steel industry remained highly fragmented at the start of the decade, particularly in Europe where large numbers of small scale producers made up the bulk of the continent's steel production. A severe recession at the beginning of the decade, and the corresponding slump in steel demand, placed the industry under extreme pressure. With prices dropping many producers boosted their production, adding to the oversupply of the market. By the middle of the decade, many of the smaller steel producers were facing bankruptcy.

MOVING TO EUROPE AT THE END OF THE DECADE

This economic situation stimulated a massive consolidation of the steel industry, especially in Europe. It also provided Duferco with the opportunity to move into the next phase of its growth. With many of its suppliers facing bankruptcy in the mid-1990s, the company opted to take the next step toward a fully integrated steel-based business model. Duferco launched an acquisition drive, buying a number of financially troubled yet viable steel producers based in Europe.

The company first targeted Italy, where it bought Ferdofin in 1996. The new subsidiary, called Duferdofin, became the focal point of the company's Italian steel holdings, growing to more than 350,000 metric tons per year. Over the next decade, Duferco added several more Italian steel producers, including Sertubi in 2000. Two smaller producers, Acciai Rivestiti Valdarno Acciaierie

KEY DATES

1979: Bruno Bolfo sets up Duferco as a steel trader focused on Brazilian steel production.
1980: Company expands focus to include other emerging markets and forms a subsidiary in Thailand.
1989: Duferco acquires first steel production holdings in Brazil.
1996: With the acquisition of Italy's Ferdofin, the production subsidiary Duferdofin is formed.
1997: Company takes over Belgium's Clabecq steel mill.
1998: Duferco enters the United States through the purchase of a steel plant in Farrell, Pennsylvania.
2006: Company spins off most steel production holdings into a joint venture with Russia's NLMK.
2007: Duferco agrees to transfer Duferdofin into a joint venture with U.S.-based Nucor.

Grigoli and San Zeno Acciai Duferco, together added more than 700,000 metric tons to the group's production.

Duferco added two new steel production markets in 1997. The group moved into the Republic of Macedonia, buying that country's Makstil Skopje. Duferco also entered Belgium, which became another major production center for the company. For its Belgian expansion, the company rescued the Clabecq works, restarting production there in 1997 and building up a total capacity of 650,000 metric tons.

Duferco's steel production wing took a leap forward in 1999 with the purchase of La Louvière steel works, which added 2.3 million metric tons to its capacity. The company also added Belgian wire producer Trebos that year. Additional presence in Belgium was gained through the creation of the Carsid joint venture with Cockerill Sambre. That project included Cockerill Sambre's mill at Charleroi in 2001. The new company, called Carsid, boasted a capacity of more than 1.8 million metric tons.

The shift in the company's focus, both toward European steel production and toward the Eastern European trade market, led Duferco to move its headquarters to Lugano, Switzerland, at the start of the new decade. In 2003 the company also added two steel producers in France—Beautor and Sorral—adding a total of 620,000 metric tons.

NEW GLOBAL MARKETS

While Europe represented the largest part of Duferco's growing steel production division, the company also targeted growth elsewhere. In the early 2000s the group moved into South Africa, launching a steel rolling and galvanizing joint venture at Saldanha Bay, in partnership with the Industrial Development Corporation. By then Duferco had also added a production arm in the United States, having purchased a hot strip mill in Farrell, Pennsylvania, from London-based Caparo Steel in 1998.

Other new markets for the company included Russia, where it bought magnetic steel producer Viz, in 1999. By 2003, Duferco had also added a production facility in London, through its purchase of Teesside Cast Products. At the same time, the company continued to build up its international trading and distribution wing, adding a number of new sites around the world. By the middle of the decade, Duferco was present in more than 40 countries.

REALIGNING TO MEET MARKET CHALLENGES

Yet Duferco had increasingly begun to question the future viability of its integration model. Despite high levels of demand through the mid-1990s, the global steel industry had begun to show clear signs of a new shift. This was due in part to new steel production capacity in China, which was expected to transform the world market during the early part of the 21st century. At the same time, the consolidation of the steel production sector had continued, resulting in a handful of truly massive companies.

Duferco was forced to recognize the difficulty of maintaining the viability of its production. With a capacity of just 7.2 million tons—out of a total of 350 million tons across the industry—Duferco's steel production was unlikely to remain competitive in the coming years. This was especially true not only because many observers expected the field to narrow to just five major producers by the middle of the next decade, but also because a majority of the world's raw materials production had by then become concentrated under the control of only three groups.

These factors led Duferco to seek a new partner for its steel production division. By the end of 2006, the company had found an ally in OJSC Novolipetsk Steel (NLMK), Russia's fourth largest steel producer with a total capacity of 8.47 million tons. The two companies agreed to form a 50-50 joint venture. In 2007 Duferco transferred most of its 22 production sites into the new company, in exchange for NLMK's payment of $805 million. The new company then boasted a total capacity, for both raw steel and finished steel products, of more than 15 million tons. Excluded from the deal was the Duferdofin plant in Italy.

EXPANSIONS AND A NEW JOINT VENTURE

The company expanded further when Duferco bought Arcelor's stakes in two Italian mills. Duferco's Louvière site in Belgium was also expanded in 2007 with the addition of a semicontinuous and push-pull pickling line. The company also launched an expansion of its Duferdofin production sites, targeting a total capacity of more than 1.6 million tons by the end of 2008.

The credit crisis that spread from the United States into Europe in 2007 led the steel industry to fear a new dip in the steel market. A number of major producers had begun to experience a drop-off in revenues. While demand for steel from fast-growing markets, especially India and China, was expected to cushion the fall in demand, Duferco took steps to further reduce its exposure to the production sector. In January 2008 the company reached an agreement to transfer 50 percent of Duferdofin into a joint venture with U.S.-based Nucor. One of the most respected names in the global steel industry, Duferco had returned to its core operations as a steel trading and distribution leader.

M. L. Cohen

PRINCIPAL SUBSIDIARIES

Cjsc "Metko" (Ukraine); Dufenergy S.A. (Luxembourg); Duferco Asia Pte Ltd.; Duferco Belgium S.A.; Duferco Coating-Sorral S.A. (France); Duferco Coating S.A. (France); Duferco Danish Steel A/S; Duferco Deutschland Gmbh (Germany); Duferco Do Brasil Ltda; Duferco España S.L. (Spain); Duferco Farrell Corporation (United States); Duferco Guatemala; Duferco Italia Holding S.P.A.; Duferco La Louvière; S.A. (Belgium); Duferco S.A. (Switzerland); Duferco Steel Inc. (United States); Duferco U.K. Ltd.; Dusiam Ltd. (Thailand); Ironet Ltd. (Mexico); Ironet Ltd. (Turkey); Korea Steel Trade and Marketing Corp. Ltd.; Profima Chile Ltda; Profima S.A. (Argentina); Rosso Steel A.S. (Czech Republic); Vitraco (Vietnam).

PRINCIPAL COMPETITORS

Mitsubishi Corporation; Sumitomo Corporation; Glencore International AG; ArcelorMittal; Steelsummit Holdings Inc.; TUI AG; Sojitz Corp.; BHP Billiton plc.

FURTHER READING

Cook, Bradley, "European Steel Makers Strike Deal," *International Herald Tribune,* November 28, 2006, p. 15.

"Gibraltar, Duferco Split Pennsylvania Processing Assets," *Metal Producing & Processing,* January–February 2004, p. 8.

Marsh, Peter, "Duferco Buys ArcelorMittal Italy Stakes," *Financial Times,* December 14, 2006, p. 24.

———, "Duferco Expects Slowdown in Steel Industry," *Financial Times,* January 11, 2008, p. 17.

———, "Duferco Looks Beyond US for Industry's Expansion," *Financial Times,* September 11, 2007, p. 28.

Randacio, E., A. Baccelli, et al., "A Wide Range Pickling Line at Duferco La Louviere," *Steel Times International,* November 2007, p. 59.

Ritchie, Martin, "Arcelor Mittal Selling Italian Mills to Duferco," *American Metal Market,* December 14, 2006, p. 6.

Duncan Aviation, Inc.

Lincoln Airport
3701 Aviation Road
Lincoln, Nebraska 68524
U.S.A.
Telephone: (402) 475-2611
Toll Free: (800) 228-4277
Fax: (402) 475-5541
Web site: http://www.duncanaviation.com

Private Company
Incorporated: 1963 as Duncan Beechcraft, Inc.
Employees: 1,900
Sales: $250 million (2000 est.)
NAIC: 488190 Other Support Activities for Air Transportation

■ ■ ■

Duncan Aviation, Inc., is a full-service maintenance center for business aircraft, or a "service station" for the jet set. The company became involved with Learjets at an early date and now services just about every kind of business aircraft. Its extensive maintenance and overhaul capabilities make it a "one-stop shop" for its time-conscious customers.

Controlled by the Duncan family, the company espouses the belief that motivated employees are the key to great customer service. It boasts a strong commitment to job training, and subsidizes college tuition, flight lessons, and some wellness programs. Such measures have made it a regular on *Fortune* magazine's annual "100 Best Companies to Work For in America" list.

Duncan's main facilities are its headquarters in Lincoln, Nebraska, and a 345,000-square-foot complex in Battle Creek, Michigan. It also has 20 avionics facilities scattered throughout the Midwest and the western United States, allowing aircraft owners to update instrumentation and other hardware quickly.

MIDWESTERN ORIGINS

Company founder Donald Duncan, born in 1922, grew up on a farm near Clarinda, Iowa, and learned to fly there as a teenager. He traded in government surplus aircraft after World War II, making enough to launch a local General Motors dealership. However, he had loftier aims.

In 1956 Duncan acquired a minority stake in Lang Aircraft, an Omaha, Nebraska, distributor of Beechcraft, a popular make of piston-engine business planes. One of the partners, Carl Lang, died three years later and another, Robert Graf, soon sold his shares to Duncan.

Duncan established a firm called Duncan Beechcraft, Inc., in December 1963. It became Duncan Aviation Company five years later, and was renamed again in February 1970 to Duncan Aviation, Inc.

ASSOCIATION WITH LEAR

Donald Duncan was able to get in on the ground floor of an industry that was about to soar after he struck up a friendship with aviation inventor Bill Lear. When the legendary Learjet was stalled for lack of development funds, Duncan and a handful of others fronted money

COMPANY PERSPECTIVES

For more than half a century, we have introduced business aircraft operators with high standards and limited time to the absolute best in turbine service, sales and support. We believe in investing in our facilities and people and in developing innovative products, services and processes to continually improve the corporate aviation industry. Duncan Aviation services all of the major business aircraft, including Falcons, Hawkers, Challengers, Gulfstreams, Astras, Westwinds, Citations and Learjets. We have specialized teams who service, paint, overhaul, install, modify, inspect, troubleshoot, fuel and repair. Above all, they work to attain the highest customer satisfaction possible in any service industry, not just in the world of corporate aviation.

to Lear to keep the project going in exchange for distribution rights.

In 1963 Duncan started an additional operation in Lincoln, Nebraska, after trying a site in Cheyenne, Wyoming. By the mid-1960s, Duncan's Omaha and Lincoln businesses were together bringing in more than $5 million a year. The company was focused on new aircraft sales, although it did perform some maintenance work and charter flights. It had 15 employees, including the founder's son Robert, who became company president in 1968 and succeeded his father as company chairman in 1981.

FOCUS ON SERVICE

Bill Lear sold Learjet to Gates Rubber in 1967 and the new owners decided to cut middlemen out of the distribution chain. Duncan Aviation then became one of a handful of authorized Learjet service centers, while continuing to maintain Beechcraft planes. AirKaman, Inc., a subsidiary of the Kaman aerospace conglomerate, acquired Duncan's Omaha dealership in 1967, but Duncan continued to service Beechcraft planes from its base in Lincoln.

The emerging jet business was central to Duncan's growth. Their speed and range made the company a practical maintenance stop for Learjet owners across the country. Lincoln, Nebraska, was no more than a three-hour flight from anywhere in the continental United States.

Originally priced at less than $500,000, the Learjet made 500 m.p.h. coast-to-coast travel affordable for businesses for the first time. The innovation was so successful that a booming aftermarket materialized. After taking off a couple of years to sell aircraft directly for Gates, Donald Duncan returned to his namesake company to start a thriving trade in preowned jets.

BOOM YEARS

Duncan began the 1970s with about 50 employees. The company's fortunes soared during the decade as the general aviation industry reached new heights. Duncan also opened a small office in Anchorage, Alaska, to service the oil exploration industry and at one point even had a sales office in Paris, France. Revenues reached $90 million in 1980, Robert Duncan told the *Omaha World-Herald.* However, a mass of product liability lawsuits, airline deregulation, and other factors would soon exact a massive toll on the general aviation industry.

As new planes became more expensive, owners diverted their funds toward keeping their existing machines in the air. More than ever, Duncan Aviation had to focus on maintenance activities in order to survive.

Duncan instituted a couple of innovative programs in the mid-1980s. It launched a network of satellite avionics centers at airports in the western half of the country, beginning with Houston's Hobby Airport. It also started a venture to resell spare parts. By the end of the decade, Duncan had about 400 employees.

Some of Duncan's ventures were less successful than others. In 1994 the company launched Alliance Engines, a joint venture with Kimberly-Clark Aviation. Based in Maryville, Tennessee, Alliance aimed to deliver quick turnarounds on extensive repairs beyond the scale of most airport mechanics. However, the founding partners withdrew from Alliance after a couple of years to concentrate on their core businesses.

BIG CHANGES

There were important shifts in the executive suite as Duncan Aviation brought in management talent from outside the family. Former banker Aaron Hilkemann became president in 1997, a year after joining the company as chief operating officer. His tenure followed a brief, somewhat controversial stint by former Omaha Mayor P. J. Morgan.

Duncan prospered in the last half of the decade, a good time for the aviation industry. By 1997, its revenues were up to $100 million, according to a

KEY DATES

1956: Chevrolet dealer Donald Duncan acquires a stake in a Beechcraft distributorship in Omaha, Nebraska.
1963: Duncan establishes a jet-servicing operation in Lincoln, Nebraska.
1981: Robert Duncan succeeds his father as company chairman.
1998: Acquisition of Kal-Aero, Inc., adds major facility in Battle Creek, Michigan.
2000: Revenues are $250 million after five years of double-digit growth.
2004: Glass Box Project combines several avionics upgrades in one system.
2007: Battle Creek facility is expanded; Todd Duncan becomes third generation of the family to lead the company as chairman.

Knight-Ridder story on the company. There were 750 employees. During the year, the company added a 20,000-square-foot building in Lincoln for its instrument repair and parts consignment operations, and bigger things were to come.

One of the biggest events in Duncan Aviation's history was the 1998 acquisition of Kal-Aero, Inc., one of the company's leading rivals, from John Ellis and Pete Parish. The purchase added a major facility at W.K. Kellogg Airport in Battle Creek, Michigan, and made the company more accessible to the East Coast. Kal-Aero was a well-established competitor, with 350 employees and 200,000 square feet of facilities including a site in Kalamazoo, Michigan. Duncan continued to expand its Lincoln facility. An additional 123,000-square-foot hangar opened there in November 2001. Built at a cost of $14 million, it provided a place to work on larger jets.

After absorbing the new addition and five years of double-digit growth, Duncan was up to revenues of $250 million in 2000. The company then had about 1,900 employees, and it had established a reputation as a great place to work. In 2001 Duncan Aviation made the first of numerous appearances on *Fortune* magazine's "Top 100 Companies to Work For" list, thanks to such attributes as its commitment to training and health and safety programs.

As technology evolved, Duncan introduced a new approach in avionics upgrades. Airframes for business aircraft had a useful life measured in decades. To keep older models relevant, the company developed its Glass Box Project. This combined a number of flight instruments in an integrated system via a common liquid crystal display, giving pilots access to state-of-the-art information and imaging technology. The first of these retrofits was completed in the fall of 2004, and the company was soon installing them at a rate of a dozen or more per year.

CELEBRATING 50 YEARS IN BUSINESS

In 2006, Duncan Aviation celebrated 50 years in business, spanning half the era of powered flight. Part of the festivities included a sweepstakes for a 1956 Chevrolet Bel Air—a nod to company founder Robert Duncan's days as a Chevy dealer in Clarinda, Iowa. By this time Duncan had more than 1,800 employees and was planning to hire hundreds more in the coming years. In September 2007 Todd Duncan, who had previously been in charge of the components division, became the third generation of his family to lead the company as chairman.

The company was continuing its ambitious growth plans. It was in the midst of a $23 million expansion of its facility in Battle Creek, Michigan, that increased the facility by a third, to 325,000 square feet. Duncan was said to be interested in adding another main facility for easier access to the West Coast.

Frederick C. Ingram

PRINCIPAL DIVISIONS

Accessory/Propeller Department; Avionics & Instrument Shop; FBO Services; Parts, Components & Services.

PRINCIPAL OPERATING UNITS

Lincoln, Nebraska; Battle Creek, Michigan.

PRINCIPAL COMPETITORS

Trego Dugan Aviation of Grand Island Inc.; Central Flying Service, Inc.

FURTHER READING

"Alliance Says, 'Come on Down,'" *Business & Commercial Aviation,* November 1, 1995, p. 38.

"Bizjet Specialists Duncan, Kal-Aero in Acquisition Deal," *Aero Safety and Maintenance,* January 23, 1998, p. 4.

Bradley, Perry, "Power Partners: Duncan Aviation and KC Aviation Have Joined Forces to Launch a Frontal Assault on the

Cost of Maintaining and Overhauling Engines," *Business & Commercial Aviation,* December 1, 1994, p. 66.

Brunkow, Angie, "Morgan Quits as President of Lincoln Firm," *Omaha World-Herald,* News Sec., January 10, 1996, p. 17.

Duncan Aviation, Inc., *Duncan Debrief,* 50th Anniversary Issue, 2006.

Emrich, Anne Bond, "Tax Exemption Gives Duncan a Lift," *Grand Rapids Business Journal,* May 15, 2006, p. SS13.

Higdon, Dave, "Aviation Company Profiles: Duncan Aviation on a Hot Streak with Awards to Show for Employees' Efforts," *AvBuyer.com,* 2002.

Hosford, Christopher, "The Sky's the Limit: A Comprehensive Education, Outreach and Recognition Program Has Given Duncan Aviation *Esprit de Corps* and Employee Referrals," *Incentive,* June 2003, pp. 56–57.

"Identical Leases Approved for Two Airport Operators," *Lincoln Star,* July 31, 1963, p. 9.

Johnson, Leonard, "Duncan Aviation Finds Its Niche," *Omaha World-Herald,* Magazine of the Midlands Sec., October 25, 1987.

"Kaman Winds Up 3 Acquisitions," *Bridgeport (Conn.) Telegram,* January 25, 1968, p. 53.

"Lincoln Firm Serious About Environment; Duncan Aviation Upgrades Paint Hangars," *Omaha World-Herald,* News Sec., March 16, 1992, p. 13.

"Lincoln Is 'Gas Station' for Some 'Jet Setters,'" *Lincoln Star,* September 17, 1971, p. 1.

Madigan, M. J., "Trade Show Exhibit: Duncan Aviation," *Interiors,* April 1, 1996, p. 64.

McConnell, Vicki P., "Duncan Aviation's Success Formula: Employees and Customers First," *Aviation Maintenance,* August 15, 2007.

Naso, Markisan, "Duncan Aviation Keeps Workers Safe on the Road and off the Job," *Safety & Health,* May 2005, p. 56.

Norris, Melinda, "Black Boxes Mean Gold for Nebraska's Duncan Aviation," *Knight-Ridder/Tribune Business News,* July 7, 1997.

———, "Duncan 'Friendship' Brings Italians to Lincoln," *Omaha World-Herald,* Bus. Sec., October 3, 1990, p. 24.

Rode, Jenny, "Strong Market, Reformed Laws Help Aircraft Company," *Associated Press Newswires,* October 23, 2000.

Russo, Ed, "Duncan Has More Room to Breathe," *Lincoln Journal Star,* June 15, 1997, p. E1.

Schmidt, J. L., "Lincoln Municipal Airport Facilities, Services Grow," *Lincoln Star,* May 19, 1976, p. 21.

Seidenman, Paul, "Duncan Opens New Facility, Eyes Growth; The New Hangar Will Relieve Cramped Conditions and Give the MRO Company Room to Expand," *Overhaul & Maintenance,* February 1, 2001, p. 57.

Smith, Eugene R., "The Lemonade Factory," *Air Progress,* January 1988, p. 10.

Egan Companies, Inc.

7625 Boone Avenue North
Brooklyn Park, Minnesota 55428-1011
U.S.A.
Telephone: (763) 544-4131
Fax: (763) 595-4380
Web site: http://www.eganco.com

Private Company
Incorporated: 2004
Employees: 700
Sales: $130 million (2005 est.)
NAIC: 238220 Plumbing, Heating, and Air-Conditioning Contractors

■ ■ ■

Egan Companies, Inc., is a Brooklyn Park, Minnesota-based privately owned group of contracting companies providing mechanical, electrical, systems, and cladding installation and maintenance services for the full life of a building project, including design, preconstruction, construction, start-up, and maintenance and repair. As a mechanical contractor, Egan handles commercial, healthcare, industrial, and institutional projects, designing and installing heating, ventilation, and air conditioning, piping, and plumbing systems.

The unit also offers millwright services, custom sheet metal fabrication capabilities, and the prefabrication of piping systems to lower costs and assure quality. Egan's electrical service subsidiary is involved in commercial, high-tech, industrial, medical, and entertainment projects, as well as outdoor projects such as traffic signals and intelligent traffic systems, roadway lighting, exterior facility lighting, landscape lighting, sports facility lighting, and tunnel electrics.

In addition, Egan maintains an industrial controls group, offering programming, installation, and service. Egan Systems provides solutions for fire and life safety, temperature control, video surveillance, and access control systems. Egan's InterClad Curtain Wall subsidiary offers integrated wall cladding systems, including metal panels made of aluminum plate or composite metal, or ornamental metals such as bronze and stainless steel. The unit also makes custom metal and glass handrails.

Egan Companies, Inc., is among the top 150 specialty contractors in the United States according to *Engineering News-Record.* It is especially adept at the complex mechanical systems required by hospitals and healthcare facilities. It also does a great deal of university work, mostly for the University of Minnesota, offering the kind of expertise needed in laboratory renovations and other high-end university projects.

EARLY 20TH-CENTURY LINEAGE

Although Egan designates 1945 as the date of its founding, the roots of the company reach back to the turn of the century. In 1903 the patriarch of the Egan family, Joseph Egan, started a pipefitting shop in northeast Minnesota, the "Iron Range." He ran the shop until the United States entered World War I, when he closed down the operation. After the war was over in 1918 and the country navigated a subsequent recession, Egan relocated to Minneapolis, where in 1919 he started a

COMPANY PERSPECTIVES

Egan is a values-based company committed to building and maintaining the best possible partnership with our customers. Our construction capabilities include design-build and prefabrication. Our 24/7 service business is a leading provider for maintenance, repair and monitoring. We are efficient, fair and enjoy lasting relationships with our customers.

plumbing business. He prospered during the economic boom of the Roaring Twenties and then hung on during the Great Depression of the 1930s. He was joined by sons Costney and Bill until World War II intervened. A shortage of materials and the military service of Costney and Bill forced Egan to once again suspend his business during wartime.

POSTWAR GROWTH

After the eldest Egan brothers were discharged from military service they returned home. With $3,000 they returned to business with their father, launching Egan & Sons Plumbing and Heating Company, which in time would evolve into the Egan Companies. With the end of war came prosperity, and following a brief recession in 1946 as the United States retooled its industry and assimilated returning service personnel, the economy boomed, as did the construction industry, leading to steady growth for Egan & Sons, which grew into a heating, ventilation, and air conditioning (HVAC) company. A third son, Gerald, the youngest, joined the family business in 1955 after completing a stint in the U.S. Air Force.

Egan & Sons moved beyond the plumbing and heating field in 1960 when the company forged a partnership with Thomas J. McKay, creating an electrical contracting company called Egan McKay Electrical Contractors. By the mid-1960s Egan & Sons looked to take advantage of its broadened capabilities by offering a package of services to customers. A novel idea at the time, packaging offered a number of advantages for everyone involved in a project. The Egan companies were able to negotiate larger contracts and leverage scale to fashion more attractive bids. At the same time, the builders, architects, and engineers engaged in major construction projects appreciated the advantage of relying on fewer subcontractors.

Moreover, Egan was well respected for its reliability and the quality of its work, thus providing customers with some peace of mind regarding a project's HVAC and electrical systems. An early example of this approach came in 1965 with the construction of Cedar-Riverside Towers, one of the largest high-rise apartment projects ever completed in Minneapolis. According to the trade newsletter *ACG Minnesota,* published by Associated General Contractors of Minnesota, "Due to the packaging of services, Egan won the contract to install everything from the big boilers in the basement to fan-coil units on the decks to wiring for the elevators."

INNOVATIONS TO SUPPORT GROWTH

Egan was a pioneer in its field in many ways. Well before most construction companies even thought to do it, Egan incorporated computer technology into its operations in the late 1960s. Given the expanding nature of the company, whose different units might be operating independently on the same project, the ability to break out payroll and job costs became imperative. As Egan grew, it also became important to retain talent as well as recruit new talent.

In 1973 it formed an employee stock ownership plan (ESOP), the first Minnesota company to do so. By giving employees an ownership stake, moreover, the company provided an incentive to improve collaboration and productivity. The results-driven culture that typifies Egan Companies was another dividend of the ESOP; it helped to spur the growth of Egan from an electrical and HVAC service provider to a prime contractor with a direct contract for an entire project.

The next step in the evolution of the Egan companies was the 1988 launch of Egan Automation to serve the energy management market. This initiative grew out of the needs of a major customer, the Minneapolis-based Target department store chain. Egan not only maintained a computer monitoring system for Target, it developed a network of contractors wherever Target opened a store in the United States. Should a store develop a problem, Egan Automation could track the situation from its base computers and then dispatch the local contractor to remedy the problem. In addition, Egan Automation provided advice to Target when it acquired stores, making recommendations for changes and cost estimates.

GERALD EGAN ERA

During the 1980s Gerald Egan took over as president and chief executive of the companies, which since 1984 no longer included Tom McKay as a principal. In 1984 McKay sold his holdings in the electrical contracting

KEY DATES

1903: Joseph Egan opens a pipefitting shop.
1945: Egan & Sons Plumbing and Heating Company is established in Minneapolis.
1960: Formation of Egan McKay Electrical Contractors.
1973: Employee stock ownership plan is instituted.
1988: Egan Automation is formed.
1997: InterClad Curtain Wall Company subsidiary is launched.
2002: Nietz Electric Inc. is acquired.
2004: Four operating units consolidate to form Egan Companies, Inc.

unit and retired, devoting the rest of his life to the hobby of trapshooting. Not only did Gerald Egan become the last of his family to run the Egan companies, he was an industry leader, serving as president of the Mechanical Contractors Association of America. He also championed education and training in the mechanical and electrical trades, endowing a scholarship fund at his alma mater, Dunwoody College of Technology in Minneapolis, for students enrolled in an HVAC or electrical program.

Gerald Egan also had a reputation as an employee-friendly boss who was especially dedicated to safety and training issues. In the late 1980s the company began holding what it called a "Tool Fair." It was conducted in-house to allow field workers, including journeymen and apprentices, to witness demonstrations from more than a dozen vendors of HVAC and piping tools and equipment on tools the company was buying. The employees were given hands-on training as well as provided with safety tips. To encourage safety, the Egan companies awarded prizes, at a formal dinner, to foremen with the best safety records. First-aid classes were also held on a regular basis and, to promote a healthy lifestyle, Egan arranged for an employee discount with an area YMCA.

By the mid-1980s Egan was comprised of five companies involved in the HVAC, electrical, mechanical, fire protection, and insulation fields. With some $70 million in annual sales it ranked among the top 25 mechanical contractors in the United States. Because of its size and diversity, opportunities to bring everyone together at events such as the Tool Fair became increasingly important in promoting the organization's success. Ideas were shared in committee meetings and among task force members, as well as at social events.

Executive committee officers met each Tuesday morning, while upper management and a committee that included a foreman from each of the Egan companies met on a quarterly basis. After the quarterly meeting the foremen gathered for their own meeting, minus management, to formulate their own recommendations. Out of this process emerged the concept of preconstruction meetings in which everyone involved in a project reviewed drawings and specifications, and clarified responsibilities, scheduling, and purchasing needs.

UNUSUAL LABOR STRIFE

Labor difficulties were not completely eliminated, however. In 1987 the Egan & Sons unit became involved in an unusual dispute that garnered national attention when Local 10 of the Sheet Metal Workers union threatened to stop representing 75 Egan workers in negotiations for a contract that was set to expire. The tactic had the effect of a strike, because it put Egan in a position in which it could not hope to win large construction projects in the Twin Cities market if it was a nonunion shop. The company would also be denied skilled workers, because in order to do sheet metal work, a competency card was required, earned by passing a city test. However, the only way to be eligible for the test was to have a great deal of experience or graduate from a Local 10 apprentice program. Egan found itself in the unusual position of going to court to force a union to act as a bargaining agent. A federal judge agreed with the company's position and Local 10 was ordered to bargain for the workers.

EGAN FAMILY ERA ENDS

The Egan family of companies expanded further in 1997 when the InterClad Curtain Wall Company was established. The Energy Services Group was also launched in 1997. By this time Gerald Egan was ready to retire. In June 2000 he sold the family business and moved with his wife to Naples, Florida, bringing an end to Egan-family control of the company. Gerald Egan died of cancer at the age of 71 in February 2003.

Under the leadership of chief executive Craig Sulentic, who had joined the organization in 1989, the Egan companies continued to expand in the new century. In 2002 the industrial controls group was added to complete the range of services required in major building projects. Also, in the fall of that year Egan-McKay expanded the territory it covered by acquiring Rochester, Minnesota-based Nietz Electric Inc., which specialized in electrical contracting for commercial and industrial projects and roads. The Nietz family business was founded in 1936 by Emil Nietz. The addition of Nietz gave Egan a toehold in the Rochester market, which Egan hoped to exploit to secure contracts for other Egan companies. Nietz brought about $7 million to the balance sheet, which approached $120 million across the Egan organization.

Egan began to reorganize in late 2003, using the move into a new 120,000-square-foot headquarters located in Brooklyn Park, Minnesota, to finally bring together six divisions in one location. In 2004 Egan Mechanical Contractors, Inc., Egan-McKay Electrical Contractors, Inc., Egan Automation, Inc., and Egan Services were consolidated to create Egan Companies, Inc. Sales reached $136 million in fiscal 2004, then dipped to $130 million in fiscal 2005.

Ed Dinger

PRINCIPAL SUBSIDIARIES

Egan Automation, Inc.; Egan Mechanical Contractors, Inc.; Egan-McKay Electrical Contractors; InterClad, Inc.

PRINCIPAL COMPETITORS

Ceco Construction Group; Penhall Company; Parsons Electric LLC.

FURTHER READING

Aronovich, Hanna, "A Wise Investment: Egan Cos. Devotes Time and Energy to Developing Its People, As Well As Leading-Edge Equipment and Facilities," *US Business Review,* November 2006.

Clepper, Irene, "Building Business on Communication, Cooperation," *Air Conditioning, Heating & Refrigeration News,* April 17, 1989, p. 32.

Freund, Bob, "Construction Contractor Egan Cos. Acquires Nietz Electric of Rochester, Minn.," *Rochester (Minn.) Post-Bulletin,* October 28, 2002.

"Gerald (Jerry) Egan, 71," *Minneapolis (Minn.) Star Tribune,* February 7, 2003, p. 6B.

Hage, Dave, "The 'Walk Away' Union Tactic Is Unusual, and So Is Confrontation," *Minneapolis (Minn.) Star Tribune,* April 8, 1987, p. 1M.

Woods, Denise, "Egan Companies, Inc," *Constructive Comments Newsletter (ACG of Minnesota),* April 2005, p. 1.

8x8, Inc.

3151 Jay Street
Santa Clara, California 95054
U.S.A.
Telephone: (408) 727-1885
Fax: (408) 980-0432
Web site: http://www.8x8.com

Public Company
Incorporated: 1987 as Integrated Information Technology, Inc. (IIT)
Employees: 160
Sales: $53.1 million (2007)
Stock Exchanges: NASDAQ
Ticker Symbol: EGHT
NAIC: 517310 Telecommunications Resellers

■ ■ ■

Based in Santa Clara, California, 8x8, Inc., is a leading provider of Internet-based telephone and videophone communications services. The company's technology relies on voice over Internet protocol (VoIP) technology. VoIP uses the Internet protocol (IP)—a communications protocol or method that is used for transmitting information between computers on the Internet—for the online transmission of voice and video data.

8x8 offers a number of different services, including the Packet8 Broadband Phone Service for residential customers with high-speed Internet connections, the Packet8 Videophone Service, and the Packet8 Virtual Office phone system for small and medium-sized businesses. The company also offers a video-enabled "softphone" device called Packet8 Softalk, which allows Packet8 subscribers to use their computers to place and receive voice and video calls directly from their personal computers, which is useful when traveling.

FORMATIVE YEARS

8x8 was established in February 1987 by two former Weitek Corp. executives as Integrated Information Technology, Inc. (IIT). According to 8x8, the company's early products consisted of programmable semiconductors and related software for the videophone and videoconferencing sectors. A May 18, 1992, *Business Wire* release further explained that IIT's early components and products were "optimized for handling numerical, text, graphics, still-image, full-motion video and audio information for the computation, communications and consumer markets."

As of early 1990, Chi-Shin Wang was IIT's president. Two years later, the company had a staff of 100 employees, regional offices in the central and eastern United States, and a subsidiary in Europe. Early competitors included the likes of C-Cube Microsystems.

It was around this time that a line of data compression products was introduced, giving computer users the ability to double the capacity of their hard drives. The introduction came at a time when the Windows operating system and compatible programs were demanding more and more disc space. Products in this category included IIT's XtraDrive Software, which sold for $99, and a related hardware product that retailed for $199.

Like so many technology start-ups, IIT was faced with legal entanglements during its early years. In June

> **COMPANY PERSPECTIVES**
>
> Since its establishment in 1987, 8x8 has contributed to the advancement of voice and video communications on both technology and service provision levels.

1992, Carlsbad, California-based Stac Electronics sued the company, alleging that its XtraDrive Plus hardware and XtraDrive software infringed upon one of Stac's data compression/decompression patents. A settlement was reached in April 1993, calling for IIT to make past and future royalty payments to Stac.

A major development occurred in 1994 when IIT forged an agreement with National Semiconductor Corporation to develop application-specific integrated circuits (ASICs), which are chips used in devices such as wireless phones, satellite systems, and radar systems. The deal involved National Semiconductor securing an 8 percent equity stake in IIT.

It also was in 1994 that IIT forged a joint effort with Siemens Corp. to produce a low-cost chipset for the personal computer-based videoconferencing market. By this time, IIT had formed a subsidiary named XTechnology, Inc., that was involved in the development and marketing of graphics processors.

A flurry of change occurred at the senior leadership level in 1995. In April the company named Joseph Parkinson—the cofounder of Boise, Idaho-based semiconductor manufacturer Micron—as president, CEO, and co-chairman. In July a reorganization effort resulted in Parkinson being named chairman, Chi-Shin Wang and Dr. Y. W. Sing vice-chairmen, and Robert Shen president and chief operating officer.

Robert Shen left the company days after the July reorganization occurred, leaving Parkinson as interim president. In October, IIT named Larry Barber as executive vice-president and chief operating officer. That same month, design group head Bryan Martin was promoted to the role of chief technical officer.

In early 1996 Sony Electronics announced that it had selected IIT's Video Communications Processor for use in the Sony TriniCom 5000, a four-way group videoconferencing system. In April of that year, IIT changed its name to 8x8, Inc.

In a March 4, 1996, *Business Wire* release, the company explained that the new name underscored its "focus on programmable solutions for the videoconferencing and MPEG markets. An 8x8 block of picture elements (pixels) is the basis of many video compression algorithms and thus enables a new generation of personal computer videoconferencing systems, video telephones, Internet video products and digital televisions using MPEG CD-players and satellite decoders. The company's family of programmable integrated circuits forms the foundation for this wide range of consumer and PC multimedia products."

The following year a breakthrough occurred when 8x8 unveiled a consumer-oriented product named ViaTV Phone, which combined a standard television set and touch-tone phone with a regular phone line to create an affordable videoconferencing system that people could use to communicate with family and friends. Other consumer and business products were introduced along with the ViaTV videophone. 8x8 went public in 1997, making its initial stock offering in July on the NASDAQ.

IP TELEPHONY FOCUS

The 1998 introduction of 8x8's Audacity Internet Telephony Processor marked the start of the company's real focus on IP telephony. 8x8 concluded the decade by acquiring telecommunications technology firm Odisei S.A. in May 1999. In early 2000, 8x8 changed its name once again, becoming Netergy Networks, Inc. At this time, the company also discontinued its consumer videophone offerings.

In a March 27, 2000, *Business Wire* release, Paul Voois, then Netergy's chairman and CEO, said: "Today we are introducing a company that will play a key role in the convergence of voice and data networks. The telecommunications industry is undergoing a fundamental transition from circuit-switched to Internet protocol (IP) based networks. We have made a series of decisive strategic decisions in the past 18 months to capitalize on this transition. Our new name is derived from the words 'network' and 'synergy,' and Netergy Networks is creating synergies out of the convergence of voice and data on IP networks."

By this time, Netergy was marketing an IP-based private branch exchange (PBX) system. A PBX system manages telecommunications between phones within a company and the external public telephone system. The Netergy Advanced Telephony System (ATS) made it possible for competitive local exchange carriers (CLECs) to offer PBX services to businesses from one location. CLECs compete with the established local phone provider in a given market in order to offer consumers additional choice in service. Dialink was the first CLEC to do so, pioneering VoIP service to the business market with the ATS in early 2000.

KEY DATES

1987: Integrated Information Technology, Inc., (IIT) is established by two former Weitek Corporation executives.
1996: IIT changes its name to 8x8, Inc.
1997: 8x8 goes public, making its initial stock offering on the NASDAQ.
2000: The company changes it name to Netergy Networks, Inc.
2001: Less than a year after becoming Netergy, the company changes its name back to 8x8.
2002: 8x8 rolls out residential VoIP (voice over Internet protocol) service to high-speed Internet subscribers under the Packet8 brand name.

For the year ended March 31, 2000, Netergy lost $24.9 million on revenues of $25.4 million. By comparison, the company lost $19.2 million on revenues of $31.7 million in 1999. On April 4, 2000, Netergy changed its ticker symbol to NTRG to reflect its new name. The following month, the company agreed to acquire Montreal-based UForce, a developer of Internet messaging products. The $51 million stock swap was completed in June.

More senior-level leadership changes occurred in early 2001. On January 16, Netergy named Sun Microsystems executive Robert Habibi as its president and chief operating officer, with Paul Voois continuing to serve as CEO. Only days later, on January 22, the company announced that both executives had tendered their resignations. Chairman Joe Parkinson was appointed interim CEO.

A new subsidiary named Netergy Microelectronics was formed in March 2001 to provide voice and video semiconductor and firmware products for the VoIP market, according to a March 12, 2001, *PR Newswire* release. Firmware consists of data and instructions written into a computer's read-only memory, which are used to control the computer's operations. Netergy also established a new subsidiary named Centile, Inc., which offered scalable VoIP-based PBX solutions (iPBX) for small and midsized businesses.

In April 2001 Netergy shuttered its Montreal office, thereby eliminating its Canadian operations altogether. For the year ended March 31, 2001, the company's revenues totaled $18.2 million, down from $25.4 million the previous year. Netergy recorded a net loss of $74.4 million, down from $24.9 million in 2000.

Less than a year after adopting the new Netergy name, the company changed its name back to 8x8 on July 17, 2001. The ticker symbol EGHT was adopted a few days later.

A major development took place in November 2002, when 8x8 rolled out residential VoIP service to high-speed Internet subscribers under the Packet8 brand name. In July of the following year, the company's Centile, Inc., business sold Centile Europe SA, a European subsidiary, to Sunleigh Investments.

By November 2003, Bryan R. Martin was in the CEO seat at 8x8. Midway through that month the company secured $5.2 million in additional financing by privately placing 1.84 million shares of its common stock. A few days later, the placement of 780,000 additional shares generated another $2.2 million. The year ended with Martin assuming the chairmanship and Joe Parkinson assuming the role of vice-chairman.

Several new product developments occurred in 2004. These included the Packet8 Virtual Office hosted IP PBX phone service in March, which was designed for small business use, followed by the Packet8 DV326 Broadband Consumer VideoPhone that summer. In an October 2004 *PR Newswire* release, the company claimed that it was the first "to ship a standalone consumer videophone that operates over a high speed Internet connection and delivers full motion video at a rate of 30 frames per second."

In September 2004, 8x8 sold about 3.5 million shares of common stock to an institutional investor, generating net proceeds of $11.2 million. Some of the funds were earmarked for the expansion of the company's Packet8 service. 8x8 rounded out the year by being named among the leading 15 VoIP providers by FierceVoIP in its annual Fierce 15 ranking.

For the 2005 fiscal year, 8x8 recorded a net loss of $19.1 million on revenues of $11.5 million, compared to a $3.0 million loss on revenues of $9.3 million for the 2004 fiscal year. E911 service was rolled out to all Packet8 subscribers in November 2005, in keeping with a mandate from the Federal Communications Commission. In December, the company ended the year on a high note when two institutional investors snapped up 7.14 million shares of 8x8 common stock for approximately $15 million, providing capital for the further expansion of Packet8 in retail and wholesale markets.

LOOKING TO THE FUTURE

By late 2006, 8x8 reported that some 5,000 businesses were using the company's Packet8 Virtual Office hosted

PBX VoIP service. Of these, 1,000 customers had signed on in the last quarter, signifying the prospect of strong future growth. In December 2006 Chairman and CEO Bryan Martin was appointed to California Governor Arnold Schwarzenegger's broadband task force, which intended to leverage the technology as a means of economic growth.

An innovative product introduction occurred in March 2007 when 8x8 unveiled its Packet8 Tango Video Terminal Adapter. The VoIP device, which was equipped with an LCD screen, allowed consumers to turn any traditional telephone into a videophone. In some respects, this product was reminiscent of the company's earlier ViaTV Phone device.

In December 2007, 8x8's Packet8 Complete Contact Center product was recognized by *Customer Interaction Solutions,* a magazine serving the call center industry, which awarded 8x8 with its 2007 Product of the Year Award. In a December 4, 2007, news release, 8x8 Vice-President of Sales and Marketing Huw Rees explained: "With the Packet8 Complete Contact Center, small businesses that need a professional, full featured call center solution can now subscribe to a pure hosted VoIP-based service and benefit from the associated lower costs and flexibility."

By early 2008 8x8 revealed that it had become the nation's second largest stand-alone VoIP service provider. The company continued to develop innovative products and technologies, with approximately 69 U.S. patents to its name and more pending. By this time, the number of businesses using 8x8's Packet8 Virtual Office hosted PBX VoIP service had reached the 10,000 mark, double the level recorded a year earlier.

Backed by its experience in VoIP technology, 8x8's prospects for continued growth in the first decade of the 21st century seemed promising.

Paul R. Greenland

PRINCIPAL SUBSIDIARIES

8x8 Europe SARL (France); 8x8 Limited (China); Netergy Microelectronics, Inc.; Netergy Networks Canada Holding Company; UForce Holding Company; Visit, Inc.

PRINCIPAL COMPETITORS

Net2Phone, Inc.; Nortel Networks, Inc.; Vonage Holdings Corporation.

FURTHER READING

"8x8 Changes Name to Netergy Networks; Name Change Signifies Company's Focus on IP Telephony," *Business Wire,* March 27, 2000.

"8x8, Inc.," *Mergent Online,* January 10, 2008, http://www.mergentonline.com.

"IIT Introduces Retail Data Compression Products; New End User Products Double Storage on PCs," *Business Wire,* May 18, 1992.

"Integrated Information Technology (IIT) to Change Name to 8x8, Inc.," *Business Wire,* March 4, 1996.

Element K Corporation

500 Canal View Boulevard
Rochester, New York 14623
U.S.A.
Telephone: (585) 240-7500
Toll Free: (800) 434-3466
Fax: (585) 240-7760
Web site: http://www.elementk.com

Wholly Owned Subsidiary of NIIT Ltd.
Incorporated: 1982 as Logical Operations, Inc.
Employees: 700
Sales: $100 million (2007 est.)
NAIC: 541512 Computer Systems Design Services

■ ■ ■

Element K Corporation is a global learning solutions company serving major corporations in such industries as information technology, financial services, hospitality, and manufacturing, as well as government agencies, universities, and training centers. A subsidiary of India's NIIT Ltd., the company is based in Rochester, New York. The company offers 1,300 print courseware titles, and 2,800 online courses in more than ten languages, both instructor-led and self-paced. They cover a wide range of information technology, computing, business management, and compliance subjects, leading to professional certification. Element K's proprietary vLabs system permits hands-on exercises on remote hardware creating a virtual training environment, while its e-Reference library provides articles and full text and abstracts of new business, marketing, and leadership books. The company also offers custom content development, and its fully hosted KnowledgeHub learning platform provides customers with a turnkey training solution, from implementation to maintenance.

COMPANY FOUNDED: 1982

Element K was founded as Logical Operations, Inc., in 1982 by two Rochester Institute of Technology professors, Dominick Fantauzzo and Barry Keesan. With a master's of business administration, Keesan served as the chief executive of the company, which started out as an onsite computer training facility with just two staff members, intended primarily to train employees on the new IBM-based personal computers that were beginning to be incorporated into the workplace. Logical Operations moved beyond the classroom in 1986 when it expanded into publishing, creating courseware and training materials that could be used by other training centers.

The company's Rochester training facility continued to grow and provide training for about 1,000 professionals each month, but its primary purpose was to serve as a laboratory to test and improve training programs and materials. In order to avoid competing against its customers, the company elected not to set up further training centers outside of Rochester. The one training center was retained because it helped the company keep tabs on what the market wanted.

For example, in 1988 Logical Operations began offering training programs for Macintosh computers, a response to increased demand for such training at its training facility. Two years earlier about one in ten

COMPANY PERSPECTIVES

Over the past 25 years, Element K has been committed to helping the world's most prestigious companies improve their business with learning and development.

customers sought Macintosh training, but that number had since increased to one in four. The year also saw Logical Operations introduce its "Train the Trainer" program, which taught outside training center personnel how to use its products, or others who could in turn train coworkers. In addition, in 1988 the company opened offices in Boston, Chicago, Los Angeles, and San Francisco in order to increase its share of the corporate, retail, education, and government markets.

COURSEWARE SOLD TO THIRD PARTIES: 1982

Logical Operations was well established in its field, and in 1987 began selling its courseware model to training operations across the country. Two years later, the company took advantage of its growing library of original curriculum and training products, making these materials available to colleges and training centers. In 1990 it drummed up further business and formalized existing relationships by establishing Training Matrix, a network of independent training companies with centers in 20 U.S. cities that used Logical Operations' classroom materials. Logical Operations became the first company to offer an alternative to vendor-authorized courseware in 1991.

COMPANY ACQUIRED BY ZIFF COMMUNICATIONS: 1991

Early in 1991 Logical Operations was acquired by Ziff Communications Company. Established in 1927 as Popular Aviation Company (to publish *Popular Aviation* magazine) by World War I flier and author William B. Ziff and business partner Bernard Davis, the company quickly changed its name to Ziff-Davis Publishing Company. It was soon publishing a wide variety of hobby and leisure and pulp magazines as well as reference, trade, and juvenile books. After William B. Ziff, Jr., took over following his father's death in 1953 and bought out Davis three years later, the company began to focus more attention on the special interest magazine business as well as trade publications. In the early 1980s the company began publishing computer magazines and acquired others, such as *PC Magazine.*

Diagnosed with cancer, Ziff sold the consumer and business publications in 1984, leaving just the computer magazines and Information Access Company, a publisher of database materials. With his cancer in remission, Ziff once again began to build up the assets of what was now called Ziff Communications. Given its interests in computer magazines and databases it was not surprising that the company would seek to become involved in personal computer training and support services.

In addition to acquiring Logical Operations, Ziff also purchased Wayne, Pennsylvania-based PC Concepts, a training and support services company providing *Fortune* 500 corporations with computer application training, help desk services, and documentation services. These two companies formed the platform for a new Ziff-Davis business group to provide end-user computer technical support. Also in 1991 Ziff-Davis acquired The Cobb Group, a Louisville, Kentucky-based publisher of technical newsletters, CDs, and journals.

Keesan became a Ziff-Davis division president and general manager, a post he held until 1994. During his tenure he forged a relationship with Applied Learning International to launch a multi-language initiative that spearheaded a global distribution effort, resulting in the opening of offices in Canada, Belgium, France, Germany, and the United Kingdom. By 1993 Logical Operations was the largest publisher of training materials for personal computers in the United States, as well as one of the largest training operations in the world.

Logical Operations experienced a major growth spurt in 1996. Early in the year it acquired the assets of Montreal-based ELIN Computer Resources, Inc., the company's Canadian distributor, and formed subsidiary Logical Operations Canada, Inc. At the same time, Logical Operations opened a Seattle sales office and assumed responsibility for a CD-ROM-based product line, Support-On-Site, taking over for a sister division, Ziff-Davis Interactive. By this time, the parent company had undergone a pair of ownership changes. In 1994 the investment firm Forstmann Little & Co. paid $1.4 billion for Ziff-Davis and then in February 1996 resold majority control to Japan's Softbank Corporation for $2.1 billion. A month later Ziff-Davis reorganized its operations, resulting in three new U.S. divisions: US Publications; Interactive Media and Development; and Training and Support Publishing, which consisted of Logical Operations and The Cobb Group. Logical Operations itself was divided into three business units: Training Center Business Unit, Publishing Business Unit, and Support Products Business Unit.

KEY DATES

1982: Company founded as Logical Operations, Inc.
1986: Publishing operation launched.
1991: Ziff Communications acquires Logical Operations.
1997: Name changed to ZD Education.
2000: Company sold and renamed Element K Corporation.
2001: KnowledgeHub introduced.
2006: Company acquired by NIIT Ltd.

KNOWLEDGE QUEST ACQUIRED: 1996

Additional changes were to follow in 1996. In May Logical Operations reached an agreement to acquire Knowledge Quest, a Southern California developer of computer-based interactive training programs, leading to the introduction of a new line of CD-ROM-based training materials marketed under the ActiveLearn name. Also in 1996 Logical Operations became the first company to introduce self-paced training delivered via the Internet. In June 1996, Logical Operations formed a new business unit to manage its online strategy, and included a new line of computer-based training products drawn from its instructor-led manuals, presented under the LearnItOnline banner.

Further restructuring occurred in 1997 when Logical Operations was renamed ZD Education and The Cobb Group became ZD Journals. ZD Education was then sold in February 2000 for $172 million in cash to U.S. Equity Partners, an affiliate of investment bank Wasserstein Perella Group, Inc. Two months later, ZD Education assumed a new name and brand, Element K, the "K" standing for Knowledge. The company's marketing executives worked closely with New York advertising agency St. Aubyn, considering hundreds of possible names before settling on Element K. In addition to the allusion to knowledge, a word that kept cropping up during market research, the company was also swayed by the availability of a web address, ElementK.com.

The branding change was intended to better reflect the company's commitment to its online learning services. The independent company also hired a new CEO, 38-year-old Bruce Barnes, former chief financial officer for Ziff Communications. In May 2000 Element K announced that it planned to make a $75 million initial public offering of stock underwritten by Credit Suisse First Boston, Chase H&Q, and Thomas Weisel Partners, LLC. The stock market, especially the tech-heavy NASDAQ, dropped, however, and Element K withdrew the offering, content to wait for better market conditions.

REORGANIZATION FOR THE 21ST CENTURY

Despite a weak economy, Element K continued to grow in the early 2000s, when it was reorganized into four business units: e-learning, courseware, newsletters and training publications, and the company's Rochester training center. The training operation was expanded by leasing space in the nearby communities of Brighton and Greece. Later in 2000 a 32,000-square-foot classroom was added close to the company's Rochester headquarters.

Most of Element K's growth at the time came from its thriving Internet business. The company's learning management platform, KnowledgeHub, was launched in 2001. In that same year, Element K formed a partnership with Harvard Business School Publishing (HBSP) to offer HBSP's Interactive Manager series online, joining Harvard ManageMentor, which was being offered online by Element K. Moreover, in 2001 Element K introduced the E-Business Library, a set of online self-study tutorials and online instructor-led training courses about corporate use of Internet technologies. Element K added the vLabs system in 2002 through the acquisition of the intellectual property related to the technology, creating a web-based learning system that allowed students to gain networking experience without the expense of setting up practice equipment or risking damage to servers or infrastructure. VLabs was also useful as a presales tool, allowing new technologies to be tried out by a company's potential customers in a real-time virtual environment.

Element K forged some major alliances in 2003. Microsoft elected to outsource the development of its e-Learning products to Element K, as well as the North American distribution of its Instructor Led Training (ILT) courseware. Also in 2003, Element K received the North American rights from Novell Training Service Partners to produce and distribute Novell Authorized Curriculum. Another development in 2003 was the introduction of an online Health Care Insurance Portability and Accountability Act (HIPAA) program to train medical personnel about the requirements of the act. Element K's entry into the medical arena brought the company to the attention of Eli Research, a Washington, D.C.-based publisher of more than 30 newsletters training medical personnel on certain coding compliance issues.

In the summer of 2005 Eli acquired Element K's journals division, which included 41 computer technology journals. The sale allowed Element K to focus on growing its learning solutions practice and services, and allowed Eli to enter the IT journals market. The two companies also reached a multiyear license agreement that would allow Element K to continue to sell and support the slate of journals.

OWNERSHIP CHANGE: 2006

Ownership of Element K changed hands once again in 2006 when New Delhi, India-based NIIT Ltd., a provider of technology-related educational services, bought the company. It was a transaction that favored both companies. Although Element K harbored global aspirations, its territory was essentially limited to the United States and Canada, and to extend its brand worldwide was cost prohibitive. NIIT, on the other hand, had operations around the globe but only a modest penetration in the North American market through outposts in Atlanta and Chicago. Thus, the addition of Element K provided instant clout in this desirable market.

NIIT elected to allow Element K to operate as an independent company under its own brand, and through NIIT Element K would be able to distribute its products and learning services around the world. Combined they fielded operations in 32 countries and generated annual sales of about $250 million. As a result of its alliance with NIIT, Element K enjoyed an immediate growth surge. It was also poised to take advantage of NIIT's strong position in China as well as other developing areas around the world.

Ed Dinger

PRINCIPAL OPERATING UNITS

Products; Services; Solutions.

PRINCIPAL COMPETITORS

Cengage Learning; Global Knowledge Training LLC; SkillSoft plc.

FURTHER READING

Armstrong, Michael W., "Magazine Publisher Buys Computer Training Firm," *Philadelphia Business Journal,* January 21, 1991, p.8.

Chao, Mary, "Element K Boosts Marketing," *Rochester Democrat and Chronicle,* October 17, 2000, p. 10D

———, "Ziff-Davis Selling Training Business," *Rochester Democrat and Chronicle,* November 18, 1999, p. 1A.

Davia, Joy, and Nishad Majmudar, "India Firms Buys Element K," *Rochester Democrat and Chronicle,* July 28, 2006, p. 10D.

Henry, Jacqueline, "Focus Is Key to Success at Logical Operations," *Computer Reseller News,* March 21, 1994, p. 119.

Mullins, Richard, "ZD Changes Its Name—Again," *Rochester Democrat and Chronicle,* April 12, 2000, p. 12D.

Thomas, Kathy Quinn, "Private Firms Map Different Roadways to Success," *Rochester Business Journal,* July 13, 2001.

Elite World S.A.

54 Boulevard Napoleon Premier L-2210
Luxembourg
Telephone: (33 0140) 44 32 22
Fax: (33 0140) 44 32 80
Web site: http://www.elitemodel-world.com

Public Company
Incorporated: 1971
Employees: 80
Sales: EUR 32.51 million (2006)
Stock Exchanges: Frankfurt
Ticker Symbol: EIM
NAIC: 711410 Agents and Managers for Artists, Athletes, Entertainers, and Other Public Figures; 533110 Lessors of Nonfinancial Intangible Assets (Except Copyrighted Works)

■ ■ ■

Elite World S.A., operates one of the top international modeling agencies, Elite Model Management; sponsors the annual Elite Model Look contest; and licenses the Elite brand name to manufacturers of clothing, eyewear, cosmetics, luggage, and other products. The firm owns nine modeling agencies and has franchised another 30, which are collectively located on five continents. Elite founder John Casablancas is largely responsible for the phenomenon of the supermodel, and over the years its roster has included such famous names as Cindy Crawford, Naomi Campbell, Gisèle Bundchen, and Heidi Klum. Although most of its famous names have moved on and its former U.S. subsidiaries are part of a separate company, the firm continues to represent more than 800 models worldwide.

BEGINNINGS

Elite World's roots date to 1969, when John Casablancas founded a modeling agency in Paris. Born in 1942 to a Spanish industrialist and a model who had settled in New York during the Spanish civil war, Casablancas traveled the globe as his parents pursued their business interests and was educated at a private school in Switzerland. After working for a Brazilian Coca-Cola bottler and Merrill Lynch, he moved to Paris. Casablancas soon started dating Danish model and beauty queen Jeanette Christiansen, who complained to him about the problems she was having with her agency. Inspired to manage her himself, in 1969 he founded an agency called Elysee 3, which would represent about 15 models in all.

Casablancas knew very little about the business, however, and when the organization began to struggle, he brought in his older brother Fernando as a partner. When the two squabbled, Fernando took control of Elysee 3. In 1971 Casablancas decided to found a new agency of his own, which he called Elite. He quickly lured away some of his former agency's best models, including Christiansen, and took a former school classmate, Alain Kittler, as his partner, which allowed him to direct his energies toward finding new clients and promoting the agency.

Though models' fees were at that time typically fixed, Casablancas' agency strove to sign only the most beautiful women and began to charge whatever the

COMPANY PERSPECTIVES

With more than 35 agencies in its network and the most powerful model scouting process in the industry (the Elite Model Look), Elite offers complete international coverage. Thirty-four years after opening its doors in Paris, Elite today manages over 800 models from 5 continents. Its approach to the business is based on a sales force capable of finding new models (such as Vanessa Hessler, Michaela H, Linda Vojtova, Leah Dewavrin) and elevating them to top models (Claudia Schiffer, Yasmine Lebon, Gisèle Bundchen, Linda Evangelista, Naomi Campbell and countless others). The Group's clients are comprised of but not limited to: leading fashion magazines, clothing designers, advertising agencies, fashion photographers. A driving force in the modeling profession and synonymous with modeling prestige, Elite is the world's leading model management company.

market would bear, receiving it because of the extraordinary quality of his models. He developed a stable of top names not only because he boosted their earnings, but also because he pampered them and treated them like stars. Unlike the more staid agencies of the day, he cultivated a youthful aura at his office, playing rock music over speakers in the lobby and keeping a refrigerator full of snacks, sodas, and wine available.

Starting with models Anne Schauffus, Gunilla Lindbald, and Beschka, and clients Dior and Mary Quant, during the 1970s Elite rose to the top of the European modeling world. Casablancas eventually formed a partnership in London called Elite Premier and became an affiliate of the famous Ford agency in New York. However, in 1977 Casablancas and longtime Ford booking agent Monique Pillard founded a branch office in New York that quickly lured away many of her former employer's models, as well as those of other agencies. The spurned agencies soon responded with lawsuits seeking more than $20 million in damages. Most were later dropped, although two were settled by arbitration.

Elite head Casablancas soon moved to New York and made it the firm's headquarters, and began traveling the United States scouting for models, leaving the European operations to partner Gerald Marie. Once a girl had been signed, Elite would train her in posing for the camera and runway. New models were often in their midteens, and the agency provided chaperones for those who moved to New York.

At that time a typical model's fee was $100 per hour or $750 per day, with top names earning double that. The agency took 15 to 20 percent of their wages in exchange for distributing photos and securing bookings. About 600 women and 300 men were employed in New York, with much of the firm's work coming from mail-order catalogs and cosmetics advertisements.

LOOK OF THE YEAR CONTEST DEBUTS IN 1983

In 1983 the company launched Look of the Year, an international model search that offered as prizes contracts worth $200,000, $150,000, and $100,000 over several years. The contest was promoted through ads in newspapers and magazines in 25 countries. Some 23,000 women entered the first contest, the finals of which were held in Acapulco. Though not a significant moneymaker, the contest would serve as an important source of new models.

During the early 1980s Casablancas also signed partnerships with top agencies in other markets and began developing a chain of more than 100 franchised modeling schools with his brother Fernando, which served as another pipeline of talent. By 1985 Elite represented 350 models, was affiliated with 14 other agencies worldwide, and had total bookings estimated at $30 million. The firm had offices in New York, Chicago, Los Angeles, Paris, London, Copenhagen, Oslo, Milan, Hamburg, Munich, and Tokyo. Elite owned some, while others were partly owned or franchised.

During this period Elite's development of top-name models helped spark a new pop culture phenomenon, the beautiful, pampered, sometimes tempestuous "supermodel." It was exemplified by client Linda Evangelista, who famously said that she would not even get out of bed for less than $10,000. Other top names of the era included Cindy Crawford, Iman, and Naomi Campbell. Although nurtured by Casablancas, they sometimes were true to their image and left after spats or were lured away by other agencies; however, the firm continued to be notorious for poaching from its rivals as well.

In 1994 the company entered the Asian market, selling the rights to China, Hong Kong, and Macao to a group of Hong Kong investors. Elite also signed a deal with Seoul Broadcasting System of Korea to host the finals of the Look of the Year contest, and agreed to produce the debut Shanghai International Fashion Culture Festival. Another new operation was the

KEY DATES

1971: John Casablancas founds Elite modeling agency in Paris.
1977: New York office opens.
1983: Look of the Year modeling contest debuts.
1985: Elite represents 350 models, has total bookings estimated at $30 million.
1995: Look of the Year contest renamed Elite Model Look.
1998: Licensing subsidiary established.
1999: Firm reorganized in Luxembourg.
2000: John Casablancas leaves the business.
2004: Stung by lawsuits, firm sells bankrupt New York agency and other U.S. operations.
2006: Company is restructured and begins offering stock on Frankfurt exchange.
2007: Name is changed to Elite World S.A.

celebrity division, which represented professional athletes and other well-known names for modeling work. Clients included Ashley Judd, Cameron Diaz, and Drew Barrymore. The firm's billings topped $70 million at that time.

In 1995 Elite Model Management Toronto was formed by the merger of two of that city's top agencies, Elmer Olsen Models and International Top Models. The Look of the Year contest was renamed Elite Model Look during that year, as well.

Casablancas had for some time been licensing the Elite name to manufacturers of clothing and accessories, and in 1995 the firm's Elite Models Fashion unit opened its first clothing store in Paris. More than a dozen licensed outlets followed in Europe, Asia, the Middle East, and the United States over the next several years.

ELITE LICENSING FOUNDED IN 1998

In 1998 a new subsidiary, Elite Licensing Company was created to manage the licensing of the company's name and logo for a variety of fashion and lifestyle products including clothes, luggage, eyewear, and cosmetics. The unit also licensed the name for cafés, beauty salons, and modeling schools. Elite owned a 15 percent stake in ABC Distribution, S.A.S., of France, distributor of some of the licensed goods. During that year the London-based Premier Model Management split from the Elite Group.

By 1999 the firm's revenues included $100 million in billings and $40 million in sales of licensed clothing and accessories endorsed by its clients. Elite had 29 affiliate agencies, employed 250, and represented 500 models worldwide. During the year a new division called Elite 3K was founded to handle the firm's web-based and interactive businesses, launching a new downloadable calendar/organizer loaded with photos of its models. Another affiliate, Illusion 2K, developed a "virtual" model called Webbie Tookay, which was licensed for use in online ads. By this time Elite models were earning from $1,000 to $50,000 per day for print work, $5,000 to $70,000 per day for television commercials, and $100 to $3,000 per hour for runway modeling.

In late November 1999 Elite became embroiled in controversy when the British Broadcasting Corporation (BBC) broadcast secretly shot film of several top executives including Look of the Year head Xavier Moreau making racist comments, and European chief Gerald Marie saying he planned to have sex with several modeling contest finalists, whose average age was 15. Elite and another agency mentioned in the show both took legal action against the BBC, but the firm suspended the four executives shown on tape before the broadcast was shown and sent apologies to models and their parents, calling the actions caught on film "shocking, unacceptable, and highly inappropriate." Marie and Moreau soon resigned, although the firm's European board voted to reinstate them and they later returned.

JOHN CASABLANCAS LEAVES IN 2000

After an attempt to sell half of Elite's holdings to a Hong Kong investment group fell through, in December 1999 the firm was reorganized in Luxembourg as Elite Model World S.A. In the summer of 2000, 57-year-old founder John Casablancas decided to quit the business, having sold his stake in the company for an amount put at $15 million to Swiss businessman Christian Larpin. He moved with his third wife, a former model, to Rio de Janeiro, where he planned to do scouting for an Elite-affiliated agency there. His franchised chain of John Casablancas Modeling and Career Centers continued to operate as well.

In June 2001 the firm reached an out-of-court settlement with the BBC over its controversial 1999 undercover television program. The BBC publicly acknowledged that Elite warned and protected young models from the dangers of sex and drugs as part of the settlement.

In 2002 Gerald Marie began boosting the firm's efforts to open new agencies around the world, and soon added agencies in Vietnam and India. The cost to join the Elite agency group was reportedly $3.5 million. During the year Elite and a dozen other top New York agencies were sued by a group of models who claimed price-fixing, the taking of kickbacks, and overcharging for commissions and expenses. Most of the defendants settled before the case went to trial, but Elite stood its ground against the suit, which had been given class-action status.

In 2003 the New York agency's legal troubles worsened when it was sued by a former executive who claimed her allergy to secondhand cigarette smoke had not been accommodated, and that she had been fired for complaining. A jury awarded her $5.27 million, including punitive damages, which was later reduced to $4.3 million. The firm quickly appealed the verdict.

BANKRUPT NEW YORK AGENCY SOLD IN 2004

Facing this settlement, and the still-unresolved class-action suit by former models, in February 2004 the U.S. branch of Elite filed for bankruptcy protection. It employed 27 and had taken in revenue of $19.4 million during 2003. The parent company, Elite Model Management Group of Switzerland, was not affected, nor were its 33 other subsidiaries and affiliates.

In August the New York agency's assets were sold at auction to Creative World Management LLC for $7.8 million. The deal included Elite offices in Los Angeles and Miami; 50 percent stakes in the Chicago, Atlanta, and Toronto offices; 60 percent of subsidiary One Model Management; and contracts with many top models. The U.S. unit was allowed to continue using the Elite name and logo, but severed all financial and operational ties to the parent firm in Switzerland.

In the summer Elite Model Management Group reportedly was restructured following a power struggle between Gerald Marie and Christian Larpin. Marie had been fired by Larpin, the firm's main shareholder, but with original Elite partner Alain Kittler had managed to buy out Larpin's stake and resume control of the company. Marie was said by some reports to be backed by Mohammed al Fayed, the owner of London retail giant Harrod's.

In the fall of 2004 an Australia/New Zealand Elite affiliate was formed, and plans were announced to hold the 2005 Elite Model Look finals in Sydney. The contest at that time was held in 50 countries and attracted more than 350,000 contestants. In 2005 a licensed Malaysian office was launched, and in December the verdict in the smoking allergy lawsuit was overturned by an appeals court on technical grounds. The firm was then also liquidating its Elite Model Look subsidiary, although the annual contest would continue to be held.

FIRM GOES PUBLIC ON FRANKFURT MARKET IN 2006

In March 2006 Elite Model World was converted from a limited liability company (S.A.R.L.) to a public limited liability company (S.A.), which required the appointment of a board of directors and an independent auditor. A private placement of stock was made on the Frankfurt exchange in May. During the year the American class-action lawsuit was settled for $1.4 million.

In 2006 new agencies opened in Turkey and Marseille, France, the latter calling itself Elite Mediterranee. In the fall the planned finals of Elite Model Look in Thailand were canceled due to political turmoil there, although the event was held in Morocco the following February. For 2006 the firm reported revenues of EUR 32.51 million, and net income of EUR 1.58 million.

Elite had licensed its name to household/beauty products maker Rowenta for the Rowenta Elite Model Look hair styling appliance line, which was distributed in more than 15 countries. Other products using the Elite name included fragrances and a telephone. The company licensed its brand to some 30 companies for use on goods that were sold in 50 countries. Licensing fees at that time amounted to only about 10 percent of the firm's total income, which continued to come primarily from hiring models out for photography and catwalk jobs.

Elite by that time had wholly owned agencies in nine countries, and franchised agencies in 30 others. Key customers included such prestigious fashion companies as Chanel, Dior, Yves Saint Laurent, Victoria's Secret, Donna Karan, Ralph Lauren, and Oscar de la Renta. Though nearly all of its most famous supermodels had long ago left the agency, the firm boasted a roster of 800 models, most of them women. More than two-thirds had been discovered in the Elite Model Look competition, which continued to be held in about 60 countries worldwide.

In February 2007 the firm's name was shortened to Elite World S.A., with Thomas Roggla named nonexecutive director. He reportedly owned 25 percent of the company's shares, and the board, which included Chief Financial Officer Andrew Gleeson and CEO Bernard Hennet, collectively owned more than 50 percent.

February 2007 also saw the firm announce a partnership with Europe Vision to create an Elite branded television network featuring fashion and lifestyle programming around the world, though the plans fell into doubt when Europe Vision suffered financial setbacks later in the year. The company was also working on a television version of its Elite Model Look contest for other networks.

More than 35 years after its founding by John Casablancas, Elite World remained one of the top international modeling agencies. Though its luster had dimmed after the sale of its key New York agency and the defection of many top names like Naomi Campbell and Cindy Crawford, the firm continued to represent a large roster of models through a network of nearly 40 agencies and remained associated with the world's top modeling contest, Elite Model Look. Elite was also working to boost its brand licensing efforts and seeking to raise its profile through increased television exposure.

Frank Uhle

PRINCIPAL SUBSIDIARIES

Elite Management S.A. (Spain; 95%); Elite Model Management Amsterdam B.V. (Holland; 80%); Elite Model Management London (U.K.); Elite Model Management S.A.R.L. (Italy; 85%); Elite Model Management S.A.R.L. (France); Nathalie S.A.R.L. (France; 55%); Inmod A.G. (Switzerland); Elite Licensing Company S.A. (Switzerland); Elite Presse/Model Look France (France); Elite Model Management Prague Sro. (Czech Republic; 60%); Elite Model Management Bratislava Sro. (Slovakia; 60%).

PRINCIPAL COMPETITORS

Models1; IMG; Ford Models, Inc.; Storm Model Management; Select Model Management; Marilyn Agency; Wilhelmina Models, Inc.; Next Model Management; 1 Model Management; MC2 Model Management; DNA Model Management, LLC.

FURTHER READING

"The BBC and Elite Model Management Have Negotiated an Out of Court Settlement," *MediaWeek,* June 15, 2001, p. 5.

Bearn, Emily, "The Man Who Loved Women," *Chicago Sun-Times,* August 6, 2000, p. 2.

Beaty, Keith, "A Man Behaving Badly," *Toronto Star,* December 6, 1999, p. 1.

Carmody, Dierdre, "The World of Models: Chaos with Glamour," *New York Times,* December 7, 1978, p. B1.

Edmonston, Peter, "Elite Falls Off Catwalk," *Daily Deal,* February 13, 2004.

Elite Model Management Lux., S.A., Frankfurt, Germany: Independent Research, 2006.

Fiber, Ben, "Elite Strategists Plan Model Campaign," *Globe and Mail,* April 10, 1985, p. B9.

Gillan, Audrey, and Gary Younge, "Race Bias Attack on Top Model Agency," *Guardian,* November 24, 1999, p. 3.

Gross, Michael, "Girls Interrupted," *New York Magazine,* January 24, 2000.

———, *Model: The Ugly Business of Beautiful Women,* New York: William Morrow, 1995.

———, "Wolfe at the Dorm," *New York Daily News,* March 23, 2003.

Hammond, Tina, "A New Junior Retailer: Elite Models," *Women's Wear Daily,* August 7, 1997, p. 9.

Low, Michelle, "Top Agency Faces Up to Asian Reality," *Business Times Singapore,* November 25, 1994.

Maull, Samuel, "Jury Awards $5.27 Million to Model Agency Employee Who Complained About Smoking," *Associated Press Newswires,* May 14, 2003.

McMorris, Robert, "Model Wars: Casablancas atop the World of Glamour," *Omaha World-Herald,* May 2, 1987.

Murray, Shanon D., "Elite Model Sold Out of Ch. 11," *TheDeal.com,* August 26, 2004.

Peterson, Helen, "4.3M Award Is Stubbed Out," *New York Daily News,* December 30, 2005, p. 39.

Prince, Dinah, "Modeling Agent Abides by Pleasure Principle," *New York Magazine,* April 3, 1988, p. 36.

Rae, Stephen, "The War of the Model Mavens," *Dallas Morning News,* December 2, 1987, p. 10E.

"Rowenta Partners with Elite Model Management to Launch New Range of Hair Styling Appliances," *Al-Bawaba News,* May 30, 2007.

Steiner, Rupert, "Girlfriend Was the Model for Success," *Sunday Times,* April 18, 1999.

Vickers, Marcia, "Not a Pretty Picture at Elite," *BusinessWeek,* June 14, 2004, p. 76.

Vranica, Suzanne, and Shelly Branch, "Fashion Models Say Agents Cheat and Fixed Fees," *Wall Street Journal,* June 27, 2002.

Fairfax Media Ltd.

One Darling Island, Level 5
Pyrmont, New South Wales 2009
Australia
Telephone: (02) 9282-2833
Fax: (02) 9282-1633
Web site: http://www.fxj.com.au

Public Company
Incorporated: 1955 as John Fairfax Ltd.
Employees: 9,474
Operating Revenue: AUD 2.1 billion ($1.84 billion) (2007)
Stock Exchanges: Sydney
Ticker Symbol: FXJ
NAIC: 511110 Newspaper Publishers; 516110 Internet Publishing and Broadcasting; 511120 Periodical Publishers; 511120 Offices of Other Holding Companies

■ ■ ■

Fairfax Media Ltd., formerly known as John Fairfax Holdings Ltd., is the holding company for an Australian publishing enterprise established more than 150 years ago. Family owned and operated until the 1990s, Fairfax is the oldest publishing group in Australia, and one of its largest. In 2007, Fairfax Media merged with Rural Press Ltd., thereby creating the largest multimedia conglomerate in Australasia with ownership of newspapers, magazines, web sites, and radio stations. Fairfax's Australian publications include the *Sydney Morning Herald,* the *Age,* and the *Australian Financial Review.* New Zealand publications include the *Dominion Post,* the *Press,* and the *Sunday Star-Times.*

EARLY HISTORY: 1841–77

The Fairfax family originated in Warwickshire, England, where the patriarch of the family publishing empire, John Fairfax, was born in 1805. At the age of 12 he went to London to work as an apprentice bookseller, librarian, and printer. Returning to Warwickshire in 1827, he started his own printing business and later established a small newspaper, the *Leamington Spa Courier.* In 1835, having converted to a "dissenter's church," he turned his energies to a less conservative paper, the *Leamington Chronicle.*

After being sued twice, however, Fairfax decided to emigrate with his family to Australia, which was then an English penal colony. In 1838 he found work in Sydney as a typesetter for the *Commercial Journal and Advertiser.* After a short stint as a librarian, he purchased an interest in the daily *Sydney Herald* and in 1841 purchased the paper with a partner, Charles Kemp, for £10,000.

With the closure of the rival *Australian* in 1848, the *Herald* dominated local journalism. By 1852 "Granny Herald," as the paper had become known, had a circulation of more than 4,000. The following year, Kemp sold his interest in the paper to Fairfax, who enlisted his son Charles as a partner.

A leader in his community, John Fairfax stood for election in 1856, but lost. Still, with circulation over 6,600 (third in the British Empire only to London's *Times* and *Telegraph*), Fairfax exercised considerable

COMPANY PERSPECTIVES

Fairfax is Australia's leading media company in print and online, serving its communities through high-quality, independent journalism and dynamic venues for commerce and information. Our mastheads include *The Sydney Morning Herald, The Age, The Australian Financial Review, BRW* and *The Sun-Herald.* In addition, Fairfax publishes regional and community newspapers, financial and consumer magazines, and provides online, interactive and e-commerce services through Fairfax Digital.

influence over public opinion. His second son, James Reading Fairfax, joined the partnership and the enterprise became John Fairfax & Sons. The company launched a second paper, the *Sydney Mail,* and installed new, more efficient Richard Hoe rotary presses.

Charles Fairfax died after being thrown from a horse in 1863 and was replaced in the partnership by a third son, Edward. The business continued to expand, particularly after the demise of another competitor, the *Empire.* John Fairfax died in 1877, leaving the business to his two sons.

SECOND-GENERATION LEADERSHIP

James Reading Fairfax strengthened the *Herald*'s reputation for evenhandedness and authority and, with his large build and Edwardian beard, was an imposing figure. It was his bold decision to turn over daily operation of the business to a capable former rival, Hugh George. Under George, the appearance of a competitor, the *Sydney Daily Telegraph,* cut into circulation but not into advertising revenue.

After George died in 1886, Edward grew openly weary of the business and sold his interest to James, who in turn brought his three sons into the company. Meanwhile, Samuel Cook, a parliamentary reporter for the *Herald,* replaced George as general manager.

Cook oversaw the conversion of the *Herald* to mechanical typesetting in 1895, an important move that lowered labor costs and sped production. Such an investment was risky, as the economy was plagued by depression, but soon paid off. Cook left the company in 1907 and was replaced by William George Conley, a former reporter.

THE THIRD GENERATION: 1900–26

James Reading Fairfax, in his seventies, began to delegate more authority to his sons James Oswald and Geoffrey. James Oswald was more domineering than his lighter spirited brother. Due to a weak voice, though, he was forced to precisely punctuate his sentences, a habit that many listeners found annoying.

In 1916, with the outbreak of war in Europe, Australia's involvement as a member of the British Empire brought hardship to the *Herald*'s readership. The Fairfax company, too, had grown beyond effective family administration. So, to limit the family's liability from litigation and facilitate the transfer of interests between family members, John Fairfax & Sons was registered as a limited corporation.

The cost of newsprint increased dramatically during World War I, forcing the company to declare its first operating loss in 1919. This was remedied by raising the sale price of the paper. With the end of the war, however, came the death of the elder James Fairfax at the age of 85. Within years, both Geoffrey, who had no children, and William Conley also died. The principal heir to the family business was James Oswald Fairfax's son Warwick; he had held only brief tenure on the board. When his father died in 1926, Warwick found himself in control of more than a third of the company's shares.

FOURTH-GENERATION LEADERSHIP

The young Warwick Fairfax placed tremendous trust in his managing director, Rupert Henderson, despite an often acrimonious relationship. A previous director, Charles Harris, was fired after four years, for drinking and gambling to excess. Another director, Athol Hugh Stuart, fared better, involving the Fairfax enterprise in a collaboration with Sir Keith Murdoch's *Herald and Weekly Times* (HWT) company to form the Australian Associated Press and a newsprint operation in Tasmania. He also oversaw Fairfax's reversion to proprietary status, eliminating the obligation to publish its balance sheet. But Stuart's demeanor grew violent, and in 1938 he too was fired.

After successive years of declining profit, Henderson reorganized Fairfax. He was so successful in shoring up the bottom line that the company's profits, when compared to the low figures of the previous years, became a source of embarrassment, especially during World War II, when after-tax profits more than doubled.

Warwick, who often wrote for the paper under pseudonyms, was frequently ill during World War II. In

KEY DATES

1841: John Fairfax and Charles Kemp take ownership of the *Sydney Herald.*
1956: John Fairfax Ltd. goes public.
1987: The company is acquired by Tryart Pty. Ltd., a shell company headed by Warwick Fairfax, Jr., after his father's death.
1992: The company is renamed John Fairfax Holdings Ltd. after being acquired by Tourang Ltd.
1998: Fred Hilmer is named CEO of Fairfax.
1999: Company launches web site, www.sold.com.au.
2003: Fairfax acquires New Zealand-based Independent News Media with its publishing and media businesses.
2005: Fairfax expands online presence with the acquisition of RSVP.COM.AU Pty Ltd.; David Kirk is named CEO.
2006: Fairfax Media and Rural Press Ltd. merge.
2007: Company is renamed Fairfax Media Ltd.

1944 one of his articles so enraged Henderson that he accused Warwick of developing "an evangelical fervor" and threatened to resign. The two made amends, however, and Henderson stayed on.

Warwick Fairfax had a troubled personal life, which led to his first divorce. While he remarried in 1948, he and Henderson became concerned about the possible loss of family control of the enterprise. They persuaded some family members to relinquish their interests in the company to them and virtually ran the company as a committee of two until 1949, when Angus Henry McLachlan was promoted to general manager.

COMPETING IN A GROWING MEDIA MARKET: 1950–70

Fairfax fought numerous battles for niche markets during this period, substantially expanding its publishing empire in and around Sydney with such papers as the *Australian Financial Review.* When rival Frank Packer made a bid to acquire several papers run by the independent Associated Newspapers, Henderson beat him to the punch, in effect merging that business with Fairfax. Later, several of the papers and their operations were consolidated into one facility, a new production house on Sydney's Broadway.

In 1955 Fairfax also acquired a license for Sydney's ATN7 television. The expansion stretched Fairfax's financial resources so thinly that the company was forced to go public on April 9, 1956.

Warwick Fairfax, meanwhile, had become embroiled in another matrimonial debacle when, it was charged, he forced the breakup of a friend's marriage. He divorced a second time, married his friend's wife, and was forced to leave the company temporarily to settle litigation. Warwick renewed his waning interest in the company, which, under Henderson's managerial direction, had obtained a second television station, QTQ in Brisbane. The company also took over its number two rival in Sydney, the *Mirror Newspapers,* through a shell company.

The *Mirror,* however, was a poor fit and was sold in 1960 to Keith Rupert Murdoch, who had inherited his father's publishing group. Murdoch used this entrée into Sydney wisely, using the *Mirror*'s publishing facilities to launch a rival national paper, the *Australian.* In 1972 Murdoch also snapped up Packer's *Daily Telegraph* and *Sunday Telegraph,* which competed directly with Fairfax.

Fairfax, however, had also been busy during the 1960s, acquiring the *Newcastle Morning Herald, Newcastle Sun,* and *Canberra Times,* an interest in Canberra television station CTC, and the Australian share of the British television group ATV. Six radio stations that came with ATV were later spun off as Macquarie Broadcasting Holdings Ltd.

Henderson retired in 1964 but retained his seat on the board. He was succeeded as chief executive officer by McLachlan. Under McLachlan, Fairfax acquired the Melbourne-based Syme company, which published the *Age* and, beginning in 1969, the 114-year-old *Illawarra Mercury.* Later that year, McLachlan suffered a coronary occlusion that forced his retirement. Unwilling to return managerial control of the paper to the 68-year-old Warwick, McLachlan, Henderson, and Warwick's cousin Vincent nominated R. P. Falkingham as the company's treasurer. Outraged, Warwick put up a good fight and later won, though from the ceremonial position of chairman. At last, he had direct editorial control and the power to fire people.

NEW GENERATION ON THE HORIZON

However, after the company launched a nationwide weekend paper, the *National Times,* in 1971, Fairfax's directors and other employees grew increasingly irritated by the arch-conservative views of Warwick. The situation came to a head in July 1976, when the directors asked Warwick to resign in favor of his son, James Fairfax, who had distinguished himself at the helm of Amalgamated Television. This time, they succeeded.

While relegated to a minor position in the company, Warwick mounted an ill-conceived attempt to take over Fairfax and was forced to cede even more power as a result. R. P. Falkingham, meanwhile, finally assumed the position of chief executive officer. He was properly suited for the job, showing no bias for Fairfax's newspaper business over its other important media divisions.

All aspects of the Fairfax Group, though, were suffering reverses in the marketplace. Falkingham responded by adopting more realistic rates and prices and, in 1977, placed D. N. Bowman in charge of the flagship *Sydney Morning Herald.* Bowman made several changes, including the implementation of the computer-based Arsycom cold type press system, which drastically reduced production costs.

In 1979 Rupert Murdoch surfaced again with a bid to take over Fairfax's other rival, the *Herald and Weekly Times.* Determined to thwart Murdoch, Fairfax began amassing a "friendly" holding in its competitor. In the end, however, the government compelled Murdoch to abandon his bid on antitrust grounds. The defense of the HWT cost Fairfax dearly, causing it to sell its interests in CTC and QTQ television.

In addition, sales of Fairfax's *Herald* and *Sun* were stagnant; the company's Sungravure magazines, acquired with Associated Newspapers during the 1950s, were in trouble; and its interest in Macquarie Broadcasting showed no gains. Perhaps out of desperation, Falkingham recommended that he be replaced as general manager by 36-year-old Gregory John Gardiner, and that Fairfax's five Sydney papers be put under the editorial direction of Maxwell Victor Suich.

LABOR ISSUES AND TAKEOVER THREATS: 1979

Warwick Fairfax, still offering his opinions, opposed the appointment of Suich and Gardiner, whom he considered too young. Nevertheless, the appointments stood. Under the direction of the two men, the tenor of the *Herald* and its sister papers became decidedly cynical, even sensational. While this was extremely distasteful to the aging board, they could not deny that circulation, if not yet profit margin, was rebounding strongly.

Despite attempts to modernize Fairfax, much of the company's labor-intensive production capacity was outdated and increasingly uncompetitive. A decision to overhaul several facilities led to serious labor trouble, particularly at Sungravure Magazines, where workers were on strike for higher pay. Gardiner championed the cause of upgrading the facilities and, in the end, succeeded, resulting in the layoff of 375 Sungravure employees. The division subsequently changed its name to Fairfax Magazines Pty. Ltd.

Opposing Gardiner in this and many other matters was Falkingham, who quickly fell out of favor with the board and was forced to resign. Rather than replace him, the board split Falkingham's responsibilities between Gardiner and Fred Benchley, a veteran of the magazine group.

The pressure for consolidation in the Australian publishing industry hit a fever pitch in the mid-1980s. Financiers such as Rupert Murdoch, Robert Holmes à Court, and Alan Bond swarmed over the market, raiding smaller companies to consolidate their operations with other papers they controlled.

After Murdoch's aborted attempt to enter Fairfax's Sydney market in 1979, Holmes à Court launched an unsuccessful bid for Fairfax in 1981. Far more serious, however, was Murdoch's second attempt at the *Herald and Weekly Times* in 1986. This time, the company's board advised its shareholders to accept the buyout offer from Murdoch's News Corporation. A combined HWT/News organization was capable of dominating advertising rates throughout Australia through network advertising.

FENDING OFF RUPERT MURDOCH: 1986

Fairfax Group was determined to foil Murdoch. So, however, was Holmes à Court, who offered nearly AUD 2 million for HWT. Murdoch countered with a AUD 2.3 million bid for HWT and its Queensland Press subsidiary. Although Fairfax offered a bid of its own, it was too low to be taken seriously. Fairfax could do little but watch. Sir Warwick was by this time gravely ill, which only complicated matters.

In January 1987 Murdoch struck a deal with Holmes à Court, in which Holmes à Court would sell all of his existing shares in HWT to Murdoch, increasing his control of HWT to 44 percent. Later, he arranged to purchase Advertising Newspaper's 11 percent share in HWT and emerged with a majority.

In order to stay ahead of regulators and make his deal work, Murdoch was forced to reorganize his television properties. In a complex deal involving Murdoch, Fairfax, Bond, Holmes à Court, and HWT's Kerry Packer, virtually every major station changed hands. Fairfax emerged with the Melbourne television station Murdoch had promised to Holmes à Court, and thus held television, radio, and newspaper interests in Sydney and Melbourne.

NEW OWNERSHIP AND REORGANIZATION

Warwick Fairfax died in 1987, but the battle for supremacy in Australian journalism was not over. Later that year, fearing that Holmes à Court would bid for Fairfax, Warwick's 26-year-old son, Warwick, Jr., launched a surprise bid for control of the company, under the belief that many of the 150 Fairfax family members would not sell their shares to Holmes à Court.

Warwick's takeover, launched through a shell company called Tryart Pty. Limited, succeeded in taking the company private. In the process, he deeply split the family and placed Tryart AUD $1.7 billion in debt. In order to service the company's heavy debt, Tryart was forced to sell several assets of the Fairfax Group.

In December 1990 the leveraged buyout failed when Tryart proved unable to meet its debt service obligations and was forced into receivership. Warwick Fairfax, Jr.'s bid to protect the company had only made it more vulnerable for a takeover. Almost immediately, a bid was made for the company, not from the Australians Murdoch or Holmes à Court, but by Canadian newspaper financier Conrad Black, in partnership with Kerry Packer, whose paper the Fairfaxes had once endeavored to rescue from such a takeover.

Black was widely despised in world banking and publishing circles, but had distinguished himself some years earlier by turning London's *Daily Telegraph* into a highly profitable venture. Upon news of the bid in 1991, Fairfax's employees went on strike, protesting Black's antilabor record and right-wing political views.

Despite the opposition, Black ironed out a deal with Tryart's creditors and assembled a consortium called Tourang Limited, which consisted of Black's Telegraph PLC, Hellman & Friedman, and Consolidated Press Holdings. Consolidated Press was forced to withdraw from Tourang after Australian regulators questioned the legality of its participation under media cross-ownership regulations.

Tourang succeeded in taking over all the assets of Tryart, including John Fairfax Pty. Ltd. On January 7, 1992, Tourang changed its name to John Fairfax Holdings Limited and gained a listing on the Australian Stock Exchange.

The ill-fated attempt to save Fairfax Group Pty. Ltd. from nonfamily interests only accelerated the family's loss of its patriarch's company. However, it may have happened soon enough to save Fairfax from several years of poor performance under what many considered to be inept "newspaper man" management. Black restored financial strength to the Fairfax organization and ensured that, if nothing else, at least the company did not fall into the hands of Rupert Murdoch.

DIVERSIFYING FOR FINANCIAL STABILITY

In Black's first year as nominal head of the resuscitated Fairfax group, the company's publications garnered numerous awards and marked respectable financial performances, in spite of the depressed Australian economy. Renamed John Fairfax Media Holdings Limited, under Black's leadership the company also began to diversify its interests.

In 1995 the company purchased interests in Australian Geographic Pty, a company that operated a popular magazine and a chain of retail stores selling books and outdoor exploration equipment. Although the company later sold *Australian Geographic* (in 1998), the purchase was one of several efforts in the 1990s to diversify the company's interests.

In 1998 Fairfax hired Fred Hilmer, former professor of business at the University of New South Wales, as the company's CEO. Hilmer inherited the business at a time when the laws surrounding Australian media ownership were in a state of flux and he attempted to streamline the company by selling several less profitable subsidiaries and funneling funds into the company's core assets. After a year with Hilmer at the helm, Fairfax was beginning to show signs of increased profitability. Advertising revenues increased by over 30 percent during 1998, and by early 1999 the company controlled 15 percent of the Australian advertising market.

Hilmer's various projects included increasing the company's focus on digital media and communication. In 1999, Fairfax launched a new web site, www.sold.com.au, to complement the company's growing digital media division. In 2000, Fairfax entered into a joint venture with the New York company News Alert LLC to create News Alert Asia-Pacific, a subsidiary company that would create a number of web sites aimed at providing financial and business information for the Asia-Pacific region and for investors and business people in the United States interested in researching opportunities in the Pacific.

REBOUNDING FROM HARD TIMES

Like many Australian companies, Fairfax suffered reduced revenues during the economic slump that followed the 2000 Olympic Games. Despite falling advertising revenues, which constituted over 80 percent of the company's revenue base, many of Fairfax's subsidiaries showed an increase in consumers. Hilmer's response was to look into selective expansion procedures and acquisitions while investing capital to reinvigorate the company's most profitable properties.

Fairfax continued to suffer from a poor advertising market in 2002 year with a 28 percent reduction in profit from the previous year. In 2003 the company strengthened its position with strategic acquisitions. In March the company gained 10 percent interest in Text Media Group Limited, which gave the company a strong presence in the online real estate advertising market. The company acquired the remaining interest in Text Media in February 2004.

The most significant development of 2003 was the completion of a major acquisition, in May, of New Zealand-based Independent News Media, which became known as Fairfax New Zealand. In addition to gaining control of two metropolitan newspapers, two Sunday papers and 53 community publications, the purchase also gave Fairfax ownership of 66 percent of Sky TV New Zealand. "The acquisition of these prime publishing assets will contribute strongly to our future growth," Hilmer said in the company's official press statements. Fairfax reportedly paid over NZD 6.6 billion for ownership of the New Zealand media outlets.

By 2004, Fairfax's financial returns were growing rapidly and profits had risen by over 60 percent from the previous year. Hilmer announced in 2004 that he would be stepping down the following year to pursue other opportunities, perhaps returning to academia for the final chapter in his professional life. While the board of directors conducted interviews to find Hilmer's replacement, the management team was in the process of engineering another string of strategic acquisitions aimed at building the company's presence in the Internet media market.

Hilmer left Fairfax a stronger company for his seven years as CEO and prepared the company for another wave of growth in his absence. However, Hilmer's departure was also controversial as some objected to his AUD 4.5 million payout as part of his retirement package. Hilmer returned to the academic community as vice-chancellor and president of the University of New South Wales, a position with over $700,000 in annual compensation.

GROWTH IN THE 21ST CENTURY

In 2005 Ron Walker, former treasurer of the Australian Liberal Party and a board member at Fairfax since 2003, took the helm as chairman of the board. In addition, the company completed its 16-month search for a new CEO when the board voted to hire David Kirk, a former professional rugby player from New Zealand with a diverse list of accomplishments to his credit. In addition to his sports career, Kirk received an advanced degree in medicine from the University of Otago and won a Rhodes Scholarship to the University of Worcester. Before accepting the position, Kirk had worked as a management consultant and a media commentator and had developed a positive reputation in the industry.

In 2005 Kirk helped to finalize acquisitions begun under Hilmer's leadership including the purchase of the leading online dating site in Australia, www.rsvp.com.au, and the acquisition of New Zealand's Rodney Times family of newspapers, which bolstered Fairfax New Zealand. The acquisition of rsvp.com reportedly cost the company in excess of AUD 38 million but it was a strategic choice aimed at helping the company enter the thriving online networking and dating industry. At the end of the year, the company further diversified its Internet offerings with the acquisition of Stayz Australia, an online travel site focusing on holiday accommodations and packages.

Kirk continued his predecessor's strategy of online growth the following year with the acquisition of Trade Me Limited, a New Zealand-based auction site that had become the country's largest and fastest-growing Internet marketplace. Kirk also negotiated the acquisition of several smaller newspaper chains, but the bulk of the year was spent in negotiations over a proposed merger with Rural Press. The merger had been proposed several times since the late 1990s but the board felt that the price was too high for consideration. Under the company's new leadership, Fairfax and Rural Press entered negotiations and the merger was completed in December 2006, forming Australia's largest media conglomerate with over AUD 9 billion in assets. The merger was significant also in that it brought the Fairfax family back to the company, as John B. Fairfax of Rural Press was named to the company's board of directors. In January of 2007 the company changed its name to Fairfax Media Limited.

By mid-2007 the company had recovered from management reshuffling following the merger and Kirk again began implementing plans for expansion, opening several new business and news sites to New Zealand and Australian audiences. In November Kirk completed an agreement to purchase Southern Star Television Production and Southern Cross Metro Radio from Macquarie Media Group. The sale, which had been in the works since 2006, marked the beginning of a new period in

Fairfax's history as the company prepared to expand further into the radio and television markets. With an estimated audience of 6 million readers daily, including print and online productions, and operating revenues exceeding AUD 2.1 billion, Fairfax had become Australia's leading media empire.

John Simley
Updated, Micah L. Issitt

PRINCIPAL SUBSIDIARIES

Associated Newspapers Ltd.; AAV New Zealand Ltd. (95%); David Syme & Co., Ltd.; Dysford Pty. Ltd.; Fairfax Community Newspapers Pty. Ltd.; Fairfax Corporation Pty. Ltd.; Fairfax Finance Pty. Ltd.; Fairfax Ian Ltd.; Fairfax Investments Pty. Ltd.; Fairfax Letterbox Australia Pty. Ltd.; Fairfax Newspaper Holdings Pty. Ltd.; Homes Pictorial Publications Ltd. (80%); Homes Pictorial Unit Trust (80%); Illawarra Newspapers Holdings Pty. Ltd.; Intercity Hire Pty. Limited; John Fairfax Group Pty. Ltd.; John Fairfax Group Finance Pty. Ltd.; John Fairfax Group Inc. (United States); John Fairfax Ltd.; John Fairfax & Sons Ltd.; John Fairfax Ltd. (New Zealand); John Fairfax Ltd. (United Kingdom); John Fairfax Ltd. (United States); Joynton Ave No. 2 Pty. Ltd.; Magazine Promotions Australia Pty. Ltd.; Magazine Properties Pty. Ltd.; Magdiss Pty. Ltd.; Manoa Investments Pty. Ltd.; Morisset Courier Unit Trust (80%); Newcastle Newspapers Pty. Ltd.; Rozelle Terminal Handling Company Pty. Ltd.; Ridge Publications Pty. Ltd.; S. Richardson (Newspapers) Pty. Ltd.; Suburban Investments Pty. Ltd.; Syme Communications Ltd. (New Zealand); Syme Electronic Communications Pty. Ltd.; Syme Media Pty. Ltd.; Syme Travel & Entertainment Pty. Ltd.; Suburban Community Newspapers Pty. Ltd.; The Rockwood Pastoral Company Pty. Ltd.; Votraint (No. 297) Pty. Ltd.; Votraint (No. 427) Pty. Ltd.; Wattle Street Properties Pty. Ltd.

PRINCIPAL COMPETITORS

APN News and Media Ltd.; Consolidated Media Holdings, Ltd.; News Corporation.

FURTHER READING

Carney, Shaun, "What Makes Ron Run," *Age,* March 11, 2006.

"Catching Up with Fred Hilmer," *McKinsey News,* December 13, 2006.

"Conrad Black Likes a Good Fight, and He's Getting One," *Business Week,* December 2, 1991.

"Fairfax Moves on NZ Media," *Australian,* April 14, 2003, 1p. 39.

"Fairfax Takes Equity Stake in News Alert LLC," *Fairfax Online,* March 15, 2000.

Foltz, Kim, "Canadian Financier Adds to Media Holdings," *New York Times,* December 18, 1991.

"John Fairfax Board Moves to Put Firm into Receivership," *Wall Street Journal,* December 11, 1990.

Ricketson, Matthew, "Executives in Place After Fairfax Merger," *Age,* June 22, 2007.

Souter, Gavin, *Heralds and Angels: The House of Fairfax, 1841–1990,* Carlton, Victoria, Australia: Melbourne University Press, 1991.

"Transcript: David Kirk, CEO of Fairfax Media," *CNN Online,* January 9, 2007.

Gartner, Inc.

56 Top Gallant Road
P.O. Box 10212
Stamford, Connecticut 06904-2212
U.S.A.
Telephone: (203) 964-0096
Fax: (203) 316-1100
Web site: http://www.gartner.com

Public Company
Incorporated: 1979 as Gartner Group, Inc.
Employees: 4,000
Sales: $1.2 billion (2007)
Stock Exchanges: New York
Ticker Symbol: IT
NAIC: 518111 Information Retrieval Services; 511210 Prepackaged Software; 541910 Marketing Research and Public Opinion Polling

■ ■ ■

Gartner, Inc., is one of the leading U.S. providers of research and analysis for the information technology (IT) industry, which is composed in part by the computer hardware, software, application, network, and communications industries. Gartner operates in four primary areas: Gartner Research provides IT companies with extensive intelligence and advice either through direct consulting or subscriptions to online research products; Gartner Events oversees conferences and programs for IT professionals; Gartner Consulting provides individual service for corporate clients in need of business plans and strategies for managing their IT operations; and Gartner Executive Programs provides programming and information for corporate CIOs (chief information officers). The company has offices located in more than 75 countries and reports that 80 percent of the Global 500 relies on Gartner for IT solutions.

THE EARLY YEARS: 1979–83

Gartner Group, Inc., was founded in 1979 by Gideon Gartner as a provider of research and analysis in the field of information technology (IT), with a specialization in information about IBM and its products. At the time that he created the company, Gartner possessed many years of experience in the IT field, after having worked for IBM in both the United States and Europe in the company's competitive intelligence operations division. Prior to that, he had received his bachelor's degree in mechanical engineering at the Massachusetts Institute of Technology, and his master's of science degree in management at the Sloan School.

Following his stint at IBM, Gartner was a partner at Oppenheimer & Co., where he worked as an analyst and developed the research methods that later came to typify Gartner Group. While at Oppenheimer, Gartner was rated as the top individual securities analyst in the technology field for seven straight years by *Institutional Investor.* As computers became more prevalent in the work world, Gartner began to research and track the computer industry more so than did other securities dealers. He attended countless trade association meetings and IBM user meetings and combined that

COMPANY PERSPECTIVES

Gartner offers the combined brainpower of 1,200 research analysts and consultants who advise executives in 75 countries every day. We publish tens of thousands of pages of original research annually and answer 200,000 client questions every year. We can help you make smarter and faster decisions. Our years of relevant experience and institutional knowledge prevent costly and avoidable errors. Be confident that with Gartner, your decisions are the right decisions. Gartner is not just bigger, more networked, or more influential than the competition. We are in a league of our own.

information with the knowledge he possessed from his time at IBM to gain an insight into the industry that other analysts did not have. Thus, his research became quite valuable to those in the business of buying and selling computer and telecommunications equipment.

After Oppenheimer failed to pay as much attention to Gartner's research as he wanted, Gartner decided to start his own company. At that point, other consulting firms such as Dataquest had established themselves as counsel for the Silicon Valley computer manufacturers, so Gartner decided instead to target his services at confused corporate computer users. He approached Oppenheimer with an opportunity for a partnership, but the company declined. Instead, Gartner teamed up with David Stein, and in 1979 the two launched Gartner Group, Inc., with only $675,000 in venture capital. Initially they had no clients, but Oppenheimer soon agreed to give them existing contracts in exchange for royalties.

Gartner and Stein then went about the business of providing advice and information to buyers and sellers of computers. Their company spent a majority of its time tracking IBM and its advances, and then delivered information to clients in a substantially different form than did most other consulting firms. In attempting to help a client make a decision regarding a product or a marketing strategy, Gartner would forgo the typical lengthy and often-ignored written study, opting instead for a straightforward and easy-to-understand one-page memo. This strategy helped the company increase its customer base, and Gartner Group was soon a well-established presence on the IT scene.

ACQUISITIONS AND ADJUSTMENTS: 1983–90

Gartner Group, Inc., soon became well known for its "insider" perspective on IBM and the comprehensive information that it possessed about the company's products and services. In 1983, Gartner Group was actually sued by IBM, who alleged that the consulting company had illegally revealed IBM trade secrets. The suit was later settled out of court. Gartner was quoted in *Intercorp* as saying that IBM was known to consistently provide Gartner Group with "enough information so we don't totally screw up, but not enough so that they are telling us what is really going on." At that time, many of Gartner Group's analysts were former employees of IBM, which may have led to the technology giant's unease at having a third party counsel its customers about its products.

Meanwhile, Gartner had been developing an addition to the company that was engaged in providing the investment community with advice and information related to the IT industry. This new brokerage and investment division was separated from Gartner Group in 1985 and became a wholly owned subsidiary called Gartner Group Securities. The following year, after seven years of steady increases in sales and earnings since its foundation, Gartner Group initiated a public offering of its stock. Within a year, the company ranked ninth on the 1987 *Business Week* list of "Best Small Companies and Corporations," and an overwhelming majority of the top *Fortune* 100 companies were part of Gartner's client list.

Just one year later, in 1988, the company was purchased for $90.3 million by the British communications firm Saatchi & Saatchi. No major changes were made within Gartner Group following the takeover, and business proceeded as usual for both entities, with Saatchi & Saatchi acting as a holding company. Gartner Group benefited from the deal because its new owner was able to offer the still-growing company any necessary capital support, as well as help the consulting firm increase market share on an international level. Meanwhile, Saatchi & Saatchi would benefit from Gartner's in-depth knowledge of the industry, in order to make wise decisions regarding future acquisitions.

By the time the acquisition by Saatchi & Saatchi was complete, Gartner Group had expanded from the one service it had offered when founded to 13 different "Continuous Services," each of which provided in-depth analysis of different high-tech industry segments. Continuous Services were available for subscription to clients on an annual basis. Revenues for the 1988 fiscal year topped off at $40 million, which gave the company a profit of $2.3 million for the year.

KEY DATES

1979: Company founded by Gideon Gartner.
1985: Company establishes financial subsidiary Gartner Group Securities.
1988: British communications firm Saatchi & Saatchi purchases company.
1990: Dun & Bradstreet purchases 54 percent interest under Information Partners group.
1993: Gideon Gartner sells his equity position and completely severs ties with the company.
1998: Gartner begins trading on the New York Stock Exchange.
2000: Company simplifies name to Gartner, Inc.
2002: Gartner begins publishing information technology (IT) books with John Wiley & Sons.
2003: Gartner introduces employee rewards and research program known as Gartner Fellows.
2006: Company sales surpass the $1 billion mark.

Just a year later, however, Saatchi & Saatchi's bid to become a business service powerhouse took a turn for the worse. After plowing through a short-lived and perhaps overzealous acquisition phase, the advertising and communications giant suddenly found itself short of cash and began making changes to avoid being taken over itself. In late 1989, it decided to begin selling many of the consulting firms that it had just purchased, including Gartner Group. Gideon Gartner himself made plans to repurchase his company. In an attempt to discourage any other potential suitors, Gartner stated that he would quit in 1991 when his contract expired if he lost the bidding, hoping that the idea of Gartner Group without its founder would be unappealing to another bidder.

NEW OWNERSHIP AND GROWTH: 1990–99

In 1990, Gartner Group management led a leveraged buyout of the company, with assistance from Dun & Bradstreet. The new owner was listed as a group called Information Partners Capital Fund, L.P., while the company itself became Gartner Group, Inc., Holding Corp. (GHC). GHC was then merged back into Gartner Group, Inc., under new management, including a new president and CEO named Manny Fernandez. At that time, Gideon Gartner left the day-to-day operations of the company. New management restructured the ailing company, which had suffered losses during its time with Saatchi & Saatchi. Although the company registered increased revenue figures during 1991 and 1992, its books remained in the red. Gideon Gartner stayed with the company—on paper only—until 1993, when he sold his equity position and completely severed ties with the company.

In 1993, Gartner Group finally registered earnings of $6.8 million on $122.5 million in sales for the year. This boost in profitability enabled the company to go public again, listing and offering shares of its stock on NASDAQ. With offices spread throughout 20 different countries, Gartner Group continued to provide its growing client base with objective research and analysis of the IT industry. The company also began positioning itself for expansion, which it initiated with the acquisition of New Science at the end of 1993, and of Real Decisions from NYNEX Worldwide Services Group, Inc., in early 1994.

If 1994 was a successful year at Gartner, with earnings more than doubling to $15 million from sales of $169 million, then 1995 was outstanding: earnings skyrocketed to $25.5 million from sales of $229.2 million. In July 1995, Gartner purchased a majority interest in Relational Courseware, Inc. (RCI), a developer of computer-based training products. RCI continued to operate as an independent company, although it took advantage of Gartner's worldwide distribution channels and could use Gartner's extensive network of research analysts. Later that year, Gartner also expanded its holdings with the formation of Gartner Group Japan, K.K., and with the purchase of longtime IT consulting rival Dataquest. The Dataquest acquisition greatly increased Gartner's share of the IT consulting market.

In 1996, Dun & Bradstreet's (D&B) 54 percent stake in Gartner Group, Inc., was transferred to a D&B subsidiary called Cognizant Corp. The transfer of holdings, however, caused no major changes in Gartner's day-to-day operations. The consulting company continued to seek out and purchase other companies that complemented its own services, including Internet vendor Fox Industries, Italian consulting entity Nomos Ricerca, J3 Learning (a leading provider of IT training products), and Mindware Technologies. In order to accommodate its rapid expansion efforts, the company increased its base of analysts by 25 percent.

The late 1990s marked a surge in popularity and use of the Internet as a means of transferring and obtaining information, and Gartner took advantage of the trend by creating a web site called @vantage. @vantage was a compilation of information about industry outlooks and research about the IT industry, in an easy-to-find and simple-to-use format. Although Gartner Group had traditionally faced very few direct competitors in its field, the end of the century drew rumors that Gideon Gartner was planning on launching his own IT consulting service, and he did launch Giga Information Group and Soundview Technologies, both later sold to larger IT firms. Even in the face of competition by its own founder, however, Gartner Group still possessed major advantages: years of experience and a stellar reputation among a client base that included almost all of the top companies in the world.

In 1997 and 1998, Gartner continued its aggressive strategy of acquiring competitors. Gartner bought French technology publisher Bouhot & LeGendre and also the Singapore-based IT vendor and information services compiler Datapro Information Services, Inc. Next, Gartner acquired Swedish company Informatics MCAB, which specialized in management consultation, and in 1998 acquired the National Institute of Management Technology in Ireland and Norbert Miconnet Information Technology Advisors in France. With a wave of European expansion, the company's position in foreign markets was greatly strengthened, and Gartner was also able to increase the range of services offered to domestic customers. Gartner also established, in 1998, a technology education program at five U.S. postsecondary institutions. The program provided classes in IT services, management, and analysis.

Also in 1998, Gartner began trading its shares on the New York Stock Exchange under the ticker symbol IT. The following year brought new leadership, as CEO William Clifford left the firm to accept a position at a start-up IT company, and the board of directors voted former Chief Financial Officer Michael Fleisher to replace Clifford as CEO. Among Fleisher's first projects was to initiate an extensive program to bring Gartner to the forefront of the emerging e-commerce industry. Gartner purchased INTECO Corporation, a company specializing in e-business research, and also invested in software for e-commerce applications. The company's own gartner.com web site went live in 2001.

GARTNER IN THE 21ST CENTURY

Gartner expanded its staff by over 400 new hires in the first quarter of 2000, which included 24 new e-commerce professionals. Under Fleisher's leadership, the company continued its expansion and thus streamlined the company's name to Gartner, Inc. While several competitors were challenged during this time by fluctuations in the Internet market (the so-called bursting of the dot-com bubble), Gartner remained strong with its core focus on analysis and research. The company's web site was redesigned and debuted in 2001. While it initially met with criticism from users, being fraught with glitches from faulty programming, Gartner moved quickly to address the problems.

In 2002, Gartner, along with publisher John Wiley & Sons, produced three books aimed at helping business managers and laypersons understand the development of business and technology. The company's first release, *World Without Secrets,* was written by Gartner analyst Richard Hunter and dealt with issues regarding computer privacy, security, crime, and the Internet era. The second book, *Achieving Business Value from Technology,* was written by company Vice-President Tony Murphy and was intended as a practical guide to using technology to fuel business growth. The company followed these up with *Consumer Evolution,* written by company research director Judy Carr and industry scientist Charles Graham, which explored the evolution of consumer psychology in the information age and provided a guide to businesses looking to maximize the potential of their expenditures on technology and e-business.

During this time Gartner introduced an employee rewards and research program known as Gartner Fellows. Employees chosen for the program were granted the title of Fellow and were given a two-year period in which to work outside their regular duties to develop between one and five of their own ideas with the support and resources of Gartner at their disposal. Each Fellow's work was published as Gartner company research, which was analyzed by competitors, clients, and industry experts. Much of the data that came from the company's Gartner Fellows program involved interviews and research sessions with industry leaders and entrepreneurs from leading technology and research companies. The data that were collected served not only to reinvigorate Gartner's existing bank of knowledge but also as a resource for educators, students, and employees of the industry.

In 2004, the company's board of directors voted to make Gene Hall CEO of the company and to eliminate the position of chief operating officer, formerly held by Maureen O'Connell, who had been named to the position in 2003. Hall praised O'Connell, who was named CFO for Barnes and Noble, Inc., the following year, for her year at the helm of Gartner but indicated that the board of directors felt the business needed a more unified executive structure.

Gartner grew significantly during the second financial quarter of 2005 by acquiring META Group, one of the company's major competitors in IT consulting and analysis. According to CEO Hall, the acquisition was intended to strengthen Gartner's core research business and to give the company stronger representation in the United Kingdom and Germany. Dale Kutnick, former chairman of META, was also asked to serve as director of research and senior vice-president for Gartner after the buyout.

In September 2005, Gartner increased its presence in the Chinese market by expanding an existing research office opened by the company in 2002. Gartner established a wholly foreign-owned enterprise in Beijing to aid in expanding the range of services and products that could be brought to Chinese consumers. In 2007, two of Gartner's leading analysts published the book *IT and Asia* in conjunction with Harvard University Business School, which focused on the development and dominance of China and India in the technology sales and development markets.

Also during this time Gartner initiated its Gartner Business Intelligence (BI) Excellence Awards to recognize companies that demonstrated leadership in the integration and analysis of business data and information. Continental Airlines was named as the recipient of the first BI Excellence Award, with AXA Financial and Cardinal Health also receiving nominations. The BI Excellence Awards also promoted Gartner's business research industry by sharing the successes and strategies of the world's leading IT businesses with a global audience.

Following its growth and global expansion, Gartner enjoyed a position of leadership among the world's IT consulting firms. Its stock reflected industry and consumer confidence, with prices rising to over $20 per share. Moreover, the company's sales increased, surpassing the $1 billion mark by 2005 and $1.2 billion by 2007. Continued growth seemed likely.

Laura E. Whiteley
Updated, Micah L. Issitt

PRINCIPAL OPERATING UNITS

Gartner Research; Gartner Executive Programs; Gartner Events; Gartner Consulting.

PRINCIPAL COMPETITORS

The Butler Group; Forrester Research, Inc.; Cutter Consortium; IDC Research, Inc.; Yankee Group Research, Inc.

FURTHER READING

Brubeck, Noreen, "Gartner Group Sold to Saatchi & Saatchi," *Fairfield County Business Journal,* June 20, 1988, p. 1.

Burke, Steven, "London Ad Agency Buys Gartner, Hopes to Be Top Consulting Firm," *PC Week,* July 11, 1988, p. 133.

"Company News: Gartner Group to Buy Back up to 15.7 Million Shares," *New York Times,* July 17, 1999.

Deutschman, Alan, "What Price Freedom?" *Fortune,* November 20, 1989, p. 213.

Ferranti, Mark, "Gartner, Align Thyself," *CIO,* November 15, 2001.

Finucane, Stephanie, "Gartner Group Revenues Climb as Market's Thirst for Research Intensifies," *Fairfield County Business Journal,* March 21, 1994, p. 7.

"Gartner Announces Business Intelligence Summit, 2007," *Business Wire,* January 16, 2007.

LaMonica, Martin, "Gartner Acquires Smaller Rival Meta," *CNet News,* December 27, 2004.

Lohr, Steve, "Millionaires by the Dozen: They Know Computers, Who Knows Them?" *New York Times,* October 1, 1995, p. F1.

Matters, Craig, "Gartner Group Tracks Big Blue for Fun and Profit," *Intercorp,* January 24, 1986, p. 13.

Popoloski, Martha, "Gideon Gartner Becomes Chairman of BIS Decisions and Giga Information Group," *PR Newswire,* June 5, 1995.

Granite City Food & Brewery Ltd.

5402 Parkdale Drive, Suite 101
Minneapolis, Minnesota 55416
U.S.A.
Telephone: (952) 215-0660
Fax: (952) 525-2021
Web site: http://www.gcfb.net

Public Company
Incorporated: 1997 as Founders Food & Firkins Ltd.
Employees: 1,955
Sales: $58.3 million (2006)
Stock Exchanges: NASDAQ
Ticker Symbol: GCFB
NAIC: 722110 Full-Service Restaurants

■ ■ ■

Granite City Food & Brewery Ltd. is a Minneapolis, Minnesota-based operator of a chain of more than 20 restaurant-breweries under the Granite City Food & Brewery name. Originally established in second-tier Midwestern cities with populations in the 150,000 range, the chain's growth plans include entering multiple large markets as well. Granite City combines made-from-scratch food with made-from-scratch beers. Menu items include a range of appetizers, flatbread pizzas, burgers, pastas, sandwiches, and such entrees as meatloaf, steaks, ribs, lasagna, chicken burrito, chicken Parmesan, North Atlantic salmon, and freshwater walleye. Granite City signature beers include Duke of Wellington, an India pale ale; Broad Axe Stout, a dry Irish beer; Brother Benedict Bock, a German-style lager; Northern Light Lager, a mild beer slanted toward U.S. tastes; and the Two Pull, a blend of the Northern Light and Bock brew. Granite City is a public company listed on the NASDAQ. It has no plans to franchise.

BREWING UP A NEW IDEA

Granite City was incorporated in Minnesota in 1997 as Founders Food & Firkins Ltd. (A firkin is an old English unit of measurement; for beer and ale it represents one-quarter of a full-size barrel, and casks this size are often referred to as firkins.) The men behind the company were friends, veteran restaurateur Steve Wagenheim and brewmaster William E. Burdick, who was a restaurateur in his own right. In the mid-1990s they began to develop a brewpub concept that would combine microbrew beer with good food. More importantly, they decided to target second-tier cities, gaining an edge over the usual casual-dining chain restaurants such as Applebee's and the like by introducing a big-city brewpub concept offering higher-end food at mid-market prices.

Unlike other brewpubs, Granite City restaurants do not maintain complete brewing facilities at all their locations. Rather, the company employs a "par-brewing" method patented as Fermentus Interruptus, in which unfermented liquid, called wort, is produced at a central brewery, where water, hops, and barley are blended. The nonalcoholic liquid is then shipped via tanker trucks to the restaurants where yeast is added and the process is completed in finishing tanks visible to customers. In this way, Granite City is able to minimize its investment in brewing equipment, giving the restaurants a competitive

COMPANY PERSPECTIVES

Our mission at Granite City is to develop and operate highly successful restaurants by consistently exceeding our guests' expectations in product, service and overall dining experience. We are committed to consistent, long-term growth in unit and overall company earnings and to superior returns for our shareholders. We will be committed to the company's vision and be guided by our stated values. We will be recognized as the leader in the casual dining industry.

edge, while also providing economies of scale and a measure of quality control. The "worthouse" also serves as the foundation for a hub-and-spoke approach to expansion: new restaurants must be located within 500 miles of a production unit, the first of which was built some 45 minutes north of Des Moines, Iowa. The construction of additional wort houses will set the stage for future expansion across the country.

BRINGING TOGETHER FOOD AND MICROBREWS

Burdick earned his undergraduate degree in microbiology from Brown University and then a master's degree in brewing science from Heriot-Watt University in Edinburgh, Scotland. He then went to work for the William Younger Brewing Company in Edinburgh to complete his education as a brewing chemist. A few years later he began developing pubs for Allied Breweries, which opened 140 pubs in northern England in just four years. Burdick came to Minneapolis in 1976, in charge of restaurant design and development for Multifoods Corporation. Over the next dozen years he was involved in the opening of more than 400 restaurants. In 1989 he struck out on his own, opening an English-style brewpub in Minnetonka, Minnesota, called Sherlock's Home Restaurant Pub and Brewery, which was the first restaurant in the state permitted to brew beer on the premises.

Wagenheim came to the brewpub field with a different sort of restaurant experience. An accounting major at Michigan State University, he began to have doubts about his career choice and met with a counselor who suggested that because of his math skills and outgoing personality he should consider focusing on the restaurant field. Wagenheim followed her advice and after graduation went to work for Laventhal & Horwath, a major accounting firm serving the hospitality industry. Working in both the Chicago and Denver offices, he focused on the restaurant industry, becoming involved in the implementation of accounting systems, organization development, productivity management, and other elements of operational management. Wagenheim was then transferred to Minneapolis to work on the account of Champps Americana, a sports restaurant-bar chain.

In 1989 Wagenheim went to work for Champps, becoming chief operating officer, heavily involved in expanding the chain. In 1992 he became chief executive officer of a Champps' franchise operator, Champps Development Group, Inc., and two years later became president of Americana Dining Corporation to operate Champps units in Minnesota and develop others in Ohio. In April 1996 he sold his interest in Americana, and formed New Brighton Ventures, Inc., to operate a Champps restaurant in New Brighton, Minnesota. "But Wagenheim and his staff had a grander vision," according to *Twin Cities Business.* Wagenheim told the business publication in 2007, "We thought that the made-from-scratch food product that we knew from the Champps days was definitely the way to go, but we wanted to get away from the sports-bar genre." Joining Wagenheim and his Champps' colleagues, including chef Art Nemoe, who had developed Champps' menu, was his brewmaster friend, Bill Burdick.

BUSINESS INCORPORATED: 1997

In June 1997 Founders Food & Firkins Ltd. was incorporated, with Wagenheim as CEO and Burdick as chairman. Late in the year the company raised seed money through a private placement of stock and arranged financing for long-term building and equipment leases. The next 18 months were devoted to working out the detail of the concept and the opening of the first unit. "To lure investors," according to *Twin Cities Business,* "Wagenheim's team crafted a distinctive positioning strategy. 'We thought we could push the story of Granite City faster if we opened up in nontraditional markets and in a variety of market sizes,' [Wagenheim] says." Hence, the first brewpub was planned for St. Cloud, Minnesota, one of the second-tier cities with the smallest population, the goal being to prove that the concept could work in any of the smaller cities—and eventually in the large urban centers as well.

FIRST RESTAURANTS OPEN: 1999–2001

Wagenheim and Burdick looked for sites close to major highways as well as regional shopping centers and hotels. In St. Cloud they opted to be part of the new Rainbow

KEY DATES

1997: Company is incorporated as Founders Food & Firkins Ltd.
1999: First Granite City restaurant opens in St. Cloud, Minnesota.
2000: Company is taken public.
2001: Fargo restaurant becomes the first to use "wort" brewed offsite.
2005: A central wort processing center opens.
2006: Brewmaster and cofounder William Burdick retires.

Village grocer and retail center located near Highway 15. The new 8,000-square-foot, 260-seat restaurant opened in June 1999 under the name Granite City Food & Brewery, a name residents associated with area quarries, and one that performed well in focus groups, which connected the name to simplicity and strength.

The St. Cloud restaurant was an immediate hit on the local scene, generating almost $2 million in sales in its first, truncated year in operation. Its success allowed Founders Food to tap into the equity markets in 2000. An initial public offering was underwritten by the Minneapolis investment firm of R.J. Steichen, which had taken several restaurant companies public. The ensuing road show was not typical of most companies looking to make their pitch to executives from banks, investment firm, and other institutions. Instead, as Wagenheim told *Restaurants & Institutions,* "We had farmers coming in straight from the fields to see our road show. ... We cooked in community centers, post offices, other local restaurants." Although the company had a limited track record, its management team was experienced and well respected, and as a result, the offering, completed in June 2000, was able to net $3.5 million. Founders Food stock then began trading on the NASDAQ.

The proceeds of the stock offer helped to fund the opening of the second Granite City restaurant, in Sioux Falls, South Dakota, in December 2000. Again, the concept proved to be both a critical and financial success, allowing Founders to continue their plans to open a third restaurant and create a multiunit, multistate operation. Sales totaled $4.1 million in 2000, and with the addition of the Sioux Falls unit that amount more than doubled to nearly $9 million in 2001. Helping to boost that total was the November 2001 opening of the third restaurant, located in Fargo, North Dakota, near West Acres Mall.

BREWING INNOVATION AND EXPANSION: 2002

The Fargo restaurant was the first unit to take advantage of the trademarked Fermentus Interruptus system, developed by Burdick. From his experience with Sherlock's Home, he knew how the cost of brewing equipment affected margins, leading him to conceive of a way to eliminate the need for extra brewing equipment and storage tanks at each restaurant. Not only did the new commissary system require a specially designed truck, the company had to secure permission from each state to transport the wort. Initially, the Sioux Falls restaurant created wort for use in Fargo, while St. Cloud continued to act as a stand-alone brewery operation. Later a central brewery would open, capable of supplying wort to a large number of Granite City units. All told, the company estimated the innovative Fermentus Interruptus system could save as much as $400,000 per new restaurant in equipment costs. To keep an edge over their competition, Granite City also applied for a patent on Fermentus Interruptus, which was eventually granted in early 2007.

With three restaurants in operation, sales increased to $11.85 million in 2002. Although no new restaurants opened during the year, the company was able to raise $5.56 million from a private placement of stock late in the year to fuel further expansion. Founders also changed its name in September 2002, taking advantage of its growing brand to become Granite City Food & Brewery Ltd.

Two new Granite City operations opened in 2003, relying on a new prototype. They would also be the first developed with a new business partner. Real estate developer Barclay Ltd. agreed to buy the land, build the restaurants, and lease the units back to Granite City. The first debuted in Des Moines, Iowa, in September. Two months later, a unit opened in the eastern part of the state in Cedar Rapids, Iowa. With contributions from these new restaurants, Granite City improved its sales to $14.1 million in 2003. A third Iowa Granite City restaurant was also in the works, opening in Davenport in January 2004. Two more units would follow in 2004: Lincoln, Nebraska, in May, followed a month later by an opening in Maple Grove, Minnesota. The Maple Grove restaurant was especially important because it was located in the Minneapolis/St. Paul metropolitan area, making it the company's first foray into a larger market. These openings were partly funded by another private placement of stock, which raised $1.9 million for expansion. With eight restaurants contributing to the balance sheet, sales jumped to $30.6 million in 2004.

NEW CORPORATE OFFICES: 2005

Three more Granite City restaurant locations were added in 2005: Wichita, Kansas, in July; Egan, Minnesota, in September; and Kansas City, Missouri, in November. The Egan unit was also within the Minneapolis/St. Paul market. Granite City made progress on other fronts as well. In February 2005 the Des Moines restaurant began serving as the site of Granite City University, a management training program. A central worthouse, capable of supplying 30 to 35 restaurants, became operational in June. Also in July 2005 Granite City formed a new store-opening team to help in the final phases of a store opening, primarily to help with staffing and training. In the fall Granite City moved into new corporate offices in Minneapolis and leased a facility in the city to serve as a test kitchen. In addition, Granite City raised $5.34 million in another private placement of newly issued stock to maintain the chain's growth.

Sales increased to $36.2 million in 2005. A year later that number grew to more than $58 million on the strength of seven restaurant openings: Kansas City, Kansas, in January; Olathe, Kansas, in March; West Wichita, Kansas, in July; St. Louis Park, Minnesota, in September; Omaha, Nebraska, the following month; Roseville, Minnesota, in November; and Madison, Wisconsin, to close out the year. The year was also noteworthy because in February, Burdick, 65 years old, elected to retire from the company.

Granite City raised more funds for expansion in 2007, netting $14 million in a March private placement of stock, and late in the year arranged a $16 million debt facility. Some of the proceeds of the stock sale were used to open three Granite City Restaurants in 2007. In July a unit debuted in Rockford, Illinois, followed in October by openings in Rogers, Arkansas, and East Peoria, Illinois. By the start of 2008 plans were also in the works to open Granite City restaurants in Toledo, Ohio; Fort Wayne, Indiana; Creve Coeur, Missouri; and Orland Park, Illinois. The unit in Creve Coeur, a St. Louis suburb, and the Orland Park unit, located in the Chicago market, were likely to factor significantly in the company's future success as a further test to see if the Granite City concept would succeed in a larger market. The planned Orland Park restaurant was also seen as a possible springboard to take the chain to Michigan, Ohio, and other states to the east of the company's core market.

Ed Dinger

PRINCIPAL COMPETITORS

Gordon Biersch Brewery Restaurant Group, Inc.; Metromedia Restaurant Group; Rock Bottom Restaurants, Inc.

FURTHER READING

Bolsta, Phil, "Steve Wagenheim: Emerging Category, Granite City Food & Brewery," *Twin Cities Business,* August 2007.

Halena, Sue, "Granite City Tests New Brewing Plan," *St. Cloud Times Metro,* October 15, 2001, p. 1B.

Licata, Elizabeth, "Granite City Food & Brewery," *Nation's Restaurant News,* September 3, 2007, p. 36.

Murphy, H. Lee, "Chicago Awash in New Brewpubs," *Crain's Chicago Business,* April 9, 2007, p. 19.

Spethmann, Betsy, "Stock Marketing (Founders Food & Firkins Ltd. Example of Restaurant IPO)," *Restaurants & Institutions,* December 15, 2000, p. 29.

Walkup, Carolyn, "Granite City Chain Takes Rock-Solid Stance on Growth," *Nation's Restaurant News,* April 26, 2004, p. 8.

Youngblood, Dick, "Granite City Founders Have Recipe for Growth," *Star Tribune,* September 7, 2005.

Zimmerman, Christine, "Rock Solid: Granite City Food & Brewery Has a Two-Tiered Approach to Growth," *Chain Leader,* March 2003, p. 26.

Grupo Planeta

Avda Diagonal 662-664
Barcelona, E-08034
Spain
Telephone: (34 93) 492 80 00
Fax: (34 93) 492 85 65
Web site: http://www.planeta.es

Private Company
Incorporated: 1949
Employees: 4,730
Sales: EUR 900 million ($1.33 billion) (2006)
NAIC: 511110 Newspaper Publishers; 424920 Book, Periodical, and Newspaper Merchant Wholesalers

■ ■ ■

Grupo Planeta has long been the Spanish-speaking world's leading publisher, not only in its native Spain, but in Latin America as well, and is the world's 12th largest publisher overall. In addition to publishing flagship Editorial Planeta Ediciones Generales, Planeta owns many of Spain's most prominent imprints. These include Editorial Espasa, Ediciones Destino, Editorial Seix Barral, Emecé, MR Ediciones, Libros Cúpula, Planeta Junior. Altogether the company operates more than 40 publishing houses and imprints, both in Spain and in Argentina, Colombia, Ecuador, Chile, Uruguay, Mexico, Venezuela, and the United States.

The company also operates a major direct-sales operation for its encyclopedias and other works, and owns Casa del Libro, the leading bookstore chain in Spain. With the deregulation of much of the Spanish media sector since the mid-1990s, Planeta has been repositioning itself as a diversified media group. The company has acquired reference shareholder status in a number of broadcasting outlets, including the Antena 3 TV, Antena Neox and AntenaNova television networks; the Onda Cero and Europa FM radio stations. The company's newspaper and magazine holdings include *La Razón,* Spain's number two national daily, the free daily *ADN,* and since 2007, Colombia's Casa Editorial El Tiempo (CEET) media group, which publishes newspapers including *El Tiempo* and *Hoy,* and magazines, including *Alo, Cambio,* and *Don Juan.* The company also owns half of Spanish magazine publisher Prisma, with titles including *Playboy, Quéfem, Historia y Vida,* and *Living Deco.*

Other Planeta operations include advertising; Internet businesses including the ADN.es portal, DVDgo.com, the leading Internet-based DVD sales specialist in Spain, and LaNetro Zed; and mail-order and distance sales operations including Planeta Directo and Shopo. The company's Training and Professional division includes CEAC, a leading long-distance vocational training center, and Home English, as well as specialized publishers such as Deusto, Alienta Editorial and Gestion 2000.

Grupo Planeta is also the company behind the Planeta Prize, which, since its introduction in 1952, has been the Spanish publishing market's most prestigious literary prize. Grupo Planeta remains controlled by the founding Lara family. José Manuel Lara, son of the company's founder, is Planeta's president. Planeta's sales topped EUR 900 million ($1.13 billion) in 2006.

COMPANY PERSPECTIVES

One of Grupo Planeta's main characteristics is its capacity for innovation in the world of business. Since it was founded, it has introduced new forms of understanding the publishing, promotion and commercialisation of contents. These contributions began in the publishing sector and have been extended to new formats for contents distribution. Planeta contents were the first to be presented in multimedia format and now they are on the Internet and digital and interactive TV. This achievement is the product of the Group's professional staff; they have ably maintained a strategic attitude beyond their own sphere of specialisation and this has put Planeta in a privileged position in the worldwide market.

BARCELONA BEGINNINGS

José Manuel Lara Hernández was born in 1915 in El Pedroso, near Seville. Lara, whose father was a doctor, was enrolled in a seminary, but ran away at the age of 15. Over several years Lara worked at a number of odd jobs before joining a chorus line as a dancer in Madrid.

At the outbreak of the Spanish civil war, Lara sided with the fascists and rose to become the youngest captain in Franco's army. Lara was to remain loyal to Franco for the rest of his life. As *Variety* reported, Lara famously boasted that "After Franco, I am the most Francoist man in Spain." Following the war, Lara was demobilized in Barcelona, where in 1941 he met his wife, Maria Teresa Bosch, a teacher. The husband and wife team founded a training academy, providing instruction for people seeking civil service jobs. Lara taught math at the academy, while Maria Teresa taught literature.

Yet Lara had begun to develop an interest in the publishing industry. In 1944 Lara acquired his first publishing company, but soon sold it. As part of that sale, Lara gained the Spanish translation rights to two British writers, Somerset Maugham and G. K. Chesterton, for which he set up a new company, called Lara.

TRUE START OF A PUBLISHING EMPIRE

By the end of the decade the Lara imprint gave way to Lara's next—and landmark—publishing venture. In 1949, Lara and Maria Teresa Bosch founded Ediciones Planeta. The new company sought to publish primarily fiction, including foreign translations. Yet the company's most significant success came from its support of Spanish writers.

Lara wisely turned over editorial decisions entirely to Maria Teresa Bosch, who soon proved to have a keen eye for commercial success. This led the company to publish the sprawling, 800-page family saga *Los Cipreses Creen en Dios* (The Cypresses Believe in God) in 1953. The manuscript for the novel had been turned down by a number of publishing houses. Bosch, however, saw its potential—and the novel became the company's first blockbuster success, selling more than six million copies in Spain and still more overseas.

Bosch's leadership of the group's fiction list brought it many more successes as the company established itself as a major up-and-comer in Spain's publishing industry. Translations of foreign writers remained an essential component of the group's success, and the company claimed credit for introducing such popular writers as Pearl Buck and Frank Yerby to the Spanish market.

Bosch's literary acumen was matched by her husband's gift for business. Lara quickly established Planeta's reputation for strong marketing and promotion efforts, but also for publishing industry innovations. Among the company's most notable early initiatives was the launch of the Planeta literary award in 1952. Lara assured the award of notoriety, endowing it with an impressive 40,000 pesetas in its first year. The Planeta prize soon became the Spanish-speaking world's most prestigious literary award, worth EUR 600,000 at the start of the 21st century. Among the award's recipients were future Nobel Prize–winner Camilo José Cela, and major international successes such as Mário Vargas Llosa and Jorge Semprun. At the same time, Planeta itself benefited from the award's notoriety—and became the publisher of many of the award winners. Significantly, despite Lara's own outspoken support for Franco, the company published works across the full spectrum of political opinion.

FOREIGN EXPANSION BEGINS

Through the 1950s and 1960s, Planeta instituted a number of other innovations. In 1956, the company created a new subsidiary, Crédito Internacional del Libro (later called Editorial Planeta Grandes Publicaciones), which pioneered the direct-sales model in Spain's publishing industry. Through Crédito Internacional, Planeta also entered encyclopedia publishing, enabling consumers in economically depressed Spain to purchase series on installment. The company's encyclopedia operations took off still further in 1967, after Planeta

KEY DATES

1949: Founding of Ediciones Planeta publishing company in Barcelona by José Manuel Lara Hernández and wife Maria Teresa Bosch.
1953: Planeta publishes *Los Cipreses Creen en Dios* (The Cypresses Believe in God), which becomes a multimillion seller.
1966: Planeta opens publishing and distribution subsidiaries in Mexico, Colombia, Argentina, and elsewhere in Latin America.
1982: Acquires Seix Barral and Ariel as part of expansion in Spain.
1994: Launches distribution subsidiary in Miami, Florida.
1998: Launch of *La Razón* daily newspaper as part of expansion of media interests.
2003: José Manuel Lara Hernández dies at the age of 88.
2008: Company increases stake in Antena 3 television network to 44.58 percent.

acquired the Spanish-language rights to publish the *Larousse Encyclopedia* in Spain. By the end of the decade, the company's encyclopedias had become fixtures in most Spanish households.

Planeta by then had launched the effort to make good on the implied scope of its name. In 1966, the company established its first foreign operations, targeting the Latin American market as a natural extension to its publishing business. The company first established publishing operations in Mexico and Colombia. At the same time, Planeta opened distribution subsidiaries in Venezuela and Argentina. Two years later, the company added a distribution subsidiary in Chile as well. The company later entered Ecuador, setting up Editorial Planeta Ecuador in 1981 as a distribution subsidiary.

Much of Planeta's early international operation consisted of publishing and/or distributing the group's Spanish catalog. Into the 1970s, however, the group's Latin American businesses turned more and more toward publishing and distributing writers from the continent. The first of the group's subsidiaries to do this was Planeta Venezuela, which began publishing Venezuelan writers at the end of the 1970s. The group's Argentinean business added its first domestic catalog in 1983. Two years later the company boosted its Mexican presence, acquiring Joaquín Mortiz, a publisher of contemporary Mexican literature. In Chile, the group launched the Biblioteca del Sur collection of Chilean literature in 1987, edited by noted literary critic Mariano Aguirre.

ADDING IMPRINTS IN THE EIGHTIES AND NINETIES

Planeta's evolution into the Spanish-speaking world's leading publishing group began in earnest in the early 1980s. Acquisitions came to play an important part in the company's growth over the next decade. In 1982 the company purchased Seix Barral, one of the most important publishers of literature in Spain. Also in 1982, Planeta bought social sciences specialist Ariel. Other acquisitions completed in the 1980s and 1990s included Ediciones Deusto, acquired in 1989, which was refocused as a producer of datebooks and corporate gifts. The company acquired Ediciones Martinez Roca in 1992, followed by Barcelona-based Editorial Espasa Calpe, one of Spain's oldest and largest publishers. In 1995, the company bought Centro Informativo de la Construccion (CIC), a company focused on providing information and related services to the construction industry.

Planeta also expanded into new markets during this time. The company had set up a mail-order business, Fasciculos Planeta, serving the collections market in 1977; in 1985 that subsidiary was merged with Editorial Delta, part of Italy's Istituto Geografico DeAgostini, forming Editorial Planeta DeAgostini. That joint venture then became an important vehicle for Planeta's expansion into other media.

In the meantime the company created a new imprint specializing in nonfiction, Ediciones Temas de Hoy, in 1987. In the early 1990s the company set its targets on the large U.S. Hispanic population, setting up a distribution subsidiary in Miami in 1994. Planeta Publishing Corp. later set up its own publishing operations, releasing its first Spanish-language books in 2001.

The company joined with Lunwerg Editores to form the Plawerg Editores joint venture in 1994. That operation focused on high-end "coffee table" books and other major works. Planeta created a new imprint, Ediciones de Bronce in 1996, specifically targeting the market for Asian, African, and other non-Western literature.

Through the end of the decade, Planeta added two new operations in Portugal. These included Placresa, Comércio de Produções Editoriais, as part of Editorial Planeta Grandes Publicaciones, added in 1997. In 1999, the company purchased Publicações Dom Quixote, a leading publisher in Portugal with a catalog of more than 2,000 titles.

MULTIMEDIA EXPANSION BEGINS

Increasingly, however, Planeta had been developing a new strategy aimed at becoming a full-fledged media group. This effort had its start in the early 1990s, when Planeta DeAgostino formed a partnership with IBM to create Multimedia Ediciones, a software and multimedia publisher, in 1992.

The 1998 creation of another subsidiary, Audiovisual Espanola 2000, marked the company's entry into newspaper publishing. The launch of *La Razón* that year introduced a new, highly conservative daily newspaper to the Spanish market. *La Razón* quickly grew in popularity, and in the next decade became the country's number two national daily.

Planeta stepped up its media diversification into the 2000s, as the next generation of the Lara family—son José Manuel Lara Bosch—took over the company's direction. Founder José Manuel Lara Hernández died in 2003, at the age of 88.

Planeta's media interests turned to television, with the acquisition of a stake in Antena 3 TV, a leading Spanish broadcaster, which also operated the Antena Neox and AntenaNova digital television networks. By mid-decade, Planeta had become a reference shareholder in that company. At the same time, Planeta extended its operations into the radio broadcasting field, with stakes in the Onda Cero and Europa FM radio stations. In 2001 the company's youth division formed the Planeta Junior television joint venture with Germany's EM.TV & Merchandising, a part of the Kirch Group. The company continued to buy shares in Antena 3, and at the beginning of 2008 increased its stake in that company to 44.58 percent.

DIVERSIFYING FOR A STRONG FUTURE

The company pursued a variety of diversified ventures in keeping with its new strategy. In 1999 Planeta acquired Ediciones Altaya, one of the world's leading installment-collectibles companies with operations in Spain, Argentina, Colombia, Mexico, Poland, and Brazil. The company launched the television- and Internet-based shopping business, Shopo, in 2005.

The following year, Planeta expanded its Internet presence again, founding DVDgo.com, which quickly became the leading Spanish online DVD retailer. The company also acquired OcioJoven.com, a leading leisure-oriented Spanish e-commerce site, in 2006. At the same time, the company launched its own free newspaper, *ADN,* as well as a sister site, ADN.com. The company's newspaper operations were expanded again in 2007 with the acquisition of Colombia's largest newspaper group, El Tiempo, for $150 million. The company had also founded a distance-learning subsidiary Home English. In 2008, the group announced plans to open 15 teaching centers in Spain by 2010.

Despite its thrust into media holdings, Planeta's publishing operations remained the core of its business and continued to grow well. In 2002 the group bought Emecé, in Argentina, and entered the Brazilian market for the first time. In 2005 the company expanded its South American presence, buying Barsa Planeta, one of the leading publishers on that continent, with operations in Argentina, Mexico, and Venezuela. That year the company added operations in Peru, as well. Planeta's presence in Brazil was expanded with the purchase of 70 percent of Editora Academia de Inteligência, a publisher specialized in the self-help category, in 2006.

Since its founding in 1949, Grupo Planeta had grown into the Spanish-speaking world's leading publishing company, and a major media group in Spain itself. With revenues of more than $1.13 billion in 2007, Planeta ranked number 12 among the global publishing industry. Planeta's long history of successful expansion promised further growth in the future.

M. L. Cohen

PRINCIPAL SUBSIDIARIES

Antena 3 Televisión; AntenaNova; Barsa Planeta Internacional, Ltda. (Brazil); Crítica; Ediciones Destino; Ediciones Generales; Ediciones Paidós; Editora Academia de Inteligência (Brazil); Editora Planeta DeAgostini, S.A. (Portugal); Editora Planeta do Brasil; Editorial Ariel; Editorial Diana (Mexico); Editorial Espasa; Editorial Joaquín Mortiz (Mexico); Editorial Planeta Argentina; Editorial Planeta Chile; Editorial Planeta Colombia; Editorial Planeta Ecuador; Editorial Planeta México; Editorial Planeta Perú; Editorial Planeta Uruguay; Emecé Editores Argentina; GeoPlaneta; Grupo Júbilo Comunicación; La Razón; Libros Cúpula; Onda Cero Radio/Europa FM; Planeta Publishing Corporation (United States).

PRINCIPAL COMPETITORS

Acciona S.A.; Grupo PRISA; Vocento; Grupo Zeta S.A.; Diario El Pais; Grupo Godo de Comunicacion; Editorial Prensa Iberica S.A.; Recoletos Compania Editorial S.A.; Unidad Editorial S.A.

FURTHER READING

"Death of Planeta Boss Leaves Behind Rapidly Growing Legacy for Son," *Europe Intelligence Wire,* May 13, 2003.

"Expansion Plans of Grupo Planeta," *Expansion,* July 19, 2000, p. 10.

Fortson, Danny, "A New Wavelength," *Daily Deal,* January 5, 2004.

Gil, Miguel, "Una Empresa, Dos Líneas Editoriales," *Epoca,* November 24, 2005, p. 86.

"Grupo Planeta Acquired Credsa," *Expansion,* February 22, 2002.

"Grupo Planeta de Agostini Raises Antena 3 Stake to 44.58 pct vs 42.54," *AFX News Limited,* February 19, 2008.

"Grupo Planeta to Open 15 New Language Schools," *Business Week,* February 6, 2008.

Lopez, Adriana, "Spain's Grupo Planeta Goes English," *School Library Journal,* August 2002, p. S7.

Lottman, Herbert, "Searching for Growth," *Bookseller,* June 30, 2003, p. 10.

Mullan, Michael, "José Manuel Lara Hernández," *Times,* May 19, 2003.

"Planeta About to Acquire Emece," *Expansion,* December 21, 2000, p. 8.

"Spain's Planeta Buys Controlling Interest in Colombia's Biggest Newspaper," *Associated Press,* August 1, 2007.

"Spanish Publisher Aims for Major AV Status," *Screen Digest,* October 1, 2002.

The Haartz Corporation

87 Hayward Road
Acton, Massachusetts 01720-3000
U.S.A.
Telephone: (978) 264-2600
Fax: (978) 264-2601
Web site: http://www.haartz.com

Private Company
Incorporated: 1924 as Auto Fabric and Specialty Company
Employees: 350
Sales: $209 million (2006)
NAIC: 313210 Broadwoven Fabric Mills

■ ■ ■

The Haartz Corporation is a privately held, Acton, Massachusetts-based company that for more than a century has been a leading manufacturer of car top materials. For convertibles the company offers three-ply cloth toppings, in either square weave or twill weave construction, and a variety of vinyl constructions. For hardtops Haartz offers roof treatments in either fabric constructions (made of its trademarked Cambria composite) or in vinyl. The company's line of road gear products includes covers for pickup truck beds, tire covers, and nose covers.

Haartz has ventured inside vehicles as well, developing a variety of automotive interior trim products, including door inserts and panels, instrument panels, and seating materials. In addition, Haartz has applied its expertise to the marine market, offering waterproof topping and seating materials. Because of its extensive history in the car top field, Haartz also promotes itself as a resource for restorers of vintage cars, publishing an online guide on car top materials and care.

As an original equipment manufacturer (OEM), Haartz commands a leading share of the market for car tops in the United States and does healthy business abroad as well. In addition to its Massachusetts' headquarters, Haartz maintains manufacturing facilities in Detroit, Michigan; Mannheim, Germany; and Shanghai, China. Haartz is owned and led by the third generation of the Haartz family.

CAR TOP MATERIALS EVOLVE

As the automobile industry took shape in the early 1900s, topping materials began to develop. Leather, simple canvas, three-ply cloth, and rubber-coated materials soon gave way to new constructions especially suited for the new extendible car roofs. Imitation leather became a common low-price option, while in the premium market, Pantasote, a surface-coated topping, gained popularity. Another premium topping, Mohair, was introduced in North America in 1907 by the founder of the Haartz Corporation, John Carl Haartz, Sr., the son of German immigrants who was about 24 years old at the time.

Automobile mohair was not quite the same material as textile industry mohair, which was strictly yarn and cloth produced from the hair of Angora goats. Automobile mohair fabric for tops combined a rubber backing with a face fabric that might be made entirely of mohair yarns or combined with cotton yarn, leading

> **COMPANY PERSPECTIVES**
>
> Our People make our Company a Great Place to Work. At the Haartz Corporation, we care about our people and that is why we have many long service employees. We provide tools to empower our employees to do their very best at work and enable them to balance professional and personal goals. Our company culture brings together a diverse set of skills and expertise to make our world-class product line. Our success is due to our dedicated employees, who have the desire to be number one in everything we do, and make this a great place to work.

marketers to coin such names as "silk mohair" and "cotton-mohair" to differentiate their products. Mohair was also used for closed-car seats, generally with a pile surface. What made mohair popular, particularly in the early 1900s, was its shiny, attractive appearance and ease of cleaning.

John Haartz established J. C. Haartz, Inc., in Boston in 1907 to produce automobile top and seat cover materials, specializing in mohair. In 1916, as World War I was creating a textile dyestuff shortage, cloth toppings gave way to surface-coated materials, two-ply for the low-price end of the market and four-ply for the premium market, a move that was also aided by advances in rubber coating technology. The company focused on rubberized fabrics for the automobile industry. In 1919 J. C. Haartz was incorporated in Delaware and became a public company with a capitalization of $750,000, an amount that would double two months later. Some of those funds were put to use in opening a new coating plant in New Haven, Connecticut, in 1920, which did business as the J.C. Haartz Rubber Company.

JOHN HAARTZ STARTS SECOND COMPANY

In 1924 John Haartz's enterprise was the victim of a hostile takeover, and Haartz was forced out. He quickly bounced back, setting up a new company in Watertown, Massachusetts, under the name Auto Fabric and Specialty Company. A year later it was renamed Haartz Auto Fabric Company. Haartz set up a second company that he also headed, cofounded with New York rubber chemist Jess Mason and James Gordon Grower, manufacturing rubber goods under the name Haartz-Mason-Grower Company. (Later renamed Haartz-Mason Inc., the company would provide single-ply synthetic rubber membranes to the roofing industry. It was sold to Medina, Ohio-based RPM Inc., a specialized protective coatings company, in 1980. The mill Haartz established would be closed in 1993.)

In the mid-1920s there was renewed interest in cloth car tops. Especially popular were the stylish premium cloth toppings used on sportier sedans and convertibles. It was John Haartz who is thought to have coined the term "sport topping" which gained such common usage that for the next 30 years people referred to any convertible topping, no matter the type of cloth (or, later, vinyl) it was made of, as sport topping.

Whether the consumer preferred sport topping or something more pedestrian and less expensive made little difference a few years later when the stock market crashed and the Great Depression cast a pall over the country's industrial sector. New car sales plummeted, as did the demand for Haartz products. The company reportedly came close to collapse but managed to hang on. By the end of the decade it had introduced a new line of tops using synthetic fibers, available in a wide variety of colors.

FOUNDER DIES: 1941

John Haartz, Sr., died from a heart attack in August 1941 at the age of 60. Succeeding him as president was his son, John Haartz, Jr. Before the end of the year, the United States would be involved in World War II, new car manufacturing would be suspended in order to ramp up the production of tanks and aircraft, and like most U.S. manufacturers, Haartz would have to find defense-related products to keep its factories busy.

After the war John Haartz, Jr., hired his brother-in-law, and former prep school and college classmate and fraternity brother, Kenneth Ritchie, who would serve as his chief lieutenant for the next 30 years. The Detroit automakers required a few years to retool, but once they did the industry soared, spurred by pent-up demand for new cars by consumers who had money in their pockets from an economy that was enjoying an extended boom in the postwar years. Haartz benefited as well, serving as a supplier to both Ford and General Motors.

FIRST EXTRUDERS INSTALLED: 1960

From the end of the war until the mid-1950s, new convertibles were mostly fitted with three-ply cloth materials, either made completely from synthetic fibers or blended with cotton. Some hardtop cars were also us-

KEY DATES

1907: John C. Haartz, Sr., launches car top company.
1924: Haartz forms new company.
1941: John Haartz, Sr., dies, succeeded by son, John Haartz, Jr.
1955: First vinyl-coated topping products offered.
1976: John Haartz, Jr., dies, replaced by brother-in-law.
1986: Eric Haartz named chief executive.
1994: Company begins offering interior trim products.
2001: Rode & Schwalenberg GmbH acquired.
2006: China office opened.

ing similar roof covers as a styling feature. Starting in the early 1950s vinyl-coated replacement tops became available for convertibles and were soon available for new cars as well. In 1955 Haartz offered its first topping products coated with vinyl. To accommodate the growing business for vinyl, Haartz installed its first extruders in 1960 to melt and shape the product.

With business growing, Haartz outgrew its facilities in the 1960s, and the company acquired property on Hayward Road in Acton, Massachusetts, which not only included factory buildings that could be adapted to the manufacture of car toppings but offered plenty of space for future expansion. The company moved into its new facilities in 1967. In time, the complex would grow to 330,000 square feet in size; a 66,000-square-foot facility would later open on nearby Craig Road.

Haartz had to contend with a changing marketplace in the mid-1960s. A number of U.S.-made hardtop cars featured vinyl landau (convertible) roofs with surface coated materials bonded to woven fabrics. To achieve more of a padded look, these tops would later resort to nonwoven "synthetic felt." The landau roof business proved to be a godsend to Haartz, which soon had to contend with convertibles falling out of favor with consumers for a time. Convertibles offered by Mercedes in the late 1970s, however, helped to revitalize the category to Haartz's benefit.

John Haartz, Jr., died in 1976, and Ritchie stepped in as chief executive while Haartz's college-age son Eric was groomed to take over the business. When Ritchie retired ten years later, the younger Haartz was ready to take charge. A host of new topping materials were available for use, and they would only increase in the 1990s as the number of convertible models multiplied. Not only would these new materials wear better, they would offer acoustical performance unmatched by once-popular materials.

INTERIOR TRIM PRODUCTS ADDED: 1994

Haartz also expanded beyond car tops in the 1990s. The company began offering foam laminate interior trim products in 1994. In addition Haartz transferred its expertise from land to water, developing cloth tops for pleasure boats. The company also looked overseas to support further growth, becoming more aggressive in Europe and Asia. By the end of the decade sales reached the $100 million level and the company was ready once again to expand its manufacturing capabilities.

In 1999 the auto industry was poised to switch auto part materials from polyvinyl chloride (PVC) foam to a more recycling-friendly thermoplastic olefin (TPO). PVC had a number of problems, including the fact that it cracked in high temperatures. In response, work began at Haartz on a $3.5 million project that would add 58,000 square feet to its facility, to house a new extruder that would produce olefinic interior panels. Another $7 million was earmarked for new TPO equipment. Later in 1999 Haartz forged an alliance with French firm Establissements Treves, the two companies agreeing to share in the design and development of TPO foam composite, TPO sheet, and other automotive interior materials. The move to TPO quickly paid dividends for Haartz, which in 2000 landed deals to produce TPO cover skins for Mazda and a TPO instrument panel for another automaker.

Also during this time Haartz became known for the new materials it developed for sheltering car passengers from the noise created by wind outside the vehicle, particularly in convertible models such as the Corvette. Using layers of newly engineered rubber amid cloth backing and facing, Haartz created car tops to address this situation effectively damping the noise and decreasing vibrations, allowing for better "cabin acoustics" in the car.

NEW CENTURY BRINGS GERMAN ACQUISITION

Haartz took a major step in securing its position in the global automotive industry in 2001 when it acquired Mannheim, Germany-based Rode & Schwalenberg GmbH, which became a Haartz subsidiary. Rode & Schwalenberg had been in business since 1897, its factory having been destroyed during World War II but rebuilt in 1945. The firm became involved in the convertible topping material business in the early 1970s and had since grown into one of the largest companies in the field, with a presence in the United States.

Instead of supplying the European market from Massachusetts, Haartz had a manufacturing operation on the continent. In addition, the German company brought with it a number of important customers, including Mercedes-Benz A.G., Porsche A.G., Saab Automobile A.B., Volvo A.B., Renault S.A., and Jaguar Cars Ltd. Although Rode & Schwalenberg would continue to operate separately under its own name, its Dover, New Hampshire, sales and warehousing operation were taken over by Haartz.

In a further development in 2001, Haartz established a relationship with Wolfsteins Pro Series to market a line of environmentally friendly convertible top cleaners and protectant products that had been developed jointly by the two companies. It was the first cleaning product Haartz had ever endorsed. "For three generations, our family had been asked how to clean convertible tops," Eric Haartz said in a prepared statement. He explained: "With the exception of soap and water, we never found a product that we felt comfortable endorsing ... until now." The four products in the new line were RAGGTOPP Cleaner and RAGGTOPP Protectant for cars, and BIMINI TOPP Cleaner and BIMINI TOPP Protectant for boats.

The area around Haartz's Acton operation had become increasingly more populated, and its facilities caused the area some concern. In 2001 Haartz paid a penalty of $11,875 to the Massachusetts Department of Environmental Protection for hazardous waste and air quality violations, marking the only time Haartz had ever been sanctioned. The problem was rectified when the hazardous material involved was moved to a Canadian disposal site. In general Haartz reported that it maintained a good relationship with the community, hosting schoolchildren on plant tours and maintaining a policy that only allowed deliveries during daylight hours. In 2005 the company made a successful bid of $165,000 for 8.4 acres of state-owned land put up for auction. Haartz requested rezoning of the land from residential to industrial use, planning to use the three acres closest to its facilities for expansion, but announcing that it would use about five acres primarily as a buffer space between the plant and nearby residences. The company did, however, retain the option to one day expand its facilities onto the land.

In the early 2000s Haartz had to contend with the escalating cost of raw materials, and of PVC resins in particular. The company absorbed the costs for as long as it felt it could before finally raising prices in late 2004. The following year, Haartz also added a 2 percent surcharge on its product to cover escalating energy costs. Controlling costs became increasing important. As part of an effort to remain competitive, in 2006 Haartz opened an office in Shanghai, China.

Ed Dinger

PRINCIPAL SUBSIDIARIES

Haartz GmbH (Germany).

PRINCIPAL COMPETITORS

Eagle Ottawa Leather Company LLC; Lear Corporation; Seton Company.

FURTHER READING

Begin, Sherri, "All Quiet on the Inside," *Rubber and Plastics News,* October 30, 2000.

———, "Haartz Buys Rode & Schwalenberg," *Rubber and Plastics News,* May 7, 2001.

Heaney, Sally, "Business to Bid on Route 2 State Land," *Boston Globe,* June 23, 2005, p. 1.

———, "Haartz Requests Rezoning," *Boston Globe,* February 12, 2006.

"John Carl Haartz," *New York Times,* August 4, 1941.

Pryweller, Joseph, "Haartz Invests $3.5 Million in Expansion," *Plastics News,* March 22, 1999.

Schiavone, Christian, "Putting the Top Down," *Acton (Mass.) Beacon,* September 20, 2007.

Simon, Bernard, "Car Parts Suppliers Driven to Distraction," *Financial Times,* November 1, 2004, p. 28.

Harkins Amusement Enterprises, Inc.

7511 East McDonald Drive
Scottsdale, Arizona 85250
U.S.A.
Telephone: (480) 627-7777
Web site: http://www.harkinstheatres.com

Private Company
Incorporated: 1933
Employees: 2,100
Sales: $79 million (2003 est.)
NAIC: 512131 Motion Picture Theaters (Except Drive-Ins)

■ ■ ■

Harkins Amusement Enterprises, Inc., operates Harkins Theatres, the biggest chain of movie theaters in Arizona. The firm has more than 400 screens at over 30 locations, most in its home state, with others located in California, Oklahoma, Colorado, and Texas. Harkins theaters are distinguished by their neon-decorated lobbies, chiropractor-designed seats, wide range of concession-stand offerings, and high-quality image and sound. A growing number of locations also offer supervised play areas that enable parents of young children to attend movies without hiring a babysitter.

EARLY YEARS

Harkins Theatres traces its beginnings to September 1933, when Dwight "Red" Harkins took over management of the State Theatre in Tempe, Arizona. Born and raised in Cincinnati, Ohio, Harkins had founded a small printing business as a teen and used the proceeds to buy a Model "A" Ford. At the age of 16 he decided to trade the car for a Harley-Davidson motorcycle and run away to Hollywood, but his plan fizzled when he ran out of money in Arizona. Settling in the small town of Tempe, just east of Phoenix, he began fronting a dance band called Einstein and the Eight Atoms, for whom he played violin and sang through a self-built public address system.

In 1933 the 18-year-old Harkins heard about a movie theater that had been shuttered by a local bank because its owner could not keep up with loans for equipment to play the new talking pictures. With $50 saved from his band earnings and the backing of area theater magnate Harry Nace, he leased it from the bank. A few months later he also established an outdoor movie theater at Tempe Beach; it was damaged by storms and shut down after one season.

Movies were a tonic to many during the Great Depression, and Harkins' business was successful enough that in the late 1930s he built a new theater called the College, located around the corner from the State. Opened on November 20, 1940, it featured a number of innovative ideas of Harkins' own devising including glow-in-the-dark carpeting; photocell-activated drinking fountains; color-changing, dimmable wall sconces; and amplified headphones for the hearing-impaired. Like many theaters of the era, it incorporated an apartment where Harkins lived. Several years later, the State Theatre was closed.

COMPANY PERSPECTIVES

Harkins Theatres is over 300 screens strong and growing. With annual attendance exceeding the capacity of Arizona's top 25 venues combined, Harkins is the Southwest's first choice for entertainment.

Red Harkins believed that business was not just about making money, and he followed three guiding principles. The first was that a sense of achievement was more important than financial success; the second, that the firm should be run in a democratic, rather than an autocratic, fashion; and the last, that he and his employees were the servants of the moviegoer.

SAGUARO THEATRE OPENS IN 1948

In 1948 Harkins opened the Saguaro Theatre in the town of Wickenburg. During the 1950s he also turned his attention to broadcasting, operating a radio station and serving as general manager of the Phoenix area's second television station, which was owned by Harry Nace. During this period the inventive Harkins developed a system for multiplex FM stereo broadcasting that was used to simulcast the television station's sound. He also installed stereo audio equipment and other new technology in the theaters as they became available.

In the early 1960s the College Theatre was sold (and later renamed the Valley Art Theatre by its new owners), and in 1973 Harkins opened the Camelview, a three-screen theater. The following April Red Harkins died suddenly at the age of 59. His son Dan, a 21-year-old prelaw student at Arizona State University who was the company's general manager, ignored the advice of bankers to sell the debt-laden firm, and decided to honor his beloved father's memory by keeping it solvent. He had grown up in the movie business, working every job from janitor to projectionist, and like his father before him was starting out as the youngest theater owner in the country.

During the mid-1970s Dan Harkins followed in his father's entrepreneurial footsteps, becoming one of the first to install video-game machines in the lobby of his theaters, and introducing a low-priced children's frequent filmgoer program and "gourmet" snack bar items that included baked goods and ice cream. To maximize ticket sales Harkins promoted his films creatively, turning titles like *Monty Python and the Holy Grail* into regional hits where other exhibitors had given up on them after short runs. Harkins Amusement, as the company was known, had begun bringing such foreign and "art" movies to its theaters in large part because of difficulties in landing top Hollywood titles.

LAWSUIT FILED IN 1977

In 1977 Harkins Amusement filed suit against a group of eight film distribution companies and three larger exhibitors, alleging that they had conspired to create a business monopoly which shut it out of booking many top first-run Hollywood titles. The firm sought $3 million in damages. The case dragged on for a decade until a summary motion for dismissal was granted.

The company had struggled to turn a profit during the 1970s and early '80s, but the 1982 reissue of the Walt Disney animated classic *Fantasia* was a turning point. Dan Harkins' careful marketing of the film as a special event brought in moviegoers, and the firm's profits grew steadily afterward, helped as well by the rapid growth of the Phoenix area.

In 1988 Harkins took over management of the 22-year-old Cine Capri in Phoenix, which had become a local landmark to moviegoers for its sleek styling, huge curved screen, and powerful sound system. On December 25 the firm also opened its biggest theater to date, the luxurious $2.4 million Arcadia 8 in Scottsdale. Its lobby featured extensive use of neon, a design element that would become a Harkins trademark. The company by this time employed about 150.

By this time the hardworking Dan Harkins had found time to get married, tying the knot at the last theater his father had built, the Camelview. His wife, Karen, was a chiropractor and nutritionist by trade, and she soon began to offer suggestions for improvements to the company's theaters. In addition to upgrading the concession stand to offer healthier snack products like juices, bottled water, yogurt, and diet foods, she also spurred the firm to begin cooking popcorn in heart-friendly canola oil and helped design wider, more comfortable theater seats that had a higher back and a cup-holder arm.

In 1990 Harkins expanded the Camelview from three to five screens, and the next year a new seven-screen theater opened in the Fashion Square Mall, which like the Arcadia 8 had a neon-decorated lobby and other distinctive touches. In 1991 the company also bought back the Valley Art Theatre, which had opened in the 1930s as the College Theatre, and leased it to former Harkins employee Krista Griffin, who would show foreign and independent films there.

In the late 1980s, with film studios legally able to buy stakes in theater chains, Harkins tried again to stop

KEY DATES

1933: Dwight "Red" Harkins begins managing the State Theatre in Tempe, Arizona.
1940: College Theatre, with numerous Harkins technical innovations, opens in Tempe.
1948: Saguaro Theatre is added in Wickenburg, Arizona.
1973: Camelview 3 opens in Scottsdale, Arizona.
1974: Red Harkins dies at 59; 21-year-old Dan Harkins takes control of firm.
1977: Harkins sues eight distributors and three exhibitors, alleging film booking collusion.
1988: New eight-screen multiplex opens in Scottsdale; company takes over the historic Cine Capri.
1991: Out-of-court settlement is reached in legal battle with film distributors.
1993: Seven theaters with 41 screens are bought from the Mann chain.
1995: Harkins buys three theaters from General Cinema, adding 21 screens.
1997: Firm opens a 25-screen theater, at the time the largest in the United States.
2004: Harkins' first out-of-state theater opens in Oklahoma City.
2006: New theaters are added in Colorado, California, and Texas.

the booking practices that kept prime Hollywood titles from him. He sought redress under the Sherman Antitrust Act and with additional suits against distributors, which were settled out of court in 1991 for an undisclosed amount that was substantial enough to help fund new expansion.

ACQUISITIONS BRING GROWTH

In May 1993 the firm bought seven Phoenix-area theaters with 41 screens from the larger Mann Theatres chain. The purchase more than doubled the number of Harkins' screens, which until then comprised 26 at five first-run multiplexes, one single-screen first-run theater, and three multiscreen "dollar movie" houses. The company soon began a program to upgrade the former Mann sites to feature Dolby stereo sound and better seating, spending about $100,000 per screen on audio and $150,000 to $200,000 per screen to upgrade seats. The price of first-run movies was dropped from $6 to the Harkins standard of $5.50, while concession prices fell about 20 percent, with the firm's wider range of snacks added. In the months after the acquisition ticket sales at the former Mann sites more than doubled.

Shortly after the Mann acquisition Harkins also opened a new theater of its own adjacent to the Valley Art in downtown Tempe. The $5.2 million, two-story, 11-screen Centerpoint Cinemas was touted as the largest theater complex in the state. Its presence also helped boost the business of restaurants and stores nearby.

In April 1995 the firm acquired three more Phoenix-area theaters with 21 screens from the General Cinema chain. In September, the Shea 14 opened in Scottsdale, replacing the closed Shea Plaza. It was followed in January 1996 by a six-screen facility in the town of Sedona, Harkins' first location outside greater Phoenix.

In early 1996, as national chain AMC Entertainment opened a new 20-plus screen "megaplex" in Phoenix, Harkins announced plans to add 111 screens in the metro area by 1998. Although competition from national concerns like United Artists and AMC was fierce, Phoenix native Dan Harkins felt his company was up to the challenge. With Americans increasingly turning to watching films on home video systems, Harkins believed that new, more attractive and luxurious theaters increased frequency of moviegoing, noting that in Sedona the typical person was spending $110 at the box office each year, compared to the national average of just $22.

To maintain its high standards of quality the firm inaugurated a "mystery shopper" program in which each theater was visited anonymously weekly to check cleanliness, projection quality, and customer service. Employee pay and bonuses were tied to theaters' performance at these inspections.

HARKINS OPENS MEGAPLEXES

Though the firm had typically relied on developers to build its facilities, and then rented them back, in 1997 it began to do this in-house to take full ownership of more theaters. In July of that year, after months of construction delays, another outlying theater was opened, an 11-screen multiplex in Flagstaff. October and November saw the debuts of the first two Harkins megaplexes, a 25-screen site in Superstition Springs and a 24-screen facility in Arizona Mills.

Built at a cost of $15 million, the Superstition Springs 25 was then the largest theater in the United States and featured 4,500 seats, four concession stands, and a 10-window ticket booth. The large number of auditoriums allowed the projection of hit movies on multiple screens, with showtimes staggered so that patrons would have only a short wait until the next start time. The theater was later recognized as "Best Designed Building" by the Arizona chapter of the American Institute of Architects. Owner Dan Harkins had also been honored numerous times by a leading exhibitors' organization as its "Showman of the Year." In addition to looking after patrons' comfort, the firm also gave as much as $800,000 per year to local charitable organizations in the form of on-screen ads and giveaways for fund-raising events.

With the concession stand providing more income than ticket sales (which distributors took the bulk of), Harkins began seeking other types of revenue. One successful method was to rent its theaters to business and community groups during the day, when fewer patrons attended films, as well as showing ads before movies.

At the start of 1999 the company took over the Valley Art Theatre when its tenant declared bankruptcy, and Dan Harkins began a thorough updating of the facility's seating and projection systems while retaining as much historic detail as possible in tribute to his father's original vision. In the spring of 1999 another new theater, the Metro 12, was opened, and during the year the company also moved to new, larger headquarters in Scottsdale; launched a frequent moviegoer program that gave customers a free ticket after buying ten via the MovieFone reservation service; and installed a new digital projection system on one screen. Harkins Amusement had always been an early adopter of new technologies like digital sound, and it was one of the first exhibitors in the United States to purchase the expensive new equipment, which was slated to eventually replace film with a high-definition video format.

Though plans were announced in 2000 to add nearly 200 screens over two years, including theaters in California and New Mexico, growth was soon scaled back as the U.S. economy stumbled and many national exhibition chains consolidated or filed for bankruptcy, the result of aggressive overbuilding. A surge of megaplex construction had increased the number of U.S. screens from 27,000 to 37,000 between 1995 and 1999.

EXPANSION IN THE 21ST CENTURY

Harkins added another theater in the metropolitan Phoenix area in 2000, the Arrowhead 18, which was followed by three in 2001: the Prescott Valley 14, the North Valley 16, and the Chandler Fashion Mall 20. The latter featured the firm's first in-house childcare facility, which enabled parents to drop their child off during a film for about the price of an admission ticket.

In the fall of 2002 the company added another 18-screen theater, and in 2003 Harkins secured a new $65 million line of credit from a consortium of banks to ramp up the pace of expansion. During the year a new Phoenix-area multiplex, the Scottsdale 101, was also opened, which included a 600-seat recreation of the beloved Cine Capri, which had been demolished in 1998 despite an aggressive local campaign to save it.

The fall of 2004 saw the company open a new theater in Oklahoma City, Oklahoma, its first outside Arizona. During the year Harkins also bought more than 200 Kodak Digital Cinema projection systems for its theaters as the industry moved closer to implementing the new format.

In 2005 the firm announced plans to add as many as 14 theaters over two years including ones in California, Texas, and Colorado. The first in the latter state, an 18-screen, $17 million facility, opened near Denver in April 2006, and it was quickly followed by the company's first California theater in Moreno Valley, and one near Dallas/Fort Worth, Texas.

In September 2006 Mike Bowers was named president and chief operating officer of Harkins Amusement Enterprises, with Dan Harkins remaining CEO. Bowers had served as vice-president since 1996. In December the State of Arizona filed suit against the company, alleging that it had failed to provide accommodations for hearing- and vision-impaired patrons at the 262 movie screens it operated in the state. Arizona had also filed suit against national chain AMC.

In the summer of 2007 it was announced that the Centerpoint development in downtown Tempe would be razed and replaced by condominiums. The firm's theater there would close, although its patrons would continue to be served by newer Harkins facilities nearby. During the year the company opened six new theaters including ones in Tucson, Mesa, and Pinal County, Arizona. More were on the drawing board for 2008.

After three-quarters of a century in business, Harkins Amusement Enterprises, Inc., had become the dominant movie exhibitor in the Phoenix area, and was branching out to serve the rest of Arizona and other states. Under the leadership of CEO Dan Harkins, the firm continued to follow the principles of showmanship, respect for audiences, and technical innovation set by his father, Dwight "Red" Harkins.

Frank Uhle

PRINCIPAL SUBSIDIARIES

Harkins Enterprises, Inc.; Harkins Camelview Theatres, Inc.; Harkins Theatres, Inc.; Harkins Centerpoint, Inc.;

Harkins Shea Cinemas, LLC; Harkins Sedona Cinemas, LLC; Harkins Cinemas, LLC; Harkins Arizona Mills Cinemas, LLC; Harkins Metro Center Cinemas, LLC; Harkins Phoenix Cinemas, LLC; Harkins Chandler Fashion Center Cinemas, LLC; Harkins Scottsdale 101 Cinemas, LLC; Harkins Yuma Palms, LLC; Harkins Tempe Marketplace LLC; Harkins Administrative Services, Inc.; Red's Moviola I, LLC; Red's Moviola, Inc.; Harkins Spectrum, LLC; Harkins Casa Grande, LLC; Harkins Investments, LLC; Harkins Parke West, LLC; Harkins Reel Deals, LLC; Harkins Santan Village, LLC; Harkins Tucson Spectrum, LLC; Harkins Chandler Crossroads, LLC; Harkins Norterra, LLC.

PRINCIPAL COMPETITORS

Regal Entertainment Group; AMC Entertainment Holdings, Inc.; Cinemark Holdings, Inc.; Starplex Operating L.P.

FURTHER READING

Ascenzi, Joseph, "Arizona-Based Theater Chain Offers Unusual Perks," *Business Press, San Bernardino,* November 6, 2006, p. 15.

Casacchia, Chris, "Deal Means More National Advertisers for Harkins," *Business Journal of Phoenix,* February 2, 2007.

Cook, Kristen, "Theater's Ticket to Success: Lobbying for Your Child Care," *Arizona Daily Star,* November 2, 2001, p. F43.

Creno, Glen, "Arizona-Based Harkins Theatres Expands Despite Industry's Troubles," *World Reporter,* August 28, 2000.

Daniels, Jeffrey, "Harkins Raising Curtain on 111 Ariz. Theaters," *Hollywood Reporter,* April 29, 1996, p. 3.

Ducey, Lynn, "Harkins Theatres Names Bowers to Lead Operations," *Business Journal of Phoenix,* September 15, 2006.

Fischer, Howard, "State Sues Harkins Theater Chain," *Arizona Daily Star,* December 19, 2006, p. D1.

Groff, Garin, "Centerpoint to Fall, Rise Anew," *Mesa Tribune,* August 10, 2007.

"Harkins Theatres Timeline," http://www.harkinstheatres.com/timeline.asp, February 14, 2008.

Klayman, Gary, "Movies Are the Reel Life for Local Cinema Mogul," *Business Journal of Phoenix,* November 12, 1990, p. 1.

Kramer, Pat, "David Smites Goliath Chains," *Variety,* January 4, 1999, p. 83.

Kress, Adam, "Harkins Theatres Grows amid Evolving Movie Industry," *Business Journal of Phoenix,* August 26, 2005.

Lally, Kevin, "Southwest Showmanship: Harkins Theatres Celebrates 70 Years of Excellence," *Film Journal International,* August, 2003, p. 26.

McDonald, Michele, "Scottsdale-Based Harkins Purchases Mann Theaters," *Scottsdale Progress,* May 21, 1993.

Reinke, Martha, "Bigger, Better; Harkins Turns Theaters into Show Places," *Mesa Tribune,* October 30, 1993.

———, "The Show Must Go On ... 25 Screens," *Business Journal of Phoenix,* April 26, 1996, p. 1.

Ringle, Hayley, "On the Big Screen," *Bulldog,* December 15, 1999.

Streuli, Ted, "Dan Harkins: A Life in the Movies," *Journal Record,* September 24, 2004.

———, "Entrepreneur Dan Harkins Builds First Theater Outside Arizona," *Journal Record,* October 1, 2004.

Tusher, Will, "MGM/UA, Harkins Chain Settle Antitrust Suits," *Variety,* August 12, 1991, p. 10.

Wagner, Eileen Brill, "Valley Movie Pioneer Gets Capital to Expand," *Business Journal of Phoenix,* February 7, 2003, p. 1.

Harland Clarke Holdings Corporation

2939 Miller Road
Decatur, Georgia 30035-4038
U.S.A.
Telephone: (770) 981-9460
Toll Free: (800) 723-3690
Fax: (770) 593-5619
Web site: http://www.harlandclarke.com

Wholly Owned Subsidiary of M & F Worldwide Corporation
Founded: 1874 as Maverick Printing Company
Employees: 5,360
Sales: $1.67 billion (2006)
NAIC: 323110 Commercial Lithographic Printing; 323118 Blankbook, Loose-leaf Binder and Device Manufacturing; 323119 Other Commercial Printing; 334119 Other Computer Peripheral Equipment Manufacturing; 511210 Software Publishers

■ ■ ■

Harland Clarke Holdings Corporation is the largest printer of paper checks in the United States. Formed from the 2007 union of John H. Harland with Clarke American, the company also provides marketing and other services to the financial industry through its Harland Financial Solutions segment, and supplies schools and companies with testing systems via Scantron. Although Harland Clarke was banking on such newly acquired businesses for its future growth, as of 2006 printed products accounted for three-quarters of its total revenues.

SAN ANTONIO ORIGINS

The Harland Clarke story begins with the Maverick Printing Company, which was started in 1874. Its founder, Samuel Maverick, also had considerable interests in ranching and banking. Robert Clarke, a printer from Galveston, Texas, bought Samuel Maverick's shares in the company in 1898, whereupon it was renamed Maverick-Clarke Litho Company. It soon moved to a site on San Antonio's West Houston Street and then a few years later to a still larger facility on Soledad. The company specialized in stationery and printed items, which it handled in its own plant. It eventually added furniture and other office supplies to its offerings.

A 1950 article in the *San Antonio Light* painstakingly chronicles Maverick-Clarke's real estate moves in the first half of the 20th century. In 1916 the company relocated to a 50,000-square-foot building on South St. Mary's Street. It was at the time the only structure on the peninsula known as Bowen's Island. An even larger building was acquired in 1929, but the company moved again eight years later to a former Southwestern Bell building on East Travis Street.

THRIVING STORES

Maverick-Clarke had two stores at the end of its first 50 years in business. The largest was the one on South St. Mary's Street in the heart of downtown San Antonio. A photo of it in the June 4, 1927, *San Antonio Light* shows a large, open room with a 12-foot ceiling, with orderly rows of merchandise arrayed over every inch of the wall-height shelves and across several tables clustered

COMPANY PERSPECTIVES

Harland Clarke was formed in 2007 by combining the products and services of Clarke American Corporation and the printed products segment of John H. Harland Company. Together, both highly respected companies have over 200 years of combined experience, each with a rich heritage, traditions of innovation and performance excellence. Harland Clarke offers an expanded suite of direct-marketing services, delivery and anti-fraud products, contact center services and checks and check-related products to the financial institution market, including banks, credit unions, thrifts, and securities firms.

in the middle. Billed as "the Office Men's Department Store," it also catered to women with a department devoted to selecting the proper stationery for social use.

In 1926 San Antonio developer Russell C. Hill was named president of the company, a position he held for more than 25 years. His son Roger C. Hill worked at Maverick-Clarke as a youth and after World War II was placed in charge of its branch operations and printing plant.

The firm spread steadily through Texas, starting with a branch opened in Corpus Christi in 1937. It bought Houston's Standard Printing and Lithographing Co. in 1944 and opened a store in Brownsville, Texas, in 1949. Maverick-Clarke also had sales agents in several other Texas cities.

NEW PLANT IN 1950

Maverick-Clarke followed industrial development toward the south of San Antonio after World War II. Its printing facilities at 215 East Travis Street were moved to a relatively new 50,000-square-foot building in 1950. This was a colossal undertaking, as some of the presses weighed more than 15 tons each and were located on the upper two floors of a five-story building. The new plant operated under the Clarke Printing Co. name. Maverick-Clarke retained its group headquarters at Travis Street, converting some of the freed space to retail floors and offices for lease to third parties.

By this time, the firm was printing checks. Its state-of-the-art print works were capable of embossing and bookbinding in addition to offset lithography and other types of printing. Clarke was one of the first to embrace the magnetic ink that allowed for automated processing of checks beginning in 1959.

In 1968, Maverick-Clarke added a third store to its San Antonio operations by buying family-owned Henderson's Office Supply. Maverick-Clarke had nine stores overall, and had expanded in Texas to Austin, Victoria, and Laredo.

A GROWING CORPORATION

The company's structure was slowly evolving. Clarke Printing began operating independently from the rest of Maverick-Clarke in the mid-1960s, and the checks division was renamed Clarke Checks in 1977. A string of several acquisitions increased Clarke's mass rapidly and the firm itself was bought out in 1985 by MB America, Inc. (MBA), the U.S. affiliate of England's MB Group Plc. MB Group was merged with Caradon Plc a few years later and was renamed Novar Plc in 2001.

A year after the change in ownership, Clarke introduced its own version of Total Quality Management, dubbed, "First in Service." The company continued to grow and ended the 1980s with 25 printing plants and annual revenues of $110 million.

CLARKE AMERICAN CREATED

Clarke's corporate parent MB Group acquired American Bank Stationery, another midsize check printing firm, for about $300 million in September 1989. Baltimore-based American Bank Stationery was almost 50 percent larger than Clarke, with annual revenues of $150 million and 21 printing plants.

Over the next two years, American Bank Stationery was gradually merged with Clarke Checks to form Clarke American Holdings, Inc. It had approximately 3,500 employees and was the third largest check printer in the United States after Minnesota-based Deluxe Corporation and John H. Harland Co., founded in 1923, of Decatur, Georgia.

In 1991 Clarke wrested the check-printing contract of NCNB Corporation away from its larger rival, John H. Harland. NCNB, based in Charlotte, had grown rapidly to more than 900 branches and was streamlining its purchasing after absorbing many smaller banks.

Clarke American's revenues were up to about $300 million in 1995. By 1999, Clarke American had 2,700 employees and was hiring more. Drawn by the North Carolina banking industry, which included such important clients as Bank of America, Clarke opened a call center in Charlotte in 1999. Clarke had several other such centers, including locations in Salt Lake City, Utah; Orlando, Florida; and Syracuse, New York.

KEY DATES

1874: Maverick Printing Company launched in San Antonio, Texas.
1898: Robert Clarke buys Samuel Maverick's shares; firm is renamed Maverick-Clarke Litho Company.
1923: John H. Harland Company launched as office supply and printed products firm.
1950: Maverick-Clarke moves into new printing plant in San Antonio.
1985: Clarke acquired by U.S. affiliate of England's MB Group PLC (later Novar plc).
1989: American Bank Stationery begins merging with Clarke Checks to form Clarke American Corporation.
2005: M & F Worldwide buys Clarke American.
2007: M & F Worldwide buys John H. Harland Company, and merges it with Clarke American to form Harland Clarke.

THE DECLINE OF PRINTED CHECKS

Although the 1990s saw record levels of checks printed, by the end of the decade it was apparent that this was a shrinking industry, as electronic debit cards and online payments were accounting for an increasing number of transactions. The CEO of rival John H. Harland, Chuck Dawson, told the *San Antonio Express-News* that 1997 was the beginning of the decline in the check printing market. Harland's stock price plunged 40 percent during the year, leading to a restructuring. Another landmark year was 2003, when according to the Federal Reserve, electronic payments outnumbered paper checks for the first time (not including checks processed electronically). Clarke American, nevertheless, continued to post impressive revenue gains in the stagnant market. Sales reached $462 million in 2000.

A period of intense industry consolidation accompanied the shrinking of the market. Clarke's larger rival Harland bought banking software provider Concentrex, Inc., in 2001 and continued to gobble up smaller rivals. In 2005, Harland bought Liberty Enterprises, a check printer specializing in credit unions, in a deal worth $160 million.

Clarke American underwent another change of ownership. Honeywell acquired Clarke American's parent company, Novar, in 2004. The next year it sold Clarke American to M & F Worldwide Corporation, the holding company associated with New York financier Ronald Perelman, for $800 million. By this time Clarke American was the third largest check printing company in the United States. Revenues were $624 million in 2006, when the company had 3,200 employees. It was printing more than 10 billion checks a year. Included in the deal were Clarke Checks, Checks in the Mail, and a couple of direct-marketing businesses, Alcott Routon and B2Direct. Checks in the Mail (formerly Checks Express), a provider of mail-order checks that dated back to 1922, had been acquired by Novar in 1993; the others were more recent acquisitions.

HARLAND CLARKE MERGER

In 2007 Clarke American's corporate parent M & F Worldwide Corporation acquired the John H. Harland Company, the country's number two check printer, for about $1.7 billion. John H. Harland Company was then merged with Clarke American, which was renamed Harland Clarke Holdings Corporation.

John H. Harland had been much bigger than Clarke American; the combined company had revenues of $1.7 billion and eclipsed Deluxe as the largest in the land. Nearly two-thirds of its business was in printed checks. The aim, according to analysts, was to achieve efficiencies of scale in a shrinking market.

John H. Harland's side ventures were also a major consideration as they offered growth prospects beyond the printed check. These businesses included Scantron, maker of standardized testing systems for schools, and software and database marketing operations tailored to the financial services industry. "We want to print the last check that's ever printed," Harland Clarke CEO Chuck Dawson later explained to the *San Antonio Express-News,* adding, "We just don't want it to be the only thing we do that day."

Frederick C. Ingram

PRINCIPAL SUBSIDIARIES

Harland Mexico SA de CV; Checks in the Mail, Inc.; Harland Checks and Services, Inc.; Clarke American Checks, Inc.; B2Direct, Inc.; HFS Scantron Holdings Corporation.

PRINCIPAL DIVISIONS

Harland Clarke; Harland Financial Solutions; Scantron.

PRINCIPAL COMPETITORS

Deluxe Corporation.

FURTHER READING

Bills, Steve, "Clarke Has Financing for Harland Purchase," *American Banker,* February 23, 2007, p. 9.

———, "Will Harland Sale to M & F Derail Tech Unit Spinoff?: A Private Equity-Style Deal Would Combine Check Printing Leaders," *American Banker,* December 21, 2006, p. 1.

Chang, Richard, *The Passion Plan at Work: Building a Passion-Driven Organization,* San Francisco: Jossey-Bass, 2001.

"Eisemann Is Manager," *San Antonio Light,* October 1, 1958, p. 3E.

Gardyasz, Joe, "Clarke American to Expand Its Ankeny Facilities: Company Sees Demand, Despite Decline in Check Usage," *Des Moines Business Record,* November 27, 2006, pp. 10f.

Hannon, David, "Diary of a Makeover," *Purchasing,* April 5, 2007, p. 33.

Howard, J. Lee, "Clarke to Add 250 Jobs," *Charlotte (N.C.) Business Journal,* April 9, 1999, pp. 1, 69.

"Keenan Plant Mgr.," *San Antonio Light,* October 1, 1950, p. 4E.

Kendrick, Tim, "How First Union Deals with a Vendor: A Case Study in Checking Conversions," *Bankers Magazine* (Boston), January/February 1995, pp. 53–56.

Kleiner, Kurt, "American Bank to Move to Texas, Cutting 190 Md. Jobs," *Baltimore Business Journal,* February 19, 1990, p. 3.

"Maverick-Clarke Christens New Plant; Public Asked to Inspect So. Side Unit," *San Antonio Light,* October 1, 1950, p. 1E.

"Maverick Clarke Cools Store, Business Gains; Cooling System Makes Large S.A. Store More Efficient," *San Antonio Light,* June 4, 1927, p. 12A.

McNeel, J. S., Jr., "S.A. Industrial District Expands: Mav.-Clarke Big Units Moved South," *San Antonio Light,* January 22, 1950, pp. D1, D3.

Newman, A. Joseph, Jr., "Check Printer Wages Campaign Against Mail-Order Competitors," *American Banker,* March 30, 1989, p. 8.

"Not Lulled by High Participation, Employer Revamps Plan to Improve Administration, Investment Education," *Employee Benefit Plan Review,* March 1997, pp. 50f.

"Office Men's Department Store—With Furniture and Equipment of Latest Designs—Also Operating Women's Stationery Department," *San Antonio Express,* February 4, 1929, p. 12.

"Office Supply Firm Sold," *San Antonio Express,* June 18, 1968, p. 8B.

Phelps, Grady, "Tom Quinn New Manager of Maverick-Clarke Firm," *Corpus Christi Times,* December 10, 1965, p. 5B.

"Plant Operates on Streamline," *San Antonio Light,* October 1, 1950, p. 5E.

Poling, Travis E., "NCNB Picks Clarke Corp. as Its Printer," *San Antonio Business Journal,* February 8, 1991, pp. 1f.

———, "San Antonio, Texas, Check-Printing Firm Is Honored for Quality," *San Antonio Express-News,* December 5, 2001.

"Roger C. Hill Organizes Units," *San Antonio Light,* October 1, 1950, p. 3E.

"Russell C. Hill; S.A. Civic Leader," *San Antonio Light,* October 1, 1950, p. 2E.

Slywotzky, Adrian J., Richard Wise, and Karl Weber, *How to Grow When Markets Don't,* New York: Warner Books, 2003.

Thiruvengadam, Meena, "A Conversation with Chuck Dawson of Harland Clarke," *San Antonio Express-News,* July 4, 2007.

———, "Rise in Electronic Banking Spurs Check-Printing Company to Add New Services," *San Antonio Express-News,* June 20, 2007.

Hobie Cat Company

4925 Oceanside Boulevard
Oceanside, California 92056
U.S.A.
Telephone: (760) 758-9100
Toll Free: (800) 462-4349
Fax: (760) 758-1841
Web site: http://www.hobiecat.com

Private Company
Incorporated: 1968 as Coast Catamaran Corporation
Employees: 125
Sales: $100 million (2003 est.)
NAIC: 336611 Ship Building and Repairing

■ ■ ■

Hobie Cat Company makes innovative vehicles for water recreation. Its founder, Hobart "Hobie" Alter, was a pioneer of polypropylene foam surfboards for the mass market. The product most synonymous with his nickname, however, is the lightweight family of catamarans he first introduced in the late 1960s. These made sailing accessible to thousands around the world.

The world fleet includes more than 100,000 Hobie Cats. However, catamaran sales have since been eclipsed by the firm's pedal-driven kayaks. Separately owned companies, Hobie Designs, Inc., and Hobie Brands International, LLC, handle licensing of sunglasses and other items. The French firm Hobie Cat Europe, which also makes sail-powered craft, is independently owned as well.

ORANGE COUNTY, CALIFORNIA, ORIGINS

The company's namesake and founder, Hobart L. Alter—better known by his nickname, "Hobie"—started out by crafting balsa wood and fiberglass surfboards in his Laguna Beach, California, garage.

In 1954, he and a partner opened a store at Dana Point that was among the first of the Orange County surf shops. Within a few years he had established a successful surfboard manufacturing operation. Alter was one of the first to work with polyurethane foam, making boards in sufficient volume for the mass market.

The "Cat" part of the company name refers to the catamarans that then captured Alter's attention. In 1967 he designed the Hobie 14 catamaran, a 14-foot, sail-powered vessel with twin fiberglass hulls suggestive of the outrigger canoes of Polynesia. At 215 pounds, it was one-third the weight of conventional catamarans and could be launched and piloted by a single person. The Hobie 14 bridged the gap between surfing and sailing. It dismantled easily for traveling, making the adventure of sailing even more accessible. A top speed of better than 20 knots made for an exciting ride.

In the middle of 1968 Alter launched a business to make the new vessels. Based in San Juan Capistrano, the company was originally known as the Coast Catamaran Corporation. Sales were very slow at first, but by the end of 1969 Alter had sold 1,000 of the catamarans at about $1,200 each. A photo spread in the February 6, 1970, *Life* magazine helped steer the Hobie Cat toward a place in the nation's consciousness.

COMPANY PERSPECTIVES

Since 1950, Hobie Cat Company has been in the business of shaping a unique lifestyle based around fun, water, and quality products. From our headquarters in Oceanside, California, we manufacture, distribute, and market an impressive collection of watercraft worldwide. These include an ever-expanding line of recreational and racing sailboats, pedal-driven and paddle sit-on-top kayaks, fishing boats, and authorized parts and accessories.

Alter quickly developed a two-person model called the Hobie 16, which, like its predecessor, was named after its length in feet. Introduced in 1969, it became the all-time bestseller of any of Hobie catamarans.

Sales were up to nearly $10 million in 1975, and the company, then publicly owned, was profitable. By this time, there were about 50,000 Hobie Cats plying the seas of the world, and Coast was by far the largest catamaran manufacturer. There were a handful of manufacturing operations overseas.

OWNERSHIP CHANGES

In 1976, Coleman Company, the Wichita, Kansas, sporting-goods conglomerate, bought Coast Catamaran, which had gone public a couple of years earlier, for $3.5 million. Hobie Alter remained on board for a time as a consultant. In 1979, manufacturing was relocated to a facility in Oceanside, California. Sales exceeded $30 million within a couple of years, but an industry-wide slowdown was just around the corner.

Annual revenues fell to about $15 million in the mid-1980s and the Coleman Company put the unprofitable unit on the auction block. A group of 130 employees fielded a bid but in November 1987 Coleman agreed to sell Coast Catamaran to Evergreen Partners of Newport Beach for $16 million. However, Evergreen canceled the deal a few months later due to deteriorating financials.

In 1989 Coleman found another buyer in Texas entrepreneur and sailing enthusiast Anthony Wilson. Wilson had two years earlier sold South Coast Terminals, Inc., a company he founded in the 1960s, to Chevron Oil Co. Coast Catamaran France, S.A., the company's French sailboat-making operation, was bought out by three of its directors in 1989. It continued to make Hobie-branded light sailing vessels under license.

There was another change of ownership in the mid-1990s. The business was acquired by R.R. Sail, Inc., which was incorporated in Missouri in 1995 and renamed Hobie Cat Company the following year. Its chairman was Richard Rogers.

A key designer was hired around this time. Greg Ketterman, a veteran of NASA, was placed in charge of design efforts. He led the development of a unique pedal-drive system that propelled Hobie into a leading position in new water sports.

SPINOFFS AND SIDE PROJECTS

As one of the oldest names in surfing, the Hobie brand was valuable to lifestyle-oriented marketers of clothing and other products. In 1981 the Great American Shirt Co. formed Hobie Apparel, Inc., to make a line of clothing for mass-market department stores. The clothing was not, however, sold at Hobie's surf shops. Annual apparel sales began at less than $3 million but were up to $65 million within a few years. The name began appearing on sunglasses in 1982 through another licensing arrangement.

A company called Hobie Designs, Inc., was formed in 1990 to handle licenses for items such as surfboards. It was based in McCall, Idaho, and Jeff Alter, son of the company founder, was the president and owner.

Hobie was known throughout its history for its relentless pace of innovation. Not all of the firm's new creations met with enduring commercial success, but when they did, they launched entire industries. Hobie Alter placed one foot in the skateboard craze of the 1970s through a joint venture called Hobie Skateboards, Inc. At one point he developed a $5,000 recumbent model for downhill racing. Among other products of the times was a radio-controlled glider called the Hobie Hawk.

In the mid-1980s the company developed single-hulled sailing craft such as the Hobie 33 and the Holder 14. The company also came out with a powerboat, called the Hobie Skiff, around 1984. After a series of changes in ownership and a new leadership team, the company found one of its greatest successes by applying its creativity to a whole new class of boat.

MAKING A SPLASH WITH KAYAKS

Paddle sports were growing in popularity when Hobie entered the market in 1997. Hobie did not invent the sit-on-top category, whose vessels were much more

KEY DATES

1950: Hobie Alter begins making surfboards in Laguna Beach, California.
1967: Alter develops the Hobie 14 catamaran, first of the Hobie Cats.
1968: Alter launches Coast Catamaran Corporation to produce catamarans.
1976: The Coleman Company buys Coast Catamaran after sales exceed $10 million.
1989: Texas entrepreneur Anthony Wilson buys Coast Catamaran from Coleman.
1995: R.R. Sail, Inc., chaired by Richard Rogers, acquires Hobie.
1996: R.R. Sail is renamed Hobie Cat Company.
1997: Hobie rolls out a line of unique pedal-driven kayaks.
2003: Sales are estimated at more than $100 million.

stable and easier to use than traditional kayaks. Its revolution lay under the surface, with a revolutionary propulsion system that freed the user's hands for tasks such as taking pictures, fishing, or hunting.

To experienced paddlers, Hobie's kayaks seemed nearly as different from other kayaks as its catamarans were from other sailing vessels 30 years earlier. Hobie's innovation was the so-called Mirage-Drive: a pair of flexible polypropylene fins linked to pedals, meant to emulate the efficient movement of penguins.

Hobie originally sourced kayak hulls from Anaheim's American Rotational Molding Group, Inc., but installed a couple of its own ovens around 2000, and its rotomolding process kept costs down. At about $4,700, the 16.5 foot Getaway had a list price of about $2,700 less than a comparable fiberglass model.

LOOKING AHEAD

The plunge into paddle sports was more than a sideline. Kayaks eclipsed Hobie's catamaran business within a couple of years. Total sales were estimated at more than $100 million in 2003, when Hobie Cat Company had 125 employees. Hobie remained synonymous with innovation. In a hint of things to come, in October 2006 Hobie entered a licensing arrangement for an electric-drive system from Florida's Solomon Technologies, Inc. Hobie was also introducing inflatable kayaks, designed to be portable enough to carry in a car or even as airline baggage. While reaching ahead, the company remained close to its roots, still working from a base near the waves of Southern California.

Frederick C. Ingram

PRINCIPAL COMPETITORS

LaserPerformance.

FURTHER READING

Bardia, Alexander, "Hobie … Hobie! … Hobie!! Surfing Sailing or Kayaking, if You Are on the Surface of the Water You Are in Hobie Territory," *Pier2Peer,* April 2005.

Bellantonio, Jennifer, "Hobie Surf Tightens Licensing; No More 'Handshake' Deals," *Orange County Business Journal,* August 2, 2004.

Bivins, Ralph, "Coleman to Sell Boat Firm; Houston Man Agrees to Purchase Coast Catamaran," *Houston Chronicle,* August 9, 1988, p. 1.

Bloomfield, Judy, "Hobie: Riding the Waves," *WWD,* March 2, 1988, p. S10.

Broderick, Pat, "Hobie-GE Deal to Be Cat's Meow," *San Diego Business Journal,* November 19, 2007, p. 12.

Bucher, Judy, "Rotomolding: Not Your Grandfather's Process Anymore … Or Your Father's, for That Matter," *Plastics World,* February 1997, pp. 28–32.

"Californian Hit Jackpot with Sailors," *Houston Chronicle,* Sports Sec., December 15, 1985, p. 23.

Caswell, C., "Ride the Wind," *Popular Mechanics,* October 1987, pp. 62–65.

"The Cat That Flies," *Life,* February 6, 1970, pp. 28–31.

Chambers, Heather, "Hobie Cat Still Making Waves," *Today's Local News* (Calif.), April 9, 2006.

"Coleman Buys 91% of Firm," *Fresno Bee,* January 26, 1976, p. B6.

DeGaspari, John, "Moves Like a Penguin," *Mechanical Engineering—CIME,* April 2001, p. 12.

Duke, B., "Hobie Powers Up," *Motor Boating & Sailing,* September 1990, pp. 142–45.

———, "Hobie's Power Trip," *Motor Boating & Sailing,* May 1988, pp. 60–63.

Fikes, Bradley J., "Hobie Cat Is 'Made in America,'" *North County (Calif.) Times,* July 26, 2007.

Foust, Tom, "Hobies Provide a New Breed of Catamaran," *Arizona Daily Star,* October 6, 1994, p. 8C.

Hansell, Craig, "Hobie Cat Builder Keeps Enjoying Sailing His Legendary Catamaran," *Salt Lake Tribune,* September 24, 1992, p. C5.

"Happiness Is a Hobie Cat," *Time,* August 3, 1981, p. 55.

Himmelspach, Darlene, "Employees Still in Running for Hobie Cat; Buyout Study OK'd," *San Diego Union-Tribune,* October 29, 1987, p. B5.

———, "Evergreen Cancels Offer for Hobie Cat," *San Diego Union-Tribune,* June 18, 1988, p. D1.

Hobie Class Association of North America, "History of Hobies," 2002, http://hcana.hobieclass.com.

Jaffe, Thomas, "Dewy and the Hobie Cats," *Forbes,* May 19, 1986, p. 228.

Kren, Lawrence, "Kayak Trades Paddles for Pedals," *Machine Design,* June 7, 2001, p. 33.

Larsen, Carl, "Hobie Cat Maker May Be Sold by Coleman Co.," *San Diego Union-Tribune,* September 10, 1987, p. AA1.

McDonald, Merete, "Houston Investor Signs Option to Buy Hobie Cat," *San Diego Union-Tribune,* August 9, 1988, p. E1.

McDowell, Edwin, "Coleman Is Growing Overseas," *New York Times,* December 9, 1991.

"Millionaire Toymaker Flying High," *San Mateo (Calif.) Times,* July 2, 1975, p. 31.

Mills, Dawson, "The People's Racing Boat," *Norfolk Virginian-Pilot and Ledger-Star,* Virginia Beach Beacon Sec., July 14, 1996, p. 12.

Morris, Jim, "Sailboat Goes Twice As Fast As the Wind," *Dayton Daily News,* September 16, 1995, p. 7D.

Ostler, Scott, "When Intelligence Runs Wild, Hobie Alter Invents Fun," *Syracuse (N.Y.) Post-Standard,* October 31, 1984, p. C1.

Renstrom, Roger, "Hobie to Rotomold Getaway Catamaran," *Plastics News,* September 2000, p. 9.

Ruben, Howle, "Hobic Sport Shops Win the West," *Daily News Record,* December 22, 1983, p. 6.

Scherer, Ron, "Ex-Surfer's Dream: 'Hobie' Means Big Success," *San Mateo (Calif.) Times,* September 19, 1977, p. 23.

Sutro, Dirk, "Hobie Cat Workers Lose in Buyout Bid," *San Diego Union-Tribune,* November 25, 1987, p. AA1.

INTERNATIONAL

ICF International, Inc.

9300 Lee Highway
Fairfax, Virginia 22031-1207
U.S.A.
Telephone: (703) 934-3603
Toll Free: (800) 532-4783
Fax: (703) 934-3740
Web site: http://www.icfi.com

Public Company
Incorporated: 1914 as Kaiser Engineers, Inc.
Employees: 2,111
Sales: $331 million (2006)
Stock Exchanges: NASDAQ
Ticker Symbol: ICFI
NAIC: 541710 Research and Development in the Physical, Engineering, and Life Sciences; 541720 Research and Development in the Social Sciences and Humanities; 541520 Computer Systems Design Services

■ ■ ■

ICF International, Inc., is one of the largest government, environmental, and energy consulting companies in the United States, with a growing international presence. Headquartered in northern Virginia, ICF partners with government and commercial clients to deliver consulting services in seven primary markets: climate change, defense, energy, homeland security, environment, transportation, and social programs. ICF developed into a leading consulting company during its ownership by Kaiser Engineers and various parent companies until splitting from the Kaiser Company in 1999 to become a separate entity focused solely on consulting services. In 2006, the company took the name ICF International, to reflect their goal of expanding beyond the U.S. market to become an international leader in the consulting industry.

EARLY HISTORY

The "Kaiser" in ICF Kaiser International traces its roots to 1914, and the founding of Henry J. Kaiser Company, Ltd., a construction company in Spokane, Washington, and the forerunner of Kaiser Aluminum & Chemical Corporation. Henry Kaiser's philosophy was "Do it faster, cheaper, and better," and he encouraged innovation among his employees. One early product of The Hobby Lobby (the company's research department) was the rubber-tired wheelbarrow. Kaiser's first big job, in 1927, was as a subcontractor building 200 miles of highway through the mountains and jungles of Cuba. The company finished a year ahead of schedule.

In the early 1930s the federal government began huge public works jobs to counter the Great Depression. In the West, this meant building dams to supply water for irrigation and power. Henry Kaiser and his engineers took part in building Bonneville (Hoover), Boulder, and Grand Coulee Dams. Even while working on the last of these giant projects, the company also was building a section of the Oakland–San Francisco Bay Bridge, tunnels, smaller dams, and a new set of locks for the Panama Canal. In 1939, when he lost out on the bid for building the Shasta Dam in northern California, Kaiser expanded into manufacturing. He designed and built

COMPANY PERSPECTIVES

ICF International partners with its clients to conceive and implement solutions and services that protect and improve the quality of life. We pride ourselves in providing lasting solutions to society's most challenging management, technology, and policy issues. We are able to fulfill this purpose because we have a passionate commitment to our work and to helping our customers achieve compelling results, we combine deep program and industry knowledge with world-class technical expertise, and we have the capability to support our customers through the entire program life cycle, from analysis and design through implementation and evaluation.

the Permanente Cement Company in just seven months and provided the gravel to the Shasta builders.

When the United States entered World War II, Kaiser moved crews and equipment from Grand Coulee to San Francisco Bay and built a shipyard that eventually produced 1,490 merchant (Liberty) ships, aircraft carriers, and other warships. He built a second shipyard in Oregon, and his engineers, according to a company publication, "designed an entire city for 35,000 people and built it in three months." Kaiser also built planes and ship engines, and his engineers built airfields and other military installations. To supply steel plate, Kaiser built a steel plant and began production. During the war, Kaiser Industries had 300,000 people working for it. Before the war ended, the engineering department decided to seek projects outside Kaiser. This was the beginning of Kaiser Engineers, Inc.

GOING INTERNATIONAL

During the 1950s Kaiser Engineers increasingly took on jobs abroad, including designing and building a car factory in Argentina to produce Willys Jeeps and Kaiser automobiles. As the lead company in a seven-firm consortium, Kaiser took on the Snowy Mountains Hydroelectic Power project in Australia, a 25-year project, with Kaiser Engineers finishing their portion on time and under budget. Domestic projects included the dual-purpose reactor at Hanford, Washington. By 1965 *Engineering News-Record* ranked Kaiser Engineers as the number one contractor in the world. When Henry Kaiser died in 1967, Kaiser Engineers was operating in 21 states and 14 countries. The company continued designing and building large projects, including steel-producing plants; cement plants; rapid transit projects in Baltimore, Maryland, and Washington, D.C.; aluminum and alumina factories; and the Great Plains Coal Gasification project in North Dakota.

A PART OF RAYMOND INTERNATIONAL

In 1977 Kaiser Industries dissolved. In June, Raymond International Inc., a Houston-based construction company, paid $30 million for Kaiser Engineers, which had $172 million in revenues. Raymond, with $254 million in revenues, was shifting from big public works projects to concentrate on private jobs. With the purchase of Kaiser Engineers, it gained the management and design capabilities it lacked to compete in the increasingly complex construction business.

In 1983 Raymond went private in a leveraged buyout, borrowing about $200 million from nine banks to pay the purchase price. When the bottom fell out of the oil and gas market soon afterward, the company began defaulting on its loans.

A SEPARATE COMPANY

In 1986 the bank consortium split Kaiser Engineers from Raymond International, forming a separate company with some $60 million of debt. At the time, Kaiser Engineers had just started building the largest copper mine in the world, the Neves-Corvo project in Portugal. Because Portugal had so little industry, almost everything for the project had to be imported. This required 680 purchase orders from 16 countries on five continents, as Kaiser built, in addition to the copper mine itself, roads, a railroad, four dams, a copper concentrator, a 40-kilometer water pipe, and a port facility. To accomplish this, the company used its Kaiser Engineers Management System, a computerized system for planning, monitoring, and cost control of huge projects.

When the company completed Neves-Corvo two years later, the bank consortium split Kaiser Engineers in two. It sold Kaiser's operations in Australia and Asia to the Australian conglomerate Elders Group IXL Ltd. The rest of Kaiser, including 2,000 employees and 1987 revenue of $300 million, was sold to tiny American Capital and Research Corp. (ACR) of Fairfax, Virginia. James O. Edwards, the chairman and president of ACR, developed the complicated transition in partnership with Elders.

KEY DATES

1914: Henry J. Kaiser Company is founded.
1939: Company expands into manufacturing industry.
1977: Kaiser Engineers is bought by Raymond International, Inc.
1988: American Capital and Research (ACR) purchases Kaiser Engineers.
1989: ACR merges Kaiser and ICFcorp International.
1990: Company acquires International Waste Energy Systems.
1993: Changes name to ICF Kaiser International, Inc.
1998: Company purchases ICT Spectrum Constructors, Inc.
1999: ICF Consulting splits from Kaiser Engineers.
2002: Company acquires two divisions of Arthur D. Little, Inc.
2005: ICF acquires Washington-based Synergy, Inc.
2006: Company changes name to ICF International.

AMERICAN CAPITAL AND RESEARCH CORP.

ACR was a new private holding company established in 1987 and run by former top federal officials. Its primary business was ICF Inc., an energy, health, and environmental consulting company founded in 1969. ICF started life as Inner City Fund, a venture capital fund that helped minority-owned businesses raise money and win government contracts. The company reorganized itself as ICF in the mid-1970s and, following the passage of the first real hazardous waste disposal bill in 1976, grew by winning government contracts for energy and environmental policy analysis.

Over the years ICF expanded to include subsidiaries handling economic analysis, biotechnology and risk assessment, defense analysis, and a computer group. In the process, it attracted senior government officials from energy, environmental, and health-related agencies. Critics complained that this created an unfair advantage in winning federal contracts, particularly in the hazardous waste field.

In the mid-1980s ICF began buying other consulting firms as part of a strategy to shift its primary business from analysis to field activities, particularly in the environmental field, and to increase its revenues to $100 million by 1990. Amendments to the hazardous waste disposal bill established "cradle to grave" liability for waste generators and required reams of documentation. "Big money was coming not from studying toxic waste dumps, but from cleaning them up," an ICF official recalled in a 1990 interview with *Diablo Business.*

Among its purchases was Clements Associates, Inc., a specialist in environmental risk assessment; K.S. Crump & Co., another risk assessment firm; SRW Associates, a small engineering firm; Buc & Associates, an economic consulting firm; and the Naisbitt Group, a trend analysis company. The purchase of Lewin and Associates Inc. made ICF the largest consulting practice in the healthcare and energy fields. In 1987 the company set up the ICF Defense Group to go after contracts in the national security and intelligence fields and established ACR.

TURNING AROUND KAISER ENGINEERS

The Kaiser acquisition in 1988 greatly strengthened ACR's (and ICF's) engineering capabilities. Kaiser's current contracts included cleaning up Boston Harbor, construction and services work at the federal government's Hanford nuclear site in Washington State, and several highway and transit projects. Yet while Kaiser added some $300 million to ACR's annual revenues, it also brought ACR between $20 million and $30 million in financial liabilities.

In less than a year, ACR trimmed Kaiser's debt through individual negotiations and slashed the company's overhead. Instead of losing $1 million a month, ICF Kaiser Engineers was profitable. ACR merged Kaiser with ICF Inc. in 1989 to form ICF Kaiser Engineers, a subsidiary of wholly owned ICFcorp International.

Later that year ACR bought CYGNA Group, a $30 million California firm that provided hazardous waste cleanup and plant reengineering services to the nuclear power industry. ACR was becoming an environmental conglomerate, providing government and industry with a single place to go for handling environmental problems.

ACR also strengthened its nonenvironmental subsidiaries. Its computer systems division, for example, acquired four local firms in barely more than a year, increasing its revenues to $37 million. The acquisitions left ACR with some $40 million in long-term debt, and in December 1989 it went public, raising about $26 million. Most of that was used to reduce the debt.

GROWTH AND FINANCIAL CHALLENGE

ACR continued to expand into other markets, such as air-quality modeling services and negotiation and mediation services for big government and private contracts. By mid-1990 ACR owned 18 companies. In September 1990 ACR acquired International Waste Energy Systems, a design firm specializing in waste incineration systems. That same month it became one of the first U.S. companies to enter the huge pollution control market in the former Soviet Union and Eastern Europe, helping design systems to monitor pollution at Soviet coke plants.

The company also purchased Kaiser Engineers Australia Pty Ltd. and Kaiser Engineers International from Elders Resources NZFP Ltd., recombining the original Kaiser Engineers. ACR had revenues of $503.9 million in fiscal 1990. Meanwhile, ICF Kaiser Engineers won a five-year, $50 million contract from the U.S. Air Force to design cleanup solutions for potentially hazardous waste sites on military bases around the world and was constructing Asia's largest high-speed railroad in Taiwan.

ICF Kaiser Engineers was one of the nation's top engineering firms specializing in toxic waste cleanup, with more than two-thirds of its contracts dealing with environmental projects. In addition to developing systems to actually clean up or destroy waste at a site, the subsidiary offered front-end services to determine the extent and nature of contamination at a site and conducted studies of alternative corrective actions.

Between 1989 and 1991, ACR's gross revenue more than doubled. The company began 1991 with a name change. To reflect both its roots and its growing international presence, the company became ICF International Inc. As it prepared for a $46 million stock offering in June, though, the fast-growing company ran into trouble. Known for its tight management controls, ICF International suddenly discovered that several of its noncore subsidiaries were performing poorly.

STOCK OFFERING PUT ON HOLD

It appeared that the company had tried to duplicate its successful shift in the environmental field to managing contracts and providing services without understanding the new fields into which it was moving. Providing services in areas such as health and information technology often meant developing products to be sold to new markets at a later date. Yet the subsidiaries continued to bill on ICF International's hourly model. As a stock analyst told the *Washington Post* in November of that year, "The company proved not particularly good at managing product-oriented businesses."

That discovery caused the company to cancel the stock offering and resulted in its first quarterly loss. Its stock prices slumped, lenders demanded renegotiations, and over the next two years ICF International sold 14 subsidiaries, although usually at a profit.

By 1993 ICF International had returned to profitability. It was a company focused on its core business of environmental and transportation/infrastructure consulting and engineering. It had laid off employees and restructured both its credit agreements and its management, moving the president of ICF Kaiser Engineers (now called the Engineering & Construction Group) from Oakland, California, to Fairfax, Virginia.

In June the company again changed its name, becoming ICF Kaiser International to underscore that it had integrated its California engineering firm with its Washington, D.C., consulting business, and in September it began trading on the New York Stock Exchange. However, 1993 was a tough year for environmental markets, particularly for hazardous waste contracting, which saw a 9 percent drop in billings by consulting firms. ICF Kaiser International registered a loss for the fiscal year.

BUILDING A CONSULTING EMPIRE

In 1994 ICF Kaiser focused increased emphasis on its domestic consulting services and set up an international company in Mexico to provide environmental consulting and engineering services in Mexico. It sold most of its Cygna Energy Services subsidiary and began unsuccessful talks to acquire a Pennsylvania-based hazardous waste cleanup company. Revenues in fiscal 1995 rose 32 percent from the previous year, but the company again reported a net loss of $1.66 million, down from $12.5 million for fiscal 1994.

The following year it won a $3.5 billion contract from the U.S. Department of Energy to clean up the Rocky Flats nuclear weapons plant in Colorado. In August, it bought EDA Inc., a Maryland engineering consulting firm, and later that year obtained the license to market a new process of making steel from steam coal, iron ore, and scrap.

In 1996 nearly 69 percent of the company's revenue came from contracts with the U.S. Department of Energy. That year ICF Kaiser lost the Hanford nuclear waste contract, which it had held for 14 years and which represented approximately $10 million a year. At the same time, Congress failed to reauthorize the Superfund cleanup law and federal projects were on hold until the Republican leadership decided the direction it would take rewriting major environmental legislation and regulations. Among the contracts ICF Kaiser won in 1996 was that with a Czech steelmaker to build a mini-mill and another with the U.S. Army Corps of Engineers to clean up federal installations in its Southern Pacific region. Following the Hanford loss, the company took severe cost-cutting steps that continued into 1997.

The company's news coverage during 1997 had little to do with its work. First the media focused on the selection of former Energy Secretary Hazel O'Leary to ICF Kaiser's board and then on CEO James Edwards's name on a list of some 150 potential contributors Vice-President Al Gore was to call for the Democratic National Committee.

FINANCIAL TROUBLES

In 1998 ICF Kaiser acquired ICT Spectrum Constructors Inc., one of the country's largest builders of semiconductor plants, in a move to broaden its construction services. ICT Spectrum had been spun off from its parent, Micron Technology Corp., in 1997. Later in the year ICF Kaiser announced a $35 million loss in the second quarter due to cost overruns at four nitric acid plant projects. In response to the company's financial difficulties, the board of directors replaced the company president and the president of the engineers and constructors group. At the same time, the company lost its contract to manage the upgrade of the Bath Iron Works in Maine, although it kept the contract for engineering work on the project.

In November, James Edwards, chairman and CEO since 1985 and a member of ICF Inc. since 1974, resigned. "I've had enough of difficult times and stress and no capital for growth," Edwards told *Engineering News-Record.* Keith Price, appointed president earlier in the year, was named CEO, and board member and former Congressman Tony Coelho was elected chairman.

In March 1999, the management of ICF Consulting teamed with CM Equity Partners L.P., a private, New York-based equity investment group, to purchase rights to the consulting division from Kaiser for $75 million. At that time, the consulting group accounted for approximately 10 percent of the company's total revenues. The sale was completed in April, just before ICF Kaiser reported losses of over $100 million for the 1998 financial year.

Sudhakar Kesavan, who was named president of ICF Consulting in 1997, was asked to serve as CEO and chairman of the independent company, while retaining his position as president of the consulting group. Kesavan also had links to the broader environmental community and served on the board of New York's Rainforest Alliance, a group dedicated to improving environmental protection through business and consumer relations.

ICF CONSULTING GOES INTERNATIONAL

In 2002, ICF Consulting finalized a deal to acquire two major consulting divisions of Arthur D. Little, Inc., a bankrupt company headquartered in Massachusetts, for a reported price of $10.5 million. ICF gained Arthur D. Little's Global Environment & Risk division, which focused on science, engineering, and environmental systems, and the company's Public Sector Program Management division, which brought a number of high-profile clients including the Federal Aviation Administration, Internal Revenue Service, U.S. Postal Service, U.S. Army, and South Carolina Research Authority. The company also gained the ability to expand geographically with new offices in Massachusetts, California, Texas, and Brazil. The acquisitions strengthened ICF's consulting capacity in four key areas; environmental, energy, program management, and applied technology.

CEO Sudhakar Kesavan said, in the company's official press release, "Both Arthur D. Little divisions reflect our firm's commitment to growth and service enhancements in our key business lines. Moreover, these services will broaden our existing technology capabilities." Kesavan also expressed the hope that the acquisitions would aid ICF in establishing a bigger global footprint as a consulting firm.

The following year, ICF won a five-year, $5.3 million contract from the Environmental Protection Agency's (EPA) National Center for Environmental Research. ICF's role was to help the EPA to develop activity summaries that served to translate EPA activities to a general audience. The high-profile contract stimulated growth in ICF's environmental consulting branch and helped to establish the company as one of the federal government's major consulting providers.

In 2004 ICF won a lucrative contract to help the U.S. General Services Administration analyze and manage data concerning the federal government's e-travel initiative. Shortly thereafter, the company finalized a contract with the Administrative Office of the U.S. Courts, to aid in the office's planning and acquisition strategies. Taken together, the company's major contracts for 2003 and 2004 brought over $40 million in potential revenue to be added to the company's existing revenue base.

ENERGY AND DEFENSE CONTRACTS

In January 2005, the company announced that it would conduct the largest purchase of renewable power made by a company representing the consulting industry. The company purchased 1.2 million kilowatt-hours of energy to offset some 24 percent of the company's electricity consumption at its U.S. offices. In official press releases, company spokespeople said that the purchase was intended to serve as an example to other large companies on how to effectively remain environmentally friendly as their need for energy increased.

ICF significantly bolstered its defense division in early 2005 with the acquisition of Synergy Inc., a Washington, D.C.-based consulting firm that focused on analysis and information technology for defense and logistics groups including the U.S. Department of Defense. The acquisition brought over 200 specialists to ICF to bolster the company's defense division and also gave the company a number of new federal and state government clients. It was estimated that the Synergy acquisition would generate over $25 million in yearly revenues through defense contracts. In the company's press releases, Kesavan said of the merger, "This allows us to combine our strengths in information technology, homeland security, and human capital management with Synergy's topflight capabilities in defense and information technology."

ACQUISITIONS AND DIVERSIFICATION

At the end of the year, ICF strengthened its energy and policy management divisions with two major acquisitions: Caliber Associates, Inc., in October and Project Technical Liaison Associates (PTL), in December. While the acquisition of PTL, a leading consulting firm specializing in Liquid Natural Gas, added to the company's energy consultation department, the acquisition of Caliber Associates, brought the company over 300 new associates and a number of clients in the health and human services industries. The company was later renamed ICF Caliber to reflect the ownership change.

In April 2006, the company changed its name to ICF International, Inc., in an effort to reflect the company's goal of marketing their consulting services to a broader audience. By this time the company had grown to manage 20 offices including international divisions in Brazil, Russia, the United Kingdom, India, and Canada.

The rapid growth and diversification of ICF's consulting capacities continued through 2007 with four major acquisitions. Arlington, Virginia-based Energy and Environmental Analysis, Inc., brought the company 27 specialists in the natural gas, alternative energy, and energy market analysis sectors while the company also acquired Maryland-based Z-Tech Corporation, which focused on software and computing technology for the healthcare industry. The company reportedly spent $27 million to acquire Z-Tech in hopes of bolstering their foothold in healthcare, which grew in 2005 with the acquisition of Caliber.

ICF also acquired Washington, D.C.-based Advanced Performance Consulting Group, which specialized in workforce consulting for government, and Simat, Helliesen & Eichner, Inc., one of the largest air transport consulting agencies, giving the company an estimated $36 million in annual contracts for the air travel industry.

Emerging from the financial decline of the Kaiser company, ICF International grew rapidly to become a profitable and internationally recognized leader in the consultation industry. The company's successful growth strategies were recognized by the *Washington Business Journal,* which ranked ICF 43rd in their list of the nation's 100 fastest-growing companies in 2007. The company was also regularly recognized as being an excellent employer, winning a number of awards in recognition for creating a satisfying workplace environment, including the 2007 Helios HR Apollo Award, which recognizes excellence in employee growth and relations. With estimated profits of over $300 million in 2006 and a growing list of high-profile clients, ICF International was well placed to remain a global leader in consultation services.

Ellen D. Wernick
Updated, Micah L. Issitt

PRINCIPAL SUBSIDIARIES

ICF Consulting Group, Inc.; ICF Consulting Pty, Ltd.; ICF Associates, L.L.C.; ICF Information Technology, L.L.C.; The K.S. Crump Group, L.L.C.; Caliber Associates, Inc.; Collins Management Consulting, Inc.; Simulation Support, Inc.; Synergy Inc.

PRINCIPAL COMPETITORS

CRA International Inc.; MTC Technologies, Inc.; Navigant Consulting, Inc.; SI International, Inc.

FURTHER READING

"ACR to Buy Elders Stake in Kaiser Australia Unit," *Journal of Commerce,* September 14, 1990, p. 5A.

"American Capital and Research Corp. to Acquire Cygna Group," *UPI,* June 20, 1989.

Berselli, Beth, "ICF Kaiser Ousts President," *Washington Post,* August 8, 1998, p. D1.

Bettelheim, Adriel, "Flats Cleanup Firm on Gore 'Call Sheet,'" *Denver Post,* September 11, 1997, p. A21.

Bredemeier, Kenneth, "ICF Kaiser Names New President," *Washington Post,* April 6, 1999, p. E3.

Chandler, Clay, "Consulting Firm Agrees to Acquisition," *Washington Post,* August 27, 1987, p. E1.

Cloud, John, "The Trouble with Hazel," *Time,* September 29, 1997, p. 28.

"A Contractor Buys Some Brains," *Forbes,* October 15, 1977, p. 32.

"Edwards out As ICF Chair," *Energy Daily,* November 6, 1998.

"Environmental Markets Are Off, but Firms Aren't Down or Out," *Engineering News-Record,* April 4, 1994, p. 41.

Gellene, Denise, "Kaiser Engineers Merging with Unit of Its Virginia Parent Firm," *Los Angeles Times,* March 2, 1989, p. D11.

Gerin, Roseanne, "ICF Consulting Picks Up Synergy," *Washington Technology,* February 2, 2005.

Hamilton, Martha, "Clean Doesn't Always Mean Green," *Washington Post,* September 29, 1996, p. H2.

———, "Cleaning Up on Environmental Concerns," *Washington Post,* July 23, 1990, p. E1.

———, "ICF Gets a New President to Lead It Through Expansion," *Washington Post,* December 6, 1993, p. F9.

———, "ICF Kaiser Plans Sale of Second Main Unit," *Washington Post,* March 10, 1999, p. E3.

———, "ICF Kaiser Reports Loss of $27 Million for Quarter," *Washington Post,* April 17, 1999, p. E2.

———, "ICF Kaiser's Consulting Unit Is Being Sold," *Washington Post,* March 9, 1999, p. E3.

———, "ICF Kaiser Sports a New Name and Attitude," *Washington Post,* September 27, 1993, p. F5.

———, "ICF Rebuilds After Effects of Stock Debacle," *Washington Post,* November 11, 1991, p. F1.

———, "Va. Company, Soviets Form Joint Venture," *Washington Post,* September 11, 1990, p. C1.

"Henry J. Kaiser: The Legacy Continues," Fairfax, Va.: ICF Kaiser International, Inc., June 1995.

"ICF Acquires Consulting Firm Energy and Environmental Analysis Inc.," *Energy Resource,* January 10, 2007.

"ICF Consulting," *Hazardous Waste Superfund Week,* November 3, 2003, p. 428.

"ICF Consulting," *Power, Finance and Risk,* November 21, 2005.

"ICF Consulting Acquired by Management-Led Team," *ICFI Online,* June 30, 1999.

"ICF Consulting Acquires Synergy Inc.," *ICFI Online,* February 1, 2005.

"ICF Consulting Becomes ICF International; Name Change Reflects Enhanced Capabilities and Expanding Geographic Presence," *Canadian Corporate News,* April 24, 2006.

"ICF Consulting Goes Green with Largest Purchase of Renewable Power by Consulting Sector," *ICFI Online,* January 31, 2005.

"ICF Consulting Has Been Awarded a 5-Year Contract for Up to $18 Million by the U.S. General Services Administration (GSA) to Support the Federal Government's New eTravel Initiative," *Government Procurement,* June 2004, p. 48.

"ICF Consulting Has Been Awarded a Contract by the Administrative Office of the U.S. Courts Under the Judiciary Multiple Awards Schedule for Information Technology (IT) Project Management Planning and Acquisition Support," *Government Procurement,* August 2004, p. 42.

"ICF Consulting Has Bought Specialist LNG Advisory Firm Project Technical Liaison Associates," *Project Finance,* December 2006.

"ICF Consulting Is Pleased to Announce the Hire of Andrew Robinson," *PR Newswire,* November 28, 2005.

"ICF Consulting to Acquire Two Divisions of Arthur D. Little, Inc.," *ICFI Online,* April 25, 2002.

"ICF International Sets $48.9 million IPO," *Europe Intelligence Wire,* September 22, 2006.

"ICF Kaiser Announces New Management Team," corporate press release, ICF Kaiser International, April 5, 1999.

"ICF Kaiser Changes Leaders but Problems Still Abound," *Engineering News-Record,* November 16, 1998, p. 14.

"ICF Kaiser Growing As Acquisitions Mount," *Engineering News-Record,* April 12, 1990, p. 22.

"ICF Kaiser Remains in Red," *Washington Times,* April 29, 1995, p. C4.

"ICF Kaiser to Buy Chip Plant Builder," *Engineering News-Record,* February 23, 1998, p. 16.

"ICF to Market Romelt Process Utilizing Steam Coal in Steelmaking," *Coal Week International,* October 24, 1995, p. 10.

"The IT Group Completes Acquisition of ICF Kaiser's Environment and Facilities Management Group," *PR Newswire,* April 12, 1999.

"James Edwards," NBC Business Video, NBC Desktop, Inc., September 17, 1997.

"Kaiser Contract Delayed; Company Is Up for Sale," *Engineering News-Record,* April 7, 1988, p. 17.

Laux, Emily, "Acquisition Campaign Changing Face, Nature of ICF's Consulting Business," *Business Review,* August 5, 1985, p. 13.

Lincoln, Taylor, "ICF Consulting to Acquire Two Arthur D. Little Divisions," *Mass High Tech: The Journal of New England Technology,* April 22, 2002.

Litvan, Laura M., "Fairfax Company out Front in Efforts to Save the Earth," *Washington Times,* May 11, 1990, p. C1.

"Managers and Investment Group to Buy ICF Kaiser Group," *New York Times,* May 25, 1999.

Menninger, Bonar, "ICF: Making of a Megafirm," *Washington Business Journal,* July 3, 1989, p. 1.

"Pension Plans," *National Journal,* June 15, 1985, p. 1441.

Rubin, Debra K., "Industry Veteran Keith Price Now President of Troubled ICF Kaiser," *Engineering News-Record,* August 17, 1998, p. 15.

Shaw, Jan, "Stock Offering Enabling Firm to Pay Debts," *San Francisco Business Times,* December 25, 1989, p. 1.

Sugawara, Sandra, "D.C. Consulting Firm Is Engineering Increasingly Big Deals," *Washington Post,* November 21, 1988, p. F5.

"Waste Incinerator Design Firm Sold," *St. Louis Post-Dispatch,* September 21, 1990, p. 3B.

Webb, Margaret, "American Capital Renamed ICF," *Washington Post,* January 23, 1991, p. C11.

Weiss, Shari, "One Man's Poison ... Is Another Man's Profit," *Diablo Business,* June 1990, p. 39.

Zonana, Victor F., "Banks Sell Kaiser Group to 2 Bidders," *Los Angeles Times,* June 17, 1988, p. D2.

IKEA Group

Bargelaan 20
Leiden, NL 2333CT
Netherlands
Telephone: (31 71) 05 65 71 00
Web site: http://www.ikea-group.ikea.com

Private Company
Incorporated: 1943 as IKEA, Ingvar Kamprad
Employees: 118,000
Sales: $28.6 billion (2007 est.)
NAIC: 442110 Furniture Stores; 442299 All Other Home Furnishings Stores

■ ■ ■

The IKEA Group is one of the world's top retailers of furniture, home furnishings, and housewares, and the largest franchisee of IKEA stores. It consists of several companies that design IKEA's own items, and sell them in their more than 242 IKEA stores that are spread throughout 24 different countries worldwide. The company also peddles its merchandise through mail order, distributing its thick catalogs in the areas surrounding its store locations. IKEA is characterized by its efforts to offer high-quality items at low prices. To save money for itself and its customers, the company buys items in bulk, ships and stores items unassembled using flat packaging, and has customers assemble many items on their own at home. INGKA Holding B.V. is the parent company for all IKEA Group companies. INGKA Holding is owned by the Netherlands-based charitable foundation, Stichting INGKA Foundation. Other franchisees own and operate an additional 29 IKEA stores outside the IKEA Group.

THE EARLY YEARS: 1943–64

Ingvar Kamprad founded IKEA in 1943 in Sweden. Kamprad was born in 1926 as the son of a farmer in Småland, a region in southern Sweden. Småland was historically one of the country's poorest regions, and its inhabitants were known for their hard work, thriftiness, and inventiveness. In 1943, at the age of 17, Kamprad upheld this characterization when he decided to become an entrepreneur and created a commercial company called IKEA, Ingvar Kamprad. The word "IKEA" was an acronym made from his name, Ingvar Kamprad, and his address, Elmtaryd, Agunnaryd, which were the names of his farm and the village it was located within. Kamprad's new company was essentially a one-man effort, and sold fish, vegetable seeds, and magazines to customers in his region. He first delivered the items to customers by bicycle.

In 1947, IKEA issued its first primitive mail-order catalog, within which the newly invented ballpoint pen was added to the assortment of products Kamprad was offering. Then in 1950, Kamprad set the foundation for the future direction of IKEA by adding furniture and home furnishings to the mail-order line. A year later, an expanded version of the IKEA catalog became available. In 1952, the stability of home furnishings in the IKEA product line was solidified when Kamprad took his items to the St. Eric's Fair in Stockholm and won over customers with the high-quality, low-priced furniture items in his line.

COMPANY PERSPECTIVES

Anybody can make a good-quality product for a high price, or a poor-quality product for a low price. But to make good products at low prices, you need to develop methods that are both cost-effective and innovative. This has been IKEA's focus since its beginnings in Småland, Sweden. Maximizing the use of raw materials and production adaptation to meet people's needs and preferences has meant that our costs are low. The IKEA way of doing things is to pass these cost savings on to you, our customers.

Up to that point, IKEA items had been obtained from other sources and sold by Kamprad, making his enterprise solely a retail operation. In 1953, however, Kamprad made the decision to buy a small furniture factory and open a small furniture and home-furnishing showroom in Älmhult. The IKEA headquarters were moved from the village of Agunnaryd to Älmhult. IKEA began designing its own furniture items in 1955, and soon began taking advantage of the benefits of flat packaging and self-assembly by customers. Success followed quickly, and in 1958 the tiny showroom was replaced by a store of 13,000 square meters, which was a giant for the times. One year later, a restaurant was added to the store, to accommodate the needs of an ever-increasing number of customers who were traveling long distances to IKEA.

The mail-order business continued to flourish as well, helping to further expand IKEA's customer range. This prompted the opening of the first IKEA store outside Sweden, near Oslo in Norway, in 1963. Business continued to increase, boosted in part by a 1964 article in the Swedish magazine *Allt i Hemmet* (All for Your Home), which listed the results of quality tests that had been run on furniture; IKEA received the highest ratings available.

INNOVATIONS AND EXPANSION: 1965–79

The event that marked the true turning point of the business, however, came in 1965 when Kamprad opened a store just outside the major city of Stockholm, to show what could be done in the way of designing and selling modern low-priced furniture in a large market. The store, located on a section of undeveloped farmland at Kungens Kurva just ten kilometers southwest of Stockholm, was extraordinary for a number of reasons. It was very large, with some 33,000 square meters of total space and 15,000 square meters of selling space, and it consisted of two connected buildings. One building, circular in shape, had four floors connected ingeniously so that customers could move easily from floor to floor. This building acted as the main display area for furniture. The second building consisted of three floors and a basement and acted as the stockroom and service unit, where there was also a selling area for smaller pieces of furniture and home furnishings. Customer services ranged from a baby carriage rental service, a children's nursery, and a restaurant with seating for 350, to cloakrooms, restrooms, a bank, and parking for 1,000 cars.

More important than the physical characteristics of the new IKEA store was the manner in which it revolutionized furniture manufacturing and selling. Kamprad continued the practice of selling most furniture in flat-pack form, as he said, "to avoid transporting and storing air." To make this possible, the furniture was specially designed by IKEA staff in workshops in the Älmhult headquarters and warehouse. For the mass production of the component parts of the flat-pack furniture, Kamprad had to bypass traditional furniture manufacturers and instead used specialist factories. Unfinished pine shelving, for example, came directly from saw mills, cabinet doors were made in door factories, metal frames came from machine shops, and upholstery materials came directly from textile mills.

The customers themselves could put almost all of the components of each piece of furniture together, but in some cases IKEA staff could help the customer assemble the furniture at home. IKEA's innovations ranged from table legs that fixed into place with snap locks, to kitchen chairs that were assembled with one screw. A large number of IKEA products carried the label of the Swedish Furniture Research Institute, a byword for good quality and design.

Another innovative marketing tool employed in the new IKEA store in Stockholm was a self-service method of selling, which was largely unknown in the furniture and home furnishing retail trades at the time. Customers were invited to walk around the whole store and select items by themselves. There were information desks and written materials about products, but no sales assistants to persuade customers to buy. In these early days of IKEA, customers had to pay for their purchases in cash to improve the finances of the firm. The customer was given a ticket for each item and collected the flat-packed merchandise at the delivery dock. There was no home delivery service; the customer had to provide his or her own transportation. Car racks could be bought, and later self-drive vans could be rented.

KEY DATES

1943: Ingvar Kamprad founds IKEA, selling fish, vegetable seeds, and magazines.
1951: First IKEA catalog featuring furniture.
1956: First flatpack packaging.
1958: First IKEA store opens.
1961: IKEA establishes Swedwood furniture factory.
1965: Kamprad opens a store just outside of Stockholm.
1973: Headquarters moves from Sweden to Denmark.
1982: IKEA Group is formed under the ownership of Stichting INGKA Foundation.
1985: First U.S. IKEA store opens in Philadelphia.
1986: Kamprad retires as group president; Anders Moberg is appointed president.
1999: Anders Dahlvig appointed president and CEO of IKEA Group.
2001: IKEA Group moves headquarters from Denmark to the Netherlands.

The IKEA formula was an instant success, particularly for kitchenware and children's furniture, and soon more IKEA stores were launched. Additional stores were opened in Sweden in 1966 and 1967, and in 1969 a store was opened in Denmark. This was followed by the first store openings outside the Scandinavian territory—in Switzerland in 1973, and in Germany in 1974. Soon there were ten IKEA stores in five European countries. The stores employed a total of 1,500 people, and sales in 1974 were SEK 616 million. Sweden remained the company's main market, accounting for 75 percent of total sales.

Kamprad soon realized the potential for IKEA's expansion into new markets worldwide. In 1973, he once again packed up and moved the company's headquarters—this time to Copenhagen, Denmark, which was a more central location for European expansion. The first major expansion was in Germany. After the first store in 1974, ten more were opened by 1980, more than were in operation in Sweden, and by 1990 there were 17 stores in Western Germany. Elsewhere in Europe, stores were opened in Austria in 1977 and in the Netherlands in 1979. The company was expanding outside of Europe, as well. In 1975 the first IKEA in Australia was opened; in 1976 a store opened in Canada; and in 1978 a store was placed in Singapore.

CONTINUED GROWTH AND NEW LEADERSHIP: 1980–90

With worldwide expansion moving along successfully, IKEA continued to enter new markets around the globe in the 1980s. Stores were placed in the Canary Islands in 1980, in France and in Iceland in 1981, in Saudi Arabia in 1983, in Belgium and in Kuwait in 1984, in the United Kingdom and in Hong Kong in 1987, and in Italy in 1989.

One of the company's most challenging expansion efforts, however, began in 1985 when a store of 15,700 square meters was opened in the United States in Philadelphia, Pennsylvania. The move was a test to see whether a European retail concept, however enterprising in its methods and outlook, could succeed in a vastly different U.S. market. The answer was yes. If anything, the U.S. consumer was more receptive to innovative ideas and merchandise than many of the more conservative European customers. The experience of the previously opened Canadian stores was useful in getting the concept on its feet in the United States.

Another major challenge was taken up in 1990 when IKEA stores were opened in Eastern Europe. A store was opened in Budapest in a joint venture with a Hungarian firm, Butorker, and in the same year another small store was opened in Warsaw, Poland. In 1991, stores were placed in the Czech Republic and the United Arab Emirates, and the following year IKEA stores appeared for the first time in Majorca and Slovakia, along with the opening of a pilot store in the Netherlands. This rapid expansion in a decade and a half helped to change the pattern of sales greatly. In 1975, the Scandinavian markets represented around 85 percent of the company's total sales. By 1990, however, the proportion had dropped to just over 26 percent, and sales in Germany alone had risen to account for more than 27 percent of the company's total. The rest of Europe contributed another large chunk of overall sales—34 percent—and stores in other regions accounted for just over 12 percent of the total.

Leadership of the company changed in 1986, when Kamprad resigned as president, to be replaced by 36-year-old Anders Moberg. In the early 1980s, Kamprad set up a family-controlled charitable foundation, Stichting INGKA Foundation, based in the Netherlands. Kamprad transferred ownership of IKEA to the foundation in 1982 as a means to ensure the continuation of the company, to ensure the family maintained control, and to minimize taxes.

While IKEA's geographic expansion provided it with more stability—the company no longer had to rely on its saturated Swedish markets for the majority of its income—the expansion also presented minor supply problems. The component parts had to be made to strict specifications, and the originality of the Kamprad approach was to replace the craftsman philosophy with an engineering philosophy.

In the early years of growth—while using Sweden, Denmark, and Finland as the main sources of supply—IKEA also saw the advantages of using supplies from Eastern European countries. Contracts were signed with state-controlled and other independent factories in East Germany, Poland, and Yugoslavia for the supply of furniture components. Since payment was made in "hard" currency, strict specifications could be enforced and the dates of payment could be flexible, thus improving IKEA's cash flow. In the 1970s, some 20 to 25 percent of total supplies came from Eastern Europe in this fashion. By 1990, however, the proportion of supplies obtained from Eastern Europe had fallen to around 15 percent, even though that portion was part of a much larger total than had been the case in the past. In 1990, there were around 1,500 suppliers in 45 different countries, presenting a problem of planning and logistics, because production took place in fewer locales.

To counter any problematic situations arising from the fact that IKEA's operations were situated all around the world, management organized the company as a whole into four different main areas with interlocking functions. The first area—product range and development—was primarily carried out by IKEA of Sweden. New or improved products had always been an essential part of the success of the company, and the work was undertaken by separate product groups within IKEA of Sweden. Thus, product development tasks were completed in a more centralized fashion, and then filtered down to all other areas of IKEA's operations. The second area—purchasing of materials for production and other small retail items—was conducted by agents responsible for placing orders to the specifications laid down by IKEA of Sweden and the product development teams. Third, the distribution service undertook the transport and distribution of the finished products to 12 regional distribution centers and stores throughout the world. Finally, retailing functions were carried out by those operating under the same retail concept, ensuring that selling methods and customer service were of the same standards in all IKEA stores.

In addition to its strong corporate organization of operations, another factor in IKEA's success during the expansion years was its effective—and at times unusual—advertising and sales promotion campaigns around the world. Targeted customers were mainly 20- to 35-year-olds, and the high quality of modern Swedish design was emphasized. The IKEA catalogs played a primary role in advertising success. The catalogs were attractive and easy to use, emphasizing quality of design and the efficiency of IKEA products. During the busy years of geographic expansion, every household in the area surrounding a new store received a copy of the catalog. Although direct mail-order sales always represented a very small portion of total sales and the catalogs did not offer the whole IKEA range, they were always a key factor in attracting new customers to the stores.

IKEA advertisements themselves were unusual in their contradiction of the traditional image of the Swedish as conservative and rather serious. In France, for example, one slogan used was "*Ils sont fous ces Suèdois*"; in Germany, it was "*unmögliche Möbelhaus aus Schweden*"; and in the United Kingdom, "the mad Swedes are coming." In the United States, advertising campaigns were even more outrageous, and almost every advertisement included a reindeer, leaving no doubt as to the origin of the campaign. The combination of offbeat advertising and well-designed merchandise had a very effective impact on the group of customers IKEA was targeting.

THE INTERNET AND THE ENVIRONMENT: 1991–99

IKEA continued to open stores in new locations throughout the world. In 1990, it had global sales of over $3 billion, from 89 stores in 21 countries. It was of note that a company that offered the same basic products at all stores did so well in so many different cultures with different tastes. In 1994, IKEA opened its first store in Taiwan. Two years later, the company placed new stores in Finland, Malaysia, and Spain. By 1998, IKEA had also opened a store in mainland China.

The following year, the company brought together in one area in a store all products for infants and children up to seven years old. Marketed as Children's IKEA, offerings ranged from cribs and dressers to toys, lamps, bedspreads, and curtains.

In 1997, IKEA, with total sales of approximately $6 billion, joined thousands of other companies online when it introduced its site on the World Wide Web, aptly named the "World Wide Living Room Web Site." The web site not only offered information about the company, its origin, and its future vision, but also made it possible for customers to see IKEA's merchandise on their computers at home. Part of the company's catalog was available for viewing online, and information about new product lines and pictures of the items were present.

The company also continued its practice of being environmentally friendly, which was actually a practice that the company had embraced since its beginnings. In the 1990s, when media hype about recycling and saving the environment was at its height, IKEA had taken steps to cut down on waste years before. In order to save money in the production phase, IKEA had long strived to be as economical as possible and to use only the amount of materials absolutely necessary when producing items. The company had also been saving money (and trees) by using flat-packaging for the storage and transport of items, which dramatically reduced the amount of cardboard packaging materials used by the company. The company's web site challenged customers to "search for new and economical uses of our precious environmental resources to adapt ourselves to the forests, lakes, air and mountains. Not the other way around." In 1999, Anders Dahlvig became president and CEO of the IKEA Group, taking over from Anders Moberg. The following year e-commerce commenced with customers in Sweden and Denmark being able to purchase IKEA goods online.

IKEA IN THE 21ST CENTURY

The IKEA model continued to work. In 2001 the company's headquarters were moved to Leiden in the Netherlands. By 2003, IKEA had stores and offices in 34 countries, including 19 stores in the United States, sales of over $10.8 billion, and more than 75,000 employees. Two years later, its 226 stores served some 410 million customers a year and brought in revenues of $17.7 billion. That year, the company was found guilty of trademark infringement by selling a flashlight with a design almost indistinguishable from the Mini Maglite made by Mag Instrument, Inc. It had to pay $44,000 in damages and $585,000 in legal costs.

In 2006, IKEA claimed it was serving 500 million visitors annually and was publishing 174 million catalogs (up from 96 million in 1999). Having saturated Europe, which accounted for over 80 percent of sales, the company was concentrating on the Asian, Russian, and U.S. markets, opening its first store in Japan that year. That same year, IKEA introduced its own food label for products sold in its stores and served in its restaurants.

In 2007, the company opened 21 stores in 11 countries and saw sales rise by 14 percent. Over 191 million copies of the IKEA catalog were printed in 27 languages and 54 editions. During this period, IKEA continued to support environmental and "green" efforts, including projects with the World Wildlife Federation to reduce greenhouse gas emissions generated by its operation. It also introduced models of prefabricated homes to provide more affordable energy-efficient housing.

IKEA was also exploring ways to expand beyond its traditional customer base. The opening of a huge 293,000-square-foot store in South Florida, for example, provided the company the opportunity to examine the market for furnishing second homes as well as to identify ways to attract older customers. Another initiative was IKEA Business, which focused on the small business market. In 23 markets worldwide, the company offered a web site for small business owners, events at IKEA stores, and furnished business settings such as a bookstore or home office within the stores. Finally, the company was going urban, opening stores in major cities, including Paris and Madrid, instead of operating in the suburbs. IKEA's affordable, well-designed products, which numbered over 9,500, had proven attractive to people all over the world. The current efforts would indicate that the company was continuing to be creative and flexible in order to be successful.

James B. Jefferys
Updated, Laura E. Whiteley; Ellen Wernick

PRINCIPAL SUBSIDIARIES

InterSwedwood Group; Inter IKEA Services B.V.; IKEA Services AB.

PRINCIPAL COMPETITORS

Target Corporation; Wal-Mart Corporation; Bed Bath & Beyond Inc.

FURTHER READING

Allegrezza, Ray, "Kid's IKEA Growing Like Weeds," *Home Textiles Today,* September 22, 2000, p. S34.

Brown-Humes, Christopher, "The Bolt That Holds the IKEA Empire Together," *Financial Times,* August 12, 2002, p. 11.

Burton, Jack, "Rearranging the Furniture," *International Management,* September 1991, p. 58.

Capell, Kerry, et al., "IKEA: How the Swedish Retailer Became a Global Cult Brand," *BusinessWeek,* November 14, 2005.

Cohen, Karen-Janine, "Ikea-Mania," *South Florida CEO,* December 2007, p. 26.

Colangelo, Michael, "IKEA's World; A Unique Structure and Philosophy Speeds This Swedish Furniture Giant Ahead," *HFD—Weekly Home Furnishings Newspaper,* May 25, 1987, p. 1.

Cowley, Deborah, and Anne Paillard-Bernier, "IKEA: Fascinating World of Furniture," *Reader's Digest* (Canada), May 1989, p. 53.

DeMott, John S., "The Store That Runs on a Wrench; An Invader from Scandinavia Creates a Build-It-Yourself Empire," *Time,* July 27, 1987, p. 54.

"Flat-Pack Accounting," *Economist.com,* May 11, 2006.

Fuhrman, Peter, "The Workers' Friend," *Forbes,* March 21, 1988, p. 124.

"Furnishing the World," *Economist* (U.S.), November 19, 1994, p. 79.

Gillespie, Andrew, "IKEA," *Business Review* (U.K.), April 2003, p. 18.

Hall, Emma, and Normandy Madden, "IKEA Courts Buyers with Offbeat Ideas," *Advertising Age,* April 12, 2004, p. 10.

Heller, Richard, "Man of the People," *Business Review Weekly,* August 25, 2000, p. 84.

"IKEA International," *Plunkett's Retail Industry Almanac,* Houston, Tex.: Plunkett Research Ltd., 2004.

"IKEA Ordered to Pay Damages for Trademark Infringement," *Nordic Business Report,* May 16, 2005.

Kelley, Bill, "The New Wave from Europe," *Sales & Marketing Management,* November 1987, p. 44.

Krienke, Mary, "IKEA=Simple Good Taste," *Stores,* April 1986, p. 56.

Kruger, Jennifer Barr, "IKEA Inspiration: Retailer IKEA Reaches Out to Businesses with Much More than Fixtures," *PMA Magazine—Connecting the Imaging Communities,* November 2007, p. 16.

"Private Man Behind Private IKEA Keeps Tight Grip on Growing Empire," *South China Morning Post,* July 30, 1998.

"Profile: Ingvar Kamprad: IKEA Always Was a Disaster to Assemble," *Sunday Times,* February 13, 2003.

Reynolds, Jonathan, "IKEA," *Retail & Distribution Management,* May–June 1988, p. 32.

Rothacher, Albrecht, "IKEA: The Småland Way Goes Global," *Corporate Cultures and Global Brands,* Singapore: World Scientific Publishing, 2004.

Solomon, Barbara, "A Swedish Company Corners the Business: Worldwide," *Management Review,* April 1991, p. 10.

Weinstein, Steve, "IKEA Furnishes More Than Homes," *Progressive Grocer,* September 1992, p. 95.

Wray, Kimberley, "Scandinavian Surprise—IKEA: Beware the Patient Giant," *HFN—Weekly Newspaper for the Home Furnishing Network,* June 22, 1998, p. 1.

Image Entertainment, Inc.

20522 Nordhoff Street, Suite 200
Chatsworth, California 91311-6104
U.S.A.
Telephone: (818) 407-9100
Fax: (818) 407-9151
Web site: http://www.image-entertainment.com

Public Company
Incorporated: 1975 as Key International Film Distributors, Inc.
Employees: 195
Sales: $99.8 million (2007)
Stock Exchanges: NASDAQ
Ticker Symbol: DISK
NAIC: 512199 Other Motion Picture and Video Industries

■ ■ ■

Image Entertainment, Inc., is an independent global distributor of DVDs. The company's library of more than 2,500 exclusive DVD titles includes theatrical releases as well as classic films, foreign films, and documentaries, and offerings in such genres as science fiction and horror. Image also distributes new and vintage television programs, special interest programming, concert videos and other music specials, stand-up comedy videos and television specials, a line of urban fare that includes hip-hop films and programming, Spanish-language films and television programming, and mature content from the likes of *Playboy* and *Penthouse.* Image also has exclusive distribution rights to about 200 audio titles. Each month the company releases 30 new exclusive DVDs and four audio titles. Image maintains its headquarters in Chatsworth, California, and domestic distribution is handled through a Las Vegas, Nevada, facility. International distribution is carried out through sublicense agreements.

COMPANY INCORPORATED AS KEY INTERNATIONAL FILM DISTRIBUTORS

The origins of Image Entertainment date to the 1975 incorporation of Key International Film Distributors, Inc., a Colorado distributor of adult films. Three years later it was taken public by Meyer Blinder, the notorious penny stockbroker. Born in New York City in 1921 to Russian immigrant parents, Blinder dropped out of school in the midst of the Great Depression to peddle a variety of wares door-to-door from a pushcart. After serving in World War II he ran a coffee machine vending route with his brother, eventually selling enough stock in the company to finance a brief retirement. Then in the 1970s he and a friend, Mac Robinson, began marketing over-the-counter stocks in Westbury, New York, under the name Blinder, Robinson & Company. After Robinson left, Blinder acquired a bankrupt Denver brokerage firm and relocated to Colorado where he became the "king of penny stocks," known for his street-tough Brooklyn accent, diamond pinkie-ring, and gold chains, as well as a stock touting operation that made him millions while leaving countless disgruntled customers and ruined companies in his wake. Eventually Blinder would be convicted on six counts of racketeering, money laundering, and securities

COMPANY PERSPECTIVES

Image Entertainment, Inc., is a leading independent home entertainment company that acquires, licenses, finances and produces exclusive content for worldwide video distribution through its direct relationships with major North American retailers and foreign sublicensees such as Sony/BMG and Warner Music.

fraud, resulting in his serving 40 months in a federal prison, but at its height his brokerage firm maintained 66 offices in 37 states.

GREENWALD GROUP ACQUIRES KEY

Key International was struggling in 1981 when it was acquired by Martin W. Greenwald, a 1964 graduate of Fairleigh Dickinson University who became a stockbroker and then manager of the Las Vegas Cinema chain of adult film theaters. He also became a partner in Miracle Film Distributors, known for producing the 1970s adult films of Marilyn Chambers, the onetime Ivory Soap girl, responsible for such works as *Insatiable* and *Saddle Tramp Women.* Years late Greenwald admitted to *Forbes,* "I have mixed shame [and] non-shame about my involvement, but it served my needs and purposes in the 1970s." He told the *Los Angeles Daily News,* "It was a business," saying further, "We were in the adult business because that's where the money was."

Among the members of the investment pool Greenwald assembled to acquire Key International were Chambers and her husband Charles Traynor. They were soon joined by another investor, adult film producer Thomas Sinopoli. The group paid $150,000 for a 90 percent stake in Key International, which at first was used to distribute the partners' adult films to video and TV. The purpose of the company began to take a different turn in 1983 when Greenwald saw a demonstration of the new Pioneer laser disk player, which played 12-inch disks and offered far superior sound and picture quality than videocassette tapes.

KEY INTERNATIONAL BECOMES IMAGE ENTERTAINMENT

Greenwald, believing that he had glimpsed the future of video format, decided to get in on the ground floor and in June 1983 renamed Key International as Image Entertainment, Inc. Because the rights were reasonable his initial laser disk releases were adult films, including *Insatiable.* Image scraped along as the laser disk player, only able to carve out a minor niche in the market, failed to replace the videocassette recorder (VCR). In order to serve a select group of videophiles, Greenwald decided he needed to find a way to represent mainstream Hollywood fare on an exclusive basis.

Greenwald offered stock options to independent film producer Dino Conte, who had extensive ties to Hollywood, as well as reported connections to organized crime. "He opened a lot of doors for us," Greenwald told *Forbes.* Needing more capital to take advantage of those open doors to acquire film rights, Greenwald sought out John Kluge, a media mogul, the chairman of Metromedia, who at the time was the richest man in the United States. Through a friend Greenwald was able to arrange a meeting with Kluge's chief lieutenant, Stuart Subotnick. Although Subotnick was interested in the pitch, he insisted that Greenwald sever his ties to adult entertainment, including his stake in Miracle Film and an adult theater for which he remained the landlord. Once Greenwald complied, Kluge began to invest in Image in late 1987. He would then sink $10 million into the business, taking an interest of about 40 percent in what was the only pure-play company in the laser disk field. Other mainstream investors would soon follow, including Capital Guardian Trust and the California State Teachers Retirement Fund.

Just as importantly, Kluge was the majority shareholder of Orion Pictures Corp. and used his influence to award exclusive laser disk rights for the company's films to Image. Kluge's involvement also provided Image, and Greenwald, with a much-needed stamp of approval that led to deals with other Hollywood studios. Image's revenues increased from $2.3 million in fiscal 1986 to $28.1 million in fiscal 1990. The company received further affirmation in the industry in 1991 when it finalized a four-year laser disk licensing deal with Walt Disney Co., which also took a warrant to buy 10 percent of Image. A few weeks later, Mitsubishi Corporation acquired a 3.5 percent stake in Image, and the two companies also reached an agreement that would have Mitsubishi provide laser disk manufacturing. Next, in April 1992 Mitsui & Co. invested $2 million in Image.

EXPLORING OTHER FORMATS

Although revenues improved to $48.2 million in fiscal 1991, the company lost $609,000, and despite the declining cost of laser disk players, Image was still waiting for the format to catch hold with mainstream consumers. In 1992 the company tried to expand its

KEY DATES

1975: Company formed as Key International Film Distributors, Inc.
1978: Company taken public by Meyer Blinder.
1981: Key International acquired by Martin Greenwald.
1983: Name changed to Image Entertainment, Inc.
1991: Image reaches laser disk distribution deal with Walt Disney Co.
1997: Image begins distribution of DVDs.
2005: Lions Gate makes unsolicited bid to buy company.
2008: Deal to sell company to David Bergstein fails.

scope by establishing a CD-ROM division and releasing karaoke laser disks, but neither move did much to pump sales. After the company posted a loss of $9 million on revenues of $59 million in fiscal 1993, Greenwald instituted a number of cost-cutting measures, which included layoffs and a 20 percent cut in the pay of executives, including his own compensation, which fell from $200,000 to $160,000 a year.

In 1994 Image decided to release full-length movies on CD-ROMs for playback on computers. While the number of home computers was growing steadily, the desire of consumers to watch movies on a small computer screen rather than their television was not great enough to provide Image with much of a market opportunity. Nevertheless, laser disk players increased in number, so that in fiscal 1994 Image was able to turn a profit of $3.4 million on sales of $65.6 million. A year later revenues increased to $85.6 million, resulting in net income of $6.3 million.

On the horizon, however, was a new, small disk format, digital video disk, or DVD, which many in the industry believed would quickly replace the VCR as the video player of choice among consumers. In preparation for the changing landscape, Image in July 1995 paid $3.1 million to acquire V.T. Laser Inc., also known as U.S. Laser Video Distributors. The 10-year-old Fairfield, New Jersey, company was a one-stop laser disk distributor that added about a 15 percent retail market share to Image's one-third wholesale share, giving Image even greater heft in the industry. The addition of U.S. Laser helped boost revenues to $95.1 million in fiscal 1996 and led to an increase in net income to $7.6 million.

DVDS BECOME AVAILABLE

The DVD format entered the domestic home video market in March 1997, and Image was forced to reinvent itself. In that same month, it began distributing DVD programming on a nonexclusive wholesale distribution basis while continuing to offer laser disks. Once DVDs became available, however, the sale of laser disks began to evaporate. Making matters worse for the company, studios decided to distribute DVDs themselves, leaving Image without any major content partners. Image responded by buying the rights to any programming that was available, whether it was old horror films, classic television shows, or Broadway shows. "We knew we had a one- to two-year window to get our act together," Greenwald explained to the *Los Angeles Daily News.* A major title during this period was the DVD of the 1994 reunion concerts of the Eagles, "Hell Freezes Over," which became Image's early bestseller as the company emphasized music programming during this time.

Also during this transitional phase, the company began moving its shipping warehouse operation from Chatsworth, California, to a much larger Las Vegas facility. Getting the state-of-the-art operation on line proved problematic and two years would pass before it was open and running smoothly. The switch to the new distribution facility, completed in May 1999, and the DVD format were felt on the balance sheet, as sales dipped to $85.6 million in fiscal 1997 and $75.5 million in fiscal 1998, and net income fell to $845,000 in fiscal 1997 and a loss of $9.6 million in fiscal 1998. A year later the situation stabilized, as sales inched up to $77.2 million and Image returned to profitability, recording earnings of $1.7 million.

In January 1999 Image was able to raise $10.6 million in a private placement of stock and a few days later completed the $7 million cash and stock acquisition of certain assets of Ken Crane's Magnavox City, Inc., an Internet and direct-to-consumer DVD and laser disk software business, operating as DVDPlanet.com. Image was also benefiting from a relationship with Internet retailers, especially Amazon.com. The Internet also provided Image with a cost-effective way to continue to distribute products to consumers who still used their laser disk players.

In the new century Image completed the transition to DVDs and laser disks were discontinued. Sales totaled $83.1 million in fiscal 2001 while net income jumped from $1.4 million the prior year to more than $8.4 million. The company's exclusive DVD programming also increased at a rapid rate in the early 2000s, as Image added to its library of programming with extreme sports, "lifestyle," and urban fare. In fiscal 2003 alone, exclusive programming sales surged 40 percent, contributing the lion's share of the company's $87 million in total revenues. CD audio programming also emerged as a new growth category.

What did not pan out was DVDPlanet.com, which in the beginning proved useful as a way to sell Image's inventory of laser disks but failed to work as a direct-to-consumer DVD business. DVDPlanet was sold in September 2003. In fiscal 2004, Image revamped its European distribution system, replacing its network of independent European distributors with a sublicensee, Bertelsmann Music Information Services, GmbH, which in addition to Europe received the rights to distribute Image programming in Africa and the Middle East.

TAKEOVER BID DEFEATED

Image's revenues increased to $118.4 million in fiscal 2005 and the company earned $5.1 million. A few months later Image found itself the object of an unsolicited takeover bid by Lions Gate Entertainment Corp. after it acquired a stake of nearly 19 percent. The offer was turned down by Image, which then added a shareholder rights plan. Lions Gate did not give up, however, and launched a hostile takeover bid that was eventually thwarted by Image. In the meantime, Image made progress in once again adding theatrical products to supplement its library of niche programming. In August 2006 it signed a ten-year distribution deal with Relativity Media, which received a 14 percent stake in Image. The company also continued to broaden its niche programming, in 2006 licensing the rights to programming of the Discovery Channel. A year later Image established a new urban division called One Village Entertainment and at the same time reached a distribution deal for the documentaries and narrative feature films of Rugged Entertainment, formed by Peter Spirer, an Academy Award–nominated director who had completed films on such rap artists as Tupac Shakur and Notorious B.I.G.

Image experienced a drop in business in fiscal 2006, with revenues decreasing to $111.9 million. The company also lost about $200,000. The following year Image lost $12.6 million as revenues slipped below $100 million. As fiscal 2007 came to a close, an agreement was reached to sell the business for $132 million to BTP Acquisition Company, LLC, an investor group led by David Bergstein, a film financier and producer who had acquired a pair of film distributors, the United Kingdom-based Capitol Films, and the North American film distributor Thinkfilm. The sale would not come to fruition, however. In February 2008, BTP backed out of the deal.

Ed Dinger

PRINCIPAL SUBSIDIARIES

Egami Media, Inc.; Image Entertainment (UK), Inc.

PRINCIPAL COMPETITORS

Alliance Entertainment; Genius Products Inc.; Navarre Corporation.

FURTHER READING

Adamson, Deborah, "Laserdisc Firm's Distribution Site Leaving Valley," *Los Angeles Daily News,* June 27, 1996, p. B1.

Apodaca, Patrice, "Laser Disc Firm Sees Turn Toward Profit," *Cleveland Plain Dealer,* January 4, 1992, p. 6F.

Armstrong, Larry, "Up from Shady Ladies," *Business Week,* May 18, 1992, p. 106.

Britt, Russ, "Big Player in a Small Market," *Los Angeles Daily News,* November 13, 1994, p. B1.

Gubernick, Lisa, "A Shady Past, a Questionable Future," *Forbes,* September 17, 1990, p. 165.

Hernandez, Greg, "An Image for Everyone," *Los Angeles Daily News,* June 13, 2002, p. B1.

Martin, Douglas, "Meyer Blinder, Penny Stock King, Dies at 82," *New York Times,* March 4, 2004, p. C16.

Yu, Deborah, "Image Entertainment Cuts Staff, Pay," *Los Angeles Daily News,* March 23, 1993, p. B2.

Jack Henry and Associates, Inc.

663 Highway 60
P.O. Box 807
Monett, Missouri 65708
U.S.A.
Telephone: (417) 235-6652
Fax: (417) 235-8406
Web site: http://www.jackhenry.com

Public Company
Incorporated: 1977
Employees: 3,583
Sales: $668 million (2007)
Stock Exchanges: NASDAQ
Ticker Symbol: JKHY
NAIC: 541512 Computer Systems Design

■ ■ ■

Jack Henry and Associates, Inc. (JHA), started as a small technology supply and consulting company and has grown to become a national leader in technology services and consultation. In 2007, JHA's products and services were used by more than 8,700 businesses and the company grossed over $600 million in annual sales. JHA operates through three principal operating units: Jack Henry Banking, which provides computer integration and automation systems for financial institutions; Symitar, which was acquired by Jack Henry in 2000 and provides service and also provides surveys and customer information; and Profitstar, which provides software and automation programs for a variety of financial institutions and services to over 6,000 domestic and international businesses.

STARTING UP: 1976–85

In 1976, John W. "Jack" Henry, Jerry D. Hall, and a third person founded Jack Henry and Associates to develop, market, maintain, and support integrated data processing systems for in-house automation of standard banking and accounting applications in commercial banks and other financial institutions. The company targeted community banks and marketed a bank automation system that used IBM's System/36 midrange computer. The firm was first incorporated in Missouri in 1977 but remained a private company until 1985. Its headquarters were established in Monett, Missouri, a small city located in the southwest corner of the state.

JHA reincorporated in Delaware on November 12, 1985, making an initial public offering on November 20 of that year. Approximately 1.1 million shares were offered at $6.75 per share, with the company realizing $6.21 per share. Henry and Hall owned about 60 percent of the outstanding common stock of the company following the public offering. Revenues by then had grown to approximately $12.5 million, up from $5.5 million the year before. The company's main sources of revenue were software licensing and installation, maintenance and support, and hardware, with hardware sales accounting for most of 1985's new revenue. By the end of 1985, JHA had 46 employees, plus 22 employees in its unconsolidated affiliates.

COMPANY PERSPECTIVES

Jack Henry's mission is to protect and increase the value of its stockholders' investment by providing quality products and services to its customers by: concentrating its activities on what it knows best—information systems and services for financial institutions; providing outstanding commitment and service to its customers so that the perceived value of its products and services is consistent with the real value; and maintaining a work environment that is personally, professionally, and financially rewarding to its employees.

GROWTH AND CHALLENGES: 1986–90

In 1986 JHA attempted to expand into financial services, acquiring FinSer Capital Corporation, a securities brokerage operation based in San Antonio, Texas. The new acquisition became a wholly owned subsidiary of JHA, but after three unprofitable years, JHA divested it in May 1989, transferring ownership to FinSer's chairman and CEO, Fred L. Baker, following a 40 percent drop in gross revenues that was attributed to generally poor performance in the industry at that time.

On March 31, 1988, JHA entered into a product development and marketing agreement with Unisys, a Detroit-based supplier of mainframe computers and related equipment. The next day IBM terminated its agreement with JHA. Under the original agreement between JHA and Unisys, JHA software would have been installed on more than 300 of the Unisys A Series computers, which were comparable to IBM System/36 midrange computers. The deal with Unisys soured, however, and JHA filed suit for breach of contract against Unisys a year later, in July 1989. Claiming that Unisys failed to pay approximately $1.7 million due on May 30, JHA sought $13.5 million, an amount that would have been due under the remaining portion of the contract. At the same time that it filed the lawsuit, JHA announced that it had reestablished a remarketing agreement with IBM.

Henceforth the company would devote practically all of its efforts to two software systems that ran on IBM hardware: the CIF 20/20, which was designed for community banks with assets of less than $200 million and ran on the IBM System/36 midrange computer; and the Silverlake System, which ran on IBM's AS/400 system, a higher-grade midrange computer than the System/36, designed for midsized institutions with $100 million to $2 billion in assets. A new generation of AS/400 computers that was introduced in the early 1990s allowed the Silverlake System to service institutions with assets of up to $10 billion. The software systems were often sold bundled with IBM System/36 or IBM AS/400 systems through the remarketing agreement with IBM.

In June 1990 JHA announced a promising merger with Peerless Systems, Inc., a bank software company based in Richardson, Texas, with about 250 customers. The merger would have resulted in a banking software vendor with revenues projected at $20 million and about 850 customers, but in July JHA unexpectedly called it off. After four weeks of negotiations, it appeared that it would have taken too long to reach an agreement. One possible problem affecting negotiations may have been JHA's continuing lawsuit against Unisys.

NEW LEADERSHIP AND ACQUISITIONS: 1990–99

In August, Colin McAllister quit as CEO at JHA, after serving for two years. Under McAllister, JHA had become embroiled in its lawsuit with Unisys, attempted to diversify into financial services by acquiring FinSer, and failed to consummate a promising merger with Peerless. President Jerry D. Hall immediately assumed the duties of CEO.

In 1990 JHA paid its first dividend, $0.28 per share, a practice it would continue to follow. The declaration may have been motivated in part as a move to bolster the stock price, which was trading in the $1.5 to $3.5 range that year. The company reported negative income on revenues of $15 million.

The next year, fiscal 1991, saw the beginning of five consecutive years of profitability. The company's stock price began to recover in 1991, trading in the $1.5 to $6.125 range. The number of employees increased by about 20 percent to 110, a trend that would continue for the next several years.

In January 1992 JHA acquired the banking software contracts of Bankers Own Software Systems (BOSS), the first of four acquisitions of bank software system businesses that it would consummate over the next few years. In December it acquired the business operations of Fremont Software, Inc., of Fremont, Indiana. Like JHA, Fremont marketed banking software and was an authorized remarketer of IBM computer equipment to small and medium-sized banks. These acquisitions served to expand JHA's customer base.

The end of 1992 also saw a favorable out-of-court settlement with Unisys, which agreed to pay $4 million

KEY DATES

1976: Company is founded with headquarters in Monett, Missouri.
1985: Company reincorporates in Delaware and goes public.
1988: A software development agreement with Unisys is forged.
1992: The banking software contracts of Bankers Own Software Systems (BOSS) are acquired.
1993: Company purchases BankVision Software Ltd. and expands to Durango, Colorado.
1994: Michael E. Henry is named chairman and CEO.
1995: Broadway & Seymour and SECTOR are acquired.
1996: Company restructures and then discontinues the BankVision division.
2003: Company acquires Symitar and forms second major operating division.
2004: Jack Prim is named chief executive officer.
2006: Profitstar becomes the company's third major operating division.
2007: Founder John W. (Jack) Henry dies.

to JHA. JHA was to receive $3,464,000 in cash, with the remaining $536,000 to be paid by eliminating charges against Unisys. JHA announced that the settlement income would be added to working capital and that the company was pleased to reach a settlement, noting that a continuing legal battle could have significantly drained its resources.

Finally, in 1992 Michael E. Henry, the son of founder Jack Henry, was named to the board of directors and became vice-president of research and development. Henry had been with the firm since 1979 and had held a number of management positions with the company. Michael R. Wallace also joined the board and was named vice-president of installation services. These two promotions marked the beginning of an orderly management change to a younger generation of executives that would be completed in 1994, when Michael E. Henry became chairman and chief executive officer and Michael R. Wallace, by then president, assumed the additional role of chief operating officer.

JHA continued to seek ways to expand its business in 1993. In January it announced the formation of a marketing alliance with BankVision Software, Ltd., of Durango, Colorado. By August JHA purchased BankVision for $2 million in stock and future payments based on earnings. BankVision added about 35 domestic customers, but its primary focus was to provide software and services for the international banking community.

By the end of 1993 JHA reported that it had software installed at more than 910 banks and financial institutions worldwide. Revenues had reached $32.6 million, net income was up to $6.259 million, and the stock was trading in the $10.25 to $17 range. For the first time the number of stockholders had dramatically increased to nearly 2,000, and the company employed some 154 workers.

By 1994 the company had more than 3,000 stockholders, but the stock price was down in the $6.5 to $11.25 range due to flat earnings. JHA bolstered its stock price by increasing the quarterly dividend and reporting an increase in earnings by the end of the calendar year. Revenues were more heavily weighted toward the two most profitable segments, software and service, a trend JHA officials expected to continue.

In mid-1994 JHA acquired CommLink Corporation, described in the company's annual report as "a rapidly growing electronic transactions company that handles automated teller machine (ATM) switching and point-of-sale (POS) technology for both financial and nonfinancial institutions." JHA paid $2.5 million, plus potential payments based on specific performance targets. CommLink, based in Houston, Texas, would operate as a subsidiary of JHA and be run by Thomas D. McCarlet, its founder, president, and CEO. CommLink had a customer base of approximately 100 customers for its ATM products and services. JHA regarded this as an important complementary service that could be marketed to its existing bank customers, to banks not served by JHA, and also to nonfinancial institutions such as gas stations and casinos that might market their own ATM cards.

In 1995 JHA made several significant deals that further expanded its customer base and added new services that it could market. The first was a "technical services alliance" with Integrated Systems Solutions Corp. (ISSC), a subsidiary of IBM. The deal stemmed from the longstanding relationship between JHA and IBM. JHA had more than 1,000 installations of software on IBM's AS/400 computer line. Under the agreement, ISSC could use JHA's Silverlake System in service bureau arrangements, whereby several banks operated out of a single data center, or in facilities management contracts, where IBM installed and maintained a computer system onsite at the bank's location. Thus, IBM was able to offer banks with assets in the $500 million to $10 billion range an outsourcing option based on the AS/400, using JHA's Silverlake software. This represented a new market for JHA software in terms of the size of the banks it could service. The first contract realized from the arrangement with ISSC resulted in a $617,000 contribution to net income in the first quarter of fiscal 1996 for JHA, and JHA expected two or three such contracts per year, not all of them of the same magnitude.

In June 1995 JHA purchased two banking software businesses, significantly increasing its customer base. The first involved the SECTOR business unit of Nationar, located in Danbury, Connecticut, with a customer base of 34 customers concentrated in the Northeast. Like JHA, SECTOR marketed software to banks. It was a cash transaction in the neighborhood of $883,000, with two possible future payments dependent on customers renewing their contracts with JHA.

The second purchase, and perhaps the most important acquisition in the history of the company, involved the community banking business of Broadway & Seymour (B&S), which JHA acquired for approximately $12 million. The transaction price included fees for certain distribution and marketing rights and fees for management services to be provided by B&S during the 12 months following the sale. Of the $12 million, JHA paid $6 million in cash and $6 million in installments through April 1, 1996.

As a result of the acquisition, JHA gained about 340 bank customers of the Liberty banking system in 35 states, thus increasing its customer base by one-third. The new subsidiary was called Liberty Software, Inc., with headquarters in Charlotte, North Carolina, and had approximately 150 employees. The subsidiary also provided revenue from service bureau contracts, disaster recovery, and a forms and supplies business.

In early 1995 JHA announced the restructuring of its unprofitable BankVision subsidiary, which was involved in developing and marketing international banking software. The unit was relocated from Durango, Colorado, to JHA's corporate headquarters in Monett, Missouri, in June. The division's president, Raymond L. Walters, was relieved of his duties as a result of the restructuring. JHA officials expected BankVision to impact negatively earnings for the current quarter and possibly the next. The BankVision unit was expected to break even or even become profitable during fiscal year 1996 beginning July 1, 1995.

William M. Caraway, senior vice-president of JHA, was named BankVision's president. He kept his sales and marketing duties for JHA. According to the company's annual report, the reorganization "eliminated significant overhead and minimized the loss potential for the BankVision operation." The reorganization gave JHA better control over its international operations and allowed the company to better focus its international marketing efforts. The company planned to expand BankVision more conservatively, and its major focus would be developing the Latin American market. However, at the end of fiscal 1996, JHA discontinued BankVision, taking a $1.68 million loss.

As a result of acquisitions and reorganization, 1995 was a major turning point for the company. Revenues increased by over 20 percent to $46.1 million and JHA led all bank technology stocks with a 154 percent gain in stock prices and stock prices trading in the $8.75 to $25.50 range. The acquisition of B&S resulted in a 33 percent increase in the company's customer base.

In March 1995, JHA announced plans to develop a home banking software system that would become available through the Internet and online service CompuServe. JHA would develop the new product for Block Financial, owner of CompuServe and a wholly owned subsidiary of H&R Block, Inc., and offer it to its banking clients. The software package would allow a bank's customers to check account balances, pay bills, and get stock quotes using their personal computers. They would also have access to nonfinancial services as well as tax software from H&R Block through Block Financial's web site. A final agreement was reached with Block Financial in May 1996.

In September 1999, JHA acquired the Financial Services Division of BankTec, Inc., a global systems integration, manufacturing, and services company. The acquisition was significant in that JHA gained access to the company's Synergy-based Windows application, Core Director, which became an important part of JHA's product and services offerings to financial institutions using a Windows-based system.

ENTERING THE CREDIT UNION INDUSTRY: 2000–03

In 2000, JHA acquired Symitar Systems, Inc., a privately owned San Francisco-based corporation focusing on data processing for credit unions. Symitar, which generated a reported $33 million during the 1999 financial period, brought a client list of 237 credit unions and gave JHA a foothold in the 2,500-company credit union industry. The purchase price was reported in company filings as $44 million, making it the largest acquisition in the company's history. Chairman Michael E. Henry said of the acquisition, "By adding our disaster recovery and service bureau offerings to Symitar's line of applications, Jack Henry will amass a superior network of UNIX products and services unparalleled in the industry." By 2003, Symitar had become the second major operating division for JHA.

In June, JHA acquired the Shawnee, Kansas-based Sys-Tech, Inc., which specialized in the construction and maintenance of computer facilities. JHA formed a product supply partnership with Sys-Tech in 1991 and eventually opted to purchase the company to expand its product lines. One of Sys-Tech's specialties was the construction of uninterruptible power supply systems, which helped companies to maintain service and data in the event of power failures. JHA hoped to market Sys-Tech's power systems as part of the company's computer management services. The purchase was completed for a reported $16 million in stock transfer.

In 2001, JHA completed an orderly shift in management as Jack Prim, who joined the company in 1995 with the acquisition of B&S, was named chief operating officer. Prior to his promotion to executive management, Prim had been serving as general manager of the company's E-Services Division. In June 2001, the company announced the 12th consecutive year of record revenues, with a 53 percent increase over the previous year and an earnings increase of more than 62 percent. Part of the company's increased profits was attributed to its acquisitions and development of the company's credit union services.

JHA posted another record-breaking year in 2002 and finished the year by acquiring, in November, CU Solutions, a South Dakota-based company that specialized in data processing for credit unions. While the acquisition of Symitar allowed the company to handle data and services for larger credit unions (those with assets over $25 million), CU Solutions specialized in catering to credit unions with assets below the $20 million mark. Entering the 2003 calendar year, JHA's credit union services had more than doubled to become the company's second largest operating division. There were additional personnel changes in 2002 as President Terry Thompson decided to retire and Jack Prim was promoted according to the company's regular plan of succession. CEO Michael Henry said of Prim's promotion, "He has demonstrated ability to lead the company. Jack is ideally suited to propel Jack Henry's continued growth."

NEW LEADERSHIP AND GROWTH FOR THE FUTURE

From 2003 to 2005, the company engaged in a number of small-scale acquisitions that broadened the company's products and services across a range of activities. The 2003 acquisition of National Bancorp Data Processing and the 2004 acquisition of SERsynergy, a division of Virginia-based SER Solutions, Inc., enhanced the company's ability to handle document management and check imaging technologies. JHA also acquired California-based Verinex Technologies, a company that handled security functions for financial technology.

Though JHA continued to grow through acquisitions, overall revenues and profits slowed as a reflection of changes in the national and international market for financial management technology. JHA responded by diversifying growth strategies and by increasing efforts in marketing. In 2004, Symitar was awarded a contract with Alliant Credit Union, the nation's seventh largest credit union, which marked a major boost for the company's visibility in the credit union industry.

In July 2004, Jack Prim became chief executive officer of the company while Michael Henry remained with the company as chairman of the board of directors. Former Chief Operating Officer Tony L. Worthington was promoted to president to replace Prim. "Jack and Tony have both been performing the responsibilities associated with these titles for well over a year now and the Board felt it was the appropriate time for the realignment," said Chairman Michael Henry in company press releases.

During the 2005 fiscal year, JHA added 49 credit unions and 60 banks to its client lists. The company also posted net income growth exceeding 21 percent. The year's most important acquisition was the purchase of Profitstar, Inc., an Omaha, Nebraska-based company specializing in financial and profitability management. Prior to the purchase, Profitstar served a client base of over 2,000 banks nationwide.

The acquisition of Profitstar became the focus for a major rebranding strategy in 2006, in which many of JHA's smaller subsidiaries, products, and services were grouped and offered under the Profitstar name, reformulated as the company's third major operating division. The company continued with its diversification strategy with the 2006 acquisition of Georgia-based US Banking Alliance, a major financial software provider, and the 2007 acquisition of Gladiator Technology Services, Inc., both of which were grouped under the company's Profitstar banner.

Founder John W. (Jack) Henry passed away in April 2007, just after the company celebrated its 30th anniversary. "Jack was not only a great businessman and leader, but he's also been a good friend to many of us," said CEO Jack Prim in official company press releases, continuing with, "His common sense approach to business and his single vision of doing what is best for our customers will continue to guide the company he started for years to come." In August 2007, Jack Prim was appointed to the company's board of directors to fill the void left by the death of Jack Henry.

At the end of the 2007 fiscal year, the company announced a 13 percent increase in revenues and a 12 percent increase in gross profits, with $668 million in total revenues for the financial period. During 30 years of business, the company increased from a single client to over 8,700 clients representing a variety of financial operations and a full-time staff of more than 3,000. With strong profits and an expanding list of services and products, JHA was in a position to continue as a leader in financial industry technology solutions.

David Bianco
Updated, Micah L. Issitt

PRINCIPAL SUBSIDIARIES

Jack Henry Banking, Inc.; Symitar, Inc.; Profitstar, Inc.; Jack Henry International, Ltd.; CommLink Corporation; Liberty Software, Inc.

PRINCIPAL COMPETITORS

CheckFree Corporation; Metavante Technologies, Inc.; MoneyGram International, Inc.; S1 Corporation.

FURTHER READING

Barthel, Matt, "Unisys Paying $4 Million to Settle Dispute with Bank Software Firm," *American Banker,* January 5, 1993, p. 3.

Bills, Steve, "Jack Henry Names CEO to Board," *American Banker,* August 2, 2007, p. 17.

———, "Jack Henry, Up 9.9%, Growing More Self-Reliant," *American Banker,* October 31, 2007, p.5.

"Block Unit, Jack Henry in Home Banking Pact," *American Banker,* March 19, 1996, p. 18.

Dyches, Kevin J., "Jack Henry & Associates, Inc.," *George K. Baum & Co. Equity Research,* March 28, 1996.

"Jack Henry Acquires BankTec," *Dallas Business Journal,* September 9, 1999.

"Jack Henry Announces Management Shift," *American Banker,* November 21, 1994, p. 14.

"Jack Henry Dies at 71," *ABA Banking Journal,* May 1, 2007, p. 52.

"Jack Henry Plans Joint Marketing with BankVision," *American Banker,* January 14, 1993, p. 3.

"Jack Henry Purchases Software Firm," *American Banker,* February 1, 1993, p. 17A.

"Jack Henry Rebrands Acquired Firms Under a New Name," *Credit Union Journal,* March 2006.

"Jack Henry, Small-Bank Software Firm, Posts Record Profit," *American Banker,* January 19, 1994, p. 23.

"John F. (Jack) Prim Appointed to Jack Henry Board of Directors," *PRS Newswire,* August 1, 2007.

Layne, Richard, "Another Blow for Jack Henry; Chief Executive Officer Quits," *American Banker,* August 8, 1990, p. 3.

———, "Jack Henry Calls Off Talks on Merger with Peerless," *American Banker,* July 5, 1990, p. 3.

———, "Likely Merger Would Create Big Vendor to Small Banks," *American Banker,* June 8, 1990, p. 3.

Marjanovic, Steven, "Broadway & Seymour Spinning Off Core Software Business to Jack Henry," *American Banker,* June 22, 1995, p. 16.

Tracey, Brian, "Hogan and Jack Henry Gained in 2Q as Demand for Software Took Off," *American Banker,* July 31, 1995, p. 14.

———, "IBM Unit Gets Access to Jack Henry Package for Outsourcing Deals," *American Banker,* January 23, 1995, p. 10.

———, "Software Firm Jack Henry to Develop Own Check Imaging Unit," *American Banker,* October 24, 1994, p. 14.

———, "Systems Developer Jack Henry Posts Earnings Gain," *American Banker,* January 25, 1995, p. 13.

Tyson, David O., "Jack Henry Claims Breach of Contract in $13.5 Million Suit Against Unisys," *American Banker,* July 20, 1989, p. 2.

———, "Jack Henry Posts Loss for Quarter," *American Banker,* June 7, 1989, p. 11.

John D. Brush Company Inc.

900 Linden Avenue
Rochester, New York 14625
U.S.A.
Telephone: (585) 381-4900
Fax: (585) 381-9408
Web site: http://www.sentrysafe.com

Private Company
Incorporated: 1930 as Brush-Punnett Safe Co.
Employees: 900
Sales: $500 million (2007 est.)
NAIC: 332999 All Other Miscellaneous Fabricated Metal Product Manufacturing

Doing business as Sentry Group, John D. Brush Company Inc. is a Rochester, New York-based privately owned maker of fireproof and waterproof safes sold under the Sentry brand as well as of Smith & Wesson label gun safes. The company makes a wide variety of safes for home and business use. They range in size from small chests to large floor safes and include file cabinet safes and wall-mounted units. Gun safes, both fireproof and non-fireproof, come in seven sizes. Sentry also provides security solutions for media, including safes with in-lid holders for DVDs and CDs, and waterproof and fireproof computer hard drives. In addition to key and combination locks, some Sentry products rely on a patented biometric fingerprint lock. Sentry is owned and operated by the third generation of the Brush family.

DEPRESSION ERA ROOTS

John D. Brush Company was founded in 1930 as Brush-Punnett Safe Co. in 1930 by John Brush and his brother-in-law Willard Punnett. Brush had been a young Massachusetts clergyman with two churches; he retired from the ministry in search of a more physically demanding occupation. With a small sum of money at his disposal, he hoped to start a manufacturing business but found it difficult to settle on a product line. In the summer of 1930 his search came to an end in Rochester, New York, where he was visiting his sister. Her husband, Punnett, told Brush of a safe he had designed some years earlier that instead of being made entirely by hand, like other safes on the market, made use of machine-stamped parts. Hence it could be produced at half the cost while offering the same features, thus gaining a tremendous price advantage in the marketplace.

Brush was intrigued and researched the safe industry upon his return home. He was advised that the time was ideal to launch a new safe-manufacturing company because the Great Depression would soon peter out and there would be a ready market for a less-expensive safe. Of course, hard times would continue into the next decade, but Brush had no way of knowing that and he decided it was the right time to go into business with Punnett.

To fund the company Brush raised $12,000, supplied equally by himself, his wife, and his sister, all of whom received a quarter-interest in the new company. For contributing the safe design and his knowledge, Punnett also received a 25 percent stake. The company

COMPANY PERSPECTIVES

A useful product, honestly made and honestly sold … that is good business.—John D. Brush Sr.

was formed in late 1930 and in the following year, 8,000 square feet of manufacturing space was secured from the Vogt Manufacturing Company of Rochester and $6,000 worth of tools were purchased, along with a massive 600-ton toggle press. The Brushes and Mrs. Punnett invested another $1,000 each for promotional costs as well as to cover the rent and pay the company's only employee while the business got under way. Unfortunately the die-maker failed to deliver the tools as promised by September and Brush-Punnett was unable to fill some 40 orders generated by the advertising. To make matters worse, Brush had hired two more men to handle the business that was coming in. By the time the tools arrived in January 1932, the orders had been canceled, no new orders were replacing them, and the company had no further money to invest in promotions.

PUNNETT LEAVES COMPANY: 1933

Although Brush took to the road to drum up some business, there was not nearly enough to keep his three employees busy. They were soon let go, and he and Punnett, neither of whom were taking a salary, had to do everything themselves. During that first difficult year, the company produced 200 safes and did less than $5,000 in business. Thoroughly discouraged, Punnett suggested that they simply walk away from the business and allow the creditors to take the tools and machinery, which they could not hope to sell because the Depression had only gotten worse, not better. Unlike Punnett, however, Brush had committed money to the enterprise, as did his wife and sister, and he felt obligated to carry on. After Punnett turned in his stock in February 1933, Brush began to run the business by himself with the occasional help of a laborer named Sam Pressley.

Brush was fortunate that Vogt Manufacturing, well aware of his situation, did not dun him for the rent, but asked only that he pay something as he was able. Only occasionally did his landlords check to see if he was still in business, content that the space was actually being put to use. In 1933 the company turned out 120 safes and took on some press work and welding, altogether generating $3,000 in income, barely enough to keep the business afloat. Pressley's ability to do job work proved especially valuable, and in 1934 his growing number of contacts led to consistent work that Brush could rely on to cover overhead. For the year, revenues improved to $5,000. Along the way, the former minister became involved in some speculative ventures, persuaded to help various inventors turn out products for a market that would never materialize, such as chicken feeders and trick ice-cream scoops.

A major turning point for Brush-Punnett came in May 1935 when the company received an order for 2,200 wall safes from Vassar College to be installed in dormitory rooms. Brush's winning bid was 90 cents each. Later he would learn that the next lowest bid was more than $2. Despite leaving a good deal of money on the table, he was grateful for the order, which allowed him to begin taking out a salary for the first time, $5 each week. The successful Vassar job also solidified the company's reputation, leading to more sales, and by the end of the year, revenues totaled about $10,000 and Brush was able to increase his salary to $10 a week.

BRUSH BUYS BUILDING: 1936

Business picked up further in 1936. By the middle of the year Brush was not only able to pay the back rent but could afford to buy the building from Vogt Manufacturing, which was more than happy to unload the property at a nominal price. Brush took over the mortgage, which he then repaid from a loan provided by his father-in-law. Sales continued to climb in 1937, when the company's six employees produced 500 safes leading to revenues of $17,000, allowing the owner to pay himself $50 a week.

Prosperity suddenly vanished in 1937, however, proving once again that the grip of the Great Depression was firm and enduring. Orders dried up and the employees had to be let go, leaving Brush to once again deny himself a paycheck and carry on the business single-handedly. Yearly sales fell to less than $9,000, and while business picked up somewhat during the remainder of the 1930s, Brush-Punnett would have to scrape by for the next few years. Due to changes in tax laws and the regulations covering corporations, it no longer made sense to remain a corporation, and so in 1939 a partnership was formed between Brush and his sister to own the company.

WAR SHORTAGES LIMIT SAFE PRODUCTION

The national economy began to pick up from defense spending and then boomed when the United States

KEY DATES

1930: Brush-Punnett Safe Co. is formed by John Brush, Willard Punnett, and their spouses.
1933: Punnett leaves the company.
1943: Brush becomes sole owner.
1955: Company is reincorporated as John D. Brush & Co. Inc.
1958: Security Wall Safe Co. is acquired.
1962: John Brush, Jr., assumes company presidency.
1968: New facilities open outside Rochester.
1979: A third generation joins the company.
1981: John Brush, Sr., dies.
1991: Douglas Brush is named president.
2006: John Brush, Jr., dies.

entered World War II in late 1941, but Brush-Punnett was unable to produce safes because its primary raw material, steel, was needed for the war effort. Brush struggled to find war work for his plant, subsisting on a handful of subcontracting jobs, and it was not until late in 1943 that he was able to secure a large order to produce steel skids for the Eastman Kodak Company in Rochester. In order to complete the job on time Brush not only had to hire dozens of new men, he had to find ways to increase their productivity, eventually resorting to a bonus system for the number of skids they produced each day. Able to double their salaries by splitting the bonus pool, the men spurred each other on to working harder and policed themselves to become punctual and eliminate absenteeism. Brush was able to buy out his sister, and in 1943 he became the sole proprietor of the company, which continued to use the Brush-Punnett name.

In order to take on more war contracts, Brush-Punnett built a warehouse behind the plant in 1944 to free up more work space. Late in the war, Brush-Punnett was granted some raw materials and allowed to begin producing safes again, about 100 each month. With the economy roaring, there was no lack of demand. Rather than take advantage of the situation to sell his modest output at the highest possible price, Brush rationed out his safes to his established dealers at the regular price, a policy creating goodwill that would be repaid many times over in the postwar years.

While Brush was growing his business he and his wife were also raising three sons, whom he wished to involve in the business. The oldest son, John, Jr., served in the U.S. Army Air Corps and after his discharge in 1946 enrolled at St. Lawrence College, where both his parents had earned degrees. After graduating in 1950 with a degree in psychology he went to work for his father for two years, and then left for Harvard University, where he earned a master's degree in business administration. He planned to seek employment at a major corporation, but at the urging of his father he returned to the family business as a principal in 1954, leading to a change in the company structure to not only accommodate him but his two younger brothers should they decide to become involved. Early in 1955 the business was once again incorporated, taking the name John D. Brush & Co. Inc.

MID-CENTURY GROWTH AND GENERATIONAL CHANGES

John Brush, Jr., purchased a one-third stake, paid out of profits over the next 15 years. Due to his influence, the company began to change the way it did business. For a quarter-century the company made safes in just one size. To open up new sales channels, it began to offer two sizes. The company also grew through acquisitions, including the 1958 purchase of Boston-based Security Wall Safe Co., a deal that brought with it the Security brand name.

In 1962 John Brush, Sr., turned 65 and retired, and his son took over day-to-day control as president. Nevertheless, the elder Brush remained chairman and continued to come into the office most days. Helping to run the business was a second son, Richard, who also graduated from St. Lawrence, class of 1952. He then attended Officer Candidate School and served in the U.S. Navy for three years before joining the company. Sales were well under $1 million per year when the new generation took charge and business began to grow at a steady pace. The factory floor had grown to about 15,000 square feet, a rabbit warren of crowded rooms that hindered productivity. The family looked for a new space, and 16 acres of land was purchased outside Rochester. In April 1968 a new 50,000-square-foot manufacturing plant with a separate administrative building was opened. With plenty of land at its disposal, the company was able to add space to the plant as the business grew.

Robert, the youngest of the elder Brush's sons, came to work for the company in 1973, having graduated from college a dozen years earlier and served in the military. Other personnel changes took place in the 1970s. Richard Brush became president in 1970, and John Brush, Jr., replaced his father as chairman in 1975. (John Brush, Sr., passed away in 1981.) A third generation also became involved during the decade. Douglas, son of John Brush, Jr., joined the company in 1979 after working as a college administrator.

DIVERSIFYING PRODUCT LINES FOR GROWTH

A number of changes to the business took place during the late 1970s. The company introduced a new line of molded fire-resistant products, including fireproof boxes to secure valuable papers and jewelry. It also began doing business as Sentry Group to bolster the Sentry brand and was exporting safes to more than 20 countries in Europe as well as to Japan.

Business began to decline somewhat in the late 1970s and early 1980s. Douglas Brush played a key role in moving the company forward. He lobbied for the removal of the sales and marketing head, whose performance he believed was greatly hurting the business. He also championed the development of a wider variety of security containers. In 1985 the new Sentry Fire-Safe Security Chest shattered all previous Sentry sales records. By 1987 the company was doing $20 million in sales. By mid-decade another member of the third generation had joined the company: Douglas's brother James. After graduating from St. Lawrence in 1977 he worked at IBM Corporation for ten years before joining the company in 1986.

Like their father and uncles, Douglas and James Brush began buying out the previous generation through company earnings, in this way avoiding heavy estate taxes. In 1991 Douglas succeeded his father as president. The company continued to grow sales by introducing innovative products and developing new sales channels. In 1994 a new mini-locker safe, the Portable LockR, was introduced for sale at home centers and mass merchants. By 1995 sales increased to $70 million. Sentry increased productivity by investing in robots to help pour insulating concrete into molds, press metal forms into shape, and weld joints. Previously, about one-quarter of the workers were needed just to clean up after the insulation was poured.

Y2K FEARS AND BEYOND

Sentry laid off some workers in 1997, but during the second half of the 1990s the company generally enjoyed a growth surge that led to increasing employment and sales increasing to about $500 million. Much of the new demand for safes came from first-time buyers, related to fears of "Y2K" calamities, the economic chaos that some predicted could ensue when the world's computers had to make the date change from 1999 to 2000. Although no major problems occurred, many people had taken the precaution of buying a home safe in which to secure copies of financial records and other important documents, and to store cash.

Sentry experienced a sudden drop in sales in 2000, partly related to the passing of Y2K fears, but mostly due to increased competition from safe manufacturers in Korea and China. As a result, Sentry pared back its workforce and instead of working around the clock, the plant operated only two shifts. Again Sentry looked to product innovation to remain competitive. It added gun safes to its product mix as well as new fire-resistant safes for the home market to secure important personal and household documents. Much of the gun safe production was done at a plant in Shanghai, China, but because of freight costs, that work would be brought back to Rochester in 2005. Later in the year, Sentry bolstered its position in this line by licensing the Smith & Wesson brand and logo for a new line of large capacity gun safes to be manufactured in the Rochester plant and available for sale in 2006. The year 2006 would also see the passing of John Brush, Jr.

Other new products and innovations would continue in the second half of the first decade of the 2000s. In 2007 Sentry introduced a fingerprint safe that used a patented biometric fingerprint lock. Also in 2007 Sentry unveiled six new data and document security products, including a pair of fireproof and waterproof computer hard drives, which also included a suite of software protection and "system restore" tools. The new product line also included data storage chests.

Ed Dinger

PRINCIPAL OPERATING UNITS

Business Safes; Home Safes; Gun Safes.

PRINCIPAL COMPETITORS

Brinks Home Security Inc.; Fireking Security Group; Honeywell Safes.

FURTHER READING

Deckert, Andrea, "John Brush Jr. Secured a Strong Future for Sentry," *Rochester Business Journal,* February 17, 2006.

Grady, Todd, "Squeezed Safe Maker Sentry Lays Off 33 More," *Rochester Democrat and Chronicle,* November 7, 2000, p. 10D.

Salibian, E. Catherine, "A Family Affair," *Rochester Business Journal,* July 23, 1993.

Stolt, Carrie, "2003 Rochester Business Hall of Fame: His Place in Rochester Business History Is Secure," *Rochester Business Journal,* September 19, 2003.

"The Story of an American Small Business," John D. Brush Company Inc., 2006.

Tyler, David, "Sentry Group Looks to Continue Growing," *Rochester Democrat and Chronicle,* November 29, 2003, p. 14D.

BAGELS AIN'T BAGELS UNLESS THEY'RE JUST BAGELS

Just Bagels Manufacturing, Inc.

527 Casanova Street
Bronx, New York 10474
U.S.A.
Telephone: (718) 328-9700
Fax: (718) 328-9997
Web site: http://www.justbagels.com

Private Company
Incorporated: 1992 as Just Bagels, Inc.
Employees: 90
Sales: $12 million (2007 est.)
NAIC: 311812 Commercial Bakeries

■ ■ ■

Based in the Bronx, New York, Just Bagels Manufacturing, Inc., is a privately owned baking company that makes bagels in a traditional manner that most large-scale producers avoid due to the cost. The bagels contain no oils, fat, cholesterol, or preservatives, and are certified as a kosher product by the Orthodox Union. In addition to using high-quality ingredients, Just Bagels makes "water bagels," which involves refrigerating the dough for six to eight hours and then boiling the bagels (rather than steaming, a short cut taken by large producers) before baking. As a result the bagels are crunchy on the outside and chewy on the inside. The company offers one-ounce cocktail bagels, two-ounce mini bagels, and three- and four-ounce bagels, as well as bagel sticks and bialys, a Jewish delicacy similar to bagels, which are baked without being boiled first and feature an indentation rather than a hole in the middle. In addition to typical varieties—plain, poppy, sesame, onion, pumpernickel, whole wheat, and cinnamon raisin—Just Bagels offers such exotic bagels as blueberry, French toast, and sun-dried tomato, and special flavors upon request. The company supplies bagels to such national customers as Starbucks and Barnes & Noble, making its products available in all 50 states. Upscale New York City customers include hotels such as the Waldorf-Astoria and the Marriott Marquis, and gourmet food shops such as Dean & DeLuca and Citarella. Individually wrapped bagels are sold to schools, airlines, cruise ships, and convenience stores. Supermarket chains that carry Just Bagels are Stop-and-Shop, Pathmark, and ShopRite. The bagels are also sold frozen in supermarkets throughout the country, cobranded as Ray's New York Bagels. New York City–area online grocer FreshDirect sells frozen par-baked bagels under the Just Bagels label. In addition, Just Bagels offers a private-label and co-packing program. Baking is done at a 44,000-square-foot facility located in the Hunts Point section of the Bronx, operating 24 hours a day.

COMPANY STARTED IN THE BRONX

Just Bagels was started in the Pelham Bay neighborhood in the Bronx in 1992 by Just Bagels president, Clifford Nordquist, and a partner. Nordquist grew up in Brooklyn, where he was a talented enough football player to attract several scholarships. He settled on Southern Connecticut State University, primarily because he was told that there were seven females to every male enrolled. While admittedly enjoying his college years, he also learned how to support himself, work-

COMPANY PERSPECTIVES

We take pride in our commitment to Quality. Our delicious bagels are prepared daily using the finest ingredients and are readily available to you at a reasonable price.

ing as a bouncer in a New Haven nightclub while earning a degree in communications. After graduating in 1990, however, he found it difficult to land a communications job in Manhattan. He tried his hand as a copier salesman and quit after spending four months without landing a single customer.

Nordquist went to work for his father's construction company, where one of the foremen suggested that they open a bagel store together. Interested in running his own business rather than being somebody's employee, Nordquist agreed, borrowing $50,000 from his mother to start a 1,500-square-foot bagel shop on Westchester Avenue in the Bronx, which took the name Just Bagels. Just three weeks after the doors opened, however, his partner left. Nordquist borrowed another $17,000 from his mother to buy out his partner, who a week later opened a bagel store elsewhere in the Bronx with someone else and tried to pilfer what few accounts Nordquist had managed to secure.

Needing help to run the business, Nordquist turned to a former roommate at Southern Connecticut, James O'Connell. Also an athlete, a wrestler, O'Connell had earned a degree in criminology and was on the waiting list to become a U.S. marshal, making ends meet by working as a security guard at a department store. He met with Nordquist and liked the shop and the prospects for the bagel business, which at the time was enjoying a surge of popularity across the country. Borrowing $13,000 from his mother, O'Connell bought into the business and took charge of the bakery.

MOVING INTO WHOLESALE

Despite their lack of baking experience, the young partners were committed to making traditional water bagels using the best available ingredients, a decision that made the small shop a success, resulting in long lines of customers. They were able to buy a second shop to sell the bagels produced at the Westchester Avenue bakery, and when the shop of Nordquist's former partner closed, they bought that as well. While they were doing well by some measures, with annual sales in the $800,000 range, Nordquist and O'Connell were also overwhelmed. They were making bagels around the clock to fill demand but they could make no more than 900 dozen a day and they had no plan to take the business to the next level. In 1996 they decided to sell the operation and placed a newspaper ad. The first person to respond was Charles Contreras, who had been involved in banking and the mortgage industry and was looking for a company in which to invest. The three men enjoyed an instant rapport, and rather than offering to buy the business, Contreras suggested that he buy a stake, bringing in a much-needed cash infusion. The three of them would then turn the retail bagel shop into a wholesale operation.

The roles of the three partners quickly fell into place. With his banking background Contreras was in charge of finances, O'Connell oversaw the bakery, and Nordquist took care of sales and marketing and served as the public face of Just Bagels. With the investment by Contreras, the company also had money to expand the operation to accommodate growth. Having outgrown the Westchester Avenue space, the partners took a 10-year lease on a new location on Zerega Avenue in the Bronx, 10,000 square feet in size. They also researched new equipment and made down payments on three new ovens, a flour silo, a bagel machine, a refrigerator, and office equipment.

HUNTS POINT BUILDING BOUGHT

The new Zerega Avenue bakery was able to produce 6,000 bagels a day, but the partners soon realized that they were unable to mass-produce the bagel they had perfected at their Westchester Avenue location. The hard-crusted bagel was preservative free but its shelf life was little more than three hours. To keep up with demand, the new bakery had to begin making bagels earlier in the day, resulting in a product that became stale early in the day. The problem would not be solved until 2000, when Just Bagels paid $2 million for a 10,000-square-foot building in Hunts Point to house their operation.

The move to Hunts Point was made to take advantage of tax incentives available to this designated economic development area as well as to set up the company to grow a frozen bagel business. Earlier, at the Zerega Avenue location, Just Bagels had begun to produce frozen bagels. They were frozen before being completely baked and then shipped for sale. End users could then complete the final five minutes of baking and enjoy a fresh-tasting product. The frozen bagel took Just Bagels into the food industry. Nordquist was able to seek wholesale accounts, playing up the company's state-

KEY DATES

1992: Just Bagels opens as retail bagel shop.
1996: Company begins transition to wholesale operation.
2000: Baking operations move to Hunts Point, the Bronx.
2001: Second Hunts Point building acquired.
2003: Branding effort begins.
2006: Sales reach $10 million.

of-the-art plant that made it a dependable supplier of high-quality bagels.

It was also at Hunts Point that Just Bagels switched from a hard-crusted bagel to a softer texture, partly because many consumers mistook a hard-crusted bagel for a stale bagel, but also in order to mass-produce the product. The bagels continued to be boiled in the traditional manner, but a new $1 million oven was able to bake them in half the time. As a result, the bagels retained more water, making them softer. Not only did customers prefer the texture, the reduction in baking time allowed Just Bagels to begin production later in the day, thus providing a fresher product. Moreover, the new bakery was able to turn out 18,000 dozen bagels a day, allowing Just Bagels to supply the needs of wholesale customers, and if need be, Just Bagels was still capable of producing the old hard-crusted bagel as well.

SECOND BUILDING ACQUIRED

In the early years of the new century, Just Bagels was able to land several major accounts, including Starbucks, Barnes & Noble, Dean & DeLuca, Citarella, and American Airlines. Believing that demand would continue to rise, Just Bagels took out a $1 million loan in 2001 to acquire a nearby 18,000-square-foot facility in Hunts Point, where it hoped to move its baking operations. The old plant was subleased, but when the tenant backed out of the deal, Just Bagels found itself saddled with the expense of two facilities. To make matters worse, the employees were having difficulty adjusting to the new high-tech ovens. In order to scrape by during this difficult period the three partners cut their own salaries. Meanwhile, Nordquist began pitching Just Bagels to food distributors. When he succeeded in winning over one major distributor, Just Bagels was able to gain entry to several major supermarket chains, including Publix, Stop-and-Shop, Pathmark, and ShopRite. Instead of having excess capacity, Just Bagels would soon be looking for more production space.

FRESHDIRECT RELATIONSHIP A TURNING POINT

While a thriving company doing business with marquee-name customers the likes of Starbucks and Barnes & Noble, Just Bagels was hardly visible to the general public until 2003. It was then that area online grocer FreshDirect urged the company to put its name on its packaging. "And that," Nordquist told *Crain's New York Business,* "put us on the map in New York." Serving the five boroughs of New York City and portions of Long Island, Westchester County, and New Jersey, FreshDirect was launched in 1999. The company did not actually position itself as an online supermarket, concentrating instead on higher margin items—fresh produce, fresh meat and seafood, baked goods, and prepared dishes—emphasizing convenience and quality over wide selection. While a typical supermarket might carry 25,000 different packaged goods and about 2,200 perishable products, FreshDirect offered 5,000 perishable products and just 3,000 packaged goods. To ensure freshness, many of its suppliers, like Just Bagels, were local. The service began to be rolled out to New York City neighborhoods in 2002 and steadily spread across the city, where it found plenty of receptive customers and began to develop something of a cult following.

Just Bagels was just one of a number of FreshDirect suppliers that benefited from the grocer's popularity to improve their local standing. While adding luster to local suppliers, FreshDirect built its own image as a provider of high-quality goods. Not only would Just Bagels' business with FreshDirect grow to about $500,000 a year, the suggestion to focus on branding was a watershed moment. "I learned that branding is everything," Nordquist told *Crain's.* "In the beginning, all I wanted to do was sell [FreshDirect] my bagels." The FreshDirect connection and the branding effort led to a large number of distribution contracts, which served to increase sales and further grow the Just Bagels brand.

To keep up with mounting demand for its product, Just Bagels acquired the building next door to its Hunts Point bakery in 2005, bringing the total amount of space in the facility to 44,000 square feet. Just Bagels posted sales of $8 million in 2005, a number that would grow to $10 million in 2006, and $12 million in 2007. The partners hoped to increase sales to $25 million by 2010. With FreshDirect interested in taking its business national, Just Bagels looked to further ride the grocer's coattails to help meet that target. Going forward, the partners also hoped to take the company public and perhaps open stores under the Just Bagels banner. Moreover, they looked to expand internationally. A deal to sell the Just Bagels product line in Israel was in the works, and in the fall of 2007 Nordquist told his alumni magazine that China might be a potential target: "They love bagels there. Not too long ago, nobody knew about bagels."

Ed Dinger

PRINCIPAL COMPETITORS

George Weston Bakeries; Pinnacle Foods Group LLC; Pepperidge Farm, Inc.

FURTHER READING

Baar, Karen, "Making Dough," *Southern Alumni Magazine,* Fall 2007.

Craigwell, Antoine, "Baking in the Glory," *Bronx Times Reporter,* November 23, 2006.

Fickenscher, Lisa, "Hitched to a Comet," *Crain's New York Business,* February 13, 2006, p. 2.

Traster, Tina, "Bagel Makers Bake Up Plan for Fast Growth," *Crain's New York Business,* August 14, 2006, p. 19.

Lewis Drug Inc.

2701 South Minnesota Avenue, Suite 1
Sioux Falls, South Dakota 57105-4746
U.S.A.
Telephone: (605) 367-2000
Toll Free: (800) 658-3620
Fax: (605) 367-2876
Web site: http://www.lewisdrug.com

Private Company
Founded: 1942
Employees: 800
Sales: $121.9 million (2006)
NAIC: 446110 Pharmacies and Drug Stores

■ ■ ■

Lewis Drug Inc. is a Sioux Falls, South Dakota-based operator of about 30 drugstores under the Lewis Drug and the Lewis Family Drug banners in South Dakota, Minnesota, and Iowa. Nimble, innovative, and highly attuned to the needs of customers, Lewis Drug has more than held its own against much larger national drug chains and mass merchants like Wal-Mart and Target, as well as supermarkets offering pharmacies. Lewis Drug units average 40,000 square feet in size, and offer customers a wide variety of merchandise and services. In addition to the mix of products most large chain drugstores carry, Lewis sells apparel, furniture, electronics, power tools, high-end grills, garden and yard ware, office supplies, sporting goods, and flowers. Customer service is an important feature of Lewis Drug locations, which offer post office substations, bill paying services, video rentals, gift wrapping, lottery tickets, Ticketmaster services, and dry cleaning drop-off.

Lewis Family Drug stores, a joint venture with Sioux Falls-based Sanford Health, are much smaller in footprint, averaging 8,000 square feet, and are unable to offer the breadth of merchandise of the large units. Nevertheless, they are successful in the smaller communities in which they are located. The company also operates pharmacies in long-term care facilities in Sioux Falls and Rock Rapids, Iowa, and four clinics affiliated with Sioux Valley Hospital. Lewis is owned by its chief executive officer, Mark E. Griffin.

WORLD WAR II–ERA ROOTS

Lewis Drug was established in downtown Sioux Falls in 1942 by partners Jesse Lewis and George Frederickson. Hired to manage the 7,000-square-foot store was Mark Griffin's father, John Griffin, a man not afraid to be an innovator. Hence, Lewis Drug was the first self-serve drugstore in South Dakota, and rather than merely serve as a pharmacy it offered a wide variety of goods, in many ways emulating the general stores that had been the commercial bedrock of rural communities for so many years.

Launching a venture just as the United States was becoming involved in World War II was not the best of timing, however. Mark Griffin told *Drug Topics* that his father "made it through the war by selling soaps, books, and popcorn. We used to get in trouble because we sold most of the popcorn in that downtown area. That was our main income flow back then. The theater people across the street were upset because we sold more

COMPANY PERSPECTIVES

At Lewis, our continual goal is to provide exceptional pricing, exemplary personal service and the ultimate in convenience. In short, our goal is to always be your first stop.

popcorn than they did. But you did what you could to get through the war years. We sold everything right to the ceiling—a lot of toys and a lot of items that were pretty unusual for a drugstore of that type."

EXPANSION BEGINS IN POSTWAR YEARS

Although John Griffin bought out the interest of Jesse Lewis in 1946, the store continued to bear the Lewis name. In partnership with Frederickson, Griffin looked to expand, opening a second store in Mankato, Minnesota, in 1947. The original Sioux Falls store prospered in the postwar years, leading to the opening of a second store in the city in 1956, located at 35th Street and Minnesota Avenue. It was then the site of a cornfield, a location that at the time puzzled residents but would one day become the home to numerous other retailers—serving as an example of the knack the Griffin family had in determining the direction in which Sioux Falls would grow. Over the years the company bought up parcels of land at strategic locations at reasonable prices and waited until the time was ripe to open a new Lewis Drug location. The real estate around the store could then be developed to bring in traffic, such as the opening of fast-food restaurants like McDonald's or Burger King.

The 1956 store was 17,000 square feet in size, a superstore for the time, one where families might gather on a Sunday afternoon. New competition emerged in the 1960s with the arrival of Kmart. Lewis Drug met the challenge by expanding the size of its stores even more, eventually growing to as large as 65,000 square feet. In 1967 the company opened its Westgate location, at 12th and Kiwanis Avenue, followed in 1974 with the Eastgate store at 10th and Cliff Avenue. The original downtown store was also closed in 1974 and converted into the company's headquarters, where it would remain until new offices were built in 1991. John Griffin took advantage of the larger format to become a quasi–mass merchandiser by expanding his product mix. He also tried his hand at selling tires and adding a bakery, neither of which panned out because the size of competitors put him at a disadvantage. He did have success with seasonal garden centers set up in the stores' parking lots, which became a yearly staple at Lewis Drug. About the only items John Griffin would not carry were beer and liquor. John Griffin's character, in truth, was as much a key to the success of Lewis Drug as was product selection and low prices. His availability and constant interaction with customers set the tone for the entire organization and established the commitment to customer service that became a hallmark of the stores.

NEXT GENERATION JOINS THE COMPANY

In 1978 Mark Griffin joined his father at Lewis Drug. The younger Griffin had been helping out since the age of 10 when he was assigned the task of cutting up cardboard boxes and cleaning a store parking lot. He worked in the warehouse and drove a truck during high school and college. After attending the University of South Dakota and Arizona State University Business School, Griffin lived in Atlanta for a while before returning to Sioux Falls to work in investment securities. His father, along with George Frederickson, persuaded him to come to work for Lewis Drug and make a career out of it. Although it involved a cut in pay, the younger Griffin finally agreed.

While Mark Griffin was learning the business, Lewis Drug continued to expand in the 1980s. The Southwest store, located at 41st Street and Marion Road in Sioux Falls, opened in 1984. Two years later John Griffin realized a long-held dream, becoming sole owner of Lewis Drug. But just two months after buying out the Frederickson family, John Griffin died, leaving the business to his son, who had learned his lessons well on how to prosper in a world increasingly dominated by giant chains. He added video rentals in the mid-1980s. Not only did low rental prices attract customers who might make additional purchases while in the store, the return of the video brought them back to the store for a second visit.

The number of stores also began to increase under Mark Griffin's leadership. In 1989 the Southeast store, at 26th Street and Sycamore, opened. A year later the chain's 1956-built store was replaced with a new unit located six blocks away on property that John Griffin had purchased in 1974 in anticipation of the city's growth. His intuition was borne out: The new Lewis Drug was positioned on the state's second busiest intersection, 41st Street and Minnesota Avenue. Although slightly smaller than the 60,000-square-foot store it replaced, the new Southgate location offered wider aisles and improved lighting and such new service

KEY DATES

1942: Jesse Lewis and George Frederickson open the first Lewis Drug store in Sioux Falls.
1946: Store manager John Griffin buys out Lewis.
1947: Store in Mankato, Minnesota, opens.
1956: Second Sioux Falls store opens.
1974: Original downtown store is closed; building is converted into firm's headquarters.
1978: Mark Griffin joins the company.
1986: John Griffin becomes sole owner, but dies two months later.
1997: Lewis Drug reaches $50 million in annual sales.
1999: Family Drug chain is acquired with a joint venture partner.
2002: Company sales for the year top $100 million mark.
2005: New distribution center opens.

offerings as money orders and check cashing, UPS and postal service substations, and a Ticketmaster outlet.

GROWTH IN AN ERA OF MANAGED HEALTH CARE

At the start of the 1990s Lewis Drug expanded into more aspects of the healthcare market in light of the increasing importance of managed healthcare. With the construction of the new Southgate store, the company reached an agreement to build a 10,000-square-foot satellite unit located adjacent to the nearby Central Plains Clinic, providing patients with the ability to conveniently fill prescriptions and make other home healthcare purchases. The success of this venture led to an alliance with Sioux Valley Hospital, the largest in South Dakota. In November 1995 a 25,000-square-foot outpatient care facility, Midwestern Health Services, was tacked onto the Westgate store. Although Midwestern Health leased the space from Lewis—to offer nurse contracting, medical training, mastectomy fittings, oxygen, and other services—the two operations were seamlessly integrated, the boundaries virtually indiscernible to Midwestern's patients. The clinic's waiting area led into Lewis Drug's pharmacy and durable medical equipment section, from which the rest of the store was accessible.

Another growing source of income for Lewis Drug in the early 1990s was the institutional sale of prescription drugs. The company started out supplying a nursing home, leading to the 1992 hiring of a salesperson to call on other nursing homes, hospitals, and medical professionals. Four years later a five-person sales force was responsible for the growing business, the customers of which included retirement communities and South Dakota's penitentiary system. Also in 1995 Lewis Drug acquired an independent pharmacy that commanded 80 percent of the Sioux Falls ostomy supplies market. Its former owner and his trained staffed then formed an ostomy department in the Eastgate store and grew the market share even further.

Although Sioux Falls was a regional shopping mecca, attracting rural customers from as far away as 120 miles in all directions, Lewis Drug was so entrenched in the market that it did not face much of a threat from national drugstore chains. Nevertheless, it still had to contend with the likes of Wal-Mart and Target, forcing it to remain nimble to stave off competition. The chain's video business continued to thrive, performing so well that a pair of video rental chains tried to persuade Griffin to allow them to operate their concepts within Lewis Drug locations. The stores continued to sell grills but dropped less-expensive charcoal grills for higher-end gas and charcoal units, leading to strong growth in this category. Pet departments were also expanded, floral departments added, and in 1997, for the first time in its history, Lewis Drug began to sell beer and wine, products that sold quite well.

Lewis Drug also remained unafraid to pursue new ventures. In 1996 Lewis Drug opened a 15,000-square-foot store within a 60,000-square-foot building housing a Jubilee Foods supermarket located in the affluent Sioux Falls–area bedroom community of Brandon, South Dakota. Both stores shared a single set of cash registers, with Lewis' computer system using universal product codes to sort out sales between the partners.

FAMILY DRUG CHAIN ACQUISITION LEADS TO NEW FORMAT STORES

Revenues reached the $50 million mark for Lewis Drug and its nine stores in 1997. The chain doubled its number of units in 1999 with the acquisition of the 11-store Family Drug chain, operating in two South Dakota, three Minnesota, and six Iowa farming communities, all located within 100 miles of Sioux Falls. Lewis Drug took on a partner in Sioux Valley Hospital (later known as Sanford Health). While the two shared ownership, Lewis ran all of the operations with the exception of home healthcare. The Family Drug name was subsequently replaced by the Lewis Family Drug banner. Although the new stores were much smaller than Lewis Drug outlets, ranging in size from 7,000 to 10,000 square feet, they also housed successful video departments and did a strong business in consumables. Nevertheless, Lewis Drug hoped to take advantage of its merchandising success to improve the front-end business of their new stores. It would take some time, however, before the company learned how to maximize sales in smaller footprint stores.

Lewis Drug maintained its pattern of steady growth in the 21st century despite a number of challenges, including a nationwide shortage of pharmacists, pharmacy margins being squeezed by managed care providers, and ever increasing competition on front-end sales. The company acquired Dell Rapids, South Dakota-based Ray's Drug Store in 2000, increasing the number of units to 21, all of which combined to generate $85 million in sales for the year. Sales reached the $100 million level in 2001, when the company added its 22nd store through acquisition. Despite a deteriorating economy, the company enjoyed a prosperous year in large part because of its sound management.

GROWTH DESPITE CHALLENGE

Discipline and creativity became even more important at this time due to the opening of four Walgreens stores and a pair of Wal-Mart Supercenters. Although Sioux Falls offered more retail outlets per capita than any other market in the United States, Lewis Drug continued to write almost half of all prescriptions in the area. Sioux Falls, repeatedly listed as one of the best places to live in the United States by *Money* magazine, was experiencing a population surge, presenting Lewis Drug with the challenge of introducing its brand to newcomers who were already well familiar with the likes of Walgreens, Wal-Mart, and Target, but were strangers to the Lewis Drug name. Moreover, the company sought to appeal to younger consumers, the major customers of the future. In order to accomplish these ends, the chain began spending more money on television advertising and began buying spots on local radio stations that catered to a younger demographic.

Lewis Drug added a pair of stores in 2002 and grew sales to $104 million. The following year it opened its tenth Lewis store, a 45,000-square-foot unit in Madison, South Dakota, replacing the store it had acquired two years earlier, remodeled another one of the large footprint stores, and opened four Lewis Family Drug stores. Two more of the smaller format stores were added through acquisition in 2004: Scott's Pharmacy in Sioux Falls and Prairie Pharmacy in Lennox, South Dakota. The company also saw plans fall through to open a larger distribution center and new headquarters outside Sioux Falls. More successful was the opening of a Gourmet Coffee Centers outlet in the Southgate store, a leased department offering specialty coffee, sandwiches, and pastries.

Sales from 26 stores totaled $115 million in 2004. More leased departments were added in 2005, including another Gourmet Coffee unit and a pair of Wells Fargo bank branches. The chain also added drive-through pharmacies to about half of its stores. Three new units were added to the chain in 2005, a Lewis Drug store in Brookings, South Dakota, and a pair of Lewis Family Drug units, one in Canton, South Dakota, and a second in a Sioux Falls clinic. The year also brought the purchase of a 130,000-square-foot warehouse/headquarters, allowing the company to vacate and sell its overcrowded 28,000-square-foot distribution center.

A FUTURE OVERSHADOWED BY MEDICAID AND MEDICARE?

Sales held steady at $115 million in 2005, the lack of growth the result of Medicaid cuts and low Medicare Part D rates, a cause of increasing concern for community pharmacies across the country. The issue continued to adversely impact the industry in 2006. Lewis Drug was able to grow revenues to $121.9 million, aided in large part by the opening of two new stores, bringing the total to 30, as well as by the chain's strong front-end sales, but Medicaid and Medicare remained a worry. Mark Griffin, a onetime chairman of the National Association of Chain Drug Stores, appealed to politicians in the states where his company did business, but parties that benefited from the status quo proved more powerful and no help was forthcoming.

To maintain its edge in the marketplace Lewis Drugs made changes to the layouts of its large stores and new merchandise was added in 2006 and 2007. The goal was to make them more shopper-friendly, in large measure to appeal to young families. Pet supplies were bolstered and upscale branded kitchen appliances were added. Always willing to buck conventional wisdom, Lewis Drug moved food and pantry items to the front of the store as a matter of convenience for customers who needed to pick up only a couple items. Traditionally such products were tucked in the back of drugstores, forcing customers to pass through a good portion of the store in hopes that they might buy other items. Despite the competitive nature of Sioux Falls, plans were in the works to open an eleventh large format Lewis Drug store in the area, although as of

2007, the company had not revealed a prospective location.

Ed Dinger

PRINCIPAL DIVISIONS

Lewis Drug; Lewis Family Drug.

PRINCIPAL COMPETITORS

ShopKo Stores; Walgreens Co.; Wal-Mart Stores, Inc.

FURTHER READING

"Family Drug Buy Doubles Lewis' Size," *Drug Store News,* August 24, 1998, p. 4.

Grauvogl, Ann, "Lewis Drug Builds on Regional Strength to Keep Growing," *Sioux Falls (S.Dak.) Argus Leader,* July 27, 2005, p. 5A.

Griffin, Marie, "Lewis Drug's Healthcare Reach Stretches Beyond Pharmacy," *Drug Store News,* April 29, 1996, p. 24.

"Innovative Approach a Hallmark of Lewis," *Chain Drug Review,* April 28, 1997, p. 244.

"Intense Competition Makes Lewis Stronger," *Chain Drug Review,* April 29, 2002, p. 236.

Johnson, Michael, "Market Advantage Lies in Ability to Adapt Quickly," *Drug Store News,* September 26, 2005.

Levy, Sandra, "What's Their Secret?" *Drug Topics,* January 7, 2002, p. 34.

"Lewis Builds Business with an Eye on the Future," *Chain Drug Review,* April 26, 2004, p. 195.

"Lewis Capitalizes on Opportunities," *Chain Drug Review,* April 26, 1999, p. 276.

"Lewis Counters Drop in Rx Margins," *Chain Drug Review,* May 1, 2006, p. 210.

"Lewis Holds Its Own in Battle with Retail Powerhouses," *Chain Drug Review,* May 2, 2005, p. 197.

"Lewis Meets Challenges," *Chain Drug Review,* April 27, 1998, p. 248.

"Lewis Meets Competitive Challenge in Sioux Falls," *Chain Drug Review,* December 18, 1995, p. 6.

"Lewis Optimistic Despite Challenges," *Chain Drug Review,* April 23, 2007, p. 208.

"Lewis Thrives Despite Competition," *Chain Drug Review,* April 28, 2003, p. 235.

"Lewis Uses 'Guerrilla Retailing' to Counteract Its Competitors," *Chain Drug Review,* April 23, 2001, p. 198.

"Roots in Community Give Lewis an Important Edge," *Chain Drug Review,* June 23, 1997, p. 301.

Swenson, Rob, "Lewis Revamps Marketing Strategy with New Campaign," *Sioux Falls Business Journal,* September 26, 2007.

Symons, Allene, "Lewis Drug's 50th Anniversary," *Drug Store News,* June 21, 1993, p. 104.

LG Corporation

LG Twin Towers
20 Yoido-dong
Yongdungpo-gu
Seoul, 150-010
Republic of Korea
Telephone: (82 02) 3773 2292
Fax: (82 02) 3773 5114
Web site: http://www.lg.net

Public Company
Incorporated: 1947 as Lucky Chemical Industrial Company
Employees: 160,000
Sales: $70.9 billion (2006)
Stock Exchanges: Korea
Ticker Symbol: 003550
NAIC: 551120 Offices of Other Holding Companies

■ ■ ■

LG Corporation is a holding company that operates worldwide through more than 30 companies in the electronics, chemical, and telecom fields. Its electronics subsidiaries manufacture and sell products ranging from electronic and digital home appliances to televisions and mobile telephones, from thin film transistor–liquid crystal displays to security devices and semiconductors. In the chemical industry, subsidiaries manufacture and sell products including cosmetics, industrial textiles, rechargeable batteries and toner products, polycarbonates, medicines, and surface decorative materials. Its telecom products include long-distance and international phone services, mobile and broadband telecommunications services, as well as consulting and telemarketing services. LG also operates the Coca-Cola Korea Bottling Company, manages real estate, offers management consulting, and operates professional sports clubs.

COSMETICS AND CHEMICALS 1947–57

The earliest predecessor of LG was the Lak Hui (Lucky) Chemical Company, founded in Korea by the Koo and Huh families in 1947. The company's first product was a line of cosmetic creams. It then expanded into other petroleum products, including caps for the cream jars and other plastic molds.

The business remained small through its early years. Korea had suffered severe economic disruption during World War II, and virtual ruin by its partition and subsequent invasion by Soviet-backed armies from North Korea. The U.S. government, however, had a strong interest in seeing both Japan and Korea transformed into large industrial economies in order to check the advance of communism in the East. With substantial foreign aid, industrial programs were created that helped companies such as Lucky to succeed and grow.

Lucky was regarded as a strategic industrial resource; it was Korea's only plastics manufacturer, and held great foreign exchange earnings potential. To that end, Lucky created an export agency in 1953. The following year, the company developed the first domestic toothpaste in Korea, Luk Hui Dental Cream, and a year later began producing the first PVC pipe in the country.

COMPANY PERSPECTIVES

The LG Way represents LG's core beliefs, values, and aspirations. It illustrates a vision structure that guides the thoughts and actions of LG people in attaining the ultimate goal of becoming No. 1 LG. It stipulates the way in which this goal is reached through the practice of *Jeong-Do* Management and the realization of LG's management principles, "Creating value for customers" and "Respecting human dignity."

ADDING CONSUMER ELECTRONICS 1958–65

Observing the success of Japanese consumer goods exporters such as Matsushita and Mitsubishi, Koo decided that Lucky was ready for diversification into electronics. Lucky created an electrical appliance manufacturer in 1958 called Goldstar Company, Ltd., whose first product was a simple electric fan.

The following year, with a new factory located at Pusan, Goldstar introduced the country's first line of domestically produced radios. These products were unsophisticated and generally unfit for sale abroad. In addition, Goldstar lacked marketing arms in foreign markets. Parallel to Matsushita's experience, Goldstar's products would first satisfy domestic demand (and thereby substitute for more expensive imports) until design changes and improvements could be incorporated. Goldstar would then enter the international market with more thoroughly tested, modern, and competitive products.

Protected from foreign competitors by rigid import restrictions, Lucky Chemical and Goldstar continued to prosper during the early 1960s. Much of the companies' profits were dedicated to the acquisition of new petrochemical technologies and the establishment of a wider market presence. New product development was delayed, hampered by limited engineering resources and expensive patent licensing. Despite these disadvantages, Goldstar managed to successfully market a refrigerator in 1965 and a television a year later. Both were the first domestically manufactured appliances of their kind. Goldstar was the first Korean manufacturer to establish a solid toehold in electronics export markets, for example, supplying televisions to various U.S. companies, such as Sears and J.C. Penney. Those buyers sold the units under their own brand names. Goldstar gradually earned a reputation as a supplier of low-cost, high-quality electronic components and appliances.

SOUTH KOREAN BUSINESS GROUP STRUCTURE

Lucky and Goldstar were divisions of a *chaebol,* or business group. Chaebol were massive groups of interrelated companies that dominated South Korean industry. Rising to prominence after the Korean War, South Korean chaebol were founded and operated by prominent, or "royal," families. Different chaebol generally concentrated on separate markets, such as those for chemicals or automobiles. Throughout the middle 1900s, chaebol were characterized by hierarchical, centralized control, which was usually exerted by members of the founding family. Chaebol traditionally had a central planning division, or secretary's office, which was directly subordinate to the chaebol chairman. The office would oversee all of the group's activities and was responsible for strategic management.

Park Chung Hee, a general who had seized power in South Korea in 1962, approached the chaebol in an effort to improve living standards in Korea. Since many government officials held financial stakes in the conglomerates (a Lucky-Goldstar director even served in Park's cabinet), the chaebol were often afforded special privileges. Lucky Chemical and Goldstar proposed that South Korea's export earnings could be increased if the chaebol had better engineers. The company asked for, and got, government funds to sponsor students at leading Western universities. It was a heavy investment whose benefits would not be realized for years, but the education scheme was essential to maintaining the company's position.

RAPID GROWTH 1966–79

During this period, Lucky Chemical established joint ventures with foreign firms, gaining access to new technology. In 1966, Lucky teamed with Continental Carbon. The company, called Lucky Continental Carbon, became the largest Korean manufacturer of carbon black, a basic raw material in rubber products. Lucky entered into a far more significant joint venture the following year when it established the Honam Oil Refinery in conjunction with Caltex Petroleum. Honam was Korea's first privately owned, as well as its largest, refinery. The complex eliminated Korea's dependence on more expensive imported oil products and even permitted substantial export earnings.

When Koo In Hwoi died in 1969, the chairmanship of Lucky and Goldstar went to his eldest son, Koo Cha Kyung. Nepotism, far from being regarded as dishonorable or unfair, was widely practiced in the company, as in many Asian companies. Members of the

KEY DATES

1947: Koo In Hwoi and Huh Joon Koo establish Lak Hui (Lucky) Chemical Industrial Corp. (later called LG Chemical Ltd.).
1958: Goldstar Co., Ltd, is. established (later called LG Electronics Inc.).
1959: Goldstar produces Korea's first radio.
1965: Goldstar develops the first refrigerator manufactured in Korea.
1969: Koo Cha-Kyung becomes LG's second chairman.
1974: Lak Hui Chemical Industry changes its name to Lucky Co. Ltd.
1977: First Goldstar branded product is exported to the United States.
1995: Lucky-Goldstar changes its name to LG Group and Koo Bon Moo becomes third chairman.
2003: LG Group shifts from *chaebol* to holding company structure.
2004: LG Group creates two holding companies, LG Corp. and GS Holdings.

Koo and Huh families occupied top management positions within both companies and their subsidiaries, although as the company grew, professional managers came to dominate. During the 1970s, the chaebol created 20 subsidiaries and established new plant space for them, mostly in extreme southern Korea, where land is flatter and there are more deepwater ports.

Goldstar's revenues continued to swell as it extended its reach into new industries and marketing channels. For example, it introduced its first product bearing the Goldstar name brand in the United States in 1977. The success of that 19-inch black-and-white television prompted it to export several lines of low-cost electronics during the late 1970s and 1980s that were sold under the Goldstar label. Importantly, Goldstar also began to advance into high-tech industry segments during the 1970s. For instance, it invested massive amounts of capital to establish its own semiconductor manufacturing division. Its initial goal was to produce microchips for use in its own electronic components. However, Goldstar's long-term strategy was to use the semiconductor division to position the company to compete in the much more advanced electronics and telecommunications industries that were emerging.

POLITICAL CHANGE FORCES REORGANIZATION 1980–85

Park, who had eventually been elected as a civilian president, was assassinated in 1979. With his death, much government favoritism was eliminated. All the chaebol had to become more self-reliant, drawing upon their own resources to guarantee markets, seal deals, and cover risks.

These new conditions precipitated an industrial reorganization for Lucky and Goldstar. Lucky Chemical and Goldstar Electronics were made subsidiaries of a larger parent company, officially referred to as Lucky-Goldstar. The company maintained a very positive public image, owing to its gentle character and ability to avoid scandal. In 1980, the Lucky-Goldstar group had sales of more than $4 billion annually.

Various chemical-related businesses still accounted for the majority of that revenue. Encouraged by the success of its electronics and appliance businesses, though, the chaebol decided to shift its focus away from chemicals. To that end, Lucky-Goldstar invested heavily in Goldstar Co. during the early and mid-1980s, boosting production capacity with both domestic and foreign production facilities. Goldstar even became the first Korean manufacturer to set up a manufacturing plant in the United States. Built in 1983, its Huntsville, Alabama, television plant was churning out more than one million color televisions and microwave ovens annually by the late 1980s. Goldstar augmented production efforts with a boost in advertising expenditures from $2 million in 1983 to $12 million in 1984.

In addition to overseas efforts, Goldstar launched an aggressive growth program at home. It expanded production capacity for virtually every one of its major products during the early and mid-1980s and broadened its product lines to include a number of high-tech goods. Most notable was Goldstar's construction of a new factory south of Seoul, in Pyongtaek. The plant, which opened in 1984, represented Goldstar's intent to become a leading global supplier of VCRs, personal computers, facsimile machines, and other relatively high-tech consumer and business devices. In fact, the company publicly announced a goal of deriving a full 40 percent of its sales by the mid-1980s from high-margin, advanced technology products, rather than from its traditional core of relatively low-tech, low-priced commodity goods.

Summing up Goldstar's basic tactic during the 1980s was one of its advertising slogans: "Expensive electronics without the expense." The strategy seemed to benefit the chaebol during the decade. Goldstar established a solid presence in domestic and international markets for microwave ovens and televisions, as well as for refrigerators, washing machines, and other major appliances. As a result, Lucky-Goldstar's revenues rocketed more than fivefold to $22 billion between 1980 and 1989. Much of that gain was attributable to electronics, which was supplying more than 30 percent of Lucky-Goldstar's revenue by the end of the decade, while 25 percent came from chemicals and 33 percent from various trade and financial services companies.

MAJOR PROBLEMS AT GOLDSTAR 1985–89

Although Goldstar's sales gains during the 1980s may have seemed impressive to the casual observer, its financial performance began to wane in the mid-1980s and the company experienced a series of setbacks. Goldstar's woes were the result of a variety of factors, including shifting global economies, labor strife, and greater domestic competition. For example, Goldstar's dominance of Korea's domestic electronics industry, which it had enjoyed since the 1960s, was challenged by the Samsung chaebol, particularly beginning in the early 1980s. Samsung's electronics division surpassed Goldstar in both sales and profits by 1984 and continued to widen its lead throughout the decade. By the late 1980s, Goldstar's domestic market share had fallen from 45 percent early in the decade to just 36 percent.

Illustrative of Goldstar's difficulties during the 1980s were its reversals in the semiconductor business. In an effort to compete with rival Samsung, Goldstar had invested heavily to develop more sophisticated chip technology. Unfortunately, the semiconductors it developed had limited market applications and Goldstar had trouble mastering the production technology. The end result was that Goldstar was unable to achieve savings by producing its chips in-house, and it also failed to establish itself as a significant global chip manufacturer. Meanwhile, Samsung successfully transitioned into new semiconductor technology and eroded Goldstar's market share.

Adding to Goldstar's technology and competition woes in the 1980s were labor and economic setbacks. Because the Korean government restricted access to overseas financing sources, Goldstar was forced to fund much of its growth during the early and mid-1980s with loans from short-term domestic financiers. The unfortunate result by the late 1980s was that Goldstar was paying out more than 85 percent of its operating income to cover interest on its massive debt load. At the same time, Goldstar's primary export market, the United States, was maturing. Ongoing competition from Japanese producers exacerbated the export dilemma. To make matters worse, Goldstar lost much of its important low-cost labor advantage in the late 1980s when its workers rebelled. Frustrated union members went on strike, which ultimately cost the company $600 million between 1988 and 1990. They forced Goldstar to greatly boost wages, and as a result the company had to raise prices an average of 8 percent.

LOSING GROUND ON QUALITY AND MARKET SHARE

Goldstar's greatest problem by the end of the 1980s, however, was that it was losing its reputation for quality. By 1990, for example, *Consumer Reports* ranked Goldstar's VCRs last in a comparison with 18 other brands. Part of Goldstar's quality problems stemmed from its reliance on outside suppliers—a faulty chip imported from Japan in 1987, for instance, nearly terminated Goldstar's American VCR operations. Nonetheless, it was also the result of Lucky-Goldstar's unwieldy organizational structure. By the late 1980s the chaebol was comprised of more than 30 different companies operating without cooperation. Research and development efforts were being duplicated in different divisions, and managers had lost touch with overall organizational objectives.

Quality and management problems, combined with a stronger won (the Korean currency unit), caused Goldstar's exports to the United States to crumble from $834 million in 1988 to just $535 million in 1990. That decline, along with plummeting domestic market share, caused Goldstar's net profit margins to drop by more than 100 percent during the period. The company was befuddled and had lost its focus. In 1984, for instance, management predicted that U.S. sales would top $1 billion by 1986. By 1990 that goal seemed like a foggy dream. Furthermore, Goldstar had fallen well short of its objective of generating 40 percent of its revenues from high-tech products—by 1990 only 12 percent of sales came from such goods.

The origin of many of Goldstar's problems in the late 1980s was the chaebol structure. Early in Lucky-Goldstar's history, the centralized, hierarchical structure of the chaebol had been an asset. The Koo family had made virtually all major decisions, and directives were regularly dispatched to executives from breakfast meetings over which the family presided. As the chaebol mushroomed in size, however, the authoritative nature of the organization became a liability. Importantly, the slow hierarchical decision-making process had become obsolete in the fast-moving global economy of the 1980s.

MANAGEMENT INNOVATIONS AND GLOBAL VISION 1990–94

Recognizing the urgency of the situation, the 62-year-old Koo took drastic measures beginning in 1989 to turn the ailing Lucky-Goldstar around. Most importantly, he handed control of Goldstar to Lee Hun Jo, a 27-year Lucky-Goldstar veteran.

Koo cemented Lee's independence when, in 1991, he gave a written guarantee of autonomy to Lee in a public ceremony. In a remarkable departure from chaebol tradition, Lee was allowed to run the company as he liked and was only required to report to Koo twice each year. Lee quickly reorganized Goldstar into two major groups: consumer electronics, and personal computers and office equipment. Products that did not fit into those divisions were spun off, distributed to contractors, or absorbed by other Lucky-Goldstar electronics companies.

During the early 1990s Lee virtually transformed Goldstar from a lagging electronics producer to a leading, global high-tech contender. Lee, who spoke both English and Japanese fluently, integrated proven Western and Japanese management techniques. His efforts permeated Goldstar's management and work force. Lee jettisoned entire layers of management and successfully forged an amiable working relationship between top management and labor. He also increased promotional spending in an effort to woo former customers, and reasserted Goldstar's plan to assume a lead role in high-technology markets.

Largely as a result of Lee's efforts, Goldstar staged a major comeback. Sales vaulted from $4 billion in 1990 to more than $6 billion in 1994, and net income rose to a record $120 million after slumping to around $12 million. More importantly, by 1994 Goldstar had regained its number one position in the South Korean market for color televisions, refrigerators, and washing machines, and it had suddenly resumed its contention for global semiconductor market share.

Among the company's pivotal breakthroughs was a unique new refrigerator, introduced in the early 1990s, which was designed to keep Korea's national dish, kimchi, fresh and odorless for a long time. Likewise, Goldstar was achieving marked gains overseas by focusing on emerging markets like Russia and Vietnam while at the same time increasing North American sales through overseas manufacturing and partnerships with U.S. companies. In fact, Goldstar's U.S. sales jumped 17 percent in 1994 to around $1.2 billion.

GROWTH THROUGH DIVERSIFICATION

Lucky-Goldstar was reorganizing and expanding in other areas as well. It combined Lucky Pharm and other of its companies into a single chemical arm, Lucky Ltd. In 1990 Lucky Ltd. formed a new manufacturing joint venture with Owens Corning Fiberglass Corp. to make products for reinforced plastics sold in various Korean markets. The following year, taking advantage of a new Korean law that allowed chaebol to become openly involved in national banking, Lucky-Goldstar became the leading shareholder in the Goldstar Investment and Finance Company.

At the same time, Goldstar Information and Communications was producing telecommunications systems and products for developing nations. Lucky Securities Company Ltd, a brokerage and underwriting provider, operated 55 offices in Korea with a subsidiary in London and branches in New York, Hong Kong, and Tokyo. As well, Lucky-Goldstar's company CD-1 was producing CDs of pop music.

Also in 1994, Goldstar invested heavily to develop technology related to advanced liquid crystal displays (LCDs), which are used in notebook computers and other applications. The Dutch electronics firm Philips invested $1.6 billion in a 50-50 joint venture to make LCDs using Philips' proprietary technology. That year, Goldstar captured about 35 percent of its sales from home appliances, 25 percent from televisions, 13 percent from computer and office equipment, and the remainder from miscellaneous audio and video gear.

CORPORATE OVERHAUL

In 1995, Koo Bon Moo, the founder's grandson, took over as the third chairman of the conglomerate. He changed the chaebol's name to LG Group, eliminated seven management levels, and paid $351 million for 58 percent of Zenith Electronics Corp., the largest electronics company and last domestic TV manufacturer in the U.S. LG's agenda for the acquisition was not only to command a significant segment of the U.S. television market, but also to have its executives learn American management techniques. By 1996, LG, the third largest chaebol, behind Hyundai and Samsung, had sales of $55 billion.

The Asian economic crisis in 1997–98 hit LG and the other big chaebol hard. With its large chaebol facing bankruptcy because of huge debts, the Korean government pushed them to consolidate duplicative and unprofitable operations and become more efficient. LG responded by trying to get rid of 90 operations. Further, in 1999, after much government pressure, LG Group agreed to sell its semiconductor business, LG Semicon Co. Ltd., to Hyundai Electronics Industries.

Later that year, LG merged LG Securities Co. with LG Merchant Banking Corp. and moved into the telecommunications field, purchasing and offering wired and wireless services to complement its own mobile telecom operations and telecom equipment manufacturing businesses. Koo used one of LG's major telecom acquisitions, Dacom Corporation, as a model for corporate transparency. Independent directors made up half of the board, and controlled the audit process. Additionally, in 2000 LG Group merged LG Electronics Co. and LG Information & Communications Co., to expand its capacity to develop and produce next generation mobile telephones.

GROWING INTO THE 21ST CENTURY

In 2001, the LG Group, with some 50 affiliates worldwide, had revenues of $81 billion; for 2002, revenues rose to $95 billion. In 2003, LG completed a 5-year radical restructuring, shifting from the chaebol model to become LG Corporation, a Western-style holding company for the LG Group. Even with the new structure, the Koo and Huh families owned enough shares to keep control of the corporation. In addition, the families also acquired several LG companies that were spun off as separate entities during the reorganization.

LG Group further restructured in 2004, splitting its components into two holding companies. LG Corporation, under the Koo family, became the holding company for the manufacturing companies, including LG Chem and LG Electronics. GS Holdings, under the Huh family assumed responsibility for LG's retail units, including LG-Caltex Oil, LG Mart and LG Home Shopping.

The year 2005 was difficult for LG, as it adjusted to the loss of the cash-generating retail divisions as well as to greater competition, higher prices, and sluggish domestic market conditions. However, the LG corporate "smiley" logo was becoming one of the most recognizable brands in the world. LG Electronics was the number one maker of home air conditioners, a top producer of other home appliances, and had 7.5 percent of the global market share of cellular handsets, making it number five in the world.

By 2008, LG, particularly its LG Electronics division, was gaining notice for its design-centered products. LG offered a touch-screen cell phone before Apple's iPhone did, built the Venus music cell phone for Verizon, and developed new designs for large-screen plasma TVs in hopes of gaining market share in the competitive U.S. market. LG aimed to be the third largest brand for consumer electronics by 2010.

Dave Mote
Updated, Ellen Wernick

PRINCIPAL SUBSIDIARIES

LG Electronics; LG Philips LCD; LG Chem; LG Household & Health Care; LG Life Sciences; LG Tele-Com; LG Dacom.

PRINCIPAL COMPETITORS

ASHAI KASEI Corporation; Electrolux AB; Matsushita Electric Industrial Co. Ltd.; Whirlpool Corporation; Samsung; Sony Corporation.

FURTHER READING

"Adapting to New Environments," *Business Korea,* September 1992, p. 54.

"Bringing in the Big Boys," *Economist* (U.S.), February 9, 1991, p. 86.

Bulik, Beth Snyder, "LG's $100 Mil Charge Apes Samsung Tack," *Advertising Age,* June 21, 2004, pp. 1–33.

Byung Hoo Suh, "S. Korea Conglomerates Move In on Record Biz," *Billboard,* April 30, 1994, p. 56.

Carson, Phil, "LG's 'Mass Premium' Phones Bring Success," *RCR Wireless News,* April 17, 2006, p. 4.

Chang, Sue, "High Tech and Meaner," *Business Korea,* January 1992, p. 35.

Clifford, Mark, "Electronic Leapfrog," *Far Eastern Economic Review,* November 1987, pp. 80–83.

———, "Seoul-Mates Again," *Far Eastern Economic Review,* March 1990, pp. 46–47.

Clifford, Mark, and Jennifer Veale, "So Much for Reform," *Business Week,* July 26, 1999, p. 46.

Crane, Geoff, "Ailing Goldstar Needs Strong Medicine," *Electronic Business,* August 20, 1990, pp. 67–69.

Darlin, Damon, "Eager to Learn," *Forbes,* August 12, 1996, p. 92.

Doebele, Justin, "Ends and Means," *Forbes,* February 17, 2003.

"Domestic Electronics Industry: Backbone of Korean Exports," *Business Korea,* October 1993, pp. 34–36.

Fitzgerald, Robert, and Young Chan Kim, "Business Strategy, Government and Globalization: Policy and Miscalculation in the Korean Electronics Industry," *Asia Pacific Business Review,* Spring/Summer 2004, pp. 441–62.

"The Giants Stumble," *Economist,* October 18, 1997, p. 67.

"Goldstar Information and Communications: Reaching Out and Touching the World," *Business Korea,* February 1992, p. 43.

Gutierrez, Carl, "Netflix Teams with LG on Streaming Video," *Forbes.com,* January 3, 2008.

Hur Nam-Il, "A Starry-Eyed Vision," *Business Korea,* April 1997, p. 52.

Ihlwan, Moon, Cliff Edwards, and Roger Crockett, "Korea's LG: The Next Samsung?" *Business Week Online,* January 13, 2005.

———, "LG Bets Big on TV Design," *BusinessWeek,* January 16, 2008.

Kennedy, Kristen, "LG Spreads Its Wings," *Digital Connect,* January 1, 2005, p. 20.

Kharif, Olga, "Verizon's Venus Is a Beauty," *Business Week Online,* December 7, 2007.

"Koo Bon Moo," *Business Week,* July 3, 2000, p. 36.

Kraar, Louis, "Korea's Comeback ... Don't Expect a Miracle," *Fortune,* May 25, 1998, p. 120.

Lee, B. J., "Out of the Box: LG Electronics Is Killer in TV Chips, but Not TVs," *Newsweek International,* June 6, 2005, p. 66.

"LG Corp.," Company Insight Center, *BusinessWeek,* http://investing.businessweek.com.

"LG Electronics: Suddenly Top Tier," *Chief Executive* (U.S.), March 2005, p. S8.

"LG Launches $13 Billion North American Product Push," *InformationWeek,* January 9, 2008.

"LG Poised to Acquire Dacom," *Network Briefing,* October 5, 1999.

"LG's 60 Years of Unstoppable Progress," *Business Korea,* January 2007, p. 68.

"Lightening the Load at the Top," *Business Korea,* April 1991, pp. 26–28.

"Making Waves," *SPC Asia,* March 2005, pp. 14–18.

Manners, David, "The Chasing Pack," *Electronics Weekly,* October 19, 1994, p. 28.

Mi Young, Ahn, "Merger to Get LGE Back on Track," *Electronic News,* June 19, 2000, p. 16.

Nakarmi, Laxmi, "At Lucky-Goldstar, the Koos Loosen the Reins," *Business Week,* February 18, 1991, pp. 72–73.

———, "Goldstar Is Burning Bright," *Business Week,* September 26, 1994, pp. 129–30.

"Owens-Corning Participate in Korean Joint Venture," *Pacific Business News,* May 21, 1990, p. 26.

Robertson, Jack, "Hyundai Out on Top—Will Acquire LG Semicon," *Electronic Buyers' News,* January 11, 1999, p. 1.

Schuman, Michael, "Outward Bound: With Plenty of Cool Gadgets, LG's Kim Ssang Su Is Building a Global Brand," *Time,* June 21, 2004, p. A4.

Shin, Yoo Keun, Richard Steer, and Gerardo R. Ungson, *The Chaebol,* New York: Harper & Row, 1989.

"South Korea's Lucky Pharm to Consolidate," *SCRIP World Pharmaceutical News,* September 20, 1991, p. 12.

Tarr, Greg, "LG Says Network Key to Firm's Future," *TWICE: This Week in Consumer Electronics,* July 25, 2004, pp. 1–12.

Tong, Alfred, "LG Chem Changes Direction," *Asian Chemical News,* June 7, 2004, p. 8.

———, "LG Group to Split Business," *Asian Chemical News,* May 3, 2004, p. 7.

———, "LG: Lots of Possibilities ... and Hope," *Asian Chemical News,* August 8, 2005, p. 9.

"Unfinished Business," *Economist,* April 19, 2003, pp. 8–10.

Verespej, Michael A., "Can Goldstar Earn Its Gold Star," *Industry Week,* November 30, 1987, pp. 33–36.

"War of the Suds," *Business Korea,* January 1993, pp. 32–33.

Macy's, Inc.

7 West Seventh Street
Cincinnati, Ohio 45202
U.S.A.
Telephone: (513) 579-7000
Toll Free: (800) 261-5385
Fax: (513) 579-7185
Web site: http://www.macysinc.com

Public Company
Incorporated: 1929 as Federated Department Stores
Employees: 188,000
Sales: $26.97 billion (2006)
Stock Exchanges: New York
Ticker Symbol: M
NAIC: 452110 Department Stores; 454113 Mail-Order Houses; 551120 Offices of Other Holding Companies

■ ■ ■

Formerly known as Federated Department Stores, Macy's, Inc., is one of the largest department store operators in the United States. Its stores, under the Macy's and Bloomingdale's names, are generally located in large shopping malls and offer men's and women's clothing, cosmetics, accessories, home furnishings, and other consumer goods. At the end of 2007, the company was operating 866 Macy's and Bloomingdale's stores in 45 states, the District of Columbia, Guam, and Puerto Rico. It also reached consumers through macys.com, bloomingdales.com, and Bloomingdale's By Mail catalog and e-commerce operations. Federated changed its name to Macy's, Inc., name in 2007.

HISTORY OF THE MACY NAME IN RETAILING

After a few failed retail ventures, Rowland H. Macy opened R.H. Macy and Co. in Manhattan in 1858. After one year in business, the store reported impressive sales of $85,000.

In a time when most stores routinely sold on credit, Macy was unique in that he instituted a cash-only policy not only for customers but for himself as well. No Macy's inventory was purchased on credit, and no Macy's credit account was issued until well into the 1950s.

The new Manhattan establishment benefited from the founder's advertising and promotional skills as well as his product line instincts. By 1870, when sales broke the $1 million mark, the loyal clientele could purchase not only dry goods, but such items as men's hosiery and ties, linens and towels, fancy imported goods, costume jewelry, silver, and clocks.

Macy's son was not interested in the retail business, so Macy passed ownership into other family hands. Through the years, the company introduced innovations now considered commonplace in the industry. In 1887, Lazarus Straus and his sons became partners in the company. Straus had for years leased space in Macy's to operate a chinaware department, which accounted for some 20 percent of the store's sales.

Under the new partnership, Macy's matched and outpriced its rivals. Macy's sales rose to $5 million within a year and subsequently continued to grow by 10 percent annually. The Straus brothers introduced their odd-price policy, now used virtually everywhere in U.S. retailing. By charging $4.98 instead of $5.00, for

COMPANY PERSPECTIVES

Macy's, Inc., is a premier national retailer with brands that reflect the spirit of America. The timeless values that made our nation strong are the same values that make our company strong: a belief in the promise of the future with the energy and determination to get us there; a belief that our heritage mirrors the optimism, inclusion and integrity that provide for both stability and growth; a belief that taking advantage of the right opportunities will continue to lead us to success in all that we do.

example, the store sought to entice consumers with prices that seemed reasonably low and thereby encourage more spending.

Following in Macy's footsteps, the Strauses brought in line after line of new merchandise, including Oriental rugs, ornate furniture, lavish stationery, bicycles, and even pianos. They also instituted the store's depositor's accounts, in which shoppers could make deposits with the store and then charge purchases against them. This, in effect, provided Macy's with interest-free loans and was a forerunner of installment buying and layaway plans.

In 1896, the Strauses became full owners of Macy's, ending the founding family's line of ownership. They relocated the store to its Herald Square location at 34th Street and Broadway in 1902. No modern convenience was lacking in the Herald Square store. It was equipped with newly designed escalators, pneumatic tubes to move cash or messages, and an air exhaust system that provided the store with a constant supply of fresh air. The store's spacious building had ample fitting rooms, accommodation desks, an information counter, and comfortable restrooms. Macy's also maintained a fleet of comparison shoppers who checked out other stores' prices to be sure Macy's merchandise was competitively priced. Sales increased to $11 million within a year of the move. Called the world's largest store, Macy's Herald Square thrilled tourists and locals alike.

RETAIL EXPANSION AND POSTWAR CHALLENGES

By the end of World War I in 1918, Macy's sales had reached $36 million, twice that of 1914. Macy's next began its expansion into other cities, acquiring LaSalles & Koch Co. in Toledo, Ohio, and Davison-Paxon-Stokes Co. in Atlanta, Georgia. In the 1920s Macy's began the tradition of sponsoring New York City's Thanksgiving Day parade. The public relations impact of the event would later go national when two major television networks began to cover the parade in 1952. Just before the Great Depression, Macy's bought L. Bamberger & Co. of Newark, New Jersey. In the 1940s, it added stores in San Francisco, California, and Kansas City, Missouri. By the late 1940s, Macy's not only ran the world's largest store but was also the largest department store chain in the country.

After World War II, Macy's beefed up its advertising campaign and sought to localize its appeal, billing their outlets as "community stores." Nevertheless, as the postwar economy picked up, New Yorkers no longer craved only the bargains that were Macy's stock in trade but also sought greater variety, doing more shopping and spending at other stores. Macy's stock fell from $3.35 per common share in fiscal 1950 to $2.51 in fiscal 1951. Further problems lay ahead.

In 1952, Schwegmann Brothers, a New Orleans, Louisiana, drugstore chain, contested the Federal Fair Trade Law of 1931 and won its case. The reversal of the 20-year-old practice that allowed some suppliers to set minimum retail prices (intended to help stabilize a Depression-era economy) undercut Macy's competitive strategy. Macy's had undersold its competitors with its six-percent-less-for-cash policy, but since fixed minimum prices were not protected by law, all retailers could lower prices without fear of reprisals by suppliers.

Macy's responded by cutting its prices even further. Still, the huge Herald Square store proved to have several weaknesses. While no one could match the giant's prices across the board, Gimbel could undersell Macy's in pharmaceuticals; Gertz of Long Island, New York, in books; and Bloomingdale's in stationery and menswear. In 1952 Macy's posted the first year of losses in its history. Its battle plan was outmoded. Macy's fumbled in directions it had previously ignored, instituting charge accounts and catering more to its suppliers.

REDEFINING MACY'S STRENGTHS: 1960–75

While the flagship Macy's store struggled, a renaissance began in what had become a division of Macy's: Bamberger's of New Jersey. Acquired by Macy's in the 1920s, the New Jersey retailer was struggling in 1955, when a turnaround and expansion plan was launched, resulting in new outlets in suburbs all over New Jersey. The chain's annual sales rose from $82 million to $500 million in 1962, with its profits being among the highest in the nation and topping even those of the mammoth New York division.

KEY DATES

1858: First successful Macy's retail store opens in Manhattan.
1872: Bloomingdale brothers open East Side Bazaar in New York City.
1896: The Straus family, of the Abraham & Straus retail chain, invests heavily in the Macy's operations.
1924: The first Macy's Thanksgiving Day parade is held.
1929: Federated Department Stores is formed as a holding company for three family-owned department stores: Abraham & Straus, F&R Lazarus & Co. and Shillito's.
1930: Bloomingdale's joins Federated.
1988: Campeau Corporation buys Federated and merges Allied Stores with it.
1989: Federated and Allied declare bankruptcy.
1992: Federated emerges from bankruptcy and goes public; R.H. Macy & Co. declares bankruptcy.
1994: Federated acquires R.H. Macy & Co.
2005: Federated acquires May Department Stores Co.
2007: Federated changes name to Macy's, Inc.

One reason was the use of new customer-oriented merchandising. Instead of buying whatever suppliers offered, Bamberger's bought the top of the line in any new group of goods, and featured that in the most glamorous displays Bamberger's customers had ever seen. The technique garnered notice not only within the Macy's organization but also from top executives at other chains as well. The store began its push out of New Jersey to the south and west in 1968 and by the 1980s had three times as many stores as in the late 1960s. Bamberger's were eventually converted to the Macy's name and format for consistency among the parent's East Coast operations.

On the West Coast, Macy's had acquired the O'Connor, Moffat & Company store as its first California outpost in 1945. This was renamed Macy's in 1947 and became a flagship location in San Francisco's then posh Union Square. By the 1960s, however, like other urban retail centers, Union Square and its surrounding complement of chic shops (including I. Magnin, Liberty House, Bonwit Teller, and Gumps) had fallen victim to urban neglect and decay. Now known as Macy's California and including a total of 12 locations, the West Coast division sought to upgrade its image, aiming its product lines at a more well-heeled buyer. The successful transformation helped Macy's surpass most of its competitors, leaving it as one of the top retailers in the region along with I. Magnin.

In the 1970s at the Herald Square store management shuttered such departments as pharmaceuticals, major appliances, sporting goods, and toys, where it found Macy's could not effectively compete. It also put an end to its focus on household durable goods, a department that suffered heavy competition from such discounters as Korvettes and Sears. In place of the discontinued departments, Macy's increased and refined presentations in certain departments, including linens and domestics, furniture, menswear, and jewelry.

The company remodeled about 35 percent of the space in New York's 16 stores, including the Herald Square store, which benefited from the installation of the Cellar in 1976. Macy's basement, which had been a no-frills depository for bargain merchandise, was transformed into a sparkling esplanade of airy specialty shops offering gourmet foods, yard goods, stationery, baskets, and contemporary housewares. Geared to a trend-conscious consumer, the cross between a European boulevard and a chic suburban mall also offered frequent cooking demonstrations, an old-fashioned apothecary, and a pottery shop complete with a working potter at the wheel. The revitalized Macy's had its biggest holiday season ever in 1976 and increased its annual earnings significantly over the previous year.

The Macy's Miracle, as the turnaround was called by some industry observers, gained momentum as annual sales soared between the years 1979 and 1982. In 1982 corporate sales gains of 20.1 percent topped the industry, and Macy's surpassed its major competitors in operating profit per square foot.

While other stores were consolidating departments under fewer buyers, Macy's added more buyers, encouraging them to find unique products. Stores were overstocked by 10 to 20 percent, so that unpredicted buying surges could be accommodated. The company also hired many executives for its training program, up to 300 per year in larger divisions. In the early 1980s, Macy's realized impressive gains. Sales for 1983 were $3.47 billion, representing a 16.4 percent increase over the previous year. In 1984, Macy's sales again rose 17.2 percent to $4.07 billion. At each of its 96 stores, Macy's averaged after-tax profits of $2.31 million. During this time Macy's common stock soared in value.

GOING PRIVATE: 1985

The boom years were soon to be eclipsed, however, industry-wide as 1985 proved tough for most retailers, including Macy's. While sales did increase for the year, the rate was more modest and, perhaps more significantly, net income dropped sharply. Sales costs had also risen, due to an aggressive advertising push and new staff training programs.

Additionally, Macy's bulky inventories had gotten out of hand. The company slashed prices, but the store could not seem to get rid of its excess, miscalculating the buying force of the public. Wall Street began to waver in its praise. Macy's had the second-best year in its history in 1985, but the radical drops were not taken kindly in an institution that had been on a steady rise for over a decade.

Mergers and acquisitions abounded in the retail industry in 1985. A company with a weak profit record was a likely target because that performance pushed its stock value down, and a change in management could improve it. Although Macy's ten-year profit history was phenomenal, questions from analysts were pushing Macy's stock prices down, and there was concern about a hostile takeover and executives leaving.

To resolve the situation, Edward S. Finkelstein, chairman of the Macy's New York division, led a group of executives in a leveraged buyout of Macy's, paying $70 per share, slightly above its market high. Some shareholders objected, and one even filed suit, but the offer was sufficiently attractive that they eventually agreed. It was the biggest takeover of a retailer at that time and the first leveraged buyout of a major retail chain.

LOSING GROUND: 1986–90

The year after the buyout, Macy's stores did so well that the chain could almost report a net profit, despite the debt service on the heavy borrowing needed to fund the buyout. In 1988 Macy's added further to its debt, however, by purchasing Bullocks, Bullocks-Wilshire, and I. Magnin chains from Federated Department Stores. The $1 billion expenditure weighed heavily on company finances, but the confident company stocked its stores with merchandise in anticipation of a strong holiday season in 1989.

Economic recession in the late 1980s, however, had lowered consumer demand for the entire retailing industry, and sales during the holidays proved disappointing. Moreover, when a troubled major competitor, the Campeau retailing empire, ran huge sales to increase its cash flow, Macy's had to follow suit to compete. Burdened with an overstocked inventory that was selling too slowly, coupled with high spending on expensive promotions, Macy's saw its earnings for the holiday season drop 50 percent.

The company sold two subsidiaries, Macy Credit Corporation and Macy Receivables Funding Corporation, to General Electric Capital Corp. for $100 million, relieving the company of $1.5 billion in debt. It also sold its equity interest in the Valley Fair Shopping Center in San Jose, California.

The company, however, still had $4 billion in long-term debt, and in early 1990 rumors of bankruptcy started to circulate. As the recession persisted, consumer confidence was low, and sales were again below expectations. Sales throughout 1991 continued to be slow and Macy's sustained further losses. To further cut its deficit, Macy's bought back $300 million of its bonds for less than 50 percent of their face value.

BANKRUPTCY: 1992–94

In early 1992 the company announced an indefinite delay in paying its suppliers. A last-minute effort by investor Laurence Tisch to buy $802 million of outstanding stock did not win creditor support. The final blow came on January 27th when Macy's filed for bankruptcy protection.

A five-year business plan included reducing the advertising budget, fewer one-day sales, more focused promotions, fewer private-label items, improved customer service, and a new computerized inventory management system.

By early 1993, the plan had begun to demonstrate its effectiveness as Macy's showed its first profit—$147. 7 million—since filing for bankruptcy. Moreover, sales during the 1992 holiday season were better than expected, reaching $1.2 billion, while revenue was 3.8 percent higher than the previous year. Macy's continued to rid itself of unprofitable operations, closing 11 stores in March 1993. As sales increased, industry analysts reported that the strategy of increasing productivity and cutting costs, in spite of the continued poor economy on the coasts, was beginning to pay off for Macy's. Further encouragement for Macy's financial picture would soon arrive in the form of a merger offer from Federated Department Stores.

THE HISTORY OF FEDERATED DEPARTMENT STORES

Federated Department Stores, Inc., was incorporated in Columbus, Ohio, in 1929 as a holding company for F & R Lazarus & Company, its subsidiary Shillito's, and the Abraham & Straus department stores. The Federated group was formed and led by Fred Lazarus, Jr., whose eponymous company was the dominant retail store in Columbus. F & R Lazarus was created by Fred's grandfather, Simon. The elder Lazarus, a Jewish refugee who fled religious persecution in Germany, founded the men's clothing store in 1851.

Shillito's, a Cincinnati-based store acquired by F & R Lazarus in 1928, was founded in 1830. While Shillito's was the oldest store west of the Allegheny Mountains, it ranked only fourth among Cincinnati stores at the time it was purchased by Lazarus. Shillito's sales grew over 50 percent during its first year under the management of the Lazarus family, and within a decade, the store had regained the top spot in its urban market. The other founding member of Federated, Abraham & Straus (A & S), was founded in 1865 in Brooklyn, New York.

Bloomingdale's joined the Federated group in 1930. Lyman and Joseph Bloomingdale had founded this revered name in retail in 1872, on New York's East Side. Although the brothers had chosen an area of the city that was underdeveloped at the time, Bloomingdale's reputation for carrying unique merchandise brought more and more patrons to the store. The department store carried European imports as early as 1886 and had quickly become a leader in home furnishings.

During the 1930s, Fred Lazarus, Jr., earned a reputation for innovation that made his family "the first name in retail," according to a 1961 *Forbes* article. In the late 1920s, he instituted an administrative division of labor that placed department managers in charge of buying and selling all of the merchandise in their particular department. This brought a spirit of entrepreneurship to the individual departments in each store. In 1934, Lazarus revolutionized retail clothing sales when he adopted a French merchandising technique in which apparel was arranged according to size, rather than by color, price, or brand. The system eventually became an industry standard. In 1939, Lazarus was a key figure in convincing President Franklin D. Roosevelt to move the Thanksgiving holiday from the last Thursday in November to one week earlier. The calendar change extended the Christmas shopping season, giving retailers more time to sell at their busiest time of year.

Federated stores helped their customers during the Great Depression by extending credit, and they therefore established a reputation for community involvement in times of crisis. The Federated organization helped support its divisions throughout the Great Depression by sharing their risks and benefits. The loosely defined coalition worked so well that by the end of World War II the holding company was making more money than it could profitably reinvest in existing stores.

FEDERATED'S POSTWAR EXPANSION

By the end of the war, Federated had reached a turning point. Faced with increasingly fierce competition from suburban shopping centers, the company had to decide whether to dissolve itself or form a central organization geared toward expansion. Chairperson Fred Lazarus, Jr., pushed for a stronger organization, which he achieved in June 1945. Federated's main office was moved to Cincinnati, and the central management team worked to capture a leading role in the retail revolution of the postwar era. Although the holding company's leadership took a more aggressive role in corporate administration after 1945, divisional autonomy remained a hallmark of the Federated organization for decades.

Federated "boomed" along with the postwar population of the 1950s through expansion and acquisition. In 1956, Burdines, of Miami, became a division of Federated through an exchange of common stock. Rikes' and Goldsmith's, the largest department stores in Dayton, Ohio, and Memphis, Tennessee, respectively, were purchased in 1959. Over the course of the decade, sales at Federated's 50 main stores and 32 branches increased over 100 percent, and the group became the largest and most profitable department store company in the country. Its members included the most prestigious department store chains in almost any given metropolitan area: Foley's of Houston, Sanger's in Dallas, and Filene's of Boston. The haute couture reputation of Federated's stores carried a high price, which translated into the high profit margins that accounted for much of the corporation's success.

Growth continued in the 1960s. In 1965, Federated purchased Bullock's and I. Magnin, two upscale department stores based in California. As a result of the antitrust concerns this acquisition generated, Federated was forced to enter into a consent decree with the Federal Trade Commission (FTC) that prohibited the company from acquiring any more department stores until 1970. By 1965 Federated's annual sales had topped the $1 billion mark. Sales increased 250 percent from 1960 to 1970, reaching $2 billion by 1970. Ralph Lazarus succeeded his father, Fred Lazarus, Jr., as chair and chief executive officer of Federated in 1967.

VENTURING INTO NEW TERRITORY: 1968–70

Since Federated's expansion by acquisition was limited, Ralph Lazarus led Federated into the supermarket industry in 1968 with the purchase of the West Coast chain Ralph's Industries. The chain had 65 stores that were accounting for 10 percent of Federated's total sales by the end of the decade. Federated also entered the mass merchandising segment during the 1960s, with the creation of Gold Circle discount stores in 1968. The small Gold Circle chain totaled five stores in Columbus and Dayton at the end of the decade.

However, Federated's success was not uninterrupted. In 1971, the group sold its Fedway chain to a competitor, Dillard Department Stores, for $6 million in cash. Fedway had been created in 1951 to take advantage of southward population shifts. Its stores represented a new direction for Federated, a move into the small, but burgeoning markets of the so-called Sun Belt: Texas, Arizona, and Southern California. Fedway peaked in the mid-1960s with 11 stores and over $30 million in annual sales. After that point, however, the chain was overcome by larger, more experienced retailers including Sears & Roebuck, Montgomery Ward, and J. C. Penney. By the time it was liquidated, Fedway's sales volume had dwindled to $13 million, and the chain had shrunk to six stores.

GROWTH AND SOME LOSSES: 1970–79

The Federated chain continued to expand in the 1970s. Net income increased from $91.1 million in 1970 to $277.7 million in 1979, and sales nearly tripled during that time to $6.3 billion. The growth was stimulated by a $2.2 billion acquisition spree that almost doubled the group's number of stores to over 350 units. This growth was even more astonishing in light of punishing recessions that cycled throughout the decade. Part of Federated's enduring success stemmed from the fact that most of its upper-income clientele was not as badly affected by economic downturns as were working-class shoppers.

The group made a pivotal acquisition in 1976, when the purchase of Rich's Inc. gave it a foothold in southeastern retail. The $157 million stock swap gave Federated control of the 109-year-old, Atlanta-based institution with its 11 department stores, three Rich's II boutiques, and 11 Richway discount stores in Atlanta, Birmingham, Alabama, and Charlotte, North Carolina. From this installed base, Federated hoped to expand its operations throughout the South.

Federated also expanded its established chains more aggressively. In 1976, Bloomingdale's opened its first full-line store outside the New York market, in a suburb of Washington, D.C. Bullock's, I. Magnin, Burdines, and other divisions were also opening regional and cross-country branches far from their traditional metropolitan markets. New stores were built 20 percent smaller than usual to squeeze more profits from less space. Federated's tradition of divisional autonomy gave way to more centralized supervision.

Federated's growth, however, was countered by troubled divisions throughout the 1970s. In the early years of the decade, Federated's biggest unit and dollar producer, the original Abraham & Straus store in Brooklyn, pulled the entire A & S division down. Some of the division's problems were out of its control, such as a demographic shift that eroded its traditionally affluent customer base. As middle-class Brooklynites escaped to the suburbs, they were replaced by an impoverished population with little interest in A & S's pricey merchandise. Many of the new residents were also drawn to a large regional mall located just a few miles away. Furthermore, the chain's management had neglected its 100-year-old, 1.5 million-square-foot Brooklyn store. By 1973, both sales and profits at A & S had leveled off, and two years later, A & S's pretax profits slid a disturbing 45 percent. The chain launched a comprehensive remodeling effort in an attempt to recapture its middle-income shoppers.

Ralph's, the 98-unit Los Angeles-based supermarket chain, faltered throughout most of the decade as well, as management made a lukewarm commitment to that competitive industry. Although Ralph's was recognized as one of the country's most productive, enterprising food stores, it fell victim to costly price wars in California in 1976 and 1977. The grocery chain eventually withdrew to its home region, closing 18 stores after failing in northern California.

Federated's long-running attempts to diversify into mass merchandising, which began in the 1960s, reaped uninspiring results in the 1970s. Gold Circle, which was projected to grow into a 200-unit upscale discounter, had only 42 units by 1981. High start-up costs and no profits in the western units disappointed Federated officials, who had underestimated the competition that came from Kmart and Target. By the end of the decade, Gold Circle was slated to retreat from the California market entirely.

Two industry trends also threatened Federated's dominant position in retail. Specialty stores started to broaden their appeal, attracting increasingly more upscale shoppers. At the same time, Sears, J. C. Penney, and other mass merchandisers were enhancing their stores to attract more affluent shoppers. Federated felt the squeeze between these two forces. The company's 1979 profits stayed level at $179.9 million, even though sales had increased 10 percent to $5.4 billion.

TOUGH TIMES FOR FEDERATED: 1980–90

When Howard Goldfeder was elevated from president to CEO, succeeding Ralph Lazarus in 1981, he set demanding return-on-investment quotas as a prerequisite for further expansion. Furthermore, he instituted seven new strategies to induce Federated to retake its position as a retail innovator. These included: enlarging market share through more aggressive promotions and deeper inventories; renovating key units in major markets; expanding department stores into the high-growth Sun Belt; cultivating new divisions; ensuring lower management turnover; repositioning and expanding Ralph's supermarkets; and disposing of or merging less profitable units.

Nevertheless, some industry analysts criticized Federated for attempting to dominate too many segments of the retail industry. While rivals Dayton-Hudson and R. H. Macy's limited their focus to either mass merchandising or upscale retail, Federated spread its investments and profit margins among a wide range of concepts. As the decade wore on, Federated's return-on-equity stagnated, and its stock price dwindled. By the late 1980s, the company was ripe for a hostile takeover; it was not strong enough to command a high stock price, yet it was not weak enough to be beyond help.

In 1988, Campeau Corporation acquired Federated. Subsequently, Federated's Bullock's and I. Magnin divisions were sold to competitor R.H. Macy, and the Foley's and Filene's divisions were sold to other retailers. Furthermore, the headquarters of Allied Stores Corporation was moved from New York to Cincinnati to be consolidated with Federated. Allied had been founded in 1935 to succeed Hahn Department Stores, Inc., a holding company that managed Boston's Jordan Marsh stores, among others. Allied had been instrumental in the establishment of the United States' first regional shopping center in 1950, and had acquired the Stern Brothers and Block's department stores over the course of its history.

Campeau Corporation's Robert Campeau acquired Allied for $3.6 billion in a 1986 hostile, debt-financed takeover. Then he borrowed $6.5 billion (97 percent of the purchase price) to buy Federated in 1988. Campeau scheduled his 1989 debt payments according to profit projections of $740 million. However, Federated only made $372 million that year, and Campeau's creditors clamored for the $627 million that was due them. On January 15, Federated and Allied filed the second largest non-bank bankruptcy on record and entered the largest, most complex restructuring in the retail trade.

BANKRUPTCY, REORGANIZATION, AND RESURGENCE

During the course of the two-year reorganization, Federated and Allied merged and cut all ties with Campeau Corporation. More than 40 stores were liquidated. Federated traded $8.2 billion in debt for $850 million in cash, plus $2.8 billion in new debt and 92 million shares of new stock valued at $2.3 billion. Over $2 billion of the debt was forgiven, but the new Federated was still stuck with $3.5 billion of debt on its balance sheet. The new entity boasted 220 department stores in 26 states and annual sales of about $7 billion. A new CEO, Allen Questrom, led the reorganization.

Together with Federated President James A. Zimmerman, Questrom instituted cost-cutting measures that benefited Federated and its customers in the first months after the reorganization. SABRE, a data-processing system, and FACS, the credit-services operation, helped centralize sales, credit, and inventory tracking while promoting economies of scale. The merger of the background operations of Abraham & Straus and Jordan Marsh saved Federated $25 million per year without disrupting either chain's image. Part of the savings realized by these measures was passed on to the choosier shopper of the 1990s. Some industry observers cited Questrom's commitment to GMROI (gross margin return on investment), a new, but reliable performance measurement for department stores, as another reason for high confidence in the new Federated.

Buoyed by these improved perceptions of the company, Federated made one of Wall Street's largest initial public offerings of 1992 within months of emerging from bankruptcy. The group had planned to offer 40 million shares and use the proceeds to prepay a chunk of its long-term debt but was pleasantly surprised when applications for 50 million shares poured in, enabling the company to generate more than $500 million. In 1992, Federated prepaid almost $1 billion of its debt. During the first six months of 1993, the company was able to retire $355 million of its most expensive bonded debt. The interest savings permitted Federated to increase its 1993–96 budget for store renovations and openings by $461 million to $1.2 billion.

THE 1994 MERGER OF MACY'S AND FEDERATED DEPARTMENT STORES

In January 1994, Federated Department Stores made a move to acquire Macy's when it bought almost $5 million of Macy's debt from Prudential Insurance Company. For seven months, Macy's officials resisted Federated's efforts to purchase it, hoping to instead turn the company around on its own. However, the company's efforts to climb out of bankruptcy were proving inadequate; despite cost-cutting measures and new marketing initiatives, it was unable to return to profitability. In July 1994, the company yielded to Federated, agreeing to be acquired and filing a joint reorganization plan. After bankruptcy court approved the reorganization in December 1994, the companies completed the merger, bringing Macy's out of its three-year bankruptcy.

During this time, Federated embarked on a series of acquisitions. Consolidation offered Federated a number of benefits as the department store industry encountered intense competition from both discount merchandisers such as Wal-Mart and such specialty retailers as The Gap. "There are certain economies of scale that size gives you," a retail analyst explained to the *Tribune Review.* By purchasing the Joseph Horne Co. of Pittsburgh in 1994, Federated added ten Pennsylvania stores to its Lazarus division. With its December 1994 purchase of R.H. Macy & Co., Federated became the largest department store company in the United States.

The company was not finished shopping. In 1995, Federated purchased the 82-store Broadway Stores, Inc., chain, which included Broadway, Emporium, and Weinstock's department stores. The Broadway acquisition, given that chain's strength on the West Coast, afforded Federated with much desired access to that part of the country, particularly the markets of populous and prosperous California.

Smoothly incorporating these diverse additions into the Federated fold presented its own challenges. In an effort to integrate Macy's operations with its own, Federated launched its Federated Logistics Division in 1994, to coordinate distribution facilities and functions in the United States. Federated then consolidated its A & S/Jordan Marsh division into Macy's East, creating a single 89-store division stretching across 15 eastern states.

On the opposite side of the country, Federated folded its Bullock's stores into a new Macy's West division. Shortly thereafter, Federated dissolved the I. Magnin chain, converting some of the 13 I. Magnin stores into Macy's or Bullock's, and selling the rest. In 1995, the company consolidated Rich's/Goldsmith's and Lazarus into a single operating unit—Rich's/Lazarus's/Goldsmith's and converted the A & S stores to the Macy's brand.

After acquiring the Broadway Stores empire, Federated converted 56 of those stores to the Macy's nameplate. Five others were slated to become Bloomingdale's, which represented the first time that upscale department store had ventured into California. In 1996, the Jordan Marsh stores in the Northeast (administered under the Macy's East division) were renamed Macy's.

Despite its larger presence, Federated still needed to concentrate on boosting sales. In an effort to distinguish its stores, the company focused on developing its own brands, such as Alfani, I.N.C., Charter Club, and Tools of the Trade. Federated rapidly expanded its Federated Merchandising Group, which was responsible for designing, manufacturing, and marketing all its private labels. At the same time, the company bolstered the presence of its unique brands by creating catchy vendor shops within its department stores. In 1997 alone, Federated built over 680 of these subunits, which served to leverage its private labels.

While Federated worked to lure customers into its diverse department stores, the company also acknowledged that commerce was evolving, as Internet sales rose exponentially each year. Federated launched macys.com in 1996. This online retail venue allowed Internet-savvy consumers to purchase many of the same items found in Macy's department stores. In 1998, Federated also introduced Macy's By Mail, a catalog business.

James M. Zimmerman, who had replaced Allen Questrom as Federated's chairman and chief executive officer in 1997, led the company to acquire Fingerhut Companies, Inc., for $1.5 billion in 1999. Federated planned to exploit Fingerhut's considerable expertise in direct-to-customer and Internet retailing.

Federated's numerous acquisitions, consolidations, and strategy shifts proved successful. Sales increased from $8.31 billion in 1994 to $15.83 billion in 1998. As consumer confidence levels surged to a 30-year high in 1999, Federated's sales in both its department stores and its direct-to-consumer operations were brisk.

2000 AND BEYOND

Federated continued to refine its image and brand. In 2003, the company closed its Stern's division and sold Fingerhut, and then it began attaching the Macy's name with those of its regional department stores. Customers were suddenly confronted with Burdines-Macy's, Lazarus-Macy's, and others. Federated next bought competitor The May Department Stores Company. When the acquisition was completed in 2005, Federated was the fourth largest non-food retailer in the United States. That same year, Federated began converting all its regional department store names to the Macy's brand and initiated its first national advertising for Macy's.

In 2006, Federated sold some chains included in the May acquisition including Lord & Taylor, David's Bridal, and Priscilla of Boston. The company also completed the sale of its credit card portfolio to Citigroup, and eventually divested its After Hours Formalwear business. In 2007 Federated's shareholders voted to change the corporate name to Macy's, Inc. In a 2007 press release, CEO Terry Lundgren explained the decision: "By aligning our corporate name with our largest brand, we will increase the visibility of the company with customers, leverage the world-famous Macy's brand name, and get more credit for our accomplishments in the marketplace."

Taking this brand-driven approach presented some challenges. The integration of the former May stores into the company and under the Macy's name took longer than expected and proved more expensive than originally anticipated. Some customers reportedly resented the loss of the recognized names of stores to which they had been loyal and looked to shop elsewhere. Macy's responded by improving dressing rooms, adding its private-label lines, and introducing food options at stores. Still, analysts noted that the difficulties encountered with the May Company integration allowed competitors such as J. C. Penney and Kohl's to infringe on their customer base.

Macy's stock prices began dropping in 2007, despite increased sales for the year, as many analysts began to question management's strategies in integrating its holdings. The 2007–08 holiday shopping sales proved disappointing, and in February 2008 the company announced it would cut its managerial workforce by 2,300 in efforts to further consolidate its divisions and, it hoped, become more attuned to the needs of customers at the local and regional levels. With a slumping U.S. economy, and with consumer discretionary spending slipping in general, Macy's and its competitors faced a challenging industry climate.

Elaine Belsito and April S. Dougal
Updated, Shawna Brynildssen; Rebecca Stanfel; Ellen Wernick

PRINCIPAL OPERATING UNITS

Bloomingdale's; Macy's East; Macy's Florida; Macy's Midwest; Macy's North; Macy's Northwest; Macy's South; Macy's West.

PRINCIPAL COMPETITORS

Saks Inc.; Dillard's, Inc.; Nordstrom, Inc.; J. C. Penney Company, Inc.

FURTHER READING

Barmash, Isadore, *Macy's for Sale,* New York: Weidenfeld & Nicolson, 1989.

Berner, Robert, "Is Federated As Flush As It Looks?" *Business Week,* May 28, 2007, pp. 71–72.

"Bloomingdale's Celebrates a Century," *Stores,* November 1972, p. 10.

Chakravarty, Subrata N., "Federated Chooses Not to Choose," *Forbes,* April 8, 1985, p. 82.

———, "Survivor on 34th St.," *Forbes,* August 6, 1990, p. 10.

Churchill, Mike, "Department Store Chain Placed on the Selling Block," *Tribune Review,* April 20, 1994.

"Fadeout for Fedway," *Dun's,* October 1971, p. 60.

"Federated: Blue Chip Retailer," *Financial World,* March 22, 1972, p. 6.

"Federated's Push to Improve Profitability," *Business Week,* July 6, 1981, pp. 44–46.

"Federated: The Most Happy Retailer Grows Faster and Better," *Business Week,* October 18, 1976, pp. 74–77, 80.

Feinberg, Phyllis, "Federated Finesses Recession," *Commercial and Financial Chronicle,* October 27, 1957, pp. 1, 3.

"The First Family of Retailing," *Forbes,* March 15, 1961, pp. 19–22.

Jereski, Laura, "Damn the Torpedoes," *Forbes,* June 10, 1991, p. 66.

Kirdahy, Matthew, "Counter Attack," *Forbes.com,* November 26, 2007.

———, "M Is Not for Microsoft," *Forbes.com,* April 1, 2007.

Klokis, Holly, "Retailing's Grande Dame: Cloaked in New Strategies," *Chain Store Age Executive,* March 1985, pp. 18–20.

Loomis, Carol J., "The Biggest, Looniest Deal Ever," *Fortune,* June 18, 1990, pp. 48–72.

Macy's New York 125th Anniversary: 1858–1983, New York: R.H. Macy & Co., Inc., 1983.

Neuborne, Ellen, "A Retail Giant in Store: Federated to Acquire Rival Macy," *USA Today,* July 15, 1994, p. 1.

"Optimism at Federated," *New York Times,* May 24, 1993, p. D3.

Peterson, Thane, "Macy's Is Trimmed in Red," *Business Week,* December 30, 1991, p. 48.

Picciola, Kimberly, "Macy's M," *Morningstar Analyst Report,* January 1, 2008.

"Ralph Lazarus of Federated," *Stores,* January 1974, pp. 2–3.

Reda, Susan, "Staying in Tune: Allen Questrom, Chairman and CEO, Federated Dept. Stores," *Stores,* September 1992, pp. 18–24.

Rosenberg, Hillary, "Life Among the Ruins," *Institutional Investor,* June 1990, pp. 92–94+.

Silverman, Edward, "End of an Error: Decision to Take on Heavy Debt Cost Macy's Its Independence," *Newsday,* July 17, 1994, p. A72.

"Southern Bastion Falls to Federated," *Business Week,* July 26, 1976, pp. 43–44.

"This Peacock Won't Be Tomorrow's Feather Duster," *Forbes,* June 15, 1957, pp. 24–33.

Trachtenberg, Jeffrey, *The Rain on Macy's Parade: How Greed, Ambition, and Folly Ruined America's Greatest Store,* New York: Times Business, 1996.

"Where 'Beautiful People' Find Fashion," *Business Week,* September 2, 1972, pp. 44, 45.

Zinn, Laura, "Prudence on 34th St.," *Business Week,* November 16, 1992, p. 44.

Zinn, Laura, and Christopher Power, "It's Too Soon to Write Macy's Obituary," *Business Week,* December 17, 1990, p. 27.

Zinn, Laura, and Michele Galen, "Short Chapter, Happy Ending," *Business Week,* February 10, 1992, pp. 126–27.

WE ARE PRINT.™

MAN Roland Druckmaschinen AG

Mühlheimer Straße 341
Offenbach am Main, 63075
Germany
Telephone: (49 69) 8305 0
Fax: (49 69) 8305 1440
Web site: http://www.man-roland.de

Private Company
Founded: 1871
Employees: 9,000
Sales: EUR 2 billion ($2.64 billion) (2007)
NAIC: 333293 Printing Machinery and Equipment Manufacturing

■ ■ ■

MAN Roland Druckmaschinen AG is the world's second largest producer of printing presses and related machinery. Its products include a line of web offset presses for newspaper printing and commercial printing; a line of sheet-fed offset presses for publishing, commercial printing, and the printing of packaging; and a line of all-purpose digital presses. MAN Roland also sells parts for all of its equipment and maintains a staff of repair and maintenance specialists. The company divides its production among four cities in Germany. Its headquarters are located in Offenbach near Frankfurt am Main and the company's sheet-fed presses for all formats are produced there as well.

A second main production site is located in the Bavarian city of Augsburg where MAN Roland's web offset presses are made. Other production sites include Plauen, where small- and medium-format newspaper presses are manufactured, and Mainhausen, where primarily small-format sheet-fed presses are made. The company maintains approximately 120 branches in 90 countries on six continents. Since 2006 MAN Roland has been owned by Allianz Capital Partners, a venture capital company established the same year for the purpose of launching an initial public offering (IPO) of MAN Roland stock.

PRINTING PRESS INNOVATIONS IN SOUTHERN GERMANY

In 1841 Carl Buz, a mechanical engineer and bridge builder for the Bavarian railway, settled in the Bavarian city of Augsburg where he married his second wife, a widow and part-owner of the G. Geiger'sche Buchdruckerei, a printing company. Buz joined the company and started working closely with Carl August Reichenbach, a partner in the company. Reichenbach was a mechanical engineer as well as the nephew of the inventor of the flatbed printing press, Friedrich Koenig. Reichenbach and Buz cast about for opportunities to expand the business to include the design and production of printing presses.

The opportunity presented itself in the form of the Sander'sche Maschinenfabrik, founded in 1840 to supply machinery to the region's textile manufacturers. By 1844 the factory was thriving and had a workforce of 56. In September of that year Reichenbach and Buz leased the company, renaming it C. Reichenbach'sche Maschinenfabrik.

COMPANY PERSPECTIVES

MAN Roland is a key player in the global market of leading-edge production systems for the world of printed media. As a team of creative specialists and competent service providers we design and commission customised printing systems for publishers and professional printers. We provide the decisive edge that ensures our customers' success. We offer our international partners a platform which contributes to the creation of a joint successful future in the new communication age. Innovation, professionalism, customer orientation, and the willingness to change are the strengths of all MAN Roland employees. These characteristics guarantee our group's success and create the foundation for job satisfaction and the personal success of each and every employee.

The new company delivered its first product in May 1845, a flatbed printing press sold to a print shop in Augsburg. That press was used for a remarkable 110 years before it was finally scrapped in 1955. From the outset, the Reichenbach'sche company worked hard at finding out what its customers and potential customers needed, and then developed products to fill those needs. In 1850 the company produced its first dual flatbed press, in 1866 its first four-sheet flatbed press, and in 1868 its first two-color machine. By 1852 the firm had sold 75 flatbed printing presses and its workforce had nearly quadrupled to about 200.

FULL OWNERSHIP BEGINS

In December 1855 the lease agreement ended when Reichenbach and Buz bought the entire company and the land it was on outright from Sander for 70,000 gulden. Two years later, hoping to raise money for research and further expansion, the partners reorganized the firm into a joint stock company, the Maschinenfabrik Augsburg, with Buz as general manager and Reichenbach head of its flatbed press manufacturing operations. By the end of the 1850s, however, the company was manufacturing more than just printing presses. It had also added steam engines, pressure vessels, and hydroelectric turbines to its production program. A major innovation was made in 1873 when the company displayed the prototype of the first German web-fed press for printing newspapers at the Vienna World Exhibition. That press went into production in 1879.

The business continued to prosper, and in April 1898 representatives of the Maschinenbau-Actien-Gesellschaft Nürnberg, a machine-building company based in Nuremberg, approached Maschinenfabrik Augsburg about a possible merger. The proposal was accepted and in December of the same year the two companies fused to form Maschinenfabrik Augsburg-Nürnberg AG. Little more than a year later the new company was employing some 9,000 workers in factories in three cities in southern Germany.

DEVELOPING AND PRODUCING OFFSET PRINTING PRESSES

Meanwhile, another company was getting started in Frankfurt. The Associationsgeschäft zur Fabrikation von Lithographischen Schnellpressen (Corporation for the Production of High-Speed Lithographic Printing Presses) was founded in 1871 by Louis Faber and Adolf Schleicher. They had gotten their start in a small factory in Paris and were soon partners in the French business.

After the German victory in the Franco-Prussian War of 1870, however, they were no longer welcome in the French capital so they returned to Frankfurt to open their own factory. It specialized in making presses that used the newly developed offset-printing process. Its first product was a high-speed lithographic press, the Albatross. The machine was a hit right away with both German and foreign printers, and within a year, Faber and Schleicher needed larger facilities to meet the high demand.

They moved to a building in Offenbach, near Frankfurt am Main, in April 1872, and in September of the same year purchased a piece of land where they built a two-story factory. Business was so good that just one year later, Louis Faber wrote his family that the new premises were already too small. In 1887, when the company found it could not reliably obtain the cast-iron part it needed, it made itself independent of its suppliers by building its own iron and steel foundry, a foundry MAN Roland continued to operate in the 2000s. It is a model of environmental efficiency, having reduced emissions to previously unheard of levels.

In July 1896 Louis Faber died of a heart attack. Upon his death, his family sold their holdings in the firm. Schleicher wanted to cut back on his involvement in the day-to-day management of the company. Because he had no adult son to inherit the business, a decision was made to transform the company into an *Aktiengesellschaft,* a joint stock company, a change reflected in the change of the company's name to Faber & Schleicher AG in 1900. One year later the reorganization was complete. Schleicher kept 1,396 of the company's 1,400

KEY DATES

1844: Carl August Reichenbach and Carl Buz acquire the Sander'sche Maschinen Fabrik.
1857: The firm is reorganized to a joint stock company, Maschinenfabrik Augsburg.
1871: Louis Faber and Adolf Schleicher found the Association for the Manufacture of Lithographic Presse.
1881: J.C. & H. Dietrich, Vogtländische Stickmaschinenfabrik is founded in Plauen.
1898: Maschinenfabrik Augsburg and Maschinenbaugesellschaft Nürnberg A.-G. merge to form Maschinenfabrik Augsburg-Nürnberg AG (later renamed MAN).
1900: Association for the Manufacture of Lithographic Presses is renamed Faber & Schleicher AG.
1911: First Roland offset press is introduced.
1920: MAN is acquired by the Gutehoffnungshütte group.
1921: MAN introduces its first web-fed offset press.
1947: PLAMAG introduces its first printing press after the end of World War II.
1950: Reconstruction of the badly damaged Offenbach plant is completed.
1951: The ULTRA-MAN, the first sheet-fed offset press built by MAN in Augsburg after World War II, is introduced.
1957: Faber & Schleicher AG is renamed Roland Offsetmaschinenfabrik Faber & Schleicher AG.
1970: Gutehoffnungshütte Aktienverein, Nürnberg/Oberhausen acquires Roland.
1972: ROLAND 800, a sheet-fed offset press that included a first ink control system is introduced.
1979: Roland and the printing division of MAN merge to establish MAN Roland Druckmaschinen AG, Offenbach/Main; MAN Roland acquires Wood Industries of Groton, CT.
1990: MAN AG acquires DIAG from the German federal government and integrates its printing division, Miller-Johannisberg Druckmaschinen GmbH, into MAN Roland Druckmaschinen AG.
1991: MAN Roland acquires the East German state-run printing press manufacturer PLAMAG.
1992: New headquarters, Senefelder-Haus, is opened.
2006: MAN Roland is sold to Allianz Capital Partners.

new shares, worth 1,000 marks each; the remaining four shares were given to four business associates.

The first six months of business in the reorganized company were prosperous, and stockholders earned dividends of 240 marks per share, 24 percent of the stock's value. When Schleicher passed away in 1910, his 1,396 shares were inherited by his young children and the stock was put in the hands of a trustee, who felt that it did not represent a secure investment. Under his instructions, the shares were sold and the proceeds used to purchase bonds.

This decision would have financially disastrous consequences for the Schleicher heirs. When the great postwar inflation hit Germany in 1923, the value of the bonds was wiped out completely, while the stock, based in real property and machinery, retained its value. As a result, by the time World War I started, control of the company had passed from the founders' families to a small group of other families who would run Faber & Schleicher until the 1970s.

INNOVATIONS IN THE TWENTIETH CENTURY

One year after Schleicher's death, the firm introduced a new product, the Roland, a sheet-fed offset press that won a gold medal at a European industrial exhibition that same year. A year later the firm introduced another Roland that used three cylinders of the same size. The Roland line was popular throughout the world, however even before its development exports accounted for a significant percentage of Faber & Schleicher's sales.

In 1914 one-third of the company's sales were to foreign customers. Eastern Europe was a particularly good market. Nearly half of the company's 1,317 exports before 1914 went there. Russia alone accounted for about half of those sales. Indeed 5 percent of Faber

& Schleicher's total sales in the period were to Russia. Exports remained a significant portion of the firm's business until the eve of World War II.

Research and development were important to Faber & Schleicher's success in the 1920s. In 1925 the company debuted a new high-speed offset press. One year later it brought out an offset press that could print on both sides of the paper. The first two-color offset press was perfected in 1928, an invention that was an essential step in the development of the five-cylinder principle in printing.

Meanwhile, in Augsburg MAN was making its own technological leaps forward. Following its acquisition by the Gutehoffnungshütte group in 1920, it launched its own its own offset press production program. By the start of the 1930s, it was making important advances in the development of dry offset processes and phototypesetting. In 1931 it introduced a high-performance, rotary web-fed press capable of printing 25,000 16-page newspapers an hour.

The strong business successes enjoyed by both Faber & Schleicher and MAN during the 1930s came largely to an end in 1939 with the start of World War II. They were abruptly cut off from essential export markets and, as the war wore on, increasingly threatened with destruction from Allied bombers. Faber & Schleicher's plant in Offenbach was nearly obliterated in air raids in 1944.

POSTWAR RECOVERY AT THE TWO COMPANIES

Faber & Schleicher resumed production in 1946, and a number of those first postwar presses went to foreign customers. Exports grew quickly, and by 1949, one year after the currency reform in the Federal Republic of Germany, exports accounted for nearly 50 percent of the firm's total sales. In 1951 the company completely rebuilt its Offenbach factories, and its workforce began to return to prewar levels. The year 1951 saw the introduction of the company's first four-color offset press that was capable of wet-on-wet printing. It was a press that remained popular with customers until 1968 when it went out of production. In October 1957, largely associated with its Roland line, Faber & Schleicher assumed the Roland name, rechristening itself Roland Offsetmaschinenfabrik Faber & Schleicher AG.

Meanwhile, 1951 was a milestone year for MAN, which began its switch from letterpress equipment to offset with the introduction of the ULTRA-MAN, a sheet-fed offset press. MAN's printing division rebounded after the war, and by 1960, three-quarters of all daily newspapers in Germany were being printed on MAN equipment. In 1967 printing press sales at MAN surpassed the DEM 200 million for the first time, while its workforce grew to more than 3,000.

In 1970, one year before Roland celebrated its 100th anniversary, it was the target of a hostile takeover by Gutehoffnungshütte Aktienverein, Nürnberg/Oberhausen, the company that had acquired the MAN group in 1920. Roland existed side-by-side with—albeit independent of—MAN in the Gutehoffnungshütte group until 1979 when Roland and MAN's printing press division were merged to establish MAN Roland Druckmaschinen AG, Offenbach/Main. That same year the new company established its first beachhead in the United States with the acquisition of Wood Industries, a printing press manufacturer located in Groton, Connecticut, that became MAN Roland Inc.

The 1970s and 1980s witnessed the introduction of a series of innovative new presses from MAN Roland. In 1972 the firm brought out the Roland 800, a large-format offset press capable of printing 10,000 sheets per hour. Within four years the 800 was being used in 20 nations worldwide. The COLORMAN, the largest offset rotary printing press available in Europe, appeared in 1974; and the company introduced the Roland-CCI in 1977. It was the world's first press with a computer-controlled inking system. In 1986 the firm introduced the LITHOMAN, a web offset press that worked at 60,000 revolutions per hour and had fully electronic press center technology.

EXPANSION AND STAGNATION

The 1990s opened with a period of further expansion at MAN Roland, but that growth was followed with the onset of financial doldrums that extended into the middle of the next decade. The expansion began in 1990 when MAN acquired Deutsche Industrieanlagen GmbH (DIAG), a group of manufacturing firms, from the German federal government. DIAG's printing division was Miller-Johannisberg Druckmaschinen GmbH, Geisenheim, a company with a history almost as long as MAN and Roland's own. After the purchase, Miller-Johannisberg was spun off and merged into MAN Roland.

One year later, in 1991, following the opening of the Berlin Wall at a time when many of the old East German state-owned companies were being sold to West German buyers, MAN Roland acquired another printing company that was rich in tradition, PLAMAG. Originally founded as the Vogtländische Maschinenbau AG, the company began producing printing presses in the Saxon city of Plauen in 1896. At the close of World War II, its production facilities were stripped clean by the Soviet army, but somehow the firm was able to resume production in 1945 as Plauener Maschinenbau AG or PLAMAG. Over the years, it developed into one of the most important printing press manufacturers behind the Iron Curtain. After its acquisition it became, with the Augsburg and Offenbach divisions, one of MAN Roland's core companies.

The early and middle 1990s were difficult for MAN Roland. The 1992–93 fiscal year was one of the worst in the company's history, with revenues dropping some 6 percent, to DEM 2.2 billion. The company continued to record losses until the end of 1997, thanks in large measure to a drop in demand that was ascribed to the rise of the Internet. Newspapers, it was said, were waiting to see how the new media affected sales before they invested in expensive new printing equipment.

As a result of those declines, MAN Roland was forced to reduce its total workforce by some 30 percent between 1992 and 1997—from 12,000 to about 8,500. By autumn 1997 rumors began to circulate in the industry that the firm would be taken over by a competitor such as Heidelberger Druckmaschinen AG. By 1998, however the company's orders had picked up once again, so that by midyear revenues were predicted to exceed DEM 3 billion for the first time in company history. That year MAN Roland reported a profit for the first time in six years.

CHALLENGES IN THE 21ST CENTURY

In 2002, however, the advertising market in Germany—another important market for printing equipment—was hit by a downturn, which sent new shockwaves through the printing industry. By the end of the year, MAN Roland was experiencing major drops in new orders—they were down 34 percent in the first half of 2002, for example. The company tried to make up those losses with new cuts to the workforce, which in the preceding four years had grown once again to more than 10,000. That set off a struggle between management and the company's labor council, which had to give its approval to any layoffs. The company cut 356 jobs in mid-2003, and foresaw even more in the coming year, despite hefty resistance from workers' representatives.

In March 2006 MAN AG took the first steps to separate itself from its financially troubled printing division. With Allianz Capital Partners, a venture capital subsidiary of the Allianz Group, a joint venture was formed, Munich-based Roland Beteiligungs GmbH, which took over all shares of MAN Roland Druckmaschinen AG. Alliance Capital acquired 65 percent of the joint venture, valued at the time at EUR 856 million; MAN AG retained the remaining 35 percent. The goal of the partnership was to make, within the next four to five years, an IPO of MAN Roland stock. In spring 2007 the firm reported a record profit of more than EUR 118 million. Observers credited the upturn to the trend among German newspaper publishers away from the broadsheet to the smaller tabloid format, a change that necessitated the purchase of new equipment. As 2007 drew to an end, with MAN Roland riding the wave of success its new profits had brought, it seemed possible that Allianz Capital Partners would make the public stock offering earlier than originally planned, possibly within the following 24 months.

Gerald E. Brennan

PRINCIPAL COMPETITORS

Goss International Corporation; Koenig & Bauer AG; Heidelberger Druckmaschinen AG; Mitsubishi Heavy Industries, Ltd.; Tokyo Kikai Seisakusho, Ltd.

FURTHER READING

Henry, Patrick, "MAN Roland's Operational Nerve Center Gets into Its Full Stride in Middlesex, N.J.," *Printing News,* January 18, 1999

The MAN Group: 150 Years of Printing Press Production, Germany: MAN Roland, 1995.

"Press Builder Previews Products for Drupa," *Graphic Arts Monthly,* April 1, 2000.

25 Jahre Druckmaschinen aus Offenbach, Germany: MAN Roland, 1996.

MARK T. WENDELL TEA COMPANY
Importers and Purveyors of Fine Teas Since 1904

Mark T. Wendell Tea Company

50 Beharrell Street
West Concord, Massachusetts 01742
U.S.A.
Telephone: (978) 369-3709
Fax: (978) 369-7972
Web site: http://www.marktwendell.com

Private Company
Incorporated: 1904
NAIC: 311423 Dried and Dehydrated Food Manufacturing

■ ■ ■

Based in West Concord, Massachusetts, Mark T. Wendell Tea Company is a venerable importer of fine teas that toiled in obscurity for many years catering to the upper crust of society in Boston, New York, and Philadelphia, but in recent years has taken advantage of the Internet to reach a far broader customer base. The company primarily offers loose tea leaves—not torn or crushed as they are in tea bags and conventional tins—although some products for the sake of customer convenience are available in bags as well. Wendell's signature tea, and a longtime favorite of Boston's Brahmin class and other wealthy families of the Northeast, is Hu-Kwa Tea, a delicately smoked Lapsang Souchong tea that has always been an acquired taste, often called the master's "poison" by servants.

Wendell also sells a wide variety of black teas, green teas, rare and delicate white teas, scented teas, oolong teas, pesticide-free organic teas, decaffeinated black and green teas, and flavored black, green, and herbal teas. The company also makes its teas available in sampler gift tins, and offers iced tea blends and herbal and fruit tisanes that do not contain traditional tea leaves.

In addition, Wendell imports a number of packaged teas, including Boston Harbour tea (produced by the British firm whose tea chests were dumped in the Boston harbor during the 1773 "Boston Tea Party"), Foojoy Gold tea from China, Sushi Chef Japanese Green Tea, and Indar tea from France. Other English teas include Heath & Heather herbal and fruit teas, Lifeboat tea, London Fruit & Herb teas, P.G. Tips tea, Ridgways teas, Typhoo tea, and the famous elephant tins of Williamson Fine Teas. To round out the tea-drinking experience, Wendell sells a broad selection of teapots, tea glasses for single-serve brewing, strainers, tea balls, filters, and Gilway brand sugars. Wendell is owned and operated by Elliot H. Johnson and his son, Hartley E. Johnson.

ORIGINS IN THE 19TH CENTURY

Mark T. Wendell Tea Company was founded in 1904 by Mark T. Wendell, but the firm was in fact a continuation of the firm established by his uncle, Richard Devens, around 1840. Devens was one of a number of U.S. and British importers who did business in the Chinese port of Canton through a dozen sanctioned merchants, who each operated large warehouses called Hongs and were responsible for paying all import duties to the emperor. The head of the so-called Hong merchants was Wu Tun-yuan, known as Houqua (or

COMPANY PERSPECTIVES

For over a century, we have taken great pride in providing our customers with the highest levels of customer service, affordable pricing and an unparalleled knowledge into the world of specialty teas.

Hu-Kwa as Wendell would spell it phonetically), who invested directly in the United States and at the time of his death may have been the wealthiest man in the world. Devens was also known for his honesty and generosity, and this legacy he would pass on through his nephew, Mark T. Wendell.

Devens imported a number of luxury items from Canton, including port, sherry, olive oil, coffee, snuff, and fine tea that he sold under the "XXX" label, an allusion to the traditional symbol for products of the highest quality. Shortly after graduating from Harvard University, Wendell took over his uncle's business, applied his name to it, and opened an office on State Street in Boston's Beacon Hill section. He continued to import the same products as his uncle but instead of marketing his smoky tea as "XXX," he recalled the tales Devens had recounted about the great Chinese merchant Hu-Kwa and adopted his name for the tea. The product became so popular among the gentry of Boston that in time Wendell dropped his other products and dedicated the company to the importation of tea, adding other teas to complement Hu-Kwa, including Cheericup Ceylon, Fancy Formosa Oolong, Jasmine, and MTW Keemun. Beyond that Wendell would not venture, for fear that additional teas might take sales away from Hu-Kwa.

Mark T. Wendell Tea Company was always a small concern, its courtly owner not willing to solicit business openly. Rather, he mailed gifts of Hu-Kwa tea, packed in distinctive black tins, to members of Boston society as well as classmates in New York City and Philadelphia, and waited for his clientele to find him. By word of mouth they did, and the gentry of Boston, New York, and Philadelphia formed the backbone for a mail-order business.

The extent of Wendell's marketing efforts was little more than the occasional mailing of postal cards, reminding his customers that supplies of Hu-Kwa were limited because it was "grown only in one little spot in the world"—in the province of Foo Kien, China—and gently suggesting that "whenever you find your supply of Hu-Kwa getting low, you let us know of your requirements as soon as possible." He would then personally attend to each order, most of the business taking place around the Christmas holidays. In time specialty shops including William Poll and A.S.J. Gentiles in New York and the Chestnut Hill Cheese Shop in Philadelphia would also carry his tea.

MARK WENDELL DIES: 1967

During World War II, when imports were cut off from China, Wendell made do by offering his customers a product called "Hu-Kwa Matte," a blend of Brazilian matte and India-Ceylon Tea. Following the war he carried on as before and continued personally to fill orders with the help of his longtime employee Joseph Shair. Known as the "Bachelor of Beacon Hill," Wendell had no heirs and as he grew elderly he gave Shair the option of inheriting $10,000 or taking over the company. Shair opted for the company, and took charge of Mark T. Wendell Tea Co. after Wendell died at the age of 85 in January 1967.

Shair carried on the business in the same manner as his predecessor, limiting his line of teas and serving a very select clientele. By 1971 Shair was ready to retire and sell the company when he was approached by brothers Alan H. Johnson, Jr., and Elliot H. Johnson, food brokers who were interested in representing Mark T. Wendell teas in the marketplace. Instead, they bought the company.

The Johnson brothers' brokerage business, Hartley S. Johnson & Son Food Brokerage, had been established by their grandfather, Hartley S. Johnson, in 1929 as Specialty Food Brokers. Covering the New England states, he represented specialty food manufacturers, placing their upscale products in department stores while also urging smaller establishments to carry them. He was joined by his son, Alan H. Johnson, Sr., and they worked together until the 1960s when the elder Johnson retired. At the same time, however, his son's health began to falter. Stepping in to help out were Alan Johnson's sons, Alan, Jr., and younger brother Elliot, the former a graduate of Babson University and the latter still enrolled at Clark University. When their father died in 1966 they took over the business. They would learn of Mark T. Wendell Tea while making a sales call to a Cambridge, Massachusetts, shop, the owner of which raved about the company's teas and suggested that the brothers seek out Mark T. Wendell to see if it needed representation.

KEY DATES

1904: Mark T. Wendell takes over uncle's import business.
1967: Wendell dies, leaving the business to Joseph Shair.
1971: Alan and Elliot Johnson acquire company.
1999: Elliot Johnson's son, Hartley, joins company.

JOHNSON BROTHERS BUY COMPANY: 1971

In 1971 the Johnson brothers acquired Wendell as a second business while continuing to run the brokerage. Elliot would become sole owner of both companies in the late 1970s after Alan left to operate a Boston Back Bay specialty food store called Malbens that he had purchased. Wendell was very much a small business from another era when the new owners took over. The inventory, packing machinery, and files were all contained in the minuscule State Street office. The rubber airmail stamp was so old that it featured a DC-3 propeller-driven airplane. Although the sale price included a large mailing list of customers, after the first mailing went out under new ownership, close to 2,000 pieces were returned, marked "Deceased." Moreover, the door to the business was always left open, to accommodate longtime customers who came in at their leisure to pack their own tea, complete their own invoices, and leave behind the proper amount of money.

The Johnson brothers did not wish to tamper with the charm of the company, lest they alienate a base of loyal customers, but they disagreed with the founder's premise that the addition of other teas would draw sales away from Hu-Kwa, and soon they added other teas, such staples as Earl Grey, Darjeeling, and English Breakfast. Of course, not all of the company's inherited clientele were hardened traditionalists. One letter they received pleaded, "You *must* put the Hu-Kwa in teabags, because the leaves are clogging up the drain in my yacht."

To drum up more business for Wendell, the Johnson brothers pitched the teas to the specialty food accounts of their other business. They also took out newspaper ads and advertised in upscale magazines. They built up a database of names and addresses and assembled a mail-order catalog to send to them. Outgrowing the State Street office they soon relocated the business to a West Concord warehouse.

LATE 20TH-CENTURY GROWTH IN TEA MARKET

Despite the changes made by new management, Wendell remained a small business, ensconced as it was in a country far more devoted to coffee than to tea. That would change in the final decades of the 20th century as mainstream consumer tastes began to become more discerning about wine, beer, and especially coffee. As coffee drinkers became enamored with gourmet coffees so too did tea drinkers begin to become more receptive to specialty teas. In addition to indulging a more adventurous spirit, many consumers of the baby boom generation were also showing an increasing interest in tea because of its reported health benefits. Hence, the tea business began to gain momentum in the late 1990s.

HARTLEY JOHNSON JOINS FATHER: 1999

Elliot Johnson's son, Hartley E. Johnson, never gave much thought to joining his father at Wendell while growing up because the company was so small that it could not support another salary. While majoring in psychology and communications at Denison University, he developed an interest in industrial/organizational studies, and after graduating in 1995 entered the management training program with Enterprise Rent-A-Car in Boston. After four years he was a branch manager, in charge of three daily rental offices, but did not believe it was a career he wanted to pursue long-term. In 1999 he approached his father about going to work for Wendell, offering to manage the warehouse and staff. By this time the business had been enjoying several years of growth, making his addition both desirable and helpful.

Having developed import connections for many years, Wendell was well positioned to take advantage of the increasing interest in specialty teas. A number of high-end teas that previously were not known in the United States became available in bulk quantities that could be resold at a reasonable price. As Elliot Johnson explained to *Tea* magazine in 2004, "I'm trying to blend good business sense with good selection. There's a point on that S-curve where quality goes up incrementally and price goes up geometrically. That's a good spot to stop." As for customers, reported *Tea,* "the Johnsons continually pitch to baby boomers, cultural creatives, and émigrés from tea-saturated cultures, as well as individuals primed for a nostalgic brew. Indeed, many of the company's new customers are the descendants of its old mainstays, having responded to Hu-Kwa's smoke vapors as a Proustian reminder of childhood."

The greatest marketing tool for Wendell in reaching a wider customer base was without doubt the Internet.

The company introduced a secure web site where customers from all over the world could place orders any time of day or night. The Internet was also far more cost-effective than the company's mail-order business, which naturally shifted to the Internet.

Increasing Internet sales in the first decade of the 21st century also led Wendell to begin importing popular packaged tea from overseas, including Boston Harbour, P.G. Tips, Typhoo, Indar, and Lifeboat tea. When consumers interested in those teas used a search engine like Google, Wendell would appear as a supplier, resulting in new sources of business. The company also began offering accessories such as teapots, strainers, and filters to round out its product offerings. Given sustained interest in quality teas, the company's reputation, and a second generation of the Johnson family waiting in the wings to carry on the tradition established by Richard Devens in the 1840s and carried on by his nephew, the future of Mark T. Wendell Tea Company appeared to be assured for some time to come.

Ed Dinger

PRINCIPAL COMPETITORS

International Tea Importers; Tea Importers, Inc.; Upton Tea Imports.

FURTHER READING

Drexler, Madeline, "Mark T. Wendell Tea Company: A Century-Long Tradition," *Tea,* Summer 2004, p. 2.

Norwich, William, "Style & Entertaining; Andy's Gang," *New York Times,* May 28, 2000.

Roberts, Nancy, "Tea Is Back, and Not Just Bagged and Black," *Specialty Coffee Retailer,* December 2000, p. 20.

Weber, Bridget, "A Healthy Take on Tea," *Specialty Coffee Retailer,* March 2005, p. 10.

MBK Industrie S.A.

BP 639, ZI de Rouvroy
Rouvroy, F-02100
France
Telephone: (33 03) 23 51 44 44
Fax: (33 03) 23 51 45 45
Web site: http://www.mbk.fr

Wholly Owned Subsidiary of Yamaha Motor Company Ltd.
Incorporated: 1923 as Motebécane; 1984 as MBK Industrie
Employees: 850
Sales: $354.5 million (2006)
NAIC: 336991 Motorcycle, Bicycle, and Parts Manufacturing; 423110 Automobile and Other Motor Vehicle Merchant Wholesalers

■ ■ ■

MBK Industrie S.A. is a leading French brand of motor scooters and small motorbikes. The company, most famously known as Motobécane, has been part of the Yamaha Motor Company since the mid-1980s. MBK maintains production facilities in Saint Quentin, in a factory complex of some 370,000 square meters, with a production space of more than 131,000 square meters. MBK produces its own scooter and motorbike models as well as rebranded versions of Yamaha's own motor vehicles. The company's core scooter line is its "Booster" line of high-performance 50 cubic centimeter (cc) scooters, originally launched in 1990. The company also produces a range of 125cc scooters and motorbikes, including the Cityliner, launched for the 2008 model year. That model is MBK's first entry into the large-wheel scooter category, marketed especially to the urban professional consumer segment. Other popular MBK models include Ovetto, Nitro, the X-Power dirt bikes, and Stunt and Waap models. MBK employs 850 people and posted revenues of approximately EUR 275 million ($350 million) in 2006. The company has no relation to U.S.-based bicycle brand Motobécane.

FRENCH MOTORCYCLE LEGEND BEGINS

The development of France's motor vehicle and motorcycle industry began in earnest in the aftermath of World War I. The high cost of automobiles at the time meant that they remained unaffordable for the vast majority of the French population, a situation that would continue to exist through the 1950s. Motorcycles and other small vehicles therefore represented a means for providing inexpensive reliable transportation to the country's increasingly urban and industrialized population. Into the 1920s, the country saw a surge in the number of new companies seeking to capitalize on this market.

Among these was a company established by Charles Benoit and Abel Bardin. The pair had worked together at a Pantin-based company, SICAM (Société Industrielle de Construction d'Automobiles et de Moteurs). That company had developed a small two-stroke motor that could be attached to bicycles to provide auxiliary motors. Benoit and Bardin had the idea that the two-stroke engine could be adapted for use in a "voiturette"

COMPANY PERSPECTIVES

Our Philosophy: Modern-day living can be stressful and rushed, as work and city travel consume more of our time. Doing things your way has never held more appeal. In fact, it's our defining passion at MBK. Which is why our philosophy is geared towards giving you mobility solutions that put the fun back into getting around.

(little car). This type of vehicle, which like an automobile was generally fully enclosed, represented a midpoint between the motorcycle and a full-size car.

Benoit and Bardin left the SICAM to found their own company in 1922. The partners designed their first vehicle, the Pélican, which was later described as a "cyclecar." Yet on its first test run, the prototype of the Pélican caught fire. Benoit and Bardin were forced to abandon that project.

Instead, the pair set to work designing a motorcycle. In 1923, the partners completed their first prototype, a motorcycle featuring a single-cylinder, two-stroke 175cc engine. This time, test runs were much more successful, and in 1924 Benoit and Bardin, joined by several others, founded a new company, Société des Ateliers de la Motobécane. The word "Motobécane" was a play on two French words: "Moto," an informal term for motorcycle, and "bécane," popularly used to refer to bicycles. The 175cc motorcycle was then dubbed the MB1. The MB1 featured the company's first patent, for a piston design that helped the engine achieve greater power over similarly classed engines.

EXPANDING THE RANGE

Motobécane launched full production of the MB1 starting in 1924 at a small, 400-square-meter factory in Pantin. The MB1 quickly became a bestseller in the entry-level range of the motorcycle market. By the end of the decade, Motobécane had become one of the best-known names in the French motorcycle market.

In order to meet the strong demand for the MB1, Motobécane launched an expansion of its production facilities, which grew to more than 6,000 square meters by 1926. The company continued to improve on the MB1 design through the end of the decade, adding a number of new features, such as a luggage rack and a muffler, as well as improvement to its engine and other systems.

The MB1 was to remain a fixture in Motobécane's catalog through the 1930s. In the meantime, the company had continued to expand its range. The company developed a 308cc motorcycle—dubbed the 308—in 1926. Like the MB1, the 308 featured a single-cylinder, two-stroke engine. However, the uncertainty of the success of the new model led Motobécane to introduce it under a different name, Motoconfort, so as not to damage the rapidly growing reputation of the Motobécane name.

In the event, the Motoconfort 308 provided the company with its second success, while also helping the company expand its network of exclusive sales agents. Motobécane was to continue to produce similar motorcycles under both the Motobécane and Motoconfort brand for many years.

SMALLER MOTORS IN THE POSTWAR PERIOD

While its early success had been built on two-stroke engine designs, Motobécane began developing its first four-stroke engines in the late 1920s. The company's first efforts produced a 500cc engine in 1929. That model failed to provide success for the company, in large part because its design generated little more power than the company's two-stroke engines.

Motobécane tried again in 1930, launching the B7, a 750cc four-stroke motorcycle. This model delivered greater power, but nonetheless achieved only poor sales. The company continued, however, to develop its line of four-strokes, adopting a single-cylinder design for the launch of a new 250cc model in 1933. By the end of the decade, the four-stroke featured prominently among the group's models. Still, two-stroke engines remained an important part of its production, particularly in its small-cylinder models. These included the Poney, introduced in 1938, initially with a 63cc engine. In 1945, that engine was replaced with a smaller 50cc design.

World War II put an end to the group's growth for the duration. Immediately following the war, the company initially sought to continue its push into larger motorcycle categories. The company began designing a new two-cylinder, four-stroke engine. By 1947, the company was able to display a prototype of the new model, called the V4C. However the company decided to abandon continued development of that model; in the aftermath of the war, there was little demand for larger motorcycles.

On the other hand, the company's smaller bikes enjoyed stronger sales. These included the 125cc D45, introduced in 1945, a single-cylinder engine adapted

KEY DATES

1924: Founding of Motobécane and launch of full-scale production of first motorcycle, the MB1.
1949: Launch of the Mobylette, which will sell more than 14 million units.
1981: Motobécane goes bankrupt and is renamed MBK Industrie in 1983.
1986: Yamaha Motor Company acquires majority control of MBK Industrie.
1990: The "Booster" line of scooters is introduced.
2007: First large-wheel scooter, the Cityliner, is introduced.

from a motorized bicycle design from the prewar period. The D45 enjoyed considerable success, and remained a popular fixture in the company's catalog into the early 1960s. Other popular Motobécane models launched in the late 1940s included the 175cc Z46C, launched in 1946, which remained in production until 1964.

LAUNCHING THE MOBYLETTE LEGEND

With all the success of its smaller motorcycles, Motobécane had not fully abandoned its efforts to develop larger models. The company made a new attempt at developing a two-cylinder engine into the mid-1950s, resulting in the introduction of the L4C in 1954. This model had the unusual distinction of sporting a two-cylinder in-line engine in a V formation. In the end, the L4C sold poorly for the company.

By then, Motobécane found itself far too occupied elsewhere to be troubled by the commercial flop of the L4C. In 1949, the company introduced a new motorcycle—or rather, a hybrid between a bicycle and a motorcycle—that was to become its biggest success. The Mobylette, as the new model was called, responded perfectly to the needs of the postwar French population. With very few automobiles in circulation, the country's workers typically traveled to and from their homes on bicycle.

Under the leadership of Charles Benoit, Motobécane had been exploring the possibility of updating the concept of the auxiliary motor, as produced by SICAM earlier in the century. In 1942, for example, the company had developed the AV2 motor, which was intended as an add-on for a bicycle.

Inspiration for the Mobylette came in 1946, with the introduction of the similarly designed Velosolex at the Paris Salon that year. The success of that model convinced Benoit to guide Motobécane into developing its own motorcycle-bicycle hybrid. For this, the company reinforced a bicycle frame. The company then adapted one of its Poney motors, which was mounted to the frame. The result was dubbed the Mobylette AV3, and was launched in 1949 under both the Motobécane and Motoconfort names.

The Mobylette featured a number of important innovations that ensured its success against the Velosolex and other competing models. The design featured a low-slung frame appropriate for both male and female riders. The company had also designed the fuel reserve and engine in a way that eliminated the risk of spattering clothing. Motobécane had also equipped the hybrid with a number of features, including a wide, comfortable seat, raised handlebars and a headlamp, that set it apart from competitors. At the same time, despite the motor's small size and limited performance—the top speed was only 30 kilometers an hour—the Mobylette was capable of climbing all but the steepest hills.

CHANGES IN THE CORE MARKET

The success of the Mobylette was immediate, transforming Motobécane from a relatively small company focused primarily on the French market, to a highly international company. Production of the Mobylette, which grew steadily through the 1950s and into the 1960s, quickly eclipsed the company's motorcycle operations. By 1964, the company had produced its last motorcycle.

In the meantime, sales of the Mobylette remained quite strong, as the company continued to expand its range and improve on its design, adding new models, colors and features. Altogether, the company sold more than 14 million Mobylettes, earning it the position as the leading producer in its class. The model's popularity was such that Mobylette became more or less a generic term for this type of motored cycle.

Yet by the late 1960s, the market for the Mobylette had begun to decline. Steady economic prosperity permitted larger numbers of French and others to replace their Mobylettes with automobiles and larger motorcycles. The introduction of new economy-class automobiles, such as Citroën's 2CV and Renault's 4L, played an important part of this development as well. At the same time, the rise of the scooter, made popular especially in Italy in the postwar period, posed another threat to Motobécane's core market.

INTRODUCING A MOTORCYCLE LINE

In response, Motobécane launched a new attempt to reenter the full-size motorcycle market, introducing a new 125cc model in 1969. Yet a number of the model's features were somewhat dated in the rapidly developing motorcycle industry. At the same time, the rapid growth of imports from the major Japanese motorcycle makers, including Yamaha, Kawasaki, Honda, and Suzuki made it all the more difficult for Motobécane to find a place in the market. This was especially true given the relatively low prices, high reliability, and especially high performance of the Japanese motorcycle designs.

Motobécane nonetheless tried again, introducing a well received 350cc three-cylinder model in 1973. However, the many advanced features included in this model also raised its base price. As a result, the company found it difficult to compete against its lower-priced Japanese competition.

Another factor in the changing world of motorcycling led to the group's downfall at the end of the 1970s. Racing had become an important, if not obligatory, means of promoting motorcycle brands at the end of the decade. This became all the more true with the rising popularity of televised racing. Motobécane developed its own racing team in the late 1970s and competed in several Grand Prix races, in the 125cc category, into the early 1980s. The company managed to score a number of victories, albeit with motorcycles that bore little resemblance to its production models.

Motobécane also continued to explore new engine and component designs. The company launched a collaboration with Germany's Bosch in order to develop a fuel-injection system for two-stroke engines. That project failed to produce results, however. By the early 1980s, Motobécane had run out of steam. After a failed attempt to merge with Italy's Motoguzzi, the company was forced to declare bankruptcy in 1981.

REBORN AS MBK

Motobécane had been sold to a group of buyers led by Xavier Maugendre in 1983. Maugendre had long been a prominent figure in France's automotive and motorcycle markets. He started his career with Citroën before introducing Kawasaki motorcycles and becoming the brand's exclusive importer to France in the 1960s. When Kawasaki moved to take control of its own distribution, Maugendre turned to Motobécane.

Renamed as MBK, the company began seeking new investors in order to rebuild its operations. By 1984, the company had succeeded in securing new financing. Its new shareholders included Yamaha Motor Company, which acquired, directly or indirectly, 40 percent of its French counterpart. By 1986, Yamaha had gained majority control of MBK, and by 1988 had succeeded in raising its stake to nearly 100 percent.

Under Yamaha's ownership, MBK was soon able to return to profitability. This was achieved in part through the transfer of parts of Yamaha's scooter production to MBK's factory. While some of the company's production was sold under the Yamaha name, it also marketed many of its models under its own MBK brand. These included the highly popular "Booster" scooter line launched in 1990.

MBK continued to produce the Mobylette through much of the 1990s, finally abandoning the line in 1997. The company also continued to produce bicycles on a small scale, although the Motobécane brand was later sold to a U.S. company, which began to market Chinese- and Korean-built bicycles under the Motobécane name.

MBK's production also included outboard motors for Yamaha's line of sports boats. Early in the first decade of the 21st century, MBK also began producing motorcycles again, including a 600cc motorcycle for Yamaha starting in 2003. Scooters, however, remained MBK's core operation into the second half of the decade. By then, the market had begun to evolve somewhat, as the scooter's economic and environmental advantages won over a growing number of urban commuters. MBK sought to position itself within this new market, launching its first large-wheel scooter, the Cityliner, for the 2008 model year. MBK inherited the Motobécane tradition while establishing itself as a leading French scooter brand in the new century.

M. L. Cohen

PRINCIPAL COMPETITORS

Honda Motor Company Ltd.; Bayerische Motoren Werke AG; Suzuki Motor Corp.; Harley-Davidson Motor Co.; Kawasaki Heavy Industries Ltd.; Guangzhou Five Rams Bicycle Import and Export Company Ltd.; Irbit Motorcycle Plant Ltd.; Hero Cycles Ltd.; Aprilia S.p.A.; MV Agusta Motorcycles S.p.A.; Bridgestone Cycle Co. Ltd.; Ducati Motor Holding S.p.A.

FURTHER READING

"Cheap and Cheerful Scooters," *Evening Times,* May 1, 1998, p. 74.

Lucot, Yves-Marie, "MBK Se Lance dans les 'Gros Cubes,'" *Les Echos,* September 12, 2003.

McAfee Inc.

3965 Freedom Circle
Santa Clara, California 95054
U.S.A.
Telephone: (408) 988-3832
Fax: (408) 970-9727
Web site: http://www.mcafee.com

Public Company
Incorporated: 1992 as McAfee Associates Inc.
Employees: 3,342
Sales: $1.15 billion (2006)
Stock Exchanges: New York
Ticker Symbol: MFE
NAIC: 511210 Software Publishers

■ ■ ■

Billing itself as the world's largest dedicated security firm, McAfee Inc. is a leading provider of Internet security software, including antivirus applications. With headquarters in Santa Clara, California, the company's reach spans the globe, with offices in 38 countries, including burgeoning markets like China and India.

McAfee's security products are organized under the umbrellas of threat prevention, compliance, online safety, and professional services and support. The company serves businesses through its Foundstone Professional Services & Education division, and provides around-the-clock support through its McAfee Customer Service and Technical Support arm. Since 1992, McAfee has been granted more than 250 patents. The company furthers innovation through McAfee Avert Labs, which employs approximately 100 research professionals on five continents.

FROM START-UP TO NASDAQ

McAfee's history dates back to 1989, when the company was established by John McAfee, a former engineer who wrestled with some of the earliest computer viruses while working for Lockheed. McAfee's experience led him to post a virus program on an online bulletin board, which he asked people to pay for if they thought it was of value. The shareware approach and electronic delivery model became McAfee's differential during the company's early years.

Relying on the honor system for sales, McAfee asked users who downloaded the company's products from electronic bulletin boards to send in payments of $25 to $35. By 1990 McAfee's sales totaled $1.6 million, of which $1.2 million was net income. The following year, sales climbed to $6.9 million, with net income of $4.5 million. During the company's first two years, John McAfee was the sole management executive for the business.

By mid-1992 McAfee employed a staff of 26. On August 14 of that year, McAfee incorporated his enterprise in Delaware, forming McAfee Associates Inc. By this time McAfee had some 10,000 licenses for its product in place at various corporations.

Although some criticized McAfee for focusing more on the promotion of virus scares and the availability of its products than on software functionality, the company continued to grow and prosper. Among its early offer-

COMPANY PERSPECTIVES

McAfee proactively secures systems and networks from known and as yet undiscovered threats worldwide. Home users, businesses, service providers, government agencies, and our partners all trust our unmatched security expertise and have confidence in our comprehensive and proven solutions to effectively block attacks and prevent disruptions.

ings were resident file infection and activity checking programs named VShield and Sentry, a file- and memory-scanning program named Scan, a disinfection program called Clean, and various software utilities.

McAfee went public on October 6, 1992, selling 2.6 million shares at $16 each. The company's stock began trading on the NASDAQ under the ticker symbol MCAF. That year, McAfee gained notoriety by warning the public of the Michelangelo virus.

ACQUISITIONS AND NEW PRODUCT DEVELOPMENT

It was around this time that McAfee began to branch out into other areas of computer software. Bill Larson was named McAfee's CEO on September 7, 1993. Formerly the vice-president of sales and marketing for SunSoft Inc., Larson had played a role in writing the business plan for Apple Computer Inc.'s Claris Corp., and was known for turning the Solaris 32-bit operating system into a viable competitor of Microsoft Windows NT. John McAfee retained his role as company chairman, and also became chief technical officer in order to focus more on new product acquisition and development.

According to an article in the August 14, 1997, issue of the *San Francisco Chronicle,* when Larson took the reins McAfee had no sales force to speak of. The company had 40 fax machines to accept incoming orders, and a ragtag 40-member workforce that included computer hackers, one of whom insisted on being paid in cash. Larson began to institute a number of changes, including the addition of a real sales force.

By the late 1990s more than ten million licensed copies of the company's software were in use, seven million of which were registered copies. A 100-machine license for an organization cost approximately $3,000.

Growth occurred via several acquisitions during the mid-1990s. In March 1994, Brightwork Development Inc. was acquired in a cash deal worth approximately $10.25 million. In August of the following year, the company acquired Dallas, Texas-based computer network design firm Saber Software Corp. in a $40.6 million stock deal. This was followed by the acquisition of College Park, Maryland-based Vycor Corporation in March 1996 for $9 million in cash.

After abandoning a $1 billion attempt to acquire Cheyenne Software Inc. in May, McAfee formed a partnership with Seagate Software in September. The two companies began working to offer McAfee's antivirus applications along with Seagate's backup products. That year, net income grew to $39 million on revenues of $181.1 million.

EARLY DOT-COM GROWTH

By 1997 McAfee was benefiting from the exploding popularity of the Internet and e-mail, which had become key channels for rapidly propagating computer viruses. By this time some 200 salespeople were selling the company's wares to those seeking protection.

McAfee's market value had grown to $2.3 billion. Growth was furthered via alliances with such companies as Security Dynamics and RSA Data Security, giving the company an edge as it competed head-to-head with rival Symantec Corporation. The competition turned ugly when Symantec sued McAfee for alleged patent infringement in April 1997. This was followed by a $1 billion defamation lawsuit in August from McAfee, claiming that false statements in a Symantec press release had caused McAfee's stock price to fall.

The company's legal wrangling with Symantec came at a time when its products were becoming more complex. More than an antivirus software developer, by the late 1990s McAfee had evolved into a provider of network management tools, firewalls, and a variety of other security software.

International growth occurred in April 1997 when McAfee shelled out $2.6 million in cash for a controlling stake in Brazil-based Compusul-Consultores de Informatica Ltd., a former distributor. In all, the deal had a total potential value of $3.6 million.

An important development unfolded in December 1997 when McAfee merged with Network General Corporation. The deal resulted in the company changing its name to Networks Associates, at which time its stock started trading under the ticker symbol NETA. The company's former name lived on in the company's McAfee Software division. It also was in December 1997 that Network Associates made a major acquisition by paying $35 million in cash for cryptographic solu-

KEY DATES

1989: John McAfee establishes company and begins offering a shareware antivirus program on an electronic bulletin board.
1992: McAfee incorporates, at which time company's name becomes McAfee Associates Inc.
1997: McAfee merges with Network General Corp. and changes its name to Networks Associates.
1998: Network Associates establishes a new consumer-focused subsidiary named McAfee.com, which offers PC security and management products and services online.
1999: McAfee.com is spun off as a separate, publicly traded company.
2002: The company reacquires McAfee.com.
2004: Network Associates changes its name to McAfee Inc.

tions developer Good Privacy Inc.

INTERNET SECURITY PROTECTION BECOMES FOCUS

In 1998 Network Associates established a new consumer-focused subsidiary named McAfee.com, which offered PC security and management products and services online. The company kicked acquisition activity into high gear that year, snapping up Anyware Seguridad Informatica S.A.; CSB Consulenza Software di Base S.r.l.; Nordic Lantools OY and AB; Syscon (Proprietary) Ltd.; Magic Solutions International Inc.; Trusted Information Systems; Secure Networks Inc.; Dr. Solomon's Group PLC; and QA Information Security Holding AB. Network Solutions also obtained a controlling stake in Cybermedia Inc. for approximately $130 million.

By mid-1998 Bill Larson had been named chairman and CEO of Network Associates. After the McAfee Software division established an Internet venture capital fund named Vulcan in January 1999, the company capped off the decade with an initial public offering for McAfee.com, which went public in December. Network Associates retained about 75 percent of McAfee.com's stock. The McAfee.com spinoff reflected the company's growing focus on network security and the business market.

With the new millennium came new product introductions. In order to provide added protection for individual users—especially those with continuous broadband connections—McAfee.com introduced a personal firewall utility. Released early in the year, the utility was added to the company's suite of diagnostic and antivirus software. In September 2000, Network Associates introduced software to identify and remove cookies from computers. Cookies are files containing personal information, which have the potential to compromise security.

CHANGING LEADERSHIP

In early 2001 an important leadership change occurred when George Samenuk was named as Network Associates' chairman and CEO. Another change occurred in December, when the company named Gene Hodges as president. Anticipating consumer market changes, Mcfee.com introduced a product called VirusScan Wireless 2.0 that provided protection for the growing number of handheld computer users.

As part of the Network Associates' focus on network security, the company began to streamline nonrelated operations. This involved the sale of its PGP and Gauntlet businesses. In addition, Network Associates devoted $19.1 million in cash to acquire Traxess, BySupport, BySecure, and Deersoft.

After making several offers to fully reacquire McAfee.com over the course of about six months, in September 2002 Network Associates sealed the deal and reclaimed the shares it did not already own. This was a sign of the company's renewed interest in the consumer Internet security sector.

The April 2003 acquisition of Entercept Security Technologies for $125.8 million in cash, followed by the acquisition of IntruVert Networks in May for $103.3 million, bolstered Network Solutions' Intrusion Prevention Solutions product line.

Change continued at Network Associates in 2004. Early in the year, BMC Software acquired the company's Magic Solutions product line in a $47.1 million cash deal. Then, on July 1, the company changed its name to McAfee Inc. as a reflection of its commitment to offering protection for the full spectrum of customers, from individuals to small and large businesses. That same month, McAfee sold its Sniffer Technologies arm to Network General Corp. in a $235 million deal. The company rounded out the year by acquiring Foundstone Inc. in October, in a cash deal worth $86 million.

The fabric of McAfee's business continued to change in the middle years of the first decade of the 2000s. In April 2005 SPARTA Inc. acquired McAfee

Research in a $1.5 million cash deal. Midway through the year McAfee acquired Wireless Security Corporation for $20.3 million.

TURMOIL AMID CONTINUED GROWTH

McAfee had a busy year in 2006. In January the company paid a $40 million fine to the Securities and Exchange Commission in order to settle charges of securities fraud that dated back to 2000. In April, McAfee acquired SiteAdvisor Inc. for $61 million in cash. A $4.8 million deal followed two months later, which resulted in the company acquiring the security risk management and security compliance reporting software firm Preventsys Inc.

A negative development occurred in 2006 when an internal investigation revealed the need to restate financial results due to improperly dated stock options, resulting in non-cash charges of $100 million to $150 million. The scandal led to the "retirement" of CEO George Samenuk and the termination of President Kevin Weiss in October. Following this setback, board member Charles Robel was named nonexecutive chairman. Board member Dale Fuller, who had previously served as the head of Borland Software, was named interim CEO.

At the same time that McAfee made significant leadership changes, the company continued to on the acquisition path. The data loss protection solutions firm Onigma Ltd. was acquired in October for $19.1 million, and McAfee ended the year by paying $60 million in cash for Citadel Security Software Inc. in December.

In early 2007, the firm Frost & Sullivan recognized McAfee with an award for its innovative efforts in the growing area of mobile security. New leadership was finally established in April of that year, when former EMC executive David DeWalt was named president and CEO. Growth continued in November when McAfee acquired enterprise security software vendor SafeBoot B.V. for $350 million in cash.

The acquisition of SafeBoot gave McAfee a leadership position in the data protection market, and was but one example of how much the company had grown since John McAfee posted a shareware antivirus utility on an electronic bulletin board almost 20 years before.

Paul R. Greenland

PRINCIPAL SUBSIDIARIES

CoreKT Security Systems Inc.; Entercept Security Technologies Europe Ltd.; Inversiones NAI Guatemala S.A.; McAfee A.G.; McAfee Consolidated Inc.; McAfee.com Limited; MyCIO.com Inc.; McAfee GmbH; McAfee (Hong Kong) Ltd.; McAfee Security LLC; McAfee Software de Mexico S.A. de C.V.; McAfee S.r.l.; NA NetTools Holding Co.; NAI International Holdings Corp.; Network Associates Holding Company Inc.; Preventsys Inc.; SA Internet Services Inc.; Wireless Security Corp.

PRINCIPAL COMPETITORS

CA Inc.; Microsoft Corporation; Symantec Corporation.

FURTHER READING

Angwin, Julia, "McAfee Sweeps Away Viruses. Software Maker Riding the Internet Boom," *San Francisco Chronicle,* August 14, 1997.

Daly, James, "McAfee to Go Public," *Computerworld,* September 28, 1992.

Howell, Donna, "McAfee Execs Latest Options Casualties; CEO Resigns; President Fired; Stock Options Backdating Scandals Continue to Spark Changes in Tech Landscape," *Investor's Business Daily,* October 12, 2006.

———, "Network Associates Goes Forward with Offer to Buy McAfee.Com. McAfee Says Offer Is Too Low. Network Associates Now Holds 75% of the Firm, but Wants to Own Whole Thing," *Investor's Business Daily,* March 26, 2002.

Kirby, Carrie, "McAfee.com Board OKs Sale of Firm," *San Francisco Chronicle,* August 24, 2002.

Microsemi Corporation

2381 Morse Avenue
Irvine, California 92614
U.S.A.
Telephone: (949) 221-7100
Toll Free: (800) 713-4113
Fax: (949) 756-0308
Web site: http://www.microsemi.com

Public Company
Incorporated: 1960 as Microsemiconductor
Employees: 2,300
Sales: $442.3 million (2007)
Stock Exchanges: NASDAQ
Ticker Symbol: MSCC
NAIC: 334413 Semiconductor and Related Device Manufacturing

■ ■ ■

Headquartered in Irvine, California, Microsemi Corporation manufactures semiconductors for several market segments, including commercial aerospace, defense, consumer electronics, medical equipment, and mobile communications. Examples of applications for the company's semiconductors include computer monitors, LCD television displays, GPS systems, set-top boxes, MRI machines, and radar systems.

According to Microsemi, close collaboration with customers and suppliers allows the company "to identify unique ways to influence future designs—beyond the scope of simple product enhancements. The resulting 'system-engineered' solutions create must-have products with competitive barriers and higher margins."

FORMATIVE YEARS

Microsemi's roots stretch back to 1960, when the company was formed in Culver City, California, as a power conditioning equipment manufacturer named Microsemiconductor. Among the company's founders was Richard L. Geiger, a World War II veteran who saw action in Pearl Harbor and retired as a U.S. Navy captain before becoming a partner in the venture capital firm of Geiger & Fialkov.

After a quiet start, the company was acquired by Standard Resources Corporation in 1969. Developments began to occur at a fast pace during the 1970s, at which time the company's annual sales were approximately $500,000, and most of its customers were in the defense sector. Philip Frey was named as president and CEO in 1971, and was at the company's helm as it embarked upon a period of rapid growth through acquisitions. Early deals included the acquisition of Houston, Texas-based Nano Systems, Inc., in March 1971, followed by a 50 percent stake in Standard Microsystems five months later.

In March 1972, Standard Resources adopted the name Microsemiconductor Corporation. That year, operations were relocated to Santa Ana, California. A 75 percent interest in Xtel, Inc., was secured in July 1973, followed by Globe-Union, Inc.'s, Centralab business in September 1974. The company rounded out the decade with two additional deals, acquiring Regubus Semiconductor Corporation in 1975 and Quest Engineering in 1978.

COMPANY PERSPECTIVES

A long-time supplier of high-reliability discrete components to military and aerospace customers, Microsemi has transformed itself into a global supplier of high performance analog, mixed-signal integrated circuits and high reliability discrete semiconductors that manage and regulate power, protect against transient voltage spikes, and transmit, receive and amplify electronic signals.

DEFENSE INDUSTRY FOCUS

Notable developments continued at Microsemiconductor during the early 1980s. The company went public in 1981 and ended the year by acquiring Sound Wave Systems, Inc.

On February 10, 1983, the company changed its name once again, opting for the shorter nameplate of Microsemi Corporation. That same year, international expansion took place when Bombay, India-based Semcon Electronics PVT Ltd. was acquired. In addition, the company offered 1.5 million common shares of stock for sale via Baker, Watts & Co. and Fahnestock & Co.

In 1985, Microsemi made plans to expand and upgrade its plant in Santa Ana, California. The company received approval from the city council to issue $6.5 million in industrial revenue bonds to finance the initiative. It was around this time that the U.S. semiconductor industry faced heightened competition from overseas competitors.

A more than ample supply of semiconductors drove prices down, and the White House launched an investigation into alleged dumping by Japanese firms who, according to the January 27, 1986, *San Diego Union-Tribune,* saw their market share rise from 19 percent in 1977 to 38 percent in 1984. During the same time frame, the market share in the United States fell from 73 percent to 55 percent. The publication referred to comments from Intel Senior Vice-President Jack Carston, who in 1985 "said the era of all-purpose U.S. chip makers" was over.

In order to ensure their survival, U.S. semiconductor firms began to specialize. In Microsemi's case, the company remained focused on the defense industry, which came to represent approximately three-quarters of its sales. The company's capabilities in this sector would be strengthened via additional acquisitions throughout the second half of the decade, of which there were plenty.

After acquiring Microcap, Inc., in August 1985, Microsemi acquired two California companies—Torrance-based Bikor Corporation and Santa Ana-based RPM Enterprises—midway through 1986. That year, the company filed to offer 2.5 million shares of common stock through Paine Webber, Inc.

Prior acquisition activity paled in comparison to 1987, when the company spent roughly $10 million on acquisitions and revenues were approximately $50 million. That year, Microsemi snapped up Power Technology Components; General Microcircuits, Inc.; Beverly, Massachusetts-based Hybrid Components, Inc.; San Diego, California-based Cernetics Corporation; San Jose, California-based Omni Technology Corporation; and Broomfield, Colorado-based Coors Components, Inc.

Other noteworthy developments occurred in 1987. In March, Philip Frey was named chairman. About five months later, the Defense Electronics Supply Center (DESC) tapped Microsemi, National Semiconductor, Texas Instruments, and Teledyne to participate in a new initiative that enabled the companies to offer parts directly to defense contractors.

After snapping up Mooresville, North Carolina-based General Microcircuits, Inc., and Orange, California-based Distributed Microtechnology, Inc., in 1988, Microsemi rounded out the decade by acquiring Sertech Labs, Inc., and Microsemi Assembly and Test, Inc., in 1989. That year, sales reached a record $104 million. The company also acquired Garland, Texas-based Varo Quality Semiconductor, Inc., in 1989 and changed Varo's name to Micro Quality Semiconductor, Inc.

It also was in 1989 that Microsemi sold three unprofitable subsidiaries in the wake of its first quarterly loss in eight years. After losing $707,000 in the third quarter, the company sold Universal Microtechnologies to Great Britain-based Dowty Electronics and Universal Microelectronics to Taiwan-based Yubo International. Then Vitarel Microelectronics was sold to a group of managers in a leveraged buyout.

DIVERSIFICATION

Microsemi continued to grow via acquisitions during the 1990s. In 1992 the company acquired the Semiconductor Products Division of Unitrode Corporation in an $8.5 million deal. In addition to facilities in Watertown, Massachusetts, Unitrode also had operations in Ennis, Ireland.

KEY DATES

1960: The company is formed in California as a power conditioning equipment manufacturer named Microsemiconductor.
1969: Standard Resources acquires the company.
1981: The company goes public.
1983: The company shortens its name to Microsemi Corporation.
1995: Microsemi begins shifting emphasis to transportation, medical, telecommunications, and computer sectors.
2000: The company begins making semiconductors for cell phones and other types of handheld devices.

Around this time, Microsemi was struggling with a cash shortfall. In March, the company failed to make a payment on a $33 million loan. This situation led Microsemi to announce a number of cost-cutting measures, including a workforce reduction and the sale of certain assets. The company sold its Bikor and Micro-CeramX units in mid-1993. Midway through the following year, Microsemi sold its Omni Technology Corporation subsidiary in a deal with Technology Marketing, Inc.

Heading into the mid-1990s, Microsemi struck a deal with Mountain View, California-based Telcom Semiconductor, Inc., and acquired its High Noise Immunity Logic product line. A positive development occurred early the following year when the DESC awarded Microsemi with a $55,000 contract for the supply of semiconductor devices. That October, the company acquired a diode assembly product line from National Semiconductor Corporation, and part of SGS Thomson Microelectronics' Montgomeryville, Pennsylvania-based Radio Frequency Semiconductor business.

Despite difficult conditions within the larger semiconductor industry, things were going well for Microsemi in 1996. In the third quarter, the company earned $5.6 million on sales of $116 million, up 40 percent and 21 percent from the same period in 1995, respectively. An important shift was under way at this time, as the company was focusing less on the defense industry and more on the transportation, medical, telecommunications, and computer sectors.

Compared to the early 1990s, when some 70 percent of sales were generated within the defense industry, by 1996 that figure had declined to 30 percent. In addition to diversifying the markets it served, CEO Philip Frey revealed that no one customer accounted for more than 4 percent of sales, according to the November 11, 1996, issue of the *Orange County Business Journal.* It was around this time that the company began to search for a potential successor to Frey, who was 69.

Microsemi headed into the late 1990s with domestic operations in Arizona, California, Colorado, and Massachusetts. In addition, the company had established international locations in Shanghai, Hong Kong, Ireland, and India. With high-profile customers like Nokia and Motorola, Microsemi faced off against notable competitors, including AT&T, Motorola, and National Semiconductor.

After selling Mooresville, North Carolina-based General Microcircuits, Inc., in a $7 million deal, Microsemi finished out the 1990s with a steady stream of acquisitions. BKC Semiconductors, Inc., was acquired in 1998, followed by Linfinity Microelectronics, Inc., in 1999. That same year, the company also acquired the semiconductor business of Narda Microwave for $5 million.

Building on some of its acquisitions in 1999, Microsemi kicked off the new millennium by focusing on chips for cell phones and other types of handheld devices. The company also began targeting markets for high-speed wireless Internet gear, as well as medical devices like pacemakers and defibrillators. In early 2000, the company acquired Los Angeles-based HBT Products Group, which made chips for wireless devices, from Infinesse Corporation for $17.9 million. Midway through the year, the company shuttered plants in Lawrence, Massachusetts, and Riviera Beach, Florida. Microsemi ended the year by naming former Linfinity President James J. Peterson as president and CEO.

In 2001, Microsemi acquired New England Semiconductor for $9.1 million and Compensated Devices, Inc., for $11.5 million, bolstering its aerospace and military business. Despite its diversification, the company's military experience was of great benefit in the wake of the terrorist attacks against the United States on September 11, 2001, and the country's substantial military presence in the Middle East. Microsemi's chips were employed in everything from laser-guided missiles and antimissile devices to electronic bomb fuses and warship radar systems.

STREAMLINING OPERATIONS

In 2002 Philip Frey retired as Microsemi's chairman, ending his long tenure with the company, and was succeeded by Nick Yocca. That year, the company shuttered its plant in Watertown, Massachusetts, as part of a continued effort to reduce expenses. The company also sold its Montgomeryville, Pennsylvania-based Microsemi RF Products, Inc., subsidiary to Bend, Oregon-based Advanced Power Technology, Inc. Microsemi's Semcon Electronics Private Limited subsidiary and Carlsbad design center were also sold. After seven consecutive years of profitability, Microsemi recorded a $4.7 million loss for the fiscal year ending September 2002.

More plant closures were announced in 2003 as Microsemi moved to boost capacity at each of its facilities. By this time, the company's factories were operating at 35 percent of capacity, compared to 20 percent only three years before. The shutdown of the Microsemi factory in Santa Ana, California, was expected to save the company up to $12 million annually and boost its per-factory capacity to 50 percent, furthering a goal to have each factory running at 70 percent capacity by 2006, according to the October 21, 2003, issue of the *Orange County Register.*

In 2004 Dennis Leibel succeeded Nick Yocca as Microsemi's chairman. The following year, plans were made to close the company's plants in Broomfield, Colorado, and Ennis, Ireland. The two closures were in addition to eight plants Microsemi had already shuttered since 2001. In addition, the company had managed to trim its workforce from 2,600 jobs to 1,398 during the same time frame, based on figures cited in the April 28, 2005, issue of the *Orange County Register.*

FOCUSED GROWTH

In April 2006, Microsemi acquired the Bend, Oregon-based semiconductor company Advance Power Technology, Inc. (APT). Upon completion of the $139 million deal, APT became part of Microsemi's Power Products Group. Six months later, Congress awarded the group a $1.8 million appropriation for its efforts to develop semiconductors made of silicon carbide. With greater capacities for power and heat, semiconductors made of this material were of great interest to customers such as Northrop Grumman for military avionics purposes. Other applications included power grids and shipbuilding. As evidence of the product line's potential, in November Microsemi announced it was devoting $3.7 million to remodel the Bend, Oregon, plant.

Several other significant developments occurred in 2006. In October, Microsemi agreed to acquire Israel's PowerDsine Ltd. in a $245 million cash and stock deal that was completed the following January. In December the company announced the opening of a new design center in Taiwan in order to be closer to customers throughout Asia.

Microsemi began 2007 with a market capitalization of $1.3 billion. Progress continued that year, and in November the company announced it would acquire Lowell, Massachusetts-based Microwave Device Technology. The $7.8 million cash deal allowed Microsemi to expand into the sensor market, furthering a pattern of growth that had continued for almost 50 years.

Paul R. Greenland

PRINCIPAL SUBSIDIARIES

Microsemi Corp. Santa Ana; Microsemi Corp. Scottsdale; Microsemi Corp. Colorado; Microsemi Corp. Massachusetts; Microsemi Corp. Analog Mixed Signal Group; Microsemi Corp. Analog Mixed Signal Group Ltd. (Israel); Microsemi Corp. Power Products Group; Microsemi Corp. RF Power Products; Microsemi Corp. Montgomeryville; Microsemi Corp. Advanced Technology Center; Microsemi Power Module Products SAS (France); Microsemi Corp. International (Cayman Islands); Microsemi Corp. Holdings (Cayman Islands); Microsemi Corp. Israel Ltd.; Micro WaveSys, Inc.; Microsemi Real Estate, Inc.; Micro Ltd. (Bermuda); Microsemi Comercial Offshore de Macau Limitada (Macao).

PRINCIPAL COMPETITORS

Maxim Integrated Products, Inc.; Texas Instruments, Inc.; Vishay Intertechnology, Inc.

FURTHER READING

Berger, Dan, "Specialization, Dumping Probe May Rescue Semiconductor Firms," *San Diego Union-Tribune,* January 27, 1986.

Detar, James, "Military Helps Chipmaker Microsemi March Ahead; Also in Consumer Electronics; The Company Stuck with Defense When Others Left Market, Now Key Supplier," *Investor's Business Daily,* October 6, 2005.

———, "Specialty Semiconductors Power Chips Spark Turnaround Small Firm Microsemi Was Fading Fast Until It Targeted Cell Phone, PDA Field," *Investor's Business Daily,* July 6, 2001.

Finkle, Jim, "Chip Maker to Shut Factory in Santa Ana, Calif.," *Orange County Register,* October 21, 2003.

Galvin, Andrew, "Microsemi's Cost-Cutting Pays Off in Profit," *Orange County Register,* April 28, 2005.

Lyster, Michael, "Do or Diode: Microsemi Converts from Defense," *Orange County Business Journal,* November 11, 1996.

"Microsemi Corp.," *Mergent Online,* December 5, 2007, http://www.mergentonline.com.

MoneyGram International, Inc.

1550 Utica Avenue South
St. Louis Park, Minnesota 55416
U.S.A.
Telephone: (952) 591-3000
Toll Free: (800) 328-5678
Web site: http://www.moneygram.com

Public Company
Incorporated: 1988
Employees: 2,076
Sales: $595.9 million (2006)
Stock Exchanges: New York
Ticker Symbol: MGI
NAIC: 522320 Financial Transactions Processing, Reserve, and Clearinghouse Activities

■ ■ ■

Based in St. Louis Park, Minnesota, MoneyGram International, Inc., is a leading provider of payment and financial services for consumers, businesses, and financial institutions. Money orders and check services are among the company's offerings, as are electronic payment or money transfer services. As its name suggests, MoneyGram is a global enterprise, with services offered at more than 125,000 locations throughout the world.

THE FIRST DATA YEARS

MoneyGram's roots stretch back to January 1988, when American Express Company established MoneyGram as a subsidiary of First Data Corporation's own subsidiary Integrated Payment Systems, Inc., a business based in Englewood, Colorado. First Data, a financial data-processing company founded by Omaha, Nebraska, banker Perry E. "Bill" Esping in 1971, was acquired by American Express in 1980 and made a division of the company.

MoneyGram, which initially allowed people to transfer funds of up to $5,000 in cash, competed head to head with Western Union, which had been an industry player for more than a century. By September 1988, the MoneyGram service was available at approximately 3,000 agent locations. This number quickly grew to 9,000 in mid-1990, at which time the service was available in 35 countries worldwide.

American Express furthered MoneyGram's expansion in 1990 by making the service available at 112 7-Eleven convenience stores. According to a 1990 article in the *New York Times,* American Express's marketing efforts during this time were focusing on lower-income consumers, particularly minorities and immigrants, who as a demographic were loyal users of money-wiring services.

First Data was spun off from American Express in 1992 and became a publicly traded company on the New York Stock Exchange. From its base in Hackensack, New Jersey, the company expanded in the Philippines by adding Rizal Commercial Banking Corporation and Philippine Commercial International Bank in Manila to its network. The MoneyGram service continued to grow, with availability climbing to approximately 12,000 sites in 62 countries.

COMPANY PERSPECTIVES

MoneyGram International is a high-performance payment and financial services company that efficiently and economically moves money around the world or close to home.

According to a company spokesperson in a November 26, 1994, article in the *New York Times,* an influx of immigrants into the United States contributed to MoneyGram's phenomenal growth in 1993, as wiring money internationally accounted for an estimated 40 percent of the all MoneyGram business. The company's business increased some 80 percent over the previous year. With 15,500 agents in 76 countries, MoneyGram faced its heaviest competition from Western Union in 1994, which then had about 24,000 agents in 79 countries.

That year, First Data competed with Atlanta-based First Financial in a bid to acquire Western Union, which held approximately 80 to 90 percent of the money-wiring market. Although First Financial was the winner, topping First Data's offer of $1.133 billion with a $1. 193 billion bid, an interesting development occurred the following year when First Data and First Financial merged in a stock deal worth $6.7 billion, forming a new company named First Data Corporation. In order to secure the Federal Trade Commission's (FTC) approval of the merger and avoid violating antimonopoly laws, First Data was required to sell either Western Union or Integrated Payment Systems, Inc., of which MoneyGram was a subsidiary.

BRIEFLY INDEPENDENT

In the end, First Data opted to spin off MoneyGram via an initial public offering (IPO) of 14.46 million shares. The spinoff created MoneyGram Payment Systems, Inc., the nation's second largest non-bank consumer money transfer business. The FTC granted its approval of the spinoff in November 1996, and the IPO took place the following month, raising $174 million.

After the sale, First Data's stake in MoneyGram was reduced to 13 percent. Valued at $225 million, MoneyGram held about 16 percent of the global money transfer business as the company headed into 1997. That January, several significant leadership changes occurred. Most notable was the appointment of former Western Union President James F. Calvano as chairman and CEO.

Another important development occurred in 1997 when MoneyGram was named as the exclusive funds provider of post offices throughout the United Kingdom, via an agreement with Post Office Counters Ltd. In addition, the company bolstered its international distribution network by establishing MoneyGram International Ltd., in which it held a 51 percent ownership stake and London's Thomas Cook Group held the remainder.

In late 1997, both Western Union and MoneyGram were sued in federal court for false advertising. Separate class-action lawsuits alleged that while the companies advertised free transfers to victims of Hurricane Pauline living in Mexico, they still charged fees for the transactions. Revenues totaled $140.9 million that year, up 2 percent from 1996, and net income totaled $11.7 million, down from $14.6 million the previous year.

THE TRAVELERS EXPRESS YEARS

By the late 1990s MoneyGram served customers at some 22,000 locations. The company, then located in Saddle Brook, New Jersey, began 1998 by acquiring Louisville, Kentucky-based Mid-America Money Order Co. from Mid-America Bancorp in a cash deal worth $15 million. Then, in April, MoneyGram found itself on the other side of the acquisition fence when Minneapolis, Minnesota-based Travelers Express Company, Inc., offered to acquire the company in a $287 million deal.

A subsidiary of Viad Corporation, Travelers was the nation's largest money order processor. The company also owned other financial enterprises, including Game Financial Corporation, a business serving casino goers in need of cash, as well as a check rebate business named Financial Services Management Corporation. Some MoneyGram shareholders initially opposed the deal, going so far as to file a lawsuit to prevent it. In May Viad upped its offer from $17 per share to $17.35, and the deal was finalized in July. MoneyGram's employee base doubled in size, swelling from 700 to 1,400.

MoneyGram ended the 1990s by tentatively settling a federal class-action lawsuit that charged that the company, along with competitors Western Union and Orlando Valuti (businesses owned by First Data), charged hidden fees to customers who needed funds converted from dollars to pesos. On May 12, the three firms agreed to issue discount coupons totaling $375 million to some one million people who had transferred money to Mexico from 1987 to 1999.

The overall settlement was approved in U.S. District Court, Northern District of Illinois, in December 2000. Totaling approximately $400 million,

KEY DATES

1988: American Express establishes MoneyGram as a subsidiary of First Data Corporation's Integrated Payment Systems, Inc.
1992: First Data is spun off from American Express and goes public on the New York Stock Exchange.
1996: First Data spins off MoneyGram via an initial public offering that raises $174 million.
1997: The company establishes MoneyGram International Ltd.
1998: Travelers Express acquires MoneyGram.
2003: Full ownership of MoneyGram network is acquired by Travelers Express when it acquires MoneyGram International.
2004: Travelers Express is spun off from Viad as independent firm and changes its name to MoneyGram International, Inc.

the settlement also included the formation of a charitable fund, national advertising, and an agreement to disclose exchange rates.

The terrorist attacks against the United States on September 11, 2001, created some challenges for MoneyGram. Laws such as the Patriot Act resulted in stricter regulations on money transfers, in order to put a clamp on attempted money laundering. The difficulties stemming from this legislation were still very clear five years later, when Bank of America cut ties with both Western Union and MoneyGram because of cost and liability issues related to the act. In the case of MoneyGram, the company lost a key international banking partner.

Full ownership of the MoneyGram network went to Travelers Express in 2003, at which time the company acquired MoneyGram International. In December of that year, Viad announced its plans to spin off Traveler's as an independent firm. In the December 12, 2003, issue of the *Star Tribune,* Viad executive Patricia Phillips said: "We believe that Travelers Express will be worth more to shareholders as a stand-alone company than as part of a conglomerate that's associated with totally unrelated businesses. They also need their own [stock] currency for growth."

INDEPENDENT AGAIN

Following the deal, Travelers Express veteran Philip W. Milne was tapped to carry on as CEO of the company. Travelers changed its name to MoneyGram International, Inc., when the spinoff was completed in June 2004. At this time, the company continued to serve customers through its own network of offices, and via the likes of U.S. Bank, Wachovia Bank, Wal-Mart, Safeway, and Albertson's. During the third quarter, MoneyGram added 3,000 new agent locations, bringing its total to 74,000, as well as some 1,700 Speedway SuperAmerica gas stations and 144 bank locations.

In early 2005 MoneyGram extended its agreement with Wal-Mart to offer money transfer and money order services at the retail giant's stores. That year, sales increased 17.5 percent, to $971.2 million, and profits soared 72.4 percent, reaching $112.2 million. The company's employee base had grown to include 2,200 workers. In addition to 28,000 locations in North America, the company had 16,500 sites in South America, followed by Europe (32,500), Australia (9,400), Asia (5,800), and Africa (3,800).

The following year, international expansion was furthered when MoneyGram agreed to acquire Rome-based Money Express, which oversaw the approximately 800 sites selling MoneyGram services throughout Italy. Money Express was added to a newly created subsidiary named MoneyGram Italy. Business in Italy also grew when the company renewed its contract to offer money transfers through Poste Italiane. Plans were made to increase the number of Poste Italiane sites offering MoneyGram from 9,000 to 13,000.

By mid-2006, international growth pushed MoneyGram's agent base to 96,000, up almost 20 percent from the same period the previous year. Growth was especially strong in Mexico, where 1,500 new locations were secured. However, other developing markets included Asia Pacific, Eastern Europe, Guatemala, Nigeria, and South Africa. By this time, MoneyGram had introduced additional services, such as bill payment, an online money transfer service named eMoney Transfer, and debit cards, in order to maintain an edge over the competition.

The world market for MoneyGram's business swelled to $281 billion in 2006, according to the September 25, 2006, issue of the *Star Tribune.* This was an increase of 77 percent from 2000, based on data from the Boston research firm Celent. MoneyGram's share of the pie was estimated at 4 percent, compared to Western Union's 18 percent share. Projections indicated the market would grow to $345 billion by 2008, which translated into great potential for MoneyGram.

CHALLENGES AND UNCERTAINTIES

MoneyGram started off 2007 on a sour note, when it revealed that hackers had accessed one of the company's servers and stolen information on as many as 79,000 of its customers. Dubbing the breach an "isolated incident," the company told the *Saint Paul Pioneer Press* that state ID numbers, driver's license numbers, and Social Security numbers were not involved, although bank account data and biller account numbers were, along with customer names and contact information.

In early 2007 MoneyGram's operations had extended to approximately 104,000 sites in 170 countries. In September, the company announced plans to acquire PropertyBridge, Inc., a payment provider that allowed people to pay their mortgage or rent electronically using cash, checks, or credit cards.

The following month, MoneyGram's stock fell 11 percent in one day when third-quarter losses totaled $230 million. The losses stemmed from heavy investments the company made in high-rate, mortgage-supported bonds, which declined in value when many homeowners failed to make mortgage payments. Several analysts were baffled as to why MoneyGram had invested almost 33 percent of its total portfolio in subprime mortgages and residential mortgage-backed securities, as opposed to lower-risk investments.

Following this negative development, MoneyGram secured the services of JPMorgan Chase & Co. to explore the possible sale of its payment systems arm. By December 2007, the company's stock had declined in value by about 50 percent. That month, Leawood, Kansas-based Euronet Worldwide extended an unsolicited offer to acquire MoneyGram for $1.65 billion in stock. When Euronet—which operated a money transfer business consisting of 67,000 locations, as well as an ATM network and other financial-related operations—refused to sign a confidentiality agreement, MoneyGram rejected its offer, according to the December 13, 2007, *St. Paul Pioneer Press.*

Blum Capital Partners, MoneyGram's second largest shareholder, urged the company to forgo the confidentiality agreement and discuss a possible deal with Euronet. However, in a December 21, 2007, letter to Blum, MoneyGram Chairman, President, and CEO Philip Milne wrote: "We specifically decided not to engage in a public dialogue on this matter because we don't believe that is the proper way to communicate, nor in the best interests of our shareholders. We believe that parties negotiating in good faith do so in a confidential manner. Unfortunately, Euronet chose to engage in an unproductive public relations campaign that simply siphons away valuable energy that could be applied to substantive discussion. ... We firmly believe confidentiality and an agreement that potential competitive and/or sensitive information cannot be used to the detriment of MoneyGram is in the best interests of our shareholders. We have worked hard to reach a compromise with Euronet, but thus far they have rejected each of our proposals."

Milne concluded that MoneyGram remained "open to genuine proposals from third parties when we can explore them on terms that provide us the ability to maximize shareholder value." Moving into 2008, it was unclear exactly how MoneyGram would improve its position as the company began its 20th year of operation.

Paul R. Greenland

PRINCIPAL SUBSIDIARIES

MoneyGram Payments Systems, Inc.; MoneyGram of New York LLC; MoneyGram Payment Systems Canada, Inc.; MoneyGram International Holdings Limited (United Kingdom).

PRINCIPAL COMPETITORS

American Express Company; First Data Corporation; PreCash, Inc.; United States Postal Service; Western Union Company.

FURTHER READING

"First Data Raises $174M, Taking MoneyGram Public," *American Banker,* December 16, 1996.

Garrison-Sprenger, Nicole, "MoneyGram Nixes $1.65B Bid," *Saint Paul Pioneer Press,* December 13, 2007.

Lee, Thomas, "Wired for Growth," *Star Tribune,* September 25, 2006.

"MoneyGram International, Inc.," *Mergent Online,* December 5, 2007, http://www.mergentonline.com.

Onaran, Yalman, and Elizabeth Hester, "Breach Affects 79,000 MoneyGram Accounts," *Saint Paul Pioneer Press,* January 13, 2007.

Ramirez, Anthony, "2 Giants Battle in Wiring Money," *New York Times,* August 14, 1990.

Ravo, Nick, "Sending Cash: In Money Transfer, Fast Costs More than Slow," *New York Times,* November 26, 1994.

St. Anthony, Neal, "Travelers Express to Change Its Name," *Star Tribune,* December 30, 2003.

———, "Viad Ready to Spin Off Travelers Express," *Star Tribune,* December 12, 2003.

Taylor, John, "First Data to Merge with Atlanta Firm First Financial," *Omaha World Herald,* June 13, 1995.

National Frozen Foods Corporation

1600 Fairview Avenue East, Suite 200
Seattle, Washington 98102
U.S.A.
Telephone: (206) 322-8900
Fax: (206) 322-4458
Web site: http://www.nationalfrozenfoods.com

Private Company
Incorporated: 1912 as the National Fruit Canning Co.
Employees: 600
Sales: $124.6 million (2007 est.)
NAIC: 311410 Frozen Food Manufacturing

■ ■ ■

National Frozen Foods Corporation is one of the largest private-label frozen vegetable producers. It processes peas, carrots, green beans, mixed vegetables, and pureed items in plants in Washington and Oregon and sells them in grocery stores nationwide. The company also sells to restaurants, hospitals, cafeterias, and to bulk buyers—industrial or reprocessing customers—who use the vegetables in frozen dinners, canned soups, and other prepared dishes. National also sells to foodservice establishments. Additionally, the family-owned company provides custom-packaging services. National processes vegetables for such chains as Boston Market, Kentucky Fried Chicken, Wal-Mart, Sysco Foods, ConAgra, and Woodstock Farms, as well as producing its own label, Valamont.

EARLY CHANGES IN OWNERSHIP: 1912 TO POST–WORLD WAR II

William McCaffray and his brother-in-law, Mark Ewald, cofounded the National Fruit Canning Co. in Seattle in 1912 with $10,000 in savings. After enlisting to serve during World War I, McCaffray sold the company to Armour & Co., a national meatpacking firm, but the war ended before he had a chance to see active duty. He returned to Seattle where he sought to buy back his former company, but Armour would sell him only a one-eighth interest in it. He did, however, get to head the National Fruit Canning Co. He purchased the remaining shares of the company in 1932 when antitrust laws forced Armour out of the canning business.

The buyback included access to none of Armour's sales outlets, so McCaffray found himself with the challenge of developing new markets for his canned goods in the midst of the Depression. He soon landed a government contract to can beef for distribution to the unemployed. At the same time, he began to explore new methods for quick-freezing vegetables and in 1936, the company installed its first fast-freezing tunnel in Chehalis, Oregon, which was capable of processing two to three tons of food per hour. As early as 1918, the company had begun to cold pack strawberries in 50-gallon wooden barrels.

World War II created business for National, which produced tens of thousands of small cans of jam and other foods for soldiers' field kits. In the aftermath of the war, while other food processors struggled to downsize their business, National was able to find a market

COMPANY PERSPECTIVES

At National, we boast comprehensive Quality Assurance policies and procedures. These programs are utilized throughout the company—from production to operations, field to harvest, distribution to customer relations. Our commitment to our clients: maintain a quality focus while exceeding customer expectations.

for its jam tins. At National's suggestion, Fisher Flouring Mills began to include a can of its jam in each box of Fisher's scone mix. Throughout the 1950s, jams and jellies became National's core products.

SWITCH FROM CANNING TO FROZEN FOODS

By the late 1950s, National enjoyed several contracts with food industry moguls. It canned concentrates of Hawaiian Punch and orange and grape juice for Kraft Co., and it had a contract with Safeway to provide up to 800,000 cases of jams and jellies a year. However, there was a surplus of agricultural products at the time, and food processors in general were hard hit financially. National had to contend with increased competition from canning plants in the East and Midwest and with high freight rates because its Seattle plant was far from the crops on which it depended.

The $3.5 million-a-year company responded by investing in its capabilities. It installed a new freezing tunnel belt in 1958 that allowed it to process five million pounds of vegetables per year. After Safeway terminated its contract with National, the company focused its production solely on frozen products, beginning in 1964. It built a $120,000 vegetable-freezing facility in 1965 and bought ten pea vining harvesting machines.

STEADY GROWTH CONTINUES

These investments led to growth for National throughout the 1970s. Production during the year 1970 was at 47 million pounds, an increase of almost 50 percent over 1965 totals. By 1975, that figure had reached 61 million, and five years later, it had soared to 90 million. In 1975, riding the wave of its success, the company purchased and moved into new, larger headquarters in Seattle.

Steady growth in frozen vegetables continued for the company throughout the next decade. In 1986, the company had revenues of $53 million. In 1987, the company changed its name to National Frozen Foods Corp., in recognition of its exclusive focus on frozen foods. By the mid-1980s, National was selling mostly to restaurants and institutions. Private retailers constituted the next largest category of customers, with bulk buyers, who used vegetables in their prepared food items, coming in a distant third. In 1984, National was earning revenues of $57 million on 131 million pounds of production annually. By 1991, when the company phased out the last of its frozen fruit from its Burlington plant, those figures had increased to $75 million on 174 million pounds. In 1992, the company was packing vegetables for 100 different labels, including Campbell's, Western Family, and Church's Fried Chicken, and exporting a significant portion of its production to Japan and Australia.

NEW MANAGEMENT, NEW PLANTS, AND NEW MACHINERY

During this time of growth, National underwent a change of command. Art McCaffray resigned as president in 1982, turning the reins over to Steve McCaffray, a third-generation family member, upon his retirement. The change in command led to a change in leadership style. According to Steve McCaffray in a 1992 *Puget Business Journal* article, "When my father, Ted, and his brothers, Art and Bill, made decisions for the company, they never argued. They just worked out plans. I've always felt maybe they didn't express all their feelings or ideas in that environment. Today I think you need a management style that includes more involvement by employees and managers, more open discussion, even arguments."

The new management invested in new plants and new machinery. In 1985, the company opened its Moses Lake plant, adding to its plants in Burlington and Chehalis, Washington. In 1989, it initiated a $2.5 million expansion and upgrade of its 50,000-square-foot packaging operation. National needed to be able to perform quick changeovers among package sizes and labels for its private-branded items. By 1992, however, sales were down from 1991 totals of $75 million on 174 million pounds of vegetables. In 1993, heavy spring rains caused further concern about crop outcomes. However, those crops yielded $82 million on close to 200 million pounds of peas, corn, carrots, beans, and lima beans.

National also purchased Cuizina Italia, a pasta and frozen sauce company in Woodinville, Washington, in 1989, but this attempt to diversify production with vegetable pasta mixes ended in 1994, when National sold Cuizina to its management and to Orca Bay, a seafood company. "It didn't fit with our program as we

KEY DATES

1912: William McCaffray and Mark Ewald cofound the National Fruit Canning Co.
1936: The company installs its first fast-freezing tunnel in Chehalis, Oregon.
1964: The company stops canning and turns completely to frozen foods.
1975: The company moves into new headquarters in Seattle.
1987: The company changes its name to National Frozen Foods Corp.
1991: The company phases out the last of its frozen fruit from its Burlington plant.
1999: Dick Grader becomes the first nonfamily member to assume the presidency.
2000: The company closes its Burlington, Washington, pea processing plant.
2001: The company expands its Moses Lake, Washington, processing plant.
2002: Grader becomes chief executive officer; the company expands its Albany, Oregon, plant.

hoped. It didn't align well with our customers," McCaffray noted in a 1994 *Puget Sound Business Journal.*

EXPANSION AND INCREASED REVENUES

What did fit was to increase production of frozen vegetables and in 1995 National purchased 130 acres between Centralia and Chehalis, Washington, for planting vegetables. In 1997, it began a multiyear expansion of its Moses Lake plant, adding a new 70,000-square-foot building and increasing its production to 279 million pounds, up about 50 million from 1996. The company added lines for processing peas and corn in 1997, corn on the cob in 1998, and lima beans, baby carrots, sugar snap peas, and pearl onions later on. Sales jumped 20 percent from 1995 to 1998 with the increase in production. Revenues reached $107.8 million. By that time, pea processing, which had once accounted for about 60 percent of National's production, had declined and processed corn accounted for half of the company's business. "The little green pea was always our backbone, but it doesn't seem to get the play anymore," Steve McCaffray reflected in a 1998 *Puget Sound Business Journal* article.

New executive headquarters, completed in 1998, accommodated this business growth and paved the way for the next change in leadership. This shift occurred in 1999 when Steve McCaffray became chairman of the board and Dick Grader became the first nonfamily member to assume the presidency of the company. Grader had joined National in 1988 as vice-president of sales and progressed to executive vice-president in 1997. By that time, National employed 1,200 people and processed 300 million pounds of vegetables at its plants in Burlington, Chehalis, and Moses Lake, Washington, and Albany, Oregon.

LABOR CONFLICTS IN THE 21ST CENTURY

By the year 2000, the market for frozen vegetables was constricting and higher energy costs, supply and capacity problems, and foreign competitors were forcing some in the industry to shutter their plants. Change in the demand for peas and lower prices for them, combined with high operating costs for agriculture and food processing in eastern Washington, led National to shut down its 74-year-old Burlington pea processing plant and to stop processing peas at its plant in Centralia, Washington. Those who worked at the Burlington plant and the farmers who supplied it with peas were hard hit by the decision. The following year, National, among the top five of the nation's private-label frozen vegetable processors, expanded freezing capacity at its Moses Lake plan so that it could process 50 tons of vegetables per hour. In total, National processed about 300 million pounds of finished products each year.

Dick Grader assumed the role of chief executive officer of National in 2002 when Steve McCaffray stepped down after 40 years at the company's helm. For the first time since its founding, there was no McCaffray leading National. "There was some jitteriness at first when we went outside for leadership, but we needed the best person for the job, and no family member was experienced or ready," said the retiring McCaffray in a 2002 *Seattle Post-Intelligencer* article. That year the company expanded its Albany, Oregon, plant and enjoyed record sales of more than $100 million.

Grader faced tension with National's workforce beginning in 2004. The company asked workers to make concessions, such as cuts in pay, fewer healthcare benefits, and an increased number of qualifying hours for certain worker benefits and pay increases. According to the Teamsters Union, it also manufactured two decertification elections in 2004 and 2007, both of which were defeated by a solid majority of workers. These moves led to tension between National and the union, which, in 2007, filed charges of unfair labor practices against the company with the National Labor Relations Board. After National cut off negotiations with the union and terminated its contract with workers, the Teamsters protested the company's actions by shutting down the Port of Seattle's Terminal 46.

Despite such bad press and the fact that demand for frozen vegetables remained flat, National's profits continued to grow. In 2004, the company had $116 million in annual revenue. In order to remain competitive, National invested throughout the next three years in software to track and maximize sales and profits, to analyze production and supply data in real time, and to schedule its workforce, which during peak season operated three shifts around the clock. The company was invested in doing all it could to cope with a business where the profit margin was low and the competition extremely high.

Carrie Rothburd

PRINCIPAL COMPETITORS

Birds Eye Foods, Inc.; General Mills, Inc.

FURTHER READING

Baker, M. Sharon, "Company's Success Is Just a Corn-Fed Line: National Frozen Foods Is Boosting Sales Thanks to a New Interest in Corn," *Puget Sound Business Journal,* June 26, 1998, p. 54.

———, "100 Largest Private Companies: Corn-Fed National Frozen Wants You to Eat Your Veggies," *Puget Sound Business Journal,* June 24, 1994, p. 33.

Larson, Melissa, "Frozen Foods Packer Demands Flexible Filling; National Frozen Foods Corp. Requires Adaptable Filling Machinery," *Packaging,* November 1992, p. 41.

Lyons-Holestine, Kate, "Frozen Food on the Grow," *Wenatchee World,* January 15, 1997, A1.

Mulady, Kathy, "CEO of Family-Run Frozen-Food Firm Is Stepping Down," *Seattle Post-Intelligencer,* June 7, 2002, p. D1.

"Teamsters Tell Colonel Sanders: Stop Your Supplier's War on Workers," *U.S. Newswire,* September 10, 2007.

Wolcott, John, "Frozen Foods: A 'Human Success Story,'" *Puget Sound Business Journal,* July 17, 1992, p. 19.

Nebraska Furniture Mart, Inc.

700 South 72nd Street
Omaha, Nebraska 68114-4614
U.S.A.
Telephone: (402) 255-6327
Toll Free: (800) 359-1200
Fax: (402) 392-3429
Web site: http://www.nebraskafurnituremart.com

Wholly Owned Subsidiary of Berkshire Hathaway Inc.
Founded: 1937
Employees: 2,408
Sales: $1 billion (2007 est.)
NAIC: 442110 Furniture Stores; 443111 Household Appliance Stores; 443112 Radio, Television, and Other Electronics Stores

■ ■ ■

A subsidiary of Berkshire Hathaway Inc., Nebraska Furniture Mart, Inc., is an Omaha, Nebraska-based operator of three mega-stores, offering a wide selection of furniture, flooring products, electronics, computers, and appliances. Nebraska Furniture also offers building solutions for built-in kitchen appliances, whirlpool baths, and custom electronics, including home security systems, multiroom audio systems, home theater systems, central vacuum systems, telephone outlets, digital satellite systems, and prewiring for new homes.

A major Nebraska tourist attraction, the flagship store, located in Omaha, is 450,000 square feet in size and includes a Burger King restaurant. Nearby on the massive campus is a 500,000-square-foot warehouse and distribution center and Mrs. B's Clearance Center and Factory Outlet Store. Almost as large is the Kansas City, Missouri, campus and its store, which features a 450,000-square-foot showroom and a Quiznos Sub outlet. On a much smaller scale is the Des Moines, Iowa, store, which sells only flooring, appliances, and electronics. Furniture sales in central Iowa are handled by Homemakers Furniture, a two-store operation in Des Moines acquired in 2000. In addition, Nebraska Furniture sells through its web site.

FOUNDER, RUSSIAN BORN: 1893

The origins of Nebraska Furniture is a quintessential immigrant success story. The company's founder, Rose Blumkin, known to her employees and customers as Mrs. B, was born Rose Gorelick in a Jewish settlement near Minsk, Russia, in 1893. She was one of eight children born to a rabbi and his wife, who ran a grocery store while her husband devoted his days to study. Rose received little formal education, yet decades later famed financier Warren E. Buffett maintained, "Put her up against the top graduates of the top business schools or chief executives of the *Fortune* 500 and, assuming an even start with the same resources, she'd run rings around them."

Starting at an early age, Rose did receive a practical business education working in her mother's store, helping out when she was just six years old. At the age of 13 she walked 18 miles to the nearest train station in order to seek work outside the settlement and then after two-dozen rejections used her powers of persuasion, which would serve her well throughout her life, to get a job as a clerk at a dry goods store. Just three years later she was manager of the store, supervising half-a-dozen men.

COMPANY PERSPECTIVES

An American legend, Rose Blumkin (Mrs. B), knew early in life that honesty and integrity would serve her well. Those beliefs laid the foundation for Nebraska Furniture Mart's rise to its status as a Midwestern retailing legend.

At the age of 20 she married Isadore Blumkin, a shoe salesman, and would have likely lived her life in obscurity as little more than a peasant had world events not intervened. With the outbreak of World War I in 1914, Isadore fled to the United States to avoid being drafted into the Russian army. The war would also hasten the end of czarist rule in Russia and ushered in the Soviet Union. In 1917, with tensions mounting in the country, Rose left to join her husband. Stopped at the Siberian-Chinese border by a Russian guard, she concocted a story that she was on a trip to purchase leather for the army. She then closed the deal by promising to bring back a bottle of vodka for the guard.

ROSE BLUMKIN AND HUSBAND MOVE TO OMAHA: 1919

Rose booked what she thought was first-class passage on a ship that turned out to be a peanut boat that made stops in China and Japan. After six weeks in transit she finally arrived in Seattle and despite an inability to speak English made her way to Fort Dodge, Iowa (with the help of the American Red Cross and the Hebrew Immigrant Aid Society) to rejoin her husband. In 1919 she and Isadore moved to Omaha, where a community of Russian Jews had formed. There her husband ran a secondhand clothing store. Rose gave birth to four children during the 1920s and learned English. She also brought over to America her parents and seven siblings.

With the advent of the Great Depression of the 1930s Rose began exercising her gifts as a shopkeeper to help her husband. According to the *Wall Street Journal,* "She rented shotguns and peddled used clothing, jewelry, fur coats, and anything else she could lay her hands on." She also displayed a gift for marketing. In one well-documented example, she offered to clothe a man from head to toe for just $5. She printed up 10,000 fliers to that effect, and a day later the secondhand clothing store did $800 in business.

In 1937 Rose decided to open her own furniture store and with $500 borrowed from her brother she rented a store in the basement of a pawn shop located across the street from her husband's clothing store. She then took the train to Chicago, the center of the wholesale furniture business at the time, and began visiting manufacturers to ask for merchandise on credit. Her perseverance and eagerness won them over and she returned home with $12,000 worth of furniture for inventory. The trip also provided her with a name for her new venture, taken from the American Furniture Mart she saw in Chicago.

FURNITURE STORE OPENS: 1937

Nebraska Furniture Mart opened in February 1937. Rose's business model was simple and effective: buy at 5 percent over wholesale and mark up the merchandise by 10 percent. She tried to meet the needs of her customers while giving them the best deal possible. It became encapsulated in a phrase that in effect became the motto for Nebraska Furniture: "Sell cheap and tell the truth."

While this was a winning formula in the long run, the business had to endure some difficult times for the first dozen years. Early on Rose sold all of the furniture and appliances in her own house in order to pay $800 to her creditors. The competition also did not look kindly on Nebraska Furniture underselling them and pressured manufacturers not to supply to her. Nor would banks lend her money. Undeterred she bought furniture as far away as New York, had it shipped to Omaha, and was still able to beat the price of her competition. In one often-repeated instance she was taken to court for unfair trade in 1950 because she was selling carpet that usually fetched $7.95 a yard for just $3.95 a yard. She pleaded with the judge, maintaining, "I sell everything 10 percent above cost, what's wrong? I don't rob my customers." Not only did the judge throw out the case, the next day he stopped by the store to buy $1,400 worth of carpeting.

Nebraska Furniture reached a major turning point in 1950 when the outbreak of the Korean War led to a sudden drop in business, leaving Rose with a lot of excessive inventory but not enough cash to meet her loan payments and other bills. A local banker offered her a $50,000 loan for 90 days, relying on the merchandise as collateral. Rose took the loan and used it to rent an auditorium and to place an ad in the local newspaper announcing a major sale. In a matter of three days she sold $250,000 worth of merchandise, allowing her to pay off all of her debts including the short-term loan. From that day forward she would never have to borrow money again, and as a result of minimal overhead Nebraska Furniture was able to keep charging lower prices and maintain a competitive advantage.

It was also in 1950 that Isadore died. Their son, Louis, had gone to work for Nebraska Furniture after

KEY DATES

1937: Rose Blumkin starts Nebraska Furniture Mart in pawn shop basement in Omaha.
1950: Company pays off debt and never borrows again.
1975: Larger operation replaces store devastated by tornado.
1983: Berkshire Hathaway acquires Nebraska Furniture.
1989: Rose Blumkin launches rival business, Mrs. B's Warehouse.
1992: Berkshire Hathaway acquires Mrs. B's.
1998: Rose Blumkin dies at age 104.
2000: Homemakers Furniture of Des Moines, Iowa, is acquired.
2003: Kansas City store opens.

serving in the military in World War II and took over management of the company as president, while as chairman Rose spent her time on the sales floor, especially devoted to the carpeting department. Louis learned the business well from his mother and soon made a name for himself as an astute buyer as well as an innovative retailer in his own right. In addition to furniture and carpeting Nebraska Furniture began selling appliances and electronics.

As the business grew during the 1950s it spread to several Omaha locations until they were consolidated into a flagship store at 2205 Farnum. A new flagship store opened on South 72nd Street in 1970, but five years later it was completely destroyed by a tornado. Undeterred, Rose and her son built a new and even larger store on the site. In 1980 the other Omaha stores was shut down and all business was thereafter conducted at this new 200,000-square-foot store.

Nebraska furniture posted sales of more than $100 million from one location in 1983. It was a remarkable total for several reasons. After the new store opened in the mid-1970s, annual sales were less than $50 million, an amount that represented about all the greater Omaha market could support. Given that the city's population was growing at only a modest rate, Nebraska Furniture, in order to enjoy such strong sales growth, simply increased its market reach farther and farther from Omaha, as customers were more than willing to make the trek to shop there. The amount of business the Omaha store generated was reportedly staggering, more than any other home furnishings store in the country. In fact, it sold more furniture, carpets, and appliances than all of its Omaha competitors combined.

WARREN BUFFETT ACQUIRES COMPANY: 1983

Nebraska's Furniture's success and the legacy of Mrs B. was not lost on another Omaha native, Warren Buffett. In the late 1960s he had offered $7 million for the business, an amount that Rose turned down while calling him cheap. In 1983 he came calling again, but Rose was 89 and more receptive, eager to raise cash for her children and grandchildren and ensure the company's future with Buffett's deep pockets. Moreover, Buffett had a reputation for keeping successful management in place and indicated no desire to replace the Blumkin family members who were involved in running the business.

Without taking inventory or an audit a deal was quickly reached and sealed with a handshake, calling for Buffett's company, Berkshire Hathaway, to purchase 90 percent of the business for $60 million. The written agreement would comprise only two pages, and legal fees related to the deal amounted to just $1,400. An option to buy back 10 percent of the company was subsequently exercised by members of the Blumkin family, so that in the end Berkshire Hathaway had in effect paid $55 million for 80 percent of Nebraska Furniture.

Although there was a change in ownership, little changed at Nebraska Furniture. Mrs. B continued to roam the carpet sales floor, albeit on a motorized cart, and sales continued to grow at a steady rate, topping $150 million in 1988. By this time her son Louis had retired as CEO and assumed the chairmanship. Louis's son Irvin had taken over as CEO and son Ronald served as chief operating officer.

The new leadership would soon, however, run into trouble with their headstrong grandmother, who believed they were meddling with her beloved carpeting department, which in the previous three years had seen a 17 percent decline in sales while the other department improved sales by 24 percent. In May 1989 she walked out and a few months later, at the age of 95, invested $2 million to open Mrs. B's Warehouse, a new business across the street that sold furniture and carpet. She leased out the home-furnishings department and ran the carpeting business herself. Although Mrs. B's Warehouse was not going to drive her grandsons out of business, within two years it was Omaha's third largest carpet retailer. In late 1991, two days before her 98th birthday, Buffett made peace with Rose, who had become angry with him after he had sided with the grandsons, bringing her roses and chocolates and a $5 million offer for the Warehouse business. She accepted and this time Buffett made sure to have Rose sign a noncompete agreement.

ROSE BLUMKIN, 104, DIES: 1998

Rose continued to work at Mrs. B's Warehouse, and a year later celebrated her 100th birthday at the store, joined by Nebraska Governor Ben Nelson, Senator Bob Kerrey, and other dignitaries. She continued to work seven days a week as long as the store was opened for business until she was 103, sometimes relying on an oxygen mask and tank connected to her cart. Even after she retired and her health began to deteriorate she continued to be driven to the store each day to be given daily briefings on how business was going on top of several phone calls she placed each day to the grandchildren she put in charge of Mrs. B's Warehouse. In time this operation would be subsumed by Nebraska Furniture, becoming Mrs. B's Clearance Center and Factory Outlet Center. On August 1998 Rose Blumkin died four months shy of her 105th birthday.

In the final years of Rose's life, Nebraska Furniture expanded on several fronts. In 1993 the company opened NFM Builder Sales in Des Moines, Iowa, selling appliances and flooring to home builders and contractors. By the end of the decade the business outgrew its space and as part of the expansion plans Nebraska Furniture decided to add a retail operation, Nebraska Furniture Mart Appliances & Flooring, which would refrain from selling furniture or general electronics equipment.

The main reason that the company did not sell furniture in Des Moines was due to an entrenched competitor, Homemakers Furniture, established a quarter-century earlier and modeled after Nebraska Furniture. Homemakers's main store was about 300,000 square feet in size, and it maintained a newer 65,000-square-foot outlet as well. The enterprise frustrated Nebraska Furniture's attempts to gain a significant share of the market in central Iowa for a time. In September 2000, however, Nebraska Furniture acquired Homemakers. Because the brand was well established in the market, Nebraska Furniture elected to allow the stores to operate under the Homemakers name.

Other changes followed in the new century. The Omaha operation was modernized in 2000 and a Mega-Mart was added to sell electronics and appliances. In 2002 Mrs. B's Clearance Center and Factory Outlet Center was renovated and a new warehouse and distribution center added to the 77-acre Omaha campus. The extra warehousing capabilities would be needed to support the opening of a third Nebraska Furniture store in 2003 in Kansas City. This 450,000-square-foot store performed so well that it soon required its own distribution operation, and in 2006 a new warehouse and distribution center was added in Kansas City. A year later the Omaha operation grew even larger with the addition of 25,000 square feet to the electronics and appliance store, originally intended to accommodate the new fixtures required by the increasingly popular flat-screen television.

In addition to increasing stock by 20 percent, the renovated store included in-store departments dedicated to Apple, Sony, Harman@Home, and Bose products. These investments were made to keep Nebraska Furniture ahead of the competition, which by then included Costco, a major seller of electronics and appliances that opened its first Nebraska store in Omaha in 2007. While not about to rest on its laurels, the company was confident that it could fend off any new competitors. "We set the standard in Omaha, and in Des Moines and Kansas City," Executive Vice-President Bob Batt told *Omaha World-Herald* in October 2007, adding, "We set the bar, not the other way around. They're chasing us. Never caught us."

Ed Dinger

PRINCIPAL OPERATING UNITS

Nebraska Furniture Mart; Homemakers Furniture; Mrs. B's Clearance Center and Factory Outlet Store.

PRINCIPAL COMPETITORS

Best Buy Co., Inc.; Circuit City Stores, Inc.; Ethan Allen Interiors Inc.

FURTHER READING

"Cheap No More; Berkshire Buys Blumkin," *Fortune,* October 17, 1983, p. 8.

Feder, Barnaby J., "A Retailer's Home-Grown Success," *New York Times,* June 17, 1994, p. D1.

———, "Rose Blumkin, Retail Queen, Dies at 104," *New York Times,* August 13, 1998, p. D19.

Hayes, John R., "The Oversight Was Understandable," *Forbes,* April 26, 1993, p. 196.

James, Frank E., "Furniture Czarina: Still a Live Wire at 90, a Retail Phenomenon Oversees Her Empire," *Wall Street Journal,* May 23, 1984, p. 1.

Johnson, Patt, "Nebraska Furniture Buys Homemakers," *Des Moines Register,* September 15, 2000, p. 1A.

Miles, Robert P., *The Warren Buffett CEO: Secrets from the Berkshire Hathaway Managers,* New York: John Wiley & Sons, Inc., 2002, 412 p.

Pinkerton, Janet, "Dealerscope Hall of Fame: The Blumkin Family," *Dealerscope,* January 2002, p. 62.

Neogen Corporation

620 Lesher Place
Lansing, Michigan 48912
U.S.A.
Telephone: (517) 372-9200
Toll Free: (800) 234-5333
Fax: (517) 372-2006
Web site: http://www.neogen.com

Public Company
Incorporated: 1981
Employees: 427
Sales: $86.2 million (2007)
Stock Exchanges: NASDAQ
Ticker Symbol: NEOG
NAIC: 325413 In-Vitro Diagnostic Substance Manufacturing

■ ■ ■

Neogen Corporation is a Lansing, Michigan-based manufacturer of products designed to protect human and animal health. The company's food safety division markets a wide range of test kits to detect the presence of bacteria, toxins, pathogens, and allergens for the bakery and cereal, beverage, dairy, feed and grain, foodservice, meat and poultry, nutraceuticals, pet food, prepared food, produce, sauces, and seafood industries. Neogen's animal safety products include diagnostics, veterinary instruments, pharmaceuticals, nutritional supplements, disinfectants, and rodenticides. Subsidiary Acumedia Manufacturers, Inc., offers dehydrated culture media for industrial, pharmaceutical, biotech, food safety, and life science uses. Neogen's life sciences unit markets forensic drug detection kits for a wide variety of prescription and illegal drugs, and research test kits to detect levels of hormones, steroids, prostaglandins, leukotrienes, thromboxanes, cyclic nucleotides, lipoxins, and histamine. Some of the tests, for example, are used to detect performance-enhancing drugs in racehorses and greyhounds. Another subsidiary, Hacco, Inc., provides contract and private-label formulation and packaging of rodenticides and other bait formulations. In addition to its corporate headquarters, Neogen maintains operations in Lexington, Kentucky; Randolph, Wisconsin; and in Europe through a Scotland office.

NEOGEN FOUNDED 1981

Neogen was incorporated in Lansing, Michigan, in June 1981, with the goal of expanding the state's economy beyond the confines of the automotive industry. During this time the automobile industry in the United States was struggling, leading to a shrinking tax base in Michigan, which was heavily dependent on the industry. A special task force sponsored by the state had identified two areas of possible growth: automated manufacturing and biotechnology. Around the same time, the nonprofit fund-raising arm of Michigan State University, the Michigan State University Foundation, formed Neogen as a vehicle to raise venture capital for limited partnerships to exploit the innovations emanating from research conducted at the school. Not only would such a company help retain faculty members who would have a way to pursue business ventures without leaving the school, it could help diversify the area's economy. Serv-

> ## COMPANY PERSPECTIVES
>
> Neogen's customers face serious consequences if their products are contaminated with any of a number of well-established or emerging threats. No other company offers the breadth of products, variety of formats, and packaging options to provide the efficient solutions that food and animal safety customers are seeking.

ing as Neogen's founder was James L. Herbert, a vice-president of agricultural genetics company DeKalb AgResearch.

FIRST RESEARCH FUNDED

The foundation purchased the first $100,000 in stock and soon invested another $130,000. Dow Chemical's former chief executive, Herbert Doan, supplied a further $250,000 and became Neogen's chairman. Looking to become involved in the emerging biotechnology field, Doan's strategy, as he explained to *Michigan Business* in 1989, was to "develop and market products designed to measure and control agricultural residues that might affect animals feeds, agricultural foods intended for human consumption or the environment."

After setting up shop in a 400-square-foot facility with just a pair of employees and some used desks, Neogen began to move beyond the concept stage in 1984 when it provided $1 million in funding to a pair of Michigan State professors to develop a simple, inexpensive diagnostic kit to screen grain used in animal feed for a carcinogen called aflatoxin. The work resulted in Neogen's first product, Agri-Screen.

Michigan State University research also led to a second product line, one that was predictive in nature. Called EnviroCaster, the battery-powered device could be installed in a field or orchard, as well as a golf course, to record environmental conditions every 15 minutes. Using this data, computer models could determine the likelihood and severity of insect infestation and fungal infection, and determine the time and amount of plant chemicals that should be applied.

In May 1985 Neogen also grew through external means, acquiring the Ideal Instruments Division of Immunogenetics Inc. The Chicago-based company had been in business for about 60 years, manufacturing veterinary instruments. While at first blush the addition of Ideal appeared unconnected to Neogen's other product lines, the company in fact shared the same overarching mission as Neogen because the accurate delivery of animal drug product is an important way to control residues of drugs that could invade the meat or milk supply. Moreover, Ideal provided a predictable revenue stream that could help support the launch of Neogen's more advanced products. In fiscal 1989, Neogen was generating about $7 million in annual sales, $4 million of which came from Ideal, $2 million from EnviroCaster, and $1 million from Agri-Screen.

FARMING MOREL MUSHROOMS

One Neogen-backed venture clearly deviated from the company's mission: the year-round commercial growing of morel mushrooms, which in the wild were harvested in North America only in May and June. It grew out of the work of Michigan State scientists, Gary Mills and James Malachowski, who built on the finding of Ronald Ower, the first person to grow the morel in captivity. The resulting Morel Mountain Mushroom Company found a partner in another Michigan-based company, Domino's Pizza Inc., which in 1989 paid $1 million for a 25 percent interest. In the early 1990s the start-up company began selling morels to gourmet shops, for about $300 a pound, although not to Domino's. In 1994 the two partners sold the business to Terry Farms, a major grower and supplier of fresh button mushrooms.

INITIAL PUBLIC STOCK OFFERING

Neogen was taken public in 1989 at $5 a share. Convincing customers that its tests, which could be conducted by almost anyone with a little training, were as reliable as the time-consuming tests conducted by professionals took some time. By the early 1990s, however, the company was established enough to accelerate the growth of its food safety business. Early in 1991 Neogen signed an agreement to provide ConAgra Inc. with kits to detect nitrates in water. A year later the company added to its capabilities by acquiring Lexington, Kentucky-based WTT Incorporated, maker of test kits used to detect performance-enhancing drugs used in horse and greyhound racing. This business was subsequently renamed ELISA Technologies.

More acquisitions followed between 1993 and 1995. In 1993 the plant diagnostics product lines of Agri-Diagnostics Associates was purchased. Later in the year the acquisition of Kansas City, Missouri-based Enzytec, Incorporated, added products and technology used to detect pesticides in food and in the environment. Camden, New Jersey-based AMPCOR, Incorporated, was purchased in 1994, adding detection

KEY DATES

1981: Neogen is incorporated.
1984: Development begins on first food safety test kit.
1985: Ideal Instruments is acquired.
1989: Company is taken public.
1995: International Diagnostics SystemCorp. is acquired.
1999: AMPCOR is acquired.
2003: Neogen Europe Ltd. is established.
2006: Secondary stock offering retires bank debt.
2007: Neogen completes a 3-for-2 stock split.

products for foodborne bacteria. Finally, in June 1995 Neogen acquired St. Joseph, Michigan-based International Diagnostic Systems Corp., whose three-dozen diagnostic tests to detect drugs of abuse in animals were folded into the ELISA unit.

Although the focus was on building up its food safety and animal safety businesses, Neogen continued to invest in veterinary instruments. In 1991 the Dynax division of Aries Manufacturing Co., was acquired and the electronic instruments it manufactured for use in small animal and equine veterinary medicine became part of Ideal Instruments. As part of a restructuring in 1996, however, electronic instruments would be phased out.

Given certain events that took place in the mid-1990s it was understandable why Neogen would want to focus more of its resources on food and animal safety. In late 1995 the U.S. Food and Drug Administration outlined new safety rules for seafood that would go into effect later in the decade, and the U.S. Department of Agriculture established a new inspection system. There were also an increasing number of foodborne illness cases reported, leading to global concerns about food safety. In July 1996, for example, Japan suffered a severe outbreak of infections from the bacteria *E. coli,* leading to an opportunity for the sale of diagnostic tests to this market. Later in 1996 Neogen's salmonella test kit received approval from a key third-party test validation organization, the Association of Official Analytical Chemists.

NEOGEN'S FIRST PROFITABLE YEARS

Neogen became profitable in fiscal 1994, netting $856,000 on total revenues of $10.7 million. Sales enjoyed steady growth, reaching $15.3 million in fiscal 1997 while profits exceeded $1.8 million. As a result, the value of Neogen approached $15 a share. Record results continued in fiscal 1998, when Neogen recorded revenues of $18.5 million and net income of $2.2 million. The company also completed two more acquisitions: Triple Crown Company, maker of pharmaceutical products for the professional equine market, and the ImmunoVet operations of France's Vetiquinak S.A., which brought a biologics production facility in Tampa, Florida.

Neogen also introduced a number of successful products in fiscal 1998, helping to grow revenues to $22.2 million in fiscal 1999, while earnings improved slightly. Nevertheless, the price of its stock began to slide in 1998 and continue to decline until reaching $7 in October 1999, about half of what the company believed it was worth. Neogen was not alone. Many small cap companies were being overlooked at the time, and management took advantage of available cash to buy back a large number of shares. It also earmarked some of the $11 million cash it had on hand and $10 million in credits to make further acquisitions in order to grow larger and command more attention from Wall Street.

Acumedia Manufacturers, Inc., was acquired in February 2000, bringing a line of media used to grow bacteria to testable levels that complemented Neogen's foodborne bacteria testing segment. Shortly after fiscal 2000 closed, Neogen bought AmVet Pharmaceuticals, adding 25 veterinary products to its portfolio of animal safety products, including a liquid antibiotic, dewormer, and a vitamin deficiency treatment. Two months later another acquisition was made, Revere, Massachusetts-based Squire Laboratories, which developed pharmaceuticals and other health products for performance horses.

Neogen's stock price rose steadily, approaching the $20 mark, while revenues increased to $23.5 million in fiscal 2000 and jumped to nearly $35 million in fiscal 2001; net income improved from $3.1 million to $3.2 million. As a result, Neogen gained even greater visibility and was named to *Forbes* magazine's Top 200 Small Companies in America.

EXPANDING DOMESTICALLY AND OVERSEAS

Neogen still had more than $7 million in cash and its lines of bank credit totaled another $10 million, allowing the company to make further acquisitions to maintain its expansion. Early in fiscal 2002, San Diego, California-based QA Life Sciences was added in a stock deal, providing Neogen with a filter membrane system. Later in the year, Neogen acquired Gene-Trak Systems of Hopkinton, Massachusetts, a maker of foodborne pathogen detection test kits that relied on DNA probe technology, giving Neogen another platform on which to build. The markets for the company's food and animal safety products were also expanding, as worries mounted about mad cow disease, foot and mouth disease, antibiotic residues in food, and bioterrorism. Revenues increased to more than $42 million in fiscal 2002, and net income improved to nearly $4 million.

Those numbers grew to $46.5 million and $4.8 million in fiscal 2003, when Neogen completed another acquisition, Adgen Ltd. of Ayr, Scotland, a manufacturer of agricultural diagnostic testing products that had also acted as Neogen's European distributor. Its name was subsequently changed to Neogen Europe Ltd., and was used to build Neogen's European sales. The company also positioned itself for growth in Asia by establishing a sales and distribution center in Shanghai, China, to tap into the emerging food safety market in that vast country. With only 20 percent of the company's sales coming from overseas, the international marketplace offered a great deal of promise for the future.

Neogen added to its roster of intervention products in fiscal 2004, spending $12 million to acquire two ConAgra companies, Hacco, Inc., and Hess & Clark, Inc. The former gave Neogen entry into the rodenticide market while the latter positioned Neogen in the disinfectant market. The following year Neogen beefed up its European operation by acquiring Germany's Biologische Analysensysteme GmbH, the distributor of its food safety test products in Germany. Its operations were folded into Neogen Europe.

POSITIONED FOR A STRONG FUTURE

Revenues grew from $55.5 million in fiscal 2004 to $62.8 million in fiscal 2005, with animal safety sales enjoying especially strong growth. Net income increased from $5.1 million to more than $5.9 million. Those numbers continued to grow at a strong pace in fiscal 2006 and fiscal 2007, increasing from $72.4 million to $86.1 million, while net income improve from $7.4 million to $9.1 million. The company was also able to make a secondary offering of stock in June 2006, netting $12.2 million in cash that was used to retire all bank debt.

Now a quarter-of-a-century old, Neogen was well positioned to achieve even greater growth. With the United States importing an increasing amount of its foods, the need for test products was growing domestically, while at the same time Neogen had barely scratched the surface of its international sales potential. The company's stock was also receiving the kind of attention management believed it deserved. In September 2007 the company repaid loyal investors with a dividend in the form of a 3-for-2 stock split that also served to make more shares available for trade and improve liquidity.

Ed Dinger

PRINCIPAL SUBSIDIARIES

Acumedia Manufacturers, Inc.; Centrus International, Inc.; Ideal Instruments, Inc.; Neogen Europe Limited; Hacco, Inc.; Hess & Clark, Inc.

PRINCIPAL COMPETITORS

Inverness Medicals Innovations, Inc.; Quidel Corp.; Abaxis, Inc.

FURTHER READING

Banas, Teri, "'Concept' Firm Grows into Leader," *Lansing State Journal,* March 26, 1999, p. 5B.

Berg, Steve, Christine Caswell, and Ann Kammerer, "Fifth Annual Event Honors Entrepreneurs," *Greater Lansing Business Monthly,* May 1999.

Commercial Biotechnology: An International Analysis, Washington, D.C.: U.S. Congress Office of Technology Assessment, January 1984.

Evenson, A. J., "Neogen's Revenue, Profits Up," *Lansing State Journal,* October 31, 1999, p. 1C.

Smith, Rod, "Neogen Reports Company-Wide Growth," *Feedstuffs,* January 17, 2005, p. 6.

Whisenhunt, Eric, "Testing Food Source for a Worried Nation," *Michigan Business,* May 1, 1989, p. 41.

NEWMONT™

The Gold Company

Newmont Mining Corporation

1700 Lincoln Street
Denver, Colorado 80203
U.S.A.
Telephone: (303) 863-7414
Fax: (303) 837-5873
Web site: http://www.newmont.com

Public Company
Incorporated: 1921 as Newmont Corporation
Employees: 15,000
Sales: $5,526 million (2007)
Stock Exchanges: New York Toronto Australia
Ticker Symbols: NEM; NMC
NAIC: 212221 Gold Ore Mining; 212234 Copper Ore and Nickel Ore Mining

■ ■ ■

Newmont Mining Corporation is one of the world's leading gold companies, with operations or assets in the United States, Australia, Peru, Indonesia, Bolivia, New Zealand, Mexico, Canada, and Ghana. It is the only gold company included in the Standard & Poor's 500 Index, *Fortune* 500, and Dow Jones Sustainability Index-World. As of December 31, 2007, the company had proven and probable equity gold reserves of 86.5 million ounces. Newmont also produces copper, primarily at its Batu Hijau project in Indonesia, and zinc.

EARLY YEARS

Newmont Mining Corporation was founded in 1921 as Newmont Corporation by Colonel William Boyce Thompson as a type of holding company for his varied financial interests. Thompson was born in 1869 in Alder Gulch, Montana, and grew up in Butte. An overweight, cigar-smoking man with a penchant for gambling (a telling hobby for someone in his line of work), Thompson eventually landed at the Columbia School of Mines, after which he made some money in the coal business. Upon selling stock in a copper mine he had bought on installments, Thompson arrived around 1905 on Wall Street where he became a successful trader, making gains in several industries, including oil, steel, and minerals. Newmont's early strategy was to establish development companies and then to sell off much of their stock. The remaining stock was accumulated in a portfolio whose income was used to finance further mining projects. Thompson had a hand in launching several companies, including Magma Copper and Texas Gulf Sulphur, but his standard policy was to make a quick profit on a new venture and to move on to the next one.

Newmont stock reached a peak of $236 in 1929, but crashed with the rest of the stock market and dropped to $37 in 1930. Thompson died the same year, never fully recovering from surgery to reduce his obesity. His personal attorney, Charles F. Ayer, took over as head of Newmont, and the company began to retain its acquired properties rather than perpetuating its earlier cycle of trading them off. Among the companies Newmont acquired in the years prior to World War II were O'okiep Copper Company, Ltd., of South Africa, and

COMPANY PERSPECTIVES

With unsurpassed financial strength and flexibility, project development and operational expertise, and portfolio management and investment skills, Newmont is "The Gold Company" of choice for employees, shareholders, host communities and governments. Newmont is committed to the highest standards and leadership in the areas of environmental management, health and safety for its employees and neighboring communities.

Colorado's Idarado Mining Corporation. Also launched during this period was Newmont Oil Company, whose aim was to explore Texas and Louisiana for oil reserves.

EXPANDING DOMESTICALLY AND GLOBALLY

By 1940, Newmont existed as an interesting hybrid of holding company and operating company. As a holding company, Newmont's investments were primarily in well-known metal and mining companies, with copper leading the way. These investments included hundreds of thousands of shares of Kennecott, Phelps Dodge, and Hudson Bay Mining and Smelting. Gold represented about 19 percent of the company's total investments. Among the significant ventures that Newmont was actively developing were O'okiep, in which Newmont held a two-thirds interest; Getch Mine, Inc., a Nevada gold mine, 18.6 percent held by Newmont; and Alder Oil Company, a wholly owned subsidiary.

Through O'okiep, Newmont launched successful ventures in southern Africa. Abandoned by its British owners, O'okiep was acquired by Newmont for the modest investment of $2 million, and Newmont subsequently took advantage of the increased demand for copper during World War II. After the war, due to high costs and a labor shortage in the United States, Newmont decided to concentrate its prospecting abroad. The result was the acquisition of an abandoned copper-lead-zinc mine at Tsumeb in the former colony of German South West Africa.

The German owners had collected an extremely rich ore at the mine, and when the site was seized in 1939 by South Africa's Custodian of Enemy Property about 800,000 tons of the ore had been left at the surface. Newmont teamed with American Metal Company and five other partners for a bid of just over $4 million, with Newmont's share at 29 percent. Tsumeb's ore reserves turned out to be much greater than anyone (including its former German operators) had imagined, and the purchase price was covered by merely processing the ore that had been dumped at the surface.

By 1950, Newmont was led by Fred Searls who, like Thompson, was a recognizable figure on Wall Street. Known for his red bow tie and yellow-topped boots, Searls disliked publicity and preferred ore exploration to sitting in an office. During this time, Newmont became involved with lucrative Sherritt Gordon Mines of Canada.

In 1951, John Drybrough, president of the Newmont Mining Corporation of Canada subsidiary, informed Newmont officials that a company run by his brother-in-law had discovered nickel deposits in Manitoba, as well as a new, more efficient method for processing the ore. With the backing of J.P. Morgan and Company, Metropolitan Life, and several other insurance companies, Newmont went ahead with the project and invested $10 million in the mining company. Eventually Sherritt Gordon became one of the largest producers of nickel in the world.

PLATO MALOZEMOFF BECOMES PRESIDENT

Plato Malozemoff became Newmont's president in 1954, beginning a 34-year period of leadership and growth. That year the company was valued at $147 million. When Malozemoff retired in 1986, Newmont was a global corporation with a market capitalization of $2.3 billion.

The son of a mining engineer, Malozemoff was born in 1909 in St. Petersburg, Russia, where his father was managing director of British-owned Lena Goldfields, Ltd., the largest gold-mining company in Russia until its seizure by the Soviets in 1920. The Malozemoff family eventually landed in San Francisco, where Plato earned a degree in mining engineering at Berkeley in 1931. After receiving his master's degree from the Montana School of Mines, Malozemoff assisted his father in the management of gold and copper mines in Argentina and Costa Rica.

He was first noticed by Newmont executives around 1943 while working for the Office of Price Administration's minerals branch in Washington, D.C., and was hired by Newmont in 1945 as an entry-level engineer. One of the driving forces behind the Sherritt Gordon deal, Malozemoff was made a vice-president as the project successfully unfolded.

Under Malozemoff's leadership, Newmont entered a period of steady growth by acquisition and diversifica-

KEY DATES

1921: Col. William Boyce Thompson founds Newmont Corporation as investment holding company.
1925: Newmont goes public, trading on the New York Stock Exchange.
1929: With the purchase of Empire Star Mine in California, Newmont becomes a mining company.
1930: Charles Ayers becomes head of the company.
1940: O'okiep Copper Company in South Africa comes into production.
1955: Newmont helps form South Peru Copper Corporation.
1962: Newmont discovers gold at Carlin, Nevada.
1987: Company divests all copper, oil, gas, and coal interests.
1997: Newmont merges with Santa Fe Pacific Gold Corporation.
1998: Newmont Mining and Newmont Gold merge.
2001: Company completes merger with Battle Mountain Gold Company.
2002: Newmont acquires Normandy Mining Limited and Franco-Nevada Mining Corp. Limited.
2007: Miramar Mining Corporation is acquired.

tion, often through joint ventures with other well-established companies. In 1955, Newmont joined Phelps Dodge, American Smelting and Refining, and Cerro de Pasco in forming the Southern Peru Copper Corporation. That same year, a uranium oxide mine was opened in Washington State with the company's majority interest in the Dawn Mining Company. Newmont also bought a 28.8 percent share in the development of a South African copper mine with Rio Tinto in Transvaal, South Africa. In 1955, a particularly active year, investments were also made in the Philippines, Canada, and Algeria. In 1957, Empire Star Mines Company, Ltd., was merged into Newmont.

DOMESTIC INVESTMENTS INCREASE

At the end of the 1950s, Newmont began to reverse its trend toward reliance on foreign investment. In 1959, $8.2 million of the company's $13 million dividend income came from foreign holdings, primarily the mines of Tsumeb and O'okiep. Newmont took action to remedy this imbalance in 1962 by trading some of its own preferred stock for a large block of stock in Magma Copper.

With this deal, Newmont's interest in Magma was raised to 80.6 percent, and suddenly the company's income from domestic holdings surpassed its foreign-generated total. Following the acquisition of additional Magma shares, Newmont was forced by the U.S. Justice Department to divest its 2.9 percent interest in Phelps Dodge on the grounds that holdings in both large copper companies violated antitrust laws. Newmont complied, and also removed two Phelps Dodge representatives from its own board of directors.

By the middle of the 1960s, over half of Newmont's income originated in North America. Most of this was in the United States, largely due to the 1965 opening of the company's new mine at Carlin, Nevada. The mine, operated by Carlin Gold Mining Company (a wholly owned subsidiary of Newmont), began operations in April 1965, producing 128,500 ounces of gold by year-end. The output was doubled the following year and Carlin quickly became the second largest gold producer in the nation, trailing only the 90-year-old Homestake Mine, also in Nevada.

More amazing than Carlin's size was the technology used to collect its difficult-to-obtain riches. In 1966, 12 tons of overburden had to be removed and 3 tons of ore milled to retrieve an ounce of gold at Carlin. Furthermore, the gold particles were the smallest ever mined, requiring an electron microscope to be seen. Despite these obstacles, Carlin became the lowest-cost gold mine in the Western world, a fact reflected in Newmont's earnings figures, which rose to $5.15 share in 1966.

MALOZEMOFF BECOMES CHAIRMAN OF THE BOARD

Malozemoff became Newmont's chairman of the board in 1966, reinforcing his position as the company's main visionary force. Between 1965 and 1967, Malozemoff and Newmont quadrupled the sum spent by the company on exploration, reaching $4.4 million in 1966. The company's Palabora Mine in South Africa also came into production in early 1966 and began paying dividends by the end of the year. Between Palabora, Tsumeb, and O'okiep, Newmont realized dividends approaching $20 million from its southern African properties. Toward the end of 1966 and into 1967, Newmont acquired a 33 percent interest in Foote Mineral Company, a major producer of iron alloys and lithium products.

Several Newmont ventures in the 1960s, however, were unsuccessful. A lead-zinc mine in Algeria became nationalized by the government; Granduc Mine, an underground copper project in Canada, encountered a series of costly construction and development delays, including an avalanche that dumped 50,000 tons of snow on the work camp and killed 26 laborers; and a joint venture with Cerro Corporation, Atlantic Cement Company, failed to turn a profit for several years, running into alternating problems with machinery and labor.

In 1969 Newmont merged completely with Magma Copper, of which it already owned 80.6 percent. Magma's minority stockholders were issued Newmont convertible preferred stock in exchange for their shares. With earnings of over $26 million at the time of the merger, Magma was the fourth largest domestic copper producer, and by 1970 about three-fourths of Newmont's revenue came from copper. The company's strategy of shifting away from reliance on foreign sources continued; by 1970, U.S. and Canadian investments accounted for 65 percent of Newmont's net income. Many in the industry considered this a positive development, since the early 1970s were a period of increased mine nationalization as well as political machinations that made foreign investments riskier than usual.

FOCUS AS AN OPERATING COMPANY

Newmont's direction in the 1970s was toward becoming more of an operating company and less of a holding company. An ambitious expansion program was undertaken at Magma, which quickly became Newmont's chief source of revenues, accounting for about 36 percent in 1972.

This expansion was largely accomplished by investing around $90 million in 1971 in two Arizona locations, Superior and San Manuel, including $18 million for a new electrolytic copper refinery at San Manuel. The expansion raised the combined output of San Manuel and Superior to 145,000 tons of copper in 1972. By that same year, 78 percent of Newmont's net income was generated by companies operating inside Canada and the United States. Foreign interests contributed about 28 percent of the company's revenues, with Tsumeb, O'okiep, Palabora, and Southern Peru Copper leading the way.

The 1970s were a roller-coaster decade for Newmont. Technical problems plagued the new smelter at San Manuel in 1972, and new antipollution laws required the installation of another $30 million worth of equipment. By 1973, however, these and other problems were largely solved. Labor problems at Granduc improved, and Newmont's other Canadian mine, Similkameen, enjoyed a smooth first year of operation, producing near its capacity.

In 1974, Newmont set a net earnings record of $113.6 million. That same year, the company paid $28.5 million to increase its interest in Foote Mineral Company to 83 percent of voting shares. The Foote acquisition gave Newmont control of the noncommunist world's largest deposit of spodumene ore (used to produce lithium), located at Kings Mountain, North Carolina.

Between 1975 and 1978 copper prices plummeted, dropping from $1.55 a pound in 1974 to as low as 50 cents, resulting in the selling price of copper falling below its production cost in the United States. In 1977, Newmont led a consortium of six companies in purchasing Peabody Coal Company from Kennecott, which had been ordered in 1971 by the Federal Trade Commission to divest itself of what was the largest coal producer in the United States. Newmont's share in the consortium, which called itself Peabody Holding Company, was 27.5 percent. With copper prices in freefall, however, Newmont's net income declined to $5.1 million in 1977, a drop in earnings also affected by a $15 million strike at Peabody and the closing of the Granduc mine.

RECOVERY AND NEW DIRECTIONS

Newmont recovered somewhat toward the end of the 1970s. Costs were cut by suspending operations at Idarado Mining Company of which Newmont owned 80 percent, as well as at the Gamsberg zinc project, a South African joint venture. In April 1978, the end of the nationwide coal strike also allowed Peabody to become profitable once again. The Newmont Oil subsidiary began to benefit from the price deregulation of new natural gas, and higher gold prices were beneficial to the wholly owned Carlin operation. Even the often sluggish Atlantic Cement Company showed a profit in 1978 after losing about $400,000 the previous year.

By 1979 gold was beginning to play an increasingly important role for Newmont. With high gold prices, it took only 30 months for the Telfer gold mine (70 percent owned by Newmont) in Australia's Great Sandy Desert to pay back the $23.5 million laid out in development costs. In fact, Newmont earned more from gold in 1979 than it had from all its operations the year before.

In 1980, Newmont began processing gold ore from its Maggie Creek mine, 14 miles south of the main area of the Carlin operation. The open pit orebodies at Maggie Creek were estimated at 4.8 million tons of ore containing about 440,000 ounces of gold. Then, less than a mile from Maggie Creek, Newmont discovered Gold Quarry (the 20th century's most important gold strike), which was estimated to contain over eight million ounces of gold.

In 1981, while Newmont was still assessing the importance of the Gold Quarry discovery, shares of Newmont were being acquired by Consolidated Gold Fields plc (CGF), a British mining company. Malozemoff was able to reach an agreement with CGF under which CGF would end up holding 26 percent interest in Newmont, but would not attempt to increase that share. This agreement was changed in 1983, allowing CGF up to a 33.3 percent interest in Newmont as well as a maximum of three representatives on Newmont's board instead of the previous limit of two.

Also in 1983 Newmont purchased the Miami, Arizona, copper operations of City Service Company. The operations included the Pinto Valley open pit mine, whose annual capacity rated about 70,000 tons of copper contained in concentrate.

CHANGES IN THE EIGHTIES

Malozemoff ended his long tenure as Newmont's chief executive officer in September 1985 and was succeeded by Gordon R. Parker, who had been named company president ten months earlier as well as president and chief executive officer of Magma. Malozemoff, 75 years old at the time, retained his chairmanship of Newmont's board.

In October 1985 Newmont reorganized its management structure, consolidating its operations into four groups headed by executives with global responsibility: nonferrous metals under David C. Ridinger; Carlin Gold Mining Company and the company's 70 percent interest in Telfer gold mine under T. Peter Philip; lithium and industrial minerals under Thomas A. Williams; and energy operations, including Peabody and Newmont Oil, under Edward P. Fontaine.

Carlin Gold Mining Company's name was changed to Newmont Gold Company in 1986. The following year, corporate raider T. Boone Pickens and his investment group, Ivanhoe Partners, attempted a takeover of Newmont, making an offer of $95-a-share for the 90 percent of Newmont they did not already control. The takeover attempt was thwarted, however, when in one day CGF raised its share of the company up to 47.7 percent, a move made possible by Newmont's announcement of a $33-a-share dividend payment as part of a new restructuring plan.

In order to compensate for the cash drain the payout created, Newmont began selling its properties. Magma Copper was spun off to Newmont shareholders, saving Newmont the costs of modernizing Magma's facilities. At the end of 1987, the company sold its 80 percent interest in Foote Mineral for about $74 million. Another $350 million was brought in by the sale of Newmont's 4.2 million shares of Du Pont stock. Finally, all four mines in South Africa held by Newmont were sold for $125 million.

FOCUSING ON GOLD

The main consequence of Newmont's restructuring was the shift of the company's focus to gold exclusively. In 1988, the company sold its interests in Newmont Oil and in both Canadian ventures, Sherritt Gordon and Similkameen. With the 1990 sale of its 55 percent interest in Peabody, Newmont had shed virtually all of its non-gold holdings and was the largest gold producer in North America. In 1991, a merger was arranged, and then collapsed, between Newmont and American Barrick Resources. American Barrick had acquired a 49 percent interest in Newmont in a deal the previous year with Hanson plc, which had acquired the shares when it took over CGF in 1989.

EXPLORATION AND ACQUISITIONS

In 1992, Newmont continued to actively explore for gold, both in North America and abroad. A joint venture was agreed upon with the Republic of Uzbekistan for producing gold at Muruntau, and similar gold exploration ventures were initiated with Costa Rica, Thailand, Peru, and Indonesia. In the United States Newmont acquired the rights to two prospective gold properties, Grassy Mountain in Oregon and Musgrove Creek in Idaho.

Gordon Parker retired in 1993 and Ronald C. Cambre assumed the CEO position. Within a year, Newmont Mining Corp and Newmont Gold Company combined assets to form a unified gold company with combined gold reserves of 26 million ounces of gold. This made the unified company the sixth largest gold producer in the world.

In 1997, Newmont Mining acquired Santa Fe Pacific Gold Corporation for $2.43 billion in stock. That same year, Newmont started the Batu Hijau copper mine project in Indonesia, with an initial investment of $1.9 billion. In October 1998, Newmont Mining bought the remaining outstanding shares of Newmont Gold creating a single, merged organization. The following year, Wayne Murdy became president. He added the CEO position in 2000 and was named chairman in 2002.

During the early part of the decade gold prices were down, bringing less than $300 an ounce. This affected mining companies' income and profits, including Newmont, which suffered losses. The company closed exploration offices around the globe and cut its exploration budget. However, low gold prices also made it less expensive to acquire other mining companies. In 2001, Newmont completed its merger with Battle Mountain Gold Company and remained the second largest gold producer in the world. That purchase brought Newmont the Phoenix project in Nevada as well as assets in Canada, Bolivia, and Australia.

RISING MARKET PRICES IN A RISKY BUSINESS

Gold prices improved in 2002, rising above $300 per ounce for the first time in two years. That year, Newmont bought Normandy Mining, an Australian company, along with its largest shareholder, Franco-Nevada Mining Company, for $5.2 billion. The deal brought Newmont two mines in Ghana and made Newmont the world's largest gold mining company at that time, with proven gold reserves of 88 million ounces and 8.2 million ounces in production.

The company's strategy at this time was to operate in a big way in just a few locations. Its major projects, including Northern Nevada, Yanacocha in Peru, and Batu Higau in Indonesia, involved big production areas, not just a single mine.

However, gold mining was a messy and risky business. To get the gold out required taking mountains apart, crushing the rock, putting it in piles, then using cyanide to leach the gold molecules out. According to a 2007 article in *Mother Jones,* it took at least 20 tons of waste and 13 pounds of toxic emissions to mine enough gold to make a one-third ounce 18-karat ring. The problem for mining companies was getting rid of these wastes and emissions without polluting the land around the mines or harming the health of the people living nearby. Local communities also became concerned about displacement of people once the mining actually began. Newmont faced challenges from governments and from environmental groups about the issues.

SEEKING NEW RESERVES

In 2006, as the price of gold rose above $500 per ounce, companies were eager to find new reserves. Newmont began producing gold and copper at its Phoenix sites in Nevada, and Richard O'Brien, Newmont's new president and CEO, announced the company would be focusing on improving its declining gold production.

To that end, Newmont planned to bring three more mines into production by 2009 in addition to the Phoenix operations. In 2007, it also closed its merchant banking business and ended its hedging practice, which had involved betting that gold prices would not continue to rise. The difference between the sale of its merchant banking and the cost of buying back its hedges left the company with some $1.9 billion for capital expenditures, including acquisitions. Shortly afterward, Newmont announced it was buying Miramar Mining Corp., a Canadian company, for $1.5 billion. That deal would bring Newmont the Hope Bay project, which included at least three gold deposits.

At the end of 2007, the average cost of mining an ounce of gold was around $400, up from $250 in 2001. The price of gold was increasing, going above $900 an ounce in 2008. With its extensive holdings and joint ventures, including the large gold system found at the Moorilda project in New South Wales, Australia, Newmont continued to focus on low-cost, long-life projects. Its geographic diversification provided some protection from geopolitical risks and it was once again branching out to include other metals, including copper and zinc.

Robert R. Jacobson
Updated, Ellen Wernick

PRINCIPAL SUBSIDIARIES

Newmont USA Ltd.; Newmont Mining B.C. Ltd.; Newmont Canada Ltd.; Newmont Capital Ltd.; Resurrection Mining Company; Newmont Yandal Operation Pty. Ltd.; Newmont Australia Ltd.; Idarado Mining Company (80.1%); P.T. Newmont Minahasa Raya (80%); Minera Yanacocha S.R.L. (51.35%); Dawn Mining Company LLC (51%).

PRINCIPAL COMPETITORS

Barrick Gold Corporation; Anglogold Ashanti Ltd.; Gold Fields Ltd.

FURTHER READING

"Alkane Resources Confirms Large Gold System in Australia," *AsiaPulse News,* February 18, 2008.

Anreder, Steven S., "Newmont Poised for '73 Recovery," *Barron's,* December 4, 1972.

Aven, Paula, "Newmont's Top Cop," *Denver Business Journal,* October 22, 1999, p. 1.

Bagli, Charles V., "Newmont Wins Santa Fe, with Further Gold Deals Expected," *New York Times,* March 11, 1997, p. D1.

Berman, Phyllis, "Will Copper Outshine Gold?" *Forbes,* November 26, 1979.

Bogoslaw, David, "Newmont Clips Its Hedges," *Business Week Online,* July 9, 2007, p. 19.

Botta, Mike, "Two Mining Firms Draw Closer," *American Metal Market,* November 3, 1983.

Brandon, Keith, "A Diversified Investment in Minerals," *Barron's,* May 26, 1941.

"Carlin Gold Mining Will Develop Its Maggie Creek Deposits," *Engineering and Mining Journal,* October 1980.

Case, David, "Mr. Clean," *Mother Jones,* September–October 2007, pp. 66+.

Davis, Jo Ellen, "One Swallow Could Make Pickens' Summer," *Business Week,* September 14, 1987.

"The Engineer Who's Domesticating Newmont," *Business Week,* October 5, 1974.

Fathi, Vahid, "Newmont Mining NEM," *Morningstar Analyst Report,* December 13, 2007.

"From Shotguns to Rifles," *Forbes,* June 15, 1971.

"Gold Fields or Mine Field?" *Forbes,* April 2, 1990.

Guerriere, Alison, "Newmont Mining Blames Loss on Weaker Prices, Lower Sales," *American Metal Market,* May 4, 2001, p. 5.

Guzzardi, Walter, "The Huge Find in Roy Ash's Backyard," *Fortune,* December 27, 1982.

Jordan, Carol L., "Newmont Mining Reorganizes and Consolidates Management," *American Metal Market,* October 3, 1985.

Knight, Danielle, "Environment: Mining Watchdog Warns Investors About Gold Giant," *Environment Bulletin,* February 8, 2001.

MacRae, Robert M., "Resourceful Investor," *Barron's,* July 31, 1967.

Maresca, Stephen, "Bright Copper Outlook Adds Luster to Newmont Mining," *Barron's,* November 27, 1978.

Mullins, Luke, Katy Marquardt, and Kirk Shinkle, "Return to a Golden Age," *U.S. News & World Report,* December 31, 2007, pp. 34–35.

"Newmont, Indonesia Reach Deal to End Civil Suit in Pollution Row," *American Metal Market,* February 17, 2006, p. 2.

"Newmont Mining a Sound Value," *Financial World,* July 1, 1970.

"Newmont Mining and Battle Mountain Gold to Merge," *E&MJ: Engineering & Mining Journal,* August 2000, pp. 13+.

"Newmont Mining CEO Murdy to Retire," *Denver Rocky Mountain News,* June 6, 2007, p. 8 Business.

"Newmont Mining Corporation," *Wall Street Transcript,* December 23, 2002, pp. 81–83.

"Newmont Mining Corporation," *2007 Form 10-K,* U.S. Securities and Exchange Commission, March 18, 2008.

"Newmont Mining's Fourth Generation of Gamblers," *Fortune,* October 1965.

"Newmont to Acquire Miramar Mining for $1.5 Billion," *E&MJ,* November 2007, pp. 10, 12.

"Newmont's Vindication," *Wall Street Journal—Eastern Edition,* December 26, 2007, p. A10.

"Peabody Terms Told," *Chemical Week,* December 8, 1976.

Rudnitsky, Howard, "Sir Jimmy's Busted Deal," *Forbes,* August 19, 1991.

———, "Sir Jimmy's Golden Deal," *Forbes,* July 8, 1991.

Sherman, Joseph V., "Over the Rainbow," *Barron's,* October 2, 1967.

Staebler, Jonathon, "Peak Results on Tap for Newmont Mining," *Barron's,* November 5, 1973.

"Striking Gold," *American Executive,* June 2007, pp. 122+.

Sudrajat, Deden, "Indonesia Cabinet to Decide on Newmont's Mining Contract," *Dow Jones Newswire,* February 20, 2008.

Viani, Laura, "Newmont Clones Itself into Twins," *American Metal Market,* December 10, 1993, p. 2.

"Wayne Murdy of Newmont Mining Corp: All That Glitters," *Institutional Investor International Edition,* March 2002, pp. 20+.

Welling, Kathryn M., "After the Raid," *Barron's,* June 6, 1988.

"Will It Recover on My Watch?" *Forbes,* December 1, 1997, pp. 98–100.

Yafie, Roberta C., "Newmont Gaining N. American Edge," *American Metal Market,* June 23, 2000, pp. 1+.

———, "Newmont Mining Agrees to Buy Cities Service Ariz. Copper Operations," *American Metal Market,* December 3, 1982.

Pacific Coast Building Products, Inc.

10600 White Rock Road, Suite 100
Rancho Cordova, California 95670-6032
U.S.A.
Telephone: (916) 631-6500
Fax: (916) 325-3630
Web site: http://www.paccoast.com

Private Company
Incorporated: 1953 as Anderson Lumber Company
Employees: 3,700
Sales: $750 million (2007 est.)
NAIC: 423310 Lumber, Plywood, Millwork, and Wood Panel Merchant Wholesalers; 238160 Roofing Contractors; 238310 Drywall and Insulation Contractors; 238990 All Other Specialty Trade Contractors; 327121 Brick and Structural Clay Tile Manufacturing; 327124 Clay Refractory Manufacturing; 327331 Concrete Block and Brick Manufacturing

■ ■ ■

Maintaining its corporate headquarters in Rancho Cordova, California, the privately held Pacific Coast Building Products Inc. is a multifaceted manufacturer and distributor of building products to professional builders and contractors. The Pacific Coast family of companies operates in ten western states, offering such products as clay, concrete, drywall, roofing, waterworks, and wood. In addition, the Transportation Services, Inc., unit provides delivery services to eight states and Canada, and Pacific Coast Jet Charter, Inc., which grew out of the company's own flight department, offers charter service in the continental United States as well as Alaska, Canada, Mexico, and the Caribbean. Pacific Coast Companies Inc. provides sister subsidiaries and outside companies with a variety of support functions, including accounting and internal audit, human resources, information technology, and legal services. Pacific Coast also develops and manages real estate projects in the western United States.

FOUNDER BORN 1924

Pacific Coast was founded by Frederick Edward Anderson in Sacramento, California, in 1924. Anderson was a third-generation American whose great-grandfather had immigrated to the country from England to work on the railroads, establishing the Anderson family as one of Sacramento's pioneering families. Anderson's father was an electrical engineer, employed mostly by the U.S. Army Corps of Engineers, and at one point he headed the Sacramento district.

The younger Anderson was both academically oriented and a devoted equestrian. He enrolled at Stanford University at just 16 years of age and paid his way by showing horses. It was at a Sacramento riding stable that he met his future wife, Pat Fuller, the daughter of George Fuller, who founded and ran Fuller Lumber Company. They married in 1944 before he began military service during World War II. Because of his academic background, Anderson was dispatched to the University of Chicago campus in Puerto Rico to train as a meteorologist.

> **COMPANY PERSPECTIVES**
>
> At Pacific Coast Building Products, we never forget that our success depends on how well we serve our customers. That's why our foremost commitment is to you. This means not only providing a wide range of products and services, but also offering the knowledge and guidance to bring each project to a successful completion.

After his service Anderson completed his degree in hydroelectric and transmission engineering in 1947, but rather than pursue a career in that field he went to work for his father-in-law and learned the lumber business. Six years later he decided to strike out on his own, starting Anderson Lumber Company. He and his wife raised money by selling their car and pledging the rest of their possessions as collateral for a loan. With that money Anderson leased property at 65th and S streets in Sacramento, purchased an inventory of lumber, and hired four men. For a delivery truck Anderson paid $90 for an old Crystal Dairy milk truck, which he stripped of its refrigeration. Often to get the truck started in the morning Pat had to tow him with another vehicle until the motor turned over.

ANDERSON LUMBER OPENS FOR BUSINESS

Anderson Lumber Company served area builders, and because his customers could buy such a basic commodity from a number of sources, Anderson early adopted an approach that emphasized service and relationship. Anderson Lumber opened its doors in February 1953. It was a good time to be in the lumber business: Sacramento was enjoying a building boom spurred by a surging postwar economy and a population explosion. Servicemen able to take advantage of the GI Bill to buy homes created a demand for new housing developments, which were supplemented by a variety of commercial buildings as well. In just two years Anderson was able to reached the million dollar mark in annual sales.

By the start of the 1960s revenues doubled to $2 million and Anderson was ready to expand. To serve drywall contractors he formed Drywall Supply in 1960. A year later he acquired a truck and launched Material Transport. His first acquisition came in 1964 when he bought Arcata, California-based Pacific Coast Woods Products, Inc., a shake and shingle manufacturer that distributed its products through a pair of company-owned yards in Santa Rosa and San Rafael, which provided him with entry to the flourishing San Francisco Bay Area market. Moreover, it offered a name he could appropriate for his expanding stable of businesses, which were all brought under the rubric of Pacific Coast Wood Products, Inc.

As Pacific Coast entered the 1970s it remained a relatively small company, generating around $10 million, but was poised for a major growth spurt, one that not only expanded its distribution business but also took it into manufacturing. The company began 1970 by acquiring Pacific Supply of Santa Clara, which distributed roofing supplies to the Silicon Valley area. Later in the year Pacific Coast launched Arcade Insulation, specializing in the installation of insulation for both residential and commercial buildings.

SON-IN-LAW JOINS BUSINESS

Another important development in 1970 was the arrival of Anderson's son-in-law, Dave Lucchetti. Born in Stockton, California, he came to Sacramento to earn a degree in physical education at California State University in 1967. He then became a high school football coach and history teacher at an area public school, and married Christine Anderson. After two years of coaching and teaching he regretted his career choice and at the suggestion of his wife asked Fred Anderson for a job with Pacific Coast Wood Products.

Despite being the husband of the boss's daughter, Lucchetti spent the first year doing manual labor, loading lumber and installing insulation, among other jobs. Only after he learned the business at the lowest levels would he be brought into the executive office, becoming president by the end of the 1970s. Lucchetti was also a pilot; his interest in aircraft led to the opening of a corporate flight department in 1978, out of which grew Pacific Coast Jet Charter.

EXPANSION AND DIVERSIFICATION IN THE SEVENTIES

While Lucchetti was learning the ropes, Pacific Coast continued to expand and diversify. In 1972 the company became involved in manufacturing with the acquisition of Newark, California-based gypsum wallboard plant. As a reflection of the changing nature of the company, in 1976 Pacific Coast Wood Products changed its name to Pacific Coast Building Products, Inc. Anderson picked up the pace of acquisitions, quick to take advantage of opportunities that arose because of poor economic conditions.

KEY DATES

1953: Fred Anderson starts a lumber yard in Sacramento, California.
1964: Company assumes the name Pacific Coast Woods Products, Inc.
1970: Pacific Supply is acquired.
1976: Company name is changed to Pacific Coast Building Products, Inc.
1988: Anderson's son-in-law Dave Lucchetti is named CEO.
1997: Fred Anderson dies.
2003: Company is reorganized into four main subsidiaries.

The 1976 acquisition of Gladding McBean & Co. was as much a sentimental purchase as it was a strategic one. The troubled company, in business since the mid-1800s, manufactured clay sewer pipe and ornamental terra-cotta with technology from a bygone era, its products used in some of the United States' most prominent buildings. Although the plant could never be adequately modernized, under Pacific Coast it found a place as a niche manufacturer in the architectural terra-cotta market.

Many more deals were completed in the 1970s. Anderson came across a struggling gypsum plant in Las Vegas and combined it in early 1977 with the Newark operation to create Pabco Gypsum. This company saw business soar when the economy began to improve. Pacific Shingle and Drywall Supply joined forces to become Pacific Supply, which then broadened the scope of its business to include insulation, masonry, and waterproofing products.

In addition, Pacific Coast acquired a truss-assembling plant in North Highlands, California, and concrete plants in California, Nevada, Oregon, and Washington. In 1979 Basalite Block and its Napa, California, block manufacturing plant was acquired. When the 1970s came to a close revenues increased to $129 million.

CONTINUED GROWTH

Pacific Coast continued to grow at a fast rate in the 1980s. The H.C. Muddox brick manufacturing company was acquired in 1980, and was subsequently combined with a large brick-making plant purchased in Utah. Next, Pacific Coast bought Camellia Valley Supply, a major Northern California distributor of underground waterworks products, seemingly unrelated to the company's other build supplies, but it in fact served a strategic purpose. Because water mains were installed well in advance of housing construction in new developments, Camellia tipped off other Pacific Coast companies to new business to pursue.

On another front in the 1980s, Pabco Gypsum secured a steady supply of wallboard paper to expand production by acquiring a Vernon, California, paper plant. A pair of shuttered roofing plants in Richmond, California, and Tacoma, Washington, were bought and merged under the Pabco Roofing Products name. The Basalite business also grew during this period, adding A.B.C. Block to its Nevada operation. A new sacking plant was opened in Carson City, California, and later the main Napa plant was replaced by a new state-of-the-art facility in Dixon, California. Pacific Coast also launched a new venture in the 1985, establishing P.C. Wholesale to act as a mill-direct lumber wholesale business.

While growing Pacific Coast, Fred Anderson became increasingly involved in the sideline of bringing sports franchises to his beloved Sacramento. In order to spend more time with these ventures—which would include buying a stake in the Sacramento Kings franchise of the National Basketball Association, attempting to lure the National Football League's Oakland Raiders to Sacramento, and owning a minor league baseball team and franchises in the Canadian Football League and the short-lived World League of American Football—he decided in 1986 to resign as Pacific Coast's chief executive. He was replaced in 1988 by Lucchetti.

GROWTH DESPITE ECONOMIC CHALLENGE

Despite poor economic conditions, Lucchetti continued to grow Pacific Coast in the 1990s. Early in 1990 it acquired the 100-year-old Utah-based Interstate Brick Company, a major producer of commercial bricks. In 1995 the Basalite unit joined forces with Portland, Oregon-based Westblock Products Company to form a joint venture under the Westblock Pacific Inc. to produce concrete products for the Oregon and Washington markets from plants located in each state. Also in the mid-1990s Pacific Supply, as well as Pacific Coast's corporate headquarters, was relocated, moving out of the first Anderson Lumber Company site into a new Rancho Cordova, California, facility.

In other deals during the 1990s, Diamond Pacific was formed to supply both contractors and retail customers with a wide range of building products, including lumber, hardware, and plumbing and electrical supplies. Dixon, California-based Latham Truss was acquired and renamed Anderson Truss. In the fall of 1996 Pacific Coast expanded its distribution reach in the western United States by acquiring three Colorado building-supply yards.

Pacific Coast considered expanding beyond wholesaling into the retail side of the business, but in the end decided that the company was better suited to catering to contractors, who, unlike general consumers, were more educated about and willing to pay for the higher-quality goods Pacific Coast had to offer.

The 1990s was also a time of sadness and transition for Pacific Coast. In March 1997, Fred Anderson died at the age of 72 after struggling with cancer and suffering a series of strokes. He left behind a company doing business in eight states, producing about $500 in annual revenues to rank No. 461 on the *Forbes* magazine's list of the 500 largest private U.S. companies. Once a Northern California–oriented company, Pacific Coast and its 19 subsidiaries generated 40 percent of its business outside of California, this geographic diversity helping it to negotiate an extended California recession in the 1990s. In addition to making his mark as a businessman, sportsman, and civic booster, Fred Anderson was also a philanthropist along with his wife, who continued to endow charities and make other contributions until her death in early 2008.

GROWTH IN THE 21ST CENTURY

In February 2003 Pacific Coast celebrated its 50th anniversary. The family of companies employed 3,200 and generated sales of $760 million. The company also took time in 2003 to reorganize the business, converting divisions into wholly owned subsidiaries or limited liability corporations which included Alcal-Arcade Contracting, Inc.; Basalite Concrete Products, LLC; Pabco Building Products, LLC; and Pacific Coast Supply LLC. Each of the subsidiaries had its own president and board, allowing the different parts of Pacific Coast to react more quickly to changing business conditions.

The new structure did not prevent the companies from continuing to grow, however. In 2003 Anderson Trust opened a new location in Marysville, California, to expand its business in the Sacramento Valley; Basalite acquired assets of Ocean Concrete Products, adding a block and landscape wall manufacturing facility in Surrey, California, and a private-label bagging plant in British Columbia, Canada; and Arden Lumber of Sacramento was acquired.

More acquisitions followed in 2005. Alcal-Arcade acquired Insulcom, Inc., which operated in California's Orange and San Diego counties providing thermal insulation and fire-stopping services. Sales topped $1 billion in 2005, giving Pacific Coast the 366th slot on the *Forbes'* list of the 500 largest private U.S. companies. A building slump caused an erosion of sales, which dipped to $1.04 billion in 2006 and dropped to $750 million in 2007, forcing the company to cut about 40 jobs. While the company expected economic conditions to continue to depress revenues in the near-term, acquisition opportunities were also likely to arise as other companies in the field were less able than Pacific Coast to manage tough times.

Ed Dinger

PRINCIPAL SUBSIDIARIES

Alcal-Arcade Contracting, Inc.; Basalite Concrete Products, LLC; Epic Plastics, Inc.; Pabco Building Products, LLC; Pacific Coast Supply, LLC; Transportation Services, Inc.; Pacific Coast Jet Charter, Inc.; Pacific Coast Companies, Inc.; PCBP Properties, Inc.

PRINCIPAL COMPETITORS

America Builders & Contractors Supply Co., Inc.; Building Materials Holding Corporation; HD Supply.

FURTHER READING

Davila, Robert D., "Philanthropist, 82, Dedicated to Kids' Causes," *Sacramento Bee,* January 26, 2008.

Delsohn, Gary, "Fred Anderson, Tycoon and Sports Booster, Dies at 72," *Sacramento Bee,* March 25, 1997, p. A1.

"Fred Anderson," *San Francisco Chronicle,* March 26, 1997, p. C3.

Goldman, Ed, "Keeping It in the Family," *Sacramento Magazine,* June 2005.

Kasler, Dale, "Top of the Heap," *Sacramento Bee,* June 1, 1997, p. E1.

Ortiz, Jon, "Business, Charities Mark His Domain," *Sacramento Bee,* January 25, 2008.

Paramount Pictures Corporation

5555 Melrose Avenue, Suite 121
Hollywood, California 90038
U.S.A.
Telephone: (323) 468-5000
Fax: (323) 956-5000
Web site: http://www.paramount.com

Wholly Owned Subsidiary of Viacom, Inc.
Incorporated: 1916 as Famous Players-Lasky Corporation
Employees: 2,500
Sales: $3.1 billion (2005 est.)
NAIC: 512110: Motion Picture and Video Production

■ ■ ■

Paramount Pictures Corporation is the last major movie studio located in Hollywood, California, the iconic locale having been vacated by Paramount's former neighbors, including MGM and Disney. With annual revenues in excess of $3.1 billion, Paramount is one of the largest film and television companies in the United States. Paramount's development from a privately owned company distributing films in California to a wholly owned subsidiary of Viacom, Inc., one of the world's largest media conglomerates, has been marked by alternating fits of financial feast and famine. Emerging from a financial low at the end of the 1990s, Paramount has been on the rise, engineering partnerships with a number of television and animation studios to produce innovative projects for the 21st century.

FOUNDATION AND EARLY HISTORY: 1912–23

Adolph Zukor, the founder of Paramount Pictures, spent most of his life establishing and supervising one of the largest and most successful motion-picture companies in the history of the entertainment industry. Zukor was born in Hungary in 1873, but immigrated to the United States at age 15. He arrived in New York with $40 hidden inside his waistcoat, and got a job sweeping floors in an East Side fur store. By the dawn of the 20th century, he was the owner of a prosperous fur business in Chicago.

Eventually Zukor returned to New York in search of new investment opportunities. There he met Mitchell Mark, an owner of penny arcades. These arcades, where customers paid pennies to see a short moving picture, were both popular and profitable. Zukor and Mark soon formed the Automatic Vaudeville Arcades Company with Zukor's friend Marcus Loew. A short time later, they were operating their own separate companies as owners of nickelodeons, where for a nickel customers could see a short movie.

It was a short step from nickelodeons to full-scale variety shows for Zukor and Loew. Combining movies and vaudeville acts, the men pooled their resources and established Loew's Consolidated Enterprises in 1910 with Loew as president and Zukor as treasurer. By 1912 they controlled a growing number of theaters, including New York's Crystal Hall on 14th Street. Zukor became intrigued by the possibilities of film production, particularly for longer shows (until that time, films had been arbitrarily kept to one reel, or ten minutes, by a

KEY DATES

1912: Adolph Zukor releases the first four-reel film in the United States.
1916: Zukor and Lasky buy controlling rights to Paramount Film Company.
1924: Zukor opens first international Paramount theater in Paris.
1929: Paramount Pictures film *Wings* wins first Academy Award for Best Picture.
1936: Barney Balaban becomes president of Paramount.
1948: Antitrust decision forces Paramount to divest public theater holdings.
1966: Gulf + Western Industries purchases Paramount.
1974: Barry Diller becomes chairman of Paramount.
1984: Martin S. Davis becomes CEO of the company.
1989: Davis renames the company Paramount Communications.
1993: Sumner Redstone's Viacom, Inc., acquires Paramount Communications.
1999: Viacom purchases CBS, becoming country's second largest media conglomerate.
2005: Paramount acquires DreamWorks SKG.
2006: Paramount divests television holdings.
2007: Paramount enters the movie download market in partnership with Apple, Inc.

consortium of the largest film distributors and licensers). He sold his interest back to Loew for a handsome profit and bought the U.S. distribution rights to a four-reel French production of *Queen Elizabeth,* starring Sarah Bernhardt.

After a tremendously successful opening of *Queen Elizabeth* at New York's Lyceum Theatre, Zukor founded a new company, Famous Players in Famous Plays (later shortened to just Famous Players), to begin producing movies. The company's first four releases—*The Count of Monte Cristo, The Prisoner of Zenda, His Neighbor's Wife,* and *Tess of the d'Urbervilles*—were moderately successful, but it was not until Zukor signed Mary Pickford that Famous Players started producing hits and making money. By 1913, his firm had increased its production to 30 pictures a year.

In 1914, Zukor met Jesse Lasky. Lasky had established the Jesse L. Lasky Feature Play Company in 1913 with himself as president and Cecil B. DeMille as director general. The firm's first production effort was *The Squaw Man,* directed by DeMille, and was soon followed by *Rose of the Rancho* and *The Virginian.* In its second year, the company released 36 pictures. When Zukor offered a 50-50 partnership in a joint Famous Players-Lasky company in 1916, Lasky did not hesitate to accept the opportunity. Flattered by the offer and foreseeing a lucrative future for the combine, Lasky allowed Zukor to appoint himself president; Lasky, vice-president in charge of production; and Cecil B. DeMille, director general. Samuel Goldfish (later Goldwyn) was made chairman of the board.

Two months later, Zukor bought a majority of the Paramount Company, the film-distribution company that both Zukor and Lasky had signed with in 1914. Meanwhile, the creative tempo was so great at Famous Players-Lasky that an average of more than two pictures emerged every week between 1916 and 1921. The awkward name of Zukor's firm was soon replaced with Paramount, the distribution company's name and trademark. One of the most familiar slogans in the film industry—"If it's a Paramount Picture it's the Best Show in Town"—was created soon after.

STRUGGLING TO BUILD AN INTERNATIONAL EMPIRE 1923–50

Paramount's large organization began to expand rapidly in the early and mid-1920s. At first Zukor began to build a large theater chain by buying or building showplaces for the company. In 1924 he went overseas and opened the Paris Paramount and the London Plaza. At the same time, Paramount developed a worldwide distribution network and opened studios in London, Berlin, and Bombay, in addition to its U.S. ones.

The studio reached its peak in the field of silent film making with DeMille's blockbuster *The Ten Commandments* in 1923. However scandal cast a shadow over Paramount and the movie industry in general when one of its stars, Fatty Arbuckle, was accused of rape and manslaughter and then acquitted in a much-publicized trial. This and several other events caused a public outcry against immorality in the movies, and DeMille's spectacular productions came under criticism. After an argument with Zukor over artistic differences and rising production costs, DeMille left the company.

Even though Paramount was making more money—a steady $5 million a year—than Warner, Fox, and Universal, Zukor was obsessed with maintaining his company's supremacy in the industry. He began a theater-buying campaign that amassed single houses and entire circuits, paying for many of the acquisitions with Paramount stock. By 1930, the firm's movie-house division had grown to include almost 2,000 units and was named Publix Theaters; that year the company's name was changed to Paramount-Publix.

The significance of the Warner Brother's 1927 movie *The Jazz Singer,* with its brief sequences of song and dialogue, was not lost on Paramount. Warner Brothers had used the Vitaphone sound system for this movie, but Zukor decided to go with Fox's new development, sound-on-film Movietone, which was more technically reliable and easier to handle. Paramount used it in *Wings* and won the first Oscar for best picture, in 1929.

In 1930 the company's stable of stars was one of the most impressive in Hollywood; it included Fredric March, Claudette Colbert, Maurice Chevalier, Kay Francis, Walter Huston, Gary Cooper, William Powell, Carole Lombard, Harold Lloyd, W. C. Fields, and the Marx Brothers. Over the next few years, Paramount also contracted Tallulah Bankhead, Marlene Dietrich, and the inimitable Mae West.

Prosperity and success at Paramount did not last long, however. In 1930 the firm recorded a profit of $18 million, but by 1932 the Great Depression was at its height and the studio ran a deficit of slightly more than $15 million. The main problem was the Publix theater chain. Many deals during its growth were made by paying owners of theaters Paramount stock, fully redeemable at a fixed price and fixed date. However, too many redemption dates came in the middle of the Depression, and the company could not pay. Hundreds of company employees were forced to leave, while others accepted huge salary cuts. Paramount-Publix went into receivership in 1933. When in 1935 it emerged from bankruptcy as Paramount Pictures Inc., John Otterson assumed the position of president, Emanuel Cohen was named studio chief, and Adolph Zukor became chairman of the board. The one bright spot during these years was the return of DeMille.

Sustained by Bing Crosby musicals, DeMille spectacles, and sexy Mae West comedies, Paramount announced a $3 million profit in 1936, a profit of $6 million the following year, and $12 million the next. Despite this turnaround, both Otterson and Cohen were drummed out of the company; Barney Balaban became president in 1936 and Y. Frank Freeman took over as vice-president in charge of production in 1938. They lasted until 1966 and 1959, respectively.

The stability that Balaban and Freeman gave Paramount led to a $13 million profit in 1941; by the end of the war, its profits had topped $15 million. The hits of Crosby, DeMille, and West in the 1930s had given way to the more sophisticated and elegant comedies of Ernst Lubitsch, Mitchell Leisen, and Preston Sturges. The number of Paramount releases also dropped, from 71 in 1936 to 19 in 1946 as the studio concentrated on quality over quantity. Leo McCarthy's *Going My Way* won the Oscar for best picture in 1944—the company's first win since *Wings*—and Billy Wilder's *Lost Weekend* won it in 1945. These successes led to a phenomenal $39 million profit for 1946.

In 1948 Paramount, along with all the other major film companies, was found guilty of antitrust-law violations and ordered by the U.S. government to divest itself of all its theater holdings. Within a year, the company had sold the properties that Zukor had collected—and profits dropped from $20 million in 1949 to $6 million in 1950.

ADJUSTING TO THE TELEVISION GENERATION 1950–93

By this time, the company was feeling the effects of a growing television audience. The entire movie industry tried to fight back with visual inventions that the smaller screen could not duplicate. Three-dimensional (3D) effects, Cinerama's huge concave screen, and Twentieth Century Fox's CinemaScope were some of the developments used to help increase box-office receipts. Paramount came up with its own panoramic big-screen system, Vista-Vision, which was acknowledged to be a significant improvement over previous systems. Nonetheless, these technical innovations failed to increase revenues. Even though Paramount reported a $12.5 million profit in 1958 (the largest since 1949), it continued to suffer from a decline in theater attendance through the 1960s.

In 1965 George Weltner, the executive vice-president of Paramount, led a group of dissident executives in a proxy battle to unseat the old management. (Freeman had retired in 1959, but Balaban had become chairman of the board in 1964.) While both sides were planning their strategies, Gulf + Western Industries (which became Paramount Communications) offered to purchase the company at $83 a share, nearly $10 more than the market price. The offer was accepted at the annual stockholders meeting, and on October 19, 1966, Paramount became the first major film company to be owned by a conglomerate.

Paramount was incorporated into Gulf + Western's leisure-time group. Charles Bluhdorn, the founder of Gulf + Western, appointed himself chairman of the board at his newest subsidiary, and Paramount began to produce hits like *True Grit, The Odd Couple, Romeo and Juliet, Love Story, Rosemary's Baby,* and *Goodbye, Columbus.*

In 1970 a deal of far-reaching significance between Paramount and Universal studios was made. Bluhdorn and Lew Wasserman, chairman of MCA, agreed to combine their companies' distribution outlets everywhere but in the United States. That new firm was enlarged ten years later when MGM became a joint owner. Since MGM had bought United Artists, foreign countries that had been served by four distribution networks were served by one, United International Pictures.

In 1974 Bluhdorn relinquished his position as chairman of the board at Paramount to Barry Diller, a change in leadership that in no way diminished the company's good fortune. The *Godfather* movies, each an Academy Award winner, were joined by *The Conversation, Chinatown, Nashville,* and *Grease* in audience popularity. It was also during this time that Gulf + Western added publisher Simon & Schuster and New York's Madison Square Garden to its leisure-time group. When Adolph Zukor died in 1976 at the age of 103, after having been chairman emeritus for 12 years, he had lived to see the rebirth of his company.

A 1980 Oscar winner for Paramount, *Ordinary People,* was a critical as well as a popular success. In 1981, the new champion of box-office profits, *Raiders of the Lost Ark,* raked in worldwide rentals totaling approximately $200 million. *Raiders* had been turned down by four other studios by the time Paramount president Michael Eisner decided to take the risk. The film's success was a tribute to his and chairman Barry Diller's instincts. Eisner told *Business Week* in 1984 that unlike other studios, Paramount did not believe in market research. "Everyone thinks they can find a magic wand. But I would rather fail on my own judgment than on the judgment of some man in Columbus, Ohio," he said. "I think about what I like not what the public likes. If I ask Miss Middle America if she wants to see a movie about religion she'll say yes. If I say 'Do you want to see a movie about sex,' she'll say no. But she'll be lying." Eisner and Diller had worked together for several years, first at the ABC television network, then at Paramount. Their instincts had brought the studio a consistent string of big successes.

In 1984, after the unexpected death of Gulf + Western Chairman Charles Bluhdorn, Martin S. Davis took the helm at the holding company. Davis clashed with Paramount chairman Diller, and in late 1984 Diller left to head Twentieth Century Fox. A day later Michael Eisner resigned to head Walt Disney Company. Half of the company's top executives followed them, leaving Paramount with a serious management crisis. Frank Mancuso, the former head of the marketing department, who had been with the company for 24 years, became Paramount's new chairman.

After a brief but severe slump in earnings (in 1985 the motion-picture group took the biggest write-off in its history) the soft-spoken Mancuso rebuilt the company's upper echelon and Paramount began churning out blockbusters once again. Hits like *Beverly Hills Cop II* and *The Untouchables* helped Paramount account for 22 percent of all box-office receipts in 1986.

Paramount's television division did extremely well in the later 1980s as well. *Entertainment Tonight,* a nightly entertainment news program, was a huge success breaking into the first-run syndication market for the company and was followed by *Star Trek: The Next Generation, War of the Worlds,* and *Hard Copy.* While a fourth network run by Rupert Murdoch's Fox Broadcasting Company provided a new outlet for Paramount's TV division, the company's network fare included such hits as *Family Ties, Cheers,* and *MacGyver.*

By the end of the decade Paramount was making consistently hefty profits on its television and motion-picture operations. Nonetheless, like many entertainment companies, Paramount was unsettled by the merger-mania that seemed to be sweeping the entertainment industry late in the decade. When Time Inc. announced its intention to merge with Warner Communications to create the world's largest media company, Paramount made its own bid for Time. Paramount's bid was ultimately rejected by Time, however, and after a brief court battle Time Warner was created.

Throughout the remainder of the 1980s and into the early 1990s, Paramount suffered from declining profits, and the company's management looked for ways to expand the revenue base. By 1993, Paramount's profits had fallen sufficiently that the board of directors was prepared to accept bids for a takeover. As news spread that the ailing studio was on the market, the stage was set for one of the most contentious acquisition scenarios of the 1990s.

ACQUISITION BY VIACOM AND NEW MANAGEMENT

New York-based Viacom, Inc., owner of several television networks including Nickelodeon, MTV, and The Movie Channel (TMC), was the first company to make a serious bid for ownership of Paramount Communications (the company having been renamed in 1989). When news of the bid circulated through the entertainment industry, Barry Diller, founder and chairman of QVC Network leveraged his assets to counter Viacom's bid. Over the course of the next six months, Viacom and QVC battled for ownership, with each month bringing a new set of offers.

Viacom eventually won the bidding battle and promised to pay a total of $10 billion for Paramount. Viacom, however, was itself in a tenuous financial situation as it was also engaged in costly negotiations over a proposed merger with Blockbuster Entertainment. Immediately following the takeover, Viacom sold several assets in an effort to raise revenues to pay off debt to fund the company's merger proposals. Ultimately, Viacom completed both mergers, and by 1995, with both Paramount and Blockbuster as subsidiaries, Viacom was one of the largest media conglomerates in the nation.

Shortly after the Viacom takeover, the Viacom board named Jonathan Dolgen as chairman of the Viacom Entertainment Group, the division controlling Paramount's movie and television production operations. Dolgen inherited control of Paramount at a time when the company's financial outlook was relatively poor, with losses amounting to over $34 million in 1994. Dolgen developed several new financial strategies that were embraced by Sherry Lansing, the executive who had served as chair of Paramount's motion-picture group since 1992. Lansing had developed a reputation in the industry for picking film projects that had the mass appeal to become highly profitable.

From 1994 to 1999, Dolgen and Lansing presided over one of the most profitable periods in Paramount's history. Blockbuster successes such as *Mission Impossible* and *Forrest Gump* helped the studio to reach the top of box-office lists. In addition, Dolgen and Lansing were seen as innovators for their efforts to finance the company's operations through joint ventures with other companies. Dolgen and Lansing's highly profitable partnership with Twentieth Century Fox, for example, resulted in the hit movie *Braveheart* as well as in *Titanic,* which was the highest-grossing film of all time to that point. Together, Dolgen and Lansing managed to increase the studio's production while simultaneously succeeding in reducing costs, as directed from Viacom Chairman Sumner Redstone after the acquisition.

In 1999, Viacom purchased a controlling interest in CBS Corporation for a reported $37.3 billion, creating the world's second largest media empire after Time Warner Entertainment. In the acquisition, Viacom obtained 15 television stations and the nation's largest family of radio stations. With the purchase of CBS, Viacom again became involved in the ongoing debate over the legality of media mergers and the dangers of media monopolies. Despite objections from antimonopoly groups, the purchase signaled a new era for Viacom and the company entered the 21st century with an estimated stock value of over $72 billion and a dominant position in the national entertainment industry.

PARAMOUNT IN THE 21ST CENTURY

After a highly profitable run in the 1990s under Dolgen's and Lansing's leadership, Paramount's profits began to decline. A string of box-office disappointments, including *The Stepford Wives* and *Sky Captain and the World of Tomorrow,* offset profits from the company's more successful films such as *Sponge Bob Square Pants* and *Lemony Snicket's A Series of Unfortunate Events.* After three years of losses, rumors began to circulate that management changes were imminent.

In 2004, Dolgen resigned from Paramount. This came shortly after the announcement that he would not succeed the retiring Paramount President Mel Karmazin. Sumner Redstone appointed two of his high-level executives, Tom Freston, chairman of MTV Networks, and Les Moonves, chairman of CBS, as joint presidents after Karmazin's departure, stating in press releases that Dolgen's future with the company would be up to Freston and Moonves to decide. Analysts speculated that Dolgen's difficulties in working with both Freston and Moonves on past projects may have prompted his decision to leave the company. The following year, Lansing also left Paramount, stating in press releases that it was time for her to move on to new opportunities.

In January 2005, shortly after the announcement of Lansing's departure, Viacom announced that Brad Grey, formerly of Brillstein-Grey Entertainment, would become the new chairman and CEO of Paramount's motion-picture group. Grey pushed Paramount's revenues to their limits, investing in expensive but ultimately successful projects with major talent, including *War of the Worlds* starring Tom Cruise and a remake of *The Longest Yard* starring Adam Sandler. In addition, Grey diversified the division's offerings by teaming with Viacom subsidiaries MTV Networks and Comedy Central to produce films based on characters and television series from both networks. The summer of 2005 was Paramount's biggest summer to that point with box-office revenues reaching over $503 million.

In October 2005, Viacom announced that it would be reorganizing into two new divisions. While Paramount was grouped with MTV and the company's other cable television networks under the Viacom label, CBS and the company's radio and network television offerings would become a separate business. Paramount was reduced to approximately one-quarter of its original size, as the company's television production division was transferred to the control of Viacom's newly partitioned CBS division. As part of the split, Sumner Redstone's daughter, Shari Redstone, who had served on the Viacom board for over 11 years, was set to replace her father as vice-chairwoman of both units. The split also ended an ongoing succession battle between Moonves and Freston, who had been serving as co-presidents since the retirement of Karmazin. Moonves was promoted to president of CBS while Freston became president of Viacom.

At the end of 2005, Paramount announced the acquisition of DreamWorks SKG Inc., a company started 11 years earlier by Steven Spielberg, Jeffrey Katzenberg, and David Geffen. The purchase, reported at $775 million, gave Paramount production rights to DreamWorks' library of animated and feature films and the rights to produce all future projects by the company. The company's most significant gain in the purchase was the acquisition of DreamWorks Animation, the division that produced many of the decade's most successful animated films including the *Shrek* franchise.

Grey instituted several new initiatives designed to help Paramount regain a leading position in the industry. In 2007, Paramount entered into an agreement with Apple to sell some of the company's movies as downloads through Apple's iTunes store. Disney was the first studio to sign an agreement with Apple and the company received over $1 million in profits from the first week of the partnership. Paramount also announced that DreamWorks would begin producing animated features in the 3D format beginning in 2009. Newly developed technology that allowed 3D adjustment to digitally remastered films brought with it the possibility of converting some of the company's previous releases to 3D format. "I believe this is the greatest opportunity for movies and for the theatrical exhibition that has come along in 30 years," DreamWorks CEO Jeffrey Katzenberg said in a press release.

In January 2008, company representatives announced that Paramount would join a growing list of production studios that officially supported the transition to Blu-Ray technology over the more standard high-definition DVD format. The debate over Blu-Ray and HD-DVD had intensified, with distribution companies and movie studios feeling pressure to side with one or the other format to simplify the distribution process. Blu-Ray technology offered significant advantages in the capacity for high-quality data storage but came at a higher price for both packaging and production.

Since ascending to the top spot in 2005, Grey helped to redefine Paramount as a company that was willing to take risks to stay ahead of industry developments. With several high-profile projects and releases during this time, Paramount remained profitable, although changes in the movie market posed a continued risk to the company's overall stability. In 2008, Paramount was the last movie studio to retain its Hollywood, California, location, after its competition had either shut down or moved to new locations. Through its transition from a pioneer in the industry to its position as part of one of the 21st century's largest media empires, Paramount remained a leader and one of the most recognized studio names in the history of U.S. cinema.

Cindy Pearlman
Updated, Micah L. Issitt

PRINCIPAL SUBSIDIARIES

Paramount Home Video Inc.; Paramount Television; Paramount Vantage; DreamWorks SKG.

PRINCIPAL COMPETITORS

Sony Pictures Entertainment Inc.; Universal Studios Inc.; Warner Bros. Entertainment Inc.; New Line Cinema Corporation; Miramax Film Corporation.

FURTHER READING

Carter, Bill, and Lorne Manly, "Talent Manager Named Paramount Chief," *New York Times,* January 7, 2005.

Dick, Bernard F., *Engulfed: The Death of Paramount Pictures and the Birth of Corporate Hollywood,* Lexington: University Press of Kentucky, 2001.

"Dreamworks Animation Goes 3D," http://www.paramount.com/paramount.php, press release, March 13, 2007.

Eames, John Douglas, *The Paramount Story,* New York: Crown, 1985.

Edmonds, J. G., and Reiko Mimura, *Paramount Pictures and the People Who Made Them,* New York: A.S. Barnes, 1980.

Fabrikant, Geraldine, "Another Viacom Executive Quits After Management Shakeup," *New York Times,* June 3, 2004.

Mack, Gracian, "Inside the Viacom-Paramount Deal," *Black Enterprise,* December 1994.

Mifflin, Lawrie, "Making a Media Giant: The Overview; Viacom to Buy CBS, Forming 2d Largest Media Company," *New York Times,* September 8, 1999.

Siklos, Richard, "Family Feud at CBS and Viacom," *New York Times,* July 20, 2007.

"Viacom Explains Split into Units," *Bloomberg News Online,* October 6, 2005.

Weinraub, Bernard, "Profiles: The New Man in the Hollywood Hot Seat," *New York Times,* July 24, 1994.

PCC Natural Markets

4201 Roosevelt Way NE
Seattle, Washington 98105
U.S.A.
Telephone: (206) 547-1222
Fax: (206) 545-7131
Web site: http://www.pccnaturalmarkets.com

Cooperative
Incorporated: 1961
Employees: 750
Revenues: $115 million
NAIC: 445110 Supermarkets and Other Grocery (Except Convenience) Stores

■ ■ ■

The largest food cooperative in the United States, PCC Natural Markets operates eight stores with an emphasis on natural foods in the Seattle neighborhoods of Seward Park, View Ridge, Greenlake, West Seattle, Fremont, and Kirkland, and in Redmond and Issaquah, Washington.

BECOMING A NATURAL FOOD CO-OP: 1953–75

In 1953 John Affolter organized 15 families in Seattle and in Renton, Washington, into a food-buying club that operated out of the "depot" in his basement. Called Puget Consumer Cooperative, the club's inventory in the early days consisted of bulk grains, dried beans, honey, and railroad-damaged canned goods that were dropped off at members' homes. In 1961, the club incorporated as a cooperative. The original 15 member households each purchased $50 membership certificates that went to build and maintain the co-op's storefront in Renton. They paid dues semiannually in return for which they received a rebate based on a percentage of their purchases each year.

By 1967 the number of families in the co-op had grown to 340, and Affolter's basement depot closed after complaints about neighborhood traffic. A new storefront opened in the mostly residential neighborhood of Madrona in east-central Seattle. The co-op's members opted to end the rebate system and to institute instead an arrangement whereby each household paid dues in proportion to its size.

Two years later, membership had almost doubled to 650 households, and a split occurred between those who wanted their co-op to focus on natural foods and those whose interest was primarily in offering cost savings to members. Those focused on natural foods split off to open a Puget Consumer Cooperative storefront in the University District of Seattle in 1969 where sales for the first year topped $66,000. (A second group of members split off in 1971 because they felt the co-op was getting too large and started the Capitol Hill Co-op; in 1973 another group of members withdrew their certificates to start the Phinney Street Co-op with a loan from Puget Consumer Cooperative.)

Puget Consumer Cooperative continued to thrive and to evolve as a cooperative. In 1971 workers began to take on some management responsibilities, marking the beginning of democratic management at the co-op.

COMPANY PERSPECTIVES

PCC is a cooperatively-owned retailer of high quality natural and organic foods. It exists to create a cooperative, sustainable environment for members and patrons in which the natural and organic supply chains thrive.

The co-op board changed the bylaws to reflect this alteration: staff members became co-op members; all workers received equal pay; and staff meetings occurred more regularly. By 1973 co-op membership had grown to 1,887. Two years later, membership had close to doubled again, and Puget Consumer Cooperative's sales exceeded $1 million.

NEW STORES, NEW CHALLENGES, AND NEW MANAGEMENT

In order to accommodate the increase in size, the store in Madrona moved to a new location in Seattle's Ravenna neighborhood in 1976; members carried boxes, pushed handcarts, and drove vans and pickups filled with the necessary items to the Ravenna store. The new site attracted more clientele, and sales more than doubled while the staff tripled. Some of the co-op's new business came from the closing of the Capitol Hill Co-op. By 1977 earnings had increased to about $48,000.

Puget Consumer Cooperative purchased another co-op, Co-op East, and opened a second branch in Kirkland, a suburb of Seattle, in 1978. The move led the co-op, in 1979, to conduct a survey of its customers, which revealed the information that many shoppers traveled a considerable distance to get to Puget Consumer Cooperative. The decision to become a multistore organization followed and brought with it centralization of some business functions. A third store in Greenlake opened in 1980 and became the new home to Puget Consumer Cooperative's corporate headquarters.

Not all went smoothly for Puget Consumer Cooperative in the early 1980s, however. Despite net earnings in 1978 of $79,000, the Kirkland store was experiencing continued financial losses, while sales at the Ravenna store began to fall. To remedy these situations, the co-op board suspended democratic management at Kirkland, remodeled the store, reopened membership at Ravenna, and decided to hire a general manager.

The first general manager came on board in 1982 and left a year later. A second general manager, Lyle Whiteman, came on board in 1984 and the co-op moved its offices to a separate building in the University District. Meanwhile workers at the Kirkland and Greenlake stores and office staff unionized, and Puget Consumer Cooperative negotiated its first contract with their union in 1983; the office staff voted to decertify in 1985, while Ravenna staff joined the union in 1987.

TURNING BUSINESS AROUND

During the second half of the 1980s, Puget Consumer Cooperative began to pursue a course of cautious expansion. Two new stores were opened in 1985 and 1987—in Seward Park and View Ridge respectively. In 1989 a store in West Seattle became store number six. In 1990 these six stores boasted combined revenues of about $26 million and more than 35,000 active members. There were more than 200 staff members.

The early 1990s continued to be a time of change in leadership, finances, and politics for the co-op. Despite several years of negative earnings from 1992 to 1994, Puget Consumer Cooperative purchased the Meat Shop, Inc., in 1991. (In 1985, it had installed a Meat Shop, Inc., counter at the Ravenna store over some members' objections.) After Lyle Whiteman left his position as general manager in 1991, Jeff Voltz replaced him in 1992. Also in 1992 Puget Consumer Cooperative opened a South Everett store, which closed in 1995. A store in Fremont opened in 1994.

By 1995, with 300 staff and sales exceeding $800,000 per week, Puget Consumer Cooperative's financial situation promised to turn itself around. That year, Puget Consumer Cooperative purchased Greenlake Market, and in 1996 it opened a co-op in the Greenlake neighborhood, its seventh store, nearby. In 1997, sales for all of Puget Consumer Cooperative reached $1 million each week with net earnings about 2 percent of sales. The year 1998, when Puget Consumer Cooperative began to do business as PCC Natural Markets, was even more profitable than 1997.

CULTIVATING GROWTH AND ENVIRONMENTAL RESPONSIBILITY

By 1998 PCC Natural Markets was the largest natural food co-op in the United States. It still held firmly to established co-op values of listening to members' wants and needs and of working closely with the communities in which it was located. All locations placed a priority on using local vendors and approximately 60 percent of the produce was organic. In the case of the new Greenlake store, both the parking lot and the merchandising emphasized environmental responsibility.

KEY DATES

1961: Fifteen families incorporate their food-buying club as Puget Consumer Cooperative.
1969: Members interested in focusing on natural foods split off to form a separate club, which retains the name Puget Consumers Co-op.
1976: The store moves to Seattle's Ravenna neighborhood.
1978: The co-op opens a store in Kirkland, Washington.
1980: A third store opens in the Greenlake neighborhood of Seattle and headquarters move from Ravenna to Greenlake.
1982: The co-op hires its first general manager.
1983: The general manager resigns; the co-op negotiates its first contract with its workers' union.
1984: Lyle Whiteman is hired as general manager; headquarters move to the University District of Seattle.
1985: A fourth store opens in Seattle's Seward Park neighborhood.
1987: A fifth store opens in the View Ridge neighborhood of Seattle.
1989: A sixth store opens in West Seattle.
1991: Puget Consumer Cooperative purchases the Meat Shop, Inc.
1992: A seventh store opens in South Everett; Jeff Voltz becomes general manager.
1994: An eighth store opens in the Fremont neighborhood of Seattle.
1995: Puget Consumer Cooperative buys Greenlake Market; the South Everett store closes.
1996: The Greenlake store moves to a new location.
1998: The co-op begins doing business as PCC Natural Markets.
1999: A store opens in Issaquah, Washington.
2001: The Ravenna store closes; Tracy Wolpert becomes chief executive.
2006: PCC opens a store in Redmond, Washington, bringing total locations back to eight.

At the same time, according to Voltz in a 1997 *Progressive Grocer* article, "Changes we've made to both product selection and the design style have helped us sell more groceries than ever. We have a professional look and style that we didn't have before." These changes translated to profits of about $1 million on about $50 million in sales in 1998 and $58 million in 1999. Still bent on bringing more stores to its then-35,000 members, PCC opened another new store in Issaquah, Washington, in 1999.

During the late 1990s, the board transitioned to a different model of governance, one that cast board members as the "servant leaders," followed by a management restructure in 2000. When Voltz left PCC in 2000, Tracy Wolpert and Randy Lee assumed the roles of co–chief executives. PCC also took active steps to support its vision of locally produced produce. The newly formed PCC Farmland Fund, a nonprofit entity, purchased a $600,000 piece of property in the Dungeness River Delta to save it from development in partnership with the state Fish and Wildlife Department. The plan called for PCC to seek reimbursement for half the purchase price from a federal grant, at which point the state would take title of the land and lease it to PCC in perpetuity for farming.

BECOMING MORE COMPETITIVE

By the first years of the new century, the market for organic and natural foods was growing fast at about 25 percent a year, although even by 2004, organic foods accounted for only 1 to 2 percent of food sales nationally. "The world is changing. Co-ops across America over the last 30 years really cultivated and supported organic agriculture. Now it's becoming mainstream," Voltz said in the *Seattle Times* in 2001.

However, PCC was once again experiencing financial losses—$1.4 million on revenues of $63 million in 2000, a decrease of about 6 percent over 1999, caused in part by the expense of opening the Issaquah store. PCC closed its Ravenna store in 2001 after competition from a neighboring QFC market led to a drop in sales of nearly 20 percent. Whole Foods arrived in Seattle in 2000 and started cutting into PCC's profits as well.

The co-op took steps to make itself more competitive in 2001. Under Wolpert, who became sole chief executive officer in the spring, it replaced many clothing and general merchandise items with perishable foods, introduced catering and a boxed lunch program, expanded the bakery line, boosted its amount of organic produce, and introduced lamb and pork items. The co-op also investigated new marketing after a 2000 survey revealed that PCC's name was not familiar to many people who shopped near PCC stores. It adopted a new logo in 2003.

PCC also invested in training for employees to boost their knowledge about products and to improve workers' attitudes. "When I got here, there was a lack of focus on sales," said Wolpert, a 20-year veteran of Von's supermarkets, in a 2001 *Puget Sound Business Journal.* He continued, "There were few consequences for doing things poorly, or rewards for doing things right. So we've restored accountability."

Efforts paid off. In 2001, revenues jumped to $67 million. The co-op did $75 million in sales in 2002, a 12 percent increase over 2001. Although a slight scandal erupted in 2003, after evidence showed that it had sold fish labeled as "environmentally friendly" that originated from unvetted sources. Although it was never clear whether the mislabeling occurred within co-op stores or before the fish reached PCC, EcoFish, Inc., the co-op's supplier of fish harvested in an environmentally approved manner, suspended its contract with PCC. In 2004, PCC switched to a new fish supplier, Ocean Bay, and partnered with Monterey Bay Aquarium to educate consumers about sustainable seafood.

CONTINUED COMMITMENT TO NATURAL FOODS AND HEALTHY CHOICES

By 2004 sales had reached $89 million, up more than 10 percent from 2003, and the number of customers shopping at PCC was up 8 percent. About 90 percent of PCC's produce was certified organic and about 60 percent of its bulk grocery items were as well. As part of its mission to educate consumers about the foods they eat, the co-op began its Kid Picks program in 2004. It put together samples of healthful foods for tasting in schools, at community events, and in stores. Those items approved by more than two-thirds of kids were labeled "Kid Picks."

The year 2005 marked the completion of extensive remodels at most of PCC's seven stores. In 2003, the Fremont store had moved to a new location. In 2006, the co-op added an eighth location in Redmond, Washington. A banner year for PCC, in 2006, sales topped $100 million as co-op membership reached 40,000, and employees numbered 700.

Even as the co-op enjoyed the boom in the organic industry and while sales in mainstream supermarkets remained flat, it remained true to its mission of affordable food, sold in accordance with its commitment to education, fair trade, and environmental stewardship. In 2007, PCC removed all products with trans-fats, BGH, and high-fructose corn syrup from its shelves and stopped using plastic bags. As part of its remodeling efforts, all stores had full recycling facilities and energy-efficient lighting and water fixtures. The co-op also voluntarily instituted country-of-origin labeling for meat, seafood, peanuts, and fresh produce. Local county government named it the "Best Workplace for Recycling 2007" and in 2008, PCC's Redmond store exceeded the U.S. Green Building Council's LEED Gold Certification for energy efficiency.

According to the company's web site, "The products we sell are not only healthier than those found in conventional sources, they're likely to be produced in a way that helps sustain the environment or that is cruelty-free, meaning animals are range-grazed without hormones or antibiotics, fish are sustainably harvested and products are not tested on animals. We encourage our members to shop this way, too." With a ninth store to be constructed in Edmonds, Washington, in mid-2008 and with interest in organic, responsibly produced food and personal items increasing, PCC Natural Markets looked toward a future of steady growth.

Carrie Rothburd

PRINCIPAL COMPETITORS

Quality Food Centers, Inc.; Whole Foods Market, Inc.; Albertsons LLC; Trader Joe's Company.

FURTHER READING

Burrows, Kate, "An Organic Success: PCC Natural Markets, the Nation's Largest Organic Food Coop, Says It Provides Seattle-Area Customers with High-Quality Organic Foods," *U.S. Business Review,* January 1, 2007, p. 164.

Denn, Rebekah, "PCC's 'Premium Fish' Was Wrongly Labeled; Some Products Sold As EcoFish Really Weren't, Say Workers," *Seattle Post-Intelligencer,* October 24, 2003, p. A1.

Engleman, Eric, "Largest 100 Private Companies: PCC Natural Marker; PCC Returns to Its Organic Roots After a Few Lean Years," *Puget Sound Business Journal,* June 20, 2003, p. 46.

"From Hippies to Hip," *Progressive Grocer,* December 1, 1997.

Holt, Gordy, "Reclaiming a Fertile Delta," *Seattle Post-Intelligencer,* May 26, 2000, p. B1.

Moriwaki, Lee, "Landmark Store Closing—Competition Squeezes Out Ravenna PCC," *Seattle Times,* January 8, 2001, p. A4.

"PCC Touts High Sales, Labor Contract at Annual Meeting," http://www.progressivegrocer.com, April 29, 2005.

Tice, Carol, "Natural Choice," *Puget Sound Business Journal,* August 31, 2001, p. 8.

Peavey Electronics Corporation

5022 Hartley Peavey Drive
Meridian, Mississippi 39305
U.S.A.
Telephone: (601) 483-5365
Fax: (601) 486-1278
Web site: http://www.peavey.com/corp

Private Company
Incorporated: 1965
Employees: 2,400
Sales: $271 million (2007 est.)
NAIC: 339992 Musical Instrument Manufacturing; 334310 Audio and Video Equipment Manufacturing; 334412 Bare Circuit Board Manufacturing; 334419 Other Electronic Component Manufacturing

■ ■ ■

Peavey Electronics Corporation, founded in 1965 by Hartley Peavey, is a major manufacturer of guitars, amplifiers, speakers, electronic keyboards, and other electronic audio-enhancement equipment. Over more than 40 years of operation, Peavey expanded his operations, with the aid of his wife Melia Peavey, to occupy 33 facilities on three continents with over 2,000 products and annual revenues exceeding $270 million. Peavey's guitars and equipment are distributed to 136 countries through its facilities in the United States, the United Kingdom, and China. Hartley Peavey has been recognized as an industry leader and innovator and is the recipient of numerous awards and honors for his contributions to the musical industry. In addition, Peavey is one of the largest manufacturers in Mississippi and has remained headquartered in Meridian, Mississippi, where the company's manufacturing plant, known as "Peavey City," is one of the region's key employers.

MUSICAL AMBITIONS LEAD TO THE FOUNDATION OF THE COMPANY: 1965–68

Hartley Peavey grew up in Meridian, Mississippi, and had early aspirations of becoming a rock and roll guitar player. As a teenager in the late 1950s, he worked in the Peavey Melody Music Store, owned by his father, J. B. "Mutt" Peavey, and tinkered with building amplifiers for local musicians. When, as he once confessed to *Inc.* magazine, he turned out to be a "pretty lousy guitarist," Peavey decided his future was in making amplifiers.

In 1965, after graduating from Mississippi State University with a degree in marketing and management, Peavey, then 23 years old, took the remaining $8,000 in his college fund and formed Peavey Electronics, working out of his parents' basement. As he later recalled in *Music and Sound's Greatest Hit,* published by Peavey Electronics for its 25th anniversary: "I would build one (amplifier) a week, go out and sell it, come back and start on another one." The amplifiers were inscribed with the lightning bolt logo that Peavey had designed as a college freshman.

A year later, Peavey moved the business from the family's basement to an attic in the building that had housed his father's music store. By then, his father had sold the music store but still owned the building. Peavey

COMPANY PERSPECTIVES

Since its founding in 1965, our company goal has always been to build the best products available while at the same time making them affordable through the use of the most modern computer-assisted design manufacturing methods available.

also hired his first employee, a salesman, so he could concentrate on building amplifiers.

In the mid-1960s, however, there were many larger, better-known companies making amplifiers, and Peavey soon expanded into building public address (PA) systems to keep his young business afloat. In the company's 25th anniversary retrospective, Peavey explained that as "I traveled and talked to music dealers, I realized there was no shortage of instrument amplifiers. But if you wanted a PA system there were essentially only two available and both were expensive systems. ... Most folks think I got into the music business with guitar amps. Not necessarily so!"

A CORNERSTONE OF THE COMMUNITY: 1968–80

By 1968, business was good enough that Peavey decided to borrow $17,500 to build a small "factory" in Meridian. Over the next five years, Peavey Electronics enlarged the building seven times, and having grown to more than 150 employees, in 1973 the company began construction on Plant #3, which would become its main manufacturing facility. To hire enough skilled employees, Peavey Electronics established training courses at Meridian Community College.

Over the years, Peavey was often asked about his decision to keep the company in Meridian. In 1985, he told *Inc.* magazine that Mississippi "unfortunately runs dead last in everything. You don't have the skilled people you need, you don't have the suppliers, you don't have the access to the freight network. ... Back in 1965, when I got into this, I was too damn dumb to know it couldn't be done." He went on to say that he had "lost count" of how often he wished he had built Peavey Electronics somewhere else. In a later interview with his hometown newspaper, the *Meridian Star,* Peavey explained, "What I tried to say in the *Inc.* article was that Mississippi presented many difficulties in starting a high-tech business. And some of these difficulties exist to this day."

It was in the early 1970s that the company began the vertical integration which would make it unique among major electronic musical equipment manufacturers. Unable to purchase reliable speaker components for its high-power amplifiers, Peavey Electronics began making its own loudspeakers. Eventually, Peavey Electronics would build everything it needed for its musical instruments, from cabinets and metalwork down to making its own circuit boards and running its own advertising agency.

Peavey explained in a 1990 interview, "If somebody local had been able to subcontract for me the things I needed to build amplifiers, I would probably still be using subcontractors. We had to learn to make our own chassis, our own circuit boards, and eventually everything 'in-house,' and while we thought it was a tremendous disadvantage, and in many ways it was, we discovered that it was the best thing that could have happened."

In the mid-1970s, Peavey Electronics also began manufacturing electric guitars, again from necessity. Several leading electronic instrument companies were absorbed by conglomerates during the 1960s, including Fender Musical Instruments, which was purchased by CBS in 1964. These companies, with their immense marketing power, began encouraging dealers to sell their guitars and amplifiers as a package deal, cutting into sales of Peavey amplifiers.

As he had when he adopted solid-state components for his first amplifiers, Peavey embraced state-of-the-art technology to produce guitars at lower cost, becoming the first manufacturer to use computer-controlled machinery to turn out guitar bodies and precision parts. Years later, Peavey recalled, "When we announced that we were making guitar bodies on computer-controlled machinery, some of the most prominent names in the industry said, 'Impossible. Everybody knows you can't make guitars with a computer.' That was a rather simplistic attitude, we thought, because, in fact, we weren't making guitars on computers. We were using ... computer-controlled machines to make precision guitar parts to tolerances that heretofore manufacturers couldn't even think about approaching. Guitar makers are always talking about handcraftsmanship. What handcraftsmanship is, in many instances, is the ability to fit together parts that are produced with a lot of 'slop' in them."

EXPANSION AND COMPUTER INTEGRATION: 1980–90

While the decision to remain in Meridian was made more out of necessity than design, Hartley Peavey's

KEY DATES

1965: Company is founded by Hartley Peavey.
1968: Peavey begins manufacturing public address systems.
1973: Construction begins on company headquarters and largest manufacturing plant.
1977: Peavey's Black Widow loudspeaker is debuted.
1982: City of Meridian, Mississippi, declares April 21 to be Hartley Peavey Day.
1987: Company initiates Audio Media Research division and enters the studio market.
1989: Peavey opens Architectural Acoustics division for commercial applications.
1990: Hartley Peavey inducted into the Rock Walk of Fame in Hollywood, California.
1999: Peavey completes acquisition of Crest Audio.
2002: Peavey launches custom guitar and bass building shop for online customers.
2003: Meridian honors founder with establishment of Hartley Peavey Drive.
2005: *Guitar Player* magazine honors Hartley Peavey with first Manufacturer Lifetime Achievement Award.

company had become a cornerstone of the local economy and the city greatly appreciated the employment opportunities and economic influx that Peavey brought to the city. In 1982, the city of Meridian honored its hometown industrialist by proclaiming April 21 as Hartley Peavey Day.

Peavey continued to expand on the use of emergent technology in the construction of the company's components and amplification systems. Engineers at the Peavey plant created a focused field geometry system to enhance the company's loudspeakers and also developed new electronics systems for mixing consoles and other equipment used primarily by sound engineers. In 1987, Peavey formed their Audio Media Research division, which gave way to new lines of products including multitrack recorders and studio amplification and recording systems. The following year, Peavey cooperated with Motorola to create the first upgradable line of keyboards, allowing keyboardists to purchase new software to upgrade their equipment rather than purchasing a new system with each development in technology.

In the late 1980s, when the company was considering building its first U.S. manufacturing facility outside of Mississippi, then-Governor Ray Mabus worked with Peavey Electronics and Meridian Community College to create The Meridian Partnership, the first private-sector use of the Job Skills Education Program, a technology and basic-skills program originally developed by the U.S. Army.

In 1989, Peavey introduced another major division, Architectural Acoustics, specializing in providing sound solutions for large, commercial clients. The division provided complete sound system solutions from installing speakers and microphones to working with institutions to craft precision audio technology for unique architectural products.

WORLD WIDE STATUS: 1990–2000

When Peavey Electronics celebrated its 25th anniversary in 1990, the *Meridian Star* published a 40-page special edition to honor the company that had become the area's largest employer. The newspaper noted that Peavey Electronics created more than 1,000 new jobs in east-central Mississippi between 1980 and 1989, including more than 850 in the Meridian area, and 73 percent of all new manufacturing jobs in Lauderdale County. Among those saluting the company was Mayor Jimmy Kemp, who said, "Of course the obvious things you think about when somebody in your community employs 1,850 people is the enormous impact it has on your city, which is fantastic. I'd hate to think what we'd do without Peavey Electronics as far as our city is concerned." Peavey Electronics was then the tenth largest manufacturing employer in the state. For his contributions to the industry, Hartley Peavey was also inducted into the Hollywood Rock Walk of Fame.

During the early 1990s, Peavey both expanded its operations, with the construction of a 58,000-square-foot training center, complete with an in-house recording studio, and continued to develop new modes of construction for its products. The introduction of the computer-integrated manufacturing system allowed the company to link all aspects of the manufacturing process through a simple control scheme. The company also began to automate much of its production process, though Hartley and his wife Melia Peavey, then president of the company, maintained an unofficial no-layoffs policy. Employees whose jobs were eliminated through technology were retrained to serve in alternate positions. In 1994, Jere Hess, then director of public relations, told the *Meridian Star*, "No one in this company has ever lost their job because of automation."

In 1991, Peavey Electronics was one of 20 companies selected by the U.S. Department of Commerce to participate in a five-year program designed to stimulate export of U.S. products to Japan. As part of the program, the Department of Commerce arranged meetings between heads of the U.S. companies and Japanese officials, including Prime Minister Toshiki Kaifu and Minister of International Trade and Industry Eiichi Nakao. Peavey Electronics, which first entered the Japanese market in the mid-1970s in a short-lived relationship with industrial giant Yamaha Corporation, also agreed to participate in at least one trade show a year in Japan.

In 1991, President George H. W. Bush chose Peavey Electronics as the site to give a speech on economic growth. The *Meridian Star* noted, "Hoping to pump fresh air into his sagging popularity, President Bush hailed the success of Meridian's Peavey Electronics Co. as proof that Americans can excel in a worldwide economic battle." The newspaper also quoted Peavey as stating that the company's "one real goal, perhaps unreachable, is to become a $1 billion company." At the time, Peavey Electronics was reported in the local media to have sales approaching $500 million a year, although company executives said that figure was greatly exaggerated. As a matter of policy, the privately held company did not release financial information, but annual sales in the mid-1990s were generally believed to be about $200 million to $220 million.

In 1993, Peavey debuted the world's first computer-based audio processing and control interface. The system, known as MediaMatrix, was used in a number of prominent installations, including the U.S. Congress building and the Sydney Opera House in Australia. MediaMatrix became an industry standard for computer integrated sound systems and other companies soon debuted similar systems. In 1998, MediaMatrix produced the Page Matrix system, an integrated paging system ideal for large organizations and buildings. The system was adopted by dozens of airports and other larger companies over the next several years.

Peavey completed their acquisition of Crest Audio, begun in 1998, just before the end of the decade. Crest Audio was a leading manufacturer of powered amplifiers and other equipment for the recording and performance industries. While acquisitions were not a common strategy for Peavey, the merger with Crest Audio helped the company to expand its share of the studio amplification market.

PEAVEY IN THE 21ST CENTURY

In the 21st century, Peavey embraced the digital age with the integration of Internet-based systems and e-commerce into the company's business model. Peavey launched an online custom guitar shop in 2002, and continued to improve on their web services each year since entering the e-commerce market. In 2006, the company debuted a new custom shop, available through a separate web site, www.peaveycustomshop.com, which provided more than 16,000 construction and equipment options for electric guitars and basses.

Peavey also embarked on a number of promotional campaigns, including teaming with famed guitarist Joe Santriani to produce a signature line of amplifiers and obtaining the rights to whiskey producer Jack Daniel's brand name for use in a line of products, debuted in 2004. In an innovative promotional campaign, the first guitars released under the Jack Daniel's label were constructed using wood from barrels made at Jack Daniel's whiskey plants.

While Peavey maintained its focus on entry-level instruments, innovative marketing strategies, such as collaborations with rock music artists and iconic brand names like Jack Daniel's, helped the company to compete in a challenging market while simultaneously maintaining credibility as a company grounded in American rock culture.

As it had been since the company's inception, Peavey's relationship with its home state of Mississippi continued to be filled with both pride and frustration. In 2003, Meridian, Mississippi, honored Peavey by naming the street on which the company's headquarters were located "Hartley Peavey Drive." In a 2003 article for the *Mississippi Business Journal,* Hartley Peavey expressed his appreciation for his home state's honors but also dissatisfaction at the challenges Mississippi placed before its established companies. "I appreciated that honor, but frankly I would have been much more appreciative if they hadn't gone up on my taxes and my water bill," Peavey said, "And they're trying to annex the Sonny Montgomery Industrial Park where we have a lot of facilities. Yes, I appreciate the honor, but at the end of the day it doesn't buy any groceries." Peavey cited difficulties and governmental regulations as part of the reason his company had been forced to conduct layoffs and other cutbacks since 2000. Despite the difficulties, Peavey expressed no plans to move his major facilities from the state and appreciated his commitment to the community. In 2001, Hartley Peavey was inducted into the Mississippi Music Hall of Fame.

As the end of the first decade of the new millennium approached, Peavey still had not reached its ultimate goal of becoming a billion-dollar company, but profits continued to rise and the company's estimated annual revenues exceeded $270 million in 2007. Peavey's commitment to integration of new technology and diversification of their electronics industry was key in the company's growth and dominance of the industry. Peavey's catalog of over 2,000 products included numerous award-winning electronic systems, musical components, and commercial applications. Industry acknowledgment continued, including *Guitar Player Magazine*'s first Manufacturer Lifetime Achievement Award in 2005. Commitment to both tradition and innovation was the key to Peavey's success and the plan for the future.

Dean Boyer
Updated, Micah L. Issitt

PRINCIPAL SUBSIDIARIES

Peavey Amplification Ltd. (United Kingdom).

PRINCIPAL COMPETITORS

Fender Musical Instruments; Harman International; Gibson Musical Instruments; Yamaha Corporation.

FURTHER READING

Achard, Ken, *The Peavey Revolution: Hartley Peavey, the Gear, the Company and the All American Success Story,* Milwaukee, Wisc.: Backbeat Books Press, 2005.

Armbruster, William, "US Guitar Maker Hopes for Big Hit in Japan," *Journal of Commerce and Commercial,* June 3, 1991, p. 1.

Deutsch, Claudia H., "Computers Turn Design on Its Prototypical Ear," *New York Times,* March 31, 1997.

Hallam, Linda, "Building Business on Caring," *Southern Living,* July 1991, pp. 67–68.

Johnson, Wilton J., Jr., "Peavey Electronics Continues to Dominate Its Field: But CEO Hartley Peavey Is Not a Happy Camper," *Mississippi Business Journal,* March 17, 2003.

"Marking 30 Years, Peavey Reaffirms Industry Commitment," *Music Trades,* March 1, 1995, p. 149.

Moulden, Philip, "Bush, Peavey Harmonize on Economy," *Meridian Star,* December 4, 1991, p. 1.

Music and Sound's Greatest Hit, Meridian, Miss.: Peavey Electronics Corporation, 1990.

"Peavey Powers Up a New Web Site," *Mississippi Business Journal,* November 3, 2003, p. 30.

"Peavey 25th Anniversary Souvenir Edition," *Meridian Star,* June 14, 1990.

Rodgers, John, "President's Visit Amplifies Peavey's Success," *Meridian Star,* December 4, 1991, p. 5A.

Sheffield, Skip, "Chilling Out in Boca," *Boca Raton News,* April 4, 1993, p. E1.

Slaughter, Jeff, "Peavey Electronics: 'Tenacious, Innovative, Responsive,'" *Mississippi Business Journal,* August 1, 1994, p. 24.

Torgerson, Stan, "Peavey Grows with Automation," *Meridian Star,* August 7, 1994, p. B1.

"What Makes Peavey Run?: With Little More than a Tablesaw, Determination, and Some Very Good Ideas, Hartley Peavey Launched Peavey Electronics in 1965," *Music Trades,* August 8, 2005, p. 118.

Wojahn, Ellen, "Homegrown: Peavey Electronics Does It All—Better and Cheaper—In Meridian, Miss.," *Inc.,* May 1985, p. 136.

Quick Restaurants S.A.

Grotesteenweg 224, Box 5
Berchem, B-2600
Belgium
Telephone: (32 03) 286 18 11
Fax: (32 03) 286 18 79
Web site: http://www.quick-restaurants.com

Private Company
Incorporated: 1971
Employees: 15,000
Sales: EUR 807 million ($1.2 billion) (2006 est.)
NAIC: 722110 Full-Service Restaurants

■ ■ ■

Quick Restaurants S.A. is a French-owned, Belgium-based operator of fast-food restaurants. The company, which features a hamburger based on McDonald's, is the sole European-owned fast-food format that has successfully resisted the arrival of the major U.S. chains. Quick has long claimed the leading position in the hamburger segment in Belgium, and holds a strong second place in France. Quick operates more than 410 restaurants, including more than 80 in Belgium and Luxembourg, and 320 in France. In 2007, the company, which operates five restaurants in the French-controlled island of Réunion, launched an effort to build a wider geographic presence. The company targeted Spain, Morocco, Algeria, and Russia for the initial phase of this effort, and has opened sites in Andorra and Algiers, and two restaurants in Morocco. The company has also announced plans for further restaurant openings in its core French and Belgian territories.

Approximately three-quarters of the company's restaurants are operated through its franchise network. Founded in 1971 as part of the Belgian GIB supermarket group, Quick went public in 1993. In 2007 France's Caisse des Dépôts et Consignations Capital Investissement (CDC CI), through its Financière Gallop holding, took full control of the company, which was subsequently delisted. Quick is led by Chairman and CEO Jean-Paul Brayer.

EMULATING THE UNITED STATES IN 1971

Quick's ability to survive and even prosper in the highly competitive European fast-food market stemmed from its early entrance into what was at the time an untouched market. The fast-food restaurant concept had been introduced in the United States in the 1950s, but the format had not reached the continent. While pioneer McDonald's and others focused on building up their networks in the United States, the restaurant sector in Europe remained dominated by traditional restaurants and eating habits through the late 1960s and into the early 1970s.

In Belgium, however, one of the continent's first fast-food chains had begun to transform the country's restaurant sector. In 1968, Baron Vaxelaire, founder and leader of Belgian supermarket group GB Entreprises, had discovered the fast-food concept while on a trip to the United States to gather new retailing ideas. GB set up a new subsidiary, called Quick Restaurants, and

COMPANY PERSPECTIVES

As an active and proactive local player, Quick moves in step with its customers, shares their passions, predicts their desires and innovates in order to surprise them with new products and restaurant architectural design. Quick is committed to the public health debate on nutrition and continues to focus its efforts on a balanced diet. These challenges call for the constant mobilization of the men and women working for the success of the brand alongside whom Quick works daily to ensure the long-term viability of its economic model.

began adapting the American hamburger-based menu to the Belgian palate. GB opened its first two Quick restaurants in 1971, in Schoten and Waterloo.

GB's supermarket network provided the framework for Quick's expansion, and the company's restaurants were typically located next to or near the group's supermarkets and hypermarkets. This network was further expanded in 1974, when GB Entreprises merged with rival Inno-BM, operator of the Innovation, Grand Bazar, and Bon Marché retail chains. The new company, called GB-Inno-BM, and later GIB, emerged as a leader in Belgium's retail sector, providing the backing for Quick's own growth.

In its early years, new Quick restaurants were wholly owned by the company. In the second half of the decade, however, Quick again looked to its U.S. models for inspiration, and began developing its own franchise network to stimulate expansion. The first Quick franchise opened in Brussels in 1978. Franchising proved a cost-efficient method for rapidly building the company's network of restaurants, which typically required two to three years to achieve profitability. By focusing much of its expansion through the franchise channel, the company was able to avoid taking on too much debt.

FRENCH EXPANSION BEGINNING IN 1979

Quick's early entry into the Belgian market enabled it to gain and keep the leading position in that country. This remained true despite the entry of McDonald's Corporation, then in the midst of its European conquest, into Belgium. Success in the small Belgian market had its limits in the long term, however. In order to secure a larger base of operations for the future, the company targeted expansion beyond Belgium for its second decade in business.

Quick's interest naturally turned to Belgium's southern neighbor, France. The company opened its first Quick restaurant in France in Aix-en-Provence in 1978. The larger scale of the French market, however, led the company to seek a local partner for the expansion of the format there. In 1979, the company entered into a joint venture with supermarket group Casino in order to launch a full-fledged chain of Quick restaurants in France. As part of that agreement, Casino acquired a 21.5 percent stake in Quick from GIB. The first Quick restaurant under the joint venture opened in 1980.

With the backing of two powerful supermarket groups, Quick prepared its next phase of expansion. The company realized the necessity of gaining scale quickly in France, in order to generate profitability, but also in order to claim the country's prime locations. With McDonald's growing strongly, and with the arrival of Burger King in France, Quick turned to acquisition to provide its own French network with a jumpstart. In 1986, the company acquired the O'Kitch chain of 20 restaurants. This was soon followed by the purchase of the Freetime chain, adding another 45 units to its French portfolio. Most of these restaurants were then remodeled into the Quick format, a process largely completed by the beginning of the next decade.

GOING PUBLIC IN 1993

Quick had also launched an aggressive expansion drive, doubling the number of restaurants in France over the course of five years. The expansion allowed the company to build its French network to 145 stores by 1993, as compared to 62 stores in Belgium. By then, the company had also opened three stores in Luxembourg.

Throughout this period, Quick continued to adapt its restaurant format and menu, in part in response to its competitors' operations. Starting in 1983, the company added takeaway service and then introduced drive-up windows to most of its restaurants. The company also adapted McDonald's Happy Meal concept for its own restaurants, while adopting the U.S. giant's strategy of marketing to children.

Casino sought an exit from its shareholding, and in 1993 Quick placed the French supermarket group's shares on the Belgium Stock Exchange. GIB remained the group's majority shareholder, with more than 57.5 percent. The initial public offering (IPO) enabled the company to restructure its capital, reducing its debt and achieving a more stable financial footing.

The IPO also enabled Quick to launch a new and more aggressive phase of its expansion. The

KEY DATES

1971: First Quick restaurants open as subsidiary of Belgium's GB supermarket group.
1978: The first Quick franchise opens in Brussels.
1979: The company enters joint venture with Casino, SA, in France.
1993: Quick goes public on Brussels Stock Exchange.
1996: Outbreak of BSE (mad cow disease) leads to crisis in food industry.
2007: France's Caisse des Dépôts acquires 100 percent control of Quick.

company's franchise operations formed the heart of its new growth strategy as it sought to increase the balance of franchises to company-owned restaurants from just 20 percent at the start of the 1990s to a target of 75 percent by the end of the decade. Quick stepped up the pace of new restaurant openings into the middle of the decade, and by 1996 had increased the number of Quick restaurants in operation to nearly 315. In this way, Quick not only maintained its leader status in Belgium, but also assured itself of the number two position in France as well.

REELING FROM THE BSE CRISIS

The second half of the 1990s proved difficult for the company. The recession that lingered throughout much of Europe resulted in record numbers of unemployed and underemployed youth—precisely Quick's primary consumer segment. The reduced spending of its core customers slowed the company's revenue growth.

At the same time, Quick was feeling the effects of its ambitious expansion strategy as a number of its new restaurants had begun to cannibalize sales at existing outlets. This in turn caused resentment among the company's franchisees, who were already hard-pressed by the aggressive expansion of competing fast-food groups. McDonald's had launched an effort to gain the top sales position in Belgium, aggressively opening new restaurants while cutting its prices. At the same time, the traditional restaurant sector was forced to fight back, and more and more restaurants began developing lower-priced menus, with many starting to feature hamburgers as well.

To these difficulties were added the difficulties of Quick's management to accommodate to its own rapid growth, and the company's costs began to spiral. The company's spending on restaurant refurbishment had slowed, with the result that restaurants in its network had increasingly begun to appear run-down and out of date. Quick finally began to address these issues in 1997, when it launched a cost-cutting initiative along with a revamped marketing drive, including refurbished store formats and new menus.

However, these efforts could do little to counter the first of a series of crises to strike the food sector beginning in the mid-1990s. The fast-food market was in particular hit by the BSE (bovine spongiform encephalopathy or "mad cow disease") crisis in 1996. An outbreak of BSE, the so-called mad cow disease, among British and then European cattle herds was at that time accompanied by the first deaths from Creutzfeldt-Jakob disease, the human form of BSE. The discovery that BSE was transmissible to humans, and the possibility of extremely long incubation periods, sparked a panic among consumers, who turned away from beef consumption in massive numbers through the end of the decade.

Quick attempted to meet consumer concerns by adapting its menu, including introducing other meat choices, such as chicken. However, the company's core business remained hamburgers, and as a result the group's sales stagnated while its store expansion slowed dramatically. Through the end of the decade, the company managed to open just 10 to 14 new stores per year.

NEW OWNERS AND NEW OBJECTIVES

The effects of the BSE crisis subsided very slowly through the end of the decade. The company, by this time with more than 400 restaurants, saw its sales start to rise again, driven by its French restaurant operations, and by 1999 the company's revenues had topped EUR 655 million. Another bright spot for the company came when Burger King announced that it was retreating from the French fast-food sector; Quick then acquired five of that company's locations in 1997. In this way, Quick remained the sole viable challenger to McDonald's in the hamburger segment, claiming nearly one-third of the market in France.

Quick then sought further international expansion. The company targeted the Netherlands in the late 1990s, opening two pilot restaurants in that country in 1999. However, the company's entry into this neighboring market came far too late, and Quick was forced to retreat from the Netherlands by 2000. The company began seeking other horizons, targeting Eastern Europe. The first Quick restaurant opened in Slovenia in 1999, while the company began negotiating with a local partner to develop the chain in Hungary as well. In the end, these efforts too proved unsuccessful. Into the early 2000s, the only foreign expansion to succeed was the group's extension into the French West Indies, where it opened five franchised restaurants starting in 2001.

A new BSE scare rocked the company at the beginning of the new century as BSE outbreaks began to appear in France and Belgium. The increasingly weakened company became the subject of takeover rumors, as it issued profit warnings in 2000. Instead, the company launched a restructuring effort, closing down 35 of its unprofitable restaurants, as well as shutting down its operations in Hungary and Slovenia in 2001. The restructuring process continued with the appointment of Jean-Paul Brayer, former head of the Flo restaurant group in France, as group CEO. The company then announced plans to shut another 35 restaurants through 2003.

As investors grew impatient with the company's struggles to restore growth, Quick's future prospects as a publicly listed company were called into question. The company also faced mounting pressure targeting the poor nutritional value of the fast-food sector, and its strategy of marketing to children. In order to deflect these concerns, Quick instituted its Value and Nutrition communication program in 2004, while adapting its menu to include fresh fruits and other items. The company also worked at reducing the fat content in a number of sauces, and experimented with allowing consumers to salt their own french fries.

In the meantime, the company launched a new expansion program targeting the North African markets. The company opened its first restaurant in Morocco in 2004. In 2005, the company signed a major franchise agreement in Algeria, calling for the opening of 20 restaurants in that country. The first of these opened in Algiers in 2006. Another potential market for the company was Spain, where the group opened its first restaurant in Andorra that same year.

Quick found a new owner at the end of 2006, when France's CDC CI agreed to buy out GIB's holding in the company through subsidiary Financière Gallop. That company then launched a full-fledged takeover offer, boosting its position to 97.2 percent by the beginning of 2007. In February of that year, Gallop then launched a minority "squeeze out," taking 100 percent control of Quick. Freed from investor pressures, Quick began developing a new strategy, including plans to resume opening new restaurants at the pace of 20 to 25 new sites per year.

M. L. Cohen

PRINCIPAL SUBSIDIARIES

Financière Quick SAS; France Quick SAS; Quick Restaurants SAS.

PRINCIPAL COMPETITORS

Casino Guichard-Perrachon S.A.; Groupe Auchan S.A.; Rallye S.A.; McDonald's Corporation; Sodexho Alliance S.A.; Buffalo Grill S.A.; Elior S.A.

FURTHER READING

"Algeria Industry: Quick Restaurants to Open Fast-Food Chain," *Economist Intelligence Unit,* September 30, 2005.

Braude, Jonathan, "Bidders Scramble for Quick," *Daily Deal,* August 4, 2004.

"European Quick Restaurant Tapping into Chinese Market," *Alestron,* July 11, 2003.

Newpoff, Laura, "Wendy's Rumored to Be Suitor for Belgian Fast-Food Chain," *Business First-Columbus,* July 7, 2000, p. 10.

"Quick Restaurants," *Euroweek,* November 3, 2006, p. 58.

"Quick Restaurants Eyeing Deal to Buy 5 Paris BKs," *Nation's Restaurant News,* November 10, 1997, p. 6.

Reiter Dairy, LLC

1961 Commerce Circle
Springfield, Ohio 45502-2011
U.S.A.
Telephone: (937) 323-5777
Toll Free: (800) 762-5905
Fax: (937) 323-2420
Web site: http://www.reiterdairy.com

Wholly Owned Subsidiary of Dean Foods Company
Incorporated: 1933
Employees: 350
Sales: $132 million (2001 est.)
NAIC: 311511 Fluid Milk Manufacturing

■ ■ ■

A subsidiary of Dean Foods Company, Reiter Dairy, LLC, is a Springfield, Ohio-based manufacturer and marketer of dairy products, nondairy creamer, fruit juices, flavored drinks, and bottled water. Although Reiter exited the ice-cream business in 2003, it continues to offer such dairy products as milk, flavored milk, cottage cheese, sour cream, buttermilk, French onion dip, half and half, and heavy whipping cream. The company also markets Hershey's-branded flavored milk drinks, and Swiss-branded iced teas, lemonade, fruit punch, and orange drink. Reiter is the leading milk brand in Ohio and also serves portions of surrounding states. In addition to its main office and plant in Springfield, the company maintains branch offices in Akron and Findlay, Ohio.

DEPRESSION-ERA ORIGINS

Reiter Dairy was founded in 1933 by Ralph Reiter, a Pennsylvania native and master baker who after World War I moved to Akron to start a bakery. He quickly changed course, deciding to sell the bakery in order to indulge in his passion for invention. According to company sources, he developed a precursor to the car gas gauge. Apparently he was unable to make a living as a tinkerer and he turned his attention to the butter business, becoming the owner of Akron's Miller-Maid Creamery. Like many companies across the country that had focused on butter and cheese production, however, Reiter decided that fluid-milk production offered a greater upside than butter. Thus, in February 1933, along with his son, Harold, he launched Reiter Dairy, located across the street from the University of Akron.

When the dairy began bottling milk supplied by hundreds of area farmers and delivered to Akron homes and businesses by horse-drawn wagons, the country was in the midst of the Great Depression, which was not particularly kind to the dairy industry. Because people could no longer afford to buy milk, demand plunged while supply remained high. As a result, prices bottomed out and producers struggled to hang on. Reiter Dairy existed from week to week, sometimes relying on loans from friends and suppliers to pay the company's 15 employees each Saturday night. When that first difficult year came to an end, the dairy posted sales of $500,000. More importantly, it remained in business for 1934.

Ralph Reiter used his penchant for innovation to good use as a milk producer. His was the first Akron

COMPANY PERSPECTIVES

Reiter Dairy invites you to enjoy life's moments ... the pause in your busy day when you take time to appreciate all of life's goodness: the warmth of the sun, a child's laughter, maybe a call from an old friend, a plate of warm cookies and a cold glass of milk. These are the moments when you feel most alive. Reiter Dairy. Rediscover Life's Goodness.

dairy to homogenize milk, making raw milk more stable and preventing cream from rising to the top. He marketed the new product as "Mello-Milk." Reiter also invented a new way to cap milk bottles, creating a machine to crown and band the mouth of the bottle with a square of plyofilm, similar to cellophane.

POSTWAR GROWTH OF STORE SALES

Reiter Dairy was able to survive the Great Depression, and as the economy roared back to life because of defense spending after the United States entered World War II in late 1941. When the servicemen and servicewomen returned home four years later, the market for milk expanded greatly. Birth rates soared, leading to the baby-boom generation, creating an increasing demand for milk. Suburbs took shape and new, large self-serve grocery stores, "supermarkets," opened to serve them. Home delivery, especially by horse-drawn wagon, began to be overshadowed by store sales. In addition, the old quart milk bottles that had been delivered to homes each morning were replaced by paper containers favored by supermarkets. Reiter began offering its milk in Pure-Pak containers as it expanded its store sales. During the postwar years, the dairy also began producing ice cream, starting in 1946.

In 1952 Harold Reiter replaced his father as the head of the family dairy. By this time annual sales reached $5 million and the workforce numbered 100. Under Harold Reiter's leadership, the company expanded in a number of directions. Reiter added to its ice-cream business by merging in 1954 with Belle Isle Dairy Farms, a major ice-cream producer owned by former Ohio State Senator Fred S. Harter. The resulting company operated under the name Reiter & Harter Dairy, Inc., and in the 1950s expanded its market reach by acquiring more than 20 small dairies across northern Ohio. Ralph Reiter remained involved in running the dairy until the end of the decade, passing away in 1959.

THIRD GENERATION ASSUMES CONTROL: 1967

Reiter & Harter continued to grow in the 1960s, so that by the time Harold Reiter died in 1967, annual sales approached $10 million and employment exceeded 200. Succeeding Harold Reiter as president was his son, Rollin S. Reiter. Under his leadership the company took the name Reiter Foods, Inc., in 1969. It also tried its hand, like many dairies, in establishing a chain of convenience stores, operating under the Stop and Go name. In order to focus on the dairy business, the stores were eventually sold, as was a frozen food institution supply company. To reflect this change in direction, the company name changed once again in 1978, becoming Reiter Dairy, Inc.

Reiter gained entry to the markets of southern Ohio in 1982 with the acquisition of a milk plant and distribution center in Springfield, Ohio, purchased from Akron's Lawson Co. In addition, Reiter added Oak Farm Dairy in Findlay, located in the north western part of Ohio, as well as a frozen food distribution center in Tallmadge, located in northwestern Ohio. The latter would prove useful in 1986 when Reiter introduced a new line of premium ice cream to compete against such brands as Häagen-Dazs and Ben & Jerry's, along with local premium brand Pierre's French Ice Cream Co. The new "Signature" line, so called because the label carried Rollin Reiter's signature, had an increased butterfat content and came in 11 flavors.

Reiter Dairy had been run by three generations of the Reiter family, but as Rollin Reiter reached his mid-50s he found that there was no one to whom he could pass the baton. One son was employed in New York City by a trade journal, *Beverage World,* while another worked as an architect in Boston. Reiter decided the time had come to sell the business. Not only would such a move provide liquidity for the family, but he also hoped to secure the future of the company and its employees by aligning it with an owner with deep-enough pockets to sustain growth. Reiter began looking for a buyer and in 1986 settled on Chicago-based Dean Foods Co. He had been impressed by Dean's chairman, Kenneth J. Douglas, who met him at the airport when Reiter paid a visit to Chicago and insisted on carrying his bags. Waiting for them was a "plain vanilla car." He felt comfortable with the down-to-earth approach and was reassured that the values of the two companies were in line.

DEAN FOODS ACQUIRES REITER: 1986

A deal was struck in October 1986 and Reiter Dairy became part of the Dean Foods family. It was a deal that

KEY DATES

1933: Reiter Dairy started in Akron, Ohio, by Ralph Reiter.
1946: Ice-cream production begins.
1952: Harold Reiter succeeds father as president.
1954: Merger with Belle Isle Dairy Farms; name is changed to Reiter & Hart Dairy, Inc.
1967: Harold Reiter dies, replaced by son Rollin Reiter.
1969: Name is changed to Reiter Foods, Inc.
1978: Reiter Dairy, Inc., name taken.
1986: Dean Foods Company acquires Reiter.
1990: Rollin Reiter leaves company to become Dean vice-president.
2001: Dallas-based Suiza Foods Corporation acquires Dean Foods.
2003: Ice-cream production ceased.
2007: Akron production plant closed; distribution facility opened.

made sense for both parties. From Reiter's perspective, as Rollin Reiter told *Smart Business Akron/Canton,* "Even though we were making $100 million in sales and had over 550 employees between our major production plants and branches, to go further constantly requires an infusion of new capital for new equipment and expanded facilities." For Dean Foods, Reiter Dairy was a desirable acquisition because it was a dominant brand in Ohio and had made inroads into surrounding states. Moreover, it fielded an excellent sales and marketing team, and owned modern facilities that possessed excess production capacity.

Little changed at Reiter Dairy after Dean assumed ownership. Rollin Reiter continued to run the business with little input from the new corporate parent, which had a reputation for granting autonomy to its local dairies. The biggest difference was the financial wherewithal Reiter possessed. Soon after the deal was completed, Dean began investing in improvements to the dairy's main plant, spending about $6 million over two years, followed by another $4.3 billion at the end of the decade. The Springfield plant was also upgraded, bringing milk production to one million gallons a week. Moreover, profitability improved, partly because overhead expenses such as accounting were handled by Dean, but also because, as Rollin Reiter told the *Akron Beacon-Journal,* they now ran a "tighter ship." Planning became more formal under Dean. "We did a lot of that by the seat of our pants and it worked," Reiter told the *Beacon-Journal.* "But you can't run a $1.5 billion operation like that."

By the start of the 1990s annual sales at Reiter Dairy topped $125 million. After running the company for more than 20 years, Rollin Reiter was ready for a new challenge. He found it at Dean headquarters in Franklin Park, Illinois. In February 1990 the 62-year-old Reiter became vice-president for milk and ice-cream sales and marketing, responsible for 29 Dean Foods plants spread across the country, a position he would hold until retiring in 1993. Replacing him at Reiter Dairy, which Reiter would continue to oversee while retaining the title of president, was Bob Livingston, a 13-year veteran of the company who would assume day-to-day responsibility as chief administrative officer.

Reiter Dairy became part of Dean's Northeast division, serving as the regional headquarters for a group of ten dairies located in Ohio, Pennsylvania, New York, and Kentucky. Being part of a large unit helped Reiter to remain competitive in the 1990s, a decade that brought consolidation among retailers. Only large suppliers like Dean could meet the needs of the expanding supermarket chains, and in its local sphere Reiter was one of the few dairies able to cover every corner of Ohio. Another, perhaps more significant challenge, was a drop in milk consumption among young people. On a national level, Dean helped to support the industry's "Got Milk?" marketing campaign that successfully halted declining sales, while in Ohio Reiter was forced to take a closer look at consumer trends.

The company soon realized that it had lost track of what the consumer wanted. Specifically, its customers no longer thought of milk as a drink for all occasions, nor did they care any longer for the company's traditional square carton. A new product was developed, Milk Chugs, colorful resealable plastic bottles geared toward the on-the-go modern consumer. Chugs were introduced in 1998, offering white, chocolate, and strawberry whole and reduced-fat milks in quarts, pints, and eight-ounce multipacks. It was a successful launch that led to the introduction of orange juice Chugs.

CHANGE IN OWNERSHIP: 2001

A major change at the corporate level took place in late 2001 when Dean Foods was acquired by Dallas-based Suiza Foods Corporation, which since the early 1990s had become a major consolidator in the dairy industry. After going public in 1996, Suiza used its stock to complete more than 40 acquisitions, so that by the start of the new century it had emerged as the United States' largest dairy processor and distributor. It grew even larger with the addition of Dean Foods, but because Dean had more brand recognition the company opted to retain the name and Suiza Foods Corporation was renamed Dean Foods.

The new Dean Foods soon initiated changes that would have an impact on Reiter Dairy. In May 2003 the company began to focus on strategic brands. In October of that year, Reiter announced that it would cease to make ice cream after nearly half a century of production. With more than 25 ice-cream plants in the Dean Foods family with plenty of excess capacity, there was simply no compelling reason for continued ice-cream production in Akron. For Reiter employees it meant the loss of 25 jobs, or 7 percent of the plant's workforce.

More changes were to follow in early 2007 when the Reiter milk-processing plant near Akron was shut down, the result of excess capacity in the area. Only sales staff and some managers would remain in Reiter's longtime home city. The operation was reduced to a branch office and the company's headquarters was moved to Springfield. At the same time, Dean Foods was still willing to invest in Reiter Dairy. In 2007 a new $1 million state-of-the-art distribution facility was opened in Akron.

Ed Dinger

PRINCIPAL COMPETITORS

Dairy Farmers of America, Inc.; Land O'Lakes, Inc.

FURTHER READING

Badillo, Francisco, "Dean Acquisition Hasn't Soured for Reiter," *Akron Beacon Journal,* February 20, 1989, p. B1.

Casey, Mike, "Reiter Puts Signature, Pop-Top on Premium Brand of Ice Cream," *Crain's Cleveland Business,* March 10, 1986, p. 10.

Harrow, Victoria, "Strength in Numbers," *Smart Business Akron/Canton,* November 1999.

Schleis, Paula, "Reiter Parent to Lay Off up to 700," *Akron Beacon Journal,* October 3, 2007, p. C9.

Vanac, Mary, "Reiter to Close Plant in Summit," *Cleveland Plain Dealer,* December 9, 2006, p. C1.

Weizel, Richard, "He Shifts to Illinois Parent Firm; Reiter Dairy Chief Gets New Challenge," *Akron Beacon Journal,* February 19, 1990.

Ritz-Craft Corporation of Pennsylvania Inc.

15 Industrial Parkway
Mifflinburg, Pennsylvania 17844
U.S.A.
Telephone: (570) 966-1053
Toll Free: (800) 326-9836
Fax: (570) 966-9428
Web site: http://www.ritz-craft.com

Private Company
Incorporated: 1954
Employees: 1,050
Sales: $115 million (2005 est.)
NAIC: 321991 Manufactured Home (Mobile Home) Manufacturing; 321992 Prefabricated Wood Building Manufacturing

■ ■ ■

Ritz-Craft Corporation of Pennsylvania Inc. is one of the United States' leading manufacturers of modular (or "systems-built") homes, offering a wide variety of ranch, cape, and two-story houses and vacation homes in more than 300 home floor plans with a multitude of custom options. Models range in price from less than $100,000 to more than $1 million. The privately held, Mifflinburg, Pennsylvania-based company maintains five strategically located plants with a combined production space of 1 million square feet in Pennsylvania, Michigan, and North Carolina in order to serve 30 states, including all states east of the Mississippi River plus Iowa, Missouri, and Louisiana. In 2008 the company had plans to establish a plant in Florida.

Ritz-Craft contends that the houses it offers are superior to onsite-built houses because the construction work is done in environmentally controlled conditions by skilled and experienced workers who specialize in one facet of construction, using top-notch materials that are protected from the weather. Because the company is able to take advantage of volume purchasing, customers are able to save money. Because the homes are weather sealed in the factory, with properly installed wall and attic insulation, caulked windows, and electrical outlets on outside walls furnished with gaskets, customers save on energy costs.

They also have their homes available faster than ones constructed onsite: the house is completed in sections and available in about a month. The parts are then delivered to the building site and assembled in less than a week. Once completed the house is indistinguishable from an onsite-built house. In addition, Ritz-Craft operates a trucking company, a building materials distribution company, and a home mortgage company. Ritz-Craft is owned and managed by brothers Paul and Eric John.

COMPANY FOUNDED: 1954

Ritz-Craft started out in 1954 as a manufacturer of travel trailers, operating a plant in Argos, Indiana. According to obituaries published in the *Rochester Sentinel* of Indiana, the company was co-owned by Carl "Pat" Hendricks and his wife Pauline. The company expanded beyond trailers to include what became known as mobile homes until the company was acquired in the early 1970s by Wickes Corporation, a Saginaw,

COMPANY PERSPECTIVES

With over 50 years of experience, we are proud to offer an extensive line of energy efficient off-site built modular and manufactured homes with hundreds of unique options—so you can customize with ease and style.

Michigan-based company that owned the largest chain of lumberyards in the United States.

Wickes was implementing an expansion program, entering the European market while diversifying into such areas as commercial construction, retail furniture, and consumer credit. The acquisition of Ritz-Craft allowed Wickes to expand into modular and manufactured homes, increasing demand for its lumber products. In 1974 Wickes became a $1 billion company.

WICKES SELLS RITZ-CRAFT: 1976

Before long, Ritz-Craft no longer fit into the Wickes corporation's long-term plan, and in 1976 Wickes elected to sell the business to four Ritz-Craft managers: Paul R. John, Don Ritzenthaler, Glenn Cunningham, and Bob Roney. The new owners consolidated the assets acquired from Wickes in Mifflinburg, Pennsylvania, where the headquarters and assembly plant were combined. Starting out with just 50 employees, the company focused on the modular and manufactured home market.

At this stage Ritz-Craft was generating about $5 million in annual sales. Fifteen years later that amount would grow to $50 million, generated from three plants in Mifflinburg employing 450 people. The "pick-a-plan-out-of-the-book" days were also coming to an end with the advent of computer-aided design and an increase in consumer demand for more customization of modular homes.

SUCCESSION PLAN INITIATED: 1991

In 1991 a succession plan was initiated that would turn over ownership and management responsibilities to a new generation. Slated to become chief executive was Paul D. John, the son of Ritz-Craft's president, Paul R. John. His brother Eric was to become vice-president, Gary Ames would take over as director of marketing, and Barbara Shady become office manager. The elder John would stay on as chairman of the board.

The John brothers had been working for the company with their father since childhood. Five years older than his brother, Paul accompanied his father to the plant on weekends by the time he was nine, helping with cleanup chores, and he spent even more time at the plant during the summers. Both of the John boys would try their hand at the production line as they grew older, becoming proficient at each of the 16 building stations. Paul continued to work at the Mifflinburg plant during the summers while attending Lycoming College, where he started out as an engineering major before switching to business administration. After Paul graduated in 1985, his brother Eric followed him to Lycoming, receiving a business degree in 1990.

LEARNING AND EXPANDING THE BUSINESS

Although the brothers were the sons of the president, they reported to another partner of the company when they joined Ritz-Craft. Moreover, they were required to become familiar with all aspects of the operation, periodically moving from one department to the next as they learned sales and purchasing in addition to production, engineering, and service. When the succession plan was implemented they were permitted to buy a 2.5 percent stake in the company between them. Over the next dozen years they would continue to add to their holdings until the brothers were full owners of Ritz-Craft.

After the second generation took expanded leadership roles, Ritz-Craft launched five new product lines. One of them was the Genesis, a cost-effective product that combined modular and panelized technology. Delivered in a single carrier, it consisted of two modules for the first floor and panelized walls and roof for an unfinished second floor. However, because the plumbing and electrical infrastructure were already in place, Genesis buyers could complete the second floor as their finances allowed or the size of their families dictated. Thus, instead of having a ranch house of less than 1,000 square feet, Genesis owners had the potential to expand their living space to 1,440 square feet. Not only were freight costs reduced but setup required less than eight hours, providing further savings in finishing the house. Minus land and improvements, the Genesis retailed for about $40,000.

INNOVATIONS IN MODULAR CONSTRUCTION

In an effort to bring innovative solutions to modular building, Ritz-Craft developed a new dormer structure that allowed Ritz-Craft to offer more elaborate two-story

KEY DATES

1954: Company is founded in Indiana.
1976: Management buyout leads to headquarters moving to Mifflinburg, Pennsylvania.
1991: Succession plan is initiated.
2000: Michigan plant opens.
2005: North Carolina plant opens.
2007: Ritz-Craft Home Mortgage, LLC, is formed.

structures. In 1993 Paul R. John and Paul D. John, along with Gregory J. Sloditskie and Robert J. Roney, received a patent on a collapsible dormer, allowing first and second stories to be shipped by tractor trailer. Previously, dormers or second story structures were unable to meet the standard trailer roadway limitations of 14 feet high, 14 feet wide, and 60 feet long. The patent also included a method of assembling the module to the base unit.

Two-story models opened up the modular home industry to a wider group of customers in the 1990s. Aside from its collapsible dormer, Ritz-Craft benefited from advances in chassis and transportation systems, allowing the company to design more attractive and affordable two-story models.

Another important development was the hinged roof system. Manufactured homes had always relied on a low roof pitch, which not only made them stand out from site-built homes, but in many cases failed to meet local zoning codes that demanded higher-pitched roofs. Like collapsible dormers, hinged roofs were made to meet roadway limitations, but when set up on site and raised to their full height, they made the homes more attractive and allowed them to pass muster with zoning codes.

In other developments in the 1990s, Ritz-Craft renovated its two assembly plants in Mifflinburg, where a new 65,000-square-foot kitchen and bathroom cabinet manufacturing plant was also opened. Moreover, Ritz-Craft opened corporate model centers in Pennsylvania, Michigan, and North Carolina to drive sales of the expanding lines of Ritz-Craft products.

MICHIGAN PLANT OPENS: 2000

In order to better serve Midwest markets, Ritz-Craft opened a 175,000-square-foot, state-of-the-art modular home manufacturing plant in Jonesville, Michigan, in 2000. The early years of the new century proved challenging, however. The sale of modular houses was already in decline in the late 1990s when low interest rates and easy credit lured many people to buy existing homes or spend money on site-built homes. Despite the many advances made in modular homes, which featured many new floor plans and offered countless custom options, as well as superior construction under controlled conditions and extreme energy efficiency, the reputation of modular homes among consumers remained tainted by the "factory-built homes" of a bygone era that were lacking in curb appeal and associated with cheap materials and construction techniques.

The housing market soured after the terrorist attacks against the United States of September 11, 2001, which caused a struggling economy to worsen. Modular homebuilders, who had hoped that the affordability of their products would help them in tougher times, continued to see sales slip. Ritz-Craft was able to carry on while others in the field fell by the wayside. In 2002 the company turned out 642 houses, generating $80 million.

NORTH CAROLINA PLANT OPENS: 2005

For growth, Ritz-Craft looked to the Southeast where the winters were milder and the homebuilding season stretched longer. In September 2004 the company agreed to build a new plant in Richmond County, North Carolina, in the town of Hamlet, a community that the company believed had ample skilled labor to offer. A year later a 200,000-square-foot modular manufacturing plant was opened to produce homes for shipping to North Carolina, South Carolina, Virginia, Georgia, and parts of Tennessee. To appeal to the southern markets, Ritz-Craft introduced a pair of new product series that offered a number of built-in porches and dormer options.

The North Carolina plant hoped to hire more than 252 people but after two years in operation, it employed only about 100 because a glut of existing homes on the market depressed sales. Overall, Ritz-Craft did $115 million in sales in 2005. While some rumors circulated that the Hamlet plant was on the verge of closing at the end of 2006, management maintained that it took a much longer view of the operation and remained optimistic about Ritz-Craft's long-term prospects in the southeast. The Hamlet location included 57 acres, so should business dictate, the company had enough space to build a second plant of the same size.

DIVERSIFYING OPERATIONS AND ENHANCING PRODUCT OPTIONS

Ritz-Craft expanded beyond manufacturing in the middle of the first decade of the 2000s. It launched

Ritz-Trans Corporation in 2006, a trucking company dedicated to transporting modular homes. Its fleet of about two dozen trucks were capable of delivering modular homes from manufacturers to building sites coast to coast. The company took advantage of its cabinet plant in Mifflinburg by establishing Legacy Building Products in 2007. The subsidiary offered kitchen cabinets, vanities, entertainment centers, flooring products, decorative light fixtures and lamps, faucet products, locks and door hardware, and exterior architectural ornament products. Also in 2007 Ritz-Craft Home Mortgage, LLC, began offering financing for construction and permanent mortgages.

Ritz-Craft did not forget its main business, however. In 2007 it gained a toehold in the potentially lucrative Florida market by forming an alliance with Integrity Homes of Chipley, located in Northwest Florida. Integrity's partners had previously acquired distressed properties and renovated them. Serving as a showcase home was a 2,600-square-foot home built by the Hamlet plant and featured at the 2007 International Builders Show in Orlando. With a Tuscan-columned entry, customer-built hearth kitchen and built-in wine chiller, it was the kind of upscale home that Ritz-Craft was promoting as a way to stimulate business and elevate the image of modular homes.

The company also made plans to build a Florida manufacturing plant. Management believed that the advantages of system-built construction would, in time, be accepted by consumers. With only about 5 percent of new homes being modular, Ritz-Craft anticipated ample room to grow.

Ed Dinger

PRINCIPAL SUBSIDIARIES

Ritz-Trans; Legacy Crafted Cabinets; Legacy Building Products; Ritz-Craft Home Mortgage LLC.

PRINCIPAL COMPETITORS

Clayton Homes, Inc.; Champion Enterprises, Inc.; New Era Building Systems, Inc.

FURTHER READING

Bady, Susan, "Modular/Panelized Hybrid Expands As Needed," *Profession Builder and Remodeler,* August 1, 1991, p. 60.

"The Business of Homes," *Lycoming College Magazine,* Spring 2005, p. 5.

Carson, Daniel, "New Modular Home Company Opens Chipley Office," *Panama City (Fla.) News Herald,* June 12, 2007.

Caulfield, John, "Building Blocks," *Builder,* February 2007, p. 226.

DeMuth, Erin, "Ritz-Craft: Local Man Hired to Lead Operations," *Richmond County (N.C.) Daily Journal,* September 24, 2004.

Peacock, Julie, "Ritz-Craft Looks to the Future," *Richmond County (N.C.) Daily Journal,* December 16, 2006.

Power, Matthew, "Factory-Built Housing: Manufactured Meltdown," *Builder,* May 2003, p. 172.

———, "Modular Makeover," *Builder,* May 2005, p. 236.

Röchling Gruppe

Richard-Wagner-Strasse 9
Mannheim, 68165
Germany
Telephone: (49 621) 44 02-0
Fax: (49 621) 44 02-284
Web site: http://www.rochling.de

Private Company
Founded: 1822
Employees: 6,041
Sales: EUR 1.05 billion ($1.38 billion) (2006)
NAIC: 325211 Plastics Material and Resin Manufacturing; 326122 Plastics Pipe and Pipe Fitting; 326199 All Other Plastics Product Manufacturing; 422610 Plastics Materials and Basic Forms

■ ■ ■

The Röchling Gruppe is one of Germany's largest producers of high-performance industrial and automotive plastics. The group consists of 52 companies in 18 countries that utilize a broad range of processes to produce a variety of plastics including standard plastics, engineering plastics, high-temperature plastics, glass fiber reinforced plastics, thermosets, laminated densified wood, and natural fiber plastic composites. Of Röchling's customers, 46 percent are located in Germany and another 33 percent in the rest of Europe; customers in the Americas account for about 12 percent of the firm's sales, and customers in Asia for 9 percent.

The Röchling-Gruppe is comprised of two divisions: High-Performance Plastics and Automotive Plastics. High-Performance Plastics produces manufacturing and processing engineering plastics. Its products are used in industries such as foods, chemicals, semiconductors, medicine, electricity, and transportation. The division has about 1,900 employees in 31 production facilities worldwide. The Automotive Plastics division produces plastic systems and components for the automobile industry, such as intake manifolds and pipes, containers for liquids, windshield cowls, fans and shrouds, air ducts, door and seat panels, center consoles, air conditioning parts, wheel arch liners, and trays. Approximately 3,900 workers are employed in the Automotive Plastics division in 23 locations in Europe, the Americas, and Asia.

In Europe Röchling-Gruppe companies are located in Germany, Austria, Spain, France, Italy, Finland, Sweden, Lithuania, Denmark, United Kingdom, Belgium, and the Czech Republic. The firm is represented in the Americas in the United States and Brazil. Its Asian branches are in China and India. The Röchling-Gruppe is a private company, owned jointly by the more than 200 members of the Röchling family.

ESTABLISHING A BUSINESS IN THE SAARLAND

In the course of its history, Röchling has made three remarkable changes of corporate focus that reflect the evolution of industry and production from its start in coal based production to the manufacture of iron and steel and, finally in the late 20th century, to the production of high-quality industrial plastics. The Röchling family traces its business activities back to

COMPANY PERSPECTIVES

The Röchling Group, founded in 1822, has been active in plastics processing for more than 80 years. Step by step, the company has extended its activities with high-quality materials and state-of-the-art technologies. This, combined with the competency of its employees, we have developed what today makes Röchling a reliable partner of customers around the world—proficiency in plastics. Three entrepreneurial cornerstones—competence, quality and innovation—have been the foundation of the Röchling Group's rise to the leading international ranks among plastics companies. Competence means that Röchling companies are leaders in their business. The Group covers the full range of quality plastics and all major plastics processing techniques. What Röchling means by a quality is that our products and services meet and exceed our customers' requirements and expectations and that there is a spirit of innovation when advising our business partners with the latest knowledge available in our fields. Röchling leads the field in technological development of products, applications and processes.

around 1731, when Johann Gottfried Röchling first moved to Saarbrücken in southeastern Germany near the French border. The move to the Saarland was one that would have immense political and economic repercussions for the Röchling family that extended well into the latter half of the 20th century. In Saarbrücken, Röchling managed an ironworks. His grandson Friedrich worked for the same company before launching his own coal trading business in 1822—the company Röchling considers to be the original forebear of the present-day conglomerate.

After Friedrich Röchling died childless in 1836, the coal firm passed into the joint ownership of his four nephews. Under their management, the company expanded, opening its first branch office in the German city of Ludwigshafen in 1850, and later additional branch offices elsewhere in the country as well as in England, France, and Switzerland. The most influential nephew proved to be Carl Röchling, who eventually took over the sole leadership of the company.

A critical event took place in 1857 when Carl Röchling married Alwine Vopelius, the daughter of a wealthy industrialist. Not only did this mark the start of Carl's own family, but Alwine also brought with her shares in a coal mine near the Saar city of Völklingen. Before long Röchling had taken over management of the mine. He increased his holdings until by the beginning of the 20th century he was the majority shareholder. As with his trading firm, Röchling expanded his mining business rapidly. He bought smaller mines scattered throughout Germany, France, and Luxembourg. By 1910, the firm employed more than 920 miners who produced approximately 146,000 tons of coal annually. The firm also began producing coke, an essential component for making iron. Alongside its sales and distribution business, production of coal, coke, and soon afterward chemicals, became Röchling's second main line of business. The company was also looking to expand greatly its production side.

EXPANSION INTO IRON PRODUCTION

In 1862 Röchling made the jump into iron and steel production. This took place when Röchling, in a partnership with another company, acquired an ironworks in Mousson in the French province of Lorraine. As with his other ventures, the Mousson works immediately grew under Carl Röchling's management. Within little more than a decade, according to company historians, Röchling had established an iron monopoly in France. He also expanded the Mousson works to four blast furnaces and built it into one of Europe's largest iron foundries. However, political tensions between Germany and France that began with the German victory in the Franco-Prussian War of 1870–71 would impinge over and over on the Röchling company for the next 80 years. They led first of all to the sale of the Mousson works in the 1890s.

By that time, however, Röchling, whose firm had been renamed Gebr. Röchling OHG, had added other steel factories to its portfolio. The major addition came in 1881 when the firm paid 270,000 marks for the Völklinger Hütte, an iron works in the city of Völklingen. The mill prospered, thanks in large part to the protectionist laws the German government had enacted for iron and steel. Growth was remarkably fast. In a single year, for instance, from 1882 to 1883, the workforce at Völklingen nearly tripled, increasing from 450 to 1,150. Between 1883 and 1907 seven new blast furnaces were constructed. During the same period, Röchling was acquiring iron mines in Lorraine to supply raw materials. By 1910, Röchling was mining coal and iron, producing coke, iron, and steel, and it was selling coal, iron, and steel. It had a foothold in every aspect of the steel-making industry—raw materials, production, and distribution.

KEY DATES

1822: Friedrich Röchling founds a coal trading company in Saarbrücken.
1857: Carl Röchling marries and acquires shares in a coal mine near Völklingen.
1862: Röchling acquires its first iron mill.
1881: Völklingen iron mill is acquired.
1918: Construction of first Röchling-Rodenhauser furnace is completed.
1919: Röchling loses all holdings in France.
1920: Buderus-Röchling AG is founded in partnership with Buderus company.
1935: French administration of Saarland ends.
1938: Hermann Röchling named Reich Minister of War Industries.
1939: Company is reorganized into two organizations, Röchling'schen Eisen- und Stahlwerke GmbH and Gebr. Röchling GmbH.
1946: Hermann Röchling is sentenced to ten years imprisonment for war crimes; Röchling companies in the Saarland put under French management.
1951: Headquarters are relocated to Mannheim.
1956: Controlling share of Rheinmetall-Borsig AG acquired.
1957: Saarland reunited with the Federal Republic of Germany and Saar holdings are returned to Röchling.
1960: Industrieverwaltung Röchling GmbH is founded.
1970: Völklinger Hütte is merged into Stahlwerke Röchling-Burbach GmbH.
1978: Shares in Stahlwerke Röchling-Burbach GmbH are sold.
1982: Acquires plastics manufacturer Sustaplast.
1984: Acquires Impact Plastics in the United States and Seeber SPA Leifers in Italy.
2004: Decision is made to focus exclusively on high-quality industrial plastics; Rheinmetall AG is sold.
2005: Telecommunications firm DeTeWe is sold.
2007: Plastics companies in Denmark and the United States are acquired.

His empire established, Carl Röchling, the firm's guiding light for nearly sixty years, passed away in 1910. With his death the management of the company passed into the hands of his son Hermann Röchling. Hermann would have just as decisive an impact on the Röchling company as his father, overseeing further expansion, survival of two world wars and the Great Depression. Hermann Röchling had significant experience in the family business. He had overseen the construction of a major ironworks in Diedenhofen, which was named Carlshütte in honor of this father. In addition, as the manager of the company's showcase ironworks at Völklingen, he had introduced new technologies that made the company a leader in the efficient production of high-quality steels. He had even helped invent important new methods for steel production, including the Röchling-Rodenhauser furnace and processes for desulfurization and cutting the usage of manganese.

WORLD WAR I AND ITS EFFECTS ON RÖCHLING

Röchling switched over to war production when World War I started in 1914. The war was good for iron producers—it opened a nearly insatiable market for armaments and a year after its start Röchling put a brand-new ironworks into operation. The war provided other unique opportunities for expansion that were not available in peacetime. As German armies penetrated into French territory, Röchling's people followed, taking over French iron and steelworks, dismantling them, and using the scrap in production.

After the armistice in November 1918, German rapaciousness in France came home to roost. One of the provisions of the peace treaty dictated that all Röchling holdings in France, especially its mines and iron and steel mills, including Carlshütte, would be taken over by the French. In addition, the French army occupied the Saarland and the area was placed under the administration of the League of Nations. In a final blow, the French charged brothers Hermann and Robert Röchling with war crimes. Robert was captured, but Hermann was able to escape to Heidelberg. He was tried in absentia and sentenced to ten years imprisonment, a fine of 10 million Francs, and a 15-year banishment from the Saarland. He was able to return to the Saarland only two years later, however, without punishment. Once back, Röchling became politically active in the movement to win the Saarland's return to Germany and joined Adolf Hitler's nascent National Socialist Party.

The first half of the 1920s was a period of financial crisis for Röchling. It was cut off from the French market—one of its most important before the war—as well as from its former French mines, which had been a major source of raw materials. The French tried to take over administration of the big iron mill in Völklingen, but the firm was able to block the attempts. The final straw was the high reparations Röchling was required to pay. In autumn 1924, pushed to the end of its resources, the Röchling management announced it was closing the Völklinger Hütte. The announcement forced the French hand—if the mill closed, the French would lose one of their biggest customers for coal. They gave in and lifted financial and other restrictions on Röchling. Able to operate once again on an equal footing with French mills, Röchling reopened the Völklinger Hütte two months later.

To keep the risk of such French interference in their business to a minimum, Röchling started looking for business opportunities outside the Saarland. In 1920, in partnership with Buderus'schen Eisenwerke AG, it founded Buderus-Röchling AG, a company that produced high-quality stainless steel. The two firms also cofounded Röchling-Buderus GmbH Ludwigsfelde, a company that would sell its steel. On its own, Röchling also acquired new iron and coal mines and iron mills in the German states of Saxony and Thuringia.

RÖCHLING DURING THE NAZI REGIME

Hitler came to power in 1933. Between 1935 and 1939, as Germany was shifting to a war economy, Röchling invested RM 48 million in its Völklinger ironworks and its subsidiaries, and after the start of the war, the company planned additional expansion. In 1939 the company was reorganized into two main groups: Röchling'schen Eisen- und Stahlwerke for its iron and steel mills and Gebrüder Röchling for its coal and steel trading and other operations unrelated to core activities, such as the Gebrüder Röchling Bank. When war broke out, the company moved a number of its administrative workers out of the Saarland. Most civilians were evacuated from the mills in Völklingen, which early in the war was located in the war zone. However, so rapid were the German victories in France that within three months the mills had resumed normal operations. Production there was changed over to war materiel, like artillery shells, gun barrels, and antiaircraft guns. Because most of Röchling's male workforce had been drafted into the military, the plants were manned primarily by prisoners of war and slave laborers.

As a so-called *alter Kämpfer* (old warrior)—a party member who had joined the Nazis before Hitler's failed *putsch* attempt in 1923, Hermann Röchling enjoyed special status within the party. He continued to enjoy that status within the Nazi government after Hitler's takeover of power. In 1938, one year before Germany began World War II, Röchling was named the Reich Minister of War Industries as well as a member of the War Industries Council of the Reich Chamber of Commerce. As the war progressed, Röchling's government responsibilities and influence grew. On his initiative, the Reich Union of Iron Producers was founded to coordinate war production by requiring every company in the iron and steel industry to join. In the middle of the war he was named Reich Commissioner for Iron and Steel in the Occupied Territories, where Röchling opened new offices and hoped to take over local businesses after the war.

POSTWAR RECOVERY

Following the German defeat, members of the Röchling upper management, including Hermann Röchling, his son-in-law Baron Hans-Lothar von Gemmingen-Hornberg, and his nephew Dr. Ernst Röchling, were convicted of war crimes by a French military court. Hermann Röchling thus had the dubious distinction of being a convicted war criminal in both world wars. He was sentenced to ten years imprisonment, but thanks to the intervention of German Chancellor Konrad Adenauer, only served six years.

The Saarland became the French zone of occupation and was put under French customs administration, making free trade with the rest of Germany impossible. Röchling once again lost its holdings in France. All German managers of the Röchling'schen Eisen- und Stahlwerke GmbH were released and barred from further employment in the industry. The Röchling operations in the Saarland were placed under French management. The Röchling family could not continue to exist economically in the Saarland under such circumstances. They had moved their administrative offices to other parts of the country during the war, and in 1951 a decision was made to move Röchling headquarters to Mannheim in the U.S. occupation zone. The German economy had finally begun to recover after the currency reform of 1948.

However, times remained difficult for Röchling. Its companies in both Mannheim and Ludwigshafen reported losses until the mid-1950s. In 1954 the coal and heating oil trading company in Ludwigshafen turned a 13 percent profit. From that point on business took off. Within three years, Röchling's annual revenues doubled. An important factor in the recovery occurred in 1956 with the acquisition from the German government of a controlling share in Rheinmetall-Borsig AG, a major German armaments producer. The acquisition took place at a time when the German army had been allowed to reform and needed to be armed. The Völklinger Hütte in the Saarland remained a major question mark, however. Röchling hoped to get the facility back, but future developments in the Saarland were unclear.

The company began casting about for a buyer. That brought its own problems since French authorities could veto any sale. Finally, in 1955, Saarland residents voted for political and economic reunification with the German Federal Republic. One year later, the French left. In 1957 the Saarland became Germany's tenth federal state. With the French exit, Röchling recovered its old holdings, in particular the mill in Völklingen with its workforce of 13,000. In exchange for the return, the company agreed to pay the French DM 36 million with the assistance of a loan from the German government.

In 1956 a law went into effect in Germany that expanded the rights of employees in decision making in the coal and steel industries. To sidestep this limitation on management autonomy, Röchling completely reorganized its operations. It left the Steel Association (Hüttenverband) and in 1960 formed Industrieverwaltung Röchling GmbH (IVR)—Röchling Industrial Administration, Ltd. IVR was an umbrella organization that included major iron and steel operations such as Röchling'schen Eisen- und Stahlwerke, Röchling-Buderus, and the renamed Rheinmetall Berlin. Other companies, such as the Gebrüder Röchling Bank, Kaltwalzwerk Oberkochen, and Lignostone Altenberg were placed within the Gebr. Röchling iron trading company in Ludwigshafen.

GOODBYE TO STEEL

In the early 1960s the iron mills in Völklingen were undergoing hard times that resulted in frequent layoffs and short-time work. In an effort to recover financial health, the company launched a DM 800 million investment plan to solidify the mill's position in the highly competitive European Coal and Steel Community. Despite the best efforts of the company management, which included the sale of various holdings, such as parts of Röchling-Buderus, the situation continued to deteriorate throughout the rest of the decade. The formation of Stahlwerke Röchling-Burbach GmbH by merging the Völklinger Hütte with nearby iron mills of the firm Burbach in 1970 provided some short-term relief.

Long-term trends in the steel industry, however, were working against Röchling. Countries like Japan and India could produce and sell steel much more inexpensively than German companies. Moreover, demand for steel was declining in Germany and the rest of the world. Röchling suffered significant losses in the second half of the 1970s. By the end of the decade, the writing on the wall was clear—the firm could no longer survive in steel. Röchling began its exit from the industry in which it had been active for over 100 years. In 1978 the firm sold its shares of Röchling-Burbach and the Völklingen iron mill.

Steel was being steadily replaced as a manufacturing component by different varieties of plastics, and when the firm management decided on a course of "diversification and decentralization" in the early 1980s, one of the prime industries upon which they set their sights was plastics producers. Fortunately, the German economy was in a period of upswing in the 1980s. As a result the firm was able to acquire a number of smaller plastics companies. In 1982, for instance, it purchased plastics maker Sustaplast, which provided an entrée into the lucrative field of industrial plastics. It strengthened its position in this industry in 1984 with the acquisition of a 50 percent share in an Italian plastics manufacturer Seeber SPA Leifers, followed by Impact Plastics in Gastonia, North Carolina, which enabled it to introduce its Polystone products in the North American market.

During the rest of the decade, it purchased additional firms in the fields of plastics, electronics, and telecommunications throughout Europe, including a 99 percent share in the Bergmann-Elektriciaets Werke AG, in Berlin, Germany, a conglomerate comprised of three major electronics and telecommunications companies. At the same time, Röchling maintained its strong presence in the defense industry with Rheinmetall GmbH. To facilitate its foreign expansion along with its penetration into the quickly unifying European economic market of the 1980s, Röchling reorganized its two main divisions, Gebr. Röchling and Röchling Industrie Verwaltung GmbH, to be able to operate as independently of one another as possible. At the beginning of the 1990s, when trade barriers were disappearing in the European Union, Röchling restructured once again, forming a holding company based in Mannheim that would enable the firm and its network of foreign subsidiaries to operate efficiently in the developing global economy.

The German economy flourished briefly with the opening of East Germany after the fall of the Berlin Wall, but it was soon followed by the worst economic downturn since the end of World War II. The recession hit Röchling hard, and the firm was forced to introduce various cost-cutting measures, including layoffs in Germany and the transfer of production to foreign sites. Nonetheless, Röchling continued to make new acquisitions in the 1990s. It purchased a majority holding in the Nuremberg electronics company ABB Metrawatt. Around the same time the firm added Casimir Kast Formteile, a plastics manufacturer, to its portfolio. By the end of the decade the financial situation had been stabilized.

By 2004 the company had some 30,000 employees, with 309 subsidiaries and affiliates in Europe, the Americas, and Asia, and about EUR 6 billion in annual revenues. That year the 200-member Röchling family made an important strategic decision: to focus the firm's activities exclusively on the production of plastics. The result over the next year or two was the systematic sell-off of holdings in other areas. In late 2004, for example, the company surprised industry watchers when it sold all of its shares in the German defense giant Rheinmetall. About six months later, it sold postage meter maker Francotyp Postalia, a company it had owned since 1989, to a British venture capital company. Finally, in July of the same year, DeTeWe, whose profits had been dropping, was sold to Aastra, a Canadian telecom company.

As a result of the sales, Röchling's annual revenues dropped about 17.4 percent in 2006. At the same time the Röchling firm began a search for new acquisitions in the plastics field. In particular Röchling hoped to strengthen its position in technical plastics, materials that were highly durable and heat, chemical, and corrosion resistant, for use in space technology, medicine, household appliances, and similar industries.

The hunt did not produce immediate results. During the first 18 months, Röchling found itself in bidding wars for choice firms, wars it pulled out of rather than pay overvalued prices. In 2007 it acquired several plastics companies with total annual revenues of approximately EUR 70 million and workforces 450 strong. These included two North American companies, Glastic Corporation of Cleveland, Ohio, and Symplastics Limited of Ontario, Canada, as well as the Danish company Meta-Plast A/S. In October 2007 a new Röchling production facility for plastics for the automobile industry went into operation in the Czech town of Koprivnice.

Gerald E. Brennan

PRINCIPAL SUBSIDIARIES

Röchling Engineering Plastics KG; Röchling Hydroma GmbH; Röchling Technische Kunststoffe KG; Röchling Sustaplast KG; Röchling Technische Teile KG; Röchling Automotive AG & Co. KG; Röchling Kaltwalzwerk KG; BEA Holding AG; BEA Elektrotechnik und Automation GmbH; BEA Elektrotechnik und Automation Technische Dienste Lausitz GmbH; Röchling Engineering S.à.r.l. (France); Röchling Engineered Plastics (United States); Röchling Permali Composites S.A.S. (France); Röchling Engineering Plastiques S.A.S. (France); Röchling Machined Plastics (United States); Röchling Engineering Plastics Pte. Ltd. (Singapore); Leripa Kunststoff GmbH & Co. KG (Austria); Leripa Papertech (Kunshan) Co. Ltd. (China); Röchling Rimito Plast Oy (Finland); Leripa Papertech LLC (United States); Röchling Engineering Plastics Italia s.r.l. (Italy); Röchling Formaterm AB (Sweden); Röchling Engineering Plastics (UK), Ltd.; Röchling Technické Plasty, s.r.o. (Czech Republic); Röchling Engineering Plastics (India) Pvt. Ltd.; Röchling Plásticos Técnicos S.A. Unipersonal (Spain).

PRINCIPAL COMPETITORS

AGC Chemicals Europe, Ltd.; Aragonesas Industrias y Energia; BASF SE; Borealis AG; Cytec Industries, Inc.; Dow Chemical Company; Koninklijke DSM N.V.; E.I. du Pont de Nemours & Co.; Huntsman International, LLC; Tessenderlo Group; Rhodia.

FURTHER READING

Braude, Jonathan, "Rochling Cedes Some Control of Rheinmetall," *Daily Deal,* December 10, 2001.

Grewenig, Meinrad Maria, ed., *Die Völklinger Hütte,* Ostfildern-Ruit, Germany: Völklingen, 2001.

Marsh, Peter, "A Conglomerate Forced to Sharpen Up Its Act," *Financial Times,* October 26, 2001, p. 14.

Nutzinger, Richard, et al., *50 Jahre Röchling Völklingen,* Saarbrücken-Völklingen, Germany: Hofer, 1931.

———, *Das Haus Röchling in Ludwigshafen am Rhein, 1849–1929,* Ludwigshafen am Rhein, Germany, 1929.

Seabury, Jane, "New Steel-Pricing Complaints Made Against Europeans," *Washington Post,* August 11, 1982, p. D7.

Seibold, Gerhard, *Röchling Kontinuität im Wandel,* Stuttgart, Germany, 2001.

Von Gemmingen-Hornberg, Hans-Lothar, *Christian Röchling 1772–1855, Ahnen und Enkel,* Mannheim, Germany, 1995.

RUDOLPH
TECHNOLOGIES

Rudolph Technologies Inc.

One Rudolph Road
Flanders, New Jersey 07836
U.S.A.
Telephone: (973) 691-1300
Fax: (973) 691-4863
Web site: http://www.rudolphtech.com

Public Company
Incorporated: 1996
Employees: 620
Sales: $201.2 million (2006)
Stock Exchanges: NASDAQ
Ticker Symbol: RTEC
NAIC: 334513 Instruments and Related Products Manufacturing for Measuring, Displaying, and Controlling Industrial Process Variables

■ ■ ■

Headquartered in Flanders, New Jersey, Rudolph Technologies Inc. (RTI) designs and manufactures process control metrology (measurement) equipment that semiconductor manufacturers use to ensure that silicon chips are of the right thickness. In addition, the company makes inspection equipment that is used during the final stages of manufacturing to ensure that computer chips are defect-free.

The company sells inspection equipment to front-end "fabs," which are the facilities where chips are actually "built." "Front-end" also is referred to as wafer processing. The company also sells inspection and other tools to "back-end" fabs. Also referred to as final manufacturing or packaging, back-end fabs are usually separate facilities from the front-end. They perform steps necessary to get the die (chip) ready to be used in the end product, such as a computer, cell phone, or automobile. There are a number of different steps performed at the back-end, including the final test step, which is the absolute "end of the back-end" where each ready-to-ship die is tested.

RUDOLPH RESEARCH 1940–95

Although RTI was established in June 1996, the company's origins can be traced back to 1940, when Otto Curt Rudolph formed O.C. Rudolph & Sons. Originally an importer of microscopes and scientific instruments, this RTI predecessor was later renamed Rudolph Research Corp. The company eventually began designing its own optical equipment for laboratories and universities, according to the April 25, 2002, issue of the *Star-Ledger.*

Otto Rudolph, who had three sons (H. Curt, Hellmuth, and Werner) and two daughters, died in Caldwell Township, New Jersey, in December 1956, at the age of 72. However, the company he established continued to evolve, making breakthroughs such as "the industry's first production-oriented ellipsometer for thin-transparent film measurements in 1977," according to RTI. (An ellipsometer is an optical measurement device that measures thickness via a polarized laser beam.)

In 1966 the company named Dr. Richard Spanier as its chairman and president. A former chemistry instructor at the Stevens Institute of Technology and Fairleigh Dickinson University, Spanier was married to

> **COMPANY PERSPECTIVES**
>
> Rudolph has a long history of technology leadership in manufacturing highly accurate quality instruments that use polarized light as a measuring medium.

the granddaughter of founder Otto Rudolph. During his tenure, he was the guiding force behind the development of the company's metrology products. Spanier authored a host of technical papers on ellipsometry and came to hold many related patents. His accomplishments culminated in a Lifetime Achievement Award from the Semiconductor Equipment and Materials International (SEMI) trade association in 2002, at which time he served as RTI's chairman emeritus.

FORMATION OF RUDOLPH TECHNOLOGIES: 1996–2001

Rudolph Technologies was formed in June 1996, when Richard Spanier decided to retire as Rudolph Research's chief executive. That year, Spanier forged a partnership agreement with Boston-based Riverside Partners and New York-based Liberty Partners who, along with other investors, poured $36.3 million in the company. In addition, executives from both investment firms joined the company's board, including Liberty's Stephen Fisher and Carl Ring, Jr.

At this time, the newly named Rudolph Technologies Inc. (RTI) was the third largest thin-film metrology firm in the world. According to a June 17, 1996, *Business Wire* release, the company's new name reflected its "expansion from ellipsometry into additional metrology technologies while at the same time demonstrating RTI's continued commitment to its large installed base of customers." Semiconductor industry veteran Paul F. McLaughlin was named as CEO at this time.

Three years later, in November 1999, RTI made its initial public offering (IPO) of common stock, offering 4.8 million shares at a price of $16 per share. The company revealed that 13.94 million shares would be outstanding following the IPO. At this time, Liberty held approximately 6.9 million shares (47%) of RTI's stock. The company's customer base had grown to include virtually all of the leading semiconductor firms, such as AMD, IBM, Fujitsu, Intel, Philips, Texas Instruments, Toshiba, and TSMC.

That year, revenues skyrocketed 90 percent over 1998, reaching a record $38.1 million. Despite an industry downturn, RTI maintained its research and development efforts. With a new facility that opened early in the year, the company continued to roll out new products, such as its MetaPULSE line of copper film measurement tools. In the fourth quarter of 1999, some 83 percent of RTI's revenues were tied to products that were not yet on the market in the first quarter of 1997, according to CEO Paul McLaughlin.

RTI ushered in the new millennium with McLaughlin assuming the additional role of chairman in January. Richard Spanier remained a director and was named chairman-emeritus. A number of important developments occurred that year. In April the company announced it had been included in the SEMIndex, a global index maintained by Semiconductor Equipment and Materials International. Midway through the year, the company also was added to the Russell 3000 Index, which ranked the performance of the leading 3,000 U.S. public companies.

There were other highlights during 2000. For the sixth straight year RTI was named as the customer satisfaction leader among thin-film metrology firms, based on a survey conducted by VLSI Research Inc. Finally, the company opened an 8,000-square-foot training center in Mount Arlington, New Jersey, near its Engineering Center.

In early 2001 RTI made a public offering of 3.5 million shares of its common stock, including 1 million company-owned shares. At this time Riverside Partners sold approximately 300,000 of its shares, valued at $12.5 million. Liberty Partners sold about 1.8 million shares, valued at almost $79 million. That year, RTI's net income totaled $11.7 million on revenues of $79.4 million.

WORLDWIDE GROWTH IN 2002

With tech industry heavyweights such as IBM and Intel among its client base, RTI's market value grew to approximately $560 million in 2002. This was wonderful news for the investors who had forked over a collective $36 million for Rudolph only six years before. As Spanier remarked in the April 25, 2002, issue of the *Star-Ledger,* "It worked out like gangbusters. The combination of Liberty Partners, Riverside Partners, (current Chairman) Paul McLaughlin and me has been a textbook, classic, wonderful case."

A major development unfolded in July 2002 when RTI agreed to acquire the Richardson, Texas-based defect control company ISOA. A spinoff from Texas Tech University's International Center for Informatics Research, ISOA had been licensing technology to the semiconductor industry for about 16 years, offering

KEY DATES

1940: Otto Curt Rudolph forms O.C. Rudolph & Sons, an importer of microscopes and scientific instruments that eventually becomes Rudolph Research Corp.
1966: Dr. Richard Spanier is named chairman and president of Rudolph Research.
1996: Spanier retires as chief executive of Rudolph Research and forms Rudolph Technologies Inc. (RTI) with investors from Riverside Partners and Liberty Partners.
1999: RTI makes its initial public offering of common stock, offering 4.8 million shares for $16 per share.
2002: Richardson, Texas-based defect control company ISOA is acquired for $24.2 million and becomes RTI's Yield Metrology Group.
2006: August Technology Corporation is acquired for $193 million in cash and stock.
2007: RTI acquires Issaquah, Washington-based Applied Precision LLC.

defect detection tools under brand names such as WaferView. The all-cash, $24.2 million deal was completed in September, with ISOA becoming RTI's Yield Metrology Group. While the business remained based in Richardson, ISOA's manufacturing operations were relocated from Japan, to Ledgewood, New Jersey.

Several months later, RTI expanded into China by establishing an office in Shanghai's Pudong industrial area. In an October 14, 2002, *PR Newswire* release, RTI Vice-President of Global Customer Support Robert DiCrosta said: "China continues to emerge as one of the world's fastest growing semiconductor markets. Rudolph has been doing business in China for well over a decade and the time was right for us to establish a strategic-presence in Shanghai to be in close proximity to our major Chinese customers." In order to ensure the new operation's success, the company hired industry veteran Wai-Man Li, who brought technical experience and local knowledge to the table.

LEGAL DISPUTES BEGIN IN 2003

In the wake of an industry downturn, RTI began 2003 by reducing its employee base by 10 percent worldwide. Later that year, the company became entangled in a legal dispute with then competitor August Technology Corp. An intellectual property dispute between RTI subsidiary ISOA Inc. and August subsidiary STI Inc. escalated when August sued both RTI and ISOA on September 23. This led RTI to file a counterclaim on September 30.

A number of positive developments also occurred in 2003, including a multimillion-dollar order for seven of the company's tools from a manufacturer in Taiwan. Spanning the MetaPULSE, WaferView, and S-ultra product lines, the order included delivery dates that ranged from the fourth quarter of 2003 through the second quarter of 2004.

After nearly one year, RTI and August ultimately settled their legal dispute. As part of the settlement, announced in August 2004, RTI received a $502,500 payment from former STI parent ASTI Holdings Ltd. The company capped off 2004 by celebrating the fifth anniversary of its listing on the NASDAQ. On Wednesday, November 24, RTI Chairman and CEO Paul McLaughlin presided over the Market Open in honor of the special milestone.

As RTI headed into the middle of the first decade of the 2000s, the company once again made headlines in connection with August Technology Corp. However, this time the news was in relation to RTI's hostile bid to acquire its chip-testing competitor. On January 27, 2005, RTI made a $190 million cash and stock bid that trumped a $150 million all-stock offer made on January 21 by Nanometrics Inc. of Milpitas, California.

Compared to a 13 percent drop when the Nanometrics offer was announced, August Technology's stock increased 18 percent following RTI's bid, which August initially rejected. Several factors then led August Technology to change its stance and consider RTI's proposal. The first was a confidentiality agreement that RTI agreed to sign. Then, on February 4, August Technology's shareholders filed a lawsuit to stop the Nanometrics deal on the grounds that it was preventing the acceptance of RTI's superior offer.

The entire situation became even more complicated when a third potential acquirer emerged. California-based KLA-Tencor Corp. offered $205 million in cash for August Technology on February 9. Ultimately, RTI was the winner when a merger agreement was reached in June for $193 million in cash and stock. The deal cleared antitrust hurdles in July. KLA-Tencor withdrew its offer for August Technology in January 2006, and the RTI–August Technology merger was completed on February 15.

POSTMERGER GROWTH IN 2006

Following the deal, RTI's workforce grew to 550 employees. The company remained based in Flanders,

New Jersey, with additional operations in Texas, Massachusetts, and Minnesota. Paul McLaughlin continued in his role as chairman and CEO, while August Technology CEO Jeff O'Dell became an RTI board member.

In an April 1, 2006, *Semiconductor International* interview with Alexander E. Braun, McLaughlin commented on the benefits of the merger, explaining: "There are three strategic benefits to be considered as a result of the merger. These are benefits to the customers, to the industry, and to the shareholders. We now offer a much broader scope and scale, we have more R&D resources and, what's very important, we have more staying power in a very dynamic—and cyclical—marketplace. This gives customers a solid choice and an alternative to the larger guys in the same space."

McLaughlin also offered some insight into how RTI would maintain the agility of a smaller enterprise despite its larger size, commenting: "We've organized into three separate business units. The metrology business unit, which will remain in New Jersey, will continue doing our transparent and metal metrology businesses. The inspection business unit, located in Bloomington, Minn., will be a combination of August Technology activities and Rudolph's in the macrodefect arena, both front and back end. Our Texas operation will report into Bloomington. And the third business unit is a software unit—data analysis and review—residing in Lowell, Mass., offering fabwide and product-specific software solutions. All three are small enough to be agile and still connect with one another, providing benefits from economy of scale."

LEADERSHIP AND ACQUISITIONS FOR THE FUTURE

Heading into the second half of the first decade of the 2000s, several significant leadership changes occurred at RTI. In November 2006, the company named Alex Oscilowski, a semiconductor industry veteran who was vice-president of strategy for the research and development consortium SEMATECH, as its chief operating officer. That year, revenues reached $201.2 million.

In January 2007 RTI made two significant appointments at Rudolph Technologies Japan KK, naming Yasuomi Uchida as chairman and Yoshiro Ogaya as president. Also in early 2007, Chairman and CEO Paul McLaughlin dubbed the aforementioned acquisition of August Technology a success. In a February 7, 2007, *Market Wire* release, McLaughlin said the integration of August exceeded expectations, commenting: "This merger was, in my estimation, a clear case of 1 + 1 equaling 3. We now have attained the scope and scale necessary to be increasingly important to our customers and to become a consolidator in our space."

RTI ended 2007 by acquiring Issaquah, Washington-based Applied Precision LLC. In a December 18, 2007, *Business Wire* release, McLaughlin indicated that the deal was beneficial on several fronts, explaining, "This acquisition combines two successful companies with complementary products and technologies, and will accelerate our efforts to be a more complete supplier of back-end equipment and software."

From its origins as an importer of microscopes and scientific instruments some 68 years before, by 2008 RTI had evolved into a leader within the semiconductor testing industry. As the company approached the twenty-first century's second decade, its prospects for continued success seemed strong.

Paul R. Greenland

PRINCIPAL SUBSIDIARIES

Yield Metrology Group.

PRINCIPAL COMPETITORS

Camtek Ltd.; KLA-Tencor Corporation; Nikon Corporation.

FURTHER READING

Braun, Alexander E., "Paul McLaughlin, Chairman & CEO, Rudolph Technologies Inc.," *Semiconductor International,* April 1, 2006.

"Rudolph Research Signs a Partnership Agreement to Support Expansion in the Semiconductor Metrology Arena; Name Change to Rudolph Technologies Reflects New Strategic Focus," *Business Wire,* June 17, 1996.

"Rudolph Technologies Acquires Semiconductor Business of Applied Precision LLC," *Business Wire,* December 18, 2007.

"Rudolph Technologies Announces Record 2006 Quarterly Earnings in Line with Guidance," *Market Wire,* February 7, 2007.

"Rudolph Technologies' Dr. Richard Spanier Receives Technology 'Lifetime Achievement' Award from SEMI," *PR Newswire,* October 4, 2002.

"Rudolph Technologies Expands into China; Hires Seasoned Semiconductor Veteran as General Manager," *PR Newswire,* October 14, 2002.

Saitz, Greg, "A $36 Million Gamble that 'Worked Like Gangbusters,'" *Star-Ledger,* April 25, 2002.

Scherer Brothers Lumber Company

9401 73rd Avenue North, Suite 400
Brooklyn Park, Minnesota 55428-1022
U.S.A.
Telephone: (612) 379-9633
Fax: (612) 627-0879
Web site: http://www.schererbros.com

Private Company
Incorporated: 1930
Employees: 45
Sales: $175 million (2007 est.)
NAIC: 444190 Other Building Material Dealers

■ ■ ■

Scherer Brothers Lumber Company is a privately held building materials supplier and manufacturer, serving both contractors and homeowners in Minnesota and western Wisconsin. Based in the Minneapolis–St. Paul area, the company operates five full-service lumberyards in Albertville, Arden Hills, Hopkins, Minneapolis, and Shakopee, Minnesota. In addition to lumber, the yards offer cabinetry, closet and storage systems, decking, doors, flooring, hardware, roofing, siding, trusses, wall panels, and windows.

Building advice is provided through Scherer Brothers Sales Centers located in the yards, four of which also include a cabinet and closet showroom where a number of major cabinet lines are represented. Scherer also offers such services as construction labor, custom millwork, and the installation of siding and replacement doors and windows. Subsidiary Allegiance Millwork Solutions manufactures a variety of finished building materials, including columns, molding, louvers, mantels, posts, stair parts, trim, shutters, and timbers.

Another unit, Alpine Capital LLC provides funding to builders and developers. The RemodSquad unit offers remodeling advice to both professionals and homeowners. Scherer Brothers is led by the third generation of the Scherer family, who along with the second generation own 85 percent of the business. Employees own the remaining 15 percent.

ORIGINS

The original Scherer brothers were Munn and Clarence Scherer, originally farmers who made their living baling hay. Minnesota did not offer the ideal climate for the business and by 1929 the young men turned to the Mississippi River as a secondary source of income. A half-century earlier the forests of northern Minnesota, until they gave out, had supplied a massive amount of lumber, which was floated down the Mississippi River in "log drives" to the sawmills operating along the banks. Because of the force generated by the large volume of logs, jams were created and many logs were driven below the silt and trapped.

About one in ten logs became what were known as "deadheads." Although not forgotten, these submerged logs were neglected. By the early 1900s foresting ceased in the area and most of the mills closed down, but in the 1920s raising deadheads from the water became an attractive source of revenue. The men who plied this dangerous trade, often former lumberjacks who were familiar with the site of the old logjams, scouted for

COMPANY PERSPECTIVES

At Scherer Brothers our vision—what drives us—is the single desire to be the outstanding materials, services and solutions provider for the residential construction industry. So, what is outstanding? That is a good question, but it is not a question for us as much as it is a question for our customers. What are outstanding services, quality, and communication to them? Certainly we must have our own standards for getting things done with excellence, but it is the customer who will define "outstanding" for us.

deadheads with long iron poles. Then they maneuvered a hook and chain beneath a log and using a winch hauled it into a boat.

Fishing for deadheads was dangerous work, especially for a nonswimmer like Munn Scherer. Nevertheless, he decide to try his luck at the trade and went to work for his brother-in-law, Joe Leuer, who hired out the two of them and his tractor to a deadheader working the Mississippi just north of Minneapolis.

While Leuer soon tired of the work and returned home, Scherer liked the prospects of the lumber business. In 1930 he recruited his brother Clarence as a partner, borrowed $240, and bought a half-interest in a lumber mill to process the deadheads they brought in. At the same time, the brothers hedged their bets by continuing to work their farms, rising early in the morning to complete the necessary farm chores and then spending the rest of the day on the water and at the mill.

MILL MOVED ACROSS THE MISSISSIPPI: 1934

The Scherer brothers did well enough with their new venture that after just one month they acquired the mill, using deadhead lumber to buy out their partner. Nonetheless, the early years, which coincided with the depth of the Great Depression, were far from easy. They were not always paid for their orders, and the brothers barely remained one step ahead of their own creditors. A large order related to the construction of a new First National Bank Building in St. Paul was a major boon, providing security for their business. By 1934 the company was doing well enough that they moved the mill to the east bank of the Mississippi, the site of the company's current Minneapolis yard. Revenues in 1934 totaled $80,000. In a few years that amount would grow to $250,000.

The treasure trove of Mississippi deadheads petered out by the early 1940s. All told, the stretch of the river worked by the Scherer brothers gave up 22 million board feet of lumber, 15 million of which they fished to the surface. Given that as many as nine deadhead operations were working the Mississippi at any one time, their production was remarkable. Moreover, they were the only ones who were still in the lumber business after the bounty gave out.

WORLD WAR II ENDS PARTNERSHIP

In late 1941 the United States entered World War II, and Munn Scherer enlisted in the U.S. Army, temporarily bringing an end to the partnership with his brother, who bought him out for $10,000 in cash and a $40,000 promissory note. Although shipped off to Europe, Munn spent the war running a sawmill in Brussels. Clarence, in the meantime, struggled to keep the stateside family sawmill in business. Not only was there a shortage in workers because of the draft and enlistments, the military commandeered most of the lumber supplies. To circumvent tight rationing, Clarence bought lots of odd-size lumber the military did not want, 50 carloads in all, and converted it into products needed for the war effort.

After his discharge Munn Scherer returned home to find the mill thriving but still in need of his services. Thus, he and his brother formed a new partnership, with Munn keeping the $10,000 he received earlier and a one-third interest in the mill, while the promissory note was canceled. During the postwar years the economy, revived by war spending, continued to roar, with the exception of a mild recession in 1946 as the country returned to a peacetime footing. Returning servicemen married, began raising families, and used the GI Bill to buy houses in the suburbs that were springing up across the country.

Scherer Brothers was able to take advantage of this postwar building boom. While the larger lumber yards catered to the major contractor developers, Scherer Brothers focused on the small professional builder, and gained a reputation for customer service and a willingness to provide credit to reliable customers. As a result, Scherer Brothers developed a deep reservoir of good will with its customers, whose sense of loyalty to the yard would pay dividends for many years to come.

By the early 1950s Scherer Brothers was posting annual sales of close to $2 million. The company had

KEY DATES

1930: Company is formed by brothers Munn and Clarence Scherer.
1934: Sawmill moves to the east bank of the Mississippi River.
1963: Hall's Island is acquired.
1980: Second-generation family member, Roger Scherer, is named chairman.
1985: Arden Hills lumber yard is acquired.
1995: Third-generation family member, Peter Scherer, is named chief executive.
2001: Justus Lumber Company is acquired.
2007: Rachael Scherer replaces father as chair.

begun providing value-added products. At the behest of the builders they served, the company began manufacturing inexpensive wooden windows under the PineCraft name in the late 1940s. The line would later add casements and patio doors as well. The brothers did not, however, fare as well when they attempted to build prefabricated homes or components. Customers preferred the work of professional builders, so Scherer Brothers refocused its attention on serving their needs with in-shop built windows, doors, and other millwork.

CREATIVE EXPANSION

Scherer Brothers expanded its operation in an unusual fashion in 1963, paying $95,000 to acquire Hall's Island, a nearby three-acre parcel of land owned by the city of Minnetonka. The company then received approval from the U.S. Army Corps of Engineers to bridge the gap between the two properties, an area that is used for timber and I-beam storage. The 1960s and early 1970s also brought a second generation of the Scherer family into the lumber business: Gary, Greg, Mike, and Roger Scherer. Not only did they gain stakes in the business, other key employees were given stock in 1976, eventually leading to the current 15 percent interest held by nonfamily members.

Being a member of Scherer family did not guarantee a job in the organization, however. In time, rules were developed to cover the addition of family members: Only after they worked for someone else for three or four years would they be considered for employment, and would be hired only if they had the proper commitment and had some talent to offer the company. A changing of the guard took place in 1980 when Roger Scherer was named chairman as well as chief executive.

By the early 1970s Scherer Brothers' revenues reached $8 million. A new way to grow sales emerged during this period when a surge in building activity resulted in extended waiting times for trusses, as long as ten weeks. Sensing an opportunity, Scherer Brothers launched the Truss Manufacturing Company in Albertville, Minnesota. Since delivery time of trusses was cut to less than a month, the new venture found a ready demand for its products. The PineCraft line of millwork products also continued to grow, leading in 1981 to an expansion of the yard by 48,000 square feet. By this stage annual sales totaled about $30 million.

DEVELOPMENTS IN THE EIGHTIES

An enterprise that did not fare as well as the company had hoped was called Scherer Brothers Westco, an attempt to sell window products in Seattle, Washington. Established in 1983, it was sold to its manager three years later. Scherer Brothers grew its Minnesota operation by focusing on its home territory. In 1983 the truss-making facility was expanded, and two years later the Arden Hills yard was acquired from Stewart Lumber Co., providing Scherer Brothers with its second yard and allowing it to extend its reach to the north and east.

That year also saw a fire at one of Scherer Brothers' large storage facilities, the blaze had been ignited by a lightning strike. Fortunately inventory had just been taken, greatly expediting a $1.2 million insurance settlement and limiting the impact on the company. Another natural disaster would visit Scherer Brothers later in the decade when heavy snows and high winds caused the collapse of a storage facility.

Scherer built upon its practice of extending credit to builders in 1988 when it established Scherer Brothers Financial Services, later renamed Alpine Capital, to provide construction financing. As Scherer Brothers entered the 1990s other new business units followed. In 1990 the company turned its attention to the manufacture and distribution of cabinets, forming Scherer Brothers Cabinet Division. With window and door sales continuing to grow and inroads made with more expensive homes, PineCraft was rebranded Scherer FarNorth. The following year housing marketer President Homes was acquired, but it did not fit in well with the operation and was sold seven years later.

A more compatible venture, Contract Property Developers Company, was established in 1992 to help contractors find suitable lots on which to build, a task that had grown more difficult because of a strong housing market. By providing customers with locations on which to build, Scherer Brothers naturally drove lumber sales. The company then entered the value-added installed products field in 1994 by acquiring a small shelving installation company, which became Scherer Brothers Installation Services and expanded to include the installation of insulation, siding, soffits, and wood flooring. To better serve the southern portion of the Twin Cities, the company opened a full-service lumber yard in Shakopee, Minnesota.

PETER SCHERER, 31, NAMED CEO

In 1995 the third generation of the Scherer family ascended to the top ranks of the organization when Roger Scherer's son, Peter, was named CEO at the age of 31. After earning a degree in finance from the University of Notre Dame, the younger Scherer spent his required period of outside employment working as a real estate lender at a St. Paul bank. After joining the family business he worked his way up through the ranks, ultimately serving as general manager before becoming chief executive. His father retained the chairmanship. Other third-generation members also joined the business in the 1990s, including: Kristopher Scherer, who became chief financial officer, and Mark Scherer, who became chief operating officer.

Peter Scherer took day-to-day control over a business generating $120 million in annual revenues. To keep pace with the growth of Minneapolis and St. Paul, Scherer Brothers continued to expand its own operations in the second half of the 1990s. In 1998 a small truss manufacturer and component designer, Component Systems, Inc., was acquired, and another yard was opened in Albertville to better serve the western side of Minneapolis. Also, near the end of the decade Scherer Brothers created a specialized remodeling service that operated under the RemodSquad banner.

At the tail end of the 1990s and in the early 2000s, Scherer Cabinet Division added custom shelving and flooring to its product lines. In 2001 a new line was added, the storage solutions of Harmony Melamine Creations. The new century also saw Scherer Brothers become involved in wall panel manufacturing. A Newport, Minnesota, lumberyard was acquired in February 2002 and converted into a wall panelization plant. In addition, the truss operations at Albertville and Newport began building wall panels, and the PerfectFIT brand of wall panels was launched and pitched to builders.

Further expansion followed in the 2000s. A 133,000-square-foot plant was opened in Champlin, Minnesota, in 2001, to increase production of FarNorth windows and doors. That same year Scherer Brothers added its fifth lumberyard, acquiring Justus Lumber Company, a 100-year-old Hopkins, Minnesota, concern. Because of its strong brand name the yard continued to operate under the Justus name until 2006 when it was converted to the Scherer Brothers banner.

Another major development in 2001 was the consolidation of all millwork under a single brand, Allegiance Millwork Solutions. The SuperAttic Truss brand was introduced in 2003, and a year later the Scherer FarNorth brand was recast as FarNorth Window and Door, dropping the Scherer name in order to widen its appeal. To help market this brand and others, and enter the window replacement market, Scherer Window & Door Consultants was launched in 2005.

DIVERSIFICATION LENDS STABILITY

Despite poor conditions in the housing market that prevailed in 2007, Scherer Brothers, because of its diversity, was better able to withstand the downturn than most companies in the industry. The company used its varied products and capabilities to cross-sell to customers, adapting to their needs, such as focusing on remodeling when new home sales dropped off.

Sales were in the $175 million range in 2007 when the second generation of the Scherer family finally left the stage. In January 2007 Roger Scherer stepped down as chairman, turning over the post to his 46-year-old daughter, Rachael Scherer. She had worked for the family business during high school in the 1970s, serving in a variety of capacities from receptionist to load dock worker. After earning degrees in history and economics from St. Mary's College in Notre Dame, Indiana, she earned a master's degree in finance from the University of Chicago. She then went to work for the Dain Bosworth stock brokerage firm, providing healthcare research, and in 1999 became vice-president of investor relations and corporate strategy at Medtronic Inc., a medical technology company. She later became vice-president of emerging-technologies marketing at Scherer, a position she would continue to hold while serving as the chairperson of the family business.

Ed Dinger

PRINCIPAL SUBSIDIARIES

Allegiance Millwork Solutions; Alpine Capital LLC; Scherer Brothers Installation Services; Scherer Window & Doors Consultants.

PRINCIPAL COMPETITORS

Home Depot Inc.; Lampert Yards Inc.; Menard, Inc.

FURTHER READING

Blanchette, Aimee, "Rachael Scherer," *Star Tribune,* January 29, 2007, p. 5D.

Cullen, Cheryl Dangel, "At Scherer Bros., Business Is Relative," *LBM Journal,* July 2007, p. 64.

Gale, Elaine, "CEO of Scherer Brothers Meeting New Job Head-On," *Star Tribune,* July 10, 1995, p. 8D.

Schouw & Company A/S

Chr Filtenborgs Plads 1
Aarhus C, DK-8000
Denmark
Telephone: (45) 86 11 22 22
Fax: (45) 86 11 33 22
Web site: http://www.schouw.dk

Public Company
Incorporated: 1878
Employees: 3,352
Sales: DKK 7.37 billion ($1.36 billion) (2006)
Stock Exchanges: Copenhagen
Ticker Symbol: SCHO-A
NAIC: 551112 Offices of Other Holding Companies

■ ■ ■

Schouw & Company A/S has evolved from a packaging-focused company to become a major Danish industrial holding company. Following the disposal of its packaging operations to Elopak in 2006, Schouw has regrouped around several industrial businesses. Grene is a major manufacturer of spare parts for agricultural machinery and equipment, as well as agricultural accessories. Grene also includes subsidiary Hydra Grene, a manufacturer of hydraulics and other electrical and technical products.

In 2006, Grene contributed nearly DKK 1.4 billion to Schouw's total revenues of DKK 7.4 billion ($1.36 billion). Another wholly owned company is Martin, the world's top producer of computer-controlled intelligent lighting and effects systems for the entertainment, amusement, "experience" and related industries; the company has also branched out into architectural lighting and security systems. Martin's revenues topped DKK 1 billion in 2006. Martin systems have been used in many Broadway theaters, and have been featured in concert tours for such acts as the Rolling Stones, Pink Floyd, Radiohead, and Madonna.

Schouw's wholly owned subsidiary Fibertex is a major producer of nonwoven textiles, operating through two divisions: Personal Care, based primarily on spunbond technology, for diapers and the like; and Industrial and Technical, using needle-punch technology, and featured in automotive fabrics, among other applications. Fibertex's revenues topped DKK 1.3 billion in 2006. Schouw is also the majority shareholder of publicly listed BioMar, the world's number three producer of fish feed for the fish farming sector, with revenues of more than DKK 3.7 billion. Schouw also holds a 50 percent share of Xergi, a major producer of turnkey biogas-driven power plants, in a joint venture with Dalgas Group. Other investments include 49 percent of investment group Incuba, and a stake in wind-farm systems manufacturer Vestas Wind Systems. Schouw itself is listed on the Copenhagen Stock Exchange. The company is led by president Jens Bjerg Sørensen.

PAPER BAG MAKER IN 1878

Victor Schouw founded a business producing paper bags by hand in Copenhagen in 1878, and over the next several decades helped lead the industrialization of Denmark's packaging sector. By the turn of the 20th

COMPANY PERSPECTIVES

We create value for our shareholders through active long-term investments in leading industrial businesses focusing on profitable growth.

century, Schouw oversaw a collection of companies, and by then had expanded to include paper production as well. Nonetheless, the production of paper bags remained the group's primary operation.

Schouw retired in 1911, converting his business into a limited liability company. Schouw remained a company chairman for the next several years, turning over the managing director's position to Hans Hornsyld. That family remained at the head of the company for the next half of a century, with Hans Hornsyld succeeded by Svend Hornsyld in 1927.

The younger Hornsyld led the company in its most significant expansion, following the acquisition of Jyllands Papir-Vaerk A/S in 1930. That company, based in Aarhus, gradually became the focus of the Schouw company's operations. The Jyllands purchase allowed Schouw & Co. to extend its operations from paper bags into the production of wax papers, cartons, and other packaging products and materials. The Jyllands works were pioneers in Denmark, becoming one of the first to introduce the industrial production of cartons. The company also experimented with color offset printing, by the 1950s emerging as one of Denmark's leading packaging groups.

INTRODUCING PURE-PAK TO EUROPEAN CONSUMERS

The presence of U.S. troops in postwar Europe, especially in West Germany, provided a new opportunity for Schouw & Co. The U.S. military had helped introduce a new packaging concept in Europe—that of the milk carton, a sector led by the Pure-Pak brand at the time. The Jyllands work's industrial packaging strength helped the company become the first European licensee for the new packaging type in 1956.

At first, Jyllands's Pure-Pak producer was focused solely on supplying the U.S. troops stationed in Germany. The rise of another U.S. concept, the supermarket, in Denmark as well as in the rest of Europe soon helped lay the groundwork for a surge in demand for new packaging formats. This led Jyllands to launch production of Pure-Pak cartons for the domestic Danish dairy sector in 1967. The development of new long-life UHT (ultrahigh-temperature) milk products also stimulated demand for the easier-to-stock milk cartons. By the end of that decade, Schouw & Co. had built a new purpose built facility in Lystrup, near Aarhus, in order to meet the growing demand for milk cartons.

The success of Pure-Pak soon came to define the company. By 1973, Schouw & Co. had moved its headquarters to the Lystrup plant. Over the next decade, the company sold its other packaging businesses. Into the middle of the 1980s, Jyllands's operations came to be focused completely on the production of Pure-Pak-branded packaging. As a result, Schouw changed the name of its subsidiary to Schouw Packaging in 1986.

BUILDING AN INDUSTRIAL HOLDINGS PORTFOLIO

The acquisition by Norway's Elopak for the global licensing rights to the Pure-Pak brand led to the next phase in Schouw & Co.'s history. Schouw, which retained the Pure-Pak license for Denmark, agreed to sell a 50 percent stake in Schouw Packaging to Elopak in 1988, forming a partnership that was to remain in place for more than 15 years.

The sale provided Schouw, which had exhibited little growth over the previous decade, with something of a kick-start. The company began to reposition itself as an industrial holding company. While packaging was to remain a major part of Schouw's operations through the 1990s and into the next century, the company began to target a more diversified portfolio of businesses.

Schouw & Co.'s first extension beyond packaging came in 1988, when the company acquired A/S P. Grene, a family-owned company that operated through two distinct businesses: Chr. C. Grene, which produced spare parts and equipment for the agricultural sector; and Hydra Grene, a company focused on the production of hydraulics systems.

Schouw next took a minority stake in Schulstad Gruppun A/S, a producer of fresh breads and ready-to-bake breads, in 1989. Schouw continued to invest in Schulstad, building up a control of more than 37 percent of the company's stock by the end of the 1990s. Into the 2000s, Schouw gained majority control of the bread manufacturing group, buying another 24 percent of its shares in 2002.

In the meantime, Schouw had continued building its diversified portfolio. The group entered the renewable energy market in 1994, acquiring 25 percent of

KEY DATES

1878: Victor Schouw founds company producing paper bags by hand in Copenhagen.
1911: Schouw & Company is incorporated as a limited liability company.
1930: Schouw & Company acquires Jyllands Papir-Vaerk, which becomes main company focus.
1956: Jyllands acquires Danish license to Pure-Pak carton technology.
1967: Company introduces Pure-Pak milk cartons to Danish market.
1986: After divesting other packaging interests, the company regroups around its core Pure-Pak operation.
1988: Schouw & Company agrees to sell 50 percent of its packaging operations to Elopak, then launches new industrial holding strategy, acquiring Als P. Green.
1994: Company acquires wind turbine producer Micon, which becomes NEG Micon in 1997.
2005: Completes largest investment, acquiring nearly 69 percent of BioMar.
2006: Company sells its 50 percent stake in Elopak to Elopak, exiting the packaging sector.

wind turbine producer Micon A/S. Over the next three years, the company increased its holding to nearly 92.5 percent. The company leveraged that investment into a merger of Micon with publicly listed Nordtank Energy Group (NEG) in 1997, creating NEG Micon. The public listing enabled Schouw to reduce its stake in NEG Micron over the next two years; nonetheless, the company remained its largest shareholder, with nearly 24 percent. That position in turn represented nearly two-thirds of Schouw's total market value.

NEW SECTORS IN THE 21ST CENTURY

Schouw's transition from industrialist to industrial holding company continued into the 21st century. The company acquired majority control of Martin Gruppen A/S, based in Aarhus, in 1999. Martin had established itself as a major producer of computer-controlled "intelligent" lighting systems. These were used to provide lighting and special effects for a variety of applications, ranging from theaters to amusement parks, large-scale concerts and other entertainment productions. By 2000, Schouw had increased its shareholding to over 69 percent, and in 2001 gained full control of Martin.

The company's next investment once again targeted the renewable energy sector. In 2001, the company agreed to contribute DKK 46 million in exchange for a 50 percent stake in Dansk Biogas. That company had been developing biogas plants—which used primarily animal manure to generate gas and heat—since the late 1990s. The investment from Schouw enabled Dansk Biogas to launch its commercial operations, selling its systems under the Smedemester name. By the end of 2001, the company had installed more than 20 biogas plants, making it a leading player in the sector in Europe. Schouw subsequently acquired full control of Dansk Biogas, then merged it into Xergi A/S, a joint venture set up with the Dalgas Group in 2004.

In 2002, Schouw paid DKK 350 million to acquire Fibertex, a Czech Republic-based specialist producer of primarily polypropylene-based nonwoven textiles founded in 1968. Fibertex incorporated two nonwoven technologies: spunbond, for use in diapers and other absorbent products, as well as bedding and cushions; and needle punch, a two-step process based on extruded fibers, used to produce flooring, bedding, and automotive fabrics and the like. As part of Schouw, Fibertex launched a DKK 270 million investment in order to add production capacity in Malaysia, in 2002. The company also established production facilities in Aalborg, Denmark, in 2005.

EXITING THE PACKAGING MARKET

Schouw completed its largest ever investment in 2005, however, when it bought the nearly 69 percent stake held by Norsk Hydro in publicly listed BioMar Holdings A/S. The acquisition gave Schouw control over the world's third largest producer of fish feeds for the fish farming industry. Biomar, formerly part of Foderstof Kompagniet, had been in operation since 1962.

The addition of BioMar produced a significant shift in Schouw's revenue base, adding more than DKK 3.75 billion to nearly double the group's annual sales. This transformation also enabled the company to launch the next phase of its historical development.

The company had continued to develop its partnership with Elopak since the early 1990s. In 1992, for example, the two companies joined together to launch an Elopak subsidiary in Poland. In 2001, Schouw acquired a 50 percent stake in Elopak Sweden, then changed the name of its own packaging division to Elopak Denmark. Finally, in 2006, Schouw agreed to sell all of its packaging operations to Elopak for DKK 505 million.

The sale marked the end of nearly 130 years in the packaging industry. Yet Schouw & Company's strategy of reinventing itself as an industrial holding company had produced dramatic results over the previous two decades. From a small-scale manufacturer with sales of just DKK 370 million in 1988, the company had transformed itself into a major Danish holding company, boasting total revenues of nearly DKK 7.5 billion ($1.4 billion) in 2007.

M. L. Cohen

PRINCIPAL SUBSIDIARIES

BioMar Holding A/S; Fibertex A/S; Incuba A/S; Martin Professional A/S; P. Grene A/S; Xergi A/S.

PRINCIPAL COMPETITORS

DSV A/S; Skandinavisk Holding A/S; FLSmidth A/S; S.A.S. Scandinavian Airlines Danmark A/S; Dalhoff Larsen and Horneman A/S; LEGO Group A/S; Bestseller A/S; DaimlerChrysler Skandinavien Holding A.S; Monberg and Thorsen A/S; NCC Construction Danmark A/S; Auriga Industries A/S.

FURTHER READING

"Danish Industrial Group Schouw & Co. A/S Completes Sales of Packaging Business to Elopak Group," *Nordic Business Report,* October 31, 2006.

"DJ Schouw & Co. Launches Mandatory Offer for Biomar," *FWN Financial News,* December 20, 2005.

"Fibertex Assumes New Ownership," *Nonwovens Industry,* May 2002, p. 10.

"Packaging Manufacturer Elopak Has Taken Over All Share in Its Joint Venture with Schouw & Co. in Denmark, Sweden and Poland," *Dairy Industries International,* November 2006, p. 6.

"Schouw & Co. A/S Divests Packaging Business," *Nordic Business Report,* Sept 20, 2006.

"Schouw & Co. to Acquire Majority Stake in Nordic Bakery Business Schulstad A/S," *Nordic Business Report,* March 13, 2002.

"Schouw & Co. to Buy 50% of Elopak," *Boersen,* February 23, 2001.

Wood, Andy, "Martin Acquired by Schouw & Co.," *Pro Sound News Europe,* July 1999, p. 29.

Scope Products, Inc.

233 Wilshire Boulevard, Suite 310
Santa Monica, California 90407-2211
U.S.A.
Telephone: (310) 458-1574
Web site: http://www.scopeproducts.com

Private Company
Incorporated: 1938 as Southern California Petroleum Corporation
Employees: 400
Sales: $77 million (2004 est.)
NAIC: 562219 Other Nonhazardous Waste Treatment and Disposal

■ ■ ■

Scope Products, Inc., is a privately held recycler of bakery waste. The Santa Monica, California-based company offers waste removal services to more than 750 food manufacturers in the 48 contiguous states, offering a number of customized removal solutions, including self-container compactors and mobile packers for low- to mid-volume producers, stationary compactors, and elevated bulk loaders that deposit waste through the roof of the unit to prevent spillage. The waste materials are then transported to a dozen plants spread across the country for reprocessing. Nonedible materials are separated from such waste items as bread, candy, chips, cookies, crackers, dough, pasta, and snack foods. The resulting mixture is then ground and dried, and sold as a high-energy Dried Bakery Product to makers of feed for poultry, cattle, and pigs. In addition to Scope Products, the company does business as ReConserve, Inc.; ReCycle to Conserve, Inc.; and International Processing Corporation.

DEPRESSION-ERA ROOTS

Scope Products was incorporated in California in February 1938 as Southern California Petroleum Corporation. The oil and gas industry remained the company's focus until Scope's chairman, Meyer Luskin, took charge in the early 1960s. A graduate of the University of California, Los Angeles, and holder of a master of business administration degree from Stanford University, Luskin was an investment broker and counselor when he joined the board of Southern California Petroleum in 1958. In October 1961 he was named president and chairman and began using the company as an investment vehicle, taking Southern California Petroleum into ventures far afield from energy.

BEAUTY SCHOOLS ACQUIRED: 1963

In 1963 Luskin acquired the Marinello beauty school chain. Although named for Giovanni Marinello, the 16th-century Italian father of cosmetology, the school was founded by a Wisconsin woman named Ruth Mauer, who in the early 1900s concocted her own face cream, which led to a host of beauty products sold around the world. To drum up further business she launched a school in 1905 to train beauticians, who could then pitch her wares to their customers, as well as a chain of Marinello Beauty Parlors. The company

COMPANY PERSPECTIVES

Scope Products, Inc., is committed to operational excellence and the highest standard of quality in customer service, environmental stewardship, and corporate responsibility. We conduct business based on solid core values of integrity, openness, accountability, teamwork, and continued evaluation and improvement.

relocated to New York City in 1925 where it remained until being acquired by Southern California Petroleum. Luskin also delved into the bakery waste business, owning and operating recycling plants under the name of Dext Company. Because of Southern California Petroleum's evolving business mix, Luskin changed its name in 1964 to Scope Industries.

In time, the company's involvement in the oil and gas business was limited to royalties and working interests with active drillers. While the main focus became waste recycling and beauty schools, Luskin continued to use Scope to make investments. The company invested in Avnet, Inc., a major distributor of electronic and electromechanical components, but in 1980 failed in a hostile bid to take over control. Luskin also invested in cement, acquiring a 14 percent stake in Stamford, Connecticut-based Lone Star Industries, a fast-growing consolidator in the 1980s that snapped up cement companies across the United States as well as in South America.

Not only did Lone Star take on too much debt, its chairman, James E. Stewart, took advantage of the business to support a lavish lifestyle. When Lone Star began to falter, Stewart stepped aside and his successor, David W. Wallace, quickly filed for Chapter 11 bankruptcy protection in 1990 and during the reorganization maneuvered to acquire Lone Star's assets at greatly reduced prices. Scope and other investors were left with the losses. Clearly upset with the turn of events, Luskin told *Forbes,* "He [Wallace] steals the company from [Stewart], does a lousy job, then gets rewarded with bonuses and options. America is beautiful."

Despite being burned by Lone Star, Luskin had developed a solid reputation with Scope shareholders, who saw him as "a poor man's Warren Buffett," someone who knew how to make investments and cash them in to provide solid and steady dividends. In fiscal 1990, for example, Scope reported net income of $1.19 per share on just $16 million in revenues, 93 percent of which came from waste material recycling. What made the difference was $2.3 million in "other income," which included some real estate projects, U.S. Treasury Bills, and other short-term investments.

BEAUTY SCHOOLS REACQUIRED: 1991

In 1988 Luskin sold Scope Beauty Enterprises, the holding company for the Marinello beauty school, but in July 1991 the 15 beauty schools returned to the fold after the buyer defaulted on a collateralized note. In fiscal 1992 Marinello's contribution to the balance sheet increased revenues to $20.8 million. Scope posted a rare loss that year, almost $700,000 in fiscal 1992, due to several factors. Although Marinello strengthened sales, the schools' operations were in disarray, resulting in an expensive overhaul of the business that included the hiring of a new management team, the retraining of personnel, and the revamping of systems and procedures.

The waste materials segment experienced a modest sales increase for the year despite poor animal feed prices. A $2 million investment to modernize and expand the recycling plants hurt the balance sheet, although the improvement in productivity would benefit the company in the long run. An investment in a new Vernon, California, plant to manufacture edible breadcrumb products for restaurant supply food processors would not bear fruit, however, and Scope would focus on the animal feed grain market.

Scope experienced a difficult fiscal 1993, when the effects of the Lone Star investment were reflected on the balance sheet. Scope owned shares worth $10.8 million but because Lone Star was operating under Chapter 11 bankruptcy protection, the Securities and Exchange Commission (SEC) mandated that Scope recognize a loss on its balance sheet, despite Luskin's desire simply to reduce the asset value to have the option of adjusting upward if the market value later improved. Because the market value of the Lone Star shares was determined to be slightly less than $4 million, Scope was forced to recognize a loss of nearly $6.9 million. As it turned out, the SEC's position was borne out by subsequent events. Writing to shareholders regarding fiscal 1994, Luskin charged, "the creditors in collaboration with the Lone Star management that got them into bankruptcy, received almost the entire company in reorganization. The creditors then granted bonuses and stock options to management. All was then approved by the courts, who, to this observer, were more interested in clearing their calendar than in seeking equity and justice."

To make matters worse for Scope in fiscal 1993, Marinello was still recovering from the mistakes of

KEY DATES

1938: Company founded as Southern California Petroleum Corporation.
1961: Meyer Luskin named president and chairman.
1963: Luskin acquires the Marinello beauty school chain.
1964: Name changed to Scope Industries.
1991: Marinello Beauty Schools reacquired.
1999: International Processing Corporation (IPC) acquired.
2004: Company delisted from American Stock Exchange.

previous management and Dext Company had to contend with lower prices for Dried Bakery Product, which was bringing the same amount as it had ten years earlier. As a result of all these factors, Scope experienced a dip in revenues to $20.7 million in fiscal 1993 while posting a net loss of $11.4 million.

Scope rebounded somewhat in fiscal 1994, although the results were somewhat mixed. Marinello fared poorly and recorded a significant loss. Investment income, which had been devastated by Lone Star the previous year, produced more than $2 million. The highlight of the year was a jump in feed commodity prices that resulted in far better results for Dext than the previous year. All told, sales increased to $23.3 million in fiscal 1994 and Scope netted $1.6 million, or $1.24 per share.

In fiscal 1995 the chief operating officer of Dext Company was fired for fraud and defalcation, a term that usually referred to embezzlement. Because Scope's insurer accepted the claim of defalcation, the losses were reimbursed and the balance sheet was not adversely impacted. Although revenues dipped below $23 million and net income decreased to $1.4 million in fiscal 1995, Scope actually fared better with the Dext Companies and Marinello, boding well for the future, but a drop in investment and other income masked those improvements. The bakery waste business enjoyed an excellent fiscal 1996, when after several years of depressed commodity prices, record corn prices led to much higher prices for Dried Bakery Product. Not only did prices increase by 36 percent, Scope was able to take advantage of the investments it had made during the lean times to improve the operations of the Dext Companies. Hence, net income for the parent company increased to almost $4 million on revenues of $30.2 million.

The Dext Companies enjoyed another strong year in fiscal 1997 while Marinello turned in a mediocre performance. Revenues improved by just over $50,000 over the previous year, yet Scope recorded net income of nearly $19 million, due almost entirely to the sale of the company's holdings in Imperial Bancorp and Mesa, Inc. As a result, net income per share approached $16, a major improvement over the $3.23 per share the previous year. The asset sell-off continued the following year, leading to more than $16 million in net income despite a decrease in revenues to $25 million, due to a drop in the price of Dried Bakery Product and poor enrollment at the Marinello schools, which never fared particularly well during periods of strong employment.

IPC ACQUIRED: 1999

With an ample amount of cash available, Scope looked to acquire a company in the recycling business, and found it in 1999 in Tucker, Georgia-based International Processing Corp. (IPC), a bakery waste recycling company. It was owned by Darling International, a Texas-based rendering company that sold IPC to focus on its core business after a difficult 1998. IPC, along with its International Transportation Services, Inc., unit, was purchased for $20.5 million, the deal closing in April 1999. Scope picked up dehydration and processing plants in Carteret, New Jersey; Lake City, Georgia; Conley, Georgia; Terre Haute, Indiana; Mt. Pleasant, Texas; and Kansas City, Kansas; along with blending and grinding plants in Fairfield, Ohio; Bedford Park, Illinois; and Durham, North Carolina.

The addition of IPC came just two months before the close of fiscal 1999, so that its impact on the balance sheet was minor. It was a difficult year for Scope's recycling business, because of plummeting commodity feed prices, and an improved performance by the beauty schools could not offset it. Although total revenues increased to more than $31 million, Scope recorded a net loss of nearly $850,000. With IPC contributing for the entire year in fiscal 2000, revenues topped $60 million and net income jumped to $6 million. The major reason for this stellar performance was in fact $15 million in investment and other income achieved through the sale of stock in Scope's holding of OSI Systems, Inc. Originally called Opto-Sensors, Inc., OSI developed optoelectronic devices used by the medical and security industries. Scope had been investing in OSI since 1990 when OSI was in its start-up phase and Luskin became a director. He had no particular interest in selling Scope's stake in OSI, but a sudden jump in stock price led him to conclude that it was in the best interests of Scope shareholders to sell a major portion of the shares. The windfall was especially welcome because of extremely low feed product prices that year.

In addition to OSI, Scope held stakes in early-stage companies in the early 2000s on whose boards Luskin sat. They included Chromagen, Inc., a gene expression technologies company; Metaprobe, LLC, developer of physiological imaging technology for possible use in drug discovery; and Stamet, Inc., a company developing a cleaner and more efficient way to burn coal. Although Luskin was not a director, Scope also owned stock in software company Myricom, Inc.

OSI STAKE SOLD: 2002

While Scope did not record a significant amount of investment income in fiscal 2001, the following year it cashed in its OSI holdings, netting a profit of more than $20 million. As a result, a loss of $4.1 million in fiscal 2001 led to net income of over $11 million in fiscal 2002. In the meantime, Scope bolstered its recycling business, rebuilding its Terre Haute, Indiana, plant and opening a new plant in the Atlanta, Georgia, area. The investment in upgrading the company's facilities paid off in fiscal 2003 when revenues increased from $63.2 million to $81.4 million. Despite recording investment income of just $666,434, Scope was able to net almost $3.2 million.

Marinello had been demonstrating some improvement, but during fiscal 2004 Scope decided the time had come to dedicate all of its resources to the waste food recycling business. In February 2004 Scope Beauty Enterprises, Inc., was sold to B&H Educations, Inc. The sale helped boost investment income for the year, resulting in net income of $9.7 million. Also during fiscal 2004 Scope elected to save money by delisting its stock on the American Stock Exchange and deregistering from the SEC. Going forward, Scope stock was relegated to over-the-counter status.

Luskin had always been reluctant to speak with the press, and information about the company had been confined mostly to the company's SEC filings. Because Scope was no longer required to make public disclosures, it became difficult to gauge how well the company was doing. What was known was that the company continued to be led by Meyer Luskin, then in his 80s. How much longer he could continue in this capacity remained to be seen, and what would happen to Scope once he left was also an open question.

Ed Dinger

PRINCIPAL SUBSIDIARIES

ReConserve, Inc.; ReCycle to Conserve, Inc.; International Processing Corporation.

PRINCIPAL COMPETITORS

Griffin Industries; Imperial Western Products; InnoPet Brands Corporation.

FURTHER READING

Dougherty, Conor, "Maverick Chief Elicits Faith with Folksy Style," *Los Angeles Business Journal,* March 11, 2002.

Norman, James R., "Was He Born on Friday the 13th?" *Forbes,* August 1, 1994, p. 38.

"Oil Concern Names President," *New York Times,* October 7, 1961.

"Scope Bids for Avnet to Sell Businesses," *New York Times,* September 4, 1980, p. D5.

Smart & Final LLC

600 Citadel Drive
City of Commerce, California 90040
U.S.A.
Telephone: (323) 869-7500
Fax: (323) 869-7858
Web site: http://www.smartandfinal.com

Wholly Owned Subsidiary of Apollo Management L.P.
Incorporated: 1871 as Hellman-Haas Grocery Company
Employees: 5,910
Sales: $2.1 billion (2006)
NAIC: 445110 Supermarkets and Other Grocery; 424410 General Line Grocery Merchant Wholesalers; 452910 Warehouse Clubs and Supercenters

■ ■ ■

Smart & Final LLC operates the largest warehouse grocery store chain in the United States with 282 retail locations, serving both the commercial wholesale and retail markets. Originating in California in 1871, the company expanded into neighboring states in the 1980s and eventually into the international market. Smart & Final operates 247 stores under the Smart & Final and Smart Foodservice banners, with stores in California, Oregon, Washington, Nevada, Arizona, Idaho, and Northern Mexico and also operates 35 farmers market stores in Southern California and Texas under the Henry's Farmers Markets and Sun Farmers Markets banners.

Unlike many so-called members markets, which offer wholesale products in a variety of categories, Smart & Final stores do not charge a membership fee and focus primarily on restaurant-quality food and supplies, averaging between 7,000 to 9,000 items in stock. The company's goal is to serve both as a public grocery and as an outlet for restaurants, catering companies, and other food-related businesses. In 2007, Smart & Final was acquired by Apollo Management L.P., Smart & Final declared sales in excess of $2 billion and the company employed more than 10,000 full-time employees at its various outlets.

GROCERY PIONEERS

Los Angeles was a dusty town of unpaved streets and wood or adobe buildings when Hellman, Haas & Co. opened as a wholesale grocer in 1871. Founded by Abraham Haas, who had arrived from Bavaria at the age of 16, along with brother Jacob Haas and partners Bernard Cohn and Herman Hellman, the two-story brick building provided bulk staple items such as flour, brown sugar, salt, rope, chewing tobacco, gunpowder, patent medicines, and shepherding supplies to the town's 6,000 residents.

The small store played an important role in the early growth of Los Angeles, adding items catering to the town's many ethnic populations, including Native and Mexican Americans, and a growing Chinese community. As the town grew, Hellman, Haas & Co. grew with it; in 1880, the store was listed among the seven names in Los Angeles's first phone directory. The partners played a role in the area's growth as well. Herman Hellman would later head the Farmers and Merchants Bank and join in the founding of the

COMPANY PERSPECTIVES

Smart & Final competes across several traditional industry classifications. It has evolved from a traditional "Cash and Carry" concept, to a hybrid serving both the wholesale and retail market for food, supplies and culinary equipment. Although it competes with supermarkets for the purchasing dollars of household consumers, its low-price, warehouse format and restaurant-quality product assortment clearly differentiate it from other competitors in that segment. It also competes with warehouse club stores, but is clearly differentiated by its smaller store size, focus on a single product category and lack of a membership fee.

University of Southern California. Abraham Haas branched out into the flour milling and cold storage businesses and was among the founders of Southern California's first gas and electric companies.

In 1889, Jacob Baruch bought Hellman's interest in the company, and the company's name changed to Haas, Baruch & Co. The store continued to prosper and, in 1895, began selling canned tomatoes under its own Iris brand name. Sales by that year had reached an impressive $2 million. By the dawn of the 20th century, Haas, Baruch was the leading grocer in a town that, over the next two decades, would swell to a population of nearly one million. Abraham Haas left Los Angeles during this period, opening a successful wholesale operation in San Francisco. Haas's son, Walter, worked in the family business, but later left to join a small clothing company, Levi Strauss, where he would serve as president for the next 30 years. Haas, Baruch continued to thrive; in 1948 the company opened its own 3.5-acre warehouse in Vernon, California.

CASH-AND-CARRY GROCERY MARKET IN THE 20TH CENTURY

Meanwhile, J. S. Smart, a banker from Saginaw, Michigan, arrived in California in 1914, where he purchased a small feed and grain supplier, the Santa Ana Wholesale Company, which had been founded two years earlier. Smart was soon joined by H. D. Final, and the partners moved their business to San Pedro, renaming the company Smart & Final Wholesale Grocers. By the end of the decade, the company's sales reached $10 million.

Competition among the area's wholesalers intensified over the next decade. The grocery industry itself was changing, as more and more retailers began purchasing directly from the manufacturers, bypassing the wholesalers altogether. However, on a trip to Ohio, Smart discovered the latest trend in grocery sales—that of allowing customers to choose their purchases, rather than having the grocery's clerks gather the items. In 1923, Smart brought this innovation to the West Coast, and Smart & Final became the first in the area to offer the "cash-and-carry" concept. Another key to the company's survival and success was its practice of locating its stores close to the businesses they served, instead of requiring customers to travel to remotely located warehouses.

Smart & Final was helped by the outbreak of World War II, winning supply contracts to support the military effort. After the war, the company expanded its customer base to include churches and local clubs and organizations and, by the beginning of the 1950s, had grown to a chain of 65 stores. Changes were occurring in the grocery industry, as improved cold storage and refrigeration techniques were making possible an expanding assortment of foods. A new type of store, the supermarket, became popular during this time, placing still more pressure on the wholesalers. In 1953, Smart & Final acquired Haas, Baruch, adding the latter's popular Iris brand to the Smart & Final name. The new company, Smart & Final Iris Co., moved its headquarters to Haas, Baruch's Vernon warehouse site. In 1955, however, Smart & Final was bought by the Thriftimart supermarket chain, founded by Roger M. Laverty.

Laverty had been active in the grocery trade since 1930, when he bought the small, Los Angeles-based chain Fitzsimmons Stores Inc. In 1947, Laverty acquired Thriftimart Inc., also based in Los Angeles, merging the two chains under the Thriftimart name. The addition of Smart & Final's warehouse stores boosted Thriftimart's sales to $168 million by 1960. When Laverty died in 1969, he was succeeded by his son, Roger Laverty II.

DECADES OF GROWTH AND EXPANSION

Under Thriftimart, the Iris brand name was expanded to include hundreds of frozen food products, paper and canned goods, and janitorial supplies. The chain of Smart & Final cash-and-carry stores, which averaged from 4,000 to 10,000 square feet, grew to 86 stores by the 1980s. Together with Thriftimart's 41 supermarkets, sales passed $250 million by the early 1970s and climbed to $500 million by the early 1980s.

KEY DATES

1871: Company is founded as Hellman-Haas Grocery Co.
1889: Company name changes to Haas, Baruch and Co.
1923: Smart & Final becomes first cash-and-carry grocer on the West Coast.
1948: Haas, Baruch opens a warehouse in Vernon, California.
1953: Smart & Final acquires Haas, Baruch.
1955: Smart & Final is acquired by Thriftimart grocery chain.
1969: Roger Laverty II becomes president of Thriftimart.
1984: Company is acquired by Casino USA.
1990: The first store in Arizona opens.
1991: Company goes public on the New York Stock Exchange.
1993: Roger Laverty III is named CEO; company opens first international locations, in Mexico.
2000: Company opens an e-commerce site.
2003: Company sells assets in Northern California and Florida.
2007: Smart & Final is purchased by Apollo Management L.P.

Despite this growth, however, Thriftimart struggled for profitability. After posting an $822,000 loss on sales of $260 million in 1972, the company climbed back into the black, only to post a $5.4 million loss on $343 million sales in 1976. Thriftimart fared better in the second half of that decade, rebuilding its bottom line to a $4.5 million net income on sales of $368 million in 1979. The following year, net income rose to a high of $7.2 million, with sales climbing to $431 million. Nevertheless, the growth of warehouse clubs such as Price Club and Costco began to pressure the supermarket industry. By 1982, when Thriftimart's sales peaked at $506 million, its net income fell to $4.8 million. Thriftimart moved to divest its struggling supermarket division, selling 23 California supermarkets to Safeway Stores, Inc., in 1983. By 1984, with sales just under $500 million, net income had dropped to $1.5 million.

In that year, Roger Laverty II, his brother Robert, and their sister Nancy Harris, who together owned 85 percent of Thriftimart's stock, sold their interest in the company to Casino USA and its parent, Établissements Economiques du Casino Guichard-Perrachon et Cie (later known as Groupe Casino), a $3 billion French-based operator of supermarkets, convenience stores, restaurants, and food production and processing facilities. Laverty II retired after the sale of the company, and Robert Emmons was named chairman, president, and CEO in 1984.

Thriftimart's 17 remaining supermarkets were liquidated after the Casino acquisition, and the focus was shifted to Smart & Final's 86-store cash-and-carry operations, which had remained profitable throughout the Thriftimart period. As Smart & Final, Inc., the company moved to refocus, modernize, and expand the chain. The new management, which included Roger Laverty III, developed the strategy that would take the company into the next decade. This strategy targeted smaller, independent foodservice and related businesses with a redesigned store concept offering a product assortment adapted to this market's needs. At the same time, the company moved to modernize its stores, closing a number of its aging stores while relocating dozens more stores to locations featuring parking, convenient access to customers, and larger size. Over the next ten years, store size would more than double to an average 17,000 square feet.

MOVING INTO A NATIONAL MARKET

By 1988, the Smart & Final chain had been pared down to 72 modern stores. Until then, the chain had served the Southern California market exclusively. In the late 1980s, however, Smart & Final began an aggressive expansion into Northern California, Nevada, and Arizona. Sales, which dropped to $335 million in 1986, rose to $498 million by 1989. One year later, sales neared $560 million, generating a net income of $9.4 million.

As the country slipped into the recession of the early 1990s, Smart & Final's growth continued. The drop in real estate prices in its core California market proved a boon to the expanding company, which numbered 99 stores by 1989 and 135 stores by 1993. In 1991, with sales of $663 million, Smart & Final went public again, offering a minority stake on the New York Stock Exchange, with Casino maintaining a 53 percent share of the company's stock.

In that year, Smart & Final expanded into foodservice distribution with the purchase of Northern California-based Port Stockton Food Distributors, Inc. The company next launched its Casino Frozen Foods, Inc., subsidiary as distributor both to its own stores and to independent customers. By 1993, that business expanded beyond frozen foods to supply delicatessen and other products as well. In that year, Roger Laverty III was named the company's president and CEO.

While Smart & Final continued to increase its presence in California, growing to 140 stores in 20 counties by the end of 1995, the company began to eye other markets. Encouraged by the passage of the North American Free Trade Agreement, and joining a growing trend among U.S. retailers, in 1993 the company formed a joint venture with Central Detallista S.A. de C.V. to bring Smart & Final stores into Mexico. The first stores opened in Baja, Mexico, and the company made plans for nine stores by 1995 and as many as 50 stores in the near future.

Smart & Final next prepared to enter the Florida market, which, with its large Hispanic population, fit well with its Californian customer base. In 1994, Smart & Final added the Henry Lee Company, which served the Florida, Central and South American, and Caribbean markets, to its distribution business. The acquisition of Henry Lee, which ranked among the largest foodservice distributors in the country, paved the way for the expansion of Smart & Final's cash-and-carry operations into Florida. In early 1996 the company opened its first six Dade and Broward county stores. In Florida, Smart & Final continued its policy of opening stores in inner-city areas typically shunned by other grocers (after the 1992 riots, for example, Smart & Final opened 11 stores in Los Angeles) while providing a product assortment geared to its customers' cultures and needs.

After expanding its geographic scope, however, Smart & Final began feeling the impact of increased competition and a slowed economy in the late 1990s. Sales slumped in 1997 and 1998, with a loss of over $16 million reported for the 1998 fiscal period. In 1999, Ross Roeder was named CEO of Smart & Final and initiated a restructuring program to help the company return to profitability. Over the course of the next year, Smart & Final posted increased earnings and profits for the 1999 fiscal year with a 14 percent increase in sales. "Our same store sales growth was the best we've seen in the past five years," Roeder said in a press releases, "and we hope to build on that growth with the marketing, merchandising, and margin improvements we've introduced. We look to the future with great confidence."

SURVIVING AS AN INDUSTRY PIONEER

In the fall of 2000, Smart & Final opened the company's first e-commerce site at www.smartandfinal.com, where private and commercial customers could purchase over 5,000 of the company's products for delivery. Geared more toward the professional market, Smart & Final's e-commerce site offered cooking and food preparation equipment, bulk ingredients, and janitorial supplies. "Our site is truly unique," said Roeder in the company's December press release, "offering easy browsing, competitive pricing and quick fulfillment, while encouraging direct customer communication with customer service specialists who can respond promptly to all queries."

In December 2000, the company's Henry Lee branch won a lucrative three-year contract to serve as a supplier to the Miami-based Royal Caribbean Cruise Lines. By the end of the year, Smart & Final's average sales had increased by more than 5 percent and the company posted earnings in excess of $30 million, a significant improvement over the company's $26 million for the previous year. In 2000, Smart & Final opened four new branches and had developed plans for an additional 15 stores, drawing on the company's increased revenues to fuel a major expansion program.

In 2003, Smart & Final's board of directors decided to sell the company's properties in Florida to an alternate vendor. While the company's Florida operations were initially profitable, poor performance and market changes in 2001 and 2002 resulted in an overall loss of revenue. In 2003, Smart & Final representatives began negotiations with Michigan-based Gordon Food Service (GFS) to sell all distribution and retail locations in Florida. In a press release Roeder said of the sale, "Progress is seldom achieved without cost. Although the bold steps we are taking to reposition Smart & Final for future growth and success required some financial pain, I am confident that we are taking the right actions to put Smart & Final on course for industry-leading performance."

That same year, Smart & Final sold some of its locations in Northern California to competitor SYSCO Corporation. Together with the sale of the company's Florida operations, Smart & Final's comprehensive divestiture program raised over $59 million in revenues. Through negotiations with both SYSCO and GFS, Smart & Final secured continued employment for more than 700 former employees. Roeder cited nationwide changes in the warehouse market as key to the company's divestiture strategies. "All of Smart & Final's resources now are focused on our most profitable and fastest-growing operations," Roeder said, adding, "We believe we have effectively repositioned our company for strong future performance."

Roeder and the board of directors conducted a management restructuring, including hiring industry veteran Etienne Snollaerts as president and chief operating officer, to serve directly under Roeder. Snollaerts previously served as an executive for Groupe Casino. Snollaerts replaced Roeder as CEO in May 2004, while Roeder remained chairman of the board of directors.

The company's financial performance improved some in 2003 and 2004, with fourth-quarter sales in 2004 of over $470 million, after the corporate restructuring and the sale of some of the company's less-profitable divisions. The company opened three new locations in 2004, including two in California, one in Arizona, and one in Baja California, Mexico. Expansion continued in 2005 with 13 new store openings in California, Arizona, and Washington and two additional stores opened in Mexico.

In 2006, Groupe Casino, the majority shareholder of Smart & Final, announced that it would be selling some of its core assets, although it was initially unclear whether Smart & Final would be sold as part of the company's divestitures. In 2007, Groupe Casino sold the company to Apollo Management L.P., a private-equity investment firm with an estimated $16 billion in investments in various businesses. The sale was completed in May 2007 for approximately $812 million. The company was subsequently delisted from the New York Stock Exchange and shareholders were paid $22 per share of common stock.

Snollaerts remained company CEO after the management shift and the transition to the Apollo board. Even as the company readjusted, growth continued and the company's total number of stores grew to 282 locations by the end of 2007. In October 2007, the company made a major acquisition of 27 Henry's Markets in Southern California and eight Sun Harvest stores in Texas. With the purchase, Smart & Final entered the thriving farmers market industry and gained a stronger foothold in Texas.

With estimated sales of over $2 billion in 2007, Smart & Final had become one of the fastest-growing wholesale chains in the United States. With the company's interest in the growing farmers market industry, Smart & Final has diversified its operations in an effort to stay ahead of the market.

M. L. Cohen
Updated, Micah L. Issitt

PRINCIPAL SUBSIDIARIES

Port Stockton Food Distributors, Inc.; Smart Foodservice; Sun Harvest Markets; Henry Harvest Markets.

PRINCIPAL COMPETITORS

Sam's Club; SYSCO Corporation; Costco Wholesale Corporation.

FURTHER READING

Berry, Kate, "Missteps, Competitors Take Toll on Aging Smart & Final Chain," *Los Angeles Times,* February 24, 2003.

Brooks, Nancy Rivera, "Growth Market: Smart & Final Celebrates 125 Years in a Big Way," *Los Angeles Times,* March 4, 1996, p. D1.

Cassano, Erik, "Retail Key Ingredients: Etienne Snollaerts Shares His Recipe for Making Smart and Final a Food Service Force," *Smart Business Los Angeles,* December 2006.

Coupe, Kevin, "Smart & Focused (& Growing Fast)," *Progressive Grocer,* September 1994, p. 44.

Goodman, Cindy Krischer, "Smart & Final Bulk Grocery Chain Targets Florida Inner Cities," *Miami Herald,* December 14, 1994.

"Smart & Final Reports 1999 Return to Profitability," *Business Wire,* February 22, 2000.

Taylor, John H., "Niche Guys Finish First," *Forbes,* October 26, 1992, p. 128.

York, Emily Bryson, "Smart & Final Stock Rises as Majority Owner Considers Sale," *Los Angeles Business Journal,* November 27, 2006.

South Dakota Wheat Growers Association

110 6th Avenue SE
Aberdeen, South Dakota 57401
U.S.A.
Telephone: (605) 225-5500
Fax: (605) 225-0859
Web site: http://www.sdwg.com

Private Cooperative
Incorporated: 1923
Employees: 270
Sales: $434.6 million (2007)
NAIC: 111140 Wheat Farming; 325311 Nitrogenous Fertilizer Manufacturing

■ ■ ■

The South Dakota Wheat Growers Association is an agricultural cooperative whose members, despite the name, now grow more corn and soybeans than they do wheat. The Aberdeen, South Dakota-based organization serves 16,000 equity holders and 3,600 farmers (who do at least $5,000 in business each year with Wheat Growers) in the James River Valley, which runs through the eastern portion of North and South Dakota. Wheat Growers provides grain-handling services that market more than 90 billion bushels of grain each year through 16 rail loading facilities, including four high-speed train loading facilities. The co-op also offers condo storage options, leasing space to members on a time-share basis; a bin probing service that takes a sample of a farm's grain, analyzes it, and offers guaranteed pricing; and an off-the-farm grain-buying program that transports a crop to the most profitable market.

Wheat Growers provides agronomy products—including fertilizers, herbicides, insecticides, and nutrients—and services, such as the delivery and application of the products, and seed treatments and inoculation. Wheat Growers also offers financing options through its Crop Input Loan and Operating Loan programs.

The organization is also involved in three joint ventures: Dakota Feeds, a feed and nutrition provider formed with partners Land O'Lakes, Farmland Feeds, and North Central Farmers Elevator; James Valley Grain, LLC, a train loading facility operated with Norway Spur Farmers Cooperative; and Petroleum Partners, LLC, a bulk petroleum products provider run by Wheat Growers and four other cooperatives, serving northeast South Dakota. Wheat Growers is governed by a 19-member board of active producers representing six districts, backed by 54 delegates who serve as the liaison with the general membership.

EARLY 20TH-CENTURY RISE OF FARMERS ELEVATORS

When the 1900s dawned, grain farmers of the upper Midwest began to band together to gain much needed economic leverage. Unable to store grain themselves, farmers were reliant on their local grain elevators, which themselves were too small and were forced to sell the grain and ship it to the regional facilities of millers or grain merchants. Because so much grain was available at harvest time, commodity prices were depressed for farm-

> **COMPANY PERSPECTIVES**
>
> Wheat Growers Mission: To provide, with integrity, our customers with reliable markets, services, and quality products through a profitable and innovative organization.

ers, but once the grain made its way to regional sites the economics changed, resulting in more realistic prices. In order to receive their rightful share of the profits that resulted from their hard labor, grain farmers responded by forming either marketing cooperatives or wheat pools.

WHEAT GROWERS FORMED: 1923

Wheat Growers was launched in 1923 when wheat prices were especially depressed, resulting in a rash of farm bankruptcies. A conference was convened in Sioux City, Iowa, where representatives from a number of states met to discuss ways of improving grain prices. Here the president of the Montana Wheat Growers Association, Dwight Cressap, told the participants how wheat pools had been successfully launched in Montana, Oregon, and Washington. One of the delegates, South Dakota Lt. Governor Carl Gunderson, was so impressed that he called for a meeting of interested participants to form a South Dakota wheat pool. About 30 members of the state legislature attended the meeting held at the state capital and a tentative agreement was reached to form the South Dakota Wheat Growers Association.

Wheat Growers established its headquarters in Aberdeen, South Dakota, and an organizational committee of 12 was selected. The number soon increased to 14 after the committee decided to divide the state into 14 districts. A wheat pool contract was drawn up, and the committee established a goal of one million bushels and a deadline to achieve it. Once enough farmers signed on, the committee hired a general manager of the association, Charles W. Croes, who was given a salary of $250 per month. Croes had attended the first organizational meeting and been selected to the organizational committee. He grew up on a farm near Wessington, South Dakota, but in addition to knowing firsthand the plight of growers, Croes was an experienced, banker, lawyer, and legislator. He would serve as Wheat Growers' general manager for the next 41 years.

The underlying tactic of the wheat pool was to withhold grain from the market, to regulate the flow to the market to improve the price—rather than have grain flood the market at harvest time and depress the price the farmers received. Initially, Wheat Growers owned no grain-handling facilities and had to rely on local elevators to ship its grain, which came from member farmers who signed commitment contracts to deliver a certain amount of grain to elevators that were allied with Wheat Growers. The improvement in prices from pooling was not especially dramatic in the early years, but a number of other factors combined to result in much better grain prices for farmers in the 1920s. Everything would change, however, when the stock market crashed in the autumn of 1929 and the country was soon plunged into the Great Depression of the 1930s.

CONVERSION FROM POOL TO CO-OP AND THE DEPRESSION

At their annual meeting held in June 1930, the members of the South Dakota Wheat Growers Association considered whether to liquidate the organization and split the organization's reserve funds among its members. Instead, they decided to convert Wheat Growers into a farmer-owned cooperative. Hence, the group conducted its last pool in 1930–31. During a transition period, elevators were acquired in Andover, Bristol, Columbia, and Frankfort, South Dakota; Wheat Growers began to operate these on a cooperative basis in 1931. As well, the federal government had stepped in to support grain prices through the creation of the Grain Stabilization Corporation, putting an end to need for wheat pools. In 1933 the Roosevelt administration formed the Commodity Credit Corporation to stabilize and support farm income and prices.

Despite federal efforts the 1930s were a dark period for U.S. agriculture, no less so for Wheat Growers, which was soon on the verge of folding. By 1934 the co-op's staff was limited to just Croes, who took a steep cut in pay to keep the co-op going. The situation was so dire that Croes was authorized by the board to shut down the elevators at his discretion. Croes and Wheat Growers hung on, however, and in 1934 Croes seized an opportunity to make use of the elevators to supply feed grains to farms, made possible by a new government loan program for feed.

This business not only provided much needed revenue but also helped to establish Wheat Growers as an elevator operator. Six elevators were leased from the Omaha Bank for Cooperatives in 1937, and another lease was taken on the Farmer's Elevator in Aberdeen. Two years later Wheat Growers was able to buy all seven of these facilities, supplemented by the acquisition of

KEY DATES

1923: Organization is formed as a wheat pool.
1930: Wheat Growers becomes an agricultural cooperative.
1940: Blue Diamond feed is introduced.
1962: Fertilizer operations are added.
1966: Petroleum products are made available to members.
1988: Wheat Growers and Farmland Industries together open a terminal to handle liquid fertilizer.
1992: A joint venture opens the cooperative's first ethanol plant.
2003: A customer-needs assessment leads to changes.

five other elevators. Another, located in Glencross, was bought from the federal government in 1940. Also in 1940 Wheat Growers introduced its own brand of feed under the Blue Diamond name.

POSTWAR GROWTH

Following the interruption of World War II in the early 1940s, Wheat Growers resumed its growth. In 1945 it acquired a pair of elevators, and the following year an elevator and additional warehouses were picked up in auction. One of the new elevators was then supplemented with a pellet mill in 1947, allowing Wheat Growers to market Blue Diamond pelleted feed. A year later, when it marked its 25th anniversary, Wheat Growers had a membership of 5,000 farmers who were served by 15 facilities. In fiscal 1948 the co-op posted record sales of more than $3.3 million.

Grain harvests were plentiful in the late 1940s, leading to surpluses and falling prices, forcing the Commodity Credit Corporation to step in and acquire large amounts of grain to stabilize the situation. As a result, the government needed storage space and in 1953 Croes reached an agreement with Commodity Credit Corporation, which contracted to use 85 percent of a new grain-storage facility in the Aberdeen area to be constructed by Wheat Growers. A 550,000-bushel terminal was ready for the 1954 harvest, but soon proved inadequate to meet the needs of both the government and the co-op's members. More space was added in 1956, capable of handling a further 600,000 bushels. Two years later another 650,000 bushels of space was tacked on to the Aberdeen terminal, followed by a 250,000-bushel building, so that by the end of the 1950s the Aberdeen complex enjoyed a capacity of more than 2 million bushels.

FERTILIZER BUSINESS ENTERED: 1964

At the start of the 1960s a new feed mill complex was completed in Bath, South Dakota. Two elevators were relocated here and production of Blue Diamond feed was transferred to the new plant. In 1962 Wheat Growers became involved in the fertilizer business, building a dry fertilizer warehouse at Bath, where other fertilizer assets would later be added to the mix. A liquid fertilizer supplier, Wheeting Farm Service, was acquired in 1964 and relocated to Bath, and anhydrous ammonia storage and the fabrication of liquid fertilizer attachments were incorporated into the business as well.

The 1960s also saw a changing of the guard in management. In 1964 the 78-year-old Croes stepped down as general manager after serving more than four decades. He passed away three years later. His replacement, Warren Grebner, wasted little time in making his mark, taking Wheat Growers in a number of directions. He expanded the co-op's reach to the south in 1965 by acquiring the 500,000-bushel elevator in Huron, South Dakota. Grebner also filled in the one gap that prevented Wheat Growers from being a full-service farmer cooperative. In 1966 the co-op began to offer members petroleum products after acquiring Tulare Oil Company.

Also during this period Wheat Growers forged an alliance with Farmland Industries, then known as Consumer Cooperative Association (CAA), which had invested considerable funds to establish research laboratories that developed "open formula" feed. Wheat Growers elected to cease production of Blue Diamond feeds and instead manufacture and market CAA feeds. Unfortunately, on the very last day of the 1960s, a fire destroyed the Bath feed mill.

WEATHERING PETROLEUM SHORTAGES

The Tulare acquisition proved to be a godsend to Wheat Growers' members in the 1970s, when the OPEC oil embargoes caused major oil companies to all but abandon rural America. Wheat Growers was able to keep its members supplied with gasoline and other products, especially during the periods of shortage. The co-op expanded its petroleum business in 1975 with the addition of Huron Oil, Andover Oil, and Langford Oil. Petroleum sales grew steadily through the remainder of the decade, increasing from 3.8 million gallons to 7.8 million gallons in 1979.

The 1970s brought changes on a number of other fronts as well. Following the fire that destroyed the Bath feed mill, Wheat Growers replaced the operation by acquiring Hub City Feed and Seed and also added a wholesale seed business. The co-op expanded its grain-handling capabilities in the 1970s, acquiring the one-million-bushel Western Grain elevator in Redfield, South Dakota, in 1971. The following year another Redfield elevator was added and two years later made into a seed-cleaning plant. Also in 1972 an elevator in Cresbard, South Dakota, was purchased and 100,000 bushels of capacity was added to the Mallette elevator. In addition, a pair of dry fertilizer plants were opened in the 1970s, and agronomy services were expanded through the acquisition of new locations.

EXPANDING TRANSPORTATION AND OTHER SERVICES

The 1980s brought new multicar freight rates by railroads. Some of the co-op's elevators laid sidetrack to accommodate the loading of multicar trains, which grew from 26 cars to 54 cars in 1983. To make unit trains even more cost-effective, some of the grain-handling facilities were expanded and renovated and switch engines were bought to speed up loading. About 60 percent of all Wheat Growers' grain was shipped on unit trains by 1986.

On other fronts in the 1980s, another 320,000 bushels of storage space was added to the Chamberlain elevator in 1987. A year later, Wheat Growers purchased Cargill elevators located in Aberdeen and Athol, while an elevator located in Milbank was sold to another cooperative. Because a pipeline would no longer carry the co-op's liquid nitrogen fertilizer to its terminal, Wheat Growers joined forces with Farmland in 1988 to establish their own two-million-gallon storage terminal that could be supplied by rail.

Wheat Growers also opened a new dry fertilizer plant in Tulare in 1986, followed a year later by the addition of a fertilizer storage plant in Cresbard. The co-op then expanded its fertilizer business into North Dakota with the acquisition of Oakes Fertilizer Company. The petroleum operation was also enlarged through the 1986 acquisition of Brown County Co-op and James Valley Co-op, and the unit closed out the decade by buying several bulk oil plants from Harms Oil Company of Aberdeen.

NEW MARKETS AND VALUE-ADDED PRODUCTS

Wheat Growers became involved in agricultural processing for the first time in the 1990s. This was in response to a 1987 survey conducted with co-op members, who indicated they wanted Wheat Growers to process their raw materials into value-added products that would open up new markets. As a result, Wheat Growers and Farmland Industries joined forces once again to form Heartland Grain Fuels, LLP, which opened an ethanol plant in late 1992 to produce a gasoline supplement.

Following the passage of the 1996 Farm Bill that eased some regulations and eliminated the requirement that farmers leave land unused in order to qualify for crop subsidies, many Wheat Growers' members began producing corn to be sold for ethanol or soy beans, which were becoming more valuable due to changes in the diets of many Americans. Some members stopped growing wheat completely, prompting the co-op to ask members if they wanted to change the organization's name. The consensus was to keep the Wheat Growers name, which the members had devoted decades to promoting.

MCLAUGHLIN FARMERS COOPERATIVE ACQUIRED

Despite its involvement with ethanol, the handling of grain, fertilizer, feed, and petroleum remained Wheat Growers' core business in the 1990s. The co-op expanded to the west in 1991 through the acquisition of the McLaughlin Farmers Cooperative, which brought with it grain, fertilizer, and seed operations. Later in the decade the Maple Valley Farmers Co-op based in Ellendale, North Dakota, was added, strengthening Wheat Growers' footprint in North Dakota, although the Maple Valley facilities were subsequently sold.

During the 1990s, Wheat Growers added new products and services for its members, including the addition of hybrid seeds; a financing program to help buy agricultural "inputs" and services; more marketing information made available to growers; a program to connect farrowing producers with farmers who finished hogs; and precision farming services, such as grid sampling and advanced variable rate fertilizer application using global positioning technology.

Not every member of Wheat Growers was satisfied with the co-op, however. In 2000 a number of farmers called for the resignation of board members who had supported the proposed construction of a 110-car grain-handling unit in one community while refusing to build a grain dryer in another. The essential complaint was that Wheat Growers favored the large producers over smaller growers who made up the bulk of the co-op's membership. Two years later more members were upset over Wheat Growers' decision to close small elevators in Stratford and Hecla, South Dakota, and Ellendale, North Dakota, thereby forcing growers to bear the additional expense of hauling their crops to the co-op's larger elevators. Wheat Growers maintained that the smaller elevators were simply no longer economically viable. The three elevators were later sold.

Wheat Growers reached out to members in 2003, conducting a customer-needs assessment. The co-op was told that it should improve on pricing, marketing, and communications. Over the next few years Wheat Growers attempted to address these concerns. It increased the marketing of ethanol by expanding plants, and instituted the Power Bin Probe program to help growers monitor and better market their grain. At the same time Wheat Growers continued to invest in more storage and additional tracks to accommodate unit trains.

Ed Dinger

PRINCIPAL SUBSIDIARIES

Dakota Feeds LLC; Heartland Grain Fuels, LLP; Petroleum Partners LLC.

PRINCIPAL COMPETITORS

Cargill, Inc.; Country Pride Cooperative; Northern Growers LLC.

FURTHER READING

"Farmers Upset with Wheat Growers Decision to Close Elevators," *Associated Press Newswires,* October 2, 2002.

Fennel, Ian H., "South Dakota Wheat Growers Co-Op Selling Grain Elevators," *Aberdeen (S.Dak.) American News,* September 26, 2002.

Keen, Russ, "Brown County, S.D., Wheat Farmers Protest Board Members' Policies," *Knight-Ridder/Tribune Business News,* February 3, 2000.

Miller, Ruth, *South Dakota Wheat Growers: The History of a Cooperative,* Sioux Falls, S.Dak.: Vista Publication, 1998, 49 p.

Schofer, Dan, "South Dakota: Great Faces, Great Places—and Great Value-Added Opportunities," *Rural Cooperatives,* September–October 2007.

"Wheat Growers Grow Corn, Soybeans but Name's the Same," *Associated Press,* October 4, 2004.

Sport Chalet, Inc.

One Sport Chalet Drive
La Cañada, California 91011
U.S.A.
Telephone: (818) 949-5300
Toll Free: (888) 801-9162
Fax: (818) 949-5301
Web site: http://www.sportchalet.com

Public Company
Incorporated: 1959
Employees: 3,600
Sales: $388.21 million (2007)
Stock Exchanges: NASDAQ
Ticker Symbols: SPCHA SPCHB
NAIC: 451110 Sporting Goods Stores

■ ■ ■

Sport Chalet, Inc., is a leading operator of full-service, specialty sporting goods superstores. A small business for decades, Sport Chalet began expanding rapidly during the late 1980s, quickly establishing its superstores throughout five counties in Southern California. In 2001 the chain began to expand to other parts of the state as well as Nevada, Arizona, and Utah.

By 2008, the chain had four-dozen stores and a central distribution facility in Ontario, California. The company is known for its attention to customer service and efficient and responsive logistics operation. The goal set out by founder Norbert Olberz was "not being the biggest, but the best," and in the eyes of many loyal patrons and industry observers, Sport Chalet was succeeding.

The company's stores stock a full line of traditional sporting goods, as well as thousands of products for nontraditional sports such as downhill skiing, bicycling, mountaineering, scuba diving, and kayaking. Many stores feature swimming pools for scuba diving and kayaking instruction and promotion. Sport Chalet tempts the uninitiated into trying new outdoor sports through a rental program that includes a credit toward purchase of the gear.

THE FOUNDER AND EARLY COMPANY HISTORY

No figure looms larger in Sport Chalet's history than Norbert J. Olberz, the company's founder, chairman, and guiding hand during its evolution from a one-store enterprise to an 18-unit chain of sporting goods superstores. Olberz superintended Sport Chalet's development over a four-decade span and was still in command as his company entered the late 1990s when he was in his early 70s. Olberz's tenure at Sport Chalet may be divided into two eras of the company's history, the first consisting of 20 years during which Sport Chalet operated as a modestly sized business, and the second consisting of another two-decade period during which Sport Chalet rapidly grew into a chain of sporting goods superstores, becoming one of the leading sporting goods chains in the United States. Through the slow years and the years of animated growth, Olberz held sway over Sport Chalet's operation, guiding the company from his office in La Cañada, California.

COMPANY PERSPECTIVES

Sport Chalet is the premier sporting goods store. We carry the best brands, but that's not all. We offer unparalleled customer service and dozens of value-added services, from rentals to repairs. With 17 specialty shops all under one roof, our full array of products and services will thrill any sports lover.

A pastry chef by trade, Olberz had immigrated from Germany. In 1959, he and his wife paid $4,000 for a ski shop in La Cañada, California, a small town north of Los Angeles. During the early years of Sport Chalet's history, Olberz, then in his early 30s, lived in a small house several blocks away from the site of his original store, which was located along Foothill Boulevard in La Cañada. The first store measured 2,000 square feet and focused on the sale of skiing gear, as the company's name suggested. Merchandise moved quickly enough, however, to enable Olberz to expand the scope of his business not long after opening the first store.

Shortly after the grand opening of the first store, Olberz branched out and moved across the street to a 25,000-square-foot facility. Although the move represented a giant leap for the start-up, the expansion did not signal continued rapid growth. Rather, Olberz and his retail business assumed a stable position in the Southern California sporting goods retail community, not mounting any aggressive assault on neighboring sporting goods retailers until the 1980s.

EXPANSION BEGINS IN 1981

Sport Chalet had already celebrated its 20th anniversary by the time it began to show intentions of capturing the lion's share of the sporting goods retail sales in Southern California. In fact, the bid to become big began exactly 21 years after the first store was opened, when Olberz established a Sport Chalet in Huntington Beach in June 1981. Another Sport Chalet was opened in June 1983, followed by the August 1986 establishment of a Sport Chalet in Mission Viejo. Stores in Point Loma and Santa Clarita were opened in 1987, and the pace of expansion picked up considerably. Olberz spearheaded the establishment of two stores in 1989, Beverly Hills and Marina del Rey, and another two in 1990, Brea and Oxnard, none of which was smaller than 30,000 square feet, widely considered the minimum size for a superstore.

During the latter part of the decade in particular, Sport Chalet began to take on the trappings of a retail powerhouse. Aside from the ambitious store expansion, the company upgraded its accounting and inventory systems and opened a 116,000-square-foot warehouse in Montclair, part of which would later be devoted to retail space for another Sport Chalet store.

GOING PUBLIC IN 1992

Following the establishment of the stores in Brea and Oxnard in 1990, both of which featured indoor pools, Olberz opened the largest Sport Chalet at the time, a 44,000-square-foot store complete with indoor pool that opened in June 1991 in West Hills. A slightly larger store was opened a little more than a year later, when customers first walked through the 45,000-square-foot Sport Chalet in Burbank in August 1992.

The two months that followed the Burbank grand opening were the last months of Sport Chalet's existence as a private company. Competition among Southern California sporting goods superstores was intensifying with each passing month, as mammoth retail outlets proliferated throughout the area. In 1992 alone, three sporting goods superstore retailers—Atlanta-based Sportstown; Tampa, Florida-based Sports & Recreation; and Niles, Illinois-based Sportmart—had completed initial public offerings to fund store expansion. By November 1992, it was Sport Chalet's turn. Olberz at the time was hoping to open 9 to 12 Sport Chalet stores during the ensuing three years, a plan that would require at least $2 million per store opening. Consequently, in November Olberz put roughly 25 percent of his 13-store company on the market, and then used the money gained from the public offering to help finance Sport Chalet's expansion.

The conversion to public ownership led to the first disclosure of Sport Chalet's financial figures in the company's 32-year history. Between 1988 and 1992, as documents filed with the Securities and Exchange Commission revealed, Sport Chalet had recorded a robust 24.9 percent annually compounded growth rate, achieving enviable sales growth during its rise to superstore chain status. Totals for fiscal 1991 reached $79.2 million in sales and $344,000 in net income, figures easily eclipsed by the totals generated in fiscal 1992, when Sport Chalet collected $94.8 million in sales and $1.85 million in net income.

Propelled by the momentum of solid financial growth, Sport Chalet entered the public spotlight in November 1992, and then proceeded to implement its ambitious expansion program that called for the establishment of three to four stores per year. Two stores

KEY DATES

1959: Norbert Olberz acquires small ski shop in La Cañada, California, called Sport Chalet.
1981: Opening of Huntington Beach store kicks off expansion drive.
1992: Company goes public as revenues approach $100 million.
1994: Rare loss prompts company to reduce its reliance on winter-related merchandise.
2001: First out-of-state store opens in Nevada.
2003: Company ventures into Northern California, then Central California a year later.
2005: First Arizona stores open.
2007: Company enters Utah with a new store in a suburb of Salt Lake City.

were opened in November 1993, one in Torrance and another in Glendora, each of which measured 40,000 square feet. The addition of these two stores followed the announcement of 1993's financial figures, which elevated Sport Chalet past the $100-million-in-sales plateau for the first time. For the year, the company generated $106.3 million in sales and earned more than $2 million in net income, fueling confidence that Sport Chalet had successfully withstood the deleterious effects of a national economic recession.

During the early 1990s, Sport Chalet stores stocked merchandise that the company categorized in nine product groups, giving each store a full spectrum of products. In addition to selling downhill skiing equipment and apparel, which had contributed the largest percentage of store sales since 1960, Sport Chalet stores stocked camping, backpacking, and mountaineering merchandise, including camping equipment rentals, and scuba gear, including air compressors to refill dive tanks. Rounding out the company's merchandise lines were fishing gear; cycling gear, including bicycle repair service; general sporting goods; shoes and in-line skates; racquet sports; and water sports, including swimwear, water skis, and kayaks. Of the company's total sales, winter-related merchandise represented Sport Chalet's largest sporting goods category, accounting for nearly 30 percent of annual sales. In ranking order, general sporting goods and water sports represented the second largest category, contributing nearly 25 percent of the company total sales, followed by the 15 percent derived from outdoor gear, the 13 percent grossed from the sale of shoes and in-line skates, and the 9 percent contributed by scuba equipment.

The stores by this point were huge, generally containing more than 30,000 square feet each, with one—the Sport Chalet in Marina del Rey—as large as 42,000 square feet. Despite their size, Sport Chalet stores avoided the trappings typically associated with massive retail stores, featuring carpeted floors and standard retail gondolas and fixtures instead of warehouse racking structures and concrete floors. Sport Chalet stores were upscale rather than spartan, and several of the company's largest stores were outfitted with glass-walled pools for scuba and kayaking instruction and promotion.

RARE LOSS IN 1994

Sport Chalet opened two more stores in 1994, one in June in Rancho Cucamonga and another in August in El Cajon, but the continued expansion of the company's retail units was the only bright spot in an otherwise dismal year. For the first time in its history Sport Chalet lost money, generating $122.2 million in sales but posting a loss of $111,127. The recession was partly to blame, but Sport Chalet executives also attributed the loss to an earthquake that temporarily closed five of the company's stores as well as below-average snowfall in Southern California. Sales of winter-related merchandise in Sport Chalet stores fell 8.7 percent during the year, while the company's other merchandise categories registered a 6 percent increase, pinning Sport Chalet's anemic profitability on its dependence on skiing equipment and apparel sales.

In the wake of 1994's loss, Sport Chalet intensified efforts to reduce its reliance on winter-related merchandise, striving to lessen its exposure to the vagaries of snowfall by expanding into other areas such as bicycling and in-line skating. In November 1995, when it opened a store in Irvine, Sport Chalet climbed out of the red and posted $292,000 in net income on $134.7 million in sales, but the return to profitability was short-lived.

In 1996, as Sport Chalet executives were charting the company's course for the future, warm and dry weather contributed to another year of below average snowfall, causing the company's winter-related merchandise sales to plummet 31 percent. As a result, total sales for the company fell 0.7 percent, slipping to $133.7 million, and net income plunged precipitously, cascading to a $1.3 million loss. With these financial totals hanging over company executives, Sport Chalet prepared for the late 1990s, hoping for steady snowfall in the years ahead and a revival of a sluggish California economy.

RECOVERING IN A DUBIOUS ECONOMY

The company posted a $2.3 million net profit in 1997 as sales edged up to $137.7 million. By the end of the year, an "operations whiz" named Craig Levra was recruited from Sports Authority to help the company continue its recovery. Results were swift.

In fiscal 1998 there was a $3.2 million surplus. Revenues were up 4 percent at $143 million. The company then had 1,300 employees. Olberz celebrated the record earnings by giving 300,000 of his own shares to a select group of 109 workers who had been with the company for a decade or more. The stock was then trading at $6, valuing the company at $39 million.

Sport Chalet largely resisted an industry trend toward consolidation led by larger rivals such as Sports Authority, Inc. At the same time, it fared relatively well as its larger competitors suffered in a declining economy.

Though its rate of adding new stores had slowed in the last half of the decade, Sport Chalet grew its revenues about 15 percent to $175.8 million in 2000. Net income was up slightly at $5.5 million. By this time, the company had a market capitalization of about $50 million.

EXPANDING TERRITORY

Sport Chalet ventured out of state for the first time in 2001 by opening a store in Nevada. The company only opened a couple of stores in the diminished economic environment of the following year. However, it did set up a 325,000-square-foot distribution center in Ontario, California. This featured state-of-the-art automation.

By fiscal 2003–04, the company was on the expansion path again, opening five stores. The chain ventured into Northern California, an area known for its rugged, "tree-hugging" populace—and discount sporting goods stores. Sport Chalet was not aiming to compete on price alone, however. The next year, the company was in Central California, following a stream of young, affluent refugees from the state's more expensive coastal zip codes. The first Arizona store opened in 2005.

Some of the growth came from acquisitions. The company acquired John Wells Golf Shops in 2000. Sport Chalet had been leasing the chain sales floor space in 14 of its own stores for four years. John Wells had established his namesake company in 1974. In August 2004 Sport Chalet added Bassco Sporting Goods, a manufacturer of team uniforms for high schools and others.

BUILDING FOR THE FUTURE

The company added a second class of stock in a 2005 recapitalization designed to resolve succession issues. The new "B" shares gave management the bulk of the voting power, while keeping most of the equity with the Olberz family. Norbert Olberz stepped down from his position as chairman emeritus in March 2007. He was 82.

Revenues were up to $309.1 million by fiscal year 2004–05. Net income rose by a third to $6.1 million. Sport Chalet was consistently managing to achieve gross margins of more than 30 percent. By this time, winter sports accounted for roughly one-sixth of total sales, down from one-third a decade before. Sport Chalet slipped into the red in fiscal 2006, thanks to the recapitalization plan. The next year it posted a $7.1 million net profit as sales rose more than 10 percent to $388.2 million.

The company entered Utah in 2007 with a new store in a suburb of Salt Lake City. This was more than a step across the border from existing territory. Utah was renowned for its outdoorsy families, and its capital was home to a number of outdoor industry manufacturers as well as the industry's largest trade shows.

Jeffrey L. Covell
Updated, Frederick C. Ingram

PRINCIPAL COMPETITORS

Recreational Equipment, Inc.; Sports Authority, Inc.; Chick's Sporting Goods, Inc.; Dick's Sporting Goods, Inc.

FURTHER READING

Adamson, Deborah, "Sharing the Wealth; Sport Chalet Chairman Gives Stock to Workers," *Los Angeles Daily News,* June 3, 1998, p. B3.

Belgum, Deborah, "Sport Chalet Founder Sets Up Stock Plan," *Los Angeles Business Journal,* January 6, 2003, p. 9.

Berry, Kate, "Expansion Plans Lift Retailer into View of Larger Investors," *Los Angeles Business Journal,* April 12, 2004, p. 27.

Brooks, Holly, "Looking In on California," *STN,* December 1992, p. 21.

Brown, Rachel, "Unsportsmanlike Conduct," *Los Angeles Business Journal,* August 22, 2005, p. 11.

"CEO Interview: Craig Levra—Sport Chalet, Inc. (SPCH)," *Wall Street Transcript,* July 19, 2004.

Cole, Benjamin Mark, "Sport Chalet Sporting Good Chain Will Take Plunge into Stock Market," *Los Angeles Business Journal,* October 26, 1992, p. 1.

Daniels, Wade, "Independent Sport Chalet Shuns Consolidation Trend," *Los Angeles Business Journal,* November 10, 1997, p. 25.

Darmiento, Laurence, "Sales and Earnings Growth Have Sport Chalet Rolling," *Los Angeles Business Journal,* April 23, 2001, p. 28.

Drickhamer, David, "First Pick," *Material Handling Management,* March 1, 2006, p. 36.

Garcia, Shelly, "Sport Chalet Acquires Firm to Extend Reach Among Team Sports," *San Fernando Valley Business Journal,* August 30, 2004.

Hogan, Donna, "Sport Chalet Gears Up for Arizona Debut," *Mesa (Ariz.) Tribune,* February 4, 2005.

Howard, Beth, "California Skiin'; Company Profile," *SportStyle,* January 1, 1997, p. SS6.

Kerr, John, "Clocking Performance; To Improve Warehouse Labor Productivity, Sport Chalet Pulled Out the Stopwatch, but Instead of Provoking a Backlash, the Time-and-Motion Studies Sparked Fairer Compensation and Higher Productivity Than Ever," *Logistics Management,* April 1, 2007, p. 47.

Lee, Louise, "More Closings in Store for Retailers in '96," *Wall Street Journal,* December 27, 1995, p. 2.

Martinez, Carlos, "Sport Chalet Heads North in Slow, Steady Expansion," *San Fernando Valley Business Journal,* June 9, 2003, p. 7.

Millstein, Marc, "Sport Chalet Improves Inventory Management," *Chain Store Age,* December 1, 2007.

Morse, Dan, "Small Can Be Beautiful for Two Sporting-Goods Retailers," *Wall Street Journal,* November 14, 2000.

Ortiz, Jon, "Retailers Head for Sacramento, Calif., as Demographics Go Young, Upscale," *Sacramento Bee,* August 30, 2004.

Russell, Joel, "Sport Chalet Staying Fit amid Growth and Leadership Challenge," *Los Angeles Business Journal,* September 11, 2006, pp. 5, 59.

Ryan, Thomas J., "Sport Chalet's Olberz Retiring," *Sporting Goods Business,* April 2007, p. 10.

Sims, Burt, "Shows Kick Off Southern California Ski Season," *STN,* January 1994, p. 14.

———, "Sport Chalet Reports Loss," *STN,* October 1994, p. 11.

Smith, Kevin, "Snowfall Heats Up Sporting Sales in California's San Gabriel Valley," *San Gabriel Valley Tribune,* December 21, 2006.

———, "Survey Rates Sport Chalet No. 1," *San Gabriel Valley Tribune,* August 29, 2006.

"Sport Chalet Announces Year End Results," *PR Newswire,* June 7, 1996, p. 60.

"Sport Chalet Execs Adopt Stock Trading Plan," *Sporting Goods Business,* September 16, 2005.

"Sport Chalet Files Public Offering," *Discount Store News,* November 16, 1992, p. 6.

"Stockholders Approve Sport Chalet Recapitalization Plan," *Sporting Goods Business,* September 21, 2005.

Taylor, Debbi, "Sporting Goods Retailer to Enter Utah Market with West Jordan Store," *Salt Lake City Enterprise,* February 12, 2007, p. 1.

Stemilt Growers Inc.

123 Ohme Garden Road
Wenatchee, Washington 98801
U.S.A.
Telephone: (509) 663-1451
Fax: (509) 665-4376
Web site: http://www.stemiltgrowers.com

Private Company
Incorporated: 1964
Employees: 1,600
Sales: $350 million (2007 est.)
NAIC: 115114 Postharvest Crop Activities (Except Cotton Ginning)

■ ■ ■

Stemilt Growers Inc. is the largest fresh-market sweet-cherry shipper in the world; Washington State's largest fruit grower, packer, and shipper for apples, cherries, and pears; and one of the nation's leading tree-fruit growers, packers, and shippers. The company owns five fruit-packing facilities in Washington State and one in Stockton, California. It also owns an orchard management division called Stemilt AgServices and a sliced-apple division called AppleSweets.

THE HOMESTEADING YEARS

In 1893, Thomas Cyle Mathison, an immigrant from Scotland, began homesteading on 160 acres on Stemilt Hill in the area south of Wenatchee, Washington. Although the land was rich and crops grew well, it was covered with sagebrush and bunch grass. Stemilt Creek, five miles away, was Mathison's only source of water. For the next five years, Mathison worked with a shovel and later a plow and team to irrigate and improve the land for cultivation. The high-elevation microclimate of Stemilt Hill offered outstanding growing conditions for fruit trees, and in 1914, he planted the family's first apple, cherry, and pear trees. He continued homesteading until 1922 when he died of pneumonia.

Chris Mathison, Thomas Mathison's son, took over the family's homestead upon his father's death, and lived there with his wife and four children. He almost lost the orchard during the Great Depression, but managed to hold on. When he died in a work-related accident in 1947, his son, third-generation family member Tom Mathison, took on the leadership role for the business, aided by his mother. His brother, Ray, kept the company's books.

BUILDING ADDITIONS AND ACQUISITIONS

The business thrived, but in 1959, its entire cherry harvest yielded a profit of only $89. Tom Mathison then decided to purchase his own equipment, and along with a small group of growers, to build a small fruit warehouse on Stemilt Hill. The 1960s thus became a decade of tremendous strides for the company. In 1960, construction of the first packinghouse on Stemilt Hill was completed, and in 1962, the first box of Stemilt Hill cherries sold at the New York Growers auction. In 1964, Stemilt Growers incorporated and built its first controlled-atmosphere storage room where lowered

COMPANY PERSPECTIVES

No other fruit shipper has orchards located in so many different locations or at so many different elevations as Stemilt Growers. From Central California, to south Central Washington, clear to the Canadian border, Stemilt grows tree fruits in the very best sites to maximize the growing conditions and production microclimates for every variety. That's why Stemilt can specialize in some of the most unique apple, pear, cherry, and stone fruit varieties. We have the locations that count—for all types of fruits.

oxygen levels kept apples from ripening. Also in the 1960s, the company outfitted a trailer park to accommodate the migrant pickers upon whom its harvesting relied.

In 1974, the company built the Olds Station warehouse as its main facility with a controlled-atmosphere storage room and packaging facilities. In 1976, it added more cold storage, and in 1978, began construction of a packaging room, common storage, and loading docks for the Olds Station facility. In 1979, after the addition of an apple pre-size room and two more large controlled atmosphere rooms, as well as an office, the company moved its headquarters from Stemilt Hill to Olds Station.

The company continued to grow through building additions and acquisitions throughout the 1980s. In 1986, Stemilt purchased the Columbia Street plant in downtown Wenatchee, Washington, from Welch Fruit, where it began to pack pears and Golden Delicious apples. About 70 percent of Washington's orchards at the time were planted in Red Delicious apples, with Golden Delicious apples making up another 22 percent.

However, 1987 and 1988 were bad years for Washington's apple industry despite the state's second largest crop on record. Stemilt, along with other growers, suffered two consecutive years of apple losses after the television news magazine *60 Minutes* reported on a claim made by the National Resources Defense Council that apples treated with Alar, a chemical used to help preserve fruit, posed a potential cancer risk to the public. Still, in 1988, Stemilt Growers had the resources to add cherry fumigation equipment, which enabled it to export cherries to Japan. In 1989, it established a research and development department.

NEW INITIATIVES FOR GROWTH

The company also developed in another, related direction in the 1980s. In 1984, it formed Stemilt Management Inc. to provide orchard property management for banks and absentee owners, or those who needed help running their growing operations. Stemilt Management allowed the company an avenue for developing relationships with other growers, which stimulated rapid growth during the first half of the 1990s. Fruit produced by those growers was packaged under the Stemilt name. By 2005, Stemilt Management worked with 75 Washington State orchards.

Also in the later 1980s, Tom Mathison introduced a program called Responsible Choice at Stemilt. This program was intended to focus on the development of sustainable agricultural practices. Sustainable agriculture refers to farming that produces quality products, reduces the use of pesticides, promotes the conservation of natural resources, and contributes positively to the environment and society. Composting, reducing carbon emissions, energy conservation, and water conservation became part of Stemilt's philosophy and practices. The company added a ladybug to the Stemilt logo in 1989, the same year that it began growing organic tree fruits, to represent its commitment to sustainability.

The company's new initiatives continued into the next decade. From 1990 to 1995, Stemilt constructed receiving and storage facilities in Pasco and Quincy, Washington, where it began to process the fruit of other growers in the Columbia Basin. In 1992, it embarked on making juice of Golden Delicious and Granny Smith apples after receiving requests from customers in Taiwan. The juice was made and bottled at Woodring Orchards in Cashmere, Washington. In 1993, Stemilt became a 25 percent partner in the newly formed Green Acres Orchard Partnership when it joined four other Wenatchee fruit-packing plants to buy the largest contiguous apple orchards in the United States, the 1,900-acre Green Acres, from Pacific First Bank of Seattle.

During the early 1990s, the export of fruit to Japan provided new opportunities for Washington growers, who had been seeking for nearly a decade to open the Japanese market to U.S. imports. In 1994, a critical tariff reduction opened the market for Washington State apples to China as well, and the first domestic fresh fruit was shipped commercially to China since 1949. Stemilt, as one of the largest domestic fruit warehousers and packers, played a leadership role in advocating the exportation of fruit to Japan and China.

KEY DATES

1893: Thomas Cyle Mathison begins homesteading on Stemilt Hill in the area south of Wenatchee, Washington.
1914: Mathison plants the family's first apple, cherry, and pear trees.
1922: Chris Mathison, Thomas Mathison's son, takes over the family's homestead upon his father's death.
1947: Chris Mathison dies in a work-related accident; his son, Tom Mathison, takes over the business.
1960: The Mathison family constructs its first packinghouse on Stemilt Hill.
1962: The first box of Stemilt Hill cherries is sold at the New York Growers auction.
1964: Stemilt Growers incorporates.
1974: The company builds the Olds Station warehouse as its main facility.
1979: Stemilt moves its headquarters from Stemilt Hill to Olds Station.
1984: The company forms Stemilt Management Inc.
1986: Stemilt purchases the Columbia Street plant from Welch Fruit.
1993: Stemilt becomes a 25 percent partner in the newly formed Green Acres Orchard partnership.
1997: The Teamsters Union files unfair labor charges against Stemilt with the National Labor Relations Board.
1998: The company acquires Chief Wenatchee.
1999: Stemilt agrees to allow a new union-organizing campaign to take place.
2003: Stemilt partners with Douglas Fruit Co.; the company earns a National Excellence Award from the Produce for Better Health Foundation.

OPPOSITION FROM THE TEAMSTERS UNION

In 1996, Stemilt became embroiled in a different battle closer to home as the United Farm Workers and the International Brotherhood of Teamsters teamed up to organize its workers in the first major campaign involving apple workers in 20 years. Stemilt, with 500 workers and annual revenues of $100 million, became a target of the campaign. Stemilt, for its part, opposed an organized workforce on the grounds that it would raise operating costs in the face of plummeting apple prices. The value of the Washington apple crop had dropped from $1 billion in 1995 to $823 million in 1997.

The unions settled into Wenatchee, holding meetings, rallies, and public protests. Stemilt responded by posting its own information and meeting with employees to deny union claims. After the Teamsters filed unfair-labor charges against Stemilt with the National Labor Relations Board (NLRB) in September 1997, the company agreed to stop posting uniformed guards on catwalks, to purge disciplinary warnings against several workers, and not to suspend other employees for supporting union activities.

Still the battle continued. The Teamsters lost the first union vote in 1998, but immediately challenged the elections. In May, the NLRB filed charges against Stemilt on the grounds that it had threatened, interrogated, and fired workers for organizing. It was on the verge of taking Stemilt to court to declare the union the official winner of the election when Stemilt agreed in May 1999 to allow a new union-organizing campaign to take place. In the vote that September, a slim margin of workers voted in favor of unionizing. By 2001, however, the Teamsters had backed off efforts to organize workers at Stemilt after workers there launched a decertification campaign.

NEW TECHNOLOGY, NEW MARKETING, NEW GROWTH

Meanwhile Stemilt's scope and profits continued to grow. In 1998, it shipped more than 8.6 million boxes of 18 varieties of apples, seven of pears, and five of cherries to 30 nations. The company also acquired Chief Wenatchee, a well-known Washington fruit packaging company. In 1999, Stemilt controlled more than a tenth of the apple industry and a quarter of the cherry industry and had relationships with 200 to 300 small growers in state. Its revenues reached a record $50 million. Stemilt Management, under the direction of David Mathison, managed more than 8,000 acres of producing orchards in Washington State.

The company sought to meet the challenges of the declining apple market as it entered the 21st century. With too many trees of the wrong variety, profit margins were slim for many apple growers around the year 2000. Stemilt responded by turning to new technology, installing a new infrared sorting system, and in 2001, it formed a statewide marketing coop. Apple prices started moving up at the end of 2001, and by 2002, the smallest apple crop since 1988 fetched the highest market prices since 1995.

In 2003, the company was experiencing a growth spurt reflected in its revenues. Its reliance on cherry orchards in Washington and California, where growing seasons overlapped, enabled it to make cherries available for longer periods. Stemilt scaled back its exports, while increasing imports from South America, allowing it to offer fruit during times when it was not available in northern climates. It also joined with Douglas Fruit Co., a leader in apricots, peaches, and nectarines, part of a general move toward consolidation in the packing industry.

Stemilt took over marketing for Douglas and began to provide a larger quantity and variety of produce to retailers. Stemilt also developed its own marketing resources, adding a number of other marketing positions to its ranks. In particular, Stemilt made efforts to promote fresh-fruit consumption and earned the 2003 National Excellence Award from the Produce for Better Health Foundation. In 2005, it again received honors from the same foundation for its work to spread healthful eating practices. By that year, it was shipping 30,000 tons of cherries, 10,000 tons of sweet cherries, and 230,000 tons of apples to customers.

In 2007, the company extended its commitment to encouraging smart food choices through a partnership with Hannaford Supermarkets and Sesame Workshop, the people responsible for Sesame Street, to feature a different variety of Stemilt produce each month along with a Sesame Street character. Wherever the 21st century would take Stemilt, it was clear the company would carry its concern for making fruit an important part of people's diets into the future.

Carrie Rothburd

PRINCIPAL DIVISIONS

Stemilt AgServices; AppleSweets.

PRINCIPAL COMPETITORS

Double S; Doves Fruit Co.; Giumarra Co.; Pacific Organic; Phillippi Fruit Co.; Taplett Fruit.

FURTHER READING

DiBenedetto, William, "U.S. Apple Growers Manage to Take Only Small Bite of Japanese Market," *Journal of Commerce,* June 7, 1996, p. 1A.

Ferrendelli, Betta, "Stemilt Growers Started with a Man and His Shovel," *Puget Sound Business Journal,* November 3, 2000, p. 52.

Freeman, Paul, "Largest 100 Private Companies: Wenatchee's Stemilt Growers Inc., Desire for Fresh Fruit Has Stemilt on Growth Spurt," *Puget Sound Business Journal,* June 20, 2003, p. 60.

Holmes, Stanley, "Packer Settles Labor Claims—Fruit Workers See Boost to Organizing," *Seattle Times,* April 11, 1997, p. A1.

Mapes, Lynda V., "Unionization of Northwest Apple Packinghouse Workers Unravels," *Seattle Times,* December 8, 2001.

Moriwaki, Lee, "Labor Board Accuses Washington State Apple Grower of Union Interference," *Seattle Times,* May 2, 1998.

Ramsey, Bruce, "Fruit Packer Stemilt Settles in Union Cases," *Seattle Post-Intelligencer,* April 11, 1997, p. C4.

———, "Teamsters Claim Win with Packers," *Seattle Post-Intelligencer,* September 17, 1999, p. B1.

Technology Research Corporation

5250 140th Avenue North
Clearwater, Florida 33760
U.S.A.
Telephone: (727) 535-0572
Toll Free: (800) 780-4324
Fax: (727) 535-4828
Web site: http://www.trci.net

Public Company
Incorporated: 1981
Employees: 429
Sales: $38 million (2007)
Stock Exchanges: NASDAQ
Ticker Symbol: TRCI
NAIC: 335313 Switchgear and Switchboard Apparatus Manufacturing

■ ■ ■

Headquartered in Clearwater, Florida, Technology Research Corporation (TRC) is a global designer and manufacturer of portable electrical safety products. Ground fault detection technology, which interrupts the flow of electricity in the event of a short circuit, is at the heart of the company's product range. TRC counts original equipment manufacturers, commercial enterprises, electrical contractors, individual consumers, and the U.S. military among its customer base.

DEFENSE AND COMMERCIAL ORIGINS

TRC was founded by Raymond H. Legatti in June 1981. During the company's early years, producing military generators for the U.S. Department of Defense was the company's bread and butter. However, it also provided ground fault circuit interrupters (GFCI)—which the National Electric Code had mandated for use in public buildings, new homes, and hotels—to the commercial market. GFCI devices protect people from electric shock or electrocution. During the early 1980s, the company also manufactured transformers, computer-related power-line filters, and products that were used for energy management purposes.

For the fiscal year ending in March 1983, TRC reported shipments worth almost $1.8 million. This figure doubled the following year, growing to approximately $4 million. By early 1984 TRC had registered an order backlog of more than $8 million, up from about $3 million in 1983.

On July 18, 1984, TRC offered 1.2 million shares of its common stock to the public at a price of $2.50 per share. Proceeds from the initial public offering were earmarked for the purchase of new equipment, plant expansion, and debt reduction. That same month, Legatti revealed that earnings during the first quarter of the fiscal year totaled $115,245, exceeding the previous year's annual total.

In September 1984, TRC received its largest contract to date when a midwestern manufacturer of military generating equipment signed a purchasing agreement worth approximately $3 million. The

COMPANY PERSPECTIVES

Technology Research Corporation (TRC), founded in June of 1981, is a Florida corporation and is internationally recognized as a leader in the design, manufacture and marketing of portable electrical safety products that save lives, protect people against serious injury from electrical shock and prevent electrical fires in the home and workplace.

contract contributed to a total of $4.3 million in military and commercial contracts received between April and November 1984.

For the fiscal year ending March 31, 1985, TRC's sales increased 34 percent, reaching $5.4 million. However, heavy costs related to the development of a new GFCI device resulted in a net loss of $264,895. The good news was that the company's new product had garnered four royalty license agreements from companies in the United States, Italy, England, and France. By mid-1985 a new offshore manufacturing facility was in place, as a means to reduce order backlog and boost profits.

ENTRY INTO THE CONSUMER MARKET

Development and marketing costs continued to put a clamp on TRC's financials in 1986. That year, revenues fell to $4.8 million and the company's net loss totaled $538,332. While this was a setback, new royalty income was expected to have a positive impact on the company's bottom line later in the decade. It also was in 1986 that TRC began expanding into the consumer market for GFCI devices. In fact, the company began marketing its GFCI products on cable television's Home Shopping Network late in the year.

Several important developments unfolded in 1987. Early in the year Australia's H.P.M. Industries was granted a royalty license to manufacture TRC's GFCI products in Australia, New Zealand, Fiji, and Papua New Guinea. In May, Raymond Legatti received Florida's 1987 Governor's New Product Award for the company's Shock Shield GFCI product. By this time, TRC employed about 165 people. In addition to these developments, the company took part in heavy negotiations over its possible sale throughout the year.

A significant leadership change occurred in March 1988, when Legatti gave up his post as chairman to former Paradyne Corp. executive Robert Wiggins, who also was named CEO. Legatti remained as president, and also assumed the role of chief marketing and engineering officer. TRC rounded out the 1980s by inking a deal with personal care and household appliance maker Windmere Corp., which planned to use the company's GFCI and immersion detection technology in its products.

Growth continued at TRC into the early 1990s. By early 1993 the company employed a workforce of 286 people and was doing better financially. For the fiscal year ending March 31, 1993, revenues totaled $12.87 million, up from $8.19 million in 1992 and $7.40 million in 1990. Net income in 1993 totaled $1.66 million, up from $183,710 in 1992 and a net loss of $849,670 in 1990.

TRC bolstered its international reach in 1993 via a new agreement with the United Kingdom's B&R Electrical Products, an existing licensee, as well as a new deal with Italian personal care products manufacturer Amidic. Driven by strong commercial and military sales, the company ended its 1994 fiscal year with record revenues of $20.49 million.

By 1995 TRC had transferred all of its high-volume manufacturing to Chinese factories owned by Windmere Corp. in an effort to cut costs. This was a key move as the company struggled with weaker military sales. Although TRC's revenues inched up to $21.8 million, profits fell slightly from $2.3 million to $1.9 million. In addition to its offshoring activities, TRC also eliminated 34 jobs in April to further contain costs.

In September 1995 TRC orchestrated a one-for-three reverse stock split that reduced the number of issued and outstanding shares from 15.84 million to 5.28 million. The move enabled the company to move its listing from the NASDAQ Small Cap Market to the NASDAQ National Market that November.

FIRE SHIELD PRODUCT LINE INTRODUCED

In early 1996 TRC unveiled its Fire Shield product line, aimed at preventing fires and electrical shocks from extension cords and electrical appliance cords. That year, the company received what would be the first of many Gold Medals from the Defense Logistics Agency's Defense Supply Center, in recognition of "superior quality and delivery performance," according to a June 21, 1996, *Business Wire* release. TRC rounded out the year by establishing an office in Kanagawa, Japan.

Heading into the late 1990s, TRC continued to increase its focus on the consumer market as sales to the

KEY DATES

1981: TRC is founded by Raymond H. Legatti.
1984: The company offers 1.2 million shares of its common stock to the public.
1995: A one-for-three reverse stock split; TRC's stock moves from the NASDAQ Small Cap Market to the NASDAQ National Market.
2006: Automated Engineering's Recreational Vehicle (RV) product line is acquired in a $678,000 cash and stock deal.

commercial and military markets began to decline. In April 1997 the company began offering its products for sale in retail stores under its own brand name. This was a departure from TRC's previous strategy of making products sold under other companies' nameplates at leading stores such as Lowe's, Sears, and Home Depot.

International expansion continued in 1997 via the formation of a new subsidiary named TRC Honduras, S.A. de C.V. A new plant was developed, providing employment for 127 workers who joined an existing employee base of 152, according to the June 22, 1997, *St. Petersburg Times.* Also of note on the international front was TRC's decision to move away from manufacturing in China at this time.

In 1998 TRC announced a deal to supply Ford Motor Co. with prototype circuits for charging electric vehicles. The company capped off the 1990s with a December 1999 plan to buy back up to 500,000 shares of common stock.

NEW PRODUCTS AND EXPANDED DISTRIBUTION

TRC ushered in the new century by expanding its distribution network. The addition of Consolidated Electrical Distributors, Inc. (CED), enabled the company to market its wares at 531 CED branches, and increased the size of TRC's North American distributor base to 1,200 firms. By this time the company had added the new HD Pro ground fault protector to its product line, as well as a cable protection system named Yellow Jacket.

In the fourth quarter of the 2001 fiscal year, TRC implemented workforce reductions at its facilities in Clearwater, Florida, and Honduras. Increased royalty income and military sales had a positive impact on annual sales, which reached $18.04 million. However, the company still suffered a net loss of $411,547. Late in the fourth quarter Acquisition Search Co., an investment banking firm based in Atlanta, was retained to explore the possible sale of TRC.

New product introductions continued in 2002. That year, the company rolled out Fire Shield, a new line of power strips that blended overload and surge protection with ground fault protection and cord fire prevention technology. The following year, TRC gained a license to market its products under the First Alert brand name via a deal with BRK Brands, Inc.

NEW LEADERSHIP FOR THE 21ST CENTURY

A series of senior-level leadership changes began in 2003, starting when founder and President Raymond Legatti revealed his plans to retire on December 31. In advance of his retirement, Legatti relinquished his president title to Jerry T. Kendall in April and became a senior vice-president for the remainder of his employment, after which time he planned to serve the company in a consulting role. Kendall also was named chief operating officer.

Developments in 2004 included a strategic alliance with Korea's Danam Communications, Inc., in order to promote the inclusion of TRC's Fire Shield cord sets in air conditioners made for the U.S. market. Progress was made on the financial front, with revenues reaching $24.34 million for the year ending March 31. This was an increase from $17.76 million in 2003. Earnings also increased during this period, climbing from $1.42 million to $3.84 million. Midway through 2004, TRC was named to *Fortune* magazine's list of America's 100 fastest-growing companies, ranking 21st.

More leadership changes occurred during the middle of the decade. In August 2004, Jerry Kendall was promoted to president and CEO, with Robert Wiggins remaining as chairman and secretary. Wiggins attempted to end his 17-year career with TRC in March 2005, at which time he retired from full-time employment. Wiggins intended to remain chairman until August. However, an unexpected leadership change occurred that month when Jerry Kendall resigned. Putting his retirement on hold, Wiggins agreed to fill the roles of president and CEO until a replacement could be found.

TRC received a Gold Medal from the Defense Supply Center for the tenth consecutive year in 2005. In April of that year, the company secured the services of Jacksonville, Florida-based Heritage Capital Group for advice on possible acquisition targets. Before this time, the two companies had worked together in the initial stages of acquisition strategy development.

THE RV ACQUISITION: 2006

TRC's acquisition plans bore fruit in April 2006 when the company acquired Automated Engineering's Recreational Vehicle (RV) product line in a $678,000 cash and stock deal that also involved DB Technologies, Inc., and DB shareholder David Bailey.

Wiggins elaborated on the deal in an April 26, 2006, *Business Wire* release, commenting: "This acquisition reinforces our commitment to provide leadership in the RV marketplace for surge and transfer switch products. It also supports our strategy of supplementing our company's internal growth with targeted investments in new technologies that advance our company's leadership position and that provide us both revenue and bottom line growth potential in this estimated $20 to $25 million segment of the RV market."

TRC ended the 2006 fiscal year with record revenues of $45.6 million, up 16 percent from $39.4 million in 2005. Net income rose slightly, reaching $2.1 million. Key investments for the company's future were being made. One element that was expected to have a positive impact on future earnings was the development of a lower-cost technology for room air conditioners.

Owen Farren was chosen as TRC's new president and CEO in January 2007. Farren was founder of a business consulting firm named StratEx, which provided interim executives to companies, and had served as temporary CEO of businesses such as Servometer and American Metal Coatings.

Wiggins retained the chairmanship at TRC until his death at age 78 on November 24, 2007. In the November 27, 2007, *St. Petersburg Times,* columnist Andrew Meacham shed light on Wiggins' character with a story that dated back to his employment at a previous company, writing: "As chief executive of Paradyne, with 3,000 employees beneath him, Mr. Wiggins abolished reserved parking spaces for executives. He parked his 1965 Buick Riviera on the outer edges of the lot, his family said. Board members eventually pressured Mr. Wiggins into driving a late-model company car. However, he never joined a country club and increasingly came to measure his achievements by the miles he walked, ran or bicycled."

Following Wiggins' death, Owen Farren assumed the additional role of chairman. The company moved toward the second decade of the 21st century under new leadership in a highly competitive industry.

Paul R. Greenland

PRINCIPAL SUBSIDIARIES

TRC Honduras, S.A. de C.V.

PRINCIPAL COMPETITORS

American Electric Technologies, Inc.; Littelfuse, Inc.; TII Network Technologies, Inc.

FURTHER READING

Greiff, James, "Paradyne's Past Chief Moves on to Research Firm," *St. Petersburg Times,* March 1, 1988.

Meacham, Andrew, "From His Late 40s on, He Ran Through Life," *St. Petersburg Times,* November 27, 2007.

"Raymond H. Legatti, President and a Founder Announces Intention to Retire from Technology Research Corporation," *Business Wire,* April 17, 2003.

Russo, Catherine M., "Electrical Safety Specialist Battles Sales Drop Shock," *St. Petersburg Times,* June 22, 1997.

"Technology Research Corp.," *Mergent Online,* January 10, 2008, http://www.mergentonline.com.

"Technology Research Corp. Announces Opening of TRC Japan," *Business Wire,* October 2, 1996.

"TRC Awarded Gold Medal by DSCR for Commitment to Quality Performance," *Business Wire,* June 21, 1996.

Technology Solutions Company

55 East Monroe, Suite 2600
Chicago, Illinois 60603
U.S.A.
Telephone: (312) 228-4500
Fax: (312) 228-4501
Web site: http://www.techsol.com

Public Company
Incorporated: 1988
Employees: 168
Sales: $42.6 million (2006)
Stock Exchanges: NASDAQ
Ticker Symbol: TSCC
NAIC: 541512 Computer Systems Design Services

■ ■ ■

Technology Solutions Company (TSC) is a Chicago-based technology consulting firm. Serving *Fortune* 1000 companies in the healthcare, financial services, and manufacturing industries, TSC helps clients solve business problems by blending business expertise with information technology (IT) strategy, planning, and the right computer applications and digital technology. TSC applies its expertise in a wide range of areas, including budgeting, finance, supply chain management, training, and customer relationship management (CRM). TSC's consultants have an average of 18 years of experience, and most have at least a decade of real-world business experience under their belt.

VOLATILE START IN 1988

TSC was formed in May 1988 when partners in the Midwestern Management Consulting Group arm of Arthur Young & Co.—an accounting firm that later became Ernst & Young—decided to establish their own national consultancy to provide both custom and packaged software for companies in the insurance and manufacturing industries.

The new enterprise set up shop in a 3,500-square-foot office on Chicago's North Michigan Avenue and moved forward with ambitious growth plans. Within a few months, TSC planned to have 100 employees. This number was expected to reach between 300 and 400 by 1991, according to the June 20, 1988, issue of *Computerworld.*

The breakaway was volatile from the start, with Arthur Young firing partners Albert D. Beedie, Jr., and Joyce Bennis on May 25 for an alleged breach of their partnership agreement. In the aforementioned issue of *Computerworld,* Arthur Young Vice Chairman John Schornack commented: "We have no objection to their starting a new business. But they all signed a covenant not to take our clients or to take our people."

After Beedie and Bennis were fired, three other Midwest partners resigned, paving the way for 27 other employees to follow suit. On June 9, TSC offered to buy the Midwest group for $50 million. The offer infuriated Arthur Young, which sued Beedie, Bennis, and the other three partners. TSC filed a $15 million countersuit that same month, charging that Arthur Young tried to prevent venture capitalists from funding

COMPANY PERSPECTIVES

From IT or business strategy and project planning to software selection, reengineering, implementation and training, our clients have access to A-team resources at each stage of the engagement. By intersecting our best practices, methodologies and tools with our industry know-how, our experienced teams help clients design and deploy business, process and technology innovation. And we always focus on solutions with measurable value and the transfer of real knowledge to our clients.

TSC and attempted to block an Arthur Young client from going with TSC.

EARLY SUCCESSES 1988–92

With Beedie as president, TSC moved ahead with its plans. Legal entanglements aside, the company found almost immediate financial success. After losses in its first two quarters, TSC began turning a profit. For the fiscal year ending May 31, 1989, TSC generated revenues of $14.7 million and posted earnings of $854,000. The following year, the company's revenues increased to $43.9 million and earnings climbed to $4.3 million.

For the 1990 fiscal year, which ended on May 31, 1991, TSC's finances improved even more, with revenues reaching $52.4 million and earnings growing to $8.5 million. A positive legal development also occurred at this time. The California Superior Court ruled in May that the non-compete clauses the company's employees had signed while with Arthur Young could not prevent them from working for former Arthur Young clients. While the decision was specific to one state, it was important because California often set the legal precedent for other states.

TSC made its initial public offering in September 1991, generating $57 million. A second stock offering followed in February, making millionaires of Albert Beedie ($4 million) and his wife Joyce Bennis ($1.5 million), who sold some of their stock at $25 per share, according to the July 9, 1992, *Chicago Sun-Times.*

In March 1992, TSC ventured into the image processing products arena through a joint marketing tie-up with Filenet Corporation, a Costa Mesa, California-based imaging systems firm. The venture was focused on the consumer products, financial services, and manufacturing industries.

ECONOMIC AND LEGAL TROUBLES 1992

Important leadership changes occurred at TSC in May 1992. At that time Vice-Chairman Melvyn E. Bergstein, another one of the company's founders, succeeded Albert Beedie as president. Beedie, who remained chairman, also began sharing the CEO post with Bergstein. William Waltrip later succeeded Beedie as chairman.

The leadership changes occurred only a few months before a rough period at TSC. In July the company found itself in a difficult position when it was forced to write off $3.6 million in uncollected receivables related to oral agreements with customers. In addition, TSC was trying to collect $8.5 million from Northrop Corp. for a systems integration project that was more than two-thirds complete, but which also was not covered by a written agreement.

On July 2, TSC's stock plunged 50 percent, to $8.75 per share. By Wednesday of the following week shares declined even further, to $7.50. This was a drastic fall from a 52-week high of $30.75. While TSC claimed oral agreements were commonplace in the computer consulting field, the situation prompted shareholders to sue Beedie, Bennis, and eight other TSC employees who had sold them stock in the secondary offering. According to the aforementioned *Chicago Sun-Times* article, the shareholders claimed they "paid 'artificially inflated prices' because the company made 'materially false and misleading statements' about when it booked revenue."

TSC generated revenues of $71 million and earnings of $12.1 million for the fiscal year ending May 1992. While this was good news, the company continued to face legal entanglements. These difficulties led TSC to announce the elimination of 75 to 100 jobs from its aerospace and defense arm. In addition, the company put seven project managers on the hook for $5.3 million of uncollected funds related to the Northrop project.

RESTRUCTURING 1993–94

Conditions within TSC deteriorated in September 1993 when founder Albert Beedie and Melvyn Bergstein were asked to leave as part of a restructuring effort. While Beedie, whose family held 18 percent of TSC's stock, ultimately remained with TSC as a consultant, Bergstein was let go. He subsequently filed a $12.5 million lawsuit against the company in October over an alleged breach of his employment and severance contracts. According

KEY DATES

1988: TSC is formed when partners in the Midwestern Management Consulting Group arm of Arthur Young & Co. decide to establish their own national consultancy.
1991: The company's initial public offering generates $57 million.
1999: TSC's Enterprise Customer Management unit becomes a wholly owned subsidiary named eLoyalty.
2000: eLoyalty is spun off as a separate, publicly traded company.
2007: A new subsidiary named Exogen Solutions LLC is formed to serve healthcare providers and manufacturers.

to the October 11, 1993, issue of *Computer Reseller News,* while TSC said the two were removed from management roles because of "head-butting" that interfered with corporate decision-making, Bergstein countered that he was let go in order to avoid a potential proxy fight from the Beedie family.

By the year's end, the *Chicago Sun-Times* reported that Beedie and Bennis had cashed in all of their TSC stock for $5 million, or just $7.93½ per share, with plans to use the money to buy property in Colorado. Bennis' relatives—brothers Jim and David, and David's wife Roberta—continued to hold about 10 percent of TSC's shares.

By this time, TSC had approximately 300 employees in Chicago, Boston, Dallas, and New York. In mid-1994 the *Chicago Sun-Times* reported that TSC's net income was a mere $35,000 for fiscal year 1994, down from $5.7 million the previous year. In its July 7, 1994, issue, the paper explained that TSC blamed its weak earnings on a "$9.5 million special charge for 1994 for the establishment of significant additional reserves for legal expenses, separation agreements, and other management changes."

NEW PROJECTS, NEW STABILITY 1995

During the mid-1990s TSC reorganized some of its operations. As part of this initiative, the company's consumer products arm was split into new geographic units. On the project front, a number of favorable developments occurred. In 1995 the company worked with the Chicago Board Options Exchange on a $4 million project to install the public automated routing system, which included 18 touch-screen terminals brokers could use to execute orders. The same year TSC secured a network systems development project from the engineering firm UOP.

For the fiscal year ending May 31, 1995, TSC's revenues totaled $64 million. In June, SAP AG named the company as an SAP Alliance Partner, which gave TSC an edge to compete against other consulting firms that were helping corporations transition away from older mainframe computer systems. The following month, a leadership change occurred when TSC named President and Chief Operating Officer John T. Kohler as CEO.

GROWTH AND EXPANSION 1996–98

A significant milestone in TSC's history was reached in March 1996, when the company finally settled the breach of contract lawsuit that Arthur Young & Co. (which by this time was Ernst & Young) had filed in 1988. That same month, the company reached a settlement with former Vice-Chairman Melvyn Bergstein.

After settling the Ernst & Young litigation, TSC embarked upon a period of growth via acquisitions and international expansion. The activity began in when the company established a European subsidiary and a London office in March. Two months later came the acquisition of British call center firm Aspen Consultancy Ltd., followed by the Schaumburg, Illinois-based strategic business consultancy McLaughlin & Associates, which was renamed TSC Strategy Group.

After TSC's common stock split three-for-two in June, a Canadian subsidiary was formed in July, followed by a German subsidiary in December. That month, TSC also established its Change & Learning Technologies business unit. Progress continued in 1997 as TSC Europe (Deutschland) GmbH acquired Geising International in February 1997. That deal was followed by the acquisition of HRM Resources Inc. in March. Three months later, The Bentley Company was acquired in a $17.5 million deal.

REORGANIZING TO BUILD BUSINESS 1998–2002

In February 1998, TSC established an Australian subsidiary. The following August, the company reorganized its operations into three strategic service lines. In addition to a unit that included the company's

European Enterprise Resource Planning and PeopleSoft practices, a new unit was formed that included the company's OrTech subsidiary with its Oracle and Baan practices. Finally, a third unit consisted of TSC's SAP, Change and Learning Technologies, and Enterprise Customer Management arms.

The last year of the decade was filled with important developments. In March TSC announced plans to eliminate 300 jobs as it sought to reduce costs. Three months later, the company transformed its Enterprise Customer Management unit into a new wholly owned subsidiary named eLoyalty. Focused on solutions in the areas of loyalty and customer relationship management, the new business received about $13 million in venture capital funding in August and was spun off as a separate, publicly traded company in February 2000. TSC rounded out the 1990s by acquiring CourseNet Systems Inc. in October for $5.2 million.

TSC began the new millennium with an effort to buy back its common stock. A plan to buy back 3 million shares was approved by the company's board in September 2000, followed by authorizations to repurchase 2 million shares in August 2001 and 3.9 million shares in April 2002.

CHANGING LEADERSHIP 2003–06

In mid-2003 TSC announced that difficult market conditions had caused it to consider strategic alternatives, including a possible merger, joint venture, or even the sale of the entire company. TSC also began planning job cuts and office closures. The company's board approved a plan to refocus the company on the provision of cost-competitive IT services.

Senior leadership changes also were implemented at this time. William H. Waltrip resigned as chairman and was succeeded by John R. Purcell, who was appointed nonexecutive chairman. Stephen B. Oresman was named CEO, succeeding President and CEO Jack Hayden. Responsibility for daily operations was given to an executive committee.

About a year later, more leadership changes occurred. In May 2004, Michael R. Gorsage was named president and CEO, and Stephen Oresman succeeded John Purcell as chairman. New services were introduced in tandem with the leadership changes. A forensics practice named Micronomics Technology Forensics was developed to "provide expert support for technology litigation, arbitration, and mediation in cases involving complex IT systems and projects," according to a May 6, 2004, company news release. Another offering was the introduction of software that could automate complex calculations of multistate use taxes. TSC capped off 2004 with the acquisition of Minneapolis-based software company Zamba Corp. for approximately $5 million.

More top-level leadership changes unfolded at TSC in late 2005, when President and CEO Michael R. Gorsage resigned in December. Carl F. Dill, Jr., the lead director of the TSC's board, was appointed chairman and acting CEO. In March 2006 TSC acquired Charter Consulting Inc. in a $3.8 million cash and stock deal. The following month, Charter Consulting CEO and founding partner David B. Benjamin was named as TSC's president. He held the position briefly, resigning in November, at which time Emageon Inc. President Milton Silva-Craig was named TSC's president and CEO.

FOCUS ON HEALTHCARE 2007–08

Progress during 2007 included growth within TSC's Healthcare Sales Team, as well as the formation of a new subsidiary named Exogen Solutions LLC in December, which was established to offer consulting services to healthcare providers and manufacturers.

In early 2008, Exogen secured a major data migration contract from North Shore–Long Island Jewish Health System, the country's third largest nonprofit secular healthcare system. The project involved the transfer of medical imaging data from the health system's old computer systems to a new system. Medical imaging data can include everything from digitized X-rays and CAT scans to MRIs and PET scans. This deal boded well for TSC's overall success, as well as its activities within the healthcare sector.

Paul R. Greenland

PRINCIPAL SUBSIDIARIES

Exogen Solutions LLC; Technology Solutions Company de Mexico S.A. de C.V.; TSC South America Inc.; TSC Colombia Inc.; TSC Asia Inc.; Technology Solutions Company Brasil Ltda.; TSC Europe (U.K.) Ltd.; TSC Canada Corporation; Zamba Solutions LLC; Zamba Solutions Canada Inc.

PRINCIPAL COMPETITORS

Accenture Ltd.; Computer Sciences Corporation; International Business Machines Corporation.

FURTHER READING

Bozman, Jean S., "Arthur Young Squabble Heats Up," *Computerworld*, June 20, 1988.

Chandler, Susan, "Investor Lawsuit on Stock Hits TSC," *Chicago Sun-Times,* July 9, 1992.

Hedlund, Kristen, "Alleges Breach of Employment—Ex-exec Sues Technology Solutions," *Computer Reseller News,* October 11, 1993.

Knowles, Francine, "TSC Co-founder Cashes In All His Stock for $5 Million," *Chicago Sun-Times,* December 3, 1993.

———, "TSC Sued by Former Vice Chairman," *Chicago Sun-Times,* October 6, 1993.

"New Business Unit Focused on Improving the Experience of Healthcare Providers and Manufacturers," Technology Solutions Co., December 11, 2007, http://www.techsol.com.

"Technology Solutions Company Appoints New CEO, Announces First Quarter Financial Results and Introduces New Service Offerings," Technology Solutions Co., May 5, 2004, http://www.techsol.com.

"TSC Net Falls," *Chicago Sun-Times,* July 7, 1994.

Terra Industries, Inc.

600 Fourth Street
P.O. Box 6000
Sioux City, Iowa 51102
U.S.A.
Telephone: (712) 277-1340
Fax: (712) 233-3648
Web site: http://www.terraindustries.com

Public Company
Incorporated: 1964 as Terra Chemicals International, Inc.
Employees: 1,238
Revenues: $1.8 billion (2006)
Stock Exchanges: New York
Ticker Symbol: TRA
NAIC: 325311 Nitrogenous Fertilizer Manufacturing; 325312 Phosphatic Fertilizer Manufacturing; 325320 Fertilizer and Other Agricultural Chemical Manufacturing

■ ■ ■

Terra Industries, Inc., is one of the largest international producers of nitrogen fertilizer and crop protection products for commercial and industrial agricultural use. Terra's agricultural products fall into seven major categories: anhydrous ammonia, urea ammonium nitrate solutions, ammonium nitrate, granular urea, urea liquor, diesel exhaust treatment, and nitric acid. The company owns and operates five nitrogen product manufacturing locations in the United States and Canada and controls 50 percent interest in nitrogen production facilities in both the Republic of Trinidad and Tobago and the United Kingdom. In 2007, the company reported assets exceeding $1.8 billion and maintained one of the largest nitrogen production businesses in the nation.

EARLY HISTORY: 1964–84

Terra Industry's roots extend to 1964, when Terra Chemicals International, Inc., broke ground for a large nitrogen fertilizer manufacturing complex at Port Neal, Iowa. Initially, Terra distributed its products through a number of small companies in Iowa and Wisconsin and in 1965 the company purchased the Grand Forks Seed Company, which became the company's principal distribution center.

The young company moved quickly to expand its product line and sales territory. By 1967, the Port Neal site was producing sizable amounts of nitrogen-based fertilizer and within a decade the company entered into a joint venture with W.R. Grace and Gulf Oil Chemical Co. to obtain an interest in another fertilizer plant in Woodward, Oklahoma. The Woodward plant developed into one of the company's largest production centers and Terra eventually became the sole owner of the plant after purchasing the rights from W.R. Grace in 1988.

Terra went public in 1974 with its first stock offering. Three years later, bolstered by investment resources, the company was ready for another expansion and decided to purchase the Memphis, Tennessee-based Riverside Chemical Company. The addition of Riverside's 45 farm service centers made Terra one of the nation's largest independent producers and distributors of fertilizer, agricultural chemicals, and seed.

COMPANY PERSPECTIVES

Terra manufactures nitrogen products that farmers need to grow crops that directly or indirectly feed the world. The demand for nitrogen products continually increases as the population grows and rising standards of living increase the demand for more, higher-protein food.

In 1981 Terra became a wholly owned subsidiary of Plateau Holdings, an umbrella company for mining and natural resources, to begin a decade of vastly accelerated growth and diversification. Plateau, which was jointly owned by Minerals and Resources Corporation Limited (Minorco Inc., U.S.A.) and Hudson Bay Mining and Smelting Co., Ltd. (HBMS), created a new company, Inspiration Resources Corporation (IRC), as a holding company for Terra and several other natural resources ventures.

Within two years, a reorganization realigned the corporate chips, making HBMS and Tren International Ltd. (TIL) wholly owned subsidiaries of Inspiration. In 1984 Inspiration traded shares of TIL and Trend Exploration Ltd. (TEL)—formerly one of its wholly owned subsidiaries—with Danville Resources, Inc., which in turn exchanged its shares of TIL and TEL for shares in Madison Resources, Inc. Thus, Terra's parent, Inspiration, ended up holding a 73 percent interest in Madison, including its wholly owned subsidiaries, TIL and TEL. Despite this session of "musical shares" and the diversification of Inspiration into everything from copper mining to ammonia production, the Terra subsidiary continued to focus primarily on agricultural markets.

GROWTH AND FINANCIAL STRAIN: 1984–92

A series of strategic acquisitions, paired with renewed emphasis on aggressive distribution channels, propelled new growth for Terra in the mid-1980s. The company began operating a dry and liquid flowable crop protection formulation facility in Blytheville, Arkansas, in 1984. In 1985 Terra acquired the agricultural products division of Sohio Chemical Company, augmenting its direct sales contact with farm customers through the division's 118 retail farm service centers across Michigan, Ohio, Indiana, Illinois, Missouri, and Kansas. That year, the company also changed its name to Terra International, Inc., in anticipation of broader markets.

As markets for base metals took a beating in the early 1980s, Terra's parent felt the heat. Inspiration suffered consecutive losses of $83 million in 1983 and $101 million in 1984, for example, largely due to sagging copper prices (which adversely affected the company's Consolidated Copper Corp. and Hudson Bay Mining & Smelting Co. Ltd. subsidiaries). A 1985 company report noted that Inspiration was attempting to lessen its dependence on copper by increasing its interests in oil, gas, agricultural, and chemical businesses. This trend spelled good news for Terra, which would benefit from the parent's search for "inspiration" in agribusiness. In a 1986 speech to shareholders, Reuben F. Richards, Inspiration's chairman, said that the corporation's prospects for profitability hinged greatly on the ability of Inspiration Copper to secure substantial labor cost reductions and a strong performance by Terra International's agricultural business.

By the early 1990s, with the base metals market still weighing down on Inspiration's recovery, the company focused its efforts on agribusiness, beginning to divest or discontinue other operations in areas such as mining and base metal refining. In 1990 the company wrote off its equity investment in western Gold Exploration and Mining Co. Limited Partnership (Westgold). That year, Inspiration also discontinued its coal operations. Such divestment continued in August 1991, when Inspiration sold its base metals business, principally its wholly owned subsidiary Hudson Bay Mining and Smelting Co. Ltd., and related metals marketing and trading operations to Minorco (U.S.A.). Within a year, the parent company also sold certain leased rail assets and by 1992 had discontinued the leasing and construction materials businesses as well as equity interests in a copper alloy producer, an undeveloped beryllium mine property, and its gold mining affiliate.

These changes were accompanied by organizational shifts as well. In August 1991, Inspiration named W. Mark Rosenbury as vice-president and chief financial officer of the newly reconstituted company, with its new emphasis on fertilizer and other agribusiness units operated by Terra International, Inc. Terra's ascent was not complete until Inspiration moved its corporate offices from New York to Sioux City, Terra's headquarters, and finally, until IRC's shareholders approved a name change for the parent company to Terra Industries, Inc., in May 1992. The new name recognized Terra's focus on agribusiness with the sale/discontinuation of its natural resources and other businesses. "We have transformed ourselves from a metal and mining company to one of the nation's leading producers and marketers of fertilizers, crop chemicals and seed. Terra, the Latin world for 'land,' has been known and respected for over 25 years

KEY DATES

1964: Company is founded as Terra Chemicals International, Inc.
1965: Grand Forks Seed Co. is purchased.
1974: Company completes its first public stock offering.
1977: Riverside Chemical Company is acquired.
1981: Company is bought out by Plateau Holdings.
1985: Company is renamed Terra International, Inc.
1992: Parent company name is changed to Terra Industries, Inc.
1993: Terra moves into Canada, with manufacturing plant in Ontario.
1999: Company sells its distribution business.
2004: Mississippi Chemical Corporation is acquired.
2007: A joint venture for European expansion is forged with Kemira GrowHow Oyj.

in the agricultural community," President and CEO Burton M. Joyce said at the annual meeting in May 1992. Essentially, the parent company had developed along the lines of its most successful subsidiary.

In 1992 Terra decided to diversify into methanol production, announcing plans on December 1 to begin production of the chemical at its Woodward, Oklahoma, nitrogen fertilizer manufacturing facility. Scheduled for completion in the first quarter of 1994, the $15.5 million project was designed for a capacity of 400 tons of methanol per day, a relatively small production quantity by industry standards. Still, the company focused not on volume but on efficiency, devising a production process by which methanol and ammonia could be processed simultaneously, using synergy to save energy. "Terra will be one of the smallest methanol producers, but likely one of the most efficient," Joyce said in a news release. By diversifying into methanol, while increasing its storage capacity, Terra hoped to reduce the impact of fertilizer market seasonality on its profits, Joyce said.

SHIFTS TO A FOCUS ON PRODUCTION: 1993–99

Terra also moved toward market stability through sheer volume, effecting a virtual explosion of growth in its nitrogen fertilizer business in 1993. With that year's acquisition of ICI Canada's Lambton Works facility near Sarnia, Ontario, Terra increased its nitrogen fertilizer capacity by 50 percent, making it the fourth largest nitrogen solutions producer and the fifth largest anhydrous ammonia producer in North America. The ICI acquisition also included interests in 32 farm service centers, or "Agromarts," in Ontario, New Brunswick, and Nova Scotia.

Terra continued to expand its geographical reach with the 1993 acquisition of the business and most of the assets of Asgrow Florida Company (AFC), a subsidiary of the Upjohn Company and a distributor of fertilizer, crop protection products, and seed to the vegetable and ornamental markets in Florida. Initially operating under the Terra Asgrow Florida name, the combined organization resulted in a broader range of products and services for Florida vegetable, citrus, ornamental, and other growers. For Terra, it marked another new frontier; in 1993 the company announced plans to broaden its agrochemical operations into the Southwest and far West as well.

Such explosive growth in fertilizers was, unfortunately, interrupted by a tragic fertilizer explosion at Terra's Port Neal plant in Iowa in December 1994. The accident took the lives of four employees, injured 19 people, unleashed a cloud of potentially dangerous ammonia gas that caused the evacuation of a nearby town, and rendered the 325,000-ton-a-year plant inoperable for nearly one year.

Terra's Port Neal explosion created shock waves on various fronts, including trading floors. While personnel tried to assess the damage and the cause of the explosion—and whether the plant would reopen—Terra stock plunged, as Terra's main competitors, Cominco Fertilizers Ltd. of Calgary and Chicago-based Vogoro Corp., saw their shares jump in brisk trading.

Tremors from the explosion also shook up investigators and regulatory boards. In January 1995, the Iowa Occupational Safety and Health Administration (IOSHA) filed an affidavit alleging that Terra had hindered inspections of the blast, whereupon Terra filed a court motion disputing the state's charges. By May, the dispute had escalated, with Terra denying IOSHA's allegations that the company hindered inspections and contesting the $460,000 fine that the state agency proposed. Into 1995, the dispute fueled other related disputes in the media, including the extent of federal regulation and oversight in an era when Congress displayed an antiregulatory mood. In 1990 Congress had created a five-member, independent Chemical Safety and Hazard Investigation Board as part of the Clean Air Act amendments. By 1995, the new panel—which would have investigated cases similar to Terra's—had not been sworn in; the Office of Management and Budget made moves to block the panel and transfer its intended responsibilities to the existing U.S.

Environmental Protection Agency and the U.S. Occupational Safety and Health Administration. Thus, the Terra explosion highlighted not only ambiguities regarding that company's safety policies, but those of the federal government as well.

Despite the legal and financial setbacks of the Port Neal explosion, Terra enjoyed a year of solid growth in 1994, reporting a net income of $56.6 million, or 78 cents a share, for the year, compared with net income of $22.8 million for 1993. Despite a $7 million charge in the fourth quarter to cover uninsured costs from the explosion, the company said business interruption insurance and property damage insurance would enable it to rebuild the facility.

Moreover, Terra continued to grow through strategic acquisitions, shooting to the top echelon of North American nitrogen product and methanol production with its 1994 acquisition of Agricultural Minerals and Chemicals Inc. (AMCI). The combination of both companies' production facilities resulted in an annual production capacity of 2.7 million tons of ammonia, of which 1.6 million tons were upgraded into 3.0 million tons of nitrogen solutions, and over 700,000 tons of urea. The combined methanol production capacity of the company reached 320 million gallons a year. To help finance the AMCI acquisition, Terra successfully issued 9.7 million common shares, raising $113 million and immediately adding to earnings per share. "Geographically, these businesses fit well, and operationally we'll realize synergies that will benefit both sides of the business combination," Joyce announced in an October 1994 company news release.

Positioning itself for still wider markets, in June 1994 Terra announced that it had signed a letter of intent to acquire a one-third interest in Royster-Clark, Inc., a farm service distribution network located on the East Coast. The terms of the agreement provided Terra with the option of increasing its ownership position to majority holder within five years. In a June 1994 news release, Joyce said that the new alliance afforded Terra Products growth potential in new markets, such as the East Coast—particularly the Carolinas—where Royster-Clark had a strong presence.

These new markets laid a fertile groundwork for Terra's continued growth into the 21st century. Moreover, the methanol market, which the company had entered in 1992, showed particular promise as requirements of the Clean Air Act caused gasoline producers to build inventories of methanol for use in formulating methyl-tertiary-butyl-ether (MTBE), a clean-burning fuel additive, in anticipation of increased demand.

In 1997, Terra expanded into the United Kingdom by purchasing two nitrogen fertilizer plants, one in Billingham and one in Severnside. The company also expanded its operations with new ammonia processing facilities at its Beaumont, Texas, location and a reconstructed, higher-capacity nitrogen production facility at Port Neal.

Over the next three years, the company endured a financial slump that convinced management to reorganize its growth strategy. In 1999, the decision was made to sell the company's distribution facilities, including approximately 400 farm service centers, to Cenex/Land O'Lakes Agronomy Company. With the sale, reported at over $390 million, the company left the farm supply business and reorganized its operations to concentrate on chemical production and sale. In company press releases, Terra said that portions of the sale would be used to pay down debt and to enhance the company's chemical manufacturing activities.

TERRA INDUSTRIES IN THE 21ST CENTURY

In 2001, Terra's board of directors named Michael L. Bennett as president and chief executive officer. Bennett began his career with Terra in 1973 as an operations technician at the company's Port Neal plant and worked his way through the company's management structure to the position of senior vice-president, which he assumed in 1997. Under Bennett's leadership, the company further streamlined its management structure, reorganizing job responsibilities and reducing the company's board of directors from 11 to seven members.

The shifting price of nitrogen and the company's other chemical products made it difficult for Terra to achieve growth. The company reported losses in 2000, 2001, 2002, and 2003, with the highest loss coming in 2002 at a reported $258 million. In response to declining dividends, the company decided in March 2004 to close their Blytheville, Arkansas, location. Bennett explained the closure in the company's press releases, saying: "We decided to permanently close our Blytheville production plants because of continuing high natural gas costs, the upcoming lull in off-season nitrogen markets and the likelihood that competition from imported ammonia and urea barged up the Mississippi River will make future major maintenance and capital investments at the Blytheville facility unsound." Although a number of Blytheville employees lost their jobs due to the closure, company management announced that they would help to find job opportunities for as many employees as possible. That same year, Terra was forced to "mothball" its Beaumont, Texas, facility, which had been operated under the terms of a five-year lease to Methenex Corporation since 2003. Approximately 40 employees were released from the Beaumont facility. As the company's financial difficulties continued, further closures were announced, including the 2005 closure of the company's Woodward, Oklahoma, location, which had previously been one of the company's largest production facilities.

In August 2004, Terra finalized a deal to purchase Mississippi Chemical Corporation, a company that had been under Chapter 11 bankruptcy, for a reported price of $268 million. With the acquisition, Terra strengthened its production and distribution capabilities and gained facilities in Houston, Texas, and Donaldsville, Louisiana. "This transaction creates a strong platform for improved efficiency and future growth," Bennett stated in an official press release, adding that the acquisition was an important step in increasing the company's sources for natural gas.

In 2007, Terra completed an agreement with Kemira GrowHow Oyj to enter into a joint venture processing and production facility in the United Kingdom. Negotiations for the deal began in 2006 and the venture was approved by stockholders in September 2007. The joint venture would combine the two companies' operations in the United Kingdom and Ireland and significantly enhance financial prospects for both companies. Kemira, one of Europe's largest producers of feed phosphates and fertilizers, had sales in 2006 of EUR 1.2 billion. Together with GrowHow, Terra would control over 40 percent of the fertilizer market in the United Kingdom. Terra's other international ventures included 50 percent ownership in a plant at Point Lisas in the Republic of Trinidad and Tobago.

While Terra's financial difficulties continued, the company's revenues increased slowly in the period from 2004 to 2007, with 2005 marking a 75 percent increase in revenues over the previous year. Although the company again posted minor losses in 2006, growth from international ventures was expected to reinvigorate the company through the remainder of the decade.

Kerstan Cohen
Updated, Micah L. Issitt

PRINCIPAL SUBSIDIARIES

Terra Nitrogen Company L. P.; GrowHow UK Ltd.; Point Lisas Nitrogen, Ltd.

PRINCIPAL COMPETITORS

PotashCorp; CF Industries, Inc.; Agrium, Inc.

FURTHER READING

Beeman, Perry, "Bumpy Ride for Terra Probe," *Des Moines Register,* January 22, 1995, p. G1.

"Blast Hits Terra Plant in U.K.," *Chemical Week,* May 31, 2006.

Hendee, David, "Iowa Says Terra Isn't Cooperating; Firm Denies Slowing Probe of Plant," *Omaha World Herald,* January 7, 1995, p. 1.

———, "Terra to Expand Through Global Sales," *Omaha World Herald,* May 3, 1995.

Jordan, Carol L., "Profit Prospects Hinge in Agri, Copper Businesses: Inspiration," *American Metal Market,* May 16, 1986, p. 5.

"Kemira GrowHow Oyj and Terra Industries, Inc., Confirm Formation of Joint Venture," *Nordic Business Report,* September 14, 2007.

Munford, Christopher, "Inspiration to Cut Costs, Staff; Consolidation Under Way After Sizable 2nd-Quarter Loss," *American Metal Market,* August 16, 1991, p. 2.

"Terra, CF Industries Join Forces in Trinidad Project," *Chemical Week,* April 27, 2005.

"Terra, GrowHow Merge in U.K," *Chemical Week,* October 25, 2006.

"Terra Industries Acquires Mississippi Chemical," *New York Times,* August 8, 2007, p. C4.

"Terra Industries, Inc., to Acquire Mississippi Chemical Corp. for 0.24 Times Revenue," *Weekly Corporate Growth Report,* August 16, 2004, p. 3.

"Terra Industries to Sell Agricultural Line to Distribution Firm," *Wall Street Journal,* May 4, 1999, p. 6.

United Parcel Service, Inc.

55 Glenlake Parkway NE
Atlanta, Georgia 30328
U.S.A.
Telephone: (404) 828-6000
Toll Free: (800) 742-5877
Fax: (404) 828-6562
Web site: http://www.ups.com

Public Company
Incorporated: 1907 as American Messenger Company
Employees: 428,000
Sales: $47.55 billion (2006)
Stock Exchanges: New York
Ticker Symbol: UPS
NAIC: 484122 General Freight Trucking, Long-Distance, Less Than Truckload; 492110 Couriers; 522220 Sales Financing

■ ■ ■

Known in the industry as "Big Brown," United Parcel Service, Inc. (UPS), is the world's largest package-delivery company. The Atlanta-based business delivered nearly seven billion items throughout more than 200 countries in 2006. In addition to its fleet of 101,000 vehicles, the company operates the world's eighth largest airline by virtue of its more than 600 company-owned and chartered aircraft. Its main hubs are in Louisville, Kentucky; Cologne, Germany; and the Philippines. UPS's embrace of technology has positioned it for a central position in the world of e-commerce. Numerous acquisitions expanded its capabilities in handling flows of "goods, funds, information." UPS even bought a bank, allowing it to finance small business transactions related to the merchandise it delivers.

EARLY 20TH-CENTURY ROOTS

UPS was founded in 1907 in Seattle, Washington, by 19-year-old Jim Casey as a six-bicycle messenger service. He set the future tone of the company by mandating that it be employee-owned. Casey delivered telegraph messages and hot lunches and sometimes took odd jobs to keep his struggling business going. By 1913 UPS consisted of seven motorcycles. With Casey's tacit approval, UPS drivers joined the International Brotherhood of Teamsters in 1916. In 1918 three Seattle department stores hired the service to deliver merchandise to purchasers on the day of the purchase. Department store deliveries remained the center of UPS's business until the late 1940s.

In 1929 UPS began air delivery through a new division, United Air Express, which put packages onto passenger planes. The Great Depression ended plans for an overnight air service, and UPS terminated United Air Express in 1931; the company did not resume air service until the 1950s. In the late 1940s the urban department stores that UPS serviced began following their clients to the new suburbs. More people owned cars and picked up their own parcels. UPS's revenue declined.

Casey decided to change direction and expand the common-carrier parcel business, picking up parcels from anyone and taking them to anyone else, charging a fixed rate per parcel. The company's initial customers were primarily industrial and commercial shippers, although

COMPANY PERSPECTIVES

As the world's largest package delivery company and a leading global provider of specialized transportation and logistics services, UPS continues to develop the frontiers of logistics, supply chain management, and e-Commerce ... combining the flows of goods, information, and funds.

the firm also served consumers. The company had offered common-carrier service in Los Angeles since 1922, and in 1953 UPS extended it to San Francisco, Chicago, and New York. UPS delivered any package meeting weight and size requirements to any location within 150 miles of these bases. After this initial expansion, UPS frequently appeared before the Interstate Commerce Commission (ICC) to expand its operating rights.

UPS scaled its operations to fit its market niche, refusing packages weighing more than 50 pounds or with a combined length and width of more than 108 inches, limitations that would increase in concert with the company's capabilities. Its average package weighed about ten pounds and was roughly the size of a briefcase, making sorting and carrying easy. UPS competed with scores of regional firms but most had not limited the size and weight of their packages. They ended up with the heavier packages, higher overheads, and lower volumes.

THE SECOND GENERATION OF LEADERSHIP

Casey resigned as chief executive officer in 1962 and was succeeded by George D. Smith. UPS more than doubled its sales and profits between 1964 and 1969, when the company made $31.9 million on sales of about $548 million. The company remained privately owned, its stock held by several hundred of its executives. UPS in 1969 served 31 states on the East and West Coasts. It had just gotten ICC approval to add nine midwestern states and soon got approval for three more states. Only the lightly populated states of Arizona, Alaska, Hawaii, Idaho, Montana, Nevada, and Utah were without UPS service. The firm kept a low profile, avoiding publicity, and refusing interviews of its chief executives. UPS officials believed only one parcel shipping company could exist in the United States, and it hoped that keeping a low profile would prevent anyone from copying its methods.

The firm's secrecy policy was possible because it was closely held. Its 3,700 stockholders (a number raised to 23,000 by 1991) were its own top and middle managers and their families. Stockholders wanting to divest would sell their stock back to the company. Because management owned UPS, the company could make long-range plans without the pressure for instant profits faced by many publicly owned firms. Most managers started as UPS drivers or sorters and came up through the ranks, creating great loyalty. The company's management structure was relatively informal, stressing partnership and the involvement of management at all levels.

In 1970 Congress considered a reform of the U.S. Postal Service that would allow it to subsidize its parcel post operations with profits from its first-class mail. This would allow it to lower prices and compete more directly with UPS. UPS hired a public relations firm and for the first time officially announced its earnings, trying to build a case that it was an integral part of the U.S. economy and that the postal reform would be disruptive. UPS handled 500 million packages in 1969, for 165,000 regular customers. The company claimed that 95 percent of all deliveries within 150 miles were delivered overnight. The company centered operations around a five-day-a-week cycle. Drivers made deliveries in the morning, made pickups in the afternoon, and returned to operations centers around 6 P.M. Their packages were immediately sorted and transferred for delivery.

UPS trucks were painted brown to avoid showing soil and were cleaned every night. Trucks were assigned to specific drivers, whom the company treated as future managers and owners. The company had 22,000 drivers in 1969, and most were kept on the same route to develop a relationship with customers. Some drivers, however, found UPS management inflexible, resulting in occasional local strikes.

In 1976 UPS tried to replace, gradually, all of its full-time employees who sorted and handled packages at warehouses with part-time workers. Teamsters locals in the South, Midwest, and West accepted the idea, but 17,000 UPS employees from Maine to South Carolina went on strike. The strike caused chaos for East Coast retailers as their suppliers were forced to send Christmas goods through the overburdened U.S. Postal Service. UPS eventually reached agreement with the Teamsters, but its labor relations continued to be spotty. Because management owned the business, it tended to drive its employees hard, and many drivers complained of the long hours and hard work. To maximize driver performance, the company kept records of the production of every driver and sorter and compared them to its

KEY DATES

1907: Jim Casey forms a Seattle bike delivery service called American Messenger Company.
1922: UPS begins operating a common carrier service in Los Angeles.
1953: Common carrier service is extended to San Francisco, Chicago, and New York.
1969: Revenues exceed $500 million; UPS handles 500 million packages.
1976: UPS launches service in Germany.
1981: Second-day air service launches to compete with Federal Express.
1987: Revenues reach $10 billion.
1991: Headquarters is relocated to Atlanta, Georgia.
1997: UPS endures its first national labor strike when drivers walk out for 15 days.
1998: UPS Capital Corporation adds a financial dimension to the business.
1999: Initial public offering on the Big Board takes in $5.5 billion for future expansion.
2001: UPS buys Mail Boxes Etc., gaining a chain of retail shipping stores.
2004: Addition of Menlo Worldwide Forwarding adds heavy air freight capabilities.
2005: Purchase of Overnite Corporation bolsters ground freight services.
2007: After 100 years in business, UPS has sales of about $50 billion and roughly 450,000 employees.

performance projections. Drivers' routes were timed in great detail.

In 1976 UPS launched service in Germany with 120 delivery vans. It quickly ran into trouble because of cultural and language differences. UPS eventually adapted by hiring some German managers and accepting the German dislike of working overtime. George C. Lamb, Jr., succeeded Harold Oberkotter as UPS chairman in 1980.

COMPETITION INTENSIFIES

UPS continued to grow rapidly, aided by trucking deregulation in 1980. By 1980 UPS earned $189 million on revenues of $4 billion, shipping 1.5 billion packages. Federal Express Corporation (FedEx), however, which began operations in 1973, was siphoning off a growing amount of UPS's business. FedEx shipped packages overnight by air, and many businesses began shipping high-priority packages with FedEx. UPS had the resources to challenge FedEx, but it meant taking on significant debt, something the conservatively run UPS was reluctant to do. In 1981 it had only $7 million in long-term debt and a net worth of $750 million. To compete with FedEx, UPS bought nine used 727 airplanes in 1981 from Braniff Airlines for $28 million. It opened an air hub in Louisville, Kentucky, but was hesitant about directly challenging FedEx because of the huge cost of building an air fleet. It decided to stick with two-day delivery rather than overnight delivery, hoping that many businesses would be willing to let packages take an extra day if it meant savings of up to 70 percent. It called its two-day delivery Blue Label Air and spent $1 million in 1981 to promote it—a large sum for UPS, which had rarely advertised. In 1982 UPS ran its first television ads, trying to convince executives that two-day service was fast enough for most packages.

The recession of the early 1980s helped UPS because many companies shifted to smaller inventories, shipping smaller lots more frequently and demanding greater reliability. Package volume grew 6 percent in 1981. Because of the recession, the Teamsters accepted a contract in 1982 that limited wage increases to a cost-of-living adjustment, which then was diverted to pay the increased cost of medical benefits. When UPS then released information showing its net income rose 74 percent in 1981, labor relations worsened. Bitterness continued between UPS management and drivers as company profits swelled 48 percent to $490 million in 1983. UPS and the Teamsters secretly negotiated for two months in 1984 and reached a three-year agreement providing for bonuses and increased wages. The move averted a probable strike by 90,000 employees. Despite this labor tension, UPS's employee turnover remained remarkably low at 4 percent. Many workers were recruited as part-time employees while college students and were offered full-time positions after graduation.

In 1982 UPS decided to offer overnight air service, charging about half of FedEx's rate. By 1983 its second-day and next-day services were shipping a combined 140,000 packages a day. In 1982 UPS earned $332 million on $5.2 billion in sales. It had a fleet of more than 62,000 trucks. Mail-order firms and catalog houses were the fastest-growing part of UPS's business. Jack Rogers became UPS chairman in 1984.

Despite labor troubles, a *Fortune* survey found UPS's reputation the highest in its industry every year from 1984 to 1991. It was by far the most profitable U.S. transportation company, making more than $700 million in 1987 on revenue of $10 billion. FedEx, however, had 57 percent of the rapidly growing overnight package business; UPS had only 15 percent. FedEx was highly automated and used electronics to track packages en route and to perform other services. UPS still did most jobs manually, but was rapidly switching to the use of electronic scanners at its sorting centers and to computers on its trucks. UPS introduced technology methodically, buying a software firm and a computer design shop to create the necessary equipment. It then field-tested its new gear at a 35-car messenger service it owned in Los Angeles. It launched a $1.5 billion five-year computerization project, trying to create a system that tracked packages door-to-door, which FedEx was doing already. UPS's healthy river of cash flow enabled it to pay $1.8 billion for 110 aircraft in 1987. The purchase made it the tenth largest U.S. airline. The company launched its first wide-range television advertising campaign in 1988, spending $35 million to publicize the slogan, "We run the tightest ship in the shipping business." Despite these expenses, the company still had only $114 million in long-term debt and continued to finance large projects out of its cash flow.

By 1988 UPS's ground service was growing 7 to 8 percent per year, and air service was growing 30 percent per year. UPS handled 2.3 billion packages per year, compared with 1.4 billion for the U.S. Postal Service. The 300-plane fleet of the UPS overnight service handled 600,000 parcels and documents per day, making $350 million on $2.2 billion in sales in 1988. UPS continued building an overseas air network, but in West Germany, where it had 6,000 employees, it delivered only on the ground. The company shipped eight million packages overseas in 1988, losing $20 million in the process. UPS bought its Italian partner, Alimondo, in 1988, hoping to use it and its German base to expand through Europe. The company also bought nine small European courier companies to expand air service. Its overseas acquisitions cost UPS less than $100 million. UPS and rival FedEx both were losing money on overseas operations, but UPS had an advantage: FedEx could not match its $6.5 billion in assets and $480 million in cash with minimal debt. UPS hoped this would give it greater staying power as the two companies struggled to build a global delivery network. Meanwhile, UPS slowly won some FedEx customers by giving volume discounts, which it previously had refused to do. The overseas shipping war escalated as FedEx bought Tiger International, Inc., a major international shipper that UPS used for some of its foreign deliveries.

INVIGORATING NEW LEADERSHIP

Kent C. Nelson succeeded Jack Rogers as chairman and CEO in 1989. Nicknamed "Oz" for 1940s-era band leader Ozzie Nelson, the 52-year-old had spent his entire working life at UPS, starting with the company only two days after graduating from college. The new leader undertook a gradual, but complete transformation of UPS that extended from its innermost workings to its public image.

Challenged by competitors large and small, UPS launched a plethora of new services in the early 1990s. These ranged from timed and same-day deliveries to less expensive two- and three-day services. The company's Worldwide Logistics subsidiary offered clients everything from inventory management to warehousing and, of course, delivery. Powerful and costly technical systems, often developed internally by a 4,000-member staff, backed up these expanded operations. UPS's DIAD (delivery information acquisition device), for example, combined a bar-code scanner, electronic signature capture, and cellular tracking network in a single hand-held tool. By 1992, the corporation was investing more money in computers than in ubiquitous brown vehicles. These internal changes reflected the company's traditional focus on super-efficiency as well as its new-found emphasis on customer satisfaction.

In contrast to its secretive early years, the UPS of the 1990s was a bold global marketer. The company embarked on the largest advertising campaign in its history in 1996, spending an estimated $100 million in conjunction with its sponsorship of the Centennial Olympics held in Atlanta, Georgia (which, not coincidentally, had become UPS's headquarters in 1991). UPS hoped that the worldwide recognition enjoyed by the Olympic rings would rub off on its brown trucks, which were not well known outside the United States.

That recognition was vital to the success of UPS's international operations, which continued to lose money into the mid-1990s. By 1995, in fact, losses on the company's European venture totaled nearly $1 billion. Nevertheless, backed by its patient and confident employee/stockholders and a hefty bank account, UPS was able to wait out publicly held FedEx, which had limited its European service to intercontinental deliveries by mid-decade. In stark contrast, UPS had expanded its international network to include 200 countries and territories worldwide. Undaunted by its massive losses, UPS announced plans to invest more than $1 billion in its European operations from 1995 to 2000, and it infused another $130 million into its Asian operations. The company hoped to profit on its piece of the $25 billion European parcel post market by the end of the century.

This global push fueled a 69 percent increase in sales over the course of Kent Nelson's first six years at the helm of UPS. At the same time, however, it played a significant role in the reduction of the company's overall profit margin from 8 percent in 1987 to 4.8 percent in 1995. As the company approached its ninetieth anniversary in 1997, it looked forward to reaping the rewards of its global investment.

A DECADE OF TRANSFORMATION: 1997–2007

UPS's ninetieth anniversary year was notable for labor unrest. In spite of its much vaunted human resources culture and employee ownership, UPS endured its first nationwide strike in 1997. The 15-day walkout by the Teamsters, protesting stagnant wages and working conditions, cost UPS an estimated $200 million to $700 million in lost business and goodwill. The pilots' union then capitalized on the moment by threatening a disruption in order to secure increases to its own members' salaries.

The impact on corporate profits proved relatively short-lived, and Big Brown was soon raking in big green again. While revenues stalled at $24.5 billion in 1997, they then began a steady climb to nearly $30 billion by 2000. Net profit was less consistent, but reached $2.9 billion in 2000. By this time, there were 359,000 employees.

"GOODS, FUNDS, INFORMATION"

While there were many doubts about in the Internet bubble, shipping companies seemed poised to develop from any growth in e-commerce. In this environment, UPS went public on November 10, 1999, gaining funds for acquisitions. The offering of about 9 percent of shares raised $5.5 billion and valued the company at more than $60 billion. UPS was undergoing a transformation from a simple shipper to a facilitator of global commerce, insinuating itself into the three flows that made up trade: "goods, funds, information."

UPS dipped into the "funds" part of the equation by creating UPS Capital Corporation in 1998. Three years later, it acquired First International Bank for $78 million in stock. The financial aspect brought UPS into such helpful activities as collecting payments and providing letters of credit and small business loans.

The company's logistics support business, or supply chain services, was another area of particular attention. A buying spree launched in the late 1990s built this up through the purchase of 20 companies that expand its capabilities as well as its hauling capacity. Fritz Companies, added in 2001 in a $437 million stock swap, was one of the bigger acquisitions. Fritz provided a global freight forwarding service, allowing UPS to ship a wide range of freight to all parts of the world.

The 2002 acquisition of Challenge Air Cargo Inc. boosted shipping capabilities in South America. However, the company felt Europe and Asia showed more promise for growth. The latter offered plenty of potential, but the sparse transportation network there favored air service. After operating a base in Taiwan, in 2003 UPS opened a new intra-Asia hub at Clark Air Force Base in the Philippines. This was expanded within a couple of years.

UPS continued to build its freight capabilities through acquisitions. It bought heavy air freight specialist Menlo Worldwide Forwarding Inc. at the end of 2004. UPS closed Menlo's Dayton, Ohio, facility in 2006, integrating the operations with other UPS facilities. The 2005 acquisition of Overnite Corporation added less-than-truckload ground freight capacity. Overnite was soon rebranded UPS Freight.

NEW SPIN ON AN OLD BRAND

In early 2001, UPS acquired Mail Boxes Etc. from U.S. Office Products Co. for $191 million. This gave the shipper a retail presence through a chain of more than 4,000 units that soon began doing business as "The UPS Store." UPS aimed not only to make its services more accessible to residential and small business customers, but to increase overall brand awareness.

In 2002 its priciest ad campaign to date asked "What can Brown do for you?" The next year the company began referring to itself by its initials instead of the full "United Parcel Service." It also modernized the 40-year-old shield logo, doing away with the strings and bow that were a hindrance to automated sorting machinery anyway. The old design did not apply to the new UPS, which was involved in much more than shipping. For example, the UPS Supply Chain Solutions could provide merchants with call center or warehousing support.

2007 CENTENNIAL

Total revenues climbed from $31.3 billion in 2002 to $47.6 billion in 2006. Net income grew less quickly, remaining at the $3 billion level from 2002 to 2004 but reaching $4.2 billion in 2006. The company was on its way to reaching the $50 billion figure by its 100th anniversary, as the headcount approached a staggering 450,000 employees.

In its first 100 years, the company had only had nine chief executives. James P. Kelly became the company's chairman and CEO in 1997. He was succeeded by former Vice-Chairman Michael Eskew in 2002.

The still-growing giant had seen tremendous change over the previous decade in particular. Not only had the company entered a wide array of new ventures, but it had substantially reworked its financial underpinnings. Privately owned since its first days, Big Brown was trading shares on the Big Board, and had taken on billions in debt.

Scott M. Lewis
Updated, April Dougal Gasbarre; Frederick C. Ingram

PRINCIPAL SUBSIDIARIES

United Parcel Service of America, Inc.; United Parcel Service General Services Co.; United Parcel Service Co.; UPS Worldwide Forwarding, Inc.; United Parcel Service, Inc. (Ohio); United Parcel Service, Inc. (New York); UPICO Corporation; UPS Supply Chain Solutions, Inc.; UPS International, Inc.; United Parcel Service Deutschland Inc. (USA); Overnite Corporation; UPS Capital Corporation.

PRINCIPAL OPERATING UNITS

The UPS Store; UPS Air Cargo; UPS Capital; UPS Consulting; UPS Freight; UPS Logistics Technologies; UPS Mail Innovations; UPS Professional Services; UPS Supply Chain Solutions.

PRINCIPAL COMPETITORS

FedEx Corporation; United States Postal Service; Deutsche Post AG.

FURTHER READING

Barron, Kelly, "Logistics in Brown," *Forbes,* January 10, 2000, p. 78.

"Behind the UPS Mystique: Puritanism and Productivity," *Business Week,* June 6, 1983.

Birger, Jon, "A Big Question for Big Brown: How Can UPS Grow When It Operates Almost Everywhere?" *Money,* June 1, 2002, p. 49.

Bonney, Joseph, "UPS Bets a Billion," *American Shipper,* January 1993, p. 26.

Brewster, Mike, and Frederick Dalzell, *Driving Change: The UPS Approach to Business,* New York: Hyperion, 2007.

Day, Charles R., Jr., "Shape Up and Ship Out," *Industry Week,* February 6, 1995, pp. 14, 17–20.

Decler, K., et al., "United Parcel Service and the Management of Change," *Business Week,* May 21, 2001.

"Delivering in Tough Times: Under CEO Mike Eskew, UPS, the Venerable Package Deliverer, Goes Global and High Tech," *Chief Executive* (U.S.), March 2003, p. 32.

Donnelly, Sally B., and Greg Fulton, "Out of the Box: UPS Still Delivers Packages, of Course, but It's Also Helping Firms Like Nike and Toshiba Assemble, Store and Repair Products. Who Knew?" *Time,* November 8, 2004, p. A2.

Duffy, Caroline A., "UPS Toes the Line with Its Package-Tracking Technologies," *PC Week,* June 28, 1993, p. 211.

Gillam, Carey, "Delivering the Dream," *Sales & Marketing Management,* June 1996, pp. 74–78.

Gillespie, Andrew, "UPS," *Business Review* (U.K.), February 2002, p. 5.

Gilpin, Kenneth N., "U.P.S. Initial Public Offering Raises $5.47 Billion," *New York Times,* November 10, 1999.

Greenwald, John, "Hauling UPS's Freight," *Time,* January 29, 1996, p. 59.

Harrison, Joan, "Making It Fit: Culture Clash and Other Issues Plague FedEx and UPS Years After Their Respective Jumps into Retail," *Mergers & Acquisitions: The Dealmaker's Journal,* October 1, 2007.

Hosea, Maeve, "Case Study—UPS: Brand Deliverance," *Brand Strategy,* November 6, 2006, p. 20.

"James E. Casey," *Puget Sound Business Journal,* April 2, 1993, p. 2A.

LaGesse, David, "Big Brown," *U.S. News & World Report,* July 31, 2006, p. 52.

Lyne, Jack, "UPS COO Jim Kelly: Bold Days for 'Big Brown,'" *Site Selection,* August 1995, pp. 53–54.

Madden, Stephen J., "Big Changes at Big Brown," *Fortune,* January 18, 1988.

Minahan, Tim, "UPS Strike Makes Shippers More Cautious, Strategic," *Purchasing,* October 23, 1997, p. 105.

Niemann, Greg, *Big Brown: The Untold Story of UPS,* San Francisco: Jossey-Bass, 2007.

"The Quiet Giant of Shipping," *Forbes,* January 15, 1970.

Walker, Karen, "Brown Is Beautiful," *Airline Business,* November 1997, p. 46.

"Why United Parcel Admits Its Size," *Business Week,* July 18, 1970.

"The Wizard Is Oz," *Chief Executive* (U.S.), March 1994, pp. 40–43.

Valhi, Inc.

Three Lincoln Centre
5430 LBJ Freeway, Suite 1700
Dallas, Texas 75240-2697
U.S.A.
Telephone: (972) 233-1700
Fax: (972) 448-1445
Web site: http://www.valhi.net

Wholly Owned Subsidiary of Contran Corporation
Incorporated: 1932
Employees: 7,950
Sales: $1.67 billion (2006)
Stock Exchanges: New York
Ticker Symbol: VHI
NAIC: 325131 Inorganic Dye and Pigment Manufacturing; 331419 Inorganic Smelting and Refining of Nonferrous Metal; 562111 Solid Waste Collection; 334119 Other Computer Peripheral Equipment Manufacturing

■ ■ ■

Valhi, Inc., is one of the least known, but most successful, multinational conglomerates located in the United States. The company has succeeded through its diversity with four primary businesses, including component products, chemicals, hazardous waste management, and titanium manufacturing. Valhi's principal operating subsidiaries are: CompX International, Inc., one of the leading U.S. manufacturers of ergonomic office workstation supplies and components, precision ball bearing drawer slides, and mechanical locks; NL Industries, Inc., one of the world's largest producers of titanium dioxide pigments; Waste Control Specialists LLC, one of the fastest-growing firms in the processing, treatment, storage, and disposal of hazardous waste materials in the United States; and Titanium Metals Corporation (TIMET), which produces titanium sponge and melted and milled titanium products. As of 2007 Valhi, Inc., was a subsidiary of Contran Corporation, a private company that owns 90 percent of Valhi, Inc., and is largely controlled by founder and Chairman Harold Simmons.

EARLY HISTORY 1932–73

Valhi, Inc., was a sleepy agricultural company with land holdings in California and Louisiana and sales totaling $21 million per year before it was transformed by Harold Clark Simmons into one of the most successful conglomerates within the United States.

Early in his business career, Simmons demonstrated a talent for reading financial reports and discovering undervalued assets. In 1974 he skillfully negotiated the purchase of Valhi for approximately $8 million, although the assets turned out to be worth more than $100 million. With the purchase of Valhi, Simmons was on his way to becoming a billionaire, having learned from previous missteps.

Born in Golden, Texas, about 80 miles east of Dallas, Harold Simmons was raised by his schoolteacher parents in the midst of the Great Depression. Hardened by his experiences on the edge of the notorious dust bowls of the 1930s, Simmons was determined to make his fortune in the world. A lackadaisical student with a

KEY DATES

1932: Valhi, Inc., founded as agricultural firm.
1974: Valhi purchased by Harold Clark Simmons.
1982: Company purchases Keystone Consolidated Industries, Inc.
1986: Company acquires controlling interest in NL Industries, Inc.
1990: TIMET purchased by Valhi's Baroid Corporation.
1993: Valhi incorporates CompX International, Inc.
1995: Valhi creates Waste Control Specialists, Inc.
1997: Sells Sybra Corporation and leaves fast-food industry.
2002: Stephen Watson named CEO of Valhi, Inc.

photographic memory, he graduated from the University of Texas at Austin with a bachelor's degree and master's degree in economics, Phi Beta Kappa key dangling around his finger.

Following his graduation, Simmons first worked with the Federal Deposit Insurance Corporation, and later with the Republic National Bank. The young man clashed with his superiors, however, and conflict arose with his boss at Republic National Bank. When Simmons suddenly quit his job, his wife was reportedly so distressed that he had thrown away a stable and lucrative future that she left him. Not knowing what to do, on a whim he gathered $5,000 of his own money and, with a note for $95,000, he purchased the University Pharmacy located adjacent to Southern Methodist University.

While he managed the store and flipped burgers, Simmons also found time to read about James Ling, the force behind the famous conglomerate LTV. Impressed with the acquisition strategy that Ling had implemented to make LTV into the giant that it was, Simmons began to copy Ling's modus operandi. His first purchase was a 100 percent leveraged buyout of seven drugstores in Waco, Texas, soon followed by the acquisition of 30 more stores in Houston, and another 11 in eastern rural Texas. By the time the 1960s came to a close, Simmons was managing the financial equivalent of a Texas oil well.

THE MAKING OF A CONGLOMERATE 1973–85

In 1973, Simmons sold all of his holdings for approximately $50 million to the Jack Eckerd Corporation. With his money, the ambitious but rather careless millionaire began to speculate in the financial services industry. In 1974, Simmons was indicted for mail and securities fraud in relation to one of the insurance companies he had purchased during this time. Although he was found not guilty by the judge, most of his money had been eaten up by court costs or spent in lavish living. As a result, his second wife also left him and, once again, he had two more daughters to take care of. He used his business acumen to win control over the undervalued Valhi, Inc., which would fuel the acquisition of future holdings.

After purchasing Valhi in 1974, Simmons established his own holding company, Contran Corporation, which controlled all of Valhi's stock, and then began using Valhi to purchase companies. Soon he had the beginnings of a conglomerate. In 1982, he purchased Keystone Consolidated Industries, Inc., for the bargain price of $25 million. Keystone, a Dallas-based manufacturer of steel, wire, and hardware, was plagued with manufacturing cost overruns, labor problems, and the expense and difficulty of disposing of hazardous waste materials. Simmons kept the management of Keystone, but implemented strict cost-cutting measures.

He also had no qualms about using approximately $15 million of Keystone's employee pension fund in his takeover bid for Amalgamated Sugar Company. Amalgamated Sugar, based in Utah, was a refiner and marketer of sugar and, most important to Simmons, had undervalued assets including $100 million in cash. In this transaction, Simmons violated pension fund regulations and was required by the State Court of Utah to sell the Amalgamated shares owned by the fund. He remained undeterred, however, and bought Amalgamated Sugar with $35 million of his own money.

FROM HOSTILE TAKEOVERS TO STRONG COMPANIES

The next major acquisition was NL Industries, a mismanaged firm with oil services and a titanium dioxide business worth more than $2 billion in sales annually. To prevent Simmons's takeover, management at NL Industries devised a poison pill defense that would dilute the shareholders' equity significantly if Simmons attacked and began buying stock. Simmons concluded that the poison pill of NL Industries was illegal and began buying the company's stock. When a federal judge agreed with Simmons that the poison pill was indeed illegal, Simmons rushed to buy the company the very same day. Upon conclusion of the purchase agreement, Simmons immediately split up the company into Baroid, an oilfield services operation, and NL Industries, Inc., a chemical company.

Although most corporate raiders like Simmons purchased companies for the specific reason of selling their operating divisions at a higher cost than the value of the firm itself, thereby reaping a healthy and quick profit, Simmons himself was not a typical raider. In fact, when he purchased a company, he devoted a good deal of his time and energy into rehabilitating its operating divisions. After having acquired Keystone Consolidated Industries, it took him seven years to revitalize it. By 1989, Keystone had opened a brand-new steel mill worth $50 million, which boosted profits to $12 million on sales of $306 million. The year before, Keystone had reported a $6 million loss on sales of $257 million.

Amalgamated Sugar Company was no different. After a hostile and extremely acrimonious takeover battle for control of the company, Simmons turned about-face and asked its management to continue on at the company. For nearly eight years he invested more and more money to buy new sugar-processing equipment. After having spent nearly $70 million, he saw productivity increase by 40 percent. Also impressive is that, although sugar prices increased only 4 percent from 1983 to 1989, Amalgamated Sugar saw its operating income jump to $38 million, a fourfold increase during those same years.

CREATING SUCCESS AND AVOIDING FAILURE

Simmons exhibited an uncanny ability to understand and act upon industry basics, as illustrated by his turnaround of NL Industries, which he bought in 1986. That year the company's oilfield services reported a loss of $324 million since its managers had failed to downsize operations during the oil bust. Simmons immediately reorganized the division into an independent company called Baroid; sold four units from the oilfield services that were losing money, including a longstanding oilfield equipment rental business; discontinued perks such as private corporate jets for management travel; and refocused on strengthening the company's main product of providing oilfield drilling fluids and measurement services. Finally, Simmons directed Baroid management to develop and introduce as quickly as possible new products to capitalize on the increased demand in horizontal drilling. In 1989, Baroid reported an unheralded increase of its operating income by 66 percent, to more than $30 million.

Simmons's careful and highly methodical analysis of financial statements enabled him to stay far away from the disastrous state of affairs in the oil, real estate, and banking sectors in Texas during the 1980s. By the end of the decade, Valhi owned and operated seven extremely profitable businesses, including NL Industries, which was involved in chemicals production; Baroid, a provider of petroleum services; Amalgamated Sugar, a producer of refined sugar; Medford, Inc., a manufacturer of forest products; Medite Corporation, a fiberboard company; Sybra, a large fast-food chain of restaurants; and its Hardware Division, a manufacturer of locks and various metal products. Total revenues for Valhi at the end of fiscal 1989 were reported at $2.2 billion. Simmons had made himself a billionaire.

BRIGHT SPOT IN A DOWNTURN 1990–92

At the beginning of the 1990s, the trend toward takeovers and leveraged buyouts within the corporate world seemed to have run its course. Junk bonds, one of the ways enormously priced leveraged buyouts were arranged throughout the 1980s, had been discredited as a long-term viable business strategy. Unfortunately, Harold Simmons, a man who was at his best during the takeover years, turned ice cold as an investor just when he most needed to infuse Valhi share earnings with another promising acquisition. In fact, during 1991 and 1992, Simmons saw the value of his stock market holdings decline precipitously, to almost $1 billion in total value.

The one bright spot in his portfolio of companies was NL Industries, one of the country's leaders in the manufacture of titanium dioxide, or TiO_2, a specialty chemical used as a brightener in paints, paper, fibers, ceramics, and also on the surface of many consumer appliances. Demand for titanium dioxide was growing at a much faster rate than could be supplied, especially in the United States where consumers wanted their appliances to have a "clean look." As demand continued to grow during the mid-1990s, NL Industries established its own subsidiary, Kronos, Inc., which constructed four new production facilities in Western Europe and one in Canada. By the end of 1995, Kronos had captured 18 percent of the total market share for titanium dioxide in Europe.

INCREASING LIQUIDITY FOR INVESTMENT POWER 1993–97

The success of NL Industries was not enough for Simmons, however, and in the mid-1990s he began to sell companies he had previously purchased, to increase Valhi's liquidity and thereby concentrate on new investment opportunities. The first company to go was Baroid, the oilfield services firm that, despite its early success, never reached the level of profitability Simmons desired. Although Simmons disposed of Baroid, Valhi remained in control of Titanium Metals Corporation (TIMET), a subsidiary purchased by Baroid in 1990 that specialized in titanium processing and manufacturing. Quick to follow was Medite Corporation and Medford, Inc. Selling the fiberboard and lumber companies for $240 million gave Simmons some of the capital he needed to begin looking for new investments. Yet the amount still was not enough to acquire a high-quality firm. Consequently, Simmons disposed of Amalgamated Sugar Company for approximately $200 million in a deal with Snake River Sugar Company, an Oregon-based agricultural cooperative.

Satisfied that he had some of the funds needed for new investments, Simmons created Waste Control Specialists in November 1995, to enter the rapidly growing market for the processing, treatment, storage, and disposal of hazardous waste materials in Texas. Money was provided for the construction of a facility in west Texas, which accepted its first waste materials for disposal in the winter of 1997. In the spring of 1997, Waste Control Specialists applied for authorization to treat, store, and dispose of low-level radioactive waste materials.

In addition to the promise of high revenues from Waste Control Specialists, Simmons also reaped rewards from CompX, his components products company, created out of Valhi's Hardware Division. Having captured a well-defined niche market, CompX grew into the largest supplier of ergonomic office workstation products in North America.

EXITING THE FAST-FOOD INDUSTRY

Simmons's fascination with the fast-food industry had also run its course by the beginning of 1997. Sybra operated more than 150 Arby's restaurants over a four-state area, including Michigan, Texas, Pennsylvania, and Florida. In fact, Sybra was the third biggest franchisee within Arby's operational network. A niche segment in the fast-food industry, Arby's sells roast beef sandwiches, chicken sandwiches, and soft drinks. However sales increased only 2 percent from 1995 to 1996, primarily because of the highly competitive nature of the fast-food industry. As a result of this disappointing performance, Simmons decided to dispose of his Sybra holdings and sold part of it to ICH Corporation and the remainder to Restaurant Property Master for a total of $84.7 million.

VALHI IN THE 21ST CENTURY

In 2002, Simmons relinquished his position as CEO of the company to Stephen L. Watson, who had worked with Valhi since the 1980s and held various board positions within Valhi's subsidiaries. Watson became president of Valhi, Inc., in 1998 and was named CEO in 2002. In 2006, Watson was named president of Titanium Metals Corporation, a position that he held while simultaneously serving as Valhi's chief executive. Simmons remained chairman of the board of directors for both Valhi and its parent company, Contran Corp.

Though Valhi rarely appeared in national news from 2000 to 2005, founder Harold Simmons's philanthropy was widely noted, including substantial gifts and donations to Republican Party candidates and judicial nominees during the first term of president George W. Bush. Simmons explained his interest in politics as largely financial and based on the belief that the Republican Party is better able to manage economic growth. In addition to political donations, Simmons and his family also donated millions to other institutions including his former high school and several hospitals in the Dallas, Texas, area. In 2006 Simmons was listed by *Forbes* magazine as number 61 in the company's annual list of the nation's 400 richest Americans. By 2007, *Forbes* increased Simmons's ranking to number 43 with a reported net worth of $7.4 billion. Simmons donated over $400 million in philanthropic gifts in 2007 while his company's annual sales rose to over 6.4 billion.

In 2005, Valhi's subsidiary CompX International acquired interest in two companies specializing in the manufacture of equipment for the marine and boating industries. The growth of CompX International significantly enhanced Valhi's gross earnings in 2006 and 2007. In addition, Valhi's waste management services experienced overall growth from 2000 to 2006.

At the end of the 2007 calendar year, Valhi remained one of the least known top companies in the United States. Valhi's diverse interests helped to keep profits high while the company continued to experience modest growth. Contran Corporation maintained controlling interest in five publicly traded companies including Valhi, Inc., and Keystone Consolidated Industries, a major producer of steel products. Although Contran's profits were unclear for 2007 and potentially totaled over $2 billion, Harold Simmons and investors consistently ranked among the nation's financial elite.

Thomas Derdak
Updated, Micah L. Issitt

PRINCIPAL SUBSIDIARIES

NL Industries, Inc.; CompX International, Inc.; Waste Control Specialists LLC; Titanium Metals Corporation (TIMET).

PRINCIPAL COMPETITORS

Allegheny Technologies; E.I. du Pont de Nemours and Company; Huntsman Corporation.

FURTHER READING

"Agreements Made to Sell Sybra Inc. for $84.7 Million," *Wall Street Journal,* February 13, 1997, p. B8(E).

"Company News: Valhi Purchases a 43.8 Percent Stock in Tremont," *New York Times,* June 20, 1998.

"400 Richest Americans 2006," *Forbes.com,* September 21, 2006.

"400 Richest Americans 2007," *Forbes.com,* September 20, 2007.

Hunter, Glenn, "I'm Going to Start Thinking Bigger," *Dallas Business Journal,* August 11, 2006.

"Investor Harold Simmons: His Personal Takeover Philosophy," *Chemical and Engineering News,* May 28, 1990, pp. 11–15.

Kelly, Kevin, "If Simmons Boards Lockheed, Can He Fly It?" *Business Week,* April 2, 1990, pp. 77–78.

Marcial, Gene, "Buying a Stake in Harold Simmons," *Business Week,* September 22, 1986, p. 88.

Mason, Todd, "Harold Simmons Is Coming Out to Play Again," *Business Week,* January 9, 1989, pp. 44–46.

Rowe, Frederick E., Jr., "The Harold Simmons Bet," *Forbes,* August 2, 1993, p. 148.

Serwer, Andrew Evan, "The Whistling Billionaire," *Fortune,* April 10, 1989, pp. 102–6.

"A Takeover Artist Takes on the Teamsters," *Business Week,* October 22, 1984, p. 46.

"Valhi Sells Fiberboard Business," *Wall Street Journal,* March 3, 1997, p. A6.

Varsity Brands, Inc.

6745 Lennox Center Court, Suite 300
Memphis, Tennessee 38115-4300
U.S.A.
Toll Free: (800) 533-8022
Fax: (800) 792-4337
Web site: http://www.varsity.com

Private Company
Incorporated: 1983 as Varsity Spirit Corporation
Employees: 700
Sales: $156.4 million (2007 est.)
NAIC: 315999 Other Apparel Accessories and Other Apparel Manufacturing; 711211 Sports Teams and Clubs; 721214 Recreational and Vacation Camps (Except Campgrounds)

■ ■ ■

Varsity Brands, Inc. (formerly known as Varsity Spirit, Inc.), sells products and services to the school spirit industry throughout the United States and in Japan. It designs and markets cheerleader, dance team, and booster club uniforms and accessories, including sweatshirts, jumpers, vests, sweaters, pompons, jackets, pins, and other paraphernalia. The company also operates and markets its products through high school and college cheerleader and dance team camps in the United States and Japan. After a largely unsuccessful merger and expansion in the late 1990s, Varsity Brands returned to its core focus on equipment and support for the cheerleading and school dance industries and has strengthened its position as the dominant company in the market.

FOUNDATION OF A NICHE MARKET

Varsity Brands is a leader in a business niche that it helped to create, the school spirit industry. When the company was launched in 1974, there was only one other significant player in the industry: National Cheerleaders Association (later dubbed National Spirit Group), a privately owned Dallas-based venture. National Cheerleaders had been founded by Lawrence Herkimer in 1948. The company had grown and profited chiefly through the operation of cheerleading camps, where high school and college students could learn cheerleading routines and hone related athletic and gymnastic skills. Among the company's employees in the early 1970s was Jeffrey Webb, the soon-to-be entrepreneur destined to pose the first serious challenge to Herkimer's enterprise.

Webb, a self-described "sports nut," had become absorbed in cheerleading during a one-year stint as a cheerleader for the University of Oklahoma's football team. While he was a student at Oklahoma he began teaching at, and directing, cheerleading training camps for National Cheerleaders Association. It was that experience that prompted him to launch a similar venture. Although Webb enjoyed cheerleading, he believed that the activity had become stagnant and, more specifically, that National Cheerleaders was missing opportunities to advance the sport. He wanted to breathe new life into cheerleading and take it in a new,

COMPANY PERSPECTIVES

Varsity Brands, Inc., is the leader in cheerleading and dance apparel, camps, and competitions.

more dynamic direction that incorporated athleticism and entertainment. "I wanted to modernize cheerleading," Webb recalled in the June 1994 issue of *Nation's Business.*

Webb left National Cheerleaders in 1974 and, at the age of 23, started a company that he called Universal Cheerleaders Association (UCA). With no business experience and a relatively unconventional business plan, Webb was unable to secure institutional financing. Instead, he raised $80,000 by establishing a limited partnership and selling $5,000 shares in his company to his family and friends. He also invested $5,000 from his own savings. At the time, the burgeoning cheerleading business was gravitating toward Texas. Webb bucked the trend by setting up his office in Memphis, Tennessee, because it was in the middle of the region where he had developed most of his contacts.

Webb's original goal was to provide high-quality, innovative instructional programs for young people on a national basis. He would attract young people to his camps by promising to shun the staid, monotonous routines taught year after year at National Cheerleaders Association, and instead teach new routines that emphasized more athletic and gymnastic stunts. "From the very beginning, he had a good vision of what cheerleading fashions and the whole school spirit industry would look like ten years down the road with the athletics and national television exposure," said Greg Webb, Jeffrey's younger brother and vice-president, in the February 22, 1993, issue of *Memphis Business Journal.* "We knew we were working with a changing environment for school spirit efforts, while some of our competitors were still holding to the traditional role and look."

After setting up his base in Memphis, Webb started scouting out and reserving college and university dormitories and athletic facilities that were empty during the summer, in anticipation of enrolling high school students interested in attending his camps. Then he mailed letters announcing the training camps, with registration forms, to every high school within 100 miles of each of the campuses where he had reserved space. The effort sapped all of the company's start-up capital, so Webb was relieved when the return mail brought a sack of registration forms. "If the registration forms didn't come in, we were out of business," he recalled in an article printed in the October 25, 1993, issue of *Forbes.* "I was yelling and screaming, throwing letters into the air. I knew we were going to survive."

With a rapidly expanding registry, Webb knew that he would be able to find the talent to teach at his camps because several of his associate instructors at National Cheerleaders Association had promised to join him once he got his venture "up and running." Webb hired 24 instructors during his first summer and operated a total of 20 of his high-energy clinics throughout the Midwest and Southeast. A total of 4,000 students attended. He sometimes slept in his car during that summer as he traveled from clinic to clinic. The venture was an immediate success. Universal Cheerleaders posted a profit in its first year and continued to do so every year thereafter into the 21st century.

Once the word spread, Universal's rosters were filled with eager students. By 1979 the company was generating $2 million from its training camps. Encouraged by the success, Webb decided that it was time to branch into a new segment of the market: fashions and supplies. Webb realized that most of the clothing being marketed by the competition at the time did not suit the style of cheerleading taught at his camps. The clothing was restrictive and often tore under the stress of more athletic cheerleading routines. Furthermore, it was outdated. Webb wanted to introduce an updated line of clothing that was durable and stylish.

In 1979 Universal Cheerleaders started a division named Varsity Spirit Fashions and Supplies. Through that unit, Webb began offering updated outfits that were less restrictive and which featured, for example, sleeveless tops, jumpers, and a variety of necklines. The uniforms contrasted with the traditional sweaters and skirts that had been worn for years. The clothing line was an instant hit, and Webb found that it was relatively easy to market through his clinics. During its first year, the Varsity Spirit division chalked up $200,000 in sales. That early gain signaled the success of a venture that soon overcame Universal's core cheerleading clinic business and vaulted the company to multimillion-dollar corporate status.

GROWTH AND INTERNATIONAL EXPANSION

Webb realized the potential of the clothing and equipment business and quickly moved to emphasize its growth. Throughout the 1980s and early 1990s he was able to boost sales rapidly through a large sales force, promotional videotapes, and full-color catalogs. At the

KEY DATES

1974: Jeffrey Webb founds Universal Cheerleaders Association (UCA).
1979: Varsity Spirit Fashions and Supplies founded as a division of the UCA.
1987: Expands to Japan through an agreement with Japan Drill & Cheer Association.
1992: Company goes public as Varsity Spirit Corp.
1996: Acquires United Spirit Associated Camp Division.
1997: Varsity Spirit is acquired in a major buyout by New York-based Riddell Sports, Inc.
2000: Company launches first web sites.
2001: Company changes name to Varsity Brands, Inc.
2003: Varsity Brands goes private.
2006: Varsity Brands merges with World Spirit Federation.
2007: Company launches new web site at www.varsity.com.

same time, he was able to increase profits steadily from the cheerleading clinics. Despite steady sales and profit growth, however, Webb was still unable to find a financial institution that was willing to back his company during the first seven years. Instead, he was forced to rely on savvy, cost-effective marketing funded directly from the company's profits.

Among his most successful efforts was the creation of several special events, many of which were televised, sponsored by UCA. Universal's nationally televised events included the National High School Cheerleading Championship, the National Dance Team Championship, the National College Cheerleading and Dance Team Championship, as well as various parade exhibitions and college football bowl half time shows. The events became a profitable advertising channel for Universal because they established goodwill toward the company and often gave national exposure to its Varsity Spirit products.

Buoyed by external financing, Universal Cheerleaders Association was able to increase its annual revenue base from barely more than $2 million in 1980 to about $10 million going into the late 1980s. Of import was the 1985 purchase of a Winona, Minnesota-based concern called Varsity Spirit Fashions. Strengthened by that addition, Universal's Varsity Spirit division and cheerleading camp unit were each capturing sales of about $5 million per year by 1987. The company was employing about 40 full-time workers as well as 350 cheerleading camp instructors who trained 60,000 cheerleaders annually.

Furthermore, Webb was beginning to expand overseas. In 1987 Universal signed an agreement to consult with the Japan Drill & Cheer Association. The agreement led to the creation of a separate licensed venture called UCA-Japan. Universal developed the firm's teaching staff and began supplying it with uniforms and equipment. The partnership was a perfect fit with Universal's U.S. operations because Japan's cheerleading camp season occurred between November and March, whereas U.S. clinics were offered between April and October. By the early 1990s, the joint venture was sponsoring more than 20 clinics in Japan annually.

By 1989 Universal was bringing in more than $20 million in annual sales. It was late in that year that the original limited partners, who had each fronted $5,000, chose to cash out. They effectively sold two-thirds of the company to a group of investors by way of a leveraged buyout. The deal loaded Universal with debt until the investment group took the company public in 1992. It sold shares in the company and used the cash to pay off all of the company's debt. Webb pocketed about $7.7 million in the deal and also managed to hold on to about 13 percent of the company. The company went public with a name change to Varsity Spirit Corp.

The name change reflected the increasing influence of the organization's clothing and supplies division. Indeed, by the early 1990s the company's uniforms and equipment were contributing more than 60 percent of total sales and more than 70 percent of profits. In fact, the cheerleading and dance clinics had become a marketing tool for the organization's products. In 1993 Varsity Spirit trained 116,000 cheerleaders at 600 camps held on campuses throughout the United States. For a four-day session, students paid only $155, which barely covered Varsity Spirit's costs. Varsity was able to profit, though, by having its instructors pass out product catalogs to the students. Because the average cheerleader spent $200 on clothes, pompons, duffel bags, megaphones, and various other items, Varsity was able to generate hefty product sales from clinic patrons.

As a result of its savvy marketing strategy and innovative clinics and products, Varsity Spirit was able to sustain steady sales and profit growth throughout the early and mid-1990s. Sales increased to $28.1 million in 1991, $33.8 million in 1992, and then to $41.6 million in 1993. Likewise, net income rose from about $623,000 in 1991 to about $2.4 million in 1993. In 1993, Varsity Spirit hosted its first international cheerleading championship in Tokyo. A total of 31 U.S. and

Japanese teams participated in the event, which was televised nationally in Japan. That effort helped Webb to win the *Memphis Business Journal*'s Small Business Executive of the Year award, among other honors.

During the 1994 summer camp season, Varsity Spirit trained 137,000 coaches and students at more than 700 camps in 50 states. It employed a staff of about 250 full-time workers, although its workforce could grow to as many as 1,000 or more during the summers. In addition to marketing goods at those camps, Varsity employed a 100-member sales force that called on 15,000 schools and colleges to sell Varsity Spirit's products and services.

OWNERSHIP BY RIDDELL SPORTS, INC.

In 1996, Varsity Spirit Corporation completed an acquisition of the United Spirit Associated Camp Division, based in California, in an effort to increase coverage of the West Coast market. In the company's press releases, Webb stated of the acquisition, "This is an excellent strategic acquisition for our company. The geographic fit is ideal, as USA has a strong position in the West and Southwest markets, with more than 30,000 participants attending their camps and events during 1995. Combining our two companies, we expect to have approximately 200,000 participants attend our cheerleader and dance team summer camps in 1996."

In the summer of 1997, Varsity Spirit was acquired in a major buyout by New York-based Riddell Sports, Inc., for a reported $91.2 million. The partnership arrangement included the sale of $4.4 million in Riddell stock to the four top executives at Varsity Spirit, including Webb. Riddell Sports issued a private stock offering amounting to $115 million to finance the purchase and to repay existing debt. Webb remained with Varsity Spirit as president and CEO of the company, which was reclassified as a subsidiary of Riddell. Webb then worked with Riddell to integrate Varsity Spirit's products into the Riddell line, which included football uniforms and various brands of sports equipment.

Both Varsity Spirit and Riddell Sports benefited from the buyout and from 1998 to 1999, profits increased by 12 percent from $189.4 million to $208.6 million. To fuel future expansion, the company also began investing in developing a web presence and an Internet marketing site and, in 1999, formed a partnership with Umbro, Inc., to sell the company's soccer equipment. Riddell reported that the sale of spirit equipment increased by 7 percent from 1997 to 1999 while revenues from camps and events also increased significantly with a total of 215,000 participants for the 1999 camp season.

In 2000, the company opened two new web sites for product marketing and community building activities. While the web site www.riddell.com focused on marketing sports collectibles for consumers, the partner site, www.varsity.com, provided resources for cheerleaders and coaches in addition to selling equipment and uniforms.

VARSITY RETURNS TO ITS ROOTS IN THE 21ST CENTURY

After disappointing revenues in 2000 and 2001, the company decided to make a number of strategic changes. In June, the company sold its sports teams division with the exception of the sports collectable division. The team sports and helmet manufacturing businesses retained the Riddell label while Varsity Spirit and the remaining portions of the former Riddell Sports division changed their combined name, in September, to Varsity Brands, Inc. At the conclusion of their restructuring, which included shifting the company's headquarters from New York to Memphis, Varsity Brands was similar to Varsity Spirit, Inc., before the merger with Riddell.

Webb was promoted from president and CEO of the Varsity Spirit division to president and CEO of the parent company, replacing former CEO David Bauer. In October, the company won a lawsuit that enabled them to end a licensing deal with Umbro two years ahead of the initial contract. According to company press releases, the shifts in company strategy reflected changes in the market. In 2001, the spirit products portion of the company's business was growing and Varsity Brands controlled approximately 65 percent of the market for school dance and cheerleading squads.

Varsity Brands formed a partnership in 2002 with the National Federation of State High School Associations. Under the development contract, Varsity Brands agreed to help develop educational programs for cheerleading and dance teams as well as an education program for high school coaches and leaders. In company press releases, Webb called the National Federation the "key organization for all sports and extracurricular activities in high school in America," and expressed his hopes that the merger would lead to increased revenues for the company.

In 2003, after several years of falling stock prices, Webb and the board of directors for Varsity Brands made the decision to take the company private. Webb partnered with Los Angeles private equity firm Leonard Green and Partners to initiate the stock repurchasing program, which was estimated at over $130 million. The price of Varsity stock had fallen from its initial public offering of $16 per share in 1991 to around $4 per share in 2002. The company agreed to pay stockholders $6.57 per share, significantly in excess of the going rate.

Over the next two years, Webb and his fellow executives concentrated on maintaining profit growth for Varsity Brands' major divisions, including sprit products and cheerleading/dance camps. By the end of 2005, Webb was looking for new opportunities to increase the company's market. In 2006, Webb found an opportunity to form a merger with the World Spirit Federation (WSF), an organization that sponsored 13 annual cheerleading competitions in the United States. The WSF structure remained intact after the merger, which significantly increased Varsity Brands' share of the market.

In 2007, Varsity Brands launched a redesigned web site, which was intended to function as a major hub for news and information pertaining to the dance and cheerleading community. The redesigned interface featured videos, cheer squad profiles, and a shopping portal for marketing the company's brands. After persevering through an economic downturn in the early years of the 21st century, by returning to the company's core focus Varsity Brands remained strong, with sales exceeding $156 million in 2006 and control over more than 60 percent of the cheerleading and high school dance industry.

Dave Mote
Updated, Micah L. Issitt

PRINCIPAL DIVISIONS

Varsity Spirit Fashions; Cheerleader and Danz Team; UCA All Star; Athletic Championships; World Spirit Federation; Universal Cheerleaders Association; American Championships; National Cheerleaders Association; Universal Dance Association; National Dance Alliance; United Spirit Association; Cheerleading Technique Camps; V.ROC!

PRINCIPAL COMPETITORS

NIKE, Inc.; Russell Corporation; Triumph Apparel Corporation.

FURTHER READING

Becker, Susan, "Cheerleading Company Will Begin Exporting Its Universal Message to Japan," *Memphis Business Journal,* February 9, 1987, p. 1.

Flaum, David, "Memphis, Tenn.-based Varsity Brands Gets National Development Deal," *Memphis Commercial Appeal,* October 3, 2002.

———, "Sports Company Gets New Name, Headquarters in Memphis, Tenn.," *Memphis Commercial Appeal,* September 20, 2001.

———, "Varsity Brands to Terminate Licensing Deal with Umbro's Soccer Products," *Memphis Commercial Appeal,* October 5, 2001.

Hopkins, Brent, "Sporting Goods Titans to Merge," *Knight-Ridder/Tribune Business News,* February 8, 2006.

Lacey, Nicole, "'93 Executive of the Year Winner Knows Value of Team Spirit," *Memphis Business Journal,* January 10, 1994, p. 1.

"Riddell Takes Swing at New E-Markets," *Sporting Goods Business,* January 4, 2000.

Rodgers, Cheryl, "Spirit! Let's Hear It!" *Nation's Business,* June 1994, p. 16.

Sullivan, R. Lee, "School for Cheerleaders," *Forbes,* October 25, 1993, p. 118.

Thompson, Richard, "Memphis, Tenn., Dance Camp, Sports Equipment Firm to Go Private," *Knight-Ridder/Tribune Business News,* April 23, 2003.

"Universal Cheerleaders Buys Minnesota Uniform Plant," *Memphis Business Journal,* December 9, 1985, p. 17.

"Varsity Spirit Corporation to Acquire United Spirit Association Camp Division," *Business Wire,* April 25, 1996.

Yawn, David, "Webb's Vision Guiding Varsity Spirit Along Route to New Markets," *Memphis Business Journal,* February 22, 1993, p. 1.

Velocity Express Corporation

1 Morningside Drive North
Building B, Suite 300
Westport, Connecticut 06880
U.S.A.
Telephone: (203) 349-4160
Toll Free: (888) 839-7669
Web site: http://www.velocityexpress.com

Public Company
Incorporated: 1993 as U.S. Delivery Systems, Inc.
Employees: 2,090
Sales: $410.1 million (2007)
Stock Exchanges: NASDAQ
Ticker Symbol: VEXP
NAIC: 551120 Offices of Other Holding Companies; 484110 General Freight Trucking, Local

■ ■ ■

Velocity Express Corporation is the largest provider of time-definite, same-day regional delivery service in the United States. Its trucks generally operate within a major metropolitan area or radius of 40 miles. Services include distributing bulk shipments to multiple locations, daily pick up and delivery on a customer's schedule, and unique deliveries as required. In contrast to the next-day delivery business, which is dominated by major national players, such as FedEx Corporation and United Parcel Service, Inc. (UPS), the same-day sector of the delivery business is highly fragmented, with close to 6,000 firms in operation in the United States, most of them conducting business only locally. Velocity Express has been a leading consolidator within this sector. By mid-2007, the company had in place a network of 180 locations in 37 states, serving about 96 percent of the major metropolitan areas. Velocity also had two locations in Canada. The wide range of businesses served by the company includes financial institutions, healthcare and medical organizations, retailers, petrochemical firms, and technology companies.

FROM IDEA TO IPO

The origins of the same-day delivery operations that are the core of Velocity Express can be traced back to those of U.S. Delivery Systems, Inc., which was founded by Clayton K. Trier, a one-time accountant who eventually developed a reputation as an acquirer and consolidator. Prior to founding U.S. Delivery, Trier had served as co-CEO in the late 1980s of a Houston firm called Allwaste, Inc., which grew rapidly through a string of acquisitions of small companies within the highly fragmented industrial waste cleaning business. In 1993 Trier was approached by his friend Michael Baker, head of a venture capital firm called Notre Capital Ventures, about taking a similar approach to the same-day, local delivery market. According to a 1995 *Forbes* article, Trier's immediate reaction was, "You mean those spiky-haired guys on bicycles?"

Of course, the market was much bigger than just the bicycle messenger business. In the mid-1990s, U.S. businesses were spending $15 billion for the services of same-day local delivery companies. This segment of the market was highly fragmented, consisting of about 10,000 companies, most of which were privately held

COMPANY PERSPECTIVES

As America's only national provider of regional shipping solutions, Velocity Express doesn't deliver on our schedule. We deliver on yours.

and operated in only one market. None of the firms held more than 2 percent of the national market share. The idea was to create a national same-day delivery service, following the example set by FedEx in the overnight delivery sector.

As he researched his friend's idea further, Trier found a number of trends that indicated that the time might be right for a national same-day delivery company. First, companies were increasingly turning to outsourcing for noncore activities, one of which was local delivery operations. Second, to maintain lower levels of inventories, companies were using sophisticated inventory control systems along with just-in-time delivery of components and materials; this increased the demand for same-day delivery services. Third, the same general trend toward a quicker pace of business that had earlier increased the demand for second-day and next-day delivery services (and that continued to be driven by the increasing speed of communication in the high-tech world) was tending to increase the demand for same-day deliveries. Finally, major companies with locations scattered around the country were clamoring for the efficiencies and cost-savings that could be realized by being able to deal with just one same-day delivery firm rather than the dozens that they had been relying on. There was also an operational advantage to building a national network in that the delivery company itself could realize savings in overhead and certain operating expenses.

Having convinced himself through his research of the merit of the idea, Trier, with the backing of Notre Capital Ventures, formed U.S. Delivery Systems, Inc., in November 1993, basing the firm in Houston. Trier was named chairman, president, and CEO. The firm had no operations at the time, but in a clever maneuver, Trier planned to complete an initial public offering (IPO) simultaneous with the acquisition of six local delivery companies and one telemarketing services firm, thereby raising the needed funding. On May 20, 1994, the company completed its IPO, selling three million shares of common stock on the New York Stock Exchange at $10 per share. This represented 40 percent of the company's equity. The remaining shares were retained by the initial investors, who saw the value of their investment skyrocket. At the time of the IPO, for example, the 10 percent stake that Baker's Notre Capital Ventures had gained for $2.3 million was worth $7.5 million. Out of the $29.2 million netted from the IPO, about $19.4 million in cash went toward purchasing the seven founding companies. In addition to the cash, the acquisitions also involved 3.4 million shares of U.S. Delivery common stock.

The seven founding companies had combined for about $108 million in revenues in 1993. The six local delivery companies had operations in a number of major markets and therefore formed a solid base upon which to grow. Eastway Transportation Services, Inc., operated in eastern Texas and Louisiana. First National Courier Systems, Inc., had locations in Woodside, New York, and in Boston. Grace Courier Service, Inc., had operations in New York City, White Plains, and Long Island City, New York; Paramus and Edison, New Jersey; Newington, Virginia, a suburb of Washington, D.C.; and Tampa and Fort Lauderdale, Florida. U.S. Courier Corporation of San Francisco had been serving the San Francisco Bay area for 15 years. U.S. Service Corporation of America had locations in Los Angeles, San Diego, Chicago, and Milwaukee. ViaNet, Inc., was serving markets in Texas, Louisiana, and Tennessee. The telemarketing firm, CallCenter Services, Inc., was based in Salisbury, Maryland, and provided inbound telemarketing services that were used to process home delivery orders for catalog retailers.

CREATING A NATIONAL NETWORK

From the start, U.S. Delivery offered several different types of same-day delivery services. Scheduled and routed delivery services were offered for time-sensitive local deliveries that were recurrent. Financial institutions were the prototypical users of this type of service, with an example being a bank needing to have canceled checks or ATM receipts picked up from various locations and then transported to a central processing center. A second type of service was "dedicated vehicle," or what the company later called "distribution services." In this case, a customer, usually a wholesale distributor, needed a bulk supply of some product divided up into smaller batches for delivery to several locations. For example, a pharmaceutical wholesaler might need a shipment of a particular drug delivered to several local drugstores. On-demand delivery comprised the third category and was usually offered 24 hours a day, seven days a week. In this case, a customer could request immediate pick up and delivery of the item(s) in question, choosing from one-hour, two-hour, and four-hour service. As part of its on-demand services, U.S. Delivery

KEY DATES

1993: U.S. Delivery Systems, Inc., is founded to establish a nationwide network of same-day delivery services.
1994: Simultaneous with an initial public offering (IPO) that raises $29.2 million, U.S. Delivery acquires seven companies, including six local delivery firms; an additional 18 local delivery companies are acquired by U.S. Delivery following the IPO.
1996: Corporate Express, Inc., acquires U.S. Delivery, creating a subsidiary known as Corporate Express Delivery Systems, Inc. (CEDS).
1998: Under new Chairman and CEO Peter Lytle, Minneapolis-based U-Ship, Inc., enters the same-day shipping business.
1999: U-Ship changes its name to United Shipping & Technology, Inc.; Corporate Express sells CEDS to United Shipping for about $60 million.
2000: United Shipping changes the name of its same-day delivery operations to Velocity Express.
2002: United Shipping reincorporates as Velocity Express Corporation.
2006: Velocity Express Corporation acquires competitor CD&L.

also offered air-courier/freight services. Other services offered by the firm included delivery management, warehousing, and just-in-time delivery services.

Working quickly toward its goal of creating a nationwide network, U.S. Delivery completed the acquisition of an additional 18 businesses by the end of 1994. Among the additional markets added via these purchases were Atlanta, Baltimore, Charlotte, Jacksonville, Orlando, Philadelphia, Phoenix, and Salt Lake City. For the year, the company reported net income of $5.3 million on revenues of $127.9 million. At this point, Trier was involved more in the acquisitions side of the business, while the day-to-day operations were being led by Gary W. Grant, who had been named senior vice-president and COO in March 1994. Grant had been one of the founders of ViaNet.

During 1995 U.S. Delivery completed more than two-dozen additional acquisitions. By the end of the year, the firm had more than 150 locations that served 70 major markets using more than 6,500 delivery vehicles. The workforce had swelled to 6,400. Also in 1995, U.S. Delivery entered the contract logistics business through the purchase of American Distribution System, Inc. Based in Keego Harbor, Michigan, American Distribution provided logistics management services, which entailed the coordination, distribution, and warehousing of products for commercial and industrial clients.

SUBSIDIARY OF CORPORATE EXPRESS

Rather than continuing to expand on its own, U.S. Delivery agreed in January 1996 to be bought by Corporate Express, Inc., in a stock swap valued at about $410 million. Since its founding in 1986, Corporate Express had grown into a national powerhouse in the supplying of large companies with office products and services the same way that U.S. Delivery had built its national delivery network: through the acquisition of small, local, privately held firms. Corporate Express completed the acquisition of U.S. Delivery on March 1, 1996. Both companies viewed the merger as a way of enhancing their national networks, and there were obvious synergies in terms of both firms serving a similar clientele. The executives at U.S. Delivery also anticipated that the merger would enable the company to grow at a faster pace through both acquisition and internal expansion and would give the firm access to highly evolved information systems that had been developed at Corporate Express.

Following the merger, Trier briefly joined the Corporate Express board of directors, and Grant also joined the firm as president of the delivery operations, which became a subsidiary of Corporate Express that was eventually renamed Corporate Express Delivery Systems, Inc. (CEDS). The headquarters for CEDS remained in Houston. For the fiscal year ending on March 2, 1996, the delivery subsidiary accounted for $342.5 million of Corporate Express's total revenues of $1.59 billion.

The pace of acquisition was initially faster for CEDS, with 20 more delivery companies acquired during the fiscal year ending on March 1, 1997. The most significant of these was the purchase of Roswell, Georgia-based United TransNet, Inc., the second largest same-day delivery company in the nation. The transaction, completed in November 1996, involved $138 million in Corporate Express stock. Founded in 1994, United TransNet had combined a number of local same-day delivery companies into a growing national concern whose 1995 revenues were about $254 million. The firm's operations were centered mainly in the eastern United States. With the addition of United TransNet and the other acquired companies, revenues for CEDS more than doubled during fiscal 1996, reaching $759.8 million.

In 1997, but particularly in 1998, Corporate Express began running into problems assimilating all of the acquisitions it had made. The acquisition pace slowed considerably, and the company stock price took a beating. The integration of United TransNet into CEDS proved especially nettlesome, and the same-day delivery subsidiary began losing money. In January 1999 Corporate Express announced it intended either to reduce its ownership interest in CEDS or sell it outright. The delivery business was declared to be a discontinued operation.

ACQUISITION BY UNITED SHIPPING

Takeover rumors began swirling around Corporate Express because of its troubles as the firm posted a net loss for fiscal 1998 and the stock continued to languish. Finally, in July 1999, the Dutch firm Buhrmann N.V. reached an agreement to purchase Corporate Express for $2.3 billion. The deal was contingent upon Corporate Express finding a buyer for CEDS. In September 1999 Corporate Express sold CEDS to Minneapolis-based United Shipping & Technology, Inc., for about $60 million.

United Shipping, which was known as U-Ship, Inc., from its founding in 1991 to May 1999, had been mainly involved in making and operating self-service, automated shipping systems that were used by consumers and small business shippers to ship packages and express letters through major carriers such as UPS. Although touted for their convenience (customers could access them 24 hours a day), the shipping centers never really caught on with consumers or businesspeople, and U-Ship posted a string of losses, including a loss of $2.5 million on revenues of just $917,000 for the fiscal year ending in June 1997. By December 1997 the company was close to running out of money and faced a possible delisting from the NASDAQ SmallCap Market. Peter Lytle, a business strategist and turnaround specialist, was brought in as chairman and CEO in early 1998 to save the firm from bankruptcy and revamp the company strategy.

Lytle quickly brought U-Ship back from the brink by raising $2.6 million in new equity through private placements. Then in July 1998 Lytle made the critical decision to expand the company's operations by moving into same-day delivery services the same way that U.S. Delivery had: by buying up existing local delivery firms and consolidating them into a larger and larger entity. Initially this was viewed as an extension of the company's shipping kiosk business, and Lytle believed that the firm's advanced shipping technology would give it a competitive advantage. In September 1998, U-Ship created a new subsidiary called Advanced Courier Services, Inc., as its platform for same-day delivery acquisitions, and in late 1998 the acquisition of JEL Trucking, Inc., which operated in the Minneapolis–St. Paul metropolitan area was completed. A second company, Twin Cities Transportation, Inc., was acquired in January 1999. U-Ship then changed its name to United Shipping & Technology in May 1999.

After learning that CEDS was for sale, Lytle boldly suggested to his board of directors that United Shipping make a bid, despite his company having revenues of less than $2 million compared to the more than $600 million of CEDS. Nevertheless, if the acquisition could be pulled off, United Shipping would instantly achieve its goal of operating a nationwide same-day delivery service. Lytle was able to pull off the deal—beating out 21 other bidders in the process—completing the acquisition of CEDS in September 1999 for about $60 million, plus the assumption of $60 million in debt. The name of CEDS was then changed to UST Delivery Systems, Inc., which was set up as a subsidiary of United Shipping.

THE NEW SAME-DAY SERVICE VELOCITY EXPRESS

Riding high on its acquisition coup and beginning to see the dividends of a new strategy aimed at going after e-commerce clients, United Shipping saw its stock trade well in excess of $10 a share by early 2000. Just two years earlier, the stock was going for 12 cents per share and the company verged on bankruptcy. The firm significantly improved its balance sheet in May 2000 by selling 2.8 million preferred shares, which were convertible to about 13 percent of the outstanding common stock, for $9 each to TH Lee. Putnam Internet Partners, a venture capital firm specializing in e-commerce. The $25.2 million thus raised was used to pay down debt that had been incurred to acquire CEDS and also provided United Shipping with additional working capital. One month later, the company unveiled its new brand for the same-day delivery service, Velocity Express; UST Delivery Systems was renamed Velocity Express, Inc. For the year ending July 1, 2000, United Shipping reported a net loss of $28.2 million on revenues of $471.2 million.

In October 2000 Jeffry J. Parell was named president and CEO of Velocity Express. Parell had been president of the North American Rental Group of AutoNation, Inc., where he was responsible for rental operations. Just four months later, Parell took over as CEO of United Shipping, with Lytle remaining chairman. Meantime, in November 2000, United Shipping sold one of its two air courier units, Tricor America, Inc., in a paring back of a noncore operation. By the early months of 2001 United Shipping was struggling again—it continued to lose money, bad winter weather and a stumbling economy were not helping matters, and the share price had made a precipitous drop to below $1 a share.

The company was forced to scale back on its ambitious growth plans—talk of becoming a $1 billion company at least temporarily disappeared—and it launched an $11 million cost-cutting program that involved the streamlining of its existing operations through the consolidation or elimination of loss-making delivery locations. Nearly 250 jobs were eliminated from the workforce as a result of this restructuring. To improve the working capital situation, United Shipping raised $15 million through another private placement of preferred shares. The revenues of $471.7 million were nearly flat for the fiscal year ending June 30, 2001, while the net loss widened to $35.3 million thanks to a $7.1 million restructuring charge.

United Shipping was able to strengthen its balance sheet in July 2001 by reaching an agreement with Corporate Express in a follow-up to the acquisition of CEDS. Through the agreement, United Shipping was able to eliminate $43 million in liabilities from its balance sheet. The company's improved financial position enabled it to stave off another threatened delisting from the NASDAQ.

In August 2001 Lytle retired from the company board and was replaced as chairman by Vince Wasik, a cofounder and principal of MCG Global, a private equity firm that had helped United Shipping with its restructuring efforts and its negotiations with Corporate Express and had also taken a stake in the company. United Shipping in October 2001 completed its exit from the air courier business by selling its remaining air unit, Air Courier Dispatch, Inc., to an investment group. One month later, United Shipping added two high-profile names to its board of directors: William S. Cohen, former U.S. Secretary of Defense, and Jack Kemp, former Secretary of Housing and Urban Development.

REORGANIZATION AS VELOCITY EXPRESS CORPORATION

In January 2002 United Shipping was merged into its Velocity Express subsidiary and was reincorporated as Velocity Express Corporation as a holding company. In April of that year, Velocity Express executed a five-for-one reverse stock split, thereby increasing the share price to a level that it was hoped would make the stock more appealing to institutional investors. Through the first nine months of the 2002 fiscal year, the company saw its income fall significantly, from $365 million to $261.7 million, as a result of the elimination of unprofitable delivery locations, the divestment of the air courier business, and the faltering U.S. economy.

On the positive side, the net loss of $11.4 million was a major improvement over the $26.7 million of the previous nine-month period, and the firm was able to report operating income of $231,000, compared to an operating loss of $21.8 million a year earlier. Although its long-term prospects still seemed somewhat shaky, Velocity Express was certainly on more solid ground as a result of its restructuring efforts and its focus on strengthening the balance sheet.

In 2003, Chairman Vince Wasik was named president and CEO. In December, the company brought on Jeff Hendrickson, who had worked with Wasik at National Car Rental, appointing him president and chief operating officer. In 2004, a federal law went into effect that, over the next few years, caused a severe decline in Velocity Express's business of transporting checks. The new law required banks and other financial institutions to move to electronic processing. For that year, losses increased fourfold, to $48 million on sales of $288 million. Despite cutting jobs, closing unprofitable locations, and initiating a new "metro-to-metro" service in partnership with Greyhound Lines, Inc., the company's financial situation continued to deteriorate. For 2005, it had losses of $50 million on sales of $257 million.

CONSOLIDATION, FRANCHISING, AND GLOBALIZATION

Hoping to improve business, Velocity turned to the traditional approach in its industry: consolidation. In the summer of 2006, the company spent $66 million to buy CD&L, a major competitor based in New Jersey. The acquisition, which doubled Velocity's size, appeared to be a good match. CD&L was strong in the West and Southwest, while Velocity provided more coverage in the Northeast. Within their territories, they served several of the same large customers. Velocity anticipated saving $39 million in operational expenses by closing duplicative offices and eliminating overlapping job positions.

The consolidation resulted in revenues more than doubling for the fiscal year ending June 2007, to $410.10 million. However, losses also doubled, to

$39,500 million. Velocity blamed the cost of integrating CD&L, the loss of several major customers, and the continuing decline of its check transporting business. During this period, Velocity continued to invest in new technology, adding automated track and trace capabilities to its services.

In June 2007, NASDAQ informed Velocity that it was in danger of being delisted if its stock price was not increased. In December, the company again turned to a 1-for-15 reverse split. At the end of the month, Velocity Express was again in compliance with NASDAQ requirements.

In September 2007, the company established a new subsidiary, Velocity Systems Franchising Corporation, and began awarding franchises. This freed Velocity from the costs involved in opening new agencies and moving into new markets. The first franchise agreements were signed in Fargo, South Dakota; Columbus, Ohio; and St. Louis and Kansas City, Missouri. Within five months, Velocity had 20 franchise markets operating. The company was also reportedly negotiating to sell its Canadian operations.

As these activities occurred, Velocity was also pursuing entry into the $20 billion international express delivery market through its Global Alliance. Velocity was focused on obtaining some of the three-quarters of that market involved in moving cargo within and between the United States, Asia, and Europe. Initially, the company hoped to help U.S. customers export goods to Asia by partnering with national and regional transportation providers in Asia. It would remain to be seen if this latest effort, combined with its franchises and more efficient U.S. operations, would lead Velocity Express Corporation into the black financially.

David E. Salamie
Updated, Ellen Wernick

PRINCIPAL SUBSIDIARIES

Velocity Express, Inc.; CD&L, Inc.; Velocity Express Leasing, Inc.; Clayton/National Courier Systems, Inc.; Click Messenger Service, Inc.; KBD Services, Inc.; Olympic Courier Systems, Inc.; Securities Courier Corporation; Silver Star Express, Inc.; CD&L Air Freight, Inc.; USDS Canada, Ltd.; Velocity Express Canada, Ltd.; Velocity Systems Franchising Corporation.

PRINCIPAL COMPETITORS

Dynamex, Inc.; Celadon Group, Inc.; USA Truck, Inc.; Dispatch Management Services Corporation.

FURTHER READING

"ALC Advisors Retained to Advance Velocity Express Global Alliance Strategy," *Business Wire,* January 22, 2008.

Barshay, Jill J., "Seeking More Growth, Edina-Based U-Ship Inc. Names Director CEO," *Minneapolis Star Tribune,* June 7, 1997, p. 2D.

Boisseau, Charles, "Delivering the Goods with Gusto," *Houston Chronicle,* June 27, 1995.

Frankston, Sherman, "Rebuilding a Strong Business After a Decade of Maximum Change," *Strategic Investor Relations,* Winter 2002, p. 37.

Gallagher, Thomas L., "Velocity Struggles to Stem Losses," *Traffic World,* November 14, 2007.

Goldberg, Laura, "Delivering the Goods: Corporate Express Caters to E-commerce," *Houston Chronicle,* May 4, 2000.

Hassell, Greg, "Houston Firm Wants to Take Local Delivery Nationwide," *Houston Chronicle,* August 15, 1994.

Hoffman, William, "Gaining Velocity by Merger," *Traffic World,* May 7, 2007, p. 16.

Jean, Sheryl, "Plymouth, Minn.-based Shipping Firm Believes Same-Day Delivery Will Grow," *St. Paul Pioneer Press,* September 6, 2000.

Ketelsen, James, "Learning the Hard Way," *Forbes,* December 18, 1995, p. 130.

Malone, Robert, "Toward Real-Time Delivery," *Forbes.com,* February 9, 2007.

Niemela, Jennifer, "Get Educated," *Minneapolis–St. Paul City-Business,* April 7, 2000, p. S14.

Pybus, Kenneth R., "Allwaste Ex-President Goes Public with Nationwide Delivery Network: U.S. Delivery Systems Seeking $48 Million to Buy Seven Businesses," *Houston Business Journal,* April 11, 1994, p. 1.

———, "Forging a Delivery Network from Fragments," *Houston Business Journal,* November 4, 1994, p. 12.

———, "U.S. Delivery Breaks New Ground in Purchasing Michigan Company," *Houston Business Journal,* February 24, 1995, p. 2.

Robbins Gentry, Connie, "Back-Room Secrets," *Chain Store Age,* March 2007, p. 66.

St. Anthony, Neal, "Cold Winter, Cool Economy Hurt United Shipping," *Minneapolis Star Tribune,* May 18, 2001, p. 1D.

———, "Stock Deal Gives Shipping Company Cash and Credibility," *Minneapolis Star Tribune,* May 19, 2000, p. 1D.

Soule, Alexander, "Growing Pains," *Fairfield County Business Journal,* November 5, 2007, pp. 1, 16.

Stone, Adam, "Gaining Velocity," *Minneapolis–St. Paul City-Business,* September 14, 2001, p. 13.

"Velocity and Greyhound to Offer Guaranteed Delivery," *Fairfield County Business Journal,* October 17, 2005, p. 41.

"Velocity Express Closes $21 Million Investment," *Fairfield County Business Journal,* January 10, 2005, p. 35.

Yip, Pamela, "U.S. Delivery Systems Offered Buyout: Colorado Firm Proposes $410 Million Deal," *Houston Chronicle,* January 8, 1996.

Youngblood, Dick, "U-Ship, Long at Sea, Tries to Set Profitable Course Under New Management," *Minneapolis Star Tribune,* June 24, 1998, p. 2D.

Virginia Dare Extract Company, Inc.

882 3rd Avenue
Brooklyn, New York 11232-1902
U.S.A.
Telephone: (718) 788-1776
Toll Free: (800) 847-4500
Fax: (718) 768-3978
Web site: http://www.virginiadare.com

Private Company
Incorporated: 1923
Employees: 175
Sales: $184.7 million (2006 est.)
NAIC: 311930 Flavoring Syrup and Concentrate Manufacturing

■ ■ ■

Virginia Dare Extract Company, Inc., is a Brooklyn, New York-based flavor manufacturer serving a wide variety of industries, including bakery, beverage, cereal, confectionery, dairy, desserts, foodservice, functional and fortified food, ice cream, pharmaceutical, prepared food, and snack food. The company's signature product is vanilla extract. Other product lines include coffee, tea, cocoa extracts and concentrates, spray-dried flavors, compounded flavors, sweetness modifiers, flavor enhancers and masking agents, "mouthfeel" and sensation flavors, clouding agents, and colors. Virginia Dare offers several hundred base flavors, ranging from the commonplace, like apple and banana, to the unusual, such as apple butter and Bananas Foster. The company's chemists can draw from the flavor library to create an unlimited number of combinations able to mimic virtually any flavor a customer might want or to create a flavor no tongue has ever tasted. Howard Smith, Jr., is the fourth generation of his family to run the company.

19TH-CENTURY LINEAGE

Virginia Dare was launched in 1923 by Bernard H. Smith as a subsidiary of Garrett & Company, a winemaker forced into other lines of business by Prohibition. The roots of Garrett date back to 1835 when Sydney Weller established Medoc Vineyard in Halifax County, North Carolina, the state's first commercial winery. Other North Carolina vintners were to follow, but the Civil War disrupted the business. Following the war, Medoc Vineyard was acquired by brothers Charles Garrett and Francis Marion Garrett, and they began producing still and sparkling wines, mostly from native American scuppernong grapes. They were joined by Francis's 14-year-old son, Paul, in 1877, and seven years later, upon the death of his uncle, the young man became the winery's salesman under new ownership.

Garrett proved to be a natural-born promoter, benefiting his firm while also championing the North Carolina wine industry and American wines in general. In 1900 he had a falling out with the winery over sales commissions and started his own company, Garrett & Company. He started out marketing both New York State wines and those made from the scuppernong grape of North Carolina but soon elected to focus on the latter. He aggressively outbid competitors for available scuppernong grapes, the juice of which he blended with New York and California wines to produce red and

> **COMPANY PERSPECTIVES**
>
> Virginia Dare is driven today by the traditions of our past. The challenge of creating exciting new flavors, and improving existing ones is our reason for being. Our ultimate success is our customer's satisfaction.

white wines he marketed under the "Virginia Dare" label.

Virginia Dare was a name, and legend, familiar to a native son of North Carolina like Paul Garrett. The story harkened back to the very origins of the state, the ill-fated Virginia Colony of Roanoke Island, established in 1587 off the coast of present-day North Carolina after a previous effort to establish a colony on the island had failed. Both ventures were backed by Sir Walter Raleigh, who named the colony Virginia after his patron, Queen Elizabeth of England, the "Virgin Queen." Serving as the colony's governor was John White, whose daughter Eleanor gave birth to the first English child on American soil two weeks after the colonists landed at Roanoke. Eleanor and her husband, Ananias Dare, christened the child Virginia Dare. Governor White soon returned home to resupply Roanoke but because England was at war with Spain, which was building a mighty invasion force, the Spanish Armada, he was compelled to wait three years until the armada was destroyed and the threat passed. When he returned to Roanoke in 1591 he found that all traces of the colony had vanished, save one word carved on a tree: Croatoan, the name of the present-day Hatteras Island and home to friendly natives. Due to the weather, White was never able to search the island, and he returned home to England. Whether the colonists were killed by Native Americans or marauding Spanish troops from Florida, relocated and married into the native population, or met some other fate became the subject of scholarly debate for centuries to come.

Because of the mystery surrounding the lost colony, it was not surprising that legends would develop, many of which centered on Virginia Dare, who was thought to be blond and fair. According to one of the most popular myths, the colonists were driven from Roanoke to Croatoan, where they were accepted into the native tribe. Virginia Dare grew into a beautiful young woman, who attracted the attention of a medicine man, Chico. When she rejected him, he vowed revenge and lured her to Roanoke Island where she turned into a snow-white deer. All the deer on the island followed her, and the creature became a prized target to the hunters, but no arrow could find the mark. The Croatoan chief's son believed that the silver-tipped arrow presented to his father by Queen Elizabeth had the power to slay the deer. He stalked the deer and just as he had hoped, the arrow found the mark. His triumph soon turned to sorrow, however, when he approach the deer, which in its final breath whispered, "Virginia Dare."

Long associated with wholesomeness and purity, Virginia Dare was a perfect brand name for Garrett, who turned his wine into the most popular U.S. brand of the day. By 1903 he was operating five North Carolina wineries. A year later Virginia Dare wine won the grand prize in the Louisiana Purchase Exhibition, leading to even greater sales. Soon it was so popular that there were not enough scuppernong grapes to meet demand and Garrett began relying on an increasing amount of California wine, until Virginia Dare offered only a tincture of the flavor.

PROHIBITION KEEPS GARRETT ON THE MOVE

A shortage of grapes was a minor problem for Garrett compared to the growth of Prohibition. In 1908 a referendum calling for the statewide prohibition of alcoholic beverages was enacted in North Carolina, and a year later it became the first southern state to go "dry." In response Garrett moved his business to Virginia, but after that state followed North Carolina's lead and enacted its own prohibition laws, he had to relocate again in 1917. This time he moved to the Finger Lakes region of New York State. Two years later the entire country went dry, leaving Garrett with no place to turn. By that time. he had developed a small business empire that included 17 processing plants located in half a dozen states capable of producing ten million gallons of wine each year.

Not believing that Prohibition could last very long, Garrett tried to keep his plants open so that they would be able to gear up quickly to once again produce wine when alcohol was again legal. He turned to manufacturing such products as Virginia Dare Tonic, a medicament that contained beef extract and pepsin. He also looked to transfer the company's ability to produce fine alcohol to the production of high-quality flavor extracts. Hired in 1919 to produce a line of flavor extracts, Virginia Dare Flavoring Secrets, was chemist Bernard H. Smith.

BROOKLYN COMPANY LAUNCHED: 1923

Smith was born in Massachusetts, where he earned undergraduate degrees from the Massachusetts

KEY DATES

1923: Company is established as a subsidiary of Garrett & Co. and is headed by Bernard H. Smith.
1951: Lloyd E. Smith succeeds father as president.
1952: Bernard Smith dies.
1960: Lloyd Smith dies, replaced by son Norman Smith.
1993: Mouthfeel Flavors introduced.
2000: Prosweet brand introduced.
2006: Product development labs expanded.

Agricultural College and Boston University. He then earned a master's degree from George Washington University in 1902, followed three years later by a law degree. While completing the latter degrees, Smith in 1901 took a job as an assistant chemist in the Bureau of Chemistry of the U.S. Department of Agriculture. After completing his law degree in 1905 he became chief of the Boston branch of the U.S. Food and Drug Inspection laboratory, a post he held for seven years. In 1912 he turned to the private sector, becoming a chemist for the Baker Extract Company in Springfield, Massachusetts. He then went to work for Garrett & Co. in 1919, and four years later was appointed president of the new Virginia Dare Extract Company in Brooklyn, located in the Bush Terminal on the waterfront of New York harbor.

The company made flavors for both home and industry use. The initial line of Virginia Dare Flavoring Secrets included 21 flavors, such as fruit and peppermint, but the flagship product, vanilla extract, was the first one developed, an item that was perfectly suited to the Virginia Dare name with its connotations of purity. Originally of Mexican origin, vanilla, the only fruit-bearing member of the orchid family, was unknown to Europeans until Spanish explorers brought it back from the New World in the early 1500s, calling it *vainilla,* or little pod. Although expensive, it became widespread, used to make chocolate, flavor tobacco, serve as an ingredient in medicines, and act as an aphrodisiac. Thomas Jefferson became familiar with vanilla while serving as ambassador to France in the late 1700s and is credited with introducing it to the United States. He also brought back with him a recipe for vanilla ice cream.

While Paul Garrett was no doubt pleased with Smith's success in Brooklyn, his passion for the wine business did not diminish. When Prohibition was repealed in 1933, he was the only winemaker ready to gear up to serve wet states, and he reintroduced Virginia Dare wine. Unfortunately, the Prohibition years had devastated once-thriving Eastern vineyards and wineries and despite his tireless efforts to persuade Southern farmers to once again plant scuppernong grapes, not enough were available to supply his needs. Because of the grape shortage, Virginia Dare lost what remained of its distinctive taste and appeal to consumers. In March 1940 the 76-year-old Garrett took ill and a week later died from pneumonia. Having no heirs, his company went out of business and the once popular Virginia Dare wine brand, aside from vintage bottle collectors, faded from popular memory.

Bernard Smith continued to make use of the Virginia Dare name, however. The Brooklyn firm did well providing flavors to the soft-drink industry. It formed a division called Korker Company which sold a lemon-lime product under the Korker label ("A corking good drink") that was produced by franchised bottlers. Its success led to a line of bottled flavors, including such exotic sounding names as South Seas (orange soda) and Vin-Vie (grape soda). During World War II the company added some other products to help consumers deal with shortages caused by the war. It offered Virginia Dare Ice Cream Powder to make a reasonable facsimile of the kind of ice cream that had been available before the war. Because of mayonnaise shortages, it also developed an oil-less French-style salad dressing that enjoyed some popularity.

BERNARD SMITH DIES: 1952

Following the war Virginia Dare gradually began to drop its consumer brands and focused an increasing amount of attention on its industrial flavor and extract business. In April 1951 there was a changing of the guard when Smith's son, Lloyd E. Smith, replaced him as president. The elder Smith stayed on as chairman of the board, a post he held until July 1952, when he died of a heart attack at the age of 73. His son, in his 50s, was well prepared to take the reins. After graduating from Dartmouth University in the early 1920s, he had gone to work for the National Biscuit Company before going to work for his father and quickly assuming an increasing amount of responsibility. He also forged a reputation in the extracts industry, being named president of the Flavoring Extract Manufacturers' Association of the United States in 1942. He would head Virginia Dare until he died of a reported heart ailment in 1960. His son Howard, a Princeton University graduate, carried on the family business, and in time Howard Smith, Jr., would be the fourth member of the clan to run the company.

Virginia Dare focused on traditional flavors, but over the years the more exotic combinations became more commonplace. In 1992 Virginia Dare Vice-President Lee Kohnstamm told *Beverage World,* "To survive, we flavor companies must have our fingers on the pulse of the pulse of the industry." It the early 1990s, for example, the iced tea market exploded, fueled by the popularity of Snapple, and customers clamored for tea flavor extract and concentrate, something Virginia Dare had been offering since the 1970s. Hybrid flavors were also in vogue, again playing to the strength of Virginia Dare and its experienced chemists. To meet growing demands in the 1990s, the company began to beef up its laboratory operation.

Other trends opened up additional opportunities. Consolidation in the beverage industry led to small beverage companies being acquired by larger players. This left a void to be filled by private-label manufacturers, which in order to compete against the remaining behemoths, looked to companies like Virginia Dare to help them launch new flavors to gain an edge. The rise of reduced-fat and low-fat products also created a niche opportunity for Virginia Dare. Because many of the properties associated with fat were not addressed by the new fat replacers, in 1993 the company introduced Mouthfeel Flavors to provide in a reduced-fat product the richer, fuller taste associated with a high-fat product, essentially fooling the brain into believing that fat was present when in reality it was not.

Mostly spurred on by the beverage industry, Virginia Dare introduced an abundance of new products in the 1990s. In response to the popularity of oolong tea, an oolong tea extract was added to the company's slate of black and green teas. Masking ingredients were not only needed when manufacturers removed fat, sugar, and caffeine, but also when they began to add poor-tasting fortifiers to create a healthier product. In the late 1990s Virginia Dare launched a line of masking agents to counteract the tastes of vitamins, herbs, minerals, soy, and oats added to nutraceutical products. The company also developed a replenishment flavor system for frozen drinks. To serve the candy industry it offered Contrasweet, to reduce sweetness without altering the product flavor.

New products continued to be rolled out at a steady pace in the early years of the 21st century. Early in 2000 Virginia Dare offered a broad line of fruit and berry flavors, including Cherry–Candy Apple Sorbet, Kiwi-Strawberry Green Tea, Blueberry Black Tea, and Fuzzy Mango lemonades. A new line of flavor enhancers and masking agents, marketed under the Prosweet brand, was also introduced in 2000. A year later Virginia Dare unveiled a pair of new frozen dessert flavors, Marshmallow Crispie Treat and Ginger Snap Cookie; Bananas Foster and Ginger Peach soft-serve ice cream flavors; a new spray-dried natural chocolate flavor; and a natural elderberry extract that could be combined with other berries to create unique flavor profiles in beverages, baked goods, and puddings.

RESEARCH FACILITY EXPANDED

To stay current with changing consumer tastes and the demand for new flavor combinations, Virginia Dare expanded its research staff and in 2006 added 5,000 square feet to its new product development laboratories to create new applications for beverages and sweet goods, and also created a beverage pilot plant. At the same time, Virginia Dare did not forget about its first, and most basic, product, vanilla. In 2007 it began to offer a new high-quality Fair Trade Vanilla of Indian origin, which not only offered a clean flavor profile but was also produced in an ethical manner from small farmers and producers. In addition, Virginia Dare was involved in research efforts to increase vanilla yields through new cultivation techniques, and improved production processes.

Ed Dinger

PRINCIPAL OPERATING UNITS

Coffee, Tea, Cocoa & Vanilla Extracts & Concentrates; Compounded Flavors; Spray Dried Flavors; Flavor Enhancers/Masking Agents; Sweetness Modifiers; Mouthfeel/Sensation Flavors; Clouding Agents; Colors.

PRINCIPAL COMPETITORS

U.S. Flavors and Fragrances, Inc.; Flavor Specialties, Inc.; Flavor Innovations Incorporated.

FURTHER READING

"Bernard H. Smith, Chemist, 73, Dead," *New York Times,* July 6, 1952.

"Lloyd E. Smith, 60, Virginia Dare Head," *New York Times,* November 29, 1960.

Mills, Joseph, and Danielle Tarmey, *A Guide to North Carolina Wineries,* Winston-Salem, N.C.: John F. Blair, Inc., 2007.

"Paul Garrett Dies; Noted Wine Maker," *New York Times,* March 20, 1940.

"Virginia Dare," *Dairy Foods,* January 2006.

"Virginia Dare Celebrates 75 Years in Beverage Flavors," *Beverage Industry,* May 1998, p. 28.

"Virginia Dare Completes R&D Lab Expansion," *Candy Industry,* September 2006, p. 13.

Vitasoy International Holdings Ltd.

1 Kin Wong Street
Tuen Mun, New Territories
Hong Kong
Telephone: (852) 2466 0333
Fax: (852) 2465 1008
Web site: http://www.vitasoy.com

Public Company
Incorporated: 1940
Employees: 2,321
Sales: HKD 2.69 billion ($345.91 million) (2007)
Stock Exchanges: Hong Kong
Ticker Symbol: 0345.HK
NAIC: 311920 Coffee and Tea Manufacturing; 311991 Perishable Prepared Food Manufacturing; 424490 Other Grocery and Other Related Products Merchant Wholesalers; 551112 Offices of Other Holding Companies

■ ■ ■

Vitasoy International Holdings Ltd. is one of the world's leading producers of soy milk and tofu. The company's two major brands are its Vitasoy line of soy drinks and tofu, and its Vita line of other drinks, including dairy milk, juices, teas, distilled water, and sodas. Headquartered in Hong Kong, Vitasoy maintains strong markets there and in the rest of China, throughout Southeast Asia, in Australia and New Zealand, and in the United States. Its U.S. subsidiary holds about 10 percent of the U.S. market in soy milk and over 50 percent of the U.S. tofu market. The company operates plants in Hong Kong, mainland China, the United States, and Australia. The business was founded in 1940 by Dr. K. S. Lo, and is run today by members of the Lo family. Vitasoy stock has been traded on the Hong Kong exchange since 1994, while the Lo family remains the major stockholders.

THE COW OF CHINA

Dr. Kwee Seong Lo founded Vitasoy in 1940 in Hong Kong to provide an answer to rising malnutrition in the area. Dr. Lo was involved in several businesses, but dropped them all to invest HKD 25,000 in the venture that became Vitasoy after hearing a talk at the U.S. embassy in Shanghai about the nutritional benefits of soy. Soy products had been key to the Chinese diet for thousands of years. Soy milk, a preparation made from heated and mashed soybeans, was well known throughout China and Japan, though it was most typically converted into its solid form, tofu. With vitamin deficiency diseases such as beriberi and pellagra rampant in China during this turbulent period, the embassy talk focused on a possible solution. This was the humble soybean, the "cow of China."

Dr. Lo immediately grasped the potential of soy milk for a populace desperately needing protein and nutrition. He opened a factory in Hong Kong's Causeway Bay and began delivering fresh soy milk door-to-door by bicycle. Lo's first day saw only six bottles sold. The business barely had time to get off the ground before changing conditions forced it to close. The Japanese invasion of Hong Kong in 1941 stopped Vitasoy's production, which by then had reached a thousand bottles a day.

COMPANY PERSPECTIVES

At Vitasoy, promoting consumer well-being is our number one priority. This is achieved through the provision of a variety of high-quality, nutritious food and beverages. Vitasoy is an innovative company, a reliable employer, and a responsible corporate citizen and is dedicated to creating value for our shareholders.

POSTWAR RELAUNCH

Lo returned to Vitasoy at the cease of hostilities in 1945, with a few changes. Rather than deliver by bicycle, Lo sought out retail outlets. The product was still positioned as a milk substitute, marketed as healthful. Vitasoy turned a significant profit by 1948. The company's business grew so quickly that by 1950, the company needed to build a new factory in Aberdeen, Hong Kong. In those years, soy milk had very short shelf life and needed refrigeration, just like cow's milk. In 1953, the company perfected a sterilization technique that allowed Vitasoy to be stocked without refrigeration. This greatly increased the product's reach, and sales climbed markedly. In 1962, the company built another new plant to handle the increased growth. This one was in Kwun Tong, Hong Kong.

GROWTH IN HONG KONG

Vitasoy thrived in its home market, where the Lo family was involved in several aspects of the food industry. Vitasoy was a Pepsi-Cola distributor from 1957 to 1977, and this helped the company understand the soft-drink market both domestically and abroad. Lo's son Victor began working for Vitasoy while still a teenager, and he returned to the company in 1960 with an advanced degree in food science from Cornell University in the United States. Victor Lo then founded a fast-food chain in Hong Kong in 1968, Café de Coral. This had become the leading Chinese fast-food chain by the beginning of the 21st century, with over 500 outlets worldwide. Son Dennis Lo also had a hand in Vitasoy and later founded his own restaurant chain.

Family know-how combined with international marketing exposure through the Pepsi franchise meant Vitasoy was able to adapt and grow. The biggest change was that Vitasoy's advertising began to portray soy milk not just as good for you, but as a "leisure" drink, like cola or lemonade. With a population no longer threatened with starvation, Vitasoy became a fun drink, a treat, rather than a protein-rich milk substitute.

DIVERSIFICATION AFTER 1974

The company faced a major challenge in the early 1970s, when rising energy costs worldwide led to escalating prices in other commodities, including sugar and soybeans. With its costs for raw materials going up, Vitasoy's profitability was affected, and the company had to compensate quickly. In 1974, with oil prices worldwide at a peak, the company was in trouble. However, Vitasoy found a technological solution that enabled it to reach wider markets. In 1975, the company debuted new packaging, the foil and paper box known as Tetra Pak. Liquids packed in Tetra Pak could withstand high heat, so Vitasoy's soy milk could be processed with ultrahigh temperature sterilization. Product shelf life was much longer with the new packaging and sterilizing, and this allowed Vitasoy to ship to farther-flung markets.

At the same time, the company began making more inroads into the leisure drinks market, selling not just soy milk but a variety of sweetened concoctions such as juices and teas. These non-soy drinks were marketed under the brand-name Vita. This quick thinking restored the company to profitability. With two distinct product lines, better equipped factories, and proven ability in wider markets, the company was poised for international market penetration.

INTERNATIONAL MARKETS

Vitasoy had a strong and loyal market in Hong Kong, but it also had waiting customer bases in other countries. It could sell relatively easily in markets with emigrant Chinese populations. Furthermore, soy products were also becoming known in the West in health-food markets. Vitasoy moved its products into beckoning foreign markets in the 1980s, eventually finding its way into 30 different countries. Vitasoy made inroads into the potentially enormous mainland China market beginning in 1979, when it arranged a joint venture to import New Zealand dairy cows to the neighboring Chinese province of Guangdong. Vitasoy sold cow milk in China, and eventually added its other product lines. People in Guangdong were close enough to Hong Kong to view Hong Kong television, so they were already seeing advertising for Vitasoy products. However, Vitasoy moved cautiously in mainland China, where political and legal uncertainties made joint ventures sometimes dicey.

At the same time, Vitasoy was moving into the U.S. market. Founder Lo's daughter Yvonne incorporated a U.S. subsidiary, Vitasoy USA, Inc., in 1979, selling at first exclusively in San Francisco's Chinatown neighborhood. Vitasoy USA slowly penetrated more of

KEY DATES

1940: Founded as bicycle-delivery soy drink company in Hong Kong.
1950: Company builds new postwar factory.
1962: Vitasoy builds second Hong Kong plant.
1975: Financial pinch reversed with introduction of new packaging.
1979: U.S. subsidiary founded in San Francisco.
1994: Sells shares to public.
1995: Founder Kwee Seong Lo dies; succeeded by son Winston Lo.
2001: Opens plant in Australia.

the U.S. market, selling through Asian grocery stores to primarily ethnic Chinese customers.

HEALTH-FOOD MARKETS

In the mid-1980s, the company reconfigured its products to appeal to non-Chinese consumers in the West. Vitasoy began selling tofu and soy milk in health-food markets in the United States and in Australia. This was a small but potentially booming market niche. Vitasoy consolidated its position in the U.S. health-food market by acquiring two existing soy products companies. In 1990, the U.S. subsidiary purchased Nasoya Foods, Inc., a Massachusetts-based maker of tofu, soy-based salad dressings, and soy mayonnaise. Then in 1993, Vitasoy USA bought the San Francisco tofu operations known as Nasoya Foods.

Consumption of soy-based foods rose 10 percent a year in the United States between 1990 and 1995, and Vitasoy seemed nicely placed to take advantage of the trend. With its two acquisitions, the company became the largest tofu manufacturer in the United States, with a market share of about 30 percent. As sales rose, Vitasoy invested $14.5 million in a new Massachusetts plant. Findings published in the *New England Journal of Medicine* in 1995 gave new backing to the healthful properties of soy, and tofu and soy milk began to move into mainstream supermarkets. Vitasoy revamped its soy milk formula to appeal to Western consumers as it prepared for abundant growth in the category over the next decade. By about 2005, Vitasoy had over 50 percent of the U.S. tofu market share, and about 10 percent of the soy milk market. Major competitors in the United States were White Wave and Edensoy.

OTHER DEVELOPMENTS AFTER 1990

Other key events happened closer to home. In 1987, Vitasoy built a new plant in Tuen Mun, Hong Kong, investing HKD 100 million in a vastly larger plant and office complex. Then in 1994, the company sold shares to the public for the first time. While Vitasoy shares were listed on the Hong Kong stock exchange, the Lo family remained the principal shareholders. Founder Kwee Seong Lo died in 1995. He was succeeded by his son Winston, while his other children were also closely involved in the business.

Though its markets were growing abroad and it had a thriving base in Hong Kong, Vitasoy ran into production problems in the mid-1990s that set its business back. The first was a problem with soy milk packed at its Hong Kong plants. Consumers began complaining of a sour taste in some Vitasoy products in 1996. Although the off taste proved not to be related to anything harmful, the company was forced to halt production temporarily, and then to recall some 14.2 million units of soy milk. The company's stock price fell rapidly, and Vitasoy's profits also fell for the year, by as much as 75 percent.

Then only two years later, Vitasoy experienced difficulties with a new soy and tofu plant it refurbished in Massachusetts. The new plant was expected to enhance greatly the company's ability to distribute to its North American market, but one snag after another dragged down profits. Profits from the company's U.S. subsidiary remained flat or negative into the early years of the new century, despite continued growth in overall soy product sales in that market. Vitasoy spent heavily on advertising and in rolling out new products. It saw this as a wise investment, as the U.S. soy market was far from mature.

NEW CEO AT U.S. SUBSIDIARY

In 2004, Vitasoy's U.S. subsidiary hired a new chief executive, Robert C. Jones. It seemed time for a new direction, as Vitasoy U.S.A.'s revenue had dropped by 6 percent in the first half of fiscal 2003, even as retail tofu and soy drink sales overall grew 10 percent. Jones had worked at several pharmaceutical companies before coming to Vitasoy, and he had also founded his own company, Advanced Functional Foods. Jones was interested in foods such as soy products that people might eat for distinct medical or nutritional advantages. Jones was not tied to traditional Chinese conceptions of soy cuisine, and under his leadership, the company brought out new convenience products such as marinated tofu that appealed to Western tastes.

PREPARATION FOR FUTURE GROWTH

Vitasoy opened its first factory in Australia in 2001. By the middle of the first decade of the 21st century, the company was well placed to sell its products both to consumers in Asia and to Westerners. Vitasoy had approximately 300 different drink products in its stable, including juices, teas, and distilled water. It sold these in more than 30 countries around the globe. It ran five factories in total, with its flagship plant in Tuen Mun, one in nearby Shenzhen and another in Shanghai, and the overseas plants in Australia and the United States. Vitasoy also began moving into another successful product line in the new century, catering lunches to Hong Kong schools. By 2005, this was a significant business, with contracts with some 300 school eateries.

Winston Lo, the founder's son, was himself near retirement age by the end of the decade. As he considered his successor, he stressed the importance of a vision for international markets. Although almost 60 percent of the company's revenue came from Hong Kong, sales in the rest of China were expected to grow in double digits over the next few years. Although the North American market had remained disappointing in terms of profits, it still held out promise of growth. The company would continue to respond to consumer needs for healthful foods and drinks, whether in China or abroad. Health consciousness was particularly acute in Vitasoy's Western markets, and would probably play an increasingly important role in its native Chinese markets as well. The company was also prepared to address environmental concerns in coming decades. All in all, Vitasoy hoped to build on its long history as the maker of nutritious and healthful products as it moved into its third generation of management.

A. Woodward

PRINCIPAL SUBSIDIARIES

Hong Kong Gourmet Ltd.; Shenzhen Vitasoy Foods and Beverage Co. Ltd.; Vitasoy Australia Products Ltd.; Vitasoy Services Ltd; Vitasoy (Shanghai) Co. Ltd.; Vitasoy USA, Inc.

PRINCIPAL COMPETITORS

WhiteWave Foods Co.; Tata Tea Ltd.; Yeo Hiap Seng Ltd.

FURTHER READING

Ackerman, Jerry, "In Ayer, Factory Rises near Tofu's 'Mecca' amid Growing U.S. Demand," *Boston Globe,* April 1, 1998, p. F4.

Chiu, Jennifer, "Vitasoy Profits Rise on U.S. Demand," *Hong Kong Standard,* July 13, 2000.

Esposito, Andy, "Healthy Competition," *Worcester (Mass.) Telegram & Gazette,* May 16, 2004, p. E1.

Flagg, Michael, "In Hong Kong: A Local Price War Turns Analysts Sour on Vitasoy," *Asian Wall Street Journal,* October 20, 1999, p. 13.

Li, Joyce, "Vitasoy Optimistic Despite SARS," *Hong Kong Mail,* July 10, 2003.

Ng, Dennis, "Losses in U.S. Drain Vitasoy Earnings," *Hong Kong Mail,* July 13, 2001, p. 1.

Reyes, Sonia, "Vitasoy Defends Organic Turf with New Tofu, TV," *Brandweek,* April 30, 2001, p. 7.

———, "Vitasoy Puts Some Meat on Tofu Pitch," *Brandweek,* September 15, 2003, p. 9.

"Soya Coming," *Economist,* August 6, 1994, pp. 56–57.

Wang, Jasmine, "Vitasoy Sets Mainland Sales Target," *South China Morning Post,* November 27, 2007, p. 4.

Webb, Sara, "In Hong Kong: Investors Remain Wary of Cloud over Vitasoy," *Asian Wall Street Journal,* January 19, 1996, p. 11.

Yiu, Enoch, "Vitasoy Chief Milks Vision of Health," *South China Morning Post,* January 15, 2007, p. 14.

Vocento

Juan Ignacio Luca de Tena 7
Madrid, E-28027
Spain
Telephone: (34 91) 339 90 00
Fax: (34 91) 320 35 55
Web site: http://www.vocento.com

Public Company
Incorporated: 1910 as Diario El Correo S.A.
Employees: 4,918
Sales: EUR 872.5 million ($1.19 billion) (2006)
Stock Exchanges: Madrid
Ticker Symbol: VOC
NAIC: 511110 Newspaper Publishers; 424920 Book, Periodical, and Newspaper Merchant Wholesalers; 515112 Radio Stations

■ ■ ■

Vocento is one of Spain's leading media groups. The Madrid-based company is active across a broad spectrum of media outlets, with operations in newspapers, television, radio, and film production and distribution. Vocento's newspaper holdings include the national daily *ABC,* the third largest in Spain, and a portfolio of 13 regional titles including *El Correo, El Diario Vasco, La Verdad, Ideal, Hoy, Sur, La Rioja,* and *La Voz de Cadiz.* Vocento also publishes the free daily *Qué!* and a number of newspaper supplements and magazines. Altogether, the company counts a readership of more than 3.5 million each day. Vocento's predecessor, El Correo, began building the group's media interests in the mid-1990s. These include a 13 percent stake in Telecinco, one of Spain's largest free-to-air channels and one of the most profitable television channels in Europe. The company holds two digital terrestrial television licenses, Net TV and Fly Music.

The company is also a leading player in multilingual Spain's important regional television market, operating 49 local and regional television stations in 39 markets, through subsidiary Punto TV. Vocento's production and distribution operations are grouped under subsidiary Veralia. The company's holdings include three of Spain's leading production companies, Group Europroducciones, BocaBoca and Group Videomedia, as well as leading independent film distributor TriPictures. Through Europroducciones, Vocento has also expanded internationally, with operations in Greece, Poland, Portugal, Italy, Turkey, and the United States. The company's radio division operates through Punto Radio, launched in 2004. Vocento also has a significant presence on the Internet, operating web sites for most of its major titles, as well as Internet service subsidiaries including Sarenet, La Trastienda Digital, and Vocento Media Trader. Vocento has been listed on the Madrid Stock Exchange since 2006. The company is led by managing director Belarmino García. Vocento's revenues reached EUR 872.5 million ($1.19 billion) in 2006.

LAUNCH OF *ABC* IN 1903

The merger of regional newspaper group Grupo El Correo with Prensa Espanola, publisher of the national daily *ABC,* one of the largest in Spain, formed the basis

COMPANY PERSPECTIVES

As a communications group, we are aware that our mission goes beyond merely disseminating content. We maintain a firm commitment to offering quality, rigorous, truthful, useful information that helps people understand the world they live in, gives faithful testimony to daily events, and serves as an essential vehicle for reflecting on the world we live in.

of the Vocento media group. Both El Correo and Prensa Espanola had begun investing in diversified media interests during the mid-1990s. Both groups, however, had their origins at the beginning of the 20th century.

Prensa Espanola was the older of the two, having been founded as a weekly newspaper publisher by Juan Ignacio Luca de Tena in 1903. The newspaper adopted the unusual name of *ABC.* In keeping with Spanish—and European—tradition, in which newspapers were generally closely aligned with a specific political ideology, *ABC* espoused a highly conservative line. The newspaper became closely associated with both the Catholic Church and the Spanish monarchy, a position the newspaper maintained even with its support of Franco's fascist government. By 1905, *ABC* had converted itself into a daily newspaper. Before long, *ABC* grew into the biggest newspaper in Madrid. The newspaper later expanded on a national level, becoming the largest in Spain.

Like all of Spain's press, *ABC* was affected by the Spanish civil war. The newspaper became a highly vocal critic of the Second Republic in the early 1930s. Juan Ignacio Luca de Tena was himself an active supporter of Franco's Nationalist movement. In 1936 Luca de Tena supplied the airplane that flew Franco to Spanish Morocco to launch the civil war. During the war, *ABC* was seized by the Frente Popular (Popular Front). The newspaper was then split into two editions. In Madrid, the newspaper's editors took up the cause of the Republicans, while the Seville edition gave its support to the Nationalists.

Following the war, ownership of *ABC* was returned to the Luca de Tena family. By then, Franco announced new regulations placing the country's press and publishing industries under the fascist government's control. The new law, passed in 1938, gave rise the following year to a new body, Prensa del Movimiento, placed under the oversight of the National Press and Propaganda Agency. In this way, the Franco government imposed more than 30 years of censorship on Spain's newspaper industry. Pro-fascist *ABC* maintained its strongly pro-monarchist stance throughout this period.

The Franco government passed new legislation governing the press in 1966. The new law relaxed some of the repressive restrictions on Spain's press. Nonetheless, the press remained highly controlled by the Franco government. Publishers and journalists taking up critical stances against the government's policies remained exposed to risk of sanctions. As a result, the country's newspaper readership dropped significantly into the early 1970s for most newspapers, with the exception of *ABC* and its Barcelona counterpart, *La Vanguardia.*

ABC continued to support the fascist government up until Franco's death in the mid-1970s. The newspaper did not, however, oppose the institution of a new democratic government, instead adopting a position that maintaining the country's monarchy was necessary for ensuring Spain's political stability. The new Spanish government passed new legislation in 1978, restoring the liberty of the press.

ABC retained its highly conservative editorial position through the next two decades. By the beginning of the 21st century, *ABC* had lost its position as Spain's largest newspaper, ceding ground on the left to *El Mundo* and on the right to the populist *La Razon.* At the same time, *ABC* faced increasing competition with the arrival of the first free dailies into the Spanish market. By about 2005, the free newspapers, including *Metro, ADN,* and Vocento's own *Qué!* had captured a 51 percent share of the total market.

ABC was merged into El Correo to form Vocento in 2001. As part of this new media giant, the third largest in Spain, *ABC* began softening its own editorial stance somewhat, adopting a more moderate conservative tone. In this way, the company hoped to attract a more youthful readership in order to replace the older readership lost to the more hard-line *La Razon.*

REGIONAL BEGINNINGS OF EL CORREO IN 1910

The merger with *ABC,* which gave El Correo majority control of the new company, was part of El Correo's effort to transform itself from a regional to a national media group. El Correo's origins lay in Bilbao, in northern Spain, where the company was founded by brothers Fernando, Gabriel, and Emilio Ybarra y de la Revilla in 1910. The company's first title was *El Pueblo Vasco* (The Basque People), and served as a Spanish-language voice supporting autonomy for the Basque region. The newspaper nonetheless remained conservative editorially, supporting the monarchy and the Catholic Church.

KEY DATES

1903: Founding of Prensa Espanola with launch of *ABC* newspaper in Madrid.
1910: Launch of *El Pueblo Vasco* in Bilbao.
1938: *El Pueblo Vasco* is merged with rival *El Correo,* forming basis of El Correo group.
1984: El Correo launches drive to become leading regional newspaper publisher in Spain.
2001: El Correo and Prensa Espanola merge, creating Vocento.
2006: Vocento completes initial public offering on Madrid Stock Exchange.

Regional newspapers played an extremely important role in Spain's press landscape. The presence of two major languages—Spanish and Catalan—as well as the Basque language in a region spanning northern Spain and southern France played a prominent role in this regionalism. Equally important were the ongoing conflicts for power among Spain's major cities, especially between Madrid and Barcelona. As a result, regional newspapers often had as much influence as the national dailies.

The chief regional rival of *El Pueblo Vasco* remained *La Gazeta del Norte* in the years leading up to the civil war. Another title joined the market in 1934, *El Diario Vasco,* which was published from San Sebastian. Competition for the regional market was heightened with the appearance of a new daily newspaper, *El Correo* (The Courier) in 1937, launched by the fascist party. As the official newspaper of the Falange, *El Correo* emerged as the instrument for the fascist government's consolidation of the region's newspapers.

In 1938, *El Correo* and *El Pueblo Vasco* were combined into a single newspaper. The following year, the company took over another competitor, *El Noticiero Bilaino.* The company grew again in 1948, when it took over *El Diario Vasco.* The company, which remained under the ownership of the Ybarra family, then changed its name, becoming Bilbao Editorial SA.

El Correo and *El Diario Vasco* remained the core of the group's publishing interests into the 1990s. *El Correo,* which later also became the company's name, emerged as its flagship in the mid-1970s, when its circulation topped that of *La Gazeta de Norte.* With the end of the Franco government and the liberalization of the Spanish newspaper market, El Correo continued to extend its presence in the Basque regions, expanding *El Correo* into nine local editions.

BECOMING A REGIONAL NEWSPAPER LEADER

The mid-1980s marked a new phase in El Correo's growth as it sought to establish itself beyond its home region for the first time. Acquisitions played a major role in the group's strategy, starting with *El Diario Montañes,* based in Cantabria, in 1984. That paper, founded in 1902, highlighted El Correo's strategy of targeting leading regional newspapers. The new title gave El Correo more than 70 percent of the Cantabria region's newspaper readership.

The year 1988 marked another major milestone for El Correo. In that year, the company acquired three major regional titles. *La Verdad,* founded in 1903, was the leading newspaper in Murcia. *Ideal,* which was launched in 1932, covered the Granada, Almería, and Jaén markets. *Hoy,* formed in 1933, brought El Correo into the Extremadura region, including local editions for the Cáceres, Badajoz, Mérida, and Plasencia markets.

El Correo continued its regional conquest into the 1990s, buying *Diario Sur,* based in Málaga, in 1990 and extending the group's coverage to the Marbella–Costa del Sol, Campo de Gibraltar, Melilla, and other markets. The fast-growing tourist market in this region later led the company to add an English-language edition of *Sur* as well.

By the middle of the 1990s, El Correo had largely completed its regional expansion. New titles added during the first half of the decade included *La Rioja,* added in 1993; *El Norte de Castilla,* acquired in 1994; and *El Commercio,* bought in 1995. This last acquisition also brought *La Voz de Avilés* into the El Correo fold. By then, El Correo had grown into one of Spain's leading regional newspaper groups.

MEDIA GIANT FOR THE 21ST CENTURY

Both El Correo and Prensa Espanola had begun investing in diversifying their holdings amid the deregulation of Spain's media markets in the late 1990s. Prensa Espanola acquired a 30 percent stake in Europroducciones, a leading producer of programming for the Spanish and international television markets. Prensa Espanola had also entered the broadcasting market, taking a 25 percent stake of newly formed digital terrestrial broadcaster Net TV.

El Correo in the meantime had acquired a 25 percent stake in Spain's leading commercial broadcaster,

Telecinco. At the same time, El Correo had also been investing in production companies, building up a 30 percent stake in BocaBoca and a 17 percent stake in Arbol.

The creation of Vocento in 2001 merged El Correo and Prensa Espanola's media and publishing interests, creating one of Spain's top media groups. The company expected to list its stock on the Madrid Stock Exchange that year. However, the terrorist attacks against the United States on September 11, 2001, and the resulting downturn in the investor market forced the group to put the offering on hold.

Vocento instead launched an effort to consolidate its holdings. In 2004, for example, the company increased its stake in Europroducciones, then in the midst of an international expansion effort, to 79 percent. Europroducciones was then incorporated into a dedicated production division, Veralia. The company also attempted to gain the majority control of Telecinco, but was beaten out by rival Mediaset. As a result, Vocento reduced its stake in Telecinco to 13 percent at mid-decade.

Vocento increased its stake in BocaBoca from 30 percent to 70 percent in 2005. The company also added a new investment that year, buying 30 percent of another leading Spanish production company, Videomedia, for EUR 10 million. These holdings were also added to the Veralia production division.

Vocento also stepped up its broadcasting holdings through the middle of the decade. The company acquired majority control of Net TV, and added a second digital license, launching Fly TV as well. Vocento also became a leading local broadcaster, building up a portfolio of more than 50 local channels by 2007. Vocento also entered the radio market, launching Punta Radio in 2004. In 2006, the group added film distribution to its credits, paying $63.8 million for a 60 percent stake in leading independent film distributor TriPictures.

Vocento finally completed its initial public offering in November 2006. The successful offering helped boost the company's treasury past EUR 500 million, while the group's 13 percent stake in Telecinco provided it with the potential of another EUR 700 million as it surveyed the media landscape for the next phase of its expansion.

For this, the group brought in a new leader, Belarmino García, formerly head of France Telecom Espana, in 2007. García took over from José María Bergareche, who during 30 years as the head of the company had transformed Vocento into Spain's largest newspaper publisher and one of its top media players.

M. L. Cohen

PRINCIPAL SUBSIDIARIES

Alava Televisión, S.L.; Canal Bilbovisión, S.L.; Canal Ideal Televisión, S.L.; Corporación de Medios de Murcia, S.A.; Diario ABC, S.L; Diario El Correo; Editorial Cantabria, S.A.; El Comercio, S.A.; Gala Ediciones, S.L.; Inversor Ediciones, S.L.; La Verdad Radio y Televisión, S.L.; Medios de Andalucía, S.A.; Nueva Rioja, S.A; Radiotelevisión Canal 8–DM, S.L.; Rioja Televisión, S.A.; S.A.U. Sociedad Vascongada de San Publicaciones, S.A.; Taller de Ediciones Corporativas, S.L.U.; Taller de Editores, S.A.

PRINCIPAL COMPETITORS

Acciona S.A.; Grupo PRISA; Grupo Planeta; Grupo Zeta S.A; Diario El Pais; Grupo Godo de Comunicacion; Editorial Prensa Iberica S.A.; Recoletos Compania Editorial S.A.; Unidad Editorial S.A.

FURTHER READING

De Pablos, Emiliano, "Digital TV's Reign Begins in Spain," *Variety,* December 5, 2005, p. 28.

———, "Fewer Hands Holding Reins in Spain's TV Biz," *Variety,* October 1, 2001, p. 64.

———, "Indie Incorporated: Vocento Buys TriPictures Majority Stake," *Daily Variety,* June 2, 2006, p. 5.

Elkin, Mike, "Spain's Correo and Prensa Groups near Deal," *Daily Deal,* September 19, 2001.

Hopewell, John, "Garcia to Manage Vocento," *Daily Variety,* April 23, 2007, p. 11.

Hopewell, John, and Emiliano De Pablos, "Vocento's Cash Deal," *Variety,* October 30, 2006, p. 31.

"Spain's Vocento to Launch Eu500m IPO via BBVA, CS," *Euroweek,* September 8, 2006, p. 28.

"Vocento, El Nuevo Nombre del Grupo Correo," *Epoca,* June 6, 2003, p. 98.

Wilh. Wilhelmsen ASA

P.O. Box 33
Strandveien 20
Lysaker, N-1324
Norway
Telephone: (47) 67 58 40 00
Fax: (47) 67 58 40 80
Web site: http://www.ww-group.com

Public Company
Incorporated: 1861
Employees: 13,443
Sales: $2.5 billion (2006)
Stock Exchanges: Oslo
Ticker Symbol: WWI
NAIC: 483111 Deep Sea Freight Transportation; 483112 Deep Sea Passenger Transportation

■ ■ ■

Wilh. Wilhelmsen ASA is one of the world's top shipping and maritime services companies. The Norwegian company, in operation since 1861, focuses on three core divisions: shipping, logistics, and maritime services. The shipping division operates through Wallenius Wilhelmsen Logistics (WWL), a shipping and logistic joint venture with Sweden's Wallenius Lines, which operates 36 carriers; Wilhelmsen Lines, with eight vessels; and Wilhelmsen Offshore & Chartering, with 35 vessels. The division is also present in the United States through a 40 percent stake in Eukor Car Carriers Inc., and a 50 percent share of American Roll-on Roll-off Carrier. Shipping remains the group's largest division, accounting for 60 percent of revenues of more than $2.5 billion, and 90 percent of group earnings in 2006.

The logistics division focuses mostly on providing logistics services to the company's shipping operations. This division, based around WWL, includes a 20 percent stake in Korea's Glovis, and 50 percent shares of both American Auto Logistics and American Auto Network, which focus on providing support services to the U.S. military. The logistics division adds 25 percent to group revenues.

Maritimes services is the company's youngest division, having been set up in 2005 in order to restructure the company's ship management, products, equipment, and financial, insurance, and other services to the maritime industry. Wilh. Wilhelmsen is listed on the Oslo stock exchange, and is based in Lysaker, Norway. The founding Wilhelmsen family remains closely associated with the company, controlling nearly 20 percent of its stock. Wilhelm Wilhelmsen, a descendant of the founder, serves as group chairman.

FIRST VESSEL IN 1865

Wilh. Wilhelmsen originated as a ship brokering and chandlering business launched by Morten Wilhelm Wilhelmsen in Tønsberg, Norway, in 1861. Wilhelmsen's entry into ship ownership came shortly after, with the purchase of a stake in a barque, the *Mathilde,* in 1865. The company added its second vessel, the ship *Aksel,* just one year later. By the end of the decade, Wilhelmsen owned shares in three ships.

Wilhelmsen continued to add to his fleet over the next decade and a half, during which time he was joined

COMPANY PERSPECTIVES

Vision and Philosophy: The WW Group will be the leading provider of maritime services. We believe that empowered employees in an innovative, learning organisation are the group's main competitive advantage in meeting the needs and wants of our customers.

by Halfdan, his eldest son. Halfdan Wilhelmsen recognized that the age of the sailing vessel was drawing to an end, as new and more powerful steam-driven ships began to appear. The younger Wilhelmsen led the company in the acquisition of its first steamship, the *Talabot,* in 1887. That vessel, built just six years earlier and bought from Liverpool's Moss SS Co., later set a naming standard for the company's fleet. Over the next century, more than 300 vessels owned by the company were given names beginning with the letter "T."

By the end of the 19th century, Wilhelmsen had converted fully to steamship, emerging as a major player in the Norwegian shipping industry, and then entering the ranks of major international shipowners. The company began developing its own regular liner service as early as 1901. This led the company to form a partnership in 1911 with Fearnley & Eger, creating the Norwegian Africa and Australia Line (NAAL).

NAAL grew quickly, adding routes to China, the Straits, Japan, and India before the outbreak of World War I. The partnership between the two companies deepened during this period with the mutual acquisition of a second liner company, Norway Mexico Gulf Line. In this way, the group already covered a large percentage of the world's major shipping routes. The operations of the two lines, which focused primarily on cargo transport, also provided the company with its first passenger business, with most ships outfitted to accommodate a dozen or more passengers.

LINER FOCUS IN THE TWENTIES

Yet cargo transport remained the group's primary business. The company entered the oil tanker market, adding its first tanker vessel in 1913. By the end of World War I the company's tanker fleet numbered ten vessels. During the war, however, a number of its U.K.-based tankers were requisitioned by the British government, and were restored to the company only after the war ended. Wilhelmsen then regrouped its tankers at its new headquarters in Oslo. Wilhelmsen became Norway's dominant tanker operator, controlling more than 90 percent of the country's total tanker fleet.

Into the 1920s, however, the company focused its expansion more narrowly on its liner operations. Leading this shift in strategy was Halfdan Wilhelmsen's younger brother, Wilhelm Wilhelmsen. When Halfdan died in 1923, the younger Wilhelmsen took over as head of the company. By then, Wilhelmsen had bought out its partner in NAAL and Norway Mexico Gulf Line, in 1920. Over the next decade, the company began selling its tankers and fleet of trampers.

In their place, Wilhelmsen launched a major fleet expansion. Over the next two decades, the company added nearly 60 newly built cargo liners. The massive investment, entirely financed by the company itself, enabled Wilhelmsen to grow into the largest shipping company in Norway by the beginning of World War II.

REBUILDING IN THE POSTWAR ERA

During the war, Wilhelmsen joined the exiled Norwegian government, placing its fleet at the disposal of the Allied war effort from bases in London and New York. The group's vessels provided troop and ammunition transport in both the European and Pacific theaters. Of particular note was the company's ship *Torrens,* put into service in the Pacific in 1942. Over the course of the war, that ship provided transport for more than 60,000 U.S. soldiers without suffering any damage.

The same could not be said for the rest of Wilhelmsen's fleet, however. By the end of World War II, the company had lost 24 ships—nearly half of its fleet. More than 50 of the company's sailors had also been killed. Returning to Oslo, the company immediately began rebuilding its fleet, and by 1946 delivery was pending on 18 new ships. The company's purchases of newly built vessels continued through the next decade, and by the beginning of the 1960s, Wilhelmsen had taken delivery on 52 new cargo liners.

The period was also marked by a diversification of the group's shipping interests. The company reentered the tanker sector, building up a fleet of nine tankers by the early 1960s. During that decade the group became one of the pioneers of the fast-growing ro-ro (roll-on, roll-off) market for vehicle transport, made possible by the development of the containership concept.

Partnerships played a major role in Wilhelmsen's growth in the new shipping market. The company reconnected with Fearnley & Eger in 1969, and, joined by another shipper, AF Klaveness, they launched the Barber Lines joint venture. That company operated

KEY DATES

1861: Morten Wilhelm Wilhelmsen founds a ship brokering and chandlering company in Tønsberg, Norway.
1865: Wilhelmsen enters ship-owning with a stake in his first vessel.
1887: Under son Halfdan Wilhelmsen, company acquires its first steam-powered vessel.
1911: Wilhelmsen forms Norwegian Africa and Australia Line (NAAL) in partnership with Fearnley & Eger, as part of expansion into cargo liner market.
1920: Acquires full control of NAAL.
1946: After losing 24 of 54 vessels during World War II, company launches fleet rebuilding with order for 18 new builds.
1969: Wilhelmsen becomes a pioneer in the ro-ro (roll-on, roll-off) market, forming Barber Lines joint venture.
1995: Company acquires Norway America Line as part of entry into car carrier market.
1999: Cargo liner joint venture Wallenius Wilhelmsen Logistics is formed.
2002: Wilhelmsen acquires 40 percent of Eukor Car Carrier partnership.
2005: Company forms new Maritime Services Division and acquires Norway's Unitor.
2007: Callenberg Group, of Sweden, is acquired as part of expansion of Maritime Services Division.

between the Far East and the United States. Before long Wilhelmsen took over full control of Barber Lines. In 1975, the company merged Barber Lines into a joint venture with Liverpool's Blue Funnel Line and Brostoms, creating Barber Blue Sea Line.

The company also targeted Australia's ro-ro market in the early 1970s. For this, the company established a partnership with East Asiatic and Transatlantic to form ScanAustral in 1972. Wilhelmsen contributed three of its own vessels to the venture.

TROUBLES IN THE NINETIES

The scramble to develop new sources of oil and natural gas during the 1970s led Wilhelmsen to attempt a rare diversification, as the company acquired a number of offshore drilling platforms in that decade. At first, the decision helped the company weather the difficult years of the early 1980s, when the Iran-Iraq war, coupled with an ongoing recession, led to a sharp drop in the international shipping industry. By the middle of the decade, Wilhelmsen's offshore division accounted for some 65 percent of the group's operating profit.

Yet this left the company vulnerable to the slump that hit the offshore industry in the second half of the decade. In response, the company was forced to restructure its operations. The company once again refocused around its core liner business, especially the ro-ro sector. A new upswing in the global shipping industry into the 1990s helped consolidate the restructuring effort, restoring Wilhelmsen's financial health. The restructuring was completed in 1995 with the sale of the group's remaining offshore operations.

Wilhelmsen took new steps to build its core operations that year. Until then 45 percent of Wilhelmsen Lines had been owned by other shareholders. In 1995, however, the company bought out the minority shareholders. Wilhelmsen then targeted external growth, buying Norway America Line. This purchase introduced the company into the car carrier market, which became a major focus of the group's ro-ro business.

PARTNERSHIPS IN THE 21ST CENTURY

The approach of the new century introduced a new phase in Wilhelmsen's growth. The group began developing a new series of partnerships in order to consolidate its position as a major player in the inherently global shipping industry. The most important of these came in 1999 when Wilhelmsen created a joint venture with Sweden's Wallenius Lines. Under the agreement, both companies agreed to transfer most of their liner operations into a new 50-50 subsidiary, Wallenius Wilhelmsen Lines (later Wallenius Wilhelmsen Logistics).

In 2002, the company added a new partnership to its list, when it joined with Wallenius, Hyundai Motor Company, and Kia Motors to acquire the car carrier operations of Hyundai Merchant Marine. Wilhelmsen held 40 percent of the new joint venture, called Eukor Car Carriers Inc. This shareholding was matched by Wallenius. Eukor's operations were then linked the operations of Wallenius Wilhelmsen Logistics, enabling the company to utilize a greater percentage of its total fleet tonnage. That company grew again in 2005, when it acquired a 50 percent stake in Distribution and Auto Service Inc., part of the Nissan America group. The deal helped boost Wilhelmsen's own position, as the company emerged as the leader of the global car carrier market.

In the meantime, Wilhelmsen had also been building a leadership position in maritime services. In 2005 the group restructured its existing operations, which included ship's agency Barwil and Barber International, a ship management and consultancy specialist, creating a new subsidiary, Wilhelmsen Maritime Services.

The company quickly expanded this division, buying 90 percent of Norwegian maritime services specialist Unitor in 2005. By the end of 2007, the company was able to attain a leadership position in the world maritime services market, through the acquisition of Sweden's Callenberg Group AB.

Wilhelmsen continued to seek new partnerships. In 2006, for example, the company joined with India's Katra Group to launch an innovative "floating port." The new joint venture, called Katra Wilhelmsen, operated a 250-meter ship in order to provide port services to larger vessels unable to enter Indian ports. After nearly 150 years, Wilhelmsen had established itself as a leading force in the global shipping industry.

M. L. Cohen

PRINCIPAL SUBSIDIARIES

AAL-American Auto Logistics Inc. (U.S.A., 50%); ALN-American Logistics Network, Inc. (U.S.A., 50%); American Roll-on Roll-off Carrier, Inc. (U.S.A., 50%); Dockwise (21%); Wallenius Wilhelmsen Logistics (50%); Wilhelmsen Lines ASA; Wilhelmsen Offshore & Chartering ASA; Wilhelmsen Ship Management; Wilhelmsen Ships Equipment; Wilhelmsen Ships Service.

PRINCIPAL COMPETITORS

A P Moller-Maersk A/S; TUI AG; Alghanim Industries; Louis Dreyfus S.A.S.; ThyssenKrupp Services AG; Suhail Bahwan Group (Holding) LLC; Dr August Oetker KG; Danzas Group; Hapag-Lloyd AG.

FURTHER READING

"Katra, Wilhelmsen Team to Launch 'Floating Port,'" *Florida Shipper,* April 24, 2006.

"Shipping Unit Aids Wilh. Wilhelmsen's Second Quarter Profit," *Pacific Shipper,* August 10, 2006.

"Wallenius Wilhelmsen Lines AS Acquires 50% of Distribution and Auto Service Inc. from Nissan North America," *Nordic Business Report,* April 15, 2005.

"Wilh. Wilhelmsen and Wallenius Lines in Talks to Acquire Korean Car Transport Business," *Nordic Business Report,* March 4, 2002.

"Wilh. Wilhelmsen ASA Acquires Swedish Maritime Services Provider Callenberg Group AG," *Nordic Business Report,* November 1, 2007.

"Wilh. Wilhelmsen ASA Acquires Unitor ASA for NOK 1.4 bn," *Nordic Business Report,* June 20, 2005.

"Wilh. Wilhelmsen Reports Profit Growth," *Pacific Shipper,* August 13, 2007.

"Wilhelmsen Rides Cargo Wave," *Traffic World,* August 21, 2006, p. 33.

Wilhelm Karmann GmbH

Karmannstrasse 1
Osnabrück, D-49084
Germany
Telephone: (49 541) 581-0
Fax: (49 541) 581-1900
Web site: http://www.karmann.com

Private Company
Incorporated: 1906 as Wagenfabrik Wilhelm Karmann
Employees: 6,958
Sales: EUR 1.9 billion ($2.4 billion) (2006)
NAIC: 336111 Automobile Manufacturing; 336399 All Other Motor Vehicle Parts Manufacturing; 333512 Machine Tool (Metal Cutting Types) Manufacturing; 333513 Machine Tool (Metal Forming Types) Manufacturing; 336370 Motor Vehicle Metal Stamping

Wilhelm Karmann GmbH is a full-service supplier to some of the world's largest car manufacturers, including Audi, BMW, Porsche, Daimler, Volkswagen, Chrysler, and Renault/Nissan. Karmann develops and manufactures anything from stamped parts to complete vehicles, from machine tools and dies to production facilities for passenger cars. The company's core competencies are the design and manufacturing of auto bodies and roof systems for convertibles and sports cars. About four-fifths of the company's workforce is employed at Karmann headquarters in Osnabrück, Germany, and at the company's second major German subsidiary in Rheine. Additional production plants are located in Brazil, Mexico, the United States, Portugal, and Poland. Karmann is owned by the Battenfeld, Boll, and Karmann families, all descendants of company founder Wilhelm Karmann.

FROM CARRIAGES TO MOTOR VEHICLES

In 1901, when Wilhelm Karmann acquired a carriage manufacturer in Osnabrück, Germany, horse-driven carriages were still the most common means of road transportation. Karmann had learned his craft as a cartwright at his father's small carriage workshop in Krefeld, but was fascinated by a new invention of the time: motor-driven vehicles called *Motorwagen.* Karmann dreamed of building such vehicles and he took classes in technical drawing on the side. His father, however, resisted the idea so Karmann decided to break out on his own. He worked as a technician in various *Motorwagen* factories and became director of operations at Heinrich Scheele electro-mobile factory in Cologne. When his employer sent him to an automobile show in Frankfurt am Main in 1900, Karmann knew that he wanted to build such vehicles himself. When he discovered that Osnabrück-based carriage manufacturer Christian Klages was for sale, the thirty-year-old found a bank in Münster that lent him the capital and he signed the purchase contract with Klages' widow on August 1, 1901.

Karmann took over a reputable business with two small buildings and a staff of 15 in Osnabrück's city center. The company continued to build and repair car-

COMPANY PERSPECTIVES

As a full-service-vehicle-supplier, we supply the international automotive industry with ideas, new solutions, products and production plants. For more than 100 years, our overall knowledge from modules to complete vehicles has made us partners with the great names in the industry.

riages of various kinds, including hunting carriages, coupes, landaus, and landaulets, for customers throughout Germany. However, it was only a few months before the start-up entrepreneur found a customer in the emerging German automobile industry.

In 1902 Karmann built his first automobile body for Dürkopp Werke in Bielefeld. Two years later his company's staff had doubled. The workshops were so busy and crowded that Karmann opened an additional showroom and sales office in Osnabrück. In 1905 Karmann presented his first catalog, featuring four different car body models, at the Berlin Auto Show. In 1906 the company was renamed Wagenfabrik Wilhelm Karmann and the name soon became well known among German motor-vehicle manufacturers. Among the company's early customers were two large carmakers, Adler and Opel. For the latter, Karmann developed his first passenger car with an enclosed body in 1908.

REGISTERING THE COMPANY'S FIRST PATENT

Ten years after its foundation, Karmann's enterprise advanced to a new level. In 1911 Karmann acquired Maschinenfabrik und Eisengießerei Lindemann, a machine tool manufacturer and iron smelter in Osnabrück. Karmann moved his operations to the new premises with modern fabrication halls and a power station. Because his staff was busy building car bodies, the company founder turned down orders for carriages for the first time. In 1913 Wilhelm Karmann registered his first patent, for a convertible roof mechanism, with the German patent office.

However, when World War I began in mid-1914, convertibles were not in demand. When half of his workers were drafted to the military service, Karmann managed to secure an initial order of 100 ambulances from the German army; these later went into mass production under much larger contracts. In addition the company supplied harness equipment for horses, artillery equipment, and Zeppelin components. After the war ended in 1918 Karmann muddled through the postwar economic depression by manufacturing chairs, handcarts, and oxcarts, in addition to carriages, which Karmann continued to build for customers throughout Germany up until the 1920s. By then, the German automobile industry began to pick up speed again and new orders for car bodies came in from Neue Automobilgesellschaft (NAG), Protos, and Allg. Gesellschaft für Automobilbau (AGA), among others.

At the invitation of the Detroit automakers' trade association, Wilhelm Karmann traveled to the United States in 1924, where he visited the factories of Detroit carmakers. Deeply impressed by the sophistication and effectiveness of production technology and by the high quality of the finished steel bodies of U.S. passenger cars, Karmann invested heavily in state-of-the-art machinery and equipment at his own company. Although car bodies in Germany were still mostly made of wood and then covered with artificial leather or tin, Karmann was convinced that the future lay in full-metal bodies and casings, and he invested large sums in spray lacquering and in the reorganization of production processes to be suitable for mass production.

CRAFTING AN INTERNATIONAL REPUTATION

In the mid-1920s Wilhelm Karmann developed a close business relationship with Heinrich Kleyer, the owner of Frankfurt am Main-based Adler-Werke, one of Germany's largest carmakers. Consequently, Karmann became intimately involved in the design and production of many legendary Adler models. In 1932 Karmann built the Adler Primus convertible with a Karmann-designed waterproof convertible roof. One year later the Adler Trumpf convertible with a Karmann body won numerous design competitions—or *Concours d'Elégance,* as they were called—the best advertising an auto manufacturer could hope for. Not surprisingly, the model turned into a bestseller. Another classic of the time built by Karmann was the representative Adler Diplomat convertible. One of Karmann's large customers was Hannoversche Maschinenbau AG, also known as Hanomag, for whom the company built half-steel and full-steel bodies for a number of sedans and convertibles.

By the 1930s Wagenfabrik Wilhelm Karmann had gained an international reputation. To handle the increasing amount of business, three large production plants were built. Their new equipment enabled Karmann to mass-produce tin casings for car bodies. Business soared until 1939 when Germany was once again at war. During World War II Karmann manufactured

KEY DATES

1901: Wilhelm Karmann acquires a horse carriage manufacturer in Osnabrück.
1902: Karmann's company builds its first body for an automobile.
1906: The company is renamed Wagenfabrik Wilhelm Karmann.
1913: Wilhelm Karmann registers his first patent for a convertible roof mechanism.
1932: The company builds the Adler Primus convertible with Karmann's convertible roof mechanism.
1939: Karmann manufactures components for fighter airplanes during World War II.
1949: The company starts manufacturing the Volkswagen Bug convertible.
1955: The Karmann Ghia is first introduced.
1960: Karmann's first foreign subsidiary is established in Brazil.
1979: Mass production of the VW Golf convertible begins.
1983: Werk Rheine begins producing the Ford Escort convertible.
1991: Karmann builds basic bodies and roof systems for Renault convertibles.
1996: The company establishes Karmann USA in Michigan.
2003: Production of Chrysler's Crossfire convertible sports car begins.
2006: A Karmann sales office opens in Yokohama, Japan.
2007: Specialty fabrics subsidiary Julius Heywinkel GmbH is sold.

components for fighter airplanes. In 78 bombing raids over Osnabrück, the company's production facilities were almost completely destroyed within a few days.

POSTWAR RECOVERY WITH VOLKSWAGEN

After almost half a century of hard work,70-year-old Wilhelm Karmann's enterprise lay in ruins. However, he was determined to do whatever was necessary to preserve his life's work. Together with his son, Wilhelm Karmann, Jr., who returned from an American prisoner camp in fall 1945, he began to rebuild his company from scratch. With the few machines and raw materials that survived the war, the company started manufacturing folding chairs for movie theaters, metal bodies for wheel barrows, 100,000 shoehorns, and several hundred thousand sets of silverware for the British occupation forces.

While the reconstruction of the company's facilities in Osnabrück was underway, Wilhelm Karmann secured the first postwar orders. The Ford Motor Company ordered 800 cargo platform frames for trucks. Soon after, Karmann started producing truck fenders for Ford as well. In spring 1946 the company received an order of 1,000 cockpits for heavy-duty trucks from prewar customer Hanomag. The British military administration asked Karmann to make 100 frames for prisoner transport vehicles. Slowly, things began to improve—too slowly for Wilhelm Karmann. After all, the company founder's vision had been to build passenger cars. Although many Germans struggled economically through the first years following the war, it was foreseeable that the demand for cars would pick up again.

In the summer of 1945, German auto company Volkswagen (VW) had started manufacturing Volkswagen Bugs (known as "Beetles" in the United States) which, in the beginning, were sold only to the Allied forces and the German Post Office. Wilhelm Karmann envisioned a compact convertible based on Volkswagen's Bug model. Convinced that his idea would be marketable, Karmann bought a Bug and put his engineers to work. As soon as the prototype was built, Karmann shipped it to Wolfsburg and presented it to Volkswagen's CEO Heinrich Nordhoff—who turned Karmann's proposal down.

Fortunately, Germany's largest VW dealer was also present at the meeting. He believed Karmann's idea had great commercial potential. Nordhoff changed his mind and ordered 1,000 VW Bug convertibles from Karmann, and mass production of the new model began in 1949. Despite the relatively high price—Karmann's version cost about 35 percent more than the standard model Bug—demand for the compact convertible grew steadily.

NEW GENERATION OF INNOVATION

In September 1952, just a few weeks after the 10,000th VW Bug convertible had been shipped, company founder Wilhelm Karmann passed away at age 81 and his only son, Wilhelm Karmann, Jr., took over the reins. The younger Karmann had joined the family business as an apprentice at age 19, and had gained additional experience working at Fiat Germany before he began studying automotive engineering at Bernau Technical College near Berlin. Under his leadership, his father's company experienced an enormous boom, which was partly due to his father's deal with Volkswagen, and which partly coincided with the years of the so-called German Economic Miracle. However, it soon became apparent that Wilhelm Karmann, Jr., was no less creative and determined than his father.

The younger Karmann had a vision of his own—a sassy two-seat sports car version of the Volkswagen Bug. Volkswagen CEO Nordhoff, however, was happy with the way things were going—demand for the standard VW Bug continued to climb—and he showed no interest in unnecessary risk-taking. After several unsuccessful attempts to persuade Volkswagen, Karmann met with his business friend Luigi Segre, the owner of the Italian car body design firm Ghia S.p.A Carozzeria, at the Genf Automobile Salon in spring 1953, and shared his idea. Well aware that if this were carried out successfully it could be a great business opportunity for him as well, Segre embraced Karmann's vision.

Six months later Segre presented Karmann with a top secret coupe prototype based on the VW Bug at the private garage of a French VW importer's home in Paris. Although Segre's coupe had a closed top, Karmann immediately fell in love with its elegant design. After a few minor changes had been made in Italy, the car was shipped to Osnabrück, where a small team of experts made a meticulous calculation of development and production costs, all under the veil of absolute secrecy.

Before approaching Nordhoff again, Karmann decided to get his right-hand man, Karl Feuereisen, involved. Feuereisen immediately liked the design and spurred Nordhoff's curiosity. At a meeting in November 1953, Nordhoff—impressed by the Italian design as well as by Karmann's calculations—decided to accept the risk. Moreover, Nordhoff also approved of the suggested name of the new vehicle: Karmann Ghia.

SUCCESS WITH THE KARMANN GHIA

Although Volkswagen CEO Nordhoff had agreed to invest in the mass production of the Karmann Ghia, his planners were fairly skeptical and forecast a total market potential of 50,000 cars. In 1955 the "Volkswagen Bug in Sunday dress" was presented to the broader public for the first time at the International Auto Show in Frankfurt am Main. Orders started coming in immediately. In fact, there were so many orders that Karmann had a hard time keeping up with them. By mid-1956, the serial production of the Karmann Ghia was up and running and the company built 11,500 coupes that year.

In 1957 a convertible version, as Wilhelm Karmann, Jr., had imagined, went into mass production as well. While demand continued to rise in Germany, the sporty coupe turned into an even bigger success overseas. The first orders from the United States and Canada rolled in before Volkswagen had even spent the first dollars on advertising. When VW finally rolled out its campaign in 1961, there were already 30,000 Karmann Ghias rolling on America's streets. The curvy little sports car that cost only half as much as a Corvette or Jaguar became especially popular among U.S. women and in California.

Due to the overwhelming success of the VW Bug convertible and the Karmann Ghia, Karmann's workforce doubled within less than five years, reaching about 3,400 by 1959. During the second half of the 1950s, production was moved to a brand-new plant on the outskirts of Osnabrück. In 1960 Karmann established its first foreign subsidiary near São Paulo in Brazil, fewer than two miles away from Volkswagen's car factory.

In 1961, a larger version of the Karmann Ghia coupe with a more powerful engine went into production. However, it never gained a following comparable to its predecessor's. Meanwhile, the ongoing demand for the original Karmann Ghia models kept the company busy for another decade. The last one was produced in 1974, eventually reaching a total of 362,585 coupes, of which 80,881 were convertibles—with two-thirds of those exported to the United States—and 42,498 were the "large" Karmann Ghia model.

Finally, after 30 years, Karmann's booming postwar success story wound down. On January 10, 1980, the last Volkswagen Beetle convertible came off the Karmann assembly line. Almost 332,000 had been built in Osnabrück since 1949. The great popularity of the Karmann Ghia, however, outlived by far the end of its production life cycle and became a legend that lived on in many Hollywood movies, including the 1958 Alfred Hitchcock thriller *Vertigo,* the 1986 teenager cult movie *Pretty in Pink,* and the 2004 action movie *Kill Bill 2.*

EXPANDING THE CUSTOMER BASE

The phaseout of the Karmann Ghia in 1974 marked the end of an era for Karmann—the era of high visibility in the world as a top German car manufacturer. As the company started producing the VW Scirocco in the same year, Karmann returned to its role as a highly competent and specialized supplier of vehicles and components, mainly to Volkswagen. After the automobile market's slowdown at the beginning of the 1980s—when the company produced losses for the first time in its history—had been overcome, Karmann's continued close partnership with VW and the resulting large business volume provided a solid basis for the company during the 1980s.

The VW Scirocco turned out to be a success, with over 500,000 cars manufactured until 1981. In 1979, shortly before the last Volkswagen Beetle convertible left Karmann's assembly line, the mass production of the new VW Golf convertible began. By far not as elegant as its predecessor—a roll bar stuck out when the roof was down—it still outdid the earlier model, and more than 388,500 Golf convertibles had been produced by 1993. However, the overwhelming success of the Volkswagen Bug convertible and Karmann Ghia had made the company strongly dependent on VW and therefore vulnerable at the same time.

Karmann had always worked with other vehicle manufacturers after World War II: it built the DKW Meisterklasse convertible for the German Auto Union and the Ford Taurus 12M station wagon in the 1950s; the Porsche 356 B hardtop coupe as well as the bodies for the Porsche 911 and 912 series; the body for the BMW-Coupe 2000 C/CS and the exclusive Opel Diplomat Coupe in the 1960s; and the VW Porsche 914, a mid-engine sports car that combined Porsche coachwork with a VW engine, in the 1970s. In addition, Karmann manufactured bodies, parts and components for BMW, Daimler-Benz, Porsche, Renault, Fiat, Peugeot, and other large automakers. The company also developed and built dies for car bodies and machine tools, and even developed whole car-body production plants for vehicle manufacturers.

While the company's ties to VW remained strong in the 1980s and 1990s, Karmann made an effort to decrease the company's dependence on just one auto manufacturer. In 1983 Karmann's plant in Rheine started producing the Ford Escort convertible, a joint development work of Karmann and Italian designer Giorgio Giugiaro; more than 188,000 were built between then and 1997. In 1989 Wilhelm Karmann, Jr., retreated from company management and put the responsibility in the hands of new CEO Rainer Thieme, who steered the company through the rough waters of the 1990s.

GLOBAL MARKET CHANGES

In the early 1990s car manufacturers faced a dramatic drop in sales in the world's major markets. In 1991 Karmann started building raw bodies and roof systems for Renault convertibles. However, sales for the VW Golf convertible, the manufacturing of which had generated a major revenue stream for Karmann for more than a decade, were sluggish. Production of the VW Scirocco was being phased out and the demand for Ford Escort convertibles dropped by 30 percent. Despite an interim contract from VW for manufacturing Golf sedans in the second half of 1993, Karmann reported losses for the second straight year. The company, which at the time still relied heavily on its main customer Volkswagen and generated over two-thirds of sales with the manufacture of complete vehicles, cut its workforce by roughly one quarter, eliminating 1,500 jobs in Osnabrück. At the same time Karmann opened new production plants abroad, one in Portugal in 1992 and one in Mexico four years later.

While the company successfully acquired new projects with Daimler-Benz and VW in Germany later in the decade, Karmann's executive management focused much of its attention and efforts on the world's largest automobile market: the United States. In 1996 the company established Karmann USA in Livonia, Michigan, where the company began to set up R&D and production capacities and to build new business relationships with America's top three automakers. When Wilhelm Karmann, Jr., passed away in 1998 at age 84, the company was back on track with over 8,500 employees in Europe and South and North America.

POSITIONING FOR THE FUTURE

In 2002, when Bernd Lieberoth-Leden became Karmann's new CEO, the company's U.S. headquarters were moved to a new location in Plymouth, Michigan, where a production plant for roof systems was set up in 2005. In 2003 Karmann began producing Chrysler's Crossfire convertible sports car in Osnabrück. To strengthen the company's core competency in roofs for convertibles, the development and manufacturing of roof systems became an independent profit center in 2002. In the years that followed, Karmann acquired ten contracts for roof systems. A major order for retractable glass roofs came from Renault for its Mégane convertible sports car, the production of which started in 2003.

In 2004 the company built a production plant for roof systems in the United States. In the same year Karmann reported a new annual production record of 94,000 Audi A4 convertibles, Mercedes CLK convertibles, Chrysler Crossfire Coupes and Roadsters, and Land Rover Defenders combined. In 2005 Karmann started making roofs for Nissan's Micra convertible.

In an effort to focus on the company's core competencies, Karmann sold its specialty fabrics subsidiary, Julius Heywinkel GmbH, in 2007. The company's hopes for the future lay in the growing niche market for specialty cars as well as in additional business from Japanese and Korean car manufacturers. For that purpose, a Karmann sales office was established in Yokohama, Japan, in 2006. The first roof system for a Japanese automaker was on track to be manufactured in 2008.

Evelyn Hauser

PRINCIPAL SUBSIDIARIES

Karmann-Rheine GmbH & Co. KG (Germany); Karmann Engineering Services GmbH (Germany); Automotive Global Service GmbH (Germany); ATP Automotive Testing Papenburg GmbH (Germany); Karmann-Ghia do Brasil Ltda. (Brazil); Karmann U.S.A., Inc.; Karmann-Ghia de México S.de R.L. de C.V.; Karmann-Ghia de Portugal Lda.; Karmann Sunderland (United Kingdom); Karmann-Ghia Zary Sp. Z o.o. (Poland); Karmann Chorzów (Poland); Karmann Japan Co., Ltd.

PRINCIPAL COMPETITORS

Webasto AG; Edscha AG; American Specialty Cars Inc (ASC); ArvinMeritor Inc.; Magna International Inc.

FURTHER READING

Alarab, Caron, "Maker of Hardtops to Bring 20 Jobs to Plymouth Twp.," *Detroit Free Press,* June 9, 2005.

Das Symbol. 50 Jahre Volkswagen Karmann Ghia, Osnabrück, Germany: Wilhelm Karmann GmbH, 2005, 104 p.

Dole, Charles E., "Karmann Tie to VW Goes Long Way Back," *Christian Science Monitor,* July 15, 1983, p. 17.

Fisher, Lawrence M., "Wilhelm Karmann Jr., 83; Ran German Car Body Maker," *New York Times,* October 31, 1998.

Karmann Cars. Eine Erfolgsgeschichte, Osnabrück, Germany: Wilhelm Karmann GmbH, 2005, 158 p.

"Karmann sieht sich nach einem Partner um," *Frankfurter Allgemeine Zeitung,* July 29, 1993, p. 12.

Moetsch, Matthias, "100 Jahre Karmann; Kutschen Karossen Cabrios," *Auto Bild,* August 24, 2001.

Steinborn, Deborah, "Speed, Outsourced," *Forbes Global,* April 28, 2003, p. 18.

"Wilhelm Karmann: 2007 Company Profile Edition 1," *just-auto.com,* April 2007.

"Wilhelm Karmann; Obituary," *Times,* November 14, 1998, p. 24.

World Wide Technology, Inc.

60 Weldon Parkway
St. Louis, Missouri 63043
U.S.A.
Telephone: (314) 569-7000
Toll Free: (800) 432-7008
Fax: (314) 569-8300
Web site: http://www.wwt.com

Private Company
Incorporated: 1990
Employees: 1,008
Sales: $2.5 billion (2007 est.)
NAIC: 541512 Computer Systems Design Services

■ ■ ■

St. Louis, Missouri-based World Wide Technology, Inc. (WWT), is a leading technology services firm. The company's capabilities fall into three main categories. Information Technology Products and Solutions include services such as systems integration. Supply Chain Services include services like warehousing and logistics. Finally, Professional Services include offerings such as planning/design, consulting, and training.

As its name suggests, WWT's footprint spans the globe. According to the company, it operates more than 1.5 million square feet of distribution, warehousing, and integration space at 19 facilities. In addition to its St. Louis headquarters, WWT's domestic operations include three distribution centers in the Texas communities of Austin, Plano, and San Antonio. Other U.S. locations include Granite City, Illinois; Livermore, California; Nashville, Tennessee; Detroit, Michigan; Reno, Nevada; Redmond, Washington; Phoenix, Arizona; High Point, North Carolina; and West Chester, Ohio.

In addition to the U.S. government, WWT's customer base includes leading organizations in the commercial and telecommunication sectors. Its customer base includes companies such as the Boeing Co., Dell Inc., Cisco Systems Inc., Computer Sciences Corp., and Microsoft Corp.

FORMATIVE YEARS

David L. Steward founded WWT. A Clinton, Missouri, native, Steward's business experience was developed in sales and marketing positions at Federal Express, Wagner Electric, and the Missouri Pacific Railroad. Prior to establishing WWT, Steward started a company named Transport Administrative Services, which provided automated transportation audit services to seven railroads. According to the June 22, 1998, *St. Louis Business Journal,* the formation of WWT enabled Steward to expand his business. "I realized we were going through one of the greatest revolutions that ever hit the history of the world—the information age—and I wanted to be a part of it," Steward explained.

Incorporated on July 23, 1990, WWT began with four employees and initial funding from a $250,000 Small Business Administration loan. The new enterprise started out as a computer hardware reseller and software developer, dabbling in everything from desktop computers to video equipment. The early years were difficult at times. In a May 16, 2001, *St. Charles County Business*

> **COMPANY PERSPECTIVES**
>
> WWT understands that today's advanced technologies, when properly planned, procured, and deployed are business solutions that reduce costs, increase profitability, and ultimately improve a company's ability to effectively serve their customers.

Record article, Steward recalled times when the company was not able to pay its bills, and an occasion when he looked out of his window and saw his car being repossessed. However, Steward's vision for the company's future, along with a passion for technology and the ability to attract the right people, would prove instrumental as his company grew.

During WWT's formative years, the company mainly worked for the U.S. government. It quickly gained a reputation for on-time delivery and quality. After forming a number of strategic alliances with other technology firms, WWT saw its commercial business begin to grow.

WWT's sales increased rapidly during the first half of the decade. From $812,000 its first year, sales reached $3 million in 1991 and $8 million the following year. Sales nearly doubled from $9 million in 1993 to $17 million in 1994, and mushroomed to $74 million in 1995. That year, Steward received the Southwestern Bell Minority Supplier of the Year Award.

A key development occurred at this time when WWT was selected to supply U.S. troops in Bosnia with computer workstations. As part of the project, it created a way for the military to track the equipment using the Internet. This led WWT to develop other Internet-based solutions for companies, from resource planning tools to customer service systems.

VALUE-ADDED RESELLER

Sales continued to climb during the second half of the 1990s, reaching $81 million in 1996. That year, WWT opened a new office in Herndon, Virginia. The company began to receive recognition from numerous trade publications, as well as regional and national organizations. In 1997, WWT ranked 394th in *Inc.* magazine's "*Inc.* 500."

It was also in 1997 that WWT secured part of a $150 million electronic component assembly and installation contract with Lucent Technologies and Southwestern Bell Telephone Co. The deal, which included work in four states, meant an additional $10 million to $12 million in annual sales. By this time the company had a workforce of approximately 100 employees and a client base that included McDonnell Douglas and Fannie May Candy Shops. WWT ended the year with sales of $135 million.

Several key developments occurred in 1998. Midway through the year, WWT acquired a four-building campus in Maryland Heights, Missouri, from Weldon Partners. The buildings joined a building the company already owned at 131 Weldon Parkway, as well as its leased facility at 127 Weldon Parkway. Together, the facilities formed what the company named its WWT/Telcobuy Campus.

WWT's physical expansion provided much needed space for its growing workforce of 175 people, and occurred at about the same time that Steward was honored with the Ernst & Young Entrepreneur of the Year Award. In addition, in 1998 *Black Enterprise* magazine ranked WWT 11th among the nation's largest 100 black-owned industrial and services firms.

After eight years in business, WWT had established itself as a leading systems integrator, providing software, hardware, and networking solutions for leading companies nationwide. Using products and components from different vendors, systems integrators build computer systems that meet specific customer requirements. Supporting WWT's success were partnerships with leading information technology (IT) firms, including Cisco, FileNET, Fujitsu, Oracle, Sun, and Lucent.

In 1999 WWT spun off its telecommunications division to create a subsidiary named Telcobuy.com LLC, which operated an online marketplace for telecommunications equipment. After raising $27.5 million in venture capital funding for the business from Summit Partners and Highland Capital, the company made its initial public offering. Telcobuy.com was led by CEO Jim Kavanaugh, who had helped Steward establish WWT a decade before.

WWT capped off the 1990s with sales of $413 million in 1999, more than double from the previous year's $202 million. In addition *Black Enterprise* ranked the company as the nation's largest black-owned company that year, an honor it would earn several times in the coming years.

The beginning of the 21st century was accompanied by a host of changes. In April 2000, the company opened a new office in Plano, Texas. On the leadership front, Joe Koenig was promoted to the role of company president, and Mark Catalano was chosen to lead Telcobuy.

KEY DATES

1990: David L. Steward incorporates World Wide Technology, Inc. (WWT).
1998: A four-building campus in Maryland Heights, Missouri, is acquired from Weldon Partners.
1999: The company spins off its telecommunications division to create a subsidiary named Telcobuy.com LLC; *Black Enterprise* ranks WWT as the nation's largest black-owned company for the first time.
2001: Annual sales reach $924 million and David Steward is named to the Small Business Administration "Hall of Fame."
2003: World Wide Technology Holding Co. Inc. is formed, and WWT and Telcobuy are combined.
2004: The company spins off its SDE Business Partnering subsidiary as an independent company, which becomes World Wide Technology–Automotive.
2006: A state-of-the-art Integration Technology Center opens near WWT's headquarters.

In September 2000 WWT received a major boost when it earned the largest IT contract in the state of Missouri, worth approximately $65 million. As part of the deal, which General Electric Co. lost after failing to meet minority-subcontracting targets established by the late Governor Mel Carnahan, WWT became the state's principal microcomputer vendor. WWT ended the year with approximately 540 employees and sales of $802 million.

The following year brought more physical expansion for WWT. In January, a new office was established in Livermore, California. Three months later, a 300,000-square-foot warehouse was secured for Telcobuy.com in Aberdeen, Maryland, to serve as its distribution center for the East Coast region. By this time Telcobuy.com's net worth was growing at a fast rate, increasing from $250 million in 1999 to $610 million in 2000. More physical expansion occurred in August when an office was established in McLean, Virginia. WWT ended 2001 with David Steward being named to the Small Business Administration "Hall of Fame," and with annual sales of $924 million.

Midway through 2002, WWT teamed with Xybernaut Corp., a leading wearable/mobile computing hardware provider, to offer Xybernaut's products and services to both civilian government organizations and the military. The company ended the year by opening new facilities in Austin, Texas, and Nashville, Tennessee.

Growth and change continued at an accelerated pace in 2003. WWT began the year by establishing an office in Reno, Nevada. This was followed by a new office in Tuscaloosa, Alabama, midway through the year, and a Rancho Dominguez, California, site in October.

In addition to physical expansion, WWT also made significant changes to its organizational structure in 2003. World Wide Technology Holding Co. Inc. was formed in January, with Jim Kavanaugh serving as CEO. WWT and Telcobuy were combined at this time.

WWT continued to receive numerous awards and recognition during the early 2000s. In 2003 the company received a number of new honors, including an Industry Partner Award from the General Services Administration, a Cisco Systems Growing with Technology Award for operational excellence, and a Best Customer Experience Supplier Award from Dell Corp.

Other key developments in 2003 included a five-year, $27 million business process outsourcing agreement for EDS Procurement Services to provide WWT with hiring and management services for contract workers. In addition, the two organizations also announced plans to market collaboratively a contract labor management solution for large organizations. Annual sales surpassed the $1 billion mark that year, reaching $1.1 billion.

Heading into the middle of the decade, David Steward published a new book titled *Doing Business by the Good Book.* In the January 2, 2004, issue of the *St. Louis Post-Dispatch,* writer David Nicklaus described the book as a blend of autobiography, Sunday school lesson, and business instruction. Discussing the book in a September 10, 2004, *St. Louis Post-Dispatch* article by Linda Tucci, Steward commented on the impact Christian principles had on the management of WWT, explaining, "At the end of the day, it's still about relationships you build along the way. I remember vividly that we were having some real challenges in this business, and we were losing a tremendous amount of money. We didn't know where the next opportunity was coming from. There are people who had faith in the vision of this business that stayed in spite of what they saw. Faith is about believing in the unseen. It's impossible to please God without faith. When you take a look at World Wide at the start, what did we call it? We had faith that this company was going to be a global player. World Wide Technology. We were professing by our words a faith about whom we would become."

Other developments in 2004 included the acquisition of a Scientific and Engineering Workstation

Procurement III (SEWP) contract from ECS Technologies Inc. In November, WWT Holding spun off its SDE Business Partnering subsidiary, which became World Wide Technology–Automotive. WWT ended the year with sales of $1.4 billion.

SOLUTIONS DEVELOPER

By 2005, WWT had expanded beyond its role as a value-added reseller and systems integrator to become a provider of supply chain solutions for large organizations in the automotive, government, and telecommunications sectors, helping them to manage the complexities associated with functions such as warehousing and logistics.

As WWT evolved on the service front, the company continued on the path of physical growth. That year, WWT expanded its existing locations in Austin, Texas; Compton, California; and Nashville, Tennessee; and established new offices in Virginia Beach, Virginia; West Chester, Ohio; Greensboro, North Carolina; Earth City, Missouri; Granite City, Illinois; and Phoenix, Arizona.

By this time, WWT remained a privately owned firm, with no plans of going public. With annual growth of 25 to 30 percent, the company was on solid footing. CEO Jim Kavanaugh attributed the company's condition to factors such as diversification, technology investments, and a skilled and productive workforce, which had grown to include 900 employees.

It was also in 2005 that WWT bought out its venture capital partners, Summit Partners and Highland Capital, at a cost of $27.5 million. The company ended the year with sales of $1.8 billion, and by making the 2005 Deloitte Technology Fast 500—a list of the fastest-growing technology firms in North America.

In 2006 WWT unveiled a new Integration Technology Center (ITC) near its headquarters. The new state-of-the-art facility provided the company with a weekly capacity to configure more than 30,000 systems. In addition to the latest features of a cutting-edge data center, such as a redundant power system, it also was equipped with a conveyor-belt box materials handling system.

In addition to the ITC, other high points during 2006 included a $110 million IT procurement contract from the state of Missouri and a $15 million IT procurement contract from Alaska's Department of Administration. Along with the Alaska deal, new offices were established in Anchorage, and 29 new employees were added to WWT's workforce there.

In addition to receiving sizable government contracts, WWT gained 420 new customers in 2006, including PepsiCo, the Microsoft Network, and the state of Arizona. A special milestone was reached when annual sales surpassed the $2 billion mark, reaching $2.1 billion and culminating 17 straight years of double-digit growth.

WWT's achievements continued into the second half of the decade. In 2007 the company received a seven-year, $5.6 billion Solutions for Enterprise-Wide Procurement contract from the National Aeronautics and Space Administration (NASA). The deal included a range of technology solutions, from storage and collaboration to wireless technology and network security.

It was also in 2007 that WWT began focusing more on the healthcare industry, with plans to market its Unified Communications at the Point of Care System to hospitals nationwide. The new system offered capabilities in the areas of equipment tracking, electronic medical record, and voice over Internet communications.

WWT ended 2007 with sales of $2.5 billion. The company headed into 2008 on the strength of 1,008 employees and a stellar track record of growth. As WWT approached a new decade, it seemed well equipped for continued innovation and success.

Paul R. Greenland

PRINCIPAL COMPETITORS

Electronic Data Systems Corporation; HP Technology Solutions Group; IBM Global Services.

FURTHER READING

Jackson, Margaret, "World Wide Technology Plans for Future, Buys Four Buildings," *St. Louis Business Journal,* June 22, 1998.

Nicklaus, David, "World Wide Chief Takes His Latest Leap of Faith," *St. Louis Post-Dispatch,* January 2, 2004.

Trask, Mike, "CEO of High-Tech Industry Tells St. Charles Business Community the Good News about Small Business," *St. Charles County Business Record,* May 16, 2001.

Tucci, Linda, "Christian Principles Guide David Steward's Growth," *St. Louis Post-Dispatch,* September 10, 2004.

Xerium Technologies, Inc.

14101 Capital Boulevard, Suite 201
Youngsville, North Carolina 27596
U.S.A.
Telephone: (508) 616-9468
Web site: http://www.xerium.com

Public Company
Incorporated: 1999
Employees: 3,846
Sales: $601.4 million (2006)
Stock Exchanges: New York
Ticker Symbol: XRM
NAIC: 313210 Broadwoven Fabric Mills

■ ■ ■

Xerium Technologies, Inc., serves the paper manufacturing industry by offering machine clothing products and roll covers. Clothing is an important part of the papermaking process, with components of it running the length of the papermaking machine. Forming fabrics carry wet slurry to form sheets, dewatering devices remove excess water, press felts transport the paper through pressing rolls, and drying fabrics take the paper through the final drying process. Xerium clothing brands include Huyck and Wangner, primarily sold in Asia, Europe, and South America; and Weavexx, mostly sold in North America.

Dozens of rolls are also used in paper production to remove excess water from the slurry and press the slurry through the clothing to form paper sheets. Xerium provides the covers to the large steel cylinders that make up the rolls of the papermaking machine, as well as spreader rolls. The company also provides repair and rebuilding services.

Roll technology brands include Stowe Woodward, sold in most of the world; Mount Hope, sold primarily in North America and South America; and Robec, found primarily in Europe. With its headquarters in Youngsville, North Carolina, Xerium is a public company with global reach, listed on the New York Stock Exchange. The company maintains 11 roll plants in North America, ten in Europe, one in South America, and licensees in Australia, India, and Korea. Three clothing plants are found in North American cities, four in South America, five in Europe, and single plants in Australia and Japan.

XERIUM TAKES SHAPE: 1976

Xerium grew out of the holdings of United Kingdom conglomerate BTR, plc, which in 1976 began to assemble what would become Xerium with the acquisition of Massachusetts-based roller companies Mount Hope Machinery and Stowe Woodward, Inc. The BTR initials stood for British Tyre and Rubber Company, a name taken in 1934 by the British subsidiary of B.F. Goodrich Company after it acquired a sister subsidiary in Denmark. In 1936 BTR established a relationship with Stowe Woodward to produce "Stonite" printing rollers. Over the next 30 years BTR acquired sports equipment manufacturer A.G. Spalding & Brothers and became

COMPANY PERSPECTIVES

Xerium Technologies is highly-recognized and highly-valued in the machine clothing and roll technologies industry. Xerium is committed to continued growth through both increased operations and acquisitions.

involved in packaging materials, the production of hoses, and polyurethane insulating foam.

BTR was not an especially distinguished company until Owen Whitley Green took over as chief executive officer in 1967 and initiated an acquisition spree that grew the company into one of Great Britain's most celebrated conglomerates, focusing on industrial companies to serve niche markets with high-quality products. Paper machine products fit nicely into that model, and both Mount Hope and Stowe Woodward were well-established companies in the field, serving as a foundation for the BTR Paper Technology Group.

Mount Hope was founded in Taunton, Massachusetts, in 1941 to serve the textile industry with weft straighteners and cloth guiding systems. The company moved into the papermaking business in 1945 when it developed the first bowed roll in North America. Mount Hope steadily expanded its market to cover the entire United States, supported by new plants opened in Massachusetts and Charlotte, North Carolina, and in 1958 established an alliance with a Swiss company to sell its products around the world. After being acquiring by BTR, all of Mount Hope's operations were moved from Massachusetts to North Carolina as the company's brand continued to grow in North America.

STOWE WOODWARD FORMED: LATE 19TH CENTURY

Stowe Woodward boasted an even deeper heritage. Founded by Newton, Massachusetts, businessman Frederick R. Woodward and his partner in 1886, the company was a rubber and polymer manufacturing company that produced rubber-covered balls and ebonite bowling balls in addition to rubber covers used to extend the life of steel rolls used in the textile and tannery industries. By the mid-1940s Stowe Woodward began making rubber covers for paper manufacturers. Over the next 20 years the company continued to develop innovative technologies and opened new plants across the country to meet increasing demand for its roll cover products, which were also manufactured internationally through licensees. In 1973 polyurethane expertise was added to the company's capabilities through the acquisition of Essex Polymer, and led to additional plant openings in Middleton, Virginia, and Sherbrooke, Canada.

HUYCK ACQUIRED: 1980

BTR added to its paper machine products holdings in 1980 with the acquisition of Huyck Corporation, one of the country's oldest machine clothing companies. Its founding dated back to 1870 when the U.S. papermaking industry was just taking shape. The company was founded in Rensselaerville near Albany, New York, and was originally known as H. Waterbury & Co., named for Henry Waterbury. Having learned the business of manufacturing clothing woolens from his father and uncle, Waterbury had come to Rensselaerville in 1860 to open his own woolen mill, using the Hudson River for power. Ten years later he became interested in producing felts for paper manufacturers, strips of material used to squeeze water from slurry and press the material into sheets. The sheets were then laid in lofts to dry but Waterbury devised a way to connect the ends of the felt together to create a loop that permitted the paper to be dried automatically.

Needing a partner with money to invest in the project, Waterbury turned to the son of a local general store owner, Francis Conkling Huyck, who was a good businessman and salesman and disenchanted with life as a shopkeeper. He borrowed $10,000 from his father and became Waterbury's partner in what would become the fourth felt mill to be opened in the United States. When the railroad bypassed Rensselaerville, hindering the mill's ability to compete, the partnership was dissolved in 1878. Waterbury relocated the operation to remote Oriskany, New York, but Huyck decided for the sake of his children's education to stay close to Albany, setting up his own business in the suburb of Kenwood. When Kenwood Mills burned down in 1894 he relocated the business to the other side of the Hudson River in Rensselaer. After his death in 1907 his sons renamed the company F.C. Huyck & Sons, later shortened to Huyck Corporation. It made a major contribution to the paper machine clothing industry in the late 1950s when it found a way to replace the bronze wire that had been traditionally combined with felt to produce paper machine clothing. Instead, Huyck relied on a textile, "plastic wire," that established the modern forming fabric industry.

Also in 1980 BTR acquired the Becker Company of West Germany. For the next several years, BTR Paper Technologies allowed its paper machine clothing companies to operate independently, but then began to

KEY DATES

1976: BTR, plc, acquires Mount Hope Machinery and Stow Woodward, Inc., to form BTR Paper Technology Group.
1980: BTR acquires Huyck Corporation.
1990: Niagara-Lockhart Industries, Inc., is acquired.
1992: Huyck and Niagara-Lockhart are merged to create Weavexx.
1999: BTR sells assets to Apax partners; Xerium is formed.
2005: Xerium is taken public.
2006: Headquarters moved to North Carolina.

act as an industry consolidator. In 1988 Nokia of Finland and Brazil's Nortelas were acquired, followed a year later by the addition of Irga of Italy and Plastex and Boettcher of Germany. Another acquisition, completed in 1990, was Canada's Niagara-Lockport Industries, Inc., which combined a pair of well-established companies, Niagara Wires of Canada, producer of the bronze wires that had once been used in paper machine clothing, and the U.S. firm of Lockport Felts, a dryer felt manufacturer. Niagara had acquired Lockport in 1977 to become a full-line supplier.

BTR merged Huyck and Niagara-Lockport in 1992, renaming the combination Weavexx. Another company, Germany's Wittler, was added to the BTR Paper Technology Group. During the 1990s the Group added to its capabilities. Stowe Woodward developed the PressManager press section management tool, PRAXAIR ceramics cover technology, and SMART roll embedded monitoring technology. Mount Hope engineers met the demand for larger and faster bowed rolls. They developed METROL metal spools capable of withstanding high temperatures; the Vari-Bow method of adjusting the bow for maximum performance; and the Multi-Bow, an automatic system that could adjust the bow while in use. Later in the 1990s Huyck developed hyperpunch technology.

In the meantime, changes were taking place with the parent company. A new CEO, Ian Strachen, took charge, and in the mid-1990s he initiated a plan to bring some focus to BTR's wide-ranging interests, divesting a number of properties over the next few years to concentrate on the conglomerate's core, industrial products. In 1999 Siebe, plc, acquired BTR and the resulting company, which took the name Invensys, plc, became the world's largest controls-automation company, with divisions covering intelligent automation, controls, power systems, industrial drives, and automotives.

APAX ACQUIRES BTR ASSETS: 1999

The assets of BTR Paper Technology did not fit in with the future of Invensys, and in 1999 the business was put up for sale. Invensys hoped it would bring well over $1 billion but finally had to settle for $819 million from Apax Funds, part of buyout firm Apax Partners & Co. Invensys did, however, elect to retain a 10 percent stake in its former unit. Apax had been founded by Alan Patricof as Alan Patricof Associates in 1969, an early venture capital firm that in the 1970s helped launch Apple Computers.

Apax completed the BTR acquisition in December 1999 and incorporated the business as Xerium Technologies, Inc., which established its headquarters in Westborough, Massachusetts. Under new ownership the company continued to develop technologies and add assets from around the world. In 2000 Stowe Woodward added nanotechnology. In that same year the venerable Germany firm of Wangner GbmH was acquired. It had started out in 1849 as a manufacturer of bronze wire, a product that naturally led to paper machine clothing. It was merged with Huyck to create a major provider of forming fabrics. In 2001 the unit developed Huyper Press Felts, the industry's first permeable press belt, followed in 2002 by Huytexx/Optiply Forming Fabrics, which stitched together two different fabric layers to accommodate the needs of both sides of the papermaking process.

Xerium made further acquisitions in the early 2000s. Italy's Trelleborg AB was added in 2001, followed a year later by Robec Walzen GmbH of Germany. Also in 2002 Apax decided to sell Xerium, hoping to receive $1 billion to $1.25 billion and take a healthy profit in less than two years of ownership. Morgan Stanley was hired to find a buyer. Bids fell short of the desired price, however, and after weighing the offers from three main suitors, Apax changed course, called off the sale, and recapitalized Xerium with $700 million in loans, making possible a sizable dividend for Apax, which continued to own a significant stake in the company.

XERIUM TAKEN PUBLIC: 2005

Xerium grew sales from $515 million in 2002 to $586.8 million in 2004. The company was losing money, primarily because the paper industry was undergoing a difficult stretch. Despite high paper consumption, paper prices were disappointing. Like many of its customers, Xerium pursued a cost reduction program. This resulted in the closing of eight plants and the shift of production from two other plants, as well as a reduction in headcount by 370. Despite losing money, Xerium was able to attract the interest of investors and in May 2005 completed an initial public offering of stock, priced at $12 per share. The proceeds were primarily used to pay down debt.

Sales dipped to $582 million in 2005 and Xerium recorded a net loss of $2.1 million. Early in the next year Xerium acquired Atlanta-based Coldwater Covers, Inc., and its Alabama manufacturing facility for $6.8 million. Coldwater Covers, which was folded into the Stowe Woodward operation, produced a wide variety of polyurethane and composite roll covers and bowed rolls. Shortly after the deal was completed, Xerium moved its headquarters from Massachusetts to Youngsville, North Carolina, where just three years earlier a Weavexx plant was closed, although an administrative office had remained open.

In 2006 Xerium began to reap the benefits of its cost reduction efforts. Revenues totaled $601.4 million and the company turned a profit of $29.5 million. The company also appeared to be well positioned to prosper for years to come. Not only was it well diversified in terms of paper sector, customers, and geography, Xerium looked to benefit from an increasing global demand for paper, leading to a greater need for the products the company provided.

Ed Dinger

PRINCIPAL SUBSIDIARIES

Coldwater Covers, Inc.; Huyck Limited; Robec Walzen GmbH; Stowe Woodward LLC; Wangner AB.

PRINCIPAL COMPETITORS

Polymer Group, Inc.; Dyersburg Corporation; Culp, Inc.; CMI Industries, Inc.

FURTHER READING

"History of the Rensselaerville Grist Mill," http://www.uhls.org/NICH/RvGristHist.htm.

Kosman, Josh, "Apax Calls Off Xerium Sales," *Daily Deal,* October 16, 2002.

———, "Apax Hires Morgan Stanley to Sell Xerium," *Daily Deal,* April 16, 2002.

Larsen, Peter Thal, "Invensys Sells Paper Side for $810m," *Financial Times,* October 14, 1999, p. 26.

"The Logic Behind Pulling a Conglomerate Apart," *Independent* (London) September 12, 1997.

Parker, Vicki Lee, "Textile Maker Moves Headquarters to Familiar Youngsville, N.C., Area," *Raleigh (N.C.) News & Observer,* February 24, 2006.

Vennochi, Joan, "BTR's Checkered Past," *Boston Globe,* March 27, 1990, p. 39.

Yara International ASA

Bygdoy alle 2
Oslo, N-0202
Norway
Telephone: (47) 24 15 70 00
Fax: (47) 24 15 70 01
Web site: http://www.yara.com

Public Company
Incorporated: 1900 as Norsk Hydro; 2004 as Yara International
Employees: 7,000
Sales: NOK 48.26 billion ($8.72 billion) (2006)
Stock Exchanges: Oslo
Ticker Symbol: YAR
NAIC: 325311 Nitrogenous Fertilizer Manufacturing; 325120 Industrial Gas Manufacturing

■ ■ ■

Yara International ASA is the world's largest specialty producer of mineral-based fertilizers. Nitrogen fertilizers represent 90 percent of the group's production, which includes products such as ammonia, urea, nitrates, and NPK (the nutrients nitrogen, phosphorus, and potassium). Nitrogen fertilizers are also the most widely used fertilizers, accounting for 60 percent of the global fertilizer market. Ammonia, derived from natural gas, represents 53 percent of the group's total production, while NPKs add 17 percent.

The company is the global leader in both categories, and is also the world's largest nitrates producer, a position further solidified by its acquisition of Kemira GrowHow in 2007. That acquisition also helped raise Yara's global market share to 7 percent of the total fertilizer market. Yara, a spinoff of oil and gas giant Norsk Hydro, has also been leading the consolidation of the fertilizer industry, completing nearly 15 acquisitions since the beginning of the 2000s. Through these acquisitions, as well as through organic growth, Yara's total production has topped 20 million tons into 2008.

The company plans to double that capacity, with a goal of boosting its total market share past 10 percent. Yara operates through a global network of production and marketing subsidiaries in more than 40 countries. The Norwegian company has been listed on the Oslo Stock Exchange since 2004 and is led by CEO and President Thorlief Enger. In 2006, Yara's sales topped NOK 48 billion ($8.7 billion).

NITROGEN FERTILIZER PIONEER IN 1904

The population explosion that resulted from the Industrial Revolution of the 19th century placed extreme pressures on Europe's food supplies. By the dawn of the 20th century, farmers found themselves hard pressed to keep up with demand. Traditional fertilizers, primarily animal manure, were not available in sufficient quantities. At the same time, the adoption of new types of crops and increasingly intensified growing techniques contributed to a steady depletion of nutrients in the soil.

Among the most important of these nutrients was nitrogen. The coal industry provided one source of nitrogen-based fertilizers, in the form of ammonium sulfate. However, production of this byproduct could

COMPANY PERSPECTIVES

Yara helps provide food and renewable energy for a growing world population. Our industrial product portfolio includes environmental protection agents with a range of applications. Vision: Aim for Industry Shaper Performance. Yara is uniquely equipped and committed to driving industry shaping performance through operational excellence, profitable growth and people development. Yara's safety and environmental record shall be of the highest standard.

not reach a sufficient level to meet the growing demand at the turn of the 20th century.

A more abundant source of nitrogen had been identified: the air. However at the beginning of the 1900s, no method for extracting that nitrogen had been perfected. Early attempts to release the nitrogen, in the form of nitrous gases, using electricity had been unsuccessful.

This problem was taken up by two Norwegians: Sam Eyde and Kristian Birkeland. The former was a prominent engineer while the latter was a professor of physics at the University of Christiania (the earlier name for the city of Oslo) as well as a prolific inventor. Birkeland had developed the idea of an electric cannon, which could make use of Norway's abundant waterfalls to provide the electric power necessary to produce the nitrogen-releasing reaction. Eyde secured the rights to build and use a hydroelectric plant at the Notodden falls, in the south of Norway. The partners then turned to Sweden's Wallenberg family for start-up funding. With the support from Marcus Wallenberg, the company, founded as Norsk Hydro-Elektrisk Kvaelstofaktieselskap (Norwegian Hydro-Electric Nitrogen Corporation, or Norsk Hydro) in 1905, secured further financing from France's Paribas Bank.

Within a year, the company's products, principally calcium nitrate, had achieved international recognition. "Norwegian nitrate" quickly set the standard for the agricultural market for its purity and efficacy in boosting crop growth. The resulting surge in crop production was to have far-reaching effects on the Western world, helping to lower food prices and raise the nutritional value of the Western diet.

Success at the Notodden plant encouraged the company to begin planning a new and still larger fertilizer complex. Preparations began in 1906 to build a new fertilizer facility at Rjukan, powered by the Skarsfoss waterfall. This time the company formed a partnership with Germany's BASF, which had been developing its own nitric acid furnace design. The Germans became majority shareholders of the Rjukan facility, imposing the use of their furnace. Yet this design proved far less efficient than the furnace developed by Norsk Hydro itself. By 1911, the German backers had agreed to sell their stake, and the Rjukan plant was instead converted to the Norwegian furnace design. Production at Rjukan was launched by 1919.

NEW TECHNOLOGIES BEFORE WORLD WAR II

Norsk Hydro's pioneering status enabled the company to maintain a competitive edge into the 1920s. Yet the company's production process required enormous amounts of energy. The company was able to improve its technology by refining its electric arc production process. Its competitors, however, especially BASF, which became one of the founders of IG Farben, had in the meantime developed a more efficient ammonia-based method for producing calcium nitrate.

By the mid-1920s, Norsk Hydro recognized the need to convert to the new technology as well. The company acquired a license for the use of IG Farben's production technology, in exchange for a 25 percent stake in the company, in 1927. By the end of that decade, Norsk Hydro had begun to modify both the Notodden and Rjukan factories. The company's production then shifted to calcium nitrate, an improved form of the original Norwegian nitrate.

These facilities, however, had been built close to the falls, making transportation of the company's fertilizers, which were sold primarily on the export market, difficult and costly. The 1920s had seen the development of Norway's electrical transmission network. This new infrastructure permitted Norsk Hydro to construct a third factory close to Norway's ports. The company chose Herøya, on the Tinnelv River near Porsgrunn, launching production of calcium nitrate in 1930. That site was later to grow into Norway's largest industrial center.

Norsk Hydro had also been building up its research and development side. This led the company to launch production of the complex fertilizer, NPK, combining nitrogen with two other essential plant nutrients, phosphorous and potassium, in 1936. By 1938, the company had refined its NPK production technology, which became known as the Hydro process, with full-scale production launched that year.

In the years leading up to World War II, Hydro continued to expand its production, adding a number of

KEY DATES

1905: Norsk Hydro is founded to produce nitrogen-based fertilizers.
1968: Norsk Hydro launches production of petrochemicals-based fertilizers.
1979: International expansion of fertilizer operations ensues with purchase of NSM of the Netherlands.
1990: Acquisition of Ceylon Oxygen Company provides access to the Asian market.
2004: Norsk Hydro spins off fertilizer operations as publicly listed Yara International.
2007: Kemira GrowHow is acquired, boosting total global market share to 7 percent.

new chemicals and minerals. These included urea, ammonium nitrate, potassium, phosphate, and calcium chloride.

The Depression era, however, placed the company under new pressure, as the market for ammonia fertilizers collapsed. A new highly protectionist era emerged in the global fertilizer industry, as countries sought to protect their domestic producers. Norsk Hydro's heavy reliance on exports, which accounted for 95 percent of its sales, left the company particularly vulnerable during this period. In order to survive, the company formed an alliance with ICI in England and IG Farben, called the DEN Cooperation.

The company returned to profit growth only toward the end of the decade. However the outbreak of World War II, and the German occupation of Norway, brought an end to the group's prosperity as an independent concern. A new shareholder base took over the company, while its managing director was taken as a prisoner of war. Norsk Hydro's operations were then turned over for the support the German war effort. The Rjukan facility, for example, was used to produce heavy water needed for the Nazi atomic research program. This led to the plant's destruction by Allied-trained saboteurs, the famed Heroes of Telemark. By the end of the war, however, the company's other sites, including Herøya, had also suffered extensive bomb damage.

MODERNIZATION IN THE POSTWAR ERA

With the end of the war, the Norwegian government moved to take control of Norsk Hydro, claiming a 51 percent stake in the company. Norsk Hydro mapped out an ambitious plan to expand its production capacity. The company launched a massive investment program, succeeding in nearly quadrupling its sales revenues between 1945 and 1955. While the period was marked by a general overcapacity in the global fertilizer industry, Norsk Hydro counted on its access to Norway's readily available and inexpensive hydroelectric power. In this way, the company was not only able to remain competitive, but also to grow to become one of the world's leading fertilizer producers.

A major factor in the group's rise was its acquisition of the Glomfjord hydroelectric plant near the polar circle. Developed in the post–World War I era, the Glomfjord site had originally powered an aluminum factory. In 1947, Norsk Hydro acquired the plant, which had been damaged during the war. The company launched construction of a new ammonia and fertilizer production facility, and production there was launched in 1949. The Glomfjord site not only provided ammonia production, but also capacity for converting ammonia into higher-value fertilizers including NPK and calcium nitrate.

The postwar era witnessed Norsk Hydro's growth into Norway's largest and most diversified conglomerate. Fertilizer production inspired much of this diversification, either through production byproducts or into related business areas. The most important of these stemmed from the company decision in the mid-1960s to convert its ammonium production processes to petrochemicals-based methods, using butane and naphtha. The first of the company's new generation plants began production at Porsgrunn in 1968.

As a result, Norsk Hydro entered the oil and gas industry during this time in order to ensure its supply of raw materials. Over time, Norsk Hydro also expanded into the production of light metals. By the turn of the century, the group's diversified operations had grown far larger than its original fertilizer business.

INTERNATIONAL EXPANSION IN THE EIGHTIES

Fertilizers nonetheless remained an important component under the company, and were later regrouped as Hydro Agri. International expansion played a prominent part of the division's growth. The company had begun establishing international sales subsidiaries, including in the United States from 1946. In 1969, the company added its first international production operations, gaining a 25 percent stake of a joint venture launched in Qatar in 1969. By 1972, Hydro Agri had entered the Asian market, starting with a sales operation in Thailand.

The surge in European agricultural production brought on by intensive agricultural techniques led to an oversupply of the market by the late 1970s. Hydro Agri took steps to lead the consolidation of the European fertilizer market, in order to maintain its role as a major player. The company's first acquisition came in 1979, when it acquired NSM, based in the Netherlands. In 1981, the group turned to Sweden, buying 75 percent of Supra AB. The United Kingdom's Fisons Group was added next, becoming Hydro Agri (UK) Ltd. in 1982. That year, Hydro Agri expanded its Scandinavian reach again, purchasing Denmark's Korn- og Foderstofkompagniet.

The company's next move onto the continent came in 1985, with the acquisition of Veba, based in Germany. The following year, Hydro Agri gained a major stake in the French market, with the purchase of 80 percent of Cofaz (Compagnie Française de L'Azote). The company acquired full control of Cofaz the following year. At the end of that decade, the company added a new sales headquarters in Brussels in order to coordinate its European marketing efforts. By 1991, the company had boosted its European production base again, acquiring a facility in Rostock, Germany.

INDEPENDENCE IN THE NEW CENTURY

Hydro Agri targeted more global expansion with the lowering of trade barriers in the early 1990s. With its European market position threatened by the influx of less-expensive Asian and South American fertilizers, the company moved to gain a stake in these markets as well. The group's first entry outside of Europe came in 1990, with the acquisition of Sri Lanka's state-owned Ceylon Oxygen Company. The company next added operations in Trinidad, then launched a joint venture in Florida, marking its entry into the North American market. That operation was later joined by a move into Canada, with the acquisition of that country's Nutrite in 1996.

By the end of the 1990s, however, Hydro Agri was once again suffering from the low margins and massive oversupply of the European and global fertilizers markets. By then the smallest part of Norsk Hydro, the Agri division continued losses had left it deprived of further investment funding. As a result, the company launched a major restructuring effort at the dawn of the 21st century. As part of its restructuring the Hydro Agri shut down a number of its plants and downsized others, while instituting tough new profitability requirements.

With the restructuring underway, the company once again targeted the further consolidation of the fertilizer industry on a more global level. The company entered South Africa in 2000, forming a 50-50 joint venture with Anglo American Industrial Corporation to take over Kynoch Fertilizers, the country's largest fertilizer producer. Also that year, Hydro Agri entered Brazil, buying a 58 percent stake in Adubos Trevo, based in Porto Allegre. Back in Europe, the company boosted its U.K. position through the purchase of 35 percent of Phosyn in 2001.

Hydo Agri's restructuring was largely completed by 2003. With the revenues and profits of its fertilizer business once again on the rise, Norsk Hydro announced its decision to spin off that division as a separate, publicly listed company in 2004. The new company became known as Yara International, the name being taken from an ancient Norse-language word similar to the English word "yield."

PLANNED DOUBLE PRODUCTION BY 2010

Yara's total production capacity reached 20 million tons by mid-decade. Already the outright leader in the global fertilizer industry, Yara mapped out a new strategy of doubling its total capacity into the next decade. For this, the company once again began shopping for new acquisitions as it celebrated its 100th anniversary.

The first of these came in 2006, when the company reached an agreement to acquire full control of Phosyn in the United Kingdom. Soon after, the company announced that it had acquired control of Fertibras, a fertilizer marketing and distribution company in Brazil. Fertibras also owned 15 percent of Fosfertil, the leading nitrogen and phosphate fertilizer producer in Brazil. By the end of 2006, Yara had bought up 50 percent of Balderton Fertilisers, in Switzerland, a leading European fertilizer trading group. The company then acquired Mexican fertilizer retailer Olmeca.

Yara added new operations in North Africa in 2007 through a joint venture with the National Oil Corporation to take over its ammonia and urea plants in Libya. The company then extended its reach into India, forming a joint venture there with Krishak Bharati Corporation.

By the end of that year, Yara had gained approval to complete a still larger purchase: Europe's number two fertilizer producer, Kemira GrowHow. The addition of the new operations were expected to add more than 20 percent to Yara's 2006 revenues of NOK 48.26 billion ($8.72 billion) and boost the company's total global market share considerably.

M. L. Cohen

PRINCIPAL SUBSIDIARIES

Yara A/S; Yara AB (Sweden); YARA Agri Czech Republic S.R.O.; Yara Agri Ltd. (United Kingdom); Yara Belgium S.A./NV; Yara Brasil Fertilizantes S.A.; Yara Colombia Ltda.; Yara France S.A.S.; YARA GmbH and Company KG (Germany); Yara Iberian S.A. (Spain); Yara Industrial GmbH (Germany); Yara Italia S.p.A.; Yara North America Inc. (United States); Yara Phosyn Ltd. (United Kingdom); Yara Rus Ltd.; Yara Sluiskil B.V (Netherlands); Yara Trinidad Ltd.

PRINCIPAL COMPETITORS

China National Chemical Corporation; Vietnam National Chemical Corporation; Norsk Hydro ASA; Royal DSM N.V.; Equistar Chemicals L.P.; Bangladesh Chemical Industries Corporation; Liaocheng Luxi Chemical Group General Corporation; Wesfarmers Ltd.; Jiangxi Damaoshan Group Company Ltd.; Bayer CropScience AG; Arkema S.A.

FURTHER READING

Bains, Elizabeth, "Yara Undertakes Indian and Libyan Ventures," *ICIS Chemical Business Weekly,* April 30, 2007.

Baker, John, "Yara Cultivates Its Fertilizer Business," *ICIS Chemical Business Weekly,* May 28, 2007.

"FGBusiness: Yara Mounts Kemira Bid," *Farmers Guardian,* June 1, 2007, p. 84.

Gibson, Jane, "Yara Buys into Mexico," *ICIS Chemical Business,* November 6, 2006, p. 17.

"Hydro Agri Faces a New Future," *Fertilizer International,* September–October 2003, p. 14.

"Hydro Agri Prepares for Demerger from Norsk," *Chemical Market Reporter,* December 8, 2003, p. 6.

"New Jewels in Hydro Agri's Network," *Fertilizer International,* July 2001, p. 14.

"New Name for Fertiliser Business," *Farmers Guardian,* March 26, 2004, p. 110.

O'Driscoll, Cath, "Successful Fertilisation," *ECN-European Chemical News,* July 25, 2005, p. 21.

"Yara Eyes Synergies from GrowHow," *Chemical Week,* December 12, 2007, p. 5.

"Yara International Takes to the Water," *Fertilizer International,* May–June 2004, p. 14.

"Yara Plans to Acquire GrowHow in Fertilizer Megadeal," *Chemical Week,* May 30, 2007, p. 5.

"Yara Restructures in Europe and Latin America," *Fertilizer International,* January–February 2007, p. 60.

"Yara Takes a Bow," *Fertilizer International,* March–April 2004, p. 52.

"Yara to Build Urea Unit at Dutch Complex," *Chemical Week,* October 31, 2007, p. 16.

Young, Ian, "Yara Will Sell Assets to Secure Clearance for GrowHow Deal," *Chemical Week,* October 3, 2007, p. 17.

Index to Companies

Listings in this index are arranged in alphabetical order under the company name. Company names beginning with a letter or proper name such as Eli Lilly & Co. will be found under the first letter of the company name. Definite articles (The, Le, La) are ignored for alphabetical purposes as are forms of incorporation that precede the company name (AB, NV). Company names printed in **bold** *type have full, historical essays on the page numbers appearing in bold. Updates to entries that appeared in earlier volumes are signified by the notation* **(upd.)**. *Company names in light type are references within an essay to that company, not full historical essays. This index is cumulative with volume numbers printed in bold type.*

A

A and A Limousine Renting, Inc., **26** 62
A & A Medical Supply, **61** 206
A&E Plastics, **12** 377
A&E Television Networks, 32 3–7
A&K Petroleum Company *see* Kerr-McGee Corp.
A&M Records, **23** 389
A&N Foods Co., *see* Nippon Suisan Kaisha, Ltd.
A&P *see* The Great Atlantic & Pacific Tea Company, Inc.
A & W Brands, Inc., 25 3–5 *see also* Cadbury Schweppes PLC.
A-dec, Inc., 53 3–5
á la Zing, **62** 259
A-Mark Financial Corporation, 71 3–6
A-1 Supply *see* International Game Technology.
A-R Technologies, **48** 275
A.A. Mathews *see* CRSS Inc.
A. Ahlström Oy *see* Ahlstrom Corp.
A.B. Chance Industries Co., Inc. *see* Hubbell Inc.
A.B.Dick Company, 28 6–8
A.B. Leasing Corp., *see* Bozzuto's, Inc.
A.B. Watley Group Inc., 45 3–5
A-BEC Mobility, **11** 487
A.C. Delco, **26** 347, 349
A.C. Moore Arts & Crafts, Inc., 30 3–5
A.C. Nielsen Company, 13 3–5 *see also* ACNielsen Corp.
A. Duda & Sons, Inc., 88 1–4
A/E/C/ Systems International, *see* Penton Media, Inc.
A.E. Fitkin & Company, **6** 592–93; **50** 37
A.E. Lottes, **29** 86
A. F. Blakemore & Son Ltd., 90 1–4
A.G. Becker, **20** 260
A.G. Edwards, Inc., 8 3–5; 32 17–21 (upd.)
A.G. Industries, Inc., *see* American Greetings Corp.
A.G. Stanley Ltd. *see* The Boots Company PLC.
A.H. Belo Corporation, 10 3–5; 30 13–17 (upd.)
A.H. Robins Co., *see* Wyeth.
A. Hirsh & Son, **30** 408
A. Hölscher GmbH, **53** 195
A. Johnson & Co. *see* Axel Johnson Group.
A.L. Pharma Inc., 12 3–5 *see also* Alpharma Inc.
A.L. Van Houtte Inc. *see* Van Houtte Inc.
A. Leon Capel and Sons, Inc. *see* Capel Inc.
A.M. Castle & Co., 25 6–8
A. Michel et Cie., **49** 84
A. Moksel AG, 59 3–6
A. Nelson & Co. Ltd., 75 3–6
A. O. Smith Corporation, 11 3–6; 40 3–8 (upd.); 93 1–9 (upd.)
A.P. Møller - Maersk A/S, 57 3–6
A.P. Orleans, Inc., *see* Orleans Homebuilders, Inc.
A.S. Abell Co., **IV** 678
A.S. Watson & Company Ltd., 84 1–4
A.S. Yakovlev Design Bureau, 15 3–6
A. Schilling & Company *see* McCormick & Company, Inc.
A. Schulman, Inc., 8 6–8; 49 3–7 (upd.)
A. Sulka & Co., **29** 457
A.T. Cross Company, 17 3–5; 49 8–12 (upd.)
A.T. Massey Coal Company, Inc., **34** 164; **57** 236
A.T. Mays, **55** 90
A-T-O Inc. *see* Figgie International, Inc.
A.W. Baulderstone Holdings Pty. Ltd., **55** 62
A.W. Faber-Castell Unternehmensverwaltung GmbH & Co., 51 3–6
A. Wilhelmsen A/S, **74** 278
AA Energy Corp., *see* AMR Corp.
AADC Holding Company, Inc., **62** 347
AAF-McQuay Incorporated, 26 3–5
AAI Corporation, **37** 399
Aai.FosterGrant, Inc., **60** 131, 133
Aalborg Industries A/S, 90 5–8
AAON, Inc., 22 3–6
AAPT, **54** 355–57
AAR Corp., 28 3–5

Aardman Animations Ltd., **61** 3–5
Aareal Bank AG *see* DEPFA BANK PLC.
Aarhus United A/S, **68** 3–5
Aaron Brothers Holdings, Inc. *see* Michaels Stores, Inc.
Aaron Rents, Inc., **14** 3–5; **35** 3–6 (upd.)
AARP, **27** 3–5
AASE SARL, **53** 32
Aavid Thermal Technologies, Inc., **29** 3–6
Aavid Thermalloy, LLC, **69** 337
AB Capital & Investment Corporation, **23** 381
AB Ingredients Limited, **41** 32
AB Metal Pty Ltd, **62** 331
Abacus Direct Corporation, **46** 156
ABACUS International Holdings Ltd., **26** 429
Abar Corporation *see* Ipsen International Inc.
Abar Staffing, **25** 434
Abaxis, Inc., **83** 1-4
Abatix Corp., **57** 7–9
ABB Asea Brown Boveri Ltd., *see* ABB Ltd.
ABB Hafo AB *see* Mitel Corp.
ABB Ltd., **II** 1–4; **22** 7–12 (upd.); **65** 3–10 (upd.)
ABB RDM Service, **41** 326
Abba Seafood AB, *see* Orkla ASA.
Abbey Home Entertainment, **23** 391
Abbey Life Group PLC, *see* Lloyds TSB Group plc.
Abbey National plc, **10** 6–8; **39** 3–6 (upd.)
Abbott Laboratories, **I** 619–21; **11** 7–9 (upd.); **40** 9–13 (upd.); **93** 10–18 (upd.)
ABC Appliance, Inc., **10** 9–11
ABC Carpet & Home Co. Inc., **26** 6–8
ABC Family Worldwide, Inc., **52** 3–6
ABC, Inc. *see* Capital Cities/ABC Inc.
ABC Learning Centres Ltd., **93** 19–22
ABC Rail Products Corporation, **18** 3–5
ABC Stores *see* MNS, Ltd.
ABC Supply Co., Inc., **22** 13–16
ABC Treadco, *see* Treadco, Inc.
Abeille Vie *see* Aviva PLC.
Les Abeilles International SA, **60** 149
Abell-Howe Construction Inc., **42** 434
Abelle Limited, **63** 182, 184
Abengoa S.A., **73** 3–5
Abercrombie & Fitch Company, **15** 7–9; **35** 7–10 (upd.); **75** 7–11 (upd.)
Abertis Infraestructuras, S.A., **65** 11–13
ABF *see* Associated British Foods plc.
ABF Freight System, Inc., **16** 39–41
ABI *see* American Furniture Company, Inc.
Abigail Adams National Bancorp, Inc., **23** 3–5
Abilis, **49** 222
Abington Shoe Company *see* The Timberland Co.
Abiomed, Inc., **47** 3–6
Abita Springs Water Co., **58** 373
Abitec Corporation, **41** 32–33
Abitibi-Consolidated, Inc., **IV** 245–47; **25** 9–13 (upd.)
ABM Industries Incorporated, **25** 14–16 (upd.)
ABN *see* Algemene Bank Nederland N.V.
ABN AMRO Holding, N.V., **50** 3–7
Above The Belt, Inc., **16** 37
AboveNet, Inc., **61** 210, 213
ABR Foods, *see* Associated British Foods plc.
Abrafract Abrasives *see* Carbo PLC.
Abraham & Straus, *see* Federated Department Stores Inc.
Abrams Industries Inc., **23** 6–8
Abraxas Petroleum Corporation, **89** 1–5
ABRY Partners LLC, **72** 36, 39
ABS Pump AB, **53** 85
Absolut Company, **31** 458, 460
Abu Dhabi National Oil Company, **IV** 363–64; **45** 6–9 (upd.)
AC Design Inc., **22** 196
AC Humko Corporation, **41** 32–33
AC Roma SpA, **44** 388
Academic Press *see* Reed Elsevier plc.
Academy of Television Arts & Sciences, Inc., **55** 3–5
Academy Sports & Outdoors, **27** 6–8
Acadia Investors, **23** 99
Acadia Partners, **21** 92
Acadian Ambulance & Air Med Services, Inc., **39** 7–10
ACC Corporation *see* AT&T Corp.
Accel, S.A. de C.V., **51** 115–17
Accenture Ltd., **59** 130; **68** 26
Access Business Group *see* Alticor Inc.
Access Graphics Technology Inc., *see* CalComp Inc.
ACCION International, **87** 1–4
Acciona S.A., **81** 1–4
Acclaim Entertainment Inc., **24** 3–8
ACCO World Corporation, **7** 3–5; **51** 7–10 (upd.)
Accolade Inc., **35** 227
Accor S.A., **10** 12–14; **27** 9–12 (upd.); **69** 3–8 (upd.)
Accord Energy, *see* Dynegy Inc.
Accredited Home Lenders Holding Co., **91** 1–4
Accres Uitgevers B.V., **51** 328
Accubuilt, Inc., **74** 3–5
Accudata Inc., **64** 237
AccuRead Limited, **42** 165, 167
Accuscan, Inc., **14** 380
AccuStaff Inc. *see* MPS Group, Inc.
AccuWeather, Inc., **73** 6–8
Ace Bag Company Limited, **70** 43
ACE Cash Express, Inc., **33** 3–6
Ace Comb Company, *see* Goody Products, Inc.
Ace Hardware Corporation, **12** 6–8; **35** 11–14 (upd.)
Ace Medical Company, **30** 164
Ace Novelty Company, **26** 374
Acer Incorporated, **16** 3–6; **73** 9–13 (upd.)
Aceralia, **42** 414
Acerinox, **59** 226
Aceros Fortuna S.A. de C.V., *see* Carpenter Technology Corp.
Acesa *see* Abertis Infraestructuras, S.A.
Aceto Corp., **38** 3–5
ACF Industries, **30** 282
ACG *see* American Cotton Growers Association.
ACH Food Companies, Inc., **74** 349
Achatz GmbH Bauunternehmung, **55** 62
AchieveGlobal Inc., **90** 9–12
Achiever Computers Pty Ltd, **56** 155
ACI *see* Advance Circuits Inc.
ACI Billing Services, Inc., **72** 36, 39
ACI Ltd., **29** 478
Aciéries de Ploërmel, *see* Varlen Corp.
Aciéries Réunies de Burbach-Eich-Dudelange S.A. *see* ARBED S.A.
Acindar Industria Argentina de Aceros S.A., **87** 5–8
Acker Drill Company, **26** 70
Ackerley Communications, Inc., **9** 3–5
Acktion Corporation *see* Morguard Corp.
ACL *see* Automotive Components Ltd.
ACLC *see* Allegheny County Light Co.
ACLU *see* American Civil Liberties Union (ACLU).
ACM *see* Advanced Custom Molders, Inc.
Acme Brick Company, *see* Justin Industries, Inc.
Acme-Cleveland Corp., **13** 6–8
Acme Market *see* American Stores Co.
Acme Quilting Co., Inc., **19** 304
Acme United Corporation, **70** 3–6
ACMI, **21** 118–19
ACNielsen Corporation, **38** 6–9 (upd.)
Acordis, **41** 10
Acorn Financial Corp., **15** 328
Acorn Products, Inc., **55** 6–9
Acosta Sales and Marketing Company,Inc., **77** 1–4
Acova S.A., **26** 4
Acquired Systems Enhancement Corporation, *see* American Power Conversion Corp.
ACR *see* American Capital and Research Corp.
AcroMed Corporation, **30** 164
ACS *see* Affiliated Computer Services, Inc.; Alaska Communications Systems Group, Inc.
Acsys, Inc., **44** 3–5
ACT Group, **45** 280
ACT Inc, **50** 48
ACT Research Center Inc., **56** 238
Actava Group, **14** 332
Actelion Ltd., **83** 5-8
Action, **6** 393
Action Gaming Inc., **44** 337
Action Labs Inc., **37** 285
Action Performance Companies, Inc., **27** 13–15
Action Temporary Services, **29** 273
Active Apparel Group *see* Everlast Worldwide Inc.
Actividades de Construcción y Servicios S.A. (ACS), **55** 179

Activision, Inc., **32** 8–11; **89** 6–11 (upd.)
Actuant Corporation, **94** 1–8 (upd.)
Acuity Brands, Inc., **90** 13–16
Acumos, **11** 57
Acushnet Company, **64** 3–5
Acuson Corporation, **10** 15–17; **36** 3–6 (upd.)
Acxiom Corporation, **35** 15–18
AD-AM Gas Company, **11** 28
AD South Africa, Inc., **60** 34
Ad Vantage Computer Systems Inc., **58** 273
Adaco, **70** 58
Adage Systems International, Inc., *see* Systems & Computer Technology Corp.
Adam, Meldrum & Anderson Company (AM&A), **16** 61–62; **50** 107
Adam Opel AG, **7** 6–8; **21** 3–7 (upd.); **61** 6–11 (upd.)
Adams/Cates Company, **21** 257
Adams Childrenswear *see* Sears plc.
The Adams Express Company, **86** 1–5
Adams Golf, Inc., **37** 3–5
Adams Media Corporation *see* F&W Publications, Inc.
Adaptec, Inc., **31** 3–6
Adar Associates, Inc. *see* Scientific-Atlanta, Inc.
ADC of Greater Kansas City, Inc., **22** 443
ADC Telecommunications, Inc., **10** 18–21; **30** 6–9 (upd.); **89** 12–17 (upd.)
Addison Communications Plc, **45** 272
Addison Corporation, **31** 399
Addison Structural Services, Inc., **26** 433
Addison Wesley, **IV** 659
Adecco S.A., **36** 7–11 (upd.)
Adeletom Aviation L.L.C., **61** 100
Adelphia Communications Corporation, **17** 6–8; **52** 7–10 (upd.)
Ademco *see* Alarm Device Manufacturing Co.
Adero Inc., **45** 202
ADESA, Inc., **71** 7–10
Adesso-Madden, Inc., **37** 372
ADI Group Limited *see* AHL Services, Inc.
Adia S.A., **6** 9–11 *see also* Adecco S.A.
Adiainvest S.A. *see* Adecco S.A.
adidas Group AG, **14** 6–9; **33** 7–11 (upd.); **75** 12–17 (upd.)
Aditya Birla Group, **79** 1–5
Adler, **23** 219
Adler Line *see* Transatlantische Dampfschiffahrts Gesellschaft.
ADM *see* Archer Daniels Midland Co.
ADME Bioanalyses SAS *see* Eurofins Scientific S.A.
Administaff, Inc., **52** 11–13
Administracion Corporativa y Mercantil, S.A. de C.V., **37** 178
Administración Nacional de Combustibles, Alcohol y Pórtland, **93** 23–27
Admiral Co. *see* Maytag Corp.
ADNOC *see* Abu Dhabi National Oil Co.
Adobe Systems Incorporated, **10** 22–24; **33** 12–16 (upd.)
Adolf Würth GmbH & Co. KG, **49** 13–15
Adolfo Dominguez S.A., **72** 3–5
Adolph Coors Company, **I** 236–38; **13** 9–11 (upd.); **36** 12–16 (upd.) *see also* Molson Coors Brewing Co.
Adolphe Lafont, *see* Vivarte SA.
ADP *see* Automatic Data Processing, Inc.
Adria Produtos Alimenticos, Ltd., **12** 411
Adrienne Vittadini, **15** 291
ADS *see* Aerospace Display Systems.
Adstaff Associates, Ltd., **26** 240
Adsteam, **60** 101
ADT Automotive, **71** 8–9
ADT Ltd., **26** 410; **28** 486; **63** 403
ADT Security Services, Inc., **12** 9–11; **44** 6–9 (upd.)
Adtran Inc., **22** 17–20
Adtranz *see* Bombardier Inc.
Advacel, **18** 20; **43** 17
Advance Auto Parts, Inc., **57** 10–12
Advance Circuits Inc., **49** 234
Advance Gems & Jewelry Co., Ltd., **62** 371
Advance/Newhouse Communications, **42** 114
Advance Publications Inc., **IV** 581–84; **19** 3–7 (upd.)
Advanced Aerodynamics & Structures Inc. *see* Mooney Aerospace Group Ltd.
Advanced Broadband, L.P., **70** 325
Advanced Casino Systems Corporation, **21** 277
Advanced Circuits Inc., **67** 3–5
Advanced Colortech Inc., **56** 238
Advanced Communications Engineering *see* Scientific-Atlanta, Inc.
Advanced Communications Inc. *see* Metrocall, Inc.
Advanced Data Management Group S.A., **23** 212
Advanced Fiberoptic Technologies, **30** 267
Advanced Fibre Communications, Inc., **63** 3–5
Advanced Gravis, **28** 244; **69** 243
Advanced Logic Research, Inc., *see* Gateway, Inc.
Advanced Marine Enterprises, Inc., **18** 370
Advanced Marketing Services, Inc., **34** 3–6
Advanced Medical Optics, Inc., **79** 6–9
Advanced Metallurgy, Inc., **29** 460
Advanced Micro Devices, Inc., **6** 215–17; **30** 10–12 (upd.)
Advanced Neuromodulation Systems, Inc., **73** 14–17
Advanced Parking Systems Ltd., **58** 184
Advanced Plasma Systems, Inc., **48** 299
Advanced Pollution Instrumentation Inc., **62** 362
Advanced Semiconductor Engineering, **73** 301
Advanced Structures, Inc., *see* Essef Corp.
Advanced System Applications, **11** 395
Advanced Technology Laboratories, Inc., **9** 6–8
Advanced Telecommunications, Inc. *see* Eschelon Telecom, Inc.
Advanced Tissue Sciences Inc., **41** 377
Advanced Web Technologies, *see* Miner Group Int.
AdvanceMed LLC, **45** 146
AdvancePCS, Inc., **63** 336
Advanstar Communications, Inc., **57** 13–17
Advanta Corporation, **8** 9–11; **38** 10–14 (upd.)
Advanta Partners, LP, **42** 322
Advantage Company, *see* LDDS-Metro Communications, Inc.
The Advantage Group, Inc., *see* Habersham Bancorp.
Advantage Health Plans, Inc., **11** 379
Advantage Health Systems, Inc., **25** 383
Advantage Publishers Group, **34** 5
Advantest Corporation, **39** 350, 353
Advantica Restaurant Group, Inc., **27** 16–19 (upd.)
Advantra International NV *see* Punch International N.V.
Adventist Health, **53** 6–8
The Advertising Council, Inc., **76** 3–6
Advertising Unlimited, Inc., *see* R.L. Polk & Co.
The Advisory Board Company, **80** 1–4 *see also* The Corporate Executive Board Co.
Advo, Inc., **6** 12–14; **53** 9–13 (upd.)
Advocat Inc., **46** 3–5
AEA *see* United Kingdom Atomic Energy Authority.
AEA Investors Inc., **22** 169, 171; **28** 380; **30** 328
AECOM Technology Corporation, **79** 10–13
AEG A.G., **I** 409–11
AEG Hausgeräte, **53** 128
Aegean Marine Petroleum Network Inc., **89** 18–21
Aegek S.A., **64** 6–8
Aegis Group plc, **6** 15–16
AEGON N.V., **III** 177–79; **50** 8–12 (upd.) *see also* Transamerica–An AEGON Company
AEI Music Network Inc., **35** 19–21
Aeneas Venture Corp., **26** 502
AEON Co., Ltd., **V** 96–99; **68** 6–10 (upd.)
AEP *see* American Electric Power Co.
AEP Industries, Inc., **36** 17–19
Aer Lingus Group plc, **34** 7–10; **89** 22–27 (upd.)
Aera Energy LLC, **41** 359
Aérazur, **36** 529
Aereos Del Mercosur, **68** 365
Aerial Communications Inc., **31** 452
Aeries Health Care Corporation, **68** 299
Aero Mayflower Transit Company *see* Mayflower Group Inc.
Aero O/Y *see* Finnair Oy.

Aeroflot - Russian Airlines JSC, 6 57–59; 29 7–10 (upd.); 89 28–34 (upd.)
Aerojet-General Corp., 63 6–9
Aerolíneas Argentinas S.A., 33 17–19; 69 9–12 (upd.)
Aeroméxico, **20** 168
Aeromotive Systems Co., **55** 31
Aeronautics Leasing, Inc., **39** 33
Aeronca Inc., 46 6–8
Aeropar Participacoes S.A., **73** 166
Aeropharm Technology, Inc., **63** 233–34
Aéroports de Paris, 33 20–22
Aéropostale, Inc., 89 35–38
Aeroquip Corporation, 16 7–9 *see also* Eaton Corp.
Aerosance Inc., **62** 362
Aerosonic Corporation, 69 13–15
Aerospace Display Systems, **36** 158
Aerospace International Services, **41** 38
Aerospace Products International, Inc., **49** 141
The Aérospatiale Group, 7 9–12; 21 8–11 (upd.) *see also* European Aeronautic Defence and Space Company EADS N.V.
Aerostar, **33** 359–61
The AES Corporation, 10 25–27; 13 12–15 (upd.); 53 14–18 (upd.)
Aetna, Inc., III 180–82; 21 12–16 (upd.); 63 10–16 (upd.)
Aetna Insulated Wire *see* The Marmon Group, Inc.
AF Insurance Agency, **44** 33
AFC *see* Advanced Fibre Communications, Inc.
AFC Enterprises, Inc., 32 12–16 (upd.); 83 9-15 (upd.)
Affiliated Computer Services, Inc., 61 12–16
Affiliated Foods Inc., 53 19–21
Affiliated Hospital Products Inc., **37** 400
Affiliated Managers Group, Inc., 79 14–17
Affiliated Paper Companies, Inc., **31** 359, 361
Affiliated Physicians Network, Inc., **45** 194
Affiliated Publications, Inc., 7 13–16
Affinity Group Holding Inc., 56 3–6
Affymetrix, Inc., **75** 70–71
AFG Industries Inc., **I** 483; **48** 42
AFIA, *see* CIGNA Corp.
Afianzadora Insurgentes Serfin, **19** 190
AFK Sistema, **59** 300
AFL *see* American Football League.
AFLAC Incorporated, 10 28–30 (upd.); 38 15–19 (upd.)
AFP *see* Australian Forest Products.
AFRA Enterprises Inc., **26** 102
AFRAM Carriers, Inc. *see* Kirby Corp.
African Rainbow Minerals, **63** 185
Africare, 59 7–10
AFT *see* Advanced Fiberoptic Technologies.
After Hours Formalwear Inc., 60 3–5
Aftermarket Technology Corp., 83 16-19
AG&E *see* American Electric Power Co.
AG Barr plc, 64 9–12
Ag-Chem Equipment Company, Inc., 17 9–11 *see also* AGCO Corp.
AG Communication Systems Corporation, **15** 194; **43** 446
Ag Services of America, Inc., 59 11–13
Aga Foodservice Group PLC, 73 18–20
Agan Chemical Manufacturers Ltd., *see* Koor Industries Ltd.
Agape S.p.A., **57** 82–83
Agasote Millboard Company *see* Homasote Co.
Agatha Christie Ltd., **31** 63 67
AGCO Corp., 13 16–18; 67 6–10 (upd.)
Age International, Inc., **62** 347
Agefi, **34** 13
AGEL&P *see* Albuquerque Gas, Electric Light and Power Co.
Agema Infrared Systems AB, **69** 171
Agence France-Presse, 34 11–14
Agency, **6** 393
Agency Rent-A-Car, *see* National Auto Credit, Inc.
Agere Systems Inc., 61 17–19
AGF *see* Assurances Generales de France.
Agfa Gevaert Group N.V., 59 14–16
Aggregate Industries plc, 36 20–22
Aggreko Plc, 45 10–13
AGI Industries, **57** 208–09
Agiba Petroleum, **IV** 414
Agie Charmilles, **61** 106, 108
Agilent Technologies Inc., 38 20–23; 93 28–32 (upd.)
Agilysys Inc., 76 7–11 (upd.)
Agip SpA *see* ENI S.p.A.
Agiv AG, **39** 40–41; **51** 25
Agnew Gold Mining Company (Pty) Ltd., **62** 164
Agnico-Eagle Mines Limited, 71 11–14
Agora S.A. Group, 77 5–8
Agouron Pharmaceuticals, Inc., **38** 365
Agr *see* Artes Grafica Rioplatense S.A.
Agra Europe Limited, **58** 191
AGRANA, *see* Südzucker AG.
AgReliant Genetics Inc. *see* Groupe Limagrain.
Agri Beef Company, 81 5–9
Agri-Foods, Inc., **60** 256
Agri-Insurance Company, Ltd., **63** 23
Agribrands International, Inc., **40** 89
Agrico Chemical Company *see* The Williams Companies.
Agricole de Roquefort et Maria Grimal, **23** 219
Agricultural Minerals and Chemicals Inc., **13** 504
Agrifull, **22** 380
Agrigenetics, Inc. *see* Mycogen Corp.
Agrilink Foods Inc., **73** 110; **76** 16
Agrilusa, Agro-Industria, **51** 54
Agrium Inc., 73 21–23
Agrobios S.A., **23** 172
Agrologica, **51** 54
Agromán S.A., **40** 218
AGTL *see* Alberta Gas Trunk Line Company, Ltd.
Agua de la Falda S.A., **38** 231
Agusta S.p.A., **46** 66
AgustaWestland N.V., 75 18–20
Agway, Inc., 7 17–18; 21 17–19 (upd.) *see also* Cargill Inc.
Aherns Holding, **60** 100
AHI Building Products *see* Carter Holt Harvey Ltd.
AHL Services, Inc., 27 20–23
Ahlstrom Corporation, 53 22–25
Ahmanson *see* H.F. Ahmanson & Co.
AHMSA *see* Altos Hornos de México, S.A. de C.V.
Ahold *see* Koninklijke Ahold NV.
AHP *see* American Home Products Corp.
AHS *see* American Hospital Supply Corp.
AHSC Holdings Corp. *see* Alco Health Services Corp.
Ahtna AGA Security, Inc., *see* The Wackenhut Corp.
AIB *see* Allied Irish Banks plc.
AIC *see* Allied Import Co.
AICA bv, *see* Randstad Holding n.v.
AICPA *see* The American Institute of Certified Public Accountants.
Aida Corporation, **11** 504
AIG *see* American International Group, Inc.
AIG Global Real Estate Investment Corp., **54** 225
AIG Latin America Equity Partners, Ltda., **74** 48
AIG/Lincoln International L.L.C., **54** 225
Aigner *see* Etienne Aigner AG.
Aikenhead's Home Improvement Warehouse, **26** 306
AIL Technologies, **46** 160
AIM Create Co., Ltd. *see* Marui Co., Ltd.
AIM Management Group Inc., **65** 43–45
AIMCO *see* Apartment Investment and Management Co.
Ainsworth Gaming Technologies, **54** 15
AIP *see* American Industrial Properties; Amorim Investimentos e Participaço.
Air & Water Technologies Corporation, 6 441–42 *see also* Aqua Alliance Inc.
Air Berlin GmbH & Co. Luftverkehrs KG, 71 15–17
Air By Pleasant, **62** 276
Air Canada, 6 60–62; 23 9–12 (upd.); 59 17–22 (upd.)
Air China, 46 9–11
Air Compak, **12** 182
Air Express International Corporation, 13 19–20
Air France *see* Groupe Air France; Societe Air France.
Air Global International, **55** 30
Air-India Limited, 6 63–64; 27 24–26 (upd.)
Air Inter *see* Groupe Air France.
Air Inuit, **56** 38–39
Air Jamaica Limited, 54 3–6
Air Lanka Catering Services Ltd. *see* Thai Airways International.
Air Liberté, **6** 208
Air Liquide *see* L'Air Liquide SA.
Air London International, **36** 190

Air Mauritius Ltd., **63** 17–19
Air Methods Corporation, **53** 26–29
Air Midwest, Inc. *see* Mesa Air Group, Inc.
Air New Zealand Limited, **14** 10–12; **38** 24–27 (upd.)
Air NorTerra Inc., **56** 39
Air Pacific Ltd., **70** 7–9
Air Partner PLC, **93** 33–36
Air Products and Chemicals, Inc., **I** 297–99; **10** 31–33 (upd.); **74** 6–9 (upd.)
Air Pub S.à.r.l., **64** 359
Air Sahara Limited, **65** 14–16
Air Sea Broker AG, **47** 286–87
Air Southwest Co. *see* Southwest Airlines Co.
Air T, Inc., **86** 6–9
Air Taser, Inc. *see* Taser International, Inc.
Air Transport International LLC, **58** 43
Air Wisconsin Airlines Corporation, **55** 10–12
Air Zimbabwe (Private) Limited, **91** 5–8
AirAsia Berhad, **93** 37–40
Airborne Freight Corporation, **6** 345–47; **34** 15–18 (upd.) *see also* DHL Worldwide Network S.A./N.V.
Airborne Systems Group, **89** 39–42
Airbus Industrie *see* G.I.E. Airbus Industrie.
AirCal, **I** 91
Airco, **26** 94
Aircraft Modular Products, **30** 73
Aircraft Turbine Center, Inc., **28** 3
AirFoyle Ltd., **53** 50
Airgas, Inc., **54** 7–10
Airguard Industries, Inc., *see* CLARCOR Inc.
AirLib *see* Société d'Exploitation AOM.
Airline Interiors Inc., **41** 368–69
Airlines of Britain Holdings, **34** 398; **38** 105–06
Airlink Pty Ltd *see* Qantas Airways Ltd.
Airopak Corporation *see* PVC Container Corp.
Airport Leather Concessions LLC, **58** 369
Airrest S.A., **64** 359
Airshop Ltd., *see* Jalate Inc.
Airstream *see* Thor Industries, Inc.
AirTouch Communications, **11** 10–12 *see also* Vodafone Group PLC.
Airtours Plc, **27** 27–29, 90, 92
AirTran Holdings, Inc., **22** 21–23
AirWair Ltd., **23** 399, 401–02
AirWays Corporation *see* AirTran Holdings, Inc.
Aisin Seiki Co., Ltd., **III** 415–16; **48** 3–5 (upd.)
AIT Worldwide, **47** 286–87
Aitchison & Colegrave *see* Bradford & Bingley PLC.
Aitken, Inc., **26** 433
AITS *see* American International Travel Service.
Aiuruoca, **25** 85
Aiwa Co., Ltd., **30** 18–20
Ajax Repair & Supply, **58** 75
Ajegroup S.A, **92** 1–4
Ajinomoto Co., Inc., **II** 463–64; **28** 9–11 (upd.)
AJS Auto Parts Inc., **15** 246
AK Steel Holding Corporation, **19** 8–9; **41** 3–6 (upd.)
Akamai Technologies, Inc., **71** 18–21
Akane Securities Co. Ltd., *see* ORIX Corp.
AKAY Flavours & Aromatics Ltd., **70** 56
Akbank TAS, **79** 18–21
Akemi, Inc. *see* FinishMaster, Inc.; Maxco Inc.
Aker RGI, **32** 99
Akerys S.A., **90** 17–20
AKG Acoustics GmbH, **62** 3–6
AKH Co. Inc., **20** 63
Akin, Gump, Strauss, Hauer & Feld, L.L.P., **33** 23–25
Akorn, Inc., **32** 22–24
Akro-Mills Inc., *see* Myers Industries, Inc.
Akron Extruders Inc., **53** 230
Aktia Sparbank Abp, **69** 177, 179
Aktiebolaget SKF, **III** 622–25; **38** 28–33 (upd.); **89** 401–09 (upd.)
Aktieselskabet Dampskibsselskabet Svendborg, **57** 3, 5
Akzo Nobel N.V., **13** 21–23; **41** 7–10 (upd.)
Al-Amin Co. For Securities & Investment Funds *see* Dallah Albaraka Group.
Al Copeland Enterprises, Inc., **7** 26–28; **32** 13–15
Al Habtoor Group L.L.C., **87** 9–12
Al-Tawfeek Co. For Investment Funds Ltd. *see* Dallah Albaraka Group.
ALA *see* Americal Library Association.
Alaadin Middle East-Ersan, **IV** 564
Alabama Farmers Cooperative, Inc., **63** 20–22
Alabama Gas Corporation, **21** 207–08
Alabama National BanCorporation, **75** 21–23
Alabama Power Company, **38** 445, 447–48
Alabama Shipyards Inc., **21** 39–40
Aladdin Mills Inc., **19** 276; **63** 300
Alagasco, **21** 207–08
Alagroup, **45** 337
Alain Afflelou SA, **53** 30–32
Alain Manoukian *see* Groupe Alain Manoukian.
Alamac Knit Fabrics, Inc., *see* WestPoint Stevens Inc.
Alamito Company, **6** 590
Alamo Group Inc., **32** 25–28
Alamo Rent A Car, **6** 348–50; **24** 9–12 (upd.); **84** 5–11 (upd.)
Alamo Water Refiners, Inc. *see* The Marmon Group, Inc.
Alan Patricof Associates *see* Apax Partners Worldwide LLP.
ALANTEC Corporation, *see* FORE Systems, Inc.
ALARIS Medical Systems, Inc., **65** 17–20
Alarm Device Manufacturing Company, *see* Pittway Corp.
Alaron Inc., *see* The Marmon Group, Inc.
Alascom, Inc. *see* AT&T Corp.
Alaska Air Group, Inc., **6** 65–67; **29** 11–14 (upd.)
Alaska Commercial Company, **12** 363
Alaska Communications Systems Group, Inc., **89** 43–46
Alaska Native Wireless LLC, **60** 264
Alaska Railroad Corporation, **60** 6–9
Alaska Steel Co., **19** 381
Alatas Mammoet, **26** 279
Alba Foods, **27** 197; **43** 218
Alba-Waldensian, Inc., **30** 21–23 *see also* E.I. du Pont de Nemours and Co.
Albany Cheese, **23** 219
Albany International Corporation, **8** 12–14; **51** 11–14 (upd.)
Albany Molecular Research, Inc., **77** 9–12
Albaugh Inc., **62** 19
Albemarle Corporation, **59** 23–25
Alberici Corporation, **76** 12–14
Albert E. Reed & Co. Ltd. *see* Reed International PLC.
The Albert Fisher Group plc, **41** 11–13
Albert Heijn NV, *see* Koninklijke Ahold N.V. (Royal Ahold).
Albert Nipon, Inc., *see* The Leslie Fay Company, Inc.
Albert's Organics, Inc. *see* United Natural Foods, Inc.
Alberta Energy Company Ltd., **16** 10–12; **43** 3–6 (upd.)
Alberta Gas Trunk Line Company, Ltd. *see* Nova Corporation of Alberta.
Alberto-Culver Company, **8** 15–17; **36** 23–27 (upd.); **91** 9–15 (upd.)
Albertson's, Inc., **II** 601–03; **7** 19–22 (upd.); **30** 24–28 (upd.); **65** 21–26 (upd.)
Albion Industries, Inc., *see* The Marmon Group, Inc.
Albright & Wilson Ltd., **12** 351; **38** 378, 380; **50** 282; **59** 25
Albuquerque Gas & Electric Company *see* Public Service Company of New Mexico.
Albuquerque Gas, Electric Light and Power Company, **6** 561–62
Alcan Aluminium Limited, **IV** 9–13; **31** 7–12 (upd.)
Alcan Inc., **60** 338
Alcatel S.A., **9** 9–11; **36** 28–31 (upd.)
Alchem Capital Corp., *see* Delta Woodside Industries, Inc.
Alchem Plastics *see* Spartech Corp.
Alco Health Services Corporation, **III** 9–10 *see also* AmeriSource Health Corp.
Alco Office Products Inc., **24** 362
Alco Standard Corporation, **I** 412–13
ALCO Trade Show Services, **26** 102
Alcoa Inc., **56** 7–11 (upd.)
Alden Merrell Corporation, **23** 169
Alderwoods Group, Inc., **68** 11–15 (upd.)
Aldi Einkauf GmbH & Co. OHG, **13** 24–26; **86** 10–14 (upd.)
Aldila Inc., **46** 12–14

Aldiscon, **37** 232
Aldus Corporation, 10 34–36 *see also* Adobe Systems Inc.
Alert Centre Inc., **32** 373
Alès Groupe, 81 10–13
Alestra, **19** 12
Alex & Ivy, *see* The Bombay Company, Inc.
Alex Lee Inc., 18 6–9; 44 10–14 (upd.)
Alexander & Alexander Services Inc., 10 37–39 *see also* Aon Corp.
Alexander & Baldwin, Inc., 10 40–42; 40 14–19 (upd.)
Alexander Hamilton Life Insurance Co., *see* Household International, Inc.
Alexander Howden Group, *see* Alexnder & Alexander Services Inc.
Alexander's, Inc., 45 14–16
Alexandra plc, 88 5–8
Alexandria Petroleum Co., **51** 113
Alfa Corporation, 60 10–12
Alfa-Laval AB, III 417–21; 64 13–18 (upd.)
Alfa Romeo, 13 27–29; 36 32–35 (upd.)
Alfa, S.A. de C.V., 19 10–12
Alfa Trading Company, **23** 358
Alfalfa's Markets, *see* Wild Oats Markets, Inc.
Alfesca hf, 82 1–4
alfi Zitzmann, **60** 364
Alfred A. Knopf, Inc., *see* Random House, Inc.
Alfred Bullows & Sons, Ltd., **21** 64
Alfred Dunhill Limited, *see* Vendôme Luxury Group plc.
Alfred Kärcher GmbH & Co KG, 94 9–14
Alfred Marks Bureau, Ltd. *see* Adia S.A.
Alfred McAlpine plc, **51** 138
Alfred Ritter GmbH & Co. KG, 58 3–7
Alfried Krupp von Bohlen und Halbach Foundation, **IV** 89
ALG *see* Arkla, Inc.
Alga, *see* BRIO AB.
Algamar, S.A., **64** 91
Algemeen Burgerlijk Pensioenfonds, **26** 421
Algemeen Dagbald BV, **53** 273
Algemene Bank Nederland N.V., II 183–84
Algerian Saudi Leasing Holding Co. *see* Dallah Albaraka Group.
Algo Group Inc., 24 13–15
ALI *see* Aeronautics Leasing, Inc.
Aliança Florestal-Sociedade para o Desenvolvimento Agro-Florestal, S.A., **60** 156
Alicia S.A. *see* Arcor S.A.I.C.
Alico, Inc., 63 23–25
Alidata SpA *see* Alitalia—Linee Aeree Italiana, S.P.A.
Alienware Corporation, 81 14–17
Aligro Inc., *see* Steinberg Inc.
Align Technology, Inc., 94 15–18
Alimentation Couche-Tard Inc., 77 13–16
Alimentos Indal S.A., **66** 9
Alitalia–Linee Aeree Italiana, S.p.A., 6 68–69; 29 15–17 (upd.)
Aljazeera Satellite Channel, 79 22–25
All American Airways *see* USAir Group, Inc.
All American Communications Inc., 20 3–7
All American Gourmet Co., **12** 199
All American Sports Co., *see* Riddell Sports Inc.
All-Clad Metalcrafters Inc., **34** 493, 496–97
The All England Lawn Tennis & Croquet Club, 54 11–13
All-Glass Aquarium Co., Inc., **58** 60
All Nippon Airways Co., Ltd., 6 70–71; 38 34–37 (upd.); 91 16–20 (upd.)
All Seasons Vehicles, Inc. *see* ASV, Inc.
Allami Biztosito, **15** 30
Alldays plc, 49 16–19
Allders plc, 37 6–8
Alleanza Assicurazioni S.p.A., 65 27–29
Alleghany Corporation, 10 43–45; 60 13–16 (upd.)
Allegheny Airlines *see* USAir Group, Inc.; US Airways Group, Inc.
Allegheny Energy, Inc., 38 38–41 (upd.)
Allegheny International, Inc., **22** 3, 436
Allegheny Ludlum Corporation, 8 18–20
Allegheny Power System, Inc., V 543–45 *see also* Allegheny Energy, Inc.
Allegheny Steel Distributors, Inc. *see* Reliance Steel & Aluminum Co.
Allegiance Life Insurance Company, *see* Horace Mann Educators Corp.
Allegis, Inc. *see* United Airlines.
Allen & Co., **12** 496; **25** 270
Allen-Bradley Co., *see* Rockwell Automation.
Allen Canning Company, 76 15–17
Allen-Edmonds Shoe Corporation, 61 20–23
Allen Foods, Inc., 60 17–19
Allen Group Inc. *see* TransPro, Inc.
Allen Organ Company, 33 26–29
Allen-Stuart Equipment Company, **49** 160
Allen Systems Group, Inc., 59 26–28
Allen Tank Ltd., **21** 499
Allerderm *see* Virbac Corp.
Allergan, Inc., 10 46–49; 30 29–33 (upd.); 77 17–24 (upd.)
ALLETE, Inc., **71** 9
Allgemeine Elektricitäts-Gesellschaft *see* AEG A.G.
Allgemeine Handelsgesellschaft der Verbraucher AG *see* AVA AG.
Allgemeine Schweizerische Uhrenindustrie, **26** 480
Allhabo AB, **53** 85
Allia S.A., **51** 324
Alliance and Leicester plc, 88 9–12
Alliance Assurance Company, *see* Royal & Sun Alliance Insurance Group plc.
Alliance Atlantis Communications Inc., 39 11–14
Alliance Boots plc, 83 20-28 (upd.)
Alliance Capital Management Holding L.P., 63 26–28
Alliance de Sud, **53** 301
Alliance Entertainment Corp., 17 12–14 *see also* Source Interlink Companies, Inc.
Alliance Gaming Corp., **15** 539
Alliance International LLC, **73** 283–84
Alliance Paper Group, *see* M-real Oyj.
Alliance Resource Partners, L.P., 81 18–21
Alliance UniChem Plc *see* Alliance Boots plc.
Alliant Energy Corp., **39** 261
Alliant Techsystems Inc., 8 21–23; 30 34–37 (upd.); 77 25–31 (upd.)
Allianz AG, III 183–86; 15 10–14 (upd.); 57 18–24 (upd.)
Allied Bakeries Limited *see* Greggs PLC.
Allied Chemical *see* General Chemical Corp.
Allied Chemical & Dye Corp., *see* AlliedSignal Inc.
Allied Color Industries, *see* M.A. Hanna Company
Allied Communications Group, **22** 297
Allied Construction Products, *see* Pubco Corp.
Allied Corporation *see* AlliedSignal Inc.
The Allied Defense Group, Inc., 65 30–33
Allied Department Stores, **50** 106
Allied Domecq PLC, 29 18–20
Allied Drink Distributors Ltd., **68** 99
Allied Gas Company, **6** 529
Allied Healthcare Products, Inc., 24 16–19
Allied Irish Banks, plc, 16 13–15; 43 7–10 (upd.); 94 19–24 (upd.)
Allied Leisure, **40** 296–98
Allied-Lyons plc, I 215–16 *see also* Carlsberg A/S.
Allied Maintenance Corp., *see* Ogden Corp.
Allied Pipe & Tube Corporation, **63** 403
Allied Plywood Corporation, *see* Ply Gem Industries Inc.
Allied Products Corporation, 21 20–22
Allied Safety, Inc. *see* W.W. Grainger, Inc.
Allied-Signal Corp., I 414–16 *see also* AlliedSignal, Inc.
Allied Signal Engines, 9 12–15
Allied Stores Corporation, **15** 94, 274; **23** 59–60; **31** 192; **37**
Allied Strategies Inc. *see* Sleeman Breweries Ltd.
Allied Structural Steel Company, *see* Alleghany Corp.
Allied Supermarkets, Inc., **28** 511
Allied Suppliers, **50** 401
Allied Telephone Company *see* Alltel Corp.
Allied Van Lines Inc. *see* Allied Worldwide, Inc.
Allied Waste Industries, Inc., 50 13–16
Allied Worldwide, Inc., 49 20–23
AlliedSignal Inc., 22 29–32 (upd.) *see also* Honeywell Inc.

Allis Chalmers Corporation, **I** 163; **11** 104; **21** 502–03; **22** 380; **50** 196
Allis-Gleaner Corp. *see* AGCO Corp.
Allison Engine Company, **21** 436
Allison Engineering Company *see* Rolls-Royce Allison.
Allison Gas Turbine Division, 9 16–19
Allmanna Svenska Elektriska Aktiebolaget *see* ABB Ltd.
Allmänna Telefonaktiebolaget L.M. Ericsson *see* Telefonaktiebolaget L.M. Ericsson.
Allmerica Financial Corporation, 63 29–31
Allou Health & Beauty Care, Inc., 28 12–14
Alloy, Inc., 55 13–15
Allparts, Inc., **51** 307
Allsport plc., **31** 216, 218
The Allstate Corporation, 10 50–52; 27 30–33 (upd.)
ALLTEL Corporation, 6 299–301; 46 15–19 (upd.)
Alltrista Corporation, 30 38–41 *see also* Jarden Corp.
Allwaste, Inc., 18 10–13
Allweiler, **58** 67
Alma Media Group, **52** 51
Almac Electronics Corporation, *see* Arrow Electronics, Inc.
Almacenes de Baja y Media, **39** 201, 204
Almacenes Exito S.A., 89 47–50
Almaden Vineyards, *see* Canandaigua Brands, Inc.
Almanacksförlaget AB, **51** 328
Almanij NV, 44 15–18 *see also* Algemeene Maatschappij voor Nijverheidskrediet.
Almay, Inc. *see* Revlon Inc.
Almeida Banking House *see* Banco Bradesco S.A.
Almost Family, Inc., 93 41–44
ALNM *see* Ayres, Lewis, Norris & May.
Aloha Airlines, Incorporated, 24 20–22
ALP *see* Associated London Properties.
Alp Sport Sandals, **22** 173
Alpargatas S.A.I.C., 87 13–17
Alpex, S.A. de C.V., **19** 12
Alpha Airports Group PLC, 77 32–35
Alpha Beta Co., *see* American Stores Co.
Alpha Engineering Group, Inc., **16** 259–60
Alpha Healthcare Ltd., *see* Sun Healthcare Group Inc.
Alpha Networks Inc. *see* D-Link Corp.
Alpha Processor Inc., **41** 349
Alpha Technical Systems, **19** 279
Alphaform, **40** 214–15
AlphaGraphics Inc. *see* G A Pindar & Son Ltd.
Alphanumeric Publication Systems, Inc., **26** 518
Alpharma Inc., 35 22–26 (upd.)
Alphonse Allard Inc., *see* Provigo Inc.
Alpine Confections, Inc., 71 22–24
Alpine Electronics, Inc., 13 30–31
Alpine Gaming *see* Century Casinos, Inc.
Alpine Lace Brands, Inc., 18 14–16 *see also* Land O'Lakes, Inc.
Alpine Securities Corporation, **22** 5
Alpnet Inc. *see* SDL PLC.
Alpre, **19** 192
Alps Electric Co., Ltd., II 5–6; 44 19–21 (upd.)
Alric Packing, *see* Associated British Foods plc.
Alrosa Company Ltd., 62 7–11
Alsco *see* Steiner Corp.
Alside Inc., 94 25–29
ALSO Holding AG, **29** 419, 422
Alsthom, *see* Alcatel S.A.
ALTA Health Strategies, Inc., **11** 113
Alta Vista Company, **50** 228
Altadis S.A., 72 6–13 (upd.)
ALTANA AG, 87 18–22
AltaSteel Ltd., **51** 352
AltaVista Company, 43 11–13
ALTEC International, **21** 107–09
Altera Corporation, 18 17–20; 43 14–18 (upd.)
Alternative Living Services *see* Alterra Healthcare Corp.
Alternative Tentacles Records, 66 3–6
Alternative Youth Services, Inc., *see* Res-Care, Inc.
Alterra Healthcare Corporation, 42 3–5
Altex, **19** 192–93
Alticor Inc., 71 25–30 (upd.)
Altiris, Inc., 65 34–36
Altman Weil Pensa, **29** 237
Alton Towers, **55** 378
Altos Hornos de México, S.A. de C.V., 42 6–8
Altra Broadband Inc., **63** 34
Altran Technologies, 51 15–18
Altron Incorporated, 20 8–10
Altura Energy Ltd. *see* Occidental Petroleum Corp.
Aluar Aluminio Argentino S.A.I.C., 74 10–12
Aluma Systems Corp., *see* Tridel Enterprises Inc.
Alumalsa *see* Aluminoy y Aleaciones S.A.
Alumax Inc., **I** 508; **22** 286; **56** 11
Aluminoy y Aleaciones S.A., **63** 303
Aluminum and Stainless, Inc. *see* Reliance Steel & Aluminum Co.
Aluminum Company of America, IV 14–16; 20 11–14 (upd.) *see also* Alcoa Inc.
Aluminum Forge Co., *see* Marmon Group, Inc.
Alupak, A.G., **12** 377
Alusuisse, **73** 212–13
Alvic Group, **20** 363
Alvin Ailey Dance Foundation, Inc., 52 14–17
Alvis Plc, 47 7–9
ALZA Corporation, 10 53–55; 36 36–39 (upd.)
Alzouman Aviation, **56** 148
AM Cosmetics, Inc., **31** 89
Am-Safe, Inc., *see* The Marmon Group, Inc.
AM-TEX Corp., Inc., **12** 443
Amagasaki Spinners Ltd. *see* Unitika Ltd.
Amalgamated Bank, 60 20–22
Amalgamated Sugar Co., **14** 18; **19** 467–68
Amana Refrigeration Company, **38** 374; **42** 159
Amaray International Corporation, **12** 264
Amarillo Gas Company *see* Atmos Energy Corp.
Amarillo Railcar Services, **6** 580
Amati Communications Corporation, **57** 409
Amax Gold, **36** 316
AMAX Inc., IV 17–19 *see also* Cyprus Amex.
Amazon.com, Inc., 25 17–19; 56 12–15 (upd.)
AMB Generali Holding AG, 51 19–23
AMB Property Corporation, 57 25–27
Ambac Financial Group, Inc., 65 37–39
Ambassadors International, Inc., 68 16–18 (upd.)
Amberg Hospach AG, **49** 436
AmBev *see* Companhia de Bebidas das Américas.
Amblin Entertainment, 21 23–27
AMBRA, Inc., **48** 209
AMC Entertainment Inc., 12 12–14; 35 27–29 (upd.)
AMCA International Corporation, *see* United Dominion Industries Ltd.
AMCC *see* Applied Micro Circuits Corp.
Amcell *see* American Cellular Network.
AMCOL International Corporation, 59 29–33 (upd.)
Amcor Ltd., IV 248–50; 19 13–16 (upd.); 78 1–6 (upd.)
AMCORE Financial Inc., 44 22–26
Amcraft Building Products Co., Inc., **22** 15
AMD *see* Advanced Micro Devices, Inc.
Amdahl Corporation, III 109–11; 14 13–16 (upd.); 40 20–25 (upd.) *see also* Fujitsu Ltd.
Amdocs Ltd., 47 10–12
AME Finanziaria, **IV** 587; **19** 19; **54** 20
Amec Spie S.A., 57 28–31
Amedysis, Inc., 53 33–36
Amer Group plc, 41 14–16
Amer Sport, **68** 245
Amerace Corporation, **54** 373
Amerada Hess Corporation, IV 365–67; 21 28–31 (upd.); 55 16–20 (upd.)
Amerchol Corporation *see* Union Carbide Corp.
AMERCO, 6 351–52; 67 11–14 (upd.)
Ameren Corporation, 60 23–27 (upd.)
AmerGen Energy LLC, **49** 65, 67
Ameri-Kart Corp., *see* Myers Industries, Inc.
America Online, Inc., 10 56–58; 26 16–20 (upd.) *see also* CompuServe Interactive Services, Inc.; AOL Time Warner Inc.
America Today, *see* Koninklijke Vendex KBB N.V. (Royal Vendex KBB N.V.)

America West Holdings Corporation, 6 72–74; 34 22–26 (upd.)
America's Car-Mart, Inc., 64 19–21
America's Favorite Chicken Company, Inc., 7 26–28 *see also* AFC Enterprises, Inc.
American & Efird, Inc., 82 5-9
American Acquisitions, Inc., **49** 279
American Air Filter, **26** 3–4
American Airlines, I 89–91; 6 75–77 (upd.) *see also* AMR Corp.
American Apparel, Inc., 90 21–24
American Association of Retired Persons *see* AARP.
American Austin Quality Foods Inc., **44** 40
American Aviation Manufacturing Corp., **15** 246
American Axle & Manufacturing Holdings, Inc., 67 15–17
American Bancshares, Inc., **11** 457
American Banknote Corporation, 30 42–45
American Bar Association, 35 30–33
American Beet Sugar Company, **11** 13–14
American Biltrite Inc., 16 16–18; 43 19–22 (upd.)
American Bio Corporation Inc., **70** 346
American Biodyne Inc., *see* Medco Containment Services Inc.
American BioScience, **69** 20–21
American Bottling, **49** 78
American Brands, Inc., V 395–97 *see also* Fortune Brands, Inc.
American Broadcasting Co. *see* ABC, Inc.; Capital Cities/ABC Inc.
American Builders & Contractors Supply Co. *see* ABC Supply Co., Inc.
American Building Maintenance Industries, Inc., 6 17–19 *see also* ABM Industries Inc.
American Bus Lines Inc., *see* Coach USA, Inc.
American Business Information, Inc., 18 21–25
American Business Interiors *see* American Furniture Company, Inc.
American Business Products, Inc., 20 15–17
American Cabinet Hardware Corp. *see* Amerock Corp.
American Cable Systems, Inc. *see* Comcast Corp.
American Campus Communities, Inc., 85 1–5
American Can Co. *see* Primerica Corp.
The American Cancer Society, 24 23–25
American Capital and Research Corp., **28** 201
American Capital Strategies, Ltd., 91 21–24
American Cast Iron Pipe Company, 50 17–20
American Cellular Corporation, **63** 131–32
American Cement Co. *see* Giant Cement Holding, Inc.
American Civil Liberties Union (ACLU), 60 28–31
American Classic Voyages Company, 27 34–37
American Coin Merchandising, Inc., 28 15–17; 74 13–16 (upd.)
American Colloid Co., 13 32–35 *see* AMCOL International Corp.
American Colonial Insurance Company, **44** 356
American Commercial Lines Inc., *see* CSX Corp.
American Commonwealths Power Corporation, **6** 579
American Computer Systems *see* American Software Inc.
American Construction Lending Services, Inc., **39** 380, 382
American Cotton Growers Association, *see* Plains Cotton Cooperative Association.
American Courier Express, Inc., *see* Consolidated Delivery & Logistics, Inc.
American Crystal Sugar Company, 11 13–15; 32 29–33 (upd.)
American Cyanamid, I 300–02; 8 24–26 (upd.)
American Digital Communications, Inc., **33** 329
American Drew, Inc., **12** 301
American Drug Company, *see* National Patient Development Corp.
American Eagle Airlines, Inc., **28** 22
American Eagle Outfitters, Inc., 24 26–28; 55 21–24 (upd.)
American Ecology Corporation, 77 36–39
American Electric Company, **22** 10; **54** 371–73
American Electric Power Company, V 546–49; 45 17–21 (upd.)
American Encaustic Tiling Co., **22** 170
American Energy Management Inc., **39** 261
American Envelope Co., **28** 251
American Equipment Co., *see* Fluor Corp.
American Express Company, II 395–99; 10 59–64 (upd.); 38 42–48 (upd.)
American Factors, Ltd. *see* Amfac/JMB Hawaii L.L.C.
American Family Corporation, III 187–89 *see also* AFLAC Inc.
American Family Publishers, **23** 393–94
American Feldmühle Corp., **II** 51; **21** 330
American Financial Group Inc., III 190–92; 48 6–10 (upd.)
American Fine Wire, Inc., **33** 248
American Fitness Products, Inc., **47** 128
American Flange, **30** 397
American Foods Group, 43 23–27
American Football League, **29** 346
American Foreign Insurance Association *see* AFIA.
American Freightways Corporation, **42** 141
American Fructose Corp., **14** 18–19
American Furniture Company, Inc., 21 32–34
American Gaming and Electronics, Inc., **43** 461
American Gas & Electric *see* American Electric Power Co.
American General Corporation, III 193–94; 10 65–67 (upd.); 46 20–23 (upd.)
American General Finance Corp., 11 16–17
American Girl, Inc., 69 16–19 (upd)
American Golf Corporation, 45 22–24
American Gramaphone LLC, 52 18–20
American Graphics, **23** 100
American Greetings Corporation, 7 23–25; 22 33–36 (upd.); 59 34–39 (upd.)
American Hardware & Supply Company *see* TruServ Corp.
American Hawaii Cruises, *see* American Classic Voyages Co.
American Healthcorp Inc., **48** 25
American Healthways, Inc., 65 40–42
American Hoechst Corporation *see* Hoechst Celanese Corp.
American Home Mortgage Holdings, Inc., 46 24–26
American Home Patients Centers Inc., **46** 4
American Home Products, I 622–24; 10 68–70 (upd.) *see also* Wyeth.
American Home Shield *see* ServiceMaster Inc.
American Homestar Corporation, 18 26–29; 41 17–20 (upd.)
American Homeware Inc., **15** 501
American Hospital Supply Co., **21** 118; **30** 496; **53** 345
American I.G. Chemical Corporation *see* GAF Corp.
American Improved Cements *see* Giant Cement Holding, Inc.
American Independent Oil Co. *see* Aminoil, Inc.
American Industrial Properties *see* Developers Diversified Realty Corp.
American Institute of Certified Public Accountants (AICPA), 44 27–30
American Insurance Group, Inc., **73** 351
American International Group, Inc., III 195–98; 15 15–19 (upd.); 47 13–19 (upd.)
American Isuzu Motors, Inc. *see* Isuzu Motors, Ltd.
American Italian Pasta Company, 27 38–40; 76 18–21 (upd.)
American Kennel Club, Inc., 74 17–19
American Land Cruiser Company *see* Cruise America Inc.
American Lawyer Media Holdings, Inc., 32 34–37
American Learning Corporation, *see* Encyclopaedia Britannica, Inc.
American Library Association, 86 15–19
American Licorice Company, 86 20–23
American Light and Traction *see* MCN Corp.
American Lightwave Systems, Inc., *see* ADC Telecommunications, Inc.

American Limousine Corp., **26** 62
American Linen Supply Company *see* Steiner Corp.
American Locker Group Incorporated, 34 19–21
American Lung Association, 48 11–14
American Machine and Metals, *see* AMETEK, Inc.
American Machine and Tool Co., Inc., **57** 160
American Machinery and Foundry, Inc., **57** 85
American Maize-Products Co., 14 17–20
American Management Association, 76 22–25
American Management Systems, Inc., 11 18–20
American Materials & Technologies Corporation, **27** 117
American Media, Inc., 27 41–44; 82 10–15 (upd.)
American Medical Association, 39 15–18
American Medical Disposal, Inc. *see* Stericycle, Inc.
American Medical Holdings, **55** 370
American Medical International, Inc., III 73–75
American Medical Response, Inc., 39 19–22
American Medical Services, *see* TW Services, Inc.
American Metal Climax, Inc. *see* AMAX.
American Metals and Alloys, Inc., **19** 432
American Metals Corporation *see* Reliance Steel & Aluminum Co.
American Modern Insurance Group *see* The Midland Co.
American Motors Corp., I 135–37 *see also* DaimlerChrysler AG.
América Móvil, S.A. de C.V., 80 5–8
American MSI Corporation *see* Moldflow Corp.
American Multi-Cinema *see* AMC Entertainment Inc.
American National Can Co., *see* Pechiney SA.
American National Insurance Company, 8 27–29; 27 45–48 (upd.)
American Natural Snacks Inc., **29** 480
American Olean Tile Company, *see* Armstrong Holdings, Inc.
American Optical Co., **38** 363–64
American Oriental Bioengineering Inc., 93 45–48
American Pad & Paper Company, 20 18–21
American Paging, *see* Telephone and Data Systems, Inc.
American Patriot Insurance, **22** 15
American Payment Systems, Inc., **21** 514
American Petrofina, Inc., *see* FINA, Inc.
American Pfauter, *see* Gleason Corp.
American Pharmaceutical Partners, Inc., 69 20–22
American Phone Centers, Inc., **21** 135
American Pop Corn Company, 59 40–43
American Port Services (Amports), **45** 29
American Power & Light Co., **6** 545, 596–97; **49** 143
American Power Conversion Corporation, 24 29–31; 67 18–20 (upd.)
American Premier Underwriters, Inc., 10 71–74
American Prepaid Professional Services, Inc. *see* CompDent Corp.
American President Companies Ltd., 6 353–55 *see also* APL Ltd.
American Printing House for the Blind, 26 13–15
American Prospecting Equipment Co., **49** 174
American Public Automotive Group, **37** 115
American Publishing Co., *see* Hollinger International Inc.
American Re Corporation, 10 75–77; 35 34–37 (upd.)
American Recreation Company Holdings, Inc., **16** 53; **44** 53–54
American Red Cross, 40 26–29
American Reprographics Company, 75 24–26
American Residential Mortgage Corporation, 8 30–31
American Residential Services, **33** 141
American Restaurant Partners, L.P., 93 49–52
American Retirement Corporation, 42 9–12 *see also* Brookdale Senior Living.
American Rice, Inc., 33 30–33
American Rug Craftsmen, *see* Mohawk Industries, Inc.
American Safety Razor Company, 20 22–24
American Salt Co., **12** 199
American Satellite Co., **15** 195
American Savings Bank, *see* Hawaiian Electric Industries, Inc.
American Science & Engineering, Inc., 81 22–25
American Sealants Company *see* Loctite Corp.
American Seating Company, 78 7–11
American Seaway Foods, Inc, *see* Riser Foods, Inc.
American Securities Capital Partners, L.P., **59** 13; **69** 138–39
American Service Corporation, **19** 223
American Ships Ltd., **50** 209
American Skiing Company, 28 18–21
American Sky Broadcasting, **27** 305; **35** 156
American Smelting and Refining Co. *see* ASARCO.
American Society for the Prevention of Cruelty to Animals (ASPCA), 68 19–22
The American Society of Composers, Authors and Publishers (ASCAP), 29 21–24
American Software Inc., 22 214; **25 20–22**
American Standard Companies Inc., III 663–65; 30 46–50 (upd.)
American States Water Company, 46 27–30
American Steamship Company *see* GATX.
American Steel & Wire Co., *see* Birmingham Steel Corp.
American Steel Foundries, **7** 29–30
American Stores Company, II 604–06; 22 37–40 (upd.) *see also* Albertson's, Inc.
American Sugar Refining Company *see* Domino Sugar Corp.
American Sumatra Tobacco Corp., **15** 138
American Superconductor Corporation, **41** 141
American Surety Co., **26** 486
American Teaching Aids Inc., **19** 405
American Technical Ceramics Corp., 67 21–23
American Technical Services Company *see* American Building Maintenance Industries, Inc.; ABM Industries Inc.
American Telephone and Telegraph Company *see* AT&T.
American Television and Communications Corp., **IV** 675
American Thermos Bottle Company *see* Thermos Co.
American Threshold, **50** 123
American Tile Supply Company, **19** 233
American Tissue Company, **29** 136
American Tobacco Co. *see* American Brands Inc.; B.A.T. Industries PLC.; Fortune Brands, Inc.
American Tool Companies, Inc., **52** 270
American Tourister, Inc., 16 19–21 *see also* Samsonite Corp.
American Tower Corporation, 33 34–38
American Trans Air, **34** 31
American Transitional Hospitals, Ltd., **65** 307
American Transport Lines, **6** 384
American Twist Drill Co., **23** 82
American Vanguard Corporation, 47 20–22
American VIP Limousine, Inc., **26** 62
American Water Works Company, Inc., 6 443–45; 38 49–52 (upd.)
American Woodmark Corporation, 31 13–16
American Yard Products, **22** 26, 28
American Yearbook Company, *see* Jostens, Inc.
Americana Entertainment Group, Inc., **19** 435
Americana Foods, LP, *see* TCBY Enterprises Inc.
Americana Healthcare Corp., **15** 522
Americana Ships Ltd., **50** 210
AmeriCares Foundation, Inc., 87 23–28
Americom, **61** 272
Americrown Service Corporation *see* International Speedway Corp.
Ameridrive, **58** 67
AmeriGas Partners, L.P., **56** 36

AMERIGROUP Corporation, **69 23–26**
Amerihost Properties, Inc., **30 51–53**
AmeriKing Corp., **36** 309
Amerin Corporation *see* Radian Group Inc.
AmeriServe Food Distribution *see* Holberg Industries, Inc.
Amerisex, **64** 198
AmeriSource Health Corporation, **37 9–11 (upd.)**
AmerisourceBergen Corporation, **64 22–28 (upd.)**
Ameristar Casinos, Inc., **33 39–42**; **69 27–31 (upd.)**
AmeriSteel Corp., **59** 202
AmeriSuites, **52** 281
Ameritech Corporation, **V 265–68**; **18 30–34 (upd.)** *see also* AT&T Corp.
Ameritech Illinois *see* Illinois Bell Telephone Co.
Ameritrade Holding Corporation, **34 27–30**
Ameritrust Corporation, **9** 476
Ameriwood Industries International Corp., **17 15–17** *see also* Dorel Industries Inc.
Amerock Corporation, **53 37–40**
Ameron International Corporation, **67 24–26**
Amerop Sugar Corporation, **60** 96
Amersham PLC, **50 21–25**
Ames Department Stores, Inc., **9 20–22**; **30 54–57 (upd.)**
AMETEK, Inc., **9 23–25**
N.V. Amev, **III 199–202** *see also* Fortis, Inc.
AMEX *see* American Stock Exchange.
Amey Plc, **47 23–25**
AMF *see* American Machinery and Foundry, Inc.
AMF Bowling, Inc., **40 30–33**
Amfac/JMB Hawaii L.L.C., **I 417–18**; **24 32–35 (upd.)**
AMFM Inc., **35** 221, 245, 248; **37** 104; **41** 384
Amgen, Inc., **10 78–81**; **30 58–61 (upd.)**; **89 51–57 (upd.)**
AMI *see* Advanced Metallurgy, Inc.
AMI Metals, Inc. *see* Reliance Steel & Aluminum Co.
AMICAS, Inc., **69 32–34**
Aminoil, Inc. *see* American Independent Oil Co.
Amisys Managed Care Information Systems, **16** 94
Amitron S.A., *see* Arrow Electronics, Inc.
Amity Leather Products Company *see* AR Accessories Group, Inc.
Amko Service Company, **74** 363
Amkor Technology, Inc., **69 35–37**
AMLI Realty Company, **33** 418, 420
Ammirati Puris Lintas, *see* Interpublic Group of Companies, Inc.
Amnesty International, **50 26–29**
Amoco Corporation, **IV 368–71**; **14 21–25 (upd.)** *see also* BP p.l.c.
AMOR 14 Corporation, **64** 95
Amorim Investimentos e Participaço, **48** 117, 119
Amorim Revestimentos, **48** 118
Amoskeag Company, **8 32–33** *see also* Fieldcrest Cannon, Inc.
Amot Controls Corporation, **15** 404; **50** 394
AMP, Inc., **II 7–8**; **14 26–28 (upd.)**
Ampacet Corporation, **67 27–29**
Ampad Holding Corporation *see* American Pad & Paper Co.
AMPAL *see* American-Palestine Trading Corp.
AMPCO Auto Parks, Inc. *see* American Building Maintenance Industries, Inc.; ABM Industries Inc.
Ampco-Pittsburgh Corporation, **79 26–29**
Ampeg Company, **48** 353
Ampersand Ventures, **73** 227–28
Ampex Corporation, **17 18–20**
Amphenol Corporation, **40 34–37**
Ampro, *see* Unison HealthCare Corp.
AMR *see* American Medical Response, Inc.
AMR Combs Inc., **36** 190
AMR Corporation, **28 22–26 (upd.)**; **52 21–26 (upd.)**
Amram's Distributing Limited, *see* Russ Berrie and Co., Inc.
AMREP Corporation, **21 35–37**
Amro *see* Amsterdam-Rotterdam Bank N.V.
Amrop International Australasia, **34** 249
AMS *see* Advanced Marketing Services, Inc.
Amsbra Limited, **62** 48
Amscan Holdings, Inc., **61 24–26**
Amsco International, **29** 450
Amserve Ltd., **48** 23
AmSouth Bancorporation, **12 15–17**; **48 15–18 (upd.)**
Amstar Sugar Corporation, **26** 122
Amsted Industries Incorporated, **7 29–31**
Amsterdam-Rotterdam Bank N.V., **II 185–86**
Amstrad plc, **III 112–14**; **48 19–23 (upd.)**
AmSurg Corporation, **48 24–27**
AMT *see* American Machine and Tool Co., Inc.; American Materials & Technologies Corp.
Amtech *see* American Building Maintenance Industries, Inc.; ABM Industries Inc.
Amtrak *see* The National Railroad Passenger Corp.
Amtran, Inc., **34 31–33**
AmTrans *see* American Transport Lines.
Amurol Confections Company, **58** 378
Amvac Chemical Corporation, **47** 20
AMVESCAP PLC, **65 43–45**
Amway Corporation, **III 11–14**; **13 36–39 (upd.)**; **30 62–66 (upd.)** *see also* Alticor Inc.
Amy's Kitchen Inc., **76 26–28**
Amylin Pharmaceuticals, Inc., **67 30–32**
ANA *see* All Nippon Airways Co., Ltd.
Anacomp, Inc., **94 30–34**
Anadarko Petroleum Corporation, **10 82–84**; **52 27–30 (upd.)**
Anaheim Angels Baseball Club, Inc., **53 41–44**
Anaheim Imaging, **19** 336
Analex Corporation, **74 20–22**
Analog Devices, Inc., **10 85–87**
Analogic Corporation, **23 13–16**
Analysts International Corporation, **36 40–42**
Analytic Sciences Corporation, **10 88–90**
Analytical Nursing Management Corporation (ANMC) *see* Amedisys, Inc.
Analytical Science Laboratories Inc., **58** 134
Analytical Surveys, Inc., **33 43–45**
Analytico Food BV *see* Eurofins Scientific S.A.
Anam Group, **23 17–19**
Anarad, Inc., *see* Tech-Sym Corp.
Anaren Microwave, Inc., **33 46–48**
Anchor Bancorp, Inc., **10 91–93**
Anchor Brewing Company, **47 26–28**
Anchor Gaming, **24 36–39**
Anchor Hocking Glassware, **13 40–42**
Anchor Motor Freight, Inc., *see* Leaseway Transportation Corp.
Anchor National Financial Services, Inc., *see* SunAmerica Inc.
Anchor National Life Insurance Company, *see* SunAmerica Inc.
Andenne Bricolage BVBA, **68** 64
Andersen, **10 94–95**; **29 25–28 (upd.)**; **68 23–27 (upd.)**
Andersen Consulting *see* Accenture Ltd
Anderson Animal Hospital, Inc., **58** 354
The Anderson-DuBose Company, **60 32–34**
Anderson Exploration Ltd., **61** 75
Anderson, Greenwood & Co., *see* Keystone International, Inc.
Anderson Packaging, Inc., **64** 27
Anderson Testing Company, Inc., **6** 441
Anderson Trucking Service, Inc., **75 27–29**
The Andersons, Inc., **31 17–21**
Andis Company, Inc., **85 6–9**
Andlinger & Co., **60** 132
Andreas Christ, **26** 243
Andreas Stihl AG & Co. KG, **16 22–24**; **59 44–47 (upd.)**
Andrew Corporation, **10 96–98**; **32 38–41 (upd.)**
Andrew Jergens Company *see* Kao Brands Company
Andrews Kurth, LLP, **71 31–34**
Andrews McMeel Universal, **40 38–41**
Andrews Office Supply and Equipment Co., *see* U.S. Office Products Co.
Andritz AG, **51 24–26**
Andronico's Market, **70 10–13**
Andrx Corporation, **55 25–27**
Angele Ghigi, **II** 475

Angelica Corporation, 15 20–22; 43 28–31 (upd.)
Angelo's Supermarkets, Inc., *see* Supermarkets General Holdings Corp.
ANGI Ltd., **11** 28
AngioDynamics, Inc., 81 26–29
Anglian Water Plc, **38** 51
Anglo-Abrasives Ltd. *see* Carbo PLC.
Anglo American Industrial Corporation, **59** 224–25
Anglo American PLC, IV 20–23; 16 25–30 (upd.); 50 30–36 (upd.)
Anglo-Canadian Telephone Company of Montreal *see* British Columbia Telephone Co.
Anglo-Dutch Unilever group, **9** 317
Anglo Energy, Ltd., **9** 364
Anglo Industries, Inc., *see* Nabors Industries, Inc.
Anglovaal Industries Ltd., **20** 263
Anheuser-Busch Companies, Inc., I 217–19; 10 99–101 (upd.); 34 34–37 (upd.)
ANI America Inc., **62** 331
Anixter International Inc., 88 13–16
Anker BV, 53 45–47
ANMC *see* Amedisys, Inc.
Ann Street Group Ltd., **61** 44–46
Anne Klein & Co., **15** 145–46; **40** 277–78; **56** 90
Annecy Béøn Carrières, **70** 343
Anneplas, **25** 464
Annie's Homegrown, Inc., 59 48–50
AnnTaylor Stores Corporation, 13 43–45; 37 12–15 (upd.); 67 33–37 (upd.)
Anocout Engineering Co., **23** 82
ANR Pipeline Co., 17 21–23
Anritsu Corporation, 68 28–30
The Anschutz Company, 12 18–20; 36 43–47 (upd.); 73 24–30 (upd.)
Ansco & Associates, LLC, **57** 119
Ansell Ltd., 60 35–38 (upd.)
Anselmo L. Morvillo S.A., **19** 336
Ansett Australia, *see* Air New Zealand Ltd.
Ansoft Corporation, 63 32–34
Answer Products, Inc., **76** 237
ANSYS Technologies Inc., **48** 410
Antalis, **34** 38, 40
AntarChile S.A., **69** 141, 143
Antares Capital Corp., **53** 213
Antares Electronics, Inc., *see* Control Data Systems, Inc.
Antenna Company, **32** 40
Anteon Corporation, 57 32–34
ANTEX *see* American National Life Insurance Company of Texas.
Anthem Electronics, Inc., 13 46–47
Anthem P&C Holdings, **15** 257
Anthony & Sylvan Pools Corporation, 56 16–18
Anthony Industries Inc. *see* K2 Inc.
Anthracite Industries, Inc. *see* Asbury Carbons, Inc.
Anthropologie, Inc. *see* Urban Outfitters, Inc.
Antinori *see* Marchesi Antinori SRL.
The Antioch Company, 40 42–45
Antique Street Lamps, **19** 212
ANTK Tupolev *see* Aviacionny Nauchno-Tehnicheskii Komplex im. A.N. Tupoleva.
Antofagasta plc, 65 46–49
Antonio Puig, S.A. *see* Puig Beauty and Fashion Group S.L.
Antonov Design Bureau, 53 48–51
ANZ *see* Australia and New Zealand Banking Group Ltd.
AO Sidanco, **45** 50
AO VimpelCom, **59** 300
Aohata Corporation, **57** 202, 204
AOK-Bundesverband (Federation of the AOK), 78 12–16
Aoki Corporation, **9** 547, 549; **29** 508
AOL Time Warner Inc., 57 35–44 (upd.)
Aon Corporation, III 203–05; 45 25–28 (upd.)
AP *see* The Associated Press.
AP&L *see* American Power & Light Co.
Apache Corporation, 10 102–04; 32 42–46 (upd.); 89 58–65 (upd.)
APACHE Medical Systems, Inc., **16** 94
Apanage GmbH & Co. KG, **53** 195
Apartment Furniture Rental, **26** 102
Apartment Investment and Management Company, 49 24–26
Apasco S.A. de C.V., 51 27–29
Apax Partners Worldwide LLP, 89 66–69
APB *see* Atlantic Premium Brands, Ltd.
APCOA/Standard Parking *see* Holberg Industries, Inc.
Apex Digital, Inc., 63 35–37
Apex Oil, **37** 310–11
Apex One Inc., **31** 137
APH *see* American Printing House for the Blind.
APi Group, Inc., 64 29–32
APL Limited, 61 27–30 (upd.)
Aplex Industries, Inc., **26** 363
APLIX S.A. *see* Velcro Industries N.V.
APM Ltd. *see* Amcor Limited
APN *see* Affiliated Physicians Network, Inc.
Apogee Enterprises, Inc., 8 34–36
Apogee Sound International LLC, **62** 39
Apollo Advisors L.P., **16** 37; **26** 500, 502; **43** 438
Apollo Group, Inc., 24 40–42
Apollo Heating & Air Conditioning Inc., **15** 411
Apollo Investment Fund Ltd., **31** 211; **39** 174
Apollo Ski Partners LP of New York, *see* Vail Associates, Inc.
Apothekernes Laboratorium A.S., **12** 3–5
Appalachian Travel Services, Inc., *see* Habersham Bancorp.
Apparel Ventures, Inc. *see* The Jordan Company, LP.
Appetifrais S.A., **51** 54
Applause Inc., 24 43–46 *see also* Russ Berrie and Co., Inc.
Apple & Eve L.L.C., 92 5–8
Apple Bank for Savings, 59 51–53
Apple Computer, Inc., III 115–16; 6 218–20 (upd.); 36 48–51 (upd.); 77 40–45 (upd.)
Apple Corps Ltd., 87 29–34
Apple Orthodontix, Inc., **35** 325
Apple South, Inc. *see* Avado Brands, Inc.
Applebee's International Inc., 14 29–31; 35 38–41 (upd.)
Applera Corporation, **74** 71
Appliance Recycling Centers of America, Inc., 42 13–16
Applica Incorporated, 43 32–36 (upd.)
Applied Beverage Systems Ltd., **21** 339
Applied Biomedical Corp., **47** 4
Applied Bioscience International, Inc., 10 105–07
Applied Biosystems, **74** 72
Applied Communications, Inc., **6** 280; **29** 477–79
Applied Data Research, Inc., **18** 31–32
Applied Engineering Services, Inc. *see* The AES Corp.
Applied Films Corporation, 48 28–31
Applied Industrial Materials Corporation, *see* Walter Industries, Inc.
Applied Laser Systems, **31** 124
Applied Learning International, **IV** 680
Applied Materials, Inc., 10 108–09; 46 31–34 (upd.)
Applied Micro Circuits Corporation, 38 53–55
Applied Network Technology, Inc., **25** 162
Applied Power Inc., 9 26–28; 32 47–51 (upd.) *see also* Actuant Corp.
Applied Signal Technology, Inc., 87 35–38
Applied Technology Solutions *see* RWD Technologies, Inc.
Applied Thermal Technologies, Inc., **29** 5
Apria Healthcare Inc., **43** 266
Aprilia SpA, 17 24–26
Aprolis, **72** 159
APS *see* Arizona Public Service Co.
APSA, **63** 214
AptarGroup, Inc., 69 38–41
Aqua Alliance Inc., 32 52–54 (upd.)
Aqua Cool Pure Bottled Water, **52** 188
Aqua de Oro Venture, **58** 23
Aquafin N.V., **12** 443; **38** 427
aQuantive, Inc., 81 30–33
Aquarion Company, 84 12–16
Aquarius Group *see* Club Mediterranee SA.
Aquarius Platinum Ltd., 63 38–40
Aquatech, **53** 232
Aquila Energy Corp., **6** 593
Aquila, Inc., 50 37–40 (upd.)
Aquitaine *see* Société Nationale des Petroles d'Aquitaine.
AR Accessories Group, Inc., 23 20–22
ARA *see* Consorcio ARA, S.A. de C.V.
ARA Services, II 607–08 *see also* Aramark.
Arab-Israel Bank Ltd., **60** 50
Arab Japanese Insurance Co., *see* Mitsui Marine and Fire Insurance Co., Ltd.
Arab Leasing International Finance, **72** 85

Arab Potash Company, 85 10–13
Arab Radio & Television, **72** 85
Arabian American Oil Co. *see* Saudi Arabian Oil Co.
Arabian Gulf Oil Company *see* Natinal Oil Corp.
Arabian Investment Banking Corp., **15** 94; **26** 53; **47** 361
Aracruz Celulose S.A., 57 45–47
Aral AG, 62 12–15
ARAMARK Corporation, 13 48–50; 41 21–24 (upd.)
Aramco *see* Arabian American Oil Co.; Saudi Arabian Oil Co.
Aramis Inc., **30** 191
Arandell Corporation, 37 16–18
Arapuã *see* Lojas Arapuã S.A.
ARBED S.A., IV 24–27; 22 41–45 (upd.) *see also* Arcelor Gent.
Arbeitsgemeinschaft der öffentlich-rechtlichen Rundfunkanstalten der Bundesrepublick *see* ARD.
The Arbitron Company, 38 56–61
Arbor Drugs Inc., 12 21–23 *see also* CVS Corp.
Arbor International *see* VeriFone Holdings, Inc.
Arbor Living Centers Inc., **6** 478
Arbor Software Corporation, **76** 188
Arby's Inc., 14 32–34
ARC *see* American Rug Craftsmen.
Arc International, 76 29–31
ARC Materials Corp., *see* CSR Ltd.
ARC Propulsion, *see* Sequa Corp.
ARCA *see* Appliance Recycling Centers of America, Inc.
Arcadia Group plc, 28 27–30 (upd.)
Arcadian Corporation, *see* Potash Corporation of Saskatchewan Inc.
Arcadian Marine Service, Inc., **6** 530
Arcadis NV, 26 21–24
Arcata Corporation, **12** 413
Arcata National Corp., **9** 305
Arcelor Gent, 80 9–12
ARCH Air Medical Service, Inc., **53** 29
Arch Chemicals, Inc., 78 17–20
Arch Mineral Corporation, 7 32–34
Arch Petroleum Inc., **39** 331
Arch Wireless, Inc., 39 23–26
Archbold Container Co., **35** 390
Archer Daniels Midland Company, I 419–21; 11 21–23 (upd.); 32 55–59 (upd.); 75 30–35 (upd.)
Archer Management Services Inc., **24** 360
Archibald Candy Corporation, **36** 309; **71** 22
Archie Comics Publications, Inc., 63 41–44
Archipelago RediBook, **48** 226, 228
Archon Corporation, 74 23–26 (upd.)
Archstone-Smith Trust, 49 27–30
Archway Cookies, Inc., 29 29–31
ArcLight, LLC, **50** 123
ARCO *see* Atlantic Richfield Co.
ARCO Chemical Company, 10 110–11 *see also* Lyondell Chemical Co.
ARCO Comfort Products Co., **26** 4
Arco Pharmaceuticals, Inc., **31** 346
Arcon Corporation, **26** 287
Arcor S.A.I.C., 66 7–9
Arcorp Properties, **70** 226
Arctco, Inc., 16 31–34
Arctic Alaska Fisheries Corporation, *see* Tyson Foods, Inc.
Arctic Cat Inc., 40 46–50 (upd.)
Arctic Enterprises, **34** 44
Arctic Slope Regional Corporation, 38 62–65
ARD, 41 25–29
Arden Group, Inc., 29 32–35
Ardent Risk Services, Inc. *see* General Re Corp.
Ardent Software Inc., **59** 54–55
AREVA NP, 90 25–30 (upd.)
Argenbright Security Inc. *see* Securicor Plc.
Argentaria Caja Postal y Banco Hipotecario S.A. *see* Banco Bilbao Vizcaya Argentaria S.A.
Argentaurum A.G. *see* Pall Corp.
Argon Medical, **12** 327
Argon ST, Inc., 81 34–37
Argos Retail Group *see* Home Retail Group plc.
Argos S.A. *see* Cementos Argos S.A.
Argos Soditic, **43** 147, 149
Argosy Gaming Company, 21 38–41 *see also* Penn National Gaming, Inc.
Argosy Group LP, **27** 197
Argus Corp., **IV** 611
Arguss Communications, Inc., **57** 120
Argyle Television Inc., **19** 204
Argyll Group PLC, II 609–10 *see also* Safeway PLC.
Aria Communications, Inc. *see* Ascend Communications, Inc.
Arianespace S.A., 89 70–73
Ariba, Inc., 57 48–51
Ariel Capital Management, **28** 421
Ariens Company, 48 32–34
Aries Technology, **25** 305
Ariete S.P.A. *see* De'Longhi S.p.A.
Aris Industries, Inc., 16 35–38
Arista Laboratories Inc., **51** 249, 251
Aristocrat Leisure Limited, 54 14–16
Aristokraft Inc. *see* MasterBrand Cabinets, Inc.
The Aristotle Corporation, 62 16–18
AriZona Beverages *see* Ferolito, Vultaggio & Sons.
Arizona Daily Star, **58** 282
Arizona Edison Co., **6** 545
Arizona Public Service Company, **6** 545–47; **19** 412; **26** 359; **28** 425–26; **54** 290
Arizona Refrigeration Supplies, *see* Kitchell Corp.
Arjo Wiggins Appleton p.l.c., 34 38–40
Ark Restaurants Corp., 20 25–27
Arkansas Best Corporation, 16 39–41; 94 35–40 (upd.)
Arkansas Louisiana Gas Company *see* Arkla, Inc.
Arkia, **23** 184, 186–87
Arkla, Inc., V 550–51
Arla Foods amba, 48 35–38
Arlington Securities plc, *see* British Aerospace plc.
Arlon, Inc., **28** 42, 45
Armani *see* Giorgio Armani S.p.A.
Armaris, **75** 126
Armco Inc., IV 28–30 *see also* AK Steel.
Armement Sapmer Distribution, **60** 149
Armin Corporation *see* Tyco International Ltd.
Armor All Products Corp., 16 42–44
Armor Holdings, Inc., 27 49–51
Armour *see* Tommy Armour Golf Co.
Armour & Company, **8** 144; **23** 173; **55** 365
Armour-Dial, **8** 144; **23** 173–74
Armstrong Air Conditioning Inc. *see* Lennox International Inc.
Armstrong Holdings, Inc., III 422–24; 22 46–50 (upd.); 81 38–44 (upd.)
Armstrong Tire Co., *see* Pirelli & C. S.p.A.
Army and Air Force Exchange Service, 39 27–29
Arnold & Porter, 35 42–44
Arnold Clark Automobiles Ltd., 60 39–41
Arnold Industries Inc., **35** 297
Arnold, Schwinn & Company *see* Schwinn Cycle and Fitness L.P.
Arnoldo Mondadori Editore S.p.A., IV 585–88; 19 17–21 (upd.); 54 17–23 (upd.)
Arnott's Ltd., 66 10–12
Aro Corp., *see* Ingersoll-Rand Company Ltd.
Aromatic Industries, *see* Blyth, Inc.
Arotech Corporation, 93 53–56
ArQule, Inc., 68 31–34
Arrendadora del Norte, S.A. de C.V., **51** 150
ARRIS Group, Inc., 89 74–77
Arriva PLC, 69 42–44
Arrosto Coffee Company, *see* Koo Koo Roo, Inc.
Arrow Air Holdings Corporation, 55 28–30
Arrow Electronics, Inc., 10 112–14; 50 41–44 (upd.)
Arrow Freight Corporation, **58** 23
Arrow Furniture Co., **21** 32
Arrow Pacific Plastics, **48** 334
Arrowhead Mills Inc., **27** 197–98; **43** 218–19
Arsam Investment Co., **26** 261
Arsenal Holdings PLC, 79 30–33
Arsynco, Inc., **38** 4
The Art Institute of Chicago, 29 36–38
Art Van Furniture, Inc., 28 31–33
Artal Luxembourg SA, **40** 51; **33** 446, 449; **73** 379
Artal NV,
Artear S.A. *see* Grupo Clarín S.A.
Artec, *see* Kimball International, Inc.
Artech Digital Entertainments, Inc., **15** 133
Artes Grafica Rioplatense S.A., **67** 202
Artesian Resources Corporation, **45** 277

Artesyn Solutions Inc., **48** 369
Artesyn Technologies Inc., 46 35–38 (upd.)
Artex Enterprises, *see* Fruit of the Loom, Inc.
ArthroCare Corporation, 73 31–33
Arthur Andersen & Company, Société Coopérative, 10 115–17 *see also* Andersen.
The Arthur C. Clarke Foundation, 92 9–12
Arthur D. Little, Inc., 35 45–48
Arthur H. Fulton, Inc., **42** 363
Arthur J. Gallagher & Co., 73 34–36
Arthur Murray International, Inc., 32 60–62
Arthur Young & Company *see* Ernst & Young.
Artigiancassa SpA, **72** 21
Artisan Entertainment Inc., 32 63–66 (upd.)
Artistic Direct, Inc., **37** 108
Artists Management Group, **38** 164
ArtMold Products Corporation, **26** 342
Artra Group Inc., **40** 119–20
Arts and Entertainment Network *see* A&E Television Networks.
Artsana SpA, 92 13–16
Arundel Corp, **46** 196
Arval *see* PHH Arval.
Arvin Industries, Inc., 8 37–40 *see also* ArvinMeritor, Inc.
ArvinMeritor, Inc., 54 24–28 (upd.)
A/S Air Baltic Corporation, 71 35–37
AS Estonian Air, 71 38–40
ASA Holdings, **47** 30
Asahi Breweries, Ltd., I 220–21; 20 28–30 (upd.); 52 31–34 (upd.)
Asahi Corporation, *see* Casio Computer Co., Ltd.
Asahi Denka Kogyo KK, 64 33–35
Asahi Glass Company, Ltd., III 666–68; 48 39–42 (upd.)
Asahi Komag Co., Ltd., *see* Komag, Inc.
Asahi Kyoei Co., *see* Asahi Breweries, Ltd.
Asahi Medix Co., Ltd., **36** 420
Asahi National Broadcasting Company, Ltd., 9 29–31
Asahi Real Estate Facilities Co., Ltd. *see* Seino Transportation Company, Ltd.
Asahi Shimbun, **9** 29–30
Asanté Technologies, Inc., 20 31–33
ASARCO Incorporated, IV 31–34; 40 220–22, 411
Asatsu-DK Inc, 82 16–20
ASB Air, **47** 286–87
Asbury Associates Inc., **22** 354–55
Asbury Automotive Group Inc., 60 42–44
Asbury Carbons, Inc., 68 35–37
ASC, Inc., 55 31–34
ASCAP *see* The American Society of Composers, Authors and Publishers.
Ascend Communications, Inc., 24 47–51 *see also* Lucent Technologies Inc.
Ascension Health, **61** 206
Ascential Software Corporation, 59 54–57
ASCO Healthcare, Inc., *see* NeighborCare, Inc.
Asco Products, Inc., **22** 413
Ascom AG, 9 32–34
ASCP *see* American Securities Capital Partners.
ASD Specialty Healthcare, Inc., **64** 27
ASDA Group Ltd., II 611–12; 28 34–36 (upd.); 64 36–38 (upd.)
ASEA AB *see* ABB Ltd.
Aseam Credit Sdn Bhd, **72** 217
ASF *see* American Steel Foundries.
ASG *see* Allen Systems Group, Inc.
Asgrow Seed Co., **29** 435; **41** 306
Ash Grove Cement Company, 94 41–44
Ash Resources Ltd., **31** 398–99
Ashanti Goldfields Company Limited, 43 37–40
Ashbourne PLC, *see* Sun Healthcare Group Inc.
Ashdown *see* Repco Corporation Ltd.
Ashland Inc., 19 22–25; 50 45–50 (upd.)
Ashland Oil, Inc., IV 372–74 *see also* Marathon.
Ashley Furniture Industries, Inc., 35 49–51
Ashtead Group plc, 34 41–43
Ashworth, Inc., 26 25–28
ASIA & PACIFIC Business Description Paid-in Capital Voting Rights, **68** 30
Asia Oil Co., Ltd., **IV** 404, 476; **53** 115
Asia Pacific Breweries Limited, 59 58–60
Asia Pulp & Paper, **38** 227
Asia Shuang He Sheng Five Star Beer Co., Ltd., **49** 418
Asia Television, **IV** 718; **38** 320
Asia Terminals Ltd., **IV** 718; **38** 319
AsiaInfo Holdings, Inc., 43 41–44
Asiamerica Equities Ltd. *see* Mercer International.
Asiana Airlines, Inc., 46 39–42
ASIX Inc. *see* Manatron, Inc.
ASICS Corporation, 57 52–55
ASK Group, Inc., 9 35–37
Ask Jeeves, Inc., 65 50–52
Ask Mr. Foster Agency, *see* Carlson Companies, Inc.
ASMI *see* Acer Semiconductor Manufacturing Inc.
ASML Holding N.V., 50 51–54
ASPCA *see* American Society for the Prevention of Cruelty to Animals (ASPCA).
Aspect Telecommunications Corporation, 22 51–53
ASPECTA Global Group AG, **53** 162
Aspen Imaging International, Inc., *see* Pubco Corp.
Aspen Mountain Gas Co., **6** 568
Aspen Publishers, *see* Wolters Kluwer NV.
Aspen Skiing Company, 15 23–26
Asplundh Tree Expert Co., 20 34–36; 59 61–65 (upd.)
Asprofos S.A., **64** 177
Asset Marketing Inc. *see* Commercial Financial Services, Inc.
Assicurazioni Generali SpA, III 206–09; 15 27–31 (upd.)
Assisted Living Concepts, Inc., 43 45–47
Associated British Foods plc, II 465–66; 13 51–53 (upd.); 41 30–33 (upd.)
Associated British Ports Holdings Plc, 45 29–32
Associated Bulk Carriers Ltd., **38** 345
Associated Container Transportation, **23** 161
Associated Cooperative Investment Trust Ltd. *see* Hammerson plc.
Associated Dry Goods Corp., **V** 134; **12** 54–55; **63** 259
Associated Estates Realty Corporation, 25 23–25
Associated Fire Marine Insurance Co., **26** 486
Associated Fresh Foods, **48** 37
Associated Gas & Electric Company *see* General Public Utilities Corp.
Associated Gas Services, Inc., **11** 28
Associated Grocers, Incorporated, 9 38–40; 31 22–26 (upd.)
The Associated Group, **10** 45
Associated Hospital Service of New York *see* Empire Blue Cross and Blue Shield.
Associated Inns and Restaurants Company of America, **26** 459
Associated International Insurance Co. *see* Gryphon Holdings, Inc.
Associated Lead Manufacturers Ltd. *see* Cookson Group plc.
Associated London Properties *see* Land Securities PLC.
Associated Madison Companies, *see* Primerica Corp.
Associated Milk Producers, Inc., 11 24–26; 48 43–46 (upd.)
Associated Natural Gas Corporation, 11 27–28
Associated Newspapers Holdings P.L.C., *see* Daily Mail and General Trust plc.
The Associated Press, 13 54–56; 31 27–30 (upd.); 73 37–41 (upd.)
Associates First Capital Corporation, **22** 207; **59** 126
Association des Centres Distributeurs E. Leclerc, 37 19–21
Association of Junior Leagues International Inc., 60 45–47
Assurances Générales de France, 63 45–48
Assured Guaranty Ltd., 93 57–60
AST Holding Corp. *see* American Standard Companies, Inc.
AST Research, Inc., 9 41–43
Astakos Terminal S.A., **64** 8
Astec Industries, Inc., 79 34–37
Astech, **18** 370
AstenJohnson Inc., 90 31–34
Asteroid, **IV** 97
Aston Brooke Software, **14** 392
Aston Villa plc, 41 34–36
Astor Holdings Inc., **22** 32
Astoria Financial Corporation, 44 31–34

Astra *see* PT Astra International Tbk.
Astra Resources, **12** 543
AstraZeneca PLC, I 625–26; 20 37–40 (upd.); 50 55–60 (upd.)
Astrium N.V., **52** 113
Astrolink International LLC, **54** 406–07
Astronics Corporation, 35 52–54
Astrotech Space Operations, L.P., **37** 365
Astrum International Corp., **12** 88; **16** 20–21; **43** 355
Asur *see* Grupo Aeropuerto del Sureste, S.A. de C.V.
Asurion Corporation, 83 29–32
ASV, Inc., 34 44–47; 66 13–15 (upd.)
ASW *see* American Steel & Wire Corp.
Asylum Records, **23** 33; **26** 150
AT&T Bell Laboratories, Inc., 13 57–59 *see also* Lucent Technologies Inc.
AT&T Corporation, V 259–64; 29 39–45 (upd.); 61 68 38–45 (upd.)
AT&T Istel Ltd., 14 35–36
AT&T Microelectronics, **63** 397
AT&T Wireless Services, Inc., 54 29–32 (upd.)
At Home Corporation, 43 48–51
AT TOKYO Corp., **74** 348
ATA Holdings Corporation, 82 21–25
Atanor S.A., 62 19–22
Atari Corporation, 9 44–47; 23 23–26 (upd.); 66 16–20 (upd.)
ATAS International, **26** 527, 530
ATC Healthcare Inc., 64 39–42
Atchison Casting Corporation, 39 30–32
ATCOR Resources Ltd., *see* Canadian Utilities Ltd.
ATD Group, *see* Arrow Electronics, Inc.
ATE Investment *see* Atlantic Energy, Inc.
Athalon Products, Ltd., *see* Lenox, Inc.
Athena Neuroscience, **63** 142
The Athlete's Foot Brands LLC, 84 17–20
Athletic Attic, **19** 230
The Athletics Investment Group, 62 23–26
Athleticum Sportmarket, **48** 279
ATI Technologies Inc., 79 38–41
Atkins Nutritionals, Inc., 58 8–10
Atkinson Candy Company, 87 39–42
ATL Group, **65** 304
Atlanta Bread Company International, Inc., 70 14–16
Atlanta Gas Light Company, 6 446–48; 23 27–30 (upd.)
Atlanta-LaSalle Corporation, **43** 54
Atlanta National League Baseball Club, Inc., 43 52–55
Atlantech Medical Devices, Ltd. *see* ArthroCare Corp.
Atlantia Offshore Limited *see* IHC Caland N.V.
Atlantic & Pacific Tea Company (A&P) *see* The Great Atlantic & Pacific Tea Company, Inc.
Atlantic Airways, **52** 167
Atlantic American Corporation, 44 35–37
Atlantic Auto Finance Corp. *see* United Auto Group, Inc.
Atlantic Cellular, **43** 341
Atlantic Coast Airlines Holdings, Inc., 55 35–37
Atlantic Coast Carton Company, *see* Caraustar Industries, Inc.
Atlantic Coast Line Railroad Company *see* CSX Corp.
Atlantic Container Lines Ltd., **23** 161
Atlantic Energy, Inc., 6 449–50
Atlantic Envelope Company, **54** 251–52, 255
The Atlantic Group, 23 31–33
Atlantic Mutual, **41** 65
Atlantic Premium Brands, Ltd., 57 56–58
Atlantic Records Group, **26** 150; **64** 115
Atlantic Refining Co. *see* Atlantic Richfield Co.
Atlantic Research Corporation, *see* Sequa Corp.
Atlantic Richfield Company, IV 375–77; 31 31–34 (upd.)
The Atlantic Seaboard Dispatch *see* GATX.
Atlantic Southeast Airlines, Inc., 47 29–31
Atlantic Southern Properties, Inc. *see* Atlantic Energy, Inc.
Atlantic Wholesalers Ltd., *see* George Weston Ltd.
Atlantis Energy Inc., **44** 182
Atlantis Group, Inc., **17** 16; **19** 50, 390
Atlantis Plastics, Inc., 85 14–17
Atlantis Resort and Casino *see* Sun International Hotels Ltd.
Atlas Air, Inc., 39 33–35
Atlas Air Worldwide Holdings, Inc., **60** 238
Atlas America, Inc., **42** 311
Atlas Bolt & Screw Company *see* The Marmon Group, Inc.
Atlas Cement Company, **31** 252
Atlas Copco AB, III 425–27; 28 37–41 (upd.); 85 18–24 (upd.)
Atlas Eléctrica S.A., *see* Electrolux AB.
Atlas Hotels, Inc., **V** 164
Atlas Securities, **47** 160
Atlas Tag & Label, *see* BISSELL, Inc.
Atlas Van Lines, Inc., 14 37–39
Atlas Ventures, **25** 96
Atlatec SA de CV, **39** 192
Atmel Corporation, 17 32–34
ATMI, Inc., 93 61–64
Atmos Energy Corporation, 43 56–58
Atmospherix Ltd. *see* Blyth Industries, Inc.
Atochem S.A., I 303–04, 676 *see also* Total-Fina-Elf.
AtoHaas Americas, **26** 425
Atoll Soft Nederland BV, **72** 35
Atomic Austria GmbH, **41** 14–16
Atos Origin S.A., 69 45–47
Atossa HealthCare, Inc. *see* Nastech Pharmaceutical Company Inc.
ATR, **7** 9, 11
Atrix Laboratories, Inc. *see* QLT Inc.
ATS *see* Magasins Armand Thiéry et Sigrand.
ATT Microelectrica España, **V** 339
Attachmate Corporation, 56 19–21
ATTC Manufacturing Inc., **48** 5
Attic Futura *see* PMP Ltd.
Attica Enterprises S.A., 64 43–45
Atwater McMillian *see* St. Paul Companies, Inc.
Atwood Mobil Products, 53 52–55
ATX Technologies, Inc., **32** 374
ATx Telecom Systems Inc., **31** 124
Au Bon Marché, **26** 160
Au Bon Pain Co., Inc., 18 35–38
AU Optronics Corporation, 67 38–40
Au Printemps S.A., V 9–11 *see also* Pinault-Printemps-Redoute S.A.
Aubert & Duval Holding *see* Eramet.
Auchan, 37 22–24
The Auchter Company, 78 21–24
Auctentia Subastas S.L., **60** 146
Audible Inc., 79 42–45
Audifon U.K. Ltd., **56** 338
Audio Accessories, Inc., **37** 301
Audio International Inc., **36** 159
Audio King Corporation, 24 52–54
Audio/Video Affiliates, Inc., *see* REX Stores Corp.
Audiofina, **44** 377
Audiovox Corporation, 34 48–50; 90 35–39 (upd.)
Audits & Surveys Worldwide Inc., **28** 501, 504
Auerhahn, **60** 364
Augat Inc., **54** 373
Aughton Group, *see* Associated British Foods plc.
August Max Woman *see* United States Shoe Corp.
August Schell Brewing Company Inc., 59 66–69
August Storck KG, 66 21–23
Ault Incorporated, 34 51–54
Auntie Anne's, Inc., 35 55–57
Aura Books plc, **34** 5
Aurea Concesiones de Infraestructuras SA *see* Abertis Infraestructuras, S.A.
Aurec Information and Directory Systems *see* Amdocs Ltd.
Aurigene Discovery Technologies Limited, **59** 168
AurionGold Limited, **61** 293
Aurora Casket Company, Inc., 56 22–24
Aurora Dairy Corporation, **37** 195, 198
Aurora Foods Inc., 32 67–69
Aurora Systems, Inc., **21** 135
Aurrera S.A., **35** 459
Aurum Corp., **38** 431
Ausimont S.p.A., *see* Solvay S.A.
Ausplay, *see* Little Tikes Co.
Aussedat-Rey, **23** 366, 368
Austal Limited, 75 36–39
The Austin Company, 8 41–44; 72 14–18 (upd.)
Austin Nichols, *see* Pernod Ricard S.A.
Austin Powder Company, 76 32–35
Austin Quality Foods, **36** 313

Austins Steaks & Saloon, Inc. *see* WesterN SizzliN Corp.
Australia and New Zealand Banking Group Limited, II 187–90; 52 35–40 (upd.)
Australian Airlines *see* Qantas Airways Ltd.
Australian and Overseas Telecommunications Corporation *see* Telecom Australia.
Australian Consolidated Press, **27** 42; **54** 299
Australian Mutual Provident Society, **IV** 61, 697
Australian Tankerships Pty. Ltd., **25** 471
Australian Telecommunications Corporation, **6** 342
Australian Wheat Board *see* AWB Ltd.
Austria Tabak, **55** 200
Austrian Airlines AG (Österreichische Luftverkehrs AG), 33 49–52
Austrian Star Gastronomie GmbH, **48** 63
Authentic Fitness Corp., 20 41–43; 51 30–33 (upd.)
Auto Helloes Co. Ltd., **76** 37
Auto Parts Wholesale, **26** 348
Auto Shack *see* AutoZone, Inc.
Auto Value Associates, Inc., 25 26–28
Autobacs Seven Company Ltd., 76 36–38
Autobytel Inc., 47 32–34
Autocam Corporation, 51 34–36
Autodesk, Inc., 10 118–20; 89 78–82 (upd.)
Autogrill SpA, 49 31–33
Autoliv, Inc., 65 53–55
Autologic Information International, Inc., 20 44–46
Automated Loss Prevention Systems, **11** 445
Automated Sciences Group, Inc. *see* CACI International Inc.
Automated Security (Holdings) PLC, *see* Sensormatic Electronics Corp.
Automatic Coil Corp., **33** 359, 361
Automatic Data Processing, Inc., III 117–19; 9 48–51 (upd.); 47 35–39 (upd.)
Automatic Liquid Packaging, **50** 122
Automatic Payrolls, Inc. *see* Automatic Data Processing, Inc.
Automatic Retailers of America, Inc., *see* Aramark Corporation
Automatic Sprinkler Corp. of America *see* Figgie International, Inc.
Automatic Toll Systems, **19** 111
Automatic Voting Machine Corporation *see* American Locker Group Inc.
AutoMed Technologies, Inc., **64** 27
Automobiles Citroën, 7 35–38
Automobili Lamborghini Holding S.p.A., 13 60–62; 34 55–58 (upd.); 91 25–30 (upd.)
Automotive Diagnostics, *see* SPX Corp.
Automotive Group *see* Lear Corp.
Automotive Industries Holding Inc., **16** 323
AutoNation, Inc., 50 61–64
Autonet, **6** 435
Autonom Computer, **47** 36
Autoridad del Canal de Panamá, 94 45–48
Autoroutes du Sud de la France SA, 55 38–40
Autosite.com, **47** 34
Autotote Corporation, 20 47–49 *see also* Scientific Games Corp.
AutoTrader.com, L.L.C., 91 31–34
Autoweb.com, **47** 34
AutoZone, Inc., 9 52–54; 31 35–38 (upd.)
AVA AG (Allgemeine Handelsgesellschaft der Verbraucher AG), 33 53–56
Avado Brands, Inc., 31 39–42
Avalon Correctional Services, Inc., 75 40–43
Avalon Publishing Group *see* Publishers Group, Inc.
AvalonBay Communities, Inc., 58 11–13
Avantel, **27** 304
Avantium Technologies BV, 79 46–49
Avaya Inc., **41** 287, 289–90
Avco *see* Aviation Corp. of the Americas.
Avco Corp., **34** 433
Avco Financial Services Inc., 13 63–65 *see also* Citigroup Inc.
Avdel, **34** 433
Avecia Group PLC, 63 49–51
Avecor Cardiovascular Inc., **22** 360
Avecor, Inc. *see*M. A. Hanna Co.
Aveda Corporation, 24 55–57
Avedis Zildjian Co., 38 66–68
Avendt Group, Inc., *see* Marmon Group, Inc.
Aventine Renewable Energy Holdings, Inc., 89 83–86
Aventis Pharmaceuticals, **34** 280, 283–84; **38** 378, 380; **63** 232, 235
Avery Communications, Inc., **72** 39
Avery Dennison Corporation, IV 251–54; 17 27–31 (upd.); 49 34–40 (upd.)
AvestaPolarit, **49** 104
Avex Electronics Inc., **40** 68
Avgain Marine A/S, **7** 40; **41** 42
Avia Group International, Inc. *see* Reebok International Ltd.
Aviacionny Nauchno-Tehnicheskii Komplex im. A.N. Tupoleva, 24 58–60
Aviacsa *see* Consorcio Aviacsa, S.A. de C.V.
Aviall, Inc., 73 42–45
Avianca Aerovías Nacionales de Colombia SA, 36 52–55
Aviation Corp. of the Americas, **9** 497–99
Aviation Inventory Management Co., **28** 5
Aviation Sales Company, 41 37–39
Aviation Services West, Inc. *see* Scenic Airlines, Inc.
Avid Technology Inc., 38 69–73
Avimo, **47** 7–8
Avionics Specialties Inc. *see* Aerosonic Corp.
Avions Marcel Dassault-Breguet Aviation, I 44–46 *see also* Groupe Dassault Aviation SA.
Avis Group Holdings, Inc., 6 356–58; 22 54–57 (upd.); 75 44–49 (upd.)
Avista Corporation, 69 48–50 (upd.)
Aviva PLC, 50 65–68 (upd.)
Avnet Inc., 9 55–57
Avocent Corporation, 65 56–58
Avon Products, Inc., III 15–16; 19 26–29 (upd.); 46 43–46 (upd.)
Avon Rubber plc, **23** 146
Avondale Industries, Inc., 7 39–41; 41 40–43 (upd.)
Avonmore Foods Plc, **59** 205
Avril Alimentaire SNC, **51** 54
Avstar, **38** 72
Avtech Corp., **36** 159
AVTOVAZ Joint Stock Company, 65 59–62
AVX Corporation, 67 41–43
AW Bruna Uitgevers BV, **53** 273
AW North Carolina Inc., **48** 5
AWA *see* America West Holdings Corp.
AWA Defence Industries (AWADI) *see* British Aerospace plc.
AwardTrack, Inc., **49** 423
AWB Ltd., 56 25–27
Awesome Transportation, Inc., **22** 549
Awrey Bakeries, Inc., 56 28–30
AXA Colonia Konzern AG, III 210–12; 49 41–45 (upd.)
AXA Financial, Inc., **63** 26–27
AXA Private Equity *see* Camaïeu S.A.
AXA UK plc, **64** 173
Axcan Pharma Inc., 85 25–28
Axe-Houghton Associates Inc., **41** 208
Axel Johnson Group, I 553–55
Axel Springer Verlag AG, IV 589–91; 20 50–53 (upd.)
Axsys Technologies, Inc., 93 65–68
Ayala Corporation, **70** 182
Ayala Plans, Inc., **58** 20
Aydin Corp., 19 30–32
Aynsley China Ltd. *see* Belleek Pottery Ltd.
Ayres, Lewis, Norris & May, Inc., **54** 184
AYS *see* Alternative Youth Services, Inc.
AZA Immobilien AG, **51** 196
Azcon Corporation, 23 34–36
Azerbaijan Airlines, 77 46–49
Azerty, **25** 13
Azienda Generale Italiana Petroli *see* ENI S.p.A.
AZL Resources, *see* Tosco Corp.
Azlan Group Limited, **74** 338
Aznar International, **14** 225
Azon Limited, *see* Illinois Tool Works Inc.
AZP Group Inc., **6** 546
Aztar Corporation, 13 66–68; 71 41–45 (upd.)
AZZ Incorporated, 93 69–72

B

B&D *see* Barker & Dobson.
B&G Foods, Inc., 40 51–54
B&J Music Ltd. *see* Kaman Music Corp.
B & K Steel Fabrications, Inc., **26** 432

B & L Insurance, Ltd., **51** 38
B&M Baked Beans, **40** 53
B & O *see* Baltimore ;amp; Ohio Railroad.
B&Q plc *see* Kingfisher plc.
B&S *see* Binney & Smith Inc.
B.A.T. Industries PLC, 22 70–73 (upd.) *see also* Brown and Williamson Tobacco Corporation
B. B. & R. Knight Brothers, *see* Fruit of the Loom, Inc.
B.C. Rail Telecommunications, **6** 311
B.C. Ziegler and Co. *see* The Ziegler Companies, Inc.
B. Dalton Bookseller Inc., 25 29–31 *see also* Barnes & Noble, Inc.
B/E Aerospace, Inc., 30 72–74
B.F. Goodrich Co. *see* The BFGoodrich Co.
B.I.C. America, **17** 15, 17
B.J. Alan Co., Inc., 67 44–46
The B. Manischewitz Company, LLC, 31 43–46
B. Perini & Sons, Inc., *see* Perini Corp.
B.R. Guest Inc., 87 43–46
B Ticino, **21** 350
B.W. Rogers Company, 94 49–52
BA *see* British Airways plc.
BAA plc, 10 121–23; 33 57–61 (upd.)
Bålforsens Kraft AB, **28** 444
Baan Company, 25 32–34
Babbage's, Inc., 10 124–25 *see also* GameStop Corp.
The Babcock & Wilcox Company, 82 26–30
Babcock International Group PLC, 69 51–54
BABE *see* British Aerospace plc.
Baby Dairy Products, **48** 438
Baby Lock USA *see* Tacony Corp.
Baby Phat *see* Phat Fashions LLC.
Baby Superstore, Inc., 15 32–34 *see also* Toys 'R Us, Inc.
Babybird Co., Ltd. *see* Nagasakiya Co., Ltd.
BabyCenter.com, **37** 130
Babyliss, S.A. *see* Conair Corp.
BAC *see* Barclays American Corp.; Beverage Associates Corp.; British Aircraft Corp.
Bacardi & Company Ltd., 18 39–42; 82 31–36 (upd.)
Baccarat, 24 61–63
Bachman Foods, **15** 139
Bachman's Inc., 22 58–60
Bachoco *see* Industrias Bachoco, S.A. de C.V.
Back Bay Investments Ltd., **64** 217
Back Bay Restaurant Group, Inc., 20 54–56
Back Yard Burgers, Inc., 45 33–36
Backer & Spielvogel, **14** 48–49; **22** 296
Backer Spielvogel Bates Worldwide *see* Bates Worldwide, Inc.
Backus y Johnston *see* Unión de Cervecerias Peruanas Backus y Johnston S.A.A.
Bacon's Information, Inc., **55** 289
Bacova Guild, Ltd., *see* Burlington Industries, Inc.
Bad Boy Worldwide Entertainment Group, 58 14–17
Badak LNG Transport Inc., **56** 181
Baddour, Inc. *see* Fred's, Inc.
Badger Illuminating Company, **6** 601
Badger Meter, Inc., 22 61–65
Badger Paper Mills, Inc., 15 35–37
Badger State Ethanol, LLC, 83 33-37
BAe *see* British Aerospace plc.
BAE-Newplan Group Ltd. *see* SNC-Lavalin Group Inc.
BAE Systems Ship Repair, 73 46–48
BAFS *see* Bangkok Aviation Fuel Services Ltd.
Bahamas Air Holdings Ltd., 66 24–26
Bahlsen GmbH & Co. KG, 44 38–41
Bailey, Banks & Biddle, *see* Zale Corp.
Bailey Nurseries, Inc., 57 59–61
Bailey Street Trading Company, **71** 60
Bailey's Pub and Grille *see* Total Entertainment Restaurant Corp.
Bain & Company, 55 41–43
Bain Capital, Inc., **16** 466; **20** 18; **26** 184; **38** 107–09; **63** 133, 137–38
Baird *see* Imo Industries Inc.
Baird & Warner Holding Company, 87 47–50
Bairnco Corporation, 28 42–45
Bajaj Auto Limited, 39 36–38
BÅKAB *see* Bålforsens Kraft AB.
Baker *see* Michael Baker Corp.
Baker and Botts, L.L.P., 28 46–49
Baker & Daniels LLP, 88 17–20
Baker & Hostetler LLP, 40 55–58
Baker & McKenzie, 10 126–28; 42 17–20 (upd.)
Baker & Taylor Corporation, 16 45–47; 43 59–62 (upd.)
Baker Cummins Pharmaceuticals Inc., **11** 208
Baker Hughes Incorporated, III 428–29; 22 66–69 (upd.); 57 62–66 (upd.)
Bakers Best Snack Food Corporation, *see* J & J Snack Foods Corp.
Bakers Square *see* VICORP Restaurants, Inc.
Bakery Feeds Inc. *see* Griffin Industries, Inc.
Bakkavör Group hf., 91 35–39
Bal-Sam India Holdings Ltd., **64** 95
Balance Bar Company, 32 70–72
Balatongáz Kft. (Ltd), **70** 195
Balchem Corporation, 42 21–23
Balco, Inc., *see* Snap-On, Inc.
Bald Eagle Corporation, **45** 126
Baldor Electric Company, 21 42–44
Baldwin & Lyons, Inc., 51 37–39
Baldwin-Ehret-Hill Inc., **28** 42
Baldwin Filters, Inc., *see* CLARCOR Inc.
Baldwin Hardware Manufacturing Co. *see* Masco Corp.
Baldwin-Montrose Chemical Co., Inc., **31** 110
Baldwin Piano & Organ Company, 18 43–46 *see also* Gibson Guitar Corp.
Baldwin Technology Company, Inc., 25 35–39
Balfour Beatty Construction Ltd., 36 56–60 (upd.)
Ball & Young Adhesives, *see* British Vita PLC.
Ball Corporation, I 597–98; 10 129–31 (upd.); 78 25–29 (upd.)
The Ball Ground Reps, Inc., **26** 257
Ball Horticultural Company, 78 30–33
Ball Industries, Inc., **26** 539
Ballantine Books, *see* Random House, Inc.
Ballantyne of Omaha, Inc., 27 56–58
Ballard Medical Products, 21 45–48 *see also* Kimberly-Clark Corp.
Ballard Power Systems Inc., 73 49–52
Ballet Makers-Europe, Ltd., **62** 59
Balli Group plc, **26** 527, 530
Ballistic Recovery Systems, Inc., 87 51–54
Bally Entertainment Corp., *see* Hilton Hotels Corp.
Bally Gaming International, **15** 539
Bally Manufacturing Corporation, III 430–32
Bally Total Fitness Corporation, 25 40–42; 94 53–57 (upd.)
Balmac International, Inc., 94 58–61
Bâloise-Holding, 40 59–62
Baltek Corporation, 34 59–61
Baltic Cable, **15** 521
Baltic International USA, **71** 35
Baltika Brewery Joint Stock Company, 65 63–66
Baltimore & Ohio Railroad *see* CSX Corp.
Baltimore Aircoil Company, Inc., 66 27–29
Baltimore Gas and Electric Company, V 552–54; 25 43–46 (upd.)
Baltimore Orioles L.P., 66 30–33
Baltimore Technologies Plc, 42 24–26
Balzers Process Systems GmbH, **48** 30
The Bama Companies, Inc., 80 13–16
Banamex *see* Banco Nacional de Mexico; Grupo Financiero Banamex S.A.
Banana Boat Holding Corp., **15** 359
Banana Brothers, **31** 229
Banana Importers of Ireland, **38** 197
Banana Republic Inc., 25 47–49 *see also* Gap, Inc.
Banc Internacional d'Andorra-Banca Mora, **48** 51
Banc One Corporation, 10 132–34 *see also* JPMorgan Chase & Co.
Banca Commerciale Italiana SpA, II 191–93
Banca del Salento, **65** 73
Banca di Roma S.p.A., **65** 86, 88
Banca Esperia, **65** 230–31
Banca Fideuram SpA, 63 52–54
Banca Intesa SpA, 65 67–70
Banca Monte dei Paschi di Siena SpA, 65 71–73
Banca Nazionale del Lavoro SpA, 72 19–21
Banca Serfin *see* Grupo Financiero Serfin, S.A.

BancBoston Capital, **48** 412
Bancen *see* Banco del Centro S.A.
BancMortgage Financial Corp., *see* Habersham Bancorp.
Banco Bilbao Vizcaya Argentaria S.A., II 194–96; 48 47–51 (upd.)
Banco Bradesco S.A., 13 69–71
Banco Central, II 197–98; 56 65 *see also* Banco Santander Central Hispano S.A.
Banco de Crédito del Perú, 9273–76
Banco Chemical (Portugal) S.A. *see* Chemical Banking Corp.
Banco Comercial de Puerto Rico, **41** 311
Banco Comercial Português, SA, 50 69–72
Banco Credito y Ahorro Ponceno, **41** 312
Banco de Chile, 69 55–57
Banco de Comercio, S.A. *see* Grupo Financiero BBVA Bancomer S.A.
Banco de Credito Local, **48** 51
Banco de Credito y Servicio, **51** 151
Banco de Galicia y Buenos Aires, S.A., **63** 178–80
Banco de Londres, Mexico y Sudamerica *see* Grupo Financiero Serfin, S.A.
Banco de Madrid, **40** 147
Banco de Ponce, **41** 313
Banco del Centro S.A., **51** 150
Banco di Roma, **II**, 257, 271
Banco di Santo Spirito, *see* Istituto per la Ricostruzione Industriale S.p.A.
Banco di Sicilia S.p.A., **65** 86, 88
Banco do Brasil S.A., II 199–200
Banco Espírito Santo e Comercial de Lisboa S.A., 15 38–40 *see also* Espírito Santo Financial Group S.A.
Banco Federal de Crédito *see* Banco Itaú.
Banco Itaú S.A., 19 33–35
Banco Mercantil del Norte, S.A., **51** 149
Banco Opportunity, **57** 67, 69
Banco Popolar *see* Popular, Inc.
Banco Santander Central Hispano S.A., 36 61–64 (upd.)
Banco Santander-Chile, **71** 143
Banco Serfin, *see* Grupo Financiero Serfin, S.A.
Bancomer S.A. *see* Grupo Financiero BBVA Bancomer S.A.
BancorpSouth, Inc., **14** 40–41
Bancrecer *see* Banco de Credito y Servicio.
Bandag, Inc., 19 36–38
Bandai Co., Ltd., 55 44–48
Bando McGlocklin Small Business Lending Corporation, **53** 222–24
Banfi Products Corp., 36 65–67
Banfield, The Pet Hospital *see* Medical Management International, Inc.
Bang & Olufsen Holding A/S, 37 25–28; 86 24–29 (upd.)
Bangkok Airport Hotel *see* Thai Airways International.
Bangkok Aviation Fuel Services Ltd. *see* Thai Airways International.
Bangladesh Krishi Bank, **31** 220
Bangor and Aroostook Railroad Company, *see* Amoskeag Company
Bangor Punta Alegre Sugar Corp., **30** 425
Banister Continental Corp. *see* BFC Construction Corp.
Bank Austria AG, 23 37–39
Bank Brussels Lambert, II 201–03
Bank Central Asia, **62** 96, 98
Bank für Elektrische Unternehmungen *see* Elektrowatt AG.
Bank Hapoalim B.M., II 204–06; 54 33–37 (upd.)
Bank Hofmann, **21** 146–47
Bank Leumi le-Israel B.M., 60 48–51
Bank of America Corporation, 46 47–54 (upd.)
Bank of Boston Corporation, II 207–09 *see also* FleetBoston Financial Corp.
Bank of Britain, **14** 46–47
Bank of China, 63 55–57
Bank of Cyprus Group, 91 40–43
Bank of Delaware, **25** 542
Bank of East Asia Ltd., 63 58–60
Bank of England, **14** 45–46; **47** 227
Bank of Granite Corporation, 89 87–91
Bank of Hawaii Corporation, 73 53–56
Bank of Ireland, 50 73–76
Bank of Italy, *see* Bank of America.
Bank of Mississippi, Inc., 14 40–41
Bank of Montreal, II 210–12; 46 55–58 (upd.)
Bank of New England Corporation, II 213–15
Bank of New South Wales *see* Westpac Banking Corp.
Bank of New York Company, Inc., II 216–19; 46 59–63 (upd.)
The Bank of Nova Scotia, II 220–23; 59 70–76 (upd.)
The Bank of Scotland *see* The Governor and Company of the Bank of Scotland.
Bank of the Ozarks, Inc., 91 44–47
Bank of the Philippine Islands, 58 18–20
Bank of Tokyo-Mitsubishi Ltd., II 224–25; 15 41–43 (upd.)
Bank of Wales plc, *see* The Governor and Company of the Bank of Scotland.
Bank One Corporation, 36 68–75 (upd.) *see also* JPMorgan Chase & Co.
BankAmerica Corporation, II 226–28 *see also* Bank of America.
BankAtlantic Bancorp., Inc., **66** 273
BankBoston *see* FleetBoston Financial Corp.
Bankers Life and Casualty Co., *see* Conseco Inc.
Bankers Life Association *see* Principal Mutual Life Insurance Co.
Bankers National Life Insurance Co., *see* Conseco Inc.
Bankers Trust Co., **38** 411
Bankers Trust New York Corporation, II 229–31
Bankhaus August Lenz AG, **65** 230, 232
Banknorth Group, Inc., 55 49–53
Bankrate, Inc., 83 38-41
Bankruptcy Services LLC, **56** 112
Banksia Wines Ltd., **54** 227, 229
BankWatch, **37** 143, 145
Banner Aerospace, Inc., 14 42–44; 37 29–32 (upd.)
Banner Life Insurance Company, *see* Legal & General Group plc
Banorte *see* Grupo Financiero Banorte, S.A. de C.V.
Banpais *see* Grupo Financiero Asemex-Banpais S.A.
BanPonce Corporation, **41** 312
Banque Bruxelles Lambert *see* Bank Brussels Lambert.
Banque de Bruxelles *see* Bank Brussels Lambert.
Banque de France, **14** 45–46
Banque de la Société Générale de Belgique *see* Generale Bank.
Banque de Paris et des Pays-Bas, **33** 179
Banque Indosuez, **52** 361–62
Banque Internationale de Luxembourg, **42** 111
Banque Lambert *see* Bank Brussels Lambert.
Banque Nationale de Paris S.A., II 232–34 *see also* BNP Paribas Group.
Banque Paribas *see* BNP Paribas Group.
Banque Sanpaolo of France, **50** 410
La Banque Suisse et Française *see* Crédit Commercial de France.
Banta Corporation, 12 24–26; 32 73–77 (upd.); 79 50–56 (upd.)
Bantam Doubleday Dell Publishing Group, *see* Random House Inc.
Banyan Systems Inc., 25 50–52
Baoshan Iron and Steel, **19** 220
Baosteel Group International Trade Corporation *see* Shanghai Baosteel Group Corp.
BAP of New York, Inc., **15** 246
Baptist Health Care Corporation, 82 37–40
Bar-S Foods Company, 76 39–41
Bar Technologies, Inc., **26** 408
Barastoc Stockfeeds Pty Ltd., **62** 307
Barat *see* Barclays PLC.
Barbara's Bakery Inc., 88 21–24
Barber Dental Supply Inc., **19** 291
Barberet & Blanc, **I** 677; **49** 350
Barcel, **19** 192
Barclay Furniture Co., *see* LADD Furniture, Inc.
Barclay White Inc., **38** 436
Barclays PLC, II 235–37; 20 57–60 (upd.); 64 46–50 (upd.)
BarclaysAmerican Mortgage Corporation, 11 29–30
Barco Manufacturing Co., **16** 8; **26** 541
Barco NV, 44 42–45
Barcolo Manufacturing, **15** 103; **26** 100
Barden Companies, Inc., 76 42–45
Bardon Group *see* Aggregate Industries plc.
Bare Escentuals, Inc., 91 48–52
Bareco Products, **15** 352
Barefoot Inc., **23** 428, 431
Barilla G. e R. Fratelli S.p.A., 17 35–37; 50 77–80 (upd.)
Baring Brothers & Co., Ltd., **39** 5
Barings PLC, 14 45–47

Barker & Dobson, **47** 367
Barlow Rand Ltd., I 422–24
Barlow Specialty Advertising, Inc., **26** 341
Barmag AG, 39 39–42
Barneda Carton SA, **41** 326
Barnes & Noble, Inc., 10 135–37; 30 67–71 (upd.); 75 50–55 (upd.)
Barnes Group, Inc., 13 72–74; 69 58–62 (upd.)
Barnett Banks, Inc., 9 58–60 *see also* Bank of America Corp.
Barnett Inc., 28 50–52
Barney's, Inc., 28 53–55
Barnstead Thermolyne Corporation, *see* Sybron International Corp.
Baroid, **19** 467–68
Baron de Ley S.A., 74 27–29
Baron Industries Corporation, **53** 298
Baron Philippe de Rothschild S.A., 39 43–46
Barr *see* AG Barr plc.
Barr & Stroud Ltd., *see* Pilkington plc.
Barr Pharmaceuticals, Inc., 26 29–31; 68 46–49 (upd.)
Barracuda Technologies, **47** 7, 9
Barratt Developments plc, I 556–57; 56 31–33 (upd.)
Barrett Business Services, Inc., 16 48–50
Barrett-Jackson Auction Company L.L.C., 88 25–28
Barricini Foods Inc., **27** 197
Barrick Gold Corporation, 34 62–65
Barris Industries, Inc., **23** 225
Barry Callebaut AG, 29 46–48; 71 46–49 (upd.)
Barry Controls, *see* Applied Power, Inc.
Barry-Wehmiller Companies, Inc., 90 40–43
Barry's Jewelers *see* Samuels Jewelers Inc.
Barsab Investment Trust *see* The South African Breweries Ltd.
Barsotti's, Inc. *see* Foster Wheeler Corp.
The Bartell Drug Company, 94 62–65
Bartlett & Co., **33** 261
Barton & Ludwig, Inc., **21** 96
Barton Beers, Ltd., **29** 219
Barton Incorporated, *see* Canandaigua Brands, Inc.
Barton Malow Company, 51 40–43
Barton Protective Services Inc., 53 56–58
Barwig Medizinische Systeme *see* OEC Medical Systems, Inc.
The Baseball Club of Seattle, LP, 50 81–85
Baseline, **58** 167
BASF Aktiengesellschaft, I 305–08; 18 47–51 (upd.); 50 86–92 (upd.)
Bashas' Inc., 33 62–64; 80 17–21 (upd.)
Basic Resources, Inc. *see* Texas Utilities Co.
BASIS Information Technologies, Inc., **11** 132
The Basketball Club of Seattle, LLC, 50 93–97
Basketball Properties Ltd, **53** 166
Baskin-Robbins Ice Cream Co., **29** 18
Bass Anglers Sportsman Society Inc., **52** 192
Bass Brewers Ltd., **15** 441; **29** 85
Bass Brothers Enterprises Inc., **28** 107; **36** 472
Bass Charington, **29** 84
Bass PLC, I 222–24; 15 44–47 (upd.); 38 74–78 (upd.)
Bass Pro Shops, Inc., 42 27–30
Bassett Boat Company, **30** 303
Bassett Furniture Industries, Inc., 18 52–55
Bassett Lowke Ltd., **60** 372
Bassett-Walker Inc. *see* VF Corp.
BAT Industries plc, I 425–27 *see also* British American Tobacco PLC.
Bata Ltd., 62 27–30
Batavia Wine Company, *see* Canandaigua Brands, Inc.
Bateaux Parisiens, **29** 442
Bates, *see* Wolverine World Wide, Inc.
Bates Manufacturing Company, **10** 314
Bates Worldwide, Inc., 14 48–51; 33 65–69 (upd.)
Batesville Casket Company *see* Hillenbrand Industries, Inc.
Bath & Body Works, **11** 41; *see also* Intimate Brands, Inc.
Bath Iron Works Corporation, 12 27–29; 36 76–79 (upd.)
Bath Plus Inc., **51** 196
Batkor Finances BV, **68** 64
Baton Rouge Gas Light Company *see* Gulf States Utilities Co.
Battelle Memorial Institute, Inc., 10 138–40
Batten Barton Durstine & Osborn *see* Omnicom Group Inc.
Battery Engineering, Inc. *see* Greatbatch Inc.
Battle Mountain Gold Company, 23 40–42 *see also* Newmont Mining Corp.
Battlefield Equipment Rentals, **21** 499, 501
BATUS Inc., *see* British American Tobacco PLC.
Baublys-Control Laser Corporation *see* Excel Technology, Inc.
Bauer + Kunzi, **64** 226
Bauer Audio Visual, Inc., **24** 96
Bauer Nike Hockey Inc. *see* NIKE, Inc.
Bauer Publishing Group, 7 42–43
Bauerly Companies, 61 31–33
Baugur Group hf, 81 45–49
Baumax AG, 75 56–58
Baume & Mercier, *see* Vendôme Luxury Group plc.
Bausch & Lomb Inc., 7 44–47; 25 53–57 (upd.)
Bavaria S.A., 90 44–47
BAX Global, **58** 43
Baxter Healthcare, **36** 497–98
Baxter International Inc., I 627–29; 10 141–43 (upd.)
The Bay *see* The Hudson's Bay Co.
Bay Area Review Course, Inc., **IV** 623
Bay Frontier Onoda Co. Ltd., **60** 301
Bay Harbour Management L.C., **28** 55
Bay Networks, Inc., **20** 33, 69; **26** 276; **36** 352
Bay Ridge Savings Bank, *see* Anchor Bancorp, Inc.
Bay Shipbuilding Corporation, *see* Manitowoc Co., Inc.
Bay State Gas Company, 38 79–82
Bay West Paper Corporation *see* Mosinee Paper Corp.
Bayard SA, 49 46–49
BayBanks, Inc., 12 30–32
Bayer A.G., I 309–11; 13 75–77 (upd.); 41 44–48 (upd.)
Bayerische Hypotheken- und Wechsel-Bank AG, II 238–40 *see also* HVB Group.
Bayerische Landesbank, **14** 170; **47** 83
Bayerische Motoren Werke A.G., I 138–40; 11 31–33 (upd.); 38 83–87 (upd.)
Bayerische Vereinsbank A.G., II 241–43 *see also* HVB Group.
Bayerische Wagnisbeteiligung GmbH, **27** 192
Bayernwerk AG, V 555–58; 23 43–47 (upd.) *see also* E.On AG.
Bayliner Marine Corporation, **22** 116
Bayou Steel Corporation, 31 47–49
Bayox, Inc. *see* Union Carbide Corp.
Baytree Investors Inc., **15** 87
Bayview Water Company, **45** 277
Bazaar & Novelty *see* Stuart Entertainment Inc.
BB&T Corporation, 79 57–61
BB Holdings Limited, 77 50–53
BBA *see* Bush Boake Allen Inc.
BBA Aviation plc, 90 48–52
BBAG Osterreichische Brau-Beteiligungs-AG, 38 88–90
BBC *see* British Broadcasting Corp.
BBC Brown, Boveri Ltd. *see* ABB Ltd.
BBDO Worldwide *see* Omnicom Group Inc.
BBGI *see* Beasley Broadcast Group, Inc.
BBME *see* British Bank of the Middle East.
BBN Corp., 19 39–42
BBO & Co., **14** 433
BBVA *see* Banco Bilbao Vizcaya Argentaria S.A.
BC Development, **16** 481
BC Natural Foods, Inc., **68** 91
BC Partners, **51** 322; **53** 138; **76** 305, 307
BC Property Management Inc., **58** 23
BC Rail Ltd., **71** 82, 88
BC TEL *see* British Columbia Telephone Co.
BCal *see* British Caledonian Airways.
BCC, *see* Kingfisher plc.
BCE, Inc., V 269–71; 44 46–50 (upd.)
BCI *see* Banca Commerciale Italiana SpA.
Bcom3 Group, Inc., **40** 142; **76** 254
BCOP *see* Boise Cascade Office Products.
BCPA *see* British Commonwealth Pacific Airways.
BDB *see* British Digital Broadcasting plc.
BDDP *see* Wells Rich Greene BDDP.

BE&K, Inc., 73 57–59
Be Free Inc., **49** 434
BEA *see* Bank of East Asia Ltd.
BEA Systems, Inc., 36 80–83
Beach Hill Investments Pty Ltd., **48** 427
Beach Patrol Inc., **29** 181
Beacon Communications Group, **23** 135
Beacon Education Management LLC *see* Chancellor Beacon Academies, Inc.
Beacon Manufacturing Company, **19** 304–05
Beacon Roofing Supply, Inc., 75 59–61
Bealls, *see* Stage Stores, Inc.
Beamach Group Ltd., **17** 182–83
Beaman Corporation, **16** 96
Bean Fiberglass Inc., **15** 247
Bear Automotive Service Equipment Company, *see* SPX Corp.
Bear Creek Corporation, 38 91–94
Bear Instruments Inc., **48** 410
Bear Stearns Companies, Inc., II 400–01; 10 144–45 (upd.); 52 41–44 (upd.)
Bearings, Inc., 13 78–80
Beasley Broadcast Group, Inc., 51 44–46
Beatrice Company, II 467–69 *see also* TLC Beatrice International Holdings, Inc.
Beatrice Foods, **21** 322–24, 507, 545; **38** 169; **43** 355
Beatrix Mines Ltd., **62** 164
Beaulieu of America, **19** 276
Beauté Prestige International S.A. *see* Shiseido Company Ltd.
BeautiControl Cosmetics, Inc., 21 49–52
Beauty Systems Group, Inc., **60** 260
Beaver Lake Concrete, Inc. *see* The Monarch Cement Co.
Beazer Homes USA, Inc., 17 38–41
Beazer Plc, *see* Hanson PLC.
bebe stores, inc., 31 50–52
BEC Group Inc., **22** 35; **60** 133
BEC Ventures, **57** 124–25
Bechstein, **56** 299
Bechtel Group, Inc., I 558–59; 24 64–67 (upd.)
Beck's North America, Inc. *see* Brauerei Beck & Co.
Becker Drill, Inc., **19** 247
Becker Group of Germany, **26** 231
Beckett Papers, 23 48–50
Beckley-Cardy Group *see* School Specialty, Inc.
Beckman Coulter, Inc., 22 74–77
Beckman Instruments, Inc., 14 52–54
BECOL *see* Belize Electric Company Ltd.
Becton, Dickinson & Company, I 630–31; 11 34–36 (upd.); 36 84–89 (upd.)
Bed Bath & Beyond Inc., 13 81–83; 41 49–52 (upd.)
Bedcovers, Inc., **19** 304
Bee Chemicals, *see* Morton International.
Bee Discount, **26** 476
Beech Aircraft Corporation, 8 49–52 *see also* Raytheon Aircraft Holdings Inc.
Beech Holdings Corp., **9** 94
Beech-Nut Nutrition Corporation, 21 53–56; 51 47–51 (upd.)
Beecham Group PLC, *see* GlaxoSmithKline plc.
Beechcroft Developments Ltd., **51** 173
Beeck-Feinkost GmbH, **26** 59
ZAO BeeOnLine-Portal, **48** 419
Beer Nuts, Inc., 86 30–33
Beerman Stores, Inc., *see* Elder-Beerman Stores Corp.
Beers Construction Company, **38** 437
Befesa *see* Abengoa S.A.
Behr GmbH & Co. KG, 72 22–25
Behring Diagnostics *see* Dade Behring Holdings Inc.
Behringwerke AG, **14** 255; **50** 249
BEI Technologies, Inc., 65 74–76
Beiersdorf AG, 29 49–53
Beijing Contact Lens Ltd., **25** 56
Beijing Dentsu, **16** 168
Beijing-Landauer, Ltd., **51** 210
Beijing ZF North Drive Systems Technical Co. Ltd., **48** 450
Beirao, Pinto, Silva and Co. *see* Banco Espírito Santo e Comercial de Lisboa S.A.
Bejam Group PLC *see* The Big Food Group plc.
Bekaert S.A./N.V., 90 53–57
Bekins Company, 15 48–50
Bel *see* Fromageries Bel.
Bel Air Markets, *see* Raley's Inc.
Bel Fuse, Inc., 53 59–62
Bel/Kaukauna USA, 76 46–48
Belco Oil & Gas Corp., 40 63–65
Belcom Holding AG, **53** 323, 325
Belden CDT Inc., 19 43–45; 76 49–52 (upd.)
Beldis, **23** 219
Beldoch Industries Corp., *see* Donnkenny, Inc.
Belgacom, 6 302–04
Belgian Rapid Access to Information Network Services, **6** 304
Belgo Group plc, **31** 41
Belize Electric Company Limited, **47** 137
Belk, Inc., V 12–13; 19 46–48 (upd.); 72 26–29 (upd.)
Bell and Howell Company, 9 61–64; 29 54–58 (upd.)
Bell Atlantic Corporation, V 272–74; 25 58–62 (upd.) *see also* Verizon Communications.
Bell Canada Enterprises Inc. *see* BCE, Inc.
Bell Canada International, Inc., 6 305–08
Bell Communications Research *see* Telcordia Technologies, Inc.
Bell Fibre Products, **12** 377
Bell Helicopter Textron Inc., 46 64–67
Bell Helmets Inc., **22** 458
Bell Industries, Inc., 47 40–43
Bell Laboratories *see* AT&T Bell Laboratories, Inc.
Bell Microproducts Inc., 69 63–65
Bell Mountain Partnership, Ltd., **15** 26
Bell-Northern Research, Ltd. *see* BCE Inc.
Bell Resources, *see* TPG NV.
Bell Sports Corporation, 16 51–53; 44 51–54 (upd.)
Bellcore *see* Telcordia Technologies, Inc.
Belleek Pottery Ltd., 71 50–53
Belleville Shoe Manufacturing Company, 92 17–20
BellSouth Corporation, V 276–78; 29 59–62 (upd.) *see also* AT&T Corp.
Bellway Plc, 45 37–39
Belmin Systems, *see* AT&T Istel Ltd.
Belo Corporation *see* A.H. Belo Corporation
Beloit Corporation, 14 55–57 *see also* Metso Corp.
Beloit Tool Company *see* Regal-Beloit Corp.
Belron International Ltd., 76 53–56
Belvedere S.A., 93 77–81
Bemis Company, Inc., 8 53–55; 91 53–60 (upd.)
Ben & Jerry's Homemade, Inc., 10 146–48; 35 58–62 (upd.); 80 22–28 (upd.)
Ben Bridge Jeweler, Inc., 60 52–54
Ben E. Keith Company, 76 57–59
Ben Franklin Retail Stores, Inc. *see* FoxMeyer Health Corp.
Ben Myerson Candy Co., Inc., **26** 468
Benair Freight International Limited *see* Gulf Agency Company
Benchmark Capital, 49 50–52
Benchmark Electronics, Inc., 40 66–69
Benchmark Tape Systems Ltd, **62** 293
Benckiser Group, **37** 269
Benckiser N.V. *see* Reckitt Benckiser plc.
Benderson Development Company, **69** 120
Bendick's of Mayfair *see* August Storck KG.
Bendix Corporation, I 141–43
Beneficial Corporation, 8 56–58
Benefits Technologies, Inc., **52** 382
Benelli Arms S.p.A., **39** 151
Benesse Corporation, 76 60–62
Bénéteau SA, 55 54–56
Benetton Group S.p.A., 10 149–52; 67 47–51 (upd.)
Benfield Greig Group plc, 53 63–65
Benguet Corporation, 58 21–24
Benihana, Inc., 18 56–59; 76 63–66 (upd.)
Benjamin Moore and Co., 13 84–87; 38 95–99 (upd.)
Benjamin Sheridan Corporation, **62** 82
Benlee, Inc., **51** 237
Benn Bros. plc, **IV** 687
Bennett's Smokehouse and Saloon, **29** 201
Bennigan's, *see* Metromedia Co.
Benpres Holdings, **56** 214
BenQ Corporation, 67 52–54
Bensdorp, **29** 47
Benson & Hedges, Ltd. *see* Gallaher Ltd.
Bentalls, **37** 6, 8
Bentex Holding S.A., **48** 209
Bentley Laboratories, **22** 360
Bentley Mills, Inc., *see* Interface, Inc.

Bentley Motor Ltd., **21** 435
Bentley's Luggage Corp., **58** 370
Bentoel, PT, **62** 97
Benton International, Inc., **29** 376
Benton Oil and Gas Company, 47 44–46
Bentwood Ltd., **62** 342
Bercy Management *see* Elior SA.
Beresford International plc, **27** 159
Beretta *see* Fabbrica D' Armi Pietro Beretta S.p.A.
Bergdorf Goodman Inc., 52 45–48
Bergen Brunswig Corporation, V 14–16; 13 88–90 (upd.) *see also* AmerisourceBergen Corp.
Berger Associates, Inc., **26** 233
Berger Bros Company, 62 31–33
Berger Manufacturing Company, **26** 405
Bergerat Monnoyeur *see* Groupe Monnoyeur.
Berges electronic GmbH, **56** 357
Beringer Blass Wine Estates Ltd., 22 78–81; 66 34–37 (upd.)
Berisford International plc *see* Enodis plc.
Berjaya Group Bhd., 67 55–57
Berk Corp., **52** 193
Berkeley Farms, Inc., 46 68–70
Berkey Photo Inc., *see* Fuqua Industries, Inc.
Berkley Dean & Co., **15** 525
Berkley Petroleum Corporation, **52** 30
Berkline Corp., **17** 183; **20** 363; **39** 267
Berkshire Hathaway Inc., III 213–15; 18 60–63 (upd.); 42 31–36 (upd.); 89 92–99 (upd.)
Berkshire Realty Holdings, L.P., 49 53–55
Berlex Laboratories, Inc., 66 38–40
BerlinDat Gesellschaft für Informationsverarbeitung und Systemtechnik GmbH, **39** 57
Berliner Kindl Brauerei, **75** 334
Berliner Stadtreinigungsbetriebe, 58 25–28
Berliner Verkehrsbetriebe (BVG), 58 29–31
Berlinwasser Holding AG, 90 58–62
Berlitz International, Inc., 13 91–93; 39 47–50 (upd.)
Berman Brothers Fur Co., **21** 525
Berman Buckskin, **21** 525
Bernard C. Harris Publishing Company, Inc., 39 51–53
Bernard Chaus, Inc., 27 59–61
Bernard Hodes Group Inc., 86 34–37
Bernard Matthews Ltd., 89 100–04
Bernard Warschaw Insurance Sales Agency, Inc., **55** 128
Bernardin Ltd., **30** 39
Berndorf Austria, **44** 206
Berndorf Switzerland, **44** 206
Berner Nut Company, **64** 110
Bernheim-Meyer: A l'Innovation *see* GIB Group.
The Bernick Companies, 75 62–65
Bernina Holding AG, 47 47–50
Bernstein-Rein,92 21–24
Berry Bearing Company, *see* Genuine Parts Co.
The Berry Company *see* L. M. Berry and Company
Berry Petroleum Company, 47 51–53
Berry Plastics Corporation, 21 57–59
Berryhill Nursery *see* Monrovia Nursery Co.
Bertelsmann A.G., IV 592–94; 43 63–67 (upd.); 91 61–68 (upd.)
Bertolini's Authentic Trattorias, **30** 329
Bertram & Graf Gmbh, **28** 45
Bertucci's Corporation, 16 54–56; 64 51–54 (upd.)
Berwick Offray, LLC, 70 17–19
Beryl Corp., **26** 149
Beryllium Resources, *see* Bush Wellman Inc.
Berzelius Umwelt-Service, *see* Metallgesellschaft AG.
Besi, **26** 498
Besix Group S.A./NV, 94 66–69
Besnier SA, 19 49–51 *see also* Groupe Lactalis
Bessemer Capital Partners L.P., **15** 505
Best Kosher Foods Corporation, 82 41–44
Best Buy Co., Inc., 9 65–66; 23 51–53 (upd.); 63 61–66 (upd.)
best energy GmbH, **39** 54, 57
Best Fabric Outlets, **16** 198
Best Holding Corporation *see* Arkansas Best Corp.
Best Manufacturing, **15** 490
Best Read Guides Franchise Corp., **36** 341
BestChoice Administrators, Inc., **51** 276–77
Bestfoods, 22 82–86 (upd.)
Bestform Group Inc., **54** 403
Bestmeat Company, **59** 3, 5
Bestop Inc., *see* Douglas & Lomason Co.
Bestseller A/S, 90 63–66
Bestway Transportation, *see* TNT Freightways Corp.
BET Holdings, Inc., 18 64–66
BETA AIR CJSC, **68** 204
Beta Analytics, Inc., **74** 22
Beth Abraham Family of Health Services, 94 70–74
Beth Israel Medical Center *see* Continuum Health Partners, Inc.
Bethesda Research Laboratories, Inc., *see* Life Technologies, Inc.
Bethlehem Steel Corporation, IV 35–37; 7 48–51 (upd.); 27 62–66 (upd.)
Betriebs- und Baugesellschaft GmbH, **53** 285
Betson Enterprises *see* H. Betti Industries Inc.
Better Brands Ltd., **32** 518–19
Better Made Snack Foods, Inc., 90 67–69
Bettis Corporation, **74** 98
Bettys & Taylors of Harrogate Ltd., 72 30–32
Betz Laboratories, Inc., I 312–13; 10 153–55 (upd.)
Beverage Associates Corp., **67** 317
Beverly Enterprises, Inc., III 76–77; 16 57–59 (upd.)
Bevis Custom Furniture, Inc., *see* Hunt Manufacturing Co.
Bevrachtingskantoor, **26** 280
Bewag AG, 39 54–57
BFC Construction Corporation, 25 63–65
The BFGoodrich Company, V 231–33; 19 52–55 (upd.) *see also* Goodrich Corp.
BFI *see* The British Film Institute; Browning-Ferris Industries, Inc.
BFP Holdings Corp. *see* Big Flower Press Holdings, Inc.
BG Freight Line Holding B.V., **30** 318
BG plc, **29** 104
BG&E *see* Baltimore Gas and Electric Co.
BGITC *see* Baosteel Group International Trade Corp.
BGJ Enterprises, Inc. *see* Brown Printing Co.
Bharti Tele-Ventures Limited, 75 66–68
BHC Communications, Inc., 26 32–34
BHP Billiton, 67 58–64 (upd.)
BHPC Marketing, Inc., **45** 41
Bhs plc, 17 42–44
BHV *see* Bazar de l'Hotel de Ville.
Bi-Lo Inc., *see* Koninklijke Ahold N.V. (Royal Ahold).
Biacore International AB, **25** 377
Bianchi International (d/b/a Gregory Mountain Products), 76 67–69
Bibb Co., **31** 199
Bibliographisches Institut & F.A. Brockhaus AG, 74 30–34
Bibop-Carire S.p.A., **65** 86, 88
BIC Corporation, 8 59–61; 23 54–57 (upd.)
BICC PLC, III 433–34 *see also* Balfour Beatty plc.
BICE Med Grille, **16** 447
Bicoastal Corporation, II 9–11
Bicycle Holding, Inc. *see* United States Playing Card Co.
Bidermann Industries, **41** 129
Biedermann Motech, **37** 112
Biesemeyer Manufacturing Corporation, **26** 363
BIFAB *see* Bibliographisches Institut & A.F. Brockhaus AG.
Biffa plc, 92 25–28
Big A Drug Stores Inc., 79 62–65
Big B, Inc., 17 45–47
Big Bear Stores Co., 13 94–96
Big Brothers Big Sisters of America, 85 29–33
Big D Construction Corporation, **42** 432
Big Dog Holdings, Inc., 45 40–42
Big Entertainment, Inc., **58** 164
Big 5 Sporting Goods Corporation, 55 57–59
Big Flower Press Holdings, Inc., 21 60–62 *see also* Vertis Communications.
Big Fluke Wine Co. *see* Click Wine Group.

The Big Food Group plc, 68 50–53 (upd.)
Big Foot Cattle Co., *see* Vienna Sausage Manufacturing Co.
Big Guns, Inc., **51** 229
Big Horn Mining Co., *see* Peter Kiewit Sons' Inc.
Big Idea Productions, Inc., 49 56–59
Big Lots, Inc., 50 98–101
Big M, *see* P&C Foods Inc.
Big O Tires, Inc., 20 61–63
Big Rivers Electric Corporation, 11 37–39
Big Sky Resort *see* Boyne USA Resorts.
Big Sky Western Bank, **35** 197, 199
Big V Supermarkets, Inc., 25 66–68
Big Y Foods, Inc., 53 66–68
BigBen Interactive S.A., 72 33–35
BigBurger Ltda., **74** 48
Bigelow-Sanford, Inc., **31** 199
BII *see* Banana Importers of Ireland.
Bike Athletics, **23** 449
BIL *see* Brierley Investments.
Bilfinger & Berger AG, I 560–61; 55 60–63 (upd.)
Bill & Melinda Gates Foundation, 41 53–55
Bill Acceptance Corporation Ltd., **48** 427
Bill Barrett Corporation, 71 54–56
Bill Blass Ltd., 32 78–80
Billabong International Ltd., 44 55–58
Billing Concepts, Inc., 26 35–38; 72 36–39 (upd.)
Billiton International, **IV** 532; **22** 237
BillPoint Inc., **58** 266
Bilsom, **40** 96–97
Bilt-Rite Chase-Pitkin, Inc., **41** 416
Biltwell Company, *see* Hartmarx Corp.
Bimar Foods Inc., **19** 192
Bimbo, *see* Grupo Industrial Bimbo.
Bimbo Bakeries USA, **29** 341
Bimbo, S.A., **36** 162, 164
Bin Zayed Group, **55** 54, 56
Binderline Development, Inc., *see* Defiance, Inc.
Bindley Western Industries, Inc., 9 67–69 *see also* Cardinal Health, Inc.
The Bing Group, 60 55–58
Bingham Dana LLP, 43 68–71
Bingo Express Co., Ltd., **64** 290
Bingo King *see* Stuart Entertainment Inc.
Binks Sames Corporation, 21 63–66
Binney & Smith Inc., 25 69–72
Binnie & Partners, **22** 89
Binter Canarias *see* Iberia.
Bio Balance Corporation *see* New York Health Care, Inc.
Bio-Clinic, **11** 486–87
Bio-Dental Technologies Corporation, **46** 466
Bio Foods Inc. *see* Balance Bar Co.
Bio-Rad Laboratories, Inc., 93 82–86
Bio Synthetics, Inc., **21** 386
Biodevelopment Laboratories, Inc., **35** 47
Biogemma, **74** 139
Biogen Idec Inc., 14 58–60; 36 90–93 (upd.); 71 57–59 (upd.)
Bioindustrias, *see* Valores Industriales S.A.
bioKinetics, **64** 18
Biokyowa, *see* Kyowa Hakko Kogyo Co., Ltd.
Biolase Technology, Inc., 87 55–58
bioMérieux S.A., 75 69–71
Biomet, Inc., 10 156–58; 93 87–94 (upd.)
Bionaire, Inc., **19** 360
BioScience Communications, **62** 115
Bioscot, Ltd., **63** 351
Biosite Incorporated, 73 60–62
Biotage, Inc. *see* Dynax.
Biovail Corporation, 47 54–56
BioWare Corporation, 81 50–53
Biralo Pty Ltd., **48** 427
Bird Corporation, 19 56–58
Birdair, Inc., **35** 99–100
Birds Eye Foods, Inc., 69 66–72 (upd.)
Birdsall, Inc. *see* Nicor Inc.
Bireley's, **22** 515
Birkenstock Footprint Sandals, Inc., 12 33–35; 42 37–40 (upd.)
Birmingham & Midland Bank *see* Midland Bank plc.
Birmingham Steel Corporation, 13 97–98; 40 70–73 (upd.) *see also* Nucor Corporation
Birra Peroni S.p.A., **59** 357
Birse Group PLC, 77 54–58
Birthdays Ltd., 70 20–22
Biscayne Bank *see* Banco Espírito Santo e Comercial de Lisboa S.A.
Bishop & Co., *see* First Hawaiian, Inc.
BISSELL, Inc., 9 70–72; 30 75–78 (upd.)
Bisset Gold Mining Company, **63** 182–83
The BISYS Group, Inc., 73 63–65
Bit LLC, **59** 303
Bit Software, Inc., **12** 62
Bitco Corporation, **58** 258
Bits & Pieces, **26** 439
Bitumen & Oil Refineries (Australia) Ltd. *see* Boral Ltd.
Bituminous Casualty Corporation, **58** 258–59
Bivac International, **55** 79
BIW *see* Bath Iron Works.
BIZ Enterprises, **23** 390
Bizarro e Milho, Lda., **64** 91
BizBuyer.com, **39** 25
Bizimgaz Ticaret Ve Sanayi A.S., **55** 346
BJ Services Company, 25 73–75
BJ's Pizza & Grill, **44** 85
BJ's Restaurant & Brewhouse, **44** 85
BJ's Wholesale Club, Inc., 94 75–78
BJK&E *see* Bozell Worldwide Inc.
BK Tag, **28** 157
BK Vision AG, **52** 357
BL Systems *see* AT&T Istel Ltd.
BL Universal PLC, **47** 168
The Black & Decker Corporation, III 435–37; 20 64–68 (upd.); 67 65–70 (upd.)
Black & Veatch LLP, 22 87–90
Black Box Corporation, 20 69–71
Black Clawson Company, *see* Thermo Fibertek, Inc.
Black Diamond Equipment, Ltd., 62 34–37
Black Entertainment Television *see* BET Holdings, Inc.
Black Hills Corporation, 20 72–74
Black Horse Agencies, *see* Lloyds TSB Group plc.
Black Pearl Software, Inc., **39** 396
Blackbaud, Inc., 85 34–37
BlackBerry *see* Research in Motion Ltd.
Blackboard Inc., 89 105–10
Blackfoot Telecommunications Group, 60 59–62
Blackhawk Holdings, Inc. *see* PW Eagle Inc.
BlackRock, Inc., 79 66–69
Blacks Leisure Group plc, 39 58–60
Blackstone Dredging Partners LP, **69** 197
The Blackstone Group, L.P., **IV** 718; **11** 177, 179; **22** 416; **26** 408; **37** 309, 311; **61** 208; **69** 101, 103; **75** 378
Blackwater USA, 76 70–73
Blackwell Publishing (Holdings) Ltd., 78 34–37
Blaine Construction Company *see* The Yates Companies, Inc.
Blair Corporation, 25 76–78; 31 53–55
Blakeman's Floor Care Parts & Equipment *see* Tacony Corp.
Blandburgh Ltd., **63** 77
Blanes, S.A. de C.V., **34** 197
BLD Europe, **16** 168
Blendax, *see* The Procter & Gamble Company
Blessings Corp., 19 59–61
Blimpie International, Inc., 15 55–57; 49 60–64 (upd.)
Bliss Manufacturing Co., *see* HMI Industries, Inc.
Blizzard Entertainment, 78 38–42
Bloch & Guggenheimer, Inc., **40** 51–52
Block Communications, Inc., 81 54–58
Block Drug Company, Inc., 8 62–64; 27 67–70 (upd.) *see also* GlaxoSmithKline plc.
Block Management, **29** 226
Block Medical, Inc., *see* Hillenbrand Industries, Inc.
Blockbuster Inc., 9 73–75; 31 56–60 (upd.); 76 74–78 (upd.)
Blodgett Holdings, Inc., 61 34–37 (upd.)
Blohm Maschinenbau GmbH, **60** 193
Blokker Holding B.V., 84 21–24
Blonder Tongue Laboratories, Inc., 48 52–55
Bloomberg L.P., 21 67–71
Bloomingdale's Inc., 12 36–38
Blount International, Inc., 12 39–41; 48 56–60 (upd.)
Blow-ko Ltd., **60** 372
BLP Group Companies *see* Boron, LePore & Associates, Inc.
BLT Ventures, **25** 270
Blue, **62** 115
Blue Arrow PLC, **9** 327; **30** 300
Blue Bell Creameries L.P., 30 79–81
Blue Bell Mattress Company, **58** 63

Blue Bird Corporation, **35 63–66**
Blue Bunny Ice Cream *see* Wells' Dairy, Inc.
Blue Byte, **41** 409
Blue Chip Stamps, **30** 412
Blue Circle Industries PLC, **III 669–71** *see also* Lafarge Cement UK.
Blue Coat Systems, Inc., **83 42–45**
Blue Cross and Blue Shield Association, **10 159–61**
Blue Cross and Blue Shield Mutual of Northern Ohio, **12** 176
Blue Cross and Blue Shield of Greater New York, *see* Empire Blue Cross & Blue Shield.
Blue Cross and Blue Shield of Minnesota, **65** 41–42
Blue Cross and Blue Shield of Ohio, **15** 114
Blue Cross of California, *see* WellPoint Health Networks Inc.
Blue Cross of Northeastern New York, *see* Empire Blue Cross & Blue Shield.
Blue Diamond Growers, **28 56–58**
Blue Dot Services, **37** 280, 283
Blue Heron Paper Company, **90 70–73**
Blue Line Distributing, *see* Little Caesar Enterprises, Inc.
Blue Martini Software, Inc., **59 77–80**
Blue Mountain Arts, Inc., **29 63–66**
Blue Mountain Springs Ltd., **48** 97
Blue Nile Inc., **61 38–40**
Blue Rhino Corporation, **56 34–37**
Blue Ribbon Packing Company, **57** 57
Blue Ridge Beverage Company Inc., **82 45–48**
Blue Ribbon Sports *see* Nike, Inc.
Blue Ridge Lumber Ltd., **16** 11
Blue Square Israel Ltd., **41 56–58**
Blue Tee Corporation, **23** 34, 36
Bluefly, Inc., **60 63–65**
Bluegreen Corporation, **80 29–32**
BlueScope Steel Limited, **62** 55
Bluewin AG, **58** 337
Blumberg Communications Inc., **24** 96
Blundstone Pty Ltd., **76 79–81**
Blyth, Inc., **18 67–69**; **74 35–38 (upd.)**
BM-Telecom, **59** 303
BMB Specialty Co., **74** 202
BMC Forestry Corporation, **58** 23
BMC Industries, Inc., **17 48–51**; **59 81–86 (upd.)**
BMC Real Estate, Inc., **62** 55
BMC Software, Inc., **55 64–67**
bmd wireless AG, **63** 204
BMG/Music *see* Bertelsmann AG.
BMHC *see* Building Materials Holding Corp.
BMI *see* Broadcast Music Inc.
BMI Systems Inc., **12** 174
BMML, Confecçoes, Lda., **64** 91
BMO Nesbitt Burns, **46** 55
BMS Laboratories Ltd., **59** 168
BMW *see* Bayerische Motoren Werke.
BNA *see* Banca Nazionale dell'Agricoltura; Bureau of National Affairs, Inc.
BNCI *see* Banque Nationale Pour le Commerce et l'Industrie.
BNE *see* Bank of New England Corp.
BNE Land & Development, **68** 54, 56
BNG, Inc., **19** 487
BNL *see* Banca Nazionale del Lavoro S.p.A.
BNP Paribas Group, **36 94–97 (upd.)**
BNS Acquisitions, **26** 247
Boa Shoe Company, **42** 325
Oy Board International AB, **56** 255
Boardwalk Pipeline Partners, LP, **87 59–62**
Boart Longyear Company, **26 39–42**
Boatmen's Bancshares Inc., **15 58–60** *see also* Bank of America Corp.
BoatsDirect.com, **37** 398
Bob Evans Farms, Inc., **9 76–79**; **63 67–72 (upd.)**
Bob's Red Mill Natural Foods, Inc., **63 73–75**
Bobbie Brooks Inc., *see* Pubco Corp.
Bobit Publishing Company, **55 68–70**
Bobro Products *see* BWP Distributors.
Bobs Candies, Inc., **70 23–25**
BOC Group plc, **I 314–16**; **25 79–82 (upd.)**; **78 43–49 (upd.)**
Boca Resorts, Inc., **37 33–36**
BOCAP Corp., **37** 372
BOCM Fish Feed Group, **56** 257
BOCOM International, **71** 366, 368
Boddie-Noell Enterprises, Inc., **68 54–56**
Boddington, **21** 247
Bodegas y Vinedos Penaflor S.A. *see* Penaflor S.A.
Bodum Design Group AG, **47 57–59**
Body Glove International LLC, **88 29–32**
The Body Shop International plc, **11 40–42**; **53 69–72 (upd.)**
Bodycote International PLC, **63 76–78**
Boehringer Gastro Profi, **60** 364
Boehringer Ingelheim GmbH *see* C.H. Boehringer Sohn.
Boehringer Mannheim Companies, **37** 111–12
The Boeing Company, **I 47–49**; **10 162–65 (upd.)**; **32 81–87 (upd.)**
Bogen Communications International, Inc., **62 38–41**
Bohemia, Inc., **13 99–101**
BÖHLER-UDDEHOLM AG, **73 66–69**
Boiron S.A., **73 70–72**
Boise Cascade Corporation, **IV 255–56**; **8 65–67 (upd.)**; **32 88–92 (upd.)**
Boizel Chanoine Champagne S.A., **94 79–82**
Bokma Distillateurs BV, **74** 41
Bolands Ltd., *see* Oshawa Group Ltd.
Boley G.m.b.H., **21** 123
Boliden AB, **80 33–36**
Bollinger Shipyards, Inc., **61 41–43**
Bollore, S.A., **65** 266–67
Bols Distilleries NV, **74 39–42**
Bolsa Mexicana de Valores, S.A. de C.V., **80 37–40**
BolsWessanen N.V. *see* Koninklijke Wessanen nv.
Bolt, Beranek & Newman Inc., **26** 520
Bolt Security, **32** 373
Bolthouse Farms, Inc., **54** 257
Bolton Group B.V., **86 38–41**
BOMAG, *see* United Dominion Industries Ltd.
Bombadier Defence Services UK, **41** 412
Bombardier Aerospace Group, **36** 190–91
Bombardier Inc., **42 41–46 (upd.)**; **87 63–71 (upd.)**
The Bombay Company, Inc., **10 166–68**; **71 60–64 (upd.)**
Bon Appetit Holding AG, **48 61–63**
Bon Dente International Inc., **39** 320
The Bon Marché, Inc., **23 58–60** *see also* Federated Department Stores Inc.
Bon Secours Health System, Inc., **24 68–71**
The Bon-Ton Stores, Inc., **16 60–62**; **50 106–10 (upd.)**
Bonanza Steakhouse, *see* Metromedia Co.
Bonaventura, **IV** 611
Bond Brewing International, **23** 405
Bond Corporation Holdings Limited, **10 169–71**
Bondex International, *see* RPM Inc.
Bonduelle SA, **51 52–54**
Bongard *see* Aga Foodservice Group PLC.
Bongrain SA, **25 83–85**
Bonhams 1793 Ltd., **72 40–42**
Bonneville International Corporation, **29 67–70**
Bonneville Power Administration, **50 102–05**
Bonnie Plant Farm, **63** 21
Bonnier AB, **52 49–52**
Bontrager Bicycles, **16** 495
Bonwit Teller, **17** 43; **54** 304–05
Book-Mart Press, Inc., **41** 111
Book-of-the-Month Club, Inc., **13 105–07**
Booker plc, **13 102–04**; **31 61–64 (upd.)**
Booker Cash & Carry Ltd., **68 57–61 (upd.)**
Booklink Technologies, **26** 19
Books-A-Million, Inc., **14 61–62**; **41 59–62 (upd.)**
Books Are Fun, Ltd. *see* The Reader's Digest Association, Inc.
Bookspan, **86 42–46**
Boole & Babbage, Inc., **25 86–88** *see also* BMC Software, Inc.
Booth Bay, Ltd., **16** 37
Booth Creek Ski Holdings, Inc., **31 65–67**
Bootprint Entertainment, **31** 240
The Boots Company PLC, **V 17–19**; **24 72–76 (upd.)** *see also* Alliance Boots plc.
Boots & Coots International Well Control, Inc., **79 70–73**
Booz Allen & Hamilton Inc., **10 172–75**
Boplan Ingénierie S.A.S. *see* SNC-Lavalin Group Inc.
Boral Limited, **III 672–74**; **43 72–76 (upd.)**

Borden, Inc., II 470–73; 22 91–96 (upd.)
Border Fine Arts, **11** 95
Border Television, **41** 352
Borders Group, Inc., 15 61–62; 43 77–79 (upd.)
Borders, Perrin and Norrander, **23** 480
Borealis AG, 94 83–86
Borg Instruments, **23** 494
Borg-Warner Australia, **47** 280
Borg-Warner Automotive, Inc., 14 63–66; 32 93–97 (upd.)
Borg-Warner Corporation, III 438–41 *see also* Burns International.
BorgWarner Inc., 85 38–44 (upd.)
Borland International, Inc., 9 80–82
Borneo Airways *see* Malaysian Airlines System BHD.
Boron, LePore & Associates, Inc., 45 43–45
Borregaard Osterreich AG, *see* Orkla ASA.
Borror Corporation *see* Dominion Homes, Inc.
Borsheim's, *see* Berkshire Hathaway Inc.
Bosch *see* Robert Bosch GmbH.
Boscov's Department Store, Inc., 31 68–70
Bose Corporation, 13 108–10; 36 98–101 (upd.)
Bosert Industrial Supply *see* W.W. Grainger, Inc.
Bossa, **55** 188
Bost Sports Clubs *see* Town Sports International, Inc.
Boston Acoustics, Inc., 22 97–99
The Boston Beer Company, Inc., 18 70–73; 50 111–15 (upd.)
Boston Celtics Limited Partnership, 14 67–69
Boston Chicken, Inc., 12 42–44 *see also* Boston Market Corp.
The Boston Consulting Group, 58 32–35
Boston Edison Company, 12 45–47
Boston Gas Company *see* Eastern Enterprises.
Boston Globe, *see* Affiliated Publications, Inc.
Boston Market Corporation, 48 64–67 (upd.)
Boston Pizza International Inc., 88 33–38
Boston Popcorn Co., **27** 197–98; **43** 218
Boston Professional Hockey Association Inc., 39 61–63
Boston Properties, Inc., 22 100–02
Boston Scientific Corporation, 37 37–40; 77 58–63 (upd.)
The Boston Symphony Orchestra Inc., 93 95–99
Boston Technology, **43** 117
Boston Ventures Management, Inc., **27** 41, 393; **65** 374
Boston Whaler, Inc. *see* Reebok International Ltd.
Bostrom Seating, Inc., **23** 306
BOTAS *see* Türkiye Petrolleri Anonim Ortakliği.
Boticas Fasa S.A., **72** 128
Botswana General Insurance Company, **22** 495
Bott SA, **72** 221
Bottu, **II** 475
BOTWEB, Inc., **39** 95
Bou-Matic, 62 42–44
Bougainville Copper Pty., **IV** 60–61
Boulanger, **37** 22
Boulder Creek Steaks & Saloon, **16** 447
Boulet Dru DuPuy Petit Group *see* Wells Rich Greene BDDP.
Boulton & Paul Ltd., **31** 398–400
Boundary Gas Inc., **6** 457; **54** 260
Bountiful Psychiatric Hospital, Inc., **68** 299
Boundary Healthcare, **12** 327
Bourbon *see* Groupe Bourbon S.A.
Bourjois, *see* Chanel.
Bourbon Corporation, 82 49-52
Bouverat Industries, **51** 36
Bouwmar N.V., **68** 64
Bouygues S.A., I 562–64; 24 77–80 (upd.)
Bovis, *see* Peninsular and Oriental Steam Navigation Company (Bovis Division)
Bovis Construction, **38** 344–45
Bovis Lend Lease, **52** 222
Bow Bangles, *see* Claire's Stores, Inc.
Bow Flex of America, Inc. *see* Direct Focus, Inc.
Bow Valley Energy Inc., **47** 397
Bowater PLC, IV 257–59
Bowdens Media Monitoring Ltd., **55** 289
Bowers and Merena Galleries Inc., **48** 99
Bowes Co., *see* George Weston Ltd.
Bowling Green Wholesale, Inc. *see* Houchens Industries Inc.
Bowman Gum, Inc., **13** 520
Bowne & Co., Inc., 23 61–64; 79 74–80 (upd.)
Bowthorpe plc, 33 70–72
The Boy Scouts of America, 34 66–69
Boyd Bros. Transportation Inc., 39 64–66
Boyd Coffee Company, 53 73–75
Boyd Gaming Corporation, 43 80–82
The Boyds Collection, Ltd., 29 71–73
Boyer Brothers, Inc., **14** 17–18
Boyer's International, Inc., **20** 83
Boyles Bros. Drilling Company *see* Christensen Boyles Corp.
Boyne USA Resorts, 71 65–68
Boys & Girls Clubs of America, 69 73–75
Bozell, Jacobs, Kenyon, and Eckhardt Inc. *see* True North Communications Inc.
Bozell Worldwide Inc., 25 89–91
Bozkurt, **27** 188
Bozzuto's, Inc., 13 111–12
BP Canada *see* Talisman Energy Inc.
BP p.l.c., 45 46–56 (upd.)
BPB plc, 83 46-49
BPI Communications, Inc., **7** 15; **19** 285; **27** 500; **61** 241
BR *see* British Rail.
Braathens ASA, 47 60–62
Brabants Dagblad BV, *see* N.V. AMEV.
Brach's Confections, Inc., 15 63–65; 74 43–46 (upd.)
Braden Manufacturing, **23** 299–301
Bradford & Bingley PLC, 65 77–80
Bradford Exchange Ltd. Inc., **21** 269
Bradington-Young LLC *see* Hooker Furniture
Bradlees Discount Department Store Company, 12 48–50
Bradley Air Services Ltd., 56 38–40
Bradley Lumber Company, *see* Potlatch Corp.
Bradstreet Co. *see* The Dun & Bradstreet Corp.
Brady Corporation, 78 50–55 (upd.)
Bragussa, **IV** 71
Braine L'Alleud Bricolage BV, **68** 64
BRAINS *see* Belgian Rapid Access to Information Network Services.
Brake Bros plc, 45 57–59
BRAL Reststoff-Bearbeitungs-GmbH, **58** 28
Bramac Dachsysteme International GmbH, **70** 363
Bramalea Ltd., 9 83–85
Brambles Industries Limited, 42 47–50
Brammer PLC, 77 64–67
The Branch Group, Inc., 72 43–45
Brand Companies, Inc., *see* Chemical Waste Management, Inc.
Branded Restaurant Group, Inc., *see* Oscar Mayer Foods Corp.
Brandeis & Sons, **19** 511
BrandPartners Group, Inc., 58 36–38
Brandt Zwieback-Biskuits GmbH, **44** 40
Brandywine Asset Management, Inc., **33** 261
Brandywine Holdings Ltd., **45** 109
Brandywine Valley Railroad Co., *see* Lukens Inc.
Braniff Airlines, **36** 231
Brannock Device Company, 48 68–70
Brascan Corporation, 67 71–73
Brasfield & Gorrie LLC, 87 72–75
Brasil Telecom Participaçoes S.A., 57 67–70
Brass-Craft Manufacturing Co. *see* Masco Corp.
Brass Eagle Inc., 34 70–72
Braud & Faucheux *see* Manitou BF S.A.
Brauerei Beck & Co., 9 86–87; 33 73–76 (upd.)
Braun GmbH, 51 55–58
Brauns Fashions Corporation *see* Christopher & Banks Corp.
Brazcot Limitada, **53** 344
Brazil Fast Food Corporation, 74 47–49
Brazos Gas Compressing, *see* Mitchell Energy and Development Corp.
Brazos Sportswear, Inc., 23 65–67
Bredel Exploitatie B.V., *see* United Dominion Industries Ltd.
Breed Corp., **63** 224
Breg, Inc. *see* Orthofix International NV.
Bremer Financial Corp., 45 60–63
Brenntag AG, 8 68–69; 23 68–70 (upd.)
Brent Walker Ltd., **49** 450–51
Brentwood Acquisition, Inc., **68** 299

Brentwood Associates Buyout Fund II LP, **44** 54
Brentwood Corporation, **61** 398
Bresler's Industries, Inc., **35** 121
Bresser Optik, **41** 264
Brewster Lines, **6** 410
Breyers Ice Cream Co. *see* Good Humor-Breyers.
BRI International *see* Quintiles Transnational Corporation
Briazz, Inc., 53 76–79
The Brickman Group, Ltd., 87 76–79
Bricorama S.A., 68 62–64
Bricotruc, **37** 259
Bridel, **19** 49–50; **25** 85
Bridge Communications Inc., **34** 442–43
The Bridge Group, **55** 41
Bridgeport Machines, Inc., 17 52–54
Bridgestone Americas Holding Inc., **64** 133
Bridgestone Corporation, V 234–35; 21 72–75 (upd.); 59 87–92 (upd.)
BridgeStreet Corporate Housing Worldwide Inc., **58** 194
Bridgewater Properties, Inc., **51** 229
Bridgeway Plan for Health, **6** 186
Bridgford Company, **13** 382
Bridgford Foods Corporation, 27 71–73
Brierly Investment Limited, **19** 156
Briggs & Stratton Corporation, 8 70–73; 27 74–78 (upd.)
Brigham Exploration Company, 75 72–74
Brigham's Inc., 72 46–48
Bright Horizons Family Solutions, Inc., 31 71–73
Bright of America Inc., **12** 426
Bright Star Technologies, **13** 92; **15** 455; **41** 362
Brighter Vision Learning Adventures, **29** 470, 472
Brighton & Hove Bus and Coach Company, **28** 155–56
Brightpoint, Inc., 18 74–77
Brightwork Development Inc., **25** 348
Briker, **23** 231
Brillianty Alrosa, **62** 9
Brillion Iron Works Inc., **23** 306
Brillstein-Grey Entertainment, 80 41–45
Brin's Oxygen Company Limited *see* BOC Group plc.
The Brink's Company, 58 39–43 (upd.)
Brinker International, Inc., 10 176–78; 38 100–03 (upd.); 75 75–79 (upd.)
Brinson Partners Inc., **41** 198
BRIO AB, 24 81–83
Brio Technology, **25** 97
Brioche Pasquier S.A., 58 44–46
Briones Alonso y Martin, **42** 19
Brioni Roman Style S.p.A., 67 74–76
BRISA Auto-estradas de Portugal S.A., 64 55–58
Brisco Engineering, **41** 412
Bristol Gaming Corporation, **21** 298
Bristol Hotel Company, 23 71–73
Bristol-Myers Squibb Company, III 17–19; 9 88–91 (upd.); 37 41–45 (upd.)
Bristow Helicopters Ltd., 70 26–28
Britannia Soft Drinks Ltd. (Britvic), 71 69–71
Britannica Software, *see* Encyclopaedia Britannica, Inc.
Britannica.com, *see* Encyclopaedia Britannica, Inc.
Britches of Georgetowne, *see* CML Group, Inc.
BRITE *see* Granada Group PLC.
Brite Voice Systems, Inc., 20 75–78
BriteSmile, Inc., **35** 325
British Aerospace plc, I 50–53; 24 84–90 (upd.)
British Airways plc, I 92–95; 14 70–74 (upd.); 43 83–88 (upd.)
British American Cosmetics, **I** 427
British American Financial Services, **42** 450
British American Tobacco PLC, 50 116–19 (upd.)
British and Foreign Steam Navigation Company, **23** 160
British and North American Royal Mail Steam Packet Company *see* Cunard Line Ltd.
British-Borneo Oil & Gas PLC, 34 73–75
British Broadcasting Corporation Ltd., 7 52–55; 21 76–79 (upd.); 89 111–17 (upd.)
British Bus Group Limited, **69** 43
British Coal Corporation, IV 38–40
British Columbia Packers, *see* George Weston Ltd.
British Columbia Telephone Company, 6 309–11
British Data Management, Ltd., **33** 212, 214
British Electric Traction Company *see* Rentokil Initial Plc.
British Energy Plc, 49 65–68 *see also* British Nuclear Fuels PLC.
British European Airways *see* Jersey European Airways (UK) Ltd.
The British Film Institute, 80 46–50
British Gas plc, V 559–63 *see also* Centrica plc.
British Home Stores PLC *see* Storehouse PLC.
British Independent Television Enterprises Ltd. *see* Granada Group PLC.
British Insulated Callender's Cables Limited *see* BICC PLC
British Interactive Broadcasting Ltd., **20** 79
British Land Plc, 54 38–41
British Leyland Motor Corporation, *see* Jaguar Cars Ltd.
British Linen Bank, *see* The Governor and Company of the Bank of Scotland.
British Midland plc, 38 104–06
The British Museum, 71 72–74
British Nuclear Fuels PLC, 6 451–54
British Oxygen Co *see* BOC Group.
The British Petroleum Company plc, IV 378–80; 7 56–59 (upd.); 21 80–84 (upd.) *see also* BP p.l.c.
British Printing and Communications Corp., *see* Maxwell Communication Corp. plc.
British Railways Board, V 421–24
British Shoe Corporation *see* Sears plc.
British Sky Broadcasting Group plc, 20 79–81; 60 66–69 (upd.)
British Steel plc, IV 41–43; 19 62–65 (upd.)
British Sugar plc, 84 25–29
British Telecommunications plc, V 279–82; 15 66–70 (upd.) *see also* BT Group plc.
British Thermoplastics and Rubber *see* BTR plc.
British Trimmings Ltd., **29** 133
British Twin Disc Ltd., **21** 504
The British United Provident Association Limited, 79 81–84
British Vita plc, 9 92–93; 33 77–79 (upd.)
British World Airlines Ltd., 18 78–80
Britt Lumber Co., Inc., *see* MAXXAM Inc.
Britvic Soft Drinks Limited *see* Britannia Soft Drinks Ltd. (Britvic)
BritWill Healthcare Corp., **25** 504
BRK Brands, Inc., **28** 134
Bro-Well, *see* Broughton Foods Co.
Broad River Power Company, **6** 575
Broadband Networks Inc., **36** 352
Broadbandtalentneet.com, **44** 164
Broadbase Software, Inc., **51** 181
Broadcast Music Inc., 23 74–77; 90 74–79 (upd.)
Broadcaster Press, **36** 341
Broadcom Corporation, 34 76–79; 90 80–85 (upd.)
Broadcom Eireann Research, *see* eircom plc.
Broadgate Property Holdings Limited, **54** 40
The Broadmoor Hotel, 30 82–85
BroadVision Inc., **38** 432
Broadway & Seymour Inc., **18** 112
Broadway.com, **58** 167
Broadway Stores, Inc., **31** 193
Broadwing Corporation, 70 29–32
Brobeck, Phleger & Harrison, LLP, 31 74–76
Brock Candy Company *see* Brach and Brock Confections, Inc.
Brockhaus *see* Bibliographisches Institut & F.A. Brockhaus AG.
Brockway Glass Co., **15** 128
Brockway Standard Holdings Corporation *see* BWAY Corp.
Brodart Company, 84 30–33
Broder Bros. Co., 38 107–09
Broderbund Software, Inc., 13 113–16; 29 74–78 (upd.)
Les broderies Lesage, **49** 83
Brok SA, **54** 315, 317
Broken Hill Proprietary Company Ltd., IV 44–47; 22 103–08 (upd.) *see also* BHP Billiton.
Bronco Drilling Company, Inc., 89 118–21

Bronner Brothers Inc., 92 29–32
Bronner Display & Sign Advertising, Inc., 82 53-57
Bronson Laboratories, Inc., **34** 460
Bronson Pharmaceuticals, **24** 257
Brookdale Senior Living, 91 69–73
Brooke Bond, **32** 475
Brooke Group Ltd., 15 71–73 *see also* Vector Group Ltd.
Brooke Partners L.P., **11** 275
Brookfield International Inc., **35** 388
Brookfield Properties Corporation, 89 122–25
Brooklyn Union Gas, 6 455–57 *see also* KeySpan Energy Co.
Brooks Brothers Inc., 22 109–12
Brooks Fashion, **29** 164
Brooks Sports Inc., 32 98–101
Brookshire Grocery Company, 16 63–66; 74 50–53 (upd.)
Brookstone, Inc., 18 81–83
Brose Fahrzeugteile GmbH & Company KG, 84 34–38
Brother Industries, Ltd., 14 75–76
Brother International, **23** 212
Brother's Brother Foundation, 93 100–04
Brothers Gourmet Coffees, Inc., 20 82–85 *see also* The Procter & Gamble Co.
Brotherton Chemicals, **29** 113
Brotherton Speciality Products Ltd., **68** 81
Broughton Foods Co., 17 55–57 *see also* Suiza Foods Corp.
Brouwerijen Alken-Maes N.V., 86 47–51
Brown & Brown, Inc., 41 63–66
Brown & Haley, 23 78–80
Brown & Root, Inc., 13 117–19 *see also* Kellogg Brown & Root Inc.
Brown & Sharpe Manufacturing Co., 23 81–84
Brown and Williamson Tobacco Corporation, 14 77–79; 33 80–83 (upd.)
Brown Boveri *see* BBC Brown Boveri.
Brown Brothers Harriman & Co., 45 64–67
Brown Cow West Corporation, **55** 360
Brown-Forman Corporation, I 225–27; 10 179–82 (upd.); 38 110–14 (upd.)
Brown Group, Inc., V 351–53; 20 86–89 (upd.) *see also* Brown Shoe Company, Inc.
Brown Institute, **45** 87
Brown Jordan International Inc., 74 54–57 (upd.)
Brown Printing Company, 26 43–45
Brown Shipbuilding Company *see* Brown & Root, Inc.
Brown, Shipley & Co., Limited, **45** 65
Brown Shoe Company, Inc., 68 65–69 (upd.)
Browning-Ferris Industries, Inc., V 749–53; 20 90–93 (upd.)
Browning International, **58** 147
Broyhill Furniture Industries, Inc., 10 183–85
BRS Ltd. *see* Ecel plc.
Bruce Foods Corporation, 39 67–69
Bruce Power LP, **49** 65, 67
Bruckmann, Rosser, Sherill & Co., **40** 51 *see also* Jitney-Jungle Stores of America, Inc.; Lazy Days RV Center, Inc.
Bruegger's Corporation, 63 79–82
Brugman, *see* Vorwerk & Co.
Bruno's Supermarkets, Inc., 7 60–62; 26 46–48 (upd.); 68 70–73 (upd.)
Brunswick Corporation, III 442–44; 22 113–17 (upd.); 77 68–75 (upd.)
Brunswick Mining, **64** 297
Brush Electrical Machines, *see* Hawker Siddeley Group PLC.
Brush Engineered Materials Inc., 67 77–79
Brush Wellman Inc., 14 80–82
Bruster's Real Ice Cream, Inc., 80 51–54
Bruxeland S.P.R.L., **64** 91
Brylane Inc., **29** 106–07; **64** 232
Bryn Mawr Stereo & Video, **30** 465
BSA *see* The Boy Scouts of America.
BSC *see* Birmingham Steel Corporation; British Steel Corp.
BSH Bosch und Siemens Hausgeräte GmbH, 67 80–84
BSkyB, **IV** 653; **29** 369, 371; **34** 85
BSN Groupe S.A., II 474–75 *see also* Groupe Danone
BSN Medical, **41** 374, 377
BT Group plc, 49 69–74 (upd.)
BTG, Inc., 45 68–70
BTG Plc, 87 80–83
BTM *see* British Tabulating Machine Co.
BTR Dunlop Holdings, Inc., **21** 432
BTR plc, I 428–30
BTR Siebe plc, 27 79–81 *see also* Invensys PLC.
B2B Initiatives Ltd. *see* O.C. Tanner Co.
Bubbles Salon *see* Ratner Companies.
Bublitz Case Company, **55** 151
Buca, Inc., 38 115–17
Buck Consultants, Inc., 55 71–73
Buck Knives Inc., 48 71–74
Buckaroo International *see* Bugle Boy Industries, Inc.
Buckbee-Mears Company *see* BMC Industries, Inc.
Buckeye Partners, L.P., 70 33–36
Buckeye Technologies, Inc., 42 51–54
Buckhorn, Inc., *see* Myers Industries, Inc.
The Buckle, Inc., 18 84–86
BUCON, Inc., **62** 55
Bucyrus International, Inc., 17 58–61
Bud Bailey Construction, **43** 400
The Budd Company, 8 74–76 *see also* ThyssenKrupp AG.
Buderus AG, 37 46–49
Budgens Ltd., 59 93–96
Budget Group, Inc., 25 92–94 *see also* Cendant Corp.
Budget Rent a Car Corporation, 9 94–95
Budgetel Inn *see* Marcus Corp.
Budweiser Budvar, National Corporation, 59 97–100
Budweiser Japan Co., **21** 320
Buena Vista Home Video *see* The Walt Disney Co.
Buena Vista Music Group, **44** 164
Bufete Industrial, S.A. de C.V., 34 80–82
Buffalo Grill S.A., 94 87–90
Buffalo News, see Berkshire Hathaway Inc.
Buffalo Paperboard, **19** 78
Buffalo Wild Wings, Inc., 56 41–43
Buffets Holdings, Inc., 10 186–87; 32 102–04 (upd.); 93 105–09 (upd.)
Bugaboo Creek Steak House Inc., **19** 342
Bugatti Automobiles S.A.S., 94 91–94
Bugle Boy Industries, Inc., 18 87–88
Buhrmann NV, 41 67–69
Buick Motor Co. *see* General Motors Corp.
Build-A-Bear Workshop Inc., 62 45–48
Builders Concrete *see* Vicat S.A.
Builders Square *see* Kmart Corp.
Building Materials Holding Corporation, 52 53–55
Building One Services Corporation *see* Encompass Services Corp.
Building Products of Canada Limited, **25** 232
Buitoni SpA, *see* Nestlé S.A.
Bulgari S.p.A., 20 94–97
Bull *see* Compagnie des Machines Bull S.A.
Bull S.A., 43 89–91 (upd.)
Bulletin Broadfaxing Network Inc., **67** 257
Bulley & Andrews, LLC, 55 74–76
Bullock's, **31** 191
Bulova Corporation, 13 120–22; 41 70–73 (upd.)
Bumble Bee Seafoods L.L.C., 64 59–61
Bundall Computers Pty Limited, **56** 155
Bundy Corporation, 17 62–65
Bunge Ltd., 62 49–51
Bunzl plc, IV 260–62; 31 77–80 (upd.)
Burbank Aircraft Supply, Inc., **14** 42–43; **37** 29, 31
Burberry Group plc, 17 66–68; 41 74–76 (upd.); 92 33–37 (upd.)
Burda Holding GmbH. & Co., 23 85–89
Burdines, Inc., 60 70–73
Bureau de Recherches de Pétrole, **21** 203–04
The Bureau of National Affairs, Inc., 23 90–93
Bureau Veritas SA, 55 77–79
Burelle S.A., 23 94–96
Burger King Corporation, II 613–15; 17 69–72 (upd.); 56 44–48 (upd.)
Burgess, Anderson & Tate Inc., *see* U.S. Office Products Co.
Burgundy Ltd., **68** 53
Bürhle, **17** 36; **50** 78
Burhmann-Tetterode, **22** 154
Buriot International, Inc., **53** 236
The Burke Company, *see* Tridel Enterprises Inc.
Burke, Inc., 88 39–42
Burke Mills, Inc., 66 41–43

BURLE Industries Inc., *see* Sensormatic Electronics Corp.
Burlington Coat Factory Warehouse Corporation, 10 188–89; 60 74–76 (upd.)
Burlington Industries, Inc., V 354–55; 17 73–76 (upd.)
Burlington Motor Holdings, **30** 114
Burlington Northern Santa Fe Corporation, V 425–28; 27 82–89 (upd.)
Burlington Resources Inc., 10 190–92 *see also* ConocoPhillips.
Burmah Castrol PLC, IV 381–84; 30 86–91 (upd.) *see also* BP p.l.c.
Burndy, **19** 166
Burney Mountain Power, **64** 95
Burns & Ricker, Inc., **40** 51, 53
Burns & Wilcox Ltd., **6** 290
Burns-Alton Corp., **21** 154–55
Burns International Security Services, 13 123–25 *see also* Securitas AB.
Burns International Services Corporation, 41 77–80 (upd.)
Burns Lumber Company, Inc., **61** 254, 256
Burns, Philp & Company Ltd., 63 83–86
Burnup & Sims, Inc., **26** 324
Burpee & Co. *see* W. Atlee Burpee & Co.
Burr-Brown Corporation, 19 66–68
Burris Industries, **14** 303; **50** 311
Burroughs & Chapin Company, Inc., 86 52–55
Burroughs Corp. *see* Unisys Corp.
Burt's Bees, Inc., 58 47–50
The Burton Corporation, V 20–22; 94 95–100 (upd.)
The Burton Group plc, *see also* Arcadia Group plc.
Burton Rubber Processing, *see* M. A. Hanna Co.
Burton Snowboards Inc., 22 118–20, 460
Burtons Gold Medal Biscuits Limited, *see* Associated British Foods plc.
Busch Entertainment Corporation, 73 73–75
Bush Boake Allen Inc., 30 92–94 *see also* International Flavors & Fragrances Inc.
Bush Brothers & Company, 45 71–73
Bush Hog, **21** 20–22
Bush Industries, Inc., 20 98–100
Bush Terminal Company, **15** 138
Business Communications Group, Inc. *see* Caribiner International, Inc.
The Business Depot, Ltd., **10** 498; **55** 353
Business Express Airlines, Inc., **28** 22
Business Information Technology, Inc., *see* Ciber, Inc.
Business Men's Assurance Company of America, 14 83–85
Business Objects S.A., 25 95–97
Business Post Group plc, 46 71–73
Business Resources Corp., **23** 489, 491
Business Software Association, **10** 35
Business Software Technology, *see* Legent Corp.
Business Wire, **25** 240
Businessland Inc., **6** 267
Buster Brown & Company *see* Brown Shoe Company, Inc.
BUT S.A., *see* Kingfisher plc.
Butler Bros., **21** 96
Butler Cox PLC, **6** 229
Butler Group, Inc., **30** 310–11
Butler Manufacturing Company, 12 51–53; 62 52–56 (upd.)
Butterfield & Butterfield *see* eBay Inc.
Butterfield & Swire *see* Swire Pacific Ltd.
Butterick Co., Inc., 23 97–99
Buttrey Food & Drug Stores Co., 18 89–91
Butzbacher Weichenbau GmbH & Co. KG, **53** 352
Buxton, **23** 21
buy.com, Inc., 46 74–77
Buzztime Entertainment, Inc. *see* NTN Buzztime, Inc.
BVR Systems (1998) Ltd., 93 110–13
BWAY Corporation, 24 91–93
BWP Distributors, **29** 86, 88
Byerly's, Inc. *see* Lund Food Holdings, Inc.
Byron Weston Company, **26** 105

C

C&A, 40 74–77 (upd.)
C&A Brenninkmeyer KG, V 23–24
C&D *see* Church & Dwight Co., Inc.
C&G *see* Cheltenham & Gloucester PLC.
C & G Systems, *see* Thermadyne Holding Corp.
C & H Distributors, Inc., *see* GEHE AG.
C&J Clark International Ltd., 52 56–59
C&K Aluminio S.A., **74** 11
C&K Market, Inc., 81 59–61
C & O *see* Chesapeake and Ohio Railway.
C&S Co., Ltd., **49** 425, 427
C&S/Sovran Corporation, *see* Bank of America Corp.
C & S Wholesale Grocers, Inc., 55 80–83
C&W *see* Cable and Wireless plc.
C-COR.net Corp., 38 118–21
C-Cube Microsystems, Inc., 37 50–54
C-Mold *see* Moldflow Corp.
C.A. Delaney Capital Management Ltd., **32** 437
C.A. La Electricidad de Caracas, **53** 18
C.A. Muer Corporation, **65** 205
C.A. Swanson & Sons *see* Vlasic Foods International Inc.
C Corp. Inc. *see* Alimentation Couche-Tard Inc.
C.D. Haupt, *see* Jefferson Smurfit Group plc.
C.E. Chappell & Sons, Inc., **16** 61–62; **50** 107
C.E.T. *see* Club Européen du Tourisme.
C.F. Burns and Son, Inc., **21** 154
C.F. Martin & Co., Inc., 42 55–58
C.F. Orvis Company *see* The Orvis Company, Inc.
The C.F. Sauer Company, 90 86–89
C. Hoare & Co., 77 76–79
C.H. Boehringer Sohn, 39 70–73
C.H. Guenther & Son, Inc., 84 39–42
C.H. Heist Corporation, 24 111–13
C.H. Masland & Sons *see* Masland Corp.
C.H. Robinson Worldwide, Inc., 11 43–44; 40 78–81 (upd.)
C.I. Traders Limited, 61 44–46
C. Itoh & Co., I 431–33 *see also* ITOCHU Corp.
C.J. Lawrence, Morgan Grenfell Inc., *see* Deutsche Bank A.G.
C.M. Barnes Company, *see* Barnes & Noble, Inc.
C.M. Life Insurance Company, **53** 213
C-MAC Industries Inc., **48** 369
C.O.M.B. Company, *see* Provell Inc.
C. Of Eko-Elda A.B.E.E., **64** 177
C.P.T. Holding B.V., **56** 152
C.P.U., Inc., *see* Ciber, Inc.
C.R. Bard, Inc., 9 96–98; 65 81–85 (upd.)
C.R. Meyer and Sons Company, 74 58–60
C-Tec Corp. *see* Commonwealth Telephone Enterprises, Inc.
C-Tech Industries Inc., 90 90–93
C.W. Costello & Associates Inc., **31** 131
C.W. Zumbiel Company, **11** 422
CAA *see* Creative Artists Agency LLC.
Cabana (Holdings) Ltd., **44** 318
Cabela's Inc., 26 49–51; 68 74–77 (upd.)
Cable & Wireless HKT, 30 95–98 (upd.)
Cable and Wireless plc, V 283–86; 25 98–102 (upd.)
Cable Design Technologies Corporation (CDT) *see* Belden CDT Inc.
Cable London, **25** 497
Cable Management Advertising Control System, **25** 497
Cable One, Inc., **73** 240
Cabletron Systems, Inc., 10 193–94
Cablevision Electronic Instruments, Inc., 32 105–07
Cablevision Systems Corporation, 7 63–65; 30 99–103 (upd.)
Cablex AG, **58** 337
CABLO Metall-Recycling & Handel GmbH, **62** 253
Cabot Corporation, 8 77–79; 29 79–82 (upd.); 91 74–80 (upd.)
Cabot Medical Corporation, **21** 117, 119
Cabot-Morgan Real Estate Co., *see* Dart Group PLC.
Cache Incorporated, 30 104–06
CACI International Inc., 21 85–87; 72 49–53 (upd.)
Cacique, *see* Intimate Brands, Inc.
Cactus Feeders, Inc., 91 81–84
Cactus S.A., 90 94–97
Cadbury Schweppes PLC, II 476–78; 49 75–79 (upd.)
CADCAM Technology Inc., **22** 196
Caddell Construction Company, **12** 41
Cademartori, **23** 219

Cadence Design Systems, Inc., **11** **45–48**; **48** **75–79 (upd.)**
Cadet Uniform Services Ltd., **21** 116
Cadillac Fairview Corporation Ltd., **61** 273, 275
Cadillac Plastic, *see* M. A. Hanna Co.
Cadmus Communications Corporation, **23** **100–03** *see also* Cenveo Inc.
CAE USA Inc., **48** **80–82**
Caere Corporation, **20** **101–03**
Caesar's Entertainment Inc., **62** 179
Caesars World, Inc., **6** **199–202**
Café Express, **47** 443
Caffè Nero Group PLC, **63** **87–89**
Cagiva Group, **17** 24; **30** 172; **39** 37
Cagle's, Inc., **20** **104–07**
Cahners Business Information, **43** **92–95**
Cahners Publishing, **22** 442
CAI Corp., **12** 79
Cain Chemical *see* Occidental Petroleum Corp.
Cain Sloan, Inc., **68** 114
Cains Marcelle Potato Chips Inc., **15** 139
Cains Pickles, Inc., **51** 232
Cairncom Pty Limited, **56** 155
Cairo Petroleum Refining Co., **51** 113
Caisse des Dépôts—Développement (C3D), **48** 107
Caisse des Dépôts et Consignations, **90** **98–101**
Caisse Nationale de Crédit Agricole, **15** 38–39
Caithness Glass Limited, **38** 402; **69** 301, 303
Cajun Bayou Distributors and Management, Inc., **19** 301
Cajun Electric Power Cooperative, Inc., **21** 470
CAK Universal Credit Corp., **32** 80
CAL *see* China Airlines.
CAL Corporation, **21** 199, 201
Cal-Maine Foods, Inc., **69** **76–78**
Cal-Van Tools *see* Chemi-Trol Chemical Co.
Calardu Pty Limited, **56** 155
CalAmp Corp., **87** **84–87**
Calavo Growers, Inc., **47** **63–66**
Calcast Ltd., **63** 304
Calcined Coke Corp., **IV** 402
CalComp Inc., **13** **126–29**
Calcot Ltd., **33** **84–87**
Calder Race Course, Inc., **29** 118
Caldera Systems Inc., **38** 416, 420
Caldor Inc., **12** **54–56**
Caledonian Airways *see* British Caledonian Airways.
Calgary Power Company *see* TransAlta Utilities Corp.
Calgene, Inc., **29** 330; **41** 155
Calgon Carbon Corporation, **73** **76–79**
Calgon Vestal Laboratories, **37** 44
Calgon Water Management, **15** 154; **40** 176
Cali Realty *see* Mack-Cali Realty Corp.
California Bank & Trust, **53** 378
California Cedar Products Company, **58** **51–53**
California Charter Inc., *see* Coach USA, Inc.
California Computer Products, Inc. *see* CalComp Inc.
California Design Studio, **31** 52
California Fruit Growers Exchange *see* Sunkist Growers, Inc.
California Pizza Kitchen Inc., **15** **74–76**; **74** **61–63 (upd.)**
California Portland Cement Co., *see* CalMat Co.
California Slim, **27** 197
California Sports, Inc., **56** **49–52**
California Steel Industries, Inc., **67** **85–87**
California Water Service Group, **79** **85–88**
Caligen, *see* British Vita PLC.
Caligor *see* Henry Schein Medical.
Caliper Life Sciences, Inc., **70** **37–40**
CALipso Sales Company, **62** 74
Call-Chronicle Newspapers, Inc., **IV** 678
Callanan Industries, Inc., **60** **77–79**
Callard and Bowser-Suchard Inc., **84** **43–46**
Callaway Golf Company, **15** **77–79**; **45** **74–77 (upd.)**
Callaway Wines, *see* Hiram Walker Resources Ltd.
Callon Petroleum Company, **47** **67–69**
Calloway's Nursery, Inc., **51** **59–61**
CalMat Co., **19** **69–72** *see also* Vulcan Materials Co.
Calor Gas Ltd., **55** 346
Calor Group, **53** 166
Calpine Corporation, **36** **102–04**
Calspan SRL Corporation, **54** 395
Caltex Petroleum Corporation, **19** **73–75** *see also* ChevronTexaco Corp.
Calumatic Group, **25** 82
Calumet Electric Company, **6** 532
Calvert Insurance Co. *see* Gryphon Holdings, Inc.
Calvin Klein, Inc., **22** **121–24**; **55** **84–88 (upd.)**
Calyx & Corolla Inc., **37** 162–63
Camaïeu S.A., **72** **54–56**
Camargo Corrêa S.A., **93** **114–18**
Camas *see* Aggregate Industries plc.
CamBar *see* Cameron & Barkley Co.
Camber Corporation, **25** 405
Camberley Enterprises Limited, **59** 261
Cambex, **46** 164
Cambrex Corporation, **16** **67–69**; **44** **59–62 (upd.)**
Cambrian Wagon Works Ltd., **31** 369
Cambridge Applied Nutrition Toxicology and Biosciences Ltd., **10** 105
Cambridge Electric Light Co., *see* Commonwealth Energy System.
The Cambridge Instrument Company, **35** 272
Cambridge SoundWorks, Inc., **48** **83–86**
Cambridge Technology Partners, Inc., **36** **105–08**
Cambridge Tool & Mfg. Co. Inc., **48** 268
Cambridge Water, **51** 389
Camden Property Trust, **77** **80–83**
Camden Wire Co., Inc., *see* Oneida Ltd.
Cameco Corporation, **77** **84–87**
Camelot Barthropp Ltd., **26** 62
Camelot Community Care, Inc., **64** 311
Camelot Group plc, **34** 140
Camelot Music, Inc., **26** **52–54**
Cameron & Barkley Company, **28** **59–61** *see also* Hagemeyer North America.
Campagnia della Fede Cattolica sotto l'Invocazione di San Paolo, **50** 407
Campbell Cereal Company *see* Malt-O-Meal Co.
Campbell, Cowperthwait & Co., *see* U.S. Trust Corp.
Campbell-Ewald Advertising, **86** **56–60**
Campbell Hausfeld *see* Scott Fetzer Co.
Campbell Industries, Inc., *see* TriMas Corp.
Campbell-Mithun-Esty, Inc., **16** **70–72** *see also* Interpublic Group of Companies, Inc.
Campbell Scientific, Inc., **51** **62–65**
Campbell Soup Company, **II** **479–81**; **7** **66–69 (upd.)**; **26** **55–59 (upd.)**; **71** **75–81 (upd.)**
Campeau Corporation, **V** **25–28**
The Campina Group, **78** **61–64**
Camping World, Inc., **56** 5
Campo Electronics, Appliances & Computers, Inc., **16** **73–75**
Campo Lindo, **25** 85
Campofrío Alimentación S.A, **59** **101–03**
CAMPSA *see* Compañia Arrendataria del Monopolio de Petróleos Sociedad Anónima.
Canada Packers Inc., **II** **482–85**
Canada Surety Co., **26** 486
Canada Trust *see* CT Financial Services Inc.
Canadair, Inc., **16** **76–78** *see also* Bombardier Inc.
Canadian Ad-Check Services Inc., **26** 270
Canadian Airlines International Ltd., **12** 192; **23** 10; **59** 20
The Canadian Broadcasting Corporation (CBC), **37** **55–58**
Canadian Electrolytic Zinc Ltd., **64** 297
Canadian Forest Products *see* Canfor Corp.
Canadian Freightways, Ltd., **48** 113
Canadian Imperial Bank of Commerce, **II** **244–46**; **61** **47–51 (upd.)**
Canadian National Railway Company, **6** **359–62**; **71** **82–88 (upd.)**
Canadian Niagara Power Company, **47** 137
Canadian Occidental Petroleum Ltd. *see* Nexen Inc.
Canadian Odeon Theatres *see* Cineplex Odeon Corp.
Canadian Pacific Railway Limited, **V** **429–31**; **45** **78–83 (upd.)**
Canadian Steel Foundries, Ltd., **39** 31
Canadian Telephones and Supplies *see* British Columbia Telephone Co.

Canadian Tire Corporation, Limited, **71 89–93 (upd.)**
Canadian Utilities Limited, **13 130–32; 56 53–56 (upd.)**
Canal Digital, **69** 344–46
Canal Electric Co., *see* Commonwealth Energy System.
Canal Plus, **10 195–97; 34 83–86 (upd.)**
CanalSatellite, **29** 369, 371
Canandaigua Brands, Inc., **13 133–35; 34 87–91 (upd.)** *see also* Constellation Brands, Inc.
Cananwill, *see* Reliance Group Holdings, Inc.
Canary Wharf Group Plc, **30 107–09**
Canatom NPM Inc. *see* SNC-Lavalin Group Inc.
Cancer Treatment Centers of America, Inc., **85 45–48**
Candela Corporation, **48 87–89**
Candie's, Inc., **31 81–84**
Candle Corporation, **64 62–65**
Candle Corporation of America *see* Blyth Industries, Inc.
Candle-Lite Inc., **61** 172
Candlewood Hotel Company, Inc., **41 81–83**
Candover Partners Limited, **70** 310
Candy SpA *see* Arcor S.A.I.C.
Canfor Corporation, **42 59–61**
Cannapp Pty Limited, **56** 155
Cannell Communications, **25** 418
Cannon Design, **63 90–92**
Cannon Express, Inc., **53 80–82**
Cannon Mills, Co., *see* Fieldcrest Cannon, Inc.
Cannondale Corporation, **21 88–90**
Canon Inc., **III 120–21; 18 92–95 (upd.); ; 79 89–95 (upd.)**
Canstar Sports Inc., **16 79–81** *see also* NIKE, Inc.
Cantel Medical Corporation, **80 55–58**
Canterbury Park Holding Corporation, **42 62–65**
Canterra Energy Ltd., **47** 180
Cantine Giorgio Lungarotti S.R.L., **67 88–90**
Canton Railway Corp., **IV** 718; **38** 320
Cantor Fitzgerald, L.P., **92 38–42**
CanWest Global Communications Corporation, **35 67–703**
Canyon Cafes, **31** 41
Canyon Offshore, Inc. *see* Helix Energy Solutions Group, Inc.
Cap Gemini Ernst & Young, **37 59–61**
Cap Rock Energy Corporation, **46 78–81**
Capacity of Texas, Inc., **33** 105–06
Caparo Group Ltd., **90 102–06**
CAPCO *see* Central Area Power Coordination Group; Custom Academic Publishing Co.
Capco Energy, Inc., **33** 296
Capcom Company Ltd., **83 50-53**
Cape Cod Potato Chip Company, **90 107–10**
Capel Incorporated, **45 84–86**
Capezio/Ballet Makers Inc., **62 57–59**
Capita Group PLC, **69 79–81**
AB Capital & Investment Corporation, **6** 108; **23** 381
Capital Bank N.A., **16** 162
Capital Cities/ABC Inc., **II 129–31**
Capital Concrete Pipe Company, **14** 250
Capital Controls Co., Inc. *see* Severn Trent PLC.
Capital Distributing Co., **21** 37
Capital Factors, Inc., **54** 387
Capital Grille, **19** 342
Capital Group, **26** 187
Capital Holding Corporation, **III 216–19** *see also* Providian Financial Corp.
Capital Management Services *see* CB Commercial Real Estate Services Group, Inc.
Capital One Financial Corporation, **52 60–63**
Capital Radio plc, **35 71–73**
Capital Senior Living Corporation, **75 80–82**
Capitalia S.p.A., **65 86–89**
Capitol Film + TV International, **IV** 591
Capitol Films, **25** 270
Capitol Records, Inc., **90 111–16**
Capitol Transamerica Corporation, **60** 16
Capstar, **62** 119
CapStar Hotel Company, **21 91–93**
Capstone Pharmacy of Delaware, Inc., **64** 27
Capstone Turbine Corporation, **75 83–85**
Captain D's, LLC, **59 104–06**
Captaris, Inc., **89 126–29**
The Carphone Warehouse Group PLC, **83 54-57**
Car Toys, Inc., **67 91–93**
Caraco Pharmaceutical Laboratories Inc., **57** 345–46
Caradco, Inc., **45** 216
Caradon plc, **20 108–12 (upd.)** *see also* Novar plc.
Carat Group *see* Aegis Group plc.
Caratti Sports, Ltd., **26** 184
Carus Publishing Company, **93 128–32**
Caraustar Industries, Inc., **19 76–78; 44 63–67 (upd.)**
Caravelle Foods, **21** 500
The Carbide/Graphite Group, Inc., **40 82–84**
Carbo PLC, **67 94–96 (upd.)**
Carbocol, **IV** 417
CarboMedics, **11** 458–60
Carbone Lorraine S.A., **33 88–90**
La Carbonique, **23** 217, 219
Carborundum Company, **15 80–82** *see also* Carbo PLC.
Cardàpio, **29** 444
Cardell Corporation, **54** 239
Cardem Insurance Co., *see* Walter Industries, Inc.
Cardiac Pacemakers, Inc., **22** 361
Cardinal Freight Carriers, Inc., **42** 365
Cardinal Health, Inc., **18 96–98; 50 120–23 (upd.)**
Cardinal Holdings Corporation, **65** 334
Cardiotronics Systems, Inc., **21** 47
Cardo AB, **53 83–85**
Cardone Industries Inc., **92 43–47**
Cardtronics, Inc., **93 119–23**
Care Advantage, Inc., **25** 383
Care Group, **22** 276
Career Education Corporation, **45 87–89**
Career Horizons Inc., **49** 265
CareerBuilder, Inc., **93 124–27**
CareerStaff Unlimited Inc., *see* Sun Healthcare Froup Inc.
Caremark Rx, Inc., **10 198–200; 54 42–45 (upd.)**
Carenes, SA, **12** 377
CareScience, Inc. *see* Quovadx Inc.
CareTel, Inc., **53** 209
CareUnit, Inc., **15** 123
CareWise, Inc., **36** 365, 367–68
Carey Diversified LLC *see* W.P. Carey & Co. LLC.
Carey International, Inc., **26 60–63**
Carey-McFall Corp. *see* Springs Industries, Inc.
Cargill, Incorporated, **II 616–18; 13 136–38 (upd.); 40 85–90 (upd.); 89 130–39 (upd.)**
Cargo Express, **16** 198
Cargo Furniture, **31** 436
Cargolux Airlines International S.A., **49 80–82**
CARGOSUR *see* Iberia.
Cargotec Corporation, **76** 225, 228
Carhartt, Inc., **30 110–12; 77 88–92 (upd.)**
Caribiner International, Inc., **24 94–97**
Caribou Coffee Company, Inc., **28 62–65**
Carisam International Corp., **29** 511
Caritas Internationalis, **72 57–59**
Carl Allers Etablissement A/S, **72 60–62**
Carl Ed. Meyer GmbH, **48** 119
Carl I. Brown and Company, **48** 178
Carl Karcher Enterprises, Inc., **19** 435; **46** 94
Carl Kühne KG (GmbH & Co.), **94 101–05**
Carl Zeiss AG, **III 445–47; 34 92–97 (upd.); 91 85–92 (upd.)**
Carl's Jr. *see* CKE Restaurants, Inc.
Carlin Foods Corporation, **62** 50
Carling O'Keefe Ltd., *see* Foster's Group Ltd.
Carlisa S.A. *see* Arcor S.A.I.C.
Carlisle Companies Inc., **8 80–82; 82 58-62 (upd.)**
Carlisle Memory Products, **14** 535
Carlon, *see* Lamson & Sessions Co.
Carlova, Inc., **21** 54
Carlsberg A/S, **9 99–101; 29 83–85 (upd.)**
Carlson Companies, Inc., **6 363–66; 22 125–29 (upd.); 87 88–95 (upd.)**
Carlson Restaurants Worldwide, **69 82–85**
Carlson Wagonlit Travel, **55 89–92**

Carlton and United Breweries Ltd., I 228–29 *see also* Foster's Group Limited
Carlton Cards Retail, Inc., **39** 87; **59** 34–35
Carlton Communications plc, 15 83–85; 50 124–27 (upd.)
Carlton Foods Corporation, **57** 56–57
Carlton Investments L.P., **22** 514
Carlyle & Co. Jewelers *see* Finlay Enterprises, Inc.
The Carlyle Group, **14** 43; **16** 47; **21** 97; **30** 472; **43** 60; **49** 444; **73** 47; **76** 315
Carlyle Management Group, **63** 226
Carma Laboratories, Inc., 60 80–82
CarMax, Inc., 55 93–95
Carmichael Lynch Inc., 28 66–68
Carmike Cinemas, Inc., 14 86–88; 37 62–65 (upd.); 74 64–67 (upd.)
Carmine's Prime Meats, Inc. *see* CBRL Group, Inc.
Carnation Company, II 486–89 *see also* Nestlé S.A.
CarnaudMetalBox, *see* Crown, Cork & Seal Company, Inc.
Carnegie Corporation of New York, 35 74–77
Carnegie Group, **41** 371–72
Carnival Corporation, 6 367–68; 27 90–92 (upd.); 78 65–69 (upd.)
Caro Produce and Institutional Foods, **31** 359–61
Carolina Energies, Inc., **6** 576
Carolina First Corporation, 31 85–87
Carolina Freight Corporation, 6 369–72
Carolina Paper Board Corporation *see* Caraustar Industries, Inc.
Carolina Power & Light Company, V 564–66; 23 104–07 (upd.) *see also* Progress Energy, Inc.
Carolina Telephone and Telegraph Company, 10 201–03
Carolinas Capital Funds Group, **29** 132
Carpenter Investment and Development Corporation, **31** 279; **76** 222
Carpenter Technology Corporation, 13 139–41
Carpets International Plc., *see* Interface, Inc.
Carpro, Inc., **65** 127
CARQUEST Corporation, 29 86–89
Carr-Gottstein Foods Co., 17 77–80
Carrabba's Italian Grill, *see* Outback Steakhouse, Inc.
CarrAmerica Realty Corporation, 56 57–59
Carre Orban International, **34** 248
Carrefour SA, 10 204–06; 27 93–96 (upd.); 64 66–69 (upd.)
Carrera-Optyl Group, **54** 319–20
Carrera y Carrera, **52** 147, 149
The Carriage House Companies, Inc., 55 96–98
Carriage Services, Inc., 37 66–68
Carrier Access Corporation, 44 68–73
Carrier Corporation, 7 70–73; 69 86–91 (upd.)
Carrington Laboratories, **33** 282
Carrington Viyella, **44** 105
Carroll County Electric Company, **6** 511
Carroll's Foods, Inc., 46 82–85
Carrols Restaurant Group, Inc., 92 48–51
Carrows, **27** 16, 19
The Carsey-Werner Company, L.L.C., 37 69–72
Carsmart.com, **47** 34
Carso Global Telecom S.A. de C.V., **34** 362
Carson, Inc., 31 88–90
Carson Pirie Scott & Company, 15 86–88
Carswell Insurance Group *see* Plamer & Cay, Inc.
CART *see* Championship Auto Racing Teams, Inc.
Cartem Wilco Group Inc., **59** 350
CarTemps USA *see* Republic Industries, Inc.
Carter & Sons Freightways, Inc., **57** 278
Carter Hawley Hale Stores, V 29–32
Carter Holt Harvey Ltd., 70 41–44
Carter Lumber Company, 45 90–92
Carter-Wallace, Inc., 8 83–86; 38 122–26 (upd.)
Cartier, *see* Vendôme Luxury Group plc.
Cartier Monde, 29 90–92
Cartiera F.A. Marsoni, **IV** 587
Cartocor S.A. *see* Arcor S.A.I.C.
Carton Titan S.A. de C.V., **37** 176–77
Cartotech, Inc., **33** 44
Carvel Corporation, 35 78–81
Carver Bancorp, Inc., 94 106–10
Carver Boat Corporation LLC, 88 43–46
Carvin Corp., 89 140–43
Cary-Davis Tug and Barge Company *see* Puget Sound Tug and Barge Co.
CASA *see* Construcciones Aeronautics S.A.
Casa Bancária Almeida e Companhia *see* Banco Bradesco S.A.
Casa Cuervo, S.A. de C.V., 31 91–93
Casa Herradura *see* Grupo Industrial Herradura, S.A. de C.V.
Casa Ley, S.A. de C.V. *see* Safeway Inc.
Casa Saba *see* Grupo Casa Saba, S.A. de C.V.
Casablanca Records, **23** 390
Casalee, Inc., **48** 406
Casarotto Security, **24** 510
Casas Bahia Comercial Ltda., 75 86–89
Cascade Communications Corp., **20** 8
Cascade Corporation, 65 90–92
Cascade Fertilizers Ltd., **25** 232
Cascade General, Inc., 65 93–95
Cascade Natural Gas Corporation, 9 102–04
Cascade Steel Rolling Mills, Inc., *see* Schnitzer Steel Industries, Inc.
Cascades Inc., 71 94–96
Cascadian Farm *see* Small Planet Foods, Inc.
CasChem, Inc. *see* Cambrex Corp.
Casco Northern Bank, 14 89–91
Casden Properties, **49** 26
Case Corporation *see* CNH Global N.V.
Case Technologies, Inc., **11** 504
Casey's General Stores, Inc., 19 79–81; 83 58-63 (upd.)
Cash & Go, Inc., **57** 139
Cash America International, Inc., 20 113–15; 61 52–55 (upd.)
Cash Systems, Inc., 93 133–36
Cash Wise Foods and Liquor, **30** 133
Casino, **23** 231; **26** 160
Casino America, Inc. *see* Isle of Capri Casinos, Inc.
Casino Frozen Foods, Inc., **16** 453
Casino Guichard-Perrachon S.A., 59 107–10 (upd.)
Casinos International Inc., **21** 300
CASIO Computer Co., Ltd., III 448–49; 16 82–84 (upd.); 40 91–95 (upd.)
Casite Intraco LLC, **56** 156–57
Caspian Pipeline Consortium, **47** 75
Cassa Risparmio Firenze, **50** 410
Cassandra Group, **42** 272
Cassco Ice & Cold Storage, Inc., **21** 534–35
CAST Inc., **18** 20; **43** 17
Cast-Matic Corporation, **16** 475
Castel MAC S.p.A., **68** 136
Castex, **13** 501
Castings, Inc., **29** 98
Castle & Cooke, Inc., II 490–92; 20 116–19 (upd.) *see also* Dole Food Company, Inc.
Castle Cement, **31** 400
Castle Harlan Investment Partners III, **36** 468, 471
Castle Rock Entertainment, **23** 392; **57** 35
Castle Rubber Co., *see* Park-Ohio Industries Inc.
Castleton Thermostats *see* Strix Ltd.
Castorama S.A. *see* Groupe Castorama-Dubois Investissements.
Castro Convertibles *see* Krause's Furniture, Inc.
Castro Model Ltd., 86 61–64
Casual Corner Group, Inc., 43 96–98
Casual Male Retail Group, Inc., 52 64–66
Casual Wear Española, S.A., **64** 91
Caswell-Massey Co. Ltd., 51 66–69
CAT Scale Company, **49** 329–30
Catalina Lighting, Inc., 43 99–102 (upd.)
Catalina Marketing Corporation, 18 99–102
Catalogue Marketing, Inc., *see* Hickory Farms, Inc.
Catalyst Rx *see* HealthExtras, Inc.
Catalyst Telecom, **29** 414–15
Catalytica Energy Systems, Inc., 44 74–77
Catalytica Pharmaceuticals Inc., **56** 95
Catamaran Cruisers, **29** 442
Catapult Learning LLC *see* Educate Inc.
Cataract, Inc., **34** 373
CATCO *see* Crowley All Terrain Corp.
Catellus Development Corporation, 24 98–101

Caterpillar Inc., III 450–53; 15 89–93 (upd.); 63 93–99 (upd.)
Cathay Pacific Airways Limited, 6 78–80; 34 98–102 (upd.)
Catherines Stores Corporation, 15 94–97
Cathodic Protection Services Co., **14** 325
Catholic Charities USA, 76 82–84
Catholic Digest, **49** 48
Catholic Health Initiatives, 91 93–98
Catholic Order of Foresters, 24 102–05
CatiCentre Ltd. Co, **48** 224
Cato Corporation, 14 92–94
Catterton Partners, **62** 137
Cattleman's, Inc., 20 120–22
Cattles plc, 58 54–56
Caudill Rowlett Scott *see* CRSS Inc.
The Caudwell Group *see* Phones 4u Ltd.
Cavalcade Holdings, Inc., **53** 146
Cavallo Pipeline Company, *see* Seagull Energy Corp.
Cavco Industries, Inc., 65 96–99
Cavendish International Holdings, **IV** 695
Caves Altovisto, *see* Marie Brizard & Roger International S.A.
Caves de Roquefort, **19** 51
Caviton Ltd. *see* Harvey Norman.
Caxton Superannuation Fund Trustee Limited, **70** 43
Cazenove Group plc, 72 63–65
CB&I, *see* Chicago Bridge & Iron Company N.V.
CB&Q *see* Chicago, Burlington and Quincy Railroad Co.
CB&T *see* Synovus Financial Corp.
CB Commercial Real Estate Services Group, Inc., 21 94–98
CB International Finance S.A.R.L. *see* Constellation Brands, Inc.
CB Richard Ellis Group, Inc., 70 45–50 (upd.)
CBE Technologies Inc., **39** 346
CBI Industries, Inc., 7 74–77 *see also* Chicago Bridge & Iron Company N.V.
CBN *see* The Christian Broadcasting Network, Inc.
CBN Cable Network, *see* International Family Entertainment Inc.
CBOT *see* Chicago Board of Trade.
CBP *see* Corporation for Public Broadcasting.
CBPI *see* Companhia Brasileira de Petróleo Ipiranga.
CBR-HCI Construction Materials Corp., **31** 253
CBRL Group, Inc., 35 82–85 (upd.); 86 65–70 (upd.)
CBS Corporation, II 132–34; 6 157–60 (upd.); 28 69–73 (upd.) *see also* CBS Television Network.
CBS.MarketWatch.com, **49** 290
CBS Radio Group, **37** 192; **48** 217
CBS Records, **22** 194; **23** 33; **28** 419
CBS Television Network, 66 44–48 (upd.)
CBSI *see* Complete Business Solutions, Inc.
CBW Inc., **42** 129
CC Beverage Corporation, **48** 97
cc:Mail, Inc., **25** 300
CCA *see* Container Corporation of America; Corrections Corporation of America.
CCA Industries, Inc., 53 86–89
CCAir Inc., **11** 300
CCB Financial Corp., **33** 293
CCC Empreendimentos e Participaçoes, **74** 48
CCC Franchising Corporation *see* Primedex Health Systems, Inc.
CCC Information Services Group Inc., 74 68–70
CCG *see* The Clark Construction Group, Inc.
CCH Inc., 14 95–97
CCL Industries, Ltd., **15** 129
CCM Inc. *see* The Hockey Co.
CCM Sport Maska, Inc., **15** 396
CCN Group Ltd., **45** 154
CCP Insurance, Inc., *see* Conseco Inc.
CCR, Inc. *see* Rica Foods, Inc.
CCS Automation Systems Inc., *see* Texas Air Corp.
CCT *see* Crowley Caribbean Transport.
CDB Infotek Inc. *see* ChoicePoint Inc.
CDC *see* Canada Development Corporation; Control Data Corp.
CDC Corporation, 71 97–99
CDG Books Canada Inc., *see* IDG Books Worldwide, Inc.
CDI *see* Centre de Dechets Industriels Group.
CDI Corporation, 6 139–41; 54 46–49 (upd.)
CDL *see* City Developments Ltd.
CDMS *see* Credit and Data Marketing Services.
CDR *see* Consortium de Realisation.
CDW Computer Centers, Inc., 16 85–87; 52 67–70 (upd.)
CE Consulting, **51** 17
CEAG AG, **23** 498
CEAT, **20** 263; **71** 210–11
Ceatech Engineering, **68** 143
Cébé, **61** 191–92
CEC Entertainment, Inc., 31 94–98 (upd.)
CECAB *see* Groupe CECAB S.C.A.
Cecil Gee, **51** 253
Ceco Doors, *see* United Dominion Industries Ltd.
Ceco Industries, Inc. *see* Robertson-Ceco Corp.
CeCorr Inc., **47** 149
CECOS International, Inc. *see* Browning-Ferris Industries, Inc.
Cedar Fair, L.P., 22 130–32
Cedarapids, Inc., **11** 413; **38** 374, 376; **40** 432
CEDC *see* Central European Distribution Corp.
Cedec S.A., **14** 43
Cederroth International AB, *see* Alberto-Culver Co.
CEDIS, **12** 153
Cedric Chivers, **35** 243–44
Cegedim S.A., **70** 72
Cegetel SA, **38** 300
Celadon Group Inc., 30 113–16
Celanese Corp., I 317–19 *see also* Hoechst Celanese Corp.
Celanese Mexicana, S.A. de C.V., 54 50–52
Celebrate Express, Inc., 70 51–53
Celebrity, Inc., 22 133–35
Celera Genomics, 74 71–74
Celeron Corporation, **20** 258, 262–63
Celestial Seasonings, Inc., 16 88–91 *see also* The Hain Celestial Group, Inc.
Celestica Inc., 80 59–62
Celestron International, **41** 262–63
Celfor Tool Company *see* Clark Equipment Co.
Celgene Corporation, 67 97–100
Celite Mineracao do Nordeste Ltda, **51** 196
Cell Technology, Inc. *see* Air Methods Corp.
Cell-Tel Monitoring, Inc., **46** 386
CellAccess Technology, Inc., **25** 162
CellLife International, **49** 280
CellStar Corporation, 83 64-67
CellularOne *see* Rural Cellular Corp.
Celluloid Studios, **63** 422
Celsius Energy Company, **6** 569
Celtrion, **62** 221
Celulosa Arauco y Constitución S.A., **69** 142
Celulosa de Levante, S.A., **68** 258
Cement Products, **46** 196
Cement Roadstone Holdings *see* CRH PLC.
Cementhai Chemicals Co., **56** 322
Cementi Centro Sud Spa, **70** 343
Cementos Apasco, S.A. de C.V., **51** 29
Cementos Argos S.A., 91 99–101
Cementos de Acapulco, S.A. de C.V., **51** 28
Cementos Portland Moctezuma, **21** 261
Cementos Veracruz, S.A. de C.V., **51** 27, 29
Cementownia Chelm, **31** 398, 400
CEMEX S.A. de C.V., 20 123–26; 59 111–16 (upd.)
CEMIG *see* Companhia Energética De Minas Gerais S.A.
Cemoi S.A., 86 71–74
Cemsto, *see* Koninklijke Vendex KBB N.V. (Royal Vendex KBB N.V.)
Cencosud S.A., **71** 144
Cencosud S.A., 69 92–94
Cendant Corporation, 44 78–84 (upd.)
Cenex Cooperative, **21** 342
Cenex Harvest States Cooperative *see* CHS Inc.
Cenex Inc., **19** 160
Centaur Communications, **43** 204, 206
Centel Corporation, 6 312–15 *see also* EMBARQ Corp.
Centennial Communications Corporation, 39 74–76
Centennial Technologies Inc., **48** 369
Center Co., Ltd., **48** 182
Center of Insurance, **51** 170

Center Rental & Sales Inc., **28** 387
Centerior Energy Corporation, V 567–68
CenterMark Properties, **57** 156
Centerplate, Inc., 79 96–100
Centerpulse AG, **68** 362
Centex Corporation, 8 87–89; 29 93–96 (upd.)
Centocor Inc., 14 98–100
CenTrade, a.s., **64** 73
Central Alloy Steel Corporation *see* Republic Engineered Steels, Inc.
Central and South West Corporation, V 569–70
Central Arizona Light & Power Company, **6** 545
Central Bancshares of the South, Inc. *see* Compass Bancshares, Inc.
Central Detallista, S.A. de C.V., **12** 154; **16** 453
Central Electric & Gas Company *see* Centel Corp.
Central Electric and Telephone Company, Inc. *see* Centel Corp.
Central Elevator Co., **19** 111
Central European Distribution Corporation, 75 90–92
Central European Media Enterprises Ltd., 61 56–59
Central Florida Investments, Inc., 93 137–40
Central Florida Press, **23** 101
Central Freight Lines, Inc., **53** 249
Central Garden & Pet Company, 23 108–10; 58 57–60 (upd.)
Central Hudson Gas And Electricity Corporation, 6 458–60
Central Illinois Public Service Company *see* CIPSCO Inc.
Central Independent Television, 7 78–80; 23 111–14 (upd.)
Central Indiana Power Company, **6** 556
Central Investment Corp., **12** 184
Central Japan Railway Company, 43 103–06
Central Maine Power, 6 461–64
Central Mining and Investment Corp., **IV** 79, 95–96, 524, 565
Central Newspapers, Inc., 10 207–09 *see also* Gannett Company, Inc.
Central Ohio Mobile Power Wash *see* MPW Industrial Services, Inc.
Central Parking Corporation, 18 103–05
Central Plains Steel Company *see* Reliance Steel & Aluminum Co.
Central Research Laboratories, **22** 194
Central Soya Company, Inc., 7 81–83
Central Sprinkler Corporation, 29 97–99
Central Supply Company *see* Granite Rock Co.
Central Telephone & Utilities Corporation *see* Centel Corp.
Central Trust Co., **11** 110
Central Vermont Public Service Corporation, 54 53–56
Central West Public Service Company *see* Centel Corp.
Centrale Verzorgingsdienst Cotrans N.V., **12** 443
Centre de Diffusion de l'Édition *see* Éditions Gallimard.
Centre Investissements et Loisirs, **48** 107
Centre Partners Management LLC, **70** 337
Centrepoint Properties Ltd., **54** 116–17
Centric Group, **69** 153
Centrica plc, 29 100–05 (upd.)
Centron DPL Company, Inc., **25** 171
Centros Commerciales Pryca, **23** 246, 248
Centrum Communications Inc., **11** 520
Centuri Corporation, 54 57–59
Centurion Brick, **14** 250
Century Aluminum Company, 52 71–74
Century Bakery *see* Dawn Food Products, Inc.
Century Brewing Company *see* Rainier Brewing Co.
Century Business Services, Inc., 52 75–78
Century Casinos, Inc., 53 90–93
Century Communications Corp., 10 210–12
Century Development *see* Camden Property Trust.
Century Manufacturing Company, **26** 363
Century Papers, Inc., *see* National Sanitary Supply Co.
Century Supply Corporation, **39** 346
Century Telephone Enterprises, Inc., 9 105–07; 54 60–63 (upd.)
Century Theatres, Inc., 31 99–101
Century 21 Real Estate, **21** 97; **59** 345; **61** 267
Century Union (Shanghai) Foods Co., **75** 372
Century Wood Door Ltd., **63** 268
CenturyTel *see* Century Telephone Enterprises, Inc.
Cenveo Inc., 71 100–04 (upd.)
CEP Industrie, **55** 79
CEPA *see* Consolidated Electric Power Asia.
CEPAM, **21** 438
CEPCO *see* Chugoku Electric Power Company Inc.
Cephalon, Inc., 45 93–96
Cepheid, 77 93–96
CEPSA *see* Compañia Española de Petroleos S.A.
Cera Trading Co. *see* Toto Ltd.
Ceradyne, Inc., 65 100–02
Ceramconsult AG, **51** 196
Ceramesh, **11** 361
Ceramic Tile International, Inc., **53** 176
Cerberus Capital Management LP, **73** 289
Cerberus Group, **69** 261
Cerberus Limited *see* Elektrowatt AG.
Cerco S.A., **62** 51
Cereal and Fruit Products, **32** 519
Cereal Industries, *see* Associated British Foods plc.
Cereal Partners Worldwide, **10** 324; **36** 234, 237; **50** 295
Cereol SA, **36** 185; **62** 51
CERES, **55** 178
Cerestar, *see* Cargill, Inc.
Ceresucre, **36** 185
Ceridian Corporation, **38** 58; **71** 262 *see also* Contral Data Systems, Inc.
Cerner Corporation, 16 92–94; 94 111–16 (upd.)
Cerprobe Corporation *see* Kulicke and Soffa Industries, Inc.
Cerro de Pasco Corp., **40** 411
Cerro E.M.S. Limited *see* The Marmon Group, Inc.
CertainTeed Corporation, 35 86–89
Certegy, Inc., 63 100–03
Certified Grocers of Florida, Inc., **15** 139
Cerulean, **51** 249, 251
Cerus, **23** 492
Cerveceria Cuahtémoc Moctezuma, **25** 281
Cerveceria Moctezuma, **23** 170
Cerveceria Polar, I 230–31 *see also* Empresas Polar SA.
Cerveceria y Malteria Quilmes S.A.I.C.A. y G., **70** 62
Ceska Nezavisla Televizni Spolecnost, **61** 56
Ceská Sporitelna a.s. *see* Erste Bank der Osterreichischen Sparkassen AG
Ceské aerolinie, a.s., 66 49–51
Cesky Telecom, a.s., 64 70–73
Cessna Aircraft Company, 8 90–93; 27 97–101 (upd.)
CET *see* Compagnie Européenne de Télésecurité.
CET 21, **61** 56, 58
Cetelem S.A., 21 99–102
Cetus Corp., **41** 201; **50** 193
CeWe Color Holding AG, 76 85–88
CFC Investment Company, **16** 104
CFM *see* Compagnie Française du Méthane.
CFP *see* Compagnie Française des Pétroles.
CFR Corporation *see* Tacony Corp.
CG&E *see* Cincinnati Gas & Electric Co.
CGE *see* Alcatel Alsthom.
CGIP, **57** 380
CGM *see* Compagnie Générale Maritime.
CGR Management Corporation, **51** 85
CH Mortgage Company I Ltd., **58** 84
Chace Precision Metals, Inc., **29** 460–61
Chaco Energy Corporation *see* Texas Utilities Co.
Chadbourne & Parke, 36 109–12
Chadwick's of Boston, Ltd., 29 106–08
Chalk Line Productions, Inc., **58** 124
Chalk's Ocean Airways *see* Flying Boat, Inc.
Challenge Corp. Ltd. *see* Fletcher Challenge Ltd.
Challenger Minerals Inc., *see* Global Marine Inc.
Challenger Series, **55** 312
Challice, **71** 238

The Chalone Wine Group, Ltd., 36 113–16
Chamberlain Group, Ltd., **23** 82
Chambon Offshore International, **60** 149
Chambosse Brokerage Co., **29** 33
Champ Industries, Inc., **22** 15
Champalimaud, **36** 63
Champcork–Rolhas de Champanhe SA, **48** 118
Champion Enterprises, Inc., 17 81–84
Champion Forge Co., **41** 366
Champion Industries, Inc., 28 74–76
Champion International Corporation, IV 263–65; 20 127–30 (upd.) *see also* International Paper Co.
Champion Modular Restaurant Company, Inc. *see* Checkers Drive-Up Restaurants Inc.
Champion Productions, **56** 74
Championship Auto Racing Teams, Inc., 37 73–75
Champps Americana, *see* Unique Casual Restaurants, Inc.
Champs Sports *see* Venator Group Inc.
Chancellor Beacon Academies, Inc., 53 94–97
Chancellor Media Corporation, 24 106–10
Chancery Law Publishing Ltd., *see* John Wiley & Sons, Inc.
Chandeleur Homes, Inc., *see* Champion Enterprises, Inc.
The Chandris Group, **11** 377
Chanel SA, 12 57–59; 49 83–86 (upd.)
Changchun Terumo Medical Products Co. Ltd., **48** 395
Channel Four Television Corporation, 93 141–44
Channel Master Corporation, **15** 134
Channel One Communications Corp., **22** 442
Channel Tunnel Group, *see* Eurotunnel PLC.
Chansam Investments, **23** 388
Chaoda Modern Agriculture (Holdings) Ltd., 87 96–99
Chaparral Boats, Inc. *see* Marine Products Corp.
Chaparral Steel Co., 13 142–44
Chapdelaine & Co., **76** 372
Chapman Printing Company *see* Champion Industries, Inc.
Chappel Music, **23** 389
Chapters Campus Bookstores Company, **58** 187
Chapters Inc., **62** 153
Charal S.A., 90 117–20
Charan Toy Co., Inc., *see* Marvel Entertainment Inc.
Chargeurs International, 6 373–75; 21 103–06 (upd.)
Charisma Brands LLC, 74 75–78
Charles Barker, plc, **25** 91
Charles D. Burnes Co., Inc. *see* The Holson Burnes Group, Inc.
Charles E. Smith Residential Realty Inc., **49** 29
Charles Krug Winery, **50** 387
Charles M. Schulz Creative Associates, **39** 95
The Charles Machine Works, Inc., 64 74–76
Charles of the Ritz Group Ltd., **64** 334
Charles Revson Inc. *see* Revlon Inc.
Charles River Laboratories International, Inc., 42 66–69
The Charles Schwab Corporation, 8 94–96; 26 64–67 (upd.); 81 62–68 (upd.)
The Charles Stark Draper Laboratory, Inc., 35 90–92
Charles Vögele Holding AG, 82 63-66
Charlesbank Capital Partners LLC, **44** 54
Charleston Consolidated Railway, Gas and Electric Company, **6** 574
Charley's Eating & Drinking Saloon, **20** 54
Charlotte Russe Holding, Inc., 35 93–96; 90 121–25 (upd.)
Charming Shoppes, Inc., 8 97–98; 38 127–29 (upd.)
Charoen Pokphand Group, 62 60–63
Charrington United Breweries, **38** 76
Chart House Enterprises, Inc., 17 85–88
Chart Industries, Inc., 21 107–09
Charter Communications, Inc., 33 91–94
Charter Consolidated, **IV** 119–20; **49** 234
Charter Golf, Inc. *see* Ashworth, Inc.
Charter Medical Corporation, **31** 356
Charter National Life Insurance Company, *see* Leucadia National Corp.
Charter Oak Capital Partners, **58** 88
Charter Publications *see* J. W. Pepper and Son Inc.
ChartHouse International Learning Corporation, 49 87–89
Chartwell Investments, **44** 54
Chartwell Land plc, *see* Kingfisher plc.
Chas. Levy Company LLC, 60 83–85
Chase General Corporation, 91 102–05
The Chase Manhattan Corporation, II 247–49; 13 145–48 (upd.) *see also* JPMorgan Chase & Co.
Chateau Communities, Inc., 37 76–79
Chateau St. Jean, *see* Beringer Blass Wine Estates Ltd.
Chateau Souverain, *see* Beringer Blass Wine Estates Ltd.
Chateau Ste. Michelle Winery, **42** 245, 247
Chateaux St. Jacques, *see* Maison Louis Jadot.
Chatham Steel Corporation *see* Reliance Steel & Aluminum Co.
Chatham Technologies Inc., **38** 189
Chatillon *see* John Chatillon & Sons Inc.
Chattanooga Bakery, Inc., 86 75–78
Chattanooga Gas Company, Inc., **6** 577
Chattanooga Gas Light Company, **6** 448; **23** 30
Chattanooga Medicine Company *see* Chattem, Inc.
Chattem, Inc., 17 89–92; 88 47–52 (upd.)
Chatto, Virago, Bodley Head & Jonathan Cape, Ltd., **31** 376
Chautauqua Airlines, Inc., 38 130–32
CHC Helicopter Corporation, 67 101–03
Check Express, **33** 4–5
Check Point Software Technologies Ltd., **20** 238
Checker Auto Parts *see* CSK Auto Corp.
Checker Motors Corp., 89 144–48
Checkers Drive-In Restaurants, Inc., 16 95–98; 74 79–83 (upd.)
CheckFree Corporation, 81 69–72
Checkpoint Systems, Inc., 39 77–80
Checkport Schweiz AG *see* Swissport International Ltd.
Chedraui *see* Grupo Comercial Chedraui S.A. de C.V.
The Cheesecake Factory Inc., 17 93–96
Cheetham Salt Ltd., **62** 307
Chef Boyardee, **10** 70; **50** 538
Chef Solutions, Inc., 89 149–52
Chelan Power Company, **6** 596
Chello Zone Ltd., 93 145–48
Chelsea Milling Company, 29 109–11
Chelsea Piers Management Inc., 86 79–82
Chelsfield PLC, 67 104–06
Cheltenham & Gloucester PLC, 61 60–62
Chem-Nuclear Systems, Inc., *see* Chemical Waste Management, Inc.
Chemcentral Corporation, 8 99–101
Chemdal Corp., *see* American Colloid Co..
Chemed Corporation, 13 149–50
Chemfab Corporation, 35 97–101
Chemgas Holding BV, **41** 340
Chemgrout, **26** 42
Chemi-Trol Chemical Co., 16 99–101
Chemical Banking Corporation, II 250–52; 14 101–04 (upd.)
Chemical Grouting Co. Ltd., **51** 179
Chemical Waste Management, Inc., 9 108–10
Chemicon International, Inc., **63** 353
Cheminor Drugs Limited, **59** 168
Chemische Werke Hüls GmbH *see* Hüls A.G.
Chemise Lacoste, *see* Crystal Brands.
ChemLawn, **23** 428, 431; **34** 153
Chemonics Industries–Fire-Trol, *see* ERLY Industries Inc.
Chemonics International–Consulting, *see* ERLY Industries Inc.
Chemquest Sdn Bhd, **57** 292, 294–95
Chemtura Corporation, 91 106–20 (upd.)
Chemviron Carbon. S.A. *see* Calgon Carbon Corp.
CHEP Pty. Ltd., 80 63–66
Cherokee Inc., 18 106–09
Cherry-Burrell Process Equipment, *see* United Dominion Industries Ltd.
Cherry Lane Music Publishing Company, Inc., 62 64–67
Cherry-Levis Co., **26** 172

Chesapeake and Ohio Railroad *see* CSX Corp.
Chesapeake Corporation, 8 102–04; 30 117–20 (upd.); 93 149–55 (upd.)
Chesapeake Microwave Technologies, Inc., **32** 41
Chesapeake Paperboard Company, **44** 66
Chesapeake Utilities Corporation, 56 60–62
Cheshire Building Society, 74 84–87
Chesebrough-Pond's USA, Inc., 8 105–07
Chessington World of Adventures, **55** 378
Cheung Kong (Holdings) Ltd., IV 693–95; 20 131–34 (upd.); 94 117–24 (upd.)
Chevignon, **44** 296
Chevrolet, **21** 153; **26** 500
Chevron U.K. Ltd., **15** 352
ChevronTexaco Corporation, IV 385–87;19 82–85 (upd.); 47 70–76 (upd.)
Chevy's, Inc., **33** 140
ChexSystems, *see* eluxe Corp.
Cheyenne Software, Inc., 12 60–62
CHF *see* Chase, Harris, Forbes.
CHF Industries, Inc., 84 47–50
Chi-Chi's Inc., 13 151–53; 51 70–73 (upd.)
CHI Construction Company, **58** 84
Chi Mei Optoelectronics Corporation, 75 93–95
Chiasso Inc., 53 98–100
Chiat/Day Inc. Advertising, 11 49–52 *see also* TBWA/Chiat/Day.
Chiba Gas Co. Ltd., **55** 375
Chiba Mitsukoshi Ltd., **56** 242
Chibu Electric Power Company, Incorporated, V 571–73
Chic by H.I.S, Inc., 20 135–37 *see also* VF Corp.
Chicago and North Western Holdings Corporation, 6 376–78 *see also* Union Pacific Corp.
Chicago and Southern Airlines Inc. *see* Delta Air Lines, Inc.
Chicago Bears Football Club, Inc., 33 95–97
Chicago Blackhawk Hockey Team, Inc. *see* Wirtz Corp.
Chicago Board of Trade, 41 84–87
Chicago Bridge & Iron Company N.V., 82 67-73 (upd.)
Chicago Cutlery, *see* General Housewares Corp.
Chicago Faucet Company, **49** 161, 163
Chicago Medical Equipment Co., **31** 255
Chicago Mercantile Exchange Holdings Inc., 75 96–99
Chicago National League Ball Club, Inc., 66 52–55
Chicago O'Hare Leather Concessions Joint Venture Inc., **58** 369
Chicago Pacific Corp., **23** 244; **34** 432
Chicago Pizza & Brewery, Inc., 44 85–88
Chicago Pneumatic Tool Co., *see* Atlas Copco AB.
Chicago Review Press Inc., 84 51–54
Chicago Rollerskate, **15** 395
Chicago Sun-Times, Inc., **62** 188
Chicago Title and Trust Co., *see* Alleghany Corp.
Chicago Title Corp., **54** 107
Chicago Tribune *see* Tribune Co.
Chichibu Concrete Industry Co. Ltd., **60** 301
Chick-fil-A Inc., 23 115–18; 90 126–31 (upd.)
Chicken of the Sea International, 24 114–16 (upd.)
Chico's FAS, Inc., 45 97–99
Chicobel S.A. Belgique *see* Leroux S.A.S.
Chieftain Development Company, Ltd., **16** 11
Childers Products Co., **21** 108
Children's Book-of-the-Month Club, *see* Book-of-the-Month Club.
Children's Comprehensive Services, Inc., 42 70–72
Children's Discovery Centers of America *see* Knowledge Learning Corp.
Children's Hospitals and Clinics, Inc., 54 64–67
The Children's Place Retail Stores, Inc., 37 80–82; 86 83–87 (upd.)
Children's Television Workshop, **35** 75
Children's World Learning Centers, *see* Aramark Corporation
Children's World Ltd. *see* The Boots Company PLC.
ChildrenFirst, Inc., 59 117–20
Childtime Learning Centers, Inc., 34 103–06 *see also* Learning Care Group, Inc.
Chiles Offshore Corporation, 9 111–13
Chili's Grill & Bar *see* Brinker International, Inc.
Chilton Corp., **25** 239
Chilton Publications *see* Cahners Business Information.
Chilton Vending Co. *see* American Coin Merchandising, Inc.
Chimney Rock Winery, **48** 392
China Airlines, 34 107–10
China Automotive Systems Inc., 87 100–103
China Coast, *see* Darden Restaurants, Inc.
China.com Corp., **49** 422
China Construction Bank Corp., 79 101–04
China Eastern Airlines Co. Ltd., 31 102–04
China International Trade and Investment Corporation *see* CITIC Pacific Ltd.
China Life Insurance Company Limited, 65 103–05
China Merchants International Holdings Co., Ltd., 52 79–82
China National Aviation Company Ltd., **18** 115; **21** 140; **66** 192
China National Cereals, Oils and Foodstuffs Import and Export Corporation (COFCO), 76 89–91
China National Heavy Duty Truck Corporation, **21** 274
China National Offshore Oil Corporation, **71** 383
China National Petroleum Corporation, 46 86–89
China Netcom Group Corporation (Hong Kong) Limited, 73 80–83
China OceanShipping Company, **50** 187
China Shenhua Energy Company Limited, 83 68-71
China Resources (Shenyang) Snowflake Brewery Co., **21** 320
China Southern Airlines Company Ltd., 33 98–100
China Telecom, 50 128–32
China Unicom, **47** 320–21
chinadotcom Corporation *see* CDC Corp.
Chinese Metallurgical Import and Export Corp., **IV** 61
Chinese Petroleum Corporation, IV 388–90; 31 105–08 (upd.)
The Chinet Company, **30** 397
Chipotle Mexican Grill, Inc., 67 107–10
CHIPS and Technologies, Inc., 9 114–17
Chiquita Brands International, Inc., 7 84–86; 21 110–13 (upd.); 83 72-79 (upd.)
ChiRex, **38** 380
Chiro Tool Manufacturing Corp., *see* Stanley Works.
Chiron Corporation, 10 213–14; 36 117–20 (upd.)
Chisholm Coal Company, **51** 352
Chisholm-Mingo Group, Inc., 41 88–90
Chittenden & Eastman Company, 58 61–64
Chock Full o'Nuts Corp., 17 97–100
Chocoladefabriken Lindt & Sprüngli AG, 27 102–05
Choice Hotels International, Inc., 14 105–07; 83 80-83 (upd.)
ChoiceCare Corporation, **24** 231
ChoicePoint Inc., 65 106–08
Chorion PLC, **75** 389–90
Chorus Line Corporation, 30 121–23
Chouinard Equipment *see* Lost Arrow Inc.
Chovet Engineering S.A. *see* SNC-Lavalin Group Inc.
Chr. Hansen Group A/S, 70 54–57
Chris-Craft Corporation, 9 118–19; 31 109–12 (upd.); 80 67–71 (upd.)
Christensen Boyles Corporation, 26 68–71
Christiaensen, **26** 160
The Christian Broadcasting Network, Inc., 52 83–85
Christian Dalloz SA, 40 96–98
Christian Dior S.A., 19 86–88; 49 90–93 (upd.)
Christian Salvesen Plc, 45 100–03
The Christian Science Publishing Society, 55 99–102
Christian Supply Centers, Inc., **45** 352
Christiana Bank og Kredietklasse, **40** 336
Christie's International plc, 15 98–101; 39 81–85 (upd.)
Christofle SA, 40 99–102

Christopher & Banks Corporation, 42 73–75
Christopher Charters, Inc. *see* Kitty Hawk, Inc.
Chromalloy American Corp., *see* Sequa Corp.
Chromalloy Gas Turbine Corp., *see* Sequa Corp.
Chromcraft Revington, Inc., 15 102–05
Chromium Corporation, **52** 103–05
Chrompack, Inc., **48** 410
The Chronicle Publishing Company, Inc., 23 119–22
Chronimed Inc., 26 72–75
Chrysalis Group plc, 40 103–06
Chrysler Corporation, I 144–45; 11 53–55 (upd.) *see also* DaimlerChrysler AG
Chrysler Financial Company, LLC, **45** 262
CHS Inc., 60 86–89
CHT Steel Company Ltd., **51** 352
CH2M Hill Ltd., 22 136–38
Chubb Corporation, III 220–22; 14 108–10 (upd.); 37 83–87 (upd.)
Chubb, PLC, 50 133–36
Chubb Security plc, **44** 258
Chubu Electric Power Company, Inc., V 571–73; 46 90–93 (upd.)
Chuck E. Cheese *see* CEC Entertainment, Inc.
Chugach Alaska Corporation, 60 90–93
Chugai Boyeki Co. Ltd., **44** 441
Chugai Pharmaceutical Co., Ltd., 50 137–40
Chugai Shogyo Shimposha *see* Nihon Keizai Shimbun, Inc.
Chugoku Electric Power Company Inc., V 574–76; 53 101–04 (upd.)
Chugoku Funai Electric Company Ltd., **62** 150
Chunghwa Picture Tubes, Ltd., 75 100–02
Chuo Rika Kogyo Corp., **56** 238
Chuo Trust & Banking Co. *see* Yasuda Trust and Banking Company, Ltd.
Chupa Chups S.A., 38 133–35
Church & Company, **45** 342, 344
Church & Dwight Co., Inc., 29 112–15; 68 78–82 (upd.)
Church's Chicken, 66 56–59
Churchill Downs Incorporated, 29 116–19
Churchill Insurance Co. Ltd., *see* Winterthur Group.
CI Holdings, Limited, **53** 120
Cia Hering, 72 66–68
Cianbro Corporation, 14 111–13
Cianchette Brothers, Inc. *see* Cianbro Corp.
Ciba-Geigy Ltd., I 632–34; 8 108–11 (upd.) *see also* Novartis AG.
CIBC *see* Canadian Imperial Bank of Commerce.
Ciber, Inc., 18 110–12
CIC *see* Commercial Intertech Corp.
CIC Investors #13 LP, **60** 130
Cie.Generale des Eaux S.A., **24** 327
CIENA Corporation, 54 68–71
Cifra, S.A. de C.V., 12 63–65 *see also* Wal-Mart de Mexico, S.A. de C.V.
Cifunsa *see* Compania Fundidora del Norte, S.A.
Ciga Group, **54** 345, 347
Cigarrera La Moderna, **21** 260; **22** 73
Cigarros la Tabacelera Mexicana (Cigatam), **21** 259
CIGNA Corporation, III 223–27; 22 139–44 (upd.); 45 104–10 (upd.)
CIGWELD, *see* Thermadyne Holding Corp.
CILCORP Energy Services Inc., **60** 27
Cilva Holdings PLC, **6** 358
CIMA Precision Spring Europa, **55** 305–06
Cimarex Energy Co., 81 73–76
Cimaron Communications Corp., **38** 54
Cimarron Utilities Company, **6** 580
CIMCO Ltd., **21** 499–501
Cimeco S.A. *see* Grupo Clarín S.A.
Cimenteries CBR S.A., **23** 325, 327
Cimentos de Portugal SGPS S.A. (Cimpor), 76 92–94
Ciments Français, 40 107–10
Ciments Lafarge France/Quebec *see* Lafarge Cement
Cimpor *see* Cimentos de Portugal SGPS S.A.
Cinar Corporation, 40 111–14
Cincinnati Bell, Inc., 6 316–18
Cincinnati Financial Corporation, 16 102–04; 44 89–92 (upd.)
Cincinnati Gas & Electric Company, 6 465–68 *see also* Duke Energy Corp.
Cincinnati Lamb Inc., 72 69–71
Cincinnati Milacron Inc., 12 66–69 *see also* Milacron, Inc.
Cincom Systems Inc., 15 106–08
Cine-Groupe, **35** 279
Cinecentrum, **IV** 591
Cinemark, **21** 362; **23** 125
Cinemas de la República, S.A. de C.V., 83 84-86
CinemaSource, **58** 167
Cinemeccanica S.p.A., 78 70–73
Cinemex, **71** 256
Cineplex Odeon Corporation, 6 161–63; 23 123–26 (upd.)
Cinépolis *see* Cinemas de la República, S.A. de C.V.
Cinerama Group, **67** 291
Cinnabon, Inc., 23 127–29; 90 132–36 (upd.)
Cinquième Saison, **38** 200, 202
Cinram International, Inc., 43 107–10
Cinsa *see* Compania Industrial del Norte, S.A.
Cintas Corporation, 21 114–16; 51 74–77 (upd.)
Cintra *see* Concesiones de Infraestructuras de Transportes, S.A.; Corporacion Internacional de Aviacion, S.A. de C.V.
Cinven, **49** 451; **63** 49–50
Ciprial S.A., **27** 260
CIPSA *see* Compañia Industrial de Parras, S.A. de C.V. (CIPSA).
CIPSCO Inc., 6 469–72 *see also* Ameren Corp.
CIR *see* Compagnie Industriali Riunite S.p.A.
Circa Pharmaceuticals, *see* Watson Pharmaceuticals Inc.
Circle International Group Inc., *see* Harper Group Inc.
The Circle K Company, II 619–20; 20 138–40 (upd.)
Circon Corporation, 21 117–20
Circuit City Stores, Inc., 9 120–22; 29 120–24 (upd.); 65 109–14 (upd.)
Circus Circus Enterprises, Inc., 6 203–05
Circus Distribution, Inc. *see* DC Shoes, Inc.
Circus Knie, **29** 126
Cirque du Soleil Inc., 29 125–28
Cirrus Design Corporation, 44 93–95
Cirrus Logic, Inc., 11 56–57; 48 90–93 (upd.)
CIS Acquisition Corporation, **56** 134
CIS Mortgage Maker Ltd., **51** 89
Cisco-Linksys LLC, 86 88–91
Cisco Systems, Inc., 11 58–60; 34 111–15 (upd.); 77 97–103 (upd.)
Cisneros Group of Companies, 54 72–75
CIT Group Inc., 76 95–98
Citadel Communications Corporation, 35 102–05
Citadel General, *see* Winterthur Group.
CitFed Bancorp, Inc., 16 105–07 *see also* Fifth Third Bancorp.
CITGO Petroleum Corporation, IV 391–93; 31 113–17 (upd.)
Citi Trends, Inc., 80 72–75
Citibank *see* Citigroup Inc
Citibank of Mexico, **34** 82
CITIC Pacific Ltd., 18 113–15
Citicasters Inc., **23** 293–94
Citicorp, II 253–55; 9 123–26 (upd.) *see also* Citigroup Inc.
Citicorp Diners Club, Inc., 90 137–40
Cities Service Company, **71** 258
CitiFinancial, **59** 121, 125
Citifor, **19** 156
Citigroup Inc., 30 124–28 (upd.); 59 121–27 (upd.)
Citivision PLC, *see* Blockbuster Inc.
Citizen Watch Co., Ltd., III 454–56; 21 121–24 (upd.); 81 77–82 (upd.)
Citizens Communications Company, 79 105–08 (upd.)
Citizens Financial Group, Inc., 42 76–80; 87 104–112 (upd.)
Citizens Gas Co., **6** 529
Citizens Gas Fuel Company *see* MCN Corp.
Citizens Gas Supply Corporation, **6** 527
Citizens Insurance Company of America, **63** 29
Citizens National Gas Company, **6** 527
Citizens Savings and Loan Society *see* Citizens Mutual Savings Bank.
Citizens State Bank, **41** 178, 180

Citizens Utilities Company, 7 87–89 *see also* Citizens Communications Company
Citrix Systems, Inc., 44 96–99
Citroën *see* Automobiles Citroën; PSA Peugeot Citroen S.A.
City and Suburban Telegraph Association *see* Cincinnati Bell Inc.
City Brewing Company LLC, 73 84–87
City Capital Associates, **31** 211
City Centre Properties Ltd. *see* Land Securities PLC.
City Collection Company, Inc., **58** 184
City Developments Limited, 89 153–56
City Light and Traction Company, **6** 593
City Light and Water Company, **6** 579
City Market Inc., *see* Dillon Companies Inc.
City National Bank of Baton Rouge, **11** 107
City of Seattle Water Department, **12** 443
City of Westminster Assurance Company Ltd., **59** 246
City Public Service, 6 473–75
Civic Parking LLC, *see* Central Parking Corp.
Civil & Civic Contractors *see* Lend Lease Corporation Ltd.
Civil Aviation Administration of China, **31** 102; **33** 98
CJ Banks *see* Christopher & Banks Corp.
CJ Corporation, 62 68–70
CJSC Transmash Holding, 93 446–49
CKE Restaurants, Inc., 19 89–93; 46 94–99 (upd.)
CKS Group Inc. *see* marchFIRST, Inc.
CKS Inc., **23** 479
Clabir Corp., **12** 199
Claire's Stores, Inc., 17 101–03; 94 125–29 (upd.)
Clairol, *see* Procter & Gamble Co.
CLAM Petroleum, *see* Louisiana Land and Exploration Co.
Clancy-Paul Inc., *see* InaCom Corp.
Clapp-Eastham Company *see* GenRad, Inc.
Clara Candy, **15** 65
CLARCOR Inc., 17 104–07; 61 63–67 (upd.)
Clare Rose Inc., 68 83–85
Claremont Technology Group Inc., **31** 131
Clariden Bank, **21** 146–47; **59** 142, 144
Clarify Corp., **38** 431
Clarion Company Ltd., 64 77–79
Clark & McKenney Hardware Co. *see* Clarcor Inc.
Clark Bar Candy Company, **53** 304
The Clark Construction Group, Inc., 8 112–13
Clark, Dietz & Associates-Engineers *see* CRSS Inc.
Clark Equipment Company, 8 114–16
Clark Filter, Inc., *see* CLARCOR Inc.
Clark Retail Enterprises Inc., **37** 311
Clark-Schwebel, Inc., **28** 195
Clarkins, Inc., **16** 35–36
Clarksburg Casket Co., **56** 23
CLASSA *see* Compañia de Líneas Aéreas Subvencionadas S.A.
Classic FM plc, **39** 198–200
Classic Vacation Group, Inc., 46 100–03
Clause/Tézier, **70** 346; **74** 139
Claxson Interactive Group, **54** 74
Clayco Construction Company, **41** 225–26
Clayton Brown Holding Company, **15** 232
Clayton Dubilier & Rice Inc., **25** 501; **29** 408; **40** 370; **49** 22
Clayton Homes Incorporated, 13 154–55; 54 76–79 (upd.)
Clayton-Marcus Co., *see* LADD Furniture, Inc.
Clayton/National Courier Systems, Inc., *see* Consolidated Delivery & Logistics, Inc.
Clayton Williams Energy, Inc., 87 113–116
CLE *see* Compagnie Laitière Européenne.
Clean Harbors, Inc., 73 88–91
Cleancoal Terminal, *see* Westmoreland Coal Co.
Clear Channel Communications, Inc., 23 130–32 *see also* Live Nation, Inc.
Clear Shield National Inc., *see* Envirodyne Industries, Inc.
Clearly Canadian Beverage Corporation, 48 94–97
Clearwire, Inc., 69 95–97
Cleary, Gottlieb, Steen & Hamilton, 35 106–09
Cleco Corporation, 37 88–91
The Clemens Family Corporation, 93 156–59
Clement Pappas & Company, Inc., 92 52–55
Clemente Capital Inc., **25** 542
Cleo Inc., **35** 131 *see also* Gibson Greetings, Inc.
Le Clerc, **21** 225–26
Clessidra SGR, **76** 326
Cleve-Co Jig Boring Co., **23** 82
Cleveland-Cliffs Inc., 13 156–58; 62 71–75 (upd.)
Cleveland Cotton Products Co., **37** 393
Cleveland Electric Illuminating Company *see* Centerior Energy Theodor.
Cleveland Fabric Centers, Inc. *see* Fabri-Centers of America Inc.
Cleveland Grinding Machine Co., **23** 82
Cleveland Indians Baseball Company, Inc., 37 92–94
Cleveland Iron Mining Company *see* Cleveland-Cliffs Inc.
Cleveland Precision Instruments, Inc., **23** 82
Cleveland Range Ltd. *see* Enodis plc.
Cleveland Twist Drill Company *see* Acme-Cleveland Corp.
Click Messenger Service, Inc., *see* Consolidated Delivery & Logistics, Inc.
Click Trips, Inc., **74** 169
Click Wine Group, 68 86–88
ClickAgents.com, Inc., **49** 433
Clicks Stores *see* New Clicks Holdings Ltd.
ClientLogic Corporation *see* Onex Corp.
Clif Bar Inc., 50 141–43
Clifford & Wills, *see* J. Crew Group Inc.
Clifford Chance LLP, 38 136–39
Cliffs Corporation, *see* Cleveland-Cliffs Inc.
Climaveneta Deutschland GmbH *see* De'Longhi S.p.A.
Clinical Partners, Inc., **26** 74
Clinical Pathology Facility, Inc., **26** 391
Clinique Laboratories, Inc., **30** 191
Clinton Cards plc, 39 86–88
Clipper Group, **12** 439
Clipper, Inc., **IV** 597
La Cloche d'Or, **25** 85
Cloetta Fazer AB, 70 58–60
Clopay Corp., **34** 195
The Clorox Company, III 20–22; 22 145–48 (upd.); 81 83–90 (upd.)
Close Brothers Group plc, 39 89–92
Clothesline Corporation, **60** 65
The Clothestime, Inc., 20 141–44
Clougherty Packing Company, 72 72–74
Clover Club, **44** 348
Clovis Water Co., **6** 580
Clow Water Systems Co., **55** 266
CLRP *see* City of London Real Property Company Ltd.
CLSI Inc., **15** 372; **43** 182
Club Corporation of America, **26** 27
Club de Hockey Canadien Inc., **26** 305
Club Méditerranée S.A., 6 206–08; 21 125–28 (upd.); 91 121–27 (upd.)
Club Monaco Inc., **62** 284
ClubCorp, Inc., 33 101–04
Cluett Corporation, *see* Celebrity, Inc.
Cluster Consulting, **51** 98
Clydesdale Group, **19** 390
CM&P *see* Cresap, McCormick and Paget.
CMAC Investment Corporation *see* Radian Group Inc.
CMC *see* Commercial Metals Co.
CME *see* Campbell-Mithun-Esty, Inc.; Central European Media Enterprises Ltd.; Chicago Mercantile Exchange Inc.
CMG Worldwide, Inc., 89 157–60
CMGI, Inc., 76 99–101
CMI International, Inc., *see* Hayes Lemmerz International, Inc.
CMIH *see* China Merchants International Holdings Co., Ltd.
CML Group, Inc., 10 215–18
CMO *see* Chi Mei Optoelectronics Corp.
CMP Media Inc., 26 76–80
CMP Properties Inc., **15** 122
CMS Energy Corporation, V 577–79; 14 114–16 (upd.)
CMS Healthcare, **29** 412
CN *see* Canadian National Railway Co.
CNA Financial Corporation, III 228–32; 38 140–46 (upd.)
CNB Bancshares Inc., **31** 207
CNBC, Inc., **28** 298

CNC Holding Corp. *see* Cole National Corp.
CNCA *see* Caisse National de Crédit Agricole.
CNEP *see* Comptoir National d'Escompte de Paris.
CNET Networks, Inc., 47 77–80
CNF Transportation *see* Consolidated Freightways, Inc.
CNG *see* Consolidated Natural Gas Co.
CNH Global N.V., 38 147–56 (upd.)
CNI *see* Community Networks Inc.
CNN *see* Cable News Network.
CNP *see* Compagnie Nationale à Portefeuille.
CNPC *see* China National Petroleum Corp.
CNS, Inc., 20 145–47 *see also* GlaxoSmithKline plc.
CNTS *see* Ceska Nezavisla Televizni Spolecnost.
Co-Counsel, Inc., **29** 364
Co-Op Blue Square Consumer Cooperative Society, **41** 56–58
Co-operative Group (CWS) Ltd., 51 86–89
Co-operative Insurance Society Ltd., **51** 89
Coach and Car Equipment Corp., **41** 369
Coach, Inc., 10 219–21; 45 111–15 (upd.)
Coach Specialties Co. *see* Fleetwood Enterprises, Inc.
Coach USA, Inc., 24 117–19; 55 103–06 (upd.)
Coachmen Industries, Inc., 77 104–07
Coal India Ltd., IV 48–50; 44 100–03 (upd.)
Coast Consolidators, Inc., *see* TNT Freightways Corp.
Coast to Coast Hardware *see* TruServ Corp.
Coastal Container Line Inc., **30** 318
Coastal Corporation, IV 394–95; 31 118–21 (upd.)
Coastline Distribution, Inc., **52** 399
Coats plc, V 356–58; 44 104–07 (upd.)
CoBank *see* National Bank for Cooperatives.
COBE Cardiovascular, Inc., 61 68–72
COBE Laboratories, Inc., 13 159–61
Coberco *see* Friesland Coberco Dairy Foods Holding N.V.
Cobham plc, 30 129–32
Coborn's, Inc., 30 133–35
Cobra Electronics Corporation, 14 117–19
Cobra Golf Inc., 16 108–10
Cobra Ventilation Products, **22** 229
Coca-Cola Bottling Co. Consolidated, 10 222–24
Coca-Cola Bottling Company of Northern New England, Inc., **21** 319
The Coca-Cola Company, I 232–35; 10 225–28 (upd.); 32 111–16 (upd.); 67 111–17 (upd.)
Coca-Cola Enterprises, Inc., 13 162–64
Cochlear Ltd., 77 108–11
Cochrane Foil Co., **15** 128
Cockburn & Campbell Ltd., **38** 501
Cockburn-Adelaide Cement, **31** 398, 400
Cockerill Sambre Group, IV 51–53; 26 81–84 (upd.) *see also* Arcelor Gent.
Coco's, **27** 16, 19
Code Hennessey & Simmons Limited, **39** 358
Codec, **19** 328
Codelco *see* Corporacion Nacional del Cobre de Chile.
Coelba *see* Companhia de Electricidade da Bahia.
Coeur d'Alene Mines Corporation, 20 148–51
COFAL *see* Compagnie financiere pour l'Amerique Latine.
COFCO *see* China National Cereals, Oils and Foodstuffs Import and Export Corp.
Coffee Club Franchise B.V., **53** 221
Coffee People, Inc., **40** 152–54
Cofica, **21** 99
Cofitel SA, **25** 466
Coflexip S.A., 25 103–05 *see also* Technip.
Cofresco Frischhalteprodukte GmbH & Co. KG, **53** 221
Cofroma, **23** 219
COGEMA Canada, **IV** 436
Cogeneracion Prat SA, **41** 325, 327
Cogeneration Development Corp., **42** 387–88
Cogent Communications Group, Inc., 55 107–10
Cogent Data Technologies, Inc., **31** 5
Cogentrix Energy, Inc., 10 229–31
Cogetex, **14** 225
Cogifer, S.A., **18** 4; **31** 156, 158
Cognex Corporation, 76 102–06
Cognitive Solutions, Inc., **18** 140
Cognizant Technology Solutions Corporation, 59 128–30
Cognos Inc., 44 108–11
Coherent, Inc., 31 122–25
Coherix Corporation, **48** 446
Cohn-Hall-Marx Co. *see* United Merchants & Manufacturers, Inc.
Cohoes Bancorp Inc., **41** 212
Cohu, Inc., 32 117–19
Coinmach Laundry Corporation, 20 152–54
Coinstar, Inc., 44 112–14
Coktel Vision, **15** 455
Colas S.A., 31 126–29
Colby Group Holdings Limited, **59** 261
Cold Spring Brewing Co. *see* Gluek Brewing Co.
Cold Spring Granite Company, 16 111–14; 67 118–22 (upd.)
Cold Stone Creamery, 69 98–100
Coldwater Creek Inc., 21 129–31; 74 88–91 (upd.)
Coldwell Banker Co. *see* CB Richard Ellis Group, Inc.
Cole Haan Holdings Incorporated, **36** 346
Cole National Corporation, 13 165–67; 76 107–10 (upd.)
Cole Sewell Corporation, **39** 322, 324
Cole's Quality Foods, Inc., 68 92–94
Coleco Industries, Inc., **21** 375
The Coleman Company, Inc., 9 127–29; 30 136–39 (upd.)
Coleman Natural Products, Inc., 68 89–91
Coleman Outdoor Products Inc., **21** 293
Colemans Ltd., **11** 241
Coles Book Stores Ltd., **58** 185 *see also* Southam Inc.
Coles Express Inc., 15 109–11
Coles Group Limited, V 33–35; 20 155–58 (upd.); 85 49–56 (upd.)
Colex Data, **14** 556
Colfax Corporation, 58 65–67
Colgate Medical Ltd. *see* Orthofix International NV.
Colgate-Palmolive Company, III 23–26; 14 120–23 (upd.); 35 110–15 (upd.); 71 105–10 (upd.)
Collaborative Care Corporation, **68** 299
Collabra Software Inc., **15** 322
Collect-a-Can (Pty) Ltd., **57** 183
Collectors Universe, Inc., 48 98–100
College Construction Loan Insurance Assoc., *see* SLM Holding Corp.
Colliers International Property Consultants Inc., 92 56–59
Collins & Aikman Corporation, 13 168–70; 41 91–95 (upd.)
Collins Industries, Inc., 33 105–07
Collins Stewart, **41** 371–72
Colo-Macco *see* CRSS Inc.
Cologne Re *see* General Re Corporation; Kölnische Rückversicherungs Gesellschaft AG.
Colonia Insurance Company (UK) Ltd., **49** 43
Colonia Versicherung Aktiengesellschaft *see* AXA Colonia Konzern AG.
Colonial Candle of Cape Cod *see* Blyth, Inc.
Colonial Companies Inc., **52** 381
Colonial National Bank, *see* Advanta Corp.
Colonial Penn Group Insurance Co., **11** 262
Colonial Properties Trust, 65 115–17
Colonial Rubber Works, *see* M. A. Hanna Co.
Colonial Sugar Refining Co. Ltd. *see* CSR Ltd.
Colonial Williamsburg Foundation, 53 105–07
Colony Gift Corporation, Ltd., *see* Blyth, Inc.
Color Corporation of America, *see* The Valspar Corp.
Color Kinetics Incorporated, 85 57–60
Color Me Mine, *see* Koo Koo Roo, Inc.
Color Tile, **31** 435
Colorado Baseball Management, Inc., 72 75–78
Colorado Belle Casino *see* Circus Circus Enterprises, Inc.

Colorado Electric Company *see* Public Service Company of Colorado.
Colorado Fuel & Iron (CF&I), *see* Oregon Steel Mills, Inc.
Colorado Gaming & Entertainment Co., **21** 335
Colorado MEDtech, Inc., 48 101–05
Colorado National Bank, **12** 165
Colorado Technical University, Inc., **41** 419
Colorfoto Inc., *see* Fuqua Industries, Inc.
Coloroll, **44** 148
ColorPlus Fashions Limited *see* Raymond Ltd.
Colorstrip, Inc., **63** 272
Colortree *see* National Envelope Corp.
ColorTyme, Inc., **45** 367
ColorWorks Salon *see* Ratner Companies.
Colt Industries Inc., I 434–36
COLT Telecom Group plc, 41 96–99
Colt's Manufacturing Company, Inc., 12 70–72
Coltec Industries Inc., **30** 158; **32** 96; **46** 213; **52** 158–59
Columbia Administration Software Publishing Corporation, **51** 244
Columbia Artists Management, Inc., **52** 199–200
Columbia Broadcasting System *see* CBS Corp.
Columbia Chemical Co. *see* PPG Industries, Inc.
Columbia Electric Street Railway, Light and Power Company, **6** 575
Columbia Forest Products Inc., 78 74–77
Columbia Gas & Electric Company *see* Columbia Gas System, Inc.
Columbia Gas Light Company, **6** 574
Columbia Gas of New York, Inc., **6** 536
The Columbia Gas System, Inc., V 580–82; 16 115–18 (upd.)
Columbia Gas Transmission Corporation, **6** 467
Columbia Hat Company *see* Columbia Sportswear Co.
Columbia/HCA Healthcare Corporation, 15 112–14
Columbia House Company, 69 101–03
Columbia Insurance Co., *see* Berkshire Hathaway Inc.
Columbia Railroad, Gas and Electric Company, **6** 575
Columbia Records, **26** 150
Columbia Sportswear Company, 19 94–96; 41 100–03 (upd.)
Columbia TriStar Motion Pictures Companies, II 135–37; 12 73–76 (upd.)
Columbian Chemicals Co., **28** 352, 356
Columbus & Southern Ohio Electric Company (CSO), **6** 467, 481–82
Columbus Bank & Trust *see* Synovus Financial Corp.
Columbus McKinnon Corporation, 37 95–98
Columbus Realty Trust, **26** 378
Columbus Stainless, **59** 226
Colwell Systems, **19** 291; **22** 181
Com Dev, Inc., **32** 435
Com Ed *see* Commonwealth Edison.
Com-Link 21, Inc., **8** LDDS-Metro Communications, Inc.
Com Tech Communications Ltd. *see* Dimension Data Holdings PLC.
Comair Holdings Inc., 13 171–73; 34 116–20 (upd.)
Comalco Ltd., **IV** 59–61, 122, 191
Comat Services Pte. Ltd., *see* System Software Associates, Inc.
Combe Inc., 72 79–82
Combined International Corporation *see* Aon Corporation
Combustion Engineering Group, **22** 11
Combustiveis Industriais e Domésticos *see* CIDLA.
Comcast Corporation, 7 90–92; 24 120–24 (upd.)
ComCore Semiconductor, Inc., **26** 330
Comdata, **19** 160
Comdial Corporation, 21 132–35
Comdisco, Inc., 9 130–32
Comerci *see* Controladora Comercial Mexicana, S.A. de C.V.
Comercial Arauco Ltda., **72** 269
Comercial Mexicana, S.A. *see* Controladora Comercial Mexicana, S.A. de C.V.
Comerica Incorporated, 40 115–17
Comesi San Luis S.A.I.C. *see* Siderar S.A.I.C.
Comet *see* Kingfisher plc.
Comet American Marketing, **33** 31
Comet Rice, Inc., **33** 31
Comfin, **60** 96
COMFORCE Corporation, 40 118–20
Comfort Inn *see* Choice Hotels International, Inc.
Comforto GmbH, *see* Haworth Inc.
ComGlobal Biosystems, Inc., **74** 22
Comilog *see* Eramet.
Cominco Ltd., 37 99–102
Comision Federal de Electricidad de Mexico (CFE), **21** 196–97
CommAir *see* American Building Maintenance Industries, Inc.
Command Security Corporation, 57 71–73
Commemorative Brands Inc., **19** 453
Commentor, **74** 143
Commerce Clearing House, Inc., 7 93–94 *see also* CCH Inc.
Commerce.TV, **42** 323
The CommerceBank of Washington, **53** 378
CommerceConnect LLC, **56** 73
Commercial Air Lines, Inc., **23** 380
Commercial Credit Company, 8 117–19 *see also* Citigroup Inc.
Commercial Federal Corporation, 12 77–79; 62 76–80 (upd.)
Commercial Financial Services, Inc., 26 85–89
Commercial Freeze Dry Ltd., **74** 229
Commercial Intertech Corporation, **57** 86
Commercial Life, *see* Continental Corp.
Commercial Metals Company, 15 115–17; 42 81–84(upd.)
Commercial Realty Services Group, **21** 257
Commercial Union plc, III 233–35 *see also* Aviva PLC.
Commercial Vehicle Group, Inc., 81 91–94
Commerzbank A.G., II 256–58; 47 81–84 (upd.)
Commerzfilm, **IV** 591
CommLink Corp., *see* Jack Henry and Associates, Inc.
Commodore International, Ltd., 7 95–97
Commonwealth Aluminium Corp., Ltd. *see* Comalco Ltd.
Commonwealth Brands, Inc., **51** 170
Commonwealth Edison, V 583–85
Commonwealth Energy System, 14 124–26
Commonwealth Industrial Gases, **25** 82
Commonwealth Industries, **11** 536
Commonwealth Insurance Co., *see* Home Insurance Co.
Commonwealth Land Title Insurance Company *see* LandAmerica Financial Group, Inc.
Commonwealth Life and Accident Insurance Company, **27** 46–47
Commonwealth Life Insurance Co. *see* Providian Financial Corporation
Commonwealth Limousine Services, Ltd., **26** 62
Commonwealth Mortgage Assurance Co., *see* Reliance Group Holdings, Inc.
Commonwealth Steel Company Ltd, **62** 331
Commonwealth Telephone Enterprises, Inc., 25 106–08
Commonwealth United Corp., **53** 364
CommQuest Technologies, **63** 199
CommScope, Inc., 77 112–15
Commtron, Inc. *see* AmerisourceBergen Corp.
Communications and Systems Specialists, *see* Nichols Research Corp.
Communications Corp. of America, **25** 418
Communications Network Consultants, **29** 400
Communications Solutions Inc., **11** 520
Communications Technology Corp. (CTC), *see* Acme-Chemical Corp.
Community Coffee Co. L.L.C., 53 108–10
Community Direct, Inc., *see* Affiliated Publications, Inc.
Community Health Systems, Inc., 71 111–13
Community HealthCare Services, **6** 182
Community Networks Inc., **45** 69
Community Newspaper Holdings, Inc., 91 128–31
Community Power & Light Company, **6** 579–80
Community Psychiatric Centers, 15 118–20

Community Public Service Company, **6** 514
Comp-Est Estimating Solutions Inc., **74** 70
Comp-U-Card of America, Inc. *see* CUC International Inc.
Compac Corp., *see* TriMas Corp.
Compagnia di Participazioni Assicurative ed Industriali S.p.A., **24** 341
Compagnia Italiana dei Jolly Hotels S.p.A., 71 114–16
Compagnie Bancaire, **21** 99–100
Compagnie de Recherche et d'Exploitation du Pétrole du Sahara, **21** 203
Compagnie de Saint-Gobain, III 675–78; 16 119–23 (upd.); 64 80–84 (upd.)
Compagnie des Alpes, 48 106–08
Compagnie des Cristalleries de Baccarat *see* Baccarat.
Compagnie des Machines Bull S.A., III 122–23 *see also* Bull S.A.; Groupe Bull.
Compagnie Européenne de Publication, **IV** 614–16
Compagnie Européenne de Télésecurité, **32** 374
Compagnie Financier Richemont AG, *see* Rothmans UK Holdings Ltd.
Compagnie Financière Belge des Pétroles *see* PetroFina S.A.
Compagnie Financiere De Bourbon, **60** 149
Compagnie Financière de Paribas, II 259–60 *see also* BNP Paribas Group.
Compagnie Financière de Richemont AG, **29** 90
Compagnie Financière de Suez *see* Suez Lyonnaise des Eaux.
Compagnie Financière du Groupe Victoire, **27** 54; **49** 44
Compagnie Financiere pour l'Amerique Latine, **67** 326
Compagnie Financière Richemont AG, 50 144–47
Compagnie Financière Sucres et Denrées S.A., 60 94–96
Compagnie Française de Manutention, *see* Manitou BF S.A.
Compagnie Française des Pétroles *see* TOTAL S.A.
Compagnie Générale d'Électricité, II 12–13
Compagnie Générale des Eaux *see* Vivendi SA.
Compagnie Générale des Établissements Michelin, V 236–39; 42 85–89 (upd.)
Compagnie Générale Maritime et Financière, 6 379–81
Compagnie Industriali Riunite S.p.A., **IV** 587–88; **54** 21
Compagnie Industrielle de Matérials de Manutention, *see* Manitou BF S.A.
Compagnie Industrielle des Fillers *see* L'Entreprise Jean Lefebvre.
Compagnie Laitière Européenne, *see* Bongrain S.A.
Compagnie Luxembourgeoise de Télédiffusion, **15** 54
Compagnie Monegasque du Banque, **65** 230, 232
Compagnie Nationale à Portefeuille, 84 55–58
Compagnie Nationale de Navigation, *see* Sequana Capital.
Compagnie Transcontinentale de Reassurance, **57** 136
Compagnie Union des Assurances de Paris (UAP), **49** 44
Compal, **47** 152–53
Companhia Brasileira de Distribuiçao, 76 111–13
Companhia Brasileira de Petróleo Ipiranga, **67** 216
Companhia de Bebidas das Américas, 57 74–77
Companhia de Celulose do Caima, **14** 250
Companhia de Electricidade da Bahia, **49** 211
Companhia de Seguros Tranquilidade Vida, S.A. *see* Banco Espírito Santo e Comercial de Lisboa S.A.
Companhia de Tecidos Norte de Minas - Coteminas, 77 116–19
Companhia Energética de Minas Gerais S.A., 65 118–20
Companhia Industrial de Papel Pirahy, **52** 301
Companhia Nordeste de Participaçoes, **73** 244
Companhia Siderúrgica Mannesmann S.A. *see* Mannesmann AG.
Companhia Siderúrgica Nacional, 76 114–17
Companhia Suzano de Papel e Celulose S.A., 94 130–33
Companhia Vale do Rio Doce, IV 54–57; 43 111–14 (upd.)
Compania Cervecerias Unidas S.A., 70 61–63
Compañia de Minas BuenaventuraS.A.A., 92160–63
Compañía de Nutrición General S.A., **72** 128
Compania Electro Metaluurgica, **67** 13
Compañia Española de Petróleos S.A. (Cepsa), IV 396–98; 56 63–66 (upd.)
Compania Fresnillo, **22** 286
Compania Fundidora del Norte, S.A., **54** 152
Compania General de Aceptaciones *see* Financiera Aceptaciones.
Compania Hulera Euzkadi, **21** 260; **23** 170
Compañia Industrial de Parras, S.A. de C.V. (CIPSA), 84 59–62
Compania Industrial de San Cristobal, S.A. de C.V., **54** 186
Compania Industrial del Norte, S.A., **54** 152
Compañia Mexicana de Transportación Aérea, **20** 167
Compania Minera de Penoles *see* Industrias Penoles, S.A. de C.V.
Compania Minera Las Torres, **22** 286
Compania Siderurgica Huachipato, **24** 209
Compañía Telefónica Nacional de España S.A. *see* Telefónica Nacional de España S.A.
Compaq Computer Corporation, III 124–25; 6 221–23 (upd.); 26 90–93 (upd.) *see also* Hewlett-Packard Co.
Comparex Holdings, **69** 127
Compart, **24** 341
Compass Bancshares, Inc., 73 92–94
Compass Design Automation, *see* VLSI Technology, Inc.
Compass Group PLC, 34 121–24
Compass Minerals International, Inc., 79 109–12
CompDent Corporation, 22 149–51
Competence ApS, **26** 240
CompHealth Inc., 25 109–12
Complete Business Solutions, Inc., 31 130–33
Complete Post, **50** 126
Completion Bond Co., **26** 487
Components Agents Ltd., *see* Arrow Electronics, Inc.
Composite Research & Management Co., *see* Washington Mutual, Inc.
Comprehensive Care Corporation, 15 121–23
Compressor Controls Corporation, **15** 404; **50** 394
Comptoir Général de la Photographie *see* Gaumont SA.
Comptoirs Modernes S.A., 19 97–99 *see also* Carrefour SA.
Compton's MultiMedia Publishing Group, Inc., *see* Encyclopaedia Britannica, Inc.
Compton's New Media, Inc., *see* Encyclopaedia Britannica, Inc.
Compu-Notes, Inc., **22** 413
CompuAdd Computer Corporation, 11 61–63
CompuChem Corporation, **11** 425
CompuCom Systems, Inc., 10 232–34
CompuDyne Corporation, 51 78–81
CompuPharm, Inc., **14** 210
CompUSA, Inc., 10 235–36; 35 116–18 (upd.)
Compuscript, Inc., **64** 27
CompuServe Interactive Services, Inc., 10 237–39; 27 106–08 (upd.) *see also* AOL Time Warner Inc.
Computer Associates International, Inc., 6 224–26; 49 94–97 (upd.)
Computer City, *see* Tandy Corp.
Computer Data Systems, Inc., 14 127–29
Computer Discount Corporation *see* Comdisco, Inc.
Computer Discount Warehouse *see* CDW Computer Centers, Inc.
Computer Learning Centers, Inc., 26 94–96
Computer Motion, Inc. *see* Intuitive Surgical, Inc.
Computer Network Technology Corporation, **75** 256

Computer Power, **6** 301
Computer Renaissance, Inc., *see* Grow Biz International, Inc.
Computer Resources Management, Inc., **26** 36
Computer Sciences Corporation, 6 227–29
Computer Systems and Applications Inc., *see* Severn Trent PLC.
Computer Terminal Corporation, *see* Datapoint Corp.
Computerized Lodging Systems, Inc., **11** 275
Computerized Waste Systems, **46** 248
ComputerLand Corp., 13 174–76
Computervision Corporation, 10 240–42
Compuware Corporation, 10 243–45; 30 140–43 (upd.); 66 60–64 (upd.)
CompX International, Inc., *see* Valhi, Inc.
Comsat Corporation, 23 133–36 *see also* Lockheed Martin Corp.
Comshare Inc., 23 137–39
Comstock Resources, Inc., 47 85–87
Comtec Information Systems Inc., **53** 374
Comtech Telecommunications Corp., 75 103–05
Comtel Electronics, Inc., *see* Palomar Medical Technologies, Inc.
Comunicaciones Avanzados, S.A. de C.V., **39** 195
Comverse Technology, Inc., 15 124–26; 43 115–18 (upd.)
Comviq GSM AB, **26** 331–33
Con Ed *see* Consolidated Edison, Inc.
ConAgra Foods, Inc., II 493–95; 12 80–82 (upd.); 42 90–94 (upd.); 85 61–68 (upd.)
Conair Corporation, 17 108–10; 69 104–08 (upd.)
Conaprole *see* Cooperativa Nacional de Productores de Leche S.A. (Conaprole).
Concentra Inc., 71 117–19
Concept, Inc., **23** 154
Concepts Direct, Inc., 39 93–96
Concepts in Community Living, Inc., **43** 46
Concert Communications Company, **15** 69; **27** 304–05; **49** 72
Concesiones de Infraestructuras de Transportes, S.A., **40** 217
Concha y Toro *see* Viña Concha y Toro S.A.
Concord Camera Corporation, 41 104–07
Concord EFS, Inc., 52 86–88
Concord Fabrics, Inc., 16 124–26
Concord Leasing, Inc., **51** 108
Concord Watch Company, S.A., **28** 291
Concorde Acceptance Corporation, **64** 20–21
Concorde Hotels & Resorts, *see* Société du Louvre.
Concrete Enterprises, Inc., **72** 233
Concrete Safety Systems, Inc., **56** 332
Concretos Apasco, S.A. de C.V., **51** 28–29
Concurrent Computer Corporation, 75 106–08
Condé Nast Publications, Inc., 13 177–81; 59 131–34 (upd.)
CONDEA Vista Company, **61** 113
Condor Systems Inc., **15** 530
Cone Communications, **25** 258
Cone Mills LLC, 8 120–22; 67 123–27 (upd.)
Conexant Systems, Inc., 36 121–25
Confecciones Cuscatlecas, S.A. de C.V., **64** 142
Confederation Freezers, **21** 501
ConferencePlus, Inc., **57** 408–09
Confiseriefabrik Richterich & Co. Laufen *see* Ricola Ltd.
Confluence Holdings Corporation, 76 118–20
Congas Engineering Canada Ltd., **6** 478
Congoleum Corp., 18 116–19
Congress Financial Corp., **19** 108
Congressional Information Services *see* Reed Elsevier.
Conic, *see* Loral Corp.
Conifer Records Ltd., **52** 429
Coniston Partners, **6** 130
CONMED Corporation, 87 117–120
Conn-Selmer, Inc., 55 111–14
Conn's, Inc., 67 128–30
Connect Group Corporation, **28** 242
Connecticut General Corporation *see* CIGNA Corp.
Connecticut Health Enterprises Network, *see* PHP Healthcare Corp.
Connecticut Light and Power Co., 13 182–84
Connecticut Mutual Life Insurance Company, III 236–38
Connecticut Telephone Company *see* Southern New England Telecommunications Corp.
Connecticut Yankee Atomic Power Company, **21** 513
The Connection Group, Inc., **26** 257
Connective Therapeutics, Inc. *see* Connetics Corp.
Connectix Corporation, **28** 245
The Connell Company, 29 129–31
Conner Corp., **15** 327
Conner Peripherals, Inc., 6 230–32
Connetics Corporation, 70 64–66
Connie Lee *see* College Construction Loan Insurance Assoc.
Connoisseur Communications, **37** 104
Connolly Data Systems, **11** 66
Connolly Tool and Machine Company, **21** 215
Connors Bros. Income Fund, **64** 61 *see also* George Weston Ltd.
Connors Steel Co., **15** 116
ConocoPhillips, IV 399–402; 16 127–32 (upd.); 63 104–15 (upd.)
ConQuest Telecommunication Services Inc., **16** 319
Conquistador Films, **25** 270
Conrad Industries, Inc., 58 68–70
Conrad International Corporation, **62** 179
Conrail Inc. *see* Consolidated Rail Corp.
Conrock Co., *see* CalMat Co.
Conseco Inc., 10 246–48; 33 108–12 (upd.)
Conseo GmbH, **68** 289
Conshu Holdings, **24** 450
Conso International Corporation, 29 132–34
Consodata S.A., **47** 345, 347
CONSOL Energy Inc., 59 135–37
Consolidated Analysis Centers, Inc. *see* CACI International Inc.
Consolidated Asset Management Company, Inc., **25** 204
Consolidated-Bathurst Inc., **26** 445
Consolidated Cigar Holdings, Inc., **15** 137–38; **28** 247
Consolidated Citrus Limited Partnership, **60** 189
Consolidated Container Company L.L.C., **73** 106
Consolidated Conversion Co., *see* Cubic Corp.
Consolidated Delivery & Logistics, Inc., 24 125–28 *see also* Velocity Express Corp.
Consolidated Edison, Inc., V 586–89; 45 116–20 (upd.)
Consolidated Electric Power Asia, **38** 448
Consolidated Electric Supply Inc., **15** 385
Consolidated Foods Corp., **29** 132
Consolidated Freightways Corporation, V 432–34; 21 136–39 (upd.); 48 109–13 (upd.)
Consolidated Gas Company *see* Baltimore Gas and Electric Co.
Consolidated Graphics, Inc., 70 67–69
Consolidated International, **50** 98
Consolidated Natural Gas Company, V 590–91; 19 100–02 (upd.) *see also* Dominion Resources, Inc.
Consolidated Papers, Inc., 8 123–25; 36 126–30 (upd.)
Consolidated Plantations Berhad, **36** 434–35
Consolidated Power & Light Company, **6** 580
Consolidated Products, Inc., 14 130–32
Consolidated Rail Corporation, V 435–37
Consolidated Restaurant Cos. *see* Landry's Restaurants, Inc.
Consolidated Specialty Restaurants, Inc., *see* Consolidated Products Inc.
Consolidated Stores Corp., **29** 311; **35** 254; **50** 98
Consolidated Theaters, Inc., **14** 87
Consolidated Tire Company, **20** 258
Consolidated TVX Mining Corporation, **61** 290
Consolidation Services, **44** 10, 13
Consorcio ARA, S.A. de C.V., 79 113–16
Consorcio Aviacsa, S.A. de C.V., 85 69–72
Consorcio G Grupo Dina, S.A. de C.V., 36 131–33
Consorcio Siderurgica Amazonia Ltd. *see* Siderar S.A.I.C.

Consortium, **34** 373
Consortium de Realisation, **35** 329
Consortium De Realization SAS, **23** 392
Constar International Inc., 64 85–88
Constellation Brands, Inc., 68 95–100 (upd.)
Constellation Enterprises Inc., **25** 46
Constitution Insurance Company, **51** 143
Construcciones Aeronáuticas SA, **7** 9 *see also* European Aeronautic Defence and Space Company EADS N.V.
Construction Developers Inc., **68** 114
Construction DJL Inc., **23** 332–33
Constructora CAMSA, C.A., **56** 383
Constructora y Administradora Uno S.A., **72** 269
Construtora Norberto Odebrecht S.A. *see* Odebrecht S.A.
Consul GmbH, **51** 58
Consumer Products Company, **30** 39
Consumer Value Stores *see* CVS Corp.
ConsumerNet, **49** 422
Consumers Cooperative Association *see* Farmland Industries, Inc.
Consumers Distributing Co. Ltd., *see* Provigo Inc.
Consumers Electric Light and Power, **6** 582
The Consumers Gas Company Ltd., 6 476–79; 43 154 *see also* Enbridge Inc.
Consumers Mutual Gas Light Company *see* Baltimore Gas and Electric Co.
Consumers Power Co., 14 133–36
Consumers Public Power District, **29** 352
Consumers Union, 26 97–99
Consumers Water Company, 14 137–39
Container Corporation of America, **V** 147; **26** 446
The Container Store, 36 134–36
Contaminant Recovery Systems, Inc., *see* Essef Corp.
CONTAQ Microsystems Inc., **48** 127
Contech, *see* SPX Corp.
Contel Corporation, **V** 296–98; **15** 192; **43** 447
Contempo Casuals, Inc. *see* The Wet Seal, Inc.
Contemporary Books, *see* Tribune Co.
Content Technologies Inc., **42** 24–25
Conti-Carriers & Terminals Inc., **22** 167
Contico International, L.L.C., **51** 190
ContiGroup Companies, Inc., 43 119–22 (upd.)
Continental AG, V 240–43; 56 67–72 (upd.)
Continental Airlines, Inc., I 96–98; 21 140–43 (upd.); 52 89–94 (upd.)
Continental American Corporation, *see* Crown Central Petroleum Corp.
Continental Baking Co., **12** 276; **38** 252
Continental Bank Corporation, II 261–63 *see also* Bank of America.
Continental Bio-Clinical Laboratories, **26** 391
Continental Cablevision, Inc., 7 98–100
Continental Can Co., Inc., 15 127–30
Continental-Caoutchouc und Gutta-Percha Compagnie *see* Continental AG.
Continental Carbon Co., **36** 146–48
Continental Casualty Co., *see* CNA Financial Corp.
Continental Corporation, III 239–44
Continental Design, **58** 194
Continental Divide Insurance Co., *see* Berkshire Hathaway Inc.
Continental Electronics Corporation, *see* Tech-Sym Corp.
Continental Gas & Electric Corporation, **6** 511
Continental General Tire Corp., 23 140–42
Continental Grain Company, 10 249–51; 13 185–87 (upd.) *see also* ContiGroup Companies, Inc.
Continental Group Co., I 599–600
Continental Hair Products, Inc. *see* Conair Corp.
Continental Homes Inc., **26** 291; **58** 84
Continental Illinois Corp. *see* Continental Bank Corp.
Continental Investment Corporation, **22** 541; **33** 407
Continental Medical Systems, Inc., 10 252–54
Continental Modules, Inc., **45** 328
Continental Oil Co. *see* ConocoPhillips.
Continental Plastic Containers, Inc., *see* Viatech Continental Can Company, Inc.
Continental Reinsurance, **11** 533
Continental Resources, Inc., 89 161–65
Continental Risk Services, *see* Continental Corp.
Continental Scale Works, *see* Health O Meter Products Inc.
Continental Telephone Company *see* GTE Corp.
Continental Wood Preservers, Inc., *see* Ply Gem Industries Inc.
ContinueCare Corporation, **25** 41
Continuum Electro-Optics, Inc. *see* Excel Technology, Inc.
Continuum Health Partners, Inc., 60 97–99
Contran Corporation, **19** 467
Contred Ltd., **20** 263
Control Data Corporation, III 126–28 *see also* Seagate Technology, Inc.
Control Data Systems, Inc., 10 255–57
Control Systemation, Inc. *see* Excel Technology, Inc.
Controladora Comercial Mexicana, S.A. de C.V., 36 137–39
Controladora Mabe, S.A. de C.V., 82 74-77
Controlled Materials and Equipment Transportation, **29** 354
Controlware GmbH, **22** 53
Converse Inc., 9 133–36; 31 134–38 (upd.)
Convotherm Ltd. *see* Enodis plc.
Conway Computer Group, *see* Nichols Research Corp.
Conwest Exploration Company Ltd., **16** 10, 12; **43** 3
Conycon *see* Construcciones y Contratas.
Conzinc Riotinto of Australia *see* CRA Ltd.
Conzzeta Holding, 80 76–79
Cook Bates Inc., **40** 347–48
Cooker Restaurant Corporation, 20 159–61; 51 82–85 (upd.)
Cookson Group plc, III 679–82; 44 115–20 (upd.)
CoolBrands International Inc., 35 119–22
CoolSavings, Inc., 77 120–24
Coop Schweiz Genossenschaftsverband, 48 114–16
Coopagri Bretagne, 88 53–56
Cooper Cameron Corporation, 20 162–66 (upd.); 58 71–75 (upd.)
The Cooper Companies, Inc., 39 97–100
Cooper Industries, Inc., II 14–17; 44 121–25 (upd.)
Cooper Tire & Rubber Company, 8 126–28; 23 143–46 (upd.)
Cooperativa Nacional de Productores de Leche S.A. (Conaprole),92 60–63
Cooperative Business International, Inc., **60** 88
Coopérative de Production et de Vente de Semences Sélectionnées du Massif Central *see* Groupe Limagrain.
Coopercredito SpA, **72** 21
Coopers & Lybrand, 9 137–38 *see also* PricewaterhouseCoopers.
Coordinados Elite, S.A. de United Apparel Ventures, **62** 353
Coordinated Caribbean Transport *see* Crowley Caribbean Transport.
Coors Company *see* Adolph Coors Co.
Copa Holdings, S.A., 93 164–67
Copart Inc., 23 147–49
Copec *see* Empresas Copec S.A.
Coperion Holding GmbH, **61** 108
Copico, **44** 273
The Copley Press, Inc., 23 150–52
Coppel, S.A. de C.V., 82 78-81
The Copps Corporation, 32 120–22
Cor Therapeutics, **47** 251
Cora S.A./NV, 94 134–37
Coral Energy, **41** 359
Corange, Ltd., **37** 111–13
Corbett Canyon *see* The Wine Group, Inc.
Corbis Corporation, 31 139–42
Corby Distilleries Limited, 14 140–42
Corchos de Mérida S.A., **48** 349
Corco *see* Commonwealth Oil Refining Co.
Corco, Inc. *see* Liqui-Box Corp.
Corcoran & Riggs *see* Riggs National Corp.
The Corcoran Group, Inc., 58 76–78
Cordant Technologies, **56** 11
Cordes, **56** 234
Cordiant plc *see* Saatchi & Saatchi plc.
Cordis Corporation, 19 103–05; 46 104–07 (upd.)

Cordon & Gotch, **IV** 619
Cordon Bleu *see* Le Cordon Bleu S.A.
Core Laboratories Inc., *see* Litton Industries Inc.
Corel Corporation, 15 131–33; 33 113–16 (upd.); 76 121–24 (upd.)
CoreStates Financial Corp, 16 111–15 *see also* Wachovia Corp.
CoreTek, Inc., **36** 353
Corfo *see* Corporación de Fomento de la Producción.
Corfuerte S.A. de C.V., **23** 171
Corin Othopedic Products, **68** 379
Corinthian Colleges, Inc., 39 101–04; 92 64–69 (upd.)
Corio Inc., **38** 188, 432
Cork Asia Pacific *see* McPherson's Ltd.
Cormetech *see* Corning Inc.
Cornelia Insurance Agency *see* Advantage Insurers, Inc.
Cornelius Nurseries, Inc., **51** 61
Cornell Corrections, **28** 255
Cornelsen Verlagsholding GmbH & Co., 90 141–46
Cornerstone Propane Partners, L.P., **37** 280, 283
Cornerstone Real Estate Advisors Inc., **53** 213
Corning Clinical Laboratories, **26** 390–92
Corning Inc., III 683–85; 44 126–30 (upd.); 90 147–53 (upd.)
La Cornue *see* Aga FoodserviceGroup PLC.
Coro International A.V.V., **39** 346
Corporación de Fomento de la Producción, **71** 210
Corporacion Durango, S.A. de C.V., **37** 178
Corporacion Energia Hidroelectrica de Navarra *see* Acciona S.A.
Corporacion Engelhard De Venezuela, C.A. *see* Engelhard Corp.
Corporacion Financiera Hipotecaria, **63** 213
Corporación Geo, S.A. de C.V., 81 95–98
Corporación Interamericana de Entretenimiento, S.A. de C.V., 83 87-90
Corporación Internacional de Aviación, S.A. de C.V. (Cintra), 20 167–69
Corporación José R. Lindley S.A., 92 70–73
Corporación Moctezuma, **21** 261
Corporación Multi-Inversiones, 94 138–42
Corporacion Nacional del Cobre de Chile, 40 121–23
Corporate Childcare Development, Inc. *see* Bright Horizons Family Solutions, Inc.
The Corporate Executive Board Company, 89 166–69
Corporate Express, Inc., 22 152–55; 47 88–92 (upd.)
Corporate Partners, **12** 391
Corporate Software Inc., 9 139–41
Corporate Wings, Inc., **75** 144–45
CorporateFamily Solutions *see* Bright Horizons Family Solutions, Inc.
Corporation for Public Broadcasting, 14 143–45; 89 170–75 (upd.)
Corporation Trust Co. *see* CCH Inc.
Corrado Passera, **IV** 588
CorrChoice, Inc. *see* Greif Inc.
Correctional Services Corporation, 30 144–46
Corrections Corporation of America, 23 153–55
Correo Argentina S.A., **63** 179; **67** 348
Correos y Telegrafos S.A., 80 80–83
Corrigan's, *see* Zale Corp.
CorrLogic, Inc., **51** 81
Corroon & Black *see* Willis Corroon Group Plc.
Corrosion Technologies de México SA de C V, **53** 285
Corrpro Companies, Inc., 20 170–73
CORT Business Services Corporation, 26 100–02
El Corte Inglés Group, 26 128–31 (upd.)
Cortefiel S.A., 64 89–91
Corticeira Amorim, Sociedade Gestora de Participaço es Sociais, S.A., 48 117–20
Corus Bankshares, Inc., 75 109–11
Corus Group plc, 49 98–105 (upd.)
Corvi *see* Grupo Corvi S.A. de C.V.
Corvis Corporation *see* Broadwing Corp.
Cory Bros & Co. Ltd., **31** 367, 369
Cory Components, **36** 158
Cory Environmental Ltd., **51** 130
Cory Orchard and Turf *see* Chemi-Trol Chemical Co.
Cosco, Inc., **59** 164
Cosco Pacific, **20** 313
Cosi, Inc., 53 111–13
Cosmair Inc., 8 129–32 *see also* L'Oreal.
Cosmar Corp., **37** 269–71
The Cosmetic Center, Inc., 22 156–58
Cosmetic Technology International, Inc., *see* Palomar Medical Technologies, Inc.
Cosmetics & More Inc., **64** 334
Cosmo Oil Co., Ltd., IV 403–04; 53 114–16 (upd.)
Cosmopolitan Cosmetics GmbH, **48** 420, 422
Cosmos International, Inc., **51** 307
Cosmotel, **46** 401
Cost Plus, Inc., 27 109–11
Cost-U-Less, Inc., 51 90–93
Costa Coffee, **63** 88
Costa Cruise Lines, **27** 29, 90, 92
Costa Rica International, Inc., **41** 329
Costain Civil Engineering Ltd., **13** 206
Costain Homes, **31** 386
CoStar Group, Inc., 73 95–98
Costco Wholesale Corporation, 43 123–25 (upd.)
Cosway Corporation Berhad *see* Berjaya Group Bhd.
Coto Centro Integral de Comercializacion S.A., 66 65–67
Cott Corporation, 52 95–98
Cotter & Company, V 37–38 *see also* TruServ Corp.
Cotter Corporation, **29** 488
Cotton Incorporated, 46 108–11
Cotton Producers Association *see* Gold Kist Inc.
Coty, Inc., 36 140–42
Coudert Brothers, 30 147–50
Coulee Region Organic Produce Pool *see* Organic Valley.
Coulter Corporation *see* Beckman Coulter, Inc.
Council on International Educational Exchange Inc., 81 99–102
Counsel Corp., **46** 3
Country Fresh, Inc., **26** 449
Country Hedging, Inc., **60** 88
Country Kitchen International, Inc., 76 125–27
Countrywide Credit Industries, Inc., 16 133–36
County Data Corporation, *see* American Business Information, Inc.
County Seat Stores Inc., 9 142–43
Courage Brewing Group, **I** 229, 438–39
Courier Corporation, 41 108–12
Courir S.A., **39** 183–85
Courrèges Parfums, *see* L'Oréal.
Court Courier Systems, Inc., *see* Consolidated Delivery & Logistics, Inc.
Courtaulds plc, V 359–61; 17 116–19 (upd.) *see also* Akzo Nobel N.V.
Courts Plc, 45 121–24
Cousins Properties Incorporated, 65 121–23
Covance Inc., 30 151–53
Covanta Energy Corporation, 64 92–95 (upd.)
Covantage, **11** 379
Coventry Health Care, Inc., 59 138–40
Covidien Ltd., 91 132–35
Coville Inc., **16** 353
Covington & Burling, 40 124–27
Covisint LLC *see* Compuware Corp.
Covol Technologies Inc. *see* Headwaters Inc.
Cowen Group, Inc., 92 74–77
Cowles Media Company, 23 156–58 *see also* Primedia Inc.
Cox Cable Communications, Inc., **42** 114
Cox Enterprises, Inc., IV 595–97; 22 159–63 (upd.); 67 131–35 (upd.)
Cox Medical Enterprises, Inc., **21** 47
Cox Pharmaceuticals, **35** 25
Cox Radio, Inc., 89 176–80
Coz Chemical Co., **21** 20, 22
CP *see* Canadian Pacific Ltd.
CP/AAON *see* AAON, Inc.
CP National, **19** 412
CP Ships Holding, Inc., **45** 80; **50** 209–10
CPAC, Inc., 86 92–95
CPC International Inc., II 496–98 *see also* Bestfoods.
CP8, **43** 89
CPI Aerostructures, Inc., 75 112–14
CPI Corp., 38 157–60
CPL *see* Carolina Power & Light Co.

CPT *see* Chunghwa Picture Tubes, Ltd.
CR England, Inc., 63 116–18
CR2A Holding, **48** 402
CRA International, Inc., 93 168–71
CRA Limited, IV 58–61 *see also* Rio Tinto plc.
Crabtree & Evelyn Ltd., **51** 67
Cracker Barrel Old Country Store, Inc., 10 258–59 *see also* CBRL Group, Inc.
Craft Brands Alliance LLC, **76** 381
Craft House Corp., *see* RPM Inc.
Craftique, Inc., **33** 350–51
Craftmade International, Inc., 44 131–33
Craftopia.com, **64** 185
craigslist, inc., 89 181–84
Crain Communications, Inc., 12 83–86; 35 123–27 (upd.)
Cram Company *see* The George F. Cram Company, Inc.
Cramer, Berkowitz & Co., 34 125–27
Cranberry Canners, Inc. *see* Ocean Spray Cranberries, Inc.
Crane & Co., Inc., 26 103–06; 30 42
Crane Carton Co., **44** 66
Crane Co., 8 133–36; 30 154–58 (upd.)
Cranium, Inc., 69 109–11
Cranswick plc, 40 128–30
Crate and Barrel, 9 144–46 *see also* Euromarket Designs Inc.
Cravath, Swaine & Moore, 43 126–28
Crawford & Company, 87 121–126
Crawford Door Försäljnings AB, **53** 85
Cray Inc., III 129–31; 16 137–40 (upd.); 75 115–21 (upd.)
Crayfish Company, Ltd., **36** 153
Crazy Eddie Inc., **23** 373
Crazy Shirts, Inc., **45** 42
CRC Holdings Corp., **51** 217
CRD Total France, **IV** 560
Creaciones Victorio & Lucchino, **60** 246
Cream City Railway Company, **6** 601
Cream Wine Company, **48** 392
Creative Artists Agency LLC, 38 161–64
Creative Artists Associates, **43** 235
Creative BioMolecules, Inc., **29** 454
Creative Business Concepts, Inc., **39** 346
Creative Forming, Inc., *see* Wellman, Inc.
Creative Gems & Jewelry, Ltd., **62** 371
Creative Hairdressers Inc. *see* Ratner Companies.
Creative Integration and Design Inc., **20** 146
Creative Memories, **40** 44
Creative Optics Inc., **61** 193
Creative Technologies Corp., **15** 401
Creative Technology Ltd., 57 78–81
Credence Systems Corporation, 90 154–57
Credit & Risk Management Associates, Inc., **18** 170
Credit Acceptance Corporation, 18 120–22
Crédit Agricole Group, II 264–66; 84 63–68 (upd.)
Crédit Communal de Belgique, **42** 111
Crédit Local de France, **42** 111
Crédit Lyonnais, 9 147–49; 33 117–21 (upd.)
Crédit National S.A., 9 150–52
Crédit Suisse Group, II 267–69; 21 144–47 (upd.); 59 141–47 (upd.) *see also* Schweizerische Kreditanstalt.
Credit Union Federation, **48** 290
CrediThrift Financial, *see* American General Finance Corp.
Credito Agrario, **65** 72
Credito Italiano, II 270–72
Creditrust Corp., **42** 259
Cree Inc., 53 117–20
Crellin Holding, Inc., *see* Sonoco Products Co.
Cremascoli Ortho Group, **61** 403
Cremonini S.p.A., 57 82–84
Creo Inc., 48 121–24
Cresap, McCormick and Paget, **32** 458
Crescent Capital, **44** 95
Crescent Real Estate Equities Company, **25** 454
Crescent Software Inc., **15** 373
Crescent Vert Company, Ltd., **II** 51; **21** 330
Crescott, Inc., **15** 501
Crest Fruit Co., *see* Standex International Corp.
Crest Ridge Homes, Inc., *see* Champion Enterprises, Inc.
Crestline, **60** 140
Cresud S.A.C.I.F. y A., 63 119–21
Creusot-Loire, **19** 166
CRH plc, 64 96–99
Cricket Communications, Inc. *see* Leap Wireless International, Inc.
Crimson Associates L.P., **26** 48
Crisnova S.A. *see* Vidrala S.A.
Crispin Porter + Bogusky, 83 91-94
Crisoba *see* Compania Industrial de San Cristobal, S.A. de C.V.
Crist Partners, **34** 249
Cristalerias de Chile S.A., 67 136–38
Crit *see* Groupe Crit S.A.
Criterion Casualty Company, *see* GEICO Corp.
Critical Care Concepts, **50** 123
Crockett Container Corporation, *see* Inland Container Corp.
Crocs, Inc., 80 84–87
Croda International Plc, 45 125–28
Croitex S.A., **26** 374
Crompton Corporation, 9 153–55; 36 143–50 (upd.) *see also* Chemtura Corp.
CROPP *see* Organic Valley.
Croscill, Inc., 42 95–97
Crosman Corporation, 62 81–83
Cross Company *see* A.T. Cross Co.
Cross-Continent Auto Retailers, **26** 501
Cross Country Group, **25** 358
Cross Creek Apparel, Inc., **30** 400
Cross Pointe Paper Corporation, **26** 363
Cross/Tessitore & Associates, **16** 259
Cross Timbers Oil Company *see* XTO Energy, Inc.
Crossair AG *see* Swiss International Air Lines Ltd.
Crossfield Foods, **61** 133
CROSSMARK, 79 117–20
Crosspoint Venture Partners, **57** 49
Crothers Properties, Ltd., **21** 500
Crouse-Hinds Co. *see* Belden CDT Inc.
Crowley Maritime Corporation, 6 382–84; 28 77–80 (upd.)
Crowley, Milner & Company, 19 106–08
Crown Advertising Agency *see* King Kullen Grocery Co., Inc.
Crown Books Corporation, 21 148–50 *see also* Random House, Inc.
Crown Casino, **54** 299
Crown Central Petroleum Corporation, 7 101–03
Crown, Cork & Seal Company, Inc., I 601–03; 13 188–90 (upd.); 32 123–27 (upd.) *see also* Crown Holdings, Inc.
Crown Crafts, Inc., 16 141–43
Crown Equipment Corporation, 15 134–36; 93 172–76 (upd.)
Crown Holdings, Inc., 83 95-102 (upd.)
Crown House Engineering, **44** 148
Crown Media Holdings, Inc., 45 129–32
Crown Pet Foods Ltd., **39** 356
Crown Point Ventures, **49** 316
Crown Publishing Group, *see* Random House, Inc.
Crown Steel Products Co. *see* TransPro, Inc.
Crown Technical Systems, Inc., **37** 215
Crown Vantage Inc., 29 135–37
Crownx Inc. *see* Extendicare Health Services, Inc.
Crowson and Son Ltd., **23** 219
CRSS Inc., 6 142–44; 23 491
CRT, **51** 199
CRTC *see* Canadian Radio-Television and Telecommunications Commission.
Cruise America Inc., 21 151–53
Cruise Associates, *see* Royal Caribbean Cruises Ltd.
Crum & Forster Holdings, Inc., *see* Xerox Corp.
Crump E & S, **6** 290
Crupo Camino Real *see* Real Turismo, S.A. de C.V.
Cruse Bekleidung GmbH & Co. KG, **53** 195
Cruzan Rum Distillery, Ltd., *see* Todhunter International, Inc.
Cruzeiro do Sul Airlines *see* Varig, SA.
Cryenco Sciences Inc., **21** 109
CryoLife, Inc., 46 112–14
Crystal Brands, Inc., 9 156–58
Crystal Choice Water Service LLC *see* SJW Corp.
Crystal d'Arques *see* Arc International.
Crystal Market, **41** 174
Crystal Rock Water Co., **51** 396
Crystal SA. *see* Dalkia Holding.
Crystaline Company Limited, **70** 234
Crystallex International Corporation, **61** 291
CS Crable Sportswear Inc., **23** 66

CS First Boston Inc., II 402–04 *see also* Credit Suisse Group.
CS Holding *see* Credit Suisse Group.
CS Life, **21** 146–47
CSA *see* China Southern Airlines Company Ltd.
CSC *see* Computer Sciences Corp.
CSC Holdings, Inc., **32** 105
CSC Service Co Ltd., **62** 245
Csemege, **53** 178
CSFB *see* Financière Crédit Suisse-First Boston; Credit Suisse Group.
CSFBdirect Inc., **46** 55
CSG Systems International, Inc., 75 122–24
CSI Computer Systems, **47** 36
CSK Auto Corporation, 38 165–67
CSM N.V., 65 124–27
CSO *see* Columbus & Southern Ohio Electric Co.
CSR Limited, III 686–88; 28 81–84 (upd.); 85 73–80 (upd.)
CSR Rinker Materials Corp., **46** 197
CSS Industries, Inc., 35 128–31
CST Office Products, **15** 36; **42** 416
CSX Corporation, V 438–40; 22 164–68 (upd.); 79 121–27 (upd.)
CSY Agri-Processing, *see* Central Soya Company, Inc.
CT Financial Services Inc., **49** 397
CT&T *see* Carolina Telephone and Telegraph Co.
CTA *see* Comptoir des Textiles Artificielles.
CTA Makro Commercial Co., Ltd., **55** 347
CTB International Corporation, 43 129–31 (upd.)
CTG, Inc., 11 64–66
CTI *see* Cosmetic Technology International, Inc.
CTN Assurance Company, **72** 117
CTR *see* Compagnie Transcontinentale de Reassurance.
CTS Corporation, 39 105–08
CTV Network, **35** 69
C2B Technologies, **45** 201
CTX Mortgage Company, *see* Centex Corp.
Cub Foods, *see* Supervalu Inc.
Cuban American Oil Company, *see* MAXXAM Inc.
Cubic Corporation, 19 109–11
CUC International Inc., 16 144–46 *see also* Cendant Corp.
Cudahy Corp., **12** 199
Cuisinart Corporation, 24 129–32
Cuisine Solutions Inc., 84 69–72
Culbro Corporation, 15 137–39 *see also* General Cigar Holdings, Inc.
Culinar Inc., **59** 364
CulinArt, Inc., 92 78–81
Culinary Foods, Inc., **14** 516; **50** 493
Cullen/Frost Bankers, Inc., 25 113–16
Culligan Water Technologies, Inc., 12 87–88; 38 168–70 (upd.)
Cullinet Software Corporation, **15** 108
Cullman Bros. *see* Culbro Corp.
Culp, Inc., 29 138–40
Culver Franchising System, Inc., 58 79–81
Cumberland Farms, Inc., 17 120–22; 84 73–77 (upd.)
Cumberland Packing Corporation, 26 107–09
Cummings-Moore Graphite Company *see* Asbury Carbons, Inc.
Cummins Cogeneration Co. *see* Cogeneration Development Corp.
Cummins Engine Co., Inc., I 146–48; 12 89–92 (upd.); 40 131–35 (upd.)
Cummins Utility Supply, **58** 334
Cumo Sports, *see* Cobra Golf Inc.
Cumulus Media Inc., 37 103–05
CUNA Mutual Group, 62 84–87
Cunard Line Ltd., 23 159–62
CUNO Incorporated, 57 85–89
CurranCare, LLC, **50** 122
Current, Inc., 37 106–09
Currys Group PLC *see* Dixons Group PLC.
Curtas Technologie SA, **58** 221
Curtice-Burns Foods, Inc., 7 104–06; 21 154–57 (upd.) *see also* Birds Eye Foods, Inc.
Curtin & Pease/Peneco, *see* Penton Media, Inc.
Curtis Circulation Co., **IV** 619
Curtis Management Group *see* CMG Worldwide, Inc.
Curtis 1000 Inc. *see* American Business Products, Inc.
Curtis Restaurant Supply, **60** 160
Curtiss-Wright Corporation, 10 260–63; 35 132–37 (upd.)
Curver-Rubbermaid *see* Newell Rubbermaid.
Curves International, Inc., 54 80–82
Cushman & Wakefield, Inc., 86 96–100
Cussons *see* PZ Cussons plc.
Custom Academic Publishing Company, **12** 174
Custom Building Products of California, Inc., **53** 176
Custom Chrome, Inc., 16 147–49; 74 92–95 (upd.)
Custom Hoists, Inc., *see* Standex International Corp.
Custom, Ltd, **46** 197
Custom Technologies Corp., *see* Fansteel Inc.
Custom Tool and Manufacturing Company, **41** 366
Custom Transportation Services, Inc., **26** 62
Custom Woodwork & Plastics Inc., **36** 159
Customized Transportation Inc., *see* CSX Corp.
AB Custos, **25** 464
Cutera, Inc., 84 78–81
Cutisin, **55** 123
Cutler-Hammer Inc., **63** 401
Cutter & Buck Inc., 27 112–14
CVC Capital Partners Limited, **49** 451; **54** 207
CVG Aviation, **34** 118
CVI Incorporated, **21** 108
CVPS *see* Central Vermont Public Service Corp.
CVRD *see* Companhia Vale do Rio Doce Ltd.
CVS Corporation, 45 133–38 (upd.)
CWA *see* City of Westminster Assurance Company Ltd.
CWM *see* Chemical Waste Management, Inc.
CWP *see* Custom Woodwork & Plastics Inc.
CXT Inc., **33** 257
Cyber Communications Inc., **16** 168
Cybermedia, Inc., 25 117–19
Cybernet Electronics Corp., **II** 51; **21** 330
Cyberonics, Inc., 79 128–31
Cybershield, Inc., **52** 103, 105
CyberSource Corp., **26** 441
CYBERTEK Corporation, **11** 395
CyberTrust Solutions Inc., **42** 24–25
Cybex International, Inc., 49 106–09
Cycle & Carriage Ltd., **20** 313; **56** 285
Cycle-Sat Inc., *see* Winnebago Industries Inc.
Cyclops Industries, *see* Alleghany Corp.
Cydsa *see* Grupo Cydsa, S.A. de C.V.
Cygne Designs, Inc., 25 120–23
Cygnus Business Media, Inc., 56 73–77
Cymbal Co., Ltd. *see* Nagasakiya Co., Ltd.
Cymer, Inc., 77 125–28
Cynosure Inc., **11** 88
Cypress Management Services, Inc., **64** 311
Cypress Semiconductor Corporation, 20 174–76; 48 125–29 (upd.)
Cyprus Airways Public Limited, 81 103–06
Cyprus Amax Minerals Company, 21 158–61
Cyprus Minerals Company, 7 107–09
Cyrix Corporation *see* National Semiconductor Corp.
Cyrk Inc., 19 112–14
Cystic Fibrosis Foundation, 93 177–80
Cytec Industries Inc., 27 115–17
Cytyc Corporation, 69 112–14
Czarnikow-Rionda Company, Inc., 32 128–30

D

D&B *see* Dun & Bradstreet Corp.
D&D Enterprises, Inc., **24** 96
D&K Wholesale Drug, Inc., 14 146–48
D Green (Electronics) Limited, **65** 141
D-Link Corporation, 83 103-106
D.B. Kaplan's, **26** 263
D.C. Heath & Co., **36** 273; **38** 374
D. de Ricci-G. Selnet et Associes, **28** 141
d.e.m.o., **28** 345
D.E. Shaw & Co., **38** 269
D.F. Stauffer Biscuit Company, 82 82-85
D.G. Yuengling & Son, Inc., 38 171–73
D.H. Holmes Company, Limited *see* Dillard's Inc.
D.I. Manufacturing Inc., **37** 351

D.K. Gold, *see* Donnkenny, Inc.
D.L. Rogers Group, **37** 363
D.L. Saslow Co., **19** 290
D.M. Nacional, **23** 170
D.R. Horton, Inc., 58 82–84
D.W. Mikesell Co. *see* Mike-Sell's Inc.
Da Gama Textiles Company, **24** 450
Dachser GmbH & Co. KG, 88 57–61
D'Addario & Company, Inc. *see* J. D'Addario & Company, Inc.
Dade Behring Holdings Inc., 71 120–22
DADG *see* Deutsch-Australische Dampfschiffs-Gesellschaft.
DAEDUK Techno Valley Company Ltd., **62** 174
Daesang Corporation, 84 82–85
Daewoo Group, III 457–59; 18 123–27 (upd.); 57 90–94 (upd.)
Daffy's Inc., 26 110–12
NV Dagblad De Telegraaf *see* N.V. Holdingmaatschappij De Telegraaf.
D'Agostino Supermarkets Inc., 19 115–17
Dagsbladunie, **IV** 611
DAH *see* DeCrane Aircraft Holdings Inc.
Dahill Industries *see* Global Imaging Systems, Inc.
Dahlonega Equipment and Supply Company, **12** 377
Dai-Ichi Kangyo Asset Management Co. Ltd., **58** 235
Dai-Ichi Kangyo Bank Ltd., II 273–75
Dai-Ichi Mutual Life Insurance Co., **26** 511; **38** 18
Dai Nippon *see also* listings under Dainippon.
Dai Nippon Ink and Chemicals, Inc., **54** 330
Dai Nippon Printing Co., Ltd., IV 598–600; 57 95–99 (upd.)
Dai Nippon Yuben Kai Kodansha *see* Kodansha Ltd.
Daido Steel Co., Ltd., IV 62–63
The Daiei, Inc., V 39–40; 17 123–25 (upd.); 41 113–16 (upd.)
Daig Corporation, **43** 349–50
Daihatsu Motor Company, Ltd., 7 110–12; 21 162–64 (upd.)
Daiichikosho Company Ltd., 86 101–04
Daikin Industries, Ltd., III 460–61
Daiko Advertising Inc., 79 132–35
Daikyo Oil Co., Ltd., **IV** 403–04, 476; **53** 114
Daily Grill *see* Grill Concepts, Inc.
Daily Mail and General Trust plc, 19 118–20
Daily Press Inc., *see* Tribune Co.
The Daimaru, Inc., V 41–42; 42 98–100 (upd.)
Daimler-Benz Aerospace AG, 16 150–52
Daimler-Benz AG, I 149–51; 15 140–44 (upd.)
DaimlerChrysler Aerospace AG *see* European Aeronautic Defence and Space Company EADS N.V.
DaimlerChrysler AG, 34 128–37 (upd.); 64 100–07 (upd.)
Dain Bosworth Inc., **15** 231–33, 486
Dain Rauscher Corporation, 35 138–41 (upd.)
Daini-Denden Kikaku Company, Ltd. *see* DDI Corp.
Dainippon *see also* listings under Dai-Nippon.
Dainippon Ink & Chemicals, Inc., **10** 466–67; **28** 194
Daio Paper Corporation, IV 266–67; 84 86–89 (upd.)
Dairy Crest Group plc, 32 131–33
Dairy Equipment Company, **62** 43
Dairy Farm Ice and Cold Storage Co., **IV** 700; **47** 176
Dairy Farmers of America, Inc., 94 143–46
Dairy Fresh, Inc., **26** 449
Dairy Mart Convenience Stores, Inc., 7 113–15; 25 124–27 (upd.) *see also* Alimentation Couche-Tard Inc.
Dairy Queen *see* International Dairy Queen, Inc.
Dairyland Healthcare Solutions, 73 99–101
Dairyworld Foods, **59** 364
Daishowa Paper Manufacturing Co., Ltd., IV 268–70; 57 100–03 (upd.)
Daisy Manufacturing Company, Inc., **34** 72; **60** 291
Daisy Outdoor Products Inc., 58 85–88
Daisy Systems Corp., **11** 46, 284–85, 489
Daisytek International Corporation, 18 128–30
Daiwa Bank, Ltd., II 276–77; 39 109–11 (upd.)
Daiwa Securities Company, Limited, II 405–06
Daiwa Securities Group Inc., 55 115–18 (upd.)
Daka, Inc. *see* Unique Casual Restaurants, Inc.
Dakin Inc., **24** 44; **33** 415
Dakota Power Company, **6** 580; **20** 73
Daksoft, Inc., **20** 74
Daktronics, Inc., 32 134–37
Dal-Tile International Inc., 22 169–71
Dale Carnegie & Associates Inc., 28 85–87; 78 78–82 (upd.)
Dale Electronics, **21** 519
Dalfort Corp., **15** 281
Dalgety PLC, II 499–500 *see also* PIC International Group PLC
Dalian, **14** 556
Dalian Dali Steel Works Co. Ltd., **53** 173
Dalian International Nordic Tire Co., **20** 263
Dalian Shide Group, 91 136–39
Dalkia Holding, 66 68–70
Dallah Albaraka Group, 72 83–86
Dallas Ceramic Co. *see* Dal-Tile International Inc.
Dallas Cowboys Football Club, Ltd., 33 122–25
Dallas-Fort Worth Suburban Newspapers, Inc., *see* A.H. Belo Corp.
Dallas Pant Manufacturing Company *see* Haggar Corporation
Dallas Semiconductor Corporation, 13 191–93; 31 143–46 (upd.)
Dalli-Werke GmbH & Co. KG, 86 105–10
Dallis Coffee, Inc., 86 111–14
Daltex General Agency, Inc., **25** 115
Damark International, Inc., 18 131–34 *see also* Provell Inc.
Damart, **25** 523
Dameron-Pierson Co., *see* U.S. Office Products Co.
Dames & Moore, Inc., 25 128–31 *see also* URS Corp.
Damon, **21** 153
Damon Clinical Laboratories Inc., **26** 392
Damon Corp., **54** 57
Dan River Inc., 35 142–46; 86 115–20 (upd.)
Dana Corporation, I 152–53; 10 264–66 (upd.)
Dana Design Ltd., *see* K2 Inc.
Danaher Corporation, 7 116–17; 77 129–33 (upd.)
Danaos Corporation, 91 140–43
Danapak Holding Ltd., **11** 422
Danapak Riverwood Multipack A/S, **48** 344
Danbury Mint, **34** 370
Danbury Phamacal Inc., **31** 254
Dancing Sandwiches, Inc. *see* Zingerman's Community of Businesses.
Dandy Ltd., **74** 121
Danfoss A/S, **61** 322
D'Angelo's Sandwich Shops Inc. *see* Papa Gino's Holdings Corporation, Inc.
Daniel James Insurance Group, **41** 64
Daniel P. Creed Co., Inc., *see* NCH Corp.
Daniel Measurement and Control, Inc., 16 153–55; 74 96–99 (upd.)
Daniel's Jewelers, *see* Zale Corp.
Daniels Pharmaceuticals, Inc., **24** 257
Danielson Holding Corporation, **64** 92
Danisco A/S, 44 134–37
Danley Machine Corp., *see* Ogden Corp.
Danner Shoe Manufacturing Company, **18** 300; **61** 164
Dannon Co., Inc., 14 149–51
Danone Group, *see* Groupe Danone.
Dansk Bioprotein, **IV** 406–07
Danske Bank Aktieselskab, 50 148–51
Danskin, Inc., 12 93–95; 62 88–92 (upd.)
Danzas Group, V 441–43; 40 136–39 (upd.)
DAP, Inc., *see* Wassall Plc.
DAP Products Inc., **36** 396
Daphne's Greek Café *see* Fili Enterprises, Inc.
Dara Michelle, *see* Claire's Stores, Inc.
D'Arcy Masius Benton & Bowles, Inc., 6 20–22; 32 138–43 (upd.)
Darden Restaurants, Inc., 16 156–58; 44 138–42 (upd.)
Darigold, Inc., 9 159–61
Darius International, Inc., **62** 296
Darling, Brown & Sharpe *see* Brown & Sharpe Manufacturing Co.
Darling International Inc., 85 81–84

Dart & Kraft Financial Corp., *see* Illinois Tool Works.
Dart Group PLC, 16 159–62; 77 134–37 (upd.)
Dart Industries *see* Premark International Inc.
Darty S.A., 27 118–20
Darvel Realty Trust, **14** 126
DASA *see* Daimler-Benz Aerospace AG; Deutsche Aerospace Airbus.
Dashwood Industries, **19** 446
DASS Die andere SystementsorgungsGesellschaft mbH, **58** 28
Dassault Aviation SA, **21** 11
Dassault-Breguet *see* Avions Marcel Dassault-Breguet Aviation.
Dassault Systèmes S.A., 25 132–34 *see also* Groupe Dassault Aviation SA.
Dastek Inc., *see* Komag, Inc.
Data-Beam Corp., **25** 301
Data Broadcasting Corporation, 31 147–50
Data Card Corporation, **IV** 680; **58** 340
Data General Corporation, 8 137–40 *see also* EMC Corp.
Data Specialties Inc. *see* Zebra Technologies Corp.
Data Systems Technology, **11** 57; **38** 375
Datac plc, **18** 140
Datacraft Asia Limited, **69** 127
DataFocus, Inc., **18** 112
DataPath Systems, **64** 246
Datapoint Corporation, 11 67–70
Dataquest Inc., **21** 235, 237
Datas Incorporated *see* Delta Air Lines, Inc.
Datascope Corporation, 39 112–14
Dataset Communications Inc., **23** 100
Datastream International Ltd., **13** 417
Datatec Ltd., **67** 392–94
DataTimes Corporation, **29** 58
Datavision Inc., **11** 444
Datek Online Holdings Corp., 32 144–46
Datsun *see* Nissan Motor Company, Ltd.
Datura Corp., **14** 391
Dauphin Deposit Corporation, 14 152–54
Dauphin Distribution Services *see* Exel Logistics Ltd.
Daut + Rietz and Connectors Pontarlier, **19** 166
Dave & Buster's, Inc., 33 126–29
Davenport Mammoet Heavy Transport Inc., **26** 280
The Davey Tree Expert Company, 11 71–73
David & Charles Group *see* F&W Publications, Inc.
The David and Lucile Packard Foundation, 41 117–19
David Brown & Son *see* Brown & Sharpe Manufacturing Co.
David Clark, **30** 357
David Hafler Company, **43** 323
The David J. Joseph Company, 14 155–56; 76 128–30 (upd.)
David Jones Ltd., 60 100–02
David Kelley Design *see* IDEO Inc.
David L. Babson & Company Inc., **53** 213
David Lloyd Leisure Ltd., **52** 412, 415–16
David Oppenheimer & Co. *see* Oppenheimer Group.
David S. Smith Ltd. *see* DS Smith Plc.
David Wilson Homes Ltd., **45** 442–43
David's Bridal, Inc., 33 130–32
Davide Campari-Milano S.p.A., 57 104–06
Davids *see* Metcash Trading Ltd.
Davidson & Associates, **16** 146
Davidson & Leigh, **21** 94
Davis Polk & Wardwell, 36 151–54
Davis Service Group PLC, 45 139–41
DaVita Inc., 73 102–05
DAW Technologies, Inc., 25 135–37
Dawn Food Products, Inc., 17 126–28
Dawson Holdings PLC, 43 132–34
Day & Zimmermann Inc., 9 162–64; 31 151–55 (upd.)
Day-Glo Color Corp., *see* RPM Inc.
Day International, Inc., 84 90–93
Day Runner, Inc., 14 157–58; 41 120–23 (upd.)
Day-Timers, Inc., **51** 9
Dayco Products, *see* Mark IV Industries, Inc.
Daylin Corporation, **46** 271
Days Inns of America, Inc., *see* Cendant Corp.
Dayton Hudson Corporation, V 43–44; 18 135–37 (upd.) *see also* Target Corp.
Dayton Power & Light Company, **6** 467, 480–82
Daytron Mortgage Systems, **11** 485
DB *see* Deutsche Bundesbahn.
DB Group, **59** 59–60
DB Reise & Touristik AG, **37** 250
DBA Holdings, Inc., **18** 24
dba Luftfahrtgesellschaft mbH, 76 131–33
DBS Transit Inc. *see* Stabler Companies Inc.
DBT Online Inc. *see* ChoicePoint Inc.
DC Comics Inc., 25 138–41
DC Shoes, Inc., 60 103–05
DCA Advertising, **16** 168
DCA Food Industries, *see* Kerry Group plc.
DCE Consultants, **51** 17
DCN S.A., 75 125–27
DDB Worldwide Communications, 14 159–61 *see also* Omnicom Group Inc.
DDD Energy, Inc., **47** 348, 350
DDI Corporation, 7 118–20
DDJ Capital, **68** 345
NV De Beer and Partners, **45** 386
De Beers Consolidated Mines Limited / De Beers Centenary AG, IV 64–68; 7 121–26 (upd.); 28 88–94 (upd.)
De Bono Industries, **24** 443
De Dietrich & Cie., 31 156–59
de Havilland Aircraft Co. *see* Bombardier Inc.
De La Rue plc, 10 267–69; 34 138–43 (upd.); **46** 251
De Leuw, Cather & Company, *see* The Parsons Corp.
De Paepe, **45** 386
De Streekkrant-De Weekkrantgroep NV, **48** 347
De Tomaso Industries, **11** 104; **50** 197
De Vito/Verdi, **26** 111
DEA Group, **23** 83
Dead Sea Works Ltd., **55** 229
Dealer Equipment and Services, *see* SPX Corp.
Dealers Wholesale Inc., **56** 230
Dean & DeLuca, Inc., 36 155–57
Dean Foods Company, 7 127–29; 21 165–68 (upd.); 73 106–15 (upd.)
Dean Witter, Discover & Co., 12 96–98 *see also* Morgan Stanley Dean Witter & Co.
Dearborn Mid-West Conveyor Company, 56 78–80
Dearborn Publishing Group, **42** 211
Death Row Records, 27 121–23 *see also* Tha Row Records.
Deb Shops, Inc., 16 163–65; 76 134–37 (upd.)
Debeka Krankenversicherungsverein auf Gegenseitigkeit, 72 87–90
Debenhams Plc, 28 95–97
Debevoise & Plimpton, 39 115–17
Debis, **26** 498
DEC *see* Digital Equipment Corp.
Decafin SpA, **26** 278, 280
Decathlon S.A., **39** 183–84
Decca Record Company Ltd., **23** 389
Deceuninck N.V., 84 94–97
Dechert, 43 135–38
Decision Systems Israel Ltd. (DSI), **21** 239
DecisionQuest, Inc., **25** 130
Decker, Howell & Co., **26** 451
Decker-Indelqui S.A., **71** 211
Deckers Outdoor Corporation, 22 172–74
Deco Industries, Inc., *see* ABC Rail Products Corp.
Deco Purchasing Company, **39** 211
Decolletage S.A. St.-Maurice, *see* AMP Inc.
Decora Industries, Inc., 31 160–62
Decorator Industries Inc., 68 101–04
DeCrane Aircraft Holdings Inc., 36 158–60
Dee Zee Inc., **61** 173
Deep Ocean Services, L.L.C., **44** 203
Deep Rock Oil Company *see* Kerr-McGee Corp.
DeepFlex Production Partners, L.P., **21** 171
DeepTech International Inc., 21 169–71
Deere & Company, III 462–64; 21 172–76 (upd.); 42 101–06 (upd.)
Deering Harvesting Machinery Company *see* Navistar.
Deering Milliken & Co. *see* Milliken & Co.

Def Jam Records, Inc., **23** 389, 391; **31** 269; **33** 373–75
Defense Technology Corporation of America, *see* Armor Holdings, Inc.
Defiance, Inc., 22 175–78
Deflecta-Shield Corporation, **40** 299–300
Deft Software, Inc., *see* Sybase, Inc.
Degussa-Hüls AG, IV 69–72; 32 147–53 (upd.)
Degussa-Metais, Catalisadores e Ceramica, Lda, **56** 127
Dehesa Baron de Ley SL *see* Baron de Ley S.A.
DEKA Research & Development Corporation *see* Segway LLC.
DeKalb Farmers Market, **23** 263–64
DeKalb Genetics Corporation, 17 129–31 *see also* Monsanto Co.
DeKalb Office Supply, *see* U.S. Office Products Co.
DeKuyper, **58** 194
Del Laboratories, Inc., 28 98–100
Del Mar Avionics, **26** 491
Del Monte Foods Company, 7 130–32; 23 163–66 (upd.)
Del Taco, Inc., 58 89–92
Del Webb Corporation, 14 162–64 *see also* Pulte Homes, Inc.
Delachaux S.A., 76 138–40
Delafield, Harvey, Tabrell, Inc., *see* U.S. Trust Corp.
Delamine B.V., **70** 329
Delaware and Hudson Railway Company, Inc., **45** 78
Delaware Charter Guarantee & Trust Co., *see* Principal Mutual Life Insurance Co.
Delaware Guarantee and Trust Co. *see* Wilmington Trust Co.
Delaware North Companies Incorporated, 7 133–36
Delchamps, Inc., *see* Jitney-Jungle Stores of America, Inc.
Delco Electronics Corporation, *see* GM Hughes Electronics Corp.
Delek Investment & Properties Ltd., **45** 170
Delhaize "Le Lion" S.A., 44 143–46
Delhi Gas Pipeline Corporation, *see* United States Steel Corp.
Deli Unique *see* Matt Prentice Restaurant Group.
Deli Universal NV, 66 71–74
dELiA*s Inc., 29 141–44
Delicato Vineyards, Inc., 50 152–55
Dell Computer Corporation, 9 165–66; 31 163–66 (upd.); 63 122–26 (upd.)
Delmarva Properties, Inc., *see* Chesapeake Corp.
Delmas-Vieljeux *see* Groupe Bolloré.
Deloitte Touche Tohmatsu International, 9 167–69; 29 145–48 (upd.)
De'Longhi S.p.A., 66 75–77
DeLorme Publishing Company, Inc., 53 121–23
Delphax Technologies Inc., 94 147–50
Delphi Automotive Systems Corporation, 45 142–44
Delphy Industries S.A.S., **53** 221
Delta and Pine Land Company, 33 133–37; 59 148–50
Delta Air Lines, Inc., I 99–100; 6 81–83 (upd.); 39 118–21 (upd.); 92 82–87 (upd.)
Delta Biologicals S.r.l., **11** 208
Delta Biotechnology Ltd., **25** 82
Delta Campground Management Corp., **33** 399
Delta Communications *see* Reed Elsevier.
Delta Education, **29** 470, 472
Delta Faucet Co. *see* Masco Corp.
Delta Health, Inc. *see* DVI, Inc.
Delta International Machinery Corp., **26** 361–63
Delta Lloyd, *see* Commercial Union PLC.
Delta Play, Ltd., **44** 261
Delta Queen Steamboat Company, **27** 34–35
Delta Resources Inc., **26** 519
Delta V Technologies, Inc., **33** 348
Delta Woodside Industries, Inc., 8 141–43; 30 159–61 (upd.)
Deltak, L.L.C., **23** 300; **52** 139
Deltec, Inc., 56 81–83
Deltic Timber Corporation, 46 115–17
Deluxe Corporation, 7 137–39; 22 179–82 (upd.); 73 116–20 (upd.)
Deluxe Media Services Inc., **64** 320
Deluxe Upholstering Ltd., **14** 303
DEMCO, Inc., 60 106–09
Demko, **30** 469
DeMoulas / Market Basket Inc., 23 167–69
Den Norske Stats Oljeselskap AS, IV 405–07 *see also* Statoil ASA.
DenAmerica Corporation, 29 149–51
Denbury Resources, Inc., 67 139–41
Denby Group plc, 44 147–50
Dendrite International, Inc., 70 70–73
Denison International plc, 46 118–20
Denker & Goodwin, *see* U.S. Trust Corp.
Denmark Tiscali A/S, **48** 398
Denner AG, 88 62–65
Dennis Publishing Ltd., 62 93–95
Dennison Manufacturing Company *see* Avery Dennison Corp.
Denny's Restaurants Inc., **27** 16–18; **50** 489
Denshi Media Services, **IV** 680
DENSO Corporation, 46 121–26 (upd.)
Dental Benefits Insurance Company, **51** 276, 278
Dental Capital Corp., **19** 290
Dental Research, **25** 56
DentiCare, Inc., *see* CompDent Corp.
Dentists Management Corporation, **51** 276–78
Dentons Green Brewery, **21** 246
Dentsply International Inc., 10 270–72
Dentsu Inc., I 9–11; 16 166–69 (upd.); 40 140–44 (upd.)
Denver & Rio Grande Railroad, **12** 18–19
Denver Gas & Electric Company *see* Public Service Company of Colorado.
Denver Nuggets, 51 94–97
Deocsa, **51** 389
DEP *see* Hellenic Petroleum SA.
DEP Corporation, 20 177–80
Depa, **69** 190, 192
Department 56, Inc., 14 165–67; 34 144–47 (upd.)
Department of Currency and Coinage, **62** 248
DEPFA BANK PLC, 69 115–17
Deposit Guaranty Corporation, 17 132–35
DePuy, Inc., 30 162–65; 37 110–13 (upd.)
Derby Cycle Corporation, **65** 297
Derby International, **69** 303
Deritend Computers, *see* AT&T Istel Ltd.
Dermablend, Inc., **31** 89
Derwent Publications, *see* The Thomson Corp.
Desai Capital Management Inc., **76** 150
Desarrolladora Homex, S.A. de C.V., 87 127–130
Desc, S.A. de C.V., 23 170–72
Deschutes Brewery, Inc., 57 107–09
Desco, **51** 120
Deseret Management Corporation, **29** 67
Deseret Pharmaceutical Company, **21** 45
Design Trend, Inc., **37** 394
Designcraft Inc. *see* Sloan's Supermarkets Inc.
Designer Holdings Ltd., 20 181–84
Designs, Inc. *see* Casual Male Retail Group, Inc.
Designtroupe, **60** 143–44
Desmonds Formalwear, **60** 5
Desnoes and Geddes Limited, 79 136–39
Desoutter Brothers plc, *see* Atlas Copco AB.
Destec Energy, Inc., 12 99–101
Desvi, S.A., **68** 258
Det Danske Rengorings Selskab A/S, **49** 221
Detroit City Gas Company *see* MCN Corp.
Detroit Diesel Corporation, 10 273–75; 74 100–03 (upd.)
The Detroit Edison Company, V 592–95 *see also* DTE Energy Co.
The Detroit Lions, Inc., 55 119–21
The Detroit Pistons Basketball Company, 41 124–27
Detroit Red Wings, 74 104–06
Detroit Steel Products Co., Inc. *see* The Marmon Group, Inc.
Detroit Stoker Company, **37** 399–401
Detroit Tigers Baseball Club, Inc., 46 127–30
Detsky Mir Group, **73** 303–04
Dettmers Industries Inc., **36** 159–60
Deutsch, Inc., 42 107–10
Deutsche Aerospace Airbus, **7** 9, 11; **21** 8; **52** 113–14
Deutsche BA, **14** 73; **26** 115
Deutsche Babcock AG, III 465–66
Deutsche Bahn AG, 46 131–35 (upd.)
Deutsche Bank AG, II 278–80; 40 145–51 (upd.)

Deutsche Börse AG, 59 151–55
Deutsche BP Aktiengesellschaft, 7 140–43
Deutsche Bundepost Telekom, V 287–90 *see also* Deutsche Telekom AG
Deutsche Bundesbahn, V 444–47
Deutsche Grammophon Gesellschaft, **23** 389
Deutsche Herold, **49** 44
Deutsche Kreditbank, **14** 170
Deutsche Lufthansa AG, I 110–11; 26 113–16 (upd.); 68 105–09 (upd.)
Deutsche Post AG, 29 152–58
Deutsche Reichsbahn *see* Deutsche Bundesbahn.
Deutsche Steinkohle AG, **60** 250
Deutsche Steinzeug Cremer & Breuer Aktiengesellschaft, 91 144–48
Deutsche Telekom AG, 48 130–35 (upd.)
Deutsche Verlags-Anstalt GmbH, **66** 123
Deutsche Vermögensberatung AG, **51** 19, 23
Deutsche Wagnisfinanzierung, **47** 83
Deutscher Kommunal-Verlag Dr. Naujoks & Behrendt, **14** 556
Deutscher Ring, **40** 61
Deutscher Sparkassen- und Giroverband (DSGV), 84 98–102
Deutz AG, 39 122–26
Deutz-Allis *see* AGCO Corp.
Devanlay SA, **48** 279
Devcon Corporation, *see* Illinois Tool Works Inc.
Deveaux S.A., 41 128–30
Developer's Mortgage Corp., **16** 347
Developers Diversified Realty Corporation, 69 118–20
Developmental Resource Center, Inc., **76** 283
Devenish, **21** 247
DeVilbiss Health Care, Inc., **11** 488
DeVito/Verdi, 85 85–88
Devoe & Raynolds Co., *see* Grow Group Inc.
Devon Energy Corporation, 61 73–75
Devonshire Group *see* OfficeTiger, LLC.
Devoteam S.A., 94 151–54
Devro plc, 55 122–24
DeVry Inc., 29 159–61; 82 86-90 (upd.)
Devtek Corporation *see* Héroux-Devtek Inc.
Dewberry, 78 83–86
Dewey Ballantine LLP, 48 136–39
Dex Media, Inc., 65 128–30
Dexer Corporation, **41** 10
Dexia NV/SA, 42 111–13; 88 66–69 (upd.)
The Dexter Corporation, I 320–22; 12 102–04 (upd.) *see also* Invitrogen Corp.
Dexter Lock Company, **45** 269
Dexter Shoe, *see* Berkshire Hathaway Inc.
Deyco, **75** 351
DFS Group Ltd., 66 78–80
DG&E *see* Denver Gas & Electric Co.
DG Bank, **33** 358
DGF Stoess & Co. GmbH *see* Gelita AG.
DGS SpA, **62** 100
DH Technology, Inc., 18 138–40
Dharma Juice, **31** 350
DHB Industries Inc., 85 89–92
DHCompounding Company, *see* M. A. Hanna Co.
DHI Corp., *see* TW Services, Inc.
DHL Worldwide Network S.A./N.V., 6 385–87; 24 133–36 (upd.); 69 121–25 (upd.)
Di Giorgio Corp., 12 105–07
Diadora SpA, 86 121–24
Diageo plc, 24 137–41 (upd.); 79 140–48 (upd.)
Diagnostic Imaging Services, Inc., **25** 384
Diagnostic Products Corporation, 73 121–24
Diagnostic/Retrieval Systems Inc. *see* DRS Technologies Inc.
Diagnostic Ventures Inc. *see* DVI, Inc.
Dial-A-Mattress Operating Corporation, 46 136–39
The Dial Corporation, 8 144–46; 23 173–75 (upd.)
Dial Home Shopping Ltd., **28** 30
Dial-Net Inc., **27** 306
Dialog Information Services, Inc., **IV** 630
Dialogic Corporation, 18 141–43
Diamandis Communications Inc., **IV** 619, 678
Diamedix, *see* IVAX Corp.
Diamond Animal Health, Inc., **39** 216
Diamond Crystal Brands, Inc., **32** 274, 277
Diamond Electronics, **24** 510
Diamond Head Resources, Inc. *see* AAON, Inc.
Diamond International Corp., **26** 446
Diamond of California, 64 108–11 (upd.)
Diamond Offshore Drilling, Inc., *see* Loews Corp.
Diamond Park Fine Jewelers, *see* Zale Corp.
Diamond Rug & Carpet Mills, **19** 276
Diamond Shamrock Corporation , IV 408–11 *see also* Ultramar Diamond Shamrock Corp.
Diamond Sparkler Manufacturing Co. Inc. *see* B.J. Alan Co., Inc.
Diamond-Star Motors Corporation, *see* Mitsubishi Motors Corp.
Diamond State Insurance Company, **63** 410–12
Diamond Walnut Growers, *see* Diamond of California.
DiamondCluster International, Inc., 51 98–101
Dianatel, *see* Dialogic Corp.
Diapositive, **44** 296
Diasonics Ultrasound, Inc., *see* OEC Medical Systems, Inc.
Diaxon A.B.E.E., **64** 177
Diavik Diamond Mines Inc., 85 93–96
Dibrell Brothers, Incorporated, 12 108–10
dick clark productions, inc., 16 170–73
Dick Corporation, 64 112–14
Dick Simon Trucking, Inc. *see* Simon Transporation Services Inc.
Dick's Sporting Goods, Inc., 59 156–59
Dickson Forest Products, Inc., **15** 305
Dickten Masch Plastics LLC, 90 158–61
Dictaphone Healthcare Solutions, 78 87–92
Didier Lamarthe, *see* Vivarte SA.
Didier-Werke AG, *see* E.On AG.
Diebold, Incorporated, 7 144–46; 22 183–87 (upd.)
Diedrich Coffee, Inc., 40 152–54
Diehl Stiftung & Co. KG, 79 149–53
Dierbergs Markets Inc., 63 127–29
Diesel Nacional, S.A. *see* Consorcio G Grupo Dina, S.A. de C.V.
Diesel SpA, 40 155–57
D'Ieteren N.V., **76** 53, 55
Dietrich & Cie. *see* De Dietrich & Cie.
Dietrich Corp., *see* Hershey Foods Corp.
Dietz and Watson, Inc., 92 88–92
DiFeo Automotive Group, **26** 500–01
Diffusion Immobilier *see* Union Financière de France Banque.
DiFranza Williamson, **6** 40
DIG Acquisition Corp., **12** 107
Digex, Inc., 46 140–43
Digi International Inc., 9 170–72
Digidesign Inc., **38** 70, 72
Digital City, Inc., *see* Tribune Co.
Digital Directory Assistance, **18** 24
Digital Entertainment Network, **42** 272
Digital Equipment Corporation, III 132–35; 6 233–36 (upd.) *see also* Compaq Computer Corp.
Digital Marketing, Inc., *see* Miner Group Int
Digital River, Inc., 50 156–59
Digitas Inc., 81 107–10
Digitel, **63** 380
Dii Group Inc., **38** 188–89
Dillard Paper Company, 11 74–76 *see also* International Paper Co.
Dillard's Inc., V 45–47; 16 174–77 (upd.); 68 110–14 (upd.)
Dillingham Construction Corporation, 44 151–54 (upd.)
Dillingham Corp., I 565–66
Dillon Companies Inc., 12 111–13
Dillon, Read, and Co., Inc., **11** 53; **20** 259
Dillons, **59** 230
DiMark, Inc., **63** 189
Dime Bancorp, **44** 32–33; **46** 316
Dime Savings Bank of New York, F.S.B., 9 173–74 *see also* Washington Mutual, Inc.
Dimeling, Schrieber & Park, **11** 63; **44** 309
Dimension Data Holdings PLC, 69 126–28
Dimension Films, **64** 285
Dimensions in Sport, Ltd., **37** 5
Dimeric Development Corporation, **14** 392
DIMON Inc., 27 124–27
Dimpex S.A., **72** 272

Dina *see* Consorcio G Grupo Dina, S.A. de C.V.
Dinamica, S.A., **19** 12
Dine S.A., **23** 170–72
Dineen Mechanical Contractors, Inc., **48** 238
Diners Club, **6** 62
Diodes Incorporated, 81 111–14
Dionex Corporation, 46 144–46
Dior *see* Christian Dior S.A.
Dippin' Dots, Inc., 56 84–86
Dirección General de Correos y Telecomunicaciónes *see* Telefónica Nacional de España S.A.
Direct Focus, Inc., 47 93–95
Direct Friends, **25** 91
Direct Marketing Technology Inc., **19** 184
Direct Merchants Credit Card Bank, N.A., **56** 224
Direct Transit, Inc., **42** 364
Direct Wines Ltd., 84 103–106
Directed Electronics, Inc., 87 131–135
Direction of Coins and Medals, **62** 248
DirectLine Insurance, **22** 52
Directorate General of Telecommunications, 7 147–49
DIRECTV, Inc., 38 174–77; 75 128–32 (upd.)
Dirk Rossmann GmbH, 94 155–59
Dirki S.A., **64** 8
Disc Go Round, *see* Grow Biz International, Inc.
Disc Manufacturing, Inc., **15** 378
Disclosure, Inc., **18** 24
Discount Auto Parts, Inc., 18 144–46
Discount Drug Mart, Inc., 14 172–73
Discount Labels, Inc., **20** 15
Discount Tire Company Inc., 84 107–110
Discovery Communications, Inc., 42 114–17
Discovery Partners International, Inc., 58 93–95
Discovery Toys, Inc., *see* Avon Products, Inc.
Discovery Zone, **31** 97
Discreet Logic Inc., 20 185–87 *see also* Autodesk, Inc.
Disctronics, Ltd., **15** 380
Disney *see* The Walt Disney Co.
Disneyland Paris *see* Euro Disney S.C.A.
Disnorte, **51** 389
Distillers Co. plc, I 239–41 *see also* Diageo PLC.
Distribución y Servicio D&S S.A., 71 123–26
Distribuidora Bega, S.A. de C.V., **31** 92
Distribuidora de Produtos de Petróleo Ipiranga, **67** 216–17
Distribution Centers Incorporated *see* Exel Logistics Ltd.
Distribution Centre Sdn. Bhd., **62** 268
Distrigaz S.A., 82 91-94
DITAS *see* Türkiye Petrolleri Anonim Ortakliği.
ditech.com, 93 181–84
Divani & Divani *see* Industrie Natuzzi S.p.A.
DIVE!, **26** 264
Diversey Corp., **I** 275, 333; **26** 305–06; **32** 476
Diversified Agency Services, *see* Omnicom Group Inc.
Diversion Entertainment, Inc., **58** 124
Diversity Consultants Inc., **32** 459
Divesco Inc., **58** 333
DiviCom, **43** 221–22
Dixie Carriers, Inc., *see* Kirby Corp.
Dixie Container Corporation, **12** 377
Dixie Crystals Brands, Inc., **32** 277
The Dixie Group, Inc., 20 188–90; 80 88–92 (upd.)
Dixie-Narco Inc., *see* Maytag Corp.
Dixie Offshore Transportation Company *see* Kirby Corp.
Dixie Power & Light Company, **6** 514
Dixie Yarns, Inc., **19** 305
Dixieland Food Stores, *see* Fleming Companies, Inc.
Dixieline *see* Lanoga Corp.
Dixon Industries, Inc., 26 117–19
Dixon Ticonderoga Company, 12 114–16; 69 129–33 (upd.)
Dixons Group plc, V 48–50; 19 121–24 (upd.); 49 110–13 (upd.)
DJ Moldings Corp., **18** 276
DJ Pharma, Inc., **47** 56
Djarum PT, 62 96–98
Djedi Holding SA, **23** 242
DKB *see* Dai-Ichi Kangyo Bank Ltd.
DKNY *see* Donna Karan International Inc.
Dl Radiators France S.A.R.L. *see* De'Longhi S.p.A.
DLC *see* Duquesne Light Co.
DLJ *see* Donaldson, Lufkin & Jenrette.
DLJ Merchant Banking Partners II, **21** 188; **36** 158–59
DLL *see* David Lloyd Leisure Ltd.
DM Associates Limited Partnership, **25** 127
DMAX-Ltd., **57** 190
DMB&B *see* D'Arcy Masius Benton & Bowles.
dmc2 Italia SrL, **56** 127
DMGT *see* Daily Mail and General Trust.
DMI Furniture, Inc., 46 147–50
DMP Mineralöl Petrochemie GmbH, **IV** 487
DMV Stainless, **54** 393
DNATA, **39** 137, 139
DNN Galvanizing Limited Partnership, *see* Dofasco Inc.
DNP DENMARK A/S, **IV** 600
Do It All, *see* Alliance Boots plc.
Do it Best Corporation, 30 166–70
Dobbs House, **21** 54
Dobbs Houses Inc., **15** 87
Dobrogea Grup S.A., 82 95-98
Dobrolet *see* Aeroflot.
Dobson Communications Corporation, 63 130–32
Dobson Park Industries, **38** 227
Doc Green's Gourmet Salads Inc., **64** 327, 329
Doc Holliday's Pawnbrokers and Jewelers, Inc., **61** 55
Docks de France, **37** 23; **39** 183–84
Doctor's Associates Inc., 67 142–45 (upd.)
The Doctors' Company, 55 125–28
Doctors Without Borders *see* Médecins Sans Frontières.
Documentum, Inc., 46 151–53
DOD Electronics Corp., **15** 215
Dodge & Day *see* Day & Zimmermann, Inc.
Dodge Motor Company, **20** 259
Doduco Corporation, **29** 460–61
Doeflex PLC, **33** 79
Dofasco Inc., IV 73–74; 24 142–44 (upd.)
Dogan Sirketler Grubu Holding A.S., 83 107-110
Dogi International Fabrics S.A., 52 99–102
Doherty, Mann & Olshan *see* Wells Rich Greene BDDP.
Dolan Design, Inc., **44** 133
Dolan Media Company, 94 160–63
Dolby Laboratories Inc., 20 191–93
Dolce & Gabbana SpA, 62 99–101
Dole Corporation, **44** 152
Dole Food Company, Inc., 9 175–76; 31 167–70 (upd.); 68 115–19 (upd.)
Dollar Bills, Inc. *see* Dollar Tree Stores, Inc.
Dollar Express Inc., **62** 104
Dollar General, **26** 533
Dollar Thrifty Automotive Group, Inc., 25 142–45
Dollar Tree Stores, Inc., 23 176–78; 62 102–05 (upd.)
Dollfus Mieg & Cie *see* Groupe DMC.
Dollond & Aitchison Group, **49** 151–52
Dollywood Corporation *see* Herschend Family Entertainment Corp.
Dolmar GmbH, **59** 272
Dolomite Franchi SpA, **53** 285
Dolphin Book Club, *see* Book-of-the-Month Club.
Dolphin Services, Inc., **44** 203
Dom Perignon, **25** 258
Domain.com, Inc. *see* StarTek, Inc.
Domain Home Fashions *see* Aga Foodservice Group PLC.
Domaine Carneros, **43** 401
Domaines Barons de Rothschild, **36** 113, 115
Doman Industries Limited, 59 160–62
Dome Petroleum, Ltd., **IV** 401, 494; **12** 364
Dominick & Dominick LLC, 92 93–96
Dominick International Corp., **12** 131
Dominick's Finer Foods, Inc., 56 87–89
Dominion Bond Rating Service Ltd., **65** 244
Dominion Bridge Company, Limited, *see* United Dominion Industries Ltd.
Dominion Homes, Inc., 19 125–27
Dominion Industries Ltd., **15** 229
Dominion Resources, Inc., V 596–99; 54 83–87 (upd.)

Dominion Salt Ltd., **62** 307
Dominion Textile Inc., 12 117–19
Domino S.p.A., **51** 324
Domino Printing Sciences PLC, 87 136–139
Domino Sugar Corporation, 26 120–22
Domino's, Inc., 7 150–53; 21 177–81 (upd.); 63 133–39 (upd.)
Domtar Corporation, IV 271–73; 89 185–91 (upd.)
Don Canham Enterprises *see* School-Tech, Inc.
Don Massey Cadillac, Inc., 37 114–16
Don's Foods, Inc., **26** 164
Donaldson Company, Inc., 16 178–81; 49 114–18 (upd.)
Donaldson, Lufkin & Jenrette, Inc., 22 188–91
Donaldson's Department Stores, **15** 274
Donatos Pizzeria Corporation, 58 96–98
Donegal Parian China Ltd. *see* Belleek Pottery Ltd.
Dong Guan Highsonic Electronic Products Company, **62** 150
Dong Yang Department Store Company, **62** 174
Dong-Myung Industrial Company Ltd., **64** 270
DongGuan Leeway Footwear Company Ltd., **68** 69
Dongguan Shilong Kyocera Optics Co., Ltd., **21** 331
Dongguan Xinda Giftware Co. Ltd., **60** 372
Dongil Frozen Foods Co., *see* Nippon Suisan Kaisha, Ltd.
Dönkasan, **55** 188
Donna Karan International Inc., 15 145–47; 56 90–93 (upd.)
Donnellon McCarthy Inc., **12** 184
Donnelly Coated Corporation, **48** 28
Donnelly Corporation, 12 120–22; 35 147–50 (upd.)
Donning Company Publishers *see* Walsworth Publishing Company, Inc.
Donnkenny, Inc., 17 136–38
Donohue Inc., *see* Quebecor Inc.
Donohue Meehan Publishing Co., *see* Penton Media, Inc.
Donruss Playoff L.P., 66 81–84
Dooney & Bourke Inc., 84 111–114
Dorel Industries Inc., 59 163–65
Dorenbecher Properties, **19** 381
Doric Corp., **19** 290
Dorling Kindersley Holdings plc, 20 194–96 *see also* Pearson plc.
Dorman Products of America, Ltd., **51** 307
Dorney Park, *see* Cedar Fair, L.P.
Dornier GmbH, *see* Daimler-Benz Aerospace AG
Dorothy Hamill International, *see* International Family Entertainment Inc.
Dorr-Oliver Inc., **35** 134–35
Dorset Capital, **49** 189
Dorsey & Whitney LLP, 47 96–99
Doskocil Companies, Inc., 12 123–25 *see also* Foodbrands America, Inc.
Dot Foods, Inc., 69 134–37
Dot Hill Systems Corp., 93 185–88
Dot Wireless Inc., **46** 422
Doty Agency, Inc., **41** 178, 180
Double A Products Co., **23** 82–83; **74** 320
Double-Cola Co.-USA, 70 74–76
DoubleClick Inc., 46 154–57
Doubleday Book Shops, Inc., **25** 31; **30** 68
Doubleday-Dell, **IV** 594, 636
Doubletree Corporation, 21 182–85
Doughty Handson, **49** 163
Douglas & Lomason Company, 16 182–85
Douglas Aircraft Co., *see* McDonnell Douglas Corp.
Douglas Dynamics L.L.C., **41** 3
Doulton Glass Industries Ltd., **IV** 659
Douwe Egberts, *see* Sara Lee Corp.
Doux S.A., 80 93–96
Dove International, *see* Mars, Inc.
Dover Corporation, III 467–69; 28 101–05 (upd.); 90 162–67 (upd.)
Dover Downs Entertainment, Inc., 43 139–41
Dover Publications Inc., 34 148–50
Dovrat Shrem, **15** 470
The Dow Chemical Company, I 323–25; 8 147–50 (upd.); 50 160–64 (upd.)
Dow Corning *see* Corning Inc.; Dow Chemical Co.; Wright Medical Group, Inc.
Dow Jones & Company, Inc., IV 601–03; 19 128–31 (upd.); 47 100–04 (upd.)
Dow Jones Telerate, Inc., 10 276–78 *see also* Reuters Group PLC.
DOW Stereo/Video Inc., **30** 466
DowElanco, **21** 385, 387
Dowell Schlumberger *see* Schlumberger Ltd.
Down River International, Inc., **15** 188
Dowty Aerospace, *see* TI Group plc.
Dowty Group plc, **58** 345
Doyle Dane Bernbach *see* Omnicom Group Inc.
Doyle Hotel Group, **64** 216
DP&L *see* Dayton Power & Light Co.
DP World, 81 115–18
dPi Teleconnect LLC, **75** 336–37
DPL Inc., 6 480–82
DPPI *see* Distribuidora de Produtos de Petróleo Ipiranga.
DQE, 6 483–85; 38 40
Dr. August Oetker KG, 51 102–06
Dr. E. Fresenius KG *see* Fresenius Aktiengesellschaft.
Dr. Gerhard Mann Pharma, **25** 56
Dr Hans Kraus d.o.o, **72** 221
Dr. Ing he F. Porsche GmbH, *see* Porsche AG.
Dr. Karl Thomae GmbH, **39** 72–73
Dr. Martens, **23** 399, 401
Dr Pepper/Seven Up, Inc., 9 177–78; 32 154–57 (upd.)
Dr. Reddy's Laboratories Ltd., 59 166–69
The Dr. Robert C. Atkins Foundation, **58** 8–9
Dr. Solomon's Software Ltd., **25** 349
Dr Specht & Partner GmbH, **70** 90
Drackett Professional Products, 12 126–28 *see also* S.C. Johnson & Son, Inc.
Draftfcb, 94 164–68
DraftDirect Worldwide, **22** 297
Draftline Engineering Co., *see* Defiance, Inc.
Dragados y Construcciones *see* Grupo Dragados SA.
Drägerwerk AG, 83 111-114
Dragoco *see* Symrise GmbH and Company KG.
Dragon Genomics Co. Ltd., **62** 347
Dragonair *see* Hong Kong Dragon Airlines Ltd.
Drake Beam Morin, Inc., 44 155–57
Draper Corporation, **15** 384
Draper Fisher Jurvetson, 91 149–52
Draw-Tite, Inc., *see* TriMas Corp.
Dräxlmaier Group, 90 168–72
DreamLand *see* Etablissements Franz Colruyt N.V.
DreamWorks SKG, 43 142–46
The Drees Company, Inc., 41 131–33
Dreher Breweries, **24** 450
Drescher Corporation *see* Dor Foods, Inc.
Dresden Papier GmbH, **64** 275
Dresdner Bank A.G., II 281–83; 57 110–14 (upd.)
Dresdner Kleinwort Wasserstein, 60 110–13 (upd.)
Dresdner RCM Global Investors, **33** 128
The Dress Barn, Inc., 24 145–46
Dresser Industries, Inc., III 470–73; 55 129–31 (upd.)
Dresser Power, **6** 555
Dressmaster GmbH, **53** 195
Drew Industries Inc., 28 106–08
Drewry Photocolor, **I** 447
Drexel Burnham Lambert Incorporated, II 407–09 *see also* New Street Capital Inc.
Drexel Heritage Furnishings Inc., 12 129–31
Dreyer's Grand Ice Cream, Inc., 17 139–41 *see also* Nestlé S.A.
The Dreyfus Corporation, 70 77–80
DRH Cambridge Homes, Inc., **58** 84
DRI *see* Dominion Resources, Inc.
Dribeck Importers Inc., *see* Brauerei Beck & Co.
Driefontein Consolidated (Pty.) Ltd., **62** 164
Dril-Quip, Inc., 81 119–21
Drinker, Biddle and Reath L.L.P., 92 97–101
Drip In Irrigation, *see* The Toro Co.
DriveTime Automotive Group Inc., 68 120–24 (upd.)
Drogueros S.A., **39** 188

Drs. Foster & Smith, Inc., 62 106–08
DRS Technologies, Inc., 58 99–101
Drug Emporium, Inc., 12 132–34 *see also* Big A Drug Stores Inc.
Drummond Lighterage *see* Puget Sound Tug and Barge Co.
DryClean U.S.A., **14** 25
Drypers Corporation, 18 147–49
DS Smith Plc, 61 76–79
DSC Communications Corporation, 12 135–37 *see also* Alcatel S.A.
DSGV *see* Deutscher Sparkassen- und Giroverband (DSGV).
DSIC *see* Diamond State Insurance Co.
DSL Group Ltd., *see* Armor Holdings, Inc.
DSM N.V., I 326–27; 56 94–96 (upd.)
DST Alliance, **63** 386
DSW Inc., 73 125–27
DTAG *see* Dollar Thrifty Automotive Group, Inc.
DTE Energy Company, 20 197–201 (upd.); 94 169–76 (upd.)
DTS, Inc., 80 97–101
Du Pareil au Même, 43 147–49
Du Pont *see* E.I. du Pont de Nemours & Co.
Du Pont Photomask, **IV** 600
Dualstar Entertainment Group LLC, 76 141–43
Duane Reade Holding Corp., 21 186–88
Dublin Corporation, **50** 74
DuBois Chemicals, **13** 149–50; **26** 306
Ducati Motor Holding SpA, 30 171–73; 86 125–29 (upd.)
Duck Head Apparel Company, Inc., 42 118–21
Duckback Products, Inc., **51** 190
Ducks Unlimited, Inc., 87 140–143
Duckwall-ALCO Stores, Inc., 24 147–49
Duco Ltd., *see* Coflexip S.A.
Ducommun Incorporated, 30 174–76
Ducros, **36** 185, 187–88
Dudley Jenkins Group Plc, **53** 362
Dudley Stationery Ltd., **25** 501
Duferco Group, 94 177–80
Duff & Phelps Credit Rating, **37** 143, 145
Duke Energy Corporation, V 600–02; 27 128–31 (upd.)
Duke Realty Corporation, 57 115–17
The Dun & Bradstreet Corporation, IV 604–05; 19 132–34 (upd.); 61 80–84 (upd.)
Dun & Bradstreet Software Services Inc., 11 77–79
Dunavant Enterprises, Inc., 54 88–90
Dunbar-Stark Drillings, Inc., **19** 247
Duncan Aviation, Inc., 94 181–84
Duncan Toys Company, 55 132–35
Duncanson & Holt, Inc., *see* UNUM Corp.
Dundee Acquisition Corp., *see* Springs Industries, Inc.
Dundee Bancorp, **36** 314
Dundee Cement Co., *see* Holnam Inc.
Dunfey Hotels Corporation, *see* Omni Hotels Corp.
Dunhill Staffing Systems, Inc., **52** 397–98
Dunkin' Donuts, **21** 323; **29** 18–19
Dunkirk Specialty Steel, LLC *see* Universal Stainless & Alloy Products, Inc.
Dunlop Coflexip Umbilicals Ltd. *see* Duco Ltd.
Dunlop Ltd., **25** 104
Dunlop Tire Corporation *see* Sumitomo Rubber Industries, Ltd.
Dunn Bennett, **38** 401
Dunn Bros., **28** 63
Dunn-Edwards Corporation, 56 97–99
Dunn Industries, Inc. *see* JE Dunn Construction Group, Inc.
Dunnes Stores Ltd., 58 102–04
Dunphy Holding Pty. Ltd., **64** 349
Dupey Enterprises, Inc., *see* Michaels Stores, Inc.
Duplex Products, Inc., 17 142–44
Dupont *see* E.I. du Pont de Nemours & Co.
Duquesne Light Company *see* DQE.
Duquesne Systems, *see* Legent Corp.
Dura Automotive Systems Inc., **53** 55; **65** 282, 284
Dura Convertible Systems, *see* Collins & Aikman Corp.
Duracell International Inc., 9 179–81; 71 127–31 (upd.)
Durachemie *see* Hexal AG.
Duraflame Inc., **58** 52
Duramed Research Inc. *see* Barr Pharmaceuticals, Inc.
Durametallic, 21 189–91 *see also* Duriron Company Inc.
Duravit AG, **51** 196
D'Urban, Inc., **41** 169
Duriron Company Inc., 17 145–47 *see also* Flowserve Corp.
Durkee Famous Foods, *see* The Glidden Co.
Dürkopp Adler AG, 65 131–34
Duro-Matic Products Co., **51** 368
Duron Inc., 72 91–93 *see also* The Sherwin-Williams Co.
Dürr AG, 44 158–61
Durr-Fillauer Medical Inc., *see* Bergen Brunswig Corp.
Dürrkopp Adler AG, **62** 132
Dutch Boy, *see* Oshawa Group Ltd.
Dutch Crude Oil Company *see* Nederlandse Aardolie Maatschappij.
Dutch State Mines *see* DSM N.V.
Duty Free International, Inc., 11 80–82 *see also* World Duty Free Americas, Inc.
Duval Corp., **25** 461
DVI, Inc., 51 107–09
Duvernay Oil Corp., 83 115-118
DVM Pharmaceuticals Inc., **55** 233
DVT Corporation *see* Cognex Corp.
DWG Corporation *see* Triarc Companies, Inc.
Dyas B.V., **55** 347
Dyax Corp., 89 192–95
Dyckerhoff AG, 35 151–54
Dycom Industries, Inc., 57 118–20
Dyersburg Corporation, 21 192–95
Dyke and Dryden, Ltd., **31** 417
Dylex Limited, 29 162–65
Dymed Corporation *see* Palomar Medical Technologies, Inc.
DYMO *see* Esselte Worldwide.
Dynatec Corporation, 87 144–147
Dynaction S.A., 67 146–48
Dynalectric Co., **45** 146
DynaMark, Inc., *see* Fair, Isaac and Co.
Dynamem Corporation, *see* Palomar Medical Technologies, Inc.
Dynamic Controls, **11** 202
Dynamic Foods, **53** 148
Dynamic Health Products Inc., **62** 296
Dynamic Homes, **61** 125–27
Dynamic Materials Corporation, 81 122–25
Dynamics Corporation of America, **39** 106
Dynamit Nobel AG, **Isee** Metallgesellschaft AG
Dynamix, **15** 455
Dynapar, *see* Danaher Corp.
Dynaplast, **40** 214–15
Dynascan AK, *see* obra Electronics Corp.
Dynatech Corporation, 13 194–96
Dynatron/Bondo Corporation, *see* RPM Inc.
DynCorp, 45 145–47
Dynea, 68 125–27
Dynegy Inc., 49 119–22 (upd.)
Dyson Group PLC, 71 132–34
Dystrybucja, **41** 340

E

E&B Marine, Inc., *see* West Marine, Inc.
E. & J. Gallo Winery, I 242–44; 7 154–56 (upd.); 28 109–11 (upd.)
E & S Retail Ltd. *see* Powerhouse.
E! Entertainment Television Inc., 17 148–50
E-Mex Home Funding Ltd. *see* Cheshire Building Society.
E-mu Systems, Inc., **57** 78–79
E-Pet Services, **74** 234
E-Stamp Corporation, **34** 474
E-Systems, Inc., 9 182–85
E*Trade Financial Corporation, 20 206–08; 60 114–17 (upd.)
E-II Holdings Inc. *see* Astrum International Corp.
E-Z Serve Corporation, 17 169–71
E-Z-EM Inc., 89 196–99
E A Rosengrens AB, **53** 158
E.B. Badger Co., **11** 413
E.B. Eddy Forest Products, *see* George Weston Ltd.
e.Biscom *see* FASTWEB S.p.A.
E.F. Hutton Group, *see* Shearson Lehman Brothers Holdings Inc.
E H Booth & Company Ltd., 90 173–76
E.I. du Pont de Nemours and Company, I 328–30; 8 151–54 (upd.); 26 123–27 (upd.); 73 128–33 (upd.)

E.J. Brach & Sons *see* Brach and Brock Confections, Inc.
E.J. Longyear Company *see* Boart Longyear Co.
E. Katz Special Advertising Agency *see* Katz Communications, Inc.
E.M. Warburg Pincus & Co., **16** 319; **29** 262
E. Missel GmbH, **20** 363
E.On AG, 50 165–73 (upd.)
E.piphany, Inc., 49 123–25
E.R.R. Enterprises, **44** 227
E. Rosen Co., **53** 303–04
E.S. International Holding S.A. *see* Banco Espírito Santo e Comercial de Lisboa S.A.
E.V. Williams Inc. *see* The Branch Group, Inc.
E.W. Howell Co., Inc., 72 94–96 *see also* Obayashi Corporation
The E.W. Scripps Company, IV 606–09; 7 157–59 (upd.); 28 122–26 (upd.); 66 85–89 (upd.)
E. Witte Verwaltungsgesellschaft GmbH, **73** 326
EADS N.V. *see* European Aeronautic Defence and Space Company EADS N.V.
EADS SOCATA, 54 91–94
Eagel One Industries, **50** 49
Eagle Airways Ltd., **23** 161
Eagle Distributing Co., **37** 351
Eagle Family Foods, Inc., **22** 95
Eagle Floor Care, Inc., *see* Tennant Co.
Eagle Gaming, L.P., **16** 263; **43** 226; **75** 341
Eagle Global Logistics *see* EGL, Inc.
Eagle Hardware & Garden, Inc., 16 186–89 *see also* Lowe's Companies, Inc.
Eagle Industries Inc., *see* Great American Management and Investment, Inc.
Eagle Managed Care Corp., *see* Rite Aid Corp.
Eagle-Picher Industries, Inc., 8 155–58; 23 179–83 (upd.) *see also* PerkinElmer Inc.
Eagle Sentry Inc., **32** 373
Eagle Trading, **55** 24
Eagle-Tribune Publishing Co., 91 153–57
Earl Scheib, Inc., 32 158–61
Earle M. Jorgensen Company, 82 99–102
Early Learning Centre, **39** 240, 242
Earth's Best, Inc., **21** 56; **36** 256
The Earthgrains Company, 36 161–65
EarthLink, Inc., 36 166–68
EAS *see* Engineered Air Systems, Inc.; Executive Aircraft Services.
Easco Hand Tools, Inc., **7** 117
Easi-Set Industries, Inc., **56** 332
Eason Oil Company, **6** 578
East African Gold Mines Limited, **61** 293
East Japan Railway Company, V 448–50; 66 90–94 (upd.)
The East New York Savings Bank, *see* First Empire State Corp.
East Penn Manufacturing Co., Inc., 79 154–57
East Tennessee Steel Supply Inc. *see* Siskin Steel & Supply Co.
East-West Federal Bank, **16** 484
East West Motor Express, Inc., **39** 377
Easter Enterprises *see* Nash Finch Co.
Easter Seals, Inc., 58 105–07
Eastern Air Group Co., **31** 102
Eastern Airlines, I 101–03
Eastern Aviation Group, **23** 408
The Eastern Company, 48 140–43
Eastern Enterprises, 6 486–88
Eastern Industries, Inc. *see* Stabler Companies Inc.
Eastern Kansas Utilities, **6** 511
Eastern Market Beef Processing Corp., **20** 120
Eastern Platinum Ltd. *see* Lonmin plc.
Eastern Shore Natural Gas Company, **56** 62
Eastern Software Distributors, Inc., **16** 125
Eastern Texas Electric *see* Gulf States Utilities Co.
Eastern Wisconsin Power, **6** 604
Eastern Wisconsin Railway and Light Company, **6** 601
EastGroup Properties, Inc., 67 149–51
Eastland Shoe Corporation, 82 103–106
Eastman Chemical Company, 14 174–75; 38 178–81 (upd.)
Eastman House *see* Chittenden & Eastman Co.
Eastman Kodak Company, III 474–77; 7 160–64 (upd.); 36 169–76 (upd.); 91 158–69 (upd.)
Easton Sports, Inc., 66 95–97
Eastpak, Inc., **30** 138; **70** 136
Eastport International Inc., **63** 318
Eastwynn Theatres, Inc., **37** 63
easyJet Airline Company Limited, 39 127–29; 52 330
Eatco, Inc., **15** 246
Eateries, Inc., 33 138–40
Eaton Corporation, I 154–55; 10 279–80 (upd.); 67 152–56 (upd.)
Eaton Vance Corporation, 18 150–53
EAudio, Inc., **48** 92
EBA Holding S.A., **63** 180
EBASCO *see* Electric Bond and Share Co.
eBay Inc., 32 162–65; 67 157–61 (upd.)
EBCO, **55** 302
Ebara Corporation, 83 119-122
Eberhard Manufacturing Company, **48** 141
EBIC *see* European Banks' International Co.
EBS *see* Electric Bond & Share Company; Electronic Bookshelf.
EBSCO Industries, Inc., 17 151–53; 40 158–61 (upd.)
EC Delaware Incorporated, **72** 117
EC Erdolchemie GmbH, *see* Deutsche BP AG.
ECAD Inc., **48** 75
ECC *see* Educational Credit Corp.
ECC Group plc, III 689–91 *see also* English China Clays plc.
ECC International Corp., 42 122–24
Ecce, **41** 129
ECCO *see* Adecco S.A.
Ecco Sko A/S, 62 109–11
Echlin Inc., I 156–57; 11 83–85 (upd.) *see also* Dana Corp.
Echo Bay Mines Ltd., IV 75–77; 38 182–85 (upd.)
The Echo Design Group, Inc., 68 128–30
Les Echos, **IV** 659
EchoStar Communications Corporation, 35 155–59
EchoStar Satellite Corp., **39** 400
ECI Telecom Ltd., 18 154–56
Eckerd Corporation, 9 186–87 *see also* J.C. Penney Company, Inc.
Eckes AG, 56 100–03
Eclipse Aviation Corporation, 87 148–151
Eclipse Candles, Ltd., *see* Blyth, Inc.
Eclipse Telecommunications, Inc., **29** 252
Eco Hotels, **14** 107
Eco SA, **48** 224
Eco-Tech Company Inc., **60** 272
Ecoiffier, **56** 335
Ecolab Inc., I 331–33; 13 197–200 (upd.); 34 151–56 (upd.); 85 97–105 (upd.)
eCollege.com, 85 106–09
Ecology and Environment, Inc., 39 130–33
Econo Lodge *see* Choice Hotels International, Inc.
Economist Group, **15** 265
The Economist Group Ltd., 67 162–65
Economy Fire & Casualty, **22** 495
Ecopetrol *see* Empresa Colombiana de Petróleos.
EcoSystems Software, Inc., *see* Compuware Corp.
EcoWater Systems, Inc., *see* The Marmon Group, Inc.
ECS S.A, 12 138–40
ECT Environmental Technologies AB, **72** 117
Ecton, Inc., **36** 5
ed bazinet international, inc., **34** 144–45
Ed S.A.S., 88 70–73
Edah, *see* Koninklijke Vendex KBB N.V. (Royal Vendex KBB N.V.).
Edasa *see* Embotelladoras del Atlántico, S.A.
Eddelbüttel & Schneider GmbH, **68** 289
Eddie Bauer Holdings, Inc., 9 188–90; 36 177–81 (upd.); 87 152–159 (upd.)
Edeka Zentrale A.G., II 621–23; 47 105–07 (upd.)
edel music AG, 44 162–65
Edelbrock Corporation, 37 117–19
Edelhoff AG & Co., **39** 415
Edelman, 62 112–15
Edenton Cotton Mills, **12** 503
EDF *see* Electricité de France.
EDGAR Online, Inc., 91 170–73

Edgars Consolidated Stores Ltd., 66 98–100
Edge Petroleum Corporation, 67 166–68
Edge Research, **25** 301
Edgell Communications Inc., **IV** 624
Edgewater Hotel and Casino *see* Circus Circus Enterprises, Inc.
EDI, **26** 441
Edipresse S.A., 82 107–110
Edison Brothers Stores, Inc., 9 191–93
Edison Electric Co., *see* General Electric Co.
Edison General Electric Co., *see* General Electric Co.
Edison International, 56 104–07 (upd.)
Edison Schools Inc., 37 120–23
Editions Dalloz, **IV** 615
Éditions Gallimard, 72 97–101
Editions Jean-Baptiste Baillière, **25** 285
Editis S.A., 78 93–97
Editorial Centro de Estudios Ramón Areces, S.A., **V** 52; **26** 130
Editorial Television, S.A. de C.V., 57 121–23
Editoriale L'Espresso, **IV** 586–87
Editoriale Le Gazzette, **IV** 587
Edivisa *see* Editorial Television, S.A. de C.V.
EDiX Corporation, **64** 191
EdK *see* Edeka Zentrale A.G.
Edmark Corporation, 14 176–78; 41 134–37 (upd.)
EDO Corporation, 46 158–61
EdoWater Systems, Inc., *see* Marmon Group, Inc.
EDP Group *see* Electricidade de Portugal, S.A.
The Edrington Group Ltd., 88 74–78
EDS *see* Electronic Data Systems Corp.
Educate Inc., 86 130–35 (upd.)
Education Association Mutual Assurance Company *see* Horace Mann Educators Corp.
The Education Finance Group, **33** 418, 420
Education Loan Processing, **53** 319
Education Management Corporation, 35 160–63
Educational Broadcasting Corporation, 48 144–47
Educational Computer International, Inc. *see* ECC International Corp.
Educational Development Corporation *see* National Heritage Academies, Inc.
Educational Loan Administration Group, Inc., **33** 420
Educational Publishing Corporation, *see* Tribune Co.
Educational Testing Service, 12 141–43; 62 116–20 (upd.)
Educor *see* Naspers Ltd.
Educorp, Inc., **39** 103
Edumond Le Monnier S.p.A., **54** 22
EduQuest, **6** 245
EduServ Technologies, Inc., **33** 420
Edusoft Ltd., **40** 113
EduTrek International, Inc., **45** 88
Edw. C. Levy Co., 42 125–27
Edward D. Jones & Company L.P., 30 177–79; 66 101–04 (upd.)
Edward Hines Lumber Company, 68 131–33
Edward J. DeBartolo Corporation, 8 159–62
Edwards & Jones, *see* United Utilities PLC.
Edwards and Kelcey, 70 81–83
Edwards Brothers, Inc., 92 102–06
Edwards Theatres Circuit, Inc., 31 171–73
Edwardstone Partners, **14** 377
EEC Environmental, Inc., **16** 259
EEGSA *see* Empresa Eléctrica de Guatemala S.A.
EEX Corporation, **65** 262
eFamily *see* Marchex, Inc.
EFJ, Inc., 81 126–29
EFM Media Management, **23** 294
Efrat Future Technology Ltd. *see* Comverse Technology, Inc.
EFS National Bank, **52** 87
EFTEC, **32** 257
EG&G Incorporated, 8 163–65; 29 166–69 (upd.)
EGAM, **IV** 422
Egan Companies, Inc., 94 185–88
EGAT *see* Electricity Generating Authority of Thailand (EGAT).
Egg plc, **48** 328
Egghead.com, Inc., 9 194–95; 31 174–77 (upd.)
EGL, Inc., 59 170–73
Egmont Group, 93 189–93
EGPC *see* Egyptian General Petroleum Corp.
eGrail Inc., **62** 142
EgyptAir, 6 84–86; 27 132–35 (upd.)
Egyptian General Petroleum Corporation, IV 412–14; 51 110–14 (upd.)
EHAPE Einheitspreis Handels Gesellschaft mbH *see* Kaufhalle AG.
eHarmony.com Inc., 71 135–38
EHN *see* Corporacion Energia Hidroelectrica de Navarra
eHow.com, **49** 290
Ehrlich-Rominger, **48** 204
Eiffage, 27 136–38
Eiffel Construction Metallique, *see* Eiffage.
8x8, Inc., 94 189–92
800-JR Cigar, Inc., 27 139–41
84 Lumber Company, 9 196–97; 39 134–36 (upd.)
Eildon Electronics Ltd., **15** 385
Eileen Fisher Inc., 61 85–87
Einstein/Noah Bagel Corporation, 29 170–73
eircom plc, 31 178–81 (upd.)
EIS, Inc., **45** 176, 179; **62** 115
EJ Financial Enterprises Inc., **48** 308–09
Ek Chor China Motorcycle, **62** 63
Eka Chemicals AB, 92 107–10
Ekco Group, Inc., 16 190–93
Eko-Elda A.B.E.E., **64** 177
Ekoterm CR *see* Dalkia Holding.
EKT, Inc., **44** 4
El Al Israel Airlines Ltd., 23 184–87
El Camino Resources International, Inc., 11 86–88
El Chico Restaurants, Inc., 19 135–38; 36 162–63
El Corte Inglés, S.A., V 51–53; 26 128–31 (upd.)
El Dorado Chemical Company*see* LSB Industries, Inc.
El Dorado Investment Company, **6** 546–47
El-Mel-Parts Ltd., **21** 499
El Nasr Petroleum Co., **51** 113
El Paso Corporation, 66 105–08 (upd.)
El Paso Electric Company, 21 196–98
El Paso Healthcare System, Ltd., **15** 112; **35** 215
El Paso Natural Gas Company, 12 144–46 *see also* El Paso Corp.
El Pollo Loco, Inc., 69 138–40
El Portal Group, Inc., **58** 370
Elamex, S.A. de C.V., 51 115–17
Elan Corporation PLC, 63 140–43
Elanco Animal Health, **47** 112
Elano Corporation, 14 179–81
Elantis, **48** 290
Elastic Reality Inc., **38** 70
Elcat Company, *see* Chattem, Inc.
Elco Corporation, **21** 329, 331
Elco Industries Inc., **22** 282
The Elder-Beerman Stores Corp., 10 281–83; 63 144–48 (upd.)
Elders IXL Ltd., I 437–39
Eldorado Gold Corporation, **22** 237
ele Corporation, **23** 251
Electra Investment Trust, **73** 340
Electra Partners, **75** 389, 391
Electrabel N.V., 67 169–71
Electric Boat Corporation, 86 136–39
Electric Bond & Share Company, **6** 596
Electric Clearinghouse, Inc., *see* Dynegy Inc.
Electric Fuels Corp. *see* Florida Progress Corp.
Electric Light Company of Atlantic City *see* Atlantic Energy, Inc.
Electric Lightwave, Inc., 37 124–27
Electric Storage Battery Co., **39** 338
Electric Transit, Inc., **37** 399–400
Electricidade de Portugal, S.A., 47 108–11
Electricité de France, V 603–05; 41 138–41 (upd.)
Electricity Generating Authority of Thailand (EGAT), 56 108–10
Electricity Metering Distribucion, S.A. DE C.V., **64** 205
Electro Rent Corporation, 58 108–10
Electrocomponents PLC, 50 174–77
Electrolux AB, 22 24–28 (upd.); 53 124–29 (upd.)
Electrolux Group, III 478–81
Electromagnetic Sciences Inc., 21 199–201
Electromedics, **11** 460
Electronic Arts Inc., 10 284–86; 85 110–15 (upd.)

Electronic Book Technologies, Inc., **26** 216 **29** 427
Electronic Data Systems Corporation, III 136–38; 28 112–16 (upd.) *see also* Perot Systems Corp.
Electronic Hair Styling, Inc., **41** 228
Electronic Processing Inc. *see* EPIQ Systems, Inc.
Electronics Boutique Holdings Corporation, 72 102–05
Electronics Corp. of Israel Ltd. *see* ECI Telecom Ltd.
Electronics for Imaging, Inc., 15 148–50; 43 150–53 (upd.)
Electrowatt Ltd., **21** 146–47
Elekom, **31** 176
Elektra *see* Grupo Elektra, S.A. de C.V.
Elektra Entertainment Group, 64 115–18
Elektriska Aktiebolaget *see* ABB Asea Brown Boveri Ltd.
Elektrizitäts-Gesellschaft Laufenburg *see* Elektrowatt AG.
Elektrizitätswerk Wesertal GmbH, **30** 206
Elektrocieplownie Warszawskie S.A., **57** 395, 397
Elektrowatt AG, 6 489–91 *see also* Siemens AG.
Element K Corporation, 94 193–96
Elementis plc, 40 162–68 (upd.)
Elephant Pharmacy, Inc., 83 123-126
Eletropaulo Metropolitana, **53** 18
Eletson Corp., **13** 374
Elettra Broadcasting Corporation, **14** 509
Elf Aquitaine SA, 21 202–06 (upd.) *see also* Société Nationale Elf Aquitaine.
Elfa International, **36** 134–35
Elgin Blenders, Inc., *see* Dean Foods Co.
Elgin Exploration, Inc., **19** 247; **26** 70
Eli Lilly and Company, I 645–47; 11 89–91 (upd.); 47 112–16 (upd.)
Eli Witt Company, **15** 137, 139; **43** 205
Elior SA, 49 126–28
Elisra Defense Group, **68** 222, 224
Elite Acquisitions, Inc., **65** 150
Elite World S.A., 94 197–201
Elizabeth Arden, Inc., 8 166–68; 40 169–72 (upd.)
Eljer Industries, Inc., 24 150–52
Elkay Manufacturing Company, 73 134–36
ElkCorp, 52 103–05
Elkjop ASA, **49** 113
Ellanef Manufacturing Corp., **48** 274
Ellen Tracy, Inc., 55 136–38
Ellerbe Becket, 41 142–45
Ellesse International S.p.A. *see* Reebok International Ltd.
Ellett Brothers, Inc., 17 154–56
Ellington Recycling Center, **12** 377
Elliot Group Limited, **45** 139–40
Elliott & Co. (Henley) Ltd. *see* Gibbs and Dandy plc.
Elliott Bay Design Group, **22** 276
Ellipse Programmes, **48** 164–65
Ellis & Everard, **41** 341
Ellis-Don Ltd., **38** 481
Ellis Park Race Course, **29** 118
Ellisco Co., **35** 130
Elma Electronic AG, 83 127-130
Elmer Candy Corporation, 88 79–82
Elmer's Products, Inc. *see* Borden, Inc.
Elmer's Restaurants, Inc., 42 128–30
Elmo Semiconductor Corp., **48** 246
Elna USA *see* Tacony Corp.
Elphinstone, **21** 501
Elpida Memory, Inc., 83 131-134
Elrick Industries, Inc., *see* Myers Industries, Inc.
Elron Industries, **75** 304–05
Elscint Ltd., 20 202–05
Elsevier NV, IV 610–11 *see also* Reed Elsevier.
Elsinore Corporation, 48 148–51
Eltra Corporation, *see* AlliedSignal Inc.
Eltron International Inc., **53** 374
Elvirasminde A/S *see* August Storck KG.
Elvis Presley Enterprises, Inc., 61 88–90
ELYO, **42** 387–88
eMachines, Inc., **63** 155
Email Ltd., **62** 331
EMAP plc, 35 164–66
Embankment Trust Ltd., **IV** 659
EMBARQ Corporation, 83 135-138
Embassy Suites, *see* Promus Companies, Inc.
Embedded Support Tools Corporation, **37** 419, 421
Embers America Restaurants, 30 180–82
Embotelladora Andina S.A., 71 139–41
Embotelladora Central, S.A., **47** 291
Embraer *see* Empresa Brasileira de Aeronáutica S.A.
Embraer-Liebherr Equipamentos do Brasil S.A., **64** 241
Embrex, Inc., 72 106–08
EMC Corporation, 12 147–49; 46 162–66 (upd.)
EMC Technology Services, Inc., **30** 469
EMCOR Group Inc., 60 118–21
EMD Holding, Inc., **64** 205
EMD Technologies, **27** 21; **40** 67
Emerson, 46 167–71 (upd.)
Emerson Electric Co., II 18–21
Emerson Radio Corp., 30 183–86
Emery Worldwide Airlines, Inc., 6 388–91; 25 146–50 (upd.)
Emge Packing Co., Inc., 11 92–93
Emhart Corp., *see* Black & Decker Corp.
EMI Group plc, 22 192–95 (upd.); 81 130–37 (upd.)
Emigrant Savings Bank, 59 174–76
Emil Moestue as, **51** 328
Emil Schlemper GmbH *see* Acme United Corp.
The Emirates Group, 39 137–39; 81 138–42 (upd.)
Emmis Communications Corporation, 47 117–21
Empaques de Carton Titan, **19** 10–11
Empi, Inc., 27 132–35
Empire Blue Cross and Blue Shield, III 245–46 *see also* WellChoice, Inc.
Empire-Cliffs Partnership, **62** 74
The Empire District Electric Company, 77 138–41
Empire Family Restaurants Inc., **15** 362
Empire Iron Mining Partnership, **62** 74
Empire of America, **11** 110
Empire of Carolina Inc., **66** 370
Empire Resorts, Inc., 72 109–12
Empire Resources, Inc., 81 143–46
Empire State Pickling Company, **21** 155
Empire Steel Castings, Inc., **39** 31–32
Empire Stores, **19** 309
Employee Solutions, Inc., 18 157–60
employeesavings.com, **39** 25
Employers General Insurance Group, **58** 259
Employers Insurance of Wausau, **59** 264
Employers Reinsurance Corp., **II** 31; **12** 197
Emporsil-Empresa Portuguesa de Silvicultura, Lda, **60** 156
Empresa Brasileira de Aeronáutica S.A. (Embraer), 36 182–84
Empresa Colombiana de Petróleos, IV 415–18
Empresa Constructora SA, **55** 182
Empresa de Distribucion Electrica de Lima Nortes SA, **73** 142
Empresa de Obras y Montajes Ovalle Moore, S.A., **34** 81
Empresa Eléctrica de Guatemala S.A., **49** 211
Empresa Nacional de Telecomunicaciones, **63** 375
Empresas Almacenes Paris S.A., 71 142–44
Empresas CMPC S.A., 70 84–87
Empresas Copec S.A., 69 141–44
Empresas Emel S.A., **41** 316
Empresas Frisco, **21** 259
Empresas ICA Sociedad Controladora, S.A. de C.V., 41 146–49
Empresas La Moderna, **21** 413; **29** 435
Empresas Penta S.A., **69** 56
Empresas Polar SA, 55 139–41 (upd.)
Empresas Públicas de Medellín S.A.E.S.P., 91 174–77
Empresas Tolteca, **20** 123
Emprise Corporation, *see* Delaware North Companies Inc.
EMS-Chemie Holding AG, **32** 257
EMS Technologies, Inc., **21** 199, 201
Enbridge Inc., 43 154–58
ENCAD, Incorporated, 25 151–53 *see also* Eastman Kodak Co.
Encompass Services Corporation, 33 141–44
Encon Safety Products, Inc., **45** 424
Encor Inc., **47** 396
Encore Acquisition Company, 73 137–39
Encore Computer Corporation, 13 201–02; 74 107–10 (upd.)
Encore Distributors Inc., **17** 12–13
Encore Wire Corporation, 81 147–50
Encryption Technology Corporation, **23** 102
Encyclopedia Britannica, Inc., 7 165–68; 39 140–44 (upd.)
Endeavor Pharmaceuticals Inc. *see* Barr Pharmaceuticals, Inc.

Endemol Entertainment Holding NV, 46 172–74; 53 154
ENDESA S.A., V 606–08; 46 175–79 (upd.)
Endevco Inc., **11** 28
Endicott Trust Company, **11** 110
Endo Pharmaceuticals Holdings Inc., 71 145–47
Endo Vascular Technologies, Inc., **11** 460
ENDOlap, Inc., **50** 122
Endovations, Inc., **21** 47
Endurance Specialty Holdings Ltd., 85 116–19
ENECO *see* Empresa Nacional Electrica de Cordoba.
Enercon, Inc., **6** 25
Energas Company, **43** 56–57
Energen Corporation, 21 207–09
Energieversorgung Ostbayern AG, **23** 47
Energis plc, 44 363; **47 122–25**
Energizer Holdings, Inc., 32 171–74
Energy & Minerals, Inc., **42** 354
Energy Absorption Systems, Inc., **15** 378
Energy Africa Limited *see* Tullow Oil plc
Energy Atlantic, LLC *see* Maine & Maritimes Corp.
Energy Biosystems Corp., **15** 352
Energy Brands Inc., 88 83–86
Energy Coatings Co., **14** 325
Energy Conversion Devices, Inc., 75 133–36
Energy Electromechanical Projects S.A., **64** 8
Energy Film Library, **31** 216, 218
Energy Foundation, **34** 386
The Energy Group, **26** 359
Energy Resource Technology, Inc. *see* Helix Energy Solutions Group, Inc.
Energy Steel Corporation, *see* Valmont Industries, Inc.
Energy Systems Group, Inc., *see* Southern Indiana Gas and Electric Co.
Energy Ventures, Inc., **49** 181
Energyline Systems, **26** 5
EnergyOne, **19** 487
Eneria *see* Groupe Monnoyeur.
Enerplus Resources, **21** 500
Enersis S.A., 73 140–43
Enesco Corporation, 11 94–96
Enet S.A., **64** 8
Enforcer Products, Inc., **54** 254
Engelhard Corporation, IV 78–80; 21 210–14 (upd.); 72 113–18 (upd.)
Engen, *see* Gold Fields Ltd.
Engenio Information Technologies, Inc., **64** 246
Engineered Support Systems, Inc., 59 177–80
Engineering for the Petroleum and Process Industries, **IV** 414
Engineering Systems, Inc., **54** 182
England Corsair Furniture, *see* La-Z-Boy Inc.
Engle Homes, Inc., 46 180–82
Engles Management Corp., **26** 448
English China Clays Ltd., 15 151–54 (upd.); 40 173–77 (upd.)
Engraph, Inc., 12 150–51 *see also* Sonoco Products Co.
Enhanced Derm Technologies, **50** 122
Enhanced Services Billing, Inc. *see* Billing Concepts Corp.
ENI S.p.A., 69 145–50 (upd.)
Enimont, **IV** 422, 525
ENMAX Corporation, 83 139-142
Ennis Business Forms, Inc., 21 215–17
Enodis plc, 68 134–37
Enogex, Inc., **6** 539–40
Enova Corporation *see* Sempra Energy.
ENPAC Corporation, *see* Essef Corp.
EnPro Industries, Inc., 93 194–98
Enquirer/Star Group, Inc., 10 287–88 *see also* American Media, Inc.
ENRECO *see* Essential Nutrient Research Corp.
Enrich International, Inc., 33 145–48
Enron Corporation, V 609–10; 19 139–41; 46 183–86 (upd.)
ENSCO International Incorporated, 57 124–26
Enserch Corp., V 611–13 *see also* Texas Utilities.
Enskilda S.A., *see* Skandinaviska Enskilda Banken AB.
Enso-Gutzeit Oy, IV 274–77 *see also* Stora Enso Oyj.
ENSTAR Corporation, *see* Seagull Energy Corp.
Ensuiko Sugar Refining Co., **75** 250–52
Ensys Environmental Products, Inc., **10** 107
Ente Nazionale Idrocarburi, IV 419–22 *see also* ENI S.p.A.
Ente Nazionale per l'Energia Elettrica, V 614–17
Entenmann's Bakery, **35** 415; **38** 364
Entercom Communications Corporation, 58 111–12
Entergy Corporation, V 618–20; 45 148–51 (upd.)
Enterprise Development Company, **15** 413
Enterprise Electronics Corporation, *see* Tech-Sym Corp.
Enterprise Federal Savings & Loan, **21** 524
Enterprise Inns plc, 59 181–83
Enterprise Metals Pty. Ltd., **IV** 61
Enterprise Oil plc, 11 97–99; 50 178–82 (upd.)
Enterprise Rent-A-Car Company, 6 392–93; 69 151–54 (upd.)
Enterra Corp., **25** 546
Entertainment Distribution Company, 89 200–03
Entertainment Publications, **16** 146
Entertainment UK Ltd, *see* Kingfisher plc.
Entertainment Zone, Inc., **15** 212
Entity Software, **11** 469
Entrada Industries Incorporated, **6** 568–69; **26** 387
Entravision Communications Corporation, 41 150–52
Entreprise Nationale Sonatrach, IV 423–25 *see also* Sonatrach.
Entrust Financial Corp., **16** 347
Envergure, *see* Société du Louvre.
Envirex, **11** 361
Envirocal Inc., **60** 223
Envirodrill Services, Inc., **19** 247
Envirodyne Industries, Inc., 17 157–60
EnviroLease, Inc., **25** 171
Enviromed, Inc., **74** 318
Environmental Defense Fund, **9** 305
Environmental Industries, Inc., 31 182–85
Environmental Mediation, Inc., **47** 20
Environmental Planning & Research *see* CRSS Inc.
Environmental Power Corporation, 68 138–40
Environmental Research and Technology, Inc., **23** 135
Environmental Systems Research Institute Inc. (ESRI), 62 121–24
Environmental Technologies Group, LLC, **56** 161
Environmentals Incorporated *see* Angelica Corp.
Envirosciences Pty. Ltd., **16** 260
EnviroSource Inc., **63** 237
EnviroTech Pumpsystems *see* Weir Group PLC.
Envision Corporation, **24** 96
Enwright Environmental Consulting Laboratories, *see* Chemical Waste Management, Inc.
Enzafruit Worldwide, **38** 202
Enzo Biochem, Inc., 41 153–55
Enzyme Bio-Systems, Ltd., **21** 386
Eon Labs, Inc., 67 172–74
Eon Systems, **38** 409
EPCOR Utilities Inc., 81 151–54
EPI *see* Essentially Pure Ingredients.
EPI Group Limited, **26** 137
Epic Express, **48** 113
Epic Systems Corporation, 62 125–28
Epiphone, *see* Gibson Guitar Corp.
EPIQ Systems, Inc., 56 111–13
Epoch Software, Plc, **49** 290
Epoch Systems Inc., *see* EMC Corp.
ePOWER International, **33** 3, 6
Eppler, Guerin & Turner, Inc., *see* Principal Mutual Life Insurance Co.
EQT Partners AB, **71** 342
Equant N.V., 52 106–08
EQUICOR-Equitable HCA Corp., **III** 80, 226; **45** 104, 109
Equicor Group Ltd., **29** 343
Equifax, Inc., 6 23–25; 28 117–21 (upd.); 90 177–83 (upd.)
Equilink Licensing Group, **22** 458
Equilon Enterprises LLC, **41** 359, 395
The Equinox Indemnity Co. Ltd. *see* SNC-Lavalin Group Inc.
Equinox Systems *see* Avocent Corp.
Equistar Chemicals, LP, 71 148–50
EquiStar Hotel Investors L.P. *see* CapStar Hotel Co.
Equitable Life Assurance Society of the United States, III 247–49
Equitable of Iowa, **76** 384

Equitable Resources, Inc., **6 492–94; 54 95–98 (upd.)**
Equitas, *see* Lloyd's.
Equitec Financial Group, **11** 483
Equity & Law, *see* AXA.
Equity Corp. International, **51** 332
Equity Corporation, **6** 599; **37** 67–68
Equity Marketing, Inc., **26 136–38**
Equity Office Properties Trust, **54 99–102**
Equity Residential, **49 129–32**
Equity Title Services Company, *see* Metropolitan Financial Corp.
Equus Capital Corp., **23** 65
Equus Computer Systems, Inc., **49 133–35**
ERA, **61** 267
Eram SA, **51 118–20**
Eramet, **73 144–47**
ERAP *see* Entreprise de Recherches et d'Activités Pétrolières.
Ercea, **41** 128–29
ERCO Systems Group, *see* Sterling Chemicals Inc.
Ercon Corp., **49** 181
Ercros S.A., **80 102–05**
ERDA Inc., **36** 160
ERE Yarmouth, **57** 234
ERGO Versicherungsgruppe AG, **44 166–69**
Erickson Retirement Communities, **57 127–30**
Ericsson *see* Telefonaktiebolaget LM Ericsson.
Eridania Béghin-Say S.A., **36 185–88**
Erie Indemnity Company, **35 167–69**
Erie Scientific Company, *see* Sybron International Corp.
ERIM International Inc., **54** 396
Erisco Managed Care Technologies, **57** 176
ERKA *see* Reichs Kredit-Gesellschaft mbH.
ERLY Industries Inc., **17 161–62**
Ermenegildo Zegna SpA, **63 149–52**
Ernest Jones (Jewelers) Plc, **61** 326
Ernie Ball, Inc., **56 114–16**
Ernst & Young, **9 198–200; 29 174–77 (upd.)**
Ernst Göhner Foundation, **47** 286–87
Ernst, Homans, Ware & Keelips, **37** 224
Eroski *see* Grupo Eroski
Ersco Corporation, *see* FinishMaster, Inc.; Mazco Inc.
Erste Bank der Osterreichischen Sparkassen AG, **69 155–57**
The Ertl Company, **37** 318
ES&A *see* English, Scottish and Australian Bank Ltd.
ES Développement SAS, **70** 90
Esaote Biomedica, **29** 298
ESCADA AG, **71 151–53**
Escalade, Incorporated, **19 142–44**
Escan, **22** 354
Eschelon Telecom, Inc., **72 119–22**
Eschweiler Bergwerks-Verein AG, **IV** 193
ESCO Technologies Inc., **87 160–163**
Escota SA, **55** 40
ESGO B.V., **49** 222
ESI Energy, Inc. *see* FPL Group Inc.
Eskay Screw Corporation, **11** 536
Eskimo Pie Corporation, **21 218–20**
Esmark, Inc., **15** 357; **19** 290
Esmerk Group, **51** 328
Espaces Gamm Vert, **70** 322
Espírito Santo Financial Group S.A., **79 158–63 (upd.)**
ESPN, Inc., **56 117–22**
Esporta plc, **35 170–72**
Esprit de Corp., **8 169–72; 29 178–82 (upd.)**
Esquire Inc., **I** 453; **IV** 672; **19** 405
ESS Technology, Inc., **22 196–98**
Essar Group Ltd., **79 164–67**
Essef Corporation, **18 161–63** *see also* Pentair, Inc.
Esselte, **64 119–21**
Esselte Leitz GmbH & Co. KG, **48 152–55**
Esselte Pendaflex Corporation, **11 100–01**
Essence Communications, Inc., **24 153–55**
Essential Nutrient Research Corporation, **72** 234
Essentially Pure Ingredients, **49** 275–76
Essex Corporation, **85 120–23**
Essex International plc, *see* Town & Country Corp.
Essex Outfitters Inc., *see* OshKosh B'Gosh, Inc.
Essilor International, **21 221–23**
Esso Petroleum *see* Exxon Corporation; Imperial Oil Limited; Standard Oil Company of New Jersey.
Essroc Corporation, **40** 108
Estat Telecom Group plc, **31** 180
Estech, Inc., **19** 290
The Estée Lauder Companies Inc., **9 201–04; 30 187–91 (upd.); 92199–207 (upd.)**
Esterline Technologies Corp., **15 155–57**
Estes Express Lines, Inc., **86 140–43**
Estes Industries Inc. *see* Centuri Corp.
Estronicks, Inc., **19** 290
Etablissements Badin-Defforey, **19** 98
Etablissements Bourgogne et Grasset, **66** 251
Etablissements Braud *see* Manitou BF S.A.
Etablissements Economiques du Casino Guichard, Perrachon et ie, S.C.A., **12 152–54** *see also* Casino Guichard-Perrachon S.A.
Etablissements Franz Colruyt N.V., **68 141–43**
Établissements Jacquot and Cie S.A.S., **92 111–14**
Etam Developpement SA, **44 170–72**
ETBD *see* Europe Through the Back Door.
Eternal Word Television Network, Inc., **57 131–34**
Ethan Allen Interiors, Inc., **12 155–57; 39 145–48 (upd.)**
Ethicon, Inc., **23 188–90**
Ethiopian Airlines, **81 155–58**
Ethyl Corp., **I 334–36; 10 289–91 (upd.)**
Etienne Aigner AG, **52 109–12**
Etihad Airways PJSC, **89 204–07**
Etkin Skanska, **38** 437
Éøile Commerciale S.A., **51** 143
Etos, *see* Koninklijke Ahold N.V. (Royal Ahold).
EToys, Inc., **37 128–30**
ETPM Entrêpose, **IV** 468
ETS *see* Educational Testing Service.
Eu-retec, **71** 393
Euralis *see* Groupe Euralis.
Eurazeo, **80 106–09**
The Eureka Company, **12 158–60** *see also* White Consolidated Industries Inc.
Eureka Technology, **18** 20; **43** 17
Eureka X-Ray Tube, Inc., *see* Dentsply International Inc.
Eurex, **41** 84, 87
Euris, **22** 365; **54** 306–07
Euro Disney S.C.A., **20 209–12; 58 113–16 (upd.)**
Euro Exhausts, **54** 206
Euro RSCG Worldwide S.A., **13 203–05**
Eurobase, **50** 48
Eurocom S.A. *see* Euro RSCG Worldwide S.A.
Eurocopter S.A., **80 110–13**
EuroCross, **48** 381
Eurodis, **46** 71
EuroDollar Rent A Car *see* Republic Industries, Inc.
Eurofind, **71** 308–09
Eurofins Scientific S.A., **70 88–90**
Euroforum BV, **58** 191
Eurogroup, **V** 65
Euroimpex SpA, *see* Essef Corp.
Euromarché SA, **23** 231
Euromarket Designs Inc., **31 186–89 (upd.)**
Euromoney Publications plc, *see* Daily Mail and General Trust plc.
Euronet Worldwide, Inc., **83 143-146**
Euronext N.V., **37 131–33; 89 208–11 (upd.)**
Euronova S.R.L., **15** 340
Europa Discount Sud-Ouest, **23** 248
Europate, S.A., **36** 162–63
Europcar Chauffeur Drive U.K. International, **26** 62
Europcar International Corporation, Limited, **25** 142, 144, **27** 9, 11
Europcar Interrent International, **69** 5, 6
Europe Computer Systems *see* ECS S.A.
Europe Craft Imports, Inc., *see* Aris Industries, Inc.
Europe Publications, **44** 416
Europe Through the Back Door Inc., **65 135–38**
European Acquisition Capital, **53** 46
European Aeronautic Defence and Space Company EADS N.V., **52 113–16 (upd.)**
European Health Spa, **46** 431
European Investment Bank, **66 109–11**

European Retail Alliance (ERA), **12** 152–53
Europene du Zirconium (Cezus), **21** 491
Europoligrafico SpA, **41** 326
Europspace Technische Entwicklungen, **51** 17
Euroquipment Ltd, **72** 221
Eurotec S.A.S., **72** 332
Eurotel Praha, spol. s.r.o., **64** 73
Eurotunnel Group, 13 206–08; 37 134–38 (upd.)
Euthenics Systems Corp. *see* Michael Baker Corp.
Euvia Media AG & Co., **54** 295, 297
EVA Airways Corporation, 51 121–23
Evac International Ltd, **51** 324
Evaluation Associates, LLC *see* Milliman USA.
Evans & Sutherland Computer Corporation, 19 145–49; 78 98–103 (upd.)
Evans Drumhead Company, **48** 232
Evans, Inc., 30 192–94
Evans Rents, **26** 101
Evansville Brewing Company *see* Pittsburgh Brewing Co.
Evansville Paint & Varnish Co. *see* Red Spot Paint & Varnish Co.
Evansville Veneer and Lumber Co., *see* Kimball International, Inc.
Evelyn Wood, Inc., *see* Encyclopaedia Britannica, Inc.
Evenflo Companies, Inc., **19** 144; **54** 73
Everan Capital Corp., **15** 257
Evercore Capital Partners, **59** 383
Everdream Corporation, **59** 12
Everex Systems, Inc., 16 194–96
Everfresh Beverages Inc., **26** 326
Evergenius, **13** 210
Evergreen Air Cargo Service Co., **51** 123
Evergreen Healthcare, Inc., **14** 210
Evergreen International Aviation, Inc., 53 130–33
Evergreen Marine Corporation (Taiwan) Ltd., 13 209–11; 50 183–89 (upd.)
Evergreen Media Corporation, **24** 106
Evergreen Resources, Inc., **11** 28
Everlast Worldwide Inc., 47 126–29
Everlaurel, **13** 210
Everyday Learning Corporation, *see* Tribune Co.
Everything for the Office, **22** 154
Everything's A Dollar Inc. (EAD), *see* Value Merchants, Inc.
EVI, Inc., **39** 416
Evity, Inc., **55** 67
EWTN *see* Eternal Word Television Network, Inc.
Ex-Lax Inc., **15** 138–39
Exabyte Corporation, 12 161–63; 40 178–81 (upd.)
Exactis.com Inc., **49** 423
ExamOne World Wide, **48** 256
Exar Corp., 14 182–84
Exbud, **38** 437
Excaliber, **6** 205
EXCEL Communications Inc., 18 164–67
Excel Corporation, *see* Cargill Inc.
Excel Industries Inc., **53** 55
Excel Technology, Inc., 65 139–42
Excelsior Life Insurance Co., **21** 14
Excelsior Printing Company, **26** 105
Excerpta Medica International *see* Reed Elsevier
Excite, Inc. *see* At Home Corp.
Execu-Fit Health Programs, **11** 379
Executive Airlines, Inc., **28** 22
Executive Gallery, Inc., **12** 264
Executive Jet, Inc., 36 189–91
Executive Life Insurance Co., *see* First Executive Corp.
Executive Money Management, **57** 269
Executive Risk Inc., **37** 86
Executone Information Systems, Inc., 13 212–14; 15 195
ExecuTrain *see* International Data Group, Inc.
Executrans, Inc., **21** 96
Exel plc, 51 124–30 (upd.)
Exelon Corporation, 48 156–63 (upd.); 49 65
Exeter & Hampton Electric Company, **37** 406
Exide Electronics Group, Inc., 20 213–15
Exito *see* Almacenes Exito S.A.
Exmark Manufacturing Company, Inc., **26** 494
Exp@nets, **37** 280, 283
Expand SA, 48 164–66
Expedia, Inc., 58 117–21
Expeditors International of Washington Inc., 17 163–65; 78 104–08 (upd.)
Experian Information Solutions Inc., 45 152–55
Experian Ltd., **47** 165, 168–69
Export & Domestic Can Co., **15** 127
Exportadora Bananera Noboa, S.A., 91 178–81
Express Airlines, Inc., **28** 266
Express Gifts Ltd., **60** 122
Express Newspapers plc, **IV** 687; **28** 503
Express Rent-a-Tire, Ltd., **20** 113
Express Scripts Inc., 17 166–68; 44 173–76 (upd.)
Expression Homes, *see* Fleetwood Enterprises, Inc.
ExpressJet Holdings Inc., **52** 89, 93
Exsa, **55** 188
ExSample Media BV, **53** 362
Extel Financial Ltd., **IV** 687
Extended Stay America, Inc., 41 156–58
Extendicare Health Services, Inc., 6 181–83
EXX Inc., 65 143–45
Exxon Mobil Corporation, IV 426–30; 7 169–73 (upd.); 32 175–82 (upd.); 67 175–86 (upd.)
Eyckeler & Malt AG, **59** 4–5
Eye Care Centers of America, Inc., 69 158–60
Eye Masters Ltd., **23** 329; **76** 243
Eyefinity *see* Vision Service Plan Inc.
Eyes Multimedia Productions Inc., **51** 286–87
EZ Direkt Marketing GmbH *see* Manutan International S.A.
Ezaki Glico Company Ltd., 72 123–25
EZCORP Inc., 43 159–61
EZPor Corporation, **12** 377

F

F&G International Insurance, *see* St. Paul Cos.
F&N Foods Ltd., **54** 116–17
F&W Publications, Inc., 71 154–56
F.A.O. Schwarz *see* FAO Schwarz
F.B. McFarren, Ltd., **21** 499–500
F.C. Internazionale Milano SpA, **44** 387
The F. Dohmen Co., 77 142–45
F.H. Tomkins Buckle Company Ltd., *see* Tomkins plc.
F. Hoffmann-La Roche & Co. A.G., I 642–44; 50 190–93 (upd.)
F. Kanematsu & Co., Ltd. *see* Kanematsu Corp.
F. Korbel & Bros. Inc., 68 144–46
F.N. Herstal *see* Groupe Herstal S.A.
F.W. Witt & Co. *see* Newly Weds foods, Inc.
F.W. Woolworth & Co. Ltd. *see* Kingfisher plc.
F.W. Woolworth Co. *see* Woolworth Corp.
F.X. Schmid Vereinigte Münchener Spielkartenfabriken GmbH & Co. KG, **64** 325
Fab-Asia, Inc., **22** 354–55
Fab Industries, Inc., 27 142–44
Fab 9, **26** 431
Fabbrica D' Armi Pietro Beretta S.p.A., 39 149–51
Faber-Castell *see* A.W. Faber-Castell Unternehmensverwaltung GmbH & Co.
Fabergé, Inc., **8** 168; **47** 114
Fabio Perini S.p.A., **60** 193
Fabri-Centers of America Inc., 16 197–99 *see also* Jo-Ann Stores, Inc.
Fabritec GmbH, **72** 221
Fabtek Inc., **48** 59
Facebook, Inc., 90 184–87
Facet International, **61** 66
Facom S.A., 32 183–85
Façonnable S.A., **67** 279–80
Facts on File, Inc., **22** 443
FactSet Research Systems Inc., 73 148–50
FAE Fluid Air Energy SA, **49** 162–63
Fafnir Bearing Company, *see* The Torrington Co.
FAG—Kugelfischer Georg Schäfer AG, 62 129–32
Fagerdala World Foams, **54** 360–61
Fair Grounds Corporation, 44 177–80
Fair, Isaac and Company, 18 168–71
Fairchild Camera and Instrument Corp., **21** 122
The Fairchild Corporation, **37** 30; **76** 318
Fairchild Dornier GmbH, 9 205–08; 48 167–71 (upd.)
Fairchild Industries, **14** 43; **15** 195; **34** 117
Fairchild Publications, **59** 133–34

Fairchild Semiconductor Corporation, **II** 63–65; **41** 201
Fairclough Construction Group plc, I 567–68
Fairey Industries Ltd., **IV** 659
Fairfax Financial Holdings Limited, 57 135–37
Fairfax Media Ltd., 94 202–08 (upd.)
Fairfield Communities, Inc., 36 192–95
The Fairfield Group, **33** 259–60
Fairfield Resorts *see* Outrigger Enterprises, Inc.
Fairmont Foods Co., **15** 139
Fairmont Hotels & Resorts Inc., 69 161–63
Fairmont Insurance Co., **26** 487
Fairway Outdoor Advertising, Inc., **36** 340, 342
Faiveley S.A., 39 152–54
Falcon Drilling Co. *see* Transocean Sedco Forex Inc.
Falcon Microsystems, Inc., **57** 172–73
Falcon Products, Inc., 33 149–51
Falconbridge Limited, 49 136–39
The Falk Corporation *see* Rexnord Corp.
Fallon Worldwide, 22 199–201; 71 157–61 (upd.)
Falmouth Fertilizer Company *see* Griffin Industries, Inc.
Family Bookstores *see* Family Christian Stores, Inc.
Family Channel *see* International Family Entertainment Inc.
Family Christian Stores, Inc., 51 131–34
Family Dollar Stores, Inc., 13 215–17; 62 133–36 (upd.)
Family Golf Centers, Inc., 29 183–85
Family Mart Group, **V** 188; **36** 418, 420
Family Preservation Services, Inc., **64** 311
Family Restaurants, Inc., *see* Foodmaker, Inc.
Family Steak Houses of Florida, Inc. *see* Ryan's Restaurant Group, Inc.
Famous Atlantic Fish Company, **20** 5
Famous-Barr, **46** 288
Famous Brands Ltd., 86 144–47
Famous Dave's of America, Inc., 40 182–84
Famous Footwear *see* Brown Shoe Company, Inc.
Famous Restaurants Inc., **33** 139–40
Fanafel Ltda., **62** 348, 350
Fancom Holding B.V., **43** 130
Fannie Mae, 45 156–59 (upd.)
Fannie May Confections Brands, Inc., 80 114–18
Fansteel Inc., 19 150–52
Fantastic Sam's, **26** 476
Fanthing Electrical Corp., **44** 132
Fanuc Ltd., III 482–83; 17 172–74 (upd.); 75 137–40 (upd.)
Fanzz, **29** 282
FAO Schwarz, 46 187–90
Faprena, **25** 85
Far-Ben S.A. de C.V., **72** 128
Far Eastern Air Transport, Inc., **23** 380
Far Eastern Bank, **56** 363
Farah Incorporated, 24 156–58
Farben *see* I.G. Farbenindustrie AG.
Farberware, Inc., *see* Lifetime Brands, Inc.
Farbro Corp., **45** 15
FAREC Fahrzeugrecycling GmbH, **58** 28
Faribault Foods, Inc., 89 212–15
Farley Northwest Industries Inc., I 440–41
Farley's & Sathers Candy Company, Inc., 62 137–39
Farm Electric Services Ltd., **6** 586
Farm Family Holdings, Inc., 39 155–58
Farm Fresh Catfish Company, **54** 167
Farm Journal Corporation, 42 131–34
Farm Power Laboratory, **6** 565; **50** 366
Farm Progress Group *see* Rural Press Ltd
Farmacias Ahumada S.A., 72 126–28
Farmacias Ahumada S.A., **69** 312
Farmcare Ltd., **51** 89
Farmer Bros. Co., 52 117–19
Farmer Jack Supermarkets, 78 109–13
Farmer Mac *see* Federal Agricultural Mortgage Corp.
Farmers Insurance Group of Companies, 25 154–56
Farmers Petroleum, Inc., **48** 175
Farmland Foods, Inc., 7 174–75
Farmland Industries, Inc., 48 172–75
Farmstock Pty Ltd., **62** 307
FARO Technologies, Inc., 87 164–167
Farouk Systems, Inc., 78 114–17
Farrar, Straus and Giroux Inc., 15 158–60
FAS Acquisition Co., **53** 142
FASC *see* First Analysis Securities Corp.
Fasco Consumer Products, **19** 360
FASCO Motors *see* Tecumseh Products Co.
Fashion Bug, *see* Charming Shoppes, Inc.
Fashion Fair Cosmetics *see* Johnson Publishing Company, Inc.
Fashion Resource, Inc. *see* Tarrant Apparel Group.
Fasint Ltd., **72** 128
Fasson *see* Avery Dennison Corp.
Fast Air, **31** 305
Fast Fare, *see* Crown Central Petroleum Corp.
Fast Trak Inc. *see* Ultimate Electronics, Inc.
Fastenal Company, 14 185–87; 42 135–38 (upd.)
FASTWEB S.p.A., 83 147-150
Fat Bastard Wine Co., **68** 86
Fat Face Ltd., 68 147–49
FAT KAT, Inc., **51** 200, 203
Fatburger Corporation, 64 122–24
Fate S.A., **74** 10
Fateco Förlag, **14** 556
FATS, Inc., *see* Firearms Training Systems, Inc.
Faultless Starch/Bon Ami Company, 55 142–45
Fauquet, **25** 85
Faurecia S.A., 70 91–93
FAvS *see* First Aviation Services Inc.
Fay's Inc., 17 175–77
Faydler Company, **60** 160
Fayette Tubular Products, *see* Danaher Corp.
Faygo Beverages Inc., 55 146–48
Fayva, *see* Morse Shoe Inc.
Fazoli's Management, Inc., 27 145–47; 76 144–47 (upd.)
FB&T Corporation, **14** 154
FBC *see* First Boston Corp.
FBO *see* Film Booking Office of America.
FBR *see* Friedman, Billings, Ramsey Group, Inc.
FBS Fuhrpark Business Service GmbH, **58** 28
FC Holdings, Inc., **26** 363
FCA Ltd. *see* Life Time Fitness, Inc.
FCC *see* Federal Communications Commission.
FCI *see* Framatome SA.
FDIC *see* Federal Deposit Insurance Corp.
Featherlite Inc., 28 127–29
Feature Enterprises Inc., **19** 452
FECR *see* Florida East Coast Railway, L.L.C.
Fedders Corporation, 18 172–75; 43 162–67 (upd.)
Federal Agricultural Mortgage Corporation, 75 141–43
Federal Cartridge, **26** 363
Federal Deposit Insurance Corporation, 93 208–12
Federal Express Corporation, V 451–53 *see also* FedEx Corp.
Federal Home Life Insurance Co., **IV** 623
Federal Home Loan Mortgage Corp. *see* Freddie Mac.
Federal Insurance Co., *see* The Chubb Corp.
Federal Laboratories, **57** 230
Federal Light and Traction Company, **6** 561–62
Federal-Mogul Corporation, I 158–60; 10 292–94 (upd.); 26 139–43 (upd.)
Federal National Mortgage Association, II 410–11 *see also* Fannie Mae.
Federal Packaging Corp., **19** 78
Federal Paper Board Company, Inc., 8 173–75
Federal Prison Industries, Inc., 34 157–60
Federal Reserve Bank of New York, **21** 68
Federal Signal Corp., 10 295–97
Federated Department Stores Inc., 9 209–12; 31 190–94 (upd.)
Federated Livestock Corporation, **64** 306
Fédération Internationale de Football Association, 27 148–51
Federation Nationale d'Achats des Cadres *see* FNAC.
Federation of Migro Cooperatives *see* Migros-Genossenschafts-Bund.
Federico Paternina S.A., 69 164–66
FedEx Corporation, 18 176–79 (upd.); 42 139–44 (upd.)
FEE Technology, **29** 461–62
Feed-Rite, Inc., *see* Hawkins Chemical, Inc.
Feed The Children, Inc., 68 150–52
FEI Company, 79 168–71

Feikes & Sohn KG, *see* PWA Group.
Felco *see* Farmers Regional Cooperative.
Feld Entertainment, Inc., 32 186–89 (upd.)
Feldmühle Nobel AG, III 692–95 *see also* Metallgesellschaft.
Fellowes Manufacturing Company, 28 130–32
Femsa *see* Formento Económico Mexicano, S.A. de C.V.
Fenaco, 86 148–51
Fendall Company, **40** 96, 98
Fendel Schiffahrts-Aktiengesellschaft, **6** 426
Fender Musical Instruments Company, 16 200–02; 43 168–72 (upd.)
Fendi S.p.A., **45** 344
Fenicia Group, *see* Lojas Arapua S.A.
Fenn, Wright & Manson, **25** 121–22
Fenton Hill American Limited, **29** 510
Fenway Partners, **47** 361
Fenwick & West LLP, 34 161–63
Ferembal S.A., *see* Viatech Continental Can Company, Inc.
Ferfin, **24** 341
Ferguson Enterprises, **64** 409, 411
Fermec Manufacturing Limited, **40** 432
Fernando Roqué, **6** 404; **26** 243
Ferolito, Vultaggio & Sons, 27 152–55
Ferragamo, **63** 151
Ferranti Business Communications, **20** 75
Ferrara Fire Apparatus, Inc., 84 115–118
Ferrara Pan Candy Company, 90 188–91
Ferrari S.p.A., 13 218–20; 36 196–200 (upd.)
Ferrellgas Partners, L.P., 35 173–75
Ferrero SpA, 54 103–05
Ferretti Group SpA, 90 192–96
Ferris Industries, **64** 355
Ferro Corporation, 8 176–79; 56 123–28 (upd.)
Ferrocarril del Noreste, S.A. de C.V. *see* Grupo Transportación Ferroviaria Mexicana, S.A. de C.V.
Ferrolux Metals Co., **63** 360
Ferrovial *see* Grupo Ferrovail
Ferruzzi Finanziaria S.p.A., **24** 341; **36** 186
Fertisere SAS, **58** 221
Fetzer Vineyards, *see* Brown-Forman Corp.
FFI Fragrances *see* Elizabeth Arden, Inc.
F5 Networks, Inc., 72 129–31
FFM Bhd, **57** 292–95
FHP International Corporation, 6 184–86
Fiamm Technologies *see* Valeo.
Fiat SpA, I 161–63; 11 102–04 (upd.); 50 194–98 (upd.)
Fibamex, *see* CLARCOR Inc.
Fibanc SA, **65** 230, 232
Fibar, **44** 261
Fiberglas Canada, *see* Owens Corning Corp.
Fiberite, Inc., **27** 117; **28** 195
FiberMark, Inc., 37 139–42; 53 24
Fibermux Corporation, *see* ADC Telecommunications, Inc.
Fibra S.A. *see* Vicunha Textil S.A.
Fibreboard Corporation, 16 203–05 *see also* Owens Corning Corp.
FibreChem, Inc., *see* M. A. Hanna Co.
Ficap S.A., **71** 211
Fichet-Bauche SA, **53** 158
Fichtel & Sachs AG, *see* Mannesmann AG.
Ficosa *see* Grupo Ficosa International.
Fidelity Exploration & Production Company, **42** 249, 253
Fidelity Investments Inc., II 412–13; 14 188–90 (upd.) *see also* FMR Corp.
Fidelity Leasing Corporation, **42** 312–13
Fidelity National Financial Inc., 54 106–08
Fidelity National Title, **19** 92
Fidelity Oil Group, *see* MDU Resources Group, Inc.
Fidelity Southern Corporation, 85 124–27
Fidenas Investment Ltd., **30** 185
Fides Holding, **21** 146
Field Enterprises Educational Corporation, **26** 15; **43** 208
Field Group plc, **30** 120
Field Limited Partnership, **22** 441
Fieldale Farms Corporation, 23 191–93
Fieldco Guide Dog Foundation, **42** 207
Fieldcrest Cannon, Inc., 9 213–17; 31 195–200 (upd.)
Fieldstone Cabinetry, *see* Masco Corp.
Fielmann AG, 31 201–03
Fiesta Restaurants Inc., **33** 139–40
FIFA *see* Fédération Internationale de Football Association.
Fifa International, **39** 58
Fifth Third Bancorp, 13 221–23; 31 204–08 (upd.)
50%Off Stores *see* LOT$OFF Corp.
Le Figaro *see* Société du Figaro S.A.
Figgie International Inc., 7 176–78
Figi's Inc., *see* Fingerhut Companies, Inc.
FII Limited, **38** 197
Fiji Water LLC, 74 111–13
Fil-Mag Group, **29** 461
Fila–Fabbrica Italiana Lapis ed Affini S.p.A., **69** 129
Fila Holding S.p.A., 20 216–18; 52 120–24 (upd.)
Filene's *see* The May Department Stores Co.
Filene's Basement *see* Value City Department Stores, Inc.
FileNet Corporation, 62 140–43
Filergie S.A., **15** 355
Fili Enterprises, Inc., 70 94–96
Filipacchi Medias S.A. *see* Hachette Filipacchi Medias S.A.
Filiz Lastex, S.A., **15** 386
Film Roman, Inc., 58 122–24
Films for the Humanities, Inc., **22** 441
Filofax Inc., **41** 120, 123
Filterfresh Corporation, **39** 409
Filtrona plc, 88 87–91
Filtros Baldwin de Mexico, *see* CLARCOR Inc.
Fimalac S.A., 37 143–45
Fimaser, **21** 101
Fimestic, **21** 101
FINA, Inc., 7 179–81 *see also* Total Fina Elf S.A.
Finaler *see* Leroux S.A.S.
Finalrealm Limited, **42** 404
Finance Oil Corp., **49** 304
Financial News Network, Inc., **31** 147
Financial Performance Corporation *see* BrandPartners Group, Inc.
Financial Security Assurance Inc., **25** 497
Financial Services Corporation of Michigan, **11** 163
The Financial Times Group, **46** 337
Financière Leroux *see* Leroux S.A.S.
Financière Saint Dominique, *see* Crédit National S.A.
Finarte Casa d'Aste S.p.A., 93 213–16
Find-A-Home Service, Inc., **21** 96
Findel plc, 60 122–24
Findlays Spring Natural Mineral Water, **64** 11
Findomestic, **21** 101
Findorff *see* J.H. Findorff and Son, Inc.
FindWhat.com *see* MIVA, Inc.
Fine Art Developments Ltd., **15** 340
Fine Fare Properties Ltd., *see* Gateway Corporation Ltd.
Fine Fragrances, *see* French Fragrances, Inc.
Finesco, LLC, **37** 200–01
Finevest Services Inc., **15** 526
Fingerhut Companies, Inc., 9 218–20; 36 201–05 (upd.)
Fininvest S.p.A., **IV** 587–88; **54** 17, 21, 23; **65** 230–31; **73** 351
Finisar Corporation, 92 115–18
The Finish Line, Inc., 29 186–88; 68 153–56 (upd.)
FinishMaster, Inc., 24 159–61
Finlay Enterprises, Inc., 16 206–08; 76 148–51 (upd.)
Finmeccanica S.p.A., 84 119–123
Finnair Oy, 6 87–89; 25 157–60 (upd.); 61 91–95 (upd.)
Finnigan Corporation, *see* Thermo Instrument Systems Inc.
Finning International Inc., 69 167–69
Finnish Chemicals Oy *see* Kemira Oyj
Finsa, **II** 196
Fired Up, Inc., 82 111–14
Firearms Training Systems, Inc., 27 156–58
Fireman's Fund Insurance Company, III 250–52
Firestone Tire and Rubber Co., **15** 355; **17** 182; **20** 259–62; **50** 316 *see also* Bridgestone Corp.
Firma Hamburger Kaffee-Import-Geschäft Emil Tengelmann *see* Tengelmann Group.
Firma Huter Vorfertigung GmbH, **49** 163
Firmenich International S.A., 60 125–27
FirmLogic, L.P., **52** 423

First & 42nd, **62** 115
First Acadiana National Bank, **11** 107
First Air *see* Bradley Air Services Ltd.
First Albany Companies Inc., 37 146–48
First Alert, Inc., 28 133–35
First American *see* Bremer Financial Corp.
First American Bank Corporation, *see* First of America Bank Corp.
The First American Corporation, 52 125–27
First Analysis Securities Corporation, **22** 5
First Atlanta Corporation, **16** 523
First Atlantic Capital, Ltd., **28** 340, 342
First Aviation Services Inc., 49 140–42
First Bank System Inc., 12 164–66 *see also* U.S. Bancorp
First Boston Corp., *see* CSFB.
First Brands Corporation, 8 180–82
First Capital Financial, *see* Great American Management and Investment, Inc.
First Cash Financial Services, Inc., 57 138–40
First Chicago Corporation, II 284–87 *see also* Bank One Corp.
First Choice Holidays PLC, 40 185–87
First Cincinnati, Inc., **41** 133
First Colony Coffee & Tea Company, 84 124–126
First Commerce Bancshares, Inc., 15 161–63 *see also* Wells Fargo & Co.
First Commerce Corporation, 11 105–07 *see also* JPMorgan Chase & Co.
First Constitution Financial Corporation *see* The Aristotle Corp.
First Consumers National Bank, *see* Spiegel, Inc.
First Data Corporation, 30 195–98 (upd.)
First Delaware Life Insurance Co., *see* First Executive Corp.
First Deposit Corp. *see* Providian Financial Corp.
First Empire State Corporation, 11 108–10
First Executive Corporation, III 253–55
First Express, **48** 177
First Fidelity Bank, N.A., New Jersey, 9 221–23
First Financial Insurance, **41** 178
First Financial Management Corporation, 11 111–13
First Hawaiian, Inc., 11 114–16
FIRST HEALTH Strategies, **11** 113
First Heights Bank, fsa, *see* Pulte Homes.
First Hospital Corp., **15** 122
First Industrial Realty Trust, Inc., 65 146–48
First Insurance Agency, Inc., *see* Washington Federal, Inc.
First International Computer, Inc., 56 129–31
First Interstate Bancorp, II 288–90 *see also* Wells Fargo & Co.
First Leisure Corporation plc *see* Esporta plc.
First Liberty Financial Corporation, **11** 457
The First Marblehead Corporation, 87 168–171
First Mississippi Corporation, 8 183–86 *see also* ChemFirst, Inc.
First National Bank in Albuquerque, **11** 119
First National Bank of Commerce, *see* First Commerce Corp.
First National Bank of Harrington, Delaware *see* J.C. Penny National Bank.
First National Bank of Houma, **21** 522
The First National Bank of Lafayette, **11** 107
First National Bankshares, Inc., **21** 524
First National City Bank, *see* Citigroup Inc.
First Nations Gaming, Ltd., **44** 334
First Nationwide Bank, 14 191–93 see also Citigroup Inc.
First Nationwide Holdings Inc., **28** 246
First Nuclear Corporation, **49** 411
First of America Bank Corporation, 8 187–89
First Omni Bank NA, **16** 14; **43** 8
First Options of Chicago, Inc., **51** 148
First Pacific Company Limited, 18 180–82
First Physician Care, Inc., **36** 367
First Private Power Corporation, **56** 215
First Quench Retailing Ltd., **52** 416
First RepublicBank Corporation, *see* NCNB Corp.
First Security Bank of Missoula, **35** 197–99
First Security Corporation, 11 117–19 see also Wells Fargo & Co.
First Sport Ltd., **39** 60
First State Bank Southwest Indiana, **41** 178–79
First Team Sports, Inc., 22 202–04
First Tennessee National Corporation, 11 120–21; 48 176–79 (upd.)
First Union Corporation, 10 298–300 *see also* Wachovia Corp.
First USA, Inc., 11 122–24
First Variable Life, **59** 246
First Virginia Banks, Inc., 11 125–26 see also BB&T Corp.
First Women's Bank of New York, **23** 3
The First Years Inc., 46 191–94
FirstAir Inc., **48** 113
Firstar Corporation, 11 127–29; 33 152–55 (upd.)
FirstGroup plc, 89 216–19
FirstMiss, Inc., *see* First Mississippi Corp.
FirstPage USA Inc., **41** 265
Fiserv Inc., 11 130–32; 33 156–60 (upd.)
Fish & Neave, 54 109–12
Fisher Broadcasting Co., **15** 164
Fisher Companies, Inc., 15 164–66
Fisher Controls International, LLC, 13 224–26; 61 96–99 (upd.)
Fisher Foods, Inc., *see* Riser Foods, Inc.
Fisher-Price Inc., 12 167–69; 32 190–94 (upd.)
Fisher Scientific International Inc., 24 162–66
Fishers Agricultural Holdings, *see* Associated British Foods plc.
Fisk Corporation, 72 132–34
Fiskars Corporation, 33 161–64
Fiskeby Board AB, **48** 344
Fisons plc, 9 224–27; 23 194–97 (upd.)
Fitch IBCA Inc., **37** 143, 145
Fitch Investor Services, **65** 243–44
Fitchburg Gas and Electric Light, **37** 406
5 & Diner Franchise Corporation, 72 135–37
Five Bros. Inc., **19** 456
Five Star Entertainment Inc., **28** 241
Five Star Group, Inc., **64** 166
546274 Alberta Ltd., **48** 97
FKI Plc, 57 141–44
FL Industries Holdings, Inc., *see* Thomas & Betts Corp.
Flagler Development Company, **59** 184–85
Flagship Resources, **22** 495
Flagstar Companies, Inc., 10 301–03 *see also* Advantica Restaurant Group, Inc.
Flagstone Hospitality Management LLC, **58** 194
Flambeau Products Corporation, **55** 132
Flanders Corporation, 65 149–51
Flanigan's Enterprises, Inc., 60 128–30
Flapdoodles, **15** 291
Flashes Publishers, Inc., **36** 341
Flatiron Construction Corporation, 92 119–22
Flatiron Mandolin Company, **16** 239
Flatow, Moore, Bryan, and Fairburn, **21** 33
Flavors Holdings Inc., **38** 294
Fleck Controls, Inc., **26** 361, 363
Fleer Corporation, 15 167–69
Fleet Aerospace Corporation *see* Magellan Aerospace Corp.
Fleet Call, Inc., *see* Nextel Communications, Inc.
Fleet Equity Partners, **62** 325, 327
Fleet Holdings, **28** 503
FleetBoston Financial Corporation, 9 228–30; 36 206–14 (upd.)
Fleetwood Enterprises, Inc., III 484–85; 22 205–08 (upd.); 81 159–64 (upd.)
Fleming Chinese Restaurants Inc., **37** 297
Fleming Companies, Inc., II 624–25; 17 178–81 (upd.)
Fleming Foodservice, **26** 504
Fletcher Challenge Ltd., IV 278–80; 19 153–57 (upd.)
Fletcher Pacific Construction Co. Ltd., **64** 113
Fleury Michon S.A., 39 159–61
Flex Elektrowerkzeuge GmbH, **26** 363
Flex Interim, *see* Randstad Holding n.v.
Flex-O-Lite, **14** 325
Flexi-Van Corporations, *see* Castle & Cooke, Inc.
Flexsteel Industries Inc., 15 170–72; 41 159–62 (upd.)
Flextronics International Ltd., 38 186–89

Flick Industrial Group *see* Feldmühle Nobel AG.
Flight Options, LLC, 75 144–46
Flight Refuelling Limited *see* Cobham plc.
FlightSafety International, Inc., 9 231–33; 29 189–92 (upd.)
Flint Ink Corporation, 13 227–29; 41 163–66 (upd.)
Flip Chip Technologies, LLC, **33** 248
FLIR Systems, Inc., 69 170–73
Flo-Pak, Inc., **57** 160
Floc'h & Marchand, 80 119–21
Flora Frey GmbH *see* Vilmorin Clause et Cie
Flora Frey/Sperling *see* Groupe Limagrain
Flora Medicinal J. Monteiro da Silva Ltda., **75** 270
Florafax International, Inc., **37** 162
Floral City Furniture Company *see* La-Z-Boy Inc.
Flori Roberts, Inc., **11** 208
Florida Crystals Inc., 35 176–78
Florida Cypress Gardens, Inc., **IV** 623
Florida Distillers Company, *see* Todhunter International, Inc.
Florida East Coast Industries, Inc., 59 184–86
Florida East Coast Railway, L.L.C., *see* The St. Joe Company
Florida Flavors, **44** 137
Florida Gaming Corporation, 47 130–33
Florida Gas Co., **15** 129
Florida Gas Transmission Company, **6** 578
Florida Panthers Hockey Club, Ltd., **37** 33, 35
Florida Power *see* Progress Energy, Inc.
Florida Power & Light Company *see* FPL Group, Inc.
Florida Progress Corp., V 621–22; 23 198–200 (upd.) *see also* Progress Energy, Inc.
Florida Public Utilities Company, 69 174–76
Florida Rock Industries, Inc., 46 195–97 *see also* Patriot Transportation Holding, Inc.
Florida's Natural Growers, 45 160–62
FloridaGulf Airlines, **11** 300
Florimex Verwaltungsgesellschaft mbH, *see* Dibrell Brothers, Inc.
Florists' Transworld Delivery, Inc., 28 136–38
Florsheim Shoe Group Inc., 9 234–36; 31 209–12 (upd.)
Flotek Industries Inc., 93 217–20
Flour City International, Inc., 44 181–83
Flow International Corporation, 56 132–34
Flow Measurement, **26** 293
Flower Time, Inc., **12** 179, 200
Flowers Industries, Inc., 12 170–71; 35 179–82 (upd.) *see also* Keebler Foods Co.
Flowserve Corporation, 33 165–68; 77 146–51 (upd.)
Floyd West & Co., **6** 290
FLSmidth & Co. A/S, 72 138–40
Fluent, Inc., **29** 4–6
Fluf N'Stuf, Inc., *see* Russ Berrie and Co., Inc.
Fluke Corporation, 15 173–75
Flunch, **37** 22
Fluor Corporation, I 569–71; 8 190–93 (upd.); 34 164–69 (upd.)
Fluor Daniel Inc., **41** 148
The Fluorocarbon Company *see* Furon Co.
FlyBE *see* Jersey European Airways (UK) Ltd.
Flying Boat, Inc. (Chalk's Ocean Airways), 56 135–37
Flying Colors Toys Inc., **52** 193
Flying Fruit Fantasy, USA, Inc., **57** 56–57
Flying J Inc., 19 158–60
Flying Tiger Line, **39** 33
FMC Corp., I 442–44; 11 133–35 (upd.); 89 220–27 (upd.)
FMR Corp., 8 194–96; 32 195–200 (upd.)
FMXI, Inc. *see* Foamex International Inc.
FNAC, 21 224–26
FNCB *see* First National City Bank of New York.
FNH USA, Inc., **58** 147
FNK *see* Finance Oil Corp.
FNMA *see* Federal National Mortgage Association.
FNN *see* Financial News Network.
Foam Creations, Inc. *see* Crocs
Foamex International Inc., 17 182–85
Focal Surgery, Inc., **27** 355
FOCUS, **44** 402
Focus Features, 78 118–22
Fodor's Travel Guides, *see* Random House, Inc.
Fog Cutter Capital Group Inc., **64** 124
Fogdog Inc., **36** 347
Fokker *see* N.V. Koninklijke Nederlandse Vliegtuigenfabriek Fokker.
Foley & Lardner, 28 139–42
Folksamerica Holding Company, Inc., **48** 431
Follett Corporation, 12 172–74; 39 162–65 (upd.)
Follis DeVito Verdi *see* De Vito/Verdi.
Follum Fabrikker, **63** 314
Fomento de Valores, S.A. de C.V., **23** 170
Fomento Economico Mexicano, S.A. de C.V. *see* Femsa.
Fonda Group, **36** 462
Fondazione Cassa di Risparmio di Venezia, **50** 408
Fonterra Co-Operative Group Ltd., 58 125–27
Food Basics *see* Farmer Jack Supermarkets
Food Circus Super Markets, Inc., 88 92–96
The Food Emporium, 64 125–27
Food Fair *see* Farmer Jack Supermarkets
Food For The Poor, Inc., 77 152–55
Food Giant, Inc. *see* Supervalu Inc.
Food Ingredients Technologies, **25** 367
Food King, **20** 306
Food Lion LLC, II 626–27; 15 176–78 (upd.); 66 112–15 (upd.)
Food Machinery Corp *see* FMC Corp.
Food Source, **58** 290
Food Town Inc., *see* Food Lion LLC.
Food World, **26** 46; **31** 372
Foodarama Supermarkets, Inc., 28 143–45 *see also* Wakefern Food Corp.
FoodBrands America, Inc., 23 201–04 *see also* Doskocil Companies, Inc.; Tyson Foods, Inc.
Foodmaker, Inc., 14 194–96 *see also* Jack in the Box Inc.
Foodtown, **V** 35; **15** 177
FoodUSA.com, **43** 24
Foot Locker, Inc., 68 157–62 (upd.)
Footaction *see* Footstar, Inc.
Foote, Cone & Belding Worldwide, I 12–15; 66 116–20 (upd.)
Footquarters, *see* Kinney Shoe Corp.
Footstar, Incorporated, 24 167–69 *see also* Foot Locker, Inc.
Foracon Maschinen und Anlagenbau GmbH & Co., **56** 134
Forbes Inc., 30 199–201; 82 115–20 (upd.)
The Ford Foundation, 34 170–72
Ford Motor Company, I 164–68; 11 136–40 (upd.); 36 215–21 (upd.); 64 128–34 (upd.)
Ford Motor Company, S.A. de C.V., 20 219–21
Ford New Holland, Inc. *see* New Holland N.V.
Fording Inc., **45** 80
FORE Systems, Inc., 25 161–63 *see also* Telefonaktiebolaget LM Ericsson.
Forefront Communications, **22** 194
Forefront Petroleum Company, **60** 160
Foreign & Colonial, **64** 303
Foremost-McKesson Inc. *see* McKesson Corp.
FöreningsSparbanken AB, 69 177–80
Forest City Auto Parts, **23** 491
Forest City Enterprises, Inc., 16 209–11; 52 128–31 (upd.)
Forest E. Olson, Inc., **21** 96
Forest Laboratories, Inc., 11 141–43; 52 132–36 (upd.)
Forest Oil Corporation, 19 161–63; 91 182–87 (upd.)
Forestal Mininco S.A. *see* Empresas CMPC S.A.
Forestal Quiñenco S.A. *see* Madeco S.A.
Forestry Corporation of New Zealand, **19** 156
Företagsfinans, **25** 464
Forethought Group, Inc., *see* Hillenbrand Industries, Inc.
Forever Living Products International Inc., 17 186–88
Forever 21, Inc., 84 127–129
Forge Books *see* Tom Doherty Associates Inc.
Forjas Metalicas, S.A. de C.V. (Formet), **44** 193
FormFactor, Inc., 85 128–31
Formica Corporation, 13 230–32

Formonix, **20** 101
Formosa Plastics Corporation, 14 197–99; 58 128–31 (upd.)
Formtec Inc., **62** 350
Formulabs, Inc., **52** 307
Forrester Research, Inc., 54 113–15
Forstmann Little & Co., 38 190–92
Fort Bend Utilities Company, *see* Imperial Sugar Co.
Fort Garry Brewery, **26** 304
Fort Howard Corporation, 8 197–99 *see also* Fort James Corp.
Fort James Corporation, 22 209–12 (upd.) *see also* Georgia-Pacific Corp.
Fort Mill Manufacturing Co. *see* Springs Industries, Inc.
Forte Plc, **15** 46; **29** 443; **64** 340
Fortis, Inc., 15 179–82; 47 134–37 (upd.); 50 4–6
Fortum Corporation, 30 202–07 (upd.) *see also* Neste Oil Corp.
Fortum Oil and Gas Oy, **68** 125–26
Fortun Foods, **26** 59
Fortune Brands, Inc., 29 193–97 (upd.); 68 163–67 (upd.)
Fortunoff Fine Jewelry and Silverware Inc., 26 144–46
Forward Air Corporation, 75 147–49
Forward Industries, Inc., 86 152–55
The Forzani Group Ltd., 79 172–76
Fosgate Electronics, **43** 322
Foss Maritime Co., *see* Totem Resources Corp.
Fossil, Inc., 17 189–91
Foster Forbes, **16** 123
Foster Grant *see* FosterGrant, Inc.
Foster Management Co., *see* NovaCare, Inc.
Foster Poultry Farms, 32 201–04
Foster-Probyn Ltd., **38** 501
Foster Wheeler Corporation, 6 145–47; 23 205–08 (upd.); 76 152–56 (upd.)
Foster's Group Limited, 7 182–84; 21 227–30 (upd.); 50 199–203 (upd.)
FosterGrant, Inc., 60 131–34
Fougerolle, *see* Eiffage.
Foundation Fieldbus, **22** 373
Foundation Health Corporation, 12 175–77
Founders of American Investment Corp., **15** 247
Fountain Powerboats Industries, Inc., 28 146–48
Four Leaf Technologies *see* Groupe Open.
Four Media Co., **33** 403
Four Paws Products, Ltd., **58** 60
Four Queens Hotel and Casino *see* The Elsinore Corp.
Four Seasons Hotels Inc., 9 237–38; 29 198–200 (upd.)
Four-Ten Corporation, **58** 378
Four Winds, **21** 153
4Kids Entertainment Inc., 59 187–89
Fournier Furniture, Inc., **12** 301
4P, **30** 396–98
Fourth Financial Corporation, 11 144–46
Fowler, Roenau & Geary, LLC, **37** 224
Fox and Hound English Pub and Grille *see* Total Entertainment Restaurant Corp.
Fox & Jacobs, *see* Centex Corp.
Fox Broadcasting Company, **21** 25, 360
Fox Children's Network, **21** 26
Fox Entertainment Group, Inc., 43 173–76
Fox Family Worldwide, Inc., 24 170–72 *see also* ABC Family Worldwide, Inc.
Fox Film Corp. *see* Twentieth Century Fox Film Corp.
Fox, Inc., *see* Twentieth Century Fox Film Corp.
Fox Network, **29** 426
Fox Paine & Company L.L.C., **63** 410, 412
Fox Ridge Homes, **70** 208
Foxboro Company, 13 233–35
Foxconn International, Inc. *see* Hon Hai Precision Industry Co., Ltd.
FoxHollow Technologies, Inc., 85 132–35
FoxMeyer Health Corporation, 16 212–14 see also McKesson Corp.
Foxmoor, **29** 163
Foxworth-Galbraith Lumber Company, 91 188–91
Foxx Hy-Reach, **28** 387
Foxy Products, Inc., **60** 287
FP&L *see* Florida Power & Light Co.
FPA Corporation *see* Orleans Homebuilders, Inc.
FPK LLC, **26** 343
FPL Group, Inc., V 623–25; 49 143–46 (upd.)
Fracmaster Ltd., **55** 294
Fragrance Corporation of America, Ltd., **53** 88
Fragrance Express Inc., **37** 271
Framatome SA, 19 164–67 aee also Alcatel S.A.; AREVA.
Franc-Or Resources, **38** 231–32
France-Loisirs, **IV** 615–16, 619
France Quick, **12** 152; **26** 160–61
France Télécom Group, V 291–93; 21 231–34 (upd.)
Franchise Finance Corp. of America, **37** 351
Franciscan Vineyards, Inc., **34** 89; **68** 99
Francisco Partners, **74** 260
Franco-American Food Company *see* Campbell Soup Co.
Francodex Laboratories, Inc., **74** 381
Francotyp-Postalia Holding AG, 92 123–27
Frank & Pignard SA, **51** 35
Frank & Schulte GmbH, *see* Stinnes AG.
Frank H. Nott Inc., *see* The David J. Joseph Co.
Frank Holton Company, **55** 149, 151
Frank J. Zamboni & Co., Inc., 34 173–76
Frank Russell Company, 46 198–200
Frank Schaffer Publications, **19** 405; **29** 470, 472
Frank W. Horner, Ltd., **38** 123
Frank's Nursery & Crafts, Inc., 12 178–79
Franke Holding AG, 76 157–59
Frankel & Co., 39 166–69
Frankfurter Allgemeine Zeitung GmbH, 66 121–24
Franklin Brass Manufacturing Company, **20** 363
Franklin Coach, **56** 223
Franklin Corp., **41** 388
Franklin Covey Company, 11 147–49; 37 149–52 (upd.)
Franklin Electric Company, Inc., 43 177–80
Franklin Electronic Publishers, Inc., 23 209–13
The Franklin Mint, 69 181–84
Franklin Mutual Advisors LLC, **52** 119, 172
Franklin National Bank, **9** 536
Franklin Plastics *see* Spartech Corp.
Franklin Resources, Inc., 9 239–40
Frans Maas Beheer BV, **14** 568
Franz Inc., 80 122–25
Franzia *see* The Wine Group, Inc.
Frape Behr S.A. *see* Behr GmbH & Co. KG.
Fraport AG Frankfurt Airport Services Worldwide, 90 197–202
Fraser & Neave Ltd., 54 116–18
Fray Data International, **14** 319
Frazer & Jones, **48** 141
FRE Composites Inc., **69** 206
Fred Campbell Auto Supply, **26** 347
Fred Meyer Stores, Inc., V 54–56; 20 222–25 (upd.); 64 135–39 (upd.)
Fred Sammons Company of Chicago, **30** 77
Fred Schmid Appliance & T.V. Co., Inc., *see* Fretter, Inc.
Fred Usinger Inc., 54 119–21
The Fred W. Albrecht Grocery Co., 13 236–38
Fred Weber, Inc., 61 100–02
Fred's, Inc., 23 214–16; 62 144–47 (upd.)
Freddie Mac, 54 122–25
Frederick Atkins Inc., 16 215–17
Frederick Gas Company, **19** 487
Frederick Manufacturing Corporation, **26** 119; **48** 59
Frederick's of Hollywood Inc., 16 218–20; 59 190–93 (upd.)
Fredrickson Motor Express, **57** 277
Free-lance Uitzendburo, **26** 240
Free People LLC *see* Urban Outfitters, Inc.
Freedom Airlines, Inc. *see* Mesa Air Group, Inc.
Freedom Communications, Inc., 36 222–25
Freedom Group Inc., **42** 10–11
Freeman Chemical Corporation, **61** 111–12
Freeman, Spogli & Co., **32** 12, 15; **35** 276; **36** 358–59; **47** 142–43; **57** 11, 242
Freemans *see* Sears plc.
FreeMark Communications, **38** 269

Freeport-McMoRan Copper & Gold, Inc., IV 81–84; 7 185–89 (upd.); 57 145–50 (upd.)
Freeport Power, **38** 448
Freescale Semiconductor, Inc., 83 151-154
Freeze.com LLC, 77 156–59
Freezer Queen Foods, Inc., **21** 509
Freight Car Services, Inc., **23** 306
Freixenet S.A., 71 162–64
Fremont Canning Company, *see* Gerber Products Co.
Fremont Group, **21** 97
Fremont Investors, **30** 268
French Connection Group plc, 41 167–69
French Fragrances, Inc., 22 213–15 *see also* Elizabeth Arden, Inc.
French Quarter Coffee Co., *see* Unique Casual Restaurants, Inc.
Frequency Electronics, Inc., 61 103–05
Fresenius AG, 56 138–42
Fresh America Corporation, 20 226–28
Fresh Choice, Inc., 20 229–32
Fresh Enterprises, Inc., 66 125–27
Fresh Express Inc., 88 97–100
Fresh Foods, Inc., 29 201–03
Fresh Start Bakeries, **26** 58
Freshbake Foods Group PLC, *see* Campbell Soup Co.
FreshDirect, LLC, 84 130–133
Freshlike, **76** 17
Fretter, Inc., 10 304–06
Freudenberg & Co., 41 170–73
Friction Products Co., **59** 222
Frictiontech Inc., **11** 84
Friday's Front Row Sports Grill, *see* Carlson Restaurants Worldwide.
Friden, Inc., **30** 418; **53** 237
Fried, Frank, Harris, Shriver & Jacobson, 35 183–86
Fried. Krupp GmbH, IV 85–89 *see also* ThyssenKrupp AG.
Friede Goldman Halter, **61** 43
Friedman, Billings, Ramsey Group, Inc., 53 134–37
Friedman's Inc., 29 204–06
Friedrich Grohe AG & Co. KG, 53 138–41
Friendly Hotels PLC, **14** 107
Friendly Ice Cream Corporation, 30 208–10; 72 141–44 (upd.)
Friesland Coberco Dairy Foods Holding N.V., 59 194–96
Frigidaire Home Products, 22 216–18
Frigoscandia AB, **57** 300
Frimont S.p.A, **68** 136
Frisby P.M.C. Incorporated, **16** 475
Frisch's Restaurants, Inc., 35 187–89; 92 128–32 (upd.)
Frisdranken Industries Winters B.V., **22** 515
Frisk Int. Nv, **72** 272
Frito-Lay North America, 32 205–10; 73 151–58 (upd.)
Fritz Companies, Inc., 12 180–82
Fritz Gegauf AG *see* Bernina Holding AG.
Fritz Schömer, **75** 56–57
Fritz W. Glitsch and Sons, Inc. *see* Glitsch International, Inc.
Frolich Intercon International, **57** 174
Fromagerie d'Illoud *see* Bongrain SA.
Fromageries Bel, 23 217–19; 25 83–84
Frome Broken Hill Co., **IV** 59
Front Range Pipeline LLC, **60** 88
Frontec, **13** 132
Frontier Airlines Holdings Inc., 22 219–21; 84 134–138 (upd.)
Frontier Communications, **32** 216, 218
Frontier Corp., 16 221–23
Frontier Expeditors, Inc., **12** 363
Frontier Natural Products Co-Op, 82 121–24
Frontier Pacific Insurance Company, **21** 263
Frontier Vision Partners L.P., **52** 9
FrontLine Capital Group, **47** 330–31
Frontline Ltd., 45 163–65
Frontstep Inc., **55** 258
Frost & Sullivan, Inc., 53 142–44
Frost National Bank *see* Cullen/Frost Bankers, Inc.
Frozen Food Express Industries, Inc., 20 233–35
Fru-Con Holding Corporation, *see* Bilfinger & Berger AG.
Fruehauf Corp., I 169–70
Fruit of the Loom, Inc., 8 200–02; 25 164–67 (upd.)
The Frustum Group Inc., **45** 280
Fruth Pharmacy, Inc., 66 128–30
Fry's Electronics, Inc., 68 168–70
Fry's Food Stores, *see* Dillon Companies Inc.
Frye Copy Systems, **6** 599
Frymaster Corporation, 27 159–62
FSA Corporation, **25** 349
FSI International, Inc., 17 192–94 *see also* FlightSafety International, Inc.
FSP *see* Frank Schaffer Publications.
FT Freeport Indonesia, **57** 145
FTD *see* Florists Transworld Delivery, Inc.
FTI Consulting, Inc., 77 160–63
FTP Software, Inc., 20 236–38
Fubu, 29 207–09
Fuddruckers, *see* Unique Casual Restaurants, Inc.
Fuel Pipeline Transportation Ltd. *see* Thai Airways International.
Fuel Resources Development Co., **6** 558–59
Fuel Resources Inc., **6** 457
Fuel Tech, Inc., 85 136–40
FuelCell Energy, Inc., 75 150–53
FuelMaker Corporation, **6** 569
Fuji Bank, Ltd., II 291–93
Fuji Electric Co., Ltd., II 22–23; 48 180–82 (upd.)
Fuji Heavy Industries, **I** 207; **23** 290; **36** 240, 243; **64** 151
Fuji Kaolin Co. *see* English China Clays Ltd.
Fuji Photo Film Co., Ltd., III 486–89; 18 183–87 (upd.); 79 177–84 (upd.)
Fuji Television Network Inc., 91 192–95
Fuji Xerox *see* Xerox Corp.
Fujisawa Pharmaceutical Company, Ltd., I 635–36; 58 132–34 (upd.)
Fujitsu-ICL Systems Inc., 11 150–51
Fujitsu Limited, III 139–41; 16 224–27 (upd.); 40 145–50 (upd.)
Fujitsu Takamisawa, **28** 131
Fukuoka Mitsukoshi Ltd., **56** 242
Fukutake Publishing Co., Ltd., *see* Benesse Corp.
Fulbright & Jaworski L.L.P., 47 138–41
The Fulfillment Corporation of America, **21** 37
Fullbright & Jaworski, **28** 48
Fuller Company *see* FLSmidth and Co. A/S.
Fuller Smith & Turner P.L.C., 38 193–95
Fulton Performance Products, Inc., *see* TriMas Corp.
Funai Electric Company Ltd., 62 148–50
Funco, Inc., 20 239–41 *see also* GameStop Corp.
Fund American Companies *see* White Mountains Insurance Group, Ltd.
Funk & Wagnalls, **22** 441
Funnel Cake Factory, **24** 241
Funtastic Limited, **52** 193
Fuqua Enterprises, Inc., 17 195–98
Fuqua Industries Inc., I 445–47
Furmanite Corporation, 92 133–36
Furnishings International Inc., **20** 359, 363; **39** 267
Furniture Brands International, Inc., 39 170–75 (upd.)
Furon Company, 28 149–51 *see also* Compagnie de Saint-Gobain.
Furr's Restaurant Group, Inc., 53 145–48
Furr's Supermarkets, Inc., 28 152–54
Furst Group, **17** 106
Furukawa Electric Co., Ltd., III 490–92
Futronix Corporation, *see* Kent Electronics Corp.
Future Diagnostics, Inc., **25** 384
Future Graphics, *see* Nu-kote Holding, Inc.
Future Now, Inc., 12 183–85
Future Shop Ltd., 62 151–53
FutureCare, **50** 123
Futurestep, Inc., **34** 247, 249
Fuyo Group, **72** 249
FX Coughlin Inc., **51** 130
Fyffes Plc, 38 196–99
Fytek, S.A. de C.V., **66** 42

G

G&G Shops, Inc., *see* Petrie Stores Corp.
G&K Services, Inc., 16 228–30
G&O Manufacturing Company, Inc. *see* TransPro, Inc.
G&R Pasta Co., Inc., *see* Hershey Foods Corp.
G A Pindar & Son Ltd., 88 101–04
G. Bruss GmbH and Co. KG, **26** 141
G.C. Industries, **52** 186
G.C. Smith Sugar Ltd., *see* Barlow Rand Ltd.

G.D. Searle & Co., I 686–89; 12 186–89 (upd.); 34 177–82 (upd.)
G.H. Bass & Co., **15** 406; *see also* Phillips-Van Heusen Corp.
G.H. Besselaar Associates, **30** 151
G. Heileman Brewing Co., I 253–55 *see also* Stroh Brewery Co.
G.I.E. Airbus Industrie, I 41–43; 12 190–92 (upd.)
G.I. Joe's, Inc., 30 221–23
G-III Apparel Group, Ltd., 22 222–24
G.J. Coles & Coy. Ltd., **20** 155
G.J. Hopkins, Inc. *see* The Branch Group, Inc.
G. Leblanc Corporation, 55 149–52
G.M. Pfaff AG, **30** 419–20
G.R. Foods, Inc. *see* Ground Round, Inc.
G.R. Herberger's Department Stores, **19** 324–25; **41** 343–44
G.S. Blodgett Corporation, 15 183–85 *see also* Blodgett Holdings, Inc.
GABA Holding AG *see* Colgate-Palmolive Co.
Gabelli Asset Management Inc., 30 211–14 *see also* Lynch Corp.
Gables Residential Trust, 49 147–49
GAC *see* The Goodyear Tire & Rubber Co.
Gadzooks, Inc., 18 188–90
GAF, I 337–40; 22 225–29 (upd.)
Gage Marketing Group, 26 147–49
Gaggenau Hausgeräte GmbH, **67** 81
Gagnon & Associates, **74** 258
Gaiam, Inc., 41 174–77
Gaines Furniture Manufacturing, Inc., **43** 315
Gainsco, Inc., 22 230–32
GalaGen Inc., **65** 216
Galardi Group, Inc., 72 145–47
Galas Harland, S.A., *see* John H. Harland Co.
Galavision, Inc. *see* Univision Communications Inc.
Galaxy Aerospace Co. L.P., **69** 216
Galaxy Carpet Mills Inc., **19** 276; **63** 300
Galaxy Energies Inc., **11** 28
Galaxy Nutritional Foods, Inc., 58 135–37
Galbreath Escott, **16** 474
Gale International Llc, 93 221–24
Gale Research Co., *see* The Thomson Corporation
Galen Health Care, **15** 112; **35** 215–16
Galenica AG, 84 139–142
Galerías Preciados, **26** 130
Galeries Lafayette S.A., V 57–59; 23 220–23 (upd.)
Galey & Lord, Inc., 20 242–45; 66 131–34 (upd.)
Gallaher Group Plc, 49 150–54 (upd.)
Gallaher Limited, V 398–400; 19 168–71 (upd.)
Gallatin Steel Company, *see* Dofasco Inc.
Galleria Shooting Team, **62** 174
Gallo Winery *see* E. & J. Gallo Winery.
Gallop Johnson & Neuman, L.C., **26** 348
The Gallup Organization, 37 153–56
Galoob Toys *see* Lewis Galoob Toys Inc.
GALP, **48** 117, 119
GALVSTAR, L.P., **26** 530
Galway Irish Crystal Ltd. *see* Belleek Pottery Ltd.
Galyan's Trading Company, Inc., 47 142–44
Gamax Holding, **65** 230, 232
The Gambrinus Company, 40 188–90
Gambro AB, 49 155–57
The GAME Group plc, 80 126–29
Gamebusters, **41** 409
Gamesa Corporacion Tecnologica S.A., **19** 192; **73** 374–75
GameStop Corp., 69 185–89 (upd.)
GameTime, Inc., *see* PlayCore, Inc.
GAMI *see* Great American Management and Investment, Inc.
Gaming Partners InternationalCorporation, 92225–28
GammaLink, *see* Dialogic Corp.
Gander Mountain Company, 20 246–48; 90 203–08 (upd.)
Gannett Company, Inc., IV 612–13; 7 190–92 (upd.); 30 215–17 (upd.); 66 135–38 (upd.)
Gano Excel Enterprise Sdn. Bhd., 89 228–31
Gantos, Inc., 17 199–201
GAP, *see* Grupo Aeroportuario del Pacífico, S.A. de C.V.
The Gap, Inc., V 60–62; 18 191–94 (upd.); 55 153–57 (upd.)
GAR Holdings, **19** 78
Garamond Press, **23** 100
Garan, Inc., 16 231–33; 64 140–43 (upd.)
Garanti Bank, **65** 69
Garantie Mutuelle des Fonctionnaires, **21** 225
Garden City Newspapers Inc., **38** 308
The Garden Company Ltd., 82 125–28
Garden Escape, **26** 441
Garden Fresh Restaurant Corporation, 31 213–15
Garden of Eatin' Inc., **27** 198; **43** 218–19
Garden Ridge Corporation, 27 163–65
Garden State Life Insurance Company, *see* GEICO Corp.
Garden State Paper, **38** 307–08
Gardenburger, Inc., 33 169–71; 76 160–63 (upd.)
Gardener's Eden, *see* Williams-Sonoma, Inc.
Gardner Advertising *see* Wells Rich Green BDDP.
Gardner Denver, Inc., 49 158–60
Gardner Merchant Ltd., **11** 325; **29** 442–44
Gardner Rubber Co. *see* Tillotson Corp.
Gardners Candies *see* Sarris Candies Inc.
Garelick Farms, Inc., **26** 449
Garena Malhas Ltda., **72** 68
Garfinckel, Brooks Brothers, Miller & Rhodes, Inc., **15** 94
Garfinckels, **37** 12
Garland Commercial Industries, Inc. *see* Enodis plc.
Garland-Compton, **42** 328
Garland Publishing, **44** 416
Garmin Ltd., 60 135–37
Garrido y Compania, Inc., **26** 448
Garst Seed Company, Inc., 86 156–59
Gart Sports Company, 24 173–75 *see also* Sports Authority, Inc.
Gartner, Inc., 21 235–37; 94 209–13 (upd.)
Garuda Indonesia, 6 90–91; 58 138–41 (upd.)
Gary Fisher Mountain Bike Company, *see* Trek Bicycle Corp.
Gary-Williams Energy Corporation, **19** 177
Gas Energy Inc., **6** 457
Gas Light and Coke Company *see* British Gas plc.
Gas Light Company *see* Baltimore Gas and Electric Co.
Gas Natural SDG S.A., 69 190–93
Gas Service Company, **6** 593; **50** 38
Gas Tech, Inc., *see* Thermo Instrument Systems Inc.
Gas Utilities Company, **6** 471
GASS *see* Grupo Ángeles Servicios de Salud, S.A. de C.V.
Gastar Co. Ltd., **55** 375
Gastronome, **70** 322
Gasunie *see* N.V. Nederlandse Gasunie.
GATC *see* General American Tank Car Co.
Gate Gourmet International AG, 70 97–100
GateHouse Media, Inc., 91 196–99
The Gates Corporation, 9 241–43
Gates Rubber, **26** 349
Gates/FA Distributing Inc., **29** 413–14
Gateway Corporation Ltd., II 628–30 *see also* Somerfield plc.
Gateway Educational Products Ltd. *see* HOP, LLC
Gateway, Inc., 10 307–09; 27 166–69 (upd.); 63 153–58 (upd.)
Gateway International Motorsports Corporation, Inc., **43** 139–40
Gateway State Bank, **39** 381–82
Gateway Technologies, Inc., **46** 387
Gatliff Coal Co., **6** 583
The Gatorade Company, 82 129–32
Gatti's Pizza, Inc. *see* Mr. Gatti's, LP.
Gattini, **40** 215
Gatwick Handling, **28** 157
GATX, 6 394–96; 25 168–71 (upd.)
Gaultier *see* Groupe Jean-Paul Gaultier.
Gaumont S.A., 25 172–75; 91 200–05 (upd.)
Gaya Motor, P.T. **23** 290
Gaylord Brothers', **60** 109
Gaylord Container Corporation, 8 203–05
Gaylord Entertainment Company, 11 152–54; 36 226–29 (upd.)
Gaymer Group, **25** 82
Gaz de France, V 626–28; 40 191–95 (upd.)
Gazelle Graphics Systems, **28** 244; **69** 243
Gazprom *see* OAO Gazprom.
GB Foods Inc., **19** 92

GB-Inno-BM *see* GIB Group.
GB s.a. *see* GIB Group.
GB Stores, Inc., *see* Schottenstein Stores Corp.
gbav Gesellschaft für Boden- und Abfallverwertung, **58** 28
GBC *see* General Binding Corp.
GC Companies, Inc., 25 176–78 *see also* AMC Entertainment Inc.
GCFC *see* General Cinema Finance Co.
GD Express Worldwide, *see* TPG NV.
GDE Systems, Inc., *see* Tracor Inc.
GDF *see* Gaz de France.
GDI *see* GO/DAN Industries, Inc.
GDS, **29** 412
GE *see* General Electric Co.
GE Aircraft Engines, 9 244–46
GE Capital Aviation Services, 36 230–33
GE Capital Corporation, **29** 428, 430; **63** 165
GE Capital Services, **49** 240
GE Medical Systems, **71** 350
GE SeaCo SRL, **29** 428, 431
GEA AG, 27 170–74
GEAC Computer Corporation Ltd., 43 181–85
Gear Products, Inc., **48** 59
Geberit AG, 49 161–64
Gebrüder Hepp, **60** 364
Gebrüder Märklin & Cie *see* Märklin Holding GmbH.
Gebrüder Sulzer Aktiengesellschaft *see* Sulzer Brothers Ltd.
GEC *see* General Electric Co.
GECAS *see* GE Capital Aviation Services.
Gecina SA, 42 151–53
Geco Mines Ltd., **64** 297
Gedney *see* M.A. Gedney Co.
Geerlings & Wade, Inc., 45 166–68
Geest Plc, 38 200–02 *see also* Bakkavör Group hf.
Gefco SA, 54 126–28
Geffen Records Inc., 26 150–52
GEHE AG, 27 175–78
Gehl Company, 19 172–74
GEICO Corporation, 10 310–12; 40 196–99 (upd.)
Geiger Bros., 60 138–41
Gel Tech LLC *see* Matrixx Initiatives, Inc.
Gelco Corporation, **53** 275
Gelco S.R.L. *see* Perfetti Van Melle S.p.A.
Gelita AG, 74 114–18
Gelman Sciences, Inc. *see* Pall Corp.
Gelsenberg AG, *see* Deutsche BP AG.
Gelson's, **29** 32
Gem State Utilities *see* Pacific Telecom, Inc.
GEMA (Gesellschaft für musikalische Aufführungs- und mechanische Vervielfältigungsrechte), 70 101–05
Gemaire Distributors, Inc., **52** 398–99
GemChem, Inc., **47** 20
Gemina S.p.A., **52** 121–22
Gemini Group Limited Partnership, **23** 10
Gemini Recycling Group LLC, **76** 130
Gemini Sound Products Corporation, 58 142–44
Gemplus International S.A., 64 144–47
Gemstar-TV Guide International, **43** 431
Gen-Probe Incorporated, 79 185–88
Gen-X Technologies Inc, **53** 285
Gencor Ltd., IV 90–93; 22 233–37 (upd.) *see also* Gold Fields Ltd.
GenCorp Inc., 9 247–49
Genencor International Inc., **44** 134, 136
Genender International Incorporated, **31** 52
Genentech, Inc., I 637–38; 8 209–11 (upd.); 32 211–15 (upd.); 75 154–58 (upd.)
General Accident plc, III 256–57 *see also* Aviva PLC.
General American Tank Car Company *see* GATX Corp.
General Aniline and Film Corporation *see* GAF Corp.
General Aquatics, Inc., **56** 16–17
General Atlantic Partners, **25** 34; **26** 94
General Atomics, 57 151–54
General Bearing Corporation, 45 169–71
General Binding Corporation, 10 313–14; 73 159–62 (upd.)
General Bussan Kaisha, Ltd. *see* TonenGeneral Sekiyu K.K.
General Cable Corporation, 40 200–03
General Casualty Co., *see* Winterthur Group.
The General Chemical Group Inc., 37 157–60
General Cigar Holdings, Inc., 66 139–42 (upd.)
General Cinema Corporation, I 245–46 *see also* GC Companies, Inc.
General DataComm Industries, Inc., 14 200–02
General Dynamics Corporation, I 57–60; 10 315–18 (upd.); 40 204–10 (upd.); 88 105–13 (upd.)
General Electric Capital Aviation Services, **48** 218–19
General Electric Capital Corporation, **15** 257, 282; **19** 190; **20** 42; **59** 265, 268; **71** 306
General Electric Company, II 27–31; 12 193–97 (upd.); 34 183–90 (upd.); 63 159–68 (upd.)
General Electric Company, PLC, II 24–26 *see also* Marconi plc.
General Electric International Mexico, S.A. de C.V., **51** 116
General Electric Mortgage Insurance Company, **52** 244
General Employment Enterprises, Inc., 87 172–175
General Export Iron and Metals Company, **15** 116
General Felt Industries Inc., **I** 202; **17** 182–83
General Finance Service Corp., **11** 447
General Fire Extinguisher Co. *see* Grinnell Corp.
General Foods Corp., **I** 608, 712; **V** 407; **26** 251; **44** 341 *see also* Kraft Foods Inc.
General Frozen Foods S.A. *see* Vivartia S.A.
General Furniture Leasing *see* CORT Business Services Corp.
General Growth Properties, Inc., 57 155–57
General Host Corporation, 12 198–200
General Housewares Corporation, 16 234–36
General Injectables and Vaccines Inc., **54** 188
General Instrument Corporation, 10 319–21 *see also* Motorola, Inc.
General Insurance Co. of America *see* SAFECO Corp.
General Maritime Corporation, 59 197–99
General Merchandise Services, Inc., **15** 480
General Mills, Inc., II 501–03; 10 322–24 (upd.); 36 234–39 (upd.); 85 141–49 (upd.)
General Motors Acceptance Corporation, **21** 146
General Motors Corporation, I 171–73; 10 325–27 (upd.); 36 240–44 (upd.); 64 148–53 (upd.)
General Nutrition Companies, Inc., 11 155–57; 29 210–14 (upd.)
General Office Products Co., *see* U.S. Office Products Co.
General Packing Service, Inc., **19** 78
General Parts Inc., **29** 86
General Petroleum Authority *see* Egyptian General Petroleum Corp.
General Physics Corporation, *see* National Patient Development Corp.
General Portland Inc., **28** 229
General Printing Ink Corp. *see* Sequa Corp.
General Public Utilities Corporation, V 629–31 *see also* GPU, Inc.
General Radio Company *see* GenRad, Inc.
General Railway Signal Company *see* General Signal Corp.
General Re Corporation, III 258–59; 24 176–78 (upd.)
General Sekiyu K.K., IV 431–33 *see also* TonenGeneral Sekiyu K.K.
General Shale Building Materials Inc. *see* Wienerberger AG.
General Signal Corporation, 9 250–52 *see also* SPX Corp.
General Telephone and Electronics Corp. *see* GTE Corp.
General Telephone Corporation *see* GTE Corp.
General Tire, Inc., 8 212–14
General Turbine Systems, **58** 75
General Utilities Company, **6** 555
General Waterworks Corporation, **40** 449
Generale Bank, II 294–95 *see also* Fortis, Inc.
Generale Biscuit Glico France S.A. *see* Ezaki Glico Company Ltd.
Genérale Biscuit S.A., **II** 475
Générale de Banque, **36** 458

Générale de Mécanique Aéronautique, *see* Avions Marcel Dassault-Breguet Aviation
Générale de Restauration, **49** 126
Générale des Eaux Group, V 632–34 *see* Vivendi Universal S.A.
Générale Occidentale, **II** 475; **IV** 614–16
Générale Restauration S.A., **34** 123
Generali *see* Assicurazioni Generali.
Génération Y2K, **35** 204, 207
Genesco Inc., 17 202–06; 84 143–149 (upd.)
Genesee & Wyoming Inc., 27 179–81
Genesee Iron Works *see* Wickes Inc.
Genesis Health Ventures, Inc., 18 195–97 *see also* NeighborCare,Inc.
Genesis Microchip Inc., 82 133–37
Genesse Hispania, **60** 246
Genetic Anomalies, Inc., **39** 395
Genetics Institute, Inc., 8 215–18
Geneva Metal Wheel Company, **20** 261
Geneva Rubber Co., *see* Park-Ohio Industries Inc.
Geneva Steel, 7 193–95
Geneve Corporation, **62** 16
GENEX Services, Inc., **52** 379
Genix Group *see* MCN Corp.
Genmar Holdings, Inc., 45 172–75
Genoc Chartering Ltd, **60** 96
Genosys Biotechnologies, Inc., **36** 431
Genovese Drug Stores, Inc., 18 198–200
Genpack Corporation, **21** 58
GenRad, Inc., 24 179–83
Gensec Bank, **68** 333
GenSet, *see* Thermadyne Holding Corp.
Genstar, **22** 14; **23** 327
Genstar Rental Electronics, Inc., **58** 110
Genstar Stone Products Co., **15** 154; **40** 176
GenSys Power Ltd., **64** 404
GenTek Inc., **37** 157; **41** 236
Gentex Corporation, 26 153–57
Genting Bhd., 65 152–55
Gentiva Health Services, Inc., 79 189–92
GenTrac, **24** 257
Gentry Associates, Inc., **14** 378
Gentry International, **47** 234
Genty-Cathiard, **39** 183–84; **54** 306
Genuardi's Family Markets, Inc., 35 190–92
Genuin Golf & Dress of America, Inc., **32** 447
Genuine Parts Company, 9 253–55; 45 176–79 (upd.)
Genzyme Corporation, 13 239–42; 38 203–07 (upd.); 77 164–70 (upd.)
Genzyme Transgenics Corp., **37** 44
Geo. H. McFadden & Bro., **54** 89
GEO SA, **58** 218
GEO Specialty Chemicals, Inc., **27** 117
geobra Brandstätter GmbH & Co. KG, 48 183–86
Geodis S.A., 67 187–90
Geofizikai Szolgáltató Kft., **70** 195
Geographics, Inc., **25** 183
GEOINFORM Mélyfúrási Információ Szolgáltató Kft., **70** 195
Geomarine Systems, **11** 202
The Geon Company, 11 158–61
Geon Industries, Inc. *see* Johnston Industries, Inc.
GeoQuest Systems Inc., **17** 419
Georesources, Inc., **19** 247
Georg Fischer AG Schaffhausen, 61 106–09
Georg Neumann GmbH, **66** 288
George A. Hormel and Company, II 504–06 *see also* Hormel Foods Corp.
George Buckton & Sons Limited, **40** 129
The George F. Cram Company, Inc., 55 158–60
The George Hyman Construction Company, *see* The Clark Construction Group, Inc.
George K. Baum & Company, **25** 433
George Kerasotes Corporation *see* Carmike Cinemas, Inc.
George P. Johnson Company, 60 142–44
George R. Rich Manufacturing Company *see* Clark Equipment Co.
George S. May International Company, 55 161–63
George Smith Financial Corporation, **21** 257
George Weston Ltd., II 631–32; 36 245–48 (upd.); 88 114–19 (upd.)
George Wimpey plc, 12 201–03; 51 135–38 (upd.)
Georgetown Group, Inc., **26** 187
Georgia Carpet Outlets, *see* The Maxim Group.
Georgia Cotton Producers Association *see* Gold Kist Inc.
Georgia Federal Bank, **I** 447; **30** 196
Georgia Gas Corporation *see* Atlanta Gas Light Company
Georgia Gulf Corporation, 9 256–58; 61 110–13 (upd.)
Georgia Hardwood Lumber Co., *see* Georgia-Pacific Corporation
Georgia-Pacific Corporation, IV 281–83; 9 259–62 (upd.); 47 145–51 (upd.)
Georgia Power & Light Co., **6** 447, 537; **23** 28
Georgia Power Company, **38** 446–48; **49** 145
Georgia Steel Supply Company, **70** 294
Georgie Pie, **V** 35
GeoScience Corporation, *see* Tech-Sym Corp.
Geosource Inc., **21** 14
Geotec Boyles Brothers, S.A., **19** 247
Geotecnia y Cimientos SA, **55** 182
Geotek Communications Inc., 21 238–40
GeoTel Communications Corp., **34** 114
GeoVideo Networks, **34** 259
Geoworks Corporation, **25** 509
Geraghty & Miller Inc., **26** 23
Gerald Stevens, Inc., 37 161–63
Gerber Products Company, 7 196–98; 21 241–44 (upd)
Gerber Scientific, Inc., 12 204–06; 84 150–154 (upd.)
Gerbes Super Markets, Inc., *see* Dillon Companies Inc.
Gerbo Telecommunicacoes e Servicos Ltda., **32** 40
Gerdau S.A., 59 200–03
Geren Associates *see* CRSS Inc.
Gerhard D. Wempe KG, 88 120–25
Gericom AG, 47 152–54
Gerling-Konzern Versicherungs-Beteiligungs-Aktiengesellschaft, 51 139–43
German American Bancorp, 41 178–80
German-American Car Company *see* GATX.
The German Society *see* The Legal Aid Society.
Germania Fluggesellschaft mbH, **76** 132
GERPI, **51** 16
Gerrard Group, **61** 270, 272
Gerresheimer Glas AG, 43 186–89
Gerrity Oil & Gas Corporation, **11** 28; **24** 379–80
Gerry Weber International AG, 63 169–72
GESA *see* General Europea S.A.
Gesbancaya, **II** 196
Gesca Ltee *see* Power Corporation of Canada.
Geschmay Group, **51** 14
Gesellschaft für musikalische Aufführungs- und mechanische Vervielfältigungsrechte *see* GEMA.
Gesellschaft für Tierernährung, **74** 117
GET Manufacturing Inc., **36** 300
Getchell Gold Corporation, **61** 292
Getrag Corporate Group, 92 137–42
Getronics NV, 39 176–78
Getty Images, Inc., 31 216–18
Getty Oil Co., **6** 457; **11** 27; **47** 436 *see also* ChevronTexaco.
Getz Bros. & Co., *see* Marmon Group, Inc.
Gevaert *see* Agfa Gevaert Group N.V.
Gevity HR, Inc., 63 173–77
Geyser Peak Winery, **58** 196
GF Health Products, Inc., 82 138–41
GFI Informatique SA, 49 165–68
GfK Aktiengesellschaft, 49 169–72
GFL Mining Services Ltd., **62** 164
GFS *see* Gordon Food Service Inc.
GFS Realty Inc., *see* Giant Food LLC.
GGT Group, **44** 198
GHI, **28** 155, 157
Ghirardelli Chocolate Company, 30 218–20
GI Export Corp. *see* Johnston Industries, Inc.
GIAG, **16** 122
Gianni Versace SpA, 22 238–40
Giant Cement Holding, Inc., 23 224–26
Giant Eagle, Inc., 86 160–64
Giant Food LLC, II 633–35; 22 241–44 (upd.); 83 155-161 (upd.)
Giant Industries, Inc., 19 175–77; 61 114–18 (upd.)

Giant Manufacturing Company, Ltd., 85 150–54
Giant TC, Inc. *see* Campo Electronics, Appliances & Computers, Inc.
Giant-Vac Manufacturing Inc., **64** 355
Giant Video Corporation, **29** 503
GIB Group, V 63–66; 26 158–62 (upd.)
Gibbons, Green, van Amerongen Ltd., **12** 28; **19** 360
Gibbs and Dandy plc, 74 119–21
Gibbs Construction, **25** 404
GIBCO Corp., *see* Life Technologies, Inc.
Gibraltar Steel Corporation, 37 164–67
Gibson, Dunn & Crutcher LLP, 36 249–52
Gibson Energy Ltd. *see* Hunting plc
Gibson Greetings, Inc., 12 207–10 *see also* American Greetings Corp.
Gibson Guitar Corp., 16 237–40
GIC *see* The Goodyear Tire & Rubber Co.
Giddings & Lewis, Inc., 10 328–30
GiFi S.A., 74 122–24
Giftmaster Inc., **26** 439–40
Gilbane, Inc., 34 191–93
Gilbert & John Greenall Limited, **21** 246
Gildan Activewear, Inc., 81 165–68
Gildemeister AG, 79 193–97
Gilead Sciences, Inc., 54 129–31
Gilkey Bros. *see* Puget Sound Tug and Barge Co.
Gillett Holdings, Inc., 7 199–201
The Gillette Company, III 27–30; 20 249–53 (upd.); 68 171–76 (upd.)
Gilliam S.A., **61** 104
Gilman & Ciocia, Inc., 72 148–50
Gilman Paper Co., **37** 178
Gilmore Steel Corporation *see* Oregon Steel Mills, Inc.
Gilroy Foods, *see* McCormick & Company, Inc.
Gimbel Brothers, Inc. *see* Saks Holdings, Inc.
Gimbel's Department Store, *see* B.A.T. Industries PLC
Gimelli Productions AG, **73** 332
Gindick Productions, **6** 28
Gingiss Group, **60** 5
Ginn & Co., **IV** 672; **19** 405
Ginnie Mae *see* Government National Mortgage Association.
Gino's East, **21** 362
Ginsber Beer Group, **15** 47; **38** 77
Giorgio Armani S.p.A., 45 180–83
Giorgio Beverly Hills, Inc., **26** 384
Giraud Restaurant System Co. Ltd. *see* Odakyu Electric Railway Co., Ltd.
Girbaud, **31** 261
Girl Scouts of the USA, 35 193–96
Giro Sport Designs International Inc., **16** 53; **44** 53–54
GiroCredit Bank, **69** 156
Girsa S.A., **23** 170
Giesecke & Devrient GmbH, 83 162-166
Girvin, Inc., *see* K2 Inc.
Git-n-Go Corporation, **60** 160
The Gitano Group, Inc., 8 219–21
La Giulia Ind. S.P.A., **72** 272
GIV *see* Granite Industries of Vermont, Inc.
Givaudan SA, 43 190–93
Given Imaging Ltd., 83 167-170
GIW Industries Inc., **62** 217
GJM International Ltd., **25** 121–22
GKH Partners, **29** 295
GKN plc, III 493–96; 38 208–13 (upd.); 89 232–41 (upd.)
Glaceau *see* Energy Brands Inc.
Glaces Thiriet S.A., 76 164–66
Gladwyne Music Publishing Corp. *see* J. W. Pepper and Son Inc.
Glitsch International, Inc., **76** 153, 155
Glacier Bancorp, Inc., 35 197–200
Glacier Park, Inc. *see* Viad Corp.
Glacier Water Services, Inc., 47 155–58
Glamar Group plc, *see* The Hartstone Group plc.
Glamis Gold, Ltd., 54 132–35
Glanbia plc, 59 204–07, 364
Glass Glover Plc, **52** 419
Glasstite, Inc., **33** 360–61
Glastron *see* Genmar Holdings, Inc.
Glatfelter Wood Pulp Company, *see* P.H. Glatfelter Company
Glaverbel Group, 80 130–33
Glaxo Holdings plc, I 639–41; 9 263–65 (upd.)
GlaxoSmithKline plc, 46 201–08 (upd.)
Glazer's Wholesale Drug Company, Inc., 82 142–45
Gleason Corporation, 24 184–87
Glemby Co. Inc., **70** 262
Glen & Co, **I** 453
Glen Alden Corp., **15** 247
Glen Dimplex, 78 123–27
Glen-Gery Corporation, *see* Ibstock plc.
Glenayre Technologies Inc. *see* Entertainment Distribution Co.
Glencairn Ltd., **25** 418
Glencore International AG, **52** 71, 73; **73** 391–92
The Glenlyte Group, **29** 469
Glenlyte Thomas Group LLC, **29** 466
Glenmoor Partners, **70** 34–35
Glenn Pleass Holdings Pty. Ltd., **21** 339
GLF-Eastern States Association, *see* Agway, Inc.
Glico *see* Ezaki Glico Company Ltd.
The Glidden Company, 8 222–24
Glimcher Co., **26** 262
Glitsch International, Inc. *see* Foster Wheeler Corp.
Global Access, **31** 469
Global Apparel Sourcing Ltd., *see* G-III Apparel Group, Ltd.
Global Berry Farms LLC, 62 154–56
Global BMC (Mauritius) Holdings Ltd., **62** 55
Global Card Holdings Inc., **68** 45
Global Communications of New York, Inc., **45** 261
Global Crossing Ltd., 32 216–19
Global Ground Support LLC *see* Air T, Inc.
Global Health Care Partners, **42** 68
Global Hyatt Corporation, 75 159–63 (upd.)
Global Imaging Systems, Inc., 73 163–65
Global Industries, Ltd., 37 168–72
Global Information Solutions, **34** 257
Global Interactive Communications Corporation, **28** 242
Global Marine Inc., 9 266–67
Global Motorsport Group, Inc. *see* Custom Chrome, Inc.
Global One, **52** 108
Global Outdoors, Inc., 49 173–76
Global Payments Inc., 91 206–10
Global Petroleum Albania S.A./Elda Petroleum Sh.P.K., **64** 177
Global Power Equipment Group Inc., 52 137–39
Global Switch International Ltd., **67** 104–05
Global TeleSystems, Inc. *see* Global Crossing Ltd.
Global Vacations Group *see* Classic Vacation Group, Inc.
Global Van Lines *see* Allied Worldwide, Inc.
GlobaLex, **28** 141
Globalia, **53** 301
GlobalSantaFe Corporation, 48 187–92 (upd.)
Globalstar Telecommunications Limited, **54** 233
GLOBALT, Inc., **52** 339
Globe Business Furniture, **39** 207
Globe Feather & Down, **19** 304
Globe Newspaper Co., *see* Affiliated Publications, Inc.
Globe Pequot Press, **36** 339, 341
Globelle Corp., **43** 368
Globenet, **57** 67, 69
Globo Comunicação e Participações S.A., 80 134–38
Globus *see* Migros-Genossenschafts-Bund.
Glock Ges.m.b.H., 42 154–56
Glon *see* Groupe Glon.
Gloria Jean's Gourmet Coffees, **20** 83
Glotel plc, 53 149–51
Glow-Tec International Company Ltd., **65** 343
Glowlite Corporation, **48** 359
Gluek Brewing Company, 75 164–66
GM *see* General Motors Corp.
GM Hughes Electronics Corporation, II 32–36 *see also* Hughes Electronics Corp.
GMH Communities Trust, 87 176–178
GMR Properties, **21** 257
GNB International Battery Group, *see* Pacific Dunlop Ltd.
GNC *see* General Nutrition Companies, Inc.
GND Holdings Corp., *see* Grand Union Co.
GNMA *see* Government National Mortgage Association.
Gnôme & Rhône, **46** 369
The Go-Ahead Group Plc, 28 155–57

GO/DAN Industries, Inc. *see* TransPro, Inc.
Go Fly Ltd., **39** 128
Go-Gro Industries, Ltd., **43** 99
Go Sport *see* Groupe Go Sport S.A.
Go-Video, Inc. *see* Sensory Science Corp.
goClick *see* Marchex, Inc.
Godfather's Pizza Incorporated, 25 179–81
Godfrey Co., *see* Fleming Companies, Inc.
Godfrey L. Cabot, Inc., *see* Cabot Corp.
Godiva Chocolatier, Inc., 64 154–57
Goelitz Confectionery Company *see* Herman Goelitz, Inc.; Jelly Belly Candy Co.
Goetze's Candy Company, Inc., 87 179–182
GOFAMCLO, Inc., **64** 160
Goggin Truck Line, **57** 277
GoGo Tours, Inc., **56** 203–04
Göhner AG, **6** 491
Gokey Company, **28** 339
Gol Linhas Aéreas Inteligentes S.A., 73 166–68
Gold Bond Stamp Company *see* Carlson Companies, Inc.
Gold Corporation, **71** 3–4
Gold Fields Ltd., IV 94–97; 62 157–64 (upd.)
Gold Kist Inc., 17 207–09; 26 166–68 (upd.) *see also* Pilgrim's Pride Corp.
Gold Lion, **20** 263
Gold Prospectors' Association of America, **49** 173
Gold Star Chili, Inc., **62** 325–26
Gold'n Plump Poultry, 54 136–38
Gold's Gym International, Inc., 71 165–68
Goldblatt's Department Stores, **15** 240–42
Goldcorp Inc., 87 183–186
Golden Bear International, **33** 103; **42** 433; **45** 300; **68** 245
Golden Belt Manufacturing Co., 16 241–43
Golden Books Family Entertainment, Inc., 28 158–61 *see also* Random House, Inc.
Golden Circle Financial Services, **15** 328
Golden Corral Corporation, 10 331–33; 66 143–46 (upd.)
Golden Enterprises, Inc., 26 163–65
Golden Gates Disposal & Recycling Co., **60** 224
Golden Grain Macaroni Co., **II** 560; **12** 411; **30** 219; **34** 366
Golden Krust Caribbean Bakery, Inc., 68 177–79
Golden Moores Finance Company, **48** 286
Golden Nugget, Inc. *see* Mirage Resorts, Inc.
Golden Ocean Group, **45** 164
Golden Peanut Company, *see* Gold Kist Inc.
Golden Poultry Company, **26** 168
Golden Press, Inc., *see* Western Publishing Group, Inc.
Golden Road Motor Inn, Inc. *see* Monarch Casino & Resort, Inc.
Golden State Foods Corporation, 32 220–22
Golden State Vintners, Inc., 33 172–74
Golden Telecom, Inc., 59 208–11
Golden West Financial Corporation, 47 159–61
Golden West Homes, **15** 328
Golden West Publishing Corp., **38** 307–08
Goldenberg Group, Inc., *see* Ply Gem Industries Inc.
Goldline Laboratories Inc., **11** 208
The Goldman Sachs Group Inc., II 414–16; 20 254–57 (upd.); 51 144–48 (upd.)
Goldner Hawn Johnson & Morrison Inc., **48** 412
Goldome Savings Bank, **11** 110
Goldsmith's, *see* Federated Department Stores Inc.
Goldstar Co., Ltd., 12 211–13 *see also* LG Corp.
Goldwin Golf, **45** 76
Goldwyn Films *see* Metro-Goldwyn-Mayer Inc.
Goleta National Bank, **33** 5
Golf Card International, **56** 5
Golin/Harris International, Inc., 88 126–30
The Golub Corporation, 26 169–71
GOME Electrical Appliances Holding Ltd., 87 187–191
Gomoljak, **14** 250
Gonnella Baking Company, 40 211–13
The Good Guys!, Inc., 10 334–35; 30 224–27 (upd.)
The Good Humor-Breyers Ice Cream Company, 14 203–05 *see also* Unilever PLC.
Good Times, Inc., *see* L.A. Gear, Inc.
Good Vibrations, Inc., **28** 345
Goodby Silverstein & Partners, Inc., 75 167–69
Goodfriend *see* Goody's Family Clothing, Inc.
Goodman Fielder Ltd., 52 140–43
Goodman Holding Company, 42 157–60
GoodMark Foods, Inc., 26 172–74
Goodrich Corporation, 46 209–13 (upd.)
Goodson Newspaper Group, **29** 262
GoodTimes Entertainment Ltd., 48 193–95
Goodwill Industries International, Inc., 16 244–46; 66 147–50 (upd.)
Goodwin, Dannenbaum, Littman & Wingfield, **16** 72
Goody Products, Inc., 12 214–16
Goody's Family Clothing, Inc., 20 265–67; 64 158–61 (upd.)
Goody's S.A. *see* Vivartia S.A.
The Goodyear Tire & Rubber Company, V 244–48; 20 259–64 (upd.); 75 170–78 (upd.)
Google, Inc., 50 204–07
Gordmans, Inc., 74 125–27
Gordon & Gotch *see* PMP Ltd.
Gordon Biersch Brewery Restaurant Group,Inc., 92229–32
Gordon Food Service Inc., 8 225–27; 39 179–82 (upd.)
Gordon Jewelry Corporation, *see* Zale Corp.
Gordon Manufacturing Co., **11** 256
Gordon Publications *see* Reed Elsevier.
Gordon S. Black Corporation, **41** 197–98
Gordy Company, **26** 314
Gorges Foodservice, Inc., **14** 516; **50** 493
Gorgonz Group, Inc., **64** 300
Gorilla Sports Club, **25** 42
The Gorman-Rupp Company, 18 201–03; 57 158–61 (upd.)
Gorton's, 13 243–44
The Gosho Co. *see* Kanematsu Corp.
Gosling Brothers Ltd., 82 146–49
Goss Holdings, Inc., 43 194–97
Gothenburg Light & Power Company, **6** 580
Gott Corp., **21** 293
Gottleib Group, **38** 437
Gottschalks, Inc., 18 204–06; 91 211–15 (upd.)
Gould Electronics, Inc., 14 206–08
Gould Paper Corporation, 82 150–53
Goulds Pumps Inc., 24 188–91
Gourmet Award Foods, **29** 480–81
Government Employees Insurance Company *see* GEICO Corp.
Government Technology Services Inc., **45** 69
Governor and Company of Adventurers of England *see* Hudson's Bay Co.
The Governor and Company of the Bank of Scotland, 10 336–38
Goya Foods Inc., 22 245–47; 91 216–21 (upd.)
GP Strategies Corporation, 64 162–66 (upd.)
GPAA *see* Gold Prospectors' Association of America.
GPE *see* General Precision Equipment Corp.
GPI *see* General Parts Inc.
GPI, **53** 46
GPM Gas Corporation, **40** 357–58
GPS Pool Supply, **29** 34
GPS Industries, Inc., 81 169–72
GPT, **15** 125
GPU *see* General Public Utilities Corp.
GPU, Inc., 27 182–85 (upd.)
Graber Industries, Inc. *see* Springs Industries, Inc.
Grace *see* W.R. Grace & Co.
Grace Drilling Company, **9** 365
Grace-Sierra Horticultural Products Co., *see* Scotts Co.
GraceKennedy Ltd., 92 143–47
Graco Inc., 19 178–80; 67 191–95 (upd.)
Gradall Industries, Inc., **52** 196
Gradco Systems, Inc., **6** 290
Gradiaz, Annis & Co., **15** 138

Graeter's Manufacturing Company, **86 165–68**
Graf, **23** 219
Graficas Monte Alban S.A., **47** 326
Graftek Press, Inc., **26** 44
Graham Corporation, **62 165–67**
Graham-Field Health Products, Inc. *see* GF Health Products, Inc.
Graham Packaging Holdings Company, **87 192–196**
Grampian Country Food Group, Ltd., **85 155–59**
Grameen Bank, **31 219–22**
GrameenPhone, **69** 344–46
Gramercy Pictures, **23** 391
Gran Central Corporation, *see* St. Joe Paper Co.
Gran Dorado, **48** 315
Granada Group PLC, **II 138–40**; **24 192–95 (upd.)**
Granaria Holdings B.V., **66 151–53**
GranCare, Inc., **14 209–11**
Grand Bazaar Innovations Bon Marché, **26** 159–60
Grand Casinos, Inc., **20 268–70**
Grand Home Furnishings *see* Grand Piano & Furniture Co.
Grand Hotel Krasnapolsky N.V., **23 227–29**
Grand Metropolitan plc, **I 247–49**; **14 212–15 (upd.)** *see also* Diageo plc.
Grand Ole Opry *see* Gaylord Entertainment Co.
Grand Piano & Furniture Company, **72 151–53**
Grand Prix Association of Long Beach, Inc., **43** 139–40
Grand Rapids Gas Light Company *see* MCN Corp.
Grand Union Company, **7 202–04**; **28 162–65 (upd.)**
Grand Valley Gas Company, **11** 28
Grand-Perret, **39** 152–53
Grandes Superficies S.A., **23** 247
Les Grands Magasins Au Bon Marché, **26** 159–60
GrandVision S.A., **43 198–200**
Grandy's, **15** 345
Grange *see* Aga Foodservice Group PLC.
Gränges, *see* Electrolux AB.
Granite Broadcasting Corporation, **42 161–64**
Granite City Food & Brewery Ltd., **94 214–17**
Granite Construction Incorporated, **61 119–21**
Granite Industries of Vermont, Inc., **73 169–72**
Granite Rock Company, **26 175–78**
Granite State Bankshares, Inc., **37 173–75**
Grant Prideco, Inc., **57 162–64**
Grant Thornton International, **57 165–67**
Grantree Corp., **14** 4; **33** 398
Granville PLC *see* Robert W. Baird & Co. Inc.
Graphic Controls Corp., **IV** 678
Graphic Industries Inc., **25 182–84**
Graphic Research, Inc., *see* Methode Electronics, Inc.
Graphix Zone, **31** 238
Grasim Industries Limited *see* Aditya Birla Group
Grass Valley Group, *see* Tektronix, Inc.
Grasso Production Management Inc., **37** 289
Grattan Plc *see* Otto-Versand (Gmbh & Co.).
The Graver Company, *see* The Marmon Group, Inc.
Gray Communications Systems, Inc., **24 196–200**
Gray Line, *see* Coach USA, Inc.
Gray Matter Holdings, L.L.C., **64** 300
Gray, Siefert & Co., Inc., **10** 44; **33** 259–60
Graybar Electric Company, Inc., **54 139–42**
Great Alaska Tobacco Co., **17** 80
Great American Bagel and Coffee Co., **27** 482
Great American Broadcasting Inc., **23** 257–58
Great American Cookie Company *see* Mrs. Fields' Original Cookies, Inc.
Great American Entertainment Company, *see* International Family Entertainment Inc.
Great American Insurance Company, **48** 9
Great American Management and Investment, Inc., **8 228–31**
The Great Atlantic & Pacific Tea Company, Inc., **II 636–38**; **16 247–50 (upd.)**; **55 164–69 (upd.)**
Great Bagel and Coffee Co., *see* Unique Casual Restaurants, Inc.
Great Harvest Bread Company, **44 184–86**
Great Lakes Bancorp, **8 232–33**
Great Lakes Chemical Corp., **I 341–42**; **14 216–18 (upd.)** *see also* Chemtura Corp.
Great Lakes Dredge & Dock Company, **69 194–97**
Great Lakes Energy Corp., **39** 261
Great Lakes Steel Corp., **26** 528
Great Lakes Transportation LLC, **71** 82
Great Lakes Window, Inc., *see* Ply Gem Industries Inc.
Great Land Seafoods, Inc., *see* Nippon Suisan Kaisha, Ltd.
Great Northern Railway Company, **6** 596
Great Plains Energy Incorporated, **65 156–60 (upd.)**
Great Plains Software Inc., **38** 432
Great Rigs, Inc., **71** 8–9
Great River Oil and Gas Corporation, **61** 111
The Great Universal Stores plc, **V 67–69**; **19 181–84 (upd.)** *see also* GUS plc.
Great-West Lifeco Inc., **III 260–61** *see also* Power Corporation of Canada.
Great Western Bank, **47** 160
Great Western Financial Corporation, **10 339–41** *see also* Washington Mutual, Inc.
Great Western Foam Co., **17** 182
Great White Shark Enterprises, Inc., **89 242–45**
Great Wolf Resorts, Inc., **91 222–26**
Great World Foods, Inc., *see* Cheesecake Factory Inc.
Greatbatch Inc., **72 154–56**
Grebner GmbH, **26** 21
Grede Foundries, Inc., **38 214–17**
Greeley Gas Company, **43** 56–57
Green Bay Food Company, *see* Dean Foods Co.
The Green Bay Packers, Inc., **32 223–26**
Green Capital Investors L.P., **23** 413–14
Green Island Cement (Holdings) Ltd. Group, **IV** 694–95
Green Mountain Coffee, Inc., **31 227–30**
Green Power & Light Company *see* UtiliCorp United Inc.
Green Siam Air Services Co., Ltd., **51** 123
Green Tree Financial Corporation, **11 162–63** *see also* Conseco, Inc.
The Greenalls Group PLC, **21 245–47**
Greenbacks Inc., **62** 104
Greenberg Traurig, LLP, **65 161–63**
The Greenbrier Companies, **19 185–87**
Greene King plc, **31 223–26**
Greene, Tweed & Company, **55 170–72**
Greenfield Healthy Foods, **26** 58
Greenham Construction Materials, **38** 451–52
Greenman Brothers Inc. *see* Noodle Kidoodle.
Greenpeace International, **74 128–30**
GreenPoint Financial Corp., **28 166–68**
Greenville Tube Corporation, **21** 108
Greenwich Air Services Inc., **73** 43
Greenwich Associates, **19** 117
Greenwood Mills, Inc., **14 219–21**
Greenwood Publishing Group *see* Reed Elsevier.
Greg Manning Auctions, Inc., **60 145–46**
Greggs PLC, **65 164–66**
Gregory Mountain Products *see* Bianchi International.
Greif Inc., **15 186–88**; **66 154–56 (upd.)**
Greiner Engineering Inc., **45** 421
Gresham Insurance Company Limited, **24** 285
Gretel's Pretzels, **35** 56
Gretsch & Brenner, **55** 150
Grévin & Compagnie SA, **56 143–45**
Grey Global Group Inc., **6 26–28**; **66 157–61 (upd.)**
Grey Wolf, Inc., **43 201–03**
Greyhound Lines, Inc., **I 448–50**; **32 227–31 (upd.)**
Griese and Ross *see* C.R. Meyer and Sons Co.
Griff Plus *see* GiFi S.A.
Griffin Bacal, **25** 381
Griffin Industries, Inc., **70 106–09**

Griffin Land & Nurseries, Inc., 43 204–06
Griffin Pipe Products Co., **7** 30–31
Griffin Press Pty. *see* PMP Ltd.
Griffin Wheel Company, **7** 29–30
Griffon Corporation, 34 194–96
Grill Concepts, Inc., 74 131–33
Grimes Aerospace, **22** 32
Grinnell Corp., 13 245–47
Grist Mill Company, 15 189–91
Gristede's Foods Inc., 68 31 231–33; 180–83 (upd.)
GRM Industries Inc., **15** 247–48
Gro-Mor Company, **60** 160
Grob Horgen AG *see* Groz-Beckert Group.
GroceryWorks Holdings, Inc, **68** 369
Grohe *see* Friedrich Grohe AG & Co. KG.
Grolier Inc., 16 251–54; 43 207–11 (upd.)
Grolier Interactive, **41** 409
Grolsch *see* Royal Grolsch NV.
Gross Brothers Laundry *see* G&K Services, Inc.
Gross Townsend Frank Hoffman, **6** 28
Grosskraftwerk Franken AG, **23** 47
Grossman's Inc., 13 248–50
Grosvenor Casinos Ltd., **64** 320
Ground Round, Inc., 21 248–51
Group Arnault, **32** 146
Group 4 Falck A/S, 42 165–68
Group Health Cooperative, 41 181–84
Group Lotus plc, **62** 268
Group Maeva SA, **48** 316
Group Maintenance America Corp. *see* Encompass Services Corp.
Group 1 Automotive, Inc., 52 144–46
Group Schneider S.A., **20** 214
Groupama S.A., 76 167–70
Groupe AB, **19** 204
Groupe Air France, 6 92–94 *see also* Air France; Societe Air France.
Groupe Alain Manoukian, 55 173–75
Groupe André, 17 210–12 *see also* Vivarte SA.
Groupe Arnault, **66** 244
Groupe Axime, **37** 232
Groupe Barrière SA, **48** 199
Groupe Bisset, **24** 510
Groupe Bolloré, 67 196–99
Groupe Bourbon S.A., 60 147–49
Groupe Bruxelles Lambert, **26** 368
Groupe Bull *see* Compagnie des Machines Bull.
Groupe Casino *see* Casino Guichard-Perrachon S.A.
Groupe Castorama-Dubois Investissements, 23 230–32 *see also* Kingfisher plc.
Groupe CECAB S.C.A., 88 131–34
Groupe Crit S.A., 74 134–36
Groupe Danone, 32 232–36 (upd.); 93 233–40 (upd.)
Le Groupe Darty, *see* Kingfisher plc.
Groupe Dassault Aviation SA, 26 179–82 (upd.)
Groupe de la Cité, IV 614–16
Groupe des Assurances Nationales, **76** 169
Groupe DMC (Dollfus Mieg & Cie), 27 186–88
Groupe Euralis, 86 169–72
Groupe Fournier SA, 44 187–89
Groupe Glon, 84 155–158
Groupe Go Sport S.A., 39 183–85
Groupe Guillin SA, 40 214–16
Groupe Herstal S.A., 58 145–48
Groupe Jean-Claude Darmon, 44 190–92
Groupe Jean Didier, **12** 413
Groupe Jean-Paul Gaultier, **34** 214
Groupe Lactalis, 78 128–32 (upd.)
Groupe Lagardère S.A., **15** 293; **21** 265, 267
Groupe Lapeyre S.A., 33 175–77
Groupe LDC *see* L.D.C. S.A.
Groupe Le Duff S.A., 84 159–162
Groupe Léa Nature, 88 135–38
Groupe Legris Industries, 23 233–35
Groupe Les Echos, 25 283–85
Groupe Limagrain, 74 137–40
Groupe Louis Dreyfus S.A., 60 150–53
Groupe Monnoyeur, 72 157–59
Groupe Open, 74 141–43
Groupe Partouche SA, 48 196–99
Groupe Pechiney, **33** 89
Groupe Pinault-Printemps-Redoute, *see* Pinault-Printemps-Redoute S.A.
Groupe Poliet, **66** 363–64
Groupe Poron, **35** 206
Groupe Promodès S.A., 19 326–28
Groupe Rallye, **39** 183–85
Groupe Rothschild, **22** 365
Groupe Rougier SA, 21 438–40
Groupe Roussin, **34** 13
Groupe Salvat, **IV** 619
Groupe SEB, 35 201–03
Groupe Sidel S.A., 21 252–55
Groupe Soufflet SA, 55 176–78
Groupe Tetra Laval, **53** 327
Groupe Vidéotron Ltée., 20 271–73
Groupe Yves Saint Laurent, 23 236–39 *see also* Gucci Group N.V.
Groupe Zannier S.A., 35 204–07
Groupement d'Achat AVP SAS, **58** 221
Groupement des Mousquetaires *see* ITM Entreprises SA.
Groupement Français pour l'Investissement Immobilier, **42** 153
Groupement pour le Financement de la Construction *see* Gecina SA.
GroupMAC *see* Encompass Services Corp.
Groux Beverage Corporation, **11** 451
Grove Manufacturing Co., *see* OshKosh B'Gosh, Inc.
Grove Worldwide, Inc., **59** 274, 278
Grow Biz International, Inc., 18 207–10 *see also* Winmark Corp.
Grow Group Inc., 12 217–19
GROWMARK, Inc., 88 139–42
Groz-Beckert Group, 68 184–86
GRS Inns Ltd *see* Punch Taverns plc.
Grubb & Ellis Company, 21 256–58
Gruma, S.A. de C.V., 31 234–36
Grumman Corp., I 61–63; 11 164–67 (upd.) *see aslo* Northrop Grumman Corp.
Grunau Company Inc., 90 209–12
Grundfos Group, 83 171-174
Grundig AG, 27 189–92
Gruner + Jahr AG & Co., **22** 442; **23** 85
Gruntal & Co., L.L.C., 20 274–76
Grupo Aeroportuario del Pacífico, S.A. de C.V., 85 160–63
Grupo Acerero del Norte, S.A. de C.V., **22** 286; **42** 6
Grupo Aeropuerto del Sureste, S.A. de C.V., 48 200–02
Grupo Ángeles Servicios de Salud, S.A. de C.V., 84 163–166
Grupo Antarctica Paulista *see* Companhia de Bebidas das Américas.
Grupo Banco Bilbao Vizcaya Argentaria S.A., **54** 147
Grupo Bimbo, S.A. de C.V., **31** 236
Grupo Bufete *see* Bufete Industrial, S.A. de C.V.
Grupo Cabal S.A., **23** 166
Grupo Campi, S.A. de C.V., **39** 230
Grupo Carso, S.A. de C.V., 21 259–61
Grupo Casa Saba, S.A. de C.V., 39 186–89
Grupo Clarín S.A., 67 200–03
Grupo Comercial Chedraui S.A. de C.V., 86 173–76
Grupo Corvi S.A. de C.V., 86 177–80
Grupo Cruzcampo S.A., **34** 202
Grupo Cuervo, S.A. de C.V., **31** 91–92
Grupo Cydsa, S.A. de C.V., 39 190–93
Grupo de Ingenieria Ecologica, **16** 260
Grupo Dina *see* Consorcio G Grupo Dina, S.A. de C.V.
Grupo Dragados SA, 55 179–82
Grupo DST, **41** 405–06
Grupo Editorial Random House Mondadori S.L., **54** 22
Grupo Elektra, S.A. de C.V., 39 194–97
Grupo Empresarial Angeles, **50** 373
Grupo Eroski, 64 167–70
Grupo Ferrovial, S.A., 40 217–19
Grupo Ficosa International, 90 213–16
Grupo Financiero Asemex-Banpais S.A., **51** 150
Grupo Financiero Banamex S.A., 54 143–46
Grupo Financiero Banorte, S.A. de C.V., 51 149–51
Grupo Financiero BBVA Bancomer S.A., 54 147–50
Grupo Financiero Galicia S.A., 63 178–81
Grupo Financiero Inbursa, **21** 259
Grupo Financiero Inverlat, S.A., **39** 188; **59** 74
Grupo Financiero Serfin, S.A., 19 188–90
Grupo Gigante, S.A. de C.V., 34 197–99
Grupo Hecali, S.A., **39** 196
Grupo Herdez, S.A. de C.V., 35 208–10
Grupo ICA, **52** 394
Grupo IMSA, S.A. de C.V., 44 193–96
Grupo Industrial Alfa, S.A. de C.V. *see* Alfa, S.A. de C.V.
Grupo Industrial Atenquique, S.A. de C.V., **37** 176

Grupo Industrial Bimbo, 19 191–93
Grupo Industrial Durango, S.A. de C.V., 37 176–78
Grupo Industrial Herradura, S.A. de C.V., 83 175-178
Grupo Industrial Lala, S.A. de C.V., 82 154–57
Grupo Industrial Maseca S.A. de C.V. (Gimsa) *see* Gruma, S.A. de C.V.
Grupo Industrial Saltillo, S.A. de C.V., 54 151–54
Grupo Irsa, **23** 171
Grupo Leche Pascual S.A., 59 212–14
Grupo Lladró S.A., 52 147–49
Grupo Marsans, **69** 9, 11–12
Grupo Martins, **59** 361
Grupo Mexico, S.A. de C.V., 40 220–23
Grupo Modelo, S.A. de C.V., 29 218–20
Grupo Nacional de Chocolates S.A. *see* Inversiones Nacional de Chocolates S.A.
Grupo Omnilife S.A. de C.V., 88 143–46
Grupo Pipsamex S.A., **37** 178
Grupo Planeta, 94 218–22
Grupo Portucel Soporcel, 60 154–56
Grupo Posadas, S.A. de C.V., 57 168–70
Grupo Pulsar *see* Pulsar Internacional S.A.
Grupo Quan, **19** 192–93
Grupo Salinas, **39** 196
Grupo Sanborns S.A. de C.V., **35** 118
Grupo Servia, S.A. de C.V., **50** 209
Grupo TACA, 38 218–20
Grupo Televisa, S.A., 18 211–14; 54 155–58 (upd.)
Grupo TMM, S.A. de C.V., 50 208–11
Grupo Transportación Ferroviaria Mexicana, S.A. de C.V., 47 162–64
Grupo Tribasa, **34** 82
Grupo Tudor, **IV** 471
Grupo Viz, S.A. de C.V., 84 167–170
Grupo Xtra, **39** 186, 188
Gruppo Banco di Napoli, **50** 410
Gruppo Buffetti S.p.A., **47** 345–46
Gruppo Coin S.p.A., 41 185–87
Gruppo Editoriale L'Espresso S.p.A., **54** 19–21
Gruppo IRI, **V** 325–27
Gruppo Riva Fire SpA, 88 147–50
Gryphon Development, *see* Intimate Brands, Inc.
Gryphon Holdings, Inc., 21 262–64
GS Financial Services L.P., **51** 148
GSC Enterprises, Inc., 86 181–84
GSD&M Advertising, 44 197–200
GSD&M's Idea City, 90 217–21
GSG&T, Inc. *see* Gulf States Utilities Co.
GSG Holdings Ltd., **39** 87
GSI *see* Geophysical Service, Inc.
GSI Commerce, Inc., 67 204–06
GSU *see* Gulf States Utilities Co.
GT Bicycles, 26 183–85
GT Global Inc. *see* AMVESCAP PLC.
GT Interactive Software, 31 237–41 *see also* Infogrames Entertainment S.A.
GTE Corporation, V 294–98; 15 192–97 (upd.) *see also* British Columbia Telephone Company; Verizon Communications.
GTE Northwest Inc., **37** 124–26
GTI Corporation, **29** 461–62
GTM-Entrepose, **23** 332
GTM Group, **43** 450, 452; **54** 392
GTO *see* Global Transport Organization.
GTS Duratek, Inc., *see* National Patient Development Corp.
GTSI *see* Government Technology Services Inc.
GTSI Corp., 57 171–73
GU Markets, **55** 83
Guangzhou Kurabo Chemicals Co. Ltd., **61** 229
Guangzhou Pearl River Piano Group Ltd., 49 177–79
Guangzhou Railway Corporation, **52** 43
Guarantee Life Cos., **69** 368
Guarantee Reserve Life Insurance Company, **59** 246
Guaranty Federal Bank, F.S.B., **31** 441
Guaranty Trust Co. *see* JPMorgan Chase & Co.
Guardforce Limited, **45** 378
Guardian Financial Services, 11 168–70; 64 171–74 (upd.)
Guardian Industries Corp., 87 197–204
Guardian Media Group plc, 53 152–55
Guardian Refrigerator Company *see* Frigidaire Home Products.
Guardsmark, L.L.C., 77 171–74
Gubor Schokoladen, **15** 221
Gucci Group N.V., 15 198–200; 50 212–16 (upd.)
Gudang Garam Tbk, PT, **62** 96–97
Guenther *see* C.H. Guenther & Son, Inc.
Guerbet Group, 46 214–16
Guerdon Homes, Inc., **41** 19
Guerlain, 23 240–42
Guess, Inc., 15 201–03; 68 187–91 (upd.)
Guest, Keen and Nettlefolds plc *see* GKN plc.
Guest Supply, Inc., 18 215–17
Guida-Seibert Dairy Company, 84 171–174
Guidant Corporation, 58 149–51
Guideoutdoors.com Inc., **36** 446
Guilbert S.A., 42 169–71
Guild Wineries, *see* Canandaigua Brands, Inc.
Guilford Industries, *see* Interface, Inc.
Guilford Mills Inc., 8 234–36; 40 224–27 (upd.)
Guilford of Maine, Inc., **29** 246
Guilford Transportation Industries, Inc., *see* Maine Central Railroad Co.
Guillemot Corporation, 41 188–91, 407, 409
Guillin *see* Groupe Guillin SA
Guinness Mahon, **36** 231
Guinness Peat Aviation, **36** 426
Guinness/UDV, I 250–52; 43 212–16 (upd.) *see also* Diageo plc.
Guinot Paris S.A., 82 158–61
Guitar Center, Inc., 29 221–23; 68 192–95 (upd.)
Guittard Chocolate Company, 55 183–85
Guizhou Tyres Inc., **71** 393
Gulf + Western Inc., I 451–53 *see also* Paramount Communications; Viacom Inc.
Gulf Air Company, 56 146–48
Gulf Agency Company Ltd., 78 133–36
Gulf Canada Ltd., **IV** 721; **6** 478
Gulf Canada Resources Ltd., **63** 110
Gulf Coast Sportswear Inc., **23** 65
Gulf Energy Development, **22** 107
Gulf Island Fabrication, Inc., 44 201–03
Gulf Marine & Maintenance Offshore Service Company, **22** 276
Gulf Oil Corp. *see* Chevron.
Gulf Power Company, **38** 446, 448
Gulf Printing Company, **70** 67
Gulf Public Service Company, Inc, **6** 580; **37** 89
Gulf Resources & Chemical Corp., **15** 464
Gulf States Utilities Company, 6 495–97 *see also* Entergy Corp.
GulfMark Offshore, Inc., 49 180–82
Gulfstream Aerospace Corporation, 7 205–06; 28 169–72 (upd.)
Gulfwind Marine USA, **30** 303
Gulistan Holdings Inc., **28** 219
Gulton Industries Inc., *see* Mark IV Industries, Inc.
Gum Base Asia Ltd., **72** 272
Gum Tech International *see* Matrixx Initiatives, Inc.
Gunderson, Inc. *see* The Greenbrier Companies.
Gunite Corporation, 51 152–55
The Gunlocke Company, 23 243–45
Gunnebo AB, 53 156–58
Gupta, **15** 492
Gurwitch Bristow Products, LLC, **49** 285
GUS plc, 47 165–70 (upd.)
Gustav Schickendanz KG *see* Karstadt Quelle AG.
Guthy-Renker Corporation, 32 237–40
Guttenplan's Frozen Dough Inc., 88 151–54
Gutzeit *see* W. Gutzeit & Co.
Guy Degrenne SA, 44 204–07
Guy Maunsell International Limited *see* AECOM Technology Corporation
Guy Pease Associates, **34** 248
Guyenne et Gascogne, 23 246–48
Guyomarc'h, **39** 356
GVN Technologies, **63** 5
Gwathmey Siegel & Associates Architects LLC, 26 186–88
GWC *see* General Waterworks Corp.
GWK GmbH, **45** 378
GWR Group plc, 39 198–200
Gymboree Corporation, 15 204–06; 69 198–201 (upd.)
Gynecare Inc., **23** 190

Gynetics, Inc., **26** 31

H

H&D *see* Hinde & Dauch Paper Co.
H&D Holdings, **64** 79
H&R Block, Inc., 9 268–70; 29 224–28 (upd.); 82 162–69 (upd.)
H.B. DeViney Company, Inc., *see* The J.M. Smucker Co.
H.B. Fenn and Company Ltd., **25** 485
H.B. Fuller Company, 8 237–40; 32 254–58 (upd.); 75 179–84 (upd.)
H. Betti Industries Inc., 88 155–58
H.C. Prange Co., **19** 511–12
H Curry & Sons *see* Currys Group PLC.
H.D. Lee Company, Inc. *see* Lee Apparel Company, Inc.
H.D. Vest, Inc., 46 217–19
H. E. Butt Grocery Company, 13 251–53; 32 259–62 (upd.); 85 164–70 (upd.)
H.E. Moss and Company Tankers Ltd., **23** 161
H.F. Ahmanson & Company, II 181–82; 10 342–44 (upd.) *see also* Washington Mutual, Inc.
H.F.T. Industrial Ltd., **62** 150
H.G. Anderson Equipment Corporation, **6** 441
H. Gringoire S.A.R.L., **70** 234
H.H. Brown Shoe Company, *see* Berkshire Hathaway Inc.
H.H. Cutler Company, *see* VF Corp.
H.H. Robertson, Inc., **19** 366
H.H. West Co., **25** 501
H.I.G. Capital L.L.C., **30** 235
H.J. Heinz Company, II 507–09; 11 171–73 (upd.); 36 253–57 (upd.)
H.J. Justin & Sons *see* Justin Industries, Inc.
H.J. Russell & Company, 66 162–65
H.L. Yoh Company *see* Day & Zimmerman, Inc.
H. Lundbeck A/S, 44 208–11
H.M. Byllesby & Company, Inc., **6** 539
H.M. Payson & Co., 69 202–04
H.M. Spalding Electric Light Plant, **6** 592; **50** 37
H N Norton Co., **11** 208
H.O. Systems, Inc., **47** 430
H-P *see* Hewlett-Packard Co.
H.P. Foods, **II** 475
H.P. Hood, **7** 17–18
H.S. Trask & Co. *see* Phoenix Footware Group, Inc.
H. Samuel Plc, **61** 326
H.W. Johns Manufacturing Co. *see* Manville Corp.
H.W.S. Solutions, **21** 37
The H.W. Wilson Company, 66 166–68
Ha-Lo Industries, Inc., 27 193–95
Häagen-Dazs, *see* Nestlé S.A.
Haan Crafts Corporation, **62** 18
Haarmann & Reimer *see* Symrise GmbH and Co. KG
The Haartz Corporation, 94 223–26
Haas, Baruch & Co. *see* Smart & Final, Inc.
Haas Publishing Companies, Inc., **22** 442
Haas Wheat & Partners, **15** 357; **65** 258–59
Habersham Bancorp, 25 185–87
Habitat for Humanity International, 36 258–61
Habitat/Mothercare PLC *see* Mothercare plc.
Hach Co., 18 218–21
Hachette Filipacchi Medias S.A., 21 265–67
Hachette S.A., IV 617–19 *see also* Matra-Hachette S.A.
Haci Omer Sabanci Holdings A.S., 55 186–89 *see also* Akbank TAS
Hacker-Pschorr Brau, **35** 331
Hackman Oyj Adp, 44 212–15
Hadco Corporation, 24 201–03
Hadron, Inc. *see* Analex Corp.
Haeger Industries Inc., 88 159–62
Haemocell, **11** 476
Haemonetics Corporation, 20 277–79
Haftpflichtverband der Deutschen Industrie Versicherung auf Gegenseitigkeit V.a.G. *see* HDI (Haftpflichtverband der Deutschen Industrie Versicherung auf Gegenseitigkeit V.a.G.).
Hagemeyer N.V., 39 201–04
Hagemeyer North America, **63** 289
Haggar Corporation, 19 194–96; 78 137–41 (upd.)
Haggen Inc., 38 221–23
Hägglunds Vehicle AB, **47** 7, 9
Hagoromo Foods Corporation, 84 175–178
Hahn Automotive Warehouse, Inc., 24 204–06
Hahn Department Stores *see* Allied Stores Corp.
Haier Group Corporation, 65 167–70
Haights Cross Communications, Inc., 84 179–182
The Hain Celestial Group, Inc., 27 196–98; 43 217–20 (upd.)
Hair Club For Men Ltd., 90 222–25
Hair Cuttery *see* Ratner Companies.
Hake Group, Inc. *see* Matrix Service Co.
Hakone Tozan Railway Co., Ltd., **68** 281
Hakuhodo, Inc., 6 29–31; 42 172–75 (upd.)
HAL Inc., 9 271–73 *see also* Hawaiian Airlines, Inc.
Hale and Dorr, **31** 75
Hale-Halsell Company, 60 157–60
Haleko Hanseatisches Lebensmittel Kontor GmbH, **29** 500
Halewood, **21** 246
Half Price Books, Records, Magazines Inc., 37 179–82
Halfords Ltd., *see* Alliance Boots plc.
Halkin Holdings plc, **49** 338–39
Hall Bros. Co. *see* Hallmark Cards, Inc.
Hall, Kinion & Associates, Inc., 52 150–52
Hall Laboratories, Inc., **45** 209
Hall-Mark Electronics, **23** 490
Hallhuber GmbH, **63** 361, 363
Halliburton Company, III 497–500; 25 188–92 (upd.); 55 190–95 (upd.)
Hallmark Cards, Inc., IV 620–21; 16 255–57 (upd.); 40 228–32 (upd.); 87 205–212 (upd.)
Hallmark Chemical Corp., *see* NCH Corp.
Hallmark Holdings, Inc., **51** 190
Hallmark Investment Corp., **21** 92
Hallmark Residential Group, Inc., **45** 221
Halo Lighting, **30** 266
Haloid Company *see* Xerox Corp.
Halstead Industries, **26** 4; **52** 258
Halter Marine, **22** 276
Hambrecht & Quist Group, **26** 66; **31** 349
Hambro Countrywide Security, **32** 374
Hambros Bank, **16** 14; **43** 7
Hamburg-Amerikanische-Packetfahrt-Actien-Gesellschaft *see* Hapag-Lloyd AG.
Hamburgische Electricitaets-Werke AG, **57** 395, 397
Hamelin Group, Inc. *see* Spartech Corp.
Hamer Hammer Service, Inc., **11** 523
Hamersley Holdings, **IV** 59–61
Hamil Textiles Ltd. *see* Algo Group Inc.
Hamilton Beach/Proctor-Silex Inc., 17 213–15
Hamilton Group Limited, **15** 478
Hamilton/Hall-Mark, **19** 313
Hamilton Oil Corp., **IV** 47; **22** 107
Hamilton Sundstrand, **76** 319
Hammacher Schlemmer & Company Inc., 21 268–70; 72 160–62 (upd.)
Hammermill Paper Co., **23** 48–49
Hammers Plastic Recycling, **6** 441
Hammerson plc, IV 696–98; 40 233–35 (upd.)
Hammery Furniture Company, *see* La-Z-Boy Inc.
Hammes Co., **38** 482
Hammond Manufacturing Company Limited, 83 179-182
Hamot Health Foundation, 91 227–32
Hampton Affiliates, Inc., 77 175–79
Hampton Industries, Inc., 20 280–82
Hampton Inns, *see* Promus Companies, Inc.
Hampton Roads Food, Inc., *see* Rally's.
Hampshire Group Ltd., 82 170–73
Hamworthy Engineering Ltd., **31** 367, 369
Han Comm Inc., **62** 174
Han-Fa Electrification Co. Ltd., **76** 139
Hancock Fabrics, Inc., 18 222–24
Hancock Holding Company, 15 207–09
Hancock Jaffe Laboratories, **11** 460
Hancock Park Associates *see* Leslie's Poolmart, Inc.
Handleman Company, 15 210–12; 86 185–89 (upd.)
Handspring Inc., 49 183–86
Handy & Harman, 23 249–52
Handy Andy Home Improvement Centers, Inc., **26** 160–61
Hanes Holding Company, **11** 256; **48** 267

Hang Seng Bank Ltd., 60 161–63
Hanger Orthopedic Group, Inc., 41 192–95
Haniel & Cie. GmbH, *see* GEHE AG.
Hanjin Group *see* Korean Ail Lines Co. Ltd.
Hanjin Shipping Co., Ltd., 50 217–21
Hankook Tyre Manufacturing Company, *see* The Yokohama Rubber Co., Ltd.
Hankyu Corporation, V 454–56; 23 253–56 (upd.)
Hankyu Department Stores, Inc., V 70–71; 62 168–71 (upd.)
Hanley Brick, **14** 250
Hanmi Financial Corporation, 66 169–71
Hanna Andersson Corp., 49 187–90
Hanna-Barbera Cartoons Inc., 23 257–59, 387
Hannaford Bros. Co., 12 220–22
Hannen Brauerei GmbH, *see* Carlsberg A/S
Hannifin Corporation *see* Parker Hannifin Corp.
HANNOVER International AG für Industrieversicherungen, **53** 162
Hannover Papier, **49** 353
Hanover Bank *see* Manufacturers Hanover Corp.
Hanover Compressor Company, 59 215–17
Hanover Direct, Inc., 36 262–65
Hanover Foods Corporation, 35 211–14
Hanover Insurance Company, **63** 29
Hansa Linie, **26** 279–80
Hansen Natural Corporation, 31 242–45; 76 171–74 (upd.)
Hansgrohe AG, 56 149–52
Hansol Paper Co., **63** 315–16
Hanson Building Materials America Inc., 60 164–66
Hanson Industries, **44** 257
Hanson PLC, III 501–03; 7 207–10 (upd.); 30 228–32 (upd.)
Hansvedt Industries Inc., **25** 195
Hanwha Group, 62 172–75
Hapag-Lloyd AG, 6 397–99
Happy Air Exchangers Ltd., **21** 499
Happy Kids Inc., 30 233–35
Haralambos Beverage Corporation, **11** 451
Harbert Corporation, 14 222–23
HARBIN Samick Corp., **56** 300
Harbison-Walker Refractories Company, 24 207–09
Harbor Group, **41** 262–63
Harborlite Corporation, *see* Alleghany Corp.
Harbour Group Industries, Inc., 90 226–29
Harco, Inc., **37** 31
Harcourt Brace and Co., 12 223–26
Harcourt Brace Jovanovich, Inc., IV 622–24
Harcourt General, Inc., 20 283–87 (upd.)
Harcros Investment Trust Ltd. *see* Harrisons & Crosfield PLC.
Hard E Beverage Co., **75** 166
Hard Rock Cafe International, Inc., 12 227–29; 32 241–45 (upd.)
Hardee's Food Systems Inc., **15** 345; **19** 93; **23** 505; **27** 16–18; **46** 98
Hardin Stockton, **21** 96
Harding Lawson Associates Group, Inc., 16 258–60
Hardinge Inc., 25 193–95
Hardware Wholesalers Inc. *see* Do it Best Corp.
Hardy Oil & Gas, **34** 75
HARIBO GmbH & Co. KG, 44 216–19
Harima Shipbuilding & Engineering Co., Ltd., *see* Ishikawajima-Harima Heavy Industries Co., Ltd.
Harkins Amusement Enterprises, Inc., 94 227–31
Harland and Wolff Holdings plc, 19 197–200
Harland Clarke Holdings Corporation, 94 232–35 (upd.)
Harlem Globetrotters International, Inc., 61 122–24
Harlequin Enterprises Limited, 52 153–56
Harley-Davidson, Inc., 7 211–14; 25 196–200 (upd.)
Harleysville Group Inc., 37 183–86
Harman International Industries Inc., 15 213–15
Harman Oilgear Ltd. *see* The Oilgear Co.
Harmon Industries, Inc., 25 201–04 *see also* General Electric Co.
Harmonic Inc., 43 221–23
Harmony Gold Mining Company Limited, 63 182–85
Harmsworth Publishing, *see* Daily Mail and General Trust plc.
Harnischfeger Industries, Inc., 8 241–44; 38 224–28 (upd.)
Harold's Stores, Inc., 22 248–50
Harp Lager Ltd., **15** 442; **35** 395, 397
Harper Group Inc., 17 216–19
Harper House, Inc. *see* Day Runner, Inc.
HarperCollins Publishers, 15 216–18
Harpers, Inc., **12** 298; **48** 245
Harpo Inc., 28 173–75; 66 172–75 (upd.)
Harrah's Entertainment, Inc., 16 261–63; 43 224–28 (upd.)
Harrell Construction Group, LLC, **75** 346
Harris & Harris Group, **59** 12
Harris Adacom Corporation B.V., **21** 239
Harris Bankcorp, **46** 55
Harris Corporation, II 37–39; 20 288–92 (upd.); 78 142–48 (upd.)
Harris InfoSource International, Inc., **61** 83
Harris Interactive Inc., 41 196–99; 92 148–53 (upd.)
Harris Manufacturing Company, **25** 464
Harris Moran Seeds Inc. *see* Vilmorin Clause et Cie.
Harris Pharmaceuticals Ltd., **11** 208
Harris Publishing *see* Bernard C. Harris Publishing Company, Inc.
The Harris Soup Company (Harry's Fresh Foods),92 154–157
Harris Teeter Inc., 23 260–62; 72 163–66 (upd.)
Harrison Salinson *see* Posterscope Worldwide.
Harrisons & Crosfield plc, III 696–700 *see also* Elementis plc.
Harrods Holdings, 47 171–74
Harron Communications Corporation, **52** 9
Harry and David *see* Bear Creek Corp.
Harry London Candies, Inc., 70 110–12
Harry N. Abrams, Inc., 58 152–55
Harry Winston Inc., 45 184–87
Harry's Farmers Market Inc., 23 263–66 *see also* Whole Foods Market, Inc.
Harry's Fresh Foods *see* The Harris Soup Company (Harry's Fresh Foods)
Harsco Corporation, 8 245–47 *see also* United Defense Industries, Inc.
Hart Schaffner & Marx *see* Hartmarx Corp.
Harte-Hanks Communications, Inc., 17 220–22; 63 186–89 (upd.)
Hartford Financial Services Group, **41** 64
Hartford Group, **63** 47
Hartford Life International Ltd., **63** 179
Hartford National Corporation, *see* Shawmut National Corp.
Hartmann & Braun, *see* Mannesmann AG.
Hartmann Elektronik GmbH, **61** 287
Hartmann Fibre, **12** 377
Hartmann Luggage, *see* Lenox, Inc.
Hartmarx Corporation, 8 248–50; 32 246–50 (upd.)
The Hartstone Group plc, 14 224–26
The Hartz Mountain Corporation, 12 230–32; 46 220–23 (upd.)
Harvard Private Capital Group Inc., **26** 500, 502
Harvard Sports, Inc., *see* Escalade, Inc.
Harvard Ventures, **25** 358
Harvest Partners, Inc., **40** 300; **52** 139
Harvest States Cooperative, **64** 307
Harvey & Thompson, **61** 53
Harvey Hotel Corporation, **23** 71, 73
Harvey Norman Holdings Ltd., 56 153–55
Harveys Casino Resorts, 27 199–201 *see also* Harrah's Entertainment, Inc.
Harwood Homes, **31** 386
Harza Engineering Company, 14 227–28
Has.net, **48** 402
Hasbro, Inc., III 504–06; 16 264–68 (upd.); 43 229–34 (upd.)
Haskel International, Inc., 59 218–20
Haslemere Estates, **26** 420
Hassenfeld Brothers Inc. *see* Hasbro, Inc.
Hastings Entertainment, Inc., 29 229–31
Hastings Manufacturing Company, 56 156–58
Hatch Grinding, **29** 86, 88
Hatfield Jewelers, **30** 408

Hatteras Yachts Inc., **45** 175
Hattori Seiko Co., Ltd. *see* Seiko Corp.
HAULOTTE, **51** 295
Hauni Maschinenbau AG, **60** 193
Hauser, Inc., 46 224–27
Hausted, Inc., **29** 451
Havas, SA, 10 345–48; 33 178–82 (upd.) *see also* Vivendi Universal Publishing
Haverty Furniture Companies, Inc., 31 246–49
Havertys, **39** 174
Haviland Candy Co., **15** 325
Haw Par Corporation, **56** 362
Hawaii World, **62** 276
Hawaiian Airlines Inc., 22 251–53 (upd.) *see also* HAL Inc.
Hawaiian Electric Industries, Inc., 9 274–77
Hawaiian Trust Company *see* Bank of Hawaii Corp.
Hawaiian Tug & Barge, *see* Hawaiian Electric Industries, Inc.
Hawk Corporation, 59 221–23
Hawk Model Co., **51** 368
Hawker Siddeley Group Public Limited Company, III 507–10
Hawkeye Holdings LLC, 86 246–49
Hawkins Chemical, Inc., 16 269–72
Haworth Inc., 8 251–52; 39 205–08 (upd.)
Haxton Foods Inc., **21** 155
Hay Group, **42** 329–30
Hay House, Inc., 93 241–45
Hayel Saeed Anam Group of Cos., 92 158–61
Hayes Aircraft Corp., **54** 283
Hayes Corporation, 24 210–14
Hayes Lemmerz International, Inc., 27 202–04
Hayes Microcomputer Products, **9** 515
Hayes Wheel Company, *see* Kelsey-Hayes Group of Companies
Haynes International, Inc., 88 163–66
Haynes Publishing Group P.L.C., 71 169–71
Hays plc, 27 205–07; 78 149–53 (upd.)
Hazel-Atlas Glass Co., **15** 128
Hazelden Foundation, 28 176–79
Hazeltine, Inc., *see* Emerson.
Hazlenut Growers of Oregon, *see* Diamond of California.
Hazleton Laboratories Corp., **30** 151
Hazlewood Foods plc, 32 251–53
Hazzard and Associates, **34** 248
HBO *see* Home Box Office Inc.
HBOS, **71** 324–26
HCA—The Healthcare Company, 35 215–18 (upd.)
HCG *see* Harrell Construction Group, LLC.
HCI *see* Holland Chemical International.
HCI Construction, **61** 125, 127
HCI Direct, Inc., 55 196–98
HCI Distribution Company, **61** 125–26
HCR Manor Care, *see* Manor Care, Inc.
HCS Technology, **26** 496–97
HDI (Haftpflichtverband der Deutschen Industrie Versicherung auf Gegenseitigkeit V.a.G.), 53 159–63
HDM Worldwide Direct, **16** 168 *see also* Euro RSCG Worldwide S.A.
HDOS Enterprises, 72 167–69
HdP *see* Holding di Partecipazioni Industriali S.p.A.
HDR Inc., 48 203–05
HDS *see* Heartland Express, Inc.
Head N.V., 55 199–201
Head Sportswear International, **15** 368; **43** 374
Heads and Threads, *see* Alleghany Corp.
Headwaters Incorporated, 56 159–62
Headway Corporate Resources, Inc., 40 236–38
Headway Technologies, Inc., **49** 392–93
Healing Arts Publishing, Inc., **41** 177
Healix Health Services Inc., **48** 310
Health and Diet Group, **29** 212
Health Care & Retirement Corporation, 22 254–56
Health Communications, Inc., 72 170–73
Health Development Corp., **46** 432
Health Maintenance Organization of Pennsylvania *see* U.S. Healthcare, Inc.
Health Management Associates, Inc., 56 163–65
Health-Mor Inc. *see* HMI Industries.
Health O Meter Products Inc., 14 229–31
Health Plan of America, **11** 379
Health Risk Management, Inc., 24 215–17
Health Services Capital Corporation, **64** 27
Health Systems International, Inc., 11 174–76
Healthcare, L.L.C., **29** 412
Healthcare Products Holdings, Inc., **70** 142
HealthCare USA, **59** 139
HealthCo International, Inc., **19** 290
Healthdyne, Inc., *see* Matria Healthcare, Inc.
HealthExtras, Inc., 75 185–87
Healthmagic, Inc., **29** 412
HealthMarkets, Inc., 88 167–72 (upd.)
HealthRider Corporation, **38** 238
HealthRite, Inc., **45** 209
Healthshares L.L.C, *see* Nichols Research Corp.
Healthsource Inc., *see* CIGNA Corp.
HealthSouth Corporation, 14 232–34; 33 183–86 (upd.)
Healthtex, Inc., 17 223–25 *see also* VF Corp.
HealthTrust, **III** 80; **15** 112; **35** 215, 217
Hearing Aid Specialists Pty Limited, **56** 338
The Hearst Corporation, IV 625–27; 19 201–04 (upd.); 46 228–32 (upd.)
Heartland Components, *see* Illinois Tool Works Inc.
Heartland Express, Inc., 18 225–27
Heartland Homes, Inc., **41** 19
Heartland Industrial Partners L.P., **41** 94
Heartland Securities Corp., **32** 145
The Heat Group, 53 164–66
Heatcraft Inc., *see* Lennox International Inc.
Heatilator Inc., *see* HNI Corp.
Heating & Cooling Supply, Inc., **52** 398–99
Hebdo Mag International, Inc. *see* Trader Classified Media N.V.
Hebei Hualong F&N Industry Group, **75** 288
Hebei Longteng Paper Corporation, **63** 316
Hechinger Company, 12 233–36
Heckett Technology Services Inc., *see* Harsco Corp.
Heckler & Koch GmbH, *see* British Aerospace plc.
Hecla Mining Company, 20 293–96
Hede Nielsen A/S, **47** 219
Heekin Can Inc., 13 254–56 *see also* Ball Corp.
Heelys, Inc., 87 213–216
Heery International, Inc., 58 156–59
Hees International Bancorp Inc. *see* Brascan Corp.
Hefei Rongshida Group Corporation, *see* Maytag Corp.
Hegenscheidt-MFD GmbH & Co. KG, **53** 352
HEI Diversified, Inc., *see* Hawaiian Electric Industries, Inc.
HEICO Corporation, 30 236–38
Heide Park, **55** 378
Heidelberger Druckmaschinen AG, 40 239–41
Heidelberger Zement AG, 31 250–53
Heidemij *see* Arcadis NV.
Heidi Bakery, *see* Giant Food LLC.
Heidrick & Struggles International, Inc., 28 180–82
Heijmans N.V., 66 176–78
Heil Company, **28** 103
Heileman Brewing Co *see* G. Heileman Brewing Co.
Heilig-Meyers Company, 14 235–37; 40 242–46 (upd.)
Heineken N.V., I 256–58; 13 257–59 (upd.); 34 200–04 (upd.); 90 230–36 (upd.)
Heinrich Bauer North America, **7** 42–43
Heinrich Bauer Verlag, **23** 85–86
Heinrich Deichmann-Schuhe GmbH & Co. KG, 88 173–77
Heinrich Koppers GmbH, **IV** 89
Heinz Co *see* H.J. Heinz Co.
Heinz Deichert KG, **11** 95
Heinz Italia S.p.A., **15** 221
Heitman Properties, **60** 184
HEL&P *see* Houston Electric Light & Power Co.
Helados La Menorquina S.A., **22** 515
Helen of Troy Corporation, 18 228–30
Helena Rubenstein, Inc., *see* L'Oréal.
Helene Curtis Industries, Inc., 8 253–54; 28 183–85 (upd.) *see also* Unilever PLC.

Helikopter Services Group AS, **67** 102
Heliotrope Studios, Inc., **39** 396
Helix Energy Solutions Group, Inc., **81 173–77**
Hella KGaA Hueck & Co., **66 179–83**
Hellenic Petroleum SA, **64 175–77**
Heller, Ehrman, White & McAuliffe, **41 200–02**
Heller Financial, Inc., **16** 37; **63** 165
Hellman & Friedman Capital Partners III, L.P., **57** 15
Hellman, Haas & Co. *see* Smart & Final, Inc.
Helly Hansen ASA, **25 205–07**
Helme Products, Inc., **15** 139
Helmerich & Payne, Inc., **18 231–33**
Helmsley Enterprises, Inc., **9 278–80; 39 209–12 (upd.)**
Helzberg Diamonds, **40 247–49**
Hemlo Gold Mines Inc., **9 281–82** *see also* Newmont Mining Corp.
Henderson Brothers Holdings, Inc., **37** 225
Henderson Investment, **73** 177–79
Henderson Land Development Company Ltd., **70 113–15**
Hendrick Motorsports, Inc., **89 250–53**
Henkel KGaA, **III 31–34; 34 205–10 (upd.)**
Henkel Manco Inc., **22 257–59**
Henkell & Söhnlein Sektkellereien KG, **51** 102, 105
Henley Drilling Company, *see* Nabors Industries, Inc.
The Henley Group, Inc., **III 511–12**
Henlys Group plc, **35** 63, 65
Hennes & Mauritz AB, **29 232–34**
Hennessy Company, *see* Mercantile Stores Company, Inc.
Henningsen Foods, Inc., **57** 202, 204
Henry Boot plc, **76 175–77**
Henry Broderick, Inc., **21** 96
Henry Crown and Company, **91 233–36**
Henry Dreyfuss Associates LLC, **88 178–82**
Henry Ford Health System, **84 183–187**
Henry Gordy International, Inc. *see* EXX Inc.
Henry Holt & Co., **IV** 622–23; **35** 451
Henry I. Siegel Co., **20** 136
Henry J. Kaiser Company, Ltd., **28** 200
Henry Lee Company, *see* Smart & Final, Inc.
Henry Modell & Company Inc., **32 263–65**
Henry Pratt Company, **7** 30–31
Henry S. Miller Companies, **21** 257
Henry Schein, Inc., **31 254–56; 70 116–19 (upd.)**
Henry Willis & Co. *see* Willis Corroon Group Plc.
Hensel Phelps Construction Company, **72 174–77**
Hensley & Company, **64 178–80**
HEPCO *see* Hokkaido Electric Power Company Inc.
Hepworth plc, **44** 438
Her Majesty's Stationery Office, **7 215–18**
Heraclio Fournier S.A., **62** 383–84
Heraeus Holding GmbH, **IV 98–100; 54 159–63 (upd.)**
Heraeus Surgical, Inc., **67** 228
Herald Media, Inc., **91 237–41**
Herald Press, Inc., *see* Engraph, Inc.
Herbalife Ltd., **17 226–29; 41 203–06 (upd.); 92 162–67 (upd.)**
Herbert Clough Inc., *see* General Re Corp.
Herby's Foods, **36** 163
Herco Technology, **IV** 680
Hercules Inc., **I 343–45; 22 260–63 (upd.); 66 184–88 (upd.)**
Hercules Offshore Drilling, **28** 347–48
Hercules Technology Growth Capital, Inc., **87 217–220**
Hereford Paper and Allied Products Ltd., *see* Sealed Air Corp.
Heritage House of America Inc. *see* Humana Inc.
Heritage Media Group, **25** 418
Heritage Springfield, **14** 245
Heritage 21 Construction, **60** 56
Herley Industries, Inc., **33 187–89**
Herman Goelitz, Inc., **28 186–88** *see also* Jelly Belly Candy Co.
Herman Miller, Inc., **8 255–57; 77 180–86 (upd.)**
Herman's World of Sports, **15** 470 *see* Gateway Corporation Ltd.
Hermès International S.A., **14 238–40; 34 211–14 (upd.)**
Hermosillo, **51** 389
Héroux-Devtek Inc., **69 205–07**
Herr Foods Inc., **84 188–191**
Herradura *see* Grupo Industrial Herradura, S.A. de C.V.
Herrick, Waddell & Reed *see* Waddell & Reed, Inc.
Herschend Family Entertainment Corporation, **73 173–76**
Hershey Foods Corporation, **II 510–12; 15 219–22 (upd.); 51 156–60 (upd.)**
F.N. Herstal *see* Groupe Herstal S.A.
Hertie Waren- und Kaufhaus GmbH, **V 72–74**
The Hertz Corporation, **9 283–85; 33 190–93 (upd.)**
Hertz-Penske Leasing *see* Penske Corp.
Hervillier, **27** 188
Heska Corporation, **39 213–16**
Hespeler Hockey Inc., **22** 204
Hess *see* Amerada Hess Corp.
Hess Department Stores Inc., **16** 61–62; **41** 343; **50** 107
Hesse Newman & Co. AG, **72** 21
Hesston Corporation, **22** 380
Hetteen Hoist & Derrick *see* Polaris Industries Inc.
Heublein Inc., **I 259–61**
Heuer *see* TAG Heuer International SA.
Hewden Stuart PLC *see* Finning International Inc.
Hewitt Associates, Inc., **77 187–90**
Hewlett-Packard Company, **III 142–43; 6 237–39 (upd.); 28 189–92 (upd.); 50 222–30 (upd.)**
Hexal AG, **69 208–10**
Hexagon AB, **78 154–57**
Hexalon, **26** 420
Hexcel Corporation, **28 193–95**
Heyer-Schulte, **26** 286
Heytesbury Party Ltd., **34** 422
HFC *see* Household Finance Corp.
HFS Inc., **21** 97; **22** 54, 56; **53** 275
HG Hawker Engineering Co. Ltd. *see* Hawker Siddeley Group PLC.
HGCC *see* Hysol Grafil Composite Components Co.
HH Finch Ltd., **38** 501
HI *see* Houston Industries Inc.
Hi-Bred Corn Company, *see* Pioneer Hi-Bred International, Inc.
Hi-Flier, Inc. *see* EXX Inc.
Hi-Lo Automotive, Inc., **26** 348–49
Hibbett Sporting Goods, Inc., **26 189–91; 70 120–23 (upd.)**
Hibbing Taconite Company, **62** 74
Hibernia Corporation, **37 187–90**
Hichens Harrison Ltd *see* Sanlam Ltd.
Hickory Farms, Inc., **17 230–32**
Hickory Specialties, Inc., **63** 69, 71
Hickorycraft, *see* Masco Corp.
HickoryTech Corporation, **92 168–71**
Hicks & Greist, **6** 40
Hicks, Muse, Tate & Furst, Inc., **24** 106; **30** 220; **36** 423; **55** 202
Hicksgas Gifford, Inc., **6** 529
Hickson International PLC *see* Arch Chemicals Inc.
Hickson Kerley *see* Tessenderlo Group.
Hidden Creek Industries, Inc., *see* Onex Corp.
HiFi Buys, **30** 465
Higgs International Ltd., **51** 130
High Falls Brewing Company LLC, **74 144–47**
High Integrity Systems, **51** 16
High Retail System Co. *see* Takashimaya Co., Ltd.
High River Limited Partnership, **73** 259
High Tech Computer Corporation, **81 178–81**
Highgate Hotels, Inc., **21** 93
Highland Distillers Ltd., **60** 355
Highland Gold Ltd., **63** 182, 184
Highland Superstores, **23** 51–52
Highland Telephone Company, **6** 334
Highlander Publications, **38** 307–08
Highmark Inc., **27 208–11**
Highsmith Inc., **60 167–70**
Highteam Public Relations Co. Ltd., **60** 143
Highveld Steel and Vanadium Corporation Limited, **59 224–27**
Hilo Hattie *see* Pomare Ltd.
Hilb, Rogal & Hobbs Company, **77 191–94**
Hildebrandt International, **29 235–38**
Hill & Knowlton Inc. *see* WPP Group PLC.

Hill Engineering *see* Comtech Telecommunications Corp.
Hill 50 Ltd., **63** 182, 184
Hill-Rom Company *see* Hillenbrand Industries, Inc.
Hill's Pet Nutrition, Inc., 27 212–14
Hillard Oil and Gas Company, Inc., **11** 523
Hillenbrand Industries, Inc., 10 349–51; 75 188–92 (upd.)
Hillerich & Bradsby Company, Inc., 51 161–64
The Hillhaven Corporation, 14 241–43 *see also* Vencor, Inc.
Hillos GmbH, **53** 169
Hills & Dales Railway Co. *see* Dayton Power & Light Co.
Hills Brothers Inc. *see* Nestlé S.A.
Hills Pet Products, *see* Colgate-Palmolive Co.
Hills Stores Company, 13 260–61
Hillsborough Holdings Corporation *see* Walter Industries, Inc.
Hillsdale Machine & Tool Company, *see* Tecumseh Products Co.
Hillsdown Holdings, PLC, II 513–14; 24 218–21 (upd.)
Hilti AG, 53 167–69
Hilton Active Apparel, *see* K2 Inc.
Hilton Group plc, III 91–93; 19 205–08 (upd.); 62 176–79 (upd.); 49 191–95 (upd.)
Hindalco Industries Limited *see* Aditya Birla Group
Hindustan Lever Limited, 79 198–201
Hines Horticulture, Inc., 49 196–98
Hino Motors, Ltd., 7 219–21; 21 271–74 (upd.)
HIP Health Plan, **22** 425
Hipercor, S.A., **V** 52; **26** 129
HiPP GmbH & Co. Vertrieb KG, 88 183–88
Hiram Walker Resources Ltd., I 262–64
Hiram Walker-Consumers' Home Ltd. *see* Consumers' Gas Company Ltd.
Hiram Walker-Gooderham & Worts Ltd., **29** 18
Hire-Purchase Company of Ireland, **16** 13; **43** 7
Hiroshima Yakult Co., **25** 449
The Hirsh Company, *see* Knape & Vogt Manufacturing Co.
Hirth-Krause Company *see* Wolverine World Wide Inc.
Hirz, **25** 85
Hispanic Broadcasting Corporation, 35 219–22
Hispanoil *see* Hispanica de Petroleos.
History Book Club, *see* Book-of-the-Month Club.
Hit de Venezuela, **54** 73
HIT Entertainment PLC, 40 250–52
Hit or Miss *see* The TJX Companies, Inc.
Hitachi, Ltd., I 454–55; 12 237–39 (upd.); 40 253–57 (upd.)
Hitachi Metals, Ltd., IV 101–02
Hitachi Zosen Corporation, III 513–14; 53 170–73 (upd.)
Hitchiner Manufacturing Co., Inc., 23 267–70
Hi3G, **63** 208
HL&P *see* Houston Lighting and Power Co.
HMI Industries, Inc., 17 233–35
HMO-PA *see* U.S. Healthcare, Inc.
HMSHost Corp., **49** 31; **63** 322
HMV Group plc, 59 228–30
HNI Corporation, 74 148–52 (upd.)
Ho-Chunk Inc., 61 125–28
Hoan Products Ltd. *see* Lifetime Hoan Corp.
HOB Entertainment, Inc., 37 191–94
Hobart Corporation *see* KitchenAid, Inc; Whirlpool Corp.
Hobby Lobby Stores Inc., 80 139–42
Hobie Cat Company, 94 236–39
Hochtief AG, 33 194–97; 88 189–94 (upd.)
The Hockey Company, 34 215–18; 70 124–26 (upd.)
Hocking Glass Company, *see* Anchor Hocking Glassware.
Hockleys Professional Limited, **55** 281
Hodes *see* Bernard Hodes Group Inc.
Hodgart Consulting *see* Hildebrandt International.
Hodgson Mill, Inc., 88 195–98
Hoechst AG, I 346–48; 18 234–37 (upd.)
Hoechst Celanese Corporation, 13 262–65
Hoenig Group Inc., 41 207–09
Hoesch AG, IV 103–06
Hofbräubierzentrale GmbH Saarbrücken, **41** 222
Hoffman Corporation, 78 158–12
Hoffman Enclosures Inc., **26** 361, 363
Hoffmann-La Roche & Co *see* F. Hoffmann-La Roche & Co.
Hoffritz, *see* Lifetime Brands, Inc.
Hofmann Herbold & Partner, **34** 249
Hogan & Hartson L.L.P., 44 220–23
Hogatron, **60** 364
Hogue Cellars, **50** 520
Hohner *see* Matth. Hohner AG.
Hojgaard & Schultz, **38** 436
HOK Group, Inc., 59 231–33
Hokkaido Electric Power Company Inc. (HEPCO), V 635–37; 58 160–63 (upd.)
Hokuriku Electric Power Company, V 638–40
Holberg Industries, Inc., 36 266–69
Holcemca B.V., **51** 29
Holcim, Ltd., **51** 27, 29; **59** 111, 115
Holco BV, **41** 12
Hold Everything, *see* Williams-Sonoma, Inc.
Holden Ltd., 62 180–83
Holden Meehan *see* Bradford & Bingley PLC.
Holderbank Financière Glaris Ltd., III 701–02 *see also* Holnam Inc
Holding di Partecipazioni Industriali S.p.A., **52** 120, 122
N.V. Holdingmaatschappij De Telegraaf, 23 271–73
Holec Control Systems, **26** 496
Holes-Webway Company, **40** 44
Holga, Inc., *see* HNI Corp.
Holiday Corp., **16** 263; **38** 76; **43** 226
Holiday Inns, Inc., III 94–95 *see also* Promus Companies, Inc.
Holiday Rambler Corporation, *see* Harley-Davidson, Inc.
Holiday Retirement Corp., 87 221–223
Holiday RV Superstores, Incorporated, 26 192–95
Holland & Holland, **49** 84
Holland & Knight LLP, 60 171–74
Holland America Line *see* Carnival Corp.
Holland Burgerville USA, 44 224–26
Holland Casino, **23** 229
Holland Chemical International, **59** 391
Holland Graphic Occasions, **64** 226
The Holland Group, Inc., 82 174–77
Holland Motor Express, *see* TNT Freightways Corp.
Holland Studio Craft, **38** 402
Holland Sweetener Company V.O.F. *see* Tosoh Corp.
Hollander Home Fashions Corp., 67 207–09
Holley Performance Products Inc., 52 157–60
Hollinger Hardware Limited *see* Home Hardware Stores Ltd.
Hollinger International Inc., 24 222–25; 62 184–88 (upd.)
Hollingsead International, Inc., **36** 158–60
Hollister Company, **75** 7
Holloway-Staubach Corporation *see* The Staubach Co.
Holly Corporation, 12 240–42
Holly Sugar Company *see* Imperial Holly Corp.
Hollywood Casino Corporation, 21 275–77
Hollywood Entertainment Corporation, 25 208–10
Hollywood Media Corporation, 58 164–68
Hollywood Park, Inc., 20 297–300
Hollywood Park Race Track, **29** 118
Hollywood Pictures, *see* Walt Disney Co.
Holme Roberts & Owen LLP, 28 196–99
Holmen AB, 52 161–65 (upd.)
Holmes International *see* Miller Industries, Inc.
Holnam Inc., 8 258–60; 39 217–20 (upd.)
Holophane Corporation, 19 209–12
Holson Burnes Group, Inc., 14 244–45
Holsten Brauerei AG, **35** 256, 258
Holt and Bugbee Company, 66 189–91
Holt, Rinehart and Winston, Inc., *see* Harcourt Brace and Co.
Holt's Cigar Holdings, Inc., 42 176–78
Holtzbrinck *see* Verlagsgruppe Georg von Holtzbrinck.
Holvis AG, **15** 229

Holyman Sally Ltd., **29** 431
Homart Development Co., **57** 156
Homasote Company, 72 178–81
Home and Community Care, Inc., **43** 46
Home Box Office Inc., 7 222–24; 23 274–77 (upd.); 76 178–82 (upd.)
Home Builders Supply, Inc. *see* Scotty's, Inc.
Home Choice Holdings, Inc., **33** 366–67
The Home Depot, Inc., V 75–76; 18 238–40 (upd.)
Home Entertainment of Texas, Inc., **30** 466
Home Hardware Stores Ltd., 62 189–91
Home Insurance Company, III 262–64
Home Interiors & Gifts, Inc., 55 202–04
Home Office Reference Laboratory, Inc., **22** 266
Home Products International, Inc., 55 205–07
Home Properties Co., Inc., **21** 95
Home Properties of New York, Inc., 42 179–81
Home Quarters Warehouse, Inc., *see* Hechinger Co.
Home Retail Group plc, 91 242–46
Home Savings of America, **28** 167; **47** 160
The Home School, Inc., **41** 111
Home Shopping Network, Inc., V 77–78; 25 211–15 (upd.) *see also* HSN.
Home Telephone Company *see* Rochester Telephone Corp.
Home Vision Entertainment Inc., **31** 339–40
HomeBase, Inc., 33 198–201 (upd.)
HomeBuyers Preferred, Inc., **51** 210
HomeChef, Inc. *see* Viking Range Corp.
HomeClub Inc. *see* HomeBase, Inc.
Homegrocer.com Inc., **38** 223
Homelite, **21** 175
Homemade Brand *see* United Dairy Farmers, Inc.
Homemakers Furniture *see* John M. Smyth Co.
HomeMax, Inc., **41** 20
Homes By Oakwood, Inc., **15** 328
Homeserve.net Ltd., **46** 72
Homestake Mining Company, 12 243–45; 38 229–32 (upd.)
Hometown Auto Retailers, Inc., 44 227–29
HomeTown Buffet, Inc. *see* Buffets, Inc
Homette Corporation, **30** 423
HomeVestors of America, Inc., 77 195–98
Homewood Suites, *see* Promus Companies, Inc.
Homex *see* Desarrolladora Homex, S.A. de C.V.
Hon Hai Precision Industry Co., Ltd., 59 234–36
HON Industries Inc., 13 266–69 *see* HNI Corp.
Honda Giken Kogyo Kabushiki Kaisha *see* Honda Motor Company Ltd.
Honda Motor Company Limited, I 174–76; 10 352–54 (upd.); 29 239–42 (upd.)
Honey Bear Tree *see* Furth Pharmacy. Inc.
Honeywell Inc., II 40–43; 12 246–49 (upd.); 50 231–35 (upd.)
Hong Kong and China Gas Company Ltd., 73 177–79
Hong Kong Dragon Airlines Ltd., 66 192–94
Hong Kong Fortune, **62** 63
Hong Kong Island Line Co., **IV** 718
Hong Kong Mass Transit Railway Corp., **19** 111
Hong Kong Ming Wah Shipping Co., **52** 80
Hong Kong Resort Co., **IV** 718; **38** 320
Hong Kong Telecommunications Ltd., 6 319–21 *see also* Cable & Wireless HKT.
Hong Kong Telephone Company, **47** 177
Hong Leong Group, **26** 3, 5; **71** 231
Hongkong & Kowloon Wharf & Godown Company, **20** 312
Hongkong and Shanghai Banking Corporation Limited, II 296–99 *see also* HSBC Holdings plc.
Hongkong Electric Holdings Ltd., 6 498–500; 23 278–81 (upd.)
Hongkong Land Holdings Ltd., IV 699–701; 47 175–78 (upd.)
Honolua Plantation Land Company, Inc., **29** 308
Honshu Paper Co., Ltd., IV 284–85 *see also* Oji Paper Co., Ltd.
Hood Rubber Company, **15** 488–89
Hoogovens *see* Koninklijke Nederlandsche Hoogovens en Staalfabricken NV.
Hooker Corp., **19** 324
Hooker Furniture Corporation, 80 143–46
Hooper Holmes, Inc., 22 264–67
Hoorcomfort Nederland B.V., **56** 338
Hoosier Insurance Company, **51** 39
Hoosier Park L.P., **29** 118
Hooters of America, Inc., 18 241–43; 69 211–14 (upd.)
The Hoover Company, 12 250–52; 40 258–62 (upd.)
Hoover Treated Wood Products, Inc., *see* Ply Gem Industries Inc.
HOP, LLC, 80 147–50
Hopkinsons Group *see* Carbo PLC.
Hopkinton LNG Corp., **14** 126
Hopper Soliday and Co. Inc., *see* Dauphin Deposit Corp.
Hops Restaurant Bar and Brewery, 46 233–36
Hopson Development Holdings Ltd., 87 224–227
Horace Mann Educators Corporation, 22 268–70; 90 237–40 (upd.)
Horizon Air Industries, Inc. *see* Alaska Air Group, Inc.
Horizon Corporation, *see* MAXXAM Inc.
Horizon Industries, *see* Mohawk Industries, Inc.
Horizon Lamps, Inc., **48** 299
Horizon Organic Holding Corporation, 37 195–99
Horizon/CMS Healthcare Corp., **25** 111, 457; **33** 185
Horizons Laitiers, **25** 85
Hormel Foods Corporation, 18 244–47 (upd.); 54 164–69 (upd.)
Horne's, **16** 62
Horsehead Industries, Inc., 51 165–67
Horseshoe Gaming Holding Corporation, 62 192–95
Horsham Corp. *see* TrizecHahn.
Horst Breuer GmbH, **20** 363
Horten, **47** 107; **50** 117, 119
Hortifrut, S.A., **62** 154
Horton Homes, Inc., 25 216–18
Horween Leather Company, 83 183-186
Hoshienu Pharmaceutical Co. Ltd., **58** 134
Hoshino Gakki Co. Ltd., 55 208–11
Hosiery Corporation International *see* HCI Direct, Inc.
Hospal SA, **49** 156
Hospira, Inc., 71 172–74
Hospital Central Services, Inc., 56 166–68
Hospital Corporation of America, III 78–80 *see also* HCA - The Healthcare Co.
Hospital Cost Consultants, **11** 113
Hospital Management Associates, Inc. *see* Health Management Associates, Inc.
Hospital Specialty Co., **37** 392
Hospitality Franchise Systems, Inc., 11 177–79 *see also* Cendant Corp.
Hospitality Worldwide Services, Inc., 26 196–98
Hosposable Products, Inc. *see* Wyant Corp.
Hoss's Steak and Sea House Inc., 68 196–98
Host America Corporation, 79 202–06
Hot Dog Construction Co., **12** 372
Hot Dog on a Stick *see* HDOS Enterprises.
Hot Sam Co. *see* Mrs. Fields' Original Cookies, Inc.
Hot Shoppes Inc. *see* Marriott.
Hot Stuff Foods, 85 171–74
Hot Topic Inc., 33 202–04; 86 190–94 (upd.)
Hotel Properties Ltd., 71 175–77
Hotel Reservations Network, Inc., **47** 420
Hotels By Pleasant, **62** 276
HotJobs.com, Ltd. *see* Yahoo! Inc.
HotRail Inc., **36** 124
HotWired, **45** 200
Houbigant, **37** 270
Houchens Industries Inc., 51 168–70
Houghton Mifflin Company, 10 355–57; 36 270–74 (upd.)
Houlihan's Restaurant Group, **25** 546
House of Blues, **32** 241, 244
House of Fabrics, Inc., 21 278–80 *see also* Jo-Ann Stores, Inc.
House of Fraser PLC, 45 188–91 *see also* Harrods Holdings.

House of Miniatures, **12** 264
House of Prince A/S, 80 151–54
Household International, Inc., II 417–20; 21 281–86 (upd.) *see also* HSBC Holdings plc.
Housing Development Finance Corporation, **20** 313
Housmex Inc., **23** 171
Houston Airport Leather Concessions LLC, **58** 369
Houston Electric Light & Power Company, **44** 368
Houston Industries Incorporated, V 641–44 *see also* Reliant Energy Inc.
Houston Oil & Minerals Corp., *see* Seagull Energy Corp.
Houston Pipe Line Company, **45** 21
Hovnanian Enterprises, Inc., 29 243–45; 89 254–59 (upd.)
Howard B. Stark Candy Co., **15** 325
Howard Flint Ink Company, *see* Flint Ink Corp.
Howard Hughes Corporation, **63** 341
Howard Hughes Medical Institute, 39 221–24
Howard Johnson International, Inc., 17 236–39; 72 182–86 (upd.)
Howard Research and Development Corporation, **15** 412, 414
Howard Schultz & Associates, Inc., **73** 266
Howard, Smith & Levin, **40** 126
Howden *see* Alexander Howden Group.
Howe & Fant, Inc., **23** 82
Howmedica, **29** 455
Howmet Corporation, 12 253–55 *see also* Alcoa Inc.
Hoyle Products, **62** 384
HP *see* Hewlett-Packard Co.
HPI Health Care Services, **49** 307–08
HQ Global Workplaces, Inc., **47** 331
HQ Office International, *see* Office Depot Inc.
HRB Business Services, **29** 227
HSBC Holdings plc, 12 256–58; 26 199–204 (upd.); 80 155–63 (upd.)
HSG *see* Helikopter Services Group AS.
Hsiang-Li Investment Corp., **51** 123
HSN, 64 181–85 (upd.)
HSS Hire Service Group PLC, **45** 139–41
HTH, **12** 464
HTM Goedkoop, **26** 278–79; **55** 200
Hua Bei Oxygen, **25** 82
Hua Yang Printing Holdings Co. Ltd., **60** 372
Huawei Technologies Company Ltd., 87 228–231
Hub Group, Inc., 38 233–35
Hub International Limited, 89 260–64
Hub Services, Inc., *see* Dynegy Inc.
Hubbard Broadcasting Inc., 24 226–28; 79 207–12 (upd.)
Hubbard Construction Co., **23** 332
Hubbell Inc., 9 286–87; 31 257–59 (upd.); 76 183–86 (upd.)
Huck Manufacturing Company, *see* Thiokol Corp.
The Hudson Bay Mining and Smelting Company, Limited, 12 259–61
Hudson Foods Inc., 13 270–72 *see also* Tyson Foods, Inc.
Hudson I.C.S., **58** 53
Hudson Pharmaceutical Corp., **31** 347
Hudson River Bancorp, Inc., 41 210–13
Hudson's *see* Target Corp.
Hudson's Bay Company, V 79–81; 25 219–22 (upd.); 83 187-194 (upd.)
Huf-North America, **73** 325
Huffman Manufacturing Company, *see* Huffy Corp.
Huffy Corporation, 7 225–27; 30 239–42 (upd.)
Hughes Aircraft Company, *see* GM Hughes Electronics Corp.
Hughes Electronics Corporation, 25 223–25
Hughes Helicopter, **26** 431; **46** 65
Hughes Hubbard & Reed LLP, 44 230–32
Hughes Markets, Inc., 22 271–73 *see also* Kroger Co.
Hughes Network Systems Inc., **21** 239
Hughes Space and Communications Company, **33** 47–48
Hughes Supply, Inc., 14 246–47
Hughes Tool Co. *see* Baker Hughes Inc.
Hugo Boss AG, 48 206–09
Hugo Neu Corporation, **19** 381–82
Hugo Stinnes GmbH, *see* Stinnes AG.
Huhtamäki Oyj, 64 186–88
HUK-Coburg, 58 169–73
The Hull Group, L.L.C., **51** 148
Hulman & Company, 44 233–36
Hüls A.G., I 349–50 *see also* Degussa-Hüls AG.
Hulsbeck and Furst GmbH, **73** 325
Hulton Getty, **31** 216–17
Human Services Computing, Inc. *see* Epic Systems Corp.
Humana Inc., III 81–83; 24 229–32 (upd.)
The Humane Society of the United States, 54 170–73
Humanetics Corporation, **29** 213
Humanities Software, **39** 341
Humberside Sea & Land Services, **31** 367
Humble Oil & Refining Company *see* Exxon.
Hummel International A/S, 68 199–201
Hummel Lanolin Corporation, **45** 126
Hummel-Reise, **44** 432
Hummer, Winblad Venture Partners, **36** 157; **69** 265; **74** 168
Humongous Entertainment, Inc., **31** 238–40
Humps' n Horns, **55** 312
Hunco Ltd., **IV** 640; **26** 273
Hungarian-Soviet Civil Air Transport Joint Stock Company *see* Malév Plc.
Hungarian Telephone and Cable Corp., 75 193–95
Hungry Howie's Pizza and Subs, Inc., 25 226–28
Hungry Minds, Inc. *see* John Wiley & Sons, Inc.
Hunt Consolidated, Inc., 7 228–30; 27 215–18 (upd.)
Hunt Manufacturing Company, 12 262–64
Hunt-Wesson, Inc., 17 240–42 *see also* ConAgra Foods, Inc.
Hunter Fan Company, 13 273–75
Hunting plc, 78 163–16
Huntingdon Life Sciences Group plc, 42 182–85
Huntington Bancshares Incorporated, 11 180–82; 87 232–238 (upd.)
Huntington Learning Centers, Inc., 55 212–14
Huntleigh Technology PLC, 77 199–202
Hunton & Williams, 35 223–26
Huntsman Chemical Corporation, 8 261–63
Huntstown Power Company Ltd., **64** 404
Hurd & Houghton, *see* Houghton Mifflin Co.
Huron Consulting Group Inc., 87 239–243
Huron Steel Company, Inc., *see* The Marmon Group, Inc.
Hurricane Hydrocarbons Ltd., 54 174–77
Husky Energy Inc., 47 179–82
Husky Oil Ltd., **IV** 695
Husqvarna AB, **53** 126–27
Husqvarna Forest & Garden Company, *see* White Consolidated Industries Inc.
Hussmann Corporation, **67** 299
Hussmann Distributing Co., Inc. *see* IC Industries Inc.
Hutcheson & Grundy, **29** 286
Hutchinson-Mapa, **IV** 560
Hutchinson Technology Incorporated, 18 248–51; 63 190–94 (upd.)
Hutchison Microtel, **11** 548
Hutchison Whampoa Limited, 18 252–55; 49 199–204 (upd.)
Huth Inc., **56** 230
Hüttenwerke Kayser AG, **62** 253
Huttepain, **61** 155
Huttig Building Products, Inc., 73 180–83
HVB Group, 59 237–44 (upd.)
Hvide Marine Incorporated, 22 274–76
HWI *see* Hardware Wholesalers, Inc.
Hy-Form Products, Inc., *see* Defiance, Inc.
Hy-Vee, Inc., 36 275–78
Hyatt-Clark Industries Inc., **45** 170
Hyatt Corporation, III 96–97; 16 273–75 (upd.) *see* Global Hyatt Corp.
Hyatt Legal Services, **20** 435; **29** 226
Hyco-Cascade Pty. Ltd. *see* Cascade Corp.
Hycor Biomedical Inc. *see* Stratagene Corp.
Hyde Athletic Industries, Inc., 17 243–45 *see also* Saucony Inc.
Hyde Company, A.L., *see* Danaher Corp.
Hyder plc, 34 219–21
Hydrac GmbH, **38** 300
Hydril Company, 46 237–39
Hydro-Carbon Light Company, *see* The Coleman Company, Inc.

Hydro Electric, **49** 363–64
Hydro-Electric Power Commission of Ontario, **6** 541
Hydro-Québec, 6 501–03; 32 266–69 (upd.)
Hydrocarbon Technologies, Inc., **56** 161
Hydrodynamic Cutting Services, **56** 134
Hygrade Operators Inc., **55** 20
Hylsa *see* Hojalata y Laminas S.A.
Hylsamex, S.A. de C.V., 39 225–27
Hynix Semiconductor Inc., **56** 173
Hyper Shoppes, Inc., *see* Supervalu Inc.
Hypercom Corporation, 27 219–21
Hyperion Software Corporation, 22 277–79
Hyperion Solutions Corporation, 76 187–91
HyperRoll Israel Ltd., **76** 190
Hyplains Beef, L.C., *see* Farmland Foods, Inc.
Hypo-Bank *see* Bayerische Hypotheken- und Wechsel-Bank AG.
Hyponex Corp., *see* Scotts Co.
Hyster Company, 17 246–48
Hyundai Group, III 515–17; 7 231–34 (upd.); 56 169–73 (upd.)

I

I Can't Believe It's Yogurt, Inc., **35** 121
I Pellettieri d'Italia S.p.A., **45** 342
I. Appel, **30** 23
I.B. Kleinert Rubber Company, **37** 399
I.C. Isaacs & Company, 31 260–62
I.D. Systems, Inc., **11** 444
I-DIKA Milan SRL, **12** 182
I. Feldman Co., **31** 359
I.G. Farbenindustrie AG, *see* BASF A.G.; Bayer A.G.; Hoechst A.G.
I.M. Pei & Associates *see* Pei Cobb Freed & Partners Architects LLP.
I. Magnin Inc., *see* R. H. Macy & Co., Inc.
I.N. Kote, *see* Inland Steel Industries, Inc.
I.N. Tek, *see* Inland Steel Industries, Inc.
I-X Corp., **22** 416
IAC/InterActive Corporation *see* Ticketmaster
Iacon, Inc., **49** 299, 301
IAL *see* International Aeradio Ltd.
Iams Company, 26 205–07
IAN S.A. *see* Viscofan S.A.
IAWS Group plc, 49 205–08
IBANCO, **26** 515
Ibanez *see* Hoshino Gakki Co. Ltd.
IBC Group plc, **58** 189, 191
IBC Holdings Corporation, **12** 276
IBCA *see* International Banking and Credit Analysis.
Iberdrola, S.A., 49 209–12
Iberia Líneas Aéreas De España S.A., 6 95–97; 36 279–83 (upd.); 91 247–54 (upd.)
IBERIABANK Corporation, 37 200–02
Iberpistas *see* Abertis Infraestructuras, S.A.
Iberswiss Catering *see* Iberia.
IBJ *see* The Industrial Bank of Japan Ltd.
IBM *see* International Business Machines Corp.
IBM Foods, Inc., **51** 280
IBP, Inc., II 515–17; 21 287–90 (upd.)
Ibstock Brick Ltd., 37 203–06 (upd.)
Ibstock plc, 14 248–50
IC Designs, Inc., **48** 127
IC Industries Inc., I 456–58 *see also* Whitman Corp.
ICA AB, II 639–40
ICA Fluor Daniel, S. de R.L. de C.V., **41** 148
Icahn Capital Corp., **35** 143
Icarus Consulting AG, **29** 376
ICEE-USA, *see* J & J Snack Foods Corp.
Iceland Group plc, 33 205–07 *see also* The Big Food Group plc.
Icelandair, 52 166–69
Icelandic Group hf, 81 182–85
ICF International, Inc., 28 200–04; 94 240–47 (upd.)
ICH Corporation, **19** 468
Ichikoh Industries Ltd., **26** 154
ICI *see* Imperial Chemical Industries plc.
ICL plc, 6 240–42
ICN Pharmaceuticals, Inc., 52 170–73
Icon Health & Fitness, Inc., 38 236–39
Icon International, **24** 445
iConcepts, Inc., **39** 95
Icreo Co., Ltd., **72** 125
ICS *see* International Care Services.
ICS, **26** 119
id Software, **31** 237–38; **32** 9
Idaho Candy Co. *see* Wagers Inc.
Idaho Power Company, 12 265–67
IDB Communications Group, Inc., 11 183–85
Idé *see* GiFi S.A.
Ideal Basic Industries, *see* Holnam Inc.
Ideal Corp., **23** 335
Ideal Loisirs Group, **23** 388
Idearc Inc., 90 241–44
Ideas Publishing Group, **59** 134
IDEC Pharmaceuticals Corporation *see* Biogen Idec Inc.
Idemitsu Kosan Co., Ltd., IV 434–36; 49 213–16 (upd.)
Identification Business, Inc., **18** 140
Identix Inc., 44 237–40
IDEO Inc., 65 171–73
IDEXX Laboratories, Inc., 23 282–84
IDG Books Worldwide, Inc., 27 222–24 *see also* International Data Group, Inc.
IDG Communications, Inc, *see* International Data Group, Inc.
IDI, **22** 365
IDI Temps, **34** 372
iDine Rewards Network *see* Rewards Network Inc.
IDO *see* Nippon Idou Tsushin.
Ido Bathroom Ltd, **51** 324
IdraPrince, Inc., 76 192–94
IDS Ltd., *see* American Express Co.
IDT Corporation, 34 222–24
IDX Systems Corporation, 64 189–92
IEC Electronics Corp., 42 186–88
Iecsa S.A. *see* Sideco Americana S.A.
IEL *see* Industrial Equity Ltd.
IFC Disposables, Inc., **30** 496–98
IFER Estamparia e Ferramentaria Ltda., **73** 326
IFF *see* International Flavors & Fragrances Inc.
IFIL, **27** 515; **71** 309
IFM, **25** 85
Ifö Sanitär AB, **51** 324
IG *see* Integrated Genetics.
IG Farben *see* I.G. Farbenindustrie AG.
IGA, **15** 479; **18** 6, 9
Igemar *see* Pesquera Iquique-Guanaye S.A.
iGetSmart.com, Inc. *see* Workflow Management, Inc.
Iggesund Paperboard AB, **52** 161, 164
Igloo Products Corp., 21 291–93
IGT, *see* International Game Technology.
IHC Caland N.V., 71 178–80
IHI *see* Ishikawajima-Harima Heavy Industries Co., Ltd.
IHOP Corporation, 17 249–51; 58 174–77 (upd.)
Ihr Platz GmbH + Company KG, 77 203–06
IHS Inc., 78 167–70
IIS, **26** 441
IJ Holdings Corp., **45** 173
IK Coach, Ltd., **23** 290
IKEA Group, V 82–84; 26 208–11 (upd.); 94 248–53 (upd.)
IKON Office Solutions, Inc., 50 236–39
Il Fornaio (America) Corporation, 27 225–28
Ilaco, **26** 22
ILC Dover Inc., **63** 318
ILFC *see* International Lease Finance Corp.
Ilitch Holdings Inc., 37 207–210; 86 195–200 (upd.)
Illco Toy Co. USA, **12** 496
Illinois Bell Telephone Company, 14 251–53
Illinois Central Corporation, 11 186–89
Illinois Lock Company, **48** 142
Illinois Power Company, 6 504–07 *see also* Ameren Corp.
Illinois Tool Works Inc., III 518–20; 22 280–83 (upd.); 81 186–91 (upd.)
Illumina, Inc., 93 246–49
Illuminet Holdings Inc., **47** 430
illycaffè SpA, 50 240–44
Ilwaco Telephone and Telegraph Company *see* Pacific Telecom, Inc.
ILX Resorts Incorporated, 65 174–76
Image Business Systems Corp., **11** 66
Image Entertainment, Inc., 94 254–57
Image Industries, Inc., *see* The Maxim Group.
Image Technologies Corporation, **12** 264
Imageline Inc., **25** 348
ImageTag Inc., **49** 290
Imaginarium Toy Centers, Inc., **57** 374
Imagine Entertainment, 91 255–58
Imagine Foods, Inc., 50 245–47
Imagine Manufacturing Solutions Inc., **48** 410
Imagine Technology Group, Inc., **73** 165
ImagiNet, **41** 97
Imaging Technologies, **25** 183

Imaje, S.A., **28** 104
IMAKE Software and Services, Inc., **49** 423–24
IMall Inc., **26** 441
Imasa Group, *see* ASARCO Inc.
Imasco Limited, V 401–02
Imation Corporation, 20 301–04 *see also* 3M Co.
Imatra Steel Oy Ab, 55 215–17
Imatran Voima Oy *see* Fortum Corporation
IMAX Corporation, 28 205–08; 78 171–76 (upd.)
IMC *see* Intertec Marine Corp.
IMC Fertilizer Group, Inc., 8 264–66
IMC Global Inc., **57** 149
ImClone Systems Inc., 58 178–81
IMCO Recycling, Incorporated, 32 270–73
IMED Corp., **38** 364
Imerys S.A., 40 176, **263–66 (upd.)**
Imetal S.A., IV 107–09
IMG, 78 177–80
Imhoff Industrie Holding GmbH, **53** 315
IMI plc, 9 288–89; 29 364
IMIWeb Bank, **50** 410
Imlo, **26** 22
Immeon Networks LLC, **54** 407
Immersion Corporation, **28** 245
Immobilier Batibail, **42** 152
Immucor, Inc., 81 192–96
Immunex Corporation, 14 254–56; 50 248–53 (upd.)
Imo Industries Inc., 7 235–37; 27 229–32 (upd.)
Imo Pump, **58** 67
Impala Platinum Holdings Ltd., **IV** 91–93; **63** 38–39
Impark Limited, **42** 433
IMPATH Inc., 45 192–94
Imperial Airways *see* British Overseas Airways Corp.
Imperial Business Forms, **9** 72
Imperial Chemical Industries plc, I 351–53; 50 254–58 (upd.)
Imperial Commodities Corporation *see* Deli Universal NV.
Imperial Feather Company, **19** 304
Imperial Holly Corporation, 12 268–70 *see also* Imperial Sugar Co.
Imperial Industries, Inc., 81 197–200
Imperial Metal Industries Ltd. *see* IMI plc.
Imperial Oil Limited, IV 437–39; 25 229–33 (upd.);
Imperial Packing Co. *see* Beech-Nut Nutrition Corp.
Imperial Parking Corporation, 58 182–84
Imperial Products, Inc., **62** 289
Imperial Sports, **19** 230
Imperial Sugar Company, 32 274–78 (upd.)
Imperial Tobacco Company *see* B.A.T. Industries PLC.
Imperial Tobacco Group PLC, 50 259–63
Implantes Y Sistemas Medicos, Inc., **72** 262
Implats *see* Impala Platinum Holdings Ltd.
IMPO Import Parfumerien, **48** 116
Imported Auto Parts, Inc., **15** 246
Impressions Software, **15** 455
Impulse Airlines Pty Ltd. *see* Qantas Airways Ltd.
Impulse Designs, **31** 435–36
IMRA America Inc., **48** 5
IMRS *see* Hyperion Software Corp.
IMS Health, Inc., 57 174–78
IMX Pharmaceuticals, **59** 285
In Focus Systems, Inc., 22 287–90
In-N-Out Burgers Inc., 19 213–15; 74 153–56 (upd.)
In-Sink-Erator, 66 195–98
INA Corporation *see* CIGNA Corp.
INA-Holding Schaeffler KG, **62** 129
InaCom Corporation, 13 276–78
Inalca S.p.A. *see* Cremonini S.p.A.
Inamed Corporation, 79 213–16
Incentive Group, **27** 269
Inchcape PLC, III 521–24; 16 276–80 (upd.); 50 264–68 (upd.)
INCO-Banco Indústria e Comércio de Santa Catarina, **13** 70
Inco Limited, IV 110–12; 45 195–99 (upd.)
Incon Research Inc., **41** 198
InControl Inc., **11** 460
Incredible Universe, **12** 470; **36** 387
Incyte Genomics, Inc., 52 174–77
Indel, Inc., 78 181–84
Indemnity Insurance Company *see* CIGNA Corp.
Independent Delivery Services, Inc., **37** 409
Independent Election Corp. of America, **47** 37
Independent Exhibitions Ltd., *see* Penton Media, Inc.
Independent Grocers Alliance *see* IGA.
Independent News & Media PLC, 61 129–31
Independent Print Media Group, **74** 283
Independent Stave Company, **28** 223
India Exotics, Inc., *see* Celebrity, Inc.
Indian Airlines Corporation *see* Air-India.
Indian Airlines Ltd., 46 240–42
Indian Archery and Toy Corp., *see* Escalade, Inc.
Indian Iron & Steel Company Ltd. *see* Steel Authority of India Ltd.
Indian Oil Corporation Ltd., IV 440–41; 48 210–13 (upd.)
Indiana Bell Telephone Company, Incorporated, 14 257–61
Indiana Electric Corporation, **6** 555
Indiana Energy, Inc., 27 233–36
Indiana Gaming Company, **21** 40
Indiana Gas & Water Company, **6** 556
Indiana Parts and Warehouse, **29** 86, 88
Indiana Power Company, **6** 555
Indiana Protein Technologies, **55** 233
Indiana Tube Co., **23** 250
Indianapolis Brush Electric Light & Power Company, **6** 508
Indianapolis Cablevision, **6** 508–09
Indianapolis Light and Power Company, **6** 508
Indianapolis Motor Speedway Corporation, 46 243–46
Indianapolis Power & Light Company, **6** 508–09
Indianapolis Pump and Tube Company, *see* Arvin Industries, Inc.
IndianOil Companies *see* Indian Oil Corporation Ltd.
Indigo Books & Music Inc., 58 185–87
Indigo NV, 26 212–14 *see also* Hewlett-Packard Co.
Indigo Systems Corp. *see* FLIR Systems, Inc.
The Inditex Group *see* Industria de Diseño Textil S.A.
Indo Mobil Ltd., **48** 212
Indosat *see* PT Indosat Tbk.
Indresco, Inc., **22** 285; **52** 215
Induba, S.A. de C.V., **39** 230
Induban, **II** 196
Indura SA Industria Y Commercio, **25** 82
Indus International Inc., 70 127–30
Industri Kapital, **27** 269; **68** 125–26
Industri Kapital 2000 Ltd., **64** 17
Industria de Diseño Textil S.A. (Inditex), 64 193–95
Industrial & Commercial Bank, **56** 363
Industrial Air Tool, **28** 387
Industrial Airsystems Inc., **56** 247
Industrial Bank of Japan, Ltd., II 300–01
Industrial Chemical and Equipment, **16** 271
Industrial Circuits, **IV** 680
Industrial Development Corp. of Zambia Ltd., *see* Zambia Industrial and Mining Corp. Ltd.
Industrial Development Corporation, **57** 185
Industrial Devices Inc., **48** 359
Industrial Exportadora Famian, S.A. de C.V., **62** 353
Industrial Gases Lagos, **25** 82
Industrial Instrument Company *see* Foxboro Co.
Industrial Light & Magic, *see* Lucasfilm Ltd.
Industrial Powder Coatings, Inc., **16** 475
Industrial Publishing Company, *see* Pittway Corp.
Industrial Resources, **6** 144
Industrial Services Group, Inc., **56** 161
Industrial Services of America, Inc., 46 247–49
Industrial Tectonics Corp., **18** 276
Industrial Tires Limited, **65** 91
Industrial Trade & Consumer Shows Inc. *see* Maclean Hunter Publishing Ltd.
Industrias Bachoco, S.A. de C.V., 39 228–31
Industrias del Atlantico SA, **47** 291
Indústrias Klabin de Papel e Celulose S.A. *see* Klabin S.A.
Industrias Nacobre, **21** 259
Industrias Negromex, **23** 170

Industrias Penoles, S.A. de C.V., 22 284–86
Industrias Resistol S.A., **23** 170–71
Industrie Natuzzi S.p.A., 18 256–58
Industrie Zignago Santa Margherita S.p.A., 67 210–12
Industriförvaltnings AB Kinnevik, **26** 331–33; **36** 335
AB Industrivärden, **32** 397
Induyco *see* Industrias y Confecciones, S.A.
Indy Lighting, **30** 266
Indy Racing League, **37** 74
Inet Technologies Inc. *see* Tektronix Inc.
Infineon Technologies AG, 50 269–73
Infinity Broadcasting Corporation, 11 190–92; 48 214–17 (upd.)
Infinity Enterprises, Inc., **44** 4
Infinity Partners, **36** 160
Inflight Sales Group Limited, **11** 82; **29** 511
InfoAsia, **28** 241
Infocom, **32** 8
InfoCure Corporation *see* AMICAS, Inc.
InFocus Corporation, 92 172–75
Infogrames Entertainment S.A., 35 227–30
Infonet Services Corporation *see* Belgacom.
Informa Group plc, 58 188–91
Information Access Company, 17 252–55
Information Builders, Inc., 22 291–93
Information Consulting Group, *see* McKinsey & Company, Inc.
Information, Dissemination and Retrieval Inc., **IV** 670
Information Holdings Inc., 47 183–86
Information International *see* Autologic Information International, Inc.
Information Management Reporting Services *see* Hyperion Software Corp.
Information Please LLC, **26** 216
Information Resources, Inc., 10 358–60
Information Spectrum Inc., **57** 34
Informix Corporation, 10 361–64; 30 243–46 (upd.) *see also* International Business Machines Corp.
Infoseek Corporation, **27** 517; **30** 490
InfoSoft International, Inc. *see* Inso Corp.
InfoSonics Corporation, 81 201–04
InfoSpace, Inc., 91 259–62
Infostrada S.p.A., **38** 300
Infosys Technologies Ltd., 38 240–43
Infotech Enterprises, Ltd., **33** 45
Infotel, Inc., **52** 342
Inframetrics, Inc., **69** 171
Infun, S.A., **23** 269
ING Australia Limited, **52** 35, 39
ING, B.V., **14** 45, 47; **69** 246, 248
Ing. C. Olivetti & C., S.p.A., III 144–46 *see also* Olivetti S.p.A
ING Groep N.V., **63** 15
Ingalls Shipbuilding, Inc., 12 271–73
Ingefico, S.A., **52** 301
Ingenico—Compagnie Industrielle et Financière d'Ingénierie, 46 250–52
Ingenious Designs Inc., **47** 420
Ingersoll-Rand Company, III 525–27; 15 223–26 (upd.); 55 218–22 (upd.)
Ingka Holding B.V. *see* IKEA International A/S.
Ingleby Enterprises Inc. *see* Caribiner International, Inc.
Inglenook Vineyards, *see* Canandaigua Brands, Inc.
Ingles Markets, Inc., 20 305–08
Inglis Ltd. *see* Whirlpool Corp.
Ingram Book Group, **30** 70
Ingram Industries, Inc., 11 193–95; 49 217–20 (upd.)
Ingram Micro Inc., 52 178–81
AB Ingredients, *see* Associated British Foods plc.
Ingres Corporation, **9** 36–37
Ingwerson and Co., **II** 356
INH *see* Instituto Nacional de Hidrocarboros.
Inha Works Ltd., **33** 164
INI *see* Instituto Nacional de Industria.
Initial Electronics, **64** 198
Initial Security, 64 196–98
Initial Towel Supply *see* Rentokil Initial Plc.
Inktomi Corporation, 45 200–04
Inland Container Corporation, 8 267–69 *see also* Temple-Inland Inc.
Inland Paperboard and Packaging, Inc., **31** 438
Inland Steel Industries, Inc., IV 113–16; 19 216–20 (upd.)
Inland Valley, **23** 321
Inmac, Inc., *see* Micro Warehouse, Inc.
Inmobiliaria e Inversiones Aconcagua S.A., **71** 143
Inmotel Inversiones, **71** 338
InnCOGEN Limited, **35** 480
The Inner-Tec Group, **64** 198
InnerCity Foods Joint Venture Company, **16** 97
Inno-BM, **26** 158, 161
Inno-France *see* Societe des Grandes Entreprises de Distribution, Inno-France.
Innova International Corporation, **26** 333
Innovacom, **25** 96
Innovation, **26** 158
Innovative Marketing Systems *see* Bloomberg L.P.
Innovative Products & Peripherals Corporation, **14** 379
Innovative Solutions & Support, Inc., 85 175–78
Innovative Sports Systems, Inc., **15** 396
Innovative Valve Technologies Inc., **33** 167
Innovex Ltd. *see* Quintiles Transnational Corp.
Innovo Group Inc., 83 195-199
Inovoject do Brasil Ltda., **72** 108
Inpaco, *see* Liqui-Box Corp.
Inprise/Borland Corporation, **33** 115; **76** 123–24
Input/Output, Inc., 73 184–87
INS *see* International News Service.
Insa, **55** 189
Inserra Supermarkets, 25 234–36
Insight Enterprises, Inc., 18 259–61
Insight Marques SARL IMS SA, **48** 224
Insignia Financial Group, Inc. *see* CB Richard Ellis Group, Inc.
Insilco Corporation, 16 281–83
Inso Corporation, 26 215–19
Inspiration Resources Corporation, *see* Terra Industries.
Inspirations PLC, **22** 129
Insta-Care Holdings Inc., **16** 59
Instant Auto Insurance, **33** 3, 5
Instant Interiors Corporation, **26** 102
Instapak Corporation, *see* Sealed Air Corp.
Instinet Corporation, 34 225–27
Insituform Technologies, Inc., 83 200-203
Institute for Professional Development, *see* Apollo Group, Inc.
Institution Food House *see* Alex Lee Inc.
Institutional Financing Services, **23** 491
Instituto Bancario San Paolo di Torino, **50** 407
Instituto Nacional de Industria, I 459–61
Instrument Systems Corp. *see* Griffon Corp.
Instrumentarium Corp., **25** 82; **71** 349
Instrumentation Scientifique de Laboratoire, S.A., **15** 404; **50** 394
Insul 8 Corporation, **76** 139
Insurance Auto Auctions, Inc., 23 285–87
Insurance Company of North America *see* CIGNA Corp.
Insurance Company of the Southeast, Ltd., **56** 165
Insurance Partners L.P., **15** 257
InsurMark, **72** 149
InSync Communications, **42** 425
Intabex Holdings Worldwide, S.A., **27** 126
Intarsia Corp., **38** 187
Intat Precision Inc., **48** 5
Integra LifeSciences Holdings Corporation, 87 244–247
Integral Corporation, **23** 446
Integrated BioPharma, Inc., 83 204-207
Integrated Computer Systems *see* Learning Tree International Inc.
Integrated Defense Technologies, Inc., 54 178–80
Integrated Genetics, *see* Genzyme Corp.
Integrated Medical Systems Inc., **12** 333; **47** 236
Integrated Resources, Inc., **11** 483; **16** 54; **19** 393
Integrated Silicon Solutions, Inc., **18** 20; **43** 17; **47** 384
Integrated Software Systems Corporation, **11** 469
Integrated Systems Engineering, Inc., **51** 382
Integrated Systems Operations *see* Xerox Corp.
Integrated Systems Solutions Corp., **11** 395
Integris Europe, **49** 382, 384

Integrity Inc., **44 241–43**
Intel Corporation, **II 44–46; 10 365–67 (upd.); 36 284–88 (upd.); 75 196–201 (upd.)**
Intelcom Support Services, Inc., *see* Michael Baker Corp.
Intelicom Solutions Corp., **6** 229
Intelig, **57** 67, 69
IntelliCorp, Inc., **45 205–07**
Intelligent Electronics, Inc., **6 243–45**
Intelligent Interactions Corp., **49** 421
Intelligent Software Ltd., **26** 275
Intelligraphics Inc., **33** 44
Intellisys, **48** 257
Inter American Aviation, Inc. *see* SkyWest, Inc.
Inter-City Products Corporation, **52** 399
Inter-City Wholesale Electric Inc., **15** 385
Inter-Comm Telephone, Inc., *see* LDDS-Metro Communications, Inc.
Inter-Continental Hotels and Resorts, **38** 77
Inter-Europa Bank in Hungary, **50** 410
Inter-Island Airways, Ltd., *see* Hawaiian Airlines, Inc.
Inter Island Telephone *see* Pacific Telecom, Inc.
Inter Link Foods PLC, **61 132–34**
Inter Parfums Inc., **35 235–38; 86 201–06 (upd.)**
Inter-Regional Financial Group, Inc., **15 231–33** *see also* Dain Rauscher Corp.
Inter Techniek, *see* Randstad Holding n.v.
Inter-Urban, Inc., **74** 370
Interactive Computer Design, Inc., **23** 489, 491
InterActive Corporation, **71** 136–37
Interactive Media CCSP AG, **61** 350
Interactive Search Holding *see* Ask Jeeves, Inc.
InterAd Holdings Ltd., **49** 422
Interbake Foods, *see* George Weston Ltd.
InterBold, *see* Diebold, Inc.
Interbrand Corporation, **70 131–33**
Interbrás, **IV** 503
Interbrew S.A., **17 256–58; 50 274–79 (upd.)**
Interceramic *see* Internacional de Ceramica, S.A. de C.V.
Interco Incorporated, **III 528–31** *see also* Furniture Brands International, Inc.
Intercontessa AG, **35** 401; **36** 294
Intercontinental Branded Apparel, *see* Hartmarx Corp.
Intercontinental Electronics Corp. *see* IEC Electronics Corp.
Intercontinentale Assicurazioni, *see* Winterthur Group.
Intercord, **22** 194
Intercorp Excelle Foods Inc., **64 199–201**
Interdesign, *see* Randstad Holding n.v.
InterDigital Communications Corporation, **61 135–37**
Interdiscount/Radio TV Steiner AG, **48** 116
Interealty Corp., **43** 184
Interep National Radio Sales Inc., **35 231–34**
Interessen Gemeinschaft Farbenwerke *see* I.G. Farbenindustrie AG.
Interface, Inc., **8 270–72; 29 246–49 (upd.); 76 195–99 (upd.)**
Interfax News Agency, **86 207–10**
Interferon Sciences, Inc., *see* National Patient Development Corp.
Interglas S.A., **22** 515
Intergraph Corporation, **6 246–49; 24 233–36 (upd.)**
INTERIM Services, Inc. *see* Spherion Corp.
Interinvest S.A., **33** 19; **69** 11
Interlabor Interim, *see* Randstad Holding n.v.
The Interlake Corporation, **8 273–75**
Interlake Steamship Company, **15** 302
Intermaco S.R.L., **43** 368
Intermarché *see* ITM Entreprises SA.
Intermark, Inc., **34** 338–39
Intermec Technologies Corporation, **72 187–91**
Intermedia, **25** 499
Intermedics, **12** 325–26; **40** 66–67
INTERMET Corporation, **32 279–82; 77 207–12 (upd.)**
Intermix Media, Inc., **83 208-211**
Intermodal Engineering Co. Ltd., **56** 181
Intermountain Health Care, Inc., **27 237–40**
Internacional de Ceramica, S.A. de C.V., **53 174–76**
International Aeradio Limited, **47** 352
International Airline Support Group, Inc., **55 223–25**
International Alliance Services, Inc. *see* Century Business Services, Inc.
International Banking and Credit Analysis (IBCA), **37** 144
International Banking Technologies, Inc., **11** 113
International Beauty Supply, Ltd. *see* L.L. Knickerbocker Co., Inc.
International Beverage Corporation *see* Clearly Canadian Beverage Corp.
International Brewing Holdings Pty., **21** 229; **50** 201
International Brotherhood of Teamsters, **37 211–14**
International Business Directories, Inc., **26** 484
International Business Machines Corporation, **III 147–49; 6 250–53 (upd.); 30 247–51 (upd.); 63 195–201 (upd.)**
International Care Services *see* Extendicare Health Services, Inc.
International Cellucotton Products Co. *see* Kimberly-Clark Corp.
International Communication Materials, Inc., *see* Nu-kote Holding, Inc.
International Computers *see* ICL plc.
International Controls Corporation, **10 368–70**
International Creative Management, Inc., **43 235–37**
International Cryogenic Equipment Corporation, **74** 363
International Dairy Queen, Inc., **10 371–74; 39 232–36 (upd.)**
International Data Group, Inc., **7 238–40; 25 237–40 (upd.)**
International Distillers & Vintners Ltd., **31** 92
International Enviroguard Systems, Inc., **57** 7–8
International Environmental Corporation *see* LSB Industries, Inc.
International Factoring Corp., *see* Nippon Shinpan Co., Ltd.
International Family Entertainment Inc., **13 279–81** *see also* ABC Family Worldwide, Inc.
International Finance Corp., **19** 192
International Financial Systems Limited, **62** 141
International Flavors & Fragrances Inc., **9 290–92; 38 244–48 (upd.)**
International Fuel Cells Inc., **39** 394
International Game Technology, **10 375–76; 41 214–16 (upd.)**
International Harvester Co. *see* Navistar International Corp.
International Home Foods, Inc., **42** 94; **64** 61
International Hotel Group, **59** 296
International House of Pancakes *see* IHOP Corp.
International Imaging Limited, **29** 58
International Insurance Company of Hannover Ltd., **53** 162
International Lease Finance Corporation, **48 218–20**
International MacGregor, **27** 269
International Management Group, **18 262–65** *see also* IMG.
International Marine Services, **22** 276
International Milling *see* International Multifoods Corp.
International Minerals and Chemical Corporation, **19** 253
International Multifoods Corporation, **7 241–43; 25 241–44 (upd.)** *see also* The J. M. Smucker Co.
International News Service *see* United Press International, Inc.
International Nickel Co. of Canada, Ltd. *see* Inco Ltd.
International Olympic Committee, **44 244–47**
International Organization of Consumers Unions, **26** 98
International Paper Company, **IV 286–88; 15 227–30 (upd.); 47 187–92 (upd.)**
International Periodical Distributors, Inc. *see* Source Interlink Companies, Inc.
International Permalite, **22** 229
International Pet Supplies and Distribution, Inc., **74** 234
International Petroleum Co., Ltd. *see* Standard Oil Co. of New Jersey.
International Pharmacy Management, Inc. *see* HealthExtras, Inc.

International Pipeline Services, Inc., **51** 248
International Playing Card Company, **62** 384
International Power PLC, 50 280–85 (upd.)
International Processing Corporation, **50** 123
International Products Corporation *see* The Terlato Wine Group.
International Profit Associates, Inc., 87 248–251
International Proteins Corporation, **21** 248
International Publishing Corp., **23** 350; **49** 407
International Raw Materials, Ltd., **31** 20
International Rectifier Corporation, 31 263–66; 71 181–84 (upd.)
International Roofing Company, **22** 13–14
International Shipbreaking Ltd. L.L.C., 67 213–15
International Shipholding Corporation, Inc., 27 241–44
International Silver Company *see* Syratech Corp.
International SMC Ltd., **60** 278
International Specialty Products, Inc., *see* GAF Corp.
International Speedway Corporation, 19 221–23; 74 157–60 (upd.)
International Talent Management, Inc. *see* Motown Records Company L.P.
International Telecommunications Satellite Organization, **46** 328
International Telephone & Telegraph Corporation, I 462–64; 11 196–99 (upd.)
International Television Corporation Entertainment Group, **23** 391
International Thomson Organisation Ltd. *see* The Thomson Corp.
International Thomson Organization Ltd., **23** 92
International Total Services, Inc., 37 215–18
The International Tourist Corporation, **68** 281
International Transmission Company *see* ITC Holdings Corp.
International Utilities Corp., **6** 444
International Well Control *see* Boots & Coots International Well Control, Inc.
International Wind Systems, **6** 581
International Wine & Spirits Ltd., *see* UST Inc.
International Wireless Inc., **21** 261
Internet Shopping Network, **26** 441
Interocean Management Corp., *see* Totem Resources Corp.
Interpac Belgium *see* Belgacom.
Interpool, Inc., 92 176–79
Interpretive Data Systems Inc. *see* IDX Systems Corp.
Interprovincial Pipe Line Ltd. *see* Enbridge Inc.
The Interpublic Group of Companies, Inc., I 16–18; 22 294–97 (upd.); 75 202–05 (upd.)
Interra Financial *see* Dain Rauscher Corp.
Interscope Music Group, 31 267–69
Intersec, Inc., *see* AHL Services, Inc.
Intersil Corporation, 93 250–54
Interstate & Ocean Transport, **6** 577
Interstate Assurance Company, **59** 246–47
Interstate Bakeries Corporation, 12 274–76; 38 249–52 (upd.)
Interstate Brick Company, **6** 568–69
Interstate Electric Manufacturing Company *see* McGraw Electric Co.
Interstate Hotels & Resorts Inc., 58 192–94
Interstate Iron and Steel Company *see* Republic Engineered Steels, Inc.
Interstate Logos, Inc. *see* Lamar Advertising Co.
Interstate Power Company, **6** 555, 605
Interstate Properties Inc., **45** 15–16
Interstate Public Service Company, **6** 555
Interstate Supply Company *see* McGraw Electric Co.
InterTAN, Inc. *see* Circuit City Stories, Inc.
Intertec Design, Inc., **34** 371–72
Intertec Publishing Corp., **22** 441
Intertechnique SA, **36** 530
InterVideo, Inc., 85 179–82
Intervision Express, **24** 510
InterVU Inc. *see* Akamai Technologies, Inc.
Intevac, Inc., 92 180–83
Intimate Brands, Inc., 24 237–39
InTouch Systems, Inc., **43** 118
Intrac Handelsgesellschaft mbH, **7** 142
Intraco Corp., **56** 157–58
Intrado Inc., 63 202–04
Intrawest Corporation, 15 234–36; 84 192–196 (upd.)
Intrepa L.L.C. *see* Manhattan Associates, Inc.
Intres B.V., 82 178–81
Intrigue Technologies, Inc., **69** 245
Intuit Inc., 14 262–64; 33 208–11 (upd.); 73 188–92 (upd.)
Intuitive Surgical, Inc., 79 217–20
Invacare Corporation, 11 200–02; 47 193–98 (upd.)
inVentiv Health, Inc., 81 205–08
Invensys PLC, 50 286–90 (upd.)
Invento Products Corporation, **21** 269
Inverfal S.A., **69** 312
Inverness Medical Innovations, Inc., 63 205–07
Inverness Medical Technology, Inc., **45** 210
Inversiones Financieras del Sud S.A., **63** 120–21
Inversiones Freire Ltda., **71** 139, 141
Inversiones Nacional de Chocolates S.A., 88 199–202
Inversiones y Desarrollo Los Andes S.A., **69** 142
INVESCO PLC *see* AMVESCAP PLC.
Invesgen S.A., **26** 129
Investcorp SA, 57 179–82
Investindustrial LP, **76** 326
Investor AB, 63 208–11
Investors Diversified Services, Inc., *see* American Express Co.
InvestorsBancorp, **53** 222, 224
Investrónica S.A., **26** 129
Invista Capital Management, *see* Principal Mutual Life Insurance Co.
Invitrogen Corporation, 52 182–84
Invivo Corporation, 52 185–87
The Invus Group, Ltd., **33** 449
Iogen Corporation, 81 209–13
Iomega Corporation, 21 294–97
IONA Technologies plc, 43 238–41
Ionatron, Inc., 85 183–86
Ionia S.A., **64** 379
Ionics, Incorporated, 52 188–90
Ionpure Technologies Corporation *see* Eastern Enterprises.
Iowa Beef Packers, **21** 287
Iowa Beef Processors, *see* IBP, Inc.
Iowa Mold Tooling Co., Inc., **16** 475
Iowa Public Service Company, **6** 524–25
Iowa Telecommunications Services, Inc., 85 187–90
IP Services, Inc., **IV** 597
IP Timberlands Ltd., *see* International Paper Co.
IP&L *see* Illinois Power & Light Corp.
IP Vista, **74** 143
Ipalco Enterprises, Inc., 6 508–09
IPC *see* International Publishing Corp.
IPC Communications, Inc., **15** 196
IPC Magazines Limited, 7 244–47
IPD *see* International Periodical Distributors.
Iphotonics Inc., **48** 369
Ipiranga S.A., 67 216–18
Ipko-Amcor, **14** 225
IPL Energy Inc. *see* Enbridge Inc.
IPM *see* International Pharmacy Management, Inc.
IPS Praha a.s., **38** 437
IPS Publishing, **39** 341–42
IPSCO Inc. *see* SSAB Svenskt Stål AB.
Ipsen International Inc., 72 192–95
Ipsos SA, 48 221–24
Ipswich Bancshares Inc., **55** 52
iQuantic Buck, **55** 73
IQUE, Inc., **21** 194
IranAir, 81 214–17
Irdeto, **31** 330
Irex Contracting Group, 90 245–48
IRI *see* Instituto per la Ricostruzione Industriale.
Irideon, Inc., **35** 435
Iridian Asset Management LLC, **52** 172
Irish Agricultural Wholesale Society Ltd. *see* IAWS Group plc.
Irish Air *see* Aer Lingus Group plc.
Irish Life & Permanent Plc, 59 245–47
Irish Life Assurance Company, **16** 14; **43** 7
Irkut Corporation, 68 202–04
iRobot Corporation, 83 212-215
Iron and Steel Industrial Corporation, **59** 224

Iron City Brewing Company *see* Pittsburgh Brewing Co.
Iron Mountain, Inc., 33 212–14
Ironside Technologies Inc., **72** 197
IronUnits LLC, **62** 74
Iroquois Gas Corporation, **6** 526
IRSA Inversiones y Representaciones S.A., 63 212–15
Irvin Aerospace, Inc. *see* Airborne Systems Group.
Irvin Feld & Kenneth Feld Productions, Inc., 15 237–39 *see also* Feld Entertainment, Inc.
Irving Tanning Company, *see* Fuqua Enterprises, Inc.
Irwin Financial Corporation, 77 213–16
Irwin Lehrhoff Associates, *see* NovaCare, Inc.
Irwin Toy Limited, 14 265–67
Isagro S.p.A., **26** 425
Isbank *see* Turkiye Is Bankasi A.S.
Iscor *see* Iron and Steel Industrial Corp.
Iscor Limited, 57 183–86
Isdin, **60** 246
Isetan Company Limited, V 85–87; 36 289–93 (upd.)
Ishikawajima-Harima Heavy Industries Company, Ltd., III 532–33; 86 211–15 (upd.)
Isis Distributed Systems, Inc., *see* Stratus Computer, Inc.
Island Def Jam Music, **57** 359
The Island ECN, Inc., 48 225–29
Island Equipment Co., **19** 381
Island Pictures Corp., **23** 389
Island Records, **23** 389
Isle of Capri Casinos, Inc., 41 217–19
Isokauf *see* SIG plc.
Isosceles PLC, **24** 270; **47** 367–68
Ispat Inland Inc., 30 252–54; 40 267–72 (upd.)
Israel Aircraft Industries Ltd., 69 215–17
Israel Chemicals Ltd., 55 226–29
ISS A/S, 49 221–23
ISS Securitas, **42** 165, 167
ISSI *see* Integrated Silicon Solutions Inc.
Istante Vesa s.r.l., *see* Gianni Versace SpA.
Istituto Farmacologico Serono S.p.A. *see* Serono S.A.
Istituto Mobiliare Italiano S.p.A., **50** 407, 409
Istituto per la Ricostruzione Industriale S.p.A., I 465–67; 11 203–06 (upd.)
Isuzu Motors, Ltd., 9 293–95; 23 288–91 (upd.); 57 187–91 (upd.)
IT Group, **28** 203
IT International, **V** 255
IT-Software Companies, **48** 402
Italcimenti Group, **40** 107–08
Italianni's, **22** 128
Italstate *see* Societa per la Infrastrutture e l'Assetto del Territoria.
Italtel, **V** 326–27
Itaú *see* Banco Itaú S.A.
Itaúsa *see* Investimentos Itaú S.A.
ITC Holdings Corp., 75 206–08
Itek Corp., *see* Litton Industries Inc.
Itel Corporation, 9 296–99
Items International Airwalk Inc., 17 259–61
Ithaca Gas & Electric *see* New York State Electric and Gas.
ITI Education Corporation, **29** 472
ITM Entreprises SA, 36 294–97
Ito Gofuku Co. Ltd. *see* Matsuzakaya Company Ltd.
Ito-Yokado Co., Ltd., V 88–89; 42 189–92 (upd.)
Itochu and Renown, Inc., **12** 281
ITOCHU Corporation, 32 283–87 (upd.)
Itochu Housing, **38** 415
Itoh *see* C. Itoh & Co.
Itoham Foods Inc., II 518–19; 61 138–40 (upd.)
Itoman & Co., **26** 456
Itron, Inc., 64 202–05
The Itsy Bitsy Entertainment Company, **51** 309
ITT *see* International Telephone and Telegraph Corp.
ITT Aerospace, **33** 48
ITT Automotive Inc. *see* Valeo.
ITT Educational Services, Inc., 33 215–17; 76 200–03 (upd.)
ITT Sheraton Corporation, III 98–101 *see also* Starwood Hotels & Resorts Worldwide, Inc.
iTurf Inc., **29** 142–43
ITV PLC, **71** 368
ITW *see* Illinois Tool Works Inc.
i2 Technologies, Inc., 87 252–257
IU International, **23** 40
IURA Edition, **14** 556
IV Therapy Associates, **16** 440
IVACO Industries Inc., *see* IVAX Corp.
Ivanhoe, Inc., *see* Steinberg Inc.
Ivar's, Inc., 86 216–19
IVAX Corporation, 11 207–09; 55 230–33 (upd.)
IVC Industries, Inc., 45 208–11
iVillage Inc., 46 253–56
Ivy and Mader Philatelic Auctions, Inc., **60** 146
Ivy Mortgage Corp., **39** 380, 382
Iwerks Entertainment, Inc., 34 228–30
IXC Communications, Inc., 29 250–52
IXI Ltd., **38** 418–19
Ixos Software AG *see* Open Text Corporation
IYG Holding Company of Japan, *see* 7-Eleven, Inc.
The IZOD Gant Corporation, *see* Phillips-Van Heusen Corp
Izod Lacoste, *see* Crystal Brands, Inc.
Izukyu Corporation, **47** 408
Izumi Fudosan *see* Sumitomo Reality & Development Co., Ltd.

J

J & J Snack Foods Corporation, 24 240–42
J&L Industrial Supply, *see* Kennametal, Inc.
J&L Steel *see* Jones & Laughlin Steel Corp.
J & M Laboratories, **48** 299
J&R Electronics Inc., 26 224–26
J&W Hardie Ltd., **62** 347
J. & W. Seligman & Co. Inc., 61 141–43
J.A. Jones, Inc., 16 284–86
J. Alexander's Corporation, 65 177–79
J.B. Hunt Transport Services Inc., 12 277–79
J.B. Ivey & Company *see* Dillard's Inc.
J.B. Lippincott & Company, *see* Wolters Kluwer NV.
J.B. McLean Publishing Co., Ltd. *see* Maclean Hunter Publishing Ltd.
J.B. Wolters Publishing Company, *see* Wolters Kluwer NV.
J. Baker, Inc., 31 270–73
J Bibby & Sons, *see* Barlow Rand Ltd.
J. Boag & Son Limited, **57** 306
J. Bulova Company *see* Bulova Corp.
J C Bamford Excavators Ltd., 83 216-222
J.C. Baxter Co., **15** 501
J.C. Hillary's, **20** 54
J.C. McCormic, Inc., **58** 334
J. C. Penney Company, Inc., V 90–92; 18 269–73 (upd.); 43 245–50 (upd.); 91 263–72 (upd.)
J.C. Potter Sausage Company, **57** 56–57
J. Crew Group, Inc., 12 280–82; 34 231–34 (upd.); 88 203–08
J.D. Bassett Manufacturing Co. *see* Bassett Furniture Industries, Inc.
J.D. Edwards & Company, 14 268–70 *see also* Oracle Corp.
J.D. Power and Associates, 32 297–301
J. D'Addario & Company, Inc., 48 230–33
J.E. Sirrine *see* CRSS Inc.
J.F. Corporation *see* Isetan Company Ltd.
J.F. Shea Co., Inc., 55 234–36
J.H. Findorff and Son, Inc., 60 175–78
J.H. Heafner Co., **20** 263
J.H. Westerbeke Corp. *see* Westerbeke Corp.
J.H. Whitney & Company, **32** 100
J. Homestock *see* R.H. Macy & Co.
J. Horner's, **48** 415
J.I.C. Group Limited, **61** 233
J.I. Case Company, 10 377–81 *see also* CNH Global N.V.
J.J. Farmer Clothing Inc., **51** 320–21
J.J. Keller & Associates, Inc., 81 2180–21
J.J. Kenney Company, Inc., **51** 244
The J. Jill Group, Inc., 35 239–41; 90 249–53 (upd.)
J.K. Starley and Company Ltd, *see* Rover Group Ltd.
J.L. Clark, Inc. *see* Clarcor Inc.
J.L. French Automotive Castings, Inc. *see* Onex Corp.
J.L. Hammett Company, 72 196–99
J.L. Hudson Company *see* Target Corp.
J.L. Shiely Co. *see* English China Clays Ltd.

J Lauritzen A/S, 90 254–57
J.M. Huber Corporation, **40** 68
The J. M. Smucker Company, 11 210–12; 87 258–265 (upd.)
J.M. Tull Metals Co., Inc., *see* Inland Steel Industries, Inc.
J.M. Voith AG, 33 222–25
J-Mar Associates, **31** 435–36
J.P. Morgan Chase & Co., II 329–32; 30 261–65 (upd.); 38 253–59 (upd.)
J.P. Stevens Inc., *see* WestPoint Stevens Inc.
J.R. Brown & Sharpe *see* Brown & Sharpe Manufacturing Co.
J.R. Simplot Company, 16 287–89; 60 179–82 (upd.)
J Sainsbury plc, II 657–59; 13 282–84 (upd.); 38 260–65 (upd.)
J. Sears & Company *see* Sears plc.
J. Spiegel and Company *see* Spiegel, Inc.
J.U. Dickson Sawmill Inc. *see* Dickson Forest Products, Inc.
J.W. Bateson, *see* Centex Corp.
J.W. Charles Financial Services Inc., **25** 542
J.W. Childs Associates, L.P., **46** 220; **64** 119
J.W. Childs Equity Partners LP, **40** 274
J.W. Foster and Sons, Inc. *see* Reebok International Ltd.
J. W. Pepper and Son Inc., 86 220–23
J.W. Spear, **25** 314
J.W. Wassall Ltd. *see* Wassall PLC.
J. Walter Thompson Co. *see* JWT Group Inc.
Jabil Circuit, Inc., 36 298–301; 88 209–14
Jack Daniel's *see* Brown-Forman Corp.
Jack Eckerd Corp., **19** 467
Jack Henry and Associates, Inc., 17 262–65; 94 258–63 (upd.)
Jack in the Box Inc., 89 265–71 (upd.)
Jack Morton Worldwide, 88 215–18
Jack Schwartz Shoes, Inc., 18 266–68
Jackpot Enterprises Inc., 21 298–300
Jackson & Perkins *see* Bear Creek Corp.
Jackson Furniture of Danville, LLC, **48** 246
Jackson Hewitt, Inc., 48 234–36
Jackson Mercantile Co. *see* Jitney-Jungle Stores of America, Inc.
Jackson National Life Insurance Company, 8 276–77
Jacmar Companies, 87 266–269
Jaco Electronics, Inc., 30 255–57
Jacob Leinenkugel Brewing Company, 28 209–11
Jacobs Brake Manufacturing Company, *see* Danaher Corp.
Jacobs Engineering Group Inc., 6 148–50; 26 220–23 (upd.)
Jacobs Suchard (AG), II 520–22 *see also* Kraft Jacobs Suchard AG.
Jacobson Stores Inc., 21 301–03
Jacoby & Meyers, **20** 435
Jacor Communications, Inc., 23 292–95
Jacques Borel International, **49** 126
Jacques Chocolaterie S.A., **53** 315
Jacques Whitford, 92 184–87
Jacquot *see* Établissements Jacquot and Cie S.A.S.
Jacuzzi Brands Inc., 23 296–98; 76 204–07 (upd.)
Jade KK, **25** 349
JAFCO Co. Ltd., 79 221–24
Jafra Cosmetics, **15** 475, 477
Jaguar Cars, Ltd., 13 285–87
JAIX Leasing Company, **23** 306
JAKKS Pacific, Inc., 52 191–94
JAL *see* Japan Airlines Company, Ltd.
Jalate Inc., 25 245–47
Jaluzot & Cie *see* Pinault-Printemps-Redoute S.A.
Jamaica Water Supply Company *see* JWP Inc.
Jamar Company, **64** 30, 32
Jamba Juice Company, 47 199–202
Jamdat Mobile *see* Electronic Arts Inc.
James Avery Craftsman, Inc., 76 208–10
James Beattie plc, 43 242–44
James Burn/American, Inc., *see* Standex International Corp.
The James C. Heintz Company, *see* Myers Industries, Inc.
James Felt Realty, Inc., **21** 257
James Fison and Sons *see* Fisons plc.
James G. Fast Company *see* Angelica Corp.
James Galt & Co. Ltd., **60** 124
James Hardie Industries N.V., 56 174–76
James Heekin and Company, *see* Heekin Can Inc.
James Industries, Inc., **61** 298
James McNaughton Ltd., *see* PWA Group.
James Original Coney Island Inc., 84 197–200
James Purdey & Sons Limited, 87 270–275
James River Corporation of Virginia, IV 289–91 *see also* Fort James Corp.
James Wellbeloved, **39** 354, 356
Jamestown Insurance Co. Ltd., **55** 20
Jamestown Publishers, *see* Tribune Co.
Jamesway Corporation, **23** 177
Jamie Scott, Inc., **27** 348
Jan Bell Marketing Inc. *see* Mayor's Jewelers, Inc.
Janata Bank, **31** 219
Janco Overseas Limited, **59** 261
Jane Jones Enterprises, **16** 422; **43** 309
Janesville Electric, **6** 604
Jani-King International, Inc., 85 191–94
Janin, S.A., **36** 163
Janna Systems Inc., **38** 433
Janssen Pharmaceutica N.V., 80 164–67
Janson Publications, *see* Tribune Co.
JanSport, Inc., 70 134–36
JANT Pty. Ltd., *see* Honshu Paper Co. Ltd.
Jantzen Inc. *see* VF Corp.
Janus Capital Group Inc., 57 192–94
Japan Airlines Company, Ltd., I 104–06; 32 288–92 (upd.)
Japan Brewery *see* Kirin Brewery Company, Ltd.
Japan Broadcasting Corporation, 7 248–50
Japan Elanco Company, Ltd., **17** 437
Japan Energy Corporation, **14** 206, 208; **59** 375
Japan Food Corporation, *see* Kikkoman Corp.
Japan Leasing Corporation, 8 278–80
Japan Medico, **25** 431
Japan Photo Holding Norge AS, **76** 85, 87
Japan Pulp and Paper Company Limited, IV 292–93
Japan Rifex Co., Ltd., **64** 261
Japan Tobacco Inc., V 403–04; 46 257–60 (upd.)
Japan Trustee Services Bank Ltd., **53** 322
Japan Vilene Company Ltd., **41** 170–72
Japan Xanpak Corporation *see* JSP Corp.
Japanese National Railway, **43** 103
Jara Enterprises, Inc., **31** 276
Jarden Corporation, 93 255–61 (upd.)
Jardine Cycle & Carriage Ltd., 73 193–95
Jardine Matheson Holdings Limited, I 468–71; 20 309–14 (upd.); 93 262–71 (upd.)
Jarvis plc, 39 237–39
Jas. D. Easton Archery *see* Easton Sports, Inc.
Jas. I. Miller Co., *see* Standard Commercial Corp.
Jason Incorporated, 23 299–301
Jasper Corporation *see* Kimball International, Inc.
Java Software *see* Sun Microsystems, Inc.
Jay Jacobs, Inc., 15 243–45
Jayco Inc., 13 288–90
Jays Foods, Inc., 90 258–61
Jazz Basketball Investors, Inc., 55 237–39
Jazzercise, Inc., 45 212–14
JB Oxford Holdings, Inc., 32 293–96
JB Pawn, Inc., **57** 139
JBA Holdings PLC, **43** 184
JCDecaux S.A., 76 211–13
JCJL *see* Java-China-Japan Line.
JCT Wireless Technology Company, **61** 233
JD Wetherspoon plc, 30 258–60
JDS Uniphase Corporation, 34 235–37
JE Dunn Construction Group, Inc., 85 195–98
The Jean Coutu Group (PJC) Inc., 46 261–65
Jean-Georges Enterprises L.L.C., 75 209–11
Jean Lassale *see* Seiko Corp.
Jean-Philippe Fragrances, Inc. *see* Inter Parfums, Inc.
Jeanmarie Creations, Inc., *see* Blyth, Inc.
Jeanneau SA, **55** 56
Jefferies Group, Inc., 25 248–51
Jefferson Bancorp, Inc., **37** 201
Jefferson-Pilot Corporation, 11 213–15; 29 253–56 (upd.)

Jefferson Properties, Inc. *see* JPI.
Jefferson Smurfit Group plc, IV 294–96; 19 224–27 (upd.); 49 224–29 (upd.) *see also* Smurfit-Stone Container Corp.
Jefferson Standard Life Insurance, *see* Jefferson-Pilot Corp.
Jefferson Ward, **12** 48–49
Jefferson Warrior Railroad Company, *see* Walter Industries, Inc.
JEGTCO *see* Japan Electricity Generation and Transmission Company (JEGTCO).
Jel Sert Company, 90 262–65
Jeld-Wen, Inc., 45 215–17
Jelly Belly Candy Company, 76 214–16
Jenkens & Gilchrist, P.C., 65 180–82
Jenn-Air Corporation *see* Maytag Corp.
Jennie-O Turkey Store, Inc., 76 217–19
Jennifer Convertibles, Inc., 31 274–76
Jenny Craig, Inc., 10 382–84; 29 257–60 (upd.); 92 188–93 (upd.)
Jeno's, **26** 436
Jenoptik AG, 33 218–21
Jenson, Woodward & Lozier, Inc., **21** 96
JEORA Co., **IV** 564
Jeppesen Sanderson, Inc., 92 194–97
Jeri-Jo Knitwear, Inc., *see* Norton McNaughton, Inc.
Jerome Foods, Inc., **54** 168
Jerome Increase Case Machinery Company *see* J.I. Case Co.
Jerry Bassin Inc., **17** 12–14
Jerry's Famous Deli Inc., 24 243–45
Jersey Central Power & Light Company, *see* GPU, Inc.
Jersey European Airways (UK) Ltd., 61 144–46
Jersey Mike's Franchise Systems, Inc., 83 223-226
Jersey Standard *see* Standard Oil Co. of New Jersey.
Jerusalem Post Publications Limited, **62** 188
Jervis B. Webb Company, 24 246–49
JESCO Inc. *see* The Yates Companies, Inc.
Jesse Jones Sausage Co. *see* GoodMark Foods, Inc.
Jet Airways (India) Private Limited, 65 183–85
JetBlue Airways Corporation, 44 248–50
Jetro Cash & Carry Enterprises Inc., 38 266–68
Jetstar Airways Pty Ltd. *see* Qantas Airways Ltd.
Jeumont-Schneider Industries, **9** 10
Jevic Transportation, Inc., **45** 448
Jewel Companies, Inc., *see* American Stores Co.
Jewett-Cameron Trading Company, Ltd., 89 272–76
JFD-Encino, *see* Jerry's Famous Deli Inc.
JFE Shoji Holdings Inc., 88 219–22
JFW Distributing Company *see* Spartan Stores Inc.
JG Industries, Inc., 15 240–42
JHT, Inc., **39** 377
Jiamusi Combine Harvester Factory, **21** 175
Jiangsu General Ball & Roller Co., Ltd., **45** 170
JIB Group plc, **20** 313
Jiffy Lube International, Inc., **IV** 490; **21** 541; **24** 339; **50** 353
Jiffy Mixes, **29** 109–10
Jiffy Packaging, *see* Sealed Air Corp.
Jil Sander A.G., **45** 342, 344
Jillian's Entertainment Holdings, Inc., 40 273–75
Jim Beam Brands Worldwide, Inc., 14 271–73; 58 194–96 (upd.)
Jim Cole Enterprises, Inc., **19** 247
The Jim Henson Company, 23 302–04
Jim Hjelm's Private Collection, Ltd. *see* JLM Couture, Inc.
The Jim Pattison Group, 37 219–22
Jim Walter Corporation *see* Walter Industries, Inc.
Jimmy Carter Work Project *see* Habitat for Humanity International.
Jimmy'Z Surf Co., Inc. *see* Aéropostale, Inc.
Jintan Taionkei Co. *see* Terumo Corp.
Jitney-Jungle Stores of America, Inc., 27 245–48
JJB Sports plc, 32 302–04
JLA Credit, *see* Japan Leasing Corp.
JLG Industries, Inc., 52 195–97
JLL *see* Jones Lang LaSalle Inc.
JLM Couture, Inc., 64 206–08
JMB Internacionale S.A., **25** 121
JMB Realty Corporation, IV 702–03 *see also* Amfac/JMB Hawaii L.L.C.
Jno. H. Swisher & Son *see* Swisher International Group Inc.
JNR *see* Japan National Railway.
Jo-Ann Stores, Inc., 72 200–03 (upd.)
Jobete Music *see* Motown Records Company L.P.
JobWorks Agency, Inc., **16** 50
Jockey International, Inc., 12 283–85; 34 238–42 (upd.); 77 217–23 (upd.)
Joe's American Bar & Grill, **20** 54
Joe's Crab Shack, **15** 279
Joe's Jeans, Inc. *see* Innovo Group Inc.
JOFA AB *see* The Hockey Co.
The Joffrey Ballet of Chicago, 52 198–202
Joh. A. Benckiser GmbH, **36** 140
John A. Frye Shoe Company, **V** 376; **26** 397–98; **36** 24
John B. Fairfax Holdings Ltd., **74** 282–84
John B. Sanfilippo & Son, Inc., 14 274–76
John Brown plc, I 572–74
John Carr Group, **31** 398–400
John Charcol *see* Bradford & Bingley PLC.
John Chatillon & Sons Inc., **29** 460
John Crane International, *see* TI Group plc.
The John D. and Catherine T. MacArthur Foundation, 34 243–46
John D. Brush Company Inc., 94 264–67
The John David Group plc, 90 266–69
John Deere *see* Deere & Co.
John Dewar & Sons, Ltd., 82 182–86
John Fairfax Holdings Limited, 7 251–54 *see also* Fairfax Media Ltd.
John Frieda Professional Hair Care Inc., 70 137–39
John H. Harland Company, 17 266–69
John H.R. Molson & Bros. *see* The Molson Companies Ltd.
John Hancock Financial Services, Inc., III 265–68; 42 193–98 (upd.)
John Labatt Ltd. *see* Labatt Brewing Company Ltd.
John Laing plc, I 575–76; 51 171–73 (upd.) *see also* Laing O'Rourke PLC.
John Lewis Partnership plc, V 93–95; 42 199–203 (upd.)
John M. Smyth Co., **15** 282
John Menzies plc, 39 240–43
John Morrell and Co., **21** 111
The John Nuveen Company, 21 304–065
John Oster Manufacturing Company *see* Sunbeam-Oster.
John Paul Mitchell Systems, 24 250–52
John Q. Hammons Hotels, Inc., 24 253–55
John Sands Ltd., *see* American Greetings Corp.
John Sexton & Co., **26** 503
John Swire & Sons Ltd. *see* Swire Pacific Ltd.
John W. Danforth Company, 48 237–39
John Wiley & Sons, Inc., 17 270–72; 65 186–90 (upd.)
John Zink Company, **22** 3–4
Johnny Carino's *see* Fired Up, Inc.
Johnny Rockets Group, Inc., 31 277–81; 76 220–24 (upd.)
Johns Manville Corporation, 64 209–14 (upd.)
Johnsen, Jorgensen & Wettre, *see* Ibstock plc.
Johnson *see* Axel Johnson Group.
Johnson & Higgins, 14 277–80 *see also* Marsh & McLennan Companies, Inc.
Johnson and Howe Furniture Corporation, **33** 151
Johnson & Johnson, III 35–37; 8 281–83 (upd.); 36 302–07 (upd.); 75 212–18 (upd.)
Johnson Controls, Inc., III 534–37; 26 227–32 (upd.); 59 248–54 (upd.)
Johnson Engineering Corporation, **37** 365
Johnson Matthey PLC, IV 117–20; 16 290–94 (upd.); 49 230–35 (upd.)
Johnson Outdoors Inc., 84 201–205 (upd.)
Johnson Products Co., Inc., **11** 208; **31** 89
Johnson Publishing Company, Inc., 28 212–14; 72 204–07 (upd.)
Johnson Wax *see* S.C. Johnson & Son, Inc.
Johnson Worldwide Associates, Inc., 28 215–17 *see also* Johnson Outdoors Inc.

Johnsonville Sausage L.L.C., 63 216–19
Johnston Coca-Cola Bottling Company of Chattanooga, *see* Coca-Cola Enterprises, Inc.
Johnston Industries, Inc., 15 246–48
Johnston, Lemon & Co., **53** 134
Johnston Press plc, 35 242–44
Johnston Sport Architecture Inc., **63** 91
Johnstown America Industries, Inc., 23 305–07
Joint Environment for Digital Imaging, **50** 322
Joker S.A., **56** 103
Jolly Hotels *see* Compagnia Italiana dei Jolly Hotels S.p.A.
Jolly Time *see* American Pop Corn Co.
Jones & Babson, Inc., *see* Business Men's Assurance Company of America.
Jones & Laughlin Steel Corp., *see* LTV Corp.
Jones Apparel Group, Inc., 11 216–18; 39 244–47 (upd.)
Jones, Day, Reavis & Pogue, 33 226–29
Jones Environmental, **11** 361
Jones Financial Companies, L.P. *see* Edward Jones.
Jones Intercable, Inc., 21 307–09
Jones Lang LaSalle Incorporated, 49 236–38
Jones Medical Industries, Inc., 24 256–58
Jones-Rodolfo Corp. *see* Cutter & Buck, Inc.
Jones Soda Co., 69 218–21
Jordache Enterprises, Inc., 23 308–10
The Jordan Company LP, 70 140–42
Jordan Industries, Inc., 36 308–10
Jordan-Kitt Music Inc., 86 224–27
Jos. A. Bank Clothiers, Inc., 31 282–85
The Joseph & Feiss Company, **48** 209
Joseph Littlejohn & Levy, **27** 204; **53** 241
Joseph T. Ryerson & Son, Inc., 15 249–51 *see also* Ryerson Tull, Inc.
Joseph Transportation Inc., **55** 347
Josephson International, **43** 235
Joshua's Christian Bookstores, **31** 435–36; **51** 132
Josiah Wedgwood and Sons Limited *see* Waterford Wedgewood plc..
Jostens, Inc., 7 255–57; 25 252–55 (upd.); 73 196–200 (upd.)
Jotcham & Kendall Ltd. *see* Seddon Group Ltd.
Jotun A/S, 80 168–71
JOULÉ Inc., 58 197–200
Journal Communications, Inc., 86 228–32
Journal Register Company, 29 261–63
Journal Star Printing Company, **64** 237
Journey's End Corporation, **14** 107
Jove Publications, Inc., *see* Harcourt Brace and Co.
Joy Technologies Inc., **II** 17; **26** 70; **38** 227
JP Realty Inc., **57** 157
JPF Holdings, Inc. *see* U.S. Foodservice.
JPI, 49 239–41
JPMorgan Chase & Co., 91 273–84 (upd.)
JPS Automotive L.P., **17** 182–84
JPS Textile Group, Inc., 28 218–20
JR & F SA, **53** 32
JR Central, **43** 103
Jr. Food Stores, Inc., **51** 170
JR Tokai, **43** 103
JSC MMC Norilsk Nickel, 48 300–02
JSP Corporation, 74 161–64
JTN Acquisition Corp., **19** 233
JTS Corporation *see* Atari Corp.
j2 Global Communications, Inc., 75 219–21
Judge & Dolph, Ltd. *see* Wirtz Corp.
The Judge Group, Inc., 51 174–76
Jugend & Volk, **14** 556
Jugos del Valle, S.A. de C.V., 85 199–202
Juice Works, **26** 57
Juicy Couture, Inc., 80 172–74
Jujo Paper Co., Ltd., IV 297–98
JuJu Media, Inc., **41** 385
Julius Baer Holding AG, 52 203–05
Julius Blüthner Pianofortefabric GmbH, 78 185–88
Julius Meinl International AG, 53 177–80
Jumbo Food Stores *see* Shoppers Food Warehouse Corp.
Jumeirah Group, 83 227-230
Juniper Networks, Inc., 43 251–55
Juno Lighting, Inc., 30 266–68
Juno Online Services, Inc., 38 269–72 *see also* United Online, Inc.
Jupiter National, **15** 247–48; **19** 166
Jupiter Partners II, **62** 265
Jupiter Tyndall, **47** 84
Jupitermedia Corporation, 75 222–24
Juristförlaget, **14** 556
Jurys Doyle Hotel Group plc, 64 215–17
Jusco Car Life Company, **23** 290
JUSCO Co., Ltd., V 96–99 *see also* AEON Co., Ltd.
Jusco Group, **31** 430
Just Bagels Manufacturing, Inc., 94 268–71
Just Born, Inc., 32 305–07
Just For Feet, Inc., 19 228–30
Just-Rite Supply, Inc. *see* Just-Rite Supply, Inc.
Just Squeezed, **31** 350
Just Toys, Inc., **29** 476
Justin Industries, Inc., 19 231–33 *see also* Berkshire Hathaway Inc.
Juventus F.C. S.p.A, 53 181–83
JVC *see* Victor Company of Japan, Ltd.
JW Aluminum Company, *see* Walter Industries, Inc.
JW Bernard & Zn., **39** 203
JWD Group, Inc., **48** 238
JWP Inc., 9 300–02 *see also* EMCOR Group Inc.
JWT Group Inc., I 19–21 *see also* WPP Group plc.
JZC *see* John Zink Co.

K

K&B Inc., 12 286–88
K&F Manufacturing *see* Fender Musical Instruments.
K & G Men's Center, Inc., 21 310–12
K&K Insurance Group, **26** 487
K&K Toys, Inc., **23** 176
K&M Associates L.P., **16** 18; **43** 19
K&U Enterprise, **75** 230
K-C Aviation, *see* Kimberly-Clark Corp.
K-Group, *see* Kesko Ltd. (Kesko Oy).
K Shoes Ltd., **52** 57–58
K-Swiss Inc., 33 243–45; 89 277–81 (upd.)
K-tel International, Inc., 21 325–28
K-III Holdings *see* Primedia Inc.
K.H.S. Musical Instrument Co. Ltd., **53** 214
K.H. Wheel Company, *see* Hayes Lemmerz International, Inc.
K. Hattori & Co., Ltd. *see* Seiko Corp.
K.J. International Inc., **70** 74, 76
k.k. Staatsbahnen *see* Österreichische Bundesbahnen GmbH.
K Line *see* Kawasaki Kisen Kaisha, Ltd.
K-Line Pharmaceuticals Ltd. *see* Taro Phramaceutical Industries Ltd.
K.O. Lester Co., **31** 359, 361
K.P. American, **55** 305
K.W. Muth Company, *see* Masland Corp.
Kabelvision AB, **26** 331–33
Kable News Company *see* AMREP Corp.
Kafte Inc., **28** 63
Kagoshima Central Research Laboratory, **21** 330
Kaiser + Kraft GmbH, *see* GEHE AG
Kaiser Aluminum Corporation, IV 121–23; 84 212–217 (upd.)
Kaiser Foundation Health Plan, Inc., 53 184–86
Kaiser Packaging, **12** 377
Kaiser Permanente Corp. *see* Kaiser Foundation Health Plan, Inc.
Kaiser Steel, **IV** 59
Kaiser's Kaffee Geschäft AG, *see* Tengelmann Group.
Kajima Corporation, I 577–78; 51 177–79 (upd.)
Kal Kan Foods, Inc., 22 298–300
Kalamazoo Limited, **50** 377
Kaldveer & Associates, **14** 228
Kaliningradnefteprodukt, **48** 378
Kaman Corporation, 12 289–92; 42 204–08 (upd.)
Kaman Music Corporation, 68 205–07
Kamewa Group, *see* Vickers plc.
Kaminski/Engles Capital Corp. *see* Suiza Foods Corp.
Kammer Valves, A.G., *see* Duriron Co. Inc.
Kampgrounds of America, Inc., 33 230–33
Kamps AG, 44 251–54
Kana Software, Inc., 51 180–83
Kanagawa Chuo Kotsu Co., Ltd., **68** 281
Kanan Enterprises Inc., **74** 167

Kanebo, Ltd., 53 187–91
Kanematsu Corporation, IV 442–44; 24 259–62 (upd.)
Kangaroo *see* Seino Transportation Company, Ltd.
Kanpai Co. Ltd., **55** 375
Kansai Paint Company Ltd., 80 175–78
The Kansai Electric Power Company, Inc., V 645–48; 62 196–200 (upd.)
Kansai Plast Corporation, **74** 163
Kansallis-Osake-Pankki, II 302–03
Kansas City Ingredient Technologies, Inc., **49** 261
Kansas City Power & Light Company, 6 510–12 *see also* Great Plains Energy Inc.
Kansas City Southern Industries, Inc., 6 400–02; 26 233–36 (upd.)
The Kansas City Southern Railway Company, 92 198–202
Kansas City White Goods Company *see* Angelica Corp.
Kansas Fire & Casualty Co., *see* Berkshire Hathaway Inc.
Kansas Sand and Concrete, Inc., **72** 233
Kansas Utilities Company, **6** 580
The Kantar Group, **48** 442
Kao Corporation, III 38–39; 20 315–17 (upd.); 79 225–30 (upd.)
Kaolin Australia Pty Ltd. *see* English China Clays Ltd.
Kapalua Land Company, Ltd., **29** 307–08
Kaplan Educational Centers, **12** 143
Kaplan, Inc., 42 209–12; 90 270–75 (upd.)
Kaplan Musical String Company, **48** 231
Kapok Computers, **47** 153
Kar Nut Products Company, 86 233–36
Karan Co. *see* Donna Karan Co.
Karastan Bigelow, **19** 276
Karl Kani Infinity, Inc., 49 242–45
Karl Schmidt Unisia, Inc., **56** 158
Karlsberg Brauerei GmbH & Co KG, 41 220–23
Karrosseriewerke Weinsberg GmbH *see* ASC, Inc.
Karstadt Aktiengesellschaft, V 100–02; 19 234–37 (upd.)
Karstadt Quelle AG, 57 195–201 (upd.)
Karsten Manufacturing Corporation, 51 184–86
Kasco Corporation, **28** 42, 45
Kash n' Karry Food Stores, Inc., 20 318–20
Kashi Company, 89 282–85
Kashima Chlorine & Alkali Co., Ltd., **64** 35
Kaspare Cohn Commercial & Savings Bank *see* Union Bank of California.
Kasper A.S.L., Ltd., 40 276–79
Kasuga Radio Company *see* Kenwood Corp.
Kasumi Co., Ltd., **68** 9
Kat-Em International Inc., **16** 125
Katabami Kogyo Co. Ltd., **51** 179
Kate Industries, **74** 202
kate spade LLC, 68 208–11
Katharine Gibbs Schools Inc., **22** 442
Katherine Beecher Candies, Inc. *see* Warrell Corp.
Katies, **V** 35
Kativo Chemical Industries Ltd., *see* H. B. Fuller Co.
Katokichi Company Ltd., 82 187–90
Katy Industries Inc., I 472–74; 51 187–90 (upd.)
Katz Communications, Inc., 6 32–34 *see also* Clear Channel Communications, Inc.
Katz Media Group, Inc., 35 245–48
Kaufhalle AG, **V** 104; **23** 311; **41** 186–87
Kaufhof Warenhaus AG, V 103–05; 23 311–14 (upd.)
Kaufman and Broad Home Corporation, 8 284–86 *see also* KB Home.
Kaufmann Department Stores, Inc. *see* The May Department Stores Co.
Kaufring AG, 35 249–52
Oy Kaukas Ab *see* UPM-Kymmene
Kaukauna Cheese Inc., **23** 217, 219
Kawai Musical Instruments Manufacturing Co.,Ltd., 78 189–92
Kawasaki Heavy Industries, Ltd., III 538–40; 63 220–23 (upd.)
Kawasaki Kisen Kaisha, Ltd., V 457–60; 56 177–81 (upd.)
Kawasaki Steel Corporation, IV 124–25
Kawsmouth Electric Light Company *see* Kansas City Power & Light Co.
Kay-Bee Toy Stores, 15 252–53 *see also* KB Toys.
Kay Jewelers Inc., **61** 327
Kaydon Corporation, 18 274–76
Kaye, Scholer, Fierman, Hays & Handler, **47** 436
Kayex, *see* General Signal Corp.
Kaytee Products Incorporated, **58** 60
KB Home, 45 218–22 (upd.)
AO KB Impuls, **48** 419
KB Investment Co., Ltd., **58** 208
KB Toys, Inc., 35 253–55 (upd.); 86 237–42 (upd.)
KBLCOM Incorporated, **V** 644
KC *see* Kenneth Cole Productions, Inc.
KC Holdings, Inc., *see* Kimco Realty Corp.
KCI Konecranes International, **27** 269
KCK Tissue S.A., **73** 205
KCPL *see* Kansas City Power & Light Co.
KCS Industries, **12** 25–26
KCSI *see* Kansas City Southern Industries, Inc.
KCSR *see* Kansas City Southern Railway.
KD Acquisition Corporation, **34** 103–04; **76** 239
KD Manitou, Inc. *see* Manitou BF S.A.
KDI Corporation, **56** 16–17
Keane, Inc., 56 182–86
Keck's *see* Decorator Industries Inc.
The Keds Corp., **37** 377, 379
Keebler Foods Company, 36 311–13
Keene Packaging Co., **28** 43
KEG Productions Ltd., **IV** 640; **26** 272
Keio Teito Electric Railway Company, V 461–62
The Keith Companies Inc., 54 181–84
Keithley Instruments Inc., 16 299–301
Kelco, **34** 281
Kelda Group plc, 45 223–26
Keliher Hardware Company, **57** 8
Kelkoo S.A. *see* Yahoo! Inc.
Kelley Blue Book Company, Inc., 84 218–221
Keller Builders, **43** 400
Keller-Dorian Graveurs, S.A., *see* Standex International Corp.
Kelley Drye & Warren LLP, 40 280–83
Kellock Holdings Ltd., *see* The Governor and Company of the Bank of Scotland.
Kellogg Brown & Root, Inc., 62 201–05 (upd.)
Kellogg Company, II 523–26; 13 291–94 (upd.); 50 291–96 (upd.)
Kellwood Company, 8 287–89; 85 203–08 (upd.)
Kelly-Moore Paint Company, Inc., 56 187–89
Kelly Services, Inc., 6 35–37; 26 237–40 (upd.)
The Kelly-Springfield Tire Company, 8 290–92
Kelsey-Hayes Group of Companies, 7 258–60; 27 249–52 (upd.)
Kelso & Co., **21** 490; **33** 92; **63** 237; **71** 145–46
Kelvinator of India, Ltd., **59** 417
KemaNobel, *see* Asko Nobel N.V.
Kemet Corp., 14 281–83
Kemira Oyj, 70 143–46
Kemper Corporation, III 269–71; 15 254–58 (upd.)
Kemper Financial Services, **26** 234
Ken's Foods, Inc., 88 223–26
Kencraft, Inc., **71** 22–23
Kendall International, Inc., 11 219–21 *see also* Tyco International Ltd.
Kendall-Jackson Winery, Ltd., 28 221–23
Kendle International Inc., 87 276–279
Kenetech Corporation, 11 222–24
Kenexa Corporation, 87 280–284
Kenhar Corporation *see* Cascade Corp.
Kenmore Air Harbor Inc., 65 191–93
Kennametal, Inc., 13 295–97; 68 212–16 (upd.)
Kennecott Corporation, 7 261–64; 27 253–57 (upd.) *see also* Rio Tinto PLC.
Kennedy-Wilson, Inc., 60 183–85
Kenner Parker Toys, Inc., **25** 488–89
Kenneth Cole Productions, Inc., 25 256–58
Kenneth O. Lester, Inc., **21** 508
Kenny Rogers' Roasters, **29** 342, 344
Kenroy International, Inc., *see* Hunter Fan Co.
Kensey Nash Corporation, 71 185–87
Kensington Associates L.L.C., **60** 146
Kensington Publishing Corporation, 84 222–225
Kent Electronics Corporation, 17 273–76
Kentrox Industries, **30** 7
Kentucky Electric Steel, Inc., 31 286–88

Kentucky Fried Chicken *see* KFC Corp.
Kentucky Institution for the Education of the Blind *see* American Printing House for the Blind.
Kentucky Utilities Company, 6 513–15
Kenwood Corporation, 31 289–91
Kenwood Silver Company, Inc., **31** 352
Kenwood Winery, **68** 146
Kenya Airways Limited, 89 286–89
Kenyon Corp., **18** 276
Kenzo, **25** 122
Keolis SA, 51 191–93
Kepco *see* Korea Electric Power Corporation; Kyushu Electric Power Company Inc.
Keppel Corporation Ltd., 73 201–03
Keramik Holding AG Laufen, 51 194–96
Kerasotes ShowPlace Theaters LLC, 80 179–83
Kernite SA, *see* NCH Corp.
Kernkraftwerke Lippe-Ems, **V** 747
Kerr Concrete Pipe Company, **14** 250
Kerr Corporation, **14** 481
Kerr Drug Stores, **32** 170
Kerr Group Inc., 24 263–65
Kerr-McGee Corporation, IV 445–47; 22 301–04 (upd.); 68 217–21 (upd.)
Kerry Group plc, 27 258–60; 87 285–291 (upd.)
Kerry Properties Limited, 22 305–08
Kerzner International Limited, 69 222–24 (upd.)
Kesa Electricals plc, 91 285–90
Kesko Ltd (Kesko Oy), 8 293–94; 27 261–63 (upd.)
Kessler Rehabilitation Corporation *see* Select Medical Corp.
Ketchikan Paper Company, **31** 316
Ketchum Communications Inc., 6 38–40
Kettle Chip Company (Australia), **26** 58
Kettle Foods Inc., 48 240–42
Kettle Restaurants, Inc., **29** 149
Kewaunee Scientific Corporation, 25 259–62
Kewpie Kabushiki Kaisha, 57 202–05
Key Industries, Inc., **26** 342
Key Pharmaceuticals, Inc., **41** 419
Key Production Company, Inc. *see* Cimarex Energy Co.
Key Safety Systems, Inc., 63 224–26
Key Tronic Corporation, 14 284–86
KeyCorp, 8 295–97; 92272–81 (upd.)
Keyes Fibre Company, 9 303–05
KeyLabs, **65** 34–35
Keypage *see* Rural Cellular Corp.
Keypoint Technology Corporation *see* ViewSonic Corp.
Keys Fitness Products, LP, 83 231-234
KeySpan Energy Co., 27 264–66
Keystone Consolidated Industries, Inc., **19** 467
Keystone Health Plans, Inc., *see* Highmark Inc.
Keystone Insurance and Investment Co., *see* Zions Bancorporation.
Keystone International, Inc., 11 225–27 *see also* Tyco International Ltd.
Keystone Life Insurance Co., **33** 419
Keystone Portland Cement Co., **23** 225
Keystone Tube Inc., **25** 8
KFC Corporation, 7 265–68; 21 313–17 (upd.); 89 290–96 (upd.)
KFF Management, **37** 350
Kforce Inc., 71 188–90
KHBB, **16** 72
KHD AG *see* Klöckner-Humboldt-Deutz AG.
KHD Konzern, III 541–44
KHF Finland Oy, **70** 126
KHL *see* Koninklijke Hollandsche Lloyd.
KI, 57 206–09
Kia Motors Corporation, 12 293–95; 29 264–67 (upd.); 56 173
Kiabi Europe, 66 199–201
Kian Dai Wools Co. Ltd., **53** 344
Kickers Worldwide, **35** 204, 207
Kidd, Kamm & Co., **21** 482; **74** 323
Kidde plc, I 475–76; 44 255–59 (upd.)
Kidder, Peabody & Co., **II** 31, 207, 430; **12** 197
Kiddie Products, Inc. *see* The First Years Inc.
Kids 'R Us *see* Toys 'R Us.
Kidz Biz Ltd., **52** 193
Kiehl's Since 1851, Inc., 52 209–12
Kien, *see* Koninklijke Vendex KBB N.V. (Royal Vendex KBB N.V.)
Kiewit Diversified Group Inc. *see* Level 3 Communications, Inc.
Kiewit Materials *see* Rinker Group Ltd.
Kiewit-Murdock Investment Corp., **15** 129
Kijkshop/Best-Sellers, *see* Koninklijke Vendex KBB N.V. (Royal Vendex KBB N.V.)
Kikkoman Corporation, 14 287–89; 47 203–06 (upd.)
Killington, Ltd., **28** 21
Kilpatrick's Department Store, **19** 511
KIM Holdings, Inc., **66** 204
Kimball International, Inc., 12 296–98; 48 243–47 (upd.)
Kimberly-Clark Corporation, III 40–41; 16 302–05 (upd.); 43 256–60 (upd.)
Kimberly-Clark de México, S.A. de C.V., 54 185–87
Kimco Realty Corporation, 11 228–30
Kimowelt Medien, **39** 13
Kincaid Furniture Company, *see* La-Z-Boy Inc.
Kindai Golf Company, **32** 447
Kinden Corporation, **7** 303
Kinder Morgan, Inc., 45 227–30
KinderCare Learning Centers, Inc., 13 298–300
Kindergard Corporation, **57** 230
Kineret Acquisition Corp. *see* The Hain Celestial Group, Inc.
Kinetek, Inc., **70** 142
Kinetic Concepts, Inc., 20 321–23
King & Spalding, 23 315–18
The King Arthur Flour Company, 31 292–95
King Bearing, Inc., *see* Bearings, Inc.
King Features Syndicate, **IV** 626; **19** 201, 203–04; **46** 232
King Hickory, **17** 183
King Kullen Grocery Co., Inc., 15 259–61
King Nut Company, 74 165–67
King Pharmaceuticals, Inc., 54 188–90
King Ranch, Inc., 14 290–92; 60 186–89 (upd.)
King Soopers Inc., *see* Dillon Companies Inc.
King World Productions, Inc., 9 306–08; 30 269–72 (upd.)
Kingbird Media Group LLC, **26** 80
Kingfisher plc, V 106–09; 24 266–71 (upd.); 83 235-242 (upd.)
Kingston Technology Corporation, 20 324–26
Kinki Nippon Railway Company Ltd., V 463–65
Kinki Piping Company Ltd., **60** 236
Kinko's Inc., 16 306–08; 43 261–64 (upd.)
Kinnevik *see* Industriförvaltnings AB Kinnevik.
Kinney Corporation, **23** 32
Kinney Shoe Corp., 14 293–95
Kinoshita Sansho Steel Co., *see* Mitsui & Co., Ltd.
Kinpo Electronic, **23** 212
Kinray Inc., 85 209–12
Kinross Gold Corporation, 36 314–16
Kintana, Inc., **59** 295
Kintec Corp., *see* Andrew Corp.
Kintera, Inc., 75 225–27
Kirby *see* Scott Fetzer Co.
Kirby Corporation, 18 277–79; 66 202–04 (upd.)
KirchMedia GmbH & Co., **54** 295–98
KirchPayTV, **46** 402
Kirin Brewery Company, Limited, I 265–66; 21 318–21 (upd.); 63 227–31 (upd.)
Kirk Stieff Company, *see* Lenox, Inc.
Kirkland & Ellis LLP, 65 194–96
Kirkland Messina, Inc., *see* The Selmer Co., Inc.
Kirsch Co., *see* Cooper Industries, Inc.
Kirshenbaum Bond + Partners, Inc., 57 210–12
Kirsten Modedesign GmbH & Co. KG, **53** 195
Kirtland Capital Partners, **67** 312–13
Kit Manufacturing Co., 18 280–82
Kitchell Corporation, 14 296–98
The Kitchen Collection, Inc. *see* Nacco Industries Inc.
Kitchen Investment Group, Inc., **76** 126
KitchenAid, 8 298–99
Kitty Hawk, Inc., 22 309–11
Kiwi International Airlines Inc., 20 327–29
Kiwi Polish Co., **15** 507
KJJ *see* Klaus J. Jacobs Holdings.
KJPCL *see* Royal Interocean Lines.
KKR *see* Kohlberg Kravis Roberts & Co.

KLA-Tencor Corporation, **11 231–33**; **45 231–34 (upd.)**
Klabin S.A., **73 204–06**
Klasky Csupo, Inc., **78 193–97**
Klaus J. Jacobs Holdings, **29** 46–47; **71** 46
Klaus Steilmann GmbH & Co. KG, **53 192–95**
KLC/New City Televentures, *see* The Kushner-Locke Co.
Klein Bicycles, **16** 495
Klein Sleep Products Inc., **32** 426
Kleiner, Perkins, Caufield & Byers, **53 196–98**
Kleinwort Benson Group PLC, **II 421–23**; **22** 55 *see also* Dresdner Kleinwort Wasserstein.
Klement's Sausage Company, **61 147–49**
KLM Royal Dutch Airlines *see* Koninklijke Luftvaart Maatschappij N.V.
Klöckner-Humboldt-Deutz AG *see* KHD Konzern.
Klöckner-Werke AG, **IV 126–28**; **58 201–05 (upd.)**
Klondike, **14** 205
Kloof Gold Mining Company Ltd., **62** 164
Klopman International S.r.l., *see* Dominion Textile Inc.
Klüber Lubrication München KG, **41** 170
Kluwer Publishers, *see* Wolters Kluwer NV.
Klynveld Peat Marwick Goerdeler *see* KPMG International.
KM&G *see* Ketchum Communications Inc.
Kmart Canada Co., **25** 222
Kmart Corporation, **V 110–12**; **18 283–87 (upd.)**; **47 207–12 (upd.)**
Kmart Mexico, **36** 139
KMI Corporation, **55** 302
KMI Europe, Inc., **68** 207
KN *see* Kühne & Nagel Group.
KN Energy *see* Kinder Morgan, Inc.
Knape & Vogt Manufacturing Company, **17 277–79**
K'Nex Industries, Inc., **52 206–08**
KNI Retail A/S, **12** 363
Knife River Coal Mining Company, *see* MDU Resources Group, Inc.
Knife River Corporation, **42** 249, 253
Knight-Ridder, Inc., **IV 628–30**; **15 262–66 (upd.)**; **67 219–23 (upd.)**
Knight Trading Group, Inc., **70 147–49**
Knight Transportation, Inc., **64 218–21**
Knightsbridge Capital Corporation, **59** 192
Knightsbridge Partners, **26** 476
Knightway Promotions Ltd., **64** 346
Knogo Corp., **11** 444; **39** 78
Knoll, Inc., **14 299–301**; **80 184–88 (upd.)**
Knorr-Bremse AG, **84 226–231**
Knorr Co. *see* C.H. Knorr Co.
Knorr Foods Co., Ltd., **28** 10
The Knot, Inc., **74 168–71**
Knott's Berry Farm, **18 288–90**
Knowledge Learning Corporation, **51 197–99**; **54** 191
Knowledge Systems Concepts, **11** 469
Knowledge Universe, Inc., **54 191–94**
KnowledgeWare Inc., **9 309–11**; **31 296–98 (upd.)**
Knox County Insurance, **41** 178
Knoxville Glove Co., **34** 159
KNP BT *see* Buhrmann NV.
KNP Leykam, **49** 352, 354
KNSM *see* Koninklijke Nederlandsche Stoomboot Maatschappij.
Knudsen & Sons, Inc., *see* The J.M. Smucker Co.
KOA *see* Kampgrounds of America, Inc.
Koala Corporation, **44 260–62**
Kobe Hankyu Company Ltd., **62** 170
Kobe Steel, Ltd., **IV 129–31**; **19 238–41 (upd.)**
Kobold *see* Vorwerk & Co.
Kobrand Corporation, **82 191–94**
Koç Holding A.S., **I 478–80**; **54 195–98 (upd.)**
Koch Enterprises, Inc., **29 215–17**
Koch Industries, Inc., **IV 448–49**; **20 330–32 (upd.)**; **77 224–30 (upd.)**
Kodak *see* Eastman Kodak Co.
Kodansha Ltd., **IV 631–33**; **38 273–76 (upd.)**
Koehring Cranes & Excavators, *see* Terex Corp.
Koei Real Estate Ltd. *see* Takashimaya Co., Ltd.
Koenig & Bauer AG, **64 222–26**
Kogaku Co., Ltd., **48** 295
Kohl's Corporation, **9 312–13**; **30 273–75 (upd.)**; **77 231–35 (upd.)**
Kohlberg Kravis Roberts & Co., **24 272–74**; **56 190–94 (upd.)**
Kohler Company, **7 269–71**; **32 308–12 (upd.)**
Kohler Mix Specialties, Inc. *see*Dean Foods.
Kohn Pedersen Fox Associates P.C., **57 213–16**
Kokkola Chemicals Oy, *see* OM Group, Inc.
Kokomo Gas and Fuel Company, **6** 533
Kokudo Corporation, **74** 301
Kokusai Kigyo Co. Ltd., **60** 301
Kolb-Lena, **25** 85
The Koll Company, **8 300–02**
Kollmorgen Corporation, **18 291–94**
Kölnische Rückversicherungs- Gesellschaft AG, *see* General Re Corp.
Komag, Inc., **11 234–35**
Komatsu Ltd., **III 545–46**; **16 309–11 (upd.)**; **52 213–17 (upd.)**
Kompass Allgemeine Vermögensberatung, **51** 23
KONE Corporation, **27 267–70**; **76 225–28 (upd.)**
Kongl. Elektriska Telegraf-Verket *see* Swedish Telecom.
Konica Corporation, **III 547–50**; **30 276–81 (upd.)**
König Brauerei GmbH & Co. KG, **35 256–58 (upd.)**
Koninklijke Ahold N.V., **II 641–42**; **16 312–14 (upd.)**
Koninklijke Bols Wessanen, N.V., **29** 480–81; **57** 105
Koninklijke Grolsch BV *see* Royal Grolsch NV.
Koninklijke Hoogovens NV *see* Koninklijke Nederlandsche Hoogovens en Staalfabrieken NV.
Koninklijke Java-China Paketvaart Lijnen *see* Royal Interocean Lines.
NV Koninklijke KNP BT *see* Buhrmann NV.
Koninklijke KPN N.V. *see* Royal KPN N.V.
Koninklijke Luchtvaart Maatschappij N.V., **I 107–09**; **28 224–27 (upd.)**
Koninklijke Nederlandsche Hoogovens en Staalfabrieken NV, **IV 132–34**
Koninklijke Nederlandsche Stoomboot Maatschappij, **26** 241
N.V. Koninklijke Nederlandse Vliegtuigenfabriek Fokker, **I 54–56**; **28 327–30 (upd.)**
Koninklijke Nedlloyd N.V., **6 403–05**; **26 241–44 (upd.)**
Koninklijke Numico N.V. *see* Royal Numico N.V.
Koninklijke Paketvaart Maatschappij, **26** 242
Koninklijke Philips Electronics N.V., **50 297–302 (upd.)**
Koninklijke PTT Nederland NV, **V 299–301** *see also* Royal KPN NV.
Koninklijke Vendex KBB N.V. (Royal Vendex KBB N.V.), **62 206–09 (upd.)**
Koninklijke Wessanen nv, **II 527–29**; **54 199–204 (upd.)**
Koninklijke West-Indische Maildienst, **26** 242
Konishiroku Honten Co., Ltd., *see* Konica Corp.
Konrad Hornschuch AG, **31** 161–62
Koo Koo Roo, Inc., **25 263–65**
Kookmin Bank, **58 206–08**
Koop Nautic Holland, **41** 412
Koor Industries Ltd., **II 47–49**; **25 266–68 (upd.)**; **68 222–25 (upd.)**
Kopin Corporation, **80 189–92**
Köpings Mekaniska Verkstad, **26** 10
Koppel Steel, **26** 407
Koppers Industries, Inc., **I 354–56**; **26 245–48 (upd.)**
Koramic Roofing Products N.V., **70** 363
Korbel Champagne Cellers *see* F. Korbel & Bros. Inc.
Körber AG, **60 190–94**
Korea Automotive Motor Corp., *see* Robert Bosch GmbH.
Korea Electric Power Corporation (Kepco), **56 195–98**
Korea Ginseng Corporation *see* KT&G Corp.
Korea Independent Energy Corporation, **62** 175

Korea Tobacco & Ginseng Corporation *see* KT&G Corp.
Korean Air Lines Co. Ltd., 6 98–99; 27 271–73 (upd.)
Korean Life Insurance Company, Ltd., **62** 175
Koret of California, Inc., 62 210–13
Kori Kollo Corp., **23** 41
Korn/Ferry International, 34 247–49
Korrekt Gebäudereinigung, *see* Randstad Holding n.v.
Kortbetalning Servo A.B., *see* Skandinaviska Enskilda Banken AB.
Kos Pharmaceuticals, Inc., 63 232–35
Koss Corporation, 38 277–79
Kosset Carpets, Ltd., *see* Shaw Industries.
Koszegi Industries Inc. *see* Forward Industries, Inc.
Kotobukiya Co., Ltd., V 113–14; 56 199–202 (upd.)
Koyland Ltd., **64** 217
KP Corporation, **74** 163
KPM *see* Koninklijke Paketvaart Maatschappij.
KPMG International, 10 385–87; 33 234–38 (upd.)
KPN *see* Koninklijke PTT Nederland N.V.
KPR Holdings Inc., **23** 203
KPS Special Situations Fund, L.P., **69** 360–62
Kraft Foods Inc., II 530–34; 7 272–77 (upd.); 45 235–44 (upd.); 91 291–306 (upd.)
Kraft Foodservice, **26** 504; **31** 359–60
Kraft Jacobs Suchard AG, 26 249–52 (upd.)
KraftMaid Cabinetry, Inc., 72 208–10
Kragen Auto Supply Co. *see* CSK Auto Corp.
Kramer Guitar, **29** 222
Kramer Machine and Engineering Company, **26** 117
Krames Communications Co., **22** 441, 443
Kransco, **25** 314; **61** 392
Krasnapolsky Restaurant and Wintergarden Company Ltd., **23** 228
Kraus-Anderson Companies, Inc., 36 317–20; 83 243-248 (upd.)
Krause Publications, Inc., 35 259–61
Krause's Furniture, Inc., 27 274–77
Krauss-Maffei AG, *see* Mannesmann AG
Kredietbank N.V., II 304–056
Kreditanstalt für Wiederaufbau, 29 268–72
Kreher Steel Co., **25** 8
Krelitz Industries, Inc., *see* D&K Wholesale Drug, Inc.
Kresge Foundation *see* Kmart Corp.
Kreymborg, *see*Koninklijke Vendex KBB N.V. (Royal Vendex KBB N.V.)
Krispy Kreme Doughnut Corporation, 21 322–24; 61 150–54 (upd.)
Kristall, **62** 10
Kroenke Sports Enterprises, **51** 97
Kroeze, **25** 82
The Kroger Company, II 643–45; 15 267–70 (upd.); 65 197–202 (upd.)
Kroll Inc., 57 217–20
Kronans Droghandel, **72** 258
Krone AG, **33** 220
Kronos, Inc., 18 295–97; 19 468
Kroy Tanning Company, *see* Fuqua Enterprises, Inc.
KRS Corporation, **57** 202–04
Krueger Insurance Company, **21** 257
Krueger International *see* KI.
Kruger Inc., 17 280–82
Kruidvat, **54** 265–67
Krung Thai Bank Public Company Ltd., 69 225–27
Krupp AG *see* Fried. Krupp GmbH; ThyssenKrupp AG.
Kruse International, 88 227–30
The Krystal Company, 33 239–42
KSB AG, 62 214–18
KT&G Corporation, 62 219–21
KT Contract Services, *see* Coach USA, Inc.
KTR *see* Keio Teito Electric Railway Co.
K2 Inc., 16 295–98; 84 206–211 (upd.)
KU Energy Corporation, 11 236–38 *see also* LG&E Energy Corp.
Kubota Corporation, III 551–53
Kudelski Group SA, 44 263–66
Kuehne & Nagel International AG, V 466–69; 53 199–203 (upd.)
Kuhlman Corporation, 20 333–35
Kühn + Bayer, *see* Fisher Scientific International Inc.
Kühne & Nagel International AG, V 466–69
Kulicke and Soffa Industries, Inc., 33 246–48; 76 229–31 (upd.)
Kumagai Gumi Company, Ltd., I 579–80
Kumba Resources, **57** 183, 186
Kumon Institute of Education Co., Ltd., 72 211–14
KUNPETROL Kiskunhalasi Szolgáltató Kft., **70** 195
Kunz-Holding GmbH & Co., **53** 216
Kuok Group, **28** 84; **57** 292, 294; **71** 331–32
Kuoni Travel Holding Ltd., 40 284–86
The Kuppenheimer Company, *see* Hartmarx Corp.
Kurabo Industries Ltd., **61** 229
Kuraray Co., Ltd., **72** 363
Kurzweil Technologies, Inc., 51 200–04
KUS *see* Karl Schmidt Unisia, Inc.
The Kushner-Locke Company, 25 269–71
Kuwait Airways Corporation, 68 226–28
Kuwait Aviation Fueling Co., **55** 243
Kuwait Flour Mills & Bakeries Company, 84 232–234
Kuwait Investment Office, **IV** 452
Kuwait Petroleum Corporation, IV 450–52; 55 240–43 (upd.)
Kvaerner ASA, 36 321–23
KW, Inc. *see* Coca-Cola Bottling Company of Northern New England, Inc.
Kwang Yang Motor Company Ltd., 80 193–96
Kwik-Fit Holdings plc, 54 205–07
Kwik Save Group plc, 11 239–41
Kwik Shop, Inc., **se** Dillon Companies Inc.
KWIM *see* Koninklijke West-Indische Maildienst.
Kyivstar GSM, **69** 344, 346
Kymco *see* Kwang Yang Motor Company Ltd.
Kymmene Corporation, IV 299–303 *see also* UPM-Kymmene Corp.
Kyocera Corporation, II 50–52; 21 329–32 (upd.); 79 231–36 (upd.)
Kyodo Kako, **IV** 680
Kyodo Kokusan K.K., **21** 271
Kyodo Veneer and Plywood Co. Ltd., *see* Toyo Sash Co., Ltd.
Kyoei Steel, **59** 202
Kyokuyo Company Ltd., 75 228–30
Kyosai Trust Co. *see* Yasuda Trust and Banking Company, Ltd.
Kyotaru Co., **66** 270–71
Kyoto Ceramic Co., Ltd. *see* Kyocera Corp.
Kyowa Hakko Kogyo Co., Ltd., III 42–43; 48 248–50 (upd.)
Kyowa Seeds, **70** 346
Kyphon Inc., 87 292–295
Kyushu Electric Power Company Inc., V 649–51

L

L&H *see* Lernout and Hauspie.
L. and J.G. Stickley, Inc., 50 303–05
L&W Supply Corp., *see* USG Corp.
L E Lundbergföretagen AB, **52** 161, 164
L-3 Communications Holdings, Inc., 48 251–53
L.A. Darling Company, 92 203–06
L.A. Dreyfus Company, **58** 378
L.A. Gear, Inc., 8 303–06; 32 313–17 (upd.)
L.A. Mex *see* Checkers Drive-Up Restaurants Inc.
L.A. T Sportswear, Inc., 26 257–59
L.B. Foster Company, 33 255–58
L. Bosendorfer Klavierfabrik, A.G., *see* Kimball International, Inc.
L.D.C. SA, 61 155–57
The L.D. Caulk Company, *see* Dentsply International Inc.
L. Grossman and Sons *see* Grossman's Inc.
L.J. Melody & Co., **21** 97
L. Kellenberger & Co. AG, *see* Hardinge Inc.
L.L. Bean, Inc., 10 388–90; 38 280–83 (upd.); 91 307–13 (upd.)
The L.L. Knickerbocker Co., Inc., 25 272–75
L. Luria & Son, Inc., 19 242–44
L. M. Berry and Company, 80 197–200
L.M. Ericsson *see* Telefonaktiebolaget LM Ericsson.

L-O-F Glass Co. *see* Libbey-Owens-Ford Glass Co.
L.S. Holding, Inc., **60** 204
L.S. Starrett Company, 13 301–03; 64 227–30 (upd.)
L.W. Pierce Co., Inc. *see* Pierce Leahy Corp.
La Banque Suisse et Française *see* Crédit Commercial de France.
La Cadena Investments, **64** 364
La Cerus, **IV** 615
La Choy Food Products Inc., 25 276–78
La Cinq, **IV** 619
La Cloche d'Or, **25** 85
La Grange Foundry, Inc., **39** 31
La Halle aux Vêtements, *see* Vivarte SA.
La Joya, **51** 389
La Madeleine French Bakery & Café, 33 249–51
La Maison du Jambon, **58** 218
La Martiniere Groupe, **58** 152
La Mesa RV Center, Inc., **69** 230
La Oroya, **22** 286
La Pizza Loca Inc., **44** 86
La Poste, V 270–72; 47 213–16 (upd.)
The La Quinta Companies, 11 242–44; 42 213–16 (upd.)
La Redoute S.A., *see* PPR SA.
La Rinascente, **12** 153
La Ruche Meridionale, **12** 153
La Senza Corporation, 66 205–07
La 7, **47** 345, 347
La Societe Anonyme Francaise Holophane, *see* Holophane Corp.
La Supercalor S.P.A. *see* De'Longhi S.p.A.
La-Z-Boy Incorporated, 14 302–04; 50 309–13 (upd.)
LAB *see* Lloyd Aereo de Bolivia.
The Lab, Inc., **37** 263
LaB Investing Co. L.L.C, **37** 224
LaBarge Inc., 41 224–26
Labatt Brewing Company Limited, I 267–68; 25 279–82 (upd.)
Labatt U.S.A., **54** 212–14
L'Abeille SA, **61** 44–45
Labeyrie SAS, 80 201–04
LabOne, Inc., 48 254–57
Labor Ready, Inc., 29 273–75; 88 231–36 (upd.)
Labor W *see* Sennheiser Electronic GmbH and Co. AG.
Laboratoire L. Lafon, **45** 94
Laboratoires Arkopharma S.A., 75 231–34
Laboratoires de Biologie Végétale Yves Rocher, 35 262–65
Laboratorio Chile S.A., **55** 233
Laboratorios Elmor S.A., **55** 233
Laboratorium Wennebostel *see* Sennheiser Electronic GmbH and Co. AG.
Laboratory Corporation of America Holdings, 42 217–20 (upd.)
LaBranche & Co. Inc., 37 223–25
Labsphere, Inc., **48** 446
Labtronics, Inc., **49** 307–08
Laci Le Beau Tea, **49** 275–76
LaCie Group S.A., 76 232–34
Lacks Enterprises Inc., 61 158–60
Laclede Steel Company, 15 271–73
Lacombe Electric *see* Public Service Company of Colorado.
LaCrosse Footwear, Inc., 18 298–301; 61 161–65 (upd.)
Lacto Ibérica, **23** 219
Lactos, **25** 85
Ladbroke Group PLC, II 141–42; 21 333–36 (upd.) *see also* Hilton Group plc.
LADD Furniture, Inc., 12 299–301 *see also* La-Z-Boy Inc.
Ladd Petroleum Corp., *see* General Electric Co.
LADECO *see* Iberia.
Ladenburg, Thalmann & Co. Inc., *see* New Valley Corp.
Ladish Co., Inc., 30 282–84
Lady Foot Locker, **V** 226
Lafarge Cement UK, 54 208–11 (upd.)
Lafarge Coppée S.A., III 703–05
Lafarge Corporation, 28 228–31
Lafayette Manufacturing Co., *see* Kimball International, Inc.
Lafuma S.A., 39 248–50
LAG&E *see* Los Angeles Gas and Electric Co.
LaGard Inc., **20** 363
Lagardère Groupe SCA, **16** 254; **34** 83
Laidlaw International, Inc., 80 205–08
Laiki Group *see* Marfin Popular Bank plc.
Laing O'Rourke PLC, 93 282–85 (upd.)
Laing's Properties Ltd. *see* John Laing plc.
L'Air Liquide SA, I 357–59; 47 217–20 (upd.)
Lake Erie Screw Corp., *see* TriMas Corp.
Lake Pacific Partners, LLC, **55** 124
Lake Superior & Ishpeming Railroad Company, **62** 74
Lake Superior Paper Industries, **26** 363
Lakehead Pipe Line Partners, L.P., **43** 155
Lakeland Industries, Inc., 45 245–48
Lakes Entertainment, Inc., 51 205–07
Lakeside Foods, Inc., 89 297–301
The Lakeside Publishing and Printing Co. *see* R.R. Donnelley & Sons Co.
Lakestone Systems, Inc., **11** 469
Lakewood Animal Hospital, Inc., **58** 354
Lala *see* Grupo Industrial Lala, S.A. de C.V.
Lalique, **55** 309
Lam Research Corporation, 11 245–47; 31 299–302 (upd.)
Lam Son Sugar Joint Stock Corporation (Lasuco), 60 195–97
Lamar Advertising Company, 27 278–80; 70 150–53 (upd.)
The Lamaur Corporation, 41 227–29
Lamb Technicon Corp., *see* Litton Industries Inc.
Lamb Weston, Inc., 23 319–21
Lambda Electronics Inc., **32** 411
Lambert Brussels Financial Corporation *see* Drexel Burnham Lambert Inc.
Lambert Frères, **33** 339
Lambert Rivière, **41** 340
Lamborghini *see* Automobili Lamborghini S.p.A.
Lamkin Brothers, Inc., *see* NCH Corp.
Lamons Metal Gasket Co., *see* TriMas Corp.
Lamonts Apparel, Inc., 15 274–76
Lampadaires Feralux, Inc., *see* Valmont Industries, Inc.
Lamplight Farms Inc. *see* W.C. Bradley Co.
The Lamson & Sessions Co., 13 304–06; 61 166–70 (upd.)
Lan Chile S.A., 31 303–06
Lancair International, Inc., 67 224–26
Lancaster Colony Corporation, 8 307–09; 61 171–74 (upd.)
Lancaster Press, **23** 102
Lance, Inc., 14 305–07; 41 230–33 (upd.)
Lancel, *see* Vendôme Luxury Group plc.
Lancer Corporation, 21 337–39
Lancey Investissement SAS, **58** 221
Land Group, **74** 283
Land O'Lakes, Inc., II 535–37; 21 340–43 (upd.); 81 222–27 (upd.)
Land-O-Sun Dairies, L.L.C., **26** 449
Land Securities PLC, IV 704–06; 49 246–50 (upd.)
Landair Corporation, **75** 148
LandAmerica Financial Group, Inc., 85 213–16
Landauer, Inc., 51 208–10
Lander Company, **21** 54
Landmark Business Products, Inc., **61** 254
Landmark Communications, Inc., 12 302–05; 55 244–49 (upd.)
Landmark Financial Services Inc., **11** 447
Landmark Theatre Corporation, 70 154–56
Landoll, Inc., *see* Tribune Co.
Landor Associates, 81 228–31
Landry's Restaurants, Inc., 15 277–79; 65 203–07 (upd.)
Lands' End, Inc., 9 314–16; 29 276–79 (upd.); 82 195–200 (upd.)
Landsbanki Islands hf, 81 232–35
Landstar System, Inc., 63 236–38
Lane Bryant, Inc., 64 231–33
The Lane Co., Inc., 12 306–08
Lane Industries Inc., **73** 160
Lane, Piper, and Jaffray, Inc. *see* Piper Jaffray Companies.
Lane Publishing Co., **IV** 676; **7** 529
Laneco, Inc., *see* Wetterau Inc.
Lang Exploratory Drilling, **26** 42
Langdon Rieder Corp., **21** 97
Lange International S.A., **15** 462; **43** 375–76
Langen Packaging Inc., **51** 249, 251
Langenpac NV, **51** 249–50
Langenscheidt KG, **74** 33
Lanier Worldwide, Inc., 75 235–38
Lanman Companies, Inc., **23** 101
Lannet Data Communications Ltd., **26** 275–77
Lanoga Corporation, 62 222–24
LAPE *see* Líneas Aéreas Postales Españolas.
Lapeyre S.A. *see* Groupe Lapeyre S.A.
LaPine Technology, **II** 51; **21** 331
Lara, **19** 192

Lareco, **26** 22
Largardère Groupe, **43** 210
Largo Entertainment, **25** 329
Largo Music Publishing, **55** 250
Lariat Petroleum, **65** 262
Larousse Group *see* Groupe de la Cité.
Larry Flynt Publishing Inc., 31 307–10
Larry H. Miller Group, 29 280–83
Larry's Food Products, **36** 163
Larsen Company, *see* Dean Foods Co.
Larson Boats *see* Genmar Holdings, Inc.
Las Vegas Sands, Inc., 50 306–08
LaSalle Investment Management, Inc., **49** 238
LaSalle Partners, **49** 28
LaSalle Steel Corporation, **28** 314
Laser Tech Color, **21** 60
Laserscope, 67 227–29
LaSiDo Inc., 58 209–11
Lasik*Plus* *see* LCA-Vision, Inc.
Lasmo, **IV** 455, 499; **65** 316–17
Lason, Inc., 31 311–13
Lassonde Industries Inc., 68 229–31
Lasuco *see* Lam Son Sugar Joint Stock Corp.
Latasa SA *see* Rexam PLC.
Latcom, Inc., **55** 302
Latham & Watkins, 33 252–54
Latin Communications Group Inc., **41** 151
Latin Percussion, Inc. *see* Kaman Music Corp.
Latitude Communications, **22** 52
Latrobe Brewing Company, 54 212–14
Lattice Semiconductor Corp., 16 315–17
Lauda Air Luftfahrt AG, 48 258–60
Laura Ashley Holdings plc, 13 307–09; 37 226–29 (upd.)
Laura Scudders, **44** 348
Laureate Enterprises Inc., **64** 190
Laurel Glen, **34** 3, 5
Laurel Pipe Line Company *see* Buckeye Partners, L.P.
The Laurel Pub Company Limited, 59 255–57
Laurel Technologies Partnership, **58** 101
Laurent-Perrier SA, 42 221–23
Laurentian Group, **48** 290
Laurus N.V., 65 208–11
LaVista Equipment Supply Co., **14** 545; **60** 326
Lavold, *see* Randstad Holding n.v.
Lavoro Bank AG *see* Banca Nazionale del Lavoro SpA.
Lawn Boy Inc., *see* Toro Co.
Lawrenceburg Gas Company *see* Cincinnati Gas & Electric Co.
Lawson Inc., **41** 113, 115
Lawson Software, 38 284–88
Lawter International Inc., 14 308–10 *see also* Eastman Chemical Co.
Lawyers Cooperative Publishing, *see* The Thomson Corp.
Lawyers Title Insurance Corporation *see* LandAmerica Financial Group, Inc.
Layer Five, **43** 252
Layne Christensen Company, 19 245–47
Layton Homes Corporation, **30** 423
Lazard LLC, 38 289–92
Lazare Kaplan International Inc., 21 344–47
Lazio *see* Societá Sportiva Lazio SpA.
Lazy Days RV Center, Inc., 69 228–30
LBO Holdings, **15** 459
LBS Communications, **6** 28
LCA Group *see* Hubbell Inc.
LCA-Vision, Inc, 85 217–20
LCC International, Inc., 84 235–238
LCI International, Inc., 16 318–20 *see also* Qwest Communications International, Inc.
LCIE, **55** 79
LCP Hotels *see* CapStar Hotel Co.
LDB Corporation, 53 204–06
LDC *see* L.D.C. S.A.
LDC, 68 232–34
LDCom Networks, **60** 151
LDDS-Metro Communications, Inc., 8 310–12 *see also* MCI WorldCom, Inc.
LDI *see* Lacy Diversified Industries, Ltd.
LDI Ltd., LLC, 76 235–37
LDMA-AU, Inc., **49** 173
Le Bon Marché *see* Bon Marché.
Le Buffet System-Gastronomie, **V** 74
Le Chameau, **39** 250
Le Chateau Inc., 63 239–41
Le Clerc, **21** 225–26
Le Cordon Bleu S.A., 67 230–32
Le Duff *see* Groupe Le Duff S.A.
Le Monde S.A., 33 308–10
Le Riche Group Ltd., **61** 44, 46
Le Touquet's, SA, **48** 197
Lea & Perrins, **II** 475
Lea County Gas Co., **6** 580
Lea Lumber & Plywood Co., **12** 300
Lea Manufacturing, **23** 299
Léa Nature *see* Groupe Léa Nature.
Leadra Design Inc., **59** 164
Leaf Candy Company, **64** 187
Leaf North America, **51** 159
Leahy & Co. *see* Pierce Leahy Corp.
Leap Wireless International, Inc., 69 231–33
LeapFrog Enterprises, Inc., 54 215–18
Lear Corporation, 16 321–23; 71 191–95 (upd.)
Lear Romec Corp., *see* Crane Co.
Lear Siegler Inc., I 481–83
Learjet Inc., 8 313–16; 27 281–85 (upd.)
Learning Care Group, Inc., 76 238–41 (upd.)
Learning Centers Inc., **51** 198
The Learning Company Inc., 24 275–78
Learning Tree International Inc., 24 279–82
LeaRonal, Inc., 23 322–24 *see also* Rohm and Haas Co.
Lease International SA, **6** 358
Leaseway Transportation Corp., 12 309–11
Leatherback Industries, **22** 229
Leatherman Tool Group, Inc., 51 211–13
Lebhar-Friedman, Inc., 55 250–52
Leblanc Corporation *see* G. Leblanc Corp.
LeBoeuf, Lamb, Greene & MacRae, L.L.P., 29 284–86
Lebr Associates Inc., **25** 246
LECG Corporation, 93 286–89
Lech Brewery, **24** 450
Leche Pascual Group *see* Grupo Leche Pascual S.A.
Lechmere Inc., 10 391–93
Lechters, Inc., 11 248–50; 39 251–54 (upd.)
Leclerc *see* Association des Centres Distributeurs E. Leclerc.
LeCroy Corporation, 41 234–37
Lectorum Publications, **29** 426
Ledcor Industries Limited, 46 266–69
Lederle Laboratories, **14** 254, 256, 423; **50** 248, 250
Lederle Standard Products, **26** 29
Ledesma Sociedad Anónima Agrícola Industrial, 62 225–27
Lee Apparel Company, Inc., 8 317–19
The Lee Company *see* VF Corp.
Lee Cooper Group Ltd., **49** 259
Lee Enterprises, Incorporated, 11 251–53; 64 234–37 (upd.)
Lee International, *see* Panavision Inc.
Lee National Corporation, **26** 234
Lee's Famous Recipe Chicken, **58** 323
Leeann Chin, Inc., 30 285–88
Leeds & Northrup Company, **28** 484; **63** 401
Lees Carpets, *see* Burlington Industries, Inc.
Leeway International Company Ltd., **68** 69
Lefrak Organization Inc., 26 260–62
Legacy Homes Ltd., **26** 290
Legacy Hotels Real Estate Investment Trust, **69** 163
Legal & General Group plc, III 272–73; 24 283–85 (upd.)
The Legal Aid Society, 48 261–64
Legal Technologies, Inc., **15** 378
Legent Corporation, 10 394–96 *see also* Computer Associates International, Inc.
Legetojsfabrikken LEGO Billund A/S *see* Lego A/S.
Legg Mason, Inc., 33 259–62
Leggett & Platt, Inc., 11 254–56; 48 265–68 (upd.)
Leggett Stores Inc., **19** 48
Lego A/S, 13 310–13; 40 287–91 (upd.)
Legrand SA, 21 348–50
Lehigh Acquisition Corp., **34** 286
Lehigh Portland Cement Company, 23 325–27
Lehman Brothers, **14** 145; **25** 301; **38** 411; **48** 59
Lehman Merchant Bank Partners, **19** 324
Lehmer Company *see* Centel Corp.
Lehser Communications, Inc., **15** 265
Leica Camera AG, 35 266–69
Leica Microsystems Holdings GmbH, 35 270–73

Leidy's, Inc., 93 290–92
Leigh-Mardon Security Group, **30** 44
Leighton Holdings Ltd., **19** 402
Leinenkugel Brewing Company *see* Jacob Leinenkugel Brewing Co.
Leiner Health Products Inc., 34 250–52
The Leisure Company, **34** 22
Leisure Concepts, Inc., **59** 187–89
Leitch Technology Corporation *see* Harris Corporation
Leitz *see* Esselte Worldwide.
Lemmerz Holding GmbH, *see* Hayes Lemmerz International, Inc.
Lemmon Co., **54** 363
Lend Lease Corporation Limited, IV 707–09; 17 283–86 (upd.); 52 218–23 (upd.)
Lender's Bagel, **32** 69
Lending Textiles, **29** 132
LendingTree, LLC, 93 293–96
Lenel Systems International Inc., **24** 510
Lennar Corporation, 11 257–59
Lennon's, *see* Gateway Corporation Ltd.
Lennox Industries, Inc., **22** 6
Lennox International Inc., 8 320–22; 28 232–36 (upd.)
Lenoir Furniture Corporation, *see* Broyhill Furniture Industries, Inc.
Lenovo Group Ltd., 80 209–12
Lenox, Inc., 12 312–13
Lens, Inc., **30** 267–68
LensCrafters Inc., 23 328–30; 76 242–45 (upd.)
L'Entreprise Jean Lefebvre, 23 331–33 *see also* Vinci.
Leo Burnett Company, Inc., I 22–24; 20 336–39 (upd.)
Leo d'Or Trading Co. Ltd., **56** 242
The Leo Group, **32** 140; **40** 140
Leon Burnett Company, Inc., **76** 254
Léon Gaumont et Cie *see* Gaumont SA.
The Leona Group LLC, 84 239–242
Leonard Bernstein Music Publishing Company, **23** 391
Leonard Parker Company, **26** 196
Leonard Silver, *see* Syratech Corp.
Leonardi Manufacturing, **48** 70
Leonardo Editore, **IV** 587
Leprino Foods Company, 28 237–39
Lernout and Hauspie, **51** 202
Leroux S.A.S., 65 212–14
Leroy Merlin SA, 54 219–21
Les Abeilles International SA, **60** 149
Les Boutiques San Francisco, Inc., 62 228–30
Les broderies Lesage, **49** 83
Les Echos *see* Groupe Les Echos.
Les Grands Magasins Au Bon Marché: Etablissements Vaxelaire-Claes, **26** 159–60
Les Papeteries du Limousin, **19** 227
Les Schwab Tire Centers, 50 314–16
Lesaffre *see* Societe Industrielle Lesaffre.
Lesco Inc., 19 248–50
The Leslie Fay Company, Inc., 8 323–25; 39 255–58 (upd.)
Leslie's Poolmart, Inc., 18 302–04
Lester of Minnesota, Inc., **62** 55
Létang et Rémy, **44** 205
Lettuce Entertain You Enterprises, **38** 103
Leucadia National Corporation, 11 260–62; 71 196–200 (upd.)
Leumi & Company Investment Bankers Ltd., **60** 50
Leuna-Werke AG, **7** 142
Leupold & Stevens, Inc., 52 224–26
Level Five Research, Inc., **22** 292
Level 13 Entertainment, Inc., **58** 124
Level 3 Communications, Inc., 67 233–35
Levenger Company, 63 242–45
Lever Brothers Company, 9 317–19 *see also* Unilever.
Leverage Group, **51** 99
Levernz Shoe Co., **61** 22
Levi Strauss & Co., V 362–65; 16 324–28 (upd.)
Leviathan Gas Pipeline Company, **21** 171
Levin Furniture *see* Sam Levin Inc.
Levine, Huntley, Vick & Beaver, **6** 28
Leviton Manufacturing Co., Inc., **54** 372
Levitt Corp., **21** 471
Levitt Investment Company, **26** 102
Levitz Furniture Inc., 15 280–82
Levolor Hardware Group, **53** 37
Levtex Hotel Ventures, **21** 363
Levy *see* Chas. Levy Company LLC.
Levy Home Entertainment, LLC, **60** 83, 85
Levy Restaurants L.P., 26 263–65
The Lewin Group, Inc., **21** 425
Lewis and Marks, **16** 27; **50** 32
Lewis Batting Company, **11** 219
Lewis Drug Inc., 94 272–76
Lewis Galoob Toys Inc., 16 329–31
Lewis Group Ltd., **58** 54–55
Lewis Homes, **45** 221
Lewis Refrigeration Company, **21** 500
Lex Service plc, **50** 42
Lexecon, Inc., **26** 187
Lexington Ice Company, **6** 514
Lexington Utilities Company, **6** 514
LEXIS-NEXIS Group, 33 263–67
Lexmark International, Inc., 18 305–07; 79 237–42 (upd.)
Leybold GmbH, **IV** 71; **48** 30
LF International, Inc., **59** 259
LFC Holdings Corp. *see* Levitz Furniture Inc.
LFE Corp., *see* Mark IV Industries, Inc.
LG&E Energy Corporation, 6 516–18; 51 214–17 (upd.)
LG Chemical Ltd., **26** 425
LG Corporation, 94 277–83 (upd.)
LG Semiconductor, **56** 173
LGT Asset Management *see* AMVESCAP PLC.
Li & Fung Limited, 59 258–61
Liaison Agency, **31** 216–17
Lianozovo Dairy, **48** 438
Libbey Inc., 49 251–54
Libbey-Owens-Ford Company, *see* TRINOVA Corp.
Liber, **14** 556
The Liberty Corporation, 22 312–14
Liberty Hardware Manufacturing Corporation, **20** 363
Liberty Life, **IV** 97
Liberty Livewire Corporation, 42 224–27
Liberty Media Corporation, 50 317–19
Liberty Mutual Holding Company, 59 262–64
Liberty Mutual Insurance Group, **11** 379; **48** 271
Liberty National Insurance Holding Company *see* Torchmark Corp.
Liberty Orchards Co., Inc., 89 302–05
Liberty Property Trust, 57 221–23
Liberty Software, Inc., *see* Jack Henry and Associates, Inc.
Liberty Surf UK, **48** 399
Liberty Tax Service, **48** 236
Liberty Travel, Inc., 56 203–06
Librairie Générale Francaise *see* Hachette.
Librairie Larousse *see* Groupe de la Cité.
Librairie Louis Hachette *see* Hachette.
Librizol India Pvt. Ltd., **48** 212
Libyan National Oil Corporation, IV 453–55 *see also* National Oil Corp.
Liebert Corp., *see* Emerson.
Liebherr Haushaltgerate GmbH, **65** 167
Liebherr-International AG, 64 238–42
Life Assurance Holding Corporation, **71** 324–26
Life Care Centers of America Inc., 76 246–48
Life Investors International Ltd., **12** 199
Life is good, Inc., 80 213–16
Life Partners Group, Inc., **33** 111
Life Retail Stores *see* Angelica Corp.
Life Savers Corp., *see* Nabisco Foods Group.
Life Science Research, Inc., *see* Applied Bioscience International, Inc.
Life Technologies, Inc., 17 287–89
Life Time Fitness, Inc., 66 208–10
Life Uniform Shops *see* Angelica Corp.
LifeCell Corporation, 77 236–39
Lifeline Systems, Inc., 32 374; **53 207–09**
LifeLock, Inc., 91 314–17
Lifemark Corp., *see* American Medical International, Inc.
LifePoint Hospitals, Inc., 69 234–36
LifeScan Inc., **63** 206
Lifestyle Fitness Clubs, **46** 432
Lifetime Brands, Inc., 27 286–89; 73 207–11 (upd.)
Lifetime Corp., **29** 363–64
Lifetime Entertainment Services, 51 218–22
Lifetouch Inc., 86 243–47
Lifeway Foods, Inc., 65 215–17
LifeWise Health Plan of Oregon, Inc., 90 276–79
Ligand Pharmaceuticals Incorporated, 10 48; **47 221–23**
Liggett & Meyers, **29** 195
Liggett-Ducat, **49** 153
Liggett Group Inc. *see* Vector Group Inc.
Light Savers U.S.A., Inc. *see* Hospitality Worldwide Services, Inc.

Lightel Inc., **6** 311
Lil' Champ Food Stores, Inc., **36** 359
LILCO *see* Long Island Lighting Co.
Lille Bonnières et Colombes, **37** 143–44
Lillian Vernon Corporation, 12 314–15; 35 274–77 (upd.); 92 207–12 (upd.)
Lillie Rubin, **30** 104–06
Lilliput Group plc, **11** 95; **15** 478
Lilly & Co *see* Eli Lilly & Co.
Lilly Endowment Inc., 70 157–59
Lilly Industries, **22** 437
Limagrain *see* Groupe Limagrain.
Limburgse Vinyl Maatschappij, **76** 346–47
Limhamns Golvindustri AB *see* Tarkett Sommer AG.
The Limited, Inc., V 115–16; 20 340–43 (upd.)
LIN Broadcasting Corp., 9 320–22
Linamar Corporation, 18 308–10
Lincare Holdings Inc., 43 265–67
Lincoln Automotive, **26** 363
Lincoln Benefit Life Company, *see* The Allstate Corp.
Lincoln Center for the Performing Arts, Inc., 69 237–41
Lincoln Electric Co., 13 314–16
Lincoln Industrial Corporation, **70** 142
Lincoln Liberty Life Insurance Co., *see* First Executive Corp.
Lincoln Marketing, Inc., *see* Total System Services, Inc.
Lincoln National Corporation, III 274–77; 25 286–90 (upd.)
Lincoln Property Company, 8 326–28; 54 222–26 (upd.)
Lincoln Snacks Company, 24 286–88
Lincoln Telephone & Telegraph Company, 14 311–13
Lindal Cedar Homes, Inc., 29 287–89
Linde AG, I 581–83; 67 236–39 (upd.)
Linde Refrigeration *see* Carrier Corp.
Lindemans *see* Southcorp Ltd.
Lindley *see* Corporación José R. Lindley S.A.
Lindsay Manufacturing Co., 20 344–46
Lindt & Sprüngli *see* Chocoladefabriken Lindt & Sprüngli AG.
Linear Corporation Bhd, **66** 28
Linear Technology, Inc., 16 332–34
Linens 'n Things, Inc., 24 289–92; 75 239–43 (upd.)
Linfood Holdings Ltd., *see* Gateway Corporation Ltd.
Ling Products, *see* Banta Corp.
Ling-Temco-Vought *see* LTV Corp.
Lingerfelt Development Corporation, **57** 223
Lingerie Time, **20** 143
Linguaphone Group, **43** 204, 206
Linificio e Canapificio Nazionale S.p.A., **67** 210–11, 246–48
Link House Publications PLC, **IV** 687
Link Motor Supply Company, **26** 347
Linroz Manufacturing Company L.P., **25** 245
LINT Company, **64** 237
Lintas: Worldwide, 14 314–16
Linz, *see* Zale Corp.
The Lion Brewery, Inc., 86 248–52
Lion Corporation, III 44–45; 51 223–26 (upd.)
Lion Match Company, **24** 450
Lion Nathan Limited, 54 227–30
Lion's Head Brewery *see* The Stroh Brewery Co.
Lionel L.L.C., 16 335–38
Lionex Corporation, *see* Anthem Electronics, Inc.
LionMark Insurance Company *see* Fidelity Southern Corp.
Lions Gate Entertainment Corporation, 35 278–81
Liontech, *see* Lionel L.L.C.
Lipman Electronic Engineering Ltd., 81 236–39
Lippincott & Margulies, *see* Marsh & McLennan Companies, Inc.
Lippincott-Raven Publishers, **14** 556
Lipschutz Bros., Inc., **29** 511
Lipson Alport Glass & Associates, **27** 195
Lipton *see* Thomas J. Lipton Co.
Liqui-Box Corporation, 16 339–41
Liquid Ag Systems Inc., **26** 494
Liquid Carbonic, *see* Chicago Bridge & Iron Company N.V.
Liquid Gas Company Ltd., **60** 236
Liquid Holdings, Inc., **45** 168
Liquidnet, Inc., 79 243–46
Liquorland, **V** 35
Liris, **23** 212
LIRR *see* The Long Island Rail Road Co.
Liscaya, **II** 196
Listening Library Inc., **31** 379
Lister, **21** 503
Litehouse Inc., 60 198–201
LiTel Communications, Inc., *see* LCI International, Inc.
Lithia Motors, Inc., 41 238–40
Lithonia Lighting, Inc., **54** 252, 254–55
LitleNet, **26** 441
Litmus Concepts, Inc. *see* Quidel Corporation
Littelfuse, Inc., 26 266–69
Little, Brown & Company, **IV** 675; **7** 528; **36** 270
Little Caesar Enterprises, Inc., 7 278–79; 24 293–96 (upd.) *see also* Ilitch Holdings Inc.
Little General, **12** 179, 200
Little Giant Pump Company, *see* Tecumseh Products Co.
Little League Baseball, Incorporated, **23** 450
Little Professor Book Centers *see* Praxis Bookstore Group LLC.
Little Switzerland, Inc., 60 202–04
Little Tikes Company, 13 317–19; 62 231–34 (upd.)
Littleton Coin Company Inc., 82 201–04
Littlewoods Financial Services, **30** 494
Littlewoods plc, V 117–19; 42 228–32 (upd.)
Litton Industries Inc., I 484–86; 11 263–65 (upd.) *see also* Avondale Industries; Northrop Grumman Corp.
Litwin Engineers & Constructors, *see* United Dominion Industries Ltd.
LIVE Entertainment Inc., 20 347–49
Live Nation, Inc., 80 217–22 (upd.)
LiveAquaria.com., **62** 108
LivePerson, Inc., 91 318–21
Liverpool Daily Post & Echo Ltd., **49** 405
Living Arts, Inc., **41** 174
LivingWell Inc., **12** 326
Liz Claiborne, Inc., 8 329–31; 25 291–94 (upd.)
LKQ Corporation, 71 201–03
Lledo Collectibles Ltd., **60** 372
LLJ Distributing Company *see* Spartan Stores Inc.
Lloyd Aereo de Bolivia, **6** 97
Lloyd Creative Staffing, *see* AHL Services, Inc.
Lloyd Instruments, Ltd., **29** 460–61
Lloyd Thompson Group plc, **20** 313
Lloyd Triestino company, **50** 187
Lloyd-Truax Ltd., **21** 499
Lloyd's, III 278–81; 22 315–19 (upd.); 74 172–76 (upd.)
Lloyds Chemists plc, *see* GEHE AG.
Lloyds TSB Group plc, II 306–09; 47 224–29 (upd.)
LLP Group plc, **58** 189
LM Ericsson *see* Telefonaktiebolaget LM Ericsson.
LME *see* Telefonaktiebolaget LM Ericsson.
LNM Group, **30** 252
Loblaw Companies Limited, 43 268–72
Lockheed Martin Corporation, I 64–66; 11 266–69 (upd.); 15 283–86 (upd.); 89 306–11 (upd.)
Locksmith Publishing Corp., **56** 75
Lockwood Banc Group, Inc., **11** 306
Lockwood Greene Engineers, Inc., *see* Philipp Holzmann AG.
Loctite Corporation, 8 332–34; 30 289–91 (upd.)
LodgeNet Entertainment Corporation, 28 240–42
The Lodging Group, **12** 297; **48** 245
Loehmann's Inc., 24 297–99
Loewe AG, 90 280–85
The Loewen Group, Inc., 16 342–44; 40 292–95 (upd.) *see also* Alderwoods Group Inc.
Loewenstein Furniture Group, Inc., **21** 531–33
Loews Cineplex Entertainment Corp., **37** 64
Loews Corporation, I 487–88; 12 316–18 (upd.); 36 324–28 (upd.); 93 297–304 (upd.)
LOF Plastics, Inc. *see* Libbey-Owens-Ford.
Loffland Brothers Company, *see* Nabors Industries, Inc.
Logan's Roadhouse, Inc., 29 290–92
Loganair Ltd., 68 235–37
Logic Modeling, **11** 491

Logica plc, **14 317–19; 37 230–33 (upd.)**
Logicon Inc., **20 350–52** *see also* Northrop Grumman Corp.
Logility, **25** 20, 22
Logistics.com, Inc. *see* Manhattan Associates, Inc.
Logistics Industries Corporation, **39** 77
Logistics Management Systems, Inc., *see* Amoskeag Co.
Logitech International S.A., **28 243–45; 69 242–45 (upd.)**
LOGIX Benelux, **74** 143
Logo Athletic, Inc., **35** 363
Logo 7, Inc., *see* Tultex Corp.
Logon, Inc., **14** 377
Lohja Corporation, **61** 295
LoJack Corporation, **48 269–73**
Lojas Americanas S.A., **77 240–43**
Lojas Arapuã S.A., **22 320–22; 61 175–78 (upd.)**
Lomak Petroleum, Inc., **24** 380
London & Hull, *see* AXA.
London & Midland Bank *see* Midland Bank plc.
London & Overseas Freighters plc *see* Frontline Ltd.
London & Rhodesia Mining & Land Company *see* Lonrho Plc.
London and Scottish Marine Oil, **11** 98
London & Western Trust, **39** 90
London Assurance Corp., **55** 331
London Brokers Ltd., **6** 290
London Buses Limited *see* London Regional Transport.
London Cargo Group, **25** 82
London Central, **28** 155–56
London Drugs Ltd., **46 270–73**
London Electricity, **12** 443; **41** 141
London Fog Industries, Inc., **29 293–96**
London Insurance Group, *see* Royal & Sun Alliance Insurance Group plc.
London International Group *see* SSL International plc.
London Precision Machine & Tool, Ltd., **39** 32
London Records, **23** 390
London Regional Transport, **6 406–08**
London Rubber Co., **49** 380
London Scottish Bank plc, **70 160–62**
London South Partnership, **25** 497
London Stock Exchange Limited, **34 253–56**
London Transport, **19** 111
Londontown Manufacturing Company *see* London Fog Industries, Inc.
Lone Star Funds, **59** 106
Lone Star Industries, **23** 326; **35** 154
Lone Star Steakhouse & Saloon, Inc., **51 227–29**
Lonely Planet Publications Pty Ltd., **55 253–55**
The Long & Foster Companies, Inc, **85 221–24**
Long Distance Discount Services, Inc., *see* LDDS-Metro Communications, Inc.
Long Island Bancorp, Inc., **16 345–47**
Long Island College Hospital *see* Continuum Health Partners, Inc.
Long Island Lighting Company, **V 652–54**
Long Island Power Authority, *see* KeySpan Energy Co.
The Long Island Rail Road Company, **68 238–40**
Long John Silver's, **13 320–22; 57 224–29 (upd.)**
Long-Term Credit Bank of Japan, Ltd., **II 310–11** *Sumitomo Mitsui Banking Corp.*
The Longaberger Company, **12 319–21; 44 267–70 (upd.)**
Longchamps, Inc., **38** 385; **41** 388
LongHorn Steakhouse, *see* Rare Hospitality International Inc.
Longman Group Ltd., **IV** 611, 658
Longs Drug Stores Corporation, **V 120; 25 295–97 (upd.); 83 249-253 (upd.)**
Longview Fibre Company, **8 335–37; 37 234–37 (upd.)**
Lonmin plc, **66 211–16 (upd.)**
Lonrho Plc, **21 351–55** *see also* Lonmin plc.
Lonza Group Ltd., **73 212–14**
Lookers plc, **71 204–06**
Loomis Armored Car Service Limited, **45** 378
Loomis Fargo Group, **42** 338
Loomis Products, Inc., **64** 349
Loop One2, **53** 240
Lor-Al, Inc., *see* Ag-Chem Equipment Company, Inc.
Loral Space & Communications Ltd., **8 338–40; 54 231–35 (upd.)**
Lord & Taylor, **15** 86; **21** 302
L'Oréal, **III 46–49; 8 341–44 (upd.); 46 274–79 (upd.)**
Lorentzen & Wettre AB, **53** 85
Lorillard Industries, **V** 407, 417; **22** 73; **29** 195
Lorimar Telepictures, *see* Time Warner Inc.
Los Angeles Lakers *see* California Sports, Inc.
Lost Arrow Inc., **22 323–25**
LOT Polish Airlines (Polskie Linie Lotnicze S.A.), **33 268–71**
LOT$OFF Corporation, **24 300–01**
Lotte Confectionery Company Ltd., **76 249–51**
Lotus Cars Ltd., **14 320–22**
Lotus Development Corporation, **6 254–56; 25 298–302 (upd.)**
Lotus Publishing Corporation, **7** 239; **25** 239
Louart Corporation, **29** 33–34
Loudcloud, Inc. *see* Opsware Inc.
Louis Allis, **15** 288
Louis Cruise Lines, **52** 298–99
Louis Dreyfus *see* Groupe Louis Dreyfus S.A.
Louis Dreyfus Energy Corp., **28** 471
Louis Kemp Seafood Company, *see* Tyson Foods, Inc.
Louis Vuitton, **10 397–99** *see also* LVMH Moët Hennessy Louis Vuitton SA.
Louisiana Corporation, **19** 301
The Louisiana Land and Exploration Company, **7 280–83**
Louisiana-Pacific Corporation, **IV 304–05; 31 314–17 (upd.)**
Louisville Gas and Electric Company *see* LG&E Energy Corp.
Loup River Public Power District, **29** 352
LoVaca Gathering Company *see* The Coastal Corp.
Love's Travel Stops & Country Stores, Inc., **71 207–09**
Lowe Group, *see* Interpublic Group of Companies, Inc.
Lowe's Companies, Inc., **V 122–23; 21 356–58 (upd.); 81 240–44 (upd.)**
Löwenbräu AG, **80 223–27**
Lower Manhattan Development Corporation, **47** 360
Lowes Food Stores *see* Alex Lee Inc.
Lowney/Moirs, *see* Hershey Foods Corp.
Lowrance Electronics, Inc., **18 311–14**
Lowrey's Meat Specialties, Inc., **21** 156
LPA Holding Corporation, **81 245–48**
LPL Investment Group, **40** 35–36
LRC International, **69** 303
LRV Corporation, **61** 173
LS Management, Inc., **51** 229
LSB Industries, Inc., **77 244–47**
LSG Sky Chefs, Inc., **68** 109
LSI *see* Lear Siegler Inc.
LSI Logic Corporation, **13 323–25; 64 243–47**
LTR Industries, **52** 301–03
LTU Group Holding GmbH, **37 238–41**
LTV Aerospace *see* Vought Aircraft Industries, Inc.
The LTV Corporation, **I 489–91; 24 302–06 (upd.)**
The Lubrizol Corporation, **I 360–62; 30 292–95 (upd.); 83 254-259 (upd.)**
Luby's, Inc., **17 290–93; 42 233–38 (upd.)**
Lucas Industries Plc, **III 554–57**
Lucas Ingredients, *see* Kerry Group plc.
Lucas-Milhaupt, Inc., **23** 250
LucasArts Entertainment Company, **32** 9
Lucasfilm Ltd., **12 322–24; 50 320–23 (upd.)**
LucasVarity plc, *see* Kelsey-Hayes Group of Companies.
Lucent Technologies Inc., **34 257–60**
Lucille Farms, Inc., **45 249–51**
Lucky-Goldstar, **II 53–54** *see also* LG Corp.
Lucky Stores Inc., **27 290–93**
Ludendo S.A., **88 237–40**
Ludi Wap S.A., **41** 409
Ludovico, **25** 85
Lufkin Industries, Inc., **78 198–202**
Luftfahrzeug-Betriebs GmbH, **60** 253
Lufthansa *see* Deutsche Lufthansa AG.
Luigino's, Inc., **64 248–50**
Luitpold-Werk GmbH & Co., **56** 303
Lukens Inc., **14 323–25** *see also* Bethlehem Steel Corp.
LUKOIL *see* OAO LUKOIL.

Lumbermens Building Centers *see* Lanoga Corp.
Lumbertown USA, **52** 232
Lumex, Inc., *see* Fuqua Enterprises, Inc.
Lumidor Safety Products, **52** 187
Luminar Plc, 40 296–98
Lummus Crest, **26** 496
Lunar Corporation, 29 297–99
Lund Boat Co. *see* Genmar Holdings, Inc.
Lund Food Holdings, Inc., 22 326–28
Lund International Holdings, Inc., 40 299–301
L'Unite Hermetique S.A., *see* Tecumseh Products Co.
Lurgei, **6** 599
LURGI *see* Metallurgische Gesellschaft Aktiengesellschaft.
Lush Ltd., 93 305–08
Lutèce, **20** 26
Lutheran Brotherhood, 31 318–21
Luxair, **49** 80
Luxor, *see* Nokia Corp.
Luxottica SpA, 17 294–96; 52 227–30 (upd.)
LuxSonor Semiconductor Inc., **48** 92
Luzianne Blue Plate Foods *see* Wm. B. Reily & Company Inc.
LVMH Moët Hennessy Louis Vuitton SA, 33 272–77 (upd.) *see also* Christian Dior S.A.
LXE Inc., **21** 199–201
Lycos *see* Terra Lycos, Inc.
Lydall, Inc., 64 251–54
Lyfra-S.A./NV, 88 241–43
Lyn Knight Currency Auctions, Inc, **48** 100
Lynch Corporation, 43 273–76
The Lynde Company, *see* Hawkins Chemical, Inc.
Lynden Incorporated, 91 322–25
Lynx Express Delivery *see* Exel plc.
Lyondell Chemical Company, IV 456–57; 45 252–55 (upd.)
Lyonnaise des Eaux-Dumez, V 655–57 *see also* Suez Lyonnaise des Eaux.
Lyons *see* J. Lyons & Co. Ltd.
Lytag Ltd., **31** 398–99

M

M & C Saatchi, **42** 330
M&C Systems Co Ltd., **62** 245
M&F Worldwide Corp., 38 293–95
M&G Group plc, **48** 328
M and H Valve Co., **55** 266
M&I Bank *see* Marshall & Ilsley Corp.
M&M Limited, *see* Mars, Inc.
M and M Manufacturing Company, **23** 143
M&M/Mars, **14** 48; **15** 63–64; **21** 219
M & S Computing *see* Intergraph Corp.
M&T Capital Corporation, *see* First Empire State Corp.
M/A Com Inc., **14** 26–27
M-Cell Ltd., **31** 329
M-R Group plc, **31** 312–13
M-real Oyj, 56 252–55 (upd.)
M-Web Holdings Ltd., **31** 329–30
M.A. Bruder & Sons, Inc., 56 207–09
M.A. Gedney Co., 51 230–32
M.A. Hanna Company, 8 345–47 *see also* PolyOne Corp.
M.B. McGerry, **21** 94
M.B. Papeles Especiales, S.A., **68** 258
M. DuMont Schauberg GmbH & Co. KG, 92 213–17
M.E.P.C. Ltd. *see* MEPC PLC.
M.F. Patterson Dental Supply Co. *see* Patterson Dental Co.
M/G Transport Inc. *see* The Midland Co.
M.G. Waldbaum Company, *see* Michael Foods, Inc.
M.H. Meyerson & Co., Inc., 46 280–83
M.L.C. Partners Limited Partnership, **22** 459
M.M. Warburg *see* SBC Warburg.
M.P. Burke PLC, *see* Southern Electric PLC.
M.P. Pumps, Inc., *see* Tecumseh Products Co.
M. Polaner Inc., **10** 70; **40** 51–52; **50** 538
M.S. Carriers, Inc., **42** 363, 365
M. Shanken Communications, Inc., 50 324–27
M. Sobol, Inc., **28** 12
M.T.G.I. Textile Manufacturers Group, **25** 121
M.W. Carr, **14** 245
M.W. Kellogg Co., **34** 81; **62** 204
MAAG Gear Wheel, **72** 138, 140
Maatschappij tot Exploitatie van de Onderneming Krasnapolsky *see* Grand Hotel Krasnapolsky N.V.
Mabe *see* Controladora Mabe, S.A. de C.V.
Mabuchi Motor Co. Ltd., 68 241–43
Mabuhay Vinyl Corporation *see* Tosoh Corp.
MAC Aviation Services LLC *see* Air T, Inc.
Mac Frugal's Bargains - Closeouts Inc., 17 297–99 *see also* Big Lots, Inc.
Mac-Gray Corporation, 44 271–73
Mac Publications LLC, **25** 240
The Macallan Distillers Ltd., 63 246–48
MacAndrews & Forbes Holdings Inc., 28 246–49; 86 253–59 (upd.)
MacArthur Foundation *see* The John D. and Catherine T. MacArthur Foundation.
Macauley & Co. *see* Greif Inc.
MacDermid Incorporated, 32 318–21
MacDonald Companies, **15** 87
MacDonald Dettwiler and Associates, **32** 436
Mace Security International, Inc., 57 230–32
The Macerich Company, 57 233–35
MacFrugal's Bargains Close-Outs Inc., **29** 312; **50** 98
MacGregor Golf Company, 68 244–46
MacGregor Sporting Goods Inc., **23** 449
Mach Performance, Inc., **28** 147
Macintosh *see* Apple Computer, Inc.
Mack-Cali Realty Corporation, 42 239–41
Mack Trucks, Inc., I 177–79; 22 329–32 (upd.); 61 179–83 (upd.)
Mack-Wayne Plastics, **42** 439
Mackay Envelope Corporation, 45 256–59
Mackays Stores Group Ltd., 92 218–21
Mackie Designs Inc., 30 406; **33 278–81**
Maclean Hunter Publishing Limited, IV 638–40; 26 270–74 (upd.) *see also* Rogers Communications Inc.
Macluan Capital Corporation, **49** 196
The MacManus Group, **32** 140; **40** 140
MacMark Corp., **22** 459
Macmillan & Co. Ltd., **35** 452
MacMillan Bloedel Limited, IV 306–09 *see also* Weyerhaeuser Co.
Macmillan, Inc., 7 284–86
The MacNeal-Schwendler Corporation, 25 303–05
MacNeil/Lehrer Productions, 87 296–299
Macquarie Bank Ltd., 69 246–49
Macromedia, Inc., 50 328–31
MACSTEEL Monroe, Inc., **62** 289
Macy's, Inc., 94 284–93 (upd.)
Mad Dog Athletics, **19** 385
Mad River Canoe *see* Confluence Holdings Corp.
MADD *see* Mothers Against Drunk Driving.
Madden's on Gull Lake, 52 231–34
Madeco S.A., 71 210–12
Madeira Wine Company, S.A., 49 255–57
Maderin ECO S.A., **51** 6
Madge Networks N.V., 26 275–77
Madison Dearborn Partners LLC, **46** 289; **49** 197; **51** 131, 282, 284; **69** 197
Madison Furniture Industries, *see* Shelby Williams Industries, Inc.
Madison Gas and Electric Company, 39 259–62
Madison-Kipp Corporation, 58 213–16
Madison Park Press *see* Bookspan.
Madrange SA, 58 217–19
Maersk Oile, **22** 167; **65** 316–17
Maersk Sealand *see* A.P. Møller - Maersk A/S.
Maes Group Breweries, **II** 475
Maeva Group *see* Club Mediterranee SA.
Mafco Holdings, Inc., **28** 248; **38** 293–95
Mag Instrument, Inc., 67 240–42
MagCorp, **28** 198
Magee Company, **31** 435–36
Magella Healthcare Corporation, **61** 284
Magellan Aerospace Corporation, 48 274–76
Magellan Corporation, **22** 403; **60** 137
Magellan et Bergerat., **72** 159
MaggieMoo's International, 89 312–16
Magic Chef Co. *see* Maytag Corp.
Magic City Food Products Company *see* Golden Enterprises, Inc.
Magic Marker, **29** 372
Magic Years Child Care, **51** 198
Magicsilk, Inc., *see* Celebrity, Inc.

Maglificio di Ponzano Veneto dei Fratelli Benetton *see* Benetton.
Magma Copper Company, 7 **287–90** *see also* BHP Billiton.
Magma Design Automation Inc., **78 203–27**
Magma Power Company, **11 270–72**
Magna Computer Corporation, *see* EMC Corp.
Magna Distribuidora Ltda., **43** 368
Magnaflux, *see* Illinois Tool Works Inc.
Magnavox Co., *see* Philips Electronics.
MagneTek, Inc., **15 287–89**; **41 241–44 (upd.)**
Magneti Marelli Holding SpA, **90 286–89**
Magnetic Peripherals Inc., **19** 513–14
Magnivision, Inc., *see* American Greetings Corp.
Magnum Hunter Resources, Inc. *see* Cimarex Energy Co.
Magro, **48** 63
Magyar Telekom Rt, **78 208–11**
Magyar Viscosa, **37** 428
Mahalo Air, **22** 252
Mahir & Numan A.S., **48** 154
MAI PLC, **28** 504
MAI Systems Corporation, **11 273–76**
Maid-Rite Corporation, **62 235–38**
Maidenform, Inc., **20 352–55**; **59 265–69 (upd.)**
Mail Boxes Etc., **18 315–17**; **41 245–48 (upd.)** *see also* U.S. Office Products Co.
Mail.com Inc., **38** 271
Mail Coups, Inc., **53** 13
Mail Finance, **53** 239
Mail Marketing Systems Inc., **53** 13
Mail-Well, Inc., **28 250–52** *see also* Cenveo Inc.
MailCoups, Inc., **53** 9
Mailtek, Inc., *see* Total System Services, Inc.
MAIN *see* Makhteshim-Agan Industries Ltd.; Mid-American Interpool Network.
Main Plaza Corporation, **25** 115
Main Street Advertising USA, **IV** 597
Maine & Maritimes Corporation, **56 210–13**
Maine Central Railroad Company, **16 348–50**
Maines Paper & Food Service Inc., **71 213–15**
Mainline Industrial Distributors, Inc., *see* Bearings, Inc.
Maison Blanche Department Stores Group, **35** 129
Maison de Valérie, **19** 309
Maison Louis Jadot, **24 307–09**
Majesco Entertainment Company, **85 225–29**
Majestic Industries, Inc., **43** 459
The Major Automotive Companies, Inc., **45 260–62**
Major SA, **53** 179
Major Video Concepts, **6** 410
Major Video Corporation, *see* Blockbuster Inc.
Makhteshim-Agan Industries Ltd., **85 230–34**
Makita Corporation, **22 333–35**; **59 270–73 (upd.)**
Makivik Corporation, **56** 38–39
Makoff R&D Laboratories, **56** 375
Malapai Resources, **6** 546
Malayan Banking Berhad, **72 215–18**
Malaysian Airlines System Berhad, **6 100–02**; **29 300–03 (upd.)**
Malcolm Pirnie, Inc., **42 242–44**
Malden Mills Industries, Inc., **16 351–53**
Malév Plc, **24 310–12**
Malew Engineering, **51** 354
Malibu, **25** 141
Mall.com, **38** 271
Mallard Bay Drilling, Inc., **28** 347–48
Mallinckrodt Group Inc., **19 251–53**
Malmö Aviation, **47** 61
Malmö Woodworking Factory *see* Tarkett Sommer AG.
Malone & Hyde, Inc., **14** 147 *see also* AutoZone, Inc.; Fleming Companies, Inc.
Malt-O-Meal Company, **22 336–38**; **63 249–53 (upd.)**
Malterie Soufflet *see* Groupe Soufflet SA
Mama Fu's Noodle House, Inc., **64** 327–28
Mama's Concept, Inc., **51** 229
Mameco International, *see* RPM Inc.
Mammoet Transport B.V., **26 278–80**
Man Aktiengesellschaft, **III 561–63**
MAN Gutehoffnungshütte AG, **15** 226
MAN Roland Druckmaschinen AG, **94 294–98**
Management and Training Corporation, **28 253–56**
Management By Information Inc., **48** 307
Management Recruiters International *see* CDI Corp.
Manatron, Inc., **86 260–63**
Manchester United Football Club plc, **30 296–98**
Manco, Inc. *see* Henkel Manco Inc.
Mancuso & Co., **22** 116
Mandabach & Simms, **6** 40
Mandalay Pictures, **35** 278–80
Mandalay Resort Group, **32 322–26 (upd.)**
Mandarin, Inc., **33** 128
Mandarin Oriental International Limited, **47** 177
Mandom Corporation, **82 205–08**
Manetta Home Fashions, Inc., *see* Pillowtex Corp.
Manhattan Associates, Inc., **67 243–45**
Manhattan Bagel Inc., **63** 80
Manhattan Construction Company *see* Rooney Brothers Co.
Manhattan Drug Company *see* Integrated BioPharma, Inc.
Manhattan Group, LLC, **80 228–31**
Manhattan International Limousine Network Ltd., **26** 62
Manheim, **88 244–48**
Manila Electric Company (Meralco), **56 214–16**
Manischewitz Company *see* B. Manischewitz Co.
Manitoba Telecom Services, Inc., **61 184–87**
Manitou BF S.A., **27 294–96**
The Manitowoc Company, Inc., **18 318–21**; **59 274–79 (upd.)**
Mann's Wine Company, Ltd., *see* Kikkoman Corp.
Mannatech Inc., **33 282–85**
Mannesmann AG, **III 564–67**; **14 326–29 (upd.)**; **38 296–301 (upd.)** *see also* Vodafone Group PLC.
Mannheim Steamroller *see* American Gramophone LLC.
Manning Selvage & Lee (MS&L), **76 252–54**
MannKind Corporation, **87 300–303**
Manor AG, **48** 279
Manor Care, Inc., **6 187–90**; **25 306–10 (upd.)**
Manor Healthcare Corporation, **26** 459
Manos Enterprises, **14** 87
Manpower Inc., **9 326–27**; **30 299–302 (upd.)**; **73 215–18 (upd.)**
Mantrec S.A., *see* Manitou BF S.A.
Mantua Metal Products *see* Tyco Toys, Inc.
Manufactured Home Communities, Inc., **22 339–41**
Manufacturera Mexicana de Partes de Automoviles S.A., **56** 247
Manufacturers and Traders Trust Company, *see* First Empire State Corp.
Manufacturers Casualty Insurance Co., **26** 486
Manufacturers Fire Insurance Co., **26** 486
Manufacturers Hanover Corporation, **II 312–14** *see also* Chemical Bank.
Manufacturers National Bank of Detroit, **40** 116
Manufacturing Management Inc., **19** 381
Manulife Financial Corporation, **85 235–38**
Manutan International S.A., **72 219–21**
Manville Corporation, **III 706–09**; **7 291–95 (upd.)** *see also* Johns Manville Corp.
Manweb plc, *see* Scottish Power plc.
Manzotin S.r.l *see* Bolton Group B.V.
Maola Milk and Ice Cream *see* Maryland & Virginia Milk Producers Cooperative Association, Inc.
MAP *see* Marathon Ashland Petroleum LLC.
MAPCO Inc., **IV 458–59**
MAPICS, Inc., **55 256–58**
Maple Grove Farms of Vermont, **88 249–52**
Maple Leaf Foods Inc., **41 249–53**
Maple Leaf Heritage Investments Acquisition Corporation *see* Hudson's Bay Co.
Maple Leaf Mills, **41** 252
Maple Leaf Sports & Entertainment Ltd., **61 188–90**
Maples Industries, Inc., **83 260-263**

MAPP *see* Mid-Continent Area Power Planner.
Mapra Industria e Comercio Ltda., **32** 40
MAR Associates, **48** 54
Mar-O-Bar Company, *see* Mars, Inc.
Marantha! Music, *see* Thomas Nelson Inc.
Marathon Ashland Petroleum LLC, **49** 329–30; **50** 49
Marathon Insurance Co., **26** 486
Marathon Oil Co., **49** 328, 330 *see also* United States Steel Corp.
Marauder Company, **26** 433
Marble Slab Creamery, Inc., 87 304–307
Marblehead Communications, Inc., **23** 101
Marbodal, **12** 464
Marc's Big Boy *see* The Marcus Corp.
Marcade Group *see* Aris Industries, Inc.
Marcam Coporation *see* MAPICS, Inc.
Marceau Investments, **II** 356
March of Dimes, 31 322–25
March Plasma Systems, Inc., **48** 299
Marchands Ro-Na Inc. *see* RONA, Inc.
Marchesi Antinori SRL, 42 245–48
Marchex, Inc., 72 222–24
marchFIRST, Inc., 34 261–64
Marco Acquisition Corporation, **62** 268
Marco Business Products, Inc., 75 244–46
Marco's Franchising LLC, 86 264–67
Marcolin S.p.A., 61 191–94
Marcon Coating, Inc., **22** 347
Marconi plc, 33 286–90 (upd.)
Marcopolo S.A., 79 247–50
The Marcus Corporation, 21 359–63
Marcy Fitness Products, Inc., *see* Escalade, Inc.
Marelli *see* Magneti Marelli Holding SpA.
Maremont Corporation, *see* Arvin Industries Inc.
Marfin Popular Bank plc, 92 222–26
Margarete Steiff GmbH, 23 334–37
Marian LLC *see* Charisma Brands LLC.
Marie Brizard & Roger International S.A., 22 342–44
Marie Callender's Restaurant & Bakery, Inc., 28 257–59
Mariella Burani Fashion Group, 92 227–30
Marina Mortgage Company, **46** 25
Marine Computer Systems, **6** 242
Marine Harvest, **56** 257
Marine Manufacturing Corporation, **52** 406
Marine Products Corporation, 75 247–49
Marine Transport Lines, Inc., **59** 323
Marine United Inc., **42** 361
Marinela, **19** 192–93
MarineMax, Inc., 30 303–05
Marinette Marine Corporation, **59** 274, 278
Marion Foods, Inc., *see* Seneca Foods Corp.
Marion Laboratories Inc., I 648–49
Marion Manufacturing, **9** 72
Marion Merrell Dow, Inc., 9 328–29 (upd.)
Marionet Corp., **IV** 680–81
Marionnaud Parfumeries SA, 51 233–35
Marisa Christina, Inc., 15 290–92
Maritime Electric Company, Limited, **15** 182; **47** 136–37
Maritz Inc., 38 302–05
Mark Controls Corporation, **30** 157
Mark Cross, Inc., **17** 4–5
Mark IV Industries, Inc., 7 296–98; 28 260–64 (upd.)
Mark T. Wendell Tea Company, 94 299–302
The Mark Travel Corporation, 80 232–35
Mark's Work Wearhouse Ltd. *see* Canadian Tire Corporation, Ltd.
Market Development Corporation *see* Spartan Stores Inc.
Market Growth Resources, **23** 480
Marketing Data Systems, Inc., **18** 24
Marketing Equities International, **26** 136
MarketSpan Corp. *see* KeySpan Energy Co.
Märklin Holding GmbH, 70 163–66
Marks and Spencer p.l.c., V 124–26; 24 313–17 (upd.); 85 239–47 (upd.)
Marks-Baer Inc., *see* CTG, Inc.
Marks Brothers Jewelers, Inc., 24 318–20 *see also* Whitehall Jewellers, Inc.
Marlene Industries Corp., **16** 36–37
Marley Co., **19** 360
Marley Holdings, L.P., **19** 246
Oy Marli Ab, **56** 103
Marlin Business Services Corp., 89 317–19
The Marmon Group, Inc., IV 135–38; 16 354–57 (upd.); 70 167–72 (upd.)
Marmon-Perry Light Company, **6** 508
Marolf Dakota Farms, Inc., **18** 14–15
Marotte, **21** 438
Marpac Industries Inc. *see* PVC Container Corp.
Marquam Commercial Brokerage Company, **21** 257
Marquette Electronics, Inc., 13 326–28
Marr S.p.A., **57** 82–84
Marriot Inc., **29** 442
Marriot Management Services, **29** 444
Marriott International, Inc., III 102–03; 21 364–67 (upd.); 83 264-270 (upd.)
Mars, Incorporated, 7 299–301; 40 302–05 (upd.)
Marsh & McLennan Companies, Inc., III 282–84; 45 263–67 (upd.)
Marsh Supermarkets, Inc., 17 300–02; 76 255–58 (upd.)
Marshall & Ilsley Corporation, 56 217–20
Marshall Amplification plc, 62 239–42
Marshall Field's, 63 254–63 *see also* Target Corp.
Marshalls Incorporated, 13 329–31
Marshfield Clinic Inc., 82 209–12
Marship Tankers (Holdings) Ltd., **52** 329
Marstons, **57** 412–13
Martank Shipping Holdings Ltd., **52** 329
Martek Biosciences Corporation, 65 218–20
Martell and Company S.A., 82 213–16
Marten Transport, Ltd., 84 243–246
Martha Stewart Living Omnimedia, Inc., 24 321–23; 73 219–22 (upd.)
Martignetti Companies, 84 247–250
Martin-Baker Aircraft Company Limited, 61 195–97
Martin Band Instrument Company, **55** 149, 151
Martin Bros. Tobacco Co., **14** 19
Martin Dunitz, **44** 416
Martin Franchises, Inc., 80 236–39
Martin Gillet Co., **55** 96, 98
Martin Guitar Company *see* C.F. Martin & Co., Inc.
Martin Hilti Foundation, **53** 167
Martin Industries, Inc., 44 274–77
Martin Marietta Corporation, I 67–69 *see also* Lockheed Martin Corp.
Martin Mathys N.V., *see* RPM Inc.
Martin Sorrell, **6** 54
Martin-Yale Industries, Inc., *see* Escalade, Inc.
MartinLogan, Ltd., 85 248–51
Martini & Rossi SpA, 63 264–66
Martinus Nijhoff, **25** 85
Martz Group, 56 221–23
Marubeni Corporation, I 492–95; 24 324–27 (upd.)
Maruha Group Inc., 75 250–53 (upd.)
Marui Company Ltd., V 127; 62 243–45 (upd.)
Marusa Co. Ltd., **51** 379
Maruti Udyog Ltd., **59** 393, 395–97
Maruzen Co., Limited, 18 322–24
Maruzen Oil Co., Ltd., **53** 114
Marva Maid Dairy *see* Maryland & Virginia Milk Producers Cooperative Association, Inc.
Marvel Entertainment, Inc., 10 400–02; 78 212–19 (upd.)
Marvin H. Sugarman Productions Inc., **20** 48
Marvin Lumber & Cedar Company, 22 345–47
Marwick, Mitchell & Company, *see* KPMG Worldwide.
Mary Ann Co. Ltd., **V** 89
Mary Ellen's, Inc., *see* The J.M. Smucker Co.
Mary Kathleen Uranium, **IV** 59–60
Mary Kay Inc., 9 330–32; 30 306–09 (upd.); 84 251–256 (upd.)
Maryland & Virginia Milk Producers Cooperative Association, Inc., 80 240–43
Maryland Medical Laboratory Inc., **26** 391
Maryland National Mortgage Corporation, *see* First Tennessee National Corp.
Maryland Square, Inc., **68** 69
Marzotto S.p.A., 20 356–58; 67 246–49 (upd.)
The Maschhoffs, Inc., 82 217–20

Maschinenfabrik Augsburg-Nürnberg *see* M.A.N.
Masco Corporation, III 568–71; 20 359–63 (upd.); 39 263–68 (upd.)
Mase Westpac Limited, **11** 418
Maserati *see* Officine Alfieri Maserati S.p.A.
Maserati Footwear, Inc., **68** 69
Mashantucket Pequot Gaming Enterprise Inc., 35 282–85
MASkargo Ltd. *see* Maladian Airlines System Bhd.
Masland Corporation, 17 303–05 *see also* Lear Corp.
Masonite International Corporation, 63 267–69
Mass Rapid Transit Corp., **19** 111
Massachusetts Electric Company, **51** 265
Massachusetts Mutual Life Insurance Company, III 285–87; 53 210–13 (upd.)
Massachusetts's General Electric Company, **32** 267
Massey Energy Company, 57 236–38
MasTec, Inc., 55 259–63 (upd.)
Master Cellars Inc., **68** 146
Master Electric Company, **15** 134
Master Lock Company, 45 268–71
Master Loom, **63** 151
Master Tek International, Inc., **47** 372
MasterBrand Cabinets, Inc., 71 216–18
MasterCard International, Inc., 9 333–35
MasterCraft Boat Company, Inc., 90 290–93
Masters-Jackson, **50** 49
Mastex Industries, **29** 132
Maszovlet *see* Malév Plc.
Matador Records, **22** 194
Matairco, *see* Applied Power, Inc.
Matalan PLC, 49 258–60
Matav *see* Magyar Telekom Rt
Match.com, LP, 87 308–311
Matchbox Toys Ltd., *see* Fisher-Price Inc.
MatchLogic, Inc., **41** 198
Matco Tools, *see* Danaher Corp.
Material Management and Services Inc., **28** 61
Material Sciences Corporation, 63 270–73
The MathWorks, Inc., 80 244–47
Matra, **IV** 617–19
Matra Aerospace Inc., **22** 402
Matra-Hachette S.A., 15 293–97 (upd.) *see also* European Aeronautic Defence and Space Company EADS N.V.
Matria Healthcare, Inc., 17 306–09
Matrix Essentials Inc., 90 294–97
Matrix Packaging, Inc. *see* Sonoco Products Co.
Matrix Science Corp., **14** 27
Matrix Service Company, 65 221–23
Matrixx Initiatives, Inc., 74 177–79
Matsumoto Medical Instruments, Inc., **11** 476; **29** 455
Matsushita Electric Industrial Co., Ltd., II 55–56; 64 255–58 (upd.)
Matsushita Electric Works, Ltd., III 710–11; 7 302–03 (upd.)
Matsuzakaya Company Ltd., V 129–31; 64 259–62 (upd.)
Matt Prentice Restaurant Group, 70 173–76
Mattel, Inc., 7 304–07; 25 311–15 (upd.); 61 198–203 (upd.)
Matth. Hohner AG, 53 214–17
Matthew Bender & Company, Inc., *see* Times Mirror Co.
Matthews International Corporation, 29 304–06; 77 248–52 (upd.)
Matthews Paint Co., **22** 437
Matussière et Forest SA, 58 220–22
Maui Land & Pineapple Company, Inc., 29 307–09
Maui Tacos International, Inc., **49** 60
Maui Wowi, Inc., 85 252–55
Mauna Loa Macadamia Nut Corporation, 64 263–65
Maus Frères SA, 48 277–79
Maus-Nordmann, **74** 245–46
Maverick Ranch Association, Inc., 88 253–56
Maverick Tube Corporation, 59 280–83
Max & Erma's Restaurants Inc., 19 258–60
Max-Grundig-Stiftung, *see* Grundig AG.
Max Media Properties LLC, **25** 419
Max Television Co., **25** 418
Maxco Inc., 17 310–11
Maxfield Candy Company *see* Alpine Confections, Inc.
Maxi-Papier-Markt, **24** 270
Maxi Vac, Inc., **9** 72
Maxicare Health Plans, Inc., III 84–86; 25 316–19 (upd.)
The Maxim Group, 25 320–22
Maxim Integrated Products, Inc., 16 358–60
MAXIMUS, Inc., 43 277–80
Maxpro Sports Inc., **22** 458
Maxpro Systems, **24** 509–10
Maxtor Corporation, 10 403–05 *see also* Seagate Technology, Inc.
Maxus Energy Corporation, 7 308–10
Maxvalu Hokkaido Co., Ltd., **68** 9
Maxwell Communication Corporation plc, IV 641–43; 7 311–13 (upd.)
Maxwell Shoe Company, Inc., 30 310–12 *see also* Jones Apparel Group, Inc.
Maxwell Travel Inc., **33** 396
MAXXAM Inc., 8 348–50
Maxxcom Inc., **63** 290–91
Maxxim Medical Inc., 12 325–27
May & Speh Inc., **35** 17
The May Department Stores Company, V 132–35; 19 261–64 (upd.); 46 284–88 (upd.)
May International *see* George S. May International Co.
Mayer & Schweitzer, **26** 66
Mayer, Brown, Rowe & Maw, 47 230–32
Mayfield Dairy Farms, Inc., 74 180–82
Mayflower Group Inc., 6 409–11
Mayo Foundation, 9 336–39; 34 265–69 (upd.)
Mayor's Jewelers, Inc., 41 254–57
Mays + Red Spot Coatings, LLC, **55** 321
Maytag Corporation, III 572–73; 22 348–51 (upd.); 82 221–25 (upd.)
Mazda Motor Corporation, 9 340–42; 23 338–41 (upd.); 63 274–79 (upd.)
Mazel Stores, Inc., 29 310–12
Mazzio's Corporation, 76 259–61
MB Group *see* Novar plc.
MBB *see* Messerschmitt-Bölkow-Blohm.
MBC *see* Middle East Broadcasting Centre, Ltd.
MBC Holding Company, 40 306–09
MBE *see* Mail Boxes Etc.
MBG Marketing, **62** 154
MBIA Inc., 73 223–26
MBK Industrie S.A., 94 303–06
MBNA Corporation, 12 328–30; 33 291–94 (upd.)
MBRD *see* Moscow Bank for Reconstruction & Development.
MC Distribution Services, Inc., **35** 298
MC Sporting Goods *see* Michigan Sporting Goods Distributors Inc.
MCA Inc., II 143–45 *see also* Universal Studios.
McAfee Inc., 94 307–10
McAlister's Corporation, 66 217–19
McBride plc, 82 226–30
MCall, **64** 57
The McAlpin Company, *see* Mercantile Stores Company, Inc.
McAndrew & Forbes Holdings Inc., **23** 407; **26** 119
MCC *see* Maxwell Communications Corporation; Morris Communications Corp.
McCain Foods Limited, 77 253–56
McCall Pattern Company, **23** 99
McCall's Corp., **23** 393
McCann-Erickson Worldwide, *see* Interpublic Group of Companies, Inc.
McCann-Erickson Hakuhodo, Ltd., **42** 174
McCarthy Building Companies, Inc., 48 280–82
McCathren Vending Corporation, **74** 14
McCaw Cellular Communications, Inc., 6 322–24 *see also* AT&T Wireless Services, Inc.
McClain Industries, Inc., 51 236–38
The McClatchy Company, 23 342–44; 92 231–35 (upd.)
McColl-Frontenac Petroleum Inc., **IV** 439; **25** 232
McCormick & Company, Incorporated, 7 314–16; 27 297–300 (upd.)
McCormick & Schmick's Seafood Restaurants, Inc., 71 219–21
McCown De Leeuw & Co., **71** 363–64
McCoy Corporation, 58 223–25
McCracken Brooks, **23** 479; **25** 91
McCrory Stores, *see* Riklis Family Corp.
McCullough Environmental Services, **12** 443
McDATA Corporation, 75 254–56

McDermott International, Inc., III 558–60; 37 242–46 (upd.)
McDonald's Corporation, II 646–48; 7 317–19 (upd.); 26 281–85 (upd.); 63 280–86 (upd.)
McDonnell Douglas Corporation, I 70–72; 11 277–80 (upd.) *see also* Boeing Co.
McDowell Energy Center, **6** 543
MCG PCS Inc., **69** 233
McGrath RentCorp, 91 326–29
McGaw Inc., **11** 208
McGraw-Edison Co., **II** 17, 87
McGraw Electric Company *see* Centel Corp.
The McGraw-Hill Companies, Inc., IV 634–37; 18 325–30 (upd.); 51 239–44 (upd.)
McGregor Corporation, **26** 102
McHugh Software International Inc. *see* RedPrairie Corp.
MCI *see* Manitou Costruzioni Industriali SRL; Melamine Chemicals, Inc.
MCI WorldCom, Inc., V 302–04; 27 301–08 (upd.) *see also* Verizon Communications Inc.
McIlhenny Company, 20 364–67
McJunkin Corporation, 63 287–89
McKechnie plc, 34 270–72
McKee Foods Corporation, 7 320–21; 27 309–11 (upd.)
McKesson Corporation, I 496–98; 12 331–33 (upd.); 47 233–37 (upd.)
McKesson General Medical, **29** 299
McKinsey & Company, Inc., 9 343–45
MCL Land *see* Jardine Cycle & Carriage Ltd.
McLane America, Inc., **29** 481
McLane Company, Inc., 13 332–34
McLean Clinic, **11** 379
McLeod's Accessories *see* Repco Corporation Ltd.
McLeodUSA Incorporated, 32 327–30
MCM Electronics, *see* Premier Industrial Corp.
MCMC *see* Minneapolis Children's Medical Center.
McMenamins Pubs and Breweries, 65 224–26
McMoRan, *see* Freeport-McMoRan Copper & Gold, Inc.
McMullen & Yee Publishing, **22** 442
MCN Corporation, 6 519–22
McNaughton Apparel Group, Inc., 92 236–41 (upd.)
McNeil Corporation, **26** 363
McNeil Laboratories *see* Johnson & Johnson
MCO Properties Inc., *see* MAXXAM Inc.
McPaper AG, **29** 152
McPherson's Ltd., 66 220–22
McQuay International *see* AAF-McQuay Inc.
McRae's, Inc., **19** 324–25; **41** 343–44
MCS, Inc., *see* Mestek, In.
MCSi, Inc., 41 258–60
MCT Dairies, Inc., **18** 14–16
MCTC *see* Medical Center Trading Corp.
McWane Corporation, 55 264–66
MD Distribution Inc., **15** 139
MD Foods (Mejeriselskabet Danmark Foods), **48** 35
MDC *see* Mead Data Central, Inc.
MDC Partners Inc., 63 290–92
MDI Entertainment, LLC, **64** 346
MDP *see* Madison Dearborn Partners LLC.
MDU Resources Group, Inc., 7 322–25; 42 249–53 (upd.)
Mead & Mount Construction Company, **51** 41
The Mead Corporation, IV 310–13; 19 265–69 (upd.) *see also* MeadWestvaco Corp.
Mead Data Central, Inc., 10 406–08 *see also* LEXIS-NEXIS Group.
Mead Johnson & Company, 84 257–262
Meade Instruments Corporation, 41 261–64
Meadowcraft, Inc., 29 313–15
MeadWestvaco Corporation, 76 262–71 (upd.)
Measurement Specialties, Inc., 71 222–25
Measurex Corporation, **14** 56; **38** 227
MEC *see* Mitsubishi Estate Company, Ltd.
Mecair, S.p.A., *see* Duriron Co. Inc.
Mecalux S.A., 74 183–85
MECAR S.A. *see* The Allied Defense Group.
Mecca Bingo Ltd., **64** 320
Mecca Bookmakers, **49** 450
Mecca Leisure PLC, **12** 229; **32** 243
Meccano S.A., **52** 207
Mecklermedia Corporation, 24 328–30 *see also* Jupitermedia Corp.
Meconic, **49** 230, 235
Medarex, Inc., 85 256–59
Medco Containment Services Inc., 9 346–48 *see also* Merck & Co., Inc.
Médecins sans Frontières, 85 260–63
Medeco Security Locks, Inc., *see* Hillenbrand Industries, Inc.
Medford, Inc., **19** 467–68
Medi Mart Drug Store Company *see* The Stop & Shop Companies, Inc.
Media Arts Group, Inc., 42 254–57
Media Exchange International, **25** 509
Media General, Inc., 7 326–28; 38 306–09 (upd.)
Media Groep West B.V., **23** 271
Media Play *see* Musicland Stores Corp.
MediaBay, **41** 61
Mediacom Communications Corporation, 69 250–52
Mediamark Research, **28** 501, 504
Mediamatics, Inc., **26** 329
MediaNews Group, Inc., 70 177–80
MediaOne Group Inc. *see* U S West, Inc.
Mediaplex, Inc., **49** 433
Mediaset SpA, 50 332–34
Media24 *see* Naspers Ltd.
Medic Computer Systems LLC, **16** 94; **45** 279–80
Medical Arts Press, Inc., **55** 353, 355
Medical Care America, Inc., **15** 112, 114; **35** 215–17
Medical China Publishing Limited, **51** 244
Medical Development Corp. *see* Cordis Corp.
Medical Device Alliance Inc., **73** 33
Medical Economics Data, **23** 211
Medical Equipment Finance Corporation, **51** 108
Medical Information Technology Inc., 64 266–69
Medical Innovations Corporation, **21** 46
Medical Learning Company, **51** 200, 203
Medical Management International, Inc., 65 227–29
Medical Marketing Group Inc., *see* Medco Containment Services Inc.
Medical Service Assoc. of Pennsylvania *see* Pennsylvania Blue Shield.
Medical Staffing Network Holdings, Inc., 89 320–23
Medical Center Trading Corporation, **70** 182
Medical Tribune Group, **IV** 591; **20** 53
Medicine Bow Coal Company, **7** 33–34
Medicine Shoppe International *see* Cardinal Health, Inc.
Medicis Pharmaceutical Corporation, 59 284–86
Medicor, Inc., **36** 496
Medicus Intercon International *see* D'Arcy Masius Benton & Bowles, Inc.
Medifinancial Solutions, Inc., **18** 370
MedImmune, Inc., 35 286–89
Medinol Ltd., **37** 39
Mediobanca Banca di Credito Finanziario SpA, **11** 205; **65** 86, 88, 230–31
Mediocredito Toscano, **65** 72
Mediolanum S.p.A., 65 230–32
The Mediplex Group, Inc., *see* Meditrust.
Medis Technologies Ltd., 77 257–60
Medite Corporation, **19** 467–68
MEDITECH *see* Medical Information Technology Inc.
Meditrust, 11 281–83
Medline Industries, Inc., 61 204–06
MedPartners, Inc. *see* Caremark Rx, Inc.
Medsep Corporation, **72** 265
Medtech, Ltd., **13** 60–62
Medtronic, Inc., 8 351–54; 30 313–17 (upd.); 67 250–55 (upd.)
Medusa Corporation, 24 331–33
Meekma Distileerderijen BV, **74** 42
Mega Bloks, Inc., 61 207–09
The MEGA Life and Health Insurance Co., **33** 418–20
MEGA Natural Gas Company, **11** 28
MegaBingo, Inc., **41** 273, 275
Megafoods Stores Inc., 13 335–37
Megahouse Corp., **55** 48
MegaKnowledge Inc., **45** 206
Megasong Publishing, **44** 164
Megasource, Inc., **16** 94
Meggitt PLC, 34 273–76
MEGTEC Systems Inc., **54** 331
Mei Foo Investments Ltd., **IV** 718; **38** 319

Meidensha Corporation, **92 242–46**
Meier & Frank Co., **23 345–47** *see also* Macy's, Inc.
Meierjohan-Wengler Inc., **56** 23
Meijer Incorporated, **7 329–31; 27 312–15 (upd.)**
Meiji Dairies Corporation, **II 538–39; 82 231–34 (upd.)**
Meiji Mutual Life Insurance Company, **III 288–89**
Meiji Seika Kaisha Ltd., **II 540–41; 64 270–72 (upd.)**
Meinecke Muffler Company, **10** 415
Meineke Discount Muffler Shops, **38** 208
Meisel *see* Samuel Meisel & Co.
Meisenzahl Auto Parts, Inc., *see* Hahn Automotive Warehouse, Inc.
Mel Farr Automotive Group, **20 368–70**
Melaleuca Inc., **31 326–28**
Melamine Chemicals, Inc., **27 316–18** *see also* Mississippi Chemical Corp.
Melbourne Engineering Co., **23** 83
Melcher Holding AG *see* Power-One.
Meldisco *see* Footstar, Inc.
Melitta Unternehmensgruppe Bentz KG, **53 218–21**
Mello Smello *see* The Miner Group International.
Mellon Financial Corporation, **II 315–17; 44 278–82 (upd.)**
Mellon-Stuart Co., **I 584–85** *see also* Michael Baker Corp.
Melroe Company, *see* Clark Equipment Co.
The Melting Pot Restaurants, Inc., **74 186–88**
Melville Corporation, **V 136–38** *see also* CVS Corp.
Melvin Simon and Associates, Inc., **8 355–57** *see also* Simon Property Group, Inc.
MEM, **37** 270–71
MEMC Electronic Materials, Inc., **81 249–52**
Memorial Sloan-Kettering Cancer Center, **57 239–41**
Memphis International Motorsports Corporation Inc., **43** 139–40
Memphis Retail Investors Limited Partnership, **62** 144
Memry Corporation, **72 225–27**
The Men's Wearhouse, Inc., **17 312–15; 48 283–87 (upd.)**
Menasha Corporation, **8 358–61; 59 287–92 (upd.)**
Mendocino Brewing Company, Inc., **60 205–07**
The Mennen Company, *see* Colgate-Palmolive Co.
Mental Health Programs Inc., **15** 122
The Mentholatum Company Inc., **32 331–33**
Mentor Corporation, **26 286–88**
Mentor Graphics Corporation, **11 284–86**
MEPC plc, **IV 710–12**
MeraBank, **6** 546
Meralco *see* Manila Electric Co.
MERBCO, Inc., **33** 456
Mercantile Bancorporation Inc., **33** 155
Mercantile Bankshares Corp., **11 287–88**
Mercantile Estate and Property Corp. Ltd. *see* MEPC PLC.
Mercantile Stores Company, Inc., **V 139; 19 270–73 (upd.)** *see also* Dillard's Inc.
Mercator & Noordstar N.V., **40** 61
Mercator Software, **59** 54, 56
Mercedes Benz *see* DaimlerChrysler AG
Mercer International Inc., **64 273–75**
Merchant Distributors, Inc., **20** 306
Merchant Investors *see* Sanlam Ltd.
Merchants Bank & Trust Co., **21** 524
Merchants Distributors Inc. *see* Alex Lee Inc.
Merchants Home Delivery Service, **6** 414
Merchants National Bank, *see* Deposit Guaranty Corp.
Mercian Corporation, **77 261–64**
Merck & Co., Inc., **I 650–52; 11 289–91 (upd.); 34 280–85 (upd.)**
Mercury Air Group, Inc., **20 371–73**
Mercury Asset Management (MAM), **14** 420; **40** 313
Mercury Communications, Ltd., **7 332–34** *see also* Cable and Wireless plc.
Mercury Drug Corporation, **70 181–83**
Mercury General Corporation, **25 323–25**
Mercury Interactive Corporation, **59 293–95**
Mercury International Ltd., **51** 130
Mercury Marine Group, **68 247–51**
Mercury Records, **23** 389, 391
Mercury Telecommunications Limited, **15** 67, 69
Mercy Air Service, Inc., **53** 29
Meredith Corporation, **11 292–94; 29 316–19 (upd.); 74 189–93 (upd.)**
Merfin International, **42** 53
Merge Healthcare, **85 264–68**
Merial, **34** 284
Meriam Instrument *see* Scott Fetzer.
Merico, Inc., **36** 161–64
Merida, **50** 445, 447
Meridian Bancorp, Inc., **11 295–97**
Meridian Emerging Markets Ltd., **25** 509
Meridian Gold, Incorporated, **47 238–40**
Meridian Healthcare Ltd., *see* NeighborCare, Inc.
Meridian Industrial Trust Inc., **57** 301
Meridian Oil Inc., **10** 190–91
Meridian Publishing, Inc., **28** 254
Merillat Industries, LLC, **13 338–39; 69 253–55 (upd.)**
Merisant Worldwide, Inc., **70 184–86**
Merisel, Inc., **12 334–36**
Merit Distribution Services, *see* McLane Company, Inc.
Merit Medical Systems, Inc., **29 320–22**
Merit Tank Testing, Inc., **IV** 411
MeritCare Health System, **88 257–61**
Merita/Cotton's Bakeries, **38** 251
Meritage Corporation, **26 289–92**
MeritaNordbanken, **40** 336
Meritor Automotive Inc. *see* ArvinMeritor Inc.
Merix Corporation, **36 329–31; 75 257–60 (upd.)**
Merkur Direktwerbegesellschaft, **29** 152
Merpati Nusantara Airlines *see* Garuda Indonesia.
Merriam-Webster Inc., **70 187–91**
Merrill Corporation, **18 331–34; 47 241–44 (upd.)**
Merrill Lynch & Co., Inc., **II 424–26; 13 340–43 (upd.); 40 310–15 (upd.)**
Merrill Lynch Capital Partners, **47** 363
Merrill Lynch Investment Managers *see* BlackRock, Inc.
Merrill, Pickard, Anderson & Eyre IV, **11** 490
Merrill Publishing, **29** 57
Merrimack Services Corp., **37** 303
Merry-Go-Round Enterprises, Inc., **8 362–64**
Merry Group *see* Boral Ltd.
Merry Maids *see* ServiceMaster Inc.
Merryhill Schools, Inc., **37** 279
The Mersey Docks and Harbour Company, **30 318–20**
Mervyn's California, **10 409–10; 39 269–71 (upd.)** *see also* Target Corp.
Merz Group, **81 253–56**
Mesa Air Group, Inc., **11 298–300; 32 334–37 (upd.); 77 265–70 (upd.)**
Mesaba Holdings, Inc., **28 265–67**
Messerschmitt-Bölkow-Blohm GmbH., **I 73–75** *see also* European Aeronautic Defence and Space Company EADS N.V.
Mestek, Inc., **10 411–13**
Met Food Corp. *see* White Rose Food Corp.
Met-Mex Penoles *see* Industrias Penoles, S.A. de C.V.
META Group, Inc., **37** 147
Metal Box plc, **I 604–06** *see also* Novar plc.
Metal-Cal *see* Avery Dennison Corp.
Metal Casting Technology, Inc., **23** 267, 269
Metal Management, Inc., **92 247–50**
AB Metal Pty Ltd, **62** 331
Metalcorp Ltd, **62** 331
Metales y Contactos, **29** 461–62
Metaleurop S.A., **21 368–71**
MetalExchange, **26** 530
Metallgesellschaft AG, **IV 139–42; 16 361–66 (upd.)**
MetalOptics Inc., **19** 212
Metalúrgica Gerdau *see* Gerdau S.A.
Metalurgica Mexicana Penoles, S.A. *see* Industrias Penoles, S.A. de C.V.
Metaphase Technology, Inc., *see* Control Data Systems, Inc.
Metatec International, Inc., **47 245–48**
Metcalf & Eddy Companies, Inc., **6** 441; **32** 52
Metcash Trading Ltd., **58 226–28**
Meteor Film Productions, **23** 391
Meteor Industries Inc., **33 295–97**

Methane Development Corporation, **6** 457
Methanex Corporation, 40 316–19
Methode Electronics, Inc., 13 344–46
MetLife *see* Metropolitan Life Insurance Co.
MetPath, Inc., *see* Corning Inc.
Metra Corporation *see* Wärtsilä Corp.
Metra Steel, **19** 381
Metragaz, **69** 191
Metrastock Ltd., **34** 5
Metric Constructors, Inc., **16** 286
Metric Systems Corporation, *see* Tech-Sym Corp.
Metris Companies Inc., 56 224–27
Metro AG, 50 335–39
Metro Distributors Inc., **14** 545
Metro-Goldwyn-Mayer Inc., 25 326–30 (upd.); 84 263–270 (upd.)
Metro Holding AG, **38** 266
Métro Inc., 77 271–75
Metro Information Services, Inc., 36 332–34
Metro International S.A., 93 309–12
Metro-Mark Integrated Systems Inc., **11** 469
Metro-North Commuter Railroad Company, **35** 292
Metro Pacific, *see* First Pacific Co. Ltd.
Metro Southwest Construction *see* CRSS Inc.
Metro Support Services, Inc., **48** 171
Metrocall, Inc., 41 265–68
Metrol Security Services, Inc., **32** 373
Metroland Printing, Publishing and Distributing Ltd., **29** 471
Metromail Corp., **IV** 661; **18** 170; **38** 370
Metromedia Company, 7 335–37; 14 298–300 (upd.); 61 210–14 (upd.)
Metronic AG, **64** 226
Metroplex, LLC, **51** 206
Métropole Télévision S.A., 76 272–74 (upd.)
Metropolis Intercom, **67** 137–38
Metropolitan Baseball Club Inc., 39 272–75
Metropolitan Clothing Co., **19** 362
Metropolitan Edison Company, *see* GPU, Inc.
Metropolitan Financial Corporation, 13 347–49
Metropolitan Life Insurance Company, III 290–94; 52 235–41 (upd.)
The Metropolitan Museum of Art, 55 267–70
Metropolitan Opera Association, Inc., 40 320–23
Metropolitan Reference Laboratories Inc., **26** 391
Metropolitan Tobacco Co., **15** 138
Metropolitan Transportation Authority, 35 290–92
MetroRed, **57** 67, 69
Metrostar Management, **59** 199
METSA, Inc., **15** 363
Metsä-Serla Oy, IV 314–16 *see also* M-real Oyj.
Metsec plc, **57** 402
Metso Corporation, 30 321–25 (upd.); 85 269–77 (upd.)
Mettler-Toledo International Inc., 30 326–28
Metwest, **26** 391
Metz Baking Company, **36** 164
Metzdorf Advertising Agency, **30** 80
Metzeler Kautschuk, **15** 354
Mexican Metal Co. *see* Industrias Penoles, S.A. de C.V.
Mexican Restaurants, Inc., 41 269–71
Meyer International Holdings, Ltd., 87 312–315
Meyerland Company, **19** 366
Meyers Motor Supply, **26** 347
Meyers Parking, *see* Central Parking Corp.
The Meyne Company, **55** 74
Meyr Melnhof Karton AG, **41** 325–27
M4 Data (Holdings) Ltd., **62** 293
M40 Trains Ltd., **51** 173
MFS Communications Company, Inc., 11 301–03 *see also* MCI WorldCom, Inc.
MG&E *see* Madison Gas & Electric.
MG Holdings *see* Mayflower Group Inc.
MGD Graphics Systems *see* Goss Holdings, Inc.
MGIC Investment Corp., 52 242–44
MGM *see* McKesson General Medical.
MGM Grand Inc., 17 316–19
MGM Mirage *see* Mirage Resorts, Inc.
MGM Studios, **50** 125
MGM/UA Communications Company, II 146–50 *see also* Metro-Goldwyn-Mayer Inc.
MGN *see* Mirror Group Newspapers Ltd.
MGT Services Inc. *see* The Midland Co.
MH Alshaya Group, **28** 96
MH Media Monitoring Limited, **26** 270
MHI Group, Inc., **16** 344
MHS Holding Corp., **26** 101
MHT *see* Manufacturers Hanover Trust Co.
MI *see* Masco Corp.
MI S.A., **66** 244
Mi-Tech Steel Inc., **63** 359–60
Miami Computer Supply Corporation *see* MCSi, Inc.
Miami Herald Media Company, 92 251–55
Miami Power Corporation *see* Cincinnati Gas & Electric Co.
Miami Subs Corp., **29** 342, 344
Mich-Wis *see* Michigan Wisconsin Pipe Line.
Michael Anthony Jewelers, Inc., 24 334–36
Michael Baker Corporation, 14 333–35; 51 245–48 (upd.)
MICHAEL Business Systems Plc, *see* Control Data Systems, Inc.
Michael C. Fina Co., Inc., 52 245–47
Michael Foods, Inc., 25 331–34
Michael Joseph, **IV** 659
Michael Page International plc, 45 272–74
Michaels Stores, Inc., 17 320–22; 71 226–30 (upd.)
MichCon *see* MCN Corp.
Michelin *see* Compagnie Générale des Établissements Michelin.
Michie Co., **33** 264–65
Michigan Automotive Compressor, Inc., *see* Toyoda Automatic Loom Works, Ltd.
Michigan Automotive Research Corporation, **23** 183
Michigan Bell Telephone Co., 14 336–38
Michigan Consolidated Gas Company *see* MCN Corp.
Michigan International Speedway *see* Penske Corp.
Michigan Livestock Exchange, **36** 442
Michigan National Corporation, 11 304–06 *see also* ABN AMRO Holding, N.V.
Michigan Packaging Company *see* Greif Inc.
Michigan Seamless Tube Company *see* Quanex Corp.
Michigan Shoe Makers *see* Wolverine World Wide Inc.
Michigan Sporting Goods Distributors, Inc., 72 228–30
Michigan Wisconsin Pipe Line, **39** 260
Mick's Inc., **30** 329
Mickey Shorr Mobile Electronics, *see* ABC Appliance, Inc.
Micrel, Incorporated, 77 276–79
Micro-Aire Surgical Instruments Corp., *see* Marmon Group, Inc.
Micro Contract Manufacturing Inc., **44** 441
Micro-Controle, **71** 248
Micro Decisionware, Inc., *see* Sybase, Inc.
Micro Focus Inc., *see* Viasoft Inc.
Micro Magic, Inc., **43** 254
Micro Metallics Corporation, **64** 297
Micro Power Systems Inc., *see* Exar Corp.
Micro Warehouse, Inc., 16 371–73
MicroAge, Inc., 16 367–70
MicroBilt Corporation, *see* First Financial Management Corp.
Microcar SA, **55** 54, 56
MicroClean Inc, **50** 49
Microcom, Inc., **26** 93; **50** 227
Microdot Inc., 8 365–68
MicroFridge, **44** 273
Micromass Ltd., **43** 455
Micromedex, **19** 268
Micron Technology, Inc., 11 307–09; 29 323–26 (upd.)
MicroPro International Corp. *see* The Learning Company Inc.
Microprose Inc., **24** 538
Micros Systems, Inc., 18 335–38
Microsemi Corporation, 94 311–14
Microsensor Systems Inc., **43** 366
Microsoft Corporation, 6 257–60; 27 319–23 (upd.); 63 293–97 (upd.)
MicroStrategy Incorporated, 87 316–320
Microtek, Inc., **22** 413

MicroUnity Systems Engineering Inc., **50** 53
Microwave Communications, Inc. *see* MCI Telecom.
Mid-America Apartment Communities, Inc., 85 278–81
Mid-America Capital Resources, Inc., **6** 508
Mid-America Dairymen, Inc., 7 338–40
Mid-America Interpool Network, **6** 602
Mid-America Packaging, Inc., *see* Gaylord Container Corp.
Mid Bus Inc., **33** 107
Mid-Continent Life Insurance Co., **23** 200
Mid-Continent Telephone Corporation *see* Alltel Corp.
Mid-Georgia Gas Company, **6** 448
Mid-Illinois Gas Co., **6** 529
Mid-Michigan Music Co., **60** 84
Mid-Pacific Airlines, **24** 21–22
Mid-Packaging Group Inc., **19** 78
Mid-South Towing, **6** 583
Mid-States Development, Inc., *see* Otter Tail Power Co.
Midas Inc., 10 414–15; 56 228–31 (upd.)
Middle East Airlines - Air Liban S.A.L., 79 251–54
Middle East Broadcasting Centre, Ltd., *see* United Press International, Inc.
Middle South Utilities *see* Entergy Corp.
Middle Wisconsin Power, **6** 604
The Middleby Corporation, 22 352–55
Middlesex Water Company, 45 275–78
Middleton Aerospace, **48** 275
The Middleton Doll Company, 53 222–25
Middleton Packaging, **12** 377
Midland Advertising & Design, Inc., **56** 332
Midland Bank plc, II 318–20; 17 323–26 (upd.) *see also* HSBC Holdings plc.
Midland Brick, **14** 250
The Midland Company, 65 233–35
Midland Enterprises Inc. *see* Eastern Enterprises.
Midland Group *see* Regency Centers Corp.
Midland Independent Newspaper plc, **23** 351
Midland United, **6** 556
Midland Utilities Company, **6** 532
Midlantic Hotels Ltd., **41** 83
Midway Airlines Corporation, 33 301–03
Midway Games, Inc., 25 335–38
Midway Manufacturing Company, **15** 539
Midwest Air Group, Inc., 35 293–95; 85 282–86 (upd.)
Midwest Agri-Commodities Company, **11** 15; **32** 29
Midwest Biscuit Company, *see* Lance, Inc.
Midwest Grain Products, Inc., 49 261–63
Midwest Realty Exchange, Inc., **21** 257
Midwest Resources Inc., 6 523–25
Midwest Staffing Systems, *see* AHL Services, Inc.
Midwest Suburban Publishing Inc., **62** 188
Miele & Cie. KG, 56 232–35
MiG *see* Russian Aircraft Corporation (MiG).
MIG Realty Advisors, Inc., **25** 23, 25
Migros-Genossenschafts-Bund, 68 252–55
MIH Limited, 31 329–32
Mikasa, Inc., 28 268–70
Mike-Sell's Inc., 15 298–300
Mikohn Gaming Corporation, 39 276–79
Milacron, Inc., 53 226–30 (upd.)
Milan AC S.p.A., 79 255–58
Milbank, Tweed, Hadley & McCloy, 27 324–27
Milchem, Inc., **63** 306
Mile-Hi Distributing, **64** 180
Miles Inc., **22** 148
Miles Laboratories, I 653–55 *see also* Bayer A.G.
Milgram Food Stores Inc., *see* Wetterau Inc.
Milgray Electronics Inc., **47** 41
Milk Specialties Co., **12** 199
Millea Holdings Inc., 64 276–81 (upd.)
Millennium & Copthorne Hotels plc, 71 231–33
Millennium Chemicals Inc., **30** 231; **45** 252, 254; **71** 149–50
Millennium Materials Inc. *see* Dyson Group PLC.
Millennium Pharmaceuticals, Inc., 47 249–52
Miller Automotive Group, **52** 146
Miller Brewing Company, I 269–70; 12 337–39 (upd.) *see also* SABMiller plc.
Miller Companies, **17** 182
Miller Exploration Company *see* Edge Petroleum Corp.
Miller Freeman, Inc., **IV** 687; **28** 501, 504
Miller Group Ltd., **22** 282
Miller Industries, Inc., 26 293–95
Miller-Meteor Company *see* Accubuilt, Inc.
Miller, Morris & Brooker (Holdings) Ltd. *see* Gibbs and Dandy plc.
Miller Plant Farms, Inc., **51** 61
Miller Publishing Group, LLC, 57 242–44
Miller, Tabak, Hirsch & Co., **28** 164
Millet, **39** 250
Millet's Leisure *see* Sears plc.
Milliken & Co., V 366–68; 17 327–30 (upd.); 82 235–39 (upd.)
Milliman USA, 66 223–26
Millipore Corporation, 25 339–43; 84 271–276 (upd.)
Mills Clothing, Inc. *see* The Buckle, Inc.
The Mills Corporation, 77 280–83
Millway Foods, **25** 85
Milne & Craighead, **48** 113
Milne Fruit Products, Inc., **25** 366
Milnot Company, 46 289–91
Milpark Drilling Fluids, Inc., **63** 306
Milsco Manufacturing Co., **23** 299, 300
Milton Bradley Company, 21 372–75
Milton CAT, Inc., 86 268–71
Milupa S.A., **37** 341
Milwaukee Brewers Baseball Club, 37 247–49
Milwaukee Electric Railway and Light Company, **6** 601–02, 604–05
Milwaukee Electric Tool, **28** 40
MIM Holdings, **73** 392
Mimi's Cafés *see* SWH Corp.
Minatome, **IV** 560
Mindpearl, **48** 381
Mindport, **31** 329
Mindset Corp., **42** 424–25
Mindspring Enterprises, Inc., **36** 168
Mine Safety Appliances Company, 31 333–35
Minebea Co., Ltd., 90 298–302
The Miner Group International, 22 356–58
Minera Loma Blanca S.A., **56** 127
Mineral Point Public Service Company, **6** 604
Minerales y Metales, S.A. *see* Industrias Penoles, S.A. de C.V.
Minerals & Metals Trading Corporation of India Ltd., IV 143–44
Minerals and Resources Corporation Limited *see* Minorco.
Minerals Technologies Inc., 11 310–12; 52 248–51 (upd.)
Minerva SA, **72** 289
Minerve, **6** 208
Minitel, **21** 233
Minneapolis Children's Medical Center, **54** 65
Minneapolis Steel and Machinery Company, **21** 502
Minnehoma Insurance Company, **58** 260
Minnesota Brewing Company *see* MBC Holding Co.
Minnesota Mining & Manufacturing Company, I 499–501; 8 369–71 (upd.); 26 296–99 (upd.) *see also* 3M Co.
Minnesota Power, Inc., 11 313–16; 34 286–91 (upd.)
Minntech Corporation, 22 359–61
Minn-Dak Farmers Cooperative, **32** 29
Minolta Co., Ltd., III 574–76; 18 339–42 (upd.); 43 281–85 (upd.)
Minorco, **IV** 97; **16** 28, 293
Minstar Inc., **15** 49; **45** 174
Minton China, **38** 401
The Minute Maid Company, 28 271–74
Minuteman International Inc., 46 292–95
Minyard Food Stores, Inc., 33 304–07; 86 272–77 (upd.)
Mippon Paper, **21** 546; **50** 58
Miquel y Costas Miquel S.A., 68 256–58
Miracle Food Mart, *see* The Great Atlantic & Pacific Tea Co., Inc.
Miracle-Gro Products, Inc., *see* Scotts Co.

Mirage Resorts, Incorporated, 6 209–12; 28 275–79 (upd.)
Miraglia Inc., **57** 139
Miramax Film Corporation, 64 282–85
Mirant, **39** 54, 57
MIRAX Corporation *see* JSP Corp.
Mircor Inc., **12** 413
Miroglio SpA, 86 278–81
Mirror Group Newspapers plc, 7 341–43; 23 348–51 (upd.)
Misonix, Inc., 80 248–51
Misr Airwork *see* EgyptAir.
Misrair *see* AirEgypt.
Miss Erika, Inc., *see* Norton McNaughton, Inc.
Miss Selfridge *see* Sears plc.
Misset Publishers, **IV** 611
Mission Group *see* SCEcorp.
Mission Jewelers, **30** 408
Mission Valley Fabrics, **57** 285
Mississippi Chemical Corporation, 39 280–83
Mississippi Gas Company, **6** 577
Mississippi Power Company, **38** 446–47
Mississippi River Recycling, **31** 47, 49
Mississippi Valley Title Insurance Company, **58** 259–60
Missoula Bancshares, Inc., **35** 198–99
Missouri Gaming Company, **21** 39
Missouri Gas & Electric Service Company, **6** 593
Missouri Public Service Company *see* UtiliCorp United Inc.
Missouri Utilities Company, **6** 580
Mist Assist, Inc. *see* Ballard Medical Products.
Misys PLC, 45 279–81; 46 296–99
Mitchell Energy and Development Corporation, 7 344–46 *see also* Devon Energy Corp.
Mitchells & Butlers PLC, 59 296–99
MiTek Industries Inc., *see* Rexam PLC.
Mitel Corporation, 18 343–46
MITRE Corporation, 26 300–02
MITROPA AG, 37 250–53
Mitsubishi Bank, Ltd., II 321–22 *see also* Bank of Tokyo-Mitsubishi Ltd.
Mitsubishi Chemical Corporation, I 363–64; 56 236–38 (upd.)
Mitsubishi Corporation, I 502–04; 12 340–43 (upd.)
Mitsubishi Electric Corporation, II 57–59; 44 283–87 (upd.)
Mitsubishi Estate Company, Limited, IV 713–14; 61 215–18 (upd.)
Mitsubishi Group, **21** 390
Mitsubishi Heavy Industries, Ltd., III 577–79; 7 347–50 (upd.); 40 324–28 (upd.)
Mitsubishi Kasei Corp., **14** 535
Mitsubishi Kasei Vinyl Company, **49** 5
Mitsubishi Materials Corporation, III 712–13
Mitsubishi Motors Corporation, 9 349–51; 23 352–55 (upd.); 57 245–49 (upd.)
Mitsubishi Oil Co., Ltd., IV 460–62 *see also* Nippon Mitsubishi Oil Corp.
Mitsubishi Rayon Co. Ltd., V 369–71
Mitsubishi Trust & Banking Corporation, II 323–24
Mitsui & Co., Ltd., I 505–08; 28 280–85 (upd.)
Mitsui Bank, Ltd., II 325–27 *see also* Sumitomo Mitsui Banking Corp.
Mitsui Group, **20** 310; **21** 72
Mitsui Marine and Fire Insurance Company, Limited, III 295–96
Mitsui Mining & Smelting Co., Ltd., IV 145–46
Mitsui Mining Company, Limited, IV 147–49
Mitsui Mutual Life Insurance Company, III 297–98; 39 284–86 (upd.)
Mitsui-no-Mori Co., Ltd., **IV** 716
Mitsui O.S.K. Lines, Ltd., V 473–76
Mitsui Petrochemical Industries, Ltd., 9 352–54
Mitsui Real Estate Development Co., Ltd., IV 715–16
Mitsui Trust & Banking Company, Ltd., II 328
Mitsukoshi Ltd., V 142–44; 56 239–42 (upd.)
Mity Enterprises, Inc., 38 310–12
MIVA, Inc., 83 271-275
Mizuho Financial Group Inc., 25 344–46; 58 229–36 (upd.)
MJ Pharmaceuticals Ltd., **57** 346
MK-Ferguson Company, *see* Morrison Knudsen Corp.
MLC *see* Medical Learning Co.
MLC Ltd., **IV** 709; **52** 221–22
MLH&P *see* Montreal Light, Heat & Power Co.
MLT Vacations Inc., **30** 446
MM Merchandising Munich, **54** 296–97
MMAR Group Inc., **19** 131
MMC Networks Inc., **38** 53, 55
MML Investors Services, *see* Massachusetts Mutual Life Insurance Co.
MMS America Corp., **26** 317
MNC Financial *see* MBNA Corp.
MNC Financial Corp., **11** 447
MND Drilling, *see* Mitchell Energy and Development Corp.
MNet, *see* First USA, Inc.
MNS, Ltd., 65 236–38
Mo och Domsjö AB, IV 317–19 *see also* Holmen AB
MOB, **56** 335
Mobil Corporation, IV 463–65; 7 351–54 (upd.); 21 376–80 (upd.) *see also* Exxon Mobil Corp.
Mobil Oil Indonesia, **56** 273
Mobile America Housing Corporation *see* American Homestar Corp.
Mobile Corporation, **25** 232
Mobile Mini, Inc., 58 237–39
Mobile Telecommunications Technologies Corp., 18 347–49
Mobile TeleSystems OJSC, 59 300–03
Mobilefone, Inc., **25** 108
MobileMedia Corp., **39** 23, 24
MobileStar Network Corp., **26** 429
Mochida Pharaceutical Co. Ltd., **II** 553
Mocon, Inc., 76 275–77
Modar, *see* Knape & Vogt Manufacturing Co.
Mode 1 Communications, Inc., **48** 305
Modell's Sporting Goods *see* Henry Modell & Company Inc.
Modeluxe Linge Services SA, **45** 139–40
Modem Media, **23** 479
Modern Controls, Inc. *see* Mocon, Inc.
Modern Food Industries Limited *see* Hindustan Lever Limited
Modern Furniture Rentals Inc., **14** 4
Modern Handling Methods Ltd., **21** 499
Modern Times Group AB, 36 335–38
Modern Woodmen of America, 66 227–29
Modine Manufacturing Company, 8 372–75; 56 243–47 (upd.)
Modis Professional Services *see* MPS Group, Inc.
MoDo *see* Mo och Domsjö AB.
MoDo Paper AB, **28** 446; **52** 164
Modtech Holdings, Inc., 77 284–87
ModusLink Corporation *see* CMGI, Inc.
Moe's Southwest Grill, LLC, **64** 327–28
Moen Incorporated, 12 344–45
Moët-Hennessy, I 271–72 *see also* LVMH Moët Hennessy Louis Vuitton SA.
Mogen David *see* The Wine Group, Inc.
The Mogul Metal Company *see* Federal-Mogul Corp.
Mohasco Corporation, **15** 102; **26** 100–01
Mohawk Carpet Corp., **26** 101
Mohawk Industries, Inc., 19 274–76; 63 298–301 (upd.)
Mohawk Rubber Co. Ltd., *see* The Yokohama Rubber Co., Ltd.
Mohegan Tribal Gaming Authority, 37 254–57
Mojave Foods Corporation, *see* McCormick & Company, Inc.
Mojo MDA Group Ltd., **11** 50–51; **43** 412
Moksel *see* A. Moskel AG.
Mokta *see* Compagnie de Mokta.
MOL *see* Mitsui O.S.K. Lines, Ltd.
MOL Rt, 70 192–95
Molabe S.A. Espagne *see* Leroux S.A.S.
Moldflow Corporation, 73 227–30
Molerway Freight Lines, Inc., **53** 250
Molex Incorporated, 11 317–19; 14 27; **54 236–41 (upd.)**
Molfino Hermanos SA, **59** 365
Moliflor Loisirs, 80 252–55
Molinera de México S.A. de C.V., **31** 236
Molinos Nacionales C.A., *see* International Multifoods Corp.
Molinos Río de la Plata S.A., 61 219–21
Molins plc, 51 249–51
Mölnlycke AB, **36** 26
The Molson Companies Limited, I 273–75; 26 303–07 (upd.)
Molson Coors Brewing Company, 77 288–300 (upd.)
Momentum Worldwide, **73** 279
Momentus Group Ltd., **51** 99

Mon-Dak Chemical Inc., *see* Hawkins Chemical, Inc.
Mona Meyer McGrath & Gavin, **47** 97
MONACA *see* Molinos Nacionales C.A.
Monaco Coach Corporation, 31 336–38
Monadnock Paper Mills, Inc., 21 381–84
Monarch Air Lines, *see* Frontier Airlines Holdings Inc.
Monarch Casino & Resort, Inc., 65 239–41
The Monarch Cement Company, 72 231–33
Monarch Development Corporation, **38** 451–52
Monarch Foods, **26** 503
Mondadori *see* Arnoldo Monadori Editore S.p.A.
Mondi Foods BV, **41** 12
Moneris Solutions Corp., **46** 55
Monet Jewelry, *see* Crystal Brands, In.
Money Access Service Corp., **11** 467
Money Management Associates, Inc., **53** 136
MoneyGram International, Inc., 94 315–18
Monfort, Inc., 13 350–52
Monitor Dynamics Inc., **24** 510
Monitor Group Inc., **33** 257
Monk-Austin Inc., **12** 110
Monnaie de Paris, 62 246–48
Monneret Industrie, **56** 335
Monnoyeur Group *see* Groupe Monnoyeur.
Monogram Aerospace Fasteners, Inc., **11** 536
Monongahela Power, **38** 40
Monoprix S.A., 86 282–85
Monro Muffler Brake, Inc., 24 337–40
Monrovia Nursery Company, 70 196–98
Monsanto Company, I 365–67; 9 355–57 (upd.); 29 327–31 (upd.); 77 301–07 (upd.)
Monsoon plc, 39 287–89
Monster Cable Products, Inc., 69 256–58
Monster Worldwide Inc., 74 194–97 (upd.)
Montabert S.A., **15** 226
Montana Alimentaria S.p.A., **57** 82
Montana Coffee Traders, Inc., 60 208–10
Montana-Dakota Utilities Co., *see* MDU Resources Group, Inc.
Montana Group, **54** 229
Montana Mills Bread Co., Inc., **61** 153
The Montana Power Company, 11 320–22; 44 288–92 (upd.)
Montana Refining Company, *see* Holly Corp.
MontBell America, Inc., **29** 279
Montblanc International GmbH, 82 240–44
Monte Paschi Vita, **65** 71–72
Montedison S.p.A., I 368–69; 24 341–44 (upd.)
Montefina, **IV** 499; **26** 367
Monterey Homes Corporation *see* Meritage Corp.
Monterey Mfg. Co., **12** 439
Monterey Pasta Company, 58 240–43
Monterey's Acquisition Corp., **41** 270
Monterrey, Compania de Seguros sobre la Vida *see* Seguros Monterrey.
Monterrey Group, **19** 10–11, 189
Montgomery Elevator Company *see* KONE Corporation.
Montgomery Ward & Co., Incorporated, V 145–48; 20 374–79 (upd.)
Montinex, **24** 270
Montreal Engineering Company, **6** 585
Montres Rolex S.A., 13 353–55; 34 292–95 (upd.)
Montrose Capital, **36** 358
Montupet S.A., 63 302–04
Moody's Corporation, 65 242–44
Moody's Investors Service,
Moog Inc., 13 356–58
Moog Music, Inc., 75 261–64
Mooney Aerospace Group Ltd., 52 252–55
Mooney Chemicals, Inc. *see* OM Group, Inc.
Moonlight Mushrooms, Inc. *see* Sylvan, Inc.
Moonstone Mountaineering, Inc., **29** 181
Moore Corporation Limited, IV 644–46 *see also* R.R. Donnelley & Sons Co.
The Moore Group Ltd., **20** 363
Moore-Handley, Inc., 39 290–92
Moore Medical Corp., 17 331–33
Moquin Breuil *see* Smoby International SA.
Moran Towing Corporation, Inc., 15 301–03
Morana, Inc., *see* International Flavors & Fragrances Inc.
More Group plc *see* JCDecaux S.A
Moretti-Harrah Marble Co. *see* English China Clays Ltd.
Morgan & Banks Limited, **30** 460
The Morgan Crucible Company plc, 82 245–50
Morgan Grampian Group, **IV** 687
Morgan Grenfell Group PLC, II 427–29 *see also* Deutsche Bank AG.
The Morgan Group, Inc., 46 300–02
Morgan Guaranty Trust Company *see* JPMorgan Chase & Co.
Morgan, Lewis & Bockius LLP, 29 332–34
Morgan, Lewis, Githens & Ahn, Inc., **6** 410
Morgan Schiff & Co., **29** 205
Morgan Stanley Dean Witter & Company, II 430–32; 16 374–78 (upd.); 33 311–14 (upd.)
Morgans Hotel Group Company, 80 256–59
Morguard Corporation, 85 287–90
Moria Informatique, **6** 229
Morinaga & Co. Ltd., 61 222–25
Morinda Holdings, Inc., 82 251–54
Morino Associates, *see* Legent Corp.
Mormac Marine Group, **15** 302
Morning Star Technologies Inc., *see* Ascend Communications, Inc.
Morning Sun, Inc., **23** 66
Morningstar Inc., 68 259–62
Morningstar Storage Centers LLC, **52** 311
Morris Communications Corporation, 36 339–42
Morris Travel Services L.L.C., 26 308–11
Morrison & Co. Ltd., **52** 221
Morrison & Foerster LLP, 78 220–23
Morrison Homes, Inc., **51** 138
Morrison Knudsen Corporation, 7 355–58; 28 286–90 (upd.) *see also* The Washington Companies.
Morrison Restaurants Inc., 11 323–25
Morrow Equipment Co. L.L.C., 87 325–327
Morse Industrial, *see* Borg-Warner Automotive, Inc.
Morse Shoe Inc., 13 359–61
Morse's Ltd., **70** 161
Mortgage Guaranty Insurance Corp. *see* MGIC Investment Corp.
MortgageRamp Inc. *see* OfficeTiger, LLC.
Morton Foods, Inc., *see* Kerry Group plc.
Morton International, Inc., 9 358–59 (upd.); 80 260–64 (upd.)
Morton Thiokol Inc., I 370–72 *see also* Thiokol Corp.
Morton's Restaurant Group, Inc., 30 329–31; 88 262–66 (upd.)
Mos Magnetics, **18** 140
The Mosaic Company, 91 330–33
Mosby-Year Book, Inc., *see* Times Mirror Co.
Moscow Bank for Reconstruction & Development, **73** 303–04
Mosinee Paper Corporation, 15 304–06 *see also* Wausau-Mosinee Paper Corp.
Moss Bros Group plc, 51 252–54
Moss-Rouse Company, **15** 412
Mossgas, **IV** 93
Mossimo, Inc., 27 328–30
Mostek Corp., **20** 175; **29** 323
Mostjet Ltd. *see* British World Airlines Ltd.
Móstoles Industrial S.A., **26** 129
Mostra Importaciones S.A., **34** 38, 40
Motel 6, 13 362–64; 56 248–51 (upd.) *see also* Accor SA
Mothercare plc, 17 334–36; 78 224–27 (upd.)
Mothers Against Drunk Driving (MADD), 51 255–58
Mothers Work, Inc., 18 350–52
Motion Factory, Inc., **38** 72
Motion Picture Association of America, **37** 353–54
Motiva Enterprises LLC, **41** 359, 395
MotivePower *see* Wabtec Corp.
The Motley Fool, Inc., 40 329–31
Moto Photo, Inc., 45 282–84
Moto S.p.A., **57** 84
Motor Cargo Industries, Inc., 35 296–99

Motor Club of America Insurance Company, **44** 354
Motor Coaches Industries International Inc., **36** 132
Motor Wheel Corporation, *see* Hayes Lemmerz International, Inc.
Motorcar Parts & Accessories, Inc., 47 **253–55**
Motoren-und-Turbinen-Union, **I** 151; **15** 142; **34** 128, 131, 133
Motorola, Inc., II 60–62; 11 326–29 (upd.); 34 296–302 (upd.); 93 313–23 (upd.)
Motorsports International Corporation, **74** 157
Motospecs *see* Repco Corporation Ltd.
Motown Records Company L.P., 26 312–14
Mott's Inc., 57 250–53
Moulinex S.A., 22 362–65 *see also* Groupe SEB.
Mound Metalcraft *see* Tonka Corp.
Mount *see also* Mt.
Mount Isa Mines, **IV** 61
Mount Vernon Group, *see* Albany International Corp.
Mount Washington Hotel *see* MWH Preservation Limited Partnership.
Mountain Air Cargo, Inc. *see* Air T, Inc.
Mountain Fuel Supply Company *see* Questar Corp.
Mountain High Casino *see* Ameristar Casinos, Inc.
Mountain Safety Research, *see* Recreational Equipment, Inc.
Mountain States Mortgage Centers, Inc., 29 335–37
Mountain States Power Company *see* PacifiCorp.
Mountain Valley Indemnity Co., **44** 356
Mountain West Bank, **35** 197
Mouvement des Caisses Desjardins, 48 288–91
Movado Group, Inc., 28 291–94
Mövenpick Holdings, **63** 328
Movie Gallery, Inc., 31 339–41
Movie Star Inc., 17 337–39
Movies To Go, Inc., *see* Blockbuster Inc.
Movil@ccess, S.A. de C.V., **39** 25, 194
Moving Co. Ltd. *see* Marui Co., Ltd.
The Moving Picture Company, **15** 83; **50** 124, 126
The Mowry Co., **23** 102
Moy Park Ltd., 78 228–31
MP3.com, **43** 109
MPB Corporation, *see* The Timken Co.
MPI *see* Michael Page International plc.
MPRG *see* Matt Prentice Restaurant Group.
MPS Group, Inc., 49 264–67
MPW Industrial Services Group, Inc., 53 231–33
Mr. Bricolage S.A., 37 258–60
Mr. Coffee, Inc., 15 307–09
Mr. Donut, **21** 323
Mr. Gasket Inc., 15 310–12
Mr. Gatti's, LP, 87 321–324
Mr. Payroll Corporation, **20** 113; **61** 52–54
MRD Gaming, **51** 206–07
M-real Oyj, 56 252–55 (upd.)
MRJ Technology Solutions, **54** 396
MRN Radio Network, **19** 223
Mrs. Baird's Bakeries, 29 338–41
Mrs. Fields' Original Cookies, Inc., 27 331–35
Mrs. Giles Country Kitchens, **63** 69, 71
Mrs. Grossman's Paper Company Inc., 84 277–280
Mrs. Paul's Kitchens *see* Campbell Soup Co.
Mrs. Smith's Frozen Foods *see* Kellogg Company
Mrs. Winner's Chicken & Biscuits, **58** 324
MS&L *see* Manning Selvage & Lee.
MS-Relais GmbH *see* Matsushita Electric Works, Ltd.
MSAS Cargo International *see* Excel plc.
MSC *see* Material Sciences Corp.
MSC Industrial Direct Co., Inc., 71 234–36
MSE Corporation, **33** 44
MSI Data Corp., **15** 482
M6 *see* Métropole Télévision S.A..
MSK Corporation *see* Suntech Power Holdings Company Ltd.
MSL Industries, *see* Alleghany Corp.
MSNBC, **28** 301
MSP, Inc., **57** 231
MSR *see* Mountain Safety Research.
MSU *see* Middle South Utilities.
Mt. *see also* Mount.
Mt. Beacon Insurance Co., **26** 486
Mt. Goldsworthy Mining Associates, **IV** 47
Mt. Olive Pickle Company, Inc., 44 293–95
MTA *see* Metropolitan Transportation Authority.
MTC *see* Management and Training Corp.
MTel *see* Mobile Telecommunications Technologies Corp.
MTG *see* Modern Times Group AB.
MTM Entertainment Inc., *see* International Family Entertainment Inc.
MTR Foods Ltd., 55 271–73
MTR Gaming Group, Inc., 75 265–67
MTS *see* Mobile TeleSystems.
MTS Inc., 37 261–64
MTV, **31** 239
MTV Asia, **23** 390
MTVi Group, **37** 194
Muehlens KG, **48** 422
Mueller Co. *see* Tyco International Ltd.
Mueller Furniture Company, *see* Haworth Inc.
Mueller Industries, Inc., 7 **359–61; 52 256–60 (upd.)**
Muench Woodworking, Inc., **68** 133
Muffler Corporation of America, **56** 230
Muir Glen *see* Small Planet Foods, Inc.
Mulberry Group PLC, 71 237–39
Mule-Hide Products Co., **22** 15
Mullen Advertising Inc., 51 259–61
Multex Systems, **21** 70
Multi-Color Corporation, 53 234–36
Multicanal S.A., **67** 200–01
Multicare Companies *see* NeighborCare, Inc.
Multicom Publishing Inc., **11** 294
Multiflex, Inc., **63** 318
Multilink, Inc., *see* PictureTel Corp.
MultiMed, **11** 379
Multimedia Cablevision Inc. *see* Gannett Company, Inc.
Multimedia Games, Inc., 41 272–76
Multimedia, Inc., 11 330–32
Multimedia Security Services, Inc., **32** 374
Multiplex, **67** 104–06
Multitech International *see* Acer Inc.
Mündener Gummiwerke GmbH, **68** 289
Munich Re (Münchener Rückversicherungs-Gesellschaft Aktiengesellschaft in München), III 299–301; 46 303–07 (upd.)
Munksjö, **19** 227
Munsingwear, Inc. *see* PremiumWear, Inc.
Munson Transportation Inc., *see* Heartland Express, Inc.
Mura Corporation, **23** 209
Murata, **37** 347
Murdock Madaus Schwabe, 26 315–19
Murfin Inc., *see* Menasha Corp.
Murphey Favre, Inc., *see* Washington Mutual, Inc.
Murphy Family Farms Inc., 22 366–68 *see also* Smithfield Foods, Inc.
Murphy Oil Corporation, 7 **362–64; 32 338–41 (upd.)**
Murphy-Phoenix Company, *see* Colgate-Palmolive Co.
Murphy's Pizza *see* Papa Murphy's International, Inc.
The Musco Family Olive Co., 91 334–37
Musco Lighting, 83 276-279
Muse, Cordero, Chen, **41** 89
Musgrave Group Plc, 57 254–57
The Music and Video Club Ltd, *see* Kingfisher plc.
Music Corporation of America *see* MCA Inc.
Music Go Round, *see* Grow Biz International, Inc.
Music Man Co., **56** 116
Musical America Publishing, Inc., **22** 441
Musician's Friend, Inc. *see* Guitar Center, Inc.
Musicland Stores Corporation, 9 360–62; 38 313–17 (upd.)
Musicmatch, Inc. *see* Yahoo! Inc.
MusicNet, Inc., **53** 282
MusicNow, Inc. *see* Circuit City Stores, Inc.
Muskegon Gas Company *see* MCN Corp.
Muskegon Wire, **55** 305
Mutual & Federal, **61** 270, 272
Mutual Benefit Life Insurance Company, III 302–04
Mutual Broadcasting System, **23** 509
Mutual Gaslight Company *see* MCN Corp.

Mutual Life Insurance Company of New York, III 305–07
Mutual Marine Office Inc., **41** 284
Mutual Savings & Loan Association, *see* Berkshire Hathaway Inc.
Muzak, Inc., 18 353–56
Muzzy-Lyon Company *see* Federal-Mogul Corp.
MVC *see* Music and Video Club.
MVF *see* Mission Valley Fabrics.
MVR Products Pte Limited, **47** 255
MWA *see* Modern Woodmen of America.
MWH Preservation Limited Partnership, 65 245–48
MWI Veterinary Supply, Inc., 80 265–68
MXL Industries, Inc., *see* National Patient Development Corp.
Myanmar Brewery Ltd., **59** 60
Mycalkyushu Corporation *see* AEON Co., Ltd.
Myco-Sci, Inc. *see* Sylvan, Inc.
Mycogen Corporation, 21 385–87 *see also* Dow Chemical Co.
Myer Emporium Ltd., **20** 156
Myers Industries, Inc., 19 277–79
Mylan Laboratories Inc., I 656–57; 20 380–82 (upd.); 59 304–08 (upd.)
MYOB Ltd., 86 286–90
Myojo Cement Co. Ltd., **60** 301
Myriad Restaurant Group, Inc., 87 328–331
Myrurgia S.A., **60** 246
MySpace.com *see* Intermix Media, Inc.

N

N.A. Woodworth, *see* Illinois Tool Works Inc.
N.C. Cameron & Sons, Ltd., **11** 95
N.C. Monroe Construction Company, *see* Cianbro Corp.
N.E.M., **23** 228
N.E. Restaurant Co. Inc. *see* Bertucci's Corpration.
N.F. Smith & Associates LP, 70 199–202
N.H. Geotech *see* New Holland N.V.
N.L. Industries, **19** 212
N M Electronics, *see* Intel Corp.
N M Rothschild & Sons Limited, 39 293–95
N. Shure Company, **15** 477
N.V. *see under first word of company name*
N.Y.P. Holdings Inc., **12** 360
Na Pali, S.A. *see* Quiksilver, Inc.
Naamloze Vennootschap tot Exploitatie van het Café Krasnapolsky *see* Grand Hotel Krasnapolsky N.V.
Nabari Kintetsu Gas Company Ltd., **60** 236
Nabisco Brands, Inc., II 542–44 *see also* RJR Nabisco.
Nabisco Foods Group, 7 365–68 (upd.) *see also* Kraft Foods Inc.
Nabisco Holdings Corporation, **42** 408; **44** 342
Nabors Industries Ltd., 9 363–65; 91 338–44 (upd.)
Nacamar Internet Services, **48** 398
NACCO Industries, Inc., 7 369–71; 78 232–36 (upd.)
Nacional de Drogas, S.A. de C.V., **39** 188
NACO Finance Corp., **33** 398
Naco-Nogales, **51** 389
Nadler Sportswear *see* Donnkenny, Inc.
Nadro S.A. de C.V., 86 291–94
Naegele Outdoor Advertising Inc., **36** 340
Naf Naf SA, 44 296–98
NAFI Corp. *see* Chris-Craft Industries, Inc.
Nagasakiya Co., Ltd., V 149–51; 69 259–62 (upd.)
Nagase & Co., Ltd., 8 376–78; 61 226–30 (upd.)
Nagase-Landauer, Ltd., **51** 210
Nagoya Mitsukoshi Ltd., **56** 242
NAI *see* Natural Alternatives International, Inc.; Network Associates, Inc.
NAI Technologies, Inc., **58** 101
Naiman Co., **25** 449
Nakano Vinegar Co. Ltd., **26** 58
Nalco Holding Company, I 373–75; 12 346–48 (upd.); 89 324–30 (upd.)
Nalge Co., *see* Sybron International Corp.
NAM *see* Nederlandse Aardolie Maatschappij.
Nam Tai Electronics, Inc., 61 231–34
Name Development Ltd. *see* Marchex, Inc.
Namibia Breweries Ltd., **33** 75
NAMM *see* North American Medical Management Company, Inc.
Namor Productions, **58** 124
Namur Re S.A., **51** 143
Nance Petroleum Corporation, **63** 347
NANCO *see* Provimi
Nancy's Notions *see* Tacony Corp.
Nanfang South China Motor Corp., **34** 132
Nanotechnologies Inc., **74** 9
Nantucket Allserve, Inc., 22 369–71
Nantucket Corporation, **6** 226
Nantucket Mills *see* Jockey International.
NAPA *see* National Automotive Parts Association.
NAPC *see* North American Philips Corp.
Napocor *see* National Power Corp.
NAPP Systems, Inc., **11** 253
Napster, Inc., 69 263–66
Narragansett Electric Company, **51** 265
NAS *see* National Audubon Society.
NASA *see* National Aeronautics and Space Administration.
NASCAR *see* National Association for Stock Car Auto Racing.
NASD, 54 242–46 (upd.)
The NASDAQ Stock Market, Inc., 92 256–60
Nash DeCamp Company, **23** 356–57
Nash Finch Company, 8 379–81; 23 356–58 (upd.); 65 249–53 (upd.)
Nashua Corporation, 8 382–84
The Nashville Network, *see* Gaylord Entertainmnet Co.
Nashville Speedway USA, Inc., **43** 139–41
Naspers Ltd., 66 230–32
NASRIN Services LLC, **64** 346
Nassco Holdings Inc., **36** 79
Nastech Pharmaceutical Company Inc., 79 259–62
Nasu Nikon Co., Ltd., **48** 295
Nat Robbins, **37** 269–70
NaTec Ltd. *see* CRSS Inc.
Nathan's Famous, Inc., 29 342–44
The National Academy of Television Arts & Sciences, **55** 3
National Acme Company *see* Acme-Cleveland Corp.
National Aeronautics and Space Administration, **11** 201, 408; **37** 364–65
National Allied Publications *see* DC Comics Inc.
National American Corporation, **33** 399
National Amusements Inc., 28 295–97
National Aquarium in Baltimore, Inc., 74 198–200
National Association for Stock Car Auto Racing, 32 342–44
National Association of Securities Dealers, Inc., 10 416–18 *see also* NASD.
National Audubon Society, 26 320–23
National Auto Credit, Inc., 16 379–81
National Automotive Fibers, Inc. *see* Chris- Craft Industries, Inc.
National Automotive Parts Association, **26** 348
National Bancard Corporation, *see* First Financial Management Corp.
National Bank of Arizona, *see* Zions Bancorporation.
National Bank of Canada, 85 291–94
National Bank of Commerce Trust & Savings Association, **15** 161
National Bank of Greece, 41 277–79
National Bank of New Zealand, *see* Lloyds TSB Group plc.
The National Bank of South Carolina, 76 278–80
National BankAmericard Inc. *see* Visa International.
National Beverage Corporation, 26 324–26; 88 267–71 (upd.)
National BioSystems, **47** 37
National Broadcasting Company, Inc., II 151–53; 6 164–66 (upd.); 28 298–301 (upd.) *see also* General Electric Co.
National Building Society, *see* Abbey National PLC.
National Can Corp., I 607–08
National Car Rental System, Inc., 10 419–20 *see also* Republic Industries, Inc.
National Carriers Ltd *see* Exel plc.
National Cash Register Company *see* NCR Corp.
National Cement Co., **35** 419; **70** 343
National Cheerleaders Association, **15** 516–18
National Chemsearch Corp. *see* NCH Corp.
National City Bancorporation, **56** 219

National City Corp., 15 313–16
National Coach, **56** 223
National Comics Publications *see* DC Comics Inc.
National Convenience Stores Incorporated, 7 372–75
National Cranberry Association *see* Ocean Spray Cranberries, Inc.
National Discount Brokers Group, Inc., 28 302–04 *see also* Deutsche Bank A.G.
National Disinfectant Company *see* NCH Corp.
National Distillers and Chemical Corporation, I 376–78 *see also* Quantum Chemical Corp.
National Economic Research Associates, *see* Marsh & McLennan Companies, Inc.
National Educational Corporation, **26** 95
National Educational Music Co. Ltd., 47 256–58
National Endowment for the Arts, **52** 15
National Enquirer, *see* American Media, Inc.
National Envelope Corporation, 32 345–47
National Equipment Services, Inc., 57 258–60
National Executive Service *see* Carey International, Inc.
National Express Group PLC, 50 340–42
National Express Laboratories, Inc., **10** 107
National Family Opinion *see* NFO Worldwide, Inc.
National Farmers Organization, **53** 260
National Fence Manufacturing Co., Inc., **45** 327
National Fidelity Life Insurance Co., *see* Conseco, Inc.
National Financial Partners Corp., 65 254–56
National Fire & Marine Insurance Co., *see* Berkshire Hathaway Inc.
National Football League, 29 345–47 *see also* NFL.
National Freight Consortium plc *see* Exel plc.
National Frozen Foods Corporation, 94 319–22
National Fuel Gas Company, 6 526–28
National Geographic Society, 9 366–68; 30 332–35 (upd.); 79 263–69 (upd.)
National Golf Properties, Inc. *see* American Golf Corporation
National Grape Co-operative Association, Inc., 20 383–85
National Grid Group plc, **11** 399–400; **13** 484; **45** 298–99; **47** 122
National Grid Transco plc, **66** 283
National Grid USA, 51 262–66 (upd.)
National Grocers Co Ltd., *see* George Weston Ltd.
National Gypsum Company, 10 421–24
National Health Laboratories Incorporated, 11 333–35 *see also* Laboratory Corporation of America Holdings.
National Healthcare Resources, Inc. *see* Concentra Inc.
National Heritage Academies, Inc., 60 211–13
National Hockey League, 35 300–03
National Home Centers, Inc., 44 299–301
National ICEE Corporation, *see* J & J Snack Foods Corp.
National Indemnity Co., *see* Berkshire Hathaway Inc.
National Inking Appliance Company, *see* Beckman Instruments, Inc.
National Instruments Corporation, 22 372–74
National Intergroup, Inc., V 152–53 *see also* FoxMeyer Health Corp.
National Iranian Oil Company, IV 466–68; 61 235–38 (upd.)
National Journal Group Inc., 67 256–58
National Key Company *see* Cole National Corp.
National Law Publishing Company, Inc., **32** 35
National Lead Co., **21** 489
National Leisure Group, **47** 421
National Liability and Fire Insurance Co., *see* Berkshire Hathaway Inc.
National Liberty Corp., *see* Capital Holding Corp.
National Life Assurance Co. of Canada, *see* Continental Corp.
National Linen Service, **54** 251, 254
National Lumber Co. *see* National Home Centers, Inc.
National Magazine Company Limited, *see* The Hearst Corp.
National Marine Service, **6** 530
National Media Corporation, 27 336–40
National Medical Care, **22** 360
National Medical Enterprises, Inc., III 87–88 *see also* Tenet Healthcare Corp.
National Medical Health Card Systems, Inc., 79 270–73
National Mobility Corp., **30** 436
The National Motor Bearing Company *see* Federal-Mogul Corp.
The National Motor Club of America, Inc., **33** 418
National Office Furniture, *see* Kimball International, Inc.
National Oil Corporation, 66 233–37 (upd.)
National Oilwell, Inc., 54 247–50
National Organization for Women, Inc., 55 274–76
National Parks Transportation Company, *see* SkyWest, Inc.
National Patent Development Corporation, 13 365–68 *see also* GP Strategies Corp.
National Periodical Publications *see* DC Comics Inc.
National Petroleum Refiners of South Africa, **47** 340
National Picture & Frame Company, 24 345–47
National Pig Development Co., **46** 84
National Power Corporation, **56** 214–15
National Power PLC, 12 349–51 *see also* International Power PLC.
National Presto Industries, Inc., 16 382–85; 43 286–90 (upd.)
National Propane Corporation, *see* Triarc Companies, Inc.
National Public Radio, 19 280–82; 47 259–62 (upd.)
National Publishing Company, **41** 110
National R.V. Holdings, Inc., 32 348–51
National Railroad Passenger Corporation (Amtrak), 22 375–78; 66 238–42 (upd.)
National Ready Mixed, **70** 343
National Realty Trust *see* NRT Inc.
National Record Mart, Inc., 29 348–50
National Register Publishing Co., **23** 442
National Reinsurance Corporation *see* General Re Corp.
National Research Corporation, 87 332–335
National Restaurants Management, Inc., **38** 385–87
National Revenue Corporation, **22** 181
National Rifle Association of America, 37 265–68
National Sanitary Supply Co., 16 386–87
National Sea Products Ltd., 14 339–41
National Security Containers LLC, **58** 238
National Semiconductor Corporation, II 63–65; 6 261–63; 26 327–30 (upd.); 69 267–71 (upd.)
National Service Industries, Inc., 11 336–38; 54 251–55 (upd.)
National-Southwire Aluminum Company, **11** 38
National Standard Co., 13 369–71
National Starch and Chemical Company, 49 268–70
National Steel Corporation, 12 352–54 *see also* FoxMeyer Health Corp.
National System Company, **11** 469
National Tea Co., *see* George Weston Ltd.
National TechTeam, Inc., 41 280–83
National Telecommunications of Austin, *see* LDDS-Metro Communications, Inc.
National Telephone and Telegraph Corporation *see* British Columbia Telephone Co.
National Thoroughbred Racing Association, 58 244–47
National Transcommunications Ltd. *see* NTL Inc.
National Weather Service, 91 345–49
National Westminster Bank PLC, II 333–35
National Wine & Spirits, Inc., 49 271–74
Nationale-Nederlanden N.V., III 308–11

Nationale Portefeuille Maatschappij (NPM) *see* Compagnie Nationale à Portefeuille.
NationsBank Corporation, **10 425–27** *see also* Bank of America Corporation
NationsRent, **28** 388
Nationwide Cellular Service, Inc., **27** 305
Nationwide Credit, Inc. *see* First Financial Management Corp.
Nationwide Logistics Corp., *see* TNT Freightways Corp.
Nationwide Mutual Insurance Co., **26** 488
NATIOVIE, **II** 234
NATM Buying Corporation, **10** 9, 468
Natref *see* National Petroleum Refiners of South Africa.
Natrol, Inc., **49 275–78**
NatSteel Electronics Ltd., **48** 369
NatTeknik, **26** 333
Natura Cosméticos S.A., **75 268–71**
Natural Alternatives International, Inc., **49 279–82**
Natural Gas Clearinghouse *see* NGC Corp.
Natural Gas Pipeline Company, **6** 530, 543
Natural Ovens Bakery, Inc., **72 234–36**
Natural Selection Foods, **54 256–58**
Natural Wonders Inc., **14 342–44**
NaturaLife International, **26** 470
Naturalizer *see* Brown Shoe Company, Inc.
Naturally Fresh, Inc., **88 272–75**
The Nature Company, *see* Discovery Communications, Inc.
The Nature Conservancy, **28 305–07**
Nature's Path Foods, Inc., **87 336–340**
Nature's Sunshine Products, Inc., **15 317–19**
Nature's Way Products Inc., **26** 315
Naturin GmbH *see* Viscofan S.A.
Naturipe Berry Growers, **62** 154
Natuzzi Group *see* Industrie Natuzzi S.p.A.
NatWest Bancorp, **38** 393
NatWest Bank *see* National Westminster Bank PLC.
Naumes, Inc., **81 257–60**
Nautica Enterprises, Inc., **18 357–60; 44 302–06 (upd.)**
Nautilus International, Inc., **30** 161
Navaho Freight Line, **16** 41
Navajo LTL, Inc., **57** 277
Navajo Refining Company, *see* Holly Corp.
Navajo Shippers, Inc., **42** 364
Navan Resources, **38** 231
Navarre Corporation, **24 348–51**
Navigant International, Inc., **47 263–66; 93 324–27 (upd.)**
The Navigators Group, Inc., **92 261–64**
Navire Cargo Gear, **27** 269
Navisant, Inc., **49** 424
Navistar International Corporation, **I 180–82; 10 428–30 (upd.)** *see also* International Harvester Co.
NAVTEQ Corporation, **69 272–75**
Navy Exchange Service Command, **31 342–45**
Navy Federal Credit Union, **33 315–17**
Naylor, Hutchinson, Vickers & Company *see* Vickers PLC.
NBC *see* National Broadcasting Company, Inc.
NBC Bankshares, Inc., **21** 524
NBC/Computer Services Corporation, **15** 163
NBD Bancorp, Inc., **11 339–41** *see also* Bank One Corp.
NBGS International, Inc., **73 231–33**
NBSC Corporation *see* National Bank of South Carolina.
NBTY, Inc., **31 346–48**
NCB *see* National City Bank of New York.
NCC Industries, Inc., **59** 267
NCC L.P., **15** 139
NCH Corporation, **8 385–87**
nChip, **38** 187–88
NCI Building Systems, Inc., **88 276–79**
NCL Corporation, **79 274–77**
NCL Holdings *see* Genting Bhd.
NCNB Corporation, **II 336–37** *see also* Bank of America Corp.
NCO Group, Inc., **42 258–60**
NCR Corporation, **III 150–53; 6 264–68 (upd.); 30 336–41 (upd.); 90 303–12 (upd.)**
NCS *see* Norstan, Inc.
NCS Healthcare Inc., **67** 262
nCube Corp., **14** 15; **22** 293
NDB *see* National Discount Brokers Group, Inc.
NDL *see* Norddeutscher Lloyd.
NE Chemcat Corporation, **72** 118
NEA *see* Newspaper Enterprise Association.
Neatherlin Homes Inc., **22** 547
Nebraska Book Company, Inc., **65 257–59**
Nebraska Furniture Mart, Inc., **94 323–26**
Nebraska Light & Power Company, **6** 580
Nebraska Public Power District, **29 351–54**
NEBS *see* New England Business Services, Inc.
NEC Corporation, **II 66–68; 21 388–91 (upd.); 57 261–67 (upd.)**
Neckermann Versand AG *see* Karstadt AG.
Nedcor, **61** 270–71
Nederland Line *see* Stoomvaart Maatschappij Nederland.
Nederlands Talen Institut, *see* Koninklijke Vendex KBB N.V. (Royal Vendex KBB N.V.)
Nederlandsche Electriciteits Maatschappij *see* N.E.M.
Nederlandsche Handel Maatschappij, **26** 242
Nederlandsche Heidenmaatschappij *see* Arcadis NV.
N.V. Nederlandse Gasunie, **V 658–61**
Nedlloyd Group *see* Koninklijke Nedlloyd N.V.
NedMark Transportation Services *see* Polar Air Cargo Inc.
Needham Harper Worldwide *see* Omnicom Group Inc.
Needleworks, Inc., **23** 66
Neenah Foundry Company, **68 263–66**
Neenah Printing, *see* Menasha Corp.
NEES *see* New England Electric System.
Neff Corp., **32 352–53**
Neff GmbH, **67** 81
NEG Micon A/S, **73** 375
Negromex, **23** 171–72
NEI *see* Northern Engineering Industries PLC.
Neico International, Inc., **67** 226
NeighborCare, Inc., **67 259–63 (upd.)**
Neilson/Cadbury, *see* George Weston Ltd.
The Neiman Marcus Group, Inc., **12 355–57; 49 283–87 (upd.)**
Nektar Therapeutics, **91 350–53**
Nelson Entertainment Group, **47** 272
Nelson Publications, **22** 442
Nelsons *see* A. Nelson & Co. Ltd.
NEMF *see* New England Motor Freight, Inc.
Neo Products Co., **37** 401
Neogen Corporation, **94 327–30**
Neopost S.A., **53 237–40**
Neos, **21** 438
Nepera, Inc., **16** 69
Neptun Maritime Oyj, **29** 431
Neptune Orient Lines Limited, **47 267–70**
NER Auction Group, **23** 148
NERCO, Inc., **7 376–79** *see also* Rio Tinto PLC.
NES *see* National Equipment Services, Inc.
Nesco Inc., **28** 6, 8
Nespak SpA, **40** 214–15
Neste Oil Corporation, **IV 469–71; 85 295–302 (upd.)**
Nestlé S.A., **II 545–49; 7 380–84 (upd.); 28 308–13 (upd.); 71 240–46 (upd.)**
Nestlé Waters, **73 234–37**
Net Investment S.A., **63** 180
NetApp *see* Network Appliance, Inc.
NetCom Systems AB, **26 331–33**
NetCreations, **47** 345, 347
NetEffect Alliance, **58** 194
Netezza Corporation, **69 276–78**
Netflix, Inc., **58 248–51**
NETGEAR, Inc., **81 261–64**
Netherlands Trading Co *see* Nederlandse Handel Maatschappij.
NetHold B.V., **31** 330
NetIQ Corporation, **79 278–81**
NetMarket Company, **16** 146
NetPlane Systems, **36** 124
Netscape Communications Corporation, **15 320–22; 35 304–07 (upd.)**
NetStar Communications Inc., **24** 49; **35** 69
Nettingsdorfer, **19** 227
Nettle Creek Corporation, *see* Pillowtex Corp.
Net2Phone Inc., **34** 224
NetWest Securities, **25** 450

Network Appliance, Inc., 58 252–54
Network Associates, Inc., 25 347–49
Network Communications Associates, Inc., **11** 409
Network Equipment Technologies Inc., 92 265–68
Network Solutions, Inc., **47** 430
Network Ten, **35** 68–69
NetZero Inc. *see* United Online, Inc.
Netzip Inc., **53** 282
Neuberger Berman Inc., 57 268–71
Neuer Markt, **59** 153
Neuro Navigational Corporation, **21** 47
NeuStar, Inc., 81 265–68
Neutrogena Corporation, 17 340–44
Nevada Bell Telephone Company, 14 345–47 *see also* AT&T Corp.
Nevada Community Bank, **11** 119
Nevada Power Company, 11 342–44
Nevada Savings and Loan Association, **19** 412
Nevada State Bank, **53** 378
Nevamar Company, 82 255–58
Nevex Software Technologies, **42** 24, 26
New Access Communications, **43** 252
New Asahi Co., *see* Asahi Breweries, Ltd.
New Balance Athletic Shoe, Inc., 25 350–52; 68 267–70 (upd.)
New Bauhinia Limited, **53** 333
New Belgium Brewing Company, Inc., 68 271–74
New Brunswick Scientific Co., Inc., 45 285–87
New Century Energies, **73** 384
New Century Equity Holdings Corporation, **72** 39
New Century Network, **13** 180; **19** 204, 285
New Clicks Holdings Ltd., 86 295–98
New CORT Holdings Corporation *see* CORT Business Services Corp.
New Daido Steel Co., Ltd., **IV** 62–63
New Dana Perfumes Company, 37 269–71
New Dimension Software, Inc., **55** 67
New England Audio Company, Inc. *see* Tweeter Home Entertainment Group, Inc.
New England Business Service, Inc., 18 361–64; 78 237–42 (upd.)
New England Confectionery Co., 15 323–25
New England CRInc, *see* Wellman Inc.
New England Electric System, V 662–64 *see also* National Grid USA.
New England Motor Freight, Inc., **53** 250
New England Mutual Life Insurance Co., III 312–14 *see also* Metropolitan Life Insurance Co.
New England Paper Tube Co., **54** 58
New England Power Association *see* National Grid USA.
New Flyer Industries Inc., 78 243–46
New Galveston Company, Inc., **25** 116
New Hampton Goldfields Ltd., **63** 182, 184
New Hampton, Inc., *see* Spiegel, Inc.
New Haven District Telephone Company *see* Southern New England Telecommunications Corp.
New Haven Electric Co., **21** 512
New Holland N.V., 22 379–81 *see also* CNH Global N.V.
New Hotel Showboat, Inc. *see* Showboat, Inc.
New Imapriver NV *see* Punch International N.V.
New Jersey Devils, 84 281–285
New Jersey Educational Music Company *see* National Educational Music Co. Ltd.
New Jersey Resources Corporation, 54 259–61
New Jersey Shale, **14** 250
New Jersey Tobacco Co., **15** 138
New Laoshan Brewery, **49** 418
New Line Cinema, Inc., 47 271–74
New Look Group plc, 35 308–10
New Market Development Company *see* Cousins Properties Inc.
New Materials Ltd., **48** 344
New Orleans Saints LP, 58 255–57
The New Piper Aircraft, Inc., 44 307–10
New Plan Realty Trust, 11 345–47
New Seasons Market, 75 272–74
New South Wales Health System, **16** 94
New Street Capital Inc., 8 388–90 (upd.) *see also* Drexel Burnham Lambert Inc.
New Times, Inc., 45 288–90
New Toyo Group, **19** 227
New Trading Company *see* SBC Warburg.
New Valley Corporation, 17 345–47
New Vanden Borre, *see* Kingfisher plc.
New Ventures Realty Corporation, **58** 272
New World Coffee-Manhattan Bagel, Inc., **32** 15
New World Communications Group, **22** 442; **28** 248
New World Development Company Limited, IV 717–19; 38 318–22 (upd.)
New World Pasta Company, 53 241–44
New World Restaurant Group, Inc., 44 311–14
New York Capital Bank, **41** 312
New York Central Railroad Company, **10** 43–44, 71–73
New York City Health and Hospitals Corporation, 60 214–17
New York City Off-Track Betting Corporation, 51 267–70
New York Community Bancorp, Inc., 78 247–50
New York Daily News, 32 357–60
New York Electric Corporation *see* New York State Electric and Gas.
New York Envelope Co., **32** 346
New York Eye and Ear Infirmary *see* Continuum Health Partners, Inc.
New York Gas Light Company *see* Consolidated Edison Company of New York.
New York Health Care, Inc., 72 237–39
New York Life Insurance Company, III 315–17; 45 291–95 (upd.)
New York Marine and Gotham Insurance, **41** 284
New York Philharmonic *see* Philharmonic-Symphony Society of New York, Inc.
New York Presbyterian Hospital *see* NewYork-Presbyterian Hospital.
New York Restaurant Group, Inc., 32 361–63
New York Shakespeare Festival Management, 92328–32
New York Sports Clubs *see* Town Sports International, Inc.
New York State Electric and Gas Corporation, 6 534–36
New York Stock Exchange, Inc., 9 369–72; 39 296–300 (upd.)
The New York Times Company, IV 647–49; 19 283–85 (upd.); 61 239–43 (upd.)
New York Zoological Society *see* Wildlife Conservation Society.
New York's Bankers Trust Co., *see* Bankers Trust Co.
New Zealand Aluminum Smelters, *see* Rio Tinto.
New Zealand Countrywide Banking Corporation, *see* The Governor and Company of the Bank of Scotland.
Newa Insurance Co. Ltd., **64** 280
Neways, Inc., 78 251–54
Newark Electronics Co., *see* Premier Industrial Corp.
Newbridge & Gilbert, **56** 285
Newco Waste Systems *see* Browning-Ferris Industries, Inc.
Newcor, Inc., 40 332–35
Newcrest Mining Ltd., **IV** 47; **22** 107
Newell Rubbermaid Inc., 9 373–76; 52 261–71 (upd.)
Newfield Exploration Company, 65 260–62
Newfoundland Brewery, **26** 304
Newfoundland Light & Power Co. *see* Fortis, Inc.
Newfoundland Processing Ltd. *see* Newfoundland Energy, Ltd.
Newhall Land and Farming Company, 14 348–50
Newly Weds Foods, Inc., 74 201–03
Newman's Own, Inc., 37 272–75
Newmark & Lewis Inc., **23** 373
Newmont Mining Corporation, 7 385–88; 94 331–37 (upd.)
NewPage Corporation, **76** 270
Newpark Resources, Inc., 63 305–07
Newport Corporation, 71 247–49
Newport News Shipbuilding Inc., 13 372–75; 38 323–27 (upd.)
News & Observer Publishing Company, **23** 343
News America Publishing Inc., 12 358–60
News Communications & Media Plc, **35** 242

News Corporation Limited, IV 650–53; 7 389–93 (upd.); 46 308–13 (upd.)
News Extracts Ltd., **55** 289
News International Corp., **20** 79
News of the World Organization (NOTW), **46** 309
News World Communications, **73** 356
Newsco NV, **48** 347
Newsquest plc, 32 354–56
Newth-Morris Box Co. *see* Rock-Tenn Co.
Newton Yarn Mills, **19** 305
NewYork-Presbyterian Hospital, 59 309–12
Nexans SA, 54 262–64
Nexar Technologies, Inc., *see* Palomar Medical Technologies, Inc.
NEXCOM *see* Navy Exchange Service Command.
Nexen Inc., 79 282–85
NexFlash Technologies, Inc. *see* Winbond Electronics Corp.
Nexity S.A., 66 243–45
Nexstar Broadcasting Group, Inc., 73 238–41
NeXstar Pharmaceuticals Inc., **54** 130
NeXT Incorporated, **34** 348
Next Media Ltd., 61 244–47
Next plc, 29 355–57
Nextel Communications, Inc., 10 431–33; 27 341–45 (upd.)
Nextera Enterprises, Inc., **54** 191, 193
NEXTLINK Communications, Inc., **38** 192
NextNet Wireless, Inc. *see* Clearwire, Inc.
Neyveli Lignite Corporation Ltd., 65 263–65
NFC Castings Inc., **68** 265
NFC plc, 6 412–14 *see also* Exel plc.
NFL *see* National Football League Inc.
NFL Films, 75 275–78
NFO Worldwide, Inc., 24 352–55
NFT Distribution Limited, **61** 258, 260–61
NGC *see* National Grid Co.
NGC Corporation, 18 365–67 *see also* Dynegy Inc.
NGK Insulators Ltd., 67 264–66
NH Hoteles S.A., 79 286–89
NHB Group Ltd. *see* MasterBrand Cabinets, Inc.
NHK *see* Japan Broadcasting Corp.
NHK Spring Co., Ltd., III 580–82
NI Industries, **20** 362
Ni-Med, **50** 122
Niagara Corporation, 28 314–16
Niagara Mohawk Holdings Inc., V 665–67; 45 296–99 (upd.)
Niagara of Wisconsin, **26** 362–63
Nice Day, Inc., *see* Meiji Dairies Corp.
NICE Systems Ltd., 83 280-283
NiceCom Ltd., **11** 520
Nichido Fire and Marine Insurance Co. *see* Millea Holdings Inc.
Nichii Co., Ltd., V 154–55
Nichimen Corporation, IV 150–52; 24 356–59 (upd.)
Nichirei Corporation, 70 203–05
Nichiro Corporation, 86 299–302
Nichols Aluminum-Golden, Inc., **62** 289
Nichols plc, 44 315–18
Nichols Research Corporation, 18 368–70
Nicholson Graham & Jones, **28** 141
Nickelodeon, **25** 381
Nickerson Machinery Company Inc., **53** 230
Nicklaus Companies, 45 300–03
Nicolet Instrument Company, *see* Thermo Instrument Systems Inc.
Nicolon N.V. *see* Royal Ten Cate N.V.
Nicor Inc., 6 529–31; 86 303–07 (upd.)
Nidec Corporation, 59 313–16
Nielsen Marketing Research *see* A.C. Nielsen Co.
Niesmann & Bischoff, **22** 207
NIF Ventures Co. Ltd., **55** 118
Nigerian National Petroleum Corporation, IV 472–74; 72 240–43 (upd.)
Nihon Keizai Shimbun, Inc., IV 654–56
Nihon Noyaku Co., **64** 35
Nihon Styrene Paper Company *see* JSP Corp.
Nihon Synopsis, **11** 491
Nihon Waters K.K., **43** 456
Nihron Yupro Corp. *see* Toto Ltd.
NII *see* National Intergroup, Inc.
NIKE, Inc., V 372–74; 8 391–94 (upd.); 36 343–48 (upd.); 75 279–85 (upd.)
Nikkei *see* Nihon Keizai Shimbun, Inc.
Nikkelverk, **49** 136
Nikken Global Inc., 32 364–67
The Nikko Securities Company Limited, II 433–35; 9 377–79 (upd.)
Nikko Trading Co., *see* Japan Airlines Company, Ltd.
Nikolaiev, **19** 49, 51
Nikon Corporation, III 583–85; 48 292–95 (upd.)
Nilpeter, **26** 540, 542
Niman Ranch, Inc., 67 267–69
Nimbus CD International, Inc., 20 386–90
Nine West Group Inc., 11 348–49; 39 301–03 (upd.)
98 Cents Clearance Centers, **62** 104
99¢ Only Stores, 25 353–55
Ningbo General Bearing Co., Ltd., **45** 170
Nintendo Co., Ltd., III 586–88; 7 394–96 (upd.); 28 317–21 (upd.); 67 270–76 (upd.)
NIOC *see* National Iranian Oil Co.
Nippon Breweries Ltd. *see* Sapporo Breweries Ltd.
Nippon Cable Company, **15** 235
Nippon Credit Bank, II 338–39
Nippon Del Monte Corporation, **47** 206
Nippon Densan Corporation *see* Nidec Corp.
Nippon Educational Television (NET) *see* Asahi National Broadcasting Company, Ltd.
Nippon Electric Company, Limited *see* NEC Corp.
Nippon Express Company, Ltd., V 477–80; 64 286–90 (upd.)
Nippon Foundation Engineering Co. Ltd., **51** 179
Nippon Gakki Co., Ltd *see* Yamaha Corp.
Nippon Global Tanker Co. Ltd., **53** 116
Nippon Gyomo Sengu Co. Ltd., **IV** 555
Nippon Hatsujo Kabushikikaisha *see* NHK Spring Co., Ltd.
Nippon Helicopter & Aeroplane Transport Co., Ltd. *see* All Nippon Airways Company Ltd.
Nippon Hoso Kyokai *see* Japan Broadcasting Corp.
Nippon Idou Tsushin, **7** 119–20
Nippon K.K *see* Nikon Corp.
Nippon Kogaku K.K. *see* Nikon Corp.
Nippon Kogyo Co. Ltd *see* Nippon Mining Co. Ltd.
Nippon Kokan K.K. *see* NKK Corp.
Nippon Life Insurance Company, III 318–20; 60 218–21 (upd.)
Nippon Light Metal Company, Ltd., IV 153–55
Nippon Meat Packers, Inc., II 550–51; 78 255–57 (upd.)
Nippon Mining Co., Ltd., IV 475–77
Nippon Mitsubishi Oil Corporation, **49** 216
Nippon Oil Corporation, IV 478–79; 63 308–13 (upd.)
Nippon Paper Industries Co., Ltd., **57** 101
Nippon Phonogram, **23** 390
Nippon Reizo Co. *see* Nichirei Corp.
Nippon Seiko K.K., III 589–90
Nippon Sekiyu Co *see* Nippon Oil Company, Ltd.
Nippon Sheet Glass Company, Limited, III 714–16
Nippon Shinpan Co., Ltd., II 436–37; 61 248–50 (upd.)
Nippon Soda Co., Ltd., 85 303–06
Nippon Steel Corporation, IV 156–58; 17 348–51 (upd.)
Nippon Suisan Kaisha, Limited, II 552–53; 92 269–72 (upd.)
Nippon Telegraph and Telephone Corporation, V 305–07; 51 271–75 (upd.)
Nippon Tire Co., Ltd. *see* Bridgestone Corp.
Nippon Unipac Holding, **57** 101
Nippon Yusen Kabushiki Kaisha (NYK), V 481–83; 72 244–48 (upd.)
Nippondenso Co., Ltd., III 591–94 *see also* DENSO Corp.
NIPSCO Industries, Inc., 6 532–33
NiSource, Inc., **38** 81
Nissan Motor Company Ltd., I 183–84; 11 350–52 (upd.); 34 303–07 (upd.); 92 273–79 (upd.)
Nissay Dowa General Insurance Company Ltd., **60** 220
Nisshin Seifun Group Inc., II 554; 66 246–48 (upd.)
Nisshin Steel Co., Ltd., IV 159–60
Nissho Iwai K.K., I 509–11

Nissin Food Products Company Ltd., 75 286–88
Nisso *see* Nippon Soda Co., Ltd.
Nissui *see* Nippon Suisan Kaisha.
Nitches, Inc., 53 245–47
Nittsu *see* Nippon Express Co., Ltd.
Niugini Mining Ltd., **23** 42
Nixdorf Computer AG, III 154–55 *see also* Wincor Nixdorf Holding GmbH.
Nixdorf-Krein Industries Inc. *see* Laclede Steel Co.
Nizhny Novgorod Dairy, **48** 438
NKI B.V., **71** 178–79
NKK Corporation, IV 161–63; 28 322–26 (upd.)
NL Industries, Inc., 10 434–36
NLG *see* National Leisure Group.
NLI Insurance Agency Inc., **60** 220
NLM City-Hopper, *see* Koninklijke Luchtvaart Maatschappij N.V.
NM Acquisition Corp., **27** 346
NMC Laboratories Inc., *see* Alpharma Inc.
NMT *see* Nordic Mobile Telephone.
NNG *see* Northern Natural Gas Co.
Noah's New York Bagels *see* Einstein/Noah Bagel Corp.
Nob Hill Foods, **58** 291
Nobel Drilling Corporation, **26** 243
Nobel Industries AB, 9 380–82 *see also* Akzo Nobel N.V.
Nobel Learning Communities, Inc., 37 276–79; 76 281–85 (upd.)
Noble Affiliates, Inc., 11 353–55
Noble Broadcast Group, Inc., **23** 293
Noble Roman's Inc., 14 351–53
Nobleza Piccardo SAICF, 64 291–93
Noboa *see also* Exportadora Bananera Noboa, S.A.
Nobody Beats the Wiz *see* Cablevision Electronic Instruments, Inc.
Nocibé SA, 54 265–68
Nocona Belt Company, **31** 435–36
Nocona Boot Co. *see* Justin Industries, Inc.
Noel Group, Inc., *see* Lincoln Snacks Co.
NOF Corporation, 72 249–51
NOK Corporation, **41** 170–72
Nokia Corporation, II 69–71; 17 352–54 (upd.); 38 328–31 (upd.); 77 308–13 (upd.)
Nokian Tyres PLC, **59** 91
NOL Group *see* Neptune Orient Lines Ltd.
Noland Company, 35 311–14
Nolo.com, Inc., 49 288–91
Nolte Mastenfabriek B.V., *see* Valmont Industries, Inc.
Nomura Securities Company, Limited, II 438–41; 9 383–86 (upd.)
Nomura Toys Ltd., *see* Hasbro, Inc.
Non-Stop Fashions, Inc., *see* The Leslie Fay Companies, Inc.
Noodle Kidoodle, 16 388–91
Noodles & Company, Inc., 55 277–79
Nooter Corporation, 61 251–53
NOP Research Group, **28** 501, 504
Nopri *see* GIB Group.
Norampac Inc., **71** 95
Norand Corporation, **72** 189
Noranda Inc., IV 164–66; 7 397–99 (upd.); 64 294–98 (upd.)
Norandex, *see* Fibreboard Corp.
Norbro Corporation *see* Stuart Entertainment Inc.
Norcal Pottery Products, Inc., **58** 60
Norcal Waste Systems, Inc., 60 222–24
Norcon, Inc., *see* VECO International, Inc.
Norcore Plastics, Inc., **33** 361
Nordbanken, **9** 382
Norddeutsche Affinerie AG, 62 249–53
Norddeutscher-Lloyd *see* Hapag-Lloyd AG.
Nordea AB, 40 336–39
Nordic Baltic Holding *see* Nordea AB.
Nordica S.r.l., **15** 396–97; **53** 24
NordicTrack, 22 382–84 *see also* Icon Health & Fitness, Inc.
Nordisk Film A/S, 80 269–73
Nordson Corporation, 11 356–58; 48 296–99 (upd.)
Nordstrom, Inc., V 156–58; 18 371–74 (upd.); 67 277–81 (upd.)
Nordwestdeutsche Kraftwerke AG *see* PreussenElektra AG.
Norelco Consumer Products Co., 26 334–36
Norelec, *see* Eiffage.
Norex Leasing, Inc., **16** 397
Norfolk Shipbuilding & Drydock Corporation, **73** 47
Norfolk Southern Corporation, V 484–86; 29 358–61 (upd.); 75 289–93 (upd.)
Norge Co., *see* Fedders Corp.
Noric Corporation, **39** 332
Norinchukin Bank, II 340–41
Norlin Industries, **16** 238–39; **75** 262
Norm Thompson Outfitters, Inc., 47 275–77
Norma AS *see* Autoliv, Inc.
Norman BV, **9** 93; **33** 78
Normandy Mining Ltd., **23** 42
Normark Corporation *see* Rapala-Normark Group, Ltd.
Norment Security Group, Inc., **51** 81
Normond/CMS, *see* Danaher Corp.
Norrell Corporation, 25 356–59
Norris Cylinder Company, *see* TriMas Corp.
Norris Oil Company, **47** 52
Norshield Corp., **51** 81
Norsk Aller A/S, **72** 62
Norsk Helikopter AS *see* Bristow Helicopters Ltd.
Norsk Hydro ASA, 10 437–40; 35 315–19 (upd.)
Norsk Rengjorings Selskap a.s., **49** 221
Norske Skog do Brasil Ltda., **73** 205
Norske Skogindustrier ASA, 63 314–16
Norstan, Inc., 16 392–94
Nortek, Inc., 34 308–12
Nortel Inversora S.A., **63** 375–77
Nortel Networks Corporation, 36 349–54 (upd.)
Nortex International, **19** 338
North African Petroleum Ltd., **IV** 455
North American Aviation, *see* Rockwell Automation.
North American Carbon, **19** 499
North American Coal Corporation, *see* NACCO Industries, Inc.
North American Company, **6** 552–53, 601–02
North American Energy Conservation, Inc., **35** 480
North American InTeleCom, Inc., **IV** 411
North American Medical Management Company, Inc., **36** 366
North American Mogul Products Co. *see* Mogul Corp.
North American Nutrition Companies Inc. (NANCO) *see* Provimi
North American Philips Corporation, *see* Philips Electronics North America Corp.
North American Plastics, Inc., **61** 112
North American Site Developers, Inc., **69** 197
North American Training Corporation *see* Rollerblade, Inc.
North American Van Lines *see* Allied Worldwide, Inc.
North American Watch Company *see* Movado Group, Inc.
North Atlantic Energy Corporation, **21** 411
North Atlantic Laboratories, Inc., **62** 391
North Atlantic Trading Company Inc., 65 266–68
North British Rubber Company, **20** 258
North Broken Hill Peko, **IV** 61
North Carolina Motor Speedway, Inc., **19** 294
North Carolina National Bank Corporation *see* NCNB Corp.
North Carolina Natural Gas Corporation, **6** 578
North Central Utilities, Inc., *see* Otter Tail Power Co.
North East Insurance Company, **44** 356
The North Face, Inc., 18 375–77; 78 258–61 (upd.)
North Fork Bancorporation, Inc., 46 314–17
North Pacific Group, Inc., 61 254–57
North Ridge Securities Corporation, **72** 149–50
North Sea Ferries, **26** 241, 243
North Shore Gas Company, **6** 543–44
North Star Communications Group Inc., **73** 59
North Star Container, Inc., **59** 290
North Star Steel Company, 18 378–81
North Star Transport Inc., **49** 402
North Star Tubes, **54** 391, 393
North Star Universal, Inc., *see* Michael Foods, Inc.
North State Supply Company, **57** 9
The North West Company, Inc., 12 361–63
North-West Telecommunications *see* Pacific Telecom, Inc.

North West Water Group plc, 11 359–62 *see also* United Utilities PLC.
Northbridge Financial Corp., **57** 137
Northbrook Holdings, Inc., **22** 495
Northcliffe Newspapers, *see* Daily Mail and General Trust plc.
Northeast Utilities, V 668–69; 48 303–06 (upd.)
Northern and Shell Network plc, 87 341–344
Northern Animal Hospital Inc., **58** 355
Northern Arizona Light & Power Co., **6** 545
Northern Dairies, *see* Northern Foods PLC.
Northern Drug Company, **14** 147
Northern Electric Company *see* Northern Telecom Ltd.
Northern Energy Resources Company *see* NERCO, Inc.
Northern Engineering Industries Plc *see* Rolls-Royce Group PLC.
Northern Fibre Products Co., **I** 202
Northern Foods plc, 10 441–43; 61 258–62 (upd.)
Northern Illinois Gas Co., *see* Nicor Inc.
Northern Indiana Power Company, **6** 556
Northern Indiana Public Service Company, **6** 532–33
Northern Infrastructure Maintenance Company, **39** 238
Northern Leisure, **40** 296–98
Northern Natural Gas Co. *see* Enron Corp.
Northern Pacific Corp., **15** 274
Northern Pacific Railroad, **26** 451
Northern Rock plc, 33 318–21
Northern Star Co., *see* Michael Foods, Inc.
Northern States Power Company, V 670–72; 20 391–95 (upd.) *see also* Xcel Energy Inc.
Northern Telecom Limited, V 308–10 *see also* Nortel Networks Corp.
Northern Trust Company, 9 387–89
Northfield Metal Products, **11** 256
Northland *see* Scott Fetzer Co.
Northland Cranberries, Inc., 38 332–34
Northland Publishing, *see* Justin Industries, Inc.
NorthPrint International, *see* Miner Group Int.
Northrop Grumman Corporation, I 76–77; 11 363–65 (upd.); 45 304–12 (upd.)
Northwest Airlines Corporation, I 112–14; 6 103–05 (upd.); 26 337–40 (upd.); 74 204–08 (upd.)
Northwest Engineering Co. *see* Terex Corp.
Northwest Express *see* Bear Creek Corp.
Northwest Industries *see* Chicago and North Western Holdings Corp.
Northwest Natural Gas Company, 45 313–15
Northwest Telecommunications Inc., **6** 598
NorthWestern Corporation, 37 280–83
Northwestern Flavors LLC, **58** 379
Northwestern Manufacturing Company, *see* Crane Co.
Northwestern Mutual Life Insurance Company, III 321–24; 45 316–21 (upd.)
Northwestern Public Service Company, **6** 524
Northwestern Telephone Systems *see* Pacific Telecom, Inc.
Norton Company, 8 395–97
Norton Healthcare Ltd., **11** 208
Norton McNaughton, Inc., 27 346–49 *see also* Jones Apparel Group, Inc.
Norton Opax PLC, **34** 140
Norton Professional Books *see* W.W. Norton & Company, Inc.
NORWEB plc, **24** 270
Norwegian Cruise Lines *see* NCL Corporation
Norweld Holding A.A., **13** 316
Norwest Bank, **19** 412
Norwest Corp., **16** 135
Norwest Mortgage Inc., **11** 29; **54** 124
Norwich & Peterborough Building Society, 55 280–82
Norwich-Eaton Pharmaceuticals, Inc. *see* The Procter & Gamble Co.
Norwood Promotional Products, Inc., 26 341–43
Nouveaux Loisirs *see* Éditions Gallimard.
Nouvelle Elastelle, **52** 100–01
Nova Corporation, *see* Dynegy Inc.
Nova Corporation of Alberta, V 673–75
Nova Mechanical Contractors, **48** 238
NovaCare, Inc., 11 366–68
Novacor Chemicals Ltd., 12 364–66
Novaction Argentina SA, **48** 224
Novagas Clearinghouse Ltd., *see* Dynegy Inc.
Novalta Resources Inc., **11** 441
Novamax Technologies Inc., **34** 209
Novanet Semiconductor, **36** 124
Novapak Corporation *see* PVC Container Corp.
Novar plc, 49 292–96 (upd.)
Novara plc, **60** 123
Novartis AG, 39 304–10 (upd.)
NovaStar Financial, Inc., 91 354–58
Novatec Plastics Corporation *see* PVC Container Corp.
Novation, **53** 346–47
Novell, Inc., 6 269–71; 23 359–62 (upd.)
Novellus Systems, Inc., 18 382–85
Noven Pharmaceuticals, Inc., 55 283–85
Noveon International, Inc. *see* The Lubrizol Corp.
Novgorodnefteprodukt, **48** 378
Novo Nordisk A/S, I 658–60; 61 263–66 (upd.)
Novobord, **49** 353
Novotel *see* Accor SA.
NOVUM *see* Industrie Natuzzi S.p.A.
NOVUS Financial Corporation, **33** 314
NOW *see* National Organization for Women, Inc.
NPBI International B.V., **56** 141
NPC International, Inc., 40 340–42
The NPD Group, Inc., 68 275–77
NPI-Omnipoint Wireless LLC, **63** 132
NPM (Nationale Portefeuille Maatschappij) *see* Compagnie Nationale à Portefeuille.
NPR *see* National Public Radio, Inc.
NRC Handelsblad BV, **53** 273
NRF B.V., **56** 247
NRG Energy, Inc., 79 290–93
NRT Incorporated, 61 267–69
NS *see* Norfolk Southern Corp.
NS Group, **31** 287
NS Petites Inc., *see* The Leslie Fay Companies, Inc.
NSF International, 72 252–55
NSK *see* Nippon Seiko K.K.
NSK Ltd., **42** 384
NSMO *see* Nederlandsche Stoomvart Maatschappij Oceaan.
NSN Network Services, **23** 292, 294
NSP *see* Northern States Power Co.
NSS Enterprises, Inc., 78 262–65
NTC Electronics Inc., **64** 198
NTC Publishing Group, *see* Tribune Co.
NTCL *see* Northern Telecom Ltd.
NTL Inc., 65 269–72
NTN Buzztime, Inc., 86 308–11
NTN Corporation, III 595–96; 47 278–81 (upd.)
NTTPC *see* Nippon Telegraph and Telephone Public Corp.
NU *see* Northeast Utilities.
The Nu-Gro Corporation *see* United Industries Corp.
Nu-kote Holding, Inc., 18 386–89
Nu Skin Enterprises, Inc., 27 350–53; 31 386–89; 76 286–90 (upd.)
Nu-West Industries, Inc. *see* Agrium Inc.
Nuance Group, **63** 361, 363
Nuclear Electric, **6** 453; **11** 399–401; **13** 484; **50** 280–81, 361–63; **66** 282
Nuclear Power International, *see* Framatome SA.
Nucor Corporation, 7 400–02; 21 392–95 (upd.); 79 294–300 (upd.)
Nucorp Energy, **59** 280–81
Nufarm Ltd., 87 345–348
NUG Optimus Lebensmittel-Einzelhandelgesellschaft mbH, **V** 74
NUMAR Corporation, **25** 192
NUMMI *see* New United Motor Manufacturing, Inc.
Nuovo Pignone, **69** 146, 148–49
Nuplex Industries Ltd., 92 280–83
NUR Touristic GmbH *see* Karstadt AG.
Nurotoco Inc. *see* Roto-Rooter Service Co.
The Nut Company NV, **66** 153
Nutmeg Industries, Inc., *see* VF Corp.
Nutraceutical International Corporation, 37 284–86
Nutrasense Australia Pty. Ltd. *see* Laboratoires Arkopharma S.A.
NutraSweet Company, 8 398–400
Nutreco Holding N.V., 56 256–59
Nutrexpa S.A., 92 284–87
Nutri-Foods International, *see* Safeskin Corp

NutriSystem, Inc., 71 250–53
Nutrition for Life International Inc., 22 385–88
Nutron Industries, **58** 75
Nuveen *see* John Nuveen Co.
NV Dagblad De Telegraaf *see* N.V. Holdingmaatschappij De Telegraaf.
NVIDIA Corporation, 54 269–73
NVR Inc., 8 401–03; 70 206–09 (upd.)
NWA, Inc. *see* Northwest Airlines Corp.
NWK *see* Nordwestdeutsche Kraftwerke AG.
NWS BANK plc, *see* The Governor and Company of the Bank of Scotland.
NWT Air, **56** 39
NY Waterway *see* Port Imperial Ferry Corp.
NYC OTB Racing Network, **51** 269
NYHC Newco Paxxon, Inc. *see* New York Health Care, Inc.
NYK *see* Nippon Yusen Kabushiki Kaisha (NYK).
Nyland Mattor, **25** 464
NYLCare Health Plans, **45** 293–94
Nylon de Mexico, S.A., **19** 10, 12
NYMAGIC, Inc., 41 284–86
NYNEX Corporation, V 311–13 *see also* Verizon Communications.
NYRG *see* New York Restaurant Group, Inc.
NYSE *see* New York Stock Exchange.
NYSEG *see* New York State Electric and Gas Corp.
NZI Corp., *see* Aviva PLC.

O

O&K Rolltreppen *see* KONE Corp.
O&Y *see* Olympia & York Developments Ltd.
O.C. Tanner Co., 69 279–81
O. Kraft & Sons, **12** 363
O.N.E. Color Communications L.L.C., **29** 306
O-Pee-Chee, **34** 447–48
O.S. Designs Inc., **15** 396
O.Y.L. Industries Berhad, **26** 3, 5
Oak Creek Homes Inc., **41** 18
Oak Harbor Freight Lines, Inc., 53 248–51
Oak Hill Investment Partners, **11** 490
Oak Hill Sportswear Corp., *see* Donnkenny, Inc.
Oak Industries Inc., 21 396–98 *see also* Corning Inc.
Oak Technology, Inc., 22 389–93 *see also* Zoran Corp.
OakBrook Investments, LLC, **48** 18
Oakhurst Dairy, 60 225–28
Oakleaf Waste Management, **74** 227
Oakley, Inc., 18 390–93; 49 297–302 (upd.)
Oakmont Investments, Inc. *see* Laboratoires Arkopharma S.A.
OakStone Financial Corporation, **11** 448
Oaktree Capital Management, LLC, 71 254–56
OakTree Health Plan Inc., **16** 404
Oakwood Homes Corporation, 13 155; **15 326–28**
OAO AVTOVAZ *see* AVTOVAZ Joint Stock Co.
OAO Gazprom, 42 261–65
OAO LUKOIL, 40 343–46
OAO NK YUKOS, 47 282–85
OAO Severstal *see* Severstal Joint Stock Co.
OAO Siberian Oil Company (Sibneft), 49 303–06
OAO Tatneft, 45 322–26
Oasis Group P.L.C., *see* Sybase, Inc.
OASYS, Inc., **18** 112
Obayashi Corporation, 78 266–69 (upd.)
ÖBB *see* Österreichische Bundesbahnen GmbH.
Oberheim Corporation, **16** 239
Oberland, **16** 122
Oberto Sausage Company, Inc., 92 288–91
Obi, **23** 231
Obie Media Corporation, 56 260–62
Object Design, Inc., **15** 372
O'Boy Inc. *see* Happy Kids Inc.
Obrascon Huarte Lain S.A., 76 291–94
O'Brien Kreitzberg, Inc., **25** 130
Observer AB, 55 286–89
OCBC *see* Overseas-Chinese Banking Corp.
Occidental Chemical Corporation, **45** 254; **71** 149
Occidental Life Insurance Company, **26** 486–87; **41** 401
Occidental Overseas Ltd., **50** 179
Occidental Petroleum Corporation, IV 480–82; 25 360–63 (upd.); 71 257–61 (upd.)
Occidental Petroleum Great Britain Inc., **21** 206
Océ N.V., 24 360–63; 91 359–65 (upd.)
Ocean Beauty Seafoods, Inc., 74 209–11
Ocean Drilling and Exploration Company *see* ODECO.
Ocean Group plc, 6 415–17 *see also* Exel plc.
Ocean Pacific Apparel Corporation, **51** 321
Ocean Reef Management, *see* L. Luria & Son, Inc.
Ocean Scientific, Inc., **15** 380
Ocean Specialty Tankers Corporation, *see* Hvide Marine Inc.
Ocean Spray Cranberries, Inc., 7 403–05; 25 364–67 (upd.); 83 284-290
Ocean Steam Ship Company *see* Malaysian Airlines System BHD.
Ocean Transport & Trading Ltd., **6** 417
Oceaneering International, Inc., 63 317–19
Oceanfast Ltd. *see* Austal Ltd.
Oceanic Steam Navigation Company, **23** 160
Oceans of Fun, *see* Cedar Fair, L.P.
Ocelet Industries Ltd., **25** 232
Ocesa *see* Corporación Interamericana de Entretenimiento, S.A. de C.V.
O'Charley's Inc., 19 286–88; 60 229–32 (upd.)
OCI *see* Orascom Construction Industries S.A.E.
OCL *see* Overseas Containers Ltd.
Oclassen Pharmaceuticals Inc., **56** 375
Octagon Group Ltd., **51** 173
Octane Software, **49** 124
Octek, *see* Foxboro Co.
Octel Messaging, 14 354–56; 41 287–90 (upd.)
Ocular Sciences, Inc., 65 273–75
Oculinum, Inc., *see* Allergan, Inc.
Odakyu Electric Railway Co., Ltd., V 487–89; 68 278–81 (upd.)
Odd Job Trading Corp., **29** 311–12
Odda Smelteverk A/S, **25** 82
Odebrecht S.A., 73 242–44
Odetics Inc., 14 357–59
ODL, Inc., 55 290–92
ODM, **26** 490
ODME *see* Toolex International N.V.
Odwalla, Inc., 31 349–51
Odyssey Marine Exploration, Inc., 91 366–70
Odyssey Partners Group, **V** 135; **12** 55; **28** 218
Odyssey Publications Inc., **48** 99
Odyssey Re Group, **57** 136–37
OEA *see* Autoliv, Inc.
OEC Medical Systems, Inc., 27 354–56
OENEO S.A., 74 212–15 (upd.)
Oetker Gruppe, **75** 332, 344
Ofek Securities and Investments Ltd., **60** 50
Off Wall Street Consulting Group, **42** 313
Office Depot, Inc., 8 404–05; 23 363–65 (upd.); 65 276–80 (upd.)
Office Electronics, Inc., **65** 371
Office Mart Holdings Corporation, *see* Staples, Inc.
Office Systems Inc., **15** 407
The Office Works, Inc., *see* U.S. Office Products Co.
OfficeMax Inc., 15 329–31; 43 291–95 (upd.)
OfficeTiger, LLC, 75 294–96
Officine Alfieri Maserati S.p.A., 13 376–78
The Offshore Company, **6** 577; **37** 243
The Offshore Drilling Co. *see* TODCO.
Offshore Logistics, Inc., 37 287–89
Offshore Transportation Corporation, **11** 523
O'Gara Company, **57** 219
Ogden Corporation, I 512–14; 6 151–53 *see also* Covanta Energy Corp.
Ogden Gas Co., **6** 568
Ogden Ground Services, **39** 240, 242
Ogilvy Group Inc., I 25–27 *see also* WPP Group.
Oglebay Norton Company, 17 355–58
Oglethorpe Power Corporation, 6 537–38
Oh la la!, **14** 107

Ohbayashi Corporation, **I 586–87**
The Ohio Art Company, **14 360–62; 59 317–20 (upd.)**
Ohio Ball Bearing *see* Bearings Inc.
Ohio Bell Telephone Company, **14 363–65**; *see also* Ameritech Corp.
Ohio Casualty Corp., **11 369–70**
Ohio Coatings Company, **58** 363
Ohio Crankshaft Co. *see* Park-Ohio Industries Inc.
Ohio Edison Company, **V 676–78**
Ohio Farmers Insurance Company *see* Westfield Group.
Ohio Mattress Co., *see* Sealy Inc.
Ohio-Sealy Mattress Mfg. Co., *see* Sealy Inc.
Ohio Valley Electric Corporation, **6** 517
Ohlmeyer Communications, *see* Molson Companies Ltd.
Ohmeda *see* BOC Group plc.
OIAG *see* Osterreichische Industrieholding AG.
Oil and Natural Gas Commission, **IV 483–84; 90 313–17 (upd.)**
Oil-Dri Corporation of America, **20 396–99; 89 331–36 (upd.)**
Oil Dynamics Inc., **43** 178
Oil Shale Corp., *see* Tosco Corp.
Oil States International, Inc., **77 314–17**
Oil Transporting Joint Stock Company Transneft, **92450–54**
The Oilgear Company, **74 216–18**
Oilinvest *see* National Oil Corp.
Oji Paper Co., Ltd., **IV 320–22; 57 272–75 (upd.)**
Ojibway Press, **57** 13
OJSC Wimm-Bill-Dann Foods, **48 436–39**
Okay, **68** 143
O'Keefe Marketing, **23** 102
Oki Electric Industry Company, Limited, **II 72–74**; **15** 125; **21** 390
Oklahoma Gas and Electric Company, **6 539–40**
Oklahoma Publishing Company, *see* Gaylord Entertainment Co.
Okuma Holdings Inc., **74 219–21**
Okura & Co., Ltd., **IV 167–68**
Olan Mills, Inc., **62 254–56**
Olathe Manufacturing, **26** 494
OLC *see* Orient Leasing Co., Ltd.
Old America Stores, Inc., **17 359–61**
Old Chicago *see* Rock Bottom Restaurants, Inc.
Old Colony Envelope Co., **32** 345–46
Old Country Buffet Restaurant Co. (OCB) *see* Buffets, Inc.
Old Dominion Freight Line, Inc., **57 276–79**
Old Dominion Power Company, **6** 513, 515
Old El Paso, *see* General Mills, Inc.
Old Harbor Candles, *see* Blyth, Inc.
Old Kent Financial Corp., **11 371–72** *see also* Fifth Third Bancorp.
Old Mutual PLC, **IV** 535; **61 270–72**
Old National Bancorp, **15 332–34**
Old Navy, Inc., **70 210–12**
Old 97 Company, **60** 287
Old Orchard Brands, LLC, **73 245–47**
Old Republic International Corporation, **11 373–75; 58 258–61 (upd.)**
Old Spaghetti Factory International Inc., **24 364–66**
Old Town Canoe Company, **74 222–24**
Oldach Window Corp., **19** 446
Oldcastle, Inc., **60** 77; **64** 98
Oldover Corp., **23** 225
Ole's Innovative Sports *see* Rollerblade, Inc.
Olean Tile Co., **22** 170
Oleochim, **IV** 498–99
OLEX *see* Deutsche BP Aktiengesellschaft.
Olga's Kitchen, Inc., **80 274–76**
Olin Corporation, **I 379–81; 13 379–81 (upd.); 78 270–74 (upd.)**
Olive Garden Italian Restaurants, *see* Darden Restaurants, Inc.
Olivetti S.p.A., **34 316–20 (upd.)**
Olivine Industries, Inc., *see* H.J. Heinz Co.
Olmstead Products Co., **23** 82
OLN *see* Outdoor Life Network.
Olsten Corporation, **6 41–43; 29 362–65 (upd.)** *see also* Adecco S.A.
Olympia & York Developments Ltd., **IV 720–21; 9 390–92 (upd.)**
Olympia Arenas, Inc., *see* Little Caesar Enterprises, Inc.
Olympia Entertainment, **37** 207
Olympic Courier Systems, Inc., *see* Consolidated Delivery & Logistics, Inc.
Olympic Insurance Co., **26** 486
Olympic Property Group LLC *see* Pope Resources LP.
Olympic Resource Management LLC *see* Pope Resources LP.
Olympus Optical Company, Ltd., **15** 483
Olympus Partners, **65** 258
Olympus Sport *see* Sears plc.
Olympus Symbol, Inc., **15** 483
OM Group, Inc., **17 362–64; 78 275–78 (upd.)**
Omaha Public Power District, **29** 353
Omaha Steaks International Inc., **62 257–59**
Omega Group *see* MasterBrand Cabinets, Inc.
Omega Protein Corporation, **25** 546
Omega Research, Inc. *see* TradeStation Group, Inc.
OmegaTech Inc. *see* Martek Biosciences Corp.
O'Melveny & Myers, **37 290–93**
OMI Corporation, **59** 321–23
Omnes, *see* Schlumberger Ltd.
Omni ApS, **56** 338
Omni Construction Company, Inc., *see* The Clark Construction Group, Inc.
Omni Hotels Corp., **12 367–69**
Omni-Pac, **12** 377
Omni Services, Inc., **51** 76
Omnicad Corporation, **48** 75
Omnicare, Inc., **13 49 307–10**
Omnicell, Inc., **89 337–40**
Omnicom Group Inc., **I 28–32; 22 394–99 (upd.); 77 318–25 (upd.)**
Omnilife *see* Grupo Omnilife S.A. de C.V.
OmniSource Corporation, **14 366–67**
OmniTech Consulting Group, **51** 99
Omnitel Pronto Italia SpA, **38** 300
OMNOVA Solutions Inc., **59 324–26**
Omron Corporation, **28 331–35 (upd.); 53** 46
Omron Tateisi Electronics Company, **II 75–77**
ÖMV Aktiengesellschaft, **IV 485–87**
On Assignment, Inc., **20 400–02**
On Command Video Corp., **23** 135
On Demand Group *see* SeaChange International, Inc.
On-Line Systems *see* Sierra On-Line Inc.
Onbancorp Inc., **11** 110
Once Upon A Child, Inc., *see* Grow Biz International, Inc.
Ondeo Nalco *see* Nalco Holding Co.
1-800-FLOWERS, Inc., **26 344–46**
1-800-GOT-JUNK? LLC, **74 225–27**
1-800-Mattress *see* Dial-A-Mattress Operating Corp.
180s, L.L.C., **64 299–301**
One For All, **39** 405
One Price Clothing Stores, Inc., **20 403–05**
17187 Yukon Inc., **74** 234
One Stop Trade Building Centre Ltd. *see* Gibbs and Dandy plc.
OneBeacon Insurance Group LLC, **48** 431
Oneida Ltd., **7 406–08; 31 352–55 (upd.); 88 280–85 (upd.)**
ONEOK Inc., **7 409–12**
Onet S.A., **92 292–95**
Onex Corporation, **16 395–97; 65 281–85 (upd.)**
OneZero Media, Inc., **31** 240
Ong First Pte Ltd., **76** 372, 374
Onion, Inc., **69 282–84**
Onitsuka Co., Ltd., **57** 52
Only One Dollar, Inc. *see* Dollar Tree Stores, Inc.
Onoda Cement Co., Ltd., **III 717–19** *see also* Taiheiyo Cement Corp.
OnResponse.com, Inc., **49** 433
Onsale Inc., **31** 177
Onstead Foods, **21** 501
OnTarget Inc., **38** 432
Ontario Hydro Services Company, **6 541–42; 32 368–71 (upd.)**
Ontario Power Generation, **49** 65, 67
Ontario Teachers' Pension Plan, **61 273–75**
OnTrack Data International, **57** 219
OnTrak Systems Inc., **31** 301
Onyx Acceptance Corporation, **59 327–29**
Onyx Software Corporation, **53 252–55**
Opel AG *see* Adam Opel AG.
Open *see* Groupe Open.
Open Cellular Systems, Inc., **41** 225–26
Open Text Corporation, **79 301–05**
OpenTV, Inc., **31** 330–31

OPENWAY SAS, **74** 143
Operadora de Bolsa Serfin *see* Grupo Financiero Serfin, S.A.
Operation Smile, Inc., 75 297–99
Operon Technologies Inc., **39** 335
Opinion Research Corporation, 46 318–22
Opp and Micolas Mills, **15** 247–48
Oppenheimer *see* Ernest Oppenheimer and Sons.
Oppenheimer & Co., Inc., **21** 235; **25** 450; **61** 50
The Oppenheimer Group, 76 295–98
Oppenheimer Wolff & Donnelly LLP, 71 262–64
Opryland USA, *see* Gaylord Entertainmnet Co.
Opsware Inc., 49 311–14
Optel S.A., **71** 211
Opti-Ray, Inc., *see* Goody Products, Inc.
Optical Corporation *see* Excel Technology, Inc.
Optilink Corporation, **12** 137
Optima Pharmacy Services, *see* Fay's Inc.
Option Care Inc., 48 307–10
Optische Werke G. Rodenstock, 44 319–23
OptiSystems Solutions Ltd., **55** 67
Opto-Electronics Corp., **15** 483
Optus Communications, **25** 102
Opus Group, 34 321–23
Oracle Corporation, 6 272–74; 24 367–71 (upd.); 67 282–87 (upd.)
Orange *see* Wanadoo S.A.
Orange and Rockland Utilities, Inc., **45** 116, 120
Orange Glo International, 53 256–59
Orange Line Bus Company, **6** 604
Orange S.A., 84 286–289
Orange Shipbuilding Company, Inc., **58** 70
Orascom Construction Industries S.A.E., 87 349–352
OraSure Technologies, Inc., 75 300–03
Orb Books *see* Tom Doherty Associates Inc.
Orb Estates, **54** 366, 368
ORBIS Corporation, **59** 289
Orbis Entertainment Co., **20** 6
Orbis Graphic Arts *see* Anaheim Imaging.
Orbital Sciences Corporation, 22 400–03
Orbitz, Inc., 61 276–78
Orbotech Ltd., 75 304–06
Orchard Supply Hardware Stores Corporation, 17 365–67
Orchid Biosciences Inc., **57** 309, 311
OrderTrust LLP, **26** 440
Ore-Ida Foods Inc., 13 382–83; 78 279–82 (upd.)
Orebehoved Fanerfabrik, **25** 464
Oregon Ale and Beer Company, *see* Boston Beer Co.
Oregon Chai, Inc., 49 315–17
Oregon Coin Company, **74** 14
Oregon Cutting Systems, **26** 119
Oregon Dental Service Health Plan, Inc., 51 276–78
Oregon Freeze Dry, Inc., 74 228–30
Oregon Metallurgical Corporation, 20 406–08
Oregon Steel Mills, Inc., 14 368–70
O'Reilly Automotive, Inc., 26 347–49; 78 283–87 (upd.)
Orenda Aerospace, **48** 274
The Organic and Natural Food Company, **74** 384
Organic Valley (Coulee Region Organic Produce Pool), 53 260–62
Organización Soriana, S.A. de C.V., 35 320–22
Organizacion Techint, **66** 293–95
Organon, **63** 141
ORI *see* Old Republic International Corp.
Orico Life Insurance Co., **48** 328
Orient, **21** 122
Orient Express Hotels Inc., **29** 429–30
Orient Leasing *see* Orix Corp.
Oriental Brewery Co., Ltd., **21** 320
Oriental Yeast Co. *see* Nisshin Seifun Group Inc.
Origin Energy Limited *see* Boral Ltd.
Origin Systems Inc., *see* Electronic Arts Inc.
Origin Technology, *see* Exar Corp.
Original Arizona Jean Company *see* J.C. Penney Company, Inc.
Original Cookie Co. *see* Mrs. Fields' Original Cookies, Inc.
Original Musical Instrument Company (O.M.I.), **16** 239
Origins Natural Resources Inc., **30** 190
Orioala, **72** 258
Orion Capital Corporation, **55** 331
Orion Food Systems *see* Hot Stuff Foods.
Orion Healthcare Ltd., *see* Guardian Royal Exchange Plc.
Orion Oyj, 72 256–59
Orion Pictures Corporation, 6 167–70 *see also* Metro-Goldwyn-Mayer Inc.
Orit Corp., *see* The Gitano Group, Inc.
ORIX Corporation, II 442–43; 44 324–26 (upd.)
Orkem, **IV** 560; **21** 205
Orkin Pest Control, *see* Rollins, Inc.
Orkla ASA, 18 394–98; 82 259–64 (upd.)
Orleans Homebuilders, Inc., 62 260–62
Orlimar Golf Equipment Co., **45** 76
Ormat Technologies, Inc., 87 353–358
Ormco Corporation, **14** 481
Ormet Corporation, 82 265–68
ÖROP, **IV** 485–86
La Oroya, **22** 286
Orrick, Herrington and Sutcliffe LLP, 76 299–301
ORSCO, Inc., **26** 363
Orszagos Takarekpenztar es Kereskedelmi Bank Rt. (OTP Bank), 78 288–91
Orthodontic Centers of America, Inc., 35 323–26
Orthofix International NV, 72 260–62
Orthopedic Services, Inc., *see* NovaCare, Inc.
Ortloff Engineers, Ltd., **52** 103–05
Orval Kent Food Company, Inc., *see* Chef Solutions.
Orville Redenbacher/Swiss Miss Foods Co., *see* Hunt-Wesson, Inc.
The Orvis Company, Inc., 28 336–39
Oryx Energy Company, 7 413–15
OSA Technologies *see* Avocent Corp.
Osaka Gas Company, Ltd., V 679–81; 60 233–36 (upd.)
Osaka Shinyo Kumiai, **15** 495
Osaka Shosen Kaisha *see* Mitsui O.S.K. Lines, Ltd.
Osborn Group Inc., **48** 256
Oscar Mayer Foods Corp., 12 370–72 *see also* Kraft Foods Inc.
Osco Drug, Inc, *see* American Stores Co.
OSF Japan Ltd., *see* Old Spaghetti Factory International Inc.
Oshawa Group Limited, II 649–50
OshKosh B'Gosh, Inc., 9 393–95; 42 266–70 (upd.)
Oshkosh Gas Light Company, *see* WPS Resources Corp.
Oshkosh Truck Corporation, 7 416–18
Oshman's Sporting Goods, Inc., 17 368–70 *see also* Gart Sports Co.
OSI Restaurant Partners, Inc., 88 286–91 (upd.)
OSi Specialties, Inc., *see* Witco Corp.
OSI Systems, Inc., **71** 348
Osiris Holding Company, **16** 344
OSK *see* Osaka Shosen Kaisha.
Osmonics, Inc., 18 399–401
Osram GmbH, 86 312–16
Oster *see* Sunbeam-Oster.
Österreichische Brau-Beteiligungs AG *see* BBAG Österreichische Brau-Beteiligungs AG.
Österreichische Bundesbahnen GmbH, 6 418–20
Österreichische Elektrizitätswirtschafts-AG, 85 307–10
Osterreichische Industrieholding AG, **73** 66
Österreichische Länderbank, **23** 37
Österreichische Luftverkehrs AG *see* Austrian Airlines AG.
Österreichische Mineralölverwaltung AG, **IV** 485
Österreichische Post- und Telegraphenverwaltung, V 314–17
Ostrada Yachts, **55** 54, 56
Ostravar A.S., **38** 77
O'Sullivan Industries Holdings, Inc., 34 313–15
Otagiri Mercantile Co., **11** 95
Otari Inc., 89 341–44
OTC, *see* SPX Corp.
Other Options, **29** 400
Otis Company, **6** 579
Otis Elevator Company, Inc., 13 384–86; 39 311–15 (upd.)
Otis Spunkmeyer, Inc., 28 340–42
Otor S.A., 77 326–29
Otosan, *see* Koç Holding A.S.
OTP Bank *see* Orszagos Takarekpenztar es Kereskedelmi Bank Rt.

OTP, Incorporated, **48** 446
OTR Express, Inc., 25 368–70
Ottakar's plc, 64 302–04
Ottaway Newspapers, Inc., 15 335–37
Otter Tail Power Company, 18 402–05
Otter-Westelaken, *see* Randstad Holding n.v.
Otto Bremer Foundation *see* Bremer Financial Corp.
Otto-Epoka mbH, **15** 340
Otto Sumisho Inc., **V** 161
Otto Versand GmbH & Co., V 159–61; 15 338–40 (upd.); 34 324–28 (upd.)
Ottumwa Daily Courier, *see* Lee Enterprises, Inc.
Ourso Investment Corporation, **16** 344
Outback Steakhouse, Inc., 12 373–75; 34 329–32 (upd.) *see also* OSI Restaurant Partners, Inc.
Outboard Marine Corporation, III 597–600; 20 409–12 (upd.) *see also* Bombardier Inc.
Outdoor Channel, Inc. *see* Global Outdoors, Inc.
The Outdoor Group Limited, **39** 58, 60
Outdoor Research, Incorporated, 67 288–90
Outdoor Systems, Inc., 25 371–73 *see also* Infinity Broadcasting Corp.
Outdoor World *see* Bass Pro Shops, Inc.
Outlet Retail Stores, Inc., *see* Lifetime Brands, Inc.
Outlook Group Corporation, 37 294–96
Outlook Window Partnership, **19** 446
OutlookSoft Corporation, **76** 190
Outokumpu Metals Group *see* OM Group, Inc.
Outokumpu Oyj, 38 335–37
Outpost.com *see* Fry's Electronics, Inc.
Outrigger Enterprises, Inc., 67 291–93
Ovation, **19** 285
Overhead Door Corporation, 70 213–16
Overhill Corporation, 51 279–81
Overnite Corporation, 14 371–73; 58 262–65 (upd.)
Overseas-Chinese Banking Corporation, **56** 363
Overseas Insurance Corporation, **58** 272
Overseas Shipholding Group, Inc., 11 376–77
Overseas Telecommunications, Inc., **27** 304
Overseas Union Bank, **56** 362–63
Overstock.com, Inc., 75 307–09
Overture Services, Inc. *see* Yahoo! Inc.
Ovonic Battery Company, Inc. *see* Energy Conversion Devices, Inc.
Ovox Fitness Clubs, **46** 432
Owen Healthcare, **50** 122
Owen Owen, **37** 8
Owen Steel Co. Inc., **15** 117
Owens & Minor, Inc., 16 398–401; 68 282–85 (upd.)
Owens Corning Corporation, III 720–23; 20 413–17 (upd.)
Owens Country Sausage, Inc., **63** 69–70
Owens-Illinois, Inc., I 609–11; 26 350–53 (upd.); 85 311–18 (upd.)
Owosso Corporation, 29 366–68
Oxfam GB, 87 359–362
Oxford Bus Company, **28** 155–56
Oxford Health Plans, Inc., 16 402–04
Oxford Industries, Inc., 8 406–08; 84 290–296 (upd.)
Oxford Learning Centres, **34** 105; **76** 240
Oxford Realty Financial Group, Inc., **49** 26
Oxford University Press, **23** 211
Oxirane Chemical Corporation, **64** 35
OXO International, *see* General Housewares Corp.
Oxycal Laboratories Inc., **46** 466
OxyChem, **11** 160
Oxygen Business Solutions Pty Limited *see* Carter Holt Harvey Ltd.
Oxygen Media Inc., **28** 175; **51** 220
Ozark Automotive Distributors, **26** 347–48
Ozark Utility Company, **6** 593; **50** 38
OZM *see* OneZero Media, Inc.

P

P&C Foods Inc., 8 409–11
P&C Groep N.V., **46** 344
P & F Industries, Inc., 45 327–29
P&F Technologies Ltd., **26** 363
P&G *see* Procter & Gamble Co.
P&L Coal Holdings Corporation, **45** 333
P & M Manufacturing Company, *see* NCH Corp.
P & O *see* Peninsular & Oriental Steam Navigation Co.
P.A. Bergner & Company, **15** 87–88
P.A. Geier Company *see* Royal Appliance Manufacturing Co.
P.C. Richard & Son Corp., 23 372–74
P.D. Associated Collieries Ltd., **31** 369
P.D. Kadi International, *see* Kumagai Gumi Company, Ltd.
P.F. Chang's China Bistro, Inc., 37 297–99; 86 317–21 (upd.)
P.H. Glatfelter Company, 8 412–14; 30 349–52 (upd.); 83 291-297 (upd.)
P.R. Mallory, *see* Duracell International, Inc.
P.T. Asurasi Tokio Marine Indonesia, **64** 280
P.T. Bridgeport Perkasa Machine Tools, *see* Bridgeport Machines, Inc.
P.T. Gaya Motor, **23** 290
P.T. GOLD Martindo, **70** 235
P.T. Indomobil Suzuki International, **59** 393, 397
P.T. Samick Indonesia, **56** 300
P.T. Satomo Indovyl Polymer, **70** 329
P.T. Unitex, **53** 344
P.V. Doyle Hotels Ltd., **64** 217
P.W.J. Surridge & Sons, Ltd., **43** 132
Paaco Automotive Group, **64** 20
Pabst Brewing Company, **I** 255; **50** 114; **74** 146
Pac-Fab, Inc., *see* Essef Corp.
PAC Insurance Services, *see* Kerry Group plc.
PACCAR Inc., I 185–86; 26 354–56 (upd.)
PacDun *see* Pacific Dunlop.
The Pace Consultants, Inc. *see* Jacobs Engineering Group Inc.
PACE Entertainment Corp., **36** 423–24
Pace Foods Ltd. *see* Campbell Soup Co.
Pace Management Service Corp., **21** 91
PACE Membership Warehouse, Inc. *see* Kmart Corp.
Pacer International, Inc., 54 274–76
Pacer Technology, 40 347–49
Pacific Advantage, **43** 253
Pacific Air Freight, Incorporated *see* Airborne Freight Corp.
Pacific Basin Shipping Ltd., 86 322–26
Pacific Bell *see* SBC Communications.
Pacific Car & Foundry Company *see* PACCAR Inc.
Pacific Clay Products Inc., 88 292–95
Pacific Coast Building Products, Inc., 94 338–41
Pacific Coast Feather Company, 67 294–96
Pacific Coast Restaurants, Inc., 90 318–21
Pacific Communication Sciences, **11** 57
Pacific Destination Services, **62** 276
Pacific Dunlop Limited, 10 444–46 *see also* Ansell Ltd.
Pacific Electric Light Company, **6** 565; **50** 365
Pacific Enterprises, V 682–84 *see also* Sempra Energy.
Pacific Ethanol, Inc., 81 269–72
Pacific Forest Products Ltd., **59** 162
Pacific Gas and Electric Company, V 685–87 *see also* PG&E Corp.
Pacific Glass Corp., **48** 42
Pacific Guardian Life Insurance Co., *see* Meiji Mutual Life Insurance Co.
Pacific Indemnity Corp., *see* The Chubb Corp.
Pacific Integrated Healthcare, **53** 7
Pacific Internet Limited, 87 363–366
Pacific Lighting Corp. *see* Sempra Energy.
Pacific Link Communication, *see* First Pacific Co. Ltd.
Pacific Lumber Company, *see* MAXXAM Inc.
Pacific Mail Steamship Company *see* APL Ltd.
Pacific Monolothics Inc., **11** 520
Pacific National Insurance Co. *see* TIG Holdings, Inc.
Pacific Northwest Laboratories, *see* Battelle Memorial Institute, Inc.
Pacific Northwest Power Company, **6** 597
Pacific Plastics, Inc., **48** 334
Pacific Power & Light Company *see* PacifiCorp.
Pacific Pride Bakeries, **19** 192
Pacific Publications, **72** 283–84
Pacific Recycling Co. Inc., **23** 225
Pacific Resources Inc., **IV** 47; **22** 107
Pacific/Southern Wine & Spirits, **48** 392
Pacific Stock Exchange, **48** 226

Pacific Sunwear of California, Inc., 28 343–45; 47 425
Pacific Telecom, Inc., 6 325–28
Pacific Telesis Group, V 318–20 *see also* SBC Communications.
Pacific Teletronics, Inc., *see* Affiliated Publications, Inc.
Pacific Towboat *see* Puget Sound Tug and Barge Co.
Pacific Trail Inc., **29** 293, 295–96
Pacific Western Extruded Plastics Company *see* PW Eagle Inc.
PacifiCare Health Systems, Inc., 11 378–80
PacifiCorp, Inc., V 688–90; 26 357–60 (upd.)
Packaged Ice, Inc., **21** 338; **26** 449
Packaging Corporation of America, 12 376–78; 51 282–85 (upd.)
Packard Bell Electronics, Inc., 13 387–89
Packerland Packing Company, *see* Gillett Holdings, Inc.
Packeteer, Inc., 81 273–76
PacNet *see* Pacific Internet Ltd.
Pact, **50** 175
PacTel *see* Pacific Telesis Group.
Paddock Publications, Inc., 53 263–65
PAFS *see* Pacific Alaska Fuel Services.
Page Plus NV *see* Punch International N.V.
PageAhead Software, **15** 492
PagesJaunes Groupe SA, 79 306–09
Paging Network Inc., 11 381–83
Pagnossin S.p.A., 73 248–50
Pagoda Trading Company, Inc. *see* Brown Shoe Company, Inc.
Paige Publications, *see* BET Holdings, Inc.
PaineWebber Group Inc., II 444–46; 22 404–07 (upd.) *see also* UBS AG.
PairGain Technologies, **36** 299
Paisley Products, **32** 255
Pak Sak Industries, *see* Maxco Inc.
Pakhoed Holding, N.V., **9** 532; **26** 420; **41** 339–40
Pakistan International Airlines Corporation, 46 323–26
Pakistan State Oil Company Ltd., 81 277–80
Pakkasakku Oy, **IV** 471
Paknet, **11** 548
Pakway Container Corporation, *see* Inland Container Corp.
PAL *see* Philippine Airlines, Inc.
Palace Station Hotel & Casino *see* Station Casinos Inc.
Paladar, **56** 116
Palais Royal, Inc., *see* Stage Stores, Inc.
Palazzo Feroni Finanziaria SpA, **62** 313
The Palestine Post Limited, **62** 188
PALIC *see* Pan-American Life Insurance Co.
Pall Corporation, 9 396–98; 72 263–66 (upd.)
Pallas Textiles, **57** 207, 209
Palm Harbor Homes, Inc., 39 316–18
Palm, Inc., 36 355–57; 75 310–14 (upd.)
Palm Management Corporation, 71 265–68
Palm Shipping Inc., *see* Teekay Shipping Corp.
Palmafina, **IV** 498–99
Palmax, **47** 153
Palmer & Cay, Inc., 69 285–87
Palmer Candy Company, 80 277–81
Palmer Co. *see* R. M. Palmer Co.
Palmer Communications, **25** 418
Palmolive Co. *see* Colgate-Palmolive Co.
Palo Alto Products International, Inc., **29** 6
Paloma Industries Ltd., 71 269–71
Palomar Medical Technologies, Inc., 22 408–10
Pamida Holdings Corporation, 15 341–43
The Pampered Chef Ltd., 18 406–08; 78 292–96 (upd.)
Pamplemousse, **14** 225
Pamplin Corp. *see* R.B. Pamplin Corp.
Pan-Alberta Gas Ltd., **16** 11
Pan-American Life Insurance Company, 48 311–13
Pan American World Airways, Inc., I 115–16; 12 379–81 (upd.)
Pan Asia Paper Company Ltd., **63** 314–16
Pan European Publishing Co., **IV** 611
PanAgora Asset Management Inc., **60** 220
Panalpina World Transport (Holding) Ltd., 47 286–88
Panamerican Beverages, Inc., 47 289–91; **54** 74
PanAmSat Corporation, 46 327–29
Panasonic, **12** 470; **43** 427
Panavia Aircraft GmbH, *see* British Aerospace plc.
Panavision Inc., 24 372–74
PanCanadian Petroleum Ltd., **45** 80
Pancho's Mexican Buffet, Inc., 46 330–32
Panda Management Company, Inc., 35 327–29
Pandick Press Inc., **23** 63
Pandrol, **76** 138, 140
PanEnergy Corporation, *see* Duke Energy Corp.
Panera Bread Company, 44 327–29
Panerai, *see* Vendôme Luxury Group plc.
Panhandle Eastern Corporation, V 691–92 *see also* CMS Energy Corp.
Panhandle Oil Corp., **IV** 498
Panhandle Power & Light Company, **6** 580
Pannon GSM *see* Telenor ASA.
Panocean Storage & Transport *see* Exel plc.
Pansophic Systems Inc., **64** 361
Pantheon Books, *see* Random House, Inc.
Pantone Inc., 53 266–69
The Pantry, Inc., 36 358–60
Pantry Pride Inc., **I** 668; **23** 407–08
Panzani, 84 297–300
Pao de Açúcar *see* Companhia Brasiliera de Distribuiçao.
Papa Aldo's Pizza *see* Papa Murphy's International, Inc.
Papa Gino's Holdings Corporation, Inc., 86 327–30
Papa John's International, Inc., 15 344–46; 71 272–76 (upd.)
Papa Murphy's International, Inc., 54 277–79
Papel e Celulose Catarinense S.A., **73** 205
Papelera del Besos, **53** 24
La Papelera del Plata S.A. *see* Empresas CMPC S.A.
Papelera General, S.A. de C.V., **39** 188
Papeleria Calparsoro S.A., *see* PWA Group.
Papeles Anoia, S.A., **68** 258
Paper Direct, **37** 107–08
The Paper Factory of Wisconsin, Inc., *see* Gibson Greetings, Inc.
Paper Magic Group, **35** 130–31
Paper Software, Inc., **15** 322
PaperMate, **23** 54
Papeteries de Golbey SA, **63** 315
Papeteries de Lancey, 23 366–68
Papeteries de Malaucene S.A.S., **52** 300–01
Les Papeteries du Limousin, **19** 227
Papetti's Hygrade Egg Products, Inc., 39 319–21
Papierfabrik Fahrbrucke GmbH, **64** 275
Papierwerke Waldhof-Aschaffenburg AG *see* PWA Group
Pappas Restaurants, Inc., 76 302–04
Papyrus Design Group, **15** 455
Par Electrical Contractors, Inc. *see* Quanta Services, Inc.
Par Pharmaceutical Companies, Inc., 65 286–88
Para-Med Health Services *see* Extendicare Health Services, Inc.
Parachute Press, **29** 426
ParaData Financial Systems, Inc., **57** 416
The Paradies Shops, Inc., 88 296–99
Paradigm Entertainment, **35** 227
Paradise Creations, **29** 373
Paradise Island Resort and Casino *see* Sun International Hotels Ltd.
Paradise Music & Entertainment, Inc., 42 271–74
Paradores de Turismo de Espana S.A., 73 251–53
Paradyne, **22** 19
Paragon Communications, **44** 372
Paragon Corporate Holdings, Inc., **28** 6, 8
Paragon Vineyard Company, **36** 114
Paragren Technologies Inc., **38** 432
Parallax Medical, Inc., **73** 33
Parallax Software Inc., **38** 70
Parametric Integrated Circuits Inc., **63** 33
Parametric Technology Corp., 16 405–07
Parametrics Corp., **25** 134
Paramount Communications Inc., **16** 338; **19** 403–04; **28** 296
Paramount Fire Insurance Co., **26** 486
Paramount Pictures Corporation, II 154–56; 94 342–47 (upd.)
Paramount Resources Ltd., 87 367–370
Parashop SA, **48** 279
Parasitix Corporation *see* Mycogen Corp.

Parasole Restaurant Holdings, Inc., **38** 117
Paravant Inc., **58** 101
PARCO Co., Ltd. *see* Seibu Department Stores, Ltd.
Parents and Children Together, Inc., **64** 311
ParentWatch, **34** 105
PAREXEL International Corporation, 84 301–304
Parfums Chanel, *see* Chanel.
Parfums Rochas S.A. *see* Wella AG.
Pargas, **I** National Distillers and Chemical Corp.
Paribas *see* Banque de Paris et des Pays-Bas, BNP Paribas Group; Compagnie Financiere de Paribas.
Paridoc and Giant, **12** 153
Paris Bourse, **34** 13
Paris Corporation, 22 411–13
Parisian, Inc., 14 374–76 *see also* Belk, Inc.
Park Acquisitions, Inc., **38** 308
Park-Brannock Shoe Company, **48** 69
Park Corp., 22 414–16
Park Inn International, **11** 178
Park-Ohio Holdings Corp., 17 371–73; 85 319–23 (upd.)
Park Tower Hotel Co. Ltd., **55** 375
Parke, Davis & Co. *see* Warner-Lambert Co.
Parker Brothers, **21** 375; **25** 489
Parker Drilling Company, 28 346–48
Parker-Hannifin Corporation, III 601–03; 24 375–78 (upd.)
Parker Lancasters & Orleans, Inc., *see* Orleans Homebuilders, Inc.
Parker Pattern Works Co., **46** 293
Parker's Pharmacy, Inc., **15** 524
Parks-Belk Co., **19** 324
The Parkside Group, **68** 244–46
Parlex Corporation, 61 279–81
Parmalat Finanziaria SpA, 50 343–46
Parque Arauco S.A., 72 267–69
Parras *see* Compañia Industrial de Parras, S.A. de C.V. (CIPSA).
Parsons Brinckerhoff, Inc., 34 333–36
The Parsons Corporation, 8 415–17; 56 263–67 (upd.)
Parsons International Trading Business, **27** 195
Partech, **28** 346, 348
Partek Corporation, **11** 312; **52** 250
Participating Annuity Life Insurance Co., **21** 14
Partlow Corporation, *see* Danaher Corp.
PartnerRe Ltd., 83 298-301
Partouche SA *see* Groupe Partouche SA.
Parts Plus, **26** 348
Party City Corporation, 54 280–82
PartyLite Gifts, Inc., *see* Blyth, Inc.
Pascagoula Lumber Company, **28** 306
Pasminco Limited *see* Zinifex Ltd.
Pasqua Inc., **28** 64
Pasquier Nutrition, **58** 46
Pass & Seymour, **21** 348–49
Passive Power Products, Inc., **32** 41
Pasta Central, **49** 60
Patagonia *see* Lost Arrow Inc.
Patch Rubber Co., *see* Myers Industries, Inc.
PATCO *see* Philippine Airlines, Inc.
Paterno Wines International, **48** 392
Paternoster Stores plc *see* Kingfisher plc; Woolworth Corp.
Paterson Candy Ltd., **22** 89
Paterson Zochonis *see* PZ Cussons plc.
Pâtes Papiers et Textilose *see* Matussière et Forest SA.
Pathe Communications Co., **IV** 676; **7** 529; **25** 329
Pathé SA, 29 369–71 *see also* Chargeurs International.
Pathfinder Pubs, **57** 411
Pathmark Stores, Inc., 23 369–71
PathoGenesis Corporation, **36** 119
Patient Care, Inc., *see* Chemed Corp.
Patina Group *see* Restaurant Associates Corp.
Patina Oil & Gas Corporation, 24 379–81
Pâtisserie Pasquier, **58** 46
Patrick Industries, Inc., 30 342–45
Patrick Raulet, S.A., **36** 164
Patricof & Company, **24** 45
Patriot American Hospitality, Inc., **21** 184
Patriot Transportation Holding, Inc., 91 371–74
PATS Inc., **36** 159
Patterson Dental Co., 19 289–91
Patterson Pump Company, **57** 159–60
Patterson-UTI Energy, Inc., 55 293–95
Patton Boggs LLP, 71 277–79
Patton Electric Company, Inc., **19** 360
Patton Paint Company *see* PPG Industries, Inc.
Paul Andra KG, **33** 393
Paul Boechat & Cie, **21** 515
Paul C. Dodge Company, **6** 579
Paul Davril, Inc., **25** 258
Paul Harris Stores, Inc., 18 409–12
Paul, Hastings, Janofsky & Walker LLP, 27 357–59
Paul Mueller Company, 65 289–91
Paul Ramsay Group, **41** 323
Paul Reed Smith Guitar Company, 89 345–48
The Paul Revere Corporation, 12 382–83
Paul Revere Insurance, **34** 433
Paul-Son Gaming Corporation, 66 249–51
Paul, Weiss, Rifkind, Wharton & Garrison, 47 292–94
Paulaner Brauerei GmbH & Co. KG, 35 330–33
Pauls Plc, *see* Elementis plc.
Pavex Construction Company *see* Granite Rock Co.
Pawnee Industries, Inc., **19** 415
Paxson Communications Corporation, 33 322–26
Pay 'N Pak Stores, Inc., 9 399–401
Pay 'n Save Corp., **15** 274
Paychex, Inc., 15 347–49; 46 333–36 (upd.)
PayConnect Solutions, **47** 39
Payless Cashways, Inc., 11 384–86; 44 330–33 (upd.)
Payless DIY *see* The Boots Company PLC.
PayLess Drug Stores, *see* Thrifty PayLess, Inc.
Payless ShoeSource, Inc., 18 413–15; 69 288–92 (upd.)
PayPal Inc., 58 266–69
PBF Corp. *see* Paris Corp.
PBL *see* Publishing and Broadcasting Ltd.
PBS *see* Public Broadcasting Stations.
The PBSJ Corporation, 82 269–73
PC Connection, Inc., 37 300–04
PC Globe, Inc., *see* Broderbund Software, Inc.
PC Home Publishing, **61** 246
PCA *see* Packaging Corporation of America.
PCA-Budafok Paperboard Ltd., **12** 377
PCA International, Inc., 62 263–65
PCAS *see* Dynaction S.A.
pcBoat.com, **37** 398
PCC *see* Papel e Celulose Catarinense S.A.
PCC Natural Markets, 94 348–51
PCI NewCo Inc., **36** 159
PCI Services, Inc. *see* Cardinal Health, Inc.
PCL Construction Group Inc., 50 347–49
PCM Uitgevers NV, 53 270–73
PCO *see* Corning Inc.
PCS *see* Potash Corp. of Saskatchewan Inc.
PCS Health Systems Inc., **12** 333; **47** 115, 235–36
PCX *see* Pacific Stock Exchange.
PDA Engineering, **25** 305
PDA Inc., **19** 290
PDI, Inc., 52 272–75
PDL BioPharma, Inc., 90 322–25
PDO *see* Petroleum Development Oman.
PDQ Food Stores Inc., 79 310–13
PDQ Machine, **58** 75
PDS Gaming Corporation, 44 334–37
PDV America, Inc., **31** 113
PDVSA *see* Petróleos de Venezuela S.A.
Peabody Energy Corporation, 10 447–49; 45 330–33 (upd.)
Peabody Holding Company, Inc., IV 169–72
Peace Arch Entertainment Group Inc., 51 286–88
Peachtree Doors, **10** 95
Peak Audio Inc., **48** 92
Peak Oilfield Service Company, *see* Nabors Industries, Inc.
The Peak Technologies Group, Inc., 14 377–80
Peapod, Inc., 30 346–48
Pearl Health Services, **I** 249
Pearl Musical Instrument Company, 78 297–300
Pearle Vision, Inc., 13 390–92
Pearson plc, IV 657–59; 46 337–41 (upd.)
Peasant Restaurants Inc., **30** 330
Pease Industries, **39** 322, 324

Peat Marwick *see* KPMG Peat Marwick.
Peavey Electronics Corporation, 16 408–10; 94 352–56 (upd.)
Peavey Paper Mills, Inc., **26** 362
Pechenganickel MMC, **48** 300
Pechiney S.A., IV 173–75; 45 334–37 (upd.)
PECO Energy Company, 11 387–90 *see also* Exelon Corp.
Pecom Nec S.A., **72** 279–80
Pediatric Services of America, Inc., 31 356–58
Pediatrix Medical Group, Inc., 61 282–85
Pedigree Petfoods, *see* Kal Kan Foods, Inc.
Peebles Inc., 16 411–13; 43 296–99 (upd.)
Peek & Cloppenburg KG, 46 342–45
Peekskill Chemical Works *see* Binney & Smith Inc.
Peet's Coffee & Tea, Inc., 38 338–40
Peg Perego SpA, 88 300–03
Pegasus Solutions, Inc., 75 315–18
PEI *see* Process Engineering Inc.
Pei Cobb Freed & Partners Architects LLP, 57 280–82
Pei Wei Asian Diner, Inc. *see* P.F. Chang's China Bistro, Inc.
Pelican Homestead and Savings, **11** 107
Pelican Products, Inc., 86 331–34
Pelikan Holding AG, 92 296–300
Pella Corporation, 12 384–86; 39 322–25 (upd.); 89 349–53 (upd.)
Pelmorex, Inc., **52** 402
Pelto Oil Corporation, **44** 362
PEM International Ltd., **28** 350
Pemco Aviation Group Inc., 54 283–86
Pemex *see* Petróleos Mexicanos.
Pen Computing Group, **49** 10
Penaflor S.A., 66 252–54
Penauille Polyservices SA, 49 318–21
Penda Corp., **19** 415
Pendaflex *see* Esselte.
Pendaries Petroleum Ltd. *see* Ultra Petroleum Corp.
Pendle Travel Services Ltd. *see* Airtours Plc.
Pendleton Grain Growers Inc., 64 305–08
Pendleton Woolen Mills, Inc., 42 275–78
Penford Corporation, 55 296–99
Pengrowth Gas Corp., **25** 232
The Penguin Group, **46** 337
Penguin Publishing Co. Ltd., **IV** 659
Penhaligon's Ltd, *see* Intimate Brands, Inc.
Peninsula Stores, Ltd. *see* Lucky Stores, Inc.
The Peninsular and Oriental Steam Navigation Company, V 490–93; 38 341–46 (upd.)
Peninsular and Oriental Steam Navigation Company (Bovis Division), I 588–89 *see also* DP World.
Peninsular Power, **6** 602
Penn Central Corp., **10** 71, 73, 547; **70** 34
Penn Champ Co., *see* BISSELL, Inc.
Penn Corp., *see* Western Publishing Group, Inc.
Penn Engineering & Manufacturing Corp., 28 349–51
Penn National Gaming, Inc., 33 327–29
Penn Traffic Company, 13 393–95
Penn Virginia Corporation, 85 324–27
Penn-Western Gas and Electric, **6** 524
PennEnergy, **55** 302
Penney's *see* J.C. Penney Company, Inc.
Pennington Seed, Inc. of Delaware, **58** 60
Pennon Group Plc, 45 338–41
Pennsy Supply, Inc., **64** 98
Pennsylvania Blue Shield, III 325–27 *see also* Highmark Inc.
Pennsylvania Dutch Candies Company *see* Warrell Corp.
Pennsylvania Electric Company, *see* GPU, Inc.
Pennsylvania Farm Bureau Cooperative Association, **7** 17–18
Pennsylvania Gas and Water Company, **38** 51
Pennsylvania General Insurance Company, **48** 431
Pennsylvania House, Inc., **12** 301
Pennsylvania International Raceway *see* Penske Corp.
Pennsylvania Power & Light Company, V 693–94
Pennsylvania Railroad, **10** 71–73; **26** 295
Pennsylvania Steel Foundry and Machine Co., **39** 32
Pennwalt Corporation, I 382–84
PennWell Corporation, 55 300–03
Penny Curtiss Baking Co., Inc., *see* Penn Traffic Co.
Pennzoil-Quaker State Company, IV 488–90; 20 418–22 (upd.); 50 350–55 (upd.)
Penobscot Shoe Company, **70** 221
Penske Corporation, V 494–95; 19 292–94 (upd.); 84 305–309 (upd.)
Pentair, Inc., 7 419–21; 26 361–64 (upd.); 81 281–87 (upd.)
Pental Insurance Company, Ltd., **11** 523
Pentastar Transportation Group, Inc. *see* Dollar Thrifty Automotive Group, Inc.
Pentax Corporation, 78 301–05
Pentech International, Inc., 29 372–74
Pentes Play, Inc., *see* PlayCore, Inc.
Pentland Group plc, 20 423–25
Penton Media, Inc., 27 360–62
Pentzer Corporation *see* Avista Corp.
Penzeys Spices, Inc., 79 314–16
People Express Airlines Inc., I 117–18
People That Love (PTL) Television, *see* International Family Entertainment Inc.
People's Radio Network, **25** 508
People's Trust Company, **49** 412
Peoples Bank & Trust Co., **31** 207
Peoples Energy Corporation, 6 543–44
Peoples Gas Light & Coke Co., **6** 529, 543–44
Peoples Heritage Financial Group, Inc. *see* Banknorth Group, Inc.
Peoples National Bank, **41** 178–79
Peoples Natural Gas Company of South Carolina, **6** 576
Peoples Security Life Insurance Co., *see* Capital Holding Corp.
Peoples Trust of Canada, **49** 411
PeopleServe, Inc., **29** 401
PeopleSoft Inc., 14 381–83; 33 330–33 (upd.) *see also* Oracle Corp.
The Pep Boys—Manny, Moe & Jack, 11 391–93; 36 361–64 (upd.); 81 288–94 (upd.)
PEPCO *see* Portland Electric Power Company; Potomac Electric Power Co.
Pepper *see* J. W. Pepper and Son Inc.
Pepper Hamilton LLP, 43 300–03
Pepperidge Farm, Incorporated, 81 295–300
The Pepsi Bottling Group, Inc., 40 350–53
PepsiAmericas, Inc., 67 297–300 (upd.)
PepsiCo, Inc., I 276–79; 10 450–54 (upd.); 38 347–54 (upd.); 93 333–44 (upd.)
Pequiven *see* Petroquímica de Venezuela S.A.
Perdigao SA, 52 276–79
Perdue Farms Inc., 7 422–24; 23 375–78 (upd.)
Perfect Fit Industries, **17** 182–84
Perfect Pizza Holdings, Ltd. *see* Papa John's International, Inc.
Perfect-Ventil GmbH, *see* Pittway Corp.
Perfetti Van Melle S.p.A., 72 270–73
Performance Food Group Company, 31 359–62
Pergamon Holdings, **15** 83; **50** 125
Pergamon Press, *see* Maxwell Communication Corporation plc; Reed Elsevier plc.
Perini Corporation, 8 418–21; 82 274–79 (upd.)
PerkinElmer, Inc., 7 425–27; 78 306–10 (upd.)
Perkins Coie LLP, 56 268–70
Perkins Engines Ltd., **19** 294
Perkins Family Restaurants, L.P., 22 417–19
Perkins Foods Holdings Ltd., 87 371–374
Perland Environmental Technologies Inc., *see* Perini Corp.
Permal Group, *see* Sequana Capital
Permaneer Corp. *see* Spartech Corp.
Permanent General Companies, Inc., *see* Ingram Industries, Inc.
Permanent Pigments Inc., **25** 71
permanent tsb, **59** 245
Pernod Ricard S.A., I 280–81; 21 399–401 (upd.); 72 274–77 (upd.)
Perot Systems Corporation, 29 375–78
Perrier Corporation of America, **16** 341
Perrier Vittel S.A., **52** 188
Perrigo Company, 12 387–89; 59 330–34 (upd.)
Perry Brothers, Inc., **24** 149
Perry Capital Corp., **28** 138
Perry Drug Stores Inc., **12** 21; **26** 476

Perry Ellis International, Inc., 41 291–94
Perry Manufacturing Co., *see* Aris Industries Inc.
Perry Sports, *see* Koninklijke Vendex KBB N.V. (Royal Vendex KBB N.V.)
Perry Tritech, **25** 103–05
Perry's Ice Cream Company Inc., 90 326–29
Perscombinatie, **IV** 611
The Perseus Books Group, 91 375–78
Personal Care Corp., *see* HMI Industries, Inc.
Personnel Pool of America, **29** 224, 26–27
Perstorp AB, I 385–87; 51 289–92 (upd.)
Pertamina, IV 491–93; 56 271–74 (upd.)
Pertec Computer Corp., **17** 49
Perusahaan Otomobil Nasional Bhd., 62 266–68
Pescanova S.A., 81 301–04
Pesquera Iquique-Guanaye S.A., **69** 142
Pet Foods Plus Inc., **39** 355
Pet Incorporated, 7 428–31
Pet Warehouse Inc., **62** 108
Petaluma Ltd., **54** 227, 229
Petco Animal Supplies, Inc., 29 379–81; 74 231–34 (upd.)
Pete's Brewing Company, 22 420–22
Peter Cundill & Associates Ltd., **15** 504
Peter Gast Shipping GmbH, **7** 40; **41** 42
Peter Kiewit Sons' Inc., 8 422–24
Peter Paul/Cadbury, *see* Hershey Foods Corp.
Peter Piper, Inc., 70 217–19
Peterbilt Motors Company, 89 354–57
Peterhouse Group PLC *see* Babcock International Group PLC.
Peters-Revington Corporation *see* Chromcraft Revington, Inc.
Petersen Cos., **52** 192
Petersen Publishing Company, 21 402–04
Peterson American Corporation, 55 304–06
Peterson Furniture Company, **51** 9
Peterson, Howell & Heather *see* PHH Arval.
Peterson Nut Company, **74** 166
Petit Bateau, **35** 263
Petite Sophisticate *see* The United States Shoe Corp.
PetMed Express, Inc., 81 305–08
Petoseed Co. Inc., **29** 435
Petrie Stores Corporation, 8 425–27
Petro-Canada Limited, IV 494–96
Petro/Chem Environmental Services, Inc., **IV** 411
Petrobrás *see* Petróleo Brasileiro S.A.
Petrobras Energia Participaciones S.A., 72 278–81
Petrocel, S.A., **19** 12
Petrochemicals Industry Co., **IV** 451; **55** 243
Petrochim, **IV** 498
PetroChina Company Ltd., **46** 86
Petrocorp *see* Petroleum Company of New Zealand.
PetroCorp, **63** 409
Petroecuador *see* Petróleos del Ecuador.
PetroFina S.A., IV 497–500; 26 365–69 (upd.)
Petrogal *see* Petróleos de Portugal.
Petrohawk Energy Corporation, 79 317–20
Petrol Ofisi Anonim Sirketi, **IV** 564
Petróleo Brasileiro S.A., IV 501–03
Petróleos de Portugal S.A., IV 504–06
Petróleos de Venezuela S.A., IV 507–09; 74 235–39 (upd.)
Petróleos del Ecuador, IV 510–11
Petróleos Mexicanos, IV 512–14; 19 295–98 (upd.)
Petroleum Authority of Thailand, **IV** 519; **56** 287
Petroleum Development Corp. of the Republic of Korea, **IV** 455
Petroleum Development Oman LLC, IV 515–16
Petroleum Helicopters, Inc., 35 334–36
Petroleum Projects Co., **IV** 414
Petrolgroup, Inc., **6** 441
Petroliam Nasional Bhd (Petronas), 56 275–79 (upd.)
Petrolite Corporation, 15 350–52 *see also* Baker Hughes Inc.
Petrolszolg Karbantartó és Szolgáltató Kft., **70** 195
Petromex *see* Petróleos de Mexico S.A.
Petromin Lubricating Oil Co., *see* Saudi Arabian Oil Co.
Petron Corporation, 58 270–72
Petronas, IV 517–20 *see also* Petroliam Nasional Bhd.
PetroNet, **70** 35
Petronor, **IV** 514, 528
Petroquímica de Venezuela S.A., **74** 236
Petrossian Inc., 54 287–89
PETsMART, Inc., 14 384–86; 41 295–98 (upd.)
Petstuff, Inc., **14** 386; **41** 297
Pettibone Corporation, **19** 365
Petzazz, **14** 386
Peugeot S.A., I 187–88 *see also* PSA Peugeot Citroen S.A.
The Pew Charitable Trusts, 35 337–40
Pez Candy, Inc., 38 355–57
Pfaff-Pegasus of U.S.A. Inc., **15** 385
Pfaltz & Bauer, Inc., **38** 3
The Pfaltzgraff Co. *see* Susquehanna Pfaltzgraff Co.
PFCI *see* Pulte Homes.
PFD Supply, Inc., **47** 304
Pfeiffer GmbH, **69** 38
PFI Acquisition Corp., **17** 184
Pfister GmbH *see* FLSmidth & Co. A/S.
Pfizer Inc., I 661–63; 9 402–05 (upd.); 38 358–67 (upd.); 79 321–33 (upd.)
PFSweb, Inc., 73 254–56
PG&E Corporation, 26 370–73 (upd.)
PGA *see* The Professional Golfers' Association.
PGG/HSC Feed Company LLC, **64** 307
PHAMIS Inc., **64** 190
Phantom Fireworks *see* B.J. Alan Co., Inc.
Phar-Mor Inc., 12 390–92
Pharma Plus Drugmarts Ltd, *see* Oshawa Group Ltd.
Pharma Services Holding Inc. *see* Quintiles Transnational Corp.
PharmaCare Management Services, Inc., **45** 136
Pharmaceutical Resources, Inc. *see* Par Pharmaceutical Companies, Inc.
Pharmacia & Upjohn Inc., I 664–65; 25 374–78 (upd.) *see also* Pfizer Inc.
Pharmacia Hospital Products, **56** 81
Pharmaco-LSR International, Inc., *see* Applied Bioscience International, Inc.
Pharmacy Corporation of America, *see* Beverly Enterprises, Inc.
Pharmanex, Inc., *see* Nu Skin Enterprises, Inc.
Pharmaplan Gruppe, **56** 141
Pharmaprix Ltd., **49** 368
Pharmion Corporation, 91 379–82
Phat Fashions LLC, 49 322–24
Phelps Dodge Corporation, IV 176–79; 28 352–57 (upd.); 75 319–25 (upd.)
PHF Life Insurance Co., **IV** 623
PHH Arval, V 496–97; 53 274–76 (upd.)
PHH Monomers, L.L.C., **61** 113
PHI *see* Pizza Hut, Inc.
PHI, Inc., 80 282–86 (upd.)
Phibro Corporation, **IV** 80; **21** 67
Philadelphia Company, **6** 484, 493
Philadelphia Eagles, 37 305–08
Philadelphia Electric Company, V 695–97 *see also* Exelon Corp.
Philadelphia Gas Works Company, 92 301–05
Philadelphia Media Holdings LLC, 92 306–10
Philadelphia Sports Clubs *see* Town Sports International, Inc.
Philadelphia Suburban Corporation, 39 326–29
Phildar, **37** 22
Phildrew Ventures, **44** 147
PhileoAviation Sdn Bhd, **65** 350
Philharmonic-Symphony Society of New York, Inc. (New York Philharmonic), 69 293–97
Philip Environmental Inc., 16 414–16
Philip Morris Companies Inc., V 405–07; 18 416–19 (upd.); 44 338–43 (upd.) *see also* Kraft Foods Inc.
Philip Services Corp., 73 257–60
Philip Smith Theatrical Enterprises *see* GC Companies, Inc.
Philipp Brothers Chemicals, Inc., **25** 82
Philipp Holzmann AG, 17 374–77
Philippine Airlines, Inc., 6 106–08; 23 379–82 (upd.)
Philippine National Oil Company, **58** 270
Philips, **V** 339; **22** 194
Philips Electronics N.V., 13 400–03 (upd.) *see also* Koninklijke Philips Electronics N.V.
Philips Electronics North America Corp., 13 396–99

N.V. Philips Gloeilampenfabriken, II 78–80 *see also* Philips Electronics N.V.
Philips Medical Systems, **29** 299
Phillip Securities, **16** 14; **43** 8
Phillippe of California, **36** 24
Phillips Colleges Inc., **22** 442; **39** 102
Phillips, de Pury & Luxembourg, 49 325–27
Phillips Foods, Inc., 63 320–22; 90 330–33 (upd.)
Phillips International, Inc., 78 311–14
Phillips Petroleum Company, IV 521–23; 40 354–59 (upd.) *see also* ConocoPhillips.
Phillips-Van Heusen Corporation, 24 382–85
Philmay Holding Inc., **72** 217
Phitech, Inc., **56** 112
PHLCorp., *see* Leucadia National Corp.
Phoenix AG, 68 286–89
Phoenix Assurance Co., *see* Royal & Sun Alliance Insurance Group plc.
Phoenix Footwear Group, Inc., 70 220–22
Phoenix Mecano AG, 61 286–88
The Phoenix Media/Communications Group, 91 383–87
Phoenix Microsystems Inc., **13** 8
PhoneCharge Inc. *see* CheckFree Corporation
Phones 4u Ltd., 85 328–31
Phonogram, **23** 389
Photo Corporation of America *see* PCA International, Inc.
Photo-Me International Plc, 83 302-306
Photo Research Inc. *see* Excel Technology, Inc.
PhotoChannel Networks, Inc., **45** 283
PhotoDisc Inc., **31** 216, 218
PHP Healthcare Corporation, 22 423–25
Phuket Air Catering Company Ltd. *see* Thai Airways International.
PhyCor, Inc., 36 365–69
Physical Measurements Information, **31** 357
Physician Corporation of America, **24** 231
Physician Sales & Service, Inc., 14 387–89
Physio-Control International Corp., 18 420–23
Physiotherapy Associates Inc., **29** 453
Piaget, *see* Vendôme Luxury Group plc.
Piaggio & C. S.p.A., 20 426–29
Piam Pty. Ltd., **48** 364
PIC International Group PLC, 24 386–88 (upd.)
Pic 'N' Save, **16** 298–99
Picard Surgeles, 76 305–07
Piccadilly Cafeterias, Inc., 19 299–302
Pick 'n Pay Stores Ltd., 82 280–83
Pick Pay, **48** 63
Pick Up Stix *see* Carlson Restaurants Worldwide.
Pickfords Ltd. *see* Exel plc.
Pickfords Removals, **49** 22
Pico Ski Area Management Company, **28** 21
Picture Classified Network, **IV** 597
PictureTel Corp., 10 455–57; 27 363–66 (upd.)
Piece Goods Shops, **16** 198
Piedmont Natural Gas Company, Inc., 27 367–69
Piedmont Pulp and Paper Co. *see* Westvaco Corp.
Pier 1 Imports, Inc., 12 393–95; 34 337–41 (upd.)
Pierburg GmbH, *see* Rheinmetall Berlin AG.
Pierce Leahy Corporation, 24 389–92 *see also* Iron Mountain Inc.
Pierce National Life, *see* Liberty Corp.
Piercing Pagoda, Inc., 29 382–84
Pierre & Vacances SA, 48 314–16
Pierre Fabre *see* bioMérieux S.A.
Pietrafesa Corporation, **29** 208
Piezo Electric Product, Inc., **16** 239
Piggly Wiggly Southern, Inc., 13 404–06
Pike Street Industries Inc. *see* Marchex, Inc.
Pilgrim House Group, **50** 134
Pilgrim's Pride Corporation, 7 432–33; 23 383–85 (upd.); 90 334–38 (upd.)
Pilkington Group Limited, II 724–27; 34 342–47 (upd.); 87 375–383 (upd.)
Pillar Corp., **52** 185
Pilliod Furniture, Inc., *see* LADD Furniture, Inc.
Pillowtex Corporation, 19 303–05; 41 299–302 (upd.)
Pillsbury Company, II 555–57; 13 407–09 (upd.); 62 269–73 (upd.)
Pillsbury Madison & Sutro LLP, 29 385–88
Pilot Air Freight Corp., 67 301–03
Pilot Corporation, 49 328–30
Pilot Pen Corporation of America, 82 284–87
Pilsa, **55** 189
PIMCO Advisors, **57** 20
Pin 'n' Save, **50** 98
Pinault-Printemps-Redoute S.A., 19 306–09 (upd.) *see also* PPR S.A.
Pindar *see* G A Pindar & Son Ltd.
Pine Tree Casting *see* Sturm, Ruger & Company, Inc.
Pinelands, Inc., **26** 33
Pinelands Water Company, **45** 275, 277
Ping An Insurance Company Ltd., **65** 104
Pinguely-Haulotte SA, 51 293–95
Pinkerton's Inc., 9 406–09 *see also* Securitas AB.
Pinnacle Airlines Corp., 73 261–63
Pinnacle Art and Frame, **31** 436
Pinnacle Distribution, **52** 429
Pinnacle Fitness, **25** 42
Pinnacle Global Group Inc. *see* Sanders Morris Harris Group Inc.
Pinnacle Ltd., **70** 325
Pinnacle West Capital Corporation, 6 545–47; 54 290–94 (upd.)
Pinole Point Steel, **63** 272
Pinto Island Metals Company, **15** 116
Pioneer Asphalt Co., **36** 146–47
Pioneer Bank, **41** 312
Pioneer Concrete Services Ltd. *see* Pioneer International Limited
Pioneer Corporations, **62** 374
Pioneer Cotton Mill, **12** 503
Pioneer Electronic Corporation, III 604–06; 28 358–61 (upd.) *see also* Agilysys Inc.
Pioneer Engineering and Manufacturing Co., **55** 32
Pioneer Federal Savings Bank, *see* First Hawaiian, Inc.
Pioneer Financial Corp., **11** 447
Pioneer Hi-Bred International, Inc., 9 410–12; 41 303–06 (upd.)
Pioneer Hotel Inc. *see* Archon Corp.
Pioneer International Limited, III 728–30
Pioneer Natural Resources Company, 59 335–39
Pioneer Plastics Corporation, **31** 399–400
Pioneer-Standard Electronics Inc., 19 310–14 *see also* Agilysys Inc.
Pipasa, **41** 329
Pipe Line Service Company *see* Plexco.
Pipelife International GmbH, **70** 363
Piper Impact, Inc., **62** 289
Piper Jaffray Companies Inc., 22 426–30 *see also* U.S. Bancorp.
Pirelli & C. S.p.A., V 249–51; 15 353–56 (upd.); 75 326–31 (upd.)
Piscines Desjoyaux S.A., 84 310–313
Pitman Company, 58 273–75
Pitney Bowes, Inc., III 156–58, 159; **19 315–18 (upd.); 47 295–99 (upd.)**
Pittman Company, **28** 350
Pittsburgh Brewing Company, 76 308–11
Pittsburgh Chemical Co. *see* United States Steel Corp.
Pittsburgh National Corporation *see* PNC Financial Corp.
Pittsburgh Paint & Glass *see* PPG Industries, Inc.
Pittsburgh Plate Glass Co. *see* PPG Industries, Inc.
Pittsburgh Steelers Sports, Inc., 66 255–57
The Pittston Company, IV 180–82; 19 319–22 (upd.) *see also* The Brink's Co.
Pittway Corporation, 9 413–15; 33 334–37 (upd.)
Pivot Rules, Inc. *see* Bluefly, Inc.
Pivotpoint, Inc., **55** 258
Pixar Animation Studios, 34 348–51
Pixel Semiconductor, **11** 57
Pixelworks, Inc., 69 298–300
Pizitz, Inc., **19** 324
Pizza Dispatch *see* Dominos's Pizza, Inc.
Pizza Hut Inc., 7 434–35; 21 405–07 (upd.)
Pizza Inn, Inc., 46 346–49
Pizzeria Uno, **25** 178
PJ's Coffee, **64** 327
PJS Publications, **22** 442
PKF International, 78 315–18
Place du Marché S.A., **76** 355
Place Two *see* Nordstrom, Inc.

Placer Dome Inc., 20 430–33; 61 289–93 (upd.)
Plain Dealer Publishing Company, 92 311–14
Plains Cotton Cooperative Association, 57 283–86
Plains Dairy, **53** 21
Planar Systems, Inc., 61 294–97
Planet Hollywood International, Inc., 18 424–26; 41 307–10 (upd.)
Planet Smoothie Franchises LLC, **64** 327–28
Planet Waves, **48** 232
Plantation Pipe Line Company, 68 290–92
Plante & Moran, LLP, 71 280–83
Plas-Techs, Inc., **15** 35
Plastibec Ltd. *see* Royal Group Technologies Ltd.
Plastic Containers, Inc., *see* Viatech Continental Can Company, Inc.
Plastic Engineered Products Company *see* Ballard Medical Products.
Plastic Parts, Inc., *see* Myers Industries, Inc.
Plastic-Plate, Inc., **61** 158, 160
Plasto Bambola *see* BRIO AB.
Plate Glass Group, **24** 450
Platinum Entertainment, Inc., 35 341–44
Platinum Holdings, **74** 146
PLATINUM Technology, Inc., 14 390–92 *see also* Computer Associates International, Inc.
Plato Learning, Inc., 44 344–47
Platte River Insurance Company, **60** 16
Play by Play Toys & Novelties, Inc., 26 374–76
Play It Again Sam (PIAS), **44** 164
Playboy Enterprises, Inc., 18 427–30
PlayCore, Inc., 27 370–72
Players International, Inc., 22 431–33
Playmates Toys, 23 386–88
Playmaxx, Inc., **55** 132
Playmobil *see* geobra Brandstätter GmbH & Co. KG.
Playskool, Inc., 25 379–81 *see also* Hasbro, Inc.
Playtex Products, Inc., 15 357–60
PLC *see* Prescription Learning Corp.
Pleasant Company, 27 373–75 *see also* American Girl, Inc.
Pleasant Holidays LLC, 62 274–76
Plessey Company, PLC, II 81–82 *see also* Marconi plc.
Plex Co., Ltd., **55** 48
Plexco, **7** 30–31
Plexus Corporation, 35 345–47; 80 287–91 (upd.)
Plezall Wipers, Inc., **15** 502
Plitt Theatres, Inc. *see* Cineplex Odeon Corp.
PLIVA d.d., 70 223–25
PLLN C.V. Partnership, **72** 265
Plough Inc. *see* Schering-Plough.
Plum Associates, **12** 270
Plum Creek Timber Company, Inc., 43 304–06
Pluma, Inc., 27 376–78
Plus Mark, Inc., *see* American Greetings Corp.
Plus-Ultra, **II** 196
Plus Vita, **36** 162
Pluto Technologies International Inc., **38** 72
Ply Gem Industries Inc., 12 396–98
Plymouth Mills Inc., **23** 66
PM Management Incorporated, **74** 234
PM Resources, Inc., **74** 381
PMC Contract Research AB, **21** 425
PMI Corporation *see* Physical Measurements Information
The PMI Group, Inc., 49 331–33
PMP Ltd., 72 282–84
PMR Corporation *see* Psychiatric Solutions, Inc.
PMS Consolidated, *see* M. A. Hanna Co.
PMT Services, Inc., 24 393–95
PN Gaya Motor, **56** 284
The PNC Financial Services Group Inc., II 342–43; 13 410–12 (upd.); 46 350–53 (upd.)
Pneumo Abex Corp., **I** 456–58; **III** 512; **38** 293–94
PNL *see* Pacific Northwest Laboratories.
PNM Resources Inc., 51 296–300 (upd.)
PNP *see* Pacific Northwest Power Co.
POAS *see* Türkiye Petrolleri Anonim Ortakliği
POB Polyolefine Burghausen GmbH, **IV** 487
Pocahontas Foods USA, **31** 359, 361
Pochet SA, 55 307–09
Poe & Associates, Inc., **41** 63–64
Pogo Producing Company, 39 330–32
Pohang Iron and Steel Company Ltd., IV 183–85 *see also* POSCO.
Poland Spring Natural Spring Water Co., **31** 229
Polar Air Cargo Inc., 60 237–39
Polar S.A., **59** 418
Polaris Industries Inc., 12 399–402; 35 348–53 (upd.); 77 330–37 (upd.)
Polaroid Corporation, III 607–09; 7 436–39 (upd.); 28 362–66 (upd.); 93 345–53 (upd.)
Polbeth Packaging Limited, **12** 377
Policy Management Systems Corporation, 11 394–95
Policy Studies, Inc., 62 277–80
Poliet S.A., 33 338–40
Polioles, S.A. de C.V., **19** 10, 12
Politos, S.A. de C.V., **23** 171
Polk Audio, Inc., 34 352–54
Pollenex Corp., **19** 360
Polo/Ralph Lauren Corporation, 12 403–05; 62 281–85 (upd.)
Polser, **19** 49, 51
Polski Koncern Naftowy ORLEN S.A., 77 338–41
Polskie Linie Lotnicze S.A. *see* LOT Polish Airlines.
Poly-Glas Systems, Inc., **21** 65
Polydesign, *see* Randstad Holding n.v.
Polydor B.V., **23** 389
Polydor KK, **23** 390
Polygon Networks Inc., **41** 73
PolyGram N.V., 23 389–92
Polyken Technologies, *see* Kendall International, Inc.
Polymer Technologies Corporation, **26** 287
PolyMedica Corporation, 77 342–45
PolyOne Corporation, 87 384–395 (upd.)
Polyphase Corporation *see* Overhill Corp.
Polysius AG, **IV** 89
Pomare Ltd., 88 304–07
Pomeroy Computer Resources, Inc., 33 341–44
Pomeroy's, **16** 61; **50** 107
Pommery et Greno, **II** 475
Pompes Guinard S.A., **62** 217
Ponderosa Steakhouse, 15 361–64
Ponderosa System Inc., **12** 199
Pont-à-Mousson S.A., *see* Compagnie de Saint-Gobain.
Pont Royal SA, **48** 316
Ponto Frio Bonzao, **22** 321
Pontos GmbH, **56** 152
Poof-Slinky, Inc., 61 298–300
Poore Brothers, Inc., 44 348–50
Pop Warner Little Scholars, Inc., 86 335–38
Pop.com, **43** 144
Pope & Talbot, Inc., 12 406–08; 61 301–05 (upd.)
Pope Cable and Wire B.V. *see* Belden CDT Inc.
Pope Resources LP, 74 240–43
Popeyes Chicken & Biscuits *see* AFC Enterprises, Inc.
Pophitt Cereals, Inc., **22** 337
Poppe Tyson Inc., **23** 479; **25** 91
Popsicle, *see* Unilever PLC.
Popular Club Plan, *see* J. Crew Group Inc.
Popular, Inc., 41 311–13
Popular Merchandise, Inc., *see* J. Crew Group Inc.
The Porcelain and Fine China Companies Ltd., 69 301–03
Poron, S.A., **42** 268–69
Porsche AG, 13 413–15; 31 363–66 (upd.)
Port Arthur Finance Corp., **37** 309
The Port Authority of New York and New Jersey, 48 317–20
Port Dickson Power Sdn. Bhd., **36** 435–36
Port Imperial Ferry Corporation, 70 226–29
Port of London Authority, **48** 317
Port Stockton Food Distributors, Inc., *see* Smart & Final, Inc.
Portage Industries Corp. *see* Spartech Corp.
El Portal Group, Inc., **58** 371
Portal Software, Inc., 47 300–03
Porter-Cable Corporation, **26** 361–63
Porter Chadburn plc, **28** 252
Portex, **25** 431
Portia Management Services Ltd., **30** 318

Portillo's Restaurant Group, Inc., 71 284–86
Portland General Corporation, 6 548–51
Portland General Electric, **45** 313; **50** 103
Portland Plastics, **25** 430–31
Portland Shipyard LLC *see* Cascade General Inc.
Portland Trail Blazers, 50 356–60
Portland-Zementwerke Heidelberg A.G., **23** 326
Portmeirion Group plc, 88 308–11
Portnet, **6** 435
Portsmouth & Sunderland, **35** 242, 244
Portucel *see* Grupo Portucel Soporcel.
Portugal Telecom SGPS S.A., 69 304–07
Portugalia, **46** 398
Posadas *see* Grupo Posadas, S.A. de C.V.
POSCO, 57 287–91 (upd.)
Posful Corporation, **68** 9
Positive Response Television, Inc., *see* National Media Corp.
Post Office Group, V 498–501
Post Properties, Inc., 26 377–79
Postabank és Takarékpénztár Rt., **69** 155, 157
La Poste, V 470–72
Posterscope Worldwide, 70 230–32
Posti- Ja Telelaitos, 6 329–31
PostScript, *see* Fay's Inc.
Potain SAS, **59** 274, 278
Potash Corporation of Saskatchewan Inc., 18 431–33
Potbelly Sandwich Works, Inc., 83 307-310
Potelco, Inc. *see* Quanta Services, Inc.
Potlatch Corporation, 8 428–30; 34 355–59 (upd.); 87 396–403 (upd.)
Potomac Edison Company, **38** 39–40
Potomac Electric Power Company, 6 552–54
Potter & Brumfield Inc., 11 396–98
Pottery Barn, *see* Williams-Sonoma, Inc.
Pottsville Behavioral Counseling Group, **64** 311
Pou Chen Corporation, 81 309–12
Poul Due Jensen Foundation *see* Grundfos Group
Poulan/Weed Eater *see* White Consolidated Industries Inc.
Powell Duffryn plc, 31 367–70
Powell Group, **33** 32
Powell's Books, Inc., 40 360–63
Power Applications & Manufacturing Company, Inc., **6** 441
Power Corporation of Canada, 36 370–74 (upd.); 85 332–39 (upd.)
Power-One, Inc., 79 334–37
Power Parts Co., **7** 358
Power Team, *see* SPX Corp.
PowerBar Inc., 44 351–53
Powercor *see* PacifiCorp.
POWEREDCOM Inc., **74** 348
Powergen PLC, 11 399–401; 50 361–64 (upd.)
Powerhouse Technologies, Inc., 27 379–81
PowerSoft Corp., **15** 374
Powerteam Electrical Services Ltd., **64** 404
Powertel Inc., **48** 130
Powerware Corporation *see* Eaton Corp.
POZEN Inc., 81 313–16
PP&L *see* Pennsylvania Power & Light Co.
PPB Group Berhad, 57 292–95
PPG Industries, Inc., III 731–33; 22 434–37 (upd.); 81 317–23 (upd.)
PPI *see* Precision Pattern Inc.
PPI Two Corporation, **64** 334
PPL Corporation, 41 314–17 (upd.)
PPR S.A., 74 244–48 (upd.)
PR Holdings, **23** 382
PR Newswire, 35 354–56
PRS *see* Paul Reed Smith Guitar Co.
Practical Business Solutions, Inc., **18** 112
PracticeWorks.com, **69** 33–34
Prada Holding B.V., 45 342–45
Prairie Farms Dairy, Inc., 47 304–07
Prairielands Energy Marketing, Inc., *see* MDU Resources Group, Inc.
Prakla Seismos, **17** 419
Pranda Jewelry plc, 70 233–35
Prandium Inc., **51** 70
Pratt & Whitney, 9 416–18
Pratt Hotel Corporation, **21** 275
Pratta Electronic Materials, Inc., **26** 425
Praxair, Inc., 11 402–04; 48 321–24 (upd.)
Praxis Bookstore Group LLC, 90 339–42
Praxis Corporation, **30** 499
Pre Finish Metals Incorporated, **63** 270–71
Pre-Paid Legal Services, Inc., 20 434–37
PreAnalytiX, **39** 335
Precept Foods, LLC, **54** 168
Precise Fabrication Corporation, **33** 257
Precise Imports Corp., **21** 516
Precision Castparts Corp., 15 365–67
Precision Engineered Products, Inc., **70** 142
Precision Husky Corporation, **26** 494
Precision IBC, Inc., **64** 20–21
Precision Interconnect Corporation, *see* AMP Inc.
Precision Moulds, Ltd., *see* Mattel, Inc.
Precision Optical Industry Company, Ltd. *see* Canon Inc.
Precision Pattern Inc., **36** 159
Precision Power, Inc., **21** 514
Precision Response Corporation, **47** 420
Precision Software Corp., **14** 319
Precision Spring of Canada, Ltd., **55** 305
Precision Stainless Inc., **65** 289
Precision Standard Inc. *see* Pemco Aviation Group Inc.
Precision Tool, Die & Machine Company Inc., **51** 116–17
Precisionaire *see* Flanders Corp.
Precoat Metals, **54** 331
Predica, **II** 266
Prefco Corporation, **57** 56–57
Preferred Medical Products *see* Ballard Medical Products.
Preferred Products, Inc., *see* Supervalu Inc.
PREINCO Holdings, Inc., *see* Transatlantic Holdings, Inc.
PREL&P *see* Portland Railway Electric Light & Power Co.
Premark International, Inc., III 610–12 *see also* Illinois Tool Works Inc.
Premcor Inc., 37 309–11
Premier Cement Ltd., **64** 98
Premier Industrial Corporation, 9 419–21
Premier Insurance Co., **26** 487
Premier Medical Services, **31** 357
Premier Milk Pte Ltd., **54** 117
Premier One Products, Inc., **37** 285
Premier Parks, Inc., 27 382–84 *see also* Six Flags, Inc.
Premier Radio Networks, Inc., **23** 292, 294
Premier Rehabilitation Centers, **29** 400
Premier Sport Group Inc., **23** 66
Premiere Labels Inc., **53** 236
Premium Standard Farms, Inc., 30 353–55
PremiumWear, Inc., 30 356–59
Premix-Marbletite Manufacturing Co. Inc. *see* Imperial Industries, Inc.
Prentice Hall Inc., **I** 453; **IV** 672; **19** 405; **23** 503
Prescott Investors, **14** 303; **50** 311
Preserver Group, Inc., 44 354–56
President Baking Co., **36** 313
President Casinos, Inc., 22 438–40
President Riverboat Casino-Mississippi Inc., **21** 300
Presidents Island Steel & Wire Company *see* Laclede Steel Co.
Presley Cos., **59** 422
Presses de la Cité *see* Groupe de la Cité.
Pressman Toy Corporation, 56 280–82
Presstar Printing, **25** 183
Presstek, Inc., 33 345–48
Pressware International, **12** 377
Prestage Farms, **46** 83
Prestel Verlag, **66** 123
Prestige Fragrance & Cosmetics, Inc., **22** 158
The Prestige Group plc., *see* Gallaher Group Plc.
Prestige International, **33** 284
Prestige Leather Creations, **31** 435–36
Prestige Properties, **23** 388
Presto Products, Inc., *see* Reynolds and Reynolds Co.; Reynolds Metals Co.
Preston Corporation, 6 421–23
Prestone Products Corp., **22** 32; **26** 349
Prestwick Mortgage Group, **25** 187
Pret A Manger, **63** 280, 284–85
Pretty Good Privacy, Inc., **25** 349
Pretty Neat Corp., *see* Goody Products, Inc.
Pretty Paper Inc., *see* Thomas Nelson Inc.
Pretzel Time *see* Mrs. Fields' Original Cookies, Inc.
Pretzelmaker *see* Mrs. Fields' Original Cookies, Inc.
Pretzels Inc., *see* J & J Snack Foods Corp.
Preussag AG, 17 378–82; 42 279–83 (upd.)

PreussenElektra Aktiengesellschaft, V 698–700 *see also* E.On AG.
Preval, **19** 49–50
Previews, Inc., **21** 96
PreVision Marketing LLC *see* Valassis Communications Inc.
PRG-Schultz International, Inc., 73 264–67
Priba, **26** 158, 160
Pribina, **25** 85
Price & Pierce International Inc. *see* Gould Paper Corporation
Price Chopper Supermarkets *see* The Golub Corp.
Price Communications Corporation, 42 284–86
Price Company Ltd *see* Abitibi-Consolidated, Inc.
The Price Company, V 162–64 *see also* Costco Wholesale Corp.
Price Enterprises, Inc., **14** 395
Price, McCormick & Co., **26** 451
Price Pfister, Inc., 70 236–39
Price Rite, **25** 67
Price Waterhouse LLP, 9 422–24 *see also* PricewaterhouseCoopers
PriceCostco, Inc., 14 393–95 *see also* Costco Wholesale Corp.
Pricel *see* Chargeurs.
Priceline.com Incorporated, 57 296–99
Priceline.com Inc., **58** 118–19
Pricesearch Ltd Co, **48** 224
PriceSmart, Inc., 71 287–90
PricewaterhouseCoopers, 29 389–94 (upd.)
PRIDE Enterprises *see* Prison Rehabilitative Industries and Diversified Enterprises, Inc.
Pride International, Inc., 78 319–23
Pride Petroleum Services *see* DeKalb Genetics Corp.
Prima Gold International Company Limited *see* Pranda Jewlry plc.
Prima S.A., **67** 201
Primagas GmbH, **55** 347
Primark Corp., 13 416–18 *see also* Thomson Corp.
Primary Coatings, Inc., **51** 190
Prime Capital Services, Inc. *see* Gilman & Ciocia, Inc.
Prime Care International, Inc., **36** 367
Prime Computer, Inc. *see* Computervision Corp.
Prime Hospitality Corporation, 52 280–83
Prime Motor Inns Inc., **IV** 718; **11** 177
Prime Service, Inc., **28** 40
Prime Telecommunications Corporation, *see* LDDS-Metro Communications, Inc.
Primedex Health Systems, Inc., 25 382–85
Primedia Inc., 22 441–43
Primera Group, **71** 151, 153
Primergy Corp., **39** 261
Primerica Corporation, I 612–14
Primerica Financial Services, Inc., **30** 124; **59** 121, 125
PriMerit Bank, **19** 412
PrimeSource, **26** 542
Primestar, **38** 176
PRIMESTAR Partners L.P., **28** 241
PrimeWood, Inc., **61** 398
Primex Fibre Ltd., *see* Sanyo-Kokusaku Pulp Co., Ltd.
Prince Co., *see* Borden, Inc.
Prince Gardner Company, **23** 21
Prince Golf International, Ltd., **23** 450
Prince Holding Corporation, **26** 231; **59** 252
Prince Sports Group, Inc., 15 368–70
Prince William Bank, **II** 337
Princes Ltd., 76 312–14
Princess Cruise Lines, 22 444–46
Princess Hotel Group, **21** 353
Princess Hotels International Inc., **45** 82
Princess Metropole, **21** 354
Princeton Gas Service Company, **6** 529
The Princeton Review, Inc., 42 287–90
Princeton Telecommunications Corporation, **26** 38
Principal Health Care, **59** 139
Principal Mutual Life Insurance Company, III 328–30
Print Technologies, Inc., *see* Miner Group Int.
PrintNation Inc., **58** 275
Printpack, Inc., 68 293–96
Printrak, A Motorola Company, 44 357–59
Printronix, Inc., 18 434–36
Priority Records, **22** 194; **69** 351
Pripps Ringnes AB, *see* Orkla ASA.
Prison Rehabilitative Industries and Diversified Enterprises, Inc. (PRIDE), 53 277–79
Prisunic SA *see* PPR SA.
Pritchard Corporation *see* Black & Veatch, Inc.
Private Colleges and Universities, Inc., **55** 15
PrivatPort, **70** 311
Prize Energy, **59** 336
Pro-Build Holdings Inc. *see* Fidelity Investments Inc.
Pro-Fac Cooperative, Inc., *see* Birds Eye Foods, Inc.
Pro-Lawn, **19** 250
Pro-Line Corporation, **36** 26
Pro-optik AG, **31** 203
Probe Exploration Inc., **25** 232
Probe Technology Corporation, **76** 231
Process Engineering Inc., **21** 108
Process Systems International, **21** 108
Processing Technologies International *see* Food Ingredients Technologies.
Procor Limited, *see* The Marmon Group, Inc.
The Procter & Gamble Company, III 50–53; 8 431–35 (upd.); 26 380–85 (upd.); 67 304–11 (upd.)
Proctor-Silex *see* Hamilton Beach/Proctor-Silex Inc.
Prodega Ltd *see* Bon Appetit Holding AG.
Prodigy Communications Corporation, 34 360–62
Prodigy Consulting Inc., **51** 198
Product Components, Inc., **19** 415
Production Association Kirishinefteorgsintez, **48** 378
Production Management Companies Inc., **65** 334
Productivity Point International Inc., **54** 192–93
Produits Jaeger, *see* Kerry Group plc.
Produits Ronald Inc. *see* Lassonde Industries Inc.
Proeza S.A. de C.V., 82 288–91
Profarmaco Nobel S.r.l., **16** 69
Profertil S.A., **73** 23
Professional Bull Riders Inc., 55 310–12
Professional Detailing, Inc. *see* PDI, Inc.
Professional Education Systems, Inc., **53** 319
The Professional Golfers' Association of America, 41 318–21
Professional Health-Care Resources, **50** 123
Professional Underwriters Liability Insurance Company, **55** 128
Proffitt's, Inc., 19 323–25 *see also* Belk, Inc.
Profile Extrusion Company, *see* Malt-O-Meal Co.
Profimatics, Inc., **11** 66
PROFITCo., *see* Bankers Trust New York Corp.
Progenx, Inc., **47** 221
Programmer's Paradise, Inc., 81 324–27
Progress Energy, Inc., 74 249–52
Progress Software Corporation, 15 371–74
Progressive Bagel Concepts, Inc. *see* Einstein/Noah Bagel Corp.
Progressive Corporation, 11 405–07; 29 395–98 (upd.)
Progressive Distributions Systems, **44** 334
Progressive Distributors, *see* Hannaford Bros. Co.
Progressive Networks, Inc. *see* RealNetworks, Inc.
Project Carriers *see* Hansa Linie.
Projexions Video Supply, Inc., **24** 96
Projiis, *see* Société Générale.
ProLab Nutrition, Inc., **49** 275, 277
Proland, *see* ECS S.A.
Proler International Corp., *see* Schnitzer Steel Industries, Inc.
ProLogis, 57 300–02
Promarkt Holding GmbH, *see* Kingfisher plc.
Promeca S.A. de C.V., **72** 262
Promodès SA, **26** 158, 161; **37** 21; **64** 66, 69
Promonte *see* Telenor ASA.
Promotional Graphics, **15** 474
Promus Companies, Inc., 9 425–27 *see also* Hilton Hotels Corp.
Propaganda Films, Inc., **23** 389, 391
Property Automation Software Corporation, **49** 290
Property Intelligence PLC, **73** 97
Prophecy Ltd., **55** 24
ProSiebenSat.1 Media AG, 54 295–98

Proskauer Rose LLP, **47** **308–10**
ProSource Distribution Services, Inc. *see* Onex Corp.
The Prospect Group, Inc., **11** 188
Prospect Provisions, Inc. *see* King Kullen Grocery Co., Inc.
Protan & Fagertun, **25** 464
Protection One, Inc., **32** **372–75**
Protective Insurance Company, **51** 37, 39
Protiviti, **70** 284
Proton *see* Perusahaan Otomobil Nasional Bhd.
Protravel S.A., **69** 7
Proveedora de Seguridad del Golfo, S.A. de C.V., **45** 425–26
Provell Inc., **58** **276–79 (upd.)**
Proventus Handels AB, **35** 362
Providence Health System, **90** **343–47**
The Providence Journal Company, **28** **367–69**; **30** 15
The Providence Service Corporation, **64** **309–12**
Providence Steam and Gas Pipe Co. *see* Grinnell Corp.
Provident Bankshares Corporation, **85** **340–43**
Provident Life and Accident Insurance Company of America, **III** **331–33** *see also* UnumProvident Corp.
Provident National Corporation *see* PNC Financial Corp.
Providian Financial Corporation, **52** **284–90 (upd.)**
Provigo Inc., **II** **651–53**; **51** **301–04 (upd.)**
Provimi S.A., **80** **292–95**
Province Healthcare Company, **69** 236
Les Provinces Réunies, *see* Commercial Union PLC.
Provincetown-Boston Airlines, **I** 118
Provincial Gas Company, **6** 526
Provincial Newspapers Ltd., **28** 502
PROWA, **22** 89
Proximity Technology, **23** 210
Prudential-Bache Trade Corporation, **II** 51; **21** 331
Prudential Financial Inc., **III** **337–41**; **30** **360–64 (upd.)**; **82** **292–98 (upd.)**
Prudential Oil & Gas, Inc. *see* Gulf States Utilities Co.
Prudential plc, **III** **334–36**; **48** **325–29 (upd.)**
Prudential Steel Ltd., **59** 280, 282
Prymetall GmbH & Co. KG, **62** 253
PS Business Parks, Inc., **52** 291
PSA *see* Pacific Southwest Airlines.
PSA Peugeot Citroen S.A., **28** **370–74 (upd.)**; **54** 126
PSB Company, **36** 517
PSCCo. *see* Public Service Company of Colorado.
PSE, Inc., *see* Destec Energy, Inc.
PSF *see* Premium Standard Farms, Inc.
PSI *see* Process Systems International.
PSI Resources, **6** **555–57**
Psion PLC, **45** **346–49**
Psychemedics Corporation, **89** **358–61**
Psychiatric Solutions, Inc., **68** **297–300**
Psychological Corp., *see* Harcourt Brace and Co.
PT Abacus Distribution System Indonesia, **58** 140
PT Aerowisata, **58** 140
PT Astra International Tbk, **56** **283–86**
PT Bank Buana Indonesia Tbk, **60** **240–42**
PT Bank MayBank Indocorp, **72** 217
PT Capura Angkasa, **58** 140
PT Indosat Tbk, **93** **354–57**
Ptarmigan Airways Ltd., **56** 39
PTI Communications, Inc. *see* Pacific Telecom, Inc.
PTN Publishing, Inc., **56** 73
PTT Nederland N.V., **30** 393–94
PTT Public Company Ltd., **56** **287–90**
PTT Telecom BV, **V** 299–301
PTV *see* Österreichische Post- und Telegraphenverwaltung.
Pubco Corporation, **17** **383–85**
Publi-Graphics, **16** 168
Public Broadcasting Stations, **29** 426; **51** 309
Public/Hacienda Resorts, Inc. *see* Santa Fe Gaming Corp.
Public Savings Insurance Co., *see* Capital Holding Corp.
Public Service Company of Colorado, **6** **558–60**
Public Service Company of Indiana *see* PSI Energy.
Public Service Company of New Hampshire, **21** **408–12**; **55** **313–18 (upd.)**
Public Service Company of New Mexico, **6** **561–64** *see also* PNM Resources Inc.
Public Service Corporation of New Jersey, **44** 360
Public Service Enterprise Group Inc., **V** **701–03**; **44** **360–63 (upd.)**
Public Service Market *see* The Golub Corp.
Public Storage, Inc., **21** **52** **291–93**
Publicaciones Citem, S.A. de C.V., **39** 188
Publicis Groupe, **19** **329–32**; **77** **346–50 (upd.)**
PubliGroupe, **49** 424
Publishers Clearing House, **23** **393–95**; **64** **313–16 (upd.)**
Publishers Group, Inc., **35** **357–59**
Publishers Paper Co., **IV** 677–78
Publishing and Broadcasting Limited, **54** **299–302**
Publix Super Markets Inc., **7** **440–42**; **31** **371–74 (upd.)**
Pubmaster Finance Ltd, **70** 242
Puck Holdings, **35** 474, 476
Puck Lazaroff Inc. *see* The Wolfgang Puck Food Company, Inc.
Pueblo Xtra International, Inc., **47** **311–13**
Puerto Rican Aqueduct and Sewer Authority, **6** 441
Puerto Rico Electric Power Authority, **47** **314–16**
Puget Mill Company, *see* Pope and Talbot, Inc.
Puget Sound Alaska Van Lines *see* Alaska Hydro-Train.
Puget Sound Energy Inc., **6** **565–67**; **50** **365–68 (upd.)**
Puig Beauty and Fashion Group S.L., **60** **243–46**
Pulaski Furniture Corporation, **33** **349–52**; **80** **296–99 (upd.)**
Pulitzer Inc., **15** **375–77**; **58** **280–83 (upd.)**
Pulsar Internacional S.A., **21** **413–15**
Pulse Engineering, Inc., **29** 461
Pulte Homes, Inc., **8** **436–38**; **42** **291–94 (upd.)**
Puma AG Rudolf Dassler Sport, **35** **360–63**
Pumpkin Masters, Inc., **48** **330–32**
Punch International N.V., **66** **258–60**
Punch Taverns plc, **70** **240–42**
Punter Southall *see* Sanlam Ltd.
Puratos S.A./NV, **92** **315–18**
Pure-Gar, Inc., **49** 276
Pure Resources, Inc., **71** 382
Pure World, Inc., **72** **285–87**
Purina Mills, Inc., **32** **376–79**
Puris Inc., **14** 316
Puritan-Bennett Corporation, **13** **419–21**
Purity Supreme, Inc., *see* Supermarkets General Holdings Corp.
Purolator Courier, Inc., **6** 390; **16** 397
Purolator Products Company, **21** **416–18**; **74** **253–56 (upd.)**
Puros de Villa Gonzales, **23** 465
Purup-Eskofot, **44** 44
Push Records, Inc., **42** 271
Putnam Investments Inc. *see* Marsh & McLennan Companies, Inc.
Putnam Plastics Corporation *see* Memry Corp.
Putt-Putt Golf Courses of America, Inc., **23** **396–98**
PVC Container Corporation, **67** **312–14**
PW Eagle, Inc., **48** **333–36**
PWA Group, **IV** **323–25** *see also* Svenska Cellulosa.
PWS Holding Corporation, **26** 47
PWT Projects Ltd., **22** 89
PWT Worldwide, *see* Thames Water plc.
Pyramid Breweries Inc., **33** **353–55**
Pyramid Communications, Inc., **IV** 623
Pyramid Companies, **54** **303–05**
Pyxis Innovations *see* Alticor Inc.
PZ Cussons plc, **72** **288–90**

Q

Q&B Foods Inc., **57** 202–03
Q.A.S. Quality Airport Services Israel Ltd., **70** 311
Q.E.P. Co., Inc., **65** **292–94**
Qantas Airways Ltd., **6** **109–13**; **24** **396–401 (upd.)**; **68** **301–07 (upd.)**
Qatar Airways Company Q.C.S.C., **87** **404–407**
Qatar General Petroleum Corporation, **IV** **524–26**

Qatar National Bank SAQ, **87 408–411**
Qatar Telecom QSA, **87 412–415**
Qdoba Restaurant Corporation, **93 358–62**
Qiagen N.V., **39 333–35**
Qingdao Haier Refrigerator Co., Ltd., **65** 167, 169
QLT Inc., **71 291–94**
QMS Ltd., **43** 284
QSC Audio Products, Inc., **56 291–93**
QSP, Inc. *see* The Reader's Digest Association, Inc.
Qtera Corporation, **36** 352
Quad/Graphics, Inc., **19 333–36**
Quad Pharmaceuticals, Inc. *see* Par Pharmaceuticals Inc.
Quail Oil Tools, **28** 347–48
Quaker Alloy, Inc., **39** 31–32
Quaker Chemical Corp., **91 388–91**
Quaker Fabric Corp., **19 337–39**
Quaker Foods North America, **II 558–60; 12 409–12 (upd.); 34 363–67 (upd.); 73 268–73 (upd.)**
Quaker State Corporation, **7 443–45; 21 419–22 (upd.)** *see also* Pennzoil-Quaker State Co.
QUALCOMM Incorporated, **20 438–41; 47 317–21 (upd.)**
Qualcore, S. de R.L. de C.V., **51** 116
Qualipac, **55** 309
QualiTROL Corporation, *see* Danaher Corp.
Quality Assurance International, **72** 255
Quality Aviation Services, Inc., **53** 132
Quality Chekd Dairies, Inc., **48 337–39**
Quality Courts Motels, Inc. *see* Choice Hotels International, Inc.
Quality Dining, Inc., **18 437–40**
Quality Food Centers, Inc., **17 386–88** *see also* Kroger Co.
Quality Inn *see* Choice Hotels International, Inc.
Quality Paperback Book Club (QPB), *see* Book-of-the-Month Club.
Quality Systems, Inc., **81 328–31**
Qualix S.A., **67** 347–48
Quanex Corporation, **13 422–24; 62 286–89 (upd.)**
Quanta Computer Inc., **47 322–24**
Quanta Display Inc., **75** 306
Quanta Services, Inc., **79 338–41**
Quanta Systems Corp., **51** 81
Quanterra Alpha L.P., **63** 347
Quantronix Corporation *see* Excel Technology Inc.
Quantum Chemical Corporation, **8 439–41**
Quantum Computer Services, Inc. *see* America Online, Inc.
Quantum Corporation, **10 458–59; 62 290–93 (upd.)**
Quantum Health Resources, **29** 364
Quantum Marketing International, Inc., *see* National Media Corp.
Quantum Restaurant Group, Inc., **30** 330
Quarex Industries, Inc. *see* Western Beef, Inc.
Quark, Inc., **36 375–79**
Quebec Credit Union League, **48** 290
Quebéc Hydro-Electric Commission *see* Hydro-Quebéc.
Quebecor Inc., **12 412–14; 47 325–28 (upd.)**
Queen City Broadcasting, **42** 162
Queens Isetan Co., Ltd. *see* Isetan Company Ltd.
Queensborough Holdings PLC, **38** 103
Queensland Alumina, **IV** 59
Queensland and Northern Territories Air Service *see* Qantas Airways Ltd.
Quelle Group, **V 165–67** *see also* Karstadt Quelle AG.
Quesarias Ibéricas, **23** 219
Quest Diagnostics Inc., **26 390–92**
Quest Education Corporation, **42** 212
Quest Pharmacies Inc., **25** 504–05
Questa Oil and Gas Co., **63** 408
Questar Corporation, **6 568–70; 26 386–89 (upd.)**
Questor Management Co. LLC, **55** 31
Questor Partners, **26** 185
The Quick & Reilly Group, Inc., **20 442–44**
Quick Pak Inc., **53** 236
Quick Restaurants S.A., **94 357–60**
Quicken Loans, Inc., **93 363–67**
Quickie Designs, **11** 202, 487–88
Quidel Corporation, **80 300–03**
The Quigley Corporation, **62 294–97**
Quik Stop Markets, Inc., *see* Dillon Companies Inc.
Quiksilver, Inc., **18 441–43; 79 342–47 (upd.)**
QuikTrip Corporation, **36 380–83**
Quill Corporation, **28 375–77**
Quillery, *see* Eiffage
Quilmes Industrial (QUINSA) S.A., **67 315–17**
Quilter Sound Company *see* QSC Audio Products, Inc.
Quimica Geral do Nordeste S.A., **68** 81
Química y Farmacia, S.A. de C.V., **59** 332
Quimicos Industriales Penoles *see* Industrias Penoles, S.A. de C.V.
Quincy Family Steak House, **27** 17, 19
Quiñenco S.A., **69** 56–57; **70** 61–62
Quintana Roo, Inc., *see* Hyde Athletic Industries, Inc.
Quintel Communications, Inc., **61** 375
Quintiles Transnational Corporation, **21 423–25; 68 308–12 (upd.)**
Quintus Computer Systems, **6** 248
Quixote Corporation, **15 378–80**
Quixtar Inc. *see* Alticor Inc.
Quixx Corporation, **6** 580
The Quizno's Corporation, **42 295–98**
Quotron Systems, Inc., **IV** 670; **30** 127; **47** 37
Quovadx Inc., **70 243–46**
QVC Inc., **9 428–29; 58 284–87 (upd.)**
Qwest Communications International, Inc., **37 312–17**
QwikSilver II, Inc., **37** 119

R

R&B Falcon Corp. *see* Transocean Sedco Forex Inc.
R&B, Inc., **51 305–07**
R&D Systems, Inc., **52** 347
R&S Home and Auto, **56** 352
R&S Technology Inc., **48** 410
R. and W. Hawaii Wholesale, Inc., **22** 15
R-Anell Custom Homes Inc., **41** 19
R-B *see* Arby's, Inc.
R-C Holding Inc. *see* Air & Water Technologies Corp.
R.B. Pamplin Corp., **45 350–52**
R.C. Bigelow, Inc., **49 334–36**
R.C. Willey Home Furnishings, **72 291–93**
R.E. Rogers, Inc. *see* Rock-It Cargo USA, Inc.
R.G. Barry Corp., **17 389–91; 44 364–67 (upd.)**
R.G. Dun-Bradstreet Corp. *see* The Dun & Bradstreet Corp.
R. Griggs Group Limited, **23 399–402; 31** 413–14
R.H. Donnelley Corporation, **61** 81–83
R.H. Macy & Co., Inc., **V 168–70; 8 442–45 (upd.); 30 379–83 (upd.)** *see also* Macy's, Inc.
R.J. Reynolds, **I** 261, 363; **15** 72–73; **21** 315; **29** 195; **32** 344 *see also* RJR Nabisco.
R.J. Reynolds Tobacco Holdings, Inc., **30 384–87 (upd.)**
R.J. Tower Corporation *see* Tower Automotive, Inc.
R.L. Crain Limited, **15** 473
R.L. Polk & Co., **10 460–62**
R. M. Palmer Co., **89 362–64**
R-O Realty, Inc., **43** 314
R.P.M., Inc., **25** 228
R.P. Scherer Corporation, **I 678–80** *see also* Cardinal Health, Inc.
R.R. Bowker Co., **23** 440
R.R. Donnelley & Sons Company, **IV 660–62; 38 368–71 (upd.)**
R.S.R. Corporation, **31** 48
R. Scott Associates, **11** 57
R-T Investors LC, **42** 323–24
R. Twining & Co., **61** 395
R.W. Beck, **29** 353
R.W. Harmon & Sons, Inc., **6** 410
Rabobank Group, **26** 419; **33 356–58**
RAC *see* Ravenswood Aluminum Company; Roy Anderson Corp.
Racal-Datacom Inc., **11 408–10**
Racal Electronics PLC, **II 83–84** *see also* Thales S.A.
Race Z, Inc. *see* Action Peformance Companies, Inc.
Rachel's Dairy Ltd., **37** 197–98
Racine Hidraulica, **21** 430
Racing Champions *see* Action Performance Companies, Inc.
Racing Champions Corporation, **37 318–20**

Racing Collectables Club of America, Inc. *see* Action Performance Companies, Inc.
Rack Room Shoes, Inc., 84 314–317
Racket Store *see* Duckwall-ALCO Stores, Inc.
Radeberger Gruppe AG, 75 332–35
Radian Group Inc., 42 299–301 *see also* Onex Corp.
Radiation Therapy Services, Inc., 85 344–47
Radio Austria A.G., **V** 314–16
Radio Cap Company *see* Norwood Promotional Products, Inc.
Radio City Productions, **30** 102
Radio Corporation of America *see* RCA Corp.
Radio Flyer Inc., 34 368–70
Radio-Keith-Orpheum, **31** 99
Radio One, Inc., 67 318–21
Radio Shack, *see* Tandy Corp.
Radio Vertrieb Fürth *see* Grundig AG.
Radiocel, **39** 194
RadioShack Canada Inc., **30** 391
RadioShack Corporation, 36 384–88 (upd.)
Radiotelevision Española, *see* Television Española, S.A.
Radisson Hotels Worldwide, *see* Carlson Companies, Inc.
Radius Inc., 16 417–19
Radix Group, Inc., **13** 20
Radman Inc., **56** 247
RadNet Managed Imaging Services, Inc., *see* Primedex Health Systems, Inc.
Radnor Venture Partners, LP, *see* Safeguard Scientifics, Inc.
RAE Systems Inc., 83 311-314
Raet, **39** 177
Raffinerie Tirlemontoise S.A., *see* Südzucker AG.
RAG AG, 35 364–67; 60 247–51 (upd.)
Rag Shops, Inc., 30 365–67
Ragdoll Productions Ltd., 51 308–11
Ragnar Benson Inc., *see* The Austin Co.
Raiffeisen Zentralbank Österreich AG, 85 348–52
Rail Link, Inc., *see* Genesee & Wyoming Inc.
Rail Van Global Logistics, **54** 276
Railtech International *see* Delachaux S.A.
RailTex, Inc., 20 445–47
Railtrack Group PLC, 50 369–72
Rain Bird Corporation, 84 318–321
Rainbow Home Shopping Ltd. *see* Otto-Versand (GmbH & Co.).
Rainbow Media, *see* Cablevision Systems Corp.
Rainbow Valley Orchards, **54** 257
RainbowBridge Communications, Inc., **25** 162
Raincoast Book Distribution, **34** 5
Rainfair, Inc., *see* LaCrosse Footwear, Inc.
Rainforest Café, Inc., 25 386–88; 88 312–16 (upd.)
Rainier Brewing Company, 23 403–05
Rainier Pulp and Paper Company *see* Rayonier Inc.
Rainy River Forest Products, Inc., **26** 445
Raky-Danubia, **IV** 485
Ralcorp Holdings, Inc., *see* Ralston Purina Co.
Raleigh UK Ltd., 65 295–97
Raley's Inc., 14 396–98; 58 288–91 (upd.)
Rally's, 25 389–91; 68 313–16 (upd.)
Rallye SA, 54 306–09
Ralph & Kacoo's *see* Piccadilly Cafeterias, Inc.
Ralph Lauren *see* Polo/Ralph Lauren Corportion.
The Ralph M. Parsons Company *see* The Parsons Corp.
Ralph Wilson Plastics, *see* Illinois Tool Works.
Ralph's Industries, **31** 191
Ralphs Grocery Company, 35 368–70
Ralston Purina Company, II 561–63; 13 425–27 (upd.) *see also* Ralcorp Holdings, Inc.; Nestlé S.A.
Ramada International Hotels & Resorts, **IV** 718; **11** 177; **21** 366; **28** 258; **38** 320; **52** 281
Rampage Clothing Co., **35** 94
Ramparts, Inc., **57** 159
Ramsay Youth Services, Inc., 41 322–24
Ramtron International Corporation, 89 365–68
Ranbar Packing, Inc. *see* Western Beef, Inc.
Ranbaxy Laboratories Ltd., 70 247–49
Ranchers Packing Corp. *see* Western Beef, Inc.
Rand Capital Corp., **35** 52–53
Rand McNally & Company, 28 378–81; 53 122
Randall's Food Markets, Inc., 40 364–67 *see also* Safeway Inc.
Randgold & Exploration, **63** 182–83
Random House, Inc., 13 428–30; 31 375–80 (upd.)
Randon Meldkamer, **43** 307
Randon S.A. Implementos e Participações, 79 348–52
Randstad Holding n.v., 16 420–22; 43 307–10 (upd.)
Range Resources Corporation, 45 353–55
The Rank Group plc, II 157–59; 14 399–402 (upd.); 64 317–21 (upd.)
Ranks Hovis McDougall Limited, II 564–65; 28 382–85 (upd.)
Ransburg Corporation, *see* Illinois Tool Works Inc.
Ransom and Randolph Company, *see* Dentsply International Inc.
Ransom Industries LP, **55** 266
RAO Unified Energy System of Russia, 45 356–60
Rapala-Normark Group, Ltd., 30 368–71
Rapides Bank & Trust Company, **11** 107
Rapidforms, Inc., **35** 130–31
Rare Hospitality International Inc., 19 340–42
RAS *see* Riunione Adriatica di Sicurtà SpA.
Rascal House, *see* Jerry's Famous Deli Inc.
Raskas Foods, Inc. *see* Shearer's Foods, Inc.
Rathbone Brothers plc, 70 250–53
RathGibson Inc., 90 348–51
Ratin A/S, **49** 376
Rational GmbH, **22** 354
ratiopharm Group, 84 322–326
Ratner Companies, 72 294–96
Raufast et Fils, **35** 205
Rauma-Repola Oy *see* Metso Corp.
Raumtechnik Messebau & Event Marketing GmbH, **60** 143
Rauscher Pierce Refsnes, Inc., **15** 233
Raven Industries, Inc., 33 359–61
Ravensburger AG, 64 322–26
Ravenseft Properties Ltd. *see* Land Securities PLC.
Ravenswood Aluminum Company, **52** 72–73
RAVIcad, **18** 20; **43** 17
Raving Brands, Inc., 64 327–29
Rawlings Sporting Goods Co., Inc., 24 402–04
Ray Industries, **22** 116
Raychem Corporation, 8 446–47
Raymond James Financial Inc., 69 308–10
Raymond International Inc., **28** 201
Raymond Ltd., 77 351–54
Raymond, Trice & Company, *see* Bank of Mississippi, Inc.
Raynet Corporation, *see* Raychem Corp.
Rayonese Textile, Inc., **29** 140
Rayonier Inc., 24 405–07
Rayovac Corporation, 13 431–34; 39 336–40 (upd.)
Raytech Corporation, 61 306–09
Raytheon Aircraft Holdings Inc., 46 354–57
Raytheon Company, II 85–87; 11 411–14 (upd.); 38 372–77 (upd.)
Razel S.A., **55** 62
Razorfish, Inc., 37 321–24
RB&W Corp., *see* Park-Ohio Industries Inc.
RBC Dominion Securities, **25** 12
RBS Global Inc. *see* Rexnord Corp.
RCA Corporation, II 88–90
RCA Global Communications, Inc., **27** 304
RCM Technologies, Inc., 34 371–74
RCN Corporation, 70 254–57
RDMS Direct Marketing BV, **53** 362
RDO Equipment Company, 33 362–65
RE/MAX International, Inc., 59 344–46
REA *see* Railway Express Agency.
Rea Construction Company, *see* Philipp Holzmann AG.
Read-Rite Corp., 10 463–64
The Reader's Digest Association, Inc., IV 663–64; 17 392–95 (upd.); 71 295–99 (upd.)
Reader's Garden Inc., **22** 441
Reading Etc., **72** 172
Reading International Inc., 70 258–60
Ready Mixed Concrete, **28** 82
Real Color Displays, **53** 117

Real Decisions, **21** 236
Real Fresh, **25** 85
Real Goods Trading Company, **41** 177
Real Madrid C.F., 73 274–76
Real Times, Inc., 66 261–65
Real Turismo, S.A. de C.V., 50 373–75
RealCom Communications Corporation, **15** 196
Realeum, Inc., **58** 11
Reality Group Limited, **47** 165, 169
Realty Information Group, Inc. *see* CoStar Group, Inc.
The Really Useful Group, 26 393–95
RealNetworks, Inc., 53 280–82
Realty Development Co. *see* King Kullen Grocery Co., Inc.
Realty Investment Group, **25** 127
Realty Parking Properties II L.P., *see* Central Parking Corp.
Reavis & McGrath, **47** 139
Rebekah W. Harkness Foundation, **52** 199
Recaro North America Inc., **26** 231
Reckitt Benckiser plc, II 566–67; 42 302–06 (upd.); 91 392–99 (upd.)
Reckson Associates Realty Corp., 47 329–31
Record Merchandisers *see* Entertainment UK.
Recordati S.p.A., **52** 135
Recording for the Blind & Dyslexic, 51 312–14
Recoton Corp., 15 381–83
Recovery Centers of America, *see* Tenet Healthcare Corp.
Recovery Engineering, Inc., 25 392–94
Recreational Equipment, Inc., 18 444–47; 71 300–03 (upd.)
Recticel S.A., **17** 182–84
Recubrimientos Interceramic, S.A. de C.V., **53** 175
Recycled Paper Greetings, Inc., 21 426–28
RED, **44** 164
The Red Adair Company, **37** 171
Red Ant Entertainment, **17** 14
Red Apple Group, Inc., 23 406–08
Red Ball, Inc., **18** 300
Red Brick Systems Inc., **30** 246
Red Bull GmbH, 60 252–54
Red Carpet Food Systems, **39** 409
Red Chisinau, **51** 389
Red McCombs Automotive Group, 91 400–03
Red-E-Food Systems, Inc. *see* Del Taco, Inc.
Red Hat, Inc., 45 361–64
Red House Books Ltd., **29** 426
Red Kap *see* VF Corp.
Red Line HealthCare Corporation, **47** 236
Red Lion Entertainment, **29** 503
Red Lobster, *see* Darden Restaurants, Inc.
Red Oak Consulting, **42** 244
Red Pepper Software Co., **59** 77
Red River Commodities, Inc. *see* Deli Universal NV.
Red Robin Gourmet Burgers, Inc., 56 294–96
Red Roof Inns, Inc., 18 448–49 *see also* Accor S.A.
Red Rooster, **V** 35
Red Spot Paint & Varnish Company, 55 319–22
Red Star Express, *see* TNT Freightways Corp.
Red Storm, **41** 409
Red Televisiva Megavision S.A., **67** 136–38
The Red Wing Co., Inc., **28** 382; **55** 96, 98
Red Wing Pottery Sales, Inc., 52 294–96
Red Wing Shoe Company, Inc., 9 433–35; 30 372–75 (upd.); 83 315-321 (upd.)
Redback Networks, Inc., 92 319–22
Redbook Florists Service, **28** 138
Reddy Ice Holdings, Inc., 80 304–07
Redgate Communications, **26** 19
Redhook Ale Brewery, Inc., 31 381–84; 88 317–21 (upd.)
Redken Laboratories Inc., 84 327–330
Redland Plasterboard, **28** 83
Redland plc, III 734–36 *see also* Lafarge Cement UK.
Redlaw Industries Inc., **15** 247
Redman Industries, Inc., *see* Champion Enterprises, Inc.
RedOctane, Inc. *see* Activision, Inc.
La Redoute, S.A. *see* PPR SA.
RedPeg Marketing, 73 277–79
RedPrairie Corporation, 74 257–60
Redrow Group plc, 31 385–87
Redwood Design Automation, **11** 47
Redwood Fire & Casualty Insurance Co., *see* Berkshire Hathaway Inc.
Redwood Systems, **48** 112
Reebok International Ltd., V 375–77; 9 436–38 (upd.); 26 396–400 (upd.)
Reed & Barton Corporation, 67 322–24
Reed Elsevier plc, 31 388–94 (upd.)
Reed-Hycalog, **57** 162, 164
Reed International PLC, IV 665–67; 17 396–99 (upd.)
Reeder Light, Ice & Fuel Company, **6** 592; **50** 38
Reeds Jewelers, Inc., 22 447–49
Reese Products, *see* TriMas Corp.
Reeves Brothers, **17** 182
Refinaria de Petróleo Ipiranga S.A., **67** 216
Refineria Metales Uboldi y Cia. S.A., **74** 11
Reflectone Inc. *see* CAE USA Inc.
Reflex Winkelmann & Pannhoff GmbH, *see* Essef Corp.
Refrigeração Paraná S.A., *see* Electrolux AB.
Refrigerantes do Oeste, SA, **47** 291
Regal-Beloit Corporation, 18 450–53
Regal Entertainment Group, 59 340–43
Regal International, **71** 232
Regal Manufacturing Co., **15** 385
The Regence Group, 74 261–63
Regency Centers Corporation, 71 304–07
Regency Health Services Inc., **25** 457
Regeneration Technologies, Inc., **68** 379
Regenerative Environmental Equipment Company, Inc., **6** 441
Regent Carolina Corporation, **37** 226
Regent Communications, Inc., 87 416–420
Regent International Hotels Limited, *see* Four Seasons Hotels Inc.
Régie Autonome des Pétroles, **IV** 544–46; **21** 202–04
Régie des Télégraphes et Téléphones *see* Belgacom.
Régie Nationale des Usines Renault, I 189–91 *see also* Renault S.A.
Regional Bell Operating Companies, **15** 125
Regis Corporation, 18 454–56; 70 261–65 (upd.)
Register & Tribune Co. *see* Cowles Media Co.
Rego Supermarkets, *see* Riser Foods, Inc.
Rehab Hospital Services Corp., *see* Tenet Healthcare Corp.
RehabClinics Inc., **11** 367
Rehrig Manufacturing, **51** 35
REI *see* Recreational Equipment, Inc.
REI Ltd. *see* CB Richard Ellis Group, Inc.
Reichhold Chemicals, Inc., 10 465–67
Reidman Corporation, **41** 65
Reiman Publications *see* The Reader's Digest Association, Inc.
Reimersholms, **31** 458–60
Reisland GmbH, **15** 340
Reiter Dairy, LLC, 94 361–64
Rejuvenation, Inc., 91 404–07
Rekkof Restart NV, **28** 327
Relational Courseware, Inc., **21** 235–36
Relational Database Systems Inc., *see* Informix Corp.
Relationship Marketing Group, Inc., **37** 409
Reliable Life Insurance Company, **58** 259
Reliance Electric Company, 9 439–42
Reliance Group Holdings, Inc., III 342–44
Reliance Industries Ltd., 81 332–36
Reliance Steel & Aluminum Company, 19 343–45; 70 266–70 (upd.)
Reliant Energy Inc., 44 368–73 (upd.)
Reliv International, Inc., 58 292–95
Relocation Central *see* CORT Business Services Corp.
Rembrandt Group Ltd., **IV** 93, 97; **50** 144
Remedy Corporation, 58 296–99
RemedyTemp, Inc., 20 448–50
Remgro, **IV** 97
Remington Arms Company, Inc., 12 415–17; 40 368–71 (upd.)
Remington Products Company, L.L.C., 42 307–10
Remington Rand, *see* Unisys Corp.
Rémy Cointreau Group, 20 451–53; 80 308–12 (upd.)
Remy Martin, **48** 348–49

REN Corp. USA, Inc., *see* COBE Laboratories, Inc.
REN Corporation, **49** 156
Renaissance Communications Corp., *see* Tribune Co.
Renaissance Connects, **16** 394
Renaissance Cosmetics Inc. *see* New Dana Perfumes Co.
Renaissance Energy Ltd., **47** 181
Renaissance Hotel Group N.V. *see* Marriott International, Inc.
Renaissance Learning Systems, Inc., 39 341–43
Renal Care Group, Inc., 72 297–99
Renal Systems, Inc. *see* Minntech Corp.
Renault Argentina S.A., 67 325–27
Renault S.A., 26 401–04 (upd.); 74 264–68 (upd.)
Rendeck International, **11** 66
René Garraud *see* Wella AG.
Renfro Corp., **25** 167
Rengo Co., Ltd., IV 326
Renishaw plc, 46 358–60
RENK AG, 37 325–28
Renner Herrmann S.A., 79 353–56
Reno Air Inc., 23 409–11
Reno de Medici S.p.A., 41 325–27
Réno-Dépôt Inc., **26** 306
Reno Technologies, **12** 124
Rent-A-Center, Inc., 45 365–67
Rent-Way, Inc., 33 366–68; 75 336–39 (upd.)
Rental Service Corporation, 28 386–88
Renters Choice Inc. *see* Rent-A-Center, Inc.
Rentokil Initial Plc, 47 332–35
Rentrak Corporation, 35 371–74
Rentz, **23** 219
Renwick Technologies, Inc., **48** 286
Reo Products *see* Lifetime Hoan Corp.
Repairmaster Canada, Inc., **53** 359
Repco Corporation Ltd., 74 269–72
Repola Oy, *see* Metso Corp.
Repsol-YPF S.A., IV 527–29; 16 423–26 (upd.); 40 372–76 (upd.)
Repubblica, **IV** 587
Republic Airlines, **28** 265
Republic Broadcasting Corp., **23** 292
Republic Corp., **I** 447
Republic Engineered Steels, Inc., 7 446–47; 26 405–08 (upd.)
Republic Industries, Inc., 26 409–11 *see also* AutoNation, Inc.
Republic Insurance, *see* Winterthur Group.
Republic New York Corporation, 11 415–19 *see also* HSBC Holdings plc.
Republic Powdered Metals, Inc., *see* RPM Inc.
Republic Services, Inc., 92 323–26
Republic Steel Corp. *see* Republic Engineered Steels, Inc.
Republic Supply Co., **63** 288
Res-Care, Inc., 29 399–402
Research Analysis Corporation, **7** 15
Research Cottrell, Inc., **6** 441
Research Genetics, Inc., **52** 183–84
Research in Motion Ltd., 54 310–14
Research Publications, *see* The Thomson Corp.
Research Triangle Institute, 83 322-325
Réseau Ferré de France, 66 266–68
Resecenter, **55** 90
Reser's Fine Foods, Inc., 81 337–40
Residence Inns, *see* Promus Companies, Inc.
ResNet Communications Inc., **28** 241
Resona Holdings Inc., **53** 322
Resorts International, Inc., 12 418–20
Resorts World Bhd *see* Genting Bhd.
Resource America, Inc., 42 311–14
The Resource Club, **32** 80
Resource Group International, **25** 207
reSOURCE PARTNER, INC., **22** 95
Resources Connection, Inc., 81 341–44
Respond Industries, Inc., **51** 76
Response Oncology, Inc., 27 385–87
Restaurant Associates Corporation, 66 269–72
The Restaurant Company, *see* Perkins Family Restaurants, L.P.
Restaurant Property Master, **19** 468
Restaurants Universal Espana S.A., **26** 374
Restaurants Unlimited, Inc., 13 435–37
Restoration Hardware, Inc., 30 376–78
Resurgens Communications Group, *see* LDDS-Metro Communications, Inc.
Retail Association Pskovnefteprodukt, **48** 378
Retail Concepts Inc., **55** 174
Retail Credit Company *see* Equifax.
Retail Ventures, Inc., 82 299–03 (upd.)
Retirement and Health Services Corporation, **57** 128
Retirement Care Associates Inc., **25** 457
Retirement Systems of Alabama, **52** 387
Retorte Ulrich Scharrer GmbH, **62** 253
Reuben H. Donnelley Corp. *see* The Dunn & Bradstreet Corp.
Reuters Group PLC, IV 668–70; 22 450–53 (upd.); 63 323–27 (upd.)
Revco D.S., Inc., V 171–73 *see also* CVS Corp.
Revell-Monogram Inc., 16 427–29
Revere Copper and Brass Co. *see* The Paul Revere Corp.
Revere Foil Containers, Inc., **12** 377
Revere Ware Corporation, 22 454–56
Revlon Inc., III 54–57; 17 400–04 (upd.); 64 330–35 (upd.)
Rewards Network Inc., 70 271–75 (upd.)
Rewe-Beteiligungs-Holding National GmbH, **53** 179; **54** 295–96
Rewe Group, **37** 241
Rewe-Liebbrand, **28** 152
Rex Re Insurance Ltd., **51** 143
REX Stores Corp., 10 468–69
Rexall Drug Co., **50** 487
Rexall Sundown, Inc., **37** 340, 342
Rexam PLC, 32 380–85 (upd.); 85 353–61 (upd.)
Rexel, Inc., 15 384–87
Rexene Products Co., **IV** 457
Rexham Inc., *see* Rexam PLC.
Rexnord Corporation, 21 429–32; 76 315–19 (upd.)
Rexroth Mecman GmbH, **74** 321
Reycan, **49** 104
Reydel Industries, **23** 95–96
Reyes Holdings, Inc., **24** 388
The Reynolds and Reynolds Company, 50 376–79
Reynolds Metals Company, IV 186–88; 19 346–48 (upd.) *see also* Alcoa Inc.
RF Micro Devices, Inc., 43 311–13
RFC Franchising LLC, 68 317–19
RFF *see* Réseau Ferré de France.
RFI Group, Inc., **54** 275
RGI *see* Rockefeller Group Inc.
RHD Holdings, **23** 413
Rheem Manufacturing, **52** 398–99; **71** 269–70
Rheem South Africa Ltd., **59** 226
Rheinbraun A.G., **73** 131
Rheinische Metallwaaren- und Maschinenfabrik AG, *see* Rheinmetall Berlin AG.
Rheinmetall Berlin AG, 9 443–46
Rhenus-Weichelt AG *see* Schenker-Rhenus AG.
RHI AG, 53 283–86
RHI Entertainment Inc., **16** 257
Rhino Entertainment Company, 18 457–60; 70 276–80 (upd.)
RHM *see* Ranks Hovis McDougall.
Rhodes Inc., 23 412–14
Rhodia SA, 38 378–80
Rhône Moulage Industrie, **39** 152, 154
Rhône-Poulenc S.A., I 388–90; 10 470–72 (upd.)
RhoxalPharma Inc., **69** 209
Rhymney Iron Company, **31** 369
Rica Foods, Inc., 41 328–30
Ricardo Gallo *see* Vidrala S.A.
Ricardo plc, 90 352–56
Rich Products Corporation, 7 448–49; 38 381–84 (upd.); 93 368–74 (upd.)
Rich's Inc., *see* Federated Department Stores Inc.
Richard A. Shaw, Inc., *see* Dean Foods Co.
Richard D. Irwin Inc. *see* Dow Jones & Company, Inc.
Richard Ginori 1735 S.p.A., **73** 248–49
Richard R. Dostie, Inc. *see* Toll Brothers Inc.
Richards & O'Neil LLP, **43** 70
The Richards Group, Inc., 58 300–02
Richardson Company, **36** 147
Richardson Electronics, Ltd., 17 405–07
Richardson Industries, Inc., 62 298–301
Richardson-Vicks Company *see* The Procter & Gamble Company
Richardson's, **21** 246
Richfood Holdings, Inc., 7 450–51; *see also* Supervalu Inc.
Richman Gordman Half Price Stores, Inc. *see* Gordmans, Inc.
Richmond Cedar Works Manufacturing Co., **19** 360
Richmond Corp., **15** 129
Richmond Paperboard Corp., **19** 78

Richton International Corporation, **39 344–46**
Richtree Inc., **63 328–30**
Richwood Building Products, Inc., *see* Ply Gem Industries Inc.
Rickel Home Centers, *see* Supermarkets General Holdings Corp.
Rickenbacker International Corp., **91 408–12**
Ricoh Company, Ltd., **III 159–61; 36 389–93 (upd.)**
Ricola Ltd., **62 302–04**
Ricolino, **19** 192
Riddarhyttan Resources AB *see* Agnico-Eagle Mines Ltd.
Riddell Inc., **33** 467
Riddell Sports Inc., **22 457–59**; **23** 449
Ridder Publications *see* Knight-Ridder, Inc.
Ride, Inc., **22 460–63**
Ridge Tool Co., *see* Emerson.
Ridgewell's Inc., **15** 87
Ridgway Co., **23** 98
Ridley Corporation Ltd., **62 305–07**
Riedel-de Haën AG, **22** 32; **36** 431
The Riese Organization, **38 385–88**
Rieter Holding AG, **42 315–17**
Riggs National Corporation, **13 438–40**
Right Associates, **27** 21; **44** 156
Right Management Consultants, Inc., **42 318–21**
Right Source, Inc., **24** 96
RightPoint, Inc., **49** 124
RightSide Up, Inc., *see* AHL Services, Inc..
Rijnhaave Information Systems, **25** 21
Riken Kagaku Co. Ltd., **48** 250
Riklis Family Corp., **9 447–50**
Rimage Corp., **89 369–72**
Rinascente S.p.A., **71 308–10**
Ring King Visibles, Inc., *see* HNI Corp.
Ring Ltd., **43** 99
Ringnes Bryggeri, *see* Orkla ASA.
Rinker Group Ltd., **65 298–301**
Rio de Janeiro Refrescos S.A., **71** 140
Rio Grande Industries, Inc., **12** 18–19
Rio Grande Servaas, S.A. de C.V., **23** 145
Rio Sportswear Inc., **42** 269
Rio Sul Airlines *see* Varig, SA.
Rio Tinto plc, **19 349–53 (upd.) 50 380–85 (upd.)**
Riocell S.A. *see* Klabin S.A.
Ripley Entertainment, Inc., **74 273–76**
Ripotot, **68** 143
Riser Foods, Inc., **9 451–54** *see also* Giant Eagle, Inc.
Risk Management Partners Ltd., **35** 36
Risk Planners, *see* Supervalu Inc.
Ritchie Bros. Auctioneers Inc., **41 331–34**
Rite Aid Corporation, **V 174–76; 19 354–57 (upd.); 63 331–37 (upd.)**
Riteway Distributor, **26** 183
Rittenhouse Financial Services, **22** 495
Ritter Co. *see* Sybron Corp.
Ritter Sport *see* Alfred Ritter GmbH & Co. KG.
Ritter's Frozen Custard *see* RFC Franchising LLC.
Ritz Camera Centers, **34 375–77**
The Ritz-Carlton Hotel Company, L.L.C., **9 455–57; 29 403–06 (upd.); 71 311–16 (upd.)**
Ritz-Craft Corporation of Pennsylvania Inc., **94 365–68**
Riunione Adriatica di Sicurtà SpA, **III 345–48**
Riva Group Plc, **53** 46
Riva Fire *see* Gruppo Riva Fire SpA.
The Rival Company, **19 358–60**
Rivaud Group, **29** 370
River City Broadcasting, **25** 418
River Metals Recycling LLC, **76** 130
River North Studios *see* Platinum Entertainment, Inc.
River Oaks Furniture, Inc., **43 314–16**
River Ranch Fresh Foods LLC, **88 322–25**
River Thames Insurance Co., Ltd., **26** 487
Riverdeep Group plc, **41** 137
Riverside Insurance Co. of America, **26** 487
Riverside Press, *see* Houghton Mifflin Co.
Riverside Publishing Company, **36** 272
Riverwood International Corporation, **11 420–23; 48 340–44 (upd.)**
Riviana Foods, **27 388–91**
Riviera Holdings Corporation, **75 340–43**
Riviera Tool Company, **89 373–76**
Riyadh Armed Forces Hospital, **16** 94
Rizzoli Publishing, **23** 88
RJMJ, Inc., **16** 37
RJR Nabisco Holdings Corp., **V 408–10** *see also* R.J Reynolds Tobacco Holdings Inc., Nabisco Brands, Inc.; R.J. Reynolds Industries, Inc.
RK Rose + Krieger GmbH & Co. KG, **61** 286–87
RKO *see* Radio-Keith-Orpheum.
RM Auctions, Inc., **88 326–29**
RMC Group p.l.c., **III 737–40; 34 378–83 (upd.)**
RMH Teleservices, Inc., **42 322–24**
Roadhouse Grill, Inc., **22 464–66**
Roadmaster Industries, Inc., **16 430–33**
Roadmaster Transport Company, **18** 27; **41** 18
RoadOne *see* Miller Industries, Inc.
Roadstone-Wood Group, **64** 98
Roadway Express, Inc., **V 502–03; 25 395–98 (upd.)**
Roanoke Capital Ltd., **27** 113–14
Roanoke Electric Steel Corporation, **45 368–70**
Robbins & Myers Inc., **15 388–90**
Robeco Group, **26** 419–20
Roberds Inc., **19 361–63**
Robert Allen Companies, *see* Masco Corp.
Robert Benson, Lonsdale & Co. Ltd. *see* Dresdner Kleinwort Wasserstein.
Robert Bosch GmbH, **I 392–93; 16 434–37 (upd.); 43 317–21 (upd.)**
Robert E. McKee Corporation, **6** 150
Robert Gair Co., **15** 128
Robert Half International Inc., **18 461–63; 70 281–84 (upd.)**
Robert Hansen Trucking Inc., **49** 402
Robert McLane Company *see* McLane Company, Inc.
Robert Mondavi Corporation, **15 391–94; 50 386–90 (upd.)**
Robert Skeels & Company, **33** 467
Robert Stigwood Organization Ltd., **23** 390
Robert Talbott Inc., **88 330–33**
Robert W. Baird & Co. Incorporated, **67 328–30**
Robert Wood Johnson Foundation, **35 375–78**
Robertet SA, **39 347–49**
Roberts Express, **V** 503
Roberts Pharmaceutical Corporation, **16 438–40**
Roberts Trading Corporation, **68** 99
Robertson Animal Hospital, Inc., **58** 355
Robertson Building Products, *see* United Dominion Industries Ltd.
Robertson-Ceco Corporation, **19 364–66**
Robin Hood Flour Mills, Ltd., *see* International Multifoods Corp.
Robin International Inc., *see* Algo Group Inc.
Robinair, *see* SPX Corp.
Robins, Kaplan, Miller & Ciresi L.L.P., **89 377–81**
Robinson & Clark Hardware *see* Clarcor Inc.
Robinson Helicopter Company, **51 315–17**
Robinson Way, **70** 160–61
Rogue Pictures *see* Focus Features
Rogue Wave Software, Inc. *see* Quovadix Inc.
Robinson's Japan Co. Ltd. *see* Ito-Yokado Co., Ltd.
Robinsons Soft Drinks Limited, **38** 77
Robotic Simulations Limited, **56** 134
ROC *see* Royal Olympic Cruise Lines Inc.
Rocawear Apparel LLC, **77 355–58**
Roccade, **39** 177
Roch, S.A., **23** 83
Roche Biomedical Laboratories, Inc., **11 424–26** *see also* Laboratory Corporation of America Holdings.
Roche Bioscience, **14 403–06 (upd.)**
Roche Holding AG, **30** 164; **32** 211, 213–14; **37** 113; **50** 421
Rocher Soleil, **48** 315
Rochester Gas And Electric Corporation, **6 571–73**
Rochester Group, Inc., **60** 267
Rochester Instrument Systems, Inc., *see* The Marmon Group, Inc.
Rochester Telephone Corporation, **6 332–34**
Röchling Gruppe, **94 369–74**
Rock Bottom Restaurants, Inc., **25 399–401; 68 320–23 (upd.)**
Rock-It Cargo USA, Inc., **86 339–42**
Rock of Ages Corporation, **37 329–32**

Rock-Tenn Company, 13 441–43; 59 347–51 (upd.)
Rockcor Inc., *see* Olin Corp.
The Rockefeller Foundation, 34 384–87
Rockefeller Group International Inc., 58 303–06
Rocket Chemical Company *see* WD-40 Co.
Rockford Corporation, 43 322–25
Rockford Products Corporation, 55 323–25
Rockhaven Asset Management, LLC, **48** 18
Rocking Horse Child Care Centers of America Inc. *see* Nobel Learning Communities, Inc.
Rockland React-Rite, Inc., *see* Interface, Inc.
Rockport Company *see* Reebok International Ltd.
RockShox, Inc., 26 412–14
Rockwell Automation, 43 326–31 (upd.)
Rockwell International Corporation, I 78–80; 11 427–30 (upd.)
Rockwell Medical Technologies, Inc., 88 334–37
Rocky Mexico, Inc., **62** 353
Rocky Mountain Chocolate Factory, Inc., 73 280–82
Rocky River Power Co. *see* Connecticut Light and Power Co.
Rocky Shoes & Boots, Inc., 26 415–18
Rod's Food Products, **36** 163
Rodale, Inc., 23 415–17; 47 336–39 (upd.)
Rodamco N.V., 26 419–21
Rodel, Inc., **26** 425
Röder & Co., **34** 38, 40
Rodeway Inn *see* Choice Hotels International, Inc.
Rodgers Instrument Corporation, **38** 391
Rodney Square Management Corp., **25** 542
Rodriguez Group S.A., 90 357–60
Rodven Records, **23** 391
Roederstein GmbH, **21** 520
ROFIN-SINAR Technologies Inc, 81 345–48
Roger Cleveland Golf Company, **15** 462; **43** 375–76
Rogers & Co., **63** 17–18
Rogers & Phillips, Inc., **56** 383
Rogers CanGuard, Inc., **32** 374
Rogers Communications Inc., 30 388–92 (upd.) *see also* Maclean Hunter Publishing Ltd.
Rogers Corporation, 61 310–13; 80 313–17 (upd.)
Rohage GmbH, **74** 117
Rohde & Schwarz GmbH & Co. KG, 39 350–53
Röhm and Haas Company, I 391–93; 26 422–26 (upd.); 77 359–66 (upd.)
ROHN Industries, Inc., 22 467–69
Rohölgewinnungs AG, **IV** 485
Rohr Gruppe, **20** 100
Rohr Incorporated, 9 458–60 *see also* Goodrich Corp.
The Rokke Group, **32** 100; **59** 431
Rokko Warehouse & Transport Co. Ltd., **56** 181
Rolamentos FAG Ltda., **62** 132
Roland Berger & Partner GmbH, 37 333–36
Roland Corporation, 38 389–91
Roland Murten A.G., 7 452–53
Roland NV, **41** 340
Rolex *see* Montres Rolex S.A.
Roll International Corporation, 37 337–39
Rollerblade, Inc., 15 395–98; 34 388–92 (upd.)
Rolling Stones Records, **23** 33
Rollins, Inc., 11 431–34
Rolls-Royce Allison, 29 407–09 (upd.)
Rolls-Royce Group PLC, 67 331–36 (upd.)
Rolls-Royce Motors Ltd., I 194–96
Rolls-Royce plc, I 81–83; 7 454–57 (upd.); 21 433–37 (upd.)
Rolm Corp., **22** 51; **34** 512
Rolodex Electronics, **23** 209, 212
Rolscreen *see* Pella Corp.
Rolta India Ltd., 90 361–64
Roly Poly Franchise Systems LLC, 83 326-328
Romacorp, Inc., 58 307–11
Roman Meal Company, 84 331–334
Romeike Ltd., **55** 289
Romper Room Enterprises, Inc., *see* Hasbro, Inc.
Ron Tonkin Chevrolet Company, 55 326–28
RONA, Inc., 73 283–86
Ronco Corporation, 15 399–401; 80 318–23 (upd.)
Ronrico, **58** 195
Ronson PLC, 49 337–39
Ronzoni Foods Corp., **15** 221
Roombar S.A., **28** 241
Rooms To Go Inc., 28 389–92
Rooney Brothers Co., 25 402–04
Roosevelt Hospital *see* Continuum Health Partners, Inc.
Roots Canada Ltd., 42 325–27
Roper Industries, Inc., 15 402–04; 50 391–95 (upd.)
Ropes & Gray, 40 377–80
RoProperty Services BV *see* Rodamco N.V.
Rorer Group, I 666–68
Rosaen Co., **23** 82
Rosarita Food Company, **25** 278
Rosauers Supermarkets, Inc., 90 365–68
Rose & Co., **26** 65
Rose Acre Farms, Inc., 60 255–57
Rose Art Industries, 58 312–14
Rose Forgrove Ltd., **51** 249, 251
Rose Foundation, *see* Medco Containment Services Inc.
Rose's Stores, Inc., 13 444–46
Roseburg Forest Products Company, 58 315–17
RoseJohnson Incorporated, **14** 303; **50** 311
Rosemount Estates *see* Southcorp Ltd.
Rosemount Inc., 15 405–08 *see also* Emerson.
Rosenbluth International Inc., 14 407–09 *see also* American Express Co.
Rosenfeld Hat Company *see* Columbia Hat Co.
Rosengrens Produktions AB, **53** 158
Rosenmund-Guèdu, **31** 158
Rosenthal A.G., **34** 493, 496
Rosetta Stone Inc., 93 375–79
Roslyn Bancorp, **46** 316
Rosno, **73** 303–04
Ross Stores, Inc., 17 408–10; 43 332–35 (upd.)
Rossendale Combining Company, *see* British Vita PLC.
Rossignol Ski Company, Inc. *see* Skis Rossignol S.A.
Rostelecom, **59** 208–11
Rostocker Brauerei VEB, *see* Brauerei Beck & Co.
Rostvertol plc, 62 308–10
Roswell Public Service Company, **6** 579
Rosy Blue N.V., 84 335–338
Rotary International, 31 395–97
Rotec Zug AG, **57** 402
Rotelcom Data Inc., **6** 334
Rotem Amfert Negev Ltd., **55** 229
Roth Freres SA, **26** 231; **59** 252
Rothmans UK Holdings Limited, V 411–13; 19 367–70 (upd.)
The Rothschild's Haberdashery Ltd., **74** 330
Roto-Rooter, Inc., 15 409–11; 61 314–19 (upd.)
Rotork plc, 46 361–64
Rotterdam Beleggings (Investment) Consortium *see* Robeco.
The Rottlund Company, Inc., 28 393–95
Rouge Steel Company, 8 448–50
Rougier *see* Groupe Rougier, SA.
Roularta Media Group NV, 48 345–47
Round Hill Foods, **21** 535
Round Table, **16** 447
Rounder Records Corporation, 79 357–61
Roundy's Inc., 14 410–12; 58 318–21 (upd.)
Rouse & Associates, **57** 221–23
The Rouse Company, 15 412–15; 63 338–41 (upd.)
Roussel Uclaf, I 669–70; 8 451–53 (upd.)
Routh Robbins Companies, **21** 96
Roux Séguéla Cayzac & Goudard *see* Euro RSCG Worldwide S.A.
Rover Group Ltd., 7 458–60; 21 441–44 (upd.)
Rowan Companies, Inc., 43 336–39
Rowe Price-Fleming International, Inc., *see* T. Rowe Price Associates, Inc.
Rowell Welding Works, **26** 433
Rowenta *see* Groupe SEB.
Rowland Communications Worldwide, **42** 328, 331

Rowntree Mackintosh PLC, II 568–70 *see also* Nestlé S.A.
Roxell, N.V., **43** 129
Roxoil Drilling, *see* Mitchell Energy and Development Corp.
Roy Anderson Corporation, 75 344–46
Roy F. Weston, Inc., 33 369–72
Royal & Sun Alliance Insurance Group plc, 55 329–39 (upd.)
Royal Ahold N.V. *see* Koninklijke Ahold N.V.
Royal Appliance Manufacturing Company, 15 416–18
The Royal Bank of Canada, II 344–46; 21 445–48 (upd.); 81 349–55 (upd.)
The Royal Bank of Scotland Group plc, 12 421–23; 38 392–99 (upd.)
Royal Bankgroup of Acadiana, Inc., **37** 201
Royal Canin S.A., 39 354–57
Royal Caribbean Cruises Ltd., 22 470–73; 74 277–81 (upd.)
Royal China and Porcelain Companies Inc. *see* The Porcelain and Fine China Companies Ltd.
Royal Copenhagen A/S, *see* Carlsberg A/S.
Royal Crown Company, Inc., 23 418–20 *see also* Cott Corp.
Royal Data, Inc. *see* King Kullen Grocery Co., Inc.
Royal Doulton plc, 14 413–15; 38 400–04 (upd.)
Royal Dutch Petroleum Company, IV 530–32 *see also* Shell Transport and Trading Company p.l.c.
Royal Dutch/Shell Group, 49 340–44 (upd.)
Royal Food Products, **36** 163
Royal Gist-brocades NV, **56** 95
Royal Grolsch NV, 54 315–18
Royal Group Technologies Limited, 73 287–89
Royal Insurance Holdings plc, III 349–51 *see also* Royal & Sun Alliance Insurance Group plc .
Royal International Optical Inc. *see* U.S. Vision, Inc.
Royal Interocean Lines *see* Koninglijke Nedlloyd N.V.
Royal KPN N.V., 30 393–95
Royal Mail Group, **6** 416
Royal Nedlloyd *see* Koninglijke Nedlloyd N.V.
Royal Nepal Airline Corporation, 41 335–38
Royal Netherlands Steamship Company *see* KNSM.
Royal Numico N.V., 37 340–42
Royal Olympic Cruise Lines Inc., 52 297–99
Royal Orchid Holidays *see* Thai Airways International.
Royal Ordnance plc, *see* British Aerospace plc.
Royal Packaging Industries Van Leer N.V., 30 396–98
Royal Pakhoed N.V., **9** 532
Royal PTT Post, **30** 463
Royal Robbins, Inc. *see* Phoenix Footwear Group, Inc.
Royal Securities Company, **6** 585
Royal Sporting House Pte. Ltd., **21** 483
Royal Ten Cate N.V., 68 324–26
Royal Vendex KBB N.V. *see* Koninklijke Vendex KBB N.V. (Royal Vendex KBB N.V.).
Royal Vopak NV, 41 339–41
Royal Wessanen *see* Koninklijke Wessanen.
Royal Worcester Spode Ltd. *see* The Porcelain and Fine China Companies Ltd.
Royce Laboratories Inc., **56** 375
RPB Venture Capital Corporation, **72** 217
RPC Group PLC, 81 356–59
RPC, Inc., 91 413–16
RPG (Aventis) S.A. *see* Ranbaxy Laboratories Ltd.
RPI *see* Research Polymers International.
RPISA *see* Refinaria de Petróleo Ipiranga S.A.
RPM International Inc., 8 454–57; 36 394–98 (upd.); 91 417–25 (upd.)
RSA Security Inc., 46 365–68
RSC *see* Rental Service Corp.
RSO Records, **23** 390
RSV, **26** 496
RTI Group, **58** 366
RTL Group SA, 44 374–78
RTM Restaurant Group, 58 322–24
RTR Funding LLC, **70** 275
RTS Packaging, LLC, **59** 347, 350
RTW Air Service(s) Pte. Ltd., **51** 123
RTZ Corporation PLC, IV 189–92 *see also* Rio Tinto plc.
Rubbermaid Incorporated, III 613–15; 20 454–57 (upd.) *see also* Newell Rubbermaid Inc.
Rubicon Group plc, **32** 50
Rubio's Restaurants, Inc., 35 379–81
Rubo Lederwaren, **14** 225
Ruby Tuesday, Inc., 18 464–66; 71 317–20 (upd.)
Rubyco, Inc., **15** 386
La Ruche Meridionale, **12** 153
Ruddick Corporation, **23** 260; **72** 163, 165
Rudolf Wolff & Co. Ltd., **64** 297
Rudolph Technologies Inc., 94 375–78
Ruel Smith Transportation Services, Inc., **39** 66
Ruff Hewn, **25** 48
The Rugby Group plc, 31 398–400
Ruger Corporation, *see* Sturm, Ruger & Co., Inc.
Ruhrgas AG, V 704–06; 38 405–09 (upd.)
Ruhrkohle AG, IV 193–95 *see also* RAG AG.
Ruiz Food Products, Inc., 53 287–89
Rumasa, **69** 165
Rural Cellular Corporation, 43 340–42
Rural/Metro Corporation, 28 396–98
Rural Press Ltd., 74 282–85
Rush Communications, 33 373–75 *see also* Phat Fashions LLC.
Rush Enterprises, Inc., 64 336–38
Russ Berrie and Company, Inc., 12 424–26; 82 304–08 (upd.)
Russell Associates Inc. *see* Pall Corp.
Russell Corporation, 8 458–59; 30 399–401 (upd.); 82 309–13 (upd.)
Russell Kelly Office Services, Inc. *see* Kelly Services Inc.
Russell Reynolds Associates Inc., 38 410–12
Russell Stover Candies Inc., 12 427–29; 91 426–32 (upd.)
Russian Aircraft Corporation (MiG), 86 343–46
Russian Avionics Design Bureau CJSC, **68** 204
Russian Railways Joint Stock Co., 93 380–83
Rust International Inc., 11 435–36
Rust-Oleum Corporation, **36** 396
Rütgers AG, **60** 250
Ruth's Chris Steak House, 28 399–401; 88 338–42 (upd.)
Rutherford Hill Winery, **48** 392
RWD Technologies, Inc., 76 320–22
RWE Group, V 707–10; 50 396–400 (upd.)
RxAmerica, **22** 40; **25** 297
Ryan Aeronautical, *see* Teledyne, Inc.
Ryan Beck & Co., Inc., 66 273–75
Ryan Homes, Inc. *see* NVR Inc.
Ryan Insurance Company, *see* Aon Corp.
Ryan Milk Company of Kentucky, *see* Dean Foods Co.
Ryan's Restaurant Group, Inc., 15 419–21; 68 327–30 (upd.)
Ryanair Holdings plc, 35 382–85
Ryder System, Inc., V 504–06; 24 408–11 (upd.)
Ryecroft Foods Limited, **61** 387–88
Ryerson Tull, Inc., 40 381–84 (upd.)
Ryko Corporation, 83 329-333
Rykoff-Sexton, Inc., **21** 497; **26** 503, 505; **74** 350
The Ryland Group, Inc., 8 460–61; 37 343–45 (upd.)
Ryobi US, **73** 332
Ryohin Keikaku Co., Ltd., **36** 420
Ryoshoku Ltd., 72 300–02
Rysher Entertainment, **22** 162; **25** 329
The Ryvita Company Limited, *see* Associated British Foods plc.
RZB *see* Raiffeisen Zentralbank Österreich AG.
RZD *see* Russian Railways Joint Stock Co.

S

S&A Restaurant Corp., *see* Metromedia Companies.
S&C Electric Company, 15 422–24
S&D Coffee, Inc., 84 339–341
S&H *see* Sperry and Hutchinson Co.
S&H Diving Corporation, **6** 578
S&K Famous Brands, Inc., 23 421–23
S&P *see* Standard & Poor's Corp.
S&S/Superior of Ohio, Inc. *see* Accubuilt, Inc.

S+T Gesellschaft fur Reprotechnik mbH, **29** 306
S.A.C.I. Falabella, 69 311–13
S.A. Cockerill Sambre *see* Cockerill Sambre Group.
S.A. de C.V., **29** 461
S.A. des Ateliers d'Aviation Louis Breguet *see* Groupe Dassault Aviation SA.
s.a. GB-Inno-BM *see* GIB Group.
S.A. Greetings Corporation, Ltd., *see* American Greetings Corp.
S.A. Innovation—Bon Marché N.V., **26** 160
S.C. Johnson & Son, Inc., III 58–59; 28 409–12 (upd.); 89 382–89 (upd.)
S.E. Rykoff & Co., **26** 503
S.G. Warburg and Co. *see* SBC Warburg.
S.Gallardo, SL., **74** 185
S. Grumbacher & Son *see* The Bon-Ton Stores, Inc.
S.I.P., Co., *see* The Parsons Corp.
S-K-I Limited, 15 457–59
S.K. Wellman Ltd., **59** 222
S.P. Richards Co., **45** 177–79
S Pearson & Son Ltd. *see* Pearson plc
S.R. Dresser Manufacturing Co. *see* Dresser Industries, Inc.
S.S. Kresge Company *see* Kmart Corp.
S.S. Pierce Company, **60** 267
S.S.V. Inc., **36** 420
S.T. Cooper & Sons, *see* Jockey International, Inc.
S.T. Dupont Company, **23** 55
SA Alliance Air, **28** 404
SA Express, **28** 404
Sa SFC NV, *see* Essef Corp.
SAA *see* South African Airways.
SAA (Pty) Ltd., 28 402–04
SAAB *see* Svenska Aeroplan Aktiebolaget.
Saab Automobile AB, 32 386–89 (upd.); 83 334-339 (upd.)
Saab-Scania A.B., I 197–98; 11 437–39 (upd.)
Saarberg-Konzern, IV 196–99 *see also* RAG AG.
Saarstahl AG, *see* Usinor SA.
Saatchi & Saatchi plc, I 33–35; 33 328–31 (upd.)
SAB *see* South African Breweries Ltd.
SAB WABCO International AB, **53** 85
Saban Entertainment, *see* Fox Family Worldwide, Inc.
Sabanci Group, **54** 197–98
Sabanci Holdings *see* Haci Omer Sabanci Holdings A.S.
Sabaté Diosos SA, 48 348–50 *see also* OENEO S.A.
Sabela Media, Inc., **49** 423
Sabena S.A./N.V., 33 376–79
Saber Software Corp., **25** 348
Sabian Ltd., **38** 68
SABIC *see* Saudi Basic Industries Corp.
Sabine Transportation Company *see* Kirby Corp.
SABMiller plc, 59 352–58 (upd.)
SABO Maschinenfabrik AG, **21** 175
Sabratek Corporation, 29 410–12
Sabre Holdings Corporation, 26 427–30; 74 286–90 (upd.)
Sabre Interactive, **46** 434
Sacer, **31** 127–28
Sach Bicycle Components *see* SRAM Corp.
Sachs-Dolmer G.m.b.H., *see* Makita Corp.
Sacilor *see* Usinor S.A.
OY Saco AB, **23** 268
SACOR, **IV** 504–06
Saddlebag Lake Resorts, Inc., **63** 23
SADE Ingenieria y Construcciones S.A., **38** 435, 437
Sadia S.A., 59 359–62
Saf-T-Hammer Corporation *see* Smith & Wesson Corp.
Safe Flight Instrument Corporation, 71 321–23
SAFECO Corporation, III 352–54
Safeguard Scientifics, Inc., 10 473–75
Safelite Glass Corp., 19 371–73
Safer, Inc., **21** 385–86
Safeskin Corporation, 18 467–70 *see also* Kimberly-Clark Corp.
Safety Components International, Inc., 63 342–44
Safety 1st, Inc., 24 412–15
Safety-Kleen Systems Inc., 8 462–65; 82 314–20 (upd.)
Safeway Inc., II 654–56; 24 416–19 (upd.); 85 362–69 (upd.)
Safeway PLC, 50 401–06 (upd.)
Saffa SpA, **41** 325–26
Saffery Champness, 80 324–27
Saffil Ltd. *see* Dyson Group PLC.
Safilo SpA, 40 155–56; 54 319–21
SAFR *see* Société Anonyme des Fermiers Reúnis.
Saga *see* Sociedad Andina de Grandes Almeneces.
Saga Communications, Inc., 27 392–94
Saga Petroleum ASA, **35** 318
Sagami Optical Co., Ltd., **48** 295
Sagamore Insurance Company, **51** 37–39
The Sage Group, 43 343–46
Sagebrush Sales, Inc., *see* Ply Gem Industries Inc.
Sagebrush Steakhouse, **29** 201
SAGEM S.A., 37 346–48
Saginaw Mining Co., *see* Oglebay Norton Co.
Sagitta Arzneimittel, **18** 51; **50** 90
Sahara Casino Partners L.P., **19** 379
Sahara Las Vegas Corp. *see* Archon Corp.
SAI *see* Stamos Associates Inc.
Saia Motor Freight Line, Inc., **6** 421–23; **45** 448
Saibu Gas, **IV** 518–19
SAIC *see* Science Applications International Corp.
SAIC Velcorex, *see* Groupe DMC (Dollfus Mieg & Cie).
Saiccor, **IV** 92; **49** 353
SalesLink Corporation *see* CMGI, Inc.
Sainco *see* Sociedad Anonima de Instalaciones de Control.
Sainsbury's *see* J Sainsbury PLC.
St. Alban Boissons S.A., **22** 515
Saint-Gobain *see* Compagnie de Saint Gobain S.A.
Saint-Gobain Weber *see* Weber et Broutin France.
St. Ives Laboratories Inc., **36** 26
St Ives plc, 34 393–95
St. James Associates, **32** 362–63
St. James's Place Capital, plc, 71 324–26
The St. Joe Company, 31 422–25
St. Joe Corporation, **59** 185
St. Joe Gold, **23** 40
St. Joe Minerals Corp., *see* Flour Corp.
St. Joe Paper Company, 8 485–88
St. John Knits, Inc., 14 466–68
St. JON Laboratories, Inc., **74** 381
St. Jude Medical, Inc., 11 458–61; 43 347–52 (upd.)
St. Laurent Paperboard Inc., **30** 119
St. Lawrence Cement Inc., *see* Holnam Inc.
Saint Louis Bread Company, **18** 35, 37; **44** 327
St. Louis Concessions Inc., **21** 39
St. Louis Music, Inc., 48 351–54
St. Louis Post-Dispatch LLC, **58** 283
St. Luke's-Roosevelt Hospital Center *see* Continuum Health Partners, Inc.
St. Martin's Press, **25** 484–85; **35** 452
St. Mary Land & Exploration Company, 63 345–47
St. Michel-Grellier S.A., **44** 40
St. Paul Bank for Cooperatives, 8 489–90
St. Paul Book and Stationery, Inc., **47** 90
St. Paul Fire and Marine Insurance Co. *see* The St. Paul Companies, Inc.
The St. Paul Travelers Companies, Inc., III 355–57; 22 492–95 (upd.); 79 362–69 (upd.)
St. Paul Venture Capital Inc., **34** 405–06
St. Regis Paper Co., **12** 377
salesforce.com, Inc., 79 370–73
Saipem S.p.A. *see* ENI S.p.A.
SAirGroup, **29** 376; **33** 268, 271; **37** 241; **46** 398; **47** 287
SAirLogistics, **49** 80–81
Saison Group, **V** 184–85, 187–89; **36** 417–18, 420; **42** 340–41
Sakae Printing Co., Ltd., **64** 261
Sako Ltd., **39** 151
Saks Inc., 24 420–23; 41 342–45 (upd.)
Sakura Bank *see* Sumitomo Mitsui Banking Corp.
Salant Corporation, 12 430–32; 51 318–21 (upd.)
Sale Knitting Company *see* Tultex Corp.
Salem Broadcasting, **25** 508
Salem Sportswear, **25** 167
Salick Health Care, Inc., 53 290–92
Salient Partners & Pinnacle Trust Co., **70** 287
Salinas Equipment Distributors, Inc., **33** 364
Salix Pharmaceuticals, Ltd., 93 384–87
Sallie Mae *see* SLM Holding Corp.; Student Loan Marketing Association.
Sally Beauty Company, Inc., 60 258–60

Salomon Inc., **II 447–49**; **13 447–50 (upd.)** *see also* Citigroup Inc.
Salomon Worldwide, **20 458–60** *see also* adidas-Salomon AG.
Salon Cielo and Spa *see* Ratner Companies.
Salon Plaza *see* Ratner Companies.
Salt River Project, **19 374–76**
Salton, Inc., **30 402–04**; **88 343–48 (upd.)**
Salvagnini Company, **22** 6
The Salvation Army USA, **32 390–93**
Salvatore Ferragamo Italia S.p.A., **62 311–13**
Salzgitter AG, **IV 200–01**
SAM *see* Sociedad Aeronáutica de Medellín, S.A.
Sam & Libby Inc., **30** 311
Sam Ash Music Corporation, **30 405–07**
Sam Goody, **63** 65
Sam Levin Inc., **80 328–31**
Sam's Club, **40 385–87**
Samancor Ltd., **IV** 92–93
Samaritan Senior Services Inc., **25** 503
Samas-Groep N.V., **47** 91
Samcor Glass *see* Corning Inc.
Samedan Oil Corporation, *see* Noble Affiliates, Inc.
Sames, S.A., **21** 65–66
Samick Musical Instruments Co., Ltd., **56 297–300**
Samim, **IV** 422
Sammy Corp., **54** 16; **73** 291
Samna Corp., **6** 256; **25** 300
Sampoerna PT, **62** 96–97
Sampson Supermarkets, Inc., *see* Hannaford Bros. Co.
Samson Technologies Corp., **30** 406
Samsonite Corporation, **13 451–53**; **43 353–57 (upd.)**
Samsung Display Co., Ltd., **59** 81
Samsung Electronics Co., Ltd., **14 416–18**; **41 346–49 (upd.)**
Samsung Group, **I 515–17**
Samuel Austin & Son Company, *see* The Austin Co.
Samuel Cabot Inc., **53 293–95**
Samuel Meisel & Company, Inc., *see* Duty Free International, Inc.
Samuels Jewelers Incorporated, **30 408–10**
San Antonio Public Service Company *see* City Public Service.
San Diego Gas & Electric Company, **V 711–14** *see also* Sempra Energy.
San Diego Padres Baseball Club L.P., **78 324–27**
San Francisco Baseball Associates, L.P., **55 340–43**
San Francisco Maillots, **62** 228
San Giorgio Macaroni Inc., **53** 242
San Jose Water Company *see* SJW Corp.
San Miguel Corporation, **15 428–30**; **57 303–08 (upd.)**
San Paolo IMI S.p.A., **63** 52–53
Sanborn Hermanos, S.A., **20 461–63**
Sanborn Manufacturing Company, **30** 138
Sanborn Map Company Inc., **82 321–24**
The Sanctuary Group PLC, **69 314–17**
Sandals Resorts International, **65 302–05**
Sandcastle 5 Productions, **25** 269–70
Sanders Morris Harris Group Inc., **70 285–87**
Sanderson Farms, Inc., **15 425–27**
Sandia National Laboratories, **49 345–48**
Sandiacre Packaging Machinery Ltd., **51** 249–50
Sandoz Ltd., **I 671–73** *see also* Novartis AG.
Sandusky Plastics, Inc., *see* Envirodyne Industries, Inc.
Sandusky Portland Cement Company, *see* Medusa Corp.
Sandvik AB, **IV 202–04**; **32 394–98 (upd.)**; **77 367–73 (upd.)**
Sandwell, Inc., **6** 491
Sandwich Chef, Inc. *see* Wall Street Deli, Inc.
Sandy's Pool Supply, Inc. *see* Leslie's Poolmart, Inc.
Sanford C. Bernstein Inc., **63** 27
Sanford L.P., **82 325–29**
Sanford-Brown College, Inc., **41** 419–20
Sanitation Systems, Inc. *see* HMI Industries.
Sanitec Corporation, **51 322–24**
Sanko Peterson Corporation, **55** 306
Sankyo Company, Ltd., **I 674–75**; **56 301–04 (upd.)**
Sanlam Ltd., **68 331–34**
SANlight Inc., **62** 293
Sano Corporation, **63** 142
The Sanofi-Synthélabo Group, **I 676–77**; **49 349–51 (upd.)**
SanomaWSOY Corporation, **51 325–28**
Sanpaolo IMI S.p.A., **50 407–11**
Sanrio Company, Ltd., **38 413–15**
Sansone Group, **69** 120
Santa Barbara Restaurant Group, Inc., **37 349–52**
The Santa Cruz Operation, Inc., **38 416–21**
Santa Fe Gaming Corporation, **19 377–79** *see also* Archon Corp.
Santa Fe Gold Corporation, **38** 232
Santa Fe Industries, **12** 19; **28** 498
Santa Fe International Corporation, **38 422–24**
Santa Fe Pacific Corporation, **V 507–09** *see also* Burlington Northern Santa Fe Corp.
Santa Fe Snyder Corp., **61** 75
Santa Fe Southern Pacific Corp., **6** 150, 599; **22** 491
Santa Isabel S.A., **69** 94
Santa Margherita S.p.A. *see* Industrie Zignago Santa Margherita S.p.A.
Santal, **26** 160
Santiago Land Development Corporation, **58** 20
Santos Ltd., **81 360–63**
Sanwa Bank, Ltd., **II 347–48**; **15 431–33 (upd.)**
Sanwa USA Inc., **70** 213
Sanyo Electric Co., Ltd., **II 91–92**; **36 399–403 (upd.)**
Sanyo-Kokusaku Pulp Co., Ltd., **IV 327–28**
Sanyo White Cement Co. Ltd., **60** 301
Sao Paulo Alpargatas S.A., **75 347–49**
SAP AG, **16 441–44**; **43 358–63 (upd.)**
Sapa AB, **84 342–345**
SAPAC *see* Société Parisienne d'Achats en Commun.
Sapeksa, **55** 189
Sapirstein Greeting Card Company *see* American Greetings Corp.
Sappi Limited, **49 352–55**
Sapporo Breweries Limited, **I 282–83**; **13 454–56 (upd.)**; **36 404–07 (upd.)**;
SAPRA-Landauer Ltd., **51** 210
Saputo Inc., **59 363–65**
Sara Lee Corporation, **II 571–73**; **15 434–37 (upd.)**; **54 322–27 (upd.)**
Saracen's Head Brewery, **21** 245
Saratoga Partners, **24** 436
Sarawak Trading, *see* Sime Darby Berhad.
Sargent & Lundy, **6** 556
Sarma, **26** 159–61
Sarmag, **26** 161
Sarnoff Corporation, **57 309–12**
Saros Corp., **15** 474; **62** 141
Sarotti GmbH, **53** 315
Sarpe, **IV** 591
Sarriò S.A., **41** 325–26
Sarris Candies Inc., **86 347–50**
Sartek Industries Inc., **44** 441
The SAS Group, **34 396–99 (upd.)**
SAS Institute Inc., **10 476–78**; **78 328–32 (upd.)**
Saskatchewan Oil and Gas Corporation, *see* Wascana Energy Inc.
Sasol Limited, **IV 533–35**; **47 340–44 (upd.)**
Sasu Ldc Sable, **68** 234
SAT *see* Stockholms Allmänna Telefonaktiebolag.
Satcom Group of Companies, **32** 40
Satellite Business Systems, **21** 14; **23** 135; **27** 304
Satellite Software International, *see* WordPerfect Corp.
Satellite Television PLC, **23** 135
Saturn Corporation, **7 461–64**; **21 449–53 (upd.)**; **80 332–38 (upd.)**
Saturn Industries, Inc., **23** 489
SATV *see* Satellite Television PLC.
Satyam Computer Services Ltd., **85 370–73**
Saucona Iron Co., *see* Bethlehem Steel Corp.
Saucony Inc., **35 386–89**; **86 351–56 (upd.)**
Sauder Woodworking Co., **12 433–34**; **35 390–93 (upd.)**
Saudi Arabian Airlines, **6 114–16**; **27 395–98 (upd.)**

Saudi Arabian Oil Company, IV 536–39; 17 411–15 (upd.); 50 412–17 (upd.) *see also* Arabian American Oil Co.
Saudi Arabian Parsons Limited, *see* The Parsons Co.
Saudi Basic Industries Corporation (SABIC), 58 325–28
Saudia *see* Saudi Arabian Airlines.
Sauer-Danfoss Inc., 61 320–22
Saul Ewing LLP, 74 291–94
Saunders, Karp, and Megrue, LP, **26** 190; **28** 258; **70** 121
Saupiquet SA *see* Bolton Group B.V.
Saur S.A.S., 92 327–30
Sauza, **31** 92
Sav-on Drug, *see* American Stores Co.
Sava Group, **20** 263
Savacentre Ltd., *see* J Sainsbury plc.
Savannah Electric & Power Company, **38** 448
Savannah Foods & Industries, Inc., 7 465–67 *see also* Imperial Sugar Co.
Savannah Gas Company, **6** 448; **23** 29
Save Mart, **27** 292
Save.com, **37** 409
Savia S.A. de C.V., **29** 435
Savio, **IV** 422
Savoy Pictures Entertainment Inc., **25** 214
Sawdust Pencil Company, **29** 372
Sawgrass Asset Management, LLC, **48** 18
Sawhill Tubular Products, **41** 3
Sawtek Inc., 43 364–66 (upd.)
Saxon Oil, *see* Enterprise Oil plc.
Saxonville USA, **61** 254, 256
Sayers & Scovill *see* Accubuilt, Inc.
SB Acquisitions, Inc., **46** 74
SBAR, Inc., **30** 4
Sbarro, Inc., 16 445–47; 64 339–42 (upd.)
SBC Communications Inc., 32 399–403 (upd.)
SBC Transportation, Inc. *see* Schwebel Baking Co.
SBC Warburg, 14 419–21 *see also* UBS AG.
Sberbank, 62 314–17
SBI *see* State Bank of India.
SBK Entertainment World, Inc., **22** 194; **26** 187
SBM Group, **71** 178–79
SBS Broadcasting, **61** 58
SBS Technologies, Inc., 25 405–07
SCA *see* Svenska Cellulosa AB.
SCAC *see* Société Commercial d'Affrètements et de Combustibles.
Scaldia Paper BV, **15** 229
Scali, McCabe & Sloves, **71** 158
Scan Screen, **IV** 600
SCANA Corporation, 6 574–76; 56 305–08 (upd.)
Scanair, **34** 397–98
Scancem, **38** 437
Scandic Hotels AB, **49** 193
Scandinavian Airlines System, I 119–20 *see also* The SAS Group.
Scandinavian Broadcasting System SA, **53** 325
Scania-Vabis *see* Saab-Scania AB.
ScanSource, Inc., 29 413–15; 74 295–98 (upd.)
Scantron Corporation, *see* John H. Harland Co.
Scarborough Public Utilities Commission, 9 461–62
SCB Computer Technology, Inc., 29 416–18
SCEcorp, V 715–17 *see also* Edison International.
Scenic Airlines, Inc., *see* SkyWest, Inc.
Scenographic Designs, **21** 277
SCG Corporation, **56** 323
Schäfer, **31** 158
Schauman Wood Oy, *see* UPM-Kymmene Corp.
Schawk, Inc., 24 424–26
SCHC, Inc. *see* Shoe Carnival Inc.
Scheels All Sports Inc., 63 348–50
Scheid Vineyards Inc., 66 276–78
Schein Pharmaceutical Inc., *see* Bayer A.G.
Schell Brewing *see* August Schell Brewing Company Inc.
Schenck Business Solutions, 88 349–53
Schenker Deutschland AG, **59** 391
Schenker-Rhenus Ag, 6 424–26
Scherer *see* R.P. Scherer.
Scherer Brothers Lumber Company, 94 379–83
Schering A.G., I 681–82; 50 418–22 (upd.)
Schering-Plough Corporation, I 683–85; 14 422–25 (upd.); 49 356–62 (upd.)
Schibsted ASA, 31 401–05
Schick Products, **41** 366
Schick Shaving, **38** 363, 365
Schick-Wilkinson Sword *see* Wilkinson Sword Ltd.
Schieffelin & Somerset Co., 61 323–25
Schindler Holding AG, 29 419–22
Schlage Lock Company, 82 330–34
Schlitz Brewing Co., **12** 338; **23** 403
Schlotzsky's, Inc., 36 408–10
Schlumberger Limited, III 616–18; 17 416–19 (upd.); 59 366–71 (upd.)
SchlumbergerSema *see* Atos Origin S.A.
Schmalbach-Lubeca-Werke A.G., **15** 128
Schmermund Verpackungstechnik GmbH, **60** 193
Schmitt Music Company, 40 388–90
Schneider National, Inc., 36 411–13; 77 374–78 (upd.)
Schneider S.A., II 93–94; 18 471–74 (upd.)
Schneiderman's Furniture Inc., 28 405–08
Schnitzer Steel Industries, Inc., 19 380–82
Schnuck Markets, Inc., **60** 256; **63** 129
Schober Direktmarketing, **18** 170
Schoeller & Co. Bank AG, **59** 239
Schoeller & Hoesch Group, **30** 349, 352
Schoenfeld Industries, **16** 511
Scholastic Corporation, 10 479–81; 29 423–27 (upd.)
Scholl Inc., **49** 359, 380
Schöller Holding GmbH & Co. KG, *see* Südzucker AG.
School Specialty, Inc., 68 335–37
School-Tech, Inc., 62 318–20
Schorghuber, **70** 61
Schott Brothers, Inc., 67 337–39
Schott Corporation, 53 296–98
Schottenstein Stores Corp., 14 426–28 *see also* Retail Ventures, Inc.
Schouw & Company A/S, 94 384–87
Schreiber Foods, Inc., 72 303–06
Schreiber Frères *see* Groupe Les Echos.
Schrock Cabinet Company, *see* White Consolidated Industries Inc.
Schroders plc, 42 332–35
Schroff Inc., **26** 361, 363
Schubach, **30** 408
Schubert & Salzer GmbH, **42** 316
Schuck's Auto Supply *see* CSK Auto Corp.
Schuff Steel Company, 26 431–34
Schuler Chocolates, **15** 65
Schuler Homes, Inc., **58** 84
Schultz Sav-O Stores, Inc., 21 454–56; 31 406–08 (upd.)
Schultz, Snyder & Steele Lumber Company, **61** 254, 256
Schwabel Corporation, **19** 453
The Schwan Food Company, 7 468–70; 26 435–38 (upd.); 83 340-346 (upd.)
Schwarze Pumpe, **38** 408
Schwebel Baking Company, 72 307–09
Schweitzer-Mauduit International, Inc., 52 300–02
Schweizerische Post-, Telefon- und Telegrafen-Betriebe, V 321–24
Schweizerische Ruckversicherungs-Gesellschaft *see* Swiss Reinsurance Co.
Schweppes Ltd. *see* Cadbury Schweppes PLC.
Schwinn Cycle and Fitness L.P., 19 383–85 *see also* Huffy Corp.
SCI *see* Service Corporation International; Société Centrale d'Investissement.
SCI 169 Rue de Rennes, **53** 32
SCI Systems, Inc., 9 463–64
Scicon International, **49** 165
SciCor Inc., **30** 152
Science Applications International Corporation, 15 438–40
Scientific-Atlanta, Inc., 6 335–37; 45 371–75 (upd.)
Scientific Games Corporation, 64 343–46 (upd.)
Scientific Research Products, Inc. of Delaware, **60** 287
Scitex Corporation Ltd., 24 427–32
Scitor, **52** 108
SCLC, Inc. *see* Shoe Carnival Inc.
SCO *see* Santa Cruz Operation, Inc.
The SCO Group Inc., 78 333–37
Scope Products, Inc., 94 388–91
Scopus Technology Inc., **38** 431
SCOR S.A., 20 464–66
The Score Board, Inc., 19 386–88
Score Entertainment *see* Donruss Playoff L.P.
Score! Learning, Inc., **42** 211
Scotch House Ltd., *see* GUS plc.

Scotiabank *see* The Bank of Nova Scotia.
Scotsman Industries, Inc., 20 467–69
Scott-Ballantyne Company *see* Ballantyne of Omaha, Inc.
Scott Fetzer Company, 12 435–37; 80 339–43 (upd.)
Scott Health Care, **28** 445
Scott Holdings, *see* Schwinn Cycle and Fitness L.P.
Scott Paper Company, IV 329–31; 31 409–12 (upd.)
Scotti Brothers, **20** 3
Scottish & Newcastle plc, 15 441–44; 35 394–97 (upd.)
Scottish and Southern Energy plc, 13 457–59; 66 279–84 (upd.)
Scottish Amicable plc, **48** 328
Scottish Brick, **14** 250
Scottish Electric, **6** 453
Scottish Media Group plc, 32 404–06; 41 350–52
Scottish Mutual plc, **39** 5–6
Scottish Power plc, 49 363–66 (upd.)
Scottish Radio Holding plc, 41 350–52
Scottish Sealand Oil Services Ltd., **25** 171
Scottish Universal Investments, **45** 189
ScottishPower plc, 19 389–91
ScottishTelecom plc, *see* Scottish Power plc
Scottrade, Inc., 85 374–77
The Scotts Company, 22 474–76
Scotty's, Inc., 22 477–80
The Scoular Company, 77 379–82
Scovill Fasteners Inc., 24 433–36
SCP Pool Corporation, 39 358–60
Screen Actors Guild, 72 310–13
Screg Group, *see* Bouygues S.A.
Scripps-Howard, Inc. *see* The E.W. Scripps Co.
The Scripps Research Institute, 76 323–25
Scrivner Inc., **17** 180
SCS *see* Southern Corrections Systems, Inc.
SCS Interactive, **44** 261
Scudder Kemper Investments *see* Zurich Financial Services.
SD Warren, **49** 352–53
SDA Systems Inc., **48** 75
SDB Espan, **51** 16
SDGE *see* San Diego Gas & Electric Co.
SDK Health Care Information Systems, **16** 94
SDL PLC, 67 340–42
SDV *see* Groupe Bolloré.
Sea Containers Ltd., 29 428–31
Sea-Land Service Inc., *see* CSX Corp.
Sea Star Line, **41** 399
Sea World Property Trust, **58** 359
Seabee Corp., **18** 276
Seaboard Air Line Railroad *see* CSX Corp.
Seaboard Corporation, 36 414–16; 85 378–82 (upd.)
Seabourn Cruise Lines, *see* Carnival Corp.
Seabulk International, Inc. *see* Hvide Marine Inc.; SEACOR Holdings Inc.
SeaCat Corporation, **59** 282
SeaChange International, Inc., 79 374–78
SEACOR Holdings Inc., 83 347-350
Seafield Capital Corporation *see* LabOne, Inc.
Seafirst *see* Seattle First National Bank, Inc.
Seagate Technology, Inc., 8 466–68; 34 400–04 (upd.)
The Seagram Company Ltd., I 284–86; 25 408–12 (upd.)
Seagull Energy Corporation, 11 440–42
Seahawk Services Ltd., **37** 289
Seal Products, Inc., **12** 264
Seal Sands Chemicals, **16** 69
Sealaska Corporation, 60 261–64
Sealed Air Corporation, 14 429–31; 57 313–17 (upd.)
Sealed Power Corporation, I 199–200 *see also* SPX Corp.
SeaLite Sciences, Inc., **52** 171
Sealright Co., Inc., 17 420–23
SealRite Windows, **19** 446
Sealtest, **14** 205
Sealy Inc., 12 438–40
Seaman Furniture Company, Inc., 32 407–09
Sean John Clothing, Inc., 70 288–90
Seaquist Manufacturing Corporation, *see* Pittway Corp.
Searle & Co *see* G.D. Searle & Co.
Sears plc, V 177–79
Sears, Roebuck and Co., V 180–83; 18 475–79 (upd.); 56 309–14 (upd.)
Sears Roebuck de México, S.A. de C.V., 20 470–72
SEAT *see* Sociedad Española de Automoviles de Turismo.
Seat Pagine Gialle S.p.A., 47 345–47
Seattle Brewing and Malting Company *see* Rainier Brewing Co.
Seattle City Light, 50 423–26
Seattle Coffee Company, **32** 12, 15
Seattle Electric Company, **6** 565; **50** 365–66
Seattle FilmWorks, Inc., 20 473–75
Seattle First National Bank Inc., 8 469–71 *see also* Bank of America Corp.
Seattle Lighting Fixture Company, 92 331–34
Seattle Pacific Industries, Inc., 92 335–38
Seattle Seahawks, Inc., 92 339–43
Seattle Times Company, 15 445–47
Seaway Food Town, Inc., 15 448–50 *see also* Spartan Stores Inc.
SeaWest, **19** 390
SEB Group *see* Skandinaviska Enskilda Banken AB.
SEB S.A. *see* Groupe SEB.
Sebastian International, **48** 422
Sebastiani Vineyards, Inc., 28 413–15
Seco Products Corporation, **22** 354
The Second City, Inc., 88 354–58
Second Harvest, 29 432–34
SecPac *see* Security Pacific Corp.
Secure Horizons, *see* PacifiCare Health Systems, Inc.
Secure Networks, Inc., **25** 349
Securicor Plc, 45 376–79
Securitas AB, 42 336–39
Securities Management & Research, Inc., *see* American National Insurance Co.
Security Capital Corporation, 17 424–27
Security Capital Group, **56** 58–59
Security Data Group, **32** 373
Security Dynamics Technologies, Inc., **46** 367
Security Pacific Corporation, II 349–50
Security State Bank, *see* Habersham Bancorp.
SED International Holdings, Inc., 43 367–69
Seddon Group Ltd., 67 343–45
Sedgwick Sales, Inc., **29** 384
***see's Candies, Inc.*, 30 411–13**
Seeburg Corporation, **15** 538
Seed Solutions, Inc., **11** 491; **69** 341
Seeman Brothers *see* White Rose, Inc.
SEEQ Technology, Inc., **13** 47; **17** 32, 34; **64** 246
SEGA Corporation, 73 290–93
Sega Enterprises, Ltd., **28** 320
Sega of America, Inc., 10 482–85
Seguros Comercial America, **21** 413
Seguros Monterrey Aetna, **45** 294
Seguros Serfin S.A., **25** 290
Segway LLC, 48 355–57
Seibert-Oxidermo, Inc., **55** 321
Seibu Department Stores, Ltd., V 184–86; 42 340–43 (upd.)
Seibu Group, **36** 417–18; **47** 408–09
Seibu Railway Company Ltd., V 510–11; 74 299–301 (upd.)
Seibu Saison, **6** 207
Seifu Co. Ltd., **48** 250
Seigle's Home and Building Centers, Inc., 41 353–55
Seihoku Packaging Company *see* JSP Corp.
Seiko Corporation, III 619–21; 17 428–31 (upd.); 72 314–18 (upd.)
Seiko Instruments USA Inc., **23** 210
Seikosha Co., **64** 261
Seimi Chemical Co. Ltd., **48** 41
Seino Transportation Company, Ltd., 6 427–29
Seirt SAU, **76** 326–27
Seismograph Service Limited, **11** 413; **17** 419
Seita, 23 424–27 *see also* Altadis S.A.
Seitel, Inc., 47 348–50
The Seiyu, Ltd., V 187–89; 36 417–21 (upd.)
Sekisui Chemical Co., Ltd., III 741–43; 72 319–22 (upd.)
Selat Marine Services, **22** 276
Selby Shoe Company, **48** 69
Select Comfort Corporation, 34 405–08
Select Energy, Inc., **48** 305
Select Medical Corporation, 65 306–08
Select Theatres Corp. *see* Shubert Organization Inc.
Selection Trust, **IV** 565
Selectour SA, 53 299–301

Selectronics Inc., **23** 210
Selectrons Ltd., **41** 367
Selee Corporation, 88 359–62
Selena Coffee Inc., **39** 409
Self Auto, **23** 232
Self-Service Drive Thru, Inc., *see* Rally's.
Selfix, Inc. *see* Home Products International, Inc.
Selfridges Plc, 34 409–11
Selig Chemical Industries, **54** 252, 254
Selkirk Communications Ltd., **26** 273
Sells-Floto, **32** 186
The Selmer Company, Inc., 19 392–94
Seltel International Inc., **35** 246
Sema plc, **59** 370
Semarca, **11** 523
SembCorp Logistics Ltd., **53** 199, 203
Sembler Company, **11** 346
SEMCO Energy, Inc., 44 379–82
Semi-Tech Global, **30** 419–20
Seminis, Inc., 29 435–37
Seminole Electric Cooperative, **6** 583
Seminole Fertilizer, *see* Tosco Corp.
Seminole National Bank, **41** 312
Semitic, Inc., **33** 248
Semitool, Inc., 18 480–82; 79 379–82 (upd.)
Sempra Energy, 25 413–16 (upd.)
Semtech Corporation, 32 410–13
Seneca Foods Corporation, 17 432–34; 60 265–68 (upd.)
Senega, **63** 365
Sengstacke Enterprises *see* Real Times LLC.
Sennheiser Electronic GmbH & Co. KG, 66 285–89
Senomyx, Inc., 83 351-354
Sensi, Inc., *see* Deckers Outdoor Corp.
Sensient Technologies Corporation, 52 303–08 (upd.)
Sensormatic Electronics Corp., 11 443–45
Sensory Science Corporation, 37 353–56
Sentry Insurance Company, **10** 210
Sentry Markets, Inc., *see* Fleming Companies, Inc.
La Senza Corporation, 66 205–07
Sepal, Ltd., **39** 152, 154
AB Separator *see* Alfa-Laval AB
Sephora Holdings S.A., 82 335–39
SEPI *see* Sociedad Estatal de Participaciones Industriales.
Sepracor Inc., 45 380–83
Sequa Corporation, 13 460–63; 54 328–32 (upd.)
Sequana Capital, 78 338–42 (upd.)
Sequel Corporation, **41** 193
Sequent Computer Systems Inc., **10** 363
Sequoia Athletic Company, **25** 450
Sera-Tec Biologicals, Inc. *see* Rite Aid Corp.
Seragen Inc., **47** 223
Serco Group plc, 47 351–53
Sereg Valves, S.A., *see* Duriron Co. Inc.
Serewatt AG, **6** 491
Serologicals Corporation, 63 351–53
Serono S.A., 47 354–57
Serta, Inc., 28 416–18
Servam Corp., *see* Service America Corp.
Service and Systems Solutions Ltd., **64** 404
Service America Corp., 7 471–73
Service Co., Ltd., **48** 182
Service Control Corp. *see* Angelica Corp.
Service Corporation International, 6 293–95; 51 329–33 (upd.)
Service Master L.P., **34** 153
Service Merchandise Company, Inc., V 190–92; 19 395–99 (upd.)
Service Products Buildings, Inc. *see* Turner Construction Co.
Service Q. General Service Co., *see* Koninklijke Luchtvaart Maatschappij N.V.
The ServiceMaster Company, 6 44–46; 23 428–31 (upd.); 68 338–42 (upd.)
Services Maritimes des Messageries Impériales *see* Compagnie des Messageries Maritimes.
ServiceWare, Inc., **25** 118
Servicios de Corte y Confeccion, S.A. de C.V., **64** 142
Servicios Financieros Quadrum S.A., **14** 156; **76** 129
Servisair Plc, **49** 320
ServiStar Coast to Coast Corporation *see* TruServ Corp.
ServoChem A.B., **I** 387
Servomation Wilbur *see* Service America Corp.
Servoplan, S.A., **8** 272
Servpro Industries, Inc., 85 383–86
SES Staffing Solutions, *see* AHL Services, Inc.
Sesamee Mexicana, **48** 142
Sessler Inc., **19** 381
Setagaya Industry Co., Ltd., **48** 295
Seton Scholl *see* SSL International plc.
7-Eleven, Inc., 32 414–18 (upd.)
Seven-Eleven Japan Co. *see* Ito-Yokado Co., Ltd.
Seven Generation, Inc., **41** 177
Seven Hills Paperboard, LLC, **59** 350
Seven Network Limited, **25** 329
SevenOne Media, **54** 297
Sevenson Environmental Services, Inc., 42 344–46
Seventh Generation, Inc., 73 294–96
Seventh Street Corporation, **60** 130
Severn Trent PLC, 12 441–43; 38 425–29 (upd.)
Severonickel Combine, **48** 300
Severstal Joint Stock Company, 65 309–12
Sextant In-Flight Systems, LLC, **30** 74
Seyfarth Shaw LLP, 93 388–91
Seymour International Press Distributor Ltd., **IV** 619
Seymour Press, **IV** 619
SF Bio, **52** 51
SF Recycling & Disposal, Inc., **60** 224
SFI Group plc, 51 334–36
SFIC Holdings (Cayman) Inc., **38** 422
SFIM Industries, **37** 348
SFNGR *see* Nouvelles Galeries Réunies.
SFS Bancorp Inc., **41** 212
SFX Broadcasting Inc., **24** 107
SFX Entertainment, Inc., 36 422–25
SG Cowen Securities Corporation, **75** 186–87
SG Racing, Inc., **64** 346
SGC *see* Supermarkets General Corp.
SGE *see* Vinci.
SGI, 29 438–41 (upd.)
SGL Carbon Group, **40** 83; **46** 14
SGS-Thomson Microelectronics, **54** 269–70
Shakespeare Company, 22 481–84
Shakey's Pizza, *see* Jacmar Companies.
Shaklee Corporation, 12 444–46; 39 361–64 (upd.)
Shampaine Industries, Inc., **37** 399
Shamrock Broadcasting Inc., **24** 107
Shamrock Holdings, **25** 268
Shan-Chih Business Association, **23** 469
Shana Corporation, **62** 142
Shandong Nichirei Foods Company Ltd. *see* Nichirei Corp.
Shandwick International, **47** 97
Shanggong Co. Ltd., **65** 134
Shanghai Asia Pacific Co., **59** 59
Shanghai Autobacs Paian Auto Service Co., **76** 38
Shanghai Baosteel Group Corporation, 71 327–30
Shanghai Dajiang, **62** 63
Shanghai General Bearing Co., Ltd., **45** 170
Shanghai International Finance Company Limited, **15** 433
Shanghai Kyocera Electronics Co., Ltd., **21** 331
Shanghai Petrochemical Co., Ltd., 18 483–85
Shanghai Shesuo UNF Medical Diagnostic Reagents Co., **61** 229
Shanghai Tobacco, **49** 150, 153
Shangri-La Asia Ltd., 71 331–33
Shanks Group plc, 45 384–87
Shannon Aerospace Ltd., 36 426–28
Shannon Group, Inc., *see* Manitowoc Co., Inc.
Shansby Group, **27** 197; **43** 218; **64** 265
Shanshin Engineering Company Ltd., **60** 236
Shared Financial Systems, Inc., **10** 501
Shared Medical Systems Corporation, 14 432–34 *see also* Siemens AG.
ShareWave Inc., **48** 92
Shari Lewis Enterprises, Inc., **28** 160
Sharmoon, **63** 151
Sharp Corporation, II 95–96; 12 447–49 (upd.); 40 391–95 (upd.)
Sharp Water, Inc., **56** 62
The Sharper Image Corporation, 10 486–88; 62 321–24 (upd.)
Sharples Separator Company, **64** 17
Shasta Beverages *see* National Beverage Corp.
Shato Holdings, Ltd., **60** 357
Shaw Communications Inc., **26** 274; **35** 69
The Shaw Group, Inc., 50 427–30

Shaw Industries, Inc., **9 465–67; 40 396–99 (upd.)**
Shaw's Supermarkets, Inc., **56 315–18**
Shea Homes *see* J.F. Shea Co., Inc.
Sheaffer Group, **23** 54, 57
Sheaffer Pen Corporation, **82 340–43**
Shearer's Foods, Inc., **72 323–25**
Shearman & Sterling, **32 419–22**
Shearson Lehman Brothers Holdings Inc., **II 450–52; 9 468–70 (upd.)**
Shedd Aquarium Society, **73 297–99**
Sheetz, Inc., **85 387–90**
Sheffield Exploration Company, **28** 470
Sheffield Forgemasters Group Ltd., **39** 32
Sheffield Silver Company, **67** 322–23
Shekou Container Terminal, **16** 481; **38** 345
Shelby Steel Processing Co., **51** 238
Shelby Williams Industries, Inc., **14 435–37**
Sheldahl Inc., **23 432–35**
Shelf Life Inc. *see* King Kullen Grocery Co., Inc.
Shell *see* Royal Dutch/Shell Group; Shell Oil Company; Shell Transport and Trading Company p.l.c.
Shell Canada Limited, **32** 45
Shell Chemical Corporation, **IV** 531–32, 540
Shell Forestry, **21** 546; **50** 58
Shell France, **12** 153
Shell Oil Company, **IV 540–41; 14 438–40 (upd.); 41 356–60 (upd.)**
Shell Transport and Trading Company p.l.c., **IV 530–32** *see also* Royal Dutch Petroleum Company; Royal Dutch/Shell.
Sheller-Globe Corporation, **I 201–02** *see also* Lear Corp.
Shells Seafood Restaurants, Inc., **43 370–72**
Shelly Brothers, Inc., **15** 65
Shenandoah Telecommunications Company, **89 390–93**
Shenhua Group *see* China Shenhua Energy Company Limited
Shenzhen Namtek Co., Ltd., **61** 232–33
Shepherd Neame Limited, **30 414–16**
Shepherd Products Ltd., *see* The Marmon Group, Inc.
Sheraton Corp. of America, *see* ITT Sheraton Corp.
The Sheridan Group, Inc., **86 357–60**
Shermag, Inc., **93 392–97**
Sherr-Gold, **23** 40
The Sherwin-Williams Company, **III 744–46; 13 469–71 (upd.); 89 394–400 (upd.)**
Sherwood Brands, Inc., **53 302–04**
Sherwood Equity Group Ltd. *see* National Discount Brokers Group, Inc.
Sherwood Medical Group, *see* American Home Porducts.
Sherwood Securities, **66** 308
Shiara Holdings, Inc., **53** 88
Shidler Group *see* First Industrial Realty Trust, Inc.
Shihen Technical Corporation, **60** 272
Shihlin Electric & Engineering Group, **49** 460
Shikoku Electric Power Company, Inc., **V 718–20; 60 269–72 (upd.)**
Shiley, Inc., **38** 361
Shillito's, **31** 192
Shimano Inc., **64 347–49**
Shimizu Construction Company Ltd., **44** 153
Shin-Nihon Glass Co., *see* Asahi Breweries, Ltd.
Shinko Rayon Ltd. *see* Mitsubishi Rayon Co., Ltd.
Shinko Securities Co. Ltd., **58** 235
Shinwa Pharmaceutical Co. Ltd., **48** 250
Shionogi & Co., Ltd., **III 60–61; 17 435–37 (upd.)**
Shipley Co. Inc., **26** 425
Shipper Group, **16** 344
Shiseido Company, Limited, **III 62–64; 22 485–88 (upd.); 81 364–70 (upd.)**
Shizuoka Itaku Co., Ltd., **64** 261
SHL Systemhouse Inc., **27** 305
Shobiz, Inc., **60** 143
Shochiku Company Ltd., **74 302–04**
Shockley Electronics, **20** 174
Shoe Carnival Inc., **14 441–43; 72 326–29 (upd.)**
Shoe Pavilion, Inc., **84 346–349**
Shoe-Town Inc., **23** 310
Shonac Corporation *see* DSW Inc.
Shoney's, Inc., **7 474–76; 23 436–39 (upd.)**
Shop 'n Save Warehouse Foods Inc., **63** 129
Shop At Home Network LLC *see* The E.W. Scripps Co.
SHOP Channel, **64** 185
Shop Rite Foods Inc. *see* Big V Supermarkets, Inc.
ShopKo Stores Inc., **21 457–59; 58 329–32 (upd.)**
Shoppers Drug Mart Corporation, **49 367–70**
Shoppers Food Warehouse Corporation, **66 290–92**
Shoppers World Stores, Inc. *see* LOT$OFF Corp.
ShopRite *see* Foodarama Supermarkets, Inc.
Shopwell/Food Emporium, *see* The Great Atlantic & Pacific Tea Co., Inc.
ShopWise.com Inc., **53** 13
Shorewood Packaging Corporation, **28 419–21**
Shorouk Airways, **68** 227
Shotton Paper Co. Ltd., *see* UPM-Kymmene.
Showa Denko, **IV** 61
Showa Shell Sekiyu K.K., **IV 542–43; 59 372–75 (upd.)**
ShowBiz Pizza Time, Inc., **13 472–74** *see also* CEC Entertainment, Inc.
Showboat, Inc., **19 400–02** *see also* Harrah's Entertainment, Inc.
Showco, Inc., **35** 436
Showscan Entertainment Inc., **34** 230
Showscan Film Corporation, **28** 206
Showtime Networks, Inc., **78 343–47**
Shred-It Canada Corporation, **56 319–21**
Shriners Hospitals for Children, **69 318–20**
Shubert Organization Inc., **24 437–39**
Shuffle Master Inc., **51 337–40**
Shure Inc., **60 273–76**
Shurfine International, **60** 302
Shurgard Storage Centers, Inc., **52 309–11**
Shuttleworth Brothers Company *see* Mohawk Industries, Inc.
Shuwa Corp., **22** 101; **36** 292
SHV Holdings N.V., **55 344–47**
SI Holdings Inc., **10** 481; **29** 425
The Siam Cement Public Company Limited, **56 322–25**
Siam Makro, **62** 63
SIAS, **19** 192
SIATA S.p.A., **26** 363
SIB Financial Services, **39** 382
Sibel, **48** 350
Siberian Moloko, **48** 438
Sibneft *see* OAO Siberian Oil Co.
SiCAP AG, **58** 338
SICC *see* Univision Communications Inc.
Sichuan Changhong Electric Co. Ltd., **63** 36
Sichuan Station Wagon Factory, **38** 462
Sick's Brewery, **26** 304
Sicma Aero Seat, **36** 529
Sideco Americana S.A., **67 346–48**
Sidel *see* Groupe Sidel S.A.
Siderar S.A.I.C., **66 293–95**
Siderca S.A.I.C., **41** 405–06
Sidley Austin Brown & Wood, **40 400–03**
Sidmar N. V. *see* Arcelor Gent
Sidney Frank Importing Co., Inc., **69 321–23**
Siebe plc *see* BTR Siebe plc.
The Siebel Group, *see* Koninklijke Vendex KBB N.V. (Royal Vendex KBB N.V.)
Siebel Marketing Group, **27** 195
Siebel Systems, Inc., **38 430–34**
Siebert Financial Corp., **32 423–25**
Siegel & Gale, **64 350–52**
Siemens AG, **II 97–100; 14 444–47 (upd.); 57 318–23 (upd.)**
Siemens Solar Industries L.P., **44** 182
The Sierra Club, **28 422–24**
Sierra Health Services, Inc., **15 451–53**
Sierra Nevada Brewing Company, **70 291–93**
Sierra On-Line, Inc., **15 454–56; 41 361–64 (upd.)**
Sierra Pacific Industries, **22 489–91; 90 369–73 (upd.)**
Sierra Precision, **52** 187
Sierrita Resources, Inc., **6** 590
Siete Oil and Gas Co., **63** 346
SIFCO Industries, Inc., **41**
Sifo Group AB *see* Observer AB.
SIG plc, **71 334–36**
Sight & Sound Entertainment, **35** 21
Sigma-Aldrich Corporation, **I 690–91; 36 429–32 (upd.); 93 398–404 (upd.)**

Sigma Alimentos, S.A. de C.V., **19** 11–12
Sigma Network Systems, **11** 464
Signal Companies, Inc. *see* AlliedSignal Inc.
Signal Corporation, **54** 395–96
Signal Pharmaceutical Inc. *see* Celgene Corp.
SignalSoft, **63** 202
Signature Bank, **54** 36
Signature Brands USA Inc., **28** 135; **30** 139
Signature Corporation, **22** 412–13
Signature Flight Support Services Corporation, **47** 450
Signature Health Care Corp., **25** 504
Signet Banking Corporation, 11 446–48 *see also* Wachovia Corp.
Signet Group PLC, 61 326–28
Signetics Co., **11** 56; **44** 127
Signode Industries, *see* Illinois Tool Works Inc.
Sika Finanz AG, **28** 195
Sikorsky Aircraft Corporation, 24 440–43
SIL&P *see* Southern Illinois Light & Power Co.
SILA *see* Swedish Intercontinental Airlines.
Silband Sports Corp., **33** 102
Silex *see* Hamilton Beach/Proctor-Silex Inc.
Silgan Holdings Inc., **26** 59
Silhouette Brands, Inc., 55 348–50
Silicon Beach Software, **10** 35
Silicon Energy Corporation, **64** 205
Silicon Engineering, **18** 20; **43** 17
Silicon Graphics Inc., 9 471–73 *see also* SGI.
Silicon Light Machines Corporation, **48** 128
Silicon Magnetic Systems, **48** 128
Silicon Microstructures, Inc., *see* Exar Corp.
Siliconware Precision Industries Ltd., 73 300–02
Silit, **60** 364
Silk-Epil S.A., **51** 58
Silkies, **55** 196
Silknet Software Inc., **51** 181
Silo Inc., **10** 306, 468
Siltronic AG, 90 374–77
Silver Burdett Co., **19** 405
Silver Cinemas Inc., **71** 256
Silver City Airways *see* British World Airlines Ltd.
Silver City Casino *see* Circus Circus Enterprises, Inc.
Silver Dollar City Corporation *see* Herschend Family Entertainment Corp.
Silver Dollar Mining Company, **20** 149
Silver Dolphin, **34** 3, 5
Silver Furniture Co., Inc., **15** 102, 104
Silver King Communications, **25** 213
Silver Screen Partners, *see* Walt Disney Co.
SilverPlatter Information Inc., 23 440–43
Silvershoe Partners, **17** 245
Silverstein Properties, Inc., 47 358–60
Simco S.A., 37 357–59
Sime Darby Berhad, 14 448–50; 36 433–36 (upd.)
Simeira Comercio e Industria Ltda., *see* Lojas Arapua S.A.
SIMEL S.A., *see* Amp Inc.
Simer Pump Company, **19** 360
Simi Winery, Inc., **34** 89
Simicon Co., **26** 153
Simmons Company, 47 361–64
Simon & Schuster Inc., IV 671–72; 19 403–05 (upd.)
Simon DeBartolo Group Inc., **26** 146; **57** 234
Simon-Hartley Ltd., *see* Thames Water plc.
Simon Marketing, Inc., *see* Cyrk Inc.
Simon Property Group Inc., 27 399–402; 84 350–355 (upd.)
Simon Transportation Services Inc., 27 403–06
Simons Inc., **26** 412
Simple Shoes, Inc., *see* Deckers Outdoor Corp.
Simplex Industries, Inc., *see* K2 Inc.
Simplex Technologies Inc., 21 460–63
Simplex Wire and Cable Co. *see* Tyco International Ltd.
Simplicity Manufacturing, Inc., 64 353–56
Simplicity Pattern Company, **I** 447; **23** 98; **29** 134
Simpson Investment Company, 17 438–41
Simpson Thacher & Bartlett, 39 365–68
Simpson Timber Company *see* PW Eagle Inc.
Simpsons *see* Hudson's Bay Co.
SIMS Deltec, Inc. *see* Deltec, Inc.
Simul International Inc. *see* Benesse Corp.
Simula, Inc., 41 368–70
Simulaids, Inc., **62** 18
SINA Corporation, 69 324–27
Sinclair Broadcast Group, Inc., 25 417–19
Sinclair Paint Company, *see* Grow Group Inc.
Sinfor Holding, **48** 402
Sing Tao Holdings Ltd., **29** 470–71
Singapore Airlines Limited, 6 117–18; 27 407–09 (upd.); 83 355-359 (upd.)
Singapore Alpine Electronics Asia Pte. Ltd., **13** 31
Singapore Petroleum Co., **IV** 452
Singapore Press Holdings Limited, 85 391–95
Singapore Shinei Sangyo Pte Ltd., **48** 369
Singapore Technologies Engineering Ltd., **61** 43
Singer & Friedlander Group plc, 41 371–73
Singer Company, **22** 4; **26** 3; **29** 190 *see also* Bicoastal Corp.
The Singer Company N.V., 30 417–20 (upd.)
Singer Supermarkets, **25** 235
The Singing Machine Company, Inc., 60 277–80
Sinister Games, **41** 409
Sinkers Inc., **21** 68
Sino Life Insurance Co., **64** 280
Sinochem *see* China National Chemicals Import and Export Corp.
Sinopec *see* China National Petroleum Corp.
Sintel, S.A., **19** 256
Sioux City Gas and Electric Company, **6** 523–24
Sioux City Newspapers, **64** 237
SIP *see* Società Italiana per L'Esercizio delle Telecommunicazioni p.A.
Siporex, S.A., **31** 253
Sir Speedy, Inc., 16 448–50
SIRCOMA, **10** 375
SIREM, **23** 95
Sirius Satellite Radio, Inc., 69 328–31
Sirrine *see* CRSS Inc.
Sirte Oil Company *see* Natinal Oil Corp.
Sirti S.p.A., 76 326–28
Siskin Steel & Supply Company, 70 294–96
Sistema JSFC, 73 303–05
Sisters of Bon Secours USA *see* Bon Secours Health System, Inc.
SIT-Siemens *see* Italtel.
SITA Telecommunications Holdings *see* Equant N.V.
Sitca Corporation, *see* K2 Inc.
Sithe Energies, Inc., **24** 327
Sitintel, **49** 383
Six Continents PLC, **54** 315; **59** 298
Six Flags, Inc., 17 442–44; 54 333–40 (upd.)
Six Industries, Inc., **26** 433
Sixt AG, 39 369–72
Sizeler Property Investors Inc., **49** 27
Sizzler International Inc. *see* Worldwide Restaurant Concepts, Inc.
SJB Equities, Inc., **30** 53
SJW Corporation, 70 297–99
The SK Equity Fund, L.P., **23** 177
SK Group, 88 363–67
Skånska Ättiksfabriken A.B. *see* Perstorp AB.
Skadden, Arps, Slate, Meagher & Flom, 18 486–88
Skaggs Companies, *see* American Stores Co.
Skaggs Drug Centers, Inc., *see* Albertson's, Inc.; American Stores Co.
Skagit Nuclear Power Plant, **6** 566
Skalli Group, 67 349–51
Skandia America Reinsurance Corp., **57** 135–36
Skandia Insurance Company, Ltd., 50 431–34
Skandinaviska Enskilda Banken AB, II 351–53; 56 326–29 (upd.)
Skanska AB, 38 435–38
Skanza Mammoet Transport Sdn Bhd, **26** 280
Skechers U.S.A. Inc., 31 413–15; 88 368–72 (upd.)
Sketchley plc, **19** 124
SKF *see* Aktiebolaget SKF.
SKF Industries Inc. *see* AB Volvo.
Ski-Doo *see* Bombardier Inc.

Skidmore, Owings & Merrill LLP, **13** 475–76; **69 332–35 (upd.)**
SkillSoft Public Limited Company, **81** 371–74
Skipton Building Society, **80 344–47**
Skis Rossignol S.A., **15 460–62; 43 373–76 (upd.)**
Skoda Auto a.s., **39 373–75**
SKODA Group, **37** 399–400
SKS Group, **20** 363
Sky Chefs, Inc., *see* see Chef Solutions.
Sky Climber Inc., **11** 436
Sky Merchant, Inc., **V** 78
SkyBox International Inc., **15** 72–73
Skylight, **25** 508
Skyline Chili, Inc., **62 325–28**
Skyline Corporation, **30 421–23**
Skyline Transportation, **57** 277
SkyMall, Inc., **26 439–41**
Skyservice Airlines Inc., **42** 327
SkyTel Corp., **23** 212
Skywalker Sound, *see* Lucasfilm Ltd.
Skyway Airlines, *see* Mesa Airlines, Inc.
SkyWest, Inc., **25 420–24**
Skyy Spirits LLC, **78 348–51**
Sl. Aves Ldc España, **68** 234
SL Green Realty Corporation, **44 383–85**
SL Holdings *see* Finlay Enterprises, Inc.
SL Industries, Inc., **77 383–86**
Slater Electric, **21** 349
Slater, Walker, **63** 76
Slautterback Corporation, **48** 299
Slavneft, **49** 306
SLCN Ltd., **64** 205
Sleeman Breweries Ltd., **74 305–08**
Sleepy's Inc., **32 426–28**
SLI, Inc., **48 358–61**
Slim Jim, Inc. *see* GoodMark Foods, Inc.
Slim-Fast Foods Company, **18 489–91; 66 296–98 (upd.)**
Slingerland Drum Company, **16** 239
Slinky, Inc. *see* Poof-Slinky, Inc.
Slip-X Safety Treads, *see* Bissell, Inc.
SLJFB Vedrenne, **22** 344
SLM Holding Corp., **25 425–28 (upd.)**
SLM International Inc. *see* The Hockey Co.
Sloan's Supermarkets Inc. *see* Gristede's Sloan's, Inc.
Sloman Neptun Schiffahrts, **26** 279
Slope Indicator Company, **26** 42
Sloss Industries Corporation *see* Walter Industries, Inc.
Slots-A-Fun *see* Circus Circus Enterprises, Inc.
Slough Estates PLC, **IV 722–25; 50 435–40 (upd.)**
Slovak Air Services S.R.O., **66** 51
Slovenská Konzultacná Firma S.R.O. V Likvidácii, **66** 51
Slovenská Sporitelna a.s., **69** 156
AB Small Business Investment Co., Inc., *see* Bozzuto's, Inc.
Small Planet Foods, Inc., **89 410–14**
Small Tube Products, Inc., **23** 517
Small World Productions, **65** 136
Smalley Transportation Company *see* Preston Corp.
SMAN *see* Societe Mecanique Automobile du Nord.
Smart & Final LLC, **16 451–53; 94 392–96 (upd.)**
Smart Choice Automotive Group, **64** 20–21
Smart Communications, *see* First Pacific Co. Ltd.
SMART Modular Technologies, Inc., **86 361–64**
Smart Products, **44** 261
Smart Shirts Ltd., *see* Kellwood Co.
Smart Talk Network, Inc., **16** 319
SmartForce PLC, **43 377–80**
SmarTTarget Marketing, **36** 342
SMBC *see* Sumitomo Mitsui Banking Corp.
Smead Manufacturing Co., **17 445–48**
Smed International, **39** 207
SMG *see* Scottish Media Group.
SMH *see* Sanders Morris Harris Group Inc.; The Swatch Group SA.
Smiles Holdings Ltd., **38** 501
Smirnoff, **14** 212
Smit International, **26** 241
Smith and Bell Insurance, **41** 178, 180
Smith & Butterfield Co., Inc., **28** 74
Smith & Hawken, Ltd., **68 343–45**
Smith & Nephew plc, **17 449–52; 41 374–78 (upd.)**
Smith & Wesson Corp., **30 424–27; 73 306–11 (upd.)**
Smith & Wollensky Operating Corp., **32** 362
Smith Barney Inc., **15 463–65** *see also* Citigroup Inc.
Smith Cattleguard *see* Smith-Midland Corp.
Smith Corona Corp., **13 477–80**
Smith International, Inc., **15 466–68; 59 376–80 (upd.)**
Smith McDonell Stone and Co., **14** 97
Smith-Midland Corporation, **56 330–32**
Smith New Court PLC, *see* Merrill Lynch & Co., Inc.
Smith Sport Optics Inc., **54** 319–20
Smith Wall Associates, **32** 145
Smith's Food & Drug Centers, Inc., **8 472–74; 57 324–27 (upd.)**
Smithfield Foods, Inc., **7** 477–78; **43 381–84 (upd.)**
SmithKline Beckman Corporation, **I 692–94** *see also* GlaxoSmithKline plc.
SmithKline Beecham plc, **III 65–67; 32 429–34 (upd.)** *see also* GlaxoSmithKline plc.
SmithMart *see* N.F. Smith & Asociates LP.
Smiths Group plc, **56** 83
Smiths Industries PLC, **25 429–31**
Smithsonian Institution, **27 410–13**
Smithway Motor Xpress Corporation, **39 376–79**
Smitty's Super Valu Inc., **12** 391
Smittybilt, Incorporated, **40** 299–300
Smoby International SA, **56 333–35**
Smoothie Island, **49** 60
Smorgon Steel Group Ltd., **62 329–32**
SMP Clothing, Inc., **22** 462
Smucker's *see* The J.M. Smucker Co.
Smurfit-Stone Container Corporation, **26 442–46 (upd.) ; 83 360-368 (upd.)**
SN Repal *see* Société Nationale de Recherche de Pétrole en Algérie.
Snack Ventures Europe, **10** 324; **36** 234, 237
Snake River Sugar Company, **19** 468
Snam *see* Società Nazionale Metanodotti.
Snam Montaggi, **IV** 420
Snam Progetti, **IV** 420, 422
Snap-On, Incorporated, **7 479–80; 27 414–16 (upd.)**
Snapfish, **83 369-372**
Snapper Inc., **64** 355
Snapple Beverage Corporation, **11 449–51**
Snappy Car Rental, Inc. *see* Republic Industries, Inc.
SnapTrack Inc., **63** 203
SNC-Lavalin Group Inc., **72 330–33**
SNCF *see* Société Nationale des Chemins de Fer Français.
SNE Enterprises, Inc., *see* Ply Gem Industries Inc.
SNEA *see* Société Nationale Elf Aquitaine.
Snecma Group, **46 369–72**
Snell & Wilmer L.L.P., **28 425–28**
Snell Acoustics, *see* Boston Acoustics, Inc.
Snelling Personnel Services, **52** 150
SNET *see* Southern New England Telecommunications Corp.
Snoqualmie Falls Plant, **6** 565
Snow Brand Milk Products Company, Ltd., **II 574–75; 48 362–65 (upd.)**
Snow White Dairies Inc. *see* Dairy Mart Convenience Stores, Inc.
Snyder Communications, **35** 462, 465
Snyder Group Company, **56** 294
Snyder Oil Company, **24** 379–81; **45** 354
Snyder's of Hanover, **35** 213
SnyderGeneral Corp. *see* AAF-McQuay Inc.
Soap Opera Magazine, *see* American Media, Inc.
Sobeys Inc., **80 348–51**
Socal *see* Standard Oil Company (California).
Socamel-Rescaset, **40** 214, 216
Socar, Incorporated, **45** 370
Socata *see* EADS SOCATA.
Sociade Intercontinental de Compressores Hermeticos SICOM, S.A., *see* Tecumseh Products Co.
La Sociale di A. Mondadori & C. *see* Arnoldo Mondadori Editore S.P.A.
Sociedad Aeronáutica de Medellín, S.A., **36** 53
Sociedad Andina de Grandes Almeneces, **69** 312
Sociedad Anonima de Instalaciones de Control, **73** 4
Sociedad Anónima Viña Santa Rita, **67** 136–37

Sociedad Anonimo de Electricidad, **72** 278
Sociedad de Inversiones Internacionales Parque Arauco S.A., **72** 269
Sociedad Española Zig Zag, S.A., **68** 258
Sociedad Estatal de Participaciones Industriales, **69** 11
Sociedad Macri S.A., **67** 346
Sociedade Anónima Concessionária de Refinacao em Portugal *see* SACOR.
Sociedade de Vinhos da Herdade de Espirra-Produçao e Comercializaçao de Vinhos, S.A., **60** 156
Società Anonima Lombarda Fabbrica Automobili, *see* Alfa Romeo
Società Finanziaria Idrocarburi, **69** 148
Società Finanziaria Telefonica per Azioni, V 325–27
Societa Industria Meccanica Stampaggio S.p.A., **24** 500
Societa Italiana Gestione Sistemi Multi Accesso *see* Alitalia—Linee Aeree Italiana, S.P.A.
Società Italiana per L'Esercizio delle Telecommunicazioni p.A., **V** 325–27
Società Meridionale Finanziaria, **49** 31
Società Sportiva Lazio SpA, 44 386–88
Société Africaine de Déroulage des Ets Rougier, **21** 439
Société Air France, 27 417–20 (upd.) *see also* Groupe Air France.
Société Anonyme Automobiles Citroën *see* PSA Peugeot Citroen S.A.
Société Anonyme Belge des Magasins Prisunic-Uniprix, **26** 159
Société Anonyme des Assurances Générales *see* Assurances Générales de France.
Société Anonyme des Fermiers Reúnis, **23** 219
Société Anonyme Française du Ferodo *see* Valeo.
La Societe Anonyme Francaise Holophane, *see* Holophane Corp.
Société, Auxiliaire d'Entrepreses SA, **13** 206
Société BIC S.A., 73 312–15
Société Centrale d'Investissement, **29** 48
Société Civil des Mousquetaires *see* ITM Entreprises SA.
Société Civile Valoptec, **21** 222
Société Commercial d'Affrètements et de Combustibles, **67** 198
Société Commerciale Citroën, *see* Automobiles Citroën
Société Congolaise des Grands Magasins Au Bon Marché, **26** 159
Société d'Emboutissage de Bourgogne *see* Groupe SEB.
Société d'Exploitation AOM Air Liberté SA (AirLib), 53 305–07
Société d'Investissement de Travaux Publics, **31** 128
Société de Développements et d'Innovations des Marchés Agricoles et Alimentaires *see* SODIMA.
Société de Diffusion de Marques *see* SODIMA.
Société de Diffusion Internationale Agro-Alimentaire *see* SODIAAL.
Société de Fiducie du Québec, **48** 289
Société des Caves et des Producteurs Reunis de Roquefort, *see* Besnier SA.
Société des Ciments Français, **33** 339
Société des Etablissements Gaumont *see* Gaumont SA.
Société des Fibres de Carbone S.A., **51** 379
Société des Grandes Entreprises de Distribution, Inno-France, **V** 58
Société des Immeubles de France, **37** 357, 359
Société des Magasins du Casino, **59** 109
Société des Moteurs Gnôme, **46** 369
Societe des Produits Marnier-Lapostolle S.A., 88 373–76
Société du Figaro S.A., 60 281–84
Société du Louvre, 27 421–23
Société Economique de Rennes, **19** 98
Société Européenne de Production de L'avion E.C.A.T. *see* SEPECAT.
Société Française de Casinos, **48** 198
Société Générale, II 354–56; 42 347–51 (upd.)
Société Générale de Banque *see* Generale Bank.
Société Générale de Belgique S.A. *see* Generale Bank.
Société Générale des Entreprises *see* Vinci.
Societe Generale du Telephones, **21** 231
Société Industrielle Belge des Pétroles, **IV** 498–99
Société Industrielle Lesaffre, 84 356–359
Société Internationale Pirelli S.A., **V** 250
Société Laitière Vendômoise, **23** 219
Société Luxembourgeoise de Navigation Aérienne S.A., 64 357–59
Societe Mecanique Automobile de l'Est/du Nord, *see* PSA Peugeot Citroen S.A.
Société Nationale de Programmes de Télévision Française 1 *see* Télévision Française 1.
Société Nationale des Chemins de Fer Français, V 512–15; 57 328–32 (upd.)
Société Nationale des Pétroles d'Aquitaine, **21** 203–05
Société Nationale Elf Aquitaine, IV 544–47; 7 481–85 (upd.)
Société Norbert Dentressangle S.A., 67 352–54
Société Nouvelle d'Achat de Bijouterie, *see* Finlay Enterprises, Inc.
Société Nouvelle des Etablissements Gaumont *see* Gaumont SA.
Société Parisienne Raveau-Cartier, **31** 128
Société pour l'Étude et la Realisation d'Engins Balistiques *see* SEREB.
Société pour le Financement de l'Industrie Laitière, **19** 51
Société Samos, **23** 219
Société Succursaliste S.A. d'Approvisonnements Guyenne et Gascogne *see* Guyenne et Gascogne.
Société Suisse de Microelectronique & d'Horlogerie *see* The Swatch Group SA.
Société Tefal *see* Groupe SEB.
Société Tunisienne de l'Air-Tunisair, 49 371–73
Society Corporation, 9 474–77
Socma *see* Sociedad Macri S.A.
Socony *see* Standard Oil Co. (New York).
Socony-Vacuum Oil Company *see* Mobil Corp.
Socpresse, **60** 281
Sodak Gaming, Inc., **41** 216
Sodexho SA, 29 442–44; 91 433–36 (upd.)
Sodiaal S.A., 19 50; **36 437–39 (upd.)**
SODIMA, II 576–77 *see also* Sodiaal S.A.
Sodimac S.A., **69** 312
La Sodis *see* Éditions Gallimard.
Sodiso, **23** 247
Soeker Exploration & Production Pty, Ltd., **59** 336–37
Soekor, **IV** 93
Sofamor Danek Group, Inc. *see* Medtronic, Inc.
Soffo, **22** 365
Soficom, *see* Eiffage.
SOFIL *see* Société pour le Financement de l'Industrie Laitière.
Sofimex *see* Sociedad Financiera Mexicana.
Sofitam, S.A., **21** 493, 495
Sofitels *see* Accor SA.
Sofora Telecomunicaciones S.A., **63** 377
Soft Sheen Products, Inc., 31 416–18
Soft*Switch, **25** 301
Softbank Corporation, 13 481–83; 38 439–44 (upd.); 77 387–95 (upd.)
Softimage Inc., **38** 71–72
SoftKat *see* Baker & Taylor, Inc.
Softsel Computer Products, *see* Merisel, Inc.
Software Architects Inc., **74** 258
Software Development Pty., Ltd., **15** 107
Software Dimensions, Inc. *see* ASK Group, Inc.
The Software Group Inc., **23** 489, 491
Software Plus, Inc., **10** 514
Software Publishing Corp., **14** 262
Softwood Holdings Ltd., *see* CSR Ltd.
Sogara S.A., **23** 246–48
Sogedis, **23** 219
Sogo Co., **42** 342
Soil Teq, Inc., *see* Ag-Chem Equipment Company, Inc.
Soilserv, Inc. *see* Mycogen Corp.
Sol Meliá S.A., 71 337–39
Sola International Inc., 71 340–42
Solair Inc., **14** 43; **37** 30–31
La Solana Corp., **IV** 726
Solar Wide Industrial Ltd., **73** 332
Solaray, Inc., **37** 284–85
Sole Technology Inc., 93 405–09
Solect Technology Group, **47** 12
Solectron Corporation, 12 450–52; 48 366–70 (upd.)
Solera Capital, **59** 50
Solid Beheer B.V., **10** 514
Solid Cement Corporation, **59** 115
Solite Corp., **23** 224–25

Söll, **40** 96, 98
Solley's Delicatessen and Bakery, *see* Jerry's Famous Deli Inc.
Solo Serve Corporation, 28 429–31
SOLOCO Inc., **63** 305
Solomon Valley Milling Company, **6** 592; **50** 37
Solutia Inc., 52 312–15
Solvay & Cie S.A., I 394–96; 21 464–67 (upd.)
Solvay S.A., 61 329–34 (upd.)
Somali Bank, **31** 220
Somerfield plc, 47 365–69 (upd.)
Somerville Packaging Group, **28** 420
Sommer-Allibert S.A., 19 406–09 *see also* Tarkett Sommer AG.
Sonat, Inc., 6 577–78 *see also* El Paso Corp.
Sonatrach, 65 313–17 (upd.)
Sonecor Systems, **6** 340
Sonera Corporation, 50 441–44 *see also* TeliaSonera AB.
Sonergy, Inc., **49** 280
Sonesta International Hotels Corporation, 44 389–91
Sonet Media AB, **23** 390
SONI Ltd., **64** 404
Sonic Automotive, Inc., 77 396–99
Sonic Corp., 14 451–53; 37 360–63 (upd.)
Sonic Duo, **48** 419
Sonic Innovations Inc., 56 336–38
Sonic Restaurants, **31** 279
Sonic Solutions, Inc., 81 375–79
SonicWALL, Inc., 87 421–424
Sonnen Basserman, **II** 475
Sonoco Products Company, 8 475–77; 89 415–22 (upd.)
Sonofon *see* Telenor ASA.
The Sonoma Group, **25** 246
Sonor GmbH, **53** 216
SonoSite, Inc., 56 339–41
Sony Corporation, II 101–03; 12 453–56 (upd.); 40 404–10 (upd.)
Sony Ericsson Mobile Communications AB, **61** 137
Soo Line Corporation *see* Canadian Pacific Ltd.
Soo Line Mills, *see* George Weston Ltd.
Sooner Trailer Manufacturing Co., **29** 367
Soparind, *see* Bongrain S.A.
Sope Creek, **30** 457
Sophus Berendsen A/S, 49 374–77
SOPORCEL, **34** 38–39
Soporcel-Sociedade Portuguesa de Papel, S.A., **60** 156
Sorbee International Ltd., 74 309–11
Sorbents Products Co. Inc., **31** 20
Sorbus, **6** 242
Sorenson Research Company, **36** 496
Sorg Paper Company *see* Mosinee Paper Corp.
Soriana *see* Organización Soriana, S.A. de C.V.
Sorin S.p.A., **61** 70, 72
Soros Fund Management LLC, 28 432–34
Sorrento, Inc., 19 51; **24 444–46**
SOS Staffing Services, 25 432–35
Sosa, Bromley, Aguilar & Associates *see* D'Arcy Masius Benton & Bowles, Inc.
Soterra, Inc., **15** 188
Sotetsu Rosen, **72** 301
Sotheby's Holdings, Inc., 11 452–54; 29 445–48 (upd.); 84 360–365 (upd.)
Soufflet SA *see* Groupe Soufflet SA.
Sound Advice, Inc., 41 379–82
Sound of Music Inc. *see* Best Buy Co., Inc.
Sound Video Unlimited, **16** 46; **43** 60
Souplantation Incorporated *see* Garden Fresh Restaurant Corp.
The Source Enterprises, Inc., 65 318–21
Source Interlink Companies, Inc., 75 350–53
Source One Mortgage Services Corp., **12** 79
Source Perrier, *see* Nestlé S.A.
Sourdough Bread Factory *see* Matt Prentice Restaurant Group.
Souriau, **19** 166
South African Airways Ltd., *see* Transnet Ltd.
The South African Breweries Limited, I 287–89; 24 447–51 (upd.) *see also* SABMiller plc.
South African Transport Services *see* Transnet Ltd.
South Asia Tyres, **20** 263
South Australian Brewing Company, **54** 228, 341
South Beach Beverage Company, Inc., 73 316–19
South Carolina Electric & Gas Company *see* SCANA Corp.
South Carolina National Corporation, **16** 523, 526
South Carolina Power Company, **38** 446–47
South Central Bell Telephone Co. *see* BellSouth Corp.
South Central Railroad Co., **14** 325
South Coast Gas Compression Company, Inc., **11** 523
South Coast Terminals, Inc., **16** 475
South Dakota Public Service Company, **6** 524
South Dakota Wheat Growers Association, 94 397–401
South Florida Neonatology Associates, **61** 284
South Fulton Light & Power Company, **6** 514
South Jersey Industries, Inc., 42 352–55
South Overseas Fashion Ltd., **53** 344
South Wales Electric Company, **34** 219
South West Water Plc *see* Pennon Group Plc.
South Western Electricity plc, **38** 448; **41** 316
South-Western Publishing Co., *see* The Thomson Corp.
Southam Inc., 7 486–89 *see also* CanWest Global Communications Corp.
Southcorp Limited, 54 341–44
Southdown, Inc., 14 454–56 *see also* CEMEX S.A. de C.V.
Southdown Press *see* PMP Ltd.
Southeast Public Service Company, *see* Triarc Companies, Inc.
Southeastern Freight Lines, Inc., **53** 249
Southeastern Personnel *see* Norrell Corp.
Southern and Phillips Gas Ltd., *see* Southern Electric PLC.
Southern Blvd. Supermarkets, Inc., **22** 549
Southern California Edison Co. *see* Edison International.
Southern California Fruit Growers Exchange *see* Sunkist Growers, Inc.
Southern California Gas Co., *see* Sempra Energy.
The Southern Company, V 721–23; 38 445–49 (upd.)
Southern Connecticut Gas Company, 84 366–370
Southern Cooker Limited Partnership, **51** 85
Southern Corrections Systems, Inc. *see* Avalon Correctional Services, Inc.
Southern Cross Paints, **38** 98
Southern Electric PLC, 13 484–86 *see also* Scottish and Southern Energy plc.
Southern Electric Supply Co., **15** 386
Southern Electronics Corp. *see* SED International Holdings, Inc.
Southern Equipment & Supply Co., **19** 344
Southern Financial Bancorp, Inc., 56 342–44
Southern Foods Group, L.P. *see* Dean Foods Co.
Southern Forest Products, Inc., **6** 577
Southern Gage, *see* Illinois Tool Works Inc.
Southern Guaranty Cos., *see* Winterthur Group.
Southern Indiana Gas and Electric Company, 13 487–89
Southern Minnesota Beet Sugar Cooperative, **32** 29
Southern National Bankshares of Atlanta, **10** 425
Southern National Corporation *see* BB&T Corporation
Southern Natural Gas Co., **6** 577
Southern New England Telecommunications Corporation, 6 338–40
Southern Oregon Broadcasting Co., *see* Affiliated Publications, Inc.
Southern Pacific Transportation Company, V 516–18 *see also* Union Pacific Corp.
Southern Peru Copper Corp.,
Southern Peru Copper Corporation, 40 411–13
Southern Phenix Textiles Inc., **15** 247–48
Southern Poverty Law Center, Inc., 74 312–15
Southern Power Company *see* Duke Energy Corp.
Southern Recycling Inc., **51** 170

Southern States Cooperative Incorporated, 36 440–42
Southern Sun Hotel Corporation *see* South African Breweries Ltd.; Sun International Hotels Ltd.
Southern Union Company, 27 424–26
Southern Water plc, *see* Scottish Power plc.
Southern Wine and Spirits of America, Inc., 84 371–375
Southgate Medical Laboratory System, **26** 391
Southington Savings Bank, **55** 52
The Southland Corporation, II 660–61; 7 490–92 (upd.) *see also* 7-Eleven, Inc.
Southland Mobilcom Inc., **15** 196
Southland Royalty Co., **10** 190
Southmark Corp., **11** 483; **33** 398
Southport, Inc., **44** 203
Southtrust Corporation, 11 455–57 *see also* Wachovia Corp.
Southwest Airlines Co., 6 119–21; 24 452–55 (upd.); 71 343–47 (upd.)
Southwest Convenience Stores, LLC, **26** 368
Southwest Gas Corporation, 19 410–12
Southwest Property Trust Inc., **52** 370
Southwest Sports Group, **51** 371, 374
Southwest Water Company, 47 370–73
Southwestern Bell Corporation, V 328–30 *see also* SBC Communications Inc.
Southwestern Bell Publications, **26** 520
Southwestern Electric Power Co., 21 468–70
Southwestern Explosives, Inc., **76** 34
Southwestern Gas Pipeline, *see* Mitchell Energy and Development Corp.
Southwestern Public Service Company, 6 579–81
Southwire Company, Inc., 8 478–80; 23 444–47 (upd.)
Souza Cruz S.A., 65 322–24
Souza Pinto Industria e Comercio de Artefatos de Borracha Ltda., **71** 393
Soviba, **70** 322
Sovintel, **59** 209, 211
Sovion NV *see* Vion Food Group NV.
Sovran Financial, **10** 425–26
Sovran Self Storage, Inc., 66 299–301
SovTransavto, **6** 410
Soyco Foods, Inc., **58** 137
SP Alpargatas *see* Sao Paulo Alpargatas S.A.
SP Pharmaceuticals, LLC, **50** 123
SP Reifenwerke, **V** 253
SP Tyres, **V** 253
Space Control GmbH, **28** 243–44
Space Craft Inc., *see* SCI Systems, Inc.
Space Systems Corporation *see* Orbital Sciences Corp.
Space Systems/Loral, *see* Loral Corp.
Spacehab, Inc., 37 364–66
Spacelabs Medical, Inc., 71 348–50
Spacesaver Corporation, **57** 208–09
Spaghetti Warehouse, Inc., 25 436–38
Spago *see* The Wolfgang Puck Food Company, Inc.
Spalding, Inc., **23** 449; **54** 73
Spanco Yarns, **62** 375
Spangler Candy Company, 44 392–95
Spanish Broadcasting System, Inc., 41 383–86
Spanish International Communications Corp. *see* Univision Communications Inc.
Spansion Inc., 80 352–55
Spanx, Inc., 89 423–27
SPAO, **39** 184
Spar Aerospace Limited, 32 435–37
SPAR Handels AG, 35 398–401
SpareBank 1 Gruppen, **69** 177, 179
Spark Networks, Inc., 91 437–40
Sparkassen-Finanzgruppe *see* Deutscher Sparkassen- und Giroverband (DSGV).
Sparks-Withington Company *see* Sparton Corp.
Sparrow Records, **22** 194
Sparta Surgical Corporation, **33** 456
Spartan Communications, **38** 308–09
Spartan Industries, Inc., **45** 15
Spartan Insurance Co., **26** 486
Spartan Motors Inc., 14 457–59
Spartan Stores Inc., 8 481–82; 66 302–05 (upd.)
Spartech Corporation, 19 413–15; 76 329–32 (upd.)
Sparton Corporation, 18 492–95
Spear & Jackson, Inc., 73 320–23
Spear, Leeds & Kellogg, 66 306–09
Spec's Music, Inc., 19 416–18 *see also* Camelot Music, Inc.
Special Olympics, Inc., 93 410–14
Special Project Films, Inc., **58** 124
Special Zone Limited, **26** 491
Specialist Computer Holdings Ltd., 80 356–59
Specialized Bicycle Components Inc., 50 445–48
Specialty Brands Inc., **25** 518
Specialty Coatings Inc., 8 483–84
Specialty Equipment Companies, Inc., 25 439–42
Specialty Foods Inc., **29** 29, 31; **74** 202
Specialty Products & Insulation Co., 59 381–83
Specialty Products Co., *see* NCH Corp.
Specialty Restaurant Group, LLC, **71** 319
Specialty Retailers, Inc., *see* Stage Stores, Inc.
Spector Photo Group N.V., 82 344–47
Spectra-Physics, Inc. *see* Newport Corp.
Spectradyne, **28** 241
Spectral Dynamics Corporation *see* Scientific- Atlanta, Inc.
Spectron MicroSystems, *see* Dialogic Corp.
Spectrum Brands *see* United Industries Corp.
Spectrum Club, *see* The Sports Club Company.
Spectrum Concepts, *see* Legent Corp.
Spectrum Control, Inc., 67 355–57
Spectrum Data Systems, Inc., **24** 96
Spectrum Health Care Services, *see* Aramark Corp.
Spectrum Medical Technologies, Inc., *see* Palomar Medical Technologies, Inc.
Spectrum Numismatics International, Inc., **60** 146
Spectrum Organic Products, Inc., 68 346–49
Spectrum Technology Group, Inc., **18** 112
Spectrumedia, **21** 361
Spee-Dee Delivery Service, Inc., 93 415–18
Speech Design GmbH, **62** 38–39
SpeeDee Oil Change and Tune-Up, 25 443–47
Speedway Motorsports, Inc., 32 438–41
Speedway SuperAmerica LLC, **49** 330
Speedy Auto Glass, **30** 501
Speedy Europe, **54** 207
Speedy Hire plc, 84 376–379
Speedy Muffler King, **10** 415
Speizman Industries, Inc., 44 396–98
Spelling Entertainment, 14 460–62; 35 402–04 (upd.)
Spenard Builders Supply *see* Lanoga Corp.
Spencer & Spencer Systems, Inc., *see* Ciber, Inc.
Spencer Gifts, Inc., **15** 464
Spencer Stuart and Associates, Inc., 14 463–65
Sperry & Hutchinson Co., **23** 243–44
Sperry Aerospace Group, **6** 283
Sperry Corporation, *see* Unisys Corp.
Sperry New Holland *see* New Holland N.V.
Sperry Top-Sider, Inc., **37** 377, 379
Spezialpapierfabrik Blankenstein GmbH, **64** 275
Sphere Drake Holdings Ltd., **57** 136
Spherion Corporation, 52 316–18
Spicecraft Co. *see* Newly Weds Foods, Inc.
Spider Software, Inc., **46** 38
Spie *see* Amec Spie S.A.
Spie Batignolles SA, **13** 206
Spiegel, Inc., 10 489–91; 27 427–31 (upd.)
SPIEGEL-Verlag Rudolf Augstein GmbH & Co. KG, 44 399–402
Spike's Holding, Inc. *see* The Finish Line, Inc.
Spin Master, Ltd., 61 335–38
SpinCircuit Inc., **38** 188
Spinelli Coffee Co., **51** 385
Spinnaker Exploration Company, 72 334–36
Spinnaker Industries, Inc., **43** 276
Spirax-Sarco Engineering plc, 59 384–86
Spire, Inc., **25** 183
Spirella Company of Great Britain Ltd. *see* Coats plc.
Spirit Airlines, Inc., 31 419–21
Spirit Cruises, **29** 442–43
Spliethoff, **26** 280
SPN Resources, LLC, **65** 334
Spode *see* The Porcelain and Fine China Companies Ltd.
Spoerle Electronic, *see* Arrow Electronics, Inc.

Spokane Falls Electric Light and Power Company *see* Edison Electric Illuminating Co.
Spokane Falls Water Power Company, **6** 595
Spokane Natural Gas Company, **6** 597
Spokane Street Railway Company, **6** 595
Spokane Traction Company, **6** 596
Spom Japan, **IV** 600
Spon Press, **44** 416
Spoornet, **6** 435
Sporis, **27** 151
Sport Chalet, Inc., 16 454–56; 94 402–06 (upd.)
Sport Developpement SCA, **33** 10
Sport Maska Inc., **70** 126
Sport Supply Group, Inc., 23 448–50
Sporting Dog Specialties, Inc., **14** 386
Sportland, **26** 160
Sportmagazine NV, **48** 347
Sportmart, Inc., 15 469–71 *see also* Gart Sports Co.
Sports & Co. *see* Hibbett Sporting Goods, Inc.
Sports & Recreation, Inc., 17 453–55
The Sports Authority, Inc., 16 457–59; 43 385–88 (upd.)
The Sports Club Company, 25 448–51
Sports Experts Inc., *see* Provigo Inc.
Sports Holdings Corp., **34** 217
Sports Inc., **14** 8; **33** 10
Sports Plus, **44** 192
Sports-Tech Inc., **21** 300
Sports Traders, Inc., **74** 393
Sportservice Corporation, *see* Delaware North Companies Inc.
The Sportsman's Guide, Inc., 36 443–46
Sportstown, Inc., **15** 470
Sportsystems Corporation, *see* Delaware North Companies Inc.
Spotless Group Limited, **62** 391
Sprague Devices, Inc., *see* Echlin Inc.
Sprague Technologies, **21** 520
Spraysafe, **29** 98
Spreckels Sugar Company, Inc., **32** 274, 277
Spring Co., **21** 96, 246
Spring Group plc, **54** 191–93
Spring Grove Services, **45** 139–40
Spring Valley Brewery *see* Kirin Brewery Company, Ltd.
Springer Verlag GmbH & Co., **IV** 611, 641
Springfield Gas Light Company, **38** 81
Springhouse Corp. *see* Reed Elsevier plc.
Springs Global US, Inc., V 378–79; 19 419–22 (upd.); 90 378–83 (upd.)
Sprint Canada Inc., **44** 49
Sprint Communications Company, L.P., 9 478–80 *see also* Sprint Corporation; US Sprint Communications.
Sprint Corporation, 46 373–76 (upd.)
Sprint PCS, **33** 34, 36–37; **38** 433
Sprocket Systems, **50** 320
Sprout Group, **37** 121
Sprout-Matador A.S., **51** 25
SPS Technologies, Inc., 30 428–30
SPSS Inc., 64 360–63
SPT Telecom *see* Cesky Telecom, a.s.
Spun Yarns, Inc., **12** 503
SPX Corporation, 10 492–95; 47 374–79 (upd.)
Spyglass Entertainment Group, LLC, 91 441–44
SPZ, Inc., **26** 257
SQL Solutions, Inc., *see* Sybase, Inc.
Square D, 90 384–89
Square Industries, *see* Central Parking Corp.
Squibb Beech-Nut *see* Beech-Nut Nutrition Corp.
Squibb Corporation, I 695–97 *see also* Bristol-Myers Squibb Co.
Squire Fashions Inc. *see* Norton McNaughton of Squire, Inc.
SR *see* Southern Railway.
SR Teleperformance S.A., 86 365–68
SRA International, Inc., 77 400–03
SRAM Corporation, 65 325–27
SRC Holdings Corporation, 67 358–60
SRI International, Inc., 57 333–36
SRI Strategic Resources Inc., **6** 310
SS&C Technologies Inc., **66** 225
SS Cars, Ltd. *see* Jaguar Cars, Ltd.
SS Lazio *see* Societá Sportiva Lazio SpA.
SSA *see* Stevedoring Services of America Inc.
SSAB Svenskt Stål AB, 89 428–31
Ssangyong Cement Industrial Co., Ltd., III 747–50; 61 339–43 (upd.)
Ssangyong Motor Company, **34** 132
SSC Benelux & Company, **52** 310–11
SSDS, Inc., *see* United Video Satellite Group.
SSI Medical Services, Inc., **10** 350
SSL International plc, 49 378–81
SSOE Inc., 76 333–35
SSP Company, Inc., *see* Seneca Foods Corp.
St. *see under* Saint
Staal Bankiers, *see* Koninklijke Vendex KBB N.V. (Royal Vendex KBB N.V.)
STAAR Surgical Company, 57 337–39
The Stabler Companies Inc., 78 352–55
Stackpole Fibers, **37** 427
Stadia Colorado Corporation, **18** 140
Stadt Corporation, **26** 109
Staefa Control System Limited *see* Elektrowatt AG.
Staff Builders Inc. *see* ATC Healthcare, Inc.
Staff International, **40** 157
StaffAmerica, Inc., **16** 50
Stafford-Lowdon, **31** 435
Stage Stores, Inc., 24 456–59; 82 348–52 (upd.)
Stagecoach Holdings plc, 30 431–33
Stags' Leap Winery, *see* Beringer Blass Wine Estates Ltd.
Stahlwerke Südwestfalen AG, **IV** 89
Stainless Fabrication Inc., **65** 289
Stakis plc, **49** 193
Stamford Drug Group, *see* Bindley Western Industries, Inc.
Stamos Associates Inc., **29** 377
Stamps.com Inc., **34** 474
Stanadyne Automotive Corporation, 37 367–70
Stanadyne, Inc., **7** 336
StanCorp Financial Group, Inc., 56 345–48
Standard & Poor's Corp., **IV** 482, 636–37; **25** 542
Standard Brands, *see* Nabisco Foods Group.
Standard Candy Company Inc., 86 369–72
Standard Chartered plc, II 357–59; 48 371–74 (upd.)
Standard Commercial Corporation, 13 490–92; 62 333–37 (upd.)
The Standard Companies, Inc., **58** 374
Standard Federal Bank, 9 481–83
Standard Fruit and Steamship Co. of New Orleans, **31** 168
Standard Gypsum Corp., *see* Caraustar Industries, Inc.
Standard Insert Co., **28** 350
Standard Life & Accident Insurance Company, **27** 47–48
Standard Life Assurance Company, III 358–61
The Standard Life Insurance Company of New York, **56** 345
Standard Microsystems Corporation, 11 462–64
Standard Motor Products, Inc., 40 414–17
Standard Oil Co., **10** 110, 289; **14** 21 *see also* Exxon Corporation; Mobil Corp.
Standard Oil Co. (California) *see* ChevronTexaco Corporation
Standard Oil Co. (Indiana) *see* Amoco Corp.
Standard Oil Co. (New York), **IV** 485, 504, 537, 549, 558 *see also* Mobil Corp.
Standard Oil Co. of New Jersey, **IV** 415–16, 419, 431–33, 438, 460, 463–64, 488, 522, 531, 537–38, 544, 558, 565, 571
Standard Oil Co. of Ohio, **IV** 452, 463, 522, 571
Standard Pacific Corporation, 52 319–22
Standard Process & Engraving, Inc., **26** 105
The Standard Register Company, 15 472–74; 93 419–25 (upd.)
Standard Screw Co., *see* Moen Inc.
Standard Telephones and Cables, Ltd., **6** 242
Standard Tin Plate Co., **15** 127
Standard-Vacuum Oil Co. *see* Mobil Corp.
Standex International Corporation, 17 456–59; 44 403–06 (upd.)
Standish Industries Inc., **61** 295
Stanhome Inc., 15 475–78
Stanhome Worldwide Direct Selling, **35** 262, 264
STANIC, **69** 145, 148
Stankiewicz GmbH *see* Phoenix AG

Stanley Furniture Company, Inc., 34 412–14
Stanley Home Products, Incorporated *see* Stanhome Inc.
Stanley Leisure plc, 66 310–12
Stanley Mining Services, Ltd., **19** 247
Stanley Smith Security *see* Initial Security.
The Stanley Works, III 626–29; 20 476–80 (upd.); 79 383–91 (upd.)
StanMont, Inc., *see* Schawk Inc.
Stant Corporation, **15** 503, 505
StanWest Equities, Inc., **56** 348
Staple Cotton Cooperative Association (Staplcotn), 86 373–77
Staples, Inc., 10 496–98; 55 351–56 (upd.)
Star, *see* American Media, Inc.
Star Air Service *see* Alaska Air Group, Inc.
Star Alliance, **26** 113; **33** 51; **38** 36
Star Banc Corporation, 11 465–67 *see also* Firstar Corp.
Star Broadcasting Network Pty. Ltd. *see* Rural Press Ltd.
Star Building Systems, Inc., **19** 366
Star Cruises Ltd. *see* Genting Bhd.
Star Enterprises, Inc., **6** 457
Star Markets Company, Inc., **23** 169; **56** 317
Star Medical Europe B.V., **56** 338
Star Medical Technologies, Inc., *see* Palomar Medical Technologies, Inc.
Star Paper Tube, Inc., *see* Caraustar Industries, Inc.
Star Sportwear Manufacturing Corp., **29** 294
Star Systems, Inc., **52** 88
Starbucks Corporation, 13 493–94; 34 415–19 (upd.); 77 404–10 (upd.)
Starcraft Corporation, 30 434–36; 66 313–16 (upd.)
Stardent Computer Inc., *see* Kubota Corp.
Starfish Software, **23** 212
StarHub Ltd., 77 411–14
Stark Record and Tape Service *see* Camelot Music, Inc.
Starkey Laboratories, Inc., 52 323–25
StarKist Foods *see* H.J. Heinz Co.
Starlen Labs, Ltd., **31** 346
Starlight Networks, Inc., **27** 366
Starrette, *see* L.S. Starrett Co.
Starrett Corporation, 21 471–74
Startech Semiconductor Inc., *see* Exar Corp.
StarTek, Inc., 79 392–95
Startel Corp., **15** 125
Starter Corp., 12 457–458
Starwood Capital, **29** 508
Starwood Hotels & Resorts Worldwide, Inc., 54 345–48
Starz LLC, 91 445–50
The Stash Tea Company, 50 449–52
State Auto Financial Corporation, 77 415–19
State Bank of India, 63 354–57
State Farm Insurance Companies, **27** 30; **29** 397; **39** 155
State Farm Mutual Automobile Insurance Company, III 362–64; 51 341–45 (upd.)
State Financial Services Corporation, 51 346–48
State Mutual Life Assurance Company, **63** 29
State-o-Maine, *see* Nautica Enterprises, Inc.
State Savings Bank and Trust Co., **42** 429
State Street Corporation, 8 491–93; 57 340–44 (upd.)
Staten Island Advance Corp. *see* Advance Publications Inc.
Staten Island Bancorp, Inc., 39 380–82
Stater Bros. Holdings Inc., 64 364–67
Static, Inc., *see* Sealed Air Corp.
Static Snowboards, Inc., **51** 393
Station Casinos, Inc., 25 452–54; 90 390–95 (upd.)
Stationers Distributing Company, **14** 523
Stationers, Inc., **28** 74
Statoil ASA, 61 344–48 (upd.)
StatScript Management Services, **26** 73
The Staubach Company, 62 338–41
Stauffer Communications, Inc., **36** 339–41
Stax Records, **23** 32
STC PLC, III 162–64 *see also* Nortel Networks Corp.
Steak & Ale, *see* Metromedia Co.
The Steak n Shake Company, 41 387–90
Steamboat Ski and Resort Corporation, **28** 21
Steamships Trading Company Ltd., 82 353–56
Stearns & Foster, *see* Sealy Inc.
Stearns Coal & Lumber, **6** 514
Stearns, Inc., 43 389–91
Steel Authority of India Ltd., IV 205–07; 66 317–21 (upd.)
Steel Co. of Canada Ltd. *see* Stelco Inc.
Steel Dynamics, Inc., 52 326–28
Steel Technologies Inc., 63 358–60
Steelcase Inc., 7 493–95; 27 432–35 (upd.)
Steen Production Services, Inc., **51** 248
Steenkolen Handelsvereniging NV, **39** 176; **50** 335
Stefanel SpA, 63 361–63
Stegbar Pty Ltd., **31** 398–400
Steiff *see* Margarete Steiff GmbH.
Steilman Group *see* Klaus Steilmann GmbH & Co. KG.
Stein Mart Inc., 19 423–25; 72 337–39 (upd.)
Stein Printing Company, **25** 183
Stein Robaire Helm, **22** 173
Steinbach Inc., *see* Schottenstein Stores Corp.
Steinbach Stores, Inc., **19** 108
Steinberg Incorporated, II 662–65
Steinberger, **16** 239
Steiner Corporation (Alsco), 53 308–11
Steinmüller Verwaltungsgesellschaft *see* Vereinigte Elektrizitaswerke Westfalen AG
Steinway Musical Properties, Inc., 19 426–29
Stelco Inc., IV 208–10; 51 349–52 (upd.)
Stella Bella Corporation, **19** 436
Stelmar Shipping Ltd., 52 329–31
Stelwire Ltd., **51** 352
Stemilt Growers Inc., 94 407–10
Stena AB, **25** 105; **29** 429–30
Stena Line AB, **38** 345
Stena-Sealink, **37** 137
Stens Corporation, **48** 34
Stentor Canadian Network Management, **6** 310
Stepan Company, 30 437–39
The Stephan Company, 60 285–88
Stephens Inc., 92 344–48
Stephens Media, LLC, 91 451–54
Stephenson Clarke and Company, **31** 368–69
Steria SA, 49 382–85
Stericycle, Inc., 33 380–82; 74 316–18 (upd.)
STERIS Corporation, 29 449–52
Sterling Capital Partners, **57** 56–57
Sterling Chemicals, Inc., 16 460–63; 78 356–61 (upd.)
Sterling Drug Inc., I 698–700
Sterling Electronics Corp., 18 496–98
Sterling Engineered Products, *see* TRINOVA Corp.
Sterling European Airlines A/S, 70 300–02
Sterling House Corp., **42** 4
Sterling Inc., **61** 326–27
Sterling Organics Ltd., **12** 351; **50** 282
Sterling Software, Inc., 11 468–70 *see also* Computer Associates International, Inc.
Sterling Winthrop, *see* Eastman Kodak Co.
Stern Bros., LLC, **37** 224
Stern Publishing, **38** 478
Stern's, *see* Federated Department Stores Inc.
Sterner Lighting, **76** 185
STET *see* Società Finanziaria Telefonica per Azioni.
Stet Hellas, **63** 378–79
Steuben Glass *see* Corning Inc.
Stevcoknit Fabrics Company, *see* Delta Woodside Industries, Inc.
Steve & Barry's LLC, 88 377–80
Steve's Ice Cream, **16** 54–55
Stevedoring Services of America Inc., 28 435–37
Steven Madden, Ltd., 37 371–73
Stevens, Thompson & Runyan, Inc. *see* CRSS Inc.
Stevens Water Monitoring Systems, **52** 226
Stew Leonard's, 56 349–51
Stewart and Richey Construction Co., **51** 170
Stewart & Stevenson Services Inc., 11 471–73
Stewart Enterprises, Inc., 20 481–83

Stewart Information Services Corporation, 78 362–65
Stewart, Tabori & Chang, **58** 155
Stewart's Beverages, 39 383–86
Stewart's Shops Corporation, 80 360–63
Stickley *see* L. and J.G. Stickley, Inc.
Stiefel Laboratories, Inc., 90 396–99
Stihl *see* Andreas Stihl AG & Co. KG.
Stillwater Mining Company, 47 380–82
Stilwell Financial Inc. *see* Janus Capital Group Inc.
Stimson Lumber Company Inc., 78 366–69
Stimsonite Corporation, **49** 38
Stinnes AG, 8 494–97; 23 451–54 (upd.); 59 387–92 (upd.)
Stirling Group plc, 62 342–44
STM Systems Corp., **11** 485
STMicroelectronics NV, 52 332–35
Stock Yards Packing Co., Inc., 37 374–76
Stockholder Systems Inc., **11** 485
Stockpack Ltd., **44** 318
Stoddard International plc, 72 340–43
Stokely Van Camp, *see* ConAgra Foods, Inc.
Stoll-Moss Theatres Ltd., 34 420–22
Stollwerck AG, 53 312–15
Stolt-Nielsen S.A., 42 356–59; 54 349–50
Stolt Sea Farm Holdings PLC, 54 349–51
Stone & Webster, Inc., 13 495–98; 64 368–72 (upd.)
Stone Container Corporation, IV 332–34 *see also* Smurfit-Stone Container Corp.
Stone Manufacturing Company, 14 469–71; 43 392–96 (upd.)
Stonega Coke & Coal Co. *see* Westmoreland Coal Co.
Stoner Associates *see* Severn Trent PLC.
Stonington Partners, **19** 318
Stonyfield Farm, Inc., 55 357–60
Stoody Co., *see* Thermadyne Holding Corp.
Stoof, **26** 278–79
Stoomvaart Maatschappij Nederland *see* Koninklijke Nedlloyd N.V.
The Stop & Shop Supermarket Company, II 666–67; 24 460–62 (upd.); 68 350–53 (upd.)
Stop N Go, *see* National Convenience Stores Inc.
Stoppenbauch Inc., **23** 202
Stora Enso Oyj, IV 335–37; 36 447–55 (upd.); 85 396–408 (upd.)
Storage Dimensions Inc., **10** 404
Storage Technology Corporation, 6 275–77
Storage USA, Inc., 21 475–77
Storebor Brux Company, **52** 406
Storehouse PLC, 16 464–66 *see also* Mothercare plc.
Storm Technology, **28** 245
Storybook, Inc., **70** 52
Storz Instruments Co., **25** 56
Stouffer Corp., 8 498–501 *see also* Nestlé S.A.
Stow Mills, Inc., **76** 360, 362
Stowe Machine Co., Inc., **30** 283
STP, **19** 223; **26** 349
STRAAM Engineers *see* CRSS Inc.
Straits Steamship Co. *see* Malaysian Airlines System.
StrataCom, Inc., 16 467–69
Stratagene Corporation, 70 303–06
Stratasys, Inc., 67 361–63
Strategic Implications International, Inc., **45** 44
Strategix Solutions, **43** 309
StrategyOne, **62** 115
Stratford Corporation, **15** 103; **26** 100
Strattec Security Corporation, 73 324–27
Stratton Oakmont Inc., **37** 372–73; **46** 282
Stratus Computer, Inc., 10 499–501
Straumann Holding AG, 79 396–99
Straus-Frank Company, **29** 86, 88
Strauss Discount Auto, 56 352–54
Strauss-Elite Group, 68 354–57
Strawberries, **30** 465
Strayer Education, Inc., 53 316–19
Stream International Inc., **48** 369
Stream Machine Co., **48** 92
Streamline Holdings, **39** 237–38
StreamScapes Media, **51** 286, 288
Stride Rite Corporation, 8 502–04; 37 377–80 (upd.); 86 378–84 (upd.)
Strine Printing Company Inc., 88 381–84
Strintzis Lines Shipping S.A., **64** 45
Strix Ltd., 51 353–55
Strobbe Graphics NV *see* Punch International N.V.
The Strober Organization, Inc., 82 357–60
Stroehmann Bakeries, Inc., *see* George Weston Ltd.
The Stroh Brewery Company, I 290–92; 18 499–502 (upd.)
Strombecker Corporation, 60 289–91
Stroock & Stroock & Lavan LLP, 40 418–21
Strouds, Inc., 33 383–86
Structural Fibers, Inc. *see* Essef Corp.
Struebel Group, **18** 170
Strydel, Inc., *see* The Ohio Art Co.
Stryker Corporation, 11 474–76; 29 453–55 (upd.); 79 400–05 (upd.)
Stuart & Sons Ltd., **34** 493, 496
Stuart C. Irby Company, 58 333–35
Stuart Entertainment Inc., 16 470–72
Stuart Medical, Inc., *see* Owens & Minor, Inc.
Student Loan Marketing Association, II 453–55 *see also* SLM Holding Corp.
StudioCanal, **48** 164–65
Studley Products Inc., *see* Ply Gem Industries Inc.
Stuffit Co., **IV** 597
Stuller Settings, Inc., 35 405–07
Sturm, Ruger & Company, Inc., 19 430–32
Stussy, Inc., 55 361–63
Style Magazine BV, **48** 347
Styleclick.com, Inc., **47** 420
SU214, **28** 27, 30
Suave Shoe Corporation *see* French Fragrances, Inc.
Sub-Zero Freezer Co., Inc., 31 426–28
Suber Suisse S.A., **48** 350
Subic Bay Energy Co., Ltd, **56** 290
The SubLine Company, Inc., **53** 340
SubLogic, **15** 455
SUBperior Distribution Systems, Inc., **53** 340
Suburban Propane Partners, L.P., 30 440–42
Subway, 32 442–44 *see also* Doctor's Associates Inc.
Successories, Inc., 30 443–45
Sucden *see* Compagnie Financière Sucres et Denrées.
Sucesora de Jose Puig y Cia C.A., **60** 246
Suchard Co. *see* Jacobs Suchard.
Sudamericana Holding S.A., **63** 180
Sudbury Inc., 16 473–75
Sudbury River Consulting Group, **31** 131
Südzucker AG, 27 436–39
Suez Lyonnaise des Eaux, 36 456–59 (upd.)
Suez Oil Processing Co., **IV** 413–14; **51** 113
Sugar Entertainment, **51** 288
Sugar Mount Capital, LLC, **33** 355
Sugarland Industries *see* Imperial Holly Corp.
SugarLoaf Creations, Inc. *see* American Coin Merchandising, Inc.
Sugarloaf Mountain Corporation, **28** 21
Suge Knight Films, Inc., **69** 350–51
The Suit Company, **51** 253
Suito Sangyo Co., Ltd. *see* Seino Transportation Company, Ltd.
SUITS *see* Scottish Universal Investments.
Suiza Foods Corporation, 26 447–50 *see also* Dean Foods Co.
Sukhoi Design Bureau Aviation Scientific-Industrial Complex, 24 463–65
Sullivan & Cromwell, 26 451–53
Sullivan-Schein Dental Products Inc. *see* Henry Schein Inc.
Sulpetro Limited, **25** 232
Sulzer Ltd., III 630–33; 68 358–62 (upd.)
Sumergrade Corporation, **19** 304; **41** 300
Sumisho Electronics Co. Ltd., **18** 170
Sumitomo Bank, Limited, II 360–62; 26 454–57 (upd.)
Sumitomo Chemical Company Ltd., I 397–98
Sumitomo Corporation, I 518–20; 11 477–80 (upd.)
Sumitomo Electric Industries, II 104–05
Sumitomo Heavy Industries, Ltd., III 634–35; 42 360–62 (upd.)
Sumitomo Life Insurance Company, III 365–66; 60 292–94 (upd.)
Sumitomo Metal Industries Ltd., IV 211–13; 82 361–66 (upd.)

Sumitomo Metal Mining Co., Ltd., IV 214–16
Sumitomo Mitsui Banking Corporation, 51 356–62 (upd.)
Sumitomo Realty & Development Co., Ltd., IV 726–27
Sumitomo Rubber Industries, Ltd., V 252–53
Sumitomo Trading, **45** 8
The Sumitomo Trust & Banking Company, Ltd., II 363–64; 53 320–22 (upd.)
Summa International, **56** 284
Summer Paper Tube, **19** 78
SummerGate Inc., **48** 148
Summers Group Inc., **15** 386
The Summit Bancorporation, 14 472–74 *see also* FleetBoston Financial Corp.
Summit Constructors *see* CRSS Inc.
Summit Family Restaurants Inc., 19 433–36
Summit Systems Inc., **45** 280
Summit Technology Inc., **30** 485
Sumolis, **54** 315, 317
Sun Alliance Group PLC, III 369–74 *see also* Royal & Sun Alliance Insurance Group plc.
Sun Apparel Inc., **39** 247
Sun Capital Partners Inc., **63** 79
Sun Chemical Corp. *see* Sequa Corp.
Sun Communities Inc., 46 377–79
Sun Company, Inc., IV 548–50 *see also* Sunoco, Inc.
Sun Country Airlines, I 30 446–49
Sun-Diamond Growers of California, 7 496–97 *see also* Diamond of California.
Sun Distributors L.P., 12 459–461
Sun Electric, **15** 288
Sun Equities Corporation, **15** 449
Sun Financial Group, Inc., **25** 171
Sun Gro Horticulture Inc., **49** 196, 198
Sun Healthcare Group Inc., 25 455–58
Sun Hydraulics Corporation, 74 319–22
Sun International Hotels Limited, 26 462–65 *see also* Kerzner International Ltd.
Sun Life Financial Inc., 85 409–12
Sun Life Group of America, *see* SunAmerica Inc.
Sun Live Co., **56** 201
Sun-Maid Growers of California, 82 367–71
Sun Mark, Inc., **21** 483
Sun Media, **29** 471–72; **47** 327
Sun Men's Shop Co., Ltd. *see* Nagasakiya Co., Ltd.
Sun Microsystems, Inc., 7 498–501; 30 450–54 (upd.); 91 455–62 (upd.)
Sun Oil Co., **IV** 424, 548–50; **11** 35; **36** 86–87 *see also* Oryx Energy Co; Sunoco, Inc.
Sun Optical Co., Ltd. *see* Nagasakiya Co., Ltd.
Sun Pac Foods, **45** 161
Sun Pharmaceutical Industries Ltd., 57 345–47
Sun-Rype Products Ltd., 76 336–38
Sun Shades 501 Ltd., **21** 483
Sun Ship, **IV** 549
Sun Sportswear, Inc., 17 460–63
Sun State Marine Services, Inc. *see* Hvide Marine Inc.
Sun Techno Services Co., Ltd. *see* Nagasakiya Co., Ltd.
Sun Technology Enterprises, *see* Sun Microsystems, Inc.
Sun Television & Appliances Inc., 10 502–03
Sun Valley Equipment Corp., **33** 363
Sun World International, LLC, 93 426–29
SunAir, **11** 300
SunAmerica Inc., 11 481–83 *see also* American International Group, Inc.
Sunbeam-Oster Co., Inc., 9 484–86
Sunbelt Beverage Corporation, **32** 520
Sunbelt Coca-Cola Bottling Co., *see* Coca-Cola Bottling Co. Consolidated.
Sunbelt Nursery Group, Inc., **12** 179, 200, 394
Sunbelt Rentals Inc., **34** 42
Sunbird *see* Nagasakiya Co., Ltd.
Sunburst Hospitality Corporation, 26 458–61
Sunburst Shutters Corporation, 78 370–72
Sunburst Technology Corporation, **36** 273
Sunco N.V., **22** 515
Suncoast Motion Picture Company, **63** 65
Suncoast Toys, Inc., **74** 14
SunCor Development Company, **6** 546–47
Suncor Energy Inc., 54 352–54
Suncorp-Metway Ltd., 91 463–66
Sundance Publishing, **IV** 609; **12** 559
Sundor Group, **54** 213
Sundstrand Corporation, 7 502–04; 21 478–81 (upd.)
Sundt Corp., 24 466–69
Sundwig Eisenhütte Maschinenfabrik GmbH & Co., **51** 25
SunGard Data Systems Inc., 11 484–85
Sunglass Hut International, Inc., 21 482–84; 74 323–26 (upd.)
Sunkiss Thermoreactors, **21** 65
Sunkist Growers, Inc., 26 466–69
Sunkus & Associates, **49** 427
Sunkus Co. Ltd. *see* Nagasakiya Co., Ltd.
Sunlight Services Group Limited, **45** 139
Sunlit Industries, **44** 132
Sunnyside Feedmill, **60** 316
Sunoco, Inc., 28 438–42 (upd.); 83 373-380 (upd.)
SunOpta Inc., 79 406–10
SunPower Corporation, 91 467–70
SunQuest HealthCare Corp. *see* Unison HealthCare Corp.
Sunquest Information Systems Inc., **45** 279, 281
The Sunrider Corporation, 26 470–74
Sunrise Greetings, 88 385–88
SunRise Imaging, **44** 358
Sunrise Inc., **55** 48
Sunrise Medical Inc., 11 486–88
Sunrise Senior Living, Inc., 81 380–83
Sunrise Test Systems, **11** 491
Sunsations Sunglass Company, **21** 483
Sunshine Biscuit Co., **35** 181; **36** 313
Sunshine Bullion Co., **25** 542
Sunshine Mining Company, **20** 149
SunSoft Inc., *see* Sun Microsystems, Inc.
Sunstate Airlines Pty Ltd. *see* Qantas Airways Ltd.
Sunsweet Growers, *see* Diamond of California.
Suntech Power Holdings Company Ltd., 89 432–35
Sunterra Corporation, 75 354–56
Suntory Ltd., 65 328–31
SunTrust Banks Inc., 23 455–58
Sunward Technologies, Inc., **10** 464
Supasnaps, **V** 50
Supelco, Inc., **36** 431
Super Bazars, **26** 159
Super Dart *see* Dart Group Corp.
Super 8 Motels, Inc., 83 381-385
Super Food Services, Inc., 15 479–81
Super 1 Stores *see* Brookshire Grocery Co.
Super Sagless Spring Corp., **15** 103
Super Sol Ltd., **41** 56–57
Superb Manufacturing, **60** 56
La Supercalor S.P.A. *see* De'Longhi S.p.A.
Supercuts Inc., 26 475–78
Superdrug plc *see* Rite Aid Corp.
Superfast Ferries SA, **64** 45
Superior Bearings Company *see* Federal-Mogul Corp.
Superior Coach Co. *see* Accubuilt, Inc.
Superior Energy Services, Inc., 65 332–34
Superior Essex Inc., 80 364–68
Superior Foam and Polymers, Inc., **44** 261
Superior Healthcare Group, Inc., **11** 221
Superior Industries International, Inc., 8 505–07
Superior Oil Co., **49** 137
Superior Recycled Fiber Industries, **26** 363
Superior Uniform Group, Inc., 30 455–57
SuperMac Technology Inc., **16** 419
Supermarchés GB, **26** 159
Supermarkets General Holdings Corporation, II 672–74 *see also* Pathmark Stores, Inc.
Supersaver Wholesale Club, Inc. *see* Wal-Mart Stores, Inc.
Supersnaps, **19** 124
SuperStation WTBS *see* Turner Broadcasting System, Inc.
SUPERVALU INC., II 668–71; 18 503–08 (upd.); 50 453–59 (upd.)
Supplyon AG, **48** 450
Suprema Specialties, Inc., 27 440–42
Supreme International Corporation, 27 443–46
Supreme Life Insurance Company of America *see* Johnson Publishing Company, Inc.
Supron Energy Corp., **15** 129
Suramericana de Inversiones S.A., 88 389–92

Surapon Nichirei Foods Company Ltd. *see* Nichirei Corp.
Surety Life Insurance Company, **10** 51
SureWay Air Traffic Corporation, *see* Consolidated Delivery & Logistics, Inc.
Surgical Plastics, **25** 430–31
Surgimedics Inc., **68** 379
OAO Surgutneftegaz, 48 375–78
Suroflex GmbH, **23** 300
Surplus Software, **31** 176
Surrey Free Inns plc *see* SFI Group plc.
Surrey Satellite Technology Limited, 83 386-390
Surridge Dawson Ltd. *see* Dawson Holdings PLC.
Survey Research Group, **10** 360
Susan Bristol, **16** 61
The Susan G. Komen Breast CancerFoundation, 78 373–76
Susan Kay Cosmetics *see* The Cosmetic Center, Inc.
SuSE Linux AG, **45** 363
Susquehanna Pfaltzgraff Company, 8 508–10
Sussex Group, **15** 449
Sutherland Lumber Co., **19** 233
Sutter Corp., **15** 113
Sutter Home Winery Inc., 16 476–78
Sutton & Towne, Inc., **21** 96
Sutton Publishing Limited *see* Haynes Publishing Group P.L.C.
Suunto Oy, **41** 14, 16
Suzannah Farms, *see* Thorn Apple Valley, Inc.
Suzhou Elevator Company, **29** 420
Suzuki Motor Corporation, 9 487–89; 23 459–62 (upd.); 59 393–98 (upd.)
Suzy Shier Limited *see* La Senza Corp.
Sveaskog AB, 93 430–33
AB Svensk Färgämnesindustri, **50** 55
Svensk Filmindustrie, **52** 49, 51
Svensk Pantbelåning, **61** 53
Svenska Aeroplan Aktiebolaget *see* Saab-Scania AB.
Svenska Aller AB, **72** 62
Svenska Cellulosa Aktiebolaget SCA, IV 338–40; 28 443–46 (upd.); 85 413–20 (upd.)
Svenska Handelsbanken AB, II 365–67; 50 460–63 (upd.)
Svenska Kullagerfabriken A.B. *see* AB Volvo.
Svenska Stålpressnings AB, **26** 11
Sverdrup Corporation, 14 475–78 *see also* Jacobs Engineering Group Inc.
SVF *see* Société des Vins de France.
SWA *see* Southwest Airlines.
SWALEC *see* Scottish and Southern Energy plc.
Swales & Associates, Inc., 69 336–38
Swank, Inc., 17 464–66; 84 380–384 (upd.)
Swarovski International Holding AG, 40 422–25
The Swatch Group SA, 26 479–81
Swedish Match AB, 12 462–64; 39 387–90 (upd.); 92 349–55 (upd.)
Swedish Telecom, V 331–33
SwedishAmerican Health System, 51 363–66
Sweedor, **12** 464
Sweeney's, *see* Zale Corp.
Sweet Candy Company, 60 295–97
Sweet Stripes, Inc. *see* Bobs Candies, Inc.
Sweet Traditions LLC, **21** 323
Sweetheart Cup Company, Inc., 36 460–64
Swenson Granite Company, Inc., **37** 331
The Swett & Crawford Group Inc., 84 385–389
SWH Corporation, 70 307–09
Swift & Company, 55 364–67
Swift Adhesives, **10** 467
Swift Denim Group, **66** 134
Swift Energy Company, 63 364–66
Swift Independent Packing Co., **42** 92
Swift Textiles, Inc., *see* Dominion Textile Inc.
Swift Transportation Co., Inc., 42 363–66
Swinerton Inc., 43 397–400
Swing-N-Slide, Inc. *see* PlayCore, Inc.
Swingline, Inc., **7** 3–5
Swire Pacific Ltd., I 521–22; 16 479–81 (upd.); 57 348–53 (upd.)
Swisher International Group Inc., 23 463–65
Swiss Air Transport Company Ltd., I 121–22
Swiss Army Brands, Inc. *see* Victorinox AG.
Swiss Banca de Gottardo, **26** 456
Swiss Bank Corporation, II 368–70 *see also* UBS AG.
Swiss Barry Callebaut AG, **53** 315
Swiss Broadcasting Corporation, **53** 325
Swiss Federal Railways (Schweizerische Bundesbahnen), V 519–22
Swiss International Air Lines Ltd., 48 379–81
Swiss Life, **52** 357–58
Swiss Reinsurance Company (Schweizerische Rückversicherungs-Gesellschaft), III 375–78; 46 380–84 (upd.)
Swiss Saurer AG, **39** 39, 41
Swiss Telecom PTT *see* Swisscom AG.
Swiss Time Australia Pty Ltd, **25** 461
Swiss Valley Farms Company, 90 400–03
Swiss Volksbank, **21** 146–47
Swissair Associated Co., **34** 397–98; **36** 426
Swissair Group, **47** 286–87; **49** 80–81
SwissCargo, **49** 81
Swisscom AG, 58 336–39
Swissport International Ltd., 70 310–12
Switchboard Inc., **25** 52
SXI Limited, *see* Standex International Corp.
Sybase, Inc., 10 504–06; 27 447–50 (upd.)
Sybra, Inc., *see* Valhi, Inc.
Sybron International Corp., 14 479–81
Sycamore Networks, Inc., 45 388–91
Sydney Electricity, **12** 443
Sydney FM Facilities Pty. Limited, **58** 359
SYDOOG, Inc., **64** 160
Sydsvenska Kemi AB, **51** 289
Sykes Enterprises, Inc., 45 392–95
Syllogic B.V., **29** 376
Sylvan, Inc., 22 496–99
Sylvan Lake Telephone Company, **6** 334
Sylvan Learning Systems, Inc., 35 408–11 *see also* Educate Inc.
Sylvania Companies, **23** 181; **50** 299
Symantec Corporation, 10 507–09; 82 372–77 (upd.)
Symbian Ltd., **45** 346, 348
Symbios Logic Inc., **31** 5
Symbiosis Corp., **10** 70; **50** 538
Symbol Technologies, Inc., 15 482–84 *see also* Motorola, Inc.
Symrise GmbH and Company KG, 89 436–40
Syms Corporation, 29 456–58; 74 327–30 (upd.)
Symtron Systems Inc., **37** 399–400
Symtronix Corporation, *see* Tech-Sym Corp.
Symyx Technologies, Inc., 77 420–23
Syn-Optics, Inc., **29** 454
Synavant Inc. *see* Dendrite International, Inc.
Synbiotics Corporation, **23** 284
Syncordia Corp., **15** 69
Syncro Ltd., **51** 89
Syncrude Canada Limited, **25** 232
Synercom Technology Inc., **14** 319
Synergy Software Inc., **31** 131
Syneron Medical Ltd., 91 471–74
Synetic, Inc., **16** 59
Synfloor SA, **25** 464
Syngenta International AG, 83 391-394
SYNNEX Corporation, 73 328–30
Synopsys, Inc., 11 489–92; 69 339–43 (upd.)
SynOptics Communications, Inc., 10 510–12
Synovus Financial Corp., 12 465–67; 52 336–40 (upd.)
Synrad, Inc. *see* Excel Technology, Inc.
Syntel, Inc., 92 356–60
Syntex Corporation, I 701–03
Syntex Pharmaceuticals Ltd., **21** 425
Synthes, Inc., 93 434–37
Synthetic Blood Corp., **15** 380
Synthomer *see* Yule Catto & Company plc.
Syntron, Inc., *see* Tech-Sym Corp.
Sypris Solutions, Inc., 85 421–25
SyQuest Technology, Inc., 18 509–12
Syratech Corp., 14 482–84
SYSCO Corporation, II 675–76; 24 470–72 (upd.); 75 357–60 (upd.)
SYSCO Security Systems, Inc., **51** 81
Syscon Corporation, **38** 227
SysScan, **V** 339
Systech Environmental Corporation, **28** 228–29
System Designers plc *see* SD-Scicon plc.
System Parking West, **25** 16
System Software Associates, Inc., 10 513–14

Systematic Business Services, Inc., **48** 256–57
Systematics Inc., **6** 301
Systemax, Inc., 52 341–44
Systembolaget, **31** 459–60
Systems & Computer Technology Corp., 19 437–39
Systems and Services Company *see* SYSCO Corp.
Systems Center, Inc., **11** 469
Systron Donner Corp. *see* BEI Technologies, Inc.
Systronics, **13** 235
Sytner Group plc, 45 396–98
Syufy Enterprises *see* Century Theatres, Inc.

T

T. and J. Brocklebank Ltd., **23** 160
T&N PLC, **26** 141
T-Fal *see* Groupe SEB.
T-Netix, Inc., 46 385–88
T-Online International AG, 61 349–51
T-Shirt Brokerage Services, Inc., **26** 257
T-Tech Industries, **26** 363
T.G.I. Friday's, *see* Carlson Restaurants Worldwide.
T.J. Falgout, **11** 523
T.J. Maxx *see* The TJX Companies, Inc.
T.L. Smith & Company, **21** 502
T. Marzetti Company, 57 354–56
T. Rowe Price Associates, Inc., 11 493–96; 34 423–27 (upd.)
T. Wear Company S.r.l., **25** 121
TA Associates Inc., **32** 146; **54** 361
TA Logistics, **49** 402
TA Media AG, **15** 31
TA Triumph-Adler AG, 48 382–85
TAB Products Co., 17 467–69
Tabacalera, S.A., V 414–16; 17 470–73 (upd.) *see also* Altadis S.A.
TABCORP Holdings Limited, 44 407–10
Table Supply Meat Co. *see* Omaha Steaks International Inc.
Tabletop Holdings, **70** 185
TACA *see* Grupo TACA.
Tachikawa Bus Co., Ltd., **68** 281
Taco Bell Corporation, 7 505–07; 21 485–88 (upd.); 74 331–34 (upd.)
Taco Cabana, Inc., 23 466–68; 72 344–47 (upd.)
Taco John's International Inc., 15 485–87; 63 367–70 (upd.)
Tacony Corporation, 70 313–15
Taft Broadcasting Co. *see* Great American Broadcasting Inc.
TAG Heuer S.A., 25 459–61; 77 424–28 (upd.)
Tag-It Pacific, Inc., 85 426–29
Tag Mex, Inc., **62** 353
Taggarts Motor Group *see* Lookers plc.
Taguchi Automobile *see* Seino Transportation Company, Ltd.
Tahitian Noni International, Inc. *see* Morinda Holdings, Inc.
Tahoe Joe's, Inc., **32** 102 **32** 249
TAI, Ltd., **34** 397
Taiheiyo Bank, **15** 495
Taiheiyo Cement Corporation, 60 298–301 (upd.)
Taiko Trading Co. Ltd., **51** 179
Taikoo Motors Limited, **57** 352
Taio Paper Mfg. Co., Ltd. *see* Daio Paper Co., Ltd.
Taisho Marine and Fire Insurance Co., Ltd., *see* Mitsui Marine and Fire Insurance Co., Ltd.
Taittinger S.A., 43 401–05
Taiwan Aerospace Corp., **24** 88
Taiwan Power Company, **22** 89
Taiwan Semiconductor Manufacturing Company Ltd., 47 383–87
Taiwan Tobacco & Liquor Corporation, 75 361–63
Taiyo Fishery Company, Limited, II 578–79 *see also* Maruha Group Inc.
Taiyo Kobe Bank, Ltd., II 371–72
Taiyo Kogyo Corporation, **35** 98, 100
Taiyo Nippon Kisen Co. Ltd., **56** 181
Taka-Q, **72** 4
Takanashi Milk Products Ltd., **37** 197
Takara Holdings Inc., 62 345–47
Takarazuka Hankyu Company Ltd., **62** 170
Takashimaya Company, Limited, V 193–96; 47 388–92 (upd.)
Take-Two Interactive Software, Inc., 46 389–91
Takeda Chemical Industries, Ltd., I 704–06; 46 392–95 (upd.)
Takeda Riken, **11** 504
Takihyo, **15** 145
Takkyubin, **V** 537
Tako Carton Plant Ltd., **56** 255
Talanx AG, **53** 162
The Talbots, Inc., 11 497–99; 31 429–32 (upd.); 88 393–98 (upd.)
Talcott National Corporation, *see* Leucadia National Corporation
Talegen Holdings Inc., **26** 546
Talent Net Inc., **44** 164
Talisman Energy Inc., 9 490–93; 47 393–98 (upd.)
Talk America Holdings, Inc., 70 316–19
TALK Corporation, **34** 48
Talk Miramax Books, **64** 285
Talk Radio Network, Inc., **23** 294
Talkline, **63** 371–72
Talley Industries, Inc., 16 482–85
Talmadge Farms, Inc., **20** 105
Taltex Ltd., **51** 379
TALX Corporation, 92 361–64
TAM Linhas Aéreas S.A., 68 363–65
Tama *see* Hoshino Gakki Co. Ltd.
Tamarind International Inc., **62** 342, 344
Tambrands Inc., 8 511–13 *see also* Procter & Gamble Co.
Tamedia AG, 53 323–26
Tamfelt Oyj Abp, 62 348–50
Tampa Electric Company, **6** 582–83
Tampax Inc. *see* Tambrands Inc.
Tamron Company Ltd., 82 378–81
TAMSA *see* Tubos de Acero de Mexico, S.A.
Tandem Computers, Inc., 6 278–80 *see also* Hewlett-Packard Co.
Tandy Corporation, II 106–08; 12 468–70 (upd.) *see also* RadioShack Corp.
Tandycrafts, Inc., 31 433–37
Tangent Industries, **15** 83; **50** 124
Tanger Factory Outlet Centers, Inc., 49 386–89
Tangiers International *see* Algo Group Inc.
Tangram Rehabilitation Network, Inc., **29** 401
Tanimura & Antle, **54** 257
Tanox, Inc., 77 429–32
Tantalum Mining Corporation, **29** 81
TAP—Air Portugal Transportes Aéreos Portugueses S.A., 46 396–99 (upd.)
Tapemark Company Inc., 64 373–75
Tapis-St. Maclou, **37** 22
Tappan *see* White Consolidated Industries Inc.
Target Corporation, 10 515–17; 27 451–54 (upd.); 61 352–56 (upd.)
Target Marketing and Promotions, Inc., **55** 15
Target Marketing Systems Inc., **64** 237
Target Rock Corporation, **35** 134–36
Tarkett Sommer AG, 25 462–64
Targetti Sankey SpA, 86 385–88
Tarmac America, **64** 379–80
Tarmac plc, III 751–54; 28 447–51 (upd.)
Taro Pharmaceutical Industries Ltd., 65 335–37
TAROM S.A., 64 376–78
Tarragon Oil and Gas Ltd. *see* Unocal Corp.
Tarragon Realty Investors, Inc., 45 399–402
Tarrant Apparel Group, 62 351–53
Tarsa, **63** 151
TASC *see* Analytical Sciences Corp.
Tascam *see* TEAC Corporation
Taser International, Inc., 62 354–57
Tasman Pulp and Paper Co. Ltd. *see* Fletcher Challenge Ltd.
Tastee Freeze, **39** 234
Tasty Baking Company, 14 485–87; 35 412–16 (upd.)
Tasukara Company Ltd., **62** 170
TAT European Airlines, *see* British Airways PLC.
Tata Airlines *see* Air-India Ltd.
Tata Industries, **20** 313; **21** 74
Tata Iron & Steel Co. Ltd., IV 217–19; 44 411–15 (upd.)
Tata Tea Ltd., 76 339–41
Tate & Lyle PLC, II 580–83; 42 367–72 (upd.)
Tatham Corporation, **21** 169, 171
Tati SA, 25 465–67
Tatneft *see* OAO Tatneft.
Tattered Cover Book Store, 43 406–09
Tatung Co., 23 469–71
Taubman Centers, Inc., 75 364–66
Taurus Exploration, **21** 208
Taurus Programming Services, **10** 196

TaurusHolding GmbH & Co. KG, 46 400–03
Tax Management, Inc., **23** 92
Taylor & Francis Group plc, 44 416–19
Taylor Aircraft Corporation, **44** 307
Taylor Corporation, 36 465–67
Taylor Guitars, 48 386–89
Taylor Made Golf Co., 23 472–74
Taylor Medical, **14** 388
Taylor Nelson Sofres plc, 34 428–30
Taylor Publishing Company, 12 471–73; 36 468–71 (upd.)
Taylor Woodrow plc, I 590–91; 38 450–53 (upd.)
Tayto Ltd., **22** 515
Tazo Tea Company, **50** 450
TB Wood's Corporation, 56 355–58
TBC Corp., **20** 63
TBS *see* Turner Broadcasting System, Inc.
TBWA/Chiat/Day, 6 47–49; 43 410–14 (upd.) *see also* Omnicom Group Inc.
TC Advertising *see* Treasure Chest Advertising, Inc.
TC Debica, **20** 264
TCA *see* Air Canada.
TCBC *see* Todays Computers Business Centers.
TCBY Enterprises Inc., 17 474–76
TCF *see* Tokyo City Finance.
TCF Financial Corporation, 47 399–402
Tchibo GmbH, 82 382–85
TCI *see* Tele-Communications, Inc.
TCI Communications, **29** 39
TCI Inc., **33** 92–93
TCI International Inc., **43** 48
TCJC *see* Charisma Brands LLC
TCM Investments, Inc., **49** 159
TCO *see* Taubman Centers, Inc.
TCPL *see* TransCanada PipeLines Ltd.
TCS Management Group, Inc., **22** 53
TD Bank *see* The Toronto-Dominion Bank.
TD Brasil, Ltda., **74** 338
TDC A/S, 63 371–74
TDK Corporation, II 109–11; 17 477–79 (upd.); 49 390–94 (upd.)
TDL Group Ltd., 46 404–06
TDL Infomedia Ltd., **47** 347
TDS *see* Telephone and Data Systems, Inc.
TEAC Corporation, 78 377–80
Teachers Insurance and Annuity Association-College Retirement Equities Fund, III 379–82; 45 403–07 (upd.)
Team Penske *see* Penske Corp.
Team Rental Group *see* Budget Group, Inc.
Teams, Inc., **37** 247
Teamsters Union, *see* International Brotherhood of Teamsters.
TearDrop Golf Company, 32 445–48
Tech Data Corporation, 10 518–19; 74 335–38 (upd.)
Tech/Ops Landauer, Inc. *see* Landauer, Inc.
Tech Pacific International, **39** 201, 203 *see also* First Pacific Co. Ltd.
Tech-Sym Corporation, 18 513–15; 44 420–23 (upd.)
Tech Textiles, USA, **15** 247–48
TechBooks Inc., 84 390–393
Techgistics, **49** 403
Techint Group, **63** 385
TECHNE Corporation, 52 345–48
Technical Coatings Co., *see* Benjamin Moore and Co.
Technical Olympic USA, Inc., 75 367–69
Technicolor Inc., **28** 246
Technip, 78 381–84
Techniques d'Avant-Garde *see* TAG Heuer International SA.
Technisch Bureau Visser, *see* Randstad Holding n.v.
Technitrol, Inc., 29 459–62
Technology Management Group, Inc., **18** 112
Technology Research Corporation, 94 411–14
Technology Solutions Company, 94 415–19
Technology Venture Investors, **11** 490; **14** 263
Techserviceavia, CJSC, **68** 204
Techsource Services, Inc., **60** 185
TechTeam Europe, Ltd., **41** 281
Techtronic Industries Company Ltd., 73 331–34
Teck Corporation, 27 455–58
Tecnacril Ltda, **51** 6
Tecnamotor S.p.A. *see* Tecumseh Products Co.
Tecneco, **IV** 422
Tecnipapel-Sociedade de Transformaçao e Distribuiçao de Papel, Lda, **60** 156
Tecnost S.p.A., **34** 319
TECO Energy, Inc., 6 582–84
Tecom Industries, Inc., *see* Tech-Sym Corp.
Tecomar S.A., **50** 209
Tecsa, **55** 182
Tecstar Inc. *see* Starcraft Corp.
Tectrix Fitness Equipment, Inc., **49** 108
Tecumseh Products Company, 8 514–16; 71 351–55 (upd.)
Ted Baker plc, 86 389–92
Ted Bates, Inc., **10** 69; **50** 537
Teddy's Shoe Store *see* Morse Shoe Inc.
Tee Vee Toons, Inc., 57 357–60
Teekay Shipping Corporation, 25 468–71; 82 386–91 (upd.)
Teepak International, **55** 123
Tees and Hartlepool, **31** 367, 369
Tefal *see* Groupe SEB.
TEFSA, **17** 182
TEIC *see* B.V. Tabak Export & Import Compagnie.
Teijin Limited, V 380–82; 61 357–61 (upd.)
Teikoku Jinken *see* Teijin Ltd.
Teikoku Oil Co., Ltd., **63** 312
Teixeira Duarte, **76** 94
Tejas Gas Co., **41** 359
Tejas Snacks LP, **44** 349
Tejon Ranch Company, 35 417–20
Tekelec, 83 395-399
Teklogix International, **45** 346, 348
Teknika Electronics Corporation, **43** 459
Tekno Books, **58** 167
Tektronix, Inc., 8 517–21; 78 385–91 (upd.)
TelAutograph Corporation, **29** 33–34
Telcon *see* Telegraph Construction and Maintenance Co.
Telcordia Technologies, Inc., 59 399–401
Tele-Communications, Inc., II 160–62
Tele Danmark *see* TDC A/S.
Télé Luxembourg, **44** 376
Tele Norte Leste Participações S.A., 80 369–72
Tele-Response and Support Services, Inc., **53** 209
Telebook, **25** 19
Telec Centre S.A., *see* Valmont Industries, Inc.
TeleCheck Services, Inc., **11** 113
TeleChef, **33** 387, 389
Telecom Argentina S.A., 63 375–77
Telecom Australia, 6 341–42 *see also* Telstra Corp. Ltd.
Telecom Canada *see* Stentor Canadian Network Management.
Telecom Corporation of New Zealand Limited, 54 355–58
Telecom Eireann, 7 508–10 *see also* eircom plc.
Telecom Finland, **57** 363
Telecom FL AG, **58** 338
Telecom Italia Mobile S.p.A., 63 378–80
Telecom Italia S.p.A., 43 415–19
Telecom-900, **59** 303
Telecom One, Inc., **29** 252
Telecom Personal S.A., **63** 376
Telecom*USA, **27** 304
Telecom Ventures, **73** 5
Telecom XXI, **59** 303
TelecomAsia, **62** 63
Telecomunicaçoes do Paraná *see* Brasil Telecom Participaçoes S.A.
Telecredit, Inc., **6** 25
Telectronic Pacing Systems, *see* Pacific Dunlop Ltd.
Teledyne Technologies Inc., I 523–25; 10 520–22 (upd.); 62 358–62 (upd.)
Teledyne Water Pik *see* Water Pik Technologies, Inc.
Teleflora LLC, **19** 12; **21** 259; **28** 138; **37** 337
Telefonaktiebolaget LM Ericsson, V 334–36; 46 407–11 (upd.)
Telefónica de Argentina S.A., 61 362–64
Telefónica de España, S.A., V 337–40
Telefonica Moviles, **69** 304, 306
Telefónica S.A., 46 412–17 (upd.)
Telefonos de Mexico S.A. de C.V., 14 488–90; 63 381–84 (upd.)
TeleFutura *see* Univision Communications Inc.
telegate AG, **47** 345, 347 *see also* ECI Telecom Ltd.

Teleklew Productions, Inc. *see* The Welk Group, Inc.
Telekom Malaysia Bhd, 76 342–44
Telekomunikacja Polska SA, 50 464–68
Telelistas Editors Ltda., **26** 520
TeleMarketing Corporation of Louisiana, *see* LDDS-Metro Communications, Inc.
Telematics International Inc., *see* ECI Telecom Ltd.
Télémécanique, **19** 166
Telemundo Communications Group Inc., **63** 161, 166
Telenet Information Services, **47** 37
Telenor ASA, 69 344–46
Teleos Communications Inc., **26** 277
Telepar *see* Brasil Telecom Participaçoes S.A.
Telephone and Data Systems, Inc., 9 494–96
Telephone Management Corporation, *see* LDDS-Metro Communications, Inc.
Telephone Utilities, Inc. *see* Pacific Telecom, Inc.
Telephone Utilities of Washington *see* Pacific Telecom, Inc.
TelePizza S.A., 33 387–89
Teleport Communications Group *see* AT&T Corp.
Telerate Systems Inc., *see* Dow Jones Telerate, Inc.
Telerent Europe *see* Granada Group PLC.
TeleRep *see* Cox Enterprises, Inc.
TeleRoss LLC, **59** 209–211
Telesat Cable TV, Inc., **23** 293
Telesis Oil and Gas, **6** 478
Telesistema, *see* Grupo Televisa, S.A.
Telesistema Mexico *see* Grupo Televisa.
TeleSite, U.S.A., Inc., **44** 442
Telesystems SLW Inc., *see* Telxon Corp.
Teletrade Inc., **60** 146
Tele2 AB, **26** 331–33
Television de Mexico, S.A., *see* Grupo Televisa, S.A.
Television Española, S.A., 7 511–12
Télévision Française 1, 23 475–77
Television Sales and Marketing Services Ltd., *see* Central Independent Television.
TeleZüri AG, **53** 324
Telfin, **V** 339
Telia AB *see* TeliaSonera AB.
Telia Mobitel, **11** 19; **26** 332
TeliaSonera AB, 57 361–65 (upd.)
Telios Pharmaceuticals, Inc., **11** 460
Tellabs, Inc., 11 500–01; 40 426–29 (upd.)
TELMARK, Inc., **57** 284
Telmex *see* Teléfonos de México S.A. de C.V.
Telpar, Inc., **14** 377
Telport, **14** 260
Telstra Corporation Limited, 50 469–72
Telrad Networks Ltd., **68** 222, 225
Teltrend, Inc., **57** 409
Telvent *see* Telecom Ventures.
Telxon Corporation, 10 523–25
Tembec Inc., 66 322–24
Temerlin McClain, **23** 479; **25** 91
TEMIC TELEFUNKEN, **34** 128, 133, 135
Temp Force, *see* Randstad Holding n.v.
Temple, Barker & Sloan/Strategic Planning Associates, *see* Marsh & McLennan Companies, Inc.
Temple Frosted Foods, **25** 278
Temple-Inland Inc., IV 341–43; 31 438–42 (upd.)
Tempo-Team, *see* Randstad Holding n.v.
Tempur-Pedic Inc., 54 359–61
Tempus Group plc, **48** 442
Ten Cate *see* Royal Ten Cate N.V.
Tenaris SA, 63 385–88
Tenby Industries Limited, **21** 350
Tencor Instruments, Inc. *see* KLA-Tencor Corp.
Tender Loving Care Health Care Services Inc., **64** 39
Tenet Healthcare Corporation, 55 368–71 (upd.)
TenFold Corporation, 35 421–23
Tengelmann Group, 27 459–62
Tengelmann Warenhandelsgesellschaft OHG, **47** 107
Tennant Company, 13 499–501; 33 390–93 (upd.)
Tenneco Inc., I 526–28; 10 526–28 (upd.)
Tennessee Eastman Corporation *see* Eastman Chemical Co.
Tennessee Gas Pipeline Co., **14** 126
Tennessee Insurance Company, *see* Ingram Industries, Inc.
Tennessee Paper Mills Inc. *see* Rock-Tenn Co.
Tennessee Restaurant Company, *see* Promus Companies, Inc.
Tennessee River Pulp & Paper Co., **51** 282–83
Tennessee Valley Authority, 50 473–77
Tennessee Woolen Mills, Inc., *see* Pillowtex Corp.
TenneT B.V., 78 392–95
Teoma Technologies, Inc., **65** 51–52
TEP *see* Tucson Electric Power Co.
TEPCO Cable Television Inc., **74** 348
TEPPCO Partners, L.P., 73 335–37
Tequila Herradura *see* Grupo Industrial Herradura, S.A. de C.V.
Tequila Sauza, **31** 91
Tequilera de Los Altos, **31** 92
Tera Computer Company, **75** 119
TeraBeam Networks Inc., **41** 261, 263–64
Teradata Corporation *see* NCR Corp.
Teradyne, Inc., 11 502–04
Terex Corporation, 7 513–15; 40 430–34 (upd.); 91 475–82 (upd.)
The Terlato Wine Group, 48 390–92
Terminix International, **25** 16
Terra Industries, Inc., 13 502–04; 94 420–24 (upd.)
Terra Lycos, Inc., 43 420–25
Terragrafics, **14** 245
Terrain King, **32** 26
Terre Haute Electric, **6** 555
Terre Lune, **25** 91
Terrena L'Union CANA CAVAL, 70 320–22
Territory Ahead, Inc., **29** 279
Terumo Corporation, 48 393–95
Tesa, S.A., **23** 82
TESC *see* The European Software Co.
Tesco plc, II 677–78; 24 473–76 (upd.); 68 366–70 (upd.)
Tesoro Petroleum Corporation, 7 516–19; 45 408–13 (upd.)
Tessenderlo Group, 76 345–48
Tesseract Inc., **33** 331
The Testor Corporation, 51 367–70
Tetley USA Inc., 88 399–402
Tetra Pak International SA, 53 327–29
Tetra Plastics Inc. *see* NIKE, Inc.
Tetra Tech, Inc., 29 463–65
Tettemer & Associates *see* The Keith Companies.
Teva Pharmaceutical Industries Ltd., 22 500–03; 54 362–65 (upd.)
Tex-Mex Partners L.C., **41** 270
Texaco Canada Inc., **25** 232
Texaco Inc., IV 551–53; 14 491–94 (upd.); 41 391–96 (upd.) *see also* ChevronTexaco Corp.
Texas Air Corporation, I 123–24
Texas Bus Lines, *see* Coach USA, Inc.
Texas Coffee Traders, **60** 210
Texas Eastern Transmission Company, **11** 28
Texas Farm LLC *see* Nippon Meat Packers Inc.
Texas Homecare, **21** 335
Texas Industries, Inc., 8 522–24
Texas Instruments Incorporated, II 112–15; 11 505–08 (upd.); 46 418–23 (upd.)
Texas International Airlines, **21** 142
Texas-New Mexico Utilities Company, **6** 580
Texas Pacific Group Inc., 36 472–74
Texas Rangers Baseball, 51 371–74
Texas Roadhouse, Inc., 69 347–49
Texas Timberjack, Inc., **51** 279–81
Texas Utilities Company, V 724–25; 25 472–74 (upd.)
Texasgulf Inc., *see* Potash Corporation of Saskatchewan Inc.
Têxtil Santa Catarina Ltda., **72** 68
Textile Diffusion, **25** 466
Textile Rubber and Chemical Company, **15** 490
Textron Inc., I 529–30; 34 431–34 (upd.); 88 403–07 (upd.)
Textron Lycoming Turbine Engine, 9 497–99
Texwood Industries, Inc., **20** 363
TFC *see* Times Fiber Communications, Inc.
TFH Publications, Inc., **58** 60
TFM *see* Grupo Transportación Ferroviaria Mexicana, S.A. de C.V.
TF1 *see* Télévision Française 1
TFP, Inc., **44** 358–59
TFS *see* Total Filtration Services, Inc.
TG Credit Service Co. Ltd., **55** 375

TGEL&PCo *see* Tucson Gas, Electric Light & Power Co.
TH:s Group, *see* Arrow Electronics, Inc.
Tha Row Records, 69 350–52 (upd.)
Thai Airways International Public Company Limited, 6 122–24; 27 463–66 (upd.)
Thai Lube Blending Co., **56** 290
Thai Nylon Co. Ltd., **53** 344
Thai Union Frozen Products PCL, 75 370–72
Thales S.A., 42 373–76
Thames Trains, **28** 157
Thames Water plc, 11 509–11; 90 404–08 (upd.)
Thameslink, **28** 157
Thane International, Inc., 84 394–397
Thanulux Public Company Limited, 86 393–96
THAW *see* Recreational Equipment, Inc.
Thelem SA, **54** 267
Therm-o-Disc, *see* Emerson.
Thermacore International Inc., **56** 247
Thermador Corporation, **67** 82
Thermadyne Holding Corporation, 19 440–43
Thermal Dynamics, *see* Thermadyne Holding Corp.
Thermal Energies, Inc., **21** 514
Thermal Snowboards, Inc., **22** 462
Thermal Transfer Ltd., *see* Southern Electric PLC.
ThermaStor Technologies, Ltd., **44** 366
Thermo BioAnalysis Corp., 25 475–78
Thermo Electron Corporation, 7 520–22
Thermo Fibertek, Inc., 24 477–79
Thermo Instrument Systems Inc., 11 512–14
Thermo King Corporation, 13 505–07 *see also* Ingersoll-Rand Company Ltd.
Thermoform Plastics, Inc., **56** 378–79
Thermogas Co., **35** 175
Thermolase Corporation, **22** 410
Thermos Company, 16 486–88
TheStreet.com, **34** 125
THHK Womenswear Limited, **53** 333
ThiemeMeulenhoff BV, **53** 273
Thiess Dampier Mitsui, **IV** 47
Things Remembered, Inc., 84 398–401
Thiokol Corporation, 9 500–02 (upd.); 22 504–07 (upd.)
Third Age Inc., **71** 137
Third Coast Capital, Inc., **51** 109
Third National Bank *see* Fifth Third Bancorp.
Third Wave Publishing Corp. *see* Acer Inc.
ThirdAge.com, **49** 290
Thirteen/WNET *see* Educational Broadcasting Corp.
Thistle Hotels PLC, 54 366–69
THM Biomedical Inc. *see* Kensey Nash Corp.
Thom McAn *see* Melville Corp.
Thomas & Betts Corporation, 11 515–17; 54 370–74 (upd.)
Thomas & Howard Company, Inc., 90 409–12
Thomas Borthwick & Sons (Australia) Pty. Ltd. *see* Nippon Meat Packers Inc.
Thomas Bros. Maps, **28** 380
Thomas Cook Group Ltd., **57** 195
Thomas Cook Travel Inc., 9 503–05; 33 394–96 (upd.)
Thomas Crosbie Holdings Limited, 81 384–87
Thomas De La Rue and Company, Ltd., **44** 357–58
Thomas H. Lee Co., 24 480–83
Thomas Industries Inc., 29 466–69
Thomas J. Lipton Company, 14 495–97
Thomas Jefferson Life Insurance Co., *see* St. Paul Cos.
Thomas Kinkade Galleries *see* Media Arts Group, Inc.
Thomas Nationwide Transport *see* TNT.
Thomas Nationwide Transport Limited *see* TNT Post Group N.V.
Thomas Nelson Inc., 14 498–99; 38 454–57 (upd.)
Thomas Publishing Company, 26 482–85
Thomas Y. Crowell, **IV** 605
Thomaston Mills, Inc., 27 467–70
Thomasville Furniture Industries, Inc., 12 474–76; 74 339–42 (upd.)
Thompson and Formby, **16** 44
Thompson Medical Company *see* Slim-Fast Nutritional Foods International Inc.
Thompson Nutritional Products, **37** 286
Thomsen Greenhouses and Garden Center, Incorporated, 65 338–40
Thomson-Brandt, **II** 13, 116–17
The Thomson Corporation, 8 525–28; 34 435–40 (upd.); 77 433–39 (upd.)
Thomson International, **37** 143
THOMSON multimedia S.A., II 116–17; 42 377–80 (upd.)
Thomson-Ramo-Woolridge *see* TRW Inc.
Thona Group *see* Hexagon AB
Thonet Industries Inc., *see* Shelby Williams Industries, Inc.
Thor Industries Inc., 39 391–94; 92 365–370 (upd.)
Thorn Apple Valley, Inc., 7 523–25; 22 508–11 (upd.)
Thorn EMI plc, I 531–32 *see also* EMI plc; Thorn plc.
Thorn plc, 24 484–87
Thornhill Inc, **64** 217
Thornton Baker *see* Grant Thornton International.
Thorntons plc, 46 424–26
Thorpe Park, **55** 378
Thorsen Realtors, **21** 96
Thos. & Wm. Molson & Company *see* The Molson Companies Ltd.
ThoughtWorks Inc., 90 413–16
Thousand Trails, Inc., 33 397–99
THQ, Inc., 39 395–97; 92 371–375 (upd.)
Threads for Life, **49** 244
Threadz, **25** 300
Three-Diamond Company *see* Mitsubishi Shokai.
The 3DO Company, 43 426–30
3 Guys, **V** 35
Three Ring Asia Pacific Beer Co., Ltd., **49** 418
Three Score, **23** 100
365 Media Group plc, 89 441–44
3 Suisses International, **12** 281
3Com Corporation, 11 518–21; 34 441–45 (upd.) *see also* Palm, Inc.
3D Planet SpA, **41** 409
3dfx Interactive Inc., **54** 269–71
3Dlabs, **57** 78, 80
3i Group PLC, 73 338–40
3M Company, 61 365–70 (upd.)
360 Youth Inc., **55** 15
360networks inc., **46** 268
Threshold Entertainment, **25** 270
Thrift Drug, **V** 92
Thrift Mart, **16** 65
Thriftimart Inc., **12** 153
Thriftway Food Drug, **21** 530
Thriftway Foods, **74** 365
Thrifty Corporation, **55** 58
Thrifty PayLess, Inc., 12 477–79 *see also* Rite Aid Corp.
Thrifty Rent-A-Car *see* Dollar Thrifty Automotive Group, Inc.
Thrustmaster S.A., **41** 190
Thummel Schutze & Partner, **28** 141
Thunder Bay Press, **34** 3–5
Thüringer Schokoladewerk GmbH, **53** 315
Thyssengas, **38** 406–07
ThyssenKrupp AG, IV 221–23; 28 452–60 (upd.); 87 425–438 (upd.)
TI *see* Texas Instruments.
TI Group plc, 17 480–83
TIAA-CREF *see* Teachers Insurance and Annuity Association-College Retirement Equities Fund.
Tianjin Automobile Industry Group, **21** 164
Tianjin Bohai Brewing Company, **21** 230; **50** 202
Tianjin Paper Net, **62** 350
Tibbett & Britten Group plc, 32 449–52
TIBCO Software Inc., 79 411–14
Tiber Construction Company, **16** 286
TIC Holdings Inc., 92 376–379
Tichenor Media System Inc., **35** 220
Ticketmaster, 13 508–10; 37 381–84 (upd.); 76 349–53 (upd.)
Ticketron, **37** 381–82
TicketsWest.com, **59** 410, 412
Ticor Title Insurance Co., *see* Alleghany Corp.
Tidewater Inc., 11 522–24; 37 385–88 (upd.)
Tidewater Utilities, Inc., **45** 275, 277
TIE *see* Transport International Express.
Tien Wah Press (Pte.) Ltd., **IV** 600
Tierco Group, Inc., *see* Premier Parks, Inc.
Tierney & Partners, **23** 480
Tiffany & Co., 14 500–03; 78 396–401 (upd.)
TIG Holdings, Inc., 26 486–88

Tiger Aspect Productions Ltd., **72** **348–50**
Tiger International, Inc., *see* FedEx Corp.
TigerDirect, Inc., **52** 342–44
Tigon Corporation, **41** 288
Tiki Corp., **69** 365
Tilcon Capaldi, Inc., **64** 98
Tilcon-Connecticut Inc., **80 373–76**
Tilia Inc., **62 363–65**
Tilley Endurables, Inc., **67 364–66**
Tillinghast, Nelson & Warren Inc., **32** 459
Tillotson Corp., **15 488–90**
TIM *see* Telecom Italia Mobile S.p.A.
Tim Horton's Restaurants *see* TDL Group Ltd.; Wendy's Inc.
Timber Lodge Steakhouse, Inc., **73** **341–43**
The Timberland Company, **13 511–14**; **54 375–79 (upd.)**
Timberline Software Corporation, **15** **491–93**
TIMCO *see* Triad International Maintenance Corp.
Time Industries, **26** 445
Time-Life Books, Inc. *see* AOL Time Warner Inc.
Time Life Music, **44** 242
Time Out Group Ltd., **68 371–73**
Time Saver Stores, Inc., *see* Dillon Companies Inc.
Time Warner Inc., **IV 673–76**; **7 526–30 (upd.)** *see also* AOL Time Warner Inc.
Timeplex, *see* Ascom AG.
Times Fiber Communications, Inc., **40** 35–36
The Times Mirror Company, **IV** **677–78**; **17 484–86 (upd.)** *see also* Tribune Co.
Times Publishing Group, **54** 116, 118
Timeshare Resale Brokers Inc. *see* ILX Resorts Inc.
TIMET *see* Titanium Metals Corp.
Timex Corporation, **7 531–33**; **25** **479–82 (upd.)**
The Timken Company, **8 529–31**; **42** **381–85 (upd.)**
Tioga Gas Plant Inc., **55** 20
Tioxide Group plc, **44** 117, 119
Tip Top Tailors, **29** 162
TIPC Network *see* Gateway 2000.
Tiphook PLC, **13** 530
Tiscali SpA, **48 396–99**
TISCO *see* Tata Iron & Steel Company Ltd.
Tishman Speyer Properties, L.P., **47** **403–06**
Tissue Technologies, Inc., *see* Palomar Medical Technologies, Inc.
Titan Acquisition Corporation, **51** 34, 36
Titan Cement Company S.A., **64** **379–81**
The Titan Corporation, **36 475–78**
Titan International, Inc., **89 445–49**
Titan Sports, Inc., **52** 192
Titanium Metals Corporation, **21** **489–92**
Titileist *see* Acushnet Co.
Title Insurance Company of America *see* LandAmerica Financial Group, Inc.
Titmuss Sainer Dechert *see* Dechert.
TiVo Inc., **75 373–75**
Tivoli Audio, **48** 85
Tivoli Systems, Inc., **14** 392
TJ International, Inc., **19 444–47**
The TJX Companies, Inc., **V 197–98**; **19 448–50 (upd.)**; **57 366–69 (upd.)**
TKR Cable Co., **15** 264
TKT *see* Transkaryotic Therapies Inc.
TL Enterprises, Inc., **56** 5
TLC Beatrice International Holdings, Inc., **22 512–15**
TLC Gift Company, **26** 375
TLO, **25** 82
TMNI International Inc., **70** 275
TMP Worldwide Inc., **30 458–60** *see also* Monster Worldwide Inc.
TMS, Inc., **7** 358
TMS Marketing, **26** 440
TMT *see* Trailer Marine Transport.
TMW Capital Inc., **48** 286
TN Technologies Inc., **23** 479
TNI Funding I Inc., **70** 275
TNT Crust, Inc., **23** 203
TNT Freightways Corporation, **14** **504–06**
TNT Grading Inc., **50** 348
TNT Limited, **V 523–25**
TNT Post Group N.V., **27 471–76 (upd.)**; **30 461–63 (upd.)** *see also* TPG N.V.
Toa Tanker Co. Ltd., **IV** 555
Tobacco Group PLC, **30** 231
Tobias, **16** 239
Tobu Railway Co Ltd, **6 430–32**
Today's Man, Inc., **20 484–87**
Todays Computers Business Centers *see* Intelligent Electronics, Inc.
The Todd-AO Corporation, **33 400–04** *see also* Liberty Livewire Corp.
Todd Shipyards Corporation, **14** **507–09**
TODCO, **87 439–442**
Toden Real Estate Company Inc., **74** 348
Todhunter International, Inc., **27** **477–79**
Todito.com, S.A. de C.V., **39** 194, 196
Toei Co. Ltd., **9** 29–30; **28** 462
Tofaş, *see* Koç Holding A.S.
Tofte Industrier, **63** 315
Toftejorg Group, **64** 18
Tofutti Brands, Inc., **64 382–84**
Togo's Eatery, **29** 19
Tohan Corporation, **84 402–405**
Toho Co., Ltd., **28 461–63**
Tohoku Alps, *see* Alps Electric Co., Ltd.
Tohoku Anritsu Co., Ltd. *see* Anritsu Corp.
Tohuku Electric Power Company, Inc., **V 726–28**
Tokai Aircraft Co., Ltd. *see* Aisin Seiki Co., Ltd.
The Tokai Bank, Limited, **II 373–74**; **15** **494–96 (upd.)**
Tokai Kogyo Co. Ltd., **I** 615; **48** 42
Tokheim Corporation, **21 493–95**
Tokio Marine and Fire Insurance Co., Ltd., **III 383–86** *see also* Millea Holdings Inc.
Tokiwa shokai Ltd., **64** 261
Tokos Medical Corporation, *see* Matria Healthcare, Inc.
Tokushima Automobile Service Company Inc., **60** 272
Tokyo City Finance, **36** 419–20
Tokyo Disneyland, **6** 176
Tokyo Electric Power Company, **V** **729–33**; **74 343–48 (upd.)**
Tokyo Gas Co., Ltd., **V 734–36**; **55** **372–75 (upd.)**
Tokyo Maritime Agency Ltd., **56** 181
Tokyo Motors *see* Isuzu Motors, Ltd.
Tokyo Stock Exchange, **34** 254
Tokyo Telecommunications Engineering Corp *see* Tokyo Tsushin Kogyo K.K.
TOKYOPOP Inc., **79 415–18**
Tokyu Corporation, **V 526–28**; **47** **407–10 (upd.)**
Tokyu Department Store Co., Ltd., **V** **199–202**; **32 453–57 (upd.)**
Tokyu Land Corporation, **IV 728–29**
Toledo Edison Company *see* Centerior Energy Corp.
Toledo Milk Processing, Inc., **15** 449
Toledo Scale Corp., **30** 327
Toll Brothers Inc., **15 497–99**; **70** **323–26 (upd.)**
Tollgrade Communications, Inc., **44** **424–27**
Tom Brown, Inc., **37 389–91**
Tom Doherty Associates Inc., **25** **483–86**
Tom Snyder Productions, **29** 470, 472
Tom Thumb, **40** 365–66
Tom's Foods Inc., **66 325–27**
Tom's of Maine, Inc., **45 414–16**
Toman Corporation, **19** 390
The Tomatin Distillery Co., Ltd., **62** 347
Tombstone Pizza Corporation, **13** **515–17** *see also* Kraft Foods Inc.
Tomcan Investments Inc., **53** 333
Tomen Corporation, **IV 224–25**; **24** **488–91 (upd.)**
Tomkins plc, **11 525–27**; **44 428–31 (upd.)**
Tommy Armour Golf Co., **32** 446–47
Tommy Bahama *see* Viewpoint International, Inc.
Tommy Hilfiger Corporation, **20** **488–90**; **53 330–33 (upd.)**
TomTom N.V., **81 388–91**
Tomy Company Ltd., **65 341–44**
Tone Brothers, Inc., **21 496–98**; **74** **349–52 (upd.)**
Tone Coca-Cola Bottling Company, Ltd., *see* Kikkoman Corp.
Tonen Corporation, **IV 554–56**; **16** **489–92 (upd.)**
TonenGeneral Sekiyu K.K., **54 380–86 (upd.)**
Tong Yang Cement Corporation, **62** **366–68**
Tonka Corporation, **25 487–89**
Tonkin, Inc., **19** 114

Tony Lama Company Inc., **19** 233
Tony Roma's, A Place for Ribs Inc. *see* Romacorp, Inc.
Tony Stone Images, **31** 216–17
Too, Inc., 61 371–73
Toolex International N.V., 26 489–91
Tootsie Roll Industries, Inc., 12 480–82; 82 392–96 (upd.)
Top End Wheelchair Sports, **11** 202
Top Glory International Group Company, **76** 89–90
Top Tool Company, Inc., **25** 75
Topack Verpackungstechnik, **60** 193
The Topaz Group, Inc., 62 369–71
Topco Associates LLC, 60 302–04
Topcon Corporation, 84 406–409
Topkapi, *see* Claire's Stores, Inc.
Toppan Printing Co., Ltd., IV 679–81; 58 340–44 (upd.)
The Topps Company, Inc., 13 518–20; 34 446–49 (upd.); 83 400-406 (upd.)
Topps Markets, **16** 314
Tops Appliance City, Inc., 17 487–89
Tops Markets LLC, 60 305–07
TopTip, **48** 116
Tor Books *see* Tom Doherty Associates Inc.
Toray Industries, Inc., V 383–86; 51 375–79 (upd.)
Torchmark Corporation, 9 506–08; 33 405–08 (upd.)
Toresco Enterprises, Inc., 84 410–413
Torfeaco Industries Limited, *see* Pillowtex Corp.
The Toro Company, 7 534–36; 26 492–95 (upd.); 77 440–45 (upd.)
Toromont Industries, Ltd., 21 499–501
The Toronto-Dominion Bank, II 375–77; 49 395–99 (upd.)
Toronto Maple Leafs *see* Maple Leaf Sports & Entertainment Ltd.
Toronto Raptors *see* Maple Leaf Sports & Entertainment Ltd.
Toronto Sun Publishing Company *see* Sun Media.
Torrent Systems, Inc., **59** 56
The Torrington Company, 13 521–24 *see also* Timken Co.
Torstar Corporation, 29 470–73 *see also* Harlequin Enterprises Ltd.
Tosco Corporation, 7 537–39 *see also* ConocoPhillips.
Toshiba Corporation, I 533–35; 12 483–86 (upd.); 40 435–40 (upd.)
Toshin Building Co. Ltd., **74** 348
Toshin Kaihatsu Ltd. *see* Takashimaya Co., Ltd.
Tosoh Corporation, 70 327–30
Tostem *see* Toyo Sash Co., Ltd.
Total Beverage Corporation, *see* Dart Group PLC.
Total Compagnie Française des Pétroles S.A., IV 557–61 *see also* Total Fina Elf S.A.
Total Entertainment Restaurant Corporation, 46 427–29
Total Filtration Services, Inc., **61** 66
Total Fina Elf S.A., 50 478–86 (upd.)
Total Global Sourcing, Inc., *see* Staples, Inc.
Total Home Entertainment (THE), **39** 240, 242
Total Petroleum Corporation, **21** 500
TOTAL S.A., 24 492–97 (upd.)
Total System Services, Inc., 18 516–18
Totem Resources Corporation, 9 509–11
Totino's Finer Foods, **26** 436
TOTO LTD., III 755–56; 28 464–66 (upd.)
Tottenham Hotspur PLC, 81 392–95
Touch America Inc., **37** 127; **44** 288
Touch-It Corp., **22** 413
Touche Remnant Holdings Ltd., **II** 356
Touche Ross *see* Deloitte Touche Tohmatsu International.
Touchstone Films *see* The Walt Disney Co.
Toupargel-Agrigel S.A., 76 354–56
Le Touquet's, SA, **48** 197
Touristik Union International GmbH. and Company K.G., II 163–65 *see also* Preussag AG.
Tourtime America, **56** 223
TOUSA *see* Technical Olympic USA, Inc.
Touton S.A., 92 380–383
Toval Japon, **IV** 680
Towa Optical Manufacturing Company, **41** 261–63
Tower Air, Inc., 28 467–69
Tower Automotive, Inc., 24 498–500
Tower Records *see* MTS Inc.
Towers Department Stores, *see* Oshawa Group Ltd.
Towers Perrin, 32 458–60
Towle Manufacturing Co., *see* Syratech Corp.
Town & Country Corporation, 19 451–53
Town Sports International, Inc., 46 430–33
Towngas *see* Hong Kong and China Gas Company Ltd.
Townsend Hook, **IV** 650, 652
Townsends, Inc., 64 385–87
Toxicol Laboratories, Ltd., **21** 424
The Toxicology Group, LLC *see* NOF Corp.
Toy Biz, Inc., 18 519–21 *see also* Marvel Entertainment, Inc.
Toy Liquidators, **50** 99
Toymax International, Inc., 29 474–76
Toyo Ink Manufacturing, **26** 213
Toyo Microsystems Corporation, **11** 464
Toyo Rayon *see* Toray Industries, Inc.
Toyo Sash Co., Ltd., III 757–58
Toyo Seikan Kaisha Ltd., I 615–16
Toyo Soda Manufacturing Co *see* Tosoh Corp.
Toyo Tire & Rubber Co., **V** 255–56
Toyo Toki Co., Ltd. *see* Toto.
Toyoda Automatic Loom Works, Ltd., III 636–39
Toyota Industrial Equipment, *see* Manitou BF S.A.
Toyota Motor Corporation, I 203–05; 11 528–31 (upd.); 38 458–62 (upd.)
Toys 'R Us, Inc., V 203–06; 18 522–25 (upd.); 57 370–75 (upd.)
TP Transportation, **39** 377
TPA *see* Aloha Airlines Inc.
TPCR Corporation *see* The Price Co.
TPG N.V., 64 388–91 (upd.)
TPS SNC, **76** 274
Trac Inc., **44** 355
Trace International Holdings, Inc., **17** 182–83; **26** 502
Tracinda Corporation, **25** 329–30
Tracker Marine *see* Bass Pro Shops, Inc.
Tracor Inc., 17 490–92
Tractebel S.A., 20 491–93 *see also* Suez Lyonnaise des Eaux.
Tractor Supply Company, 57 376–78
Trade Secret Development Corp. *see* Regis Corp.
Trade Source International, **44** 132
Trade-Winds Environmental Restoration, Inc., **62** 389
Trademark Metals Recycling LLC, **76** 130
Trader Classified Media N.V., 57 379–82
Trader Joe's Company, 13 525–27; 50 487–90 (upd.)
Trader Media Group, **53** 152
Trader Publications, Inc., **IV** 597
TradeStation Group, Inc., 83 407-410
Trading Cove Associates *see* Kerzner International Ltd.
Trading Post Group Pty Ltd., **57** 381
Tradition Financial Services *see* Viel & Cie.
Trafalgar House Investments Ltd., **IV** 711; **20** 313; **23** 161; **36** 322
Trafalgar House PLC, **47** 178
TrafficLeader *see* Marchex, Inc.
Traffix, Inc., 61 374–76
Trafford Park Printers, **53** 152
Trafiroad NV, **39** 239
Trailer Bridge, Inc., 41 397–99
Trak Auto Corporation, *see* Dart Group PLC.
TRAK Communications Inc., **44** 420
TRAK Microwave Corporation, *see* Tech-Sym Corp
Trammell Crow Company, 8 532–34; 57 383–87 (upd.)
Trane, 78 402–05
Trans-Canada Air Lines *see* Air Canada.
Trans-Continental Leaf Tobacco Company, (TCLTC), *see* Standard Commercial Corp.
Trans Continental Records, **52** 430
Trans International Airlines, **41** 402
Trans Louisiana Gas Company, **43** 56–57
Trans-Lux Corporation, 51 380–83
Trans-Mex, Inc. S.A. de C.V., **42** 365
Trans-Natal Coal Corp., **IV** 93
Trans-Pacific Airlines *see* Aloha Airlines Inc.
Trans Tech Electric Inc. *see* Quanta Services, Inc.
Trans Thai-Malaysia, **56** 290

Trans Union Corp., *see* Marmon Group, Inc.
Trans World Airlines, Inc., I 125–27; 12 487–90 (upd.); 35 424–29 (upd.)
Trans-World Corp., **19** 456; **47** 231
Trans World Entertainment Corporation, 24 501–03; 68 374–77 (upd.)
Trans World International, *see* International Management Group.
Trans World Life Insurance Company, **27** 46–47
Transaction Systems Architects, Inc., 29 477–79; 82 397–402 (upd.)
TransAlta Utilities Corporation, 6 585–87
Transamerica—An AEGON Company, I 536–38; 13 528–30 (upd.); 41 400–03 (upd.)
Transamerica Pawn Holdings *see* EZCORP Inc.
Transamerica Retirement Services, **63** 176
TransAmerican Waste Industries Inc., **41** 414
Transat *see* Compagnie Générale Transatlantique (Transat).
Transatlantic Holdings, Inc., 11 532–33
Transatlantische Gruppe, *see* Winterthur Group.
Transax, **63** 102
TransBrasil S/A Linhas Aéreas, 31 443–45
TransCanada Corporation, V 737–38; 93 438–45 (upd.)
Transco Energy Company, V 739–40 *see also* The Williams Companies.
Transcontinental Air Transport, *see* Trans World Airlines, Inc.
Transcontinental Gas Pipe Line Corporation *see* Transco Energy Co.
TransCor America, Inc., **23** 154
Transfer Drivers, Inc., **46** 301
Transfracht, **6** 426
Transiciel SA, 48 400–02
Transit Homes of America, Inc., **46** 301
Transitions Optical, Inc., 83 411-415
Transkaryotic Therapies Inc., **54** 111
Transking Inc. *see* King Kullen Grocery Co., Inc.
Transkrit Corp., **IV** 640; **26** 273
Translittoral, **67** 353
Transmanche-Link, *see* Eurotunnel PLC.
CJSC Transmash Holding, 93 446–49
Transmedia Network Inc., 20 494–97 *see also* Rewards Network Inc.
Transmedica International, Inc., **41** 225
Transmisiones y Equipos Mecanicos, S.A. de C.V., **23** 171
TransMontaigne Inc., 28 470–72
Transmontane Rod and Gun Club, **43** 435–36
Transnation Title Insurance Company *see* LandAmerica Financial Group, Inc.
Oil Transporting Joint Stock Company Transneft, 92450–54
Transnet Ltd., 6 433–35
Transocean Sedco Forex Inc., 45 417–19
Transport Corporation of America, Inc., 49 400–03
Transport International Pool, **58** 239
TransPoint L.L.C. *see* CheckFree Corporation
Transportacion Ferroviaria Mexicana, **50** 209
Transportacion Maritima Mexicana S.A. de C.V., **12** 279; **26** 236; **47** 162; **50** 208
Transportation Technologies Industries Inc., **51** 155
Transportation.com, **45** 451
Transportes Aéreas Centro-Americanos *see* Grupo TACA.
Transportes Aereos Portugueses, S.A., 6 125–27 *see also* TAP—Air Portugal Transportes Aéreos Portugueses S.A.
Transportes Aeromar, **39** 188
TransPro, Inc., 71 356–59
Transrack S.A., **26** 363
TransWestern Holdings L.P. *see* Yell Group PLC
Transworld Communications, **35** 165
Transworld Drilling Company Limited *see* Kerr-McGee Corp.
The Tranzonic Companies, 15 500–02; 37 392–95 (upd.)
Trasgo, S.A. de C.V., **14** 516; **50** 493
Travel Inc., **26** 309
Travel Ports of America, Inc., 17 493–95
Travelers/Aetna Property Casualty Corp., **63** 14
Travelers Book Club, *see* Book-of-the-Month Club.
Travelers Corporation, III 387–90 *see also* Citigroup Inc.
Travelers Property Casualty Corp. *see* The St. Paul Travelers Companies, Inc.
Travelocity.com, Inc., 46 434–37
Travelzoo Inc., 79 419–22
Travers Morgan Ltd., **42** 183
Travis Boats & Motors, Inc., 37 396–98
Travis Perkins plc, 34 450–52
TRC *see* Tennessee Restaurant Co.
TRC Companies, Inc., 32 461–64
TRE Corp., **23** 225
Treadco, Inc., 19 454–56
Treasure Chest Advertising Company, Inc., 32 465–67
Treatment Centers of America, **11** 379
Tredegar Corporation, 52 349–51
Tree of Life, Inc., 29 480–82
Tree Sweet Products Corp., **26** 325
Tree Top, Inc., 76 357–59
TreeHouse Foods, Inc., 79 423–26
Trego Systems Inc., **64** 190
Trek Bicycle Corporation, 16 493–95; 78 406–10 (upd.)
Trelleborg AB, 93 455–64
Tremec *see* Transmisiones y Equipos Mecanicos, S.A. de C.V.
Tremont Corporation, **21** 490
Trenchwood Plc, **45** 443
Trend-Lines, Inc., 22 516–18
Trends Magazine NV, **48** 347
Trendwest Resorts, Inc., 33 409–11 *see also* Jeld-Wen, Inc.
TrentonWorks Limited *see* The Greenbrier Companies.
Trevor Sorbie of America, Inc., **60** 287
Trex Company, Inc., 71 360–62
Tri-City Utilities Company, **6** 514
Tri-Miller Packing Company, *see* Thorn Apple Valley, Inc.
Tri-State Baking, **53** 21
Tri-State Improvement Company *see* Cincinnati Gal & Electric Co.
Tri-State Publishing & Communications, Inc., **22** 442
Tri-State Recycling Corporation, **15** 117
Tri-Union Seafoods LLC, *see* Chicken of the Sea International.
Tri Valley Growers, 32 468–71
Tri-Village Developments BV, **58** 359
Triad Artists Inc., **23** 514
Triad Systems Corp., **38** 96
The Triangle Group, *see* The Marmon Group, Inc.
Triangle Pharmaceuticals, Inc., **54** 131
Triangle Sheet Metal Works, Inc., **45** 327
Triarc Companies, Inc., 8 535–37; 34 453–57 (upd.)
Triax Midwest Associates L.P. *see* Mediacom Communications Corp.
Tribe Computer Works *see* Zoom Technologies, Inc.
Tribeca Grill *see* Myriad Restaurant Group, Inc.
Tribune Company, IV 682–84; 22 519–23 (upd.); 63 389–95 (upd.)
Tricap Restructuring Fund, **59** 162
Trick & Murray, **22** 153
Trico Marine Services, Inc., 89 450–53
Trico Products Corporation, 15 503–05
Tricon Global Restaurants, Inc. *see* Yum! Brands Inc.
Tricor Direct Inc. *see* Brady Corporation
Tridel Enterprises Inc., 9 512–13
Trident Data Systems, **54** 396
Trident II, Inc., **64** 253
Trident NGL Holdings Inc., *see* Dynegy Inc.
Trident Seafoods Corporation, 56 359–61
Tridon Ltd., **69** 206
Trigen Energy Corporation, 42 386–89
Trigon Industries, *see* Dynatech Corp.
Trilan Developments Ltd., *see* Tridel Enterprises Inc.
Trilogy Fabrics, Inc., **16** 125
Trilogy Retail Enterprises L.P., **58** 186
Trilon Financial Corporation, II 456–57
TriMas Corp., 11 534–36
Trimble Navigation Limited, 40 441–43
Trimel Corp., **47** 54
Trinc Company, **59** 320
Třinecké Železárny A.S., 92 384–87
TriNet Corporate Realty Trust, Inc., **65** 146
Trinity Beverage Corporation, **11** 451
Trinity Broadcasting, *see* International Family Entertainment Inc.
Trinity Distributors, **15** 139

Trinity Industries, Incorporated, 7 540–41
Trinity Mirror plc, 49 404–10 (upd.)
TRINOVA Corporation, III 640–42
TriPath Imaging, Inc., 77 446–49
Triple Five Group Ltd., 49 411–15
Triple P N.V., 26 496–99
TriQuest-Nypro Plastics, **60** 264
TriQuint Semiconductor, Inc., 63 396–99
Trisko Jewelry Sculptures, Ltd., 57 388–90
TriStar Pictures, **23** 275; **28** 462 *see also* Columbia TriStar Motion Pictures Companies.
Triton Cellular Partners, L.P., **43** 341
Triton Energy Corporation, 11 537–39
Triton Systems Corp., **22** 186
Triumph-Adler *see* TA Triumph-Adler AG.
Triumph American, Inc., **12** 199
Triumph, Finlay, and Philips Petroleum, **11** 28
Triumph Group, Inc., 31 446–48
Triumph LOR, Inc., **63** 305–06
Triumph Motorcycles Ltd., 53 334–37
Trivest, Inc., **21** 531–32; **74** 54–55
Trix Modelleisenbahn GmbH & Co. KG, **70** 166
Trizec Corporation Ltd., 10 529–32
TrizecHahn, **37** 311; **63** 341
The TriZetto Group, Inc., 83 416-419
TRM Copy Centers Corporation, 18 526–28
Trolley Barn Brewery Inc., **25** 401
Tropical Marine Centre, **40** 128–29
Tropical Shipping, Inc., **6** 529, 531
Tropical Sportswear Int'l Corporation, **42** 120
Tropicana Products, Inc., 28 473–77; 73 344–49 (upd.)
Trotter, Inc., **49** 108
Trottner-McJunkin SA de CV, **63** 287–88
Troutman Sanders L.L.P., 79 427–30
Trouw Nutrition USA, **56** 258
Troxel Cycling, **16** 53
Troy & Nichols, Inc., **13** 147
Troy Design Group, **55** 32
Troy Metal Products *see* KitchenAid.
TRT Communications, Inc., **6** 327; **11** 185
Tru-Stitch, *see* Wolverine World Wide, Inc.
Truck Components Inc., **23** 306
True Form Foundations Corporation, **59** 267
True North Communications Inc., 23 478–80 *see also* Foote, Cone & Belding Worldwide.
True Religion Apparel, Inc., 79 431–34
True Temper Hardware Co., **30** 241–42
True Value Company, 74 353–57 (upd.)
TruGreen, **23** 428, 430
Trump Organization, 23 481–84; 64 392–97 (upd.)
TRUMPF GmbH + Co. KG, 86 397–02
Trunkline LNG Co., **IV** 425
Trus Joist Corporation *see* TJ International, Inc.
TruServ Corporation, 24 504–07 *see* True Value Co.
Trussdeck Corporation *see* TJ International, Inc.
Trust Company of the West, *see* Spartech Corp.
Trustcorp, Inc., *see* Society Corp.
Trusted Information Systems, Inc., **25** 349
Trusthouse Forte PLC, III 104–06
TRW Automotive Holdings Corp., I 539–41; 11 540–42 (upd.); 14 510–13 (upd.); 75 376–82 (upd.)
TSA *see* Transaction Systems Architects, Inc.
Tsakos Energy Navigation Ltd., 91 483–86
TSB Group plc, 12 491–93
TSC *see* Tractor Supply Co.
TSI Inc., **38** 206
TSI Soccer Corporation, **29** 142–43
Tsingtao Brewery Group, 49 416–20
TSMC *see* Taiwan Semiconductor Manufacturing Company Ltd.
TSO *see* Teacher's Service Organization, Inc.
TSP *see* Tom Snyder Productions.
TSR Inc., **24** 538
TSYS *see* Total System Services, Inc.
TT Acquisitions, Inc., **56** 361
TTK *see* Tokyo Tsushin Kogyo K.K.
TTL *see* Taiwan Tobacco & Liquor Corp.
TTX Company, 6 436–37; 66 328–30 (upd.)
Tubby's, Inc., 53 338–40
Tube Fab Ltd., *see* HMI Industries, Inc.
Tube Forming, Inc., **23** 517
Tube Service Co., *see* Reliance Steel & Aluminum Co.
Tubed Chemicals Corporation, *see* McCormick & Company, Inc.
Tuborg, *see* Carlsberg A/S.
Tubos de Acero de Mexico, S.A. (TAMSA), 41 404–06
Tuboscope, **42** 420
Tucker, Lynch & Coldwell *see* CB Commercial Real Estate Services Group, Inc.
Tucker Rocky Distributing, **76** 235
TUCO, Inc., *see* Cabot Corp.
Tucows Inc., 78 411–14
Tucson Electric Power Company, 6 588–91
Tuesday Morning Corporation, 18 529–31; 70 331–33 (upd.)
TUF *see* Thai Union Frozen Products PCL.
Tuff Stuff Publications, **23** 101
TUI *see* Touristik Union International GmbH. and Company K.G.
TUI Group GmbH, 42 283; **44 432–35**
TUJA, *see* AHL Services, Inc.
Tulip Ltd., 89 454–57
Tullow Oil plc, 83 420-423
Tully's Coffee Corporation, 51 384–86
Tultex Corporation, 13 531–33
Tumaro's Gourmet Tortillas, 85 430–33
Tumbleweed, Inc., 33 412–14; 80 377–81 (upd.)
Tunisair *see* Société Tunisienne de l'Air-Tunisair.
Tupolev Aviation and Scientific Technical Complex, 24 58–60
Tupperware Brands Corporation, 28 478–81; 78 415–20 (upd.)
Turbine Engine Asset Management LLC, **28** 5
TurboChef Technologies, Inc., 83 424-427
TurboLinux Inc., **45** 363
Turk Telecom, **63** 378, 380
Turkish Airlines Inc. (Türk Hava Yollari A.O.), 72 351–53
Turkish Petroleum Co. *see* Türkiye Petrolleri Anonim Ortakliği.
Turkiye Is Bankasi A.S., 61 377–80
Türkiye Petrolleri Anonim Ortakliği, IV 562–64
Turner Broadcasting System, Inc., II 166–68; 6 171–73 (upd.); 66 331–34 (upd.)
Turner Construction Company, 66 335–38
The Turner Corporation, 8 538–40; 23 485–88 (upd.)
Turnstone Systems, **44** 426
TURPAS *see* Türkiye Petrolleri Anonim Ortakliği
Turtle Wax, Inc., 15 506–09; 93 465–70 (upd.)
Tuscarora Inc., 29 483–85
The Tussauds Group, 55 376–78
Tutogen Medical, Inc., 68 378–80
Tutor Time Learning Centers Inc., **76** 238, 241
Tutt Bryant Industries PLY Ltd., **26** 231
Tuttle, Oglebay and Company *see* Oglebay Norton Co.
Tuttle Publishing, 86 403–06
TV Azteca, S.A. de C.V., 39 398–401
TV Guide, Inc., 43 431–34 (upd.)
TVA *see* Tennessee Valley Authority.
TVE *see* Television Española, S.A.
TVH Acquisition Corp., *see* Home Insurance Co.
TVI, Inc., 15 510–12
TVN Entertainment Corporation, **32** 239
TVSN Ltd., **64** 185
TVT Records *see* Tee Vee Toons, Inc.
TW Services, Inc., II 679–80
TWA *see* Trans World Airlines; Transcontinental & Western Airways.
TWC *see* The Weather Channel, Inc.
Tweco Co., *see* Thermadyne Holding Corp.
Tweedy, Browne Company L.L.C. *see* Affiliated Managers Group, Inc.
Tweeter Home Entertainment Group, Inc., 30 464–66
Twentieth Century Fox Film Corporation, II 169–71; 25 490–94 (upd.)
"21" International Holdings, **17** 182
21 Invest International Holdings Ltd., **14** 322

21st Century Food Products *see* Hain Food Group, Inc.
21st Century Mortgage, *see* American Homestar Corp.
21st Century Oncology *see* Radiation Therapy Services, Inc.
21st Century Telecom Services, Inc. *see* RCN Corp.
Twenty-third Publications, **49** 48
24 Hour Fitness Worldwide, Inc., 71 363–65
24/7 Real Media, Inc., 49 421–24
TWI *see* Trans World International.
Twin City Wholesale Drug Company, **14** 147
Twin Disc, Inc., 21 502–04
Twin Hill Acquisition Company, Inc., **48** 286
Twinings Tea, **41** 31
Twinlab Corporation, 34 458–61
II-VI Incorporated, 69 353–55
2ndhead Oy, **51** 328
21st Century Mortgage, **41** 18, 20
TWW Plc, **26** 62
TXEN, Inc., *see* Nichols Research Corp.
TxPort Inc., *see* Acme-Cleveland Corp.
Ty Inc., 33 415–17; 86 407–11 (upd.)
Tyco International Ltd., III 643–46; 28 482–87 (upd.); 63 400–06 (upd.)
Tyco Submarine Systems Ltd., **32** 217
Tyco Toys, Inc., 12 494–97 *see also* Mattel, Inc.
Tyler Corporation, 23 489–91
Tyndale House Publishers, Inc., 57 391–94
Tyndall's Formal Wear, **60** 5
Tyrolean Airways, **33** 50
Tyskie Brewery, **24** 450
Tyson Foods, Inc., II 584–85; 14 514–16 (upd.); 50 491–95 (upd.)

U

U.B. TUFF., **67** 339
U.C.L.A.F *see* Roussel-Uclaf.
U-Haul International Inc. *see* Amerco.
U.S. *see also* US.
U.S. Aggregates, Inc., 42 390–92
U.S. Appliances, **26** 336
U.S. Army Corps of Engineers, 91 491–95
U.S. Bancorp, 14 527–29; 36 489–95 (upd.)
U.S. Bank of Washington, *see* U.S. Bancorp.
U.S. Banknote Company, **30** 43
U.S. Bearings Company *see* Federal-Mogul Corp.
U.S. Billing, Inc. *see* Billing Concepts Corp.
U.S. Bioscience, Inc., **35** 286, 288
U.S. Borax, Inc., 42 393–96
U.S. Brass., *see* Eljer Industries, Inc.
U.S. Can Corporation, 30 474–76
U.S. Cellular Corporation, 31 449–52 (upd.); 88 408–13 (upd.)
U.S. Computer of North America Inc., **43** 368
U.S. Delivery Systems, Inc., 22 531–33 *see also* Velocity Express Corp.
U.S. Foodservice, 26 503–06
U.S. Generating Company, **26** 373
U.S. Graphite *see* Wickes Inc.
U.S. Healthcare, Inc., 6 194–96
U.S. Home Corporation, 8 541–43; 78 421–26 (upd.)
U.S. Industries, Inc., **23** 296; **76** 185, 204, 206
U.S. Intec, **22** 229
U.S. International Reinsurance, *see* Home Insurance Co.
U.S. Investigations Services Inc., **35** 44
U.S. Journal Training, Inc., **72** 172
U.S. Lawns, **31** 182, 184
U.S. Lock Corporation, **28** 50–52
U.S. Long Distance Corp. *see* Billing Concepts Corp.
U.S. News & World Report Inc., 30 477–80; 89 458–63 (upd.)
U.S. Office Products Company, 25 500–02
U.S. Physical Therapy, Inc., 65 345–48
U.S. Plywood Corp *see* United States Plywood Corp.
U.S. Premium Beef LLC, 91 487–90
U.S. RingBinder Corp., *see* General Binding Corp.
U.S. Robotics Corporation, 9 514–15; 66 339–41 (upd.)
U.S. Satellite Broadcasting Company, Inc., 20 505–07 *see also* DIRECTV, Inc.
U.S. Shoe Corporation, **43** 98; **44** 365
U.S. Software Inc., **29** 479
U.S. Steel Corp *see* United States Steel Corp.
U.S. Timberlands Company, L.P., 42 397–400
U.S. Trust Corp., 17 496–98
U.S. Venture Partners, **15** 204–05
U.S. Vision, Inc., 66 342–45
U S West, Inc., V 341–43; 25 495–99 (upd.)
U.S. Windpower, *see* Kenetech Corp.
U.S. Xpress Enterprises, Inc., **75** 148
UA *see* Metro- Goldwyn-Mayer Inc., MGM/UA Communications Company; United Artists Corp.
UAA *see* EgyptAir.
UAL Corporation, 34 462–65 (upd.)
UAP *see* Union des Assurances de Paris.
UAP Inc., **45** 179
UARCO Inc., **15** 473–74
UAT *see* UTA.
UAW (International Union, United Automobile, Aerospace and Agricultural Implement Workers of America), 72 354–57
Ube Industries, Ltd., III 759–61; 38 463–67 (upd.)
Ubi Soft Entertainment S.A., 41 407–09
Ubique Ltd, **25** 301
UBL Educational Loan Center, **42** 211
UBS AG, 52 352–59 (upd.)
UCAR International, Inc., **40** 83
UDRT *see* United Dominion Realty Trust, Inc.
UDV *see* United Distillers and Vintners.
Ueda Kotsu Company, **47** 408
UETA Inc., **29** 510–11
Ufa Sports, **44** 190
UFA TV & Film Produktion GmbH, 80 382–87
UFJ Bank, **61** 250
Ugg Holdings, Inc., *see* Deckers Outdoor Corp.
UGI *see* United Gas Improvement.
UGI Corporation, 12 498–500
Ugine S.A., 20 498–500
Ugly Duckling Corporation, 22 524–27 *see also* DriveTime Automotive Group Inc.
UHU GmbH *see* Bolton Group B.V.
UI International, **6** 444
UIB *see* United Independent Broadcasters, Inc.
UICI, 33 418–21 *see also* HealthMarkets, Inc.
Uinta Co., **6** 568
UIS Co., **15** 324
Uitgeversmaatschappij Elsevier *see* Reed Elsevier plc.
Uitzendbureau Amstelveen *see* Randstad Holding n.v.
Ukbetting Plc *see* 365 Media Group plc.
UKF *see* Unie van Kunstmestfabrieken.
Ukrop's Super Market's, Inc., 39 402–04
UL *see* Underwriters Laboratories, Inc.
Ullrich Copper, Inc. *see* Foster Wheeler Corp.
Ullstein Langen Müller, **IV** 591
ULN *see* Union Laitière Normande.
Ulstein Holding ASA, *see* Vickers plc.
Ulster Television PLC, 71 366–68
Ulta Salon, Cosmetics & Fragrance, Inc., 92471–73
Ultimate Electronics, Inc., 18 532–34; 69 356–59 (upd.)
Ultimate Leisure Group PLC, 75 383–85
Ultra Mart, **16** 250
Ultra Pac, Inc., 24 512–14
Ultra Petroleum Corporation, 71 369–71
UltraCam *see* Ultrak Inc.
UltraCare Products, *see* Drypers Corp.
Ultrak Inc., 24 508–11
Ultralife Batteries, Inc., 58 345–48
Ultramar Diamond Shamrock Corporation, IV 565–68; 31 453–57 (upd.)
ULVAC, Inc., 80 388–91
Umberto's of New Hyde Park Pizzeria, **16** 447
Umbro plc, 88 414–17
UMC *see* United Microelectronics Corp.
UMG *see* Universal Music Group.
UMI Company, **29** 58
NV Umicore SA, 47 411–13
Umpqua Holdings Corporation, 87 443–446

Unadulterated Food Products, Inc., *see* Snapple Beverage Corp.
Unbrako Socket Screw Company Ltd., **30** 429
UNCF *see* United Negro College Fund, Inc.
Uncle Ben's Inc., 22 528–30
Uncle Ray's LLC, 90 417–19
Under Armour Performance Apparel, 61 381–83
Underberg AG, 92 388–393
Underwriter for the Professions Insurance Company, **55** 128
Underwriters Laboratories, Inc., 30 467–70
Underwriters Reinsurance Co., *see* Alleghany Corp.
Unefon, S.A., **39** 194, 196
UNELCO *see* Union Electrica de Canarias S.A.
UNG *see* United National Group, Ltd.
Ungaro SA, **62** 313
Uni-Cast *see* Sturm, Ruger & Company, Inc.
Uni-Marts, Inc., 17 499–502
Uni-President Group, **49** 460
Unibail SA, 40 444–46
Unibanco Holdings S.A., 73 350–53
Unibank, **40** 336; **50** 149–50
Unic *see* GIB Group.
Unica Corporation, 77 450–54
Unicapital, Inc., **15** 281
UNICARE, *see* WellPoint Health Networks Inc.
Unicco Security Services, **27** 22
Unice, **56** 335
UNICEF *see* United Nations International Children's Emergency Fund (UNICEF).
Unicel *see* Rural Cellular Corp.
Unicer, *see* Carlsberg A/S.
Unicharm Corporation, 84 414–417
Unicom Corporation, 29 486–90 (upd.) *see also* Exelon Corp.
Unicoolait, **19** 51
UNICOR *see* Federal Prison Industries, Inc.
Unicord Company, **64** 60
UniCredito Italiano, **50** 410
Unidrive, **47** 280
Uniface Holding B.V., *see* Compuware Corp.
Unifi, Inc., 12 501–03; 62 372–76 (upd.)
Unified Energy System of Russia *see* RAO Unified Energy System of Russia.
Unified Grocers, Inc., 93 474–77
Unified Western Grocers, **31** 25
UniFirst Corporation, 21 505–07
Uniflex Corporation, **53** 236
Uniforce Services Inc., **40** 119
Unigate PLC, II 586–87; 28 488–91 (upd.) *see also* Uniq Plc.
Uniglory, **13** 211
Unigro *see* Laurus N.V.
Unigroup, **15** 50
UniHealth America, **11** 378–79
Unijoh Sdn, Bhd, **47** 255
Unik S.A., **23** 170–171
Unilab Corp., **26** 391
Unilever, II 588–91; 7 542–45 (upd.); 32 472–78 (upd.); 89 464–74 (upd.)
UniLife Insurance Co., *see* CompDent Corp.
Unilog SA, 42 401–03
Uniloy Milacron Inc., **53** 230
UniMac Companies, **11** 413
Unimetal, **30** 252
Union Aéromaritime de Transport *see* UTA.
Union Bag–Camp Paper Corp. *see* Union Camp Corp.
Union Bank *see* State Street Boston Corp.
Union Bank of California, 16 496–98 *see also* UnionBanCal Corp.
Union Bank of Switzerland, II 378–79 *see also* UBS AG.
Union Biscuits *see* Leroux S.A.S.
Union Camp Corporation, IV 344–46
Union Carbide Corporation, I 399–401; 9 516–20 (upd.); 74 358–63 (upd.)
Union Colliery Company *see* Union Electric Co.
Union Commerciale, **19** 98
Union Corporation *see* Gencor Ltd.
Unión de Cervecerias Peruanas Backus y Johnston S.A.A.,92 394–397
Union des Assurances de Paris, III 391–94
Union des Coopératives Bressor, **25** 85
Union des Cooperatives Laitières *see* Unicoolait.
Union des Mines, **52** 362
Union des Transports Aériens *see* UTA.
Union Electric Company, V 741–43 *see also* Ameren Corp.
Unión Electrica Fenosa *see* Unión Fenosa S.A.
Unión Fenosa, S.A., 51 387–90
Union Financière de France Banque SA, 52 360–62
Union Fork & Hoe Company *see* Acorn Products, Inc.
Union Gas & Electric Co., **6** 529
l'Union Générale des Pétroles, **IV** 560
Union Laitière Normande *see* Compagnie Laitière Européenne.
Union Light, Heat & Power Company *see* Cincinnati Gas & Electric Co.
Union Minière *see* NV Umicore SA.
Union Mutual Life Insurance Company *see* UNUM Corp.
Union Oil Co. of California *see* Unocal Corp.
Union Pacific Corporation, V 529–32; 28 492–500 (upd.); 79 435–46 (upd.)
Union Pacific Resources Group, **52** 30
Union Paper & Co. AS, **63** 315
Union Planters Corporation, 54 387–90
Union Power Construction Co. *see* Quanta Services, Inc.
Union Pub Company, **57** 411, 413
Union Savings and Loan Association of Phoenix, **19** 412
Union Suisse des Coopératives de Consommation *see* Coop Schweiz.
Union Tank Car Co., *see* Marmon Group, Inc.
Union Telecard Alliance, LLC, **34** 223
Union Texas Petroleum Holdings, Inc., 9 521–23
The Union Underwear Company, *see* Fruit of the Loom, Inc.
Union Verwaltungsgesellschaft mbH, **66** 123
UnionBanCal Corporation, 50 496–99 (upd.)
Unione Manifatture, S.p.A., **19** 338
Uniphase Corporation *see* JDS Uniphase Corp.
Uniplex Business Software, **41** 281
Uniq plc, 83 428-433 (upd.)
Unique Casual Restaurants, Inc., 27 480–82
Unique Pub Company, **59** 182
Uniroy of Hempstead, Inc. *see* Aris Industries, Inc.
Uniroyal Chemical Corporation, **36** 145
Uniroyal Corp., **20** 262
Uniroyal Goodrich, **42** 88
Uniroyal Holdings Ltd., **21** 73
Unishops, Inc. *see* Aris Industries, Inc.
Unison HealthCare Corporation, 25 503–05
Unisource Worldwide, Inc., **47** 149
Unistar Radio Networks, **23** 510
Unisys Corporation, III 165–67; 6 281–83 (upd.); 36 479–84 (upd.)
Unit Corporation, 63 407–09
Unitech plc, *see* Invensys PLC.
United AgriSeeds, Inc., **21** 387
United Air Express *see* United Parcel Service of America Inc.
United Air Fleet, **23** 408
United Aircraft and Transportation Co., **21** 140
United Airlines, I 128–30; 6 128–30 (upd.) *see also* UAL Corp.
United Alloy Steel Company, **26** 405
United American Insurance Company, *see* Torchmark Corp.
United Arab Airlines *see* EgyptAir.
United Artists Corp., **IV** 676; **12** 13; **21** 362; **23** 389; **26** 487; **36** 47; **41** 402 *see also* MGM/UA Communications Company; Metro-Goldwyn-Mayer Inc.
United Artists Theatre Circuit, Inc., **37** 63–64; **59** 341
United Australian Automobile Industries, **62** 182
United Auto Group, Inc., 26 500–02; 68 381–84 (upd.)
United Biscuits (Holdings) plc, II 592–94; 42 404–09 (upd.)
United Brands Company, II 595–97
United Breweries International, Ltd., **60** 207
United Breweries Ltd. *see* Carlsberg A/S.
United Broadcasting Corporation Public Company Ltd., **31** 330
United Building Centers *see* Lanoga Corp.
United Business Media plc, 52 363–68 (upd.)

United Cable Television Corporation, **43** 431; **76** 75
United Capital Corporation, **56** 136
The United Center *see* Wirtz Corp.
United Cigar Manufacturers Company, *see* Culbro Corp.
United Cities Gas Company, **43** 56, 58
United Communications Systems, Inc. **V** 346
United Dairy Farmers, Inc., 74 364–66
United Defense Industries, Inc., 30 471–73; 66 346–49 (upd.)
United Distillers and Vintners *see* Diageo plc.
United Distillers Glenmore, Inc., **34** 89
United Dominion Industries Limited, 8 544–46; 16 499–502 (upd.)
United Dominion Realty Trust, Inc., 52 369–71
United Electronic Services, Inc., **72** 29
United Engineers & Constructors, **11** 413
United Farm Workers of America, 88 418–22
United Foods, Inc., 21 508–11
United Fruit Co., **44** 152
United Gas and Electric Company of New Albany, **6** 555
United Gas Improvement Co., **6** 523
United Graphics, *see* Banta Corp.
United Health, Inc. *see* Extendicare Health Services, Inc.
United HealthCare Corporation, 9 524–26 *see also* Humana Inc.
The United Illuminating Company, 21 512–14
United Image Entertainment, *see* BET Holdings, Inc.
United Industrial Corporation, 37 399–402
United Industries Corporation, 68 385–87
United Information Systems, Inc., **V** 346
United International Holdings Inc., **28** 198
United Investors Life Insurance Company, **22** 540; **33** 407
United Iron & Metal Co., **14** 156
United Jewish Communities, 33 422–25
United Kingdom Hotel Investments Ltd., **64** 217
United Knitting, Inc., **21** 192, 194
United Life & Accident Insurance Co., **14** 109
United Light and Power, **6** 511
United Machinery Co., **15** 127
United Media, **22** 442
United Merchants & Manufacturers, Inc., 13 534–37
United Microelectronics Corporation, **22** 197; **47** 384, 386; **67** 38; **73** 300; **74** 389
United National Group, Ltd., 63 410–13
United Nations International Children's Emergency Fund (UNICEF), 58 349–52
United Natural Foods, Inc., 32 479–82; 76 360–63 (upd.)
United Natural Gas Company, **6** 526
United Negro College Fund, Inc., 79 447–50
United Netherlands Navigation Company *see* Vereenigde Nederlandsche Scheepvaartmaatschappij.
United News & Media plc, 28 501–05 (upd.) *see also* United Business Media plc.
United Newspapers plc, IV 685–87 *see also* United Business Media plc.
United Online, Inc., 71 372–77 (upd.)
United Overseas Bank Ltd., 56 362–64
United Pacific Financial Services, *see* Reliance Group Holdings, Inc.
United Pan-Europe Communications NV, 47 414–17
United Paper Mills Ltd., IV 347–50 *see also* UPM-Kymmene Corp.
United Paramount Network, **25** 418–19; **26** 32; **31** 109
United Parcel Service, Inc., V 533–35; 17 503–06 (upd.); 63 414–19; 94 425–30 (upd.)
United Payors and United Providers, **75** 185
United Pet Group, Inc. *see* United Industries Corp.
United Plantations Berhad *see* Aarhus United A/S.
United Presidential Life Insurance Company, *see* Washington National Corp.
United Press International, Inc., 25 506–09; 73 354–57 (upd.)
United Refining Co., **23** 406, 408
United Rentals, Inc., 34 466–69
United Resources, Inc., **21** 514
United Retail Group Inc., 33 426–28
United Road Services, Inc., 69 360–62
United Scientific Holdings, **47** 8
United Service Organizations, 60 308–11
United Shipping & Technology, Inc., **49** 440
United Shirt Shops, Inc. *see* Aris Industries, Inc.
United States Aviation Underwriters, Inc., *see* General Re Corp.
United States Can Co., **15** 127, 129
United States Cellular Corporation, 9 527–29 *see also* U.S. Cellular Corp.
United States Fidelity and Guaranty Co. *see* USF&G Corp.
United States Filter Corporation, 20 501–04 *see also* Siemens AG.
United States Football League, **29** 347
United States Gypsum Co. *see* USG Corp.
United States Health Care Systems, Inc. *see* U.S. Healthcare, Inc.
United States Mail Steamship Co., **23** 160
United States Marine Repair, Inc. *see* BAE Systems Ship Repair.
United States National Bank of Galveston *see* Cullen/Frost Bankers, Inc.
United States National Bank of Oregon, *see* U.S. Bancorp.
United States Pipe and Foundry Company, 62 377–80
United States Playing Card Company, 62 381–84
United States Postal Service, 14 517–20; 34 470–75 (upd.)
United States Satellite Broadcasting Company Inc. *see* Hubbard Broadcasting Inc.
United States Shoe Corporation, V 207–08
United States Steel Corporation, 50 500–04 (upd.)
United States Surgical Corporation, 10 533–35; 34 476–80 (upd.)
United States Tobacco Company, *see* UST Inc.
United Stationers Inc., 14 521–23
United Talent Agency, Inc., 80 392–96
United Technologies Automotive Inc., 15 513–15
United Technologies Corporation, I 84–86; 10 536–38 (upd.); 34 481–85 (upd.)
United Telecommunications, Inc., V 344–47 *see also* Sprint Corp.
United Telephone System, Inc., **V** 346
United Television, Inc., **26** 32
United Thermal Corp., **42** 388
United Truck Lines, *see* TNT Freightways Corp.
United Utilities PLC, 52 372–75 (upd.)
United Van Lines, **14** 37; **15** 50
United Video Satellite Group, 18 535–37 *see also* TV Guide, Inc.
United Water Resources, Inc., 40 447–50; 45 277
United Way of America, 36 485–88
United Westburne Inc., **19** 313
United Wholesale Grocery Company *see* Spartan Stores Inc.
United-A.G. Cooperative Inc., **65** 252
Unitel Communications Inc., **6** 311; **44** 49; **46** 401; **47** 136
Unitika Ltd., V 387–89; 53 341–44 (upd.)
Unitil Corporation, 37 403–06
Unitog Co., 19 457–60 *see also* Cintas Corp.
Unitpool, **70** 311
Unitrin Inc., 16 503–05; 78 427–31 (upd.)
Unitron Medical Communications, **29** 412
Unity Cellular Systems, Inc. *see* Rural Cellular Corp.
Univar Corporation, 9 530–32
Univas, **23** 171
Univasa, **39** 229
Univel Inc., **38** 418
Universal Cheerleaders Association *see* Varsity Spirit Corp.
Universal Cigar Corp., **14** 19
Universal Compression, Inc., 59 402–04
Universal Consumer Products Group, **30** 123
Universal Corporation, V 417–18; 48 403–06 (upd.)

Universal Electronics Inc., **39** **405–08**
Universal Foods Corporation, **7** **546–48** *see also* Sensient Technologies Corp.
Universal Footcare Products Inc., **31** 255
Universal Forest Products, Inc., **10** **539–40**; **59** **405–09 (upd.)**
Universal Frozen Foods, **23** 321
Universal Health Services, Inc., **6** **191–93**
Universal International, Inc., **25** **510–11**
Universal Juice Co., **21** 55
Universal Leaf Tobacco Company *see* Universal Corp.
Universal Manufacturing Company, **88** **423–26**
Universal Match, **12** 464
Universal Matchbox Group, **12** 495
Universal Music Group, **22** 194; **26** 152; **37** 193
Universal Pictures *see* Universal Studios, Inc.
Universal Press Syndicate, **40** 38
Universal Reinsurance Corporation, **58** 20
Universal Resources Corporation, **6** 569; **26** 388
Universal Stainless & Alloy Products, Inc., **75** **386–88**
Universal Studios, Inc., **33** **429–33**
Universal Tea Co., Inc., **50** 449
Universal Technical Institute, Inc., **81** **396–99**
Universe Tankships, **59** 198
UNIVERSELLE Engineering U.N.I. GmbH, **60** 194
University HealthSystem Consortium, **53** 346
The University of Chicago Press, **79** **451–55**
University of Phoenix, *see* Apollo Group, Inc.
Univision Communications Inc., **24** **515–18**; **83** **434-439 (upd.)**
Unix System Laboratories Inc., **25** 20–21; **38** 418
UNM *see* United News & Media plc.
Uno-e Bank, **48** 51
Uno Restaurant Holdings Corporation, **18** **538–40**; **70** **334–37 (upd.)**
Uno-Ven, *see* Unocal Corp.
Unocal Corporation, **IV** **569–71**; **24** **519–23 (upd.)**; **71** **378–84 (upd.)**
Unova Manufacturing Technologies Inc., **72** 69, 71
UNR Industries, Inc. *see* ROHN Industries, Inc.
Unterberg Harris, **25** 433
UNUM Corp., **13** **538–40**
UnumProvident Corporation, **52** **376–83 (upd.)**
Uny Co., Ltd., **V** **209–10**; **49** **425–28 (upd.)**
UO Fenwick, Inc., **74** 370
UOB *see* United Overseas Bank Ltd.
UPC *see* United Pan-Europe Communications NV.
UOD Inc. *see* Urban Outfitters, Inc.
UPI *see* United Press International.
Upjohn Company, **I** **707–09**; **8** **547–49 (upd.)** *see also* Pharmacia & Upjohn Inc.; Pfizer Inc.
UPM-Kymmene Corporation, **19** **461–65**; **50** **505–11 (upd.)**
UPN *see* United Paramount Network.
Upper Deck Company, LLC, **34** 448; **37** 295
Upper Peninsula Power Co., **53** 369
UPS *see* United Parcel Service, Inc.
UPS Aviation Technologies, Inc., **60** 137
UPSHOT, **27** 195
Urban Outfitters, Inc., **14** **524–26**; **74** **367–70 (upd.)**
Urbaser SA, **55** 182
Urbi Desarrollos Urbanos, S.A. de C.V., **81** **400–03**
Urbium PLC, **75** **389–91**
URS Corporation, **45** **420–23**; **80** **397–400 (upd.)**
URSI *see* United Road Services, Inc.
US *see also* U.S.
US Airways Group, Inc., **I** **131–32**; **6** **131–32 (upd.)**; **28** **506–09 (upd.)**; **52** **384–88 (upd.)**
US Industries Inc., **30** 231
US Monolithics, **54** 407
US 1 Industries, Inc., **89** **475–78**
US Order, Inc., *see* WorldCorp, Inc.
US Repeating Arms Co., **58** 147
US Sprint Communications Company *see* Sprint Communications Company, L.P.
US West Communications Services, Inc. *see* Regional Bell Operating Companies.
USA Cafes, *see* Metromedia Companies.
USA Interactive, Inc., **47** **418–22 (upd.)**
USA Networks Inc., **25** 330, 411; **33** 432; **37** 381, 383–84; **43** 422
USA Security Systems, Inc., *see* AHL Services, Inc.
USA Truck, Inc., **42** **410–13**
USAA, **10** **541–43**; **62** **385–88 (upd.)**
USANA, Inc., **29** **491–93**
USCC *see* United States Cellular Corp.
Usego AG., **48** 63
USF&G Corporation, **III** **395–98** *see also* The St. Paul Companies.
USFL *see* United States Football League.
USFreightways Corporation, **49** 402
USG Corporation, **III** **762–64**; **26** **507–10 (upd.)**; **81** **404–10 (upd.)**
USH *see* United Scientific Holdings.
Ushio Inc., **91** **496–99**
Usinas Siderúrgicas de Minas Gerais S.A., **77** **454–57**
Usinger's Famous Sausage *see* Fred Usinger Inc.
Usinor SA, **IV** **226–28**; **42** **414–17 (upd.)**
USLD Communications Corp. *see* Billing Concepts Corp.
USO *see* United Service Organizations.
Usource LLC, **37** 406
USPS *see* United States Postal Service.
USSC *see* United States Surgical Corp.
USSI *see* U.S. Software Inc.
UST Inc., **9** **533–35**; **50** **512–17 (upd.)**
UST Wilderness Management Corporation, **33** 399
Usutu Pulp Company, **49** 353
USWeb/CKS *see* marchFIRST, Inc.
USX Corporation, **IV** **572–74**; **7** **549–52 (upd.)** *see also* United States Steel Corp.
UT Starcom, **44** 426
Utah Gas and Coke Company, **6** 568
Utah Medical Products, Inc., **36** **496–99**
Utah Mines Ltd., **IV** 47; **22** 107
Utah Power and Light Company, **27** **483–86** *see also* PacifiCorp.
UTI Energy, Inc. *see* Patterson-UTI Energy, Inc.
Utilicom, **6** 572
Utilicorp United Inc., **6** **592–94** *see also* Aquilla, Inc.
UtiliTech Solutions, **37** 88
Utility Constructors Incorporated, **6** 527
Utility Engineering Corporation, **6** 580
Utility Line Construction Service, Inc., **59** 65
Utility Service Affiliates, Inc., **45** 277
Utility Services, Inc., **42** 249, 253
Utility Supply Co. *see* United Stationers Inc.
Utopian Leisure Group, **75** 385
UTStarcom, Inc., **77** **458–61**
UTV *see* Ulster Television PLC.
Utz Quality Foods, Inc., **72** **358–60**
UUNET, **38** **468–72**
Uwajimaya, Inc., **60** **312–14**

V

V&S Vin & Sprit AB, **91** **504–11 (upd.)**
V.L. Churchill Group, *see* SPX Corp.
VA Linux Systems, **45** 363
VA Systeme *see* Diehl Stiftung & Co. KG
VA TECH ELIN EBG GmbH, **49** **429–31**
VA Technologie AG, **57** 402
Vacheron Constantin, *see* Vendôme Luxury Group plc.
Vaco, **38** 200, 202
Vaculator Division *see* Lancer Corp.
Vacuum Oil Co. *see* Mobil Corp.
VAE AG, **57** 402
VAE Nortrak Cheyenne Inc., **53** 352
Vail Resorts, Inc., **11** **543–46**; **43** **435–39 (upd.)**
Vaillant GmbH, **44** **436–39**
Val Corp., **24** 149
Val-Pak Direct Marketing Systems, Inc., **22** 162
Valassis Communications, Inc., **8** **550–51**; **37** **407–10 (upd.)**; **76** **364–67 (upd.)**
ValCom Inc. *see* InaCom Corp.
Valdi Foods Inc., *see* Steinberg Inc.
Vale do Rio Doce Navegacao SA—Docenave, **43** 112
Vale Harmon Enterprises, Ltd., **25** 204
Valenciana de Cementos, **59** 112
Valentine & Company, *see* The Valspar Corp.
Valentino, **67** 246, 248
Valeo, **23** **492–94**; **66** **350–53 (upd.)**

Valero Energy Corporation, 7 553–55; 71 385–90 (upd.)
Valhi, Inc., 19 466–68; 94 431–35 (upd.)
Valid Logic Systems Inc., **11** 46, 284; **48** 77
Vality Technology Inc., **59** 56
Vallen Corporation, 45 424–26
Valley Bank of Helena, **35** 197, 199
Valley Bank of Maryland, **46** 25
Valley Crest Tree Company, **31** 182–83
Valley Federal of California, **11** 163
Valley Fig Growers, *see* Diamond of California.
Valley Media Inc., 35 430–33
Valley Milk Products LLC *see* Maryland & Virginia Milk Producers Cooperative Association, Inc.
Valley National Gases, Inc., 85 434–37
Valley of the Moon, **68** 146
Valley Proteins, Inc., 91 500–03
Valleyfair, *see* Cedar Fair, L.P.
ValleyCrest Companies, 81 411–14 (upd.)
Vallourec SA, 54 391–94
Valmet Oy, III 647–49 *see also* Metso Corp.
Valmont Industries, Inc., 19 469–72
Valois S.A. *see* AptarGroup, Inc.
VALOR Communications Group *see* Windstream Corp.
Valorem S.A., 88 427–30
Valores Industriales S.A., 19 473–75
The Valspar Corporation, 8 552–54; 32 483–86 (upd.); 77 462–68 (upd.)
Valtek International, Inc., *see* Duriron Co. Inc.
Value America, **29** 312
Value City Department Stores, Inc., 38 473–75 *see also* Retail Ventures, Inc.
Value Line, Inc., 16 506–08; 73 358–61 (upd.)
Value Merchants Inc., 13 541–43
ValueClick, Inc., 49 432–34
ValueVision International, Inc., 22 534–36
ValuJet, Inc. *see* AirTran Holdings, Inc.
Valvtron, *see* Keystone International, Inc.
VAMED Gruppe, **56** 141
Van Camp Seafood Company, Inc., 7 556–57 *see also* Chicken of the Sea International.
Van Cleef & Arpels Inc., **26** 145
Van der Moolen Holding NV, **37** 224
Van Houtte Inc., 39 409–11
Van Lanschot NV, 79 456–59
Van Leer Containers Inc., **30** 397
Van Leer Holding, Inc., **9** 303, 305
Van Leer N.V. *see* Royal Packaging Industries Van Leer N.V.; Greif Inc.
Van Ommeren, **41** 339–40
Van Sickle, **IV** 485
Van Wezel, **26** 278–79
Van's Aircraft, Inc., 65 349–51
Vance Publishing Corporation, 64 398–401
Vanderbilt Mortgage and Finance, *see* Clayton Homes Inc.
Vanessa and Biffi, *see* Keystone International, Inc.
The Vanguard Group, Inc., 14 530–32; 34 486–89 (upd.)
Vanguard Health Systems Inc., 70 338–40
Vanguard International Semiconductor Corp., **47** 385
Vanity Fair *see* VF Corp.
Vans, Inc., 16 509–11; 47 423–26 (upd.)
Vantage Analysis Systems, Inc., **11** 490
Vantage Components *see* Bell Microproducts Inc.
Vantive Corporation, **33** 333; **38** 431–32
Varco International, Inc., 42 418–20
Varco-Pruden, Inc., *see* United Dominion Industries Ltd.
Vari-Lite International, Inc., 35 434–36
Varian Associates Inc., 12 504–06
Varian, Inc., 48 407–11 (upd.)
Varibus Corporation *see* Gulf States Utilities Co.
Variety Wholesalers, Inc., 73 362–64
Variflex, Inc., 51 391–93
Variform, Inc., *see* Ply Gem Industries Inc.
VARIG S.A. (Viação Aérea Rio-Grandense), 6 133–35; 29 494–97 (upd.)
Varity Corporation, III 650–52 *see also* AGCO Corp.
Varlen Corporation, 16 512–14
Varney Speed Lines *see* Continental Airlines, Inc.
Varo, *see* Imo Industries Inc.
Varsity Brands, Inc., 15 516–18; 94 436–40 (upd.)
Varta AG, 23 495–99
VASCO Data Security International, Inc., 79 460–63
Vaserie Trevigiane International S.p.A., **73** 248–49
VASP (Viaçao Aérea de Sao Paulo), **31** 444–45
Vasset, S.A., *see* OM Group, Inc.
Vast Solutions, **39** 24
Vastar Resources, Inc., 24 524–26
Vattenfall AB, 57 395–98
Vaughan Harmon Systems Ltd., **25** 204
Vaughan Printers Inc., **23** 100
Vauxhall Motors Limited, 73 365–69
Vax Ltd., **73** 331–32
VBA - Bloemenveiling Aalsmeer, 88 431–34
VBB Viag-Bayernwerk-Beteiligungs-Gesellschaft mbH, *see* E.On AG.
VCA Antech, Inc., 58 353–55
VCH Publishing Group *see* John Wiley & Sons, Inc.
VDM Nickel-Technologie AG, **IV** 89
VEAG, **57** 395, 397
Veba A.G., I 542–43; 15 519–21 (upd.) *see also* E.On AG.
Vebego International BV, 49 435–37
VECO International, Inc., 7 558–59 *see also* CH2M Hill Ltd.
Vector Casa de Bolsa, **21** 413
Vector Group Ltd., 35 437–40 (upd.)
Vectra Bank Colorado, **53** 378
Vectura Holding Company L.L.C., **69** 197
Veda International, **54** 395–96
Vedelectric, *see* Koninklijke Vendex KBB N.V. (Royal Vendex KBB N.V.).
Vedior NV, 35 441–43
Veeco Instruments Inc., 32 487–90
Veeder-Root Company, *see* Danaher Corp.
VeggieTales *see* Big Idea Productions, Inc.
Veit Companies, 43 440–42; 92 398–402 (upd.)
Velcro Industries N.V., 19 476–78; 72 361–64 (upd.)
Velda Farms, Inc., **26** 448
Velocity Express Corporation, 49 438–41; 94 441–46 (upd.)
Velva-Sheen Manufacturing Co., **23** 66
Velux A/S, 86 412–15
Venator Group Inc., 35 444–49 (upd.) *see also* Foot Locker Inc.
Venbo Comercio de Alimentos Ltda., **74** 48
Vencemos, **20** 124
Vencor, Inc., 16 515–17
Vendex International N.V., 13 544–46 *see also* Koninklijke Vendex KBB N.V. (Royal Vendex KBB N.V.).
Vendôme Luxury Group plc, 27 487–89
Vendors Supply of America, Inc., *see* International Multifoods Corp.
Venetian Casino Resort, LLC, 47 427–29
Venevision, **54** 72–73, 75
Ventana Medical Systems, Inc., 75 392–94
Ventshade Company, **40** 299–300
Ventura Foods LLC, 90 420–23
Venture Out RV, **26** 193
Venture Stores Inc., 12 507–09
Ventures Limited, **49** 137
Venturi, Inc., **9** 72
Veolia Environnement SA, **66** 68
Vepco *see* Virginia Electric and Power Co.
Vera Imported Parts, **11** 84
Veragon Corporation *see* Drypers Corp.
VeraSun Energy Corporation, 87 447–450
Veratex Group, *see* Chemed Corp.
Veravision, **24** 510
Verbatim Corporation, 14 533–35; 74 371–74 (upd.)
Verbund *see* Österreichische Elektrizitätswirtschafts-AG.
Verbundnetz Gas AG, **38** 408
Verdugt, **70** 143, 145
Vereinigte Elektrizitäts und Bergwerke A.G. *see* VEBA A.G.
Vereinigte Elektrizitätswerke Westfalen AG, IV V 744–47
Vereinigte Industrie-Unternehmungen Aktiengesellschaft *see* VIAG
Vereinigte Papierwerke Schickedanz AG, **26** 384
Verenigde Bedrijven Bredero, **26** 280
Verenigde Nederlandse Uitgeverijen *see* VNU N.V.

Verenigde Spaarbank Groep *see* VSB Groep.
Veri-Best Baking Co., **56** 29
Veridian Corporation, 54 395–97
Verifact Inc. (IVI), **46** 251
VeriFone, Inc., 18 541–44; 76 368–71 (upd.)
Verint Systems Inc., 73 370–72
VeriSign, Inc., 47 430–34
Verispan LLC, **68** 308
Veritas Capital Fund L.P., **26** 408; **44** 420, 423; **54** 178; **59** 192
Veritas Software Corporation, 45 427–31
Veritec Technologies, Inc., **48** 299
Veritus Inc., *see* Highmark Inc.
Verity Inc., 68 388–91
Verizon Communications Inc., 43 443–49 (upd.); 78 432–40 (upd.)
Verizon Wireless, Inc., **42** 284; **63** 131
Verlagsgruppe Georg von Holtzbrinck GmbH, 35 450–53
Verlagsgruppe Märkische Verlags- und Druckgesellschaft mbH, **66** 123
Vermeer Manufacturing Company, 17 507–10
The Vermont Country Store, 93 478–82
Vermont General Insurance Company, **51** 248
Vermont Pure Holdings, Ltd., 51 394–96
The Vermont Teddy Bear Co., Inc., 36 500–02
Verneuil Holding Co, **21** 387
Vernon and Nelson Telephone Company *see* British Columbia Telephone Co.
Vernors, Inc., **25** 4
Verreries Brosse S.A.S., **67** 210, 212
Verreries Pochet et du Courval, **55** 309
Versace *see* Gianni Versace SpA.
Versatile Farm and Equipment Co., **22** 380
Versax, S.A. de C.V., **19** 12
Verson Allsteel Press Co., **21** 20, 22
Vert Baudet, **19** 309
Vertex Data Science Limited, **52** 372, 374–75
Vertex Pharmaceuticals Incorporated, 83 440-443
Vertical Technology Industries, **14** 571
Vertis Communications, 84 418–421
Vertrue Inc., 77 469–72
Verve Records, **23** 389
Vesa Energy, **57** 397
Vessel Management Services, Inc., **28** 80
Vestas Wind Systems A/S, 73 373–75
Vestek Systems, Inc., *see* Primark Corp.
Vestro, **19** 309
Veszpremtej, **25** 85
Veterinary Cos. of America, *see* Colgate-Palmolive Co.
VEW AG, 39 412–15
VF Corporation, V 390–92; 17 511–14 (upd.); 54 398–404 (upd.)
VH Serviços e Construçoes Ltda., **72** 68
VHA Inc., 53 345–47
VHA Long Term Care, **23** 431
VH1 Inc., **23** 503
Via Cariane *see* Keolis SA.
Via-Générale de Transport et d'Industrie SA, **28** 155
Via Verde, **64** 57
ViaAfrika *see* Naspers Ltd.
Viacao Aerea Rio Grandense of South America *see* VARIG, SA.
Viacom Inc., 7 560–62; 23 500–03 (upd.); 67 367–71 (upd.) *see also* Paramount Pictures Corp.
Viad Corp., 73 376–78
Viag AG, IV 229–32 *see also* E.On AG.
Viajes El Corte Inglés, S.A., **26** 129
VIASA *see* Iberia.
ViaSat, Inc., 54 405–08
Viasoft Inc., 27 490–93; 59 27
VIASYS Healthcare, Inc., 52 389–91
Viasystems Group, Inc., 67 372–74
Viatech Continental Can Company, Inc., 25 512–15 (upd.)
Vibracoustic GmbH & Co. KG, **68** 289
Vicat S.A., 70 341–43
Vickers plc, 27 494–97
VICOM, **48** 415
Vicon Industries, Inc., 44 440–42
VICORP Restaurants, Inc., 12 510–12; 48 412–15 (upd.)
Victoire Delage, **62** 229
Victor Company of Japan, Limited, II 118–19; 26 511–13 (upd.); 83 444-449 (upd.)
Victor Equipment Co., *see* Thermadyne Holding Corp.
Victoria & Co., **39** 247
Victoria Coach Station *see* London Regional Transport.
Victoria Creations Inc., *see* United Merchants & Manufacturers, Inc.
Victoria Group, III 399–401; 44 443–46 (upd.)
Victoria Ward, Limited, **57** 157
Victoria's Secret *see* The Limited, Inc.
Victorinox AG, 21 515–17; 74 375–78 (upd.)
Vicunha Têxtil S.A., 78 441–44
Victory Refrigeration, Inc., 82 403–06
Victory Supermarket *see* Big V Supermarkets, Inc.
Video News International, **19** 285
Video Trend, **60** 84
VideoFusion, Inc., **16** 419
Videojet Technologies, Inc., 90 424–27
Videotex Network Japan, **IV** 680
Videotron, **25** 102
Vidrala S.A., 67 375–77
Vie de France Yamazaki Inc., **58** 380–82
Viel & Cie, 76 372–74
Vienna Sausage Manufacturing Co., 14 536–37
Viessmann Werke GmbH & Co., 37 411–14
Vietnam International Assurance Co., **64** 280
Vietnam LPG Co., Ltd., **56** 290
Viewlogic, **11** 490
Viewpoint International, Inc., 66 354–56
ViewSonic Corporation, 72 365–67
ViewStar Corp., **20** 103
Viewtel Holdings Ltd, *see* AT&T Istel Ltd.
ViewTrade Holding Corp., **46** 282
Vigilant Insurance Co., *see* The Chubb Corp.
Viking, **IV** 659
Viking Building Products, **22** 15
Viking Computer Services, Inc., *see* D&K Wholesale Drug, Inc.
Viking Consolidated Shipping Corp, **25** 470
Viking Industries, **39** 322, 324
Viking Office Products, Inc., 10 544–46 *see also* Office Depot, Inc.
Viking Penguin, **IV** 611
Viking Pump Company, **21** 499–500
Viking Range Corporation, 66 357–59
Viking Star Shipping, Inc. *see* Teekay Shipping Corp.
Village Inn *see* VICORP Restaurants, Inc.
Village Roadshow Ltd., 58 356–59
Village Super Market, Inc., 7 563–64
Village Voice Media, Inc., 38 476–79
Villeroy & Boch AG, 37 415–18
Vilmorin Clause et Cie, 70 344–46
VILPAC, S.A., **26** 356
AO VimpelCom, 48 416–19
Vimto *see* Nichols plc.
Vin & Spirit AB, 31 458–61 *see also* V&S Vin & Sprit AB.
Viña Concha y Toro S.A., 45 432–34
Vina San Pedro S.A., **70** 62–63
Vinci, 27 54; **43 450–52; 49** 44
Vincor International Inc., 50 518–21
Vinedos Baron de Ley SL *see* Baron de Ley S.A.
Vinewood Companies, **53** 232
Vingaarden A/S, *see* Carlsberg A/S.
Vining Industries, **12** 128
Viniprix SA, **19** 309
Vinita Rock Company, **50** 49
Vinland Web-Print, *see* Menasha Corp.
Vinson & Elkins L.L.P., 30 481–83
Vintage Petroleum, Inc., 42 421–23
Vintage Yarns, **62** 374
Vintners International, **34** 89
Vinton Studios, 63 420–22
Vion Food Group NV, 85 438–41
Vipond, Inc., **64** 31
VIPS, **11** 113
Viratec Thin Films, Inc., **22** 347
Virbac Corporation, 74 379–81
Virco Manufacturing Corporation, 17 515–17
Virgin Atlantic Airlines *see* Virgin Group PLC.
Virgin Express, **35** 384
Virgin Group Ltd., 12 513–15; 32 491–96 (upd.); 89 479–86 (upd.)
The Virgin Islands Telephone Co., **19** 256
Virgin Music Group Worldwide, **52** 429
Virginia Dare Extract Company, Inc., 94 447–50
Virginia Eastern Shore Sustainable Development Corporation, **28** 307
Virginia Electric and Power Company *see* Dominion Resources, Inc.

Virginia Fibre Corporation *see* Greif Inc.
Virginia Mason Medical Center, **41** 183
Virginia Railway and Power Company (VR&P) *see* Dominion Resources, Inc.
Viridian Group plc, 64 402–04
Viridor Waste Limited, **45** 338
Visa *see* Valores Industriales S.A.
Visa International, 9 536–38; 26 514–17 (upd.)
Viscofan S.A., 70 347–49
Vishay Intertechnology, Inc., 21 518–21; 80 401–06 (upd.)
Visible Impact Target Company, **62** 82
Visio Corporation, **63** 296
Vision Hardware Group *see* Acorn Products, Inc.
Vision Service Plan Inc., 77 473–76
Vision Technologies Kinetics Inc., **61** 43
Vision Technology Group Ltd., **19** 124; **49** 113
Visionware Ltd., **38** 419
Viskase Companies, Inc., 55 379–81
Vista Alegre, **69** 303
Vista Bakery, Inc., 56 365–68
Vista Chemical Company, I 402–03
Vista Resources, Inc., *see* Fuqua Enterprises, Inc.
Vista 2000, Inc., **36** 444
Vistana, Inc., 22 537–39
VistaPrint Limited, 87 451–454
Vistar Inc., **76** 54
Visual Action Holdings plc, **24** 96, 374
Visual Information Technologies, **11** 57
VISX, Incorporated, 30 484–86
Vita-Achter, *see* British Vita PLC.
Vita Plus Corporation, 60 315–17
Vitafoam Incorporated, **9** 93; **33** 78
Vital Images, Inc., 85 442–45
Vital S.A., **71** 140
Vitalink Communications Corp., **11** 520; **34** 444
Vitalink Pharmacy Services, Inc., 15 522–24
Vitalscheme, **38** 426
VitalWorks, Inc. *see* AMICAS, Inc.
The Vitamin Factory *see* Integrated BioPharma, Inc.
Vitamin Shoppe Industries, Inc., 60 318–20
Vitamin World, **31** 346–48
Vitasoy International Holdings Ltd., 94 451–54
Vitesse Semiconductor Corporation, 32 497–500
Vitoria-Minas Railroad, **43** 111
Vitramon, Inc., **54** 371–72
Vitro Corp., 10 547–48
Vitro Corporativo S.A. de C.V., 34 490–92
VIVA, **23** 390
Vivarte SA, 54 409–12 (upd.)
Vivartia S.A., 82 407–10
Vivendi Universal S.A., 46 438–41 (upd.)
Vivendia, **40** 449
Vivra, Inc., 18 545–47 *see also* Gambro AB.
VKI Technologies Inc., **39** 409
Vladivostok Dairy, **48** 438
Vlasic Foods International Inc., 25 516–19
VLSI Technology, Inc., 16 518–20
VMG Products *see* Drypers Corp.
VMware, Inc., 90 428–31
VMX Inc., *see* Octel Messaging.
VNG *see* Verbundnetz Gas AG.
VNS *see* Vereenigde Nederlandsche Scheepvaartmaatschappij.
VNU N.V., 27 498–501
Vobis Microcomputer, **20** 103; **23** 311
Vocento, 94 455–58
Vodac, **11** 548
Vodacom World Online Ltd, **48** 399
Vodafone Group Plc, 11 547–48; 36 503–06 (upd.); 75 395–99 (upd.)
Vodapage, **11** 548
Vodata, **11** 548
voestalpine AG, IV 233–35; 57 399–403 (upd.)
Voegel *see* Charles Vögele Holding AG.
Vogel Peterson Furniture Company, **7** 4–5
Voice Data Systems, **15** 125
Voice Powered Technology International, Inc., **23** 212
Voice Response, Inc., **11** 253
VoiceStream Wireless Corporation, **48** 130
Voith Sulzer Papiermaschinen GmbH *see* J.M. Voith AG.
Volcan Compañia Minera S.A.A., 92 403–06
Volcom, Inc., 77 477–80
Volga-Dnepr Group, 82 411–14
Volition, Inc., **39** 395
Volkswagen Aktiengesellschaft, I 206–08; 11 549–51 (upd.); 32 501–05 (upd.)
Volt Information Sciences Inc., 26 518–21
Volume Distributors *see* Payless ShoeSource, Inc.
Volume Service Company *see* Restaurants Unlimited, Inc.
Volume Services America, Inc. *see* Centerplate, Inc.
Volume Shoe Corporation *see* Payless ShoeSource,Inc.
Volunteer Leather Company, *see* Genesco Inc.
Volunteers of America, Inc., 66 360–62
AB Volvo, I 209–11; 7 565–68 (upd.); 26 9–12 (upd.); 67 378–83 (upd.)
Volvo-Penta, **21** 503
Von Maur Inc., 64 405–08
von Roll, **6** 599
Vonage Holdings Corp., 81 415–18
The Vons Companies, Incorporated, 7 569–71; 28 510–13 (upd.)
Vornado Realty Trust, 20 508–10
Voroba Hearing Systems, **25** 56
Vortex Management, Inc., **41** 207
Vorwerk & Co., 27 502–04
Vosper Thornycroft Holding plc, 41 410–12
Vossloh AG, 53 348–52
Votorantim Participaçoes S.A., 76 375–78
Vought Aircraft Industries, Inc., 49 442–45
Vox, **58** 195
Voyageur Travel Insurance Ltd., **21** 447
VR&P *see* Virginia Railway and Power Co.
Vratislavice A.S., **38** 77
VRG International *see* Roberts Pharmaceutical Corp.
Vriesco Plastics B.V., **53** 221
Vroom & Dreesmann, *see* Koninklijke Vendex KBB N.V. (Royal Vendex KBB N.V.).
VSA *see* Vendors Supply of America, Inc.
VSB Groep, *see* N.V. AMEV.
VSD Communications, Inc., **22** 443
VSK Group *see* The Allied Defense Group, Inc.
VSM *see* Village Super Market, Inc.
VST *see* Vision Technology Group Ltd.
VTech Holdings Ltd., 77 481–84
VTR Incorporated, **16** 46; **43** 60
Vu-Tech Communications, Inc., **48** 54
Vulcan Materials Company, 7 572–75; 52 392–96 (upd.)
Vulcan Ventures Inc., **32** 145; **43** 144
Vulcraft, *see* Nucor Corp.
VW&R *see* Van Waters & Rogers.
VWR Textiles & Supplies, Inc., **11** 256
VWR United Company, *see* Univar Corp.
Vycor Corporation, **25** 349
Vyvx, **31** 469

W

W&A Manufacturing Co., LLC, **26** 530
W & J Sloane Home Furnishings Group, **35** 129
W + K *see* Wieden + Kennedy.
W de Argentina–Inversiones S.L., **63** 377
W.A. Whitney Company, 53 353–56
W. Atlee Burpee & Co., 27 505–08
W.B Doner & Co., 56 369–72
W.B. Saunders Co., **IV** 623–24
W.C. Bradley Co., 69 363–65
W.C.G. Sports Industries Ltd. *see* Canstar Sports Inc.
W.E. Dillon Company, Ltd., **21** 499
W.F. Kaiser, **60** 364
W.F. Linton Company, *see* Newell Rubbermaid Inc.
W.G. Yates & Sons Construction Company *see* The Yates Companies, Inc.
W.H. Brady Co., 16 518–21 *see also* Brady Corp.
W. H. Braum, Inc., 80 407–10
W.H. Gunlocke Chair Co. *see* Gunlocke Co.
W.H. Smith & Son (Alacra) Ltd., **15** 473
W H Smith Group PLC, V 211–13
W Jordan (Cereals) Ltd., 74 382–84
W.L. Gore & Associates, Inc., 14 538–40; 60 321–24 (upd.)
W.M. Bassett Furniture Co. *see* Bassett Furniture Industries, Inc.
W.P. Carey & Co. LLC, 49 446–48
W.R. Berkley Corporation, 15 525–27; 74 385–88 (upd.)

W.R. Case & Sons Cutlery Company *see* Zippo Manufacturing Co.
W.R. Grace & Company, I 547–50; 50 522–29 (upd.)
W.S. Barstow & Company, **6** 575
W.W. Grainger, Inc., V 214–15; 26 537–39 (upd.); 68 392–95 (upd.)
W.W. Norton & Company, Inc., 28 518–20
Waban Inc., 13 547–49 *see also* HomeBase, Inc.
Wabash National Corp., 13 550–52
Wabash Valley Power Association, **6** 556
Wabtec Corporation, 40 451–54
Wachbrit Insurance Agency, **21** 96
Wachovia Bank of Georgia, N.A., 16 521–23
Wachovia Bank of South Carolina, N.A., 16 524–26
Wachovia Corporation, 12 516–20; 46 442–49 (upd.)
Wachtell, Lipton, Rosen & Katz, 47 435–38
The Wackenhut Corporation, 14 541–43; 63 423–26 (upd.)
Wacker-Chemie GmbH, 35 454–58
Wacker Oil Inc., *see* Seagull Energy Corp.
Wacoal Corp., 25 520–24
Waddell & Reed, Inc., 22 540–43
Wade Smith, **28** 27, 30
Wadsworth Inc., *see* The Thomspn Corp.
WaferTech, **18** 20; **43** 17; **47** 385
Waffle House Inc., 14 544–45; 60 325–27 (upd.)
Wagers Inc. (Idaho Candy Company), 86 416–19
Waggener Edstrom, 42 424–26
Wagner Castings Company, **16** 474–75
Wagon plc, 92 407–10
Wagonlit Travel, *see* Carlson Wagonlit Travel.
Wagons-Lits, **27** 11; **29** 443; **37** 250–52
Wah Chang, 82 415–18
Waha Oil Company *see* National Oil Corp.
Wahl Clipper Corporation, 86 420–23
AB Wahlbecks, **25** 464
Waitrose Ltd. *see* John Lewis Partnership plc.
Wakefern Food Corporation, 33 434–37
Wako Shoji Co. Ltd. *see* Wacoal Corp.
Wal-Mart de Mexico, S.A. de C.V., 35 459–61 (upd.)
Wal-Mart Stores, Inc., V 216–17; 8 555–57 (upd.); 26 522–26 (upd.); 63 427–32 (upd.)
Walbridge Aldinger Co., 38 480–82
Walbro Corporation, 13 553–55
Walchenseewerk AG, **23** 44
Waldbaum, Inc., 19 479–81
Waldenbooks, 17 522–24; 86 424–28 (upd.)
Waldorf Corporation, **59** 350
Walgreen Co., V 218–20; 20 511–13 (upd.); 65 352–56 (upd.)
Walk Haydel & Associates, Inc., **25** 130
Walk Softly, Inc., **25** 118
Walker Dickson Group Limited, **26** 363
Walker Digital, **57** 296–98
Walker Manufacturing Company, 19 482–84
Walkers Shortbread Ltd., 79 464–67
Walkers Snack Foods Ltd., 70 350–52
Wall Drug Store, Inc., 40 455–57
Wall Street Deli, Inc., 33 438–41
Wallace & Tiernan Group, **11** 361; **52** 374
The Wallace Berrie Company *see* Applause Inc.
Wallace Computer Services, Inc., 36 507–10
Wallace International Silversmiths, *see* Syratech Corp.
Wallin & Nordstrom *see* Nordstrom, Inc.
Wallis *see* Sears plc.
Wallis Arnold Enterprises, Inc., **21** 483
Wallis Tractor Company, **21** 502
Walnut Capital Partners, **62** 46–47
Walrus, Inc., *see* Recreational Equipment, Inc.
Walsworth Publishing Company, Inc., 78 445–48
The Walt Disney Company, II 172–74; 6 174–77 (upd.); 30 487–91 (upd.); 63 433–38 (upd.)
Walter Bau, *see* Eiffage.
Walter Herzog GmbH, *see* Varlen Corp.
Walter Industries, Inc., III 765–67; 22 544–47 (upd.); 72 368–73 (upd.)
Walter Kidde & Co., **73** 208
Walter Wilson, **49** 18
Walter Wright Mammoet, **26** 280
Walton Monroe Mills, Inc., 8 558–60 *see also* Avondale Industries.
WaMu *see* Washington Mutual, Inc.
Wanadoo S.A., 75 400–02
Wang Global, **39** 176–78
Wang Laboratories, Inc., III 168–70; 6 284–87 (upd.) *see also* Getronics NV.
WAP, **26** 420
Warbasse-Cogeneration Technologies Partnership, **35** 479
Warburg Pincus, **14** 42; **61** 403; **73** 138
Warburg USB, **38** 291
Warburtons Ltd., 89 487–90
Ward's Communications, **22** 441
Wards *see* Circuit City Stores, Inc.
Waremart *see* WinCo Foods.
WARF *see* Wisconsin Alumni Research Foundation.
Warman International *see* Weir Group PLC.
The Warnaco Group Inc., 12 521–23; 46 450–54 (upd.) *see also* Authentic Fitness Corp.
Warner Chilcott Limited, 85 446–49
Warner Communications Inc., II 175–77 *see also* AOL Time Warner Inc.
Warner Electric, **58** 67
Warner-Lambert Co., I 710–12; 10 549–52 (upd.) *see also* Pfizer Inc.
Warner Music Group Corporation, 90 432–37 (upd.)
Warner Roadshow Film Distributors Greece SA, **58** 359
Warners' Stellian Inc., 67 384–87
Warrantech Corporation, 53 357–59
Warrell Corporation, 68 396–98
Warren Apparel Group Ltd., **39** 257
Warren Bancorp Inc., **55** 52
Warren Frozen Foods, Inc., **61** 174
Warren, Gorham & Lamont, *see* The Thomson Corp.
Warren Petroleum, *see* Dynegy Inc.
Warrick Industries, **31** 338
Warrington Products Ltd. *see* Canstar Sports Inc.
Warwick International Ltd., *see* Sequa Corp.
Warwick Valley Telephone Company, 55 382–84
Wasatch Gas Co., **6** 568
Wascana Energy Inc., 13 556–58
Washburn Graphics Inc., **23** 100
The Washington Companies, 33 442–45
Washington Federal, Inc., 17 525–27
Washington Football, Inc., 35 462–65
Washington Gas Light Company, 19 485–88
Washington Inventory Service, **30** 239
Washington Mutual, Inc., 17 528–31; 93 483–89 (upd.)
Washington National Corporation, 12 524–26
Washington Natural Gas Company, 9 539–41 *see also* Puget Sound Energy Inc.
The Washington Post Company, IV 688–90; 20 515–18 (upd.)
Washington Public Power Supply System, **50** 102
Washington Railway and Electric Company, **6** 552–53
Washington Scientific Industries, Inc., 17 532–34
Washington Sports Clubs *see* Town Sports International, Inc.
Washington Steel Corp., *see* Lukens Inc.
Washington Water Power Company, 6 595–98 *see also* Avista Corp.
Washtenaw Gas Company *see* MCN Corp.
Wassall Plc, 18 548–50
Waste Connections, Inc., 46 455–57
Waste Control Specialists LLC, *see* alhi, Inc.
Waste Holdings, Inc., 41 413–15
Waste Management, Inc., V 752–54
Water Pik Technologies, Inc., 34 498–501; 83 450-453 (upd.)
The Waterbury Companies, *see* Talley Industries, Inc.
Waterford Foods Plc, **59** 206
Waterford Wedgwood plc, 12 527–29; 34 493–97 (upd.)
Waterhouse Investor Services, Inc., 18 551–53
Waterman Marine Corporation, *see* International Shipholding Corporation, Inc.
The Waterman Pen Company *see* BIC Corp.
Watermark Paddlesports Inc., **76** 119
Waterpark Management Inc., **73** 231

WaterPro Supplies Corporation *see* Eastern Enterprises.
Waters Corporation, 43 453–57
Waterstone's, **42** 444 *see also* HMV Group plc.
Watkins-Johnson Company, 15 528–30
Watsco Inc., 52 397–400
Watson & Philip *see* Alldays plc.
Watson Group, **55** 52
Watson-Haas Lumber Company, **33** 257
Watson-Marlow Bredel, **59** 384
Watson Pharmaceuticals Inc., 16 527–29; 56 373–76 (upd.)
Watson Wyatt Worldwide, 42 427–30
Watt & Shand, **16** 61; **50** 107
Watt AG, **6** 491
The Watt Stopper, **21** 348, 350
Wattie Industries, **52** 141
Wattie's Ltd., 7 576–78
Watts Industries, Inc., 19 489–91
Watts of Lydney Group Ltd., 71 391–93
Watts/Silverstein, Inc., **24** 96
Waukesha Engine Servicenter, **6** 441
Wausau Sulphate Fibre Co. *see* Mosinee Paper Corp.
Wausau-Mosinee Paper Corporation, 60 328–31 (upd.)
Waverly, Inc., 16 530–32
Waverly Pharmaceutical Limited, **11** 208
Wawa Inc., 17 535–37; 78 449–52 (upd.)
The Wawanesa Mutual Insurance Company, 68 399–401
Waxman Industries, Inc., 9 542–44
Wayfinder Group Inc., **51** 265
Waymaker Oy, **55** 289
Wayne Home Equipment *see* Scott Fetzer Co.
WAZ Media Group, 82 419–24
WB *see* Warner Communications Inc.
WBI Holdings, Inc., **42** 249, 253
WCI Holdings Corporation, **V** 223; **41** 94
WCM Beteilingungs- und Grundbesitz AG, **58** 202, 205
WCPS Direct, Inc., **53** 359
WCRS Group plc *see* Aegis Group plc.
WD-40 Company, 18 554–57; 87 455–460 (upd.)
We Energies *see* Wisconsin Energy Corp.
WearGuard, *see* Aramark Corp.
The Weather Channel Companies, 52 401–04 *see also* Landmark Communications, Inc.
Weatherford International, Inc., 39 416–18
Weaver Popcorn Company, Inc., 89 491–93
Webb Corbett and Beswick, **38** 402
Webber Oil Company, 61 384–86
WeBco International LLC, **26** 530
Webco Securities, Inc., **37** 225
Weber, **16** 488
Weber Aircraft Inc., **41** 369
Weber et Broutin France, 66 363–65
Weber Metal, **30** 283–84
Weber-Stephen Products Co., 40 458–60
WebEx Communications, Inc., 81 419–23
WebLogic Inc., **36** 81
WebMD Corporation, 65 357–60
WebTrends Corporation, **76** 189
Webvan Group Inc., **38** 223
Weddingpages, Inc. *see* The Knot, Inc.
Wedgwood *see* Waterford Wedgewood Holdings PLC.
Weeres Industries Corporation, 52 405–07
Weetabix Limited, 61 387–89
Weg S.A., 78 453–56
Wegener NV, 53 360–62
Wegert Verwaltungs-GmbH and Co. Beteiligungs-KG, **24** 270
Wegmans Food Markets, Inc., 9 545–46; 41 416–18 (upd.)
Weichenwerk Brandenburg GmbH, **53** 352
Weider Health and Fitness, Inc., **38** 238
Weider Nutrition International, Inc., 29 498–501
Weight Watchers Gourmet Food Co., **43** 218
Weight Watchers International Inc., 12 530–32; 33 446–49 (upd.); 73 379–83 (upd.)
Weil Ceramics & Glass, **52** 148
Weil, Gotshal & Manges LLP, 55 385–87
Weiner's Stores, Inc., 33 450–53
Wieden + Kennedy, 75 403–05
Wienerberger AG, 70 361–63
Weingut Robert Weil, **65** 328, 330
The Weir Group PLC, 85 450–53
Weirton Steel Corporation, IV 236–38; 26 527–30 (upd.)
Weis Markets, Inc., 15 531–33; 84 422–426 (upd.)
The Weitz Company, Inc., 42 431–34
Welbilt Corp., 19 492–94; *see also* Enodis plc.
Welborn Transport Co., **39** 64, 65
Welch Engineering Ltd. *see* Swales & Associates, Inc.
Welch's, **25** 366
Welco Feed Manufacturing Company, **60** 316
Welcome Wagon International Inc., 82 425–28
Weleda AG, 78 457–61
The Welk Group, Inc., 78 462–66
Wella AG, III 68–70; 48 420–23 (upd.)
Welland Pipe Ltd., **51** 352
Wellborn Paint Manufacturing Company, **56** 98
WellChoice, Inc., 67 388–91 (upd.)
Wellco Enterprises, Inc., 84 427–430
Wellcome Foundation Ltd., I 713–15 *see also* GlaxoSmithKline plc.
Wellington Management Company, **23** 226 *see also* The Vanguard Group of Investment Companies.
Wellington Sears Co., **15** 247–48
Wellman, Inc., 8 561–62; 52 408–11 (upd.)
Wellness Co., Ltd., **IV** 716
WellPath Community Health Plans, Inc., **59** 140
WellPoint Health Networks Inc., 25 525–29
Wellrose Limited, **53** 333
Wells Fargo & Company, II 380–84; 12 533–37 (upd.); 38 483–92 (upd.) *see also* American Express Co.
Wells Fargo HSBC Trade Bank, **26** 203
Wells-Gardner Electronics Corporation, 43 458–61
Wells Rich Greene BDDP, 6 50–52
Wells' Dairy, Inc., 36 511–13
Wellspring Associates L.L.C., **16** 338
Wellspring Resources LLC, **42** 429
Welsh Associated Collieries Ltd., **31** 369
Welsh, Carson, Anderson & Stowe, **65** 128–30; **71** 117–19
Welsh Water *see* Hyder plc.
Wendel Investissement, **57** 381
Wendy's International, Inc., 8 563–65; 23 504–07 (upd.); 47 439–44 (upd.)
Wenger S.A., **21** 515; **74** 375–77
Wenmac Corp., **51** 368
Wenner Bread Products Inc., 80 411–15
Wenner Media, Inc., 32 506–09
Werco, Inc., **54** 7
Werkhof GmbH, *see* Standard Commercial Corp.
Werknet, *see* Randstad Holding n.v.
Werner Baldessarini Design GmbH, **48** 209
Werner Die & Stamping, **69** 38
Werner Enterprises, Inc., 26 531–33
Werner International, **14** 225
Weru Aktiengesellschaft, 18 558–61
Wesco Financial Corp., *see* Berkshire Hathaway Inc.
Wescot Decisison Systems, **6** 25
Weseley Software Development Corp. *see* RedPrairie Corp.
Wesley Jessen VisionCare Inc., **65** 274
Wesley's Quaker Maid, Inc. *see* Farmer Jack Supermarkets
Wesper Co., **26** 4
Wesray Capital Corporation, **47** 363
Wessanen *see* Koninklijke Wessanen nv.
Wessanen USA, **29** 480
Wesson/Peter Pan Foods Co., *see* Hunt-Wesson, Inc.
West Australia Land Holdings, Limited, *see* Bond Corporation Holdings Ltd.
West Bend Co., 14 546–48
West Coast Entertainment Corporation, 29 502–04
West Company, **53** 298
West Corporation, 42 435–37
West End Family Pharmacy, Inc., **15** 523
West Fraser Timber Co. Ltd., 17 538–40; 91 512–18 (upd.)
West Group, 34 502–06 (upd.)
West Harrison Gas & Electric Company *see* Cincinnati Gas & Electric Co.
West Linn Paper Company, 91 519–22
West Los Angeles Veterinary Medical Group, Inc., **58** 355
West Lynn Creamery, Inc., **26** 450

West Marine, Inc., 17 541–43; 90 438–42 (upd.)
West Missouri Power Company *see* UtiliCorp United Inc.; Aquilla, Inc.
West One Bancorp, 11 552–55 *see also* U.S. Bancorp.
West Penn Electric *see* Allegheny Power System, Inc.
West Penn Power Company, **38** 38–40
West Pharmaceutical Services, Inc., 42 438–41
West Point-Pepperell, Inc., 8 566–69 *see also* WestPoint Stevens Inc.; JPS Textile Group, Inc.
West Publishing Co., 7 579–81
West Shore Pipe Line Company, **70** 35
West TeleServices Corporation *see* West Corp.
West Texas LPG Pipeline Limited Partnership, **70** 35
West Texas Utilities Company, **6** 580
West Virginia Pulp and Paper Co. *see* Westvaco Corp.
Westaff Inc., 33 454–57
WestAir Holding Inc., **11** 300; **25** 423; **32** 336
Westamerica Bancorporation, 17 544–47
Westar Energy, Inc., 57 404–07 (upd.)
Westbrae Natural, Inc., *see* Hain Celestial Group, Inc.
Westchester Specialty Group, Inc., **26** 546
WestCoast Hospitality Corporation, 59 410–13
Westcon Group, Inc., 67 392–94
Westcor Realty, **57** 235
Westcorp Financial Services *see* WFS Financial Inc.
Westcott Communications Inc., **22** 442
Westdeutsche Landesbank Girozentrale, II 385–87; 46 458–61 (upd.)
Westec Corporation *see* Tech-Sym Corp.
Westell Technologies, Inc., 57 408–10
Westerbeke Corporation, 60 332–34
Western Air Lines, **I** 98, 100, 106; **21** 142
Western Areas Ltd., **61** 292
Western Atlas Inc., 12 538–40
Western Auto, **19** 223; **57** 11
Western Beef, Inc., 22 548–50
Western Brands Holding Company, Inc. *see* Crocs
Western Company of North America, 15 534–36
Western Digital Corporation, 25 530–32; 92 411–15 (upd.)
Western Edison, **6** 601
Western Electric Co., **II** 57, 66, 88, 101, 112; **49** 346
Western Electric Manufacturing Company, **54** 139
Western Empire Construction *see* CRSS Inc.
Western Equities, Inc. *see* Tech-Sym Corp.
Western Family Foods, **47** 457; **53** 21
Western Forest Products Ltd., **59** 161
Western Gas Resources, Inc., 45 435–37
Western Geophysical Co., *see* Western Atlas Inc.
Western Glucose Co., *see* American Maize-Products Co.
Western Graphics Corporation, **58** 314
Western Hotels Inc. *see* Westin Hotels and Resorts Worldwide.
Western International Communications, **35** 68
Western International Media, *see* Interpublic Group of Companies, Inc.
Western International University, *see* Apollo Group, Inc.
Western Kentucky Gas Company, **43** 56–57
Western Light & Telephone Company *see* Western Power & Gas Co.
Western Light and Power *see* Public Service Company of Colorado.
Western Lithograph Company *see* Consolidated Graphics, Inc.
Western Medical Services, **33** 456
Western Merchandisers, Inc., **29** 229–30
Western Metals Recycling LLC, **76** 130
Western Mining Corp., **IV** 61, 95
Western National Corp., *see* Conseco, Inc.
Western Newell Manufacturing Company *see* Newell Co.
Western Oil Sands Inc., 85 454–57
Western Pacific, **22** 220
Western Pioneer, Inc., *see* Kirby Corp.
Western Platinum, **21** 353
Western Platinum Ltd. *see* Lomin plc.
Western Power & Gas Company *see* Centel Corp.
Western Public Service Corporation, **6** 568
Western Publishing Group, Inc., 13 559–61 *see also* Thomson Corp.
Western Reflections LLC, **55** 291
Western Reserve Telephone Company *see* Alltel Corp.
Western Resources, Inc., 12 541–43
The WesterN SizzliN Corporation, 60 335–37
Western Slope Gas, **6** 559
Western States Fire Protection Company, **64** 30–32
Western Steel Group, **26** 407
Western Steer Family Restaurant, *see* Alex Lee Inc.
Western Union Corporation, **12** 9; **15** 72; **21** 25
Western Union Financial Services, Inc., 54 413–16
Western Wireless Corporation, 36 514–16
Westfälische Metall-Industrie Aktien-Gesellschaft *see* Hella KGaA Hueck & Co.
Westfälische Transport AG, **6** 426
Westfield Group, 69 366–69
Westin Hotels and Resorts Worldwide, 9 547–49; 29 505–08 (upd.)
Westinghouse Air Brake Company *see* Wabtec Corp.
Westinghouse Cubic Ltd., **19** 111
Westinghouse Electric Corporation, II 120–22; 12 544–47 (upd.) *see also* CBS Radio Group.
WestJet Airlines Ltd., 38 493–95
WestLB *see* Westdeutsche Landesbank Girozentrale.
Westmark Realty Advisors, **21** 97
Westmark Systems, Inc., **26** 268
Westminster Press Ltd. *see* Pearson plc.
Westmoreland Coal Company, 7 582–85
Weston Bakeries Ltd., *see* George Weston Ltd.
Weston Engineering, **53** 232
Weston Foods Inc. *see* George Weston Ltd.
Weston Presidio, **49** 189; **65** 257, 259
Westpac Banking Corporation, II 388–90; 48 424–27 (upd.)
WestPoint Stevens Inc., 16 533–36 *see also* JPS Textile Group, Inc.
Westport Resources Corporation, 63 439–41
Westport Woman, *see* Dress Barn, Inc.
Westvaco Corporation, IV 351–54; 19 495–99 (upd.) *see also* MeadWestvaco Corp.
The Westwood Group, **20** 54
Westwood One, Inc., 23 508–11
Westworld Resources Inc., **23** 41
Westwynn Theatres, **14** 87
The Wet Seal, Inc., 18 562–64; 70 353–57 (upd.)
Wet'n Wild Inc., **64** 94
Wetterau Incorporated, II 681–82 *see also* Supervalu Inc.
Wexpro Company, **6** 568–69
Weyco Group, Incorporated, 32 510–13
Weyerhaeuser Company, IV 355–56; 9 550–52 (upd.); 28 514–17 (upd.); 83 454-461 (upd.)
WFP *see* Western Forest Products Ltd.
WFS Financial Inc., 70 358–60
WFSC *see* World Fuel Services Corp.
WGBH Educational Foundation, 66 366–68
WGM Safety Corp., **40** 96–97
WH Smith PLC, 42 442–47 (upd.)
Wham-O, Inc., 61 390–93
Wharf Holdings Limited, **12** 367–68
Whatman plc, 46 462–65
Wheat, First Securities, **19** 304–05
Wheaton Industries, 8 570–73
Wheaton Science Products, 60 338–42 (upd.)
Wheel Horse, *see* Toro Co.
Wheel to Wheel Inc., **66** 315
Wheelabrator Technologies, Inc., 6 599–600; 60 343–45 (upd.)
Wheeled Coach Industries, Inc., **33** 105–06
Wheeling-Pittsburgh Corporation, 7 586–88; 58 360–64 (upd.)
Whemco, *see* Park Corp.
Where Magazines International, **57** 242
Wherehouse Entertainment Incorporated, 11 556–58
WHI Inc., **14** 545; **60** 326

Whippoorwill Associates Inc., **28** 55
Whirlpool Corporation, III 653–55; 12 548–50 (upd.); 59 414–19 (upd.)
Whitbread PLC, I 293–94; 20 519–22 (upd.); 52 412–17 (upd.)
White & Case LLP, 35 466–69
White Automotive, *see* ABC Appliance, Inc.
White Brothers, **39** 83, 84
White Castle Management Company, 12 551–53; 36 517–20 (upd.); 85 458–64 (upd.)
White Consolidated Industries Inc., 13 562–64 *see also* Electrolux.
The White House, Inc., 60 346–48
White Lily Foods Company, 88 435–38
White Mountain Freezers, **19** 360
White Mountains Insurance Group, Ltd., 48 428–31
White-New Idea, *see* AGCO Corp.
White Rock Corp., **27** 198; **43** 218
White Rose, Inc., 24 527–29
White Star Line, **23** 161
White Wave, 43 462–64
White-Westinghouse *see* White Consolidated Industries Inc.
Whitehall Jewellers, Inc., 82 429–34 (upd.)
WhiteWave Foods Company *see* Dean Foods Co.
Whitewear Manufacturing Company *see* Angelica Corp.
Whiting Petroleum Corporation, 81 424–27
Whitman Corporation, 10 553–55 (upd.) *see also* PepsiAmericas, Inc.
Whitman Education Group, Inc., 41 419–21
Whitmire Distribution *see* Cardinal Health, Inc.
Whitney Group, **40** 236–38
Whitney Holding Corporation, 21 522–24
Whitney Partners, L.L.C., **40** 237
Whittaker Corporation, I 544–46; 48 432–35 (upd.)
Whittard of Chelsea Plc, 61 394–97
Whittman-Hart Inc. *see* marchFIRST, Inc.
Whole Foods Market, Inc., 20 523–27; 50 530–34 (upd.)
Wholesale Cellular USA *see* Brightpoint, Inc.
The Wholesale Club, Inc., *see* Wal-Mart Stores, Inc.
Wholesome Foods, L.L.C., **32** 274, 277
Wholly Harvest, **19** 502
WHSC Direct, Inc., **53** 359
WHX Corporation, **58** 360
Whyte & Mackay Distillers Ltd., *see* Gallaher Group Plc.
Wicanders Group, **48** 119
Wicell Research Institute, **65** 367
Wickes Inc., V 221–23; 25 533–36 (upd.)
Wicor, Inc., **54** 419
Widmer Brothers Brewing Company, 76 379–82
Wiener Städtische, **58** 169
Wiesner, Inc., **22** 442
Wight Nurseries *see* Monrovia Nursery Co.
Wikimedia Foundation, Inc., 91 523–26
Wilbert, Inc., 56 377–80
Wilbur Chocolate Company, 66 369–71
Wilco Farm Stores, 93 490–93
Wild by Nature *see* King Cullen Grocery Co., Inc.
Wild Harvest, **56** 317
Wild Leitz G.m.b.H., **23** 83
Wild Oats Markets, Inc., 19 500–02; 41 422–25 (upd.)
WildBlue Communications Inc., **54** 406
Wilderness Systems *see* Confluence Holdings Corp.
Wildlife Conservation Society, 31 462–64
Wildlife Land Trust, **54** 172
Wildwater Kingdom, *see* Cedar Fair, L.P.
Wiles Group Ltd. *see* Hanson PLC.
Oy Wilh. Schauman AB *see* UPM-Kymmene
Wilh. Wilhelmsen ASA, 94 459–62
Wilhelm Karmann GmbH, 94 463–68
Wilhelm Weber GmbH, **22** 95
Wilhelm Wilhelmsen Ltd., **7** 40; **41** 42
Wilkinson Hardware Stores Ltd., 80 416–18
Wilkinson Sword Ltd., 60 349–52
Willamette Falls Electric Company *see* Portland General Corp.
Willamette Industries, Inc., IV 357–59; 31 465–68 (upd.) *see also* Weyerhaeuser Co.
Willamette Valley Vineyards, Inc., 85 465–69
Willbros Group, Inc., 56 381–83
Willcox & Gibbs Sewing Machine Co., **15** 384
Willey Brothers, Inc. *see* BrandPartners Group, Inc.
William Benton Foundation, *see* Encyclopaedia Britannica, Inc.
The William Brooks Shoe Company *see* Rocky Shoes & Boots, Inc.
William Byrd Press Inc., **23** 100
William Cory & Son Ltd., **6** 417
William Esty Company, **16** 72
William George Company, **32** 519
William Grant & Sons Ltd., 60 353–55
William Hewlett, **41** 117
William Hill Organization Limited, 49 449–52
William Hodges & Company, **33** 150
William Hollins & Company Ltd., **44** 105
William L. Bonnell Company, Inc., 66 372–74
William Lyon Homes, 59 420–22
William Morris Agency, Inc., 23 512–14
William P. Young Contruction, **43** 400
William Penn Life Insurance Company of New York, *see* Legal & General Group plc.
William Reed Publishing Ltd., 78 467–70
William Underwood Co., *see* Pet Inc.
William Zinsser & Company, Inc., 58 365–67
Williams & Connolly LLP, 47 445–48
Williams & Wilkins *see* Waverly, Inc.
Williams Advanced Materials Inc., *see* Brush Wellman Inc.
Williams Communications Group, Inc., 34 507–10
The Williams Companies, Inc., IV 575–76; 31 469–72 (upd.)
Williams Electronics Games, Inc., **15** 539
The Williams Manufacturing Company, *see* Escalade, Inc.
Williams/Nintendo Inc., **15** 537
Williams Oil-O-Matic Heating Corporation, **21** 42
Williams plc, **44** 255
Williams Printing Company *see* Graphic Industries Inc.
Williams Scotsman, Inc., 65 361–64
Williams-Sonoma, Inc., 17 548–50; 44 447–50 (upd.)
Williamsburg Restoration, Incorporated, **53** 106
Williamson-Dickie Manufacturing Company, 14 549–50; 45 438–41 (upd.)
Williamsport Barber and Beauty Corp., **60** 287
Willie G's, **15** 279
Willis Corroon Group plc, 25 537–39
Willis Group Holdings Ltd., **73** 36
Willis Stein & Partners, **21** 404; **58** 318, 321; **73** 397
Williston Basin Interstate Pipeline Company, *see* MDU Resources Group, Inc.; WBI Holdings, Inc.
Wilmington Trust Corporation, 25 540–43
Wilsdorf & Davis, *see* Montres Rolex S.A.
Wilshire Real Estate Investment Trust Inc., **30** 223
Wilshire Restaurant Group Inc., **28** 258
Wilson Bowden Plc, 45 442–44
Wilson Brothers, *see* Triarc Companies, Inc.
Wilson Foods Corp., *see* Doskocil Companies, Inc.
Wilson Greatbatch Technologies Ltd *see* Greatbatch Inc.
Wilson Jones Company, **7** 4–5
Wilson Sonsini Goodrich & Rosati, 34 511–13
Wilson Sporting Goods Company, 24 530–32; 84 431–436 (upd.)
Wilson's Supermarkets, *see* Hannaford Bros. Co.
Wilsons The Leather Experts Inc., 21 525–27; 58 368–71 (upd.)
Wimbledon Tennis Championships *see* The All England Lawn Tennis & Croquet Club.
Win-Chance Foods, *see* H.J. Heinz Co.
Winbond Electronics Corporation, 74 389–91
Wincanton plc, 52 418–20
Winchell's Donut Houses Operating Company, L.P., 60 356–59

WinCo Foods Inc., 60 360–63
Wincor Nixdorf Holding GmbH, 69 370–73 (upd.)
Wind River Systems, Inc., 37 419–22
Windmere Corporation, 16 537–39 *see also* Applica Inc.
Windmere-Durable Holdings, Inc., **30** 404
WindowVisions, Inc., **29** 288
Windsong Exports, **52** 429
Windsor Forestry Tools, Inc., **48** 59
Windstar Sail Cruises *see* Carnival Corp.
Windstream Corporation, 83 462-465
Windsurfing International, **23** 55
Windswept Environmental Group, Inc., 62 389–92
Windward Capital Partners, **28** 152, 154
The Wine Group, Inc., 39 419–21
Winegard Company, 56 384–87
Winfire, Inc., **37** 194
Wingate Partners, *see* United Stationers Inc.
Winget Ltd. *see* Seddon Group Ltd.
Wings & Wheels Express, Inc., *see* Air Express International Corp.
WingspanBank.com, **38** 270
Winkelman Stores, Inc., *see* Petrie Stores Corp.
Winlet Fashions, **22** 223
Winmark Corporation, 74 392–95
Winn-Dixie Stores, Inc., II 683–84; 21 528–30 (upd.); 59 423–27 (upd.)
Winnebago Industries Inc., 7 589–91; 27 509–12 (upd.)
Winners Apparel Ltd. *see* The TJX Companies, Inc.
Winning International, **21** 403
WinsLoew Furniture, Inc., 21 531–33 *see also* Brown Jordan International Inc.
Winston & Strawn, 35 470–73
Winston Furniture Company, Inc., **21** 531–33
Winter Hill Frozen Foods and Services, **55** 82
WinterBrook Corp., **26** 326
Winterflood Securities Limited, **39** 89, 91
Wintershall AG, **IV** 485; **38** 408
Winterthur Group, III 402–04; 68 402–05 (upd.)
Winyah Concrete & Block, **50** 49
Wipro Limited, 43 465–68
Wire and Plastic Products PLC *see* WPP Group PLC.
Wireless Hong Kong *see* Hong Kong Telecommunications Ltd.
Wireless Management Company, **11** 12
The Wiremold Company, 81 428–34
Wiretel, **76** 326–27
Wiron Prefabricados Modulares, S.A., **65** 363
Wirtz Corporation, 72 374–76
Wisconsin Alumni Research Foundation, 65 365–68
Wisconsin Bell, Inc., 14 551–53 *see also* AT&T Corp.
Wisconsin Central Transportation Corporation, 24 533–36
Wisconsin Dairies, 7 592–93
Wisconsin Energy Corporation, 6 601–03; 54 417–21 (upd.)
Wisconsin Gas Company, **17** 22–23
Wisconsin Power and Light, **22** 13; **39** 260
Wisconsin Public Service Corporation, 9 553–54 *see also* WPS Resources Corp.
Wisconsin Steel, *see* Envirodyne Industries, Inc.
Wisconsin Wire and Steel, *see* FinishMaster, Inc.; Maxco Inc.
Wise Foods, Inc., 79 468–71
Wise Solutions, Inc. *see* Altiris, Inc.
Wispark Corporation, **6** 601, 603
Wistron Corporation *see* Acer Inc.
Wisvest Corporation, **6** 601, 603
WiSys Technology Foundation, **65** 367
Witco Corporation, I 404–06; 16 540–43 (upd.) *see also* Chemtura Corp.
Wite-Out Products, Inc., **23** 56–57
Witech Corporation, **6** 601, 603
Withington Company *see* Sparton Corp.
Witness Systems, Inc., 87 461–465
Wittgensteiner Kliniken Gruppe, **56** 141
The Wiz *see* Cablevision Electronic Instruments, Inc.
Wizards of the Coast Inc., 24 537–40
WizardWorks Group, Inc., **31** 238–39
WL Ross & Co., **67** 125
WLIW-TV *see* Educational Broadcasting Corp.
WLR Foods, Inc., 21 534–36
Wm. B. Reily & Company Inc., 58 372–74
WM Investment Company, **34** 512
Wm. Morrison Supermarkets PLC, 38 496–98
Wm. Underwood Company, **40** 53
Wm. Wrigley Jr. Company, 7 594–97; 58 375–79 (upd.)
WMC, Limited, 43 469–72
WMF *see* Württembergische Metallwarenfabrik AG (WMF).
WMS Industries, Inc., 15 537–39; 53 363–66 (upd.)
WMX Technologies Inc., 17 551–54
Wolfe & Associates, **25** 434
Wolfgang Puck Worldwide, Inc., 26 534–36; 70 364–67 (upd.)
Wolohan Lumber Co., 19 503–05 *see also* Lanoga Corp.
Wolseley plc, 64 409–12
Wolters Kluwer NV, 14 554–56; 33 458–61 (upd.)
The Wolverhampton & Dudley Breweries, PLC, 57 411–14
Wolverine Equities Company, **62** 341
Wolverine Insurance Co., **26** 487
Wolverine Tube Inc., 23 515–17
Wolverine World Wide, Inc., 16 544–47; 59 428–33 (upd.)
Womacks Saloon and Gaming Parlor, **53** 91
Womble Carlyle Sandridge & Rice, PLLC, 52 421–24
Women's Specialty Retailing Group *see* Casual Corner Group, Inc.
Women's World, **15** 96
Wonderware Corp., **22** 374
Wood Hall Trust plc, I 592–93
Wood-Metal Industries, Inc. *see* Wood-Mode, Inc.
Wood-Mode, Inc., 23 518–20
Wood River Oil and Refining Company, *see* Ingram Industries, Inc.
Wood Wyant Inc., **30** 496–98
Woodbridge Winery, **50** 388
Woodcraft Industries Inc., 61 398–400
Woodland Publishing, Inc., **37** 286
Woodlands Venture Capital Co., *see* Mitchell Energy and Development Corp.
Woodmen of the World Life Insurance Society, **66** 227–28
Woods Equipment Company, **32** 28
Woodside Petroleum, **63** 440
Woodside Travel Trust, **26** 310
Woodward-Clyde Group Inc., **45** 421
Woodward Foodservice Ltd. *see* The Big Food Group plc.
Woodward Governor Company, 13 565–68; 49 453–57 (upd.)
Woolco Department Stores *see* Woolworth Corp.
Woolrich Inc., 62 393–96
The Woolwich plc, 30 492–95
Woolworth Corporation, V 224–27; 20 528–32 (upd.) *see also* Kingfisher plc; Venator Group Inc.
Woolworths Group plc, 83 466-473
Woolworth Holdings *see* Kingfisher plc.
Woolworth's Ltd., *see* Kingfisher plc.
Word, Inc., *see* Thomas Nelson Inc.
Word Publishing, **71** 401
WordPerfect Corporation, 10 556–59 *see also* Corel Corp.
WordStar International, **15** 149; **43** 151 *see also* The Learning Company Inc.
Workflow Management, Inc., 65 369–72
Working Assets Funding Service, 43 473–76
Working Title Films, **23** 389
Workman Publishing Company, Inc., 70 368–71
Workscape Inc., **42** 430
World Acceptance Corporation, 57 415–18
World Airways, *see* WorldCorp, Inc.
World Bank Group, 33 462–65
World Book Group *see* Scott Fetzer Co.
World Book, Inc., 12 554–56
World Championship Wrestling (WCW), **32** 516
World Color Press Inc., 12 557–59 *see also* Quebecor Inc.
World Commerce Corporation, **25** 461
World Duty Free Americas, Inc., 29 509–12 (upd.)
World Duty Free plc, **33** 59
World Flight Crew Services, Inc., *see* WorldCorp, Inc.
World Fuel Services Corporation, 47 449–51
World Machinery Company, **45** 170–71
World Minerals Inc., **60** 16

World Online, **48** 398–39
World Poker Tour, LLC, **51** 205, 207
World Publications, LLC, 65 373–75
World Savings and Loan, **19** 412; **47** 159–60
World Trade Corporation *see* International Business Machines Corp.
World Trans, Inc., **33** 105
World Vision International, Inc., 93 494–97
World Wide Technology, Inc., 94 469–72
World Wrestling Federation Entertainment, Inc., 32 514–17
The World's Biggest Bookstore, **58** 185
World's Finest Chocolate Inc., 39 422–24
WorldCom, Inc. *see* MCI WorldCom, Inc.
WorldCorp, Inc., 10 560–62
The WorldMark Club, **33** 409
Worldmark of Wisconsin Inc. *see* Brady Corporation< /idx>
Worlds of Fun, *see* Cedar Fair, L.P.
Worlds of Wonder, Inc., **25** 381; **26** 548
Worldview Systems Corporation, **26** 428; **46** 434
WorldWay Corporation, **16** 41
Worldwide Fiber Inc., **46** 267
Worldwide Insurance Co., **48** 9
Worldwide Restaurant Concepts, Inc., 47 452–55
Worldwide Semiconductor Manufacturing Co., **47** 386
Worldwide Underwriters Insurance Co., *see* Capital Holding Corp.
Wormald International Ltd., *see* Grinnell Corp.
Worms et Cie, 27 513–15 *see also* Sequana Capital.
Worthen Banking Corporation, **15** 60
Worthington Foods, Inc., 14 557–59 *see also* Kellogg Co.
Worthington Industries, Inc., 7 598–600; 21 537–40 (upd.)
WP Spinnaker Holdings, Inc. *see* Spinnaker Exploration Co.
WPL Holdings, 6 604–06
WPM *see* Wall Paper Manufacturers.
WPP Group plc, 6 53–54; 48 440–42 (upd.) *see also* Ogilvy Group Inc.
WPS Resources Corporation, 53 367–70 (upd.)
Wrafton Laboratories Ltd., **59** 332
WRG *see* Wells Rich Greene BDDP.
Wright & Company Realtors, **21** 257
Wright Express Corporation, 80 419–22
Wright Group Publishing Inc., *see* Tribune Co.
Wright Medical Group, Inc., 61 401–05
Wright Plastic Products, *see* FinishMaster, Inc.; Maxco Inc.
Writers Guild of America, West, Inc., 92 416–20
WS Atkins Plc, 45 445–47
WSI *see* Weather Services International.
WSMC *see* Worldwide Semiconductor Manufacturing Co.
WSMP, Inc., **29** 202
WTD Industries, Inc., 20 533–36
Wunderman, 86 429–32
Württembergische Metallwarenfabrik AG (WMF), 60 364–69
WVPP *see* Westvaco Corp.
WVT Communications *see* Warwick Valley Telephone Co.
WWT, Inc., **58** 371
Wyant Corporation, 30 496–98
Wycombe Bus Company, **28** 155–56
Wyeth, 50 535–39 (upd.)
Wyeth-Ayerst Laboratories, **25** 477
Wyle Electronics, 14 560–62 *see also* Arrow Electronics, Inc.
Wyman-Gordon Company, 14 563–65
Wymar, **76** 347
Wynkoop Brewing Company, **43** 407
Wynn's International, Inc., 33 466–70
Wyse Technology, Inc., 15 540–42

X

X-Acto, *see* Hunt Manufacturing Co.
X-Rite, Inc., 48 443–46
XA Systems Corporation, *see* Compuware Corp.
Xaver Fendt GmbH & Co. KG *see* AGCO Corp.
XCare.net, Inc. *see* Quovadx Inc.
Xcel Energy Inc., 73 384–89 (upd.)
Xcor International, **15** 538; **53** 364–65
Xeikon NV, 26 540–42
Xenell Corporation, **48** 358
Xenotech, *see* Ballantyne of Omaha, Inc.
Xerium Technologies, Inc., 94 473–76
Xeron, Inc., **56** 62
Xerox Corporation, III 171–73; 6 288–90 (upd.); 26 543–47 (upd.); 69 374–80 (upd.)
Xetra, **59** 151
Xiamen Airlines, **33** 99
Xilinx, Inc., 16 548–50; 82 435–39 (upd.)
Xing Technology Corp., **53** 282
XM Satellite Radio Holdings, Inc., 69 381–84
XMR, Inc., **42** 361
Xpect First Aid Corp., **51** 76
Xpert Recruitment, Ltd., **26** 240
Xpress Automotive Group, Inc., **24** 339
XR Ventures LLC, **48** 446
XRAL Storage and Terminaling Co., **IV** 411
Xros, Inc., **36** 353
Xstrata PLC, 73 390–93
XTO Energy Inc., 52 425–27
Xtra Limited New Zealand, **54** 355–57
Xuzhuo Liebherr Concrete Machinery Co. Ltd., **64** 241
Xynetics, *see* General Signal Corp.

Y

Yacimientos Petrolíferos Fiscales Sociedad Anónima *see* Repsol-YPF SA.
Yageo Corporation, 16 551–53
Yahoo! Inc., 27 516–19; 70 372–75 (upd.)
Yakima Products Inc., **76** 120
Yale and Valor, PLC, **50** 134–35
Yamada Denki Co., Ltd., 85 470–73
Yamagata Enterprises, **26** 310
Yamaha Corporation, III 656–59; 16 554–58 (upd.); 40 461–66 (upd.)
Yamaha Motor Co., Ltd., **59** 393, 397
Yamaichi Capital Management, **42** 349
Yamaichi Securities Company, Limited, II 458–59
Yamamotoyama Co., Ltd., **50** 449
Yamanouchi Consumer Inc., **39** 361
Yamanouchi Pharmaceutical Co., Ltd., **12** 444–45; **38** 93
Yamato Transport Co. Ltd., V 536–38; 49 458–61 (upd.)
Yamazaki Baking Co., Ltd., 58 380–82
Yanbian Industrial Technology Training Institute, **12** 294
Yangzhou Motor Coach Manufacturing Co., **34** 132
The Yankee Candle Company, Inc., 37 423–26; 38 192
Yankee Gas Services Company, **48** 305
YankeeNets LLC, 35 474–77
Yankton Gas Company, **6** 524
Yara International ASA, 94 477–81
Yarnell Ice Cream Company, Inc., 92 421–24
Yasuda Fire and Marine Insurance Company, Limited, III 405–07
Yasuda Mutual Life Insurance Company, III 408–09; 39 425–28 (upd.)
The Yasuda Trust and Banking Company, Limited, II 391–92; 17 555–57 (upd.)
The Yates Companies, Inc., 62 397–99
Yell Group PLC, 79 472–75
Yellow Corporation, 14 566–68; 45 448–51 (upd.) *see also* YRC Worldwide Inc.
Yellow Freight System, Inc. of Deleware, V 539–41
Yeo Hiap Seng Malaysia Bhd., 75 406–09
YES! Entertainment Corporation, 26 548–50
YES Solutions *see* Bookspan.
Yeti Cycles Inc., **19** 385
YGK Inc. *see* Cincinnati Gas & Electric Co.
Yhtyneet Paperitehtaat Oy *see* United Paper Mills Ltd.
YHS *see* Yeo Hiap Seng Malaysia Bhd.
YMCA of the USA, 31 473–76
Ymos A.G., **IV** 53; **26** 83
YOCREAM International, Inc., 47 456–58
Yogen Fruz World-Wide, Inc. *see* CoolBrands International Inc.
Yokado Co. Ltd *see* Ito-Yokado Co. Ltd.
Yoko Sangyo Co., **64** 35
Yokohama Bottle Plant, **21** 319
The Yokohama Rubber Company, Limited, V 254–56; 19 506–09 (upd.); 91 527–33 (upd.)
Yokohama Tokyu Deppartment Store Co., Ltd., **32** 457
Yondenko Corporation, **60** 272

Yongpyong Resort Co., **61** 342
Yoosung Enterprise Co., Ltd., **23** 269
Yoplait S.A. *see* Sodiaal S.A.
The York Bank and Trust Company, **16** 14; **43** 8
The York Group, Inc., 50 540–43
York International Corp., 13 569–71; *see also* Johnson Controls, Inc.
York Research Corporation, 35 478–80
York Wastewater Consultants, Inc., **6** 441
Yorkshire Energies, **45** 21
Yorkshire Group, **61** 133
Yorkshire Television Ltd., **IV** 659
Yorkshire Water Services Ltd. *see* Kelda Group plc.
Yoshinoya D & C Company Ltd., 88 439–42
Youbet.com, Inc., 77 485–88
Young & Co.'s Brewery, P.L.C., 38 499–502
Young & Rubicam, Inc., I 36–38; 22 551–54 (upd.); 66 375–78 (upd.)
Young Broadcasting Inc., 40 467–69
Young Chang Akki Company, **51** 201
Young Innovations, Inc., 44 451–53
Young's Bluecrest Seafood Holdings Ltd., 81 435–39
Young's Market Company, LLC, 32 518–20
Youngjin Pharmaceutical, **62** 221
Youngstown Sheet & Tube, *see* LTV Corp.
Younkers, 76 19 510–12; 383–86 (upd.)
Your Communications Limited, **52** 372, 374
Youth Services International, Inc., 21 541–43; 30 146
Youthtrack, Inc., **29** 399–400
YouTube, Inc., 90 443–46
YPF Sociedad Anónima, IV 577–78 *see also* Repsol-YPF S.A.
YRC Worldwide Inc., 90 447–55 (upd.)
Yside Investment Group, **16** 196
YTT *see* Yorkshire-Tyne Tees Television.
The Yucaipa Cos., 17 558–62
Yue Yuen Industrial (Holdings) Ltd. *see* Pou Chen Corporation
Yugraneft, **49** 306
Yukon Pacific Corporation, *see* CSX Corp.
YUKOS, **49** 305–06 *see also* OAO NK YUKOS.
Yule Catto & Company plc, 54 422–25
Yum! Brands Inc., 58 383–85
Yutaka Co., Ltd., **55** 48
Yves Bertelin SAS., **72** 35
Yves Rocher *see* Laboratoires de Biologie Végétale Yves Rocher.
Yves Soulié, **II** 266
YWCA of the U.S.A., 45 452–54

Z

Z Media, Inc., **49** 433
Z-Spanish Media Corp., **35** 220; **41** 151
Z.C. Mines, **IV** 61
Zacky Farms LLC, 74 396–98
Zagara's Inc., **35** 190–91
Zale Corporation, 16 559–61; 40 470–74 (upd.); 91 534–41 (upd.)
Zambia Industrial and Mining Corporation Ltd., IV 239–41
Zamboni *see* Frank J. Zamboni & Co., Inc.
Zanett, Inc., 92 425–28
Zanussi, *see* Electrolux AB.
Zany Brainy, Inc., 31 477–79
Zap, Inc., **25** 546
Zapata Corporation, 25 544–46
Zapata Gulf Marine Corporation, **11** 524
Zappos.com, Inc., 73 394–96
Zara International, Inc., 83 474-477
Zaring Premier Homes, **41** 133
Zastron Electronic (Shenzhen) Co. Ltd., **61** 233
Zatarain's, Inc., 64 413–15
Zausner, *see* Bongrain S.A.
Zayre Corp., *see* The TJX Companies, Inc.
ZCE Platinum, **63** 40
ZCMI *see* Zion's Cooperative Mercantile Institution.
ZDF, **41** 28–29
ZDNet, **36** 523
Zealand Mines S.A., **23** 41
Zebco Corp. *see* W.C. Bradley Co.
Zebra Technologies Corporation, 14 569–71; 53 371–74 (upd.)
Zecco, Inc., **6** 441
Zed Group, 93 498–501
Zee Medical, Inc., **47** 235
ZeFer, **63** 151
Zell Bros., *see* Zale Corp.
Zellers *see* Hudson's Bay Co.
Zellstoff-und Papierfabrik Rosenthal Gmbh & Co KG., **64** 275
Zeneca Group PLC, 21 544–46 *see also* AstraZeneca PLC.
Zengine, Inc., **41** 258–59
Zenit Bank, **45** 322
Zenith Data Systems, Inc., 10 563–65
Zenith Electronics Corporation, II 123–25; 13 572–75 (upd.); 34 514–19 (upd.); 89 494–502 (upd.)
Zenith Media, **42** 330–31
Zentralsparkasse und Kommerzialbank Wien, **23** 37
Zentronics, **19** 313
Zep Manufacturing Company, **54** 252, 254
Zeppelin Luftschifftechnik GmbH, **48** 450
Zerex, **50** 48
Zergo Holdings, **42** 24–25
ZERO Corporation, 17 563–65; 88 443–47 (upd.)
Zero First Co Ltd., **62** 245
Zero Plus Dialing, Inc. *see* Billing Concepts Corp.
Zetor s.p., **21** 175
Zeus Components, Inc., *see* Arrow Electronics, Inc.
Zexel Valeo Compressor USA Inc. *see* Valeo.
ZF Friedrichshafen AG, 48 447–51
Zhenjiang Zhengmao Hitachi Zosen Machinery Co. Ltd., **53** 173
Zhong Yue Highsonic Electron Company, **62** 150
Zhongbei Building Material Products Company, **26** 510
Zhongde Brewery, **49** 417
Zicam LLC *see* Matrixx Initiatives, Inc.
Ziebart International Corporation, 30 499–501; 66 379–82 (upd.)
The Ziegler Companies, Inc., 24 541–45; 63 442–48 (upd.)
Ziff Davis Media Inc., 12 560–63; 36 521–26 (upd.); 73 397–403 (upd.)
Zignago Vetro S.p.A., **67** 210–12
Zila, Inc., 46 466–69
Zildjian *see* Avedis Zildjian Co.
Zilkha & Company, **12** 72
ZiLOG, Inc., 15 543–45; 72 377–80 (upd.)
Zimmer Holdings, Inc., 45 455–57
Zinc Products Company, **30** 39
Zindart Ltd., 60 370–72
Zingerman's Community of Businesses, 68 406–08
Zinifex Ltd., 85 474–77
Zinsser *see* William Zinsser & Company, Inc.
Zio's Italian Kitchens *see* Mazzio's Corp.
Zion Foods, **23** 408
Zion's Cooperative Mercantile Institution, 33 471–74
Zions Bancorporation, 12 564–66; 53 375–78 (upd.)
Zipcar, Inc., 92 429–32
Zippo Manufacturing Company, 18 565–68; 71 394–99 (upd.)
Zipps Drive-Thru, Inc., *see* Rally's.
Zodiac S.A., 36 527–30
Zolfo Cooper LLC, **57** 219
Zoll Foods, **55** 366
Zoloto Mining Ltd., **38** 231
Zoltek Companies, Inc., 37 427–30
Zomba Records Ltd., 52 428–31
Zondervan Corporation, 24 546–49; 71 400–04 (upd.)
Zones, Inc., 67 395–97
Zoom Technologies, Inc., 18 569–71; 53 379–82 (upd.)
Zoran Corporation, 77 489–92
Zotos International, Inc., *see* Shiseido Company, Ltd.
ZPT Radom, **23** 427
Zuari Cement, **40** 107, 109
Zuellig Group N.A., Inc., **46** 226
Zuffa L.L.C., 89 503–07
Zuivelcooperatie De Seven Provincien UA, **59** 194
Zuka Juice, **47** 201
Zumiez, Inc., 77 493–96
Zumtobel AG, 50 544–48
Zurich Financial Services, III 410–12; 42 448–53 (upd.); 93 502–10 (upd.)
Zurich Insurance Group, **15** 257
Zvezda Design Bureau, **61** 197
Zweckform Büro-Produkte G.m.b.H., **49** 38
Zycad Corp., **11** 489–91; **69** 340–41
Zycon Corporation, *see* Hadco Corp.
Zygo Corporation, 42 454–57
ZymoGenetics Inc., **61** 266

Zytec Corporation, **19 513–15** *see also* Artesyn Technologies Inc.

Index to Industries

Accounting

American Institute of Certified Public Accountants (AICPA), 44
Andersen, 29 (upd.); 68 (upd.)
Automatic Data Processing, Inc., III; 9 (upd.); 47 (upd.)
CROSSMARK, 79
Deloitte Touche Tohmatsu International, 9; 29 (upd.)
Ernst & Young, 9; 29 (upd.)
FTI Consulting, Inc., 77
Grant Thornton International, 57
Huron Consulting Group Inc., 87
KPMG International, 33 (upd.)
L.S. Starrett Co., 13
McLane Company, Inc., 13
NCO Group, Inc., 42
Paychex, Inc., 15; 46 (upd.)
PKF International 78
Plante & Moran, LLP, 71
PRG-Schultz International, Inc., 73
PricewaterhouseCoopers, 9; 29 (upd.)
Resources Connection, Inc., 81
Robert Wood Johnson Foundation, 35
Saffery Champness, 80
Schenck Business Solutions, 88
StarTek, Inc., 79
Travelzoo Inc., 79
Univision Communications Inc., 24; 83 (upd.)

Advertising & Other Business Services

ABM Industries Incorporated, 25 (upd.)
AchieveGlobal Inc., 90
Ackerley Communications, Inc., 9
ACNielsen Corporation, 13; 38 (upd.)
Acosta Sales and Marketing Company, Inc., 77
Acsys, Inc., 44
Adecco S.A., 36 (upd.)
Adia S.A., 6
Administaff, Inc., 52
The Advertising Council, Inc., 76
The Advisory Board Company, 80
Advo, Inc., 6; 53 (upd.)
Aegis Group plc, 6
Affiliated Computer Services, Inc., 61
AHL Services, Inc., 27
Alloy, Inc., 55
Amdocs Ltd., 47
American Building Maintenance Industries, Inc., 6
American Library Association, 86
The American Society of Composers, Authors and Publishers (ASCAP), 29
Amey Plc, 47
Analysts International Corporation, 36
aQuantive, Inc., 81
The Arbitron Company, 38
Ariba, Inc., 57
Armor Holdings, Inc., 27
Asatsu-DK Inc., 82
Ashtead Group plc, 34
The Associated Press, 13
Avalon Correctional Services, Inc., 75
Bain & Company, 55
Barrett Business Services, Inc., 16
Barton Protective Services Inc., 53
Bates Worldwide, Inc., 14; 33 (upd.)
Bearings, Inc., 13
Berlitz International, Inc., 13
Bernard Hodes Group Inc., 86
Bernstein-Rein, 92
Big Flower Press Holdings, Inc., 21
Billing Concepts, Inc., 26; 72 (upd.)
The BISYS Group, Inc., 73
Boron, LePore & Associates, Inc., 45
The Boston Consulting Group, 58
Bozell Worldwide Inc., 25
BrandPartners Group, Inc., 58
Bright Horizons Family Solutions, Inc., 31
Broadcast Music Inc., 23; 90 (upd.)
Buck Consultants, Inc., 55
Bureau Veritas SA, 55
Burke, Inc., 88
Burns International Services Corporation, 13; 41 (upd.)
Cambridge Technology Partners, Inc., 36
Campbell-Ewald Advertising, 86
Campbell-Mithun-Esty, Inc., 16
Cannon Design, 63
Capita Group PLC, 69
Cardtronics, Inc., 93
Career Education Corporation, 45
Carmichael Lynch Inc., 28
Cash Systems, Inc., 93
Cazenove Group plc, 72
CCC Information Services Group Inc., 74
CDI Corporation, 6; 54 (upd.)
Central Parking Corporation, 18
Century Business Services, Inc., 52
Chancellor Beacon Academies, Inc., 53
ChartHouse International Learning Corporation, 49
Chiat/Day Inc. Advertising, 11
Chicago Board of Trade, 41
Chisholm-Mingo Group, Inc., 41
Christie's International plc, 15; 39 (upd.)
Cintas Corporation, 21
CMG Worldwide, Inc., 89
COMFORCE Corporation, 40
Command Security Corporation, 57
Computer Learning Centers, Inc., 26
Concentra Inc., 71

Corporate Express, Inc., 47 (upd.)
CoolSavings, Inc., 77
The Corporate Executive Board Company, 89
CORT Business Services Corporation, 26
Cox Enterprises, Inc., 22 (upd.)
CRA International, Inc., 93
craigslist, inc., 89
Creative Artists Agency LLC, 38
Crispin Porter + Bogusky, 83
CSG Systems International, Inc., 75
Cyrk Inc., 19
Daiko Advertising Inc., 79
Dale Carnegie & Associates Inc. 28; 78 (upd.)
D'Arcy Masius Benton & Bowles, Inc., 6; 32 (upd.)
Dawson Holdings PLC, 43
DDB Needham Worldwide, 14
Deluxe Corporation, 22 (upd.); 73 (upd.)
Dentsu Inc., I; 16 (upd.); 40 (upd.)
Deutsch, Inc., 42
Deutsche Post AG, 29
DeVito/Verdi, 85
Dewberry 78
DHL Worldwide Network S.A./N.V., 69 (upd.)
Digitas Inc., 81
DoubleClick Inc., 46
Draftfcb, 94
Drake Beam Morin, Inc., 44
The Dun & Bradstreet Corporation, 61 (upd.)
Earl Scheib, Inc., 32
eBay Inc., 67 (upd.)
EBSCO Industries, Inc., 17
Ecolab Inc., I; 13 (upd.); 34 (upd.); 85 (upd.)
Ecology and Environment, Inc., 39
Edelman, 62
Edison Schools Inc., 37
Educate Inc., 86 (upd.)
Education Management Corporation, 35
Electro Rent Corporation, 58
Employee Solutions, Inc., 18
Ennis Business Forms, Inc., 21
Equifax Inc., 6; 28 (upd.); 90 (upd.)
Equity Marketing, Inc., 26
ERLY Industries Inc., 17
Euro RSCG Worldwide S.A., 13
Expedia, Inc., 58
Fallon Worldwide, 22; 71 (upd.)
FileNet Corporation, 62
Finarte Casa d'Aste S.p.A., 93
Fiserv, Inc., 33 (upd.)
FlightSafety International, Inc., 29 (upd.)
Florists' Transworld Delivery, Inc., 28
Foote, Cone & Belding Worldwide, I; 66 (upd.)
Forrester Research, Inc., 54
Frankel & Co., 39
Franklin Covey Company, 37 (upd.)
Freeze.com LLC, 77
Frost & Sullivan, Inc., 53
FTI Consulting, Inc., 77
Gage Marketing Group, 26
The Gallup Organization, 37
Gartner, Inc., 21; 94 (upd.)
GEMA (Gesellschaft für musikalische Aufführungs- und mechanische Vervielfältigungsrechte), 70
General Employment Enterprises, Inc., 87
George P. Johnson Company, 60
George S. May International Company, 55
Gevity HR, Inc., 63
GfK Aktiengesellschaft, 49
Glotel plc, 53
Golin/Harris International, Inc., 88
Goodby Silverstein & Partners, Inc., 75
Grey Global Group Inc., 6; 66 (upd.)
Group 4 Falck A/S, 42
Groupe Crit S.A., 74
Groupe Jean-Claude Darmon, 44
GSD&M Advertising, 44
GSD&M's Idea City, 90
GSI Commerce, Inc., 67
Guardsmark, L.L.C., 77
Gwathmey Siegel & Associates Architects LLC, 26
Ha-Lo Industries, Inc., 27
Hakuhodo, Inc., 6; 42 (upd.)
Hall, Kinion & Associates, Inc., 52
Handleman Company, 15; 86 (upd.)
Harris Interactive Inc., 41; 92 (upd.)
Harte-Hanks, Inc., 63 (upd.)
Havas SA, 33 (upd.)
Hays plc, 27; 78 (upd.)
Headway Corporate Resources, Inc., 40
Heidrick & Struggles International, Inc., 28
Henry Dreyfuss Associates LLC, 88
Hewitt Associates, Inc., 77
Hildebrandt International, 29
Idearc Inc., 90
IKON Office Solutions, Inc., 50
IMS Health, Inc., 57
Interbrand Corporation, 70
Interep National Radio Sales Inc., 35
International Brotherhood of Teamsters, 37
International Management Group, 18
International Profit Associates, Inc., 87
International Total Services, Inc., 37
The Interpublic Group of Companies, Inc., I; 22 (upd.); 75 (upd.)
inVentiv Health, Inc., 81
Ipsos SA, 48
Iron Mountain, Inc., 33
ITT Educational Services, Inc., 39; 76 (upd.)
J.D. Power and Associates, 32
Jack Morton Worldwide, 88
Jackson Hewitt, Inc., 48
Jani-King International, Inc., 85
Japan Leasing Corporation, 8
JCDecaux S.A., 76
Jostens, Inc., 25 (upd.)
JOULÉ Inc., 58
JWT Group Inc., I
Katz Communications, Inc., 6
Katz Media Group, Inc., 35
Keane, Inc., 56
Kelly Services Inc., 6; 26 (upd.)
Ketchum Communications Inc., 6
Kforce Inc., 71
Kinko's Inc., 16; 43 (upd.)
Kirshenbaum Bond + Partners, Inc., 57
Kohn Pedersen Fox Associates P.C., 57
Korn/Ferry International, 34
Kroll Inc., 57
L. M. Berry and Company, 80
Labor Ready, Inc., 29; 88 (upd.)
Lamar Advertising Company, 27; 70 (upd.)
Landor Associates, 81
Le Cordon Bleu S.A., 67
Learning Care Group, Inc., 76 (upd.)
Learning Tree International Inc., 24
LECG Corporation, 93
Leo Burnett Company Inc., I; 20 (upd.)
The Leona Group LLC, 84
Lintas: Worldwide, 14
LivePerson, Inc., 91
Mail Boxes Etc., 18; 41 (upd.)
Manhattan Associates, Inc., 67
Manning Selvage & Lee (MS&L), 76
Manpower Inc., 30 (upd.); 73 (upd.)
Marchex, Inc., 72
marchFIRST, Inc., 34
Marco Business Products, Inc., 75
Maritz Inc., 38
Marlin Business Services Corp., 89
MAXIMUS, Inc., 43
MDC Partners Inc., 63
Mediaset SpA, 50
Milliman USA, 66
MIVA, Inc., 83
Monster Worldwide Inc., 74 (upd.)
Moody's Corporation, 65
MPS Group, Inc., 49
Mullen Advertising Inc., 51
Napster, Inc., 69
National Equipment Services, Inc., 57
National Media Corporation, 27
Navigant Consulting, Inc., 93
NAVTEQ Corporation, 69
Neopost S.A., 53
New England Business Services Inc., 18; 78 (upd.)
New Valley Corporation, 17
NFO Worldwide, Inc., 24
Nobel Learning Communities, Inc., 37; 76 (upd.)
Norrell Corporation, 25
Norwood Promotional Products, Inc., 26
The NPD Group, Inc., 68
O.C. Tanner Co., 69
Obie Media Corporation, 56
Observer AB, 55
OfficeTiger, LLC, 75
The Ogilvy Group, Inc., I
Olsten Corporation, 6; 29 (upd.)
Omnicom Group, I; 22 (upd.); 77 (upd.)
On Assignment, Inc., 20
1-800-FLOWERS, Inc., 26
Opinion Research Corporation, 46
Oracle Corporation, 67 (upd.)
Orbitz, Inc., 61
Outdoor Systems, Inc., 25
Paris Corporation, 22
Paychex, Inc., 15; 46 (upd.)
PDI, Inc., 52
Pegasus Solutions, Inc., 75

Pei Cobb Freed & Partners Architects LLP, 57
Penauille Polyservices SA, 49
PFSweb, Inc., 73
Philip Services Corp., 73
Phillips, de Pury & Luxembourg, 49
Pierce Leahy Corporation, 24
Pinkerton's Inc., 9
Plante & Moran, LLP, 71
PMT Services, Inc., 24
Posterscope Worldwide, 70
Priceline.com Incorporated, 57
Publicis Groupe, 19; 77 (upd.)
Publishers Clearing House, 23; 64 (upd.)
Quintiles Transnational Corporation, 68 (upd.)
Quovadx Inc., 70
Randstad Holding n.v., 16; 43 (upd.)
RedPeg Marketing, 73
RedPrairie Corporation, 74
RemedyTemp, Inc., 20
Rental Service Corporation, 28
Rentokil Initial Plc, 47
Research Triangle Institute, 83
Resources Connection, Inc., 81
Rewards Network Inc., 70 (upd.)
The Richards Group, Inc., 58
Right Management Consultants, Inc., 42
Ritchie Bros. Auctioneers Inc., 41
Robert Half International Inc., 18
Roland Berger & Partner GmbH, 37
Ronco Corporation, 15; 80 (upd.)
Russell Reynolds Associates Inc., 38
Saatchi & Saatchi, I; 42 (upd.)
Schenck Business Solutions, 88
Securitas AB, 42
ServiceMaster Limited Partnership, 6
Servpro Industries, Inc., 85
Shared Medical Systems Corporation, 14
Sir Speedy, Inc., 16
Skidmore, Owings & Merrill LLP, 13; 69 (upd.)
SmartForce PLC, 43
SOS Staffing Services, 25
Sotheby's Holdings, Inc., 11; 29 (upd.); 84 (upd.)
Source Interlink Companies, Inc., 75
Spencer Stuart and Associates, Inc., 14
Spherion Corporation, 52
Steiner Corporation (Alsco), 53
Strayer Education, Inc., 53
Superior Uniform Group, Inc., 30
Sykes Enterprises, Inc., 45
Sylvan Learning Systems, Inc., 35
TA Triumph-Adler AG, 48
Taylor Nelson Sofres plc, 34
TBWA/Chiat/Day, 6; 43 (upd.)
Thomas Cook Travel Inc., 33 (upd.)
Ticketmaster, 76 (upd.)
Ticketmaster Group, Inc., 13; 37 (upd.)
TMP Worldwide Inc., 30
TNT Post Group N.V., 30
Towers Perrin, 32
Trader Classified Media N.V., 57
Traffix, Inc., 61
Transmedia Network Inc., 20
Treasure Chest Advertising Company, Inc., 32
TRM Copy Centers Corporation, 18
True North Communications Inc., 23
24/7 Real Media, Inc., 49
Tyler Corporation, 23
U.S. Office Products Company, 25
Unica Corporation, 77
UniFirst Corporation, 21
United Business Media plc, 52 (upd.)
United News & Media plc, 28 (upd.)
Unitog Co., 19
Valassis Communications, Inc., 37 (upd.); 76 (upd.)
ValleyCrest Companies, 81 (upd.)
ValueClick, Inc., 49
Vebego International BV, 49
Vedior NV, 35
Vertis Communications, 84
Vertrue Inc., 77
Viad Corp., 73
W.B Doner & Co., 56
The Wackenhut Corporation, 14; 63 (upd.)
Waggener Edstrom, 42
Warrantech Corporation, 53
WebEx Communications, Inc., 81
Welcome Wagon International Inc., 82
Wells Rich Greene BDDP, 6
Westaff Inc., 33
Whitman Education Group, Inc., 41
Wieden + Kennedy, 75
William Morris Agency, Inc., 23
Williams Scotsman, Inc., 65
Workflow Management, Inc., 65
WPP Group plc, 6; 48 (upd.)
Wunderman, 86
Xerox Corporation, 69 (upd.)
Young & Rubicam, Inc., I; 22 (upd.); 66 (upd.)

Aerospace

A.S. Yakovlev Design Bureau, 15
Aerojet-General Corp., 63
Aeronca Inc., 46
Aerosonic Corporation, 69
The Aerospatiale Group, 7; 21 (upd.)
AgustaWestland N.V., 75
Airborne Systems Group, 89
Alliant Techsystems Inc., 30 (upd.)
Antonov Design Bureau, 53
Arianespace S.A., 89
Aviacionny Nauchno-Tehnicheskii Komplex im. A.N. Tupoleva, 24
Aviall, Inc., 73
Avions Marcel Dassault-Breguet Aviation, I
B/E Aerospace, Inc., 30
Ballistic Recovery Systems, Inc., 87
Banner Aerospace, Inc., 14
BBA Aviation plc, 90
Beech Aircraft Corporation, 8
Bell Helicopter Textron Inc., 46
The Boeing Company, I; 10 (upd.); 32 (upd.)
Bombardier Inc., 42 (upd.); 87 (upd.)
British Aerospace plc, I; 24 (upd.)
CAE USA Inc., 48
Canadair, Inc., 16
Cessna Aircraft Company, 8
Cirrus Design Corporation, 44
Cobham plc, 30
CPI Aerostructures, Inc., 75
Daimler-Benz Aerospace AG, 16
DeCrane Aircraft Holdings Inc., 36
Diehl Stiftung & Co. KG, 79
Ducommun Incorporated, 30
Duncan Aviation, Inc., 94
EADS SOCATA, 54
Eclipse Aviation Corporation, 87
EGL, Inc., 59
Empresa Brasileira de Aeronáutica S.A. (Embraer), 36
European Aeronautic Defence and Space Company EADS N.V., 52 (upd.)
Fairchild Aircraft, Inc., 9
Fairchild Dornier GmbH, 48 (upd.)
Finmeccanica S.p.A., 84
First Aviation Services Inc., 49
G.I.E. Airbus Industrie, I; 12 (upd.)
General Dynamics Corporation, I; 10 (upd.); 40 (upd.); 88 (upd.
GKN plc, III; 38 (upd.); 89 (upd.)
Goodrich Corporation, 46 (upd.)
Groupe Dassault Aviation SA, 26 (upd.)
Grumman Corporation, I; 11 (upd.)
Grupo Aeropuerto del Sureste, S.A. de C.V., 48
Gulfstream Aerospace Corporation, 7; 28 (upd.)
HEICO Corporation, 30
International Lease Finance Corporation, 48
Irkut Corporation, 68
Israel Aircraft Industries Ltd., 69
N.V. Koninklijke Nederlandse Vliegtuigenfabriek Fokker, I; 28 (upd.)
Lancair International, Inc., 67
Learjet Inc., 8; 27 (upd.)
Lockheed Martin Corporation, I; 11 (upd.); 15 (upd.); 89 (upd.)
Loral Space & Communications Ltd., 54 (upd.)
Magellan Aerospace Corporation, 48
Martin Marietta Corporation, I
Martin-Baker Aircraft Company Limited, 61
McDonnell Douglas Corporation, I; 11 (upd.)
Meggitt PLC, 34
Messerschmitt-Bölkow-Blohm GmbH., I
Moog Inc., 13
Mooney Aerospace Group Ltd., 52
The New Piper Aircraft, Inc., 44
Northrop Grumman Corporation, I; 11 (upd.); 45 (upd.)
Orbital Sciences Corporation, 22
Pemco Aviation Group Inc., 54
Pratt & Whitney, 9
Raytheon Aircraft Holdings Inc., 46
Robinson Helicopter Company, 51
Rockwell International Corporation, I; 11 (upd.)
Rolls-Royce Allison, 29 (upd.)
Rolls-Royce plc, I; 7 (upd.); 21 (upd.)
Rostvertol plc, 62
Russian Aircraft Corporation (MiG), 86
Safe Flight Instrument Corporation, 71

Sequa Corp., 13
Shannon Aerospace Ltd., 36
Sikorsky Aircraft Corporation, 24
Smiths Industries PLC, 25
Snecma Group, 46
Société Air France, 27 (upd.)
Spacehab, Inc., 37
Spar Aerospace Limited, 32
Sukhoi Design Bureau Aviation Scientific-Industrial Complex, 24
Sundstrand Corporation, 7; 21 (upd.)
Surrey Satellite Technology Limited, 83
Swales & Associates, Inc., 69
Teledyne Technologies Inc., 62 (upd.)
Textron Lycoming Turbine Engine, 9
Thales S.A., 42
Thiokol Corporation, 9; 22 (upd.)
United Technologies Corporation, I; 10 (upd.)
Van's Aircraft, Inc., 65
Vought Aircraft Industries, Inc., 49
Whittaker Corporation, 48 (upd.)
Woodward Governor Company, 49 (upd.)
Zodiac S.A., 36

Airlines

Aer Lingus Group plc, 34; 89 (upd.)
Aeroflot - Russian Airlines JSC, 6; 29 (upd.); 89 (upd.)
Aerolíneas Argentinas S.A., 33; 69 (upd.)
Air Berlin GmbH & Co. Luftverkehrs KG, 71
Air Canada, 6; 23 (upd.); 59 (upd.)
Air China, 46
Air Jamaica Limited, 54
Air Mauritius Ltd., 63
Air New Zealand Limited, 14; 38 (upd.)
Air Pacific Ltd., 70
Air Partner PLC, 93
Air Sahara Limited, 65
Air Wisconsin Airlines Corporation, 55
Air Zimbabwe (Private) Limited, 91
Air-India Limited, 6; 27 (upd.)
AirAsia Berhad, 93
AirTran Holdings, Inc., 22
Alaska Air Group, Inc., 6; 29 (upd.)
Alitalia-Linee Aeree Italiana, S.p.A., 6; 29 (upd.)
All Nippon Airways Co., Ltd., 6; 38 (upd.); 91 (upd.)
Aloha Airlines, Incorporated, 24
America West Holdings Corporation, 6; 34 (upd.)
American Airlines, I; 6 (upd.)
AMR Corporation, 28 (upd.); 52 (upd.)
Amtran, Inc., 34
Arrow Air Holdings Corporation, 55
A/S Air Baltic Corporation, 71
AS Estonian Air, 71
Asiana Airlines, Inc., 46
ATA Holdings Corporation, 82
Atlantic Coast Airlines Holdings, Inc., 55
Atlantic Southeast Airlines, Inc., 47
Atlas Air, Inc., 39
Austrian Airlines AG (Österreichische Luftverkehrs AG), 33
Aviacionny Nauchno-Tehnicheskii Komplex im. A.N. Tupoleva, 24
Avianca Aerovías Nacionales de Colombia SA, 36
Azerbaijan Airlines, 77
Bahamas Air Holdings Ltd., 66
Banner Aerospace, Inc., 37 (upd.)
Braathens ASA, 47
Bradley Air Services Ltd., 56
Bristow Helicopters Ltd., 70
British Airways PLC, I; 14 (upd.); 43 (upd.)
British Midland plc, 38
British World Airlines Ltd., 18
Cargolux Airlines International S.A., 49
Cathay Pacific Airways Limited, 6; 34 (upd.)
Ceské aerolinie, a.s., 66
Chautauqua Airlines, Inc., 38
China Airlines, 34
China Eastern Airlines Co. Ltd., 31
China Southern Airlines Company Ltd., 33
Comair Holdings Inc., 13; 34 (upd.)
Consorcio Aviacsa, S.A. de C.V., 85
Continental Airlines, Inc., I; 21 (upd.); 52 (upd.)
Copa Holdings, S.A., 93
Corporación Internacional de Aviación, S.A. de C.V. (Cintra), 20
Cyprus Airways Public Limited, 81
dba Luftfahrtgesellschaft mbH, 76
Delta Air Lines, Inc., I; 6 (upd.); 39 (upd.); 92 (upd.)
Deutsche Lufthansa AG, I; 26 (upd.); 68 (upd.)
Eastern Airlines, I
easyJet Airline Company Limited, 39
EgyptAir, 6; 27 (upd.)
El Al Israel Airlines Ltd., 23
The Emirates Group, 39; 81 (upd.)
Ethiopian Airlines, 81
Etihad Airways PJSC, 89
Eurocopter S.A., 80
EVA Airways Corporation, 51
Finnair Oyj, 6; 25 (upd.); 61 (upd.)
Flight Options, LLC, 75
Flying Boat, Inc. (Chalk's Ocean Airways), 56
Frontier Airlines Holdings Inc., 22; 84 (upd.)
Garuda Indonesia, 6
Gol Linhas Aéreas Inteligentes S.A., 73
Groupe Air France, 6
Grupo Aeroportuario del Pacífico, S.A. de C.V., 85
Grupo TACA, 38
Gulf Air Company, 56
HAL Inc., 9
Hawaiian Airlines, Inc., 22 (upd.)
Hong Kong Dragon Airlines Ltd., 66
Iberia Líneas Aéreas de España S.A., 6; 36 (upd.); 91 (upd.)
Icelandair, 52
Indian Airlines Ltd., 46
IranAir, 81
Japan Air Lines Company Ltd., I; 32 (upd.)
Jersey European Airways (UK) Ltd., 61
Jet Airways (India) Private Limited, 65
JetBlue Airways Corporation, 44
Kenmore Air Harbor Inc., 65
Kenya Airways Limited, 89
Kitty Hawk, Inc., 22
Kiwi International Airlines Inc., 20
Koninklijke Luchtvaart Maatschappij, N.V. (KLM Royal Dutch Airlines), I; 28 (upd.)
Korean Air Lines Co., Ltd., 6; 27 (upd.)
Kuwait Airways Corporation, 68
Lan Chile S.A., 31
Lauda Air Luftfahrt AG, 48
Loganair Ltd., 68
LOT Polish Airlines (Polskie Linie Lotnicze S.A.), 33
LTU Group Holding GmbH, 37
Malév Plc, 24
Malaysian Airlines System Berhad, 6; 29 (upd.)
Mesa Air Group, Inc., 11; 32 (upd.); 77 (upd.)
Mesaba Holdings, Inc., 28
Middle East Airlines - Air Liban S.A.L., 79
Midway Airlines Corporation, 33
Midwest Air Group, Inc., 35; 85 (upd.)
Northwest Airlines Corporation, I; 6 (upd.); 26 (upd.); 74 (upd.)
Offshore Logistics, Inc., 37
Pakistan International Airlines Corporation, 46
Pan American World Airways, Inc., I; 12 (upd.)
Panalpina World Transport (Holding) Ltd., 47
People Express Airlines, Inc., I
Petroleum Helicopters, Inc., 35
PHI, Inc., 80 (upd.)
Philippine Airlines, Inc., 6; 23 (upd.)
Pinnacle Airlines Corp., 73
Preussag AG, 42 (upd.)
Qantas Airways Ltd., 6; 24 (upd.); 68 (upd.)
Qatar Airways Company Q.C.S.C., 87
Reno Air Inc., 23
Royal Nepal Airline Corporation, 41
Ryanair Holdings plc, 35
SAA (Pty) Ltd., 28
Sabena S.A./N.V., 33
The SAS Group, 34 (upd.)
Saudi Arabian Airlines, 6; 27 (upd.)
Scandinavian Airlines System, I
Singapore Airlines Limited, 6; 27 (upd.); 83 (upd.)
SkyWest, Inc., 25
Société d'Exploitation AOM Air Liberté SA (AirLib), 53
Société Luxembourgeoise de Navigation Aérienne S.A., 64
Société Tunisienne de l'Air-Tunisair, 49
Southwest Airlines Co., 6; 24 (upd.); 71 (upd.)
Spirit Airlines, Inc., 31
Sterling European Airlines A/S, 70
Sun Country Airlines, 30
Swiss Air Transport Company, Ltd., I
Swiss International Air Lines Ltd., 48
TAM Linhas Aéreas S.A., 68

TAP—Air Portugal Transportes Aéreos Portugueses S.A., 46
TAROM S.A., 64
Texas Air Corporation, I
Thai Airways International Public Company Limited, 6; 27 (upd.)
Tower Air, Inc., 28
Trans World Airlines, Inc., I; 12 (upd.); 35 (upd.)
TransBrasil S/A Linhas Aéreas, 31
Transportes Aereos Portugueses, S.A., 6
Turkish Airlines Inc. (Türk Hava Yollari A.O.), 72
TV Guide, Inc., 43 (upd.)
UAL Corporation, 34 (upd.)
United Airlines, I; 6 (upd.)
US Airways Group, Inc., I; 6 (upd.); 28 (upd.); 52 (upd.)
VARIG S.A. (Viação Aérea Rio-Grandense), 6; 29 (upd.)
Virgin Group Ltd., 12; 32 (upd.); 89 (upd.)
Volga-Dnepr Group, 82
WestJet Airlines Ltd., 38

Automotive

AB Volvo, I; 7 (upd.); 26 (upd.); 67 (upd.)
Accubuilt, Inc., 74
Adam Opel AG, 7; 21 (upd.); 61 (upd.)
ADESA, Inc., 71
Advance Auto Parts, Inc., 57
Aftermarket Technology Corp., 83
Aisin Seiki Co., Ltd., 48 (upd.)
Alamo Rent A Car, Inc., 6; 24 (upd.); 84 (upd.)
Alfa Romeo, 13; 36 (upd.)
Alvis Plc, 47
America's Car-Mart, Inc., 64
American Motors Corporation, I
Applied Power Inc., 32 (upd.)
Arnold Clark Automobiles Ltd., 60
ArvinMeritor, Inc., 8; 54 (upd.)
Asbury Automotive Group Inc., 60
ASC, Inc., 55
Autobacs Seven Company Ltd., 76
Autocam Corporation, 51
Autoliv, Inc., 65
Automobiles Citroen, 7
Automobili Lamborghini Holding S.p.A., 13; 34 (upd.); 91 (upd.)
AutoNation, Inc., 50
AutoTrader.com, L.L.C., 91
AVTOVAZ Joint Stock Company, 65
Bajaj Auto Limited, 39
Bayerische Motoren Werke AG, I; 11 (upd.); 38 (upd.)
Belron International Ltd., 76
Bendix Corporation, I
Blue Bird Corporation, 35
Bombardier Inc., 42 (upd.)
BorgWarner Inc., 14; 32 (upd.); 85 (upd.)
The Budd Company, 8
Bugatti Automobiles S.A.S., 94
Canadian Tire Corporation, Limited, 71 (upd.)
CarMax, Inc., 55
CARQUEST Corporation, 29
Caterpillar Inc., 63 (upd.)
Checker Motors Corp., 89
China Automotive Systems Inc., 87
Chrysler Corporation, I; 11 (upd.)
Commercial Vehicle Group, Inc., 81
CNH Global N.V., 38 (upd.)
Consorcio G Grupo Dina, S.A. de C.V., 36
Crown Equipment Corporation, 15; 93 (upd.)
CSK Auto Corporation, 38
Cummins Engine Company, Inc., I; 12 (upd.); 40 (upd.)
Custom Chrome, Inc., 16
Daihatsu Motor Company, Ltd., 7; 21 (upd.)
Daimler-Benz A.G., I; 15 (upd.)
DaimlerChrysler AG, 34 (upd.); 64 (upd.)
Dana Corporation, I; 10 (upd.)
Danaher Corporation, 77 (upd.)
Deere & Company, 42 (upd.)
Delphi Automotive Systems Corporation, 45
Directed Electronics, Inc., 87
Discount Tire Company Inc., 84
Don Massey Cadillac, Inc., 37
Donaldson Company, Inc., 49 (upd.)
Douglas & Lomason Company, 16
Dräxlmaier Group, 90
DriveTime Automotive Group Inc., 68 (upd.)
Ducati Motor Holding SpA, 30; 86 (upd.)
Eaton Corporation, I; 10 (upd.); 67 (upd.)
Echlin Inc., I; 11 (upd.)
Edelbrock Corporation, 37
Faurecia S.A., 70
Federal-Mogul Corporation, I; 10 (upd.); 26 (upd.)
Ferrara Fire Apparatus, Inc., 84
Ferrari S.p.A., 13; 36 (upd.)
Fiat SpA, I; 11 (upd.); 50 (upd.)
FinishMaster, Inc., 24
Ford Motor Company, I; 11 (upd.); 36 (upd.); 64 (upd.)
Ford Motor Company, S.A. de C.V., 20
Fruehauf Corporation, I
General Motors Corporation, I; 10 (upd.); 36 (upd.); 64 (upd.)
Gentex Corporation, 26
Genuine Parts Company, 9; 45 (upd.)
GKN plc, III; 38 (upd.); 89 (upd.)
Group 1 Automotive, Inc., 52
Grupo Ficosa International, 90
Guardian Industries Corp., 87
Harley-Davidson Inc., 7; 25 (upd.)
Hastings Manufacturing Company, 56
Hayes Lemmerz International, Inc., 27
Hendrick Motorsports, Inc., 89
The Hertz Corporation, 33 (upd.)
Hino Motors, Ltd., 7; 21 (upd.)
Holden Ltd., 62
Holley Performance Products Inc., 52
Hometown Auto Retailers, Inc., 44
Honda Motor Company Limited (Honda Giken Kogyo Kabushiki Kaisha), I; 10 (upd.); 29 (upd.)
Hyundai Group, 56 (upd.)
Insurance Auto Auctions, Inc., 23
Isuzu Motors, Ltd., 9; 23 (upd.); 57 (upd.)
INTERMET Corporation, 77 (upd.)
Jardine Cycle & Carriage Ltd., 73
Kawasaki Heavy Industries, Ltd., 63 (upd.)
Kelsey-Hayes Group of Companies, 7; 27 (upd.)
Key Safety Systems, Inc., 63
Kia Motors Corporation, 12; 29 (upd.)
Kwik-Fit Holdings plc, 54
Lazy Days RV Center, Inc., 69
Lear Corporation, 71 (upd.)
Lear Seating Corporation, 16
Les Schwab Tire Centers, 50
Lithia Motors, Inc., 41
LKQ Corporation, 71
Lookers plc, 71
Lotus Cars Ltd., 14
Lund International Holdings, Inc., 40
Mack Trucks, Inc., I; 22 (upd.); 61 (upd.)
The Major Automotive Companies, Inc., 45
Marcopolo S.A., 79
Masland Corporation, 17
Mazda Motor Corporation, 9; 23 (upd.); 63 (upd.)
Mel Farr Automotive Group, 20
Metso Corporation, 30 (upd.)
Midas Inc., 10; 56 (upd.)
Mitsubishi Motors Corporation, 9; 23 (upd.); 57 (upd.)
Monaco Coach Corporation, 31
Monro Muffler Brake, Inc., 24
Montupet S.A., 63
National R.V. Holdings, Inc., 32
Navistar International Corporation, I; 10 (upd.)
New Flyer Industries Inc. 78
Nissan Motor Company Ltd., I; 11 (upd.); 34 (upd.); 92 (upd.)
O'Reilly Automotive, Inc., 26; 78 (upd.)
Officine Alfieri Maserati S.p.A., 13
Oshkosh Truck Corporation, 7
Paccar Inc., I
PACCAR Inc., 26 (upd.)
Park-Ohio Holdings Corp., 17; 85 (upd.)
Pennzoil-Quaker State Company, IV; 20 (upd.); 50 (upd.)
Penske Corporation, V; 19 (upd.); 84 (upd.)
The Pep Boys—Manny, Moe & Jack, 11; 36 (upd.); 81 (upd.)
Perusahaan Otomobil Nasional Bhd., 62
Peterbilt Motors Company, 89
Peugeot S.A., I
Piaggio & C. S.p.A., 20
Pirelli & C. S.p.A., 75 (upd.)
Porsche AG, 13; 31 (upd.)
PSA Peugeot Citroen S.A., 28 (upd.)
R&B, Inc., 51
Randon S.A., 79
Red McCombs Automotive Group, 91
Regie Nationale des Usines Renault, I
Renault Argentina S.A., 67
Renault S.A., 26 (upd.); 74 (upd.)
Repco Corporation Ltd., 74

Republic Industries, Inc., 26
The Reynolds and Reynolds Company, 50
Riviera Tool Company, 89
Robert Bosch GmbH., I; 16 (upd.); 43 (upd.)
RockShox, Inc., 26
Rockwell Automation, I; 11 (upd.); 43 (upd.)
Rolls-Royce plc, I; 21 (upd.)
Ron Tonkin Chevrolet Company, 55
Rover Group Ltd., 7; 21 (upd.)
Saab Automobile AB, I; 11 (upd.); 32 (upd.); 83 (upd.)
Safelite Glass Corp., 19
Safety Components International, Inc., 63
Saturn Corporation, 7; 21 (upd.); 80 (upd.)
Sealed Power Corporation, I
Sheller-Globe Corporation, I
Sixt AG, 39
Skoda Auto a.s., 39
Sonic Automotive, Inc., 77
Spartan Motors Inc., 14
SpeeDee Oil Change and Tune-Up, 25
SPX Corporation, 10; 47 (upd.)
Standard Motor Products, Inc., 40
Strattec Security Corporation, 73
Superior Industries International, Inc., 8
Suzuki Motor Corporation, 9; 23 (upd.); 59 (upd.)
Sytner Group plc, 45
Titan International, Inc., 89
Toresco Enterprises, Inc., 84
Tower Automotive, Inc., 24
Toyota Motor Corporation, I; 11 (upd.); 38 (upd.)
CJSC Transmash Holding, 93
TransPro, Inc., 71
Triumph Motorcycles Ltd., 53
TRW Automotive Holdings Corp., 75 (upd.)
TRW Inc., 14 (upd.)
Ugly Duckling Corporation, 22
United Auto Group, Inc., 26; 68 (upd.)
United Technologies Automotive Inc., 15
Universal Technical Institute, Inc., 81
Valeo, 23; 66 (upd.)
Vauxhall Motors Limited, 73
Volkswagen Aktiengesellschaft, I; 11 (upd.); 32 (upd.)
Wagon plc, 92
Walker Manufacturing Company, 19
Wilhelm Karmann GmbH, 94
Winnebago Industries Inc., 7; 27 (upd.)
Woodward Governor Company, 49 (upd.)
The Yokohama Rubber Company, Limited, V; 19 (upd.); 91 (upd.)
ZF Friedrichshafen AG, 48
Ziebart International Corporation, 30; 66 (upd.)

Beverages

A & W Brands, Inc., 25
Adolph Coors Company, I; 13 (upd.); 36 (upd.)
AG Barr plc, 64
Ajegroup S.A., 92
Allied Domecq PLC, 29
Allied-Lyons PLC, I
Anchor Brewing Company, 47
Anheuser-Busch Companies, Inc., I; 10 (upd.); 34 (upd.)
Apple & Eve L.L.C., 92
Asahi Breweries, Ltd., I; 20 (upd.); 52 (upd.)
Asia Pacific Breweries Limited, 59
August Schell Brewing Company Inc., 59
Bacardi & Company Ltd., 18; 82 (upd.)
Baltika Brewery Joint Stock Company, 65
Banfi Products Corp., 36
Baron de Ley S.A., 74
Baron Philippe de Rothschild S.A., 39
Bass PLC, I; 15 (upd.); 38 (upd.)
Bavaria S.A., 90
BBAG Osterreichische Brau-Beteiligungs-AG, 38
Belvedere S.A., 93
Beringer Blass Wine Estates Ltd., 22; 66 (upd.)
The Bernick Companies, 75
Blue Ridge Beverage Company Inc., 82
Boizel Chanoine Champagne S.A., 94
Bols Distilleries NV, 74
The Boston Beer Company, Inc., 18; 50 (upd.)
Brauerei Beck & Co., 9; 33 (upd.)
Britannia Soft Drinks Ltd. (Britvic), 71
Brown-Forman Corporation, I; 10 (upd.); 38 (upd.)
Brouwerijen Alken-Maes N.V., 86
Budweiser Budvar, National Corporation, 59
Cadbury Schweppes PLC, 49 (upd.)
Canandaigua Brands, Inc., 13; 34 (upd.)
Cantine Giorgio Lungarotti S.R.L., 67
Carlsberg A/S, 9; 29 (upd.)
Carlton and United Breweries Ltd., I
Casa Cuervo, S.A. de C.V., 31
Central European Distribution Corporation, 75
Cerveceria Polar, I
The Chalone Wine Group, Ltd., 36
City Brewing Company LLC, 73
Clearly Canadian Beverage Corporation, 48
Clement Pappas & Company, Inc., 92
Click Wine Group, 68
Coca Cola Bottling Co. Consolidated, 10
The Coca-Cola Company, I; 10 (upd.); 32 (upd.); 67 (upd.)
Companhia de Bebidas das Américas, 57
Compania Cervecerias Unidas S.A., 70
Constellation Brands, Inc., 68 (upd.)
Corby Distilleries Limited, 14
Cott Corporation, 52
D.G. Yuengling & Son, Inc., 38
Dallis Coffee, Inc., 86
Davide Campari-Milano S.p.A., 57
Dean Foods Company, 21 (upd.)
Delicato Vineyards, Inc., 50
Deschutes Brewery, Inc., 57
Desnoes and Geddes Limited, 79
Diageo plc, 79 (upd.)
Direct Wines Ltd., 84
Distillers Company PLC, I
Double-Cola Co.-USA, 70
Dr Pepper/Seven Up, Inc., 9; 32 (upd.)
E. & J. Gallo Winery, I; 7 (upd.); 28 (upd.)
Eckes AG, 56
The Edrington Group Ltd., 88
Embotelladora Andina S.A., 71
Empresas Polar SA, 55 (upd.)
Energy Brands Inc., 88
F. Korbel & Bros. Inc., 68
Faygo Beverages Inc., 55
Federico Paternina S.A., 69
Ferolito, Vultaggio & Sons, 27
Fiji Water LLC, 74
Florida's Natural Growers, 45
Foster's Group Limited, 7; 21 (upd.); 50 (upd.)
Freixenet S.A., 71
Fuller Smith & Turner P.L.C., 38
G. Heileman Brewing Company Inc., I
The Gambrinus Company, 40
Gano Excel Enterprise Sdn. Bhd., 89
The Gatorade Company, 82
Geerlings & Wade, Inc., 45
General Cinema Corporation, I
Glazer's Wholesale Drug Company, Inc., 82
Gluek Brewing Company, 75
Golden State Vintners, Inc., 33
Gosling Brothers Ltd., 82
Grand Metropolitan PLC, I
Green Mountain Coffee, Inc., 31
The Greenalls Group PLC, 21
Greene King plc, 31
Groupe Danone, 32 (upd.); 93 (upd.)
Grupo Industrial Herradura, S.A. de C.V., 83
Grupo Modelo, S.A. de C.V., 29
Guinness/UDV, I; 43 (upd.)
The Hain Celestial Group, Inc., 43 (upd.)
Hansen Natural Corporation, 31; 76 (upd.)
Heineken N.V, I; 13 (upd.); 34 (upd.); 90 (upd.)
Heublein, Inc., I
High Falls Brewing Company LLC, 74
Hiram Walker Resources, Ltd., I
illycaffè SpA, 50
Imagine Foods, Inc., 50
Interbrew S.A., 17; 50 (upd.)
Jacob Leinenkugel Brewing Company, 28
JD Wetherspoon plc, 30
Jim Beam Brands Worldwide, Inc., 58 (upd.)
John Dewar & Sons, Ltd., 82
Jones Soda Co., 69
Jugos del Valle, S.A. de C.V., 85
Karlsberg Brauerei GmbH & Co KG, 41
Kendall-Jackson Winery, Ltd., 28
Kikkoman Corporation, 14
Kirin Brewery Company, Limited, I; 21 (upd.); 63 (upd.)
Kobrand Corporation, 82
König Brauerei GmbH & Co. KG, 35 (upd.)
Labatt Brewing Company Limited, I; 25 (upd.)
Latrobe Brewing Company, 54
Laurent-Perrier SA, 42

The Lion Brewery, Inc., 86
Lion Nathan Limited, 54
Löwenbräu AG, 80
The Macallan Distillers Ltd., 63
Madeira Wine Company, S.A., 49
Maison Louis Jadot, 24
Marchesi Antinori SRL, 42
Marie Brizard & Roger International S.A., 22
Mark T. Wendell Tea Company, 94
Martell and Company S.A., 82
Martignetti Companies, 84
Martini & Rossi SpA, 63
Maui Wowi, Inc., 85
MBC Holding Company, 40
Mendocino Brewing Company, Inc., 60
Mercian Corporation, 77
Miller Brewing Company, I; 12 (upd.)
The Minute Maid Company, 28
Mitchells & Butlers PLC, 59
Moët-Hennessy, I
Molson Coors Brewing Company, I; 26 (upd.); 77 (upd.)
Montana Coffee Traders, Inc., 60
Mott's Inc., 57
National Beverage Corporation, 26; 88 (upd.)
National Grape Cooperative Association, Inc., 20
National Wine & Spirits, Inc., 49
Nestlé Waters, 73
New Belgium Brewing Company, Inc., 68
Nichols plc, 44
Ocean Spray Cranberries, Inc., 7; 25 (upd.); 83 (upd.)
Odwalla, Inc., 31
OENEO S.A., 74 (upd.)
Old Orchard Brands, LLC, 73
Oregon Chai, Inc., 49
Panamerican Beverages, Inc., 47
Parmalat Finanziaria SpA, 50
Paulaner Brauerei GmbH & Co. KG, 35
Peet's Coffee & Tea, Inc., 38
Penaflor S.A., 66
The Pepsi Bottling Group, Inc., 40
PepsiAmericas, Inc., 67 (upd.)
PepsiCo, Inc., I; 10 (upd.); 38 (upd.); 93 (upd.)
Pernod Ricard S.A., I; 21 (upd.); 72 (upd.)
Pete's Brewing Company, 22
Philip Morris Companies Inc., 18 (upd.)
Pittsburgh Brewing Company, 76
Pyramid Breweries Inc., 33
Quilmes Industrial (QUINSA) S.A., 67
R.C. Bigelow, Inc., 49
Radeberger Gruppe AG, 75
Rainier Brewing Company, 23
Red Bull GmbH, 60
Redhook Ale Brewery, Inc., 31; 88 (upd.)
Rémy Cointreau Group, 20; 80 (upd.)
Robert Mondavi Corporation, 15; 50 (upd.)
Royal Crown Company, Inc., 23
Royal Grolsch NV, 54
S&D Coffee, Inc., 84
SABMiller plc, 59 (upd.)
San Miguel Corporation, 57 (upd.)
Sapporo Breweries Limited, I; 13 (upd.); 36 (upd.)
Scheid Vineyards Inc., 66
Schieffelin & Somerset Co., 61
Scottish & Newcastle plc, 15; 35 (upd.)
The Seagram Company Ltd., I; 25 (upd.)
Sebastiani Vineyards, Inc., 28
Shepherd Neame Limited, 30
Sidney Frank Importing Co., Inc., 69
Sierra Nevada Brewing Company, 70
Skalli Group, 67
Skyy Spirits LLC 78
Sleeman Breweries Ltd., 74
Snapple Beverage Corporation, 11
Societe des Produits Marnier-Lapostolle S.A., 88
The South African Breweries Limited, I; 24 (upd.)
South Beach Beverage Company, Inc., 73
Southcorp Limited, 54
Southern Wine and Spirits of America, Inc., 84
Starbucks Corporation, 13; 34 (upd.); 77 (upd.)
The Stash Tea Company, 50
Stewart's Beverages, 39
The Stroh Brewery Company, I; 18 (upd.)
Suntory Ltd., 65
Sutter Home Winery Inc., 16
Taittinger S.A., 43
Taiwan Tobacco & Liquor Corporation, 75
Takara Holdings Inc., 62
Tata Tea Ltd., 76
The Terlato Wine Group, 48
Tetley USA Inc., 88
Todhunter International, Inc., 27
Triarc Companies, Inc., 34 (upd.)
Tropicana Products, Inc., 73 (upd.)
Tsingtao Brewery Group, 49
Tully's Coffee Corporation, 51
Underberg AG, 92
Unilever, II; 7 (upd.); 32 (upd.); 89 (upd.)
Unión de Cervecerias Peruanas Backus y Johnston S.A.A., 92
V&S Vin & Sprit AB, 91 (upd.)
Van Houtte Inc., 39
Vermont Pure Holdings, Ltd., 51
Vin & Spirit AB, 31
Viña Concha y Toro S.A., 45
Vincor International Inc., 50
Whitbread and Company PLC, I
Widmer Brothers Brewing Company, 76
Willamette Valley Vineyards, Inc., 85
William Grant & Sons Ltd., 60
The Wine Group, Inc., 39
The Wolverhampton & Dudley Breweries, PLC, 57
Young & Co.'s Brewery, P.L.C., 38

Bio-Technology

Actelion Ltd., 83
Amersham PLC, 50
Amgen, Inc., 10; 30 (upd.)
ArQule, Inc., 68
Bio-Rad Laboratories, Inc., 93
Biogen Idec Inc., 71 (upd.)
Biogen Inc., 14; 36 (upd.)
bioMérieux S.A., 75
BTG Plc, 87
Caliper Life Sciences, Inc., 70
Cambrex Corporation, 44 (upd.)
Celera Genomics, 74
Centocor Inc., 14
Charles River Laboratories International, Inc., 42
Chiron Corporation, 10; 36 (upd.)
Covance Inc., 30
CryoLife, Inc., 46
Cytyc Corporation, 69
Delta and Pine Land Company, 33
Dionex Corporation, 46
Dyax Corp., 89
Embrex, Inc., 72
Enzo Biochem, Inc., 41
Eurofins Scientific S.A., 70
Gen-Probe Incorporated, 79
Genentech, Inc., 32 (upd.)
Genzyme Corporation, 38 (upd.)
Gilead Sciences, Inc., 54
Howard Hughes Medical Institute, 39
Huntingdon Life Sciences Group plc, 42
IDEXX Laboratories, Inc., 23
ImClone Systems Inc., 58
Immunex Corporation, 14; 50 (upd.)
IMPATH Inc., 45
Incyte Genomics, Inc., 52
Inverness Medical Innovations, Inc., 63
Invitrogen Corporation, 52
The Judge Group, Inc., 51
Kendle International Inc., 87
Life Technologies, Inc., 17
LifeCell Corporation, 77
Lonza Group Ltd., 73
Martek Biosciences Corporation, 65
Medarex, Inc., 85
Medtronic, Inc., 30 (upd.)
Millipore Corporation, 25; 84 (upd.)
Minntech Corporation, 22
Mycogen Corporation, 21
Nektar Therapeutics, 91
New Brunswick Scientific Co., Inc., 45
Pacific Ethanol, Inc., 81
Pharmion Corporation, 91
Qiagen N.V., 39
Quintiles Transnational Corporation, 21
Seminis, Inc., 29
Senomyx, Inc., 83
Serologicals Corporation, 63
Sigma-Aldrich Corporation, I; 36 (upd.); 93 (upd.)
Starkey Laboratories, Inc., 52
STERIS Corporation, 29
Stratagene Corporation, 70
Tanox, Inc., 77
TECHNE Corporation, 52
TriPath Imaging, Inc., 77
Waters Corporation, 43
Whatman plc, 46
Wisconsin Alumni Research Foundation, 65

Wyeth, 50 (upd.)

Chemicals

A. Schulman, Inc., 8
Aceto Corp., 38
Air Products and Chemicals, Inc., I; 10 (upd.); 74 (upd.)
Airgas, Inc., 54
Akzo Nobel N.V., 13; 41 (upd.)
Albemarle Corporation, 59
AlliedSignal Inc., 22 (upd.)
ALTANA AG, 87
American Cyanamid, I; 8 (upd.)
American Vanguard Corporation, 47
Arab Potash Company, 85
Arch Chemicals Inc. 78
ARCO Chemical Company, 10
Asahi Denka Kogyo KK, 64
Atanor S.A., 62
Atochem S.A., I
Avantium Technologies BV, 79
Avecia Group PLC, 63
Baker Hughes Incorporated, 22 (upd.); 57 (upd.)
Balchem Corporation, 42
BASF Aktiengesellschaft, I; 18 (upd.); 50 (upd.)
Bayer A.G., I; 13 (upd.); 41 (upd.)
Betz Laboratories, Inc., I; 10 (upd.)
The BFGoodrich Company, 19 (upd.)
BOC Group plc, I; 25 (upd.); 78 (upd.)
Brenntag AG, 8; 23 (upd.)
Burmah Castrol PLC, 30 (upd.)
Cabot Corporation, 8; 29 (upd.); 91 (upd.)
Calgon Carbon Corporation, 73
Caliper Life Sciences, Inc., 70
Cambrex Corporation, 16
Catalytica Energy Systems, Inc., 44
Celanese Corporation, I
Celanese Mexicana, S.A. de C.V., 54
Chemcentral Corporation, 8
Chemi-Trol Chemical Co., 16
Chemtura Corporation, 91 (upd.)
Church & Dwight Co., Inc., 29
Ciba-Geigy Ltd., I; 8 (upd.)
The Clorox Company, III; 22 (upd.); 81 (upd.)
Croda International Plc, 45
Crompton Corporation, 9; 36 (upd.)
Cytec Industries Inc., 27
Degussa-Hüls AG, 32 (upd.)
DeKalb Genetics Corporation, 17
The Dexter Corporation, I; 12 (upd.)
Dionex Corporation, 46
The Dow Chemical Company, I; 8 (upd.); 50 (upd.)
DSM N.V., I; 56 (upd.)
Dynaction S.A., 67
E.I. du Pont de Nemours & Company, I; 8 (upd.); 26 (upd.)
Eastman Chemical Company, 14; 38 (upd.)
Ecolab Inc., I; 13 (upd.); 34 (upd.); 85 (upd.)
Eka Chemicals AB, 92
Elementis plc, 40 (upd.)
Engelhard Corporation, 72 (upd.)
English China Clays Ltd., 15 (upd.); 40 (upd.)
Enterprise Rent-A-Car Company, 69 (upd.)
Equistar Chemicals, LP, 71
Ercros S.A., 80
ERLY Industries Inc., 17
Ethyl Corporation, I; 10 (upd.)
Ferro Corporation, 8; 56 (upd.)
Firmenich International S.A., 60
First Mississippi Corporation, 8
FMC Corporation, 89 (upd.)
Formosa Plastics Corporation, 14; 58 (upd.)
Fort James Corporation, 22 (upd.)
G.A.F., I
The General Chemical Group Inc., 37
Georgia Gulf Corporation, 9; 61 (upd.)
Givaudan SA, 43
Great Lakes Chemical Corporation, I; 14 (upd.)
GROWMARK, Inc., 88
Guerbet Group, 46
H.B. Fuller Company, 32 (upd.); 75 (upd.)
Hauser, Inc., 46
Hawkins Chemical, Inc., 16
Henkel KGaA, 34 (upd.)
Hercules Inc., I; 22 (upd.); 66 (upd.)
Hoechst A.G., I; 18 (upd.)
Hoechst Celanese Corporation, 13
Huls A.G., I
Huntsman Chemical Corporation, 8
IMC Fertilizer Group, Inc., 8
Imperial Chemical Industries PLC, I; 50 (upd.)
International Flavors & Fragrances Inc., 9; 38 (upd.)
Israel Chemicals Ltd., 55
Kemira Oyj, 70
Koppers Industries, Inc., I; 26 (upd.)
L'Air Liquide SA, I; 47 (upd.)
Lawter International Inc., 14
LeaRonal, Inc., 23
Loctite Corporation, 30 (upd.)
Lonza Group Ltd., 73
The Lubrizol Corporation, I; 30 (upd.); 83 (upd.)
Lyondell Chemical Company, 45 (upd.)
M.A. Hanna Company, 8
MacDermid Incorporated, 32
Makhteshim-Agan Industries Ltd., 85
Mallinckrodt Group Inc., 19
MBC Holding Company, 40
Melamine Chemicals, Inc., 27
Methanex Corporation, 40
Minerals Technologies Inc., 52 (upd.)
Mississippi Chemical Corporation, 39
Mitsubishi Chemical Corporation, I; 56 (upd.)
Mitsui Petrochemical Industries, Ltd., 9
Monsanto Company, I; 9 (upd.); 29 (upd.)
Montedison SpA, I
Morton International Inc., I; 9 (upd.); 80 (upd.)
The Mosaic Company, 91
Nagase & Company, Ltd., 8
Nalco Holding Company, I; 12 (upd.); 89 (upd.)
National Distillers and Chemical Corporation, I
National Sanitary Supply Co., 16
National Starch and Chemical Company, 49
NCH Corporation, 8
Nippon Soda Co., Ltd., 85
Nisshin Seifun Group Inc., 66 (upd.)
NL Industries, Inc., 10
Nobel Industries AB, 9
NOF Corporation, 72
Norsk Hydro ASA, 35 (upd.)
Novacor Chemicals Ltd., 12
Nufarm Ltd., 87
NutraSweet Company, 8
Occidental Petroleum Corporation, 71 (upd.)
Olin Corporation, I; 13 (upd.); 78 (upd.)
OM Group, Inc., 17; 78 (upd.)
OMNOVA Solutions Inc., 59
Penford Corporation, 55
Pennwalt Corporation, I
Perstorp AB, I; 51 (upd.)
Petrolite Corporation, 15
Pfizer Inc., 79 (upd.)
Pioneer Hi-Bred International, Inc., 41 (upd.)
PolyOne Corporation, 87 (upd.)
Praxair, Inc., 11
Quaker Chemical Corp., 91
Quantum Chemical Corporation, 8
Reichhold Chemicals, Inc., 10
Renner Herrmann S.A., 79
Rhodia SA, 38
Rhône-Poulenc S.A., I; 10 (upd.)
Robertet SA, 39
Rohm and Haas Company, I; 26 (upd.); 77 (upd.)
Roussel Uclaf, I; 8 (upd.)
RPM International Inc., 8; 36 (upd.); 91 (upd.)
RWE AG, 50 (upd.)
S.C. Johnson & Son, Inc., III; 28 (upd.); 89 (upd.)
The Scotts Company, 22
SCP Pool Corporation, 39
Sequa Corp., 13
Shanghai Petrochemical Co., Ltd., 18
Sigma-Aldrich Corporation, I; 36 (upd.); 93 (upd.)
Solutia Inc., 52
Solvay S.A., I; 21 (upd.); 61 (upd.)
Stepan Company, 30
Sterling Chemicals, Inc., 16; 78 (upd.)
Sumitomo Chemical Company Ltd., I
Takeda Chemical Industries, Ltd., 46 (upd.)
Terra Industries, Inc., 13
Tessenderlo Group, 76
Teva Pharmaceutical Industries Ltd., 22
Tosoh Corporation, 70
Total Fina Elf S.A., 24 (upd.); 50 (upd.)
Ube Industries, Ltd., 38 (upd.)
Union Carbide Corporation, I; 9 (upd.); 74 (upd.)
United Industries Corporation, 68

Univar Corporation, 9
The Valspar Corporation, 32 (upd.); 77 (upd.)
VeraSun Energy Corporation, 87
Vista Chemical Company, I
Witco Corporation, I; 16 (upd.)
Yule Catto & Company plc, 54
WD-40 Company, 87 (upd.)
Zeneca Group PLC, 21

Conglomerates

A.P. Møller - Maersk A/S, 57
Abengoa S.A., 73
Acciona S.A., 81
Accor SA, 10; 27 (upd.)
Aditya Birla Group, 79
Administración Nacional de Combustibles, Alcohol y Pórtland, 93
AEG A.G., I
Al Habtoor Group L.L.C., 87
Alcatel Alsthom Compagnie Générale d'Electricité, 9
Alco Standard Corporation, I
Alexander & Baldwin, Inc., 10, 40 (upd.)
Alfa, S.A. de C.V., 19
Alleghany Corporation, 60 (upd.)
Allied Domecq PLC, 29
Allied-Signal Inc., I
AMFAC Inc., I
The Anschutz Company, 73 (upd.)
The Anschutz Corporation, 36 (upd.)
Antofagasta plc, 65
Apax Partners Worldwide LLP, 89
APi Group, Inc., 64
Aramark Corporation, 13
ARAMARK Corporation, 41
Archer Daniels Midland Company, I; 11 (upd.); 75 (upd.)
Arkansas Best Corporation, 16
Associated British Ports Holdings Plc, 45
BAA plc, 33 (upd.)
Barlow Rand Ltd., I
Barratt Developments plc, 56 (upd.)
Bat Industries PLC, I
Baugur Group hf, 81
BB Holdings Limited, 77
Berjaya Group Bhd., 67
Berkshire Hathaway Inc., III; 18 (upd.); 42 (upd.); 89 (upd.)
Block Communications, Inc., 81
Bond Corporation Holdings Limited, 10
Brascan Corporation, 67
BTR PLC, I
Bunzl plc, 31 (upd.)
Burlington Northern Santa Fe Corporation, 27 (upd.)
Business Post Group plc, 46
C. Itoh & Company Ltd., I
C.I. Traders Limited, 61
Camargo Corrêa S.A., 93
Cargill, Incorporated, II; 13 (upd.); 40 (upd.); 89 (upd.)
CBI Industries, Inc., 7
Charoen Pokphand Group, 62
Chemed Corporation, 13
Chesebrough-Pond's USA, Inc., 8
China Merchants International Holdings Co., Ltd., 52
Cisneros Group of Companies, 54
CITIC Pacific Ltd., 18
CJ Corporation, 62
Colgate-Palmolive Company, 71 (upd.)
Colt Industries Inc., I
Compagnie Financiere Richemont AG, 50
The Connell Company, 29
Conzzeta Holding, 80
Cox Enterprises, Inc., 67 (upd.)
Cristalerias de Chile S.A., 67
CSR Limited, III; 28 (upd.); 85 (upd.)
Daewoo Group, 18 (upd.); 57 (upd.)
Dallah Albaraka Group, 72
De Dietrich & Cie., 31
Deere & Company, 21 (upd.)
Delaware North Companies Incorporated, 7
Desc, S.A. de C.V., 23
The Dial Corp., 8
Dogan Sirketler Grubu Holding A.S., 83
Dr. August Oetker KG, 51
E.I. du Pont de Nemours and Company, 73 (upd.)
EBSCO Industries, Inc., 40 (upd.)
El Corte Inglés Group, 26 (upd.)
Elders IXL Ltd., I
Empresas Copec S.A., 69
Engelhard Corporation, 21 (upd.); 72 (upd.)
Essar Group Ltd., 79
Farley Northwest Industries, Inc., I
Fimalac S.A., 37
First Pacific Company Limited, 18
Fisher Companies, Inc., 15
Fletcher Challenge Ltd., 19 (upd.)
Florida East Coast Industries, Inc., 59
FMC Corporation, I; 11 (upd.)
Fortune Brands, Inc., 29 (upd.); 68 (upd.)
Fraser & Neave Ltd., 54
Fuqua Industries, Inc., I
General Electric Company, 34 (upd.); 63 (upd.)
Genting Bhd., 65
GIB Group, 26 (upd.)
Gillett Holdings, Inc., 7
The Gillette Company, 68 (upd.)
Granaria Holdings B.V., 66
Grand Metropolitan PLC, 14 (upd.)
Great American Management and Investment, Inc., 8
Greyhound Corporation, I
Groupe Bolloré, 67
Groupe Louis Dreyfus S.A., 60
Grupo Carso, S.A. de C.V., 21
Grupo Clarín S.A., 67
Grupo Industrial Bimbo, 19
Grupo Industrial Saltillo, S.A. de C.V., 54
Gulf & Western Inc., I
Haci Omer Sabanci Holdings A.S., 55
Hagemeyer N.V., 39
Hankyu Corporation, 23 (upd.)
Hanson PLC, III; 7 (upd.)
Hanwha Group, 62
Harbour Group Industries, Inc., 90
Hawk Corporation, 59
Henry Crown and Company, 91
Hitachi Zosen Corporation, 53 (upd.)
Hitachi, Ltd., I; 12 (upd.); 40 (upd.)
Ho-Chunk Inc., 61
Hutchison Whampoa Limited, 18; 49 (upd.)
Hyundai Group, 56 (upd.)
IC Industries, Inc., I
Ilitch Holdings Inc., 37; 86 (upd.)
Inchcape PLC, 16 (upd.); 50 (upd.)
Industria de Diseño Textil S.A. (Inditex), 64
Industrie Zignago Santa Margherita S.p.A., 67
Ingram Industries, Inc., 11; 49 (upd.)
Instituto Nacional de Industria, I
International Controls Corporation, 10
International Telephone & Telegraph Corporation, I; 11 (upd.)
Investor AB, 63
Ishikawajima-Harima Heavy Industries Company, Ltd., III; 86 (upd.)
Istituto per la Ricostruzione Industriale, I
ITOCHU Corporation, 32 (upd.)
J.R. Simplot Company, 60 (upd.)
Jardine Matheson Holdings Limited, I; 20 (upd.); 93 (upd.)
Jason Incorporated, 23
Jefferson Smurfit Group plc, 19 (upd.)
The Jim Pattison Group, 37
Jordan Industries, Inc., 36
Justin Industries, Inc., 19
Kanematsu Corporation, 24 (upd.)
Kao Corporation, 20 (upd.)
Katy Industries, Inc., I
Keppel Corporation Ltd., 73
Kesko Ltd. (Kesko Oy), 8; 27 (upd.)
Kidde plc, I; 44 (upd.)
King Ranch, Inc., 60 (upd.)
Knowledge Universe, Inc., 54
Koç Holding A.S., I; 54 (upd.)
Koch Industries, Inc., 77 (upd.)
Koninklijke Nedlloyd N.V., 26 (upd.)
Koor Industries Ltd., 25 (upd.); 68 (upd.)
Körber AG, 60
K2 Inc., 16; 84 (upd.)
The L.L. Knickerbocker Co., Inc., 25
Lancaster Colony Corporation, 8; 61 (upd.)
Larry H. Miller Group, 29
LDI Ltd., LLC, 76
Lear Siegler, Inc., I
Lefrak Organization Inc., 26
Leucadia National Corporation, 11; 71 (upd.)
Linde AG, 67 (upd.)
Litton Industries, Inc., I; 11 (upd.)
Loews Corporation, I; 12 (upd.); 36 (upd.); 93 (upd.)
Loral Corporation, 8
LTV Corporation, I; 24 (upd.)
LVMH Moët Hennessy Louis Vuitton SA, 33 (upd.)
The Marmon Group, Inc., 70 (upd.)
Marubeni Corporation, I; 24 (upd.)
MAXXAM Inc., 8
McKesson Corporation, I
McPherson's Ltd., 66
Melitta Unternehmensgruppe Bentz KG, 53
Menasha Corporation, 8

Metallgesellschaft AG, 16 (upd.)
Metromedia Company, 7; 61 (upd.)
Minnesota Mining & Manufacturing Company (3M), I; 8 (upd.); 26 (upd.)
Mitsubishi Corporation, I; 12 (upd.)
Mitsubishi Heavy Industries, Ltd., 40 (upd.)
Mitsui & Co., Ltd., I; 28 (upd.)
The Molson Companies Limited, I; 26 (upd.)
Montedison S.p.A., 24 (upd.)
NACCO Industries, Inc., 7; 78 (upd.)
Nagase & Co., Ltd., 61 (upd.)
National Service Industries, Inc., 11; 54 (upd.)
New Clicks Holdings Ltd., 86
New World Development Company Limited, 38 (upd.)
Nichimen Corporation, 24 (upd.)
Nichirei Corporation, 70
Nissho Iwai K.K., I
Norsk Hydro A.S., 10
Novar plc, 49 (upd.)
Ogden Corporation, I
Onex Corporation, 16; 65 (upd.)
Orkla ASA, 18; 82 (upd.)
Park-Ohio Holdings Corp., 17; 85 (upd.)
Pentair, Inc., 7; 26 (upd.); 81 (upd.)
Petrobras Energia Participaciones S.A., 72
Philip Morris Companies Inc., 44 (upd.)
Poliet S.A., 33
Powell Duffryn plc, 31
Power Corporation of Canada, 36 (upd.); 85 (upd.)
PPB Group Berhad, 57
Preussag AG, 17
The Procter & Gamble Company, III; 8 (upd.); 26 (upd.); 67 (upd.)
Proeza S.A. de C.V., 82
PT Astra International Tbk, 56
Pubco Corporation, 17
Pulsar Internacional S.A., 21
R.B. Pamplin Corp., 45
The Rank Organisation Plc, 14 (upd.)
Raymond Ltd., 77
Red Apple Group, Inc., 23
Roll International Corporation, 37
Rubbermaid Incorporated, 20 (upd.)
Samsung Group, I
San Miguel Corporation, 15
Sara Lee Corporation, 15 (upd.); 54 (upd.)
S.C. Johnson & Son, Inc., III; 28 (upd.); 89 (upd.)
Schindler Holding AG, 29
Scott Fetzer Company, 12; 80 (upd.)
Sea Containers Ltd., 29
Seaboard Corporation, 36; 85 (upd.)
Sealaska Corporation, 60
Sequa Corporation, 54 (upd.)
Sequana Capital, 78 (upd.)
ServiceMaster Inc., 23 (upd.)
SHV Holdings N.V., 55
Sideco Americana S.A., 67
Sime Darby Berhad, 14; 36 (upd.)
Sistema JSFC, 73
SK Group, 88
Société du Louvre, 27
Standex International Corporation, 17; 44 (upd.)
Steamships Trading Company Ltd., 82
Stinnes AG, 23 (upd.)
Sudbury Inc., 16
Sumitomo Corporation, I; 11 (upd.)
Swire Pacific Limited, I; 16 (upd.); 57 (upd.)
Talley Industries, Inc., 16
Tandycrafts, Inc., 31
TaurusHolding GmbH & Co. KG, 46
Teijin Limited, 61 (upd.)
Teledyne, Inc., I; 10 (upd.)
Tenneco Inc., I; 10 (upd.)
Textron Inc., I; 34 (upd.); 88 (upd.)
Thomas H. Lee Co., 24
Thorn Emi PLC, I
Thorn plc, 24
TI Group plc, 17
Time Warner Inc., IV; 7 (upd.)
Tokyu Corporation, 47 (upd.)
Tomen Corporation, 24 (upd.)
Tomkins plc, 11; 44 (upd.)
Toshiba Corporation, I; 12 (upd.); 40 (upd.)
Tractebel S.A., 20
Transamerica–An AEGON Company, I; 13 (upd.); 41 (upd.)
The Tranzonic Cos., 15
Triarc Companies, Inc., 8
Triple Five Group Ltd., 49
TRW Inc., I; 11 (upd.)
Tyco International Ltd., 63 (upd.)
Unilever, II; 7 (upd.); 32 (upd.); 89 (upd.)
Unión Fenosa, S.A., 51
United Technologies Corporation, 34 (upd.)
Universal Studios, Inc., 33
Valhi, Inc., 19
Valorem S.A., 88
Valores Industriales S.A., 19
Veba A.G., I; 15 (upd.)
Vendôme Luxury Group plc, 27
Viacom Inc., 23 (upd.); 67 (upd.)
Virgin Group Ltd., 12; 32 (upd.); 89 (upd.)
Vivartia S.A., 82
Votorantim Participaçoes S.A., 76
W.R. Grace & Company, I; 50
Walter Industries, Inc., 72 (upd.)
The Washington Companies, 33
Watsco Inc., 52
Wheaton Industries, 8
Whitbread PLC, 20 (upd.)
Whitman Corporation, 10 (upd.)
Whittaker Corporation, I
Wirtz Corporation, 72
WorldCorp, Inc., 10
Worms et Cie, 27
Yamaha Corporation, 40 (upd.)

Construction

A. Johnson & Company H.B., I
ABC Supply Co., Inc., 22
Abertis Infraestructuras, S.A., 65
Abrams Industries Inc., 23
Aegek S.A., 64
Alberici Corporation, 76
Amec Spie S.A., 57
AMREP Corporation, 21
Anthony & Sylvan Pools Corporation, 56
Asplundh Tree Expert Co., 59 (upd.)
Astec Industries, Inc., 79
ASV, Inc., 34; 66 (upd.)
The Auchter Company, 78
The Austin Company, 8
Autoroutes du Sud de la France SA, 55
Balfour Beatty plc, 36 (upd.)
Baratt Developments PLC, I
Barton Malow Company, 51
Bauerly Companies, 61
BE&K, Inc., 73
Beazer Homes USA, Inc., 17
Bechtel Group, Inc., I; 24 (upd.)
Bellway Plc, 45
BFC Construction Corporation, 25
Bilfinger & Berger AG, I; 55 (upd.)
Bird Corporation, 19
Birse Group PLC, 77
Black & Veatch LLP, 22
Boral Limited, 43 (upd.)
Bouygues S.A., I; 24 (upd.)
The Branch Group, Inc., 72
Brasfield & Gorrie LLC, 87
BRISA Auto-estradas de Portugal S.A., 64
Brown & Root, Inc., 13
Bufete Industrial, S.A. de C.V., 34
Building Materials Holding Corporation, 52
Bulley & Andrews, LLC, 55
C.R. Meyer and Sons Company, 74
CalMat Co., 19
Cavco Industries, Inc., 65
Centex Corporation, 8; 29 (upd.)
Chugach Alaska Corporation, 60
Cianbro Corporation, 14
The Clark Construction Group, Inc., 8
Colas S.A., 31
Consorcio ARA, S.A. de C.V., 79
Corporación Geo, S.A. de C.V., 81
D.R. Horton, Inc., 58
Day & Zimmermann, Inc., 31 (upd.)
Desarrolladora Homex, S.A. de C.V., 87
Dick Corporation, 64
Dillingham Construction Corporation, I; 44 (upd.)
Dominion Homes, Inc., 19
The Drees Company, Inc., 41
Dycom Industries, Inc., 57
E.W. Howell Co., Inc., 72
Edw. C. Levy Co., 42
Eiffage, 27
Ellerbe Becket, 41
EMCOR Group Inc., 60
Empresas ICA Sociedad Controladora, S.A. de C.V., 41
Encompass Services Corporation, 33
Engle Homes, Inc., 46
Environmental Industries, Inc., 31
Eurotunnel PLC, 13
Fairclough Construction Group PLC, I
Flatiron Construction Corporation, 92
Fleetwood Enterprises, Inc., III: 22 (upd.); 81 (upd.)
Fluor Corporation, I; 8 (upd.); 34 (upd.)

Forest City Enterprises, Inc., 52 (upd.)
Fred Weber, Inc., 61
Furmanite Corporation, 92
George Wimpey plc, 12; 51 (upd.)
Gilbane, Inc., 34
Granite Construction Incorporated, 61
Granite Rock Company, 26
Great Lakes Dredge & Dock Company, 69
Grupo Dragados SA, 55
Grupo Ferrovial, S.A., 40
H.J. Russell & Company, 66
Habitat for Humanity International, 36
Heery International, Inc., 58
Heijmans N.V., 66
Henry Boot plc, 76
Hensel Phelps Construction Company, 72
Hillsdown Holdings plc, 24 (upd.)
Hochtief AG, 33; 88 (upd.)
Hoffman Corporation 78
Horton Homes, Inc., 25
Hospitality Worldwide Services, Inc., 26
Hovnanian Enterprises, Inc., 29; 89 (upd.)
IHC Caland N.V., 71
Irex Contracting Group, 90
J.A. Jones, Inc., 16
J C Bamford Excavators Ltd., 83
J.F. Shea Co., Inc., 55
J.H. Findorff and Son, Inc., 60
Jarvis plc, 39
JE Dunn Construction Group, Inc., 85
JLG Industries, Inc., 52
John Brown PLC, I
John Laing plc, I; 51 (upd.)
John W. Danforth Company, 48
Kajima Corporation, I; 51 (upd.)
Kaufman and Broad Home Corporation, 8
KB Home, 45 (upd.)
Kellogg Brown & Root, Inc., 62 (upd.)
Kitchell Corporation, 14
The Koll Company, 8
Komatsu Ltd., 16 (upd.)
Kraus-Anderson Companies, Inc., 36; 83 (upd.)
Kumagai Gumi Company, Ltd., I
L'Entreprise Jean Lefebvre, 23
Laing O'Rourke PLC, 93 (upd.)
Ledcor Industries Limited, 46
Lennar Corporation, 11
Lincoln Property Company, 8
Lindal Cedar Homes, Inc., 29
Linde A.G., I
MasTec, Inc., 55
Matrix Service Company, 65
McCarthy Building Companies, Inc., 48
Mellon-Stuart Company, I
Michael Baker Corp., 14
Modtech Holdings, Inc., 77
Morrison Knudsen Corporation, 7; 28 (upd.)
Morrow Equipment Co. L.L.C., 87
New Holland N.V., 22
Newpark Resources, Inc., 63
NVR Inc., 70 (upd.)
NVR L.P., 8
Obayashi Corporation 78
Obrascon Huarte Lain S.A., 76
Ohbayashi Corporation, I
Opus Group, 34
Orascom Construction Industries S.A.E., 87
Orleans Homebuilders, Inc., 62
The Parsons Corporation, 56 (upd.)
PCL Construction Group Inc., 50
The Peninsular & Oriental Steam Navigation Company (Bovis Division), I
Perini Corporation, 8; 82 (upd.)
Peter Kiewit Sons' Inc., 8
Philipp Holzmann AG, 17
Post Properties, Inc., 26
Pulte Homes, Inc., 8; 42 (upd.)
Pyramid Companies, 54
Redrow Group plc, 31
Rinker Group Ltd., 65
RMC Group p.l.c., 34 (upd.)
Rooney Brothers Co., 25
The Rottlund Company, Inc., 28
Roy Anderson Corporation, 75
The Ryland Group, Inc., 8; 37 (upd.)
Sandvik AB, 32 (upd.)
Schuff Steel Company, 26
Seddon Group Ltd., 67
Shorewood Packaging Corporation, 28
Simon Property Group Inc., 27; 84 (upd.)
Skanska AB, 38
Skidmore, Owings & Merrill LLP, 69 (upd.)
SNC-Lavalin Group Inc., 72
Speedy Hire plc, 84
Stabler Companies Inc. 78
Standard Pacific Corporation, 52
Stone & Webster, Inc., 64 (upd.)
Sundt Corp., 24
Swinerton Inc., 43
Taylor Woodrow plc, I; 38 (upd.)
Technical Olympic USA, Inc., 75
Terex Corporation, 7; 40 (upd.); 91 (upd.)
ThyssenKrupp AG, IV; 28 (upd.); 87 (upd.)
TIC Holdings Inc., 92
Toll Brothers Inc., 15; 70 (upd.)
Trammell Crow Company, 8
Tridel Enterprises Inc., 9
Turner Construction Company, 66
The Turner Corporation, 8; 23 (upd.)
U.S. Aggregates, Inc., 42
U.S. Home Corporation, 8; 78 (upd.)
Urbi Desarrollos Urbanos, S.A. de C.V., 81
VA TECH ELIN EBG GmbH, 49
Veit Companies, 43; 92 (upd.)
Walbridge Aldinger Co., 38
Walter Industries, Inc., 22 (upd.)
The Weitz Company, Inc., 42
Willbros Group, Inc., 56
William Lyon Homes, 59
Wilson Bowden Plc, 45
Wood Hall Trust PLC, I
The Yates Companies, Inc., 62

Containers

Ball Corporation, I; 10 (upd.); 78 (upd.)
BWAY Corporation, 24
Chesapeake Corporation, 8; 30 (upd.); 93 (upd.)
Clarcor Inc., 17
Continental Can Co., Inc., 15
Continental Group Company, I
Crown Cork & Seal Company, Inc., I; 13 (upd.); 32 (upd.)
Crown Holdings, Inc., 83 (upd.)
Gaylord Container Corporation, 8
Golden Belt Manufacturing Co., 16
Graham Packaging Holdings Company, 87
Greif Inc., 15; 66 (upd.)
Grupo Industrial Durango, S.A. de C.V., 37
Hanjin Shipping Co., Ltd., 50
Inland Container Corporation, 8
Interpool, Inc., 92
Kerr Group Inc., 24
Keyes Fibre Company, 9
Libbey Inc., 49
Liqui-Box Corporation, 16
The Longaberger Company, 12
Longview Fibre Company, 8
The Mead Corporation, 19 (upd.)
Metal Box PLC, I
Molins plc, 51
National Can Corporation, I
Owens-Illinois, Inc., I; 26 (upd.); 85 (upd.)
Packaging Corporation of America, 51 (upd.)
Primerica Corporation, I
PVC Container Corporation, 67
Rexam PLC, 32 (upd.); 85 (upd.)
Reynolds Metals Company, 19 (upd.)
Royal Packaging Industries Van Leer N.V., 30
RPC Group PLC, 81
Sealright Co., Inc., 17
Shurgard Storage Centers, Inc., 52
Smurfit-Stone Container Corporation, 26 (upd.); 83 (upd.)
Sonoco Products Company, 8; 89 (upd.)
Thermos Company, 16
Toyo Seikan Kaisha, Ltd., I
U.S. Can Corporation, 30
Ultra Pac, Inc., 24
Viatech Continental Can Company, Inc., 25 (upd.)
Vidrala S.A., 67
Vitro Corporativo S.A. de C.V., 34

Drugs & Pharmaceuticals

A. Nelson & Co. Ltd., 75
A.L. Pharma Inc., 12
Abbott Laboratories, I; 11 (upd.); 40 (upd.); 93 (upd.)
Actelion Ltd., 83
Akorn, Inc., 32
Albany Molecular Research, Inc., 77
Allergan, Inc., 77 (upd.)
Alpharma Inc., 35 (upd.)
ALZA Corporation, 10; 36 (upd.)
American Home Products, I; 10 (upd.)
American Oriental Bioengineering Inc., 93
American Pharmaceutical Partners, Inc., 69

AmerisourceBergen Corporation, 64 (upd.)
Amersham PLC, 50
Amgen, Inc., 10; 89 (upd.)
Amylin Pharmaceuticals, Inc., 67
Andrx Corporation, 55
AstraZeneca PLC, I; 20 (upd.); 50 (upd.)
Axcan Pharma Inc., 85
Barr Pharmaceuticals, Inc., 26; 68 (upd.)
Bayer A.G., I; 13 (upd.)
Berlex Laboratories, Inc., 66
Biovail Corporation, 47
Block Drug Company, Inc., 8
Boiron S.A., 73
Bristol-Myers Squibb Company, III; 9 (upd.); 37 (upd.)
BTG Plc, 87
C.H. Boehringer Sohn, 39
Caremark Rx, Inc., 10; 54 (upd.)
Carter-Wallace, Inc., 8; 38 (upd.)
Celgene Corporation, 67
Cephalon, Inc., 45
Chiron Corporation, 10
Chugai Pharmaceutical Co., Ltd., 50
Ciba-Geigy Ltd., I; 8 (upd.)
D&K Wholesale Drug, Inc., 14
Discovery Partners International, Inc., 58
Dr. Reddy's Laboratories Ltd., 59
Elan Corporation PLC, 63
Eli Lilly and Company, I; 11 (upd.); 47 (upd.)
Endo Pharmaceuticals Holdings Inc., 71
Eon Labs, Inc., 67
Express Scripts Inc., 44 (upd.)
F. Hoffmann-La Roche Ltd., I; 50 (upd.)
Fisons plc, 9; 23 (upd.)
Forest Laboratories, Inc., 52 (upd.)
FoxMeyer Health Corporation, 16
Fujisawa Pharmaceutical Company Ltd., I
G.D. Searle & Co., I; 12 (upd.); 34 (upd.)
Galenica AG, 84
GEHE AG, 27
Genentech, Inc., I; 8 (upd.); 75 (upd.)
Genetics Institute, Inc., 8
Genzyme Corporation, 13, 77 (upd.)
Glaxo Holdings PLC, I; 9 (upd.)
GlaxoSmithKline plc, 46 (upd.)
Groupe Fournier SA, 44
Groupe Léa Nature, 88
H. Lundbeck A/S, 44
Hauser, Inc., 46
Heska Corporation, 39
Hexal AG, 69
Hospira, Inc., 71
Huntingdon Life Sciences Group plc, 42
ICN Pharmaceuticals, Inc., 52
Immucor, Inc., 81
Integrated BioPharma, Inc., 83
IVAX Corporation, 55 (upd.)
Janssen Pharmaceutica N.V., 80
Johnson & Johnson, III; 8 (upd.)
Jones Medical Industries, Inc., 24
The Judge Group, Inc., 51
King Pharmaceuticals, Inc., 54
Kinray Inc., 85
Kos Pharmaceuticals, Inc., 63
Kyowa Hakko Kogyo Co., Ltd., 48 (upd.)
Laboratoires Arkopharma S.A., 75
Leiner Health Products Inc., 34
Ligand Pharmaceuticals Incorporated, 47
MannKind Corporation, 87
Marion Merrell Dow, Inc., I; 9 (upd.)
Matrixx Initiatives, Inc., 74
McKesson Corporation, 12; 47 (upd.)
Medicis Pharmaceutical Corporation, 59
MedImmune, Inc., 35
Merck & Co., Inc., I; 11 (upd.); 34 (upd.)
Merz Group, 81
Miles Laboratories, I
Millennium Pharmaceuticals, Inc., 47
Monsanto Company, 29 (upd.), 77 (upd.)
Moore Medical Corp., 17
Murdock Madaus Schwabe, 26
Mylan Laboratories Inc., I; 20 (upd.); 59 (upd.)
Nadro S.A. de C.V., 86
Nastech Pharmaceutical Company Inc., 79
National Patent Development Corporation, 13
Natrol, Inc., 49
Natural Alternatives International, Inc., 49
Nektar Therapeutics, 91
Novartis AG, 39 (upd.)
Noven Pharmaceuticals, Inc., 55
Novo Nordisk A/S, I; 61 (upd.)
Omnicare, Inc., 49
Par Pharmaceutical Companies, Inc., 65
PDL BioPharma, Inc., 90
Perrigo Company, 59 (upd.)
Pfizer Inc., I; 9 (upd.); 38 (upd.); 79 (upd.)
Pharmacia & Upjohn Inc., I; 25 (upd.)
Pharmion Corporation, 91
PLIVA d.d., 70
PolyMedica Corporation, 77
POZEN Inc., 81
QLT Inc., 71
The Quigley Corporation, 62
Quintiles Transnational Corporation, 21
R.P. Scherer, I
Ranbaxy Laboratories Ltd., 70
ratiopharm Group, 84
Reckitt Benckiser plc, II; 42 (upd.); 91 (upd.)
Roberts Pharmaceutical Corporation, 16
Roche Bioscience, 14 (upd.)
Rorer Group, I
Roussel Uclaf, I; 8 (upd.)
Salix Pharmaceuticals, Ltd., 93
Sandoz Ltd., I
Sankyo Company, Ltd., I; 56 (upd.)
The Sanofi-Synthélabo Group, I; 49 (upd.)
Schering AG, I; 50 (upd.)
Schering-Plough Corporation, I; 14 (upd.); 49 (upd.)
Sepracor Inc., 45
Serono S.A., 47
Shionogi & Co., Ltd., 17 (upd.)
Sigma-Aldrich Corporation, I; 36 (upd.); 93 (upd.)
SmithKline Beecham plc, I; 32 (upd.)
Solvay S.A., 61 (upd.)
Squibb Corporation, I
Sterling Drug, Inc., I
Stiefel Laboratories, Inc., 90
Sun Pharmaceutical Industries Ltd., 57
The Sunrider Corporation, 26
Syntex Corporation, I
Takeda Chemical Industries, Ltd., I
Taro Pharmaceutical Industries Ltd., 65
Teva Pharmaceutical Industries Ltd., 22; 54 (upd.)
The Upjohn Company, I; 8 (upd.)
Vertex Pharmaceuticals Incorporated, 83
Virbac Corporation, 74
Vitalink Pharmacy Services, Inc., 15
Warner Chilcott Limited, 85
Warner-Lambert Co., I; 10 (upd.)
Watson Pharmaceuticals Inc., 16; 56 (upd.)
The Wellcome Foundation Ltd., I
Zila, Inc., 46

Electrical & Electronics

ABB ASEA Brown Boveri Ltd., II; 22 (upd.)
ABB Ltd., 65 (upd.)
Acer Incorporated, 16; 73 (upd.)
Acuson Corporation, 10; 36 (upd.)
ADC Telecommunications, Inc., 30 (upd.)
Adtran Inc., 22
Advanced Micro Devices, Inc., 30 (upd.)
Advanced Technology Laboratories, Inc., 9
Agere Systems Inc., 61
Agilent Technologies Inc., 38; 93 (upd.)
Agilysys Inc., 76 (upd.)
Aiwa Co., Ltd., 30
AKG Acoustics GmbH, 62
Akzo Nobel N.V., 13; 41 (upd.)
Alienware Corporation, 81
Alliant Techsystems Inc., 30 (upd.); 77 (upd.)
AlliedSignal Inc., 22 (upd.)
Alpine Electronics, Inc., 13
Alps Electric Co., Ltd., II
Altera Corporation, 18; 43 (upd.)
Altron Incorporated, 20
Amdahl Corporation, 40 (upd.)
American Power Conversion Corporation, 24; 67 (upd.)
American Technical Ceramics Corp., 67
Amkor Technology, Inc., 69
AMP Incorporated, II; 14 (upd.)
Amphenol Corporation, 40
Amstrad plc, 48 (upd.)
Analog Devices, Inc., 10
Analogic Corporation, 23
Anam Group, 23
Anaren Microwave, Inc., 33
Andrew Corporation, 10; 32 (upd.)
Anixter International Inc., 88
Anritsu Corporation, 68
Apex Digital, Inc., 63
Apple Computer, Inc., 36 (upd.); 77 (upd.)
Applied Power Inc., 32 (upd.)
Applied Signal Technology, Inc., 87
Argon ST, Inc., 81
Arotech Corporation, 93
ARRIS Group, Inc., 89
Arrow Electronics, Inc., 10; 50 (upd.)

Ascend Communications, Inc., 24
Astronics Corporation, 35
Atari Corporation, 9; 23 (upd.); 66 (upd.)
ATI Technologies Inc., 79
Atmel Corporation, 17
ATMI, Inc., 93
AU Optronics Corporation, 67
Audiovox Corporation, 34; 90 (upd.)
Ault Incorporated, 34
Autodesk, Inc., 10; 89 (upd.)
Avnet Inc., 9
AVX Corporation, 67
Axsys Technologies, Inc., 93
Ballard Power Systems Inc., 73
Bang & Olufsen Holding A/S, 37; 86 (upd.)
Barco NV, 44
Bell Microproducts Inc., 69
Benchmark Electronics, Inc., 40
Bicoastal Corporation, II
Blonder Tongue Laboratories, Inc., 48
Blue Coat Systems, Inc., 83
BMC Industries, Inc., 59 (upd.)
Bogen Communications International, Inc., 62
Bose Corporation, 13; 36 (upd.)
Boston Acoustics, Inc., 22
Bowthorpe plc, 33
Braun GmbH, 51
Broadcom Corporation, 34; 90 (upd.)
Bull S.A., 43 (upd.)
Burr-Brown Corporation, 19
BVR Systems (1998) Ltd., 93
C-COR.net Corp., 38
Cabletron Systems, Inc., 10
Cadence Design Systems, Inc., 48 (upd.)
Cambridge SoundWorks, Inc., 48
Canon Inc., 18 (upd.); 79 (upd.)
Carbone Lorraine S.A., 33
Cardtronics, Inc., 93
Carl Zeiss AG, III; 34 (upd.); 91 (upd.)
Cash Systems, Inc., 93
CASIO Computer Co., Ltd., 16 (upd.); 40 (upd.)
CDW Computer Centers, Inc., 52 (upd.)
Celestica Inc., 80
Checkpoint Systems, Inc., 39
Chi Mei Optoelectronics Corporation, 75
Chubb, PLC, 50
Chunghwa Picture Tubes, Ltd., 75
Cirrus Logic, Inc., 48 (upd.)
Cisco Systems, Inc., 34 (upd.); 77 (upd.)
Citizen Watch Co., Ltd., III; 21 (upd.); 81 (upd.)
Clarion Company Ltd., 64
Cobham plc, 30
Cobra Electronics Corporation, 14
Coherent, Inc., 31
Cohu, Inc., 32
Color Kinetics Incorporated, 85
Compagnie Générale d'Électricité, II
Concurrent Computer Corporation, 75
Conexant Systems, Inc., 36
Cooper Industries, Inc., II
Cray Inc., 75 (upd.)
Cray Research, Inc., 16 (upd.)
Cree Inc., 53
CTS Corporation, 39
Cubic Corporation, 19
Cypress Semiconductor Corporation, 20; 48 (upd.)
D-Link Corporation, 83
Dai Nippon Printing Co., Ltd., 57 (upd.)
Daiichikosho Company Ltd., 86
Daktronics, Inc., 32
Dallas Semiconductor Corporation, 13; 31 (upd.)
De La Rue plc, 34 (upd.)
Dell Computer Corporation, 31 (upd.)
DH Technology, Inc., 18
Dictaphone Healthcare Solutions 78
Diehl Stiftung & Co. KG, 79
Digi International Inc., 9
Diodes Incorporated, 81
Directed Electronics, Inc., 87
Discreet Logic Inc., 20
Dixons Group plc, 19 (upd.)
Dolby Laboratories Inc., 20
Dot Hill Systems Corp., 93
DRS Technologies, Inc., 58
Dynatech Corporation, 13
E-Systems, Inc., 9
Electronics for Imaging, Inc., 15; 43 (upd.)
Elma Electronic AG, 83
Elpida Memory, Inc., 83
Emerson, II; 46 (upd.)
Emerson Radio Corp., 30
ENCAD, Incorporated, 25
Equant N.V., 52
Equus Computer Systems, Inc., 49
ESS Technology, Inc., 22
Essex Corporation, 85
Everex Systems, Inc., 16
Exabyte Corporation, 40 (upd.)
Exar Corp., 14
Exide Electronics Group, Inc., 20
Finisar Corporation, 92
Fisk Corporation, 72
Flextronics International Ltd., 38
Fluke Corporation, 15
FormFactor, Inc., 85
Foxboro Company, 13
Freescale Semiconductor, Inc., 83
Frequency Electronics, Inc., 61
FuelCell Energy, Inc., 75
Fuji Electric Co., Ltd., II; 48 (upd.)
Fuji Photo Film Co., Ltd., 79 (upd.)
Fujitsu Limited, 16 (upd.); 42 (upd.)
Funai Electric Company Ltd., 62
Gateway, Inc., 63 (upd.)
General Atomics, 57
General Dynamics Corporation, I; 10 (upd.); 40 (upd.); 88 (upd.
General Electric Company, II; 12 (upd.)
General Electric Company, PLC, II
General Instrument Corporation, 10
General Signal Corporation, 9
Genesis Microchip Inc., 82
GenRad, Inc., 24
GM Hughes Electronics Corporation, II
Goldstar Co., Ltd., 12
Gould Electronics, Inc., 14
GPS Industries, Inc., 81
Grundig AG, 27
Guillemot Corporation, 41
Hadco Corporation, 24
Hamilton Beach/Proctor-Silex Inc., 17
Harman International Industries Inc., 15
Harris Corporation, II; 20 (upd.); 78 (upd.)
Hayes Corporation, 24
Herley Industries, Inc., 33
Hewlett-Packard Company, 28 (upd.); 50 (upd.)
Holophane Corporation, 19
Hon Hai Precision Industry Co., Ltd., 59
Honeywell Inc., II; 12 (upd.); 50 (upd.)
Hubbell Incorporated, 9; 31 (upd.)
Hughes Supply, Inc., 14
Hutchinson Technology Incorporated, 18; 63 (upd.)
Hypercom Corporation, 27
IDEO Inc., 65
IEC Electronics Corp., 42
Illumina, Inc., 93
Imax Corporation, 28
In Focus Systems, Inc., 22
Indigo NV, 26
InFocus Corporation, 92
Ingram Micro Inc., 52
Innovative Solutions & Support, Inc., 85
Integrated Defense Technologies, Inc., 54
Intel Corporation, II; 10 (upd.); 75 (upd.)
Intermec Technologies Corporation, 72
International Business Machines Corporation, III; 6 (upd.); 30 (upd.); 63 (upd.)
International Rectifier Corporation, 31; 71 (upd.)
Intersil Corporation, 93
Ionatron, Inc., 85
Itel Corporation, 9
Jabil Circuit, Inc., 36; 88 (upd.)
Jaco Electronics, Inc., 30
JDS Uniphase Corporation, 34
Johnson Controls, Inc., 59 (upd.)
Juno Lighting, Inc., 30
Katy Industries, Inc., 51 (upd.)
Keithley Instruments Inc., 16
Kemet Corp., 14
Kent Electronics Corporation, 17
Kenwood Corporation, 31
Kesa Electricals plc, 91
Kimball International, Inc., 48 (upd.)
Kingston Technology Corporation, 20
KitchenAid, 8
KLA-Tencor Corporation, 45 (upd.)
KnowledgeWare Inc., 9
Kollmorgen Corporation, 18
Konica Corporation, 30 (upd.)
Koninklijke Philips Electronics N.V., 50 (upd.)
Koor Industries Ltd., II
Kopin Corporation, 80
Koss Corporation, 38
Kudelski Group SA, 44
Kulicke and Soffa Industries, Inc., 33; 76 (upd.)
Kyocera Corporation, II; 79 (upd.)
LaBarge Inc., 41
The Lamson & Sessions Co., 61 (upd.)
Lattice Semiconductor Corp., 16
LeCroy Corporation, 41

Legrand SA, 21
Lenovo Group Ltd., 80
Lexmark International, Inc., 79 (upd.)
Linear Technology, Inc., 16
Littelfuse, Inc., 26
Loewe AG, 90
Loral Corporation, 9
Lowrance Electronics, Inc., 18
LSI Logic Corporation, 13; 64
Lucent Technologies Inc., 34
Lucky-Goldstar, II
Lunar Corporation, 29
Mackie Designs Inc., 33
MagneTek, Inc., 15; 41 (upd.)
Magneti Marelli Holding SpA, 90
Marconi plc, 33 (upd.)
Marquette Electronics, Inc., 13
Matsushita Electric Industrial Co., Ltd., II
Maxim Integrated Products, Inc., 16
McDATA Corporation, 75
Measurement Specialties, Inc., 71
Medis Technologies Ltd., 77
Merix Corporation, 36; 75 (upd.)
Methode Electronics, Inc., 13
Mitel Corporation, 18
MITRE Corporation, 26
Mitsubishi Electric Corporation, II; 44 (upd.)
Molex Incorporated, 54 (upd.)
Monster Cable Products, Inc., 69
Motorola, Inc., II; 11 (upd.); 34 (upd.); 93 (upd.)
N.F. Smith & Associates LP, 70
Nam Tai Electronics, Inc., 61
National Instruments Corporation, 22
National Presto Industries, Inc., 16; 43 (upd.)
National Semiconductor Corporation, II; 26 (upd.); 69 (upd.)
NEC Corporation, II; 21 (upd.); 57 (upd.)
Network Equipment Technologies Inc., 92
Nexans SA, 54
Nintendo Co., Ltd., 28 (upd.)
Nokia Corporation, II; 17 (upd.); 38 (upd.); 77 (upd.)
Nortel Networks Corporation, 36 (upd.)
Northrop Grumman Corporation, 45 (upd.)
Oak Technology, Inc., 22
Océ N.V., 24; 91 (upd.)
Oki Electric Industry Company, Limited, II
Omnicell, Inc., 89
Omron Corporation, II; 28 (upd.)
Orbotech Ltd., 75
Otari Inc., 89
Otter Tail Power Company, 18
Palm, Inc., 36; 75 (upd.)
Palomar Medical Technologies, Inc., 22
Parlex Corporation, 61
The Peak Technologies Group, Inc., 14
Peavey Electronics Corporation, 16
Philips Electronics N.V., II; 13 (upd.)
Philips Electronics North America Corp., 13
Pioneer Electronic Corporation, 28 (upd.)
Pioneer-Standard Electronics Inc., 19
Pitney Bowes Inc., 47 (upd.)
Pittway Corporation, 9
Pixelworks, Inc., 69
Planar Systems, Inc., 61
The Plessey Company, PLC, II
Plexus Corporation, 35; 80 (upd.)
Polk Audio, Inc., 34
Polaroid Corporation, III; 7 (upd.); 28 (upd.); 93 (upd.)
Potter & Brumfield Inc., 11
Premier Industrial Corporation, 9
Protection One, Inc., 32
Quanta Computer Inc., 47; 79 (upd.)
Racal Electronics PLC, II
RadioShack Corporation, 36 (upd.)
Radius Inc., 16
RAE Systems Inc., 83
Ramtron International Corporation, 89
Raychem Corporation, 8
Rayovac Corporation, 13
Raytheon Company, II; 11 (upd.); 38 (upd.)
RCA Corporation, II
Read-Rite Corp., 10
Redback Networks, Inc., 92
Reliance Electric Company, 9
Research in Motion Ltd., 54
Rexel, Inc., 15
Richardson Electronics, Ltd., 17
Ricoh Company, Ltd., 36 (upd.)
Rimage Corp., 89
The Rival Company, 19
Rockford Corporation, 43
Rogers Corporation, 61
S&C Electric Company, 15
SAGEM S.A., 37
St. Louis Music, Inc., 48
Sam Ash Music Corporation, 30
Samsung Electronics Co., Ltd., 14; 41 (upd.)
SANYO Electric Co., Ltd., II; 36 (upd.)
Sarnoff Corporation, 57
ScanSource, Inc., 29; 74 (upd.)
Schneider S.A., II; 18 (upd.)
SCI Systems, Inc., 9
Scientific-Atlanta, Inc., 45 (upd.)
Scitex Corporation Ltd., 24
Seagate Technology, Inc., 34 (upd.)
SEGA Corporation, 73
Semitool, Inc., 79 (upd.)
Semtech Corporation, 32
Sennheiser Electronic GmbH & Co. KG, 66
Sensormatic Electronics Corp., 11
Sensory Science Corporation, 37
SGI, 29 (upd.)
Sharp Corporation, II; 12 (upd.); 40 (upd.)
Sheldahl Inc., 23
Shure Inc., 60
Siemens AG, II; 14 (upd.); 57 (upd.)
Silicon Graphics Incorporated, 9
Siltronic AG, 90
SL Industries, Inc., 77
SMART Modular Technologies, Inc., 86
Smiths Industries PLC, 25
Solectron Corporation, 12; 48 (upd.)
Sony Corporation, II; 12 (upd.); 40 (upd.)
Spansion Inc., 80
Spectrum Control, Inc., 67
SPX Corporation, 47 (upd.)
Square D, 90
Sterling Electronics Corp., 18
STMicroelectronics NV, 52
Strix Ltd., 51
Stuart C. Irby Company, 58
Sumitomo Electric Industries, Ltd., II
Sun Microsystems, Inc., 7; 30 (upd.); 91 (upd.)
Sunbeam-Oster Co., Inc., 9
SunPower Corporation, 91
Suntech Power Holdings Company Ltd., 89
Syneron Medical Ltd., 91
SYNNEX Corporation, 73
Synopsys, Inc., 69 (upd.)
Sypris Solutions, Inc., 85
SyQuest Technology, Inc., 18
Tandy Corporation, II; 12 (upd.)
Tatung Co., 23
TDK Corporation, II; 17 (upd.); 49 (upd.)
TEAC Corporation 78
Tech-Sym Corporation, 18
Technitrol, Inc., 29
Tektronix, Inc., 8
Teledyne Technologies Inc., 62 (upd.)
Telxon Corporation, 10
Teradyne, Inc., 11
Texas Instruments Inc., II; 11 (upd.); 46 (upd.)
Thales S.A., 42
Thomas & Betts Corporation, 11; 54 (upd.)
THOMSON multimedia S.A., II; 42 (upd.)
THQ, Inc., 92 (upd.)
The Titan Corporation, 36
TomTom N.V., 81
Tops Appliance City, Inc., 17
Toromont Industries, Ltd., 21
Trans-Lux Corporation, 51
Trimble Navigation Limited, 40
TriQuint Semiconductor, Inc., 63
Tweeter Home Entertainment Group, Inc., 30
Ultimate Electronics, Inc., 69 (upd.)
Ultrak Inc., 24
Universal Electronics Inc., 39
Varian Associates Inc., 12
Veeco Instruments Inc., 32
VIASYS Healthcare, Inc., 52
Viasystems Group, Inc., 67
Vicon Industries, Inc., 44
Victor Company of Japan, Limited, II; 26 (upd.); 83 (upd.)
Vishay Intertechnology, Inc., 21; 80 (upd.)
Vitesse Semiconductor Corporation, 32
Vitro Corp., 10
VLSI Technology, Inc., 16
VTech Holdings Ltd., 77
Wells-Gardner Electronics Corporation, 43

Westinghouse Electric Corporation, II; 12 (upd.)
Winbond Electronics Corporation, 74
Wincor Nixdorf Holding GmbH, 69 (upd.)
Wyle Electronics, 14
Xerox Corporation, 69 (upd.)
Yageo Corporation, 16
York Research Corporation, 35
Zenith Data Systems, Inc., 10
Zenith Electronics Corporation, II; 13 (upd.); 34 (upd.); 89 (upd.)
Zoom Telephonics, Inc., 18
Zoran Corporation, 77
Zumtobel AG, 50
Zytec Corporation, 19

Engineering & Management Services

AAON, Inc., 22
Aavid Thermal Technologies, Inc., 29
AECOM Technology Corporation, 79
Alliant Techsystems Inc., 30 (upd.)
Altran Technologies, 51
Amey Plc, 47
American Science & Engineering, Inc., 81
Analytic Sciences Corporation, 10
Arcadis NV, 26
Arthur D. Little, Inc., 35
The Austin Company, 8; 72 (upd.)
Babcock International Group PLC, 69
Balfour Beatty plc, 36 (upd.)
BE&K, Inc., 73
Birse Group PLC, 77
Brown & Root, Inc., 13
Bufete Industrial, S.A. de C.V., 34
C.H. Heist Corporation, 24
CDI Corporation, 6; 54 (upd.)
CH2M Hill Ltd., 22
The Charles Stark Draper Laboratory, Inc., 35
Coflexip S.A., 25
Corrections Corporation of America, 23
CRSS Inc., 6
Dames & Moore, Inc., 25
DAW Technologies, Inc., 25
Day & Zimmermann Inc., 9; 31 (upd.)
Donaldson Co. Inc., 16
Dycom Industries, Inc., 57
Edwards and Kelcey, 70
EG&G Incorporated, 8; 29 (upd.)
Eiffage, 27
Essef Corporation, 18
FKI Plc, 57
Fluor Corporation, 34 (upd.)
Forest City Enterprises, Inc., 52 (upd.)
Foster Wheeler Corporation, 6; 23 (upd.)
Foster Wheeler Ltd., 76 (upd.)
Framatome SA, 19
Fraport AG Frankfurt Airport Services Worldwide, 90
Gale International Llc, 93
Georg Fischer AG Schaffhausen, 61
Gilbane, Inc., 34
Great Lakes Dredge & Dock Company, 69
Grupo Dragados SA, 55
Halliburton Company, 25 (upd.)
Harding Lawson Associates Group, Inc., 16
Harza Engineering Company, 14
HDR Inc., 48
HOK Group, Inc., 59
ICF Kaiser International, Inc., 28
IHC Caland N.V., 71
Jacobs Engineering Group Inc., 6; 26 (upd.)
Jacques Whitford, 92
The Judge Group, Inc., 51
JWP Inc., 9
The Keith Companies Inc., 54
Klöckner-Werke AG, 58 (upd.)
Kvaerner ASA, 36
Layne Christensen Company, 19
The MacNeal-Schwendler Corporation, 25
Malcolm Pirnie, Inc., 42
McDermott International, Inc., 37 (upd.)
McKinsey & Company, Inc., 9
Michael Baker Corporation, 51 (upd.)
Nooter Corporation, 61
Oceaneering International, Inc., 63
Odebrecht S.A., 73
Ogden Corporation, 6
Opus Group, 34
PAREXEL International Corporation, 84
Parsons Brinckerhoff, Inc., 34
The Parsons Corporation, 8; 56 (upd.)
The PBSJ Corporation, 82
Quanta Services, Inc., 79
RCM Technologies, Inc., 34
Renishaw plc, 46
Ricardo plc, 90
Rosemount Inc., 15
Roy F. Weston, Inc., 33
Royal Vopak NV, 41
Rust International Inc., 11
Sandia National Laboratories, 49
Sandvik AB, 32 (upd.)
Sarnoff Corporation, 57
Science Applications International Corporation, 15
Serco Group plc, 47
Siegel & Gale, 64
Siemens AG, 57 (upd.)
SRI International, Inc., 57
SSOE Inc., 76
Stone & Webster, Inc., 13; 64 (upd.)
Sulzer Ltd., 68 (upd.)
Susquehanna Pfaltzgraff Company, 8
Sverdrup Corporation, 14
Tech-Sym Corporation, 44 (upd.)
Technip 78
Tetra Tech, Inc., 29
ThyssenKrupp AG, IV; 28 (upd.); 87 (upd.)
Towers Perrin, 32
Tracor Inc., 17
TRC Companies, Inc., 32
Underwriters Laboratories, Inc., 30
United Dominion Industries Limited, 8; 16 (upd.)
URS Corporation, 45; 80 (upd.)
U.S. Army Corps of Engineers, 91
VA TECH ELIN EBG GmbH, 49
VECO International, Inc., 7
Vinci, 43
The Weir Group PLC, 85
Willbros Group, Inc., 56
WS Atkins Plc, 45

Entertainment & Leisure

A&E Television Networks, 32
Aardman Animations Ltd., 61
ABC Family Worldwide, Inc., 52
Academy of Television Arts & Sciences, Inc., 55
Acclaim Entertainment Inc., 24
Activision, Inc., 32; 89 (upd.)
AEI Music Network Inc., 35
Affinity Group Holding Inc., 56
Airtours Plc, 27
Alaska Railroad Corporation, 60
All American Communications Inc., 20
The All England Lawn Tennis & Croquet Club, 54
Alliance Entertainment Corp., 17
Alternative Tentacles Records, 66
Alvin Ailey Dance Foundation, Inc., 52
Amblin Entertainment, 21
AMC Entertainment Inc., 12; 35 (upd.)
American Golf Corporation, 45
American Gramaphone LLC, 52
American Kennel Club, Inc., 74
American Skiing Company, 28
Ameristar Casinos, Inc., 33; 69 (upd.)
AMF Bowling, Inc., 40
Anaheim Angels Baseball Club, Inc., 53
Anchor Gaming, 24
AOL Time Warner Inc., 57 (upd.)
Applause Inc., 24
Apple Corps Ltd., 87
Aprilia SpA, 17
Argosy Gaming Company, 21
Aristocrat Leisure Limited, 54
Arsenal Holdings PLC, 79
The Art Institute of Chicago, 29
The Arthur C. Clarke Foundation, 92
Artisan Entertainment Inc., 32 (upd.)
Asahi National Broadcasting Company, Ltd., 9
Aspen Skiing Company, 15
Aston Villa plc, 41
The Athletics Investment Group, 62
Atlanta National League Baseball Club, Inc., 43
The Atlantic Group, 23
Autotote Corporation, 20
Aztar Corporation, 13
Bad Boy Worldwide Entertainment Group, 58
Baker & Taylor Corporation, 16; 43 (upd.)
Bally Total Fitness Holding Corp., 25
Baltimore Orioles L.P., 66
Barden Companies, Inc., 76
The Baseball Club of Seattle, LP, 50
The Basketball Club of Seattle, LLC, 50
Bertelsmann A.G., IV; 15 (upd.); 43 (upd.); 91 (upd.)
Bertucci's Inc., 16
Big Idea Productions, Inc., 49
BigBen Interactive S.A., 72
BioWare Corporation, 81
Blockbuster Inc., 9; 31 (upd.); 76 (upd.)

Boca Resorts, Inc., 37
Bonneville International Corporation, 29
Booth Creek Ski Holdings, Inc., 31
Boston Celtics Limited Partnership, 14
Boston Professional Hockey Association Inc., 39
The Boston Symphony Orchestra Inc., 93
The Boy Scouts of America, 34
Boyne USA Resorts, 71
Brillstein-Grey Entertainment, 80
British Broadcasting Corporation Ltd., 7; 21 (upd.); 89 (upd.)
The British Film Institute, 80
The British Museum, 71
British Sky Broadcasting Group plc, 20; 60 (upd.)
Brunswick Corporation, III; 22 (upd.); 77 (upd.)
Busch Entertainment Corporation, 73
Cablevision Systems Corporation, 7
California Sports, Inc., 56
Callaway Golf Company, 45 (upd.)
Canterbury Park Holding Corporation, 42
Capcom Company Ltd., 83
Capital Cities/ABC Inc., II
Capitol Records, Inc., 90
Carlson Companies, Inc., 6; 22 (upd.); 87 (upd.)
Carlson Wagonlit Travel, 55
Carmike Cinemas, Inc., 14; 37 (upd.); 74 (upd.)
Carnival Corporation, 6; 27 (upd.); 78 (upd.)
The Carsey-Werner Company, L.L.C., 37
CBS Inc., II; 6 (upd.)
Cedar Fair, L.P., 22
Central European Media Enterprises Ltd., 61
Central Independent Television, 7; 23 (upd.)
Century Casinos, Inc., 53
Century Theatres, Inc., 31
Championship Auto Racing Teams, Inc., 37
Channel Four Television Corporation, 93
Chello Zone Ltd., 93
Chelsea Piers Management Inc., 86
Chicago Bears Football Club, Inc., 33
Chicago National League Ball Club, Inc., 66
Chris-Craft Corporation, 9, 31 (upd.); 80 (upd.)
Chrysalis Group plc, 40
Churchill Downs Incorporated, 29
Cinar Corporation, 40
Cinemas de la República, S.A. de C.V., 83
Cineplex Odeon Corporation, 6; 23 (upd.)
Cinram International, Inc., 43
Cirque du Soleil Inc., 29
Classic Vacation Group, Inc., 46
Cleveland Indians Baseball Company, Inc., 37
Club Mediterranée S.A., 6; 21 (upd.); 91 (upd.)
ClubCorp, Inc., 33
CMG Worldwide, Inc., 89
Colonial Williamsburg Foundation, 53
Colorado Baseball Management, Inc., 72
Columbia Pictures Entertainment, Inc., II
Columbia TriStar Motion Pictures Companies, 12 (upd.)
Comcast Corporation, 7
Compagnie des Alpes, 48
Confluence Holdings Corporation, 76
Continental Cablevision, Inc., 7
Corporación Interamericana de Entretenimiento, S.A. de C.V., 83
Corporation for Public Broadcasting, 14; 89 (upd.)
Cox Enterprises, Inc., 22 (upd.)
Cranium, Inc., 69
Crown Media Holdings, Inc., 45
Cruise America Inc., 21
Cunard Line Ltd., 23
Dallas Cowboys Football Club, Ltd., 33
Dave & Buster's, Inc., 33
Death Row Records, 27
Denver Nuggets, 51
The Detroit Lions, Inc., 55
The Detroit Pistons Basketball Company, 41
Detroit Red Wings, 74
Detroit Tigers Baseball Club, Inc., 46
dick clark productions, inc., 16
DIRECTV, Inc., 38; 75 (upd.)
Dover Downs Entertainment, Inc., 43
DreamWorks SKG, 43
Dualstar Entertainment Group LLC, 76
E! Entertainment Television Inc., 17
edel music AG, 44
Educational Broadcasting Corporation, 48
Edwards Theatres Circuit, Inc., 31
Egmont Group, 93
Electronic Arts Inc., 10; 85 (upd.)
Elektra Entertainment Group, 64
Elsinore Corporation, 48
Elvis Presley Enterprises, Inc., 61
Empire Resorts, Inc., 72
Endemol Entertainment Holding NV, 46
Entertainment Distribution Company, 89
Equity Marketing, Inc., 26
ESPN, Inc., 56
Esporta plc, 35
Euro Disney S.C.A., 20; 58 (upd.)
Europe Through the Back Door Inc., 65
Fair Grounds Corporation, 44
Family Golf Centers, Inc., 29
FAO Schwarz, 46
Fédération Internationale de Football Association, 27
Feld Entertainment, Inc., 32 (upd.)
Film Roman, Inc., 58
First Choice Holidays PLC, 40
First Team Sports, Inc., 22
Fisher-Price Inc., 32 (upd.)
Florida Gaming Corporation, 47
Focus Features 78
4Kids Entertainment Inc., 59
Fox Entertainment Group, Inc., 43
Fox Family Worldwide, Inc., 24
Fuji Television Network Inc., 91
The GAME Group plc, 80
GameStop Corp., 69 (upd.)
Gaumont SA, 25; 91 (upd.)
Gaylord Entertainment Company, 11; 36 (upd.)
GC Companies, Inc., 25
Geffen Records Inc., 26
Gibson Guitar Corp., 16
Girl Scouts of the USA, 35
Global Outdoors, Inc., 49
GoodTimes Entertainment Ltd., 48
Granada Group PLC, II; 24 (upd.)
Grand Casinos, Inc., 20
Great Wolf Resorts, Inc., 91
The Green Bay Packers, Inc., 32
Grévin & Compagnie SA, 56
Groupe Partouche SA, 48
Grupo Televisa, S.A., 54 (upd.)
H. Betti Industries Inc., 88
Hallmark Cards, Inc., IV; 16 (upd.); 40 (upd.); 87 (upd.)
Hanna-Barbera Cartoons Inc., 23
Hard Rock Cafe International, Inc., 32 (upd.)
Harlem Globetrotters International, Inc., 61
Harpo Inc., 28; 66 (upd.)
Harrah's Entertainment, Inc., 16; 43 (upd.)
Harveys Casino Resorts, 27
Hasbro, Inc., 43 (upd.)
Hastings Entertainment, Inc., 29
The Hearst Corporation, 46 (upd.)
The Heat Group, 53
Hendrick Motorsports, Inc., 89
Herschend Family Entertainment Corporation, 73
Hilton Group plc, III; 19 (upd.); 49 (upd.)
HIT Entertainment PLC, 40
HOB Entertainment, Inc., 37
Hollywood Casino Corporation, 21
Hollywood Entertainment Corporation, 25
Hollywood Media Corporation, 58
Hollywood Park, Inc., 20
Home Box Office Inc., 7; 23 (upd.); 76 (upd.)
Horseshoe Gaming Holding Corporation, 62
Imagine Entertainment, 91
IMAX Corporation 28; 78 (upd.)
IMG 78
Indianapolis Motor Speedway Corporation, 46
Infinity Broadcasting Corporation, 48 (upd.)
Infogrames Entertainment S.A., 35
Integrity Inc., 44
International Creative Management, Inc., 43
International Family Entertainment Inc., 13
International Game Technology, 41 (upd.)
International Olympic Committee, 44
International Speedway Corporation, 19; 74 (upd.)
Interscope Music Group, 31
Intrawest Corporation, 15; 84 (upd.)
Irvin Feld & Kenneth Feld Productions, Inc., 15

Isle of Capri Casinos, Inc., 41
iVillage Inc., 46
Iwerks Entertainment, Inc., 34
Jackpot Enterprises Inc., 21
Japan Broadcasting Corporation, 7
Jazz Basketball Investors, Inc., 55
Jazzercise, Inc., 45
Jillian's Entertainment Holdings, Inc., 40
The Jim Henson Company, 23
The Joffrey Ballet of Chicago, 52
Jurys Doyle Hotel Group plc, 64
Juventus F.C. S.p.A, 53
K'Nex Industries, Inc., 52
Kampgrounds of America, Inc. (KOA), 33
Kerasotes ShowPlace Theaters LLC, 80
Kerzner International Limited, 69 (upd.)
King World Productions, Inc., 9; 30 (upd.)
Klasky Csupo Inc. 78
Knott's Berry Farm, 18
Kuoni Travel Holding Ltd., 40
The Kushner-Locke Company, 25
Ladbroke Group PLC, II; 21 (upd.)
Lakes Entertainment, Inc., 51
Landmark Theatre Corporation, 70
Las Vegas Sands, Inc., 50
Lego A/S, 13; 40 (upd.)
Liberty Livewire Corporation, 42
Liberty Media Corporation, 50
Liberty Travel, Inc., 56
Life Time Fitness, Inc., 66
Lifetime Entertainment Services, 51
Lincoln Center for the Performing Arts, Inc., 69
Lionel L.L.C., 16
Lions Gate Entertainment Corporation, 35
LIVE Entertainment Inc., 20
Live Nation, Inc., 80 (upd.)
LodgeNet Entertainment Corporation, 28
Lucasfilm Ltd., 12; 50 (upd.)
Luminar Plc, 40
Majesco Entertainment Company, 85
Manchester United Football Club plc, 30
Mandalay Resort Group, 32 (upd.)
Maple Leaf Sports & Entertainment Ltd., 61
The Marcus Corporation, 21
The Mark Travel Corporation, 80
Märklin Holding GmbH, 70
Martha Stewart Living Omnimedia, Inc., 73 (upd.)
Mashantucket Pequot Gaming Enterprise Inc., 35
MCA Inc., II
McMenamins Pubs and Breweries, 65
Media General, Inc., 7
Mediaset SpA, 50
Mega Bloks, Inc., 61
Metro-Goldwyn-Mayer Inc., 25 (upd.); 84 (upd.)
Metromedia Companies, 14
Métropole Télévision, 33
Métropole Télévision S.A., 76 (upd.)
Metropolitan Baseball Club Inc., 39
The Metropolitan Museum of Art, 55
Metropolitan Opera Association, Inc., 40
MGM Grand Inc., 17
MGM/UA Communications Company, II
Midway Games, Inc., 25
Mikohn Gaming Corporation, 39
Milan AC, S.p.A., 79
Milwaukee Brewers Baseball Club, 37
Miramax Film Corporation, 64
Mizuno Corporation, 25
Mohegan Tribal Gaming Authority, 37
Moliflor Loisirs, 80
Monarch Casino & Resort, Inc., 65
Motown Records Company L.P., 26
Movie Gallery, Inc., 31
Mr. Gatti's, LP, 87
MTR Gaming Group, Inc., 75
Multimedia Games, Inc., 41
Muzak, Inc., 18
National Amusements Inc., 28
National Aquarium in Baltimore, Inc., 74
National Association for Stock Car Auto Racing, 32
National Broadcasting Company, Inc., II; 6 (upd.)
National Football League, 29
National Hockey League, 35
National Public Radio, Inc., 19; 47 (upd.)
National Rifle Association of America, 37
National Thoroughbred Racing Association, 58
Navarre Corporation, 24
Navigant International, Inc., 47
NBGS International, Inc., 73
NCL Corporation, 79
New Jersey Devils, 84
New Line Cinema, Inc., 47
New Orleans Saints LP, 58
New York City Off-Track Betting Corporation, 51
New York Shakespeare Festival Management, 93
News Corporation Limited, 46 (upd.)
NFL Films, 75
Nicklaus Companies, 45
Nintendo Company, Ltd., 28 (upd.); 67 (upd.)
Nordisk Film A/S, 80
O'Charley's Inc., 19
Orion Pictures Corporation, 6
Outrigger Enterprises, Inc., 67
Paradise Music & Entertainment, Inc., 42
Paramount Pictures Corporation, II
Pathé SA, 29
Paul Reed Smith Guitar Company, 89
Paul-Son Gaming Corporation, 66
PDS Gaming Corporation, 44
Peace Arch Entertainment Group Inc., 51
Penn National Gaming, Inc., 33
Philadelphia Eagles, 37
Philharmonic-Symphony Society of New York, Inc. (New York Philharmonic), 69
Pierre & Vacances SA, 48
Pittsburgh Steelers Sports, Inc., 66
Pixar Animation Studios, 34
Platinum Entertainment, Inc., 35
Play by Play Toys & Novelties, Inc., 26
Players International, Inc., 22
Pleasant Holidays LLC, 62
PolyGram N.V., 23
Poof-Slinky, Inc., 61
Pop Warner Little Scholars, Inc., 86
Portland Trail Blazers, 50
Powerhouse Technologies, Inc., 27
Premier Parks, Inc., 27
President Casinos, Inc., 22
Preussag AG, 42 (upd.)
Princess Cruise Lines, 22
Professional Bull Riders Inc., 55
The Professional Golfers' Association of America, 41
Promus Companies, Inc., 9
ProSiebenSat.1 Media AG, 54
Publishing and Broadcasting Limited, 54
Putt-Putt Golf Courses of America, Inc., 23
Radio One, Inc., 67
Ragdoll Productions Ltd., 51
Rainforest Café, Inc., 25; 88 (upd.)
The Rank Group plc, II; 64 (upd.)
Rawlings Sporting Goods Co., Inc., 24
Real Madrid C.F., 73
The Really Useful Group, 26
Regal Entertainment Group, 59
Rentrak Corporation, 35
Rhino Entertainment Company, 18; 70 (upd.)
Ride, Inc., 22
Ripley Entertainment, Inc., 74
Riviera Holdings Corporation, 75
Rollerblade, Inc., 34 (upd.)
Roularta Media Group NV, 48
Rounder Records Corporation, 79
Royal Caribbean Cruises Ltd., 22; 74 (upd.)
Royal Olympic Cruise Lines Inc., 52
RTL Group SA, 44
Rush Communications, 33
Ryko Corporation, 83
S-K-I Limited, 15
Sabre Holdings Corporation, 74 (upd.)
Salomon Worldwide, 20
San Diego Padres Baseball Club LP 78
San Francisco Baseball Associates, L.P., 55
The Sanctuary Group PLC, 69
Santa Fe Gaming Corporation, 19
Schwinn Cycle and Fitness L.P., 19
Scientific Games Corporation, 64 (upd.)
Scottish Radio Holding plc, 41
Seattle FilmWorks, Inc., 20
Seattle Seahawks, Inc., 92
The Second City, Inc., 88
SEGA Corporation, 73
Sega of America, Inc., 10
Selectour SA, 53
SFX Entertainment, Inc., 36
Shedd Aquarium Society, 73
Shochiku Company Ltd., 74
Showboat, Inc., 19
Showtime Networks Inc. 78
Shubert Organization Inc., 24
Shuffle Master Inc., 51
The Singing Machine Company, Inc., 60
Sirius Satellite Radio, Inc., 69
Six Flags, Inc., 17; 54 (upd.)
Smithsonian Institution, 27
Società Sportiva Lazio SpA, 44
Sony Corporation, 40 (upd.)

Speedway Motorsports, Inc., 32
Spelling Entertainment Group, Inc., 14
Spin Master, Ltd., 61
The Sports Club Company, 25
Spyglass Entertainment Group, LLC, 91
Stanley Leisure plc, 66
Starz LLC, 91
Station Casinos, Inc., 25; 90 (upd.)
Stoll-Moss Theatres Ltd., 34
Stuart Entertainment Inc., 16
TABCORP Holdings Limited, 44
Take-Two Interactive Software, Inc., 46
Tee Vee Toons, Inc., 57
Tele-Communications, Inc., II
Television Española, S.A., 7
Texas Rangers Baseball, 51
Tha Row Records, 69 (upd.)
Thomas Cook Travel Inc., 9
The Thomson Corporation, 8
Thousand Trails, Inc., 33
THQ, Inc., 39
365 Media Group plc, 89
Ticketmaster Corp., 13
Tiger Aspect Productions Ltd., 72
The Todd-AO Corporation, 33
Toho Co., Ltd., 28
TOKYOPOP Inc., 79
Tomy Company Ltd., 65
The Topps Company, Inc., 13, 34 (upd.); 83 (upd.)
Tottenham Hotspur PLC, 81
Touristik Union International GmbH. and Company K.G., II
Town Sports International, Inc., 46
Toy Biz, Inc., 18
Trans World Entertainment Corporation, 24
Travelocity.com, Inc., 46
Tribune Company, 63 (upd.)
TUI Group GmbH, 44
Turner Broadcasting System, Inc., II; 6 (upd.); 66 (upd.)
The Tussauds Group, 55
Twentieth Century Fox Film Corporation, II; 25 (upd.)
24 Hour Fitness Worldwide, Inc., 71
Ubi Soft Entertainment S.A., 41
Ulster Television PLC, 71
Ultimate Leisure Group PLC, 75
United Pan-Europe Communications NV, 47
United States Playing Card Company, 62
United Talent Agency, Inc., 80
Universal Studios, Inc., 33
Univision Communications Inc., 24; 83 (upd.)
Urbium PLC, 75
USA Interactive, Inc., 47 (upd.)
Vail Resorts, Inc., 11; 43 (upd.)
Venetian Casino Resort, LLC, 47
Viacom Inc., 7; 23 (upd.)
Village Roadshow Ltd., 58
Vinton Studios, 63
Vivendi Universal S.A., 46 (upd.)
The Walt Disney Company, II; 6 (upd.); 30 (upd.); 63 (upd.)
Warner Communications Inc., II
Warner Music Group Corporation, 90 (upd.)
Washington Football, Inc., 35
The Welk Group Inc., 78
West Coast Entertainment Corporation, 29
WGBH Educational Foundation, 66
Wham-O, Inc., 61
Wherehouse Entertainment Incorporated, 11
Whitbread PLC, 52 (upd.)
Wildlife Conservation Society, 31
William Hill Organization Limited, 49
Wilson Sporting Goods Company, 24; 84 (upd.)
Wizards of the Coast Inc., 24
WMS Industries, Inc., 53 (upd.)
World Wrestling Federation Entertainment, Inc., 32
Writers Guild of America, West, Inc., 92
XM Satellite Radio Holdings, Inc., 69
YankeeNets LLC, 35
YES! Entertainment Corporation, 26
YMCA of the USA, 31
Youbet.com, Inc., 77
Young Broadcasting Inc., 40
Zomba Records Ltd., 52
Zuffa L.L.C., 89

Financial Services: Banks

Abbey National plc, 10; 39 (upd.)
Abigail Adams National Bancorp, Inc., 23
ABN AMRO Holding, N.V., 50
Affiliated Managers Group, Inc., 79
Akbank TAS, 79
Alabama National BanCorporation, 75
Algemene Bank Nederland N.V., II
Alliance and Leicester plc, 88
Allianz AG, 57 (upd.)
Allied Irish Banks, plc, 16; 43 (upd.)
Almanij NV, 44
Amalgamated Bank, 60
AMCORE Financial Inc., 44
American Residential Mortgage Corporation, 8
AmSouth Bancorporation,12; 48 (upd.)
Amsterdam-Rotterdam Bank N.V., II
Anchor Bancorp, Inc., 10
Apple Bank for Savings, 59
Astoria Financial Corporation, 44
Australia and New Zealand Banking Group Limited, II; 52 (upd.)
Banca Commerciale Italiana SpA, II
Banca Fideuram SpA, 63
Banca Intesa SpA, 65
Banca Monte dei Paschi di Siena SpA, 65
Banca Nazionale del Lavoro SpA, 72
Banco Bilbao Vizcaya Argentaria S.A., II; 48 (upd.)
Banco Bradesco S.A., 13
Banco Central, II
Banco Comercial Português, SA, 50
Banco de Chile, 69
Banco de Crédito del Perú, 93
Banco do Brasil S.A., II
Banco Espírito Santo e Comercial de Lisboa S.A., 15
Banco Itaú S.A., 19
Banco Santander Central Hispano S.A., 36 (upd.)
Bank Austria AG, 23
Bank Brussels Lambert, II
Bank Hapoalim B.M., II; 54 (upd.)
Bank Leumi le-Israel B.M., 60
Bank of America Corporation, 46 (upd.)
Bank of Boston Corporation, II
Bank of China, 63
Bank of Cyprus Group, 91
Bank of East Asia Ltd., 63
Bank of Granite Corporation, 89
Bank of Hawaii Corporation, 73
Bank of Ireland, 50
Bank of Mississippi, Inc., 14
Bank of Montreal, II; 46 (upd.)
Bank of New England Corporation, II
The Bank of New York Company, Inc., II; 46 (upd.)
The Bank of Nova Scotia, II; 59 (upd.)
Bank of the Ozarks, Inc., 91
Bank of the Philippine Islands, 58
Bank of Tokyo-Mitsubishi Ltd., II; 15 (upd.)
Bank One Corporation, 10; 36 (upd.)
BankAmerica Corporation, II; 8 (upd.)
Bankers Trust New York Corporation, II
Banknorth Group, Inc., 55
Banque Nationale de Paris S.A., II
Barclays plc, II; 20 (upd.); 64 (upd.)
BarclaysAmerican Mortgage Corporation, 11
Barings PLC, 14
Barnett Banks, Inc., 9
BayBanks, Inc., 12
Bayerische Hypotheken- und Wechsel-Bank AG, II
Bayerische Vereinsbank A.G., II
BB&T Corporation, 79
Beneficial Corporation, 8
BNP Paribas Group, 36 (upd.)
Boatmen's Bancshares Inc., 15
Bremer Financial Corp., 45
Brown Brothers Harriman & Co., 45
C. Hoare & Co., 77
Caisse des Dépôts et Consignations, 90
Canadian Imperial Bank of Commerce, II; 61 (upd.)
Capitalia S.p.A., 65
Carolina First Corporation, 31
Casco Northern Bank, 14
The Chase Manhattan Corporation, II; 13 (upd.)
Cheltenham & Gloucester PLC, 61
Chemical Banking Corporation, II; 14 (upd.)
China Construction Bank Corp., 79
Citicorp, II; 9 (upd.)
Citigroup Inc., 30 (upd.); 59 (upd.)
Citizens Financial Group, Inc., 42; 87 (upd.)
Close Brothers Group plc, 39
Commercial Credit Company, 8
Commercial Federal Corporation, 12; 62 (upd.)
Commerzbank A.G., II; 47 (upd.)
Compagnie Financiere de Paribas, II
Compass Bancshares, Inc., 73

Continental Bank Corporation, II
CoreStates Financial Corp, 17
Corus Bankshares, Inc., 75
Countrywide Credit Industries, Inc., 16
Crédit Agricole Group, II; 84 (upd.)
Crédit Lyonnais, 9; 33 (upd.)
Crédit National S.A., 9
Credit Suisse Group, II; 21 (upd.); 59 (upd.)
Credito Italiano, II
Cullen/Frost Bankers, Inc., 25
CUNA Mutual Group, 62
The Dai-Ichi Kangyo Bank Ltd., II
The Daiwa Bank, Ltd., II; 39 (upd.)
Danske Bank Aktieselskab, 50
Dauphin Deposit Corporation, 14
DEPFA BANK PLC, 69
Deposit Guaranty Corporation, 17
Deutsche Bank AG, II; 14 (upd.); 40 (upd.)
Deutscher Sparkassen- und Giroverband (DSGV), 84
Dexia NV/SA, 42; 88 (upd.)
Dime Savings Bank of New York, F.S.B., 9
Donaldson, Lufkin & Jenrette, Inc., 22
Dresdner Bank A.G., II; 57 (upd.)
Emigrant Savings Bank, 59
Erste Bank der Osterreichischen Sparkassen AG, 69
Espèrito Santo Financial Group S.A., 79 (upd.)
European Investment Bank, 66
Fidelity Southern Corporation, 85
Fifth Third Bancorp, 13; 31 (upd.)
First Bank System Inc., 12
First Chicago Corporation, II
First Commerce Bancshares, Inc., 15
First Commerce Corporation, 11
First Empire State Corporation, 11
First Fidelity Bank, N.A., New Jersey, 9
First Hawaiian, Inc., 11
First Interstate Bancorp, II
First Nationwide Bank, 14
First of America Bank Corporation, 8
First Security Corporation, 11
First Tennessee National Corporation, 11; 48 (upd.)
First Union Corporation, 10
First Virginia Banks, Inc., 11
Firstar Corporation, 11; 33 (upd.)
Fleet Financial Group, Inc., 9
FleetBoston Financial Corporation, 36 (upd.)
FöreningsSparbanken AB, 69
Fourth Financial Corporation, 11
The Fuji Bank, Ltd., II
Generale Bank, II
German American Bancorp, 41
Glacier Bancorp, Inc., 35
Golden West Financial Corporation, 47
The Governor and Company of the Bank of Scotland, 10
Grameen Bank, 31
Granite State Bankshares, Inc., 37
Great Lakes Bancorp, 8
Great Western Financial Corporation, 10
GreenPoint Financial Corp., 28
Grupo Financiero Banamex S.A., 54
Grupo Financiero Banorte, S.A. de C.V., 51
Grupo Financiero BBVA Bancomer S.A., 54
Grupo Financiero Galicia S.A., 63
Grupo Financiero Serfin, S.A., 19
H.F. Ahmanson & Company, II; 10 (upd.)
Habersham Bancorp, 25
Hancock Holding Company, 15
Hang Seng Bank Ltd., 60
Hanmi Financial Corporation, 66
Hibernia Corporation, 37
The Hongkong and Shanghai Banking Corporation Limited, II
HSBC Holdings plc, 12; 26 (upd.); 80 (upd.)
Hudson River Bancorp, Inc., 41
Huntington Bancshares Incorporated, 11; 87 (upd.)
HVB Group, 59 (upd.)
IBERIABANK Corporation, 37
The Industrial Bank of Japan, Ltd., II
Irish Life & Permanent Plc, 59
Irwin Financial Corporation, 77
J Sainsbury plc, 38 (upd.)
J.P. Morgan & Co. Incorporated, II; 30 (upd.)
J.P. Morgan Chase & Co., 38 (upd.)
Japan Leasing Corporation, 8
JPMorgan Chase & Co., 91 (upd.)
Julius Baer Holding AG, 52
Kansallis-Osake-Pankki, II
KeyCorp, 8; 93 (upd.)
Kookmin Bank, 58
Kredietbank N.V., II
Kreditanstalt für Wiederaufbau, 29
Krung Thai Bank Public Company Ltd., 69
Landsbanki Islands hf, 81
Lloyds Bank PLC, II
Lloyds TSB Group plc, 47 (upd.)
Long Island Bancorp, Inc., 16
Long-Term Credit Bank of Japan, Ltd., II
Macquarie Bank Ltd., 69
Malayan Banking Berhad, 72
Manufacturers Hanover Corporation, II
Manulife Financial Corporation, 85
Marfin Popular Bank plc, 92
Marshall & Ilsley Corporation, 56
MBNA Corporation, 12
Mediolanum S.p.A., 65
Mellon Bank Corporation, II
Mellon Financial Corporation, 44 (upd.)
Mercantile Bankshares Corp., 11
Meridian Bancorp, Inc., 11
Metropolitan Financial Corporation, 13
Michigan National Corporation, 11
Midland Bank PLC, II; 17 (upd.)
The Mitsubishi Bank, Ltd., II
The Mitsubishi Trust & Banking Corporation, II
The Mitsui Bank, Ltd., II
The Mitsui Trust & Banking Company, Ltd., II
Mizuho Financial Group Inc., 58 (upd.)
Mouvement des Caisses Desjardins, 48
N M Rothschild & Sons Limited, 39
National Bank of Greece, 41
National Bank of Canada, 85
The National Bank of South Carolina, 76
National City Corp., 15
National Westminster Bank PLC, II
NationsBank Corporation, 10
NBD Bancorp, Inc., 11
NCNB Corporation, II
New York Community Bancorp Inc. 78
Nippon Credit Bank, II
Nordea AB, 40
Norinchukin Bank, II
North Fork Bancorporation, Inc., 46
Northern Rock plc, 33
Northern Trust Company, 9
NVR L.P., 8
Old Kent Financial Corp., 11
Old National Bancorp, 15
Orszagos Takarekpenztar es Kereskedelmi Bank Rt. (OTP Bank) 78
PNC Bank Corp., II; 13 (upd.)
The PNC Financial Services Group Inc., 46 (upd.)
Popular, Inc., 41
Provident Bankshares Corporation, 85
PT Bank Buana Indonesia Tbk, 60
Pulte Corporation, 8
Qatar National Bank SAQ, 87
Rabobank Group, 33
Raiffeisen Zentralbank Österreich AG, 85
Republic New York Corporation, 11
Riggs National Corporation, 13
Royal Bank of Canada, II; 21 (upd.); 81 (upd.)
The Royal Bank of Scotland Group plc, 12; 38 (upd.)
The Ryland Group, Inc., 8
St. Paul Bank for Cooperatives, 8
Sanpaolo IMI S.p.A., 50
The Sanwa Bank, Ltd., II; 15 (upd.)
SBC Warburg, 14
Sberbank, 62
Seattle First National Bank Inc., 8
Security Capital Corporation, 17
Security Pacific Corporation, II
Shawmut National Corporation, 13
Signet Banking Corporation, 11
Singer & Friedlander Group plc, 41
Skandinaviska Enskilda Banken AB, II; 56 (upd.)
Société Générale, II; 42 (upd.)
Society Corporation, 9
Southern Financial Bancorp, Inc., 56
Southtrust Corporation, 11
Standard Chartered plc, II; 48 (upd.)
Standard Federal Bank, 9
Star Banc Corporation, 11
State Bank of India, 63
State Financial Services Corporation, 51
State Street Corporation, 8; 57 (upd.)
Staten Island Bancorp, Inc., 39
The Sumitomo Bank, Limited, II; 26 (upd.)
Sumitomo Mitsui Banking Corporation, 51 (upd.)
The Sumitomo Trust & Banking Company, Ltd., II; 53 (upd.)

The Summit Bancorporation, 14
Suncorp-Metway Ltd., 91
SunTrust Banks Inc., 23
Svenska Handelsbanken AB, II; 50 (upd.)
Swiss Bank Corporation, II
Synovus Financial Corp., 12; 52 (upd.)
The Taiyo Kobe Bank, Ltd., II
TCF Financial Corporation, 47
The Tokai Bank, Limited, II; 15 (upd.)
The Toronto-Dominion Bank, II; 49 (upd.)
TSB Group plc, 12
Turkiye Is Bankasi A.S., 61
U.S. Bancorp, 14; 36 (upd.)
U.S. Trust Corp., 17
UBS AG, 52 (upd.)
Umpqua Holdings Corporation, 87
Unibanco Holdings S.A., 73
Union Bank of California, 16
Union Bank of Switzerland, II
Union Financière de France Banque SA, 52
Union Planters Corporation, 54
UnionBanCal Corporation, 50 (upd.)
United Overseas Bank Ltd., 56
USAA, 62 (upd.)
Van Lanschot NV, 79
Wachovia Bank of Georgia, N.A., 16
Wachovia Bank of South Carolina, N.A., 16
Washington Mutual, Inc., 17; 93 (upd.)
Wells Fargo & Company, II; 12 (upd.); 38 (upd.)
West One Bancorp, 11
Westamerica Bancorporation, 17
Westdeutsche Landesbank Girozentrale, II; 46 (upd.)
Westpac Banking Corporation, II; 48 (upd.)
Whitney Holding Corporation, 21
Wilmington Trust Corporation, 25
The Woolwich plc, 30
World Bank Group, 33
The Yasuda Trust and Banking Company, Ltd., II; 17 (upd.)
Zions Bancorporation, 12; 53 (upd.)

Financial Services: Excluding Banks

A.B. Watley Group Inc., 45
A.G. Edwards, Inc., 8; 32 (upd.)
ACCION International, 87
Accredited Home Lenders Holding Co., 91
ACE Cash Express, Inc., 33
Advanta Corporation, 8; 38 (upd.)
Ag Services of America, Inc., 59
Alliance Capital Management Holding L.P., 63
Allmerica Financial Corporation, 63
Ambac Financial Group, Inc., 65
America's Car-Mart, Inc., 64
American Capital Strategies, Ltd., 91
American Express Company, II; 10 (upd.); 38 (upd.)
American General Finance Corp., 11
American Home Mortgage Holdings, Inc., 46
Ameritrade Holding Corporation, 34
AMVESCAP PLC, 65
Apax Partners Worldwide LLP, 89
Arthur Andersen & Company, Société Coopérative, 10
Avco Financial Services Inc., 13
Aviva PLC, 50 (upd.)
Bankrate, Inc., 83
Bear Stearns Companies, Inc., II; 10 (upd.); 52 (upd.)
Benchmark Capital, 49
Bill & Melinda Gates Foundation, 41
BlackRock, Inc., 79
Bolsa Mexicana de Valores, S.A. de C.V., 80
Bozzuto's, Inc., 13
Bradford & Bingley PLC, 65
Cantor Fitzgerald, L.P., 92
Capital One Financial Corporation, 52
Cardtronics, Inc., 93
Carnegie Corporation of New York, 35
Cash America International, Inc., 20; 61 (upd.)
Cash Systems, Inc., 93
Cattles plc, 58
Cendant Corporation, 44 (upd.)
Certegy, Inc., 63
Cetelem S.A., 21
The Charles Schwab Corporation, 8; 26 (upd.); 81 (upd.)
CheckFree Corporation, 81
Cheshire Building Society, 74
Chicago Mercantile Exchange Holdings Inc., 75
CIT Group Inc., 76
Citfed Bancorp, Inc., 16
Citicorp Diners Club, Inc., 90
Coinstar, Inc., 44
Comerica Incorporated, 40
Commercial Financial Services, Inc., 26
Compagnie Nationale à Portefeuille, 84
Concord EFS, Inc., 52
Coopers & Lybrand, 9
Cowen Group, Inc., 92
Cramer, Berkowitz & Co., 34
Credit Acceptance Corporation, 18
Cresud S.A.C.I.F. y A., 63
CS First Boston Inc., II
Dain Rauscher Corporation, 35 (upd.)
Daiwa Securities Group Inc., II; 55 (upd.)
Datek Online Holdings Corp., 32
The David and Lucile Packard Foundation, 41
Dean Witter, Discover & Co., 12
Deutsche Börse AG, 59
ditech.com, 93
Dominick & Dominick LLC, 92
Dow Jones Telerate, Inc., 10
Draper Fisher Jurvetson, 91
Dresdner Kleinwort Wasserstein, 60 (upd.)
Drexel Burnham Lambert Incorporated, II
The Dreyfus Corporation, 70
DVI, Inc., 51
E*Trade Financial Corporation, 20; 60 (upd.)
Eaton Vance Corporation, 18
Edward D. Jones & Company L.P., 66 (upd.)
Edward Jones, 30
Eurazeo, 80
Euronet Worldwide, Inc., 83
Euronext N.V., 37; 89 (upd.)
Experian Information Solutions Inc., 45
Fair, Isaac and Company, 18
Fannie Mae, 45 (upd.)
Federal Agricultural Mortgage Corporation, 75
Federal Deposit Insurance Corporation, 93
Federal National Mortgage Association, II
Fidelity Investments Inc., II; 14 (upd.)
First Albany Companies Inc., 37
First Data Corporation, 30 (upd.)
The First Marblehead Corporation, 87
First USA, Inc., 11
FMR Corp., 8; 32 (upd.)
Forstmann Little & Co., 38
Fortis, Inc., 15
Frank Russell Company, 46
Franklin Resources, Inc., 9
Freddie Mac, 54
Friedman, Billings, Ramsey Group, Inc., 53
Gabelli Asset Management Inc., 30
Gilman & Ciocia, Inc., 72
Global Payments Inc., 91
The Goldman Sachs Group Inc., II; 20 (upd.); 51 (upd.)
Grede Foundries, Inc., 38
Green Tree Financial Corporation, 11
Gruntal & Co., L.L.C., 20
Grupo Financiero Galicia S.A., 63
H&R Block, Inc., 9; 29 (upd.); 82 (upd.)
H.D. Vest, Inc., 46
H.M. Payson & Co., 69
Hercules Technology Growth Capital, Inc., 87
Hoenig Group Inc., 41
Household International, Inc., II; 21 (upd.)
Huron Consulting Group Inc., 87
Ingenico—Compagnie Industrielle et Financière d'Ingénierie, 46
Instinet Corporation, 34
Inter-Regional Financial Group, Inc., 15
Investcorp SA, 57
The Island ECN, Inc., 48
Istituto per la Ricostruzione Industriale S.p.A., 11
J. & W. Seligman & Co. Inc., 61
JAFCO Co. Ltd., 79
Janus Capital Group Inc., 57
JB Oxford Holdings, Inc., 32
Jefferies Group, Inc., 25
John Hancock Financial Services, Inc., 42 (upd.)
The John Nuveen Company, 21
Jones Lang LaSalle Incorporated, 49
The Jordan Company LP, 70
Kansas City Southern Industries, Inc., 26 (upd.)
Kleiner, Perkins, Caufield & Byers, 53
Kleinwort Benson Group PLC, II
Knight Trading Group, Inc., 70
Kohlberg Kravis Roberts & Co., 24; 56 (upd.)

KPMG Worldwide, 10
La Poste, 47 (upd.)
LaBranche & Co. Inc., 37
Lazard LLC, 38
Legg Mason, Inc., 33
LendingTree, LLC, 93
LifeLock, Inc., 91
Lilly Endowment Inc., 70
Liquidnet, Inc., 79
London Scottish Bank plc, 70
London Stock Exchange Limited, 34
M.H. Meyerson & Co., Inc., 46
MacAndrews & Forbes Holdings Inc., 28; 86 (upd.)
MasterCard International, Inc., 9
MBNA Corporation, 33 (upd.)
Merrill Lynch & Co., Inc., II; 13 (upd.); 40 (upd.)
Metris Companies Inc., 56
Morgan Grenfell Group PLC, II
Morgan Stanley Dean Witter & Company, II; 16 (upd.); 33 (upd.)
Mountain States Mortgage Centers, Inc., 29
NASD, 54 (upd.)
The NASDAQ Stock Market, Inc., 92
National Association of Securities Dealers, Inc., 10
National Auto Credit, Inc., 16
National Discount Brokers Group, Inc., 28
National Financial Partners Corp., 65
Navy Federal Credit Union, 33
Neuberger Berman Inc., 57
New Street Capital Inc., 8
New York Stock Exchange, Inc., 9; 39 (upd.)
The Nikko Securities Company Limited, II; 9 (upd.)
Nippon Shinpan Co., Ltd., II; 61 (upd.)
Nomura Securities Company, Limited, II; 9 (upd.)
Norwich & Peterborough Building Society, 55
NovaStar Financial, Inc., 91
Oaktree Capital Management, LLC, 71
Old Mutual PLC, 61
Ontario Teachers' Pension Plan, 61
Onyx Acceptance Corporation, 59
ORIX Corporation, II; 44 (upd.)
PaineWebber Group Inc., II; 22 (upd.)
PayPal Inc., 58
The Pew Charitable Trusts, 35
Piper Jaffray Companies Inc., 22
Pitney Bowes Inc., 47 (upd.)
Providian Financial Corporation, 52 (upd.)
Prudential Financial Inc., III; 30 (upd.); 82 (upd.)
The Quick & Reilly Group, Inc., 20
Quicken Loans, Inc., 93
Rathbone Brothers plc, 70
Raymond James Financial Inc., 69
Resource America, Inc., 42
Robert W. Baird & Co. Incorporated, 67
Ryan Beck & Co., Inc., 66
Safeguard Scientifics, Inc., 10
St. James's Place Capital, plc, 71
Salomon Inc., II; 13 (upd.)
Sanders Morris Harris Group Inc., 70
Sanlam Ltd., 68
SBC Warburg, 14
Schroders plc, 42
Scottrade, Inc., 85
Shearson Lehman Brothers Holdings Inc., II; 9 (upd.)
Siebert Financial Corp., 32
Skipton Building Society, 80
SLM Holding Corp., 25 (upd.)
Smith Barney Inc., 15
Soros Fund Management LLC, 28
Spear, Leeds & Kellogg, 66
State Street Boston Corporation, 8
Stephens Inc., 92
Student Loan Marketing Association, II
Sun Life Financial Inc., 85
T. Rowe Price Associates, Inc., 11; 34 (upd.)
Teachers Insurance and Annuity Association-College Retirement Equities Fund, 45 (upd.)
Texas Pacific Group Inc., 36
3i Group PLC, 73
Total System Services, Inc., 18
TradeStation Group, Inc., 83
Trilon Financial Corporation, II
United Jewish Communities, 33
The Vanguard Group, Inc., 14; 34 (upd.)
VeriFone Holdings, Inc., 18; 76 (upd.)
Viel & Cie, 76
Visa International, 9; 26 (upd.)
Wachovia Corporation, 12; 46 (upd.)
Waddell & Reed, Inc., 22
Washington Federal, Inc., 17
Waterhouse Investor Services, Inc., 18
Watson Wyatt Worldwide, 42
Western Union Financial Services, Inc., 54
WFS Financial Inc., 70
Working Assets Funding Service, 43
World Acceptance Corporation, 57
Yamaichi Securities Company, Limited, II
The Ziegler Companies, Inc., 24; 63 (upd.)
Zurich Financial Services, 42 (upd.); 93 (upd.)

Food Products

A. Duda & Sons, Inc., 88
A. Moksel AG, 59
Agri Beef Company, 81
Agway, Inc., 7
Ajinomoto Co., Inc., II; 28 (upd.)
Alabama Farmers Cooperative, Inc., 63
The Albert Fisher Group plc, 41
Alberto-Culver Company, 8; 36 (upd.); 91 (upd.)
Alfred Ritter GmbH & Co. KG, 58
Alfesca hf, 82
Allen Canning Company, 76
Alpine Confections, Inc., 71
Alpine Lace Brands, Inc., 18
American Crystal Sugar Company, 11; 32 (upd.)
American Foods Group, 43
American Italian Pasta Company, 27; 76 (upd.)
American Licorice Company, 86
American Maize-Products Co., 14
American Pop Corn Company, 59
American Rice, Inc., 33
Amfac/JMB Hawaii L.L.C., 24 (upd.)
Amy's Kitchen Inc., 76
Annie's Homegrown, Inc., 59
Archer-Daniels-Midland Company, 32 (upd.)
Archway Cookies, Inc., 29
Arcor S.A.I.C., 66
Arla Foods amba, 48
Arnott's Ltd., 66
Associated British Foods plc, II; 13 (upd.); 41 (upd.)
Associated Milk Producers, Inc., 11; 48 (upd.)
Atkinson Candy Company, 87
Atlantic Premium Brands, Ltd., 57
August Storck KG, 66
Aurora Foods Inc., 32
Awrey Bakeries, Inc., 56
B&G Foods, Inc., 40
The B. Manischewitz Company, LLC, 31
Bahlsen GmbH & Co. KG, 44
Bakkavör Group hf., 91
Balance Bar Company, 32
Baltek Corporation, 34
The Bama Companies, Inc., 80
Bar-S Foods Company, 76
Barbara's Bakery Inc., 88
Barilla G. e R. Fratelli S.p.A., 17; 50 (upd.)
Barry Callebaut AG, 71 (upd.)
Bear Creek Corporation, 38
Beatrice Company, II
Beech-Nut Nutrition Corporation, 21; 51 (upd.)
Beer Nuts, Inc., 86
Bel/Kaukauna USA, 76
Ben & Jerry's Homemade, Inc., 10; 35 (upd.); 80 (upd.)
Berkeley Farms, Inc., 46
Bernard Matthews Ltd., 89
Besnier SA, 19
Best Kosher Foods Corporation, 82
Bestfoods, 22 (upd.)
Better Made Snack Foods, Inc., 90
Bettys & Taylors of Harrogate Ltd., 72
Birds Eye Foods, Inc., 69 (upd.)
Blue Bell Creameries L.P., 30
Blue Diamond Growers, 28
Bob's Red Mill Natural Foods, Inc., 63
Bobs Candies, Inc., 70
Bolton Group B.V., 86
Bonduelle SA, 51
Bongrain SA, 25
Booker PLC, 13; 31 (upd.)
Borden, Inc., II; 22 (upd.)
Boyd Coffee Company, 53
Brach and Brock Confections, Inc., 15
Brake Bros plc, 45
Bridgford Foods Corporation, 27
Brigham's Inc., 72
Brioche Pasquier S.A., 58
British Sugar plc, 84
Brothers Gourmet Coffees, Inc., 20
Broughton Foods Co., 17

Brown & Haley, 23
Bruce Foods Corporation, 39
Bruegger's Corporation, 63
Bruster's Real Ice Cream, Inc., 80
BSN Groupe S.A., II
Bumble Bee Seafoods L.L.C., 64
Bunge Brasil S.A. 78
Bunge Ltd., 62
Bourbon Corporation, 82
Burns, Philp & Company Ltd., 63
Bush Boake Allen Inc., 30
Bush Brothers & Company, 45
The C.F. Sauer Company, 90
C.H. Robinson Worldwide, Inc., 40 (upd.)
C.H. Guenther & Son, Inc., 84
Cactus Feeders, Inc., 91
Cadbury Schweppes PLC, II; 49 (upd.)
Cagle's, Inc., 20
Cal-Maine Foods, Inc., 69
Calavo Growers, Inc., 47
Calcot Ltd., 33
Callard and Bowser-Suchard Inc., 84
Campbell Soup Company, II; 7 (upd.); 26 (upd.); 71 (upd.)
The Campina Group, 78
Campofrío Alimentación S.A, 59
Canada Packers Inc., II
Cape Cod Potato Chip Company, 90
Cargill, Incorporated, II; 13 (upd.); 40 (upd.); 89 (upd.)
Carnation Company, II
The Carriage House Companies, Inc., 55
Carroll's Foods, Inc., 46
Carvel Corporation, 35
Castle & Cooke, Inc., II; 20 (upd.)
Cattleman's, Inc., 20
Celestial Seasonings, Inc., 16
Cemoi S.A., 86
Central Soya Company, Inc., 7
Chaoda Modern Agriculture (Holdings) Ltd., 87
Charal S.A., 90
Chase General Corporation, 91
Chattanooga Bakery, Inc., 86
Chef Solutions, Inc., 89
Chelsea Milling Company, 29
Chicken of the Sea International, 24 (upd.)
China National Cereals, Oils and Foodstuffs Import and Export Corporation (COFCO), 76
Chiquita Brands International, Inc., 7; 21 (upd.); 83 (upd.)
Chock Full o'Nuts Corp., 17
Chocoladefabriken Lindt & Sprüngli AG, 27
Chr. Hansen Group A/S, 70
CHS Inc., 60
Chupa Chups S.A., 38
The Clemens Family Corporation, 93
Clif Bar Inc., 50
Cloetta Fazer AB, 70
The Clorox Company, III; 22 (upd.); 81 (upd.)
Clougherty Packing Company, 72
Coca-Cola Enterprises, Inc., 13
Cold Stone Creamery, 69
Coleman Natural Products, Inc., 68
Community Coffee Co. L.L.C., 53
ConAgra Foods, Inc., II; 12 (upd.); 42 (upd.); 85 (upd.)
The Connell Company, 29
ContiGroup Companies, Inc., 43 (upd.)
Continental Grain Company, 10; 13 (upd.)
CoolBrands International Inc., 35
Coopagri Bretagne, 88
Cooperativa Nacional de Productores de Leche S.A. (Conaprole), 92
Corporación José R. Lindley S.A., 92
CPC International Inc., II
Cranswick plc, 40
CSM N.V., 65
Cuisine Solutions Inc., 84
Cumberland Packing Corporation, 26
Curtice-Burns Foods, Inc., 7; 21 (upd.)
Czarnikow-Rionda Company, Inc., 32
D.F. Stauffer Biscuit Company, 82
Daesang Corporation, 84
Dairy Crest Group plc, 32
Dalgery, PLC, II
Danisco A/S, 44
Dannon Co., Inc., 14
Darigold, Inc., 9
Dawn Food Products, Inc., 17
Dean Foods Company, 7; 21 (upd.); 73 (upd.)
DeKalb Genetics Corporation, 17
Del Monte Foods Company, 7; 23 (upd.)
Di Giorgio Corp., 12
Diageo plc, 24 (upd.)
Diamond of California, 64 (upd.)
Dietz and Watson, Inc., 92
Dippin' Dots, Inc., 56
Dobrogea Grup S.A., 82
Dole Food Company, Inc., 9; 31 (upd.); 68 (upd.)
Domino Sugar Corporation, 26
Doskocil Companies, Inc., 12
Dot Foods, Inc., 69
Doux S.A., 80
Dreyer's Grand Ice Cream, Inc., 17
The Earthgrains Company, 36
Elmer Candy Corporation, 88
Emge Packing Co., Inc., 11
Empresas Polar SA, 55 (upd.)
Eridania Béghin-Say S.A., 36
ERLY Industries Inc., 17
Eskimo Pie Corporation, 21
Établissements Jacquot and Cie S.A.S., 92
Exportadora Bananera Noboa, S.A., 91
Ezaki Glico Company Ltd., 72
Faribault Foods, Inc., 89
Farley's & Sathers Candy Company, Inc., 62
Farmland Foods, Inc., 7
Farmland Industries, Inc., 48
Ferrara Pan Candy Company, 90
Ferrero SpA, 54
Fieldale Farms Corporation, 23
First Colony Coffee & Tea Company, 84
Fleer Corporation, 15
Fleury Michon S.A., 39
Floc'h & Marchand, 80
Florida Crystals Inc., 35
Flowers Industries, Inc., 12; 35 (upd.)
Fonterra Co-Operative Group Ltd., 58
FoodBrands America, Inc., 23
Foster Poultry Farms, 32
Fred Usinger Inc., 54
Fresh America Corporation, 20
Fresh Express Inc., 88
Fresh Foods, Inc., 29
FreshDirect, LLC, 84
Friesland Coberco Dairy Foods Holding N.V., 59
Frito-Lay Company, 32
Frito-Lay North America, 73 (upd.)
Fromageries Bel, 23
Frontier Natural Products Co-Op, 82
Fyffes Plc, 38
Galaxy Nutritional Foods, Inc., 58
Gano Excel Enterprise Sdn. Bhd., 89
The Garden Company Ltd., 82
Gardenburger, Inc., 33; 76 (upd.)
Geest Plc, 38
General Mills, Inc., II; 10 (upd.); 36 (upd.); 85 (upd.)
George A. Hormel and Company, II
George Weston Ltd., II; 36 (upd.); 88 (upd.)
Gerber Products Company, 7; 21 (upd.)
Ghirardelli Chocolate Company, 30
Givaudan SA, 43
Glaces Thiriet S.A., 76
Glanbia plc, 59
Global Berry Farms LLC, 62
Godiva Chocolatier, Inc., 64
Goetze's Candy Company, Inc., 87
Gold Kist Inc., 17; 26 (upd.)
Gold'n Plump Poultry, 54
Golden Enterprises, Inc., 26
Gonnella Baking Company, 40
Good Humor-Breyers Ice Cream Company, 14
Goodman Fielder Ltd., 52
GoodMark Foods, Inc., 26
Gorton's, 13
Goya Foods Inc., 22; 91 (upd.)
Graeter's Manufacturing Company, 86
Grampian Country Food Group, Ltd., 85
Great Harvest Bread Company, 44
Grist Mill Company, 15
Groupe CECAB S.C.A., 88
Groupe Danone, 32 (upd.); 93 (upd.)
Groupe Euralis, 86
Groupe Glon, 84
Groupe Lactalis, 78 (upd.)
Groupe Limagrain, 74
Groupe Soufflet SA, 55
Gruma, S.A. de C.V., 31
Grupo Comercial Chedraui S.A. de C.V., 86
Grupo Herdez, S.A. de C.V., 35
Grupo Industrial Lala, S.A. de C.V., 82
Grupo Leche Pascual S.A., 59
Grupo Viz, S.A. de C.V., 84
Guida-Seibert Dairy Company, 84
Guittard Chocolate Company, 55
Guttenplan's Frozen Dough Inc., 88
H.J. Heinz Company, II; 11 (upd.); 36 (upd.)
Hagoromo Foods Corporation, 84

The Hain Celestial Group, Inc., 27; 43 (upd.)
Hanover Foods Corporation, 35
HARIBO GmbH & Co. KG, 44
The Harris Soup Company (Harry's Fresh Foods), 92
Harry London Candies, Inc., 70
The Hartz Mountain Corporation, 12
Hayel Saeed Anam Group of Cos., 92
Hazlewood Foods plc, 32
Herman Goelitz, Inc., 28
Herr Foods Inc., 84
Hershey Foods Corporation, II; 15 (upd.); 51 (upd.)
Hill's Pet Nutrition, Inc., 27
Hillsdown Holdings plc, II; 24 (upd.)
HiPP GmbH & Co. Vertrieb KG, 88
Hodgson Mill, Inc., 88
Horizon Organic Holding Corporation, 37
Hormel Foods Corporation, 18 (upd.); 54 (upd.)
Hot Stuff Foods, 85
Hudson Foods Inc., 13
Hulman & Company, 44
Hunt-Wesson, Inc., 17
Iams Company, 26
IAWS Group plc, 49
IBP, Inc., II; 21 (upd.)
Iceland Group plc, 33
Icelandic Group hf, 81
Imagine Foods, Inc., 50
Imperial Holly Corporation, 12
Imperial Sugar Company, 32 (upd.)
Industrias Bachoco, S.A. de C.V., 39
Intercorp Excelle Foods Inc., 64
International Multifoods Corporation, 7; 25 (upd.)
Interstate Bakeries Corporation, 12; 38 (upd.)
Inversiones Nacional de Chocolates S.A., 88
Itoham Foods Inc., II; 61 (upd.)
J & J Snack Foods Corporation, 24
The J. M. Smucker Company, 11; 87 (upd.)
J.R. Simplot Company, 16
Jacobs Suchard A.G., II
Jays Foods, Inc., 90
Jel Sert Company, 90
Jelly Belly Candy Company, 76
Jennie-O Turkey Store, Inc., 76
Jim Beam Brands Co., 14
John B. Sanfilippo & Son, Inc., 14
Johnsonville Sausage L.L.C., 63
Julius Meinl International AG, 53
Just Born, Inc., 32
Kal Kan Foods, Inc., 22
Kamps AG, 44
Kar Nut Products Company, 86
Kashi Company, 89
Katokichi Company Ltd., 82
Keebler Foods Company, 36
Kellogg Company, II; 13 (upd.); 50 (upd.)
Ken's Foods, Inc., 88
Kerry Group plc, 27; 87 (upd.)
Kettle Foods Inc., 48
Kewpie Kabushiki Kaisha, 57
Kikkoman Corporation, 14; 47 (upd.)
The King Arthur Flour Company, 31
King Nut Company, 74
King Ranch, Inc., 14
Klement's Sausage Company, 61
Koninklijke Wessanen nv, II; 54 (upd.)
Kraft Foods Inc., II; 7 (upd.); 45 (upd.); 91 (upd.)
Kraft Jacobs Suchard AG, 26 (upd.)
Krispy Kreme Doughnuts, Inc., 21; 61 (upd.)
Kuwait Flour Mills & Bakeries Company, 84
Kyokuyo Company Ltd., 75
L.D.C. SA, 61
La Choy Food Products Inc., 25
Labeyrie SAS, 80
Lakeside Foods, Inc., 89
Lam Son Sugar Joint Stock Corporation (Lasuco), 60
Lamb Weston, Inc., 23
Lance, Inc., 14; 41 (upd.)
Land O'Lakes, Inc., II; 21 (upd.); 81 (upd.)
Lassonde Industries Inc., 68
LDC, 68
Ledesma Sociedad Anónima Agrícola Industrial, 62
Leidy's, Inc., 93
Leprino Foods Company, 28
Leroux S.A.S., 65
Lifeway Foods, Inc., 65
Liberty Orchards Co., Inc., 89
Lincoln Snacks Company, 24
Litehouse Inc., 60
Lotte Confectionery Company Ltd., 76
Lucille Farms, Inc., 45
Luigino's, Inc., 64
M.A. Gedney Co., 51
Madrange SA, 58
Malt-O-Meal Company, 22; 63 (upd.)
Maple Grove Farms of Vermont, 88
Maple Leaf Foods Inc., 41
Marble Slab Creamery, Inc., 87
Mars, Incorporated, 7; 40 (upd.)
Maruha Group Inc., 75 (upd.)
Maryland & Virginia Milk Producers Cooperative Association, Inc., 80
The Maschhoffs, Inc., 82
Maui Land & Pineapple Company, Inc., 29
Mauna Loa Macadamia Nut Corporation, 64
Maverick Ranch Association, Inc., 88
McCain Foods Limited, 77
McCormick & Company, Incorporated, 7; 27 (upd.)
McIlhenny Company, 20
McKee Foods Corporation, 7; 27 (upd.)
Mead Johnson & Company, 84
Meiji Dairies Corporation, II; 82 (upd.)
Meiji Seika Kaisha, Ltd., II
Merisant Worldwide, Inc., 70
Michael Foods, Inc., 25
Mid-America Dairymen, Inc., 7
Midwest Grain Products, Inc., 49
Mike-Sell's Inc., 15
Milnot Company, 46
Molinos Río de la Plata S.A., 61
Monfort, Inc., 13
Morinda Holdings, Inc., 82
Morinaga & Co. Ltd., 61
Moy Park Ltd. 78
Mrs. Baird's Bakeries, 29
Mt. Olive Pickle Company, Inc., 44
MTR Foods Ltd., 55
Murphy Family Farms Inc., 22
The Musco Family Olive Co., 91
Nabisco Foods Group, II; 7 (upd.)
Nantucket Allserve, Inc., 22
Nathan's Famous, Inc., 29
National Presto Industries, Inc., 43 (upd.)
National Sea Products Ltd., 14
Natural Ovens Bakery, Inc., 72
Natural Selection Foods, 54
Naturally Fresh, Inc., 88
Nature's Path Foods, Inc., 87
Naumes, Inc., 81
Nestlé S.A., II; 7 (upd.); 28 (upd.); 71 (upd.)
New England Confectionery Co., 15
New World Pasta Company, 53
Newhall Land and Farming Company, 14
Newly Weds Foods, Inc., 74
Newman's Own, Inc., 37
Nichiro Corporation, 86
Niman Ranch, Inc., 67
Nippon Meat Packers, Inc., II; 78 (upd.)
Nippon Suisan Kaisha, Ltd., II; 92 (upd.)
Nisshin Seifun Group Inc., II; 66 (upd.)
Nissin Food Products Company Ltd., 75
Northern Foods plc, 10; 61 (upd.)
Northland Cranberries, Inc., 38
Nutraceutical International Corporation, 37
NutraSweet Company, 8
Nutreco Holding N.V., 56
Nutrexpa S.A., 92
NutriSystem, Inc., 71
Oakhurst Dairy, 60
Oberto Sausage Company, Inc., 92
Ocean Beauty Seafoods, Inc., 74
Ocean Spray Cranberries, Inc., 7; 25 (upd.); 83 (upd.)
OJSC Wimm-Bill-Dann Foods, 48
Olga's Kitchen, Inc., 80
Omaha Steaks International Inc., 62
Ore-Ida Foods Inc., 13; 78 (upd.)
Oregon Freeze Dry, Inc., 74
Organic Valley (Coulee Region Organic Produce Pool), 53
Orkla ASA, 18; 82 (upd.)
Oscar Mayer Foods Corp., 12
Otis Spunkmeyer, Inc., 28
Overhill Corporation, 51
Palmer Candy Company, 80
Panzani, 84
Papetti's Hygrade Egg Products, Inc., 39
Parmalat Finanziaria SpA, 50
Pendleton Grain Growers Inc., 64
Penford Corporation, 55
Penzeys Spices, Inc., 79
Pepperidge Farm, Incorporated, 81
PepsiCo, Inc., I; 10 (upd.); 38 (upd.); 93 (upd.)

Perdigao SA, 52
Perdue Farms Inc., 7; 23 (upd.)
Perfetti Van Melle S.p.A., 72
Perkins Foods Holdings Ltd., 87
Perry's Ice Cream Company Inc., 90
Pescanova S.A., 81
Pet Incorporated, 7
Petrossian Inc., 54
Pez Candy, Inc., 38
Philip Morris Companies Inc., 18 (upd.)
Phillips Foods, Inc., 63
PIC International Group PLC, 24 (upd.)
Phillips Foods, Inc., 90 (upd.)
Pilgrim's Pride Corporation, 7; 23 (upd.); 90 (upd.)
The Pillsbury Company, II; 13 (upd.); 62 (upd.)
Pioneer Hi-Bred International, Inc., 9
Pizza Inn, Inc., 46
Poore Brothers, Inc., 44
PowerBar Inc., 44
Prairie Farms Dairy, Inc., 47
Premium Standard Farms, Inc., 30
Princes Ltd., 76
The Procter & Gamble Company, III; 8 (upd.); 26 (upd.); 67 (upd.)
Provimi S.A., 80
Punch Taverns plc, 70
Puratos S.A./NV, 92
Purina Mills, Inc., 32
Quaker Foods North America, 73 (upd.)
Quaker Oats Company, II; 12 (upd.); 34 (upd.)
Quality Chekd Dairies, Inc., 48
R. M. Palmer Co., 89
Ralston Purina Company, II; 13 (upd.)
Ranks Hovis McDougall Limited, II; 28 (upd.)
Reckitt Benckiser plc, II; 42 (upd.); 91 (upd.)
Reddy Ice Holdings, Inc., 80
Reser's Fine Foods, Inc., 81
Rica Foods, Inc., 41
Rich Products Corporation, 7; 38 (upd.); 93 (upd.)
Richtree Inc., 63
Ricola Ltd., 62
Ridley Corporation Ltd., 62
River Ranch Fresh Foods LLC, 88
Riviana Foods Inc., 27
Rocky Mountain Chocolate Factory, Inc., 73
Roland Murten A.G., 7
Roman Meal Company, 84
Rose Acre Farms, Inc., 60
Rowntree Mackintosh, II
Royal Numico N.V., 37
Ruiz Food Products, Inc., 53
Russell Stover Candies Inc., 12; 91 (upd.)
Sadia S.A., 59
Sanderson Farms, Inc., 15
Saputo Inc., 59
Sara Lee Corporation, II; 15 (upd.); 54 (upd.)
Sarris Candies Inc., 86
Savannah Foods & Industries, Inc., 7
Schlotzsky's, Inc., 36
Schreiber Foods, Inc., 72
The Schwan Food Company, 7; 26 (upd.); 83 (upd.)
Schwebel Baking Company, 72
Seaboard Corporation, 36; 85 (upd.)
See's Candies, Inc., 30
Seminis, Inc., 29
Seneca Foods Corporation, 60 (upd.)
Sensient Technologies Corporation, 52 (upd.)
Shearer's Foods, Inc., 72
Silhouette Brands, Inc., 55
Skalli Group, 67
Slim-Fast Foods Company, 18; 66 (upd.)
Small Planet Foods, Inc., 89
Smithfield Foods, Inc., 7; 43 (upd.)
Snow Brand Milk Products Company, Ltd., II; 48 (upd.)
Société Industrielle Lesaffre, 84
Sodiaal S.A., 36 (upd.)
SODIMA, II
Sorbee International Ltd., 74
Sorrento, Inc., 24
Spangler Candy Company, 44
Spectrum Organic Products, Inc., 68
Standard Candy Company Inc., 86
Starbucks Corporation, 77 (upd.)
Stock Yards Packing Co., Inc., 37
Stollwerck AG, 53
Stolt Sea Farm Holdings PLC, 54
Stolt-Nielsen S.A., 42
Stonyfield Farm, Inc., 55
Stouffer Corp., 8
Strauss-Elite Group, 68
Südzucker AG, 27
Suiza Foods Corporation, 26
Sun-Diamond Growers of California, 7
Sun-Maid Growers of California, 82
Sun-Rype Products Ltd., 76
Sun World International, LLC, 93
Sunkist Growers, Inc., 26
SunOpta Inc., 79
Supervalu Inc., 18 (upd.); 50 (upd.)
Suprema Specialties, Inc., 27
Sweet Candy Company, 60
Swift & Company, 55
Swiss Valley Farms Company, 90
Sylvan, Inc., 22
Symrise GmbH and Company KG, 89
Syngenta International AG, 83
T. Marzetti Company, 57
Taiyo Fishery Company, Limited, II
Tasty Baking Company, 14; 35 (upd.)
Tate & Lyle PLC, II; 42 (upd.)
TCBY Enterprises Inc., 17
TDL Group Ltd., 46
Terrena L'Union CANA CAVAL, 70
Thai Union Frozen Products PCL, 75
Thomas J. Lipton Company, 14
Thorn Apple Valley, Inc., 7; 22 (upd.)
Thorntons plc, 46
TLC Beatrice International Holdings, Inc., 22
Tofutti Brands, Inc., 64
Tom's Foods Inc., 66
Tombstone Pizza Corporation, 13
Tone Brothers, Inc., 21; 74 (upd.)
Tootsie Roll Industries, Inc., 12; 82 (upd.)
Touton S.A., 92
Townsends, Inc., 64
Tree Top, Inc., 76
TreeHouse Foods, Inc., 79
Tri Valley Growers, 32
Trident Seafoods Corporation, 56
Tropicana Products, Inc., 28
Tulip Ltd., 89
Tumaro's Gourmet Tortillas, 85
Tyson Foods, Inc., II; 14 (upd.); 50 (upd.)
U.S. Foodservice, 26
U.S. Premium Beef LLC, 91
Uncle Ben's Inc., 22
Uncle Ray's LLC, 90
Unigate PLC, II; 28 (upd.)
Unilever, II; 7 (upd.); 32 (upd.); 89 (upd.)
Uniq plc, 83 (upd.)
United Biscuits (Holdings) plc, II; 42 (upd.)
United Brands Company, II
United Farm Workers of America, 88
United Foods, Inc., 21
Universal Foods Corporation, 7
Utz Quality Foods, Inc., 72
Van Camp Seafood Company, Inc., 7
Ventura Foods LLC, 90
Vienna Sausage Manufacturing Co., 14
Vilmorin Clause et Cie, 70
Vion Food Group NV, 85
Vista Bakery, Inc., 56
Vlasic Foods International Inc., 25
W Jordan (Cereals) Ltd., 74
Wagers Inc. (Idaho Candy Company), 86
Walkers Shortbread Ltd., 79
Walkers Snack Foods Ltd., 70
Warburtons Ltd., 89
Warrell Corporation, 68
Wattie's Ltd., 7
Weaver Popcorn Company, Inc., 89
Weetabix Limited, 61
Weis Markets, Inc., 84 (upd.)
Wells' Dairy, Inc., 36
Wenner Bread Products Inc., 80
White Lily Foods Company, 88
White Wave, 43
Wilbur Chocolate Company, 66
Wimm-Bill-Dann Foods, 48
Wisconsin Dairies, 7
Wise Foods, Inc., 79
WLR Foods, Inc., 21
Wm. B. Reily & Company Inc., 58
Wm. Wrigley Jr. Company, 7; 58 (upd.)
World's Finest Chocolate Inc., 39
Worthington Foods, Inc., 14
Yamazaki Baking Co., Ltd., 58
Yarnell Ice Cream Company, Inc., 92
Yeo Hiap Seng Malaysia Bhd., 75
YOCREAM International, Inc., 47
Young's Bluecrest Seafood Holdings Ltd., 81
Zacky Farms LLC, 74
Zatarain's, Inc., 64

Food Services & Retailers

A. F. Blakemore & Son Ltd., 90
Advantica Restaurant Group, Inc., 27 (upd.)

AFC Enterprises, Inc., 32 (upd.); 83 (upd.)
Affiliated Foods Inc., 53
Albertson's, Inc., II; 7 (upd.); 30 (upd.); 65 (upd.)
Aldi Einkauf GmbH & Co. OHG, 13; 86 (upd.)
Alex Lee Inc., 18; 44 (upd.)
Allen Foods, Inc., 60
Almacenes Exito S.A., 89
Alpha Airports Group PLC, 77
America's Favorite Chicken Company, Inc., 7
American Restaurant Partners, L.P., 93
American Stores Company, II
Andronico's Market, 70
Applebee's International, Inc., 14; 35 (upd.)
ARA Services, II
Arby's Inc., 14
Arden Group, Inc., 29
Argyll Group PLC, II
Ark Restaurants Corp., 20
Asahi Breweries, Ltd., 20 (upd.)
ASDA Group Ltd., II; 28 (upd.); 64 (upd.)
Associated Grocers, Incorporated, 9; 31 (upd.)
Association des Centres Distributeurs E. Leclerc, 37
Atlanta Bread Company International, Inc., 70
Au Bon Pain Co., Inc., 18
Auchan, 37
Auntie Anne's, Inc., 35
Autogrill SpA, 49
Avado Brands, Inc., 31
B.R. Guest Inc., 87
Back Bay Restaurant Group, Inc., 20
Back Yard Burgers, Inc., 45
Bashas' Inc., 33; 80 (upd.)
Bear Creek Corporation, 38
Ben E. Keith Company, 76
Benihana, Inc., 18; 76 (upd.)
Bertucci's Corporation, 64 (upd.)
Bettys & Taylors of Harrogate Ltd., 72
Big Bear Stores Co., 13
The Big Food Group plc, 68 (upd.)
Big V Supermarkets, Inc., 25
Big Y Foods, Inc., 53
Blimpie International, Inc., 15; 49 (upd.)
Bob Evans Farms, Inc., 9; 63 (upd.)
Bob's Red Mill Natural Foods, Inc., 63
Boddie-Noell Enterprises, Inc., 68
Bon Appetit Holding AG, 48
Boston Market Corporation, 12; 48 (upd.)
Boston Pizza International Inc., 88
Brazil Fast Food Corporation, 74
Briazz, Inc., 53
Brinker International, Inc., 10; 38 (upd.); 75 (upd.)
Brookshire Grocery Company, 16; 74 (upd.)
Bruegger's Corporation, 63
Bruno's Supermarkets, Inc., 7; 26 (upd.); 68 (upd.)
Buca, Inc., 38
Budgens Ltd., 59
Buffalo Wild Wings, Inc., 56
Buffets Holdings, Inc., 10; 32 (upd.); 93 (upd.)
Burger King Corporation, II; 17 (upd.); 56 (upd.)
Busch Entertainment Corporation, 73
C&K Market, Inc., 81
C & S Wholesale Grocers, Inc., 55
C.H. Robinson, Inc., 11
Caffè Nero Group PLC, 63
California Pizza Kitchen Inc., 15; 74 (upd.)
Captain D's, LLC, 59
Cargill, Incorporated, II; 13 (upd.); 40 (upd.); 89 (upd.)
Caribou Coffee Company, Inc., 28
Carlson Companies, Inc., 6; 22 (upd.); 87 (upd.)
Carlson Restaurants Worldwide, 69
Carr-Gottstein Foods Co., 17
Carrols Restaurant Group, Inc., 92
Casey's General Stores, Inc., 19; 83 (upd.)
Casino Guichard-Perrachon S.A., 59 (upd.)
CBRL Group, Inc., 35 (upd.); 86 (upd.)
CEC Entertainment, Inc., 31 (upd.)
Centerplate, Inc., 79
Chart House Enterprises, Inc., 17
Checkers Drive-In Restaurants, Inc., 16; 74 (upd.)
The Cheesecake Factory Inc., 17
Chi-Chi's Inc., 13; 51 (upd.)
Chicago Pizza & Brewery, Inc., 44
Chick-fil-A Inc., 23; 90 (upd.)
Chipotle Mexican Grill, Inc., 67
Church's Chicken, 66
Cinnabon Inc., 23; 90 (upd.)
The Circle K Corporation, II
CKE Restaurants, Inc., 19; 46 (upd.)
Coborn's, Inc., 30
Cold Stone Creamery, 69
Coles Group Limited, V; 20 (upd.); 85 (upd.)
Compass Group PLC, 34
Comptoirs Modernes S.A., 19
Consolidated Products Inc., 14
Controladora Comercial Mexicana, S.A. de C.V., 36
Cooker Restaurant Corporation, 20; 51 (upd.)
The Copps Corporation, 32
Cosi, Inc., 53
Cost-U-Less, Inc., 51
Coto Centro Integral de Comercializacion S.A., 66
Country Kitchen International, Inc., 76
Cracker Barrel Old Country Store, Inc., 10
Cremonini S.p.A., 57
CulinArt, Inc., 92
Culver Franchising System, Inc., 58
D'Agostino Supermarkets Inc., 19
Dairy Mart Convenience Stores, Inc., 7; 25 (upd.)
Darden Restaurants, Inc., 16; 44 (upd.)
Dean & DeLuca, Inc., 36
Del Taco, Inc., 58
Delhaize "Le Lion" S.A., 44
DeMoulas / Market Basket Inc., 23
DenAmerica Corporation, 29
Denner AG, 88
Deschutes Brewery, Inc., 57
Diedrich Coffee, Inc., 40
Dierbergs Markets Inc., 63
Distribución y Servicio D&S S.A., 71
Doctor's Associates Inc., 67 (upd.)
Dominick's Finer Foods, Inc., 56
Domino's, Inc., 7; 21 (upd.); 63 (upd.)
Donatos Pizzeria Corporation, 58
E H Booth & Company Ltd., 90
Eateries, Inc., 33
Ed S.A.S., 88
Edeka Zentrale A.G., II; 47 (upd.)
Einstein/Noah Bagel Corporation, 29
El Chico Restaurants, Inc., 19
El Pollo Loco, Inc., 69
Elior SA, 49
Elmer's Restaurants, Inc., 42
Embers America Restaurants, 30
Etablissements Economiques du Casino Guichard, Perrachon et Cie, S.C.A., 12
Famous Brands Ltd., 86
Famous Dave's of America, Inc., 40
Farmer Jack Supermarkets 78
Fatburger Corporation, 64
Fazoli's Management, Inc., 27; 76 (upd.)
Fili Enterprises, Inc., 70
Fired Up, Inc., 82
5 & Diner Franchise Corporation, 72
Flagstar Companies, Inc., 10
Flanigan's Enterprises, Inc., 60
Fleming Companies, Inc., II
Food Circus Super Markets, Inc., 88
The Food Emporium, 64
Food Lion LLC, II; 15 (upd.); 66 (upd.)
Foodarama Supermarkets, Inc., 28
Foodmaker, Inc., 14
The Fred W. Albrecht Grocery Co., 13
Fresh Choice, Inc., 20
Fresh Enterprises, Inc., 66
Fresh Foods, Inc., 29
Friendly Ice Cream Corporation, 30; 72 (upd.)
Frisch's Restaurants, Inc., 35; 92 (upd.)
Fuller Smith & Turner P.L.C., 38
Furr's Restaurant Group, Inc., 53
Furr's Supermarkets, Inc., 28
Galardi Group, Inc., 72
Garden Fresh Restaurant Corporation, 31
Gate Gourmet International AG, 70
The Gateway Corporation Ltd., II
Genuardi's Family Markets, Inc., 35
George Weston Ltd., II; 36 (upd.); 88 (upd.)
Ghirardelli Chocolate Company, 30
Giant Eagle, Inc., 86
Giant Food LLC, II; 22 (upd.); 83 (upd.)
Godfather's Pizza Incorporated, 25
Golden Corral Corporation, 10; 66 (upd.)
Golden Krust Caribbean Bakery, Inc., 68
Golden State Foods Corporation, 32
The Golub Corporation, 26
Gordon Biersch Brewery Restaurant Group, Inc., 93
Gordon Food Service Inc., 8; 39 (upd.)

The Grand Union Company, 7; 28 (upd.)
The Great Atlantic & Pacific Tea Company, Inc., II; 16 (upd.); 55 (upd.)
Greggs PLC, 65
Grill Concepts, Inc., 74
Gristede's Foods Inc., 31; 68 (upd.)
Ground Round, Inc., 21
Groupe Le Duff S.A., 84
Groupe Promodès S.A., 19
Grupo Corvi S.A. de C.V., 86
Guyenne et Gascogne, 23
H.E. Butt Grocery Company, 13; 32 (upd.); 85 (upd.)
Haggen Inc., 38
Hannaford Bros. Co., 12
Hard Rock Cafe International, Inc., 12
Harris Teeter Inc., 23; 72 (upd.)
Harry's Farmers Market Inc., 23
HDOS Enterprises, 72
Hickory Farms, Inc., 17
Holberg Industries, Inc., 36
Holland Burgerville USA, 44
Hooters of America, Inc., 18; 69 (upd.)
Hops Restaurant Bar and Brewery, 46
Hoss's Steak and Sea House Inc., 68
Host America Corporation, 79
Hotel Properties Ltd., 71
Houchens Industries Inc., 51
Hughes Markets, Inc., 22
Hungry Howie's Pizza and Subs, Inc., 25
Hy-Vee, Inc., 36
ICA AB, II
Iceland Group plc, 33
IHOP Corporation, 17; 58 (upd.)
Il Fornaio (America) Corporation, 27
In-N-Out Burger, 19
In-N-Out Burgers Inc., 74 (upd.)
Ingles Markets, Inc., 20
Inserra Supermarkets, 25
Inter Link Foods PLC, 61
International Dairy Queen, Inc., 10; 39 (upd.)
ITM Entreprises SA, 36
Ito-Yokado Co., Ltd., 42 (upd.)
Ivar's, Inc., 86
J Sainsbury plc, II; 13 (upd.); 38 (upd.)
J. Alexander's Corporation, 65
Jack in the Box Inc., 89 (upd.)
Jacmar Companies, 87
Jamba Juice Company, 47
James Original Coney Island Inc., 84
JD Wetherspoon plc, 30
Jean-Georges Enterprises L.L.C., 75
Jerry's Famous Deli Inc., 24
Jersey Mike's Franchise Systems, Inc., 83
Jitney-Jungle Stores of America, Inc., 27
John Lewis Partnership plc, 42 (upd.)
Johnny Rockets Group, Inc., 31; 76 (upd.)
KFC Corporation, 7; 21 (upd.); 89 (upd.)
King Kullen Grocery Co., Inc., 15
Koninklijke Ahold N.V. (Royal Ahold), II; 16 (upd.)
Koo Koo Roo, Inc., 25
The Kroger Co., II; 15 (upd.); 65 (upd.)
The Krystal Company, 33
Kwik Save Group plc, 11
La Madeleine French Bakery & Café, 33
Landry's Restaurants, Inc., 15; 65 (upd.)
The Laurel Pub Company Limited, 59
Laurus N.V., 65
LDB Corporation, 53
Leeann Chin, Inc., 30
Levy Restaurants L.P., 26
Little Caesar Enterprises, Inc., 7; 24 (upd.)
Loblaw Companies Limited, 43
Logan's Roadhouse, Inc., 29
Lone Star Steakhouse & Saloon, Inc., 51
Long John Silver's, 13; 57 (upd.)
Luby's, Inc., 17; 42 (upd.)
Lucky Stores, Inc., 27
Lund Food Holdings, Inc., 22
Madden's on Gull Lake, 52
MaggieMoo's International, 89
Maid-Rite Corporation, 62
Maines Paper & Food Service Inc., 71
Marble Slab Creamery, Inc., 87
Marco's Franchising LLC, 86
Marie Callender's Restaurant & Bakery, Inc., 28
Marsh Supermarkets, Inc., 17; 76 (upd.)
Matt Prentice Restaurant Group, 70
Maui Wowi, Inc., 85
Max & Erma's Restaurants Inc., 19
Mayfield Dairy Farms, Inc., 74
Mazzio's Corporation, 76
McAlister's Corporation, 66
McCormick & Schmick's Seafood Restaurants, Inc., 71
McDonald's Corporation, II; 7 (upd.); 26 (upd.); 63 (upd.)
Megafoods Stores Inc., 13
Meijer Incorporated, 7
The Melting Pot Restaurants, Inc., 74
Metcash Trading Ltd., 58
Métro Inc., 77
Metromedia Companies, 14
Mexican Restaurants, Inc., 41
The Middleby Corporation, 22
Minyard Food Stores, Inc., 33; 86 (upd.)
MITROPA AG, 37
Monterey Pasta Company, 58
Morrison Restaurants Inc., 11
Morton's Restaurant Group, Inc., 30; 88 (upd.)
Mr. Gatti's, LP, 87
Mrs. Fields' Original Cookies, Inc., 27
Musgrave Group Plc, 57
Myriad Restaurant Group, Inc., 87
Nash Finch Company, 8; 23 (upd.); 65 (upd.)
Nathan's Famous, Inc., 29
National Convenience Stores Incorporated, 7
New Seasons Market, 75
New World Restaurant Group, Inc., 44
New York Restaurant Group, Inc., 32
Noble Roman's Inc., 14
Noodles & Company, Inc., 55
NPC International, Inc., 40
O'Charley's Inc., 19; 60 (upd.)
Old Spaghetti Factory International Inc., 24
The Oshawa Group Limited, II
OSI Restaurant Partners, Inc., 88 (upd.)
Outback Steakhouse, Inc., 12; 34 (upd.)
P&C Foods Inc., 8
P.F. Chang's China Bistro, Inc., 37; 86 (upd.)
Pacific Coast Restaurants, Inc., 90
Palm Management Corporation, 71
Pancho's Mexican Buffet, Inc., 46
Panda Management Company, Inc., 35
Panera Bread Company, 44
Papa Gino's Holdings Corporation, Inc., 86
Papa John's International, Inc., 15; 71 (upd.)
Papa Murphy's International, Inc., 54
Pappas Restaurants, Inc., 76
Pathmark Stores, Inc., 23
Peapod, Inc., 30
Penn Traffic Company, 13
Performance Food Group Company, 31
Perkins Family Restaurants, L.P., 22
Peter Piper, Inc., 70
Petrossian Inc., 54
Phillips Foods, Inc., 63
Picard Surgeles, 76
Piccadilly Cafeterias, Inc., 19
Piggly Wiggly Southern, Inc., 13
Pizza Hut Inc., 7; 21 (upd.)
Planet Hollywood International, Inc., 18; 41 (upd.)
Players International, Inc., 22
Ponderosa Steakhouse, 15
Portillo's Restaurant Group, Inc., 71
Potbelly Sandwich Works, Inc., 83
Provigo Inc., II; 51 (upd.)
Publix Super Markets Inc., 7; 31 (upd.)
Pueblo Xtra International, Inc., 47
Qdoba Restaurant Corporation, 93
Quality Dining, Inc., 18
Quality Food Centers, Inc., 17
The Quizno's Corporation, 42
Rainforest Café, Inc., 25; 88 (upd.)
Rally's, 25; 68 (upd.)
Ralphs Grocery Company, 35
Randall's Food Markets, Inc., 40
Rare Hospitality International Inc., 19
Raving Brands, Inc., 64
Red Robin Gourmet Burgers, Inc., 56
Restaurant Associates Corporation, 66
Restaurants Unlimited, Inc., 13
RFC Franchising LLC, 68
Richfood Holdings, Inc., 7
Richtree Inc., 63
The Riese Organization, 38
Riser Foods, Inc., 9
Roadhouse Grill, Inc., 22
Rock Bottom Restaurants, Inc., 25; 68 (upd.)
Roly Poly Franchise Systems LLC, 83
Romacorp, Inc., 58
Rosauers Supermarkets, Inc., 90
Roundy's Inc., 58 (upd.)
RTM Restaurant Group, 58
Rubio's Restaurants, Inc., 35
Ruby Tuesday, Inc., 18; 71 (upd.)
Ruth's Chris Steak House, 28; 88 (upd.)
Ryan's Restaurant Group, Inc., 15; 68 (upd.)

Safeway Inc., II; 24 (upd.); 50 (upd.); 85 (upd.)
Santa Barbara Restaurant Group, Inc., 37
Sbarro, Inc., 16; 64 (upd.)
Schlotzsky's, Inc., 36
Schultz Sav-O Stores, Inc., 21
The Schwan Food Company, 26 (upd.); 83 (upd.)
Seaway Food Town, Inc., 15
Second Harvest, 29
See's Candies, Inc., 30
Seneca Foods Corporation, 17
Service America Corp., 7
SFI Group plc, 51
Shaw's Supermarkets, Inc., 56
Shells Seafood Restaurants, Inc., 43
Shoney's, Inc., 7; 23 (upd.)
ShowBiz Pizza Time, Inc., 13
Skyline Chili, Inc., 62
Smart & Final, Inc., 16
Smith's Food & Drug Centers, Inc., 8; 57 (upd.)
Sobeys Inc., 80
Sodexho SA, 29; 91 (upd.)
Somerfield plc, 47 (upd.)
Sonic Corporation, 14; 37 (upd.)
The Southland Corporation, II; 7 (upd.)
Spaghetti Warehouse, Inc., 25
SPAR Handels AG, 35
Spartan Stores Inc., 8
Starbucks Corporation, 77 (upd.)
Stater Bros. Holdings Inc., 64
The Steak n Shake Company, 41
Steinberg Incorporated, II
Stew Leonard's, 56
The Stop & Shop Supermarket Company, II; 68 (upd.)
Subway, 32
Super Food Services, Inc., 15
Supermarkets General Holdings Corporation, II
Supervalu Inc., II; 18 (upd.); 50 (upd.)
SWH Corporation, 70
SYSCO Corporation, II; 24 (upd.); 75 (upd.)
Taco Bell Corporation, 7; 21 (upd.); 74 (upd.)
Taco Cabana, Inc., 23; 72 (upd.)
Taco John's International, Inc., 15; 63 (upd.)
Tchibo GmbH, 82
TelePizza S.A., 33
Tesco PLC, II
Texas Roadhouse, Inc., 69
Thomas & Howard Company, Inc., 90
Timber Lodge Steakhouse, Inc., 73
Tops Markets LLC, 60
Total Entertainment Restaurant Corporation, 46
Toupargel-Agrigel S.A., 76
Trader Joe's Company, 13; 50 (upd.)
Travel Ports of America, Inc., 17
Tree of Life, Inc., 29
Triarc Companies, Inc., 34 (upd.)
Tubby's, Inc., 53
Tully's Coffee Corporation, 51
Tumbleweed, Inc., 33; 80 (upd.)
TW Services, Inc., II
Ukrop's Super Market's, Inc., 39
Unified Grocers, Inc., 93
Unique Casual Restaurants, Inc., 27
United Dairy Farmers, Inc., 74
United Natural Foods, Inc., 32; 76 (upd.)
Uno Restaurant Holdings Corporation, 18; 70 (upd.)
Uwajimaya, Inc., 60
Vail Resorts, Inc., 43 (upd.)
VICORP Restaurants, Inc., 12; 48 (upd.)
Victory Refrigeration, Inc., 82
Village Super Market, Inc., 7
The Vons Companies, Incorporated, 7; 28 (upd.)
W. H. Braum, Inc., 80
Waffle House Inc., 14; 60 (upd.)
Wakefern Food Corporation, 33
Waldbaum, Inc., 19
Wall Street Deli, Inc., 33
Wawa Inc., 17; 78 (upd.)
Wegmans Food Markets, Inc., 9; 41 (upd.)
Weis Markets, Inc., 15
Wendy's International, Inc., 8; 23 (upd.); 47 (upd.)
The WesterN SizzliN Corporation, 60
Wetterau Incorporated, II
White Castle Management Company, 12; 36 (upd.); 85 (upd.)
White Rose, Inc., 24
Whittard of Chelsea Plc, 61
Whole Foods Market, Inc., 50 (upd.)
Wild Oats Markets, Inc., 19; 41 (upd.)
Winchell's Donut Houses Operating Company, L.P., 60
WinCo Foods Inc., 60
Winn-Dixie Stores, Inc., II; 21 (upd.); 59 (upd.)
Wm. Morrison Supermarkets PLC, 38
Wolfgang Puck Worldwide, Inc., 26, 70 (upd.)
Worldwide Restaurant Concepts, Inc., 47
Yoshinoya D & C Company Ltd., 88
Young & Co.'s Brewery, P.L.C., 38
Yucaipa Cos., 17
Yum! Brands Inc., 58
Zingerman's Community of Businesses, 68

Health & Personal Care Products

Abaxis, Inc., 83
Abbott Laboratories, I; 11 (upd.); 40 (upd.); 93 (upd.)
Advanced Medical Optics, Inc., 79
Advanced Neuromodulation Systems, Inc., 73
Akorn, Inc., 32
ALARIS Medical Systems, Inc., 65
Alberto-Culver Company, 8; 36 (upd.); 91 (upd.)
Alco Health Services Corporation, III
Alès Groupe, 81
Allergan, Inc., 10; 30 (upd.); 77 (upd.)
American Oriental Bioengineering Inc., 93
American Safety Razor Company, 20
American Stores Company, 22 (upd.)
Amway Corporation, III; 13 (upd.)
AngioDynamics, Inc., 81
ArthroCare Corporation, 73
Artsana SpA, 92
Atkins Nutritionals, Inc., 58
Aveda Corporation, 24
Avon Products, Inc., III; 19 (upd.); 46 (upd.)
Bally Total Fitness Holding Corp., 25
Bare Escentuals, Inc., 91
Bausch & Lomb Inc., 7; 25 (upd.)
Baxter International Inc., I; 10 (upd.)
BeautiControl Cosmetics, Inc., 21
Becton, Dickinson & Company, I; 11 (upd.)
Beiersdorf AG, 29
Big B, Inc., 17
Bindley Western Industries, Inc., 9
Biolase Technology, Inc., 87
Biomet, Inc., 10; 93 (upd.)
Biosite Incorporated, 73
Block Drug Company, Inc., 8; 27 (upd.)
The Body Shop International plc, 53 (upd.)
Boiron S.A., 73
Bolton Group B.V., 86
The Boots Company PLC, 24 (upd.)
Boston Scientific Corporation, 77 (upd.)
Bristol-Myers Squibb Company, III; 9 (upd.)
Bronner Brothers Inc., 92
C.R. Bard Inc., 9
Candela Corporation, 48
Cantel Medical Corporation, 80
Cardinal Health, Inc., 18; 50 (upd.)
Carl Zeiss AG, III; 34 (upd.); 91 (upd.)
Carson, Inc., 31
Carter-Wallace, Inc., 8
Caswell-Massey Co. Ltd., 51
CCA Industries, Inc., 53
Chattem, Inc., 17; 88 (upd.)
Chesebrough-Pond's USA, Inc., 8
Chronimed Inc., 26
Church & Dwight Co., Inc., 68 (upd.)
Cintas Corporation, 51 (upd.)
The Clorox Company, III; 22 (upd.); 81 (upd.)
CNS, Inc., 20
Colgate-Palmolive Company, III; 14 (upd.); 35 (upd.)
Combe Inc., 72
Conair Corp., 17
CONMED Corporation, 87
Connetics Corporation, 70
Cordis Corp., 19
Cosmair, Inc., 8
Coty, Inc., 36
Covidien Ltd., 91
Cybex International, Inc., 49
Cytyc Corporation, 69
Dade Behring Holdings Inc., 71
Dalli-Werke GmbH & Co. KG, 86
Datascope Corporation, 39
Del Laboratories, Inc., 28
Deltec, Inc., 56
Dentsply International Inc., 10
DEP Corporation, 20
DePuy, Inc., 30
DHB Industries Inc., 85

Diagnostic Products Corporation, 73
The Dial Corp., 23 (upd.)
Direct Focus, Inc., 47
Drackett Professional Products, 12
Drägerwerk AG, 83
E-Z-EM Inc., 89
Elizabeth Arden, Inc., 8; 40 (upd.)
Empi, Inc., 26
Enrich International, Inc., 33
The Estée Lauder Companies Inc., 9; 30 (upd.); 93 (upd.)
Ethicon, Inc., 23
Farouk Systems Inc. 78
Forest Laboratories, Inc., 11
Forever Living Products International Inc., 17
FoxHollow Technologies, Inc., 85
French Fragrances, Inc., 22
Gambro AB, 49
General Nutrition Companies, Inc., 11; 29 (upd.)
Genzyme Corporation, 13; 77 (upd.)
GF Health Products, Inc., 82
The Gillette Company, III; 20 (upd.)
Given Imaging Ltd., 83
Groupe Yves Saint Laurent, 23
Grupo Omnilife S.A. de C.V., 88
Guerlain, 23
Guest Supply, Inc., 18
Guidant Corporation, 58
Guinot Paris S.A., 82
Hanger Orthopedic Group, Inc., 41
Helen of Troy Corporation, 18
Helene Curtis Industries, Inc., 8; 28 (upd.)
Henkel KGaA, III
Henry Schein, Inc., 31; 70 (upd.)
Herbalife Ltd., 17; 41 (upd.); 92 (upd.)
Huntleigh Technology PLC, 77
Immucor, Inc., 81
Inamed Corporation, 79
Integra LifeSciences Holdings Corporation, 87
Integrated BioPharma, Inc., 83
Inter Parfums Inc., 35; 86 (upd.)
Intuitive Surgical, Inc., 79
Invacare Corporation, 11
IVAX Corporation, 11
IVC Industries, Inc., 45
The Jean Coutu Group (PJC) Inc., 46
John Paul Mitchell Systems, 24
Johnson & Johnson, III; 8 (upd.); 36 (upd.); 75 (upd.)
Kanebo, Ltd., 53
Kao Corporation, III; 79 (upd.)
Kendall International, Inc., 11
Kensey Nash Corporation, 71
Keys Fitness Products, LP, 83
Kimberly-Clark Corporation, III; 16 (upd.); 43 (upd.)
Kyowa Hakko Kogyo Co., Ltd., III
Kyphon Inc., 87
L'Oréal SA, III; 8 (upd.); 46 (upd.)
Laboratoires de Biologie Végétale Yves Rocher, 35
The Lamaur Corporation, 41
Lever Brothers Company, 9
Lion Corporation, III; 51 (upd.)
Lush Ltd., 93
Luxottica SpA, 17; 52 (upd.)
Mandom Corporation, 82
Mannatech Inc., 33
Mary Kay Inc., 9; 30 (upd.); 84 (upd.)
Matrix Essentials Inc., 90
Maxxim Medical Inc., 12
Medco Containment Services Inc., 9
Medline Industries, Inc., 61
Medtronic, Inc., 8; 67 (upd.)
Melaleuca Inc., 31
The Mentholatum Company Inc., 32
Mentor Corporation, 26
Merck & Co., Inc., I; 11 (upd.); 34 (upd.)
Merit Medical Systems, Inc., 29
Merz Group, 81
Natura Cosméticos S.A., 75
Nature's Sunshine Products, Inc., 15
NBTY, Inc., 31
NeighborCare, Inc., 67 (upd.)
Neutrogena Corporation, 17
New Dana Perfumes Company, 37
Neways Inc. 78
Nikken Global Inc., 32
NutriSystem, Inc., 71
Nutrition for Life International Inc., 22
Ocular Sciences, Inc., 65
OEC Medical Systems, Inc., 27
OraSure Technologies, Inc., 75
Orion Oyj, 72
Patterson Dental Co., 19
Perrigo Company, 12
Pfizer Inc., 79 (upd.)
Physician Sales & Service, Inc., 14
Playtex Products, Inc., 15
PolyMedica Corporation, 77
The Procter & Gamble Company, III; 8 (upd.); 26 (upd.); 67 (upd.)
PZ Cussons plc, 72
Quidel Corporation, 80
Reckitt Benckiser plc, II; 42 (upd.); 91 (upd.)
Redken Laboratories Inc., 84
Reliv International, Inc., 58
Revlon Inc., III; 17 (upd.)
Roche Biomedical Laboratories, Inc., 11
S.C. Johnson & Son, Inc., III; 28 (upd.); 89 (upd.)
Safety 1st, Inc., 24
Schering-Plough Corporation, 14 (upd.)
Sephora Holdings S.A., 82
Shaklee Corporation, 39 (upd.)
Shionogi & Co., Ltd., III
Shiseido Company, Limited, III; 22 (upd.); 81 (upd.)
Slim-Fast Foods Company, 18; 66 (upd.)
Smith & Nephew plc, 17
SmithKline Beecham PLC, III
Soft Sheen Products, Inc., 31
Sola International Inc., 71
Spacelabs Medical, Inc., 71
STAAR Surgical Company, 57
Straumann Holding AG, 79
Stryker Corporation, 79 (upd.)
Sunrise Medical Inc., 11
Syneron Medical Ltd., 91
Synthes, Inc., 93
Tambrands Inc., 8
Terumo Corporation, 48
Thane International, Inc., 84
Tom's of Maine, Inc., 45
Transitions Optical, Inc., 83
The Tranzonic Companies, 37
Turtle Wax, Inc., 15; 93 (upd.)
Tutogen Medical, Inc., 68
Unicharm Corporation, 84
United States Surgical Corporation, 10; 34 (upd.)
USANA, Inc., 29
Utah Medical Products, Inc., 36
Ventana Medical Systems, Inc., 75
VHA Inc., 53
VIASYS Healthcare, Inc., 52
Vion Food Group NV, 85
VISX, Incorporated, 30
Vitamin Shoppe Industries, Inc., 60
Water Pik Technologies, Inc., 34; 83 (upd.)
Weider Nutrition International, Inc., 29
Weleda AG 78
Wella AG, III; 48 (upd.)
West Pharmaceutical Services, Inc., 42
Wright Medical Group, Inc., 61
Wyeth, 50 (upd.)
Zila, Inc., 46
Zimmer Holdings, Inc., 45

Health Care Services

Acadian Ambulance & Air Med Services, Inc., 39
Adventist Health, 53
Advocat Inc., 46
Almost Family, Inc., 93
Alterra Healthcare Corporation, 42
Amedysis, Inc., 53
The American Cancer Society, 24
American Healthways, Inc., 65
American Lung Association, 48
American Medical Association, 39
American Medical International, Inc., III
American Medical Response, Inc., 39
American Red Cross, 40
AMERIGROUP Corporation, 69
AmeriSource Health Corporation, 37 (upd.)
AmSurg Corporation, 48
Applied Bioscience International, Inc., 10
Assisted Living Concepts, Inc., 43
ATC Healthcare Inc., 64
Baptist Health Care Corporation, 82
Beverly Enterprises, Inc., III; 16 (upd.)
Bon Secours Health System, Inc., 24
Brookdale Senior Living, 91
C.R. Bard, Inc., 65 (upd.)
Cancer Treatment Centers of America, Inc., 85
Capital Senior Living Corporation, 75
Caremark Rx, Inc., 10; 54 (upd.)
Catholic Health Initiatives, 91
Children's Comprehensive Services, Inc., 42
Children's Hospitals and Clinics, Inc., 54
Chronimed Inc., 26
COBE Laboratories, Inc., 13

Columbia/HCA Healthcare Corporation, 15
Community Health Systems, Inc., 71
Community Psychiatric Centers, 15
CompDent Corporation, 22
CompHealth Inc., 25
Comprehensive Care Corporation, 15
Continental Medical Systems, Inc., 10
Continuum Health Partners, Inc., 60
Coventry Health Care, Inc., 59
Cystic Fibrosis Foundation, 93
DaVita Inc., 73
Easter Seals, Inc., 58
Erickson Retirement Communities, 57
Express Scripts Incorporated, 17
Extendicare Health Services, Inc., 6
Eye Care Centers of America, Inc., 69
FHP International Corporation, 6
Fresenius AG, 56
Genesis Health Ventures, Inc., 18
Gentiva Health Services, Inc., 79
GranCare, Inc., 14
Group Health Cooperative, 41
Grupo Ángeles Servicios de Salud, S.A. de C.V., 84
Hamot Health Foundation, 91
Hazelden Foundation, 28
HCA - The Healthcare Company, 35 (upd.)
Health Care & Retirement Corporation, 22
Health Management Associates, Inc., 56
Health Risk Management, Inc., 24
Health Systems International, Inc., 11
HealthSouth Corporation, 14; 33 (upd.)
Henry Ford Health System, 84
Highmark Inc., 27
The Hillhaven Corporation, 14
Holiday Retirement Corp., 87
Hooper Holmes, Inc., 22
Hospital Central Services, Inc., 56
Hospital Corporation of America, III
Howard Hughes Medical Institute, 39
Humana Inc., III; 24 (upd.)
Intermountain Health Care, Inc., 27
Jenny Craig, Inc., 10; 29 (upd.); 92 (upd.)
Kinetic Concepts, Inc. (KCI), 20
LabOne, Inc., 48
Laboratory Corporation of America Holdings, 42 (upd.)
LCA-Vision, Inc., 85
Life Care Centers of America Inc., 76
Lifeline Systems, Inc., 53
LifePoint Hospitals, Inc., 69
Lincare Holdings Inc., 43
Manor Care, Inc., 6; 25 (upd.)
March of Dimes, 31
Marshfield Clinic Inc., 82
Matria Healthcare, Inc., 17
Maxicare Health Plans, Inc., III; 25 (upd.)
Mayo Foundation, 9; 34 (upd.)
McBride plc, 82
Médecins sans Frontières, 85
Medical Management International, Inc., 65
Medical Staffing Network Holdings, Inc., 89
Memorial Sloan-Kettering Cancer Center, 57
Merge Healthcare, 85
Merit Medical Systems, Inc., 29
MeritCare Health System, 88
National Health Laboratories Incorporated, 11
National Medical Enterprises, Inc., III
National Research Corporation, 87
New York City Health and Hospitals Corporation, 60
New York Health Care, Inc., 72
NewYork-Presbyterian Hospital, 59
NovaCare, Inc., 11
NSF International, 72
Operation Smile, Inc., 75
Option Care Inc., 48
Orthodontic Centers of America, Inc., 35
Oxford Health Plans, Inc., 16
PacifiCare Health Systems, Inc., 11
Palomar Medical Technologies, Inc., 22
Pediatric Services of America, Inc., 31
Pediatrix Medical Group, Inc., 61
PHP Healthcare Corporation, 22
PhyCor, Inc., 36
PolyMedica Corporation, 77
Primedex Health Systems, Inc., 25
Providence Health System, 90
The Providence Service Corporation, 64
Psychemedics Corporation, 89
Psychiatric Solutions, Inc., 68
Quest Diagnostics Inc., 26
Radiation Therapy Services, Inc., 85
Ramsay Youth Services, Inc., 41
Renal Care Group, Inc., 72
Res-Care, Inc., 29
Response Oncology, Inc., 27
Rural/Metro Corporation, 28
Sabratek Corporation, 29
St. Jude Medical, Inc., 11; 43 (upd.)
Salick Health Care, Inc., 53
The Scripps Research Institute, 76
Select Medical Corporation, 65
Shriners Hospitals for Children, 69
Sierra Health Services, Inc., 15
Smith & Nephew plc, 41 (upd.)
Special Olympics, Inc., 93
The Sports Club Company, 25
SSL International plc, 49
Stericycle Inc., 33
Sun Healthcare Group Inc., 25
Sunrise Senior Living, Inc., 81
Susan G. Komen Breast Cancer Foundation 78
SwedishAmerican Health System, 51
Tenet Healthcare Corporation, 55 (upd.)
Twinlab Corporation, 34
U.S. Healthcare, Inc., 6
U.S. Physical Therapy, Inc., 65
Unison HealthCare Corporation, 25
United HealthCare Corporation, 9
United Nations International Children's Emergency Fund (UNICEF), 58
United Way of America, 36
Universal Health Services, Inc., 6
Vanguard Health Systems Inc., 70
VCA Antech, Inc., 58
Vencor, Inc., 16
VISX, Incorporated, 30
Vivra, Inc., 18
Volunteers of America, Inc., 66
WellPoint Health Networks Inc., 25
World Vision International, Inc., 93
YWCA of the U.S.A., 45

Hotels

Accor S.A., 69 (upd.)
Amerihost Properties, Inc., 30
Ameristar Casinos, Inc., 69 (upd.)
Archon Corporation, 74 (upd.)
Aztar Corporation, 13; 71 (upd.)
Bass PLC, 38 (upd.)
Boca Resorts, Inc., 37
Boyd Gaming Corporation, 43
Boyne USA Resorts, 71
Bristol Hotel Company, 23
The Broadmoor Hotel, 30
Caesars World, Inc., 6
Candlewood Hotel Company, Inc., 41
Carlson Companies, Inc., 6; 22 (upd.); 87 (upd.)
Castle & Cooke, Inc., 20 (upd.)
Cedar Fair, L.P., 22
Cendant Corporation, 44 (upd.)
Choice Hotels International, Inc., 14; 83 (upd.)
Circus Circus Enterprises, Inc., 6
City Developments Limited, 89
Club Mediterranée S.A., 6; 21 (upd.); 91 (upd.)
Compagnia Italiana dei Jolly Hotels S.p.A., 71
Doubletree Corporation, 21
Extended Stay America, Inc., 41
Fairmont Hotels & Resorts Inc., 69
Fibreboard Corporation, 16
Four Seasons Hotels Inc., 9; 29 (upd.)
Fuller Smith & Turner P.L.C., 38
Gables Residential Trust, 49
Gaylord Entertainment Company, 11; 36 (upd.)
Global Hyatt Corporation, 75 (upd.)
Granada Group PLC, 24 (upd.)
Grand Casinos, Inc., 20
Grand Hotel Krasnapolsky N.V., 23
Great Wolf Resorts, Inc., 91
Grupo Posadas, S.A. de C.V., 57
Helmsley Enterprises, Inc., 9
Hilton Hotels Corporation, III; 19 (upd.); 49 (upd.); 62 (upd.)
Holiday Inns, Inc., III
Hospitality Franchise Systems, Inc., 11
Hotel Properties Ltd., 71
Howard Johnson International, Inc., 17; 72 (upd.)
Hyatt Corporation, III; 16 (upd.)
ILX Resorts Incorporated, 65
Interstate Hotels & Resorts Inc., 58
ITT Sheraton Corporation, III
JD Wetherspoon plc, 30
John Q. Hammons Hotels, Inc., 24
Jumeirah Group, 83
Kerzner International Limited, 69 (upd.)
The La Quinta Companies, 11; 42 (upd.)
Ladbroke Group PLC, 21 (upd.)
Landry's Restaurants, Inc., 65 (upd.)

Las Vegas Sands, Inc., 50
Madden's on Gull Lake, 52
Mandalay Resort Group, 32 (upd.)
Manor Care, Inc., 25 (upd.)
The Marcus Corporation, 21
Marriott International, Inc., III; 21 (upd.); 83 (upd.)
McMenamins Pubs and Breweries, 65
Millennium & Copthorne Hotels plc, 71
Mirage Resorts, Incorporated, 6; 28 (upd.)
Monarch Casino & Resort, Inc., 65
Morgans Hotel Group Company, 80
Motel 6, 13; 56 (upd.)
MTR Gaming Group, Inc., 75
MWH Preservation Limited Partnership, 65
NH Hoteles S.A., 79
Omni Hotels Corp., 12
Paradores de Turismo de Espana S.A., 73
Park Corp., 22
Players International, Inc., 22
Preussag AG, 42 (upd.)
Prime Hospitality Corporation, 52
Promus Companies, Inc., 9
Real Turismo, S.A. de C.V., 50
Red Roof Inns, Inc., 18
Resorts International, Inc., 12
The Ritz-Carlton Hotel Company, L.L.C., 9; 29 (upd.); 71 (upd.)
Riviera Holdings Corporation, 75
Sandals Resorts International, 65
Santa Fe Gaming Corporation, 19
The SAS Group, 34 (upd.)
SFI Group plc, 51
Shangri-La Asia Ltd., 71
Showboat, Inc., 19
Sol Meliá S.A., 71
Sonesta International Hotels Corporation, 44
Starwood Hotels & Resorts Worldwide, Inc., 54
Sun International Hotels Limited, 26
Sunburst Hospitality Corporation, 26
Super 8 Motels, Inc., 83
Thistle Hotels PLC, 54
Trusthouse Forte PLC, III
Vail Resorts, Inc., 43 (upd.)
WestCoast Hospitality Corporation, 59
Westin Hotels and Resorts Worldwide, 9; 29 (upd.)
Whitbread PLC, 52 (upd.)
Young & Co.'s Brewery, P.L.C., 38

Information Technology

A.B. Watley Group Inc., 45
AccuWeather, Inc., 73
Acxiom Corporation, 35
Adaptec, Inc., 31
Adobe Systems Incorporated, 10; 33 (upd.)
Advanced Micro Devices, Inc., 6
Agence France-Presse, 34
Agilent Technologies Inc., 38; 93 (upd.)
Akamai Technologies, Inc., 71
Aldus Corporation, 10
Allen Systems Group, Inc., 59
AltaVista Company, 43
Altiris, Inc., 65
Amdahl Corporation, III; 14 (upd.); 40 (upd.)
Amdocs Ltd., 47
America Online, Inc., 10; 26 (upd.)
American Business Information, Inc., 18
American Management Systems, Inc., 11
American Software Inc., 25
AMICAS, Inc., 69
Amstrad PLC, III
Analex Corporation, 74
Analytic Sciences Corporation, 10
Analytical Surveys, Inc., 33
Anker BV, 53
Ansoft Corporation, 63
Anteon Corporation, 57
AOL Time Warner Inc., 57 (upd.)
Apollo Group, Inc., 24
Apple Computer, Inc., III; 6 (upd.); 77 (upd.)
aQuantive, Inc., 81
The Arbitron Company, 38
Ariba, Inc., 57
Asanté Technologies, Inc., 20
Ascential Software Corporation, 59
AsiaInfo Holdings, Inc., 43
ASK Group, Inc., 9
Ask Jeeves, Inc., 65
ASML Holding N.V., 50
The Associated Press, 73 (upd.)
AST Research Inc., 9
At Home Corporation, 43
AT&T Bell Laboratories, Inc., 13
AT&T Corporation, 29 (upd.)
AT&T Istel Ltd., 14
Atos Origin S.A., 69
Attachmate Corporation, 56
Autodesk, Inc., 10; 89 (upd.)
Autologic Information International, Inc., 20
Automatic Data Processing, Inc., III; 9 (upd.); 47 (upd.)
Autotote Corporation, 20
Avantium Technologies BV, 79
Avid Technology Inc., 38
Avocent Corporation, 65
Aydin Corp., 19
Baan Company, 25
Baltimore Technologies Plc, 42
Bankrate, Inc., 83
Banyan Systems Inc., 25
Battelle Memorial Institute, Inc., 10
BBN Corp., 19
BEA Systems, Inc., 36
Bell and Howell Company, 9; 29 (upd.)
Bell Industries, Inc., 47
Billing Concepts, Inc., 26; 72 (upd.)
Blackbaud, Inc., 85
Blackboard Inc., 89
Blizzard Entertainment 78
Bloomberg L.P., 21
Blue Martini Software, Inc., 59
BMC Software, Inc., 55
Boole & Babbage, Inc., 25
Booz Allen & Hamilton Inc., 10
Borland International, Inc., 9
Bowne & Co., Inc., 23
Brite Voice Systems, Inc., 20
Broderbund Software, 13; 29 (upd.)
BTG, Inc., 45
Bull S.A., 43 (upd.)
Business Objects S.A., 25
C-Cube Microsystems, Inc., 37
CACI International Inc., 21; 72 (upd.)
Cadence Design Systems, Inc., 11
Caere Corporation, 20
Cahners Business Information, 43
CalComp Inc., 13
Cambridge Technology Partners, Inc., 36
Candle Corporation, 64
Canon Inc., III
Cap Gemini Ernst & Young, 37
Captaris, Inc., 89
CareerBuilder, Inc., 93
Caribiner International, Inc., 24
Catalina Marketing Corporation, 18
CDC Corporation, 71
CDW Computer Centers, Inc., 16
Cerner Corporation, 16
CheckFree Corporation, 81
Cheyenne Software, Inc., 12
CHIPS and Technologies, Inc., 9
Ciber, Inc., 18
Cincom Systems Inc., 15
Cirrus Logic, Incorporated, 11
Cisco-Linksys LLC, 86
Cisco Systems, Inc., 11; 77 (upd.)
Citizen Watch Co., Ltd., III; 21 (upd.); 81 (upd.)
Citrix Systems, Inc., 44
CMGI, Inc., 76
CNET Networks, Inc., 47
Cogent Communications Group, Inc., 55
Cognizant Technology Solutions Corporation, 59
Cognos Inc., 44
Commodore International Ltd., 7
Compagnie des Machines Bull S.A., III
Compaq Computer Corporation, III; 6 (upd.); 26 (upd.)
Complete Business Solutions, Inc., 31
CompuAdd Computer Corporation, 11
CompuCom Systems, Inc., 10
CompUSA, Inc., 35 (upd.)
CompuServe Interactive Services, Inc., 10; 27 (upd.)
Computer Associates International, Inc., 6; 49 (upd.)
Computer Data Systems, Inc., 14
Computer Sciences Corporation, 6
Computervision Corporation, 10
Compuware Corporation, 10; 30 (upd.); 66 (upd.)
Comshare Inc., 23
Conner Peripherals, Inc., 6
Control Data Corporation, III
Control Data Systems, Inc., 10
Corbis Corporation, 31
Corel Corporation, 15; 33 (upd.); 76 (upd.)
Corporate Software Inc., 9
CoStar Group, Inc., 73
craigslist, inc., 89
Cray Research, Inc., III
Credence Systems Corporation, 90
CSX Corporation, 79 (upd.)
CTG, Inc., 11

Cybermedia, Inc., 25
Dairyland Healthcare Solutions, 73
Dassault Systèmes S.A., 25
Data Broadcasting Corporation, 31
Data General Corporation, 8
Datapoint Corporation, 11
Dell Computer Corp., 9
Dendrite International, Inc., 70
Deutsche Börse AG, 59
Dialogic Corporation, 18
DiamondCluster International, Inc., 51
Digex, Inc., 46
Digital Equipment Corporation, III; 6 (upd.)
Digital River, Inc., 50
Digitas Inc., 81
Dimension Data Holdings PLC, 69
ditech.com, 93
Documentum, Inc., 46
The Dun & Bradstreet Corporation, IV; 19 (upd.)
Dun & Bradstreet Software Services Inc., 11
DynCorp, 45
E.piphany, Inc., 49
EarthLink, Inc., 36
eCollege.com, 85
ECS S.A, 12
EDGAR Online, Inc., 91
Edmark Corporation, 14; 41 (upd.)
Egghead Inc., 9
El Camino Resources International, Inc., 11
Electronic Arts Inc., 10; 85 (upd.)
Electronic Data Systems Corporation, III; 28 (upd.)
Electronics for Imaging, Inc., 43 (upd.)
EMC Corporation, 12; 46 (upd.)
Encore Computer Corporation, 13; 74 (upd.)
Environmental Systems Research Institute Inc. (ESRI), 62
Epic Systems Corporation, 62
EPIQ Systems, Inc., 56
Evans and Sutherland Computer Company 19, 78 (upd.)
Exabyte Corporation, 12
Experian Information Solutions Inc., 45
Facebook, Inc., 90
FactSet Research Systems Inc., 73
FASTWEB S.p.A., 83
F5 Networks, Inc., 72
First Financial Management Corporation, 11
Fiserv Inc., 11
FlightSafety International, Inc., 9
FORE Systems, Inc., 25
Franklin Electronic Publishers, Inc., 23
Franz Inc., 80
FTP Software, Inc., 20
Fujitsu Limited, III; 42 (upd.)
Fujitsu-ICL Systems Inc., 11
Future Now, Inc., 12
Gartner, Inc., 21; 94 (upd.)
Gateway, Inc., 10; 27 (upd.)
GEAC Computer Corporation Ltd., 43
Gericom AG, 47
Getronics NV, 39
GFI Informatique SA, 49
Global Imaging Systems, Inc., 73
Google, Inc., 50
Groupe Open, 74
GSI Commerce, Inc., 67
GT Interactive Software, 31
Guthy-Renker Corporation, 32
Handspring Inc., 49
Hewlett-Packard Company, III; 6 (upd.)
Hyperion Software Corporation, 22
Hyperion Solutions Corporation, 76
ICL plc, 6
Identix Inc., 44
IDX Systems Corporation, 64
IKON Office Solutions, Inc., 50
Imation Corporation, 20
Indus International Inc., 70
Infineon Technologies AG, 50
Information Access Company, 17
Information Builders, Inc., 22
Information Resources, Inc., 10
Informix Corporation, 10; 30 (upd.)
InfoSpace, Inc., 91
Infosys Technologies Ltd., 38
Ing. C. Olivetti & C., S.p.a., III
Inktomi Corporation, 45
Input/Output, Inc., 73
Inso Corporation, 26
Intel Corporation, 36 (upd.)
IntelliCorp, Inc., 45
Intelligent Electronics, Inc., 6
Interfax News Agency, 86
Intergraph Corporation, 6; 24 (upd.)
Intermix Media, Inc., 83
International Business Machines Corporation, III; 6 (upd.); 30 (upd.); 63 (upd.)
InterVideo, Inc., 85
Intrado Inc., 63
Intuit Inc., 14; 33 (upd.); 73 (upd.)
Iomega Corporation, 21
IONA Technologies plc, 43
i2 Technologies, Inc., 87
J.D. Edwards & Company, 14
Jack Henry and Associates, Inc., 17
Janus Capital Group Inc., 57
The Judge Group, Inc., 51
Juniper Networks, Inc., 43
Juno Online Services, Inc., 38
Jupitermedia Corporation, 75
Kana Software, Inc., 51
Keane, Inc., 56
Kenexa Corporation, 87
Kintera, Inc., 75
KLA Instruments Corporation, 11
Knight Ridder, Inc., 67 (upd.)
KnowledgeWare Inc., 31 (upd.)
Komag, Inc., 11
Kronos, Inc., 18
Kurzweil Technologies, Inc., 51
LaCie Group S.A., 76
Lam Research Corporation, 11
Landauer, Inc., 51
Lason, Inc., 31
Lawson Software, 38
The Learning Company Inc., 24
Learning Tree International Inc., 24
Legent Corporation, 10
LendingTree, LLC, 93
LEXIS-NEXIS Group, 33
LifeLock, Inc., 91
Logica plc, 14; 37 (upd.)
Logicon Inc., 20
Logitech International S.A., 28; 69 (upd.)
LoJack Corporation, 48
Lotus Development Corporation, 6; 25 (upd.)
The MacNeal-Schwendler Corporation, 25
Macromedia, Inc., 50
Madge Networks N.V., 26
Magma Design Automation Inc. 78
MAI Systems Corporation, 11
Manatron, Inc., 86
MAPICS, Inc., 55
Match.com, LP, 87
The MathWorks, Inc., 80
Maxtor Corporation, 10
Mead Data Central, Inc., 10
Mecklermedia Corporation, 24
Medical Information Technology Inc., 64
Mentor Graphics Corporation, 11
Mercury Interactive Corporation, 59
Merge Healthcare, 85
Merisel, Inc., 12
Metatec International, Inc., 47
Metro Information Services, Inc., 36
Micro Warehouse, Inc., 16
Micron Technology, Inc., 11; 29 (upd.)
Micros Systems, Inc., 18
Microsoft Corporation, 6; 27 (upd.); 63 (upd.)
MicroStrategy Incorporated, 87
Misys plc, 45; 46
MITRE Corporation, 26
MIVA, Inc., 83
Moldflow Corporation, 73
Morningstar Inc., 68
The Motley Fool, Inc., 40
National Research Corporation, 87
National Semiconductor Corporation, 6
National TechTeam, Inc., 41
National Weather Service, 91
Navarre Corporation, 24
NAVTEQ Corporation, 69
NCR Corporation, III; 6 (upd.); 30 (upd.); 90 (upd.)
Netezza Corporation, 69
NetIQ Corporation, 79
Netscape Communications Corporation, 15; 35 (upd.)
Network Appliance, Inc., 58
Network Associates, Inc., 25
Nextel Communications, Inc., 10
NFO Worldwide, Inc., 24
NICE Systems Ltd., 83
Nichols Research Corporation, 18
Nimbus CD International, Inc., 20
Nixdorf Computer AG, III
Novell, Inc., 6; 23 (upd.)
NVIDIA Corporation, 54
Océ N.V., 24; 91 (upd.)
Odetics Inc., 14
Onyx Software Corporation, 53
Open Text Corporation, 79
Opsware Inc., 49

Oracle Corporation, 6; 24 (upd.); 67 (upd.)
Orbitz, Inc., 61
Packard Bell Electronics, Inc., 13
Packeteer, Inc., 81
Parametric Technology Corp., 16
PC Connection, Inc., 37
Pegasus Solutions, Inc., 75
PeopleSoft Inc., 14; 33 (upd.)
Perot Systems Corporation, 29
Phillips International Inc. 78
Pitney Bowes Inc., III
PLATINUM Technology, Inc., 14
Policy Management Systems Corporation, 11
Policy Studies, Inc., 62
Portal Software, Inc., 47
Primark Corp., 13
The Princeton Review, Inc., 42
Printrak, A Motorola Company, 44
Printronix, Inc., 18
Prodigy Communications Corporation, 34
Programmer's Paradise, Inc., 81
Progress Software Corporation, 15
Psion PLC, 45
Quality Systems, Inc., 81
Quantum Corporation, 10; 62 (upd.)
Quark, Inc., 36
Quicken Loans, Inc., 93
Racal-Datacom Inc., 11
Razorfish, Inc., 37
RCM Technologies, Inc., 34
RealNetworks, Inc., 53
Red Hat, Inc., 45
Remedy Corporation, 58
Renaissance Learning Systems, Inc., 39
Reuters Group PLC, 22 (upd.); 63 (upd.)
The Reynolds and Reynolds Company, 50
Ricoh Company, Ltd., III
Rocky Mountain Chocolate Factory, Inc., 73
Rolta India Ltd., 90
RSA Security Inc., 46
RWD Technologies, Inc., 76
SABRE Group Holdings, Inc., 26
The Sage Group, 43
salesforce.com, Inc., 79
The Santa Cruz Operation, Inc., 38
SAP AG, 16; 43 (upd.)
SAS Institute Inc., 10; 78 (upd.)
Satyam Computer Services Ltd., 85
SBS Technologies, Inc., 25
SCB Computer Technology, Inc., 29
Schawk, Inc., 24
The SCO Group Inc., 78
SDL PLC, 67
Seagate Technology, Inc., 8
Siebel Systems, Inc., 38
Sierra On-Line, Inc., 15; 41 (upd.)
SilverPlatter Information Inc., 23
SINA Corporation, 69
SkillSoft Public Limited Company, 81
SmartForce PLC, 43
Softbank Corp., 13; 38 (upd.); 77 (upd.)
Sonic Solutions, Inc., 81
SonicWALL, Inc., 87
Spark Networks, Inc., 91
Specialist Computer Holdings Ltd., 80
SPSS Inc., 64
SRA International, Inc., 77
Standard Microsystems Corporation, 11
STC PLC, III
Steria SA, 49
Sterling Software, Inc., 11
Storage Technology Corporation, 6
Stratus Computer, Inc., 10
Sun Microsystems, Inc., 7; 30 (upd.); 91 (upd.)
SunGard Data Systems Inc., 11
Sybase, Inc., 10; 27 (upd.)
Sykes Enterprises, Inc., 45
Symantec Corporation, 10; 82 (upd.)
Symbol Technologies, Inc., 15
SYNNEX Corporation, 73
Synopsys, Inc., 11; 69 (upd.)
Syntel, Inc., 92
System Software Associates, Inc., 10
Systems & Computer Technology Corp., 19
T-Online International AG, 61
TALX Corporation, 92
Tandem Computers, Inc., 6
TenFold Corporation, 35
Terra Lycos, Inc., 43
The Thomson Corporation, 34 (upd.); 77 (upd.)
ThoughtWorks Inc., 90
3Com Corporation, 11; 34 (upd.)
The 3DO Company, 43
TIBCO Software Inc., 79
Timberline Software Corporation, 15
TomTom N.V., 81
TradeStation Group, Inc., 83
Traffix, Inc., 61
Transaction Systems Architects, Inc., 29; 82 (upd.)
Transiciel SA, 48
Triple P N.V., 26
The TriZetto Group, Inc., 83
Tucows Inc. 78
Ubi Soft Entertainment S.A., 41
Unica Corporation, 77
Unilog SA, 42
Unisys Corporation, III; 6 (upd.); 36 (upd.)
United Business Media plc, 52 (upd.)
United Online, Inc., 71 (upd.)
United Press International, Inc., 73 (upd.)
UUNET, 38
VASCO Data Security International, Inc., 79
Verbatim Corporation, 14
Veridian Corporation, 54
VeriFone Holdings, Inc., 18; 76 (upd.)
Verint Systems Inc., 73
VeriSign, Inc., 47
Veritas Software Corporation, 45
Verity Inc., 68
Viasoft Inc., 27
Vital Images, Inc., 85
VMware, Inc., 90
Volt Information Sciences Inc., 26
Wanadoo S.A., 75
Wang Laboratories, Inc., III; 6 (upd.)
WebMD Corporation, 65
WebEx Communications, Inc., 81
West Group, 34 (upd.)
Westcon Group, Inc., 67
Western Digital Corporation, 25; 92 (upd.)
Wikimedia Foundation, Inc., 91
Wind River Systems, Inc., 37
Wipro Limited, 43
Witness Systems, Inc., 87
Wolters Kluwer NV, 33 (upd.)
WordPerfect Corporation, 10
Wyse Technology, Inc., 15
Xerox Corporation, III; 6 (upd.); 26 (upd.)
Xilinx, Inc., 16; 82 (upd.)
Yahoo! Inc., 27; 70 (upd.)
YouTube, Inc., 90
Zanett, Inc., 92
Zapata Corporation, 25
Ziff Davis Media Inc., 36 (upd.)
Zilog, Inc., 15

Insurance

AEGON N.V., III; 50 (upd.)
Aetna Inc., III; 21 (upd.); 63 (upd.)
AFLAC Incorporated, 10 (upd.); 38 (upd.)
Alexander & Alexander Services Inc., 10
Alfa Corporation, 60
Alleanza Assicurazioni S.p.A., 65
Alleghany Corporation, 10
Allianz AG, III; 15 (upd.); 57 (upd.)
Allmerica Financial Corporation, 63
The Allstate Corporation, 10; 27 (upd.)
AMB Generali Holding AG, 51
American Family Corporation, III
American Financial Group Inc., III; 48 (upd.)
American General Corporation, III; 10 (upd.); 46 (upd.)
American International Group, Inc., III; 15 (upd.); 47 (upd.)
American National Insurance Company, 8; 27 (upd.)
American Premier Underwriters, Inc., 10
American Re Corporation, 10; 35 (upd.)
N.V. AMEV, III
AOK-Bundesverband (Federation of the AOK) 78
Aon Corporation, III; 45 (upd.)
Arthur J. Gallagher & Co., 73
Assicurazioni Generali SpA, III; 15 (upd.)
Assurances Générales de France, 63
Assured Guaranty Ltd., 93
Atlantic American Corporation, 44
Aviva PLC, 50 (upd.)
Axa, III
AXA Colonia Konzern AG, 27; 49 (upd.)
B.A.T. Industries PLC, 22 (upd.)
Baldwin & Lyons, Inc., 51
Bâloise-Holding, 40
Benfield Greig Group plc, 53
Berkshire Hathaway Inc., III; 18 (upd.); 42 (upd.); 89 (upd.)
Blue Cross and Blue Shield Association, 10
British United Provident Association Limited (BUPAL), 79
Brown & Brown, Inc., 41

Business Men's Assurance Company of America, 14
Capital Holding Corporation, III
Catholic Order of Foresters, 24
China Life Insurance Company Limited, 65
ChoicePoint Inc., 65
The Chubb Corporation, III; 14 (upd.); 37 (upd.)
CIGNA Corporation, III; 22 (upd.); 45 (upd.)
Cincinnati Financial Corporation, 16; 44 (upd.)
CNA Financial Corporation, III; 38 (upd.)
Commercial Union PLC, III
Connecticut Mutual Life Insurance Company, III
Conseco Inc., 10; 33 (upd.)
The Continental Corporation, III
Crawford & Company, 87
Debeka Krankenversicherungsverein auf Gegenseitigkeit, 72
The Doctors' Company, 55
Empire Blue Cross and Blue Shield, III
Enbridge Inc., 43
Endurance Specialty Holdings Ltd., 85
Engle Homes, Inc., 46
The Equitable Life Assurance Society of the United States Fireman's Fund Insurance Company, III
ERGO Versicherungsgruppe AG, 44
Erie Indemnity Company, 35
Fairfax Financial Holdings Limited, 57
Farm Family Holdings, Inc., 39
Farmers Insurance Group of Companies, 25
Federal Deposit Insurance Corporation, 93
Fidelity National Financial Inc., 54
The First American Corporation, 52
First Executive Corporation, III
Foundation Health Corporation, 12
Gainsco, Inc., 22
GEICO Corporation, 10; 40 (upd.)
General Accident PLC, III
General Re Corporation, III; 24 (upd.)
Gerling-Konzern Versicherungs-Beteiligungs-Aktiengesellschaft, 51
GraceKennedy Ltd., 92
Great-West Lifeco Inc., III
Groupama S.A., 76
Gryphon Holdings, Inc., 21
Guardian Financial Services, 64 (upd.)
Guardian Royal Exchange Plc, 11
Harleysville Group Inc., 37
HDI (Haftpflichtverband der Deutschen Industrie Versicherung auf Gegenseitigkeit V.a.G.), 53
HealthExtras, Inc., 75
HealthMarkets, Inc., 88 (upd.)
Hilb, Rogal & Hobbs Company, 77
The Home Insurance Company, III
Horace Mann Educators Corporation, 22; 90 (upd.)
Household International, Inc., 21 (upd.)
Hub International Limited, 89
HUK-Coburg, 58
Irish Life & Permanent Plc, 59
Jackson National Life Insurance Company, 8
Jefferson-Pilot Corporation, 11; 29 (upd.)
John Hancock Financial Services, Inc., III; 42 (upd.)
Johnson & Higgins, 14
Kaiser Foundation Health Plan, Inc., 53
Kemper Corporation, III; 15 (upd.)
LandAmerica Financial Group, Inc., 85
Legal & General Group plc, III; 24 (upd.)
The Liberty Corporation, 22
Liberty Mutual Holding Company, 59
LifeWise Health Plan of Oregon, Inc., 90
Lincoln National Corporation, III; 25 (upd.)
Lloyd's, 74 (upd.)
Lloyd's of London, III; 22 (upd.)
The Loewen Group Inc., 40 (upd.)
Lutheran Brotherhood, 31
Manulife Financial Corporation, 85
Marsh & McLennan Companies, Inc., III; 45 (upd.)
Massachusetts Mutual Life Insurance Company, III; 53 (upd.)
MBIA Inc., 73
The Meiji Mutual Life Insurance Company, III
Mercury General Corporation, 25
Metropolitan Life Insurance Company, III; 52 (upd.)
MGIC Investment Corp., 52
The Midland Company, 65
Millea Holdings Inc., 64 (upd.)
Mitsui Marine and Fire Insurance Company, Limited, III
Mitsui Mutual Life Insurance Company, III; 39 (upd.)
Modern Woodmen of America, 66
Munich Re (Münchener Rückversicherungs-Gesellschaft Aktiengesellschaft in München), III; 46 (upd.)
The Mutual Benefit Life Insurance Company, III
The Mutual Life Insurance Company of New York, III
National Medical Health Card Systems, Inc., 79
Nationale-Nederlanden N.V., III
The Navigators Group, Inc., 92
New England Mutual Life Insurance Company, III
New York Life Insurance Company, III; 45 (upd.)
Nippon Life Insurance Company, III; 60 (upd.)
Northwestern Mutual Life Insurance Company, III; 45 (upd.)
NYMAGIC, Inc., 41
Ohio Casualty Corp., 11
Old Republic International Corporation, 11; 58 (upd.)
Oregon Dental Service Health Plan, Inc., 51
Palmer & Cay, Inc., 69
Pan-American Life Insurance Company, 48
PartnerRe Ltd., 83
The Paul Revere Corporation, 12
Pennsylvania Blue Shield, III
The PMI Group, Inc., 49
Preserver Group, Inc., 44
Principal Mutual Life Insurance Company, III
The Progressive Corporation, 11; 29 (upd.)
Provident Life and Accident Insurance Company of America, III
Prudential Financial Inc., III; 30 (upd.); 82 (upd.)
Prudential plc, III; 48 (upd.)
Radian Group Inc., 42
The Regence Group, 74
Reliance Group Holdings, Inc., III
Riunione Adriatica di Sicurtà SpA, III
Royal & Sun Alliance Insurance Group plc, 55 (upd.)
Royal Insurance Holdings PLC, III
SAFECO Corporaton, III
The St. Paul Travelers Companies, Inc. III; 22 (upd.); 79 (upd.)
SCOR S.A., 20
Skandia Insurance Company, Ltd., 50
StanCorp Financial Group, Inc., 56
The Standard Life Assurance Company, III
State Auto Financial Corporation, 77
State Farm Mutual Automobile Insurance Company, III; 51 (upd.)
State Financial Services Corporation, 51
Stewart Information Services Corporation 78
Sumitomo Life Insurance Company, III; 60 (upd.)
The Sumitomo Marine and Fire Insurance Company, Limited, III
Sun Alliance Group PLC, III
Sun Life Financial Inc., 85
SunAmerica Inc., 11
Suncorp-Metway Ltd., 91
Suramericana de Inversiones S.A., 88
Svenska Handelsbanken AB, 50 (upd.)
The Swett & Crawford Group Inc., 84
Swiss Reinsurance Company (Schweizerische Rückversicherungs-Gesellschaft), III; 46 (upd.)
Teachers Insurance and Annuity Association-College Retirement Equities Fund, III; 45 (upd.)
Texas Industries, Inc., 8
TIG Holdings, Inc., 26
The Tokio Marine and Fire Insurance Co., Ltd., III
Torchmark Corporation, 9; 33 (upd.)
Transatlantic Holdings, Inc., 11
The Travelers Corporation, III
UICI, 33
Union des Assurances de Pans, III
United National Group, Ltd., 63
Unitrin Inc., 16; 78 (upd.)
UNUM Corp., 13
UnumProvident Corporation, 52 (upd.)
USAA, 10
USF&G Corporation, III

Victoria Group, 44 (upd.)
VICTORIA Holding AG, III
Vision Service Plan Inc., 77
W.R. Berkley Corporation, 15; 74 (upd.)
Washington National Corporation, 12
The Wawanesa Mutual Insurance Company, 68
WellChoice, Inc., 67 (upd.)
Westfield Group, 69
White Mountains Insurance Group, Ltd., 48
Willis Corroon Group plc, 25
Winterthur Group, III; 68 (upd.)
The Yasuda Fire and Marine Insurance Company, Limited, III
The Yasuda Mutual Life Insurance Company, III; 39 (upd.)
Zurich Financial Services, 42 (upd.); 93 (upd.)
Zürich Versicherungs-Gesellschaft, III

Legal Services

Akin, Gump, Strauss, Hauer & Feld, L.L.P., 33
American Bar Association, 35
American Lawyer Media Holdings, Inc., 32
Amnesty International, 50
Andrews Kurth, LLP, 71
Arnold & Porter, 35
Baker & Daniels LLP, 88
Baker & Hostetler LLP, 40
Baker & McKenzie, 10; 42 (upd.)
Baker and Botts, L.L.P., 28
Bingham Dana LLP, 43
Brobeck, Phleger & Harrison, LLP, 31
Cadwalader, Wickersham & Taft, 32
Chadbourne & Parke, 36
Cleary, Gottlieb, Steen & Hamilton, 35
Clifford Chance LLP, 38
Coudert Brothers, 30
Covington & Burling, 40
CRA International, Inc., 93
Cravath, Swaine & Moore, 43
Davis Polk & Wardwell, 36
Debevoise & Plimpton, 39
Dechert, 43
Dewey Ballantine LLP, 48
Dorsey & Whitney LLP, 47
Drinker, Biddle and Reath L.L.P., 92
Fenwick & West LLP, 34
Fish & Neave, 54
Foley & Lardner, 28
Fried, Frank, Harris, Shriver & Jacobson, 35
Fulbright & Jaworski L.L.P., 47
Gibson, Dunn & Crutcher LLP, 36
Greenberg Traurig, LLP, 65
Heller, Ehrman, White & McAuliffe, 41
Hildebrandt International, 29
Hogan & Hartson L.L.P., 44
Holland & Knight LLP, 60
Holme Roberts & Owen LLP, 28
Hughes Hubbard & Reed LLP, 44
Hunton & Williams, 35
Jenkens & Gilchrist, P.C., 65
Jones, Day, Reavis & Pogue, 33
Kelley Drye & Warren LLP, 40
King & Spalding, 23
Kirkland & Ellis LLP, 65
Latham & Watkins, 33
LeBoeuf, Lamb, Greene & MacRae, L.L.P., 29
LECG Corporation, 93
The Legal Aid Society, 48
Mayer, Brown, Rowe & Maw, 47
Milbank, Tweed, Hadley & McCloy, 27
Morgan, Lewis & Bockius LLP, 29
Morrison & Foerster LLP 78
O'Melveny & Myers, 37
Oppenheimer Wolff & Donnelly LLP, 71
Orrick, Herrington and Sutcliffe LLP, 76
Patton Boggs LLP, 71
Paul, Hastings, Janofsky & Walker LLP, 27
Paul, Weiss, Rifkind, Wharton & Garrison, 47
Pepper Hamilton LLP, 43
Perkins Coie LLP, 56
Pillsbury Madison & Sutro LLP, 29
Pre-Paid Legal Services, Inc., 20
Proskauer Rose LLP, 47
Robins, Kaplan, Miller & Ciresi L.L.P., 89
Ropes & Gray, 40
Saul Ewing LLP, 74
Seyfarth Shaw LLP, 93
Shearman & Sterling, 32
Sidley Austin Brown & Wood, 40
Simpson Thacher & Bartlett, 39
Skadden, Arps, Slate, Meagher & Flom, 18
Snell & Wilmer L.L.P., 28
Southern Poverty Law Center, Inc., 74
Stroock & Stroock & Lavan LLP, 40
Sullivan & Cromwell, 26
Troutman Sanders L.L.P., 79
Vinson & Elkins L.L.P., 30
Wachtell, Lipton, Rosen & Katz, 47
Weil, Gotshal & Manges LLP, 55
White & Case LLP, 35
Williams & Connolly LLP, 47
Wilson Sonsini Goodrich & Rosati, 34
Winston & Strawn, 35
Womble Carlyle Sandridge & Rice, PLLC, 52

Manufacturing

A-dec, Inc., 53
A. Schulman, Inc., 49 (upd.)
A.B.Dick Company, 28
A.O. Smith Corporation, 11; 40 (upd.); 93 (upd.)
A.T. Cross Company, 17; 49 (upd.)
A.W. Faber-Castell Unternehmensverwaltung GmbH & Co., 51
AAF-McQuay Incorporated, 26
Aalborg Industries A/S, 90
AAON, Inc., 22
AAR Corp., 28
Aarhus United A/S, 68
ABB Ltd., 65 (upd.)
ABC Rail Products Corporation, 18
Abiomed, Inc., 47
ACCO World Corporation, 7; 51 (upd.)
Accubuilt, Inc., 74
Acindar Industria Argentina de Aceros S.A., 87
Acme United Corporation, 70
Acme-Cleveland Corp., 13
Acorn Products, Inc., 55
Acuity Brands, Inc., 90
Acushnet Company, 64
Acuson Corporation, 36 (upd.)
Adams Golf, Inc., 37
Adolf Würth GmbH & Co. KG, 49
Advanced Circuits Inc., 67
Advanced Neuromodulation Systems, Inc., 73
AEP Industries, Inc., 36
Aftermarket Technology Corp., 83
Ag-Chem Equipment Company, Inc., 17
Aga Foodservice Group PLC, 73
AGCO Corporation, 13; 67 (upd.)
Agfa Gevaert Group N.V., 59
Agrium Inc., 73
Ahlstrom Corporation, 53
Airgas, Inc., 54
Aisin Seiki Co., Ltd., III
AK Steel Holding Corporation, 41 (upd.)
AKG Acoustics GmbH, 62
Aktiebolaget Electrolux, 22 (upd.)
Aktiebolaget SKF, III; 38 (upd.); 89 (upd.)
Alamo Group Inc., 32
ALARIS Medical Systems, Inc., 65
Alberto-Culver Company, 8; 36 (upd.); 91 (upd.)
Aldila Inc., 46
Alfa Laval AB, III; 64 (upd.)
Allen Organ Company, 33
Allen-Edmonds Shoe Corporation, 61
Alliant Techsystems Inc., 8; 30 (upd.); 77 (upd.)
The Allied Defense Group, Inc., 65
Allied Healthcare Products, Inc., 24
Allied Products Corporation, 21
Allied Signal Engines, 9
AlliedSignal Inc., 22 (upd.)
Allison Gas Turbine Division, 9
Alltrista Corporation, 30
Alps Electric Co., Ltd., 44 (upd.)
Alticor Inc., 71 (upd.)
Aluar Aluminio Argentino S.A.I.C., 74
Alvis Plc, 47
Amer Group plc, 41
American Axle & Manufacturing Holdings, Inc., 67
American Biltrite Inc., 43 (upd.)
American Business Products, Inc., 20
American Cast Iron Pipe Company, 50
American Greetings Corporation, 59 (upd.)
American Homestar Corporation, 18; 41 (upd.)
American Locker Group Incorporated, 34
American Power Conversion Corporation, 67 (upd.)
American Seating Company 78
American Standard Companies Inc., 30 (upd.)
American Technical Ceramics Corp., 67
American Tourister, Inc., 16
American Woodmark Corporation, 31

Ameriwood Industries International Corp., 17
Amerock Corporation, 53
Ameron International Corporation, 67
AMETEK, Inc., 9
AMF Bowling, Inc., 40
Ampacet Corporation, 67
Ampco-Pittsburgh Corporation, 79
Ampex Corporation, 17
Amway Corporation, 30 (upd.)
Analogic Corporation, 23
Anchor Hocking Glassware, 13
Andersen Corporation, 10
The Andersons, Inc., 31
Andis Company, Inc., 85
Andreas Stihl AG & Co. KG, 16; 59 (upd.)
Andritz AG, 51
Ansell Ltd., 60 (upd.)
Anthem Electronics, Inc., 13
Apasco S.A. de C.V., 51
Apex Digital, Inc., 63
Applica Incorporated, 43 (upd.)
Applied Films Corporation, 48
Applied Materials, Inc., 10; 46 (upd.)
Applied Micro Circuits Corporation, 38
Applied Power Inc., 9; 32 (upd.)
AptarGroup, Inc., 69
ARBED S.A., 22 (upd.)
Arc International, 76
Arctco, Inc., 16
Arctic Cat Inc., 40 (upd.)
AREVA NP, 90 (upd.)
Ariens Company, 48
The Aristotle Corporation, 62
Armor All Products Corp., 16
Armstrong Holdings, Inc., III; 22 (upd.); 81 (upd.)
Arotech Corporation, 93
Artesyn Technologies Inc., 46 (upd.)
ArthroCare Corporation, 73
ArvinMeritor, Inc., 54 (upd.)
Asahi Glass Company, Ltd., 48 (upd.)
Ashley Furniture Industries, Inc., 35
ASICS Corporation, 57
ASML Holding N.V., 50
Astec Industries, Inc., 79
Astronics Corporation, 35
ASV, Inc., 34; 66 (upd.)
Atlantis Plastics, Inc., 85
Atlas Copco AB, III; 28 (upd.); 85 (upd.)
ATMI, Inc., 93
Atwood Mobil Products, 53
AU Optronics Corporation, 67
Aurora Casket Company, Inc., 56
Austal Limited, 75
Austin Powder Company, 76
Avedis Zildjian Co., 38
Avery Dennison Corporation, 17 (upd.); 49 (upd.)
Avocent Corporation, 65
Avondale Industries, 7; 41 (upd.)
AVX Corporation, 67
AZZ Incorporated, 93
B.J. Alan Co., Inc., 67
The Babcock & Wilcox Company, 82
Badger Meter, Inc., 22
BAE Systems Ship Repair, 73
Baker Hughes Incorporated, III
Baldor Electric Company, 21
Baldwin Piano & Organ Company, 18
Baldwin Technology Company, Inc., 25
Balfour Beatty plc, 36 (upd.)
Ballantyne of Omaha, Inc., 27
Ballard Medical Products, 21
Ballard Power Systems Inc., 73
Bally Manufacturing Corporation, III
Baltek Corporation, 34
Baltimore Aircoil Company, Inc., 66
Bandai Co., Ltd., 55
Barmag AG, 39
Barnes Group Inc., 13; 69 (upd.)
Barry Callebaut AG, 29
Barry-Wehmiller Companies, Inc., 90
Bassett Furniture Industries, Inc., 18
Bath Iron Works, 12; 36 (upd.)
Beckman Coulter, Inc., 22
Beckman Instruments, Inc., 14
Becton, Dickinson & Company, 36 (upd.)
Behr GmbH & Co. KG, 72
BEI Technologies, Inc., 65
Beiersdorf AG, 29
Bekaert S.A./N.V., 90
Bel Fuse, Inc., 53
Belden CDT Inc., 76 (upd.)
Belden Inc., 19
Bell Sports Corporation, 16; 44 (upd.)
Belleek Pottery Ltd., 71
Belleville Shoe Manufacturing Company, 92
Beloit Corporation, 14
Bemis Company, Inc., 8; 91 (upd.)
Bénéteau SA, 55
Benjamin Moore & Co., 13; 38 (upd.)
BenQ Corporation, 67
Berger Bros Company, 62
Bernina Holding AG, 47
Berry Plastics Corporation, 21
Berwick Offray, LLC, 70
Bianchi International (d/b/a Gregory Mountain Products), 76
BIC Corporation, 8; 23 (upd.)
BICC PLC, III
Billabong International Ltd., 44
The Bing Group, 60
Binks Sames Corporation, 21
Binney & Smith Inc., 25
bioMérieux S.A., 75
Biomet, Inc., 10; 93 (upd.)
Biosite Incorporated, 73
BISSELL Inc., 9; 30 (upd.)
The Black & Decker Corporation, III; 20 (upd.); 67 (upd.)
Black Diamond Equipment, Ltd., 62
Blodgett Holdings, Inc., 61 (upd.)
Blount International, Inc., 12; 48 (upd.)
Blue Nile Inc., 61
Blundstone Pty Ltd., 76
Blyth Industries, Inc., 18
Blyth, Inc., 74 (upd.)
BMC Industries, Inc., 17; 59 (upd.)
Bodum Design Group AG, 47
BÖHLER-UDDEHOLM AG, 73
Bombardier Inc., 42 (upd.); 87 (upd.)
Boral Limited, 43 (upd.)
Borden, Inc., 22 (upd.)
Borg-Warner Corporation, III
BorgWarner Inc., 14; 32 (upd.); 85 (upd.)
Boston Scientific Corporation, 37; 77 (upd.)
Bou-Matic, 62
The Boyds Collection, Ltd., 29
BPB plc, 83
Brach's Confections, Inc., 74 (upd.)
Brady Corporation 78 (upd.)
Brammer PLC, 77
Brannock Device Company, 48
Brass Eagle Inc., 34
Bridgeport Machines, Inc., 17
Briggs & Stratton Corporation, 8; 27 (upd.)
BRIO AB, 24
British Vita plc, 33 (upd.)
Brose Fahrzeugteile GmbH & Company KG, 84
Brother Industries, Ltd., 14
Brown & Sharpe Manufacturing Co., 23
Brown Jordan International Inc., 74 (upd.)
Brown-Forman Corporation, 38 (upd.)
Broyhill Furniture Industries, Inc., 10
Brunswick Corporation, III; 22 (upd.); 77 (upd.)
BSH Bosch und Siemens Hausgeräte GmbH, 67
BTR Siebe plc, 27
Buck Knives Inc., 48
Buckeye Technologies, Inc., 42
Bucyrus International, Inc., 17
Bugle Boy Industries, Inc., 18
Building Materials Holding Corporation, 52
Bulgari S.p.A., 20
Bulova Corporation, 13; 41 (upd.)
Bundy Corporation, 17
Burelle S.A., 23
Burton Snowboards Inc., 22
Bush Boake Allen Inc., 30
Bush Industries, Inc., 20
Butler Manufacturing Company, 12; 62 (upd.)
C&J Clark International Ltd., 52
C.F. Martin & Co., Inc., 42
C.R. Bard, Inc., 65 (upd.)
C-Tech Industries Inc., 90
California Cedar Products Company, 58
California Steel Industries, Inc., 67
Callaway Golf Company, 15; 45 (upd.)
Campbell Scientific, Inc., 51
Cannondale Corporation, 21
Canon Inc., 79 (upd.)
Capstone Turbine Corporation, 75
Caradon plc, 20 (upd.)
The Carbide/Graphite Group, Inc., 40
Carbo PLC, 67 (upd.)
Carbone Lorraine S.A., 33
Cardo AB, 53
Cardone Industries Inc., 92
Carhartt, Inc., 77 (upd.)
Carl Zeiss AG, III; 34 (upd.); 91 (upd.)
Carma Laboratories, Inc., 60
Carrier Corporation, 7; 69 (upd.)
Carter Holt Harvey Ltd., 70
Carver Boat Corporation LLC, 88

Carvin Corp., 89
Cascade Corporation, 65
Cascade General, Inc., 65
CASIO Computer Co., Ltd., III; 40 (upd.)
Catalina Lighting, Inc., 43 (upd.)
Caterpillar Inc., III; 15 (upd.); 63 (upd.)
Cavco Industries, Inc., 65
Cementos Argos S.A., 91
CEMEX S.A. de C.V., 59 (upd.)
Central Garden & Pet Company, 58 (upd.)
Central Sprinkler Corporation, 29
Centuri Corporation, 54
Century Aluminum Company, 52
Cenveo Inc., 71 (upd.)
Cepheid, 77
Ceradyne, Inc., 65
Cessna Aircraft Company, 27 (upd.)
Champion Enterprises, Inc., 17
Chanel SA, 12; 49 (upd.)
Charisma Brands LLC, 74
The Charles Machine Works, Inc., 64
Chart Industries, Inc., 21
Chicago Bridge & Iron Company N.V., 82 (upd.)
Chittenden & Eastman Company, 58
Chris-Craft Corporation, 9, 31 (upd.); 80 (upd.)
Christian Dalloz SA, 40
Christofle SA, 40
Chromcraft Revington, Inc., 15
Cinemeccanica SpA 78
Ciments Français, 40
Cincinnati Lamb Inc., 72
Cincinnati Milacron Inc., 12
Cinram International, Inc., 43
Circon Corporation, 21
Cirrus Design Corporation, 44
Citizen Watch Co., Ltd., III; 21 (upd.); 81 (upd.)
CLARCOR Inc., 17; 61 (upd.)
Clark Equipment Company, 8
Clayton Homes Incorporated, 13; 54 (upd.)
The Clorox Company, III; 22 (upd.); 81 (upd.)
CNH Global N.V., 38 (upd.)
Coach, Inc., 45 (upd.)
Coachmen Industries, Inc., 77
COBE Cardiovascular, Inc., 61
Cobra Golf Inc., 16
Cochlear Ltd., 77
Cockerill Sambre Group, 26 (upd.)
Cognex Corporation, 76
Cohu, Inc., 32
Colas S.A., 31
The Coleman Company, Inc., 30 (upd.)
Colfax Corporation, 58
Collins & Aikman Corporation, 41 (upd.)
Collins Industries, Inc., 33
Color Kinetics Incorporated, 85
Colorado MEDtech, Inc., 48
Colt's Manufacturing Company, Inc., 12
Columbia Sportswear Company, 19
Columbus McKinnon Corporation, 37
CommScope, Inc., 77
Compagnie de Saint-Gobain, 64 (upd.)
Compass Minerals International, Inc., 79
CompuDyne Corporation, 51
Conair Corporation, 69 (upd.)
Concord Camera Corporation, 41
Congoleum Corp., 18
Conn-Selmer, Inc., 55
Conrad Industries, Inc., 58
Conso International Corporation, 29
Consorcio G Grupo Dina, S.A. de C.V., 36
Constar International Inc., 64
Controladora Mabe, S.A. de C.V., 82
Converse Inc., 9
Cooper Cameron Corporation, 58 (upd.)
The Cooper Companies, Inc., 39
Cooper Industries, Inc., 44 (upd.)
Cordis Corporation, 46 (upd.)
Corning, Inc., III; 44 (upd.); 90 (upd.)
Corrpro Companies, Inc., 20
Corticeira Amorim, Sociedade Gestora de Participaço es Sociais, S.A., 48
CPAC, Inc., 86
Crane Co., 8; 30 (upd.)
Cranium, Inc., 69
Creative Technology Ltd., 57
Creo Inc., 48
CRH plc, 64
Crosman Corporation, 62
Crown Equipment Corporation, 15; 93 (upd.)
CTB International Corporation, 43 (upd.)
Cuisinart Corporation, 24
Culligan Water Technologies, Inc., 12; 38 (upd.)
Cummins Engine Company, Inc., 40 (upd.)
CUNO Incorporated, 57
Curtiss-Wright Corporation, 10; 35 (upd.)
Custom Chrome, Inc., 74 (upd.)
Cutera, Inc., 84
Cutter & Buck Inc., 27
Cyberonics, Inc., 79
Cybex International, Inc., 49
Cymer, Inc., 77
Dade Behring Holdings Inc., 71
Daewoo Group, III
Daikin Industries, Ltd., III
Daisy Outdoor Products Inc., 58
Dalian Shide Group, 91
Danaher Corporation, 7; 77 (upd.)
Daniel Industries, Inc., 16
Daniel Measurement and Control, Inc., 74 (upd.)
Danisco A/S, 44
Day Runner, Inc., 41 (upd.)
DC Shoes, Inc., 60
DCN S.A., 75
De'Longhi S.p.A., 66
Dearborn Mid-West Conveyor Company, 56
Deceuninck N.V., 84
Decora Industries, Inc., 31
Decorator Industries Inc., 68
DeCrane Aircraft Holdings Inc., 36
Deere & Company, III; 42 (upd.)
Defiance, Inc., 22
Delachaux S.A., 76
Dell Inc., 63 (upd.)
Deluxe Corporation, 73 (upd.)
DEMCO, Inc., 60
Denby Group plc, 44
Denison International plc, 46
DENSO Corporation, 46 (upd.)
Department 56, Inc., 14
DePuy Inc., 37 (upd.)
Detroit Diesel Corporation, 10; 74 (upd.)
Deutsche Babcock A.G., III
Deutsche Steinzeug Cremer & Breuer Aktiengesellschaft, 91
Deutz AG, 39
Devro plc, 55
DHB Industries Inc., 85
Dial-A-Mattress Operating Corporation, 46
Diadora SpA, 86
Diebold, Incorporated, 7; 22 (upd.)
Diehl Stiftung & Co. KG, 79
Diesel SpA, 40
Dixon Industries, Inc., 26
Dixon Ticonderoga Company, 12; 69 (upd.)
Djarum PT, 62
DMI Furniture, Inc., 46
Domino Printing Sciences PLC, 87
Donaldson Company, Inc., 49 (upd.)
Donnelly Corporation, 12; 35 (upd.)
Dorel Industries Inc., 59
Dot Hill Systems Corp., 93
Douglas & Lomason Company, 16
Dover Corporation, III; 28 (upd.); 90 (upd.)
Dresser Industries, Inc., III
Drew Industries Inc., 28
Drexel Heritage Furnishings Inc., 12
Dril-Quip, Inc., 81
Drypers Corporation, 18
DTS, Inc., 80
Ducommun Incorporated, 30
Duncan Toys Company, 55
Dunn-Edwards Corporation, 56
Duracell International Inc., 9; 71 (upd.)
Durametallic, 21
Duriron Company Inc., 17
Dürkopp Adler AG, 65
Duron Inc., 72
Dürr AG, 44
Dynea, 68
Dyson Group PLC, 71
E-Z-EM Inc., 89
EADS SOCATA, 54
Eagle-Picher Industries, Inc., 8; 23 (upd.)
East Penn Manufacturing Co., Inc., 79
The Eastern Company, 48
Eastman Kodak Company, III; 7 (upd.); 36 (upd.); 91 (upd.)
Easton Sports, Inc., 66
Eaton Corporation, I; 10 (upd.); 67 (upd.)
Ebara Corporation, 83
ECC International Corp., 42
Ecolab Inc., I; 13 (upd.); 34 (upd.); 85 (upd.)
Eddie Bauer Holdings, Inc., 9; 36 (upd.); 87 (upd.)
EDO Corporation, 46
EG&G Incorporated, 29 (upd.)

Ekco Group, Inc., 16
Elamex, S.A. de C.V., 51
Elano Corporation, 14
Electric Boat Corporation, 86
Electrolux AB, III; 53 (upd.)
Eljer Industries, Inc., 24
Elkay Manufacturing Company, 73
Elscint Ltd., 20
Empire Resources, Inc., 81
Encompass Services Corporation, 33
Encore Computer Corporation, 13; 74 (upd.)
Encore Wire Corporation, 81
Energizer Holdings, Inc., 32
Energy Conversion Devices, Inc., 75
Enesco Corporation, 11
Engineered Support Systems, Inc., 59
English China Clays Ltd., 40 (upd.)
Enodis plc, 68
EnPro Industries, Inc., 93
Entertainment Distribution Company, 89
Ernie Ball, Inc., 56
Escalade, Incorporated, 19
ESCO Technologies Inc., 87
Esselte, 64
Esselte Leitz GmbH & Co. KG, 48
Essilor International, 21
Esterline Technologies Corp., 15
Ethan Allen Interiors, Inc., 12; 39 (upd.)
The Eureka Company, 12
Everlast Worldwide Inc., 47
Excel Technology, Inc., 65
EXX Inc., 65
Fabbrica D' Armi Pietro Beretta S.p.A., 39
Facom S.A., 32
FAG—Kugelfischer Georg Schäfer AG, 62
Faiveley S.A., 39
Falcon Products, Inc., 33
Fannie May Confections Brands, Inc., 80
Fanuc Ltd., III; 17 (upd.); 75 (upd.)
Farah Incorporated, 24
Farmer Bros. Co., 52
FARO Technologies, Inc., 87
Fastenal Company, 42 (upd.)
Faultless Starch/Bon Ami Company, 55
Featherlite Inc., 28
Fedders Corporation, 18; 43 (upd.)
Federal Prison Industries, Inc., 34
Federal Signal Corp., 10
FEI Company, 79
Fellowes Manufacturing Company, 28
Fender Musical Instruments Company, 16; 43 (upd.)
Ferretti Group SpA, 90
Ferro Corporation, 56 (upd.)
Figgie International Inc., 7
Firearms Training Systems, Inc., 27
First Alert, Inc., 28
First Brands Corporation, 8
First International Computer, Inc., 56
The First Years Inc., 46
Fisher Controls International, LLC, 13; 61 (upd.)
Fisher Scientific International Inc., 24
Fisher-Price Inc., 12; 32 (upd.)
Fiskars Corporation, 33
Fisons plc, 9
Flanders Corporation, 65
Fleetwood Enterprises, Inc., III; 22 (upd.); 81 (upd.)
Flexsteel Industries Inc., 15; 41 (upd.)
Flextronics International Ltd., 38
Flint Ink Corporation, 41 (upd.)
FLIR Systems, Inc., 69
Florsheim Shoe Company, 9
Flour City International, Inc., 44
Flow International Corporation, 56
Flowserve Corporation, 33; 77 (upd.)
FLSmidth & Co. A/S, 72
Fort James Corporation, 22 (upd.)
Forward Industries, Inc., 86
FosterGrant, Inc., 60
Fountain Powerboats Industries, Inc., 28
Foxboro Company, 13
Framatome SA, 19
Francotyp-Postalia Holding AG, 92
Frank J. Zamboni & Co., Inc., 34
Franke Holding AG, 76
Franklin Electric Company, Inc., 43
The Franklin Mint, 69
Freudenberg & Co., 41
Friedrich Grohe AG & Co. KG, 53
Frigidaire Home Products, 22
Frymaster Corporation, 27
FSI International, Inc., 17
Fuel Tech, Inc., 85
Fuji Photo Film Co., Ltd., III; 18 (upd.); 79 (upd.)
Fujisawa Pharmaceutical Company, Ltd., 58 (upd.)
Fuqua Enterprises, Inc., 17
Furniture Brands International, Inc., 39 (upd.)
Furon Company, 28
The Furukawa Electric Co., Ltd., III
G. Leblanc Corporation, 55
G.S. Blodgett Corporation, 15
Gaming Partners International Corporation, 93
Gardner Denver, Inc., 49
The Gates Corporation, 9
GE Aircraft Engines, 9
GEA AG, 27
Geberit AG, 49
Gehl Company, 19
Gelita AG, 74
Gemini Sound Products Corporation, 58
Gemplus International S.A., 64
Gen-Probe Incorporated, 79
GenCorp Inc., 8; 9 (upd.)
General Atomics, 57
General Bearing Corporation, 45
General Binding Corporation, 73 (upd.)
General Cable Corporation, 40
General Dynamics Corporation, I; 10 (upd.); 40 (upd.); 88 (upd.
General Housewares Corporation, 16
Genmar Holdings, Inc., 45
geobra Brandstätter GmbH & Co. KG, 48
Georg Fischer AG Schaffhausen, 61
The George F. Cram Company, Inc., 55
Georgia Gulf Corporation, 61 (upd.)
Gerber Scientific, Inc., 12; 84 (upd.)
Gerresheimer Glas AG, 43
Getrag Corporate Group, 92
Giant Manufacturing Company, Ltd., 85
Giddings & Lewis, Inc., 10
Gildemeister AG, 79
The Gillette Company, 20 (upd.)
GKN plc, III; 38 (upd.); 89 (upd.)
Glaverbel Group, 80
Gleason Corporation, 24
Glen Dimplex 78
The Glidden Company, 8
Global Power Equipment Group Inc., 52
Glock Ges.m.b.H., 42
Goodman Holding Company, 42
Goodrich Corporation, 46 (upd.)
Goody Products, Inc., 12
The Gorman-Rupp Company, 18; 57 (upd.)
Goss Holdings, Inc., 43
Goulds Pumps Inc., 24
Graco Inc., 19; 67 (upd.)
Graham Corporation, 62
Granite Industries of Vermont, Inc., 73
Grant Prideco, Inc., 57
Greatbatch Inc., 72
Greene, Tweed & Company, 55
Greif Inc., 66 (upd.)
Griffin Industries, Inc., 70
Griffon Corporation, 34
Grinnell Corp., 13
Groupe André, 17
Groupe Guillin SA, 40
Groupe Herstal S.A., 58
Groupe Legis Industries, 23
Groupe SEB, 35
Grow Group Inc., 12
Groz-Beckert Group, 68
Grunau Company Inc., 90
Grundfos Group, 83
Grupo Cydsa, S.A. de C.V., 39
Grupo IMSA, S.A. de C.V., 44
Grupo Industrial Saltillo, S.A. de C.V., 54
Grupo Lladró S.A., 52
Guangzhou Pearl River Piano Group Ltd., 49
Guardian Industries Corp., 87
Gulf Island Fabrication, Inc., 44
Gunite Corporation, 51
The Gunlocke Company, 23
Guy Degrenne SA, 44
H.B. Fuller Company, 8; 32 (upd.); 75 (upd.)
Hach Co., 18
Hackman Oyj Adp, 44
Haeger Industries Inc., 88
Haemonetics Corporation, 20
Haier Group Corporation, 65
Halliburton Company, III
Hallmark Cards, Inc., IV; 16 (upd.); 40 (upd.); 87 (upd.)
Hammond Manufacturing Company Limited, 83
Hansgrohe AG, 56
Hanson PLC, 30 (upd.)
Hardinge Inc., 25
Harland and Wolff Holdings plc, 19
Harmon Industries, Inc., 25
Harnischfeger Industries, Inc., 8; 38 (upd.)
Harsco Corporation, 8

Hartmarx Corporation, 32 (upd.)
The Hartz Mountain Corporation, 46 (upd.)
Hasbro, Inc., III; 16 (upd.)
Haskel International, Inc., 59
Hastings Manufacturing Company, 56
Hawker Siddeley Group Public Limited Company, III
Haworth Inc., 8; 39 (upd.)
Head N.V., 55
Headwaters Incorporated, 56
Health O Meter Products Inc., 14
Heekin Can Inc., 13
HEICO Corporation, 30
Heidelberger Druckmaschinen AG, 40
Hella KGaA Hueck & Co., 66
Henkel Manco Inc., 22
The Henley Group, Inc., III
Heraeus Holding GmbH, 54 (upd.)
Herman Miller, Inc., 8; 77 (upd.)
Hermès International S.A., 34 (upd.)
Héroux-Devtek Inc., 69
Hexagon AB 78
High Tech Computer Corporation, 81
Hillenbrand Industries, Inc., 10; 75 (upd.)
Hillerich & Bradsby Company, Inc., 51
Hillsdown Holdings plc, 24 (upd.)
Hilti AG, 53
Hindustan Lever Limited, 79
Hitachi Zosen Corporation, III
Hitchiner Manufacturing Co., Inc., 23
HMI Industries, Inc., 17
HNI Corporation, 74 (upd.)
The Hockey Company, 70
The Holland Group, Inc., 82
Hollander Home Fashions Corp., 67
Holnam Inc., 8
Holson Burnes Group, Inc., 14
Home Products International, Inc., 55
HON INDUSTRIES Inc., 13
Hooker Furniture Corporation, 80
The Hoover Company, 12; 40 (upd.)
Horween Leather Company, 83
Hoshino Gakki Co. Ltd., 55
Host America Corporation, 79
Hubbell Inc., 76 (upd.)
Huffy Corporation, 7; 30 (upd.)
Huhtamäki Oyj, 64
Hummel International A/S, 68
Hunt Manufacturing Company, 12
Hunter Fan Company, 13
Huntleigh Technology PLC, 77
Hydril Company, 46
Hyster Company, 17
Hyundai Group, III; 7 (upd.)
Icon Health & Fitness, Inc., 38
IDEO Inc., 65
IdraPrince, Inc., 76
Igloo Products Corp., 21
Illinois Tool Works Inc., III; 22 (upd.); 81 (upd.)
Illumina, Inc., 93
Imatra Steel Oy Ab, 55
IMI plc, 9
Imo Industries Inc., 7; 27 (upd.)
In-Sink-Erator, 66
Inchcape PLC, III; 16 (upd.); 50 (upd.)
Indel Inc. 78
Industrie Natuzzi S.p.A., 18
Infineon Technologies AG, 50
Ingalls Shipbuilding, Inc., 12
Ingersoll-Rand Company Ltd., III; 15 (upd.); 55 (upd.)
Insilco Corporation, 16
Insituform Technologies, Inc., 83
Interco Incorporated, III
Interface, Inc., 8
The Interlake Corporation, 8
INTERMET Corporation, 77 (upd.)
Internacional de Ceramica, S.A. de C.V., 53
International Controls Corporation, 10
International Flavors & Fragrances Inc., 38 (upd.)
International Game Technology, 10
Intevac, Inc., 92
Intuitive Surgical, Inc., 79
Invacare Corporation, 47 (upd.)
Invensys PLC, 50 (upd.)
Invivo Corporation, 52
Ionatron, Inc., 85
Ionics, Incorporated, 52
Ipsen International Inc., 72
iRobot Corporation, 83
Irwin Toy Limited, 14
Ishikawajima-Harima Heavy Industries Co., Ltd., III; 86 (upd.)
Itron, Inc., 64
J C Bamford Excavators Ltd., 83
J. D'Addario & Company, Inc., 48
J.I. Case Company, 10
J.M. Voith AG, 33
Jabil Circuit, Inc., 36; 88 (upd.)
Jacuzzi Brands Inc., 76 (upd.)
Jacuzzi Inc., 23
JAKKS Pacific, Inc., 52
James Avery Craftsman, Inc., 76
James Hardie Industries N.V., 56
James Purdey & Sons Limited, 87
JanSport, Inc., 70
Japan Tobacco Inc., 46 (upd.)
Jarden Corporation, 93 (upd.)
Jayco Inc., 13
Jeld-Wen, Inc., 45
Jenoptik AG, 33
Jervis B. Webb Company, 24
JLG Industries, Inc., 52
John Frieda Professional Hair Care Inc., 70
Johns Manville Corporation, 64 (upd.)
Johnson Controls, Inc., III; 26 (upd.); 59 (upd.)
Johnson Matthey PLC, 49 (upd.)
Johnson Outdoors Inc., 28; 84 (upd.)
Johnstown America Industries, Inc., 23
Jones Apparel Group, Inc., 11
Jostens, Inc., 7; 25 (upd.); 73 (upd.)
Jotun A/S, 80
JSP Corporation, 74
Julius Blüthner Pianofortefabrik GmbH 78
K'Nex Industries, Inc., 52
Kaman Corporation, 12; 42 (upd.)
Kaman Music Corporation, 68
Kansai Paint Company Ltd., 80
Karsten Manufacturing Corporation, 51
Kasper A.S.L., Ltd., 40
Katy Industries, Inc., 51 (upd.)
Kawai Musical Instruments Mfg Co. Ltd. 78
Kawasaki Heavy Industries, Ltd., III; 63 (upd.)
Kaydon Corporation, 18
KB Toys, Inc., 35 (upd.); 86 (upd.)
Kelly-Moore Paint Company, Inc., 56
Kenmore Air Harbor Inc., 65
Kennametal Inc., 68 (upd.)
Keramik Holding AG Laufen, 51
Kerr Group Inc., 24
Kewaunee Scientific Corporation, 25
Key Safety Systems, Inc., 63
Key Tronic Corporation, 14
Keystone International, Inc., 11
KHD Konzern, III
KI, 57
Kimball International, Inc., 12; 48 (upd.)
Kit Manufacturing Co., 18
Knape & Vogt Manufacturing Company, 17
Knoll Group Inc., 14; 80 (upd.)
Knorr-Bremse AG, 84
Koala Corporation, 44
Kobe Steel, Ltd., IV; 19 (upd.)
Koch Enterprises, Inc., 29
Koenig & Bauer AG, 64
Kohler Company, 7; 32 (upd.)
Komatsu Ltd., III; 16 (upd.); 52 (upd.)
KONE Corporation, 27; 76 (upd.)
Konica Corporation, III
Kyocera Corporation, 79 (upd.)
KraftMaid Cabinetry, Inc., 72
KSB AG, 62
Kubota Corporation, III; 26 (upd.)
Kuhlman Corporation, 20
Kwang Yang Motor Company Ltd., 80
Kyocera Corporation, 21 (upd.)
L-3 Communications Holdings, Inc., 48
L. and J.G. Stickley, Inc., 50
L.A. Darling Company, 92
L.B. Foster Company, 33
L.S. Starrett Company, 64 (upd.)
La-Z-Boy Incorporated, 14; 50 (upd.)
LaCie Group S.A., 76
Lacks Enterprises Inc., 61
LADD Furniture, Inc., 12
Ladish Co., Inc., 30
Lafarge Cement UK, 28; 54 (upd.)
Lafuma S.A., 39
Lakeland Industries, Inc., 45
Lam Research Corporation, 31 (upd.)
The Lamson & Sessions Co., 13; 61 (upd.)
Lancer Corporation, 21
The Lane Co., Inc., 12
Laserscope, 67
LaSiDo Inc., 58
LeapFrog Enterprises, Inc., 54
Lear Corporation, 71 (upd.)
Leatherman Tool Group, Inc., 51
Leggett & Platt, Inc., 11; 48 (upd.)
Leica Camera AG, 35
Leica Microsystems Holdings GmbH, 35
Lennox International Inc., 8; 28 (upd.)
Lenox, Inc., 12

Leupold & Stevens, Inc., 52
Lexmark International, Inc., 18; 79 (upd.)
Liebherr-International AG, 64
Lifetime Brands, Inc., 73 (upd.)
Linamar Corporation, 18
Lincoln Electric Co., 13
Lindal Cedar Homes, Inc., 29
Lindsay Manufacturing Co., 20
Lipman Electronic Engineering Ltd., 81
Little Tikes Company, 13; 62 (upd.)
Loctite Corporation, 8
Logitech International S.A., 28; 69 (upd.)
The Longaberger Company, 12; 44 (upd.)
Louis Vuitton, 10
LSB Industries, Inc., 77
Lucas Industries PLC, III
Lufkin Industries Inc. 78
Luxottica SpA, 17; 52 (upd.)
Lydall, Inc., 64
Lynch Corporation, 43
M&F Worldwide Corp., 38
M.A. Bruder & Sons, Inc., 56
Mabuchi Motor Co. Ltd., 68
MacAndrews & Forbes Holdings Inc., 28; 86 (upd.)
Mace Security International, Inc., 57
MacGregor Golf Company, 68
Mackay Envelope Corporation, 45
Madeco S.A., 71
Madison-Kipp Corporation, 58
Mag Instrument, Inc., 67
Maidenform, Inc., 59 (upd.)
Mail-Well, Inc., 28
Makita Corporation, 22; 59 (upd.)
MAN Aktiengesellschaft, III
Manhattan Group, LLC , 80
Manitou BF S.A., 27
The Manitowoc Company, Inc., 18; 59 (upd.)
Mannesmann AG, III; 14 (upd.)
Marcolin S.p.A., 61
Margarete Steiff GmbH, 23
Marine Products Corporation, 75
Marisa Christina, Inc., 15
Mark IV Industries, Inc., 7; 28 (upd.)
Märklin Holding GmbH, 70
The Marmon Group, 16 (upd.)
Marshall Amplification plc, 62
Martin-Baker Aircraft Company Limited, 61
Martin Industries, Inc., 44
MartinLogan, Ltd., 85
Marvin Lumber & Cedar Company, 22
Mary Kay Inc., 9; 30 (upd.); 84 (upd.)
Masco Corporation, III; 20 (upd.); 39 (upd.)
Masonite International Corporation, 63
Master Lock Company, 45
MasterBrand Cabinets, Inc., 71
MasterCraft Boat Company, Inc., 90
Material Sciences Corporation, 63
Matsushita Electric Industrial Co., Ltd., 64 (upd.)
Mattel, Inc., 7; 25 (upd.); 61 (upd.)
Matth. Hohner AG, 53
Matthews International Corporation, 29; 77 (upd.)
Maverick Tube Corporation, 59
Maxco Inc., 17
Maxwell Shoe Company, Inc., 30
Maytag Corporation, III; 22 (upd.); 82 (upd.)
McClain Industries, Inc., 51
McDermott International, Inc., III
McKechnie plc, 34
McWane Corporation, 55
Meade Instruments Corporation, 41
Meadowcraft, Inc., 29
Measurement Specialties, Inc., 71
Mecalux S.A., 74
Medtronic, Inc., 67 (upd.)
Meggitt PLC, 34
Meidensha Corporation, 92
Meiji Seika Kaisha Ltd., 64 (upd.)
MEMC Electronic Materials, Inc., 81
Memry Corporation, 72
Menasha Corporation, 59 (upd.)
Merck & Co., Inc., I; 11 (upd.); 34 (upd.)
Mercury Marine Group, 68
Merillat Industries Inc., 13
Merillat Industries, LLC, 69 (upd.)
Mestek Inc., 10
Metso Corporation, 30 (upd.); 85 (upd.)
Mettler-Toledo International Inc., 30
Meyer International Holdings, Ltd., 87
Michael Anthony Jewelers, Inc., 24
Micrel, Incorporated, 77
Microdot Inc., 8
The Middleton Doll Company, 53
Midwest Grain Products, Inc., 49
Miele & Cie. KG, 56
Mikasa, Inc., 28
Mikohn Gaming Corporation, 39
Milacron, Inc., 53 (upd.)
Miller Industries, Inc., 26
Millipore Corporation, 25; 84 (upd.)
Milton Bradley Company, 21
Mine Safety Appliances Company, 31
Minebea Co., Ltd., 90
Minolta Co., Ltd., III; 18 (upd.); 43 (upd.)
Minuteman International Inc., 46
Misonix, Inc., 80
Mitsubishi Heavy Industries, Ltd., III; 7 (upd.)
Mity Enterprises, Inc., 38
Mobile Mini, Inc., 58
Mocon, Inc., 76
Modine Manufacturing Company, 8; 56 (upd.)
Modtech Holdings, Inc., 77
Moen Incorporated, 12
Mohawk Industries, Inc., 19; 63 (upd.)
Molex Incorporated, 11
The Monarch Cement Company, 72
Monnaie de Paris, 62
Monster Cable Products, Inc., 69
Montblanc International GmbH, 82
Montres Rolex S.A., 13; 34 (upd.)
Montupet S.A., 63
Moog Music, Inc., 75
The Morgan Crucible Company plc, 82
Morrow Equipment Co. L.L.C., 87
Motorcar Parts & Accessories, Inc., 47
Moulinex S.A., 22
Movado Group, Inc., 28
Mr. Coffee, Inc., 15
Mr. Gasket Inc., 15
Mueller Industries, Inc., 7; 52 (upd.)
Multi-Color Corporation, 53
Musco Lighting, 83
Nashua Corporation, 8
National Envelope Corporation, 32
National Gypsum Company, 10
National Oilwell, Inc., 54
National Picture & Frame Company, 24
National Semiconductor Corporation, 69 (upd.)
National Standard Co., 13
National Starch and Chemical Company, 49
Natrol, Inc., 49
Natural Alternatives International, Inc., 49
NCI Building Systems, Inc., 88
NCR Corporation, III; 6 (upd.); 30 (upd.); 90 (upd.)
Neenah Foundry Company, 68
Neopost S.A., 53
NETGEAR, Inc., 81
New Balance Athletic Shoe, Inc., 25
New Holland N.V., 22
Newcor, Inc., 40
Newell Rubbermaid Inc., 9; 52 (upd.)
Newport Corporation, 71
Newport News Shipbuilding Inc., 13; 38 (upd.)
Nexans SA, 54
NGK Insulators Ltd., 67
NHK Spring Co., Ltd., III
Nidec Corporation, 59
NIKE, Inc., 36 (upd.)
Nikon Corporation, III; 48 (upd.)
Nintendo Company, Ltd., III; 7 (upd.); 67 (upd.)
Nippon Seiko K.K., III
Nippondenso Co., Ltd., III
NKK Corporation, 28 (upd.)
NOF Corporation, 72
NordicTrack, 22
Nordson Corporation, 11; 48 (upd.)
Nortek, Inc., 34
Norton Company, 8
Norton McNaughton, Inc., 27
Novellus Systems, Inc., 18
NSS Enterprises Inc. 78
NTN Corporation, III; 47 (upd.)
Nu-kote Holding, Inc., 18
O'Sullivan Industries Holdings, Inc., 34
Oak Industries Inc., 21
Oakley, Inc., 49 (upd.)
Oakwood Homes Corporation, 15
ODL, Inc., 55
The Ohio Art Company,14; 59 (upd.)
Oil-Dri Corporation of America, 20; 89 (upd.)
The Oilgear Company, 74
Okuma Holdings Inc., 74
Old Town Canoe Company, 74
180s, L.L.C., 64
Oneida Ltd., 7; 31 (upd.); 88 (upd.)
Optische Werke G. Rodenstock, 44
Orange Glo International, 53
Orbotech Ltd., 75

Orthofix International NV, 72
Osmonics, Inc., 18
Osram GmbH, 86
Otis Elevator Company, Inc., 13; 39 (upd.)
Otor S.A., 77
Outboard Marine Corporation, III; 20 (upd.)
Outdoor Research, Incorporated, 67
Overhead Door Corporation, 70
Owens Corning Corporation, 20 (upd.)
Owosso Corporation, 29
P & F Industries, Inc., 45
Pacer Technology, 40
Pacific Coast Feather Company, 67
Pacific Dunlop Limited, 10
Pagnossin S.p.A., 73
Pall Corporation, 9; 72 (upd.)
Palm Harbor Homes, Inc., 39
Paloma Industries Ltd., 71
Panavision Inc., 24
Park Corp., 22
Park-Ohio Holdings Corp., 17; 85 (upd.)
Parker-Hannifin Corporation, III; 24 (upd.)
Parlex Corporation, 61
Patrick Industries, Inc., 30
Paul Mueller Company, 65
Pearl Corporation 78
Pechiney SA, IV; 45 (upd.)
Peg Perego SpA, 88
Pelican Products, Inc., 86
Pelikan Holding AG, 92
Pella Corporation, 12; 39 (upd.); 89 (upd.)
Penn Engineering & Manufacturing Corp., 28
Pentair, Inc., 7; 26 (upd.); 81 (upd.)
Pentax Corporation 78
Pentech International, Inc., 29
PerkinElmer Inc. 7; 78 (upd.)
Peterson American Corporation, 55
Phillips-Van Heusen Corporation, 24
Phoenix AG, 68
Phoenix Mecano AG, 61
Photo-Me International Plc, 83
Physio-Control International Corp., 18
Pilkington Group Limited, III; 34 (upd.); 87 (upd.)
Pilot Pen Corporation of America, 82
Pinguely-Haulotte SA, 51
Pioneer Electronic Corporation, III
Pirelli & C. S.p.A., 75 (upd.)
Piscines Desjoyaux S.A., 84
Pitney Bowes, Inc., 19
Pittway Corporation, 33 (upd.)
Planar Systems, Inc., 61
PlayCore, Inc., 27
Playmates Toys, 23
Playskool, Inc., 25
Pleasant Company, 27
Ply Gem Industries Inc., 12
Pochet SA, 55
Polaris Industries Inc., 12; 35 (upd.); 77 (upd.)
Polaroid Corporation, III; 7 (upd.); 28 (upd.); 93 (upd.)
The Porcelain and Fine China Companies Ltd., 69
Portmeirion Group plc, 88
Pou Chen Corporation, 81
PPG Industries, Inc., III; 22 (upd.); 81 (upd.)
Prada Holding B.V., 45
Pranda Jewelry plc, 70
Praxair, Inc., 48 (upd.)
Precision Castparts Corp., 15
Premark International, Inc., III
Pressman Toy Corporation, 56
Presstek, Inc., 33
Price Pfister, Inc., 70
Prince Sports Group, Inc., 15
Printpack, Inc., 68
Printronix, Inc., 18
Puig Beauty and Fashion Group S.L., 60
Pulaski Furniture Corporation, 33; 80 (upd.)
Pumpkin Masters, Inc., 48
Punch International N.V., 66
Pure World, Inc., 72
Puritan-Bennett Corporation, 13
Purolator Products Company, 21; 74 (upd.)
PVC Container Corporation, 67
PW Eagle, Inc., 48
Q.E.P. Co., Inc., 65
QSC Audio Products, Inc., 56
Quixote Corporation, 15
R. Griggs Group Limited, 23
Racing Champions Corporation, 37
Radio Flyer Inc., 34
Rain Bird Corporation, 84
Raleigh UK Ltd., 65
Rapala-Normark Group, Ltd., 30
RathGibson Inc., 90
Raven Industries, Inc., 33
Raychem Corporation, 8
Rayovac Corporation, 39 (upd.)
Raytech Corporation, 61
Recovery Engineering, Inc., 25
Red Spot Paint & Varnish Company, 55
Red Wing Pottery Sales, Inc., 52
Red Wing Shoe Company, Inc., 9; 30 (upd.); 83 (upd.)
Reed & Barton Corporation, 67
Regal-Beloit Corporation, 18
Reichhold Chemicals, Inc., 10
Remington Arms Company, Inc., 12; 40 (upd.)
Remington Products Company, L.L.C., 42
RENK AG, 37
Renner Herrmann S.A., 79
Revell-Monogram Inc., 16
Revere Ware Corporation, 22
Revlon Inc., 64 (upd.)
Rexam PLC, 32 (upd.); 85 (upd.)
Rexnord Corporation, 21; 76 (upd.)
RF Micro Devices, Inc., 43
Rheinmetall Berlin AG, 9
RHI AG, 53
Richardson Industries, Inc., 62
Rickenbacker International Corp., 91
Riddell Sports Inc., 22
Rieter Holding AG, 42
River Oaks Furniture, Inc., 43
Riviera Tool Company, 89
RMC Group p.l.c., 34 (upd.)
Roadmaster Industries, Inc., 16
Robbins & Myers Inc., 15
Robertson-Ceco Corporation, 19
Rock-Tenn Company, 59 (upd.)
Rockford Products Corporation, 55
RockShox, Inc., 26
Rockwell Automation, I; 11 (upd.); 43 (upd.)
Rockwell Medical Technologies, Inc., 88
Rodriguez Group S.A., 90
ROFIN-SINAR Technologies Inc., 81
Rogers Corporation, 61
Rohde & Schwarz GmbH & Co. KG, 39
Rohm and Haas Company, 77 (upd.)
ROHN Industries, Inc., 22
Rohr Incorporated, 9
Roland Corporation, 38
Rollerblade, Inc., 15; 34 (upd.)
Rolls-Royce Group PLC, 67 (upd.)
Ronson PLC, 49
Roper Industries, Inc., 15; 50 (upd.)
Rose Art Industries, 58
Roseburg Forest Products Company, 58
Rotork plc, 46
Royal Appliance Manufacturing Company, 15
Royal Canin S.A., 39
Royal Doulton plc, 14; 38 (upd.)
Royal Group Technologies Limited, 73
RPC Group PLC, 81
RPM International Inc., 8; 36 (upd.); 91 (upd.)
Rubbermaid Incorporated, III
Russ Berrie and Company, Inc., 12; 82 (upd.)
S.C. Johnson & Son, Inc., III; 28 (upd.); 89 (upd.)
Sabaté Diosos SA, 48
Safe Flight Instrument Corporation, 71
Safeskin Corporation, 18
Safety Components International, Inc., 63
Safilo SpA, 54
Salant Corporation, 12; 51 (upd.)
Salton, Inc., 30; 88 (upd.)
Samick Musical Instruments Co., Ltd., 56
Samsonite Corporation, 13; 43 (upd.)
Samuel Cabot Inc., 53
Sandvik AB, 32 (upd.); 77 (upd.)
Sanford L.P., 82
Sanitec Corporation, 51
Sanrio Company, Ltd., 38
Sapa AB, 84
Sauder Woodworking Company, 12; 35 (upd.)
Sauer-Danfoss Inc., 61
Sawtek Inc., 43 (upd.)
Schindler Holding AG, 29
Schlage Lock Company, 82
Schlumberger Limited, III
School-Tech, Inc., 62
Schott Corporation, 53
Scotsman Industries, Inc., 20
Scott Fetzer Company, 12; 80 (upd.)
The Scotts Company, 22
Scovill Fasteners Inc., 24
SeaChange International, Inc., 79

Sealed Air Corporation, 14; 57 (upd.)
Sealy Inc., 12
Seattle Lighting Fixture Company, 92
Segway LLC, 48
Seiko Corporation, III; 17 (upd.); 72 (upd.)
Select Comfort Corporation, 34
Selee Corporation, 88
The Selmer Company, Inc., 19
Semitool, Inc., 18
Sequa Corp., 13
Serta, Inc., 28
Severstal Joint Stock Company, 65
Shakespeare Company, 22
Shanghai Baosteel Group Corporation, 71
The Shaw Group, Inc., 50
Sheaffer Pen Corporation, 82
Shelby Williams Industries, Inc., 14
Shermag, Inc., 93
The Sherwin-Williams Company, III; 13 (upd.); 89 (upd.)
Sherwood Brands, Inc., 53
Shimano Inc., 64
Shorewood Packaging Corporation, 28
Shuffle Master Inc., 51
Shurgard Storage Centers, Inc., 52
SIFCO Industries, Inc., 41
Siliconware Precision Industries Ltd., 73
Simmons Company, 47
Simplicity Manufacturing, Inc., 64
Simula, Inc., 41
The Singer Company N.V., 30 (upd.)
The Singing Machine Company, Inc., 60
Skis Rossignol S.A., 15; 43 (upd.)
Skyline Corporation, 30
SL Industries, Inc., 77
SLI, Inc., 48
Smead Manufacturing Co., 17
Smith & Wesson Corp., 30; 73 (upd.)
Smith Corona Corp., 13
Smith International, Inc., 15
Smith-Midland Corporation, 56
Smiths Industries PLC, 25
Smoby International SA, 56
Snap-On, Incorporated, 7; 27 (upd.)
Société BIC S.A., 73
Sola International Inc., 71
Sonic Innovations Inc., 56
Sonoco Products Company, 8; 89 (upd.)
SonoSite, Inc., 56
Spacelabs Medical, Inc., 71
Sparton Corporation, 18
Spear & Jackson, Inc., 73
Specialized Bicycle Components Inc., 50
Specialty Equipment Companies, Inc., 25
Specialty Products & Insulation Co., 59
Spectrum Control, Inc., 67
Speizman Industries, Inc., 44
Spin Master, Ltd., 61
Spirax-Sarco Engineering plc, 59
SPS Technologies, Inc., 30
SPX Corporation, 47 (upd.)
SRAM Corporation, 65
SRC Holdings Corporation, 67
Stanadyne Automotive Corporation, 37
The Standard Register Company, 15; 93 (upd.)
Standex International Corporation, 17
Stanley Furniture Company, Inc., 34
The Stanley Works, III; 20 (upd.); 79 (upd.)
Starcraft Corporation, 66 (upd.)
Stearns, Inc., 43
Steel Authority of India Ltd., 66 (upd.)
Steel Dynamics, Inc., 52
Steel Technologies Inc., 63
Steelcase, Inc., 7; 27 (upd.)
Steinway Musical Properties, Inc., 19
Stelco Inc., 51 (upd.)
The Stephan Company, 60
Stewart & Stevenson Services Inc., 11
STMicroelectronics NV, 52
Stratasys, Inc., 67
Strattec Security Corporation, 73
Straumann Holding AG, 79
Strombecker Corporation, 60
Stryker Corporation, 11; 29 (upd.); 79 (upd.)
Sturm, Ruger & Company, Inc., 19
Sub-Zero Freezer Co., Inc., 31
Sudbury Inc., 16
Sulzer Brothers Limited (Gebruder Sulzer Aktiengesellschaft), III
Sumitomo Heavy Industries, Ltd., III; 42 (upd.)
Sun Hydraulics Corporation, 74
Sunburst Shutter Corporation 78
Superior Essex Inc., 80
Susquehanna Pfaltzgraff Company, 8
Swank, Inc., 17; 84 (upd.)
Swarovski International Holding AG, 40
The Swatch Group SA, 26
Swedish Match AB, 12; 39 (upd.); 92 (upd.)
Sweetheart Cup Company, Inc., 36
Sybron International Corp., 14
Synthes, Inc., 93
Syratech Corp., 14
Systemax, Inc., 52
TAB Products Co., 17
Tacony Corporation, 70
TAG Heuer International SA, 25; 77 (upd.)
Tag-It Pacific, Inc., 85
Taiheiyo Cement Corporation, 60 (upd.)
Taiwan Semiconductor Manufacturing Company Ltd., 47
Tamron Company Ltd., 82
Targetti Sankey SpA, 86
Tarkett Sommer AG, 25
Taser International, Inc., 62
Taylor Guitars, 48
Taylor Made Golf Co., 23
TB Wood's Corporation, 56
TDK Corporation, 49 (upd.)
TearDrop Golf Company, 32
Techtronic Industries Company Ltd., 73
Tecumseh Products Company, 8; 71 (upd.)
Tektronix Inc., 8; 78 (upd.)
Tempur-Pedic Inc., 54
Tenaris SA, 63
Tennant Company, 13; 33 (upd.)
Terex Corporation, 7; 40 (upd.); 91 (upd.)
The Testor Corporation, 51
Tetra Pak International SA, 53
Thales S.A., 42
Thermadyne Holding Corporation, 19
Thermo BioAnalysis Corp., 25
Thermo Electron Corporation, 7
Thermo Fibertek, Inc., 24
Thermo Instrument Systems Inc., 11
Thermo King Corporation, 13
Thiokol Corporation, 22 (upd.)
Thomas & Betts Corp., 11; 54 (upd.)
Thomas Industries Inc., 29
Thomasville Furniture Industries, Inc., 12; 74 (upd.)
Thor Industries Inc., 39; 92 (upd.)
3M Company, 61 (upd.)
ThyssenKrupp AG, IV; 28 (upd.); 87 (upd.)
Tilia Inc., 62
Timex Corporation, 7; 25 (upd.)
The Timken Company, 8; 42 (upd.)
Titan Cement Company S.A., 64
Titan International, Inc., 89
TiVo Inc., 75
TJ International, Inc., 19
Todd Shipyards Corporation, 14
Tokheim Corporation, 21
Tomy Company Ltd., 65
Tong Yang Cement Corporation, 62
Tonka Corporation, 25
Toolex International N.V., 26
The Topaz Group, Inc., 62
Topcon Corporation, 84
Topps Company, Inc., 13; 34 (upd.)
Toray Industries, Inc., 51 (upd.)
The Toro Company, 7; 26 (upd.); 77 (upd.)
The Torrington Company, 13
TOTO LTD., 28 (upd.)
Town & Country Corporation, 19
Toymax International, Inc., 29
Toyoda Automatic Loom Works, Ltd., III
Trane 78
CJSC Transmash Holding, 93
TransPro, Inc., 71
Tredegar Corporation, 52
Trek Bicycle Corporation, 16; 78 (upd.)
Trelleborg AB, 93
Trex Company, Inc., 71
Trico Products Corporation, 15
TriMas Corp., 11
Trinity Industries, Incorporated, 7
TRINOVA Corporation, III
TriPath Imaging, Inc., 77
TriQuint Semiconductor, Inc., 63
Trisko Jewelry Sculptures, Ltd., 57
Triumph Group, Inc., 31
TRUMPF GmbH + Co. KG, 86
TRW Automotive Holdings Corp., 75 (upd.)
Tubos de Acero de Mexico, S.A. (TAMSA), 41
Tultex Corporation, 13
Tupperware Corporation, 28
TurboChef Technologies, Inc., 83
Turtle Wax, Inc., 15; 93 (upd.)
Twin Disc, Inc., 21
II-VI Incorporated, 69
Ty Inc., 33; 86 (upd.)

Tyco International Ltd., III; 28 (upd.)
Tyco Toys, Inc., 12
U.S. Robotics Corporation, 9; 66 (upd.)
Ube Industries, Ltd., 38 (upd.)
Ultralife Batteries, Inc., 58
ULVAC, Inc., 80
United Defense Industries, Inc., 30; 66 (upd.)
United Dominion Industries Limited, 8; 16 (upd.)
United Industrial Corporation, 37
United States Filter Corporation, 20
United States Pipe and Foundry Company, 62
Unitika Ltd., 53 (upd.)
Unitog Co., 19
Universal Manufacturing Company, 88
Ushio Inc., 91
Usinas Siderúrgicas de Minas Gerais S.A., 77
Utah Medical Products, Inc., 36
UTStarcom, Inc., 77
VA TECH ELIN EBG GmbH, 49
Vaillant GmbH, 44
Valley National Gases, Inc., 85
Vallourec SA, 54
Valmet Corporation (Valmet Oy), III
Valmont Industries, Inc., 19
The Valspar Corporation, 8
Vari-Lite International, Inc., 35
Varian, Inc., 48 (upd.)
Variflex, Inc., 51
Varity Corporation, III
Varlen Corporation, 16
Varta AG, 23
Velcro Industries N.V., 19; 72 (upd.)
Velux A/S, 86
Ventana Medical Systems, Inc., 75
Verbatim Corporation, 74 (upd.)
Vermeer Manufacturing Company, 17
Vestas Wind Systems A/S, 73
Viasystems Group, Inc., 67
Vickers plc, 27
Victor Company of Japan, Limited, II; 26 (upd.); 83 (upd.)
Victorinox AG, 21; 74 (upd.)
Videojet Technologies, Inc., 90
Vidrala S.A., 67
Viessmann Werke GmbH & Co., 37
ViewSonic Corporation, 72
Viking Range Corporation, 66
Villeroy & Boch AG, 37
Virco Manufacturing Corporation, 17
Viscofan S.A., 70
Viskase Companies, Inc., 55
Vita Plus Corporation, 60
Vitro Corporativo S.A. de C.V., 34
voestalpine AG, 57 (upd.)
Vorwerk & Co., 27
Vosper Thornycroft Holding plc, 41
Vossloh AG, 53
VTech Holdings Ltd., 77
W.A. Whitney Company, 53
W.C. Bradley Co., 69
W.H. Brady Co., 17
W.L. Gore & Associates, Inc., 14; 60 (upd.)
W.W. Grainger, Inc., 26 (upd.); 68 (upd.)
Wabash National Corp., 13
Wabtec Corporation, 40
Wahl Clipper Corporation, 86
Walbro Corporation, 13
Walter Industries, Inc., 72 (upd.)
Washington Scientific Industries, Inc., 17
Wassall Plc, 18
Waterford Wedgwood plc, 12; 34 (upd.)
Water Pik Technologies, Inc., 34; 83 (upd.)
Waters Corporation, 43
Watts Industries, Inc., 19
Watts of Lydney Group Ltd., 71
WD-40 Company, 18
Weber-Stephen Products Co., 40
Weeres Industries Corporation, 52
Weg S.A. 78
The Weir Group PLC, 85
Welbilt Corp., 19
Wellman, Inc., 8; 52 (upd.)
Weru Aktiengesellschaft, 18
West Bend Co., 14
Westell Technologies, Inc., 57
Westerbeke Corporation, 60
Western Digital Corporation, 25; 92 (upd.)
Wheaton Science Products, 60 (upd.)
Wheeling-Pittsburgh Corporation, 58 (upd.)
Whirlpool Corporation, III; 12 (upd.); 59 (upd.)
White Consolidated Industries Inc., 13
Wilbert, Inc., 56
Wilkinson Sword Ltd., 60
William L. Bonnell Company, Inc., 66
William Zinsser & Company, Inc., 58
Williamson-Dickie Manufacturing Company, 45 (upd.)
Wilson Sporting Goods Company, 24; 84 (upd.)
Wincor Nixdorf Holding GmbH, 69 (upd.)
Windmere Corporation, 16
Winegard Company, 56
WinsLoew Furniture, Inc., 21
The Wiremold Company, 81
WMS Industries, Inc., 15; 53 (upd.)
Wolverine Tube Inc., 23
Wood-Mode, Inc., 23
Woodcraft Industries Inc., 61
Woodward Governor Company, 13; 49 (upd.)
Wright Medical Group, Inc., 61
Württembergische Metallwarenfabrik AG (WMF), 60
Wyant Corporation, 30
Wyman-Gordon Company, 14
Wynn's International, Inc., 33
X-Rite, Inc., 48
Xerox Corporation, 69 (upd.)
Yamaha Corporation, III; 16 (upd.)
The Yokohama Rubber Company, Limited, V; 19 (upd.); 91 (upd.)
The York Group, Inc., 50
York International Corp., 13
Young Innovations, Inc., 44
Zebra Technologies Corporation, 53 (upd.)
ZERO Corporation, 17; 88 (upd.)
ZiLOG, Inc., 72 (upd.)
Zindart Ltd., 60
Zippo Manufacturing Company, 18; 71 (upd.)
Zodiac S.A., 36
Zygo Corporation, 42

Materials

AK Steel Holding Corporation, 19
American Biltrite Inc., 16
American Colloid Co., 13
American Standard Inc., III
Ameriwood Industries International Corp., 17
Apasco S.A. de C.V., 51
Apogee Enterprises, Inc., 8
Asahi Glass Company, Limited, III
Asbury Carbons, Inc., 68
Bairnco Corporation, 28
Bayou Steel Corporation, 31
Blessings Corp., 19
Blue Circle Industries PLC, III
Bodycote International PLC, 63
Boral Limited, III
British Vita PLC, 9
Brush Engineered Materials Inc., 67
California Steel Industries, Inc., 67
Callanan Industries, Inc., 60
Cameron & Barkley Company, 28
Carborundum Company, 15
Carl Zeiss AG, III; 34 (upd.); 91 (upd.)
Carlisle Companies Inc., 8; 82 (upd.)
Carter Holt Harvey Ltd., 70
Cementos Argos S.A., 91
Cemex SA de CV, 20
Century Aluminum Company, 52
CertainTeed Corporation, 35
Chargeurs International, 6; 21 (upd.)
Chemfab Corporation, 35
Cimentos de Portugal SGPS S.A. (Cimpor), 76
Cold Spring Granite Company Inc., 16; 67 (upd.)
Columbia Forest Products Inc. 78
Compagnie de Saint-Gobain S.A., III; 16 (upd.)
Cookson Group plc, III; 44 (upd.)
Corning Inc., III; 44 (upd.); 90 (upd.)
CSR Limited, III; 28 (upd.); 85 (upd.)
Dal-Tile International Inc., 22
The David J. Joseph Company, 14; 76 (upd.)
The Dexter Corporation, 12 (upd.)
Dickten Masch Plastics LLC, 90
Dyckerhoff AG, 35
Dynamic Materials Corporation, 81
Dyson Group PLC, 71
ECC Group plc, III
Edw. C. Levy Co., 42
84 Lumber Company, 9; 39 (upd.)
ElkCorp, 52
Empire Resources, Inc., 81
English China Clays Ltd., 15 (upd.); 40 (upd.)
Envirodyne Industries, Inc., 17
Feldmuhle Nobel A.G., III
Fibreboard Corporation, 16

Filtrona plc, 88
Florida Rock Industries, Inc., 46
Foamex International Inc., 17
Formica Corporation, 13
GAF Corporation, 22 (upd.)
The Geon Company, 11
Giant Cement Holding, Inc., 23
Gibraltar Steel Corporation, 37
Granite Rock Company, 26
Groupe Sidel S.A., 21
Harbison-Walker Refractories Company, 24
Harrisons & Crosfield plc, III
Heidelberger Zement AG, 31
Hexcel Corporation, 28
Holderbank Financière Glaris Ltd., III
Holnam Inc., 39 (upd.)
Holt and Bugbee Company, 66
Homasote Company, 72
Howmet Corp., 12
Huttig Building Products, Inc., 73
Ibstock Brick Ltd., 14; 37 (upd.)
Imerys S.A., 40 (upd.)
Imperial Industries, Inc., 81
Internacional de Ceramica, S.A. de C.V., 53
International Shipbreaking Ltd. L.L.C., 67
Joseph T. Ryerson & Son, Inc., 15
Lafarge Coppée S.A., III
Lafarge Corporation, 28
Lehigh Portland Cement Company, 23
Manville Corporation, III; 7 (upd.)
Material Sciences Corporation, 63
Matsushita Electric Works, Ltd., III; 7 (upd.)
McJunkin Corporation, 63
Medusa Corporation, 24
Mitsubishi Materials Corporation, III
Nevamar Company, 82
Nippon Sheet Glass Company, Limited, III
North Pacific Group, Inc., 61
Nuplex Industries Ltd., 92
OmniSource Corporation, 14
Onoda Cement Co., Ltd., III
Otor S.A., 77
Owens-Corning Fiberglass Corporation, III
Pacific Clay Products Inc., 88
Pilkington Group Limited, III; 34 (upd.); 87 (upd.)
Pioneer International Limited, III
PolyOne Corporation, 87 (upd.)
PPG Industries, Inc., III; 22 (upd.); 81 (upd.)
Redland plc, III
Rinker Group Ltd., 65
RMC Group p.l.c., III
Rock of Ages Corporation, 37
Rogers Corporation, 80 (upd.)
Royal Group Technologies Limited, 73
The Rugby Group plc, 31
Schuff Steel Company, 26
Sekisui Chemical Co., Ltd., III; 72 (upd.)
Severstal Joint Stock Company, 65
Shaw Industries, 9
The Sherwin-Williams Company, III; 13 (upd.); 89 (upd.)
The Siam Cement Public Company Limited, 56
SIG plc, 71
Simplex Technologies Inc., 21
Siskin Steel & Supply Company, 70
Solutia Inc., 52
Sommer-Allibert S.A., 19
Southdown, Inc., 14
Spartech Corporation, 19; 76 (upd.)
Ssangyong Cement Industrial Co., Ltd., III; 61 (upd.)
Steel Technologies Inc., 63
Sun Distributors L.P., 12
Symyx Technologies, Inc., 77
Tarmac plc, III, 28 (upd.)
Tilcon-Connecticut Inc., 80
TOTO LTD., III; 28 (upd.)
Toyo Sash Co., Ltd., III
Tuscarora Inc., 29
U.S. Aggregates, Inc., 42
Ube Industries, Ltd., III
United States Steel Corporation, 50 (upd.)
USG Corporation, III; 26 (upd.); 81 (upd.)
Usinas Siderúrgicas de Minas Gerais S.A., 77
Vicat S.A., 70
voestalpine AG, 57 (upd.)
Vulcan Materials Company, 7; 52 (upd.)
Wacker-Chemie GmbH, 35
Walter Industries, Inc., III
Waxman Industries, Inc., 9
Weber et Broutin France, 66
Wienerberger AG, 70
Wolseley plc, 64
ZERO Corporation, 17; 88 (upd.)
Zoltek Companies, Inc., 37

Mining & Metals

A.M. Castle & Co., 25
Acindar Industria Argentina de Aceros S.A., 87
Aggregate Industries plc, 36
Agnico-Eagle Mines Limited, 71
Aktiebolaget SKF, III; 38 (upd.); 89 (upd.)
Alcan Aluminium Limited, IV; 31 (upd.)
Alcoa Inc., 56 (upd.)
Alleghany Corporation, 10
Allegheny Ludlum Corporation, 8
Alliance Resource Partners, L.P., 81
Alrosa Company Ltd., 62
Altos Hornos de México, S.A. de C.V., 42
Aluminum Company of America, IV; 20 (upd.)
AMAX Inc., IV
AMCOL International Corporation, 59 (upd.)
Amsted Industries Incorporated, 7
Anglo American Corporation of South Africa Limited, IV; 16 (upd.)
Anglo American PLC, 50 (upd.)
Aquarius Platinum Ltd., 63
ARBED S.A., IV, 22 (upd.)
Arcelor Gent, 80
Arch Mineral Corporation, 7
Armco Inc., IV
ASARCO Incorporated, IV
Ashanti Goldfields Company Limited, 43
Atchison Casting Corporation, 39
Barrick Gold Corporation, 34
Battle Mountain Gold Company, 23
Benguet Corporation, 58
Bethlehem Steel Corporation, IV; 7 (upd.); 27 (upd.)
BHP Billiton, 67 (upd.)
Birmingham Steel Corporation, 13; 40 (upd.)
Boart Longyear Company, 26
Bodycote International PLC, 63
Boliden AB, 80
Boral Limited, 43 (upd.)
British Coal Corporation, IV
British Steel plc, IV; 19 (upd.)
Broken Hill Proprietary Company Ltd., IV, 22 (upd.)
Brush Engineered Materials Inc., 67
Brush Wellman Inc., 14
Buderus AG, 37
Cameco Corporation, 77
Caparo Group Ltd., 90
Carpenter Technology Corporation, 13
Chaparral Steel Co., 13
China Shenhua Energy Company Limited, 83
Christensen Boyles Corporation, 26
Cleveland-Cliffs Inc., 13; 62 (upd.)
Coal India Ltd., IV; 44 (upd.)
Cockerill Sambre Group, IV; 26 (upd.)
Coeur d'Alene Mines Corporation, 20
Cold Spring Granite Company Inc., 16; 67 (upd.)
Cominco Ltd., 37
Commercial Metals Company, 15; 42 (upd.)
Companhia Siderúrgica Nacional, 76
Companhia Vale do Rio Doce, IV; 43 (upd.)
Compañia de Minas Buenaventura S.A.A., 93
CONSOL Energy Inc., 59
Corporacion Nacional del Cobre de Chile, 40
Corus Group plc, 49 (upd.)
CRA Limited, IV
Cyprus Amax Minerals Company, 21
Cyprus Minerals Company, 7
Daido Steel Co., Ltd., IV
De Beers Consolidated Mines Limited/De Beers Centenary AG, IV; 7 (upd.); 28 (upd.)
Degussa Group, IV
Diavik Diamond Mines Inc., 85
Dofasco Inc., IV; 24 (upd.)
Dynatec Corporation, 87
Earle M. Jorgensen Company, 82
Echo Bay Mines Ltd., IV; 38 (upd.)
Engelhard Corporation, IV
Eramet, 73
Falconbridge Limited, 49
Fansteel Inc., 19
Fluor Corporation, 34 (upd.)
Freeport-McMoRan Copper & Gold, Inc., IV; 7 (upd.); 57 (upd.)
Fried. Krupp GmbH, IV
Gencor Ltd., IV, 22 (upd.)

Geneva Steel, 7
Gerdau S.A., 59
Glamis Gold, Ltd., 54
Gold Fields Ltd., IV; 62 (upd.)
Goldcorp Inc., 87
Grupo Mexico, S.A. de C.V., 40
Gruppo Riva Fire SpA, 88
Handy & Harman, 23
Hanson Building Materials America Inc., 60
Hanson PLC, 30 (upd.)
Harmony Gold Mining Company Limited, 63
Haynes International, Inc., 88
Hecla Mining Company, 20
Hemlo Gold Mines Inc., 9
Heraeus Holding GmbH, IV
Highveld Steel and Vanadium Corporation Limited, 59
Hitachi Metals, Ltd., IV
Hoesch AG, IV
Homestake Mining Company, 12; 38 (upd.)
Horsehead Industries, Inc., 51
The Hudson Bay Mining and Smelting Company, Limited, 12
Hylsamex, S.A. de C.V., 39
IMCO Recycling, Incorporated, 32
Imerys S.A., 40 (upd.)
Imetal S.A., IV
Inco Limited, IV; 45 (upd.)
Industrias Penoles, S.A. de C.V., 22
Inland Steel Industries, Inc., IV; 19 (upd.)
Intermet Corporation, 32
Iscor Limited, 57
Ispat Inland Inc., 30; 40 (upd.)
JFE Shoji Holdings Inc., 88
Johnson Matthey PLC, IV; 16 (upd.)
JSC MMC Norilsk Nickel, 48
Kaiser Aluminum Corporation, IV; 84 (upd.)
Kawasaki Heavy Industries, Ltd., 63 (upd.)
Kawasaki Steel Corporation, IV
Kennecott Corporation, 7; 27 (upd.)
Kentucky Electric Steel, Inc., 31
Kerr-McGee Corporation, 22 (upd.)
Kinross Gold Corporation, 36
Klockner-Werke AG, IV
Kobe Steel, Ltd., IV; 19 (upd.)
Koninklijke Nederlandsche Hoogovens en Staalfabrieken NV, IV
Laclede Steel Company, 15
Layne Christensen Company, 19
Lonmin plc, 66 (upd.)
Lonrho Plc, 21
The LTV Corporation, I; 24 (upd.)
Lukens Inc., 14
Magma Copper Company, 7
The Marmon Group, IV; 16 (upd.)
Massey Energy Company, 57
MAXXAM Inc., 8
Meridian Gold, Incorporated, 47
Metaleurop S.A., 21
Metallgesellschaft AG, IV
Minerals and Metals Trading Corporation of India Ltd., IV
Minerals Technologies Inc., 11; 52 (upd.)
Mitsui Mining & Smelting Co., Ltd., IV
Mitsui Mining Company, Limited, IV
Mueller Industries, Inc., 52 (upd.)
National Steel Corporation, 12
NERCO, Inc., 7
Newmont Mining Corporation, 7
Neyveli Lignite Corporation Ltd., 65
Niagara Corporation, 28
Nichimen Corporation, IV
Nippon Light Metal Company, Ltd., IV
Nippon Steel Corporation, IV; 17 (upd.)
Nisshin Steel Co., Ltd., IV
NKK Corporation, IV; 28 (upd.)
Noranda Inc., IV; 7 (upd.); 64 (upd.)
Norddeutsche Affinerie AG, 62
North Star Steel Company, 18
Nucor Corporation, 7; 21 (upd.); 79 (upd.)
Oglebay Norton Company, 17
Okura & Co., Ltd., IV
Oregon Metallurgical Corporation, 20
Oregon Steel Mills, Inc., 14
Ormet Corporation, 82
Outokumpu Oyj, 38
Park Corp., 22
Peabody Coal Company, 10
Peabody Energy Corporation, 45 (upd.)
Peabody Holding Company, Inc., IV
Pechiney SA, IV; 45 (upd.)
Peter Kiewit Sons' Inc., 8
Phelps Dodge Corporation, IV; 28 (upd.); 75 (upd.)
The Pittston Company, IV; 19 (upd.)
Placer Dome Inc., 20; 61 (upd.)
Pohang Iron and Steel Company Ltd., IV
POSCO, 57 (upd.)
Potash Corporation of Saskatchewan Inc., 18
Quanex Corporation, 13; 62 (upd.)
RAG AG, 35; 60 (upd.)
Reliance Steel & Aluminum Co., 19
Republic Engineered Steels, Inc., 7; 26 (upd.)
Reynolds Metals Company, IV
Rio Tinto PLC, 19 (upd.); 50 (upd.)
RMC Group p.l.c., 34 (upd.)
Roanoke Electric Steel Corporation, 45
Rouge Steel Company, 8
The RTZ Corporation PLC, IV
Ruhrkohle AG, IV
Ryerson Tull, Inc., 40 (upd.)
Saarberg-Konzern, IV
Salzgitter AG, IV
Sandvik AB, IV
Saudi Basic Industries Corporation (SABIC), 58
Schnitzer Steel Industries, Inc., 19
Severstal Joint Stock Company, 65
Shanghai Baosteel Group Corporation, 71
Siderar S.A.I.C., 66
Smorgon Steel Group Ltd., 62
Southern Peru Copper Corporation, 40
Southwire Company, Inc., 8; 23 (upd.)
SSAB Svenskt Stål AB, 89
Steel Authority of India Ltd., IV
Stelco Inc., IV
Stillwater Mining Company, 47
Sumitomo Metal Industries Ltd., IV; 82 (upd.)
Sumitomo Metal Mining Co., Ltd., IV
Tata Iron & Steel Co. Ltd., IV; 44 (upd.)
Teck Corporation, 27
Tenaris SA, 63
Texas Industries, Inc., 8
ThyssenKrupp AG, IV; 28 (upd.); 87 (upd.)
The Timken Company, 8; 42 (upd.)
Titanium Metals Corporation, 21
Tomen Corporation, IV
Total Fina Elf S.A., 50 (upd.)
Třinecké Železárny A.S., 92
U.S. Borax, Inc., 42
Ugine S.A., 20
NV Umicore SA, 47
Universal Stainless & Alloy Products, Inc., 75
Usinor SA, IV; 42 (upd.)
Usinor Sacilor, IV
VIAG Aktiengesellschaft, IV
Voest-Alpine Stahl AG, IV
Volcan Compañia Minera S.A.A., 92
Vulcan Materials Company, 52 (upd.)
Wah Chang, 82
Walter Industries, Inc., 22 (upd.)
Weirton Steel Corporation, IV; 26 (upd.)
Westmoreland Coal Company, 7
Wheeling-Pittsburgh Corp., 7
WMC, Limited, 43
Worthington Industries, Inc., 7; 21 (upd.)
Xstrata PLC, 73
Zambia Industrial and Mining Corporation Ltd., IV
Zinifex Ltd., 85

Paper & Forestry

Abitibi-Consolidated, Inc., IV; 25 (upd.)
Albany International Corporation, 51 (upd.)
Amcor Ltd, IV; 19 (upd.); 78 (upd.)
American Greetings Corporation, 59 (upd.)
American Pad & Paper Company, 20
Aracruz Celulose S.A., 57
Arjo Wiggins Appleton p.l.c., 34
Asplundh Tree Expert Co.,20; 59 (upd.)
Avery Dennison Corporation, IV
Badger Paper Mills, Inc., 15
Beckett Papers, 23
Bemis Company, Inc., 8; 91 (upd.)
Blue Heron Paper Company, 90
Bohemia, Inc., 13
Boise Cascade Corporation, IV; 8 (upd.); 32 (upd.)
Bowater PLC, IV
Bunzl plc, IV
Canfor Corporation, 42
Caraustar Industries, Inc., 19; 44 (upd.)
Carter Lumber Company, 45
Cascades Inc., 71
Champion International Corporation, IV; 20 (upd.)
Chesapeake Corporation, 8; 30 (upd.); 93 (upd.)
Consolidated Papers, Inc., 8; 36 (upd.)
Crane & Co., Inc., 26

Crown Vantage Inc., 29
CSS Industries, Inc., 35
Daio Paper Corporation, IV; 84 (upd.)
Daishowa Paper Manufacturing Co., Ltd., IV; 57 (upd.)
Deltic Timber Corporation, 46
Dillard Paper Company, 11
Doman Industries Limited, 59
Domtar Corporation, IV; 89 (upd.)
DS Smith Plc, 61
Empresas CMPC S.A., 70
Enso-Gutzeit Oy, IV
Esselte Pendaflex Corporation, 11
Federal Paper Board Company, Inc., 8
FiberMark, Inc., 37
Fletcher Challenge Ltd., IV
Fort Howard Corporation, 8
Fort James Corporation, 22 (upd.)
Georgia-Pacific Corporation, IV; 9 (upd.); 47 (upd.)
Gould Paper Corporation, 82
Groupe Rougier SA, 21
Grupo Portucel Soporcel, 60
Guilbert S.A., 42
Hampton Affiliates, Inc., 77
Holmen AB, 52 (upd.)
Honshu Paper Co., Ltd., IV
International Paper Company, IV; 15 (upd.); 47 (upd.)
James River Corporation of Virginia, IV
Japan Pulp and Paper Company Limited, IV
Jefferson Smurfit Group plc, IV; 49 (upd.)
Jujo Paper Co., Ltd., IV
Kimberly-Clark Corporation, 16 (upd.); 43 (upd.)
Kimberly-Clark de México, S.A. de C.V., 54
Klabin S.A., 73
Kruger Inc., 17
Kymmene Corporation, IV
Longview Fibre Company, 8; 37 (upd.)
Louisiana-Pacific Corporation, IV; 31 (upd.)
M-real Oyj, 56 (upd.)
MacMillan Bloedel Limited, IV
Matussière et Forest SA, 58
The Mead Corporation, IV; 19 (upd.)
MeadWestvaco Corporation, 76 (upd.)
Mercer International Inc., 64
Metsa-Serla Oy, IV
Metso Corporation, 30 (upd.); 85 (upd.)
Miquel y Costas Miquel S.A., 68
Mo och Domsjö AB, IV
Monadnock Paper Mills, Inc., 21
Mosinee Paper Corporation, 15
Nashua Corporation, 8
National Envelope Corporation, 32
NCH Corporation, 8
Norske Skogindustrier ASA, 63
Oji Paper Co., Ltd., IV
P.H. Glatfelter Company, 8; 30 (upd.); 83 (upd.)
Packaging Corporation of America, 12
Papeteries de Lancey, 23
Plum Creek Timber Company, Inc., 43
Pope & Talbot, Inc., 12; 61 (upd.)
Pope Resources LP, 74
Potlatch Corporation, 8; 34 (upd.); 87 (upd.)
PWA Group, IV
Rayonier Inc., 24
Rengo Co., Ltd., IV
Reno de Medici S.p.A., 41
Rexam PLC, 32 (upd.); 85 (upd.)
Riverwood International Corporation, 11; 48 (upd.)
Rock-Tenn Company, 13; 59 (upd.)
Rogers Corporation, 61
St. Joe Paper Company, 8
Sanyo-Kokusaku Pulp Co., Ltd., IV
Sappi Limited, 49
Schweitzer-Mauduit International, Inc., 52
Scott Paper Company, IV; 31 (upd.)
Sealed Air Corporation, 14
Sierra Pacific Industries, 22; 90 (upd.)
Simpson Investment Company, 17
Smurfit-Stone Container Corporation, 83 (upd.)
Sonoco Products Company, 8; 89 (upd.)
Specialty Coatings Inc., 8
Stimson Lumber Company 78
Stone Container Corporation, IV
Stora Enso Oyj, IV; 36 (upd.); 85 (upd.)
Svenska Cellulosa Aktiebolaget SCA, IV; 28 (upd.); 85 (upd.)
Sveaskog AB, 93
Tapemark Company Inc., 64
Tembec Inc., 66
Temple-Inland Inc., IV; 31 (upd.)
Thomsen Greenhouses and Garden Center, Incorporated, 65
TJ International, Inc., 19
U.S. Timberlands Company, L.P., 42
Union Camp Corporation, IV
United Paper Mills Ltd. (Yhtyneet Paperitehtaat Oy), IV
Universal Forest Products, Inc., 10; 59 (upd.)
UPM-Kymmene Corporation, 19; 50 (upd.)
Wausau-Mosinee Paper Corporation, 60 (upd.)
West Fraser Timber Co. Ltd., 17; 91 (upd.)
West Linn Paper Company, 91
Westvaco Corporation, IV; 19 (upd.)
Weyerhaeuser Company, IV; 9 (upd.); 28 (upd.); 83 (upd.)
Wickes Inc., 25 (upd.)
Willamette Industries, Inc., IV; 31 (upd.)
WTD Industries, Inc., 20

Personal Services

AARP, 27
ABC Learning Centres Ltd., 93
ADT Security Services, Inc., 12; 44 (upd.)
Africare, 59
Alderwoods Group, Inc., 68 (upd.)
Ambassadors International, Inc., 68 (upd.)
American Civil Liberties Union (ACLU), 60
American Management Association, 76
American Retirement Corporation, 42
American Society for the Prevention of Cruelty to Animals (ASPCA), 68
AmeriCares Foundation, Inc., 87
Arthur Murray International, Inc., 32
Association of Junior Leagues International Inc., 60
Benesse Corporation, 76
Berlitz International, Inc., 39 (upd.)
Big Brothers Big Sisters of America, 85
Blackwater USA, 76
Bonhams 1793 Ltd., 72
Boys & Girls Clubs of America, 69
The Brickman Group, Ltd., 87
The Brink's Company, 58 (upd.)
Brother's Brother Foundation, 93
CareerBuilder, Inc., 93
Caritas Internationalis, 72
Carriage Services, Inc., 37
Catholic Charities USA, 76
CDI Corporation, 6; 54 (upd.)
CeWe Color Holding AG, 76
ChildrenFirst, Inc., 59
Childtime Learning Centers, Inc., 34
Chubb, PLC, 50
Corinthian Colleges, Inc., 39; 92 (upd.)
Correctional Services Corporation, 30
Correos y Telegrafos S.A., 80
Council on International Educational Exchange Inc., 81
CUC International Inc., 16
Curves International, Inc., 54
Cystic Fibrosis Foundation, 93
Davis Service Group PLC, 45
DeVry Inc., 29; 82 (upd.)
Educational Testing Service, 12; 62 (upd.)
eHarmony.com Inc., 71
Feed The Children, Inc., 68
Food For The Poor, Inc., 77
The Ford Foundation, 34
Franklin Quest Co., 11
Gold's Gym International, Inc., 71
Goodwill Industries International, Inc., 16; 66 (upd.)
GP Strategies Corporation, 64 (upd.)
Greenpeace International, 74
Greg Manning Auctions, Inc., 60
Gunnebo AB, 53
Hair Club For Men Ltd., 90
Herbalife Ltd., 17; 41 (upd.); 92 (upd.)
The Humane Society of the United States, 54
Huntington Learning Centers, Inc., 55
Imperial Parking Corporation, 58
Initial Security, 64
Jazzercise, Inc., 45
The John D. and Catherine T. MacArthur Foundation, 34
Kaplan, Inc., 42; 90 (upd.)
KinderCare Learning Centers, Inc., 13
Knowledge Learning Corporation, 51
Kumon Institute of Education Co., Ltd., 72
Labor Ready, Inc., 29; 88 (upd.)
Learning Care Group, Inc., 76 (upd.)
Lifetouch Inc., 86
The Loewen Group Inc., 16; 40 (upd.)
LPA Holding Corporation, 81
Mace Security International, Inc., 57
Management and Training Corporation, 28

Manpower, Inc., 9
Martin Franchises, Inc., 80
Match.com, LP, 87
Michael Page International plc, 45
Mothers Against Drunk Driving (MADD), 51
National Heritage Academies, Inc., 60
National Organization for Women, Inc., 55
Nobel Learning Communities, Inc., 37; 76 (upd.)
Oxfam GB, 87
Prison Rehabilitative Industries and Diversified Enterprises, Inc. (PRIDE), 53
Recording for the Blind & Dyslexic, 51
Regis Corporation, 18; 70 (upd.)
Robert Half International Inc., 70 (upd.)
The Rockefeller Foundation, 34
Rollins, Inc., 11
Rosenbluth International Inc., 14
Rosetta Stone Inc., 93
Rotary International, 31
The Salvation Army USA, 32
Screen Actors Guild, 72
Service Corporation International, 6; 51 (upd.)
The ServiceMaster Company, 68 (upd.)
SOS Staffing Services, 25
Spark Networks, Inc., 91
Special Olympics, Inc., 93
SR Teleperformance S.A., 86
Stewart Enterprises, Inc., 20
Supercuts Inc., 26
24 Hour Fitness Worldwide, Inc., 71
UAW (International Union, United Automobile, Aerospace and Agricultural Implement Workers of America), 72
United Negro College Fund, Inc., 79
United Service Organizations, 60
Weight Watchers International Inc., 12; 33 (upd.); 73 (upd.)
The York Group, Inc., 50
Youth Services International, Inc., 21
YWCA of the U.S.A., 45
World Vision International, Inc., 93

Petroleum

Abraxas Petroleum Corporation, 89
Abu Dhabi National Oil Company, IV; 45 (upd.)
Aegean Marine Petroleum Network Inc., 89
Agway, Inc., 21 (upd.)
Alberta Energy Company Ltd., 16; 43 (upd.)
Amerada Hess Corporation, IV; 21 (upd.); 55 (upd.)
Amoco Corporation, IV; 14 (upd.)
Anadarko Petroleum Corporation, 10; 52 (upd.)
ANR Pipeline Co., 17
Anschutz Corp., 12
Apache Corporation, 10; 32 (upd.); 89 (upd.)
Aral AG, 62
Arctic Slope Regional Corporation, 38
Ashland Inc., 19; 50 (upd.)
Ashland Oil, Inc., IV
Atlantic Richfield Company, IV; 31 (upd.)
Aventine Renewable Energy Holdings, Inc., 89
Badger State Ethanol, LLC, 83
Baker Hughes Incorporated, 22 (upd.); 57 (upd.)
Belco Oil & Gas Corp., 40
Benton Oil and Gas Company, 47
Berry Petroleum Company, 47
BHP Billiton, 67 (upd.)
Bill Barrett Corporation, 71
BJ Services Company, 25
Blue Rhino Corporation, 56
Boardwalk Pipeline Partners, LP, 87
Boots & Coots International Well Control, Inc., 79
BP p.l.c., 45 (upd.)
Brigham Exploration Company, 75
The British Petroleum Company plc, IV; 7 (upd.); 21 (upd.)
British-Borneo Oil & Gas PLC, 34
Broken Hill Proprietary Company Ltd., 22 (upd.)
Bronco Drilling Company, Inc., 89
Burlington Resources Inc., 10
Burmah Castrol PLC, IV; 30 (upd.)
Callon Petroleum Company, 47
Caltex Petroleum Corporation, 19
ChevronTexaco Corporation, IV; 19 (upd.); 47 (upd.)
Chiles Offshore Corporation, 9
Cimarex Energy Co., 81
China National Petroleum Corporation, 46
Chinese Petroleum Corporation, IV; 31 (upd.)
CITGO Petroleum Corporation, IV; 31 (upd.)
Clayton Williams Energy, Inc., 87
The Coastal Corporation, IV; 31 (upd.)
Compañia Española de Petróleos S.A. (Cepsa), IV; 56 (upd.)
Comstock Resources, Inc., 47
Conoco Inc., IV; 16 (upd.)
ConocoPhillips, 63 (upd.)
CONSOL Energy Inc., 59
Continental Resources, Inc., 89
Cooper Cameron Corporation, 20 (upd.)
Cosmo Oil Co., Ltd., IV; 53 (upd.)
Crown Central Petroleum Corporation, 7
DeepTech International Inc., 21
Den Norse Stats Oljeselskap AS, IV
Denbury Resources, Inc., 67
Deutsche BP Aktiengesellschaft, 7
Devon Energy Corporation, 61
Diamond Shamrock, Inc., IV
Distrigaz S.A., 82
Dril-Quip, Inc., 81
Duvernay Oil Corp., 83
Dynegy Inc., 49 (upd.)
E.On AG, 50 (upd.)
Edge Petroleum Corporation, 67
Egyptian General Petroleum Corporation, IV; 51 (upd.)
El Paso Corporation, 66 (upd.)
Elf Aquitaine SA, 21 (upd.)
Empresa Colombiana de Petróleos, IV
Enbridge Inc., 43
Encore Acquisition Company, 73
Energen Corporation, 21
ENI S.p.A., 69 (upd.)
Enron Corporation, 19
ENSCO International Incorporated, 57
Ente Nazionale Idrocarburi, IV
Enterprise Oil PLC, 11; 50 (upd.)
Entreprise Nationale Sonatrach, IV
Equitable Resources, Inc., 54 (upd.)
Exxon Corporation, IV; 7 (upd.); 32 (upd.)
Exxon Mobil Corporation, 67 (upd.)
Ferrellgas Partners, L.P., 35
FINA, Inc., 7
Flying J Inc., 19
Flotek Industries Inc., 93
Forest Oil Corporation, 19; 91 (upd.)
OAO Gazprom, 42
General Sekiyu K.K., IV
Giant Industries, Inc., 19; 61 (upd.)
Global Industries, Ltd., 37
Global Marine Inc., 9
GlobalSantaFe Corporation, 48 (upd.)
Grey Wolf, Inc., 43
Halliburton Company, 25 (upd.); 55 (upd.)
Hanover Compressor Company, 59
Hawkeye Holdings LLC, 89
Helix Energy Solutions Group, Inc., 81
Hellenic Petroleum SA, 64
Helmerich & Payne, Inc., 18
Holly Corporation, 12
Hunt Consolidated, Inc., 7; 27 (upd.)
Hunting plc 78
Hurricane Hydrocarbons Ltd., 54
Husky Energy Inc., 47
Idemitsu Kosan Co., Ltd., 49 (upd.)
Idemitsu Kosan K.K., IV
Imperial Oil Limited, IV; 25 (upd.)
Indian Oil Corporation Ltd., IV; 48 (upd.)
Input/Output, Inc., 73
Iogen Corporation, 81
Ipiranga S.A., 67
Kanematsu Corporation, IV
Kerr-McGee Corporation, IV; 22 (upd.); 68 (upd.)
Kinder Morgan, Inc., 45
King Ranch, Inc., 14
Koch Industries, Inc., IV; 20 (upd.), 77 (upd.)
Koppers Industries, Inc., 26 (upd.)
Kuwait Petroleum Corporation, IV; 55 (upd.)
Libyan National Oil Corporation, IV
The Louisiana Land and Exploration Company, 7
OAO LUKOIL, 40
Lyondell Petrochemical Company, IV
MAPCO Inc., IV
Maxus Energy Corporation, 7
McDermott International, Inc., 37 (upd.)
Meteor Industries Inc., 33
Mitchell Energy and Development Corporation, 7
Mitsubishi Oil Co., Ltd., IV

Mobil Corporation, IV; 7 (upd.); 21 (upd.)
MOL Rt, 70
Murphy Oil Corporation, 7; 32 (upd.)
Nabors Industries Ltd., 9; 91 (upd.)
National Iranian Oil Company, IV; 61 (upd.)
National Oil Corporation, 66 (upd.)
Neste Oil Corporation, IV; 85 (upd.)
Newfield Exploration Company, 65
Nexen Inc., 79
NGC Corporation, 18
Nigerian National Petroleum Corporation, IV; 72 (upd.)
Nippon Oil Corporation, IV; 63 (upd.)
OAO NK YUKOS, 47
Noble Affiliates, Inc., 11
Occidental Petroleum Corporation, IV; 25 (upd.); 71 (upd.)
Odebrecht S.A., 73
Oil and Natural Gas Corporation Ltd., IV; 90 (upd.)
Oil States International, Inc., 77
ÖMV Aktiengesellschaft, IV
Oryx Energy Company, 7
Pacific Ethanol, Inc., 81
Pakistan State Oil Company Ltd., 81
Paramount Resources Ltd., 87
Parker Drilling Company, 28
Patina Oil & Gas Corporation, 24
Patterson-UTI Energy, Inc., 55
Penn Virginia Corporation, 85
Pennzoil-Quaker State Company, IV; 20 (upd.); 50 (upd.)
Pertamina, IV; 56 (upd.)
Petro-Canada Limited, IV
Petrobras Energia Participaciones S.A., 72
PetroFina S.A., IV; 26 (upd.)
Petrohawk Energy Corporation, 79
Petróleo Brasileiro S.A., IV
Petróleos de Portugal S.A., IV
Petróleos de Venezuela S.A., IV; 74 (upd.)
Petróleos del Ecuador, IV
Petróleos Mexicanos, IV; 19 (upd.)
Petroleum Development Oman LLC, IV
Petroliam Nasional Bhd (Petronas), IV; 56 (upd.)
Petron Corporation, 58
Phillips Petroleum Company, IV; 40 (upd.)
Pioneer Natural Resources Company, 59
Pogo Producing Company, 39
Polski Koncern Naftowy ORLEN S.A., 77
Premcor Inc., 37
Pride International Inc. 78
PTT Public Company Ltd., 56
Qatar General Petroleum Corporation, IV
Quaker State Corporation, 7; 21 (upd.)
Range Resources Corporation, 45
Reliance Industries Ltd., 81
Repsol-YPF S.A., IV; 16 (upd.); 40 (upd.)
Resource America, Inc., 42
Rowan Companies, Inc., 43
Royal Dutch/Shell Group, IV; 49 (upd.)
RPC, Inc., 91
RWE AG, 50 (upd.)
St. Mary Land & Exploration Company, 63
Santa Fe International Corporation, 38
Santos Ltd., 81
Sasol Limited, IV; 47 (upd.)
Saudi Arabian Oil Company, IV; 17 (upd.); 50 (upd.)
Schlumberger Limited, 17 (upd.); 59 (upd.)
Seagull Energy Corporation, 11
Seitel, Inc., 47
Shanghai Petrochemical Co., Ltd., 18
Shell Oil Company, IV; 14 (upd.); 41 (upd.)
Showa Shell Sekiyu K.K., IV; 59 (upd.)
OAO Siberian Oil Company (Sibneft), 49
Smith International, Inc., 59 (upd.)
Société Nationale Elf Aquitaine, IV; 7 (upd.)
Sonatrach, 65 (upd.)
Spinnaker Exploration Company, 72
Statoil ASA, 61 (upd.)
Suburban Propane Partners, L.P., 30
Sun Company, Inc., IV
Suncor Energy Inc., 54
Sunoco, Inc., 28 (upd.); 83 (upd.)
Superior Energy Services, Inc., 65
OAO Surgutneftegaz, 48
Swift Energy Company, 63
Talisman Energy Inc., 9; 47 (upd.)
OAO Tatneft, 45
TEPPCO Partners, L.P., 73
Tesoro Petroleum Corporation, 7; 45 (upd.)
Texaco Inc., IV; 14 (upd.); 41 (upd.)
Tidewater Inc., 37 (upd.)
TODCO, 87
Tom Brown, Inc., 37
Tonen Corporation, IV; 16 (upd.)
TonenGeneral Sekiyu K.K., 54 (upd.)
Tosco Corporation, 7
TOTAL S.A., IV; 24 (upd.)
TransCanada Corporation, 93 (upd.)
TransMontaigne Inc., 28
Oil Transporting Joint Stock Company Transneft, 93
Transocean Sedco Forex Inc., 45
Travel Ports of America, Inc., 17
Triton Energy Corporation, 11
Tullow Oil plc, 83
Türkiye Petrolleri Anonim Ortakliği, IV
Ultra Petroleum Corporation, 71
Ultramar Diamond Shamrock Corporation, IV; 31 (upd.)
Union Texas Petroleum Holdings, Inc., 9
Unit Corporation, 63
Universal Compression, Inc., 59
Unocal Corporation, IV; 24 (upd.); 71 (upd.)
USX Corporation, IV; 7 (upd.)
Valero Energy Corporation, 7; 71 (upd.)
Valley National Gases, Inc., 85
Varco International, Inc., 42
Vastar Resources, Inc., 24
VeraSun Energy Corporation, 87
Vintage Petroleum, Inc., 42
Wascana Energy Inc., 13
Weatherford International, Inc., 39
Webber Oil Company, 61
Western Atlas Inc., 12
Western Company of North America, 15
Western Gas Resources, Inc., 45
Western Oil Sands Inc., 85
Westport Resources Corporation, 63
Whiting Petroleum Corporation, 81
The Williams Companies, Inc., IV; 31 (upd.)
World Fuel Services Corporation, 47
XTO Energy Inc., 52
YPF Sociedad Anonima, IV

Publishing & Printing

A.B.Dick Company, 28
A.H. Belo Corporation, 10; 30 (upd.)
AccuWeather, Inc., 73
Advance Publications Inc., IV; 19 (upd.)
Advanced Marketing Services, Inc., 34
Advanstar Communications, Inc., 57
Affiliated Publications, Inc., 7
Agence France-Presse, 34
Agora S.A. Group, 77
Aljazeera Satellite Channel, 79
American Banknote Corporation, 30
American Girl, Inc., 69
American Greetings Corporation, 7, 22 (upd.)
American Media, Inc., 27; 82 (upd.)
American Printing House for the Blind, 26
American Reprographics Company, 75
Andrews McMeel Universal, 40
The Antioch Company, 40
AOL Time Warner Inc., 57 (upd.)
Arandell Corporation, 37
Archie Comics Publications, Inc., 63
Arnoldo Mondadori Editore S.p.A., IV; 19 (upd.); 54 (upd.)
The Associated Press, 31 (upd.); 73 (upd.)
The Atlantic Group, 23
Audible Inc., 79
Axel Springer Verlag AG, IV; 20 (upd.)
Banta Corporation, 12; 32 (upd.); 79 (upd.)
Bauer Publishing Group, 7
Bayard SA, 49
Berlitz International, Inc., 13
Bernard C. Harris Publishing Company, Inc., 39
Bertelsmann A.G., IV; 15 (upd.); 43 (upd.); 91 (upd.)
Bibliographisches Institut & F.A. Brockhaus AG, 74
Big Flower Press Holdings, Inc., 21
Blackwell Publishing Ltd. 78
Blue Mountain Arts, Inc., 29
Bobit Publishing Company, 55
Bonnier AB, 52
Book-of-the-Month Club, Inc., 13
Bowne & Co., Inc., 23; 79 (upd.)
Broderbund Software, 13; 29 (upd.)
Brown Printing Company, 26
Burda Holding GmbH. & Co., 23
The Bureau of National Affairs, Inc., 23
Butterick Co., Inc., 23
Cadmus Communications Corporation, 23
Cahners Business Information, 43

Carl Allers Etablissement A/S, 72
Carus Publishing Company, 93
CCH Inc., 14
Central Newspapers, Inc., 10
Champion Industries, Inc., 28
Cherry Lane Music Publishing Company, Inc., 62
Chicago Review Press Inc., 84
ChoicePoint Inc., 65
The Christian Science Publishing Society, 55
The Chronicle Publishing Company, Inc., 23
Chrysalis Group plc, 40
CMP Media Inc., 26
Commerce Clearing House, Inc., 7
Community Newspaper Holdings, Inc., 91
Concepts Direct, Inc., 39
Condé Nast Publications, Inc., 13; 59 (upd.)
Consolidated Graphics, Inc., 70
Consumers Union, 26
The Copley Press, Inc., 23
Cornelsen Verlagsholding GmbH & Co., 90
Courier Corporation, 41
Cowles Media Company, 23
Cox Enterprises, Inc., IV; 22 (upd.)
Crain Communications, Inc., 12; 35 (upd.)
Current, Inc., 37
Cygnus Business Media, Inc., 56
Dai Nippon Printing Co., Ltd., IV; 57 (upd.)
Daily Mail and General Trust plc, 19
Dawson Holdings PLC, 43
Day Runner, Inc., 14
DC Comics Inc., 25
De La Rue plc, 10; 34 (upd.)
DeLorme Publishing Company, Inc., 53
Deluxe Corporation, 7; 22 (upd.); 73 (upd.)
Dennis Publishing Ltd., 62
Dex Media, Inc., 65
Donruss Playoff L.P., 66
Dorling Kindersley Holdings plc, 20
Dover Publications Inc., 34
Dow Jones & Company, Inc., IV; 19 (upd.); 47 (upd.)
The Dun & Bradstreet Corporation, IV; 19 (upd.)
Duplex Products Inc., 17
The E.W. Scripps Company, IV; 7 (upd.); 28 (upd.); 66 (upd.)
Eagle-Tribune Publishing Co., 91
The Economist Group Ltd., 67
Edipresse S.A., 82
Éditions Gallimard, 72
Editis S.A. 78
Edmark Corporation, 14
Edwards Brothers, Inc., 92
Egmont Group, 93
Electronics for Imaging, Inc., 43 (upd.)
Elsevier N.V., IV
EMAP plc, 35
EMI Group plc, 22 (upd.); 81 (upd.)
Encyclopaedia Britannica, Inc., 7; 39 (upd.)
Engraph, Inc., 12
Enquirer/Star Group, Inc., 10
Entravision Communications Corporation, 41
Essence Communications, Inc., 24
F&W Publications, Inc., 71
Farm Journal Corporation, 42
Farrar, Straus and Giroux Inc., 15
Flint Ink Corporation, 13
Follett Corporation, 12; 39 (upd.)
Forbes Inc., 30; 82 (upd.)
Frankfurter Allgemeine Zeitung GmbH, 66
Franklin Electronic Publishers, Inc., 23
Freedom Communications, Inc., 36
G A Pindar & Son Ltd., 88
Gannett Company, Inc., IV; 7 (upd.); 30 (upd.); 66 (upd.)
GateHouse Media, Inc., 91
Geiger Bros., 60
Gibson Greetings, Inc., 12
Giesecke & Devrient GmbH, 83
Golden Books Family Entertainment, Inc., 28
Goss Holdings, Inc., 43
Graphic Industries Inc., 25
Gray Communications Systems, Inc., 24
Grolier Incorporated, 16; 43 (upd.)
Groupe de la Cite, IV
Groupe Les Echos, 25
Grupo Clarín S.A., 67
Grupo Televisa, S.A., 54 (upd.)
Guardian Media Group plc, 53
The H.W. Wilson Company, 66
Hachette, IV
Hachette Filipacchi Medias S.A., 21
Haights Cross Communications, Inc., 84
Hallmark Cards, Inc., IV; 16 (upd.); 40 (upd.); 87 (upd.)
Harcourt Brace and Co., 12
Harcourt Brace Jovanovich, Inc., IV
Harcourt General, Inc., 20 (upd.)
Harlequin Enterprises Limited, 52
HarperCollins Publishers, 15
Harris Interactive Inc., 41; 92 (upd.)
Harry N. Abrams, Inc., 58
Harte-Hanks Communications, Inc., 17
Havas SA, 10; 33 (upd.)
Hay House, Inc., 93
Haynes Publishing Group P.L.C., 71
Hazelden Foundation, 28
Health Communications, Inc., 72
The Hearst Corporation, IV; 19 (upd.); 46 (upd.)
Her Majesty's Stationery Office, 7
Herald Media, Inc., 91
N.V. Holdingmaatschappij De Telegraaf, 23
Hollinger International Inc., 24; 62 (upd.)
HOP, LLC, 80
Houghton Mifflin Company, 10; 36 (upd.)
IDG Books Worldwide, Inc., 27
IHS Inc. 78
Independent News & Media PLC, 61
Informa Group plc, 58
Information Holdings Inc., 47
International Data Group, Inc., 7; 25 (upd.)
IPC Magazines Limited, 7
J.J. Keller & Associates, Inc., 81
Jeppesen Sanderson, Inc., 92
John Fairfax Holdings Limited, 7
John H. Harland Company, 17
John Wiley & Sons, Inc., 17; 65 (upd.)
Johnson Publishing Company, Inc., 28; 72 (upd.)
Johnston Press plc, 35
Jostens, Inc., 25 (upd.); 73 (upd.)
Journal Communications, Inc., 86
Journal Register Company, 29
Jupitermedia Corporation, 75
Kaplan, Inc., 42
Kelley Blue Book Company, Inc., 84
Kensington Publishing Corporation, 84
Kinko's, Inc., 43 (upd.)
Knight Ridder, Inc., 67 (upd.)
Knight-Ridder, Inc., IV; 15 (upd.)
The Knot, Inc., 74
Kodansha Ltd., IV; 38 (upd.)
Krause Publications, Inc., 35
Landmark Communications, Inc., 12; 55 (upd.)
Larry Flynt Publishing Inc., 31
Le Monde S.A., 33
Lebhar-Friedman, Inc., 55
Lee Enterprises Inc., 11; 64 (upd.)
LEXIS-NEXIS Group, 33
Lonely Planet Publications Pty Ltd., 55
M. DuMont Schauberg GmbH & Co. KG, 92
M. Shanken Communications, Inc., 50
Maclean Hunter Publishing Limited, IV; 26 (upd.)
Macmillan, Inc., 7
Martha Stewart Living Omnimedia, Inc., 24; 73 (upd.)
Marvel Entertainment Inc., 10; 78 (upd.)
Matra-Hachette S.A., 15 (upd.)
Maxwell Communication Corporation plc, IV; 7 (upd.)
The McClatchy Company, 23; 92 (upd.)
The McGraw-Hill Companies, Inc., IV; 18 (upd.); 51 (upd.)
Mecklermedia Corporation, 24
Media General, Inc., 38 (upd.)
MediaNews Group, Inc., 70
Menasha Corporation, 59 (upd.)
Meredith Corporation, 11; 29 (upd.); 74 (upd.)
Merriam-Webster Inc., 70
Merrill Corporation, 18; 47 (upd.)
Metro International S.A., 93
Miami Herald Media Company, 92
Miller Publishing Group, LLC, 57
The Miner Group International, 22
Mirror Group Newspapers plc, 7; 23 (upd.)
Moore Corporation Limited, IV
Morris Communications Corporation, 36
Mrs. Grossman's Paper Company Inc., 84
Multimedia, Inc., 11
MYOB Ltd., 86
Naspers Ltd., 66

National Audubon Society, 26
National Geographic Society, 9; 30 (upd.); 79 (upd.)
National Journal Group Inc., 67
New Times, Inc., 45
New York Daily News, 32
The New York Times Company, IV; 19 (upd.); 61 (upd.)
News America Publishing Inc., 12
News Corporation Limited, IV; 7 (upd.)
Newsquest plc, 32
Next Media Ltd., 61
Nihon Keizai Shimbun, Inc., IV
Nolo.com, Inc., 49
Northern and Shell Network plc, 87
Oji Paper Co., Ltd., 57 (upd.)
Onion, Inc., 69
Ottaway Newspapers, Inc., 15
Outlook Group Corporation, 37
PagesJaunes Groupe SA, 79
Pantone Inc., 53
PCM Uitgevers NV, 53
Pearson plc, IV; 46 (upd.)
PennWell Corporation, 55
Penton Media, Inc., 27
The Perseus Books Group, 91
Petersen Publishing Company, 21
Philadelphia Media Holdings LLC, 92
The Phoenix Media/Communications Group, 91
Plain Dealer Publishing Company, 92
Plato Learning, Inc., 44
Playboy Enterprises, Inc., 18
Pleasant Company, 27
PMP Ltd., 72
PR Newswire, 35
Primedia Inc., 22
The Providence Journal Company, 28
Publishers Group, Inc., 35
Publishing and Broadcasting Limited, 54
Pulitzer Inc., 15; 58 (upd.)
Quad/Graphics, Inc., 19
Quebecor Inc., 12; 47 (upd.)
R.L. Polk & Co., 10
R.R. Donnelley & Sons Company, IV; 9 (upd.); 38 (upd.)
Rand McNally & Company, 28
Random House Inc., 13; 31 (upd.)
Ravensburger AG, 64
The Reader's Digest Association, Inc., IV; 17 (upd.); 71 (upd.)
Real Times, Inc., 66
Recycled Paper Greetings, Inc., 21
Reed Elsevier plc, IV; 17 (upd.); 31 (upd.)
Reuters Group PLC, IV; 22 (upd.); 63 (upd.)
Rodale, Inc., 23; 47 (upd.)
Rogers Communications Inc., 30 (upd.)
Rural Press Ltd., 74
St Ives plc, 34
Sanborn Map Company Inc., 82
SanomaWSOY Corporation, 51
Schawk, Inc., 24
Schibsted ASA, 31
Scholastic Corporation, 10; 29 (upd.)
Scott Fetzer Company, 12; 80 (upd.)
Scottish Media Group plc, 32
Seat Pagine Gialle S.p.A., 47
Seattle Times Company, 15
The Sheridan Group, Inc., 86
The Sierra Club, 28
Simon & Schuster Inc., IV; 19 (upd.)
Singapore Press Holdings Limited, 85
Sir Speedy, Inc., 16
SkyMall, Inc., 26
Société du Figaro S.A., 60
Softbank Corp., 13
The Source Enterprises, Inc., 65
Southam Inc., 7
SPIEGEL-Verlag Rudolf Augstein GmbH & Co. KG, 44
The Standard Register Company, 15; 93 (upd.)
Stephens Media, LLC, 91
Strine Printing Company Inc., 88
Sunrise Greetings, 88
Tamedia AG, 53
Taylor & Francis Group plc, 44
Taylor Corporation, 36
Taylor Publishing Company, 12; 36 (upd.)
TechBooks Inc., 84
Thomas Crosbie Holdings Limited, 81
Thomas Nelson, Inc., 14; 38 (upd.)
Thomas Publishing Company, 26
The Thomson Corporation, 8; 34 (upd.); 77 (upd.)
Time Out Group Ltd., 68
The Times Mirror Company, IV; 17 (upd.)
Tohan Corporation, 84
TOKYOPOP Inc., 79
Tom Doherty Associates Inc., 25
Toppan Printing Co., Ltd., IV; 58 (upd.)
The Topps Company, Inc., 13; 34 (upd.); 83 (upd.)
Torstar Corporation, 29
Trader Classified Media N.V., 57
Tribune Company, IV, 22 (upd.); 63 (upd.)
Trinity Mirror plc, 49 (upd.)
Tuttle Publishing, 86
Tyndale House Publishers, Inc., 57
U.S. News & World Report Inc., 30; 89 (upd.)
United Business Media plc, 52 (upd.)
United News & Media plc, IV; 28 (upd.)
United Press International, Inc., 25; 73 (upd.)
The University of Chicago Press, 79
Valassis Communications, Inc., 8
Value Line, Inc., 16; 73 (upd.)
Vance Publishing Corporation, 64
Verlagsgruppe Georg von Holtzbrinck GmbH, 35
Village Voice Media, Inc., 38
VistaPrint Limited, 87
VNU N.V., 27
Volt Information Sciences Inc., 26
W.W. Norton & Company, Inc., 28
Wallace Computer Services, Inc., 36
Walsworth Publishing Co. 78
The Washington Post Company, IV; 20 (upd.)
Waverly, Inc., 16
WAZ Media Group, 82
Wegener NV, 53
Wenner Media, Inc., 32
West Group, 7; 34 (upd.)
Western Publishing Group, Inc., 13
WH Smith PLC, V; 42 (upd.)
William Reed Publishing Ltd. 78
Wolters Kluwer NV, 14; 33 (upd.)
Workman Publishing Company, Inc., 70
World Book, Inc., 12
World Color Press Inc., 12
World Publications, LLC, 65
Xeikon NV, 26
Yell Group PLC, 79
Zebra Technologies Corporation, 14
Ziff Davis Media Inc., 12; 36 (upd.); 73 (upd.)
Zondervan Corporation, 24; 71 (upd.)

Real Estate

Akerys S.A., 90
Alexander's, Inc., 45
Alico, Inc., 63
AMB Property Corporation, 57
American Campus Communities, Inc., 85
Amfac/JMB Hawaii L.L.C., 24 (upd.)
Apartment Investment and Management Company, 49
Archstone-Smith Trust, 49
Associated Estates Realty Corporation, 25
AvalonBay Communities, Inc., 58
Baird & Warner Holding Company, 87
Berkshire Realty Holdings, L.P., 49
Bluegreen Corporation, 80
Boston Properties, Inc., 22
Bramalea Ltd., 9
British Land Plc, 54
Brookfield Properties Corporation, 89
Burroughs & Chapin Company, Inc., 86
Camden Property Trust, 77
Canary Wharf Group Plc, 30
CapStar Hotel Company, 21
CarrAmerica Realty Corporation, 56
Castle & Cooke, Inc., 20 (upd.)
Catellus Development Corporation, 24
CB Commercial Real Estate Services Group, Inc., 21
CB Richard Ellis Group, Inc., 70 (upd.)
Central Florida Investments, Inc., 93
Chateau Communities, Inc., 37
Chelsfield PLC, 67
Cheung Kong (Holdings) Limited, IV; 20 (upd.)
City Developments Limited, 89
Clayton Homes Incorporated, 54 (upd.)
Colliers International Property Consultants Inc., 92
Colonial Properties Trust, 65
The Corcoran Group, Inc., 58
CoStar Group, Inc., 73
Cousins Properties Incorporated, 65
CSX Corporation 79 (upd.)
Cushman & Wakefield, Inc., 86
Del Webb Corporation, 14
Desarrolladora Homex, S.A. de C.V., 87
Developers Diversified Realty Corporation, 69
Duke Realty Corporation, 57
Ducks Unlimited, Inc., 87
EastGroup Properties, Inc., 67

The Edward J. DeBartolo Corporation, 8
Enterprise Inns plc, 59
Equity Office Properties Trust, 54
Equity Residential, 49
Erickson Retirement Communities, 57
Fairfield Communities, Inc., 36
First Industrial Realty Trust, Inc., 65
Forest City Enterprises, Inc., 16; 52 (upd.)
Gale International Llc, 93
Gecina SA, 42
General Growth Properties, Inc., 57
GMH Communities Trust, 87
Great White Shark Enterprises, Inc., 89
Griffin Land & Nurseries, Inc., 43
Grubb & Ellis Company, 21
The Haminerson Property Investment and Development Corporation plc, IV
Hammerson plc, 40
Harbert Corporation, 14
Helmsley Enterprises, Inc., 39 (upd.)
Henderson Land Development Company Ltd., 70
Home Properties of New York, Inc., 42
HomeVestors of America, Inc., 77
Hongkong Land Holdings Limited, IV; 47 (upd.)
Holiday Retirement Corp., 87
Hopson Development Holdings Ltd., 87
Hovnanian Enterprises, Inc., 29; 89 (upd.)
Hyatt Corporation, 16 (upd.)
ILX Resorts Incorporated, 65
IRSA Inversiones y Representaciones S.A., 63
J.F. Shea Co., Inc., 55
Jardine Cycle & Carriage Ltd., 73
JMB Realty Corporation, IV
Jones Lang LaSalle Incorporated, 49
JPI, 49
Kaufman and Broad Home Corporation, 8
Kennedy-Wilson, Inc., 60
Kerry Properties Limited, 22
Kimco Realty Corporation, 11
The Koll Company, 8
Land Securities PLC, IV; 49 (upd.)
Lefrak Organization Inc., 26
Lend Lease Corporation Limited, IV; 17 (upd.); 52 (upd.)
Liberty Property Trust, 57
Lincoln Property Company, 8; 54 (upd.)
The Loewen Group Inc., 40 (upd.)
The Long & Foster Companies, Inc., 85
The Macerich Company, 57
Mack-Cali Realty Corporation, 42
Manufactured Home Communities, Inc., 22
Maui Land & Pineapple Company, Inc., 29
Maxco Inc., 17
Meditrust, 11
Melvin Simon and Associates, Inc., 8
MEPC plc, IV
Meritage Corporation, 26
Mid-America Apartment Communities, Inc., 85
The Middleton Doll Company, 53
The Mills Corporation, 77
Mitsubishi Estate Company, Limited, IV; 61 (upd.)
Mitsui Real Estate Development Co., Ltd., IV
Morguard Corporation, 85
The Nature Conservancy, 28
New Plan Realty Trust, 11
New World Development Company Ltd., IV
Newhall Land and Farming Company, 14
Nexity S.A., 66
NRT Incorporated, 61
Olympia & York Developments Ltd., IV; 9 (upd.)
Park Corp., 22
Parque Arauco S.A., 72
Perini Corporation, 8
Pope Resources LP, 74
Post Properties, Inc., 26
Potlatch Corporation, 8; 34 (upd.); 87 (upd.)
ProLogis, 57
Public Storage, Inc., 52
Railtrack Group PLC, 50
RE/MAX International, Inc., 59
Reading International Inc., 70
Reckson Associates Realty Corp., 47
Regency Centers Corporation, 71
Rockefeller Group International Inc., 58
Rodamco N.V., 26
The Rouse Company, 15; 63 (upd.)
Shubert Organization Inc., 24
The Sierra Club, 28
Silverstein Properties, Inc., 47
Simco S.A., 37
SL Green Realty Corporation, 44
Slough Estates PLC, IV; 50 (upd.)
Sovran Self Storage, Inc., 66
Starrett Corporation, 21
The Staubach Company, 62
Storage USA, Inc., 21
Sumitomo Realty & Development Co., Ltd., IV
Sun Communities Inc., 46
Sunterra Corporation, 75
Tanger Factory Outlet Centers, Inc., 49
Tarragon Realty Investors, Inc., 45
Taubman Centers, Inc., 75
Taylor Woodrow plc, 38 (upd.)
Technical Olympic USA, Inc., 75
Tejon Ranch Company, 35
Tishman Speyer Properties, L.P., 47
Tokyu Land Corporation, IV
Trammell Crow Company, 8; 57 (upd.)
Trendwest Resorts, Inc., 33
Tridel Enterprises Inc., 9
Trizec Corporation Ltd., 10
The Trump Organization, 23; 64 (upd.)
Unibail SA, 40
United Dominion Realty Trust, Inc., 52
Vistana, Inc., 22
Vornado Realty Trust, 20
W.P. Carey & Co. LLC, 49
William Lyon Homes, 59

Retail & Wholesale

A-Mark Financial Corporation, 71
A.C. Moore Arts & Crafts, Inc., 30
A.S. Watson & Company Ltd., 84
A.T. Cross Company, 49 (upd.)
Aaron Rents, Inc., 14; 35 (upd.)
Abatix Corp., 57
ABC Appliance, Inc., 10
ABC Carpet & Home Co. Inc., 26
Abercrombie & Fitch Company, 15; 75 (upd.)
Academy Sports & Outdoors, 27
Ace Hardware Corporation, 12; 35 (upd.)
Action Performance Companies, Inc., 27
ADESA, Inc., 71
Adolfo Dominguez S.A., 72
AEON Co., Ltd., 68 (upd.)
Aéropostale, Inc., 89
After Hours Formalwear Inc., 60
Alabama Farmers Cooperative, Inc., 63
Alain Afflelou SA, 53
Alba-Waldensian, Inc., 30
Alberto-Culver Company, 8; 36 (upd.); 91 (upd.)
Albertson's, Inc., 65 (upd.)
Alimentation Couche-Tard Inc., 77
Alldays plc, 49
Allders plc, 37
Alliance Boots plc (updates Boots Group PLC), 83 (upd.)
Allou Health & Beauty Care, Inc., 28
Almacenes Exito S.A., 89
Alpha Airports Group PLC, 77
Alrosa Company Ltd., 62
Alticor Inc., 71 (upd.)
Amazon.com, Inc., 25; 56 (upd.)
AMERCO, 67 (upd.)
American Coin Merchandising, Inc., 28; 74 (upd.)
American Eagle Outfitters, Inc., 24; 55 (upd.)
American Furniture Company, Inc., 21
American Girl, Inc., 69 (upd.)
American Stores Company, 22 (upd.)
AmeriSource Health Corporation, 37 (upd.)
Ames Department Stores, Inc., 9; 30 (upd.)
Amscan Holdings, Inc., 61
Amway Corporation, 13; 30 (upd.)
The Anderson-DuBose Company, 60
The Andersons, Inc., 31
AnnTaylor Stores Corporation, 13; 37 (upd.); 67 (upd.)
Appliance Recycling Centers of America, Inc., 42
Arbor Drugs Inc., 12
Arcadia Group plc, 28 (upd.)
Army and Air Force Exchange Service, 39
Art Van Furniture, Inc., 28
ASDA Group plc, 28 (upd.)
Ashworth, Inc., 26
Au Printemps S.A., V
Audio King Corporation, 24
Authentic Fitness Corporation, 20; 51 (upd.)
Auto Value Associates, Inc., 25
Autobytel Inc., 47
AutoNation, Inc., 50
AutoTrader.com, L.L.C., 91
AutoZone, Inc., 9; 31 (upd.)

AVA AG (Allgemeine Handelsgesellschaft der Verbraucher AG), 33
Aveda Corporation, 24
Aviall, Inc., 73
Aviation Sales Company, 41
AWB Ltd., 56
B. Dalton Bookseller Inc., 25
Babbage's, Inc., 10
Baby Superstore, Inc., 15
Baccarat, 24
Bachman's Inc., 22
Bailey Nurseries, Inc., 57
Ball Horticultural Company 78
Banana Republic Inc., 25
Bare Escentuals, Inc., 91
Barnes & Noble, Inc., 10; 30 (upd.); 75 (upd.)
Barnett Inc., 28
Barney's, Inc., 28
Barrett-Jackson Auction Company L.L.C., 88
Bass Pro Shops, Inc., 42
Baumax AG, 75
Beacon Roofing Supply, Inc., 75
Bear Creek Corporation, 38
Bearings, Inc., 13
bebe stores, inc., 31
Bed Bath & Beyond Inc., 13; 41 (upd.)
Belk Stores Services, Inc., V; 19 (upd.)
Belk, Inc., 72 (upd.)
Ben Bridge Jeweler, Inc., 60
Benetton Group S.p.A., 67 (upd.)
Bergdorf Goodman Inc., 52
Bergen Brunswig Corporation, V; 13 (upd.)
Bernard Chaus, Inc., 27
Best Buy Co., Inc., 9; 23 (upd.); 63 (upd.)
Bestseller A/S, 90
Bhs plc, 17
Big A Drug Stores Inc., 79
Big Dog Holdings, Inc., 45
Big 5 Sporting Goods Corporation, 55
The Big Food Group plc, 68 (upd.)
Big Lots, Inc., 50
Big O Tires, Inc., 20
Birkenstock Footprint Sandals, Inc., 42 (upd.)
Birthdays Ltd., 70
Black Box Corporation, 20
Blacks Leisure Group plc, 39
Blair Corporation, 25; 31 (upd.)
Blokker Holding B.V., 84
Bloomingdale's Inc., 12
Blue Nile Inc., 61
Blue Square Israel Ltd., 41
Bluefly, Inc., 60
Blyth Industries, Inc., 18
The Body Shop International PLC, 11
The Bombay Company, Inc., 10; 71 (upd.)
The Bon Marché, Inc., 23
The Bon-Ton Stores, Inc., 16; 50 (upd.)
Booker Cash & Carry Ltd., 68 (upd.)
Books-A-Million, Inc., 14; 41 (upd.)
Bookspan, 86
The Boots Company PLC, V; 24 (upd.)
Borders Group, Inc., 15; 43 (upd.)
Boscov's Department Store, Inc., 31
Bozzuto's, Inc., 13
Bradlees Discount Department Store Company, 12
Brambles Industries Limited, 42
Bricorama S.A., 68
Brioni Roman Style S.p.A., 67
Brodart Company, 84
Broder Bros. Co., 38
Bronner Display & Sign Advertising, Inc., 82
Brooks Brothers Inc., 22
Brookstone, Inc., 18
Brown Shoe Company, Inc., 68 (upd.)
Brunswick Corporation, 77 (upd.)
The Buckle, Inc., 18
Buhrmann NV, 41
Build-A-Bear Workshop Inc., 62
Building Materials Holding Corporation, 52
Burdines, Inc., 60
Burlington Coat Factory Warehouse Corporation, 10; 60 (upd.)
Burt's Bees, Inc., 58
The Burton Group plc, V
Buttrey Food & Drug Stores Co., 18
buy.com, Inc., 46
C&A, V; 40 (upd.)
C&J Clark International Ltd., 52
Cabela's Inc., 26; 68 (upd.)
Cablevision Electronic Instruments, Inc., 32
Cache Incorporated, 30
Cactus S.A., 90
Caldor Inc., 12
Calloway's Nursery, Inc., 51
Camaïeu S.A., 72
Camelot Music, Inc., 26
Campeau Corporation, V
Campo Electronics, Appliances & Computers, Inc., 16
Car Toys, Inc., 67
The Carphone Warehouse Group PLC, 83
Carrefour SA, 10; 27 (upd.); 64 (upd.)
Carson Pirie Scott & Company, 15
Carter Hawley Hale Stores, Inc., V
Carter Lumber Company, 45
Cartier Monde, 29
Casas Bahia Comercial Ltda., 75
Casey's General Stores, Inc., 19; 83 (upd.)
Castro Model Ltd., 86
Casual Corner Group, Inc., 43
Casual Male Retail Group, Inc., 52
Catherines Stores Corporation, 15
Cato Corporation, 14
CDW Computer Centers, Inc., 16
Celebrate Express, Inc., 70
Celebrity, Inc., 22
CellStar Corporation, 83
Cencosud S.A., 69
Central European Distribution Corporation, 75
Central Garden & Pet Company, 23
Cenveo Inc., 71 (upd.)
Chadwick's of Boston, Ltd., 29
Charlotte Russe Holding, Inc., 35; 90 (upd.)
Charming Shoppes, Inc., 38
Chas. Levy Company LLC, 60
ChevronTexaco Corporation, 47 (upd.)
Chiasso Inc., 53
The Children's Place Retail Stores, Inc., 37; 86 (upd.)
Christian Dior S.A., 49 (upd.)
Christopher & Banks Corporation, 42
Cifra, S.A. de C.V., 12
The Circle K Company, 20 (upd.)
Circuit City Stores, Inc., 9; 29 (upd.); 65 (upd.)
Clare Rose Inc., 68
Clinton Cards plc, 39
The Clothestime, Inc., 20
CML Group, Inc., 10
Co-operative Group (CWS) Ltd., 51
Coach, Inc., 45 (upd.)
Coborn's, Inc., 30
Coinmach Laundry Corporation, 20
Coldwater Creek Inc., 21; 74 (upd.)
Cole National Corporation, 13; 76 (upd.)
Cole's Quality Foods, Inc., 68
Coles Group Limited, V; 20 (upd.); 85 (upd.)
Collectors Universe, Inc., 48
Columbia House Company, 69
Comdisco, Inc., 9
Compagnie Financière Sucres et Denrées S.A., 60
Companhia Brasileira de Distribuiçao, 76
CompUSA, Inc., 10
Computerland Corp., 13
Concepts Direct, Inc., 39
Conn's, Inc., 67
The Container Store, 36
Controladora Comercial Mexicana, S.A. de C.V., 36
CoolSavings, Inc., 77
Coop Schweiz Genossenschaftsverband, 48
Coppel, S.A. de C.V., 82
Corby Distilleries Limited, 14
Corporate Express, Inc., 22; 47 (upd.)
Cortefiel S.A., 64
The Cosmetic Center, Inc., 22
Cost Plus, Inc., 27
Costco Wholesale Corporation, V; 43 (upd.)
Cotter & Company, V
County Seat Stores Inc., 9
Courts Plc, 45
CPI Corp., 38
Crate and Barrel, 9
Croscill, Inc., 42
CROSSMARK, 79
Crowley, Milner & Company, 19
Crown Books Corporation, 21
Cumberland Farms, Inc., 17; 84 (upd.)
CVS Corporation, 45 (upd.)
Daffy's Inc., 26
The Daiei, Inc., V; 17 (upd.); 41 (upd.)
The Daimaru, Inc., V; 42 (upd.)
Dairy Mart Convenience Stores, Inc., 25 (upd.)
Daisytek International Corporation, 18
Damark International, Inc., 18
Dart Group Corporation, 16
Darty S.A., 27
David Jones Ltd., 60

David's Bridal, Inc., 33
Dayton Hudson Corporation, V; 18 (upd.)
Deb Shops, Inc., 16; 76 (upd.)
Debenhams Plc, 28
Deli Universal NV, 66
dELiA*s Inc., 29
Department 56, Inc., 34 (upd.)
Designer Holdings Ltd., 20
Deveaux S.A., 41
DFS Group Ltd., 66
Dick's Sporting Goods, Inc., 59
Diesel SpA, 40
Digital River, Inc., 50
Dillard Department Stores, Inc., V; 16 (upd.)
Dillard's Inc., 68 (upd.)
Dillon Companies Inc., 12
Discount Auto Parts, Inc., 18
Discount Drug Mart, Inc., 14
Dixons Group plc, V; 19 (upd.); 49 (upd.)
Do it Best Corporation, 30
Dollar Tree Stores, Inc., 23; 62 (upd.)
Donna Karan International Inc., 56 (upd.)
The Dress Barn, Inc., 24; 55 (upd.)
Drs. Foster & Smith, Inc., 62
Drug Emporium, Inc., 12
DSW Inc., 73
Du Pareil au Même, 43
Duane Reade Holding Corp., 21
Duckwall-ALCO Stores, Inc., 24
Dunnes Stores Ltd., 58
Duron Inc., 72
Duty Free International, Inc., 11
Dylex Limited, 29
E-Z Serve Corporation, 17
Eagle Hardware & Garden, Inc., 16
Eastman Kodak Company, III; 7 (upd.); 36 (upd.); 91 (upd.)
eBay Inc., 32
Eckerd Corporation, 9; 32 (upd.)
Eddie Bauer Holdings, Inc., 9; 36 (upd.); 87 (upd.)
Edgars Consolidated Stores Ltd., 66
Edward Hines Lumber Company, 68
Egghead.com, Inc., 31 (upd.)
Eileen Fisher Inc., 61
El Corte Inglés Group, V
The Elder-Beerman Stores Corp., 10; 63 (upd.)
Electrocomponents PLC, 50
Electronics Boutique Holdings Corporation, 72
Elephant Pharmacy, Inc., 83
Ellett Brothers, Inc., 17
EMI Group plc, 22 (upd.); 81 (upd.)
Empresas Almacenes Paris S.A., 71
Ermenegildo Zegna SpA, 63
ESCADA AG, 71
The Estée Lauder Companies Inc., 9; 30 (upd.); 93 (upd.)
Etablissements Franz Colruyt N.V., 68
Ethan Allen Interiors, Inc., 39 (upd.)
EToys, Inc., 37
Euromarket Designs Inc., 31 (upd.)
Evans, Inc., 30
Eye Care Centers of America, Inc., 69
EZCORP Inc., 43
The F. Dohmen Co., 77
Family Christian Stores, Inc., 51
Family Dollar Stores, Inc., 13; 62 (upd.)
Fannie May Confections Brands, Inc., 80
Farmacias Ahumada S.A., 72
Fastenal Company, 14; 42 (upd.)
Faultless Starch/Bon Ami Company, 55
Fay's Inc., 17
Federated Department Stores, Inc., 9; 31 (upd.)
Fenaco, 86
Fielmann AG, 31
Fila Holding S.p.A., 20; 52 (upd.)
Finarte Casa d'Aste S.p.A., 93
Findel plc, 60
Fingerhut Companies, Inc., 9; 36 (upd.)
The Finish Line, Inc., 29; 68 (upd.)
Finlay Enterprises, Inc., 16; 76 (upd.)
Finning International Inc., 69
First Cash Financial Services, Inc., 57
Fleming Companies, Inc., 17 (upd.)
Florsheim Shoe Group Inc., 9; 31 (upd.)
FNAC, 21
Follett Corporation, 12
Foot Locker, Inc., 68 (upd.)
Footstar, Incorporated, 24
Forever 21, Inc., 84
Fortunoff Fine Jewelry and Silverware Inc., 26
The Forzani Group Ltd., 79
Foxworth-Galbraith Lumber Company, 91
Frank's Nursery & Crafts, Inc., 12
Fred Meyer Stores, Inc., V; 20 (upd.); 64 (upd.)
Fred's, Inc., 23; 62 (upd.)
Frederick Atkins Inc., 16
Frederick's of Hollywood, Inc., 59 (upd.)
Freeze.com LLC, 77
Fretter, Inc., 10
Friedman's Inc., 29
Fruth Pharmacy, Inc., 66
Fry's Electronics, Inc., 68
Funco, Inc., 20
Future Shop Ltd., 62
G.I. Joe's, Inc., 30
Gadzooks, Inc., 18
Gaiam, Inc., 41
Galeries Lafayette S.A., V; 23 (upd.)
Galyan's Trading Company, Inc., 47
GameStop Corp., 69 (upd.)
Gander Mountain, Inc., 20; 90 (upd.)
Gantos, Inc., 17
The Gap, Inc., V; 18 (upd.); 55 (upd.)
Garden Ridge Corporation, 27
Garst Seed Company, Inc., 86
Gart Sports Company, 24
GEHE AG, 27
General Binding Corporation, 10
General Host Corporation, 12
Genesco Inc., 17; 84 (upd.)
Genovese Drug Stores, Inc., 18
Genuine Parts Company, 45 (upd.)
Gerald Stevens, Inc., 37
Gerhard D. Wempe KG, 88
Giant Food Inc., 22 (upd.)
GIB Group, V; 26 (upd.)
Gibbs and Dandy plc, 74
GiFi S.A., 74
Glacier Water Services, Inc., 47
Global Imaging Systems, Inc., 73
GOME Electrical Appliances Holding Ltd., 87
The Good Guys, Inc., 10; 30 (upd.)
Goodwill Industries International, Inc., 16
Goody's Family Clothing, Inc., 20; 64 (upd.)
Gordmans, Inc., 74
Gottschalks, Inc., 18; 91 (upd.)
Grand Piano & Furniture Company, 72
GrandVision S.A., 43
Graybar Electric Company, Inc., 54
The Great Universal Stores plc, V; 19 (upd.)
Griffin Land & Nurseries, Inc., 43
Grossman's Inc., 13
Groupe Alain Manoukian, 55
Groupe Castorama-Dubois Investissements, 23
Groupe DMC (Dollfus Mieg & Cie), 27
Groupe Go Sport S.A., 39
Groupe Lapeyre S.A., 33
Groupe Monnoyeur, 72
Groupe Zannier S.A., 35
Grow Biz International, Inc., 18
Grupo Casa Saba, S.A. de C.V., 39
Grupo Elektra, S.A. de C.V., 39
Grupo Eroski, 64
Grupo Gigante, S.A. de C.V., 34
Gruppo Coin S.p.A., 41
GSC Enterprises, Inc., 86
GT Bicycles, 26
GTSI Corp., 57
Gucci Group N.V., 15; 50 (upd.)
Guilbert S.A., 42
Guitar Center, Inc., 29; 68 (upd.)
GUS plc, 47 (upd.)
Gymboree Corporation, 69 (upd.)
Hahn Automotive Warehouse, Inc., 24
Hale-Halsell Company, 60
Half Price Books, Records, Magazines Inc., 37
Hallmark Cards, Inc., IV; 16 (upd.); 40 (upd.); 87 (upd.)
Hammacher Schlemmer & Company Inc., 21; 72 (upd.)
Hancock Fabrics, Inc., 18
Hankyu Department Stores, Inc., V; 62 (upd.)
Hanna Andersson Corp., 49
Hanover Compressor Company, 59
Hanover Direct, Inc., 36
Harold's Stores, Inc., 22
Harrods Holdings, 47
Harry Winston Inc., 45
Harvey Norman Holdings Ltd., 56
Hasbro, Inc., 43 (upd.)
Haverty Furniture Companies, Inc., 31
Hechinger Company, 12
Heilig-Meyers Company, 14; 40 (upd.)
Heinrich Deichmann-Schuhe GmbH & Co. KG, 88
Helzberg Diamonds, 40
Hennes & Mauritz AB, 29
Henry Modell & Company Inc., 32
Hensley & Company, 64

Hertie Waren- und Kaufhaus GmbH, V
Hibbett Sporting Goods, Inc., 26; 70 (upd.)
Highsmith Inc., 60
Hills Stores Company, 13
Hines Horticulture, Inc., 49
HMV Group plc, 59
Hobby Lobby Stores Inc., 80
The Hockey Company, 34
Holiday RV Superstores, Incorporated, 26
Holt's Cigar Holdings, Inc., 42
The Home Depot, Inc., V; 18 (upd.)
Home Hardware Stores Ltd., 62
Home Interiors & Gifts, Inc., 55
Home Retail Group plc, 91
Home Shopping Network, Inc., V; 25 (upd.)
HomeBase, Inc., 33 (upd.)
Hot Topic Inc., 33; 86 (upd.)
House of Fabrics, Inc., 21
House of Fraser PLC, 45
HSN, 64 (upd.)
Hudson's Bay Company, V; 25 (upd.); 83 (upd.)
Huttig Building Products, Inc., 73
Ihr Platz GmbH + Company KG, 77
IKEA International A/S, V; 26 (upd.)
InaCom Corporation, 13
Indigo Books & Music Inc., 58
Insight Enterprises, Inc., 18
Intermix Media, Inc., 83
International Airline Support Group, Inc., 55
Intimate Brands, Inc., 24
Intres B.V., 82
Isetan Company Limited, V; 36 (upd.)
Ito-Yokado Co., Ltd., V; 42 (upd.)
J&R Electronics Inc., 26
J. Baker, Inc., 31
The J. Jill Group Inc., 35; 90 (upd.)
J. C. Penney Company, Inc., V; 18 (upd.); 43 (upd.); 91 (upd.)
J.L. Hammett Company, 72
J. W. Pepper and Son Inc., 86
Jack Schwartz Shoes, Inc., 18
Jacobson Stores Inc., 21
Jalate Inc., 25
James Beattie plc, 43
Jay Jacobs, Inc., 15
Jennifer Convertibles, Inc., 31
Jetro Cash & Carry Enterprises Inc., 38
Jewett-Cameron Trading Company, Ltd., 89
JG Industries, Inc., 15
JJB Sports plc, 32
Jo-Ann Stores, Inc., 72 (upd.)
John Lewis Partnership plc, V; 42 (upd.)
Jordan-Kitt Music Inc., 86
JUSCO Co., Ltd., V
Just For Feet, Inc., 19
K & B Inc., 12
K & G Men's Center, Inc., 21
K-tel International, Inc., 21
Karstadt Aktiengesellschaft, V; 19 (upd.)
Kash n' Karry Food Stores, Inc., 20
Kasper A.S.L., Ltd., 40
kate spade LLC, 68
Kaufhof Warenhaus AG, V; 23 (upd.)
Kaufring AG, 35
Kay-Bee Toy Stores, 15
Keys Fitness Products, LP, 83
Kiabi Europe, 66
Kiehl's Since 1851, Inc., 52
Kingfisher plc, V; 24 (upd.); 83 (upd.)
Kinney Shoe Corp., 14
Kmart Corporation, V; 18 (upd.); 47 (upd.)
Knoll Group Inc., 14
Kohl's Corporation, 9; 30 (upd.); 77 (upd.)
Koninklijke Vendex KBB N.V. (Royal Vendex KBB N.V.), 62 (upd.)
Kotobukiya Co., Ltd., V; 56 (upd.)
Krause's Furniture, Inc., 27
Krispy Kreme Doughnuts, Inc., 21; 61 (upd.)
Kruse International, 88
L. and J.G. Stickley, Inc., 50
L. Luria & Son, Inc., 19
L.A. T Sportswear, Inc., 26
L.L. Bean, Inc., 10; 38 (upd.); 91 (upd.)
La Senza Corporation, 66
La-Z-Boy Incorporated, 14; 50 (upd.)
Lamonts Apparel, Inc., 15
Lands' End, Inc., 9; 29 (upd.); 82 (upd.)
Lane Bryant, Inc., 64
Lanier Worldwide, Inc., 75
Lanoga Corporation, 62
Laura Ashley Holdings plc, 37 (upd.)
Lazare Kaplan International Inc., 21
Le Chateau Inc., 63
Lechmere Inc., 10
Lechters, Inc., 11; 39 (upd.)
LensCrafters Inc., 23; 76 (upd.)
Leroy Merlin SA, 54
Les Boutiques San Francisco, Inc., 62
Lesco Inc., 19
Leslie's Poolmart, Inc., 18
Leupold & Stevens, Inc., 52
Levenger Company, 63
Levitz Furniture Inc., 15
Lewis Galoob Toys Inc., 16
Li & Fung Limited, 59
Liberty Orchards Co., Inc., 89
Life is Good, Inc., 80
Lifetime Brands, Inc., 27; 73 (upd.)
Lillian Vernon Corporation, 12; 35 (upd.); 92 (upd.)
The Limited, Inc., V; 20 (upd.)
Linens 'n Things, Inc., 24; 75 (upd.)
Little Switzerland, Inc., 60
Littleton Coin Company Inc., 82
Littlewoods plc, V; 42 (upd.)
LivePerson, Inc., 91
Liz Claiborne, Inc., 25 (upd.)
LKQ Corporation, 71
Loehmann's Inc., 24
Lojas Americanas S.A., 77
Lojas Arapuã S.A., 22; 61 (upd.)
London Drugs Ltd., 46
Longs Drug Stores Corporation, V; 25 (upd.); 83 (upd.)
Lookers plc, 71
Lost Arrow Inc., 22
LOT$OFF Corporation, 24
Love's Travel Stops & Country Stores, Inc., 71
Lowe's Companies, Inc., V; 21 (upd.); 81 (upd.)
Ludendo S.A., 88
Luxottica SpA, 17; 52 (upd.)
Lyfra-S.A./NV, 88
Mac Frugal's Bargains - Closeouts Inc., 17
Mac-Gray Corporation, 44
Mackays Stores Group Ltd., 92
Manheim, 88
Manutan International S.A., 72
Maples Industries, Inc., 83
MarineMax, Inc., 30
Marionnaud Parfumeries SA, 51
Marks and Spencer Group p.l.c., V; 24 (upd.); 85 (upd.)
Marks Brothers Jewelers, Inc., 24
Marlin Business Services Corp., 89
Marshall Field's, 63
Marshalls Incorporated, 13
Marui Company Ltd., V; 62 (upd.)
Maruzen Co., Limited, 18
Mary Kay Inc., 9; 30 (upd.); 84 (upd.)
Matalan PLC, 49
Matsuzakaya Company Ltd., V; 64 (upd.)
Maus Frères SA, 48
The Maxim Group, 25
The May Department Stores Company, V; 19 (upd.); 46 (upd.)
Mayor's Jewelers, Inc., 41
Mazel Stores, Inc., 29
McCoy Corporation, 58
McGrath RentCorp, 91
McJunkin Corporation, 63
McKesson Corporation, 47 (upd.)
McLane Company, Inc., 13
McNaughton Apparel Group, Inc., 92 (upd.)
MCSi, Inc., 41
Media Arts Group, Inc., 42
Meier & Frank Co., 23
Meijer Incorporated, 27 (upd.)
Melville Corporation, V
The Men's Wearhouse, Inc., 17; 48 (upd.)
Menard, Inc., 34
Mercantile Stores Company, Inc., V; 19 (upd.)
Mercury Drug Corporation, 70
Merry-Go-Round Enterprises, Inc., 8
Mervyn's California, 10; 39 (upd.)
Metal Management, Inc., 92
Metro AG, 50
Michael C. Fina Co., Inc., 52
Michaels Stores, Inc., 17; 71 (upd.)
Michigan Sporting Goods Distributors, Inc., 72
Micro Warehouse, Inc., 16
MicroAge, Inc., 16
Migros-Genossenschafts-Bund, 68
Milton CAT, Inc., 86
Mitsukoshi Ltd., V; 56 (upd.)
MNS, Ltd., 65
Monoprix S.A., 86
Monrovia Nursery Company, 70
Monsoon plc, 39
Montgomery Ward & Co., Incorporated, V; 20 (upd.)

Moore-Handley, Inc., 39
Morrow Equipment Co. L.L.C., 87
Morse Shoe Inc., 13
Moss Bros Group plc, 51
Mothercare plc, 78 (upd.)
Mothers Work, Inc., 18
Moto Photo, Inc., 45
Mr. Bricolage S.A., 37
MSC Industrial Direct Co., Inc., 71
MTS Inc., 37
Mulberry Group PLC, 71
Musicland Stores Corporation, 9; 38 (upd.)
MWI Veterinary Supply, Inc., 80
Nagasakiya Co., Ltd., V; 69 (upd.)
Nash Finch Company, 65 (upd.)
National Educational Music Co. Ltd., 47
National Home Centers, Inc., 44
National Intergroup, Inc., V
National Record Mart, Inc., 29
National Wine & Spirits, Inc., 49
Natura Cosméticos S.A., 75
Natural Wonders Inc., 14
Navy Exchange Service Command, 31
Nebraska Book Company, Inc., 65
Neff Corp., 32
NeighborCare, Inc., 67 (upd.)
The Neiman Marcus Group, Inc., 12; 49 (upd.)
Netflix, Inc., 58
New Look Group plc, 35
Next plc, 29
Nichii Co., Ltd., V
NIKE, Inc., 36 (upd.)
Nine West Group Inc., 11
99;ct Only Stores, 25
Nocibé SA, 54
Noland Company, 35
Noodle Kidoodle, 16
Nordstrom, Inc., V; 18 (upd.); 67 (upd.)
Norelco Consumer Products Co., 26
Norm Thompson Outfitters, Inc., 47
North Pacific Group, Inc., 61
The North West Company, Inc., 12
Norton McNaughton, Inc., 27
Nu Skin Enterprises, Inc., 27; 76 (upd.)
Oakley, Inc., 49 (upd.)
Office Depot, Inc., 8; 23 (upd.); 65 (upd.)
OfficeMax, Inc., 15; 43 (upd.)
Olan Mills, Inc., 62
Old America Stores, Inc., 17
Old Navy, Inc., 70
One Price Clothing Stores, Inc., 20
The Oppenheimer Group, 76
Orchard Supply Hardware Stores Corporation, 17
Organización Soriana, S.A. de C.V., 35
The Orvis Company, Inc., 28
OshKosh B'Gosh, Inc., 42 (upd.)
Oshman's Sporting Goods, Inc., 17
Ottakar's plc, 64
Otto Versand (GmbH & Co.), V; 15 (upd.); 34 (upd.)
Overstock.com, Inc., 75
Owens & Minor, Inc., 16; 68 (upd.)
P.C. Richard & Son Corp., 23
Pamida Holdings Corporation, 15
The Pampered Chef, Ltd., 18; 78 (upd.)
The Pantry, Inc., 36
The Paradies Shops, Inc., 88
Parisian, Inc., 14
Party City Corporation, 54
Paul Harris Stores, Inc., 18
Pay 'N Pak Stores, Inc., 9
Payless Cashways, Inc., 11; 44 (upd.)
Payless ShoeSource, Inc., 18; 69 (upd.)
PCA International, Inc., 62
PDQ Food Stores, Inc., 79
Pearle Vision, Inc., 13
Peebles Inc., 16; 43 (upd.)
Peet's Coffee & Tea, Inc., 38
Penzeys Spices, Inc., 79
The Pep Boys—Manny, Moe & Jack, 11; 36 (upd.); 81 (upd.)
Petco Animal Supplies, Inc., 29; 74 (upd.)
Petrie Stores Corporation, 8
PetMed Express, Inc., 81
PETsMART, Inc., 14; 41 (upd.)
PFSweb, Inc., 73
Phar-Mor Inc., 12
Phones 4u Ltd., 85
Photo-Me International Plc, 83
Pick 'n Pay Stores Ltd., 82
Pier 1 Imports, Inc., 12; 34 (upd.)
Piercing Pagoda, Inc., 29
Pilot Corporation, 49
Pinault-Printemps Redoute S.A., 19 (upd.)
Pitman Company, 58
Pomeroy Computer Resources, Inc., 33
Powell's Books, Inc., 40
PPR S.A., 74 (upd.)
Praxis Bookstore Group LLC, 90
The Price Company, V
PriceCostco, Inc., 14
PriceSmart, Inc., 71
Proffitt's, Inc., 19
Provell Inc., 58 (upd.)
Provigo Inc., 51 (upd.)
Publishers Clearing House, 64 (upd.)
Puig Beauty and Fashion Group S.L., 60
Purina Mills, Inc., 32
Quelle Group, V
QuikTrip Corporation, 36
Quiksilver, Inc., 79 (upd.)
Quill Corporation, 28
QVC Inc., 58 (upd.)
R.C. Willey Home Furnishings, 72
R.H. Macy & Co., Inc., V; 8 (upd.); 30 (upd.)
RadioShack Corporation, 36 (upd.)
Rag Shops, Inc., 30
Raley's Inc., 14; 58 (upd.)
Rallye SA, 54
Rapala-Normark Group, Ltd., 30
Ratner Companies, 72
RDO Equipment Company, 33
Reckitt Benckiser plc, II; 42 (upd.); 91 (upd.)
Recoton Corp., 15
Recreational Equipment, Inc., 18; 71 (upd.)
Red McCombs Automotive Group, 91
Red Wing Shoe Company, Inc., 9; 30 (upd.); 83 (upd.)
Reeds Jewelers, Inc., 22
Rejuvenation, Inc., 91
Reliance Steel & Aluminum Company, 70 (upd.)
Rent-A-Center, Inc., 45
Rent-Way, Inc., 33; 75 (upd.)
Restoration Hardware, Inc., 30
Retail Ventures, Inc., 82 (upd.)
Revco D.S., Inc., V
REX Stores Corp., 10
Rhodes Inc., 23
Richton International Corporation, 39
Riklis Family Corp., 9
Rinascente S.p.A., 71
Rite Aid Corporation, V; 19 (upd.); 63 (upd.)
Ritz Camera Centers, 34
RM Auctions, Inc., 88
Roberds Inc., 19
Rocky Shoes & Boots, Inc., 26
Rogers Communications Inc., 30 (upd.)
RONA, Inc., 73
Ronco Corporation, 15; 80 (upd.)
Rooms To Go Inc., 28
Roots Canada Ltd., 42
Rose's Stores, Inc., 13
Ross Stores, Inc., 17; 43 (upd.)
Rosy Blue N.V., 84
Roundy's Inc., 14
Rush Enterprises, Inc., 64
Ryoshoku Ltd., 72
S&K Famous Brands, Inc., 23
S.A.C.I. Falabella, 69
Saks Inc., 24; 41 (upd.)
Sally Beauty Company, Inc., 60
Sam Ash Music Corporation, 30
Sam Levin Inc., 80
Sam's Club, 40
Samuels Jewelers Incorporated, 30
Sanborn Hermanos, S.A., 20
SanomaWSOY Corporation, 51
Scheels All Sports Inc., 63
Schmitt Music Company, 40
Schneiderman's Furniture Inc., 28
School Specialty, Inc., 68
Schottenstein Stores Corp., 14
Schultz Sav-O Stores, Inc., 31
The Score Board, Inc., 19
Scotty's, Inc., 22
The Scoular Company, 77
SCP Pool Corporation, 39
Seaman Furniture Company, Inc., 32
Sean John Clothing, Inc., 70
Sears plc, V
Sears Roebuck de México, S.A. de C.V., 20
Sears, Roebuck and Co., V; 18 (upd.); 56 (upd.)
SED International Holdings, Inc., 43
Seibu Department Stores, Ltd., V; 42 (upd.)
Seigle's Home and Building Centers, Inc., 41
The Seiyu, Ltd., V; 36 (upd.)
Selfridges Plc, 34
Service Merchandise Company, Inc., V; 19 (upd.)
7-Eleven, Inc., 32 (upd.)
Seventh Generation, Inc., 73

Shaklee Corporation, 12
The Sharper Image Corporation, 10; 62 (upd.)
Sheetz, Inc., 85
The Sherwin-Williams Company, 89 (upd.)
Shoe Carnival Inc., 14; 72 (upd.)
ShopKo Stores Inc., 21; 58 (upd.)
Shoppers Drug Mart Corporation, 49
Shoppers Food Warehouse Corporation, 66
SIG plc, 71
Signet Group PLC, 61
SkyMall, Inc., 26
Sleepy's Inc., 32
Smith & Hawken, Ltd., 68
Snapfish, 83
Solo Serve Corporation, 28
Sophus Berendsen A/S, 49
Sound Advice, Inc., 41
Source Interlink Companies, Inc., 75
Southern States Cooperative Incorporated, 36
Spartan Stores Inc., 66 (upd.)
Spec's Music, Inc., 19
Spector Photo Group N.V., 82
Spiegel, Inc., 10; 27 (upd.)
Sport Chalet, Inc., 16
Sport Supply Group, Inc., 23
Sportmart, Inc., 15
Sports & Recreation, Inc., 17
The Sports Authority, Inc., 16; 43 (upd.)
The Sportsman's Guide, Inc., 36
Stage Stores, Inc., 24; 82 (upd.)
Stanhome Inc., 15
Staple Cotton Cooperative Association (Staplcotn), 86
Staples, Inc., 10; 55 (upd.)
Starbucks Corporation, 34 (upd.)
Starcraft Corporation, 30
Stefanel SpA, 63
Stein Mart Inc., 19; 72 (upd.)
Steve & Barry's LLC, 88
Stewart's Shops Corporation, 80
Stinnes AG, 8
The Stop & Shop Companies, Inc., 24 (upd.)
Storehouse PLC, 16
Strauss Discount Auto, 56
Stride Rite Corporation, 8
The Strober Organization, Inc., 82
Strouds, Inc., 33
Stuller Settings, Inc., 35
Successories, Inc., 30
Sun Television & Appliances Inc., 10
Sunglass Hut International, Inc., 21; 74 (upd.)
Supreme International Corporation, 27
Swarovski International Holding AG, 40
Syms Corporation, 29; 74 (upd.)
Systemax, Inc., 52
Takashimaya Company, Limited, V; 47 (upd.)
The Talbots, Inc., 11; 31 (upd.); 88 (upd.)
Target Corporation, 61 (upd.)
Target Stores, 10; 27 (upd.)
Tati SA, 25
Tattered Cover Book Store, 43
Tech Data Corporation, 10; 74 (upd.)
Tengelmann Group, 27
Tesco plc, 24 (upd.); 68 (upd.)
Things Remembered, Inc., 84
Thomsen Greenhouses and Garden Center, Incorporated, 65
Thrifty PayLess, Inc., 12
Tiffany & Co., 14; 78 (upd.)
The Timberland Company, 54 (upd.)
The TJX Companies, Inc., V; 19 (upd.); 57 (upd.)
Today's Man, Inc., 20
Tokyu Department Store Co., Ltd., V; 32 (upd.)
Too, Inc., 61
Topco Associates LLC, 60
Tops Appliance City, Inc., 17
Total Fina Elf S.A., 50 (upd.)
Toys 'R' Us, Inc., V; 18 (upd.); 57 (upd.)
Tractor Supply Company, 57
Trans World Entertainment Corporation, 68 (upd.)
Travis Boats & Motors, Inc., 37
Travis Perkins plc, 34
Trend-Lines, Inc., 22
True Value Company, 74 (upd.)
TruServ Corporation, 24
Tuesday Morning Corporation, 18; 70 (upd.)
Tupperware Corporation, 28; 78 (upd.)
TVI, Inc., 15
Tweeter Home Entertainment Group, Inc., 30
U.S. Vision, Inc., 66
Ulta Salon, Cosmetics & Fragrance, Inc., 93
Ultimate Electronics, Inc., 18; 69 (upd.)
Ultramar Diamond Shamrock Corporation, 31 (upd.)
Uni-Marts, Inc., 17
United Rentals, Inc., 34
The United States Shoe Corporation, V
United Stationers Inc., 14
Universal International, Inc., 25
Uny Co., Ltd., V; 49 (upd.)
Urban Outfitters, Inc., 14; 74 (upd.)
Uwajimaya, Inc., 60
Vallen Corporation, 45
Valley Media Inc., 35
Value City Department Stores, Inc., 38
Value Merchants Inc., 13
ValueVision International, Inc., 22
Vans, Inc., 47 (upd.)
Variety Wholesalers, Inc., 73
VBA - Bloemenveiling Aalsmeer, 88
Venator Group Inc., 35 (upd.)
Vendex International N.V., 13
Venture Stores Inc., 12
The Vermont Country Store, 93
The Vermont Teddy Bear Co., Inc., 36
VF Corporation, 54 (upd.)
Viewpoint International, Inc., 66
Viking Office Products, Inc., 10
Vivarte SA, 54 (upd.)
Volcom, Inc., 77
Von Maur Inc., 64
Vorwerk & Co., 27
W. Atlee Burpee & Co., 27
W.W. Grainger, Inc., V
Waban Inc., 13
Wacoal Corp., 25
Wal-Mart de Mexico, S.A. de C.V., 35 (upd.)
Wal-Mart Stores, Inc., V; 8 (upd.); 26 (upd.); 63 (upd.)
Waldenbooks, 17; 86 (upd.)
Walgreen Co., V; 20 (upd.); 65 (upd.)
Wall Drug Store, Inc., 40
Warners' Stellian Inc., 67
Weiner's Stores, Inc., 33
West Marine, Inc., 17; 90 (upd.)
Western Beef, Inc., 22
The Wet Seal, Inc., 18; 70 (upd.)
Weyco Group, Incorporated, 32
WH Smith PLC, V; 42 (upd.)
The White House, Inc., 60
Whitehall Jewellers, Inc., 82 (upd.)
Whole Foods Market, Inc., 20
Wickes Inc., V; 25 (upd.)
Wilco Farm Stores, 93
Wilkinson Hardware Stores Ltd., 80
Williams Scotsman, Inc., 65
Williams-Sonoma, Inc., 17; 44 (upd.)
Wilsons The Leather Experts Inc., 21; 58 (upd.)
Windstream Corporation, 83
Winmark Corporation, 74
Wolohan Lumber Co., 19
Wolverine World Wide, Inc., 59 (upd.)
Woolworth Corporation, V; 20 (upd.)
Woolworths Group plc, 83
World Duty Free Americas, Inc., 29 (upd.)
Yamada Denki Co., Ltd., 85
The Yankee Candle Company, Inc., 37
Young's Market Company, LLC, 32
Younkers, 76 (upd.)
Younkers, Inc., 19
Zale Corporation, 16; 40 (upd.); 91 (upd.)
Zany Brainy, Inc., 31
Zappos.com, Inc., 73
Zara International, Inc., 83
Ziebart International Corporation, 30
Zion's Cooperative Mercantile Institution, 33
Zipcar, Inc., 92
Zones, Inc., 67
Zumiez, Inc., 77

Rubber & Tires

Aeroquip Corporation, 16
Bandag, Inc., 19
The BFGoodrich Company, V
Bridgestone Corporation, V; 21 (upd.); 59 (upd.)
Canadian Tire Corporation, Limited, 71 (upd.)
Carlisle Companies Incorporated, 8
Compagnie Générale des Établissements Michelin, V; 42 (upd.)
Continental AG, V; 56 (upd.)
Continental General Tire Corp., 23
Cooper Tire & Rubber Company, 8; 23 (upd.)

Day International, Inc., 84
Elementis plc, 40 (upd.)
General Tire, Inc., 8
The Goodyear Tire & Rubber Company, V; 20 (upd.); 75 (upd.)
The Kelly-Springfield Tire Company, 8
Les Schwab Tire Centers, 50
Myers Industries, Inc., 19
Pirelli S.p.A., V; 15 (upd.)
Safeskin Corporation, 18
Sumitomo Rubber Industries, Ltd., V
Trelleborg AB, 93
Tillotson Corp., 15
Treadco, Inc., 19
Ube Industries, Ltd., 38 (upd.)
The Yokohama Rubber Company, Limited, V; 19 (upd.); 91 (upd.)

Telecommunications

A.H. Belo Corporation, 30 (upd.)
Abertis Infraestructuras, S.A., 65
Acme-Cleveland Corp., 13
ADC Telecommunications, Inc., 10; 89 (upd.)
Adelphia Communications Corporation, 17; 52 (upd.)
Adtran Inc., 22
Advanced Fibre Communications, Inc., 63
AEI Music Network Inc., 35
AirTouch Communications, 11
Alaska Communications Systems Group, Inc., 89
Alcatel S.A., 36 (upd.)
Alliance Atlantis Communications Inc., 39
ALLTEL Corporation, 6; 46 (upd.)
América Móvil, S.A. de C.V., 80
American Tower Corporation, 33
Ameritech Corporation, V; 18 (upd.)
Amstrad plc, 48 (upd.)
AO VimpelCom, 48
AOL Time Warner Inc., 57 (upd.)
Arch Wireless, Inc., 39
ARD, 41
ARRIS Group, Inc., 89
Ascom AG, 9
Aspect Telecommunications Corporation, 22
Asurion Corporation, 83
AT&T Bell Laboratories, Inc., 13
AT&T Corporation, V; 29 (upd.); 68 (upd.)
AT&T Wireless Services, Inc., 54 (upd.)
BCE Inc., V; 44 (upd.)
Beasley Broadcast Group, Inc., 51
Belgacom, 6
Bell Atlantic Corporation, V; 25 (upd.)
Bell Canada, 6
BellSouth Corporation, V; 29 (upd.)
Bertelsmann A.G., IV; 15 (upd.); 43 (upd.); 91 (upd.)
BET Holdings, Inc., 18
Bharti Tele-Ventures Limited, 75
BHC Communications, Inc., 26
Blackfoot Telecommunications Group, 60
Bonneville International Corporation, 29
Bouygues S.A., 24 (upd.)
Brasil Telecom Participaçoes S.A., 57
Brightpoint, Inc., 18
Brite Voice Systems, Inc., 20
British Broadcasting Corporation Ltd., 7; 21 (upd.); 89 (upd.)
British Columbia Telephone Company, 6
British Telecommunications plc, V; 15 (upd.)
Broadwing Corporation, 70
BT Group plc, 49 (upd.)
C-COR.net Corp., 38
Cable & Wireless HKT, 30 (upd.)
Cable and Wireless plc, V; 25 (upd.)
Cablevision Systems Corporation, 30 (upd.)
CalAmp Corp., 87
The Canadian Broadcasting Corporation (CBC), 37
Canal Plus, 10; 34 (upd.)
CanWest Global Communications Corporation, 35
Capital Radio plc, 35
Carlton Communications PLC, 15; 50 (upd.)
Carolina Telephone and Telegraph Company, 10
The Carphone Warehouse Group PLC, 83
Carrier Access Corporation, 44
CBS Corporation, 28 (upd.)
CBS Television Network, 66 (upd.)
Centel Corporation, 6
Centennial Communications Corporation, 39
Central European Media Enterprises Ltd., 61
Century Communications Corp., 10
Century Telephone Enterprises, Inc., 9; 54 (upd.)
Cesky Telecom, a.s., 64
Chancellor Media Corporation, 24
Channel Four Television Corporation, 93
Charter Communications, Inc., 33
Chello Zone Ltd., 93
China Netcom Group Corporation (Hong Kong) Limited, 73
China Telecom, 50
Chris-Craft Corporation, 9, 31 (upd.); 80 (upd.)
The Christian Broadcasting Network, Inc., 52
Chrysalis Group plc, 40
Chugach Alaska Corporation, 60
CIENA Corporation, 54
Cincinnati Bell, Inc., 6
Citadel Communications Corporation, 35
Citizens Communications Company, 79 (upd.)
Clear Channel Communications, Inc., 23
Clearwire, Inc., 69
Cogent Communications Group, Inc., 55
COLT Telecom Group plc, 41
Comcast Corporation, 24 (upd.)
Comdial Corporation, 21
Commonwealth Telephone Enterprises, Inc., 25
CommScope, Inc., 77
Comsat Corporation, 23
Comtech Telecommunications Corp., 75
Comverse Technology, Inc., 15; 43 (upd.)
Corning Inc., III; 44 (upd.); 90 (upd.)
Corporation for Public Broadcasting, 14; 89 (upd.)
Cox Radio, Inc., 89
Craftmade International, Inc., 44
Cumulus Media Inc., 37
DDI Corporation, 7
Deutsche Telekom AG, V; 48 (upd.)
Dialogic Corporation, 18
Directorate General of Telecommunications, 7
DIRECTV, Inc., 38; 75 (upd.)
Discovery Communications, Inc., 42
Dobson Communications Corporation, 63
DSC Communications Corporation, 12
EchoStar Communications Corporation, 35
ECI Telecom Ltd., 18
Egmont Group, 93
eircom plc, 31 (upd.)
Electric Lightwave, Inc., 37
Electromagnetic Sciences Inc., 21
EMBARQ Corporation, 83
Emmis Communications Corporation, 47
Empresas Públicas de Medellín S.A.E.S.P., 91
Energis plc, 47
Entercom Communications Corporation, 58
Entravision Communications Corporation, 41
Equant N.V., 52
Eschelon Telecom, Inc., 72
ESPN, Inc., 56
Eternal Word Television Network, Inc., 57
EXCEL Communications Inc., 18
Executone Information Systems, Inc., 13
Expand SA, 48
Facebook, Inc., 90
FASTWEB S.p.A., 83
4Kids Entertainment Inc., 59
Fox Family Worldwide, Inc., 24
France Télécom Group, V; 21 (upd.)
Frontier Corp., 16
Fuji Television Network Inc., 91
Gannett Co., Inc., 30 (upd.)
Garmin Ltd., 60
General DataComm Industries, Inc., 14
Geotek Communications Inc., 21
Getty Images, Inc., 31
Global Crossing Ltd., 32
Globo Comunicação e Participações S.A., 80
Golden Telecom, Inc., 59
Granite Broadcasting Corporation, 42
Gray Communications Systems, Inc., 24
Groupe Vidéotron Ltée., 20
Grupo Televisa, S.A., 18; 54 (upd.)
GTE Corporation, V; 15 (upd.)
Guthy-Renker Corporation, 32
GWR Group plc, 39
Harmonic Inc., 43
Havas, SA, 10
HickoryTech Corporation, 92
Hispanic Broadcasting Corporation, 35
Hong Kong Telecommunications Ltd., 6
Huawei Technologies Company Ltd., 87
Hubbard Broadcasting Inc., 24; 79 (upd.)
Hughes Electronics Corporation, 25

Hungarian Telephone and Cable Corp., 75
IDB Communications Group, Inc., 11
IDT Corporation, 34
Illinois Bell Telephone Company, 14
Indiana Bell Telephone Company, Incorporated, 14
PT Indosat Tbk, 93
Infineon Technologies AG, 50
Infinity Broadcasting Corporation, 11
InfoSonics Corporation, 81
InterDigital Communications Corporation, 61
Iowa Telecommunications Services, Inc., 85
IXC Communications, Inc., 29
Jacor Communications, Inc., 23
Jones Intercable, Inc., 21
j2 Global Communications, Inc., 75
Koninklijke PTT Nederland NV, V
Landmark Communications, Inc., 55 (upd.)
LCC International, Inc., 84
LCI International, Inc., 16
LDDS-Metro Communications, Inc., 8
Leap Wireless International, Inc., 69
Level 3 Communications, Inc., 67
LIN Broadcasting Corp., 9
Lincoln Telephone & Telegraph Company, 14
LodgeNet Entertainment Corporation, 28
Loral Space & Communications Ltd., 54 (upd.)
MacNeil/Lehrer Productions, 87
Magyar Telekom Rt. 78
Manitoba Telecom Services, Inc., 61
Mannesmann AG, 38
MasTec, Inc., 19; 55 (upd.)
McCaw Cellular Communications, Inc., 6
MCI WorldCom, Inc., V; 27 (upd.)
McLeodUSA Incorporated, 32
Mediacom Communications Corporation, 69
Mercury Communications, Ltd., 7
Metrocall, Inc., 41
Metromedia Companies, 14
Métropole Télévision, 33
Métropole Télévision S.A., 76 (upd.)
MFS Communications Company, Inc., 11
Michigan Bell Telephone Co., 14
MIH Limited, 31
MITRE Corporation, 26
Mobile Telecommunications Technologies Corp., 18
Mobile TeleSystems OJSC, 59
Modern Times Group AB, 36
The Montana Power Company, 44 (upd.)
Motorola, Inc., II; 11 (upd.); 34 (upd.); 93 (upd.)
Multimedia, Inc., 11
National Broadcasting Company, Inc., 28 (upd.)
National Grid USA, 51 (upd.)
National Weather Service, 91
NCR Corporation, III; 6 (upd.); 30 (upd.); 90 (upd.)
NetCom Systems AB, 26
NeuStar, Inc., 81
Nevada Bell Telephone Company, 14
New Valley Corporation, 17
Nexans SA, 54
Nexstar Broadcasting Group, Inc., 73
Nextel Communications, Inc., 27 (upd.)
Nippon Telegraph and Telephone Corporation, V; 51 (upd.)
Nokia Corporation, 77 (upd.)
Norstan, Inc., 16
Nortel Networks Corporation, 36 (upd.)
Northern Telecom Limited, V
NTL Inc., 65
NTN Buzztime, Inc., 86
NYNEX Corporation, V
Octel Messaging, 14; 41 (upd.)
Ohio Bell Telephone Company, 14
Olivetti S.p.A., 34 (upd.)
Orange S.A., 84
Österreichische Post- und Telegraphenverwaltung, V
Pacific Internet Limited, 87
Pacific Telecom, Inc., 6
Pacific Telesis Group, V
Paging Network Inc., 11
PanAmSat Corporation, 46
Paxson Communications Corporation, 33
The Phoenix Media/Communications Group, 91
PictureTel Corp., 10; 27 (upd.)
Portugal Telecom SGPS S.A., 69
Posti- ja Telelaitos, 6
Price Communications Corporation, 42
ProSiebenSat.1 Media AG, 54
Publishing and Broadcasting Limited, 54
Qatar Telecom QSA, 87
QUALCOMM Incorporated, 20; 47 (upd.)
QVC Network Inc., 9
Qwest Communications International, Inc., 37
RCN Corporation, 70
Regent Communications, Inc., 87
Research in Motion Ltd., 54
RMH Teleservices, Inc., 42
Rochester Telephone Corporation, 6
Rogers Communications Inc., 30 (upd.)
Royal KPN N.V., 30
Rural Cellular Corporation, 43
Saga Communications, Inc., 27
Sawtek Inc., 43 (upd.)
SBC Communications Inc., 32 (upd.)
Schweizerische Post-, Telefon- und Telegrafen-Betriebe, V
Scientific-Atlanta, Inc., 6; 45 (upd.)
Seat Pagine Gialle S.p.A., 47
Securicor Plc, 45
Shenandoah Telecommunications Company, 89
Sinclair Broadcast Group, Inc., 25
Sirius Satellite Radio, Inc., 69
Sirti S.p.A., 76
Società Finanziaria Telefonica per Azioni, V
Softbank Corporation, 77 (upd.)
Sonera Corporation, 50
Southern New England Telecommunications Corporation, 6
Southwestern Bell Corporation, V
Spanish Broadcasting System, Inc., 41
Spelling Entertainment, 35 (upd.)
Sprint Corporation, 9; 46 (upd.)
StarHub Ltd., 77
StrataCom, Inc., 16
Swedish Telecom, V
Swisscom AG, 58
Sycamore Networks, Inc., 45
SynOptics Communications, Inc., 10
T-Netix, Inc., 46
Talk America Holdings, Inc., 70
TDC A/S, 63
Tekelec, 83
Telcordia Technologies, Inc., 59
Tele Norte Leste Participações S.A., 80
Telecom Argentina S.A., 63
Telecom Australia, 6
Telecom Corporation of New Zealand Limited, 54
Telecom Eireann, 7
Telecom Italia Mobile S.p.A., 63
Telecom Italia S.p.A., 43
Telefonaktiebolaget LM Ericsson, V; 46 (upd.)
Telefónica de Argentina S.A., 61
Telefónica S.A., V; 46 (upd.)
Telefonos de Mexico S.A. de C.V., 14; 63 (upd.)
Telekom Malaysia Bhd, 76
Telekomunikacja Polska SA, 50
Telenor ASA, 69
Telephone and Data Systems, Inc., 9
Télévision Française 1, 23
TeliaSonera AB, 57 (upd.)
Tellabs, Inc., 11; 40 (upd.)
Telstra Corporation Limited, 50
Thomas Crosbie Holdings Limited, 81
Tiscali SpA, 48
The Titan Corporation, 36
Tollgrade Communications, Inc., 44
TV Azteca, S.A. de C.V., 39
U.S. Satellite Broadcasting Company, Inc., 20
U S West, Inc., V; 25 (upd.)
U.S. Cellular Corporation, 9; 31 (upd.); 88 (upd.)
UFA TV & Film Produktion GmbH, 80
United Pan-Europe Communications NV, 47
United Telecommunications, Inc., V
United Video Satellite Group, 18
Univision Communications Inc., 24; 83 (upd.)
USA Interactive, Inc., 47 (upd.)
UTStarcom, Inc., 77
Verizon Communications Inc. 43 (upd.); 78 (upd.)
ViaSat, Inc., 54
Vivendi Universal S.A., 46 (upd.)
Vodafone Group Plc, 11; 36 (upd.); 75 (upd.)
Vonage Holdings Corp., 81
The Walt Disney Company, II; 6 (upd.); 30 (upd.); 63 (upd.)
Wanadoo S.A., 75
Watkins-Johnson Company, 15
The Weather Channel Companies, 52
West Corporation, 42

Western Union Financial Services, Inc., 54
Western Wireless Corporation, 36
Westwood One, Inc., 23
Williams Communications Group, Inc., 34
The Williams Companies, Inc., 31 (upd.)
Wipro Limited, 43
Wisconsin Bell, Inc., 14
Working Assets Funding Service, 43
XM Satellite Radio Holdings, Inc., 69
Young Broadcasting Inc., 40
Zed Group, 93
Zoom Technologies, Inc., 53 (upd.)

Textiles & Apparel

Abercrombie & Fitch Company, 35 (upd.); 75 (upd.)
adidas Group AG, 75 (upd.)
adidas-Salomon AG, 14; 33 (upd.)
Adolfo Dominguez S.A., 72
Aéropostale, Inc., 89
Alba-Waldensian, Inc., 30
Albany International Corp., 8
Alexandra plc, 88
Algo Group Inc., 24
Alpargatas S.A.I.C., 87
American & Efird, Inc., 82
American Apparel, Inc., 90
American Safety Razor Company, 20
Amoskeag Company, 8
Angelica Corporation, 15; 43 (upd.)
AR Accessories Group, Inc., 23
Aris Industries, Inc., 16
ASICS Corporation, 57
AstenJohnson Inc., 90
The Athlete's Foot Brands LLC, 84
Authentic Fitness Corporation, 20; 51 (upd.)
Banana Republic Inc., 25
Bata Ltd., 62
Benetton Group S.p.A., 10; 67 (upd.)
Bill Blass Ltd., 32
Birkenstock Footprint Sandals, Inc., 12
Blair Corporation, 25
Body Glove International LLC, 88
Brazos Sportswear, Inc., 23
Brioni Roman Style S.p.A., 67
Brooks Brothers Inc., 22
Brooks Sports Inc., 32
Brown Group, Inc., V; 20 (upd.)
Bugle Boy Industries, Inc., 18
Burberry Group plc, 17; 41 (upd.); 92 (upd.)
Burke Mills, Inc., 66
Burlington Industries, Inc., V; 17 (upd.)
Calcot Ltd., 33
Calvin Klein, Inc., 22; 55 (upd.)
Candie's, Inc., 31
Canstar Sports Inc., 16
Capel Incorporated, 45
Capezio/Ballet Makers Inc., 62
Carhartt, Inc., 30, 77 (upd.)
Cato Corporation, 14
Chargeurs International, 6; 21 (upd.)
Charles Vögele Holding AG, 82
Charming Shoppes, Inc., 8
Cherokee Inc., 18
CHF Industries, Inc., 84
Chic by H.I.S, Inc., 20
Chico's FAS, Inc., 45
Chorus Line Corporation, 30
Christian Dior S.A., 19; 49 (upd.)
Christopher & Banks Corporation, 42
Cia Hering, 72
Cintas Corporation, 51 (upd.)
Citi Trends, Inc., 80
Claire's Stores, Inc., 17
Coach Leatherware, 10
Coats plc, V; 44 (upd.)
Collins & Aikman Corporation, 13
Columbia Sportswear Company, 19; 41 (upd.)
Companhia de Tecidos Norte de Minas - Coteminas, 77
Compañia Industrial de Parras, S.A. de C.V. (CIPSA), 84
Concord Fabrics, Inc., 16
Cone Mills LLC, 8; 67 (upd.)
Converse Inc., 31 (upd.)
Cotton Incorporated, 46
Courtaulds plc, V; 17 (upd.)
Crocs, Inc., 80
Croscill, Inc., 42
Crown Crafts, Inc., 16
Crystal Brands, Inc., 9
Culp, Inc., 29
Cygne Designs, Inc., 25
Dan River Inc., 35; 86 (upd.)
Danskin, Inc., 12; 62 (upd.)
Deckers Outdoor Corporation, 22
Delta and Pine Land Company, 59
Delta Woodside Industries, Inc., 8; 30 (upd.)
Designer Holdings Ltd., 20
The Dixie Group, Inc., 20; 80 (upd.)
Dogi International Fabrics S.A., 52
Dolce & Gabbana SpA, 62
Dominion Textile Inc., 12
Donna Karan International Inc., 15; 56 (upd.)
Donnkenny, Inc., 17
Dooney & Bourke Inc., 84
Duck Head Apparel Company, Inc., 42
Dunavant Enterprises, Inc., 54
Dyersburg Corporation, 21
Eastland Shoe Corporation, 82
Ecco Sko A/S, 62
The Echo Design Group, Inc., 68
Edison Brothers Stores, Inc., 9
Eileen Fisher Inc., 61
Ellen Tracy, Inc., 55
Eram SA, 51
Ermenegildo Zegna SpA, 63
ESCADA AG, 71
Esprit de Corp., 8; 29 (upd.)
Etam Developpement SA, 44
Etienne Aigner AG, 52
Evans, Inc., 30
Fab Industries, Inc., 27
Fabri-Centers of America Inc., 16
Fat Face Ltd., 68
Fieldcrest Cannon, Inc., 9; 31 (upd.)
Fila Holding S.p.A., 20
Florsheim Shoe Group Inc., 31 (upd.)
Fossil, Inc., 17
Frederick's of Hollywood Inc., 16
French Connection Group plc, 41
Fruit of the Loom, Inc., 8; 25 (upd.)
Fubu, 29
G&K Services, Inc., 16
G-III Apparel Group, Ltd., 22
Galey & Lord, Inc., 20; 66 (upd.)
Garan, Inc., 16; 64 (upd.)
Gerry Weber International AG, 63
Gianni Versace SpA, 22
Gildan Activewear, Inc., 81
Giorgio Armani S.p.A., 45
The Gitano Group, Inc. 8
Gottschalks, Inc., 18; 91 (upd.)
Great White Shark Enterprises, Inc., 89
Greenwood Mills, Inc., 14
Groupe DMC (Dollfus Mieg & Cie), 27
Groupe Yves Saint Laurent, 23
Gucci Group N.V., 15; 50 (upd.)
Guess, Inc., 15; 68 (upd.)
Guilford Mills Inc., 8; 40 (upd.)
Gymboree Corporation, 15; 69 (upd.)
Haggar Corporation, 19; 78 (upd.)
Hampshire Group Ltd., 82
Hampton Industries, Inc., 20
Happy Kids Inc., 30
Hartmarx Corporation, 8
The Hartstone Group plc, 14
HCI Direct, Inc., 55
Healthtex, Inc., 17
Heelys, Inc., 87
Helly Hansen ASA, 25
Hermès S.A., 14
The Hockey Company, 34
Horween Leather Company, 83
Hugo Boss AG, 48
Hummel International A/S, 68
Hyde Athletic Industries, Inc., 17
I.C. Isaacs & Company, 31
Industria de Diseño Textil S.A., 64
Innovo Group Inc., 83
Interface, Inc., 8; 29 (upd.); 76 (upd.)
Irwin Toy Limited, 14
Items International Airwalk Inc., 17
J. Crew Group, Inc., 12; 34 (upd.); 88 (upd.)
JLM Couture, Inc., 64
Jockey International, Inc., 12; 34 (upd.); 77 (upd.)
The John David Group plc, 90
Johnston Industries, Inc., 15
Jones Apparel Group, Inc., 39 (upd.)
Jordache Enterprises, Inc., 23
Jos. A. Bank Clothiers, Inc., 31
JPS Textile Group, Inc., 28
Juicy Couture, Inc., 80
K-Swiss, Inc., 33; 89 (upd.)
Karl Kani Infinity, Inc., 49
Kellwood Company, 8; 85 (upd.)
Kenneth Cole Productions, Inc., 25
Kinney Shoe Corp., 14
Klaus Steilmann GmbH & Co. KG, 53
Koret of California, Inc., 62
L.A. Gear, Inc., 8; 32 (upd.)
L.L. Bean, Inc., 10; 38 (upd.); 91 (upd.)
LaCrosse Footwear, Inc., 18; 61 (upd.)
Laura Ashley Holdings plc, 13
Lee Apparel Company, Inc., 8

The Leslie Fay Company, Inc., 8; 39 (upd.)
Levi Strauss & Co., V; 16 (upd.)
Liz Claiborne, Inc., 8
London Fog Industries, Inc., 29
Lost Arrow Inc., 22
Maidenform, Inc., 20; 59 (upd.)
Malden Mills Industries, Inc., 16
Maples Industries, Inc., 83
Mariella Burani Fashion Group, 92
Marzotto S.p.A., 20; 67 (upd.)
Milliken & Co., V; 17 (upd.); 82 (upd.)
Miroglio SpA, 86
Mitsubishi Rayon Co., Ltd., V
Mossimo, Inc., 27
Mothercare plc, 17; 78 (upd.)
Movie Star Inc., 17
Mulberry Group PLC, 71
Naf Naf SA, 44
Nautica Enterprises, Inc., 18; 44 (upd.)
New Balance Athletic Shoe, Inc., 25; 68 (upd.)
NIKE, Inc., V; 8 (upd.); 75 (upd.)
Nine West Group, Inc., 39 (upd.)
Nitches, Inc., 53
The North Face Inc., 18; 78 (upd.)
Oakley, Inc., 18
Ormat Technologies, Inc., 87
OshKosh B'Gosh, Inc., 9; 42 (upd.)
Oxford Industries, Inc., 8; 84 (upd.)
Pacific Sunwear of California, Inc., 28
Peek & Cloppenburg KG, 46
Pendleton Woolen Mills, Inc., 42
Pentland Group plc, 20
Perry Ellis International, Inc., 41
Phat Fashions LLC, 49
Phoenix Footwear Group, Inc., 70
Pillowtex Corporation, 19; 41 (upd.)
Plains Cotton Cooperative Association, 57
Pluma, Inc., 27
Polo/Ralph Lauren Corporation, 12; 62 (upd.)
Pomare Ltd., 88
Prada Holding B.V., 45
PremiumWear, Inc., 30
Puma AG Rudolf Dassler Sport, 35
Quaker Fabric Corp., 19
Quiksilver, Inc., 18; 79 (upd.)
R.G. Barry Corporation, 17; 44 (upd.)
Rack Room Shoes, Inc., 84
Raymond Ltd., 77
Recreational Equipment, Inc., 18
Red Wing Shoe Company, Inc., 9; 30 (upd.); 83 (upd.)
Reebok International Ltd., V; 9 (upd.); 26 (upd.)
Reliance Industries Ltd., 81
Rieter Holding AG, 42
Robert Talbott Inc., 88
Rocawear Apparel LLC, 77
Rollerblade, Inc., 15
Royal Ten Cate N.V., 68
Russell Corporation, 8; 30 (upd.); 82 (upd.)
St. John Knits, Inc., 14
Salant Corporation, 51 (upd.)
Salvatore Ferragamo Italia S.p.A., 62
Sao Paulo Alpargatas S.A., 75
Saucony Inc., 35; 86 (upd.)
Schott Brothers, Inc., 67
Seattle Pacific Industries, Inc., 92
Shaw Industries, Inc., 40 (upd.)
Shelby Williams Industries, Inc., 14
Shoe Pavilion, Inc., 84
Skechers U.S.A. Inc., 31; 88 (upd.)
Sole Technology Inc., 93
Sophus Berendsen A/S, 49
Spanx, Inc., 89
Springs Global US, Inc., V; 19 (upd.); 90 (upd.)
Starter Corp., 12
Stefanel SpA, 63
Steiner Corporation (Alsco), 53
Steven Madden, Ltd., 37
Stirling Group plc, 62
Stoddard International plc, 72
Stone Manufacturing Company, 14; 43 (upd.)
Stride Rite Corporation, 8; 37 (upd.); 86 (upd.)
Stussy, Inc., 55
Sun Sportswear, Inc., 17
Superior Uniform Group, Inc., 30
Tag-It Pacific, Inc., 85
The Talbots, Inc., 11; 31 (upd.); 88 (upd.)
Tamfelt Oyj Abp, 62
Tarrant Apparel Group, 62
Ted Baker plc, 86
Teijin Limited, V
Thanulux Public Company Limited, 86
Thomaston Mills, Inc., 27
Tilley Endurables, Inc., 67
The Timberland Company, 13; 54 (upd.)
Tommy Hilfiger Corporation, 20; 53 (upd.)
Too, Inc., 61
Toray Industries, Inc., V
True Religion Apparel, Inc., 79
Tultex Corporation, 13
Under Armour Performance Apparel, 61
Unifi, Inc., 12; 62 (upd.)
United Merchants & Manufacturers, Inc., 13
United Retail Group Inc., 33
Unitika Ltd., V
Umbro plc, 88
Vans, Inc., 16; 47 (upd.)
Varsity Spirit Corp., 15
VF Corporation, V; 17 (upd.); 54 (upd.)
Vicunha Têxtil S.A. 78
Volcom, Inc., 77
Walton Monroe Mills, Inc., 8
The Warnaco Group Inc., 12; 46 (upd.)
Wellco Enterprises, Inc., 84
Wellman, Inc., 8; 52 (upd.)
West Point-Pepperell, Inc., 8
WestPoint Stevens Inc., 16
Weyco Group, Incorporated, 32
Williamson-Dickie Manufacturing Company, 14
Wolverine World Wide, Inc., 16; 59 (upd.)
Woolrich Inc., 62
Zara International, Inc., 83

Tobacco

Altadis S.A., 72 (upd.)
American Brands, Inc., V
B.A.T. Industries PLC, 22 (upd.)
British American Tobacco PLC, 50 (upd.)
Brooke Group Ltd., 15
Brown & Williamson Tobacco Corporation, 14; 33 (upd.)
Culbro Corporation, 15
Dibrell Brothers, Incorporated, 12
DIMON Inc., 27
800-JR Cigar, Inc., 27
Gallaher Group Plc, V; 19 (upd.); 49 (upd.)
General Cigar Holdings, Inc., 66 (upd.)
Holt's Cigar Holdings, Inc., 42
House of Prince A/S, 80
Imasco Limited, V
Imperial Tobacco Group PLC, 50
Japan Tobacco Incorporated, V
KT&G Corporation, 62
Nobleza Piccardo SAICF, 64
North Atlantic Trading Company Inc., 65
Philip Morris Companies Inc., V; 18 (upd.)
R.J. Reynolds Tobacco Holdings, Inc., 30 (upd.)
RJR Nabisco Holdings Corp., V
Rothmans UK Holdings Limited, V; 19 (upd.)
Seita, 23
Souza Cruz S.A., 65
Standard Commercial Corporation, 13; 62 (upd.)
Swedish Match AB, 12; 39 (upd.); 92 (upd.)
Swisher International Group Inc., 23
Tabacalera, S.A., V; 17 (upd.)
Taiwan Tobacco & Liquor Corporation, 75
Universal Corporation, V; 48 (upd.)
UST Inc., 9; 50 (upd.)
Vector Group Ltd., 35 (upd.)

Transport Services

Abertis Infraestructuras, S.A., 65
The Adams Express Company, 86
Aegean Marine Petroleum Network Inc., 89
Aéroports de Paris, 33
Air Express International Corporation, 13
Air Partner PLC, 93
Air T, Inc., 86
Airborne Freight Corporation, 6; 34 (upd.)
Alamo Rent A Car, Inc., 6; 24 (upd.); 84 (upd.)
Alaska Railroad Corporation, 60
Alexander & Baldwin, Inc., 10, 40 (upd.)
Allied Worldwide, Inc., 49
AMCOL International Corporation, 59 (upd.)
Amerco, 6
AMERCO, 67 (upd.)
American Classic Voyages Company, 27
American President Companies Ltd., 6

Anderson Trucking Service, Inc., 75
Anschutz Corp., 12
APL Limited, 61 (upd.)
Aqua Alliance Inc., 32 (upd.)
Arriva PLC, 69
Atlas Van Lines, Inc., 14
Attica Enterprises S.A., 64
Avis Group Holdings, Inc., 75 (upd.)
Avis Rent A Car, Inc., 6; 22 (upd.)
BAA plc, 10
Bekins Company, 15
Berliner Verkehrsbetriebe (BVG), 58
Bollinger Shipyards, Inc., 61
Boyd Bros. Transportation Inc., 39
Brambles Industries Limited, 42
The Brink's Company, 58 (upd.)
British Railways Board, V
Broken Hill Proprietary Company Ltd., 22 (upd.)
Buckeye Partners, L.P., 70
Budget Group, Inc., 25
Budget Rent a Car Corporation, 9
Burlington Northern Santa Fe Corporation, V; 27 (upd.)
C.H. Robinson Worldwide, Inc., 40 (upd.)
Canadian National Railway Company, 71 (upd.)
Canadian National Railway System, 6
Canadian Pacific Railway Limited, V; 45 (upd.)
Cannon Express, Inc., 53
Carey International, Inc., 26
Carlson Companies, Inc., 6; 22 (upd.); 87 (upd.)
Carolina Freight Corporation, 6
Celadon Group Inc., 30
Central Japan Railway Company, 43
Chargeurs International, 6; 21 (upd.)
CHC Helicopter Corporation, 67
CHEP Pty. Ltd., 80
Chicago and North Western Holdings Corporation, 6
Christian Salvesen Plc, 45
Coach USA, Inc., 24; 55 (upd.)
Coles Express Inc., 15
Compagnie Générale Maritime et Financière, 6
Consolidated Delivery & Logistics, Inc., 24
Consolidated Freightways Corporation, V; 21 (upd.); 48 (upd.)
Consolidated Rail Corporation, V
CR England, Inc., 63
Crowley Maritime Corporation, 6; 28 (upd.)
CSX Corporation, V; 22 (upd.); 79 (upd.)
Dachser GmbH & Co. KG, 88
Danaos Corporation, 91
Danzas Group, V; 40 (upd.)
Dart Group PLC, 77
Deutsche Bahn AG, V; 46 (upd.)
DHL Worldwide Network S.A./N.V., 6; 24 (upd.); 69 (upd.)
Dollar Thrifty Automotive Group, Inc., 25
Dot Foods, Inc., 69
DP World, 81
East Japan Railway Company, V; 66 (upd.)
EGL, Inc., 59
Emery Air Freight Corporation, 6
Emery Worldwide Airlines, Inc., 25 (upd.)
Enterprise Rent-A-Car Company, 6
Estes Express Lines, Inc., 86
Eurotunnel Group, 37 (upd.)
EVA Airways Corporation, 51
Evergreen International Aviation, Inc., 53
Evergreen Marine Corporation (Taiwan) Ltd., 13; 50 (upd.)
Executive Jet, Inc., 36
Exel plc, 51 (upd.)
Expeditors International of Washington Inc., 17; 78 (upd.)
Federal Express Corporation, V
FedEx Corporation, 18 (upd.); 42 (upd.)
FirstGroup plc, 89
Forward Air Corporation, 75
Fritz Companies, Inc., 12
Frontline Ltd., 45
Frozen Food Express Industries, Inc., 20
Garuda Indonesia, 58 (upd.)
GATX Corporation, 6; 25 (upd.)
GE Capital Aviation Services, 36
Gefco SA, 54
General Maritime Corporation, 59
Genesee & Wyoming Inc., 27
Geodis S.A., 67
The Go-Ahead Group Plc, 28
The Greenbrier Companies, 19
Greyhound Lines, Inc., 32 (upd.)
Groupe Bourbon S.A., 60
Grupo Aeroportuario del Pacífico, S.A. de C.V., 85
Grupo TMM, S.A. de C.V., 50
Grupo Transportación Ferroviaria Mexicana, S.A. de C.V., 47
Gulf Agency Company Ltd. 78
GulfMark Offshore, Inc., 49
Hanjin Shipping Co., Ltd., 50
Hankyu Corporation, V; 23 (upd.)
Hapag-Lloyd AG, 6
Harland and Wolff Holdings plc, 19
Harper Group Inc., 17
Heartland Express, Inc., 18
The Hertz Corporation, 9
Holberg Industries, Inc., 36
Hospitality Worldwide Services, Inc., 26
Hub Group, Inc., 38
Hvide Marine Incorporated, 22
Illinois Central Corporation, 11
International Shipholding Corporation, Inc., 27
J.B. Hunt Transport Services Inc., 12
J Lauritzen A/S, 90
John Menzies plc, 39
Kansas City Southern Industries, Inc., 6; 26 (upd.)
The Kansas City Southern Railway Company, 92
Kawasaki Kisen Kaisha, Ltd., V; 56 (upd.)
Keio Teito Electric Railway Company, V
Keolis SA, 51
Kinki Nippon Railway Company Ltd., V
Kirby Corporation, 18; 66 (upd.)
Knight Transportation, Inc., 64
Koninklijke Nedlloyd Groep N.V., 6
Kuehne & Nagel International AG, V; 53 (upd.)
La Poste, V; 47 (upd.)
Laidlaw International, Inc., 80
Landstar System, Inc., 63
Leaseway Transportation Corp., 12
London Regional Transport, 6
The Long Island Rail Road Company, 68
Lynden Incorporated, 91
Maine Central Railroad Company, 16
Mammoet Transport B.V., 26
Marten Transport, Ltd., 84
Martz Group, 56
Mayflower Group Inc., 6
Mercury Air Group, Inc., 20
The Mersey Docks and Harbour Company, 30
Metropolitan Transportation Authority, 35
Miller Industries, Inc., 26
Mitsui O.S.K. Lines, Ltd., V
Moran Towing Corporation, Inc., 15
The Morgan Group, Inc., 46
Morris Travel Services L.L.C., 26
Motor Cargo Industries, Inc., 35
National Car Rental System, Inc., 10
National Express Group PLC, 50
National Railroad Passenger Corporation (Amtrak), 22; 66 (upd.)
Neptune Orient Lines Limited, 47
NFC plc, 6
Nippon Express Company, Ltd., V; 64 (upd.)
Nippon Yusen Kabushiki Kaisha (NYK), V; 72 (upd.)
Norfolk Southern Corporation, V; 29 (upd.); 75 (upd.)
Oak Harbor Freight Lines, Inc., 53
Ocean Group plc, 6
Odakyu Electric Railway Co., Ltd., V; 68 (upd.)
Odyssey Marine Exploration, Inc., 91
Oglebay Norton Company, 17
Old Dominion Freight Line, Inc., 57
OMI Corporation, 59
The Oppenheimer Group, 76
Österreichische Bundesbahnen GmbH, 6
OTR Express, Inc., 25
Overnite Corporation, 14; 58 (upd.)
Overseas Shipholding Group, Inc., 11
Pacer International, Inc., 54
Pacific Basin Shipping Ltd., 86
Patriot Transportation Holding, Inc., 91
The Peninsular and Oriental Steam Navigation Company, V; 38 (upd.)
Penske Corporation, V; 19 (upd.); 84 (upd.)
PHH Arval, V; 53 (upd.)
Pilot Air Freight Corp., 67
Plantation Pipe Line Company, 68
Polar Air Cargo Inc., 60
The Port Authority of New York and New Jersey, 48
Port Imperial Ferry Corporation, 70
Post Office Group, V
Preston Corporation, 6
RailTex, Inc., 20
Railtrack Group PLC, 50

Réseau Ferré de France, 66
Roadway Express, Inc., V; 25 (upd.)
Rock-It Cargo USA, Inc., 86
Royal Olympic Cruise Lines Inc., 52
Royal Vopak NV, 41
Russian Railways Joint Stock Co., 93
Ryder System, Inc., V; 24 (upd.)
Santa Fe Pacific Corporation, V
Schenker-Rhenus AG, 6
Schneider National, Inc., 36; 77 (upd.)
Seaboard Corporation, 36; 85 (upd.)
SEACOR Holdings Inc., 83
Securicor Plc, 45
Seibu Railway Company Ltd., V; 74 (upd.)
Seino Transportation Company, Ltd., 6
Simon Transportation Services Inc., 27
Smithway Motor Xpress Corporation, 39
Société Nationale des Chemins de Fer Français, V; 57 (upd.)
Société Norbert Dentressangle S.A., 67
Southern Pacific Transportation Company, V
Spee-Dee Delivery Service, Inc., 93
Stagecoach Holdings plc, 30
Stelmar Shipping Ltd., 52
Stevedoring Services of America Inc., 28
Stinnes AG, 8; 59 (upd.)
Stolt-Nielsen S.A., 42
Sunoco, Inc., 28 (upd.); 83 (upd.)
Swift Transportation Co., Inc., 42
The Swiss Federal Railways (Schweizerische Bundesbahnen), V
Swissport International Ltd., 70
Teekay Shipping Corporation, 25; 82 (upd.)
Tibbett & Britten Group plc, 32
Tidewater Inc., 11; 37 (upd.)
TNT Freightways Corporation, 14
TNT Post Group N.V., V; 27 (upd.); 30 (upd.)
Tobu Railway Co Ltd, 6
Tokyu Corporation, V
Totem Resources Corporation, 9
TPG N.V., 64 (upd.)
Trailer Bridge, Inc., 41
Transnet Ltd., 6
Transport Corporation of America, Inc., 49
Trico Marine Services, Inc., 89
Tsakos Energy Navigation Ltd., 91
TTX Company, 6; 66 (upd.)
U.S. Delivery Systems, Inc., 22
Union Pacific Corporation, V; 28 (upd.); 79 (upd.)
United Parcel Service of America Inc., V; 17 (upd.)
United Parcel Service, Inc., 63
United Road Services, Inc., 69
United States Postal Service, 14; 34 (upd.)
US 1 Industries, Inc., 89
USA Truck, Inc., 42
Velocity Express Corporation, 49
Werner Enterprises, Inc., 26
Wincanton plc, 52
Wisconsin Central Transportation Corporation, 24
Wright Express Corporation, 80
Yamato Transport Co. Ltd., V; 49 (upd.)
Yellow Corporation, 14; 45 (upd.)
Yellow Freight System, Inc. of Delaware, V
YRC Worldwide Inc., 90 (upd.)

Utilities

AES Corporation, 10; 13 (upd.); 53 (upd.)
Aggreko Plc, 45
Air & Water Technologies Corporation, 6
Alberta Energy Company Ltd., 16; 43 (upd.)
Allegheny Energy, Inc., V; 38 (upd.)
Ameren Corporation, 60 (upd.)
American Electric Power Company, Inc., V; 45 (upd.)
American States Water Company, 46
American Water Works Company, Inc., 6; 38 (upd.)
Aquarion Company, 84
Aquila, Inc., 50 (upd.)
Arkla, Inc., V
Associated Natural Gas Corporation, 11
Atlanta Gas Light Company, 6; 23 (upd.)
Atlantic Energy, Inc., 6
Atmos Energy Corporation, 43
Avista Corporation, 69 (upd.)
Baltimore Gas and Electric Company, V; 25 (upd.)
Bay State Gas Company, 38
Bayernwerk AG, V; 23 (upd.)
Berlinwasser Holding AG, 90
Bewag AG, 39
Big Rivers Electric Corporation, 11
Black Hills Corporation, 20
Bonneville Power Administration, 50
Boston Edison Company, 12
Bouygues S.A., 24 (upd.)
British Energy Plc, 49
British Gas plc, V
British Nuclear Fuels plc, 6
Brooklyn Union Gas, 6
California Water Service Group, 79
Calpine Corporation, 36
Canadian Utilities Limited, 13; 56 (upd.)
Cap Rock Energy Corporation, 46
Carolina Power & Light Company, V; 23 (upd.)
Cascade Natural Gas Corporation, 9
Centerior Energy Corporation, V
Central and South West Corporation, V
Central Hudson Gas and Electricity Corporation, 6
Central Maine Power, 6
Central Vermont Public Service Corporation, 54
Centrica plc, 29 (upd.)
Chesapeake Utilities Corporation, 56
China Shenhua Energy Company Limited, 83
Chubu Electric Power Company, Inc., V; 46 (upd.)
Chugoku Electric Power Company Inc., V; 53 (upd.)
Cincinnati Gas & Electric Company, 6
CIPSCO Inc., 6
Citizens Utilities Company, 7
City Public Service, 6
Cleco Corporation, 37
CMS Energy Corporation, V, 14
The Coastal Corporation, 31 (upd.)
Cogentrix Energy, Inc., 10
The Coleman Company, Inc., 9
The Columbia Gas System, Inc., V; 16 (upd.)
Commonwealth Edison Company, V
Commonwealth Energy System, 14
Companhia Energética de Minas Gerais S.A. CEMIG, 65
Compañia de Minas Buenaventura S.A.A., 93
Connecticut Light and Power Co., 13
Consolidated Edison, Inc., V; 45 (upd.)
Consolidated Natural Gas Company, V; 19 (upd.)
Consumers Power Co., 14
Consumers Water Company, 14
Consumers' Gas Company Ltd., 6
Covanta Energy Corporation, 64 (upd.)
Dalkia Holding, 66
Destec Energy, Inc., 12
The Detroit Edison Company, V
Dominion Resources, Inc., V; 54 (upd.)
DPL Inc., 6
DQE, Inc., 6
DTE Energy Company, 20 (upd.)
Duke Energy Corporation, V; 27 (upd.)
E.On AG, 50 (upd.)
Eastern Enterprises, 6
Edison International, 56 (upd.)
El Paso Electric Company, 21
El Paso Natural Gas Company, 12
Electrabel N.V., 67
Electricidade de Portugal, S.A., 47
Electricité de France, V; 41 (upd.)
Electricity Generating Authority of Thailand (EGAT), 56
Elektrowatt AG, 6
The Empire District Electric Company, 77
Empresas Públicas de Medellín S.A.E.S.P., 91
Enbridge Inc., 43
ENDESA S.A., V; 46 (upd.)
Enersis S.A., 73
ENMAX Corporation, 83
Enron Corporation, V; 46 (upd.)
Enserch Corporation, V
Ente Nazionale per L'Energia Elettrica, V
Entergy Corporation, V; 45 (upd.)
Environmental Power Corporation, 68
EPCOR Utilities Inc., 81
Equitable Resources, Inc., 6; 54 (upd.)
Exelon Corporation, 48 (upd.)
Florida Progress Corporation, V; 23 (upd.)
Florida Public Utilities Company, 69
Fortis, Inc., 15; 47 (upd.)
Fortum Corporation, 30 (upd.)
FPL Group, Inc., V; 49 (upd.)
Gas Natural SDG S.A., 69
Gaz de France, V; 40 (upd.)
General Public Utilities Corporation, V
Générale des Eaux Group, V
GPU, Inc., 27 (upd.)

Great Plains Energy Incorporated, 65 (upd.)
Gulf States Utilities Company, 6
Hawaiian Electric Industries, Inc., 9
Hokkaido Electric Power Company Inc. (HEPCO), V; 58 (upd.)
Hokuriku Electric Power Company, V
Hong Kong and China Gas Company Ltd., 73
Hongkong Electric Holdings Ltd., 6; 23 (upd.)
Houston Industries Incorporated, V
Hyder plc, 34
Hydro-Québec, 6; 32 (upd.)
Iberdrola, S.A., 49
Idaho Power Company, 12
Illinois Bell Telephone Company, 14
Illinois Power Company, 6
Indiana Energy, Inc., 27
International Power PLC, 50 (upd.)
IPALCO Enterprises, Inc., 6
ITC Holdings Corp., 75
The Kansai Electric Power Company, Inc., V; 62 (upd.)
Kansas City Power & Light Company, 6
Kelda Group plc, 45
Kenetech Corporation, 11
Kentucky Utilities Company, 6
KeySpan Energy Co., 27
Korea Electric Power Corporation (Kepco), 56
KU Energy Corporation, 11
Kyushu Electric Power Company Inc., V
LG&E Energy Corporation, 6; 51 (upd.)
Long Island Lighting Company, V
Lyonnaise des Eaux-Dumez, V
Madison Gas and Electric Company, 39
Magma Power Company, 11
Maine & Maritimes Corporation, 56
Manila Electric Company (Meralco), 56
MCN Corporation, 6
MDU Resources Group, Inc., 7; 42 (upd.)
Middlesex Water Company, 45
Midwest Resources Inc., 6
Minnesota Power, Inc., 11; 34 (upd.)
The Montana Power Company, 11; 44 (upd.)
National Fuel Gas Company, 6
National Grid USA, 51 (upd.)
National Power PLC, 12
Nebraska Public Power District, 29
N.V. Nederlandse Gasunie, V
Nevada Power Company, 11
New England Electric System, V
New Jersey Resources Corporation, 54
New York State Electric and Gas, 6
Neyveli Lignite Corporation Ltd., 65
Niagara Mohawk Holdings Inc., V; 45 (upd.)
Nicor Inc., 6; 86 (upd.)
NIPSCO Industries, Inc., 6
North West Water Group plc, 11
Northeast Utilities, V; 48 (upd.)
Northern States Power Company, V; 20 (upd.)
Northwest Natural Gas Company, 45
NorthWestern Corporation, 37
Nova Corporation of Alberta, V
NRG Energy, Inc., 79
Oglethorpe Power Corporation, 6
Ohio Edison Company, V
Oklahoma Gas and Electric Company, 6
ONEOK Inc., 7
Ontario Hydro Services Company, 6; 32 (upd.)
Osaka Gas Company, Ltd., V; 60 (upd.)
Österreichische Elektrizitätswirtschafts-AG, 85
Otter Tail Power Company, 18
Pacific Enterprises, V
Pacific Gas and Electric Company, V
PacifiCorp, V; 26 (upd.)
Panhandle Eastern Corporation, V
PECO Energy Company, 11
Pennon Group Plc, 45
Pennsylvania Power & Light Company, V
Peoples Energy Corporation, 6
PG&E Corporation, 26 (upd.)
Philadelphia Electric Company, V
Philadelphia Gas Works Company, 92
Philadelphia Suburban Corporation, 39
Piedmont Natural Gas Company, Inc., 27
Pinnacle West Capital Corporation, 6; 54 (upd.)
PNM Resources Inc., 51 (upd.)
Portland General Corporation, 6
Potomac Electric Power Company, 6
Power-One, Inc., 79
Powergen PLC, 11; 50 (upd.)
PPL Corporation, 41 (upd.)
PreussenElektra Aktiengesellschaft, V
Progress Energy, Inc., 74
PSI Resources, 6
Public Service Company of Colorado, 6
Public Service Company of New Hampshire, 21; 55 (upd.)
Public Service Company of New Mexico, 6
Public Service Enterprise Group Inc., V; 44 (upd.)
Puerto Rico Electric Power Authority, 47
Puget Sound Energy Inc., 6; 50 (upd.)
Questar Corporation, 6; 26 (upd.)
RAO Unified Energy System of Russia, 45
Reliant Energy Inc., 44 (upd.)
Rochester Gas and Electric Corporation, 6
Ruhrgas AG, V; 38 (upd.)
RWE AG, V; 50 (upd.)
Salt River Project, 19
San Diego Gas & Electric Company, V
SCANA Corporation, 6; 56 (upd.)
Scarborough Public Utilities Commission, 9
SCEcorp, V
Scottish and Southern Energy plc, 66 (upd.)
Scottish Hydro-Electric PLC, 13
Scottish Power plc, 19; 49 (upd.)
Seattle City Light, 50
SEMCO Energy, Inc., 44
Sempra Energy, 25 (upd.)
Severn Trent PLC, 12; 38 (upd.)
Shikoku Electric Power Company, Inc., V; 60 (upd.)
SJW Corporation, 70
Sonat, Inc., 6
South Jersey Industries, Inc., 42
The Southern Company, V; 38 (upd.)
Southern Connecticut Gas Company, 84
Southern Electric PLC, 13
Southern Indiana Gas and Electric Company, 13
Southern Union Company, 27
Southwest Gas Corporation, 19
Southwest Water Company, 47
Southwestern Electric Power Co., 21
Southwestern Public Service Company, 6
Suez Lyonnaise des Eaux, 36 (upd.)
TECO Energy, Inc., 6
Tennessee Valley Authority, 50
Tennet BV 78
Texas Utilities Company, V; 25 (upd.)
Thames Water plc, 11; 90 (upd.)
Tohoku Electric Power Company, Inc., V
The Tokyo Electric Power Company, 74 (upd.)
The Tokyo Electric Power Company, Incorporated, V
Tokyo Gas Co., Ltd., V; 55 (upd.)
TransAlta Utilities Corporation, 6
TransCanada PipeLines Limited, V
Transco Energy Company, V
Trigen Energy Corporation, 42
Tucson Electric Power Company, 6
UGI Corporation, 12
Unicom Corporation, 29 (upd.)
Union Electric Company, V
The United Illuminating Company, 21
United Utilities PLC, 52 (upd.)
United Water Resources, Inc., 40
Unitil Corporation, 37
Utah Power and Light Company, 27
UtiliCorp United Inc., 6
Vattenfall AB, 57
Vereinigte Elektrizitätswerke Westfalen AG, V
VEW AG, 39
Viridian Group plc, 64
Warwick Valley Telephone Company, 55
Washington Gas Light Company, 19
Washington Natural Gas Company, 9
Washington Water Power Company, 6
Westar Energy, Inc., 57 (upd.)
Western Resources, Inc., 12
Wheelabrator Technologies, Inc., 6
Wisconsin Energy Corporation, 6; 54 (upd.)
Wisconsin Public Service Corporation, 9
WPL Holdings, Inc., 6
WPS Resources Corporation, 53 (upd.)
Xcel Energy Inc., 73 (upd.)

Waste Services

Allied Waste Industries, Inc., 50
Allwaste, Inc., 18
American Ecology Corporation, 77
Appliance Recycling Centers of America, Inc., 42
Azcon Corporation, 23
Berliner Stadtreinigungsbetriebe, 58
Biffa plc, 92
Brambles Industries Limited, 42
Browning-Ferris Industries, Inc., V; 20 (upd.)

Chemical Waste Management, Inc., 9
Clean Harbors, Inc., 73
Copart Inc., 23
Darling International Inc., 85
E.On AG, 50 (upd.)
Ecolab Inc., I; 13 (upd.); 34 (upd.); 85 (upd.)
Ecology and Environment, Inc., 39
Empresas Públicas de Medellín S.A.E.S.P., 91
Fuel Tech, Inc., 85
Industrial Services of America, Inc., 46
Ionics, Incorporated, 52
ISS A/S, 49
Jani-King International, Inc., 85
Kelda Group plc, 45
MPW Industrial Services Group, Inc., 53
Newpark Resources, Inc., 63
Norcal Waste Systems, Inc., 60
1-800-GOT-JUNK? LLC, 74
Onet S.A., 92
Pennon Group Plc, 45
Philip Environmental Inc., 16
Philip Services Corp., 73
Republic Services, Inc., 92
Roto-Rooter, Inc., 15; 61 (upd.)
Safety-Kleen Systems Inc., 8; 82 (upd.)
Saur S.A.S., 92
Sevenson Environmental Services, Inc., 42
Severn Trent PLC, 38 (upd.)
Servpro Industries, Inc., 85
Shanks Group plc, 45
Shred-It Canada Corporation, 56
Stericycle, Inc., 33; 74 (upd.)
TRC Companies, Inc., 32
Valley Proteins, Inc., 91
Veit Companies, 43; 92 (upd.)
Waste Connections, Inc., 46
Waste Holdings, Inc., 41
Waste Management, Inc., V
Wheelabrator Technologies, Inc., 60 (upd.)
Windswept Environmental Group, Inc., 62
WMX Technologies Inc., 17

Geographic Index

Algeria
Sonatrach, IV; 65 (upd.)

Argentina
Acindar Industria Argentina de Aceros S.A., 87
Aerolíneas Argentinas S.A., 33; 69 (upd.)
Alpargatas S.A.I.C., 87
Aluar Aluminio Argentino S.A.I.C., 74
Arcor S.A.I.C., 66
Atanor S.A., 62
Coto Centro Integral de Comercializacion S.A., 66
Cresud S.A.C.I.F. y A., 63
Grupo Clarín S.A., 67
Grupo Financiero Galicia S.A., 63
IRSA Inversiones y Representaciones S.A., 63
Ledesma Sociedad Anónima Agrícola Industrial, 62
Molinos Río de la Plata S.A., 61
Nobleza Piccardo SAICF, 64
Penaflor S.A., 66
Petrobras Energia Participaciones S.A., 72
Quilmes Industrial (QUINSA) S.A., 67
Renault Argentina S.A., 67
Sideco Americana S.A., 67
Siderar S.A.I.C., 66
Telecom Argentina S.A., 63
Telefónica de Argentina S.A., 61
YPF Sociedad Anonima, IV

Australia
ABC Learning Centres Ltd., 93
Amcor Limited, IV; 19 (upd.), 78 (upd.)
Ansell Ltd., 60 (upd.)
Aquarius Platinum Ltd., 63
Aristocrat Leisure Limited, 54
Arnott's Ltd., 66
Austal Limited, 75
Australia and New Zealand Banking Group Limited, II; 52 (upd.)
AWB Ltd., 56
BHP Billiton, 67 (upd.)
Billabong International Ltd., 44
Blundstone Pty Ltd., 76
Bond Corporation Holdings Limited, 10
Boral Limited, III; 43 (upd.)
Brambles Industries Limited, 42
Broken Hill Proprietary Company Ltd., IV; 22 (upd.)
Burns, Philp & Company Ltd., 63
Carlton and United Breweries Ltd., I
Coles Group Limited, V; 20 (upd.); 85 (upd.)
Cochlear Ltd., 77
CRA Limited, IV; 85 (upd.)
CSR Limited, III; 28 (upd.)
David Jones Ltd., 60
Elders IXL Ltd., I
Fairfax Media Ltd., 94 (upd.)
Foster's Group Limited, 7; 21 (upd.); 50 (upd.)
Goodman Fielder Ltd., 52
Harvey Norman Holdings Ltd., 56
Holden Ltd., 62
James Hardie Industries N.V., 56
John Fairfax Holdings Limited, 7
Lend Lease Corporation Limited, IV; 17 (upd.); 52 (upd.)
Lion Nathan Limited, 54
Lonely Planet Publications Pty Ltd., 55
Macquarie Bank Ltd., 69
McPherson's Ltd., 66
Metcash Trading Ltd., 58
MYOB Ltd., 86
News Corporation Limited, IV; 7 (upd.); 46 (upd.)
Nufarm Ltd., 87
Pacific Dunlop Limited, 10
Pioneer International Limited, III
PMP Ltd., 72
Publishing and Broadcasting Limited, 54
Qantas Airways Ltd., 6; 24 (upd.); 68 (upd.)
Repco Corporation Ltd., 74
Ridley Corporation Ltd., 62
Rinker Group Ltd., 65
Rural Press Ltd., 74
Santos Ltd., 81
Smorgon Steel Group Ltd., 62
Southcorp Limited, 54
Suncorp-Metway Ltd., 91
TABCORP Holdings Limited, 44
Telecom Australia, 6
Telstra Corporation Limited, 50
Village Roadshow Ltd., 58
Westpac Banking Corporation, II; 48 (upd.)
WMC, Limited, 43
Zinifex Ltd., 85

Austria
AKG Acoustics GmbH, 62
Andritz AG, 51
Austrian Airlines AG (Österreichische Luftverkehrs AG), 33
Bank Austria AG, 23
Baumax AG, 75
BBAG Osterreichische Brau-Beteiligungs-AG, 38
BÖHLER-UDDEHOLM AG, 73
Borealis AG, 94
Erste Bank der Osterreichischen Sparkassen AG, 69

Gericom AG, 47
Glock Ges.m.b.H., 42
Julius Meinl International AG, 53
Lauda Air Luftfahrt AG, 48
ÖMV Aktiengesellschaft, IV
Österreichische Bundesbahnen GmbH, 6
Österreichische Elektrizitätswirtschafts-AG, 85
Österreichische Post- und Telegraphenverwaltung, V
Raiffeisen Zentralbank Österreich AG, 85
Red Bull GmbH, 60
RHI AG, 53
VA TECH ELIN EBG GmbH, 49
voestalpine AG, IV; 57 (upd.)
Wienerberger AG, 70
Zumtobel AG, 50

Azerbaijan

Azerbaijan Airlines, 77

Bahamas

Bahamas Air Holdings Ltd., 66
Kerzner International Limited, 69 (upd.)
Sun International Hotels Limited, 26
Teekay Shipping Corporation, 25; 82 (upd.)

Bahrain

Gulf Air Company, 56
Investcorp SA, 57

Bangladesh

Grameen Bank, 31

Belgium

Agfa Gevaert Group N.V., 59
Almanij NV, 44
Arcelor Gent, 80
Bank Brussels Lambert, II
Barco NV, 44
Bekaert S.A./N.V., 90
Belgacom, 6
Besix Group S.A./NV, 94
Brouwerijen Alken-Maes N.V., 86
C&A, 40 (upd.)
Cockerill Sambre Group, IV; 26 (upd.)
Compagnie Nationale à Portefeuille, 84
Cora S.A./NV, 94
Deceuninck N.V., 84
Delhaize "Le Lion" S.A., 44
Dexia NV/SA, 88 (upd.)
DHL Worldwide Network S.A./N.V., 69 (upd.)
Distrigaz S.A., 82
Electrabel N.V., 67
Etablissements Franz Colruyt N.V., 68
Generale Bank, II
GIB Group, V; 26 (upd.)
Glaverbel Group, 80
Groupe Herstal S.A., 58
Interbrew S.A., 17; 50 (upd.)
Janssen Pharmaceutica N.V., 80
Kredietbank N.V., II
Lyfra-S.A./NV, 88
PetroFina S.A., IV; 26 (upd.)
Punch International N.V., 66
Puratos S.A./NV, 92
Quick Restaurants S.A., 94
Rosy Blue N.V., 84
Roularta Media Group NV, 48
Sabena S.A./N.V., 33
Solvay S.A., I; 21 (upd.); 61 (upd.)
Spector Photo Group N.V., 82
Tessenderlo Group, 76
Tractebel S.A., 20
NV Umicore SA, 47
Xeikon NV, 26

Belize

BB Holdings Limited, 77

Bermuda

Assured Guaranty Ltd., 93
Bacardi & Company Ltd., 18; 82 (upd.)
Central European Media Enterprises Ltd., 61
Covidien Ltd., 91
Endurance Specialty Holdings Ltd., 85
Frontline Ltd., 45
Gosling Brothers Ltd., 82
Jardine Matheson Holdings Limited, I; 20 (upd.); 93 (upd.)
Nabors Industries Ltd., 91 (upd.)
PartnerRe Ltd., 83
Sea Containers Ltd., 29
Tyco International Ltd., III; 28 (upd.); 63 (upd.)
VistaPrint Limited, 87
Warner Chilcott Limited, 85
White Mountains Insurance Group, Ltd., 48

Brazil

Aracruz Celulose S.A., 57
Banco Bradesco S.A., 13
Banco Itaú S.A., 19
Brasil Telecom Participaçoes S.A., 57
Brazil Fast Food Corporation, 74
Bunge Brasil S.A. 78
Camargo Corrêa S.A., 93
Casas Bahia Comercial Ltda., 75
Cia Hering, 72
Companhia Brasileira de Distribuiçao, 76
Companhia de Bebidas das Américas, 57
Companhia de Tecidos Norte de Minas - Coteminas, 77
Companhia Energética de Minas Gerais S.A. CEMIG, 65
Companhia Siderúrgica Nacional, 76
Companhia Suzano de Papel e Celulose S.A., 94
Companhia Vale do Rio Doce, IV; 43 (upd.)
Empresa Brasileira de Aeronáutica S.A. (Embraer), 36
Gerdau S.A., 59
Globo Comunicação e Participações S.A., 80
Gol Linhas Aéreas Inteligentes S.A., 73
Ipiranga S.A., 67
Klabin S.A., 73
Lojas Americanas S.A., 77
Lojas Arapua S.A., 22; 61 (upd.)
Marcopolo S.A. 79
Natura Cosméticos S.A., 75
Odebrecht S.A., 73
Perdigao SA, 52
Petróleo Brasileiro S.A., IV
Randon S.A. 79
Renner Herrmann S.A. 79
Sadia S.A., 59
Sao Paulo Alpargatas S.A., 75
Souza Cruz S.A., 65
TAM Linhas Aéreas S.A., 68
Tele Norte Leste Participações S.A., 80
TransBrasil S/A Linhas Aéreas, 31
Unibanco Holdings S.A., 73
Usinas Siderúrgicas de Minas Gerais S.A., 77
VARIG S.A. (Viaçâo Aérea Rio-Grandense), 6; 29 (upd.)
Vicunha Têxtil S.A. 78
Votorantim Participaçoes S.A., 76
Weg S.A. 78

Canada

Abitibi-Consolidated, Inc., V; 25 (upd.)
Abitibi-Price Inc., IV
Agnico-Eagle Mines Limited, 71
Agrium Inc., 73
Air Canada, 6; 23 (upd.); 59 (upd.)
Alberta Energy Company Ltd., 16; 43 (upd.)
Alcan Aluminium Limited, IV; 31 (upd.)
Alderwoods Group, Inc., 68 (upd.)
Algo Group Inc., 24
Alimentation Couche-Tard Inc., 77
Alliance Atlantis Communications Inc., 39
ATI Technologies Inc. 79
Axcan Pharma Inc., 85
Ballard Power Systems Inc., 73
Bank of Montreal, II; 46 (upd.)
The Bank of Nova Scotia, II; 59 (upd.)
Barrick Gold Corporation, 34
Bata Ltd., 62
BCE Inc., V; 44 (upd.)
Bell Canada, 6
BFC Construction Corporation, 25
BioWare Corporation, 81
Biovail Corporation, 47
Bombardier Inc., 42 (upd.); 87 (upd.)
Boston Pizza International Inc., 88
Bradley Air Services Ltd., 56
Bramalea Ltd., 9
Brascan Corporation, 67
British Columbia Telephone Company, 6
Brookfield Properties Corporation, 89
Cameco Corporation, 77
Campeau Corporation, V
Canada Packers Inc., II
Canadair, Inc., 16
The Canadian Broadcasting Corporation (CBC), 37
Canadian Imperial Bank of Commerce, II; 61 (upd.)
Canadian National Railway Company, 6, 71 (upd.)
Canadian Pacific Railway Limited, V; 45 (upd.)
Canadian Tire Corporation, Limited, 71 (upd.)

Canadian Utilities Limited, 13; 56 (upd.)
Canfor Corporation, 42
Canstar Sports Inc., 16
CanWest Global Communications Corporation, 35
Cascades Inc., 71
Celestica Inc., 80
CHC Helicopter Corporation, 67
Cinar Corporation, 40
Cineplex Odeon Corporation, 6; 23 (upd.)
Cinram International, Inc., 43
Cirque du Soleil Inc., 29
Clearly Canadian Beverage Corporation, 48
Cognos Inc., 44
Cominco Ltd., 37
Consumers' Gas Company Ltd., 6
CoolBrands International Inc., 35
Corby Distilleries Limited, 14
Corel Corporation, 15; 33 (upd.); 76 (upd.)
Cott Corporation, 52
Creo Inc., 48
Diavik Diamond Mines Inc., 85
Discreet Logic Inc., 20
Dofasco Inc., IV; 24 (upd.)
Doman Industries Limited, 59
Dominion Textile Inc., 12
Domtar Corporation, IV; 89 (upd.)
Dorel Industries Inc., 59
Duvernay Oil Corp., 83
Dynatec Corporation, 87
Dylex Limited, 29
Echo Bay Mines Ltd., IV; 38 (upd.)
Enbridge Inc., 43
ENMAX Corporation, 83
EPCOR Utilities Inc., 81
Extendicare Health Services, Inc., 6
Fairfax Financial Holdings Limited, 57
Fairmont Hotels & Resorts Inc., 69
Falconbridge Limited, 49
Finning International Inc., 69
Fortis, Inc., 15; 47 (upd.)
The Forzani Group Ltd. 79
Four Seasons Hotels Inc., 9; 29 (upd.)
Future Shop Ltd., 62
GEAC Computer Corporation Ltd., 43
George Weston Ltd, II; 36 (upd.); 88 (upd.)
Gildan Activewear, Inc., 81
Goldcorp Inc., 87
GPS Industries, Inc., 81
Great-West Lifeco Inc., III
Groupe Vidéotron Ltée., 20
Hammond Manufacturing Company Limited, 83
Harlequin Enterprises Limited, 52
Hemlo Gold Mines Inc., 9
Héroux-Devtek Inc., 69
Hiram Walker Resources, Ltd., I
The Hockey Company, 34; 70
Hollinger International Inc., 62 (upd.)
Home Hardware Stores Ltd., 62
The Hudson Bay Mining and Smelting Company, Limited, 12
Hudson's Bay Company, V; 25 (upd.); 83 (upd.)
Hurricane Hydrocarbons Ltd., 54
Husky Energy Inc., 47
Hydro-Québec, 6; 32 (upd.)
Imasco Limited, V
IMAX Corporation 28, 78 (upd.)
Imperial Oil Limited, IV; 25 (upd.)
Imperial Parking Corporation, 58
Inco Limited, IV; 45 (upd.)
Indigo Books & Music Inc., 58
Intercorp Excelle Foods Inc., 64
Intrawest Corporation, 15; 84 (upd.)
Iogen Corporation, 81
Irwin Toy Limited, 14
Jacques Whitford, 92
The Jean Coutu Group (PJC) Inc., 46
The Jim Pattison Group, 37
Kinross Gold Corporation, 36
Kruger Inc., 17
La Senza Corporation, 66
Labatt Brewing Company Limited, I; 25 (upd.)
LaSiDo Inc., 58
Lassonde Industries Inc., 68
Le Chateau Inc., 63
Ledcor Industries Limited, 46
Les Boutiques San Francisco, Inc., 62
Linamar Corporation, 18
Lions Gate Entertainment Corporation, 35
Loblaw Companies Limited, 43
The Loewen Group, Inc., 16; 40 (upd.)
London Drugs Ltd., 46
Maclean Hunter Publishing Limited, IV; 26 (upd.)
MacMillan Bloedel Limited, IV
Magellan Aerospace Corporation, 48
Manitoba Telecom Services, Inc., 61
Manulife Financial Corporation, 85
Maple Leaf Foods Inc., 41
Maple Leaf Sports & Entertainment Ltd., 61
Masonite International Corporation, 63
McCain Foods Limited, 77
MDC Partners Inc., 63
Mega Bloks, Inc., 61
Methanex Corporation, 40
Métro Inc., 77
Mitel Corporation, 18
The Molson Companies Limited, I; 26 (upd.)
Moore Corporation Limited, IV
Morguard Corporation, 85
Mouvement des Caisses Desjardins, 48
National Bank of Canada, 85
National Sea Products Ltd., 14
Nature's Path Foods, Inc., 87
New Flyer Industries Inc. 78
Nexen Inc. 79
Noranda Inc., IV; 7 (upd.); 64 (upd.)
Nortel Networks Corporation, 36 (upd.)
The North West Company, Inc., 12
Northern Telecom Limited, V
Nova Corporation of Alberta, V
Novacor Chemicals Ltd., 12
Olympia & York Developments Ltd., IV; 9 (upd.)
1-800-GOT-JUNK? LLC, 74
Onex Corporation, 16; 65 (upd.)
Ontario Hydro Services Company, 6; 32 (upd.)
Ontario Teachers' Pension Plan, 61
Open Text Corporation 79
The Oppenheimer Group, 76
The Oshawa Group Limited, II
Paramount Resources Ltd., 87
PCL Construction Group Inc., 50
Peace Arch Entertainment Group Inc., 51
Petro-Canada Limited, IV
Philip Environmental Inc., 16
Placer Dome Inc., 20; 61 (upd.)
Potash Corporation of Saskatchewan Inc., 18
Power Corporation of Canada, 36 (upd.); 85 (upd.)
Provigo Inc., II; 51 (upd.)
QLT Inc., 71
Quebecor Inc., 12; 47 (upd.)
Research in Motion Ltd., 54
Richtree Inc., 63
Ritchie Bros. Auctioneers Inc., 41
RM Auctions, Inc., 88
Rogers Communications Inc., 30 (upd.)
RONA, Inc., 73
Roots Canada Ltd., 42
Royal Bank of Canada, II; 21 (upd.), 81 (upd.)
Royal Group Technologies Limited, 73
Saputo Inc., 59
Scarborough Public Utilities Commission, 9
The Seagram Company Ltd., I; 25 (upd.)
Shermag, Inc., 93
Shoppers Drug Mart Corporation, 49
Shred-It Canada Corporation, 56
Sleeman Breweries Ltd., 74
SNC-Lavalin Group Inc., 72
Sobeys Inc., 80
Southam Inc., 7
Spar Aerospace Limited, 32
Spin Master, Ltd., 61
Steinberg Incorporated, II
Stelco Inc., IV; 51 (upd.)
Sun Life Financial Inc., 85
Sun-Rype Products Ltd., 76
Suncor Energy Inc., 54
SunOpta Inc. 79
Talisman Energy Inc., 9; 47 (upd.)
TDL Group Ltd., 46
Teck Corporation, 27
Tembec Inc., 66
The Thomson Corporation, 8; 34 (upd.); 77 (upd.)
Tilley Endurables, Inc., 67
Toromont Industries, Ltd., 21
The Toronto-Dominion Bank, II; 49 (upd.)
Torstar Corporation, 29
TransAlta Utilities Corporation, 6
TransCanada Corporation, V; 93 (upd.)
Tridel Enterprises Inc., 9
Trilon Financial Corporation, II
Triple Five Group Ltd., 49
Trizec Corporation Ltd., 10
Tucows Inc. 78
Van Houtte Inc., 39
Varity Corporation, III

Vincor International Inc., 50
Wascana Energy Inc., 13
The Wawanesa Mutual Insurance Company, 68
West Fraser Timber Co. Ltd., 17; 91 (upd.)
Western Oil Sands Inc., 85
WestJet Airlines Ltd., 38

Cayman Islands

Garmin Ltd., 60
Herbalife Ltd., 92 (upd.)
United National Group, Ltd., 63

Chile

Banco de Chile, 69
Cencosud S.A., 69
Compania Cervecerias Unidas S.A., 70
Corporacion Nacional del Cobre de Chile, 40
Cristalerias de Chile S.A., 67
Distribución y Servicio D&S S.A., 71
Embotelladora Andina S.A., 71
Empresas Almacenes Paris S.A., 71
Empresas CMPC S.A., 70
Empresas Copec S.A., 69
Enersis S.A., 73
Farmacias Ahumada S.A., 72
Lan Chile S.A., 31
Madeco S.A., 71
Parque Arauco S.A., 72
S.A.C.I. Falabella, 69
Viña Concha y Toro S.A., 45

China

Air China, 46
American Oriental Bioengineering Inc., 93
Asia Info Holdings, Inc., 43
Bank of China, 63
China Automotive Systems Inc., 87
China Construction Bank Corp. 79
China Eastern Airlines Co. Ltd., 31
China Life Insurance Company Limited, 65
China National Cereals, Oils and Foodstuffs Import and Export Corporation (COFCO), 76
China National Petroleum Corporation, 46
China Netcom Group Corporation (Hong Kong) Limited, 73
China Shenhua Energy Company Limited, 83
China Southern Airlines Company Ltd., 33
China Telecom, 50
Chinese Petroleum Corporation, IV; 31 (upd.)
Dalian Shide Group, 91
Egmont Group, 93
Guangzhou Pearl River Piano Group Ltd., 49
Haier Group Corporation, 65
Huawei Technologies Company Ltd., 87
Li & Fung Limited, 59
Shanghai Baosteel Group Corporation, 71
Shanghai Petrochemical Co., Ltd., 18
SINA Corporation, 69
Suntech Power Holdings Company Ltd., 89
Tsingtao Brewery Group, 49
Zindart Ltd., 60

Colombia

Almacenes Exito S.A., 89
Avianca Aerovías Nacionales de Colombia SA, 36
Bavaria S.A., 90
Cementos Argos S.A., 91
Empresa Colombiana de Petróleos, IV
Empresas Públicas de Medellín S.A.E.S.P., 91
Inversiones Nacional de Chocolates S.A., 88
Suramericana de Inversiones S.A., 88
Valorem S.A., 88

Croatia

PLIVA d.d., 70

Cyprus

Bank of Cyprus Group, 91
Cyprus Airways Public Limited, 81
Marfin Popular Bank plc, 92

Czech Republic

Budweiser Budvar, National Corporation, 59
Ceské aerolinie, a.s., 66
Cesky Telecom, a.s., 64
Skoda Auto a.s., 39
Třinecké Železárny A.S., 92

Denmark

A.P. Møller - Maersk A/S, 57
Aalborg Industries A/S, 90
Aarhus United A/S, 68
Arla Foods amba, 48
Bang & Olufsen Holding A/S, 37; 86 (upd.)
Bestseller A/S, 90
Carl Allers Etablissement A/S, 72
Carlsberg A/S, 9; 29 (upd.)
Chr. Hansen Group A/S, 70
Danisco A/S, 44
Danske Bank Aktieselskab, 50
Ecco Sko A/S, 62
FLSmidth & Co. A/S, 72
Group 4 Falck A/S, 42
Grundfos Group, 83
H. Lundbeck A/S, 44
House of Prince A/S, 80
Hummel International A/S, 68
IKEA International A/S, V; 26 (upd.)
ISS A/S, 49
J Lauritzen A/S, 90
Lego A/S, 13; 40 (upd.)
Nordisk Film A/S, 80
Novo Nordisk A/S, I; 61 (upd.)
Schouw & Company A/S, 94
Sophus Berendsen A/S, 49
Sterling European Airlines A/S, 70
TDC A/S, 63
Velux A/S, 86
Vestas Wind Systems A/S, 73

Ecuador

Exportadora Bananera Noboa, S.A., 91
Petróleos del Ecuador, IV

Egypt

EgyptAir, 6; 27 (upd.)
Egyptian General Petroleum Corporation, IV; 51 (upd.)
Orascom Construction Industries S.A.E., 87

El Salvador

Grupo TACA, 38

Estonia

AS Estonian Air, 71

Ethiopia

Ethiopian Airlines, 81

Fiji

Air Pacific Ltd., 70

Finland

Ahlstrom Corporation, 53
Amer Group plc, 41
Dynea, 68
Enso-Gutzeit Oy, IV
Finnair Oyj, 6; 25 (upd.); 61 (upd.)
Fiskars Corporation, 33
Fortum Corporation, 30 (upd.)
Hackman Oyj Adp, 44
Huhtamäki Oyj, 64
Imatra Steel Oy Ab, 55
Kansallis-Osake-Pankki, II
Kemira Oyj, 70
Kesko Ltd. (Kesko Oy), 8; 27 (upd.)
KONE Corporation, 27; 76 (upd.)
Kymmene Corporation, IV
M-real Oyj, 56 (upd.)
Metsa-Serla Oy, IV
Metso Corporation, 30 (upd.); 85 (upd.)
Neste Oil Corporation, IV; 85 (upd.)
Nokia Corporation, II; 17 (upd.); 38 (upd.); 77 (upd.)
Orion Oyj, 72
Outokumpu Oyj, 38
Posti- ja Telelaitos, 6
Sanitec Corporation, 51
SanomaWSOY Corporation, 51
Sonera Corporation, 50
Stora Enso Oyj, 36 (upd.); 85 (upd.)
Tamfelt Oyj Abp, 62
United Paper Mills Ltd. (Yhtyneet Paperitehtaat Oy), IV
UPM-Kymmene Corporation, 19; 50 (upd.)
Valmet Corporation (Valmet Oy), III

France

Accor S.A., 10; 27 (upd.); 69 (upd.)
Aéroports de Paris, 33
The Aerospatiale Group, 7; 21 (upd.)
Agence France-Presse, 34

Akerys S.A., 90
Alain Afflelou SA, 53
Alcatel S.A., 9; 36 (upd.)
Alès Groupe, 81
Altran Technologies, 51
Amec Spie S.A., 57
Arc International, 76
AREVA NP, 90 (upd.)
Arianespace S.A., 89
Association des Centres Distributeurs E. Leclerc, 37
Assurances Générales de France, 63
Atochem S.A., I
Atos Origin S.A., 69
Au Printemps S.A., V
Auchan, 37
Automobiles Citroen, 7
Autoroutes du Sud de la France SA, 55
Avions Marcel Dassault-Breguet Aviation, I
Axa, III
Baccarat, 24
Banque Nationale de Paris S.A., II
Baron Philippe de Rothschild S.A., 39
Bayard SA, 49
Belvedere S.A., 93
Bénéteau SA, 55
Besnier SA, 19
BigBen Interactive S.A., 72
bioMérieux S.A., 75
BNP Paribas Group, 36 (upd.)
Boiron S.A., 73
Boizel Chanoine Champagne S.A., 94
Bonduelle SA, 51
Bongrain SA, 25
Bouygues S.A., I; 24 (upd.)
Bricorama S.A., 68
Brioche Pasquier S.A., 58
BSN Groupe S.A., II
Buffalo Grill S.A., 94
Bugatti Automobiles S.A.S., 94
Bull S.A., 43 (upd.)
Bureau Veritas SA, 55
Burelle S.A., 23
Business Objects S.A., 25
Camaïeu S.A., 72
Caisse des Dépôts et Consignations, 90
Canal Plus, 10; 34 (upd.)
Cap Gemini Ernst & Young, 37
Carbone Lorraine S.A., 33
Carrefour SA, 10; 27 (upd.); 64 (upd.)
Casino Guichard-Perrachon S.A., 59 (upd.)
Cemoi S.A., 86
Cetelem S.A., 21
Chanel SA, 12; 49 (upd.)
Charal S.A., 90
Chargeurs International, 6; 21 (upd.)
Christian Dalloz SA, 40
Christian Dior S.A., 19; 49 (upd.)
Christofle SA, 40
Ciments Français, 40
Club Mediterranée S.A., 6; 21 (upd.); 91 (upd.)
Coflexip S.A., 25
Colas S.A., 31
Compagnie de Saint-Gobain, III; 16 (upd.); 64 (upd.)
Compagnie des Alpes, 48
Compagnie des Machines Bull S.A., III
Compagnie Financiere de Paribas, II
Compagnie Financière Sucres et Denrées S.A., 60
Compagnie Générale d'Électricité, II
Compagnie Générale des Établissements Michelin, V; 42 (upd.)
Compagnie Générale Maritime et Financière, 6
Comptoirs Modernes S.A., 19
Coopagri Bretagne, 88
Crédit Agricole Group, II; 84 (upd.)
Crédit Lyonnais, 9; 33 (upd.)
Crédit National S.A., 9
Dalkia Holding, 66
Darty S.A., 27
Dassault Systèmes S.A., 25
DCN S.A., 75
De Dietrich & Cie., 31
Delachaux S.A., 76
Deveaux S.A., 41
Devoteam S.A., 94
Dexia Group, 42
Doux S.A., 80
Du Pareil au Même, 43
Dynaction S.A., 67
EADS SOCATA, 54
ECS S.A, 12
Ed S.A.S., 88
Éditions Gallimard, 72
Editis S.A. 78
Eiffage, 27
Electricité de France, V; 41 (upd.)
Elf Aquitaine SA, 21 (upd.)
Elior SA, 49
Eram SA, 51
Eramet, 73
Eridania Béghin-Say S.A., 36
Essilor International, 21
Etablissements Economiques du Casino Guichard, Perrachon et Cie, S.C.A., 12
Établissements Jacquot and Cie S.A.S., 92
Etam Developpement SA, 44
Eurazeo, 80
Euro Disney S.C.A., 20; 58 (upd.)
Euro RSCG Worldwide S.A., 13
Eurocopter S.A., 80
Eurofins Scientific S.A., 70
Euronext Paris S.A., 37
Expand SA, 48
Facom S.A., 32
Faiveley S.A., 39
Faurecia S.A., 70
Fimalac S.A., 37
Fleury Michon S.A., 39
Floc'h & Marchand, 80
FNAC, 21
Framatome SA, 19
France Télécom Group, V; 21 (upd.)
Fromageries Bel, 23
G.I.E. Airbus Industrie, I; 12 (upd.)
Galeries Lafayette S.A., V; 23 (upd.)
Gaumont S.A., 25; 91 (upd.)
Gaz de France, V; 40 (upd.)
Gecina SA, 42
Gefco SA, 54
Générale des Eaux Group, V
Geodis S.A., 67
GFI Informatique SA, 49
GiFi S.A., 74
Glaces Thiriet S.A., 76
GrandVision S.A., 43
Grévin & Compagnie SA, 56
Groupama S.A., 76
Groupe Air France, 6
Groupe Alain Manoukian, 55
Groupe André, 17
Groupe Bolloré, 67
Groupe Bourbon S.A., 60
Groupe Castorama-Dubois Investissements, 23
Groupe CECAB S.C.A., 88
Groupe Crit S.A., 74
Groupe Danone, 32 (upd.); 93 (upd.)
Groupe Dassault Aviation SA, 26 (upd.)
Groupe de la Cite, IV
Groupe DMC (Dollfus Mieg & Cie), 27
Groupe Euralis, 86
Groupe Fournier SA, 44
Groupe Glon, 84
Groupe Go Sport S.A., 39
Groupe Guillin SA, 40
Groupe Jean-Claude Darmon, 44
Groupe Lactalis 78 (upd.)
Groupe Lapeyre S.A., 33
Groupe Le Duff S.A., 84
Groupe Léa Nature, 88
Groupe Legris Industries, 23
Groupe Les Echos, 25
Groupe Limagrain, 74
Groupe Louis Dreyfus S.A., 60
Groupe Monnoyeur, 72
Groupe Monoprix S.A., 86
Groupe Open, 74
Groupe Partouche SA, 48
Groupe Promodès S.A., 19
Groupe Rougier SA, 21
Groupe SEB, 35
Groupe Sequana Capital 78 (upd.)
Groupe Sidel S.A., 21
Groupe Soufflet SA, 55
Groupe Yves Saint Laurent, 23
Groupe Zannier S.A., 35
Guerbet Group, 46
Guerlain, 23
Guilbert S.A., 42
Guillemot Corporation, 41
Guinot Paris S.A., 82
Guy Degrenne SA, 44
Guyenne et Gascogne, 23
Hachette, IV
Hachette Filipacchi Medias S.A., 21
Havas, SA, 10; 33 (upd.)
Hermès International S.A., 14; 34 (upd.)
Imerys S.A., 40 (upd.)
Imetal S.A., IV
Infogrames Entertainment S.A., 35
Ingenico—Compagnie Industrielle et Financière d'Ingénierie, 46
ITM Entreprises SA, 36
JCDecaux S.A., 76
Keolis SA, 51
Kiabi Europe, 66
L'Air Liquide SA, I; 47 (upd.)
L'Entreprise Jean Lefebvre, 23

L'Oréal SA, III; 8 (upd.); 46 (upd.)
L.D.C. SA, 61
La Poste, V; 47 (upd.)
Labeyrie SAS, 80
Laboratoires Arkopharma S.A., 75
Laboratoires de Biologie Végétale Yves Rocher, 35
LaCie Group S.A., 76
Lafarge Coppée S.A., III
Lafuma S.A., 39
Laurent-Perrier SA, 42
Lazard LLC, 38
LDC, 68
Le Cordon Bleu S.A., 67
Le Monde S.A., 33
Legrand SA, 21
Leroux S.A.S., 65
Leroy Merlin SA, 54
Ludendo S.A., 88
LVMH Möet Hennessy Louis Vuitton SA, I; 10; 33 (upd.)
Lyonnaise des Eaux-Dumez, V
Madrange SA, 58
Maison Louis Jadot, 24
Manitou BF S.A., 27
Manutan International S.A., 72
Marie Brizard & Roger International S.A., 22
Marionnaud Parfumeries SA, 51
Martell and Company S.A., 82
Matra-Hachette S.A., 15 (upd.)
Matussière et Forest SA, 58
MBK Industrie S.A., 94
Metaleurop S.A., 21
Métropole Télévision, 33
Métropole Télévision S.A., 76 (upd.)
Moliflor Loisirs, 80
Monnaie de Paris, 62
Montupet S.A., 63
Moulinex S.A., 22
Mr. Bricolage S.A., 37
Naf Naf SA, 44
Neopost S.A., 53
Nestlé Waters, 73
Nexans SA, 54
Nexity S.A., 66
Nocibé SA, 54
OENEO S.A., 74 (upd.)
Onet S.A., 92
Otor S.A., 77
PagesJaunes Groupe SA 79
Panzani, 84
Papeteries de Lancey, 23
Pathé SA, 29
Pechiney SA, IV; 45 (upd.)
Penauille Polyservices SA, 49
Pernod Ricard S.A., I; 21 (upd.); 72 (upd.)
Peugeot S.A., I
Picard Surgeles, 76
Pierre & Vacances SA, 48
Pinault-Printemps Redoute S.A., 19 (upd.)
Pinguely-Haulotte SA, 51
Piscines Desjoyaux S.A., 84
Pochet SA, 55
Poliet S.A., 33
PPR S.A., 74 (upd.)
Provimi S.A., 80
PSA Peugeot Citroen S.A., 28 (upd.)
Publicis S.A., 19; 77 (upd.)
Rallye SA, 54
Regie Nationale des Usines Renault, I
Rémy Cointreau Group, 20, 80 (upd.)
Renault S.A., 26 (upd.); 74 (upd.)
Réseau Ferré de France, 66
Rhodia SA, 38
Rhône-Poulenc S.A., I; 10 (upd.)
Robertet SA, 39
Rodriguez Group S.A., 90
Roussel Uclaf, I; 8 (upd.)
Royal Canin S.A., 39
Sabaté Diosos SA, 48
SAGEM S.A., 37
Salomon Worldwide, 20
The Sanofi-Synthélabo Group, I; 49 (upd.)
Saur S.A.S., 92
Schneider S.A., II; 18 (upd.)
SCOR S.A., 20
Seita, 23
Selectour SA, 53
Sephora Holdings S.A., 82
Simco S.A., 37
Skalli Group, 67
Skis Rossignol S.A., 15; 43 (upd.)
Smoby International SA, 56
Snecma Group, 46
Société Air France, 27 (upd.)
Société BIC S.A., 73
Société d'Exploitation AOM Air Liberté SA (AirLib), 53
Societe des Produits Marnier-Lapostolle S.A., 88
Société du Figaro S.A., 60
Société du Louvre, 27
Société Générale, II; 42 (upd.)
Société Industrielle Lesaffre, 84
Société Nationale des Chemins de Fer Français, V; 57 (upd.)
Société Nationale Elf Aquitaine, IV; 7 (upd.)
Société Norbert Dentressangle S.A., 67
Sodexho SA, 29; 91 (upd.)
Sodiaal S.A., 36 (upd.)
SODIMA, II
Sommer-Allibert S.A., 19
SR Teleperformance S.A., 86
Steria SA, 49
Suez Lyonnaise des Eaux, 36 (upd.)
Taittinger S.A., 43
Tati SA, 25
Technip 78
Télévision Française 1, 23
Terrena L'Union CANA CAVAL, 70
Thales S.A., 42
THOMSON multimedia S.A., II; 42 (upd.)
Total Fina Elf S.A., IV; 24 (upd.); 50 (upd.)
Toupargel-Agrigel S.A., 76
Touton S.A., 92
Transiciel SA, 48
Ubi Soft Entertainment S.A., 41
Ugine S.A., 20
Unibail SA, 40
Unilog SA, 42
Union des Assurances de Pans, III
Union Financière de France Banque SA, 52
Usinor SA, IV; 42 (upd.)
Valeo, 23; 66 (upd.)
Vallourec SA, 54
Vicat S.A., 70
Viel & Cie, 76
Vilmorin Clause et Cie, 70
Vinci, 43
Vivarte SA, 54 (upd.)
Vivendi Universal S.A., 46 (upd.)
Wanadoo S.A., 75
Weber et Broutin France, 66
Worms et Cie, 27
Zodiac S.A., 36

Germany

A. Moksel AG, 59
A.W. Faber-Castell Unternehmensverwaltung GmbH & Co., 51
Adam Opel AG, 7; 21 (upd.); 61 (upd.)
adidas Group AG, 14; 33 (upd.); 75 (upd.)
Adolf Würth GmbH & Co. KG, 49
AEG A.G., I
Air Berlin GmbH & Co. Luftverkehrs KG, 71
Aldi Einkauf GmbH & Co. OHG 13; 86 (upd.)
Alfred Kärcher GmbH & Co KG, 94
Alfred Ritter GmbH & Co. KG, 58
Allianz AG, III; 15 (upd.); 57 (upd.)
ALTANA AG, 87
AMB Generali Holding AG, 51
Andreas Stihl AG & Co. KG, 16; 59 (upd.)
AOK-Bundesverband (Federation of the AOK) 78
Aral AG, 62
ARD, 41
August Storck KG, 66
AVA AG (Allgemeine Handelsgesellschaft der Verbraucher AG), 33
AXA Colonia Konzern AG, 27; 49 (upd.)
Axel Springer Verlag AG, IV; 20 (upd.)
Bahlsen GmbH & Co. KG, 44
Barmag AG, 39
BASF Aktiengesellschaft, I; 18 (upd.); 50 (upd.)
Bauer Publishing Group, 7
Bayer A.G., I; 13 (upd.); 41 (upd.)
Bayerische Hypotheken- und Wechsel-Bank AG, II
Bayerische Motoren Werke AG, I; 11 (upd.); 38 (upd.)
Bayerische Vereinsbank A.G., II
Bayernwerk AG, V; 23 (upd.)
Behr GmbH & Co. KG, 72
Beiersdorf AG, 29
Berliner Stadtreinigungsbetriebe, 58
Berliner Verkehrsbetriebe (BVG), 58
Berlinwasser Holding AG, 90
Bertelsmann A.G., IV; 15 (upd.); 43 (upd.); 91 (upd.)
Bewag AG, 39

Bibliographisches Institut & F.A. Brockhaus AG, 74
Bilfinger & Berger AG, I; 55 (upd.)
Brauerei Beck & Co., 9; 33 (upd.)
Braun GmbH, 51
Brenntag AG, 8; 23 (upd.)
Brose Fahrzeugteile GmbH & Company KG, 84
BSH Bosch und Siemens Hausgeräte GmbH, 67
Buderus AG, 37
Burda Holding GmbH. & Co., 23
C&A Brenninkmeyer KG, V
C.H. Boehringer Sohn, 39
Carl Kühne KG (GmbH & Co.), 94
Carl Zeiss AG, III; 34 (upd.); 91 (upd.)
CeWe Color Holding AG, 76
Commerzbank A.G., II; 47 (upd.)
Continental AG, V; 56 (upd.)
Cornelsen Verlagsholding GmbH & Co., 90
Dachser GmbH & Co. KG, 88
Daimler-Benz Aerospace AG, 16
DaimlerChrysler AG, I; 15 (upd.); 34 (upd.); 64 (upd.)
Dalli-Werke GmbH & Co. KG, 86
dba Luftfahrtgesellschaft mbH, 76
Debeka Krankenversicherungsverein auf Gegenseitigkeit, 72
Degussa Group, IV
Degussa-Huls AG, 32 (upd.)
Deutsche Babcock A.G., III
Deutsche Bahn AG, 46 (upd.)
Deutsche Bank AG, II; 14 (upd.); 40 (upd.)
Deutsche BP Aktiengesellschaft, 7
Deutsche Bundesbahn, V
Deutsche Bundespost TELEKOM, V
Deutsche Börse AG, 59
Deutsche Lufthansa AG, I; 26 (upd.); 68 (upd.)
Deutsche Post AG, 29
Deutsche Steinzeug Cremer & Breuer Aktiengesellschaft, 91
Deutsche Telekom AG, 48 (upd.)
Deutscher Sparkassen- und Giroverband (DSGV), 84
Deutz AG, 39
Diehl Stiftung & Co. KG 79
Dirk Rossmann GmbH, 94
Dr. August Oetker KG, 51
Drägerwerk AG, 83
Dräxlmaier Group, 90
Dresdner Bank A.G., II; 57 (upd.)
Dürkopp Adler AG, 65
Dürr AG, 44
Dyckerhoff AG, 35
E.On AG, 50 (upd.)
Eckes AG, 56
Edeka Zentrale A.G., II; 47 (upd.)
edel music AG, 44
ERGO Versicherungsgruppe AG, 44
ESCADA AG, 71
Esselte Leitz GmbH & Co. KG, 48
Etienne Aigner AG, 52
FAG—Kugelfischer Georg Schäfer AG, 62
Fairchild Dornier GmbH, 48 (upd.)
Feldmuhle Nobel A.G., III
Fielmann AG, 31
Francotyp-Postalia Holding AG, 92
Frankfurter Allgemeine Zeitung GmbH, 66
Fraport AG Frankfurt Airport Services Worldwide, 90
Fresenius AG, 56
Freudenberg & Co., 41
Fried. Krupp GmbH, IV
Friedrich Grohe AG & Co. KG, 53
GEA AG, 27
GEHE AG, 27
Gelita AG, 74
GEMA (Gesellschaft für musikalische Aufführungs- und mechanische Vervielfältigungsrechte), 70
geobra Brandstätter GmbH & Co. KG, 48
Gerhard D. Wempe KG, 88
Gerling-Konzern Versicherungs-Beteiligungs-Aktiengesellschaft, 51
Gerresheimer Glas AG, 43
Gerry Weber International AG, 63
Getrag Corporate Group, 92
GfK Aktiengesellschaft, 49
Giesecke & Devrient GmbH, 83
Gildemeister AG 79
Groz-Beckert Group, 68
Grundig AG, 27
Hansgrohe AG, 56
Hapag-Lloyd AG, 6
HARIBO GmbH & Co. KG, 44
HDI (Haftpflichtverband der Deutschen Industrie Versicherung auf Gegenseitigkeit V.a.G.), 53
Heidelberger Druckmaschinen AG, 40
Heidelberger Zement AG, 31
Heinrich Deichmann-Schuhe GmbH & Co. KG, 88
Hella KGaA Hueck & Co., 66
Henkel KGaA, III; 34 (upd.)
Heraeus Holding GmbH, IV; 54 (upd.)
Hertie Waren- und Kaufhaus GmbH, V
Hexal AG, 69
HiPP GmbH & Co. Vertrieb KG, 88
Hochtief AG, 33; 88 (upd.)
Hoechst A.G., I; 18 (upd.)
Hoesch AG, IV
Hugo Boss AG, 48
HUK-Coburg, 58
Huls A.G., I
HVB Group, 59 (upd.)
Ihr Platz GmbH + Company KG, 77
Infineon Technologies AG, 50
J.M. Voith AG, 33
Jenoptik AG, 33
Julius Blüthner Pianofortefabrik GmbH 78
Kamps AG, 44
Karlsberg Brauerei GmbH & Co KG, 41
Karstadt Quelle AG, V; 19 (upd.); 57 (upd.)
Kaufhof Warenhaus AG, V; 23 (upd.)
Kaufring AG, 35
KHD Konzern, III
Klaus Steilmann GmbH & Co. KG, 53
Klöckner-Werke AG, IV; 58 (upd.)
Knorr-Bremse AG, 84
Koenig & Bauer AG, 64
König Brauerei GmbH & Co. KG, 35 (upd.)
Körber AG, 60
Kreditanstalt für Wiederaufbau, 29
KSB AG, 62
Leica Camera AG, 35
Leica Microsystems Holdings GmbH, 35
Linde AG, I; 67 (upd.)
Loewe AG, 90
Löwenbräu AG, 80
LTU Group Holding GmbH, 37
M. DuMont Schauberg GmbH & Co. KG, 92
MAN Aktiengesellschaft, III
MAN Roland Druckmaschinen AG, 94
Mannesmann AG, III; 14 (upd.); 38 (upd.)
Margarete Steiff GmbH, 23
Märklin Holding GmbH, 70
Matth. Hohner AG, 53
Melitta Unternehmensgruppe Bentz KG, 53
Merz Group, 81
Messerschmitt-Bölkow-Blohm GmbH., I
Metallgesellschaft AG, IV; 16 (upd.)
Metro AG, 50
Miele & Cie. KG, 56
MITROPA AG, 37
Montblanc International GmbH, 82
Munich Re (Münchener Rückversicherungs-Gesellschaft Aktiengesellschaft in München), III; 46 (upd.)
Nixdorf Computer AG, III
Norddeutsche Affinerie AG, 62
Optische Werke G. Rodenstock, 44
Osram GmbH, 86
Otto Versand GmbH & Co., V; 15 (upd.); 34 (upd.)
Paulaner Brauerei GmbH & Co. KG, 35
Peek & Cloppenburg KG, 46
Philipp Holzmann AG, 17
Phoenix AG, 68
Porsche AG, 13; 31 (upd.)
Preussag AG, 17; 42 (upd.)
PreussenElektra Aktiengesellschaft, V
ProSiebenSat.1 Media AG, 54
Puma AG Rudolf Dassler Sport, 35
PWA Group, IV
Qiagen N.V., 39
Quelle Group, V
Radeberger Gruppe AG, 75
RAG AG, 35; 60 (upd.)
ratiopharm Group, 84
Ravensburger AG, 64
RENK AG, 37
Rheinmetall Berlin AG, 9
Robert Bosch GmbH, I; 16 (upd.); 43 (upd.)
Röchling Gruppe, 94
Rohde & Schwarz GmbH & Co. KG, 39
Roland Berger & Partner GmbH, 37
Ruhrgas AG, V; 38 (upd.)
Ruhrkohle AG, IV
RWE AG, V; 50 (upd.)
Saarberg-Konzern, IV
Salzgitter AG, IV

SAP AG, 16; 43 (upd.)
Schenker-Rhenus AG, 6
Schering AG, I; 50 (upd.)
Sennheiser Electronic GmbH & Co. KG, 66
Siemens AG, II; 14 (upd.); 57 (upd.)
Siltronic AG, 90
Sixt AG, 39
SPAR Handels AG, 35
SPIEGEL-Verlag Rudolf Augstein GmbH & Co. KG, 44
Stinnes AG, 8; 23 (upd.); 59 (upd.)
Stollwerck AG, 53
Südzucker AG, 27
Symrise GmbH and Company KG, 89
T-Online International AG, 61
TA Triumph-Adler AG, 48
Tarkett Sommer AG, 25
TaurusHolding GmbH & Co. KG, 46
Tchibo GmbH, 82
Tengelmann Group, 27
ThyssenKrupp AG, IV; 28 (upd.); 87 (upd.)
Touristik Union International GmbH. and Company K.G., II
TRUMPF GmbH + Co. KG, 86
TUI Group GmbH, 44
UFA TV & Film Produktion GmbH, 80
Vaillant GmbH, 44
Varta AG, 23
Veba A.G., I; 15 (upd.)
Vereinigte Elektrizitätswerke Westfalen AG, V
Verlagsgruppe Georg von Holtzbrinck GmbH, 35
VEW AG, 39
VIAG Aktiengesellschaft, IV
Victoria Group, III; 44 (upd.)
Viessmann Werke GmbH & Co., 37
Wilhelm Karmann GmbH, 94
Villeroy & Boch AG, 37
Volkswagen Aktiengesellschaft, I; 11 (upd.); 32 (upd.)
Vorwerk & Co., 27
Vossloh AG, 53
Wacker-Chemie GmbH, 35
WAZ Media Group, 82
Wella AG, III; 48 (upd.)
Weru Aktiengesellschaft, 18
Westdeutsche Landesbank Girozentrale, II; 46 (upd.)
Wincor Nixdorf Holding GmbH, 69 (upd.)
Württembergische Metallwarenfabrik AG (WMF), 60
ZF Friedrichshafen AG, 48

Ghana

Ashanti Goldfields Company Limited, 43

Greece

Aegean Marine Petroleum Network Inc., 89
Aegek S.A., 64
Attica Enterprises S.A., 64
Danaos Corporation, 91
Hellenic Petroleum SA, 64
National Bank of Greece, 41
Royal Olympic Cruise Lines Inc., 52
Stelmar Shipping Ltd., 52
Titan Cement Company S.A., 64
Tsakos Energy Navigation Ltd., 91
Vivartia S.A., 82

Guatemala

Corporación Multi-Inversiones, 94

Hong Kong

A.S. Watson & Company Ltd., 84
Bank of East Asia Ltd., 63
Cable & Wireless HKT, 30 (upd.)
Cathay Pacific Airways Limited, 6; 34 (upd.)
CDC Corporation, 71
Chaoda Modern Agriculture (Holdings) Ltd., 87
Cheung Kong (Holdings) Ltd., IV; 20 (upd.); 94 (upd.)
China Merchants International Holdings Co., Ltd., 52
CITIC Pacific Ltd., 18
First Pacific Company Limited, 18
The Garden Company Ltd., 82
GOME Electrical Appliances Holding Ltd., 87
Hang Seng Bank Ltd., 60
Henderson Land Development Company Ltd., 70
Hong Kong and China Gas Company Ltd., 73
Hong Kong Dragon Airlines Ltd., 66
Hong Kong Telecommunications Ltd., 6
The Hongkong and Shanghai Banking Corporation Limited, II
Hongkong Electric Holdings Ltd., 6; 23 (upd.)
Hongkong Land Holdings Limited, IV; 47 (upd.)
Hopson Development Holdings Ltd., 87
Hutchison Whampoa Limited, 18; 49 (upd.)
Kerry Properties Limited, 22
Meyer International Holdings, Ltd., 87
Nam Tai Electronics, Inc., 61
New World Development Company Limited, IV; 38 (upd.)
Next Media Ltd., 61
Pacific Basin Shipping Ltd., 86
Playmates Toys, 23
Shangri-La Asia Ltd., 71
The Singer Company N.V., 30 (upd.)
Swire Pacific Limited, I; 16 (upd.); 57 (upd.)
Techtronic Industries Company Ltd., 73
Tommy Hilfiger Corporation, 20; 53 (upd.)
Vitasoy International Holdings Ltd., 94
VTech Holdings Ltd., 77

Hungary

Magyar Telekom Rt. 78
Malév Plc, 24
MOL Rt, 70
Orszagos Takarekpenztar es Kereskedelmi Bank Rt. (OTP Bank) 78

Iceland

Alfesca hf, 82
Bakkavör Group hf., 91
Baugur Group hf, 81
Icelandair, 52
Icelandic Group hf, 81
Landsbanki Islands hf, 81

India

Aditya Birla Group 79
Air Sahara Limited, 65
Air-India Limited, 6; 27 (upd.)
Bajaj Auto Limited, 39
Bharti Tele-Ventures Limited, 75
Coal India Limited, IV; 44 (upd.)
Dr. Reddy's Laboratories Ltd., 59
Essar Group Ltd. 79
Hindustan Lever Limited 79
Indian Airlines Ltd., 46
Indian Oil Corporation Ltd., IV; 48 (upd.)
Infosys Technologies Ltd., 38
Jet Airways (India) Private Limited, 65
Minerals and Metals Trading Corporation of India Ltd., IV
MTR Foods Ltd., 55
Neyveli Lignite Corporation Ltd., 65
Oil and Natural Gas Corporation Ltd., IV; 90 (upd.)
Ranbaxy Laboratories Ltd., 70
Raymond Ltd., 77
Reliance Industries Ltd., 81
Rolta India Ltd., 90
Satyam Computer Services Ltd., 85
State Bank of India, 63
Steel Authority of India Ltd., IV; 66 (upd.)
Sun Pharmaceutical Industries Ltd., 57
Tata Iron & Steel Co. Ltd., IV; 44 (upd.)
Tata Tea Ltd., 76
Wipro Limited, 43

Indonesia

Djarum PT, 62
Garuda Indonesia, 6; 58 (upd.)
PERTAMINA, IV
Pertamina, 56 (upd.)
PT Astra International Tbk, 56
PT Bank Buana Indonesia Tbk, 60
PT Indosat Tbk, 93

Iran

IranAir, 81
National Iranian Oil Company, IV; 61 (upd.)

Ireland

Aer Lingus Group plc, 34; 89 (upd.)
Allied Irish Banks, plc, 16; 43 (upd.); 94 (upd.)
Baltimore Technologies Plc, 42
Bank of Ireland, 50
CRH plc, 64
DEPFA BANK PLC, 69

Dunnes Stores Ltd., 58
eircom plc, 31 (upd.)
Elan Corporation PLC, 63
Fyffes Plc, 38
Glanbia plc, 59
Glen Dimplex 78
Harland and Wolff Holdings plc, 19
IAWS Group plc, 49
Independent News & Media PLC, 61
IONA Technologies plc, 43
Irish Life & Permanent Plc, 59
Jefferson Smurfit Group plc, IV; 19 (upd.); 49 (upd.)
Jurys Doyle Hotel Group plc, 64
Kerry Group plc, 27; 87 (upd.)
Musgrave Group Plc, 57
Ryanair Holdings plc, 35
Shannon Aerospace Ltd., 36
SkillSoft Public Limited Company, 81
Telecom Eireann, 7
Thomas Crosbie Holdings Limited, 81
Waterford Wedgwood plc, 34 (upd.)

Israel

Amdocs Ltd., 47
Bank Hapoalim B.M., II; 54 (upd.)
Bank Leumi le-Israel B.M., 60
Blue Square Israel Ltd., 41
BVR Systems (1998) Ltd., 93
Castro Model Ltd., 86
ECI Telecom Ltd., 18
El Al Israel Airlines Ltd., 23
Elscint Ltd., 20
Given Imaging Ltd., 83
Israel Aircraft Industries Ltd., 69
Israel Chemicals Ltd., 55
Koor Industries Ltd., II; 25 (upd.); 68 (upd.)
Lipman Electronic Engineering Ltd., 81
Makhteshim-Agan Industries Ltd., 85
NICE Systems Ltd., 83
Orbotech Ltd., 75
Scitex Corporation Ltd., 24
Strauss-Elite Group, 68
Syneron Medical Ltd., 91
Taro Pharmaceutical Industries Ltd., 65
Teva Pharmaceutical Industries Ltd., 22; 54 (upd.)

Italy

AgustaWestland N.V., 75
Alfa Romeo, 13; 36 (upd.)
Alitalia-Linee Aeree Italiana, S.p.A., 6; 29 (upd.)
Alleanza Assicurazioni S.p.A., 65
Aprilia SpA, 17
Arnoldo Mondadori Editore S.p.A., IV; 19 (upd.); 54 (upd.)
Artsana SpA, 92
Assicurazioni Generali SpA, III; 15 (upd.)
Autogrill SpA, 49
Automobili Lamborghini Holding S.p.A., 13; 34 (upd.); 91 (upd.)
Banca Commerciale Italiana SpA, II
Banca Fideuram SpA, 63
Banca Intesa SpA, 65
Banca Monte dei Paschi di Siena SpA, 65
Banca Nazionale del Lavoro SpA, 72
Barilla G. e R. Fratelli S.p.A., 17; 50 (upd.)
Benetton Group S.p.A., 10; 67 (upd.)
Brioni Roman Style S.p.A., 67
Bulgari S.p.A., 20
Cantine Giorgio Lungarotti S.R.L., 67
Capitalia S.p.A., 65
Cinemeccanica SpA 78
Compagnia Italiana dei Jolly Hotels S.p.A., 71
Credito Italiano, II
Cremonini S.p.A., 57
Davide Campari-Milano S.p.A., 57
De'Longhi S.p.A., 66
Diadora SpA, 86
Diesel SpA, 40
Dolce & Gabbana SpA, 62
Ducati Motor Holding SpA, 30; 86 (upd.)
ENI S.p.A., 69 (upd.)
Ente Nazionale Idrocarburi, IV
Ente Nazionale per L'Energia Elettrica, V
Ermenegildo Zegna SpA, 63
Fabbrica D' Armi Pietro Beretta S.p.A., 39
FASTWEB S.p.A., 83
Ferrari S.p.A., 13; 36 (upd.)
Ferrero SpA, 54
Ferretti Group SpA, 90
Fiat SpA, I; 11 (upd.); 50 (upd.)
Fila Holding S.p.A., 20; 52 (upd.)
Finarte Casa d'Aste S.p.A., 93
Finmeccanica S.p.A., 84
Gianni Versace SpA, 22
Giorgio Armani S.p.A., 45
Gruppo Coin S.p.A., 41
Gruppo Riva Fire SpA, 88
Guccio Gucci, S.p.A., 15
illycaffè SpA, 50
Industrie Natuzzi S.p.A., 18
Industrie Zignago Santa Margherita S.p.A., 67
Ing. C. Olivetti & C., S.p.a., III
Istituto per la Ricostruzione Industriale S.p.A., I; 11
Juventus F.C. S.p.A, 53
Luxottica SpA, 17; 52 (upd.)
Magneti Marelli Holding SpA, 90
Marchesi Antinori SRL, 42
Marcolin S.p.A., 61
Mariella Burani Fashion Group, 92
Martini & Rossi SpA, 63
Marzotto S.p.A., 20; 67 (upd.)
Mediaset SpA, 50
Mediolanum S.p.A., 65
Milan AC, S.p.A. 79
Miroglio SpA, 86
Montedison SpA, I; 24 (upd.)
Officine Alfieri Maserati S.p.A., 13
Olivetti S.p.A., 34 (upd.)
Pagnossin S.p.A., 73
Parmalat Finanziaria SpA, 50
Peg Perego SpA, 88
Perfetti Van Melle S.p.A., 72
Piaggio & C. S.p.A., 20
Pirelli & C. S.p.A., 75 (upd.)
Pirelli S.p.A., V; 15 (upd.)
Reno de Medici S.p.A., 41
Rinascente S.p.A., 71
Riunione Adriatica di Sicurtè SpA, III
Safilo SpA, 54
Salvatore Ferragamo Italia S.p.A., 62
Sanpaolo IMI S.p.A., 50
Seat Pagine Gialle S.p.A., 47
Sirti S.p.A., 76
Società Finanziaria Telefonica per Azioni, V
Società Sportiva Lazio SpA, 44
Stefanel SpA, 63
Targetti Sankey SpA, 86
Telecom Italia Mobile S.p.A., 63
Telecom Italia S.p.A., 43
Tiscali SpA, 48

Jamaica

Air Jamaica Limited, 54
Desnoes and Geddes Limited 79
GraceKennedy Ltd., 92

Japan

AEON Co., Ltd., 68 (upd.)
Aisin Seiki Co., Ltd., III; 48 (upd.)
Aiwa Co., Ltd., 30
Ajinomoto Co., Inc., II; 28 (upd.)
All Nippon Airways Co., Ltd., 6; 38 (upd.); 91 (upd.)
Alpine Electronics, Inc., 13
Alps Electric Co., Ltd., II; 44 (upd.)
Anritsu Corporation, 68
Asahi Breweries, Ltd., I; 20 (upd.); 52 (upd.)
Asahi Denka Kogyo KK, 64
Asahi Glass Company, Ltd., III; 48 (upd.)
Asahi National Broadcasting Company, Ltd., 9
Asatsu-DK Inc., 82
ASICS Corporation, 57
Autobacs Seven Company Ltd., 76
Bandai Co., Ltd., 55
Bank of Tokyo-Mitsubishi Ltd., II; 15 (upd.)
Benesse Corporation, 76
Bourbon Corporation, 82
Bridgestone Corporation, V; 21 (upd.); 59 (upd.)
Brother Industries, Ltd., 14
C. Itoh & Company Ltd., I
Canon Inc., III; 18 (upd.); 79 (upd.)
Capcom Company Ltd., 83
CASIO Computer Co., Ltd., III; 16 (upd.); 40 (upd.)
Central Japan Railway Company, 43
Chubu Electric Power Company, Inc., V; 46 (upd.)
Chugai Pharmaceutical Co., Ltd., 50
Chugoku Electric Power Company Inc., V; 53 (upd.)
Citizen Watch Co., Ltd., III; 21 (upd.); 81 (upd.)
Clarion Company Ltd., 64
Cosmo Oil Co., Ltd., IV; 53 (upd.)
Dai Nippon Printing Co., Ltd., IV; 57 (upd.)
The Dai-Ichi Kangyo Bank Ltd., II
Daido Steel Co., Ltd., IV
The Daiei, Inc., V; 17 (upd.); 41 (upd.)

Daihatsu Motor Company, Ltd., 7; 21 (upd.)
Daiichikosho Company Ltd., 86
Daikin Industries, Ltd., III
Daiko Advertising Inc. 79
The Daimaru, Inc., V; 42 (upd.)
Daio Paper Corporation, IV, 84 (upd.)
Daishowa Paper Manufacturing Co., Ltd., IV; 57 (upd.)
The Daiwa Bank, Ltd., II; 39 (upd.)
Daiwa Securities Group Inc., II; 55 (upd.)
DDI Corporation, 7
DENSO Corporation, 46 (upd.)
Dentsu Inc., I; 16 (upd.); 40 (upd.)
East Japan Railway Company, V; 66 (upd.)
Ebara Corporation, 83
Elpida Memory, Inc., 83
Ezaki Glico Company Ltd., 72
Fanuc Ltd., III; 17 (upd.); 75 (upd.)
The Fuji Bank, Ltd., II
Fuji Electric Co., Ltd., II; 48 (upd.)
Fuji Photo Film Co., Ltd., III; 18 (upd.); 79 (upd.)
Fuji Television Network Inc., 91
Fujisawa Pharmaceutical Company, Ltd., I; 58 (upd.)
Fujitsu Limited, III; 16 (upd.); 42 (upd.)
Funai Electric Company Ltd., 62
The Furukawa Electric Co., Ltd., III
General Sekiyu K.K., IV
Hakuhodo, Inc., 6; 42 (upd.)
Hankyu Department Stores, Inc., V; 23 (upd.); 62 (upd.)
Hagoromo Foods Corporation, 84
Hino Motors, Ltd., 7; 21 (upd.)
Hitachi, Ltd., I; 12 (upd.); 40 (upd.)
Hitachi Metals, Ltd., IV
Hitachi Zosen Corporation, III; 53 (upd.)
Hokkaido Electric Power Company Inc. (HEPCO), V; 58 (upd.)
Hokuriku Electric Power Company, V
Honda Motor Company Limited, I; 10 (upd.); 29 (upd.)
Honshu Paper Co., Ltd., IV
Hoshino Gakki Co. Ltd., 55
Idemitsu Kosan Co., Ltd., IV; 49 (upd.)
The Industrial Bank of Japan, Ltd., II
Isetan Company Limited, V; 36 (upd.)
Ishikawajima-Harima Heavy Industries Company, Ltd., III; 86 (upd.)
Isuzu Motors, Ltd., 9; 23 (upd.); 57 (upd.)
Ito-Yokado Co., Ltd., V; 42 (upd.)
ITOCHU Corporation, 32 (upd.)
Itoham Foods Inc., II; 61 (upd.)
Japan Airlines Company, Ltd., I; 32 (upd.)
JAFCO Co. Ltd. 79
Japan Broadcasting Corporation, 7
Japan Leasing Corporation, 8
Japan Pulp and Paper Company Limited, IV
Japan Tobacco Inc., V; 46 (upd.)
JFE Shoji Holdings Inc., 88
JSP Corporation, 74
Jujo Paper Co., Ltd., IV
JUSCO Co., Ltd., V
Kajima Corporation, I; 51 (upd.)
Kanebo, Ltd., 53
Kanematsu Corporation, IV; 24 (upd.)
The Kansai Electric Power Company, Inc., V; 62 (upd.)
Kansai Paint Company Ltd., 80
Kao Corporation, III; 20 (upd.); 79 (upd.)
Katokichi Company Ltd., 82
Kawai Musical Instruments Mfg Co. Ltd. 78
Kawasaki Heavy Industries, Ltd., III; 63 (upd.)
Kawasaki Kisen Kaisha, Ltd., V; 56 (upd.)
Kawasaki Steel Corporation, IV
Keio Teito Electric Railway Company, V
Kenwood Corporation, 31
Kewpie Kabushiki Kaisha, 57
Kikkoman Corporation, 14; 47 (upd.)
Kinki Nippon Railway Company Ltd., V
Kirin Brewery Company, Limited, I; 21 (upd.); 63 (upd.)
Kobe Steel, Ltd., IV; 19 (upd.)
Kodansha Ltd., IV; 38 (upd.)
Komatsu Ltd., III; 16 (upd.); 52 (upd.)
Konica Corporation, III; 30 (upd.)
Kotobukiya Co., Ltd., V; 56 (upd.)
Kubota Corporation, III; 26 (upd.)
Kumagai Gumi Company, Ltd., I
Kumon Institute of Education Co., Ltd., 72
Kyocera Corporation, II; 21 (upd.); 79 (upd.)
Kyokuyo Company Ltd., 75
Kyowa Hakko Kogyo Co., Ltd., III; 48 (upd.)
Kyushu Electric Power Company Inc., V
Lion Corporation, III; 51 (upd.)
Long-Term Credit Bank of Japan, Ltd., II
Mabuchi Motor Co. Ltd., 68
Makita Corporation, 22; 59 (upd.)
Mandom Corporation, 82
Marubeni Corporation, I; 24 (upd.)
Maruha Group Inc., 75 (upd.)
Marui Company Ltd., V; 62 (upd.)
Maruzen Co., Limited, 18
Matsushita Electric Industrial Co., Ltd., II; 64 (upd.)
Matsushita Electric Works, Ltd., III; 7 (upd.)
Matsuzakaya Company Ltd., V; 64 (upd.)
Mazda Motor Corporation, 9; 23 (upd.); 63 (upd.)
Meidensha Corporation, 92
Meiji Dairies Corporation, II; 82 (upd.)
The Meiji Mutual Life Insurance Company, III
Meiji Seika Kaisha Ltd., II; 64 (upd.)
Mercian Corporation, 77
Millea Holdings Inc., 64 (upd.)
Minebea Co., Ltd., 90
Minolta Co., Ltd., III; 18 (upd.); 43 (upd.)
The Mitsubishi Bank, Ltd., II
Mitsubishi Chemical Corporation, I; 56 (upd.)
Mitsubishi Corporation, I; 12 (upd.)
Mitsubishi Electric Corporation, II; 44 (upd.)
Mitsubishi Estate Company, Limited, IV; 61 (upd.)
Mitsubishi Heavy Industries, Ltd., III; 7 (upd.); 40 (upd.)
Mitsubishi Materials Corporation, III
Mitsubishi Motors Corporation, 9; 23 (upd.); 57 (upd.)
Mitsubishi Oil Co., Ltd., IV
Mitsubishi Rayon Co., Ltd., V
The Mitsubishi Trust & Banking Corporation, II
Mitsui & Co., Ltd., 28 (upd.)
The Mitsui Bank, Ltd., II
Mitsui Bussan K.K., I
Mitsui Marine and Fire Insurance Company, Limited, III
Mitsui Mining & Smelting Co., Ltd., IV
Mitsui Mining Company, Limited, IV
Mitsui Mutual Life Insurance Company, III; 39 (upd.)
Mitsui O.S.K. Lines, Ltd., V
Mitsui Petrochemical Industries, Ltd., 9
Mitsui Real Estate Development Co., Ltd., IV
The Mitsui Trust & Banking Company, Ltd., II
Mitsukoshi Ltd., V; 56 (upd.)
Mizuho Financial Group Inc., 58 (upd.)
Mizuno Corporation, 25
Morinaga & Co. Ltd., 61
Nagasakiya Co., Ltd., V; 69 (upd.)
Nagase & Co., Ltd., 8; 61 (upd.)
NEC Corporation, II; 21 (upd.); 57 (upd.)
NGK Insulators Ltd., 67
NHK Spring Co., Ltd., III
Nichii Co., Ltd., V
Nichimen Corporation, IV; 24 (upd.)
Nichirei Corporation, 70
Nichiro Corporation, 86
Nidec Corporation, 59
Nihon Keizai Shimbun, Inc., IV
The Nikko Securities Company Limited, II; 9 (upd.)
Nikon Corporation, III; 48 (upd.)
Nintendo Co., Ltd., III; 7 (upd.); 28 (upd.); 67 (upd.)
Nippon Credit Bank, II
Nippon Express Company, Ltd., V; 64 (upd.)
Nippon Life Insurance Company, III; 60 (upd.)
Nippon Light Metal Company, Ltd., IV
Nippon Meat Packers Inc., II, 78 (upd.)
Nippon Oil Corporation, IV; 63 (upd.)
Nippon Seiko K.K., III
Nippon Sheet Glass Company, Limited, III
Nippon Shinpan Co., Ltd., II; 61 (upd.)
Nippon Soda Co., Ltd., 85
Nippon Steel Corporation, IV; 17 (upd.)
Nippon Suisan Kaisha, Ltd., II; 92 (upd.)
Nippon Telegraph and Telephone Corporation, V; 51 (upd.)
Nippon Yusen Kabushiki Kaisha (NYK), V; 72 (upd.)

Nippondenso Co., Ltd., III
Nissan Motor Company Ltd., I; 11 (upd.); 34 (upd.); 92 (upd.)
Nisshin Seifun Group Inc., II; 66 (upd.)
Nisshin Steel Co., Ltd., IV
Nissho Iwai K.K., I
Nissin Food Products Company Ltd., 75
NKK Corporation, IV; 28 (upd.)
NOF Corporation, 72
Nomura Securities Company, Limited, II; 9 (upd.)
Norinchukin Bank, II
NTN Corporation, III; 47 (upd.)
Obayashi Corporation 78
Odakyu Electric Railway Co., Ltd., V; 68 (upd.)
Ohbayashi Corporation, I
Oji Paper Co., Ltd., IV; 57 (upd.)
Oki Electric Industry Company, Limited, II
Okuma Holdings Inc., 74
Okura & Co., Ltd., IV
Omron Corporation, II; 28 (upd.)
Onoda Cement Co., Ltd., III
ORIX Corporation, II; 44 (upd.)
Osaka Gas Company, Ltd., V; 60 (upd.)
Otari Inc., 89
Paloma Industries Ltd., 71
Pearl Corporation 78
Pentax Corporation 78
Pioneer Electronic Corporation, III; 28 (upd.)
Rengo Co., Ltd., IV
Ricoh Company, Ltd., III; 36 (upd.)
Roland Corporation, 38
Ryoshoku Ltd., 72
Sankyo Company, Ltd., I; 56 (upd.)
Sanrio Company, Ltd., 38
The Sanwa Bank, Ltd., II; 15 (upd.)
SANYO Electric Company, Ltd., II; 36 (upd.)
Sanyo-Kokusaku Pulp Co., Ltd., IV
Sapporo Breweries, Ltd., I; 13 (upd.); 36 (upd.)
SEGA Corporation, 73
Seibu Department Stores, Ltd., V; 42 (upd.)
Seibu Railway Company Ltd., V; 74 (upd.)
Seiko Corporation, III; 17 (upd.); 72 (upd.)
Seino Transportation Company, Ltd., 6
The Seiyu, Ltd., V; 36 (upd.)
Sekisui Chemical Co., Ltd., III; 72 (upd.)
Sharp Corporation, II; 12 (upd.); 40 (upd.)
Shikoku Electric Power Company, Inc., V; 60 (upd.)
Shimano Inc., 64
Shionogi & Co., Ltd., III; 17 (upd.)
Shiseido Company, Limited, III; 22 (upd.), 81 (upd.)
Shochiku Company Ltd., 74
Showa Shell Sekiyu K.K., IV; 59 (upd.)
Snow Brand Milk Products Company, Ltd., II; 48 (upd.)
Softbank Corp., 13; 38 (upd.)
Sony Corporation, II; 12 (upd.); 40 (upd.)
The Sumitomo Bank, Limited, II; 26 (upd.)
Sumitomo Chemical Company Ltd., I
Sumitomo Corporation, I; 11 (upd.)
Sumitomo Electric Industries, Ltd., II
Sumitomo Heavy Industries, Ltd., III; 42 (upd.)
Sumitomo Life Insurance Company, III; 60 (upd.)
The Sumitomo Marine and Fire Insurance Company, Limited, III
Sumitomo Metal Industries Ltd., IV; 82 (upd.)
Sumitomo Metal Mining Co., Ltd., IV
Sumitomo Mitsui Banking Corporation, 51 (upd.)
Sumitomo Realty & Development Co., Ltd., IV
Sumitomo Rubber Industries, Ltd., V
The Sumitomo Trust & Banking Company, Ltd., II; 53 (upd.)
Suntory Ltd., 65
Suzuki Motor Corporation, 9; 23 (upd.); 59 (upd.)
Taiheiyo Cement Corporation, 60 (upd.)
Taiyo Fishery Company, Limited, II
The Taiyo Kobe Bank, Ltd., II
Takara Holdings Inc., 62
Takashimaya Company, Limited, V; 47 (upd.)
Takeda Chemical Industries, Ltd., I; 46 (upd.)
Tamron Company Ltd., 82
TDK Corporation, II; 17 (upd.); 49 (upd.)
TEAC Corporation 78
Teijin Limited, V; 61 (upd.)
Terumo Corporation, 48
Tobu Railway Co Ltd, 6
Tohan Corporation, 84
Toho Co., Ltd., 28
Tohoku Electric Power Company, Inc., V
The Tokai Bank, Limited, II; 15 (upd.)
The Tokio Marine and Fire Insurance Co., Ltd., III
The Tokyo Electric Power Company, 74 (upd.)
The Tokyo Electric Power Company, Incorporated, V
Tokyo Gas Co., Ltd., V; 55 (upd.)
Tokyu Corporation, V; 47 (upd.)
Tokyu Department Store Co., Ltd., V; 32 (upd.)
Tokyu Land Corporation, IV
Tomen Corporation, IV; 24 (upd.)
Tomy Company Ltd., 65
TonenGeneral Sekiyu K.K., IV; 16 (upd.); 54 (upd.)
Topcon Corporation, 84
Toppan Printing Co., Ltd., IV; 58 (upd.)
Toray Industries, Inc., V; 51 (upd.)
Toshiba Corporation, I; 12 (upd.); 40 (upd.)
Tosoh Corporation, 70
TOTO LTD., III; 28 (upd.)
Toyo Sash Co., Ltd., III
Toyo Seikan Kaisha, Ltd., I
Toyoda Automatic Loom Works, Ltd., III
Toyota Motor Corporation, I; 11 (upd.); 38 (upd.)
Ube Industries, Ltd., III; 38 (upd.)
ULVAC, Inc., 80
Unicharm Corporation, 84
Unitika Ltd., V; 53 (upd.)
Uny Co., Ltd., V; 49 (upd.)
Ushio Inc., 91
Victor Company of Japan, Limited, II; 26 (upd.); 83 (upd.)
Wacoal Corp., 25
Yamada Denki Co., Ltd., 85
Yamaha Corporation, III; 16 (upd.); 40 (upd.)
Yamaichi Securities Company, Limited, II
Yamato Transport Co. Ltd., V; 49 (upd.)
Yamazaki Baking Co., Ltd., 58
The Yasuda Fire and Marine Insurance Company, Limited, III
The Yasuda Mutual Life Insurance Company, III; 39 (upd.)
The Yasuda Trust and Banking Company, Ltd., II; 17 (upd.)
The Yokohama Rubber Company, Limited, V; 19 (upd.); 91 (upd.)
Yoshinoya D & C Company Ltd., 88

Jordan

Arab Potash Company, 85

Kenya

Kenya Airways Limited, 89

Kuwait

Kuwait Airways Corporation, 68
Kuwait Flour Mills & Bakeries Company, 84
Kuwait Petroleum Corporation, IV; 55 (upd.)

Latvia

A/S Air Baltic Corporation, 71

Lebanon

Middle East Airlines - Air Liban S.A.L. 79

Libya

National Oil Corporation, IV; 66 (upd.)

Liechtenstein

Hilti AG, 53

Luxembourg

ARBED S.A., IV; 22 (upd.)
Cactus S.A., 90
Cargolux Airlines International S.A., 49
Elite World S.A., 94
Espèrito Santo Financial Group S.A. 79 (upd.)
Gemplus International S.A., 64
Metro International S.A., 93
RTL Group SA, 44
Société Luxembourgeoise de Navigation Aérienne S.A., 64

Tenaris SA, 63

Malaysia

AirAsia Berhad, 93
Berjaya Group Bhd., 67
Gano Excel Enterprise Sdn. Bhd., 89
Genting Bhd., 65
Malayan Banking Berhad, 72
Malaysian Airlines System Berhad, 6; 29 (upd.)
Perusahaan Otomobil Nasional Bhd., 62
Petroliam Nasional Bhd (Petronas), IV; 56 (upd.)
PPB Group Berhad, 57
Sime Darby Berhad, 14; 36 (upd.)
Telekom Malaysia Bhd, 76
Yeo Hiap Seng Malaysia Bhd., 75

Mauritius

Air Mauritius Ltd., 63

Mexico

Alfa, S.A. de C.V., 19
Altos Hornos de México, S.A. de C.V., 42
América Móvil, S.A. de C.V., 80
Apasco S.A. de C.V., 51
Bolsa Mexicana de Valores, S.A. de C.V., 80
Bufete Industrial, S.A. de C.V., 34
Casa Cuervo, S.A. de C.V., 31
Celanese Mexicana, S.A. de C.V., 54
CEMEX S.A. de C.V., 20; 59 (upd.)
Cifra, S.A. de C.V., 12
Cinemas de la República, S.A. de C.V., 83
Compañia Industrial de Parras, S.A. de C.V. (CIPSA), 84
Consorcio ARA, S.A. de C.V. 79
Consorcio Aviacsa, S.A. de C.V., 85
Consorcio G Grupo Dina, S.A. de C.V., 36
Controladora Comercial Mexicana, S.A. de C.V., 36
Controladora Mabe, S.A. de C.V., 82
Coppel, S.A. de C.V., 82
Corporación Geo, S.A. de C.V., 81
Corporación Interamericana de Entretenimiento, S.A. de C.V., 83
Corporación Internacional de Aviación, S.A. de C.V. (Cintra), 20
Desarrolladora Homex, S.A. de C.V., 87
Desc, S.A. de C.V., 23
Editorial Television, S.A. de C.V., 57
Empresas ICA Sociedad Controladora, S.A. de C.V., 41
Ford Motor Company, S.A. de C.V., 20
Gruma, S.A. de C.V., 31
Grupo Aeroportuario del Pacífico, S.A. de C.V., 85
Grupo Aeropuerto del Sureste, S.A. de C.V., 48
Grupo Ángeles Servicios de Salud, S.A. de C.V., 84
Grupo Carso, S.A. de C.V., 21
Grupo Casa Saba, S.A. de C.V., 39
Grupo Comercial Chedraui S.A. de C.V., 86
Grupo Corvi S.A. de C.V., 86
Grupo Cydsa, S.A. de C.V., 39
Grupo Elektra, S.A. de C.V., 39
Grupo Financiero Banamex S.A., 54
Grupo Financiero Banorte, S.A. de C.V., 51
Grupo Financiero BBVA Bancomer S.A., 54
Grupo Financiero Serfin, S.A., 19
Grupo Gigante, S.A. de C.V., 34
Grupo Herdez, S.A. de C.V., 35
Grupo IMSA, S.A. de C.V., 44
Grupo Industrial Bimbo, 19
Grupo Industrial Durango, S.A. de C.V., 37
Grupo Industrial Herradura, S.A. de C.V., 83
Grupo Industrial Lala, S.A. de C.V., 82
Grupo Industrial Saltillo, S.A. de C.V., 54
Grupo Mexico, S.A. de C.V., 40
Grupo Modelo, S.A. de C.V., 29
Grupo Omnilife S.A. de C.V., 88
Grupo Posadas, S.A. de C.V., 57
Grupo Televisa, S.A., 18; 54 (upd.)
Grupo TMM, S.A. de C.V., 50
Grupo Transportación Ferroviaria Mexicana, S.A. de C.V., 47
Grupo Viz, S.A. de C.V., 84
Hylsamex, S.A. de C.V., 39
Industrias Bachoco, S.A. de C.V., 39
Industrias Penoles, S.A. de C.V., 22
Internacional de Ceramica, S.A. de C.V., 53
Jugos del Valle, S.A. de C.V., 85
Kimberly-Clark de México, S.A. de C.V., 54
Nadro S.A. de C.V., 86
Organización Soriana, S.A. de C.V., 35
Petróleos Mexicanos, IV; 19 (upd.)
Proeza S.A. de C.V., 82
Pulsar Internacional S.A., 21
Real Turismo, S.A. de C.V., 50
Sanborn Hermanos, S.A., 20
Sears Roebuck de México, S.A. de C.V., 20
Telefonos de Mexico S.A. de C.V., 14; 63 (upd.)
Tubos de Acero de Mexico, S.A. (TAMSA), 41
TV Azteca, S.A. de C.V., 39
Urbi Desarrollos Urbanos, S.A. de C.V., 81
Valores Industriales S.A., 19
Vitro Corporativo S.A. de C.V., 34
Wal-Mart de Mexico, S.A. de C.V., 35 (upd.)

Nepal

Royal Nepal Airline Corporation, 41

Netherlands

ABN AMRO Holding, N.V., 50
AEGON N.V., III; 50 (upd.)
Akzo Nobel N.V., 13; 41 (upd.)
Algemene Bank Nederland N.V., II
Amsterdam-Rotterdam Bank N.V., II
Arcadis NV, 26
ASML Holding N.V., 50
Avantium Technologies BV 79
Baan Company, 25
Blokker Holding B.V., 84
Bols Distilleries NV, 74
Bolton Group B.V., 86
Buhrmann NV, 41
The Campina Group, The 78
Chicago Bridge & Iron Company N.V., 82 (upd.)
CNH Global N.V., 38 (upd.)
CSM N.V., 65
Deli Universal NV, 66
DSM N.V., I; 56 (upd.)
Elsevier N.V., IV
Endemol Entertainment Holding NV, 46
Equant N.V., 52
Euronext N.V., 89 (upd.)
European Aeronautic Defence and Space Company EADS N.V., 52 (upd.)
Friesland Coberco Dairy Foods Holding N.V., 59
Getronics NV, 39
Granaria Holdings B.V., 66
Grand Hotel Krasnapolsky N.V., 23
Greenpeace International, 74
Gucci Group N.V., 50
Hagemeyer N.V., 39
Head N.V., 55
Heijmans N.V., 66
Heineken N.V., I; 13 (upd.); 34 (upd.); 90 (upd.)
IHC Caland N.V., 71
IKEA Group, 94 (upd.)
Indigo NV, 26
Intres B.V., 82
Ispat International N.V., 30
Koninklijke Ahold N.V. (Royal Ahold), II; 16 (upd.)
Koninklijke Luchtvaart Maatschappij, N.V. (KLM Royal Dutch Airlines), I; 28 (upd.)
Koninklijke Nederlandsche Hoogovens en Staalfabrieken NV, IV
Koninklijke Nedlloyd N.V., 6; 26 (upd.)
Koninklijke Philips Electronics N.V., 50 (upd.)
Koninklijke PTT Nederland NV, V
Koninklijke Vendex KBB N.V. (Royal Vendex KBB N.V.), 62 (upd.)
Koninklijke Wessanen nv, II; 54 (upd.)
KPMG International, 10; 33 (upd.)
Laurus N.V., 65
Mammoet Transport B.V., 26
MIH Limited, 31
N.V. AMEV, III
N.V. Holdingmaatschappij De Telegraaf, 23
N.V. Koninklijke Nederlandse Vliegtuigenfabriek Fokker, I; 28 (upd.)
N.V. Nederlandse Gasunie, V
Nationale-Nederlanden N.V., III
New Holland N.V., 22
Nutreco Holding N.V., 56
Océ N.V., 24; 91 (upd.)
PCM Uitgevers NV, 53
Philips Electronics N.V., II; 13 (upd.)
PolyGram N.V., 23
Prada Holding B.V., 45
Qiagen N.V., 39

Rabobank Group, 33
Randstad Holding n.v., 16; 43 (upd.)
Rodamco N.V., 26
Royal Dutch/Shell Group, IV; 49 (upd.)
Royal Grolsch NV, 54
Royal KPN N.V., 30
Royal Numico N.V., 37
Royal Packaging Industries Van Leer N.V., 30
Royal Ten Cate N.V., 68
Royal Vopak NV, 41
SHV Holdings N.V., 55
Tennet BV 78
TNT Post Group N.V., V, 27 (upd.); 30 (upd.)
Toolex International N.V., 26
TomTom N.V., 81
TPG N.V., 64 (upd.)
Trader Classified Media N.V., 57
Triple P N.V., 26
Unilever N.V., II; 7 (upd.); 32 (upd.)
United Pan-Europe Communications NV, 47
Van Lanschot NV 79
VBA - Bloemenveiling Aalsmeer, 88
Vebego International BV, 49
Vedior NV, 35
Velcro Industries N.V., 19
Vendex International N.V., 13
Vion Food Group NV, 85
VNU N.V., 27
Wegener NV, 53
Wolters Kluwer NV, 14; 33 (upd.)

Netherlands Antilles
Orthofix International NV, 72
Velcro Industries N.V., 72

New Zealand
Air New Zealand Limited, 14; 38 (upd.)
Carter Holt Harvey Ltd., 70
Fletcher Challenge Ltd., IV; 19 (upd.)
Fonterra Co-Operative Group Ltd., 58
Nuplex Industries Ltd., 92
Telecom Corporation of New Zealand Limited, 54
Wattie's Ltd., 7

Nigeria
Nigerian National Petroleum Corporation, IV; 72 (upd.)

Norway
Braathens ASA, 47
Den Norse Stats Oljeselskap AS, IV
Helly Hansen ASA, 25
Jotun A/S, 80
Kvaerner ASA, 36
Norsk Hydro ASA, 10; 35 (upd.)
Norske Skogindustrier ASA, 63
Orkla ASA, 18; 82 (upd.)
Schibsted ASA, 31
Statoil ASA, 61 (upd.)
Stolt Sea Farm Holdings PLC, 54
Telenor ASA, 69
Wilh. Wilhelmsen ASA, 94
Yara International ASA, 94

Oman
Petroleum Development Oman LLC, IV

Pakistan
Pakistan International Airlines Corporation, 46
Pakistan State Oil Company Ltd., 81

Panama
Autoridad del Canal de Panamá, 94
Copa Holdings, S.A., 93
Panamerican Beverages, Inc., 47
Willbros Group, Inc., 56

Papua New Guinea
Steamships Trading Company Ltd., 82

Peru
Ajegroup S.A., 92
Banco de Crédito del Perú, 93
Compañia de Minas Buenaventura S.A.A., 93
Corporación José R. Lindley S.A., 92
Southern Peru Copper Corporation, 40
Unión de Cervecerias Peruanas Backus y Johnston S.A.A., 92
Volcan Compañia Minera S.A.A., 92

Philippines
Bank of the Philippine Islands, 58
Benguet Corporation, 58
Manila Electric Company (Meralco), 56
Mercury Drug Corporation, 70
Petron Corporation, 58
Philippine Airlines, Inc., 6; 23 (upd.)
San Miguel Corporation, 15; 57 (upd.)

Poland
Agora S.A. Group, 77
LOT Polish Airlines (Polskie Linie Lotnicze S.A.), 33
Polski Koncern Naftowy ORLEN S.A., 77
Telekomunikacja Polska SA, 50

Portugal
Banco Comercial Português, SA, 50
Banco Espírito Santo e Comercial de Lisboa S.A., 15
BRISA Auto-estradas de Portugal S.A., 64
Cimentos de Portugal SGPS S.A. (Cimpor), 76
Corticeira Amorim, Sociedade Gestora de Participaço es Sociais, S.A., 48
Electricidade de Portugal, S.A., 47
Grupo Portucel Soporcel, 60
Madeira Wine Company, S.A., 49
Petróleos de Portugal S.A., IV
Portugal Telecom SGPS S.A., 69
TAP—Air Portugal Transportes Aéreos Portugueses S.A., 46
Transportes Aereos Portugueses, S.A., 6

Puerto Rico
Puerto Rico Electric Power Authority, 47

Qatar
Aljazeera Satellite Channel 79
Qatar Airways Company Q.C.S.C., 87
Qatar General Petroleum Corporation, IV
Qatar National Bank SAQ, 87
Qatar Telecom QSA, 87

Republic of Yemen
Hayel Saeed Anam Group of Cos., 92

Romania
Dobrogea Grup S.A., 82
TAROM S.A., 64

Russia
A.S. Yakovlev Design Bureau, 15
Aeroflot - Russian Airlines JSC, 6; 29 (upd.); 89 (upd.)
Alrosa Company Ltd., 62
AO VimpelCom, 48
Aviacionny Nauchno-Tehnicheskii Komplex im. A.N. Tupoleva, 24
AVTOVAZ Joint Stock Company, 65
Baltika Brewery Joint Stock Company, 65
Golden Telecom, Inc., 59
Interfax News Agency, 86
Irkut Corporation, 68
JSC MMC Norilsk Nickel, 48
Mobile TeleSystems OJSC, 59
OAO Gazprom, 42
OAO LUKOIL, 40
OAO NK YUKOS, 47
OAO Siberian Oil Company (Sibneft), 49
OAO Surgutneftegaz, 48
OAO Tatneft, 45
OJSC Wimm-Bill-Dann Foods, 48
RAO Unified Energy System of Russia, 45
Rostvertol plc, 62
Russian Aircraft Corporation (MiG), 86
Russian Railways Joint Stock Co., 93
Sberbank, 62
Severstal Joint Stock Company, 65
Sistema JSFC, 73
Sukhoi Design Bureau Aviation Scientific-Industrial Complex, 24
CJSC Transmash Holding, 93
Oil Transporting Joint Stock Company Transneft, 93
Volga-Dnepr Group, 82

Saudi Arabia
Dallah Albaraka Group, 72
Saudi Arabian Airlines, 6; 27 (upd.)
Saudi Arabian Oil Company, IV; 17 (upd.); 50 (upd.)
Saudi Basic Industries Corporation (SABIC), 58

Scotland
Arnold Clark Automobiles Ltd., 60
Distillers Company PLC, I
General Accident PLC, III
The Governor and Company of the Bank of Scotland, 10
The Royal Bank of Scotland Group plc, 12
Scottish & Newcastle plc, 15
Scottish Hydro-Electric PLC, 13
Scottish Media Group plc, 32
ScottishPower plc, 19

Stagecoach Holdings plc, 30
The Standard Life Assurance Company, III

Singapore

Asia Pacific Breweries Limited, 59
City Developments Limited, 89
Creative Technology Ltd., 57
Flextronics International Ltd., 38
Fraser & Neave Ltd., 54
Hotel Properties Ltd., 71
Jardine Cycle & Carriage Ltd., 73
Keppel Corporation Ltd., 73
Neptune Orient Lines Limited, 47
Pacific Internet Limited, 87
Singapore Airlines Limited, 6; 27 (upd.); 83 (upd.)
Singapore Press Holdings Limited, 85
StarHub Ltd., 77
United Overseas Bank Ltd., 56

South Africa

Anglo American Corporation of South Africa Limited, IV; 16 (upd.)
Barlow Rand Ltd., I
De Beers Consolidated Mines Limited/De Beers Centenary AG, IV; 7 (upd.); 28 (upd.)
Dimension Data Holdings PLC, 69
Edgars Consolidated Stores Ltd., 66
Famous Brands Ltd., 86
Gencor Ltd., IV; 22 (upd.)
Gold Fields Ltd., IV; 62 (upd.)
Harmony Gold Mining Company Limited, 63
Highveld Steel and Vanadium Corporation Limited, 59
Iscor Limited, 57
Naspers Ltd., 66
New Clicks Holdings Ltd., 86
Pick 'n Pay Stores Ltd., 82
SAA (Pty) Ltd., 28
Sanlam Ltd., 68
Sappi Limited, 49
Sasol Limited, IV; 47 (upd.)
The South African Breweries Limited, I; 24 (upd.)
Transnet Ltd., 6

South Korea

Anam Group, 23
Asiana Airlines, Inc., 46
CJ Corporation, 62
Daesang Corporation, 84
Daewoo Group, III; 18 (upd.); 57 (upd.)
Electronics Co., Ltd., 14
Goldstar Co., Ltd., 12
Hanjin Shipping Co., Ltd., 50
Hanwha Group, 62
Hyundai Group, III; 7 (upd.); 56 (upd.)
Kia Motors Corporation, 12; 29 (upd.)
Kookmin Bank, 58
Korea Electric Power Corporation (Kepco), 56
Korean Air Lines Co., Ltd., 6; 27 (upd.)
KT&G Corporation, 62
LG Corporation, 94 (upd.)
Lotte Confectionery Company Ltd., 76
Lucky-Goldstar, II
Pohang Iron and Steel Company Ltd., IV
POSCO, 57 (upd.)
Samick Musical Instruments Co., Ltd., 56
Samsung Electronics Co., Ltd., I; 41 (upd.)
SK Group, 88
Ssangyong Cement Industrial Co., Ltd., III; 61 (upd.)
Tong Yang Cement Corporation, 62

Spain

Abengoa S.A., 73
Abertis Infraestructuras, S.A., 65
Acciona S.A., 81
Adolfo Dominguez S.A., 72
Altadis S.A., 72 (upd.)
Banco Bilbao Vizcaya Argentaria S.A., II; 48 (upd.)
Banco Central, II
Banco do Brasil S.A., II
Banco Santander Central Hispano S.A., 36 (upd.)
Baron de Ley S.A., 74
Campofrío Alimentación S.A, 59
Chupa Chups S.A., 38
Compañia Española de Petróleos S.A. (Cepsa), IV; 56 (upd.)
Cortefiel S.A., 64
Correos y Telegrafos S.A., 80
Dogi International Fabrics S.A., 52
El Corte Inglés Group, V; 26 (upd.)
ENDESA S.A., V; 46 (upd.)
Ercros S.A., 80
Federico Paternina S.A., 69
Freixenet S.A., 71
Gas Natural SDG S.A., 69
Grupo Dragados SA, 55
Grupo Eroski, 64
Grupo Ferrovial, S.A., 40
Grupo Ficosa International, 90
Grupo Leche Pascual S.A., 59
Grupo Lladró S.A., 52
Grupo Planeta, 94
Iberdrola, S.A., 49
Iberia Líneas Aéreas de España S.A., 6; 36 (upd.); 91 (upd.)
Industria de Diseño Textil S.A., 64
Instituto Nacional de Industria, I
Mecalux S.A., 74
Miquel y Costas Miquel S.A., 68
NH Hoteles S.A. 79
Nutrexpa S.A., 92
Obrascon Huarte Lain S.A., 76
Paradores de Turismo de Espana S.A., 73
Pescanova S.A., 81
Puig Beauty and Fashion Group S.L., 60
Real Madrid C.F., 73
Repsol-YPF S.A., IV; 16 (upd.); 40 (upd.)
Sol Meliá S.A., 71
Tabacalera, S.A., V; 17 (upd.)
Telefónica S.A., V; 46 (upd.)
TelePizza S.A., 33
Television Española, S.A., 7
Terra Lycos, Inc., 43
Unión Fenosa, S.A., 51
Vidrala S.A., 67
Viscofan S.A., 70
Vocento, 94
Zara International, Inc., 83
Zed Group, 93

Sweden

A. Johnson & Company H.B., I
AB Volvo, I; 7 (upd.); 26 (upd.); 67 (upd.)
Aktiebolaget Electrolux, 22 (upd.)
Aktiebolaget SKF, III; 38 (upd.); 89 (upd.)
Alfa Laval AB, III; 64 (upd.)
Astra AB, I; 20 (upd.)
Atlas Copco AB, III; 28 (upd.); 85 (upd.)
Autoliv, Inc., 65
Boliden AB, 80
Bonnier AB, 52
BRIO AB, 24
Cardo AB, 53
Cloetta Fazer AB, 70
Electrolux AB, III; 53 (upd.)
Eka Chemicals AB, 92
FöreningsSparbanken AB, 69
Gambro AB, 49
Gunnebo AB, 53
Hennes & Mauritz AB, 29
Hexagon AB 78
Holmen AB, 52 (upd.)
ICA AB, II
Investor AB, 63
Mo och Domsjö AB, IV
Modern Times Group AB, 36
NetCom Systems AB, 26
Nobel Industries AB, 9
Nordea AB, 40
Observer AB, 55
Perstorp AB, I; 51 (upd.)
Saab Automobile AB, I; 11 (upd.); 32 (upd.); 83 (upd.)
Sandvik AB, IV; 32 (upd.); 77 (upd.)
Sapa AB, 84
The SAS Group, 34 (upd.)
Scandinavian Airlines System, I
Securitas AB, 42
Skandia Insurance Company, Ltd., 50
Skandinaviska Enskilda Banken AB, II; 56 (upd.)
Skanska AB, 38
SSAB Svenskt Stål AB, 89
Stora Kopparbergs Bergslags AB, IV
Sveaskog AB, 93
Svenska Cellulosa Aktiebolaget SCA, IV; 28 (upd.); 85 (upd.)
Svenska Handelsbanken AB, II; 50 (upd.)
Swedish Match AB, 12; 39 (upd.); 92 (upd.)
Swedish Telecom, V
Telefonaktiebolaget LM Ericsson, V; 46 (upd.)
TeliaSonera AB, 57 (upd.)
Trelleborg AB, 93
Vattenfall AB, 57
V&S Vin & Sprit AB, 91 (upd.)
Vin & Spirit AB, 31

Switzerland

ABB ASEA Brown Boveri Ltd., II; 22 (upd.)

ABB Ltd., 65 (upd.)
Actelion Ltd., 83
Adecco S.A., 36 (upd.)
Adia S.A., 6
Arthur Andersen & Company, Société Coopérative, 10
Ascom AG, 9
Bâloise-Holding, 40
Barry Callebaut AG, 29; 71 (upd.)
Bernina Holding AG, 47
Bodum Design Group AG, 47
Bon Appetit Holding AG, 48
Charles Vögele Holding AG, 82
Chocoladefabriken Lindt & Sprüngli AG, 27
Ciba-Geigy Ltd., I; 8 (upd.)
Compagnie Financiere Richemont AG, 50
Conzzeta Holding, 80
Coop Schweiz Genossenschaftsverband, 48
Credit Suisse Group, II; 21 (upd.); 59 (upd.)
Danzas Group, V; 40 (upd.)
De Beers Consolidated Mines Limited/De Beers Centenary AG, IV; 7 (upd.); 28 (upd.)
Denner AG, 88
Duferco Group, 94
Edipresse S.A., 82
Elektrowatt AG, 6
Elma Electronic AG, 83
F. Hoffmann-La Roche Ltd., I; 50 (upd.)
Fédération Internationale de Football Association, 27
Fenaco, 86
Firmenich International S.A., 60
Franke Holding AG, 76
Galenica AG, 84
Gate Gourmet International AG, 70
Geberit AG, 49
Georg Fischer AG Schaffhausen, 61
Givaudan SA, 43
Holderbank Financière Glaris Ltd., III
International Olympic Committee, 44
Jacobs Suchard A.G., II
Julius Baer Holding AG, 52
Keramik Holding AG Laufen, 51
Kraft Jacobs Suchard AG, 26 (upd.)
Kudelski Group SA, 44
Kuehne & Nagel International AG, V; 53 (upd.)
Kuoni Travel Holding Ltd., 40
Liebherr-International AG, 64
Logitech International S.A., 28; 69 (upd.)
Lonza Group Ltd., 73
Maus Frères SA, 48
Médecins sans Frontières, 85
Mettler-Toledo International Inc., 30
Migros-Genossenschafts-Bund, 68
Montres Rolex S.A., 13; 34 (upd.)
Nestlé S.A., II; 7 (upd.); 28 (upd.); 71 (upd.)
Novartis AG, 39 (upd.)
Panalpina World Transport (Holding) Ltd., 47
Pelikan Holding AG, 92
Phoenix Mecano AG, 61
Ricola Ltd., 62
Rieter Holding AG, 42
Roland Murten A.G., 7
Sandoz Ltd., I
Schindler Holding AG, 29
Schweizerische Post-, Telefon- und Telegrafen-Betriebe, V
Serono S.A., 47
STMicroelectronics NV, 52
Straumann Holding AG 79
Sulzer Ltd., III; 68 (upd.)
Swarovski International Holding AG, 40
The Swatch Group SA, 26
Swedish Match S.A., 12
Swiss Air Transport Company, Ltd., I
Swiss Bank Corporation, II
The Swiss Federal Railways (Schweizerische Bundesbahnen), V
Swiss International Air Lines Ltd., 48
Swiss Reinsurance Company (Schweizerische Rückversicherungs-Gesellschaft), III; 46 (upd.)
Swisscom AG, 58
Swissport International Ltd., 70
Syngenta International AG, 83
Synthes, Inc., 93
TAG Heuer International SA, 25; 77 (upd.)
Tamedia AG, 53
Tetra Pak International SA, 53
UBS AG, 52 (upd.)
Underberg AG, 92
Union Bank of Switzerland, II
Victorinox AG, 21; 74 (upd.)
Weleda AG 78
Winterthur Group, III; 68 (upd.)
Xstrata PLC, 73
Zurich Financial Services, 42 (upd.); 93 (upd.)
Zürich Versicherungs-Gesellschaft, III

Taiwan

Acer Incorporated, 16; 73 (upd.)
AU Optronics Corporation, 67
BenQ Corporation, 67
Chi Mei Optoelectronics Corporation, 75
China Airlines, 34
Chunghwa Picture Tubes, Ltd., 75
D-Link Corporation, 83
Directorate General of Telecommunications, 7
EVA Airways Corporation, 51
Evergreen Marine Corporation (Taiwan) Ltd., 13; 50 (upd.)
First International Computer, Inc., 56
Formosa Plastics Corporation, 14; 58 (upd.)
Giant Manufacturing Company, Ltd., 85
High Tech Computer Corporation, 81
Hon Hai Precision Industry Co., Ltd., 59
Kwang Yang Motor Company Ltd., 80
Pou Chen Corporation, 81
Quanta Computer Inc., 47
Siliconware Precision Industries Ltd., 73
Taiwan Semiconductor Manufacturing Company Ltd., 47
Taiwan Tobacco & Liquor Corporation, 75
Tatung Co., 23
Winbond Electronics Corporation, 74
Yageo Corporation, 16

Thailand

Charoen Pokphand Group, 62
Electricity Generating Authority of Thailand (EGAT), 56
Krung Thai Bank Public Company Ltd., 69
Pranda Jewelry plc, 70
PTT Public Company Ltd., 56
The Siam Cement Public Company Limited, 56
Thai Airways International Public Company Limited, 6; 27 (upd.)
Thai Union Frozen Products PCL, 75
Thanulux Public Company Limited, 86
The Topaz Group, Inc., 62

Tunisia

Société Tunisienne de l'Air-Tunisair, 49

Turkey

Akbank TAS 79
Dogan Sirketler Grubu Holding A.S., 83
Haci Omer Sabanci Holdings A.S., 55
Koç Holding A.S., I; 54 (upd.)
Turkish Airlines Inc. (Türk Hava Yollari A.O.), 72
Turkiye Is Bankasi A.S., 61
Türkiye Petrolleri Anonim Ortakliği, IV

Ukraine

Antonov Design Bureau, 53

United Arab Emirates

Abu Dhabi National Oil Company, IV; 45 (upd.)
Al Habtoor Group L.L.C., 87
DP World, 81
The Emirates Group, 39; 81 (upd.)
Etihad Airways PJSC, 89
Gulf Agency Company Ltd. 78
Jumeirah Group, 83

United Kingdom

A. F. Blakemore & Son Ltd., 90
A. Nelson & Co. Ltd., 75
Aardman Animations Ltd., 61
Abbey National plc, 10; 39 (upd.)
Aegis Group plc, 6
AG Barr plc, 64
Aga Foodservice Group PLC, 73
Aggregate Industries plc, 36
Aggreko Plc, 45
AgustaWestland N.V., 75
Air Partner PLC, 93
Airtours Plc, 27
The Albert Fisher Group plc, 41
Alexandra plc, 88
The All England Lawn Tennis & Croquet Club, 54
Alldays plc, 49
Allders plc, 37
Alliance and Leicester plc, 88
Alliance Boots plc, 83 (upd.)

Allied Domecq PLC, 29
Allied-Lyons PLC, I
Alpha Airports Group PLC, 77
Alvis Plc, 47
Amersham PLC, 50
Amey Plc, 47
Amnesty International, 50
Amstrad plc, III; 48 (upd.)
AMVESCAP PLC, 65
Anglo American PLC, 50 (upd.)
Anker BV, 53
Antofagasta plc, 65
Apax Partners Worldwide LLP, 89
Apple Corps Ltd., 87
Arcadia Group plc, 28 (upd.)
Argyll Group PLC, II
Arjo Wiggins Appleton p.l.c., 34
Arriva PLC, 69
Arsenal Holdings PLC 79
ASDA Group Ltd., II; 28 (upd.); 64 (upd.)
Ashtead Group plc, 34
Associated British Foods plc, II; 13 (upd.); 41 (upd.)
Associated British Ports Holdings Plc, 45
Aston Villa plc, 41
AstraZeneca PLC, 50 (upd.)
AT&T Istel Ltd., 14
Avecia Group PLC, 63
Aviva PLC, 50 (upd.)
BAA plc, 10; 33 (upd.)
Babcock International Group PLC, 69
Balfour Beatty plc, 36 (upd.)
Barclays plc, II; 20 (upd.); 64 (upd.)
Barings PLC, 14
Barratt Developments plc, I; 56 (upd.)
Bass PLC, I; 15 (upd.); 38 (upd.)
Bat Industries PLC, I; 20 (upd.)
BBA Aviation plc, 90
Belleek Pottery Ltd., 71
Bellway Plc, 45
Belron International Ltd., 76
Benfield Greig Group plc, 53
Bernard Matthews Ltd., 89
Bettys & Taylors of Harrogate Ltd., 72
Bhs plc, 17
BICC PLC, III
Biffa plc, 92
The Big Food Group plc, 68 (upd.)
Birse Group PLC, 77
Birthdays Ltd., 70
Blacks Leisure Group plc, 39
Blackwell Publishing Ltd. 78
Blue Circle Industries PLC, III
BOC Group plc, I; 25 (upd.); 78 (upd.)
The Body Shop International plc, 11; 53 (upd.)
Bodycote International PLC, 63
Bonhams 1793 Ltd., 72
Booker Cash & Carry Ltd., 13; 31 (upd.); 68 (upd.)
The Boots Company PLC, V; 24 (upd.)
Bowater PLC, IV
Bowthorpe plc, 33
BP p.l.c., 45 (upd.)
BPB plc, 83
Bradford & Bingley PLC, 65
Brake Bros plc, 45
Brammer PLC, 77
Bristow Helicopters Ltd., 70
Britannia Soft Drinks Ltd. (Britvic), 71
British Aerospace plc, I; 24 (upd.)
British Airways PLC, I; 14 (upd.); 43 (upd.)
British American Tobacco PLC, 50 (upd.)
British Broadcasting Corporation Ltd., 7; 21 (upd.); 89 (upd.)
British Coal Corporation, IV
British Energy Plc, 49
The British Film Institute, 80
British Gas plc, V
British Land Plc, 54
British Midland plc, 38
The British Museum, 71
British Nuclear Fuels plc, 6
The British Petroleum Company plc, IV; 7 (upd.); 21 (upd.)
British Railways Board, V
British Sky Broadcasting Group plc, 20; 60 (upd.)
British Steel plc, IV; 19 (upd.)
British Sugar plc, 84
British Telecommunications plc, V; 15 (upd.)
British United Provident Association Limited (BUPA) 79
British Vita plc, 9; 33 (upd.)
British World Airlines Ltd., 18
British-Borneo Oil & Gas PLC, 34
BT Group plc, 49 (upd.)
BTG Plc, 87
BTR PLC, I
BTR Siebe plc, 27
Budgens Ltd., 59
Bunzl plc, IV; 31 (upd.)
Burberry Group plc, 17; 41 (upd.); 92 (upd.)
Burmah Castrol PLC, IV; 30 (upd.)
The Burton Group plc, V
Business Post Group plc, 46
C&J Clark International Ltd., 52
C. Hoare & Co., 77
C.I. Traders Limited, 61
Cable and Wireless plc, V; 25 (upd.)
Cadbury Schweppes PLC, II; 49 (upd.)
Caffè Nero Group PLC, 63
Canary Wharf Group Plc, 30
Caparo Group Ltd., 90
Capita Group PLC, 69
Capital Radio plc, 35
Caradon plc, 20 (upd.)
Carbo PLC, 67 (upd.)
Carlton Communications PLC, 15; 50 (upd.)
The Carphone Warehouse Group PLC, 83
Cartier Monde, 29
Cattles plc, 58
Cazenove Group plc, 72
Central Independent Television, 7; 23 (upd.)
Centrica plc, 29 (upd.)
Channel Four Television Corporation, 93
Chello Zone Ltd., 93
Chelsfield PLC, 67
Cheltenham & Gloucester PLC, 61
Cheshire Building Society, 74
Christian Salvesen Plc, 45
Christie's International plc, 15; 39 (upd.)
Chrysalis Group plc, 40
Chubb, PLC, 50
Clifford Chance LLP, 38
Clinton Cards plc, 39
Close Brothers Group plc, 39
Co-operative Group (CWS) Ltd., 51
Coats plc, V; 44 (upd.)
Cobham plc, 30
COLT Telecom Group plc, 41
Commercial Union PLC, III
Compass Group PLC, 34
Cookson Group plc, III; 44 (upd.)
Corus Group plc, 49 (upd.)
Courtaulds plc, V; 17 (upd.)
Courts Plc, 45
Cranswick plc, 40
Croda International Plc, 45
Daily Mail and General Trust plc, 19
Dairy Crest Group plc, 32
Dalgety, PLC, II
Dart Group PLC, 77
Davis Service Group PLC, 45
Dawson Holdings PLC, 43
De La Rue plc, 10; 34 (upd.)
Debenhams Plc, 28
Denby Group plc, 44
Denison International plc, 46
Dennis Publishing Ltd., 62
Devro plc, 55
Diageo plc, 24 (upd.); 79 (upd.)
Direct Wines Ltd., 84
Dixons Group plc, V; 19 (upd.); 49 (upd.)
Domino Printing Sciences PLC, 87
Dorling Kindersley Holdings plc, 20
Dresdner Kleinwort Wasserstein, 60 (upd.)
DS Smith Plc, 61
Dyson Group PLC, 71
E H Booth & Company Ltd., 90
easyJet Airline Company Limited, 39
ECC Group plc, III
The Economist Group Ltd., 67
The Edrington Group Ltd., 88
Electrocomponents PLC, 50
Elementis plc, 40 (upd.)
EMAP plc, 35
EMI Group plc, 22 (upd.); 81 (upd.)
Energis plc, 47
English China Clays Ltd., 15 (upd.); 40 (upd.)
Enodis plc, 68
Enterprise Inns plc, 59
Enterprise Oil PLC, 11; 50 (upd.)
Esporta plc, 35
Eurotunnel Group, 13; 37 (upd.)
Exel plc, 51 (upd.)
Fairclough Construction Group PLC, I
Fat Face Ltd., 68
Filtrona plc, 88
Findel plc, 60
First Choice Holidays PLC, 40
FirstGroup plc, 89
Fisons plc, 9; 23 (upd.)
FKI Plc, 57
French Connection Group plc, 41
Fuller Smith & Turner P.L.C., 38

G A Pindar & Son Ltd., 88
Gallaher Group Plc, 49 (upd.)
Gallaher Limited, V; 19 (upd.)
The GAME Group plc, 80
The Gateway Corporation Ltd., II
Geest Plc, 38
General Electric Company PLC, II
George Wimpey PLC, 12; 51 (upd.)
Gibbs and Dandy plc, 74
GKN plc, III; 38 (upd.); 89 (upd.)
GlaxoSmithKline plc, I; 9 (upd.); 46 (upd.)
Glotel plc, 53
The Go-Ahead Group Plc, 28
Grampian Country Food Group, Ltd., 85
Granada Group PLC, II; 24 (upd.)
Grand Metropolitan PLC, I; 14 (upd.)
The Great Universal Stores plc, V; 19 (upd.)
The Greenalls Group PLC, 21
Greene King plc, 31
Greggs PLC, 65
Guardian Financial Services, 64 (upd.)
Guardian Media Group plc, 53
Guardian Royal Exchange Plc, 11
Guinness/UDV, I; 43 (upd.)
GUS plc, 47 (upd.)
GWR Group plc, 39
Hammerson plc, 40
The Hammerson Property Investment and Development Corporation plc, IV
Hanson PLC, III; 7 (upd.); 30 (upd.)
Harrisons & Crosfield plc, III
Harrods Holdings, 47
The Hartstone Group plc, 14
Hawker Siddeley Group Public Limited Company, III
Haynes Publishing Group P.L.C., 71
Hays Plc, 27; 78 (upd.)
Hazlewood Foods plc, 32
Henry Boot plc, 76
Her Majesty's Stationery Office, 7
Hillsdown Holdings plc, II; 24 (upd.)
Hilton Group plc, 49 (upd.)
HIT Entertainment PLC, 40
HMV Group plc, 59
Home Retail Group plc, 91
House of Fraser PLC, 45
HSBC Holdings plc, 12; 26 (upd.); 80 (upd.)
Hunting plc 78
Huntingdon Life Sciences Group plc, 42
Huntleigh Technology PLC, 77
Ibstock Brick Ltd., 14; 37 (upd.)
ICL plc, 6
IMI plc, 9
Imperial Chemical Industries PLC, I; 50 (upd.)
Imperial Tobacco Group PLC, 50
Inchcape PLC, III; 16 (upd.); 50 (upd.)
Informa Group plc, 58
Inter Link Foods PLC, 61
International Power PLC, 50 (upd.)
Invensys PLC, 50 (upd.)
IPC Magazines Limited, 7
J C Bamford Excavators Ltd., 83
J Sainsbury plc, II; 13 (upd.); 38 (upd.)
James Beattie plc, 43
James Purdey & Sons Limited, 87
Jarvis plc, 39
JD Wetherspoon plc, 30
Jersey European Airways (UK) Ltd., 61
JJB Sports plc, 32
John Brown PLC, I
The John David Group plc, 90
John Dewar & Sons, Ltd., 82
John Laing plc, I; 51 (upd.)
John Lewis Partnership plc, V; 42 (upd.)
John Menzies plc, 39
Johnson Matthey PLC, IV; 16 (upd.); 49 (upd.)
Johnston Press plc, 35
Kelda Group plc, 45
Kennecott Corporation, 7; 27 (upd.)
Kesa Electricals plc, 91
Kidde plc, 44 (upd.)
Kingfisher plc, V; 24 (upd.); 83 (upd.)
Kleinwort Benson Group PLC, II
Kvaerner ASA, 36
Kwik-Fit Holdings plc, 54
Ladbroke Group PLC, II; 21 (upd.)
Lafarge Cement UK, 54 (upd.)
Land Securities PLC, IV; 49 (upd.)
Laing O'Rourke PLC, 93 (upd.)
Laura Ashley Holdings plc, 13; 37 (upd.)
The Laurel Pub Company Limited, 59
Legal & General Group plc, III; 24 (upd.)
Littlewoods plc, V; 42 (upd.)
Lloyd's, III; 22 (upd.); 74 (upd.)
Lloyds TSB Group plc, II; 47 (upd.)
Loganair Ltd., 68
Logica plc, 14; 37 (upd.)
London Regional Transport, 6
London Scottish Bank plc, 70
London Stock Exchange Limited, 34
Lonmin plc, 66 (upd.)
Lonrho Plc, 21
Lookers plc, 71
Lotus Cars Ltd., 14
Lucas Industries PLC, III
Luminar Plc, 40
Lush Ltd., 93
The Macallan Distillers Ltd., 63
Mackays Stores Group Ltd., 92
Madge Networks N.V., 26
Manchester United Football Club plc, 30
Marconi plc, 33 (upd.)
Marks and Spencer Group p.l.c., V; 24 (upd.); 85 (upd.)
Marshall Amplification plc, 62
Martin-Baker Aircraft Company Limited, 61
Matalan PLC, 49
Maxwell Communication Corporation plc, IV; 7 (upd.)
McBride plc, 82
McKechnie plc, 34
Meggitt PLC, 34
MEPC plc, IV
Mercury Communications, Ltd., 7
The Mersey Docks and Harbour Company, 30
Metal Box PLC, I
Michael Page International plc, 45
Midland Bank PLC, II; 17 (upd.)
Millennium & Copthorne Hotels plc, 71
Mirror Group Newspapers plc, 7; 23 (upd.)
Misys plc, 45; 46
Mitchells & Butlers PLC, 59
Molins plc, 51
Monsoon plc, 39
The Morgan Crucible Company plc, 82
Morgan Grenfell Group PLC, II
Moss Bros Group plc, 51
Mothercare plc, 17; 78 (upd.)
Moy Park Ltd. 78
Mulberry Group PLC, 71
N M Rothschild & Sons Limited, 39
National Express Group PLC, 50
National Power PLC, 12
National Westminster Bank PLC, II
New Look Group plc, 35
Newsquest plc, 32
Next plc, 29
NFC plc, 6
Nichols plc, 44
North West Water Group plc, 11
Northern and Shell Network plc, 87
Northern Foods plc, 10; 61 (upd.)
Northern Rock plc, 33
Norwich & Peterborough Building Society, 55
Novar plc, 49 (upd.)
NTL Inc., 65
Ocean Group plc, 6
Old Mutual PLC, 61
Orange S.A., 84
Ottakar's plc, 64
Oxfam GB, 87
Pearson plc, IV; 46 (upd.)
The Peninsular & Oriental Steam Navigation Company (Bovis Division), I
The Peninsular and Oriental Steam Navigation Company, V; 38 (upd.)
Pennon Group Plc, 45
Pentland Group plc, 20
Perkins Foods Holdings Ltd., 87
Phones 4u Ltd., 85
Photo-Me International Plc, 83
PIC International Group PLC, 24 (upd.)
Pilkington Group Limited, III; 34 (upd.); 87 (upd.)
PKF International 78
The Plessey Company, PLC, II
The Porcelain and Fine China Companies Ltd., 69
Portmeirion Group plc, 88
Post Office Group, V
Posterscope Worldwide, 70
Powell Duffryn plc, 31
Powergen PLC, 11; 50 (upd.)
Princes Ltd., 76
Prudential plc, 48 (upd.)
Psion PLC, 45
Punch Taverns plc, 70
PZ Cussons plc, 72
R. Griggs Group Limited, 23
Racal Electronics PLC, II
Ragdoll Productions Ltd., 51
Railtrack Group PLC, 50
Raleigh UK Ltd., 65

The Rank Group plc, II; 14 (upd.); 64 (upd.)
Ranks Hovis McDougall Limited, II; 28 (upd.)
Rathbone Brothers plc, 70
The Really Useful Group, 26
Reckitt Benckiser plc, II; 42 (upd.); 91 (upd.)
Redland plc, III
Redrow Group plc, 31
Reed Elsevier plc, IV; 17 (upd.); 31 (upd.)
Renishaw plc, 46
Rentokil Initial Plc, 47
Reuters Group PLC, IV; 22 (upd.); 63 (upd.)
Rexam PLC, 32 (upd.); 85 (upd.)
Ricardo plc, 90
Rio Tinto PLC, 19 (upd.); 50 (upd.)
RMC Group p.l.c., III; 34 (upd.)
Rolls-Royce Group PLC, 67 (upd.)
Rolls-Royce plc, I; 7 (upd.); 21 (upd.)
Ronson PLC, 49
Rothmans UK Holdings Limited, V; 19 (upd.)
Rotork plc, 46
Rover Group Ltd., 7; 21 (upd.)
Rowntree Mackintosh, II
Royal & Sun Alliance Insurance Group plc, 55 (upd.)
The Royal Bank of Scotland Group plc, 38 (upd.)
Royal Doulton plc, 14; 38 (upd.)
Royal Dutch Petroleum Company/ The Shell Transport and Trading Company p.l.c., IV
Royal Insurance Holdings PLC, III
RPC Group PLC, 81
The RTZ Corporation PLC, IV
The Rugby Group plc, 31
Saatchi & Saatchi PLC, I
SABMiller plc, 59 (upd.)
Safeway PLC, 50 (upd.)
Saffery Champness, 80
The Sage Group, 43
St. James's Place Capital, plc, 71
The Sanctuary Group PLC, 69
SBC Warburg, 14
Schroders plc, 42
Scottish & Newcastle plc, 35 (upd.)
Scottish and Southern Energy plc, 66 (upd.)
Scottish Power plc, 49 (upd.)
Scottish Radio Holding plc, 41
SDL PLC, 67
Sea Containers Ltd., 29
Sears plc, V
Securicor Plc, 45
Seddon Group Ltd., 67
Selfridges Plc, 34
Serco Group plc, 47
Severn Trent PLC, 12; 38 (upd.)
SFI Group plc, 51
Shanks Group plc, 45
Shepherd Neame Limited, 30
SIG plc, 71
Signet Group PLC, 61
Singer & Friedlander Group plc, 41
Skipton Building Society, 80
Slough Estates PLC, IV; 50 (upd.)
Smith & Nephew plc, 17;41 (upd.)
SmithKline Beecham plc, III; 32 (upd.)
Smiths Industries PLC, 25
Somerfield plc, 47 (upd.)
Southern Electric PLC, 13
Specialist Computer Holdings Ltd., 80
Speedy Hire plc, 84
Spirax-Sarco Engineering plc, 59
SSL International plc, 49
St Ives plc, 34
Standard Chartered plc, II; 48 (upd.)
Stanley Leisure plc, 66
STC PLC, III
Stirling Group plc, 62
Stoddard International plc, 72
Stoll-Moss Theatres Ltd., 34
Stolt-Nielsen S.A., 42
Storehouse PLC, 16
Strix Ltd., 51
Surrey Satellite Technology Limited, 83
Sun Alliance Group PLC, III
Sytner Group plc, 45
Tarmac plc, III; 28 (upd.)
Tate & Lyle PLC, II; 42 (upd.)
Taylor & Francis Group plc, 44
Taylor Nelson Sofres plc, 34
Taylor Woodrow plc, I; 38 (upd.)
Ted Baker plc, 86
Tesco plc, II; 24 (upd.); 68 (upd.)
Thames Water plc, 11; 90 (upd.)
Thistle Hotels PLC, 54
Thorn Emi PLC, I
Thorn plc, 24
Thorntons plc, 46
3i Group PLC, 73
365 Media Group plc, 89
TI Group plc, 17
Tibbett & Britten Group plc, 32
Tiger Aspect Productions Ltd., 72
Time Out Group Ltd., 68
Tomkins plc, 11; 44 (upd.)
Tottenham Hotspur PLC, 81
Travis Perkins plc, 34
Trinity Mirror plc, 49 (upd.)
Triumph Motorcycles Ltd., 53
Trusthouse Forte PLC, III
TSB Group plc, 12
Tulip Ltd., 89
Tullow Oil plc, 83
The Tussauds Group, 55
Ulster Television PLC, 71
Ultimate Leisure Group PLC, 75
Ultramar PLC, IV
Umbro plc, 88
Unigate PLC, II; 28 (upd.)
Unilever, II; 7 (upd.); 32 (upd.); 89 (upd.)
Uniq plc, 83 (upd.)
United Biscuits (Holdings) plc, II; 42 (upd.)
United Business Media plc, 52 (upd.)
United News & Media plc, IV; 28 (upd.)
United Utilities PLC, 52 (upd.)
Urbium PLC, 75
Vauxhall Motors Limited, 73
Vendôme Luxury Group plc, 27
Vickers plc, 27
Virgin Group Ltd., 12; 32 (upd.); 89 (upd.)
Viridian Group plc, 64
Vodafone Group Plc, 11; 36 (upd.); 75 (upd.)
Vosper Thornycroft Holding plc, 41
W Jordan (Cereals) Ltd., 74
Wagon plc, 92
Walkers Shortbread Ltd. 79
Walkers Snack Foods Ltd., 70
Warburtons Ltd., 89
Wassall Plc, 18
Waterford Wedgwood Holdings PLC, 12
Watson Wyatt Worldwide, 42
Watts of Lydney Group Ltd., 71
Weetabix Limited, 61
The Weir Group PLC, 85
The Wellcome Foundation Ltd., I
WH Smith PLC, V, 42 (upd.)
Whatman plc, 46
Whitbread PLC, I; 20 (upd.); 52 (upd.)
Whittard of Chelsea Plc, 61
Wilkinson Hardware Stores Ltd., 80
Wilkinson Sword Ltd., 60
William Grant & Sons Ltd., 60
William Hill Organization Limited, 49
William Reed Publishing Ltd. 78
Willis Corroon Group plc, 25
Wilson Bowden Plc, 45
Wincanton plc, 52
Wm. Morrison Supermarkets PLC, 38
Wolseley plc, 64
The Wolverhampton & Dudley Breweries, PLC, 57
Wood Hall Trust PLC, I
The Woolwich plc, 30
Woolworths Group plc, 83
WPP Group plc, 6; 48 (upd.)
WS Atkins Plc, 45
Xstrata PLC, 73
Yell Group PLC 79
Young & Co.'s Brewery, P.L.C., 38
Young's Bluecrest Seafood Holdings Ltd., 81
Yule Catto & Company plc, 54
Zeneca Group PLC, 21
Zomba Records Ltd., 52

United States

A & E Television Networks, 32
A & W Brands, Inc., 25
A-dec, Inc., 53
A-Mark Financial Corporation, 71
A. Schulman, Inc., 8; 49 (upd.)
A.B. Watley Group Inc., 45
A.B.Dick Company, 28
A.C. Moore Arts & Crafts, Inc., 30
A. Duda & Sons, Inc., 88
A.G. Edwards, Inc., 8; 32
A.H. Belo Corporation, 10; 30 (upd.)
A.L. Pharma Inc., 12
A.M. Castle & Co., 25
A.O. Smith Corporation, 11; 40 (upd.); 93 (upd.)
A.T. Cross Company, 17; 49 (upd.)
AAF-McQuay Incorporated, 26
AAON, Inc., 22
AAR Corp., 28

Aaron Rents, Inc., 14; 35 (upd.)
AARP, 27
Aavid Thermal Technologies, Inc., 29
Abatix Corp., 57
Abaxis, Inc., 83
Abbott Laboratories, I; 11 (upd.); 40 (upd.); 93 (upd.)
ABC Appliance, Inc., 10
ABC Carpet & Home Co. Inc., 26
ABC Family Worldwide, Inc., 52
ABC Rail Products Corporation, 18
ABC Supply Co., Inc., 22
Abercrombie & Fitch Company, 15; 35 (upd.); 75 (upd.)
Abigail Adams National Bancorp, Inc., 23
Abiomed, Inc., 47
ABM Industries Incorporated, 25 (upd.)
Abrams Industries Inc., 23
Abraxas Petroleum Corporation, 89
Academy of Television Arts & Sciences, Inc., 55
Academy Sports & Outdoors, 27
Acadian Ambulance & Air Med Services, Inc., 39
ACCION International, 87
Acclaim Entertainment Inc., 24
ACCO World Corporation, 7; 51 (upd.)
Accredited Home Lenders Holding Co., 91
Accubuilt, Inc., 74
AccuWeather, Inc., 73
ACE Cash Express, Inc., 33
Ace Hardware Corporation, 12; 35 (upd.)
Aceto Corp., 38
AchieveGlobal Inc., 90
Ackerley Communications, Inc., 9
Acme United Corporation, 70
Acme-Cleveland Corp., 13
ACNielsen Corporation, 13; 38 (upd.)
Acorn Products, Inc., 55
Acosta Sales and Marketing Company, Inc., 77
Acsys, Inc., 44
Action Performance Companies, Inc., 27
Activision, Inc., 32; 89 (upd.)
Actuant Corporation, 94 (upd.)
Acuity Brands, Inc., 90
Acushnet Company, 64
Acuson Corporation, 10; 36 (upd.)
Acxiom Corporation, 35
The Adams Express Company, 86
Adams Golf, Inc., 37
Adaptec, Inc., 31
ADC Telecommunications, Inc., 10; 30 (upd.); 89 (upd.)
Adelphia Communications Corporation, 17; 52 (upd.)
ADESA, Inc., 71
Administaff, Inc., 52
Adobe Systems Inc., 10; 33 (upd.)
Adolph Coors Company, I; 13 (upd.); 36 (upd.)
ADT Security Services, Inc., 12; 44 (upd.)
Adtran Inc., 22
Advance Auto Parts, Inc., 57
Advance Publications Inc., IV; 19 (upd.)
Advanced Circuits Inc., 67
Advanced Fibre Communications, Inc., 63
Advanced Marketing Services, Inc., 34
Advanced Medical Optics, Inc. 79
Advanced Micro Devices, Inc., 6; 30 (upd.)
Advanced Neuromodulation Systems, Inc., 73
Advanced Technology Laboratories, Inc., 9
Advanstar Communications, Inc., 57
Advanta Corporation, 8; 38 (upd.)
Advantica Restaurant Group, Inc., 27 (upd.)
Adventist Health, 53
The Advertising Council, Inc., 76
The Advisory Board Company, 80
Advo, Inc., 6; 53 (upd.)
Advocat Inc., 46
AECOM Technology Corporation 79
AEI Music Network Inc., 35
AEP Industries, Inc., 36
Aerojet-General Corp., 63
Aeronca Inc., 46
Aéropostale, Inc., 89
Aeroquip Corporation, 16
Aerosonic Corporation, 69
The AES Corporation, 10; 13 (upd.); 53 (upd.)
Aetna Inc., III; 21 (upd.); 63 (upd.)
AFC Enterprises, Inc., 32; 83 (upd.)
Affiliated Computer Services, Inc., 61
Affiliated Foods Inc., 53
Affiliated Managers Group, Inc. 79
Affiliated Publications, Inc., 7
Affinity Group Holding Inc., 56
AFLAC Incorporated, 10 (upd.); 38 (upd.)
Africare, 59
After Hours Formalwear Inc., 60
Aftermarket Technology Corp., 83
Ag Services of America, Inc., 59
Ag-Chem Equipment Company, Inc., 17
AGCO Corporation, 13; 67 (upd.)
Agere Systems Inc., 61
Agilent Technologies Inc., 38; 93 (upd.)
Agilysys Inc., 76 (upd.)
Agri Beef Company, 81
Agway, Inc., 7; 21 (upd.)
AHL Services, Inc., 27
Air & Water Technologies Corporation, 6
Air Express International Corporation, 13
Air Methods Corporation, 53
Air Products and Chemicals, Inc., I; 10 (upd.); 74 (upd.)
Air T, Inc., 86
Air Wisconsin Airlines Corporation, 55
Airborne Freight Corporation, 6; 34 (upd.)
Airborne Systems Group, 89
Airgas, Inc., 54
AirTouch Communications, 11
AirTran Holdings, Inc., 22
AK Steel Holding Corporation, 19; 41 (upd.)
Akamai Technologies, Inc., 71
Akin, Gump, Strauss, Hauer & Feld, L.L.P., 33
Akorn, Inc., 32
Alabama Farmers Cooperative, Inc., 63
Alabama National BanCorporation, 75
Alamo Group Inc., 32
Alamo Rent A Car, 6; 24 (upd.); 84 (upd.)
ALARIS Medical Systems, Inc., 65
Alaska Air Group, Inc., 6; 29 (upd.)
Alaska Communications Systems Group, Inc., 89
Alaska Railroad Corporation, 60
Alba-Waldensian, Inc., 30
Albany International Corporation, 8; 51 (upd.)
Albany Molecular Research, Inc., 77
Albemarle Corporation, 59
Alberici Corporation, 76
Alberto-Culver Company, 8; 36 (upd.); 91 (upd.)
Albertson's, Inc., II; 7 (upd.); 30 (upd.); 65 (upd.)
Alco Health Services Corporation, III
Alco Standard Corporation, I
Alcoa Inc., 56 (upd.)
Aldila Inc., 46
Aldus Corporation, 10
Alex Lee Inc., 18; 44 (upd.)
Alexander & Alexander Services Inc., 10
Alexander & Baldwin, Inc., 10; 40 (upd.)
Alexander's, Inc., 45
Alfa Corporation, 60
Alico, Inc., 63
Alienware Corporation, 81
Align Technology, Inc., 94
All American Communications Inc., 20
Alleghany Corporation, 10; 60 (upd.)
Allegheny Energy, Inc., 38 (upd.)
Allegheny Ludlum Corporation, 8
Allegheny Power System, Inc., V
Allen Canning Company, 76
Allen Foods, Inc., 60
Allen Organ Company, 33
Allen Systems Group, Inc., 59
Allen-Edmonds Shoe Corporation, 61
Allergan, Inc., 10; 30 (upd.); 77 (upd.)
Alliance Capital Management Holding L.P., 63
Alliance Entertainment Corp., 17
Alliance Resource Partners, L.P., 81
Alliant Techsystems Inc., 8; 30 (upd.); 77 (upd.)
The Allied Defense Group, Inc., 65
Allied Healthcare Products, Inc., 24
Allied Products Corporation, 21
Allied Signal Engines, 9
Allied Waste Industries, Inc., 50
Allied Worldwide, Inc., 49
AlliedSignal Inc., I; 22 (upd.)
Allison Gas Turbine Division, 9
Allmerica Financial Corporation, 63
Allou Health & Beauty Care, Inc., 28
Alloy, Inc., 55
The Allstate Corporation, 10; 27 (upd.)
ALLTEL Corporation, 6; 46 (upd.)
Alltrista Corporation, 30
Allwaste, Inc., 18
Almost Family, Inc., 93
Aloha Airlines, Incorporated, 24
Alpharma Inc., 35 (upd.)
Alpine Confections, Inc., 71
Alpine Lace Brands, Inc., 18

Alside Inc., 94
AltaVista Company, 43
Altera Corporation, 18; 43 (upd.)
Alternative Tentacles Records, 66
Alterra Healthcare Corporation, 42
Alticor Inc., 71 (upd.)
Altiris, Inc., 65
Altron Incorporated, 20
Aluminum Company of America, IV; 20 (upd.)
Alvin Ailey Dance Foundation, Inc., 52
ALZA Corporation, 10; 36 (upd.)
Amalgamated Bank, 60
AMAX Inc., IV
Amazon.com, Inc., 25; 56 (upd.)
AMB Property Corporation, 57
Ambac Financial Group, Inc., 65
Ambassadors International, Inc., 68 (upd.)
Amblin Entertainment, 21
AMC Entertainment Inc., 12; 35 (upd.)
AMCOL International Corporation, 59 (upd.)
AMCORE Financial Inc., 44
Amdahl Corporation, III; 14 (upd.); 40 (upd.)
Amdocs Ltd., 47
Amedysis, Inc., 53
Amerada Hess Corporation, IV; 21 (upd.); 55 (upd.)
Amerco, 6
AMERCO, 67 (upd.)
Ameren Corporation, 60 (upd.)
America Online, Inc., 10; 26 (upd.)
America West Holdings Corporation, 6; 34 (upd.)
America's Car-Mart, Inc., 64
America's Favorite Chicken Company, Inc., 7
AmeriCares Foundation, Inc., 87
American & Efird, Inc., 82
American Airlines, I; 6 (upd.)
American Apparel, Inc., 90
American Axle & Manufacturing Holdings, Inc., 67
American Banknote Corporation, 30
American Bar Association, 35
American Biltrite Inc., 16; 43 (upd.)
American Brands, Inc., V
American Building Maintenance Industries, Inc., 6
American Business Information, Inc., 18
American Business Products, Inc., 20
American Campus Communities, Inc., 85
The American Cancer Society, 24
American Capital Strategies, Ltd., 91
American Cast Iron Pipe Company, 50
American Civil Liberties Union (ACLU), 60
American Classic Voyages Company, 27
American Coin Merchandising, Inc., 28; 74 (upd.)
American Colloid Co., 13
American Crystal Sugar Company, 9; 32 (upd.)
American Cyanamid, I; 8 (upd.)
American Eagle Outfitters, Inc., 24; 55 (upd.)
American Ecology Corporation, 77
American Electric Power Company, Inc., V; 45 (upd.)
American Express Company, II; 10 (upd.); 38 (upd.)
American Family Corporation, III
American Financial Group Inc., III; 48 (upd.)
American Foods Group, 43
American Furniture Company, Inc., 21
American General Corporation, III; 10 (upd.); 46 (upd.)
American General Finance Corp., 11
American Girl, Inc., 69 (upd.)
American Golf Corporation, 45
American Gramaphone LLC, 52
American Greetings Corporation, 7; 22 (upd.); 59 (upd.)
American Healthways, Inc., 65
American Home Mortgage Holdings, Inc., 46
American Home Products, I; 10 (upd.)
American Homestar Corporation, 18; 41 (upd.)
American Institute of Certified Public Accountants (AICPA), 44
American International Group, Inc., III; 15 (upd.); 47 (upd.)
American Italian Pasta Company, 27; 76 (upd.)
American Kennel Club, Inc., 74
American Lawyer Media Holdings, Inc., 32
American Library Association, 86
American Licorice Company, 86
American Locker Group Incorporated, 34
American Lung Association, 48
American Maize-Products Co., 14
American Management Association, 76
American Management Systems, Inc., 11
American Media, Inc., 27; 82 (upd.)
American Medical Association, 39
American Medical International, Inc., III
American Medical Response, Inc., 39
American Motors Corporation, I
American National Insurance Company, 8; 27 (upd.)
American Pad & Paper Company, 20
American Pharmaceutical Partners, Inc., 69
American Pop Corn Company, 59
American Power Conversion Corporation, 24; 67 (upd.)
American Premier Underwriters, Inc., 10
American President Companies Ltd., 6
American Printing House for the Blind, 26
American Re Corporation, 10; 35 (upd.)
American Red Cross, 40
American Reprographics Company, 75
American Residential Mortgage Corporation, 8
American Restaurant Partners, L.P., 93
American Retirement Corporation, 42
American Rice, Inc., 33
American Safety Razor Company, 20
American Science & Engineering, Inc., 81
American Seating Company 78
American Skiing Company, 28
American Society for the Prevention of Cruelty to Animals (ASPCA), 68
The American Society of Composers, Authors and Publishers (ASCAP), 29
American Software Inc., 25
American Standard Companies Inc., III; 30 (upd.)
American States Water Company, 46
American Stores Company, II; 22 (upd.)
American Technical Ceramics Corp., 67
American Tourister, Inc., 16
American Tower Corporation, 33
American Vanguard Corporation, 47
American Water Works Company, Inc., 6; 38 (upd.)
American Woodmark Corporation, 31
AMERIGROUP Corporation, 69
Amerihost Properties, Inc., 30
AmeriSource Health Corporation, 37 (upd.)
AmerisourceBergen Corporation, 64 (upd.)
Ameristar Casinos, Inc., 33; 69 (upd.)
Ameritech Corporation, V; 18 (upd.)
Ameritrade Holding Corporation, 34
Ameriwood Industries International Corp., 17
Amerock Corporation, 53
Ameron International Corporation, 67
Ames Department Stores, Inc., 9; 30 (upd.)
AMETEK, Inc., 9
AMF Bowling, Inc., 40
Amfac/JMB Hawaii L.L.C., I; 24 (upd.)
Amgen, Inc., 10; 30 (upd.); 89 (upd.)
AMICAS, Inc., 69
Amkor Technology, Inc., 69
Amoco Corporation, IV; 14 (upd.)
Amoskeag Company, 8
AMP Incorporated, II; 14 (upd.)
Ampacet Corporation, 67
Ampco-Pittsburgh Corporation 79
Ampex Corporation, 17
Amphenol Corporation, 40
AMR Corporation, 28 (upd.); 52 (upd.)
AMREP Corporation, 21
Amscan Holdings, Inc., 61
AmSouth Bancorporation, 12; 48 (upd.)
Amsted Industries Incorporated, 7
AmSurg Corporation, 48
Amtran, Inc., 34
Amway Corporation, III; 13 (upd.); 30 (upd.)
Amy's Kitchen Inc., 76
Amylin Pharmaceuticals, Inc., 67
Anacomp, Inc., 94
Anadarko Petroleum Corporation, 10; 52 (upd.)
Anaheim Angels Baseball Club, Inc., 53
Analex Corporation, 74
Analog Devices, Inc., 10
Analogic Corporation, 23
Analysts International Corporation, 36
Analytic Sciences Corporation, 10
Analytical Surveys, Inc., 33
Anaren Microwave, Inc., 33
Anchor Bancorp, Inc., 10
Anchor Brewing Company, 47

Anchor Gaming, 24
Anchor Hocking Glassware, 13
Andersen, 10; 29 (upd.); 68 (upd.)
Anderson Trucking Service, Inc., 75
The Anderson-DuBose Company, 60
The Andersons, Inc., 31
Andis Company, Inc., 85
Andrew Corporation, 10; 32 (upd.)
Andrews Kurth, LLP, 71
Andrews McMeel Universal, 40
Andronico's Market, 70
Andrx Corporation, 55
Angelica Corporation, 15; 43 (upd.)
AngioDynamics, Inc., 81
Anheuser-Busch Companies, Inc., I; 10 (upd.); 34 (upd.)
Anixter International Inc., 88
Annie's Homegrown, Inc., 59
AnnTaylor Stores Corporation, 13; 37 (upd.); 67 (upd.)
ANR Pipeline Co., 17
The Anschutz Company, 12; 36 (upd.); 73 (upd.)
Ansoft Corporation, 63
Anteon Corporation, 57
Anthem Electronics, Inc., 13
Anthony & Sylvan Pools Corporation, 56
The Antioch Company, 40
AOL Time Warner Inc., 57 (upd.)
Aon Corporation, III; 45 (upd.)
Apache Corporation, 10; 32 (upd.); 89 (upd.)
Apartment Investment and Management Company, 49
Apex Digital, Inc., 63
APi Group, Inc., 64
APL Limited, 61 (upd.)
Apogee Enterprises, Inc., 8
Apollo Group, Inc., 24
Applause Inc., 24
Apple & Eve L.L.C., 92
Apple Bank for Savings, 59
Apple Computer, Inc., III; 6 (upd.); 36 (upd.); 77 (upd.)
Applebee's International Inc., 14; 35 (upd.)
Appliance Recycling Centers of America, Inc., 42
Applica Incorporated, 43 (upd.)
Applied Bioscience International, Inc., 10
Applied Films Corporation, 48
Applied Materials, Inc., 10; 46 (upd.)
Applied Micro Circuits Corporation, 38
Applied Power, Inc., 9; 32 (upd.)
Applied Signal Technology, Inc., 87
AptarGroup, Inc., 69
Aqua Alliance Inc., 32 (upd.)
aQuantive, Inc., 81
Aquarion Company, 84
Aquila, Inc., 50 (upd.)
AR Accessories Group, Inc., 23
ARA Services, II
ARAMARK Corporation, 13; 41 (upd.)
Arandell Corporation, 37
The Arbitron Company, 38
Arbor Drugs Inc., 12
Arby's Inc., 14
Arch Chemicals Inc. 78
Arch Mineral Corporation, 7
Arch Wireless, Inc., 39
Archer Daniels Midland Company, I; 11 (upd.); 32 (upd.); 75 (upd.)
Archie Comics Publications, Inc., 63
Archon Corporation, 74 (upd.)
Archstone-Smith Trust, 49
Archway Cookies, Inc., 29
ARCO Chemical Company, 10
Arctco, Inc., 16
Arctic Cat Inc., 40 (upd.)
Arctic Slope Regional Corporation, 38
Arden Group, Inc., 29
Argon ST, Inc., 81
Argosy Gaming Company, 21
Ariba, Inc., 57
Ariens Company, 48
Aris Industries, Inc., 16
The Aristotle Corporation, 62
Ark Restaurants Corp., 20
Arkansas Best Corporation, 16; 94 (upd.)
Arkla, Inc., V
Armco Inc., IV
Armor All Products Corp., 16
Armor Holdings, Inc., 27
Armstrong Holdings, Inc., III; 22 (upd.); 81 (upd.)
Army and Air Force Exchange Service, 39
Arnold & Porter, 35
Arotech Corporation, 93
ArQule, Inc., 68
ARRIS Group, Inc., 89
Arrow Air Holdings Corporation, 55
Arrow Electronics, Inc., 10; 50 (upd.)
The Art Institute of Chicago, 29
Art Van Furniture, Inc., 28
Artesyn Technologies Inc., 46 (upd.)
ArthroCare Corporation, 73
The Arthur C. Clarke Foundation, 92
Arthur D. Little, Inc., 35
Arthur J. Gallagher & Co., 73
Arthur Murray International, Inc., 32
Artisan Entertainment Inc., 32 (upd.)
ArvinMeritor, Inc., 8; 54 (upd.)
Asanté Technologies, Inc., 20
ASARCO Incorporated, IV
Asbury Automotive Group Inc., 60
Asbury Carbons, Inc., 68
ASC, Inc., 55
Ascend Communications, Inc., 24
Ascential Software Corporation, 59
Ash Grove Cement Company, 94
Ashland Inc., 19; 50 (upd.)
Ashland Oil, Inc., IV
Ashley Furniture Industries, Inc., 35
Ashworth, Inc., 26
ASK Group, Inc., 9
Ask Jeeves, Inc., 65
Aspect Telecommunications Corporation, 22
Aspen Skiing Company, 15
Asplundh Tree Expert Co., 20; 59 (upd.)
Assisted Living Concepts, Inc., 43
Associated Estates Realty Corporation, 25
Associated Grocers, Incorporated, 9; 31 (upd.)
Associated Milk Producers, Inc., 11; 48 (upd.)
Associated Natural Gas Corporation, 11
The Associated Press, 13; 31 (upd.); 73 (upd.)
Association of Junior Leagues International Inc., 60
AST Research Inc., 9
Astec Industries, Inc. 79
AstenJohnson Inc., 90
Astoria Financial Corporation, 44
Astronics Corporation, 35
Asurion Corporation, 83
ASV, Inc., 34; 66 (upd.)
At Home Corporation, 43
AT&T Bell Laboratories, Inc., 13
AT&T Corporation, V; 29 (upd.); 68 (upd.)
AT&T Wireless Services, Inc., 54 (upd.)
ATA Holdings Corporation, 82
Atari Corporation, 9; 23 (upd.); 66 (upd.)
ATC Healthcare Inc., 64
Atchison Casting Corporation, 39
The Athlete's Foot Brands LLC, 84
The Athletics Investment Group, 62
Atkins Nutritionals, Inc., 58
Atkinson Candy Company, 87
Atlanta Bread Company International, Inc., 70
Atlanta Gas Light Company, 6; 23 (upd.)
Atlanta National League Baseball Club, Inc., 43
Atlantic American Corporation, 44
Atlantic Coast Airlines Holdings, Inc., 55
Atlantic Energy, Inc., 6
The Atlantic Group, 23
Atlantic Premium Brands, Ltd., 57
Atlantic Richfield Company, IV; 31 (upd.)
Atlantic Southeast Airlines, Inc., 47
Atlantis Plastics, Inc., 85
Atlas Air, Inc., 39
Atlas Van Lines, Inc., 14
Atmel Corporation, 17
ATMI, Inc., 93
Atmos Energy Corporation, 43
Attachmate Corporation, 56
Atwood Mobil Products, 53
Au Bon Pain Co., Inc., 18
The Auchter Company, The 78
Audible Inc. 79
Audio King Corporation, 24
Audiovox Corporation, 34; 90 (upd.)
August Schell Brewing Company Inc., 59
Ault Incorporated, 34
Auntie Anne's, Inc., 35
Aurora Casket Company, Inc., 56
Aurora Foods Inc., 32
The Austin Company, 8; 72 (upd.)
Austin Powder Company, 76
Authentic Fitness Corporation, 20; 51 (upd.)
Auto Value Associates, Inc., 25
Autobytel Inc., 47
Autocam Corporation, 51
Autodesk, Inc., 10; 89 (upd.)
Autologic Information International, Inc., 20
Automatic Data Processing, Inc., III; 9 (upd.); 47 (upd.)
AutoNation, Inc., 50

Autotote Corporation, 20
AutoTrader.com, L.L.C., 91
AutoZone, Inc., 9; 31 (upd.)
Avado Brands, Inc., 31
Avalon Correctional Services, Inc., 75
AvalonBay Communities, Inc., 58
Avco Financial Services Inc., 13
Aveda Corporation, 24
Avedis Zildjian Co., 38
Aventine Renewable Energy Holdings, Inc., 89
Avery Dennison Corporation, IV; 17 (upd.); 49 (upd.)
Aviall, Inc., 73
Aviation Sales Company, 41
Avid Technology Inc., 38
Avis Group Holdings, Inc., 75 (upd.)
Avis Rent A Car, Inc., 6; 22 (upd.)
Avista Corporation, 69 (upd.)
Avnet Inc., 9
Avocent Corporation, 65
Avon Products, Inc., III; 19 (upd.); 46 (upd.)
Avondale Industries, 7; 41 (upd.)
AVX Corporation, 67
Awrey Bakeries, Inc., 56
Axsys Technologies, Inc., 93
Aydin Corp., 19
Azcon Corporation, 23
Aztar Corporation, 13; 71 (upd.)
AZZ Incorporated, 93
B&G Foods, Inc., 40
B. Dalton Bookseller Inc., 25
The B. Manischewitz Company, LLC, 31
B/E Aerospace, Inc., 30
B.J. Alan Co., Inc., 67
B.R. Guest Inc., 87
B.W. Rogers Company, 94
Babbage's, Inc., 10
The Babcock & Wilcox Company, 82
Baby Superstore, Inc., 15
Bachman's Inc., 22
Back Bay Restaurant Group, Inc., 20
Back Yard Burgers, Inc., 45
Bad Boy Worldwide Entertainment Group, 58
Badger Meter, Inc., 22
Badger Paper Mills, Inc., 15
Badger State Ethanol, LLC, 83
BAE Systems Ship Repair, 73
Bailey Nurseries, Inc., 57
Bain & Company, 55
Baird & Warner Holding Company, 87
Bairnco Corporation, 28
Baker & Daniels LLP, 88
Baker & Hostetler LLP, 40
Baker & McKenzie, 10; 42 (upd.)
Baker & Taylor Corporation, 16; 43 (upd.)
Baker and Botts, L.L.P., 28
Baker Hughes Incorporated, III; 22 (upd.); 57 (upd.)
Balance Bar Company, 32
Balchem Corporation, 42
Baldor Electric Company, 21
Baldwin & Lyons, Inc., 51
Baldwin Piano & Organ Company, 18
Baldwin Technology Company, Inc., 25
Ball Corporation, I; 10; 78 (upd.)
Ball Horticultural Company 78
Ballantyne of Omaha, Inc., 27
Ballard Medical Products, 21
Ballistic Recovery Systems, Inc., 87
Bally Manufacturing Corporation, III
Bally Total Fitness Corporation, 25; 94 (upd.)
Balmac International, Inc., 94
Baltek Corporation, 34
Baltimore Aircoil Company, Inc., 66
Baltimore Gas and Electric Company, V; 25 (upd.)
Baltimore Orioles L.P., 66
The Bama Companies, Inc., 80
Banana Republic Inc., 25
Bandag, Inc., 19
Banfi Products Corp., 36
Bank of America Corporation, 46 (upd.)
Bank of Boston Corporation, II
Bank of Granite Corporation, 89
Bank of Hawaii Corporation, 73
Bank of Mississippi, Inc., 14
Bank of New England Corporation, II
The Bank of New York Company, Inc., II; 46 (upd.)
Bank of the Ozarks, Inc., 91
Bank One Corporation, 10; 36 (upd.)
BankAmerica Corporation, II; 8 (upd.)
Bankers Trust New York Corporation, II
Banknorth Group, Inc., 55
Bankrate, Inc., 83
Banner Aerospace, Inc., 14; 37 (upd.)
Banta Corporation, 12; 32 (upd.); 79 (upd.)
Banyan Systems Inc., 25
Baptist Health Care Corporation, 82
Bar-S Foods Company, 76
BarclaysAmerican Mortgage Corporation, 11
Barbara's Bakery Inc., 88
Barden Companies, Inc., 76
Bare Escentuals, Inc., 91
Barnes & Noble, Inc., 10; 30 (upd.); 75 (upd.)
Barnes Group Inc., 13; 69 (upd.)
Barnett Banks, Inc., 9
Barnett Inc., 28
Barney's, Inc., 28
Barr Pharmaceuticals, Inc., 26; 68 (upd.)
Barrett Business Services, Inc., 16
Barrett-Jackson Auction Company L.L.C., 88
Barry-Wehmiller Companies, Inc., 90
The Bartell Drug Company, 94
Barton Malow Company, 51
Barton Protective Services Inc., 53
The Baseball Club of Seattle, LP, 50
Bashas' Inc., 33; 80 (upd.)
The Basketball Club of Seattle, LLC, 50
Bass Pro Shops, Inc., 42
Bassett Furniture Industries, Inc., 18
Bates Worldwide, Inc., 14; 33 (upd.)
Bath Iron Works, 12; 36 (upd.)
Battelle Memorial Institute, Inc., 10
Battle Mountain Gold Company, 23
Bauerly Companies, 61
Bausch & Lomb Inc., 7; 25 (upd.)
Baxter International Inc., I; 10 (upd.)
Bay State Gas Company, 38
BayBanks, Inc., 12
Bayou Steel Corporation, 31
BB&T Corporation 79
BBN Corp., 19
BE&K, Inc., 73
BEA Systems, Inc., 36
Beacon Roofing Supply, Inc., 75
Bear Creek Corporation, 38
Bear Stearns Companies, Inc., II; 10 (upd.); 52 (upd.)
Bearings, Inc., 13
Beasley Broadcast Group, Inc., 51
Beatrice Company, II
BeautiControl Cosmetics, Inc., 21
Beazer Homes USA, Inc., 17
bebe stores, inc., 31
Bechtel Group, Inc., I; 24 (upd.)
Beckett Papers, 23
Beckman Coulter, Inc., 22
Beckman Instruments, Inc., 14
Becton, Dickinson & Company, I; 11 (upd.); 36 (upd.)
Bed Bath & Beyond Inc., 13; 41 (upd.)
Beech Aircraft Corporation, 8
Beech-Nut Nutrition Corporation, 21; 51 (upd.)
Beer Nuts, Inc., 86
BEI Technologies, Inc., 65
Bekins Company, 15
Bel Fuse, Inc., 53
Bel/Kaukauna USA, 76
Belco Oil & Gas Corp., 40
Belden CDT Inc., 76 (upd.)
Belden Inc., 19
Belk Stores Services, Inc., V; 19 (upd.)
Belk, Inc., 72 (upd.)
Bell and Howell Company, 9; 29 (upd.)
Bell Atlantic Corporation, V; 25 (upd.)
Bell Helicopter Textron Inc., 46
Bell Industries, Inc., 47
Bell Microproducts Inc., 69
Bell Sports Corporation, 16; 44 (upd.)
Belleville Shoe Manufacturing Company, 92
BellSouth Corporation, V; 29 (upd.)
Beloit Corporation, 14
Bemis Company, Inc., 8; 91 (upd.)
Ben & Jerry's Homemade, Inc., 10; 35 (upd.); 80 (upd.)
Ben Bridge Jeweler, Inc., 60
Ben E. Keith Company, 76
Benchmark Capital, 49
Benchmark Electronics, Inc., 40
Bendix Corporation, I
Beneficial Corporation, 8
Benihana, Inc., 18; 76 (upd.)
Benjamin Moore & Co., 13; 38 (upd.)
Benton Oil and Gas Company, 47
Bergdorf Goodman Inc., 52
Bergen Brunswig Corporation, V; 13 (upd.)
Berger Bros Company, 62
Beringer Blass Wine Estates Ltd., 66 (upd.)
Beringer Wine Estates Holdings, Inc., 22
Berkeley Farms, Inc., 46

Berkshire Hathaway Inc., III; 18 (upd.); 42 (upd.); 89 (upd.)
Berkshire Realty Holdings, L.P., 49
Berlex Laboratories, Inc., 66
Berlitz International, Inc., 13; 39 (upd.)
Bernard C. Harris Publishing Company, Inc., 39
Bernard Chaus, Inc., 27
Bernard Hodes Group Inc., 86
The Bernick Companies, 75
Bernstein-Rein, 92
Berry Petroleum Company, 47
Berry Plastics Corporation, 21
Bertucci's Corporation, 16; 64 (upd.)
Berwick Offray, LLC, 70
Best Buy Co., Inc., 9; 23 (upd.); 63 (upd.)
Best Kosher Foods Corporation, 82
Bestfoods, 22 (upd.)
BET Holdings, Inc., 18
Beth Abraham Family of Health Services, 94
Bethlehem Steel Corporation, IV; 7 (upd.); 27 (upd.)
Better Made Snack Foods, Inc., 90
Betz Laboratories, Inc., I; 10 (upd.)
Beverly Enterprises, Inc., III; 16 (upd.)
The BFGoodrich Company, V; 19 (upd.)
BHC Communications, Inc., 26
Bianchi International (d/b/a Gregory Mountain Products), 76
BIC Corporation, 8; 23 (upd.)
Bicoastal Corporation, II
Big A Drug Stores Inc. 79
Big B, Inc., 17
Big Bear Stores Co., 13
Big Brothers Big Sisters of America, 85
Big Dog Holdings, Inc., 45
Big 5 Sporting Goods Corporation, 55
Big Flower Press Holdings, Inc., 21
Big Idea Productions, Inc., 49
Big Lots, Inc., 50
Big O Tires, Inc., 20
Big Rivers Electric Corporation, 11
Big V Supermarkets, Inc., 25
Big Y Foods, Inc., 53
Bill & Melinda Gates Foundation, 41
Bill Barrett Corporation, 71
Bill Blass Ltd., 32
Billing Concepts Corp., 26
Billing Concepts, Inc., 72 (upd.)
Bindley Western Industries, Inc., 9
The Bing Group, 60
Bingham Dana LLP, 43
Binks Sames Corporation, 21
Binney & Smith Inc., 25
Bio-Rad Laboratories, Inc., 93
Biogen Idec Inc., 71 (upd.)
Biogen Inc., 14; 36 (upd.)
Biolase Technology, Inc., 87
Biomet, Inc., 10; 93 (upd.
Biosite Incorporated, 73
Bird Corporation, 19
Birds Eye Foods, Inc., 69 (upd.)
Birkenstock Footprint Sandals, Inc., 12; 42 (upd.)
Birmingham Steel Corporation, 13; 40 (upd.)
BISSELL Inc., 9; 30 (upd.)
The BISYS Group, Inc., 73
BJ Services Company, 25
BJ's Wholesale Club, Inc., 94
The Black & Decker Corporation, III; 20 (upd.); 67 (upd.)
Black & Veatch LLP, 22
Black Box Corporation, 20
Black Diamond Equipment, Ltd., 62
Black Hills Corporation, 20
Blackbaud, Inc., 85
Blackboard Inc., 89
Blackfoot Telecommunications Group, 60
BlackRock, Inc. 79
Blackwater USA, 76
Blair Corporation, 25; 31
Blessings Corp., 19
Blimpie International, Inc., 15; 49 (upd.)
Blizzard Entertainment 78
Block Communications, Inc., 81
Block Drug Company, Inc., 8; 27 (upd.)
Blockbuster Inc., 9; 31 (upd.); 76 (upd.)
Blodgett Holdings, Inc., 61 (upd.)
Blonder Tongue Laboratories, Inc., 48
Bloomberg L.P., 21
Bloomingdale's Inc., 12
Blount International, Inc., 12; 48 (upd.)
Blue Bell Creameries L.P., 30
Blue Bird Corporation, 35
Blue Coat Systems, Inc., 83
Blue Cross and Blue Shield Association, 10
Blue Diamond Growers, 28
Blue Heron Paper Company, 90
Blue Martini Software, Inc., 59
Blue Mountain Arts, Inc., 29
Blue Nile Inc., 61
Blue Rhino Corporation, 56
Blue Ridge Beverage Company Inc., 82
Bluefly, Inc., 60
Bluegreen Corporation, 80
Blyth, Inc., 18; 74 (upd.)
BMC Industries, Inc., 17; 59 (upd.)
BMC Software, Inc., 55
Boardwalk Pipeline Partners, LP, 87
Boart Longyear Company, 26
Boatmen's Bancshares Inc., 15
Bob Evans Farms, Inc., 9; 63 (upd.)
Bob's Red Mill Natural Foods, Inc., 63
Bobit Publishing Company, 55
Bobs Candies, Inc., 70
Boca Resorts, Inc., 37
Boddie-Noell Enterprises, Inc., 68
Body Glove International LLC, 88
The Boeing Company, I; 10 (upd.); 32 (upd.)
Bogen Communications International, Inc., 62
Bohemia, Inc., 13
Boise Cascade Corporation, IV; 8 (upd.); 32 (upd.)
Bollinger Shipyards, Inc., 61
The Bombay Company, Inc., 10; 71 (upd.)
The Bon Marché, Inc., 23
Bon Secours Health System, Inc., 24
The Bon-Ton Stores, Inc., 16; 50 (upd.)
Bonneville International Corporation, 29
Bonneville Power Administration, 50
Book-of-the-Month Club, Inc., 13
Books-A-Million, Inc., 14; 41 (upd.)
Bookspan, 86
Boole & Babbage, Inc., 25
Booth Creek Ski Holdings, Inc., 31
Boots & Coots International Well Control, Inc. 79
Booz Allen & Hamilton Inc., 10
Borden, Inc., II; 22 (upd.)
Borders Group, Inc., 15; 43 (upd.)
Borg-Warner Corporation, III
BorgWarner Inc., 14; 32 (upd.); 85 (upd.)
Borland International, Inc., 9
Boron, LePore & Associates, Inc., 45
Boscov's Department Store, Inc., 31
Bose Corporation, 13; 36 (upd.)
Boston Acoustics, Inc., 22
The Boston Beer Company, Inc., 18; 50 (upd.)
Boston Celtics Limited Partnership, 14
The Boston Consulting Group, 58
Boston Edison Company, 12
Boston Market Corporation, 12; 48 (upd.)
Boston Professional Hockey Association Inc., 39
Boston Properties, Inc., 22
Boston Scientific Corporation, 37; 77 (upd.)
The Boston Symphony Orchestra Inc., 93
Bou-Matic, 62
Bowne & Co., Inc., 23; 79 (upd.)
The Boy Scouts of America, 34
Boyd Bros. Transportation Inc., 39
Boyd Coffee Company, 53
Boyd Gaming Corporation, 43
The Boyds Collection, Ltd., 29
Boyne USA Resorts, 71
Boys & Girls Clubs of America, 69
Bozell Worldwide Inc., 25
Bozzuto's, Inc., 13
Brach and Brock Confections, Inc., 15
Brach's Confections, Inc., 74 (upd.)
Bradlees Discount Department Store Company, 12
Brady Corporation 78 (upd.)
The Branch Group, Inc., 72
BrandPartners Group, Inc., 58
Brannock Device Company, 48
Brasfield & Gorrie LLC, 87
Brass Eagle Inc., 34
Brazos Sportswear, Inc., 23
Bremer Financial Corp., 45
Briazz, Inc., 53
The Brickman Group, Ltd., 87
Bridgeport Machines, Inc., 17
Bridgford Foods Corporation, 27
Briggs & Stratton Corporation, 8; 27 (upd.)
Brigham Exploration Company, 75
Brigham's Inc., 72
Bright Horizons Family Solutions, Inc., 31
Brightpoint, Inc., 18
Brillstein-Grey Entertainment, 80
The Brink's Company, 58 (upd.)
Brinker International, Inc., 10; 38 (upd.); 75 (upd.)

Bristol Hotel Company, 23
Bristol-Myers Squibb Company, III; 9 (upd.); 37 (upd.)
Brite Voice Systems, Inc., 20
Broadcast Music Inc., 23; 90 (upd.)
Broadcom Corporation, 34; 90 (upd.)
The Broadmoor Hotel, 30
Broadwing Corporation, 70
Brobeck, Phleger & Harrison, LLP, 31
Brodart Company, 84
Broder Bros. Co., 38
Broderbund Software, Inc., 13; 29 (upd.)
Bronco Drilling Company, Inc., 89
Bronner Brothers Inc., 92
Bronner Display & Sign Advertising, Inc., 82
Brookdale Senior Living, 91
Brooke Group Ltd., 15
Brooklyn Union Gas, 6
Brooks Brothers Inc., 22
Brooks Sports Inc., 32
Brookshire Grocery Company, 16; 74 (upd.)
Brookstone, Inc., 18
Brother's Brother Foundation, 93
Brothers Gourmet Coffees, Inc., 20
Broughton Foods Co., 17
Brown & Brown, Inc., 41
Brown & Haley, 23
Brown & Root, Inc., 13
Brown & Sharpe Manufacturing Co., 23
Brown & Williamson Tobacco Corporation, 14; 33 (upd.)
Brown Brothers Harriman & Co., 45
Brown Jordan International Inc., 74 (upd.)
Brown Printing Company, 26
Brown Shoe Company, Inc., V; 20 (upd.); 68 (upd.)
Brown-Forman Corporation, I; 10 (upd.); 38 (upd.)
Browning-Ferris Industries, Inc., V; 20 (upd.)
Broyhill Furniture Industries, Inc., 10
Bruce Foods Corporation, 39
Bruegger's Corporation, 63
Bruno's Supermarkets, Inc., 7; 26 (upd.); 68 (upd.)
Brunswick Corporation, III; 22 (upd.); 77 (upd.)
Brush Engineered Materials Inc., 67
Brush Wellman Inc., 14
Bruster's Real Ice Cream, Inc., 80
BTG, Inc., 45
Buca, Inc., 38
Buck Consultants, Inc., 55
Buck Knives Inc., 48
Buckeye Partners, L.P., 70
Buckeye Technologies, Inc., 42
The Buckle, Inc., 18
Bucyrus International, Inc., 17
The Budd Company, 8
Budget Group, Inc., 25
Budget Rent a Car Corporation, 9
Buffalo Wild Wings, Inc., 56
Buffets Holdings, Inc., 10; 32 (upd.); 93 (upd.)
Bugle Boy Industries, Inc., 18
Build-A-Bear Workshop Inc., 62
Building Materials Holding Corporation, 52
Bulley & Andrews, LLC, 55
Bulova Corporation, 13; 41 (upd.)
Bumble Bee Seafoods L.L.C., 64
Bundy Corporation, 17
Bunge Ltd., 62
Burdines, Inc., 60
The Bureau of National Affairs, Inc., 23
Burger King Corporation, II; 17 (upd.); 56 (upd.)
Burke, Inc., 88
Burke Mills, Inc., 66
Burlington Coat Factory Warehouse Corporation, 10; 60 (upd.)
Burlington Industries, Inc., V; 17 (upd.)
Burlington Northern Santa Fe Corporation, V; 27 (upd.)
Burlington Resources Inc., 10
Burns International Services Corporation, 13; 41 (upd.)
Burr-Brown Corporation, 19
Burroughs & Chapin Company, Inc., 86
Burt's Bees, Inc., 58
The Burton Corporation, 22; 94 (upd.)
Busch Entertainment Corporation, 73
Bush Boake Allen Inc., 30
Bush Brothers & Company, 45
Bush Industries, Inc., 20
Business Men's Assurance Company of America, 14
Butler Manufacturing Company, 12; 62 (upd.)
Butterick Co., Inc., 23
Buttrey Food & Drug Stores Co., 18
buy.com, Inc., 46
BWAY Corporation, 24
C&K Market, Inc., 81
C & S Wholesale Grocers, Inc., 55
C-COR.net Corp., 38
C-Cube Microsystems, Inc., 37
C.F. Martin & Co., Inc., 42
The C.F. Sauer Company, 90
C.H. Guenther & Son, Inc., 84
C.H. Heist Corporation, 24
C.H. Robinson Worldwide, Inc., 11; 40 (upd.)
C.R. Bard, Inc., 9; 65 (upd.)
C.R. Meyer and Sons Company, 74
C-Tech Industries Inc., 90
Cabela's Inc., 26; 68 (upd.)
Cabletron Systems, Inc., 10
Cablevision Electronic Instruments, Inc., 32
Cablevision Systems Corporation, 7; 30 (upd.)
Cabot Corporation, 8; 29 (upd.); 91 (upd.)
Cache Incorporated, 30
CACI International Inc., 21; 72 (upd.)
Cactus Feeders, Inc., 91
Cadence Design Systems, Inc., 11; 48 (upd.)
Cadmus Communications Corporation, 23
Cadwalader, Wickersham & Taft, 32
CAE USA Inc., 48
Caere Corporation, 20
Caesars World, Inc., 6
Cagle's, Inc., 20
Cahners Business Information, 43
Cal-Maine Foods, Inc., 69
CalAmp Corp., 87
Calavo Growers, Inc., 47
CalComp Inc., 13
Calcot Ltd., 33
Caldor Inc., 12
Calgon Carbon Corporation, 73
California Cedar Products Company, 58
California Pizza Kitchen Inc., 15; 74 (upd.)
California Sports, Inc., 56
California Steel Industries, Inc., 67
California Water Service Group 79
Caliper Life Sciences, Inc., 70
Callanan Industries, Inc., 60
Callard and Bowser-Suchard Inc., 84
Callaway Golf Company, 15; 45 (upd.)
Callon Petroleum Company, 47
Calloway's Nursery, Inc., 51
CalMat Co., 19
Calpine Corporation, 36
Caltex Petroleum Corporation, 19
Calvin Klein, Inc., 22; 55 (upd.)
Cambrex Corporation, 16; 44 (upd.)
Cambridge SoundWorks, Inc., 48
Cambridge Technology Partners, Inc., 36
Camden Property Trust, 77
Camelot Music, Inc., 26
Cameron & Barkley Company, 28
Campbell-Ewald Advertising, 86
Campbell-Mithun-Esty, Inc., 16
Campbell Scientific, Inc., 51
Campbell Soup Company, II; 7 (upd.); 26 (upd.); 71 (upd.)
Campo Electronics, Appliances & Computers, Inc., 16
Canandaigua Brands, Inc., 13; 34 (upd.)
Cancer Treatment Centers of America, Inc., 85
Candela Corporation, 48
Candie's, Inc., 31
Candle Corporation, 64
Candlewood Hotel Company, Inc., 41
Cannon Design, 63
Cannon Express, Inc., 53
Cannondale Corporation, 21
Cantel Medical Corporation, 80
Canterbury Park Holding Corporation, 42
Cantor Fitzgerald, L.P., 92
Cap Rock Energy Corporation, 46
Cape Cod Potato Chip Company, 90
Capel Incorporated, 45
Capezio/Ballet Makers Inc., 62
Capital Cities/ABC Inc., II
Capital Holding Corporation, III
Capital One Financial Corporation, 52
Capitol Records, Inc., 90
Capital Senior Living Corporation, 75
CapStar Hotel Company, 21
Capstone Turbine Corporation, 75
Captain D's, LLC, 59
Captaris, Inc., 89
Car Toys, Inc., 67
Caraustar Industries, Inc., 19; 44 (upd.)

The Carbide/Graphite Group, Inc., 40
Carborundum Company, 15
Cardinal Health, Inc., 18; 50 (upd.)
Cardone Industries Inc., 92
Cardtronics, Inc., 93
Career Education Corporation, 45
CareerBuilder, Inc., 93
Caremark Rx, Inc., 10; 54 (upd.)
Carey International, Inc., 26
Cargill, Incorporated, II; 13 (upd.); 40 (upd.); 89 (upd.)
Carhartt, Inc., 30; 77 (upd.)
Caribiner International, Inc., 24
Caribou Coffee Company, Inc., 28
Carlisle Companies Inc., 8; 82 (upd.)
Carlson Companies, Inc., 6; 22 (upd.); 87 (upd.)
Carlson Restaurants Worldwide, 69
Carlson Wagonlit Travel, 55
Carma Laboratories, Inc., 60
CarMax, Inc., 55
Carmichael Lynch Inc., 28
Carmike Cinemas, Inc., 14; 37 (upd.); 74 (upd.)
Carnation Company, II
Carnegie Corporation of New York, 35
Carnival Corporation, 6; 27 (upd.); 78 (upd.)
Carolina First Corporation, 31
Carolina Freight Corporation, 6
Carolina Power & Light Company, V; 23 (upd.)
Carolina Telephone and Telegraph Company, 10
Carpenter Technology Corporation, 13
CARQUEST Corporation, 29
Carr-Gottstein Foods Co., 17
CarrAmerica Realty Corporation, 56
The Carriage House Companies, Inc., 55
Carriage Services, Inc., 37
Carrier Access Corporation, 44
Carrier Corporation, 7; 69 (upd.)
Carroll's Foods, Inc., 46
Carrols Restaurant Group, Inc., 92
The Carsey-Werner Company, L.L.C., 37
Carson Pirie Scott & Company, 15
Carson, Inc., 31
Carter Hawley Hale Stores, Inc., V
Carter Lumber Company, 45
Carter-Wallace, Inc., 8; 38 (upd.)
Carus Publishing Company, 93
Carvel Corporation, 35
Carver Bancorp, Inc., 94
Carver Boat Corporation LLC, 88
Carvin Corp., 89
Cascade Corporation, 65
Cascade General, Inc., 65
Cascade Natural Gas Corporation, 9
Casco Northern Bank, 14
Casey's General Stores, Inc., 19; 83 (upd.)
Cash America International, Inc., 20; 61 (upd.)
Cash Systems, Inc., 93
Castle & Cooke, Inc., II; 20 (upd.)
Casual Corner Group, Inc., 43
Casual Male Retail Group, Inc., 52
Caswell-Massey Co. Ltd., 51
Catalina Lighting, Inc., 43 (upd.)
Catalina Marketing Corporation, 18
Catalytica Energy Systems, Inc., 44
Catellus Development Corporation, 24
Caterpillar Inc., III; 15 (upd.); 63 (upd.)
Catherines Stores Corporation, 15
Catholic Charities USA, 76
Catholic Health Initiatives, 91
Catholic Order of Foresters, 24
Cato Corporation, 14
Cattleman's, Inc., 20
Cavco Industries, Inc., 65
CB Commercial Real Estate Services Group, Inc., 21
CB Richard Ellis Group, Inc., 70 (upd.)
CBI Industries, Inc., 7
CBRL Group, Inc., 35 (upd.); 86 (upd.)
CBS Corporation, II; 6 (upd.); 28 (upd.)
CBS Television Network, 66 (upd.)
CCA Industries, Inc., 53
CCC Information Services Group Inc., 74
CCH Inc., 14
CDI Corporation, 6; 54 (upd.)
CDW Computer Centers, Inc., 16; 52 (upd.)
CEC Entertainment, Inc., 31 (upd.)
Cedar Fair, L.P., 22
Celadon Group Inc., 30
Celanese Corporation, I
Celebrate Express, Inc., 70
Celebrity, Inc., 22
Celera Genomics, 74
Celestial Seasonings, Inc., 16
Celgene Corporation, 67
CellStar Corporation, 83
Cendant Corporation, 44 (upd.)
Centel Corporation, 6
Centennial Communications Corporation, 39
Centerior Energy Corporation, V
Centerplate, Inc. 79
Centex Corporation, 8; 29 (upd.)
Centocor Inc., 14
Central and South West Corporation, V
Central European Distribution Corporation, 75
Central Florida Investments, Inc., 93
Central Garden & Pet Company, 23; 58 (upd.)
Central Hudson Gas and Electricity Corporation, 6
Central Maine Power, 6
Central Newspapers, Inc., 10
Central Parking Corporation, 18
Central Soya Company, Inc., 7
Central Sprinkler Corporation, 29
Central Vermont Public Service Corporation, 54
Centuri Corporation, 54
Century Aluminum Company, 52
Century Business Services, Inc., 52
Century Casinos, Inc., 53
Century Communications Corp., 10
Century Telephone Enterprises, Inc., 9; 54 (upd.)
Century Theatres, Inc., 31
Cenveo Inc., 71 (upd.)
Cephalon, Inc., 45
Cepheid, 77
Ceradyne, Inc., 65
Cerner Corporation, 16; 94 (upd.)
CertainTeed Corporation, 35
Certegy, Inc., 63
Cessna Aircraft Company, 8; 27 (upd.)
Chadbourne & Parke, 36
Chadwick's of Boston, Ltd., 29
The Chalone Wine Group, Ltd., 36
Champion Enterprises, Inc., 17
Champion Industries, Inc., 28
Champion International Corporation, IV; 20 (upd.)
Championship Auto Racing Teams, Inc., 37
Chancellor Beacon Academies, Inc., 53
Chancellor Media Corporation, 24
Chaparral Steel Co., 13
Charisma Brands LLC, 74
The Charles Machine Works, Inc., 64
Charles River Laboratories International, Inc., 42
The Charles Schwab Corporation, 8; 26 (upd.); 81 (upd.)
The Charles Stark Draper Laboratory, Inc., 35
Charlotte Russe Holding, Inc., 35; 90 (upd.)
Charming Shoppes, Inc., 8; 38
Chart House Enterprises, Inc., 17
Chart Industries, Inc., 21
Charter Communications, Inc., 33
ChartHouse International Learning Corporation, 49
Chas. Levy Company LLC, 60
Chase General Corporation, 91
The Chase Manhattan Corporation, II; 13 (upd.)
Chateau Communities, Inc., 37
Chattanooga Bakery, Inc., 86
Chattem, Inc., 17; 88 (upd.)
Chautauqua Airlines, Inc., 38
Checker Motors Corp., 89
Checkers Drive-In Restaurants, Inc., 16; 74 (upd.)
CheckFree Corporation, 81
Checkpoint Systems, Inc., 39
The Cheesecake Factory Inc., 17
Chef Solutions, Inc., 89
Chelsea Milling Company, 29
Chelsea Piers Management Inc., 86
Chemcentral Corporation, 8
Chemed Corporation, 13
Chemfab Corporation, 35
Chemi-Trol Chemical Co., 16
Chemical Banking Corporation, II; 14 (upd.)
Chemical Waste Management, Inc., 9
Chemtura Corporation, 91 (upd.)
CHEP Pty. Ltd., 80
Cherokee Inc., 18
Cherry Lane Music Publishing Company, Inc., 62
Chesapeake Corporation, 8; 30 (upd.); 93 (upd.)
Chesapeake Utilities Corporation, 56
Chesebrough-Pond's USA, Inc., 8
ChevronTexaco Corporation, IV; 19 (upd.); 47 (upd.)

Cheyenne Software, Inc., 12
CHF Industries, Inc., 84
Chi-Chi's Inc., 13; 51 (upd.)
Chiasso Inc., 53
Chiat/Day Inc. Advertising, 11
Chic by H.I.S, Inc., 20
Chicago and North Western Holdings Corporation, 6
Chicago Bears Football Club, Inc., 33
Chicago Board of Trade, 41
Chicago Mercantile Exchange Holdings Inc., 75
Chicago National League Ball Club, Inc., 66
Chicago Review Press Inc., 84
Chick-fil-A Inc., 23; 90 (upd.)
Chicken of the Sea International, 24 (upd.)
Chico's FAS, Inc., 45
Children's Comprehensive Services, Inc., 42
Children's Hospitals and Clinics, Inc., 54
The Children's Place Retail Stores, Inc., 37; 86 (upd.)
ChildrenFirst, Inc., 59
Childtime Learning Centers, Inc., 34
Chiles Offshore Corporation, 9
Chipotle Mexican Grill, Inc., 67
CHIPS and Technologies, Inc., 9
Chiquita Brands International, Inc., 7; 21 (upd.); 83 (upd.)
Chiron Corporation, 10; 36 (upd.)
Chisholm-Mingo Group, Inc., 41
Chittenden & Eastman Company, 58
Chock Full o' Nuts Corp., 17
Choice Hotels International Inc., 14; 83 (upd.)
ChoicePoint Inc., 65
Chorus Line Corporation, 30
Chris-Craft Corporation, 9; 31 (upd.); 80 (upd.)
Christensen Boyles Corporation, 26
The Christian Broadcasting Network, Inc., 52
The Christian Science Publishing Society, 55
Christopher & Banks Corporation, 42
Chromcraft Revington, Inc., 15
The Chronicle Publishing Company, Inc., 23
Chronimed Inc., 26
Chrysler Corporation, I; 11 (upd.)
CHS Inc., 60
CH2M Hill Ltd., 22
The Chubb Corporation, III; 14 (upd.); 37 (upd.)
Chugach Alaska Corporation, 60
Church & Dwight Co., Inc., 29; 68 (upd.)
Church's Chicken, 66
Churchill Downs Incorporated, 29
Cianbro Corporation, 14
Ciber, Inc., 18
CIENA Corporation, 54
CIGNA Corporation, III; 22 (upd.); 45 (upd.)
Cimarex Energy Co., 81
Cincinnati Bell, Inc., 6
Cincinnati Financial Corporation, 16; 44 (upd.)
Cincinnati Gas & Electric Company, 6
Cincinnati Lamb Inc., 72
Cincinnati Milacron Inc., 12
Cincom Systems Inc., 15
Cinnabon, Inc., 23; 90 (upd.)
Cintas Corporation, 21; 51 (upd.)
CIPSCO Inc., 6
The Circle K Company, II; 20 (upd.)
Circon Corporation, 21
Circuit City Stores, Inc., 9; 29 (upd.); 65 (upd.)
Circus Circus Enterprises, Inc., 6
Cirrus Design Corporation, 44
Cirrus Logic, Inc., 11; 48 (upd.)
Cisco-Linksys LLC, 86
Cisco Systems, Inc., 11; 34 (upd.); 77 (upd.)
CIT Group Inc., 76
Citadel Communications Corporation, 35
Citfed Bancorp, Inc., 16
CITGO Petroleum Corporation, IV; 31 (upd.)
Citi Trends, Inc., 80
Citicorp Diners Club, Inc., 90
Citigroup Inc., II; 9 (upd.); 30 (upd.); 59 (upd.)
Citizens Communications Company 7; 79 (upd.)
Citizens Financial Group, Inc., 42; 87 (upd.)
Citrix Systems, Inc., 44
City Brewing Company LLC, 73
City Public Service, 6
CKE Restaurants, Inc., 19; 46 (upd.)
Claire's Stores, Inc., 17; 94 (upd.)
CLARCOR Inc., 17; 61 (upd.)
Clare Rose Inc., 68
The Clark Construction Group, Inc., 8
Clark Equipment Company, 8
Classic Vacation Group, Inc., 46
Clayton Homes Incorporated, 13; 54 (upd.)
Clayton Williams Energy, Inc., 87
Clean Harbors, Inc., 73
Clear Channel Communications, Inc., 23
Clearwire, Inc., 69
Cleary, Gottlieb, Steen & Hamilton, 35
Cleco Corporation, 37
The Clemens Family Corporation, 93
Clement Pappas & Company, Inc., 92
Cleveland Indians Baseball Company, Inc., 37
Cleveland-Cliffs Inc., 13; 62 (upd.)
Click Wine Group, 68
Clif Bar Inc., 50
The Clorox Company, III; 22 (upd.); 81 (upd.)
The Clothestime, Inc., 20
Clougherty Packing Company, 72
ClubCorp, Inc., 33
CMG Worldwide, Inc., 89
CMGI, Inc., 76
CML Group, Inc., 10
CMP Media Inc., 26
CMS Energy Corporation, V, 14
CNA Financial Corporation, III; 38 (upd.)
CNET Networks, Inc., 47
CNS, Inc., 20
Coach, Inc., 10; 45 (upd.)
Coach USA, Inc., 24; 55 (upd.)
Coachmen Industries, Inc., 77
The Coastal Corporation, IV, 31 (upd.)
COBE Cardiovascular, Inc., 61
COBE Laboratories, Inc., 13
Coborn's, Inc., 30
Cobra Electronics Corporation, 14
Cobra Golf Inc., 16
Coca Cola Bottling Co. Consolidated, 10
The Coca-Cola Company, I; 10 (upd.); 32 (upd.); 67 (upd.)
Coca-Cola Enterprises, Inc., 13
Coeur d'Alene Mines Corporation, 20
Cogent Communications Group, Inc., 55
Cogentrix Energy, Inc., 10
Cognex Corporation, 76
Cognizant Technology Solutions Corporation, 59
Coherent, Inc., 31
Cohu, Inc., 32
Coinmach Laundry Corporation, 20
Coinstar, Inc., 44
Cold Spring Granite Company, 16
Cold Spring Granite Company Inc., 67 (upd.)
Cold Stone Creamery, 69
Coldwater Creek Inc., 21; 74 (upd.)
Cole National Corporation, 13; 76 (upd.)
Cole's Quality Foods, Inc., 68
The Coleman Company, Inc., 9; 30 (upd.)
Coleman Natural Products, Inc., 68
Coles Express Inc., 15
Colfax Corporation, 58
Colgate-Palmolive Company, III; 14 (upd.); 35 (upd.); 71 (upd.)
Collectors Universe, Inc., 48
Colliers International Property Consultants Inc., 92
Collins & Aikman Corporation, 13; 41 (upd.)
Collins Industries, Inc., 33
Colonial Properties Trust, 65
Colonial Williamsburg Foundation, 53
Color Kinetics Incorporated, 85
Colorado Baseball Management, Inc., 72
Colorado MEDtech, Inc., 48
Colt Industries Inc., I
Colt's Manufacturing Company, Inc., 12
Columbia Forest Products Inc., 78
The Columbia Gas System, Inc., V; 16 (upd.)
Columbia House Company, 69
Columbia Sportswear Company, 19; 41 (upd.)
Columbia TriStar Motion Pictures Companies, II; 12 (upd.)
Columbia/HCA Healthcare Corporation, 15
Columbus McKinnon Corporation, 37
Comair Holdings Inc., 13; 34 (upd.)
Combe Inc., 72
Comcast Corporation, 7; 24 (upd.)

Comdial Corporation, 21
Comdisco, Inc., 9
Comerica Incorporated, 40
COMFORCE Corporation, 40
Command Security Corporation, 57
Commerce Clearing House, Inc., 7
Commercial Credit Company, 8
Commercial Federal Corporation, 12; 62 (upd.)
Commercial Financial Services, Inc., 26
Commercial Metals Company, 15; 42 (upd.)
Commercial Vehicle Group, Inc., 81
Commodore International Ltd., 7
Commonwealth Edison Company, V
Commonwealth Energy System, 14
Commonwealth Telephone Enterprises, Inc., 25
CommScope, Inc., 77
Community Coffee Co. L.L.C., 53
Community Health Systems, Inc., 71
Community Newspaper Holdings, Inc., 91
Community Psychiatric Centers, 15
Compaq Computer Corporation, III; 6 (upd.); 26 (upd.)
Compass Bancshares, Inc., 73
Compass Minerals International, Inc. 79
CompDent Corporation, 22
CompHealth Inc., 25
Complete Business Solutions, Inc., 31
Comprehensive Care Corporation, 15
CompuAdd Computer Corporation, 11
CompuCom Systems, Inc., 10
CompuDyne Corporation, 51
CompUSA, Inc., 10; 35 (upd.)
CompuServe Interactive Services, Inc., 10; 27 (upd.)
Computer Associates International, Inc., 6; 49 (upd.)
Computer Data Systems, Inc., 14
Computer Learning Centers, Inc., 26
Computer Sciences Corporation, 6
Computerland Corp., 13
Computervision Corporation, 10
Compuware Corporation, 10; 30 (upd.); 66 (upd.)
Comsat Corporation, 23
Comshare Inc., 23
Comstock Resources, Inc., 47
Comtech Telecommunications Corp., 75
Comverse Technology, Inc., 15; 43 (upd.)
ConAgra Foods, Inc., II; 12 (upd.); 42 (upd.); 85 (upd.)
Conair Corporation, 17; 69 (upd.)
Concentra Inc., 71
Concepts Direct, Inc., 39
Concord Camera Corporation, 41
Concord EFS, Inc., 52
Concord Fabrics, Inc., 16
Concurrent Computer Corporation, 75
Condé Nast Publications, Inc., 13; 59 (upd.)
Cone Mills LLC, 8; 67 (upd.)
Conexant Systems, Inc., 36
Confluence Holdings Corporation, 76
Congoleum Corp., 18
CONMED Corporation, 87
Conn's, Inc., 67
Conn-Selmer, Inc., 55
Connecticut Light and Power Co., 13
Connecticut Mutual Life Insurance Company, III
The Connell Company, 29
Conner Peripherals, Inc., 6
Connetics Corporation, 70
ConocoPhillips, IV; 16 (upd.); 63 (upd.)
Conrad Industries, Inc., 58
Conseco, Inc., 10; 33 (upd.)
Conso International Corporation, 29
CONSOL Energy Inc., 59
Consolidated Delivery & Logistics, Inc., 24
Consolidated Edison, Inc., V; 45 (upd.)
Consolidated Freightways Corporation, V; 21 (upd.); 48 (upd.)
Consolidated Graphics, Inc., 70
Consolidated Natural Gas Company, V; 19 (upd.)
Consolidated Papers, Inc., 8; 36 (upd.)
Consolidated Products Inc., 14
Consolidated Rail Corporation, V
Constar International Inc., 64
Constellation Brands, Inc., 68 (upd.)
Consumers Power Co., 14
Consumers Union, 26
Consumers Water Company, 14
The Container Store, 36
ContiGroup Companies, Inc., 43 (upd.)
Continental Airlines, Inc., I; 21 (upd.); 52 (upd.)
Continental Bank Corporation, II
Continental Cablevision, Inc., 7
Continental Can Co., Inc., 15
The Continental Corporation, III
Continental General Tire Corp., 23
Continental Grain Company, 10; 13 (upd.)
Continental Group Company, I
Continental Medical Systems, Inc., 10
Continental Resources, Inc., 89
Continuum Health Partners, Inc., 60
Control Data Corporation, III
Control Data Systems, Inc., 10
Converse Inc., 9; 31 (upd.)
Cooker Restaurant Corporation, 20; 51 (upd.)
CoolSavings, Inc., 77
Cooper Cameron Corporation, 20 (upd.); 58 (upd.)
The Cooper Companies, Inc., 39
Cooper Industries, Inc., II; 44 (upd.)
Cooper Tire & Rubber Company, 8; 23 (upd.)
Coopers & Lybrand, 9
Copart Inc., 23
The Copley Press, Inc., 23
The Copps Corporation, 32
Corbis Corporation, 31
The Corcoran Group, Inc., 58
Cordis Corporation, 19; 46 (upd.)
CoreStates Financial Corp, 17
Corinthian Colleges, Inc., 39; 92 (upd.)
Corning Inc., III; 44 (upd.); 90 (upd.)
The Corporate Executive Board Company, 89
Corporate Express, Inc., 22; 47 (upd.)
Corporate Software Inc., 9
Corporation for Public Broadcasting, 14; 89 (upd.)
Correctional Services Corporation, 30
Corrections Corporation of America, 23
Corrpro Companies, Inc., 20
CORT Business Services Corporation, 26
Corus Bankshares, Inc., 75
Cosi, Inc., 53
Cosmair, Inc., 8
The Cosmetic Center, Inc., 22
Cost Plus, Inc., 27
Cost-U-Less, Inc., 51
CoStar Group, Inc., 73
Costco Wholesale Corporation, V; 43 (upd.)
Cotter & Company, V
Cotton Incorporated, 46
Coty, Inc., 36
Coudert Brothers, 30
Council on International Educational Exchange Inc., 81
Country Kitchen International, Inc., 76
Countrywide Credit Industries, Inc., 16
County Seat Stores Inc., 9
Courier Corporation, 41
Cousins Properties Incorporated, 65
Covance Inc., 30
Covanta Energy Corporation, 64 (upd.)
Coventry Health Care, Inc., 59
Covington & Burling, 40
Cowen Group, Inc., 92
Cowles Media Company, 23
Cox Enterprises, Inc., IV; 22 (upd.); 67 (upd.)
Cox Radio, Inc., 89
CPAC, Inc., 86
CPC International Inc., II
CPI Aerostructures, Inc., 75
CPI Corp., 38
CR England, Inc., 63
CRA International, Inc., 93
Cracker Barrel Old Country Store, Inc., 10
Craftmade International, Inc., 44
craigslist, inc., 89
Crain Communications, Inc., 12; 35 (upd.)
Cramer, Berkowitz & Co., 34
Crane & Co., Inc., 26
Crane Co., 8; 30 (upd.)
Cranium, Inc., 69
Crate and Barrel, 9
Cravath, Swaine & Moore, 43
Crawford & Company, 87
Cray Inc., 75 (upd.)
Cray Research, Inc., III; 16 (upd.)
Creative Artists Agency LLC, 38
Credence Systems Corporation, 90
Credit Acceptance Corporation, 18
Cree Inc., 53
Crispin Porter + Bogusky, 83
Crocs, Inc., 80
Crompton Corporation, 9; 36 (upd.)
Croscill, Inc., 42
Crosman Corporation, 62
CROSSMARK 79

Crowley Maritime Corporation, 6; 28 (upd.)
Crowley, Milner & Company, 19
Crown Books Corporation, 21
Crown Central Petroleum Corporation, 7
Crown Crafts, Inc., 16
Crown Equipment Corporation, 15; 93 (upd.)
Crown Holdings, Inc., 83 (upd.)
Crown Media Holdings, Inc., 45
Crown Vantage Inc., 29
Crown, Cork & Seal Company, Inc., I; 13; 32 (upd.)
CRSS Inc., 6
Cruise America Inc., 21
CryoLife, Inc., 46
Crystal Brands, Inc., 9
CS First Boston Inc., II
CSG Systems International, Inc., 75
CSK Auto Corporation, 38
CSS Industries, Inc., 35
CSX Corporation, V; 22 (upd.); 79 (upd.)
CTB International Corporation, 43 (upd.)
CTG, Inc., 11
CTS Corporation, 39
Cubic Corporation, 19
CUC International Inc., 16
Cuisinart Corporation, 24
Cuisine Solutions Inc., 84
Culbro Corporation, 15
CulinArt, Inc., 92
Cullen/Frost Bankers, Inc., 25
Culligan Water Technologies, Inc., 12; 38 (upd.)
Culp, Inc., 29
Culver Franchising System, Inc., 58
Cumberland Farms, Inc., 17; 84 (upd.)
Cumberland Packing Corporation, 26
Cummins Engine Company, Inc., I; 12 (upd.); 40 (upd.)
Cumulus Media Inc., 37
CUNA Mutual Group, 62
Cunard Line Ltd., 23
CUNO Incorporated, 57
Current, Inc., 37
Curtice-Burns Foods, Inc., 7; 21 (upd.)
Curtiss-Wright Corporation, 10; 35 (upd.)
Curves International, Inc., 54
Cushman & Wakefield, Inc., 86
Custom Chrome, Inc., 16; 74 (upd.)
Cutera, Inc., 84
Cutter & Buck Inc., 27
CVS Corporation, 45 (upd.)
Cybermedia, Inc., 25
Cyberonics, Inc. 79
Cybex International, Inc., 49
Cygne Designs, Inc., 25
Cygnus Business Media, Inc., 56
Cymer, Inc., 77
Cypress Semiconductor Corporation, 20; 48 (upd.)
Cyprus Amax Minerals Company, 21
Cyprus Minerals Company, 7
Cyrk Inc., 19
Cystic Fibrosis Foundation, 93
Cytec Industries Inc., 27
Cytyc Corporation, 69
Czarnikow-Rionda Company, Inc., 32
D&K Wholesale Drug, Inc., 14
D'Agostino Supermarkets Inc., 19
D'Arcy Masius Benton & Bowles, Inc., VI; 32 (upd.)
D.F. Stauffer Biscuit Company, 82
D.G. Yuengling & Son, Inc., 38
D.R. Horton, Inc., 58
Dade Behring Holdings Inc., 71
Daffy's Inc., 26
Dain Rauscher Corporation, 35 (upd.)
Dairy Farmers of America, Inc., 94
Dairy Mart Convenience Stores, Inc., 7; 25 (upd.)
Dairyland Healthcare Solutions, 73
Daisy Outdoor Products Inc., 58
Daisytek International Corporation, 18
Daktronics, Inc., 32
Dal-Tile International Inc., 22
Dale Carnegie & Associates Inc. 28; 78 (upd.)
Dallas Cowboys Football Club, Ltd., 33
Dallas Semiconductor Corporation, 13; 31 (upd.)
Dallis Coffee, Inc., 86
Damark International, Inc., 18
Dames & Moore, Inc., 25
Dan River Inc., 35; 86 (upd.)
Dana Corporation, I; 10 (upd.)
Danaher Corporation, 7; 77 (upd.)
Daniel Industries, Inc., 16
Daniel Measurement and Control, Inc., 74 (upd.)
Dannon Co., Inc., 14
Danskin, Inc., 12; 62 (upd.)
Darden Restaurants, Inc., 16; 44 (upd.)
Darigold, Inc., 9
Darling International Inc., 85
Dart Group Corporation, 16
Data Broadcasting Corporation, 31
Data General Corporation, 8
Datapoint Corporation, 11
Datascope Corporation, 39
Datek Online Holdings Corp., 32
Dauphin Deposit Corporation, 14
Dave & Buster's, Inc., 33
The Davey Tree Expert Company, 11
The David and Lucile Packard Foundation, 41
The David J. Joseph Company, 14; 76 (upd.)
David's Bridal, Inc., 33
Davis Polk & Wardwell, 36
DaVita Inc., 73
DAW Technologies, Inc., 25
Dawn Food Products, Inc., 17
Day & Zimmermann Inc., 9; 31 (upd.)
Day International, Inc., 84
Day Runner, Inc., 14; 41 (upd.)
Dayton Hudson Corporation, V; 18 (upd.)
DC Comics Inc., 25
DC Shoes, Inc., 60
DDB Needham Worldwide, 14
Dean & DeLuca, Inc., 36
Dean Foods Company, 7; 21 (upd.); 73 (upd.)
Dean Witter, Discover & Co., 12
Dearborn Mid-West Conveyor Company, 56
Death Row Records, 27
Deb Shops, Inc., 16; 76 (upd.)
Debevoise & Plimpton, 39
Dechert, 43
Deckers Outdoor Corporation, 22
Decora Industries, Inc., 31
Decorator Industries Inc., 68
DeCrane Aircraft Holdings Inc., 36
DeepTech International Inc., 21
Deere & Company, III; 21 (upd.); 42 (upd.)
Defiance, Inc., 22
DeKalb Genetics Corporation, 17
Del Laboratories, Inc., 28
Del Monte Foods Company, 7; 23 (upd.)
Del Taco, Inc., 58
Del Webb Corporation, 14
Delaware North Companies Incorporated, 7
dELiA*s Inc., 29
Delicato Vineyards, Inc., 50
Dell Inc., 9; 31 (upd.); 63 (upd.)
Deloitte Touche Tohmatsu International, 9; 29 (upd.)
DeLorme Publishing Company, Inc., 53
Delphax Technologies Inc., 94
Delphi Automotive Systems Corporation, 45
Delta Air Lines, Inc., I; 6 (upd.); 39 (upd.); 92 (upd.)
Delta and Pine Land Company, 33; 59
Delta Woodside Industries, Inc., 8; 30 (upd.)
Deltec, Inc., 56
Deltic Timber Corporation, 46
Deluxe Corporation, 7; 22 (upd.); 73 (upd.)
DEMCO, Inc., 60
DeMoulas / Market Basket Inc., 23
DenAmerica Corporation, 29
Denbury Resources, Inc., 67
Dendrite International, Inc., 70
Denison International plc, 46
Dentsply International Inc., 10
Denver Nuggets, 51
DEP Corporation, 20
Department 56, Inc., 14; 34 (upd.)
Deposit Guaranty Corporation, 17
DePuy Inc., 30; 37 (upd.)
Deschutes Brewery, Inc., 57
Designer Holdings Ltd., 20
Destec Energy, Inc., 12
Detroit Diesel Corporation, 10; 74 (upd.)
The Detroit Edison Company, V
The Detroit Lions, Inc., 55
The Detroit Pistons Basketball Company,41
Detroit Red Wings, 74
Detroit Tigers Baseball Club, Inc., 46
Deutsch, Inc., 42
Developers Diversified Realty Corporation, 69
DeVito/Verdi, 85
Devon Energy Corporation, 61
DeVry Inc., 29; 82 (upd.)
Dewberry 78

Dewey Ballantine LLP, 48
Dex Media, Inc., 65
The Dexter Corporation, I; 12 (upd.)
DFS Group Ltd., 66
DH Technology, Inc., 18
DHB Industries Inc., 85
DHL Worldwide Express, 6; 24 (upd.)
Di Giorgio Corp., 12
Diagnostic Products Corporation, 73
The Dial Corp., 8; 23 (upd.)
Dial-A-Mattress Operating Corporation, 46
Dialogic Corporation, 18
Diamond of California, 64 (upd.)
Diamond Shamrock, Inc., IV
DiamondCluster International, Inc., 51
Dibrell Brothers, Incorporated, 12
dick clark productions, inc., 16
Dick Corporation, 64
Dick's Sporting Goods, Inc., 59
Dickten Masch Plastics LLC, 90
Dictaphone Healthcare Solutions 78
Diebold, Incorporated, 7; 22 (upd.)
Diedrich Coffee, Inc., 40
Dierbergs Markets Inc., 63
Dietz and Watson, Inc., 92
Digex, Inc., 46
Digi International Inc., 9
Digital Equipment Corporation, III; 6 (upd.)
Digital River, Inc., 50
Digitas Inc., 81
Dillard Paper Company, 11
Dillard's Inc., V; 16 (upd.); 68 (upd.)
Dillingham Construction Corporation, I; 44 (upd.)
Dillon Companies Inc., 12
Dime Savings Bank of New York, F.S.B., 9
DIMON Inc., 27
Diodes Incorporated, 81
Dionex Corporation, 46
Dippin' Dots, Inc., 56
Direct Focus, Inc., 47
Directed Electronics, Inc., 87
DIRECTV, Inc., 38; 75 (upd.)
Discount Auto Parts, Inc., 18
Discount Drug Mart, Inc., 14
Discount Tire Company Inc., 84
Discovery Communications, Inc., 42
Discovery Partners International, Inc., 58
ditech.com, 93
The Dixie Group, Inc., 20; 80 (upd.)
Dixon Industries, Inc., 26
Dixon Ticonderoga Company, 12; 69 (upd.)
DMI Furniture, Inc., 46
Do it Best Corporation, 30
Dobson Communications Corporation, 63
Doctor's Associates Inc., 67 (upd.)
The Doctors' Company, 55
Documentum, Inc., 46
Dolan Media Company, 94
Dolby Laboratories Inc., 20
Dole Food Company, Inc., 9; 31 (upd.); 68 (upd.)
Dollar Thrifty Automotive Group, Inc., 25
Dollar Tree Stores, Inc., 23; 62 (upd.)
Dominick & Dominick LLC, 92
Dominick's Finer Foods, Inc., 56
Dominion Homes, Inc., 19
Dominion Resources, Inc., V; 54 (upd.)
Domino Sugar Corporation, 26
Domino's Pizza, Inc., 7; 21 (upd.)
Domino's, Inc., 63 (upd.)
Don Massey Cadillac, Inc., 37
Donaldson Company, Inc., 16; 49 (upd.)
Donaldson, Lufkin & Jenrette, Inc., 22
Donatos Pizzeria Corporation, 58
Donna Karan International Inc., 15; 56 (upd.)
Donnelly Corporation, 12; 35 (upd.)
Donnkenny, Inc., 17
Donruss Playoff L.P., 66
Dooney & Bourke Inc., 84
Dorsey & Whitney LLP, 47
Doskocil Companies, Inc., 12
Dot Foods, Inc., 69
Dot Hill Systems Corp., 93
Double-Cola Co.-USA, 70
DoubleClick Inc., 46
Doubletree Corporation, 21
Douglas & Lomason Company, 16
Dover Corporation, III; 28 (upd.); 90 (upd.)
Dover Downs Entertainment, Inc., 43
Dover Publications Inc., 34
The Dow Chemical Company, I; 8 (upd.); 50 (upd.)
Dow Jones & Company, Inc., IV; 19 (upd.); 47 (upd.)
Dow Jones Telerate, Inc., 10
DPL Inc., 6
DQE, Inc., 6
Dr Pepper/Seven Up, Inc., 9; 32 (upd.)
Drackett Professional Products, 12
Draftfcb, 94
Drake Beam Morin, Inc., 44
Draper Fisher Jurvetson, 91
DreamWorks SKG, 43
The Drees Company, Inc., 41
The Dress Barn, Inc., 24; 55 (upd.)
Dresser Industries, Inc., III
Drew Industries Inc., 28
Drexel Burnham Lambert Incorporated, II
Drexel Heritage Furnishings Inc., 12
Dreyer's Grand Ice Cream, Inc., 17
The Dreyfus Corporation, 70
Dril-Quip, Inc., 81
Drinker, Biddle and Reath L.L.P., 92
DriveTime Automotive Group Inc., 68 (upd.)
DRS Technologies, Inc., 58
Drs. Foster & Smith, Inc., 62
Drug Emporium, Inc., 12
Drypers Corporation, 18
DSC Communications Corporation, 12
DSW Inc., 73
DTE Energy Company, 20 (upd.); 94 (upd.)
DTS, Inc., 80
Dualstar Entertainment Group LLC, 76
Duane Reade Holding Corp., 21
Duck Head Apparel Company, Inc., 42
Ducks Unlimited, Inc., 87
Duckwall-ALCO Stores, Inc., 24
Ducommun Incorporated, 30
Duke Energy Corporation, V; 27 (upd.)
Duke Realty Corporation, 57
The Dun & Bradstreet Corporation, IV; 19 (upd.); 61 (upd.)
Dun & Bradstreet Software Services Inc., 11
Dunavant Enterprises, Inc., 54
Duncan Aviation, Inc., 94
Duncan Toys Company, 55
Dunn-Edwards Corporation, 56
Duplex Products Inc., 17
Duracell International Inc., 9; 71 (upd.)
Durametallic, 21
Duriron Company Inc., 17
Duron Inc., 72
Duty Free International, Inc., 11
DVI, Inc., 51
Dyax Corp., 89
Dycom Industries, Inc., 57
Dyersburg Corporation, 21
Dynamic Materials Corporation, 81
Dynatech Corporation, 13
DynCorp, 45
Dynegy Inc., 49 (upd.)
E! Entertainment Television Inc., 17
E*Trade Financial Corporation, 20; 60 (upd.)
E. & J. Gallo Winery, I; 7 (upd.); 28 (upd.)
E.I. du Pont de Nemours and Company, I; 8 (upd.); 26 (upd.); 73 (upd.)
E.piphany, Inc., 49
E-Systems, Inc., 9
E.W. Howell Co., Inc., 72
The E.W. Scripps Company, IV; 7 (upd.); 28 (upd.); 66 (upd.)
E-Z Serve Corporation, 17
E-Z-EM Inc., 89
Eagle Hardware & Garden, Inc., 16
Eagle-Picher Industries, Inc., 8; 23 (upd.)
Eagle-Tribune Publishing Co., 91
Earl Scheib, Inc., 32
Earle M. Jorgensen Company, 82
The Earthgrains Company, 36
EarthLink, Inc., 36
East Penn Manufacturing Co., Inc. 79
Easter Seals, Inc., 58
Eastern Airlines, I
The Eastern Company, 48
Eastern Enterprises, 6
EastGroup Properties, Inc., 67
Eastland Shoe Corporation, 82
Eastman Chemical Company, 14; 38 (upd.)
Eastman Kodak Company, III; 7 (upd.); 36 (upd.); 91 (upd.)
Easton Sports, Inc., 66
Eateries, Inc., 33
Eaton Corporation, I; 10 (upd.); 67 (upd.)
Eaton Vance Corporation, 18
eBay Inc., 32; 67 (upd.)
EBSCO Industries, Inc., 17; 40 (upd.)
ECC International Corp., 42
Echlin Inc., I; 11 (upd.)
The Echo Design Group, Inc., 68

EchoStar Communications Corporation, 35
Eckerd Corporation, 9; 32 (upd.)
Eclipse Aviation Corporation, 87
Ecolab Inc., I; 13 (upd.); 34 (upd.); 85 (upd.)
eCollege.com, 85
Ecology and Environment, Inc., 39
Eddie Bauer, Inc., 9; 36 (upd.); 87 (upd.)
Edelbrock Corporation, 37
Edelman, 62
EDGAR Online, Inc., 91
Edge Petroleum Corporation, 67
Edison Brothers Stores, Inc., 9
Edison International, 56 (upd.)
Edison Schools Inc., 37
Edmark Corporation, 14; 41 (upd.)
EDO Corporation, 46
Educate Inc. 86 (upd.)
Education Management Corporation, 35
Educational Broadcasting Corporation, 48
Educational Testing Service, 12; 62 (upd.)
Edw. C. Levy Co., 42
Edward D. Jones & Company L.P., 30; 66 (upd.)
Edward Hines Lumber Company, 68
The Edward J. DeBartolo Corporation, 8
Edwards and Kelcey, 70
Edwards Brothers, Inc., 92
Edwards Theatres Circuit, Inc., 31
EFJ, Inc., 81
EG&G Incorporated, 8; 29 (upd.)
Egan Companies, Inc., 94
Egghead.com, Inc., 9; 31 (upd.)
EGL, Inc., 59
eHarmony.com Inc., 71
8x8, Inc., 94
84 Lumber Company, 9; 39 (upd.)
800-JR Cigar, Inc., 27
Eileen Fisher Inc., 61
Einstein/Noah Bagel Corporation, 29
Ekco Group, Inc., 16
El Camino Resources International, Inc., 11
El Chico Restaurants, Inc., 19
El Paso Corporation, 66 (upd.)
El Paso Electric Company, 21
El Paso Natural Gas Company, 12
El Pollo Loco, Inc., 69
Elamex, S.A. de C.V., 51
Elano Corporation, 14
The Elder-Beerman Stores Corp., 10; 63 (upd.)
Electric Boat Corporation, 86
Electric Lightwave, Inc., 37
Electro Rent Corporation, 58
Electromagnetic Sciences Inc., 21
Electronic Arts Inc., 10; 85 (upd.)
Electronic Data Systems Corporation, III; 28 (upd.)
Electronics Boutique Holdings Corporation, 72
Electronics for Imaging, Inc., 15; 43 (upd.)
Elektra Entertainment Group, 64
Element K Corporation, 94
Elephant Pharmacy, Inc., 83
Eli Lilly and Company, I; 11 (upd.); 47 (upd.)
Elizabeth Arden, Inc., 8; 40 (upd.)
Eljer Industries, Inc., 24
Elkay Manufacturing Company, 73
ElkCorp, 52
Ellen Tracy, Inc., 55
Ellerbe Becket, 41
Ellett Brothers, Inc., 17
Elmer Candy Corporation, 88
Elmer's Restaurants, Inc., 42
Elsinore Corporation, 48
Elvis Presley Enterprises, Inc., 61
EMBARQ Corporation, 83
Embers America Restaurants, 30
Embrex, Inc., 72
EMC Corporation, 12; 46 (upd.)
EMCOR Group Inc., 60
Emerson, II; 46 (upd.)
Emerson Radio Corp., 30
Emery Worldwide Airlines, Inc., 6; 25 (upd.)
Emge Packing Co., Inc., 11
Emigrant Savings Bank, 59
Emmis Communications Corporation, 47
Empi, Inc., 26
Empire Blue Cross and Blue Shield, III
The Empire District Electric Company, 77
Empire Resorts, Inc., 72
Empire Resources, Inc., 81
Employee Solutions, Inc., 18
ENCAD, Incorporated, 25
Encompass Services Corporation, 33
Encore Acquisition Company, 73
Encore Computer Corporation, 13; 74 (upd.)
Encore Wire Corporation, 81
Encyclopaedia Britannica, Inc., 7; 39 (upd.)
Endo Pharmaceuticals Holdings Inc., 71
Energen Corporation, 21
Energizer Holdings, Inc., 32
Energy Brands Inc., 88
Energy Conversion Devices, Inc., 75
Enesco Corporation, 11
Engelhard Corporation, IV; 21 (upd.); 72 (upd.)
Engineered Support Systems, Inc., 59
Engle Homes, Inc., 46
Engraph, Inc., 12
Ennis Business Forms, Inc., 21
EnPro Industries, Inc., 93
Enquirer/Star Group, Inc., 10
Enrich International, Inc., 33
Enron Corporation, V, 19; 46 (upd.)
ENSCO International Incorporated, 57
Enserch Corporation, V
Entercom Communications Corporation, 58
Entergy Corporation, V; 45 (upd.)
Enterprise Rent-A-Car Company, 6; 69 (upd.)
Entertainment Distribution Company, 89
Entravision Communications Corporation, 41
Envirodyne Industries, Inc., 17
Environmental Industries, Inc., 31
Environmental Power Corporation, 68
Environmental Systems Research Institute Inc. (ESRI), 62
Enzo Biochem, Inc., 41
Eon Labs, Inc., 67
Epic Systems Corporation, 62
EPIQ Systems, Inc., 56
Equifax Inc., 6; 28 (upd.); 90 (upd.)
Equistar Chemicals, LP, 71
Equitable Life Assurance Society of the United States, III
Equitable Resources, Inc., 6; 54 (upd.)
Equity Marketing, Inc., 26
Equity Office Properties Trust, 54
Equity Residential, 49
Equus Computer Systems, Inc., 49
Erickson Retirement Communities, 57
Erie Indemnity Company, 35
ERLY Industries Inc., 17
Ernie Ball, Inc., 56
Ernst & Young, 9; 29 (upd.)
Escalade, Incorporated, 19
Eschelon Telecom, Inc., 72
ESCO Technologies Inc., 87
Eskimo Pie Corporation, 21
ESPN, Inc., 56
Esprit de Corp., 8; 29 (upd.)
ESS Technology, Inc., 22
Essef Corporation, 18
Esselte, 64
Esselte Pendaflex Corporation, 11
Essence Communications, Inc., 24
Essex Corporation, 85
The Estée Lauder Companies Inc., 9; 30 (upd.); 93 (upd.)
Esterline Technologies Corp., 15
Estes Express Lines, Inc., 86
Eternal Word Television Network, Inc., 57
Ethan Allen Interiors, Inc., 12; 39 (upd.)
Ethicon, Inc., 23
Ethyl Corporation, I; 10 (upd.)
EToys, Inc., 37
The Eureka Company, 12
Euromarket Designs Inc., 31 (upd.)
Euronet Worldwide, Inc., 83
Europe Through the Back Door Inc., 65
Evans and Sutherland Computer Company 19; 78 (upd.)
Evans, Inc., 30
Everex Systems, Inc., 16
Evergreen International Aviation, Inc., 53
Everlast Worldwide Inc., 47
Exabyte Corporation, 12; 40 (upd.)
Exar Corp., 14
EXCEL Communications Inc., 18
Excel Technology, Inc., 65
Executive Jet, Inc., 36
Executone Information Systems, Inc., 13
Exelon Corporation, 48 (upd.)
Exide Electronics Group, Inc., 20
Expedia, Inc., 58
Expeditors International of Washington Inc., 17; 78 (upd.)
Experian Information Solutions Inc., 45
Express Scripts Inc., 17; 44 (upd.)
Extended Stay America, Inc., 41
EXX Inc., 65

Exxon Corporation, IV; 7 (upd.); 32 (upd.)
Exxon Mobil Corporation, 67 (upd.)
Eye Care Centers of America, Inc., 69
EZCORP Inc., 43
F&W Publications, Inc., 71
The F. Dohmen Co., 77
F. Korbel & Bros. Inc., 68
Fab Industries, Inc., 27
Fabri-Centers of America Inc., 16
Facebook, Inc., 90
FactSet Research Systems Inc., 73
Fair Grounds Corporation, 44
Fair, Isaac and Company, 18
Fairchild Aircraft, Inc., 9
Fairfield Communities, Inc., 36
Falcon Products, Inc., 33
Fallon McElligott Inc., 22
Fallon Worldwide, 71 (upd.)
Family Christian Stores, Inc., 51
Family Dollar Stores, Inc., 13; 62 (upd.)
Family Golf Centers, Inc., 29
Famous Dave's of America, Inc., 40
Fannie Mae, 45 (upd.)
Fannie May Confections Brands, Inc., 80
Fansteel Inc., 19
FAO Schwarz, 46
Farah Incorporated, 24
Faribault Foods, Inc., 89
Farley Northwest Industries, Inc., I
Farley's & Sathers Candy Company, Inc., 62
Farm Family Holdings, Inc., 39
Farm Journal Corporation, 42
Farmer Bros. Co., 52
Farmer Jack Supermarkets 78
Farmers Insurance Group of Companies, 25
Farmland Foods, Inc., 7
Farmland Industries, Inc., 48
FARO Technologies, Inc., 87
Farouk Systems Inc. 78
Farrar, Straus and Giroux Inc., 15
Fastenal Company, 14; 42 (upd.)
Fatburger Corporation, 64
Faultless Starch/Bon Ami Company, 55
Fay's Inc., 17
Faygo Beverages Inc., 55
Fazoli's Management, Inc., 76 (upd.)
Fazoli's Systems, Inc., 27
Featherlite Inc., 28
Fedders Corporation, 18; 43 (upd.)
Federal Agricultural Mortgage Corporation, 75
Federal Deposit Insurance Corporation, 93
Federal Express Corporation, V
Federal National Mortgage Association, II
Federal Paper Board Company, Inc., 8
Federal Prison Industries, Inc., 34
Federal Signal Corp., 10
Federal-Mogul Corporation, I; 10 (upd.); 26 (upd.)
Federated Department Stores Inc., 9; 31 (upd.)
FedEx Corporation, 18 (upd.); 42 (upd.)
Feed The Children, Inc., 68
FEI Company 79
Feld Entertainment, Inc., 32 (upd.)
Fellowes Manufacturing Company, 28
Fender Musical Instruments Company, 16; 43 (upd.)
Fenwick & West LLP, 34
Ferolito, Vultaggio & Sons, 27
Ferrara Fire Apparatus, Inc., 84
Ferrara Pan Candy Company, 90
Ferrellgas Partners, L.P., 35
Ferro Corporation, 8; 56 (upd.)
F5 Networks, Inc., 72
FHP International Corporation, 6
FiberMark, Inc., 37
Fibreboard Corporation, 16
Fidelity Investments Inc., II; 14 (upd.)
Fidelity National Financial Inc., 54
Fidelity Southern Corporation, 85
Fieldale Farms Corporation, 23
Fieldcrest Cannon, Inc., 9; 31 (upd.)
Fifth Third Bancorp, 13; 31 (upd.)
Figgie International Inc., 7
Fiji Water LLC, 74
FileNet Corporation, 62
Fili Enterprises, Inc., 70
Film Roman, Inc., 58
FINA, Inc., 7
Fingerhut Companies, Inc., 9; 36 (upd.)
Finisar Corporation, 92
The Finish Line, Inc., 29; 68 (upd.)
FinishMaster, Inc., 24
Finlay Enterprises, Inc., 16; 76 (upd.)
Firearms Training Systems, Inc., 27
Fired Up, Inc., 82
Fireman's Fund Insurance Company, III
First Albany Companies Inc., 37
First Alert, Inc., 28
The First American Corporation, The 52
First Aviation Services Inc., 49
First Bank System Inc., 12
First Brands Corporation, 8
First Cash Financial Services, Inc., 57
First Chicago Corporation, II
First Colony Coffee & Tea Company, 84
First Commerce Bancshares, Inc., 15
First Commerce Corporation, 11
First Data Corporation, 30 (upd.)
First Empire State Corporation, 11
First Executive Corporation, III
First Fidelity Bank, N.A., New Jersey, 9
First Financial Management Corporation, 11
First Hawaiian, Inc., 11
First Industrial Realty Trust, Inc., 65
First Interstate Bancorp, II
The First Marblehead Corporation, 87
First Mississippi Corporation, 8
First Nationwide Bank, 14
First of America Bank Corporation, 8
First Security Corporation, 11
First Team Sports, Inc., 22
First Tennessee National Corporation, 11; 48 (upd.)
First Union Corporation, 10
First USA, Inc., 11
First Virginia Banks, Inc., 11
The First Years Inc., 46
Firstar Corporation, 11; 33 (upd.)
Fiserv Inc., 11; 33 (upd.)
Fish & Neave, 54
Fisher Companies, Inc., 15
Fisher Controls International, LLC, 13; 61 (upd.)
Fisher Scientific International Inc., 24
Fisher-Price Inc., 12; 32 (upd.)
Fisk Corporation, 72
5 & Diner Franchise Corporation, 72
Flagstar Companies, Inc., 10
Flanders Corporation, 65
Flanigan's Enterprises, Inc., 60
Flatiron Construction Corporation, 92
Fleer Corporation, 15
FleetBoston Financial Corporation, 9; 36 (upd.)
Fleetwood Enterprises, Inc., III; 22 (upd.); 81 (upd.)
Fleming Companies, Inc., II; 17 (upd.)
Flexsteel Industries Inc., 15; 41 (upd.)
Flight Options, LLC, 75
FlightSafety International, Inc., 9; 29 (upd.)
Flint Ink Corporation, 13; 41 (upd.)
FLIR Systems, Inc., 69
Florida Crystals Inc., 35
Florida East Coast Industries, Inc., 59
Florida Gaming Corporation, 47
Florida Progress Corporation, V; 23 (upd.)
Florida Public Utilities Company, 69
Florida Rock Industries, Inc., 46
Florida's Natural Growers, 45
Florists' Transworld Delivery, Inc., 28
Florsheim Shoe Group Inc., 9; 31 (upd.)
Flotek Industries Inc., 93
Flour City International, Inc., 44
Flow International Corporation, 56
Flowers Industries, Inc., 12; 35 (upd.)
Flowserve Corporation, 33; 77 (upd.)
Fluke Corporation, 15
Fluor Corporation, I; 8 (upd.); 34 (upd.)
Flying Boat, Inc. (Chalk's Ocean Airways), 56
Flying J Inc., 19
FMC Corporation, I; 11 (upd.); 89 (upd.)
FMR Corp., 8; 32 (upd.)
Foamex International Inc., 17
Focus Features 78
Foley & Lardner, 28
Follett Corporation, 12; 39 (upd.)
Food Circus Super Markets, Inc., 88
The Food Emporium, 64
Food For The Poor, Inc., 77
Food Lion LLC, II; 15 (upd.); 66 (upd.)
Foodarama Supermarkets, Inc., 28
FoodBrands America, Inc., 23
Foodmaker, Inc., 14
Foot Locker, Inc., 68 (upd.)
Foote, Cone & Belding Worldwide, I; 66 (upd.)
Footstar, Incorporated, 24
Forbes Inc., 30; 82 (upd.)
The Ford Foundation, 34
Ford Motor Company, I; 11 (upd.); 36 (upd.); 64 (upd.)
FORE Systems, Inc., 25
Forest City Enterprises, Inc., 16; 52 (upd.)
Forest Laboratories, Inc., 11; 52 (upd.)

Forest Oil Corporation, 19; 91 (upd.)
Forever Living Products International Inc., 17
Forever 21, Inc., 84
FormFactor, Inc., 85
Formica Corporation, 13
Forrester Research, Inc., 54
Forstmann Little & Co., 38
Fort Howard Corporation, 8
Fort James Corporation, 22 (upd.)
Fortune Brands, Inc., 29 (upd.); 68 (upd.)
Fortunoff Fine Jewelry and Silverware Inc., 26
Forward Air Corporation, 75
Forward Industries, Inc., 86
Fossil, Inc., 17
Foster Poultry Farms, 32
Foster Wheeler Corporation, 6; 23 (upd.)
Foster Wheeler Ltd., 76 (upd.)
FosterGrant, Inc., 60
Foundation Health Corporation, 12
Fountain Powerboats Industries, Inc., 28
4Kids Entertainment Inc., 59
Fourth Financial Corporation, 11
Fox Entertainment Group, Inc., 43
Fox Family Worldwide, Inc., 24
Foxboro Company, 13
FoxHollow Technologies, Inc., 85
FoxMeyer Health Corporation, 16
Foxworth-Galbraith Lumber Company, 91
FPL Group, Inc., V; 49 (upd.)
Frank J. Zamboni & Co., Inc., 34
Frank Russell Company, 46
Frank's Nursery & Crafts, Inc., 12
Frankel & Co., 39
Franklin Covey Company, 11; 37 (upd.)
Franklin Electric Company, Inc., 43
Franklin Electronic Publishers, Inc., 23
The Franklin Mint, 69
Franklin Resources, Inc., 9
Franz Inc., 80
Fred Meyer Stores, Inc., V; 20 (upd.); 64 (upd.)
Fred Usinger Inc., 54
The Fred W. Albrecht Grocery Co., 13
Fred Weber, Inc., 61
Fred's, Inc., 23; 62 (upd.)
Freddie Mac, 54
Frederick Atkins Inc., 16
Frederick's of Hollywood, Inc., 16; 59 (upd.)
Freedom Communications, Inc., 36
Freeport-McMoRan Copper & Gold, Inc., IV; 7 (upd.); 57 (upd.)
Freescale Semiconductor, Inc., 83
Freeze.com LLC, 77
French Fragrances, Inc., 22
Frequency Electronics, Inc., 61
Fresh America Corporation, 20
Fresh Choice, Inc., 20
Fresh Enterprises, Inc., 66
Fresh Express Inc., 88
Fresh Foods, Inc., 29
FreshDirect, LLC, 84
Fretter, Inc., 10
Fried, Frank, Harris, Shriver & Jacobson, 35
Friedman's Inc., 29
Friedman, Billings, Ramsey Group, Inc., 53
Friendly Ice Cream Corporation, 30; 72 (upd.)
Frigidaire Home Products, 22
Frisch's Restaurants, Inc., 35; 92 (upd.)
Frito-Lay North America, 32; 73 (upd.)
Fritz Companies, Inc., 12
Frontier Airlines Holdings Inc., 22; 84 (upd.)
Frontier Corp., 16
Frontier Natural Products Co-Op, 82
Frost & Sullivan, Inc., 53
Frozen Food Express Industries, Inc., 20
Fruehauf Corporation, I
Fruit of the Loom, Inc., 8; 25 (upd.)
Fruth Pharmacy, Inc., 66
Fry's Electronics, Inc., 68
Frymaster Corporation, 27
FSI International, Inc., 17
FTI Consulting, Inc., 77
FTP Software, Inc., 20
Fubu, 29
Fuel Tech, Inc., 85
FuelCell Energy, Inc., 75
Fujitsu-ICL Systems Inc., 11
Fulbright & Jaworski L.L.P., 47
Funco, Inc., 20
Fuqua Enterprises, Inc., 17
Fuqua Industries, Inc., I
Furmanite Corporation, 92
Furniture Brands International, Inc., 39 (upd.)
Furon Company, 28
Furr's Restaurant Group, Inc., 53
Furr's Supermarkets, Inc., 28
Future Now, Inc., 12
G&K Services, Inc., 16
G-III Apparel Group, Ltd., 22
G. Heileman Brewing Company Inc., I
G. Leblanc Corporation, 55
G.A.F., I
G.D. Searle & Company, I; 12 (upd.); 34 (upd.)
G.I. Joe's, Inc., 30
G.S. Blodgett Corporation, 15
Gabelli Asset Management Inc., 30
Gables Residential Trust, 49
Gadzooks, Inc., 18
GAF Corporation, 22 (upd.)
Gage Marketing Group, 26
Gaiam, Inc., 41
Gainsco, Inc., 22
Galardi Group, Inc., 72
Galaxy Nutritional Foods, Inc., 58
Gale International Llc, 93
Galey & Lord, Inc., 20; 66 (upd.)
The Gallup Organization, 37
Galyan's Trading Company, Inc., 47
The Gambrinus Company, 40
GameStop Corp., 69 (upd.)
Gaming Partners International Corporation, 93
Gander Mountain Company, 20; 90 (upd.)
Gannett Company, Inc., IV; 7 (upd.); 30 (upd.); 66 (upd.)
Gantos, Inc., 17
The Gap, Inc., V; 18 (upd.); 55 (upd.)
Garan, Inc., 16; 64 (upd.)
Garden Fresh Restaurant Corporation, 31
Garden Ridge Corporation, 27
Gardenburger, Inc., 33; 76 (upd.)
Gardner Denver, Inc., 49
Gart Sports Company, 24
Gartner, Inc., 21; 94 (upd.)
Garst Seed Company, Inc., 86
GateHouse Media, Inc., 91
The Gates Corporation, 9
Gateway, Inc., 10; 27 (upd.); 63 (upd.)
The Gatorade Company, 82
GATX Corporation, 6; 25 (upd.)
Gaylord Container Corporation, 8
Gaylord Entertainment Company, 11; 36 (upd.)
GC Companies, Inc., 25
GE Aircraft Engines, 9
GE Capital Aviation Services, 36
Geerlings & Wade, Inc., 45
Geffen Records Inc., 26
Gehl Company, 19
GEICO Corporation, 10; 40 (upd.)
Geiger Bros., 60
Gemini Sound Products Corporation, 58
Gen-Probe Incorporated 79
GenCorp Inc., 8; 9
Genentech, Inc., I; 8 (upd.); 32 (upd.); 75 (upd.)
General Atomics, 57
General Bearing Corporation, 45
General Binding Corporation, 10; 73 (upd.)
General Cable Corporation, 40
The General Chemical Group Inc., 37
General Cigar Holdings, Inc., 66 (upd.)
General Cinema Corporation, I
General DataComm Industries, Inc., 14
General Dynamics Corporation, I; 10 (upd.); 40 (upd.); 88 (upd.)
General Electric Company, II; 12 (upd.); 34 (upd.); 63 (upd.)
General Employment Enterprises, Inc., 87
General Growth Properties, Inc., 57
General Host Corporation, 12
General Housewares Corporation, 16
General Instrument Corporation, 10
General Maritime Corporation, 59
General Mills, Inc., II; 10 (upd.); 36 (upd.); 85 (upd.)
General Motors Corporation, I; 10 (upd.); 36 (upd.); 64 (upd.)
General Nutrition Companies, Inc., 11; 29 (upd.)
General Public Utilities Corporation, V
General Re Corporation, III; 24 (upd.)
General Signal Corporation, 9
General Tire, Inc., 8
Genesco Inc., 17; 84 (upd.)
Genesee & Wyoming Inc., 27
Genesis Health Ventures, Inc., 18
Genesis Microchip Inc., 82
Genetics Institute, Inc., 8
Geneva Steel, 7
Genmar Holdings, Inc., 45
Genovese Drug Stores, Inc., 18
GenRad, Inc., 24

Gentex Corporation, 26
Gentiva Health Services, Inc. 79
Genuardi's Family Markets, Inc., 35
Genuine Parts Company, 9; 45 (upd.)
Genzyme Corporation, 13; 38 (upd.); 77 (upd.)
The Geon Company, 11
George A. Hormel and Company, II
The George F. Cram Company, Inc., 55
George P. Johnson Company, 60
George S. May International Company, 55
Georgia Gulf Corporation, 9; 61 (upd.)
Georgia-Pacific Corporation, IV; 9 (upd.); 47 (upd.)
Geotek Communications Inc., 21
Gerald Stevens, Inc., 37
Gerber Products Company, 7; 21 (upd.)
Gerber Scientific, Inc., 12; 84 (upd.)
German American Bancorp, 41
Getty Images, Inc., 31
Gevity HR, Inc., 63
GF Health Products, Inc., 82
Ghirardelli Chocolate Company, 30
Giant Cement Holding, Inc., 23
Giant Eagle, Inc., 86
Giant Food LLC, II; 22 (upd.); 83 (upd.)
Giant Industries, Inc., 19; 61 (upd.)
Gibraltar Steel Corporation, 37
Gibson Greetings, Inc., 12
Gibson Guitar Corp., 16
Gibson, Dunn & Crutcher LLP, 36
Giddings & Lewis, Inc., 10
Gilbane, Inc., 34
Gilead Sciences, Inc., 54
Gillett Holdings, Inc., 7
The Gillette Company, III; 20 (upd.); 68 (upd.)
Gilman & Ciocia, Inc., 72
Girl Scouts of the USA, 35
The Gitano Group, Inc., 8
Glacier Bancorp, Inc., 35
Glacier Water Services, Inc., 47
Glamis Gold, Ltd., 54
Glazer's Wholesale Drug Company, Inc., 82
Gleason Corporation, 24
The Glidden Company, 8
Global Berry Farms LLC, 62
Global Crossing Ltd., 32
Global Hyatt Corporation, 75 (upd.)
Global Imaging Systems, Inc., 73
Global Industries, Ltd., 37
Global Marine Inc., 9
Global Outdoors, Inc., 49
Global Payments Inc., 91
Global Power Equipment Group Inc., 52
GlobalSantaFe Corporation, 48 (upd.)
Gluek Brewing Company, 75
GM Hughes Electronics Corporation, II
GMH Communities Trust, 87
Godfather's Pizza Incorporated, 25
Godiva Chocolatier, Inc., 64
Goetze's Candy Company, Inc., 87
Gold Kist Inc., 17; 26 (upd.)
Gold'n Plump Poultry, 54
Gold's Gym International, Inc., 71
Golden Belt Manufacturing Co., 16
Golden Books Family Entertainment, Inc., 28
Golden Corral Corporation, 10; 66 (upd.)
Golden Enterprises, Inc., 26
Golden Krust Caribbean Bakery, Inc., 68
Golden State Foods Corporation, 32
Golden State Vintners, Inc., 33
Golden West Financial Corporation, 47
The Goldman Sachs Group Inc., II; 20 (upd.); 51 (upd.)
Golin/Harris International, Inc., 88
The Golub Corporation, 26
Gonnella Baking Company, 40
The Good Guys, Inc., 10; 30 (upd.)
Good Humor-Breyers Ice Cream Company, 14
Goodby Silverstein & Partners, Inc., 75
Goodman Holding Company, 42
GoodMark Foods, Inc., 26
Goodrich Corporation, 46 (upd.)
GoodTimes Entertainment Ltd., 48
Goodwill Industries International, Inc., 16; 66 (upd.)
Goody Products, Inc., 12
Goody's Family Clothing, Inc., 20; 64 (upd.)
The Goodyear Tire & Rubber Company, V; 20 (upd.); 75 (upd.)
Google, Inc., 50
Gordmans, Inc., 74
Gordon Biersch Brewery Restaurant Group, Inc., 93
Gordon Food Service Inc., 8; 39 (upd.)
The Gorman-Rupp Company, 18; 57 (upd.)
Gorton's, 13
Goss Holdings, Inc., 43
Gottschalks, Inc., 18; 91 (upd.)
Gould Electronics, Inc., 14
Gould Paper Corporation, 82
Goulds Pumps Inc., 24
Goya Foods Inc., 22; 91 (upd.)
GP Strategies Corporation, 64 (upd.)
GPU, Inc., 27 (upd.)
Graco Inc., 19; 67 (upd.)
Graeter's Manufacturing Company, 86
Graham Corporation, 62
Graham Packaging Holdings Company, 87
GranCare, Inc., 14
Grand Casinos, Inc., 20
Grand Piano & Furniture Company, 72
The Grand Union Company, 7; 28 (upd.)
Granite Broadcasting Corporation, 42
Granite City Food & Brewery Ltd., 94
Granite Construction Incorporated, 61
Granite Industries of Vermont, Inc., 73
Granite Rock Company, 26
Granite State Bankshares, Inc., 37
Grant Prideco, Inc., 57
Grant Thornton International, 57
Graphic Industries Inc., 25
Gray Communications Systems, Inc., 24
Graybar Electric Company, Inc., 54
Great American Management and Investment, Inc., 8
The Great Atlantic & Pacific Tea Company, Inc., II; 16 (upd.); 55 (upd.)
Great Harvest Bread Company, 44
Great Lakes Bancorp, 8
Great Lakes Chemical Corporation, I; 14 (upd.)
Great Lakes Dredge & Dock Company, 69
Great Plains Energy Incorporated, 65 (upd.)
Great Western Financial Corporation, 10
Great White Shark Enterprises, Inc., 89
Great Wolf Resorts, Inc., 91
Greatbatch Inc., 72
Grede Foundries, Inc., 38
The Green Bay Packers, Inc., 32
Green Mountain Coffee, Inc., 31
Green Tree Financial Corporation, 11
Greenberg Traurig, LLP, 65
The Greenbrier Companies, 19
Greene, Tweed & Company, 55
GreenPoint Financial Corp., 28
Greenwood Mills, Inc., 14
Greg Manning Auctions, Inc., 60
Greif Inc., 15; 66 (upd.)
Grey Advertising, Inc., 6
Grey Global Group Inc., 66 (upd.)
Grey Wolf, Inc., 43
Greyhound Lines, Inc., I; 32 (upd.)
Griffin Industries, Inc., 70
Griffin Land & Nurseries, Inc., 43
Griffon Corporation, 34
Grill Concepts, Inc., 74
Grinnell Corp., 13
Grist Mill Company, 15
Gristede's Foods Inc., 31; 68 (upd.)
Grolier Incorporated, 16; 43 (upd.)
Grossman's Inc., 13
Ground Round, Inc., 21
Group 1 Automotive, Inc., 52
Group Health Cooperative, 41
Grow Biz International, Inc., 18
Grow Group Inc., 12
GROWMARK, Inc., 88
Grubb & Ellis Company, 21
Grumman Corporation, I; 11 (upd.)
Grunau Company Inc., 90
Gruntal & Co., L.L.C., 20
Gryphon Holdings, Inc., 21
GSC Enterprises, Inc., 86
GSD&M Advertising, 44
GSD&M's Idea City, 90
GSI Commerce, Inc., 67
GT Bicycles, 26
GT Interactive Software, 31
GTE Corporation, V; 15 (upd.)
GTSI Corp., 57
Guangzhou Pearl River Piano Group Ltd., 49
Guardian Industries Corp., 87
Guccio Gucci, S.p.A., 15
Guess, Inc., 15; 68 (upd.)
Guest Supply, Inc., 18
Guida-Seibert Dairy Company, 84
Guidant Corporation, 58
Guilford Mills Inc., 8; 40 (upd.)
Guitar Center, Inc., 29; 68 (upd.)
Guittard Chocolate Company, 55
Gulf & Western Inc., I
Gulf Island Fabrication, Inc., 44

Gulf States Utilities Company, 6
GulfMark Offshore, Inc., 49
Gulfstream Aerospace Corporation, 7; 28 (upd.)
Gunite Corporation, 51
The Gunlocke Company, 23
Guardsmark, L.L.C., 77
Guthy-Renker Corporation, 32
Guttenplan's Frozen Dough Inc., 88
Gwathmey Siegel & Associates Architects LLC, 26
Gymboree Corporation, 15; 69 (upd.)
H&R Block, Inc., 9; 29 (upd.); 82 (upd.)
H.B. Fuller Company, 8; 32 (upd.); 75 (upd.)
H. Betti Industries Inc., 88
H.D. Vest, Inc., 46
H.E. Butt Grocery Company, 13; 32 (upd.); 85 (upd.)
H.F. Ahmanson & Company, II; 10 (upd.)
H.J. Heinz Company, II; 11 (upd.); 36 (upd.)
H.J. Russell & Company, 66
H.M. Payson & Co., 69
The H.W. Wilson Company, 66
Ha-Lo Industries, Inc., 27
The Haartz Corporation, 94
Habersham Bancorp, 25
Habitat for Humanity International, 36
Hach Co., 18
Hadco Corporation, 24
Haeger Industries Inc., 88
Haemonetics Corporation, 20
Haggar Corporation, 19; 78 (upd.)
Haggen Inc., 38
Hahn Automotive Warehouse, Inc., 24
Haights Cross Communications, Inc., 84
The Hain Celestial Group, Inc., 27; 43 (upd.)
Hair Club For Men Ltd., 90
HAL Inc., 9
Hale-Halsell Company, 60
Half Price Books, Records, Magazines Inc., 37
Hall, Kinion & Associates, Inc., 52
Halliburton Company, III; 25 (upd.); 55 (upd.)
Hallmark Cards, Inc., IV; 16 (upd.); 40 (upd.); 87 (upd.)
Hamilton Beach/Proctor-Silex Inc., 17
Hammacher Schlemmer & Company Inc., 21; 72 (upd.)
Hamot Health Foundation, 91
Hampshire Group Ltd., 82
Hampton Affiliates, Inc., 77
Hampton Industries, Inc., 20
Hancock Fabrics, Inc., 18
Hancock Holding Company, 15
Handleman Company, 15; 86 (upd.)
Handspring Inc., 49
Handy & Harman, 23
Hanger Orthopedic Group, Inc., 41
Hanmi Financial Corporation, 66
Hanna Andersson Corp., 49
Hanna-Barbera Cartoons Inc., 23
Hannaford Bros. Co., 12
Hanover Compressor Company, 59
Hanover Direct, Inc., 36
Hanover Foods Corporation, 35
Hansen Natural Corporation, 31; 76 (upd.)
Hanson Building Materials America Inc., 60
Happy Kids Inc., 30
Harbert Corporation, 14
Harbison-Walker Refractories Company, 24
Harbour Group Industries, Inc., 90
Harcourt Brace and Co., 12
Harcourt Brace Jovanovich, Inc., IV
Harcourt General, Inc., 20 (upd.)
Hard Rock Cafe International, Inc., 12; 32 (upd.)
Harding Lawson Associates Group, Inc., 16
Hardinge Inc., 25
Harkins Amusement, 94
Harland Clarke Holdings Corporation, 94 (upd.)
Harlem Globetrotters International, Inc., 61
Harley-Davidson Inc., 7; 25 (upd.)
Harleysville Group Inc., 37
Harman International Industries Inc., 15
Harmon Industries, Inc., 25
Harmonic Inc., 43
Harnischfeger Industries, Inc., 8; 38 (upd.)
Harold's Stores, Inc., 22
Harper Group Inc., 17
HarperCollins Publishers, 15
Harpo Inc., 28; 66 (upd.)
Harrah's Entertainment, Inc., 16; 43 (upd.)
Harris Corporation, II; 20 (upd.); 78 (upd.)
Harris Interactive Inc., 41; 92 (upd.)
The Harris Soup Company (Harry's Fresh Foods), 92
Harris Teeter Inc., 23; 72 (upd.)
Harry London Candies, Inc., 70
Harry N. Abrams, Inc., 58
Harry Winston Inc., 45
Harry's Farmers Market Inc., 23
Harsco Corporation, 8
Harte-Hanks, Inc., 17; 63 (upd.)
Hartmarx Corporation, 8; 32 (upd.)
The Hartz Mountain Corporation, 12; 46 (upd.)
Harveys Casino Resorts, 27
Harza Engineering Company, 14
Hasbro, Inc., III; 16 (upd.); 43 (upd.)
Haskel International, Inc., 59
Hastings Entertainment, Inc., 29
Hastings Manufacturing Company, 56
Hauser, Inc., 46
Haverty Furniture Companies, Inc., 31
Hawaiian Airlines, Inc., 22 (upd.)
Hawaiian Electric Industries, Inc., 9
Hawk Corporation, 59
Hawkeye Holdings LLC, 89
Hawkins Chemical, Inc., 16
Haworth Inc., 8; 39 (upd.)
Hay House, Inc., 93
Hayes Corporation, 24
Hayes Lemmerz International, Inc., 27
Haynes International, Inc., 88
Hazelden Foundation, 28
HCA - The Healthcare Company, 35 (upd.)
HCI Direct, Inc., 55
HDOS Enterprises, 72
HDR Inc., 48
Headwaters Incorporated, 56
Headway Corporate Resources, Inc., 40
Health Care & Retirement Corporation, 22
Health Communications, Inc., 72
Health Management Associates, Inc., 56
Health O Meter Products Inc., 14
Health Risk Management, Inc., 24
Health Systems International, Inc., 11
HealthExtras, Inc., 75
HealthMarkets, Inc., 88 (upd.)
HealthSouth Corporation, 14; 33 (upd.)
Healthtex, Inc., 17
The Hearst Corporation, IV; 19 (upd.); 46 (upd.)
Heartland Express, Inc., 18
The Heat Group, 53
Hechinger Company, 12
Hecla Mining Company, 20
Heekin Can Inc., 13
Heelys, Inc., 87
Heery International, Inc., 58
HEICO Corporation, 30
Heidrick & Struggles International, Inc., 28
Heilig-Meyers Company, 14; 40 (upd.)
Helen of Troy Corporation, 18
Helene Curtis Industries, Inc., 8; 28 (upd.)
Helix Energy Solutions Group, Inc., 81
Heller, Ehrman, White & McAuliffe, 41
Helmerich & Payne, Inc., 18
Helmsley Enterprises, Inc., 9; 39 (upd.)
Helzberg Diamonds, 40
Hendrick Motorsports, Inc., 89
Henkel Manco Inc., 22
The Henley Group, Inc., III
Henry Crown and Company, 91
Henry Dreyfuss Associates LLC, 88
Henry Ford Health System, 84
Henry Modell & Company Inc., 32
Henry Schein, Inc., 31; 70 (upd.)
Hensel Phelps Construction Company, 72
Hensley & Company, 64
Herald Media, Inc., 91
Herbalife International, Inc., 17; 41 (upd.)
Hercules Inc., I; 22 (upd.); 66 (upd.)
Hercules Technology Growth Capital, Inc., 87
Herley Industries, Inc., 33
Herman Goelitz, Inc., 28
Herman Miller, Inc., 8; 77 (upd.)
Herr Foods Inc., 84
Herschend Family Entertainment Corporation, 73
Hershey Foods Corporation, II; 15 (upd.); 51 (upd.)
The Hertz Corporation, 9; 33 (upd.)
Heska Corporation, 39

Heublein, Inc., I
Hewitt Associates, Inc., 77
Hewlett-Packard Company, III; 6 (upd.); 28 (upd.); 50 (upd.)
Hexcel Corporation, 28
Hibbett Sporting Goods, Inc., 26; 70 (upd.)
Hibernia Corporation, 37
Hickory Farms, Inc., 17
HickoryTech Corporation, 92
High Falls Brewing Company LLC, 74
Highmark Inc., 27
Highsmith Inc., 60
Hilb, Rogal & Hobbs Company, 77
Hildebrandt International, 29
Hill's Pet Nutrition, Inc., 27
Hillenbrand Industries, Inc., 10; 75 (upd.)
Hillerich & Bradsby Company, Inc., 51
The Hillhaven Corporation, 14
Hills Stores Company, 13
Hilton Hotels Corporation, III; 19 (upd.); 62 (upd.)
Hines Horticulture, Inc., 49
Hispanic Broadcasting Corporation, 35
Hitchiner Manufacturing Co., Inc., 23
HMI Industries, Inc., 17
HNI Corporation, 74 (upd.)
Ho-Chunk Inc., 61
HOB Entertainment, Inc., 37
Hobby Lobby Stores Inc., 80
Hobie Cat Company, 94
Hodgson Mill, Inc., 88
Hoechst Celanese Corporation, 13
Hoenig Group Inc., 41
Hoffman Corporation 78
Hogan & Hartson L.L.P., 44
HOK Group, Inc., 59
Holberg Industries, Inc., 36
Holiday Inns, Inc., III
Holiday Retirement Corp., 87
Holiday RV Superstores, Incorporated, 26
Holland & Knight LLP, 60
Holland Burgerville USA, 44
The Holland Group, Inc., 82
Hollander Home Fashions Corp., 67
Holley Performance Products Inc., 52
Hollinger International Inc., 24
Holly Corporation, 12
Hollywood Casino Corporation, 21
Hollywood Entertainment Corporation, 25
Hollywood Media Corporation, 58
Hollywood Park, Inc., 20
Holme Roberts & Owen LLP, 28
Holnam Inc., 8; 39 (upd.)
Holophane Corporation, 19
Holson Burnes Group, Inc., 14
Holt and Bugbee Company, 66
Holt's Cigar Holdings, Inc., 42
Homasote Company, 72
Home Box Office Inc., 7; 23 (upd.); 76 (upd.)
The Home Depot, Inc., V; 18 (upd.)
The Home Insurance Company, III
Home Interiors & Gifts, Inc., 55
Home Products International, Inc., 55
Home Properties of New York, Inc., 42
Home Shopping Network, Inc., V; 25 (upd.)
HomeBase, Inc., 33 (upd.)
Homestake Mining Company, 12; 38 (upd.)
Hometown Auto Retailers, Inc., 44
HomeVestors of America, Inc., 77
HON INDUSTRIES Inc., 13
Honda Motor Company Limited, I; 10 (upd.); 29 (upd.)
Honeywell Inc., II; 12 (upd.); 50 (upd.)
Hooker Furniture Corporation, 80
Hooper Holmes, Inc., 22
Hooters of America, Inc., 18; 69 (upd.)
The Hoover Company, 12; 40 (upd.)
HOP, LLC, 80
Hops Restaurant Bar and Brewery, 46
Horace Mann Educators Corporation, 22; 90 (upd.)
Horizon Organic Holding Corporation, 37
Hormel Foods Corporation, 18 (upd.); 54 (upd.)
Horsehead Industries, Inc., 51
Horseshoe Gaming Holding Corporation, 62
Horton Homes, Inc., 25
Horween Leather Company, 83
Hospira, Inc., 71
Hospital Central Services, Inc., 56
Hospital Corporation of America, III
Hospitality Franchise Systems, Inc., 11
Hospitality Worldwide Services, Inc., 26
Hoss's Steak and Sea House Inc., 68
Host America Corporation 79
Hot Stuff Foods, 85
Hot Topic, Inc., 33; 86 (upd.)
Houchens Industries Inc., 51
Houghton Mifflin Company, 10; 36 (upd.)
House of Fabrics, Inc., 21
Household International, Inc., II; 21 (upd.)
Houston Industries Incorporated, V
Hovnanian Enterprises, Inc., 29; 89 (upd.)
Howard Hughes Medical Institute, 39
Howard Johnson International, Inc., 17; 72 (upd.)
Howmet Corp., 12
HSN, 64 (upd.)
Hub Group, Inc., 38
Hub International Limited, 89
Hubbard Broadcasting Inc., 24; 79 (upd.)
Hubbell Inc., 9; 31 (upd.); 76 (upd.)
Hudson Foods Inc., 13
Hudson River Bancorp, Inc., 41
Huffy Corporation, 7; 30 (upd.)
Hughes Electronics Corporation, 25
Hughes Hubbard & Reed LLP, 44
Hughes Markets, Inc., 22
Hughes Supply, Inc., 14
Hulman & Company, 44
Humana Inc., III; 24 (upd.)
The Humane Society of the United States, 54
Hungarian Telephone and Cable Corp., 75
Hungry Howie's Pizza and Subs, Inc., 25
Hunt Consolidated, Inc., 27 (upd.)
Hunt Manufacturing Company, 12
Hunt Oil Company, 7
Hunt-Wesson, Inc., 17
Hunter Fan Company, 13
Huntington Bancshares Incorporated, 11; 87 (upd.)
Huntington Learning Centers, Inc., 55
Hunton & Williams, 35
Huntsman Chemical Corporation, 8
Huron Consulting Group Inc., 87
Hutchinson Technology Incorporated, 18; 63 (upd.)
Huttig Building Products, Inc., 73
Hvide Marine Incorporated, 22
Hy-Vee, Inc., 36
Hyatt Corporation, III; 16 (upd.)
Hyde Athletic Industries, Inc., 17
Hydril Company, 46
Hypercom Corporation, 27
Hyperion Software Corporation, 22
Hyperion Solutions Corporation, 76
Hyster Company, 17
I.C. Isaacs & Company, 31
Iams Company, 26
IBERIABANK Corporation, 37
IBP, Inc., II; 21 (upd.)
IC Industries, Inc., I
ICF International, Inc., 28; 94 (upd.)
ICN Pharmaceuticals, Inc., 52
Icon Health & Fitness, Inc., 38
Idaho Power Company, 12
IDB Communications Group, Inc., 11
Idearc Inc., 90
Identix Inc., 44
IDEO Inc., 65
IDEXX Laboratories, Inc., 23
IDG Books Worldwide, Inc., 27
IdraPrince, Inc., 76
IDT Corporation, 34
IDX Systems Corporation, 64
IEC Electronics Corp., 42
Igloo Products Corp., 21
IHOP Corporation, 17; 58 (upd.)
IHS Inc. 78
IKON Office Solutions, Inc., 50
Il Fornaio (America) Corporation, 27
Ilitch Holdings Inc., 37; 86 (upd.)
Illinois Bell Telephone Company, 14
Illinois Central Corporation, 11
Illinois Power Company, 6
Illinois Tool Works Inc., III; 22 (upd.); 81 (upd.)
Illumina, Inc., 93
ILX Resorts Incorporated, 65
Image Entertainment, Inc., 94
Imagine Entertainment, 91
Imagine Foods, Inc., 50
Imation Corporation, 20
IMC Fertilizer Group, Inc., 8
ImClone Systems Inc., 58
IMCO Recycling, Incorporated, 32
IMG 78
Immucor, Inc., 81
Immunex Corporation, 14; 50 (upd.)
Imo Industries Inc., 7; 27 (upd.)
IMPATH Inc., 45
Imperial Holly Corporation, 12

Imperial Industries, Inc., 81
Imperial Sugar Company, 32 (upd.)
IMS Health, Inc., 57
In Focus Systems, Inc., 22
In-N-Out Burgers Inc., 19; 74 (upd.)
In-Sink-Erator, 66
InaCom Corporation, 13
Inamed Corporation 79
Incyte Genomics, Inc., 52
Indel Inc. 78
Indiana Bell Telephone Company, Incorporated, 14
Indiana Energy, Inc., 27
Indianapolis Motor Speedway Corporation, 46
Indus International Inc., 70
Industrial Services of America, Inc., 46
Infinity Broadcasting Corporation, 11; 48 (upd.)
InFocus Corporation, 92
Information Access Company, 17
Information Builders, Inc., 22
Information Holdings Inc., 47
Information Resources, Inc., 10
Informix Corporation, 10; 30 (upd.)
InfoSonics Corporation, 81
InfoSpace, Inc., 91
Ingalls Shipbuilding, Inc., 12
Ingersoll-Rand Company Ltd., III; 15 (upd.); 55 (upd.)
Ingles Markets, Inc., 20
Ingram Industries, Inc., 11; 49 (upd.)
Ingram Micro Inc., 52
Initial Security, 64
Inktomi Corporation, 45
Inland Container Corporation, 8
Inland Steel Industries, Inc., IV; 19 (upd.)
Innovative Solutions & Support, Inc., 85
Innovo Group Inc., 83
Input/Output, Inc., 73
Inserra Supermarkets, 25
Insight Enterprises, Inc., 18
Insilco Corporation, 16
Insituform Technologies, Inc., 83
Inso Corporation, 26
Instinet Corporation, 34
Insurance Auto Auctions, Inc., 23
Integra LifeSciences Holdings Corporation, 87
Integrated BioPharma, Inc., 83
Integrated Defense Technologies, Inc., 54
Integrity Inc., 44
Intel Corporation, II; 10 (upd.); 36 (upd.); 75 (upd.)
IntelliCorp, Inc., 45
Intelligent Electronics, Inc., 6
Inter Parfums Inc., 35; 86 (upd.)
Inter-Regional Financial Group, Inc., 15
Interbrand Corporation, 70
Interco Incorporated, III
InterDigital Communications Corporation, 61
Interep National Radio Sales Inc., 35
Interface, Inc., 8; 29 (upd.); 76 (upd.)
Intergraph Corporation, 6; 24 (upd.)
The Interlake Corporation, 8
Intermec Technologies Corporation, 72
INTERMET Corporation, 32, 77 (upd.)
Intermix Media, Inc., 83
Intermountain Health Care, Inc., 27
International Airline Support Group, Inc., 55
International Brotherhood of Teamsters, 37
International Business Machines Corporation, III; 6 (upd.); 30 (upd.); 63 (upd.)
International Controls Corporation, 10
International Creative Management, Inc., 43
International Dairy Queen, Inc., 10; 39 (upd.)
International Data Group, Inc., 7; 25 (upd.)
International Family Entertainment Inc., 13
International Flavors & Fragrances Inc., 9; 38 (upd.)
International Game Technology, 10; 41 (upd.)
International Lease Finance Corporation, 48
International Management Group, 18
International Multifoods Corporation, 7; 25 (upd.)
International Paper Company, IV; 15 (upd.); 47 (upd.)
International Profit Associates, Inc., 87
International Rectifier Corporation, 31; 71 (upd.)
International Shipbreaking Ltd. L.L.C., 67
International Shipholding Corporation, Inc., 27
International Speedway Corporation, 19; 74 (upd.)
International Telephone & Telegraph Corporation, I; 11 (upd.)
International Total Services, Inc., 37
Interpool, Inc., 92
The Interpublic Group of Companies, Inc., I; 22 (upd.); 75 (upd.)
Interscope Music Group, 31
Intersil Corporation, 93
Interstate Bakeries Corporation, 12; 38 (upd.)
Interstate Hotels & Resorts Inc., 58
InterVideo, Inc., 85
Intevac, Inc., 92
Intimate Brands, Inc., 24
Intrado Inc., 63
Intuit Inc., 14; 33 (upd.); 73 (upd.)
Intuitive Surgical, Inc. 79
Invacare Corporation, 11; 47 (upd.)
inVentiv Health, Inc., 81
Inverness Medical Innovations, Inc., 63
Invitrogen Corporation, 52
Invivo Corporation, 52
Iomega Corporation, 21
Ionatron, Inc., 85
Ionics, Incorporated, 52
Iowa Telecommunications Services, Inc., 85
IPALCO Enterprises, Inc., 6
Ipsen International Inc., 72
Irex Contracting Group, 90
iRobot Corporation, 83
Iron Mountain, Inc., 33
Irvin Feld & Kenneth Feld Productions, Inc., 15
Irwin Financial Corporation, 77
The Island ECN, Inc., 48
Isle of Capri Casinos, Inc., 41
Ispat Inland Inc., 40 (upd.)
ITC Holdings Corp., 75
Itel Corporation, 9
Items International Airwalk Inc., 17
Itron, Inc., 64
ITT Educational Services, Inc., 33; 76 (upd.)
ITT Sheraton Corporation, III
i2 Technologies, Inc., 87
Ivar's, Inc., 86
IVAX Corporation, 11; 55 (upd.)
IVC Industries, Inc., 45
iVillage Inc., 46
Iwerks Entertainment, Inc., 34
IXC Communications, Inc., 29
J & J Snack Foods Corporation, 24
J&R Electronics Inc., 26
J. & W. Seligman & Co. Inc., 61
J. Alexander's Corporation, 65
J. Baker, Inc., 31
J. Crew Group. Inc., 12; 34 (upd.); 88 (upd.)
J. C. Penney Company, Inc., V; 18 (upd.); 43 (upd.); 91 (upd.)
J. D'Addario & Company, Inc., 48
The J. Jill Group, Inc., 35; 90 (upd.)
J.A. Jones, Inc., 16
J.B. Hunt Transport Services Inc., 12
J.D. Edwards & Company, 14
J.D. Power and Associates, 32
J.F. Shea Co., Inc., 55
J.H. Findorff and Son, Inc., 60
J.I. Case Company, 10
J.J. Keller & Associates, Inc., 81
J.L. Hammett Company, 72
The J. M. Smucker Company, 11; 87 (upd.)
J.P. Morgan Chase & Co., II; 30 (upd.); 38 (upd.)
J.R. Simplot Company, 16; 60 (upd.)
J. W. Pepper and Son Inc., 86
Jabil Circuit, Inc., 36; 88 (upd.)
Jack Henry and Associates, Inc., 17; 94 (upd.)
Jack in the Box Inc., 89 (upd.)
Jack Morton Worldwide, 88
Jack Schwartz Shoes, Inc., 18
Jackpot Enterprises Inc., 21
Jackson Hewitt, Inc., 48
Jackson National Life Insurance Company, 8
Jacmar Companies, 87
Jaco Electronics, Inc., 30
Jacob Leinenkugel Brewing Company, 28
Jacobs Engineering Group Inc., 6; 26 (upd.)
Jacobson Stores Inc., 21
Jacor Communications, Inc., 23
Jacuzzi Brands Inc., 76 (upd.)
Jacuzzi Inc., 23
JAKKS Pacific, Inc., 52
Jalate Inc., 25
Jamba Juice Company, 47

James Avery Craftsman, Inc., 76
James Original Coney Island Inc., 84
James River Corporation of Virginia, IV
Jani-King International, Inc., 85
JanSport, Inc., 70
Janus Capital Group Inc., 57
Jarden Corporation, 93 (upd.)
Jason Incorporated, 23
Jay Jacobs, Inc., 15
Jayco Inc., 13
Jays Foods, Inc., 90
Jazz Basketball Investors, Inc., 55
Jazzercise, Inc., 45
JB Oxford Holdings, Inc., 32
JDS Uniphase Corporation, 34
JE Dunn Construction Group, Inc., 85
Jean-Georges Enterprises L.L.C., 75
Jefferies Group, Inc., 25
Jefferson-Pilot Corporation, 11; 29 (upd.)
Jel Sert Company, 90
Jeld-Wen, Inc., 45
Jelly Belly Candy Company, 76
Jenkens & Gilchrist, P.C., 65
Jennie-O Turkey Store, Inc., 76
Jennifer Convertibles, Inc., 31
Jenny Craig, Inc., 10; 29 (upd.); 92 (upd.)
Jeppesen Sanderson, Inc., 92
Jerry's Famous Deli Inc., 24
Jersey Mike's Franchise Systems, Inc., 83
Jervis B. Webb Company, 24
JetBlue Airways Corporation, 44
Jetro Cash & Carry Enterprises Inc., 38
Jewett-Cameron Trading Company, Ltd., 89
JG Industries, Inc., 15
Jillian's Entertainment Holdings, Inc., 40
Jim Beam Brands Worldwide, Inc., 14; 58 (upd.)
The Jim Henson Company, 23
Jitney-Jungle Stores of America, Inc., 27
JLG Industries, Inc., 52
JLM Couture, Inc., 64
JMB Realty Corporation, IV
Jo-Ann Stores, Inc., 72 (upd.)
Jockey International, Inc., 12; 34 (upd.); 77 (upd.)
The Joffrey Ballet of Chicago, The 52
John B. Sanfilippo & Son, Inc., 14
The John D. and Catherine T. MacArthur Foundation, 34
John D. Brush Company Inc., 94
John Frieda Professional Hair Care Inc., 70
John H. Harland Company, 17
John Hancock Financial Services, Inc., III; 42 (upd.)
The John Nuveen Company, 21
John Paul Mitchell Systems, 24
John Q. Hammons Hotels, Inc., 24
John W. Danforth Company, 48
John Wiley & Sons, Inc., 17; 65 (upd.)
Johnny Rockets Group, Inc., 31; 76 (upd.)
Johns Manville Corporation, 64 (upd.)
Johnson & Higgins, 14
Johnson & Johnson, III; 8 (upd.); 36 (upd.); 75 (upd.)
Johnson Controls, Inc., III; 26 (upd.); 59 (upd.)
Johnson Outdoors Inc., 28; 84 (upd.)
Johnson Publishing Company, Inc., 28; 72 (upd.)
Johnsonville Sausage L.L.C., 63
Johnston Industries, Inc., 15
Johnstown America Industries, Inc., 23
Jones Apparel Group, Inc., 11; 39 (upd.)
Jones, Day, Reavis & Pogue, 33
Jones Intercable, Inc., 21
Jones Lang LaSalle Incorporated, 49
Jones Medical Industries, Inc., 24
Jones Soda Co., 69
Jordache Enterprises, Inc., 23
The Jordan Company LP, 70
Jordan Industries, Inc., 36
Jordan-Kitt Music Inc., 86
Jos. A. Bank Clothiers, Inc., 31
Joseph T. Ryerson & Son, Inc., 15
Jostens, Inc., 7; 25 (upd.); 73 (upd.)
JOULÉ Inc., 58
Journal Communications, Inc., 86
Journal Register Company, 29
JPI, 49
JPMorgan Chase & Co., 91 (upd.)
JPS Textile Group, Inc., 28
j2 Global Communications, Inc., 75
Juicy Couture, Inc., 80
The Judge Group, Inc., 51
Juniper Networks, Inc., 43
Juno Lighting, Inc., 30
Juno Online Services, Inc., 38
Jupitermedia Corporation, 75
Just Bagels Manufacturing, Inc., 94
Just Born, Inc., 32
Just For Feet, Inc., 19
Justin Industries, Inc., 19
JWP Inc., 9
JWT Group Inc., I
K & B Inc., 12
K & G Men's Center, Inc., 21
K'Nex Industries, Inc., 52
K-Swiss, Inc., 33; 89 (upd.)
K-tel International, Inc., 21
Kaiser Aluminum Corporation, IV; 84 (upd.)
Kaiser Foundation Health Plan, Inc., 53
Kal Kan Foods, Inc., 22
Kaman Corporation, 12; 42 (upd.)
Kaman Music Corporation, 68
Kampgrounds of America, Inc. 33
Kana Software, Inc., 51
Kansas City Power & Light Company, 6
Kansas City Southern Industries, Inc., 6; 26 (upd.)
The Kansas City Southern Railway Company, 92
Kaplan, Inc., 42; 90 (upd.)
Kar Nut Products Company, 86
Karl Kani Infinity, Inc., 49
Karsten Manufacturing Corporation, 51
Kash n' Karry Food Stores, Inc., 20
Kashi Company, 89
Kasper A.S.L., Ltd., 40
kate spade LLC, 68
Katy Industries, Inc., I; 51 (upd.)
Katz Communications, Inc., 6
Katz Media Group, Inc., 35
Kaufman and Broad Home Corporation, 8
Kaydon Corporation, 18
KB Home, 45 (upd.)
KB Toys, 15; 35 (upd.); 86 (upd.)
Keane, Inc., 56
Keebler Foods Company, 36
The Keith Companies Inc., 54
Keithley Instruments Inc., 16
Kelley Blue Book Company, Inc., 84
Kelley Drye & Warren LLP, 40
Kellogg Brown & Root, Inc., 62 (upd.)
Kellogg Company, II; 13 (upd.); 50 (upd.)
Kellwood Company, 8; 85 (upd.)
Kelly Services Inc., 6; 26 (upd.)
Kelly-Moore Paint Company, Inc., 56
The Kelly-Springfield Tire Company, 8
Kelsey-Hayes Group of Companies, 7; 27 (upd.)
Kemet Corp., 14
Kemper Corporation, III; 15 (upd.)
Ken's Foods, Inc., 88
Kendall International, Inc., 11
Kendall-Jackson Winery, Ltd., 28
Kendle International Inc., 87
Kenetech Corporation, 11
Kenexa Corporation, 87
Kenmore Air Harbor Inc., 65
Kennametal Inc., 68 (upd.)
Kennedy-Wilson, Inc., 60
Kenneth Cole Productions, Inc., 25
Kensey Nash Corporation, 71
Kensington Publishing Corporation, 84
Kent Electronics Corporation, 17
Kentucky Electric Steel, Inc., 31
Kentucky Utilities Company, 6
Kerasotes ShowPlace Theaters LLC, 80
Kerr Group Inc., 24
Kerr-McGee Corporation, IV; 22 (upd.); 68 (upd.)
Ketchum Communications Inc., 6
Kettle Foods Inc., 48
Kewaunee Scientific Corporation, 25
Key Safety Systems, Inc., 63
Key Tronic Corporation, 14
KeyCorp, 8; 93 (upd.)
Keyes Fibre Company, 9
Keys Fitness Products, LP, 83
KeySpan Energy Co., 27
Keystone International, Inc., 11
KFC Corporation, 7; 21 (upd.); 89 (upd.)
Kforce Inc., 71
KI, 57
Kidde, Inc., I
Kiehl's Since 1851, Inc., 52
Lewis Drug Inc., 94
Lifetouch Inc., 86
LifeWise Health Plan of Oregon, Inc., 90
Kikkoman Corporation, 47 (upd.)
Kimball International, Inc., 12; 48 (upd.)
Kimberly-Clark Corporation, III; 16 (upd.); 43 (upd.)
Kimco Realty Corporation, 11
Kinder Morgan, Inc., 45
KinderCare Learning Centers, Inc., 13
Kinetic Concepts, Inc. (KCI), 20

King & Spalding, 23
The King Arthur Flour Company, 31
King Kullen Grocery Co., Inc., 15
King Nut Company, 74
King Pharmaceuticals, Inc., 54
King Ranch, Inc., 14; 60 (upd.)
King World Productions, Inc., 9; 30 (upd.)
Kingston Technology Corporation, 20
Kinko's, Inc., 16; 43 (upd.)
Kinney Shoe Corp., 14
Kinray Inc., 85
Kintera, Inc., 75
Kirby Corporation, 18; 66 (upd.)
Kirkland & Ellis LLP, 65
Kirshenbaum Bond + Partners, Inc., 57
Kit Manufacturing Co., 18
Kitchell Corporation, 14
KitchenAid, 8
Kitty Hawk, Inc., 22
Kiwi International Airlines Inc., 20
KLA-Tencor Corporation, 11; 45 (upd.)
Klasky Csupo Inc. 78
Kleiner, Perkins, Caufield & Byers, 53
Klement's Sausage Company, 61
Kmart Corporation, V; 18 (upd.); 47 (upd.)
Knape & Vogt Manufacturing Company, 17
Knight Ridder, Inc., 67 (upd.)
Knight Trading Group, Inc., 70
Knight Transportation, Inc., 64
Knight-Ridder, Inc., IV; 15 (upd.)
Knoll, Inc., 14; 80 (upd.)
The Knot, Inc., 74
Knott's Berry Farm, 18
Knowledge Learning Corporation, 51
Knowledge Universe, Inc., 54
KnowledgeWare Inc., 9; 31 (upd.)
Koala Corporation, 44
Kobrand Corporation, 82
Koch Enterprises, Inc., 29
Koch Industries, Inc., IV; 20 (upd.); 77 (upd.)
Kohl's Corporation, 9; 30 (upd.); 77 (upd.)
Kohlberg Kravis Roberts & Co., 24; 56 (upd.)
Kohler Company, 7; 32 (upd.)
Kohn Pedersen Fox Associates P.C., 57
The Koll Company, 8
Kollmorgen Corporation, 18
Komag, Inc., 11
Koo Koo Roo, Inc., 25
Kopin Corporation, 80
Koppers Industries, Inc., I; 26 (upd.)
Koret of California, Inc., 62
Korn/Ferry International, 34
Kos Pharmaceuticals, Inc., 63
Koss Corporation, 38
Kraft Foods Inc., II; 7 (upd.); 45 (upd.); 91 (upd.)
KraftMaid Cabinetry, Inc., 72
Kraus-Anderson Companies, Inc., 36; 83 (upd.)
Krause Publications, Inc., 35
Krause's Furniture, Inc., 27
Krispy Kreme Doughnuts, Inc., 21; 61 (upd.)
The Kroger Company, II; 15 (upd.); 65 (upd.)
Kroll Inc., 57
Kronos, Inc., 18
Kruse International, 88
The Krystal Company, 33
K2 Inc., 16; 84 (upd.)
KU Energy Corporation, 11
Kuhlman Corporation, 20
Kulicke and Soffa Industries, Inc., 33; 76 (upd.)
Kurzweil Technologies, Inc., 51
The Kushner-Locke Company, 25
Kyphon Inc., 87
L-3 Communications Holdings, Inc., 48
L. and J.G. Stickley, Inc., 50
L. Luria & Son, Inc., 19
L.A. Darling Company, 92
L.A. Gear, Inc., 8; 32 (upd.)
L.A. T Sportswear, Inc., 26
L.B. Foster Company, 33
L.L. Bean, Inc., 10; 38 (upd.); 91 (upd.)
The L.L. Knickerbocker Co., Inc., 25
L. M. Berry and Company, 80
L.S. Starrett Company, 13; 64 (upd.)
La Choy Food Products Inc., 25
La Madeleine French Bakery & Café, 33
The La Quinta Companies, 11; 42 (upd.)
La-Z-Boy Incorporated, 14; 50 (upd.)
LaBarge Inc., 41
LabOne, Inc., 48
Labor Ready, Inc., 29; 88 (upd.)
Laboratory Corporation of America Holdings, 42 (upd.)
LaBranche & Co. Inc., 37
Lacks Enterprises Inc., 61
Laclede Steel Company, 15
LaCrosse Footwear, Inc., 18; 61 (upd.)
LADD Furniture, Inc., 12
Ladish Co., Inc., 30
Lafarge Corporation, 28
Laidlaw International, Inc., 80
Lakeland Industries, Inc., 45
Lakes Entertainment, Inc., 51
Lakeside Foods, Inc., 89
Lam Research Corporation, 11; 31 (upd.)
Lamar Advertising Company, 27; 70 (upd.)
The Lamaur Corporation, 41
Lamb Weston, Inc., 23
Lamonts Apparel, Inc., 15
The Lamson & Sessions Co., 13; 61 (upd.)
Lancair International, Inc., 67
Lancaster Colony Corporation, 8; 61 (upd.)
Lance, Inc., 14; 41 (upd.)
Lancer Corporation, 21
Land O'Lakes, Inc., II; 21 (upd.); 81 (upd.)
LandAmerica Financial Group, Inc., 85
Landauer, Inc., 51
Landmark Communications, Inc., 12; 55 (upd.)
Landmark Theatre Corporation, 70
Landor Associates, 81
Landry's Restaurants, Inc., 65 (upd.)
Landry's Seafood Restaurants, Inc., 15
Lands' End, Inc., 9; 29 (upd.); 82 (upd.)
Landstar System, Inc., 63
Lane Bryant, Inc., 64
The Lane Co., Inc., 12
Lanier Worldwide, Inc., 75
Lanoga Corporation, 62
Larry Flynt Publishing Inc., 31
Larry H. Miller Group, 29
Las Vegas Sands, Inc., 50
Laserscope, 67
Lason, Inc., 31
Latham & Watkins, 33
Latrobe Brewing Company, 54
Lattice Semiconductor Corp., 16
Lawson Software, 38
Lawter International Inc., 14
Layne Christensen Company, 19
Lazare Kaplan International Inc., 21
Lazy Days RV Center, Inc., 69
LCA-Vision, Inc., 85
LCC International, Inc., 84
LCI International, Inc., 16
LDB Corporation, 53
LDDS-Metro Communications, Inc., 8
LDI Ltd., LLC, 76
Leap Wireless International, Inc., 69
LeapFrog Enterprises, Inc., 54
Lear Corporation, 71 (upd.)
Lear Seating Corporation, 16
Lear Siegler, Inc., I
Learjet Inc., 8; 27 (upd.)
Learning Care Group, Inc., 76 (upd.)
The Learning Company Inc., 24
Learning Tree International Inc., 24
LeaRonal, Inc., 23
Leaseway Transportation Corp., 12
Leatherman Tool Group, Inc., 51
Lebhar-Friedman, Inc., 55
LeBoeuf, Lamb, Greene & MacRae, L.L.P., 29
LECG Corporation, 93
Lechmere Inc., 10
Lechters, Inc., 11; 39 (upd.)
LeCroy Corporation, 41
Lee Apparel Company, Inc., 8
Lee Enterprises Inc., 11; 64 (upd.)
Leeann Chin, Inc., 30
Lefrak Organization Inc., 26
The Legal Aid Society, 48
Legent Corporation, 10
Legg Mason, Inc., 33
Leggett & Platt, Inc., 11; 48 (upd.)
Lehigh Portland Cement Company, 23
Leidy's, Inc., 93
Leiner Health Products Inc., 34
LendingTree, LLC, 93
Lennar Corporation, 11
Lennox International Inc., 8; 28 (upd.)
Lenovo Group Ltd., 80
Lenox, Inc., 12
LensCrafters Inc., 23; 76 (upd.)
Leo Burnett Company Inc., I; 20 (upd.)
The Leona Group LLC, 84
Leprino Foods Company, 28
Les Schwab Tire Centers, 50
Lesco Inc., 19

The Leslie Fay Companies, Inc., 8; 39 (upd.)
Leslie's Poolmart, Inc., 18
Leucadia National Corporation, 11; 71 (upd.)
Leupold & Stevens, Inc., 52
Level 3 Communications, Inc., 67
Levenger Company, 63
Lever Brothers Company, 9
Levi Strauss & Co., V; 16 (upd.)
Levitz Furniture Inc., 15
Levy Restaurants L.P., 26
Lewis Galoob Toys Inc., 16
LEXIS-NEXIS Group, 33
Lexmark International, Inc., 18; 79 (upd.)
LG&E Energy Corporation, 6; 51 (upd.)
Libbey Inc., 49
The Liberty Corporation, 22
Liberty Livewire Corporation, 42
Liberty Media Corporation, 50
Liberty Mutual Holding Company, 59
Liberty Orchards Co., Inc., 89
Liberty Property Trust, 57
Liberty Travel, Inc., 56
Life Care Centers of America Inc., 76
Life is Good, Inc., 80
Life Technologies, Inc., 17
Life Time Fitness, Inc., 66
LifeCell Corporation, 77
Lifeline Systems, Inc., 53
LifeLock, Inc., 91
LifePoint Hospitals, Inc., 69
Lifetime Brands, Inc., 73 (upd.)
Lifetime Entertainment Services, 51
Lifetime Hoan Corporation, 27
Lifeway Foods, Inc., 65
Ligand Pharmaceuticals Incorporated, 47
Lillian Vernon Corporation, 12; 35 (upd.); 92 (upd.)
Lilly Endowment Inc., 70
The Limited, Inc., V; 20 (upd.)
LIN Broadcasting Corp., 9
Lincare Holdings Inc., 43
Lincoln Center for the Performing Arts, Inc., 69
Lincoln Electric Co., 13
Lincoln National Corporation, III; 25 (upd.)
Lincoln Property Company, 8; 54 (upd.)
Lincoln Snacks Company, 24
Lincoln Telephone & Telegraph Company, 14
Lindal Cedar Homes, Inc., 29
Lindsay Manufacturing Co., 20
Linear Technology, Inc., 16
Linens 'n Things, Inc., 24; 75 (upd.)
Lintas: Worldwide, 14
The Lion Brewery, Inc., 86
Lionel L.L.C., 16
Liqui-Box Corporation, 16
Liquidnet, Inc. 79
Litehouse Inc., 60
Lithia Motors, Inc., 41
Littelfuse, Inc., 26
Little Caesar Enterprises, Inc., 7; 24 (upd.)
Little Tikes Company, 13; 62 (upd.)
Littleton Coin Company Inc., 82
Litton Industries, Inc., I; 11 (upd.)
LIVE Entertainment Inc., 20
Live Nation, Inc., 80 (upd.)
LivePerson, Inc., 91
Liz Claiborne, Inc., 8; 25 (upd.)
LKQ Corporation, 71
Lockheed Martin Corporation, I; 11 (upd.); 15 (upd.); 89 (upd.)
Loctite Corporation, 8; 30 (upd.)
LodgeNet Entertainment Corporation, 28
Loehmann's Inc., 24
Loews Corporation, I; 12 (upd.); 36 (upd.); 93 (upd.)
Logan's Roadhouse, Inc., 29
Logicon Inc., 20
LoJack Corporation, 48
London Fog Industries, Inc., 29
Lone Star Steakhouse & Saloon, Inc., 51
The Long & Foster Companies, Inc., 85
Long Island Bancorp, Inc., 16
Long Island Lighting Company, V
The Long Island Rail Road Company, 68
Long John Silver's, 13; 57 (upd.)
The Longaberger Company, 12; 44 (upd.)
Longs Drug Stores Corporation, V; 25 (upd.); 83 (upd.)
Longview Fibre Company, 8; 37 (upd.)
Loral Space & Communications Ltd., 8; 9; 54 (upd.)
Lost Arrow Inc., 22
LOT$OFF Corporation, 24
Lotus Development Corporation, 6; 25 (upd.)
The Louisiana Land and Exploration Company, 7
Louisiana-Pacific Corporation, IV; 31 (upd.)
Love's Travel Stops & Country Stores, Inc., 71
Lowe's Companies, Inc., V; 21 (upd.); 81 (upd.)
Lowrance Electronics, Inc., 18
LPA Holding Corporation, 81
LSB Industries, Inc., 77
LSI Logic Corporation, 13; 64
The LTV Corporation, I; 24 (upd.)
The Lubrizol Corporation, I; 30 (upd.); 83 (upd.)
Luby's, Inc., 17; 42 (upd.)
Lucasfilm Ltd., 12; 50 (upd.)
Lucent Technologies Inc., 34
Lucille Farms, Inc., 45
Lucky Stores, Inc., 27
Lufkin Industries Inc. 78
Luigino's, Inc., 64
Lukens Inc., 14
Lunar Corporation, 29
Lund Food Holdings, Inc., 22
Lund International Holdings, Inc., 40
Lutheran Brotherhood, 31
Lydall, Inc., 64
Lynch Corporation, 43
Lynden Incorporated, 91
Lyondell Chemical Company, IV; 45 (upd.)
M&F Worldwide Corp., 38
M. Shanken Communications, Inc., 50
M.A. Bruder & Sons, Inc., 56
M.A. Gedney Co., 51
M.A. Hanna Company, 8
M.H. Meyerson & Co., Inc., 46
Mac Frugal's Bargains - Closeouts Inc., 17
Mac-Gray Corporation, 44
MacAndrews & Forbes Holdings Inc., 28; 86 (upd.)
MacDermid Incorporated, 32
Mace Security International, Inc., 57
The Macerich Company, 57
MacGregor Golf Company, 68
Mack Trucks, Inc., I; 22 (upd.); 61 (upd.)
Mack-Cali Realty Corporation, 42
Mackay Envelope Corporation, 45
Mackie Designs Inc., 33
Macmillan, Inc., 7
MacNeil/Lehrer Productions, 87
The MacNeal-Schwendler Corporation, 25
Macromedia, Inc., 50
Macy's, Inc., 94 (upd.)
Madden's on Gull Lake, 52
Madison Gas and Electric Company, 39
Madison-Kipp Corporation, 58
Mag Instrument, Inc., 67
MaggieMoo's International, 89
Magma Copper Company, 7
Magma Design Automation Inc. 78
Magma Power Company, 11
MagneTek, Inc., 15; 41 (upd.)
MAI Systems Corporation, 11
Maid-Rite Corporation, 62
Maidenform, Inc., 20; 59 (upd.)
Mail Boxes Etc., 18; 41 (upd.)
Mail-Well, Inc., 28
Maine & Maritimes Corporation, 56
Maine Central Railroad Company, 16
Maines Paper & Food Service Inc., 71
Majesco Entertainment Company, 85
The Major Automotive Companies, Inc., 45
Malcolm Pirnie, Inc., 42
Malden Mills Industries, Inc., 16
Mallinckrodt Group Inc., 19
Malt-O-Meal Company, 22; 63 (upd.)
Management and Training Corporation, 28
Manatron, Inc., 86
Mandalay Resort Group, 32 (upd.)
Manhattan Associates, Inc., 67
Manhattan Group, LLC, 80
Manheim, 88
The Manitowoc Company, Inc., 18; 59 (upd.)
Mannatech Inc., 33
Manning Selvage & Lee (MS&L), 76
MannKind Corporation, 87
Manor Care, Inc., 6; 25 (upd.)
Manpower Inc., 9; 30 (upd.); 73 (upd.)
Manufactured Home Communities, Inc., 22
Manufacturers Hanover Corporation, II
Manville Corporation, III; 7 (upd.)
MAPCO Inc., IV
MAPICS, Inc., 55
Maple Grove Farms of Vermont, 88
Maples Industries, Inc., 83
Marble Slab Creamery, Inc., 87
March of Dimes, 31

Marchex, Inc., 72
marchFIRST, Inc., 34
Marco Business Products, Inc., 75
Marco's Franchising LLC, 86
The Marcus Corporation, 21
Marie Callender's Restaurant & Bakery, Inc., 28
Marine Products Corporation, 75
MarineMax, Inc., 30
Marion Laboratories, Inc., I
Marisa Christina, Inc., 15
Maritz Inc., 38
Mark IV Industries, Inc., 7; 28 (upd.)
Mark T. Wendell Tea Company, 94
The Mark Travel Corporation, 80
Marks Brothers Jewelers, Inc., 24
Marlin Business Services Corp., 89
The Marmon Group, Inc., IV; 16 (upd.); 70 (upd.)
Marquette Electronics, Inc., 13
Marriott International, Inc., III; 21 (upd.); 83 (upd.)
Mars, Incorporated, 7; 40 (upd.)
Marsh & McLennan Companies, Inc., III; 45 (upd.)
Marsh Supermarkets, Inc., 17; 76 (upd.)
Marshall & Ilsley Corporation, 56
Marshall Field's, 63
Marshalls Incorporated, 13
Marshfield Clinic Inc., 82
Martek Biosciences Corporation, 65
Marten Transport, Ltd., 84
Martha Stewart Living Omnimedia, Inc., 24; 73 (upd.)
Martignetti Companies, 84
Martin Franchises, Inc., 80
Martin Industries, Inc., 44
Martin Marietta Corporation, I
MartinLogan, Ltd., 85
Martz Group, 56
Marvel Entertainment Inc., 10; 78 (upd.)
Marvin Lumber & Cedar Company, 22
Mary Kay Inc., 9; 30 (upd.); 84 (upd.)
Maryland & Virginia Milk Producers Cooperative Association, Inc., 80
The Maschhoffs, Inc., 82
Masco Corporation, III; 20 (upd.); 39 (upd.)
Mashantucket Pequot Gaming Enterprise Inc., 35
Masland Corporation, 17
Massachusetts Mutual Life Insurance Company, III; 53 (upd.)
Massey Energy Company, 57
MasTec, Inc., 19; 55 (upd.)
Master Lock Company, 45
MasterBrand Cabinets, Inc., 71
MasterCard International, Inc., 9
MasterCraft Boat Company, Inc., 90
Match.com, LP, 87
Material Sciences Corporation, 63
The MathWorks, Inc., 80
Matria Healthcare, Inc., 17
Matrix Essentials Inc., 90
Matrix Service Company, 65
Matrixx Initiatives, Inc., 74
Matt Prentice Restaurant Group, 70
Mattel, Inc., 7; 25 (upd.); 61 (upd.)
Matthews International Corporation, 29; 77 (upd.)
Maui Land & Pineapple Company, Inc., 29
Maui Wowi, Inc., 85
Mauna Loa Macadamia Nut Corporation, 64
Maverick Ranch Association, Inc., 88
Maverick Tube Corporation, 59
Max & Erma's Restaurants Inc., 19
Maxco Inc., 17
Maxicare Health Plans, Inc., III; 25 (upd.)
The Maxim Group, 25
Maxim Integrated Products, Inc., 16
MAXIMUS, Inc., 43
Maxtor Corporation, 10
Maxus Energy Corporation, 7
Maxwell Shoe Company, Inc., 30
MAXXAM Inc., 8
Maxxim Medical Inc., 12
The May Department Stores Company, V; 19 (upd.); 46 (upd.)
Mayer, Brown, Rowe & Maw, 47
Mayfield Dairy Farms, Inc., 74
Mayflower Group Inc., 6
Mayo Foundation, 9; 34 (upd.)
Mayor's Jewelers, Inc., 41
Maytag Corporation, III; 22 (upd.); 82 (upd.)
Mazel Stores, Inc., 29
Mazzio's Corporation, 76
MBC Holding Company, 40
MBIA Inc., 73
MBNA Corporation, 12; 33 (upd.)
MCA Inc., II
McAfee Inc., 94
McAlister's Corporation, 66
McCarthy Building Companies, Inc., 48
McCaw Cellular Communications, Inc., 6
McClain Industries, Inc., 51
The McClatchy Company, 33; 92 (upd.)
McCormick & Company, Incorporated, 7; 27 (upd.)
McCormick & Schmick's Seafood Restaurants, Inc., 71
McCoy Corporation, 58
McDATA Corporation, 75
McDermott International, Inc., III; 37 (upd.)
McDonald's Corporation, II; 7 (upd.); 26 (upd.); 63 (upd.)
McDonnell Douglas Corporation, I; 11 (upd.)
McGrath RentCorp, 91
The McGraw-Hill Companies, Inc., IV; 18 (upd.); 51 (upd.)
MCI WorldCom, Inc., V; 27 (upd.)
McIlhenny Company, 20
McJunkin Corporation, 63
McKee Foods Corporation, 7; 27 (upd.)
McKesson Corporation, I; 12; 47 (upd.)
McKinsey & Company, Inc., 9
McLane Company, Inc., 13
McLeodUSA Incorporated, 32
McMenamins Pubs and Breweries, 65
McNaughton Apparel Group, Inc., 92 (upd.)
MCN Corporation, 6
MCSi, Inc., 41
McWane Corporation, 55
MDU Resources Group, Inc., 7; 42 (upd.)
The Mead Corporation, IV; 19 (upd.)
Mead Data Central, Inc., 10
Mead Johnson & Company, 84
Meade Instruments Corporation, 41
Meadowcraft, Inc., 29
MeadWestvaco Corporation, 76 (upd.)
Measurement Specialties, Inc., 71
Mecklermedia Corporation, 24
Medarex, Inc., 85
Medco Containment Services Inc., 9
Media Arts Group, Inc., 42
Media General, Inc., 7; 38 (upd.)
Mediacom Communications Corporation, 69
MediaNews Group, Inc., 70
Medical Information Technology Inc., 64
Medical Management International, Inc., 65
Medical Staffing Network Holdings, Inc., 89
Medicis Pharmaceutical Corporation, 59
MedImmune, Inc., 35
Medis Technologies Ltd., 77
Meditrust, 11
Medline Industries, Inc., 61
Medtronic, Inc., 8; 30 (upd.); 67 (upd.)
Medusa Corporation, 24
Megafoods Stores Inc., 13
Meier & Frank Co., 23
Meijer Incorporated, 7; 27 (upd.)
Mel Farr Automotive Group, 20
Melaleuca Inc., 31
Melamine Chemicals, Inc., 27
Mellon Bank Corporation, II
Mellon Financial Corporation, 44 (upd.)
Mellon-Stuart Company, I
The Melting Pot Restaurants, Inc., 74
Melville Corporation, V
Melvin Simon and Associates, Inc., 8
MEMC Electronic Materials, Inc., 81
Memorial Sloan-Kettering Cancer Center, 57
Memry Corporation, 72
The Men's Wearhouse, Inc., 17; 48 (upd.)
Menard, Inc., 34
Menasha Corporation, 8; 59 (upd.)
Mendocino Brewing Company, Inc., 60
The Mentholatum Company Inc., 32
Mentor Corporation, 26
Mentor Graphics Corporation, 11
Mercantile Bankshares Corp., 11
Mercantile Stores Company, Inc., V; 19 (upd.)
Mercer International Inc., 64
Merck & Co., Inc., I; 11 (upd.); 34 (upd.)
Mercury Air Group, Inc., 20
Mercury General Corporation, 25
Mercury Interactive Corporation, 59
Mercury Marine Group, 68
Meredith Corporation, 11; 29 (upd.); 74 (upd.)
Merge Healthcare, 85
Meridian Bancorp, Inc., 11
Meridian Gold, Incorporated, 47

Merillat Industries Inc., 13
Merillat Industries, LLC, 69 (upd.)
Merisant Worldwide, Inc., 70
Merisel, Inc., 12
Merit Medical Systems, Inc., 29
MeritCare Health System, 88
Meritage Corporation, 26
Merix Corporation, 36; 75 (upd.)
Merrell Dow, Inc., I; 9 (upd.)
Merriam-Webster Inc., 70
Merrill Corporation, 18; 47 (upd.)
Merrill Lynch & Co., Inc., II; 13 (upd.); 40 (upd.)
Merry-Go-Round Enterprises, Inc., 8
Mervyn's California, 10; 39 (upd.)
Mesa Air Group, Inc., 11; 32 (upd.); 77 (upd.)
Mesaba Holdings, Inc., 28
Mestek Inc., 10
Metal Management, Inc., 92
Metatec International, Inc., 47
Meteor Industries Inc., 33
Methode Electronics, Inc., 13
Metris Companies Inc., 56
Metro Information Services, Inc., 36
Metro-Goldwyn-Mayer Inc., 25 (upd.); 84 (upd.)
Metrocall, Inc., 41
Metromedia Company, 7; 14; 61 (upd.)
Metropolitan Baseball Club Inc., 39
Metropolitan Financial Corporation, 13
Metropolitan Life Insurance Company, III; 52 (upd.)
The Metropolitan Museum of Art, 55
Metropolitan Opera Association, Inc., 40
Metropolitan Transportation Authority, 35
Mexican Restaurants, Inc., 41
MFS Communications Company, Inc., 11
MGIC Investment Corp., 52
MGM Grand Inc., 17
MGM/UA Communications Company, II
Miami Herald Media Company, 92
Michael Anthony Jewelers, Inc., 24
Michael Baker Corporation, 14; 51 (upd.)
Michael C. Fina Co., Inc., 52
Michael Foods, Inc., 25
Michaels Stores, Inc., 17; 71 (upd.)
Michigan Bell Telephone Co., 14
Michigan National Corporation, 11
Michigan Sporting Goods Distributors, Inc., 72
Micrel, Incorporated, 77
Micro Warehouse, Inc., 16
MicroAge, Inc., 16
Microdot Inc., 8
Micron Technology, Inc., 11; 29 (upd.)
Micros Systems, Inc., 18
Microsemi Corporation, 94
Microsoft Corporation, 6; 27 (upd.); 63 (upd.)
MicroStrategy Incorporated, 87
Mid-America Apartment Communities, Inc., 85
Mid-America Dairymen, Inc., 7
Midas Inc., 10; 56 (upd.)
The Middleby Corporation, 22
Middlesex Water Company, 45
The Middleton Doll Company, 53
The Midland Company, 65
Midway Airlines Corporation, 33
Midway Games, Inc., 25
Midwest Air Group, Inc., 35; 85 (upd.)
Midwest Grain Products, Inc., 49
Midwest Resources Inc., 6
Mikasa, Inc., 28
Mike-Sell's Inc., 15
Mikohn Gaming Corporation, 39
Milacron, Inc., 53 (upd.)
Milbank, Tweed, Hadley & McCloy, 27
Miles Laboratories, I
Millennium Pharmaceuticals, Inc., 47
Miller Brewing Company, I; 12 (upd.)
Miller Industries, Inc., 26
Miller Publishing Group, LLC, 57
Milliken & Co., V; 17 (upd.); 82 (upd.)
Milliman USA, 66
Millipore Corporation, 25; 84 (upd.)
The Mills Corporation, 77
Milnot Company, 46
Milton Bradley Company, 21
Milton CAT, Inc., 86
Milwaukee Brewers Baseball Club, 37
Mine Safety Appliances Company, 31
The Miner Group International, 22
Minerals Technologies Inc., 11; 52 (upd.)
Minnesota Mining & Manufacturing Company (3M), I; 8 (upd.); 26 (upd.)
Minnesota Power, Inc., 11; 34 (upd.)
Minntech Corporation, 22
The Minute Maid Company, 28
Minuteman International Inc., 46
Minyard Food Stores, Inc., 33; 86 (upd.)
Mirage Resorts, Incorporated, 6; 28 (upd.)
Miramax Film Corporation, 64
Misonix, Inc., 80
Mississippi Chemical Corporation, 39
Mitchell Energy and Development Corporation, 7
MITRE Corporation, 26
Mity Enterprises, Inc., 38
MIVA, Inc., 83
MNS, Ltd., 65
Mobil Corporation, IV; 7 (upd.); 21 (upd.)
Mobile Mini, Inc., 58
Mobile Telecommunications Technologies Corp., 18
Mocon, Inc., 76
Modern Woodmen of America, 66
Modine Manufacturing Company, 8; 56 (upd.)
Modtech Holdings, Inc., 77
Moen Incorporated, 12
Mohawk Industries, Inc., 19; 63 (upd.)
Mohegan Tribal Gaming Authority, 37
Moldflow Corporation, 73
Molex Incorporated, 11; 54 (upd.)
Molson Coors Brewing Company, 77 (upd.)
Monaco Coach Corporation, 31
Monadnock Paper Mills, Inc., 21
Monarch Casino & Resort, Inc., 65
The Monarch Cement Company, 72
MoneyGram International, Inc., 94
Monfort, Inc., 13
Monro Muffler Brake, Inc., 24
Monrovia Nursery Company, 70
The Mosaic Company, 91
Monsanto Company, I; 9 (upd.); 29 (upd.); 77 (upd.)
Monster Cable Products, Inc., 69
Monster Worldwide Inc., 74 (upd.)
Montana Coffee Traders, Inc., 60
The Montana Power Company, 11; 44 (upd.)
Monterey Pasta Company, 58
Montgomery Ward & Co., Incorporated, V; 20 (upd.)
Moody's Corporation, 65
Moog Inc., 13
Moog Music, Inc., 75
Mooney Aerospace Group Ltd., 52
Moore Medical Corp., 17
Moore-Handley, Inc., 39
Moran Towing Corporation, Inc., 15
The Morgan Group, Inc., 46
Morgan, Lewis & Bockius LLP, 29
Morgan Stanley Dean Witter & Company, II; 16 (upd.); 33 (upd.)
Morgans Hotel Group Company, 80
Morinda Holdings, Inc., 82
Morningstar Inc., 68
Morris Communications Corporation, 36
Morris Travel Services L.L.C., 26
Morrison & Foerster LLP 78
Morrison Knudsen Corporation, 7; 28 (upd.)
Morrison Restaurants Inc., 11
Morrow Equipment Co. L.L.C., 87
Morse Shoe Inc., 13
Morton International Inc., I; 9 (upd.); 80 (upd.)
Morton Thiokol, Inc., I
Morton's Restaurant Group, Inc., 30; 88 (upd.)
Mosinee Paper Corporation, 15
Mossimo, Inc., 27
Motel 6, 13; 56 (upd.)
Mothers Against Drunk Driving (MADD), 51
Mothers Work, Inc., 18
The Motley Fool, Inc., 40
Moto Photo, Inc., 45
Motor Cargo Industries, Inc., 35
Motorcar Parts & Accessories, Inc., 47
Motorola, Inc., II; 11 (upd.); 34 (upd.); 93 (upd.)
Motown Records Company L.P., 26
Mott's Inc., 57
Mountain States Mortgage Centers, Inc., 29
Movado Group, Inc., 28
Movie Gallery, Inc., 31
Movie Star Inc., 17
MPS Group, Inc., 49
MPW Industrial Services Group, Inc., 53
Mr. Coffee, Inc., 15
Mr. Gasket Inc., 15
Mr. Gatti's, LP, 87
Mrs. Baird's Bakeries, 29
Mrs. Fields' Original Cookies, Inc., 27
Mrs. Grossman's Paper Company Inc., 84
MSC Industrial Direct Co., Inc., 71
Mt. Olive Pickle Company, Inc., 44

MTR Gaming Group, Inc., 75
MTS Inc., 37
Mueller Industries, Inc., 7; 52 (upd.)
Mullen Advertising Inc., 51
Multi-Color Corporation, 53
Multimedia Games, Inc., 41
Multimedia, Inc., 11
Murdock Madaus Schwabe, 26
Murphy Family Farms Inc., 22
Murphy Oil Corporation, 7; 32 (upd.)
The Musco Family Olive Co., 91
Musco Lighting, 83
Musicland Stores Corporation, 9; 38 (upd.)
The Mutual Benefit Life Insurance Company, III
The Mutual Life Insurance Company of New York, III
Muzak, Inc., 18
MWH Preservation Limited Partnership, 65
MWI Veterinary Supply, Inc., 80
Mycogen Corporation, 21
Myers Industries, Inc., 19
Mylan Laboratories Inc., I; 20 (upd.); 59 (upd.)
Myriad Restaurant Group, Inc., 87
N.F. Smith & Associates LP, 70
Nabisco Foods Group, II; 7 (upd.)
Nabors Industries, Inc., 9
NACCO Industries Inc., 7; 78 (upd.)
Nalco Holding Company, I; 12 (upd.); 89 (upd.)
Nantucket Allserve, Inc., 22
Napster, Inc., 69
NASD, 54 (upd.)
The NASDAQ Stock Market, Inc., 92
Nash Finch Company, 8; 23 (upd.); 65 (upd.)
Nashua Corporation, 8
Nastech Pharmaceutical Company Inc. 79
Nathan's Famous, Inc., 29
National Amusements Inc., 28
National Aquarium in Baltimore, Inc., 74
National Association for Stock Car Auto Racing, 32
National Association of Securities Dealers, Inc., 10
National Audubon Society, 26
National Auto Credit, Inc., 16
The National Bank of South Carolina, 76
National Beverage Corporation, 26; 88 (upd.)
National Broadcasting Company, Inc., II; 6 (upd.); 28 (upd.)
National Can Corporation, I
National Car Rental System, Inc., 10
National City Corp., 15
National Convenience Stores Incorporated, 7
National Discount Brokers Group, Inc., 28
National Distillers and Chemical Corporation, I
National Educational Music Co. Ltd., 47
National Envelope Corporation, 32
National Equipment Services, Inc., 57
National Financial Partners Corp., 65
National Football League, 29
National Frozen Foods Corporation, 94
National Fuel Gas Company, 6
National Geographic Society, 9; 30 (upd.); 79 (upd.)
National Grape Cooperative Association, Inc., 20
National Grid USA, 51 (upd.)
National Gypsum Company, 10
National Health Laboratories Incorporated, 11
National Heritage Academies, Inc., 60
National Hockey League, 35
National Home Centers, Inc., 44
National Instruments Corporation, 22
National Intergroup, Inc., V
National Journal Group Inc., 67
National Media Corporation, 27
National Medical Enterprises, Inc., III
National Medical Health Card Systems, Inc. 79
National Oilwell, Inc., 54
National Organization for Women, Inc., 55
National Patent Development Corporation, 13
National Picture & Frame Company, 24
National Presto Industries, Inc., 16; 43 (upd.)
National Public Radio, Inc., 19; 47 (upd.)
National R.V. Holdings, Inc., 32
National Railroad Passenger Corporation (Amtrak), 22; 66 (upd.)
National Record Mart, Inc., 29
National Research Corporation, 87
National Rifle Association of America, 37
National Sanitary Supply Co., 16
National Semiconductor Corporation, II; VI, 26 (upd.); 69 (upd.)
National Service Industries, Inc., 11; 54 (upd.)
National Standard Co., 13
National Starch and Chemical Company, 49
National Steel Corporation, 12
National TechTeam, Inc., 41
National Thoroughbred Racing Association, 58
National Weather Service, 91
National Wine & Spirits, Inc., 49
NationsBank Corporation, 10
Natrol, Inc., 49
Natural Alternatives International, Inc., 49
Natural Ovens Bakery, Inc., 72
Natural Selection Foods, 54
Natural Wonders Inc., 14
Naturally Fresh, Inc., 88
The Nature Conservancy, 28
Nature's Sunshine Products, Inc., 15
Naumes, Inc., 81
Nautica Enterprises, Inc., 18; 44 (upd.)
Navarre Corporation, 24
Navigant Consulting, Inc., 93
Navigant International, Inc., 47
The Navigators Group, Inc., 92
Navistar International Corporation, I; 10 (upd.)
NAVTEQ Corporation, 69
Navy Exchange Service Command, 31
Navy Federal Credit Union, 33
NBD Bancorp, Inc., 11
NBGS International, Inc., 73
NBTY, Inc., 31
NCH Corporation, 8
NCI Building Systems, Inc., 88
NCL Corporation 79
NCNB Corporation, II
NCO Group, Inc., 42
NCR Corporation, III; 6 (upd.); 30 (upd.); 90 (upd.)
Nebraska Book Company, Inc., 65
Nebraska Furniture Mart, Inc., 94
Nebraska Public Power District, 29
Neenah Foundry Company, 68
Neff Corp., 32
NeighborCare, Inc., 67 (upd.)
The Neiman Marcus Group, Inc., 12; 49 (upd.)
Nektar Therapeutics, 91
Neogen Corporation, 94
NERCO, Inc., 7
Netezza Corporation, 69
Netflix, Inc., 58
NETGEAR, Inc., 81
NetIQ Corporation 79
Netscape Communications Corporation, 15; 35 (upd.)
Network Appliance, Inc., 58
Network Associates, Inc., 25
Network Equipment Technologies Inc., 92
Neuberger Berman Inc., 57
NeuStar, Inc., 81
Neutrogena Corporation, 17
Nevada Bell Telephone Company, 14
Nevada Power Company, 11
Nevamar Company, 82
New Balance Athletic Shoe, Inc., 25; 68 (upd.)
New Belgium Brewing Company, Inc., 68
New Brunswick Scientific Co., Inc., 45
New Dana Perfumes Company, 37
New England Business Service Inc., 18; 78 (upd.)
New England Confectionery Co., 15
New England Electric System, V
New England Mutual Life Insurance Company, III
New Jersey Devils, 84
New Jersey Resources Corporation, 54
New Line Cinema, Inc., 47
New Orleans Saints LP, 58
The New Piper Aircraft, Inc., 44
New Plan Realty Trust, 11
New Seasons Market, 75
New Street Capital Inc., 8
New Times, Inc., 45
New Valley Corporation, 17
New World Pasta Company, 53
New World Restaurant Group, Inc., 44
New York City Health and Hospitals Corporation, 60
New York City Off-Track Betting Corporation, 51
New York Community Bancorp Inc. 78
New York Daily News, 32
New York Health Care, Inc., 72

New York Life Insurance Company, III; 45 (upd.)
New York Restaurant Group, Inc., 32
New York Shakespeare Festival Management, 93
New York State Electric and Gas, 6
New York Stock Exchange, Inc., 9; 39 (upd.)
The New York Times Company, IV; 19 (upd.); 61 (upd.)
Neways Inc. 78
Newcor, Inc., 40
Newell Rubbermaid Inc., 9; 52 (upd.)
Newfield Exploration Company, 65
Newhall Land and Farming Company, 14
Newly Weds Foods, Inc., 74
Newman's Own, Inc., 37
Newmont Mining Corporation, 7; 94 (upd.)
Newpark Resources, Inc., 63
Newport Corporation, 71
Newport News Shipbuilding Inc., 13; 38 (upd.)
News America Publishing Inc., 12
NewYork-Presbyterian Hospital, 59
Nexstar Broadcasting Group, Inc., 73
Nextel Communications, Inc., 10; 27 (upd.)
NFL Films, 75
NFO Worldwide, Inc., 24
NGC Corporation, 18
Niagara Corporation, 28
Niagara Mohawk Holdings Inc., V; 45 (upd.)
Nichols Research Corporation, 18
Nicklaus Companies, 45
Nicor Inc., 6; 86 (upd.)
NIKE, Inc., V; 8 (upd.); 36 (upd.); 75 (upd.)
Nikken Global Inc., 32
Niman Ranch, Inc., 67
Nimbus CD International, Inc., 20
Nine West Group, Inc., 11; 39 (upd.)
99¢ Only Stores, 25
NIPSCO Industries, Inc., 6
Nitches, Inc., 53
NL Industries, Inc., 10
Nobel Learning Communities, Inc., 37; 76 (upd.)
Noble Affiliates, Inc., 11
Noble Roman's Inc., 14
Noland Company, 35
Nolo.com, Inc., 49
Noodle Kidoodle, 16
Noodles & Company, Inc., 55
Nooter Corporation, 61
Norcal Waste Systems, Inc., 60
NordicTrack, 22
Nordson Corporation, 11; 48 (upd.)
Nordstrom, Inc., V; 18 (upd.); 67 (upd.)
Norelco Consumer Products Co., 26
Norfolk Southern Corporation, V; 29 (upd.); 75 (upd.)
Norm Thompson Outfitters, Inc., 47
Norrell Corporation, 25
Norstan, Inc., 16
Nortek, Inc., 34
North Atlantic Trading Company Inc., 65
The North Face, Inc., 18; 78 (upd.)
North Fork Bancorporation, Inc., 46
North Pacific Group, Inc., 61
North Star Steel Company, 18
Northeast Utilities, V; 48 (upd.)
Northern States Power Company, V; 20 (upd.)
Northern Trust Company, 9
Northland Cranberries, Inc., 38
Northrop Grumman Corporation, I; 11 (upd.); 45 (upd.)
Northwest Airlines Corporation, I; 6 (upd.); 26 (upd.); 74 (upd.)
Northwest Natural Gas Company, 45
NorthWestern Corporation, 37
Northwestern Mutual Life Insurance Company, III; 45 (upd.)
Norton Company, 8
Norton McNaughton, Inc., 27
Norwood Promotional Products, Inc., 26
NovaCare, Inc., 11
NovaStar Financial, Inc., 91
Novell, Inc., 6; 23 (upd.)
Novellus Systems, Inc., 18
Noven Pharmaceuticals, Inc., 55
NPC International, Inc., 40
The NPD Group, Inc., 68
NRG Energy, Inc. 79
NRT Incorporated, 61
NSF International, 72
NSS Enterprises Inc. 78
NTN Buzztime, Inc., 86
Nu Skin Enterprises, Inc., 27; 76 (upd.)
Nu-kote Holding, Inc., 18
Nucor Corporation, 7; 21 (upd.); 79 (upd.)
Nutraceutical International Corporation, 37
NutraSweet Company, 8
NutriSystem, Inc., 71
Nutrition for Life International Inc., 22
NVIDIA Corporation, 54
NVR Inc., 8; 70 (upd.)
NYMAGIC, Inc., 41
NYNEX Corporation, V
O.C. Tanner Co., 69
Oak Harbor Freight Lines, Inc., 53
Oak Industries Inc., 21
Oak Technology, Inc., 22
Oakhurst Dairy, 60
Oakley, Inc., 18; 49 (upd.)
Oaktree Capital Management, LLC, 71
Oakwood Homes Corporation, 15
Oberto Sausage Company, Inc., 92
Obie Media Corporation, 56
Occidental Petroleum Corporation, IV; 25 (upd.); 71 (upd.)
Ocean Beauty Seafoods, Inc., 74
Ocean Spray Cranberries, Inc., 7; 25 (upd.); 83 (upd.)
Oceaneering International, Inc., 63
O'Charley's Inc., 19; 60 (upd.)
Octel Messaging, 14; 41 (upd.)
Ocular Sciences, Inc., 65
Odetics Inc., 14
ODL, Inc., 55
Odwalla, Inc., 31
Odyssey Marine Exploration, Inc., 91
OEC Medical Systems, Inc., 27
Office Depot, Inc., 8; 23 (upd.); 65 (upd.)
OfficeMax, Inc., 15; 43 (upd.)
OfficeTiger, LLC, 75
Offshore Logistics, Inc., 37
Ogden Corporation, I; 6
The Ogilvy Group, Inc., I
Oglebay Norton Company, 17
Oglethorpe Power Corporation, 6
The Ohio Art Company, 14; 59 (upd.)
Ohio Bell Telephone Company, 14
Ohio Casualty Corp., 11
Ohio Edison Company, V
Oil-Dri Corporation of America, 20; 89 (upd.)
Oil States International, Inc., 77
The Oilgear Company, 74
Oklahoma Gas and Electric Company, 6
Olan Mills, Inc., 62
Old America Stores, Inc., 17
Old Dominion Freight Line, Inc., 57
Old Kent Financial Corp., 11
Old National Bancorp, 15
Old Navy, Inc., 70
Old Orchard Brands, LLC, 73
Old Republic International Corporation, 11; 58 (upd.)
Old Spaghetti Factory International Inc., 24
Old Town Canoe Company, 74
Olga's Kitchen, Inc., 80
Olin Corporation, I; 13 (upd.); 78 (upd.)
Olsten Corporation, 6; 29 (upd.)
OM Group Inc. 17; 78 (upd.)
Omaha Steaks International Inc., 62
O'Melveny & Myers, 37
OMI Corporation, 59
Omni Hotels Corp., 12
Omnicare, Inc., 49
Omnicell, Inc., 89
Omnicom Group, Inc., I; 22 (upd.); 77 (upd.)
OmniSource Corporation, 14
OMNOVA Solutions Inc., 59
On Assignment, Inc., 20
180s, L.L.C., 64
One Price Clothing Stores, Inc., 20
1-800-FLOWERS, Inc., 26
Oneida Ltd., 7; 31 (upd.); 88 (upd.)
ONEOK Inc., 7
Onion, Inc., 69
Onyx Acceptance Corporation, 59
Onyx Software Corporation, 53
Operation Smile, Inc., 75
Opinion Research Corporation, 46
Oppenheimer Wolff & Donnelly LLP, 71
Opsware Inc., 49
Option Care Inc., 48
Opus Group, 34
Oracle Corporation, 6; 24 (upd.); 67 (upd.)
Orange Glo International, 53
OraSure Technologies, Inc., 75
Orbital Sciences Corporation, 22
Orbitz, Inc., 61
Orchard Supply Hardware Stores Corporation, 17

Ore-Ida Foods Inc., 13; 78 (upd.)
Oregon Chai, Inc., 49
Oregon Dental Service Health Plan, Inc., 51
Oregon Freeze Dry, Inc., 74
Oregon Metallurgical Corporation, 20
Oregon Steel Mills, Inc., 14
O'Reilly Automotive, Inc., 26; 78 (upd.)
Organic Valley (Coulee Region Organic Produce Pool), 53
Orion Pictures Corporation, 6
Orleans Homebuilders, Inc., 62
Ormat Technologies, Inc., 87
Ormet Corporation, 82
Orrick, Herrington and Sutcliffe LLP, 76
Orthodontic Centers of America, Inc., 35
The Orvis Company, Inc., 28
Oryx Energy Company, 7
Oscar Mayer Foods Corp., 12
OshKosh B'Gosh, Inc., 9; 42 (upd.)
Oshkosh Truck Corporation, 7
Oshman's Sporting Goods, Inc., 17
OSI Restaurant Partners, Inc., 88 (upd.)
Osmonics, Inc., 18
O'Sullivan Industries Holdings, Inc., 34
Otis Elevator Company, Inc., 13; 39 (upd.)
Otis Spunkmeyer, Inc., 28
OTR Express, Inc., 25
Ottaway Newspapers, Inc., 15
Otter Tail Power Company, 18
Outback Steakhouse, Inc., 12; 34 (upd.)
Outboard Marine Corporation, III; 20 (upd.)
Outdoor Research, Incorporated, 67
Outdoor Systems, Inc., 25
Outlook Group Corporation, 37
Outrigger Enterprises, Inc., 67
Overhead Door Corporation, 70
Overhill Corporation, 51
Overnite Corporation, 14; 58 (upd.)
Overseas Shipholding Group, Inc., 11
Overstock.com, Inc., 75
Owens & Minor, Inc., 16; 68 (upd.)
Owens Corning Corporation, III; 20 (upd.)
Owens-Illinois, Inc., I; 26 (upd.); 85 (upd.)
Owosso Corporation, 29
Oxford Health Plans, Inc., 16
Oxford Industries, Inc., 8; 84 (upd.)
P&C Foods Inc., 8
P & F Industries, Inc., 45
P.C. Richard & Son Corp., 23
P.F. Chang's China Bistro, Inc., 37; 86 (upd.)
P.H. Glatfelter Company, 8; 30 (upd.); 83 (upd.)
Paccar Inc., I; 26 (upd.)
Pacer International, Inc., 54
Pacer Technology, 40
Pacific Clay Products Inc., 88
Pacific Coast Building Products, Inc., 94
Pacific Coast Feather Company, 67
Pacific Coast Restaurants, Inc., 90
Pacific Ethanol, Inc., 81
Pacific Enterprises, V
Pacific Gas and Electric Company, V
Pacific Sunwear of California, Inc., 28
Pacific Telecom, Inc., 6
Pacific Telesis Group, V
PacifiCare Health Systems, Inc., 11
PacifiCorp, V; 26 (upd.)
Packaging Corporation of America, 12; 51 (upd.)
Packard Bell Electronics, Inc., 13
Packeteer, Inc., 81
Paddock Publications, Inc., 53
Paging Network Inc., 11
PaineWebber Group Inc., II; 22 (upd.)
Pall Corporation, 9; 72 (upd.)
Palm Harbor Homes, Inc., 39
Palm Management Corporation, 71
Palm, Inc., 36; 75 (upd.)
Palmer & Cay, Inc., 69
Palmer Candy Company, 80
Palomar Medical Technologies, Inc., 22
Pamida Holdings Corporation, 15
The Pampered Chef, Ltd., 18; 78 (upd.)
Pan American World Airways, Inc., I; 12 (upd.)
Pan-American Life Insurance Company, 48
Panamerican Beverages, Inc., 47
PanAmSat Corporation, 46
Panavision Inc., 24
Pancho's Mexican Buffet, Inc., 46
Panda Management Company, Inc., 35
Panera Bread Company, 44
Panhandle Eastern Corporation, V
Pantone Inc., 53
The Pantry, Inc., 36
Papa Gino's Holdings Corporation, Inc., 86
Papa John's International, Inc., 15; 71 (upd.)
Papa Murphy's International, Inc., 54
Papetti's Hygrade Egg Products, Inc., 39
Pappas Restaurants, Inc., 76
Par Pharmaceutical Companies, Inc., 65
The Paradies Shops, Inc., 88
Paradise Music & Entertainment, Inc., 42
Parametric Technology Corp., 16
Paramount Pictures Corporation, II; 94 (upd.)
PAREXEL International Corporation, 84
Paris Corporation, 22
Parisian, Inc., 14
Park Corp., 22
Park-Ohio Industries Inc., 17; 85 (upd.)
Parker Drilling Company, 28
Parker-Hannifin Corporation, III; 24 (upd.)
Parlex Corporation, 61
Parsons Brinckerhoff, Inc., 34
The Parsons Corporation, 8; 56 (upd.)
Party City Corporation, 54
Pathmark Stores, Inc., 23
Patina Oil & Gas Corporation, 24
Patrick Industries, Inc., 30
Patriot Transportation Holding, Inc., 91
Patterson Dental Co., 19
Patterson-UTI Energy, Inc., 55
Patton Boggs LLP, 71
Paul Harris Stores, Inc., 18
Paul, Hastings, Janofsky & Walker LLP, 27
Paul Mueller Company, 65
Paul Reed Smith Guitar Company, 89
The Paul Revere Corporation, 12
Paul, Weiss, Rifkind, Wharton & Garrison, 47
Paul-Son Gaming Corporation, 66
Paxson Communications Corporation, 33
Pay 'N Pak Stores, Inc., 9
Paychex, Inc., 15; 46 (upd.)
Payless Cashways, Inc., 11; 44 (upd.)
Payless ShoeSource, Inc., 18; 69 (upd.)
PayPal Inc., 58
The PBSJ Corporation, 82
PC Connection, Inc., 37
PCA International, Inc., 62
PCC Natural Markets, 94
PDI, Inc., 52
PDL BioPharma, Inc., 90
PDQ Food Stores, Inc. 79
PDS Gaming Corporation, 44
Peabody Coal Company, 10
Peabody Energy Corporation, 45 (upd.)
Peabody Holding Company, Inc., IV
The Peak Technologies Group, Inc., 14
Peapod, Inc., 30
Pearle Vision, Inc., 13
Peavey Electronics Corporation, 16; 94 (upd.)
PECO Energy Company, 11
Pediatric Services of America, Inc., 31
Pediatrix Medical Group, Inc., 61
Peebles Inc., 16; 43 (upd.)
Peet's Coffee & Tea, Inc., 38
Pegasus Solutions, Inc., 75
Pei Cobb Freed & Partners Architects LLP, 57
Pelican Products, Inc., 86
Pella Corporation, 12; 39 (upd.); 89 (upd.)
Pemco Aviation Group Inc., 54
Pendleton Grain Growers Inc., 64
Pendleton Woolen Mills, Inc., 42
Penford Corporation, 55
Penn Engineering & Manufacturing Corp., 28
Penn National Gaming, Inc., 33
Penn Traffic Company, 13
Penn Virginia Corporation, 85
Pennsylvania Blue Shield, III
Pennsylvania Power & Light Company, V
Pennwalt Corporation, I
PennWell Corporation, 55
Pennzoil-Quaker State Company, IV; 20 (upd.); 50 (upd.)
Penske Corporation, V; 19 (upd.); 84 (upd.)
Pentair, Inc., 7; 26 (upd.); 81 (upd.)
Pentech International, Inc., 29
Penton Media, Inc., 27
Penzeys Spices, Inc. 79
People Express Airlines, Inc., I
Peoples Energy Corporation, 6
PeopleSoft Inc., 14; 33 (upd.)
The Pep Boys—Manny, Moe & Jack, 11; 36 (upd.); 81 (upd.)
Pepper Hamilton LLP, 43

Pepperidge Farm, Incorporated, 81
The Pepsi Bottling Group, Inc., 40
PepsiAmericas, Inc., 67 (upd.)
PepsiCo, Inc., I; 10 (upd.); 38 (upd.); 93 (upd.)
Perdue Farms Inc., 7; 23 (upd.)
Performance Food Group Company, 31
Perini Corporation, 8; 82 (upd.)
PerkinElmer Inc. 7; 78 (upd.)
Perkins Coie LLP, 56
Perkins Family Restaurants, L.P., 22
Perot Systems Corporation, 29
Perrigo Company, 12; 59 (upd.)
Perry Ellis International, Inc., 41
Perry's Ice Cream Company Inc., 90
The Perseus Books Group, 91
Pet Incorporated, 7
Petco Animal Supplies, Inc., 29; 74 (upd.)
Pete's Brewing Company, 22
Peter Kiewit Sons' Inc., 8
Peter Piper, Inc., 70
Peterbilt Motors Company, 89
Petersen Publishing Company, 21
Peterson American Corporation, 55
PetMed Express, Inc., 81
Petrie Stores Corporation, 8
Petrohawk Energy Corporation 79
Petroleum Helicopters, Inc., 35
Petrolite Corporation, 15
Petrossian Inc., 54
PETsMART, Inc., 14; 41 (upd.)
The Pew Charitable Trusts, 35
Pez Candy, Inc., 38
Pfizer Inc., I; 9 (upd.); 38 (upd.); 79 (upd.)
PFSweb, Inc., 73
PG&E Corporation, 26 (upd.)
Phar-Mor Inc., 12
Pharmacia & Upjohn Inc., I; 25 (upd.)
Pharmion Corporation, 91
Phat Fashions LLC, 49
Phelps Dodge Corporation, IV; 28 (upd.); 75 (upd.)
PHH Arval, V; 53 (upd.)
PHI, Inc., 80 (upd.)
Philadelphia Eagles, 37
Philadelphia Electric Company, V
Philadelphia Gas Works Company, 92
Philadelphia Media Holdings LLC, 92
Philadelphia Suburban Corporation, 39
Philharmonic-Symphony Society of New York, Inc. (New York Philharmonic), 69
Philip Morris Companies Inc., V; 18 (upd.); 44 (upd.)
Philip Services Corp., 73
Philips Electronics North America Corp., 13
Phillips, de Pury & Luxembourg, 49
Phillips Foods, Inc., 63; 90 (upd.)
Phillips International Inc. 78
Phillips Petroleum Company, IV; 40 (upd.)
Phillips-Van Heusen Corporation, 24
Phoenix Footwear Group, Inc., 70
The Phoenix Media/Communications Group, 91
PHP Healthcare Corporation, 22
PhyCor, Inc., 36
Physician Sales & Service, Inc., 14
Physio-Control International Corp., 18
Piccadilly Cafeterias, Inc., 19
PictureTel Corp., 10; 27 (upd.)
Piedmont Natural Gas Company, Inc., 27
Pier 1 Imports, Inc., 12; 34 (upd.)
Pierce Leahy Corporation, 24
Piercing Pagoda, Inc., 29
Piggly Wiggly Southern, Inc., 13
Pilgrim's Pride Corporation, 7; 23 (upd.); 90 (upd.
Pillowtex Corporation, 19; 41 (upd.)
The Pillsbury Company, II; 13 (upd.); 62 (upd.)
Pillsbury Madison & Sutro LLP, 29
Pilot Air Freight Corp., 67
Pilot Corporation, 49
Pilot Pen Corporation of America, 82
Pinkerton's Inc., 9
Pinnacle Airlines Corp., 73
Pinnacle West Capital Corporation, 6; 54 (upd.)
Pioneer Hi-Bred International, Inc., 9; 41 (upd.)
Pioneer Natural Resources Company, 59
Pioneer-Standard Electronics Inc., 19
Piper Jaffray Companies Inc., 22
Pitman Company, 58
Pitney Bowes Inc., III; 19; 47 (upd.)
Pittsburgh Brewing Company, 76
Pittsburgh Steelers Sports, Inc., 66
The Pittston Company, IV; 19 (upd.)
Pittway Corporation, 9; 33 (upd.)
Pixar Animation Studios, 34
Pixelworks, Inc., 69
Pizza Hut Inc., 7; 21 (upd.)
Pizza Inn, Inc., 46
Plain Dealer Publishing Company, 92
Plains Cotton Cooperative Association, 57
Planar Systems, Inc., 61
Planet Hollywood International, Inc., 18; 41 (upd.)
Plantation Pipe Line Company, 68
Plante & Moran, LLP, 71
Platinum Entertainment, Inc., 35
PLATINUM Technology, Inc., 14
Plato Learning, Inc., 44
Play by Play Toys & Novelties, Inc., 26
Playboy Enterprises, Inc., 18
PlayCore, Inc., 27
Players International, Inc., 22
Playskool, Inc., 25
Playtex Products, Inc., 15
Pleasant Company, 27
Pleasant Holidays LLC, 62
Plexus Corporation, 35; 80 (upd.)
Plum Creek Timber Company, Inc., 43
Pluma, Inc., 27
Ply Gem Industries Inc., 12
The PMI Group, Inc., 49
PMT Services, Inc., 24
The PNC Financial Services Group Inc., II; 13 (upd.); 46 (upd.)
PNM Resources Inc., 51 (upd.)
Pogo Producing Company, 39
Polar Air Cargo Inc., 60
Polaris Industries Inc., 12; 35 (upd.); 77 (upd.)
Polaroid Corporation, III; 7 (upd.); 28 (upd.); 93 (upd.)
Policy Management Systems Corporation, 11
Policy Studies, Inc., 62
Polk Audio, Inc., 34
Polo/Ralph Lauren Corporation, 12; 62 (upd.)
PolyGram N.V., 23
PolyMedica Corporation, 77
PolyOne Corporation, 87 (upd.)
Pomare Ltd., 88
Pomeroy Computer Resources, Inc., 33
Ponderosa Steakhouse, 15
Poof-Slinky, Inc., 61
Poore Brothers, Inc., 44
Pop Warner Little Scholars, Inc., 86
Pope & Talbot, Inc., 12; 61 (upd.)
Pope Resources LP, 74
Popular, Inc., 41
The Port Authority of New York and New Jersey, 48
Port Imperial Ferry Corporation, 70
Portal Software, Inc., 47
Portillo's Restaurant Group, Inc., 71
Portland General Corporation, 6
Portland Trail Blazers, 50
Post Properties, Inc., 26
Potbelly Sandwich Works, Inc., 83
Potlatch Corporation, 8; 34 (upd.); 87 (upd.)
Potomac Electric Power Company, 6
Potter & Brumfield Inc., 11
Powell's Books, Inc., 40
Power-One, Inc. 79
PowerBar Inc., 44
Powerhouse Technologies, Inc., 27
POZEN Inc., 81
PPG Industries, Inc., III; 22 (upd.); 81 (upd.)
PPL Corporation, 41 (upd.)
PR Newswire, 35
Prairie Farms Dairy, Inc., 47
Pratt & Whitney, 9
Praxair, Inc., 11; 48 (upd.)
Praxis Bookstore Group LLC, 90
Pre-Paid Legal Services, Inc., 20
Precision Castparts Corp., 15
Premark International, Inc., III
Premcor Inc., 37
Premier Industrial Corporation, 9
Premier Parks, Inc., 27
Premium Standard Farms, Inc., 30
PremiumWear, Inc., 30
Preserver Group, Inc., 44
President Casinos, Inc., 22
Pressman Toy Corporation, 56
Presstek, Inc., 33
Preston Corporation, 6
PRG-Schultz International, Inc., 73
Price Communications Corporation, 42
The Price Company, V
Price Pfister, Inc., 70
PriceCostco, Inc., 14
Priceline.com Incorporated, 57
PriceSmart, Inc., 71

PricewaterhouseCoopers, 9; 29 (upd.)
Pride International Inc. 78
Primark Corp., 13
Prime Hospitality Corporation, 52
Primedex Health Systems, Inc., 25
Primedia Inc., 22
Primerica Corporation, I
Prince Sports Group, Inc., 15
Princess Cruise Lines, 22
The Princeton Review, Inc., 42
Principal Mutual Life Insurance Company, III
Printpack, Inc., 68
Printrak, A Motorola Company, 44
Printronix, Inc., 18
Prison Rehabilitative Industries and Diversified Enterprises, Inc. (PRIDE), 53
The Procter & Gamble Company, III; 8 (upd.); 26 (upd.); 67 (upd.)
Prodigy Communications Corporation, 34
Professional Bull Riders Inc., 55
The Professional Golfers' Association of America, 41
Proffitt's, Inc., 19
Programmer's Paradise, Inc., 81
Progress Energy, Inc., 74
Progress Software Corporation, 15
The Progressive Corporation, 11; 29 (upd.)
ProLogis, 57
Promus Companies, Inc., 9
Proskauer Rose LLP, 47
Protection One, Inc., 32
Provell Inc., 58 (upd.)
Providence Health System, 90
The Providence Journal Company, 28
The Providence Service Corporation, 64
Provident Bankshares Corporation, 85
Provident Life and Accident Insurance Company of America, III
Providian Financial Corporation, 52 (upd.)
Prudential Financial Inc., III; 30 (upd.); 82 (upd.)
PSI Resources, 6
Psychemedics Corporation, 89
Psychiatric Solutions, Inc., 68
Pubco Corporation, 17
Public Service Company of Colorado, 6
Public Service Company of New Hampshire, 21; 55 (upd.)
Public Service Company of New Mexico, 6
Public Service Enterprise Group Inc., V; 44 (upd.)
Public Storage, Inc., 52
Publishers Clearing House, 23; 64 (upd.)
Publishers Group, Inc., 35
Publix Supermarkets Inc., 7; 31 (upd.)
Pueblo Xtra International, Inc., 47
Puget Sound Energy Inc., 6; 50 (upd.)
Pulaski Furniture Corporation, 33; 80 (upd.)
Pulitzer Inc., 15; 58 (upd.)
Pulte Corporation, 8
Pulte Homes, Inc., 42 (upd.)
Pumpkin Masters, Inc., 48
Pure World, Inc., 72
Purina Mills, Inc., 32
Puritan-Bennett Corporation, 13
Purolator Products Company, 21; 74 (upd.)
Putt-Putt Golf Courses of America, Inc., 23
PVC Container Corporation, 67
PW Eagle, Inc., 48
Pyramid Breweries Inc., 33
Pyramid Companies, 54
Q.E.P. Co., Inc., 65
Qdoba Restaurant Corporation, 93
QSC Audio Products, Inc., 56
Quad/Graphics, Inc., 19
Quaker Chemical Corp., 91
Quaker Fabric Corp., 19
Quaker Foods North America, 73 (upd.)
The Quaker Oats Company, II; 12 (upd.); 34 (upd.)
Quaker State Corporation, 7; 21 (upd.)
QUALCOMM Incorporated, 20; 47 (upd.)
Quality Chekd Dairies, Inc., 48
Quality Dining, Inc., 18
Quality Food Centers, Inc., 17
Quality Systems, Inc., 81
Quanex Corporation, 13; 62 (upd.)
Quanta Services, Inc. 79
Quantum Chemical Corporation, 8
Quantum Corporation, 10; 62 (upd.)
Quark, Inc., 36
Quest Diagnostics Inc., 26
Questar Corporation, 6; 26 (upd.)
The Quick & Reilly Group, Inc., 20
Quicken Loans, Inc., 93
Quidel Corporation, 80
The Quigley Corporation, 62
Quiksilver, Inc., 18; 79 (upd.)
QuikTrip Corporation, 36
Quill Corporation, 28
Quintiles Transnational Corporation, 21; 68 (upd.)
Quixote Corporation, 15
The Quizno's Corporation, 42
Quovadx Inc., 70
QVC Inc., 9; 58 (upd.)
Qwest Communications International, Inc., 37
R&B, Inc., 51
R.B. Pamplin Corp., 45
R.C. Bigelow, Inc., 49
R.C. Willey Home Furnishings, 72
R.G. Barry Corporation, 17; 44 (upd.)
R.H. Macy & Co., Inc., V; 8 (upd.); 30 (upd.)
R.J. Reynolds Tobacco Holdings, Inc., 30 (upd.)
R.L. Polk & Co., 10
R. M. Palmer Co., 89
R.P. Scherer, I
R.R. Donnelley & Sons Company, IV; 9 (upd.); 38 (upd.)
Racal-Datacom Inc., 11
Racing Champions Corporation, 37
Rack Room Shoes, Inc., 84
Radian Group Inc., 42
Radiation Therapy Services, Inc., 85
Radio Flyer Inc., 34
Radio One, Inc., 67
RadioShack Corporation, 36 (upd.)
Radius Inc., 16
RAE Systems Inc., 83
Rag Shops, Inc., 30
RailTex, Inc., 20
Rain Bird Corporation, 84
Rainforest Café, Inc., 25; 88 (upd.)
Rainier Brewing Company, 23
Raley's Inc., 14; 58 (upd.)
Rally's, 25; 68 (upd.)
Ralphs Grocery Company, 35
Ralston Purina Company, II; 13 (upd.)
Ramsay Youth Services, Inc., 41
Ramtron International Corporation, 89
Rand McNally & Company, 28
Randall's Food Markets, Inc., 40
Random House, Inc., 13; 31 (upd.)
Range Resources Corporation, 45
Rapala-Normark Group, Ltd., 30
Rare Hospitality International Inc., 19
RathGibson Inc., 90
Ratner Companies, 72
Raven Industries, Inc., 33
Raving Brands, Inc., 64
Rawlings Sporting Goods Co., Inc., 24
Raychem Corporation, 8
Raymond James Financial Inc., 69
Rayonier Inc., 24
Rayovac Corporation, 13; 39 (upd.)
Raytech Corporation, 61
Raytheon Aircraft Holdings Inc., 46
Raytheon Company, II; 11 (upd.); 38 (upd.)
Razorfish, Inc., 37
RCA Corporation, II
RCM Technologies, Inc., 34
RCN Corporation, 70
RDO Equipment Company, 33
RE/MAX International, Inc., 59
Read-Rite Corp., 10
The Reader's Digest Association, Inc., IV; 17 (upd.); 71 (upd.)
Reading International Inc., 70
Real Times, Inc., 66
RealNetworks, Inc., 53
Reckson Associates Realty Corp., 47
Recording for the Blind & Dyslexic, 51
Recoton Corp., 15
Recovery Engineering, Inc., 25
Recreational Equipment, Inc., 18; 71 (upd.)
Recycled Paper Greetings, Inc., 21
Red Apple Group, Inc., 23
Red Hat, Inc., 45
Red McCombs Automotive Group, 91
Red Robin Gourmet Burgers, Inc., 56
Red Roof Inns, Inc., 18
Red Spot Paint & Varnish Company, 55
Red Wing Pottery Sales, Inc., 52
Red Wing Shoe Company, Inc., 9; 30 (upd.); 83 (upd.)
Redback Networks, Inc., 92
Reddy Ice Holdings, Inc., 80
Redhook Ale Brewery, Inc., 31; 88 (upd.)
Redken Laboratories Inc., 84
RedPeg Marketing, 73

Reebok International Ltd., V; 9 (upd.); 26 (upd.)
Reed & Barton Corporation, 67
Reeds Jewelers, Inc., 22
Regal Entertainment Group, 59
Regal-Beloit Corporation, 18
The Regence Group, 74
Regency Centers Corporation, 71
Regent Communications, Inc., 87
Regis Corporation, 18; 70 (upd.)
Reichhold Chemicals, Inc., 10
Reiter Dairy, LLC, 94
Rejuvenation, Inc., 91
Reliance Electric Company, 9
Reliance Group Holdings, Inc., III
Reliance Steel & Aluminum Company, 19; 70 (upd.)
Reliant Energy Inc., 44 (upd.)
Reliv International, Inc., 58
Remedy Corporation, 58
RemedyTemp, Inc., 20
Remington Arms Company, Inc., 12; 40 (upd.)
Remington Products Company, L.L.C., 42
Renaissance Learning Systems, Inc., 39
Renal Care Group, Inc., 72
Reno Air Inc., 23
Rent-A-Center, Inc., 45
Rent-Way, Inc., 33; 75 (upd.)
Rental Service Corporation, 28
Rentrak Corporation, 35
Republic Engineered Steels, Inc., 7; 26 (upd.)
Republic Industries, Inc., 26
Republic New York Corporation, 11
Republic Services, Inc., 92
Res-Care, Inc., 29
Research Triangle Institute, 83
Reser's Fine Foods, Inc., 81
Resorts International, Inc., 12
Resource America, Inc., 42
Resources Connection, Inc., 81
Response Oncology, Inc., 27
Restaurant Associates Corporation, 66
Restaurants Unlimited, Inc., 13
Restoration Hardware, Inc., 30
Retail Ventures, Inc., 82 (upd.)
Revco D.S., Inc., V
Revell-Monogram Inc., 16
Revere Ware Corporation, 22
Revlon Inc., III; 17 (upd.); 64 (upd.)
Rewards Network Inc., 70 (upd.)
REX Stores Corp., 10
Rexel, Inc., 15
Rexnord Corporation, 21; 76 (upd.)
The Reynolds and Reynolds Company, 50
Reynolds Metals Company, IV; 19 (upd.)
RF Micro Devices, Inc., 43
RFC Franchising LLC, 68
Rhino Entertainment Company, 18; 70 (upd.)
Rhodes Inc., 23
Rica Foods, Inc., 41
Rich Products Corporation, 7; 38 (upd.); 93 (upd.)
The Richards Group, Inc., 58
Richardson Electronics, Ltd., 17
Richardson Industries, Inc., 62
Richfood Holdings, Inc., 7
Richton International Corporation, 39
Rickenbacker International Corp., 91
Riddell Sports Inc., 22
Ride, Inc., 22
The Riese Organization, 38
Riggs National Corporation, 13
Right Management Consultants, Inc., 42
Riklis Family Corp., 9
Rimage Corp., 89
Ripley Entertainment, Inc., 74
Riser Foods, Inc., 9
Rite Aid Corporation, V; 19 (upd.); 63 (upd.)
Ritz Camera Centers, 34
The Ritz-Carlton Hotel Company, L.L.C., 9; 29 (upd.); 71 (upd.)
Ritz-Craft Corporation of Pennsylvania Inc., 94
The Rival Company, 19
River Oaks Furniture, Inc., 43
River Ranch Fresh Foods LLC, 88
Riverwood International Corporation, 11; 48 (upd.)
Riviana Foods Inc., 27
Riviera Holdings Corporation, 75
Riviera Tool Company, 89
RJR Nabisco Holdings Corp., V
RMH Teleservices, Inc., 42
Roadhouse Grill, Inc., 22
Roadmaster Industries, Inc., 16
Roadway Express, Inc., V; 25 (upd.)
Roanoke Electric Steel Corporation, 45
Robbins & Myers Inc., 15
Robins, Kaplan, Miller & Ciresi L.L.P., 89
Roberds Inc., 19
Robert Half International Inc., 18; 70 (upd.)
Robert Mondavi Corporation, 15; 50 (upd.)
Robert Talbott Inc., 88
Robert W. Baird & Co. Incorporated, 67
Robert Wood Johnson Foundation, 35
Roberts Pharmaceutical Corporation, 16
Robertson-Ceco Corporation, 19
Robinson Helicopter Company, 51
Rocawear Apparel LLC, 77
Roche Bioscience, 11; 14 (upd.)
Rochester Gas and Electric Corporation, 6
Rochester Telephone Corporation, 6
Rock Bottom Restaurants, Inc., 25; 68 (upd.)
Rock-It Cargo USA, Inc., 86
Rock of Ages Corporation, 37
Rock-Tenn Company, 13; 59 (upd.)
The Rockefeller Foundation, 34
Rockefeller Group International Inc., 58
Rockford Corporation, 43
Rockford Products Corporation, 55
RockShox, Inc., 26
Rockwell Automation, 43 (upd.)
Rockwell International Corporation, I; 11 (upd.)
Rockwell Medical Technologies, Inc., 88
Rocky Mountain Chocolate Factory, Inc., 73
Rocky Shoes & Boots, Inc., 26
Rodale, Inc., 23; 47 (upd.)
ROFIN-SINAR Technologies Inc., 81
Rogers Corporation, 61; 80 (upd.)
Rohm and Haas Company, I; 26 (upd.); 77 (upd.)
ROHN Industries, Inc., 22
Rohr Incorporated, 9
Roll International Corporation, 37
Rollerblade, Inc., 15; 34 (upd.)
Rollins, Inc., 11
Rolls-Royce Allison, 29 (upd.)
Roly Poly Franchise Systems LLC, 83
Romacorp, Inc., 58
Roman Meal Company, 84
Ron Tonkin Chevrolet Company, 55
Ronco Corporation, 15; 80 (upd.)
Rooms To Go Inc., 28
Rooney Brothers Co., 25
Roper Industries, Inc., 15; 50 (upd.)
Ropes & Gray, 40
Rorer Group, I
Rosauers Supermarkets, Inc., 90
Rose Acre Farms, Inc., 60
Rose Art Industries, 58
Rose's Stores, Inc., 13
Roseburg Forest Products Company, 58
Rosemount Inc., 15
Rosenbluth International Inc., 14
Rosetta Stone Inc., 93
Ross Stores, Inc., 17; 43 (upd.)
Rotary International, 31
Roto-Rooter, Inc., 15; 61 (upd.)
The Rottlund Company, Inc., 28
Rouge Steel Company, 8
Rounder Records Corporation 79
Roundy's Inc., 14; 58 (upd.)
The Rouse Company, 15; 63 (upd.)
Rowan Companies, Inc., 43
Roy Anderson Corporation, 75
Roy F. Weston, Inc., 33
Royal Appliance Manufacturing Company, 15
Royal Caribbean Cruises Ltd., 22; 74 (upd.)
Royal Crown Company, Inc., 23
RPC, Inc., 91
RPM International Inc., 8; 36 (upd.); 91 (upd.)
RSA Security Inc., 46
RTM Restaurant Group, 58
Rubbermaid Incorporated, III; 20 (upd.)
Rubio's Restaurants, Inc., 35
Ruby Tuesday, Inc., 18; 71 (upd.)
Rudolph Technologies Inc., 94
Ruiz Food Products, Inc., 53
Rural Cellular Corporation, 43
Rural/Metro Corporation, 28
Rush Communications, 33
Rush Enterprises, Inc., 64
Russ Berrie and Company, Inc., 12; 82 (upd.)
Russell Corporation, 8; 30 (upd.); 82 (upd.)
Russell Reynolds Associates Inc., 38
Russell Stover Candies Inc., 12; 91 (upd.)
Rust International Inc., 11
Ruth's Chris Steak House, 28; 88 (upd.)
RWD Technologies, Inc., 76
Ryan Beck & Co., Inc., 66

Ryan's Restaurant Group, Inc., 15; 68 (upd.)
Ryder System, Inc., V; 24 (upd.)
Ryerson Tull, Inc., 40 (upd.)
Ryko Corporation, 83
The Ryland Group, Inc., 8; 37 (upd.)
S&C Electric Company, 15
S&D Coffee, Inc., 84
S&K Famous Brands, Inc., 23
S-K-I Limited, 15
S.C. Johnson & Son, Inc., III; 28 (upd.); 89 (upd.)
Saatchi & Saatchi, 42 (upd.)
Sabratek Corporation, 29
SABRE Group Holdings, Inc., 26
Sabre Holdings Corporation, 74 (upd.)
Safe Flight Instrument Corporation, 71
SAFECO Corporaton, III
Safeguard Scientifics, Inc., 10
Safelite Glass Corp., 19
Safeskin Corporation, 18
Safety Components International, Inc., 63
Safety 1st, Inc., 24
Safety-Kleen Systems Inc., 8; 82 (upd.)
Safeway Inc., II; 24 (upd.); 85 (upd.)
Saga Communications, Inc., 27
The St. Joe Company, 31
St. Joe Paper Company, 8
St. John Knits, Inc., 14
St. Jude Medical, Inc., 11; 43 (upd.)
St. Louis Music, Inc., 48
St. Mary Land & Exploration Company, 63
St. Paul Bank for Cooperatives, 8
The St. Paul Travelers Companies, Inc. III; 22 (upd.); 79 (upd.)
Saks Inc., 24; 41 (upd.)
Salant Corporation, 12; 51 (upd.)
salesforce.com, Inc. 79
Salick Health Care, Inc., 53
Salix Pharmaceuticals, Ltd., 93
Sally Beauty Company, Inc., 60
Salomon Inc., II; 13 (upd.)
Salt River Project, 19
Salton, Inc., 30; 88 (upd.)
The Salvation Army USA, 32
Sam Ash Music Corporation, 30
Sam Levin Inc., 80
Sam's Club, 40
Samsonite Corporation, 13; 43 (upd.)
Samuel Cabot Inc., 53
Samuels Jewelers Incorporated, 30
San Diego Gas & Electric Company, V
San Diego Padres Baseball Club LP 78
Sanborn Map Company Inc., 82
Sandals Resorts International, 65
Sanders Morris Harris Group Inc., 70
Sanderson Farms, Inc., 15
Sandia National Laboratories, 49
Sanford L.P., 82
Santa Barbara Restaurant Group, Inc., 37
The Santa Cruz Operation, Inc., 38
Santa Fe Gaming Corporation, 19
Santa Fe International Corporation, 38
Santa Fe Pacific Corporation, V
Sara Lee Corporation, II; 15 (upd.); 54 (upd.)
Sarnoff Corporation, 57
Sarris Candies Inc., 86
SAS Institute Inc., 10; 78 (upd.)
Saturn Corporation, 7; 21 (upd.); 80 (upd.)
Saucony Inc., 35; 86 (upd.)
Sauder Woodworking Company, 12; 35 (upd.)
Sauer-Danfoss Inc., 61
Saul Ewing LLP, 74
Savannah Foods & Industries, Inc., 7
Sawtek Inc., 43 (upd.)
Sbarro, Inc., 16; 64 (upd.)
SBC Communications Inc., 32 (upd.)
SBS Technologies, Inc., 25
SCANA Corporation, 6; 56 (upd.)
ScanSource, Inc., 29; 74 (upd.)
SCB Computer Technology, Inc., 29
SCEcorp, V
Schawk, Inc., 24
Scheels All Sports Inc., 63
Scheid Vineyards Inc., 66
Scherer Brothers Lumber Company, 94
Schering-Plough Corporation, I; 14 (upd.); 49 (upd.)
Schieffelin & Somerset Co., 61
Schlage Lock Company, 82
Schlotzsky's, Inc., 36
Schlumberger Limited, III; 17 (upd.); 59 (upd.)
Schmitt Music Company, 40
Schenck Business Solutions, 88
Schneider National, Inc., 36; 77 (upd.)
Schneiderman's Furniture Inc., 28
Schnitzer Steel Industries, Inc., 19
Scholastic Corporation, 10; 29 (upd.)
School Specialty, Inc., 68
School-Tech, Inc., 62
Schott Brothers, Inc., 67
Schott Corporation, 53
Schottenstein Stores Corp., 14
Schreiber Foods, Inc., 72
Schuff Steel Company, 26
Schultz Sav-O Stores, Inc., 21; 31 (upd.)
The Schwan Food Company, 83 (upd.)
Schwan's Sales Enterprises, Inc., 7; 26 (upd.)
Schwebel Baking Company, 72
Schweitzer-Mauduit International, Inc., 52
Schwinn Cycle and Fitness L.P., 19
SCI Systems, Inc., 9
Science Applications International Corporation, 15
Scientific Games Corporation, 64 (upd.)
Scientific-Atlanta, Inc., 6; 45 (upd.)
The SCO Group Inc. 78
Scope Products, Inc., 94
The Score Board, Inc., 19
Scotsman Industries, Inc., 20
Scott Fetzer Company, 12; 80 (upd.)
Scott Paper Company, IV; 31 (upd.)
The Scotts Company, 22
Scottrade, Inc., 85
Scotty's, Inc., 22
The Scoular Company, 77
Scovill Fasteners Inc., 24
SCP Pool Corporation, 39
Screen Actors Guild, 72
The Scripps Research Institute, 76
Seaboard Corporation, 36; 85 (upd.)
SeaChange International, Inc. 79
SEACOR Holdings Inc., 83
Seagate Technology, Inc., 8; 34 (upd.)
Seagull Energy Corporation, 11
Sealaska Corporation, 60
Sealed Air Corporation, 14; 57 (upd.)
Sealed Power Corporation, I
Sealright Co., Inc., 17
Sealy Inc., 12
Seaman Furniture Company, Inc., 32
Sean John Clothing, Inc., 70
Sears, Roebuck and Co., V; 18 (upd.); 56 (upd.)
Seattle City Light, 50
Seattle FilmWorks, Inc., 20
Seattle First National Bank Inc., 8
Seattle Lighting Fixture Company, 92
Seattle Pacific Industries, Inc., 92
Seattle Seahawks, Inc., 92
Seattle Times Company, 15
Seaway Food Town, Inc., 15
Sebastiani Vineyards, Inc., 28
The Second City, Inc., 88
Second Harvest, 29
Security Capital Corporation, 17
Security Pacific Corporation, II
SED International Holdings, Inc., 43
See's Candies, Inc., 30
Sega of America, Inc., 10
Segway LLC, 48
Seigle's Home and Building Centers, Inc., 41
Seitel, Inc., 47
Select Comfort Corporation, 34
Select Medical Corporation, 65
Selee Corporation, 88
The Selmer Company, Inc., 19
SEMCO Energy, Inc., 44
Seminis, Inc., 29
Semitool, Inc., 18; 79 (upd.)
Sempra Energy, 25 (upd.)
Semtech Corporation, 32
Seneca Foods Corporation, 17; 60 (upd.)
Senomyx, Inc., 83
Sensient Technologies Corporation, 52 (upd.)
Sensormatic Electronics Corp., 11
Sensory Science Corporation, 37
Sepracor Inc., 45
Sequa Corporation, 13; 54 (upd.)
Serologicals Corporation, 63
Serta, Inc., 28
Service America Corp., 7
Service Corporation International, 6; 51 (upd.)
Service Merchandise Company, Inc., V; 19 (upd.)
The ServiceMaster Company, 6; 23 (upd.); 68 (upd.)
Servpro Industries, Inc., 85
7-11, Inc., 32 (upd.)
Sevenson Environmental Services, Inc., 42
Seventh Generation, Inc., 73
Seyfarth Shaw LLP, 93
SFX Entertainment, Inc., 36
SGI, 29 (upd.)
Shakespeare Company, 22

Shaklee Corporation, 12; 39 (upd.)
Shared Medical Systems Corporation, 14
The Sharper Image Corporation, 10; 62 (upd.)
The Shaw Group, Inc., 50
Shaw Industries, Inc., 9; 40 (upd.)
Shaw's Supermarkets, Inc., 56
Shawmut National Corporation, 13
Sheaffer Pen Corporation, 82
Shearer's Foods, Inc., 72
Shearman & Sterling, 32
Shearson Lehman Brothers Holdings Inc., II; 9 (upd.)
Shedd Aquarium Society, 73
Sheetz, Inc., 85
Shelby Williams Industries, Inc., 14
Sheldahl Inc., 23
Shell Oil Company, IV; 14 (upd.); 41 (upd.)
Sheller-Globe Corporation, I
Shells Seafood Restaurants, Inc., 43
Shenandoah Telecommunications Company, 89
The Sheridan Group, Inc., 86
The Sherwin-Williams Company, III; 13 (upd.); 89 (upd.)
Sherwood Brands, Inc., 53
Shoe Carnival Inc., 14; 72 (upd.)
Shoe Pavilion, Inc., 84
Shoney's, Inc., 7; 23 (upd.)
ShopKo Stores Inc., 21; 58 (upd.)
Shoppers Food Warehouse Corporation, 66
Shorewood Packaging Corporation, 28
ShowBiz Pizza Time, Inc., 13
Showboat, Inc., 19
Showtime Networks Inc. 78
Shriners Hospitals for Children, 69
Shubert Organization Inc., 24
Shuffle Master Inc., 51
Shure Inc., 60
Shurgard Storage Centers, Inc., 52
Sidley Austin Brown & Wood, 40
Sidney Frank Importing Co., Inc., 69
Siebel Systems, Inc., 38
Siebert Financial Corp., 32
Siegel & Gale, 64
The Sierra Club, 28
Sierra Health Services, Inc., 15
Sierra Nevada Brewing Company, 70
Sierra On-Line, Inc., 15; 41 (upd.)
Sierra Pacific Industries, 22; 90 (upd.)
SIFCO Industries, Inc., 41
Sigma-Aldrich Corporation, I; 36 (upd.); 93 (upd.)
Signet Banking Corporation, 11
Sikorsky Aircraft Corporation, 24
Silhouette Brands, Inc., 55
Silicon Graphics Incorporated, 9
SilverPlatter Information Inc., 23
Silverstein Properties, Inc., 47
Simmons Company, 47
Simon & Schuster Inc., IV; 19 (upd.)
Simon Property Group Inc., 27; 84 (upd.)
Simon Transportation Services Inc., 27
Simplex Technologies Inc., 21
Simplicity Manufacturing, Inc., 64
Simpson Investment Company, 17
Simpson Thacher & Bartlett, 39
Simula, Inc., 41
Sinclair Broadcast Group, Inc., 25
The Singing Machine Company, Inc., 60
Sir Speedy, Inc., 16
Sirius Satellite Radio, Inc., 69
Siskin Steel & Supply Company, 70
Six Flags, Inc., 17; 54 (upd.)
SJW Corporation, 70
Skadden, Arps, Slate, Meagher & Flom, 18
Skechers U.S.A. Inc., 31; 88 (upd.)
Skidmore, Owings & Merrill LLP, 13; 69 (upd.)
Skyline Chili, Inc., 62
Skyline Corporation, 30
SkyMall, Inc., 26
SkyWest, Inc., 25
Skyy Spirits LLC 78
SL Green Realty Corporation, 44
SL Industries, Inc., 77
Sleepy's Inc., 32
SLI, Inc., 48
Slim-Fast Foods Company, 18; 66 (upd.)
SLM Holding Corp., 25 (upd.)
Small Planet Foods, Inc., 89
Smart & Final LLC, 16; 94 (upd.)
SMART Modular Technologies, Inc., 86
SmartForce PLC, 43
Smead Manufacturing Co., 17
Smith & Hawken, Ltd., 68
Smith & Wesson Corp., 30; 73 (upd.)
Smith Barney Inc., 15
Smith Corona Corp., 13
Smith International, Inc., 15; 59 (upd.)
Smith's Food & Drug Centers, Inc., 8; 57 (upd.)
Smith-Midland Corporation, 56
Smithfield Foods, Inc., 7; 43 (upd.)
SmithKline Beckman Corporation, I
Smithsonian Institution, 27
Smithway Motor Xpress Corporation, 39
Smurfit-Stone Container Corporation, 26 (upd.); 83 (upd.)
Snap-On, Incorporated, 7; 27 (upd.)
Snapfish, 83
Snapple Beverage Corporation, 11
Snell & Wilmer L.L.P., 28
Society Corporation, 9
Soft Sheen Products, Inc., 31
Softbank Corporation, 77 (upd.)
Sola International Inc., 71
Sole Technology Inc., 93
Solectron Corporation, 12; 48 (upd.)
Solo Serve Corporation, 28
Solutia Inc., 52
Sonat, Inc., 6
Sonesta International Hotels Corporation, 44
Sonic Automotive, Inc., 77
Sonic Corp., 14; 37 (upd.)
Sonic Innovations Inc., 56
Sonic Solutions, Inc., 81
SonicWALL, Inc., 87
Sonoco Products Company, 8; 89 (upd.)
SonoSite, Inc., 56
Sorbee International Ltd., 74
Soros Fund Management LLC, 28
Sorrento, Inc., 24
SOS Staffing Services, 25
Sotheby's Holdings, Inc., 11; 29 (upd.); 84 (upd.)
Sound Advice, Inc., 41
The Source Enterprises, Inc., 65
Source Interlink Companies, Inc., 75
South Beach Beverage Company, Inc., 73
South Dakota Wheat Growers Association, 94
South Jersey Industries, Inc., 42
Southdown, Inc., 14
The Southern Company, V; 38 (upd.)
Southern Connecticut Gas Company, 84
Southern Financial Bancorp, Inc., 56
Southern Indiana Gas and Electric Company, 13
Southern New England Telecommunications Corporation, 6
Southern Pacific Transportation Company, V
Southern Poverty Law Center, Inc., 74
Southern States Cooperative Incorporated, 36
Southern Union Company, 27
Southern Wine and Spirits of America, Inc., 84
The Southland Corporation, II; 7 (upd.)
Southtrust Corporation, 11
Southwest Airlines Co., 6; 24 (upd.); 71 (upd.)
Southwest Gas Corporation, 19
Southwest Water Company, 47
Southwestern Bell Corporation, V
Southwestern Electric Power Co., 21
Southwestern Public Service Company, 6
Southwire Company, Inc., 8; 23 (upd.)
Sovran Self Storage, Inc., 66
Spacehab, Inc., 37
Spacelabs Medical, Inc., 71
Spaghetti Warehouse, Inc., 25
Spangler Candy Company, 44
Spanish Broadcasting System, Inc., 41
Spansion Inc., 80
Spanx, Inc., 89
Spark Networks, Inc., 91
Spartan Motors Inc., 14
Spartan Stores Inc., 8; 66 (upd.)
Spartech Corporation, 19; 76 (upd.)
Sparton Corporation, 18
Spear & Jackson, Inc., 73
Spear, Leeds & Kellogg, 66
Spec's Music, Inc., 19
Special Olympics, Inc., 93
Specialized Bicycle Components Inc., 50
Specialty Coatings Inc., 8
Specialty Equipment Companies, Inc., 25
Specialty Products & Insulation Co., 59
Spectrum Control, Inc., 67
Spectrum Organic Products, Inc., 68
Spee-Dee Delivery Service, Inc., 93
SpeeDee Oil Change and Tune-Up, 25
Speedway Motorsports, Inc., 32
Speizman Industries, Inc., 44
Spelling Entertainment, 14; 35 (upd.)
Spencer Stuart and Associates, Inc., 14
Spherion Corporation, 52
Spiegel, Inc., 10; 27 (upd.)

Spinnaker Exploration Company, 72
Spirit Airlines, Inc., 31
Sport Chalet, Inc., 16; 94 (upd.)
Sport Supply Group, Inc., 23
Sportmart, Inc., 15
Sports & Recreation, Inc., 17
The Sports Authority, Inc., 16; 43 (upd.)
The Sports Club Company, 25
The Sportsman's Guide, Inc., 36
Springs Global US, Inc., V; 19 (upd.); 90 (upd.)
Sprint Corporation, 9; 46 (upd.)
SPS Technologies, Inc., 30
SPSS Inc., 64
SPX Corporation, 10; 47 (upd.)
Spyglass Entertainment Group, LLC, 91
Square D, 90
Squibb Corporation, I
SRA International, Inc., 77
SRAM Corporation, 65
SRC Holdings Corporation, 67
SRI International, Inc., 57
SSOE Inc., 76
STAAR Surgical Company, 57
Stabler Companies Inc. 78
Stage Stores, Inc., 24; 82 (upd.)
Stanadyne Automotive Corporation, 37
StanCorp Financial Group, Inc., 56
Standard Candy Company Inc., 86
Standard Commercial Corporation, 13; 62 (upd.)
Standard Federal Bank, 9
Standard Microsystems Corporation, 11
Standard Motor Products, Inc., 40
Standard Pacific Corporation, 52
The Standard Register Company, 15, 93 (upd.)
Standex International Corporation, 17; 44 (upd.)
Stanhome Inc., 15
Stanley Furniture Company, Inc., 34
The Stanley Works, III; 20 (upd.); 79 (upd.)
Staple Cotton Cooperative Association (Staplcotn), 86
Staples, Inc., 10; 55 (upd.)
Star Banc Corporation, 11
Starbucks Corporation, 13; 34 (upd.); 77 (upd.)
Starcraft Corporation, 30; 66 (upd.)
Starkey Laboratories, Inc., 52
Starrett Corporation, 21
StarTek, Inc. 79
Starter Corp., 12
Starwood Hotels & Resorts Worldwide, Inc., 54
Starz LLC, 91
The Stash Tea Company, 50
State Auto Financial Corporation, 77
State Farm Mutual Automobile Insurance Company, III; 51 (upd.)
State Financial Services Corporation, 51
State Street Corporation, 8; 57 (upd.)
Staten Island Bancorp, Inc., 39
Stater Bros. Holdings Inc., 64
Station Casinos, Inc., 25; 90 (upd.)
The Staubach Company, 62
The Steak n Shake Company, 41
Stearns, Inc., 43
Steel Dynamics, Inc., 52
Steel Technologies Inc., 63
Steelcase, Inc., 7; 27 (upd.)
Stein Mart Inc., 19; 72 (upd.)
Steiner Corporation (Alsco), 53
Steinway Musical Properties, Inc., 19
Stemilt Growers Inc., 94
Stepan Company, 30
The Stephan Company, 60
Stephens Media, LLC, 91
Stephens Inc., 92
Stericycle, Inc., 33; 74 (upd.)
STERIS Corporation, 29
Sterling Chemicals Inc., 16; 78 (upd.)
Sterling Drug, Inc., I
Sterling Electronics Corp., 18
Sterling Software, Inc., 11
Steve & Barry's LLC, 88
Stevedoring Services of America Inc., 28
Steven Madden, Ltd., 37
Stew Leonard's, 56
Stewart & Stevenson Services Inc., 11
Stewart Enterprises, Inc., 20
Stewart Information Services Corporation 78
Stewart's Beverages, 39
Stewart's Shops Corporation, 80
Stiefel Laboratories, Inc., 90
Stillwater Mining Company, 47
Stimson Lumber Company 78
Stock Yards Packing Co., Inc., 37
Stone & Webster, Inc., 13; 64 (upd.)
Stone Container Corporation, IV
Stone Manufacturing Company, 14; 43 (upd.)
Stonyfield Farm, Inc., 55
The Stop & Shop Supermarket Company, II; 24 (upd.); 68 (upd.)
Storage Technology Corporation, 6
Storage USA, Inc., 21
Stouffer Corp., 8
StrataCom, Inc., 16
Stratagene Corporation, 70
Stratasys, Inc., 67
Strattec Security Corporation, 73
Stratus Computer, Inc., 10
Strauss Discount Auto, 56
Strayer Education, Inc., 53
The Stride Rite Corporation, 8; 37 (upd.); 86 (upd.)
Strine Printing Company Inc., 88
The Strober Organization, Inc., 82
The Stroh Brewery Company, I; 18 (upd.)
Strombecker Corporation, 60
Stroock & Stroock & Lavan LLP, 40
Strouds, Inc., 33
Stryker Corporation, 11; 29 (upd.); 79 (upd.)
Stuart C. Irby Company, 58
Stuart Entertainment Inc., 16
Student Loan Marketing Association, II
Stuller Settings, Inc., 35
Sturm, Ruger & Company, Inc., 19
Stussy, Inc., 55
Sub-Zero Freezer Co., Inc., 31
Suburban Propane Partners, L.P., 30
Subway, 32
Successories, Inc., 30
Sudbury Inc., 16
Suiza Foods Corporation, 26
Sullivan & Cromwell, 26
The Summit Bancorporation, 14
Summit Family Restaurants, Inc. 19
Sun Communities Inc., 46
Sun Company, Inc., IV
Sun Country Airlines, 30
Sun-Diamond Growers of California, 7
Sun Distributors L.P., 12
Sun Healthcare Group Inc., 25
Sun Hydraulics Corporation, 74
Sun-Maid Growers of California, 82
Sun Microsystems, Inc., 7; 30 (upd.); 91 (upd.)
Sun Sportswear, Inc., 17
Sun Television & Appliances Inc., 10
Sun World International, LLC, 93
SunAmerica Inc., 11
Sunbeam-Oster Co., Inc., 9
Sunburst Hospitality Corporation, 26
Sunburst Shutter Corporation 78
Sundstrand Corporation, 7; 21 (upd.)
Sundt Corp., 24
SunGard Data Systems Inc., 11
Sunglass Hut International, Inc., 21; 74 (upd.)
Sunkist Growers, Inc., 26
Sunoco, Inc., 28 (upd.); 83 (upd.)
SunPower Corporation, 91
The Sunrider Corporation, 26
Sunrise Greetings, 88
Sunrise Medical Inc., 11
Sunrise Senior Living, Inc., 81
Sunterra Corporation, 75
SunTrust Banks Inc., 23
Super 8 Motels, Inc., 83
Super Food Services, Inc., 15
Supercuts Inc., 26
Superior Essex Inc., 80
Superior Energy Services, Inc., 65
Superior Industries International, Inc., 8
Superior Uniform Group, Inc., 30
Supermarkets General Holdings Corporation, II
SUPERVALU Inc., II; 18 (upd.); 50 (upd.)
Suprema Specialties, Inc., 27
Supreme International Corporation, 27
Susan G. Komen Breast Cancer Foundation 78
Susquehanna Pfaltzgraff Company, 8
Sutter Home Winery Inc., 16
Sverdrup Corporation, 14
Swales & Associates, Inc., 69
Swank, Inc., 17; 84 (upd.)
SwedishAmerican Health System, 51
Sweet Candy Company, 60
Sweetheart Cup Company, Inc., 36
The Swett & Crawford Group Inc., 84
SWH Corporation, 70
Swift & Company, 55
Swift Energy Company, 63
Swift Transportation Co., Inc., 42
Swinerton Inc., 43
Swisher International Group Inc., 23
Swiss Valley Farms Company, 90

Sybase, Inc., 10; 27 (upd.)
Sybron International Corp., 14
Sycamore Networks, Inc., 45
Sykes Enterprises, Inc., 45
Sylvan Learning Systems, Inc., 35
Sylvan, Inc., 22
Symantec Corporation, 10; 82 (upd.)
Symbol Technologies, Inc., 15
Syms Corporation, 29; 74 (upd.)
Symyx Technologies, Inc., 77
SYNNEX Corporation, 73
Synopsys, Inc., 11; 69 (upd.)
SynOptics Communications, Inc., 10
Synovus Financial Corp., 12; 52 (upd.)
Syntel, Inc., 92
Syntex Corporation, I
Sypris Solutions, Inc., 85
SyQuest Technology, Inc., 18
Syratech Corp., 14
SYSCO Corporation, II; 24 (upd.); 75 (upd.)
System Software Associates, Inc., 10
Systemax, Inc., 52
Systems & Computer Technology Corp., 19
T-Netix, Inc., 46
T. Marzetti Company, 57
T. Rowe Price Associates, Inc., 11; 34 (upd.)
TAB Products Co., 17
Taco Bell Corporation, 7; 21 (upd.); 74 (upd.)
Taco Cabana, Inc., 23; 72 (upd.)
Taco John's International, Inc., 15; 63 (upd.)
Tacony Corporation, 70
Tag-It Pacific, Inc., 85
Take-Two Interactive Software, Inc., 46
The Talbots, Inc., 11; 31 (upd.); 88 (upd.)
Talk America Holdings, Inc., 70
Talley Industries, Inc., 16
TALX Corporation, 92
Tambrands Inc., 8
Tandem Computers, Inc., 6
Tandy Corporation, II; 12 (upd.)
Tandycrafts, Inc., 31
Tanger Factory Outlet Centers, Inc., 49
Tanox, Inc., 77
Tapemark Company Inc., 64
Target Corporation, 10; 27 (upd.); 61 (upd.)
Tarragon Realty Investors, Inc., 45
Tarrant Apparel Group, 62
Taser International, Inc., 62
Tasty Baking Company, 14; 35 (upd.)
Tattered Cover Book Store, 43
Taubman Centers, Inc., 75
Taylor Corporation, 36
Taylor Guitars, 48
Taylor Made Golf Co., 23
Taylor Publishing Company, 12; 36 (upd.)
TB Wood's Corporation, 56
TBWA/Chiat/Day, 6; 43 (upd.)
TCBY Enterprises Inc., 17
TCF Financial Corporation, 47
Teachers Insurance and Annuity Association-College Retirement Equities Fund, III; 45 (upd.)
TearDrop Golf Company, 32
Tech Data Corporation, 10; 74 (upd.)
Tech-Sym Corporation, 18; 44 (upd.)
TechBooks Inc., 84
TECHNE Corporation, 52
Technical Olympic USA, Inc., 75
Technitrol, Inc., 29
Technology Research Corporation, 94
Technology Solutions Company, 94
TECO Energy, Inc., 6
Tecumseh Products Company, 8; 71 (upd.)
Tee Vee Toons, Inc., 57
Tejon Ranch Company, 35
Tekelec, 83
Tektronix Inc., 8; 78 (upd.)
Telcordia Technologies, Inc., 59
Tele-Communications, Inc., II
Teledyne Technologies Inc., I; 10 (upd.); 62 (upd.)
Telephone and Data Systems, Inc., 9
Tellabs, Inc., 11; 40 (upd.)
Telxon Corporation, 10
Temple-Inland Inc., IV; 31 (upd.)
Tempur-Pedic Inc., 54
Tenet Healthcare Corporation, 55 (upd.)
TenFold Corporation, 35
Tennant Company, 13; 33 (upd.)
Tenneco Inc., I; 10 (upd.)
Tennessee Valley Authority, 50
TEPPCO Partners, L.P., 73
Teradyne, Inc., 11
Terex Corporation, 7; 40 (upd.); 91 (upd.)
The Terlato Wine Group, 48
Terra Industries, Inc., 13; 94 (upd.)
Tesoro Petroleum Corporation, 7; 45 (upd.)
The Testor Corporation, 51
Tetley USA Inc., 88
Tetra Tech, Inc., 29
Texaco Inc., IV; 14 (upd.); 41 (upd.)
Texas Air Corporation, I
Texas Industries, Inc., 8
Texas Instruments Inc., II; 11 (upd.); 46 (upd.)
Texas Pacific Group Inc., 36
Texas Rangers Baseball, 51
Texas Roadhouse, Inc., 69
Texas Utilities Company, V; 25 (upd.)
Textron Inc., I; 34 (upd.); 88 (upd.)
Textron Lycoming Turbine Engine, 9
Tha Row Records, 69 (upd.)
Thane International, Inc., 84
Thermadyne Holding Corporation, 19
Thermo BioAnalysis Corp., 25
Thermo Electron Corporation, 7
Thermo Fibertek, Inc., 24
Thermo Instrument Systems Inc., 11
Thermo King Corporation, 13
Thermos Company, 16
Things Remembered, Inc., 84
Thiokol Corporation, 9; 22 (upd.)
Thomas & Betts Corporation, 11; 54 (upd.)
Thomas & Howard Company, Inc., 90
Thomas Cook Travel Inc., 9; 33 (upd.)
Thomas H. Lee Co., 24
Thomas Industries Inc., 29
Thomas J. Lipton Company, 14
Thomas Nelson, Inc., 14; 38 (upd.)
Thomas Publishing Company, 26
Thomaston Mills, Inc., 27
Thomasville Furniture Industries, Inc., 12; 74 (upd.)
Thomsen Greenhouses and Garden Center, Incorporated, 65
Thor Industries Inc., 39; 92 (upd.)
Thorn Apple Valley, Inc., 7; 22 (upd.)
ThoughtWorks Inc., 90
Thousand Trails, Inc., 33
THQ, Inc., 39; 92 (upd.)
3Com Corporation, 11; 34 (upd.)
The 3DO Company, 43
3M Company, 61 (upd.)
Thrifty PayLess, Inc., 12
TIBCO Software Inc. 79
TIC Holdings Inc., 92
Ticketmaster, 76 (upd.)
Ticketmaster Group, Inc., 13; 37 (upd.)
Tidewater Inc., 11; 37 (upd.)
Tiffany & Co., 14; 78 (upd.)
TIG Holdings, Inc., 26
Tilia Inc., 62
Tillotson Corp., 15
Timber Lodge Steakhouse, Inc., 73
The Timberland Company, 13; 54 (upd.)
Timberline Software Corporation, 15
Time Warner Inc., IV; 7 (upd.)
The Times Mirror Company, IV; 17 (upd.)
Timex Corporation, 7; 25 (upd.)
The Timken Company, 8; 42 (upd.)
Tishman Speyer Properties, L.P., 47
The Titan Corporation, 36
Titan International, Inc., 89
Titanium Metals Corporation, 21
TiVo Inc., 75
TJ International, Inc., 19
The TJX Companies, Inc., V; 19 (upd.); 57 (upd.)
TLC Beatrice International Holdings, Inc., 22
TMP Worldwide Inc., 30
TNT Freightways Corporation, 14
Today's Man, Inc., 20
TODCO, 87
Todd Shipyards Corporation, 14
The Todd-AO Corporation, 33
Todhunter International, Inc., 27
Tofutti Brands, Inc., 64
Tokheim Corporation, 21
TOKYOPOP Inc. 79
Toll Brothers Inc., 15; 70 (upd.)
Tollgrade Communications, Inc., 44
Tom Brown, Inc., 37
Tom Doherty Associates Inc., 25
Tom's Foods Inc., 66
Tom's of Maine, Inc., 45
Tombstone Pizza Corporation, 13
Tone Brothers, Inc., 21; 74 (upd.)
Tonka Corporation, 25
Too, Inc., 61

Tootsie Roll Industries, Inc., 12; 82 (upd.)
Topco Associates LLC, 60
The Topps Company, Inc., 13; 34 (upd.); 83 (upd.)
Tops Appliance City, Inc., 17
Tops Markets LLC, 60
Torchmark Corporation, 9; 33 (upd.)
Toresco Enterprises, Inc., 84
The Toro Company, 7; 26 (upd.); 77 (upd.)
The Torrington Company, 13
Tosco Corporation, 7
Total Entertainment Restaurant Corporation, 46
Total System Services, Inc., 18
Totem Resources Corporation, 9
Tower Air, Inc., 28
Tower Automotive, Inc., 24
Towers Perrin, 32
Town & Country Corporation, 19
Town Sports International, Inc., 46
Townsends, Inc., 64
Toy Biz, Inc., 18
Toymax International, Inc., 29
Toys 'R Us, Inc., V; 18 (upd.); 57 (upd.)
Tracor Inc., 17
Tractor Supply Company, 57
Trader Joe's Company, 13; 50 (upd.)
TradeStation Group, Inc., 83
Traffix, Inc., 61
Trailer Bridge, Inc., 41
Trammell Crow Company, 8; 57 (upd.)
Trane 78
Trans World Airlines, Inc., I; 12 (upd.); 35 (upd.)
Trans World Entertainment Corporation, 24; 68 (upd.)
Trans-Lux Corporation, 51
Transaction Systems Architects, Inc., 29; 82 (upd.)
Transamerica–An AEGON Company, I; 13 (upd.); 41 (upd.)
Transatlantic Holdings, Inc., 11
Transco Energy Company, V
Transitions Optical, Inc., 83
Transmedia Network Inc., 20
TransMontaigne Inc., 28
Transocean Sedco Forex Inc., 45
Transport Corporation of America, Inc., 49
TransPro, Inc., 71
The Tranzonic Companies, 37
Travel Ports of America, Inc., 17
The Travelers Corporation, III
Travelocity.com, Inc., 46
Travelzoo Inc. 79
Travis Boats & Motors, Inc., 37
TRC Companies, Inc., 32
Treadco, Inc., 19
Treasure Chest Advertising Company, Inc., 32
Tredegar Corporation, 52
Tree of Life, Inc., 29
Tree Top, Inc., 76
TreeHouse Foods, Inc. 79
Trek Bicycle Corporation, 16; 78 (upd.)
Trend-Lines, Inc., 22
Trendwest Resorts, Inc., 33
Trex Company, Inc., 71
Tri Valley Growers, 32
Triarc Companies, Inc., 8; 34 (upd.)
Tribune Company, IV; 22 (upd.); 63 (upd.)
Trico Products Corporation, 15
Trico Marine Services, Inc., 89
Tilcon-Connecticut Inc., 80
Trident Seafoods Corporation, 56
Trigen Energy Corporation, 42
TriMas Corp., 11
Trimble Navigation Limited, 40
Trinity Industries, Incorporated, 7
TRINOVA Corporation, III
TriPath Imaging, Inc., 77
Triple Five Group Ltd., 49
TriQuint Semiconductor, Inc., 63
Trisko Jewelry Sculptures, Ltd., 57
Triton Energy Corporation, 11
Triumph Group, Inc., 31
The TriZetto Group, Inc., 83
TRM Copy Centers Corporation, 18
Tropicana Products, Inc., 28; 73 (upd.)
Troutman Sanders L.L.P. 79
True North Communications Inc., 23
True Religion Apparel, Inc. 79
True Value Company, 74 (upd.)
The Trump Organization, 23; 64 (upd.)
TruServ Corporation, 24
TRW Automotive Holdings Corp., 75 (upd.)
TRW Inc., I; 11 (upd.); 14 (upd.)
TTX Company, 6; 66 (upd.)
Tubby's, Inc., 53
Tucson Electric Power Company, 6
Tuesday Morning Corporation, 18; 70 (upd.)
Tully's Coffee Corporation, 51
Tultex Corporation, 13
Tumaro's Gourmet Tortillas, 85
Tumbleweed, Inc., 33; 80 (upd.)
Tupperware Corporation, 28; 78 (upd.)
TurboChef Technologies, Inc., 83
Turner Broadcasting System, Inc., II; 6 (upd.); 66 (upd.)
Turner Construction Company, 66
The Turner Corporation, 8; 23 (upd.)
Turtle Wax, Inc., 15; 93 (upd.)
Tuscarora Inc., 29
Tutogen Medical, Inc., 68
Tuttle Publishing, 86
TV Guide, Inc., 43 (upd.)
TVI, Inc., 15
TW Services, Inc., II
Tweeter Home Entertainment Group, Inc., 30
Twentieth Century Fox Film Corporation, II; 25 (upd.)
24 Hour Fitness Worldwide, Inc., 71
24/7 Real Media, Inc., 49
Twin Disc, Inc., 21
Twinlab Corporation, 34
II-VI Incorporated, 69
Ty Inc., 33; 86 (upd.)
Tyco Toys, Inc., 12
Tyler Corporation, 23
Tyndale House Publishers, Inc., 57
Tyson Foods, Inc., II; 14 (upd.); 50 (upd.)
U S West, Inc., V; 25 (upd.)
U.S. Aggregates, Inc., 42
U.S. Army Corps of Engineers, 91
U.S. Bancorp, 14; 36 (upd.)
U.S. Borax, Inc., 42
U.S. Can Corporation, 30
U.S. Cellular Corporation, 31 (upd.); 88 (upd.)
U.S. Delivery Systems, Inc., 22
U.S. Foodservice, 26
U.S. Healthcare, Inc., 6
U.S. Home Corporation, 8; 78 (upd.)
U.S. News & World Report Inc., 30; 89 (upd.)
U.S. Office Products Company, 25
U.S. Physical Therapy, Inc., 65
U.S. Premium Beef LLC, 91
U.S. Robotics Corporation, 9; 66 (upd.)
U.S. Satellite Broadcasting Company, Inc., 20
U.S. Timberlands Company, L.P., 42
U.S. Trust Corp., 17
U.S. Vision, Inc., 66
UAL Corporation, 34 (upd.)
UAW (International Union, United Automobile, Aerospace and Agricultural Implement Workers of America), 72
UGI Corporation, 12
Ugly Duckling Corporation, 22
UICI, 33
Ukrop's Super Market's, Inc., 39
Ulta Salon, Cosmetics & Fragrance, Inc., 93
Ultimate Electronics, Inc., 18; 69 (upd.)
Ultra Pac, Inc., 24
Ultra Petroleum Corporation, 71
Ultrak Inc., 24
Ultralife Batteries, Inc., 58
Ultramar Diamond Shamrock Corporation, 31 (upd.)
Umpqua Holdings Corporation, 87
Uncle Ben's Inc., 22
Uncle Ray's LLC, 90
Under Armour Performance Apparel, 61
Underwriters Laboratories, Inc., 30
Uni-Marts, Inc., 17
Unica Corporation, 77
Unicom Corporation, 29 (upd.)
Unifi, Inc., 12; 62 (upd.)
Unified Grocers, Inc., 93
UniFirst Corporation, 21
Union Bank of California, 16
Union Camp Corporation, IV
Union Carbide Corporation, I; 9 (upd.); 74 (upd.)
Union Electric Company, V
Union Pacific Corporation, V; 28 (upd.); 79 (upd.)
Union Planters Corporation, 54
Union Texas Petroleum Holdings, Inc., 9
UnionBanCal Corporation, 50 (upd.)
Unique Casual Restaurants, Inc., 27
Unison HealthCare Corporation, 25
Unisys Corporation, III; 6 (upd.); 36 (upd.)
Unit Corporation, 63

United Airlines, I; 6 (upd.)
United Auto Group, Inc., 26; 68 (upd.)
United Brands Company, II
United Dairy Farmers, Inc., 74
United Defense Industries, Inc., 30; 66 (upd.)
United Dominion Industries Limited, 8; 16 (upd.)
United Dominion Realty Trust, Inc., 52
United Farm Workers of America, 88
United Foods, Inc., 21
United HealthCare Corporation, 9
The United Illuminating Company, 21
United Industrial Corporation, 37
United Industries Corporation, 68
United Jewish Communities, 33
United Merchants & Manufacturers, Inc., 13
United National Group, Ltd., 63
United Nations International Children's Emergency Fund (UNICEF), 58
United Natural Foods, Inc., 32; 76 (upd.)
United Negro College Fund, Inc. 79
United Online, Inc., 71 (upd.)
United Parcel Service of America Inc., V; 17 (upd.)
United Parcel Service, Inc., 63; 94 (upd.)
United Press International, Inc., 25; 73 (upd.)
United Rentals, Inc., 34
United Retail Group Inc., 33
United Road Services, Inc., 69
United Service Organizations, 60
United States Cellular Corporation, 9
United States Filter Corporation, 20
United States Pipe and Foundry Company, 62
United States Playing Card Company, 62
United States Postal Service, 14; 34 (upd.)
The United States Shoe Corporation, V
United States Steel Corporation, 50 (upd.)
United States Surgical Corporation, 10; 34 (upd.)
United Stationers Inc., 14
United Talent Agency, Inc., 80
United Technologies Automotive Inc., 15
United Technologies Corporation, I; 10 (upd.); 34 (upd.)
United Telecommunications, Inc., V
United Video Satellite Group, 18
United Water Resources, Inc., 40
United Way of America, 36
Unitil Corporation, 37
Unitog Co., 19
Unitrin Inc., 16; V
Univar Corporation, 9
Universal Compression, Inc., 59
Universal Corporation, V; 48 (upd.)
Universal Electronics Inc., 39
Universal Foods Corporation, 7
Universal Forest Products, Inc., 10; 59 (upd.)
Universal Health Services, Inc., 6
Universal International, Inc., 25
Universal Manufacturing Company, 88
Universal Stainless & Alloy Products, Inc., 75
Universal Studios, Inc., 33
Universal Technical Institute, Inc., 81
The University of Chicago Press 79
Univision Communications Inc., 24; 83 (upd.)
Uno Restaurant Corporation, 18
Uno Restaurant Holdings Corporation, 70 (upd.)
Unocal Corporation, IV; 24 (upd.); 71 (upd.)
UnumProvident Corporation, 13; 52 (upd.)
The Upjohn Company, I; 8 (upd.)
Urban Outfitters, Inc., 14; 74 (upd.)
URS Corporation, 45; 80 (upd.)
US Airways Group, Inc., I; 6 (upd.); 28 (upd.); 52 (upd.)
US 1 Industries, Inc., 89
USA Interactive, Inc., 47 (upd.)
USA Truck, Inc., 42
USAA, 10; 62 (upd.)
USANA, Inc., 29
USF&G Corporation, III
USG Corporation, III; 26 (upd.); 81 (upd.)
UST Inc., 9; 50 (upd.)
USX Corporation, IV; 7 (upd.)
Utah Medical Products, Inc., 36
Utah Power and Light Company, 27
UtiliCorp United Inc., 6
UTStarcom, Inc., 77
Utz Quality Foods, Inc., 72
UUNET, 38
Uwajimaya, Inc., 60
Vail Resorts, Inc., 11; 43 (upd.)
Valassis Communications, Inc., 8; 37 (upd.); 76 (upd.)
Valero Energy Corporation, 7; 71 (upd.)
Valhi, Inc., 19; 94 (upd.)
Vallen Corporation, 45
Valley Media Inc., 35
Valley National Gases, Inc., 85
Valley Proteins, Inc., 91
ValleyCrest Companies, 81 (upd.)
Valmont Industries, Inc., 19
The Valspar Corporation, 8; 32 (upd.); 77 (upd.)
Value City Department Stores, Inc., 38
Value Line, Inc., 16; 73 (upd.)
Value Merchants Inc., 13
ValueClick, Inc., 49
ValueVision International, Inc., 22
Van Camp Seafood Company, Inc., 7
Van's Aircraft, Inc., 65
Vance Publishing Corporation, 64
The Vanguard Group, Inc., 14; 34 (upd.)
Vanguard Health Systems Inc., 70
Vans, Inc., 16; 47 (upd.)
Varco International, Inc., 42
Vari-Lite International, Inc., 35
Varian, Inc., 12; 48 (upd.)
Variety Wholesalers, Inc., 73
Variflex, Inc., 51
Varlen Corporation, 16
Varsity Spirit Corp., 15
VASCO Data Security International, Inc. 79
Vastar Resources, Inc., 24
VCA Antech, Inc., 58
VECO International, Inc., 7
Vector Group Ltd., 35 (upd.)
Veeco Instruments Inc., 32
Veit Companies, 43; 92 (upd.)
Velocity Express Corporation, 49; 94 (upd.)
Venator Group Inc., 35 (upd.)
Vencor, Inc., 16
Venetian Casino Resort, LLC, 47
Ventana Medical Systems, Inc., 75
Ventura Foods LLC, 90
Venture Stores Inc., 12
VeraSun Energy Corporation, 87
Verbatim Corporation, 14; 74 (upd.)
Veridian Corporation, 54
VeriFone Holdings, Inc., 18; 76 (upd.)
Verint Systems Inc., 73
VeriSign, Inc., 47
Veritas Software Corporation, 45
Verity Inc., 68
Verizon Communications, 43 (upd.); 78 (upd.)
Vermeer Manufacturing Company, 17
The Vermont Country Store, 93
Vermont Pure Holdings, Ltd., 51
The Vermont Teddy Bear Co., Inc., 36
Vertex Pharmaceuticals Incorporated, 83
Vertis Communications, 84
Vertrue Inc., 77
VF Corporation, V; 17 (upd.); 54 (upd.)
VHA Inc., 53
Viacom Inc., 7; 23 (upd.); 67 (upd.)
Viad Corp., 73
ViaSat, Inc., 54
Viasoft Inc., 27
VIASYS Healthcare, Inc., 52
Viasystems Group, Inc., 67
Viatech Continental Can Company, Inc., 25 (upd.)
Vicon Industries, Inc., 44
VICORP Restaurants, Inc., 12; 48 (upd.)
Victory Refrigeration, Inc., 82
Videojet Technologies, Inc., 90
Vienna Sausage Manufacturing Co., 14
Viewpoint International, Inc., 66
ViewSonic Corporation, 72
Viking Office Products, Inc., 10
Viking Range Corporation, 66
Village Super Market, Inc., 7
Village Voice Media, Inc., 38
Vinson & Elkins L.L.P., 30
Vintage Petroleum, Inc., 42
Vinton Studios, 63
Virbac Corporation, 74
Virco Manufacturing Corporation, 17
Virginia Dare Extract Company, Inc., 94
Visa International, 9; 26 (upd.)
Vishay Intertechnology, Inc., 21; 80 (upd.)
Vision Service Plan Inc., 77
Viskase Companies, Inc., 55
Vista Bakery, Inc., 56
Vista Chemical Company, I
Vistana, Inc., 22
VISX, Incorporated, 30
Vita Plus Corporation, 60
Vital Images, Inc., 85
Vitalink Pharmacy Services, Inc., 15

Vitamin Shoppe Industries, Inc., 60
Vitesse Semiconductor Corporation, 32
Vitro Corp., 10
Vivra, Inc., 18
Vlasic Foods International Inc., 25
VLSI Technology, Inc., 16
VMware, Inc., 90
Volcom, Inc., 77
Volt Information Sciences Inc., 26
Volunteers of America, Inc., 66
Von Maur Inc., 64
Vonage Holdings Corp., 81
The Vons Companies, Incorporated, 7; 28 (upd.)
Vornado Realty Trust, 20
Vought Aircraft Industries, Inc., 49
Vulcan Materials Company, 7; 52 (upd.)
W. Atlee Burpee & Co., 27
W.A. Whitney Company, 53
W.B Doner & Co., 56
W.C. Bradley Co., 69
W. H. Braum, Inc., 80
W.H. Brady Co., 17
W.L. Gore & Associates, Inc., 14; 60 (upd.)
W.P. Carey & Co. LLC, 49
W.R. Berkley Corporation, 15; 74 (upd.)
W.R. Grace & Company, I; 50 (upd.)
W.W. Grainger, Inc., V; 26 (upd.); 68 (upd.)
W.W. Norton & Company, Inc., 28
Waban Inc., 13
Wabash National Corp., 13
Wabtec Corporation, 40
Wachovia Bank of Georgia, N.A., 16
Wachovia Bank of South Carolina, N.A., 16
Wachovia Corporation, 12; 46 (upd.)
Wachtell, Lipton, Rosen & Katz, 47
The Wackenhut Corporation, 14; 63 (upd.)
Waddell & Reed, Inc., 22
Waffle House Inc., 14; 60 (upd.)
Wagers Inc. (Idaho Candy Company), 86
Waggener Edstrom, 42
Wah Chang, 82
Wahl Clipper Corporation, 86
Wakefern Food Corporation, 33
Wal-Mart Stores, Inc., V; 8 (upd.); 26 (upd.); 63 (upd.)
Walbridge Aldinger Co., 38
Walbro Corporation, 13
Waldbaum, Inc., 19
Waldenbooks, 17; 86 (upd.)
Walgreen Co., V; 20 (upd.); 65 (upd.)
Walker Manufacturing Company, 19
Wall Drug Store, Inc., 40
Wall Street Deli, Inc., 33
Wallace Computer Services, Inc., 36
Walsworth Publishing Co. 78
The Walt Disney Company, II; 6 (upd.); 30 (upd.); 63 (upd.)
Walter Industries, Inc., II; 22 (upd.); 72 (upd.)
Walton Monroe Mills, Inc., 8
Wang Laboratories, Inc., III; 6 (upd.)
The Warnaco Group Inc., 12; 46 (upd.)
Warner Communications Inc., II
Warner Music Group Corporation, 90 (upd.)
Warner-Lambert Co., I; 10 (upd.)
Warners' Stellian Inc., 67
Warrantech Corporation, 53
Warrell Corporation, 68
Warwick Valley Telephone Company, 55
The Washington Companies, 33
Washington Federal, Inc., 17
Washington Football, Inc., 35
Washington Gas Light Company, 19
Washington Mutual, Inc., 17; 93 (upd.)
Washington National Corporation, 12
Washington Natural Gas Company, 9
The Washington Post Company, IV; 20 (upd.)
Washington Scientific Industries, Inc., 17
Washington Water Power Company, 6
Waste Connections, Inc., 46
Waste Holdings, Inc., 41
Waste Management, Inc., V
Water Pik Technologies, Inc., 34; 83 (upd.)
Waterhouse Investor Services, Inc., 18
Waters Corporation, 43
Watkins-Johnson Company, 15
Watsco Inc., 52
Watson Pharmaceuticals Inc., 16; 56 (upd.)
Watson Wyatt Worldwide, 42
Watts Industries, Inc., 19
Wausau-Mosinee Paper Corporation, 60 (upd.)
Waverly, Inc., 16
Wawa Inc., 17; 78 (upd.)
Waxman Industries, Inc., 9
WD-40 Company, 18; 87 (upd.)
The Weather Channel Companies, The 52
Weatherford International, Inc., 39
Weaver Popcorn Company, Inc., 89
Webber Oil Company, 61
Weber-Stephen Products Co., 40
WebEx Communications, Inc., 81
WebMD Corporation, 65
Weeres Industries Corporation, 52
Wegmans Food Markets, Inc., 9; 41 (upd.)
Weider Nutrition International, Inc., 29
Weight Watchers International Inc., 12; 33 (upd.); 73 (upd.)
Weil, Gotshal & Manges LLP, 55
Weiner's Stores, Inc., 33
Weirton Steel Corporation, IV; 26 (upd.)
Weis Markets, Inc., 15; 84 (upd.)
The Weitz Company, Inc., 42
Welbilt Corp., 19
Welcome Wagon International Inc., 82
The Welk Group Inc. 78
WellChoice, Inc., 67 (upd.)
Wellco Enterprises, Inc., 84
Wellman, Inc., 8; 52 (upd.)
WellPoint Health Networks Inc., 25
Wells Fargo & Company, II; 12 (upd.); 38 (upd.)
Wells Rich Greene BDDP, 6
Wells' Dairy, Inc., 36
Wells-Gardner Electronics Corporation, 43
Wendy's International, Inc., 8; 23 (upd.); 47 (upd.)
Wenner Bread Products Inc., 80
Wenner Media, Inc., 32
Werner Enterprises, Inc., 26
West Bend Co., 14
West Coast Entertainment Corporation, 29
West Corporation, 42
West Group, 34 (upd.)
West Linn Paper Company, 91
West Marine, Inc., 17; 90 (upd.)
West One Bancorp, 11
West Pharmaceutical Services, Inc., 42
West Point-Pepperell, Inc., 8
West Publishing Co., 7
Westaff Inc., 33
Westamerica Bancorporation, 17
Westar Energy, Inc., 57 (upd.)
WestCoast Hospitality Corporation, 59
Westcon Group, Inc., 67
Westell Technologies, Inc., 57
Westerbeke Corporation, 60
Western Atlas Inc., 12
Western Beef, Inc., 22
Western Company of North America, 15
Western Digital Corporation, 25; 92 (upd.)
Western Gas Resources, Inc., 45
Western Publishing Group, Inc., 13
Western Resources, Inc., 12
The WesterN SizzliN Corporation, 60
Western Union Financial Services, Inc., 54
Western Wireless Corporation, 36
Westfield Group, 69
Westin Hotels and Resorts Worldwide, 9; 29 (upd.)
Westinghouse Electric Corporation, II; 12 (upd.)
Westmoreland Coal Company, 7
WestPoint Stevens Inc., 16
Westport Resources Corporation, 63
Westvaco Corporation, IV; 19 (upd.)
Westwood One, Inc., 23
The Wet Seal, Inc., 18; 70 (upd.)
Wetterau Incorporated, II
Weyco Group, Incorporated, 32
Weyerhaeuser Company, IV; 9 (upd.); 28 (upd.); 83 (upd.)
WFS Financial Inc., 70
WGBH Educational Foundation, 66
Wham-O, Inc., 61
Wheaton Industries, 8
Wheaton Science Products, 60 (upd.)
Wheelabrator Technologies, Inc., 6; 60 (upd.)
Wheeling-Pittsburgh Corporation, 7; 58 (upd.)
Wherehouse Entertainment Incorporated, 11
Whirlpool Corporation, III; 12 (upd.); 59 (upd.)
White & Case LLP, 35
White Castle Management Company, 12; 36 (upd.); 85 (upd.)
White Consolidated Industries Inc., 13
The White House, Inc., 60
White Lily Foods Company, 88

White Rose, Inc., 24
Whitehall Jewellers, Inc., 82 (upd.)
Whiting Petroleum Corporation, 81
Whitman Corporation, 10 (upd.)
Whitman Education Group, Inc., 41
Whitney Holding Corporation, 21
Whittaker Corporation, I; 48 (upd.)
Whole Foods Market, Inc., 20; 50 (upd.)
Wickes Inc., V; 25 (upd.)
Widmer Brothers Brewing Company, 76
Wieden + Kennedy, 75
Wilbert, Inc., 56
Wilbur Chocolate Company, 66
Wilco Farm Stores, 93
Wild Oats Markets, Inc., 19; 41 (upd.)
Wildlife Conservation Society, 31
Wikimedia Foundation, Inc., 91
Willamette Industries, Inc., IV; 31 (upd.)
Willamette Valley Vineyards, Inc., 85
William L. Bonnell Company, Inc., 66
William Lyon Homes, 59
William Morris Agency, Inc., 23
William Zinsser & Company, Inc., 58
Williams & Connolly LLP, 47
Williams Communications Group, Inc., 34
The Williams Companies, Inc., IV; 31 (upd.)
Williams Scotsman, Inc., 65
Williams-Sonoma, Inc., 17; 44 (upd.)
Williamson-Dickie Manufacturing Company, 14; 45 (upd.)
Wilmington Trust Corporation, 25
Wilson Sonsini Goodrich & Rosati, 34
Wilson Sporting Goods Company, 24; 84 (upd.)
Wilsons The Leather Experts Inc., 21; 58 (upd.)
Winchell's Donut Houses Operating Company, L.P., 60
WinCo Foods Inc., 60
Wind River Systems, Inc., 37
Windmere Corporation, 16
Windstream Corporation, 83
Windswept Environmental Group, Inc., 62
The Wine Group, Inc., 39
Winegard Company, 56
Winmark Corporation, 74
Winn-Dixie Stores, Inc., II; 21 (upd.); 59 (upd.)
Winnebago Industries Inc., 7; 27 (upd.)
WinsLoew Furniture, Inc., 21
Winston & Strawn, 35
The Wiremold Company, 81
Wirtz Corporation, 72
Wisconsin Alumni Research Foundation, 65
Wisconsin Bell, Inc., 14
Wisconsin Central Transportation Corporation, 24
Wisconsin Dairies, 7
Wisconsin Energy Corporation, 6; 54 (upd.)
Wisconsin Public Service Corporation, 9
Wise Foods, Inc. 79
Witco Corporation, I; 16 (upd.)
Witness Systems, Inc., 87
Wizards of the Coast Inc., 24
WLR Foods, Inc., 21
Wm. B. Reily & Company Inc., 58
Wm. Wrigley Jr. Company, 7; 58 (upd.)
WMS Industries, Inc., 15; 53 (upd.)
WMX Technologies Inc., 17
Wolfgang Puck Worldwide, Inc., 26, 70 (upd.)
Wolohan Lumber Co., 19
Wolverine Tube Inc., 23
Wolverine World Wide, Inc., 16; 59 (upd.)
Womble Carlyle Sandridge & Rice, PLLC, 52
Wood-Mode, Inc., 23
Woodcraft Industries Inc., 61
Woodward Governor Company, 13; 49 (upd.)
Woolrich Inc., 62
Woolworth Corporation, V; 20 (upd.)
WordPerfect Corporation, 10
Workflow Management, Inc., 65
Working Assets Funding Service, 43
Workman Publishing Company, Inc., 70
World Acceptance Corporation, 57
World Bank Group, 33
World Book, Inc., 12
World Color Press Inc., 12
World Duty Free Americas, Inc., 29 (upd.)
World Fuel Services Corporation, 47
World Publications, LLC, 65
World Vision International, Inc., 93
World Wide Technology, Inc., 94
World Wrestling Federation Entertainment, Inc., 32
World's Finest Chocolate Inc., 39
WorldCorp, Inc., 10
Worldwide Restaurant Concepts, Inc., 47
Worthington Foods, Inc., 14
Worthington Industries, Inc., 7; 21 (upd.)
WPL Holdings, Inc., 6
WPS Resources Corporation, 53 (upd.)
Writers Guild of America, West, Inc., 92
Wright Express Corporation, 80
Wright Medical Group, Inc., 61
WTD Industries, Inc., 20
Wunderman, 86
Wyant Corporation, 30
Wyeth, 50 (upd.)
Wyle Electronics, 14
Wyman-Gordon Company, 14
Wynn's International, Inc., 33
Wyse Technology, Inc., 15
X-Rite, Inc., 48
Xcel Energy Inc., 73 (upd.)
Xerium Technologies, Inc., 94
Xerox Corporation, III; 6 (upd.); 26 (upd.); 69 (upd.)
Xilinx, Inc., 16; 82 (upd.)
XM Satellite Radio Holdings, Inc., 69
XTO Energy Inc., 52
Yahoo! Inc., 27; 70 (upd.)
Yarnell Ice Cream Company, Inc., 92
The Yankee Candle Company, Inc., 37
YankeeNets LLC, 35
The Yates Companies, Inc., 62
Yellow Corporation, 14; 45 (upd.)
Yellow Freight System, Inc. of Delaware, V
YES! Entertainment Corporation, 26
YMCA of the USA, 31
YOCREAM International, Inc., 47
The York Group, Inc., 50
York International Corp., 13
York Research Corporation, 35
Youbet.com, Inc., 77
YouTube, Inc., 90
Young & Rubicam, Inc., I; 22 (upd.); 66 (upd.)
Young Broadcasting Inc., 40
Young Innovations, Inc., 44
Young's Market Company, LLC, 32
Younkers, 76 (upd.)
Younkers, Inc., 19
Youth Services International, Inc., 21
YRC Worldwide Inc., 90 (upd.)
Yucaipa Cos., 17
Yum! Brands Inc., 58
YWCA of the United States, 45
Zacky Farms LLC, 74
Zale Corporation, 16; 40 (upd.); 91 (upd.)
Zanett, Inc., 92
Zany Brainy, Inc., 31
Zapata Corporation, 25
Zappos.com, Inc., 73
Zatarain's, Inc., 64
Zebra Technologies Corporation, 14; 53 (upd.)
Zenith Data Systems, Inc., 10
Zenith Electronics Corporation, II; 13 (upd.); 34 (upd.); 89 (upd.)
ZERO Corporation, 17; 88 (upd.)
Ziebart International Corporation, 30; 66 (upd.)
The Ziegler Companies, Inc., 24; 63 (upd.)
Ziff Davis Media Inc., 12; 36 (upd.); 73 (upd.)
Zila, Inc., 46
ZiLOG, Inc., 15; 72 (upd.)
Zimmer Holdings, Inc., 45
Zingerman's Community of Businesses, 68
Zion's Cooperative Mercantile Institution, 33
Zions Bancorporation, 12; 53 (upd.)
Zipcar, Inc., 92
Zippo Manufacturing Company, 18; 71 (upd.)
Zoltek Companies, Inc., 37
Zondervan Corporation, 24; 71 (upd.)
Zones, Inc., 67
Zoom Technologies, Inc., 18; 53 (upd.)
Zoran Corporation, 77
Zuffa L.L.C., 89
Zumiez, Inc., 77
Zygo Corporation, 42
Zytec Corporation, 19

Uruguay

Administración Nacional de Combustibles, Alcohol y Pórtland, 93

Cooperativa Nacional de Productores de Leche S.A. (Conaprole), 92

Vatican City
Caritas Internationalis, 72

Venezuela
Cerveceria Polar, I
Cisneros Group of Companies, 54
Empresas Polar SA, 55 (upd.)
Petróleos de Venezuela S.A., IV; 74 (upd.)

Vietnam
Lam Son Sugar Joint Stock Corporation (Lasuco), 60

Virgin Islands
Little Switzerland, Inc., 60

Wales
Hyder plc, 34
Iceland Group plc, 33
Kwik Save Group plc, 11

Zambia
Zambia Industrial and Mining Corporation Ltd., IV

Zimbabwe
Air Zimbabwe (Private) Limited, 91